ALMANAC OF CHINA'S ECONOMY™ 1981

ALMANAC OF CHINA'S ECONOMY™ 1981

WITH ECONOMIC STATISTICS FOR 1949-1980

Compiled by
The Economic Research Centre,
The State Council of the People's Republic of China
and
The State Statistical Bureau

——

XUE MUQIAO, Editor-in-Chief

Published by: MODERN CULTURAL COMPANY LIMITED
Distributed by: BALLINGER PUBLISHING COMPANY
A Subsidiary of Harper & Row, Publishers, Inc.

In Association with

EURASIA PRESS
New York and Hong Kong

Copyright © 1982 by Modern Cultural Company Limited
All rights reserved.
No part of this publication may be reproduced, stored in a retrieval system, or transmitted in any form or by any means, electronic, mechanical, photocopying recording or otherwise, without the prior written consent of the publisher.

Publisher: Modern Cultural Company Limited
Address: 58, Electric Road, 1/F., Hong Kong
Telex: 71942 MCTDP HX
Cable: 4718
Tel: 5-8910493

Distributed by Ballinger Publishing Company
A subsidiary of Harper & Row, Publishers Inc.
Address: 54 Church Street, Cambridge, MA 02138

**English Language Rights Distribution
In Association with Eurasia Press, Inc.**
Address: 302 Fifth Avenue, New York, NY 10001

Printed in Hong Kong by Tai Dao Publishing Co.
Address: 113, Wanchai Road, Tak Lee Commercial Bldg.,
13/F., Block D, Hong Kong

ISBN 0-932030-14-9
ISBN 0731-1257

EDITORIAL BOARD OF THE ALMANAC OF CHINA'S ECONOMY

Editor-in-Chief: Xue Muqiao

Deputy Editors-in-Chief: Ma Hong, Chen Xian

Editorial Board (The names are listed according to the stroke order of the Chinese surname):

Yu Guangyuan
  Vice-President, Chinese Academy of Social Sciences
Ma Hong
  Vice-President, Chinese Academy of Social Sciences; Director, Institute of Industrial Economy
Lu Hanchuan
  Vice-President, Agricultural Bank of China; Director, Rural Banking Institute
Xu Dixin
  Vice-President, Chinese Academy of Social Sciences; Director, Institute of Economics

Xu Yi
  Director, Institute of Financial Science, Ministry of Finance
Liu Mingfu
  Director, Institute of Finance and Trade, Chinese Academy of Social Sciences
Liu Guoguang
  Deputy Director, Institute of Economics, Chinese Academy of Social Sciences
Liu Zhicheng
  Leading Cadre, Institute of Agricultural Economy, Chinese Academy of Agricultural Science
Sun Yefang
  Advisor, Chinese Academy of Social Sciences
Ren Tao
  Leading Cadre, Technical Economic Research Department, Economic Institute of the State Planning Commission
Chen Xian
  Director, State Bureau of Statistics
He Jianzhang
  Deputy Director, Economic Institute of the State Planning Commission
Li Gengxin
  Deputy Director, Institute of Finance and Trade, Chinese Academy of Social Sciences
Li Hao
  Special Member, State Administrative Commission on Import and Export Affairs
Du Xinyuan
  Secretary-General, State Council; Secretary-General, Leading Group of Finance and Economy of the State Council

Yang Peixin
  Deputy Director, Institute of Banking, People's Bank of China
Shen Jingnong
  Deputy Director, Institute of Financial Science, Ministry of Finance
Li Deren
  Deputy Director, Institute of Technological Economics, Chinese Academy of Social Sciences
Xiao Fan
  Director, Commercial Economics Institute, Ministry of Commerce
Lo Yuanzheng
  Deputy Director, Institute of World Economy, Chinese Academy of Social Sciences
Lin Senmu
  Deputy Director, Economic Institute, State Capital Construction Commission
Lin Zixin
  Deputy Director, Chinese Institute of Scientific and Technical Information, Chinese Academy of Sciences
Zhang Peiji
  Deputy Director, Institute of International Trade, Ministry of Foreign Trade
Zhang Siqi
  Director, Institute of Comprehensive Transportation, State Economic Commission
Fang Weizhong
  Vice-Minister, State Planning Commission
Liu Suinian
  Deputy Director, General Bureau, State Planning Commission; Deputy Director, Economic Institute, State Planning Commission
Hao Chengming
  Leading Cadre, General Research Section, State Statistical Bureau
Qian Junrui
  Director, Institute of World Economy, Chinese Academy of Social Sciences
Yao Yunfang
  Vice General-Director, Research Department, Bank of China
Mei Xing
  Deputy Director, Research Department, Secretariat of the Central Committee of the Communist Party of China

Jiang Yiwei
   Deputy Director, Institute of Industrial Economics, Chinese Academy of Social Sciences; Director, Economic Management Magazine Bureau

Zhan Wu
   Director, Institute of Agricultural Economy, Chinese Academy of Social Sciences

Liao Jili
   Deputy Director, System Reform Office, State Council; Member, State Planning Commission

Xue Muqiao
   Advisor, State Planning Commission; Director, Economic Institute, State Planning Commission

Xue Baoding
   Director, Capital Construction Economic Institute, State Capital Construction Commission; Deputy Director, Institute of Industrial Economy, Chinese Academy of Social Sciences

CONSULTANTS FOR THE ALMANAC OF CHINA'S ECONOMY (1981) (ENGLISH EDITION)

Jiang Yiwei	Vice-Director, Institute of Industrial Economics, Chinese Academy of Social Sciences; Director, Economic Management Magazine Bureau
J. C. Hsiao	Professor of Agricultural Economics Department, Southern Connecticut State College
Fung Shiu Lam	Certified Public Account, Hong Kong. Justice of the Peace, Hong Kong. Fellow of the Institute of Chartered Accountants in England and Wales, Member of the Institute of Chartered Accountants of Ontario, Canada
Fredric M. Kaplan	President and Publisher, Eurasia Press, Inc.
Peter Carton	General Manager, Publications Division, South China Morning Post Limited.
Michael Connolly	President, Ballinger Publishing Company

EDITORIAL STAFF FOR THE 1981 ENGLISH EDITION

Chief Editor: Tam Wai Ming
Editors: Jia Dingzhi
　　　　Zhang Tingquan
　　　　Hu Genkang
　　　　Fredric M. Kaplan
Managing Editors: Wong Hok Man (Hong Kong)
　　　　　　　　May Wu (New York)
　　　　　　　　Gillian Bryant (Hong Kong)
Editorial Staff: Geoffrey Bonsall
　　　　　　　Wu Kim Ching
　　　　　　　Geralyn Donahue
　　　　　　　Rosalyn Friedman (Index)
　　　　　　　Sal J. Foderaro
　　　　　　　Walter Fox
　　　　　　　Anissa Ip
　　　　　　　David Levi
　　　　　　　Leung Wai
　　　　　　　Tse Man Chun
Leading Cadre of Publishing: Tam Fung (Hong Kong)
　　　　　　　　　　　　　　Chang Kecen (China)

Front Cover Design: May Tong
Text Design: Fredric M. Kaplan
Cover Chop Design: Wong Siu Tsun
Production Executive: Wong Wing Hong

Conversion Table for Chinese Units of Measure

Length:
1 kilometre (1,000 m.) = 2 *li* = 0.621 mile
                          = 0.540 nautical mile
1 metre (m.) = 3 *chi* = 3.281 feet

1 *li* = 0.5 kilometre = 0.311 mile
      = 0.270 nautical mile
1 *chi* = 0.333 metre = 1.094 feet

1 mile = 1.609 kilometres = 3.219 *li*
        = 0.868 nautical mile
1 foot = 0.305 metre = 0.914 *chi*
1 nautical mile = 1.852 kilometres = 3.704 *li*
                  = 1.150 miles

Area:
1 hectare = 15 *mu* = 2.47 acres
1 *mu* = 6.667 hectares = 0.164 acre
1 acre = 0.405 hectare = 6.070 *mu*

Weight:
1 kilogramme = 2 *jin* = 2.205 pounds
1 *jin* = 0.5 kilogramme = 1.102 pounds
1 pound = 0.454 kilogramme = 0.907 *jin*

Volume:
1 litre (metric system) = 1 *sheng*
                        = 0.220 gallon (British)
1 gallon (British) = 4.546 litres = 4.546 *sheng*

CONTENTS

	Page
CONVERSION TABLE FOR CHINESE UNITS OF MEASURE	VIII
LISTING OF CHARTS AND TABLES	XVII
FOREWORD By Xue Muqiao	XXI
EDITOR'S NOTES	XXIII
MAP OF CHINA	XXIV

SECTION I: GENERAL SURVEY OF CHINA

1. An Outline of Chinese History — By Zhu Jiazhen — 3
2. An Outline of China's Natural Geography — By Niu Wenyuan and Zhao Songchiao — 11
3. An Outline of China's Economic Geography — By Deng Jingzhong and Li Wenyun — 22
4. China's Minority Nationalities — By Hua Juxian — 34
5. The Constitution of the Communist Party of China — 43
6. The Constitution of the People's Republic of China — 49
7. The Central People's Government (The State Council) — 57
8. Administrative Divisions of Provinces, Autonomous Regions, Municipalities and Counties of the People's Republic of China — 59

SECTION II: MAJOR ECONOMIC DOCUMENTS, WORKS OF ECONOMIC POLICY, LAWS AND DECREES (1978–1981)

1. Communique of the Sixth Plenary Session of the 11th Central Committee of the Communist Party of China — 75
2. Resolution on Certain Questions in the History of Our Party Since the Founding of the People's Republic of China — 77
3. Speech at the Meeting in Celebration of the 60th Anniversary of the Founding of the Communist Party of China by Hu Yaobang — 105
4. Opening Speech at the Third Session of the Fifth National People's Congress by Ye Jianying — 115
5. Report on the Arrangements for the National Economic Plans for 1980 and 1981 by Yao Yilin — 116
6. Report on the Final State Accounts for 1979, the Draft State Budget for 1980 and Financial Estimates for 1981 by Wang Bingqian — 128
7. Resolution of the Third Session of the Fifth National People's Congress of the People's Republic of China on the Arrangements for the National Economic Plans for 1980 and 1981, the Final State Accounts for 1979, the State Budget for 1980 and the Financial Estimates for 1981 — 139
8. Report of the Budget Committee of the Fifth National People's Congress on the Examination of the Final State Accounts for 1979, the Draft State Budget for 1980 and the Financial Estimates for 1981 — 140

Agriculture

9. Regulations on Breeding and Protection of Aquatic Resources — 143
10. The Forest Law of the People's Republic of China (*For Trial Implementation*) — 146
11. Regulations on Some Questions Concerning the Development of Enterprises Run by Rural People's Communes and Production Brigades (*Draft for Trial Use*) — 152

12. Decision of the Central Committee of the Communist Party of China on Some Questions Concerning the Acceleration of Agricultural Development — 161

Industry

13. Decisions of the Central Committee of the Communist Party of China on Some Questions Concerning the Acceleration of Industrial Development (*Draft*) — 175
14. Regulations on Awards for Quality Products of the People's Republic of China — 194
15. Regulations on Standardization Control of the People's Republic of China — 196
16. Tentative Regulations on Bonuses for Saving Specially Designated Fuels and Raw Materials in State-Owned Industrial and Transport Enterprises, Issued by the Ministry of Finance, the State Bureau of Labour and the State Administration of Supplies (*Draft*) — 200
17. Tentative Measures Concerning the Sharing of Profits in State-Owned Industrial Enterprises, Issued by the State Economic Commission and the Ministry of Finance — 202
18. Provisional Regulations for Total Quality Control in Industrial Enterprises — 205
19. Provisional Regulations of the State Capital Construction Commission, the State Planning Commission, the Ministry of Finance, the State Bureau of Labour and the State Administration of Supplies on Problems Related to the Broadening of the Management Decision-Making Power of Construction Enterprises — 211
20. Provisional Regulations Approved by the State Council on Strengthening the Work of Tapping Potential, Renovation and Transformation in Existing Industrial and Transport Enterprises — 214
21. Provisional Regulations Concerning the Promotion of Economic Combination — 218
22. Provisional Regulations Concerning the Development and Protection of Socialist Competition — 220

Finance and Taxes

23. The State Council's Circular on the Introduction of a Financial Management System by Which the Scope of Revenue and Expenditure Will Be Defined for the Central and Local Governments Respectively and Each will be Responsible for the Balance of Its Own Budget — 223
24. Regulations Concerning the Work of Financial Supervision — 226
25. The Income Tax Law of the People's Republic of China Concerning Joint Ventures with Chinese and Foreign Investment — 228
26. Detailed Rules and Regulations for the Implementation of the Income Tax Law of the People's Republic of China Concerning Joint Ventures with Chinese and Foreign Investment — 230
27. Individual Income Tax Law of the People's Republic of China — 234
28. Detailed Rules and Regulations for the Implementation of the Individual Income Tax Law of the People's Republic of China — 236
29. Circular on Improving the Payment of Industrial and Commercial Income Tax by Cooperative Stores and Individual Economic Units — 239

Banking

30. Provisional Regulations on Providing Loans for Capital Construction Projects — 240
31. Provisional Regulations on Granting Loans to and Opening Accounts by the Unemployed Youth in Cities and Towns for Setting up Enterprises of Collective Ownership — 243
32. Provisional Regulations on Providing Special Short- and Medium-Term Loans for the Light and Textile Industries by the People's Bank of China — 245
33. Provisional Regulations of the Bank of China on Foreign Exchange Certificates — 248
34. Regulations for Providing Short-Term Loans in Foreign Currency by the Bank of China — 249

35.	Provisional Regulations for Exchange Control of the People's Republic of China	252

Regulation of Foreign Investment

36.	The Law of the People's Republic of China on Joint Ventures Using Chinese and Foreign Investment	256
37.	Regulations on Labour Management in Joint Ventures Using Chinese and Foreign Investment	259
38.	Regulations on the Registration of Joint Ventures Using Chinese and Foreign Investment	261
39.	Regulations on Special Economic Zones in Guangdong Province	263
40.	Interim Regulations of the People's Republic of China Concerning the Control of Resident Offices of Foreign Enterprises	266
41.	Announcement of the General Administration for Industry and Commerce of the People's Republic of China Concerning the Registration of Resident Offices of Foreign Enterprises	268

Foreign Trade

42.	Provisional Regulations Concerning the Export License System, Issued by the Import and Export Commission and the Ministry of Foreign Trade	269

Customs

43.	Provisional Customs Regulations for Inward and Outward Baggage of Overseas Chinese and Other Passengers	271
44.	Rules of the People's Republic of China Governing the Levying of Import Duty on Articles of Passengers' Baggage and Personal Postal Parcels	273
45.	Regulation for Customs Control over Baggage of Passengers Coming from or Going to Hong Kong and Macao	275

Labour and Wages

46.	Provisional Regulations Concerning Piece-Rate Wages in State-Owned Enterprises (*Draft*), Issued by the State Planning Commission, the State Economic Commission and the State Bureau of Labour	277

Administration of Industry and Commerce

47.	A Joint Circular of the State Economic Commission, the General Administration of Industry and Commerce and the People's Bank of China on a Number of Questions Regarding the Supervision of Economic Contracts	279
48.	Regulations on Control of the Purchasing Power of Social Groups	282

Environmental Protection

49.	The Environmental Protection Law of the People's Republic of China (*For Trial Implentation*)	285

Science and Technology

50.	Regulations Regarding the Natural Science Awards of the People's Republic of China	289

SECTION III: MONOGRAPHIC STUDES ON CURRENT ECONOMIC POLICY

1.	How to Look at the Present Economic Situation	By Xue Muqiao	293
2.	On China's New Strategy for Economic Development	By Ma Hong	299
3.	China's Economic Readjustment and Reorientation	By Fang Weizhong	319
4.	On the Question of the Restructuring of China's Economic System	By Liao Jili	332

5. The Advancement of Industrial Enterprises Amidst Consolidation By Yuan Baohua 340
6. What to Do After We Have Decided on the Reform By Yu Guangyuan 346
7. Socialist Economic Democracy — The Essence of Restructuring Economic Management By Jiang Yiwei 350
8. Reform of the Industrial Management System in Sichuan Province By Lin Ling, Vice-President, Academy of Social Sciences, Sichuan Province 357
9. The System of Responsibility in Agricultural Production in Anhui Province By Zhou Yueli, Deputy Director, Anhui Provincial Agricultural Commission 368

SECTION IV: SURVEY OF CHINA'S ECONOMY

1. China's Economy in 1980 By Wei Liqun 379

Agriculture, Fishing and Forestry

2. China's Agriculture in 1980 By Zhang Siqian, Institute of Agricultural Economics, Chinese Academy of Social Sciences 392
3. China's State Farm and Land Reclamation Sector By Guo Chunhua, National Institute of Agricultural Economy, (Ministry of State Farms and Land Reclamation) 407
4. China's Water Conservancy By the Editorial Office of *Water Conservancy in China* 419
5. China's Forestry in 1980 By the Propaganda Bureau, Ministry of Forestry 427
6. China's Fisheries By Jin Shui, State Administration of Aquatic Products 432
7. China's Animal Husbandry By Zheng Xingjie, State Bureau of Animal Husbandry, Ministry of Agriculture 438

Industry

8. China's Industry in 1980 By Wang Haibo and Wu Jiajun, Institute of Industrial Economics, Chinese Academy of Social Sciences 444
9. China's Light Industry By the Policy Research Office, Ministry of Light Industry 456
10. China's Textile Industry By the Research Office, Ministry of Textile Industry 466
11. China's Handicrafts Industry By the Policy Research Office, Ministry of Light Industry 473
12. Commune-and-Brigade-Run Industry in China's Rural Areas By Qi Zong, Bureau of Commune-Run Enterprises, Ministry of Agriculture 481
13. China's Petroleum Industry By the Research Office, Ministry of Petroleum Industry 486
14. China's Coal Industry By the Research Division, General Office, Ministry of Coal Industry 494
15. China's Electric Power Industry By Chen Zengqing, Ministry of Power Industry 503
16. China's Chemical Industry By the Research Office, Ministry of Chemical Industry 508
17. China's Machine-Building Industry (First Ministry) By Yan Qiushi, Policy Research Office, First Ministry of Machine-Building 516
18. China's Shipbuilding Industry By Hong Lun, Policy Research Office, Sixth Ministry of Machine-Building 519
19. China's Agricultural Machinery Industry and Agricultural Mechanization By Long Jiyan, Ministry of Agricultural Machinery 523
20. China's Electronics Industry By the Policy Research Office, Fourth Ministry of Machine-Building 532
21. China's Metallurgical Industry By Chen Lei and Zhang Xinchuan, Research Institute of Metallurgical Economy, Ministry of Metallurgical Industry 540

22. China's Capital Construction in 1980
        By Kang Zhixin, Institute of Economic Research, State Capital Construction Commission 549
23. China's Building Materials Industry
        By Zhong Jianwen, Research Office, Ministry of Building Materials Industry 554
24. China's Building Industry
        By the Research Office, General Administration of Building Construction 560
25. China's Pharmaceutical Industry
        By Jin Tongzhen and Ma Ding, State Pharmaceutical Administration 565

Transport and Communications

26. China's Communications and Transport
        By the Institute of Comprehensive Transportation, State Economic Commission 573
27. China's Railway Transportation   By the General Office, Ministry of Railways 582
28. China's Highway Transportation
        By Cheng Yinghua, Highway Administration Bureau, Ministry of Communications 590
29. China's Water Transportation
        By Sui Qiren, Bureau of Water Transport, Ministry of Communications 592
30. China's Civil Aviation   By Wu Erer, General Administration of Civil Aviation of China 598
31. China's Posts and Telecommunications
        By the Research Office, Ministry of Posts and Telecommunications 604

Commerce and Trade

32. China's Commerce in 1980   By the Commerce Research Institute, Ministry of Commerce 608
33. How China Manages Its Supplies   By Li Kaixin, State Bureau of Supplies 613
34. Growth of China's Foreign Trade
        By Zhang Peiji, Research Institute of International Trade, Ministry of Foreign Trade 621
35. China's Importation of Technology
        By the Research Department, State Administrative Commission on Export and Import Affairs 625
36. China's Absorption of Foreign Investment
        By the Research Department, Foreign Investment Commission 627
37. China's Aid in Development Projects to Other Countries
        By Wei Jing, Ministry of Economic Relations with Foreign Countries 631
38. China's Customs Service   By the General Office, Customs General Administration 635

Finance and Banking

39. China's Financial System
        By Shen Jingnang and Chen Baosen, Finance Research Institute, Ministry of Finance 643
40. China's Taxation in 1980   By Liu Zhicheng, General Taxation Bureau, Ministry of Finance 655
41. China's Banking System   By the Research Institute of Finance and Banking 657
42. China's Rural Banking   By Cao Jiren, Agricultural Bank of China 665
43. The Development of China's International Banking
        By the Research Department, Bank of China 667
44. Prices in China   By Duan Jianke, State Administration Bureau for Commodity Prices 671
45. Rapid Development of Tourism
        By the General Office, General Administration of Travel and Tourism of China 677
46. China's Sciences in 1980   By the Policy Research Office, Chinese Academy of Sciences 683
47. Standardization in China   By Huang Weijian, State Administration of Standards 691

Labour

48. Employment, Wages, Workers' Welfare and Labour Protection China
By Zheng Ji, Policy Research Department, State Bureau of Labour — 698
49. China's Trade Unions By the Research Office, All-China Federation of Trade Unions — 707

Culture and Social Services

50. China's Cultural Achievements in 1980
By Cui Yongsheng, Policy Research Department, Ministry of Culture — 717
51. Publishing in China By the Editorial Department, Chinese Publications Yearbook — 722
52. China's Journalism in 1980
By the Press Research Institute, Chinese Academy of Social Sciences — 728
53. China's Film Industry By Ji Hong, Film Bureau, Ministry of Culture — 732
54. Education in China By Ji Hua, Ministry of Education — 743
55. China's Health Services By Wei Zhi, Ministry of Public Health — 753
56. Family Planning in China
By the Policy Research Section, Family Planning Office, State Council — 761
57. Environmental Protection in China
By the Research Section, Environmental Protection Leading Group of the State Council — 766

Provincial Survey

58. Economic Development in Anhui Province
By the Economic Research Institute, Anhui Provincial Planning Commission — 781
59. Economic Development in Beijing
By the Research Office, Beijing Municipal People's Government — 787
60. Economic Development in Fujian Province
By the General Office, Fujian Provincial People's Government — 791
61. Economic Development in Gansu Province
By the General Office, People's Government of Gansu Province — 797
62. Economic Development in Guangdong Province
By the Geography and Population Investigation and Research Division, General Office, Guangdong Provincial People's Government — 802
63. Economic Development in Guangxi Zhuang Autonomous Region
By the Institute of Economic Research, Planning Commission of Guangxi Zhuang Autonomous Region — 807
64. Economic Development in Guizhou Province By Jin Yanshi — 811
65. Economic Development in Hebei Province By the Hebei Provincial Planning Commission — 817
66. Economic Development in Heilongjiang Province
By Zhong He, Heilongjiang Provincial People's Government — 822
67. Economic Development in Henan Province
By the Financial and Economic Department, General Office of the Henan Provincial People's Government — 826
68. Economic Development in Hubei Province
By the Research Division, General Office, Hubei Provincial People's Government — 830
69. Economic Development in Hunan Province
By the Research Division, General Office, Hunan Provincial People's Government — 835
70. Economic Development, Inner Mongolian Autonomous Region
By the General Office, Inner Mongolia Autonomous Region People's Government — 841

71.	Economic Development in Jiangsu Province		
		By Mao Junyi, Jiangsu Provincial Statistical Bureau	851
72.	Economic Development in Jiangxi Province	By Zhen Yanchu	857
73.	Economic Development in Jilin Province		
		By the General Office, Jilin Provincial People's Government	861
74.	Economic Development Liaoning Province		
		By the Liaoning Provincial Statistical Bureau	866
75.	Economic Development in Ningxia Hui Autonomous Region		
		By the Research Division, General Office of the Ningxi Hui Autonomous Region People's Government	872
76.	Economic Devleopment in Qinghai Province		
		By the Economic Research Office, Qinghai Provincial Planning Commission	877
77.	Economic Development in Shaanxi Province		
		By the General Office, Shaanxi Provincial People's Government	882
78.	Economic Development in Shandong Province		
		By the Economic Research Centre, Shandong Provincial Planning Commission	887
79.	Economic Development in Shanghai		
		By He Gaosheng, General Office, Shanghai Municipal Economic Research Centre	892
80.	Economic Development in Shanxi Province		
		By the Shanxi Provincial Planning Commission	897
81.	Economic Development in Sichuan Province		
		By the Institute of Economics, Academy of Social Sciences, Sichuan Province and the Institute of Economics, Sichuan Provincial Planning Commission	901
82.	Economic Development in Tianjin		
		By the Institute of Economics, Tianjin Academy of Social Sciences	905
83.	Economic Development in Tibet Autonomous Region		
		By the General Office, Tibet Autonomous Region People's Government	913
84.	Economic Development in Xinjiang Uygur Autonomous Region		
		By the Investigation and Research Division, General Office, Xinjiang Uygur Autonomous Region People's Government	918
85.	Economic Development in Yunnan Province		
		By the General Office, Yunnan Provincial People's Government	923
86.	Economic Development in Zhejiang Province		
		By Ji Wei and Zhong He, Synthesizing Office, Zhejiang Provincial Planning Commission	927

Addenda:

A.	Survey Taiwan Province's Economy in 1980	By Gao Lingzhen	933
B.	Economic Development in Hong Kong	By Gu Nianliang and Yuan Shibang	939
C.	Economic Development in Macao	By Huang Weiliang	942

SECTION V: CHINESE ECONOMIC THEORY

Theoretical Studies by Chinese Economic Circles in Recent Years: Progress and Future Trends
  By Zhao Renwei and Xiang Qiyuan, Institute of Economics, Chinese Academy of Social Sciences 947

SECTION VI: ECONOMIC STATISTICS

1. Selected Economic Statistical Data, Compiled by the State Statistical Bureau of the People's Republic of China 959

2.	Communique of the State Statistical Bureau of the People's Republic of China on Fulfilment of China's 1980 National Economic Plan	989
3.	Monetary Statistics, 1980	997

SECTION VII: CHRONOLOGY OF MAJOR ECONOMIC EVENTS IN CHINA: 1001
December 1978 – December 1980

APPENDIX

1.	Directory of China's National Foreign Trade Corporations: Head Offices, Branches and Major Commodities Traded	1025
2.	Listing of China's Major Economic Research Institutes	1046
3.	Listing of China's Colleges Specializing in Finance and Economics; Other Universities and Colleges with Departments and Specialities in Finance, Economics and Management	1055
4.	Listing of China's Profesional Secondary Schools of Finance and Economics	1064
5.	Listing of Economic Societies in China	1072
6.	Annotated Survey of China's Major Economic Periodicals	1077
7.	Bibliography of China's Publications in Economics (1980)	1086
8.	Articles of Association of the Bank of China, Including International Branches of the People's Insurance Company	1106
9.	Exchange Rates of RMB Yuan Against Foreign Currencies, 1977–1980	1110

INDEX 1111

SUMMARY CONTENTS FOR 1982 EDITION, ALMANAC OF CHINA'S ECONOMY 1140

LISTING OF CHARTS AND TABLES

	Page
Brief Chronology of Chinese History	9
China's Climate Extremes	14
China's Temperature Zones	15
Distribution of China's River Basins	16
Balance of Water Volume in China	16
Distribution of Regional Types of China's Seed Plant Genera	18
Principal Components of China's Natural Geographic Zones	20
Membership of the Central People's Government (State Council)	57
Administrative Divisions of China	59
Individual Income Tax Rates	235
Import/Export Limits for Duty-free or Dutiable Articles	271
Schedule of Import Duty Rates (for personal baggage and postal parcels)	273
Limits for Duty-free and Dutiable Articles Carried by Passengers from Hong Kong and Macao	275
Prohibited Import/Export Articles of the PRC	276
China's Crude Oil and Natural Gas Production (1950-80)	490
Financial Statistics for the Petroleum Industry (1950-80)	491
Structure of Output in State-Owned Mines (1980)	497
Partial Production Figures for Working Faces of State-Owned Mines (1980)	497
Partial Index for Prepared Face of State-Owned Mines (1980)	497
Selected Technical-Economic Index of State-Owned Mines (1980)	497
Growth Rate of China's Chemical Industry (1950-78)	508
Investment in China's Chemical Industry (1949-79)	509
Annual Output of Chemical Fertilizers (1979)	510
Chemical Fertilizer Production (1950-79)	510
Raw Materials and Processing Industries (1953-80)	511
Production of Synthetic Materials (1965-79)	511
Production of Selected Organic Chemicals (1965-79)	513
Output of Major Chemical Products (1980)	513
Rate of Energy Consumption (per ton ammonia)	514
Economic Performance by the Chemical Industry (1976-80)	514
Output of Principal Agricultural Machinery Products (1980)	527
1980 Production of Some Key Metals	543
Technical-Economic Indices for Changzhou and Nanning	562
Growth of Various Means of Transport (1949-80)	573
Passenger Traffic Volume (1949-80)	574
Freight Traffic Volume (1949-80)	575
Passenger Turnover (1949-80)	575

(Cont'd next page)

XVII

LISTING OF CHARTS AND TABLES

(Cont'd)   Page

Freight Turnover (1949-80)	575
Average Passenger Haulage (1949-80)	576
Average Freight Haulage (1949-80)	576
Changes in Proportions of Different Modes of Transport for Passengers and Freight (1949-80)	576,577
Indices of Transportation Efficiency (1950-80)	577
Development of Railway Transportation in China (1949-79)	582
Main Goods Transported by Rail (1980)	584
Main Index of Railway Transport (1980)	505
Repair and Manufacture of Locomotives and Rolling Stock (1980)	587
Current Interest Rates on Savings Deposits	662
Current Interest Rates on Deposits and Loans	663
Varieites and Specifications of Commemorative Coins	663
Old and New Purchase Prices for Gold, Silver and Platinum (March 1, 1980)	664
General Price Index (1979)	672
Classified Index of Retail Prices (1980)	676
Cities and Areas Open to Foreign Tourists (1980)	677
Diagram of Organization Structure in Charge of Standardization	693
Numbers of National Standards for Industrial and Agricultural Products Before and After 1966	694
Comparisons of Economic Performance for Fasteners in Shanghai	696
Volume of Books Published (1971-80)	725
Categories of Books Published (1971-80)	725
Decline in Publishing Between 1956 and 1980	726
Catalogue of Feature and Stage-Art Films (1980)	734
Output of Industrial Crops, Zhejiang Province (1980)	928
Output of Industrial Products, Zhejiang Province (1980)	929
Changes in Taiwan's Economic Structure (1952-77)	934
Output of Taiwan's Principal Industrial Products (1952-78)	935
Product Composition of Taiwan's Foreign Trade (1952-79)	937
Distribution of Population and Natural Resources (end 1979)	959
Population (1949-79)	959
Main Indicators of China's National Economy (Absolute Figures) (1949-79)	960
Main Indicators of China's National Economy (Rate of Increase) (1957-79)	961
Average Daily Figures for Selected Main Economic Indicators (1949-79)	962
Birth, Death and Natural Growth Rates (1949-79)	962
National Labour Force Employment (1952-79)	963
Employment in State-Owned Sectors, By Sector (1952-79)	963
Wages and Employment in State-Owned Sectors (1952-79)	963
Wages and Employment in Collectively Owned Sectors in Cities and Towns (1965-79)	964
Fixed Assets of State-Owned Enterprises (1952-79)	964

(Cont'd next page)

LISTING OF CHARTS AND TABLES

(Cont'd)   Page

Use of Quota Circulating Funds by State-Owned Enterprises (1952-79)	964
National Income, Consumption and Accmulation (1952-79)	965
People's Communes in Rural Areas (1958-79)	965
Area of Cultivated Land (1949-79)	965
Gross Agricultural Output Value (1949-79)	966
Gross Output Value of Farm Products, Forestry, Animal Husbandry, Sideline Occupations and Fisheries (1949-79)	966
Output of Major Farm Products, Aquatic Products and Forest Products (1949-79)	967
Output Index of Farm Products, Aquatic Products and Forest Products (1957-79)	967
Hogs, Sheep and Goats and Meat Production (1952-79)	968
Major Farm Products, Average Output per Hectare (1949-79)	968
Per Capita Output of Grain, Cotton, Oil-Bearing Crops, Hogs and Aquatic Products (1949-79)	969
Large Animal Population (1949-79)	969
Major Agricultural Machinery (1957-79)	970
Agricultural Modernization (1952-79)	970
Index of Gross Output Value of Heavy and Light Industry (1949-79)	971
Gross Industrial Output Value (1952-79)	972
Index of Gross Industrial Output Value (1957-79)	972
Output Index of Major Industrial Products (1957-79)	973
Output of Major Industrial Products (1949-79)	974
Overall Labour Productivity of State-Owned Industrial Enterprises Using Independent Accounting (1952-79)	976
Main Financial Indicators for State-Owned Industrial Enterprises Using Independent Accounting (1952-79)	976
Postal and Telecommunications Transactions	976
Transportation Routes (1949-79)	977
Volume of Freight Transport (1949-79)	977
Volume of Passenger Transport (1949-79)	978
Freight and Passenger Transport (1952-79)	978
Main Indicators of Capital Construction for State-Owned Units (1950-79)	979
Retail Sales (1952-79)	980
Index of Retail Sales Value (1952-79)	980
Retail Sales of Consumer Goods (1952-79)	981
Index of Consumer Goods Retail Sales (1957-79)	981
Imports and Exports (Value) (1952-79)	982
Imports and Exports (Commodity Composition) (1952-79)	982
General Price Index (1952-79)	983
Price Indexes (at state list prices) (1952-79)	983
Price Index for State Retail List (by Commodity Groups) (1952-79)	984
Price Index for Purchasing List of Farm and Sideline Products (by Commodities) (1952-79)	984
State Revenues and Expenditures of Public Finance (1952-79)	985

(Cont'd next page)

LISTING OF CHARTS AND TABLES

(Cont'd)   Page

Savings Deposits in Urban and Rural Areas (1952-79)	985
Annual Consumption Per Capita (1952-79)	985
Basic Conditions of Families of Workers and Staff Members (1957-80)	986
Per Capita Consumption of Households in Rural People's Communes (1978, 1979)	986
Number of Enrolled Students in Schools at Various Levels (1949-79)	987
Teacher-Student Ratios in Schools of Various Levels (1952-79)	987
Health Institutions and Hospital Beds (1949-79)	987
Growth Indicators for Culture, Radio and Television Broadcasting (1949-79)	988
Industrial Output in 1980	989
Agricultural Output in 1980	991
Receipts and Payments of State Credit Funds (1979, 1980)	997
Deposits and Loans by Rural Credit Cooperatives (1979, 1980)	997
Exchange Rates, Foreign Exchange and Gold Reserves (1979, 1980)	997
Exchange Rates of RMB Yuan Against Foreign Currencies (1977-80)	1110

FOREWORD
By Xue Muqiao

This work is the first economic almanac of China to be published since the founding of the People's Republic of China. At the beginning of 1980, all units participating in the Economic Research Centre of the State Council decided to edit and publish this *Almanac of China's Economy*. With the support and cooperation of all ministries and commissions of the State Council and of the people's governments at provincial and municipal levels and in all autonomous regions, and thanks to the active efforts of staff members of the Economic Management Magazine, this almanac is at last ready for its readers. With the support of Japanese and American friends, the Japanese and English editions of the book are also being published. Comrades and friends both at home and abroad who are concerned about the development of China's economy should welcome this book.

Under the leadership of the Communist Party of China, the Chinese people overcame many hardships and difficulties, overthrew the three big mountains of imperialism, feudalism and bureaucrat-capitalism, emerged victorious in the revolution and, in 1949, founded the People's Republic of China. During the past 31 years, we have been carrying out socialist revolution and socialist construction in our poor, backward, and overpopulated country and have won unprecedented successes. However, our revolutionary path has not always gone smoothly. It has gone through many twists and turns and we have experienced successes as well as failures along the way.

After the smashing of the counter-revolutionary cliques of Lin Biao and Jiang Qing, the party's correct line was re-established along with the principle of readjustment, restructuring, consolidation and improvement formulated at the Third Plenary Session of the Party's 11th Central Committee. Thus, a new historical period began, emphasizing economic construction. Over the past two years a tremendous amount of work has been done. A series of principles and policies were formulated and experiences and lessons gleaned from economic construction during the past 30 years were summed up. As a result, China's socialist construction has embarked on a new road of seeking truth from facts. So far, it has been advancing steadily.

At this historic turning point, it is of great significance for us to edit and publish the first economic almanac since the founding of the People's Republic.

The party and government have shifted the emphasis of their work to economic construction. The whole Chinese people are confidently building a modern, powerful socialist country with a higher developed democratic structure and culture. Economic construction is not only a task for those who work in economic departments or who do research in this field. It is a task in which the entire Chinese people are engaged.

China's economic construction is an important component of the world economy. With the growth of its own economy, China will play an increasingly important role in the world's economy. Consequently, more people abroad will be taking an interest in how China's economy is faring.

Thus, in view of both domestic and international requirements, it is necessary to have an *Almanac of China's Economy* so as to systematically and accurately record China's general economic situation. Owing to lack of experience and the pressure of time, the contents of this almanac may not be comprehensive enough and there are bound to be mistakes. For the first time ever, however, this almanac is designed to provide a relatively complete picture of China's general economic situation, including statistical data which will be helpful to comrades and friends at home and abroad who are interested in China's economic development.

As the 1981 *Almanac* is also the first edition, it covers not only the economic situation of China in 1980, but also contains a general introduction to the basic situation during the years since 1949, including statistical information for that period. The *Almanac* will be published annually from now on and will serve as a historical record of the development of our national economy.

Our economy is now undergoing a great reform in its structure, system and organization. Reform must be guided by theory. The leading comrades in the Party Central Committee and in the State Council attach great importance to theoretical research. The Third Plenary Session of Party's 11th Central Committee reaffirmed the principle that practice is the only criterion of truth. It put forward the policy of emancipating our minds and seeking truth from facts. As a result, an unprecedentedly lively atmosphere has emerged in economic circles in which a hundrd flowers are in blossom and a hundred schools of thought are contending. This *Almanac* also includes some articles published since the Third Plenary

Session. Owing to time limitations, the selection may not be comprehensive, but these articles do reflect the latest developments in theory during the current period. In this respect, we hope that this *Almanac* will also serve as an "Almanac of Economics."

Everything is difficult at the beginning. We came across a host of difficulties in soliciting contributions and editing and in printing and publishing the 1981 *Almanac*. All those difficulties were overcome with the support and co-operation of all parties concerned. The publication of this book within a few months' time shows that under the socialist system, by relying on cooperation, anything can be done and can be done efficiently.

Owing to our lack of experience and to negligence in our work, this book has many shortcomings, such as in accepting or rejecting materials, in checking and co-ordinating statistical data, as well as in designing the format, collating the book and overseeing its printing quality. All criticisms and suggestions will be appreciated. We hope that as the *Almanac* is published in each successive year our economic construction will forge ahead. With the support and cooperation of our readers, we will make our almanac series richer in content and better in quality with each edition, and in this way contribute to the socialist modernization of our country.

EDITOR'S NOTES

1. The *Almanac of China's Economy* will be published annually. The contents of future issues will not repeat those of previous issues.

2. The 1981 *Almanac*, the first issued, takes 1980 data as the primary focus of its contents. It also gives a brief account of the general situation during the 30 years from 1949 to 1979. Part of the book carries data from the period following the Third Plenary Session of the 11th Party Central Committee held in December 1978.

3. The 1981 *Almanac* consists of eight sections:
   I. General Survey of China
   II. Major Economic Documents, Works of Economic Policy, Laws and Decrees (1978-81)
   III. Monographic Studies on Current Economic Policy
   IV. Survey of China's Economy
   V. Chinese Economic Theory
   VI. Economic Statistics
   VII. Chronology of Major Economic Events in China
   VIII. Appendix

4. Section I, "General Survey of China," provides materials on China's history, geography, party, government and mass organizations.

5. Section II, "Major Economic Documents, Works of Economic Policy, Laws and Decrees," is a chronological compilation of materials for the period dating from the Third Plenary Session of the 11th Party Central Committee up to the end of 1980.

While this book was being prepared, the Sixth Plenary Session of the 11th Central Committee was held and "Resolutions on Certain Historical Problems Within the Party Since the Founding of the People's Republic of China" and the important speech of Comrade Hu Yaobang were published. For chronological purposes, these important documents should have been part of the 1982 *Almanac;* however, because of their relevance, they have been included in this edition and placed at the beginning of Section II.

6. Monographic Studies on Current Economic Policy (Section III) were written especially for the *Almanac* by well-known Chinese economists. They express the personal opinions of the authors about the main problems facing our national economy.

7. The section on the "Survey of China's Economy" gives a general review of the economic situation in the different sectors and regions of China during the past 31 years, with emphasis on the situation in 1980. This section was prepared by experts who deal mainly with historical events but also express their personal views on current problems and trends. The general economic situation in 1981 will be dealt with in the 1982 edition of the *Almanac*.

8. Section V, "Chinese Economic Theory," broadly outlines our research on economic theory since the Third Plenary Session.

9. Section VI, "Economic Statistics," includes the bulletin of statistics for 1980 as well as principal statistics for the years 1949 to 1979. This data has been approved and verified by the State Statistical Bureau. This is the first occasion that these statistics have been made public.

Readers should note that Section IV, "Survey of China's Economy," includes statistics that may have been compiled through different methods. Thus, there may be discrepancies between these figures and those in Section VI. Readers studying a particular topic should take the statistics reported in Section VI as definitive.

10. Section VII, "Chronology of Major Economic Events in China," consists of events from the Third Plenary Session (December 1978) to the end of 1980.

11. This *Almanac* follows the principle of "letting a hundred flowers blossoms and a hundred schools of thought contend." The authors themselves are responsible for what they have written. They were required to base their writing on facts and to be accurate, but their views may differ. The editors have made changes only in wording and style.

12. Due to the complexity of the translation process, occasional discrepancies may occur between data published in the Chinese and English editions of the 1981 *Almanac*. In such cases, the Chinese-language edition should be regarded as definitive.

Editorial Department, *Almanac of China's Economy*   July 1982
Beijing

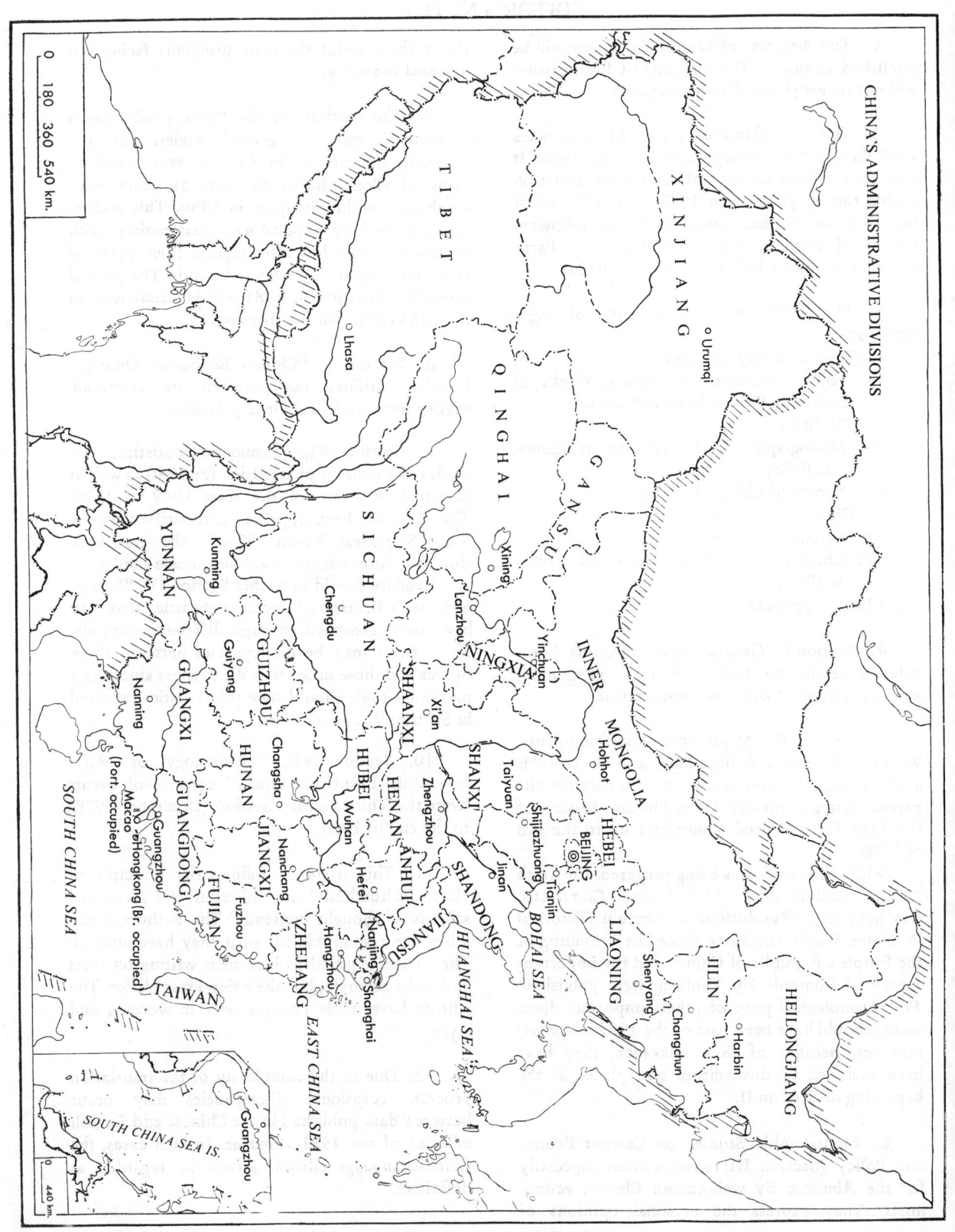

SECTION I:
GENERAL SURVEY OF CHINA

SECTION I:

GENERAL SURVEY OF CHINA

1. AN OUTLINE OF CHINESE HISTORY
By Zhu Jiazhen
*Institute of Economics,
Chinese Academy of Social Sciences*

China's Geographical Setting. Our great motherland is one of the largest countries in the world. Stretching from the Pamirs on the west to the Pacific Ocean on the east, from the Heilongjiang River in the north to the Nansha Islands in the south, China covers some 9,600,000 square kilometres in area, nearly equal in size to Europe. Within this vast territory, there are undulating mountains, criss-crossing rivers and expanses of rich land. The varied topography and climate give rise to widely different natural features in various areas as well as to abundant natural resources. Fertile plains produce rice, wheat, millet, corn, sorghum and beans, as well as cash crops, such as cotton, hemp, oilseeds and sugar. Luxuriant forests carpet the mountainous areas. Herds of cattle, sheep, horses, and camels are raised on extensive grasslands. Numerous rivers and lakes yield a variety of fish and aquatic products and are rich in hydroelectric power potential. Coal, iron, oil and other rare mineral resources lie hidden in the earth. From ancient times, the forefathers of the Chinese nation have laboured, lived and multiplied on this rich and beautiful land.

China's People. China's population of one billion includes many nationalities. Over 90% of the population are Hans, who inhabit about 40% of the country; the areas inhabited by the more than 50 minority races account for nearly 60%. Although their cultural development has differed, the nationalities all have long histories of their own. Throughout the long periods of historical development, the different nationalities, through mutual influence, constant intermingling, separation and merging, have together created China's splendid national culture.

Our motherland is also an important site in the development of mankind. The discovery of Peking Man, who lived about 500,000 years ago, and of the even earlier Lantian Man and Yuanmou Man, who lived about 1.7 million years ago, have testified to the presence of human activity in our vast country since remote antiquity.

Early Chinese Societies

Similar to many other nations of the world, the Chinese nation went through a long period as a society of primitive communes. Some 40-50,000 years ago, the primitive society entered a new stage of matrilineal clan communes, as evidenced by the remains of Liujiang Man, found in Guangxi, Ziyang Man, found in Sichuan, Hetao Man, found in Inner Mongolia, and Upper Cave Man, found at Zhoukoudian near Beijing. Evidence that the matrilineal clan communes were still thriving and prosperous about 6-7,000 years ago came to light with the discovery of the Yangshao Culture in the Huanghe River Valley.

Five thousand years ago, matrilineal clan communes gave way to patrilineal clan communes, an example of which was the Longshan Culture in the Huanghe River Valley. But, in ancient China, the pace of development of primitive society was uneven; the clan systems in the area from the middle and lower reaches of the Huanghe (Yellow) River to the Changjiang (Yangtze) River Valley developed more rapidly than those in other areas. Even in the same area, different clans developed in dissimilar ways. The Huangdi clan, which lived in the middle area and the later were revered as the ancestors of the Huaxia clan, was said to have developed more rapidly than all the others. Tang Yao and Yu Shun in ancient China, and the Xia, Shang and Zhou dynasties are all said to be descendants of the Huangdi clan.

Hereditary Kingships. The tradition of the crown being handed over by Yao to Shun and then to Yu reflected the rules and regulations of the primitive commune society. Around the 21st century B.C., Qi, son of Yu, broke with the tradition of handing over the crown and established the Xia Dynasty on a hereditary basis. This marked the collapse of the primitive commune system and the emergence of a society with the earliest slave-owning system. In the 16th century B.C., the Xia Dynasty was overthrown by the Shang clan living in the lower reaches of the Huanghe River. The rise of the Shang further advanced the slave-owning system. Then in the 11th century B.C., the Zhou clan in the middle reaches of the Huanghe River overthrew the Shang Dynasty and founded the Western Zhou Dynasty, with its system of enfeoffment. Later came the Spring and Autumn and Warring States periods, an era in which dukes and princes broke away from the central authorities and exercised their powers locally.

The Feudal Period. In 221 B.C., the Qin

Dynasty succeeded the Zhou Dynasty. After Qin Shihuang, the first Emperor of the Qin Dynasty, unified China, he set up an autocratic government with centralized power. From that time until the beginning of the Opium War in 1840, China remained a feudal society dominated by landlords. China's feudal society lasted more than 3,000 years after the Zhou and Qin dynasties; it was one of the longest periods of feudalism in the history of the world.

The Onset of Imperialism. After the Opium War, the capitalist and imperialist powers launched a series of aggressive wars against China and forced her to sign many unequal treaties, in order to occupy her territories by force, plunder her resources, extort war reparations, dominate her customs and communication lines, open banks, set up enterprises, monopolize her finances, and meddle in her internal affairs. As a result, China was reduced to the status of a semi-colony. At the same time, imperialist aggression wrecked China's self-centred national economy, hastened the disintegration of China's feudal economy, and spurred the development of her national bourgeoisie. But under the oppression of imperialism and feudalism, the development of China's national bourgeoisie was seriously hindered. Moreover, China's feudal forces formed an alliance with the imperialists to become the mainstay of the latter's rule over China. The combination of feudal exploitation and compradore capital — which served as capital for the imperialists as well as the usurers — turned China into a semi-feudal society. Imperialism and feudalism brought great suffering to the Chinese people, who struggled heroically against this twofold oppression.

The Taiping Rebellion and the Republic of China. In 1851, the Taiping Rebellion led by Hong Xiuquan established the revolutionary power of the peasants. The rebellion lasted for 14 years and its influence spread to 18 provinces; it demonstrated the Chinese people's indomitable spirit of revolt. After the failure of the Taiping movement, the Revolution of 1911 led by Dr. Sun Yat-sen overthrew the ruling Qing Dynasty and established the Republic of China, a bourgeois-democratic republic. However, faced with the opposition of the warlords and their manipulators — the imperialist powers — the democratic revolution of the old type led by Dr. Sun Yat-sen soon failed. China was thrown into long drawn-out wars among warlords.

The Russian Revolution in October 1917 brought Marxism-Leninism to China, and produced great repercussions. In 1919, the May 4th Movement broke out in opposition to imperialism and feudalism. The movement's thoroughness and lack of compromise demonstrated that the anti-imperialist and anti-feudalist bourgeois-democratic revolution had entered a new stage; it marked the beginning of the new democratic revolution led by the proletariat of China. After the May 4th Movement, came the gradual integration of Marxism-Leninism and the Chinese Workers' Movement. In July 1921, the first group of Marxists in China held the First National Congress of the Chinese Communist Party in Shanghai. The establishment of the Chinese Communist Party brought the disaster-ridden Chinese people their most reliable leadership. Thereafter, the Chinese revolution took on an entirely new look.

Growth of the Revolutionary Movement. In 1924, with the help of the Chinese Communist Party, Dr. Sun Yat-sen reshuffled his party, the Kuomingtang, convened its first National Congress, and formulated his three main policies: "Ally with the Russians, with the Chinese Communist Party and help the workers and peasants." The formation of the united front between the Chinese Communist Party and the Kuomingtang enabled the revolutionary movements of workers and peasants to make great strides forward.

After Dr. Sun Yat-sen's death in 1925, the Guangdong Revolutionary Government was reorganized to form the National Government. The following year, the National Government, pushed by the Chinese Communist Party, launched the Northern Expedition, aimed at overthrowing imperialists, warlords, and wiping out feudal forces. Warmly welcomed and sincerely supported by workers, peasant and revolutionaries, the revolutionary tide spread to the Changjiang and Huanghe river valleys in less than six months. The successful advance of the Northern Expedition and the rapid development of revolutionary movements seriously undermined the reactionary rule of imperialists and their lackeys.

While restorting directly to armed intervention, the imperialists lured the bourgeoisie into betraying the revolution. In April 1927, Chiang Kai-shek, who usurped the post of commander-in-chief of the national revolutionary forces, staged a counter-revolutionary coup d'etat and slaughtered many Communists and revolutionaries. Hence, the First Revolutionary Civil War ended in failure. Later on, the Chinese Workers and Peasants Red Army established a revolutionary base in the Jinggang Mountains near the Hunan-Jiangxi border and its central revolutionary base at Ruijin in Jiangxi Province. There it formulated its strategy of conducting far-reaching agrarian reform in the rural areas and then encircling and capturing the cities.

The Long March. In October 1934, the Central Red Army withdrew from its base in Jiangxi and began its world-famous Long March, which covered 25,000 *li**. In October 1935, the Red Army succeeded in reaching Northern Shaanxi. During the Second Revolutionary Civil War, which lasted from 1927 to 1937, the Chinese people, under the leadership of the Chinese Communist Party, waged an extremely arduous and heroic struggle.

The Lugouqiao Incident, staged by the Japanese imperialists on July 7, 1937, marked the beginning of a nationwide war against Japanese aggression. During the eight-year anti-Japanese war, the Chinese Communist Party beat back three anti-Communist offensives launched by the Kuomintang and exposed their plots to surrender to the Japanese imperialists. In August 1945, with Japan's unconditional surrender, the Chinese people won a great victory. But in 1946, shortly after the victory over Japan, Chiang Kai-shek, backed by the U.S. imperialists, launched on all-out civil war. After three years of people's war, the Chinese people finally wiped out Chiang Kai-shek's armed forces and overthrew his reactionary rule.

Founding of the People's Republic of China

In October 1949, the People's Republic of China was founded and the Chinese people, led by the Chinese Communist Party, marched into a new era of socialism.

Within three years of its founding, New China had healed the wounds of long drawn-out wars, successfully completed the agrarian reform movement and the movement to suppress counter-revolutionaries left over from the democratic revolution, and launched campaigns to eradicate the "three evils" and the "five evils."

During the war to resist U.S. aggression and aid Korea, China's economy was restored to the highest level it had achieved under the old regime. Upon this foundation began the First Five-Year Plan to develop the national economy. In the countryside, the completion of agrarian reform was followed by a series of measures based on the principle of voluntary participation and mutual benefit. With some units setting an example, the transition was made from mutual aid teams to elementary and advanced agricultural producers' cooperatives. Thus the peasants were led smoothly onto the road of agricultural cooperation. In the cities, the socialist transformation of capitalist industry and commerce was carried out as follows: state orders were placed with private enterprises for the processing of materials or the supply of manufactured goods; a state monopoly was set up for purchase and marketing; products of state-owned enterprises were marked by private shops; and joint state-private ownership of enterprises was started. The historical task of peaceful transformation of the capitalist sector of the economy was thus successfully accomplished.

Socialist Transformation of the Economy. In 1957, following the successful completion of the First Five-Year Plan, China embarked on the socialist transformation of agriculture, handicrafts and capitalist industry and commerce.

In the 31 years since Liberation, China's socialist economy has achieved tremendous successes. Compared with the years immediately after Liberation, production of grain has increased by 2.7 times, cotton by 4.9 times; meanwhile, the iron and steel, power, oil, coal, chemical, engineering, light and textile industries have developed greatly and many new industries have emerged. Especially in the vast inland and minority nationality regions, where there were few industries before Liberation, a great many new industrial bases have been built. Industrial enterprises in China now number 350,000. Fixed assets of state-owned enterprises amount to 320,000 billion yuan, 25 times the total industrial fixed assets accumulated in the last 100 years prior to Liberation. Progress in communications and transportation, as well as posts and telecommunications has opened up many places which were once inaccessible. Domestic and foreign trade are flourishing, and the people's living standard has risen considerably.

With the development of the socialist economy, the ranks of intellectuals are growing steadily. The total number of students in school amounts to 210 million, more than seven times the number in the peak year before Liberation. China's achievements in science and technology are evidenced by the successful tests of the atom bomb, hydrogen bomb and guided missiles, the launching and retrieving of man-made satellites and the production of synthetic bovine insulin, etc. China's system of free medical service and cooperative medical service has virtually eradicated acute infectious diseases; as a result, mortality has dropped greatly while the general health of the population has markedly improved. The tremendous achievements and experiences gained in socialist construction have laid a solid foundation for the realization of the four modernizations, and for the building of a socialist society with high economic and moral standards.

China's Scientific Achievements

The Contributions of Ancient China. China,

---

*One *li* equals half a kilometre.

one of the world's most ancient countries, has a civilization over 4,000 years old. Early in the Xia Dynasty, about 4,000 years ago, the first astronomic calendar, the Lunar Calendar, was invented and the earliest system of characters was formed. In the Shang Dynasty, more than 3,000 years ago, the technology for smelting bronze and then iron was developed. In ceramics, China's white pottery and glazed pottery achieved a quality close to that of primitive chinaware. The flourishing art of silk weaving led to the earliest jacquard weaving in the world. Significant technical achievements were also made in the manufacture of lacquerware, tanning hides, working with wood and bamboo, building vessels and vehicles, architecture, etc. Musical instruments were made of gold, stone, bamboo, wood, leather, silk, pottery and other materials. In the wake of the division of labour and exchange, metal money and copper coins as well as historical documents, ancient books and records in written form came into being. Much knowledge concerning the astronomic calendar, mathematical formulas, medical science and hygiene was contained in oracle instructions.

In the Western Zhou Dynasty, bronze tools were widely employed in farming, and iron-smelting and tile-making became specialized. The technological level of glazed pottery approached that of chinaware. Both the vehicle and ship building industries were further developed, and articles crafted of jade, such as "Guibi," reflected a very high level of technological sophistication. With the development of the exchange economy in this period, markets appeared in big cities.

During the Spring and Autumn Period, steelmaking came into existence; mathematics became an independent subject; achievements in geometry were quite successful, while other branches of learning, such as geography, biology, medical science, materia medica and veterinary science all developed considerably. Prior to the Warring States Period, great advances were made in mathematics, mechanics, mechanical manufacturing, medical science and astronomy. Among the achievements were: "Ju Gao," an artificial irrigation device operating on the level principle; a crossbow device constructed on the basis of a wheel axle; and the chronograph called the "Dripping-Hourglass" by later generations. The invention of the compass made a particularly brilliant contribution to the civilization of mankind. In astronomy, a tremendous achievement was "Gan Shi Xing Jing," the first list of fixed stars in the world which recorded 800 fixed stars and gave the positions of 120 of them. In medical science, there was "Huang Di Nei Jing," the first medical book in Chinese history. The period also produced the famous artisan Gong Shuban, and the renowned doctor Bian Que.

Han Dynasty Contributions. During the Han Dynasty, the outstanding astronomer, Zhang Heng, invented the armillary sphere, to study astronomical phenomena, and the surmograph, to detect earthquakes. Cai Lun invented the science of papermaking, which spread from China to Japan via Korea in the 7th Century, to Arabia in the 8th century and to Europe in the 12th century, making a great contribution to culture and science the world over.

In the Eastern Han Dynasty, the famous "Arithmetic of Nine Chapters" was completed, making an important contribution to the history of mathematics in the world while marking the formation of a perfect system in China's ancient mathematics. The first complete work on materia medica and botany, "Shen Nong Ben Cao Jing," was also written at this time. It was during the Han Dynasty, the first stable and prosperous period in China's history under centralized rule, that large-scale water-conservation projects were built, opening up and irrigating vast areas of land, and newly developed farming tools and techniques were popularized, thus promoting the advancement of agriculture. Further advances were made in the iron and steel, ceramics, silk weaving and other handicraft industries. For example, the invention of the picture-weaving machine toward the end of the Western Han and the beginning of the Eastern Han Dynasty made it possible to weave truly exquisite silks.

During the Han Dynasty, both domestic and foreign trade flourished, turning many large cities like Luoyang, Handan, Linzi, and Chengdu into commercial centres, while Chang'an became the national centre of domestic and foreign trade. Having defeated the Xiongnu aggressors many times, the Han Dynasty sent large numbers of people to settle in the border areas and open up vast farm lands, thus pacifying the frontiers, promoting the development of economy and culture in border areas, and paving the way for economic and cultural exchange with foreign countries. Zhang Qian travelled to the Western Regions in the Western Han Dynasty, and Ban Chao was sent there as an envoy in the Eastern Han Dynasty. Both rendered memorable service in cementing relations between the Han Empire and the nations of the Western Regions.

Thereafter, various kinds of products, musical instruments and Indian Buddhist philosophy and arts were brought from the West to China, while many aspects of Western Han culture travelled to the West. In return, the transmission of China's advanced production technology to the Western

Regions accelerated the latter's economic and cultural development. The sons of nobles in the Western Regions frequently were sent to Chang'an to study Han culture. China's elegant and gorgeous silk articles, shipped to Europe through Persia, were prized by Europeans, and the road from China to Persia became famous as the "Silk Road," a symbol for the exchange of economy, culture and friendship between the Chinese and Western peoples. China's steel-making technology was also disseminated to the West at that time, promoting the development of Western civilization.

At the time of the Northern and Southern dynasties, the famous scientist Zu Chongzhi was the first to calculate accurately the numerical valve of the ratio of the circumference of a circle to its diameter as between 3.1415926 and 3.1415927. He was the first person in the world who arrived at seven figures after the decimal point. The "Da Ming Calendar," also worked out by Zu Chongzhi, determined the exact number of days of one tropical year as 365.24281481, and the period in which the moon circles the earth as 29.21222 days. Compared with the results obtained by using modern means of calculation, his error was merely a few seconds.

In the Northern Wei Dynasty, Li Daoyuan produced the "Shui Jing Zhu," an outstanding work on the history and geography of ancient China, and Jia Sisi completed his "Important Principles for Farmers," China's first comprehensive text about farming. The technique of steel-pouring, developed during the Northern Qi Dynasty, greatly improved steelmaking.

Contributions of the Sui, Tang, Song, Yuan, Ming and Qing. The technology of block printing was developed during the 6th century, under the Sui Dynasty. At the beginning of this dynasty, the artisan Li Chun built the Zhaozhou Bridge, the world's oldest single-arch stone bridge still in existence. Constructed 700 years before the Selei Bridge was built in France in 1312, the Zhaozhou Bridge remained in good condition even after the big earthquake in Xingtai in 1966.

The Tang Dynasty, another great period in Chinese history, was marked by a thriving economy and culture, flourishing agriculture, advanced handicrafts and brisk trade. At that time, weaving, dyeing, ceramics, smelting, metalcasting, printing, papermaking, shipbuilding and other industries all developed considerably. Many large, densely populated cities with a multitude of shops sprang up and a network of land and water communication lines, with over a thousand posts, extended all over the country. Also during the Tang Dynasty, the monk Yixing edited the "Da Yan Calendar" and discovered the phenomenon of the movement of fixed stars. He was also the first man in the world to survey the meridian line.

As a result of repeated victories in repulsing invasions by the Western and Eastern Tujue, the Tang Dynasty cleared up frontier troubles and extended the land and water routes leading to foreign countries. Among them were the route leading to Central Asia and Europe, the route from Sichuan to Nepal and India and the route from Yunnan to Burma. China's huge ships navigated the turbulent waves of the Persian Gulf. Communications with foreign countries in the Tang Dynasty expanded beyond the "Silk Road." Numerous economic and cultural contacts were established with Korea, Japan, India, Pakistan, Ceylon, Afghanistan, Iran, Arabia, etc. Contacts with Japan were especially profuse; on 13 occasions, Japan sent large numbers of students and Buddhist monks to China to study the Han culture, and the Chinese monk Jian Zhen made several voyages to Japan. The areas influenced by Tang China's politics, economy and culture extended from Japan in the east across Congling in the west to the eastern coast of the Caspian Sea. The Eastern Roman Empire (called Da Qin since the time of the Han Dynasty) frequently sent diplomatic envoys to China. The brilliant culture of the Sui and Tang dynasties profoundly infuenced the ancient civilizatons of Europe and Asia.

During the Northern Song Dynasty, Bi Sheng invented typography 400 years before the Europeans; Shen Kuo compiled the "Meng Xi Bi Tan," China's first encyclopedia, which covered the development of ancient science and technology; and Wang Weiyi, a medical scientist in acupuncture and moxibustion, devised the "Chart of Acupunctural Curing Points on a Copper Model," a great contribution to this subject.

In the Yuan Dynasty, the methods of tin and wood-block printing were perfected on the basis of Bi Sheng's typography. This achievement soon spread to Iran, then to Europe and all over the world, contributing greatly to the development of the world's culture. In 1280, the scientist Guo Shoujing worked out the "Shou Shi Calendar," which took 365.2425 days as one year, the same as the present-day Gregorian calendar. In 1313, the agronomist Wang Zhen wrote the massive 300,000-word "Book on Agriculture," the most comprehensive encyclopedia on farming after Jia Sisi's "Important Principles for Farmers."

Gunpowder, which was invented long ago in China, was first used for military purposes in the Tang Dynasty. In the Southern Song Dynasty, its use spread to Arabia and then to Europe. But the application of gunpowder and firearms in Europe came at least 300 years later than in China. In the

Yuan Dynasty, cannons cast with copper pipes appeared, a turning point in the world's history of weaponry.

In the Ming Dynasty, China produced a great number of important works in science and technology, including: "The Compendium of Materia Medica" by Li Shizhen; "The Encyclopedia of Agricultural Management" by the agronomist Xu Guangqi; "The Adventure of Xu Xiake" by the geographer Xu Hongzu; and "Tian Gong Kai Wu," a book on agriculture and handicrafts by Song Yingxing.

In the Qing Dynasty, further contributions to the development of modern science and technology were made by the mathematician Wang Xichan, astronomer Mei Wending, botanist Wu Qijun, and especially railway engineer Zhan Tianyou and hydraulic engineer Li Yirang.

Contributions Under the People's Republic. Since the founding of the People's Republic of China, many scientists and technical specialists like Li Siquang have made great contributions on different fronts to China's socialist construction. For thousands of years, the valiant and industrious Chinese people have enriched the treasure-house of science and human civilization with their intelligence and wisdom.

China is a nation which ardently loves liberty and is imbued with revolutionary traditions. During the thousands of years of feudal rule, there were hundreds of peasant uprisings and wars against aggression. Many revolutionary leaders and national heroes, such as Yue Fei, Wen Tianxiang, Qi Jiquang, and Zheng Chenggong have emerged. Their unswerving loyalty to the motherland and dauntless heroism in struggle embodied the great patriotism of the Chinese people. The Chinese nation has always been a nation with glorious revolutionary traditions and patriotic spirit.

The Chinese people have in their long history fashioned a very rich culture and civilization. For thousands of years, China has produced many outstanding thinkers, statesmen, military strategists, writers, historians, and revolutionaries. Among the thinkers are: Lao Dan, Kong Qiu (Confucius), Me Di, Shang Yang, Meng Ke (Mencius), Zhuang Zhou, Xun Kuang, Han Fei, Lu Jia, Ja Yi, Dong Zhongshu, Wang Chong, Ran Ji, Ji Kang, Fan Zhen, Xuan Zhuang, Li Gou, Wang Anshi, Ye Shi, Zhu Xi, Li Zhi, Huang Zongxi, Gu Yanwu, Wang Fuzhi, Dai Zhen, Gong Zizhen, Hong Rengan, Yan Fu, Kang Youwei, Liang Qichao, Tan Sitong, Zhu Zhixin and Zhang Taiyan. Among the writers and historians are: Qu Yuan, Si Maqian, Ban Gu, Zheng Xuan, Tao Qian, Liu Zhiji, Li Bai, Du Fu, Han Yu, Liu Zongyuan, Liu Yuxi, Si Maguang, Ou Yangxiu, Su Shi, Li Qingzhao, Lu You, Xin Qiji, Wang Shifu, Guan Hanqing, Shi Naian, Luo Guanzhong, Wu Chengen, Pu Songling, Cao Xueqin, Lu Xun, and Guo Moruo. Chinese statesmen include: Ying Zhen, Liu Bang, Cao Cao, Zhu Geliang, Li Shimin, Songzan Ganbu, Zhu Yuanzhang, Aixin Jueluo Xuan Hua. Some military strategists are: Sun Wu, Wu Qi, Sun Bin, Wei Qing, Huo Qubing, Gengis Khan. And famous revolutionaries include: Chen Sheng, Wu Guang, Zhang Jiao, Hunag Chao, Zhong Xiang Li Zicheng, Hong Xiuquan, Sun Yatsen, Li Dazhao, Qu Qiubai, Mao Zedong, Zhou Enlai, Liu Shaoqi and Zhu De. Their outstanding thoughts and deeds as well as their talented administration and military accomplishments in history have radiated for thousands of years with the brilliance of thought and culture of the great Chinese nation.

Countless Chinese sages had made great contributions to enrich the culture and civilization of mankind. Enslavement and invasion by capitalist powers in the last hundred years seriously hindered the development of China's social economy, science and culture. But the Chinese people fought heroically and, eventually, under the leadership of the Chinese Communist Party, overthrew the three big mountains (imperialism, feudalism, bureaucrat capitalism) and paved the way for the rejuvenation of the Chinese nation. Comrade Mao Zedong said in 1949: "Since they learned Marxism-Leninism, the Chinese people have ceased to be passive in spirit and seized the initiative. That period of modern world history in which the Chinese and Chinese culture were looked down upon should have ended from that moment. The great, victorious Chinese People's War of Liberation and the people's revolution have rejuvenated and are rejuvenating the great culture of the Chinese people."

In the past 31 years, the Chinese people, led by the Chinese Communist Party, have made gratifying achievements in socialist revolution and construction despite twists and turns. While assimilating the advanced science and culture of foreign countries, the Chinese people are determined to uphold the glorious traditions of their own time-honoured culture and to struggle to realize the modernization of socialism as well as the prosperity of the motherland. Comrade Mao Zedong once predicted: "By the year 2001, at the beginning of the 21st century, China will have undergone an even greater change. It will have become a powerful industrial socialist country. And that is as it should be. China is a country with an area of 9,600,000 square kilometres and a population of 600 million, and it ought to make a greater contribution to humanity." The 21st century is bound to be an age in which the Chinese people will write even more brilliant pages in history.

A BRIEF CHRONOLOGY OF CHINESE HISTORY

	Xia Dynasty		circa 2100–1600 B.C.
	Shang Dynasty		circa 1600–1066 B.C.
Zhou Dynasty	Western Zhou Dynasty		circa 1066–771 B.C.
	Eastern Zhou Dynasty Spring and Autumn Period Warring States		770–256 B.C. 722–481 B.C. 403–221 B.C.
	Qin Dynasty		221–206 B.C.
Han Dynasty	Western Han		206 B.C. – 23 A.D.
	Eastern Han		25–220
Three Kingdoms	Wei		220–265
	Shu		221–263
	Wu		221–280
	Western Jin Dynasty		265–316
Eastern Jin Sixteen Kingdoms	Eastern Jin Dynasty		317–420
	Sixteen Kingdoms		304–439
Northern and Southern Dynasties	Southern Dynasties	Song	420–479
		Qi	479–502
		Liang	502–557
		Chen	557–589
	Northern Dynasties	Northern Wei	386–534
		Eastern Wei	534–550
		Northern Qi	550–577
		Western Wei	535–557
		Northern Zhou	557–581
	Sui Dynasty		581–618
	Tang Dynasty		618–907
Five Dynasties and Ten Kingdoms	Later Liang		907–923
	Later Tang		923–936
	Later Jin		936–946
	Later Han		947–950
	Later Zhou		951–960
	Ten Kingdoms		902–979

(continued next page)

Song Dynasty	Northern Song Dynasty	960–1127
	Southern Song Dynasty	1127–1279
	Liao Dynasty	916–1125
	Western Xia	1032–1227
	Jin Dynasty	1115–1234
	Yuan Dynasty	1279–1368
	Ming Dynasty	1368–1644
	Qing Dynasty	1644–1911
	Republic of China	1912–1949

2. AN OUTLINE OF CHINA'S NATURAL GEOGRAPHY
By Niu Wenyuan and Zhao Songchiao
*Institute of Geography,
Chinese Academy of Sciences*

I. Territory and Location

China has a territory of 9.6 million square kilometres, which accounts for 6.5% of the total land area on the globe. Next to the Soviet Union and Canada, it is the third largest of the more than 150 countries of the world. Its territory is about the size of Europe, which embraces 32 countries.

The eastern tip of China's territory is located at longitude 135°5′E., at the confluence of the Usuli River and the Heilongjiang River to the east of Fuyuan County, in Heilongjiang Province. The western tip is at 73°40′E., in the Pamirs, west of Wuqia County in the Xinjiang Uygur Autonomous Region. From east to west, the country extends for 5,200 kilometres, straddling 62 degrees of longitude, with a time difference of more than four hours. China's territory from north to south measures over 5,500 kilometres, starting in the north from the middle section of the Heilongjiang River north of Mohe in Heilongjiang Province, reaching in the south the Zengmu Reef on the southern tip of the Nansha Islands. The entire land boundary measures 22,800 kilometres.

Territorial Waters and Coastline. In addition to vast land territory, China has immense territorial waters and numerous islands. To the east of China's mainland, from north to south, are the Yellow Sea, the East China Sea and the South China Sea. The Bohai Sea, enclosed by the Shandong Peninsula and the Liaodong Peninsula, is the country's inland sea. The entire coastline from the mouth of the Yalu River in the north to the mouth of the Beilun River in the south extends for more than 18,000 kilometres. If the coastline of the offshore islands is included, the total length of China's boundaries exceeds 32,000 kilometres, one of the longest coastlines in the world.

Islands. China has more than 5,000 islands, big and small, with a total area of some 80,000 square kilometres. Taiwan is the biggest island, with an area of 35,760 square kilometres, followed by Hainan Island, with an area of 32,200 square kilometres.

China occupies a unique position on the globe: (1) Its land area in the Northern Hemisphere totals 9.56×10^7 square kilometres, almost twice as big as the area of 5.32×10^7 square kilometres located in the Southern Hemisphere. The former is usually regarded as the hemisphere of land and the latter as the hemisphere of water. (2) Two-thirds of China is located in the Eastern Hemisphere, which has a land area of 10.23×10^7 square kilometres, and one-third of it is in the Western Hemisphere, with an area of 4.65×10^7 square kilometres. The former is called the hemisphere of land and the latter the hemisphere of water. (3) The land area located in the eastern half of the Northern Hemisphere measures 7.14×10^7 square kilometres, three times as large as that in the western part, which is 2.42×10^7 square kilometres. From the above, one can see that China is situated in an area of the world where land is most concentrated.

China is situated in the eastern part of Asia, the largest continent on the globe, on the western edge of the world's biggest ocean, the Pacific Ocean, and most of its territory is in the middle latitudes. This location explains the extraordinary features of China's natural geography: the monsoon climate prevails, temperate and subtropical zones together account for 71.7% of the country's total area, and humid (plus semi-humid) areas and arid (plus semi-arid) areas each make up 50% of the country's total land mass.

Korea borders China in the northeast; the Soviet Union in the northeast and southwest; the People's Republic of Mongolia in the north; Afghanistan and Pakistan in the west; India, Nepal, Bhutan and Sikkim in the southwest; and Burma, Laos and Vietnam in the south. To the east and southeast, across the sea, China faces Japan, the Philippines, Malaysia, Indonesia, etc.

II. Contours of the Landform

Generally speaking, China's terrain is high in the west and low in the east, sloping down like a staircase. There are roughly four stairs from west to east: The Qinghai-Tibet Plateau in the southwest forms the highest stair with an average altitude of more than 4,000 metres above sea level; it is known as "the roof of the world." The second stair starts from the outer rim of the Qinghai-Tibet Plateau and extends eastward to the Da Xinggan, Taihang, Wushan and Xuefeng mountains. It includes vast plateaus such as the Inner Mongolia Plateau, the Loess Plateau and the Yunnan-Guizhou Plateau, and broad basins such as the

Tarim Basin, the Junggar Basin and the Sichuan Basin, with an average height of 1,000–2,000 metres. The third stair starts from the line linking the above-mentioned mountains and stretches eastward to the coast. Basically it comprises areas where low mountains, hills and plains alternate with each other, most areas being below 500 metres. At this level are China's biggest plains, such as the Northeast Plain, the North China Plain and the Middle-Lower Changjiang Plain. The fourth stair is an extension of the China mainland into the ocean, or the continental shelf, forming China's inland sea, the Bohai Sea, and the marginal seas — the Yellow, East China and South China seas — with waters generally less than 200 metres deep.

If a line is drawn from the Helan Mountains through the Liupan and Longmen mountains to the Ailau Mountains, dividing China into eastern and western parts, the areas west of this line have huge differences in topographical heights and marked vertical zonality, while the areas east of this line display relatively small differences in topographical heights but great latitudinal zonation.

Mountainous Areas. China has a complex terrain and numerous mountains. Mountains, plateaus and hills together make up 65% of the country's total area. Calculated in terms of their height, the areas less than 500 metres above sea level account for only 16% of the country's total land; areas between 500 and 1,000 metres above sea level make up about 19%; those between 1,000 and 2,000 metres about 28%; those between 2,000 and 5,000 metres about 18%; and those exceeding 5,000 metres 19%. There are 12 peaks in the world surpassing 8,000 metres above sea level and 7 of them are in China. Mount Qomolangma [Mount Everest – Ed.], the world's highest peak, is located on the border between China and Nepal. After repeated measuring by various means, Chinese surveyors have established the absolute height of the world's highest peak to be 8,848.13 metres. Between Mount Qomolongma and Lake Aydingkol (a dried up lake ed at 154 metres below sea level) in the Turpan Depression of Xinjiang, which is the second lowest point on the globe, the difference in topographical height is great than 9,000 metres, a phenomemon unknown in other parts of the world.

According to their arrangement and orientations, China's mountains can be divided into the following systems:

A. *East–west ranges:* Mainly the Tianshan-Yinshan-Yanshan Mountains, the Kunlun-Qinling-Dabie Mountains, the Nanling Mountains.

B. *North–south ranges:* Mainly the Helan Mountains, the Liupan Mountains and the Hengquan Mountains.

C. *North–east ranges:* Mainly mountains controlled by the Cathysian tectonic system, such as the Changbai, Da Hinggan, Taihang and Wushan mountains.

D. *North–west ranges:* These include and the Altay Mountains and the Qilian Mountains.

E. *Arc-shaped ranges:* Chiefly the Himalaya Mountains and the mountains in Taiwan.

The interweaving of different ranges forms a huge network of mountains, which constitutes the basic framework of China's topographical pattern.

In macrostructure, China's terrain can be divided into three zones: (1) The eastern humid moonsoon zone, in which running water plays a key role; (2) the northwest arid zone, in which denudation by wind and running water play an equally important role; and (3) the Qinghai-Tibet Plateau zone, where frost plays a major role.

III. China's Coastal Seas

Contiguous to China's mainland are four seas, namely, the Bohai Sea, the Yellow Sea, the East China Sea and the South China Sea. The Bohai is China's only inland sea.

The four seas form an arc running from northeast to southwest, encircling the country's eastern and southeastern coasts. They straddle temperate, subtropical and tropical zones with a total area of over 4.7 million square kilometres. The dividing line between the Bohai Sea and the Yellow Sea runs from the Laotieshan Cape on the southern end of the Liaodong Peninsula through the Miaodao Islands to the Penglai Cape on the northern end of the Shandong Peninsula. The Yellow Sea is divided from the East China Sea by a line running from the northern bank of the mouth of the Changjiang (Yangtze) River to the southwestern corner of Korea's Cheju-do Island. The division between the South China Sea and the East China Sea runs from the southern tip of Dongshan Island in Fujian Province through the southern side of the Taiwan shoals to Eluanbi on the southern tip of Taiwan Island.

Bohai Sea. The Bohai Sea is an almost completely enclosed shallow body of water encircled by the mainland on the west, north and south, and linking up with the Yellow Sea in the east through the Bohai Straits, which are 57 nautical miles wide. With an area of 77,000 square kilometres, the Bohai Sea has an average depth of 18 metres, the deepest place being 70 metres. The three big bays of the Bohai Sea are Liaodong Bay in the north, Bohai Bay in the west and Laizhou Bay in the south.

The Yellow Sea is a half-enclosed shallow sea with an area of some 380,000 square kilometres. Situated entirely on the continental shelf, it has an average depth of 44 metres, the deepest place being about 140 metres. Adjoining the China mainland to the west and facing Haizhou Bay and Jiaozhou Bay, the Yellow Sea touches on the Korean Peninsula in the east and meets the East China Sea in the south.

East China Sea. The East China Sea is an open shallow sea with an area of 770,000 square kilometres and an average depth of 370 metres, the deepest place being 2,719 metres. To the east of the China mainland, it adjoins the Yellow Sea in the north and links up with the South China Sea through the Taiwan Straits in the south.

South China Sea. The South China Sea is a large deep sea basin with an area of 3.5 million square kilometres and an average depth of 1,212 metres, the deepest place being 5,559 metres. Touching the China mainland in the north, it faces the Pacific Ocean beyond the Philippine Islands and the Indian Ocean beyond the Sunda Islands, and borders on the Indo-China Peninsula and the Malay Peninsula in the west. It links up with the East China Sea through the Taiwan Straits, with the Pacific Ocean through the Bashi Channel and Balintang Channel, with the Sulu Sea through the Mindoro Strait and the Balabac Strait, with the Java Sea through the Karimata Strait and the Gelasa (Gaspar) Strait, and with the Indian Ocean through the Straits of Malacca and the Singapore Strait.

If a line is drawn from Hainan Island through Taiwan to the Wudao Islands, we find a gentle continental shelf area, or extension of the China mainland northwest of this line; and an area with complex terrain, including continental slopes, sea troughs or deep sea basins southeast of this line. The continental shelf takes up a large proportion of China's offshore seas. It is generally more than 100 nautical miles wide, with a gradient of less than 0°02' and a depth of around 100 metres.

China's offshore seas are studded with numerous islands, a multitude of harbours, good fishing grounds and wide beaches; they are also rich in oil resources, raw materials for the chemical industry and marine life. All this adds up to excellent potential for the development of China's marine industry.

IV. Monsoonal Climate

China's vast territory embraces a wide variety of climates. On the basis of temperature, the country can be divided into six temperature zones from south to north: the equatorial zone, tropical zone, subtropical zone, warm-temperate zone, temperate zone and frigid-temperate zone. This division was made by the Natural Regionalization Committee of the Academy of Sciences of China in accordance with the aggregate active temperature of the period in which the average daily temperature equals or exceeds 10°C. The natural features corresponding to each zone are shown in Table 2.

According to moisture conditions, the area from the East China coasts to the northwest hinterlands can be divided into humid, semi-humid, semi-arid and arid regions. If aridity is taken as the main reference index, the country can be divided into: (1) A humid region, accounting for 32.2% of the country's total area, in which aridity is less than 1.0, precipitation exceeds evaporation, and natural vegetation is forest; (2) A semi-humid region, accounting for 14.5% of the country's total area, in which aridity is 1.0–1.5, precipitation roughly equals evaporation, and natural vegetation is forest grassland; (3) A semi-arid region, accounting for 21.7% of the country's total area, in which aridity is 1.5–2.0, evaporation exceeds precipitation, and natural vegetation is dry grassland; and (4) An arid region, accounting for 30.8% of the country's total area, in which aridity is greater than 2.0, evaporation far exceeds precipitation, and natural vegetation is desert grassland and desert.

Monsoonal Characteristics. Owing to differences in the heat-absorbing capacity of the continent and the ocean, the seasonal displacement of the planetary wind belt and other factors, China has a typical monsoonal climate: in winter, northeast and northwest winds prevail; in summer, southeast and southwest winds prevail. Due to the cyclical movement of the monsoons and the terrain, the country has four distinct seasons with rainfall concentrated in the hot season. The cold wave, cylones, seasonal rains and typhoons are responsible for the types of climate usually seen in China. As southeastern China is close to the ocean, the humid southeast monsoon not only directly affects the southern provinces in summer, causing humid and hot weather, but also penetrates into the hinterland. The increase in precipitation along with the rise in temperature creates the most favourable conditions for agriculture. In most areas, rainfall is concentrated mainly in the six summer months from May to October — particularly July, August and September. From southeast to northwest, precipitation decreases, the rainy season becomes progressively shorter and more concentrated, and precipitation variability becomes greater. For instance, the isopleth of average annual precipitation of 400 mm between the Songliao Plain in the northeast and the Inner Mongolia Plateau divides the region into two parts: the eastern part belongs to the humid and semi-humid region, while the western part belongs to the semi-arid and arid region.

Continental Factors. Another outstanding feature of China's climate is its strong continental character. This is not only manifested strikingly in the northwest hinterlands which are scarcely affected by the oceanic air stream, but also shows clearly in the eastern and southern humid regions which are close to the ocean. It finds expression mainly in the country's highly variable temperatrue and precipitation and the great differences between their extremes. Take the mean temperature of January and July, for instance. Winter temperatures in China are much lower than those on other continents at the same latitudes while summer temperatures are much higher. The mean January temperature of Huma in Heilongjiang Province is −27.7°C while that of London, which is on the same latitude, is 4°C, a difference of 31.7°C.

Tibet has winter all year round; most other areas are cold in winter and hot in summer with four distinct seasons.

V. Land Hydrology

China is rich in surface water. Take rivers for example, The country has more than 50,000 rivers each with a drainage basin of over 100 square kilometres, more than 1,600 rivers each with a drainage basin of over 1,000 square kilometres, 20 rivers each with a length of over 1,000 kilometres. In addition, there are lakes, marshes, glaciers and snowfields as well as subterranean water. The total length of China's rivers is estimated at 226,800 kilometres. The total runoff volume is 260,000 million cubic metres, 6.8% of the total runoff volume of all the rivers on the globe or 20% of the total runoff volume in Asia, ranking third in the world after Brazil and the Soviet Union. With a reserve of 680 million kilowatts, China tops the world in water resources.

Rivers. China's numerous rivers form a host of drainage sytems: the Heilongjiang River, Liaohe River, Haihe River, Huanghe (Yellow) River, Huaihe River, Changjiang (Yangtze) River, Jujiang

Table 1: China's Climatic Extremes

1.	Lowest mean temperature in January	−30.9°C	Mohe, Heilongjiang
2.	Absolute lowest temperature	−52.3°C	Mohe, Heilongjiang
3.	Extreme highest temperature	48.1°C	Turpan, Xinjiang
4.	Maximum annual precipitation	8,408 mm	Huoshaoliao, Taiwan Province
5.	Minimum average annual precipitation over the years	3.9 mm (only 0.5 mm in 1968)	Toksun, Xinjiang
6.	Maximum rainy days	274 days	Tongzi, Guizhou
7.	Maximum foggy days	327 days	Emei, Sichuan
8.	Maximum average cloud volume over the years	8.9	Guiyang, Guizhou
9.	Maximum strong wind days	217.2 days	Jiuxian Mountain, Qinghua, Fujian
10.	Maximum days of fresh gale and above	138.2 days	Magong Island of the Penghu Islands
11.	Maximum sunshine hours	3,370 hours	Gar and Tingri, Tibet
12.	Maximum sunshine value	1.729 calories/mm^2	Dong Rongbu Glacier, Tibet

The overall picture of China's climate is as follows: the South China Sea islands enjoy summer all year round; Guangdong, Guangxi, Fujian, Taiwan and southern Yunnan have long summers and no winters; Heilongjiang Province and the Inner Mongolia Autonomous Region, the Changbai, Tianshan and Altay mountains and the surrounding areas of the Qinghai-Tibet Plateau have long winters and no summers with spring and autumn linked together; the Qiangtang Plateau in

(Pearl) River, southeast coastal rivers, island rivers of Taiwan and Hainan Island, southwest rivers, Arctic Ocean rivers, inland rivers of the North Tibet Plateau, inland rivers of Xinjiang, inland rivers of Qaidam in Qinghai, and inland rivers of Gansu and Inner Mongolia. Table 3 lists the drainage areas of China's exterior rivers, i.e., rivers that flow into the sea, and those of enclosed inland rivers.

Most of the trunk streams of China's exterior

river system originate in the three modern geological rising belts: (1) Rising in the eastern part and the southern rim of the Qinghai-Tibet Plateau are such well-known great rivers as the Changjiang, Huanghe, Lancang, Nujiang and Yarlung Zangbo; (2) rising in the belt linking the Da Xinggan Mountains, the mountains in Hebei and Shanxi, the mountains in western Henan and the Yunnan-Guizhou Plateau are the Heilongjiang, Liaohe, Haihe, Huaihe and Xijiang rivers; (3) rising in the belt joining the Changbai Mountains, the Shandong hills and the southeastern hills are the Tumen, Yalu, Xinmu, Qiantang, Minjiang, Jiulong and Hanjiang rivers as well as the Dongjiang and Beijing tributaries of the Zhujiang River.

As precipitation decreases gradually from the southeast to the northwest, the distribution of surface runoff also shows obvious signs of zonation. (1) The abundant water region, with a runoff deeper than 900 mm, corresponds to the subtropical and tropical evergreen forest area; (2) the adequate water region, with a runoff depth between 220 and 900 mm corresponds to the deciduous broadleaf and evergreen broadleaf forests area; (3) the transitional region, with a runoff depth between 50 and 200 mm, corresponds to the mixed deciduous broadleaf and evergreen broadleaf forest area; (4) the scarce water region, with a runoff depth between 10 and 50 mm, corresponds to the semi-desert and grassland area; and (5) the arid region, with a runoff depth of less than 10 mm, corresponds to the desert area. The balance of water volume in China is shown in Table 4.

Table 2. China's Temperature Zones

Temperature Zone	Latitude	Aggregate Active Temperature in Period $\geqslant 10°C$	Major Natural Features
Equatorial zone	South of 15°N	Around 9,500°C	Sweltering heat all year round; tropical rain forest; latosol.
Tropical zone	15°–23°N	8,000°–9,000°C	Average temperature of the coldest month is above 16°C; tropical monsoon rain forest; three crops of rice a year; latosol.
Subtropical zone	22°–34°N	4,500°–8,000°C	Average temperature of the coldest month is 0°–16°C; tropical monsoon rain forest and evergreen broad-leaf forest; two crops of rice a year; red soil and yellow soil.
Warm–temperate zone	32°–43°N	3,200°–4,500°C	Average temperature of the coldest month is –8°–0°C; deciduous broad-leaf forest; three crops in two years; brown soil, cinnamon earth, black earth and brown desert soil.
Temperate zone	36°–52°N	1,700°–3,200°C	Average temperature of the coldest month is around –24°C; mixed coniferous and deciduous broad-leaf forests; one crop a year; podzolized brown soil, chernozem, chestnut soil, greyish-brown desert soil.
Frigid–temperate zone	North of 50°N	Below 1,700°C	Average temperature of the coldest month is below –24°C; spring wheat, potatoes, etc., can be grown with effort; taiga; cold, brown soil.

Table 3. Distribution of China's River Drainage Basins

	Drainage Basins		Drainage Area (in millions of sq. km.)	Percentage of China's Total Area
Drainage basins of exterior rivers	Flowing into the Pacific Ocean	Sea of Okhotsk	86	8.9
		Sea of Japan	3	0.3
		Yellow Sea, Bohai Sea	167	17.4
		East China Sea	204	21.3
		South China Sea	83	8.7
		Directly flowing into Pacific Ocean	1	0.1
		Sub-total	545	56.7
	Flowing into the Indian Ocean	Andaman Sea, Bay of Bengal	56	5.8
		Arabian Sea	7	0.7
		Sub-total	63	6.5
	Flowing into the Arctic Ocean	Kara Sea	5	0.5
		Total	612	63.8
Inland river drainage basins	Inner Mongolia area		33	3.4
	North Tibet and south Tibet areas		73	7.6
	Songhua River inland drainage basin		5	0.5
	Gansu, Xinjiang and Qaidam areas		237	24.7
	Total		348	36.2

Table 4. Balance of Water Volume in China

Drainage Basin		Percentage of China's Total Area	Precipitation		Runoff Volume		Evaporation Volume		Runoff Co-Efficient
			mm	100 million cu. m.	mm	100 million cu. m.	mm	100 million cu. m.	(%)
Drainage basins of exterior rivers	Pacific Ocean	56.8	918	49,926	391	21,347	527	28,579	42.8
	Indian Ocean	6.5	739	4,530	519	3,239	220	1,291	71.5
	Arctic Ocean	0.5	357	144	216	110	141	34	76.3
	Total (average)	63.8	894	54,600	403	24,696	492	29,904	45.2
Drainage basins of interior rivers		36.2	164	5,720	34	1,177	130	4,547	20.6
National total (average)		100	629	60,320	369	25,873	359	34,451	42.9

Lakes. China has a vast number of lakes. It is estimated that the country has more than 2,800 natural lakes larger than one square kilometre each, with a total area of 80,000 square kilometres. Of these lakes, 13 are larger than 1,000 square kilometres. In addition, there are thousands of man-made reservoirs. Most of the lakes are concentrated in five areas, viz., the eastern plain, the Qinghai-Tibet Plateau, the Yunnan-Guizhou Plateau, the Mongolia-Xinjiang area and the Northeast area. In accordance with their geographical environment and the conditions of their formation, lakes can also be divided into interior drainage basin lakes and exterior drainage basin lakes.

Most of China's interior drainage basin lakes are saltwater lakes and salt lakes. Lop Nur and the Qinghai Lake are the two largest saltwater lakes. Ebi Nur, Dujiali Lake, and Chaka Salt Lake are salt lakes which produce many important chemical raw materials. Saltwater lakes and salt lakes account for 55% of the total area of the country's lakes. Most of the exterior drainage basin lakes are fresh water lakes such as the Boyang, Dongting, Hongze and Taihu lakes.

Glaciers and Permanent Snow. Glaciers and permanent snow are also component parts of China's surface water. Statistics show that modern glaciers and permanent snow on the high mountains in western China cover an area of 44,000 square kilometres. The total water reserve of the glaciers amounts to 2,300,000 million square metres, almost equivalent to the country's total runoff volume in a year. Distributed over the sources of many rivers, glaciers play an important role in replenishing and regulating the rivers.

VI. Weathering Crust and Soil

Soil formation and evolution in China is closely connected with the country's monsoonal climate, the weathering crust of all types of chemicals, the mountainous terrain, different kinds of vegetation and human activities. Generally speaking, the gradual transition from the arid northwest to the humid southeast determines the geochemical process of China's soil and the weathering crust, which gradually intensifies from the northwest to the southeast.

1. The Qinghai-Tibet Plateau and the high mountains in the northwest are areas which have been violently thrust up since the Quaternary Period; both the weathering process and soil formation process there are in a primary stage. These areas have developed clastic weathering crusts and infant alpine soils such as severe cold meadow soil, severe cold steppe soil, etc.

2. In the arid region in the northwest hinterland, insufficient water hampers the geochemical process and large quantities of lime, gypsum and other easily soluble salts remain in the soil and the weathering crust. The result is salt-containing weathering crust and desert soil with very high salt content, namely, greyish-brown desert soil, brown desert soil, severe cold desert soil and large areas of saline-alkali soil.

3. In the semi-arid region, where rainfall is greater, most of the easily soluble salts in the soil and the weathering crust are bleached out. But lime, which is hard to dissolve, remains and there is an obvious calcification process in the soil and the weathering crust. Carbonate weathering crust and steppe soil of varying calcification processes, such as chernozem, chestnut soil and sierozem are found in this area.

4. In the eastern humid region, there is abundant rainfall and ample moisture and the geochemical process can be carried out fully. Easily soluble salts are bleached out of the soil and the weathering crust, and varying degrees of migration and accumulation occur in elements which have difficulty migrating, e.g., silicon, aluminium and iron. The process of adhering and allitic weathering dominate, siallitic weathering crust and allitic weathering crust developed. The soil in this region is mainly acid forest soil. Furthermore, because the terrain in the eastern part of China is relatively flat and the zonal character is distinct, the process of adhering and allitic weathering of the soil gradually intensifies with the increase in heat. From north to south one finds brown coniferous forest soil, dark brown soil, brown soil, yellow brown soil, yellow soil, red soil, lateritic red soil and latosol.

Since China has a typical monsoonal climate with a strong continental character, winters are cold and dry, evaporation is rapid, and there is a strong rising water current in the earth. During the hot and rainy summers, there is a stronger permeating water current in the earth and the bleaching of active minerals dominates. As a result, the processes of adhering, desilicification and allitic weathering in the soil prevail. Acid soil predominates: the area of soil with a PH value less than 6–6.5 is greater than that of neutral soil and alkali soil. About one third of the country's farmland is covered with soil that has a PH value less than 5.

In the course of soil formation, from the desert soil in the arid northwest to the forest soil in the humid east, the biological process as well as the chemical process increases regularly. This finds expression in the constant changes of the quantity and composition of organic matter in the soil. Generally speaking, arid desert soil has a shallow humus layer, only 20–30 mm, and contains 0.15–0.5% of organic matter; in chestnut soil from the grassland, the humus layer is 30–80 mm thick and contains 1.5–3.8% of organic matter; the humus layer of chernozem is generally 30–50 mm thick, with surface organic matter reaching 3–4% and even as much as 6–10%; as for soil formed on forest grassland and black soil, the humus layer can be as thick as 70 mm and sometimes more than one metre, with 3–6% and even as much as 15% of surface organic matter. The accumulation of organic matter in forest soil is also very active, the organic matter content of brown soil being 2–9%, yellow soil 5–10%. Although red soil is exposed to strong bleaching and allitic weathering, its organic matter content still reaches 1–4%; in latosol organic matter, content can be as high as 8–10%.

Thanks to the complex conditions of soil formation, the variety of soil-forming parent material and the regional character of soil formation, China has a rich variety of soil types.

VII. Vegetation and Animal Geography

China has a vast territory, complex natural conditions, a long natural history and was scarcely covered by continental glaciers in the Quaternary Period. Consequently, China's vegetation has the following four characteristics:

1. *A great variety of plants:* According to the latest statistics, China has 301 families, 2,980 genera and over 24,500 species of seed plants, ranking third in the world after Malaysia (about 45,000 species) and Brazil (about 40,000 species) It has 106 families, 480 genera and 2,100 species of bryophytic plants, which account for 70% of the families, 50% of the genera and 10% of the species of such plants in the world. Among the seed plants, there are 291 families, 2,940 genera and 24,300 species of angiosperm, making up 60% of the total number of the families, and 10% of the species of such plants in the world. With the exception of plants of the araucaria family, 10 of the 11 families of gymnosperm in the world are distributed in China, having 34 genera and over 190 species.

2. *Complex geographical factors:* As China faces Europe and Africa in the west, North America in the east and adjoins the land from India to Malaysia in the south, and since south China used to be an area where Laurasia land plants and Gondvana land plants once abounded, there are very rich geographical elements in China's plant zonation. The known seed plants can be divided into 15 "distribution region types" and 29 variations (Table 5).

Table 5. Distribution of Regional Types of China's Seed Plant Genera

Distribution of Regional Types	Number of Genera	Percentage of the Total Number of Genera
1. Worldwide distribution	108	—
2. Distribution in the tropical zone	372	13
3. Intermittent distribution in tropical America and tropical Asia	89	3.1
4. Distribution in the tropical zone of the old world	163	5.6
5. Distribution in tropical Asia to tropical Oceania	150	5.2
6. Distribution in tropical Asia to tropical Africa	151	5.2
7. Distribution in tropical Asia (India-Malaysia)	542	18.9
8. Distribution in the north temperate zone	296	10.3
9. Intermittent distribution in East Asia and North America	117	4.1
10. Distribution in the temperate zone of the old world	157	5.5
11. Distribution in temperate Asia	63	2.2
12. Distribution in the Mediterranean, West Asia to Central Asia	166	5.8
13. Distribution in Central Asia	112	3.9
14. Distribution in East Asia	298	10.4
15. Distribution special to China	196	6.8
Total	2,980	100.0

3. *Large numbers of plants of monotype and oligotype families and genera and relic plants:* China has many old relic plants and primary or isolated families and genera in evolution. Of the 2,980 genera existing in China, monotype (422) and oligotype (713) total 1,135, accounting for 38% of the total number of genera in the country.

4. *A great variety of plants special to China:* China has 196 genera of plants special to China, accounting for 6.8% of the country's total genera, of which relic plants such as water pine, ginko and Chinese tulip tree have become "living fossils" attracting worldwide attention.

China has an agricultural history of several thousand years and many wild plants have become cultivated plants. These plus the rich variety of natural plants make China one of the countries of the world with the richest plant resources. Divided according to their economic use, there are more than 1,000 kinds of timber wood, over 4,000 kinds of medical plants, over 300 kinds of fruit plants, over 500 kinds of fibre plants, over 300 kinds of starch plants, over 600 kinds of oil plants and over 80 kinds of vegetable plants.

The eight main types of vegetation in China are listed below:

1. *Coniferous forest:* From the Da Xinggan Mountains to the Himalaya Mountains, from Taiwan to the Altay Mountains are widely distributed all kinds of coniferous forests and mixed coniferous and broadleaf forests, which have an outstanding place in China's natural vegetation and forest resources. The main community plants belong to the pine, cypress and China fir families.

2. *Broadleaf forest:* Deciduous broadleaf forests are widely distributed on the high mountains and sub-high mountains in the temperate, subtropical and tropical zones. They are regional plants of the temperate zone of north China and belong mainly to the fagaceae, betulaceae, willow, hazel, elm and ulmaceae families. Mixed evergreen and deciduous broadleaf forests are distributed on acid rock and limestone mountains in the north and central subtropical zones. Since this is a transitional-type zone, the composition of the plants is complex and the community plants include all kinds of evergreen and deciduous trees. The evergreen broadleaf forests are regional plants of the subtropical zone of China. Monsoon rain forest and rain forest are distributed in the tropical regions of southwest and south China and Taiwan; they belong mainly to the dipterocarpacea, mulberry, sterculiaceae and anacardiaceae families.

3. *Bushes:* Severe cold evergreen bushes are mainly distributed in the Qinghai-Tibet Plateau, the northwest arid area and high mountains and sub-high mountains in the subtropical zone. Deciduous broadleaf bushes are distributed in the forest area of the temperate zone and in the mountains, valleys, plains and sandy land of the northeast arid area. Evergreen broadleaf bushes, most being secondary vegetation, are distributed on low hills and dry valleys in the tropical and subtropical zones as well as along some seashores.

4. *Grassland:* Widely distributed in the western part of China's northeast, the central and eastern part of Inner Mongolia and the central and northern part of the Qinghai-Tibet Plateau, China's grassland is part of the Eurasia grassland.

5. *Desert:* Distributed in the northwest arid zone and the northwestern part of the north Tibet plateau.

6. *Alpine tundra:* Alpine tundra vegetation is seen only in the alpine area of the Changbai Mountains in northeast China, rising over 2,100 metres above sea level, and in alpine areas in the northwestern part of the Altay Mountains, over 3,000 metres above sea level.

7. *Meadows:* Universally distributed on the low flatland, foothills, high mountains and sub-high mountains, from the temperate zone to the subtropical zone.

8. *Marshes:* Universally distributed along lakes and rivers and on low-lying land of big river deltas.

China's Natural Fauna. China is one of the countries of the world with the richest animal life. The country covers 6.5% of the world's land area while its wild animals make up 11.2% of the total number of the world's animals (over 420 kinds); China's birds account for 15.3% of the world's bird species (1,166 species); reptiles and amphibious animals account for 8% of all species in the world (over 510 species). Quite a few rare animals of the world are unique to China, such as the giant panda, the golden-haired monkey, the white-finned dolphin, the white-lipped deer and the Yangtze crocodile.

China's animals can be divided into three ecological geographical animal groups corresponding to three entirely different natural regions: In the eastern monsoon zone is the humidity-resistant animal group; in the northwestern arid zone is the ardity-resistant animal group; and in the Qinghai-Tibet Plateau zone is the cold-resistant animal group.

VIII. Natural Geographic Divisions

In accordance with the differences in temperature, moisture and topographical conditions, China can be divided into three natural geographical zones: the eastern monsoon zone, the northwest arid zone and the Qinghai-Tibet Plateau zone. The three natural geographical zones roughly touch on each other in the Wuqiao Ridge area west of Lanzhou in Gansu Province.

1. **Eastern Monsoon Zone**: This region accounts for some 46% of China's total land area and 96% of its population. Markedly affected by the summer monsoon, it has humid and semi-humid climate. It is located on the second and third stairs of China's landform. The region did not rise sharply in the new tectonic movement. It has numerous rivers and the river waters are active in erosion and accumulation. The areas divided according to temperature conditions from north to south are obvious and regular. Deeply and extensively affected by human activity, it is the country's industrial and agricultural centre.

2. **Northwest Arid Zone**: This region accounts for 27.3% of the country's total land and 3% of its population. Scarcely affected by the monsoons, it has arid and semi-arid climate. Most of the region belongs to the hinterland. From east to west, distinctly demarcated according to differences in moisture, are dry grassland, desert grassland and desert. This region constitutes the country's major pastoral area.

3. **Qinghai-Tibet Plateau Zone**: This region accounts for 26.7% of the country's total land area and 1% of its population. Vertical zonality that changes with the altitude is clear. In geological history, the region underwent steep upwarped movement in modern times. It has high altitude, low temperature, many glaciers and lakes and is little affected by human activity.

On the basis of the regional differences of the three natural zones, the country can be subdivided into 7 "natural regions" and 33 "natural areas" which provide the material basis for the development of China's economy in line with local conditions.

Principal components of China's three natural geographic zones are as follows:

I. Eastern Monsoon Zone
  A. *The humid and semi-humid temperate zone region of the northeast*
  1. The coniferous forest area in the northeastern part of the Da Xinggan Mountain.
  2. The mixed coniferous and broadleaf forest area in the eastern mountains of the northeast.
  3. The forest grassland area on the Northeast Plain.
  B. *The humid and semi-humid warm to temperate zone region of north China*
  4. The deciduous broadleaf forest area on the Liaodong and Shandong peninsulas.
  5. The semi-zerophyte deciduous broadleaf forest area on the north China Plain.
  6. The semi-zerophyte deciduous broadleaf forest and forest grassland area in the Hebei-Shanxi mountains.
  7. The forest grassland and arid grassland area on the Loess Plateau.
  C. *The humid subtropical region of central and south-China*
  (a) The north subtropical zone
  8. The mixed deciduous broadleaf and evergreen broadleaf forest area in the middle and lower Changjiang valley.
  9. The mixed deciduous broadleaf and evergreen broadleaf forest area in the Chinling and Daba mountains.
  (b) The central subtropical zone
  10. The evergreen broadleaf forest area in the Zhejiang and Fujian coastal mountains.
  11. The evergreen broadleaf forest area on the Jiangnan Plain and hills.
  12. The Sichuan basin evergreen broadleaf forest area.
  13. The Guizhou Plateau evergreen broadleaf forest area.
  14. The Yunnan Plateau evergreen broadleaf forest area.
  (c) The tropical zone in South Asia
  15. The evergreen broadleaf forest area in the Lingnan Hills.
  16. The evergreen broadleaf forest and monsoon forest area on Taiwan Island.
  D. *The humid tropical region of South China*
  17. The monsoon forest area of the Leizhou Peninsula and Hainan Island.
  18. The monsoon rain forest area in the southern Yunnan valley.
  19. The monsoon rain forest and rain forest area of the South China Sea islands.

II. Northwest Arid Zone
  E. *The temperate zone grassland region of Inner Mongolia*
  20. The dry grassland area of the Xiliao River basin.
  21. The dry grassland and desert grassland area on the Inner Mongolia Plateau.
  22. The dry grassland and desert grassland area on the Ordos Plateau.
  F. *The temperate zone and warm temperate zone desert region of the northwest*
  23. The Alxa highlands temperate zone desert

area.
24. The Junggar Basin temperate zone desert area.
25. The Altay Mountains coniferous forest area.
26. The dry grassland and coniferous forest area of the Tianshan Mountains.
27. The warm temperate zone desert area in the Tarim Basin.

III. Qinghai-Tibet Severe Cold Zone
   G. *The Qinghai-Tibet Plateau region*
   28. The tropical and subtropical forest area on the southern side of the Himalaya Mountains.
   29. The coniferous forest and alpine meadow area on the dissected mountains in eastern Tibet.
   30. The bushes and grassland area on the south Tibet mountains.
   31. The severe cold grassland and mountain grassland area on the Qiangtang Plateau and the Qingnan Mountains.
   32. The Qaidam Basin desert area.
   33. The alpine desert grassland and desert area on the Ali and Kunlun Mountains.

3. AN OUTLINE OF CHINA'S ECONOMIC GEOGRAPHY
By Deng Jingzhong and Li Wenyan
Institute of Geology, Chinese Academy of Sciences

I. Natural Conditions and Population

China is situated in the eastern part of Eurasia, on the west coast of the Pacific Ocean. It has an area of 9.60 million square kilometres and a population of one billion (at the end of 1979, the continental provinces and regions had 970,927 million people and Taiwan had 17.47 million). In the last 30 years, the hard-working Chinese people have made use of the country's favourable natural conditions and natural resources to develop the national economy under the socialist system. Building on the basis of the old China, the people have carried out socialist construction on an unprecedented scale and made great advances in agriculture, industry, communications and transportation.

1. Natural Conditions and Natural Resources

Natural resources, such as light, heat, water, earth, living beings, minerals, etc. abound in our country, offering greatly possibilities for the development of various sectors of the national economy. However, the uneven regional distribution of such resources, coupled with insufficient regional coordination, has hampered the development and distribution of industrial and agricultural production. The major characteristics of the natural conditions and resources in our country are as follows:

(1) *Temperate and subtropical zones predominate in China, providing abundant heat and light.* Aside from the 1.2% of the territory that lies in the frigid temperate zone and the 26.7% occupied by the Qinghai-Tibet Plateau, which belongs to the high frigid zone, the remaining 72.1% (divided into temperate zone, 25.9%; warm temperate zone, 18.5%; subtropical zone, 26.1%; and tropical zone, 1.6%) enjoys favourable thermal conditions. Almost all the crops in the world can be cultivated in China. A wide variety of thermophilic plants grow in large parts of the country in the summer half of the year, and double-cropping prevails in the warm temperate zone and its southern regions.

(2) *Water resources are abundant, thanks to the monsoon climate, but the regional distribution is by no means even and the rate of variability very great.* In the humid and sub-humid areas in the southeast part of China, 48% of the whole territory, the total precipitation is in excess of 80%, and the runoff of rivers over 90%. The correspondence of the high temperature season with the rainy season favours the cultivation of crops. Over 90% of China's farmlands and forests are concentrated in this area, and local rivers provide a rich store of hydroelectric potential. Nevertheless, the wide fluctuation between the seasons and between years of precipitation and runoff, plus their irregularity, lead to frequent periods flood and drought, which seriously affect agricultural production. The arid and semi-arid regions in the northwest of China, covering 52% of the whole territory, are seriously short of water resources, with vast stretches of steppe and desert prohibiting the development of agriculture.

(3) *Mountainous areas occupy two-thirds of the total area of the country, while plains occupy only one-third.* This is disadvantageous to the agricultural utilization of land. The characteristics of the mountain areas are: high altitude, low temperature, and short growing periods. This is especially true of high ranges and plateaus over 3,000 m. in elevation, which cover 25.9% of China's total area. The high altitude and frigid climate discourage the utilization of the land for the development of agriculture, forestry and animal husbandry. Moreover, the steep slopes and the thin soil layer of the mountain areas disturb the ecological balance. Mountains also compound the difficulty of communication and transportation. Owing to the complex natural conditions in the mountain areas, mono-economy is impracticable, and other uses for the land, suitable to local conditions, must be developed.

(4) *The inadequate coordination of the natural resources of light, heat, water, earth, etc., in different localities has resulted in disadvantages as well as local advantages.* Northeastern China has large areas of plains, extremely fertile soil, subhumid climate and rich forest resources, but the air temperature there is comparatively low, the growing season short and frigidity often causes damage. North China is commonly characterized as having broad plains, warm summers and cold winters, insufficient water resources with great variability and large areas of arid, floods and alkaline lands. In Northwestern China, there is plenty of land, strong sunlight and heat, but the land is arid, with deserts, gobies, salinized and alkaline lands scattered here and there. South China has plenty of thermal energy, abundant water, rapid

plant growth and rich biological resources, but hills and uplands predominate, farmland is scarce, precipitation is variable and liability to flood damage is great. The Qinghai-Tibet region, being high, receives the most intense solar radiation in the whole country, but the climate is frigid and the cumulative active temperature very low. Suitable measures must be taken to develop agriculture according to the features of different regions, so as to make full use of their advantages and overcome their defects.

(5) *China's mineral resources are rich and varied with confirmed reserves of 132 kinds of minerals.* The country is especially rich in nonferrous metals, rare earth metals, coal and some non-metal minerals. China ranks first in the world in reserves of tungsten, antimony, zinc, rare earths, lithium, pyrite, magnesite and borax; second in phosphorus; and third in coal. Deposits of iron, copper and manganese ores are also considerable, but they are mostly lean rather than rich ores. Petroleum prospects are excellent and certain reserves have been verified through prospecting. The distribution of most minerals is by no means even, many are found in combination with other minerals, and some kinds of minerals are deficient.

2. Population, Nationalities and Cities

China has about 23% of the world's population. She is, therefore, very rich in resources of labour for production. On the other hand, the country's requirements for sources of subsistence are very great. Population density averages 103/km^2, but the distribution of population is very uneven. If we draw a line from Aihui County through Lanzhou to Tengchong, dividing the country into a southeast part and a northwest part, the southeast part has over 95% of the population with an average density in excess of 200. In the Changjiang Delta, Changdu Plain and Zhujiang Delta, the density exceeds 100/km^2. Population density in the North China Plain averages 400-500/km^2, while in the southern and northern mountain areas, it is less than 100 km^2. In the northwest part the average population density is less than 10; in some irrigated oases it is 50–100/km^2, while in the extensive gobi, desert and high mountains, it is less than 1.

China is a multinational country, consisting of more than 50 nationalities. The Han are most numerous, making up 94% of the total population in China; the other 50 or more nationalities are less numerous, about 6% of the total. The Zhuang, the Hui, the Uygur and the Yi nationalities each have a population of over three million; the Mongolian, Tibetan, Manchu, Buyi, Korean and Miao, over one million; the Yao, Dong, Tujia, Kazak, Bai, Dai, over 500,000; the Hani, Li and others, altogether 10 nationalities, over 100,000. Other nationalities besides those mentioned above have smaller populations with the smallest down to hundreds of people. The minority nationalities live predominately in the Southwest, Northwest and Northwest border regions. They generally concentrate in a definite region, although some of them live scattered among other nationalities. In 70% of the counties in China, more than two nationalities live together. Differences in lifestyles, in customs of production, in characteristics of the economy and in the culture of different nationalities are important factors contributing to the differentiation of regional economic features. Communications and living in proximity facilitates close ties among the nationalities and mutual interdependence, as well as the country's economic and cultural development.

The rural population makes up 86.8% of the total population and the urban population the remaining 13.2%. There are more than 3,400 cities and towns, in which the municipalities number more than 200. The urban population exceeds 85 million, 63% of which are concentrated in 43 large and medium-sized cities, each with a population of over 500,000. There are six metropolises, each with a population of more than two million, viz. Shanghai, Beijing, Tianjin, Shenyang, Wuhan, Guangzhou; nine large-sized cities each with a population of one to two million, viz. Chongqing, Harbin, Nanjing, Xi'an, Chengdu, Changchun, Taiyuan, Dalian, Lanzhou; and 28 medium-sized cities with populations between 500,000 and 1,000,000. The large and medium-sized cities are China's chief centres of industry and communication.

II. The Distribution of Agriculture, Industry, Communications and Transportation

1. Agriculture

Agriculture is the basis of the national economy. The rural population accounts for 86.8% of the total population, and cultivated land, forests and grassland account for 70% of the China's territory. To the total output value of agriculture crop cultivation contributes 66.9%, animal husbandry 14%, forestry 2.8%, fishing 1.2% and sideline occupations 15.1%.

Cultivated land contributes only about 10.4% of all land for agricultural use. The proportion of forested land is small compared to China's total land area, with woodlands covering only 12.7%; but land for pastoral use is extensive, including meadows (29.8%) and grassy hills and slopes in the south prairies (4.6%). Areas suitable for forestry are large, including sparse woodland, 1.6%; shrub land, 3.1%; young forest and woodless land, 9.4%.

The inland water area has a percentage of 2.8%. The distribution of various types of agricultural lands tends to be concentrated in certain parts of the country. Over 95% of the cultivated land in China is distributed in an area to the east of a line drawn from the Da Xinggan Mountains through the Great Wall to the eastern border of the Qinghai-Tibet Plateau. The northwestern part of China is arid, with very little cultivated land scattered around oases; but it has extensive grasslands for pastoral use. Forested land and land suitable for wood-growing predominate in hilly regions in the northwest, southwest and south. Inland water areas prevail in the southeastern part of China, where rainfall is comparatively abundant, and in the western part, where interior lakes are scattered here and there.

Differences between the natural, technical and economic conditions of various regions give rise to great differentiation in productivity. The multiple crop index of the country averages 151%, but the Northeast China and Inner Mongolia regions can only produce one crop a year, the index there being less than 100%. Most of North China can produce three crops in two years, the multiple crop index being 120–150%. The Changjiang Basin and South China can support two to three crops a year, the index increasing to 180–250%. Of all cultivated land, paddy fields make up 25.6% and available irrigated areas 45%. Roughly one-third of all cultivated land is low-yield, either because the soil is thin or because it is sandy, clayey, salinized, alkaline or acidic. About 30% of the cultivated land is distributed on the slopes, liable to loss of water and soil erosion. The best way to develop China's agriculture, in consideration of the deficiency of cultivable waste land, is to improve production conditions and increase the unit-yield. China's monsoon climate, the great variability of precipitation and the constant threat of flood and drought cause great differences in the unit-yields of paddy fields and dry lands, irrigated and non-irrigated lands. Hence, the principal measures for developing agriculture and agricultural investment since the founding of New China have been the building of water-conservation projects, the development of irrigation, the improvement of low-yield fields, the development of farmlands capable of ensuring stable and high yields despite drought or excessive rain. By 1979, farmlands capable of stable and high yields despite drought and excessive rain have been built up to 340 million *mu**, making up 22.8% of all cultivated land.

Grain production is the main part of agriculture, making up 70% of the total output value of crop cultivation and occupying 80% of all land under cultivation. The main food crops are rice, wheat, maize, kaoliang, millet, potatoes and soyabeans. Rice, wheat and maize are grown most extensively and yield the largest output, making up 80% of China's total food production. China is the world's largest rice producer. The average yield per unit area of rice is the highest of the food crops and the rice output constitutes 43% of total output of food crops. About 94% of China's rice is grown in the regions south of the Huaihe River and the Qinling Mountains. To their north, less rice is cultivated, except in Northeast China. Wheat, which makes up 19% of total food production, is cultivated all over the country, but particularly in the Changjiang Basin and the plains of the Huanghe, Huaihe and Haihe rivers. Cultivation of maize has greatly increased since Liberation, and now comprises 18% of total food production. Predominantly grown in the belt extending from Heilongjiang Province southwestward to Sichuan, Yunnan and Guizhou, kaoliang, millet and soybeans are chiefly grown in northern and northeastern China. The areas under cultivation have been greatly reduced since Liberation, thus reducing their proportion in total food production. Sweet potatoes are grown in the lower reaches of the Huanghe River and the hilly southern regions, while potatoes are the predominant crop in the regions of mild and cool climate north of the Great Wall.

China's food production has greatly increased since Liberation. The total output in 1979 was 332,115 million tons, 2.93 times greater than that in 1949. Food production has increased at an average rate of 3.65% a year in the past three decades, yet because of the large population and the big proportion of rural population, per capita output of grain averages only 344 kg. and commodity grain only amounts to 15% of the total output. Production levels and rates of marketable grain of different regions in China differ enormously. For instance, the Taihu Plain, Zhujiang Delta, Chengdu Plain and Dongting Lake Plain, the regions with the highest yield, have a great amount of surplus grain to sell to the state. The Songliao Plain and Sangjiang Plain, with more land and less people, also have a significant grain surplus. Regions with low levels of production and unstable output, such as the Loess Plateau, the Guizhou and Guangxi mountain areas, as well as regions with large non-rural populations, such as Liaoning Province, are all deficient in food. It is of strategical significance, therefore, to select in a planned way some regions with favourable conditions, solid foundations and great potential to build up as major bases of commodity food crops, as well as to facilitate the overall increase of food

---

*one *mu* equals 1/15 of a hectare.

production.

China's chief industrial crops include cotton, oil-bearing crops, sugar, tobacco, bast fibre, medicine plants. Other industrial crops include tea, mulberry, fruit, rubber, and various woody plant crops. The area under industrial crops, 8–9% of the total cultivated area, is far smaller than that under food crops, but industrial crops play an important role in increasing the income of the peasants, providing raw material for light industries (60% of the material coming from industrial crops) and supplying commodities for export. Of the industrial crops, cotton and oil-bearing crops occupy the largest cultivated areas, about 80% of the total. Cotton is cultivated most extensively, chiefly in the Changjiang Delta, middle Changjiang Plain, and plains of the Huanghe, Huaihe and Haihe rivers. China is the world's third largest cotton-producing country; its output of ginned cotton was 2,207 million tons in 1979. Many species of oil-bearing crops are widely distributed. Peanuts, for example, in which China ranks as the second largest producer in the world, are grown mainly in the hilly regions of Shandong, the plains of Huanghe, Huaihe and Haihe rivers, Fujian, Guangdong and Guangxi. The rapeseed grown in China is largely winter rapes, over 70% of which is cultivated in the regions of the Changjiang Basin. Spring rapes are cultivated in Inner Mongolia, Northwest China and Qinghai-Tibet region, where the growth season is relatively short. Sesame mainly grows in the provinces of Henan, Hubei and Anhui. Sugar crops, including sugarcane and beets, occupy cultivated areas of 62% and 38% respectively, but in the country's overall sugar output, cane sugar and beet sugar account for 85% and 15% respectively. Sugarcane grows in Guangdong, Guangxi, Fujian, Sichuan, Yunnan and other subtropical regions, whereas sugar beets grow mainly in Heilongjiang, Jilin, Inner Mongolia, Xinjiang and other temperate regions. China is well-known for her silk and tea. Silk is produced in the Taihu Plain, Sichuan Basin and Zhujiang Delta, and tussah silk largely in Liaoning and Shandong provinces. Tea is commonly planted in the provinces south of the Huaihe River and Qinling Mountains, such as Zhejiang, Hunan, Anhui and Sichuan. Temperate fruits, such as apples, pears, persimmons and Chinese dates, rank first in output of fruits in China; next to them are subtropical fruits, such as oranges and tangerines, and tropical fruits, such as bananas and pineapples. Tropical cash crops, chiefly rubber, are concentrated on Hainan Island and the Leizhou Peninsula, and secondarily, in southern Yunnan Province.

Most of the industrial crops are extensively cultivated in scattered planting areas, so the yield per unit area is not high. However, a small part of industrial crops are concentrated in cultivation and produce relatively high yields. Production of cotton, plant oil and sugar is still insufficient to meet the needs of the country. The production potentials of tea, silk, fruits, etc. have not been fully tapped. Today, the distribution of the production of industrial crops is being readjusted step by step in line with local conditions and concentrated bases of various industrial crops have increased their output.

Animal husbandry is a weak link in the agricultural economy. The number of livestock is great, but the commodity rate is low, and there are very few meat products per capita. In 1979, China's large and small livestock amounted to 597,438 million head, 15% of the world total but only 7% of the world's output of meat products. China has 319.710 million pigs, about 41% of the pigs in stock in the world, but it produces only 15% of the world's output of pork. Each person in China gets an average 10.95 kg. of meat annually, 2 kg. of eggs, 1 kg. of milk and 0.6 kg. of wool, far lower than the world's average level. The main reasons for the scarcity of livestock products are: the low rate of marketable livestock (the rate for pigs is only 55%, for cattle, 7%); low dressing percentages; and high death rates. The development of animal husbandry depends, on the one hand, upon paying great attention to the eastern agricultural regions which possess 86% of the country's total livestock, upon promoting the rate of marketable livestock and that of meat production, raising larger numbers of cows, sheep, rabbits, geese and other grass-feeding livestock and poultry, as well as upon developing animal husbandry in agricultural areas; and, on the other hand, upon improvement of grasslands in the western pastoral regions, combining animal husbandry with agriculture, depending less on nature and accelerating the distribution of livestock. It is also necessary to build and develop modernized animal husbandry in the suburbs of the cities and in the manufacturing and mining regions in order to increase the production of meat, milk, eggs and poultry.

China is also weak in forestry due to the scarcity of woods, the low rate of forest cover and uneven regional distribution. The average rate of forest cover for the whole country is only 12.7%, that of Heilongjiang and the provinces south of the Changjiang River is over 30%, and that of the northwestern arid areas less than 1%. Timber forest makes up 80% of the existing forest area; economic forest, shelter forest, fuel forest, bamboo forest, etc. make up the rest. Natural forest is largely timber forest. Heilongjiang, Tibet, Sichuan, Yunnan and Jilin provinces possess more than 70% of the timber resources in China. Economic forest includes mainly oil-bearing trees, such as tea-oil trees, tung-oil trees, walnut and various kinds of fruit trees. Shelter forests are those which are used to check winds and control sand in the northern part of the country as well as those for the conservation of water and soil. To develop our forestry, it is necessary to improve the management and utilization of existing forests, strengthen the work of tending woods, raise the productivity of timber forests, reconstruct the northeast and the southwest forest areas, plant trees on the mountains and wastelands fit for afforestation, build bases for timber forest and oil-bearing trees, intersperse farmlands with trees in North China as well as build shelter forests in the northern arid areas.

Aquatic products have made rapid progress since Liberation. The total amount of aquatic products in 1979 was 4.7 times that in 1950, but the average per capita amount was only 4.5 kg. Aquatic product resources abound in the Bohai Sea, Yellow Sea, East China Sea and South China Sea. Marine products comprise 74% of the country's total output of aquatic products, largely by catching (87%) instead of aquiculture (13%). Freshwater aquatic products represent 26% of the total, largely by aquiculture (73%) instead of catching (27%) Over 60% of fresh-water aquatic products come from the numerous freshwater lakes and dense waterways in the Changjiang and Huaihe river basins; the rest from the Zhujiang River basin. To further develop aquatic products, it is necessary to protect aquatic product resources and utilize them fully, to limit the catch, to develop aquiculture and build up marine and fresh water aquiculture bases.

2. Industry

Before Liberation, China's industry was relatively undeveloped, contributing only 10% to the combined gross output value of industry and agriculture. The branches of industry were incomplete. Consumer goods industries, mainly the textile and food industries, accounted for 70% of the total value of industrial output. Heavy industry was represented by several coal mines, cement factories, machine-repair factories, and a few medium- and small-sized steel plants and chemical plants. Almost all of the industrial branches were ill-equipped and their range of products limited. The distribution of industry was also very uneven. More than 70% of total industrial output value came from the coastal regions, actually a few cities, including Shanghai, Qingdao, Tianjin, Guangzhou, Shenyang, Anshan, Fushun and Dalian.

Thirty years after the founding of the People's Republic, remarkable growth has been made in industrial production. The sectoral composition of industry has become more complete, the level of technology higher, and the distribution of industry more rational. In 1979, industry's share of the combined output value of industry and agriculture came to 74%. Industries producing energy, raw materials and various manufactures have developed rapidly. Quite a few branches of industry were built almost from scratch, such as the oil industry, rare metals, organic chemicals, motor vehicles, locomotive and aircraft manufacturing, shipbuilding, heavy machine-building, precision instruments, electronics, etc., so that China now has a relatively complete industrial system of considerable scale. Meanwhile, the distribution of industry in the whole country has been improved in the following ways:

(1) Three large previously industrialized areas (i.e. Liaoning Province, the lower Changjiang Delta and the Beijing-Tianjin-Tangshan region, as well as other industrial centres along the coast, have been greatly strengthened, so that they have become base areas for the industrialization of China;

(2) Priority was given to the development of a number of new industrial areas and centres in central China and the hinterland of Northeast China. They include Wuhan, central Hunan, central Henan, central Hebei, Taiyuan, Xi'an, Changchun, Jilin, Harbin, etc.

(3) In the inland areas previously almost cut off from the rest of the country, several industrial areas or bases, e.g. Baotou, Lanzhou, Chengdu, Chongqing and Dukou, have been built in a planned way;

(4) In the economically backward border areas and regions mainly inhabited by minority nationalities, large numbers of local industrial enterprises have been developed.

China's abundant and varied energy resources provide ample guarantees that the requirements of industry, other production and the people's standard of living can be met. Verified geological reserves of coal in China total more than 600,000 million tons and total hydroelectrical potential, according to the latest estimate, is 680 million kw., of which 380 million kw. is exploitable. Considerable reserves of oil have been verified. The distribution of these three kinds of energy resources complement and coordinate with each other. Since Liberation, the production of energy has undergone overall growth.

China's coal resources are widely distributed and are particularly abundant in Shaanxi, Inner Mongolia, Hebei, Shaanxi, Henan, Shandong,

Anhui, Heilongjiang, Xinjiang, Guizhou, and Yunnan. Shansi Province alone accounts for one-third of the national total. Annual coal output in the past few years has topped 600 million tons. All of the large economic regions have their own large coal bases: Fushun, Fuxin, Jixi, and Hegang in the Northeast; Datong, Kailuan, Fengfeng and Yangquan in North China; Huainan and Huaibei, Xuzhou and Yanzhou in East China; Pingdingshan in Central-south China; Liuzhi-Panxian-Shuicheng in the Southwest; and Helanshan in the Northwest. If account is taken of the development of medium- and small-sized coal collieries, the Northwest, Southwest and Northeast have, or have virtually, achieved self-sufficiency in coal. Because the largest reserves and the most favourable exploiting conditions are found in North China, this area supplies tens of million of tons of flame coal, coking coal and anthracite every year to East China, Central-south China and Liaoning Province in the Northeast. Shanxi Province, the largest coal-bearing area, alone produces more than 100 million tons annually.

The oil industry, previously with only one small oilfield and a few refineries, has developed rapidly. Since Liberation, a number of large oil (and natural gas) fields have been discovered and opened up in Heilongjiang, Liaoning, Hebei, Shandong, Xinjiang, Qinghai and Sichuan. Among them, the Daqing Oilfield of Heilongjiang is the first and largest oil base, built in the 1960's. Crude oil from Daqing is transported to refineries in the Northeast and to most refineries in the rest of the country and part of it is exported through Dalian. Apart from those refineries attached to oilfields (such as Daqing, Karamay and Yumen), many large refineries were built in Fushun, Jinzhou, Dalian, Beijing, Tianjin, Zibo, Shanghai, Nanjing, Lanzhou, Wuhan, Guangzhou and other places, with convenient transport facilities near oilfields or pipelines and close to the oil-consuming centres.

The large-scale development of the fuel industry has enabled the power industry to develop in step with the wider distribution of industries.

At present, thermal electricity accounts for 82% of China's total annual output of electricity, and hydroelectricity accounts for 18%. Three-fourths of the existing thermal power stations are located at the power-consuming centres and the rest in the fuel (mainly coal) producing regions. The existing large and medium-sized hydropower stations are located on the main tributaries in the upper reaches of the Huanghe and Changjiang rivers, on the Songhua River and some rivers in the southeastern coastal provinces. Nevertheless, the rate of exploitation of hydroelectric potential is still a mere 2.6%. Large regional power grids serving the Northeast, East China, Beijing-Tianjin-Tangshan, Shaanxi-Gansu-Qinghai, Hubei-Henan, etc. have been built.

The metallurgical industry has undergone large-scale development during the last 30 years. To supply the iron and steel industries with adequate raw materials, more than 40,000 million tons of iron ore reserves have been verified throughout the whole country; these reserves are concentrated in central Liaoning, eastern Hebei and western Sichuan. At present, all of the large economic regions except the Northwest have large iron and steel bases, including Anshan, Benxi, Beijing, Tianjin, Tangshan, Baotou, Taiyuan, Shanghai, Maanshan, Wuhan, Panzhihua, Chongqing, etc. In addition, dozens of medium-sized iron and steel plants and special steel plants have been constructed in most provinces, municipalities and autonomous regions.

The iron and steel industry of the Northeast, developed on the strongest foundation in China, boasts the largest productive capability and the greatest variety of steel products. Iron and steel production in Liaoning Province is particularly concentrated, with the Anshan Iron and Steel Complex alone turning out annually more than 6 million tons of steel. But the Northeast is short of coking coal and must be supplied from Hebei Province.

In North China there are more major iron and steel enterprises in scattered locations. This region has abundant coal and ore reserves for the future growth of iron and steel production.

The annual steel output of East China is second to that of Northeast China. In this vast region, Shanghai has the highest level of technology and the most comprehensive varieties and specifications of rolled steel products. But most provinces in East China (except Shandong and Anhui) are poor in coal and ore reserves and must be supplied from outside.

The major iron and steel base of Central-south China, the Wuhan Iron and Steel Complex, produces mainly steel plates of various types. All of the large and medium-sized iron and steel plants in this region get the coking coal they need from North China. The ore reserves of this region also seem to be insufficient for the future.

In Southwest China, large and medium-sized enterprises, except the old Chongqing Iron and Steel Company, were built during the 1960's and most of them still lack complete production facilities. Although the abundant ore and coal reserves favour the future development of the iron and steel industry in this region, difficulties in transportation and the shortage of flat land constitute major constraints on production and construction.

Finally, in Northwest China, there are only a few newly built medium-sized iron and steel plants with rather weak foundations for industrial development.

Before Liberation, China had a very elementary chemical industry and only a few small-scale chemical enterprises located in a few cities, such as Tianjin, Dalian, Shanghai, and Nanjing. During the last three decades, production of basic industrial chemicals, chemical fertilizers, pesticides, medicine, rubber, etc. has developed rapidly throughout the country, the few existing acid and soda plants have been greatly expanded and over a dozen large nitrogenous fertilizer plants have been set up. At the same time, the organic chemicals industry, especially the petrochemical industry, was developed from scratch. There are now large petrochemical complexes in Beijing, Shanghai, Tianjin, Daqing, Zibo, Wuhan, Jilin, Liaoyang, Lanzhou, and Luzhou. Production of the three main synthesis chemicals has also increased enormously.

Before Liberation, 70% of China's light industry was concentrated in a few coastal cities, especially Shanghai, Tianjin and Qingdao, far away from raw material sources and inland markets. After Liberation, these cities, Shanghai in particular, have undergone reconstruction and expansion and have become the country's main bases for production of high-grade and middle-grade consumer goods and for the exporting of light industrial goods. They have played an important part in supplying the national market and accumulating capital for construction.

In the same period in the inland regions — rich in raw materials, easily accessible and densely populated — and in the regions inhabited by minority nationalities, large numbers of new textile, foodstuffs, paper-making and other light industrial centres have emerged. On the whole, East China, North China and Central-south China are the most highly developed and diversified in light industry. Paper, sugar, and dairy and meat products are the major branches of light industry in Northeast China. Industries processing livestock products and producing cotton textiles are more important in Northwest China, while various foodstuff industries are more developed in Southwest China. With the readjustment of the national economy in the near future, further development of light industry throughout the country can be expected.

Old China's so-called machine-building industry undertook only repair work and as much as 85% of the plants were concentrated in a few coastal cities. As a result of construction during the last three decades, this backward state has largely changed. China has developed in an all-around way the production of general and special equipment for various industries, power equipment, machine tools, locomotives and carriages, ships, various machinery for agriculture, instruments and meters, communication materials, broadcast and television equipment and household electrical appliances, so that it is now basically self-sufficient in the various kinds of machinery and equipment needed for developing the national economy. Moreover, the geographical distribution of the machine-building industry has been extended throughout the country. Building on their previous industrial foundation, Liaoning Province, the Shanghai-Nanjing region and the Tianjin-Beijing region have developed into the most powerful bases of machine-building industry. At the same time, dozens of machine-building centres focused on different specialities have been built up in most provinces and regions. Taking into account the network of machine-repairing factories scattered in China's medium-sized and small cities, China now boasts a relatively complete machine-building industry.

3. Transport and Communications

To meet the needs for developing industrial and agricultural production and strengthen economic links among provinces and regions, great efforts have been made on to develop the country's transportation system. Whereas previously China had very limited localized lines, a handful of motor vehicles and steamboats and largely inaccessible regions, now she has a nationwide transport system with railways as the framework, connecting highways, inland navigation, marine transport and pipelines.

At present, the total length of railway lines is to 60,000 kilometres. With the exception of Tibet, every province and autonomous region has railway transport. In Southwest and Northwest China, the total length of lines accounts for 25% of the nation's entire network, compared with 5% in 1949. In the eastern part of the country, original trunk lines have undergone the necessary technological improvements and new trunk lines and feeder railways have been built in the last 30 years. Spanning the country are six vertical arteries, i.e. Beijing-Guangzhou, Tianjin-Pukou, Harbin-Dalian, Taiyuan-Jiaozuo-Zhicheng-Liuzhou, Baoji-Chengdu-Kunming and Chengdu-Chongqing-Guiyang; and four lateral arteires, i.e. Manzhouli-Harbin-Suifenhe, Shenyang-Beijing-Baotou-Lanzhou, Lianyuangang-Lanzhou-Urumqi and Shanghai-Hangzhou-Zhuzhou-Guiyang-Kunming.

The total length of highways now amounts to 876,000 km., of which 110,000 km. belong to 70 state trunk lines that link up the provincial administrative and economic centres and reach all the important communication hubs and industrial and agricultural bases.

There has been marked growth of navigation — mainly marine, but also on the main course of the Changjiang River. Some 100,000 km. of rivers are open to navigation, of which more than 20,000 km. are navigable by 100-ton ships. The most important navigable rivers are the Changjiang (more than 9,000 km.), the Zhujiang (more than 2,000 km.) and the Huaihe (more than 2,000 km.). Main inland ports include Nanjing, Wuhan, Chenglingji, Chongqing, Yuxikou, Jiujiang, Yichang, Changsha, and Guangzhou. China's marine navigation, including coastal and ocean transport, has rapidly developed to meet the needs of transporting bulky goods, such as coal and oil from north to south and phosphorites from south to north, and of foreign trade. Dalian, Qinhuangdao, Tianjin, Qingdao, Lianyungang, Shanghai, Huangpu and Zhanjiang have become large modern ports.

The total length of oil pipelines amounts to more than 9,100 km., with the most important pipelines running from Daqing Oilfield to Dalian and Beijing, from Renqiu Oilfield to Shandong and Nanjing and from Shengli Oilfield to Qingdao.

Considerable progress has been made in civil aviation. An airline network covering some 16,000 km. is now in service. All provincial capitals are linked with Beijing by direct flights. In addition, China has established business relations with more than 100 foreign aviation companies. Today, 13 international lines connect China with 15 countries. International airports with modern equipment have been built in Beijing, Shanghai, Guangzhou, Urumqi and other cities.

III. A Brief Account of the Regions

1. North China

North China comprises two municipalities (Beijing and Tianjin), two provinces (Hebei and Shanxi) and the western portion of Inner Mongolia Autonomous Region. The Hebei Plain covers the southwestern part of North China, and the Shanxi Plateau and Inner Mongolia Plateau occupy its western and northern parts. The whole region lies slightly northward, but it is the country's communications centre. In this region, industry is more developed than agriculture, and heavy industry more than light industry. It is rich in mineral resources, especially coal, the verified reserves of which make up over 60% of the country's total reserves. It also produces over 25% of the country's raw coal and is the largest industrial fuel and power base. Most of North China's coalfields, represented by such large-scale coal fields as Datong, Kailuan, Yangquan, etc., are distributed in the Shanxi Plateau, the south and north slopes of the Yenshan Mountains, the face of the Yanshan Mountains, and the eastern base of the Taihang Mountains. The Dagang and Renqiu oilfields are the major oil-producing areas. North China is the second largest base of the iron and steel industry in China, with Beijing, Baotou, Taiyuan, Tianjin, Tangshan as its centres. Both in reserves of iron ore and in iron and steel output, this region ranks second in the country. The machine-building industries (including heavy machinery, mining machinery, metallurgical equipment, dynamic machinery, agricultural machinery) and the chemical industry (basic chemicals, chemical fertilizers and organic synthesis) are both well developed in this region, with Beijing, Tianjin and Taiyuan as centres. Light and textile industries, represented by the cotton and wool textile industries, have solid bases in Beijing, Tianjin and Hebei Province. Significant quantities of sea salt are produced along the Bohai Gulf, and the processing of livestock products is of considerable importance in Inner Mongolia.

North China's agriculture lags behind its industry. Hebei, Shanxi and the middle and southern parts of Inner Mongolia produce mainly wheat, corn, millet and kaoliang. The low and unstable yields of food crops, a consequence of frequent floods and drought and the high ratio of non-agricultural population to total population (second-highest after the Northeast), make it impossible for this region to become self-sufficient in food. Cotton is a significant industrial crop, distributed largely in the central and southern parts of Hebei and the southern part of the Fen River Valley in Shanxi. Other industrial crops are: peanuts, which grow in the Hebei Plain; oil flax, in Northern Hebei, northern Shanxi and the central and southern parts of Inner Mingolia; and sugar beets, cultivated in Hetao, Inner Mongolia and Yanbei Prefecture, Shanxi. One of the most important pastoral regions in China extends from the Inner Mongolia Plateau to the adjacent regions of northern Hebei and northern Shanxi; this region provides large amounts of meat, milk, hides and fur for the cities and the light and textile industries. However, the extensive management of animal husbandry, and the serious deficiency of fodder in winter and spring, make the improvement of natural pasture imperative.

There are three metropolises in North China: Beijing, Tianjin, and Taiyuan. Beijing is not only China's capital and a political and cultural centre, but also a comprehensive industrial base with an important iron and steel industry, petrochemical industry, machine-building industry and light and textile industries. The urban population is over 4.3 million, second only to Shanghai. Tianjin is an old industrial centre with the largest harbour in the northern coastal region. It has been transformed from a centre for light and textile industries into a comprehensive industrial base focusing mainly on machinery, chemicals, textiles and light industries and metallurgy. Tianjin's urban population exceeds 3.6 million, making it the third largest metropolis in China. Taiyuan is a centre of heavy industry in the western part of North China. Other important industrial cities are Tangshan, Shijiazhuang and Baotou.

2. Northeast Region

The Northeast region embraces three provinces — Liaoning, Jilin, and Heilongjiang, and the eastern part of the Inner Mongolia Autonomous Region, which consists of a vast fertile plain (with mild and cool temperatures, medium humidity, and rich minerals), surrounded by mountains and rivers on three sides. In this region are abundant forests, large-scale oil fields, and the richest verified iron reserves in China. There are also vast expanses of wasteland suitable for agriculture. In the past hundred years, but especially after Liberation, Northeast China has been transformed into China's most important heavy industrial base, commodity food base, forest-cutting base and modern communication and transportation hub. It forms an integrated economic system under geographical conditions peculiar to northeast China.

Since cultivation in the Songliao Plain and Sanjiang Plain is rather highly mechanized, the rate of marketable agricultural products is also high. Major food crops grown in this region are spring wheat, corn, kaoliang, millet, rice, etc. and industrial crops include soybeans (over one-third of the country's total output) and sugar beets (which is grown predominantly in the northern part). Vast stretches of grassland extend along the two slopes of the Xinggan Mountains, forming an important pastoral region. There is also forestry and hunting in the mountain areas, cultivation of fruit in the southern part of Liaoning Province and fishing along the coast, all of which contribute to the potential development of agriculture in Northeast China.

Northeast China was the first base for heavy industry constructed after Liberation. Now, a fairly complete industrial system has been built up with iron and steel, machinery, oil and chemical industries as its base, and including well-developed coal, electricity, building-materials textile, paper-making and sugar industries. The output of steel in the Northeast accounts for 25% of the country's total output; metallurgical equipment and motor vehicles, 50%; mining and electric installations, 33.5%; oil and timber, over 50%, respectively.

The region's light industry is rather weak. Coal has to be supplied from North China. The region's only outlets for communication and transportation with the rest of China are the Beijing-Shenyang Railway and Dalian Harbour, which are inadequate and in need of improvement.

The heart of this economic region is the industrial area in central Liaoning Province. It is a dense conurbation comprising five cities: Shenyang, Fushun, Anshan, Benxi, Liaoyang and other industrial points in their suburbs. The aggregate population is approximately two-thirds that of the whole province, and its industrial output value 30% that of the Northeast. Shenyang is the biggest city in the region, with an urban population of 2.7 million. Its major industries are machinery and nonferrous metallurgy. It is also a junction of the railway network in Northeast China, and a political and cultural centre. Anshan is China's "Steel Capital," with an output equal to 20% of the country's total. Fushun is a centre of heavy industries, mainly coal-mining, oil-refining, electric power and machine-building. Benxi is known as a "Steel City" second to Anshan and is famous for its fine-quality pig iron. Liaoyang is a newly developed centre of the petrochemical industry. Harbin is the largest economic centre and communications hub in the northern part of this region, with a population second only to Shenyang's and a developed electrical machine-building industry. Changchun and Jilin are situated in Jilin Province; the former is important for its motor-vehicle industry; the latter for its chemical industry. Dalian lies at the southern end of the region; it is an important industrial port city with relatively developed machine-building chemical, light and textile industries.

3. East China

The East China region includes Shanghai and six provinces: Jiangsu, Zhejiang, Anhui, Jiangxi, Fujian and Shangdong. It is situated on the lower reaches of three great rivers: the Changjiang, the Huaihe, and the Huanghe, and faces the sea on its east. East China is home of 30% of China's total population but its area is only 8.2% of the country. It has the largest number of cities, the most developed industries and the most intensive management of agriculture.

The processing industry is most developed in this region, with Shanghai as the most important centre, followed by Jiangsu and Shandong. The region's machine-building, electrical equipment, textile, chemical and light industries are of paramount importance. Due to the solid technical base developed over a long period of history, East China possesses complete branches of industry, capable of producing a multitude of high-quality products. It has become a production base for various kinds of mechanical equipment and high-grade consumer goods. Raw material industries, iron and steel and basic chemical industries have also developed considerably in this region. Except for the coal fields in the southwestern part of

Shandong, the northern parts of Anhui and Jiangsu and the oil field of Shengli, which can supply only part of its needs. East China lacks sufficient resources to meet its huge energy demands, making it indispensable to bring in large amounts of coal and oil from the north.

The vast expanse of fertile plains, crisscrossed with rivers and lakes, the mild and humid climate in large parts of the region, particularly the Changjiang Delta, have long rendered it a region of dense population and intensive agriculture. The yield of crops per unit area is the highest in the country, while the hilly region here is favourable for diversified economy of crops, forestry, fruit and tea. Therefore, the region's annual production of food, cotton, rapeseed, peanuts, tea and silk, marine and fresh-water aquatic products ranks first in China. Rice, cotton, silk, and aquatic products abound in the Changjiang Delta, wheat and peanuts in Shangdong Province. Industrial woods flourish in the hilly areas of Zhajiang and Fujian, as well as in the southern part of Anhui and in Jiangxi, alongside the cultivation of rice and rapeseed. However, despite the intensive cultivation of agriculture, the dense population of the region — especially in the cities — and the rapid development of the textile industry together account for the insufficiency of cotton, flax and wool which have to be sent in from other regions; East China is self-sufficient only in foodgrains, while tea and silk are produced in quantities adequate for export.

Communications and transportation are highly developed in East China, as a result of the import of large amounts of raw materials and fuel to Jiangsu, Zhejiang and especially Shanghai, which is the centre of the region, and as a result of the export of industrial products. Railways lead mainly to the harbours, particularly to Shanghai. The bulk of the regional flow of commodities is handled by the Changjiang River, its tributaries and the network of waterways along the Changjiang and the Huaihe, as well as by sea routes. Roughly 70% of the materials enter and leave Shanghai by way of rivers and sea ports.

Shanghai, with its urban population of roughly 6 million, is the biggest metropolis in China, the most solid industrial base, the sea port with the largest handling capacity and the country's most important scientific, technological and cultural centre. It also constitutes the most densely concentrated conurbation, together with Nanjing (population 1,600,000), Zhenjiang, Changzhou, Wuxi and Suzhou along the Shanghai-Nanjing Railway. Other important cities in this region are: Qingdao, a port and industrial city; Jinan, a centre of manufacturing industry; and Hangzhou, the most famous city for tourism.

4. Central-south China

The Central-south region inludes Henan, Hubei, Hunan, and Guangdong and the Guangxi Zhuang Autonomous Region. It is situated in the middle of the country, a little to the south of the centre, with adequate land and water communications and relatively developed industry and agriculture. The iron and steel industry centred in the Wuhan Iron and Steel Company and the non-ferrous metallurgical industry (predominantly of antimony, lead and zinc, tungsten, tin) of central Hunan and Nanling region are all significant. Many important machine-building industries such as transportation machines, motor-driven machines, metallurgical and mining equipment, machines, and agricultural machines, are distributed over such cities as Wuhan, Zhengzhou, Luoyang, Xiangtan, Zhuzhou, Guangzhou, Liuzhou. Coal must be supplied from North China, but hydroelectric potential abounds here, and many medium- and small-sized hydroelectric power stations have been built up at Sanmenxia, Danjiangkou, and Xinfengjiang. When the Gezhouba hydroelectric power station is finished it will be the largest in China. Light industries are represented by textiles in Wuhan and Zhengzhou and sugar-refining in Guangdong and Guangxi.

The Central-south region is one of the most developed agriculturally, a multitude of production bases of commodity crops. Except for Henan Province, where wheat predominates, paddy rice is the region's principal food crop. The largest rice-growing area in China lies south of the Huaihe River. The Jiangshan Plain, the Dongting Lake Plain and the Zhujiang Delta are all significant centres of commodity food production. Peanuts are grown in Guangdong, Guangxi and Henan; half of the country's output of sesame, in Henan and Hubei. Hunan and Hubei are important producers of rapeseed. The former is also the largest producer of tung oil in the country. Approximately 60% of the country's sugar cane is grown in Guangdong and Guangxi. Cured tobacco from Hunan, silk from the Zhujiang Delta, tea from Hunan and Hubei, and freshwater aquatic products from the middle Changjiang Plain and Zhujiang Delta are all important commodity crops. Hainan Island and Leizhou Peninsula in the southern part of Guangdong Province are the only tropical areas in China where tropical crops, such as rubber, are cultivated. Forestry is relatively well-developed in this region. The rate of forest cover in Guangdong and Henan exceeds 13%; timber forest and economic forest prevail; and vast expanses of land suitable for afforestation hold promise of future development. Almost all the cities in this region are key communication centres by virtue of the region's geographical location. Wuhan, situated at the junction of waterways and land routes in central China, is also a comprehensive industrial base, with iron and steel, machinery, textile and chemical industries and well-developed food production. Guangzhou became an economic centre of South China on the basis of foreign trade in predominantely light industrial products. Zhengzhou, Changsha and Nanning are all important industrial cities as well as provincial capitals.

5. Southwest China

The Southwest China region includes three provinces: Sichuan, Guizhou and Yunnan, and also the Tibet Autonomous Region. The topography is complex, with large areas of mountains, hills and plateaus. Natural resources are abundant and diverse. It is the home of many minority nationalities. It is one of the important agricultural regions in China, producing many regionally specialized products in its agriculture, forestry and animal husbandry. Rice, wheat, maize, rapeseed, peanuts, sugar cane, tobacco, silk, tea, tung-oil, raw lacquer, pigs, hide, timber, medicinal materials and fruit are all produced in significant quantities. The extent of agricultural production in various places differs greatly. The Sichuan Basin is dense in population, intensive in agriculture and abundant in food production, various industrial crops, pigs and fruits. In this basin, the Changdu Plain is an important base of commodity crops for the whole country. On the Yunnan-Guizhou Plateau, where there are more mountains than plains, agricultural production is limited, but the potential in forestry is high. The western part of Sichuan and the Tibet Plateau are mountainous, sparsely populated, and have a severely cold climate; this area is important for its animal husbandry. Natural forest resources abound in large parts of west Sichuan and southeast Tibet; the timber reserves here account for 41% of the country's total.

Industry in Southeast China has mostly grown up since Liberation. Development of heavy industry has been especially rapid. Sichuan Province, which is abundant in energy and mineral resources, is the region's best developed industrial base. Its hydroelectric potential exceeds 70% of China's total, but has so far been little utilized. The region's coal reserves, largely in Guizhou, rank second in China, next to North China, but at present coal-mining is more developed in Sichuan. The Sichuan Basin has plentiful natural gas, an important resource for the chemical industry; thus it leads the country in the production of chemical fertilizers. Deposits of iron ore are distributed from the Anning River in the southwestern part of Sichuan to central Yunnan. At the centre of this area is Dukou, where a large-scale iron and steel industry is being developed. Large and medium-sized iron and steel plants are also located in Chongqing, Kunming, Shuicheng, etc. Machine-building is the region's major industrial activity; Chongqing and Chengdu are its centres. The chemical industry is fairly well developed in Chongqing, Chengdu, Zigong, Luzhou, etc. Mining and smelting of non-ferrous metals such as tin, copper, lead, zinc, aluminium and mercury are also important. Railway communication has developed rapidly in this region. The construction of Chengdu-Chongqing, Baoji-Chengdu, Guizhou-Guangxi, Sichuan-Guizhou, Guizhou-Kunming, Hunan-Guizhou, Chengdu-Kunming and Xiangyang-Chongqing railways, coupled with the realignment of the upper reaches of the Changjiang, gave rise to an integrated network of all points both inside and outside the region.

Chongqing and Chengdu, as a result of the development of industry and communications, have become particularly large cities, each with a population of over one million. Chongqing, located at the junction of waterways and overland routes on the upper reaches of the Changjiang River, is the largest comprehensive industrial base in the Southwest and has a population of about 1.8 million. Machine-building and light industries have developed fairly well in Chengdu, which is also the largest scientific and cultural centre in the Southwest. Kunming, the largest city on the Yunnan-Guizhou Plateau, is a well-known place for tourism.

6. Northwest China

The Northwest region includes the provinces of Shaanxi, Gangsu and Qinghai, and Ningxia Hui and Xinjiang Uygur autonomous regions. With an area equal to 32% of the whole country, but a population less than 7% of the total population, the density of population is only 20% of the national average population density. It is a multi-national region with a low standard of economic development, but great potential. The southern part of this region, south of Wuqiao Mountain and east of Riyue Mountain, is the major agricultural area producing wheat and millet. The Guanzhong Plain is an important food and cotton base. But a large part of the farmland here is situated on the Loess Plateau, where steep slopes are under cultivation but where serious loss of water and soil erosion render outputs low and unstable. Large areas west of Wuqiao Mountain belong climatically to arid desert, where agriculture depends entirely on irrigation. Farmlands are restricted to small irrigated patches of oases distributed at the foot of mountain ranges. Crops include wheat, cotton, melons and other fruit, well-known for their high yield and superior quality. But the development of agriculture is restricted by the scarcity of water and threatened by salinization, alkalination and sandstorms. Moreover, deserts and mountain areas prevail over a vast expanse of land. Most of the pastureland is poor and the raising of livestock remains at the mercy of the elements.

Most of the industry in this area developed after Liberation. There are oil fields at Karamay, Yumen and Lenghu; petrochemical industries in Lanzhou and Yumen; coal mining north of the Weihe River valley, in the Helan Mountains, in eastern and central parts of Gansu Province and Urumqi; large hydroelectric power stations in the gorges of the Huanghe River in Qinghai, Gansu and Ningxia; industries in non-ferrous metals (nickel, molybdenum, rare metals), copper, iron and steel, represented by the Jiuquan Iron and Steel Company; machine-building industries in Xi'an and Lanzhou; and cotton and woolen textile industries. The construction of the Tianshui-Lanzhou, Baoji-Chengdu, Baotou-Lanzhou, Gansu-Xinjiang and Gansu-Qinghai railways considerably improved communications and transportation in the region and facilitated its economic development. Xi'an and Lanzhou each have populations of more than one million and are major industrial centres — the former predominating in cotton textiles and machinery; the latter in petrochemicals, machinery, aluminium smelting and woolen textiles.

4. CHINA'S MINORITY NATIONALITIES
By Hua Juxian
State Nationalities Affairs Commission

China's valiant and industrious minority nationalities are imbued with a glorious revolutionary tradition. Throughout their long historic development, they have joined forces with the Han nationality to open up the border areas and develop a prosperous economy. They have made contributions in creating our country's brilliant culture and in founding the People's Republic of China.

I. General Situation of the Minority Nationalities

China is a unitary multinational state. Apart from the Han nationality, there are 55 minority nationalities. Up to 1978, they accounted for 55.8 million, or 6%, of the total population.

Population. The populations of various minority nationalities differ greatly. The 12 million Zhuangs constitute the largest minority nationality in China while the Hoche and Russian nationalities are the smallest, with populations of less than 1,000 each.

Thirteen nationalities have populations above 1 million: the Mongolians, Hui, Tibetans, Uygurs, Miao, Yi, Zhuang, Buyi, Koreans, Manchu, Dong, Yao and Bai.

Fifteen nationalities have populations above 100,000: the Tujia, Kazak, Hani, Dai, Li, Lisu Wa, She, Gaoshan, Lahu, Shui, Dongxiang, Naxi, Tu and Luoba.

Eighteen nationalities have a population between 10,000 and 100,000: the Kirgiz, Jingpo, Daur, Mulao, Qiang, Bulang, Sala, Maonan, Gelao, Xibo, Achang, Tajik, Nu, Ewenki, Benglong, Pumi, Monba and Jinuo.

Nine nationalities have a population below 10,000: the Uzbeks, Baoan, Yugur, Jing, Tartars, Dulong, Oroqen, Hezhe and Russians.

In addition, there are groups of people in Yunnan, Tibet and other provinces awaiting conclusive definitions of their nationality origins.

Land Areas. Although relatively small in number, the minority nationalities inhabit large areas, amounting to 50–60% of the total area of China. They are distributed mainly over the Inner Mongolia Autonomous Region, the Xinjiang Uygur Autonomous Region, the Tibet Autonomous Region, the Guangxi Zhuang Autonomous Region, the Ningxia Hui Autonomous Region and the provinces of Heilongjiang, Jilin, Liaoning, Gansu, Qinghai, Sichuan, Yunnan, Guizhou, Guangdong, Hunan, Hebei, Hubei, Fujian and Taiwan. Over 20 minority nationalities live in Yunnan Province, more than in any other province. The Gaoshan nationality lives in a compact community in Taiwan Province.

In addition to those who live in compact communities, 10 million people of minority nationalities live among other nationalities or are scattered among cities, towns and the countryside throughout the country. At present, minority nationalities live in every province and city and in over 70% of China's counties. In regions where minority nationalities live in compact communities, the Hans reside there together with them. In regions such as Inner Mongolia, Ningxia and Guangxi, the Han are in the majority. The mixing of various nationalities and the living together of various nationalities as ethnic groups with the Han as the core is one of the characteristics of our country's distribution of nationalities.

The principal areas where minority nationalities live are vast and rich in natural resources. This includes cultivated areas of more than 200 million *mu*, while over 700 million *mu* of wasteland are available for development. Some areas, such as the Hetao Plain in Ningxia and Inner Mongolia, are among China's important grain producing regions. As for industrial crops, Xinjiang is the main area for producing long-staple cotton; Guangxi is a sugar-cane growing area; Yunnan and Hainan Island of Guangdong Province produce coffee, rubber and other tropical crops.

Animal husbandry is of national significance in many areas inhabited by people of minority nationalities who live in compact communities. Grasslands, where China's five natural grazing regions are located, cover 29% of the country's territory.

Natural Resources. Areas where minority nationalities live also abound in rare birds and animals, such as pandas, rhinoceros, elephants and peacock; precious traditional medications, such as the bulb of fritillary, Chinese catepillar fungus, musk, pilose antler of young stags, tubers of elevated gastrodia, fruit of Chinese wolfberry, safflower and snow lotus are also found in these areas. Forests in these regions come to 45 million hectares, accounting for 37% of the country's total forest area. Timber stands amount to 4,300 million cubic metres, or 49.7% of the national total. Water resources are abundant, with a total hydroelectric potential of 300 million kw. The area of freshwater covers about 46 million *mu*. Within the boundaries of these areas are located several famous lakes, such as Qinghai Lake, Lop Nor, Hulunbuir Lake, Namou Lake and Er Hai Lake. The world-famous Changjiang (Yangtze) River, as well as the Huanghe, Zhujiang, Heilongjiang, Sunghua, Tarim, Yarlung Zangbo and Nujiang rivers rise in and flow through these areas.

Mineral Resources. Rich varieties of mineral resources and abundant mineral deposits include coal, petroleum, ferrous and non-ferrous metals, rare metals and nonmetallic mineral resources. The oil fields of Baise in Guangxi, Majiatan in Ningxia and Qaidam in Qinghai are quite well-known. Abundant geothermal energy resources in Tibet have begun to be exploited. There are rich tin ore deposits in Guangxi, ranking first in China. Bauxite also occupies an important place in Guangxi, Gejiu City, capital of the Han-Yi Autonomous Prefecture on the Honghe River of Yunnan Province, is traditionally known as "the tin capital." Inner Mongolia's mineral resources of aluminium, zinc and copper play an important role in north China. In addition, mica in Xinjiang, gypsum in Ningxia and marble in Yunnan are well-known in China.

All of this wealth belongs to the people of all nationalities of our country. They constitute indispensable material bases on which to build our great motherland into a powerful modernized country.

Language and Culture. Prior to Liberation, only 21 nationalities practiced their own cultures. Fifty minority nationalities have their own languages. The Han spoken language and written characters [i.e., the Chinese language] are commonly used among the Hui, Manchu and She nationalities. Eleven nationalities — the Mongolians, Tibetans, Uygurs, Koreans, Kazaks, Xibo, Dai, Uzbeks, Kirgiz, Tartars and Russians — have their own commonly used written languages; although seven nationalities — the Yi, Naxi, Miao, Jingpo, Lisu, Lahu and Wa — have their own written languages, these languages are not in common use. The remaining 34 nationalities prior to Liberation had no written languages of their own.

After Liberation, the party and state helped ten of these nationalities to create their own written languages, including Zhuang, Buyi, Miao, Dong, Hani, Li; they helped other nationalities such as the Uygurs, Kazaks, Jingpo, Lahu and Dai to reform their written languages.

The languages of 29 nationalities belong to the Han-Tibetan language family; 18 belong to the Altay language family; 3 belong to the South Asian language family; and 2 to the Indo-European language family. The language of the Gaoshan nationality in Taiwan Province belongs to the Southern Island language family. The language of one nationality has yet to be classified.

Customs and Religion. Throughout their long historical development, the minority nationalities have evolved their own customs and habits in matters of diet, dress and personal adornment, housing, marriage, burial, holidays and celebrations, entertainment, taboos and other aspects. The ten nationalities that adhere to Islam do not eat pork. Every nationality celebrates its own traditional holidays, such as "the water splashing festival" of the Dai, the "torch festival" of the Yi and the "Tibetan New Year's Day" of the Tibetan people. These holidays to varying degrees mirror each nationality's historic traditions and intellectual qualities in realms of morals, arts and religious concepts. Such observances have become an important aspect of the distinguishing features of different nationalities. Religions, including Buddhism and Islam in particular, have a profound influence among minority nationalities. Before Liberation, the ten nationalities of Hui, Uygurs, Kazaks, Kirgiz, Tartars, Uzbeks, Tajiks, Dongxiang, Sala and Baoans took Islam as their faith. The Tibetans, Mongolians, Dai and Yugur professed Buddhism (including Lamaism). Quite a number of Miao, Yao, Yi and other nationalities followed Catholicism and other forms of Christianity. The Oroqen, Ewinki and Daur believed in shamanic religion. It was or that reason that prior to Liberation in China, nationality problems often became intertwined with religious problems.

Social Development. Uneven social development among different nationalities was quite common, even among different areas within one nationality. Generally speaking, the standard of development in Han-inhabited areas was higher. This was due to the fact that before Liberation, there was advanced feudalist agricultural economy in the Han-inhabited areas, where modern capitalist industry and commerce had also developed to a considerable extent. Therefore, in areas where the Hans and other minority nationalities lived together, or in those areas of national minority concentration which bordered on or overlapped those areas inhabited by the Han people, the local economy reached or nearly reached the economic levels of Han-inhabited areas.

Conversely, the stages of social development were comparatively backward in places far from areas inhabited by the Han people. Examples of the backwardness of these minority nationalities is illustrated by the "slash-and-burn" cultivation practiced among the Miao, Yao, Jingpo, Lisu and Wa; the nomadic life of the Mongolians, Tibetans, Kazaks and Yugurs; the simple fishing and hunting life of the Oroqin, Ewenki, Hezhe and Jinuo. Some nationalities have not yet brought about a division of labour between animal husbandry and farming, between agriculture and the handicrafts industry. In other cases, economic division of labour has been carried out not within one nationality but among different nationalities.

To the extent that they are closely linked with stagnant and semi-stagnant production, the cultures of the minority nationalities are generally also backward. Although many minority nationalities possess unique styles in architecture, handicrafts, arts, music and dance, as well as in cultural heritage, and although these traditions have enriched our country's cultural wealth, most minority nationalities either have no intellectuals of their own or have only some intellectuals in the midst: of a majority in the nationality who are illiterate. Some nationalities are still in a primitive stage of keeping records — performing these functions by notching wood or tying knots.

In line with economic development at the time, the social structures of the minority nationalities before Liberation were quite complex and represented various stages of historical development. The social and economic structures of 30 minority nationalities, including the Zhuang, Hui, Uygurs, Koreans, Manchu, Buyi, Bai, Tujia, Dong and Miao; most Mongolians, Yi and Li; and a small portion of Tibetans more or less resembled that of the Han. The feudal serf system existed among the Tibetan, Dai and Hani nationalities; the herding and farming system existed in some pasturelands in Inner Mongolia. The majority of the Yi nationality had long entered into feudal landlord economy, but in Sichuan and the greater and lesser Liangshan Mountain areas of Yunnan, the slave system was still being practiced. Up to Liberation, several minority nationalities preserved systems of primitive communes. These nationalities included the Oreqen, Weinki, Hezhe, Dulong, Nu, Lisu, Wa, Bulang, Benglong, Jingpo, Jinuo, Monba and Li.

During the long process of historic development, the Han and people of the minority nationalities developed economic ties. The introduction of advanced technologies such as iron-smelting, pottery, wine-making and paper-making from the Han-inhabited central plains promoted economic development in the border areas. At the same time, the Han people imported new varieties of crops, cultivation techniques and livestock products. In turn, the Han gained valuable experiences in animal husbandry from people of minority nationalities, thus bringing about significant advances in agricultural and livestock production in the central plains. But due to the conditions of national oppression, these ties and exchanges had often to be carried out in the midst of national conflict.

II. Policies Towards Minority Nationalities

Since Liberation, the Communist Party of China and the people's government have formulated and implemented many policies towards nationalities that have taken account of Marxist-Leninist theories on nationality and of the actual conditions of minority nationalities in China. These policies have included:

1. *Adherence to the equality of all nationalities and opposition to national discrimination and oppression.*

The Communist Party of China has consistently stood for the principle that all of the nationalities are equal, be they large or small; the people of minority nationalities and scattered members of minority nationalities, whether living in compact communities or living together with other nationalities, enjoy equal rights. In line with this consistent stand, the party and government drew up a series of policies, decrees and measures on national equality. In the early days of the People's Republic, the Common Programme clearly stipulated that all the nationalities living in the territory of the People's Republic of China are equal. National discrimination, oppression and acts that undermine national unity are strictly forbidden. In the spirit of the provisions of the Common Programme, the State Council of the Central People's Government in 1951 issued its Instructions on Handling Addresses, Names of Places, Steles and Horizontal Inscribed Boards Which Have the Nature of Discriminating Against or Insulting Minority Nationalities; in 1952, it issued the Programme on the Implementation of National Regional Autonomy of the People's Republic of China and the Decision on Guaranteeing to All Scattered Members of the Minority Nationalities the Enjoyment of Equal National Rights. Thereafter, the state constitutions issued by all subsequent National People's Congresses clearly defined that all nationalities enjoy equal rights.

In order to enable the majority nationalities to participate in the management of state affairs on an equal footing with the Han and to guarantee that they enjoy equal rights in organs of state power at all levels, the party and government made special provisions with regard to the number of deputies to be elected to the National People's Congress and to local people's congresses at each level. Generally speaking, the percentage of deputies of minority nationality surpassed their proportion in the national population. The party and government have seen to it that all minority nationalities including those with populations of less than 1,000 have their own representatives in the congresses. At the same time, in areas where people of the minority nationalities live in compact communities, regional autonomy has been implemented to guarantee that the people of minority nationalities enjoy the right to manage their own national affairs within the unified extended family of the motherland.

In light of the provisions of the Constitution and other statutes, all minority nationalities have the freedom to develop their own oral and written languages. In court, the people of minority nationalities may bring lawsuits and defend cases in their own national oral or written languages. They have the freedom to retain or to reform their own customs and habits and no one has the right to interfere. They have the freedom to participate in people's organizations and in all kinds of professional work and may not be excluded on grounds of nationality. If subjected to nationality discrimination or abuse, the minority nationalities have the freedom to file charges with the people's government. All these measures have enabled dozens of minority nationalities which were not recognized by the Guomingdang reactionary government and were in a powerless condition, to appear on our country's political scene and become equal members in the great family of the motherland.

For the sake of implementing the above-mentioned stipulations, the government has taken many concrete measures such as permitting all nationalities to have their days off during their own holidays; not encouraging pig breeding among minority nationalities who do not eat pork; opening up separate dining halls or giving food allowances to the workers and staff of the Hui and Uygur natonalities, so that they may have their meals in neighbourhood Muslim canteens.

During the ten years of turmoil [i.e., the "cultural revolution"] policies regarding the minority nationalities were sabotaged by Lin Biao and the Gang of Four. After restoring order out of the chaos, the Chinese government quickly corrected the errors and restored all effective measures guaranteeing equal national rights. China's criminal law, promulgated in 1979, stipulated that those who have committed serious offences of illegally depriving citizens of their legitimate freedom of religious belief and violating the customs and habits of the minority nationalities will be sentenced to two years' imprisonment or hard-labour detention. This stipulation guarantees by law the implementation of equal national rights.

2. *The implementation of regional national autonomy.*

This is China's basic policy in resolving nationality issues. Regional national autonomy means the setting up within a united motherland under the unified leadership of the party and government and within the areas where people of the minority nationalities live in compact communities, corresponding autonomous local governments in which the minority nationalities are the masters over their own internal affairs.

The autonomous rights and characteristics of the national autonomous local government are:

A. The national autonomous governments are to be mainly formed by members of the nationalities which exercise autonomy.

B. The written languages of the minority nationalities in common use locally are to be used as instruments to exercise functions and powers.

C. In exercising their functions and powers, the autonomous governments are to fully respect national characteristics, customs and habits.

D. Autonomous and special regulations are to be formulated in accord with conditions of autonomous localities.

E. The autonomous governments are to enjoy greater financial privileges than non-autonomous local governments.

In the areas where people of the minority nationalities live in compact communities, over 90% of the population have adopted national regional autonomy. There are five autonomous regions in China: the Inner Mongolia Autonomous Region, the Xinjiang Uygur Autonomous Region, the Ningxia Hui Autonomous Region, the Guangxi Zhuang Autonomous Region and the Tibet Autonomous Region; there are also 29 autonomous prefectures and 75 autonomous counties (i.e., Inner Mongolian "banners").

The policy of national autonomy has strengthened national unity, enhanced unity between the people of all nationalities, aroused the enthusiasm of the minority nationalities, and promoted all levels of development in the national autonomous regions. But this policy had been sabotaged by Lin Biao and the Gang of Four during the ten years of turmoil. After the smashing of the Gang of Four, and especially after the Third Plenary Session of the 11th Central Committee of the Communist Party of China, the government reaffirmed this policy, did a lot of work to correct the wrongs, and adopted many important regulations; for example, the original boundaries of the Inner Mongolia Autonomous Region were restored and the abnormal situation that existed in some of its autonomous areas — where Han cadres occupied the leading positions — was corrected. At present, the promulgation of laws on national regional autonomy is going on in all parts of the country to strengthen the participation of the nationalities in autonomous organs, and especially to increase the proportion of nationality cadres. These measures will gradually perfect the policy of national autonomy, so that the minority nationalities may fully enjoy their rights as masters of their own affairs.

3. *Devoting major efforts to fostering and training cadres of minority nationalities.*

The party and government have always attached great importance to the work of fostering and training minority nationality cadres. During each stage of development of the revolution, our party trained a large number of cadres of minority nationalities. The Institute for Nationalities, founded in Yanan, was the first school to train national cadres under the leadership of the Communist Party of China. After the founding of New China, the party and government drew up the policy of "training cadres of minority nationalities thoroughly and on large scale." In addition to training them in conventional universities and colleges, ten institutes have been established for the nationalities: Central, Southwest, Northwest, Qinghai, Yunnan, Guizhou, Tibet, Guangdong, Guangxi and South-central Institutes for Nationalities. The provinces and regions run their own national cadres' schools and training centres and train and appoint cadres of minority nationalities through various campaigns and practical work.

According to incomplete data through 1977, there were over 800,000 cadres of minority nationalities throughout the country, an increase of more than 80-fold over 1949. Among them, some were assigned to leading posts in party and government organs; some worked in the departments of economy, culture, science and other special fields; and some were scientific and technical personnel. Cadres of minority nationalities maintain broad contact with the people of their nationalities; they are familiar with local conditions; and they play an important role in the development of the national autonomous areas. Thus, they are valuable assets for the party and the state.

Lin Biao and the Gang of Four wantonly dissolved eight institutes for nationalities; disrupted the work of training national cadres; fabricated a large number of unjust, false and misjudged cases; and ruthlessly persecuted and dealt mercilessly with numerous cadres of minority nationalities. After the downfall of the Gang of Four, the majority of unjust, false and misjudged cases were corrected and many cadres of minority nationalities were reinstated. In the course of reopening the eight institutes for nationalities, the Nationalities Affairs Commission convened a meeting of presidents of institutes for nationalities. The conference focused its discussions on policies and measures to train cadres and specialists of minority nationalities in the goals of the four modernizations. In order to strengthen the training of cadres of minority nationalities, the Organization Department of the Central Committee of the Communist Party of China and the Nationalities Affairs Commission convened a series of special meetings. Despite these efforts, however, the quantity and calibre of nationalities cadres is as yet unable to meet the needs of revolution and construction in the areas inhabited by national minorities. The population of minority nationalities accounts for 6% of the country's total, while cadres of minority nationalities account for only 4.8% of all cadres. There are few cadres from minority nationalities in leading posts above the county level, and scientific and technical cadres are particularly lacking. These circumstances require further improvement.

4. *Since Liberation, the party and state have undertaken positive and prudent measures to assist minority nationalities achieve democratic reform and socialist transformation.*

In the process of reform, by pursuing all cases from the standpoint of actual conditions in the areas of the minority nationalities, the party and state formulated and adopted a series of correct principles and policies. In light of these principles and policies, the party and state carried out social reforms in stock-raising areas by adopting policies distinct from those in agricultural areas where the government did not distribute cattle and sheep. In the realm of democratic reform, it abolished feudal exploitation and carried out socialization of grazing land. Herdsmen enjoyed freedom to graze sheep and cattle. These policies were beneficial both to herdsmen and to herd owners. Afterwards, with a view to developing production, it carried out transformation among the herd owners and herdsmen through different means, set up socialist collective ownership and ownership by the whole people [i.e., state ownership].

As to those areas inhabited by minority nationalities where class polarization was not clear, where standards of production were very low and where primitive commune systems had survived, the party and state provided energetic assistance by aiding progress in production and culture and by helping them to gradually pass over to socialism by directly taking to the collective road while at the same time undertaking socialist transformation and necessary reforms. For those minority nationalities in the early stage of capitalist development, the party and state upheld the policy of achieving reform through consultation — exercising the policy of redemption for those upper-class elements who accepted socialist reform. For those regions which had achieved social and economic structures roughly comparable to those of the Han nationality, more moderate policies were adopted.

In this way in less than 20 years the minority nationalities had crossed one or many stages of social development and had passed over to socialism, thus opening up broader prospects for the development of their productive forces.

5. *Constantly readjusting and improving relations between various nationalities and strengthening national unity.*

Since the founding of New China, the party and government have done much to strengthen national unity. On the whole, relations between various nationalities have been good and the unity between various nationalities has stood up to all tests. While guarding against and opposing external sabotage to split national unity, the party and government have paid constant attention to and resolved problems that threatened unity, making steady efforts to overcome the two tendencies of great Han chauvinism and local nationalism — the former tendency in particular. To this end the party, in 1952 and 1953, twice promoted education in nationality policies throughout the party and the country. Along with this educational programme, the party and government carried out general follow-ups on the implementation of policies towards nationalities, resolved a number of problems, improved relations between various nationalities and achieved excellent results.

After 1958, due to the influence of the "Left" ideology — especially during the ten years of turmoil under the reactionary policies of the Gang of Four towards the nationalities — national unity suffered great damage. The reactionary features of these policies were that instead of stressing opposition to great Han chauvinism, they opposed local nationalism. This weakened the cordial links between the party and the minority nationalities and damaged the friendly unity between various nationalities.

After the downfall of the Gang of Four, under the direction of the Party Central Committee and in combination with the condemnation of crimes committed by Lin Biao and the Gang of Four, reeducation and review of policies towards the nationalities were carried out throughout China to eliminate the Gang's negative influence on the work towards nationalities and to correct mistakes of infringing on the right of national equality and violating policies towards nationalities.

In 1980, the Central Committee of the Communist Party of China, in a document prepared for a symposium on Tibetan problems, pointed out: "It is an important task of great historical and strategic significance to cement national unity between the Han, Tibetan, Uygur and other minority nationalities in the border areas and the hinterland." At present, all areas where people of various nationalities live in compact communities are making great efforts to implement the spirit of this document so as to improve relations between various nationalities and resolve problems.

III. Tremendous Achievements in Economic Construction

Policy Achievements. Our country's fundamental tasks in solving national problems are to ernestly and sincerely help the minority nationalities to develop economically and culturally and to gradually eliminate actual inequalities inherited through historical circumstances. Since the founding of the People's Republic, the party and government have adopted many policies and measures with regard to manpower, material and technical assistance, for example:

1. *In the field of capital construction, the state invested large sums of money in districts inhabited by national minorities.* From 1950 to 1979, investments in capital construction in these areas amounted to 63,400 million yuan.

2. *In the financial field, the state annually provides huge subsidies to minority nationalities areas by granting credits, relief funds and production allowances.*

During the past few years, the total amount of special funds for regional subsidies to underdeveloped areas inhabited by national minorities was 1,000 million yuan. The total included subsidies for the development of border areas; for capital construction in border areas and areas where people of minority nationalities live in compact communities; special funds in support of the developments in under-developed areas amounted to 1,000 million yuan. In some areas where production was extremely backward, a policy of reducing or remitting taxes was carried out. In some areas short of production tools, free distribution of farm tools was carried out. Since the early period of Liberation, the party and government have assisted the growth of domestic trade by implementing a policy of rational pricing, price differences between industrial and agricultural products were readjusted so as to increase the income of peoples of minority nationalities and to promote production in areas inhabited by various nationalities.

3. *Each year the people's government allocates and transfers large quantities of industrial and agricultural products, raw materials and machinery to areas inhabited by the people of minority nationalities.*

It is clearly stipulated that all industrial products required throughout the country should be given priority in distribution to areas inhabited by the people of minority nationalities. These areas are also given special consideration in regard to some commodities.

4. *In order to enhance economic and cultural development in areas inhabited by the people of minority nationalities, the party and state have sent large numbers of cadres and technicians to work in these areas.* Hinterland workers and youth have been methodically mobilized to help construction in the border areas. Moreover, members of the People's Liberation Army stationed in areas inhabited by the people of minority nationalities also actively participate in local projects.

5. *In recent years, the state has made special provision for some provinces and municipalities with relatively advanced development in industry and science and technology to provide direct one-on-one assistance to areas inhabited by the people of minority nationalities.* For example: Beijing assists work in Inner Mongolia; Shanghai helps Yunnan and Ningxia; Tianjin helps Gansu; Hebei helps Yunnan and Ningxia; Tianjin helps Gansu; Hebei helps Guizhou; Jiangsu helps Guangxi and Xinjiang; Shandong helps Qinghai; and the whole country helps Tibet. Assistance covers a wide range of activities, including industrial and agricultural production and stock-raising, culture, education, science and public health. According to the specific conditions of the two sides, each relationship has its own emphasis, such as training cadres, disseminating techniques and providing equipment.

Thanks to the assistance from the state and plain living and hard work of the people of minority nationalities, the look of the areas inhabited by the people of minority nationalities have undergone marked changes.

Quantitative Achievements in Minority Nationalities Areas. By 1979, the total value of industry and agriculture in the areas inhabited by minority nationalities had increased by over tenfold since 1949, reaching 38,000 million yuan.

Agriculture. Since the founding of the People's Republic, strenuous efforts in capital construction on the farms in national autonomous areas have produced an extensive area of cultivated land with high, stable yields.

Irrigated areas increased by 154.1% between 1949 and 1979. The proportion of cultivated land under irrigation rose from 22.7% in 1949 to 41% in 1979. Primitive farming methods such as the use of bamboo and wooden farm tools and slash-and-burn cultivation have long become things of the past. Animal husbandry continues to be the main element in agricultural production. Nevertheless, several hundred thousand agricultural machines are in place, including tractors, rice transplanters, reapers and lorries. Chemical fertilizers and electricity used in the countryside has increased progressively while great stress has been attached to scientific farming.

In 1979, the total output of agricultural production in the national autonomous areas reached 16,800 million yuan, making up 10.6% of the national total and marking an increase of 279.1% compared with 1949; grain output was 33.17 million tons, making up 10% of the national total and an increase of 186.9% over 1949; cotton output was 56,700 tons, an increase of 455.9% over 1949; and timber output was 15.90 million cubic metres, an increase of 582.4% over 1949. The output of oil-bearing crops, roasted tobacco, tea, sub-tropical industrial crops, local and special products and medicinal herbs has also increased rapidly.

Livestock raising plays an important role in the economic development of areas inhabited by the people of minority nationalities, and occupies a large proportion of the country's animal husbandry output.

By the end of 1979, the total number of head of domestic animals in farming and stockbreeding areas of the autonomous regions reached 171.38 million, amounting to 28.8% of the national total and representing a four-fold increase over 1949; of these, draught animals reached 38.88 million head, making up 41.1% of the national total and an increase of 136.2% as compared with 1949; sheep totalled 98.57 million, accounting for 53.8% of the national total and almost six times greater than 1949; and pigs were 33.93 million, or 10.6% of the national total and four times higher than the total of 1949.

Since the founding of the People's Republic, the minority nationalities have supplied the state with large quantities of farm animals, meat-producing animals, draught animals and livestock products. These have provided significant support to national development. Initial results have been achieved in development of grasslands through the mechanization and quasi-mechanization of stock-raising, as well as through veterinary science and improvements in breeding domestic animals.

Industry. During the old society, the areas of minority nationalities had only small-scale handicrafts industries, or no industries at all. Today, a large number of modern industries have been established, including textiles, steel, coal, electric power, petroleum, machinery, chemicals and building materials industries. The state has constructed world-famous projects in Inner Mongolia, Xinjiang, Gansu and other regions inhabited by the people of minority nationalities; these include the Baotou Iron and Steel Company, the Karamay Oilfield and the Liujiaxia and Qintongxia hydroelectric power stations. In 1979, the total output of industry in the national autonomous areas was 42 times greater than that of 1949. During the three decades from 1950 to 1979, the annual growth-rate for total industrial output in the national autonomous areas was impressively high, averaging 13.3%.

Before Liberation, the people of minority nationalities had no steel industry whatsoever. By 1979, however, iron and steel output in these areas had reached 1.5 million tons. Coal output increased from 1.7 million tons in 1952 to 57.30 million tons in 1979; crude oil from 52,000 tons to 6.2 million tons; electricity from less than 100 million kwh to 18,000 million kwh; and cotton cloth from 35,000 metres to 395 million metres.

Transportation. Transportation has grown rapidly. Except for Tibet, where a railway is now under construction, trains can now travel straight to Inner Mongolia, Ningxia, Guangxi and Xinjiang. By 1979, the total mileage of railroad traffic in the autonomous areas was 3.3 times greater than in 1949. Highway construction in areas inhabited by minority nationalities has been expanding by leaps and bounds. By 1979, the total mileage of highways opened to traffic in autonomous areas was 18.5 times that of 1949. Bus services reach nearly every county town and every commune. Civil air service extends to the capitals of the autonomous regions and to some autonomous prefectures. In short, the underdeveloped conditions in transportation in these areas have been markedly improved.

Commerce. Sectors of national trade that have a direct bearing on production and life among the people of minority nationalities has also made great headway. According to incomplete data, total purchasing value in the autonomous regions in 1979 had increased by 23-fold over 1952; the total value of retail commodities increased 17-fold and the number of workers and staff engaged in national trade increased 5 times, with workers and staff of minority nationalities engaged in this sector having increased by 112 times. At present, in areas inhabited by the people of minority nationalities, administrative organs for commerce are being set up in stages.

Education. Today, each of the 55 minority nationalities has students in colleges. In 1980, there were 460,000 teachers and 9,700,000 students from minority nationalities enrolled at all levels of education. The number of students has increased by 980% over the early Liberation period; primary-school students increased by 8-fold, middle school students 46-fold and college students 20-fold. In some advanced areas, education developed more rapidly. In the Yanbian Korean Autonomous Prefecture in Jilin Province, primary-school and junior-middle-school education have been widespread for a long time, while senior-middle-school education has become quite well-developed.

Health Care. Medical organizations have for the most part been established in those areas of minority nationalities where doctors and medicines were lacking and where there had been widespread illness and high mortality rates in the past. Nearly all counties (and banners in Inner Mongolia) and most communes have hospitals or commune clinics. According to statistics through 1979, medical and public-health facilities in the autonomous areas totalled 25,027, an increase of 32.6% over 1949. Of the total, 10,254 were hospitals, an increase of 4,458.2% as compared with that of 1949. Along with growth in medical services, endemic or persistent diseases in these areas have been brought under effective prevention and control; these include malaria, snail fever, undulant fever, leprosy, keshan disease and fluorine poisoning.

Obstacles to Rapid Development. Although the people of minority nationalities have gained remarkable achievements in production since the founding of the People's Republic, differences remain vast when compared with areas inhabited by the Han people. Agriculture and stock-breeding have developed slowly; they are low in management levels and weak in their ability to combat natural calamities. Given this production basis, the living standards of peasants and herdsmen cannot be expected to grow rapidly. In some poor mountainous areas, the people's life is yet more difficult, requiring long-term state assistance. In industry and transport, conditions remain relatively backward. School enrollments, the extent of universal education and qualification rates are much lower than in Han-inhabited areas. In some remote mountainous and pastoral areas, the illiteracy rate is about 70–80% among young people.

Moreover, some contradictions exist owing to the fact that the exploitation of natural resources in areas inhabited by minority nationalities has not been linked to the interests of the local minority nationalities. Some of these problems have been handled properly, while others are now being addressed by the departments concerned and are in the process of being settled.

Since the Third Plenary Session of the 11th Central Committee of the Communist Party of China, the party and government have taken many measures in these areas and done much to exploit favourable local conditions, to implement policies, to respect the right of self-management of the communes and brigades, to promote various systems of responsibility in production and to reduce or wave taxation burdens on the people. All of these measure have been welcomed by the people of minority nationalities and have had the effect of arousing the enthusiasm of the masses. The situation in areas inhabited by people of minority nationalities has changed for the better. So long as we persist in implementing the party's principles and policies and in further strengthening unity between the nationalities, economic development is sure to leap forward in the areas inhabited by the people of minority nationalities.

5. THE CONSTITUTION OF THE COMMUNIST PARTY OF CHINA
(Adopted by the 11th National Congress of the Communist Party of China on August 18, 1977)

GENERAL PROGRAMME

The Communist Party of China is the political party of the proletariat, the highest form of its class organization. It is a vigorous vanguard organization composed of the advanced elements of the proletariat, which leads the proletariat and the revolutionary masses in their fight against the class enemy.

The basic programme of the Communist Party of China for the entire historical period of socialism is to persist in continuing the revolution under the dictatorship of the proletariat, eliminate the bourgeoisie and all other exploiting classes step by step and bring about the triumph of socialism over capitalism. The ultimate aim of the Party is the realization of communism.

Marxism-Leninism-Mao Zedong Thought is the guiding ideology and theoretical basis of the Communist Party of China. The Party persists in combating revisionism, and dogmatism and empiricism. The Party upholds dialectical materialism and historical materialism as its world outlook and opposes the idealist and metaphysical world outlook.

Our great leader and teacher Chairman Mao Zedong was the founder of the Communist Party of China and the greatest Marxist-Leninist of our time. Integrating the universal truth of Marxism-Leninism with the concrete practice of the revolution, Chairman Mao inherited, defended and developed Marxism-Leninism in the struggles against imperialism and the domestic reactionary classes, against Right and "Left" opportunist lines in the Party and against international modern revisionism. He led our Party, our army and our people in winning complete victory in the new-democratic revolution and in founding the People's Republic of China, a state of the dictatorship of the proletariat, through protracted revolutionary struggles and revolutionary wars, and then in achieving tremendous victories in the socialist revolution and socialist construction through fierce and complex struggles between the proletariat and the bourgeoisie, and through the unparalleled Great Proletarian Cultural Revolution. The banner of Chairman Mao is the great banner guiding our Party to victory through united struggle.

Socialist society covers a historical period of considerable length. In this period, classes, class contradictions and class struggle, the struggle between the socialist road and the capitalist road and the danger of capitalist restoration invariably continue to exist, and there is the threat of subversion and aggression by imperialism and social-imperialism. The resolution of these contradictions depends solely on the theory and practice of continued revolution under the dictatorship of the proletariat.

China's Great Proletarian Cultural Revolution was a political revolution carried out under socialism by the proletariat against the bourgeoisie and all other exploiting classes to consolidate the dictatorship of the proletariat and prevent the restoration of capitalism. Political revolutions of this nature will be carried out many times in the future.

The Communist Party of China adheres to its basic line for the entire historical period of socialism. It must correctly distinguish and handle the contradictions among the people and those between ourselves and the enemy, and consolidate and strengthen the dictatorship of the proletariat. The Party must rely on the working class wholeheartedly and rely on the poor and lower-middle peasants, unite with the vast numbers of intellectuals and other working people, mobilize all positive factors and expand the revolutionary united front led by the working class and based on the worker-peasant alliance. It must uphold the proletarian nationality policy and strengthen the great unity of the people of all nationalities in China. It must carry on the three great revolutionary movements of class struggle, the struggle for production and scientific experiment, it must adhere to the principle of building our country independently, with the initiative in our own hands, and through self-reliance, diligence and thrift, and to the principle of being prepared against war and natural disasters and doing everything for the people, so as to build socialism by going all out, aiming high and achieving greater, faster, better and more economical results. The Party must lead the people of all nationalities in making China a powerful socialist country with a modern agriculture, industry, national defence and science and technology by the end of the century.

The Communist Party of China upholds proletarian internationalism and opposes great-nation chauvinism; it unites firmly with the genuine Marxist-Leninist Parties and organizations the world over; unites with the proletariat, the oppressed people and nations of the whole world and fights shoulder to shoulder with them to oppose the hegemonism of the two superpowers, the Soviet Union and the United States, to overthrow imperialism, modern revisionism and all reaction; and to wipe the system of exploitation of man by man off the face of the earth, so that all mankind will be emancipated.

The correctness or incorrectness of the ideological and political line decides everything. All Party comrades must implement Chairman Mao's proletarian revolutionary line comprehensively and correctly and adhere to the three basic principles: Practice Marxism, and not revisionism; unite, and don't split; be open and aboveboard, and don't intrigue and conspire. They must have the revolutionary boldness in daring to go against any tide that runs counter to these three basic principles.

The whole Party must adhere to the organizational principle of democratic centralism and practice centralism on the basis of democracy and democracy under centralized guidance. It must give full scope to inner-Party democracy and encourage the initiative and creativeness of all Party members and Party organizations at all levels, and combat bureaucracy, commandism and warlordism. The whole Party must strictly observe Party discipline, safeguard the Party's centralization, strengthen its unity, oppose all splittist and factional activities, oppose the assertion of independence from the Party and oppose anarchism. In relations among comrades in the Party, all members should apply the principle of "Say all you know and say it without reserve" and "Blame not the speaker but be warned by his words," adopt the dialectical method, start from the desire for unity, distinguish between right and wrong through criticism or struggle and arrive at a new unity. The Party must strive to create a political situation in which there are both centralism and democracy, both discipline and freedom, both unity of will and personal ease of mind and liveliness.

The Party must conscientiously follow the proletarian line on cadres, the line of "appointing people on their merit," and oppose the bourgeois line on cadres, the line of "appointing people by favouritism." It must train and bring up in mass struggles millions of successors in the revolutionary cause of the proletariat in accordance with the five requirements put forward by Chairman Mao. Special vigilance must be exercised against careerists, conspirators and double-dealers so as to prevent such bad types from usurping the leadership of the Party and the state at any level and ensure purity of the leadership at all levels.

The whole Party must keep to and carry forward its fine tradition of following the mass line and seeking truth from facts, keep to and carry forward the style of work characterized by integration of theory with practice, close ties with the masses and criticism and self-criticism, the style of modesty, prudence and freedom from arrogance and impetuosity, and the style of plain living and hard struggle; and the whole Party must prevent Party members, especially leading Party cadres, from exploiting their position to seek privileges, and wage a resolute struggle against burgeois ideology and the bourgeois style of work.

A member of the Communist Party of China should at all times and in all circumstances subordinate his personal interests to the interests of the Party and the people; he should fear no difficulties and sacrifices, work actively for the fulfilment of the programme of the Party and devote his whole life to the struggle for communism.

The Communist Party of China is a great, glorious and correct Party, and it is the core of leadership of the whole Chinese people. The whole Party must always hold high and resolutely defend the great banner of Marxism-Leninism-Mao Zedong Thought and ensure that our Party's cause will continue to advance triumphantly along the Marxist line.

Chapter I. Membership

Article 1. Any Chinese worker, poor peasant, lower-middle peasant, revolutionary soldier or any other revolutionary who has reached the age of 18 and who accepts the Constitution of the Party and is willing to join a Party organization and work actively in it, carry out the Party's decisions, observe Party discipline and pay membership dues may become a member of the Communist Party of China.

Article 2. The Communist Party of China demands that its members should:

1. Conscientiously study Marxism-Leninism-Mao Zedong Thought, criticize capitalism and revisionism and strive to remould their world outlook;

2. Serve the people whole-heartedly and pursue no private interests either for themselves or for a small number of people;

3. Unite with all the people who can be united inside and outside the Party, including those who have wrongly opposed them;

4. Maintain close ties with the masses and consult with them when matters arise;

5. Earnestly practice criticism and self-criticism, be bold in correcting their shortcomings and mistakes and dare to struggle against words and deeds that run counter to Party principles;

6. Uphold the Party's unity, refuse to take part in and moreover oppose any factional organization or activity which splits the Party;

7. Be truthful and honest to the Party, observe Party discipline and the laws of the state and strictly guard Party and state secrets; and

8. Actively fulfil the tasks assigned them by the Party and play an exemplary vanguard role in the three great revolutionary movements of class struggle, the struggle for production and scientific experiment.

Article 3. Applicants for Party membership must go through the procedure for admission individually. An applicant must be recommended by two full Party members, fill in an application form for Party membership and be examined by a Party branch, which must seek opinions extensively inside and outside the Party; he or she may become a probationary member after being accepted by the general membership meeting of the Party branch and being approved by the next higher Party committee.

Before approving the admission of an applicant for Party membership, the higher Party committee must appoint someone specially to talk with the applicant and carefully examine his or her case.

Article 4. The probationary period of a probationary member is one year. The Party organization concerned should make further efforts to educate and observe him or her.

When the probationary period has expired, the Party branch to which the probationary member belongs must promptly discuss whether he or she is qualified for full membership. If qualified, he or she should be given full membership as scheduled; if it is necessary to continue to observe him or her, the probationary period may be extended but no more than one year; if he or she is found to be really unfit for Party membership, his or her status as a probationary member should be annulled. Any decision either to transfer a probationary member to full membership, to prolong the probationary period, or to annul his or her status as a probationary member must be adopted by the general membership meeting of the Party branch and approved by the next higher Party committee.

The probationary period of a probationary member begins from the day when the higher Party committee approves the applicant's admission. The Party standing of a Party member begins from the day when he or she is transferred to full membership.

A probationary member does not have the right to vote and to elect or be elected enjoyed by a full member.

Article 5. When a Party member violates Party discipline, the Party organization concerned should give the member education and, on the merits of the case, may take any of the following disciplinary measures — a warning, a serious warning, removal from his or her post in the Party, being placed on probation within the Party, and expulsion from the Party.

The period for which the Party member concerned is placed on probation should not exceed two years. During this period, he or she does not have the right to vote and to elect or be elected. If the Party member concerned has been through the period of probation and has corrected his or her mistake, these rights should be restored; if the member clings to the mistake instead of correcting it, he or she should be expelled from the Party.

Proven renegades, enemy agents, absolutely unrepentant persons in power taking the capitalist road, alien class elements, degenerates and new bourgeois elements must be expelled from the Party and not be re-admitted.

Article 6. Any disciplinary measure taken against a Party member must be decided on by a general membership meeting of the Party branch to which the member belongs and should be submitted to the next higher Party committee for approval. Under special circumstances, a primary Party committee or a higher Party committee has the power to take disciplinary action against a Party member.

Any decision to remove a member from a local Party committee at any level, to place on probation or to expel the member from the Party must be made by the said Party committee and be submitted to the next higher Party committee for approval.

Corresponding provisions on disciplinary measures against members of the Party committees at all levels in the army units should be laid down by the Military Commission of the Central Committee in accordance with the Party Constitution.

Any decision to take a disciplinary measure against a Member or Alternate Member of the Central Committee must be made by the Central Committee or its Political Bureau.

When a Party organization takes a decision on a disciplinary measure against a member, it must, barring special circumstances, notify the member that he or she should attend the meeting. If the member disagrees with the decision, he or she may ask for a review of the case and has the right to appeal to higher Party committees, up to and including the Central Committee.

Article 7. A Party member whose revolutionary will has degenerated, who fails to function as a Communist and remains unchanged despite repeated education may be persuaded to withdraw from the Party. The case must be decided by the general membership meeting of the Party branch concerned and submitted to the next higher Party committee for approval.

A Party member who fails to take part in Party life, to do the work assigned by the Party and to pay membership dues over six months and without proper reason is regarded as having given up membership.

When a Party member asks to withdraw from the Party or has given up membership, the Party branch concerned should, with the approval of its general membership meeting, remove his or her name from the Party rolls and report the case to the next higher Party committee for the record.

Chapter II. Organizational System of the Party

Article 8. The Party is organized on the principle of democratic centralism.

The whole Party must observe democratic centralist discipline: The individual is subordinate to the organization, the minority is subordinate to the majority, the lower level is subordinate to the higher level, and the entire Party is subordinate to the Central Committee.

Article 9. Delegates to Party congresses and members of Party committees at all levels should be elected by secret ballot after democratic consultation and in accordance with the five requirements for successors in the revolutionary cause of the proletariat and with the principle of combining the old, the middle-aged and the young.

Article 10. The highest leading body of the Party is the National Congress and, when it is not in session, the Central Committee elected by it. The leading bodies of Party organizations at all levels in the localities and in the army units are the Party congresses or general membership meetings at their respective levels and the Party committees elected by them. Party congresses at all levels are convened by Party committees at their respective levels. The convocation of Party congresses at all levels in the localities and in the army units and the composition of the Party committees they elect are subject to approval by the next higher Party committee.

Article 11. Party committees at all levels operate on the principle of combining collective leadership with individual responsibility under a division of labour. They should rely on the political experience and wisdom of the collective; all important issues are to be decided collectively, and at the same time each individual is to be enabled to play his or her due part.

Party committees at all levels should set up their working bodies in accordance with the principles of close ties with the masses and of structural simplicity and efficiency. Party committees at the county level and upwards may send out their representative organs when necessary.

Article 12. Party committees at all levels should report regularly on their work to Party congresses or general membership meetings, constantly listen to the opinions of the masses both inside and outside the Party and put themselves under their supervision.

Party members have the right to criticize Party organizations and working personnel in leading posts at all levels and make proposals to them and also the right to bypass the immediate leadership and present their appeals and complaints to higher levels, up to and including the Central Committee and the Chairman of the Central Committee. It is absolutely impermissible for anyone to suppress criticism or to retaliate. Those guilty of doing so should be investigated and punished.

If a Party member holds different views with regard to the decisions or directives of the Party organizations, he or she is allowed to reserve these views and has the right to bring up the matter for discussion at Party meetings and the right to bypass the immediate leadership and report to higher levels, up to and including the Central Committee and the Chairman of the Central Committee, but the member must resolutely carry out these decisions and directives.

Article 13. The Central Committee of the Party, local Party committees at the county level and upwards and Party committees in the army units at the regimental level and upwards should set up commissions for inspecting discipline.

The commissions for inspecting discipline at all levels are to be elected by the Party committees at the respective levels and, under their leadership, should strengthen Party members' education on discipline, be responsible for checking on the observance of discipline by Party members and Party cadres and struggle against all breaches of Party discipline.

Article 14. State organs, the People's Liberation Army and the militia and revolutionary mass organizations, such as trade unions, the Communist Youth League, poor and lower-middle peasant associations and women's federations, must all accept the absolute leadership of the Party.

Leading Party groups should be set up in state organs and people's organizations. Members of leading Party groups in state organs and people's organizations at the national level are to be appointed by the Central Committee of the Party. Members of leading Party groups in state organs and people's organizations at all levels in the localities are to be appointed by the corresponding Party committees.

Chapter III. Central Organizations of the Party

Article 15. The National Congress of the Party should be convened every five years. Under special circumstances, it may be convened before its due date or postponed.

Article 16. The plenary session of the Central Committee of the Party elects the Political Bureau of the Central Committee, the Standing Committee of the Political Bureau of the Central Committee and the Chairman and Vice-Chairmen of the Central Committee.

The plenary session of the Central Committee of the Party is convened by the Political Bureau of the Central Committee.

When the Central Committee is not in plenary session, the Political Bureau of the Central Committee and its Standing Committee exercise the functions and powers of the Central Committee.

Chapter IV. Party Organizations in the Localities and the Army Units

Article 17. Local Party congresses at the county level and upwards and Party congresses in the army units at the regimental level and upwards should be convened every three years. Under special circumstances, they may be convened before their due date or postponed, subject to approval by the next higher Party committees.

Local Party committees at the county level and upwards and Party committees in the army units at the regimental level and upwards elect their standing committees, secretaries and deputy secretaries.

Chapter V. Primary Organizations of the Party

Article 18. Party branches, general Party branches or primary Party committees should be set up in factories, mines and other enterprises, people's communes, offices, schools, shops, neighbourhoods, companies of the People's Liberation Army and other primary units in accordance with the need of the revolutionary struggle and the size of their Party membership, subject to approval by the next higher Party committees.

Committees of Party branches should be elected annually, committees of general Party branches and primary Party committees should be elected every two years. Under special circumstances, the election may take place before its due date or be postponed, subject to approval by the next higher Party committees.

Article 19. The primary organizations of the Party should play the role of a fighting bastion. Their main tasks are:

1. To lead Party members and people outside the Party in studying Marxism-Leninism-Mao Zedong Thought conscientiously, educate them in the ideological and political line and in the Party's fine tradition and give them basic knowledge about the Party;

2. To lead and unite the broad masses of the people in adhering to the socialist road, in criticizing capitalism and revisionism, in correctly distinguishing and handling the contradictions among the people and those between ourselves and the enemy and in waging a resolute struggle against the class enemy;

3. To propagate and carry out the line, policies and decisions of the Party, and fulfil every task assigned by the Party and the state;

4. To maintain close ties with the masses, constantly listen to their opinions and demands and faithfully report these to higher Party organizations and be concerned about their political, economic and cultural life;

5. To promote inner-Party democracy, practice criticism and self-criticism, expose and get rid of shortcomings and mistakes in work, and wage struggles against violations of the law and breaches of discipline, against corruption and waste, and against bureaucracy and all other undesirable tendencies; and

6. To admit new Party members, enforce

Party discipline, and consolidate the Party organizations, getting rid of the stale and taking in the fresh, so as to purify the Party's ranks and constantly enhance the Party's fighting power.

6. THE CONSTITUTION OF THE PEOPLE'S REPUBLIC OF CHINA
(Adopted by the First Session of the Fifth National People's Congress of the People's Republic of China on March 5, 1978)

PREAMBLE

After more than a century of heroic struggle the Chinese people, led by the Communist Party of China headed by our great leader and teacher Chairman Mao Zedong, finally overthrew the reactionary rule of imperialism, feudalism and bureaucrat-capitalism by means of people's revolutionary war, winning complete victory in the new-democratic revolution, and in 1949 founded the People's Republic of China.

The founding of the People's Republic of China marked the beginning of the historical period of socialism in our country. Since then, under the leadership of Chairman Mao and the Chinese Communist Party, the people of all our nationalities have carried out Chairman Mao's proletarian revolutionary line in the political, economic, cultural and military fields and in foreign affairs and have won great victories in socialist revolution and socialist construction through repeated struggles against enemies both at home and abroad and through the Great Proletarian Cultural Revolution. The dictatorship of the proletariat in our country has been consolidated and strengthened, and China has become a socialist country with the beginnings of prosperity.

Chairman Mao Zedong was the founder of the People's Republic of China. All our victories in revolution and construction have been won under the guidance of Marxism-Leninism-Mao Zedong Thought. The fundamental guarantee that the people of all our nationalities will struggle in unity and carry the proletarian revolution through to the end is always to hold high and staunchly to defend the great banner of Chairman Mao.

The triumphant conclusion of the first Great Proletarian Cultural Revolution has ushered in a new period of development in China's socialist revolution and socialist construction. In accordance with the basic line of the Chinese Communist Party for the entire historical period of socialism, the general task for the people of the whole country in this new period is: To persevere in continuing the revolution under the dictatorship of the proletariat, carry forward the three great revolutionary movements of class struggle, the struggle for production and scientific experiment, and make China a great and powerful socialist country with modern agriculture, industry, national defence and science and technology by the end of the century.

We must persevere in the struggle of the proletariat against the bourgeoisie and in the struggle for the socialist road against the capitalist road. We must oppose revisionism and prevent the restoration of capitalism. We must be prepared to deal with subversion and aggression against our country by social-imperialism and imperialism.

We should consolidate and expand the revolutionary united front which is led by the working class and based on the worker-peasant alliance, and which unites the large numbers of intellectuals and other working people, patriotic democratic parties, patriotic personages, our compatriots in Taiwan, Hong Kong and Macao, and our countrymen residing abroad. We should enhance the great unity of all the nationalities in our country. We should correctly distinguish and handle the contradictions among the people and those between ourselves and the enemy. We should endeavour to create among the people of the whole country a political situation in which there are both centralism and democracy, both discipline and freedom, both unity of will and personal ease of mind and liveliness, so as to help bring all positive factors into play, overcome all difficulties, better consolidate the proletarian dictatorship and build up our country more rapidly.

Taiwan is China's sacred territory. We are determined to liberate Taiwan and accomplish the great cause of unifying our motherland.

In international affairs, we should establish and develop relations with other countries on the basis of the Five Principles of mutual respect for sovereignty and territorial integrity, mutual non-aggression, non-interference in each other's internal affairs, equality and mutual benefit, and peaceful coexistence. Our country will never seek hegemony, or strive to be a superpower. We should uphold proletarian internationalism. In accordance with the theory of the three worlds, we should strengthen our unity with the proletariat and the oppressed people and nations throughout the world, the socialist countries, and the third world countries, and we should unite with all countries subjected to aggression, subversion, interference, control and bullying by the social-imperialist and imperialist superpowers to form the broadest possible international united front against the hegemonism of the superpowers and against a new world war, and strive for the progress and emancipation of humanity.

Chapter I. General Principles

Article 1. The People's Republic of China is a socialist state of the dictatorship of the proletariat led by the working class and based on the alliance of workers and peasants.

Article 2. The Communist Party of China is the core of leadership of the whole Chinese people. The working class exercises leadership over the state through its vanguard, the Communist Party of China.

The guiding ideology of the People's Republic of China is Marxism-Leninism-Mao Zedong Thought.

Article 3. All power in the People's Republic of China belongs to the people. The organs through which the people exercise state power are the National People's Congress and the local people's congresses at various levels.

The National People's Congress, the local people's congresses at various levles and all other organs of state practice democratic centralism.

Article 4. The People's Republic of China is a unitary multi-national state.

All the nationalities are equal. There should be unity and fraternal love among the nationalities and they should help and learn from each other. Discrimination against, or oppression of, any nationality, and acts which undermine the unity of the nationalities are prohibited. Big-nationality chauvinism and local-nationality chauvinism must be opposed.

All the nationalities have the freedom to use and develop their own spoken and written languages, and to preserve or reform their own customs and ways.

Regional autonomy applies in an area where a minority nationality lives in a compact community. All the national autonomous areas are inalienable parts of the People's Republic of China.

Article 5. There are mainly two kinds of ownership of the means of production in the People's Republic of China at the present stage: socialist ownership by the whole people and socialist collective ownership by the working people.

The state allows non-agricultural individual labourers to engage in individual labour involving no exploitation of others, within the limits permitted by law and under unified arrangement and management by organizations at the basic level in cities and towns or in rural areas. At the same time, it guides these individual labourers step by step into the road of socialist collectivization.

Article 6. The state sector of the economy, that is, the socialist sector owned by the whole people, is the leading force in the national economy.

Mineral resources, waters and those forests, undeveloped lands and other marine and land resources owned by the state are the property of the whole people.

The state may requisition by purchase, take over for use, or nationalize land under conditions prescribed by law.

Article 7. The rural people's commune sector of the economy is a socialist sector collectively owned by the masses of working people. At present, it generally takes the form of three-level ownership, that is, ownership by the commune, the production brigade and the production team, with the production team as the basic accounting unit. A production brigade may become the basic accounting unit when its conditions are ripe.

Provided that the absolute predominance of the collective economy of the people's commune is ensured, commune members may farm small plots of land for personal needs, engage in limited household side-line production, and in pastoral areas they may also keep a limited number of livestock for personal needs.

Article 8. Socialist public property shall be inviolable. The state ensures the consolidation and development of the socialist sector of the economy owned by the whole people and of the socialist sector collectively owned by the masses of working people.

The state prohibits any person from using any means whatsoever to disrupt the economic order of the society, undermine the economic plans of the state, encroach upon or squander state and collective property, or injure the public interest.

Article 9. The state protects the right of citizens to own lawfully earned income, savings, houses and other means of livelihood.

Article 10. The state applies the socialist principles: "He who does not work, neither shall he eat" and "from each according to his ability, to each according to his work."

Work is an honourable duty for every citizen able to work. The state promotes socialist labour emulation, and, putting proletarian politics in command, it applies the policy of combining moral encouragement with material reward, with the stress on the former, in order to heighten the citizens' socialist enthusiasm and creativeness in work.

Article 11. The state adheres to the general line of going all out, aiming high and achieving greater, faster, better and more economical results in building socialism, it undertakes the planned, proportionate and high-speed development of the national economy, and it continuously develops the productive forces, so as to consolidate the country's independence and security and improve the people's material and cultural life step by step.

In developing the national economy, the state adheres to the principle of building our country independently, with the initiative in our own hands and through self-reliance, hard struggle, diligence and thrift, it adheres to the principle of taking agriculture as the foundation and industry as the leading factor, and it adheres to the principle of bringing the initiative of both the central and local authorities into full play under the unified leadership of the central authorities.

The state protects the environment and natural resources and prevents and eliminates pollution and other hazards to the public.

Article 12. The state devotes major efforts to developing science, expands scientific research, promotes technical innovation and technical revolution and adopts advanced techniques wherever possible in all departments of the national economy. In scientific and technological work we must follow the practice of combining professional contingents with the masses, and combining learning from others with our own creative efforts.

Article 13. The state devotes major efforts to developing education in order to raise the cultural and scientific level of the whole nation. Education must serve proletarian politics and be combined with productive labour and must enable everyone who receives an education to develop morally, intellectually and physically and become a worker with both socialist consciousness and culture.

Article 14. The state upholds the leading position of Marxism-Leninism-Mao Zedong Thought in all spheres of ideology and culture. All cultural undertakings must serve the workers, peasants and soldiers and serve socialism.

The state applies the policy of "letting a hundred flowers blossom and a hundred schools of thought contend" so as to promote the development of the arts and sciences and bring about a flourishing socialist culture.

Article 15. All organs of state must constantly maintain close contact with the masses of the people, rely on them, heed their opinions, be concerned for their weal and woe, streamline administration, practice economy, raise efficiency and combat bureaucracy.

The leading personnel of state organs at all levels must conform to the requirements for successors in the proletarian revolutionary cause and their composition must conform to the principle of the three-in-one combination of the old, the middle-aged and the young.

Article 16. The personnel of organs of state must earnestly study Marxism-Leninism-Mao Zedong Thought, wholeheartedly serve the people, endeavour to perfect their professional competence, take an active part in collective productive labour, accept supervision by the masses, be models in observing the Constitution and the law, correctly implement the policies of the state, seek the truth from facts, and must not have recourse to deception or exploit their position and power to seek personal gain.

Article 17. The state adheres to the principle of socialist democracy, and ensures to the people the right to participate in the management of state affairs and of all economic and cultural undertakings, and the right to supervise the organs of state and their personnel.

Article 18. The state safeguards the socialist system, suppresses all treasonable and counter-revolutionary activities, punishes all traitors and counter-revolutionaries, and punishes new-born bourgeois elements and other bad elements.

The state deprives of political rights, as prescribed by law, those landlords, rich peasants and reactionary capitalists who have not yet been reformed, and at the same time it provides them with the opportunity to earn a living so that they may be reformed through labour and become law-abiding citizens supporting themselves by their own labour.

Article 19. The Chairman of the Central Committee of the Communist Party of China commands the armed forces of the People's Republic of China.

The Chinese People's Liberation Army is the workers' and peasants' own armed force led by the Communist Party of China; it is the pillar of the dictatorship of the proletariat. The state devotes major efforts to the revolutionization and modernization of the Chinese People's Liberation Army, strengthens the building of the militia and adopts a system under which our armed forces are a combination of the field armies, the regional forces and the militia.

The fundamental task of the armed forces of

the People's Republic of China is: To safeguard the socialist revolution and socialist construction, to defend the sovereignty, territorial integrity and security of the state, and to guard against subversion and aggression by social-imperialism, imperialism and their lackeys.

Chapter II. The Structure of the State
Section I
The National People's Congress

Article 20. The National People's Congress is the highest organ of state power.

Article 21. The National People's Congress is composed of deputies elected by the people's congresses of the provinces, autonomous regions, and municipalities directly under the Central Government, and by the People's Liberation Army. The deputies should be elected by secret ballot after democratic consultation.

The National People's Congress is elected for a term of five years. Under special circumstances, its term of office may be extended or the succeeding National People's Congress may be convened before its due date.

The National People's Congress holds one session each year. When necessary, the session may be advanced or postponed.

Article 22. The National People's Congress exercises the following functions and powers:
1. To amend the Constitution;
2. To make laws;
3. To supervise the enforcement of the Constitution and the law;
4. To decide on the choice of the Premier of the State Council upon the recommendation of the Central Committee of the Communist Party of China;
5. To decide on the choice of other members of the State Council upon the recommendation of the Premier of the State Council;
6. To elect the President of the Supreme People's Court and the Chief Procurator of the Supreme People's Procuratorate;
7. To examine and approve the national economic plan, the state budget and the final state accounts;
8. To confirm the following administrative divisions: provinces, autonomous regions, and municipalities directly under the Central Government;
9. To decide on questions of war and peace; and
10. To exercise such other functions and powers as the National People's Congress deems necessary.

Article 23. The National People's Congress has the power to remove from office the members of the State Council, the President of the Supreme People's Court and the Chief Procurator of the Supreme People's Procuratorate.

Article 24. The Standing Committee of the National People's Congress is the permanent organ of the National People's Congress. It is responsible and accountable to the National People's Congress.

The Standing Committee of the National People's Congress is composed of the following members:

the Chairman;
the Vice-Chairmen;
the Secretary-General; and
other members.

The National People's Congress elects the Standing Committee of the National People's Congress and has the power to recall its members.

Article 25. The Standing Committee of the National People's Congress exercises the following functions and powers:
1. To conduct the election of deputies to the National People's Congress;
2. To convene the sessions of the National People's Congress;
3. To interpret the Constitution and laws and to enact decrees;
4. To supervise the work of the State Council, the Supreme People's Court and the Supreme People's Procuratorate.
5. To change and annul inappropriate decisions adopted by the organs of state power of provinces, autonomous regions, and municipalities directly under the Central Government;
6. To decide on the appointment and removal of individual members of the State Council upon the recommendation of the Premier of the State Council when the National People's Congress is not in session;
7. To appoint and remove Vice-Presidents of the Supreme People's Court and Deputy Chief Procurators of the Supreme People's Procuratorate;
8. To decide on the appointment and removal of plenipotentiary representatives abroad;
9. To decide on the ratification and abrogation of treaties concluded with foreign states;
10. To institute state titles of honour and decide on their conferment;
11. To decide on the granting of pardons;
12. To decide on the proclamation of a state of war in the event of armed attack on the country when the National People's Congress is not in session; and

13. To exercise such other functions and powers as are vested in it by the National People's Congress.

Article 26. The Chairman of the Standing Committee of the National People's Congress presides over the work of the Standing Committee; receives foreign diplomatic envoys; and in accordance with the decisions of the National People's Congress or its Standing Committee promulgates laws and decrees, dispatches and recalls plenipotentiary representatives abroad, ratifies treaties concluded with foreign states and confers state titles of honour.

The Vice-Chairmen of the Standing Committee of the National People's Congress assist the Chairman in his work and may exercise part of the Chairman's functions and powers on his behalf.

Article 27. The National People's Congress and its Standing Committee may establish special committees as deemed necessary.

Article 28. Deputies to the National People's Congress have the right to address inquiries to the State Council, the Supreme People's Court, the Supreme People's Procuratorate, and the ministries and commissions of the State Council, which are all under obligation to answer.

Article 29. Deputies to the National People's Congress are subject to supervision by the units which elect them. These electoral units have the power to replace at any time the deputies they elect, as prescribed by law.

Section II
The State Council

Article 30. The State Council is the Central People's Government and the executive organ of the highest organ of state power; it is the highest organ of state administration.

The State Council is responsible and accountable to the National People's Congress, or, when the National People's Congress is not in session, to its Standing Committee.

Article 31. The State Council is composed of the following members:
the Premier;
the Vice-Premiers;
the ministers; and
the ministers heading the commissions.

The Premier presides over the work of the State Council and the Vice-Premiers assist the Premier in his work.

Article 32. The State Council exercises the following functions and powers:
1. To formulate administrative measures, issue decisions and orders and verify their execution, in accordance with the Constitution, laws and decrees;
2. To submit proposals on laws and other matters to the National People's Congress or its Standing Committee;
3. To exercise unified leadership over the work of the ministries and commissions and other organizations under it;
4. To exercise unified leadership over the work of local organs of state administration at various levels throughout the country;
5. To draw up and put into effect the national economic plan and the state budget;
6. To protect the interests of the state, maintain public order and safeguard the rights of citizens;
7. To confirm the following administrative divisions: autonomous prefectures, counties, autonomous counties, and cities;
8. To appoint and remove administrative personnel according to the provisions of the law; and
9. To exercise such other functions and powers as are vested in it by the National People's Congress or its Standing Committee.

Section III
The Local People's Congresses and the Local Revolutionary Committees at Various Levels

Article 33. The administrative division of the People's Republic of China is as follows:
1. The country is divided into provinces, autonomous regions, and municipalities directly under the Central Government;
2. Provinces and autonomous regions are divided into autonomous prefectures, counties, autonomous counties, and cities; and
3. Counties and autonomous counties are divided into people's communes and towns.

Municipalities directly under the Central Government and other large cities are divided into districts and counties. Autonomous prefectures are divided into counties, autonomous counties, and cities.

Autonomous regions, autonomous prefectures and autonomous counties are all national autonomous areas.

Article 34. People's congresses and revolutionary committees are established in provinces, municipalities directly under the Central Government, counties, cities, municipal districts, people's communes and towns.

People's congresses and revolutionary committees of the people's communes are organizations of political power at the grass-roots level, and are also leading organs of collective economy.

Revolutionary committees at the provincial level may establish administrative offices as their agencies in prefectures.

Organs of self-government are established in autonomous regions, autonomous prefectures and autonomous counties.

Article 35. Local people's congresses at various levels are local organs of state power.

Deputies to the people's congresses of provinces, municipalities directly under the Central Government, counties, and cities divided into districts are elected by people's congresses at the next lower level by secret ballot after democratic consultation; deputies to the people's congresses of cities not divided into districts, and of municipal districts, people's communes and towns are directly elected by the voters by secret ballot after democratic consultation.

The people's congresses of provinces and municipalities directly under the Central Government are elected for a term of five years. The people's congresses of counties, cities and municipal districts are elected for a term of three years. The people's congresses of people's communes and towns are elected for a term of two years.

Local people's congresses at various levels hold at least one session each year, which is to be convened by revolutionary committees at the corresponding levels.

The units and electorates which elect the deputies to the local people's congresses at various levels have the power to supervise, remove and replace their deputies at any time according to the provisions of the law.

Article 36. Local people's congresses at various levels, in their respective administrative areas, ensure the observance and enforcement of the Constitution, laws and decrees; ensure the implementation of the state plan; make plans for local economic and cultural development and for public utilities; examine and approve local economic plans, budgets and final accounts; protect public property; maintain public order; safeguard the rights of citizens and the equal rights of minority nationalities; and promote the development of socialist revolution and socialist construction.

Local people's congresses may adopt and issue decisions within the limits of their authority as prescribed by law.

Local people's congresses elect, and have the power to recall, members of revolutionary committees at the corresponding levels. People's congresses at county levels and above elect, and have the power to recall, the presidents of the people's courts and the chief procurators of the people's procuratorates at the corresponding levels.

Deputies to local people's congresses at various levels have the right to address inquiries to the revolutionary committees, people's courts, people's procuratorates and organs under the revolutionary committees at the corresponding levels, which are all under obligation to answer.

Article 37. Local revolutionary committees at various levels, that is, local people's governments, are the executive organs of local people's congresses at the corresponding levels and they are also local organs of state administration.

A local revolutionary committee is composed of a chairman, vice-chairmen and other members.

Local revolutionary committees carry out the decisions of people's congresses at the corresponding levels as well as the decisions and orders of the organs of state administration at higher levels, direct the administrative work of their respective areas, and issue decisions and orders within the limits of their authority as prescribed by law. Revolutionary committees at country levels and above appoint or remove the personnel of organs of state according to the provisions of the law.

Local revolutionary committees are responsible and accountable to people's congresses at the corresponding levels and to the organs of state administration at the next higher level, and work under the unified leadership of the State Council.

Section IV
The Organs of Self-Government of National Autonomous Areas

Article 38. The organs of self-government of autonomous regions, autonomous prefectures and autonomous counties are people's congresses and revolutionary committees.

The election of the people's congresses and revolutionary committees of national autonomous areas, their terms of office, their functions and powers and also the establishment of their agencies should conform to the basic principles governing the organization of local organs of state as specified in Section III, Chapter Two, of the Constitution.

In autonomous areas where a number of nationalities live together, each nationality is entitled to appropriate representation in the organs of self-government.

Article 39. The organs of self-government of national autonomous areas exercise autonomy within the limits of their authority as prescribed by law, in addition to exercising the functions and powers of local organs of state as specified by the Constitution.

The organs of self-government of national autonomous areas may, in the light of the political, economic and cultural characteristics of the nationality or nationalities in a given area, make regulations on the exercise of autonomy and also specific regulations and submit them to the Standing Committee of the National People's Congress for approval.

In performing their functions, the organs of self-government of national autonomous areas employ the spoken and written language or languages commonly used by the nationality or nationalities in the locality.

Article 40. The higher organs of state shall fully safeguard the exercise of autonomy by the organs of self-government of national autonomous areas, take into full consideration the characteristics and needs of the various minority nationalities, make a major effort to train cadres of the minority nationalities, and actively support and assist all the minority nationalities in their socialist revolution and construction and thus advance their socialist economic and cultural development.

Section V
The People's Courts and the People's Procuratorates

Article 41. The Supreme People's Court, local people's courts at various levels and special people's courts exercise judicial authority. The people's courts are formed as prescribed by law.

In accordance with law, the people's courts apply the system whereby representatives of the masses participate as assessors in administering justice. With regard to major counter-revolutionary or criminal cases, the masses should be drawn in for discussion and suggestions.

All cases in the people's courts are heard in public except those involving special circumstances as prescribed by law. The accused has the right to defence.

Article 42. The Supreme People's Court is the highest judicial organ.

The Supreme People's Court supervises the administration of justice by local people's courts at various levels and by special people's courts; people's courts at the higher levels supervise the administration of justice by people's courts at the lower levels.

The Supreme People's Court is responsible and accountable to the National People's Congress and its Standing Committee. Local people's courts at various levels are responsible and accountable to local people's congresses at the corresponding levels.

Article 43. The Supreme People's Procuratorate exercises procuratorial authority to ensure observance of the Constitution and the law by all the departments under the State Council, the local organs of state at various levels, the personnel of organs of state and the citizens. Local people's procuratorates and special people's procuratorates exercise procuratorial authority within the limits prescribed by law. The people's procuratorates are formed as prescribed by law.

The Supreme People's Procuratorate supervises the work of local people's procuratorates at various levels and of special people's procuratorates; people's procuratorates at the higher levels supervise the work of those at the lower levels.

The Supreme People's Procuratorate is responsible and accountable to the National People's Congress and its Standing Committee. Local people's procuratorates at various levels are responsible and accountable to people's congresses at the corresponding levels.

Chapter III. The Fundamental Rights and Duties of Citizens

Article 44. All citizens who have reached the age of 18 have the right to vote and to stand for election, with the exception of persons deprived of these rights by law.

Article 45. Citizens enjoy freedom of speech, correspondence, the press, assembly, association, procession, demonstration and the freedom to strike, and have the right to "speak out freely, air their views fully, hold great debates and write big-character posters."

Article 46. Citizens enjoy freedom to believe in religion and freedom not to believe in religion and to propagate atheism.

Article 47. The citizens' freedom of person and their homes are inviolable.

No citizen may be arrested except by decision of a people's court or with the sanction of a people's procuratorate, and the arrest must be made by a public security organ.

Article 48. Citizens have the right to work. To ensure that citizens enjoy this right, the state provides employment in accordance with the principle of overall consideration, and, on the basis of increased production, the state gradually increases payment for labour, improves working conditions, strengthens labour protection and expands collective welfare.

Article 49. Working people have the right to rest. To ensure that working people enjoy this right, the state prescribes working hours and systems of vacations and gradually expands material facilities for the working people to rest and recuperate.

Article 50. Working people have the right to material assistance in old age, and in case of illness or disability. To ensure that working people enjoy this right, the state gradually expands social insurance, social assistance, public health services, cooperative medical services, and other services.

The state cares for and ensures the livelihood of disabled revolutionary armymen and the families of revolutionary martyrs.

Article 51. Citizens have the right to education. To ensure that citizens enjoy this right, the state gradually increases the number of schools of various types and of other cultural and educational institutions and popularizes education.

The state pays special attention to the healthy development of young people and children.

Article 52. Citizens have the freedom to engage in scientific research, literary and artistic creation and other cultural activities. The state encourages and assists the creative endeavours of citizens engaged in science, education, literature, art, journalism, publishing, public health, sports and other cultural work.

Article 53. Women enjoy equal rights with men in all spheres of political, economic, cultural, social and family life. Men and women enjoy equal pay for equal work.

Men and women shall marry of their own free will. The state protects marriage, the family, and the mother and child.

The state advocates and encourages family planning.

Article 54. The state protects the just rights and interests of overseas Chinese and their relatives.

Article 55. Citizens have the right to lodge complaints with organs of state at any level against any person working in an organ of state, enterprise or institution for transgression of law or neglect of duty. Citizens have the right to appeal to organs of state at any level against any infringement of their rights. No one shall suppress such complaints and appeals or retaliate against persons making them.

Article 56. Citizens must support the leadership of the Communist Party of China, support the socialist system, safeguard the unification of the motherland and the unity of all nationalities in our country and abide by the Constitution and the law.

Article 57. Citizens must take care of and protect public property, observe labour discipline, observe public order, respect social ethics and safeguard state secrets.

Article 58. It is the lofty duty of every citizen to defend the motherland and resist aggression.

It is the honourable obligation of citizens to perform military service and to join the militia according to the law.

Article 59. The People's Republic of China grants the right of residence to any foreign national persecuted for supporting a just cause, for taking part in revolutionary movements or for engaging in scientific work.

Chapter IV. The National Flag, The National Emblem and the Capital

Article 60. The national flag of the People's Republic of China has five stars on a field of red.

The national emblem of the People's Republic of China is: Tian An Men in the centre, illuminated by five stars and encircled by ears of grain and a cogwheel.

The capital of the People's Republic of China is Beijing.

7. THE CENTRAL PEOPLE'S GOVERNMENT
(THE STATE COUNCIL)
(Compiled by the State Personnel Bureau of the State Council, April 31, 1981)

I. Listing of Premiers, Vice-Premiers, Advisers and the General Secretary of the State Council

Premier: Zhao Ziyang

Vice-Premiers: Wan Li   Yu Qiuli   Geng Biao
                  Fang Yi   Gu Mu   Yao Yilin
                  Kang Shien   Chen Muhua (female) Bo Yibo
                  Ji Pengfei   Yang Jingren   Zhang Aiping
                  Huang Hua

Advisors: Qian Zhiguang   Liu Linbo   Li Qiang   Zeng Sheng

General Secretary: Du Xingyuan

II. Listing of Ministers in Charge of Ministries and Commissions of the State Council

Minister of Foreign Affairs:	Huang Hua	(concurrently)
Minister of National Defence:	Geng Biao	(concurrently)
Minister in Charge of the State Planning Commission:	Yao Yilin	(concurrently)
Minister in Charge of the State Agricultural Commission:	Wan Li	(concurrently)
Minister in Charge of the State Economic Commission:	Yuan Baohua	
Minister in Charge of the State Capital Construction Commission:	Han Guang	
Minister in Charge of the State Scientific and Technological Commission:	Fang Yi	(concurrently)
Minister in Charge of the Foreign Investment Commission:	Gu Mu	(concurrently)
Minister in Charge of the Administrative Commission on Import and Export Affairs:	Gu Mu	(concurrently)
Minister in Charge of the Machine-Building Industry Commission of the State Council	Bo Yibo	(concurrently)
Minister in Charge of the State Energy Commission:	Yu Qiuli	(concurrently)
Minister in Charge of the State Nationalities Affairs Commission:	Yang Jingren	(concurrently)
Minister of Public Security:	Zhao Cangbi	
Minister of Civil Affairs:	Cheng Zihua	
Minister of Justice:	Wei Wenbo	
Minister of Foreign Trade:	Li Qiang	
Minister of Economic Relations with Foreign Countries:	Chen Muhua (female, concurrently)	
Minister of Agriculture:	Lin Hujia	
Minister of State Farms and Land:	Gao Yang	
Minister of Forestry:	Yong Wentao	
Minister of Water Conservancy:	Qian Zhengying	(female)
Minister of Metallurgical Industry:	Tang Ke	
Minister of the First Ministry of Machine-Building:	Rao Bin	
Minister of the Second Ministry of Machine-Building:	Liu Wei	
Minister of the Third Ministry of Machine-Building:	Lu Dong	
Minister of the Fourth Ministry of Machine-Building:	Qian Min	
Minister of the Fifth Ministry of Machine-Building:	Zhang Zhen	
Minister of the Sixth Ministry of Machine-Building:	Chai Shufan	
Minister of the Seventh Ministry of Machine-Building:	Zheng Tianxiang	
Minister of the Eighth Ministry of Machine-Building:	Jiao Ruoyu	

Minister of Agricultural Machinery:	Yang Ligong	
Minister of Coal Industry:	Gao Yangwen	
Minister of Petroleum Industry:	Kang Shien	(concurrently)
Minister of Chemical Industry:	Sun Jingwen	
Minister of Power Industry:	Li Peng	
Minister of Geology:	Sun Daguang	
Minister of Building Materials Industry:	Song Yangchu	
Minister of Light Industry:		
Minister of Railways:	Guo Weicheng	
Minister of Communications:	Peng Deqing	
Minister of Posts and Telecommunications:	Wen Minsheng	
Minister of Finance:	Wang Bingqian	
President of the People's Bank of China:	Li Baohua	
Minister of Commerce:	Wang Lei	
Minister of Food:	Zhao Xinchu	
Director of the All-China Federation of Supply and Marketing Cooperatives:	Niu Yinguan	
Minister of Textile Industry	Hao Jianxiu	(female)
Minister of Culture:	—	
Minister of Education:	Jiang Nanxiang	
Minister of Public Health:	Qian Xinzhong	
Minister in Charge of the State Physical Culture and Sports Commission:	Wang Meng	
Minister in Charge of the Commission for Cultural Relations with Foreign Countries:	Huang Zhen	
Minister in Charge of the State Family-Planning Commission:	Chen Muhua	(female)

8. ADMINISTRATIVE DIVISIONS OF PROVINCES, AUTONOMOUS REGIONS, MUNICIPALITIES AND COUNTIES OF THE PEOPLE'S REPUBLIC OF CHINA
(1980)

The Municipality of Beijing

Districts under the Jurisdiction of the Municipality:
Dongcheng, Xuanwu, Haidian, Fengtai, Shijingshan, Xicheng, Chongwen, Chaoyang, Mentougou, Yanshan.
Counties:
Changping, Yanqing, Huairou, Miyun, Shunyi, Pinggu, Tongxian, Daxing, Fanshan.

The Municipality of Shanghai

Districts under the Jurisdiction of the Municipality:
Huangpu, Luwan, Changning, Jingan, Yangpu, Wusong, Nanshi, Xuhui, Zhabei, Hongkou, Putou.
Counties:
Shanghai, Jiading, Baoshan, Chusha, Nanhui, Fengxian, Songjiang, Jinshan, Qingpu, Chongming.

The Municipality of Tianjin

Districts under the Jurisdiction of the Municipality:
Heping, Hebei, Hongqiao, Hangu, Nanjiao, Beijiao, Hedong, Nankai, Tanggu, Dongjiao, Xijiao, Dagang, Hexi.
Counties:
Jixian, Baodi, Wuqing, Jinghai, Ninghe.

Anhui Province

Hefei City: Changfeng County
Huainan City: Fengtai County
Huaibei City: Suixi County
Bengbu City
Ma'anshan City
Wuhu City: Wuhu County
Anqing City
Tongling City: Tongling County
Suxian Prefecture: The City of Suzhou, Suxian County, Dangshan County, Xiaoxian County, Lingbi County, Sixian County, Wuhe County, Guzhen County, Huaiyuan County.

Chuxian Prefecture: Chuxian County, Jiashan County, Tianchang County, Lai'an County, Quanjiao County, Dingyuan County, Fengyang County.
Chaohu Prefecture: Chaoxian County, Feidong County, Hanshan County, Hexian County, Wuwei County, Lujiang County.
Xuancheng Prefecture: Xuancheng County, Dangtu County, Langxi County, Guangde County, Jingxian County, Nanling County, Fanchang County, Ningguo County, Qingyang County.
Huizhou Prefecture: Tunxi City, Xiuning County, Jingde County, Jixi County, Taiping County, Shexian County, Qimen County, Yixian County, Shitai County.
Anqing Prefecture: Tongcheng County, Zongyang County, Huaining County, Wangjiang County, Dongzhi County, Susong County, Taihu County, Yuexi County, Qianshan County, Guichi County.
Lu'an Prefecture: Lu'an City, Lu'an County, Huoqiu County, Shouxian County, Feixi County, Shucheng County, Huoshan County, Jinzhai County.
Fuyang Prefecture: Fuyang City, Fuyang County, Boxian County, Guoyang County, Mengcheng County, Lixin County, Yingshang County, Funan County, Linquan County, Jieshou County, Taihe County.

Fujian Province

Fuzhou City: Minhou County
Xiamen City: Tong'an County
Jianyang Prefecture: Nanping City, Jianyang County, Jian'ou County, Pucheng County, Shaowu County, Shunchang County, Chongan County, Guangze County, Songxi County, Zhenghe County.
Ningde Prefecture: Ningde County, Fu'an County, Lianjiang County, Fuding County, Xiapu County, Gudian County, Luoyuan County, Shouning County, Zhouning County, Pingnan County, Zherong County.
Putian Prefecture: Putian County, Xianyou County, Fuqing County, Changle County, Yongtai County, Pingtan County, Minqing County.

Jinjiang Prefecture: Quanzhou City, Jinjiang County, Nan'an County, Hui'an County, Anxi County, Yongchun County, Dehua County, Jinmen County.

Longxi Prefecture: Zhangzhou City, Longhai County, Zhangpu County, Zhao'an County, Pinghe County, Yunxiao County, Nanjing County, Changtai County, Dongshan County, Hua'an County.

Longyan Prefecture: Longyan County, Shanghang County, Yongding County, Changting County, Wuping County, Liancheng County, Zhangping County.

Sanming Prefecture: Sanming City, Longxi County, Ninghua County, Dadian County, Yong'an County, Shaxian County, Jiangle County, Qingliu County, Jianning County, Taining County, Mingxi County, Jinmen County to be returned to the motherland.

Gansu Province

Lanzhou City: Yongdeng County, Yuzhong County, Gaolan County.

Jiayuguan City

Dingxi Prefecture: Dingxi County, Huining County, Longxi County, Lintao County, Jingyuan County, Tongwei County, Weiyuan County.

Pingliang Prefecture: Pingliang County, Lingtai County, Huating County, Jingning County, Jingchuan County, Chongxin County, Zhuanglang County.

Qingyang Prefecture: Qingyang County, Huachi County, Zhengning County, Zhenyuan County, Huanxian County, Heshui County, Ningxian County.

Tianshui Prefecture: Tianshui City, Changjiachuan Autonomous County for Hui Nationality, Tianshui County, Huixian County, Lixian County, Wushan County, Tai'an County, Qingshui County, Liangdang County, Xihe County, Gangu County, Zhangxian County.

Wudu Prefecture: Wudu County, Dangchang County, Kangxian County, Minxian County, Chengxian County, Wenxian County.

Gannan Autonomous Prefecture for Tibetan Nationality: Lintan County, Zhouqu County, Maqu County, Xiahe County, Jone County, Tewo County, Luqu County.

Linxia Autonomous Prefecture for Hui Nationality: Linxia County, Yongjing County, Hezheng County, Autonomous County for Dongxiang Nationality, Kangle County, Guanghe County,

Wuwei Prefecture: Wuwei County, Minqiu County, Gulang County, Yongchang County, Jintai County, Tianzhu Autonomous County for Tibetan Nationality, Jishishan Autonomous County for Bao'an, Dongxiang and Sala Nationalities.

Zhangye Prefecture: Zhangye County, Minle County, Linze County, Shandan County, Sunan Autonomous County for Yugur Nationality, Gaotai County.

Jiuquan Prefecture: Yumen city, Jiuquan County, Aksay Kazak Autonomous County, Dunhuang County, Jinta County, Subei Mongolian Autonomous County, Anxi County.

Qinghai Province

Xining City: Datong County

Haidong Prefecture: Ping'an County, Huzhu Autonomous County for Tu Nationality, Huangzhong County, Ledu County, Minhe County, Hualong Autonomous County for Hui Nationality, Xunhua Autonomous County for Sala Nationality, Huangyuan County.

Haibei Autonomous Prefecture For Tibetan Nationality: Menyuan Autonomous County for Hui Nationality, Haiyan County, Gangca County, Qilian County.

Huangnan Autonomous Prefecture For Tibetan Nationality: Tongren County, Jianza County, Zekog County.

Hainan Autonomous Prefecture for Tibetan Nationality: Gonghe County, Guide County, Guinan County, Tongde County, Xinghai County.

Golog Autonomous Prefecture for Tibetan Nationality: Maqen County, Gade County, Jigzhi County, Baima County, Daria County, Madoi County.

Yushu Autonomous Prefecture for Tibetan Nationality: Yushu County, Chindu County, Nangqen County, Zadoi County, Zhidoi County, Qumarleb County.

Haixi Autonomous Prefecture for Mongolian, Tibetan and Kazak Nationalities: Golmud City, Ulan County, Tianjun, Dulan County.

Guangdong Province

Guangzhou City:

Huaxian County, Xinfeng County, Zengcheng County, Conghua County, Longmen County, Panyu County.

Haikou City
Shantou City
Zhanjiang City
Maoming City
Foshan City
Jiangmen City
Shenzhen City
Zhuhai City
Shaoguan City: Qujiang County

Shaoguan Prefecture: Lechang County, Renhua County, Nanxiong County, Sixing County, Wengyuan County, Fogang County, Yingde County, Qingyuan County, Yangshan County, Lianshan Autonomous County for Zhuang and Yao Nationalities, Liannan Autonomous County for Yao Nationality, Lianxian County, Ruyuan Autonomous County for Yao Nationality.

Huiyang Prefecture: Huizhou City, Huiyang County, Bolou County, Heyuan County, Lianping County, Heping County, Longchuan County, Zijin County, Huidong County, Dongguan County.

Meixian Prefecture: Meizhou City, Meixian County, Pingyuan County, Jiaoling County, Dapu County, Fengshun County, Wuhua County, Xingning County.

Shantou Prefecture: Chaozhou City, Chenghai County, Chao'an County, Raoping County, Nan'ao County, Chaoyang County, Huilai County, Lufeng County, Haifeng County, Puning County, Jiexi County, Jieyang County.

Foshan Prefecture: Nanhai County, Sanshui County, Shunde County, Zhongshan County, Doumen County, Xinhui County, Gaohe County, Kaiping County, Taishan County, Enping County.

Administrative Units Directly under the Jurisdiction of Hainan Administrative District: Qiongshan County, Wenchang County, Ding'an County, Qionghai County, Wanning County, Tunchang County, Chengmai County, Danxian County, Lingao County.

Hainan Autonomous Prefecture for Li and Miao Nationalities under the Hainan Administrative District: Baoting County, Baisha County, Qiongzhong County, Lingshui County, Yaxian County, Ledong County, Dongfang County, Changjiang County.

Zhanjiang Prefecture: Lianjiang County, Huazhou County, Gaozhou County, Xinyi County, Yangchun County, Yangjiang County, Dianbai County, Wuchuan County, Xuwen County, Haikang County, Suixi County.

Zhaoqing Prefecture: Zhaoqing City, Gaoyao County, Huaiji County, Guangning County, Sihui County, Xinxing County, Yunfu County, Louding County, Yunan County, Deqing County, Fengkai County.

Guizhou Province

Guiyang City
Lupanshui City: Shuicheng Special Region, Luzhi Special Region, Panxian Special Region.

Zunyi Prefecture: Zunyi City, Zunyi County, Suiyang County, Daozhen County, Fenggang County, Yuqing County, Chishui County, Tongzi County, Zheng'an County, Wuchuan County, Meitan County, Renhuai County, Xishui County.

Tongren Prefecture: Tongren County, Yuiping County, Sinan County, Dejiang County, Songtao Autonomous County for Miao Nationality, Wanshan Special Region, Jiangkou County, Shiqian County, Yinjiang County, Yanhe County.

Xingyi Prefecture: Xingyi County, Pu'an County, Zhenfeng Autonomous County for Buyi and Miao Nationalities, Wangmo Autonomous County for Buyi and Miao Nationalities, Ceheng Autonomous County for Buyi Nationality, Anlong Autonomous County for Buyi and Miao Nationalities, Xingren County, Qinglong County.

Bijie Prefecture: Bijie County, Qianxi County, Zhijin County, Weining Autonomous County for Yi, Hui and Miao Nationalities, Hezhang County, Dafang County, Jinsha County, Nayong County.

Anshun Prefecture: Anshun City, Anshun County, Xifeng County, Qingzhen County, Puding County, Zhenning Autonomous County for Buyi and Miao Nationalities, Ziyun Autonomous County for Miao and Buyi Nationalities, Kaiyang County, Xiuwen County, Pingba County, Guanling County.

Qiandongnan Autonomous Prefecture for Miao and Dong Nationalities: Kaili County, Shibing County, Zhenyuan County, Tianzhu County, Qianhe County, Liping County, Congjiang County, Majiang County, Huangping County, Sansui County, Cengong County, Jinping County, Taijiang County, Rongjiang County,

Leishan County, Danzhai County.

Qiannan Autonomous Prefecture for Buyi and Miao Nationalities: Duyun City, Duyun County, Guiding County, Weng'an County, Pingtang County, Changshun County, Huishui County, Sandu Autonomous County for Shui Nationality, Lipo County, Fuquan County, Dushan County, Luodian County, Longli County.

Hebei Province

Shijiazhuang City
Tangshan City

Shijiazhuang Prefecture: Xingtang County, Lingshou County, Shulu County, Jinxian County, Gaocheng County, Gaoyi County, Zhaoxian County, Jingxing County, Huolu County, Xinlu County, Zhengding County, Shenze County, Wuji County, Zanhuang County, Yuanshi County, Luancheng County, Pingshan County.

Handan Prefecture: Handan City, Yongnian County, Quzhou County, Guantao County, Weixian County, Chengan County, Daming County, Shexian County, Handan County, Jize County, Qiuxian County, Guangping County, Feixiang County, Linzhang County, Cixian County, Wu'an County.

Xingtai Prefecture: Xingtai City, Xingtai County, Baixiang County, Ningjin County, Longyao County, Linxi County, Nangong County, Julu County, Renxian County, Shahe County, Lincheng County, Neiqiu County, Xinhe County, Qinghe County, Weixian County, Guangzong County, Pingxiang County, Nanhe County.

Baoding Prefecture: Baoding City, Laishui County, Zhuoxian County, Dingxing County, Rongcheng County, Anxin County, Lixian County, Yixian County, Xincheng County, Fuping County, Tangxian County, Laiyuan County, Zhuoxian County, Dingxing County, Xiongxian County, Xushui County, Gaoyan County, Anguo County, Qingyuan County, Wangdu County, Quyang County, Wanxian County, Mancheng County.

Zhangjiakou Prefecture: Zhangjiakou City, Kangbao County, Chicheng County, Huailai County, Yuxian County, Xuanhua County, Zhangbei County, Guyuan County, Chongli County, Zhuolu County, Yangyuan County, Huai'an County, Shangyi County, Wanquan County.

Chengde Prefecture: Chengde City, Weichang County, Pingquan County, Kuancheng County, Xinlong County, Luanping County, Longhua County, Qinglong County, Chengde County, Fengning County.

Tangshan Prefecture: Qinhuangdao City, Qianxi County, Qian'an County, Changli County, Lulong County, Luannan County, Yutian County, Zunhua County, Funing County, Leting County, Luanxian County, Fengnan County, Fengrun County.

Langfang Prefecture: Anci County, Sanhe County, Xianghe County, Baxian County, Gu'an County, Dachang Autonomous County for Hui Nationality, Dacheng County, Wenan County, Yongqing County.

Cangzhou Prefecture: Cangzhou City, Cangxian County, Huanghua County, Yanshan County, Wuqiao County, Dongguang County, Suning County, Hejian County, Jiaohe County, Qingxian County, Haixin County, Mengcun Autonomous County for Hui Nationality, Nanpi County, Renqiu County, Xianxian County.

Hengshui Prefecture: Hengshui County, Raoyang County, Fucheng County, Jingxian County, Zaoqiang County, Shenxian County, Anping County, Wuqiang County, Wuyi County, Gucheng County, Jixian County.

Heilongjiang Province

Harbin City
Qiqihar City
Hegang City
Shuangyashan City
Jixi City
Daqing City
Yichun City: Jiayin County, Tieli County.

Suihua Prefecture: Suihua County, Suileng County, Hailun County, Qing'an County, Lanxi County, Zhaodong County, Zhaozhou County, Zhaoyuan County, Anda County, Mingshui County, Qinggang County, Wangkui County.

Heihe Prefecture: Heihe City, Anhui County, Bei'an County, Dedu County, Sunwu County, Xunke County, Nanjiang County.

Hejiang Prefecture: Jiamusi City, Qitaihe City, Huachuan County, Luobei County, Suibin County, Fujin County, Tongjiang County, Fuyuan County, Raohe County, Baoqing County, Jixian County, Boli County, Huanan County, Yilan County, Tangyuan County.

Mudanjiang Prefecture: Mudanjiang City, Suifenhe City, Linkou County, Jidong County, Mishan County, Hulin County, Dongning County, Muling County, Ningan County, Hailin County.

Songhuajiang Prefecture: Acheng County, Hulan County, Bayan County, Binxian County, Mulan County, Tonghe County, Fengzheng County, Yanshou County, Shangzhi County, Wuchang County, Shuangcheng County.

Nenjiang Prefecture: Fuyu County, Nehe County, Keshan County, Kedong County, Baiquan County, Yi'an County, Lindian County, Dorbod Autonomous County for Mongolian Nationality, Tailai County, Longjiang County, Gannan County.

Da Hinggan Ling Prefecture: Huma County.

Henan Province

Zhengzhou City: Xingyang County
Kaifeng City
Pingdingshan City
Luoyang City
Jiaozuo City
Hebi City

Kaifeng Prefecture: Kaifeng County, Qixian County, Weishi County, Xinzheng County, Dengfeng County, Tongxu County, Zhongmou County, Mixian County, Gongxian County, Lankao County.

Xinxiang Prefecture: Xinxiang City, Xinxiang County, Jixian County, Fengqiu County, Huojia County, Wenxian County, Jiyuan County, Bo'ai County, Huixian County, Yanjin County, Yuanyang County, Wuzhi County, Mengxian County, Qinyang County, Xiuwu County.

Anyang Prefecture: Anyang City, Anyang County, Nanle County, Yuanxian County, Taiqian County, Huaxian County, Xunxian County, Qixian County, Neihuang County, Qingfeng County, Puyang County, Changyuan County, Tangyin County, Linxian County.

Shangqiu Prefecture: Shangqiu City, Shangqiu County, Xiayi County, Zhecheng County, Suixian County, Yucheng County, Yongcheng County, Ningling County, Minquan County.

Zhoukou Prefecture: Zhoukou City, Shangshui County, Fugou County, Luyi County, Huaiyang County, Shenqiu County, Xihua County, Taikang County, Dancheng County, Xiangcheng County.

Xuchang Prefecture: Xuchang City, Luohe City, Xuchang County, Yanling County, Yancheng County, Xiangcheng County, Lushan County, Jiaxian County, Changge County, Linying County, Wuyang County, Yexian County, Baofeng County, Yuxian County.

Zhumadian Prefecture: Zhumadian City, Queshan County, Xiping County, Runan County, Xincai County, Qinyang County, Suiping County, Shangcai County, Pingyu County, Zhengang County.

Xinyang Prefecture: Xinyang City, Xinyang County, Xixian County, Gushi County, Huangchuan County, Xinxian County, Loushan County, Huaibin County, Shangcheng County, Guangshan County.

Nanyang Prefecture: Nanyang City, Nanyang County, Fancheng County, Tanghe County, Xinye County, Dengxian County, Xichuan County, Nanzhao County, Sheqi County, Tongbai County, Zhenping County, Neixiang County, Xixia County.

Luoyang Prefecture: Sanmenxia City, Mengjin County, Linru County, Ruyang County, Songxian County, Luanchuan County, Lingbao County, Mianchi County, Yanshi County, Yichuan County, Yiyang County, Luoning County, Lushi County, Shanxian County, Xin'an County.

Hubei Province

Wuhan City: Wuchang County, Hanyang County
Huangshi City: Daye County
Shiyan City
Shashi City
Yichang City
Xiangfan City

Xiaogan Prefecture: Xiaogan County, Huangpi County, Hanchuan County, Yunmeng County, Yingshan County, Dawu County, Yingcheng County, Anlu County.

Huanggang Prefecture: Echeng City, Huanggang County, Xinzhou County, Hongan County, Macheng County, Loutian County, Echeng County, Xishui County, Qichun County, Huangmei County, Guangji County, Yingshan County.

Xianning Prefecture: Xianning County, Yangxin County, Tongshan County, Tongcheng County, Jiayu County, Chongyang County, Puqi County.

Jingzhou Prefecture: Jingzhou City, Jiangling County, Jingmen County, Zhongxiang County, Jingshan County, Jianli County, Shishou

County, Tianmen County, Qianjiang County, Mianyang County, Honghu County, Gong'an County, Songzi County.

Yichang Prefecture: Yichang County, Yuan'an County, Dangyang County, Yidu County, Zhijiang County, Wufeng County, Changyang County, Zigui County, Xingshan County.

Enshi Prefecture: Enshi County, Jianshi County, Badong County, Hengfeng Autonomous County for Tujia Nationality, Xuan'en County, Laifeng Autonomous County for Tujia Nationality, Xianfeng County, Lichun County.

Yunyang Prefecture: Yunxian County, Fangxian County, Zhuxi County, Junxian County, Zhushan County, Yunxi County, Shennongjia Forest Area.

Xiangyang Prefecture: Suizhou City, Laohekou City, Xiangyang County, Suixian County, Nanzhang County, Gucheng County, Zaoyang County, Yicheng County, Baokang County, Guanghua County.

Hunan Province

Changsha City: Changsha County, Wangcheng County
Zhuzhou City: Zhuzhou County
Xiangtan City
Hengyang City
Shaoyang City
Yueyang Prefecture: Yueyang City, Yueyang County, Linxiang County, Pingjiang County, Miluo County, Xiangyin County, Huarong County.
Xiangtan Prefecture: Xiangtan County, Liuyang County, Liling County, Youxian County, Chaling County, Lingxian County, Xianxiang County.
Chenzhou Prefecture: Chenzhou City, Chenxian County, Anren County, Yongxing County, Zixing County, Guidong County, Rucheng County, Yizhang County, Linwu County, Jiahe County, Guiyang County, Laiyang County.
Hengyang Prefecture: Hengnan County, Hengshan County, Hengdong County, Changning County, Qiyang County, Qidong County, Hengyang County.
Lingling Prefecture: Lingling County, Xintian County, Ningyuan County, Lanshan County, Jianghua Autonomous County for Yao Nationality, Shuangpai County, Jiangyong County, Daoxian County, Dong'an County.
Shaoyang Prefecture: Shaoyang County, Xinning County, Wugang County, Longhui County, Chengbu Autonomous County for Miao Nationality, Suining County, Dongkou County.
Lianyuan Prefecture: Loudi City, Lengshuijiang City, Lianyuan County, Xinshao County, Shuangfeng County, Shaodong County, Xinhua County.
Qianyang Prefecture: Huaihua City, Hongjiang County, Huaihua County, Qianyang County, Chenxi County, Yuanling County, Xupu County, Huitong County, Jingxian County, Tongdao Autonomous County for Dong Nationality, Xinhuang Autonomous County for Dong Nationality, Zhijiang County, Mayang County.
Xiangxi Autonomous Prefecture for Tujia and Miao Nationalities: Jishou County, Yongshun County, Sangzhi County, Dayong County, Guzhang County, Luxi County, Fenghuang County, Huayuan County, Baojing County, Longshan County.
Changde Prefecture: Changde City, Jinshi City, Changde County, Linli County, Lixian County, Anxiang County, Hanshou County, Taoyuan County, Cili County, Shimen County.
Yiyang Prefecture: Yiyang City, Yiyang County, Nanxian County, Yuanjiang County, Ningxiang County, Anhua County, Taojiang County.

Jiangsu Province

Nanjing City: Jiangning County, Liuhe County, Jiangpu County.
Xuzhou City
Lianyungang City
Nantong City
Suzhou City
Wuxi City
Changzhou City
Xuzhou Prefecture: Fengxian County, Peixian County, Ganyu County, Donghai County, Xinyi County, Peixian County, Suining County, Tongshan County.
Huaiyin Prefecture: Qingjiang County, Guanyun County, Guannan County, Shuyang County, Suqian County, Siyang County, Xuyi County, Lianshui County, Huaiyin County, Huai'an County, Hongze County, Sihong County, Jinhu County.
Yancheng Prefecture: Yancheng County, Binhai County, Funing County, Sheyang County, Jianhu County, Xiangshui County, Dafeng County, Dongtai County.

Nantong Prefecture: Hai'an County, Rugao County, Rudong County, Qidong County, Haimen County, Nantong County.

Yangzhou Prefecture: Yangzhou City, Taizhou City, Baoying County, Xinghua County, Gaoyou County, Taixing County, Taixian County, Jingjiang County, Jiangdu County, Hanjiang County, Yizheng County.

Zhenjiang Prefecture: Zhenjiang City, Dantu County, Yangzhong County, Danyang County, Wujin County, Yixing County, Jintan County, Liyang County, Jurong County, Lishui County, Goachun County.

Suzhou Prefecture: Jiangyin County, Shazhou County, Changshu County, Taicang County, Kunshan County, Wuxian County, Wujiang County, Wuxi County.

Jiangxi Province

Nanchang City: Xinjian County, Nanchang County
Jingdezhen City
Pingxiang City
Jiujiang City

Administrative Unit directly under the Jurisdiction of the Province: Jinggangshan

Jiujiang Prefecture: Jiujiang County, Pengze County, Hukou County, Duchang County, Xingzi County, Yongxiu County, De'an County, Ruichang County, Wuning County, Xiushui County.

Shangrao Prefecture: Shangrao City, Yingtan City, Shangrao County, Wuyuan County, Dexing County, Yushan County, Guangfeng County, Yanshan County, Hengfeng County, Guixi County, Yujiang County, Wannian County, Leping County, Boyang County, Yugan County, Yiyang County.

Yichun Prefecture: Yichun City, Yichun County, Wanzai County, Tonggu County, Yifeng County, Shanggao County, Anyi County, Fengxin County, Gao'an County, Fengcheng County, Qingjiang County, Xinyu County, Fenyi County, Jing'an County.

Fuzhou Prefecture: Fuzhou City, Linchuan County, Jinxi County, Zixi County, Lichuan County, Nanfeng County, Nancheng County, Yihuang County, Chongren County, Le'an County, Dongxiang County, Jinxian County.

Ji'an Prefecture: Ji'an City, Ji'an County, Xingan County, Xiajiang County, Jishui County, Yongfeng County, Taihe County, Wan'an County, Suichuan County, Ninggan County, Yongxin County, Lianhua County, Anfu County.

Ganzhou Prefecture: Ganzhou City, Guangchang County, Shicheng County, Ningdu County, Xinggao County, Yudu County, Ruijin County, Huichang County, Anyuan County, Xunwu County, Dingnan County, Longnan County, Quannan County, Xinfeng County, Ganxian County, Nankang County, Shangyou County, Chongyi County, Dayu County.

Jilin Province

Changchun City: Nongan County, Dehui County, Yushu County, Jiutai County, Shuangyang County.

Jilin City: Yongji County, Shulan County, Jiaohe County, Huadian County, Panshi County.

Yanbian Autonomous Prefecture for Korean Nationality: Yanji City, Tumen City, Yanji County, Wangqing County, Hunchun County, Helong County, Antu County, Dunhua County.

Tonghua Prefecture: Tonghua City, Hunjiang City, Tonghua County, Liuhe County, Hailong County, Huinan County, Jingyu County, Fusong County, Changbai Autonomous County for Korean Nationality, Ji'an County.

Siping Prefecture: Siping City, Liaoyuan City, Lishu County, Huaide County, Yitong County, Dongfeng County, Shuangliao County.

Baicheng Prefecture: Baicheng City, Zhenlai County, Da'an County, Qian Gorlos Mongolian Autonomous County, Fuyu County, Qian'an County, Changling County, Tongyu County, Tao'an County.

Liaoning Province

Shenyang City: Xinmin County, Liaozhong County

Dalian City: Jinxian County, Fuxian County, Xinjin County, Zhuanghe County, Changhai County.

Anshan City: Haicheng County, Tai'an County

Fushun City: Fushun County, Xinbin County, Qingyuan County

Benxi City: Benxi County, Huanren County

Jinzhou City: Jinxian County, Yixian County, Heishan County, Beizhen County, Jinxi County, Xingcheng County, Shuizhong County.

Dandgong City: Donggou County, Xiuyan County, Fengcheng County, Kuandian County.
Fuxin City: Mongolian Autonomous County of Fuxin, Zhangwu County.
Yingkou City: Yingkou County, Gaixian County, Panshan County, Dawa County.
Liaoyang City: Liaoyang County, Dengta County.
Tieling Prefecture: Tieling City, Tieling County, Kaiyuan County, Changtu County, Kangping County, Faku County, Xifeng County.
Chaoyang Prefecture: Chaoyang City, Chaoyang County, Jianchang County, Beipiao County, Lingyuan County, Jianping County, Harqin Left Wing Mongolian Autonomous County.

Shaanxi Province

Xi'an City: Chang'an County
Tongchuan City: Yaoxian County
Baoji City: Baoji County, Fengxiang County, Qianyang County, Longxian County, Linyou County, Qishan County, Fufeng County, Wugong County, Meixian County, Taibai County, Fengxian County.
Yulin Prefecture: Yulin County, Shenmu County, Fugu County, Jiaxian County, Mizhi County, Wubu County, Suide County, Qingjian County, Zizhou County, Hengshan County, Jingbian County, Dingbian County.
Yan'an Prefecture: Yan'an City, Ansai County, Zichang County, Yanchuan County, Yanchang County, Yichuan County, Huanglong County, Luochuan County, Yijun County, Huangling County, Fuxian County, Ganquan County, Zhidan County, Wuqi County.
Xianyang Prefecture: Xianyang City, Liquan County, Yongshou County, Binxian County, Changwu County, Xunyi County, Chunhua County, Jingyang County, Sanyuan County, Gaoling County, Huxian County, Zhouzhi County, Xingping County, Qianxian County.
Weinan Prefecture: Weinan County, Pucheng County, Baishui County, Chengcheng County, Hancheng County, Heyang County, Dali County, Tongguan County, Huayin County, Huaxian County, Lantian County, Lintong County, Fuping County.
Shangluo Prefecture: Shangxian County, Luonan County, Danfeng County, Shangnan County, Shanyang County, Zhen'an County, Zhashui County.
Ankang Prefecture: Ankang County, Xunyang County, Baihe County, Pingli County, Zhenping County, Lan'gao County, Ziyang County, Hanyin County, Shiquan County, Ningshan County.
Hanzhong Prefecture: Hanzhong County, Liuba County, Chenggu County, Yangxian County, Foping County, Xixiang County, Zhenba County, Nanzheng County, Ningjiang County, Mianxian County, Lueyang County.

Shandong Province

Jinan City: Licheng County, Changqing County, Zhangqiu County.
Qingdao City: Laoshan County, Jiaonan County, Jimo County, Jiaoxian County.
Zibo City

Zaozhuang City: Tengxian County.
Dezhou Prefecture: Dezhou City, Ningjin County, Leling County, Shanghe County, Jiyang County, Yucheng County, Xiajin County, Lingxian County, Qingyun County, Linyi County, Qihe County, Pingyuan County, Wucheng County.
Huimin Prefecture: Binxian County, Kenli County, Guangrao County, Huantai County, Zouping County, Yangxin County, Zhanhua County, Lijin County, Boxing County, Gaoqing County, Huimin County, Wudi County.
Changwei Prefecture: Weifang City, Weixian County, Pingdu County, Zhucheng County, Anqiu County, Linqu County, Shouguang County, Changyi County, Gaomi County, Wulian County, Changle County, Yidu County.
Yantai Prefecture: Yantai City, Weihai City, Mouping County, Wendeng County, Haiyang County, Laiyang County, Qixia County, Yexian County, Changdao County, Fushan County, Rongcheng County, Rushan County, Laixi County, Zhaoyuan County, Huangxian County, Penglai County.
Linyi Prefecture: Linyi County, Yishui County, Rizhao County, Lianshu County, Cangshan County, Pingyi County, Yiyuan County, Yinan County, Juxian County, Junan County, Tancheng County, Feixian County, Mengying County.
Tai'an Prefecture: Tai'an County, Laiwu County, Xinwen County, Feicheng County, Pingying

County, Xintai County, Ningyang County, Dongping County.

Jining Prefecture: Jining City, Jining County, Yanzhou County, Sishui County, Yutai County, Jiaxiang County, Wenshang County, Qufu County, Zouxian County, Weishan County, Jinxiang County.

Heze Prefecture: Heze County, Yuncheng County, Juye County, Shanxian County, Caoxian County, Juancheng County, Liangshan County, Chengwu County, Dingtao County, Dongming County.

Liaocheng Prefecture: Liaocheng County, Gaotang County, Dong'e County, Xinxian County, Linqing County, Chiping County, Yanggu County, Guanxian County.

Shanxi Province

Taiyuan City: Yangqu County, Loufan County Qingxu County.
Datong City
Yangquan City
Changzhi City

Yanbei Prefecture: Datong County, Tanzhen County, Lingqiu County, Huairen County, Shanyin County, Pinglu County, Youyu County, Yanggao County, Guangling County, Hunyuan County, Yingxian County, Shuoxian County, Zuoyun County.

Xinxian Prefecture: Xinxian County, Daixian County, Wutai County, Jingle County, Baode County, Hequ County, Shenchi County, Yuanping County, Fanshi County, Dingxiang County, Kelan County, Wuhan County, Pianguan County, Nianwu County.

Jinzhong Prefecture: Yuci City, Yuci County, Yuxian County, Xiyang County, Znoquan County, Taigu County, Pingyao County, Lingshi County, Shouyang County, Pingding County, Heshun County, Yushe County, Qixian County, Jiexiu County.

Luliang Prefecture: Lishi County, Xingxian County, Fanshan County, Lanxian County, Jiaocheng County, Wenshui County, Fenyang County, Xiaoyi County, Jiaokou County, Shilou County, Zhongyang County, Linxian County, Liulin County.

Jindongnan Prefecture: Changzhi County, Xiangyuan County, Licheng County, Huguan County, Gaoping County, Yangcheng County, Zhangzi County, Qinyuan County, Lucheng County, Wuxiang County, Pingshun County, Lingchuan County, Jincheng County, Qinshui County, Tunliu County, Qinxian County.

Linfen Prefecture: Linfen City, Houma City, Linfen County, Fenxi County, Anze County, Guxian County, Yicheng County, Quwo County, Jixian County, Daning County, Xixian County, Yonghe County, Hongdong County, Huoxian County, Fushan County, Xiangfen County, Xiangning County, Puxian County.

Yuncheng Prefecture: Yuncheng County, Wenxi County, Yuanqu County, Ruicheng County, Linyi County, Xinjiang County, Hejin County, Xiaxian County, Jiangxian County, Pinglu County, Yongji County, Wanrong County, Jishan County.

Sichuan Province

Chengdu City: Jintang County, Shuangliu County
Chongqing City: Changshou County, Baxian County, Qijiang County, Jiangbei County

Zigong City: Rongxian County
Dukou City: Miyi County, Yanbian County

Wenjiang Prefecture: Wenjiang County, Pixian County, Guanxian County, Pengxian County, Shifang County, Guanghan County, Xindu County, Xinjin County, Pujiang County, Qionglai County, Dayi County, Chongqing County.

Mianyang Prefecture: Mianyang City, Jiangyou County, Qingchuan County, Pingwu County, Guangyuan County, Wangcang County, Jian'ge County, Zitong County, Santai County, Yanting County, Shehong County, Suining County, Pengxi County, Zhongjiang County, Deyang County, Mianzhu County, Anxian County, Beichuan County.

Neijiang Prefecture: Neijiang City, Neijiang County, Leizhi County, Anyue County, Weiyuan County, Zizhong County, Ziyang County, Jianyang County, Longchang County.

Yibin Prefecture: Yibin City, Luzhou City, Yibin County, Fushun County, Nanxi County, Jiang'an County, Naxi County, Luxian County, Hejiang County, Gulin County, Xuyong County, Changning County, Xingwen County, Gongxian County, Gaoxian County, Yunlian County, Pingshan County.

Leshan Prefecture: Leshan City, Jiajiang County, Hongya County, Danling County, Qingshen County, Meishan County, Pengshan County, Jingyan County, Renshou County, Jianwei County, Muchuan County, Emei County, Jinkouhe Industrial and Agricultural District, Mabian County, Ebian County.

Jiangjin Prefecture: Yongchuan County, Dazhu County, Tongliang County, Hechuan County, Tongnan County, Bishan County, Jiangjin County, Rongchang County.

Fuling Prefecture: Fuling County, Dianjiang County, Fengdu County, Shizhu County, Xiushan County, Youyang County, Qianjiang County, Pengshui County, Wulong County, Nanchuan County.

Wanxian Prefecture: Wanxian City, Wanxian County, Kaixian County, Chengkou County, Wuxi County, Wushan County, Fengjie County, Yunyang County, Zhongxian County, Liangping County.

Nanchong Prefecture: Nanchong City, Nanchong County, Cangxi County, Langzhong County, Yilong County, Nanbu County, Xichong County, Yingshan County, Peng'an County, Guang'an County, Yuechi County, Wusheng County, Huayun Industrial and Agricultural District.

Daxian Prefecture: Daxian City, Daxian County, Wanyuan County, Xuanhan County, Kaijing County, Linshui County, Dazhu County, Quxian County, Nanjiang County, Bazhong County Pingchang County, Tongjiang County, Baisha Industrial and Agricultural District.

Ya'an Prefecture: Ya'an County, Lushan County, Mingshan County, Xingjing County, Hanyuan County, Shimian County, Tianquan County, Baoxing County.

Aba Autonomous Prefecture for Tibetan Nationality: Barkam County, Hongyuan County, Aba County, Zoige County, Heishui County, Songpan County, Nanping County, Maowen Autonomous County for Qiang Nationality, Wenchuan County, Lixian County, Xiaojin County, Jinchuan County, Zamtang County.

Garze Autonomous Prefecture for Tibetan Nationality: Kangding County, Luhao County, Garze County, Xinlong County, Baiyu County, Dege County, Serxu County, Sertar County, Luding County, Danba County, Jiulong County, Yajiang County, Dawu County, Litang County, Xiangcheng County, Daocheng County, Batang County, Derong County.

Liangshan Autonomous Prefecture for Yi Nationality: Xichang City, Xichang County, Zhaojue County, Ganluo County, Leibo County, Ningnan County, Huidong County, Huili County, Dechang County, Meigu County, Jinyang County, Butuo County, Puge County, Xide County, Yuexi County, Yanyuan County, Muli Autonomous County for Tibetan Nationality, Mianning County.

Taiwan Province
(Materials are left vacant for the time being)

Yunnan Province

Kunming City: Fumin County, Jinning County, Chenggong County, Anning County

Dongchuan City

Zhaotong Prefecture: Zhaotong County, Yongshan County, Daguan County, Yiliang County, Ludian County, Suijiang County, Yanjin County, Weixin County, Zhenxiong County, Qiaojia County.

Qujing Prefecture: Qujing County, Xuanwei County, Fuyuan County, Shizong County, Lunan Autonomous County for Yi Nationality, Songming County, Xundian Autonomous County for Hui and Yi Nationalities, Huize County, Zhanyi County, Luoping County, Luliang County, Yiliang County, Malong County.

Yuxi Prefecture: Yuxi County, Huaning County, Tonghai County, Yuanjiang Autonomous County for Hani, Yi and Dai Nationalities, Xinping Autonomous County for Yi and Dai Nationalities, Chengjiang County, Jiangchuan County, Eshan Autonomous County for Yi Nationality, Yimen County.

Simao Prefecture: Pu'er County, Zhenyuan County, Mojiang Autonomous County for Hani Nationality, Lancang Autonomous County for Lahu Nationality, Ximeng Autonomous County for Wa Nationality, Jingdong County, Jinggu County, Jiangcheng Autonomous County for Hani and Yi Nationalities, Menglian Autonomous County for Dai, Lahu and Wa Nationalities.

Lincang Prefecture: Lincang County, Yunxian County, Cangyuan Autonomous County for Wa Nationality, Zhenkang County, Yongde County, Fengqing County, Shuangjiang County, Gengma Autonomous County for Dai and Wa Nationalities.

Baoshan Prefecture: Baoshan County, Shidian County, Tengchong County, Changning County, Longling County.

Lijiang Prefecture: Lijiang Autonomous County for Naxi Nationality, Huaping County, Ninglang Autonomous County for Yi Nationality, Yongsheng County.

Wenshan Autonomous Prefecture for Zhuang and Miao Nationalities: Wenshan County, Guangnan County, Xichou County, Malipo County,

Maguan County, Qiubei County, Yanshan County, Funing County.

Honghe Autonomous Prefecture for Hani and Yi Nationalities: Gejiu County, Mile County, Kaiyuan County, Mengzi County, Hekou Autonomous County for Yao Nationality, Yuanyang County, Honghe County, Shiping County, Luxi County, Pingbian Autonomous County for Miao Nationality, Jinping County, Luchun County, Jianshui County.

Xishuangbanna Autonomous Prefecture for Dai Nationality: Jinghong County, Menghai County, Mengla County.

Chuxiong Autonomous Prefecture for Yi Nationality: Chuxiong County, Yuanmou County, Wuding County, Lufeng County, Nanhua County, Dayao County, Yongren County, Luquan County, Mouding County, Shuangbo County, Yao'an County.

Dali Autonomous Prefecture for Bai Nationality: Xiaguan City, Jianchuan County, Eryuan County, Binchuan County, Midu County, Weishan Autonomous County for Yi and Bai Nationalities, Yongping County, Heqing County, Dali County, Xiangyun County, Nanjian Autonomous County for Yi Nationability, Yangbi County, Yunlong County.

Dehong Autonomous Prefecture for Dai and Jingpo Nationalities: Luxi County, Longchuan County, Yingjiang County, Wandingzhen, Ruili County, Lianghe County.

Nujiang Autonomous Prefecture for Lisu Nationality: Lushui County, Pijiang County, Fugong County, Lanping County, Gongshan Autonomous County for Drung and Nu Nationalities.

Diqing Autonomous Prefecture for Tibetan Nationality: Zhongdian County, Deqen County, Weixi County.

Zhejiang Province

Hangzhou City: Yuhang County, Fuyang County, Jiande County, Lin'an County, Xiaoshan County, Tonglu County, Chun'an County
Ningbo City
Wenzhou City

Jiaxing Prefecture: Huzhou City, Jiaxing City, Wuxing County, Pinghu County, Jiaxing County, Tongxiang County, Anji County, Jiashan County, Haiyan County, Haining County, Deqing County, Changxing County.

Zhoushan Prefecture: Dinghai County, Daishan County, Shengsi County, Putuo County.

Ningbo Prefecture: Yinxian County, Xiangshan County, Fenghua County, Cixi County, Zhenhai County, Ninghai County, Yuyao County.

Shaoxing Prefecture: Shaoxing City, Shaoxing County, Xinchang County, Zhuji County, Shangyu County, Shengxian County.

Taizhou Prefecture: Linhai County, Shanmen County, Wenling County, Xianju County, Tiantai County, Huangyan County, Yuhuan County.

Wenzhou Prefecture: Yongjia County, Tongtou County, Pingyang County, Taishun County, Leqing County, Rui'an County, Wencheng County.

Lishui Prefecture: Lishui County, Qingtian County, Qingyuan County, Suichang County, Jinyun County, Yunhe County, Longquan County.

Jinhua Prefecture: Jinhua City, Quzhou City, Jinhua County, Pujiang County, Dongyang County, Wuyi County, Jiangshan County, Kaihua County, Lanxi County, Yiwu County, Yongkang County, Quxian County, Changshan County.

Guangxi Zhuang Autonomous Region

Nanning City
Liuzhou City
Guilin City
Wuzhou City

Nanning Prefecture: Pingxiang City, Yongning County, Wuming County, Mashan County, Shanglin County, Binyang County, Hengxian County, Fusui County, Chongzuo County, Ningming County, Longzhou County, Daxin County, Tiandeng County, Long'an County.

Hechi Prefecture: Hechi County, Huanjiang County, Loucheng County, Yishan County, Du'an Autonomous County for Yao Nationality, Bama Autonomous County for Yao Nationality, Donglan County, Fengshan County, Tian'e County, Nandan County.

Liuzhou Prefecture: Liucheng County, Rongshui Autonomous County for Miao Nationality, Rong'an County, Sanjiang Autonomous County for Dong Nationality, Luzhai County, Jinxiu Autonomous County for Yao Nationality, Xiangzhou County, Wuxuan County, Liujiang County, Laibin County, Xincheng County.

Guilin Prefecture: Lingui County, Lingchuan County, Xing'an County, Ziyuan County,

Quanzhou County, Guanyang County, Gongcheng County, Pingle County, Yangshuo County, Lipu County, Yongfu County, Longsheng Multinational Autonomous County.

Wuzhou Prefecture: Cangwu County, Zhongshan County, Fuchuan County, Hexian County, Cenxi County, Dengxian County, Mengshan County, Zhaoping County.

Yulin Prefecture: Yulin County, Guiping County, Pingnan County, Rongxian County, Beiliu County, Luchuan County, Bobai County, Guixian County.

Qinzhou Prefecture: Beihai County, Qinzhou County, Lingshan County, Pubei County, Hepu County, Fangcheng Multinational Autonomous County, Shangsi County.

Bose Prefecture: Bose County, Lingyun County, Leye County, Tianyang County, Tiandong County, Pingguo County, Debao County, Jingxi County, Napo County, Xilin County, Longlin Multinational Autonomous County, Tianlin County.

Inner Mongolian Autonomous Region

Hohhot City: Tumd Left Banner, Togtoh County
Baotou City: Tumd Right Banner, Guyang County
Wuhai City

Ulanqab Leaque: Jining City, Xinghe County, Qingshuihe County, Wuchuan County, Zhuozi County, Qahar Right Wing Rear Banner, Qahar Right Wing Middle Banner, Qahar Right Wing Front Banner, Darhan Muminggan Joint Banner, Siziwang Banner, Shangdu County, Fengzhen County, Liangcheng County, Horinger County, Huade County.

Xilin Gol League: Erenhot City, Abagnar Banner, Duolun County, Abag Banner, Xi Ujimqin Banner, Dong Ujimqin Banner, Sonid Left Banner, Taibus Banner, Zhengxiangbai Banner, Zhenglan Banner, Xianghuang Banner, Sonid Right Banner.

Hulun Buir League: Hailar City, Manzhouli City, Chen Barag Banner, Ergun Right Banner, Ergun Left Banner, Xuguit Banner, Arun Banner, Butha Banner, Ewenki Autonomous Banner, Xin Barag Left Banner, Xin Barag Right Banner, Oroqen Autonomous Banner, Daur Autonomous Banner of Morin Dawa.

Jirem League: Tongliao City, Tongliao County, Horqin Right Wing Middle Banner, Horqin Left Wing Rear Banner, Hure Banner, Naiman Banner, Kailu Banner, Karud Banner.

Ju Ud League: Chifeng City, Chifeng County, Ningcheng County, Linxi County, Harqin Banner, Aohen Banner, Ongniud Banner, Bairin Right Banner, Bairin Left Banner, Ar Horqin Banner, Hexigten Banner.

Ih Ju League: Dongsheng County, Jungar Banner, Uxin Banner, Ejinhoro Banner, Otog Banner, Hanggin Banner, Dalad Banner, Otog Front Banner.

Bayannur League: Linhe County, Wuyuan County, Hanggin Rear Banner, Urad Middle and Rear Joint Banner, Urad Front Banner, Qog Banner, Dengkou County.

Alxa Leaque: Alxa Left Banner, Alxa Right Banner, Ejin Banner.

Xingan Leaque: Ulan Hot City, Tuquan County, Jalaid Banner, Horqin Right Wing Front Banner, Horqin Right Wing Middle Banner.

Ningxia Hui Autonomous Region

Yingchuan City: Yongning County, Helan County.
Shizuishan City: Pingluo County, Taole County.

Yinnan Prefecture: Wuzhong County, Tongxin County, Lingwu County, Zhongning County, Yanchi County, Zhongwei County, Qingtongxia County.

Guyuan Prefecture: Guyuan County, Xiji County, Jingyuan County, Haiyuan County, Longde County.

Tibet Autonomous Region

Lhasa City: Lhunzhub County, Damxung County, Maizhokunggar County, Nyemo County, Mainling County, Medog County, Dagze County, Quxu County, Doilungdeqen County, Nyingchi County, Gongbogyamda County.

Nagqu Prefecture: Nagqu County, Baqen County, Biru County, Boingoin County, Lhari County, Nyainrong County, Sog County, Amdo County, Xainza County.

Qamdo Prefecture: Qamdo County, Gonjo County, Zogang County, Zayu County, Lhorong County, Dengqen County, Bomi County, Jomda County, Chag'yab County, Markam County, Baxoi County, Banbar County, Riwoqe County.

Shannan Prefecture: Nedong County, Gyaca

County, Qusum County, Cona County, Qonggyai County, Gongga County, Nagarze County, Sangri County, Nangxian County, Lhunze County, Coma County, Lhozhag County, Zhanang County.

Xigaze Prefecture: Xigaze County, Dinggye County, Lhaze County, Nyalam County, Xaitongmoin County, Zhongba County, Kangmar County, Yadong County, Gamba County, Namling County, Sa'gya County, Tingri County, Gyirong County, Ngamring County, Gyangze County, Rinbung County, Bainang County, Sa'gya County.

Ngari Prefecture: Gar County, Ge'gya County, Zanda County, Coqen County, Rutog County, Gerze County, Burang County.

Xinjiang Uygur Autonomous Region

Urumqi City: Urumqi County
Karamay City
Shihezi City

Turpan Prefecture: Turpan County, Toksun County, Shanshan County.

Hami Prefecture: Hami City, Hami County, Barkol Autonomous County for Kazak Nationality, Yiwu County.

Bayinglin Autonomous Prefecture for Mongolian Nationality: Korla City, Korla County, Hejing County, Yanqi Autonomous County for Hui Nationality, Hoxud County, Bohu County, Ruoqiang County, Yuli County, Qiemo County, Luntai County.

Hotan Prefecture: Hotan County, Minfeng County, Qira County, Yutian County, Lop County, Pishan County, Moyu County.

Aksu Prefecture: Aksu County, Wensu County, Baicheng County, Kuqa County, Xinhe County, Xayar County, Awat County, Kalpin County, Wushi County.

Kashi Prefecture: Kashi City, Bachu County, Jiashi County, Yopurga County, Markit County, Shache County, Zepu County, Yecheng County, Shule County, Yengisar County, Taxkorgan Autonomous County for Tajik Nationality, Shufu County.

Kizilsu Autonomous Prefecture for Kirgiz Nationality: Artux County, Akqi County, Akto County, Wuqia County.

Changji Autonomous Prefecture for Hui Nationality: Changji County, Fukang County, Qitai County, Jimsar County, Miquan County, Mori Autonomous County for Kazak Nationality, Manas County, Hutubi County.

Bortala Autonomous Prefecture for Mongolian Nationality: Bole County, Jinghe County, Wenquan County.

Ili Autonomous Prefecture for Kazak Nationality (Administrative Units under Its Jurisdiction): Yining City, Kuiytun City, Yining County, Nilka County, Xinyuan County, Gongliu County, Tekes County, Zhaosu County, Qapqal Autonomous County for Xibo Nationality, Korgas County.

Ili Autonomous Prefecture for Kazak Nationality (Tacheng Prefecture): Tacheng County, Hobksar Autonomous County for Mongolian Nationality; Emin County, Usu County, Toli County, Yumin County, Shawan County.

Ili· Autonomous Prefecture for Kazak Nationality (Alta Prefecture): Alta County, Qinghe County, Fuyun County, Jeminay County, Burqin County, Habahe County.

SECTION II:

MAJOR ECONOMIC DOCUMENTS, WORKS OF ECONOMIC POLICY, LAWS AND DECREES (1978-1981)

1. COMMUNIQUE OF THE SIXTH PLENARY SESSION OF THE 11th CENTRAL COMMITTEE OF THE COMMUNIST PARTY OF CHINA

(Adopted on June 29, 1981)

The 11th Central Committee of the Communist Party of China held its Sixth Plenary Session in Beijing from June 27 to 29, 1981. It was attended by 195 members and 114 alternate members of the Central Committee and 53 non-voting participants. Members of the Standing Committee of the Political Bureau of the Central Committee, Comrades Hu Yaobang, Ye Jianying, Deng Xiaoping, Zhao Ziyang, Li Xiannian, Chen Yun and Hua Guofeng, presided at the session.

Items on the agenda of the plenary session were: 1. Discussion and approval of the Resolution on Certain Questions in the History of Our Party Since the Founding of the People's Republic of China; 2. Re-election of principal leading members of the Central Committee and election of new members. The above-mentioned agenda was thoroughly deliberated and conscientiously discussed at a preparatory meeting held before the plenary session. This session is another meeting of great significance in the history of our party following the Third Plenary Session of the 11th Central Committee, a meeting for summing up experience and closing the ranks to press forward. This session will go down in history for fulfilling the historic mission of setting right things which have been thrown into disorder in the guiding ideology of the party.

Applying Marxist dialectical materialism and historical materialism, the Resolution on Certain Questions in the History of Our Party Since the Founding of the People's Republic of China unanimously adopted by the plenary session correctly sums up the major historical events of the party in the 32 years since the founding of the People's Republic of China, particularly the "cultural revolution." The resolution scientifically analyses the rights and wrongs in the party's guiding ideology during these events, analyses the subjective factors and social causes that gave rise to mistakes, realistically evaluates the historical role played by Comrade Mao Zedong, the great leader and teacher, in the Chinese revolution and fully elaborates the great significance of Mao Zedong Thought as the guiding ideology of our party. The resolution affirms the correct path for building a modern and powerful socialist country, a path which has been gradually established since the Third Plenary Session and which conforms to realities in China, and further points out the orientation for the continued advance of our country's socialist cause and the work of our party. The plenary session believes that the adoption and publication of the resolution will exert great and far-reaching influence on unifying the thinking and understanding of the party, the army and the people of all nationalities throughout the country so that they will strive with one heart and one mind to carry out our new, historical task.

The plenary session unanimously approved Comrade Hua Guofeng's request to resign his posts as Chairman of the Central Committee and Chairman of its Military Commission. The plenary session re-elected the principal leading members of the Central Committee and elected new ones by secret ballot. The results of the elections are:

  1. Comrade Hu Yaobang — Chairman of the Central Committee;
  2. Comrade Zhao Ziyang — Vice-Chairman of the Central Committee;
  3. Comrade Hua Guofeng — Vice-Chairman of the Central Committee;
  4. Comrade Deng Xiaoping — Chairman of the Military Commission of the Central Committee;
  5. A Standing Committee of the Political Bureau of the Central Committee made up of the Chairman and Vice-Chairman of the Central Committee. They are Hu Yaobang, Ye Jianying, Deng Xiaoping, Zhao Ziyang, Li Xiannian, Chen Yun and Hua Guofeng;
  6. Comrade Xi Zhongxun — Member of the Secretariat of the Central Committee.

The plenary session holds that the election and re-election of the principal leading members of the Central Committee will play an important part in strengthening the Central Committee's collective leadership and unity on the basis of Marxism and ensuring the full implementation of the party's correct line and policies formulated since the Third Plenary Session.

The plenary session gave full play to democracy. All comrades present spoke out freely, followed the scientific approach of seeking truth from facts and displayed the spirit of criticism and self-criticism in summing up historical experience and discussing and deciding the choice of persons as leading members of the Central Committee. This restored and carried forward the fine tradition formed by our party during the Yan'an rectification period. The session vividly demonstrates our party's strong unity and fully reflects the growth and flourishing of our cause.

The plenary session believes that, just as the party's correct summing up of historical experience in the period of the democratic revolution brought great revolutionary victories, the correct summing up of the party's historical experience since the founding of the People's Republic of China will help bring about new great victories in our future socialist construction. The plenary session calls on the party, the army and the people of all nationalities throughout the country to hold high the banner of Marxism-Leninism and Mao Zedong Thought, to rally more closely around the Party Central Committee, to carry forward the spirit of the legendary Foolish Old Man who removed mountains, to be resolute, to surmount all difficulties and work hard to turn China step by step into a modern and powerful socialist country with a high degree of democracy and civilization.

2. RESOLUTION ON CERTAIN QUESTIONS IN THE HISTORY OF OUR PARTY SINCE THE FOUNDING OF THE PEOPLE'S REPUBLIC OF CHINA

Adopted by the Sixth Plenary Session of the 11th Central Committee of the Communist Party of China (June 27, 1981)

Review of the History of the 28 Years Before the Founding of the People's Republic

1. The Communist Party of China has traversed 60 years of glorious struggle since its founding in 1921. In order to sum up its experience in the 32 years since the founding of the People's Republic, we must briefly review the previous 28 years in which the party led the people in waging the revolutionary struggle for New Democracy.

2. The Communist Party of China was the product of the integration of Marxism-Leninism with the Chinese workers' movement and was founded under the influence of the October Revolution in Russia and the May 4th Movement in China and with the help of the Communist International led by Lenin. The Revolution of 1911, led by Dr. Sun Yat-sen, the great revolutionary forerunner, overthrew the Qing Dynasty, thus bringing to an end over 2,000 years of feudal monarchical rule. However, the semi-colonial and semi-feudal nature of Chinese society remained unchanged. Neither the Kuomintang nor any of the bourgeois or petty-bourgeois political groupings and factions found any way out for the country and the nation, nor was it possible for them to do so. The Communist Party of China and the Communist Party of China alone was able to show the people that China's salvation lay in overthrowing once and for all the reactionary rule of imperialism and feudalism and then switching over to socialism. When the Communist Party of China was founded, it had less than 60 members. But it initiated the vigorous workers' movement and the people's anti-imperialist and anti-feudal struggle and grew rapidly, soon becoming a leading force such as the Chinese people had never before known.

3. In the course of leading the struggle of the Chinese people with its various nationalities for New Democracy, the Communist Party of China went through four stages: the Northern Expedition (1924-27) conducted with the co-operation of the Kuomintang, the Agrarian Revolutionary War (1927-37), the War of Resistance Against Japan (1937-45) and the nationwide War of Liberation (1946-49). On two occasions, first in 1927 and then in 1934, it endured major setbacks. It was not until 1949 that it finally triumphed in the revolution, thanks to the long years of armed struggle in conjunction with other forms of struggle in other fields closely coordinated with it.

In 1927, despite the resolute opposition of the left wing of the Kuomintang with Soong Ching Ling as its outstanding representative, the Kuomintang, controlled by Chiang Kai-shek and Wang Jingwei, betrayed the policies of Kuomintang-Communist cooperation and of anti-imperialism and anti-feudalism decided on by Dr. Sun Yat-sen and, in collusion with the imperialists, massacred Communists and other revolutionaries. The Communist Party was still quite inexperienced and, moreover, was dominated by Chen Duxiu's Right capitulationism, so that the revolution suffered a disastrous defeat under the surprise attack of a powerful enemy. The total membership of the party, which had grown to more than 60,000, fell to just over 10,000.

However, our party continued to fight tenaciously. Launched under the leadership of Zhou Enlai and several other comrades, the Nanchang Uprising of 1927 fired the opening shot for armed resistance against the Kuomintang reactionaries. The meeting of the Central Committee of the Party held on August 7, 1927 decided on the policy of carrying out agrarian revolution and organizing armed uprisings.

Shortly afterwards, the Autumn Harvest and Guangzhou uprisings and uprisings in many other areas were organized. Led by Comrade Mao Zedong, the Autumn Harvest Uprising in the Hunan-Jiangxi border area gave birth to the First Division of the Chinese Workers' and Peasants' Revolutionary Army and to the first rural revolutionary base area in the Jinggang Mountains. Before long, the insurgents, led by Comrade Zhu De, arrived at the Jinggang Mountains and joined forces with it. With the progress of the struggle, the party set up the Jiangxi central revolutionary base area and Western Hunan-Hubei, Haifeng-Lufeng, Hubei-Henan-Anhui, Qiongya, Fujian-Zhejiang-Jiangxi, Hunan-Hubei-Jiangxi, Hunan-Jiangxi, Zuojiang-Youjiang, Sichuan-Shaanxi, Shaanxi-Gansu and Hunan-Hubei-Sichuan-Guizhou and other base areas. The First, Second and Fourth Front armies of the Workers' and Peasants' Red Army were also born, as were many other Red Army units. In addition, party organizations and other revolutionary organizations were established and revolutionary mass struggles unfolded under difficult conditions in the Kuomintang areas.

In the Agrarian Revolutionary War, the First Front Army of the Red Army and the central revolutionary base area under the direct leadership of comrades Mao Zedong and Zhu De played the most important role. The front armies of the Red Army in turn defeated a number of "encirclement and suppression" campaigns launched by Kuomintang troops. But because of Wang Ming's "Left" adventurist leadership, the struggle against the Kuomintang's fifth "encirclement and suppression" campaign ended in failure.

The First Front Army was forced to embark on the 25,000-*li* Long March and made its way to northern Shaanxi to join forces with units of the Red Army, which had been perservering in struggles there, and with its 25th Army, which had arrived earlier. The Second and Fourth Front Armies also went on their long march, first one and then the other arriving in northern Shaanxi. Guerrilla warfare was carried on under difficult conditions in the base areas in south China from which the main forces of the Red Army had withdrawn. As a result of the defeat caused by Wang Ming's "Left" errors, the revolutionary base areas and the revolutionary forces in the Kuomintang areas sustained enormous losses. The Red Army of 300,000 men was reduced to about 30,000 and the Communist Party of 300,000 members to about 40,000.

In January 1935, the Political Bureau of the Central Committee of the Party convened a meeting in Zunyi during the Long March, which established the leading position of Comrade Mao Zedong in the Red Army and the Central Committee of the Party. This saved the Red Army and the Central Committee of the Party — which were then in critical danger — and subsequently made it possible to defeat Zhang Guotao's splittism, to bring the Long March to a triumphant conclusion and to open up new vistas for the Chinese revolution. It was a vital turning point in the history of the party.

At a time of national crisis of unparalleled gravity when the Japanese imperialists were intensifying their aggression against China, the Central Committee of the Party headed by Comrade Mao Zedong decided on and carried out the correct policy of forming an anti-Japanese national united front. Our party led the students' movement of December 9, 1935 and organized the powerful mass struggle to demand an end to the civil war and to demand resistance against Japan so as to save the nation. The Xi'an Incident, organized by generals Zhang Xueliang and Yang Hucheng on December 12, 1936, and its peaceful settlement which our party promoted, played a crucial historical role in bringing about renewed cooperation between the Kuomintang and the Communist Party and in achieving national unity for resistance against Japanese aggression.

During the war of resistance, the ruling clique of the Kuomintang continued to oppose the Communist Party and the people and was passive in resisting Japan. As a result, the Kuomintang suffered defeat after defeat in front operations against the Japanese invaders. Our party persevered in the policy of maintaining its independence and initiative within the united front, closely relied on the masses of the people, conducted guerrilla warfare behind enemy lines and set up many anti-Japanese base areas.

The Eighth Route Army and the New Fourth Army — the reorganized Red Army — grew rapidly and became the mainstay in the war of resistance. The Northeast Anti-Japanese United Army sustained its operations amid formidable difficulties. Diverse forms of anti-Japanese struggle were unfolded on a broad scale in areas occupied by Japan or controlled by the Kuomintang. Consequently, the Chinese people were able to hold out in the war for eight long years and win final victory, in cooperation with the people of the Soviet Union and other countries in the anti-fascist war.

During the anti-Japanese war, the party conducted a rectification movement — a movement of Marxist education. Launched in 1942, it was a tremendous success. It was on this basis that the enlarged Seventh Plenary Session of the Sixth Central Committee of the Party in 1945 adopted the Resolution on Certain Questions in the History of Our Party and soon afterwards the party's Seventh National Congress was convened. These meetings summed up our historical experience and laid down our correct line, principles and policies for building a new-democratic New China, enabling the party to attain an unprecedented ideological, political and organizational unity and solidarity.

After the conclusion of the War of Resistance Against Japan, the Chiang Kai-shek government, with the aid of U.S. imperialism, flagrantly launched an all-out civil war, disregarding the just demand of our party and the people of the whole country for peace and democracy. With the wholehearted support of the people in all the Liberated Areas, with the powerful backing of the students' and workers' movements and the struggles of the people of various strata in the Kuomintang areas and with the active cooperation of the democratic parties and non-party democrats, our party led the People's Liberation Army in fighting the three-year War of Liberation and — following the Liaoxi-Shenyang, Beijing-Tianjin and Huai-Hai campaigns and the successful crossing of the Changjiang (Yangtse) River — in wiping out a total of 8,000,000 Chiang Kai-shek troops. The end result was the overthrow of the reactionary Kuomintang government and the establishment of the great People's Republic of China. The Chinese people had stood up.

4. The victories gained in the 28 years of struggle fully show that:

1) *Victory in the Chinese revolution was won under the guidance of Marxism-Leninism.* Our party had creatively applied the basic principles of Marxism-Leninism and integrated them with the concrete practice of the Chinese revolution. In this way, the great system of Mao Zedong Thought came into being and the correct path to victory for the Chinese revolution was charted. This is a major contribution to the development of Marxism-Leninism.

2) *As the vanguard of the Chinese proletariat, the Communist Party of China is a party serving the people whole-heartedly, with no selfish aim of its own.* It is a party with both the courage and the ability to lead the people in their indomitable struggle against any enemy. Convinced of all this by virtue of their own experience, the Chinese people of every nationality came to rally around the party and to form a broad united front, thus forging a strong political unity unparalleled in Chinese history.

3) *The Chinese revolution was victorious mainly because we relied on a people's army led by the party — an army of a completely new type and one enjoying flesh-and-blood ties with the people — to defeat a formidable enemy through protracted people's war.* Without such an army, it would have been impossible to achieve the liberation of our people and the independence of our country.

4) *The Chinese revolution had the support of the revolutionary forces in other countries at every stage, a fact which the Chinese people will never forget.* Yet, it must be said that, fundamentally, victory in the Chinese revolution was won because the Chinese Communist Party adhered to the principle of independence and self-reliance and depended on the efforts of all of the Chinese people, whatever their nationality, after they underwent untold hardships and surmounted innumerable difficulties and obstacles together.

5) *The victorious Chinese revolution put an end to the rule of a handful of exploiters over the masses of the working people and to the enslavement of the multinational Chinese people by the imperialists and colonialists.* The working people have become the masters of the new state and the new society. While changing the balance of forces in world politics, the people's victory in so large a country — having nearly one-quarter of the world's population — has inspired the people in countries similarly subjected to imperialist and colonialist exploitation and oppression with heightened confidence in their forward march. The triumph of the Chinese revolution is the most important political event since World War II and has exerted a profound and far-reaching impact on the international situation and the development of the people's struggle throughout the world.

5. Victory in the new-democratic revolution was won through long years of struggle and sacrifice by countless martyrs, party members and people of all nationalities. We should by no means give all the credit to the leaders of the revolution, but at the same time we should not underrate the significant role these leaders have played.

Among the many outstanding leaders of the party, Comrade Mao Zedong was the most prominent. Prior to the failure of the revolution in 1927, he had clearly pointed out the paramount importance of the leadership of the proletariat over the peasants' struggle and the danger of a Right deviation in this regard. After its failure, he was the chief representative of those who succeeded in shifting the emphasis in the party's work from the city to the countryside and in preserving, restoring and promoting the revolutionary forces in the countryside.

In the 22 years from 1927 to 1949, Comrade Mao Zedong and other party leaders managed to overcome innumerable difficulties and gradually worked out an overall strategy and specific policies and directed their implementation, so that the revolution was able to switch from staggering defeats to great victory. Our party and people would have had to grope in the dark much longer had it not been for Comrade Mao Zedong, who more than once rescued the Chinese revolution from grave danger, and for the Central Committee of the Party which was headed by him and which charted the firm, correct political course for the whole party, the whole people and the people's army. Just as the Communist Party of China is recognized as the central force leading the entire people forward, so Comrade Mao Zedong is recognized as the great leader of the Chinese Communist Party and the whole Chinese people, and Mao Zedong Thought, which came into being through the collective struggle of the party and the people, is recognized as the guiding ideology of the party. This is the inevitable outcome of the 28 years of historical development preceding the founding of the People's Republic of China.

Basic Appraisal of the History of the 32 Years Since the Founding of the People's Republic

6. Generally speaking, the years since the founding of the People's Republic of China are years in which the Chinese Communist Party, guided by Marxism-Leninism and Mao Zedong Thought, has very successfully led the whole people in carrying out socialist revolution and socialist construction. The establishment of the socialist system represents the greatest and most profound social change in Chinese history and is the foundation for the country's future progress and development.

7. Our major achievements in the 32 years since the founding of the People's Republic are the following:

1) *We have established and consolidated the people's democratic dictatorship led by the working class and based on the worker-peasant alliance, namely, the dictatorship of the proletariat.* It is a new type of state power, unknown in Chinese history, in which the people are the masters of their own domain. It constitutes the fundamental guarantee for the building of a modern socialist country, prosperous and powerful, democratic and culturally advanced.

2) *We have achieved and consolidated nationwide unification of the country — with the exception of Taiwan and other islands — and have thus put an end to the state of disunity characteristic of old China.* We have achieved and consolidated the great unity of the people of all nationalities and have forged and expanded a socialist relationship of equality and mutual help among the more than 50 nationalities. And we have achieved and consolidated the great unity of the workers, peasants, intellectuals and people of other strata and have strengthened and expanded the broad united front which is led by the Chinese Communist Party in full cooperation with the patriotic democratic parties and people's organizations, and comprises all socialist working people and all patriots who support socialism and patriots who stand for the unification of the motherland, including our compatriots in Taiwan, Xianggang (Hong Kong) and Aomen (Macao) and Chinese citizens overseas.

3) *We have defeated aggression, sabotage and armed provocations by the imperialists and hegemonists, safeguarded our country's security and independence and fought successfully in defence of our border regions.*

4. *We have built and developed a socialist economy and have in the main completed the socialist transformation of the private ownership of the means of production into public ownership and put into practice the principle of "to each according to his work."* The system of exploitation of man by man has been eliminated, and exploiters no longer exist as classes since the overwhelming majority have been remoulded and now live by their own labour.

5) *We have scored signal successes in industrial construction and have gradually set up an independent and fairly comprehensive industrial base and economic system.* Compared with 1952 when economic rehabilitation was completed, fixed industrial assets — calculated on the basis of their original price — were more than 27 times greater in 1980, exceeding 410,000 million yuan; the output of cotton yarn was 4.5 times greater, reaching 2,930,000 tons; that of coal, 9.4 times, reaching 620 million tons; that of electricity, 41 times, exceeding 300,000 million kwh.; the output of crude oil exceeded 105,000,000 tons and that of steel, 37 million tons; and the output value of the engineering industry was 54 times greater, exceeding 127,000 million yuan. A number of new industrial bases have been built in our vast hinterland and the regions inhabited by our minority nationalities. National defence industry started from scratch and is gradually being built up. Much has been done in prospecting for natural resources. There has been a tremendous growth in railway, highway, water and air transport and in posts and telecommunications.

6) *The conditions prevailing in agricultural production have experienced remarkable change, giving rise to big increases in production.* The amount of land under irrigation has grown from 300 million *mu* in 1952 to over 670 million *mu*. Flooding by large rivers such as the Changjiang (Yangtse), Huanghe (Yellow River), Huaihe, Haihe, Zhujiang (Pearl River), Liaohe and Songhuajiang has been brought under initial control. In our rural areas, where farm machinery, chemical fertilizers and electricity were practically nonexistent before Liberation, there has now been a big increase in the number of agriculture-related tractors and irrigation and drainage equipment and in the quantity of chemical fertilizers applied, and the amount of electricity consumed is now 7.5 times the amount generated in the whole country in the early years of Liberation. In 1980, the total

of grain was nearly double that in 1952 and that of cotton, more than double. Despite the excessive rate of growth in our population, which is now nearly one billion, we have succeeded by our own efforts in basically meeting the needs of our people in food and clothing.

7) *There has been substantial growth in urban and rural commerce and in foreign trade.* The total value of commodities purchased by enterprises owned by the whole people rose from 17.5 billion yuan in 1952 to 226.3 billion yuan in 1980, registering a nearly 13-fold increase; retail sales rose from 27.7 billion yuan to 214 billion yuan, an increase of 7.7 times. The total value of the state's foreign trade in 1980 was 8.7 times that of 1952. With the growth in industry, agriculture and commerce, the people's livelihood has improved very markedly as compared with pre-Liberation days. In 1980, average consumption per capita in both town and country was nearly twice as much as in 1952, allowing for price changes.

8) *Considerable progress has been made in education, science, culture, public health and physical culture.* In 1980, enrollment in the various kinds of full-time schools totalled 204 million, 3.7 times the number in 1952. In the past 32 years, institutions of higher education and vocational schools have turned out nearly 9 million graduates with specialized knowledge or skills. Our achievements in nuclear technology, man-made satellites, rocketry, etc. represented substantial advances in the field of science and technology. In literature and art, large numbers of fine works have appeared to cater to the needs of the people and of socialism. With the participation of the masses, sports have developed vigorously, and records have been achieved in quite a few events. Epidemic diseases with their high mortality rates have been eliminated or largely eliminated; the health of the rural and urban populations has greatly improved, and average life expectancy is now much longer.

9) *Under the new historical conditions, the People's Liberation Army has grown in strength and in quality.* No longer composed only of ground forces, it has become a composite army, including naval and air forces and various technical branches. Our armed forces, which are a combination of field armies, regional forces and the militia, have been strengthened. Their quality is now much higher and their technical equipment much better. The PLA is serving as the solid pillar of the people's democratic dictatorship in defending and participating in the socialist revolution and socialist construction.

10) *Internationally, we have steadfastly pursued an independent socialist foreign policy,* advocated and upheld the Five Principles of Peaceful Coexistence, entered into diplomatic relations with 124 countries and promoted trade and economic and cultural exchanges with still more countries and regions. Our country's place in the United Nations and the Security Council has been restored to us. Adhering to proletarian internationalism, we are playing an increasingly influential and active role in international affairs by enhancing our friendship with the peoples of other countries; by supporting and assisting the oppressed nations in their cause of liberation, the newly independent countries in their national construction and the people of various countries in their just struggles; and by staunchly opposing imperialism, hegemonism, colonialism and racism in defence of world peace. All of this has served to create favourable international conditions for our socialist construction and contributes to the development of a world situation favourable to people everywhere.

8. New China has not been in existence for very long, and our successes are still preliminary. Our party has made mistakes owing to its meagre experience in leading the cause of socialism and to subjective errors in the party leadership's analysis of the situation and its understanding of Chinese conditions. Before the "cultural revolution" there were mistakes of enlarging the scope of class struggle and of impetuosity and rashness in economic construction. Later, there was the comprehensive, long-drawn-out and grave blunder of the "cultural revolution". All these errors prevented us from scoring the greater achievements of which we should have been capable. It is impermissible to overlook or whitewash mistakes; this in itself would be a mistake and would give rise to more and greater mistakes.

But, after all, our achievements in the past 32 years is the main thing. It would be a no less serious error to overlook or deny our achievements. Our achievements and successful experiences are the products of the creative application of Marxism-Leninism by our party and people. They are the manifestation of the superiority of the socialist system and the base from which the entire party and people will continue to advance. "Uphold truth and rectify errors" — this is the basic stand of dialectical-materialism our party must take. It was by taking this stand that we saved our cause from danger and defeat and won victory in the past. By taking the same stand, we will certainly win still greater victories in the future.

The Seven Years of Basic Completion of the Socialist Transformation

9. From the inception of the People's Republic of China in October 1949 to 1956, our party led the whole people in gradually realizing the transition from new democracy to socialism, in rapidly rehabilitating the country's economy, in undertaking planned economic construction and in the main accomplishing the socialist transformation of private ownership of the means of production in most sectors of the country. The guidelines and basic policies defined by the party in this historical period were correct and have led to brilliant successes.

10. In the first three years of the People's Republic, we cleared the mainland of bandits and the remnant armed forces of the Kuomintang reactionaries; peacefully liberated Tibet; established people's governments at all levels throughout the country; confiscated bureaucrat-capitalist enterprises and transformed them into state-owned socialist enterprises; unified the country's financial and economic work; stabilized commodity prices; carried out agrarian reform in the new liberated areas; suppressed counter-revolutionaries; and unfolded the movements against the "three evils" of corruption, waste and bureaucracy and against the "five evils" of bribery, tax evasion, theft of state property, cheating on government contracts and stealing of economic information — the latter being a movement to beat back the attack mounted by the bourgeoisie. We effectively transformed the educational, scientific and cultural institutions of old China. While successfully carrying out the complex and difficult task of social reform and simultaneously undertaking the great war to resist U.S. aggression and aid Korea, to protect our homes and to defend the country, we rapidly rehabilitated the country's economy which had been devastated in old China. By the end of 1952, the country's industrial and agricultural production had attained record levels.

11. On the proposal of Comrade Mao Zedong in 1952, the Central Committee of the Party advanced the general line for the transition period, which was to realize the country's socialist industrialization and socialist transformation of agriculture, handicrafts and capitalist industry and commerce step by step over a fairly long period of time. This general line was a reflection of historical necessity.

1) *Socialist industrialization is an indispensable prerequisite to the country's independence and prosperity.*

2) *With nationwide victory in the new-democratic revolution and completion of the agrarian reform, the contradiction between the working class and the bourgeoisie and between the socialist road and the capitalist road became the principal internal contradiction.* The country needed a certain expansion of capitalist industry and commerce which were beneficial to its economy and to the people's livelihood. But in the course of their expansion, things detrimental to the national economy and the people's livelihood were bound to emerge. Consequently, a struggle between restriction and opposition to restriction was inevitable. The conflict of interests became increasingly apparent between capitalist enterprises on the one hand, and the economic policies of the state, the socialist state-owned economy, the workers and staff in these capitalist enterprises, and the people as a whole, on the other. An integrated series of necessary measures and steps — such as the fight against speculation and profiteering, the readjustment and restructuring of industry and commerce, the movement against the "five evils," workers' supervision of production and state monopoly of the purchase and marketing of grain and cotton — were bound gradually to bring backward, anarchic, lopsided and profit-oriented capitalist industry and commerce into the orbit of socialist transformation.

3) *Among the individual peasants, and particularly poor and lower-middle peasants who had just acquired land in the agrarian reform but lacked other means of production, there was a genuine desire for mutual aid and cooperation in order to avoid borrowing at usurious rates and even mortgaging or selling their land again with consequent polarization, and in order to expand production, undertake water conservancy projects, ward off natural calamities and make use of farm machinery and new techniques.* The progress of industrialization, while demanding agricultural products in ever increasing quantities, would provide increasingly stronger support for the technological transformation of agriculture, and this also would constitute a motive force behind the transformation from individual to cooperative farming.

As is borne out by history, the general line for the transition period set forth by our party was entirely correct.

12. During the period of transition, our party creatively charted a course for socialist transformation that suited China's specific conditions. In dealing with capitalist industry and commerce, we devised a whole series of transitional forms of state capitalism from lower to higher levels, such as the placing of state orders with private enter-

prises for the processing of materials or the manufacture of goods, state monopoly of the purchase and marketing of the products of private enterprise, the marketing of products of state-owned enterprises by private shops, and joint state-private ownership of individual enterprises or enterprises of a whole trade. Thus, we eventually realized the peaceful redemption of the bourgeoisie, a possibility envisaged by Marx and Lenin. In dealing with individual farming, we devised transitional forms of cooperation, proceeding from temporary or all-year-round mutual-aid teams, to elementary agricultural producers' cooperatives of a semi-socialist nature and then to advanced agricultural producers' cooperatives of a fully socialist nature, always adhering to the principles of voluntariness and mutual benefit, demonstration through advanced examples, the extension of state help. Similar methods were used in transforming individual handicrafts industries. In the course of such transformation, the state-capitalist and cooperative economies displayed their unmistakable superiority over forms of the past. By 1956, the socialist transformation of the private ownership of the means of production had been largely completed in most regions.

But there had been shortcomings and errors. From the summer of 1955 onwards, we were over-hasty in pressing on with agricultural cooperation and the transformation of private handicrafts and commercial establishments; we were far from meticulous, the changes were too fast, and we did our work in a somewhat summary, stereotyped manner, leaving open a number of questions for a long time. Following the basic completion of the transformation of capitalist industry and commerce in 1956, we failed to do a proper job in employing and dealing with some of the former industrialists and businessmen. But, on the whole, it was decidedly a historic victory for us to have effected, and to have effected fairly smoothly, so difficult, complex and profound a social change in so vast a country with its several hundred million people — a change, moreover, which promoted the growth of industry, agriculture and the economy as a whole.

13. In economic construction under the First Five-Year Plan (1953-57), we likewise scored major successes through our own efforts and with the assistance of the Soviet Union and other friendly countries. A number of basic industries, essential for the country's industrialization and yet very weak in the past, were built up. Between 1953 and 1956, the average annual increases in the total value of industrial and agricultural output were 19.6% and 4.8%, respectively. Economic growth was quite rapid, with satisfactory economic results, and the key economic sectors were well-balanced. The market prospered and prices were stable. The people's livelihood improved perceptibly. In April 1956, Comrade Mao Zedong made his speech *On the Ten Major Relationships,* in which he initially summed up our experiences in socialist construction and set forth the task of exploring a way of building socialism suited to the specific conditions of our country.

14. The First National People's Congress was convened in September 1954, and it enacted the Constitution of the People's Republic of China. In March 1955, a national conference of the party reviewed the major struggle against the plots of the careerists Gao Gang and Rao Shushi to split the party and usurp supreme power in the party and the state; in this way it strengthened party unity. In January 1956, the Central Committee of the Party called a conference on the question of the intellectuals. Subsequently, the policy of "letting a hundred flowers blossom and a hundred schools of thought contend" was advanced. These measures spelled out the correct policy regarding intellectuals and the work in education, science and culture and thus brought about a significant advance in these fields. Owing to the party's correct policies, fine style of work and the consequent high prestige it enjoyed among the people, the vast numbers of cadres, masses, youth and intellectuals earnestly studied Marxism-Leninism and Mao Zedong Thought and participated enthusiastically in revolutionary and construction activities under the leadership of the party, so that a healthy and virile revolutionary morality prevailed throughout the country.

15. The Eighth National Congress of the Party held in September 1956 was very successful. The congress declared that the socialist system had been basically established in China; that while we must strive to liberate Taiwan, thoroughly complete socialist transformation, ultimately eliminate the system of exploitation and continue to wipe out the remnant forces of counter-revolution, the principal contradiction within the country was no longer the contradiction between the working class and the bourgeoisie but between the demand of the people for rapid economic and cultural development and the existing state of our economy and culture, which fell short of the needs of the people; that the chief task confronting the whole nation was to concentrate all efforts on developing productive forces, industrializing the country and gradually meeting the people's incessantly growing material and cultural needs; and that although class struggle still existed and the people's democratic dictator-

ship had to be further strengthened, the basic task of the dictatorship was now to protect and develop the productive forces in the context of the new relations of production. The congress adhered to the principle put forward by the Central Committee of the Party in May 1956, the principle of opposing both conservatism and rash advance in economic construction — that is, of making steady progress by striking an over-all balance. It emphasized the problem of the building of the party in office and the need to uphold democratic centralism and collective leadership, oppose the personality cult, promote democracy within the party and among the people and strengthen the party's ties with the masses. The line laid down by the Eighth National Congress of the Party was correct and it charted the path for the development of the cause of socialism and for party building in the new period.

The Ten Years of Initially Building Socialism in All Spheres

16. After the basic completion of socialist transformation, our party led the entire people in shifting our work to all-round, large-scale socialist construction. In the ten years preceding the "cultural revolution" we achieved very big successes despite serious setbacks. By 1966, the value of fixed industrial assets, calculated on the basis of their original price, was four times greater than in 1956. The output of such major industrial products as cotton yarn, coal, electricity, crude oil, steel and mechanical equipment all recorded impressive increases. Beginning in 1965, China became self-sufficient in petroleum. New industries such as the electronic and petrochemical industries were established one after the other. The distribution of industry over the country became better balanced. Capital construction in agriculture and its technical transformation began on a massive scale and yielded better and better results. Both the number of tractors for farming and the quantity of chemical fertilizers applied increased over 7 times and rural consumption of electricity 71 times. The number of graduates from institutions of higher education was 4.9 times that of the previous seven years. Educational work was improved markedly through consolidation. Scientific research and technological work also produced notable results.

In the ten years from 1956 to 1966, the party accumulated precious experience in leading socialist construction. In the spring of 1957, Comrade Mao Zedong stressed the necessity of correctly handling and distinguishing between the two types of social contradictions differing in nature in a socialist society, and made the correct handling of contradictions among the people the main content of the country's political life. Later, he called for the creation of "a political situation in which we have both centralism and democracy, both discipline and freedom, both unity of will and personal ease of mind and liveliness." In 1958, he proposed that the focus of party and government work be shifted to technical revolution and socialist construction. All this was the continuation and development of the line adopted by the Eighth National Congress of the Party and was to go on serving as a valuable guide. While leading the work of correcting the errors in the Great Leap Forward and the movement to organize people's communes, Comrade Mao Zedong pointed out that there must be no expropriation of the peasants; that a given stage of social development should not be skipped; that equalitarianism must be opposed; that we must stress commodity production, observe the law of value and strike an over-all balance in economic planning; and that economic plans must be arranged with the priority proceeding from agriculture to light industry and then to heavy industry. Comrade Liu Shaoqi said that a variety of means of production could be put into circulation as commodities and that there should be a double-track system for labour as well as for education* in socialist society. Comrade Zhou Enlai said, among other things, that the overwhelming majority of Chinese intellectuals had become intellectuals belonging to the working people and that science and technology would play a key role in China's modernization. Comrade Chen Yun held that plan targets should be realistic, that the scale of construction should correspond to national capability and considerations should be given to both the people's livelihood and the needs of state construction, and that the material, financial and credit balances should be maintained in drawing up plans. Comrade Deng Xiaoping held that industrial enterprises should be consolidated and their management improved and strengthened, and that the system of workers' conferences should be introduced. Comrade Zhu De stressed the need to pay attention to the development of handicrafts and of diverse undertakings in agriculture. Deng Zihui and other comrades pointed out that a system of production responsibility should be introduced in agriculture. All these views were not only of vital significance then, but have remained so ever since. In the course of economic readjustment, the Central Committee drew up draft rules governing the work of the rural people's communes and work in industry, commerce, education, science and literature and art. These rules which were a more or less systematic summation of our experience in socialist construction and embodied specific policies suited to the prevailing conditions remain important as a source of reference for us to this very day.

In short, the material and technical basis for modernizing our country was largely established during that period. It was also largely in the same period that the core personnel for our work in the economic, cultural and other spheres were trained and that they gained their experience. This was the principal aspect of the party's work in that period.

17. In the course of this decade, there were serious faults and errors in the guidelines of the party's work which developed through twists and turns.

The year 1957 was one of the years that saw the best results in economic work since the founding of the People's Republic owing to the conscientious implementation of the correct line formulated at the Eighth National Congress of the Party.To start a rectification campaign throughout the party in that year and to urge the masses to offer criticisms and suggestions were normal steps in developing socialist democracy. In the rectification campaign, a handful of bourgeois Rightists seized the opportunity to advocate what they called "speaking out and airing views in a big way" and to mount a wild attack against the party and the nascent socialist system in an attempt to replace the leadership of the Communist Party. It was therefore entirely correct and necessary to launch a resolute counter-attack. But the scope of this struggle was made far too broad and a number of intellectuals, patriotic people and party cadres were unjustifiably labelled "Rightists," with unfortunate consequences.

In 1958, the Second Plenum of the Eighth National Congress of the Party adopted the general line for socialist construction. The line and its fundamental aspects were correct in that it reflected the masses' pressing demand for a change in the economic and cultural backwardness of our country. Its shortcoming was that it overlooked objective economic laws. Both before and after the plenum, all comrades in the party and people of all nationalities displayed high enthusiasm and intiative for socialism and achieved certain results in production and construction. However, "Left" errors, characterized by excessive targets, the issuing of arbitrary directions, boastfulness and the stirring up of a "communist wind," spread unchecked throughout the country. This was due to lack of experience in socialist construction and inadequate understanding of the laws of economic development and of the basic economic conditions in China.

More important, it was due to the fact that Comrade Mao Zedong and many leading comrades, both at the centre and in the localities, had become smug about their successes, were impatient for quick results and overestimated the role of man's subjective will and efforts. After the general line was formulated, the Great Leap Forward and the movement for rural people's communes were initiated without careful investigation and study and without prior experimentation. From the end of 1958 to the early stage of the Lushan Meeting of the Political Bureau of the Party's Central Committee in July 1959, Comrade Mao Zedong and the Central Committee led the whole party in energetically rectifying the errors which had already been recognized. However, in the later part of the meeting, he erred in initiating criticism of Comrade Peng Dehuai and then in launching a party-wide struggle against "Right opportunism." The resolution passed by the Eighth Plenary Session of the Eighth Central Committee of the Party concerning the so-called anti-party group of Peng Dehuai, Huang Kecheng, Zhang Wentian and Zhou Xiaozhou was entirely wrong. Politically, this struggle gravely undermined inner-party democracy from the central level down to the grassroots; economically, it cut short the process of the rectification of "Left" errors, thus prolonging their influence. It was mainly due to the errors of the Great Leap Forward and of the struggle against "Right opportunism" — together with a succession of natural calamities and the perfidious scrapping of contracts by the Soviet government — that our economy encountered serious difficulties between 1959 and 1961, causing serious losses to our country and people.

In the winter of 1960, the Central Committee of the Party and Comrade Mao Zedong set about rectifying the "Left" errors in rural work and decided on the principle of "readjustment, consolidation, filling out and raising standards" for the economy as a whole. A number of correct policies and resolute measures were worked out and put into effect with comrades Liu Shaoqi, Zhou Enlai, Chen Yun and Deng Xiaoping in charge. All this constituted a crucial turning point in that historical phase. In January 1962, the enlarged Central Work Conference, attended by 7,000 people, made a preliminary summing-up of the positive and negative experience of the Great Leap Forward and unfolded criticism and self-criticism. A majority of the comrades who had been unjustifiably criticized during the campaign against "Right opportunism" were rehabilitated before or after the conference. In addition, most of the "Rightists" had their label removed. Thanks to these economic and political measures, the national economy recovered and developed fairly smoothly between 1962 and 1966.

Nevertheless, "Left" errors in the principles

guiding economic work were not only not eradicated, but actually grew in the spheres of politics, ideology and culture. At the Tenth Plenary Session of the Party's Eighth Central Committee in September 1962, Comrade Mao Zedong widened and absolutized the class struggle — which exists only within certain limits in socialist society — and carried forward the viewpoint he had advanced after the anti-Rightist struggle in 1957 that the contradiction between the proletariat and the bourgeoisie remained the principal contradiction in our society. He went a step further and asserted that throughout the historical period of socialism, the bourgeoisie would continue to exist and would attempt a comeback and become the source of revisionism inside the party. The socialist education movement that unfolded between 1963 and 1965 in some rural areas and at the grassroots level in a small number of cities did help to some extent to improve the cadres' style of work and economic management. However, in the course of the movement, problems differing in nature were all treated as forms of class struggle or its reflections inside the party. As a result, quite a number of the cadres at the grassroots level were unjustly dealt with in the latter half of 1964, and early in 1965 the erroneous thesis was advanced that the main target of the movement should be "those party persons in power taking the capitalist road."

In the ideological sphere, a number of literary and art works and schools of thought and a number of representative personages in artistic, literary and academic circles were subjected to unwarranted, inordinate political criticism. And there was an increasingly serious "Left" deviation on the question of intellectuals and on the question of education, science and culture. These errors eventually culminated in the "cultural revolution," although they had not yet become dominant.

Thanks to the fact that the entire party and people had concentrated on carrying out the correct principle of economic readjustment since the winter of 1960, socialist construction gradually flourished again. The party and the people were united in sharing weal and woe. They overcame difficulties at home, stood up to the pressure of the Soviet leading clique and repaid all the debts owed to the Soviet Union, which were chiefly incurred through purchasing Soviet arms during the movement to resist U.S. aggression and aid Korea. In addition, they did what they could to support the revolutionary struggles of the people of many countries and assist them in their economic construction. The Third National People's Congress, which met between the end of 1964 and the first days of 1965, announced that the task of national economic readjustment had in the main been accomplished and that the economy as a whole would soon enter a new stage of development. It called for energetic efforts to build China step by step into a socialist power with modern agriculture, industry, national defence and science and technology. This call was not fulfilled owing to the "cultural revolution."

18. All the successes in these ten years were achieved under the collective leadership of the Central Committee of the Party headed by Comrade Mao Zedong. Likewise, responsibility for the errors committed in the work of this period rested with the same collective leadership. Although Comrade Mao Zedong must be held chiefly responsible, we cannot lay the blame for all those errors on him alone. During this period, his theoretical and practical mistakes concerning class struggle in a socialist society became increasingly serious, his personal arbitrariness gradually undermined democratic centralism in party life and the personality cult grew graver and graver. The Central Committee of the Party failed to rectify these mistakes in good time. Careerists like Lin Biao, Jiang Qing and Kang Sheng, harbouring ulterior motives, took advantage of these errors and inflated them. This led to the inauguration of the "cultural revolution."

The Decade of the "Cultural Revolution"

19. The "cultural revolution," which lasted from May 1966 to October 1976, was responsible for the most severe setbacks and the heaviest losses suffered by the party, the state and the people since the founding of the People's Republic. It was initiated and led by Comrade Mao Zedong. His principal theses were that many representatives of the bourgeoisie and counter-revolutionary revisionists had infiltrated the party, the government, the army and cultural circles, and that the leadership in a fairly large majority of organizations and departments was no longer in the hands of Marxists and the people; that party persons in power taking the capitalist road had formed a bourgeois headquarters inside the Central Committee which pursued a revisionist political and organizational line and had agents in all provinces, municipalities and autonomous regions, as well as in all central departments; that since the forms of struggle adopted in the past had been unable to solve this problem, the power usurped by the capitalist-roaders could be recaptured only by carrying out a great cultural revolution, by openly and fully mobilizing the broad masses from the bottom up to expose these sinister phenomena; and that the cultural revolution was in fact a great political

revolution in which one class would overthrow another, a revolution that would have to be waged time and again. These theses appeared mainly in the May 16 Circular, which served as the programmatic document of the "cultural revolution," as well as in the political report to the Ninth National Congress of the Party of April 1969. They were incorporated into a general theory — the "theory of continued revolution under the dictatorship of the proletariat" — which then took on a specific meaning. These erroneous "Left" theses, upon which Comrade Mao Zedong based himself in initiating the "cultural revolution," were obviously inconsistent with the system of Mao Zedong Thought, which is the integration of the universal principles of Marxism-Leninism with the concrete practice of the Chinese revolution. These theses must be clearly distinguished from Mao Zedong Thought. As for Lin Biao, Jiang Qing and others, who were placed in important positions by Comrade Mao Zedong, the matter is of an entirely different nature. They rigged up two counter-revolutionary cliques in an attempt to seize supreme power and, taking advantage of Comrade Mao Zedong's errors, committed many crimes behind his back, bringing disaster to the country and the people. As their counter-revolutionary crimes have been fully exposed, this resolution will not go into them at great length.

20. The history of the "cultural revolution" has proved that Comrade Mao Zedong's principal theses for initiating this revolution conformed neither to Marxism-Leninism nor China's reality. They represent an entirely erroneous appraisal of the prevailing class relations and political situation in the party and state.

1) *The "cultural revolution" was defined as a struggle against the revisionist line or the capitalist road.* There were no grounds at all for this definition. It led to the confusing of right and wrong on a series of important theories and policies. Many things denounced as revisionist or capitalist during the "cultural revolution" were actually Marxist and socialist principles, many of which had been set forth or supported by Comrade Mao Zedong himself. The "cultural revolution" negated many of the correct principles, policies and achievements of the 17 years after the founding of the People's Republic. In fact, it negated much of the work of the Central Committee of the Party and the People's Government, including Comrade Mao Zedong's own contribution. It negated the arduous struggles the entire people had conducted in socialist construction.

2) *The confusing of right and wrong in-*

evitably led to confusing the people with the enemy. The "capitalist-roaders" overthrown in the "cultural revolution" were leading cadres of party and government organizations at all levels, who formed the core force of the socialist cause. The so-called bourgeois headquarters inside the party headed by Liu Shaoqi and Deng Xiaoping simply did not exist. Irrefutable facts have proved that labelling Comrade Liu Shaoqi a "renegade, disguised traitor and scab" was nothing but a frame-up by Lin Biao, Jiang Qing and their followers. The political conclusion concerning Comrade Liu Shaoqi drawn by the 12th Plenary Session of the Eighth Central Committee of the Party and the disciplinary measures it meted out to him were both utterly wrong. The criticism of the so-called reactionary academic authorities in the "cultural revolution" — during which many capable and accomplished intellectuals were attacked and persecuted — also badly muddled up the distinction between the people and the enemy.

3) *Nominally the "cultural revolution" was conducted by directly relying on the masses. In fact, it was divorced both from the party organizations and from the masses.* After the movement started, party organizations at different levels were attacked and became partially or wholly paralyzed, the party's leading cadres at various levels were subjected to criticism and struggle, inner-party life came to a standstill, and many activists and large numbers of the basic masses upon whom the party has long relied on were rejected. At the beginning of the "cultural revolution," the vast majority of participants in the movement acted out of their faith in Comrade Mao Zedong and the party. Except for a handful of extremists, however, they did not approve of launching ruthless struggles against leading party cadres at all levels. With the lapse of time, following their own circuitous paths, they eventually attained a heightened political consciousness and consequently began to adopt a sceptical or wait-and-see attitude towards the "cultural revolution," or even resisted and opposed it. Many people were assailed more or less severely for this very reason. Such a state of affairs could not but provide openings to be exploited by opportunists, careerists and conspirators, not a few of whom were escalated to high or even key positions.

4) *Practice has shown that the "cultural revolution" did not in fact constitute a revolution or social progress in any sense, nor could it possibly have done so.* It was we and not the enemy at all who were thrown into disorder by the "cultural revolution." Therefore, from beginning to end, it did not turn "great disorder under heaven" into

"great order under heaven," nor could it conceivably have done so. After state power in the form of the people's democratic dictatorship was established in China, and especially after socialist transformation was basically completed and the exploiters were eliminated as classes, the socialist revolution represented a fundamental break with the past in both content and method, even though its tasks remained to be completed. Of course, it was essential to take proper account of certain undesirable phenomena that undoubtedly existed in party and state organs and to remove them by correct measures in conformity with the state Constitution, the laws and the Party Constitution. But on no account should the theories and methods of the "cultural revolution" have been applied. Under socialist conditions, there is no economic or political basis for carrying out a great political revolution in which "one class overthrows another." It decidely could not come up with any constructive programme, but could only bring grave disorder, damage and retrogression in its wake. History has shown that the "cultural revolution," initiated by a leader labouring under a misapprehension and capitalized on by counter-revolutionary cliques, led to domestic turmoil and brought catastrophe to the party, the state and the whole people.

21. The "cultural revolution" can be divided into three stages:

1) *From the initiation of the "cultural revolution" to the Ninth National Congress of the Party in April 1969.* The convening of the enlarged Political Bureau meeting of the Central Committee of the Party in May 1966 and the 11th Plenary Session of the Eighth Central Committee in August of that year marked the launching of the "cultural revolution" on a full scale. These two meetings adopted the May 16 Circular and the Decision of the Central Committee of the Communist Party of China Concerning the Great Proletarian Cultural Revolution, respectively. They launched an erroneous struggle against the so-called anti-party clique of Peng Zhen, Luo Ruiqing, Lu Dingyi and Yang Shangkun and the so-called headquarters of Liu Shaoqi and Deng Xiaoping. They wrongly reorganized the central leading organs, set up the "Cultural Revolution Group Under the Central Committee of the Chinese Communist Party" and gave it a major part of the power of the Central Committee. In fact, Comrade Mao Zedong's personal leadership characterized by "Left" errors took the place of the collective leadership of the Central Committee, and the cult of Comrade Mao Zedong was frenziedly pushed to an extreme. Lin Biao, Jiang Qing, Kang Sheng, Zhang Chunqiao and others, acting chiefly in the name of the "Cultural Revolution Group," exploited the situation to incite people to "overthrow everything and to wage full-scale civil war." Around February 1967, at various meetings, Tan Zhenlin, Chen Yi, Ye Jianying, Li Fuchun, Li Xiannian, Xu Xiangqian, Nie Rongzhen and other Political Bureau members and leading comrades of the Military Commission of the Central Committee sharply criticized the mistakes of the "cultural revolution." This was labelled the "February adverse current," and those involved were attacked and repressed. Comrades Zhu De and Chen Yun were also wrongly criticized. Almost all leading party and government departments in the different spheres and localities were stripped of their power or reorganized. The chaos was such that it was necessary to send in the People's Liberation Army to support the Left, the workers and the peasants and to institute military control and military training. This played a positive role in stabilizing the situation, but it also produced some negative consequences. The Ninth Congress of the Party legitimatized the erroneous theories and practices of the "cultural revolution," and so reinforced the positions of Lin Biao, Jiang Qing, Kang Sheng and others in the Central Committee of the Party. The guidelines of the Ninth Congress were wrong — ideologically, politically and organizationally.

2) *From the Ninth National Congress of the Party to its Tenth National Congress in August 1973.* In 1970-71, the counter-revolutionary Lin Biao clique plotted to capture supreme power and attempted an armed counter-revolutionary coup d'etat. Such was the outcome of the "cultural revolution" which overturned a series of fundamental party principles. Objectively, it announced the failure of the theories and practices of the "cultural revolution." Comrades Mao Zedong and Zhou Enlai ingenuiously thwarted the plotted coup. Supported by Comrade Mao Zedong, Comarde Zhou Enlai took charge of the day-to-day work of the Central Committee and things began to improve in all fields. During the criticism and repudiation of Lin Biao in 1972, he correctly proposed criticism of the ultra-"Left" trend of thought. In fact, this was an extension of the correct proposals put forward around February 1967 by many leading comrades of the Central Committee who had called for the correction of the errors of the "cultural revolution." Comrade Mao Zedong, however, erroneously held that the task was still to oppose the "ultra-Right." The Tenth Congress of the Party perpetuated the "Left" errors of the Ninth Congress and made Wang Hongwen a vice-chairman of the party. Jiang Qing, Zhang Chunqiao, Yao Wenyuan and Wang

Hongwen formed a Gang of Four inside the Political Bureau of the Central Committee, thus strengthening the influence of the counter-revolutionary Jiang Qing clique.

3) *From the Tenth Congress of the Party to October 1976.* Early in 1974, Jiang Qing, Wang Hongwen and others launched a campaign to "criticize Lin Biao and Confucius." Jiang Qing and the others directed the spearhead at Comrade Zhou Enlai, which was different in nature from the campaign conducted in some localities and organizations where individuals involved in and incidents connected with the conspiracies of the counter-revolutionary Lin Biao clique were investigated. Comrade Mao Zedong approved the launching of the movement to "criticize Lin Biao and Confucius." When he found that Jiang Qing and the others were turning it to their advantage in order to seize power, he severely criticized them. He declared that they had formed a "gang of four" and pointed out that Jiang Qing harboured the wild ambition of making herself chairman of the Central Committee and "forming a cabinet" by political manipulation.

In 1975, when Comrade Zhou Enlai was seriously ill, Comrade Deng Xiaoping, with the support of Comrade Mao Zedong, took charge of the day-to-day work of the Central Committee. He convened an enlarged meeting of the Military Commission of the Central Committee and several other important meetings with a view to solving problems in industry, agriculture, transport and science and technology, and began to straighten out the work in many fields so that the situation took an obvious turn for the better.

However, Comrade Mao Zedong could not bear to accept systematic correction of the errors of the "cultural revolution" by Comrade Deng Xiaoping and triggered the movement to "criticize Deng and counter the Right deviationist trend to reverse correct verdicts," once again plunging the nation into turmoil.

In January of 1976, Comrade Zhou Enlai passed away. Comrade Zhou Enlai was utterly devoted to the party and the people and stuck to his post till his dying day. He found himself in an extremely difficult situation throughout the "cultural revolution." He always kept the general interest in mind, bore the heavy burden of office without complaint, racking his brains and untiringly endeavouring to keep the normal work of the party and the state going, to minimize the damage caused by the "cultural revolution" and to protect many party and non-party cadres. He waged all forms of struggle to counter sabotage by the counter-revolutionary Lin Biao and Jiang Qing cliques. His death left the whole party and people in the most profound grief. In April of the same year, a powerful movement of protest signalled by the Tian An Men Incident swept the whole country, a movement to mourn for the late Premier Zhou Enlai and oppose the Gang of Four. In essence, the movement was a demonstration of support for the party's correct leadership as represented by Comrade Deng Xiaoping. It laid the ground for massive popular support for the subsequent overthrow of the counter-revolutionary Jiang Qing clique. The Political Bureau of the Central Committee and Comrade Mao Zedong wrongly assessed the nature of the Tian An Men Incident and dismissed Comrade Deng Xiaoping from all his posts inside and outside the party. As soon as Comrade Mao Zedong passed away in September 1976, the counter-revolutionary Jiang Qing clique stepped up its plot to seize supreme party and state leadership.

Early in October of the same year, the Political Bureau of the Central Committee, executing the will of the party and the people, resolutely smashed the clique and brought the catastrophic "cultural revolution" to an end. This was a great victory won by the entire party, army and people after prolonged struggle. Hua Guofeng, Ye Jianying, Li Xiannian and other comrades played a vital part in the struggle to crush the clique.

22. Chief responsibility for the grave "Left" error of the "cultural revolution" — an error comprehensive in magnitude and protracted in duration — does indeed lie with Comrade Mao Zedong. But, after all, it was the error of a great proletarian revolutionary. Comrade Mao Zedong paid constant attention to overcoming shortcomings in the life of the party and state. In his later years, however, far from making a correct analysis of many problems, he confused right and wrong and the people with the enemy during the "cultural revolution." While making serious mistakes, he repeatedly urged the whole party to study the works of Marx, Engels and Lenin conscientiously and imagined that his theory and practice were Marxist and that they were essential for the consolidation of the dictatorship of the proletariat. Herein lies his tragedy. While persisting in the comprehensive error of the "cultural revolution," he checked and rectified some of its specific mistakes, protected some leading party cadres and non-party public figures and enabled some leading cadres to return to important leading posts. He led the struggle to smash the counter-revolutionary Lin Biao clique. He made major criticisms and exposures of Jiang Qing, Zhang Chunqiao and others, frustrating their sinister ambition to seize supreme leadership. All this was crucial to the subsequent and relatively painless overthrow of the Gang of Four by our party. In his later years, he still remained alert to

safeguarding the security of our country, stood up to the pressure of the social-imperialists, pursued a correct foreign policy, firmly supported the just struggles of all peoples, outlined the correct strategy of the three worlds and advanced the important principle that China would never seek hegemony. During the "cultural revolution," our party was not destroyed, but maintained its unity. The State Council and the People's Liberation Army were still able to do much of their essential work. The Fourth National People's Congress, which was attended by deputies from all nationalities and all walks of life, was convened and it determined the composition of the State Council with comrades Zhou Enlai and Deng Xiaoping as the core of its leadership. The foundation of China's socialist system remained intact and it was possible to continue socialist economic construction. Our country remained united and exerted a significant influence on international affairs. All these important facts are inseparable from the great role played by Comrade Mao Zedong. For these reasons, and particularly for his vital contributions to the cause of the revolution over the years, the Chinese people have always regarded Comrade Mao Zedong as their respected and beloved great leader and teacher.

23. The struggle waged by the party and the people against "Left" errors and against the counter-revolutionary Lin Biao and Jiang Qing cliques during the "cultural revolution" was arduous and full of twists and turns, and it never ceased. Rigorous tests throughout the "cultural revolution" have proved that standing on the correct side in the struggle were the overwhelming majority of the members of the Eighth Central Committee of the Party and the members it elected to its Political Bureau, Standing Committee and Secretariat. Most of our party cadres, whether they were wrongly dismissed or remained at their posts, whether they were rehabilitated early or late, are loyal to the party and people and steadfast in their belief in the cause of socialism and communism. Most of the intellectuals, model workers, patriotic democrats, patriotic overseas Chinese and cadres and masses of all strata and all nationalities who had been wronged and persecuted did not waver in their love for the motherland and in their support for the party and socialism. Party and state leaders such as comrades Liu Shaoqi, Peng Dehuai, He Long and Tao Zhu and all other party and non-party comrades who were persecuted to death in the "cultural revolution" will live forever in the memories of the Chinese people.

It was through the joint struggles waged by the entire party and the masses of workers, peasants, PLA officers and men, intellectuals, educated youths and cadres that the havoc wrought by the "cultural revolution" was somewhat mitigated. Some progress was made in our economy despite tremendous losses. Grain output increased rather steadily. Significant achievements were scored in industry, communications and capital construction and in science and technology. New railways were built and the Changjiang River Bridge at Nanjing was completed; a number of large enterprises using advanced technology went into operation; hydrogen bomb tests were successfully undertaken and man-made satellites successfully launched and retrieved; and new hybrid strains of long-grained rice were developed and popularized. Despite the domestic turmoil, the People's Liberation Army bravely defended the security of the motherland. And new prospects were opened up in the sphere of foreign affairs.

Needless to say, none of these successes can be attributed in any way to the "cultural revolution," without which we would have scored far greater achievements for our cause. Although we suffered from sabotage by the counter-revolutionary Lin Biao and Jiang Qing cliques during the "cultural revolution," we won out over them in the end. The party, the people's political power, the people's army and Chinese society on the whole remained unchanged in nature. Once again history has proved that our people are a great people and that our party and socialist system have enormous vitality.

24. In addition to the above-mentioned immediate cause of Comrade Mao Zedong's mistakes in leadership, there are complex social and historical causes underlying the "cultural revolution" which dragged on for as long as a decade. The main causes are as follows:

1) *The history of the socialist movement is not long and that of the socialist countries even shorter.* Some of the laws governing the development of socialist society are relatively clear, but many more remain to be explored. Our party had long existed in circumstances of war and fierce class struggle. It was not fully prepared, either ideologically or in terms of scientific study, for the swift advent of the new-born socialist society and for socialist construction on a national scale. The scientific works of Marx, Engels, Lenin and Stalin are our guide to action, but can in no way provide ready-made answers to the problems we may encounter in our socialist cause. Even after the basic completion of socialist transformation, given the guiding ideology, we were liable, owing to the historical circumstances in which our party grew, to continue to regard issues unrelated to class struggle as its manifestations when observing and

handling new contradictions and problems which cropped up in political, economic, cultural and other spheres in the course of the development of socialist society. And when confronted with actual class struggle under the new conditions, we habitually fell back on the familiar methods and experiences of the large-scale, turbulent mass struggle of the past, which should no longer have been mechanically followed. As a result, we substantially broadened the scope of class struggle.

Moreover, this subjective thinking and practice, divorced from reality, seemed to have a "theoretical basis" in the writings of Marx, Engels, Lenin and Stalin, since certain ideas and arguments set forth in them were misunderstood or dogmatically interpreted. For instance, it was thought that equal right, which reflects the exchange of equal amounts of labour and is applicable to the distribution of the means of consumption in socialist society, or "bourgeois right" as it was designated by Marx, should be restricted and criticized, and thus the principle of "to each according to his work" and that of material interest should be restricted and criticized; that small production would continue to engender capitalism and the bourgeoisie daily and hourly on a large scale, even after the basic completion of socialist transformation, and thus a series of "Left" economic policies and policies on class struggle in urban and rural areas were formulated; and that all ideological differences inside the party were reflections of class struggle in society, and thus frequent and acute inner-party struggles were conducted. All this led us to regard the error in broadening the scope of class struggle as an act in defence of the purity of Marxism. Furthermore, Soviet leaders started a polemic between China and the Soviet Union, and turned the arguments between the two parties on matters of principle into a conflict between the two nations, bringing enormous pressure to bear upon China politically, economically and militarily. So we were forced to wage a just struggle against the big-nation chauvinism of the Soviet Union. In these circumstances, a campaign to prevent and combat revisionism inside the country was launched, which spread the error of broadening the scope of class struggle in the party, so that normal differences among comrades inside the party came to be regarded as manifestations of the revisionist line or of the struggle between the two lines. This resulted in growing tension in inner-party relations. Thus it became difficult for the party to resist certain "Left" views put forward by Comrade Mao Zedong and others, and the development of these views led to the outbreak of the protracted "cultural revolution."

2) *Comrade Mao Zedong's prestige reached a peak and he began to became arrogant at the very time when the party was confronted with the new task of shifting the focus of its work to socialist construction, a task for which the utmost caution was required.* He gradually divorced himself from practice and from the masses, acted more and more arbitrarily and subjectively, and increasingly put himself above the Central Committee of the Party. The result was a steady weakening and even undermining of the principle of collective leadership and democratic centralism in the political life of the party and the country. This state of affairs took shape only gradually and the Central Committee of the Party should be held partly responsible. From the Marxist viewpoint, this complex phenomenon was the product of given historical conditions. Blaming this on only one person or on only a handful of people will not provide a deep lesson for the whole party or enable it to find practical ways to change the situation. In the communist movement, leaders play quite an important role. This has been borne out by history time and again and leaves no room for doubt. However, certain grievous deviations, which occurred in the history of the international communist movement owing to the failure to handle the relationship between the party and its leaders correctly, also had an adverse effect on our party. Feudalism in China has had a very long history. Our party fought in the firmest and most thoroughgoing way against it, and particularly against the feudal system of land ownership and the landlords and local tyrants, and it fostered a fine tradition of democracy in the anti-feudal struggle. But it remains difficult to eliminate the evil ideological and political influence of centuries of feudal autocracy. And for various historical reasons, we failed to institutionalize and legalize inner-party democracy and democracy in the political and social life of the country, or else we drew up the relevant laws but without granting them due authority. This meant that conditions were present for the overconcentration of party power in the hands of individuals and for the development of arbitrary individual rule and personality cults in the party. Thus, it was hard for the party and state to prevent the initiation of the "cultural revolution" or to check its development.

A Great Turning Point in History

25. The victory won in overthrowing the counter-revolutionary Jiang Qing clique in October 1976 saved the party and the revolution from disaster and enabled our country to enter a new historical period of development. In the two years from October 1976 to December 1978, when the

Third Plenary Session of the 11th Central Committee of the Party was convened, large numbers of cadres and other people most enthusiastically devoted themselves to all kinds of revolutionary work and the task of construction. Notable results were achieved in exposing and repudiating the crimes of the counter-revolutionary Jiang Qing clique and in uncovering their factional set-up. The consolidation of party and state organizations and the redress of wrongs suffered by those who were unjustly, falsely and wrongly charged began in some places. Industrial and agricultural production was fairly quickly restored. Work in education, science and culture began to return to normal. Comrades inside and outside the party were more and more insistent that the errors of the "cultural revolution" be corrected, but such demands met with serious resistance.

This, of course, was partly due to the fact that the political and ideological confusion created in the decade-long "cultural revolution" could not be eliminated overnight, but it was also due to the "Left" errors in the guiding ideology that Comrade Hua Guofeng continued to commit in his capacity as Chairman of the Central Committee of the Communist Party of China. On the proposal of Comrade Mao Zedong, Comrade Hua Guofeng had become First Vice-Chairman of the Central Committee of the Party and concurrently Premier of the State Council during the "movement to criticize Deng Xiaoping" in 1976. He contributed to the struggle to overthrow the counter-revolutionary Jiang Qing clique and did useful work after that. But he promoted the erroneous "two-whatever's" policy, that is, "we firmly uphold whatever policy decisions Chairman Mao made, and we unswervingly adhere to whatever instructions Chairman Mao gave," and he took a long time to rectify this error. He tried to suppress the discussions on the criterion of truth that unfolded in the country in 1978, which were very significant in setting things right. He procrastinated and obstructed the work of reinstating veteran cadres in their posts and of redressing the injustices left over from the past (including the case of the "Tian An Men Incident" of 1976). He accepted and fostered the personality cult around himself while continuing the personality cult of the past. The 11th National Congress of the Communist Party of China convened in August 1977 played a positive role in exposing and repudiating the Gang of Four and in mobilizing the whole party for building China into a powerful modern socialist state. However, owing to the limitations imposed by the prevailing historical conditions and the influence of Comrade Hua Guofeng's mistakes, it reaffirmed the erroneous theories, policies and slogans of the "cultural revolution" instead of correcting them.

He also had his share of responsibility for impetuously seeking quick results in economic work and for continuing certain other "Left" policies. Obviously, under his leadership it was impossible to correct "Left" errors within the party, and all the more impossible to restore the party's fine traditions.

26. The Third Plenary Session of the 11th Central Committee in December 1978 marked a crucial turning point of far-reaching significance in the history of our party since the birth of the People's Republic. It put an end to the situation in which the party had been advancing haltingly in its work since October 1976 and began to correct conscientiously and comprehensively the "Left" errors of the "cultural revolution" and earlier. The plenary session resolutely criticized the erroneous "two-whatever's" policy and fully affirmed the need to grasp Mao Zedong Thought comprehensively and accurately as a scientific system. It highly evaluated the forum on the criterion of truth and decided on the guiding principles of emancipating the mind, using our brains, seeking truth from facts and uniting as one in looking forward to the future. It firmly discarded the slogan "Take class struggle as the key link," which had become unsuitable for a socialist society, and made the strategic decision to shift the focus of work to socialist modernization. It declared that attention should be paid to solving the problem of serious imbalances between the major branches of he economy and drafted decisions on the acceleration of agricultural development. It stressed the task of strengthening socialist democracy and the socialist legal system. It examined and redressed a number of major unjust, false and wrong cases in the history of the party and settled the controversy on the merits and demerits, the rights and wrongs, of some prominent leaders. The plenary session also elected additional members to the party's central leading organs.

These momentous changes in the work of leadership signified that the party had re-established the correct line of Marxism ideologically, politically and organizationally. Since then, it has gained the initiative in setting things right and has been able to solve step by step many problems left over since the founding of the People's Republic and the new problems cropping up in the course of practice and to carry out the heavy tasks of construction and reform, so that things are going very well in both the economic and political spheres.

1) *In response to the call of the Third Plenary Session of the 11th Central Committee of the Party for emancipating the mind and seeking truth*

from facts, large numbers of cadres and other people have freed themselves from the spiritual shackles of the personality cult and the dogmatism that prevailed in the past. This has stimulated thinking inside and outside the party, giving rise to a lively situation where people try their best to study new things and to seek solutions to new problems. To carry out the principle of emancipating the mind properly, the party reiterated in good time the four fundamental principles of upholding the socialist road, the people's democratic dictatorship (i.e., the dictatorship of the proletariat), the leadership of the Communist Party, and Marxism-Leninism and Mao Zedong Thought. It reaffirmed the principle that neither democracy nor centralism can be practiced at each other's expense and pointed out the basic fact that, although the exploiters had been eliminated as classes, class struggle continues to exist within certain limits.

In his speech at the meeting in celebration of the 30th anniversary of the founding of the People's Republic of China, which was approved by the Fourth Plenary Session of the 11th Central Committee of the Party, Comrade Ye Jianying fully affirmed the gigantic achievements of the party and people since the inauguration of the People's Republic, while making self-criticism on behalf of the party for errors in its work and outlining our country's bright prospects. This helped to unify the thinking of the whole party and people. At its meeting in August 1980, the Political Bureau of the Central Committee set itself the historic task of combating corrosion by bourgeois ideology and of eradicating the evil influence of feudalism in the political and ideological fields which is still present. A work conference convened by the Central Committee in December of the same year resolved to strengthen the party's ideological and political work, make greater efforts to build a socialist civilization, criticize the erroneous ideological trends running counter to the four fundamental principles and strike at the counter-revolutionary activities disrupting the cause of socialism. This exerted a most salutary countrywide influence in fostering a political situation characterized by stability, unity and liveliness.

2) *At a work conference called by the Central Committee in April 1979, the party formulated the principle of "readjusting, restructuring, consolidating and improving" the economy as a whole in a decisive effort to correct the shortcomings and mistakes of the previous two years in our economic work and to eliminate the influence of "Left" errors that had persisted in this field.* The party indicated that economic construction must be carried out in the light of China's conditions and in conformity with economic and natural laws; that it must be carried out within the limits of our own resources, step by step, after due deliberation and with emphasis on practical results, so that the development of production will be closely connected with the improvement of the people's livelihood; and that active efforts must be made to promote economic and technical cooperation with other countries on the basis of independence and self-reliance. Guided by these principles, light industry has quickened its rate of growth and the structure of industry is becoming more rational and better coordinated.

Reforms in the system of economic management, including extension of the decision-making powers of enterprises, restoration of the workers' congresses, strengthening of democratic management of enterprises and transference of financial management responsibilities to the various levels, have gradually been carried out in conjunction with economic readjustment. The party has worked conscientiously to remedy the errors in rural work since the latter stage of the movement of agricultural cooperation, with the result that the purchase prices of farm and sideline products have been raised, various forms of production responsibility introduced whereby remuneration is determined by farm output, family plots have been restored and appropriately extended, village fairs have been revived, and sideline occupations and diverse undertakings have been developed. All these have greatly enhanced the peasants' enthusiasm. Grain output in the last two years reached an all-time high, and at the same time industrial crops and other farm and sideline products registered a big increase. Thanks to the development of agriculture and the economy as a whole, the living standards of the people have improved.

3) *After detailed and careful investigation and study, measures were taken to clear the name of Comrade Liu Shaoqi, former Vice-Chairman of the Central Committee of the Communist Party of China and Chairman of the People's Republic of China, those of other party and state leaders, national minority leaders and leading figures in different circles who had been wronged, and to affirm their historical contributions to the party and the people in protracted revolutionary struggle.*

4) *Large numbers of unjust, false and wrong cases were re-examined and their verdicts reversed.* Cases in which people had been wrongly labelled bourgeois Rightists were also corrected. Announcements were made to the effect that former businessmen and industrialists, having undergone remoulding, are now working people; that small

tradespeople, peddlers and handicraftsmen who were originally labourers have been differentiated from businessmen and industrialists who were members of the bourgeoisie; and that the status of the vast majority of former landlords and rich peasants, who have become working people through remoulding, has been redefined. These measures have appropriately resolved many contradictions inside the party and among the people.

5) *People's congresses at all levels are doing their work better and those at the provincial and county levels have set up permanent organs of their own.* The system according to which deputies to the people's congresses at and below the county level are directly elected by the voters is now universally practiced. Collective leadership and democratic centralism are being perfected in party and state organizations. The powers of local and primary organizations are steadily being extended. The so-called right to "speak out, air views and hold debates in a big way and write big-character posters," which actually obstructs the promotion of socialist democracy, was deleted from the Constitution. A number of important laws, decrees and regulations have been reinstated, enacted or enforced, including the Criminal Law and the Law of Criminal Procedure — neither of which had been drawn up since the founding of the People's Republic. The work of the judicial, procuratorial and public security departments has improved and telling blows have been dealt to all types of criminals guilty of serious offences. The ten principal members of the counter-revolutionary Lin Biao and Jiang Qing cliques were publicly tried according to law.

6) *The party has striven to readjust and strengthen the leading bodies at all levels.* The Fifth Plenary Session of the 11th Central Committee of the Party, held in February 1980, elected additional members to the Standing Committee of its Political Bureau and re-established the Secretariat of the Central Committee, greatly strengthening the central leadership. Party militancy has been enhanced by the establishing of the Central Commission for Inspecting Discipline and of discipline inspection commissions at the lower levels, by the formulation of the Guiding Principles for Inner-Party Political Life and other related inner-party regulations, and by the effort made by leading party organizations and discipline inspection bodies at the different levels to rectify unhealthy practices. The party's mass media have also contributed immensely in this respect. The party has decided to put an end to the virtually lifelong tenure of leading cadres, change the over-concentration of power and, on the basis of revolutionization, gradually reduce the average age of the leading cadres at all levels and raise their level of education and professional competence, and has initiated this process. With the reshuffling of the leading personnel of the State Council and the division of labour between party and government organizations, the work of the central and local governments has improved.

In addition, there have been significant successes in the party's efforts to implement our policies in education, science, culture, public health, physical culture, nationality affairs, united front work, Overseas Chinese affairs and military and foreign affairs.

In short, the scientific principles of Mao Zedong Thought and the correct policies of the party have been revived and developed under new conditions and all aspects of party and government work have been flourishing again since the Third Plenary Session of the 11th Central Committee. Our work still suffers from shortcomings and mistakes, and we are still confronted with numerous difficulties. Nevertheless, the road of victorious advance is open, and the party's prestige among the people is rising day by day.

Comrade Mao Zedong's Historical Role and Mao Zedong Thought

27. Comrade Mao Zedong was a great Marxist and a great proletarian revolutionary, strategist and theorist. It is true that he made gross mistakes during the "cultural revolution," but, if we judge his activities as a whole, his contributions to the Chinese revolution far outweigh his mistakes. His merits are primary and his errors secondary. He rendered indelible meritorious service in founding and building up our party and the Chinese People's Liberation Army, in winning victory for the cause of liberation of the Chinese people, in founding the People's Republic of China and in advancing our socialist cause. He made major contributions to the liberation of the oppressed nations of the world and to the progress of mankind.

28. The Chinese Communists, with Comrade Mao Zedong as their chief representative, made a theoretical synthesis of China's unique experience in its protracted revolution in accordance with the basic principles of Marxism-Leninism. This synthesis constituted a scientific system of guidelines befitting China's conditions, and it is this synthesis which is Mao Zedong Thought, the product of the integration of the universal principles of Marxism-Leninism with the concrete practice of the Chinese revolution. Making revolution in a

large Eastern semi-colonial, semi-feudal country is bound to meet with many special, complicated problems which cannot be solved by reciting the general principles of Marxism-Leninism or by copying foreign experience in every detail. The erroneous tendency of making Marxism a dogma and deifying Comintern resolutions and the experience of the Soviet Union prevailed in the international communist movement and in our party mainly in the late 1920's and early 1930's, and this tendency pushed the Chinese revolution to the brink of total failure. It was in the course of combating this erroneous tendency and in making a profound summary of our historical experience in this respect that Mao Zedong Thought took shape and developed. It was systematized and extended in a variety of fields and reached maturity in the latter part of the Agrarian Revolutionary War and the War of Resistance Against Japan, and it was further developed during the War of Liberation and after the founding of the People's Republic of China. Mao Zedong Thought is Marxism-Leninism as applied and developed in China; it constitutes a correct theory, a body of correct principles and a summary of the experiences that have been confirmed in the practice of the Chinese revolution, a crystallization of the collective wisdom of the Chinese Communist Party. Many outstanding leaders of our party made important contributions to the formation and development of Mao Zedong Thought, and their ideas are synthesized in the scientific works of Comrade Mao Zedong.

29. Mao Zedong Thought is wide-ranging in content. It is an original theory which has enriched and developed Marxism-Leninism in the following respects:

1) *On the new-democratic revolution.*

Proceeding from China's historical and social conditions, Comrade Mao Zedong made a profound study of the characteristics and laws of the Chinese revolution, applied and developed the Marxist-Leninist thesis of the leadership of the proletariat in the democratic revolution, and established the theory of new-democratic revolution — a revolution against imperialism, feudalism and bureaucrat-capitalism waged by the masses of the people on the basis of the worker-peasant alliance under the leadership of the proletariat. His main works on this subject include: *Analysis of the Classes in Chinese Society; Report on an Investigation of the Peasant Movement in Hunan; A Single Spark Can Start a Prairie Fire; Introducing "The Communist;" On New Democracy; On Coalition Government;* and *The Present Situation and Our Tasks.* The basic points of this theory are:

i) China's bourgeoisie consisted of two sections, the big bourgeoisie (that is, the comprador bourgeoisie, or the bureaucrat-bourgeoisie), which was dependent on imperialism, and the national bourgeoisie, which had revolutionary leanings but wavered. The proletariat should endeavour to get the national bourgeoisie to join in the united front under its leadership and in special circumstances to include even part of the big bourgeoisie in the united front, so as to isolate the main enemy to the greatest possible extent. When forming a united front with the bourgeoisie, the proletariat must preserve its own independence and pursue the policy of "unity, struggle, unity through struggle;" when forced to split with the bourgeoisie, chiefly the big bourgeoisie, the proletariat should have the courage and ability to wage a resolute armed struggle against the big bourgeoisie, while continuing to win the sympathy of the national bourgeoisie or keep it neutral.

ii) Since there was no bourgeois democracy in China and the reactionary ruling classes enforced their terroristic dictatorship over the people by armed force, the revolution could not but essentially take the form of protracted armed struggle. China's armed struggle was a revolutionary war led by the proletariat with the peasants as the principal force. The peasantry was the most reliable ally of the proletariat. Through its vanguard, it was possible and necessary for the proletariat, with its progressive ideology and its sense of organization and discipline, to raise the political consciousness of the peasant masses, to establish rural base areas, to wage a protracted revolutionary war and to build up and expand the revolutionary forces. Comrade Mao Zedong pointed out that "the united front and armed struggle are the two basic weapons for defeating the enemy." Together with party building, they constituted the "three magic weapons" of the revolution. They were the essential basis which enabled the Chinese Communist Party to become the core of leadership for the whole nation and to chart the course of encircling the cities from the countryside and of finally winning countrywide victory.

2) *On the socialist revolution and socialist construction.*

On the basis of the economic and political conditions for the transition to socialism ensuing from victory in the new-democratic revolution, Comrade Mao Zedong and the Chinese Communist Party followed the path of effecting socialist industrialization simultaneously with socialist transformation and adopted concrete policies for the gradual transformation of the private ownership of the means of production, thereby providing a theoretical as well as practical solution to the difficult task of building socialism in a large country such as China, a country which was economically and culturally backward, with a population accounting for nearly one-fourth of the world's total. By putting forward the thesis that the combination of democracy for the people and dictatorship over the reactionaries constitutes the people's democratic dictatorship, Comrade Mao Zedong enriched the Marxist-Leninist theory of the dictatorship of the proletariat. After the establishment of the socialist system, Comrade Mao Zedong pointed out that under socialism the people had the same fundamental interests, but that all kinds of contradictions still existed among them, and that contradictions between the enemy and the people and contradictions among the people should be strictly distinguished from each other and correctly handled. He proposed that among the people we should follow a set of correct policies. We should follow the policy of "unity — criticism — unity" in political matters, the policy of "long-term coexistence and mutual supervision" in the party's relations with the democratic parties, the policy of "let a hundred flowers blossom, let a hundred schools of thought contend" in science and culture, and, in the economic sphere, the policy of over-all arrangement with regard to the different strata in town and country and of consideration for the interests of the state, the collective and the individual — all three. He repeatedly stressed that we should not mechanically transplant the experience of foreign countries, but should find our own way to industrialization, a way suited to China's conditions, by proceeding from the fact that China is a large agricultural country, taking agriculture as the foundation of the economy, correctly handling the relationship between heavy industry on the one hand and agriculture and light industry on the other, and attaching due importance to the development of the latter. He stressed that in socialist construction we should properly handle the relationships between economic construction and building up defence, between large-scale enterprises and small and medium-scale enterprises, between the Han nationality and the minority nationalities, between the coastal regions and the interior, between the central and the local authorities, and between self-reliance and learning from foreign countries, and that we should properly handle the relationship between accumulation and consumption and pay attention to over-all balance. Moreover, he stressed that the workers were the masters of their enterprises and that cadres must take part in physical labour and workers in management, that irrational rules and regulations must be reformed and that the three-in-one combination of technical personnel, workers and cadres must be effected. And he formulated the strategic idea of bringing all positive factors into play and turning negative factors into positive ones so as to unite the whole Chinese people and build a powerful socialist country.

The important ideas of Comrade Mao Zedong concerning the socialist revolution and socialist construction are mainly contained in such major works as *Report to the Second Plenary Session of the Seventh Central Committee of the Communist Party of China; On the People's Democratic Dictatorship; On the Ten Major Relationships; On the Correct Handling of Contradictions Among the People;* and *Talk at an Enlarged Work Conference Convened by the Central Committee of the Communist Party of China.*

3) *On the building of the revolutionary army and military strategy.*

Comrade Mao Zedong methodically solved the problem of how to turn a revolutionary army chiefly made up of peasants into a new type of people's army which is proletarian in character, observes strict discipline and forms close ties with the masses. He stressed that the sole purpose of the people's army is to serve the people wholeheartedly; he put forward the principle that the party commands the gun and not the other way around; he advanced the Three Main Rules of Discipline and the Eight Points for Attention and stressed the practice of political, economic and military democracy and the principles of the unity of officers and soldiers, the unity of army and people and the disintegration of the enemy forces, thus formulating by way of summation a set of policies and methods concerning political work in the army. In his military writings such as *On Correcting Mistaken Ideas in the Party; Problems of Strategy in China's Revolutionary War; Problems of Strategy in Guerrilla War Against Japan; On Protracted War;* and *Problems of War and Strategy,* Comrade Mao Zedong summed up the experience of China's protracted revolutionary wars and advanced the comprehensive concept of building a people's army and of building rural base areas and waging people's war by employing the people's army as the main force and relying on the masses. In raising guerrilla war to the strategic plane, he maintained that guerrilla warfare and mobile warfare of a guerrilla character would for a long time be the main forms of operation in China's revolutionary wars. He explained that it would be necessary to effect an appropriate change in military strategy simultaneously with the changing balance of forces between the enemy and ourselves and with the progress of the war. He worked out a set of strategies and tactics for the revolutionary army to wage people's war in conditions when the enemy was strong and we were weak. These strategies and tactics include fighting a protracted war strategically and campaigns and battles of quick decision, turning strategic inferiority into superiority in campaigns and battles and concentrating a superior force to destroy the enemy forces one by one. During the War of Liberation, he formulated the celebrated ten major principles of operation.

All these ideas constitute Comrade Mao Zedong's outstanding contribution to the military theory of Marxism-Leninism. After the founding of the People's Republic, he put forward the important guideline that we must strengthen our national defence and build modern revolutionary armed forces (including the navy, the air force and technical branches) and develop modern defence technology (including the making of nuclear weapons for self-defence).

4) *On policy and tactics.*
Comrade Mao Zedong penetratingly elucidated the vital importance of policy and tactics in revolutionary struggles. He pointed out that policy and tactics were the life of the party, that they were both the starting-point and the end-result of all the practical activities of a revolutionary party and that the party must formulate its policies in the light of the existing political situation, class relations, actual circumstances and the changes in them, combining principle and flexibility. He made many valuable suggestions concerning policy and tactics in the struggle against the enemy, in the united front and other questions. Among other things he pointed out that under changing subjective and objective conditions a weak revolutionary force could ultimately defeat a strong reactionary force; that we should despise the enemy strategically and take him seriously tactically; that we should keep our eyes on the main target of struggle and not strike out in all directions; that we should differentiate among and disintegrate our enemies, and adopt the tactic of making use of contradictions, winning over the many, opposing the few and crushing our enemies one by one; that in areas under reactionary rule, we should combine legal and illegal struggle and, organizationally, adopt the policy of assigning picked cadres to work underground; that, as for members of the defeated reactionary classes and reactionary elements, we should give them a chance to earn a living and to become working people living by their own labour, so long as they do not rebel or create trouble; and that the proletariat and its party must fulfil two conditions in order to exercise leadership over their allies: (a) Lead their followers in waging resolute struggles against the common enemy and achieving victories; (b) Bring material benefits to their followers or at least avoid damaging their interests and at the same time give them political education.

These ideas of Comrade Mao Zedong's concerning policy and tactics are embodied in many of his writings, particularly in such works as *Current Problems of Tactics in the Anti-Japanese United Front; On Policy; Conclusions on the Repulse of the Second Anti-Communist Onslaught; On Some Important Problems of the Party's Present Policy; Don't Hit Out in All Directions;* and *On the Question of Whether Imperialism and All Reactionaries Are Real Tigers.*

5) *On ideological and political work and on cultural work.*

In his *On New Democracy,* Comrade Mao Zedong stated that any given culture (as an ideological form) is a reflection of the politics and economics of a given society, and the former in turn has a tremendous influence and effect upon the latter; economics is the base and politics the concentrated expression of economics. In accordance with this basic view, he put forward many important ideas of far-reaching and long-term significance. For instance, the thesis that ideological and political work is the life-blood of economic and all other work and that it is necessary to unite politics and economics and to unite politics and professional skills, and to be both red and expert; the policy of developing a national, scientific and mass culture and of letting a hundred flowers blossom, weeding through the old to bring forth the new, and making the past serve the present and foreign things serve China; and the thesis that intellectuals have an important role to play in revolution and construction, that intellectuals should identify themselves with the workers and peasants and that they should acquire the proletarian world outlook by studying Marxism-Leninism, by studying society and through practical work. He pointed out that "this question of 'for whom?' is fundamental; it is a question of principle" and stressed that we should serve the people whole-heartedly, be highly responsible in revolutionary work, wage arduous struggle and fear no sacrifice.

Many notable works written by Comrade Mao Zedong on ideology, politics and culture, such as *The Orientation of the Youth Movement; Recruit Large Numbers of Intellectuals; Talks at the Yan'an Forum of Literature and Art; In Memory of Norman Bethune; Serve the People;* and *The Foolish Old Man Who Removed the Mountains,* are of tremendous significance even today.

6) *On party building.* It was a most difficult task to build a Marxist, proletarian party of a mass character in a country where the peasantry and other sections of the petty bourgeoisie constituted

the majority of the population, while the proletariat was small in number yet strong in combat effectiveness. Comrade Mao Zedong's theory on party building provided a successful solution to this question. His main works in this area include *Combat Liberalism; The Role of the Chinese Communist Party in the National War; Reform Our Study; Rectify the Party's Style of Work; Oppose Stereotyped Party Writing; Our Study and the Current Situation; On Strengthening the Party Committee System;* and *Methods of Work of Party Committees.*

He laid particular stress on building the party ideologically, saying that a party member should join the party not only organizationally but also ideologically and should constantly try to reform his non-proletarian ideas and replace them with proletarian ideas. He indicated that the style of work which entailed integrating theory with practice, forging close links with the masses and practicing self-criticism was the hallmark distinguishing the Chinese Communist Party from all other political parties in China. To counter the erroneous "Left" policy of "ruthless struggle and merciless blows" once followed in inner-party struggle, he proposed the correct policy of "learning from past mistakes to avoid future ones and curing the sickness to save the patient," emphasizing the need to achieve the objective of clarity in ideology and unity among comrades in inner-party struggle. He initiated the rectification campaign as a form of ideological education in Marxism-Leninism throughout the party, which applied the method of criticism and self-criticism. In view of the fact that our party was about to become and then became a party in power leading the entire country, Comrade Mao Zedong urged time and again, first on the eve of the founding of the People's Republic and then later, that we should remain modest and prudent, guard against arrogance and rashness and keep to plain living and hard struggle in our style of work, and that we should be on the lookout against the corrosive influence of bourgeois ideology and should oppose bureaucratism which would alienate us from the masses.

30. The living soul of Mao Zedong Thought is the stand, viewpoint and method embodied in its component parts mentioned above.

This stand, viewpoint and method boil down to three basic points: to seek truth from facts, the mass line, and independence. Comrade Mao Zedong applied dialectical and historical materialism to the entire work of the proletarian party, giving shape to the stand, viewpoint and method so characteristic of Chinese Communists in the course of the Chinese revolution and its arduous, protracted struggles and thus enriching Marxism-Leninism.

They find expression not only in such important works as *Oppose Book Workship; On Practice; On Contradiction; Preface and Postscript to "Rural Surveys;" Some Questions Concerning Methods of Leadership;* and *Where Do Correct Ideas Come From?* — but also in all his scientific writings and in the revolutionary activities of the Chinese Communists.

1) *Seeking truth from facts.*

This means proceeding from reality and combining theory with practice, that is, integrating the universal principles of Marxism-Leninism with the concrete practice of the Chinese revolution. Comrade Mao Zedong was always against studying Marxism in isolation from the realities of Chinese society and the Chinese revolution. As early as 1930, he opposed blind book worship by emphasizing that investigation and study is the first step in all work and that one has no right to speak without investigation. On the eve of the rectification movement in Yan'an, he affirmed that subjectivism is a formidable enemy of the Communist Party, a manifestation of impurity in party spirit. These brilliant theses helped people break through the shackles of dogmatism and to greatly emancipate their minds. While summarizing the experience and lessons of the Chinese revolution in his philosophical works and many other works rich in philosophical content, Comrade Mao Zedong showed great profundity in expounding and enriching the Marxist theory of knowledge and dialectics. He stressed that the dialectical materialist theory of knowledge is the dynamic, revolutionary theory of reflection and that full scope should be given to man's conscious dynamic role when it is based on and is in conformity with objective reality. Basing himself on social practice, he comprehensively and systematically elaborated the dialectical materialist theory on the sources, the process and the purpose of knowledge and on the criterion of truth. He said that, as a rule, correct knowledge can be arrived at and developed only after many repetitions of the process leading from matter to consciousness and then back to matter; that is, leading from practice to knowledge and then back to practice. He pointed out that truth exists by contrast with falsehood and grows in struggle with it, that truth is inexhaustible and that the truth of any piece of knowledge — namely, whether it corresponds to objective reality — can ultimately be decided only through social practice.

He further elaborated the law of the unity of opposites, the nucleus of Marxist dialectics. He indicated that we should not only study the universality of contradiction in objective existence, but, more importantly, we should study the particularity of contradiction, and that we should resolve contradictions which are different in nature by different methods. Therefore, dialectics should not be viewed as a formula to be learned by rote and then applied mechanically, but should be closely linked with practice and with investigation and study and should be applied flexibly. He forged philosophy into a sharp weapon in the hands of the proletariat and the people for knowing and changing the world.

His distinguished works on China's revolutionary war, in particular, provide outstandingly shining examples of applying and developing the Marxist theory of knowledge and dialectics in practice. Our party must always adhere to the above ideological line formulated by Comrade Mao Zedong.

2) *The mass line means everything for the masses, reliance on the masses in everything, and "from the masses, to the masses."* The party's mass line in all its work has come into being through the systematic application in all its activities of the Marxist-Leninist principle that the people are the makers of history. It is a summation of our party's invaluable historical experience in conducting revolutionary activities over the years under difficult circumstances in which the enemy's strength far outstripped ours. Comrade Mao Zedong stressed time and again that as long as we rely on the people, believe firmly in the inexhaustible creative power of the masses and hence trust and identify ourselves with them, no enemy can crush us — while we can eventually crush every enemy and overcome every difficulty. He also pointed out that in leading the masses in all practical work, the leadership can form its correct ideas only by adopting the method of "from the masses, to the masses" and by combining the leadership with the masses and the general call with particular guidance. This means concentrating the ideas of the masses and turning them into systematic ideas, then going to the masses so that the ideas are persevered in and carried through, and testing the correctness of these ideas in the practice of the masses. And this process goes on, over and over again, so that the understanding of the leadership becomes more correct, keener and richer each time. This is how Comrade Mao Zedong united the Marxist theory of knowledge with the party's mass line.

As the vanguard of the proletariat, the party exists and fights for the interests of the people. But it always constitutes only a small part of the people, so that isolation from the people will render all the party's struggles and ideals devoid of content as well as impossible of success. To persevere in the revolution and advance the socialist cause, our party must uphold the mass line.

3) *Independence and self-reliance are the inevitable corollary of carrying out the Chinese revolution and construction by proceeding from Chinese reality and relying on the masses.*

The proletarian revolution is an internationalist cause which calls for the mutual support of the proletariat of different countries. But in order for its cause to triumph, each proletariat should base itself primarily on its own country's realities, rely on the efforts of its own masses and revolutionary forces, integrate the universal principles of Marxism-Leninism with the concrete practice of its own revolution and thus achieve victory. Comrade Mao Zedong always stressed that our policy should rest on our own strength and that we should find our own rate of advance in accordance with our own conditions. In a vast country like China, it is all the more imperative for us to rely mainly on our own efforts to promote the revolution and construction. We must be determined to carry the struggle through to the end and must have faith in the hundreds of millions of Chinese people and rely on their wisdom and strength; otherwise, it will be impossible for our revolution and construction to succeed or to be consolidated even if success is won.

Of course, China's revolution and national construction are not and cannot be carried out in isolation from the rest of the world. It is always necessary for us to try to win foreign aid and, in particular, to learn all that is advanced and beneficial from other countries. The closed-door policy, blind opposition to everything foreign and any theory or practice of great-nation chauvinism are all entirely wrong. At the same time, although China is still comparatively backward economically and culturally, we must maintain our own national dignity and confidence, and there must be no slavishness or submissiveness in any form in dealing with big, powerful or rich countries. Under the leadership of the party and Comrade Mao Zedong, no matter what difficulty we encountered, we never wavered, whether before or after the founding of New China, in our determination to remain independent and self-reliant and we never submitted to any pressure from outside; we showed the dauntless and heroic spirit of the Chinese Communist Party and the Chinese people. We stand for the peaceful co-existence of the people of all countries and their mutual assistance on an equal footing. While upholding our own independence, we respect other people's right to independence. The road of revolution and construction suited to the characteristics of a country has to be explored, decided on and blazed by its own people. No one has the right to impose his views on others. Only under these conditions can there be genuine internationalism. Otherwise, there can only be hegemonism. We will always adhere to this principled stand in our international relations.

31. Mao Zedong Thought is the valuable spiritual asset of our party. It will be our guide to action for a long time to come. The party leaders and the large group of cadres nurtured by Marxism-Leninism and Mao Zedong Thought were the backbone forces in winning great victories for our cause; they are and will remain our treasured mainstay in the cause of socialist modernization. While many of Comrade Mao Zedong's important works were written during the periods of new-democratic revolution and of socialist transformation, we must still constantly study them. This is not only because one cannot cut the past off from the present and because failure to understand the past will hamper our understanding of present-day problems, but also because many of the basic theories, principles and scientific approaches set forth in these works are of universal significance and provide us with invaluable guidance now and will continue to do so in the future. Therefore, we must continue to uphold Mao Zedong Thought, study it in earnest and apply its stand, viewpoint and method in studying the new situaion and solving the new problems arising in the course of practice. Mao Zedong Thought has added much that is new to the treasure-house of Marxist-Leninist theory. We must combine our study of the scientific works of Comrade Mao Zedong with that of the scientific writings of Marx, Engels, Lenin and Stalin.

It is entirely wrong to try to negate the scientific value of Mao Zedong Thought and to deny its guiding role in our revolution and construction just because Comrade Mao Zedong made mistakes in his later years. And it is likewise entirely wrong to adopt a dogmatic attitude towards the sayings of Comrade Mao Zedong, to regard whatever he said as the immutable truth which must be mechanically applied everywhere, and to be unwilling to admit honestly that he made mistakes in his later years, and even try to stick to them in our new activities. Both these attitudes fail to make a distinction between Mao Zedong Thought — a scientific theory formed and tested over a long period of time — and the mistakes Comrade Mao Zedong made in his later years. And it is absolutely necessary that this distinction should be made. We must treasure all the positive experience obtained in the course of integrating the universal principles of Marxism-Leninism with the concrete practice of China's revolution and construction over 50 years or so, apply and carry forward this experience in our new work and enrich and develop party theory with new principles and new conclusions corresponding to reality, so as to ensure the continued progress of our cause along the scientific course of Marxism-Leninism and Mao Zedong Thought.

Unite and Strive to Build a Powerful, Modern Socialist China

32. The objective of our party's struggle in the new historical period is to turn China step by step into a powerful socialist country, with modern agriculture, industry, national defence and science and technology and with a high level of democracy and culture. We must also accomplish the great cause of reunification of the country by getting Taiwan to return to the embrace of the motherland. The fundamental aim of summing up the historical experience of the 32 years since the founding of the People's Republic is to accomplish the great objective of building a powerful and modern socialist country by further rallying the will and strength of the whole party, the whole army and the whole people on the basis of upholding the four fundamental principles, namely, upholding the socialist road, the people's democratic dictatorship (i.e., the dictatorship of the proletariat), the leadership of the Communist Party, and Marxism-Leninism and Mao Zedong Thought. These four principles constitute the common political basis of the unity of the whole party and the unity of the whole people as well as the basic guarantee for the realization of socialist modernization. Any word or deed which deviates from these four principles is wrong. Any word or deed which denies or undermines these four principles cannot be tolerated.

33. Socialism and socialism alone can save China. This is the unalterable conclusion drawn by all our people from their own experience over the past century or so; it likewise constitutes our fundamental historical experience in the 32 years since the founding of our People's Republic. Although our socialist system is still in its early phase of development, China has undoubtedly established a socialist system and entered the stage of socialist society. Any view denying this basic fact is wrong. Under socialism, we have achieved successes which were absolutely impossible in old China. This is a preliminary but at the same time a compelling manifestation of the superiority of the socialist system. The fact that we have been and are able to overcome all kinds of difficulties through our own efforts testifies to its great vitality. Of course, our system will have to undergo a long process of development before it can be perfected. Given

the premise that we uphold the basic system of socialism, we must therefore strive to reform those specific features which are not in keeping with the expansion of the productive forces and the interests of the people, and to combat staunchly all activities detrimental to socialism. With the development of our cause, the immense superiority of socialism will become more and more apparent.

34. Without the Chinese Communist Party, there would have been no New China. Likewise, without the Chinese Communist Party, there would be no modern socialist China. The Chinese Communist Party is a proletarian party armed with Marxism-Leninism and Mao Zedong Thought and imbued with a strict sense of discipline and the spirit of self-criticism, and its ultimate historical mission is to realize communism. Without the leadership of such a party, without the flesh-and-blood ties it has formed with the masses through protracted struggles and without its painstaking and effective work among the people and the high prestige it consequently enjoys, our country — for a variety of reasons, both internal and external — would inexorably fall apart and the future of our nation and people would inexorably be forfeited. The party leadership cannot be exempt from mistakes, but there is no doubt that it can correct them by relying on the close unity between the party and the people, and in no case should one use the party's mistakes as a pretext for weakening, breaking away from or even sabotaging its leadership. That would only lead to even greater mistakes and court grievous disasters. We must improve party leadership in order to uphold it. We must resolutely overcome the many shortcomings that still exist in our party's style of thinking and work, in its system of organization and leadership and in its contacts with the masses. So long as we earnestly uphold and constantly improve party leadership, our party will assuredly be better able to undertake the tremendous tasks entrusted to it by history.

35. Since the Third Plenary Session of its 11th Central Committee, our party has gradually mapped out the correct path for socialist modernization as suited to China's conditions. In the course of practice, the path will be broadened and become more clearly defined, but, in essence, the key pointers can already be determined on the basis of the summing up of the negative as well as positive experiences since the founding of the People's Republic, and particularly of the lessons of the "cultural revolution."

1) *After socialist transformation was fundamentally completed, the principal contradiction our country has had to resolve is that between the growing material and cultural needs of the people and the backwardness of social production.*

It was imperative that the focus of party and government work be shifted to socialist modernization centering on economic construction and that the people's material and cultural life be gradually improved by means of an immense expansion of the productive forces. In the final analysis, the mistake we made in the past was that we failed to persevere in making this strategic shift. What is more, the preposterous view opposing the so-called "theory of the unique importance of productive forces" — a view diametrically opposed to historical materialism — was put forward during the "cultural revolution." We must never deviate from this focus, except in the event of large-scale invasion by a foreign enemy (and even then it will still be necessary to carry on such economic construction as wartime conditions require and permit). All party work must be subordinated to and serve this central task — economic construction. All party cadres, and particularly those in economic departments, must diligently study economic theory and economic practice as well as science and technology.

2) *In our socialist economic construction, we must strive to reach the goal of modernization systematically and in stages, according to the conditions and resources of our country.*

The prolonged "Left" mistakes we made in our economic work in the past consisted chiefly in departing from China's realities, in trying to exceed our actual capabilities and in ignoring the economic returns of construction and management as well as the scientific confirmation of our economic plans, policies and measures, with their concomitants of colossal waste and losses. We must adopt a scientific attitude, gain a thorough knowledge of the realities and make a deep analysis of the situation, earnestly listen to the opinions of the cadres, masses and specialists in the various fields and try our best to act in accordance with objective economic and natural laws and bring about a proportionate and harmonious development of the various branches of our economy. We must keep in mind the fundamental fact that China's economy and culture are still relatively backward. At the same time, we must keep in mind such favourable domestic and international conditions as the achievements we have already scored and the experience we have gained in our economic construction and the expansion of economic and technological exchanges with foreign countries, and we must make full use of these favourable conditions. We must oppose both impetuosity and passivity.

3) *The reform and improvement of the socialist relations of production must be in conformity with the level of the productive forces and conducive to the expansion of production.*

The state economy and the collective economy are the basic forms of the Chinese economy. The working people's individual economy within certain prescribed limits is a necessary complement to public economy. It is necessary to establish specific systems of management and distribution suited to the various sectors of the economy. It is necessary to have a planned economy and at the same time give play to the supplementary, regulatory role of the market on the basis of public ownership. We must strive to promote commodity production and exchange on a socialist basis. There is no rigid pattern for the development of the socialist relations of production. At every stage, our task is to create those specific forms of the relations of production that correspond to the needs of the growing productive forces and facilitate their continued advance.

4) *Class struggle no longer constitutes the principal contradiction after the exploiters have been eliminated as classes.*

However, owing to certain domestic factors and influences from abroad, class struggle will continue to exist within certain limits for a long time to come and may even grow acute under certain conditions. It is necessary to oppose both the view that the scope of class struggle must be enlarged and the view that it has died out. It is imperative to maintain a high level of vigilance and conduct effective struggle against all those who are hostile to socialism and try to sabotage it in the political, economic, ideological and cultural fields and in community life. We must correctly understand that there are diverse social contradictions in Chinese society which do not fall within the scope of class struggle and that methods other than class struggle must be used for their appropriate resolution. Otherwise, social stability and unity will be jeopardized. We must unswervingly unite with all forces that can be united and consolidate and expand the patriotic united front.

5) *A fundamental task of the socialist revolution is gradually to establish a highly democratic socialist political system.*

Inadequate attention was paid to this matter after the founding of the People's Republic, and this was one of the major factors contributing to the initiation of the "cultural revolution." Here is a grievous lesson for us to learn. It is necessary to strengthen the building of state organs at all levels in accordance with the principle of democratic centralism, to make the people's congresses at all levels and their permanent organs authoritative organs of the people's political power, to gradually realize direct popular participation in the democratic process at the grassroots of political power and community life and, in particular, to stress democratic management by the working masses in urban and rural enterprises over the affairs of their establishments. It is essential to consolidate the people's democratic dictatorship, to improve our Constitution and laws and to ensure their strict observance and inviolability. We must turn the socialist legal system into a powerful instrument for protecting the rights of the people, for ensuring order in production, work and other activities and for punishing criminals and cracking down on the disruptive activities of class enemies. The kind of chaotic situation that obtained in the "cultural revolution" must never be allowed to happen again in any sphere.

6) *Life under socialism must attain a high ethical and cultural level.*

We must firmly eradicate such gross fallacies as the denigration of education, science and culture and discrimination against intellectuals — fallacies which had long existed and found extreme expression during the "cultural revolution;" we must strive to raise the status and expand the role of education, science and culture in our drive for modernization. We unequivocally affirm that, together with the workers and peasants, the intellectuals are a force to rely on in the cause of socialism and that it is impossible to carry out socialist construction without culture and the intellectuals. It is imperative for the whole party to engage in a more diligent study of Marxist theories, of the past and present, in China and abroad, and of the different branches of the natural and social sciences. We must strengthen and improve ideological and political work and educate the people and youth in the Marxist world outlook and communist morality. We must persistently carry out the educational policy which calls for all-around development morally, intellectually and physically; for being both red and expert; for integration of the intellectuals with the workers and peasants; and for the combination of mental and physical labour. We must counter the influence of decadent bourgeois ideology and the decadent remnants of fedual ideology, overcome the influence of petty-bourgeois ideology and foster the patriotism which puts the interests of the motherland above everything else and promote the pioneer spirit of selfless devotion to modernization.

7) *The improvement and promotion of socialist relations among our various nationalities and the strengthening of national unity are of*

profound significance to our multinational country.

In the past, particularly during the "cultural revolution," we made a grave mistake on the question of nationalities— the mistake of widening the scope of class struggle; and we wronged a large number of cadres and masses of the minority nationalities. In our work among them, we did not show due respect for their right to autonomy. We must never forget this lesson. We must have a clear understanding that relations among our nationalities today are mainly relations among the working people of the various nationalities. It is necessary to adhere to their regional autonomy and to enact laws and regulations to ensure this autonomy and their decision-making power in applying party and government policies according to the actual conditions in their regions. We must take effective measures to assist economic and cultural development in regions inhabited by minority nationalities, actively train and promote cadres from among them and resolutely oppose all words and deeds undermining national unity and equality. It is imperative to continue to implement the policy of freedom of religious belief. To uphold the four fundamental principles does not mean that religious believers should renounce their faith but that they must not engage in propaganda against Marxism-Leninism and Mao Zedong Thought and that they must not interfere with politics and education in their religious activities.

8) *In the present international situation in which the danger of war still exists, it is necessary to strengthen the modernization of our national defence.*

The building up of national defence must be in keeping with the building up of the economy. The People's Liberation Army should strengthen its military training, political work, logistic service and study of military science and further raise its combat effectiveness so as gradually to become a still more powerful modern revolutionary army. It is necessary to restore and carry forward the fine tradition of unity inside the army, between the army and the government and between the army and the people. The building of the people's militia must also be further strengthened.

9) *In our external relations, we must continue to oppose imperialism, hegemonism, colonialism and racism, and safeguard world peace.*

We must actively promote relations and economic and cultural exchanges with other countries on the basis of the Five Principles of Peaceful Coexistence. We must uphold proletarian internationalism and support the cause of the liberation of oppressed nations, the national construction of newly independent countries and the just struggles of the peoples everywhere.

10) *In the light of the lessons of the "cultural revolution" and the present situation in the party, it is imperative to build up a sound system of democratic centralism inside the party.*

We must carry out the Marxist principle of the exercise of collective party leadership by leaders who have emerged from mass struggles and who combine political integrity with professional competence, and we must prohibit personality cults in any form. It is imperative to uphold the prestige of party leaders and at the same time to ensure that their activities come under the supervision of the party and the people. We must have a high degree of centralism based on a high degree of democracy and insist that the minority is subordinate to the majority, the individual to the organization, the lower to the higher level and the entire membership to the Central Committee. The style of work of a political party in power is a matter that determines its very existence. Party organizations at all levels and all party cadres must go deep among the masses, plunge themselves into practical struggle, remain modest and prudent, share weal and woe with the masses and firmly overcome bureaucratism. We must properly wield the weapon of criticism and self-criticism, overcome erroneous ideas that deviate from the party's correct principles, uproot factionalism, oppose anarchism and ultra-individualism and eradicate such unhealthy tendencies as the practice of seeking perquisites and privileges. We must consolidate the party organization, purify the party ranks and weed out degenerate elements who oppress and bully the people. In exercising leadership over state affairs and work in the economic and cultural fields as well as in community life, the party must correctly handle its relations with other organizations, ensure by every means the effective functioning of the organs of state power and of administrative, judicial and economic and cultural organizations and see to it that trade unions, the Youth League, the Women's Federation, the Science and Technology Association, the Federation of Literary and Art Circles and other mass organizations carry out their work responsibly and on their own initiative. The party must strengthen its co-operation with public figures outside the party, give full play to the role of the Chinese People's Political Consultative Conference, hold conscientious consultations with democratic parties and personages without party affiliation on major issues of state affairs and respect their opinions and the opinions of specialists in various fields. As with other social organizations, party organizations at all levels must conduct their activities within the limits permitted by the Constitution and the law.

36. In firmly correcting the mistake of the so-called "continued revolution under the dictatorship of the proletariat" — a slogan which was advanced during the "cultural revolution" and which called for the overthrow of one class by another — we absolutely do not mean that the tasks of the revolution have been accomplished and that there is no need to carry on revolutionary struggles with determination. Socialism aims not just at eliminating all systems of exploitation and all exploiting classes but also at greatly expanding the productive forces, improving and developing the socialist relations of production and the superstructure and, on this basis, gradually eliminating all class differences and all major social distinctions and inequalities — which are chiefly due to the inadequate development of the productive forces — until communism is finally realized. This is a great revolution, unprecedented in human history. Our present endeavour to build a modern socialist China constitutes but one stage of this great revolution. Differing from the revolutions before the overthrow of the system of exploitation, this revolution is carried out not through fierce class confrontation and conflict, but through the strength of the socialist system itself, under leadership, step by step and in an orderly way. This revolution, which has entered the period of peaceful development, is more profound and arduous than any previous revolution and will not only take a very long historical period to accomplish but also demand many generations of unswerving and disciplined hard work and heroic sacrifice. In this historical period of peaceful development, revolution can never be plain sailing. There are still overt and covert enemies and other saboteurs who watch for opportunities to create trouble. We must maintain high revolutionary vigilance and be ready at all times to come out boldly to safeguard the interests of the revolution. In this new historical period, the whole membership of the Chinese Communist Party and the whole people must never cease to cherish lofty revolutionary ideals, maintain a dynamic revolutionary fighting spirit and carry China's great socialist revolution and socialist construction through to the end.

37. Repeated assessment of our successes and failures, of our correct and incorrect practices, of the 32 years since the founding of our People's Republic, and particularly deliberation over and review of the events of the past few years, have helped to raise immensely the political consciousness of all party comrades and of all patriots. Obviously, our party now has a higher level of understanding of socialist revolution and construction than at any other period since Liberation. Our party has both the courage to acknowledge and correct its mistakes and the determination and ability to prevent repetition of the serious mistakes of the past. In the last analysis, from a longterm historical point of view, the mistakes and setbacks of our party were only temporary whereas the consequent steeling of our party and people, the greater maturity of the core force formed among our party cadres through protracted struggle, the growing superiority of our socialist system and the increasingly keen and common aspiration of our party, army and people for the prosperity of the motherland will be decisive factors in the long run. A great future is in store for our socialist cause and for the Chinese people in their hundreds of millions.

38. Inner-party unity and unity between the party and the people are the basic guarantee for new victories in our socialist modernization. Whatever the difficulties, as long as the party is closely united and remains closely united with the people, our party and the cause of socialism it leads, will certainly prosper day by day.

The Resolution on Certain Questions in the History of Our Party, unanimously adopted in 1945 by the Enlarged Seventh Plenary Session of the Sixth Central Committee of the Party, unified the thinking of the whole party, consolidated its unity, promoted the rapid advance of the people's revolutionary cause and accelerated its eventual triumph. The Sixth Plenary Session of the 11th Central Committee of the Party believes that the present resolution which it has unanimously adopted will play a similar historical role. This session calls upon the whole party, the whole army and the people of all nationalities to act under the great banner of Marxism-Leninism and Mao Zedong Thought, to closely rally around the Central Committee of the Party, to preserve the spirit of the legendary Foolish Old Man who removed mountains and to work together as one in defiance of all difficulties so as to turn China step by step into a powerful modern socialist country which is highly democratic and highly cultured. Our goal must be attained! Our goal unquestionably can be attained!

---

*The double-track system for labour refers to a combination of the system of the eight-hour day in factories, rural areas and government offices with a system of part-time work and part-time study in factories and rural areas. The double-track system for education means a system of full-time schooling combined with a system of part-time work and part-time study.

3. SPEECH AT THE MEETING IN CELEBRATION OF THE 60TH ANNIVERSARY OF THE FOUNDING OF THE COMMUNIST PARTY OF CHINA
By Hu Yaobang
(July 1, 1981)

Comrades and Friends:

We are gathered here today to celebrate the 60th anniversary of the founding of the Communist Party of China. At this moment, we are all deeply aware that our party and state find themselves in an important historical period, a period in which we are bringing order out of chaos, carrying on our cause and forging ahead.

To bring order out of chaos, to carry on our cause and to forge ahead, we must undo all the negative consequences of the "cultural revolution," advance the great cause pioneered by the party under the leadership of Comrade Mao Zedong and other proletarian revolutionaries of the older generation, and facilitate the Chinese people's way to socialism and communism.

The Sixth Plenary Session of the 11th Central Committee of the Communist Party of China, which has just ended, adopted the Resolution on Certain Questions in the History of Our Party Since the Founding of the People's Republic of China. The resolution reviews the party's 60 years of struggle, sums up the basic experience it has gained in the 32 years since the founding of the People's Republic; it makes a concrete and realistic evaluation of a whole train of crucial historical events; it analyses what was right and what was wrong in the ideology behind these events and the subjective factors and social roots giving rise to them; it evaluates Comrade Mao Zedong's role in history and expounds Mao Zedong Thought scientifically; and it indicates our way forward more clearly. The plenary session also made decisions on other important matters. History will prove that it too was a meeting of paramount importance for our party — a new milestone for our party and state in the course of bringing order out of chaos, carrying on our cause and forging ahead.

Looking back over the path our party has traversed, we are acutely conscious of the fact that the Chinese revolution has not been smooth sailing. We can say that the 60 years since the founding of the Communist Party of China have been years of unflinching, heroic struggle for the liberation of the Chinese nation and the happiness of the Chinese people, years of ever closer integration, through repeated application, of the universal truth of Marxism-Leninism with the concrete practice of the Chinese revolution, and years when right prevailed over wrong and positive aspects prevailed over negative aspects in the party. They have been years during which we marched on to a number of victories despite untold hardships and setbacks.

Why do we say that the history of the Chinese Communist Party is one of unflinching, heroic struggle for the liberation of the Chinese nation and the happiness of the Chinese people?

In modern Chinese history, between the Opium War of 1840-42 and the outbreak of the May 4th Movement of 1919, the Chinese people waged protracted, heroic struggles against imperialism and feudalism. The 1911 Revolution led by the great revolutionary Dr. Sun Yatsen overthrew the Qing Dynasty monarchy, thus terminating more than 2,000 years of feudal autocracy. However, the way to China's salvation was not discovered through any of these struggles. It was not until the Communist Party of China was born after the October Socialist Revolution in Russia and the May 4th Movement in China that new vistas were opened up for the Chinese revolution — as a result of the integration of Marxism-Leninism with the rising workers' movement in China, and with the help of the international proletariat.

The enemies of the Chinese revolution were formidable and ferocious. But no hardship could overwhelm the Chinese people and the Communist Party of China. In a dauntless revolutionary spirit, our party led the people in rising up to fight the enemy. We Communists and the people depended on each other for survival; we relied closely on the people, and the people had deep faith in us. Our party steeled itself in grim struggle and became the most advanced and most powerful leading force in the history of the Chinese revolution and built a new and well-trained people's army. After 28 years of arduous struggle in four great people's revolutionary wars (the Northern Expedition, 1924-27; the Agrarian Revolutionary War, 1927-37; the War of Resistance Against Japan, 1937-45; and the War of Liberation, 1946-49), our party led the people of all our nationalities in finally overthrowing the reactionary rule of imperialism, feudalism and bureaucrat-capitalism in 1949 and winning victory in the new-democratic revolution, a tremendous victory which led to the founding of the People's Republic of China, a state of the people's democratic dictatorship.

After the founding of the People's Republic, our party led the entire people in sustained advance. We thwarted the threats, attempts at subversion, sabotage and armed provocations of the imperialists and hegemonists, and safeguarded the independence and security of our great motherland. Except for Taiwan Province and a few other islands, we have achieved and consolidated the unification of our country. We have achieved and strengthened the great unity of the Chinese people of all nationalities and of the workers, peasants and intellectuals throughout the country. We have formed and consolidated the broadest possible united front of all socialist workers, all patriots who support socialism and all other patriots who uphold the reunification of the motherland — a united front led by the Chinese Communist Party in full cooperation with all the democratic parties. And we smoothly effected the decisive transition of our society from new democracy to socialism. Thanks to the arduous struggle of the whole party and people, we essentially completed the socialist transformation of the private ownership of the means of production and embarked on large-scale, planned socialist economic construction. Thus, our economy and culture registered an advance unparalleled in Chinese history. However numerous the shortcomings and mistakes in our work and however imperfect certain aspects of our social system, we have eliminated the system of exploitation and the exploiting classes and have established the socialist system. Hence, with nearly a quarter of the world's population, China has entered upon a socialist state of society, a state of society new in the history of mankind. Beyond a shadow of a doubt, this is the most radical social change in Chinese history. It is a leap of the most far-reaching significance in the progress of mankind and an immense victory for and a further development of Marxism.

The change is indeed striking. In the four score years between the Opium War and the birth of the Chinese Communist Party, the ceaseless struggles of the people had all failed despite their heroism, and their hopes and lofty aspirations were sadly frustrated. The picture has been altogether different in the 60 years since the birth of the Chinese Communist Party. A new epoch in Chinese history has been ushered in. The Chinese people have taken their destiny into their own hands; they have stood up in the East. Never again will the Chinese nation be bullied and oppressed.

In celebrating the 60th anniversary of the founding of the Chinese Communist Party, we feel with deep emotion that the splendid fruits of the Chinese people's revolution have been truly hardwon. They have been won by the Chinese people in 60 long years of hard struggle under the leadership of the Chinese Communist Party. They have been nurtured by the blood of millions of Communists and non-party revolutionaries who died before the firing squad, on the battlefield or at their posts.

Let us rise and pay our sincere tribute to the memory of all the revolutionary martyrs, all the revolutionary leaders and cadres, Communists and Communist Youth League members, veteran revolutionaries and young fighters, non-party comrades-in-arms and foreign friends who laid down their lives for the Chinese people at different stages of the Chinese revolution over the past six decades.

Why do we say that the history of the Chinese Communist Party is one of ever closer integration, through repeated application, of the universal truth of Marxism-Leninism with the concrete practice of the Chinese revolution?

From the moment of its inception, our party adopted Marxism-Leninism as its guiding ideology. However, the general principles of Marxism provide no ready-made recipe for revolution in a particular country, especially a large oriental, semi-feudal and semi-colonial country like China. During its formative years, in the 1920's and 1930's, our party suffered again and again from the "infantile malady" of turning Marxism into a dogma and deifying foreign experience — a malady which could not but leave the Chinese revolution groping in the dark and even lead it into a blind alley. Comrade Mao Zedong's great contribution lies in the fact that, in the course of combating this erroneous tendency and in the struggles waged collectively by the party and the people, he succeeded in integrating the universal truth of Marxism with the concrete practice of the Chinese revolution and in summing up freshly gained experiences. In this way, Mao Zedong Thought took shape as the guiding scientific ideology conforming to Chinese conditions. It is this scientific ideology that has guided the sweeping advance of the Chinese revolution from one triumph to another.

Mao Zedong Thought, coming into being and developing in the course of the Chinese revolution, is the crystallization of the collective wisdom of our party and a summing-up of the victories in the gigantic struggles of the Chinese people. Its theories on the new-democratic revolution, on the socialist revolution and socialist construction, on the strategy and tactics of revolutionary struggle, on the building of a revolutionary army, on military strategy, on ideological and political work, on cultural work, and on the building of the party, as well as its theories concerning scientific modes of thought, work and leadership which will be even more important in guiding all our work in the future, have all added new and original ideas to the treasure-house of Marxism. As a theory and as the summing-up of experiences varified in practice, as the application and development of Marxism in

China, Mao Zedong Thought has been and will remain the guiding ideology of our party.

However, Comrade Mao Zedong had his shortcomings and made mistakes just as many other outstanding figures in the forefront of the march of history. Chiefly in his later years, having been admired and loved for so long by the whole party and people, he became over-confident and more and more divorced from reality and the masses and, in particular, from the party's collective leadership, and often rejected and even suppressed correct opinions that differed from his. Thus, he inevitably made mistakes, including the comprehensive, long-drawn-out and gross blunder of initiating the "cultural revolution." This was a tremendous misfortune for the party and the people. Of course, it must be admitted that, both before the "cultural revolution" and at its inception, the party failed to prevent Comrade Mao Zedong's erroneous tendency from growing more serious but, instead, accepted and approved of some of his wrong theses. We veterans who had been working together with him for a long time as his comrades-in-arms, or who had long been following him in revolutionary struggle as his disciples, are keenly aware of our own responsibility in this matter, and we are determined never to forget this lesson.

Although Comrade Mao Zedong made grave mistakes in his later years, it is clear that if we consider his life work as a whole, his contributions to the Chinese revolution far outweigh his errors. He had dedicated himself to the Chinese revolution since his youth and had fought for it all his life. He was one of the founders of our party and the chief architect of the glorious Chinese People's Liberation Army. At the most trying times in the Chinese revolution, he was the first to discover the correct road for the revolution, to work out a correct over-all strategy and to gradually formulate a whole set of correct theories and tactics, thus guiding the revolution from defeat to victory. After the founding of the People's Republic, under the leadership of the Central Committee of the Party and Comrade Mao Zedong, New China quickly consolidated its position and embarked on the great cause of socialism. Even in the last few years of his life, when his errors had become very serious, Comrade Mao Zedong still remained alert to the nation's independence and security and had a correct grasp of the new developments in the world situation. He led the party and people in standing up to all pressures from hegemonism and instituted a new pattern for our foreign relations. In the long years of struggle, all comrades in our party drew wisdom and strength from Comrade Mao Zedong and Mao Zedong Thought, which nurtured successive generations of our party's leaders and large numbers of its cadres and educated the whole Chinese people. Comrade Mao Zedong was a great Marxist, a great proletarian revolutionary, theorist and strategist, and the greatest national hero in Chinese history. He made major contributions to the cause of the liberation of the world's oppressed nations and to the cause of human progress. His immense contributions are immortal.

While celebrating the 60th anniversary of the founding of the Communist Party of China, we deeply cherish the memory of Comrade Mao Zedong. We deeply cherish the memory of the great Marxists, comrades Zhou Enlai, Liu Shaoqi and Zhu De, and the memory of comrades Ren Bishi, Dong Biwu, Peng Dehuai, He Long, Chen Yi, Luo Ronghuan, Lin Boqu, Li Fuchun, Wang Jiaxiang, Zhang Wentian, Tao Zhu and others, who were all outstanding leaders of our party and who, together with Comrade Mao Zedong, made important contributions to the victorious Chinese revolution and to the formation and development of Mao Zedong Thought. We deeply cherish the memory of comrades Li Dazhao, Qu Qiubai, Cai Hesen, Xiang Jingyu, Deng Zhongxia, Su Zhaozheng, Peng Pai, Chen Yannian, Yun Daiying, Zhao Shiyan, Zhang Tailei, Li Lisan and other prominent leaders of our party in its formative years. We deeply cherish the memory of comrades Fang Zhimin, Liu Zhidan, Huang Gonglue, Xu Jishen, Wei Baqun, Zhao Bosheng, Dong Zhentang, Duan Dechang, Yang Jingyu, Zuo Quan, Ye Ting and other outstanding commanders of the people's army who early laid down their lives for the party and the country. We deeply cherish the memory of Comrade Soong Ching Ling, a great contemporary woman fighter who fought together with us over a long period of time and became a member of the glorious Chinese Communist Party before her death; of Cai Yuanpei, the prominent Chinese intellectual forerunner; and of Lu Xun, the great standard-bearer of our proletarian revolutionary culture. We deeply cherish the memory of Liao Zhongkai, He Xiangning, Deng Yanda, Yang Xingfo, Shen Junru and other close non-party comrades-in-arms of ours who consistently supported our party. We deeply cherish the memory of comrades Zou Taofen, Guo Moruo, Mao Dun and Li Siguang, Mr. Wen Yiduo and other distinguished fighters in the fields of science and culture. We deeply cherish the memory of Yang Hucheng, Tan Kah Kee, Zhang Zhizhong, Fu Zuoyi and other renowned patriots who made significant contributions to the victorious Chinese people's revolution. We deeply cherish the memory of Norman Bethune, Agnes Smedley, Anna Louise Strong, Dwarkanath S. Kotnis, Edgar Snow, Inejiro Asanuma, Kenzo Nakajima and other close friends of the Chinese people and eminent internationalist fighters.

Why do we say that the history of the Chinese Communist Party is also the history of the triumph of right over wrong and of the triumph of the party's positive over its negative aspects?

The revolutionary cause our party has embarked upon is a sacred cause involving the radical transformation of Chinese society, a completely new cause never undertaken by our forefathers. The enemy of the revolution was formidable and the social conditions under which the revolution took place were extremely complex. Therefore, it was only natural that we should make mistakes of one kind or another, even grievous ones, in the course of our revolutionary struggles. The important thing is to be good at learning through practice once a mistake has been made; to wake up in good time and endeavour to correct it; to strive to avoid a blunder which is long-drawn-out and comprehensive in character; and to avoid repetition of the same grievous blunder.

Our party was born and grew to maturity in the old society. At the high tide of the revolution, large numbers of revolutionaries joined our ranks. This boosted our strength; however, a few careerists and opportunists, too, wormed their way into the party. This could hardly be avoided. The point is that while transforming society, our party must pay attention to remoulding itself, must be good at educating and remoulding those who have diverse non-proletarian ideas when they join our party, and must recognize careerists and conspirators for what they are so as to be able to foil their schemes and conspiracies.

The greatness of the party does not lie in any readiness to guarantee complete freedom from any negative phenomena, but in its ability to overcome shortcomings and rectify errors and to defeat sabotage by all alien forces. Let us look back: Isn't this precisely how our party has fought in the past? Its history contains the blunders of Chen Duxiu's Right capitulationism and Wang Ming's "Left" dogmatism. There were also conspiracies to split the party hatched by Zhang Guotao and by Gao Gang and Rao Shushi. There were even the Lin Biao and Jiang Qing counter-revolutionary cliques. However, none succeeded in destroying our party. The extremely treacherous careerists and conspirators Lin Biao and Jiang Qing exploited the "cultural revolution" to seize supreme power; they committed every conceivable crime against our nation and people, with the gravest consequences. Yet they were finally unmasked and swept into the garbage bin of history by the party and the people. Isn't this an incontrovertible historical fact? Instead of being destroyed by sabotage or crippled by reverses of one kind or another, our party has emerged each time refreshed and reinvigorated from the struggle to overcome mistakes and prevail over what is negative. It is our party that is invincible.

The past 60 years prove that our party is indeed a proletarian party armed with Marxism-Leninism and Mao Zedong Thought and a party that wholeheartedly serves the people, entirely dedicated to their interests and with no particular interest of its own. It is truly a long-tested party which has acquired rich experience, learned many lessons and is capable of leading the people in braving difficulties to win victory after victory in the revolution. The role of this great party as the force at the core of the Chinese people's revolutionary cause and its leadership in this cause is the dictate of history and of the will and interests of the people of all our nationalities, a dictate which no force on earth can alter or shake.

Comrades and Friends!

With widespread popular support, our party smashed at one stroke the Jiang Qing counter-revolutionary clique in October 1976. This saved the revolution and our socialist state and ushered in a new period of historical development. Two years later, in December, 1978, the Third Plenary Session of the 11th Central Committee marked a decisive turning point in the post-1949 history of our party.

The tremendous significance of this plenary session lies in the fact that it genuinely began to correct matters in an all-around, determined and well-considered way by relying on the masses. Since then, right through the Fourth, Fifth and Sixth Plenary Sessions, our party has been working hard with concentrated energy and attention and under difficult and complex conditions, and has adopted and implemented step by step a series of major policy decisions in ideological, political and organizational matters and all aspects of socialist construction, thus correcting the erroneous "Left" orientation. Moreover, in the light of the new historical conditions, our party has gradually charted a correct course for socialist modernization that is suited to China's conditions.

The most striking change of all is the shift of the focus of work of the whole party and nation after the liquidation and repudiation of the Lin Biao and Jiang Qing counter-revolutionary cliques. Leading organs — from the central down to local levels — are now concentrating their energy and attention on socialist modernization. Now that liquidation of the long prevalent "Left" deviationist guiding ideology is under way, our socialist economic and cultural construction has shifted to a course of development that takes into account the basic conditions of the country and the limits of our ability, that proceeds step by step, and that seeks practical results and steady advance. With the implementation of the party's policies, the introduction of the system of production responsibilities and the development of a diversified economy, an excellent situation has developed in the vast rural areas in particular — a dynamic and progressive situation seldom seen since the founding of the People's Republic.

In socio-political relations, our party has resolutely and appropriately solved many important issues which had been wrongly handled over a long period of time, eliminated a number of major factors detrimental to stability and unity and put an end to the social unrest and upheaval fomented during the "cultural revolution." We are now striving to foster socialist democracy, to improve the socialist legal system and to reform and perfect the socialist political system. This gives a powerful impetus to the consolidation and development of a political situation of stability, unity and liveliness.

Through organizational consolidation and rectification of the style of work, tangible progress has been made in the normalization of party life, the development of inner-party democracy and the strengthening of the party's ties with the masses. The party's prestige, grievously damaged during the "cultural revolution," is gradually being restored.

To ensure the proper implementation of the principle of emancipating the mind, our party has reinterated that it is necessary to uphold the four fundamental principles of adhering to the socialist road, the people's democratic dictatorship (i.e., the dictatorship of proletariat), the Communist Party's leadership, and Marxism-Leninism and Mao Zedong Thought. These principles constitute the common political basis for the unity of the whole party and the unity of the entire people and provide the fundamental guarantee for the success of socialist modernization.

The great change which began with the Third Plenary Session of the Party's 11th Central Committee and our correct line and policies fulfil the common aspirations of the people and the party. Speaking of the general orientation and major policy decisions taken since the session, many comrades have said, "They suit us fine." These words reflect the thoughts and feelings of the masses and of the majority of cadres. They explain why this change is so dynamic and irresistible.

Needless to say, many difficulties confront us. We have yet to finish the process of correction, and in various fields many problems remain to be solved. Our material resources, expertise and experience are far from adequate for the achievements of the four modernizations. The people's living standards are still very low and many pressing problems demand solution. We have yet to introduce further improvements in the party's leadership and style of work. It is wrong to take these difficulties lightly. Only by taking them into full account will we be invincible. The road before us is still long and tortuous. It is like climbing the Taishan Mountain; when we have reached the Half-Way Gate to Heaven, we find that the Three 18 Flights of Steps lie ahead of us, demanding herculean efforts. Until we have negotiated these Flights of Steps, however, we won't be able to reach the South Gate to Heaven. Still climbing, we will find it relatively easy to mount the Peak of the Jade Emperor, our destination, and only then can we claim to have accomplished the splendid cause of socialist modernization. Once at the South Gate to Heaven, we shall be in a position to appreciate the great Tang Dynasty poet Du Fu's well-known lines, "Viewed from the topmost summit, / All mountains around are dwarfed." The hardships that once towered like "mountains" will then look small and we will be able to negotiate the obstacles on the way to the "topmost summit" more or less easily. In the course of our long journey, we will certainly be able to conquer these Flights of Steps, reach the South Gate to Heaven and then ascend the Peak of the Jade Emperor. Once there, we shall push towards new summits.

Comrades and Friends!

The historical experience of the past 60 years can be summed up in one sentence: there must be a Marxist, revolutionary line and a proletarian party capable of formulating and upholding this line. Faced with the gigantic task of socialist modernization centering around economic construction in the new historical period, we are deeply aware that the key to the fulfilment of this task lies in our party.

Now, the entire people have placed their hopes on our party, and other peoples of the world are closely watching it. Whether or not we can steer the ship of the Chinese revolution onward through storm and stress in the new historical period, whether or not we can modernize our agriculture, industry, national defence and science and technology fairly smoothly, avoid suffering such serious setbacks and paying huge prices as in the past, and achieve results that will satisfy the people and win the praise of posterity — all this depends on the efforts of all comrades in the party in the next decade or two. We must not let our people down.

With higher political awareness, we must make our party a solid core which is more mature politically, more unified ideologically and more consolidated organizationally, and more able to unite with all our nationalities and lead them in socialist modernization.

1. *All members of the party must work with*

selfless devotion for China's socialist modernization and in the service of the people.

We Chinese Communists must always proceed from our basic standpoint with the objective of wholeheartedly serving the people. Serving the people in essence means that our party must rally the masses round it and — by virtue of its correct guidelines and policies, its close ties with the masses, its members' exemplary role and its propaganda and organizational work — help them to see where their fundamental interests lie and to become united to strive for them.

The people are the makers of history. Both the people's revolution and the construction of socialism led by our party are the people's very own cause. At all times, party members comprise only a small minority of the population; so we must rely on the people in all of our work, have faith in them, draw wisdom from them, set store by their creativeness and subject ourselves to their supervision. Otherwise, we will accomplish nothing; we will fail. Since victory was won in the revolution, the people have become the masters of the country and society. To organize and support them in fulfilling this role and in building a new life under socialism is the quintessence of the party's leadership over the affairs of state.

For us Communists, serving the people means primarily dedication to the cause of communism and readiness to sacrifice ourselves for the interests of the people. In the years of war, many of our party members were the first to charge at the enemy and the last to pull back; they remained staunch and unyielding in captivity, dying as martyrs; and they were invariably the first to bear hardships and the last to enjoy comforts. What an inspiration and encouragement they were to millions upon millions of our people! Today, in peacetime construction, and particularly after the decade of havoc of the "cultural revolution," we need this revolutionary spirit even more. Although our party's fine style of work was corroded by the counter-revolutionary cliques of Lin Biao and Jiang Qing, there are still large numbers of fine party members who have maintained and carried forward this revolutionary spirit characterized by readiness to sacrifice one's individual interests and one's very life for the interests of the people. They have won high praise from the people, and they have earned it. It is utterly wrong to think and act as though the revolutionary spirit may be discarded in peacetime construction and as if party members no longer needed to share weal and woe with the masses whose interests they may subordinate to their own. That would be to debase our party spirit.

The style of work of a party in power vitally affects its very existence. As Comrade Mao Zedong pointed out in 1942, "Once our party's style of work is put completely right, the people all over the country will learn from our example. Those outside the party who have the same kind of bad style will, if they are good and honest people, learn from our example and correct their mistakes, and thus the whole nation will be influenced. So long as our Communist ranks are in good order and march in step, so long as our troops are picked troops and our weapons are good weapons, any enemy, however powerful, can be overthrown." Let us firmly resolve to strive to our utmost to restore and carry forward the fine style of work which our party and Comrade Mao Zedong cultivated, and to lead the whole Chinese nation in building a high level of socialist civilization.

2. *We must be good at carrying forward Marxism-Leninism and Mao Zedong Thought in the light of the new historical conditions.*

We have obtained great success in revolution and construction in the past under the guidance of Marxism-Leninism and Mao Zedong Thought, We will obtain new and greater success in our long march into the future by relying on Marxism-Leninism and Mao Zedong Thought for guidance. If we Communists have any family heirlooms to speak of, by far the most important one is Marxism-Leninism and Mao Zedong Thought. It has always been our basic and unshakable principle to uphold Marxism-Leninism and Mao Zedong Thought and to persist in taking the tenets of Marxism as our guideline.

Marxism is the crystallization of scientific thinking on proletarian revolution; it is our most powerful weapon for understanding and transforming the objective world. Its tenets are truths that have been repeatedly verified in practice. However, it does not exhaust all the truths of human history in its unending course, nor can it possibly do so. For us revolutionaries, the theory of Marxism is a guide to action and by no means a rigid dogma to be followed unthinkingly. All revolutionaries true to Marxism have the responsibility to ensure that it does not become divorced from social life and does not stagnate, wither or ossify; they must enrich it with fresh revolutionary experiences so that it will remain full of vitality. Therefore, our fundamental approach to Marxism is that we should apply and advance Marxism-Leninism and Mao Zedong Thought; such is our unshirkable historical duty as Chinese Communists. This is not easy of course. It requires us to make strenuous, lifelong efforts to achieve a better integration of the tenets of Marxism with the concrete practice of China's socialist modernization.

We must continue to apply ourselves to the

study and investigation of the history of the Chinese revolution. For the China of today has grown out of the China of yesterday, a China of which we know not too much, but too little. We should especially study present-day China because our efforts to create a radiant future must first of all be based on a comparatively correct understanding of the present. And the trouble is that we don't know much — in fact, we still know very little about Chinese realities today and the objective laws governing the building of socialism.

Our cause is an integral whole and has a single goal. Yet, ours is a vast country with extremely diverse conditions. Therefore, our study and understanding of the over-all situation and of the situation in different regions must be closely coordinated. If we overlook the whole and disregard uniformity, we shall make the mistake of acting blindly and thoughtlessly and with no consideration for the whole in directing the work in specific regions. If we ignore the regions' specific conditions in directing the work of the whole country, we shall make the mistake of being guided by our own conjectures and fancies which may have no bearing in reality. We Chinese Communists should be revolutionaries who are at once far-sighted and realistic in our approach.

We lay stress on self-reliance and strive to solve our problems by our own efforts and treasure our own experience. But we must never be conceited and underrate the experience of others. We should through analysis absorb whatever is useful in others' experience and lessons. We must therefore earnestly study and analyse the experience of other countries, other regions and other people while studying and summing up our own.

The integration of the universal truth of Marxism with Chinese reality is a long process of repeated cycles of practice, knowledge, again practice and again knowledge. In the new historical period, we should emancipate our minds and constantly identify and grapple with the new conditions and problems in our practice and thus equip ourselves with rich, varied, living, perceptual knowledge. At the same time, we must set our minds to work and learn more social and natural science and their methods in order to raise perceptual knowledge to the plane of rational knowledge, logical knowlege that is more or less systematic, and verify it again and again in practice. We must therefore study diligently, learn from specialists and heed differing views and opinions and, at the same time, delve deep into reality and carry out thorough, systematic investigations and study so as to successfully synthesize our direct and indirect experience.

So long as we proceed in study and work in accordance with this stand, viewpoint and method, we shall be able to put all our party work on a scientific foundation, make discoveries and function creatively for socialist modernization, thus ensuring the triumphant advance of our great cause.

3. *We must put democratic life in the party on a sounder basis and strengthen party organization and discipline.*

One of the fundamental reasons why the grievous errors of the "cultural revolution" remained unrectified for so long was that the regular political life of our party, inner-party democratic centralism and the collective leadership of the Central Committee in particular, had been disrupted. As a result, personality cults, anarchism and ultra-individualism all prevailed. This afforded the Lin Biao and Jiang Qing counter-revolutionary cliques and other scoundrels an opportunity they exploited to the full. No comrade in the party must ever forget this bitter lesson and we must all take a warning from it.

We are historical materialists. We do not deny the singificant role that outstanding individuals play in history or the significant role of outstanding leaders in a proletarian party. But at the same time, we maintain that our party must be placed under collective leadership exercised by those who combine ability with political integrity and who have emerged in the course of mass struggle, and that we must ban all forms of personality cults. Party organizations should commend all comrades, irrespective of their rank or position, who have made special contributions and achieved outstanding results in their work, so as to encourage other party members and people to learn from their example. But such public commendation must be truthful and unvarnished.

Appropriate relationships should be established between the leaders and the led in our party organizations at all levels. Comrades at a lower level must respect and obey the leadership of comrades at a higher level. They must not feign compliance while actually violating or resisting instructions from the higher level. On the other hand, comrades at a higher level must heed the opinions of their subordinates, respect their functions and powers and accept their supervision. Leaders should take part in inner-party activities just like ordinary party members, abide by party rules and discipline and the law of the state, and maintain their ties with the rank-and-file and the masses in general; they must not put themselves in a special category just because they are in leading positions.

Decisions concerning important matters must be made after collective discussions by the appropriate party committee, and no one individual is allowed to have the final say. All members of a party committee must abide by its decisions. Party committees at all levels must practice a division of labour and responsibilities to be discharged under the collective leadership of the party committee, with each member doing his share conscientiously and responsibly and in the best and most efficient way possible.

All party members are entitled to criticize, at party meetings, any individuals within the party, including leading members of the Central Committee; retaliation is impermissible. Party organizations at all levels and all party members should give full play to their initiative and dare to work independently and conscientiously in a spirit characterized by boldness in thinking and action. But no party member is allowed to impair the party's interests and the common goal by turning the department or unit entrusted to him by the party into his own independent kingdom.

Our party's fighting strength lies in its vitality and strict discipline. Now that we are committed to the socialist modernization of the country and our tasks are so challenging and difficult, we have still greater need to promote this fine party tradition.

4. *We must be good at keeping ourselves politically pure and healthy and under all circumstances maintain our revolutionary vigour as members of a party in power.*

Ours is a large party with a membership of 39 million and it is a party in power. This can easily make some of our comrades feel conceited and succumb to bureaucratic practices. Confronted as we are with so many new things and new problems, we can hardly avoid making mistakes. Besides, class struggle continues to exist to a certain extent in our society, and the ideological influences of the exploiting and other non-proletarian classes still survive. These facts, combined as they are with the complexities of contemporary international relations, put us in daily contact with the undesirable phenomena of capitalism, feudalism and small-scale production. The contradictions between proletarian and non-proletarian ideology and between correct and erroneous thinking within our party demand that we make more effective use of the best weapon Communists have for remoulding themselves, namely, the practice of criticism and self-criticism.

Communists should take a clear-cut stand on questions of principle and should uphold truth. Every party member should uphold the party spirit and be unequivocal in his position on questions of right and wrong which involve the interests of the party and the people and should show clearly what he is for and what he is against. The vile and vulgar practice of trying to be on good terms with everybody at the expense of principle is incompatible with the proletarian character of our party.

Our party's fine tradition of criticism and self-criticism, gravely undermined in previous years, is now being revived and carried forward, and new and useful experience has been gained in this respect. In making either criticism or self-criticism, one should base oneself on facts and should rectify existing mistakes without trying to hide or magnify them. Criticism should be offered in a well-reasoned way and should be instructive so that it can help the comrades concerned raise their level of political consciousness; it must not be based on speculation or aimed at intimidating others. We should induce the comrades concerned voluntarily to examine themselves and to correct their mistakes. In our criticisms, we must not make far-fetched interpretations and unduly involve other comrades at a higher or lower level. So long as the comrades concerned have recognized their mistakes and are willing to correct them, we should encourage them to go on working boldly. Our main mistake in the past was to engage in excessive struggle which yielded results contrary to our expectations; people became reluctant to make self-criticism and were afraid to criticize others. We must change this unhealthy tendency.

We Communists need to practice criticism and self-criticism so that our party will become more, not less, united and militant. Provided we fully revive and carry forward this fine tradition, our party will undoubtedly continue to show endless vitality and will never show signs of decay.

5. *We must select more cadres who combine ability and political integrity and who are in the prime of life, and appoint them to leading posts at all levels.*

Insofar as experience in struggle is concerned, it may be said that our party's cadres belong to three or four generations, which shows that ours is a long-standing and well-established cause. It is indeed fortunate that our leading cadres at all fronts are largely veterans who have been tempered in prolonged revolutionary struggle. If cadres can be called valuable party assets, then these numerous senior comrades are indeed most valuable.

But the laws of nature cannot be changed and, after all, most of our senior comrades are physically not as strong and active as before. In order to make sure that there is an adequate number of successors to carry on our cause and guarantee continuity in our party's guidelines and policies, we must devote much of our energy from now on to the selection and training of thousands upon thousands of cadres who combine ability and political integrity and who are in their prime, and give these comrades the opportunity to take part in leadership in various fields so that they may be better and more effectively tempered through practice. It is now a pressing strategic task facing the whole party to build up a large contingent of revolutionary, well-educated, professionally competent and younger cadres.

Older comrades have an especially significant role to play in fulfilling this strategic task. Comrades Ye Jianying, Deng Xiaoping, Chen Yun and Li Xiannian have said more than once that although old comrades may be pardoned for other mistakes, they would be committing an unforgivable historical error if they did not redouble their efforts to train younger successors. The old comrades should work personally with the organizational departments of the party and the masses in the selection and training of younger cadres and should eagerly and enthusiastically guide them to frontline posts of leadership. At the same time, they should free themselves from the onerous pressure of day-to-day work and advance their views and judgments on key and long-range problems. The Central Committee of the Party earnestly hopes that all veteran party comrades will have the vision to discharge this crucial historic responsibility to the best of their ability. Meanwhile, it hopes that party organizations at all levels and all comrades in their prime who have been selected for higher posts will respect and take good care of our veterans and learn as much as possible from them.

At present, we are facing the major task of learning anew. It is the hope of the Central Committee of the Party that all party comrades, and the younger comrades in particular, will brace up, strengthen their party spirit, enhance their political consciousness, set stricter demands on themselves, diligently study Marxist-Leninist works and works by Mao Zedong and the history of the party, our nation and the world, acquire more theoretical and practical knowledge, and learn more about management and technology as required by their own occupations and specific jobs. The results of our study will determine the quality of our leadership and work and will have a direct bearing on the progress of the socialist modernization of our country. Since we have successfully learned to destroy the old world, we can surely learn even more successfully how to build a new one.

6. *We must forever uphold internationalism and cast in our lot with the proletariat and the people of the whole world.*

We Chinese Communists have always integrated patriotism with internationalism.

We are patriots. We have invariably fought might and main for our national liberation, for the well-being of our people and for the unification and prosperity of our motherland. We have never knuckled under to any pressure from any foreign power. We have never flinched in our determination to be independent and to rely on ourselves, no matter how formidable the difficulties we have faced. Our country is still relatively backwards economically and culturally; but we have always maintained our national self-respect in the face of hegemonist threats of force and in our relations with all stronger and richer countries, and we will not tolerate any servility in thought or deed. We are resolved to strive together with the people of the whole country, not least including those in Taiwan, for its return and for the sacred cause of the complete reunification of our motherland.

At the same time, we are proletarian internationalists. We have always cast in our lot with other peoples of the world in their just struggles and with the cause of human progress. Throughout, our struggles have enjoyed the support of the other peoples of the world, and we on our part have always supported the struggles of the world's oppressed nations and peoples for emancipation, the cause of world peace and the cause of human progress, and we have consistently opposed imperialism, hegemonism, colonialism and racism. Our cause of socialist modernization is at once patriotic and internationalist. Its success will be a tremendous contribution to the cause of world peace and human progress. We hereby wish solemnly to proclaim once again that the Communist Party of China will always live in friendship and cooperation and on an equal footing with all the political parties and organizations in the world which are dedicated to human progress and to national liberation and will learn from their useful experience, and that we will never interfere in the internal affairs of any foreign political party. Even when it becomes stronger and more prosperous, socialist China will belong to the third world and will forever stand by the other peoples of the world, will strive for world peace and friendly intercourse among peoples, will abide faithfully by the Five Principles of Peaceful Co-existence, and will continue to promote increased economic, cultural, scientific and technological exchange and cooperation with other nations; it will never seek advantage at the expense of others or bully weaker nations and will never under any circumstances seek hegemony.

Comrades and Friends!

The decisions of the Sixth Plenary Session of the 11th Central Committee of the Party were adopted after ample and extensive exchanges of views and discussions both prior to and during the session. Its outcome fully testifies to our party's ability to safeguard and strengthen its unity on the basis of Marxist principles and to the fact that the political life of our party has now become much healthier.

Some well-intentioned friends at home and abroad have been worried about our party's ability to achieve complete unity, while a handful of people harbouring evil designs placed their hopes on successfully sowing dissension so as to undermine the unity of our party. Now reality has given them a clear answer: No force on earth can break the Chinese Communist Party's strong unity based on Marxist principles.

Comrades and Friends!

We, the proletariat, are the class which commands the future, and our party has lofty ideals and aspirations. The best way for us to celebrate our party's birthday and to celebrate this grand festival is to learn from historical experience and thus unite and look to the future, focusing our attention on problems awaiting solution.

Socialist modernization is a great revolution. We are undertaking this great revolution in a huge oriental nation left economically and culturally backward by ruthless imperialist oppression and plunder. The fact that China embarked upon socialism before developed capitalist countries is due to China's specific historical conditions, to the correct leadership exercised by our party and to the arduous struggles of the entire people. It represents a development of scientific socialism and is a credit to our party and the Chinese people. On the other hand, our socialist cause is bound to meet many difficulties arising from our economic and cultural backwardness. This in turn calls for more strenuous and protracted struggle. We are still living under the threat of aggression and sabotage from outside. Therefore, our whole party, our whole army and our whole people must more actively apply their revolutionary spirit, heighten their revolutionary vigilance and steel their revolutionary will so as to win victory in this great revolution.

We have suffered severe setbacks in our advance to socialism and have paid heavily for our errors. However, these errors and setbacks have made us more resolute, more experienced, more sensitive to our actual conditions, more sober and more powerful. We have learned much from our reverses and mistakes and shall go on learning. In this sense, our grievous errors and reverses are but fleeting phenomena. We must not overlook the fact that we have a vast contingent of cadres steeled in struggle, that we have built up a substantial material base, that the whole party, army and people fervently desire a prosperous motherland, and that we enjoy the superiority of our socialist system. All of these things, together with the fact that we now have correct ideological, political and organizational lines, constitute the decisive factors that will apply for a long time to come. There is no doubt whatsoever that our socialist cause and the hundreds of millions of Chinese people have a bright future.

The internal unity of the party and the party's unity with the people are the essential condition for the triumph of our cause. While celebrating the 60th anniversary of the founding of the Communist Party of China, we wish to pay our sincere respects to the workers, peasants and intellectuals who are fighting valiantly on the different fronts, to the glorious People's Liberation Army, the Great Wall of steel that defends our motherland, to the vast numbers of hard-working cadres, to our Party's close aides — the Communist Youth League members who are full of vigour and vitality, and to our fellow-countrymen in Taiwan, Hong Kong and Macao and to Chinese citizens overseas! We wish to extend our heartfelt thanks to all the democratic parties and non-party personages and friends of all circles who have cooperated with our party and rendered invaluable support to the people's revolution and to construction.

The unity of the Chinese people with the other peoples of the world is another essential condition for the triumph of our cause. In celebrating the 60th anniversary of the founding of the Communist Party of China, we wish to express our deep gratitude to all friendly countries which have entered into relations of equality and mutual assistance with us, and to all our foreign friends and comrades who have rendered invaluable assistance to our party and people.

Let all comrades in the party and the people of all nationalities in our country unite as one under the great banner of Marxism-Leninism and Mao Zedong Thought and work hard to make China a modern and powerful socialist country, a country which is prosperous, highly democratic and culturally advanced! Let us all strive for the supreme ideal of communism!

4. OPENING SPEECH
(At the Third Session of the Fifth National People's Congress of the People's Republic of China on August 30, 1980)

By Ye Jianying

Fellow Deputies,

Since the conclusion of the Second Session of the Fifth National People's Congress, there has been tremendous progress in all spheres of our work, thanks to the concerted efforts of the people of all nationalities in the country. The readjustment of the national economy has achieved marked success; socialist democracy and the legal system have been strengthened; and political stability and unity have been further consolidated. The great undertaking of the four modernizations in socialist construction is making steady progress. The people of the whole country are happy about these changes as we advance triumphantly in the first year of the 1980's.

Fellow Deputies,

At this session we will examine and approve the Report of the State Council on the Arrangements for the National Economic Plans for 1980 and 1981 and the Report of the State Council on the Final State Accounts for 1979, the Draft State Budget for 1980 and the Financial Estimates for 1981.

The present session will deliberate on the Proposal for an Amendment to Article 45 of the Constitution of the People's Republic of China, put forward by the Standing Committee of the National People's Congress on the recommendation of the Central Committee of the Communist Party of China, and the drafts of the Nationality Law of the People's Republic of China, the revised Marriage Law of the People's Republic of China, the Income Tax Law of the People's Republic of China Concerning Joint Ventures with Chinese and Foreign Investment, and the Individual Income Tax Law of the People's Republic of China.

The present session will hear and deliberate on the Report on the Work of the Standing Committee of the National People's Congress and deliberate on the Report on the Work of the Supreme People's Court and the Report on the Work of the Supreme People's Procuratorate.

Another important item on the agenda of the session is to hear a speech by Hua Guofeng, Premier of the State Council, and to decide on the appointment of the Premier of the State Council on the proposal of the Central Committee of the Communist Party of China, as well as decide on or elect some other leading state personnel. The session will also examine and discuss another important proposal of the Central Committee of the Communist Party of China for the revision of the Constitution of the People's Republic of China and the setting up of the Committee for the Revision of the Constitution.

Fellow Deputies,

In order to meet the requirements of socialist modernization, we must further promote socialist democracy and improve our socialist legal system. We must institute necessary laws one after another, and in particular, speed up the work of legislation concerning the economy and the nationalities. In order to strengthen and improve the leadership of our party and government, perfect our state apparatus and raise our efficiency, we must take effective measures to change the state of affairs wherein leading personnel hold too many posts with the consequence that power becomes too concentrated, and we must select and appoint to leading posts those cadres who have distinguished themselves in practical work, who enjoy popular support and who are in the prime of life. This session will discuss the proposal of the Central Committee of the Communist Party of China with regard to the change of a number of leading personnel of the Standing Committee of the National People's Congress and the State Council.

This session is of great significance as it will discuss and make decisions on matters of major import to our country. I am convinced that at this session the deputies will fully reflect and sum up the opinions of the workers, peasants, soldiers, intellectuals and all other patriots of the country, offer criticisms and suggestions with regard to the work of the government in every field, and, after thorough deliberations, make proper decisions on the proposals submitted to the session. Let us work together to accomplish the various tasks facing this session and make it a success.

5. REPORT ON THE ARRANGEMENTS FOR THE NATIONAL ECONOMIC PLANS FOR 1980 AND 1981

(Delivered at the Third Session of the Fifth National People's Congress on August 30, 1980)

By Yao Yilin

Vice-Premier of the State Council and Concurrently Minister in Charge of the State Planning Commission

Fellow Deputies,

I have been entrusted by the State Council to submit a report on the arrangements for the national economic plans for 1980 and 1981 to this congress for deliberation and approval.

In regard to the arrangements for the national economic plan for 1980, Comrade Li Renjun. Vice-Minister in Charge of the State Planning Commission, was entrusted by the State Council to report to the 14th Session of the Standing Committee of the National People's Congress, which he did on April 8 this year. The plan is being smoothly implemented, and it is expected that the targets set in the plan for the gross output value of both agriculture and industry will be overfulfilled. Copies of the report have been distributed for your deliberation, so I will not elaborate here. In view of the fact that previous annual plans were adopted rather late and this inconvenienced the various localities and government departments in their efforts to make timely arrangements, the State Council decided that the national economic plan for 1981 should be drawn up in advance and submitted to this congress for deliberation and approval this year. The localities and government departments will then be called on to compile their specific plans.

I will now focus on the implementation of the policy of the readjustment, restructuring, consolidation and improvement of the economy since 1979 and on the arrangements for the 1981 national economic plan.

I. Progress Made in the Readjustment, Restructuring, Consolidation and Improvement of the Economy

The Second Session of the Fifth National People's Congress called upon the people of all nationalities in China, under the leadership of the party and the government, resolutely to effect the great strategic shift of the focus of our work to modernization and to carry out the policy of the readjustment, restructuring, consolidation and improvement of the economy. Through well over a year of arduous and concerted effort, the people of all nationalities have made marked progress in all aspects of economic readjustment.

1. The relationships between the major sectors of the economy are moving towards balance, and there is sustained economic growth.

The pace of development of agriculture and light industry has quickened, while the relationship between agriculture, light industry and heavy industry has improved. Since the Third Plenary Session of the Party's 11th Central Committee, a series of rural policies have been put into effect and the state has given greater financial and material support to agriculture, considerably raised the purchase price of a number of major farm products, and reduced or remitted the grain purchase quotas for poorer communes, production brigades and production teams. All this has greatly fired the enthusiasm of vast numbers of peasants for production, triggering a faster growth in agricultural production. In 1979, gross agricultural output value registered an increase of 8.6% over 1978. The total grain output was 332.12 million tons, 27.37 million tons more than the bumper harvest of 1978. The increase in grain output in 1978 and 1979 totalled over 49 million tons — an increase unparalleled since the founding of the People's Republic. In 1979, the output of oil-bearing crops was 6.44 million tons, 1.22 million tons more than in 1978; the output of meat was 10.62 million tons, 2.06 million tons more than in 1978. These are both substantial increases. The output of cotton, hemp, silk, tea and other cash crops has also increased in varying degrees. The sluggish growth in agricultural production which prevailed for many years has begun to change.

Thanks to the priority given to light industry in the supply of raw materials, fuel and power, its gross output value increased by 9.6% in 1979 over 1978 and by 24.2% in the first half of this year over the same period last year. Both increases eclipsed those in heavy industry. Major light industry items such as cotton yarn and cloth, synthetic fibres, paper, detergents, bicycles, sewing machines and wrist-watches all recorded comparatively big increases in output, and many have been improved markedly in both quality and variety. In the first half of this year, the output value of collectively owned industrial enterprises increased by 23.6% over the same period last year.

In heavy industry, continued advance has been made in the course of the readjustment. The production of goods which were in excessive supply was curtailed and that of readily marketable items boosted, while a number of enterprises which had turned out high-cost, low-quality, unwanted goods or had long operated at a loss were shut down or suspended operations or were amalgamated or switched to the manufacture of other products. The gross output value of heavy industry in 1979 showed a 7.7% increase over the previous year and another 6% increase in the first half of this year as compared with the same period last year. The rate of growth of production in the coal and oil industries has been slowed down as a result of readjusting the relationship between extraction and tunnelling and between extraction and reserves. While increasing generating capacity, we have improved management in the power industry, thus putting an end to the serious frequency fluctuation and low voltage operation which have persisted for years. In the iron and steel industry, steel output in 1979 increased by 2.7 million tons over 1978, while total energy consumption (taking the standard of one kilogramme of coal producing 7,000 kilocalories of heat) dropped by one million tons. At the same time, overall energy consumption per ton of steel fell from 2.51 tons of coal to 2.28 tons. In machine-building we have done much in adjusting service orientation and in changing the product lineup. The enterprises under the First Ministry of Machine-Building alone successfully trial-produced 945 major new products, a single-year record unmatched in the last decade. In the chemical and building materials industries, the output of many major items such as chemical fertilizers, plastics, cement and plate glass has risen considerably. The defence industry has succeeded in raising the quality of military supplies. In addition, it turned out more products for civilian use, which accounted for about 20% of its total output value in 1979. We have also scored new successes in transport, posts and telecommunications and in geological prospecting.

The ratio between accumulation and consumption has improved. The national income in 1979 was 7% higher than that of the preceding year. Of the national income of 333.1 billion yuan, 221.1 billion yuan went to consumption and 112 billion yuan to accumulation. Thus the rate of accumulation dropped from 36.5% in 1978 to 33.6% and, under the 1980 plan, it may drop further to around 30%. This lower rate of accumulation is mainly the result of an increase in the consumption fund for the rural and urban population, of limiting the scope of capital construction and of economizing on the circulating fund. It has played a positive role in the correct handling of the relationship between national construction and the people's livelihood and in the promotion of the planned, proportionate growth of the economy.

We have achieved initial successes in curtailing capital construction and getting better results from investment. In 1979, the total investment in capital construction within and outside the state budget was held at 50 billion yuan and 295 large and medium-sized projects were suspended or deferred. The plan called for the commissioning of 118 large and medium-sized projects but 128 projects were actually completed. This has changed the situation in which the number of completed projects fell short of the plan year after year. The planned total investment in capital construction for 1980 is to be limited to 50 billion yuan, and a further 238 large or medium-sized projects are to be suspended or deferred. Of the total investment in capital construction, the portion allocated for housing for workers and staff, science, culture, education, public health and city construction is to be increased. It was 17.4% in 1978 and 27% in 1979 and will reach 29% in 1980.

2. *We have introduced a number of new economic policies and initiated certain measures to reform economic management; the economy as a whole is thus livening up.*

In the rural areas, new trails have been blazed in introducing more flexible policies and in exploiting favourable local conditions. In accordance with the Decisions of the Central Committee of the Communist Party of China on Some Questions Concerning the Acceleration of Agricultural Development, the localities have adopted measures to ensure the right of the communes, production brigades and production teams to make their own decisions, striven to carry out the policy of distribution according to work, implemented various systems of responsibility in production, developed diversified production and household sideline occupations and encouraged village fairs, thus greatly reinvigorating the rural economy. In accordance with the principle of adapting measures to local conditions, many localities have begun to make adjustments both in the internal structure of agriculture and in the overall crop pattern. While raising the production of food grains, they have given attention to the development of forestry, animal husbandry, sideline occupations and fisheries. As for crop pattern, the acreage devoted to cash crops has increased both in 1979 and in 1980. The structure of agriculture and the patterning of crops which have been irrational for a long time have begun to show some change.

Industry has made a good start in establishing various forms of association and producing for demand. Under the precondition that ownership and affiliation are not altered, different forms of association which take into account the economic interests of all the parties concerned have been established on a trial basis in various localities. We now have specialized associations, joint investment ventures breaking through the conventional confines of different trades, joint undertakings embracing processing factories in one region and raw material producers in another, and so on. Through associated operation, the enterprises involved have been able to tap their potentials better, create new productive forces, open up new sources of raw material supply and achieve better results. Many local administrations and enterprises have tried to become more familiar with the market, and have organized sales exhibitions or sales through their own channels or on a commission basis. This has promoted the integration of industry and commerce and the linking of production with demand, and as a result readily marketable commodities have gradually increased. To meet market demand, the iron and steel industry has increased production and turned out more than 2 million tons of rolled steel products in short supply, such as small-sized steel products, wire, sheet steel and welded pipe. With undercapacity production quotas in 1979, the machine-building industry started to produce according to demand and sought and found more markets. Its gross output for the year registered an increase of 81.% over the preceding year, while export volume rose by 30.8%.

We have actively yet prudently initiated experiments in restructuring economic management in selected enterprises on the basis of prior investigation. In the first half of this year, about 6,600 industrial enterprises experimented with added decision-making powers, their total output value accounting for some 45% of the gross output value of all state-run industrial enterprises. These experiments have done much to arouse the enthusiasm of the enterprises and their workers and staff, making them more mindful of management, markets, services and competition, and thus improving operational management, expanding production, improving quality and increasing profit. The rates of increase in output, output value and profits turned in by such enterprises generally surpassed their earlier levels and also those of other enterprises in the same trades which have yet to engage in such experiments. According to data from 84 local enterprises in Sichuan Province where experiments are being carried out, in 1979 average output value showed an increase of 14.9%, profits 33% and profits turned in to the state 24.2% over 1978. This year all of Shanghai's textile enterprises are experimenting with retention of a portion of profits. Output value for the first half of the year was 14.1% higher than that for the same period last year and the profits turned in to the state increased by 16.3%, both increases being higher than the average increases for the city as a whole. In the rural areas, more than 100 state farms and a number of counties have formed associations on a trial basis embracing agricultural, industrial and commercial enterprises; the results have been generally good. In the financial sector, we have introduced the practice under which the central and local authorities "each apportions its revenues and expenditures and fixes its responsibilities," which has strengthened the motivation of the localities to boost receipts and cut down expenditures. In the foreign trade sector we have begun a number of experimental reforms, appropriately increasing the power of the localities and certain industrial departments to engage in import and export trade, and introducing the practice of allowing the retention of a share of the foreign currency earned. All such experiments give expression to the principle of combining regulation through planning with regulation by the market, the principle of taking into account the interests of the central and local authorities, the enterprises and the individual workers and the principle of closely linking the material interests of the workers with their enterprise's success, so as to stimulate the enthusiasm and initiative of the enterprises and workers in improving management, increasing producton and practicing economy. Generally speaking, the results of these experiments are good, though quite a few new problems have cropped up in the process, and these will have to be solved in future.

3. *We have achieved better economic results in various sectors with the progress in adjusting the relationships between the sectors of the economy, in introducing reforms in management and in consolidating enterprises.*

In agricultural production and capital construction, fewer arbitrary orders are issued, and there is less inefficient use of labour and more regard for production costs. Production expenses took up a smaller share of the total proceeds of agriculture in 1979. State farms, some of which had long been running at a loss, showed over 300 million yuan profit last year as against a loss of 90 million yuan in 1978. In industrial production, measures for economizing on energy consumption have begun to take effect. Last year, with an increase in energy of less than 3%, gross industrial output value rose 8.5%. With only a slight increase in the supply of energy it was 13.6% higher in the first half of this year than in the same period last year. 62% of the increased output value of state-run industrial enterprises is due to higher labour productivity. Every 100 yuan of net fixed assets produced 31.5 yuan in taxes and profits for the state in 1977, 35.5 yuan in 1978 and 36.3 yuan in 1979. The turnover of circulating funds has been speeded up. The amount of such circulating funds used by state-run industrial and commercial enterprises in 1979 fell by 6.4 billion yuan as compared with 1978. In the first half of 1980, it was another 16 billion yuan less than in the same period last year. In the field of capital construction, the ratio of operational fixed assets to total investment increased from 74.3% in 1978 to 83.7% in 1979.

4. *The party and government have made strenuous efforts to increase the income of the urban and rural population and to improve living standards.*

With growing agricultural production and higher state purchase prices for major farm products, peasant income increased 10.8 billion yuan in 1979. The peasants have benefited to the extent of 2 billion yuan from the reduction or remission of agricultural tax and taxes paid by enterprises run by the communes, production brigades and production teams. Their per capita income from the collective economy averaged 83.4 yuan in 1979, up 9.4 yuan over 1978, as against a total increase of only 10.5 yuan over the entire 11 years between 1965 and 1976 (these figures do not include their income from household sideline occupations). In 1979, a total of 9,030,000 people were provided with jobs in cities and towns, and we raised the wage-scales of 40% of the workers and staff and readjusted wage classifications for some regions. Moreover, all workers and staff now receive a monthly subsidy to cover the price increases in non-staple food, and the system of rewards was universally introduced in enterprises. Last year's total outlay on wages (bonuses included) for workers and staff in state-run enterprises and establishments was 6 billion yuan more than in the preceding year, with annual per capita wages averaging 705 yuan, 61 yuan above the 1978 figure. 1979 witnessed the biggest addition to housing for workers and staff since the founding of the People's Republic, totalling 62,560,000 square metres of floor space (a 66% increase over 1978). Construction of another 73,710,000 square metres of housing began in January-June this year, again more than in the same period in 1979.

5. *We have enjoyed steady increases in purchases and sales, a brisk retail trade in urban and rural areas and a fairly big increase in foreign trade.*

The total value of commodities purchased by commercial departments in 1979 was 199.2 billion yuan, or 14.5% more than in 1978. It rose again by 17.9% in the first six months of this year as against the same period last year. Thanks to the higher income of the majority of workers and staff as well as of peasants, the people's purchasing power has grown substantially. With retail sales totalling 175.3 billion yuan, 22.5 billion yuan or 14.7% more than in 1978, 1979 witnessed the biggest increase in such sales in many years. In the first half of this year there was another 18.5% increase above the corresponding period last year. Since 1979, urban and rural consumption of major consumer items has been rising. Pork, long in short supply, can now be bought without any restriction. There has also been a substantial increase in the sales of knitted and cotton goods, bicycles, sewing machines, radio sets, wristwatches, TV sets, tape recorders, etc.

The total value of imports and exports rose by 28% in 1979 and by another 20.2% in the first half of 1980 as against the same period last year. Foreign exchange earnings from non-trade channels such as tourism, remittances by overseas Chinese and harbour services have also recorded a fairly rapid increase.

6. *Science, culture, education and public health have made further progress.*

Altogether 103 inventions were approved by the state in 1979, and good results were obtained in more than 3,000 major scientific and technological research projects. New successes were scored in the popularization of hybrid paddy-rice over large areas, in the extensive use of methane gas, and in surveying China's agricultural resources, regional planning for agricultural growth, etc. The industrial departments have succeeded in trial-manufacturing some 1,000 important products, and heartening progress has been reported in scientific research into the multipurpose use of associated ores in the three big mines at Panzhihua, Baotou and Jinchuan. In the field of scientific research for national defence, new advances have been made in the development and manufacture of carrier rockets, nuclear weapons, man-made satellites, and so on. China's successful launching of a carrier rocket over the Pacific Ocean in the first half of this year signifies that our scientific and technological development has reached a new level. A lively atmosphere now prevails in the realm of social science, and many useful ideas have been put forth in studies of the theory and practice of socialist economy.

In 1979, the number of students in the colleges and universities reached 1,020,000, an all-time high. There were 1,200,000 students in secondary technical schools and 59,050,000 in ordinary middle schools. Another 860,000 students were enrolled in various kinds of adult institutions of higher learning. New achievements have been registered in the fields of culture, art, broadcasting, television, the press, publishing, public health and physical culture. We have made some headway in family planning, with the natural growth rate of our population dropping from 1.2% in 1978 to 1.17% in 1979.

Things have been going fairly well in the implementation of this year's national economic plan. Owing to severe natural calamities in many areas the output of summer crops dropped by over 10%, but the autumn crops are now at the height of their growth and if there are no more severe natural calamities they will probably approach the 1979 output. It is expected that cotton and sugar crops will be bigger than in 1979 and that the output of oil-bearing crops, meat and aquatic products will reach state quotas. In industry, it is estimated that the output of major products such as coal, crude oil, electricity, steel, cement, chemical fertilizer, cotton yarn, synthetic fibres, paper, sugar, bicycles and TV sets will reach or exceed state quotas and that the planned 6% increase in gross industrial output value for the year will be exceeded.

Practice has proved that the economic policies adopted by the party and government in the past year or more are correct and have the support of the people. The readjustment of the national economy has been carried out smoothly and the people are pleased with what has been achieved. Nevertheless, we still face a lot of problems in our march forward. The living standards of the majority of peasants and workers have improved, but for people living in the outlying regions and in the minority nationality areas, where the pace of economic development has been slow over the years, or for people living in disaster-stricken areas, life is still very hard. For those scientific research workers, teachers, and medical and government workers who receive little or no bonus, income has increased very little or not at all, and for some of them living standards have actually declined. With the purchasing power of the people rising in both town and country, some commodities are in short supply because time is required for the reform of the industrial structure. The problems accumulated over the years in housing, health facilities, public utilities and environmental protection can only be solved step by step through sustained efforts. Generally speaking, capital construction is still over-extended. On the one hand, some major projects have not been cut back as they should have been. On the other hand, in areas such as energy, transport, building materials and science and education where spending should be increased, the demands cannot be met owing to shortage of funds. In the process of readjustment, certain heavy industrial enterprises, especially in the machine-building industry, are now operating under capacity. The problem of stockpiling is quite serious within some categories of means of production. Financially, we are still operating and in the red. The readjustment of the national economy is a highly complex and difficult task and some contradictions and difficulties are bound to appear. So long as we earnestly implement the various policies laid down by the Central Committee of the Party and the State Council and work hard to increase production and practice economy, these problems can be solved step by step.

II. The Task and Main Targets for the National Economic Plan for 1981

The main task in developing the economy in 1981 is to carry on with the policy of readjustment, restructuring, consolidation and improvement so as to bring about the co-ordinated development of industrial and agricultural production and all other undertakings. Specifically, we should strive to speed up the growth of agriculture and light industry so that the supply of consumer goods will be in general balance with the rise in the people's purchasing power and that commodity prices will remain stable on the whole. We should strive to develop and conserve energy, to promote communications services and the building industry, to speed up the reorganization and technical transformation of the machine-building industry, to rationally readjust production in the metallurgical, chemical and other heavy industries, to increase the production of raw and semi-finished materials in short supply and of new types of such materials, so as to do a better job in serving agriculture, the people's livelihood, export, national defence and the economy as a whole. We should continue to exercise strict control over the scale of capital construction and strive to shorten the building cycle so as to get more projects completed and into operation. We should develop foreign trade and expand international economic exchange. We should step up our efforts in science and technology, education and public health, urban construction, environmental preservation and labour protection. We should give overall consideration to economic results, do our best to find new financial resources, increase revenues and reduce expenditures. We should further adjust the ratio between accumulation and consumption, so that a further improvement in the people's standards of living will be possible with increased production.

In accordance with the above requirements, the main targets for the national economic plan for 1981 are as follows:

The total output value of industry and agriculture is expected to increase by 5.5% as compared with 1980, with that of agriculture increasing by 4% and that of industry by 6%.

Agriculture: The output of grain will be 342.5 million tons, with an estimated increase of 10 million tons over 1980; cotton output will be 2.55 million tons, with an estimated increase of 250,000 tons over 1980. The output of other cash crops, meat and aquatic products and the acreage for afforestation will also register new increases.

Light Industry: It is estimated that total output value will increase by 8%, with light industry continuing to maintain a higher rate of growth than heavy industry. The output of cotton yarn will be 2.865 million tons, an estimated increase of 90,000 tons over 1980; that of paper, 5.2 million tons, an increase of 200,000 tons; sugar 2.6 million tons, an increase of 100,000 tons; bicycles, 14.84 million, an increase of 2.24 million; sewing machines, 8.6 million, up 1.4 million; wrist-watches, 23.6 million, an increase of 2.6 million; and detergents, 480,000 tons, an increase of 50,000 tons. The output of other light industrial products will all be increased to varying degrees.

Energy Industry: The output of coal will be 620 million tons, an estimated increase of 10 million tons over 1980; that of petroleum, 106 million tons, maintaining the same level as 1978 and 1979; and that of electricity, 312 billion kwh, an estimated increase of 12 billion kwh over 1980.

Raw and Semi-Finished Materials Industry: The output of steel will be 35 million tons; 10 nonferrous metals, 1.08 million tons; cement, 78 million tons; chemical fertilizer, 12.3 million tons; and timber, 49.1 million cubic metres.

Machine-Building Industry: It will produce 97,500 tractors, internal-combustion engines with 20 million hp. and 160,000 automobiles. These figures are fixed in accordance with need and the likely available fuel supplies.

Transport and Communications: The volume of rail freight will be 1,060 million tons; that of ship and barge freight, 390 million tons; and that of truck freight, 540 million tons. The total volumes of civilian passenger and freight transport by air and of postal and telecommunication services will also be increased.

Capital Construction: Total investment will be held at 55 billion yuan, including direct investments under the state budget plus those made by the departments and localities, loans from Chinese banks and construction projects utilizing foreign capital.

Foreign Trade: The total volume of imports and exports will be 55.9 billion yuan, an estimated rise of 4.2 billion yuan over 1980.

Home Market: The total volume of retail sales will be 220 billion yuan, an estimated increase of 15 billion yuan over 1980.

Science and Technology: Over 400 items have been listed in the national scientific and technological plan. These include trial-manufacture of new products, intermediate tests and major scientific research projects.

Education: As students admitted into institutions of higher learning in 1977 began the academic year later than usual and will not graduate and make room for new students until the winter vacation of 1981, the enrollment of new students in 1981 will be 270,000, or the same as in 1978 and 1979.

Employment: 6 million people will be given jobs in cities and towns.

Family Planning: The natural population growth rate will be 1%.

People's Livelihood: The income of communes, production brigades, production teams and individual peasants will increase by approximately 10 billion yuan. The urban population's income will increase by more than 4 billion yuan, and urban housing and collective welfare and everyday services will continue to be improved. Beginning from 1981, we shall gradually and suitably raise the income of people engaged in scientific research, teaching, medicine and office work who receive small bonuses or none at all.

In making plans for 1981, we should pay attention to the solution of the following questions:

The growth of light industry has been hampered by the slow increase in cash crops in recent years. Therefore, in agriculture, we must do a better job in surveying resources and in regional planning, suiting measures to local conditions in order to achieve all-around progress. In regions suitable for growing cash crops, we must develop them in a planned way, giving top priority to the production of cotton and sugar. Simultaneously, we must strive to increase the output of grain wherever conditions are suitable. In the grain-producing regions of Heilongjiang, Jilin and other provinces, we must expand commodity grain-producing bases in a planned way to provide the state with more marketable grain. We must actively promote growth in forestry, animal husbandry, sideline production and fisheries. In light industry, we must strive to expand the sources of raw materials and processing capacity since growth lags behind the increase in the people's purchasing power. We must also increase variety in product design, size and colour and raise the proportion of medium- and high-grade goods.

The planned increase in the production of energy for next year is 0.9%, whereas the planned increase for industrial production as a whole is 6%. We must try hard to save energy and, at the same time, ship out more quickly the coal stockpiled at a number of coal mines. In the rural areas, we must actively promote the utilization of methane gas and the planting of forests for fuel.

In the field of transport and communications, we must step up our efforts to renovate and expand the major harbours and wharves and those railway sections which are unable to handle large traffic volumes.

We must continue to do a good job of tapping the potential of existing enterprises and of renovating and transforming them with the emphasis on saving energy and raw and semi-finished materials, on producing raw and semi-finished materials in short supply and those which are needed but have not yet been produced as well as new types of materials.

There are numerous demands from every quarter for capital construction funds, but as our financial and material resources are limited, we must act according to our capabilities and rationalize the use of the construction funds from various channels through planning and guidance so that the needs of key projects are fully met.

Both in industry and agriculture, we must attach importance to popularizing the achievements of scientific research and energetically apply new technology. We should make overall arrangements for the introduction of key technology urgently needed in our economic construction and for scientific research projects aimed at meeting the needs of long-term development.

In the field of education, we must open up new avenues of schooling, reinforce higher education, reform the system of secondary education and promote vocational and technical education. We must continue to universalize elementary school education and improve our work in child-care and preschool education.

In health work, we must continue to unfold patriotic sanitation campaigns so as to improve sanitary conditions in both town and country and reduce the incidence of disease, thus raising the people's level of health.

With respect to the questions of employment, we must modify the current labour administrative system step by step, adopt more flexible policies and open up new avenues of employment. We must combine employment on the recommendation of state labour departments with employment through voluntary self-organization and the individual search for jobs. We must vigorously develop the economy of collective ownership in which enterprises assume sole responsibility for their profits and losses, and must appropriately develop individual economy involving no exploitation of others.

We should promote labour protection. All production and construction units, enterprises and establishments should conscientiously draw on the profound lessons to be learned from the capsizing of the oil rig *Bohai No. 2* and should perfect and strictly abide by the rules for safety in production and the various systems of job responsibilities, respect science, improve their technical knowledge, modestly heed the opinions of the workers and technicians, submit themselves to supervision by the masses and guarantee the workers' safety of person.

As for family planning, we must regard it as a task of strategic importance and allow of no relaxation of effort. We should conduct intensive and meticulous publicity work and forbid any resort to compulsion. We should constantly improve birth control techniques and take the utmost care to prevent accidents resulting in injury or disablement.

III. Take Vigorous Measures to Ensure the Fulfilment of the Plans for 1980 and 1981

To fulfil the national economic plans for 1980 and 1981 successfully, it is necessary to proceed from the actual conditions and adopt effective and vigorous measures. In agriculture, all local authorities should conscientiously carry out the policies laid down by the Central Committee of the Party, energetically promote and popularize science and technology, increase their aid to agriculture so as to ensure the continued all-round development of agricultural production. The whole nation should continue to pay attention to light industry and boost its production by every possible means, so that its prospects will become ever broader.

I would now like to explain the principal measures that are needed in four areas: the exploitation and conserving of energy; the readjustment of heavy industry, especially the readjustment and transformation of the machine-building industry; the strengthening of the raw and semi-finished materials industry; and the restructuring of economic management.

1. *We should lay equal stress on exploiting energy and practicing economy in its consumption. In the near future, however, it is imperative to give priority to saving energy and make every endeavour to carry out technical transformation and structural reform to this end. The first steps should be taken next year.*

We shall adopt the following measures to exploit energy and increase its production:

In the coal mining industry, we should strive, through state investments in capital construction, bank credits and associations of various forms, to engage in the construction of new collieries having a total capacity of 120 million tons next year, with those put into operation having a capacity of 10 million tons. Simultaneously, beginning next year we shall appropriately increase expenditures on maintaining simple reproduction so as to better tap the potential of existing coal mines and bring about their renovation. We shall also take necessary measures to improve the work system and ensure the safety of the coal miners.

In the petroleum industry, agreements on marine prospecting have been signed with a number of foreign oil companies, and geophysical surveys have been conducted over an area of 410,000 square kilometres in China's Nanhai Sea (South China Sea) and southern Huanghai Sea (Yellow Sea). On this basis we will begin issuing successive calls for tenders on joint exploration and exploitation. Moreover, we have signed contracts with foreign oil companies to carry out joint exploration and exploitation of oil and gas in parts of the Bohai Sea and Beibu Gulf. With regard to onshore oil prospecting, while work continues in the eastern part of the country, progress is being made in the continental sedimentary basins of Jungar, Qaidam, Tarim, Shaanxi-Gansu-Ningxia and Sichuan.

In the power industry, we shall strive to install new generating sets with a total capacity of over 3 million kw next year. This will be done through state investment in capital construction and by attracting funds from the localities and getting more bank credits. In the meantime, we shall speed up surveying and designing and other preparatory work for the construction of a number of big hydropower stations.

We shall continue to step up research and experiments in nuclear power, solar energy and other new sources of energy:

And we shall take the following measures to conserve energy:

We shall continue to improve energy management. Quota management will be strengthened and a balance between power and heat loss will be struck next year for those enterprises with an annual comprehensive consumption of over 50,000 tons of standard coal. Economic methods will also be utilized to impel the enterprises to further reduce their energy consumption. We must do all this well and strive to save 7 to 8 million tons of standard coal next year.

We shall alter the structure of industry and the product mix step by step. The plan calls for an increase in the proportion of the output value of light industry to the total output value of industry from an estimated 44% this year to 45% next year. By an increase of 1%, we can save 6 million tons of standard coal. The planned ratio of the amount of pig iron to the output of steel will fall from 1.03:1 this year to 1:1 next year, which will mean a further saving of 2 million tons of standard coal. Every locality and government department must adopt effective ways and means to change the structure of industry and the product mix in order to save as much energy as possible.

We shall endeavour to carry out technical transformation with the focus on energy saving. This will be an avenue for conserving energy for a long time to come and an important step towards modernizing our industry. Preparations will be made next yeat to renovate medium and low voltage generating units which are characterized by high coal consumption and to introduce the centralized supply of heating and integrated power generation and heat supply, so as gradually to replace small boiler units. Other measures will also be enforced that will yield prompt and effective results in energy conservation in the metallurgical, chemical, building material, petroleum, communications and transport and other major departments.

We shall update motorized machines and tools with high energy consumption. Experiments will start with trucks next year. Some will be replaced, others put into storage and still others eliminated in order to save oil.

We shall keep on trying to convert oil consumers into coal consumers. The focus will be on those power stations and factory boilers which were originally designed to use coal but were later changed over to oil consumption. Plans call for the conversion of power stations and factory boilers with a total consumption of 2.5 million tons of oil next year.

We shall institute laws and regulations setting standards for energy consumption together with relevant regulations for rewards and penalties.

2. *We shall further readjust the structure of heavy industry, especially the machine-building industry, so as better to serve economic development.*

With the readjustment of the ratio between accumulation and consumption, the scope of capital construction is being brought under control and the demand for some kinds of means of production is on the decline; the income of the urban and rural population is steadily rising and so is their demand for consumer goods. These are new conditions to which the present structure of industry finds it hard to adapt itself. Part of the machine-building industry now has idle capacity, whereas supplies of some consumer goods are inadequate; this has an adverse effect on the harmonious development of the entire economy. The key to settling this problem is for us to actively undertake a substantial readjustment in heavy industry, and especially the machine-building sector, as far as its service orientation is concerned.

The machine-building industry, including the electrical engineering and electronics industries, supplies all branches of the economy with technical equipment and carries a heavy burden in the four modernizations programme. In order to utilize its capacity to the full and raise its level of production and skills, we must undertake comprehensive planning, gradually break down all sorts of barriers between different departments and regions and accelerate the readjustment and transformation of the industry in accordance with the principles of coordination among specialized departments, standardization, serialization and interchangeability. We must step up scientific research and the import of technology in order increasingly to master the world's advanced production technology and product designing. We must make great efforts to improve the quality of basic parts and raise the level of basic process technology. We should work hard to trial-produce and manufacture new-type machines and electronic products and optical instruments including lasers, which are urgently needed, highly efficient, of good quality, and low in consumption of energy and cost of production, for light and heavy industries and other departments. We should strive to increase the production of consumer goods. We must make ever wider use of such new technology as integrated circuits and electronic computers, and particularly small and medium-sized computers and microprocessors, in industrial and agricultural production and in producing articles for daily use. We must get large-scale integrated circuits into mass production. In the machine-building industry, we must energetically raise our ability to supply complete sets of machinery and improve technical services. All departments and all the people should show concern for our machine-building industry and should be keen on using Chinese products. Administrative and economic measures should be taken to promote the growth of our machine-building industry, at the same time reducing its dependence on imports and increasing its exports.

In line with technical transformation centred on energy conservation, the machine-building industry should develop energy-saving mechanical and electrical products and quicken the pace of replacement of those with high rates of energy consumption. Particularly with respect to those motorized machines and tools which consume large amounts of energy, such as factory boilers, internal-combustion engines, automobiles, pneumatic machines, pumps, and motors, we should actively study, design and manufacture new types that meet energy-saving targets.

We should transfer, in a planned way, a part of the productive capacity and technical forces of the heavy and defence industries to the production of consumer goods and other urgently needed merchandise. We hope that the localities and departments will make solid market investigations and forecasts and, basing themselves on economic rationality and allowing for technical suitability and supplies of raw materials, concretely carry out these transfers.

3. *We must strengthen the materials industry, increase variety and improve quality and make every effort to promote comprehensive utilization.*

Materials are vital to the economy, defence and the development of science and technology. The levels achieved in their variety, quality and output are major indicators of the degree of development of our economy and science and technology. Technical transformation, with its focus on energy saving, the growth of industrial and agricultural production and science and technology, the modernization of national defence and the gradual improvement in living standards — all this will make more and new demands on the materials industry. Therefore, we must pay adequate attention to its development.

We should produce more varieties of better metallic materials and gradually raise the share of alloy steel in steel production to meet our social needs. At the same time, given China's wealth of polymetallic associated ores, we should exploit and utilize such ores in a planned and comprehensive way. Our rich deposits of vanadium, titanium, nickel, cobalt, niobium and rare-earth metals should be exploited so as to increase the varieties of iron, steel and nonferrous metals.

We should systematically put such nonferrous metals as tungsten, molybdenum, tin, aluminium and copper to multipurpose use and improve the quality of their products. We should step by step turn from the export of nonferrous metals themselves to the export of their products.

Wherever possible, we should energetically develop the manufacture of plastics, synthetic fibres and synthetic rubber and gradually increase their level in the raw material mix used by industry, and by light industry in particular.

New construction materials are important for shortening construction cycles in the building industry, lessening the structural weight of buildings, cutting costs, utilizing industrial residues and saving energy. We should give special help to their development.

Our country abounds in non-metallic mineral deposits such as graphite, asbestos, gympsum and kaolin. We should gradually modernize the existing technology in prospecting for, extracting and processing these minerals, which is still backward.

We should continue to develop new materials. As the cause of modernization progresses, there will be an increasing demand for more new materials of better quality, more variety and improved properties. This work will be most challenging. We must consider it an important task and render all necessary financial and material assistance to the development of new materials to which we must given special help in matters of pricing and taxation.

4. *We must expedite our experiments in restructuring the economic managerial system, give full play to favourable conditions, ensure competition, promote integration and mobilize the initiative of all concerned.*

We should try to enlarge the decision-making power of all enterprises in state-owned industry. Under the guidance of the state plan, enterprises should enjoy greater power than they do today to decide matters concerning personnel, financial and material resources, production, supply and marketing. On condition that it ensures the supply of goods as required by the state, an enterprise may fix production plans according to market demand or undertake tasks in co-operation with other units. Aside from materials provided under the state plan, an enterprise may also purchase what it needs according to its own choosing. Contracts and agreements signed between enterprises should be protected by law. Any rules and regulations now in force which are incompatible with the principle of enlarging the decision-making power of enterprises should be gradually revised. Congresses or conferences of representatives of workers and staff should be instituted in every enterprise or establishment. They have the right to discuss and take decisions on important matters concerning their unit. They have the right to submit to the higher authorities proposals for the removal of any leading member of the administration who is not equal to his duty, and they can gradually undertake the election of leading personnel at appropriate levels.

We should actively develop various types of economic integration. All localities, departments and enterprises should give full scope to their respective specialities and strong points and, taking the road of integration, develop economic co-operation, complement each other, fostering strengths and circumventing weaknesses so that they may obtain the maximum economic results at minimum costs. Organizational linkups should be arranged on the principles of equality, mutual benefit and due consideration of the economic interests of all parties concerned. Though such linkups need not be limited to the same trade, region, sphere of ownership, or affiliation, the ownership, affiliation and financial relations of the participants must not be changed at will. Each enterprise within an association should keep its separate accounts, which means no "sharing of food from the same big pot." The association is entitled to market those goods produced over and above its plan quota. A joint committee consisting of representatives of all parties concerned should be set up to act as the overall authority.

Extensive competition is to be encouraged under the guidance of the state plan. Given adherence to the socialist planned economy, competition between enterprises will spur them to improve management, strengthen cost accounting and raise economic efficiency and quality. To unfold competition, it is necessary to do away with regional blockades and interdepartmental barriers and combat monopoly so as to allow goods to flow freely in all directions. It is wrong to shield backwardness, blockade the market and impede the normal circulation of merchandise by administrative means, and this should be stopped. While competing, we should encourage the socialist spirit of co-operation and the exchange of technical know-how. As for important new technology, a scheme of royalties should be worked out.

Banks are to be run independently. Under the guidance of the state plan we should promote to the full their role in economic development. We should enlarge their decision-making power step by step, so that they are entitled to decide on the extension and supervision of loans in accordance with credit policies, loan ceilings and lending priorities stipulated by the state. All banks should improve their work, make full use of interest rates as leverage, broaden the sources of credit funds, support the expansion of production, assist enterprises in making careful plans and economize in the use of capital funds by speeding up their turnover.

We should gradually reform the system of taxation. In accordance with the laws to be adopted at the present session, we shall impose an income tax on ventures involving joint Chinese and foreign investment and an individual income tax, and we must do a good job of taxation where foreigners are involved. In the machine-building and farm machinery industries, we shall experiment with a tax on added value so as to solve the problem of double taxation on some industrial products. We shall revise the laws concerning taxes on income of collectively owned urban enterprises and appropriately adjust their taxes so as to facilitate the development of the collective economy. Beginning from 1981, we shall try out collecting fees from state-owned enterprises for the use of fixed funds so as to promote the rational use of state assets. We shall extend to more state-owned enterprises the experimental changeover from the transfer of profits to the state to a tax on income, and we shall also impose regulatory taxes and taxes on natural resources. In capital construction, investment by the state should be replaced by bank loans wherever repayment is possible.

We should encourage market regulation under the guidance of the state plan. The state plan should bring about overall balance. Some of the targets assigned to the enterprises are of a mandatory nature and must be fulfilled; there will be a gradual reduction in targets of this kind. Others perform the function of guidance or forecasting. Through its economic policies and decrees and the use of certain economic levers, the state gives guidance to the enterprises regarding production and expansion so as to stimulate their initiative. There will be more and more targets of this kind. Except for those materials which are very important and in short supply and must be distributed in a planned way and those which are subject to priority purchase by supplies departments, the means of production can be put on the market for free circulation. Except for those consumer goods which are subject to unified purchase and marketing or unified purchase and distribution, the state monopoly over the selling of consumer goods will be replaced by planned purchases, by placing orders or by exercising choice. It is necessary to reduce the number of links in the chain of circulation and open up more channels of circulation. It is necessary to break down the barriers separating different administrative departments and divisions and to organize rational circulation of the means of production and consumer goods within the economic zones. We should sum up experience concerning the existing forms of distribution used by various regions and departments, such as commodity fairs, wholesale markets, trade centres, trade warehouses, enterprise-operated street outlets and combined exhibition and sales departments. Those forms of circulation must continue to be run well so as to promote industrial and agricultural production and improve the people's living standards.

We should continue with the restructuring of the management of foreign trade. We should entrust all areas and departments engaged in foreign trade with greater operational powers. We should effectively strengthen economic accounting. At the same time, certain large enterprises and associations can begin, upon approval, to experiment with direct foreign trade. It is imperative to formulate necessary decrees, rules and regulations in accordance with the principle of unified policies, unified planning and unified international stance and the principle of expanding the power of departments at all levels to make decisions with respect to foreign trade. Goods will be imported or exported under license and exchange controls will be tightened.

We should strengthen legislation and the administration of justice in the economic field. With the gradual restructuring of our economic management and with the increasing application of economical methods in managing our economy, there is an urgent need for reinforcing both economic legislation and its administration. It is imperative to conscientiously study and sum up experience in economic construction at home and abroad, gradually to formulate laws and rules governing the planning and management of our socialist economy in the light of our party's lines, principles and policies, and actively to train legal personnel. It is imperative to reinforce economic arbitration, and we suggest that an economic tribunal be quickly set up with adequate personnel.

All the economic reform measures mentioned

above are aimed at promoting the readjustment of the economy, arousing general enthusiasm, using our economic potential, increasing production and practicing economy. But these measures are only of a preliminary nature. The overall restructuring of management of our economy calls for further investigation and study, the summing-up of experience, deeper theoretical exploration and the absorption of the strong points of other countries which are relevant and useful. It will take a period of deliberation and preparation before it can be unfolded.

Fellow Deputies! Thanks to our conscientious implementation of the policy of readjustment, restructuring, consolidation and improvement for well over a year, our economy has made major progress. Practice proves that it can advance steadily in the process of readjustment. We are convinced that our national construction will continue to advance triumphantly and the prospects for realizing socialist modernization by the turn of the century are very good, so long as, under the leadership of the Central Committee of the Party, we continue to carry out this policy, give more scope to the people's wisdom and talent and earnestly solve new problems as they crop up in our advance. We must emancipate our minds, seek truth from facts, work with one heart, study diligently, go all out to make the country strong, enthusiastically and steadily make a success of our work and strive to fulfil and overfulfil our national economic plans for 1980 and 1981!

6. REPORT ON THE FINAL STATE ACCOUNTS FOR 1979, THE DRAFT STATE BUDGET FOR 1980 AND FINANCIAL ESTIMATES FOR 1981

(Delivered at the Third Session of the Fifth National People's Congress on August 30, 1980)

By Wang Bingqian
Minister of Finance

Fellow Deputies,

I have been entrusted by the State Council with making the report on the final state accounts for 1979, the draft state budget for 1980 and the financial estimates for 1981 which I now submit for your examination.

I. The Final State Accounts for 1979

In 1979, the people of all our nationalities, led by the Chinese Communist Party, strove conscientiously to implement the policy decisions of the Third Plenary Session of the 11th Central Committee of the Party and the decisions of the Second Session of the Fifth National People's Congress; they brought about a great shift of emphasis in the work of the whole nation and began the task of readjusting, restructuring, consolidating and improving the economy. The serious disproportions in our economy were somewhat corrected, and new advances were made in production and construction. In state finances, a series of important measures were adopted last year that led to notable results in readjusting the ratio between accumulation and consumption, promoting industrial and agricultural production and bettering the livelihood of the people, and also in reforming the financial system, increasing the financial powers of the local authorities and enterprises, and encouraging initiative in all quarters. While doing all this we paid a certain price in terms of state expenditure in order to correct the serious disproportions in our economy caused by the sabotage of Lin Biao and the Gang of Four, and gradually to solve the problems in production and in the people's livelihood left outstanding over the years.

In the state budget for 1979 adopted by the Second Session of the Fifth National People's Congress last year, revenues and expenditures were balanced at 112 billion yuan. The final state accounts for 1979 as prepared on the basis of the actual implementation of the budget break down essentially as follows:

Revenues totalled 110.33 billion yuan. Deducting the 3.53 billion yuan of foreign loans not originally included in the budget, domestic revenues amounted to 106.8 billion yuan, or 95.4% of the budgeted figure. Of this, revenues from industrial enterprises totalled 49.29 billion yuan, or 88.6% of the budgeted figure; taxes totalled 53.78 billion yuan, or 99.7%; other revenues totalled 650 million yuan, or 272.5%, while 2.46 billion yuan, or 112%, consisted of depreciation funds turned in to the central financial authorities by the various enterprises.

Expenditures totalled 127.39 billion yuan. Deducting the 7.09 billion yuan not originally included in the budget but appropriated out of foreign loans, for capital construction and other purposes, domestic expenditures amounted to 120.3 billion yuan, or 107.4% of the budgeted figure. This included 44.38 billion yuan, or 113.8%, for domestic capital construction; 7.2 billion yuan, or 128.6%, for tapping the potential of existing enterprises, and for subsidizing their transformation and the trial-manufacture of new products; 5.2 billion yuan, or 106.2%, for additional allocations of circulating funds to enterprises, and of credit funds to banks; 9.01 billion yuan, or 127.8%, for financing rural people's communes and other agricultural undertakings; 13.21 billion yuan, or 109.4%, for culture, education, health work and science; 22.27 billion yuan, or 110.1%, for national defence and preparations against war; and 5.69 billion yuan, or 124.2%, for administrative expenses.

In the final state accounts for 1979, expenditures exceeded income by 17.06 billion yuan. To make up the difference, we drew on the surplus of the past years to the sum of 8.04 billion yuan, and took out an overdraft of 9.02 billion yuan from the People's Bank of China.

This deficit is mainly the result of the measures taken for economic readjustment. These measures, which led to reduced revenues and increased expenditures, were indispensable for helping to lay the foundation for sustained economic growth in the future. They have already achieved obvious and heartening results and contributed to the consolidation and improvement of the political situation in which unity and stability go hand in hand with liveliness and vitality.

1. *The purchase prices of farm and sideline products were increased by a fairly big margin and some taxes in the rural areas were reduced or remitted.*

This helped bring about recovery in the rural areas in a relatively short time and contributed to the strengthening of agriculture which is the foundation of the economy. Beginning from the summer harvest of last year, the state raised the purchase prices of 18 major farm and sideline products, including grain, cotton, edible oils, hemp, sugar cane, beets, pigs, cattle, sheep, fish, eggs and cocoons, and instituted the policy of offering higher prices for grain, cotton and edible oils sold over and above quota. The state subsidy for such purposes amounted to 7.8 billion yuan in the year, or 1.3 billion yuan over the budgeted figure. For low-yielding, grain-deficient areas, the state set a level below which agricultural tax was to be remitted. As a result, the total amount of agricultural tax collected in 1979 was reduced by 4.7 billion *jin* (2.35 million tons) of grain. Moreover, the minimum taxable income level was appropriately raised for industrial and commercial income tax to be paid by enterprises run by communes, production brigades and production teams; the time limit for the reduction or remission of taxes to be paid by the newly established enterprises in the same category was appropriately extended; and it was stipulated that such enterprises located in minority nationality autonomous counties (or banners) and border counties should be exempted from industrial and commercial income tax for a period of five years. The total amount of taxes thus reduced and remitted came to 2 billion yuan in 1979, exceeding the budgeted figure by 300 million yuan. Thanks to the expansion of agricultural production and the rise in the price paid by the state for farm and sideline products, the peasants' per capita income from the collective economy averaged 83.4 yuan in 1979, an increase of 9.4 yuan over the previous year. Naturally, the situation differed from locality to locality. The above measures, nevertheless, were some of the most important ones taken in any year since the founding of the People's Republic to readjust the relationship between industry and agriculture, and to readjust the distribution of the national income and state finances. This is of positive, far-reaching significance for the development of the economy.

2. *Great efforts were made to increase employment, and steps were taken to increase the wages and salaries of a proportion of the workers and staff and introduce the system of rewards.*

As a result, their income rose to some extent. In 1979, jobs were provided through various channels for a total of 9,030,000 people in cities and towns, including students who, graduating during the year from colleges and secondary vocational schools, were given jobs under a unified state plan. Altogether 40% of workers and staff got pay rises, and wage scales were readjusted in certain regions. A system of rewards was introduced in all state enterprises, and a monthly subsidy to offset the increased prices of non-staple foodstuffs given to all workers and staff. The average annual per capita wage of workers and staff in all state-run enterprises and establishments rose to 705 yuan, an increase of 61 yuan over 1978. State expenditures on all these items totalled 7.5 billion yuan, or 2.5 billion yuan more than the budgeted figure. In addition, the state allocated special funds out of capital construction investment which were combined with the reserve funds of local authorities and enterprises to build housing for workers and staff. By the end of last year, a total floor space of 62,560,000 square metres had been completed in cities, towns and mining areas. This figure shows a 66% increase over 1978, making 1979 the year which saw the greatest amount of housing built since the birth of the People's Republic. It should be noted that the state made strenuous efforts to provide this considerable sum in a year in which certain proportions in the economy were being readjusted and the state was in financial difficulty. However, there are a number of people in urban areas who are yet to be provided with jobs; earnings in some scientific, educational and public health establishments and administrative organs where no bonuses are given have increased only a little, or not at all, and the actual living standards of some have even fallen to a certain extent; moreover, housing is still a headache in urban, industrial and mining areas. We must make further efforts to solve all these problems.

3. *The financial powers and reserve funds of the local authorities and enterprises were increased.*

This is conducive to reinvigorating the national economy, promoting production and increasing revenue, and gradually correcting the serious disproportion between the productive and non-productive sectors. In 1979, the state specified that the authorities of 49 big and medium-sized cities could draw 5% from their industrial and commercial profits for urban construction, and that all other local authorities could utilize a certain portion of the earnings of their county-run industrial enterprises. As a result, the reserve funds of the local authorities were increased by 2 billion yuan. Meanwhile, a system was introduced whereby all state enterprises may set up enterprise funds, and in over 4,000 industrial and commercial enterprises the policy of allowing the enterprise to keep a portion of its profits was tried out. As a result, these enterprises obtained 4 billion yuan as reserve funds. The state earmarked more than 6 billion yuan for the above purposes, which involved 2 billion yuan in excess of the budgeted figure.

4. *Funds devoted to developing agriculture and light industry were increased by a fairly big margin.*

This helped to readjust the proportions between agriculture, light industry and heavy industry, enliven the market and meet the people's rising purchasing power. In 1979, the state used 9.01 billion yuan, or 1.96 billion yuan more than the budgeted figure, to aid the communes and finance various agricultural undertakings. At the same time, apart from the 2.3 billion yuan set aside as investment in capital construction for the textile and other light industries, the state appropriated an additional 1.5 billion yuan for them as funds for tapping their potential and carrying out their transformation, or as special-purpose loans. To boost production, the state adopted the policy of giving them priority as regards supplies of fuel, power and raw and semi-finished materials. Last year saw a growth rate of 9.6% in the textile and other light industries, as against 7.7% in the case of heavy industry. There was a significant increase, seldom seen in past years, in the production of such manufactured consumer goods as cotton cloth, synthetic-fibre knitwear, paper, bicycles, sewing machines, wrist-watches, TV sets and synthetic detergents, all of which were in great demand.

5. *There were increased expenditures on national defence and preparations against war.*

In 1979, spending for such purposes reached 22.27 billion yuan, or 2.04 billion yuan in excess of the budgeted figure. In order to oppose hegemonism and ensure a peaceful environment for the realization of our socialist modernization, it was absolutely necessary that we increase our defence spending to some extent in 1979.

6. *It should also be mentioned that since the Third Plenary Session of the 11th Central Committee of the Party, we have, in line with the principle of seeking truth from facts, redressed on a nationwide scale the wrongs done to many people who were unjustly, falsely or wrongfully accused.*

This is of great significance in consolidating a political situation of stability and unity. It will also help to mobilize our whole people to work for the four modernizations with one heart and one mind. In accordance with regulations laid down, the state has given the back pay due to rehabilitated cadres, workers and staff, and given subsidies to those in special difficulties. According to incomplete statistics, state expenditures in this regard have amounted to well over 1 billion yuan.

State expenditures in the six above-mentioned categories exceeded the budgeted figure by more than 11 billion yuan. These major measures taken by the state are very significant and have yielded remarkable results. That in a single year we did so much that had to be done is something unheard of for many years. The state spent more than the sum budgeted for improving the people's livelihood by readjusting prices, increasing wages and expanding employment. Moreover, despite reductions in spending on domestic capital construction, the necessary readjustment in expenditures could not be completed all at once and the scope of such construction is still too big. For these reasons state expenditures exceeded the budgeted figure by 5.3 billion yuan, and there is a deficit in the final state accounts for 1979. This is the price we have had to pay for the measures adopted. But people have already seen that with these measures, the relationships between the major sectors in our economy have begun to move towards better co-ordination, an excellent situation of all-round increase has been brought about in industrial and agricultural production and in commodity circulation, and a relatively big increase has been achieved in the purchasing power of both the urban and the rural population together with an improvement in living standards. In a word, things are thriving in all fields. Of course, our work is not free from shortcomings and mistakes, for in the implementation of the 1979 budget, we underestimated the serious consequences of the sabotage by Lin Biao and the Gang of Four. To cite some examples: there was a dislocation between the import of capital construction projects and budgetary arrangements; we failed to give top priority to the plan to lower costs in enterprises and to help those running at a loss to change for the better and make a profit; our financial management was not strict enough so that some profits and taxes were not turned in to the state as they should have been, and economy was not practised as it could have been with regard to some items of expenditure; our financial discipline was lax, and there were fairly serious cases of losses and waste with which we did not deal effectively. We have to improve our work and remedy the shortcomings in all these respects.

It should also be explained that a considerable part of last year's deficit was covered by drawing on the accumulated surpluses, and partly by a bank overdraft. However this did not lead to any big increase in the issue of paper money, because, first, the total value of agricultural output last year was 8.6% higher than in the previous year, the total value of the output of light industry increased by 9.6%, and the total volume of retail sales rose by 14.7%. For many years past such big increases have been rare. Thanks to the good harvests and the increased output of the textile and other light industries, generally speaking, supplies of food, clothing and articles of daily use, with a few exceptions, were quite sufficient. Therefore people felt reassured, and the market was virtually stable and also healthy.

Second, the savings deposits of the urban and rural population rose by 9.7 billion yuan during the year, and this is also a big increase, unheard of for many years. On the one hand, it shows that the masses are industrious and thrifty and are eager to support national construction; on the other, it also indicates that the people's currency, the Renminbi, enjoys high prestige.

Third, as a consequence of the restructuring of the financial system, part of the state's financial resources was converted into reserve funds of various local authorities and enterprises. The unspent part of these funds in turn became bank deposits. By the end of 1979, the deposits originally earmarked for specific uses by enterprises, the extra-budgetary deposits of local authorities, and the deposits of capital construction units, government departments, mass organizations and army units were some 6.7 billion yuan larger than at the beginning of the year. These funds helped to reduce the effects of the state financial deficit. The three aforesaid factors played an important role in forestalling any grave consequences that last year's financial deficit might have had on the economic life of the nation. There may well be repercussions sooner or later. The rise in the prices of certain commodities in recent years is a symptom of this. We must never treat this matter casually, but should pay great attention to and really solve it.

In our financial work, our policy has all along been one of ensuring a balance of revenue and expenditure with a slight surplus, and of striving to avoid deficit financing. In the final analysis, our financial deficit last year resulted from the severe damage done to the economy by Lin Biao and the Gang of Four over the ten catastrophic years and from the many problems ensuing therefrom. Experience has made us keenly aware that these problems which have accumulated over the years are much more serious than we first estimated and cannot be solved once and for all within a short period. Furthermore, our shortcomings and mistakes in construction will also take their toll by adding to the price we will have to pay. None of the major measures for economic readjustment we adopted last year, including price readjustment, wage increases, bonus payments and the provision of employment, are temporary measures which are be completed in a single year. They must be pursued and will inevitably impede our efforts to balance state revenue and expenditure for the next year or two. We must continue to do well in agricultural and light industrial production, keep prices basically stable and, in the course of implementing the budget, take vigorous measures to tap potential, increase revenues and economize on expenditures. While solving the problem of the unified collection of revenue and unified spending, we must further improve our financial system to meet the needs of the structural reform of the economy. Success in these respects will enable us gradually to reduce, and finally do away with, financial deficits and to strike a balance between revenue and expenditure. We believe that by following this economic readjustment and with advances in production and construction, we shall definitely be able to achieve our goal.

II. The Draft State Budget for 1980

In 1980, our financial work faces most serious tasks. We must continue to implement the policy of readjustment, restructuring, consolidation and improvement and further correct the serious disproportions in our economy. At the same time, we must conscientiously give full play to favourable conditions, ensure competition and promote integration so as to invigorate the economy. We must do what we can to accelerate the development of production, tap potential, explore more sources of revenue and increase receipts. We must firmly control investment in capital construction, reduce the rate of accumulation step by step and in a planned way, and gradually improve the people's livelihood on the basis of increased production and productivity. We must give more and more assistance to agriculture and light industry, strengthen such weak links as the coal, power, petroleum and building-materials industries and the transport services, and aid progress in the fields of culture, education, public health and science. We must, actively but prudently, continue to keep tight control over the restructuring of the financial system and the reform of the financial management of enterprises and the taxation system in order to improve our financial work.

To meet the above requirements, the 1980 budget sets state revenues at 106.29 billion yuan and expenditures at 114.29 billion yuan, the latter exceeding the former by 8 billion yuan. It should be possible to reduce this gap somewhat in the course of implementing the budget by increasing production and practicing economy. The remainder of the deficit we plan to make up by obtaining loans at interest from the People's Bank of China.

At the 14th Session of the Standing Committee of the National People's Congress in April this year, the State Council submitted the Report on the Implementation of the 1979 National Economic Plan and the Arrangements for the 1980 National Economic Plan, in which it estimated that state revenues in 1980 would be 98.2 billion yuan and expenditures 102.2 billion yuan, the difference being 4 billion yuan. A new estimate has now been made in the light of the implementation of the 1980 budget during the first half of this year, and the fresh problems that have cropped up. Moreover, new items have been included: for instance, revenue in the form of foreign loans and allocations for capital construction out of foreign loans, outlay for repaying principal and interest within the current year, additional allocations for investment in the power industry and for combating unusually serious floods and droughts, necessary expenditures for the increase of personnel in the public security, procuratorial and judicial organs, and subsidies for the reduction in the price of pork. Therefore, there has been an increase in both revenues and expenditures, with a bigger gap between them.

Of the total budgetary revenues for 1980, receipts from enterprises amount to 46.06 billion yuan, taxes 54.4 billion yuan, receipts from other sources 240 million yuan, depreciation funds turned in by enterprises to the central financial departments 2.2 billion yuan, and receipts in the form of foreign loans 3.39 billion yuan.

Compared with the previous year, total revenues for 1980 are 4.04 billion yuan lower. This is because the higher prices paid for farm and sideline products, the wage increases, the expansion of employment, etc., which were successively introduced in the middle of last year had an impact on revenues for only a few months in 1979, but this effect will continue to be seen throughout the year of 1980. Furthermore, the year 1980 will also see the prices of cotton, medicines, pig iron, coke, etc., readjusted and the depreciation rate raised for the railways as well as for those enterprises which are experimenting with profit sharing. Calculated in terms of comparable items, revenues in 1980 will increase by 6.4 billion yuan, or 6% over last year. This target is basically in keeping with the 5.5% increase in the gross value of industrial and agricultural output. It is ambitious yet realizable.

It is necessary to add that at present there is a wide variety of state subsidies to offset price increases, and these subsidies will exceed 20 billion yuan in 1980. Some totalling about 12 billion yuan cover such basic consumer commodities as grain, cotton, edible oils, meat, eggs, vegetables and coal for household use; others, which are for the increased purchase prices of agricultural products sold above quota, amount to over 5 billion yuan; still others costing 3 billion yuan or so are for ensuring preferential prices of the means of agricultural production and of industrial products which aid agriculture. The total figure will be much bigger, if subsidies for house rent, transport and other items are included. All these price subsidies eat up part of the state's revenue and will naturally affect its increase adversely. Nonetheless, it must be affirmed that, in the conditions prevailing in our country, such subsidies are essential for ensuring a secure and better life for the people and for promoting national stability and unity. We must do an even better job in this regard.

Total budgetary expenditures for 1980 were cut by 13.1 billion yuan as compared with last year. The breakdown is essentially as follows:

1. *Appropriations for capital construction total 37.35 billion yuan, 14.1 billion yuan less than last year.*

Of this sum, capital construction investment directly provided for in the state budget comprises 24.15 billion yuan; capital construction investment provided by stand-by financial resources in the localities plus the investments placed at the disposal of Tangshan comprise 2.13 billion yuan; outlays such as reserve funds for capital construction comprise 4.74 billion yuan; and appropriations for capital construction derived from foreign loans comprise 6.33 billion yuan. Here some explanations are in order. Investment in capital construction arranged by the state has been reduced, while construction outlays from extra-budgetary funds raised by the localities and enterprises themselves, as well as various loans earmarked for capital construction, have increased. Therefore, the projected scope of capital construction still remains at the level of 50 billion yuan. This requires an overall arrangement which takes account of both budgetary and extra-budgetary investments, both financial resources and credit, and both domestic funds and foreign loans, which can channel scattered funds into the production and construction projects most vital to the state, and which can exercise a strict control over the scope of capital construction. From now on it is necessary to draw up a comprehensive financial plan and improve the overall balance of our financial and material resources.

2. *Funds allocated for tapping the potential of enterprises or for transforming enterprises, plus those for subsidizing the trial-manufacture of new*

products, amount to 6.98 billion yuan, 220 million yuan less than last year.

Apart from these funds which fall within the category of direct state appropriations, the depreciation funds collected by the state-owned enterprises according to the relevant stipulations plus profits kept by the enterprises for expanding production amount to 16 billion yuan. Added together, all these funds amount to a considerable sum. If they are put to rational use through an overall arrangement, they can yield substantial results.

3. *Additional allocations of circulating funds to enterprises and of credit funds to banks account for 3.72 billion yuan, 1.48 billion yuan less than last year.*

They are intended mainly to meet the needs of newly commissioned enterprises and certain special reserves. Considering that overstocking of materials is a common problem in enterprises so that too large a percentage of their funds is lying idle, the funds needed for expanding production in the existing enterprises should be obtained mainly through improving management, reducing stocks and exploiting financial potential.

4. *Expenditures for aiding the communes and other operating expenses for agriculture total 7.74 billion yuan, 1.27 billion yuan less than that for last year.*

If we add to this the 6.66 billion yuan that will flow to the countryside from the investments in capital construction, circulating funds and rural relief funds, and another 2.4 billion yuan in agricultural loans, the amount earmarked for agriculture in 1980 comes to 16.8 billion yuan, which represents a considerable sum.

5. *Allocations for culture, education, health work and science amount to 14.83 billion yuan, an increase of 1.62 billion yuan over 1979.*

Speeding up the development of education and science is the key to the realization of the four modernizations. Since these two fields have been starved of funds for a number of years, outlay ought to be increased. Therefore the funds allocated have been increased as much as the country's financial resources will allow. Owing to our present limited financial and material resources, some problems in science and education will have to be solved step by step.

6. *Expenditures on national defence and preparations against war account for 19.33 billion yuan, 2.94 billion yuan less than last year.*

7. *Expenditures on administration and management amount to 5.78 billion yuan, an increase of 90 million yuan over 1979.*

8. *Development funds in aid to economically underdeveloped areas take 500 million yuan.*

These funds have been established for the first time in this year's budget for the purpose of boosting production mainly in the old revolutionary base areas, remote border areas, autonomous localities inhabited by minority nationalities and places with a relatively poor economic base.

9. *The general reserve funds account for 1.88 billion yuan.*

10. *Payments on the principal and interest of foreign loans take 2.17 billion yuan.*

They cover mainly the proportion borrowed and to be repaid by the state for financing contracts signed during the last few years to import equipment and technology with foreign funds, and payments of principal and interest starting as from this year.

As for foreign debts, it is estimated that up to the end of 1980, the total amount borrowed by the state will be U.S.$3.4 billion after deducting the matured principal that will be paid off. In order to bring about the quickest possible economic results from foreign loans, we must conscientiously strengthen our planning and management in the import of advanced technology and equipment. Especially in the coming years this work must be linked with the readjustment of the economy and with the elimination of some of its weak links. At the same time, full consideration must be given to the terms and conditions of loans, to our ability to manufacture the necessary accessories in China and our ability to repay. From now on the proportion of loans to be repaid from the state coffers must be borrowed by the state financial institutions and included in the national plan. A system of clearly defined job responsibility should be set up, and management must be properly strengthened so that the present state of lax management and poor co-ordination can be firmly dealt with.

Fellow Deputies, more than seven months of the year 1980 have elapsed. During this period, the national economic plan has been implemented very satisfactorily. Industrial production has surpassed the planned rate of growth; the textile and other light industries, in particular, have increased output by a big margin as compared with the same period of last year. In commerce, both sales and purchases have been brisk and the market is active. With the gradual raising of the people's income, urban savings deposits have shown an increase of 4.7 billion yuan compared with the end of last year. The situation as regards revenues and expenditures from January to July was also fairly good. Revenues were 57.7 billion yuan, or 54.3% of the sum budgeted for the whole year, while expenditures were 58.26 billion yuan, or 51% of the sum budgeted for the whole year; thus expenditures exceeded revenues by 560 million yuan.

According to the pattern prevailing over the years, the greater part of expenditures is incurred in the second half of the year, especially in the last quarter. Furthermore, the impact of most of the factors that will result in a reduction in revenue this year, such as enterprises retaining part of their profits, wage increases, and price adjustment for cotton and so on, will only be felt in the last few months of the year. So we must not relax in the coming months just because the situation as regards revenues and expenditures in the first seven months is not bad. In order to fulfil the budgetary plan for the whole year, we should exert still greater efforts to increase revenues and cut expenditures and narrow the gap between the two.

III. Financial Estimates for 1981

Nineteen eighty-one will be the first year of the Sixth Five-Year Plan. According to the guiding principles and policies laid down by the state and the requirements of the national economic plan for 1981, the state financial departments must, on the basis of the continued readjustment of the economy and growth of production, rationally arrange the various revenues and expenditures so as to promote the co-ordinated development of various undertakings and to improve the people's livelihood. Our efforts to narrow the gap between revenue and expenditure in 1980 should be carried on through 1981 so as to lay the foundation for sound and balanced finances. We should continue to reform financial administration, the system of taxation and the management of finance in enterprises, thus improving financial work, and co-ordinate all this with the restructuring of the economic system so as to meet the needs of the four modernizations.

The projected state financial estimates for 1981 are as follows: State revenues are put at 115.46 billion yuan and state expenditures at 120.46 billion yuan, with a deficit of 5 billion yuan. These estimates take into account the money to be borrowed from abroad, the appropriations for capital construction provided by foreign loans and payments on principal and interest for the year.

Estimated state revenues for 1981 show an increase of 9.17 billion yuan compared with 1980. This is calculated in terms of the rate of growth of industrial and agricultural production after the increase in revenue resultant from reducing costs and tapping the potential of the enterprises has been taken into account. Of the total revenues, 49.62 billion yuan is to come from the enterprises, 59 billion yuan from taxation and 240 million yuan from other sources, while the depreciation funds of enterprises to be turned in to the central financial authorities will amount to 2.1 billion yuan.

Estimated state expenditures for 1981 are 6.17 billion yuan more than in 1980. This is in line with the need to continue the readjustment of the national economy. The breakdown of the total is as follows: appropriations for capital construction, 37.58 billion yuan; additional allocations of circulating funds to enterprises, 2 billion yuan; funds to be allocated for tapping the potential of enterprises, for transforming them and for subsidizing the trial-manufacture of new products, 6.7 billion yuan; aid to the communes and other operating expenses for agriculture, 8.8 billion yuan; allocations for culture, education, health work and science, 16.95 billion yuan; national defence and preparations against war, 20.17 billion yuan; administrative expenses, 6.06 billion yuan and general reserve funds, 2.6 billion yuan.

According to these estimates, the increase in revenues in 1981 will be greater than in expenditures, and thus the difference between them will be smaller than in 1980. During 1981, the state will gradually provide for appropriate increases in the incomes of staff members in scientific research, educational and health institutions as well as in government departments where very small or no bonuses are given, and will find work for several million more people who are waiting for jobs. The living standards of both the urban and rural population will be further raised.

Since the plan for the development of the economy in the period of the Sixth Five-Year Plan is still being worked out, necessary readjustments will be made in the state financial estimates for 1981 in accordance with the finalized plan. If there are major changes, these estimates will be submitted to the Standing Committee of the National People's Congress for re-examination.

I would now like to go into the question of reforming the system of financial administration. The concentration and distribution of financial resources must be suited to the restructuring of the economic system. At present, we are carrying out a step-by-step restructuring of the economic system in accordance with the principle of combining regulation by planning with regulation by the market. We will give the enterprises greater power to make decisions, organize various forms of economic integration and encourage competition guided by planning. The reform of the financial administration system began in 1978. In the latter half of that year, the systems of establishing enterprise funds and giving awards to workers and staff were put into effect in state-owned enterprises. In 1979, we tried out three systems under which some state-owned enterprises retained a share of their profits, loans replaced appropriations in some capital construction projects, and some administrative establishments took responsibility for their surpluses or deficits; we instituted a system of holding agricultural reclamation enterprises responsible for their own finances; and we adjusted and improved the tax system relating to agriculture as well as to industry and commerce. In 1980, we have undertaken the reform of the financial structure and also launched some experiments in the reform of the taxation system. In general, these reforms have aroused the initiative of the parties concerned and have achieved good results. However, they are only preliminary reforms. We should continue to carry out reforms in the next few years and co-ordinate the reform of the financial administration system with that of the economic system. For the next year and a half we will concentrate our efforts on the following reforms:

1. The Restructuring of the Financial System. Starting this year, we have instituted a special system for the two provinces of Guangdong and Fujian under which the provincial authorities are to be held responsible for their own finances after handing in a fixed sum to the state. For the other provinces, municipalities and autonomous regions we are trying out a system of "apportioning revenues and expenditures between the central and local authorities, while holding the latter responsible for their own profit and loss." That is to say, whereas in the past "everybody shared food from the same big pot," now each will "eat from his own pot." The localities will be able to spend more when their revenues rise but should spend less when they fall. They must balance their own revenues and expenditures. For the five minority nationality autonomous regions, Xinjiang, Ningxia, Inner Mongolia, Tibet and Guangxi, and the three provinces, Yunnan, Guizhou and Qinghai, the preferential treatment they have enjoyed will remain unchanged and the subsidies provided by the central authorities will be increased progressively at a rate of 10% a year. In 1981, we should sum up the experience gained in experimenting with these new systems and improve them.

2. Reform of the System of Enterprise Finance Management. The system of letting enterprises keep part of their profits is being tried out this year in 6,600 state-owned industrial and transport and communications enterprises. It will be extended to all state-owned enterprises in 1981. In order to make rational use of state assets, the state financial departments will charge state-owned enterprises for the use of circulating funds allocated to them beginning from the latter half of this year, and starting in 1981 will charge them for the use of the fixed assets on a trial bais. As for investments in capital construction, from 1981 we will implement a system of bank loans instead of appropriations from the state coffers for all units except administrative establishments and a few projects. We shall have to see how integrated complexes develop and operate before we can work out a system for their financial management.

3. Reform of the Taxation System. In 1980, we shall pass legislation and begin to collect an income tax from joint ventures involving Chinese and foreign investment and an income tax from individuals. We should do a good job in collecting taxes concerning foreign nationals. In order to solve the problem of double taxation on some industrial products, we shall try out a value-added tax in the machinery and farm machinery industries. We shall also amend the income tax law on urban collectively owned enterprises so as to appropriately reduce their tax burden in an equitable manner and promote the development of the collective economy. Starting from 1981, we shall experiment with having state-owned enterprises pay a business tax instead of turning their profits over to the state, and accordingly begin to levy the regulatory business tax and resources tax.

The above reforms, particularly the reform of the tax system, will inevitably affect the distribution of revenue and other aspects of the economy. They are therefore important policy issues and involve a wide range of problems. They require thorough investigation and study, experimentation, and co-ordination with the reform of the economic system as a whole. We must vigorously but prudently push ahead with these reforms in order to meet the requirements of economic development.

IV. Go All Out to Increase Production and Practice Economy, Combat Extravagance and Waste, and Improve Economic Performance, in Order to Carry Out Our Financial Tasks for This Year and the Next

The political and economic situation in our whole country today is very satisfactory. After more than a year of strenuous effort, the ideological, political and organizational lines adopted at the Third Plenary Session of the 11th Central Committee of the Party are being conscientiously put into effect. The readjustment and restructuring of the national economy are making good progress and notable results have been achieved. However, there are still some weak links in the chain of our financial and economic work, and losses and waste are not uncommon. Consequently, there is an enormous potential to tap with respect to increasing production and practicing economy. In order to fulfil the financial tasks for this year and the next, we must inspire and organize the cadres and the people to work even harder to increase production and practice economy, combat extravagance and waste and vastly improve economic performance so that the national economy may develop steadily and harmoniously.

Production is the foundation of finance. The active promotion of production together with increases in tax revenues and in profits will provide important guarantees for the fulfilment of the financial tasks for 1980 and 1981. In many enterprises at present the rate of consumption of energy and raw materials is high, waste great, the rate of profit low and losses are heavy. Every one hundred yuan's worth of products sold by state-run enterprises yielded 25 yuan in tax revenue and profit in 1979 which is 5 yuan, or 16% less than in 1965. The total losses incurred by industrial enterprises in the first six months of this year were still as high as 1.4 billion yuan. Such losses must be eliminated as quickly as possible. The success or failure of industrial as well as agricultural undertakings in future should be judged by their economic performance. Every undertaking must take the actual conditions into full account, make the best possible use of favourable conditions and avoid the unfavourable and must use the available manpower, material, and financial resources where they can yield the maximum results. Each enterprise must tap its own potential to the maximum and increase the variety of its products and expand their sales to make sure that the increase in production and in tax revenue and profit required by the state plan is attained. Priority in the supply of raw and semi-finished materials, fuel and power must be given to the textile and other light industries to ensure more and better products for the market, and to keep prices basically stable. Measures must be taken to cut down the consumption of energy, and to reach the targets set by the state for the economical use of energy. Energetic efforrts must be made to develop foreign trade, tourism and the service trades, and a conscientious job must be done with regard to remittances from Chinese nationals residing abroad. The masses of workers and staff must be aroused to improve management and business accounting in their enterprises so as to lower costs and increase profits and thus contribute more to the state.

Increasing the returns on investment while strictly controlling the magnitude of capital construction is of first-rate importance to the more rapid growth of production and construction. During the First Five-Year Plan, it generally took four or five years to build a large or medium-sized project. Now, it averages a dozen years. During the First Five-Year Plan it took an average of three to four years to recoup the sum invested in some industries, and now, it averages more than eight years. Some completed projects were not commissioned for a long period of time. Others have operated at a loss year after year ever since they were commissioned. How much can we accomplish in the 20 years before the end of this century if it takes ten years to build a large or medium-sized project and more than eight years to recoup the sum invested and if, still worse, some of the projects continue to depend on state subsidies for their operations? And where can we acquire all the funds needed for our modernization programme? We must conscientiously draw lessons from such undeniable historical facts as are presented by instances of excess in capital construction, huge waste and unsatisfactory economic results, and resolutely cut out projects which are unrealistic in terms of construction possibilities or which are not badly needed, and use our limited financial and material resources for those projects which will yield the best economic results. We very much need to frame legislation to check the results of investment in capital construction and to apply strict discipline to capital construction. It should be stipulated, among other things, that no project can be undertaken before its feasibility has been studied, before the advisability of importing advanced technology and equipment financed by foreign funds has been considered, before alternative construction plans are drawn up and compared and the best is chosen. The projects chosen should be undertaken strictly according to the procedure for capital construction. Those who act irresponsibly, make the investment inefficient, or cause heavy losses or waste in construction, shall be held economically responsible, and disciplinary actions shall be taken against them or, where warranted, they shall be punished according to law. They must not be allowed to get away unpunished.

Enterprises must use their circulating funds with meticulous care so as to achieve the best possible economic results. The turnover of enterprise circulating funds was speeded up last year and in the first half of this year, thus saving a considerable sum. But generally speaking, there are still large sums lying idle, serious overstocking of materials and huge losses and waste. For every hundred yuan's worth of manufactured goods sold, 33 yuan of circulating funds was needed in 1979, eight yuan more than in 1965. Despite constant appeals, the stockpile of rolled steel and mechanical and electrical engineering products has swollen year after year. The country's stockpile of mechanical and electrical engineering products has now reached 60 billion yuan in value and that of rolled steel has now increased to nearly 20 million tons. Business establishments also have a considerable quantity of unsalable or slow-selling goods on hand, which are tying down large funds. In coordination with the general checkup on enterprise assets now under way, it is necessary to give scope to the regulatory role of the market by various means so as to dispose of these overstocked materials and bring about a quicker turnover of materials and funds. Commercial enterprises should organize the circulation of commodities according to the economic regions of the country, cut down the number of intermediate links, reduce circulation expenses and speed up the turnover of funds.

In the non-productive sectors we must continue to practice strict economy and combat waste. Since the beginning of the year, local authorities, departments and units have put into effect the "Circular on Reducing Non-Productive Spending and Combating Waste" issued by the Central Committee of the Party and the State Council; good results have already begun to be seen, and many models have emerged. However, extravagance and waste still exist in a number of enterprises and establishments as well as in government departments, mass organizations and army units. The squandering of state funds on the purchase of luxury goods by some units which take advantage of their dealings with foreign personnel and foreign visitors is still rather serious. The unhealthy tendency of some leading cadres to use their positions to pursue personal perquisites and privileges has not yet been completely brought in check. We must continue to take vigorous action in the spirit of the circular and give fuller play to the fine tradition of building the country through diligence, thrift and hard work. We must streamline our administration step by step and in a planned way, exercise strict control over institutional purchases, drastically reduce various kinds of non-productive spending and make earnest efforts to solve the problems of overstaffing and inefficiency.

To increase production and practice economy, combat extravagance and waste and achieve better economic results, it is necessary to strengthen financial control and enforce strict financial and economic discipline. In April and May this year, a general countrywide checkup on the enforcement of financial and economic discipline was carried out. This yielded good results, and we found that certain local authorities, departments and enterprises had arbitrarily held back state revenues, had reduced or remitted taxes without authorization, had taken it upon themselves to raise prices, extend the scope of cost outlays and raise the ceilings on their spending, or had handed out bonuses without regard to merit and subsidies without regard to need. Some of the offences were quite serious. While it is true that the root of these problems lies in lax party discipline and a weak sense of legality resulting from the long interference and sabotage perpetrated by Lin Biao and the Gang of Four, the tendency among some leading cadres to attempt the impossible, seek quick results and only concern themselves with a part to the neglect of the whole must also be considered an important cause. In order to strengthen financial and economic discipline, we must first see to it that leading cadres at various levels are guided by the principles of attempting only what is possible and taking the whole country and the overall situation into account. Leading cadres at all levels must draw the lessons from the capsizing of the oil rig *Bohai No. 2* and improve their work. They must set an example in abiding by the law and in having a scientific approach and take the lead in enforcing all financial and economic rules and regulations. To ensure that laws are observed, their enforcement must be strict and law-breakers must be punished; violations of financial and economic discipline must be investigated and sternly dealt with. No violation should be tolerated, not even with the excuse that it "will not serve as a precedent," for such an excuse actually means a precedent is being set which can pave the way for more and more violations of law and discipline. Financial personnel, tax collectors and accountants must be supported in performing their duties and encouraged to go about their work boldly. We must back up those comrades who are subjected to retaliation for upholding principles or for reporting matters truthfully and severely punish those who seek revenge so as to promote healthy tendencies and combat unhealthy ones.

Fellow Deputies,

The current political and economic situation in our country provides very favourable conditions for the fulfilment of the national economic plans and the state budgets for 1980 and 1981. Although we will encounter all manner of difficulties as we advance, the prospects for development are good and it is entirely possible to bring about a steady growth of the economy and gradually strike a balance between revenue and expenditure. Led by the Chinese Communist Party and relying closely on the workers, peasants and intellectuals of all nationalities as well as all the democratic parties, patriotic personages and patriotic overseas Chinese, let us emancipate our minds, seek truth from facts, unite and work as one and strive for the successful fulfilment of the financial tasks set for 1980 and 1981.

7. RESOLUTION OF THE THIRD SESSION OF THE FIFTH NATIONAL PEOPLE'S CONGRESS OF THE PEOPLE'S REPUBLIC OF CHINA ON THE ARRANGEMENTS FOR THE NATIONAL ECONOMIC PLANS FOR 1980 AND 1981, THE FINAL STATE ACCOUNTS FOR 1979, THE STATE BUDGET FOR 1980 AND THE FINANCIAL ESTIMATES FOR 1981

(Adopted on September 10, 1980)

The Third Session of the Fifth National People's Congress of the People's Republic of China, after deliberation and examination, approves the arrangements for the national economic plans for 1980 and 1981 and the Report on the Arrangements for the National Economic Plans for 1980 and 1981 delivered by Yao Yilin, Vice-Premier of the State Council and concurrently Minister in charge of the State Planning Commission. The session, in accordance with the Examination Report submitted by the Budget Committee, approves the final state accounts for 1979, the state budget for 1980 and the financial estimates for 1981, and approves the Report on the Final State Accounts for 1979, the Draft State Budget for 1980 and the Financial Estimates for 1981 delivered by Wang Bingqian, Minister of Finance.

The session holds that the National Economic Plan for 1979 was implemented satisfactorily in the main and the economy as a whole made steady advances in the course of readjustment. The state financial departments did a lot of work to support the readjustment of the economy and did much that had to be done to correct the serious disproportions in our economy caused by the sabotage of Lin Biao and the Gang of Four and gradually to solve the problems in production and in the people's livelihood left outstanding over the years, thus promoting the stability and unity of the whole country and the growth of the national economy and resulting in some improvement in the lives of the majority of the urban and rural population.

The successes scored in our national economy prove that the policies of shifting the focus of the work of the whole country and of readjusting, restructuring, consolidating and improving the national economy, which were put forward by the Central Committee of the Communist Party of China and the State Council and adopted at the Second Session of the Fifth National People's Congress, and a series of new policies are correct and that our economic work in various aspects are fruitful.

On the other hand, the session, having conscientiously studied the problem of deficits in the final state accounts for 1979, points out certain shortcomings and mistakes that occurred in the performance of work. The session enjoins the relevant departments under the State Council to make further efforts to implement the guiding principle of proceeding from reality, acting according to our capabilities and paying attention to economic results; to adopt effective measures to increase production, practice economy, combat waste, curtail capital construction, strengthen financial control; and to enforce strict financial and economic discipline so as gradually to reduce our financial deficit and achieve a balance between revenues and expenditures.

The session holds that the arrangements for the national economic plans for 1980 and 1981, the state budget and financial estimates embody the requirements of the continued readjustment of the national economy and the betterment of the people's lives; that the main targets are ambitious yet prudent and the measures are efficient. The fulfilment of the plans, budget and financial estimates will certainly lead to new advances in our socialist construction and create favourable conditions for the continued restructuring of our economic management and for the sustained growth of the national economy in the future.

The session calls on the people of all nationalities in the country, under the leadership of the Communist Party of China and the People's Government, to emancipate the mind, to seek truth from facts, to work with one mind and one heart, and to strive to fulfil the national economic plans and financial tasks for 1980 and 1981.

8. REPORT OF THE BUDGET COMMITTEE OF THE FIFTH NATIONAL PEOPLE'S CONGRESS ON THE EXAMINATION OF THE FINAL STATE ACCOUNTS FOR 1979, THE DRAFT STATE BUDGET FOR 1980 AND THE FINANCIAL ESTIMATES FOR 1981

(Adopted by the Presidium of the Third Session of the Fifth National People's Congress at its Second Meeting on September 1, 1980)

The Budget Committee of the Fifth National People's Congress, after hearing the Report on the Final State Accounts for 1979, the Draft State Budget for 1980 and the Financial Estimates for 1981 delivered by the Minister of Finance, Wang Bingqian, on behalf of the State Council, discussed and examined the final accounts for 1979, the draft state budget for 1980 and the financial estimates for 1981, in the light of the opinions raised by the deputies. I am now submitting a report on the result of the examination on behalf of the Budget Committee:

According to the final state accounts for 1979 prepared by the State Council, revenues totalled 110,330 million yuan, expenditures totalled 127,390 million yuan, and expenditures exceeded income by 17,060 million yuan. To make up the difference, the state drew on the surplus of the previous years to the sum of 8,040 million yuan and took out an overdraft of 9,020 million yuan from the People's Bank of China. The Budget Committee holds that the state financial departments did a lot of work in 1979 to implement the policy of readjustment, restructuring, consolidation and improvement, and scored great successes. That year, the purchase prices of major farm and sideline products were increased by a fairly big margin; some taxes in the rural areas were reduced or remitted; 40% of workers and staff got pay rises; jobs were provided for more than 9 million people; a total floor space of 60 million square metres of housing for workers and staff were completed; back pay was given to rehabilitated cadres, workers and staff after their wrongs had been redressed, etc. At the same time, in accordance with the requirements of the economic readjustment and restructuring, the state increased fairly substantially its expenditures for developing agriculture, light industry and educational and scientific undertakings, and enlarged the financial powers of the localities and enterprises.

It is indeed something unheard of for many years that the state adopted so many significant measures and did so much that had to be done in a single year. This was necessitated by the effort to correct the serious disproportions in the national economy caused by the sabotage of Lin Biao and the Gang of Four and by the effort to gradually solve the problems in production and in the people's livelihood left outstanding over the years. Although there was a considerable deficit in the final state accounts for 1979 and there were certain shortcomings and mistakes in our work, our financial work on the whole did promote economic readjustment and growth and the achievements were primary.

The draft state budget for 1980, put forward by the State Council, sets revenues at 106,290 million yuan and expenditures at 114,290 million yuan, the latter exceeding the former by 8,000 million yuan. The financial estimates for 1981 put the revenues at 115,460 million yuan and the expenditures at 120,460 million yuan, with a deficit of 5,000 million yuan. The Budget Committee holds that while 1979 saw a deficit of 17,000 million yuan, the difference would be narrowed to 8,000 million yuan for 1980 and further to 5,000 million yuan for 1981; this is in line with the need of national construction in this year and the next and with the possibility of increasing income and retrenching spending. These will be the results of tremendous efforts.

Judging by the economic and financial development in this year and the next, it is impossible to attain big increases in state revenues in these two years, because the failure to push energy industry up will affect the speed of growth of production to a certain extent, coupled with factors of temporary cuts in incomes resulting from the continued readjustment of the proportions in the national economy. On the other hand, drastic cuts in spending and an abrupt about-turn will also do harm to the national economy. Although necessary retrenchments have been made in appropriations for capital construction, in allocations of circulating funds to enterprises and in funds for national defence and preparations against war, overall expenditures cannot be reduced too much because of appropriate increases in allocations for culture, education, health work and science and for the maintenance of urban construction; for the establishment of a new development assistance fund for economically underdeveloped areas; for payments on principal and interest for foreign loans and appropriate arrangements for aid expenditures to agriculture; for tapping the potential of enterprises; for transforming enterprises; for trial-manufacturing new products; and for allocations related to the improvement of the life of the urban and rural population. In these circumstances, it is realistic to require a gradual narrowing and final elimination of deficits in this year and the next. On the whole, the arrangements for revenues and expenditures for these two years embody the requirement to continue to readjust the ratio between accumulation and consumption and gradually lower the rate of accumulation; they embody the requirement to effect a gradual improvement in the material and cultural life of the people on the basis of increased production; and they embody the requirement both to ensure the minimum need for the immediate production and construction and to prepare the conditions necessary for the sustained development of the national economy in the future.

On the basis of the above analysis, the Budget Committee proposes that the National People's Congress approve the final state accounts for 1979 and the state budget for 1980, adopt in principle the financial estimates for 1981, and approve the Report on the Final State Accounts for 1979, the Draft State Budget for 1980 and the Financial Estimates for 1981, delivered by the Minister of Finance, Wang Bingqian, on behalf of the State Council.

The stability and balance of state finances is an important condition for the four modernizations and also a significant hallmark for accomplishing the task of readjusting the national economy. The Budget Committee thinks that there will still be a deficit in this year and the next and that successive deficits will eventually affect the economic life. On the other hand, a number of unexpected problems may turn up in the course of economic readjustment and restructuring. Therefore, it will be a strenuous task to carry out the 1980 state budget and the 1981 financial estimates and to strive to narrow the gap between revenues and expenditures. The Budget Committee proposes that the present session of the National People's Congress raise the following demands on the departments concerned, all our personnel and the people of all nationalities in the country:

1. Work harder to increase production, practice economy, increase the varieties of products and expand sales, tap potential, improve economic performance, make sure that industry and agriculture will develop harmoniously and steadily; energetically develop foreign trade and tourism, do a good job with regard to remittances from Chinese nationals residing abroad, and explore more sources of revenue. On this basis, be sure to fulfil and strive to overfulfil the revenue tasks for this year and the next.

2. Continue to expand textile and light industries energetically and increase the commodity supplies on the market to suit the needs of the ever-growing purchasing power of the urban and rural population. At the same time, it is necessary to advocate among the people diligence and thrift in running the family and to encourage them to deposit their savings in the banks and to exercise strict control over institutional purchases and reduce the issuance of bank notes. Powerful measures should be taken to keep the prices basically stable and to resolutely correct the erroneous practice in some areas or units to willfully raise the prices of consumer goods or to effect increases in a disguised form.

3. Implement the principle of building the country through diligence, thrift and hard work, and firmly combat extravagance and waste. At present, in the sectors of capital construction, production and distribution, it is not uncommon to neglect business accounting or economic performance, to stockpile goods and to incur losses and waste; it is very serious in some cases. All departments must take effective measures to get rid of these, strive to do more with less money, and do it well so as to divert money in order to aid the speedy development of science and education.

4. In line with the need to give full play to favourable conditions and to ensure competition and promote integration, it is necessary to speed up the pace of structural reform on the basis of trials and thus to further invigorate the economy. With regard to plans already set for reforms of the financial, taxation and enterprise finance systems, preparations must be hastened so that they can be put into effect step by step in this year and the next, and so that the reform of the financial administration system is coordinated with that of the economic system.

5. Be guided by the principle of attempting only what is possible and taking the overall situation into account, and strengthen overall balance. In economic work, we must be realistic and scientific and act in accordance with objective economic laws; combine the need of construction with our financial resources; and combine overall interests with local interests so as to do our production and construction work better.

6. Strengthen financial control and enforce strict financial and economic discipline. Violations of financial and economic discipline or those who act irresponsibly to render investments inefficient

or to cause heavy losses or waste, must be investigated and dealt with sternly as in the case of the capsizing of the oil rig *Bohai No. 2*. These cases should be used to educate our cadres as a warning and to urge them to heighten their sense of responsibility to the cause of the people and their awareness to observe law and discipline and to perform their duties well.

The above is put to this congress for examination.

9. REGULATIONS ON BREEDING AND PROTECTION OF AQUATIC RESOURCES

(Promulgated by the State Council of the People's Republic of China on February 10, 1979)

Chapter I. General Principles

Article 1. In accordance with Article 6 in the Constitution of the People's Republic of China that "mineral resources, waters and those forests, undeveloped land and other marine and land resources owned by the state are the property of the whole people" and with Article 11 that "the state protects the environment and natural resources and prevents and eliminates pollution and other hazards to the public," and in order to breed and protect aquatic resources and expand the aquatic production to meet the needs of the socialist modernization, these regulations have been enacted.

Article 2. Aquatic animals and plants of economic value in all stages of development, including their parents, younglings, roes and spore, as well as their environment, should all be protected under the stipulations in these regulations.

Article 3. The State Administration of Aquatic Products, fishing headquarters in all sea areas, and revolutionary committees at all local levels should strengthen their organizational work and leadership over the breeding and protection of aquatic resources, fully arouse and rely on the masses and conscientiously carry out the regulations.

Chapter II. What Is To Be Protected and Principles for Catching and Gathering

Article 4. Special attention should be paid to the protection of the following important and valuable aquatic animals and plants.

(1) Fishes. Sea fishes: hairtail, yellow croakers, small yellow croakers, round scad, sardine, Pacific herring, long-finned herring, and porgy, black sea bream, red-fin pargo, snapper, mullet, left-eyed flounder, right-eyed flounder, sole, grouper, codfish, lizard fish, golden thread, pomfrets, slat cod croaker, white Chinese croaker, spotted maigre, chub mackerel, mackerel, sharp-toothed eel.

Fresh-water fishes: Common carp, black carp, grass carp, silver carp, big head, white fish, red-fin cutler, mud carp, golden carp, reeves shad, mandarin fish, triangular bream, bream, salmon, Yangtze sturgeon, Chinese sturgeon, sturgeon, scaleless carp of the Qinghai Lake, Coilia nasus, whitebait, river eel, ricefield eel and silver chub.

(2) Shrimps and Crabs. Prawn, small shrimp, freshwater shrimp, sea shrimp, Mitten crab, swimming crab and fresh-water crab.

(3) Shellfishes. Abalone, razor calm, ark shell, oyster, Mactra (double-shelled Scallop), sea scallop, pen shell, hard clam, varietgated calm, green mussel, blue mussel, hard-shell mussel, pearl shell, river mussel.

(4) Seaweeds. Laver, Undaria, Gracilaria, kelp, Eucheuma spinosa.

(5) Freshwater Edible Plants. Lotus-root, water chestnut, Gorgon fruit.

(6) Others. Chinese river dolphin, whale, giant salamander, green turtle, hark's bill turtle, sea cucumber, cuttlefish, squid, tortoise and turtle.

The revolutionary committees of provinces, autonomous regions and municipalities may make necessary additions to or subtractions from the above list according to the local aquatic resources.

Article 5. Aquatic animals must not be caught until they are sexually mature. Standards for catching (length or weight) and the maximum specific gravity of caught products below standards should be worked out for various kinds of animals. Adequate numbers of parent animals should be preserved to ensure the steady growth of aquatic animals.

All kinds of valuable seaweeds and freshwater edible plants must not be gathered until they are mature. Attention should be paid to reserving seeds and plants for rational rotation gathering.

Article 6. Various measures suited to local conditions should be taken in all areas to increase aquatic resources, such as improving the water conditions, putting fish fry and roe into water, drawing more water into rivers and streams for fish fry, rescuing fingerlings, transplanting and taming, eliminating harmful effects and introducing new varieties for cultivation.

Chapter III. Forbidden Fishing Zones and Periods

Article 7. Rational forbidden fishing zones and periods should be defined for some important fishes, prawns, shrimps and shells to spawn, winter or for the fingerlings to feed.

Fishing operations should be prohibited or restricted to some kinds of fishes or the number of certain fishing gear should be restricted, depending on the different conditions.

Article 8. Rivers where fishes and crabs migrate for spawning must not be entirely blocked for catching. Passages of a given width should be left to ensure that adequate numbers of parent fishes and crabs go upstream or downstream for spawning. Young fishes and crabs and parents migrating for spawning must not be caught at sluice-gates and, if necessary, forbidden fishing periods should be defined. Those who want to catch fish or crab fry for breeding must obtain approval from the aquatic products departments of provinces, autonomous regions and municipalities and carry out fishing operations in designated water areas and periods of time.

Chapter IV. Fishing Gear and Fishing Methods

Article 9. Minimum mesh sizes for all fishing nets should be stated separately for different kinds of aquatic products. The minimum mesh sizes for the trawl nets and purse nets of motor vessels and motorized junks' trawl nets shall be specified by the State Administration of Aquatic Products.

Manufacturing or selling of fishing gear not up to standard is prohibited.

Article 10. Existing fishing gear and fishing methods harmful to aquatic resources should be dealt with differently according to the degree of harm they do to resources. Those which do a little harm to resources should be improved step by step in a planned way. Those which do serious harm to resources should be prohibited or eliminated within a limited time. Areas and periods for operations should be restricted properly until they are all eliminated.

Small-mesh fishing nets for catching small mature fishes and shrimps are permitted for use only in designated areas and periods.

Article 11. Catching by blasting, poisoning, electric shock or other practices that seriously jeopardize aquatic resources must be strictly prohibited.

Chapter V. Protection of Water Environments

Article 12. Sewage, oils, oil compounds and other pollutants and discarded materials that are harmful to aquatic resources must not be discharged into the fishing water. All factories and mines must strictly implement the "Tentative Standard for Discharging Industrial Wastes," the "Regulations on Prevention and Protection Against Radioactivity" and other relevant stipulations promulgated by the state.

Attention should be paid to the breeding and protection of aquatic resources when drugs or pesticides have to be injected into the fishing waters in order to prevent or eliminate epidemic diseases and pests. Flax retting in rural areas should be concentrated in designated water areas.

Article 13. Attention must be paid to the protection of the fishing waters when water conservancy projects are built. Proper fish passes should be built when dams are constructed across the rivers where fishes and crabs migrate. Wherever the built water conservancy projects obstruct the spawning migration of fishes and crabs, departments in charge of aquatic products and water conservancy projects should hold consultations to open the sluice-gates for the fry to come in or to catch fry for transplanting, provided the level, volume and quality of the water permits.

Reclamation on sea beaches and lakesides must be taken into overall consideration and proceed in a planned way on the condition that it does not jeopardize aquatic resources.

Chapter VI. Rewards and Penalties

Article 14. Units and individuals who do outstanding work in implementing the regulations should be recommended or given proper material rewards by the State Administration of Aquatic Products, the fishing headquarters in all sea areas or the revolutionary committees at all local levels as they see appropriate.

Article 15. Those who contravene the regulations should be criticized or be made to pay for the losses, or their catches and fishing gear should be confiscated or they should be fined, depending on the severity of the case. Actions must be taken against leaders who instigate people in contravening the regulations, or administrative or disciplinary penalties should be given if necessary. Criminal sanctions will be imposed on those who seriously impair and cause great damage to resources, or defy supervision or commit physical assault against and hurt supervisors. Resolute blows must be dealt to the sabotage of bad people and punishment must be given to them according to law.

Chapter VII. Leadership and Responsibility

Article 16. The breeding and protection of aquatic resources throughout the country is managed by the State Administration of Aquatic Products, assisted by other departments concerned. The revolutionary committees at all local levels should assign the administrative departments in charge of aquatic products and other departments concerned to see that the regulations are implemented, and set up fishery management organs in case of need. The fishing headquarters in all sea areas and the provinces, autonomous regions and municipalities should provide patrol vessels.

Management organs for the breeding and protection of aquatic resources or mass management committees may be set up at some of the bays, lakes, rivers and water reservoirs in case of need, with the approval of the revolutionary committees of provinces, autonomous regions and municipalities.

Article 17. Administrative departments in charge of aquatic products at all levels and the fishery management organs under them should earnestly strengthen the management over the breeding and protection of aquatic resources, establish a fishery licence system, check the number of fishing boats and fishing gear and their types of fishing operations, register the fishing-boats and strengthen supervision and inspection so as to ensure the rational utilization of aquatic resources.

Aquatic research departments should make important surveys and protect aquatic resources and improve fishing gear and fishing methods, and should put forward proposals for the breeding and protection of aquatic resources and provide scientific data for working out the details of implementation of the regulations.

Article 18. Those who carry out fishery production in the waters outside their own provinces, autonomous regions and municipalities shall adhere to the local regulations on the breeding and protection of aquatic resources.

Those who engage in activities needed in scientific research but contravening the regulations or the local regulations on the breeding and protection of aquatic resources must report in advance to the administrative departments of aquatic products in the provinces, autonomous regions and municipalities for approval.

Chapter VIII. Appendix

Article 19. Revolutionary committees at all local levels should work out details of implementation of the regulations in light of the concrete conditions in their own localities and report them to the leading organs at the upper levels for the record.

Article 20. The regulations will take effect the day they are promulgated.

10. THE FOREST LAW OF THE PEOPLE'S REPUBLIC OF CHINA

(For Trial Implementation)

Approved in Principle at the Sixth Session of the Standing Committee of the Fifth National People's Congress on February 23, 1979

Chapter I. General Principles

Article 1. Forests are important resources of the country. They can provide timber and other forest products to meet the needs of national economic construction and the people's livelihood; they help to regulate the climate, conserve soil and water for streamflow, protect the land against windstorms and shifting sands and ensure the development of agriculture and animal husbandry; and they can prevent air pollution, protect and beautify the environment and improve people's mental and physical health. It is for the purpose of speeding up afforestation, strengthening forest protection and administration and ensuring the rational exploitation and utilization of forest resources that the Forest Law is formulated.

Article 2. Forest resources include woods, bamboos, woodlands as well as plants and animals in forest zones.

Forests are divided into the following five categories according to the different benefits they produce:

(1) Shelter forests: Those used mainly for providing protection. They include forests for soil and water conservation, forests for the preservation of water for streamflow, windbreaks and sand-fixing forests, shelter belts for farmland and grazing grounds, and trees planted to protect embankments and roads and for defence purposes.

(2) Timber forests: Those used mainly for the production of timber and bamboo.

(3) Economic forests: Those used mainly for the production of fruit, edible oil, industrial materials, and medicinal herbs.

(4) Fuel forests: Trees and shrubs for the production of fuel.

(5) Forests for special purposes: Forests and trees used mainly for such special purposes as environmental protection and scientific experiment. They include experimental forests, maternal forests, environment protection forests, landscape forests, woods around scenic spots, historical sites and sacred places of the revolution, and forests in natural preserves.

Article 3. According to the provisions in the Constitution concerning ownership of the means of production at the present stage, forests are owned by the people as a whole or by the working people collectively — both of a socialist nature.

Trees planted by members of people's communes around their houses or at places designated by their production teams belong to the commune members themselves.

Trees planted by such units as government departments, people's organizations, army units, schools, factories, mines and agricultural and pastoral farms at places designated by local revolutionary committees belong to these units.

Ownership of forests and trees by the state, the collective and the individual is protected against encroachment. It is forbidden to transfer state-owned forests to collective or non-forestry units, to divide collectively owned forests among individuals or to appropriate the woods owned by communes or their subdivisions or trees owned by individual commune members without payment.

Article 4. The guideline for forest-zone counties, communes and their subdivisions is to engage mainly in forestry while developing the economy in an all-around way. As to which counties, communes, production brigades and production teams should be included in this category, it shall be determined by the revolutionary committees of the provinces, autonomous regions and municipalities directly under the central authorities [*Hereinafter, "municipalities" for short — Translator*].

Article 5. The guideline for the development of forestry is to take afforestation as the basis, put equal stress on tree planting and management, plant more trees than have been cut, combine seed collection with nursery of plants and make multiple use of the resources.

Article 6. In the development of forestry, the basic tasks are: making strenuous efforts in afforestation to increase forest cover and timber reserves continuously; improving forest protection, ensuring rational cutting, and reforesting the cutover areas promptly; speeding up the development of forest zones and improving forest management and administration to hasten the growth of trees and make rational use of forest resources; strengthening education in the science of forestry to train forestry technicians and stepping up scientific research to accelerate the modernization of forest production.

Article 7. Planting, cherishing and protecting trees is a glorious duty and a right of the people throughout the country. All localities should organize the masses to plant trees on the annual Arbour Day and in other seasons that are fit for tree planting.

Revolutionary committees at all levels should constantly publicize the need to cherish and protect trees and should mobilize the masses to protect forests and trees.

Chapter II. Forest Administration

Article 8. A Ministry of Forestry shall be set up under the State Council to take charge of the development of forestry throughout the country. Forestry administrations shall be set up by the revolutionary committees of the provinces, autonomous regions, municipalities, autonomous prefectures, counties, autonomous counties and cities to take charge of forestry in their localities.

Specialized or joint companies may be set up to deal in seeds and engage in investigation, planning and designing, capital construction, timber production and processing, the production of chemicals, the supply of materials and the manufacture and maintenance of machines and equipment relating to the development of forestry. These companies shall operate as enterprises.

Article 9. State procuratorial departments shall appoint one to three spare-time forestry inspectors for each of the forestry departments of forest-zone counties, state-run forestry bureaux and major state-run forestry centres to check up on the implementation of government policies and decrees relating to forestry. The terms of reference of forestry inspectors shall be defined by the state procuratorial departments in a unified way.

The revolutionary committees of the provinces and autonomous regions, if need be, should set up public security bureaux and police stations, staffed with forest police, in major forestry centres to strengthen public security and protect forests.

Article 10. Revolutionary committees at all levels should strengthen the administration of forests. State-owned forests shall be under the unified management and administration of state-run forestry bureaux and state-run forestry centres. Forests and trees planted by government departments, organizations, army units, schools, factories, mines and agricultural and pastoral farms shall be managed and administered by these organizations themselves. Collectively owned forests shall be managed and administered by the tree farms or specialized teams of people's communes or their subdivisions, or by their appointees.

Article 11. State-run forestry bureaux and forestry centres shall be administered at various levels. State-run forestry bureaux in major state-owned forest zones shall be led by the Ministry of Forestry or by the forestry departments of the provinces and autonomous regions where they are located. Large state-run forestry centres shall be led by the provincial, autonomous regional and municipal forestry departments.

All state-run forestry bureaux and forestry centres shall be run as enterprises. For forestry centres engaged mainly in afforestation, the whole process of operation before the start of timber production — including the collection of seeds, the nursing of saplings and the planting, tending and protection of trees — shall be regarded as the development stage in checking up on the results of investment.

Article 12. The provincial and autonomous regional forestry departments may set up specialized forestry companies in areas where there are many collectively-owned forests. These companies shall give guidance to communes and their subdivisions in the development of forestry by signing contracts with them or by other economic means.

Article 13. The state and the revolutionary committees at all levels should work out long-term forestry development programmes.

Forestry departments at all levels should, in accordance with state regulations, conduct periodic surveys of forest resources to keep abreast of the changing situation, such as the depletion or expansion of forests.

State-run forestry bureaux and forestry centres should draw up forest management plans in accordance with the long-term development programmes. These plans shall be submitted to the competent authorities for approval before they are implemented.

Forestry departments at all levels should give guidance to communes and their subdivisions and to government departments, organizations, army units, schools, factories, mines and agricultural and pastoral farms in mapping out their own forestry development plans.

Article 14. With regard to engineering and mining projects in forest zones which have to clear forests or trees or occupy woodlands, the construction departments should consult the forest management and administration departments and report to the provincial, autonomous regional or municipal revolutionary committees for approval.

In case more than 1,000 *mu* of woodlands would be occupied, this must be reported to the Ministry of Forestry for approval. The trees cut down shall be handled in a unified way by the forest management and administration departments. The losses caused by the occupation of woodlands or devastation of forests shall be made up for by the construction departments.

Article 15. Road construction in forest zones should be speeded up in order to improve forest management and administration. In state-owned forest zones, it should enjoy priority in the allocation of capital investment. In collectively owned forest zones, roads shall be built by the collective themselves or with government help.

Article 16. Considering the prolonged forest production cycle and the need to make up for the losses caused to forest resources by prolonged excessive cutting in the past, a forest development funding system shall be established by levying certain amounts of fees on sales of timber, bamboo and other forest products.

Forest development funds shall be used mainly for reforestation but may also be used for new afforestation projects. Their use shall be supervised by the financial and banking departments.

Such funds are divided into two kinds: those for state-owned forests and those for collectively owned forests. Funds for state-owned forests shall be controlled by provincial, autonomous regional and municipal forestry departments while the Ministry of Forestry has the power to redistribute them. The control of funds for collectively owned forests shall be stipulated by the provincial, autonomous regional and municipal revolutionary committees.

Coal-mining and paper-making departments may draw certain amounts of forest development fees in proportion to their output of coal and paper to be used for the cultivation of forests as sources of pit props and raw material for paper mills.

Specific measures governing the collection of forest development funds shall be formulated by the ministries of forestry and finance.

Chapter III. Forest Protection

Article 17. The revolutionary committees of the provinces, autonomous regions, municipalities and forest-zone counties, if need be, may organize the departments concerned to set up forest protection commands. Forest-zone communes and their subdivisions, state-run forestry centres and agricultural and pastoral farms, and factories and mines should set up grassroots forest protection organizations of a mass character. In forest zones located at the junctures of different administrative areas, joint forest protection organizations should be set up under the leadership of the revolutionary committees concerned.

Forest protection responsibility zones, staffed by full-time or part-time rangers, shall be designated under the leadership of county revolutionary committees for forest-zone communes and their subdivisions as well as for state-run forestry centres, agricultural and pastoral farms, factories, mines and other units.

The main duties of the rangers are:

(1) Patrolling forests.

(2) Stopping any actions that may cause damage to forests.

(3) Bringing the law-breakers who have caused forest fires or other damage to forests to the local public security departments for handling.

Article 18. Revolutionary committees at all levels and other departments concerned must adopt effective measures to prevent forest fires and safeguard forests:

(1) They must fix forest fire prevention periods, during which precautionary measures must be adopted to enforce strict control on all outdoor uses of fire in forest zones and all other activities that may cause a fire.

(2) They must set up forest protecting and fire preventing facilities in forest zones. Where there are large tracts of state-owned forests, the civil aviation departments should set up specialized aviation teams to protect forests from the air.

(3) In case a forest fire breaks out, they must promptly organize forces in an all-out effort to fight the fire. Local army units and commercial, food and public health departments should give them energetic support. In fighting a forest fire, the departments concerned have priority in using the transport and communications facilities of the railway, highway, shipping, aviation and posts and telecommunications departments.

(4) In case a forest fire breaks out, they must ascertain the causes, investigate into the losses, find out who are to blame and deal with them seriously.

(5) The state shall provide medical treatment for those injured and pensions for the families of those who have died in fighting forest fires.

Article 19. Destruction of forests for land reclamation or for the development of side occupations is strictly forbidden. In case such destruction occurs, the forest-destroying units or persons shall be ordered to reforest the areas within the designated time limit.

It is forbidden to cut firewood, graze animals

or excavate sand or stone in areas of young growth, in areas where the hillsides are closed to facilitate afforestation, in windbreaks or sand-fixing forests, or in forests for special purposes.

Article 20. In areas where precious or rare animals and plants grow and propagate, the state and the provincial, autonomous regional and municipal revolutionary committees should mark out natural preserves and set up organizations to strengthen their protection and management and engage in scientific research.

Article 21. All persons entering forest zones must abide by the following regulations:

(1) *They must observe the rules for forest protection and fire prevention during the forest fire prevention periods.*

(2) *They must refrain from damaging forests, trees, roads, streams or other forestry facilities.*

(3) *Herdsmen must keep a close watch on their animals to prevent them from damaging trees.*

(4) *Hunters must observe the rules for the control of hunting.*

Article 22. Revolutionary committees at all levels, if need be, should set up institutions to actively prevent and treat plant diseases and insect pests, determine which tree seeds or saplings should be held in quarantine, delimit epidemic and protection zones, perform quarantine on tree seeds and saplings and prevent the spread of dangerous plant diseases and insect pests.

Chapter IV. Tree Planting

Article 23. The state and the revolutionary committees at all levels should work out afforestation programmes to be carried out within the appointed time-limits in accordance with the following provisions:

(1) *Nationally, the area under forest should reach 30% of the land. All provinces, autonomous regions and municipalities as well as autonomous prefectures, counties and autonomous counties should calculate the forested area, which in general should exceed 40% of the land in mountainous counties, 20% in hilly counties and 10% in counties on the plains.*

(2) *Shelter belts shall be built in agricultural and pastoral areas, at places suffering severely from soil erosion or wind and sand storms, on both sides of railways, highways and rivers, around reservoirs and along sea coasts and lakesides.*

(3) *The state and the provinces, autonomous regions and municipalities should systematically develop new timber forests and economic forests. Forest-deficient provinces and autonomous regions must achieve self-sufficiency in timber supply within fixed time limits.*

(4) *Cities and industrial and mining areas, where conditions permit, should develop parks and environmental protection forests according to the requirement that there should be an average of no less than five square meters of green area for every person.*

(5) *In afforestation, it is essential to strictly follow the technical regulations and ensure the survival of trees. In large-scale afforestation and reforestation, attention should be paid to changing the species of trees and developing forests of mixed species.*

Article 24. Revolutionary committees at all levels should work out programmes for the afforestation, within fixed time limits, of the barren hills and land fit for this purpose. In case the work is not accomplished before the deadline without legitimate reasons, the leadership concerned shall be held responsible if the hills and land are state-owned and, if they are collectively owned, the state shall arrange for their afforestation and the benefits from this shall go to the tree-planting units.

Article 25. Along railways, highways, rivers and canals, around reservoirs, in industrial and mining areas, in the vicinity of government departments, schools and army barracks as well as in areas managed by agricultural and pastoral farms, trees should be planted by the organizations in charge within the time limits set by local revolutionary committees.

Coal mining, paper-making and other enterprises should make use of all possible conditions to develop timber forests.

Article 26. Renewal of cutover areas must be carried out, mainly by artificial means, in the same or the next year according to state regulations.

Article 27. The cultivation and felling of trees in state-owned forests and the improvement of low-yield forests should be included in state plans. Measures should be adopted according to local conditions to speed up the growth and to increase the yields of forests.

Article 28. Forestry departments at all levels should vigorously popularize fine-quality and fast-growing species of trees, set up maternal forests and seed farms and breed fine strains and robust saplings so that such strains are used everywhere.

Chapter V. The Opening Up and Utilization of Forests

Article 29. Forests should be opened up rationally. The annual cuts should not exceed the amount of growth, which shall be calculated on the basis of each county or state-run forestry bureau. All timber production by the state and the localities should be included in state plans. No cutting outside the plan is permitted.

For state-owned forests, the felling of trees should be carried out by state-run forestry bureaux and forestry centres according to the quota assigned by the state. For collectively owned forests, it should be carried out by the owners under the guidance of state plans and according to the contracts they have signed with forestry departments.

Felling of trees by communes and their sub-divisions in their own forests and for their own use must be reported to the county revolutionary committees for approval if the annual cut exceeds ten cubic metres. The felling of trees by government departments, organizations, army units, schools, factories, mines and agricultural and pastoral farms in their own forests and for their own use must be reported to the provincial, autonomous regional and municipal forestry departments for approval if the annual cut exceeds 100 cubic metres.

Article 30. Felling of trees in forests must abide by the following regulations:

(1) For timber forests, felling of trees must proceed rationally according to state regulations to ensure the quality of the operation.

(2) For shelter, environmental protection, landscape and maternal forests, felling of trees is permitted only as is necessary for cultivating or renewing the forests.

(3) All tree felling is forbidden for forests in natural preserves.

The forestry departments have the power to stop an operation that violates the above-mentioned regulations.

Article 31. Bamboos, firewood, charcoal and finished and semi-finished wood and bamboo products to be sold in batches shall be put under the unified management and control of the specialized companies set up by forestry departments; or the forestry department shall be responsible for organizing the production of these goods and the supply and marketing department shall be responsible for their marketing under the plans which are worked out jointly by the two departments in accordance with the principle of protecting forest resources and rational utilization of odds-and-ends materials, and which are approved by the provincial, autonomous regional and municipal planning commissions. No other organizations or individuals are allowed to enter forest zones for the purpose of felling trees, processing or purchasing forest products.

Article 32. Shipment of timber, bamboo or their products, either finished or semi-finished, out of a county must have the permits issued by the county forestry department; shipment of these products out of a province or autonomous region must have the permits issued by the provincial or autonomous regional forestry department.

Article 33. Positive efforts should be made to promote the multiple use of timber, set up timber processing and forest chemical enterprises in forest zones in a planned way, and raise the utilization rates of forest resources and timber.

Article 34. Timber for construction projects shall be standardized step by step. Timber processing enterprises in forest zones shall produce according to demands and their products shall be supplied to appointed places. As to timber processing enterprises in cities, their production shall be concentrated and the supply of their products unified.

Chapter VI. Awards and Punishment

Article 35. Spiritual encouragement or material awards shall be given by the state or by revolutionary committees at various levels, according to the contributions made, to those organizations which have performed one of the following exemplary deeds:

(1) Having conscientiously implemented the principles and policies relating to forestry, fulfilled state plans in an all-around way for three consecutive years and attained advanced domestic levels in major economic-technical indices.

(2) Having made outstanding achievements in forest protection or prevented the outbreak of any forest fires for three consecutive years.

(3) Having achieved high output, fine quality and low cost in nursing saplings and fulfilled their tasks for three consecutive years.

(4) Having achieved fine quality and high speed with less investment in afforestation and fulfilled all their afforestation tasks ahead of schedule.

(5) Having achieved remarkable results in speeding up the growth and increasing the yields of forests and trees through timely cultivation and positive efforts to improve low-yield forests.

(6) Having made remarkable achievements in ensuring rational cutting and timely renewal.

(7) Having increased timber utilization rates remarkably through positive efforts to make multiple and economic use of timber.

(8) Having made remarkable achievements in forestry education and scientific research.

Article 36. Spiritual encouragement or material awards shall be given by the state or by revolutionary committees at various levels, according to the contributions made, to those individuals who have performed one of the following exemplary deeds:

(1) Having worked at grassroots forestry units for 15 years or more, shown ardent love for the work and made remarkable achievements.

(2) Having made discoveries, inventions or important innovations in forest production, teaching and scientific research.

(3) Having stuck to their posts, observed discipline and fulfilled their forest production tasks with honours.

(4) Having exemplarily implemented forestry policies and decrees, firmly combated law-breaking actions and rendered remarkable meritorious services.

(5) Having distinguished themselves by their heroism, tenacity and selflessness in fighting forest fires.

(6) Having rendered meritorious services in preventing accidents and rescuing operations and protected the property of the state and the people from grave losses.

Article 37. Different disciplinary sanctions, up to discharge from public service, shall be applied on the merits of each case to those government functionaries who have been found derelict of their duties in one of the following aspects:

(1) Causing losses to forest production for failure to exercise effective leadership or inefficiency in management and administration.

(2) Violating forestry policies, decrees, rules or regulations, causing damage to forests or serious waste of timber.

(3) Ignoring state regulations in felling trees or reforestation.

(4) Diverting forest development funds for other uses.

(5) Making false reports of achievements by resorting to deceit or deception.

Article 38. Anyone who destroys trees in cities and towns, around villages, along roads and streams or around houses must plant three trees (counting only the surviving ones) for every tree destroyed or shall be fined.

Article 39. Anyone who commits one of the following offences against the Forest Law shall, if the offence is minor, be ordered to compensate for the losses or be fined, and all illegal earnings shall be confiscated; those who commit serious offences shall be punished according to law:

(1) Causing forest fires.

(2) Destroying forests for land reclamation or for the development of side occupations, or causing damage to forests or trees while grazing animals.

(3) Cutting firewood, grazing animals or excavating sand or stones in areas of young growth, in areas where the hillsides are closed to facilitate afforestation, in windbreaks or sand-fixing forests, or in forests for special purposes.

(4) Violating the regulations governing the administration of natural preserves or the regulations for the control of hunting.

(5) Entering forest zones for unauthorized purchase of timber, bamboo, firewood, charcoal or wood or bamboo products, either finished or unfinished.

(6) Seizing or stealing trees, robbing or stealing timber.

(7) Speculating and profiteering in timber.

(8) Violating the Forest Law and causing physical harm to rangers in disregard of admonitions.

(9) Serious negligence of duty causing damage to forests.

Article 40. Those who deliberately set fire to forests, gang up to destroy forests or murder rangers shall be seriously punished according to law.

Article 41. If the offenders against the Forest Law have acted on the instructions of their superiors, both they and their superiors should be held at fault for their offences and dealt with seriously on the merits of each case.

Chapter VII. Appendix

Article 42. Detailed regulations for the implementation of the Forest Law shall be formulated by the Ministry of Forestry and reported to the State Council for approval. Specific measures for the implementation of the Forest Law shall be formulated by the provincial, autonomous regional and municipal revolutionary committees in accordance with the Forest Law and the detailed regulations.

11. REGULATIONS ON SOME QUESTIONS CONCERNING THE DEVELOPMENT OF ENTERPRISES RUN BY RURAL PEOPLE'S COMMUNES AND PRODUCTION BRIGADES

Promulgated by the State Council (Draft for Trial Use)
(July 3, 1979)

I. The Significance of Developing Commune- and Brigade-Run Enterprises

In accordance with the Decision on Some Questions Concerning the Acceleration of Agricultural Development (Draft) adopted at the Third Plenary Session of the Eleventh Central Committee of the Communist Party of China, there should be a big expansion of enterprises run by rural people's communes and production brigades. The expansion of such enterprises can, above all, better serve the development of agricultural production, strengthen the collective economy at the commune and brigade levels and provide the funds required for mechanization. At the same time, it will open up new avenues of employment in production for the labour power which will be released by mechanization, make fuller use of local resources, aid the development of a diversified rural economy, increase collective income and raise the living standards of commune members. It will also gradually create the conditions for the people's communes to undergo the transition from the system of small-scale collective ownership to that of large-scale collective ownership and then to the system of ownership by the whole people. A big expansion of industries run by rural people's communes can provide society in general with large amounts of raw and semi-finished materials and industrial products, thus accelerating the development of China's industry as a whole; it can also avoid the disadvantage of overconcentration of industry in large and medium-sized cities. It is an important way gradually to narrow the differences between town and country, worker and peasant, and manual and mental labour.

II. Guiding Principles for Development

Commune- and brigade-run enterprises must persist in the socialist orientation and strive to produce what is needed by society, serving mainly agricultural production and the people's livelihood and also the needs of large-scale industry and for exports.

These enterprises must develop in line with local conditions and in accordance with local resources and social needs, and they must grow from small to big and from a lower to a higher stage. They must not be initiated if their machines cannot be 'fed', nor, in the case of processing industries, should they be built with excessive production capacity. They must not compete with large-scale, advanced industries for raw materials and energy, and they must not cause damage to the natural resources of the country.

They must persist in self-reliance and hard struggle, democratic management and thrift, and must practice strict economic accounting.

Active attempts must be made to run enterprises which combine agricultural, industrial and commercial functions.

III. Business Scope

Crop cultivation, animal husbandry and fish-breeding must be expanded energetically. Where local conditions are favourable, forestry centres, orchards, tea plantations, silkworm farms, medicinal herb plantations, seed-production centres, edible-mushroom farms, livestock and poultry farms, and fish hatcheries must be set up. All these can provide the basis for developing processing industries for farm and side-line products. Farms can be set up where there is virgin territory.

Efforts must be made to develop processing industries for farm and side-line products. In accordance with the principle of economic rationality, all farm, forestry, animal husbandry and fishery products and special local products which are suitable for processing by communes and brigades can be processed by them. As to those products already being processed by factories set up by the state, whether they should be handed over to commune and brigade-run enterprises is to be decided by the revolutionary committees of provinces or autonomous regions in consultation with the departments concerned and after weighing both advantages and disadvantages.

Efforts must be made to run agriculture-related industries well. Small and medium-sized farm tool manufacturing and repair shops must be set up to process spare parts under the unified plans for local farm machinery undertakings. Where the necessary conditions exist, enterprises can be set up to produce humic acid fertilizer, bacterial fertilizer, insecticides and herbicides, and veterinary medicines, and to process fodder.

In line with local conditions, more fuel and raw materials extraction industries such as bio-gas stations, small coal fields, small iron, non-ferrous metal and other mines must be initiated, and small works for producing building materials — brick yards, lime kilns, quarries and cement plants — set up. Saltworks and saline chemical works can be set up where there are abundant resources of bittern.

A major effort must be made to develop the power industry. In the light of concrete conditions, hydro- and thermal-power stations with generating capacities of 12,000 kilowatts and less can be set up.

Localities with the necessary conditions can undertake the production of spare parts or certain products subcontracted to them by large-scale industries. In accordance with the demands of the market and with the availability of energy, small chemical works, hardware factories, smelters, and workshops turning out daily necessities must be set up to make use of leftover bits and pieces of industrial material, urban and rural wastes and old materials, as well as waste residue, waste water and waste gas.

Where it is necessary and feasible, building squads and transport teams can be organized to undertake certain tasks in urban and rural capital construction, transport and loading.

Efforts must be made to produce traditional handicrafts and goods for export where there are local resources or favourable technical conditions. Production bases for export commodities must be built up step by step, based on the requirements of foreign trace. When conditions permit, compensatory trade should be promoted.

Service trades such as sewing and repair, hotel and restaurant operation, should be initiated where they are needed.

IV. Plans for the Readjustment and Development of Enterprises

In the light of the spirit of the Third Plenary Session of the Eleventh Central Committee of the Communist Party, the percentage of income from nationwide commune-and brigade-run enterprises in the total income of rural people's communes at three levels should increase from 29.7% in 1978 to around 50% in 1985. The various provinces, municipalities, autonomous regions and counties must work out long-term plans for the development of commune-and brigade-run enterprises, plans which are tied closely to local plans for production in farming, forestry, animal husbandry and fisheries, industrial and transportation undertakings and for urban and rural construction, and they must see to it that these plans are implemented at the commune level. In mapping out such plans, they must seek truth from facts, take the overall situation into account, and aim at rational distribution.

The first thing in working out development plans is to adhere to the general policy for readjusting the national economy, pursuing both progress and consolidation in the course of readjustment, and accomplishing the readjustment of commune- and brigade-run enterprises as soon as possible. Efforts must be made to increase the production of raw and semi-finished materials, fuels and power, and of all badly needed commodities for the home market and for export. Enterprises with excessive capacity for spare-part production and those where the technology is not up to standard or where the problem of supplies and marketing cannot be solved must readjust the orientation of their production, merge or close down according to the unified arrangement of the county revolutionary committees.

New enterprises must not be initiated blindly, but must be set up in a planned way with the approval of the departments in charge of commune- and brigade-run enterprises, and they must be rationally distributed. Industrial and commercial enterprises must be approved and licensed by the departments in charge of industry and commerce.

V. Sources of Funds

1. Capital must be accumulated mainly by the enterprises themselves through their own efforts. When an enterprise is first started, or where the necessary conditions prevail, appropriate sums can be drawn from the public reserve funds of production brigades or teams and treated as shares with the approval of the congresses of commune or brigade members.

2. Local revolutionary committees at the various levels must do their best to support commune- and brigade-run enterprises by allocating part of their reserve funds to the departments in charge of such enterprises for this purpose.

3. Normally, not less than half of the investment made by the state to support rural people's communes must be allocated to the departments in charge of commune-and brigade-run enterprises to support the poorer brigades in their effort to set up enterprises. The departments in charge may entrust these investment funds and those provided by local financial departments to the banks for disbursement and retrieval for continued use.

4. The Agricultural Bank must assign a certain proportion of annual agricultural loans as low-interest loans to support commune-and brigade-run enterprises. Those loans which are spent on buying equipment are normally to be repaid over a period of 3 to 5 years.

VI. Ownership

Commune-and brigade-run enterprises are collectively owned socialist enterprises. Those run by communes are owned by those communes, and those run by brigades are owned by the brigades. Economic exchanges between state enterprises and those run by communes and brigades, or between commune- and brigade-run enterprises and other collective economic units, should be exchanges of equal values. No organization or individual may obtain funds, products, equipment, or raw or semi-finished materials from commune- and brigade-run enterprises without compensation, or borrow money from them. The power of these enterprises to make their own decisions must be respected.

Nationalization of commune- and brigade-run enterprises is forbidden. Those enterprises taken over by the state after the First National Conference on Learning from Dazhai in Agriculture must be returned to their original owners; the pay and working conditions of workers and staff need not be affected.

In order to improve rational distribution, strengthen co-ordination, raise quality and reduce costs, it is necessary to encourage joint enterprises. These can be run by several communes or brigades, or by communes and brigades together. Hereafter, industrial enterprises should be run mainly by communes or by several communes jointly under the auspices of county authorities with cadres appointed by the county authorities and economic activities carried on in the capacity of county-run factories.

Joint enterprises can also be set up on a trial basis between communes and counties, the profits made to be shared between the two sides according to an agreed ratio. It is forbidden to nationalize joint enterprises, either those involving several communes which resemble county-owned factories in form or those run by counties and communes.

The revolutionary committees of various provinces, municipalities and autonomous regions should readjust unreasonable management fees and administrative charges levied against commune- and brigade-run enterprises by the departments concerned.

VII. The Farming Out of Production by Urban Industries

According to the needs of expanding production and the capacity of communes and brigades, urban industries can divert the production of some products or spare parts to rural communes.

When organizing the farming out of certain products from urban industries, it is necessary to give good technical guidance and in some cases to transfer special equipment and tools at fixed prices. For cooperation between urban industries and rural people's communes and brigades to be maintained, supplies of raw and semi-finished materials and marketing channels must not be interrupted. Commune- and brigade-run enterprises must guarantee the quality of products and fulfil their assumed tasks on time. Contracts must be signed and strictly observed by both parties. An overall solution to the problem of duplicated taxation must be worked out by the Ministry of Finance with respect to products turned out through such co-operative efforts.

Only after effective measures have been taken to prevent or deal with the discharge of poisonous substances in the production process can commune- and brigade-run enterprises be assigned the tasks of such production. Those goods that are unsalable and those that are already obsolete must not be assigned to commune- and brigade-run enterprises for production.

Urban industrial equipment lying idle or discarded in the course of retooling but suitable for use in commune- and brigade-run enterprises should be transferred to such enterprises at reasonable prices and may be paid for in a single or in several installments.

VIII. Improved Planning in Production, Supply and Marketing

Commune- and brigade-run enterprises are becoming an increasingly important component of the national economy. The planning commissions at all levels and all departments concerned, especially the industrial departments, must take charge of state and commune- and brigade-run enterprises. Every possible means must be employed to improve planning as related to the production, supply and marketing of commune- and brigade-run enterprises so that their plans dovetail with state economic plans at the various levels.

1. The departments in charge of commune- and brigade-run enterprises and the other departments concerned should give guidance to the people's communes when plans are being worked out

for the production of such enterprises. For some products, the production plans proposed by the departments concerned are to be brought into overall balance by the State Planning Commission and directly incorporated into the state economic plans at the various levels. The production plans for other products can be indirectly incorporated into the state economic plans at the various levels through contracts signed with the clients. As for those products which are not included in one or another level of the state economic plans but which are needed by society and are assured of raw and semi-finished materials and power supply, production plans can be worked out by the people's communes themselves.

Medium-sized and small farm tools, building materials and processed farm and side-line products turned out by commune- and brigade-run enterprises should be managed by the departments in charge of such enterprises. State and local funds and materials used for this purpose should also be managed and distributed by them. As to which other products can also be managed by the local departments in charge of commune-and brigade-run enterprises, this is a question to be decided by the revolutionary committees of the same level according to the terms of their jurisdiction.

Planning commissions at the various levels should pool the output value and revenue figures of commune- and brigade-run enterprises as well as the investment indices for agricultural production and capital construction and incorporate them into their respective comprehensive plans.

2. Materials required for the production of products directly included in the plans of various levels should be allocated according to plan by the planning commissions and departments responsible for arranging production. Special-use equipment should be provided by the departments in charge of the product category concerned. Materials required for the production of products which are only indirectly included in the plans should be provided by those ordering the products according to the terms of their contracts.

Local planning commissions at the various levels are to list the materials required by commune and brigade-run enterprises for capital construction, the maintenance of equipment and technical improvement which are to be allotted by the state, and the means of transportation to be acquired by the enterprises themselves, and to work out overall arrangements; the State Planning Commission is to give them the necessary allotments. A certain amount of substandard steels and other waste materials recovered by the localities is to be allotted by the local planning commissions to commune-and brigade-run enterprises.

The departments in charge of commune-and brigade-run enterprises are to apply to the departments concerned (in accordance with the supplies system provisions) for the second and third-category materials and for labour protection articles required by the enterprises in order to fulfil production plans. Such materials can also be acquired through exchanges organized by offices of the same level in charge of co-ordination of materials, or can be purchased directly by commune- and brigade-run enterprises and the departments in charge of such enterprises.

3. Products which are directly included in the plans at various levels are to be purchased by the departments concerned and contracts are to be signed between the concerned parties on production and marketing. Products which are indirectly involved in the plans at various levels are to be purchased by those ordering the products according to contract. Products which are produced according to the plans of commune-and brigade-run enterprises themselves and surplus products which are produced according to the plans of various levels or according to contract and which are not to be allocated by the state are to be sold by the departments in charge of commune-and brigade-run enterprises or by the enterprises themselves. If such products are not purchased within the localities concerned, no restrictions should be placed on their sale outside.

With the approval of the state, a certain proportion of the products to be allotted by the state can be kept by the commune- and brigade-run enterprises themselves provided there is a genuine need for such products within the production process.

4. Applications by commune- and brigade-run enterprises for the transportation of the required raw and semi-finished materials, fuels, equipment and of finished products should be arranged by railway, transport and shipping authorities and such transportation should be included in their plans.

Departments in charge of commune- and brigade-run enterprises can sign contracts for production, supply, marketing and transportation with the departments or units concerned on behalf of such enterprises.

IX. All Trades and Lines of Work Must Actively Support Commune- and Brigade-Run Enterprises

All trades and lines of work must treat support for the development of commune-and brigade-run enterprises as an important task. They must work out plans, adopt measures and do their part in greatly expanding commune- and brigade-run enterprises.

Planning departments must take all factors into consideration and make overall arrangements to see that commune- and brigade-run enterprises mesh with state enterprises, each displaying its own strong points and developing in close coordination with the other.

The various industrial departments must have regard for those commune- and brigade-run industrial enterprises which turn out the same line of products as themselves or which cooperate to produce spare parts as their competent assistants; they must guide these enterprises in developing in a planned way, help them to raise their technical levels, and provide them with special equipment and the necessary materials. The state should not set up new factories to produce products which can be produced by commune- and brigade-run industries.

Departments engaged in capital construction must guide and assist the communes and production brigades in their efforts to run construction enterprises, and must make overall arrangements for construction tasks, train construction teams for them and gradually mechanize these teams.

The railway, transport and shipping departments must guide and assist communes and brigades in their efforts to run transport and loading enterprises and must help commune- and brigade-run enterprises to solve effectively the problems of materials transportation.

Departments of commerce, supply and marketing, and foreign trade must guide commune- and brigade-run enterprises in their efforts to determine the needs of the market, to improve the quality of their products and to increase their variety, and must support them in the supply of materials and in product marketing. Commune- and brigade-run enterprises must be given their shares of the profits made from the sale of export commodities in foreign currency, in accordance with the unified regulations of the state.

Financial departments, banks and credit cooperatives must support commune- and brigade-run enterprises with funds while strengthening their guidance and supervision over the use of such funds. The banks should assist the departments in charge of such enterprises to do a good job of coaching in accounting so as to help the commune- and brigade-run enterprises institute business accounting; and the banks should make it convenient for them to open or close accounts.

Departments in charge of farming, forestry and aquatic products must help communes and brigades to expand planting and breeding activities, to develop the processing and comprehensive use of forest and aquatic products. Commune- and brigade-run enterprises must be encouraged to produce the agriculture-related industrial products which fall within the jurisdiction of farming and forestry departments.

Scientific and technological departments and educational institutions must help communes and brigade-run enterprises train management and technical personnel, conduct scientific research, and exchange scientific and technological information.

Labour and public health departments must actively aid commune- and brigade-run enterprises in improving dust and poison prevention work so as to guarantee safety in production and protection of the environment.

Geological departments must help the people's communes solve problems arising in mineral prospecting so as to promote the expansion of mining by communes and brigades.

Administrative departments in charge of industry and commerce must actively help coordinate production, supply and marketing relationships and ensure the conduct of business in accordance with law through the registration of enterprises and the management of contracts.

X. Pricing Policy and Subsidies to Encourage Sales

Commune- and brigade-run enterprises must follow state pricing policies. In principle, products to be purchased by the state must be priced the same as those of similar quality turned out by state enterprises. The prices of products to be sold by the enterprises themselves are to be fixed through discussion between the buying and selling parties within the price limits set by the pricing departments.

Materials allotted by the state to commune- and brigade-run enterprises according to plan must be paid for at the state-determined prices for allotted or supplied materials; large batches of raw materials supplied by the market may be paid for at wholesale prices.

Awards, subsidies and advance purchases of certain products of commune- and brigade-run enterprises by the state and departments concerned must be continued and honoured. Materials awarded to encourage the sale of certain products and subsidies or compensatory materials which should be turned over to the production units must not be intercepted by the departments handling them or, indeed, by any other department.

XI. Tax Policy

The state applies reduced-tax or tax-exemption policies to the commune-and brigade-run enterprises. They, in turn, are duty-bound to pay state taxes according to the regulations and not to default or evade.

According to the concrete conditions prevailing in the localities, and with the approval of the revolutionary committees of the various provinces, municipalities or autonomous regions, those commune- and brigade-run enterprises directly serving agricultural production and the livelihood of the commune members may register specific products and services for exemption from industrial, commercial and income taxes.

In accordance with the stipulations set forth in Document Cai Shui Zi No. 21 issued by the Ministry of Finance in 1978, small iron mines, coal fields, power stations, and cement works are to be exempt from industrial, commercial and income taxes for a period of three years commencing in 1978. New enterprises of this kind are to be exempt from taxes for a period of three years from the time they are established. Other new enterprises which have difficulty in paying taxes in the initial stage may be exempted from industrial, commercial and income taxes for a period of 2-3 years with the approval of the revolutionary committees of the provinces, municipalities or autonomous regions.

In order to accelerate the growth of the rural economy in border areas and in areas inhabited by the minority nationalities, commune- and brigade-run enterprises in counties, autonomous counties or banners in such areas are to be exempt from income tax for a period of five years as from 1979. The revolutionary committees of the various provinces, municipalities and autonomous regions should also make up lists of those old revolutionary base areas which still suffer from difficult economic conditions and which should therefore be similarly exempted from taxes; these lists should be submitted to the State Council for approval.

Self-help undertakings run by communes and brigades in areas struck by natural disasters may be exempt from some or all industrial, commercial and income taxes for a set period of time, with the approval of the revolutionary committees of the provinces, municipalities or autonomous regions.

Commune- and brigade-run enterprises are to be taxed at the present tax rate of 20%. This rate will also apply to the income tax to be paid by the supply and marketing organs of the departments in charge of commune- and brigade-run enterprises or of specialized corporations.

XII. The Labour System, Labour Remuneration and Labour Protection

The labour system of the commune- and brigade-run enterprises involves both industrial and agricultural aspects. The labour force required by the enterprises is to be provided by communes or brigades in accordance with the principle of overall consideration and arrangement and through the transfer of personnel in consultation with the basic accounting units, on the precondition that a sufficient labour force remains in agricultural production. This labour force will gradually grow as the mechanization of agriculture goes forward. Enterprises should not recruit workers on their own or hand out jobs to friends or relatives.

Payment for labour in commune- and brigade-run enterprises must follow the principle of "to each according to his work." The common practice is "to have workers' grades determined by the factories, their work-points calculated by their production teams, their remuneration worked out by the factories and teams together, and their earnings distributed to them by their teams." Other systems can also be implemented. Where conditions are ripe, a wage system can be implemented. In the case of personnel whose registered permanent residence is in an urban area and who live on commodity grain, the wage system should apply. Technical subsidies should be granted by the enterprises to those personnel who are highly skilled and who contribute the most to the enterprises. The system of fixed production quotas should be implemented and material incentives given as appropriate to those groups or individuals who overfulfil their quotas and who guarantee the quality of the products. Men and women should enjoy equal pay for equal work.

An extra allowance for living expenses should be given to personnel who engage in high-temperature operations; work in mines or high above the ground; work at jobs detrimental to the health or in particularly heavy labour; and to those who cannot take meals at home. The extra grain ration for these jobs is to be drawn from the extra grain put aside by the collectives for extra-grain subsidies.

Payment by the enterprises to the production teams for labour should in general be higher than the distribution levels in the teams and, as far as possible, rich teams must not be left at a disadvantage. Accounts must be settled on time and obligations must be honoured. In the case of enterprises which are temporarily without income and, therefore, have difficulty in honouring payrolls, the communes or brigades can use the profits handed in by other enterprises, or can keep clear accounts and wait for such time as these enterprises begin to acquire an income.

Commune- and brigade-run enterprises should attach importance to production safety and strengthen education in this respect. Continued efforts must be made in improving working conditions, labour protection must be handled well, care must be given to the health of personnel, and attention paid to the special needs of women workers. Accidents resulting in injury or death in the course of duty must be reported and investigated promptly and dealt with seriously. Medical treatment should be provided to those injured while on duty and to those contracting occupational diseases; extra living allowances should be given to those who are disabled and pensions given to the families of any deceased.

The environment must be well protected. New enterprises must not pollute the environment, and existing ones should make an effort to eliminate pollution. Those that cause serious pollution must be required to provide remedies within fixed time-limits.

In those rural handicraft enterprises that have been transferred to commune management in accordance with Document No. 66 issued by the State Council in 1977, the wages of workers and staff, their grain rations, and the regulations concerning withdrawal or retirement, labour protection and other welfare conditions remain the same as before the transfer.

XIII. The Use of Profits

The use of the profits of the commune- and brigade-run enterprises is to be decided by the conferences of the representatives of members of the brigades and communes, and then approved by the communes or counties respectively. Leaders are strictly forbidden to give arbitrary personal instructions on the use of profits. Apart from expanded reproduction and the setting up of new enterprises, profits must be expended mainly on farm capital construction, the mechanization of agriculture and in giving support to the poor teams. A certain proportion may also be distributed among the commune members or spent on commune or brigade welfare undertakings. Waste and extravagance are prohibited and it is forbidden to spend profits on entertainment or gifts.

A certain proportion of the profits made can be left as enterprise funds in the hands of those enterprises which have fulfilled or overfulfilled their production plans.

XIV. The Establishment and Perfection of a System of Management Rules and Regulations

Commune- and brigade-run enterprises must persist in the principles of democratic management and thrift, give full play to the initiative of their personnel, and establish and perfect rules and regulations of business management.

Planning must be strengthened. Plans must be made by relying on the masses and regular checks must be conducted to guarantee their fulfilment. As production expands and management skills improve, the eight economic and technical indices — output, variety, quality, consumption, labour productivity, costs, profits, fixed assets and circulating funds — should be worked out and assessment procedures initiated.

Labour management must be strengthened. The labour force must be organized rationally and a system of fixed production quotas implemented. A system in which specialized groups or individuals take responsibility for each section of a production line must be established. Discipline must be strict, and awards and punishments fair.

Technical management must be improved. A system of personal responsibility for technical matters must be set up. Operational regulations must be worked out in accord with the special characteristics of the enterprises. Enterprise personnel should be graded according to technical proficiency as determined through regular assessments and they should be granted the titles appropriate for technical personnel.

Product quality control must be strengthened and the principle of "quality first" adhered to. Production must be organized according to the demands of variety, specification and quality. Strict product inspection rules must be formulated so that quality can catch up or surpass advanced levels for the various product lines. Substandard products must not be allowed to leave the factories and must not be included in total output values.

Materials management must be strengthened. There must be fixed quotas for the consumption of raw and semi-finished materials and other goods and there must be detailed rules governing the stocking or removal of materials from storehouses. Fixed assets such as machinery, equipment and means of transportation must be maintained by people especially assigned for the job and must be overhauled regularly. As regards abnormal losses, it is necessary to find out where the responsibility lies and to deal with such cases seriously.

Financial management must be strengthened. State regulations governing financial matters and the management of cash must be strictly implemented. The magnitude of circulating funds must be fixed and the depreciation funds for fixed assets set aside; mining operations must also set aside funds for technical transformation. Accounting must be improved and efforts must be made to practice strict economy while increasing production so as to reduce costs and boost profits. Commune- and brigade-run enterprises must make public their income and expenditures regularly and must report to the congresses or conferences of the representatives of commune members, accepting the supervision of the masses.

XV. Technical Innovation and Transformation

Commune- and brigade-run enterprises must actively engage in technical innovation and technical transformation, make an effort to tap production potentials and constantly raise production levels. Small groups or individuals that make contributions to technical innovation and technical transformation must be commended and awarded.

Depreciation funds generally and the technical transformation funds for mines must be expended on the renewal of equipment and on technical transformation; the surplus must be deposited in banks and must not be used otherwise. Departments in charge of commune-and brigade-run enterprises and other departments concerned must give active support to such enterprises in the renewal of equipment involved in their technical transformation so as to help change their production step by step. Those enterprises which have the necessary conditions can make use of their shares of foreign-currency profits to import advanced technology and equipment from abroad.

The study of science and training in technology must be strengthened, with commune- and brigade-run enterprises becoming schools for helping raise the scientific and cultural level of the rural population.

XVI. Consolidation of Enterprises

It is necessary to make a real effort to consolidate commune- and brigade-run enterprises this year and next. Consolidation must be centered on production and mainly on the improvement of management and the establishment of a national production order so as to lay the foundation for large-scale development.

It is necessary to teach cadres to work in close cooperation with technical personnel and all other personnel in the enterprises, to encourage rationalization proposals, to set up a proper production order, and to establish and perfect business management, especially the system of fixed responsibility for each section of the production line and the system of democratic management of financial matters. It is imperative that all waste and extravagance, graft and embezzlement, speculation and profiteering be combatted.

It is necessary to help the cadres to learn production skills and business management, to persist in ideological work, to take the lead in observing rules and regulations and discipline, and to accept the supervision of the masses.

It is necessary to establish the system of electing the leading cadres of the enterprises democratically and to form good leading groups through consolidation. The leading cadres of an enterprise are to be elected by the personnel of that enterprise and approved by the leading organ at the higher level. Government functionaries who are assigned work in factories jointly run by several communes continue to enjoy remuneration and other conditions as state functionaries and, just as everybody else, they can assume leading posts only when elected to them and when their election is approved by leading organs of a higher level.

From now on, we must check the work of the enterprises regularly, sum up experiences and solve problems as they arise so as to enable commune- and brigade-run enterprises to develop in a healthy manner.

XVII. The Establishment of Efficient Administrative Organs

Commune- and brigade-run enterprises have broad prospects for development involving many sectors of the economy, and it is therefore necessary to set up powerful and efficient organs to take charge.

A General Administration for Commune- and Brigade-Run Enterprises is being established under the Ministry of Agriculture to take direct charge of the investments, materials and equipment allotted to such enterprises by the State Planning Commission and the State General Administration for Materials. Administrative bureaus for these enterprises are to be set up at the provincial and county levels, with corresponding organs at the prefectural level. The people's communes must assign persons to take special charge of commune- and brigade-run enterprises. Planning commissions at the various levels and the other departments concerned should also set up functional organs or assign persons to take special charge.

Departments in charge of commune- and brigade-run enterprises at various levels must implement the line, policies and principles formulated by the party and state for the development of these enterprises, work out and fulfil annual and long-term plans, do a good job of managing the products entrusted to them and of the materials and funds allotted to the enterprises. They must co-ordinate their relations with the other departments concerned, mediate between producers, suppliers and sellers, and help the enterprises to improve management, popularize new techniques and sum up and exchange experiences.

The staff of the departments in charge of commune- and brigade-run enterprises at the various levels must be kept as small as possible (their actual size to be decided by the revolutionary committees of the various provinces, municipalities and autonomous regions) and must be drawn from existing staff. Expenses are to be included in the general financial expenditures at the various levels.

Departments in charge of commune- and brigade-run enterprises at the various levels must set up supply and marketing agencies and specialized corporations, which are themselves in the nature of enterprises. The tasks of such agencies and corporations are to organize production, exchange economic information, mediate between producers, suppliers and sellers, organize co-operative ventures, and do a good job of procuring materials and selling products. The expenses of their staffs must be paid out of commissions collected. The circulating funds required are to be provided through allocations by financial departments or through bank loans.

XVIII. The Strengthening of Leadership

Commune- and brigade-run enterprises are forging ahead and changing day by day. New circumstances, problems and experiences will inevitably keep presenting themselves. The leading organs at all levels must make unified plans and strengthen their leadership; they must listen to reports regularly, study and solve major problems, and sum up and popularize advanced experience.

It is necessary, under the leadership of the party committees of the various levels, to strengthen the political work in commune- and brigade-run enterprises and to arouse the masses in unfolding socialist labour emulation drives and campaigns to increase production and practice economy, and in exerting themselves to turn their enterprises into advanced operations and become model workers themselves. It is important to build up party and youth league organizations and give full play to the role of the party organizations as fighting bastions and the role of the youth league as the party's aide.

In accordance with the instructions of the Party Central Committee and Comrade Hua Guofeng, the leadership at all levels must display the spirit of the foolish old man who removed the mountains and make persistent and redoubled efforts to turn all bright hopes into reality as soon as possible.

The revolutionary committees of the various provinces, municipalities and autonomous regions should work out concrete plans for the implementation of the above regulations.

12. DECISION OF THE CENTRAL COMMITTEE OF THE COMMUNIST PARTY OF CHINA ON SOME QUESTIONS CONCERNING THE ACCELERATION OF AGRICULTURAL DEVELOPMENT

Adopted at the Fourth Plenary Session of the 11th Central Committee of the Party
(September 28, 1979)

The Chinese people have entered the new historical stage of realizing the four modernizations in the great cause of socialist construction. In 1979, the focus of the work of our party and state was shifted to socialist modernization. The first and foremost task now confronting us is to concentrate our efforts on speeding up the development of our still backward agriculture. As agriculture is the foundation of the national economy, its rapid development provides the essential guarantee for the realization of modernization. Only by speeding up agricultural production and bringing about modernization in agriculture step by step can our peasants, who comprise 80% of the population, become rich; and only then can the national economy as a whole prosper, the worker-peasant alliance be strengthened and the socialist system and dictatorship of the proletariat be consolidated in China. For this reason, the Central Committee has made a decision on the following questions:

I. Unifying Understanding in the Party on the Question of Agriculture

In order to speed up our agricultural development, it is essential for all comrades in the party to have a unified and correct understanding of the conditions prevailing in agriculture at present and of our past experience.

Since the founding of our People's Republic, the peasants in their millions and the large numbers of cadres, guided by Marxism-Leninism and Mao Zedong Thought, have worked hard and scored tremendous achievements. The socialist transformation of our agriculture has been a triumphant success. Grain output in 1978 showed a 2.7-fold increase over that in 1949, and cash crops, forestry, animal husbandry, side-line occupations, fisheries and enterprises run by the people's communes, production brigades and teams have all registered increases in output. Some areas have witnessed a striking expansion in agriculture. Many big, medium- and small-sized water conservancy projects have been completed throughout the country and large areas of farmland with stable high yields have been cultivated. There has been a considerable increase in the production of chemical fertilizers, farm machinery, drainage and irrigation machinery and electricity. However, our overall agricultural development has not progressed very rapidly in the last 20 years and is highly incompatible with the needs of the people and of the four modernizations. From 1957 to 1978, our population increased by 300 million and the number of people not engaged in agricultural production increased by 40 million, whereas the acreage of cultivated land decreased because, among other reasons, more land was used for capital construction purposes. Although there has been a rise both in per-*mu* and in total grain yields, the average amount of grain per capita throughout the country in 1978 was more or less the same as in 1957. The average annual income of our agricultural population per capita was no more than 70-odd yuan; in nearly a quarter of the production teams, the members' average income was less than 50 yuan. The collective accumulation funds of the production brigades averaged less than 10,000 yuan, and in some places things were so bad that it was hard to go on with simple reproduction. Without an acceleration in agricultural development, any increase in industrial production or other forms of construction will be out of the question, as will be the four modernizations. The vital and pressing nature of this question merits the close attention of our comrades throughout the party.

In the past 29 years, China has followed a tortuous course in the development of agriculture. During the three years of rehabilitation and the period of the First Five-Year Plan after Liberation, we carried out agrarian reform on a nationwide scale, won the great victory in the socialist transformation of our agriculture, embarked on large-scale construction of the socialist economy in an orderly manner, and developed agricultural production to a fairly considerable extent. In these eight years, grain yields increased at an average rate of 7% a year. In the drive to establish people's communes and in the great leap forward in 1958, the masses of the people were imbued with lofty revolutionary zeal; they overcame blind faith, emanicpated their minds and dared to think and act. Yet, at the end of the

1950's and the beginning of the 1960's, our agriculture suffered disastrous setbacks. Apart from natural calamities, annulment of contracts by the government of the Soviet Union and withdrawal of its experts, the reason for these setbacks lay in our lack of experience in giving nationwide leadership to collectivized, socialist agriculture and also in our failure to remain cool-headed, and thus the mistakes of giving arbitrary directions, being boastful and stirring up a "communist wind" were made. Under the leadership of the Central Committee of the Party and of Comrades Mao Zedong and Zhou Enlai and through the efforts by the entire party and the whole nation, we overcame the shortcomings and mistakes in our work and surmounted the difficulties in a relatively short period of time; as a result, agricultural production was rapidly rehabilitated and new developments were attained. During the ten years of the "cultural revolution," the counter-revolutionary, conspiratorial cliques of Lin Biao and the Gang of Four pushed an ultra-"Left" line, gravely undermining the various levels of the party organizations in the rural areas, the party's rural policies and its traditional fine style of work, disrupting the collective economy, and the worker-peasant alliance, and drastically checking the enthusiasm of the peasants and cadres. Nevertheless, thanks to resistance on the part of the cadres and masses to the perverse acts of Lin Biao and the Gang of Four, our agricultural production continued to increase to a certain extent in the 1970's.

Our 20 years of experience in agricultural development show us that, with the completion of socialist transformation, a correct appraisal of the class struggle should be made, correct policies adopted, and profound attention paid to maintaining political stability in our society; otherwise, the productive forces and the relations of production in socialist agriculture will be disrupted and rapid development in agriculture will be impossible. At the same time, we must do our work in accordance with natural and economic laws. In the past, in some specific aspects of our work, we failed to take agriculture as the foundation of the national economy, some of our policies and measures were unfavourable to the all-around development of farming, forestry, animal husbandry, side-line occupations and fisheries and to the promotion of the peasants' enthusiasm for socialist production, the state failed to give enough aid to agriculture or that aid failed to be efficiently utilized, technical transformation was not really grasped as a central task, scientific research and education in agriculture were not duly emphasized, and the principle of all-around development of farming, forestry, animal husbandry, side-line occupations and fisheries was not implemented satisfactorily. All this impaired rapid development in agriculture. Therefore, in order to accelerate rehabilitation and development in agriculture, we must bear in mind the major lessons derived from our experience as follows:

1. We must maintain long-term political stability and unity. Without this prerequisite, neither the modernization of agriculture nor the realization of the four modernizations by the end of the century will be possible. Since the smashing of the Gang of Four, there has been stability and unity throughout the country. This has not been won easily. We must cherish it, safeguard it and do everything in our power to promote the excellent situation.

2. We must correctly understand and handle the class struggle in the rural areas and in the country as a whole, correctly conduct socialist education among the peasants, guard against interference by "Left" or Right deviations and pay special attention to eliminating the pernicious influence of the ultra-"Left" line of Lin Biao and the Gang of Four. After the co-operative transformation of agriculture, class struggle still exists in the rural areas, although class enemies who are hostile to and who sabotage socialism constitute only a very tiny fraction of the entire population. Therefore, it is wrong either to neglect or exaggerate class struggle. We shall firmly discourage the disruptive activities engaged in by the handful of class enemies, whose existence is an objective fact; but it is absolutely impermissible to wilfully confuse the two different types of contradictions, arbitrarily exaggerate class struggle, or artificially create it so as to undermine unity and harm fine people. Long years of practice in struggle have proven that the masses of peasants in China firmly support the leadership of the party and are willing to take the socialist road. In the course of our endeavour to modernize agriculture, we should rely more firmly on their enthusiasm and give it fuller play. As to the spontaneous tendency towards capitalism found among a small number of peasants, it is imperative to use painstaking persuasion and education to help them overcome it of their own accord. Here it is essential to clarify, first and foremost, what socialism is and what capitalism is. The diversified production engaged in by the communes and production brigades constitutes part of the socialist sector of the economy, and the small plots of land planted by commune members for their personal needs and the limited number of livestock raised by them for the same purpose, household side-line occupations and village fairs are subordinate and supplemental to the socialist economy; they definitely cannot be re-

garded as a form of capitalist economics and must not be repudiated and outlawed as such. "To each according to his work" and "more pay for more work" constitute the socialist principle of distribution, which must not be opposed as a capitalist principle. The three-level system of ownership by the commune, the production brigade and the production team, with the production team as the basic accounting unit, is suitable to the present-day stage of development of the productive forces in our agriculture, and it is absolutely impermissible to alter it arbitrarily in order to effect a premature transition in ownership.

3. We must concentrate our efforts on technical transformation in agriculture to develop agriculture's productive forces. Technical transformation is to be accomplished on the basis of collectivization in agricultural production. This is the fundamental line of our party on the question of agriculture and must never be forgotten. If it is forgotten, the worker-peasant alliance will not be consolidated, nor will capitalism be defeated by socialism, and that will mean departure from the vital interests of the party and the people. We must attach importance to the fact that the expansion of capital construction in different aspects of agriculture (including the increase of water conservancy works, farmland, pastures, forestry, fishing grounds, livestock sheds, fodder processing centres, slaughterhouses, storehouses, grain-drying grounds, roads, methane-generating pits and other natural resources) and the expansion of the commune- and brigade-run enterprises in the rural areas have played a remarkable role in transforming natural conditions in agricultural production and in increasing the material capacity of the peasants for expanded reproduction.

4. We must implement the party's rural policies for the present stage in a sustained and steady way. On no account must we make random changes in the policies that have been proved to be effective in practice, lest we thus lose the people's confidence and dampen the peasants' enthusiasm. However, we must resolutely alter and set right erroneous policies that are not conducive to promoting the peasants' enthusiasm for production and to developing the productive forces in agriculture.

5. We must steadfastly adhere to the policy of taking agriculture as the foundation. The Central Committee of the Party, the State Council and the various ministries and commissions in charge of economic work must pay special attention to ensuring effective implementation of this policy. In formulating plans for the national economy, they must truly abide by the order of priorities in which agriculture is primary, followed by light industry and heavy industry, and they must maintain the balance between agriculture and industry, first taking into consideration whether agriculture can bear the burden for additional construction projects. The state and the municipalities, the departments of industry and communications, trade and finance, science and technology, culture, education and public health, and the People's Liberation Army must increase their material and technical assistance to agriculture.

6. We must correctly and comprehensively carry out the policies of "simultaneous development of farming, forestry, animal husbandry, side-line occupations and fisheries" and "taking grain as the key link, ensuring all-around development, suiting measures to local conditions and appropriately concentrating on specialized planting." Close attention must be given to grain production since it has a direct bearing on the livelihood of our 900 million people and on our preparedness against war and natural calamities. We were correct in going all out to promote grain production in the past, but in so doing we neglected and thus hindered production in cash crops, forestry, animal husbandry and fisheries, and failed to pay attention to maintaining the ecological balance. This has been a tremendous lesson to us. We must make the best use of favourable natural conditions in our country and fully tap the potential in all fields, so as to bring about large-scale growth in farming, forestry, animal husbandry, side-line occupations and fisheries. In the light of the special features of different localities, appropriate efforts should be made to increase the production of food grains and cash crops. A gradual and planned change should be effected in the present structuring of our agriculture and in our people's diet, and we should correct the emphasis on planting food grains to the neglect of production in cash crops, forestry, animal husbandry, side-line occupations and fisheries.

7. In guiding agricultural production, we must proceed from reality, act in accordance with natural and economic laws, and bear in mind the interests of the masses. We must firmly persist in the principle of running the people's communes democratically and respect and protect the democratic rights of the commune members. There must be no abuse of the right to issue administrative orders, nor must there be the delivering of arbitrary directions; and complex situations are not to be dealt with in a sweeping manner.

By smashing the Gang of Four, we removed the biggest obstacle on our march forward. We are in a position to make full use of all favourable conditions and we are confident that we shall succeed in speeding up the development of our agriculture. Ours is the superior socialist system; we are rich in natural resources and have 800 million courageous and industrious peasants and a large contingent of long-tempered rural cadres, agricultural scientists and technicians. A relatively solid foundation has been laid for our industry, which will gradually be able to provide our agriculture with modern technology. In addition to 1.5 billion *mu* of cultivated land, we have wide stretches of wasteland, grassland, forest and mountain areas which are suitable for afforestation and grazing. We also have large bodies of fresh water and seas which are suitable for aquatic production. In short, there are amply favourable conditions for agricultural development. As long as we persist in the socialist road, the dictatorship of the proletariat, the party's leadership and Marxism-Leninism and Mao Zedong Thought, and as long as we are truly good at summing up both the positive and negative experience of the past, always adhere to the ideological line of dialectical materialism, uphold the Marxist principle of taking practice as the sole criterion for testing truth, continue to study new problems and sum up new experience, we shall certainly be able to mobilize all positive factors and realize the great goal of modernizing our agriculture by the turn of the century.

II. Twenty-Five Policies and Measures for Developing the Productive Forces in Agriculture at Present

In order to effect a rapid change in the backwardness of our agriculture, we must focus on implementing a series of policies and measures in the coming two or three years; policies and measures for accelerating agricultural development, lightening the burden of the peasants, and increasing their income. On this basis we shall gradually modernize our agriculture.

In formulating our agricultural and rural economic policies, our starting point is to bring into full play the superiority of our socialist system and the enthusiasm shared by our 800 million peasants. While strengthening ideological education in socialism among the peasants, we must show concern for them, both economically and politically, by protecting their material interests and guaranteeing their democratic rights. Enthusiasm on the part of any social class cannot rise of its own accord without ensuring certain material interests and political rights. Whether or not any of our policies meet the needs of the development of the productive force will be determined by whether they serve to mobilize the working people's enthusiasm in production. The state, however, must also give more effective material and technical assistance to agriculture, provide it with advanced techniques and gradually raise the peasants' mastery of science and technology. Without such assistance and with sole reliance on the peasants' own material strength and enthusiasm, rapid development in agriculture will be impossible, as will modernization. Only when the state provides agriculture with more assistance will the peasants' enthusiasm rise; and only when the peasants' enthusiasm is fully aroused will assistance from the state yield better results. The two sides of the matter are complementary.

With the foregoing as a guideline, the Central Committee holds that the following 25 recommendations on policies for agriculture, economic policies for the rural areas and measures for increasing production must be adopted:

1. The ownership rights and decision-making power of the people's communes, production brigades and production teams must be effectively protected by the laws of the state, and no unit or individual shall deprive them of their interests or encroach upon them at will. Provided that it persists in the socialist orientation, carries out state policies, laws and decrees and accepts the guidelines of state plans, the basic accounting unit of a people's commune has the power to decide on the kinds of crops that shall be planted in the light of local conditions in different seasons, on the measures for increasing production and on ways of operation and management; it has the power to distribute its products and earnings in cash and the right to reject arbitrary directions issued by any leading organs or individuals.

2. No unit or individual is permitted to requisition or take possession of a production team's labour power, farmland, livestock, machines, funds, products or other materials. No enterprise or establishment run by a department of the state in the rural areas (excluding those set up by the peasants of their own free will) is permitted to increase the burden of the collective or of any individual member, except in cases stipulated by state laws and decrees. The principle of voluntary participation and mutual benefit must be upheld in carrying out capital construction in agriculture and in expanding enterprises run by the communes, production brigades or production teams. No unit is permitted to transfer labour power out of the communes, production brigades or production teams, except as in accordance with state plans; a contract, specifying rational terms for payment,

must be signed with contracted-for or temporary workers transferred in accordance with state plans.

3. The economic organizations at different levels in the people's communes must conscientiously carry out the distribution principle of "from each according to his ability, to each according to his work," "more pay for more work, less pay for less work," and "equal pay for equal work" irrespective of sex. There must be stricter control over production quotas, work should be paid according to the quantity and quality of products, a requisite system of rewards and penalties must be formulated, and egalitarianism must be overcome resolutely. Workpoints should be calculated on the basis of the fulfilment of fixed quotas or on a time-rate basis plus appraisal. On the premise of unified accounting and distribution at the production team level, it is also possible for quotas to be assigned to a production group and for payment to be worked out according to output of production, with rewards offered for overfulfilled quotas. No land shall be redistributed for individual farming. No output quotas shall be fixed on a household basis, except in certain cases in order to meet special requirements in side-line production or in outlying mountain areas where there are scattered, solitary households and where communication is inconvenient. Generally speaking, the amount of grain distributed to a commune member is fixed in accordance with the amount allotted for his or her workpoints in addition to the basic ration, or that which is allotted as preferential consideration. Another method is for distributed quantities to be decided upon by the majority of the commune members. The basic grain ration per member is fixed according to age groups. With the expansion of the collective economy, improvements must be made in the running of collective welfare undertakings, so that the livelihood of the old and the weak, the childless, and widowers, widows, orphans, members with disabilities, disabled demobilized armymen and the families of revolutionary martyrs and armymen will be better ensured.

4. The farming of small plots of land and the keeping of a limited number of livestock for commune members' personal needs, household side-line occupations and village fairs constitute an appendage of the socialist economy and supplement it, and must not be repudiated as vestiges of capitalism. On the contrary, while consolidation and expansion of the collective economy must be guaranteed, the peasants should be encouraged and supported to engage in household side-line occupations so as to increase their personal income and invigorate the rural economy.

5. The people's communes must continue to adhere steadily to the three-level system of ownership, that is, ownership by the commune, the production brigade and the production team, with the production team as the basic accounting unit, and concentrate their efforts on developing the productive forces in the rural areas. The basic accounting unit shall not be changed from the production team to the production brigade before conditions are ripe and the majority of the members agree; even when conditions are ripe and the vast majority of the members agree, the change shall not be made until approval by a leading organ at the provincial level is obtained. Where a production brigade is already the basic accounting unit and is able to manage as such, further efforts should be made to ensure its success.

6. In the next three to five years, investments by the state in agriculture will gradually rise to about 18% of its total investment in capital construction; expenditures for financing agricultural undertakings and assisting communes, production brigades and teams will gradually rise to about 8% of total state expenditures. Local financial revenues should go mainly to agriculture and those industries that serve agriculture.

7. From now until 1985, loans granted to agriculture will amount to more than twice as much as in the past. The state will provide, in a planned way, long-term loans for special purposes at low or very little interest, some of which may be repaid in 10 years, some in 15 years and others at the turn of the century. To meet the needs of developing the credit business in rural areas, the Agricultural Bank of China should do a good job of providing credit in the countryside.

8. From the time when the summer grain comes on the market in 1979, state purchase prices for grain will be raised by 20%, and the price of grain purchased in excess of quotas will be raised by 50% over the new prices. The purchase price for cotton, edible oils, sugar cane, livestock, aquatic and forest products will be raised correspondingly, step by step, according to the merits of each kind of product. On the basis of reduced production costs, wholesale and retail prices for manufactured products for agricultural use, such as farm machinery, chemical fertilizers, agricultural pesticides and plastics will gradually be lowered, with the peasants mainly benefitting from the reduced production costs. After state purchase prices for agricultural products have been raised, the sales price of grain to the consumer will remain unchanged; the sales prices of other agricultural products needed by the masses must be kept more

or less stable; and appropriate subsidies must be granted to the consumer in instances where the prices of some products must be increased. In the future, we shall continue to make necessary readjustments in the price parities between industrial and agricultural products in light of the development of the national economy and in accordance with the principle of exchange at equal value.

9. For a fairly long time to come, the total annual purchase quota of grain will be kept at the figure set for the five-year period from 1971 through 1975, and will even be reduced by 5 billion catties from 1979 onward so as to lighten the burden of the peasants and to spur production. No grain will be purchased by the state in those rice-planting areas where the grain ration per capita is less than 400 catties and in areas where food grains other than wheat and rice are planted and where the grain ration is less than 300 catties. In no case shall the purchase quota be increased.

10. While adapting measures to local conditions, firm and vigorous efforts must be kept up to do a good job of agricultural capital construction, which is indispensible for production, storing, transportation and processing in farming, forestry, animal husbandry, side-line occupations and fishing. The agricultural areas which chiefly produce food grains should continue to focus on water control and soil improvement; should go all out to plant trees and grass; should tackle problems relating to the utilization of mountains, rivers, farmland, forests and roads in an all-round way; and should actively and gradually change production conditions, enhance their ability to combat natural calamities, and increase the acreage of farmland with guaranteed stable and high yields irrespective of drought or water-logging. In the light of local conditions in different seasons, overall consideration should be given to production in cash crops, forestry, animal husbandry, side-line occupations and fisheries. By 1985, there should be a relatively noticeable increase in the total area of irrigated land and of farmland with stable and high yields all over the country. While the state will continue to build a number of key, large-scale water conservancy projects, the main task of the localities is to build medium- and small-sized conservancy projects and conveyance systems, thus combining the construction of large-, medium- and small-sized projects and integrating the efforts of specialized teams and the masses. Stress must be placed on actual results and quality must be guaranteed. Formalism should be eschewed. In all agricultural capital construction projects, the masses must be fully mobilized to conduct democratic discussions and, in accordance with actual local conditions, comprehensive arrangements should be made and long-term plans worked out to be put into effect step by step. Capital construction and production should be considered comprehensively.

11. While making full use of available cultivated land, the state farms and people's communes should begin, where possible, to open up wasteland in a planned way. For the first five years, no purchase quota will be set for harvests gathered from newly-cultivated land by the people's communes, production brigades, or production teams. In the process of land reclamation, no forests, grasslands or water conservancy works are to be destroyed, neither shall flood water storage or release projects be hindered. Where possible, dykes can be built to reclaim land from the sea for planting, on condition that this will not affect or disrupt the production of sea salt. This does not apply to inland lakes or inshore areas which are better suited to aquatic or other products. Factories, mines and enterprises should make a conscientious effort to solve the problem of pollution, so as to prevent contamination of water, air and other natural resources, and damage to agriculture. No government offices, people's organizations, army units, enterprises or schools are permitted to appropriate at will farmland, pastures and forest land belonging to the people's communes and the state farms. Where capital construction projects must be carried out, it is still necessary to economize strictly on the use of land and most advisable to use little or no cultivated land at all. The Land Law should be adopted and promulgated as soon as possible.

12. Efforts must be made to operate the state farms well, so that they will provide the state with more commodity grain, cash crops and other farm and side-line products. The state farms that still show a deficit must make a change in the situation and start to earn profits within a time limit. The staff and workers of the farms that have been successful and have earned profits may increase their personal incomes. State farms are not required to turn over their profits to the state before 1985, but can use them to expand reproduction, diversify the economy, build processing centres for farm and livestock products, expand trade for the sale of their own products, and thus move as quickly as possible towards becoming integrated agricultural-industrial-commercial complexes. In this way they will play an exemplary role in the modernization of agriculture.

13. While guaranteeing quality, the production of chemical fertilizers, agricultural pesticides and plastics, and various kinds of weed killers must

be rapidly increased. Large quantities of farm manure must be stored, more green-manure crops planted, more beancake fertilizer and other organic fertilizers made, and more stalks returned to the fields after threshing. In increasing the production of chemical fertilizers, attention should be paid to keeping nitrogen, potassium and phosphorus in rational proportion. The production of different kinds of agricultural chemicals, weed killers and plastic materials for agricultural use should be increased by a large margin. It is necessary in order to popularize the scientific application of fertilizers and pesticides, make the best use of them and, at the same time, conscientiously work out effective ways of preventing and treating the pollution of crops, water and the environment that might result from their use. Active efforts should also be made to spread the use of biological controls.

14. Seed selection and breeding must be carried out, and improved varieties introduced and disseminated. The seed-breeding fields of production brigades and teams along with the seed multiplication farms of the counties and people's communes should continue to be run well and, at the same time, seed-producing bases at the provincial, prefectural and county levels should be set up — so that seed production can gradually become specialized, processing mechanized and quality standardized — so that plant varieties can be allocated to specified areas. A sound operational system for seed corporations should be set up; adequate rules and regulations should be drawn up for examining and approving varieties of seed, multiplying and popularizing fine strains, and for operational management, testing of seeds, and preventing degeneration and hybridization of seeds. The Seed Law should be adopted and promulgated at an early date. Prices for fine strains should be set according to their quality, so as to ensure increased production of grain.

15. Mechanization should be promoted in farming, forestry, animal husbandry, side-line production and fishing in the light of local conditions, and there should be more mechanized stock raising. Active efforts should be made to manufacture machines needed by agriculture for transportation, loading and unloading. We should carry out readjustment, restructuring, consolidation and improvement in the manufacture of farm machines, improve the quality of products, reduce production costs, gradually bring about standardization, serialization and interchangeability of machine parts, and conscientiously facilitate the supply of complete sets of farm machines and of spare parts for farm tools. The problem of supplying accessories and spare parts for farm machines and tools must be solved within the next two or three years. The efficiency of existing farm machines will thus be greatly raised.

From now on, the main parts, accessories and spare parts of farm machines must be manufactured in a proportionate way. The Ministry of Farm Machine-Building should do a good job of unifying administration of scientific studies relating to farm machines, their design and manufacture, operation and management, maintenance and repair, supply and marketing, and also of the training of personnel and so on and so forth. There are two ways to set up tractor stations: 1. The people's communes, production brigades or teams can buy their own tractors for their stations, and those that are short of funds can apply for state loans; 2. The state can set up stations to provide tractors to the communes, production brigades or teams at a reasonable fee. The first way is considered preferable.

16. While stepping up the production of grain, conscientious efforts should be made to produce cotton, edible oils, sugar and other cash crops, to develop forestry, animal husbandry, sideline production and fisheries, and to promote their simultaneous development. All positive factors should be fully mobilized and all resources that can be brought into use should be gradually exploited and utilized for the flourishing of our rural economy as a whole.

17. Energetically go in for afforestation and try to ensure a high survival rate. We should focus on building a shelter belt from the Northwest to the Northeast, create networks of farmland skirted by trees and plant trees around every house and village, by roadsides and watersides in North China, the Central Plains and the Northeast. Among other key projects, quick-growing trees that can be used for timber should be planted in the ten provinces south of the Changjiang (Yangtse) River, cash forest regions should be established both in the north and south, and the old forest areas in the Northeast should be reforested. All localities should act realistically and should work out feasible plans to afforest wasteland and barren hills within a given time limit. Efforts should be made to adopt advanced techniques, make comprehensive use of lumber resources and fell trees in a rational way. Improved seedlings should be actively cultivated, introduced and popularized, and stress should be placed on planting more oil-bearing and edible fruit trees. We should conscientiously abide by the Forest Law and effectively protect the forests, strictly forbid arbitrary cutting and felling of trees, resolutely correct the

practice of felling trees without reforesting, and take strict precautions against forest fires.

18. Go all out to develop animal husbandry and increase its role in agricultural production. Special attention should be paid to the raising of herbivorous animals such as cattle, sheep and rabbits. In animal husbandry, importance should be attached not simply to numbers of livestock bred and kept, but to increasing the numbers immediately available for slaughter and the amount of meat produced. We should continue to encourage commune members to raise pigs, cattle and sheep on a household basis and actively increase the number of collectively-raised pigs, cattle and sheep. We should improve livestock breeds, redouble efforts to improve the condition of pastures, grass hills and slopes in agricultural regions, build water conservancy works, improve grass seeds, make rational use of pastures, adopt rotation grazing and expand grazing capacity. We should do a good job in preventing animal diseases. The Pasture Law should be promulgated as soon as possible. It is essential to establish a number of modernized livestock and poultry farms in the livestock-raising areas and in the suburbs of large and medium-sized cities in a planned way and to build a number of modernized slaughterhouses, cold storage plants and processing plants for animal products.

19. Make rational use of aquatic product resources; rapidly increase fishery production and the output of aquatic products. We should fully utilize and exploit waters and seacoasts and go all out to develop the breeding of freshwater and seawater animals and plants, such as fish, shrimps and prawns, shellfish, frogs, kelp and laver, and steadily expand artificial breeding areas. It is necessary for specialized institutions and personnel to take charge of making practical arrangements for investigation and utilization of resources, and of providing financial and material assistance, technical guidance and product processing, so as to ensure rapid growth in breeding different kinds of fish. Effective readjustments should be made with regard to inshore fishing and to opening up midsea fishing grounds. The Regulations for Reproduction and Protection of Aquatic Resources should be carried out, and the Fishery Law should be promulgated as soon as possible in order to strengthen administration and management of fisheries. We should adopt advanced techniques and equipment to promote modernized fishing, breeding, processing, storage and transportation in fisheries. A number of fishing grounds should gradually be built up. Great efforts should be made to develop breeding of various kinds of aquatic animals in the suburbs of cities; centres for fish and shrimp breeding can be set up where conditions permit.

20. There should be a major expansion of the enterprises run by the communes, production brigades and teams, so that earnings from the enterprises will constitute a gradually increasing proportion of the total income of the three-level economy. The processing of farm and side-line products should gradually be taken up by these enterprises in those rural areas where it is suitable, economical and rational. Where feasible, urban factories should transfer part of the processing of products and spare parts to rural enterprises in a planned way, providing them with equipment and technical guidance. In keeping with the economic plans made at various levels, different methods should be developed to facilitate the production, supply and marketing of products by these enterprises, to ensure smooth supply and marketing. As regards these enterprises, the state should pursue a policy of reducing or remitting taxes, as conditions may dictate.

21. In commerce, the principle of exchange of equal values must be conscientiously applied to facilitate interflow of commodities between town and country. When purchasing farm and side-line products from the rural areas, prices should be fixed according to quality; it is strictly forbidden for buyers to force down grades and prices for goods. The means of production and of subsistence needed in the rural areas must be supplied in time, with quality guaranteed and at reasonable prices. Contracts must be signed for purchasing grain, cotton, edible oils and other commodities subject to unified purchase, and for unified, allotted or negotiated purchasing of other farm and side-line products. Contracts must be respected. There shall be no resorting to coercion or commandism.

22. It is imperative to make an effort to turn out more agricultural products for export. The state has decided to allocate a certain amount of foreign currency specifically for the purpose of assisting the provinces, municipalities and autonomous regions to expand production of cash crops and special local products, animal husbandry, side-line production and fisheries, to build corresponding processing industries, and, under unified state plans, to turn out products which will find a good market abroad and bring quick returns and earn foreign exchange. Specific measures will be worked out by the State Planning Commission together with the departments concerned.

23. Parts of the northwest and southwest, some old revolutionary base areas, outlying mountain areas, minority nationality regions and frontier areas have long been low-yield, grain-deficient areas where the population is impoverished. The slow speed of development in production in these areas presents not only an economic problem, but also a political one. The State Council is going to set up a special commission, composed of responsible comrades from relevant departments, to formulate an overall plan and to organize forces to focus on providing these areas with financial, material and technical assistance, and to help them to increase production and lift themselves out of poverty. The commission will also help poor communes, production brigades and teams to bring about a change as quickly as possible. Impoverished production brigades and teams must guarantee to use state allotted funds for production and cosntruction.

24. Resolute efforts must continue to be made to practice family planning; conscientious propaganda and education must be conducted for this purpose; arbitrary and unsuitable methods must be corrected; and medicare services and medicinal supplies must be ensured. It is imperative to adopt more effective policies and measures, and chiefly economic measures, to bring down the population growth rate over the years; it is expected to drop to 0.5% by 1985.

25. Protecting and mobilizing the initiative of the large numbers of cadres at the grassroots level in the rural areas is vital to accelerating agricultural development. The overwhelming majority of rural cadres are good or fairly good. They live together with the masses all year around, braving the elements and working hard without complaint, and they have made magnificent contributions to our agriculture. Towards those cadres who have made mistakes, except for a handful of bad elements, it is absolutely necessary to rely on education to help them correct their mistakes and to continue to make progress. Many mistakes made by cadres at the grassroots can be attributed to authorities at higher levels or to the central authorities who set tasks and drew up policies that were unsuitable or inexplicit. Efforts must be redoubled to examine and redress the wrongs done to cadres at the grassroots level in past political movements. Salary and welfare problems of commune cadres and agricultural technicians should be gradually and appropriately solved. The income of chief production brigade cadres should be a bit higher in labour capacity than that of their peers. Those cadres who are successful in work should be commended and rewarded. Specific plans should be made for their training and education in politics, culture, management and special skills. All cadres at the commune, brigade and production-team levels must be elected at regular intervals at congresses of the commune members or at general meetings of the commune members and they must put themselves under constant supervision by the masses. The various kinds of economic accounts should be published regularly. Democratic management should be upheld in running the communes, production brigades and teams, the cadres should carry forward a democratic style of work, and they should persist in taking part in collective productive labour. It is not advisable to change cadres too often.

The Party Committees at all levels should continue to guide the large numbers of cadres and peasants in learning from the basic experience of Dazhai, that is, in adhering to the principle of putting politics in command and placing Mao Zedong Thought in the lead, to the spirit of self-reliance and hard struggle and to the communist style of loving the country and the collective. At the same time, they must firmly carry out the party's policies for agriculture and the rural economy, learn from successful domestic and foreign experience, exert themselves to master advanced sciences and technology, and learn how to run modern agriculture on a large scale. Our cause is forging ahead with each passing day, a large number of advanced units have emerged in the Learn-from-Dazhai Campaign, and new ones will continue to emerge, one after another. Dazhai Brigade and other advanced units throughout the country should take an analytical approach towards themselves, and do their best to achieve new successes, acquire new experience, and make new contributions to the acceleration of the development of agriculture in China.

III. Arrangements for the Modernization of Agriculture

The overall modernization of agriculture and thorough transformation of China's rural areas is a revolution of unprecedented scale. In order to attain this goal we must proceed from existing conditions: our large population, limited arable land, weak foundation and low scientific and cultural levels — but vast territory, relatively rich natural resources and great labour reserves. We must earnestly sum up our own experience, modestly learn from the advanced experience of foreign countries, avoid insofar as possible the evils which have cropped up in the technically advanced countries, and follow a course of agricultural modernization suitable to our own national circumstances. While conscientiously implementing the 25 policies and measures outlined above. we must continue to investigate and study, to carefully work out a plan for realizing agricultural modernization stage by stage and step by step and to resolutely work out arrangements for solving problems once a definite understanding of them is arrived at, all the while organizing our various forces and doing down-to-earth work so as to guarantee success.

1. The modernization of agriculture urgently requires that we arm our rural cadres and agro-technical personnel with modern scientific and technical knowledge, that we have a large contingent of specialists who understand modern agricultural science and technology, an enormous scientific and technical agricultural army, and sufficient numbers of good agricultural colleges and schools to train agro-technical and management personnel. At the same time, it requires that we greatly raise the scientific, technical and cultural levels of the entire peasantry, first and foremost the young peasants. These tasks will require several years — even a dozen or more years — to complete, and we must begin to take them firmly in hand right now, and not relax our efforts even for a moment. We must thoroughly correct the mistaken view that agricultural modernization can get along without the most modern scientific research and education, that agro-science research organs and advanced agricultural schools are optional, and that agricultural development can do without the active participation of specialists — and we must quickly restore and strengthen the research and educational conditions which they require. We must organize the scientific and technical forces of the entire nation to study and solve the scientific and technical problems involved in agricultural modernization. The central organs must do a good job of running key higher-level agro-science research institutes and higher agriculture schools such as the Chinese Academy of Agricultural Science and the Beijing Agricultural University and, on the basis of the plans of different agricultural regions, the various provinces, municipalities and autonomous regions must set up and operate a group of agro-science research organs, institutes and agro-technical secondary schools so as to gradually form a comprehensive, rationally-distributed agro-science research system. At the same time, we must work conscientiously to strengthen technical popularization. The agro-science experimentation network encompassing counties, communes, brigades and teams is our network for agro-technical promotion, and from the county on down we should do a good job with experimentation, demonstration, popularization and technical training. We should lay down plans as quickly as possible and set about training county, commune and brigade cadres by rotation, and urgently-required agricultural equipment operators, agro-technicians and financial and accounting personnel. Over the next few years, virtually all cadres should undergo a stint of training and every commune and brigade should acquire sufficient numbers of qualified machinery operators, agro-technicians and financial and accounting personnel. Educated youth who are posted to, or return to, the countryside all have a certain cultural level and some practical experience and should be encouraged to engage in farming. According to their different levels and circumstances, they should be accepted for study at agricultural institutes, agro-technical secondary schools or various kinds of training classes, and efforts should be made to train them into a backbone force for large-scale agricultural modernization.

2. In order to modernize agriculture, we must actively push agricultural mechanization forward in a planned way. Agricultural mechanization must conform to the needs of production and be premised on realities. We should bring in, manufacture and popularize advanced agricultural machinery suited to China's particular conditions, run parts and repair services properly, and give full play to the potential of agricultural equipment so as to raise labour productivity by a wide margin. On the basis of available resources, we should strive to set up small rural hydro-electric and thermal power stations. We should popularize the use of marsh gas. Each region, depending on local conditions, should determine the steps and concrete requirements of popularization, include it in their plans for agricultural capital construction, allot the necessary funds, provide the necessary materials, and organize technical training. We should actively utilize wind and solar energy and adopt every practicable measure for expanding energy resources to serve agriculture. Taking local conditions into account, we should develop water conservancy and grassland irrigation and, differentiating between north and south, mountain and plain, paddy field and dry farmland, bring in water, store it, or pump it up where possible, and systematically develop sprinkler irrigation, so as to realize an irrigated agriculture — one in which we can freely increase or reduce the amount of water and thus achieve high and stable yields. We must speed up production of agriculture-related chemical products, and steadily provide our agricultural sector with chemical fertilizers, pesticides, plastic sheeting, herbicides and other products of fine quality and wide variety and at reasonable prices,

so as to facilitate the rapid development of agriculture. In light of the needs of agricultural modernization, the ministries of Agriculture, Forestry, State Farms and Land Reclamation, Agricultural Machinery, Water Conservancy, Power Industry and Chemical Industry should co-operate closely and, during 1980, should work out their own, all-around, long-term plans for modernizing agriculture and workable annual implementation schedules — and then apply themselves to implementing them.

3. To modernize agriculture, agricultural production as a whole must be rationally arranged, and we must progressively implement regionalization and specialization, continuously raising the level of socialization of agricultural production. If we don't do this, it won't be possible to carry out large-scale, all-around mechanization or to adopt advanced science and technology comprehensively and on an extensive scale. At the same time, we must ensure the balanced development of farming, forestry and animal husbandry, with different regions engaging in these activities as local natural conditions permit or, taking one as primary, pursuing a diversified economy. The relevant departments under the State Council and the various regions should organize their forces to complete, within three years, nationwide investigations into natural resources and natural conditions of soil, climate and so on, and into social conditions such as population, transport and communications, industry, commerce, science and education. On this basis they can put their heads together with peasants and rural cadres rich in local experience and work out plans for the progressive implementation of regional specialization varying in scope and magnitude, and make plans which coordinate farming, forestry, animal husbandry, fisheries, industry, side-line production, local and external trade, transport and communications, scientific education, and finance. On the basis of carefully worked out plans, we should also run experiments in a down-to-earth manner, sum up experiences, and advance in an orderly and step-by-step way.

4. State agricultural investment must be concentrated in the construction of a number of bases for producing marketable grain, cash crops, livestock, fish and forest products. These bases may be expanded versions of present state-run agricultural enterprises; they may be new state or collective farms set up in virgin territories; or they may be set up as joint enterprises by the people's communes. They should all acquire advanced equipment and adopt scientific methods in production and management step by step, and become large, modern agricultural enterprises with high labour productivity and a high degree of commodity production. In addition to agriculture, some of these bases should go in for processing and marketing farm and side-line products, and should gradually develop into integrated agricultural-industrial-commercial complexes. Agricultural and forestry departments and relevant scientific and technical research institutions should establish close relations with these bases, co-operate with them, and help improve their production technology. A group of such bases will provide a more reliable guarantee for the supply to the state of required commodity grains, cotton, oil and sugar crops, fruit, animal, marine and forest products. The development of commodity agricultural bases is an important strategic measure for building a large-scale, modern, socialist agriculture, and we must concentrate the necessary state funds and do our utmost to run them well.

5. Agricultural modernization can't do without modern industry or transport and communications for a single instant. Basing ourselves on the characteristics of China's agriculture and on the demands of modernization and on the different conditions and production requirements of the various regions, within two or three years we must make overall arrangements and, while adhering to the principle of co-operative specialization, organize a rational national distribution of agriculture-related industry. We should see that various kinds of agricultural machinery and various kinds of agriculture-related chemical products are put into economically rational mass production, that their quality is continuously raised and that their costs are lowered. In the light of actual needs, each of the departments concerned, such as the ministries of Agricultural Machinery and Chemical Industry, should set up a number of specialized companies with strong management and attention to economic results; and effectively promote agriculture-related industry. The Ministry of Agricultural Machinery should orient itself toward the rural grassroots and, taking into consideration the needs of different economic zones, set up and flesh out agricultural mechanization service companies which progressively unify the management of provisioning, repair, rental and recall of agricultural machinery and various kinds of agriculture-related chemical products, and the management of technical training and application services, thereby offering convenient and timely service, and reducing commune and brigade expenditures. As for transport and communications, we should strive to build highways linking cities, towns and communes so that by 1985 it is generally possible to get from one county to another and from com-

mune to commune by motor vehicle. At the same time, we should strengthen the construction of communications links in herding, forest and fishing regions.

6. We must strive to establish modern agricultural and animal product processing industries based on principles of economic rationality – industries which meet the needs of and promote agricultural modernization. Such processing industries must be established in areas where production is concentrated, for the convenience of utilizing the products and resources of those areas and going as far as possible in comprehensive utilization. What is more, they must be in keeping with the transportation and communications conditions of these regions, be rationally distributed, and facilitate the commerce and supply requirements of both city and countryside. Only then will they be fully efficient economically. The ministries of Agriculture, State Farms and Land Reclamation, Light Industry, Textile Industry and Commerce, and the Federation of Supply and Marketing Co-operatives, together with other departments concerned under the State Council, should, through earnest discussions with the provinces, municipalities and autonomous regions, lay down development plans for this purpose as quickly as possible.

7. We must develop the construction of small towns in a planned way and must strengthen support for the countryside by the cities. This is the path we must take in order to hasten the modernization of agriculture and the four modernizations generally, and to gradually reduce the differences between town and country and between worker and peasant. At present, China has 800 million people in the countryside, 300 million of them agricultural labourers. With the advance of agricultural modernization, a great amount of agricultural labour power is bound to be saved. The labourers involved cannot and need not all enter the existing large and medium-sized cities, and neither can or should all our industrial and other construction undertakings be located in these cities. We must pay full attention to strengthening the construction of small towns and gradually build them up as advanced centres with modern industry and communications, modern commerce and services, modern educational, scientific, cultural and sanitation undertakings, centres for transforming the appearance of the entire countryside. First and foremost, stress should be placed on the planning for step-by-step construction of the more than 2,000 county towns and the economically more developed sub-county market towns and commune seats, based on the needs and possibilities of economic development. The strengths of the existing big cities can also be utilized in the construction of some satellite towns in the surrounding countryside and in increased support for agriculture generally. Beijing, Shanghai, Tianjin, Shenyang, Wuhan, and all other cities strong enough to follow this course should, under the unified leadership of local party committees, take responsibility for helping several counties in their agricultural modernization.

8. In order to realize the modernization of agriculture, we must adhere to the general policy of concentrating our strength to fight wars of annihilation, going ahead piece by piece, a bit at a time. This is to say we should proceed in a wave-like advance and not take on everything at once. There should be unified management and employment of agricultural machines of which there should be complete sets; funds and materials allotted to agriculture must be used for key projects; only thus will it be possible to get maximum effects. Places where necessary conditions exist can go ahead first and procure more machines. For production to increase significantly and for peasant incomes to rise rapidly in places which go ahead first isn't a bad thing, but a good one; it can play a great demonstrative and motivational role for the entire country. In the first few years, if we concentrate on doing a good job in regions with, say, 5% of the national population, that would mean the raising of the incomes of more than 40 million people first; that is equivalent to a relatively large country in world terms, and domestically it would mean a great expansion in the internal market – it would be a remarkable achievement and of great encouragement to the whole of the 800 million peasants.

The Central Committee holds that agricultural modernization is an entirely new undertaking for us, and the above points cannot yet be said to be completely mature views, but are to be supplemented, corrected and perfected in the course of practice. The Central Committee hopes that party committees and governments at the various levels, and especially the agricultural departments and masses of rural cadres and workers in agricultural science, technology and education, will continue to immerse themselves in reality, will conscientiously carry on investigation and research, and will exert themselves even more practically and effectively to push forward the great cause of agricultural modernization.

IV. Strengthen Party and Government

The rapid development of agricultural production and the active construction of an extensively modernized agriculture is a grand undertaking involving the entire party and people. The whole party and nation must be mobilized to put their all into agriculture. Party committees and governments at the various levels, from the centre to the localities, must all give priority to agricultural work, make the modernization of agriculture an important goal of long-term struggle, conscientiously strengthen their leadership, and lead an enormous and mighty army into this great, unprecedented battle.

For a long time in their direction and management of agriculture, some party committees, government organs, and departments concerned with agricultural work have been accustomed to rely solely on the issuing of administrative orders with general measures, indiscriminately demanding that subordinate levels down to the rural communes and brigades carry them out. Since this approach is divorced both from reality and from the masses, things often turn out contrary to their intentions, blunting the enthusiasm of the masses, causing losses in agricultural production and construction, and jeopardizing the liveliness and development of the rural economy. We must strive to change this.

Party committees at the various levels must pay close attention to the implementation of the party's line, principles and policies, and take firm hold of the major policies of rapidly developing agriculture and gradually realizing its modernization. They must strengthen the building of rural party branches and give play to the exemplary leading role of party members. At the same time, they must conscientiously carry out ideological and political work among the masses of cadres and peasants and do a good job of linking political with economic work so as to guarantee the smooth fulfilment of the various production and construction tasks. In the concrete operations of agricultural production and construction, they should give full play to the functions of the professional organs at different levels, letting them go about their work independently and responsibly; party committees should not concern themselves with everything or try to run everything. If the party committees get immersed in detailed professional matters, they will neglect party affairs and begin to replace governments; then not only will government departments and agricultural enterprises and operations have no way to carry on planned and orderly work with defined jobs, powers and responsibilities, but the party's leadership will also certainly be weakened, even to the point of losing its leading function.

In managing agriculture, state administrative departments should act independently and responsibly and must undertake a whole series of tasks successfully; for example, the planning of production and construction of a national or regional character; the control of major water systems and the construction of large- and medium-scale water conservancy projects; the construction of bases for commodity grains, cash crops, livestock and fisheries production; the construction of key forest regions and pasturelands; the research, planning and implementation of practical mechanization for agricultural modernization; investigation into natural resources and soil conditions and the planning of their utilization and transformation; research into and promotion of agro-science and technology; planning and conduct of agricultural education; the correct utilization and distribution of agricultural funds and materials; planning for the establishment and running of seed, fertilizer, fodder and agricultural machinery services companies; and so on. These are all things which agricultural and related departments at the various levels should and must tackle. In order to conscientiously strengthen work in these fields, the State Agriculture Commission should take responsibility for studying and putting forth the guidelines and policies for agricultural production and construction for the whole country; should, together with the State Planning Commission, give joint leadership to the departments concerned in laying down long-term and annual plans for agriculture; make overall arrangements for the distribution and use of agricultural funds and materials; examine, approve and direct the construction of major agricultural projects of national scope or involving the co-operation of a number of provinces and regions or a number of departments; co-ordinate work between agriculture-related ministries, between agricultural and other departments, and between the central departments and the localities; and resolve major problems arising in the course of agricultural work.

In the management of agriculture, the central and local departments should have clear divisions of labour and job responsibility. Those matters which affect the entire country or involve the joint efforts of several provinces are the responsibility of the central departments. Those things which affect an entire province or involve the joint efforts of a number of counties are the responsibility of the provincial departments. And so on for districts and counties. The upper levels must not take charge of everything for the lower levels but should give full play to the initiative of the lower levels.

The various administrative organs should and must provide the necessary planning and guidance to the rural collective economic units in their production and construction, but in determining plans they must follow the mass line, carrying out full investigation at the base, deliberating and discussing things and achieving overall balance; aside from those things determined by law, it is impermissible to resort to administrative orders to compel communes and brigades to comply; they should be allowed to work out their own measures in the light of local conditions in different seasons, under the guidance of the state's unified plans; and their decision-making powers in this respect must be guaranteed if their initiative is to be brought into play. When giving guidance to the communes, production brigades and teams in scientific farming, the professional departments and scientific research institutions concerned should do their best to see that their guidance is truly scientific and suited to local conditions, and they too must abide by the principle of voluntary participation by the masses and must adopt the method of demonstration by model units which has proved effective over the years. Compulsion, commandism and arbitrary directions are to be guarded against.

To meet the needs of modernizing our agriculture, we must drastically transform our style and methods of leadership, restoring and upholding the fine traditions of seeking truth from facts, keeping close ties with the masses and promoting democracy, so as to raise the level and art of leadership and our ability to lead the extensive modernization of agriculture through practice. We must consciously act in accordance with natural and economic laws and resolutely overcome undesirable practices, such as failure to start from reality, lack of attention to practical economic results, lack of respect for science, and failure to follow the mass line. We must resolutely oppose subjectivism, bureaucratism and formalism, as well as any meeting, slogan, report, inspection tour, visit or circulation of documents which fails to solve problems but squanders human and material resources. We must be resolute in implementing a system of job responsibility; there should be a person charged with special responsibility for each and every task, and any phenomenon of a link for which no one is held to account must be eliminated.

The important thing is to study. Not only must our cadres at every level — and especially leading cadres — continue to study Marxist-Leninist theories and strive to attain a comprehensive and accurate understanding of Mao Zedong Thought as a scientific system and the party's line and policies, but they must also possess the necessary scientific and technical knowledge and scientific economic knowledge, learn advanced agricultural management methods, and strive to make themselves experts in a particular post. We must carry out regular and strict assessments of cadres, particularly leading cadres, distinguishing between right and wrong, achievements and errors, rewards and penalties. Those cadres who study hard, work well, have a good style of work, are bold in liberating their minds and in raising, studying and solving problems, should be given rewards and be promoted. Those cadres who never study, remain amateurs, parrot others and bungle their work should be shifted to other posts or subjected to the appropriate criticisms or disciplinary measures. Our tasks being enormous and complex, if we are to complete this great revolution on China's agricultural front we must pay full attention to discovering, training and using talent in order to create a huge cadre contingent, both able and politically solid, capable of leading and managing the modernization of agriculture.

13. DECISIONS OF THE CENTRAL COMMITTEE OF THE COMMUNIST PARTY OF CHINA ON SOME QUESTIONS CONCERNING THE ACCELERATION OF INDUSTRIAL DEVELOPMENT (Draft)

(July 1978)

The 11th National Congress of the Communist Party of China and the Fifth National People's Congress defined the general task for the Chinese people in the new period of development in socialist revolution and socialist construction as: Firmly carry out the line of the 11th Party Congress; steadfastly continue the revolution under the dictatorship of the proletariat; deepen the three great revolutionary movements of class struggle, the struggle for production and scientific experiment, and transform China into a great and powerful socialist country with modern agriculture, industry, national defence and science and technology by the end of the century.

Industry is the leading factor in the national economy. To speed up industrial growth and bring about its modernization is decisive to the modernization of agriculture, national defence and science and technology. Our aims are: To establish an independent and fairly comprehensive industrial system by 1980; to set up 14 fairly strong industrial bases throughout the country and build up main industrial complexes in the six greater regions with varying levels and different characteristics by 1985; and to bring the output of China's major industrial products and their production techniques close to the levels achieved by the advanced countries by the year 2000. In a few industries, we will equal or outstrip the advanced nations, and our industry will be able to provide agriculture and other branches of the national economy with ample and diversified sources of energy, a multitude of new raw and semi-finished materials, large quantities of sophisticated modern equipment and a rich variety of manufactured goods for daily use, thus promoting the rapid growth of the national economy as a whole.

Tremendous achievements have been made in industrial production and construction since Liberation. The rate of industrial growth was absolutely unattainable in old China and was faster than that in many capitalist countries. This is a great victory for Chairman Mao's revolutionary line, which has held sway on the industrial front throughout the past 28 years. But, owing to the interference and sabotage by Lin Biao and especially by the Gang of Four — Wang Hongwen, Zhang Chunqiao, Jiang Qing and Yao Wenyuan, our industry did not grow at the anticipated rate and the present level of our industrial production lags far behind that of developed capitalist countries. We will not be able to approach or overtake them in the next 22 years if we do not press ahead at a much faster rate.

Quickening the tempo of industrial development is essential to the enlargment of the socialist economic base and the consolidation of the dictatorship of the proletariat in our country, to the strengthening of defence capabilities and safeguarding our socialist motherland, and to the continual improvement of the standards of material and cultural life of the people and their well-being. Our party committees at every level, our industrial departments and industrial enterprises should all draw up their programs of action and arrange their work with a view to accelerating the development of industry and the national economy as a whole and turning China into a mighty socialist state by the end of this century. All our comrades should start up the machine, be bold in thinking, give full play to their wisdom and abilities, and strive to make outstanding contributions to the acceleration of the rate of growth.

In speeding up industrial development, it is fundamental to raise high the great banner of Chairman Mao under the leadership of the Party Central Committee headed by our wise leader Chairman Hua; to keep to the party's basic line, to the general line of going all out, aiming high and achieving greater, faster, better and more economical results in building socialism, and to the series of policies of walking on two legs; and to build up our country independently by means of our own initiative, self-reliance, hard work, diligence and thrift.

At present, it is necessary to grasp well the struggle to expose and criticize the Gang of Four and shake up the country's 3,000 or more big and medium-sized industrial enterprises and its 200,000 or more small industrial enterprises by stages and in groups in line with the "Charter of the Anshan Iron and Steel Company"[1] and the requirements set at the National Conference on Learning from Daqing in industry. At the same time, great efforts should be made to consolidate and strengthen leadership in and management of industry as a whole, implement Chairman Mao's line for running socialist industry and various policies correctly and, in a general way, translate into reality the goal put forth by Chairman Hua of achieving within three years marked and anticipated success in grasping the key link of class struggle and running the country well, and lay a solid foundation for still faster development of industry in future.

The following decisions have been made on some questions concerning the acceleration of industrial development:

Chapter I. Expose and Criticize the Gang of Four

To do a thorough check-up of the enterprises and industrial management, speed up industrial growth and ensure the advance of our industry along the socialist road, it is imperative to grasp firmly the key link of the struggle between the two classes and between the two roads. At present and for some time to come, we must grasp firmly the struggle to expose and criticize the Gang of Four and carry it through to the end.

Great victory has been won in this struggle. By and large, the country-wide investigation has been successfully concluded. Investigation into the individuals and incidents associated with the gang's conspiracy to usurp party and state power has in the main been completed in most of the localities and departments. In a few localities and units where it got off to a late start or where the Gang of Four had their fingers deep in the pie, problems abound, resistance is strong and investigation is still an arduous task. These units must carry the investigation firmly and successfully through to the end and must not stop half way. All units must pay attention to the party's policies, strictly distinguish between the two different types of contradictions, help more people through education and narrow the target of attack.

A host of counter-revolutionary, revisionist fallacies spread by Lin Biao and the Gang of Four over the decade or so have seriously corroded our ranks like germs and wrought grave damage. Their pernicious influence must not be underestimated. All units must, in accordance with the plan of the Party Central Committee, mobilize the masses to conduct a scathing criticism of these fallacies one by one in close conjunction with the "ten needs and need nots"[2] on the economic front and with their own specific conditions, and rectify all their reversals of right and wrong in the matter of line. This is a solemn struggle on the ideological and political front. The struggle must be waged in an organized way under proper leadership, rather than perfunctorily or superficially. Unless we succeed in this struggle and shatter the mental manacles the Gang of Four tried to fasten on the people, there can be neither emancipation of the mind nor substantial growth of productive forces.

The "three talks"[3] and "comparison of the lines" launched in Daqing and the petroleum departments provide a good model for conducting mass exposure and criticism of the crimes perpetrated by the Gang of Four, for clearing up right and wrong in the matter of line, and for carrying out class education. This model should be popularized in all localities and units in the light of their specific conditions. In the struggle, it is necessary to keep firmly to the general orientation, direct the spearhead of the struggle at all times at the bourgeois factional setup of the Gang of Four and their followers, and unite with over 95% of the cadres and the masses in a common fight against the enemy.

Dealing resolute blows to the class enemies for their disruptive activities and clamping down on the corrupt elements, embezzlers and profiteers is an important component of the movement to settle accounts with the crimes of the Gang of Four, strike at the Gang's social base and make a clean sweep of its pernicious influence. In the course of exposing and criticizing the Gang of Four thoroughly, all localities and units must, on the basis of consolidating the leading bodies and in light of their realities, devote a period of time to boldly arousing the masses to carry to success the "double blow" struggle in a guided and systematic way under the unified leadership and plan of the provincial, municipal and autonomous region party committees. The main target is the handful of class enemies engaged in disruptive activities, smash-and-grabbers, and those guilty of serious corruption, embezzlement and profiteering. Penalties must be meted out to them, and they must not be allowed to remain at large. Those who engage in graft, embezzlement or speculation and those who take advantage of their position of power to practice jobbery or bribery should be sternly criticized, educated and given help in mending their ways. Serious offenders must be dealt with. Economically, they must return or pay compensation for what they have unlawfully taken. Restitution should not be perfunctory, but it should be reasonable. As for those who fail to distinguish between public and private property, commit petty theft, or eat or take more than their share, the stress should be on self-education. They are encouraged to return public property. Once they have done so, no recurrences are permitted.

Chapter II. Learn from Daqing in a Thorough Way

A broader and sustained mass movement to learn from Daqing in industry and to popularize Daqing-type enterprises is the fundamental guarantee for shaking up and running well socialist enterprises and speeding up industrial development.

Daqing serves as a model for studying Mao Zedong Thought and applying to industry the theory of continuing the revolution under the dictatorship of the proletariat, and as a model for putting revolutionization in command of industrialization and following our own road of industrial development. Party committees of all provinces, municipalities and autonomous regions and all industrial departments should continue to increase their understanding of the need to learn from Daqing, strengthen leadership in the movement to learn from Daqing, and earnestly solve the problem of whether the units under them are learning truly or for show. In learning from Daqing, we must learn the essentials and grasp the three great revolutionary movements simultaneously. There must be meticulous work and down-to-earth measures to ensure that the movement advances soundly.

All localities and departments should work out plans for learning from Daqing in industry and popularizing Daqing-type enterprises, and make earnest efforts to sum up the experience, assess and compare the results and examine and approve them. By 1980, one-third of the industrial enterprises, first of all the key enterprises, must be turned into Daqing-type enterprises that measure up to the six standards. In building Daqing-type enterprises, we must maintain high standards and strict demands. Enterprises that already follow the Daqing model should continue to advance towards still higher goals; those which are not up to Daqing standards should try hard to catch up. A few enterprises should be stripped of the title of Daqing-type enterprise.

Chapter III. Consolidate Leading Bodies of Enterprises

Consolidation of the leading bodies of enterprises is the key to shaking up enterprises. It is also essential to the successful overhaul of party organizations and of the work style in enterprises.

Currently, leading bodies in our enterprises roughly fall into four categories: (1) good; (2) fairly good; (3) "soft, lazy or lax" to a serious degree with many problems; and (4) leadership is usurped by bad elements. Very few leading bodies fall into the last category.

In consolidating the leading bodies, the good should sum up their experience and continue to advance. If there are problems, they should be tackled in earnest. An active ideological struggle should be waged against those leading bodies that have erred but can still be won over; they should be changed ideologically and not pushed aside. Those who refuse to mend their ways must be reorganized with a firm hand. Where the power of leadership has been usurped by bad elements, it must be resolutely seized back. Work teams should be sent to enterprises where problems abound. The relevant departments under the State Council and the provinces, municipalities and autonomous regions should share the responsibility for the consolidation of key enterprises.

A leading body that firmly implements Chairman Mao's revolutionary line, enjoys the support of the masses and is competent and dynamic should be set up in each enterprise in accordance with the five requirements for revolutionary successors and the principle of the three-in-one combination of the old, the middle-aged and the young. All leading bodies in enterprises must adhere to the basic principles of "three dos and three don'ts" [*practice Marxism, and not revisionism; unite, and do not split; be open and aboveboard, and do not intrigue or conspire* — Tr.].

Party committee secretaries and managers of the enterprises must cadres who are strong in party spirit, full of drive, good in work style and familiar with their work. People who harbour wild ambitions, are politically deviant and have an obnoxious work style must not be allowed to sit in leading bodies or be given important jobs. Veteran cadres must do a good job of passing on their experience to young cadres, warm-heartedly helping and guiding the latter.

Leading bodies must not be overstaffed, and the situation in which "secretaries are counted by the squad and standing committee members are counted by the platoon" must be changed. Proper arrangements should be made for cadres who are too advanced in age or too poor in health to work in enterprises. The composition of leading bodies, once consolidated, should remain stable so that the cadres can accumulate experience.

We must attach great importance to and do a good job of building grassroots party branches, workshops, teams and groups, as well as give full play to the role of the party branches as bastions and to the role of party members as vanguards of the struggle. Party branch secretaries and workshop directors should be politically advanced and active in production; they should be good at organizing and maintaining close ties with the masses. Team and group leaders should be dynamic at production, politically and ideologically adept and skilled in technical matters. We must give warm-hearted support and help to the grassroots cadres in enterprises so that they can take the lead both politically and in production and win the support of the masses.

All work and all political movements in each

enterprise must be placed under the unified leadership of the party committee. The party committee must conscientiously carry out the principle of combining collective leadership and division of responsibility, avoiding or overcoming the unhealthy tendency of making arbitrary decisions or shirking responsibility. The party committee should strengthen its leadership over the trade union, the Communist Youth League and other mass organizations, support their work and bring their due role into full play. The trade union should be made into an able aide to the party in maintaining ties with the masses in the enterprise; a mass organization to encourage the participation of the entire workforce and staff in management; and a school of communism.

Chapter IV. Build Up Our Ranks

It is impossible to develop industry at high speed or accomplish socialist modernization without contingents of workers able to stand stiff tests. All party committees in our enterprises must devote much effort to building up our ranks just as Daqing has done. Arm vast numbers of workers and staff with Marxism-Leninism-Mao Zedong Thought, and continue to educate them in the basic line, in classes and class struggle, in the general situation and in revolutionary traditions. Commend the advanced by great publicity, award model workers, and strive to effect a change of the backward workers and staff members. In the course of the three great revolutionary movements, gradually build up a huge army of industrial workers who are ideologically sound, full of drive, technically proficient, have a good work style, are closely united and strictly observe discipline.

All enterprises must rely whole-heartedly on the working class, implement the party's mass line and launch vigorous mass movements, criticize and overcome the erroneous thinking and practice of running enterprises by relying on a handful of isolated people instead of relying on the broad masses. Pay more attention to old workers and give full play to their role as the mainstay; be concerned about the growth of young workers and bring into play their role as a shock force. Apprentices should respect their masters, and masters should love their apprentices. Do work among the wives and other dependents of workers.

Enhance the revolutionary solidarity of the working class. Continue to criticize bourgeois factionalism. Those who encourage bourgeois factionalism should be criticized and educated and should not be allowed to split the workers' ranks. Action shall be taken against those who refuse to mend their ways. Party members are absolutely prohibited from taking part in bourgeois factionalist activity. Disciplinary action will be taken against those who persist in so doing despite repeated admonition.

Chapter V. System Whereby the Factory Director Takes Charge of Production and Administration under the Leadership of the Party Committee, and Several Other Basic Systems in Enterprises

The following basic systems must be established and perfected in all our enterprises after summing up the experience, both positive and negative, of enterprise management in our country in line with Chairman Mao's consistent teachings:

1. *The system whereby the factory director takes charge of production and administration under the leadership of the party committee.* All major issues in the enterprise must be discussed and decided upon by the party committee collectively. It is the responsibility of the factory director to organize the implementation of decisions made by the party committee on important matters concerning production, technique, finance and welfare. The party committee of the enterprise should energetically support the factory's unified chain of command in production and administration headed by the director in performing its functions, and supervise and check its work. In case urgent matters arise in production, the factory director may and must deal with them without delay before reporting them to the party committee.

In units where government administration is integrated with factory management, the chairman of the revolutionary committee takes charge of production and administration in the enterprise under the leadership of the party committee.

The party committee of the enterprise should guarantee the fulfilment of state plans and the implementation of decisions made and directives issued by the higher authorities. If the enterprise party committee has differing views on any decision or directive of the higher authorities, it may raise the matter with the higher party committee, but must still act as directed pending any change.

2. *System of responsibility for chief engineer, chief accountant, etc.* Engineers and technicians in an enterprise shall have the power commensurate with their posts so that they shoulder real responsibility in technical matters.

3. *System of workers' congresses or conferences under the leadership of the party committee.* Congresses or conferences of workers in an enterprise should be convened at regular intervals so that workers may hear reports on work made by the leaders of the enterprise, discuss major issues of the enterprise, offer criticisms or suggestions on the work, and supervise the leading cadres of the enterprise. The workers' congress or conference has the right to suggest to the higher authorities the removal or the taking of disciplinary action against certain leading pesonnel who seriously neglect their duties or have an obnoxious work style.

4. *System of worker participation in management, cadre participation in labor, and three-in-one combination of leading cadres, workers and technicians.*

These basic systems ensure the successful management of enterprises and control over planning, production, technology, equipment, materials, labour and finance, the establishment and improvement of responsibility systems in various fields and the system of personal responsibility involving cadres, workers and technicians at all levels. In this way, nothing will be neglected, each person has clear-cut responsibilities, and the phenomenon of shirking responsibility will be thoroughly eliminated. The basic tasks of enterprises, such as meeting various quotas, keeping original records and measurements, must be established and perfected rapidly. All enterprises must organize production along rational lines, ensure clean conditions, reduce noise levels, and maintain good order. It is all the more necessary for scientific research and design units to have a quiet and good environment.

Leading cadres at all levels in the enterprises and technical and professional personnel shall be examined and assessed once every year. The good ones shall be commended and the bad ones criticized. Those who neglect their duties or are incompetent shall be removed or readjusted.

All enterprises must have strict, scientific rules and regulations. Irrational rules and regulations must be reformed in good time while rational ones must be preserved and enforced. The formulation or revision of rules and regulations should be conducted with the participation of the masses. The formulation or revision of important rules and regulations should be reported to the higher authorities for approval.

Chapter VI. Criteria for Shaking Up Enterprises

The shake-up of enterprises should be conducted in the same way as we conducted the "four clean-ups" [*namely, the political, economic, organizational and ideological clean-ups* — Tr.] It is imperative to take the struggle to expose and criticize the Gang of Four as the key link; to continue to learn from Daqing in industry; to arrange the consolidation of leading bodies, the building of contingents of workers, the overhaul of the management of enterprises and the "double blow" struggle; to carry out these measures step by step in a planned way, and link them closely with the consolidation of the party and the rectification of work style. Capable and strong work teams should be sent to enterprises that have many problems. The shake-up of enterprises should be carried out in stages and in groups, with the emphasis on putting the key enterprises in order in 1978.

Whether an enterprise is effectively shaken up should be appraised by the masses and strictly inspected and approved by the higher authorities. It should be judged by the following criteria: (1) whether the struggle to expose and criticize the Gang of Four is fruitful and whether the investigation into individuals and incidents associated with the Gang's conspiratorial activities has been successfully concluded; (2) whether a good leading body that firmly implements Chairman Mao's revolutionary line has been established; (3) whether the enthusiasm for socialism of the workers, technical personnel and cadres has been brought into play; (4) whether the disruptive activities of class enemies and such capitalist activities as graft, embezzlement and speculation have been dealt a blow and whether an end has been put to evil trends and practices of the bourgeoisie; (5) whether various rules and regulations centred around the system of job responsibility have been instituted and strictly enforced, whether the administrative structure of the enterprise has been streamlined, and whether the surplus non-productive personnel have returned to the frontline of production; (6) whether marked progress has been made in production, in the eight economic and technical norms — output, variety, quality, consumption of material, labour productivity, costs, profits and use of the circulating fund — and in the maintenance of all kinds of equipment and installations.

If these criteria are met, an enterprise can be considered as put in order. If not, work should be done to put the enterprise in order. These are the minimum requirements for a socialist enterprise. We must press ahead on this basis to build Daqing-type enterprises.

Chapter VII. Tasks for Industrial Enterprises

It is on this question that the Gang of Four

created a great mess. The tasks should be redefined in accordance with Chairman Mao's consistent instructions.

Socialist industrial and transport enterprises are production units under socialist public ownership and are important bastions for consolidating the dictatorship of the proletariat. The routine work of an enterprise must be to put politics in command, grasp production as the key task, and fulfil or overfulfil the state plan in an all-around way. This task is shared by the enterprise's party organizations, its administration, trade union and Communist Youth League. Whether or not this task is fulfilled is the main criterion for judging the success of all work of an enterprise. By exercising leadership in everything, the party should not only provide able leadership in ideological and political work, but also guide production and construction work to success. To do well in production under the command of politics is the sacred duty of all members of the party and the Communist Youth League and all workers and staff in the enterprise, and the realization of its task of consolidating the dictatorship of the proletariat down to every grass-roots organization. The Gang of Four misrepresented the task of grasping production as "the theory of the productive forces" and spread the nonsense that "factories may not necessarily turn out products." Their aim was to undermine our socialist economy and the dictatorship of the proletariat. Their fallacies must be thoroughly repudiated and their pernicious influence eliminated. Every enterprise should engage in production with perfect justification and contribute its share to the accomplishment of the four modernizations.

Chapter VIII. Political Work in Industrial Enterprises

Politics commands everything; it is the soul in everything. Ideological and political work is the life-blood of economic work and guarantees its success. Putting politics in command means putting the party's line, its principles and policies in command. Only by firmly implementing Chairman Mao's line, conscientiously carrying out the "Charter of the Anshan Iron and Steel Company" and launching powerful ideological and political work is it possible for enterprises to keep to the socialist orientation, arouse the revolutionary spirit of their workers and staff and increase production so as to achieve greater, faster, better and more economical results.

Politics is the concentrated expression of the economy; it must reflect the requirements of the economy. In enterprises, political work must serve production; politics must be translated into action in all work and in production. How can politics command if it fails to reflect the requirements of the economy or to advance production and technique? If we pay no attention to politics and bury ourselves in day-to-day routine, production will not increase and may even go astray. If we babble on about putting politics in command while making a mess of production, we are liars. When Lin Biao and the Gang of Four opposed translating politics into action in production and using politics to propel production, they intended to abolish putting proletarian politics in command and to use their bourgeois politics to disrupt socialist production.

Political work in the enterprises must be done alongside economic work. Political work must carry over into production processes, scientific experiments and the life of the workers and staff so that its mighty force of promoting production can truly be brought into play. The separation of political work from economic work as "two different skins" must be firmly rectified.

Every enterprise must, like Daqing, learn from and apply the experience gained by the People's Liberation Army by instituting a strong system of political work. Political departments and instructors should be set up. Routine ideological and political work must be performed in a lively and meticulous fashion in light of the actual conditions of production and the ideological conditions of the masses. The corrosive influence of bourgeois ideology of all stripes must be combatted to ensure that the ranks of workers and staff are united as one, vigorous and in high morale ready to carry on the revolution and the struggle for production. The personnel in the political departments should be dynamic, have a decent work style, remain modest and prudent, familiarize themselves with professional work — both political work and production work, participate regularly in productive labour and, through their work, ensure the fulfilment of the tasks of production and construction.

Chapter IX. Fix Five Norms for Enterprises and Create Enterprise Funds

We would do well to fix five norms for enterprises to ensure stable production conditions. These norms govern:

1. The product line and the scope of production;

2. The size of the workforce and staff and their structure;

3. The consumption quotas of raw materials,

semi-finished materials, fuel, power and tools as well as the sources of supply;

4. The enterprise's fixed assets and circulating funds; and

5. The relations of coordination.

This work shall be conducted in groups by the ministries and commissions under the central government, together with local departments and enterprises, and shall be done on the basis of overall balance and regional distribution in combination with the mapping out of the long-term programme. We must strive to complete this work with the big and medium-sized enterprises in two years or a little longer. Once set, these norms will not be changed in the main, but they may be readjusted against the annual state plan. Any change, if necessary, shall be approved by the central and local departments in charge after consultation. In designing documents for new enterprises these five norms must be included; otherwise they will not be approved.

Enterprises must guarantee all-around fulfilment of the eight economic and technical targets set by the state and of the contracts for supply of goods. Enterprises that fulfil or overfulfil state plans in an all-around way may retain a portion of their profits as the enterprise fund, to be used mainly for collective welfare facilities in these enterprises. The portion of profits to be retained as the enterprise fund should vary from trade to trade, from enterprise to enterprise, and the specific provisions shall be worked out by the Ministry of Finance in conjunction with the relevant departments. When enterprises fail to fulfil state plans, investigations shall be made. If the failure is due to poor leadership, bureaucracy or other subjective causes, the leaders of the enterprise or the relevant units in charge shall be held responsible and even be removed from office.

Chapter X. Reorganize Industry According to the Principle of Coordination Between Specialized Departments

The fixing of five norms for enterprises should be combined with efforts to encourage coordination between specialized departments and raise the degree of organization in industry.

Coordination between specialized departments is an inevitable trend of the development of modern industry. All-embracing plants, whether large or small, lead to enormous waste; they also seriously handicap the progress in production techniques and the increase of labour productivity. It is high time to make up our mind and change this backward form of enterprise organization.

Given our experience and the need to develop industrial production, we must, at present, undertake extensive work in the following areas:

— Strive to improve the standardization, serialization and interchangeability of products. Without this, there can be no specialized production, nor high quality, nor speed. The electronics, meters and instruments and machinery trades in particular must make earnest efforts to carry out this work on the basis of simplifying the types of machinery and reorganizing the present products, so as to use the least possible series of products to satisfy the needs of all consumers and use as many interchangeable parts as possible in the assembly of diverse products. Parts and accessories should be supplied by the manufacturers, or they should be made by specialized units at several locations so as to avoid their being produced by every user on its own.

— On the basis of unified planning, readjust the production schemes for enterprises engaged in the same line of production, institute a rational division of work among them and raise the level of specialized production. Specialized companies may be formed in one locality by incorporating similar enterprises and the small ones directly serving them.

— Organize around the manufacture of one or several products, the relevant enterprises found in one locality — including enterprises under collective ownership and run by communes and their subdivisions — so as to streamline production from raw materials to semi-finished goods to finished goods, and fix this relation of coordination.

— Gradually group the similar auxiliary workshops found in one locality, such as repairing and tools shops, into repair centres or tools supply centres. Foundry and forging, electroplating, heat-treatment and other centres can be set up in big cities.

— Gradually develop associations spanning provinces, cities and trades on the basis of coordination between specialized units.

The reorganization of industry is a very painstaking and complex task which requires various departments, localities and enterprises to make concerted efforts, adopt a firm attitude and proceed step by step in a planned way. The experience of Shanghai Municipality in organizing a variety of specialized companies, the experience of Zhangzhou city in streamlining and coordinating production and the experience of the Ministry of Chemical Industry in helping localities work out plans for the development of chemical industry and coordinate specialized chemical enterprises should be assessed and generalized.

The work of overall planning and coordination between specialized units in the machine-building industry must be tackled rapidly and to good account. The organizational form of industrial management must be in keeping with the specialized production of the enterprises. When central departments are chiefly responsible for organizing coordination between specialized units that span provinces and cities, localities should support them; when localities are chiefly responsible for organizing coordination between specialized units in their respective areas, central departments should support them. In case contradictions arise, they should be settled by the localities and departments through consultation in accordance with the principle of developing production with greater, faster, better and more economical results. National taxation and pricing policies should be conducive to coordination between specialized departments.

All localities and departments in charge should examine one by one the existing relations of coordination among enterprises. The rational ones should be adopted, the irrational ones readjusted and new ones that are needed quickly set up. Coordinating parties must sign economic contracts, and stable relations of coordination should gradually lead to the signing of long-term contracts. Contracts, once signed, must be honoured strictly. Violation of coordination agreements or contracts is tantamount to undermining the socialist planned economy. Those who fail to act in accordance with the provisions of the contract and wilfully terminate relations of coordination shall be held responsible and compensate for the losses incurred. Disputes arising from the implementation of the economic contracts shall be arbitrated and handled by economic commissions at various levels.

Chapter XI. Initiative from Both Sides and the Industrial Management System

To strengthen leadership and management in industry, it is necessary to bring into play the initiative of both the central and the local authorities, provided the unified central leadership is consolidated. While the former must have absolute control over major issues, power should devolve on the latter with respect to minor ones. Power is to be centralized or devolved as the case may be.

The management system of industrial enterprises shall follow the principle of management by different levels under unified leadership. Industrial enterprises can be classified into three categories: key enterprises that have a bearing on the economy as a whole (the field armies); other enterprises owned by the people as a whole (the regional forces); and collectively-owned enterprises run by the communes and their subdivisions, neighbourhoods and streets (the guerrilla units). These three categories should be managed by different levels under unified leadership.

A few key enterprises and research and design units that have a bearing on the economy as a whole should be put under dual leadership, with the central departments concerned assuming the chief responsibility. Where these key enterprises are concerned, the relevant central departments are responsible for drawing up their production and construction plans and financial plans, supplying them with the principal materials, assigning norms for labour power, and carrying out state plans for the distribution and transfer of products. The localities are responsible for improving party work and ideological and political work, organizing coordination and support from relevant circles, supervising and checking the key enterprises' implementation of the party's line, principles and policies and state plans, and ensuring the supply of materials distributed by the localities as well as of consumer goods. The appointment, removal or transfer of the principal leaders of these key enterprises are to be decided by the relevant departments together with party committees of the provinces, municipalities and autonomous regions. These enterprises must respect the leadership of the local party committees. For the fulfilment of state plans, processing enterprises can undertake some processing tasks for the localities if they have surplus processing capacity and the localities have raw materials. Enterprises engaged in the production of fuel and raw and semi-finished materials may, in general, give a certain portion of their products to the localities. The variety of products and the actual proportions to be given to the localities are to be decided by the State Planning Commission in conjunction with the relevant departments and localities. The list of enterprises that will be put under dual leadership, with the central departments concerned assuming the chief responsibility, shall be agreed upon through consultation by the departments in charge and the localities, and the list shall be submitted to the State Council for approval after examination by the State Economic Commission, the State Capital Construction Commission and the State Scientific and Technological Commission respectively. We must not retract power over every enterprise simply for the sake of strengthening centralization and unified leadership.

The other large and medium-sized enterprises should be managed by the localities or be put under dual leadership with the localities assuming the chief responsibility. Enterprises whose management is to be transferred from the central departments should be put into the hands of the provincial authority or the municipal authority under the province; they must not be transferred from one level to another further down. The localities should be responsible for the production and construction plans of these enterprises, the balance between supply of raw materials, the production and sale of products and the distribution of labour power, but they must observe unified state plans and guarantee the fulfilment of the tasks for the production and transfer of auxiliary products. The relevant central departments should give guidance and support in planning, production and technology instead of washing their hands of these enterprises.

As for enterprises run by communes and their subdivisions and neighbourhoods and streets, the localities should strengthen leadership over them and assist them to develop in a planned way.

In capital construction, key projects that have a bearing on the economy as a whole shall be arranged by the state and the departments concerned; local projects shall be arranged by the provinces, municipalities and autonomous regions and included in state plans after nationwide balancing.

The system of control over materials should be in keeping with the system of enterprise management and the system of allocating investment in capital construction. Materials are, in principle, allocated according to the affiliation of enterprises. Enterprises whose materials are supplied by central departments and construction projects that are arranged by central departments receive materials from the central departments. Enterprises managed by the localities and construction items arranged by the localities receive the materials they need from the provinces, municipalities and autonomous regions. The principal materials needed in production by those local enterprises whose production plans are worked out by central departments and whose products are transferred on a national scale, may also be supplied by the central departments in charge. All materials shall be controlled in unified warehouses gradually set up by the supplies departments. They shall be supplied at the nearest possible location according to the quotas specified in national plans. Bulk materials are to be supplied at a fixed location and delivered directly. A network of stations shall be organized to supply materials in small quantities against the presentation of certificates. Industrial and mining enterprises will not be allowed to sell their products as they are or in a disguised form. The scope of products under unified state distribution shall be enlarged. Sales agencies under various industrial departments shall gradually be put under the dual leadership of the departments concerned and the State Administration of Supplies, with the latter assuming chief responsibility. Continued efforts should be made to evaluate the operation of the system of material control and perfect it step by step.

Localities and central departments must be mindful of the overall interest, work in close coordination and in concert, and support each other. The initiative from both sides should be combined to do things well. While managing the enterprises under them well, central departments should make an effort to study policy matters, keep abreast of trends in production techniques at home and abroad, determine the direction for technical development in their respective trades, map out annual and long-term plans for all trades, and help the localities work out their plans and organize all types of enterprises along different trades so that they become streamlined. The central departments should also help the localities solve problems that the localities cannot solve on their own. The localities should not only run the enterprises under them well but also try by every possible means to support the key enterprises and projects that have a bearing on the whole situation as well as those enterprises that work in coordination with them, and push forward the production and construction of these enterprises and projects.

Chapter XII. Unified Planning

An important aspect of checking up industrial management is to strengthen unified state planning and to overcome the anarchy that still exists to a serious extent.

Production, construction, labour, wages, materials, prices, finance and other economic activities in both central and local units, in both units owned by the whole people and collectively owned units, including industrial enterprises run by communes and their subdivisions and streets and neighbourhoods, must all be included in the unified plans at revelant levels in one form or another and through one channel or another.

All regions and departments should endeavour to strike an overall balance in planning; should properly arrange the proportions between various sectors; should ensure smooth linking of supply, production, transportation and marketing; and should pay special attention to achieving a balance between the needs for raw and semi-finished materials, fuel and power and the possibility of their supply. The departments are responsible for the overall balance in each of the trades; the provinces, municipalities and autonomous regions are responsible for the overall balance in their respective areas. The State Planning Commission works out the overall balance for the whole country.

Every region, department and enterprise must arouse the masses to draw up its long-range plan in the light of needs and possibilities and in accordance with the state's Ten-Year Programme and Five-Year Plan, so that their vision will not be confined to the immediate step they are going to take.

In formulating plans, we must follow the mass line. Plans must be scientific and precise and they should reflect objective economic laws as much as possible. Different plans should be linked with one another. Targets set in plans should be forward-looking and reliable and have some leeway. Production tasks and construction projects listed in the plans must be assured of funds, materials and manpower.

Production and construction plans of the provinces, municipalities and autonomous regions and of the departments shall be submitted for examination and approval by the state as scheduled. Annual state plans must be made known to the enterprises before the beginning of the year. Plans must be serious. As for state plans made known to the lower levels upon the approval of the Central Committee, all regions, departments and enterprises must implement them with a firm hand and fulfil them in an all-around way. Readjustments to be made in the plans must be submitted for approval. Regular checks will be made to see how the plans are being carried out.

We must strengthen statistical work. Statistics must be made in good time and true to fact. Cheating or making false reports is not permitted. Such cases shall be sternly dealt with.

Chapter XIII. Chain of Command in Industry

A strong and able chain of command must be set up from top to bottom if we are to organize our massive industry to proceed with production and construction at high speed and in an orderly manner according to unified state plans.

Economic commissions should be formed and strengthened at all levels to take up the following tasks: specifically guide the movement to Learn from Daqing in Industry and do a good job of the political and ideological work in the industrial and transport enterprises, organize production, perform well in day-to-day command and control in production, and popularize advanced techniques; study and solve certain policy matters in industrial management and enterprise management, sum up and exchange experience in this respect.

Economic commissions at every level must ensure the implementation of state plans. They should work in close coordination with planning commissions, capital construction commissions and scientific and technological commissions at corresponding levels under the unified leadership of party committees. We should avoid a situation of each going its own way.

The leading body of every central and provincial department should also be consolidated and strengthened. We should resolutely streamline those that are overstaffed and add more technical and professional cadres if they are weak.

Chapter XIV. Aid Agriculture Energetically

All industrial and communications departments and industrial enterprises must firmly foster the idea of taking agriculture as the foundation, must render better service to agriculture, and must contribute to the effort to popularize Dazhai-type counties, bring about the mechanization and modernization of agriculture and consolidate the worker-peasant alliance.

All industrial departments and enterprises must, in accordance with state plans, endeavour to provide agriculture with all kinds of means of production, help the peasants master modern science and technology and fulfil without fail the task of accomplishing the mechanization of agriculture in the main by 1980. Be sure to improve the quality of all products for rural use, reduce costs from time to time, and accordingly lower their factory and selling prices so as to impart the benefit by lowering costs to the peasants. The state will appropriately increase its investment in agriculture and in the industries aiding agriculture and, with regard to the distribution of financial and material resources, give more consideration to agriculturally backward and industrially weak areas and to areas inhabited by minority nationalities.

Every industrial city should, on the basis of achieving an overall balance and in line with its capabilities, take along one to several counties and help them develop agriculture and the small industries serving agricultural production.

Industrial and mining enterprises should do what they can to help nearby communes and their subdivisions increase the production of grain and non-staple foodstuffs and to run their industries well. But a clear line of distinction must be drawn between the two kinds of ownership, and no transfer of property between them is allowed.

Expansion of industries run by the communes

and their subdivisions is of great importance to consolidating and developing the collective economy in the people's communes; promoting the mechanization of agriculture; increasing the accumulation of the communes and their subdivisions and the income of commune members; narrowing the differences between town and country, between worker and peasant; and supporting national construction, the market and export trade. These industries must develop under unified plans and stronger leadership; they must keep to the socialist orientation, use local resources, engage in production at the original site, and serve mainly agriculture. These industries must not contend with big industries for fuel, power and raw and semi-finished materials. They should engage in both industry and agriculture.

We should educate the rural cadres and vast numbers of commune members so that they give warm support to industrial construction and care for the factories and state property. No commune, brigade, team or individual is permitted to seize state property.

Chapter XV. Give Prominence to Developing Fuel, Power, Raw and Semi-Finished Materials Industries and Transport and Communications Services

At present, fuel, power and raw and semi-finished materials industries lag behind the processing industries, especially in the acute shortages of electricity and coal and in the tensions in communications which seriously handicap speedy industrial growth. The state and the localities must direct their main forces to effect a faster development in these sectors.

Vigorous efforts must be made to tap the potentials of existing enterprises, to constantly raise efficiency and produce more coal, electricity, petroleum, iron and steel, non-ferrous metals, chemicals and building materials. The state should select places to build in stages and by groups a number of large bases of fuel, power, raw and semi-finished materials industries that use advanced technologies. Their layout should be considered from a strategic point of view and for the purpose of solving the question of speed in the long run. The localities should make full use of local resources, should actively develop medium-sized and small coal mines and power stations, consolidate and upgrade medium-sized and small iron and steel enterprises and non-ferrous metals enterprises, and boost the production of chemicals and non-metal materials. Medium-sized and small enterprises should be renovated technically and should pay attention to economic results.

Geological work should be strengthened. We should employ advanced prospecting techniques without delay to make a success of regional geological surveys and the general exploration of mineral resources. We should endeavour to find resources in the vicinity of existing industrial and mining areas and in the hinterland. The stress is on oil, gas, high-grade iron ore, non-ferrous metals and rare metals, on underground water resources, phosphur, sulphur and potassium and, in the south, on coal, low-calorie fuels including bone coal, lignite, oil shale, etc. We should strive for a major breakthrough in these field as soon as possible. We should continue to develop mines on a large scale. Efforts should be made to shorten the time needed in opening new mines, to develop advanced and huge mining machinery, to raise by a large margin the extraction capacity of existing mines, and to solve the problem of mineral ores. We should not try to "cook a meal without rice."

We should step up the construction and technical transformation of railways, highways and water transport facilities, organize transportation in a rational way and do a good job of short-distance transport. It is necessary to strengthen coordination between production and communications departments, to continue to raise the efficiency of existing means of transportation, and to rapidly change the present passiveness resulting from backward transport and communications services. We should pay attention to the development of water transport so that it can carry more goods.

Machine-building and electronics industries should be organized under overall planning to speed-up coordination between specialized units and to bring about a rapid growth. We should vigorously turn out all types of top-quality and highly efficient machinery and equipment, raise the production levels of large-scale, precision and modern plants, greatly increase the output of computers and other electronic products to equip basic industries and other branches of the economy.

Along with the strengthening of basic industries, there should be a vigorous development of light industry. We should explore and open up more sources of raw materials, strive to increase the supply of agricultural raw materials, substantially increase the ratio of petrochemically produced raw materials such as chemical fibres and plastics to all raw materials used in light industry, produce a rich variety of light industrial goods that are cheap and beautiful so that light and heavy industry will develop in harmony. We should also pay attention to the development of handicrafts production and efficiently arrange the manufacture of articles for daily use, miscellaneous goods and commodities specially needed by the minority nationalities. Handicrafts products concern vast numbers of families and are needed by the people at home and by international markets. They must not be overlooked.

Chapter XVI. Energy Policy

Energy is a problem of strategic importance. The speed of industrial development will in a large measure be determined by how we solve the energy problem.

We should exert efforts to explore all types of energy and use them rationally. While increasing the production of coal, oil and natural gas, we should energetically develop the generation of hydroelectric power, make full use of bone coal, gangue, peat, lignite, oil shale and various exhaust thermals, and develop bio-gas in a big way. It is also necessary to develop nuclear power generating in a planned way, to study the utilization of solar energy, geothermal power, wind and tidal energy, to explore and study new sources of energy, and to combine the exploration and utilization of energy sources appropriately with the distribution of industry.

We should use as much low-calorie fuels as possible in industrial boilers and for civilian purposes so as to save high-quality coal and crude oil — this is an important policy. Oil must not be used where it should not. Boilers using oil should be converted as soon as possible. We should mount extensive studies and experiments in using low-calorie fuels, in manufacturing equipment and in converting oil- and coal-burning equipment. We should mobilize scientific and technical personnel and workers to give full play to their abilities in this field. Marked results must be achieved in 1978 in the use of low-calorie fuels.

Rigid measures should be adopted to save energy. The state and the relevant departments should set up energy research institutes. All enterprises should achieve a balance in the use of heat and make full use of all kinds of exhaust heat. The system of supplying fuel and power under fixed quotas must be strictly implemented. Those who save energy shall be rewarded; those who waste energy shall be criticized, and the grave cases shall be penalized. We shall institute a pricing policy that facilitates the exploration of energy sources, encourages economy and inhibits waste.

Chapter XVII. Tapping Potential, Renovation and Transformation

All industrial and communications departments and enterprises must proceed from existing conditions and take the tapping of potentials, renovation and transformation as the primary ways to speed up industrial development.

All enterprises must fully arouse the masses to put forward rational proposals, to introduce technical innovations and to go on creating new production levels. Enterprises which have not reached their designed capacity or have not attained their previous good levels must reach or surpass them within given time limits. Those already up to their designed capacity or previous good levels should attempt to scale new heights. As for those enterprises whose production has stagnated and who have failed to reach their designed capacity over a long time, the relevant authorities should look into the matter, take appropriate measures and urge and help them to change the situation within given time limits instead of letting things drift.

In tapping the potential of enterprises and in renovating and transforming them, there must be overall planning and strengthened leadership. The stress is on increasing fuel, power, raw and semi-finished materials, and products in short supply, on improving the quality of products and reducing consumption. A number of enterprises in the processing industries that have surplus production capacity can be changed over to manufacture products in short supply. Expenses for renewal or technical transformation should be included in plans and put to good use. In distributing materials, equipment and funds, priority should be given to the need of tapping potential, renovation and transformation. Transformation items that can recoup investment and gain results the same year may obtain small loans from the financial departments if they are short of funds.

Experiences useful to tapping potential, renovation and transformation should be summed up and spread without delay, and earnest efforts made to solve problems that surface in the course of their popularization. Proven experiences should be included in rules of operation or product designs. Production capacity to be added in the future — except the new plants necessitated by changing industrial distribution or objective conditions — shall be obtained from existing enterprises, primarily from tapping their potential and upgrading them, or from reconstructing and expanding them if necessary.

Military enterprises should turn their production capacity to good account by integrating military with civilian needs and peace-time production with preparedness against war. Civilian enterprises that are in a position to do so should actively undertake military mobilization tasks.

Chapter XVIII. Multiple Utilization, Environmental Protection

Although the Central Committee raised this

problem on several occasions, it still has not aroused the attention of all of our comrades. Many valuable resources have yet to be used comprehensively and there is worsening pollution of the environment in some places. Every region and department should make a conscientious investigation into this matter and take necessary organizational and technical measures and tighten rules and regulations.

All departments and enterprises should bear the overall interest in mind, break the barriers between different trades and undertake multiple utilization. In geological work, we must do comprehensive prospecting and assessment; all resources must be explored and utilized in a comprehensive way according to state requirements. Multiple utilization involving different trades shall be organized by the relevant regions and departments.

All departments, enterprises, units and cities must work out plans and solve the treatment of "three wastes" [*waste water, waste gas and industrial residue* – Tr.] within given time limits. Certain enterprises that have caused serious damage to local inhabitants and to the environment and that have failed to solve the problem over a long period should be resolutely ordered to suspend operations and to solve the pollution problem within given time limits before resuming production. If no effort is made to solve those pollution problems arising from the "three wastes" that can be solved, it shall be judged a manifestation of indifference towards the interests of the people. Such enterprises cannot be cited as Daqing-type enterprises, and their leaders shall be held responsible. Newly built and reconstructed enterprises must resolutely observe the ruling that principal construction and the building of auxiliary facilities for treatment of the "three wastes" must go hand in hand and that their design, construction and commissioning should be simultaneous. The State Capital Construction Commission and Environmental Protection Office are asked to supervise and check up on this matter.

A law of environmental protection shall be formulated and promulgated by the state for implementation.

Projects for the comprehensive use and treatment of the "three wastes" should be included in departmental or regional plans. Big projects shall be listed in state plans. Alloted funds and materials should be guaranteed and must not be diverted to other purposes. The state will draw up certain policies to encourage and support these undertakings.

Chapter XIX. Give First Priority to Quality, Variety and Specifications

Major problems in industrial production at present are poor quality, rapid-rate of consumption, inadequate variety, low efficiency and lack of spare parts. If these are not solved there can be no rapid acceleration, no technological advance, no realization of the four modernizations. We must follow Chairman Mao's teachings to bring our industrial work truly into the "quality first" orbit, seeking greater and faster results on the basis of better and more economical results, and achieving the unity of greater, faster, better and more economical results.

All enterprises should constantly improve the quality of products and produce goods that are highly efficient, have a long service life and a low consumption rate; add new varieties and specifications in a planned way; and engage in production with the needs of the users in mind. Trial production and manufacture of new products should be encouraged and supported. Industrial enterprises should improve packaging and be responsible for the losses resulting from poor packing. Transport enterprises should improve services and be responsible for losses caused in loading and unloading. We must oppose all bad practices that pay no heed to quality, produce substandard goods and incur enormous waste of state funds and property, practices that are irresponsible to the state and the people.

Products that fail to meet the standards in quality, variety, specification or the requirements set in contracts shall not be considered as part of the fulfilled quotas, or calculated in output value, or allowed to leave the factory. Users have the right to reject such products. Manufacturers are obliged to repair, replace or compensate for those that have already left the factory. Shops and stores are responsible for exchanging substandard goods sold through them if the buyers so demand. Investigations must be made into cases involving serious incidents to ascertain the responsibility and deal with them sternly. Criminal sanctions shall be imposed in some cases. Enterprises that turn out very low quality goods shall suspend operations to tidy things up and to make improvements within specified time limits.

All products that fail to reach previous required levels in quality are required to do so within a year. Those already up to previous levels should press ahead to catch up with and surpass domestic and international advanced levels.

A campaign should be launched on an extensive scale among the workshop teams and groups to turn out products of guaranteed quality. We should tighten operating rules, strengthen quality control and perform strict check-ups on every work process from the admission of raw materials into the factory through the delivery of products and on all spare parts and accessories. We should compare and assess quality from time to time, commending the advanced and criticizing the backward.

We should seriously enforce the system of trademark registration. Products without trademarks are not allowed to leave the factory or to be put on sale. We should make efforts to manufacture brand-name products. In pricing policy, higher prices will be fixed for better goods.

Output value serves only as a calculation figure for the convenience of higher authorities, and cannot be used as a yardstick to judge the performance of an enterprise. Regions or departments are not allowed to allocate false norms in terms of output value to the enterprises.

Chapter XX. Increase Accumulation, Practice Economy

All industrial and transport enterprises must carry out state plans in an all-around way and fulfil or overfulfil the tasks set by the state for turning over profits and paying taxes, contributing more to the accumulation of the state. They must earnestly implement the policy of building up the country with diligence and thrift, and strictly enforce the system of economic accounting. Such acts as doing no business accounting, paying no regard to production costs, indulging in extravagance and waste and raising or lowering prices at will must be criticized severely and resolutely stopped.

All enterprises must do a good job of fixing the numbers of their staff and labour quotas, and strive to raise labour productivity. They should simplify the administrative structure, cut down on the number of non-production personnel and increase the ratio of production personnel. All those who should not be divorced from productive work must go back to their production posts without exception. Activities designed to be done in spare time should not be done during ordinary work hours. No labour power in excess of planned quotas shall be employed.

All enterprises must strictly control their consumption of materials according to quotas. Beginning from 1978, fuel, power and raw and semi-finished materials will be supplied on the strength of certificates according to minimum consumption levels previously attained by each enterprise. The quotas will be revised from time to time in accordance with technological progress and improved management. We should resolutely change the present situation in which no quotas are set for consumption and where materials and fuel are supplied without limit and where overstocking or waste goes unchecked. This matter should be grasped by industrial, communications and supplies departments at all levels. Failure to do a good job in this respect constitutes negligence. The method of giving a certain subsidy to the collection of used and waste material as practised in the past should be continued.

Every enterprise must retrench non-productive expenses and endeavour to lower production costs. On no account should spendings not itemized under the production costs be so listed. Enterprises that show deficits because of poor management must arrest these losses by the end of 1978. Those which fail to do so within the time limit will receive no subsidies from financial departments or credits from the banks. Effective measures should be adopted to check losses incurred by factors other than the enterprises, and notable results should be attained this year. Losses permitted under state policies shall be kept to the minimum.

We should speed up the turnover of circulating funds. Financial departments should work in conjunction with industrial departments to verify the amount of circulating funds for the enterprises one by one; the banks shall supervise this work.

Leading organs at all levels shall observe state plans and financial discipline, and they are not allowed to draw labour power, funds, materials or equipment from enterprises at will. If they do so, those enterprises have the right to resist.

Chapter XXI. Fight a Battle of Annihilation in Capital Construction

Capital construction plans must be decided upon in the light of our material, financial and manpower resources. We shall match our undertakings with the amount of money available and strive to get more done with less money. We must ensure the construction of key projects while giving due consideration to the other ones. Projects listed in the annual plans must be assured of planned investment, appropriations, equipment, materials and a construction work force.

Each project must give consideration to the auxiliary facilities and secure the supplies of water, electricity, raw and semi-finished materials and transport facilities once it goes into operation; otherwise it will not be approved. Arrangements must be made in advance for the acquisition of complete units of equipment needed in the newly constructed large and medium-sized projects.

In building a project, we must pay attention to the results from investment, shorten building time, reduce construction costs, and completely correct the erroneous tendency of grabbing for investment and projects to the neglect of investment results. From now on, every new construction project shall be strictly reviewed according to the following indices: newly-acquired production capacity, building time, actual amount of construction, quality of construction, consumption of materials, construction costs, the proportion turned into fixed assets, time limits set to recoup investments after the project goes into operation, and the time needed to reach the designed capacity. All construction projects should be completed quickly, leaving nothing unsettled. Inspection and testing must be strictly carried out upon their completion.

All capital construction items, including those built with funds raised by the localities and departments themselves, must be listed in the unified plan. No locality, department or unit is allowed to change the amount of capital construction for a project, enlarge the scope of construction, change the construction standards, alter the tempo of construction or erect buildings, guest houses and auditoriums without authorization or stand in violation of the state plan.

Funds not earmarked for capital construction shall not be used in capital construction. The People's Bank of Capital Construction is enjoined to control all appropriations for capital construction. It may refuse to disburse the sum requested to cover spending that goes against state regulations.

All construction work must follow strictly the procedures concerning capital construction.

We must continue to revolutionize design and actively use new techniques, technologies and materials that have proved effective. Capital construction units should undergo technical transformation in a planned way and raise their level of mechanization step by step. Strict rules and regulations and responsibility systems should be instituted concerning geological prospecting, design, construction and inspection.

Chapter XXII. Strengthen Scientific Research, Adopt Advanced Techniques

It is necessary to step up scientific research, adopt advanced techniques and catch up with and surpass advanced world levels. This goal must be put high on the agenda.

All industrial and transport enterprises are required to study and work out their own plans for technical development and technical policies in light of China's conditions and of new technical achievements in the world.

Every department, every industrial city and every big or medium-sized enterprise must have its own or joint scientific research and design units where necessary technical personnel are concentrated to study and solve the major technical and design problems in production in conjunction with mass scientific experimentation. Necessary pilot plants should be set up. Every enterprise must strengthen its technical back-up service and increase the proportion of technical personnel engaged in this work. Materials, funds, time and other conditions needed for scientific experiments should be guaranteed.

Industrial and communications departments at all levels should conscientiously popularize all new techniques, technologies and materials that have been successfully tested. Items to be popularized should be listed in plans at various levels and verified.

While maintaining independence and self-reliance, we should earnestly study what is good from other countries and import badly needed advanced technologies and equipment in a planned and selective way to make foreign things serve China. We should organize and train the necessary technical forces to quickly master the imported advanced technologies; they should not only know the how but also the why. We should assiduously study and learn to operate them before ever trying to improve and develop them.

We should strengthen scientific information work, oppose the practice of refusing to share information with others or make a monopoly of information.

Appropriate commendations and material awards should be given to those collectives and individuals who have achieved marked success in making inventions and technical innovations.

Chapter XXIII. Train Cadres, Workers and Technicians

To accomplish the four modernizations, we must raise the scientific and cultural level of the entire Chinese nation. It is a pressing task to train cadres, workers and technicians on a large scale and bring up more people who are both red and expert. Modernization of industry will remain empty talk if we fail to solve this problem, if we fail to make scores of millions of our industrial workers, millions of technicians and tens of thousands of cadres directing our industries at various levels master both modern technology and the expertise in managing modern industry.

All cadres, including leading cadres in industrial departments and enterprises, must assiduously study Marxism-Leninism-Mao Zedong Thought as well as technology and professionalism so as to become experts and raise their level in managing and organizing modern production. It is necessary to sponsor cadre training courses extensively and run schools of every description to make plans to organize the principal leading cadres of industrial and communications departments and key enterprises on study tours abroad and to invite specialists, both domestic and foreign, and those who have returned from study tours abroad to give lectures.

Workers must energetically study politics and technique and sharpen their basic skills by all means. They should run well "July 21" colleges, workers' schools and technical evening schools, and make arrangements so that all the workers can get necessary technical training; they should institute a system of technical examinations and tests. Those who pass them can operate at their posts; those who fail must make up for it. In future, workers must pass technical and operating tests before being promoted. Every worker must study technique in their spare time at least twice a week.

Scientific and technical personnel must persist in their integration with workers and peasants, remould their world outlook, and at the same time diligently study the new technologies of the time and become proficient in their professions. Leaders at all levels should give them the time and opportunity to study. Scientists and technicians who have been improperly transferred to other trades should return to do what they were trained for. College graduates should be assigned to do technical work. Technical personnel shall be put to technical tests, and their jobs shall be readjusted according to their actual technical levels. We should restore the necessary financial schools and faculties to train financial cadres. We should make efforts to publish books on industrial management, enterprise management and all kinds of technical literature as well as popular readings to spread scientific and technical knowledge. We should make full use of the radio and television services to sponsor technical lectures.

Party committees at every level must commend those advanced elements who are both red and expert; restore and formulate the technical titles for technical personnel and professional managerial personnel and the system of promotion. In 1978, a group of outstanding technicians and skilled workers shall be promoted to engineers or assistant engineers. Educate those people who pay no heed to politics or do not study technique or professionalism.

Chapter XXIV. Labour Emulation and Revolutionary Contests

We should launch socialist labour emulation and revolutionary contests in a vigorous but down-to-earth manner and keep at it, bringing about an upsurge in aiming high, emulating, learning from, catching up with and overtaking the advanced and helping the less advanced. In emulation and contests, the workers and staff members are encouraged to learn from and help each other, make up each other's deficiencies and make common progress, so that the advanced levels created by a few individuals and units will rapidly spread throughout the society.

All regions, departments and enterprises must make regular inspection, comparison and appraisal of work done, boldly compare contributions, elect models and pace-setters, cite the advanced, sum up and popularize their experience. In labour emulation, we must pay attention to practical results and prevent formalism. In organizing study tours and exchanges of experience, we must not go in for ostentation and extravagance.

Economic commissions, departments and trade union organizations at every level must grasp this work in earnest under the leadership of the party committees.

Chapter XXV. From Each According to His Ability, To Each According to His Work

In line with Chairman Mao's consistent teachings, we should combine communist ideological education and the economic policies for the present stage, and combine moral encouragement and material reward with stress on the former. We must persist in putting politics in command and encourage every worker to cultivate the communist attitude towards labour — exerting one's all in whole-hearted service to the people regardless of remuneration. In distribution, we shall adhere to the principle of to each according to his work, more pay for more work and less pay for less work. While opposing a wide wage spread, we recognize necessary differences and oppose egalitarianism. In this regard, the following methods and measures will have to be adopted:

1. Institute the normal system of pay increases. Wage increases will be effected after discussion by the masses and approval by the leadership according to the worker's political record, labour attitude, technical skills and contributions.

2. The time-wage system is to apply in most cases. A restricted version of the piece-wage system may be applied to a few jobs that involve heavy manual labour and strenuous hand operation.

3. Apply the system of payment by the hour with additional bonuses.

4. Step by step there should be pecuniary allowances for jobs requiring higher labour intensity or that are performed under poor working conditions.

5. Gradually reduce the wage disparity between different regions so that wages will be in keeping with price levels in the locality.

In applying the piece-wage system and the reward system, we must conscientiously sum up the past experience and avoid past drawbacks. Disparities should not be too great, appraisal for rewards should not be too frequent, and bonuses should not be too multifarious. It is necessary to step up ideological and political work and to prevent and discard the idea of solving every problem with bonuses. Labour departments shall make a comprehensive study of this work and put forth some methods for trial in selected places within 1978 before implementation.

We must explain to the masses that ours is still a developing socialist country and our life can only be improved step by step on the basis of increased production and higher labour productivity. In the absence of increased production, improvement of life is unrealistic and impossible. We must carry forward the fine tradition of plain living and hard struggle and endeavour to boost production.

Chapter XXVI. Be Concerned with the Well-Being of the Workers

Leaders at every level must carry forward the party's fine tradition of being concerned with the well-being of the masses, and of grasping production and the well-being of the people at the same time. In the enterprise, a deputy director should be put in charge of the well-being of the workers.

We should build more housing for the workers in a planned way. The state, the locality and the enterprise should join forces to draw up concrete plans and work in concert to appropriately resolve within several years the problem of providing living quarters for those workers and staff members in need. Workers' housing in cities should be included in urban construction plans.

We should vigorously improve the supply of non-staple foodstuffs in the cities and in the industrial and mining enterprises. Big and medium-sized cities should build the basis for producing non-staple foodstuffs, run mechanized pig and poultry farms, and effect notable improvements in one or two years in the supply of such non-staple foodstuffs as meat, eggs and vegetables. Industrial and mining enterprises which are in a position to do so should act as the Daqing Oil Field and organize the workers and their family members to engage in farming, forestry, livestock breeding, side-line production and fishing so as to improve the workers' lives with their own hands.

We should take step-by-step measures to solve the problem of those husbands and wives who have worked and lived in separate places over a long period. We should vigorously create conditions to solve the problem within several years for those working in the strategically important interior areas.

Measures should be taken to run canteens, nurseries, medical and health units and other collective welfare facilities well and to organize sparetime recreational and sports activities. We should do a good job of family planning. We should check up on the methods of passing out welfare allowances as practiced in various regions and enterprises, and appropriate regulations should be formulated by the departments concerned.

We should do well in labour protection and improve working conditions. We should ensure safety in production; major incidents must be sternly dealt with.

We should combine work with adequate rest. We should do a good job in protecting women workers.

Chapter XXVII. City Work Should Serve Production and Workers

All cities must implement the principle of serving production and the workers, and run cultural and educational facilities, health undertakings, urban public utilities, commercial and service trades well, so as to facilitate production and provide amenities for the people. We shouldn't importune the enterprises to run those undertakings and services that cities should and can establish; we should not draw labour power will fully from the enterprises so that the enterprises can concentrate their energy on pushing the revolution and production forward. Funds earmarked by the state for urban construction are not to be diverted to any other purpose. A fairly large portion of the reserve fund in the cities should be used in urban construction.

Vast numbers of workers and staff members engaged in commercial and service trades, urban public utilities as well as educational and health work are components of the working class. Their labour is indispensable to society and their work should command the respect of society. Workers and staff members in these trades should love their work, should constantly improve their services and should contribute their share to the accomplishment of the four modernizations.

Chapter XXVIII. Discipline

Owing to the interference and sabotage by the Gang of Four, discipline in many fields is lax and anarchism exists to a serious extent, causing much harm. It is imperative to strengthen organization, tighten discipline and wage a struggle against all acts in contravention with policies, systems or unified plans, or in breach of financial discipline and labour discipline.

The workers and staff must consciously observe discipline and protect public property.

Members of the Communist Party and the Communist Youth League and particularly leading cadres at all levels should be models in observing discipline. Support and commend those comrades who conscientiously implement the policies and systems and who dare to stick to principle; retaliation against them is absolutely impermissible.

Sternly criticize and educate those in breach of discipline. As for those who commit serious breaches and refuse to mend their ways despite repeated education, the following actions may be taken against them — the recording of a demerit, removal from post, demotion in rank and salary, being placed on probation within the factory (during this period the offender will get only the minimum living expenses) and expulsion. The last measure must be taken with prudence.

Chapter XXIX. Methods and Style of Work

In the great struggle to accelerate industrial development and bring about the modernization of industry, whether the cadres on the industrial front have correct methods and style of work is of important significance. We must restore and develop the party's fine tradition and style of work — seeking truth from facts and following the mass line.

All cadres, especially leading cadres at every level, must go to work at the frontline, take part in labour, do investigation and study among the masses, listen to each other's opinions and refrain from issuing arbitrary orders. They should earnestly sum up and spread the advanced experience created by the masses. While encouraging the advanced, they should be sure to work among the backward units and effect a change in them.

We should work in a down-to-earth manner and guard against empty talk. We should cut down on meetings and make meetings and speeches short. Economic work must be performed in a meticulous way; we should oppose carelessness and flashiness. We should be responsible and keep improving; oppose shifting responsibility onto others or muddling through one's work. We should pay attention to efficiency; oppose being slack or dilatory. We should go in for "three honests and four stricts"[4] and be honest and speak and act honestly; oppose boastfulness or deception.

We should promote materialist dialectics; oppose metaphysics and one-sidedness. Approach everything analytically. Be sure to criticize what is wrong and protect what is right. Take care that one tendency conceals another. Stick to the viewpoint of one dividing into two. Learn the good experience of other places and units, and overcome the erroneous idea of being complacent, conservative and parochially arrogant.

Chapter XXX. Overall Planning, Stronger Leadership

Overall planning and stronger leadership are indispensable to the accomplishment of the tasks mentioned above.

Since we have a lot of things to do, they must be tackled in close coordination. Under the unified leadership of the party committee, every region and department must make overall arrangements in the light of its actual conditions. We should give priority to the key points and avoid attending to too many things at the same time.

In line with Chairman Mao's instruction "formulate a whole set of concrete principles, policies and measures under the guidance of the general line," the central departments concerned shall, together with the localities, draw up rules and regulations for work in every trade and profession and in the industrial enterprises on the basis of making investigation and study and summing up the experience on the principles set out in this document.

The situation on the industrial front is getting better and better under the leadership of Chairman Hua and the Party Central Committee and under the guidance of Chairman Mao's revolutionary line. Our future is infinitely bright. All difficulties we may encounter on our road of advance are temporary and can be overcome. All cadres, workers and technicians on the industrial front must call forth all their vigour, work hard, and boldly shoulder the great historical mission of quickening the pace of industrial development and building up our mighty socialist country. Unite to win still greater victories!

Translator's Notes:

1. The "Charter of the Anshan Iron and Steel Company" is a set of guiding principles approved by Chairman Mao for running socialist enterprises, namely; keep politics firmly in command; strengthen party leadership; launch vigorous mass movements; institute the system of cadre participation in productive labour and worker participation in management, of reform of irrational rules and regulations, and of close cooperation among cadres, workers and technicians; and go full steam ahead with technical innovations and the technical revolution.

2. The "ten needs and need nots" are: need we or needn't we adhere to the party's basic line; need we or needn't we have party leadership; need we or needn't we rely whole-heartedly on the working class; need we or needn't we do well in production; need we or needn't we have rules and regulations; need we or needn't we have socialist accumulation; need we or needn't we apply the principle "From each according to his ability, to each according to his work"; need we or needn't we train the proletariat's own experts; need we or needn't we import new technology; and need we or needn't we stick to planned economy.

3. The "three talks" are: talk about the history of the struggle between the two lines; talk about what we suffered from the Gang of Four; and talk about what we did under the Gang's pernicious influence.

4. The "three honests and four stricts" are: be honest in thought, word and deed; set strict standards for work, organization, attitude and observance of discipline.

14. REGULATIONS ON AWARDS FOR QUALITY PRODUCTS OF THE PEOPLE'S REPUBLIC OF CHINA

((Approved by the State Council and Promulgated by the State Economic Commission on June 30, 1979)

Chapter I. General Principles

Article 1. In order to encourage industrial enterprises to keep improving the quality of their products and strive to make more high-quality goods as required by China's socialist modernization programme and the need to steadily raise the people's living standards and increase exports, the state has decided to confer State Quality Awards on fine-quality industrial products.

Article 2. State Quality Awards are issued annually after evaluation, selection, consideration and approval of the eligible products. The awards are divided into two classes: Class A — gold medals; and Class B — silver medals.

Chapter II. Qualifications

Article 3. All products to be granted State Quality Awards must conform to the following qualifications:
1. They are suited to the needs of, are reliable and satisfactory to the users, and are sought for and appreciated in domestic and world markets;
2. Their quality indices are higher than those laid down in all existing technical standards, on a par with or close to the advanced international standards for the same category or products, or the products are unique and original in design and possess fine traditional qualities;
3. The products are placed first in quality contests among Chinese products of the same kind; and
4. Their designs have been finalized and approved for serial production, and the quality of the products improves steadily.

Chapter III. Selection and Approval

Article 4. Applications for State Quality Awards shall be submitted by the producers of high-quality products and studied by the organizations concerned under the auspices of the revolutionary committees of the provinces, municipalities and autonomous regions. If the applications are accepted, the products shall be tested, evaluated and selected nationally by the departments in charge under the State Council. The results shall be re-examined by the State Administration of Standards and the General Administration for Industry and Commerce and reported to the State Quality Award Board for consideration and approval.

Article 5. The selection and approval of products for State Quality Awards must follow the principal of "high standards and strict demands." Resort to deceit or deception is strictly forbidden and offenders shall be dealt with seriously on the merits of each case.

Chapter IV. Awards

Article 6. All State Quality Awards shall be issued by the State Economic Commission, generally during the annual "Quality Promotion Month."

Article 7. The issuing of State Quality Awards represents a major policy to encourage the development of fine-quality products and must be regarded seriously. The localities, departments and units shall no longer issue medals, badges or cups as prizes for any industrial products.

Chapter V. Symbols of Honour

Article 8. Symbols of honour indicative of medal-winning high-quality products may be affixed to the products which have won State Quality Awards and to their directions and trademarks.

Article 9. The quality of all award-winning products may only be improved and not lowered. No unqualified products are allowed to use the symbols for State Quality Awards.

Article 10. If the quality of any award-winning products should deteriorate, the producer should immediately stop using the symbols for State Quality Awards and promptly report this to the relevant authorities. When the original quality is restored through improvement, the producer may apply to the departments concerned for using these symbols again.

Chapter VI. Appendices

Article 11. The policy toward quality products is to give them higher prices and priority in the supply of raw and semi-processed materials, fuel and electricity.

Article 12. The expenses involved in the issuance of State Quality Awards shall be defrayed by special allocations from the state treasury.

Article 13. The right of interpretation of these Regulations is vested in the State Economic Commission.

Article 14. These Regulations shall come into force from the day they are promulgated.

15. REGULATIONS ON STANDARDIZATION CONTROL OF THE PEOPLE'S REPUBLIC OF CHINA

Promulgated by the State Council
(July 31, 1979)

Chapter I. General Principles

Article 1. Standardization is an important means of organizing modern production and an essential part of scientific management. Promoting standardization in the course of socialist construction is a major technical-economic policy of the state. Without standardization, there will be neither specialization, nor high quality, nor high-speed growth. These Regulations are formulated to strengthen standardization control, raise the level of standardization and bring its role into full play in the modernization of agriculture, industry, national defence, and science and technology.

Article 2. Technical standards (hereinafter, standards for short) provide a common technical basis for production, construction and the circulation of commodities. Standards must be worked out and implemented for all industrial goods in regular production, major farm products, engineering projects, and for environmental protection, safety, sanitation and other matters where the technical requirements should be unified.

Chapter II. Formulation and Revision of Standards

Article 3. In formulating or revising standards, full consideration should be given to the needs of the users, to natural conditions and to the rational utilization of the country's resources, so that the standards shall be technically advanced, economically sound, and reliable for safe operation.

Article 4. The formulation or revision of standards must be based on a selection, proper classification and serialization of the varieties and specifications of the products of the same category; the scope of application should be enlarged as far as possible for widely used spare parts, components, elements, apparatus, structural parts and fittings so as to improve their interchangeability. Different types of standards should be well-coordinated and be complementary to one another; attention should be paid to their applicability for both military and civilian purposes.

Article 5. With regard to the quality indices for industrial and agricultural products, proper grading rules may be included in the relevant standards as required.

Article 6. Packaging standards should be worked out simultaneously with product standards and they must meet the quality and safety requirements, taking into consideration the conditions of loading, unloading, transportation and storage and paying attention to the economical use of materials.

Article 7. Internationally accepted standards and advanced foreign standards should be studied conscientiously and adopted as far as possible.

Article 8. With regard to products for export and the engineering projects China undertakes to build in foreign countries, standards geared to the needs of foreign trade markets should be worked out, if necessary, by the authorities in charge of production and construction, in cooperation with the departments in charge of foreign trade and foreign economic relations.

Article 9. Standards should be revised in time to keep pace with technical and economic development. They should be reviewed once every three to five years to see whether they should be reaffirmed, revised or abrogated.

Article 10. Standardization promoting programmes and plans shall be included in the national economic programmes and plans at all levels. The experimental and research projects necessary for the formulation of standards shall be included in the relevant scientific research plans of various levels.

Chapter III. Classification, Endorsement and Promulgation of Standards

Article 11. Standards are divided into three classes: state standards, ministry standards (specialized standards) and enterprise standards. Ministry standards should be replaced by specialized standards step by step. Neither ministry standards (specialized standards) nor enterprise standards should contravene state standards; and no enterprise standards should contravene ministry standards (specialized standards).

Article 12. State standards refer to those which are of cardinal importance to China's economic and technical development and which must be uniform throughout the country. They include mainly: standards for basic raw materials and semi-processed materials; standards for major industrial and agricultural products which are vital to the people's livelihood, used extensively and in large quantities and produced inter-departmentally; safety and sanitation standards for the protection of the public and the environment; basic standards for interchangeability and common technical terminology; standards for general-purpose spare parts, components, elements, apparatus, structural parts, fittings, tools and measuring instruments; standards for commonly adopted experimental and testing methods; and international standards adopted in China.

Article 13. State standards shall be drafted by the departments in charge under the State Council (or the technical committees in charge of specialized standardization) and, depending on the scope of application of the standards, reported to the following departments for examination, endorsement and promulgation:

- —The State Administration of Standards (for standards relating to industrial and agricultural products and products for both military and civilian uses);
- —The State Capital Construction Commission (for standards relating to engineering projects and environmental protection);
- —The Ministry of Public Health (for standards relating to pharmaceuticals, public health and disease prevention); and
- —The defence industry departments (for standards relating to defence industries).

Important standards shall be reported to the State Council for examination and approval.

Article 14. Ministry standards (specialized standards) refer mainly to those which are unified for a specialized trade throughout the country. They shall be drafted under the auspices of, and endorsed and promulgated by, the competent authorities and reported to the State Administration of Standards to be put on record.

Article 15. Enterprise standards should be worked out for all products that are not covered by state standards or ministry standards (specialized standards). To ensure constant improvement of their products, enterprises may draw up higher quality standards than those laid down in state and ministry standards (specialized standards). Measures governing enterprise standards shall be formulated separately by the State Administration of Standards.

Article 16. All organizations and individuals may propose draft standards. Proposals for state and ministry standards (specialized standards) shall be considered by the national organizations in charge of technical matters relating to specialized standardization; proposals for enterprise standards shall be considered by the higher authorities of the enterprises concerned.

Article 17. The revision or abrogation of standards shall be endorsed and announced by the departments which approved the standards in question. These departments or the organizations they appoint are responsible for the interpretation of the said standards.

Chapter IV. Implementation of Standards

Article 18. As soon as standards are endorsed and promulgated, they become technical decrees, which must be strictly observed by all departments in charge of production, construction, scientific research and design and by all enterprises and undertakings; no organizations are allowed to alter or lower standards without authorization. Anyone who acts in violation of standards and thus causes ill consequences or even grave accidents shall be criticized, disciplined, given economic sanctions or brought to court, depending on the merits of each case.

Where there are real difficulties in implementing standards, the reasons must be explained and a report made on the time allowance requested and the measures to be adopted to apply the standards. After examination and endorsement by the higher authorities, the report shall be submitted to the standard-promulgating departments for approval.

Article 19. The material and technical conditions necessary for the implementation of standards should be guaranteed by the higher authorities; the major items should be included as part of the technical measures that are planned at various levels.

Article 20. All production enterprises must adhere to standards when checking raw materials, semi-processed materials and parts made by other enterprises, examining semi-finished products and inspecting finished products. Up-to-standard products shall be certified as such by the inspection departments; substandard products shall all be excluded from the statistics showing the fulfilment of plans and from output values, and are not allowed to be checked out.

Article 21. All engineering projects must be designed and built in accordance with standards. No project should start on substandard designs and no substandard project should be accepted as passed in final inspection.

Article 22. Full consideration should be given to the requirements of standardization in designing new products and projects, and the letters of designing assignments as well as the design papers must undergo standardization checks; the standardization control departments must be represented in such checks when a design is being examined and finalized.

No new product is allowed to go into serial production unless the standards for that product have been worked out.

Article 23. Full attention should be paid to standardization in reorganizing and improving old products, and the standardization control departments must be represented in the standardization checks.

Article 24. Full consideration must be given to the requirements of domestic standardization when importing equipment and techniques from abroad. There must be prior standardization checks by the departments concerned under the State Council, by the provincial, municipal or autonomous regional standardization control organizations or, if the imported items greatly affect domestic standardization, by the departments concerned under the auspices of the State Administration of Standards.

Chapter V. Quality Supervision and Inspection

Article 25. The State Administration of Standards and the provincial, municipal and autonomous regional bureaus of standards are in charge of the work of supervising and inspecting the quality of products, and they shall coordinate and guide the specialized inspection organizations concerned in carrying out the task. Specific measures shall be drawn up separately by the State Administration of Standards in cooperation with the other departments concerned.

The provinces, municipalities and autonomous regions should establish and improve the organizations charged with quality supervision and inspection in those cities where industries are concentrated. These organizations shall work under the leadership of the standardization control departments of the same level.

Article 26. The tasks of the organizations charged with quality supervision and inspection are: supervising and inspecting the quality of products against the standards; acting as arbiter-inspector when there are disputes over the quality of products between the producer and the seller; keeping the higher authorities informed of the situation and problems in implementing standards, and proposing improvements to the quality of products; giving guidance and help to enterprises in checking up on the quality of products.

Article 27. The departments in charge of quality supervision and inspection have the power to conduct regular and irregular check-ups on the quality of products, either directly or by proxy. They have the power to stop the issuance of quality certificates by those enterprises which do not produce according to standards and the products of which are of low quality; for especially serious cases, they have the power to propose to the competent authorities the application of economic sanctions on the enterprises and the personnel concerned, or to order the enterprises to suspend operation, pending improvement.

Article 28. A new product must be certified up-to-standard by the organizations in charge of quality supervision and inspection before an application for the registration of its trademark is made.

Article 29. With regard to fine-quality products, a quality-indicating system, an award system and a policy of higher price for better quality are adopted. Symbols for good-quality products shall be issued if the products have been certified as such by the organizations in charge of quality supervision and inspection, recognized by the departments concerned and approved by the higher authorities in charge. Specific measures for this shall be formulated separately by the State Administration of Standards together with the other departments concerned.

Chapter VI. Standardization Control Organizations and Personnel

Article 30. The main tasks of the standardization control departments are: enforcing the relevant principles and policies of the state; organizing the formulation and revision of standards; supervising and speeding up the implementation of standards; supervising and inspecting the quality of products and engineering projects; supervising and checking up on the work of standardization relating to the design of new products; the reorganization of old products and the importation of equipment and techniques.

Article 31. The State Administration of Standards is the functional department under the State Council in charge of all standardization work in the country. Its responsibility is to put forward principles and policies for standardization, organize the formulation and implementation of national standardization programmes and plans, and take charge of all standardization work and quality supervision and inspection in the country.

Article 32. The bureaus of standards of the provinces, municipalities, autonomous regions and industrial cities and the standardization control organizations of autonomous prefectures and counties are the functional departments under the revolutionary committees of the same level and are responsible for standardization control and quality supervision and inspection in their localities.

Article 33. The standardization control organizations of the departments concerned under the State Council and in the People's Liberation Army are responsible for standardization control within their respective departments.

Article 34. The standardization control organizations or standardization control personnel in the specialized bureaus, companies, enterprises and undertakings of the departments concerned under the State Council and of the provinces, municipalities and autonomous regions are under the direct leadership of the officials in charge of technical work (or the chief engineers) and are responsible for standardization work in their own units or as assigned by the higher authorities.

Article 35. The State Administration of Standards and the departments concerned under the State Council should set up and strengthen standardization research institutes and standardization information and data-processing centres. The provincial, municipal and autonomous regional bureaus of standards should set up and strengthen standardization information and data-processing centres.

Article 36. The national technical committees in charge of specialized standardization, the standardization research institutes of the departments concerned under the State Council and other organizations in charge of technical matters relating to specialized standardization shall conduct relevant scientific research, organize and undertake the formulation and revision of state standards and ministry standards (specialized standards), and participate in relevant international activities.

Article 37. Standardization and quality inspection are productive technical work. The scientists and technicians engaged in this work are part of the scientific and technical contingent, and they should enjoy the same political and economic treatment as the scientists and technicians of other departments. Those who have made outstanding achievements or important contributions should be awarded.

Chapter VII. Appendices

Article 38. Measures for the implementation of these regulations shall be worked out by the revolutionary committees of the provinces, municipalities and autonomous regions, the departments concerned under the State Council, and the departments concerned of the People's Liberation Army.

Article 39. The State Administration of Standards is responsible for the interpretation of these regulations.

Article 40. These regulations shall come into force from the day they are promulgated, and the former "Measures Governing Technical Standards for Industrial and Agricultural Products and Engineering Projects" shall cease to be effective.

16. TENTATIVE REGULATIONS (DRAFT) ON BONUSES FOR SAVING SPECIALLY DESIGNATED FUELS AND RAW MATERIALS IN STATE-OWNED INDUSTRIAL AND TRANSPORT ENTERPRISES, ISSUED BY THE MINISTRY OF FINANCE, THE STATE BUREAU OF LABOUR AND THE STATE ADMINISTRATION OF SUPPLIES

(Promulgated on November 10, 1979)

To increase production and practice economy is a common and long-range task in carrying out socialist modernization. With a view to increasing production and practicing economy in a far-reaching and sustained way and encouraging the staff and workers of enterprises to save funds and materials for the state, reduce the cost of production, increase the profits of enterprises and speed up the development of production, we have formulated the following regulations:

Article 1. All enterprises which consume large quantities of fuels, electricity, non-ferrous metals and other much-wanted products and precious materials in production and which have established management systems (including consumption quotas, consumption measurements, keeping original records, making regular inventories, checking product quality and assessing economic results) may, with the approval of the ministries which they are under, introduce a single-item bonus system for saving specially-designed fuels and raw materials on a trial basis in line with the specific requirements of the respective enterprises. Enterprises which do not have the above-mentioned requisites shall not introduce the system. Administrative action shall be taken against anyone who introduces this bonus system in enterprises which do not have the above-mentioned requisites.

Article 2. The fuels and raw materials that are designated for single-item bonuses are the ten categories that are consumed in large quantities, namely: coal, coke, electricity, gasoline, diesel oils, heavy oils, crude oil, timber, rare and precious metals or other non-ferrous metals that cannot be produced at home in large quantities, and high-quality rolled steel. The bonuses will be paid from the amount of value saved and counted as part of the production cost.

The saving of fuels and raw materials other than those mentioned above should be taken into consideration in issuing regular production bonuses, which shall be paid from the regular bonus funds drawn according to the percentages permitted by the state and shall not be paid again from the amount of value saved as a single-item saving bonus.

Article 3. The savings of fuels and raw materials in the enterprises should be counted according to the quotas set by the state. The actual consumption under a set quota is the saved amount.

The consumption quotas for the above-mentioned fuels and raw materials as a whole will be fixed by the respective ministries on the basis of the average best level of consumption ever achieved in the respective industries or trades. If some ministries have difficulties in fixing their quotas, the municipalities, provinces and autonomous regions may fix quotas on the basis of the local average best levels of consumption ever achieved. In principle, quotas should be revised once a year on the basis of the new level of consumption achieved so as to maintain the most advanced and rational levels.

Article 4. The rates of bonuses for the savings, worked out on the basis of the prices of the fuels, electricity and raw materials consumed and the degree of difficulty in reducing the consumption quotas, are defined as follows:

1–3% of the amount of value saved for non-ferrous metals and high-quality rolled steels;

3–8% of the amount of value saved for gasoline, diesel oils, heavy oils, crude oil and coke;

8–15% of the amount of value saved for coal, electricity and timber.

The ministries must obtain approval from the Ministry of Finance, the State Bureau of Labour and the State Administration of Supplies in working out the details of the rates of bonuses for each industry.

Article 5. Savings shall be assessed annually. Bonuses for savings may be given quarterly or monthly according to the actual amount saved. If more fuels, electricity and raw materials are consumed than the quotas permit in a quarter or a month, no bonus will be given for that quarter or that month, and the above-quota amount will be deducted from the amount saved in the next quarter or the next month, and bonuses will be given on the basis of the amount saved after deduction and according to the fixed rates of bonuses.

In the case of a combined operation in which a group of people doing different kinds of work take part, a shift, a group or a section will be taken as a counting unit. In the case of an operation by an individual, the individual will be taken as the counting unit. The collective receiving the award should distribute the bonus to its members according to their contributions: bigger shares for bigger contributions, smaller shares for smaller contributions and no share for no contribution.

Article 6. Enterprises which introduce the single-item saving bonus system must check the quality of products strictly and must not alter the quality of products for the sake of saving fuels or raw materials. Bonuses shall be suspended if frauds are discovered and the quality of products drops. If bonuses are given in this case, the same amount of money shall be deducted from wages. Action shall be taken against those who are responsible for fraud. Disciplinary action shall be taken against individuals involved in serious cases.

Article 7. The departments of supplies and planning should, in accordance with the policy of "savings to factories," leave to the factories the fuels and raw materials saved by reducing the factories' consumption quotas for above-quota production. The increased part of production will be distributed according to the relevant state regulations.

Article 8. The savings and the issued bonuses must be made known to the workers and staff from time to time in the interest of democratic management and mass supervision.

Article 9. Details may be worked out by the ministries under the State Council and the governments of provinces, municipalities and autonomous regions in line with this regulation. They should be sent to the Ministry of Finance, the State Bureau of Labour and the State Administration of Supplies for the records. Regulations previously published by the local governments and ministries which contravene this regulation should be abrogated.

17. TENTATIVE MEASURES CONCERNING THE SHARING OF PROFITS IN STATE-OWNED INDUSTRIAL ENTERPRISES, ISSUED BY THE STATE ECONOMIC COMMISSION AND THE MINISTRY OF FINANCE

Approved by the State Council on January 22, 1980

In July 1979 the State Council issued the "Regulations on the Sharing of Profits in State-Owned Enterprises," and the Ministry of Finance, the State Economic Commission and the People's Bank also published the "Opinions Concerning Some Concrete Problems in the Experimental Work Of Putting into Effect the State Council Document on Restructuring the Enterprise Management System." These two documents have helped to bring into play the initiative of enterprises and to encourage enterprises to show interest in production and increase their profits.

In order to improve the experimental work, ensure the collection of state revenues and give consideration to the interests of the state, the enterprises and individual workers, the measures concerning the sharing of profits in state-owned industrial enterprises were revised after problems and opinions collected from various parts of the country in the course of the experiment were discussed at the National Planning Meeting. The revised measures are as follows:

Article 1. State-owned industrial enterprises which have maintained normal production order and management after consolidation, retained independent economic accounting and have profits may, with approval, try out the profit-sharing system in accordance with the Measures.

Article 2. The original method of drawing shares from the total profit is changed to the method of drawing shares from the basic profit and the increase in profit. If the profit of an enterprise in the current year is bigger than that in the preceding year, the enterprise may draw a share from the basic profit, which is equivalent to its profit in the preceding year, according to the assessed proportions, and then draw another share from the increase in profit, that is, the part above the profit in the preceding year, according to the proportions defined by the state.

If the profit of an enterprise in the current year is smaller than that in the preceding year, the enterprise may draw a basic share from its actual profit in the current year according to the assessed proportions. In calculating the shares to be drawn from the basic profit or from the increase in profit, the amount of increased profit attributable to technical measures adopted with depreciation funds and funds pooled by the enterprise itself should be included.

An enterprise may use the shares drawn from the basic profit and the increase in profit for its production development fund, workers' welfare fund and workers' bonus fund.

Article 3. When an enterprise obtains approval to start the experiment, the proportions of shares it draws from the basic profit shall be determined by the percentage of the following expenses in the preceding year to the total amount of profit in the same year:

(1) Enterprises assigned to develop new products may, on the whole, calculate the cost of new product development at 1% of the total profit. Those enterprises which have been assigned to develop more new products may calculate the cost of new product development at 2% of the total profit. Machine-building plants may calculate the cost at 3% of the total profit. Enterprises which are not assigned to develop new products, e.g., coal mines, oilfields, power plants, power stations, lumber centres, railways and other communications, and other mining enterprises, shall not calculate this cost.

(2) An enterprise's expenses for scientific research and for workers' technical training are calculated on the basis of the government's actual allocations to the enterprise (not including the three special appropriations given by the government for scientific and technical work and expenses for adopting technical measures). The expenses not included in the production cost of an enterprise or its business turnover shall be calculated according to the formula stated above.

(3) The workers' welfare fund to be drawn from the cost of production shall be calculated at 11% of total wages.

(4) Workers' bonuses, paid from the cost of production as a whole, shall be calculated at 10% of the total basic wages of an enterprise. The percentage may be raised proportionately for a limited number of advanced enterprises, but it shall not constitute more than 12% of total basic wages.

(5) The percentage of enterprise funds to be drawn from the profit by a basic level enterprise shall be stated separately by the authorities and shall constitute no more than 5% of total wages, depending on varying conditions in enterprises.

The sums in items (1) and (2) constitute the production development fund. The amount in item (3) and 80% of the amount in item (5) constitute the workers' welfare fund. The amount in item (4) and 20% of the amount in item (5) the workers' bonus fund. Proportional shares of profits to be drawn by enterprises shall be assessed separately for the three funds.

The total profit for calculating the proportional share from the basic part is the amount of profit after the loan for technical measures to be returned is deducted. After the system of drawing the workers' welfare fund and bonus fund from the cost of production is replaced by the system of drawing them from profit, the total profit for calculating the proportion share from the basic part should be increased correspondingly.

After the profit-sharing system is introduced, the government shall no longer make appropriations for the expenses which should be paid from the share of profit, and enterprises shall no longer include expenses as part of the production cost nor draw enterprise funds.

Article 4. The proportions of shares which enterprises will draw from the increased part of profit are separately stated for different industries as follows:

(1) 10% for petroleum, power, and petrochemical enterprises and enterprises with complete plants imported from abroad which earn considerably more profits;

(2) 20% for metallurgical, machine-building, electronic, chemical, light industry, textile, building materials, timber, railway and other communications and other enterprises;

(3) 30% for coal mining, post and telecommunications, civil aviation and farm machinery enterprises.

Article 5. The proportions of shares from the basic part of profit shall be assessed level by level from top to bottom. The total proportions of shares of profits retained by the provinces, municipalities, autonomous regions and the ministries in charge of production shall be assessed by the State Economic Commission and the Ministry of Finance. The provinces, municipalities, autonomous regions and the ministries in charge of production may separately assess the proportions of shares of profits retained by the enterprises (or corporations) under them within the limits of the total proportions of shares assessed by the state.

Article 6. The assessed proportions of shares from the basic part of profit shall, in principle, remain unchanged for three years. Adjustments may be made under the following circumstances:

(1) The readjustment of the prices of products, the prices of major raw materials and the restructuring of the taxation system lead to big increases or decreases in the profits of enterprises;

(2) The readjustment of the enterprises in the industrial reorganization leads to big increases or decreases in the profits of enterprises;

(3) The operation of workshops, branch factories and attached factories that are newly-built or expanded with government investment leads to big increases in the profits of enterprises;

(4) The profits of enterprises decrease after they pay taxes on fixed assets and interest on fixed loans.

Article 7. An industrial enterprise can draw a full share of profit as stated only when it reaches the four planned targets for output, quality, profit and fulfilment of its contracts to supply goods. If an enterprise fails to reach one of the four planned quotas, a deduction of 10% shall be made from its share of profit (including both the share from the basic part of profit and the share from the increased part of profit).

Quotas for assessment in the railway and other land and water transport, post and telecommunications and civil aviation enterprises shall be defined separately by the ministries in charge of these enterprises and the Ministry of Finance through consultation.

Article 8. An enterprise shall draw a full share from the basic part of profit as stated if it fulfills its monthly target; it shall draw 80% of its share in advance for the month if it fails to fulfil its monthly target. An enterprise may draw 50% of its share in advance from the increased part of profit as stated if it fulfils 50% or more of its annual quota in the first six months, but it is not permitted to draw any shares from the increased part of profit in advance if it fails to fulfil 50% of the annual quota. The share of profit an enterprise is entitled to shall be included in its final accounts at the end of a year. A surplus shall be refunded and a deficiency made up when the final accounts are settled after an examination by the department above in charge and by the financial department at the same level.

When an enterprise draws a share of profit, the profit shall be calculated after the enterprise repays its loan for technical measures.

Article 9. An enterprise shall draw its share from the basic part of profit according to the assessed percentages separately for the production development fund, the workers' welfare fund and the workers' bonus fund, and shall also manage and use them separately for these purposes. The amount drawn by an enterprise from the increased part of profit to be used for development of production shall not be less than 60% and the amount used for workers' welfare facilities and bonuses shall not be more than 40%. The production development fund may be used together with the capital fund for replacing or revamping old equipment, but not for workers' welfare or bonuses. The bonuses issued to workers shall be paid from the workers' bonus fund, except the savings bonus stated separately by the government. An enterprise should draw the workers' bonus fund before using it and the bonus fund shall not exceed the quota. Total bonuses issued to the workers of an enterprise which draws a greater bonus fund than others, calculated on the basis of the enterprise as a unit, shall not exceed an amount equivalent to the basic wages of the workers in the enterprise for two months. The surplus of the bonus fund shall be carried over to the following year.

Article 10. An enterprise's plan for the use of the funds drawn from profit must be submitted to the workers' congress of the enterprise for discussion. The funds must be placed under full democratic management and mass supervision.

Article 11. The quantity of materials and equipment needed by an enterprise for adopting production measures or for improving welfare facilities with the retained share of profit should be reported to the planning commissions and departments in charge of surplus at all levels and should be included in the plans for settlement.

Article 12. In practising the profit-sharing sytem, enterprises must conscientiously carry out the party's policies and principles and state plans, and must adhere to financial guidelines; they must not resort to fraud and deception. If an enterprise violates the guidelines, the departments above in charge of the work should make a deduction from the share of profit accruing to the enterprise or suspend the enterprise's right to draw the share of profit in a given period, depending on the severity of the case, and the leaders of the enterprise and other people involved shall be dealt with sternly.

Subject to approval, these measures shall be adopted on an experimental basis in state-owned industrial enterprises beginning in 1980. Enterprises which have already started the experiment according to local measures must all change to adopt these measures as of 1980.

18. PROVISIONAL REGULATIONS FOR TOTAL QUALITY CONTROL IN INDUSTRIAL ENTERPRISES
Promulgated by the State Economic Commission
(March 18, 1980)

Chapter I. General Principles

Article 1. The present regulations are formulated for the purposes of popularizing total quality control in industrial enterprises, carrying out the policy of putting "quality in first place" and improving the quality of products steadily so as to meet the needs of the programme of Four Modernizations and the continuous rise in the people's living standards.

Article 2. Total quality control is a central link in enterprise management as well as a scientific method of quality control in modern industry. It means control of the quality of products in the entire process from designing, trial-production, manufacture through post-sale service. All the workers and staff of an enterprise and all the departments therein should learn and take part in quality control.

Article 3. The tasks for those involved in total quality control are: keep abreast of the needs of national reconstruction and the people's livelihood and investigate the developments of similar products in China and other countries and their market conditions; educate the workers and staff to foster the concept of putting "quality in first place" and correctly carry out advanced and rational technical standards; adopt scientific methods (including mathematical statistics) and, through specialized technical research, control various factors affecting product quality; undertake technico-economic analysis of the quality of products; offer technical services to users; constantly improve product quality in line with the requirements in their use and strive to turn out products that are good in quality, low in price, suited to buyer's requirements, satisfactory to users and competitive on both the domestic and overseas markets.

Chapter II. Planning for Product Quality

Article 4. Planning for the product quality is a constant and effective means of organizing total quality control. Such planning calls for a programme of action involving departments engaged in quality control. All industrial enterprises need to map out comprehensive plans for improving product quality, as well as specific plans for different items, periods and departments in line with the principle of achieving greater, faster, better and more economical results.

Article 5. Planning for product quality consists of:

1. Planning for catching up with or surpassing advanced levels in product quality. This means drafting plans for catching up with or surpassing advanced levels in trial-producing and manufacturing new products and improving existing products in line with users' requirements and the orientation of technological development. This requires the defining of concrete targets for catching up with or surpassing advanced levels in China and abroad and the setting of a time limit and rate of progress for fulfilling the targets.

2. Planning for quality targets. The comprehensive economic plan of an enterprise should embody the policy of putting "quality in first place." A separate plan defining the rates of first-grade and fine quality products should be drafted and examined in the light of specific circumstances.

3. Planning for measures to improve quality. This kind of plan defines the measures for quality improvement to be taken during the year and in each quarter and the departments to take the main responsibilities. The annual outlay for technical measures should, first of all, be spent on improvement of product quality and development of new products.

Article 6. Stress should be laid on the implementation of plans. Various plans for the quality of products should be carried out by all departments, brigades and individual workers, and their implementation should be linked up with examination, emulation, assessment, rewards and punishments.

Chapter III. Quality Control at Design and Trial-Production Stage

Article 7. The stage of designing and trial-production means the whole process of technical preparations prior to the stage of regular production of a product. It covers investigation and research, programme drafting, product designing, technical designing, trial-production, testing and appraisal.

1. Investigation, research and drafting of programme. This means investigating users' requirements with respect to product quality, collecting relevant technical data in China and other countries, and studying ways of solving key technological problems. The work also includes the drafting of targets for quality and technical requirements that are suitable and reliable, satisfactory to customers, economic and rational.

2. Organization of users, sales, research, manufacturing, and quality control departments and a "three-in-one" combination of leading officials, technicians and workers for the examination of designs. Efforts should be made through such examination to meet the requirements of users, solve problems that may arise in the course of production, and select suitable design.

3. Work must be done well in the trial-production, testing and assessment of new products. After the completion of the trial-production of new products (including major improvements in existing products), the enterprise concerned should organize relevant personnel to make strict tests and appraisals. With regard to important products, the department in charge should organize user and other relevant units for appraisal and all-round technical and economic assessment.

4. Work must be done well in the examination of standardization. It is essential to ensure that product designs are up to or even above the various technical standards stipulated by the state and to raise the level of standardization, serialization and inter-changeability of products.

Article 8. The following requirements must be met before a new product can go into serial production:

1. The technical standards of the product have been drawn up and gone through the formalities of report and approval;

2. The technical papers must be complete, accurate and clear;

3. A certificate of quality must be obtained from the authorities for supervising and inspecting the product, and a product ready to go into the market must have its trade mark registered;

4. There must be complete sets of equipment and devices for examining and testing product quality;

5. It must be in conformity with the requirements for environmental protection, security and sanitation.

Article 9. It is essential to adopt a scientific approach to the process of designing and trial-production and to act strictly according to the stipulated procedures; it is forbidden to proceed with designing, experimenting and manufacturing simultaneously.

Chapter IV. Quality Control in Course of Production

Article 10. The tasks for those involved in quality control in the course of production are: establish a production system capable of constantly turning out qualified and top quality products, and do a good job of quality control at each link of the chain of production; strictly follow the technical standards, make sure that the quality of products reaches or surpasses all these standards, strive to turn out top quality products, and try to cut down rejects as far as possible.

Article 11. Close attention should be given to the following points if success is to be achieved in quality control in the course of production:

1. Establish or improve the system of responsibility for each and every workpost, map out or revise rules for various operations in good time, implement them strictly, and get everyone to observe technical discipline.

2. Do a really good job of working in a scientific way and, in particular, maintaining good order in production, rationally equip the work places with tools and make sure that the passageways for production are free from obstacles and that the work sites are tidy and clean. Trees should be planted in the surroundings and pollution and dust prevented.

3. Make good preparations before production starts and arrange production plans rationally; improve production management, strengthen weak links in time, and take steps to achieve a harmonious flow in production.

4. Make full use and flexible employment of mathematical statistics and other methods of quality control to maintain the quality of products in the course of production and prevent rejects.

5. Map out or revise technical standards for existing products. Enterprises which do not have such standards should institute their standards and those whose standards are backward should revise them; all enterprises should strictly implement their standards after they are submitted to and approved by the appropriate authorities.

6. Strengthen metrological work. To ensure the quality of products, all enterprises should institute special metrological organizations or personnel to be responsible for unified control of metrological work in measurement, temperature, mechanics, electricity, chemistry, etc., to implement metrological laws and decrees and the system

of metrological control, and to be responsible for the examination and maintenance of metrological instruments and the work of testing. It is essential to equip the enterprises with all necessary metrological devices and testing instruments and equipment and keep them constantly in good repair.

7. Establish or improve various systems for quality control centred round the system of responsibility for each workpost. Unqualified raw and other materials must not be used in production, unqualified semi-finished products must not be used, unqualified products must not be allowed to leave the factory as qualified products, nor must they be included in calculating the value and volume of production. Workpieces from one working procedure which are not up to standard must not be allowed to move to the next procedure; workers on the next shift have the right to refuse to take over if they find the equipment, the job being worked on and the environmental sanitation are not up to the standards for quality control. The principle of combining inspection by the workers themselves and by full-time personnel should be adopted in the inspection of product quality. Self-inspection and mutual inspection among the workers should be the main practice in the course of production whereas semi-finished and finished products should mainly be inspected by professional personnel. Records on quality should be established or improved and a good job should be done in keeping primary records about product quality and in making statistics and analysis.

8. Do a good job of quality control in the supply of materials. Examination and acceptance of materials going into storage should be done strictly according to rule. Materials that are not up to standard or not in conformity with the provisions of contracts may be returned or rejected. The care-takers of materials should take effective steps to avoid damage and deterioration. The quality of service should be raised so as to ensure timely supply of materials. Departments in charge of materials supply should assume total responsibility for the quality of those products whose purchase and marketing are monopolized by these departments.

9. Strengthen maintenance service so as to keep all equipment in good technical condition. Repaired equipment should be up to the specified requirements for quality. Tools and equipment should be kept well to ensure the required precision of tools, fixtures, measuring instruments and cutting tools.

10. Improve the quality of packing. Standards for packing should be instituted in line with the characteristics of products, packing and examination should be done in strict accordance with the standards, and packing of products that is not up to standard must be done over again. Packing and decoration of products should be improved continuously to make them attractive.

11. Delivery of products should be handled in line with the specific contracts signed with the customers. It is impermissible to compel the customers to accept them on the pretext that they are up to certain general norms or to accept a mixture of quality and inferior products.

Chapter V. Quality in the Course of Use

Article 12. The assessment of product quality depends mainly on the users' evaluation. Quality control in the course of use is an extension of the work of an enterprise in quality control. The enterprise should constantly study and seek to improve product quality through visits to users and technical service for them.

Article 13. Active steps should be taken to develop technical service:

1. Compile manuals explaining the use of products. The contents of such manuals should generally include the characteristics, structure, installation, use and maintenance of the products, points for attention, the period of guarantee and conditions under which they are to be kept and transported, etc. Manuals for export products should be translated into foreign languages

2. Impart techniques about the installation, use and maintenance of products and help train technicians in a variety of ways, and undertake to resolve knotty technical problems in the use of products.

3. Provide blueprints for the manufacture of parts that are easily worn out and supply users according to their needs with spare parts and accessories for maintenance purposes (assembly plants responsible for supplying users; factories making elements and components and factories rendering assistance responsible for supplying assembly plants).

4. Set up a network of repair shops or retail shops and in certain cases take service to users' doorsteps.

5. Manufacturers should help users with the installation and trial run of certain complex products or provide technical guidance.

Article 14. Introduce and maintain such practices as visiting users, manning sales counters or holding users' discussions regularly. Links between industry and commerce, and between production and marketing, should be strengthened. Every enterprise should try through all possible channels to investigate the effects and requirements of its products in use, find out their flaws and problems, and feed these back in good time while comparing its own products with those of other enterprises and countries, so as to improve designs and raise product quality.

Article 15. All users (including units in the following working procedures) should, in the spirit of responsibility to the country and people and mutual assistance between enterprises, keep the manufacturing and supplying units informed of the quality of raw and other materials, parts and whole products. Assembly plants should keep abreast of the work of the quality control systems of supplying units and suggest improvements with respect to existing problems and take the initiative to solve the problems. All units involved should be organized in a coordinated effort to guarantee the quality of the end products. Manufacturing units should handle conscientiously problems concerning the quality of its ex-factory products. They should give prompt answers to criticisms and demands raised by users. They should enthusiastically help users acquire the techniques of using the products where problems have arisen because of inappropriate handling. In case of problems due to faulty manufacturing, the assembly plants should be responsible for repairing or substituting the parts concerned or for refunding, no matter whether the parts in question were made by themselves or bought from other factories. Damages should be paid in case of accidents occurring during the period of guarantee because of inferior product quality. Economic contracts should be concluded between assembly plants and factories supplying raw and other materials and accessories. The supplying units should deliver their consignments according to the quality, quantity and date of delivery specified in the contracts; those which fail to honor contracts should be held responsible for the economic losses thus incurred.

Chapter VI. System of Quality Control

Article 16. All enterprises should conscientiously implement the principles, policies, rules and regulations for quality control laid down by the party and state. Its is essential to give full play to the enthusiasm and initiative of the technical personnel and the workers in quality control and define explicitly the tasks that must be fulfilled by each department, unit and individual worker, the responsibilities they are charged with and the limits of their authority. All departments and units should draft their own standards for high quality work so as to use the high quality of work done to ensure the quality of products. A complete system for total quality control should be established, under which there should be people responsible for each product, each working procedure and each relevant piece of work.

Article 17. All enterprises should put total quality control as an important item on the agenda, and the managers or factory directors should bear full responsibility for the quality of products manufactured by their own enterprises. The chief engineers should, under the leadership of the factory directors, be responsible for the development and manufacture of new products, the drafting of plans for catching up with or surpassing advanced levels in product quality, and the solving of major technical problems concerning product quality.

Article 18. Establish comprehensive quality control organizations or full-time personnel whose major functions are: under the leadership of the managers or factory directors, assist the leadership in comprehensive, day-to-day work of quality control; be responsible for the tabulation of comprehensive statistics and examination of the implementation of the plans for quality control; study and popularize advanced methods of quality control; coordinate the work of quality control in related departments; organize investigations of the effects and requirements of use of products; take part in the assessment of new products; carry out publicity and education with regard to quality control; and organize mass participation in quality control.

All enterprises should establish or improve quality inspection organizations which are responsible for supervising the implementation of the standards for product quality. Their main tasks are: make strict inspection of product quality in accordance with the technical standards and orders for goods; undertake the inspection of the quality of raw and other materials, purchased parts, semi-finished products, finished products, and the principal working procedures; make comments on whether a new product can be put into regular production; sign certificates of inspection for products leaving the factory; and report to the managers or factory directors and the higher authorities on the actual quality of products manufactured by their own enterprises and parts supplied by support factories. The appointment and removal of chiefs of quality inspection divisions or sections should be done with the approval of the next higher authorities.

Article 19. Departments of distribution, materials supply and transportation should set up a system of responsibility for guaranteeing the quality of products during transportation and for improving the work of factories, workshops, warehouses and storage and transport facilities in this regard.

Chapter VII. Mass Participation in Quality Control

Article 20. All enterprises should, in the light of their own characteristics, mobilize the masses extensively and carry out various forms of activity for quality control. Quality control groups in different forms should be set up on a voluntary basis and with reference to the actual conditions, and they should carry out constant activities concerning quality control and tackle major problems in order to improve quality. Records should be kept on the establishment of quality control groups and their activities.

Article 21. The workers should be organized to take an active part in the "quality month" drive, emulation campaigns should be launched to turn out high quality products, pace-setters in improving quality elected, and all kinds of meetings on the work of quality control held to exchange experience, commend advanced workers and promote the steady improvement of products.

Chapter VIII. Education and Training

Article 22. Education in total quality control should be carried out in all enterprises, and leading cadres at various levels should take the lead in study and application. First of all, it is necessary to train a number of people as the backbone force in quality control.

Article 23. All workers should be given constant, repeated education in quality control. The contents and time of study should be stipulated according to the workers' different trades and needs. Education inside and outside of the factory should be integrated so that all concerned will be able to acquire the basic knowledge and methods of total quality control and apply them in a flexible way in the light of their own jobs.

Article 24. Effective steps should be taken to run technical schools and various types of technical training courses. A variety of methods such as on-site training, technical demonstrations, competitions of skills and election of skilled hands should be adopted in conjunction with everyday production activities to encourage the workers to study techniques and raise their technical standards.

Article 25. New workers should be given basic technical training and education in total quality control following their recruitment. They must first pass the examination and acquire a certificate of qualification for operation before they are allowed to take over workposts and operate.

Article 26. All workers are subjected to technical and professional examinations on the improving of product quality according to rule. The results are to be entered in their records as an important basis for their promotion or upgrading

Chapter IX. Rewards and Punishments

Article 27. The principle to be followed is: high price for high quality, low price for low quality, and priority for advanced units in the supply of raw materials, fuel and power.

Article 28. The system of rewards in all enterprises should embody the policy of "putting quality in first place." Contributions to quality should be regarded as the foremost condition for winning overall rewards.

Separate terms should be drafted for rewarding full-time inspectors in enterprises. Examination of inspectors' records should be concentrated on the quality and amount of inspection they have done.

Article 29. Improvement of product quality should be integrated with the interests of the enterprises and the workers themselves. Outstanding groups and individuals who have made signal contributions to quality control and improvement of product quality should be given honorary diplomas and annual material rewards. Quality products up to the required standards may apply for regional, departmental or national rewards for quality.

Article 30. Those enterprises whose products are of inferior quality for long periods of time due to chaotic business management and therefore incur strong criticisms from users, must be ordered to make improvements within a set time. They should be ordered to stop production and straighten things out where necessary, and the wages of their leading cadres may be reduced appropriately and the bonuses for the workers suspended in the light of the circumstances, until the quality of their products attains the standard.

Article 31. Where accidents pertaining to product quality have occurred, the enterprises concerned should find out the causes, handle them seriously, and report to the departments in charge promptly in accordance with relevant stipulations. In case of major accidents pertaining to quality, the leadership should be held responsible and those who are directly responsible should be criticized or punished according to the seriousness of their cases and their own attitudes. Those whose cases are serious and whose attitudes are bad should be dealt with according to law. Anyone who practises fraud on product quality, trumps up data, palms off inferior products as qualified ones, cheats customers, or retaliates upon inspectors and others who expose his fraudulence, will be held responsible and dealt with severely.

Chapter X. Supplementary Articles

Article 32. The present regulations shall go into force from the day of their promulgation. Various regions and departments concerned may formulate their own by-laws for application according to their specific circumstances.

Article 33. The right of explanation of these regulations rests with the State Economic Commission.

19. PROVISIONAL REGULATIONS OF THE STATE CAPITAL CONSTRUCTION COMMISSION, THE STATE PLANNING COMMISSION, THE MINISTRY OF FINANCE, THE STATE BUREAU OF LABOUR AND THE STATE ADMINISTRATION OF SUPPLIES ON PROBLEMS RELATED TO THE BROADENING OF THE MANAGEMENT DECISION-MAKING POWER OF CONSTRUCTION ENTERPRISES
(May 4, 1980)

It is essential to broaden appropriately the decision-making power of construction enterprises in matters of management in order to operate them as basic units of material production with independent management and accounting, to further arouse the enthusiasm of the construction enterprises and their workers and staff, to improve management, to increase economic returns, and to fulfil capital construction tasks with greater, faster, better and more economic results. Following are the relevant regulations:

1. Broaden the power of decision of the enterprises in the management of production. The drafting of production plans for construction enterprises should, under the guidance of the unified state plan, be changed over step by step to the practice of taking contracts as the basis. While assigning construction tasks to the enterprises, the department in charge should guarantee the material conditions they require in order to fulfil the tasks. So long as they guarantee the fulfilment of the tasks assigned by the state, the enterprises should have the right to contract on their own certain construction jobs or to develop the provision of multiple services to construction work in the light of their own conditions and social needs. No unit or individual should interfere with the normal business of production and management within the enterprises.

2. Reform the methods of material supply. Building materials, forms, tools and materials for erecting large provisional facilities needed in capital construction projects should be supplied within the overall consideration of manpower, funds and material supplies. Before major reforms are made in the entire system of material supply, the following three methods can be adopted in the contracting of jobs and material supplies for construction enterprises:

A. Materials needed by construction enterprises under the ministries of metallurgical, coal, power, railways, communications, petroleum, second machine-building and chemical industries are allocated to the ministries concerned according to existing regulations and then distributed by the ministries directly to the construction units in line with the needs of the projects to be built.

B. With regard to projects whose budgets are covered by the central government, the materials needed are to be determined by the central government in accordance with the progress of the projects, and the practice of delivering materials to the construction sites is to be adopted step by step.

C. The supply of materials for construction projects undertaken by enterprises under the State Bureau of Building Industry is to be handled in the following ways:

For local projects belonging to provinces, municipalities or autonomous regions, the practice of allocating materials to the departments in charge of construction or directly to the construction units is to be adopted by the related departments in the provinces, municipalities or autonomous regions concerned; for projects directly belonging to various departments under the State Council, the departments in charge may earmark quotas for material consumption or supply materials to the construction units directly; the construction units may use the materials in a flexible way in line with the order of priority of the projects.

3. Restore the practice of retaining legal profits. All state-run construction enterprises that practice independent accounting are entitled, beginning from 1980, to draw a legal profit equivalent, for the time being, to 2.5% of the budgeted cost of the project. The legal profit does not have to be turned over to the higher authorities but is kept entirely by the enterprises themselves in the first three years. After the first three years, the profit will be handled according to the ratio of distribution specified in Item 4. Following the adoption of the practice of retaining the legal profit, construction units will no longer charge the departments owning the projects for funds to operate schools for workers' children.

4. Introduce the practice of reserving part of the building cost saved in construction. The amount of building costs saved by the construction enterprises together with other income that remains after non-business expenditures and stipulated enterprise funds are duly deducted, will be divided in half, one of which is to be turned over to the financial authorities and the other to be kept by the enterprise. When the profits to be turned over by an enterprise to the higher authorities on a 50/50 basis exceeds the amount handed over in the previous year, the enterprise is then required to hand over only 20% of the excess portion while retaining the rest. In order to foster development in areas populated by national minorities and in remote provinces, construction enterprises belonging to the provinces and autonomous regions of Yunnan, Guizhou, Tibet, Xinjiang, Qinghai, Ningxia and Inner Mongolia, together with enterprises for constructing hydroelectric projects under the Ministry of Power Industry, are allowed to hand in to the financial authorities only 30% of the year's profits while keeping the rest. They do not have to follow the practice of reserving part of the excess portion of above-quota profits.

Those units which have been authorized by provincial, municipal or autonomous regional governments to practice the system of sole responsibility for profit or loss may continue to act according to existing rules.

The legal profit and the share of saved building costs reserved by construction enterprises should be used mainly for expanding production and for the workers' collective welfare facilities.

5. Replace the practice of receiving government investments by charging fees for construction tasks as payment for technical equipment needed by local state-run construction enterprises. Beginning from 1981, the government will no longer make investments to cover the expenses of technical equipment for local state-run construction enterprises. They can charge fees equivalent to 3% of the budgeted cost of the projects contracted and, if this is insufficient, borrow money from the Construction Bank to cover the balance. This practice may be introduced this year (1980) in those provinces, municipalities and autonomous regions which generally have not yet allocated funds for the purchase of technical equipment for construction enterprises. Funds earmarked for technical equipment must be used for this purpose only. The surplus left over from one year can be used during the following year. Departments in charge of construction enterprises in various areas should control an appropriate amount of such funds in their hands, make an overall arrangement and use them flexibly according to the level of equipment and the tasks of different enterprises under them.

Regulations governing the equipment funds of those construction units directly under the departments of the State Council will be studied and formulated separately.

6. Introduce a quota system for expenditures on large temporary facilities and building materials. Specific quotas will be determined by the State Planning Commission, the State Capital Construction Commission, the Ministry of Finance and the State Bureau of Supplies in line with the circumstances of different construction enterprises and will be assigned to them separately. Surpluses can be used by the construction enterprises for building houses to improve the workers' living conditions.

7. Broaden the scope of authority of the enterprises in the management of labour and wages. In view of the fact that construction tasks change frequently, that workers are constantly on the move and are scattered and that construction projects often involve work high above ground and field operations, the enterprises may recruit temporary workers directly through local labour departments to meet the needs of the projects. When recruiting permanent workers in line with the state employment plan, the enterprises have the right to choose the best through examination according to the needs of production. In view of the characteristics of construction enterprises, the labour departments should allot to them as few women workers as possible. The enterprises may, on the principle of "to each according to his work" and in the light of specific tasks, adopt the system of time-wages plus bonuses or piece-rate wages. Bonuses may be given to those who complete their projects ahead of schedule while meeting the requirements for engineering quality, material consumption and safety in operation; bonuses are to be paid by project-owning units out of their own revenues. Bonuses may also be given to those who economize on the three major categories of building materials — 8 to 15% of the cost saved for timber; 3 to 8% of the cost saved for cement; and 1 to 3% of the cost saved for rolled steel. These bonuses are to be paid out of the money saved. The specific regulations for these matters will be drafted by the State Capital Construction Commission after consultation with the Ministry of Finance and the State Bureau of Labour.

8. Reduce the added burdens on construction enterprises. No unit or individual is permitted to apportion expenses to construction enterprises

or to transfer their personnel, equipment or funds to other uses beyond the explicit stipulations of the state. Or, the enterprises have the right to reject them. When personnel are transferred with authorization, their wages and expenses are to be borne by the units that employ them.

9. Uphold the principle of combining right and responsibility and fulfil obligations strictly. All enterprises must, under the leadership of the department in charge and under the supervision of the workers' congresses, correctly exercise their righs and strictly fulfil the following obligations:

A. Uphold the four basic principles (Communist Party leadership, the dictatorship of the proletariat, the socialist road, and Marxism-Leninism-Mao Zedong Thought); conscientiously implement state principles, policies, laws and decrees; and safeguard state property from encroachment.

B. Try in every way to fulfil the state construction plans, conscientiously honour contracts and strictly observe financial regulations.

C. Keep to the work processes of capital construction, continuously improve management, raise the quality of projects, shorten construction time, lower building costs, accelerate the turnover of funds and increase work efficiency.

D. Strive to train qualified personnel, adopt advanced technology and scientific managerial methods, and work hard to raise technical and managerial levels.

E. Make rational use of basic depreciation funds, funds for major overhauls, legal profits and shares of saved building costs, tap potential and revamp enterprises systematically so as to expand production.

F. Ensure safety in operation, improve environmental protection, and improve the workers' physical fitness.

G. Correctly handle relationships among the state, the enterprises and the individual workers with regard to their material interests, and improve the workers' livelihood and welfare amenities step by step on the basis of expanded production.

H. Strengthen political and ideological work, continuously raise the workers' ideological awareness and communist ethics, educate them to observe state laws and decrees and labour discipline in an exemplary way.

The broadening of the decision-making power of construction enterprises in matters of management, which involves a wide range of complex problems, must be done actively and appropriately. All departments concerned should closely coordinate their efforts while consciously summing up experience so as to achieve success.

20. PROVISIONAL REGULATIONS APPROVED BY THE STATE COUNCIL ON STRENGTHENING THE WORK OF TAPPING POTENTIAL, RENOVATION AND TRANSFORMATION IN EXISTING INDUSTRIAL AND TRANSPORT ENTERPRISES
(June 21, 1980)

The State Council has approved the "Provisional Regulations on Strengthening the Work of Tapping Potential, Renovation and Transformation in Existing Industrial and Transport Enterprises" drafted by the State Economic Commission, the State Planning Commission and the Ministry of Finance and is now transmitting these regulations to you with the hope that you will study and implement them conscientiously.

Provisional Regulations on Strengthening the Work of Tapping Potential, Renovation and Transformation in Existing Industrial and Transport Enterprises

China has established the beginnings of an independent and fairly comprehensive industrial complex through 30 years of socialist construction. Relying on existing enterprises, tapping their potential, renovating and transforming them and giving full play to their role — this is the starting point of our modernization programme and the "base area" from which we set out on a new "Long March." During the period of the readjustment of the national economy, in particular, the growth of our industry and transport, the increase of commodities for the domestic market and for export, and the expansion of accumulated funds will mainly rely on the tapping of the potential of existing enterprises. Adhering to the principle of "production before capital construction and tapping potential before building new enterprises" and doing a good job of tapping the potential, renovating and transforming existing industrial and transport enterprises is, therefore, a cardinal issue which has a direct bearing on the overall situation. It is of special importance for winning success in the first campaign of the new "Long March" and for accelerating the advance of the modernization programme.

1. The potential-tapping renovation and transformation of existing enterprises must be linked up with the restructuring of our country's system of economic management, with the broadening of the decision-making power of the enterprises in matters of management. Along with the restructuring of the system of economic management, the enterprises should be given greater decision-making power in management, including the right to improve their production techniques continuously and to accelerate the expansion of production through the tapping of potential, renovation and transformation in line with the state plans, market demands and their own economic interests.

2. The tapping of potential, renovation and transformation of existing enterprises means carrying out technical renovation and transformation of present factory buildings and equipment by adopting new technologies and processes while maintaining simple reproduction so as to tap the production potential of the enterprises to the fullest possible extent and increase their economic returns comprehensively.

3. In tapping potential and in carrying out renovation and transformation during the period of economic readjustment, emphasis should be placed on: A. Saving energy by giving first priority to such measures as reducing oil consumption, substituting coal for oil in use as boiler fuel, using exhaust heat for power generating and other purposes, developing central heating and conserving power; B. Giving priority to the development of light, textile and handicraft industries; C. Strengthening weak links in communications and transport, chiefly the bottleneck sections of several old railway lines and several harbours; D. Improving the quality of products, increasing varieties and designs, raising the production of raw and other materials in short supply and expanding the production capacity of export commodities.

4. Formulation and examination of programmes for tapping of potential, renovation and transformation.

Programmes should be drawn up before projects for these purposes are carried out. All areas and departments should conscientiously map out their own programmes for tapping of potential, renovation and transformation in line with the aim of the readjustment of the national economy and the principles and tasks of the long-range programme, in the interest of coordination between different specialities and the requirements for the reorganization of industry and in conformity with the orientation and emphasis of the national drive for potential, renovation and transformation. All areas and departments should provide guidelines for their subordinate enterprises in drafting their programmes for these purposes, be responsible for examining these programmes and organize efforts to carry them out.

All enterprises which need to carry out such projects should draw up their own economical, rational and practical programmes in accordance with the requirements specified in the programmes of their areas and industries, and with reference to their own orientation in production and specific circumstances and in the light of the problems that exist in their production and management, technological processes, factory buildings and equipment. These enterprises should try to make their products readily marketable while avoiding increases in their average consumption of fuel, power and raw materials. They should not try to expand themselves into integrated enterprises. No project should be included in such a programme unless the related geological resources have been clearly established, the technological processes and techniques are up to standard, the supplies of fuel, power and raw materials and transport facilities are guaranteed and the problems of environmental pollution have been solved. No projects of tapping potential, renovation and transformation involving large amounts of work are allowed to start unless they have been included in the programmes of an area or department so that blindness in action can be avoided.

Unified programmes should be drawn up by the relevant local authorities or departments in charge for certain comprehensive regional projects and those involving several industries. Local authorities and relevant departments of the State Council should cooperate closely and support each other in this regard. Before assigning projects to various areas, the departments concerned should first obtain approval from the planning and economic commissions of the relevant provinces, municipalities or autonomous regions; on the other hand, various localities should submit for examination to the departments in charge those projects they intend to apply for inclusion in the national programme.

All areas and departments should map out programmes and annual plans for tapping potential, renovation and transformation with the following contents: A. Names and contents of the projects; B. The funds needed and their sources; C. The equipment and materials needed and their sources; D. The sources of fuel, power and raw materials needed and ways to achieve a balance in their supply; E. The economic returns expected; F. The time limits set for the projects.

Systematic steps should be taken to carry out the projects included in the programmes and plans according to their order of priority, on the principle of easy ones before difficult ones and with a view to minimizing the cost, shortening the time, increasing returns and achieving satisfactory results. Efforts should be made to acquire the funds, equipment, materials and labour power needed for those projects already included in the annual plans. Those enterprises which cannot solve the problem of labour power may request the capital construction commissions at various levels to make an overall arrangement.

As to the procedures of examining and approving programmes and plans for tapping potential, renovation and transformation, those projects which fall in line with the requirements of regional and departmental programmes and whose expenses can be covered by the sponsoring enterprises out of their reserve funds need only be reported to the local authorities or departments in charge for the record; those projects which need to go through the procedures of requisitioning land, call for a unified balance in the supply of fuel, power and raw materials or have to apply for bank loans or government subsidies, should first go through examination by the departments in charge (and by the bank as well in instances where loans are required) and then be submitted for approval to the economic and planning commissions and financial departments at various levels. Major projects should be handled with reference to the procedures for capital construction. Small loans and odd construction items are to be handled according to existing rules.

In drafting their programmes and plans for tapping potential, renovation and transformation, the enterprises should fully practise democracy, follow the mass line, adopt the "three-in-one combination" of leading cadres, technical personnel and workers. The programmes and plans should be submitted to the workers' congresses for discussion and approval, and their execution should be reported to the congresses regularly.

5. Ways of acquiring and using funds for tapping potential, renovation and transformation. Pending an all-round reform of the system of economic management, funds needed for these purposes may be obtained from the following sources:

A. That part of the basic depreciation funds reserved for these purposes. The State Council document Guo Fa (1978) No. 12 and the document (1979) Cai Qi No. 675 jointly issued by the Ministry of Finance and the State Economic Commission, stipulate that a certain portion of basic depreciation funds should continue to be set aside in the state budget mainly for the purpose of ensuring the conservation of energy and other such important projects. Basic depreciation funds in the hands of various departments and local authorities should be spent entirely on the renewal of existing equipment and major projects of tapping potential, renovation and transformation. Similar funds reserved by the enterprises and those deducted according to the quantity of production should also be spent entirely on renewing and transforming fixed assets (including development and extension in mining) and must not be diverted to other purposes.

In order to accelerate the renewal and technical transformation of machinery and equipment, those enterprises which have been authorized by the State Economic Commission and the Ministry of Finance to experiment with the broadening of their decision-making power in management may raise their rate of basic depreciation for machinery and equipment by 0.05% in 1980 on the basis of increased profits.

B. The share of profits kept by the enterprises that may be used for the purposes of tapping potential, renovation and transformation.

C. Loans that may be provided by the banks (including small loans for introducing technological measures and loans for special purposes).

D. Small sums in subsidies granted by the state or local authorities.

E. Funds pooled in partnership. Comprehensive regional projects like central heating may be started with funds pooled by the enterprises being benefited. Specialized items, such as the multiple utilization of timber, can be started as joint ventures between central and local authorities, between different provinces, between different cities and counties within the same province, or between enterprises under ownership by the whole people and those under collective ownership by breaking the bounds of different localities, trades and systems of ownership. The products, profits and other revenues of such joint ventures may be shared among the partners on the principle of mutual benefit and according to reasonable proportions agreed upon through consultation. Enterprises may apply for reduction or exemption of tax on those products they have increased through the treatment of industrial wastes and may reserve part of the profits thus increased in accordance with relevant state regulations.

Those enterprises which carry out technical transformation in connection with major overhauls may combine the use of funds for major overhauls with funds for the renewal and transformation of equipment. Funds for the purposes of tapping potential, renovation and transformation not in use for the time being should be deposited in banks under separate accounts; departments in charge of the enterprises may cooperate with the banks in using such deposits as loans to those enterprises which are short of funds for these purposes. Enterprises that raise loans should make sure to repay them. A low rate of interest is to be adopted on both deposits and loans in this regard. No department has the right to transfer or to divert to other uses funds of enterprises for the said purposes.

6. Enterprises should first of all make full use of over-stocked goods in their warehouses in providing the equipment and materials needed for the said purposes. In case such goods fall short of needs, central or local departments in charge of the enterprises should draw up unified plans for supply on the principle that whichever level provides them with funds shall provide materials as well, and shall apply for help separately to departments of supplies at various levels in accordance with the present system of material distribution. Departments of supplies at various levels should, in line with plans for tapping potential, renovation and transformation approved by the central or local authorities, treat materials needed for these purposes in the same way as production, maintenance and capital construction, open separate accounts, include them in the plans for the distribution of materials at different levels, give them priority and see to it that the relevant plans are carried out. When various areas, departments and enterprises under them start up projects for the said purposes using funds raised by themselves, they should in principle solve the problems regarding equipment and materials on their own; those which cannot solve these problems may apply for help. Projects for which the materials needed cannot be obtained should not be included in the annual plans. Economic commissions at various levels should participate in examining and approving plans for distributing materials and should assist departments of supplies with the work of coordination in the course of executing the plans.

7. Enterprises should make full use of existing labour power, improve their labour organization and raise labour productivity in tapping their potential, renovating and transforming themselves. If it becomes essential to increase the numbers of some workers, the quotas should be examined and determined by labour departments at various levels

through consultation with the planning and economic commissions at the same level and should be included in the plans for the distribution of labour power at different levels.

8. Projects for the said purposes should be linked up with the popularization of advanced techniques developed in China and the introduction of advanced techniques from abroad. Importance should be attached to the systematic application of existing advanced techniques in China to the technical transformation of old enterprises. Imported advanced technologies and equipment should be used first of all in the transformation of old enterprises.

9. Funds for the said purposes are to be managed by the Construction Bank. Special loans issued by the People's Bank for introducing technical measures should continue to be managed by the People's Bank. Funds raised by enterprises on their own should be used on the principle of depositing before using.

Foreign exchange needed by enterprises for importing technical patents and equipment should be included in the state plan for balance in foreign exchange, and the enterprises concerned should raise loans in foreign exchange in accordance with the "Regulations Governing Short-Term Loans in Foreign Exchange" approved and transmitted by the State Council.

10. Strengthening of leadership. Economic commissions at various levels are responsible for supervising the entire work of tapping potential, renovation and transformation. They should supervise the drafting of programmes and plans, organize efforts to carry them out and strive for good economic results. All industrial and communication departments under the State Council should also take practical steps to do this work well. Financial departments and banks at various levels should strengthen management and supervision of the use of funds for these purposes. Departments in charge of enterprises should report to the economic commissions and financial, banking and statistical departments at the same level on the results of the use of funds. Provincial, municipal and autonomous regional economic commissions and financial bureaus should pool information on the way local enterprises use their funds for the said purposes and report it to the State Economic Commission and the Ministry of Finance. Statistical departments and departments in charge of enterprises at all levels should strengthen their statistical force and establish or improve their system of statistics and reports on the implementation of plans for tapping potential, renovation and transformation.

21. PROVISIONAL REGULATIONS CONCERNING THE PROMOTION OF ECONOMIC COMBINATION

Adopted by Executive Meeting of the State Council
(July 1, 1980)

Following the preliminary reform of the system of economic management, certain forms of economic combination have emerged in many places. Such combination helps to make full use of the advantages of each economic unit, while making up for its deficiencies, achieving greater economic results and speeding up production and construction. It helps to channel the material and financial resources of the local governments and enterprises into serving the urgent needs of the nation's construction. It helps to build up the horizontal connections between different areas and departments according to economic laws and to break down regional blockades and unreasonable division of production and distribution by the various departments. It facilitates the reorganization of industry according to the principle of specialized co-operation, avoiding such practices as small factories squeezing out big ones, duplication in the building of plants and blindness in production. To take the path of combination and to organize various forms of economic combination is a requirement of the readjustment of our economy and of the further reform of our economic system. It represents an inevitable trend of development in our national economy. With a view to promoting economic combination, the following provisional regulations have been worked out:

1. In organizing economic combination, one must proceed from the urgent needs of the development of production, adhere to the principle of voluntary participation and must not use administrative orders to force various enterprises to combine. Generally, the combination of enterprises should start at the lower level, although in some cases it may also begin at the top. It should proceed gradually, from the easier to the more difficult and should expand step by step. The combination should not be accomplished in haste.

The combination of enterprises should not be restricted by trades, territories and ownership or by their relationship of subordination. However, the ownership, relationship of subordination and financial relations of the combined enterprises must not be changed arbitrarily. These enterprises must not change their original arrangement for handing over their income, or their credit and debt relationships with banks. If changes must be made, they should obtain the prior agreement of the relevant financial department and bank.

Combination must be effected according to the principle of equality and mutual benefit, and consideration must be given to the economic interests of all parties concerned. On the basis of their respective contributions, including funds, raw materials, technology, labour power, sites, equipment and installations, the parties to the combination will determine the proportion in which the proceeds of their operation (profit and products) will be divided among themselves and an agreement or contract will be signed accordingly.

The form of combination should conform to actual conditions. Many different forms are allowed and no one particular type should be enforced.

2. Provided that targets set by the state are met, the combinations of various types may dispose of their products in excess of the planned targets, as well as products manufactured with materials arranged by themselves, in the following ways: They may ask the commercial and supply departments to purchase certain kinds of their products. For others, they may market them directly according to state policy, with each supplying what the others need.

3. Combinations of producers and processors of raw materials should be promoted. First of all, the tasks set by the state for the transfer of raw materials must be fulfilled. For some raw materials it has supplied to the processer in excess of planned targets, the producer may be compensated through consultation by receiving a suitable share of the profit or processed goods from the processor. As for others, they may be processed on the spot under the joint management of the processor and the producer of the raw materials.

If one of the combined enterprises requires raw materials produced by another, it may obtain them directly from the latter without going through the intermediate links of commercial, supply and marketing and materials distribution departments. As for certain kinds of materials that are distributed by the state, these can still be sent to the processor by the producer directly, or through the commercial, supply and marketing and materials distribution departments. This is to be done according to the original relation of subordination of each party and according to principles of economy and rationality.

4. All combined enterprises must guarantee their payment of taxes and profits to the state so as to fulfil their obligations. They are not allowed to make inroads in state revenue.

The parties to the combination should continue to carry out their original regulations concerning wages and welfare benefits for the workers and staff, and may not change these regulations as they please.

5. The leadership of the combined enterprises should practice democratic and scientific management in a spirit of co-operation and of taking joint responsibility. The enterprises should have a combination committee as the organ of authority consisting of the representatives of all parties concerned. None of these parties has the right to change the decisions made by the committee, and arbitrary interference by the administrative departments is not allowed.

The parties to a combination shall not interrupt their co-operative relationships with other departments without mutual agreement through consultation. While fulfilling their contracts of co-operation, they may establish business relations with other enterprises outside the combination. Enterprises which have joined a combination for specialized co-operation should not "eat the rice cooked in one big pot" and each should be responsible for its own income and expenditure.

6. After an agreement on combination has been reached, each party to the combination should report to its own department in charge and to the concerned department of administration of industry and commerce for the record. The combination agreement and contract signed by the parties to the combination shall be protected by the law of the state, and its funds, equipment and materials shall not be appropriated or transferred by any person or organization. If any party to the combination fails to fulfil the agreement or contract or in the event of a dispute in the process of executing it, the department in charge will mediate between the parties. Should the mediation fail to produce any result, the dispute shall be settled by arbitration by the court.

7. With regard to an economic combination involving several provinces, municipalities or regions, or of different trades, the constituent parties may work out temporary arrangements on problems of administrative leadership, material supply and the distribution of products.

8. The governments at all levels should give competent leadership to economic combination. They should support and encourage all forms of economic combination which facilitate the development of production, accelerate supplies and marketing and promote economic prosperity. The governments should respect the power of the enterprises to make their own decisions, and should not cause any unjustified administrative interference in the affairs of the enterprises. To speed up our socialist construction, the governments at all levels should be good at guiding the enterprises to adapt their enthusiasm for economic combination to the sound development of production in society.

Along with the development of various types of economic combination, a series of new problems may crop up which require the departments concerned to make corresponding improvements in policies, regulations and measures so as to promote the consolidation and expansion of economic combination. The planning departments should strengthen overall balance. The departments in charge of the administration of industry and commerce should improve their work to make the various forms of combination beneficial to the readjustment and development of the national economy. The banks should use such means as credit and interest rates to support the different combinations, giving priority to those that operate more successfully. The banks should organize account-settling work and try out various kinds of trust agreements according to the characteristics of the various forms of economic combination. The financial and tax authorities should improve the taxation system and solve the problem of double taxation on components which are produced by one of the enterprises within the economic combination, and which are used in the assembly of a complete piece of equipment produced by another, etc. Promoting economic combination is an important policy of our country. All localities and departments should enthusiastically protect and support it and continuously sum up experiences so as to enable this policy to develop healthy.

We hope that all localities and departments will carry out the present provisional regulations in light of their specific conditions.

22. PROVISIONAL REGULATIONS CONCERNING THE DEVELOPMENT AND PROTECTION OF SOCIALIST COMPETITION
Adopted by Executive Meeting of the State Council
(October 17, 1980)

Since the Third Plenary Session of the 11th Central Committee of the Chinese Communist Party, competition has developed steadily with the implementation of the policy of "readjustment, restructuring, consolidation and improvement" of our economy, especially with the expansion of the rights of enterprises to make their own decisions and the utilization of the regulating role of the market. Having displayed its vitality in our economic life, competition is giving an impetus to economic development and technological progress. There are essential differences between socialist competition and capitalist competition. The former, being developed on the basis of the public ownership of the means of production and under the guidance of the state plan, serves the socialist economy. It plays an important role in bringing into play the initiative and creativity of production and business units and of the workers, in making full use of their strongpoints and avoiding their weaknesses, in promoting the combination of enterprises and further activating our economy so as to constantly meet the people's demands and speed up the four modernizations. We should gradually reform the existing system of economic management, energetically develop competition and protect its smooth progress. For this purpose, the following provisional regulations have been worked out:

1. In the course of developing competition, all production and business units should ensure the fulfilment of their production and sales plans as set by the state and make great efforts to improve management, strengthen business accounting, increase the varieties of their products, raise their quality, reduce the consumption of energy, raw and processed materials, cut down costs and expenses, raise labour efficiency and improve their services. They should try to compete with each other, steadily raising the level of production and technology and the level of business management so as to achieve good economic results.

2. To develop competition, an enterprise must be granted greater power to make its own decisions and its status as a relatively independent commodity producer should be respected. No local authority or department is allowed to interfere with the rights which an enterprise is entitled to enjoy under government policies, laws and regulations, rights with regard to production, supply and marketing, personnel, finance and materials. Agreements and contracts concluded between enterprises will be honoured by both parties and protected by the laws of the state. If a party breaks a contract, it shall be held responsible economically and legally. An enterprise may work out its own production plan or undertake tasks in co-operation with other enterprises according to market demand, provided that such plans ensure the supply of goods as required by the state. In addition to materials to be allocated by the state, an enterprise may purchase the materials it needs from other areas and units, insofar as this is permitted by government policies and laws. The areas and departments concerned must not hinder them. As for materials that are allocated by the state according to plan, steps should be taken gradually to give enterprises some freedom in choosing where to buy them. An enterprise has the right to resist all attempts to violate its power to make its own decisions and may lodge complaints with higher authorities.

3. While the socialist public ownership plays the dominant role in the economy, competition shall be allowed and encouraged among the various economic sectors and among the enterprises, enabling each to bring its own advantages into play. In economic activities, no monopoly of commodities shall be allowed, except those which the state has specified to be handled exclusively by certain departments and units. Tenders may be invited and submitted for the construction of production and business projects which can be undertaken by contractors. Those collective and individual economic units which are beneficial to the national economy and the people's livelihood should be given help after they have registered and started business. With overall arrangements in place, they should be given lenient treatment with regard to the supply of goods, payments for goods, taxation, labour power, marketing of products, etc. Their legitimate rights and interests should be protected by the laws of the state. No department or person shall appropriate their assets, impose irrational burdens on them or encroach on their interests.

4. Channels of commodity circulation shall be increased to open ground for competition. In

principle, an enterprise may market products that are its own in excess of the planned target, those turned out with raw and processed materials arranged by itself, and goods it has trial-produced. Goods in short supply and those to be purchased, marketed and allocated exclusively by the state must be first of all purchased by the state. The enterprise may be permitted to market a portion of certain products itself. The prices of the products thus sold should be fixed according to the relevant stipulations. Distribution channels shall be increased while the number of intermediate links reduced. The enterprises shall be permitted to use various distribution channels and to reduce the number of intermediate links, to adopt diverse forms of operation to link up production with demand and to speed up the circulation of commodities. With a view to promoting the marketing of their goods, enterprises of a certain area may set up marketing offices in other areas, hold trade fairs there, or commission others to act as their agents. Urban enterprises may do the same in rural districts, and vice versa.

5. To develop competition, irrational prices must be readjusted gradually. The prices of certain commodities selected by the state are allowed to fluctuate within a prescribed range. In accordance with state policies and the changes in the condition of supply and demand on the market, the enterprises have the power to lower the prices of the capital goods they have turned out, provided that this will not affect their delivery of profit to the state. If an enterprise wants to raise the prices of its goods, it must obtain the approval of the relevant authorities as stipulated by the division of power in price management. The prices of all major commodities which are closely related to the people's livelihood must be kept basically stable.

6. To promote competition, regional blockades must be broken and the partition of the market by different departments must be stopped. No area or department is allowed to enforce a blockade or to forbid the sale of outside products in its own area or department. It must ensure the export of the raw and processed materials it produces according to the state plan, and any blockade is impermissible. To facilitate competition, the departments in charge of industry, communications, finance and trade must revise that part of existing regulations and rules which hinders competition. It is illegal to adopt administrative means to protect the backward and to restrict the advanced, obstructing the normal circulation of commodities; such practices must be abolished.

7. In order to encourage technological innovation and inventions, and to protect the economic benefits due to the departments and personnel concerned, compensation should be made for the transfer of the possession of important technological achievements. For this purpose, the State Council departments concerned shall draw up relevant policies and regulations. Before such documents are formulated, the problem should be solved through consultation between the enterprises. In the course of competition, we should promote technical exchange in the spirit of socialist co-operation.

8. To engage in competition, enterprises should strictly observe government policies and laws and practise lawful means. Attention should be paid to building up reputation and observing business morality. It is impermissible to practise fraud, to offer and accept bribes, to engage in speculation and to seek exorbitant profits at the expense of the interest of the state and the people. Those who violate law and discipline should be dealt with by law according to the severity of the circumstances.

9. Government at all levels and the departments in charge of different enterprises should deepen their understanding, keep abreast of the current situation and give better leadership to competition as the circumstances demand. They should work in a down-to-earth way to render services, coordinate, plan as a whole and supervise, grasp the new situation and resolve new contradictions and problems in good time. In order to ensure that competition develops soundly, they should learn to master the law of economics and work out the necessary economic laws and regulations by making use of such economic links as prices, taxes, credit and rates of interest. Those enterprises which consume less energy and materials in turning out good-quality products at low cost should enjoy priority in obtaining raw and processed materials and energy resources. With regard to backward enterprises, some should be consolidated and helped to improve their management and administration so as to catch up with the others. In the course of readjusting the national economy, others shall be reorganized, change their line of production or merge with other enterprises. They shall be encouraged to take the path of combination. The economically developed areas should pay attention to helping the underdeveloped areas. Economic management departments at various levels must give better guidance to planning and market management, do a good job in making market investigation and forecasts, make comprehensive analyses of the trends of develop-

ment of products and the market situation so as to guide the enterprises to improve their production and management and avoid blindness in production and construction that may arise in the course of competition.

10. It is hoped that all economic enterprises will earnestly try out the above provisional regulations in the light of their specific conditions. Every area and department may work out implementing rules on the basis of these regulations, to protect the development of competition.

23. THE STATE COUNCIL'S CIRCULAR ON THE INTRODUCTION OF A FINANCIAL MANAGEMENT SYSTEM BY WHICH THE SCOPE OF REVENUE AND EXPENDITURE WILL BE DEFINED FOR THE CENTRAL AND LOCAL GOVERNMENTS RESPECTIVELY AND EACH WILL BE RESPONSIBLE FOR THE BALANCE OF ITS OWN BUDGET

(February 1, 1980)

In order to carry out the policy of "readjustment, restructuring, consolidation and improvement" of our economy, to bring the initiative of both the central and the local governments into full play, and to meet the need of gradually realizing the modernization programme, the State Council has decided to introduce from 1980 a system of financial management by which the scope of revenues and expenditures will be defined for the central and local governments respectively and each will be responsible for the balancing of its own budget. The recently held national planning conference has discussed and decided on the basic norms of revenue and expenditure fixed for local governments, the ratio between that part of revenues to be handed over to the central government and the part to be used locally, and the fixed amounts of subsidies for areas entitled to such help. Herewith, we are transmitting a copy of the Provisional Regulations Concerning the Introduction of a Financial Management System by Which the Scope of Revenue and Expenditure Will Be Defined for Central and Local Governments Respectively and Each Will Be Responsible for Balancing Its Own Budget, hoping you will abide by them.

To define the scope of revenues and expenditures for central and local governments and to make each responsible for the balance of its own budget is an important reform of the system of financial management by the state, a reform which will not only affect the structure of revenues and expenditures, the division of financial powers and the readjustment and improvement of the distribution of financial resources, but will also affect the readjustment and improvement of the system of management of planning, capital construction, materials supply, enterprises and public undertakings. To make this reform a success is of great significance to promoting the development of the national economy and the gradual realization of the Four Modernizations. All localities and departments must pay great attention to this question, give better guidance and ask the cadres to take the overall situation into consideration and correctly handle the relationship between the whole and the part and between national and regional interests. In combination with this reform, they should properly readjust and improve relevant systems and regulations concerning economic management so as to facilitate our work in all fields. In the course of introducing the new financial system, they must promptly grasp the current situation, sum up experiences and study and solve any new problems that may crop up in order to make a success of the work of reforming the system of financial management.

Appendix

Provisional Regulations Concerning the Introduction of a Financial System by Which the Scope of Revenue and Expenditure Will Be Defined for the Central and Local Governments Respectively and Each Will Be Responsible for Balancing Its Own Budget

In order to carry out the policy of "readjustment, restructuring, consolidation and improvement" of our economy, and meet the need of gradually realizing our modernization programme, beginning in 1980 the state will introduce for the provinces, municipalities and autonomous regions a system of financial management by which the scope of revenues and expenditures will be defined for central and local governments respectively and each will be responsible for balancing its own budget. The basic principle is that under the condition that the unified leadership and planning by the central government is consolidated and that the indispensable expenditure of the central government is ensured, the power and responsibility of governments at various levels in financial affairs should be made clear, so that each will exercise its function and shoulder its responsibility, and the initiative of both central and local governments will be brought into full play.

1. Clearly divide the different kinds of revenue and expenditure between the central and local governments according to their relationship of subordination as specified under the system of economic management.

Revenue: income of the enterprises under the administration of the central government; custom duties and other income of the central government belong to the Ministry of Finance, as its regular sources of revenue. Income of enterprises under local administration; salt tax; agricultural and animal breeding taxes; industrial and commercial income tax; local taxes and other income of the local governments belong to the local financial departments as their regular sources of revenue. The income of those local enterprises which have been placed under the direct administration of the central ministries, with the approval of the State Council, will be divided according to a fixed ratio — 80% will be handed over to the Ministry of Finance and 20% to the local financial departments. Industrial and commercial taxes will be used to supplement the revenue of the central and local governments.

Expenditure: capital investments handled by the central government; the circulating funds of the enterprises under central administration; expenses for the tapping of potential and the technological transformation of the enterprises; and trial manufacture of new products for geological prospecting; national defence; foreign aid, material reserve of the state; operating expenses for cultural, educational, health and scientific undertakings at the central level; those for agriculture, forestry, irrigation and meteorology and those for the industrial, communications and commercial departments will be disbursed from state revenues. The capital investment handled by the localities, the circulating funds of the local enterprises (including those of the projects built by the central government for them); funds for the tapping of potential and the technological transformation of enterprises; funds for the trial manufacture of new products; financial aid to rural people's communes; operating expenses for agriculture, forestry, irrigation, meteorology, etc.; operating expenses for industrial, communications and commercial departments; maintenance fees for the cities; funds for building anti-air-raid defence works; funds for moving people from the cities into the countryside; operating expenses for cultural, educational, health and scientific undertakings; social relief funds; and pensions for the disabled and for families of the deceased; administrative expenses, etc. will be disbursed from the revenue of the local governments.

Expenditures on a few particular items, such as relief fees for extraordinary natural disasters, subsidies for campaigns against extraordinary droughts and floods and developing funds in support of underdeveloped regions will be earmarked by the central government and will not be included in the budgets of the local governments.

2. The basic norms fixed for the revenue and expenditure of a local government will be calculated and worked out on the basis of estimated revenues and expenditures for 1979, with suitable readjustments made according to the aforesaid division of the scope of revenues and expenditures. Where local revenues are larger than expenditures, a part of the surplus will be handed over to the central government according to a fixed ratio. Where revenues are not enough to cover expenditures, the deficiency will be made by allowing the local government to keep a portion of the industrial and commercial tax. In places where revenues are still insufficient to cover expenditures even if income from the industrial and commercial taxes has been left entirely with the local government, the Ministry of Finance will give the local government a fixed amount of subsidies. Once the ratio by which the local government divides its revenues with the central government and the amount of the subsidies are fixed, they will, as a rule, remain unchanged for five years; should the local government earn more, it may spend more.

After the introduction of the system by which the scope of revenues and expenditures is defined for central and local governments and each is responsible for the balance of its own budget, if an enterprise or public undertaking originally administered by the central government is placed under local leadership, if a large enterprise which has been newly put into operation is put under local administration, or if a new kind of tax is levied and, as a result, the revenues and expenditures of the central and local governments are seriously affected, the division of local revenues and the amount of subsidies granted by the central authorities should be readjusted. Or, as an alternative, the central financial authorities will settle accounts with the local authorities. When other economic measures are adopted in accordance with decisions of the central government, including the readjustment of prices, increases of wages for factory and office workers, readjustments of tax rates, and tax reductions and exemptions, the aforesaid division of local revenues and expenditures and the amount of subsidies shall not be changed, unless otherwise stipulated. In the case of an exceptional natural disaster, the central government will give aid to the affected areas according to the consequences of the disaster.

3. In order to help step up production in remote border areas, the autonomous areas of minority nationalities, former revolutionary bases and other economically underdeveloped areas, the central government will, as far as its financial capacity permits, establish development funds for the

economically underdeveloped areas. Such funds will gradually increase to account for 2% of state expenditures; these funds will be allocated by the Ministry of Finance. They will be earmarked for special purposes and used on more important projects.

4. The autonomous regions of the nationalities will continue to adopt the system of financial management that has been stipulated for the nationalities autonomous areas. The special provisions laid down for their finances will remain unchanged. But the amount of subsidies granted to them by the central government will remain unchanged for a period of five years once it is fixed, instead of being changed every year. Within the five years, their increased income will be entirely retained for local use. In the meantime, to give special consideration to the needs of the nationalities autonomous areas in developing their production, construction and culture and education, the central government will increase the amount of subsidies to the autonomous areas at a rate of 10% each year.

5. After the reform of the system of financial management has been effected, all provinces, municipalities and autonomous regions should make overall arrangements for the production, construction and expenditure of their respective areas according to the guidelines, policies and plans of the state. In working out its budget, the local government must act cautiously and not over extend itself, see to it that revenues and expenditures are balanced, with a small surplus on the credit side. They must not make a budget with a deficit, issue local bonds, or appropriate the funds of and apportion expenses to enterprises under them. The budgets of the localities shall be compiled by the local governments and, after being collected and examined by the Ministry of Finance, submitted to the State Council for approval.

The central departments in charge of the enterprises and public undertakings will no longer make overall arrangements for expenses of enterprises of the same trade, or allocate expenditure targets to the localities as before. However, the various central departments shall continue to formulate guidelines and point to the orientation of work, adopt policies and measures and check up on the economic effects so as to help the local governments to do their work well. The provinces, municipalities and autonomous regions should take the interests of the whole into account, and respect the opinions of the central departments. Those expenses which have been assigned to a local government and which serve the production and construction of the whole country or of the area concerned must be included in the local budget. The local government must guarantee the transfer from its own area of materials and commodities as required by the state.

6. In executing both the central and the local budgets, all income must be collected according to government policies, all expenses paid must conform to the budgets, and all additional expenses must be made through proper procedures. All income that should be included in the budgets must be treated accordingly. On important questions that concern the whole country such as the taxation system, price policy, the issuance of public bonds, wages and bonus standards, the scope of payment of the costs of enterprises, the proportions of the profit to be used as special funds and the standards of important expenditures, all localities and departments must follow the provisions that apply to the whole country. No changes shall be allowed unless they are approved by the proper authorities. Discipline in economic and financial affairs must be enforced. To grant tax reductions or exemptions, or to encroach on state revenues by going beyond the limits of one's authority as prescribed by the state, is strictly prohibited. All localities and departments must strive to increase production, practise economy, increase their income and cut down expenses, so as to fulfil their tasks with regard to revenues and expenditures and to make greater contributions to the state.

7. The specific kind of system of financial management which a province, municipality or autonomous region adopts in relation to counties and cities under its administration shall be decided by the province, municipality or autonomous region concerned in conformity with the spirit of the present regulations.

24. REGULATIONS CONCERNING THE WORK OF FINANCIAL SUPERVISION
Promulgated by the Ministry of Finance
(Approved for Transmission by the State Council on July 2, 1980)

To strengthen supervision over financial affairs is an important guarantee for upholding financial discipline, for promoting the increase of revenues and the economy of expenditure and for accelerating the socialist modernization of our country. With a view to combatting graft, embezzlement, extravagance, waste and all violations against financial discipline, to correctly carrying out the financial policies, laws and regulations of the state, and to successfully realizing the state budget, the following regulations have been worked out:

1. **The Setting Up of Financial Supervisory Organizations.**

A financial supervisory department will be set up under the Ministry of Finance. Financial supervisory offices will also be set up under the financial department (bureau) of each province, autonomous region and municipality directly under the central government. A financial supervisory section will be set up under the financial bureau of each prefectural administrative office, city directly under the province and autonomous *zhou*. Under the financial section of each county (city) and autonomous county there will be a sub-section or persons in charge of financial supervision.

The financial departments of the ministries, commissions and departments directly under the State Council and of the provinces, autonomous regions, and municipalities directly under the central government may set up financial supervisory offices or sections or may appoint persons in charge of such work according to the requirements of the work.

Where the required conditions exist, the financial departments may engage financial supervisory correspondents from among the accountants in enterprises, public undertakings and government organizations.

2. **The Tasks of the Financial Supervisory Organizations.**

The tasks of the financial supervisory organizations are as follows:

a) To supervise and check up on government organizations, public bodies, enterprises and public undertakings in their carrying out of the financial policies, laws and regulations, and to discover existing problems;

b) To supervise and check up on the financial departments and related personnel to see whether they are abiding by financial policies, laws and regulations, and to discover the existing problems;

c) To take up and investigate cases of disruption of financial regulations and of violations against financial discipline as well as cases in which people suffered from retaliation for having persisted in following financial regulations;

d) To make proposals for the improvement of financial management and administration on the basis of the problems discovered;

e) To conduct education in socialist legality and financial discipline.

3. **Leadership Over the Financial Supervisory Organizations.**

Administratively, the financial supervisory organizations are under the leadership of the financial departments at their corresponding levels. In professional matters, they are guided by higher financial supervisory organizations. The lower financial supervisory organizations should periodically report their work to the higher financial supervisory organizations. If necessary, they may bypass their immediate leadership and report to the higher authorities. The financial supervisory organizations at a higher level have the right to check up on the work of the financial supervisory organizations at lower levels.

The appointment, dismissal and transfer of the chief responsible personnel of a financial supervisory organization should be reported for the record to the financial department at the next higher level.

4. **Rights of the Personnel in Charge of Financial Supervision.**

The personnel in charge of financial supervision have the right:

a) To ask the leaders and other persons concerned in the unit under investigation to provide the necessary information and to attend the relevant meetings;

b) To examine the budget and final accounts, and to plan for revenues and expenditures, reports and forms of statistics, account books, original vouchers, and other related records and files of the unit being investigated; and, if necessary, to Xerox or duplicate some of the important material;

c) To check up on the cash, materials and bank deposits of the unit under investigation, and go to the building-sites, workshops and storehouses concerned to investigate;

d) To make investigations and collect materials from units involved in the case;

e) To inquire about any person who is involved in the case and ask him to give an answer on the spot or write down his answer.

When a person in charge of financial supervision performs the above functions, the units under investigation and the people concerned should cooperate voluntarily and give a truthful account of the facts, and should not obstruct the process in any way.

5. The Handling of Cases Under Financial Supervision.

In handling a case it has accepted, the financial supervisory organization concerned should carefully determine the facts and promptly write a report on the result of its investigations. And, according to the specific nature and circumstances of the case, it should make a proposal for its settlement and submit it to the unit under investigation or the department in charge of the unit so as to settle the case. If the case being handled calls for disciplinary action against the offenders, the case should be handed over to the relevant authorities which are in charge of these cadres. If the case is a serious one that calls for punishment by law, it should be handed over to judicial organs to be judged according to law. The financial supervisory organizations should propose to the units concerned the commendation of people who adhere to financial regulations, or provide awards to those who protect state property and dare to combat violations against financial discipline.

The investigation report must be shown to the unit and persons under investigation to ask for their opinions. If they do not agree with the report they are allowed to state their reasons and to present a written statement, which should be appended to the report.

After a case has been dealt with, the unit under investigation or the department in charge should send a copy of its decisions on the case to the financial supervisory organization concerned. If the latter has differing views regarding the handling of the case, it may present its views to the department which has made decisions on the case or report to the higher authorities.

6. Requirements for Personnel in Charge of Financial Supervision.

a) They must conscientiously study the financial and economic policies, laws and regulations of the state, be knowledgeable about financial affairs and accounting, and love their work;

b) They must closely rely on the masses, intimately cooperate with the relevant departments, combine their own work with supervision by the masses;

c) They must adhere to principle, abide by law and discipline, be unintimidated by the powerful and the influential, be not swayed by personal considerations, and dare to combat all violations against financial discipline;

d) They must seek truth from facts, pay serious attention to evidence and investigation, be scrupulous about every detail and heed the opinion of everyone concerned, including the units and people who are being investigated.

25. THE INCOME TAX LAW OF THE PEOPLE'S REPUBLIC OF CHINA CONCERNING JOINT VENTURES WITH CHINESE AND FOREIGN INVESTMENT

Adopted on September 10, 1980 by the Fifth National People's Congress of the People's Republic of China at its Third Session.

Article 1. Income tax shall be levied in accordance with this Law on the income derived from production, business and other sources by any joint venture with Chinese and foreign investment (hereinafter called joint venture for short) in the People's Republic of China.

Income tax on the income derived from production, business and other sources by branches within or outside the territory of China of such joint ventures shall be paid by their head office.

Article 2. The taxable income of a joint venture shall be the net income in a tax year after deduction of costs, expenses and losses in that year.

Article 3. The income tax rate on joint ventures shall be 30%. In addition, a local surtax of 10% of the assessed income tax shall be levied.

The income tax rate on joint ventures exploiting petroleum, natural gas and other resources shall be stipulated separately.

Article 4. In the case of a foreign participant in a joint venture remitting its share of profit from China, an income tax of 10% shall be levied on the remitted amount.

Article 5. A newly established joint venture scheduled to operate for a period of 10 years or more may, upon approval of the tax authorities for an application filed by the enterprise, be exempted from income tax in the first profit-making year and allowed a 50% reduction in the second and third years.

With the approval of the Ministry of Finance of the People's Republic of China, joint ventures engaged in such low-profit operations as farming and forestry or located in remote, economically underdeveloped outlying areas may be allowed a 15–30% reduction in income tax for a period of 10 years following the expiration of the term for exemptions and reductions mentioned in the preceding paragraph.

Article 6. A participant in a joint venture which reinvests its share of profit in China for a period of not less than five years may, upon approval of the tax authorities for an application filed by the said participant, obtain a refund of 40% of the income tax paid on the reinvested amount. A participant which withdraws its reinvested funds within five years shall pay back the tax amount refunded.

Article 7. Loss incurred in a joint venture in a tax year may be carried over to the next tax year and made up with an equal amount drawn from that year's income. Should the income in the subsequent tax year be insufficient to make up for the said loss, the balance may be made up with further deductions from income year by year over a period not exceeding five years.

Article 8. Income tax on joint ventures shall be levied on an annual basis and paid in quarterly installments. Such provisional payment shall be made within 15 days after the end of each quarter. The final settlement shall be made within 3 months after the end of a tax year. Excess payments shall be refunded by the tax authorities or deficiencies made good by the taxpayer.

Article 9. Joint ventures shall file their provisional income tax returns with the local tax authorities within the period prescribed for provisional payments. The taxpayer shall file its final annual income tax return together with its final accounts within 3 months after the end of the tax year.

Article 10. Income tax levied on joint ventures shall be computed in terms of Renminbi (RMB). Income in foreign currency shall be assessed according to the exchange rate quoted by the State General Administration of Exchange Control of the People's Republic of China and shall be taxed in Renminbi.

Article 11. When joint ventures go into operation or when they change the nature of their business, change their address, close down, and change or transfer registered capital, such joint ventures shall register with the General Administrative Bureau for Industry and Commerce of the People's Republic of China, and within 30 days of such registration, present the relevant certificates to the local tax authorities for tax registration.

Article 12. The tax authorities have the right to investigate the financial affairs, account books and tax situation of any joint venture. Such joint venture must make reports according to the facts and provide all relevant information and shall not refuse or conceal the facts.

Article 13. A joint venture must pay its tax within the prescribed time limit. In case of failure to pay within the prescribed time limit, the appropriate tax authorities, in addition to setting a new time limit for tax payment, shall surcharge overdue payments at one half of one per cent of the overdue tax for every day in arrears, starting from the first day of default.

Article 14. The tax authorities may, acting at their discretion, impose a penalty on any joint venture which has violated the provisions of Articles 9, 11 and 12 of this Law.

In dealing with any joint venture which has evaded or refused to pay tax, the tax authorities may, in addition to pursuing the tax, impose a penalty of not more than five times the amount of tax underpaid or not paid, according to the seriousness of the offence. Cases of gross violation shall be handled by the local people's courts according to law.

Article 15. In case of disputes with tax authorities about tax payment, joint ventures must pay tax according to the relevant regulations first before applying to higher tax authorities for reconsideration. If they do not accept the decisions made after such reconsideration, they can bring the matter before the local people's courts.

Article 16. Income tax paid by a joint venture or its branch in other countries may be credited against the assessed income tax of the head office as foreign tax credit.

Where agreements on avoidance of double taxation have been concluded between the Government of the People's Republic of China and the government of another country, income tax credits shall be handled in accordance with the provisions of the related agreements.

Article 17. Detailed rules and regulations for the implementation of this Law shall be formulated by the Ministry of Finance of the People's Republic of China.

Article 18. This Law shall come into force from the date of promulgation.

26. DETAILED RULES AND REGULATIONS FOR THE IMPLEMENTATION OF THE INCOME TAX LAW OF THE PEOPLE'S REPUBLIC OF CHINA CONCERNING JOINT VENTURES WITH CHINESE AND FOREIGN INVESTMENT

Approved by the State Council on December 10, 1980

Article 1. These detailed rules and regulations are formulated in accordance with the provisions of Article 17 of the Income Tax Law of the People's Republic of China concerning Joint Ventures with Chinese and Foreign Investment (hereinafter called Tax Law for short).

Article 2. "Income derived from production and business" mentioned in article 1 of the Tax Law means income from the production and business operations in industry, mining, communications, transportation, agriculture, forestry, animal husbandry, fisheries, poultry farming, commerce, tourism, food and drink, service and other trades.

"Income from other sources" mentioned in Article 1 of the Tax Law covers dividends, bonuses, interest and income from lease or transfer of property, patent right, ownership of trade marks, proprietary technology, copyright, and other sources.

Article 3. "A local surtax of 10 per cent of the assessed income tax" in Article 3 of the Tax Law means a surtax to be computed and levied according to the actual amount of income tax paid by joint ventures.

Reduction or exemption of local surtax on account of special circumstances shall be decided by the people's government of the province, municipality or autonomous region in which the joint venture is located.

Article 4. A foreign participant in a joint venture, who wants to remit its share of profits from China, shall report to the local tax authorities; the remitting agency shall withhold an income tax of 10% from the remittance. No tax shall be levied on that part of its share of profits which is not remitted from China.

Article 5. "The first profit-making year" mentioned in Article 5 of the Tax Law means the year in which a joint venture has begun making profit after its losses in the initial stage of operation have been made up in accordance with the provisions of Article 7 of the Tax Law.

Article 6. A participant in a joint venture, who reinvests its share of profit in this enterprise or in other joint ventures with Chinese and foreign investment for a period of not less than five years in succession, may receive a refund of 40% of the income tax already paid on the reinvested amount upon the examination and approval of the certificate of the invested enterprise by the tax authorities to which the tax was paid.

Article 7. The tax year for joint ventures starts from January 1 and ends on December 31 on the Gregorian calendar.

Article 8. The amount of taxable income shall be computed by the following formulae:

1. Industry:

A. Cost of production of the year is equal to direct material used in production of the year plus direct wages plus manufacturing expenses.

B. Cost of production of the year is equal to inventory of semi-finished product at the beginning of the year and in-production product plus cost of production of the year minus inventory of semi-finished product at the end of the year and in-production product.

C. Cost of sale of product is equal to cost of product of the year plus inventory of product at the beginning of the year minus inventory of product at the end of the year.

D. Net volume of sale of product is equal to total volume of sale of product minus (sales returns plus sales allowance).

E. Profit from sale of product is equal to net volume of sale of product minus taxes on sales minus cost of sale of product minus (selling expenses plus administrative expenses).

F. Amount of taxable income is equal to profit from sale of product plus profit from other operations plus non-operating income minus non-operating expenditure.

2. Commerce:

A. Net volume of sale is equal to total volume of sale minus (sales returns plus sales allowance).

B. Cost of sales is equal to inventory of merchandise at the beginning of the year plus [purchase of the year minus (purchase returns plus purchase discount) plus purchase expenses] minus inventory of merchandise at the end of the year.

C. Sale profit is equal to net volume of sale minus sale tax minus cost of sales minus (selling expenses plus overhead expenses).

D. Amount of taxable income is equal to sale profit plus profit from other operations plus non-operating income minus non-operating expenditure.

3. Service trades:

A. Net business income is equal to gross business income minus [business tax plus operating expenses plus overhead expenses).

B. Amount of taxable income is equal to net business income plus non-operating income minus non-operating expenditure.

4. Other lines of operation:

For other lines of operations, refer to the above-mentioned formulae for calculation.

Article 9. The following items shall not be counted as cost, expense or loss in computing the amount of taxable income:

1. Expenditure on the purchase or construction of machinery, equipment, buildings, facilities and other fixed assets;
2. Expenditure on the purchase of intangible assets;
3. Interest on capital;
4. Income tax payment and local surtax payment;
5. Penalty for illegal operations and losses in the form of confiscated property;
6. Overdue tax payment and tax penalty;
7. Losses from windstorms, floods and fire risks covered by insurance indemnity;
8. Donations and contributions other than those for public welfare and relief purposes;
9. That part of the entertainment expenses for operating purposes above the quota of three per thousand of the total sale income in the tax year or above the quota of ten per thousand of the total operational income and those entertainment expenses that are not relevant to production and operation.

Article 10. Depreciation of fixed assets in use shall be calculated on an annual basis. Fixed assets of joint ventures cover houses, buildings, machinery and other mechanical apparatus, means of transport and other equipment for the purpose of production with useful life of more than one year. But items with a per-unit value of less than 500 yuan and a short useful life can be itemized as expenses according to the actual number in use.

Article 11. Fixed assets shall be assessed according to the original price.

For fixed assets used as investment, the original price shall be the price agreed upon by the participants at the time of investment.

For purchased fixed assets, the original price shall be the purchase price plus transport fees, installation expenses and other related expenses incurred before they are put to use.

For self-made and self-built fixed assets, the original price shall be the actual expenditures incurred in the course of manufacture or construction.

Article 12. In depreciating fixed assets, the residual value shall be assessed first and deducted from the original price, the principle being making the residual value at 10% of the original price; those requiring to retain a little or no residual value, shall be submitted for approval to the local tax authorities.

The depreciation of fixed assets shall generally be computed in average by the method of straight line.

Article 13. The useful life for computing depreciation of fixed assets is as follows:

1. The minimum useful life for houses and buildings is 20 years;
2. The minimum useful life for trains, ships, machines and equipment and other facilities for the purpose of production is 10 years;
3. The minimum useful life for electronic equipment and means of transport other than trains and ships is 5 years.

For cases where the fixed assets of joint ventures, owing to special reasons, need to accelerate depreciation or where methods of depreciation need to be modified, applications shall be submitted by the said ventures to the local tax authorities for examination and then relayed level by level to the Ministry of Finance of the People's Republic of China for approval.

Article 14. Expenditures arising from the increase of value of fixed assets in use as a result of technical reform shall not be listed as expense.

The fixed assets continuing in use after full depreciation shall no longer be depreciated.

Article 15. The balance of the gain of joint ventures derived from sale of fixed assets at the current price after the net sum of non-depreciated assets or the residual value is deducted shall enter the year's loss and gain account.

Article 16. Intangible assets such as technical know-how, patent right, ownership of trade marks, copyright, ownership of sites and other royalties used as investment shall be assessed by amortization according to the sums provided in the agreements or contracts from the year they begin in use; for the intangible assets that are bought in at a fixed price, the actual payment shall be assessed from the year they are put in use.

The above-mentioned intangible assets with provision of time limit for use, shall be assessed by amortization according to the provision of time limit for use; those without the provision shall be assessed by amortization in ten years.

Article 17. Expenses arising during the period of preparation for a joint venture shall be amortized after it goes into production or business, with the amount of amortization not exceeding 20% each year.

Article 18. Inventory of merchandise, raw materials, in-production products, semi-finished products, finished products and by-products shall be computed according to the cost price. For the method of computation, the joint ventures may choose one of the following: First-in first-out, shifting average and weighted average. In those cases where a change in the method of computation is necessary, it shall be submitted for approval to the local tax authorities.

Article 19. Income tax to be paid in quarterly installments as prescribed in Article 8 of the Tax Law may be computed as one-fourth of the planned annual profit or the actual income in the preceding year.

Article 20. Joint ventures shall file their income tax returns and their final accounting statements with the local tax authorities within the prescribed period irrespective of profit or loss in the tax year and send the reports on auditing by the chartered public accountants registered in the People's Republic of China.

The accounting statements submitted by branches of joint ventures within China to their head offices shall be submitted to the local tax authorities at the same time for reference.

Article 21. Joint ventures shall file tax returns within the time limit set by the Tax Law. In case of failure to submit the tax returns within the prescribed time limit owing to special circumstances, application should be submitted in the said time limit, and the time limit may be appropriately extended upon the approval of the local tax authorities.

The final day of the time limit for tax payment and filing tax returns may be extended if it falls upon an official holiday.

Article 22. Income of joint ventures in foreign currency shall be assessed according to the exchange rate quoted by the State General Administration of Exchange Control on the day when the tax payment certificates are made out and shall be taxed in Renminbi.

Article 23. The accounting on the accrual basis shall be practised for revenue and expenditure of joint ventures. All accounting records shall be accurate and perfect and shall have lawful vouchers as the basis for entry account.

Article 24. The method of finance and accounting of joint ventures shall be submitted to local tax authorities for reference.

When the method of finance and accounting of joint ventures contradicts the provisions of the Tax Law, tax payments shall be computed according to the provisions of the Tax Law.

Article 25. Vouchers for accounting, accounting books and reports used for joint ventures shall be recorded in the Chinese language or in both Chinese and foreign language.

Accounting vouchers, accounting books and reports shall be kept for at least 15 years.

Article 26. Sales invoices and business receipts shall be submitted for approval to the local tax authorities before they are used.

Article 27. Officials sent by tax authorities shall produce identification cards when investigating the financial affairs, accounting books and tax situation of a joint venture and undertake to keep secret.

Article 28. Tax authorities may impose a penalty of not more than 5,000 yuan on a joint venture which has violated the provisions of Articles 9, 11 and 12 of the Tax Law according to the seriousness of the case.

Article 29. Tax authorities may impose a penalty of not more than 5,000 yuan on a joint venture which has violated the provisions of Paragraph 2 of Article 25, and Article 26 of these detailed rules and regulations.

Article 30. Tax authorities shall serve notices on cases involving penalty in accordance with the relevant provisions of the Tax Law and these detailed rules and regulations.

Article 31. When a joint venture applies for reconsideration in accordance with the provisions of Article 15 of the Tax Law, the tax authorities concerned are required to make decisions within three months after receiving the application.

Article 32. Income tax paid abroad by joint ventures or its branches on their income earned outside China may be credited against the amount of income tax to be paid by their head offices upon presenting the foreign tax payment certificate. But the credit amount shall not exceed the payable tax on the income abroad computed according to the tax rate prescribed by China's Tax Law.

Article 33. Income tax returns and tax payment certificates used by joint ventures are to be printed by the General Tax Bureau of the Ministry of Finance of the People's Republic of China.

Article 34. The right of interpretating the provisions of these detailed rules and regulations resides in the Ministry of Finance of the People's Republic of China.

Article 35. These detailed rules and regulations come into force on the same date as the publication and enforcement of the "Income Tax Law of the People's Republic of China Concerning Joint Ventures with Chinese and Foreign Investment."

27. INDIVIDUAL INCOME TAX LAW OF THE PEOPLE'S REPUBLIC OF CHINA

Adopted by the Fifth National People's Congress of the People's Republic of China at its Third Session on September 10, 1980

Article 1. An individual income tax shall be levied in accordance with the provisions of this Law on the incomes gained within or outside China by any individual residing for one year or more in the People's Republic of China.

For individuals not residing in the People's Republic of China or individuals residing in China less than one year, individual income tax shall be levied only on that income gained within China.

Article 2. Individual income tax shall be levied on the following categories of income:
1. Wages and salaries;
2. Remuneration for personal services;
3. Royalties;
4. Interest, dividends and bonuses;
5. Income from lease of property; and
6. Other kinds of income specified as taxable by the Ministry of Finance of the People's Republic of China.

Article 3. Individual income tax rates:
1. Income from wages and salaries in excess of specific amounts shall be taxed at progressive rates ranging from 5% to 45% (see appended tax rate table).
2. Income from remuneration for personal services, royalties, interest, dividends, bonuses and lease of property, and other kinds of income shall be taxed at a flat rate of 20%.

Article 4. The following categories of income shall be exempted from individual income tax:
1. Prizes and awards for scientific, technological or cultural achievements;
2. Interest on savings deposits in the state banks and credit co-operatives of the People's Republic of China;
3. Welfare benefits, survivors' pensions and relief payments;
4. Insurance indemnities;
5. Military severance pay, decommission or demobilization pay for cadres and fighters of the armed forces;
6. Severance pay or retirement pay for cadres, staff members and workers;
7. Salaries of diplomatic officials of foreign embassies and consulates in China;
8. Tax-free incomes as stipulated in international conventions to which China is a party or as stipulated in agreements China has signed;
9. Incomes approved as tax-free by the Ministry of Finance of the People's Republic of China.

Article 5. The amount of taxable income shall be computed as follows:
1. For income from wages or salaries, a monthly deduction of 800 yuan shall be allowed; that part in excess of 800 yuan shall be taxed.
2. For income from remuneration for personal services, royalties or lease of property, a deduction of 800 yuan shall be allowed for expenses if the amount in a single payment is less than 4,000 yuan; for single payments in excess of 4,000 yuan a deduction of 20% shall be allowed. The balance remaining after deduction shall be taxed.
3. Interest, dividends, bonuses or other kinds of income shall be taxed on the full amount received in each payment.

Article 6. For individual income tax, the income earner shall be the taxpayer and the paying unit shall be the withholding agent. Taxpayers not covered by withholding are required personally to file declarations of their income and pay tax themselves.

Article 7. Taxes withheld each month by a withholding agent and those to be paid each month by taxpayers filing personal returns shall be turned in to the state treasury and the tax return submitted to the tax authorities within the first seven days of the following month.

Any taxpayer who earns income outside China shall pay the tax due to the state treasury and submit a tax return to the tax authorities within 30 days of the end of each year.

Article 8. All incomes shall be computed in terms of Renminbi (RMB). Income in foreign currency shall be assessed according to the exchange rate quoted by the State General Administration of Exchange Control of the People's Republic of China, and shall be taxed in Renminbi.

Article 9. The tax authorities have the right to conduct investigations concerning the payment of tax. Withholding agents and taxpayers filing personal returns must report according to the facts and provide all relevant information and shall not refute or conceal the facts.

Article 10. A commission of 1% of the tax amount withheld shall be paid to the withholding agents.

Article 11. A withholding agent or a taxpayer filing personal returns must pay the tax due within the prescribed time limits. In case of failure to pay within the prescribed time limits, the appropriate tax authorities, in addition to setting a new time limit for tax payment, shall surcharge overdue payments at one half of 1% of the overdue tax for every day in arrears, starting from the first day of default.

Article 12. The tax authorities may, acting at their discretion, impose a penalty on a withholding agent or on a taxpayer filing personal returns who has violated the provisions of Article 9 of this Law.

In dealing with those who have concealed income or evaded or refused to pay tax, the tax authorities may, in addition to pursuing the tax, impose a penalty not more than five times the amount of tax underpaid or not paid, according to the seriousness of the offence. Cases of gross violation shall be handled by the local people's courts according to law.

Article 13. In case of disputes with the tax authorities on the payment of taxes, the withholding agent or taxpayer filing personal returns must pay taxes according to the relevant regulations first before applying to higher tax authorities for reconsideration. If they do not accept the decisions made after such reconsideration, they can bring the matter before the local people's courts.

Article 14. Detailed rules and regulations for the implementation of this Law shall be formulated by the Ministry of Finance of the People's Republic of China.

Article 15. This law shall come into force from the date of promulgation.

Individual Income Tax Rates
(Applicable to wages and salaries)

Grade	Range of Income	Tax Rate (%)
1	Monthly income of 800 yuan and less	Exempt
2	That part of monthly income from 801 yuan to 1,500 yuan	5
3	That part of monthly income from 1,501 yuan to 3,000 yuan	10
4	That part of monthly income from 3,001 yuan to 6,000 yuan	20
5	That part of monthly income from 6,001 yuan to 9,000 yuan	30
6	That part of monthly income from 9,001 yuan to 12,000 yuan	40
7	That part of monthly income above 12,001 yuan	45

28. DETAILED RULES AND REGULATIONS FOR THE IMPLEMENTATION OF THE INDIVIDUAL INCOME TAX LAW OF THE PEOPLE'S REPUBLIC OF CHINA

Approved by State Council
(December 10, 1980)

Article 1. These detailed rules and regulations are drawn up in accordance with the provisions of Article 14 of the Individual Income Tax Law of the People's Republic of China (hereinafter called Tax Law for short).

Article 2. "Any individual residing for one year or more in the People's Republic of China" mentioned in Article 1 of the Tax Law means any individual who resides in China for a full 365 days within a tax year. No subtractions shall be made of the number of days of temporary absence from Chinese territory within the tax year.

A tax year starts from January 1 and ends on December 31 on the Gregorian calendar.

Article 3. Individuals residing in the People's Republic of China for one year or more but less than five years shall pay tax only on that part of their income gained abroad which is remitted to China; individuals whose period of residence in China exceeds five years shall pay tax on all their income gained outside China beginning from the sixth year of residence.

Article 4. The range of the various categories of income mentioned in Article 2 of the Tax Law is as follows:

a) "Wages and salaries" means wages, salaries, bonuses and year-end extras gained from work in offices, organizations, schools, enterprises, undertakings and other units.

Bonuses mentioned in the preceding paragraph do not include prizes and awards for scientific, technological or cultural achievements.

b) "Compensation for personal services" means earnings from personal services in designing, installation, drafting, medical treatment, practising law, accounting, consultation, lecturing, news reporting radio and television broadcasting, contributions to publications, translation, calligraphy and painting, sculpture, cinema, drama and opera, music, dancing, acrobatics, ballad singing and comic talk, sports and technical services.

c) "Royalties" means income from the provision and transfer of patent right, copyright, the right to use proprietary technology and other rights.

d) "Interest, dividends and bonuses" means interest on deposits, loans and various kinds of securities and dividends and bonuses from investments.

e) "Income from lease of property" means income from lease of houses, warehouses, machinery and equipment, motor vehicles and boats, and other kinds of property.

f) "Other kinds of income" means income specified as taxable by the Ministry of Finance of the People's Republic of China other than that provided in the preceding items.

Article 5. The following categories of income from sources in China, regardless of whether the place of payment is in China or not, shall be taxed according to the Tax Law:

a) Individual income from work and compensation for services within China. But, for individuals whose period of residence in China does not exceed 90 days, the above compensation paid by employers outside China shall be exempted from taxation.

b) Dividends and bonuses gained by any individual within China. But dividends and bonuses derived from joint ventures and from urban and rural cooperative organizations shall be exempted from taxation.

c) Remuneration for staff members sent to work abroad by governmental offices at all levels of the People's Republic of China.

d) Royalties and interest derived by any individual within China and income from lease of property within China as well as other kinds of income specified as taxable by the Ministry of Finance of the People's Republic of China.

Article 6. For a taxpayer, who has two or more categories of taxable income as provided in Article 2 of the Tax Law, income tax shall be computed and levied separately.

Article 7. If a taxpayer's taxable income is paid in kind or in marketable securities, that part of the income thus paid shall be computed in terms of money according to the market price at the time of its acquirement.

Article 8. "Prizes and awards for scientific, technological or cultural achievements" mentioned in item 1, Article 4, of the Tax Law mean prizes and awards given to individuals by the Chinese

Government or Chinese or foreign scientific, technological or cultural organizations for inventions or creations in the fields of science, technology and culture.

Article 9. "Interest on savings deposits in the state banks and credit cooperatives of the People's Republic of China" mentioned in Item 2, Article 4, of the Tax Law includes interest on savings deposits in Renminbi and foreign currency and interest on savings deposit in other banks entrusted by the state banks.

Dividends in investments by individuals in local construction (investment) companies in China, which pay no bonuses and whose dividends are not higher than the interest on savings deposits in state banks and credit cooperatives, are also exempt from tax.

Article 10. "Salaries of diplomatic officials of foreign embassies and consulates in China" mentioned in Item 7, Article 4, refer to salaries of diplomats in foreign embassies, consuls and other persons enjoying the same treatment as diplomats.

Tax exemption for salaries earned by other persons in foreign embassies and consulates in China shall be kept at the same level as the tax exemption for persons of similar status in Chinese embassies and consulates granted by the relevant countries.

Article 11. Compensation for personal services, royalties and income from lease of property gained in China by individuals not residing in China shall be taxed on the full amount received in such payment.

Article 12. "Income from compensation for personal services, royalties or lease of property" "in a single payment" mentioned in Article 5 of the Tax Law means income gained on one single occasion or income from performance of only one piece of task of matter, and the amount so paid is counted as a single payment. For succeeding income from the same item that cannot be obviously divided into separate payments, such income received within a month is combined and counted as a single payment.

Article 13. For the same item of income gained by two or more persons in collaboration, deduction for expenses, if eligible according to the Tax Law, may be made from each share separately.

Article 14. The withholding agents in making various kinds of taxable payment shall withhold the taxes according to the Tax Law, turn them in to the state treasury in time and put them in itemized records for future reference.

The various kinds of taxable payment referred to in the preceding paragraph includes payment in cash, payment by remittance, payment by the transfer of accounts and payment in marketable securities or in kind, the value of which is computed in terms of money.

Article 15. Withholding agents and taxpayers filing personal returns shall submit tax returns within the time limit prescribed by the Tax Law. In cases of failure to submit the returns within the prescribed time limit on account of special circumstances, applications for extension shall be submitted within the prescribed time limit for approval to the local tax authorites.

The final day for tax payment and submission of tax returns may be extended if it falls upon an official holiday.

Article 16. For individuals residing in China for one year or more, the income gained outside China shall be computed and taxed separately from the taxable income earned within China. The amount of taxable income shall be computed after deducting expenses for different categories as provided in Article 5 of the Tax Law.

Income tax paid by taxpayers outside China for income earned abroad may be credited against the amount of income tax computed according to the tax rate prescribed by the Tax Law of China through applications by presenting tax payment certificate.

Article 17. Individual income in foreign currency shall be assessed according to the exchange rate quoted by the State General Administration of Exchange Control on the day when the tax payment certificate is made out and shall be taxed in Renminbi.

Article 18. Individuals liable to the tax in China who desire to leave the country are required to pay off the tax to the local tax authorities seven days before departure from China and only then can they go through exit formalities.

Article 19. In conducting investigations concerning the payment of tax by withholding agents or taxpayers filing personal returns, the tax officials sent by tax authorities are required to produce identification cards and undertake to keep secret.

Article 20. For the commission of 1% of the tax amount paid to the withholding agents provided in Article 10 of the Tax Law, the local tax authorities shall make out refund notice for the withholding agents on the monthly basis in accordance with the actual amount of tax withheld and the withholding agents may go through refunding formalities at the designated banks.

Article 21. A withholding agent or taxpayer filing personal returns who has violated the provisions of Article 9 of the Tax Law shall be penalized 500 yuan or less by the tax authorities according to the seriousness of the case.

Article 22. A withholding agent or a taxpayer filing personal returns who has violated the provisions of Article 14 and 15 of these detailed rules and regulations shall be penalized 500 yuan or less by the tax authorities.

Article 23. The tax authorities shall serve notices on cases involving penalty in accordance with the relevant provisions of the Tax Law and these detailed rules and regulations.

Article 24. For cases of applying for reconsideration by a withholding agent or a taxpayer filing personal returns according to the provisions of Article 13 of the Tax Law the tax authorities concerned are required to make decisions within three months after the application is received.

Article 25. Tax returns and tax payment certificates for individual income tax are to be printed by the General Tax Bureau of the Ministry of Finance of the People's Republic of China.

Article 26. The right of explanation of the present detailed rules and regulations resides in the Ministry of Finance of the People's Republic of China.

Article 27. These detailed rules and regulations come into force on the same date as the publication and enforcement of the "Individual Income Tax Law of the People's Republic of China."

29. CIRCULAR ON IMPROVING THE PAYMENT OF INDUSTRIAL AND COMMERCIAL INCOME TAX BY COOPERATIVE STORES AND INDIVIDUAL ECONOMIC UNITS

Promulgated by the Ministry of Finance
(October 9, 1980)

The existing regulations concerning the levying of income tax on cooperative stores and individual economic units were ratified by the State Council in 1963 for trial implementation. A 9-grade progressive tax rate is imposed upon cooperative stores on their income over and above a specified limit, and a 14-grade one on the gross income of individual economic units. It is also stipulated that a higher tax rate applies to those whose yearly income has exceeded the specified figure. In 1979, the Ministry of Finance abolished the stipulation of imposing a higher income tax rate on cooperative stores whose yearly income has surpassed the specified sum. At the same time, it made it clear that the provinces, municipalities and autonomous regions may allow those stores with difficulties tax reductions or exemptions, provided that they do not pay less tax than the handicraft cooperatives. But no changes have been made with regard to the above-mentioned 9-grade progressive tax, the 14-grade one and the higher tax rate for individual economic units.

At present, the government encourages the development of the collective economy and permits individual economy to expand to a certain extent, so as to promote economic prosperity, enliven the market and create more work opportunities for young people awaiting jobs in cities and towns. Certain departments in charge and local governments, however, have reported that the tax burdens of cooperative stores are still too heavy. Although the stores are no longer required to pay according to a higher tax rate when their yearly income exceeds the specified figure, they are still encountering difficulties in operation. Therefore, the departments and local governments demanded that the 8-grade progressive tax rate that is imposed on incomes in excess of the specified limit of collectively owned handicraft industry be applied to these stores. For individual economic units, they proposed to abrogate the stipulation of collecting a higher rate of tax from them if their annual income is more than the specified sum, and to lower their tax rate.

To appropriately lighten the income tax burden of cooperative stores and individual economic units, the Ministry of Finance, upon approval of the State Council, has decided to take the following interim measures before a new income tax law is enacted:

1. Starting on October 1, 1980, income tax will be levied on cooperative stores in cities, towns and the countryside according to the 8-grade progressive tax rate which has been imposed on the income of the collectively owned handicraft industry in excess of the specified limit. The provinces, municipalities and autonomous regions shoud act according to the spirit of this regulation and make proper arrangements for implementation in the light of their local conditions.

2. To those cooperative stores engaged in catering, services and repair trades which still have difficulties after the aforesaid 8-grade progressive tax rate has applied to them, the provinces, municipalities and autonomous regions may, after examining their cases, allow appropriate tax reductions.

3. The 14-grade progressive taxation on gross income and the current practice of collecting income tax at a higher rate from those units whose yearly income has surpassed the specified limit may not be applied to individual economic units for the time being. The provinces, municipalities and autonomous regions may, with local conditions in mind, determine the actual standard of the tax burden of these units according to the principle that it will correspond to the 8-grade progressive tax rate that has been imposed on the income of handicrafts industry. Regulations concerning the management and collection of taxes shall likewise be formulated for implementation by the various localities.

30. PROVISIONAL REGULATIONS ON PROVIDING LOANS FOR CAPITAL CONSTRUCTION PROJECTS

Approved for Transmission by the State Council
(August 28, 1979)

For the purpose of speeding up socialist modernization, upgrading the financial management of capital construction and making the most of the investment capital, provisional regulations are hereby issued to provide loans for some capital construction projects.

Chapter I. The Lending Institution

Article 1. The institution authorized to grant loans for capital construction projects is the People's Construction Bank of China (hereinafter called the Construction Bank).

Chapter II. The Eligible Borrowers and the Purposes For Wich the Loans Are to be Used

Article 2. The Construction Bank shall grant loans for investment capital to enterprises engaged in industry, transport, land reclamation, animal husbandry, marine products, commerce, tourism, etc. who have instituted an independent accounting system and are able to repay the loans.

Investment capital required by government organizations and non-profit institutions and for construction projects specified in the state plans shall be allocated by the Ministry of Finance.

Article 3. The borrower must be an independent entity who assumes economic responsibility for production. Where loans are to be used for renovations or extension of existing plants, it is the responsibility of the existing enterprise to apply for and repay the loans; in case of establishing a new enterprise, it is the responsibility of the preparatory organ who will be in charge of production after the project is in operation. If the borrower has been incorporated into a specialized or regional enterprise, it is the responsibility of that specialized or regional enterprise.

Chapter III. Prerequisites for Borrowing

Article 4. Before a project is financed by the Construction Bank, the borrower shall submit a target plan duly approved by the competent authorities and a preliminary design of the project that has been included in the state plans for capital construction for the current year.

The planning commissions at all levels and the departments in charge must invite the Construction Bank to join them in examining and approving the target plan for the project and in deciding on the current-year plan for capital construction. The capital construction commissions at all levels and the departments in charge must do likewise when examining and approving the preliminary design of the project.

When approved, a copy each of the target plan, the preliminary design and the current-year plan for capital construction shall be provided to the head office of the Construction Bank or its branch, whichever is involved in the financing.

Article 5. The projects must meet the following conditions before they are financed:

1) The production technique is up to standard and the products in good demand;

2) Factors of production such as raw materials, fuel, power, water supply, transport are in place and ready to be used;

3) An acceptable estimate of the time it takes to generate enough returns to pay for the investment, and an assurance that repayment of the loan will be made when due;

4) The construction site, equipment, materials and construction manpower have been duly arranged.

Chapter IV. Application, Examination and Approval of the Loan

Article 6. After the approval of the target plan, the borrower may submit a preliminary application to the Construction Bank who shall, if agreeable, sign an agreement with the borrower. Funds needed for the preparatory stage before the start of the project may be borrowed from the Construction Bank, if the department in charge stands surety for the borrower.

Article 7. After the preliminary design is approved, the borrower will ask the department in charge to include the project in the current-year plan for capital construction and simultaneously submit a formal application to the Construction Bank with supportive documents such as an estimate of the total cost for the preliminary design duly approved by the authorities higher up, a yearly construction plan and an agreement signed with other enterprises to work in cooperation during the construction of the project. When the documents are found in order, the Construction Bank shall sign a loan contract with the borrower.

Article 8. The loan contract shall set forth the term of the loan, the total loan amount, interest rate and the purposes for which the loan is granted. The contract shall also include yearly plans for the drawdown and repayment. The contract specifies the responsibilities of both parties: the borrower undertakes to use the loan for the purposes as stated in the contract, to make repayment when due and the Construction Bank undertakes to provide loanable funds according to the progress of the project.

The contract is legally binding on both parties. Either party in a breach of the contract shall indemnify the other party for the losses incurred.

Article 9. For the project in progress for which a loan contract has been signed, the planning commissions at all levels and the departments in charge shall guarantee the continuity in construction in the subsequent years so that the project will be completed on time or ahead of schedule. The materials and equipment needed for construction shall be provided by the departments in charge of supplies.

Article 10. The Construction Bank may provide loans to finance small-size projects that do not take long to construct with all factors of production in place and ready for use, that will turn out products in urgent demand, and that will yield quick returns and larger profits. Such loans are to be provided within the Bank's quota of freely disposable loanable funds.

Chapter V. Drawdown and Supervision of the Loan

Article 11. According to the progress of the project, the borrower shall make out an annual drawdown plan up to the total amount of the loan and present it to the Construction Bank who shall, if agreeable, provide the funds according to the plan.

If the amount that needs to be drawn out in any one year exceeds the amount listed in the annual drawdown plan, the matter is to be settled between the Bank and the borrower. In case the total drawdown exceeds the total loan amount but comes within the estimate of the total cost of the project, a supplementarty loan contract may be signed. For drawings in excess of the said estimate, consent must be obtained from the departments who have respectively approved the preliminary design and the target plan for the project.

Article 12. The Construction Bank shall supervise the performance of the borrower and oversee how the loan is being utilized. Upon discovering that the borrower has diverted funds to unauthorized construction work, to aimless purchases of materials and equipment or has violated financial regulations, the Construction Bank shall give warnings and demand such misbehaviour be corrected within a specific period of time. If not heeded, the Bank has the right to suspend the loan before maturity and report to authorities higher up.

The borrower shall provide financial statements and statistics to the Construction Bank. The Bank should be given access to materials it needs for examination.

Chapter VI. Repayment of the Loan

Article 13. The borrower must repay the loan plus interest on maturity as set out in the loan contract.

The term of the loan is to be counted from the date of the loan contract to the date of full repayment. For enterprises in heavy industry, it shall not be longer than 15 years; for others no longer than 10 years, except those referred to in Article 10 for which the term shall not exceed 5 years. The term of the loan is to be determined according to the specific case and set out in the loan contract.

Article 14. Interest shall be charged on an annual basis as from the date of the drawdown. Normally, the interest rate is 3% per annum. The specific rate is to be determined by the borrower's line of trade, its importance in the development of the national economy and according to the government economic policies.

Where the loan is not fully repaid on maturity, interest rate on the overdue loan shall be charged at double the rate. In case the loan is diverted to unauthorized projects, interest rate on the diverted portion shall be tripled.

Article 15. Sources of funds for repayment: During the period of repayment, newly established enterprises may repay the principal and interest out of the depreciation reserves for fixed assets, charges payable to the government for the use of the fixed assets and profits to be turned over to the government after the project is in operation. This shall also apply to existing enterprises that have borrowed from the Bank for renovations or extension of existing plants provided that they have instituted an accounting scheme to assess the economic gains from the borrowings. If not, they must repay out of profits to be turned over to the government corresponding to the proportion of the new fixed assets to the entire fixed assets as well as out of the depreciation reserves for the new fixed assets and charges payable to the government for the use of the new fixed assets.

For enterprises that have difficulty in repaying the loan out of the above-mentioned funds because of heavy tax and low profits, the industrial-commercial tax may be exempted during the period of repayment, if recommended by the provincial internal revenue department and approved by the Ministry of Finance.

Prior to the completion of the project, interest may be paid out of the loan and the portion so used shall be free of interest.

Borrowers that have completed construction on time or ahead of schedule and are thus able to repay the loan before maturity may use the funds set aside for repayment to expand production and improve the welfare of their workers and staff. In case borrowers fail to make repayment when due, they shall repay out of funds earmarked for making technological innovations or from capital accounts. They are not permitted to make repayment by way of including the loan in the cost of products or out of profits previously accumulated.

Chapter VII. Supplementary Regulations

Article 16. Where a dispute over the implementation of the loan contract cannot be settled between the borrower and the Bank, the case shall be submitted to an economic court for arbitration. If the court has not been established, the matter shall be dealt with by the Capital Construction Commission in their locality.

Article 17. The present regulations are applicable to state-owned enterprises. Loans to collectively owned enterprises may be handled on the principle of these regulations.

Article 18. The head office of the Construction Bank shall formulate and make public detailed rules for implementing these Provisional Regulations.

Article 19. Loans granted by the Construction Bank before these regulations become effective shall continue to be handled according to the provisions previously issued.

Article 20. The present regulations shall come into force on the date of issue.

31. PROVISIONAL REGULATIONS ON GRANTING LOANS TO AND OPENING ACCOUNTS BY THE UNEMPLOYED YOUTH IN CITIES AND TOWNS FOR SETTING UP ENTERPRISES OF COLLECTIVE OWNERSHIP

Issued by the People's Bank of China
(October 12, 1979)

1. Enterprises of collective ownership that are in operation with the approval of the competent authorities at a level not lower than the county or district (part of city) under licences issued by the Administration of Industry and Commerce, that have a certain amount of working capital, that have instituted an independent accounting system and are responsible for their own profits and losses may open accounts with the People's Bank of China (hereinafter called "the Bank").

2. Industrial enterprises of collective ownership who have opened accounts with the Bank, and met the requirements mentioned in (1) above, and provided their products are of fine quality, in good demand and profit-yielding may apply for industrial loans to cover shortage of working capital to pay for the concentrated arrival of raw materials they ordered. The Bank shall extend credit facilities to such enterprises consistent with the regulations for granting loans to collective industrial enterprises in cities and towns.

Enterprises that need to buy machines and equipment to expand production or upgrade the quality of products may apply for loans for purchasing equipment, provided that their investments will bring economic returns and the borrowers are able to repay the loans when due. The Bank shall extend support to such enterprises consistent with the regulations for granting loans to collective industrial enterprises in cities and towns for buying equipment.

3. Commercial enterprises of collective ownership that have opened accounts with the Bank and met the requirements mentioned in (1) above may apply for marketing loans to cover a temporary shortage of funds to stock up for the busy seasons, festivals or for urgent needs. The accounts to be opened thereunder should be kept separate from the deposit accounts they have opened, i.e., transactions of loans and deposits should be passed to the respective loan and deposit accounts.

No loans will be granted by the Bank to commercial enterprises of collective ownership who are subsidiaries of the state commercial enterprises, or who act as sales/purchase agents of the supply and marketing cooperatives, or who have obtained from them initial capital to launch themselves.

4. Collectively owned enterprises engaged in catering, services and repairs who have opened accounts with the Bank and met the requirements mentioned in (1) above, may obtain funds from the Bank to finance the purchases of raw materials they need. In addition, the Bank may provide a temporary credit facility, but for once only, to finance the purchases of simple equipment and tools vital to their business operations. Applications for such loans should be submitted by the enterprises with the departments in charge standing surety for them. The term of the loan is to be determined by the specific circumstances but no longer than two years. Repayment is to be made by installments.

5. To provide funds for production and business operations, the enterprises mentioned in (2), (3) and (4) above should improve their business management, make a sound distribution of profits and have an increasing accumulation of surplus. The surplus should be set aside first to repay the loans and replenish their working capital.

6. Collectively owned enterprises failing to meet the requirements mentioned in (1) above, must have their accounts opened en bloc with the Bank in the name of the street administrative office, neighbourhood committee or the business entity with which the enterprises are affiliated. Generally, no loans are to be granted to them.

7. The Bank may provide loans to cooperative shops not only to stock up for the busy seasons or festivals but to cover temporary shortage of funds to keep the shops stocked in order to increase sales.

The Bank and its branches shall give active support to and exercise strict supervision over the collectively owned enterprises run by the unemployed youth in cities and towns. In providing loans, the Bank should stick to the principle of "three assessments" (i.e. to assess the creditworthiness of the borrowers, to assess their applications for loans and to assess the effectiveness of the loans after they are granted); the term of the loan must be set and repayment made when due, so as to ensure the healthy development of the enterprises.

No credit will be granted to those enterprises that operate at a loss. Interest for the loans is to be charged at the prevailing rates for industrial/commercial loans.

The Bank's branches in the provinces, cities and autonomous regions may grant loans within the quotas allocated to them for industrial/commercial loans.

32. PROVISIONAL REGULATIONS ON PROVIDING SPECIAL SHORT- AND MEDIUM-TERM LOANS FOR THE LIGHT AND TEXTILE INDUSTRIES BY THE PEOPLE'S BANK OF CHINA

(January 14, 1980)

For the purpose of carrying out the policy of "readjustment, restructuring, consolidation and improvement" and taking special measures to boost the light and textile industries so as to meet market demands at home and abroad, provisional regulations are hereby issued for the People's Bank of China and the Bank of China to provide special short- and medium-term loans and foreign-currency loans in the form of buyers' credits to the light and textile industries.

Chapter I. Eligible Borrowers and the Purposes for Which Loans Are to be Used

Article 1. Loans are to be granted to state-owned and collectively owned enterprises in the light and textile industries (including specialized companies responsible for their own profits and losses). The loans are to be used primarily for the purposes of tapping production potential (including raw material potential), making technological innovations and launching small-scale construction and renovation projects related to such purposes.

Article 2. No loans shall be granted for construction of new factories or for extension of existing factories.

Chapter II. Prerequisites for Borrowing

Article 3. Applicants must meet the following requirements:

a) They must be able to generate quick returns, more profits and more foreign exchange earnings in proportion to the money borrowed.

b) They must have the necessary materials, equipment, design and construction manpower in place and ready to be used for the project undertaken, and must be assured of the availability of raw materials, power and labour force once the project is in operation. They must be able to find markets to sell their products.

c) Their production techniques must be up to standard.

d) They must promise economic yields and must be able to repay the loan with operating profits when due.

e) They must be able to take effective measures to prevent environmental pollution.

Chapter III. Term and Repayment of Loans

Article 4. A loan is normally available for one to two years but not longer than three years.

Article 5. A borrower must institute a separate accounting system to monitor the economic gains from the loan. Repayment of the loan plus interest shall be made out of earnings attributed to the loan, not from previous earnings.

State-owned enterprises must repay loans out of the profits from new projects or from the depreciation reserves for fixed assets or from the charges payable to the government for the use of fixed assets. If the above-mentioned funds are not sufficient for repayment, the deficit may be covered by the industrial-commercial tax that would otherwise be collected by the government on the increased output attributed to the loan.

Collectively owned enterprises must repay loans out of the accumulated profits from the new project after tax (during the period of repayment, the department in charge is not allowed to collect profits or other funds from the borrower for tax purposes) or from the depreciation reserves for fixed assets. If these funds are inadequate for repayment, the deficit may be covered by the income tax and industrial-commercial tax that would otherwise be collected by the government on the increased output attributed to the loan.

Article 6. If a loan cannot be repaid when it falls due, owing to suspension of the project in the course of construction or to failure of the borrower to generate the expected returns, repayment must be made out of the depreciation reserves for fixed assets and other reserves.

Article 7. The interest rate to be charged for a loan is 4.2% per month and interest is to be paid as soon as the financed project is in operation.

Chapter IV. Applications for Loans, Examination and Approval of Applications

Article 8. Plans for borrowing shall be examined and approved as follows:

The Bureau of Light Industry, the Bureau of Light Industry No. 2 (handicrafts) and the Bureau

245

of Textile Industry in the provinces, municipalities and autonomous regions (hereinafter called "local departments in charge") shall submit annual plans for borrowing on the basis of their programmes for tapping production potential and for making technological innovations duly approved by the Economic Commission in their locality. Plans for borrowing are to be examined by the local branches of the People's Bank of China (hereinafter called "bank branches"). They are to be submitted for re-examination by the head office of the People's Bank of China (hereinafter called "bank head office") and the ministries of light and textile industries (hereinafter called the "responsible ministries") who will, after adding their comments, submit the plans for further approval to a joint conference chaired by the State Economic Commission and attended by the bank head office, the State Planning Commission, responsible ministries and the Ministry of Finance. Then, the responsible ministries and the bank head office shall send back to the local departments in charge the approved plans for borrowing involving maximum project financing of over two million yuan for the textile industry and over one million yuan for light industries, with copies sent to the bank branches, the local economic commissions, planning commissions and finance bureaus. As for loans below the said maximum amounts, the bank head office and responsible ministries shall send back the approved plans for borrowing to the bank branches with copies sent to the local departments in charge.

Article 9. Authority to deal with applications for loans: Borrowers shall submit their applications to the bank branch where they keep an account. If a loan is below the said maximum amount, the bank branch has the right to approve the application in consultation with the local departments in charge. A report shall be sent to the responsible ministries and bank head office and a copy sent to the local economic commission, planning commission and finance bureau. For a loan over the maximum amount, the application shall be examined by the bank branch together with the local departments in charge and then, if agreeable, submitted to the bank head office and the responsible ministries for approval. The bank head office and the responsible ministries shall send back the approved application to the bank branches and local departments in charge with copies sent to the State Economic Commission, State Planning Commission and Ministry of Finance and their respective organizations.

Article 10. After approval of the project to be financed, the borrower and the bank shall sign a loan agreement whereby the bank is to provide funds within the approved amount in accordance with the progress of the project.

Article 11. A loan that has not been completely drawn down in the current year may continue to be available in the next year. Repayment received during the current year may be used for lending by the bank within its jurisdiction.

Chapter V. Supply of Materials for Projects to Be Financed

Article 12. The planning commission and supply administration at different levels shall be responsible for the supply of materials such as steel, timber, cement, etc. needed by the projects to be financed. These materials shall first be supplied from the local stockpile. The State Administration of Supplies will provide half of the necessary amount, which is then included in its distribution plans for tapping production potential and technological innovation. The ministries of light and textile industries shall make suggestions on the allocations of materials to be provided by the State Administration of Supplies. Accordingly, the State Administration of Supplies will instruct its local branches to supply the materials on the spot. The remaining supplies are to be provided, in principle, by the local authorities.

Article 13. Special equipment shall be supplied by the ministries of light and textile industries; general equipment by the State Administration of Supplies and its local branches; and optional equipment by the local authorities.

Chapter VI. Periodic Review and Supervision of Loans

Article 14. The People's Bank of China and the departments in charge shall inquire into each project before financing it and oversee the performance of the borrower after the loan is granted. They must carefully check whether the project conforms to the provisions of Articles 1, 2 and 3 and see to it that all necessary measures have been taken, giving preference to those borrowers who promise good returns and have the ability to repay loans.

Article 15. The loan must be used to finance the project for which it is granted. The bank has the right to suspend the loan before maturity in case the borrower changes its plans and raises its expenditure without the bank's consent or diverts the loan and construction materials to projects other than those agreed upon by the bank.

Article 16. The People's Bank of China and the departments in charge should work in close cooperation to help the borrower run its enterprise and regularly check the progress of the project and how the loan is being utilized so as to urge the enterprise to make the most of the loan with early returns.

Article 17. The borrower must submit to the departments in charge and the bank branch quarterly and annual reports on the progress of the project and how the loan is being used, with supporting statements and statistics. On the basis of these reports, the ministries of light and textile industries shall submit a quarterly consolidated report to the State Economic Commission and State Planning Commission with a copy sent to the bank head office.

Chapter VII. Loans in Convertible Foreign Currency

Article 18. When light and textile industrial enterprises require loans in foreign currency, such loans shall generally be in the form of buyers' credits. In addition to the funds from buyers' credits, the Bank of China may, if necessary, grant a supplementary loan in convertible foreign currency to cover down payment for imported equipment plus freight and insurance, or to import major components to fit the equipment to be manufactured by the borrower, or to import such things that are not covered by buyers' credits, thereby accelerating the development of light and textile industries.

Article 19. Foreign currency loans are to be applied for and granted according to the regulations issued by the Bank of China.

Chapter VIII. Supplementary Regulations

Article 20. These regulations are to be formulated and amended by the head office of the People's Bank of China. Branch banks in the provinces, municipalities and autonomous regions may issue supplementary rules to suit local conditions and submit a report to the head office for the record.

These regulations shall come into force on the date of issue.

33. PROVISIONAL REGULATIONS OF THE BANK OF CHINA ON FOREIGN EXCHANGE CERTIFICATES

(March 19, 1980)

1. With a view to strengthening exchange control, the State Council has authorized the Bank of China to issue Foreign Exchange Certificates (hereinafter called "Exchange Certificates").

2. Exchange Certificates are in seven denominations, namely, 100 yuan, 50 yuan, 10 yuan, 5 yuan, 1 yuan, 5 jiao and 1 jiao. The yuan expressed in them is equivalent in value to the renminbi yuan. No refund is allowed in case of loss.

3. Exchange Certificates are usable only in China for specific purposes. They are to be used by short-time visitors (foreigners, overseas Chinese, Hongkong and Macao compatriots), personnel of the diplomatic corps and foreign representative offices in China at the following places or for making the following payments:

a) at travel services dealing exclusively with foreigners, overseas Chinese, Hongkong and Macao compatriots, friendship stores, companies provisioning foreign ships, arts and crafts stores, curios shops, foreign trade centres and special shop counters for selling imported goods;

b) at guest houses, hotels and clubs accommodating exclusively foreigners, overseas Chinese, Hongkong and Macao compatriots;

c) payment of fares for through train or ship to Hongkong or Macao, and charges for transporting luggage or personal effects;

d) payment of fares for domestic or international flights and charges for transporting luggage or personal effects;

e) payment of international telecommunication charges and international parcels post;

f) at places where Exchange Certificates are required for payment as approved by the State General Administration of Exchange Control (or its branches) or according to official regulations.

4. Convertible foreign banknotes, bills of exchange or payment instruments in foreign currency that are immediately cashable or remittances from abroad may be exchanged by the above-mentioned categories of persons for Exchange Certificates at the Bank of China or its designated exchange centres throughout the country. When handing out Exchange Certificates, the Bank of China (or its exchange centres) shall issue to the customer an "exchange memo."

5. Holders of Exchange Certificates may within six months and against the "exchange memo," convert the Exchange Certificates into Renminbi special deposits or foreign currency deposits with the Bank of China, or into foreign currency, or take them out of the country.

6. No private dealings in Exchange Certificates are permitted. Speculation in or counterfeit of Exchange Certificates is strictly prohibited. Voilators will be punished for undermining the socialist economic order according to Chapter 3 of the Criminal Law of the People's Republic of China.

34. REGULATIONS FOR PROVIDING SHORT-TERM LOANS IN FOREIGN CURRENCY BY THE BANK OF CHINA

Approved for Transmission by the State Council on August 30, 1980

With the funds it raises from abroad, the Bank of China is ready to provide loans in foreign currency to export-oriented industries and other enterprises in order to boost their foreign exchange earnings on the basis of self-reliance, thereby speeding up the socialist modernization of our country. It is for these purposes that the following regulations are formulated.

Chapter I. Eligible Borrowers and the Purposes for Which Loans Are To Be Used

Article 1. Loans are to be granted to export-oriented industries and other enterprises earning foreign exchange income directly or indirectly who can meet the prerequisites for borrowing. The loans are primarily for encouraging export-oriented industries to tap production potential and renovate obsolete plants and equipment.

Article 2. The loans are to be used for:

a) financing imports of advanced technology, equipment and materials essential to upgrading the borrower's productivity and the quality, variety and packaging of export goods;

b) financing imports of raw materials and components to be processed for export;

c) developing transportation and tourism and carrying out engineering projects contracted with foreign firms;

d) supporting the processing of raw materials and assembling of parts supplied by foreign buyers, and for supporting compensatory trade; and

e) providing short-term working capital to production that earns foreign exchange directly or indirectly.

Chapter II. Prerequisites for Borrowing

Article 3. Applicants must meet the following requirements:

a) Effective productivity of the loan: Preference is given to borrowers who are able to earn more foreign exchange in proportion to the money invested and repay bank loans sooner. Borrowers should be able to run their enterprises efficiently, make the most of the imported advanced technology, equipment and raw materials, tap their production potential, renovate obsolete plants and equipment, enhance the competitiveness of their export goods in the international markets, thereby earning more foreign exchange for the country.

b) Assurance of repayment: Borrowers must give evidence of a reliable source of foreign exchange income and the ability to repay loans plus interest for which they are required to submit a schedule of repayment.

Where loans are granted to the export-goods industry, the increased output attributed to the loan should be primarily for export and not be included in the state domestic marketing plan. The income from the increased output and the export proceeds in foreign exchange should first be set aside for repayment of the bank loan. In case the goods are to be turned over to a foreign trade corporation for export, the borrower should sign a sales contract with this corporation which commits the latter to repay the bank loan in foreign exchange for the borrower.

Enterprises not directly related to the export trade must submit a document of approval signed by the department in charge committing the latter to repay the loan from its own foreign exchange income. When necessary, the bank may demand that some organization that has a regular foreign exchange income stand surety for the borrower.

c) Readiness of domestic factors of production to make imported materials and equipment operational. Domestic factors of production refer to factory buildings, equipment, steam, water, electricity and fuel, raw materials, labour force, technological expertise and counterpart funds in Renminbi requisite to making the imported equipment and materials operational. These items must be duly arranged and approved by the Planning Commission or the authorities in charge who have to list them in their plans or sign contracts with the borrower.

d) With respect to the items mentioned above, borrowers should obtain prior approval of higher authorities for those items that require allotment of funds for capital construction or technological installations.

Chapter III. Applications for Loans, Examination and Approval of Applications and Drawdowns of the Loans

Article 4. Application for loans should be submitted to the Bank of China (or People's Bank of China where the Bank of China does not exist) together with the following supporting documents: a document evidencing the approval of the proposed project by the department in charge; a list of imports the loan is to finance; a schedule proving the domestic factors of production are in readiness or a copy of the relevant contract; a document approved by the department in charge showing that counterpart funds in Renminbi have been earmarked for repayment of the loan (if the borrower is not directly involved in the export trade); a copy of the sales contract signed with a foreign trade corporation which commits itself to repay the loan in foreign exchange for the borrower (if the borrower is to repay the loan with export proceeds).

Article 5. Applications for loans by the departments under the State Council shall be examined item by item against the prerequisites for borrowing by the head office of the Bank of China. Applications by local departments and enterprises shall be reviewed by the Bank of China's regional branches in the provinces, municipalities and autonomous regions within the bounds of their respective loan quotas assigned by the head office. Cases that need to be reviewed by the head office or ministries concerned should be submitted to them for approval. In examining the applications, the bank should keep in touch with the departments in charge and work in cooperation with them.

Article 6. After the application is approved, the borrower should sign a loan agreement, open a loan account with the Bank of China and place an order for imports. If the borrower fails to sign the loan agreement or submit a list of imports within the specified time, the bank may revoke its approval of the loan. The list of imports must be signed by the bank before the order is placed. Without the approval of the bank, neither the purpose for which the loan is to be used nor the descriptions and quantities of imports should be changed. The borrower should submit to the bank a copy of the contract signed with the foreign trader who provides the goods. The bank should help the borrower to make the most of the loan.

Article 7. For a substantial loan, the borrower should submit a quarterly drawdown plan according to which the bank will raise the funds. In case the plan needs to be adjusted because of miscalculation or unexpected changes of circumstances, the borrower should apply to the bank for adjustment a month before the end of the quarter. For failure to carry out the plan, the borrower shall bear additional bank charges on the amount of the drawdown falling short of, or in excess of, the planned amounts so as to compensate the bank for losses in raising funds from abroad.

Chapter IV. Term of Loans and Rates of Interest

Article 8. The term of the loan is to be counted from the day of the drawdown to the day of repayment. Loans for importing raw materials and components to be processed for export are normally available for one year. Loans for importing equipment or materials to be used in making equipment, and loans for other purposes shall not exceed three years. Where loans take the form of buyers' credits, the maturity shall not exceed five years.

Article 9. The interest rates for loans are to be determined and made public by the head office of the Bank of China on the basis of the cost of raising funds on the international money markets plus its handling charges.

Chapter V. Repayment of Loans

Article 10. Full repayment must be made on the due date specified in the loan agreement. If the borrower fails to repay, the surety is responsible for repayment. If necessary, the Bank of China or the People's Bank of China may force repayment by debiting the foreign currency deposit account of the borrower or the surety (or by writing off the foreign exchange quota alloted to the borrower and seizing his counterpart funds in Renminbi earmarked for the purchase of the foreign exchange quota).

Article 11. A borrower who has a regular foreign exchange income should repay the loan from foreign exchange earnings. A borrower who is not directly involved in the export trade should repay the loan from export proceeds received through a foreign trade corporation. This corporation or some other organization which stands surety for the borrower should issue a certificate to "repay foreign exchange quota" against which the borrower may purchase foreign exchange with Renminbi from the Bank of China to repay the loan. Foreign exchange earnings from the processing of raw materials and assembling of parts provided by foreign buyers or earnings from compensatory trade must first be set aside for repayment of the loan.

Article 12. Loans made to finance a construction project by a state-owned enterprise may be repaid out of profits derived from the increased output, out of depreciation reserves for fixed assets, or out of charges payable to the government for the use of fixed assets. Enterprises that are authorized to retain a portion of their profits may make repayment from the retained profits after deductions for the staff's welfare fund and bonus fund. However, deductions for the production development fund and for retention of increased profits are not allowed. Loans to collectively owned urban enterprises may be repaid out of profits derived from the increased output (profits before tax) or from depreciation reserves for fixed assets. The department in charge is not allowed to collect profits or demand payment out of the project financed by the bank loan so long as the loan remains to be repaid.

If the above-mentioned funds are sufficient to repay the loan and a surplus remains, income tax shall be paid on the surplus or a percentage of profits shall be turned over to the government as required. If not, the deficit may, with the consent of the Internal Revenue Bureau, be covered by the industrial-and-commercial tax on the increased output which would otherwise be collected by the Bureau. When applying for the loan, the borrower should send a copy of the application to the Bureau for its reference.

Chapter VI. Buyers' Credits

Article 13. When loans are provided in the form of the buyers' credits, the following rules shall apply, apart from other provisions in the regulations:

a) The borrower must abide by the provisions in the buyer's credit agreement that the Bank of China has signed with a foreign bank and must place orders for imports from the country in which the foreign bank is located.

b) The borrower must indicate in the order for imports that the buyer's credit is to be used for payment. The sales contract signed between the Chinese foreign trade corporation and the foreign seller should indicate the name of the bank providing the buyer's credit.

c) At the time the sales contract is signed, the Bank of China shall negotiate with the foreign bank providing the buyer's credit and sign an agreement on the drawdown of the credit. The agreement shall be signed by the Bank of China head office or by one of its branches with its authorization.

Chapter VII. Bank Supervision

Article 14. The borrower must maximize the effective productivity of the loan by relying on cost accounting. Preference is given to the borrower who earns more foreign exchange in proportion to the amount of the loan granted and makes repayment sooner. The borrower who performs poorly or who is unable to repay his loan upon maturity, will not receive further loans until he shows improvement in management.

Article 15. Both the bank and the borrower shall abide by the loan agreement: The bank undertakes to provide the loanable funds; the borrower undertakes to draw on the loan and utilize its productive potential effectively. The bank shall raise the interest by 10—50% for overdue loans counting from the maturity date, and by 100% for loans diverted to uses other than those authorized by the bank.

Article 16. The bank shall inquire into each project before financing it, examine the borrower's application before approving it and oversee the performance of the borrower after the loan is granted. The bank has the duty to help the borrower achieve its economic goals. In this way the bank shall fulfil its role of promoting, regulating and supervising the economic activities of the borrower.

For large loans, the bank shall sit in on the negotiations between the borrower and the foreign supplier and make suggestions as to the preferred currency for making payment and the method of payment. The borrower must provide the bank with all necessary information, documents, statistics and a duplicate of the relevant contract.

The borrower shall be held accountable for violation of government decrees and policies; failure to abide by the regulations, the contract or the agreement; dissipation of foreign exchange; or failure to repay the loan when due. At the same time the bank may take such disciplinary actions as suspending or recalling the loan before maturity, raising the interest rate or even suing the borrower in a court of law.

Chapter VIII. Supplementary Regulations

Article 17. On the date the regulations come into force, "Regulations for Providing Short-term Loans in Foreign Currency," issued by the Ministry of Finance on September 29, 1978, shall no longer be valid except for loans and loan agreements previously approved and signed. Detailed rules for the enforcement of the regulations shall be formulated separately by the Bank of China.

35. PROVISIONAL REGULATIONS FOR EXCHANGE CONTROL OF THE PEOPLE'S REPUBLIC OF CHINA

Promulgated by the State Council
(December 18, 1980)

Chapter I. General Provisions

Article 1. These provisional regulations are formulated for the purpose of strengthening exchange control, increasing national foreign exchange income and economizing on foreign exchange expenditure so as to expedite national economic growth and safeguard the rights and interests of the country.

All foreign exchange income and expenditure, the issuance and circulation of all kinds of payment instruments in foreign currency, dispatch and carriage into and out of the People's Republic of China of foreign exchange, precious metals and payment instruments in foreign currency shall be governed by these regulations.

Article 2. Foreign exchange herein mentioned refers to:
 a) Foreign currencies, including banknotes, coins, etc.
 b) Securities in foreign currency, including government bonds, treasury bills, corporate bonds and debentures, shares, interest and dividend coupons, etc.
 c) Instruments payable in foreign currency, including bills, drafts, cheques, bank deposit certificates, postal savings certificates, etc.
 d) Other foreign exchange funds.

Article 3. The People's Republic of China pursues the policy of centralized control and unified management of foreign exchange by the state.

The administrative organ in charge of exchange control of the People's Republic of China is the State General Administration of Exchange Control (SGAEC) and its branch offices.

The specialized foreign exchange bank of the People's Republic of China is the Bank of China. No other financial institution shall engage in foreign exchange business, unless approved by the SGAEC.

Article 4. All Chinese and foreign organizations and individuals in the People's Republic of China must, unless otherwise stipulated by law or decree or in these regulations, sell their foreign exchange proceeds to the Bank of China. Any foreign exchange required is to be sold to them by the Bank of China in accordance with the quota approved by the state or with relevant regulations.

The circulation, use and mortgage of foreign currency in the People's Republic of China are prohibited. Unauthorized sales and purchases of foreign exchange and unlawful seizure and possession of foreign exchange in whatever ways and by whatever means are prohibited.

Chapter II. Exchange Control Relating to State Organizations and Collective Economic Units

Article 5. Foreign exchange income and expenditure of state organs, units of the armed forces, non-governmental bodies, educational institutions, state enterprises, government establishments, and urban and rural collective economic units in China (hereinafter referred to as domestic organizations) are all subject to control according to plan.

Domestic organizations are permitted to retain a proportion of their foreign exchange receipts in accordance with relevant regulations.

Article 6. Unless approved by the SGAEC or its branch offices, domestic organizations shall not possess foreign exchange; deposit foreign exchange abroad; offset foreign exchange expenditure against foreign exchange income; or use the foreign exchange belonging to state organs stationed abroad or Chinese enterprises and establishments resident in foreign countries or in the Hong Kong and Macao regions, by way of borrowing or acquisition.

Article 7. Unless approved by the State Council, domestic organizations shall not issue securities with foreign exchange value inside or outside China.

Article 8. Departments under the State Council and people's governments of various provinces, municipalities and autonomous regions shall compile annual overall plans for domestic organizations under their respective jurisdiction whereby loans may be accepted from banks or enterprises in foreign countries or in the Hong Kong and Macao regions. These plans shall be submitted to the SGAEC and the Foreign Investment Control Commission for examination and forwarding to the State Council for approval.

The procedure for examining and approving individual borrowings shall be prescribed separately.

Article 9. The portion of foreign exchange retained by domestic organizations, non-trade foreign exchange and foreign exchange under compensatory trade received in advance for later payments, funds borrowed in convertible foreign currency, and other foreign exchange held with the approval of the SGAEC or its branch offices, must be placed in foreign currency deposit accounts or foreign currency quota accounts to be opened with the Bank of China, and must be used within the prescribed scope and be subject to the supervision of the Bank of China.

Article 10. When domestic organizations import or export goods, the banks handling the transactions shall check their foreign exchange receipts and payments either against the import or export' licences duly verified by the Customs or against the Customs declaration forms for imports or exports.

Article 11. State organs stationed abroad must use foreign exchange according to the plan approved by the state.

The operating profits of enterprises and establishments in foreign countries or in the Hongkong and Macao regions must, except for the portion kept locally as working funds according to the plan approved by the state, be transferred back on schedule and be sold to the Bank of China.

No Chinese organization stationed abroad is permitted to keep foreign exchange for domestic organizations without authorization.

Article 12. Delegations and workgroups sent temporarily to foreign countries or to the Hongkong and Macao regions must use foreign exchange according to their respective specific plans, and must, upon their return, promptly transfer back to China their surplus foreign exchange to be checked by and sold to the Bank of China.

Foreign exchange earned in their various business activities by the delegations and workgroups referred to in the above paragraph and by members thereof, must be promptly transferred back to China and must not be kept abroad without the approval of the SGAEC or its branch offices.

Chapter III. Exchange Control Relating to Individuals

Article 13. Foreign exchange remitted from foreign countries or from the Hongkong and Macao regions to Chinese or foreign nationals or stateless persons residing in China must be sold to the Bank of China, except the portion retained as permitted by the state.

Article 14. Chinese and foreign nationals and stateless persons residing in China are permitted to keep in their own possession foreign exchange already in China.

The foreign exchange referred to in the above paragraph shall not, without authorization, be carried or sent out of China either in person or by others or by post. If the owners wish to sell the foreign exchange, they must sell it to the Bank of China and are permitted to retain a portion thereof as convertible foreign currency according to the percentage prescribed by the state.

Article 15. When foreign exchange that has been kept in foreign countries or in the Hong Kong and Macao regions by Chinese residents in China prior to the founding of the People's Republic of China, by overseas Chinese prior to their returning to and settling down in China, by Hongkong and Macao compatriots prior to their returning to and settling down in their home places, is transferred to China, the owners are permitted to retain a portion thereof as convertible foreign currency according to the percentage prescribed by the state.

Article 16. When foreign exchange belonging personally to individuals sent to work or study in foreign countries or in the Hong Kong and Macao regions is remitted or brought back to China, the owners returning after completion of their missions are permitted to retain the entire amount as convertible foreign currency.

Article 17. The percentages of foreign exchange retention permitted under Articles 13, 14 and 15 of these regulations shall be prescribed separately.

Foreign exchange retained by individuals as permitted under Articles 13, 14, 15 and 16 of these regulations must be deposited with the Bank of China. These foreign exchange deposits may be sold to the Bank of China or remitted out of China through the Bank of China, or taken out of China against certification by the Bank of China. It is however not permitted, without authorization, to carry or send deposit certificates out of China either in person or by others or by post.

Article 18. Foreign exchange remitted or brought into China from foreign countries or from the Hong Kong and Macao regions by foreign nationals coming to China, by overseas Chinese and Hongkong and Macao compatriots returning for a short stay, by foreign experts, technicians, staff members and workers engaged to work in domestic organizations, and by foreign students and trainees, may be kept in their own possession, or sold to or deposited with the Bank of China, or remitted or taken out of China.

Article 19. Chinese and foreign nationals and stateless persons residing in China may apply to the local branch offices of the SGAEC for the purchase of foreign exchange to be remitted or taken out of China. When approved, the required foreign exchange will be sold to the applicants by the Bank of China.

When foreign experts, technicians, staff members and workers engaged to work in domestic organizations require foreign exchange to be remitted or taken out of China, the Bank of China will deal with their applications in accordance with the stipulations in the contracts or agreements.

Chapter IV. Exchange Control Relating to Foreign Representations in China and Their Personnel

Article 20. Foreign exchange remitted or brought into China from foreign countries or from the Hong Kong and Macao regions by foreign diplomatic missions, consulates, official commercial offices, offices of international organizations and nongovernmental bodies resident in China, diplomatic officials and consuls as well as members of the permanent staff of the above units, may be kept in their own possession, or sold to or deposited with the Bank of China, or remitted or taken out of China.

Article 21. The conversion into foreign currency, if required, of visa and certification fees received in Renminbi from Chinese citizens by foreign diplomatic missions and consulates in China, is subject to approval by the SGAEC or its branch offices.

Chapter V. Exchange Control Relating to Enterprises with Overseas Chinese Capital, Enterprises with Foreign Capital, and Chinese and Foreign Joint Ventures and Their Personnel

Article 22. All foreign exchange receipts of enterprises with overseas Chinese capital, enterprises with foreign capital and Chinese and foreign joint ventures, must be deposited with the Bank of China, and all their foreign exchange disbursements must be paid from their foreign exchange deposit accounts.

The enterprises referred to in the above paragraph must submit periodic reports and statements of their foreign exchange business to the SGAEC or its branch offices, all of which are empowered to inspect their activities in respect to their foreign exchange receipts and payments.

Article 23. Except where otherwise approved by the SGAEC or its branch offices, Renminbi should in all cases be used in the settlement of accounts between enterprises with overseas Chinese capital, enterprises with foreign capital, Chinese and foreign joint ventures and other enterprises and individuals residing in the People's Republic of China.

Article 24. Enterprises with overseas Chinese capital, enterprises with foreign capital and foreign partners in Chinese and foreign joint ventures may apply to the Bank of China for remitting abroad their net profits after tax as well as other legitimate earnings by debiting the foreign exchange deposit accounts of the enterprises concerned.

The enterprises and foreign partners referred to in the above paragraph should apply to the SGAEC or its branch offices for transferring foreign exchange capital abroad by debiting the foreign exchange deposit accounts of the enterprises concerned.

Article 25. An amount not exceeding 50% of their net wages and other legitimate earnings after tax may be remitted or taken out of China in foreign currency by staff members and workers of foreign nationality and those from the Hongkong and Macao regions employed by enterprises with overseas Chinese capital, enterprises with foreign capital and Chinese and foreign joint ventures.

Article 26. Enterprises with overseas Chinese capital, enterprises with foreign capital and Chinese and foreign joint ventures which wind up operations in accordance with legal procedure, should be responsible for the liquidation within the scheduled period of their outstanding liabilities and taxes due in China, under the joint supervision of the relevant departments in charge and the SGAEC or its branch offices.

Chapter VI. Control Relating to Carrying Foreign Exchange, Precious Metals and Payment Instruments in Foreign Currency into and out of China

Article 27. No restriction as to the amount is

imposed on the carrying into China of foreign exchange, precious metals and objects made from them, but declaration to the Customs is required at the place of entry.

To carry foreign exchange out of China or to carry out of China the foreign exchange previously brought in shall be permitted by the Customs against certification by the Bank of China or against the original declaration form at the time of entry.

To carry out of China precious metals and objects made from them or to carry out of China precious metals and objects made from them previously brought in shall be permitted by the Customs according to the specific circumstances as prescribed by government regulations or against the original declaration form at the time of entry.

Article 28. Renminbi traveller's cheques, traveller's letters of credit and other Renminbi payment instruments convertible into foreign currency may be brought into China against declaration to the Customs, and taken out of China against certification by the Bank of China or against the original declaration form at the time of entry.

Article 29. Unless otherwise approved by the SGAEC or its branch offices, the carrying or sending out of China either in person or by others or by post of the following documents and securities held by Chinese residing in China is not permitted:

Bonds, debentures, share certificates issued abroad;

Title deeds for real estate abroad;

Documents or deeds necessary in dealing with creditor's right or owner's right to possession regarding inheritance, real estate and other foreign exchange assets abroad.

Article 30. The carrying or sending out of China of Renminbi cheques, drafts, passbooks, deposit certificates and other Renminbi instruments held by Chinese or foreign nationals or stateless persons residing in China, is not permitted, either in person or by others or by post.

Chapter VII. Supplementary Provisions

Article 31. All units and individuals have the right to report any violation of these regulations. Reward shall be given to such units or individuals according to the merit of the report. Violators shall be penalized by the SGEAC, its branch offices or by the departments of public security, or by the departments of Administration of Industry and Commerce, or by the Customs. According to the seriousness of the offence, the penalties may take the form of compulsory exchange of the foreign currency for Renminbi, or fine or confiscation of the properties or both, or punishment by judicial authorities according to law.

Article 32. The exchange control regulations for special economic zones, for trade in border areas, and for personal dealings between inhabitants across the border shall be formulated by the people's governments of the provinces, municipalities and autonomous regions concerned in the spirit of these regulations and in the light of specific local conditions, and shall be enforced upon the approval of the State Council.

Article 33. Detailed provisions for the enforcement of these regulations shall be formulated by the SGEAC.

Article 34. These regulations shall come into force on March 1, 1981.

36. THE LAW OF THE PEOPLE'S REPUBLIC OF CHINA ON JOINT VENTURES USING CHINESE AND FOREIGN INVESTMENT

Approved on July 1, 1979 by the Fifth National People's Congress of the People's Republic of China at its Second Session

Article 1. With a view to expanding international economic cooperation and technological exchange, the People's Republic of China permits foreign companies, enterprises, other economic entities or individuals (hereinafter referred to as "foreign participants") to incorporate themselves, within the territory of the People's Republic of China, into joint ventures with Chinese companies, enterprises or other economic entities (hereinafter referred to as "Chinese participants") on the principle of equality and mutual benefit and subject to authorization by the Chinese Government.

Article 2. The Chinese Government protects, by the legislation in force, the resources invested by a foreign participant in a joint venture and the profits due him pursuant to the agreements, contracts and articles of association authorized by the Chinese Government as well as his other lawful rights and interests.

All the activities of a joint venture shall be governed by the laws, decrees and pertinent rules and regulations of the People's Republic of China.

Article 3. A joint venture shall apply to the Foreign Investment Commission of the People's Republic of China for authorization of the agreements and contracts concluded between the parties to the venture and the articles of association of the venture formulated by them, and the commission shall authorize or reject these documents within three months. When authorized, the joint venture shall register with the General Administration for Industry and Commerce of the People's Republic of China and start operations under licence.

Article 4. A joint venture shall take the form of a limited liability company.

In the registered capital of a joint venture, the proportion of the investment contributed by the foreign participant(s) shall in general not be less than 25 per cent.

The profits, risks and losses of a joint venture shall be shared by the parties to the venture in proportion to their contributions to the registered capital.

The transfer of one party's share in the registered capital shall be effected only with the consent of the other parties to the venture.

Article 5. Each party to a joint venture may contribute cash, capital goods, industrial property rights, etc., as its investment in the venture.

The technology or equipment contributed by any foreign participant as investment shall be truly advanced and appropriate to China's needs. In cases of losses caused by deception through the intentional provision of outdated equipment or technology, compensation shall be paid for the losses.

The investment contributed by a Chinese participant may include the right to the use of a site provided for the joint venture during the period of its operation. In case such a contribution does not constitute a part of the investment from the Chinese participant, the joint venture shall pay the Chinese Government for its use.

The various contributions referred to in the present article shall be specified in the contracts concerning the joint venture or in its articles of association, and the value of each contribution (excluding that of the site) shall be ascertained by the parties to the venture through joint assessment.

Article 6. A joint venture shall have a board of directors with a composition stipulated in the contracts and the articles of association after consultation between the parties to the venture, and each director shall be appointed or removed by his own side. The board of directors shall have a chairman appointed by the Chinese participant and one or two vice-chairmen appointed by the foreign participant(s). In handling an important problem, the board of directors shall reach decision through consultation by the participants on the principle of equality and mutual benefit.

The board of directors is empowered to discuss and take action on, pursuant to the provisions of the articles of association of the joint venture, all fundamental issues concerning the venture, namely, expansion projects, production and business programmes, the budget, distribution of profits, plans concerning manpower and pay scales, the termination of business, the appointment or hiring of the president, the vice-president(s), the chief engineer, the treasurer and the auditors as well as their functions and powers and their remuneration, etc.

The president and vice-president(s) (or the

general manager and assistant general manager(s) in a factory) shall be chosen from the various parties to the joint venture.

Procedures covering the employment and discharge of the workers and staff members of a joint venture shall be stipulated according to law in the agreement or contract concluded between the parties to the venture.

Article 7. The net profit of a joint venture shall be distributed between the parties to the venture in proportion to their respective shares in the registered capital after the payment of a joint venture income tax on its gross profit pursuant to the tax laws of the People's Republic of China and after the deductions therefrom as stipulated in the articles of association of the venture for the reserve funds, the bonus and welfare funds for the workers and staff members and the expansion funds of the venture.

A joint venture equipped with up-to-date technology by world standards may apply for a reduction of or exemption from income tax for the first two to three profit making years.

A foreign participant who reinvests any part of his share of the net profit within Chinese territory may apply for the restitution of a part of the income taxes paid.

Article 8. A joint venture shall open an account with the Bank of China or a bank approved by the Bank of China.

A joint venture shall conduct its foreign exchange transactions in accordance with the Foreign Exchange Regulations of the People's Republic of China.

A joint venture may, in its business operations, obtain funds from foreign banks directly.

The insurances appropriate to a joint venture shall be furnished by Chinese insurance companies.

Article 9. The production and business programmes of a joint venture shall be filed with the authorities concerned and shall be implemented through business contracts.

In its purchase of required raw and semi-processed materials, fuels, auxiliary equipment, etc., a joint venture should give first priority to Chinese sources, but may also acquire them directly from the world market with its own foreign exchange funds.

A joint venture is encouraged to market its products outside China. It may distribute its export products on foreign markets through direct channels or its associated agencies or China's foreign trade establishments. Its products may also be distributed on the Chinese market.

Wherever necessary, a joint venture may set up affiliated agencies outside China.

Article 10. The net profit which a foreign participant receives as his share after executing his obligations under the pertinent laws and agreements and contracts, the funds he receives at the time when the joint venture terminates or winds up its operations, and his other funds may be remitted abroad through the Bank of China in accordance with the foreign exchange regulations and in the currency or currencies specified in the contracts concerning the joint venture.

A foreign participant shall receive encouragements for depositing in the Bank of China any part of the foreign exchange which he is entitled to remit abroad.

Article 11. The wages, salaries or other legitimate income earned by a foreign worker or staff member of a joint venture, after payment of the personal income tax under the tax laws of the People's Republic of China, may be remitted abroad through the Bank of China in accordance with the foreign exchange regulations.

Article 12. The contract period of a joint venture may be agreed upon between the parties to the venture according to its particular line of business and circumstances. The period may be extended upon expiration through agreement between the parties, subject to authorization by the Foreign Investment Commission of the People's Republic of China. Any application for such extension shall be made six months before the expiration of the contract.

Article 13. In cases of heavy losses, the failure of any party to a joint venture to execute its obligations under the contracts or the articles of association of the venture, force majeure, etc., prior to the expiration of the contract period of a joint venture, the contract may be terminated before the date of expiration by consultation and agreement between the parties and through authorization by the Foreign Investment Commission of the People's Republic of China and registration with the General Administration for Industry and Commerce. In cases of losses caused by breach of the contract(s) by a party to the venture, the financial responsibility shall be borne by the said party.

Article 14. Disputes arising between the parties to a joint venture which the board of directors fails to settle through consultation may be settled through conciliation or arbitration by an arbitral body of China or through arbitration by an arbitral body agreed upon by the parties.

Article 15. The present law comes into force on the date of its promulgation. The power of amendment is vested in the National People's Congress.

37. REGULATIONS ON LABOUR MANAGEMENT IN JOINT VENTURES USING CHINESE AND FOREIGN INVESTMENT

Approved by the State Council of the People's Republic of China
(July 26, 1980)

Article 1. Labour management problems concerning joint ventures using Chinese and foreign investment (hereinafter referred to as "joint ventures") should be handled in accordance with the regulations, in addition to the pertinent stipulations in Article 6 of the "Law of the People's Republic of China on Joint Ventures Using Chinese and Foreign Investment."

Article 2. Matters pertaining to employment, dismissal and resignation of the workers and staff members, tasks of production and other work, wages and awards and punishment, working time and vacation, labour insurance and welfare, labour protection and labour discipline in joint ventures shall be stipulated in the labour contracts signed.

A labour contract is to be signed collectively by a joint venture and the trade union organization formed in the joint venture. A relatively small joint venture may sign contracts with the workers and staff members individually.

A signed labour contract must be submitted to the labour management department of the provincial, autonomous regional or municipal people's government for approval.

Article 3. The workers and staff members of a joint venture either recommended by the authorities in the locality in charge of the joint venture or the labour management department, or recruited by the joint venture itself with the consent of the labour management department, should all be selected by the joint venture through examination for their qualification.

Joint ventures may run workers' schools and training courses for the training of managerial personnel and skilled workers.

Article 4. With regard to the surplus workers and staff members as a result of changes in production and technical conditions of the joint venture, those who fail to meet the requirements after training and are not suitable for other work can be discharged. However, this must be done in line with the stipulations in the labour contract and the enterprise must give compensation to these workers.

The dismissed workers and staff members will receive assignments for other work from the authorities in charge of the joint venture or the labour management department.

Article 5. The joint venture may, according to the degree of seriousness of the case, take action against those workers or staff members who have violated rules and regulations of the enterprise that result in certain bad consequences. Punishment by discharges must be reported to the authorities in charge of the joint venture and the labour management department for approval.

Article 6. With regard to the dismissal and punishment of workers and staff members by the joint venture, the trade union has the right to raise an objection if it considers them unreasonable, and send representatives to seek a solution through consultation with the board of directors. Should the consultation fail to arrive at a solution, the matter will be handled in accordance with the procedures set forth in Article 14 of the present regulations.

Article 7. When workers and staff members of a joint venture, on account of special conditions, submit their resignation to the enterprise through the trade union in accordance with the labour contract, the enterprise should give its consent.

Article 8. The wage levels of workers and staff members in a joint venture will be determined at 120 to 150% of the real wages of workers and staff members of state-owned enterprises of the same trade in the locality.

Article 9. The wage standards, the forms of wages paid, and bonus and subsidy systems are to be discussed and decided upon by the board of directors.

Article 10. The bonuses and welfare funds drawn by the joint venture from the profits must be used as bonuses, awards and collective welfare and should not be misappropriated.

Article 11. A joint venture must pay for the Chinese workers' and staff members' labour insurance, cover their medical expenses and various kinds of government subsidies in line with the standards prevailing in state-owned enterprises.

Article 12. The employment of foreign workers and staff members and their dismissal, resignation, pay, welfare and social insurances and other relevant matters should all be stipulated in the employment contracts.

Article 13. Joint ventures must implement the relevant rules and regulations of the Chinese Government on labour protection and ensure safety in production and civilized production. The labour management department of the Chinese Government is authorized to supervise and inspect their implementation.

Article 14. Labour disputes occurring in a joint venture should first of all be solved through consultation by both parties. If consultation fails to arrive at a solution, either party or both parties may request arbitration by the labour management department of the people's government of the province, autonomous region or municipality where the joint venture is located. Either party that disagrees to the arbitration may file a suit at the people's court.

Article 15. The right of interpretation of the present regulations belongs to the State Bureau of Labour of the People's Republic of China.

Article 16. The regulations come into force on the date of their promulgation.

38. REGULATIONS ON THE REGISTRATION OF JOINT VENTURES USING CHINESE AND FOREIGN INVESTMENT

Approved by the State Council of the People's Republic of China
(July 26, 1980)

Article 1. The present regulations are worked out in accordance with stipulations laid down in the "Law of the People's Republic of China on Joint Ventures Using Chinese and Foreign Investment" and for the purpose of registering such ventures to protect their legitimate operations.

Article 2. A joint venture using Chinese and foreign investment should, within one month after approval by the Foreign Investment Commission of the People's Republic of China, register with the General Administration for Industry and Commerce of the People's Republic of China.

The General Administration for Industry and Commerce authorizes the administrative bureaus for industry and commerce in the provinces, municipalities and autonomous regions to register joint ventures using Chinese and foreign investment in their localities. Licences for operations shall be issued to the said joint ventures after examination by the General Administration for Industry and Commerce of the People's Republic of China.

Article 3. In applying for registration, a joint venture using Chinese and foreign investment should produce the following documents:

a) The document of approval issued by the Foreign Investment Commission of the People's Republic of China;

b) The agreement on the joint venture reached by the various parties involved, the contract and the articles of association of the venture, in both Chinese and foreign language and each in triplicate;

c) A duplicate of the licence and other documents issued by the departments concerned under the government of the country (or region) from which the foreign participants in the joint venture come.

Article 4. In applying for registration of a joint venture using Chinese and foreign investment, a registration form, in triplicate, shall be completed in Chinese and the relevant foreign language. Items to be registered include the name of the venture, its address, scope of production and business, forms of production and business, registered capital of the parties concerned, chairman and vice-chairmen of the board of directors, general manager and deputy general managers or general director and deputy directors of the plant, the number and date of approval on the document, the size of the entire staff, and the number of foreign workers and staff members.

Article 5. A joint venture using Chinese and foreign investment is regarded as having officially been established the day when the license for its operation is issued, and the legitimate production and business shall be protected by the law of the People's Republic of China.

An unregistered enterprise shall not be permitted to begin operation.

Article 6. A joint venture using Chinese and foreign investment shall, by producing the licence for its operation, open an account with the Bank of China or another bank approved by the Bank of China, and register with the local tax bureau for payment of taxes.

Article 7. In cases where a joint venture using Chinese and foreign investment desires to move to a new site, shift its production, increase or cut or transfer the registered capital, or extend the contract period, the said venture shall, within one month after approval by the Foreign Investment Commission of the People's Republic of China, register the changes with the Administrative Bureau for Industry and Commerce in the province, municipality or autonomous region where it is located.

In cases where changes to other items are effected, the said venture shall have to forward at the end of the year a written report about these changes to the Administrative Bureau for Industry and Commerce in the province, municipality or autonomous region where it is located.

Article 8. In registering or getting its changes registered, a joint venture using Chinese and foreign investment shall pay the registration fee or the fee for getting its changes registered, the sum of which is to be fixed by the General Administration for Industry and Commerce of the People's Republic of China.

Article 9. A joint venture using Chinese and foreign investment, upon the expiration of the contract period of the venture or desirous of terminating the contract before its expiration date, shall upon production of the document of approval issued by the Foreign Investment Commission of the People's Republic of China register for the nullification of the contract with the Administrative Bureau for Industry and Commerce in the province, municipality or autonomous region where it is located. The licence of the said venture shall be handed in for cancellation after examination by the General Administration for Industry and Commerce of the People's Republic of China.

Article 10. The General Administration for industry and Commerce of the People's Republic of China and the Administrative Bureaus for Industry and Commerce in the provinces, municipalities and autonomous regions are authorized to supervise and inspect the joint ventures using Chinese and foreign investment in the areas they govern. In cases of violations of the present regulations the violator shall be given a warning or be fined in accordance with the varying degrees of seriousness in each specific case.

Article 11. The present regulations come into force on the date of their promulgation.

39. REGULATIONS ON SPECIAL ECONOMIC ZONES IN GUANGDONG PROVINCE

(Approved by the 15th Session of the Standing Committee of the Fifth National People's Congress on August 26, 1980)

Chapter I. General Principles

Article 1. Certain areas are delineated from the three cities of Shenzhen, Zhuhai and Shantou in Guangdong Province to form special economic zones (hereinafter referred to as "special zones") in order to develop external economic cooperation and technical exchanges and promote the socialist modernization programme. In the special zones, foreign citizens, overseas Chinese, compatriots in Hong Kong and Macao and their companies and enterprises (hereinafter referred to as "investors") are encouraged to open factories or set up enterprises and other establishments with their own investment or undertake joint ventures with Chinese investment, and their assets, due profits and other legitimate rights and interests are legally protected.

Article 2. Enterprises and individuals in the special zones must abide by the laws, decrees and related regulations of the People's Republic of China. Where there are specific provisions contained in the present regulations, they have to be observed as stipulated herewith.

Article 3. A Guangdong Provincial Administration of Special Economic Zones is set up to exercise unified management of the special zones on behalf of the Guangdong Provincial People's Government.

Article 4. In the special zones investors are offered a wide scope of operation, favourable conditions for such operation are created, and stable business sites are guaranteed. All items of industry, agriculture, livestock breeding, fish breeding and poultry farming, tourism, housing and construction, research and manufacture involving high technologies and techniques that have positive significance in international economic cooperation and technical exchanges, as well as other trades of common interest to investors and the Chinese side, can be established with foreign investment or in joint venture with Chinese investment.

Article 5. Land-levelling projects and various public utilities in the special zones such as water supply, drainage, power supply, roads, wharves, communications and warehouses, are undertaken by the Guangdong Provincial Administration of Special Economic Zones. When necessary, foreign capital participation in their development can be considered.

Article 6. Specialists at home and abroad and persons who are enthusiastic about China's modernization programme will be invited by each of the special zones to form an advisory board as a consultative body for that special zone.

Chapter II. Registration and Operation

Article 7. Investors wishing to open factories or take up various economic undertakings with their investment should apply to the Guangdong Provincial Administration of the Special Economic Zones, and will be issued licences of registry and use of land after examination and approval.

Article 8. Investors can open accounts and deal with matters related to foreign exchange at the Bank of China in the special zones or other banks set up in the special zones with China's approval.

Investors can apply for insurance policies at the People's Insurance Company of China in the special zones and other insurance companies set up in the special zones with China's approval.

Article 9. Products of the enterprises in the special zones are to be sold on the international market. If an enterprise wants to sell its products in the domestic market in China, it must have the approval of the Guangdong Provincial Administration of Special Economic Zones and pay Customs duties.

Article 10. Investors can operate their enterprises independently in the special zones and employ foreign personnel for technical and administrative work.

Article 11. If investors want to terminate their business in the special zones, they should submit the reasons for termination to the Guangdong Provincial Administration of Special Economic Zones, go through related procedures and clear all debts. The assets of the closed enterprises can be transferred and the funds can be remitted out of China.

Chapter III. Preferential Treatment

Article 12. The land in the special zones remains the property of the People's Republic of China. Land to be used by investors will be provided according to actual needs, and the length of tenure, rent and method of payment will be given favourable consideration according to different trades and uses. Concrete methods will be specified separately.

Article 13. Machinery, spare parts, raw materials, vehicles and other means of production for the enterprises in the special zones are exempted from import duties. The necessary consumer goods shall be subjected to full or lower import duties or exempted, depending on the merits of each case. Imports of the above-mentioned goods and exports of products of the special zones must go through existing Customs procedures.

Article 14. The rate of income tax levied on the enterprises in the special zones is to be 15%. Special preferential treatment will be given to enterprises established within two years of the promulgation of these regulations, enterprises with an investment of US$5 million or more, and enterprises involving higher technologies or having a longer cycle of capital turnover.

Article 15. Legitimate after-tax profits of the investors, salaries and other proper earnings of the foreign, overseas Chinese and Hong Kong and Macao workers and staff members of the enterprises in the special zones after deduction of personal income tax can be remitted out of China through the Bank of China or other banks in the special zones in line with the zone's foreign exchange control measures.

Article 16. Investors who reinvest their profits in the special zones for five years and longer may apply for exemption of income tax on profits from such reinvestment.

Article 17. Enterprises in the special zones are encouraged to use China-made machinery, raw materials and other goods. Preferential prices will be offered on the basis of the export prices of China's similar commodities and settled in foreign exchange. These products and materials can be shipped directly to the special zones with the vouchers of the selling units.

Article 18. Entry and exit procedures will be simplified and convenience offered to foreigners, overseas Chinese and compatriots in Hong Kong and Macao going in and out of the special zones.

Chapter IV. Labour Management

Article 19. Labour service companies are to be set up in each of the special zones. Chinese staff members and workers to be employed by enterprises in the special zones are to be recommended by the local labour service companies or recruited by the investors with the consent of the Guangdong Provincial Administration of Special Economic Zones. Enterprises can test them before employment and sign labour contracts with them.

Article 20. Employees of the enterprises in the special zones are to be managed by the enterprises according to their business requirements, and, if necessary, can be dismissed in line with the provisions of the labour contracts.

Employees of enterprises in the special zones can submit resignation to their enterprises according to the provisions of the labour contracts.

Article 21. Wage scales and forms of wages, award methods, labour insurance and various state subsidies for Chinese staff members and workers in the enterprises are to be included in the contracts signed between the enterprises and the employees in accordance with the stipulations of the Guangdong Provincial Administration of Special Economic Zones.

Article 22. Enterprises in the special zones should take the necessary measures for labour protection to ensure that the staff members and workers work in safe and hygienic conditions.

Chapter V. Administration

Article 23. The Guangdong Provincial Administration of Special Economic Zones is to exercise the following functions:

a) Draw up development plans for the special zones and organize their implementation;

b) Examine and approve investment projects of investors in the special zones;

c) Handle the registration of industrial and commercial enterprises in the special zones and land allotment;

d) Coordinate the working relations among the banking, insurance, taxation, Customs, frontier inspection, postal and telecommunications and other organizations in the special zones;

e) Provide staff members and workers needed by the enterprises in the special zones and protect the legitimate rights and interests of these staff members and workers;

f) Run education, cultural, health and other

public welfare facilities in the special zones;

g) Maintain law and order in the special zones and protect according to law the persons and properties in the special zones from encroachment.

Article 24. The Shenzhen Special Zone is under the direct jurisdiction of the Guangdong Provincial Administration of Special Economic Zones. Necessary agencies are to be set up in the Zhuhai and Shantou Special Zones.

Article 25. A Guangdong Provincial Special Economic Zones Development Company is to be set up to cope with the economic activities in the special zones. Its scope of business includes fund-raising and trust investment, operating enterprises or joint ventures with investors in the special zones, acting as agents for the investors in the special zones in matters related to sales and purchases with other parts of China outside the special zones, and providing services for business talks.

Chapter VI. Appendix

Article 26. These regulations shall be enforced after their adoption by the Guangdong Provincial People's Congress and after they have been submitted to and approved by the Standing Committee of the National People's Congress of the People's Republic of China.

40. INTERIM REGULATIONS OF THE PEOPLE'S REPUBLIC OF CHINA CONCERNING THE CONTROL OF RESIDENT OFFICES OF FOREIGN ENTERPRISES
Promulgated by the State Council
(October 30, 1980)

Article 1. The regulations hereunder are formulated with a view to facilitating the development of international economic and trade contacts and the control of resident offices in China of foreign companies, enterprises and other economic organizations (hereinafter referred to as "foreign enterprises").

Article 2. Any foreign enterprise desiring to establish a resident office in China should first apply for permission and then, after securing approval, go through the registration procedure.

No foreign enterprise is allowed to start business activities in the nature of those of a resident office before approval is granted and the registration procedure completed.

Article 3. When applying for permission to establish a resident office in China, a foreign enterprise should produce the following documents and reference materials:

a) An application form signed by the chairman of the board of directors or the general manager of the enterprise. The application form should include such details as the name of the resident office to be established, the name(s) of the responsible member(s), the scope of activity, duration and site of the office;

b) The legal document sanctioning the operation of that enterprise issued by the authorities of the country or the region in which that enterprise operates;

c) The capital creditability document issued by the banking institution(s) having business contacts with that enterprise; and

d) The credentials and brief biographies of the members of the resident office appointed by that enterprise.

A banking or insurance institution which desires to open a resident office should, apart from producing the documents and reference materials as specified in Paragraphs a, b and d above, produce at the same time an annual report showing the assets and liabilities and losses and profits of the head office of that enterprise, its constitution and the composition of its board of directors.

Article 4. Applications of foreign enterprises for permission to establish resident offices are to be submitted to one of the following organizations for approval:

a) A trader, manufacturer or a shipping agent should apply to the Ministry of Foreign Trade of the People's Republic of China;

b) A banking or insurance institution should apply to the People's Bank of China;

c) A maritime shipping operator or a maritime shipping agent should apply to the Ministry of Communications of the People's Republic of China;

d) An air transport enterprise should apply to the General Administration of Civil Aviation of China;

e) Enterprises outside these lines of activity should, according to the nature of their operations, apply to the proper commissions, ministries or bureaus under the Government of the People's Republic of China.

Article 5. When granted approval to establish a resident office, a foreign enterprise should, within 30 days of the date of approval, go to the General Administration for Industry and Commerce of the People's Republic of China on the strength of the approval document and go through the registration procedure. The enterprise must fill in a registration form and pay registration fees before it is issued a registration certificate. The original approval document should be recalled in case of failure to register within the deadline.

Article 6. After approval for the establishment of a resident office is granted in accordance with the stipulations in Article 4, the members of that office and their families should, on the strength of the approval document, apply to the local public security organ for residence permission before they are issued residence permits.

Article 7. When a resident office desires to change its name, its responsible member(s), scope of operation, or duration or site, it should apply to the original approval-issuing organization and, after securing approval, go to the General Administration for Industry and Commerce of the People's Republic of China on the strength of the approval document and go through the procedure for effecting a change in registration and pay the fees. It should also go through the procedure with the local public security organ for changing the residence permits.

Article 8. A resident office should, on the

strength of the registration certificate and in accordance with the relevant stipulations of the Bank of China, open an account at the Bank of China or at any bank which the Bank of China may designate.

Article 9. A resident office and its members should, in accordance with the stipulations of Chinese tax laws, go through the tax registration procedure with the local tax office and pay taxes in accordance with the regulations.

Article 10. A resident office and its members should declare to China's House of Customs the imported office articles, articles for daily use and means of transport and pay customs duties and the unified industrial and commercial tax as stipulated.

Imported vehicles and ships should be registered with the local public security organ before the licence plates and permits are issued. Fees should be paid to the local tax office for the use of the

Unauthorized transfer or sale of the above-mentioned imported goods are not permitted. In the event of a necessary transfer or sale, an application should be put forward to the House of Customs and approval obtained before such a transfer or sale can be effected. Imported goods can be sold only to designated shops.

Article 11. A resident office should entrust local service units for foreigners or other such units as may be designated by the Chinese Government with such matters as renting a house or engaging the service of Chinese personnel.

Article 12. The Government of the People's Republic of China undertakes to protect, in accordance with law, the legitimate rights and interests of resident offices and their members and facilitate their normal business activities.

Article 13. Resident offices are not allowed to set up radio stations on Chinese territory. They should apply to the local telecommunications bureaus for the renting of such commercial communications lines or communications equipment as may be necessary for their business operations.

Article 14. The members of a resident office and their families should abide by Chinese laws, decrees and relevant regulations in all their activities in China and in entering and leaving China.

Article 15. In case a resident office and its members violate the "Interim Regulations" or engage in other law-breaking activities, the proper Chinese authorities have the power to look into the cases and deal with them in accordance with law.

Article 16. A resident office, when the duration of its operation expires, or if it decides to end its business activities before the due date, should notify in writing the original approval-granting organization 30 days in advance of the termination of its operation. After clearing up its debts, paying its taxes and winding up other related matters, the resident office should go through the formalities with the original registration certificate-issuing organization for cancelling the registration and turn in the certificate.

The foreign enterprise which the said resident office represented, should continue to be held responsible for any matter that the said resident office may leave unfinished at the time of its termination.

Article 17. Those resident offices that have already been established with approval should, within 30 days of the promulgation of the "Interim Regulations," go through the procedure of registration with the General Administration for Industry and Commerce of the People's Republic of China on the strength of the documents of approval.

Article 18. Any other matter that may not be covered in the "Interim Regulations" should be handled in accordance with the relevant Chinese laws, decrees and regulations.

Article 19. The "Interim Regulations" should apply to all foreign enterprises which desire to appoint a resident representative or representatives as well as to those desiring to establish resident offices.

Article 20. The "Interim Regulations" enter into effect on the day of promulgation.

41. ANNOUNCEMENT OF THE GENERAL ADMINISTRATION FOR INDUSTRY AND COMMERCE OF THE PEOPLE'S REPUBLIC CHINA CONCERNING THE REGISTRATION OF RESIDENT OFFICES OF FOREIGN ENTERPRISES

(December 8, 1980)

The Interim Regulations of the State Council of the People's Republic of China Concerning the Control of Resident Offices of Foreign Enterprises (hereinafter called "Interim Regulations") have been promulgated for implementation. The present announcement concerns matters relating to registration:

1. As stipulated in the Interim Regulations, resident offices or representatives of foreign enterprises, having secured the approval of the departments in charge under the State Council, should register at this Administration. To enable resident offices or representatives of foreign enterprises to go through the registration procedure at convenient and nearby places, this Administration, upon approval of the State Council, entrusts the administrations for industry and commerce in various provinces, municipalities and autonomous regions to take up this work on its behalf.

2. Resident offices or representatives of foreign enterprises, approved by the departments in charge under the State Council before the promulgation of the Interim Regulations, must go through the registration procedure before December 20, 1980, at the administrations for industry and commerce in the provinces, municipalities and autonomous regions where they are located, on the strength of the approval documents of the departments concerned and copies or duplicates of the documents listed in Article 3 of the Interim Regulations, and obtain a Registration Certificate for Resident Offices of Foreign Enterprises issued by the General Administration for Industry and Commerce of the People's Republic of China.

3. Resident Offices or representatives of overseas Chinese, Hong Kong and Macao enterprises that have been granted approval by the departments in charge under the State Council before and after this announcement is made, must also register in accordance with the Interim Regulations and obtain a Registration Certificate for Resident Offices of Overseas Chinese, Hong Kong and Macao Enterprises issued by the General Administration for Industry and Commerce of the People's Republic of China.

4. Resident offices or representatives of foreign enterprises approved by people's governments of various provinces, municipalities and autonomous regions or departments under them, must go through the registration procedure with the administrations for industry and commerce in the relevant provinces, municipalities or autonomous regions in accordance with the regulations of the respective provinces, municipalities or autonomous regions, and obtain a Registration Certificate for Resident Offices of Foreign Enterprises issued by the administrations of industry and commerce of the provinces, municipalities or autonomous regions.

5. When going through the registration procedure, the resident office or representative of a foreign enterprise, upon approval, should pay a registration fee of 600 yuan. When going through the procedure for changing the registration certificate, it should pay a registration fee of 300 yuan. When going through the procedure for effecting a change in name, responsible member, scope of operation, duration or site, it should pay a fee of 100 yuan.

6. The period of validity of a Registration Certificate for Resident Offices of Foreign Enterprise is the same as the approved duration of operation, beyond which the registration should be renewed. Offices approved to operate for more than one year should go through the registration procedure once every year.

42. PROVISIONAL REGULATIONS CONCERNING THE EXPORT LICENCE SYSTEM

Issued by the Import and Export Commission and the Ministry of Foreign Trade

(June 3, 1980)

The following regulations have been formulated with a view to strengthening the control of foreign trade:

Article 1. The introduction of the export licensing system by the People's Republic of China is a necessary measure to strengthen the control of export commodities and to coordinate foreign trade transactions and exports of different localities and departments, so as to achieve unity in dealing with foreign countries. The Ministry of Foreign Trade of the People's Republic of China (hereinafter referred to as the "Ministry of Foreign Trade") and the foreign trade bureaus of provinces, municipalities and autonomous regions that have been authorized by the Ministry are designated by the state as the organizations which shall carry out the export licensing system.

Article 2. The general import and export corporations under the Ministry of Foreign Trade and their branches, as well as the corporations authorized by the Import and Export Commission to engage in export business, have the right to conduct export business within a prescribed sphere. Any corporation that wishes to export certain commodities must first make an application and can start business only after it has received approval from the Import and Export Commission and has registered with the Ministry of Foreign Trade or the foreign trade bureaus of the province, municipality or autonomous region and with the customs office concerned, while presenting to it its document of authorization.

Article 3. According to the provisions of Article 2, a corporation which has been authorized to engage in export business, when exporting commodities within the prescribed sphere, is generally regarded as having obtained authorization to export, and customs give clearance to the export commodities according to the "export declaration" filled in by the corporation. It is not necessary for the corporation to apply for an export licence. But an export licence should be applied for in any of the following cases:

a) When commodities are limited by the countries and regions to which they are exported (specific rules shall be worked out separately by the Ministry of Foreign Trade);

b) In case of commodities to which the Ministry of Foreign Trade thinks it necessary to apply the export licence system and of which the Ministry has fixed the amounts to be exported by different localities and departments, so as to ensure that the total amount of such commodities exported by different localities and departments will not exceed the marketing capacity of the countries and regions to which the commodities are exported;

c) In the case of commodities to which the Ministry of Foreign Trade thinks it necessary to apply the export licence system and for which minimum export prices must be fixed in order to prevent the export prices from being set too low;

d) In the case of commodities which are to be exported under control or which are forbidden for export as explicitly declared by the relevant departments of the State Council;

e) In the case of export commodities which the Ministry of Foreign Trade thinks should be suitably controlled within a certain period of time because of changes in the world market or because of the need to carry out policies towards some specific countries.

Article 4. Export licences are necessary in the cases as follows:

a) Goods to be sent abroad by enterprises, state organs, public organizations, schools or individuals who are not authorized to conduct export business;

b) Goods for sale at exhibitions organized by Chinese departments, enterprises or public organizations in foreign countries;

c) Commodities which are produced by various enterprises, factories or mines on the basis of contracts signed with foreign countries on the basis of compensatory trade, on the processing of goods with materials supplied by clients and on loan grants and which they want to export directly without going through the foreign trade corporations;

d) Goods sent abroad by foreign diplomatic missions, business representatives, citizens and tourists;

e) Goods in excess of the reasonable amount to be taken out of China by foreign citizens and tourists for their own use.

Article 5. In the following cases, the Ministry of Foreign Trade may notify any enterprise at any time to stop, postpone or reduce its export of any commodity to any country or region:

a) If the exports do not conform to the policies of China towards the countries or regions to which the exports are directed;

b) If the exports do not conform to the content and spirit of bilateral trade agreements or payment agreements between China and the countries or regions to which the exports are directed;

c) If the exports have to be postponed or reduced in order to achieve a balance of foreign exchange in bilateral trade;

d) If inspection by the General Bureau for Imports and Exports Inspection has shown that the quality of the export commodities are not up to the standard fixed by the state, or do not conform to the provisions of the contract.

Article 6. Export licences should be applied for, respectively, by enterprises, government organizations, public bodies, schools, people's communes and individuals. Entries in the application include the names of the commodities (or goods), specifications, the countries and regions to which they are to be exported, quantity, unit price, total value of the exports, date of delivery and method of payment (i.e., how foreign currency is to be collected for the exports. Export licence application form will be issued separately). Application must be submitted for examination and approval by the Ministry of Foreign Trade or the authorized foreign trade bureau of the province, municipality or autonomous region concerned before the dispatch of the goods.

In applying for export licences, the applicants shall not try to obtain the licences through deception or by making false entries in the application form. Those who do so must be investigated and held responsible. Serious cases must be dealt with according to law.

Article 7. After the application has been examined and approved by the department concerned, the applicant will be issued a "licence for the exportation of goods" (hereinafter referred to as "export licence") in triplicate copies. One copy will be kept by the applying unit or individual. The other two will be handed over, together with the "export declaration," to customs, which will examine it and give clearance accordingly. Customs will keep one of these two copies, while the third one, after being signed by customs, will be sent to the local branch of the Bank of China, which will check it, settle the account and collect foreign currency accordingly.

Article 8. The customs of the People's Republic of China at various levels should exericse supervision and control over export commodities and goods in accordance with these provisional regulations and other relevant provisions. When passing commodities and goods that require an export licence through the customs, the exporter must present the export licence to customs for inspection. If customs find that the export commodities do not tally with the export licence, they should urge the unit concerned to apply for a new export licence or correct the errors before they give clearance. Those commodities which require an export licence shall not be passed until the licence is granted for them.

Article 9. The term of validity of an export licence should be fixed on the basis of the time goods are to be delivered as prescribed in the contract and according to other factors. The term of a licence should not exceed six months starting from the date the licence is issued, and the licence will become invalid after the specified date. If the applicant cannot deliver the goods within the period of validity he may apply for an extension, unless the export licence has stipulated otherwise. The licence may be extended only once, and for a period of two months. If the applicant still cannot send the goods abroad within the extended period but still needs to export them, he should apply for a new licence. The authorities responsible for its approval should examine the application again in the light of the conditions then prevailing.

Article 10. The list of commodities which require an export licence as stipulated in these regulations will be drawn up by the Ministry of Foreign Trade and will be readjusted from time to time according to the actual situation and distributed to units concerned for them to abide by.

43. PROVISIONAL CUSTOMS REGULATIONS FOR INWARD AND OUTWARD BAGGAGE OF OVERSEAS CHINESE AND OTHER PASSENGERS

Promulgated by the Ministry of Foreign Trade
(July 1, 1979)

1. To effectively implement foreign trade control policy as well as serve the needs of those passengers having relatives in China or abroad, viz. overseas Chinese, foreigners of Chinese origin, permanent aliens residents in China and Chinese nationals on visits to relatives abroad, Customs shall deal with their inward and outward baggage according to the present regulation, subject to the "Rules for Customs Supervision and Control over Inward and Outward Passengers' Baggage."

2. Baggage carried by the above-mentioned passengers, if within the prescribed limit set on the attached table, shall be released on entry or departure either free of duty or on payment of duty. In case the imported articles listed as items Nos. 1 to 14 of the table exceed the import duty-free limit, they may still be released on payment of duty, provided they are in reasonable quantities for personal use and their total value does not exceed 200 yuan.

Articles exceeding duty-free and dutiable limits shall be returned abroad or to places in China as the case may be, except watches, radios, cameras and other items necessary for the journey, which shall be registered with Customs and taken

Table of Import/Export Limits for Duty-free or Dutiable Articles

Category	Item	Import Limit	Export Limit
	1. Overcoats	3	3
	2. Underwear	20 pcs.	20 pcs.
	3. Other clothes	20 pcs.	20 pcs.
	4. Bedding	1 pc. of each kind	1 pc. of each kind
	5. Woollen yarn and manufactures made thereof	4 kg.	4 kg.
	6. Scarves	6 pcs.	6 pcs.
	7. Shoes/Socks	12 prs. for each	12 prs. for each
	8. Dress material	30 m. (single width)	15 m. (single width)
Duty-free	woollens	5 m. (double width)	—
	9. Foodstuffs*	50 kg	25 kg
	10. Cigarettes	600	600
	11. Wine/spirits	4 bottles	4 bottles
	12. Pharmaceutical products	50 yuan	25 yuan
	13. Ginseng/deer antlers	50 g.	50 g.
	14. Daily necessities	100 yuan	50 yuan
	15. Watches	1	
	16. Bicycles	1	
	17. Radios**	1	any 2 of these 6 items
	18. Sewing machines	1	
	19. Electric fans	1	
	20. Pocket calculators	1	
	1. Watches	1	
	2. Recorders (including combinations)	1	
Dutiable	3. TV sets	1	
	4. Cameras	1	
	5. Musical instruments (accordions or violins)	1	
	6. Ginseng/deer antlers	150 g.	

* Luxuries are dutiable   **Without recording facility out of or brought back to China by the passengers at the time of exit or entry.

The provisions of this Article also apply to baggage carried by the accompanying spouse and children of passengers. For children under 16 years of age, only half of the quantities specified under items Nos. 1 to 14 shall be duty-free. For children between the ages of 12 and 15, one watch per person may also be released duty free.

3. The above-mentioned passengers shall be subject to the Customs Rules for Short-term Visitors from the second time of entry or departure if they enter or leave China more than once within a year.

4. The limits prescribed in the table attached to the present regulation do not apply to baggage carried by the above-mentioned passengers who are coming to China or going abroad for resettlement. Their baggage may be released free of duty on entry or departure provided it is in reasonable quantities for personal use.

5. New handicrafts bought at state-owned shops, cultural relics (ascertained by the authorities in charge of cultural relics as permissible for export), old handicrafts, jewellery, gold and silver ornaments, etc., bought at Friendship Stores or Relics Stores by overseas Chinese or foreigners of Chinese origin with Renminbi obtained by the exchanging of foreign currencies, shall be presented on departure to Customs together with the relevant invoices and foreign exchange certificates, on the strength of which Customs shall release the articles concerned.

6. The present regulation came into force on April 5, 1978.

44. RULES OF THE PEOPLE'S REPUBLIC OF CHINA GOVERNING THE LEVYING OF IMPORT DUTY ON ARTICLES OF PASSENGERS' BAGGAGE AND PERSONAL POSTAL PARCELS

Article 1. These rules have been drawn up with a view to implementing the policy of State control of foreign trade, protecting the country's socialist economy, and simplifying the procedures for the collection of customs duties so as to facilitate regular traffic.

Article 2. Import duties on dutiable articles carried by inward passengers, imported by means of personal parcels, carried by crew members of inward means of conveyance for personal use or imported by any other means for personal use (all hereunder referred to as "imported articles") are to be levied by Customs according to these rules.

The import duty referred to in these rules includes both customs duty and the industrial and commercial consolidated tax.

Article 3. The schedule of import duty rates is as follows:

Tariff No.	Description of Articles	Rate of Import Duty
1.	Cereals, cereal flours	20%
2.	Medical equipment, scientific instruments and electronic computers	20%
3.	Pharmaceutical products and preparations, medicinal and aromatic substances of animal or vegetable origin	50%
4.	Office or household machines, recorders, cutting tools, hand tools, hand farm implements, and parts or accessories thereof	50%
	Television sets and parts or accessories thereof	50%
	Sports equipment, musical instruments	50%
5.	Foodstuffs and beverages	100%
6.	Deer antlers, musk, ginseng	100%
7.	Cotton cloth, linen, clothing and other articles for personal wear made of cotton or linen, cotton or linen fabrics and other cotton products	100%
8.	Radio sets, record-players, and parts or accessories thereof	100%
	Bicycles and other vehicles, and parts or accessories thereof	100%
9.	Fabrics of woollen, silk, artificial and synthetic fibres and clothing and other articles for personal wear made thereof, clothing and articles for personal wear made of other materials (such as leather, fur, plastics, etc.)	150%
	Cameras, photographic supplies or materials, video recorders, and parts or accessories thereof	150%
10.	Birds' nests, sharks' fins, beche-de-mer, awabi, compoy, fish maws, fish lips	200%
	Tobacco and products thereof, wine and spirits	200%
	Cosmetics and perfumes	200%
11.	Wrist-watches, pocket-watches and parts or accessories thereof	200%
12.	Duty-free articles: 1. Books, newspapers, periodicals, educational films and lantern-slides, and language records which are allowed to be imported; 2. Contraceptive devices and medications; 3. Gold and silver, and articles made thereof.	
13.	Articles not otherwise provided for in the above tariff numbers	100%

Article 4. Articles not enumerated in the above schedule shall be classified by Customs under the most appropriate tariff number.

Import duty on an article is to be levied at the tariff rate in force on the date of issue of the Customs Duty Memorandum.

Article 5. Imported articles are liable to ad valorem duties. An articles duty-paying value shall be assessed by Customs on the basis of its c.i.f. value. If the c.i.f. value cannot be ascertained, the duty-paying value shall be assessed by Customs in light of domestic prices.

Article 6. Should a duty-payer be dissatisfied with the tariff classification and/or the duty-paying values of the imported articles as determined by Customs, he shall first pay the import duty in full and then file an appeal in writing with

Customs within 14 days of the date on which the duty is paid. On receipt of the written appeal, Customs shall reconsider the case within 7 days. If the original decision is maintained, Customs shall, within 14 days of the date of receipt of the original appeal, transmit the appeal, together with its comments, to the Customs Administration of the People's Republic of China for consideration. If the original decision is modified, the duty-payer is to be duly notified and the duty adjusted accordingly. Should the duty-payer still be dissatisfied with the modified decision, he may file another appeal within 7 days of the date of receipt of the notification of the modified decision. Customs shall, within 7 days of the date of receipt of the second appeal, forward the case to the Customs Administration of the People's Republic of China for consideration. The decision of the Customs Administration of the People's Republic of China shall be final.

Article 7. After approval by the State Council, these rules shall be promulgated and put into force by the Ministry of Foreign Trade.

45. REGULATION FOR CUSTOMS CONTROL OVER BAGGAGE OF PASSENGERS COMING FROM OR GOING TO HONG KONG AND MACAO
Promulgated by the Ministry of Foreign Trade
(July 1, 1979)

Article 1. Baggage carried by passengers coming from or going to Hong Kong and Macao (hereinafter referred to as "passengers"), if in reasonable quantities for personal use and within the limit specified in the "Table of Duty-free and Dutiable Articles Carried by Passengers" (see Appendix 1), shall be released either free of duty or on payment of duty after Customs inspection.

Article 2. Inward passengers carrying baggage which is within the import duty-free limit as specified in the attached table may pass through "Green Channel" where it is so provided by Customs. Should articles carried by such a "Green Channel" passenger be found exceeding the import duty-free limit, which is deemed a violation of Customs regulations, Customs shall inflict on the offender a fine not greater than 500 yuan according to the nature of the case. In addition, the articles exceeding the import duty-free limit shall be returned to Hong Kong or Macao. Should dutiable articles be found in such a case, it shall be

Appendix 1:

Table of Limits for Duty-free and Dutiable Articles Carried by Passengers

Category	Item	Import Limit	Export Limit
Duty-free	Total weight in which:	30 kg.	30 kg.
	1. Clothes of all kinds	35 pcs. (in reasonable quantities)	Total value not exceeding 15 yuan for traditional Chinese medicines, in which the total weight of Chinese medicinal herbs shall not exceed 1 kg.; each kind of medicine 250g.; Yunnanbaiyao 12 g.
	2. Shoes/socks/scarves	10 prs./pcs. of each	
	3. Bedding	1 pc. or pr. of each kind, but 3 pcs. or prs. in all	
	4. Dress material (single width)	10 m.	
	5. Foodstuffs	15 kg.	
	6. Wine and spirits (including medicated wine)	2 bottles (not exceeding 750 g. each)	
	7. Cigarettes	400 pcs.	
	8. Therapeutic medicines and home remedies	in reasonable quantities for personal use only	
	9. Daily necessities	RMB 20 yuan (in reasonable quantities for each kind)	
Dutiable	1. Pocket calculators	1 pc.	
	2. Watches, radios, TV sets, recorders (including combinations), cameras, electric fans, bicycles, sewing machines, and accessories thereof	1 pc. per person a year with a reasonable quantity of accessories.	
	3. Ginseng/Deer antlers	100 g. of each	
Remarks	1. For children under 16 years of age, only articles necessary for personal use shall be released free of duty.		
	2. Furniture or unsanitary old clothes shall not be allowed to be brought into China.		
	3. Musks, toad cake, cinnabar, eucommia, gastrodia elata, Chinese caterpillar fungus, Pianzihuang, Angongnuihuang pills, Liushen pills and unappraised cultural relics shall not be allowed to be taken out of China.		
	4. Articles bought with Renminbi obtained through the exchanging of foreign currencies may be taken out on the strength of the relevant commercial invoices.		

deemed an act of smuggling and dealt with accordingly.

Article 3. Inward passengers carrying articles which are dutiable and/or over the import duty-free limit as specified in the table shall pass through "Red Channel," where it is so provided by Customs, and declare their articles to Customs, who shall release the articles after inspection according to the present regulation.

Article 4. Baggage carried by outward passengers may be released at the time of exit provided it does not exceed the limit as specified in the attached table.

Article 5. For passengers who will return within 24 hours, only items necessary for their personal use on the journey shall be released.

Article 6. For passengers coming in or going out for resettlement in China or Hongkong or Macao, Customs shall, on the strength of the relevant papers, deal with their baggage according to the provisions of the "Rules for Customs Supervision and Control over Inward and Outward Passengers' Baggage."

Article 7. Articles carried by outward passengers, if found to be in excess of the prescribed export limit, shall not be permitted to be taken out whereas articles carried by inward passengers, if found to be in excess of the prescribed import limit, shall be detained by Customs. In the latter case, the detained articles may be reclaimed and returned to Hongkong or Macao within a month. On expiry of the time limit, the Customs shall dispose of the articles and remit to the national treasury the proceeds realized from their disposal. However, passengers may make a request to bring along articles necessary for the journey guaranteeing the re-importation or re-exportation of such articles. With Customs approval and registration, such articles shall be released but must be brought back to or taken out of China at the time of re-entry or exit.

Article 8. Passengers shall be forbidden to bring into or take out of China certain prohibited articles (see Appendix 2). However, jewelry and gold and silver ornaments brought in by passengers at the time of entry and registered with Customs may be taken out at the time of exit.

Article 9. Selling for profit of the Articles released by Customs for inward passengers' personal use shall be strictly forbidden.

Article 10. Offenders of the present regulation shall be dealt with according to the relevant provisions of the regulations.

Appendix 2:

List of Prohibited Import/Export Articles of the People's Republic of China

Prohibited Import Articles

(1) Arms, ammunition and explosives of all kinds;
(2) Radio transmitter-receivers and principal parts;
(3) Renminbi;
(4) Manuscripts, printed matter, films, photographs, phonograph records, cinematographic films, loaded recording tapes and video-tapes, etc. detrimental to Chinese political, economic, cultural and moral interests;
(5) Deadly poison, addictive narcotics, opium, morphia, heroin, etc.;
(6) Animals, plants, and products thereof infected with or carrying harmful germs and insect pests;
(7) Unsanitary foodstuffs and germ-carrying foodstuffs from infected areas;
(8) Other articles the importation of which is prohibited by national regulations.

Prohibited Export Articles

(1) Arms, ammunition and explosives of all kinds;
(2) Radio transmitter-receivers and principal pests;
(3) Renminbi and securities in Renminbi;
(4) Foreign currencies, bills and securities in foreign currencies (with the exception of those allowed to be taken out);
(5) Manuscripts, printed matter, films, photographs, phonograph recods, cinematographic films, loaded recording tapes and video-tapes, etc. which contain state secrets or otherwise not permissible for export;
(6) Valuable cultural relics and rare books relating to China's revolution, Chinese history, culture and art;
(7) Rare animals, rare plants and their seeds;
(8) Precious metals and articles made thereof, jewelry and ornaments made thereof (with the exception of those within the quantity allowed to be taken out by outward passengers);
(9) Other articles the exportation of which is prohibited by national regulations.

46. PROVISIONAL REGULATIONS CONCERNING PIECE-RATE WAGES IN STATE-OWNED ENTERPRISES (DRAFT)

Issued by the State Planning Commission, the State Economic Commission and the State Bureau of Labour
(April 1, 1980)

With a view to better carrying out the principle of "from each according to his ability, to each according to his work," to arousing the labour enthusiasm of the workers and staff members, to enhancing labour productivity and impeling the enterprises to improve their management so as to speed up the development of socialist production and construction, the present regulations have been worked out:

1. Those enterprises which carry out the piece-rate wage system must possess the following conditions:

a) They should have adequate production tasks and a normal supply of raw and processed materials, fuels and power and a stable market for their products;

b) They should have advanced, rational production quotas and strict standards for measuring the quantity of products and for checking on their quality;

c) They should have a fairly sound management system (with original records of production, statistical data, check-up and acceptance of products and economic accounting).

2. The enterprises which possess the necessary conditions for the implementation of the piece-rate wage system may apply it to all workers for whom the system is suitable.

3. In the course of carrying out the piece-rate wage system, the enterprises must guarantee that their products are up to the fixed standards, and that the quota for material consumption is not exceeded, and they must bring about a clear-cut reduction in the costs of per-unit products and wages. If, after an enterprise has adopted the piece-rate wage system, the quality of its products is lowered, its consumption of materials exceeds the fixed quota, or the costs of per-unit products and wages are increased, it should immediately stop practising the system. Meanwhile, the leadership of the enterprise must to a certain degree be held responsible for resultant economic losses and must recover that portion of wages that should not have been paid to the workers.

4. In practising the piece-rate wage system, an enterprise must strengthen the management of production quotas. Wherever there are unified production quotas set by the department in charge, the enterprise should adopt these quotas for its workers. Where there are no unified quotas, the enterprise may set its own quotas, but it must report them for approval to the higher authorities in charge before adopting these production quotas.

The production quotas of an enterprise, be they stipulated by the department in charge or set by the enterprise itself, must always be advanced, rational quotas. As a rule, they should be re-examined and revised every six months or each year. A timely revision must be made if any of the following cases arises:

a) Major changes made in the specifications of products or raw materials;

b) Major changes made in production equipment, instruments and in the technological process;

c) The worksite or geological conditions have changed obviously;

d) The level of some quotas have been set too low or too high;

e) The level of quotas is seriously affected by the adoption of inventions, technical innovations or rationalization proposals (the collective or individuals who have made the inventions, innovations or rationalization proposals may be allowed to keep the original level of quotas unchanged for half a year, in addition to receiving the bonuses due to them).

When production quotas are introduced by an enterprise, they first should be tried out for a certain period, but generally for not more than three months.

5. In practising the piece-rate wage system, an enterprise should fix reasonable piece prices per unit. The unit piece price of a product will be fixed on the basis of production quotas to be fulfilled by workers within a prescribed time, the standard-time wages corresponding to the equivalent grade of the object of work and the current level of workers' wages. The grade of the object of work is determined by the technical complexity, the strenuousness of the work, the weight of responsibility and the condition of the production equipment involved.

When a production quota has been revised, the unit piece price must be changed accordingly.

6. To encourage workers to raise the quality of products, the piece prices of all products that are classified according to quality of all products should be fixed according to the principle of "higher price for better quality." The piece prices of high-quality products should be set a little higher than that of average up-to-standard products.

To facilitate the upgrading and renewal of products, the piece price of a new variety of product may also be set higher when it is trial-produced.

7. An enterprise may apply the piece-rate wage system to the collective or to the individual according to the characteristics of its production. But among the workers of the same group or team, it shall not apply the collective piece-rate wage system to some and a time wage system to others.

8. Whether the piece-rate wage system is applied to a collective or to individual workers, an enterprise should pay the wages on the basis of piece price according to how well the collective or the workers fulfil their production quotas.

Provided that production quotas are advanced and rational, no limit should be imposed on extra wages earned by workers who overfulfil their quotas.

9. In groups or teams to which the collective piece-rate wage system is applied, the piece-rate wage received should be distributed according to the respective contributions of their members in production. It should not be distributed on a basis of equal portions.

10. The workers to whom the piece-rate wage system is applied may be given economy bonuses in accordance with the Tentative Regulations (Draft) on Bonuses for Saving Specially Designated Fuels and Raw Materials in State-Owned Industrial and Transport Enterprises as jointly promulgated on December 10, 1979 by the Ministry of Finance, the State Bureau of Labour and the State Administration of Supplies. But they shall no longer receive regular production bonuses.

11. When a worker who is paid according to the piece-rate wage system produces items that are rejected due to his own fault, the enterprise concerned shall not pay wages for the rejects but shall ask him to compensate for a part or the whole of the loss according to the seriousness of the loss he has caused. While a basic living standard is guaranteed to the worker, the maximum amount of the compensation he pays per month should not exceed 25% of his standard monthly wage and generally the compensation should be paid off within a period not exceeding six months.

12. Before an enterprise introduces the piece-rate wage system, it must make a plan and send it to the department in charge for approval and then report the system to the local labour management department for the record.

13. An enterprise practising the piece-rate wage system should at three-month intervals inform the bank with whom it has opened an account how the system is being carried out so that the bank may supervise its execution. If the bank discovers that the unit costs of a product and wages have increased after the enterprise introduced the piece-rate wage system, it has the right to examine the financial affairs of the enterprise and refuse to pay the piece wages.

14. While practising the piece-rate wage system, the enterprises should strengthen political ideological work among the workers and staff members, educating them to adopt a communist attitude towards labour, to co-operate well with each other in production, and to strictly observe labour discipline and the operating rules. Those who practise fraud, who damage equipment and tools and who waste too much raw material should be given disciplinary sanctions in accordance with the relevant regulations. The portion of wages received through fraud should be ascertained and all of it returned.

15. The provinces, municipalities and autonomous regions as well as the various departments of the State Council may, in light of their specific conditions, work out concrete rules according to the provisions of these regulations to be transmitted to their subordinate units and, at the same time, send copies of these rules to the State Planning Commission, the State Economic Commission and the State Bureau of Labour for the record.

47. A JOINT CIRCULAR OF THE STATE ECONOMIC COMMISSION, THE GENERAL ADMINISTRATION OF INDUSTRY AND COMMERCE AND THE PEOPLE'S BANK OF CHINA ON A NUMBER OF QUESTIONS REGARDING THE SUPERVISION OF ECONOMIC CONTRACTS

(August 8, 1979)

To the Administrations of Industry and Commerce, the Economic Commissions and Branches of the People's Bank of All Provinces, Municipalities and Autonomous Regions:

To practise the contract system, i.e., to stipulate in the form of a contract the details of contact and coordination between enterprises in the production, supply, shipment and marketing of goods, to stipulate each other's economic commitments and responsibilities and to seriously carry out these stipulations, is an important measure for raising the level of management of enterprises, strengthening business accounting, guaranteeing the fulfilment of the state plan and managing the economy by economic measures. This system should be actively pursued in the realization of the Four Modernizations in socialist construction. In order to strengthen the supervision of contracts, to urge the enterprises to execute their contracts strictly and to defend the just interests of both sides, the following circular on a number of major questions regarding the supervision of economic contracts is made in the light of the documents concerned as issued by the Central Committee of the Chinese Communist Party and the State Council:

1. In accordance with the State Council Document No. 102 (1979), the economic contracts on goods supply, production and sales, processing, shipment, etc. are to be supervised by the following authorities on the basis of division of work:

The economic contracts between units belonging to the same department or economic sector, such as industry, agriculture, material administration, communications and transport, commerce (which includes foreign trade, grain and supply and marketing cooperatives, here and below), are to be supervised by the authorities in charge of that department or sector.

Economic contracts between different industrial departments; between industrial enterprises and material administration, building industry and agricultural departments; between industrial, agricultural, commercial, material administration and building units and communications and transport departments; as well as those between industrial, communications and transport departments and government organs, mass organizations, army units and institutions; are to be supervised by economic commissions at various levels or by other corresponding authorities.

Economic contracts between different commercial departments, between commercial units and units of industrial and agricultural departments as well as government organs, mass organizations, army units and institutions are to be supervised by the administrations of industry and commerce at various levels.

2. Before signing a contract, the enterprises or units concerned must conduct realistic and full consultations on an equal footing on the basis of the policies, decrees and laws and plans of the state and in the spirit of the principles of producing according to needs, ensuring supplies and promoting development of the national economy. A contract must have specific details, clear commitments and responsibilities of each side and unequivocal wording.

The main contents of a contract should include: name of the product, its model, specification, quality, quantity, measuring unit, the technical specification of industrial products, package requirements and the supply and retrieval of packing materials, means of delivery and destination, shipment, date of delivery (and taking delivery) of the goods, the price of the product, modes of settlement of accounts, settling bank, the bank account number of the units, economic commitments and responsibilities, etc.

3. For the guarantee of contracts, we do not make any unified stipulations for the time being. The contract supervisory authorities of each province, municipality and autonomous region can make their own decisions in this connection in accordance with actual conditions. But if both the supplier and buyer sides of a contract demand a guarantee, the contract should be guaranteed.

For all the guaranteed contracts, the guarantor authorities should be responsible for the checkup of the contracts' legality and their main contents, and those which do not conform to the policies or stipulations of the state should be corrected.

The guarantor authorities should be the contract supervisory authorities of the region where the supplier side of the contract is located.

4. Once a contract is signed, it has a legal effect. Both sides must scrupulously keep their word and strictly execute the contract. If any side does not execute the contract seriously and causes losses to the other side, it should bear the economic and legal responsibilities.

5. Once a contract is signed, neither side can change it or terminate it on its own authority. If it is necessary to make any changes or terminate the contract, it should be agreed on by both sides through consultations and an agreement should be signed on the amendment to the contract or on its termination. If an important product controlled by the state plan is involved, such an agreement should be reported for the record to the authorities in charge of the product; if a guaranteed contract is involved, it should be reported for the record without exception to the guarantor authorities. Before such an agreement is signed, the original contract remains valid and neither side can refuse to execute it on any excuse. Any losses incurred by the amendment or termination of the contract should be compensated on a fair and reasonable basis by the side which asked for the change or termination.

6. If any disputes arise during the execution of the contract, the two contracting sides should actively consult each other and do their best to find out a reasonable solution. If they fail to agree with each other, any side may apply for arbitration to the Economic Commission (or corresponding authorities) or the Administration of Industry and Commerce of the county or the district, in the case of a big or medium-sized city, where the other side is located, in accordance with the division of work among the contract supervisory authorities. If any side refuses to accept the ruling, it may apply to the next higher supervisory authorities for reconsideration within ten days after the day the notice on the ruling is received. If it still remains unconvinced by the reconsidered ruling, it may sue at the people's court within ten days after the day the notice on the reconsidered ruling is received. In case one side concerned does not apply for reconsideration or does not sue at the court within the ten-day period while refusing to execute the ruling, the People's Bank should transfer the sum of money and the contract-breaking side should pay for the goods or compensate for the losses to the other side's account in accordance with the ruling notice.

For disputes or economic contracts between units belonging to the same department or sector, the mediation and arbitration procedure can be decided by the authorities in charge of that department or sector.

During the period of mediation and arbitration, the arbitrating authorities, in the light of the actual situation, may notify both contractors to stop executing the contract for the time being.

7. The People's Bank is to supervise all enterprises' execution of their economic contracts by means of credit and settlement management. The People's Bank will gradually take the measure of granting loans to enterprises in accordance with their economic contracts, on the basis of the state plan. The rules of settlement must be conscientiously followed and settlement discipline strictly adhered to. Both contractors must settle the account in accordance with the mode of settlement specified in the economic contract, and the bank should handle acceptance or refusal of payments, or deduct the required sum of money from the account of the enterprise which delays payment for the goods or payment of compensation, in accordance with the specific regulations of the rules of settlement.

8. The money paid in compensation caused by an enterprise's own errors should not be included in the cost of production of the goods, but should be paid out of the enterprise's share of the profits or out of its own funds. If a serious violation of this rule occurs, a fine will be deducted from the wages of those who are responsible for it, and an investigation into their administrative or legal responsibilities should be made.

For any failure in executing the contract caused by force majeure or other reasons which are really not brought about by the enterprise itself, the enterprise can be freed from economic responsibilities when the above causes are proved through investigation by the arbitrating authorities. The authorities in charge can take other measures to recoup as much of those economic losses as possible.

9. In order to supervise enterprises and to encourage them to execute their contracts conscientiously, the supervisory authorities have the right to verify both the statistics and data concerned and the actual execution of the contract. If problems that hamper the execution of the contract are discovered, the departments concerned should be asked to take effective steps to solve the problem in time. Any violations of the law — such as performing shoddy work or using inferior materials, making profits by acting as a broker, selling a contract at a profit, or purposely avoiding

supervision — should be put to the Administration of Industry and Commerce for investigation and punishment. If it is a serious case, it should be handed over to the judiciary for punishment by law.

10. Economic contracts are major business documents. All enterprises should establish files, compile ledgers and keep them properly. For a guaranteed contract, the enterprise should give a copy to the guarantor authorities for special filing.

11. In their work, the contract supervisory authorities should closely cooperate with judicial, planning and other business departments concerned. Necessary liaison systems should be established for exchanging information, coordinating actions and strengthening collaboration.

12. All parts of the country are asked to adopt the above points as experiments, to sum up their experiences and to offer suggestions for further amendments.

48. REGULATIONS ON CONTROL OF THE PURCHASING POWER OF SOCIAL GROUPS

(Revised by the Financial and Trade Group of the State Council, the State Planning Commission, the State Commission, the Ministry of Finance, the People's Bank of China, the Ministry of Commerce, the All-China Federation of Supply and Marketing Cooperatives and the State Statistical Bureau on November 17, 1980.)

Economizing on non-production expenses, by limiting the purchasing power of social groups, is an important measure for the implementation of the policy of "building the country industriously and thriftily" and speeding up the process of the Four Modernizations. This measure should be enforced over a long period of time. In light of the development and changes of the economic situation, we have revised the "Regulations on Control of the Purchasing Power of Social Groups" adopted in 1977 as follows:

I. The Scope of Control

The purchasing power of social groups refers to the public funds spent by social groups in the market for non-production commodities. Its scope is defined in the "Provisions on the Scope of the Purchasing Power of Social Groups," an appendix to the "Regulations on Control of the Purchasing Power of Social Groups" issued by the State Planning Commission and three other departments in 1977.

Except for some specially controlled commodities, no control quotas are imposed on neighbourhood offices in the cities, on districts, towns and people's communes of the counties and their affiliated enterprises and establishments, or on units of the People's Liberation Army below battalion level. The provinces, municipalities and autonomous regions, the General Logistics Department and the General Bureau of Frontiers can work out their own regulations on control of the purchasing power of social groups.

II. Control Measures

The purchasing power of social groups shall be controlled through planning, quotas, authorization for specially controlled commodities and supply quotas. Concrete measures are as follows:

A. **Control through Planning.** The state will fix annually the purchasing power quotas of social groups and decide on the extent of their increase or decrease as part of the national economic plan in accordance with the needs of developing the national economy and of maintaining balance in the market. The quotas should be implemented at all levels.

When making plans for the production, importation and distribution of commodities, the departments of planning, materials, commerce and foreign trade at various level should keep an overall balance between production, supply and marketing. With regard to those commodities specially produced for social groups, the departments should decide on the quotas after consultations with relevant departments at the same levels.

B. **Control Through Quotas.** All provinces, municipalities and autonomous regions should allocate the quotas distributed by the higher authorities to the independent accounting units at the grass-roots level before the beginning of a new fiscal year with reference to the actual fulfilment of the quotas of the previous year, in proportion to the number of workers and staff members and with the expansion of the units in mind. The quotas can be allocated at one time or at several times; when the base figure is not available, it is better to allocate the quotas quarterly. Allocating the quotas it is necessary to deal with each case on its own merit. Efforts should be made to control the quotas in the spirit of practising strict economy while not interfering in the work of the units concerned. Purchasing power quotas should be closely integrated with financial quotas.

The purchasing power quotas of social groups are completely·controlled. However, quotas for such commodities as medicines, medical apparatus and instruments, labour safety supplies, coal for drinking water, bathing and heating, and fuel for cars used for non-production purposes can be allocated to grassroots units or kept at the provincial, municipal or autonomous regional level. The purchasing power of local enterprises and establishments located outside the capital belonging to the central government departments and the standing organs of the central government departments should be controlled by the local department concerned.

All units should deal properly with the quotas allocated by the higher authorities in accordance with the actual situation and distribute them to those departments in need of the commodities. The departments in need of the commodities should regularly work out plans for purchasing non-production commodities and purchase the commodities within the framework of the quotas. The accounting section of the units that purchase commodities under the purchasing power of social groups should enter the purchased items according to the invoice in the subsidiary account book for the purchasing power of social groups. Commodities purchased by the enterprises and establishments as production commodities but later used for non-production purposes should also be entered in the subsidiary account book. The finance section should strictly check and supervise non-production expenses and see that they do not exceed the quotas. Meanwhile, it should submit the precise statistical figures to the higher authorities as required.

C. Authorization for Specially Controlled Commodities. The purchase of specially controlled commodities should be authorized on the basis of the "Regulations on the Purchase of Specially Controlled Commodities by Social Groups" issued by the Ministry of Finance and four other central government departments in 1980, and related documents. All units which purchase commodities under special control should go through the necessary procedures and refrain from fraudulently purchasing these commodities without the authorization of the department concerned. A unit which purchases specially controlled commodities in other provinces should have an "authorization paper" issued by the authorities of the province in which the unit is located.

D. Supply by Quota. All units supplying commodities under the purchasing power of social groups should supply those items strictly on the basis of the quota and relevant regulations. Supply in excess of the quota and plan is not allowed. The supply unit should submit the marketing plan for these commodities and the actual marketing situation to the local office in charge of controlling the purchasing power of social groups.

All regions and departments should establish step by step the quota system for the commodities and expenses which can be put under quota control.

III. Relying on the Masses

The method of combining professional management with mass administration shall be put into effect. The significance of controlling the purchasing power of social groups should be repeatedly made known to the masses. It is necessary to rely on the masses to work out thrift measures, draw up warehouse inventories, tap the latent potential of enterprises, repair and utilize old or discarded articles, use substitute materials to practise thrift and actively further the movement to increase production and practise economy.

When planning its expenses related to the purchasing power of social groups and reporting specially controlled commodities to the higher authorities, each unit shall consult democratic management and supervisory setups, regularly publicize the implementation of the regulations on the purchasing power of social groups, solicit opinions and suggestions from the broad masses and place itself under the surveillance of the masses.

IV. Strict Discipline

All government and mass organisations, PLA units, schools, enterprises and institutions must observe the financial and economic discipline of the state, act according to the present regulations and various other provisions. In case of statutory violations, financial departments have the power to reject accounts to be rendered, banks have the power to refuse to pay and transfer accounts, commodity supply units have the power to refuse to supply goods, departments of public security and traffic supervision and control have the power to refuse to issue car licences, and the office of controlling purchasing power of social groups and financial organs have the power to confiscate the indiscriminately purchased commodities. In serious cases, reports will go to the leadership for taking disciplinary actions against the violators.

A regular inspection system shall be set up with one or two general and special inspections organized by each province, municipality and autonomous region per year. Various units and departments shall undertake regular book-keeping activities and carry out joint auditing and mutual inspections so as to learn from and supervise each other.

V. Strengthening the Leadership

Leading groups and offices of controlling purchasing power of social groups shall be established by the people's governments above the county level. Leading groups shall consist of leading comrades from the State Council Financial Office, the State Planning Commission, the State Economic

Commission, financial, banking, commercial, supply and marketing, statistical and other departments. Each group leader is to be selected from among the leading comrades by the people's government. The leading group is to hold regular meetings, review its work and strengthen the leadership in earnest. The offices of controlling purchasing power of social groups are standing executive organs of the said leading groups. Each office must have a regular authorized size and enough staff members to suit the needs of its work.

All responsible departments, enterprises, institutions and administrative units must appoint special persons to take charge of the work of controlling the purchasing power of social groups.

All departments of planning, finance, banking, commerce, supply and marketing, materials, statistics, public security, transportation and communications at various levels shall adopt a clear-cut division of labour, work in close coordination, support and cooperate with each other. The implementation of the present regulations must be included in the system of personal responsibility for checking on and appraising through comparison cadres in charge of finance and taxes, financial accountants, employees of commodity supply units, bank bookkeepers, cashiers, public security personnel, and workers of traffic supervision and control.

The regulations on control of the purchasing power of social groups for the Chinese People's Liberation Army and the People's Armed Frontiers Police of China shall be prepared separately, in the light of the present regulations, by the General Logistics Department of the Military Commission of the Central Committee of the Chinese Communist Party and the General Bureau of Frontiers of the Ministry of Public Security.

The present regulations shall come into force as of January 1, 1981. In case of any contravention between the present regulations and previous regulations, the present regulations shall hold.

49. THE ENVIRONMENTAL PROTECTION LAW OF THE PEOPLE'S REPUBLIC OF CHINA
(For Trial Implementation)
(Adopted in Principle at the 11th Meeting of the Standing Committee of the Fifth National People's Congress on September 13, 1979)

Chapter I. General Provisions

Article 1. This law is established in accordance with Article 11 of the Constitution of the People's Republic of China which provides that "the State protects the environment and natural resources and prevents and eliminates pollution and other hazards to the public."

Article 2. The function of the Environmental Protection Law of the People's Republic of China is to ensure, during the construction of a modernized socialist state, rational use of natural environment, prevention and elimination of environmental pollution and damage to ecosystems, in order to create a clean and favourable living and working environment, protect the health of the people and promote economic development.

Article 3. For the purposes of this law, "environment" means: the atmosphere, water, land, mineral resources, forests, grassland, wildlife, wild plants, aquatic plants and animals, famous spots and historic sites, scenic spots for sightseeing, hot springs, health resorts, nature conservation areas, residential districts, etc.

Article 4. The guidelines governing environmental protection work are: overall planning, rational layout, comprehensive utilization, conversion of harm into good, reliance upon the masses with everybody taking part in the protection of the environment for the benefit of the people.

Article 5. The State Council and its subordinate bodies, and the local people's governments at all levels shall endeavour to carry out environmental protection work in earnest and do a good job of it. They shall make overall plans for the protection and improvement of the environment in planning for national economic development and take practical measures for its implementation. Where pollution of the environment and other hazards to the public have already been caused, plans should be worked out to eliminate such in a systematic and orderly manner.

Article 6. All enterprises and institutes shall pay adequate attention to the prevention of pollution and damage to the environment when selecting their sites, designing, constructing and planning production. In planning new construction, reconstruction and extension projects, a report on the potential environmental effects shall be submitted to the environmental protection department and other relevant departments for examination and approval before designing can be started. The installations for the prevention of pollution and other hazards to the public should be designed, built and put into operation at the same time as the main project. Discharge of all kinds of harmful substances shall be in compliance with the criteria set down by the State.

The units which have caused pollution and other hazards to the environment shall, according to the principle of "whoever causes pollution shall be responsible for its elimination," make plans to actively eliminate such, or alternatively submit an application to the competent authorities for approval to transfer the property or move to some other place.

Article 7. In rebuilding old cities or building new ones, assessments shall be made of the potential environmental effects in industrial and residential areas, public utility facilities, and green belts by reference to the meteorological, geographical, hydrological and ecological conditions; and overall planning and rational layout shall be made to prevent pollution and other hazards to the public so as to build a clean modern city in a planned way.

Article 8. The citizen has the right to supervise, accuse and bring a complaint before the court against the unit or the individual who has caused pollution and damage to the environment. The unit or the individual thus accused and charged shall not take any retaliatory action.

Article 9. Foreigners or foreign aircraft, ships, vehicles, goods, plants and animals, etc. entering or passing Chinese territory, territorial waters, or airspace shall be subject to the present law and other regulations and rules relating to the protection of the environment.

Chapter II. Protection of Natural Environment

Article 10. Use the land rationally according to local conditions, improve the soil and increase the vegetation to prevent soil erosion, hardening, alkalinization, desertification, and water losses.

Comprehensive scientific surveys shall be carried out before going ahead with plans to reclaim wasteland, put up dykes along the seacoast or lakes, and construct new large- or medium-sized water conservancy facilities. Practical measures for protection and improvement of the environment shall be taken to prevent damage to the ecosystems.

Article 11. Keep bodies of waters such as rivers, lakes, seas, reservoirs, etc., from being polluted so as to preserve the quality of water in a good state.

Protect, develop and utilize aquatic flora and fauna in a rational way. Fishing to the extent of threatening extinction of, and damage to, living resources is prohibited.

Exercise tight control over, and economize, use of water in industry, agriculture, and in daily life. Exploit rationally the subsoil waters to prevent exhaustion of water resources and surface subsidence.

Article 12. In exploiting mineral resources, comprehensive surveying, evaluation and utilization should be carried out. Excavating and mining at random is strictly forbidden, and tailings and slags should be appropriately diposed of, to prevent damage to resources and pollution of the natural environment.

Article 13. Strictly adhere to the National Forestry Law; protect and develop forest resources; fell trees in a rational way; tend trees and reforest at the appropriate time. Destroying forest to reclaim land and arbitrary cutting and felling are strictly forbidden. Preventive measures should be taken against forest fires.

Efforts should be made to plant trees everywhere and make barren hills, wasteland, desert areas and semi-desert areas green; tree planting should be vigorously carried out in villages, towns, and industrial and mining districts. Make good use of all available scattered open spaces inside and outside factory compounds, mining districts, school campuses, office compounds, along roadsides, river banks, and around villages and houses by planting trees and grass so as to turn the whole country into a big park.

Article 14. Protect and develop forage resources. Actively plan and carry out the grassland development programme; herd sheep and cattle rationally; maintain and improve the regenerating capacity of the grasslands, and prevent the grasslands from deteriorating. Abusive exploitation of grassland is strictly forbidden. Efforts should be made to prevent grassland fires.

Article 15. Protect, develop, and utilize rationally wildlife and wild plant resources. National regulations forbid hunting of rare animals and felling of precious trees.

Chapter III. Prevention and Elimination of Pollution and Other Hazards to the Public

Article 16. Actively prevent and control noxious substances from factories, mines, enterprises and urban life, such as waste gas, waste water, waste residues, dust, garbage, radioactive material, etc., as well as noise, vibration, and bad odours from polluting and damaging the environment.

Article 17. Enterprises or institutions that will cause pollution of the environment shall not be set up in the residential areas of the cities and towns, water resource protection zones, places of historic interest and scenic beauty, scenic spots for sightseeing, hot springs, health resorts and nature conservation areas. Where such units have been established, a target date shall be set for elimination and control of the pollution, or making necessary adjustments, or removal.

Article 18. Actively conduct experiments and adopt new technology, techniques and devices which are pollution-free or will reduce pollution.

Strengthen business management and carry out civilized production; make comprehensive use of such environment-polluting substances as waste gas, waste water and waste residues, and transform them into useful things. Discharge of such substances where necessary shall be in compliance with the criteria laid down by the State. Where such national criteria cannot be met for the time being, a later date will be set for compliance; if national standards still cannot be met by the deadline, a limit shall be set to production.

In cases where release of pollutants goes beyond the limits of the specified national standards, a fee shall be charged towards dealing with the release of such pollutants according to the quantities and concentrations of the pollutants released as specified in the relevant regulations.

Article 19. All smoke-discharging devices, industrial furnaces, motor vehicles, ships, etc. shall take effective measures to eliminate smoke and dust, and discharge of noxious gas shall be in compliance with the standards laid down by the State.

Develop and use on a large scale coal gas, liquefied petroleum gas (LPG), natural gas, marsh gas, solar energy, terrestrial heat and other non-polluting or less polluting energy sources. In the cities, district central heating should be promoted.

Article 20. Dumping garbage and waste residues into the waters is prohibited. Discharge of sewage shall be in compliance with the standards set down by the State.

Ships are prohibited from discharging substances containing oil, poison, and other harmful wastes into the waters protected by the law of this country.

It is strictly prohibited to discharge poisonous and harmful waste water by way of seepage pits, crevices, lava holes, or dilution methods. Prevent seepage of water containing industrial filth to ensure that subsoil water is not contaminated.

Take strong measures to protect sources of drinking water from contamination and gradually perfect the sewage discharge piping system and sewage purification facilities.

Article 21. Actively develop effective, low-toxin and low-residue agricultural pesticides. Promote comprehensive and biological methods of prevention and control; use rationally sewage for irrigation so as to prevent pollution of the soil and crops.

Article 22. Step up control of noise and vibration in urban and industrial districts. All kinds of noisy machines, motor vehicles, aircraft, etc. with heavy vibrations are required to install noise suppressors and antivibration devices.

Article 23. The units which emit harmful gases or dust should actively adopt sealed production equipment and technology, and install ventilating, dust collecting and purifying, and recovery facilities. The amount of harmful gases and dust in the working environment must conform with the standards for industrial hygiene specified by the law of this country.

Article 24. Registration and control of toxic chemicals must be strictly carried out. Highly toxic substances should be tightly sealed to prevent leakage during storage and transportation.

Radioactive materials, electro-magnetic radiation, etc. should be strictly monitored and controlled according to the applicable law of this country.

Article 25. Strict precautions shall be taken to prevent pollution of food in the course of production, processing, packing, transportation, storage, and marketing. Food inspection shall be strengthened, and the sale, export and import of foods not meeting the requirements of national hygienic standards shall be prohibited.

Chapter IV. Environmental Protection Office and its Functions

Article 26. The State Council has established an Environmental Protection Office whose main functions are:

a) To implement and supervise the carrying out of national guidelines, policies, laws and acts relating to environmental protection;

b) To draft regulations, rules, standards, economic and technical policies relating to environmental protection in conjunction with relevant departments;

c) To develop long-term programmes and annual plans for protection of the environment in conjunction with relevant departments and to encourage and supervise their implementation;

d) To make unified plans for organizing the monitoring of the environment; carry out investigations and keep under review the environmental situation and development trends of the whole country, and recommend improvement measures;

e) To organize and coordinate, in conjunction with relevant departments, research and educational programmes in environmental science, and actively promote foreign as well as domestic advanced experiences and techniques in the field of environmental protection;

f) To direct the environmental protection work of all the departments under the State Council, and of the provinces, autonomous regions, and municipalities directly under the central government;

g) To organize and coordinate international cooperation and communication in the field of environmental protection.

Article 27. The people's governments of the provinces, autonomous regions, and municipalities directly under the central government shall establish environmental protection bureaus in their respective areas. The people's governments of the municipalities, autonomous prefectures, counties, and autonomous counties may establish environmental protection organizations as required.

The main functions of the local environmental protection organizations at every level are: To supervise and urge the implementation of the national guidelines, policies, laws and acts relating to the protection of environment in the various departments and units within their jurisdictions; to draft applicable local standards and specifications concerning environmental protection; to organize monitoring of the environment and keep under review the local environmental situation and development trends; to develop long-term programmes and annual plans applicable locally for the protection of the environment in conjunction with the relevant departments, and supervise their implementation; to organize local research and educational programmes in environmental science in conjunction with relevant departments; to actively promote foreign as well as domestic advanced experiences and techniques in the field of environmental protection.

Article 28. The relevant departments under the State Council, the local people's governments at all levels, large- and medium-size enterprises, and relevant institutions shall establish, as required, environmental protection offices separately responsible for the protection of the environment within their own system of affiliated organizations, departments, and units.

Chapter V. Scientific Research, Propaganda and Education

Article 29. China Environmental Science Research Institute, relevant scientific institutes, universities and colleges should devote major efforts to research in the following areas: fundamental principles of environmental science, environmental management, environmental economics, comprehensive control techniques, environmental quality evaluation, environmental pollution and human health, rational use and protection of natural environment, etc.

Article 30. Cultural and publicity departments should actively carry out publicity and educational programmes to disseminate the knowledge of environmental science so as to enhance the understanding of the general public about the significance of environmental protection work and to raise the scientific and technical standards in the environmental field.

Environmental protection specialists should be trained in a planned way. The educational departments should establish a required course or speciality in environmental protection in the relevant departments of the universities and colleges. Middle and primary school textbooks should include appropriate texts relating to environmental protection.

Chapter VI. Rewards and Punishments

Article 31. The State will give commendations and rewards to units and individuals who have made outstanding achievements and contributions to the work of environmental protection.

The State will grant tax reductions or exemptions on, and apply a preferential pricing policy to, products manufactured by utilizing waste gas, waste water, and waste residues as main material, and the profits originating therefrom need not be turned over to the higher authorities but will be used by the manufacturers concerned to control pollution and improve the environment.

Article 32. Units which have violated this law and other environmental protection regulations and rules by polluting and damaging the environment and causing hazards to the people's health shall, according to the merit of each case, be criticized, warned, fined, or ordered to pay damages and stop production and control and eliminate such pollution, by the environmental protection organizations at various levels subject to the approval of the people's government of the corresponding level.

Unit leaders, persons directly responsible or other citizens who have caused serious pollution and damage to the environment resulting in casualties or substantial damage to farming forestry, animal husbandry, side-line production and fishery shall be held responsible administratively, economically, and even criminally, as the case may be, according to law.

Chapter VII. Supplementary Articles

Article 33. The State Council may establish regulations and rules relating to environmental protection according to the present law.

50. REGULATIONS REGARDING THE NATURAL SCIENCE AWARDS OF THE PEOPLE'S REPUBLIC OF CHINA

Promulgated by the State Council
(December 21, 1979)

Article 1. In order to encourage and bring into full play the initiative and creativeness of scientific workers, speed up the development of China's sciences and promote socialist modernization, the present regulations are hereby formulated.

Article 2. Awards for natural sciences shall be conferred on those collectives or individuals whose research into the phenomena, characteristics or laws of nature have produced results with great significance for scientific and technological development.

Article 3. Awards for natural sciences are divided into four grades:

First-class awards include a certificate of honour, a first-class medal and a monetary award of 10,000 yuan.

Second-class awards include a certificate of honour, a second-class medal and a monetary award of 5,000 yuan.

Third-class awards include a certificate of honour, a third-class medal and a monetary award of 2,000 yuan.

Fourth-class awards include a certificate of honour, a fourth-class medal and a monetary award of 1,000 yuan.

Article 4. A special award shall be given to those whose scientific research results, as provided in Article 2, are of specially great significance. Separate awards for such cases shall be reported by the Scientific and Technological Commission of China to the State Council for approval.

Article 5. Recommendations for awards can be made by research institutes, institutions of higher learning, national academic societies or by a group of over ten scientific workers at or above the level of associate research fellows.

Article 6. Preliminary examination of the items recommended for award shall be organized, in accordance with their special fields, by the Chinese Academy of Sciences, the Ministry of Education, the Scientific and Technological Association of China, the State Agriculture Commission, the Ministry of Public Health, the State Economic Commission, the Science and Technology Commissions for National Defence and the Office in Charge of National Defence Industry of the State Council. In the preliminary examination, the related units should hold meetings, with the participation of those in the same trade or occupation, to choose items for award through public evaluation and make suggestions on the grade of the award.

Article 7. The issuance of awards is under the unified leadership of the Scientific and Technological Commission.

The Natural Science Awards Committee under the Commission is in charge of evaluating items and grades for awards. Its recommendations will be examined and approved by the Commission which will confer the awards.

Article 8. When the natural science award belongs to an individual, the certificate of honour, medal and monetary award will be conferred on the individual; when the award belongs to a collective, the certificate of honour will go to the collective, the medal will go to the collective and the personnel who made the biggest contributions in the scientific research, and the monetary award will be distributed among the participants in the research effort in proportion to their contributions.

Article 9. The natural science awards may be conferred, in accordance with the regulations, upon those Chinese nationals residing in foreign countries and foreigners who are engaged in natural science research and whose outstanding achievements have contributed enormously to the development of science and technology in the People's Republic of China.

Article 10. Recommendation and assessment of items for awards should be practical, realistic and serious. Cases of malpractice for selfish ends and deception will be dealt with sternly according to the seriousness of each case.

Article 11. The regulations will enter into effect on the date of promulgation. In cases of contravention with previous regulations regarding the natural science awards, the present regulation will hold.

SECTION III:

MONOGRAPHIC STUDIES ON CURRENT ECONOMIC POLICY

1. HOW TO LOOK AT THE PRESENT ECONOMIC SITUATION
By Xue Muqiao

I. The Economic Situation Is Excellent

The present economic situation is excellent. It is an excellent situation rarely seen since the founding of New China. Why do we say it is an excellent economic situation?

Achievements in Economic Growth. Firstly, we base our conclusion on the record of economic growth. The rate of industrial growth in 1979 and 1980, 8.5% and 8.7% respectively, was lower than in 1977 and 1978 (14.3% and 13.5%). However, the high rate of growth in 1977 and 1978 included some misleading elements. A considerable part of what was produced was not needed by the market, but was stocked in warehouses. As in previous years, little attention was paid to the needs of the people's livelihood; moreover, light industrial production was limited to the development of heavy industry. Thus, the bigger the growth rate, the more serious the economic imbalance.

No high quotas were set in drawing the 1979 and 1980 economic plans and heavy industrial production was limited to the development of light industry. This was why economic growth in 1979 was sounder than in the two previous years. Growth was even sounder in 1980. Unlike previous years, in 1979 the growth rate of light industry surpassed that of heavy industry. In 1980, heavy industry grew by 1.4% while light industry increased by 18.4%. This marked the beginning of economic development in a direction more suited to conditions in China. Agricultural production grew by 9% in 1978 after corrections of "Left" deviationist mistakes in relevant policies. It went up again by 8.6% in 1979, thus producing major growth in two successive years. Last year the drought in the north and water-logging in the south were more serious than in several decades. Nevertheless, total agricultural output value was 2.7% higher than in 1979. Moreover, the proportional balance among the different branches of the national economy has become more rational.

Improvements in the Livelihood of the People. Secondly, our conclusion is based on the improved livelihood of the people. The Third Plenary Session of the 11th Central Committee of the Communist Party of China held towards the end of 1978 decided to cut back the scale of capital construction, raise the purchasing prices of agricultural produce, increase pay for a portion of the work force and provide bonuses. Under the original plan, capital investment for 1979 was to be 9,000 million yuan less than in 1978 and the income of both workers and peasants would be increased by 10,000 million yuan (not including pay for new workers and income from extra purchases of agricultural produce). By the end of 1979, however, total capital investment was not less than the 1978 figure, but in fact exceeded it (increasing from 48,000 million yuan in 1978 to 50,000 million yuan in 1979). On the other hand, the income of the workers and peasants increased by 14,000 million yuan.

Social purchasing power has grown by large margins during these years. In this way, the income of both urban and rural people has risen greatly. Between 1970 and 1977, social purchasing power increased by an average of 8,400 million yuan a year, but it rose by 14,800 million yuan in 1978, and by 32,200 million yuan in 1979. The preliminary calculated increase for 1980 was 35,400 million yuan (about 24,000 million yuan after deducting the price rise). The increase in social purchasing power roughly equalled the increase in national income. In other words, almost all of the increased part of national income in the past three years went to improve the livelihood of the people. The average per capita income of Chinese peasants increased from 117 yuan in 1977 to 170 yuan in 1980 (a 45% increase over three years). The average wage of the workers increased from 620 yuan in 1977 to 781 yuan in 1980 (a 30% increase over three years). Last year, the workers in most of the enterprises received bonuses and subsidies amounting to two months basic pay, while office workers also received extra monthly pay in the form of bonuses. What the people are lining up for in front of the shops are no longer foodstuffs, but luxury goods. At the same time, bank savings deposits also went up greatly.

Which should serve as the universal index for a good or bad economic situation — the growth rate of production or improvement in the people's livelihood? It is true that improvement of the people's livelihood must be based on production growth, but in the past 30 years in China, attention was often paid to growth in the rate of production rather than improvement of the people's livelihood. Therefore, the principle mark for a good or bad economic situation should be the living conditions of the people, and especially the living conditions of the peasants who constitute the overwhelming majority of the

Chinese population. There were two periods in the past 30 years in which China's economy grew at a high rate:

The Period of Economic Rehabilitation. The first period was the three years of economic rehabilitation right after the founding of New China. During this period, industrial production grew at an average rate of 34.8% per year and agricultural production at 14.1% per year. However, this high growth was of a rehabilitative nature. After three years of rehabilitation, the national economy that had been wrecked by wars surpassed the previous record level. We had a very poor economic foundation at that time. Although the people's livelihood was considerably improved during those three years, there was a far cry between those levels and the present living standard. Ministers could not afford to buy a wristwatch in 1952 or a vacuum-tube radio set in 1954. Today, almost every worker has a wristwatch and most of their families have bought radio sets and some even have television sets. Production growth rates were also high during the First Five-Year Plan period (1953-1957). Industrial production grew at an annual rate of 18% and agricultural production at 4.5%, and the people's livelihood also improved notably. The superiority of socialism was clearly demonstrated and none of the Chinese people doubted it.

"The Three Years of the Great Leap Forward." Nevertheless, the second period of high-rate development failed. That was the so-called "three years of the great leap forward" beginning in 1958. During those years, heavy industry grew by 49% a year and light industry by 14%; but agricultural production dropped and the people's livelihood worsened. Of course, this was hardly an excellent situation, but rather a very bad situation. During the 20 years between 1957 and 1976 — excluding the period of readjustment (1961–1965) — the scale of capital construction became greater and greater due to the stress on a high growth rate. As a result, industrial production grew very quickly, but, again, the people's livelihood was not at all improved. It was stated each year that the situation was excellent but, in fact, it was not good in many of these years.

The Present Situation. Although the growth rate of industrial production in the two years just past was not as high as before, the people's livelihood improved considerably indeed, and especially that of the peasants, while the livelihood of low-paid workers also improved. In this sense, the present economic situation is truly an excellent one and one rarely seen since the founding of New China. Of course, this is only the beginning, and the situation will become better and better.

Correction of "Left" Deviationist Mistakes. This excellent situation is not only manifested in production growth and the improvement of the people's livelihood but, even more important, in the fact that we have begun to correct the "Left" deviationist mistakes and are making efforts to eliminate the serious economic imbalance. The national economy was seriously out of balance in the past 20 years because we failed to build our economy on the basis of China's actual conditions. Rather, we blindly sought for higher growth rates. It is impossible to restore the normal balance among the different branches of the national economy in two or three years. Although it was already two years since the policy of readjusting the national economy was adopted, the results were not satisfactory because many comrades failed to understand the policy deeply or to implement it firmly. The old difficulties were not yet overcome and new difficulties emerged. A practical programme of further readjusting the national economy was adopted last year at the Working Meeting of the Central Committee of the Communist Party of China. It was pointed out that the scale of capital construction was still too big, the proportions among agriculture, light industry and heavy industry were not yet balanced, and energy production and transport capacity were still behind the present production and construction scale. It was pointed out that not only must the scale of capital construction continue to be reduced, but the growth rate of some industrial departments must also be kept down. Heavy industrial production must be limited and the production of agriculture and light industry would in turn be boosted. Owing to the large financial deficit and the resultant price increases, the improvement of the people's livelihood could not but be rigidly controlled. Otherwise, the whole plan for the further improvement of the people's livelihood would be of no avail. In short, we will still have to traverse a difficult and tortuous road in the course of economic readjustment. However, as long as we have a correct direction, we will be able to sail over the dangerous shoals and continue to move forward. Therefore, it is not enough to assess the excellent situation merely in terms of production growth and improvements in the people's livelihood during the past three years. What is more important is that we have become sober-minded, have begun to correct the "Left" deviationist mistakes and are regaining our initiative again. A truly bright future is unfolding before us.

II. There Are Grave Difficulties in This Excellent Situation

How do we account for our statement that the situation is excellent on the one hand and that there are grave difficulties on the other? The root cause for the difficulties, of course, is the "Left" deviationist mistakes that prevailed for 20 years. The ten years of calamity during the "cultural revolution" brought the national economy to the brink of collapse. We failed to correct the "Left" deviationist mistakes promptly after the Gang of Four was smashed. On the contrary, in 1977 we raised the slogan of achieving agricultural mechanization in the main by 1980, and in 1978 another industrial upsurge was started. Government appropriations for capital construction increased by more than 40% as compared with 1977 and many complete plants were purchased from abroad. This brought the economic imbalance further to the surface. The Third Plenary Session of the 11th Central Committee of the CPC held in the winter of 1978 and the Working Meeting of the CPC Central Committee held in the following spring adopted in good time the policy of readjusting, restructuring, consolidating and improving the national economy with emphasis on economic readjustment, and we began to correct the "Left" deviationist mistakes in an all-around way. The Working Meeting decided to cut back capital investment in 1979 from 45,000 million yuan to 36,000 million yuan and to spend the saved amount of money in raising the purchasing prices of agricultural produce and in increasing the workers' pay.

Problems of Financial Deficits and Price Stability. As the people's livelihood remained unimproved for 20 years, it was entirely necessary to raise the purchasing prices of agricultural produce and to increase the workers' pay by a relatively big margin. However, the question is as stated above: because many comrades failed to understand the necessity of readjusting the economy in face of the excellent economic situation (this was different from the economic readjustment of the early 1960's), the policy of readjustment was not firmly implemented and the scale of capital investment was not reduced as required; however, the improvement of the people's livelihood exceeded the planned quota. This resulted in a large financial deficit and it became impossible to keep prices stable in 1980.

Attention was drawn to this question in drawing up the 1980 economic plan. Planned capital investment was further cut back from 36,000 million yuan to 24,000 million yuan, but the predetermined goal was not reached. Because local governments and enterprises had more money at their own disposal, capital investments not included in the plan increased considerably and a good number of small and new but unnecessary enterprises were built. Some 40% of the workers were supposed to receive pay increases in 1979, but increased pay was given to them retroactively in the summer or autumn of 1980. More bonuses and subsidies were issued, and the amount of bonuses in many enterprises was equivalent to a pay increase of one grade for all low-paid workers. The planned prices of agricultural produce were raised only a little, but many communes and their subdivisions reduced their base quotas for compulsory purchases by the state at planned prices and increased by 50% the quantity of grains sold at prices for "above-base quota purchases." Many communes and subdivisions sold grain and other agricultural products at even higher negotiable prices. In other words, the government had to pay 5,000 million yuan more for the same quantity of grain it purchased from the peasants. Although agricultural products were purchased at higher prices, their selling prices were not raised. As a result, price subsidies by the government rose to 20,000 million yuan. With their livelihood unimproved for 20 years, the people had many difficulties and the various departments paid more attention to the livelihood of the workers and peasants.

This was quite understandable. The question was that the purchasing power of the people rose by more than 30,000 million yuan a year for two successive years, not only exceeding the government's financial capability, but also exceeding production growth. In 1979, national income increased by 6.9% (calculated at constant prices) and the volume of retail sales of social commodities rose by 18.9% (12.2% after deducting the price rise), but social purchasing power rose by 20%. In 1980, the national income also increased by 6.9%, the same as in 1979. The financial deficit in 1980 was 12,000 million yuan, exceeding the planned quota. Therefore, commodity prices went up by 6% last year, 8.1% in urban areas and 4.4% in rural areas.

Reductions in Capital Expenditures and Investment. In order to get rid of the deficit, to control the issuance of currency and to keep the market prices stable, the Party Central Committee has decided to reduce capital investment for 1981 by all means and to reduce expenditures in all fields. A nationwide discussion is now under way on readjusted quotas for this year and it will be possible to hold down capital investments. The question is: Should the improvement of the people's livelihood also be properly controlled? Some comrades propose that the workers' wages should continue to be raised and bonuses issued on a wider scale. Others say that to stimulate agricultural production, the purchasing prices of agricultural produce should be raised further. These suggestions are reasonable in a limited sense. But, in an overall sense, if we issue more bonuses (or subsidies) to offset price rises, the greater circulation of money might in turn work to stimulate price rises. If the purchasing prices of agricultural produce are further raised while selling prices remain the same, price subsidies from the government will rise even more quickly and the financial deficit will become even larger. This will make it even more difficult to control prices. If prices rise sharply, the benefits we gave to the people in the past two years will be lost once again. Therefore, treating the question in an overall way, we must adhere to the correct policy of eliminating the financial deficit and of stabilizing market prices. To achieve this, not only capital investment must be kept down, but growth in the people's purchasing power must be controlled.

The economic situation at present is quite different from that of the early 1960's: production has continued to grow steadily instead of dropping and the people have notably improved their livelihood rather than continuing to live in serious difficulties. What then is the real problem? It is that the accumulation of funds cannot be reduced according to plan while the growth of consumption funds surpasses planned targets. State expenditures, combining both accumulation funds and consumption funds, exceeded total national income. This accounted for the financial deficit. The imbalance between revenues and expenditures, between credit receipts and payments and between supply and demand has created difficulties in keeping market prices stable in the midst of an excellent economic situation. The measures that should be taken to overcome this difficulty are to continue to reduce capital investment and administrative expenses according to the plan of readjustment, to rigidly control the overgrowth of the people's purchasing power, to get rid of the serious waste in our economic work by various means and to increase economic results. If this is achieved, the financial deficit will be eliminated, market prices will remain stable and the potential danger will surely disappear.

Inflation Cannot Help China. Some Western economists and economic circles have found it difficult to understand why we have paid so much attention to the question of financial deficits and price increases. They say that according to Western experience, a minor degree of financial deficits, inflation and price rises, as long as they do not exceed given limits, offer more advantages than disadvantages to economic growth. A very small number of economists in our country also hold to the same view. They do not understand that although both China and the Western countries may have economic difficulties, the difficulties are different in nature. Their difficulty is the shrinkage of demand arising from basic contradictions in the capitalist system (including investment and living standards) and to overproduction. A small rate of inflation can stimulate growth in demand, alleviate over-production and prevent economic recession. Our economic difficulty is the swelling of demand (over-investment and surplus purchasing power), and the fact that production of all commodities lags behind demand. The present supply of market commodities in China (including capital goods) is already short enough. If prices continue to rise, the people will rush to purchase all kinds of commodities (as in the early 1960's) and market prices might undergo utter confusion. Inflation can help capitalist countries out of economic difficulties temporarily under given conditions, but it cannot help China out of its economic difficulty. On the contrary, inflation will only aggravate our difficulties. The prescription of the Keynesians, which proved unsuccessful in the West, is not applicable in China.

III. By Earnestly Readjusting and Restructuring the National Economy, the Difficulty Can Be Overcome

The imbalance in China's national economy has existed for a long time. Before the Party Central Committee adopted the policy of economic readjustment, the supply of most capital goods and consumer goods was even shorter than it is today, causing great difficulties in production, construction and the people's livelihood. On the other hand, more and more unwanted goods were overstocked in warehouses and the national economy had already fallen into distress. After the economic readjustment began, the supply of both capital goods and consumer goods became better than in the early or mid-1970's as a result of the reduced scale of capital construction and the priority given to the development of agricultural and light industrial production. In the past, the market supply became shorter and shorter, but now it has improved year by year. The notable improvement in the livelihood of the people, and of the peasants in particular, is solid proof of the initial results achieved by the policy of readjustment.

Today, although the central government is encountering financial difficulties, the local governments have more money, and many enterprises in particular have funds at their own disposal. This makes it possible for them to arrange production by themselves to a certain extent, to encourage technical innovations and to improve the livelihood of their workers. Bank savings in urban and rural areas have greatly increased. Is this not a good thing that has rarely been seen since the founding of New China? It is a good thing, not a bad thing, that the enterprises and the people have more money in their hands. The problem is that managerial work has lagged behind. The local governments and enterprises have spent their money on the construction of unnecessary projects. The increased income of the workers and peasants has exceeded the possibility of market commodity supply to such an extent that even expensive goods have sold out in a rush. So unexpected grave difficulties emerged in the midst of the excellent situation. From an overall point of view, our economy has begun to improve. But from a partial point of view, energetic measures must be taken to quickly overcome financial and credit difficulties.

Strengthening the Planned Management of the Macroeconomy. The principal measure to overcome these difficulties is, first of all, to strengthen the planned management of the macroeconomy. The specific content of this is to further cut back capital investment, and especially to check the construction of unnecessary projects by local governments and the enterprises. The more than 300,000 existing industrial enterprises must be reorganized through integration to reduce redundancy and waste in production. At the same time, the improvement of the people's livelihood must also be controlled. In the past, Comrade Zhou Enlai and Comrade Chen Yun often paid attention to controlling total employment. As wage standards were constant at that time, total wages would not be exceeded as long as employment was controlled. Today, not only is employment not rigidly controlled, but wage standards are also out of control due to the excessive issuance of bonuses by some enterprises. The overissuance of bonuses has led to price rises, forcing government offices to give subsidies to their staffs. In order to raise the purchasing prices of farm products, the state paid out more than 8,000 million yuan in 1979 alone. Planned prices were not raised in 1980, but prices for above-quota purchases and negotiable prices were greatly increased.

Bonuses play an important role in enhancing the workers' enthusiasm in production, and we should not oppose them. But we must oppose the overissuance of bonuses. Negotiable prices have also played a beneficial role in increasing the market supply of farm products in the third category, the cancellation of negotiable prices would again place the enlivened rural fairs into a corner, but we must prevent a drop in state purchase quotas just for the sake of raising negotiable prices. As regards bonuses and negotiable prices, we must strengthen our policy of management, but we must not take rash actions.

We must stop thinking of solely using administrative measures to solve such complicated questions. Instead, we must undertake intensive investigations and rely on the masses to help us with supervision and inspection. Once the difficulties of the government are explained clearly to the masses, they will help us to overcome them.

Eliminating the financial deficit, controlling the issuance of currency and keeping market prices stable are the urgent questions that must be solved at present. But our economic readjustment will not stop at this. We must go on to fundamentally restructure the economy, that is, to change the ratio among agriculture, light industry and heavy industry so as to meet actual conditions in China — we have 1,000 million people, including 800 million peasants, and their living standards are low. Our economic work must, first of all, ensure that the 1,000 million people — and the 800 million peasants in particular — have enough food and clothing and that they gradually improve their living standards as production increases. Today, most of the people have notably raised their level of consumption, gradually turning their attention from wristwatches, radio sets, bicycles and sewing machines to televisions, tape recorders, washing machines and electric fans. We must speed up the development of agriculture and light industry to satisfy the needs of the people. Every paper note issued must be guaranteed in kind.

In recent years, our agriculture has grown fast and, moreover, the growth of light industry has begun to surpass that of heavy industry. There is still great room for the development of agriculture and light industry and we must take various effective measures to speed up their growth. As to heavy industry, we must step up capital construction in the energy production and transport sectors and change their irrational internal proportions. As the scale of capital construction has been reduced, many machine-building plants are operating under capacity. They should be encouraged to help those existing factories with technical innovations instead of producing equipment for new plants. The machine-building industry should be readjusted, reorganized and restructured. From a long-term point of view, the purpose of the readjustment is not only to strike a balance between revenues and expenditures but, more important, to reorganize the whole economic structure rationally. It is obviously impossible to achieve the healthy development of the national economy without this readjustment.

Changing the Economic Management System. If we look still farther, we will have to restructure the economic management system. Many economists point out that the chief characteristics of China's national economy are high growth rate and high accumulation, but low results and low consumption. The ultimate purpose of our economic construction is to gradually satisfy the growing needs of the material and cultural life of the people throughout the country. What's the point of our economic construction if the result of the high growth rate is low consumption? There are two root causes for this abnormal situation. One is the imbalance of the national economy as stated above and the other is that we adopted the over-centralized Soviet system of economic management — that is, centralized revenues and expenditures and monopoly purchases and sales of industrial products by the state, or what we often call "sharing porridge from the same pot." If we fail to establish a system of responsibility for accounting at all levels, but continue to "share porridge from the same pot," it will be impossible for us to get rid of the enormous wastes in production, distribution and economic construction, or to increase economic results. In the long run, if we do not change this situation, it will be impossible for our finances to get out of the current awkward situation. In this sense, the ultimate purposes of both readjustment and restructuring are identical and complementary to each other. It is short-sighted to think that restructuring the system would obstruct economic readjustment and create economic difficulties.

Of course, the principles guiding the restructuring of the system are correct, but if we do not handle it properly, it might produce a negative effect on the readjustment. We should exercise bi-level control over the revenues and expenditures of central and local governments, give more power to the enterprises in management and introduce a profit-sharing system so that local authorities and enterprises have more funds for arranging their production and for increasing the livelihood of their workers. This is an entirely correct orientation. Generally speaking, local governments have too few reserve funds and most of the enterprises do not have sufficient reserve funds. However, state revenues are limited and revenues at the lower levels can only be increased gradually after the enterprises receive more power in management. If both the local governments and enterprises ask for more reserve funds than they deserve, it will inevitably affect state revenue. If the local governments and enterprises have more reserve funds at their own disposal and use them to build unnecessary projects instead of investing in projects most needed by the country, it will not only be detrimental to the readjustment but also place obstacles to the progress of readjustment. In the past two years, we neglected this tendency and failed to exercise tight control over capital construction, thus retarding the progress in readjustment. In order to correct this tendency, we have decided this year to concentrate the surplus funds of local governments and enterprises in the hands of the central government by issuing treasury bonds so that funds can be directed to the most needed projects. Ours is a socialist country. Even if revenues and expenditures are managed at different levels, they are owned by the whole people. Whenever necessary, decentralized revenues can be consolidated by the central government for use with compensation. Moreover, we must study how to improve the system of financial management at different levels so as to ensure that revenues and expenditures can be balanced at the central level. In short, to overcome economic difficulties in the end, we must completely change the present economic management system. This is essential to eliminating waste and to increasing economic results. This is also our strategic principle from a long-term point of view.

Our difficulty is a difficulty that has emerged in the course of our advance, and one which we are sure to overcome. All pessimistic views are unfounded.

2. ON CHINA'S NEW STRATEGY FOR ECONOMIC DEVELOPMENT
By Ma Hong

I. The Advancement of a New Strategy of Economic Development and Its Significance

The Third Plenary Session of the 11th Central Committee of the Chinese Communist Party, held in the winter of 1978, rectified the prolonged "Left" mistakes in the party, eliminated the pernicious ideological political influence of Lin Biao and the Gang of Four in distorting and tampering with Marxism-Leninism-Mao Zedong Thought, and at the same time resolutely and clearly called for a shift of focus of party work to economic construction and to socialist modernization. This brought the party line back to the correct road of Marxism-Leninism.

In order to implement the resolutions adopted at the Third Plenary Session of the 11th Party Central Committee, to save the economy from collapse and to find a new way of developing the socialist economy in China in line with the four fundamental principles of upholding the socialist road, the dictatorship of the proletariat, the leadership of the Communist Party and Marxism-Leninism and Mao Zedong Thought, the Party Central Committee formulated the principle of "readjusting, restructuring, consolidating and improving" the economy, with the primary focus on readjustment. This is a great strategic change in the development of socialist economic construction in China and is therefore of great theoretical and practical significance.

We are very hopeful of finding a new road of developing the socialist economy in our country by readjusting, restructuring, consolidating and improving the economy. The practical experience in the past two years has shown us a bright prospect. We should be confident in this regard.

The Rationale for Readjustment. The advancement and implementation of the principle of economic readjustment represents a fundamental change in our prevailing ideology for economic work as a whole. This change has two aspects: a change in the strategic goal of economic development and a change in the road taken to reach this goal.

For a long time, our understanding of the basic economic laws of socialism was not deep. For many years, under the influence of "Left" mistakes, our economic work departed more or less from the purpose of socialist production. We often said that the purpose of socialist production was to satisfy the needs of the people but, in fact, our actions failed in this regard with the result that there existed a certain tendency towards production for production's sake. The present economic readjustment and reform is meant to thoroughly correct the tendency of production for production's sake so that economic work as a whole will take the road of satisfying the material and cultural needs of the people.

Owing to mistakes in the selection of the strategic goal of economic development and owing to our failure to have a sober understanding of basic conditions in our country, we made many serious mistakes concerning the road of economic development, mostly "Left" mistakes.

1. In production and construction, we blindly sought high plan targets and high growth rates to the neglect of returns.

2. Undue emphasis was laid on the development of heavy industry to the neglect of agriculture and light industry.

3. We depended merely on the construction of new projects for expanded reproduction to the neglect of tapping potentials in existing enterprises.

4. Attention was paid only to the output of steel and other primary and intermediate products to the total neglect of the variety and quality of the products, and especially to the total neglect of the production of end-of-line consumer goods.

5. Undue emphasis was placed on the high accumulation rate to the neglect of the necessary consumption of the people.

6. We were overly anxious to bring about a transition in the relationships of production and blindly sought after bigness in size and completeness in socialist nature.

We were overanxious to make the transition from collective ownership to ownership by the whole people, prematurely negated the role of the individual economy in urban and rural areas and adopted an overconcentrated economic management system within the sector of ownership by the whole people. All these mistakes contributed to a vicious circle of "high growth rate, high accumulation rate, low efficiency and low consumption level" in the economy.

Purpose of the Current Readjustment. The purpose of our current economic readjustment is to overcome the "Left" mistakes concerning the road of economic construction, to truly proceed from the basic conditions in China and to find a new road of developing its socialist economy simultaneously with the change in the strategic goal of economic development.

Such a change means that the fundamental purpose of China's socialist economic construction is to satisfy the needs of the people.

Such a change means that we are no longer blindly seeking a high growth rate to the neglect of returns. In other words, we will attach great importance to increasing economic returns. Only this approach can serve the purpose of satisfying the needs of the people.

Such a change means that we are no longer merely seeking to produce steel and other primary and intermediate products to the neglect of quality, variety and the production of end-of-line consumer goods. We must guide production according to the needs of consumers, the needs of the market and the needs of defending the fruits of socialism. In this way, we can more effectively satisfy the needs of the people and the needs of society, including the needs of national defence.

Such a change means that we will alter the erroneous practice of laying undue stress on the development of heavy industry, blindly seeking high growth rates and restricting the consumption of the people. Rather, we shall gradually build, through readjustment, a rational economic structure that suits basic conditions in China. Only in this way will it be possible to achieve high growth rates, more accumulation and better results, and thus still better satisfy the needs of the people.

Such a change means that we will gradually change the irrational economic system and build a rational economic system. We will give full play to the initiative and enthusiasm of enterprises and the working people, promote the development of productive forces and ensure that the rational needs of the people will be satisfied. Such a change also means that we will make the relations of production conform with the character and level of productive forces and allow a multiplicity of economic sectors and multiple modes of business operation to co-exist, all on the prerequisite that socialist public ownership is predominant.

Such a change means that we must do our economic work in accordance with objective economic laws. The principle of economic readjustment is precisely adopted to serve the requirements of socialist economic laws.

In short, through the implementation of the principle of readjustment, restructuring, consolidation and improvement, the Chinese economy will gradually begin to follow the model described recently by a leading comrade of the State Council: "an economy which will develop in a coordinated way, make steady progress, grow healthy, fully display the superiority of the socialist system and offer more benefits to the people."

It is thus obvious that our purpose of readjusting, restructuring, consolidating and improving the economy is to correct past mistakes committed in the strategic goal of economic development and the road of economic construction so that the socialist economic construction will develop along a new road, namely, the road of increasing economic results and serving the needs of the people. Therefore, this is a change of great theoretical and practical significance, a change of historical significance. We must fully understand the strategic significance of this change.

A Correct Strategy for Socialist Economic Construction. We are not unfamiliar with the question of strategy. By strategy we mean overall and fundamental questions of a perpetual character. Comrade Mao Zedong wrote a number of well-known articles, including "Problems of Strategy in China's Revolutionary War." They were of great importance to the victory in the Chinese revolutionary wars. We all know that the Chinese revolutionary wars suffered serious setbacks before the final victory was won. One of the fundamental reasons was the change from an erroneous strategy to a correct strategy. Without a correct strategy in a revolutionary war, it is impossible to win it. Likewise, without a correct strategy in socialist economic construction, it is impossible to achieve economic success.

In short, we should fully understand the significance of the period and principle of economic readjustment from the high plane of the strategy of economic development. If we approach the question this way, we will be able to understand how important the period of readjustment is and how important readjustment and restructuring are. Our party experienced several strategic changes of great historic significance during the periods of the revolutionary wars — one at the Zunyi meeting, one on the eve of the War of Resistance to Japanese aggression and one after the War of Liberation. We all know very well about the great victories of these strategic changes. The current change in economic development strategy is likewise of great historic significance and will lead to great victory.

In order to further raise our awareness of the importance of the principle of economic readjustment, I now present my views for discussion.

A leading comrade of the State Council said recently: "We will gradually achieve a rational economic structure, a rational management system and a rational enterprise organization and break a new path in developing the economy of our country through readjustment and reforms and on the basis of stabilizing the economy." Here, I would like to deal separately with the questions relating to rational economic structure, rational management system and rational enterprise organization.

On the Readjustment and a Rational Economic Structure

The purpose of our economic readjustment, from a fundamental point of view, is to readjust the economic structure, thoroughly redress the serious imbalances among the major portions of the national economy and place the economy on the healthy road of planned and proportionate development so as to satisfy the needs of the people.

Problems in China's Economic Structure and the Requirements of Economic Readjustment

In order to deal with the necessity of readjusting the economic structure, to make readjustment work proceed step by step and to render the readjustment measures more effective, it is necessary to make an analysis of the existing economic structure and its problems.

For many years, our economic work fell under the influence of "Left" mistakes. Undue emphasis was laid on the development of heavy industry to the neglect of agriculture and light industry. Increases in total output value and in state revenues and an expansion of employment were achieved mainly by investing large funds, consuming large quantities of energy, expanding the scale of capital construction and constructing a large number of new factories. For this reason, industry was built, but it could not be integrated with agriculture into one unitary production system; heavy industry was built, but it could not be integrated with light industry into one unitary production system. On the question of the development of heavy industry, undue emphasis was laid on construction of the steel industry. In order to expand the iron and steel industry, large quantities of energy were consumed and a great part of transport facilities and large capital funds were used. This not only hampered the development of agriculture and light industry, but also impeded the development of the energy industry and of communications. It resulted in an imbalanced development of heavy industry per se. Energy production and communications became weak links in the national economy and the iron and steel industry itself was not duly developed. As time passed, a lopsided economic structure took shape. Some branches of heavy industry were rapidly developed, but agriculture, light industry, energy, communications, construction, commerce and service trades remained underdeveloped. Moreover, the localities developed self-sufficient economic systems, and the ministries and enterprises also built all-embracing production systems. Therefore, economic imbalance, loose structure, ineffective mechanisms, low efficiency and great waste became the special features of this economic structure.

It is obvious that this method of economic construction required large-scale investments and high consumption. But it yielded less returns and gave fewer benefits to the people. Moreover, it often brings about a vicious circle in economic development. In the future, we must break a new path in developing China's economy that can make the best of existing economic resources and bring the national economy into the orbit of sound development.

Sound Development and Vicious Cycles. For the past 30 years, sound development and vicious cycles have alternated with each other in China's economic growth. During the First Five-Year Plan period, China achieved good returns. After the "Great Leap Forward," we took a road of "high growth rate, high accumulation rate, low efficiency and low consumption." We directed the strategic target of economic development at an impractical "high growth rate." In order to reach such impractical targets, it was necessary to set high plan targets in production, over-extended scales in capital construction and high accumulation rates in the distribution of the national income, which caused a serious imbalance between accumulation and consumption. No attention was paid to the returns from capital funds. Owing to high consumption of fuels and raw materials, a large proportion of these were wasted and no actual returns were obtained from the investment. As a result, the national income grew very slowly, the poverty and backwardness were not changed and the livelihood of the people was little improved. In order to remedy this backwardness, we were overly anxious to achieve success by seeking a high growth rate and by expanding the scale of capital construction. Therefore, high plan targets were set, a huge construction programme was drafted, the accumulation rate was raised and wastage became even more serious. As this repeated itself in endless cycles, it led to a vicious circle in economic development.

Balancing the Relationship of Proportions. After 30 years of construction, the industrial scale is no longer small, nor is the growth rate of the total industrial output value very low — it now averages about 13% a year. However, neither the variety nor the quality of many products as yet meet the needs of consumers. There are more intermediate products, the proportion of final products is low and the quantities of consumer goods that can be used to meet the material and cultural needs of the people are limited, and for this the people have paid a very heavy cost. Moreover, the country remains poor and the people's livelihood has not been improved adequately.

The superiority of the socialist relations of production not only lies in the fact that it opens up the possibility of planned development of the national economy, but derives also from the fact that after an erroneous macroeconomic decision has led to an imbalance in the national economy, it is still possible to balance the relationship of proportions again through planned readjustment. The purpose of economic readjustment is to transform an irrational, dislocated and lopsided economic structure into a rational economic structure. Such a rational economic structure calls for a change from the guiding principle of building up heavy industry as the target to the target of increasing the production of final consumer goods, of producing final consumer goods according to the needs of the people's consumption and social consumption, and of producing intermediate products and primary products such as raw materials according to the needs of production of the final consumer goods. The changed focus includes the construction of a well-balanced economic structure, including industry and agriculture, with the production of final consumer goods as its target.

Once such an economic structure is established, the raw materials industries and the industries producing semi-finished goods both serve the final products, and every industry or every enterprise has a definite target to which it provides services. In this way, the products they manufacture become products needed in the course of reproduction so as to better gear the supply of social products to the social demand for such products. Thus, maximum returns will be obtained from the manpower, material power and financial power that society invests and thus the growing material and cultural needs of the people will be satisfied still better. Such an economic structure is one which can take greatest advantage of manpower, material power and natural resources in China so as to facilitate well-coordinated development of the different divisions of the national economy (especially agriculture, light industry and heavy industry) and the different parts of social reproduction and thus achieve a sound development of the national economy.

Some Theoretical Questions Concerning the Readjustment of the National Economy

In line with the requirements dealt with in the proceeding paragraphs, some theoretical questions on the readjustment of the national economy must be discussed. Apart from achieving a correct understanding of the purpose of socialist production and continuing the criticism of the erroneous tendencies of production for its own sake, some other theoretical questions are open to discussion.

For many years, we have regarded the priority of the development of heavy industry as a universal law in socialist construction and as a road to and a way of socialist industrialization. The prolonged undue emphasis on the priority of developing heavy industry in China has been closely related to this guiding ideology. In readjusting the national economy and establishing a rational economic structure, and in calling for a change from the target of building up heavy industry to the target of increasing the production of final consumer goods, we must make a reassessment of this guiding ideology.

The experience of many economically developed countries in the world shows that heavy industry was developed on the basis of the development of agriculture and light industry and to keep abreast of the demand of agriculture, light industry and other production sectors related to the means of production.

The General Relationship Between Production and Consumption. Some people argue, however, that this is the capitalist road of industrialization. This approach to the question does not conform with fact. The key to the question lies in the fact that the objective process of economic development is not necessarily connected with this particular relationship of production — or, capitalism. Rather, we would say that this relationship is a requirement of the universal law of development of modern industrial production. Marx once said: "Without consumption, there is no production ... since in that case production would be useless." (Karl Marx, "A Contribution to the Critique of Political Economy," p. 196. Moscow: Progress Publishers, 1970). So far as the ultimate purpose is concerned, production in any society is for consumption. This is the general relationship between production and consumption, the universal law of social production. As to the relation between the production of means of production and the production of means of consumption, this universal law finds its expression in the fact that the production of means of production always in the end serves the production of means of consumption. As for modern industrial production, this universal law finds expression in the fact that heavy industry, which mainly produces means of production, always ultimately serves agriculture, light industry, communications and transport, commerce and other service trades that mainly produce means of consumption.

It is worth mentioning that in his first section, "Development of Machinery," in Chapter 13 of "Das Capital," Marx made a detailed analysis of the expressions of these universal laws from the angle of the history of development of the modern machinery industry. In the past, however, people often regarded the development from light industry to heavy industry in the course of the capitalist industrial revolution described by Marx as the outcome of the operation of the capitalist law of surplus value. However, in this they neglected his analysis of the universal laws of modern industrial production. It is true that Marx, in describing the development of the modern machine-building industry, said: "Machinery is a means for producing surplus value." (Karl Marx, *Das Capital*, Vol. 1, p. 371. Moscow: Foreign Languages Publishing House, 1958). When he dealt with the development of modern industry (including light industry), calling for the development of modern machine-building industry, he also said that the machines produced by manual labour were dearer than those produced by the machine-building industry. But here he was mainly expounding the idea that "at certain stages of its development, Modern Industry became technologically incompatible with the basis furnished for it by handicraft and manufacture... Modern Industry had therefore to take in hand itself the machine, the characteristic instrument of production, and to construct machines by machines. It was not till it did this, that it built up for itself a fitting technical foundation, and stood on its own feet." (Karl Marx, *Das Capital*, Vol. 1, p. 383-384. Moscow: Foreign Languages Publishing House, 1958.) This tells us that when modern light industry develops to a certain stage, it calls for the development of modern machine-building industry, the most important part of heavy industry. In other words, the latter is developed on the basis of the former and is developed to suit the needs of the former.

These theoretical analyses by Marx coincided completely with the historical course of modern industrial development in England. If the invention and application of the steam engine marked the beginning of the industrial revolution, then modern light industry in England began to develop in the 1760's. In the words of Marx, however, it was not until the development of machinery in the early decades of the 19th century that the machine-building industry actually mastered the skills required for the construction of machine tools. It was only during the proceeding decade (the first volume of "Das Capital" was published at the end of the 1860's) that the construction of railways and ocean steamers on a stupendous scale called into existence the cyclopean machines now employed in the construction of primary movers.

In Vol. II, Part III, of "Das Capital," Marx again made an overall analysis of the expression of this universal law from the angle of the reproduction and circulation of aggregate social capital. In Vol. III of the same book, Marx summed up his analysis in these words: "As we have seen (Book II, Part III), continuous circulation takes place between constant capital and constant capital (even regardless of accelerated accumulation). It is at first independent of individual consumption because it never enters the latter. But this consumption definitely limits it nevertheless, since constant capital is never produced for its own sake but solely because more of it is needed in spheres of production whose products go into individual consumption." (Karl Marx, *Das Capital*, Vol. III, p. 299. Moscow: Foreign Languages Publishing House, 1958.) If "constant capital" as described by Marx is changed to "means of production," this principle is not only applicable to, but is most effective for socialism. This is because the direct purpose of socialist production is to satisfy the needs of the people.

It is thus obvious that the history of the development of modern industry as well as the general course of social reproduction both show that the production of means of production definitely serves the production of means of subsistence; and that, therefore, heavy industry must be developed on the basis of the development of agriculture, light industry and communications and so as to satisfy their demand for means of production. This is the requirement of the universal law of the development of modern industrial production. It is by no means different because of the social economic system being capitalist or socialist.

It is thus obvious that the economic readjustment, the establishment of a rational economic structure and the change from the building of heavy industry as the target to the increased production of final consumer goods not only coincide with the requirements of the basic economic laws of socialism, but also correspond to the requirements of the universal law of the development of modern industrial production.

The Experience of the Soviet Union. However, some people argue that the Soviet Union persisted in giving priority to the development of heavy industry for a certain period and that the Soviet experience shows that priority given to the development of heavy industry is the socialist road of industrialization. It is true that the Soviet Union did do things that way. However, it should be noted that the Soviet Union was once the only socialist country in the world, surrounded and threatened by capitalism. The policy used at that time was actually a special measure adopted under particular historical conditions. It was not the universal law of socialist industrialization. Moreover, because the Soviet Union laid prolonged and undue emphasis on the development of heavy industry and went against the requirements of the universal law of the development of modern industrial production, it also inevitably suffered from the imbalance of its economic structure despite the important role it had played in the development of Soviet industry, and especially in the development of military strength for the defence against Hitler's fascism. It should be stressed that if we say that the Soviet Union had persisted in giving priority to the development of heavy industry for the sake of strengthening its economic independence and national defence capabilities during the Stalin era, then it must also be said that, after Khrushchev and Brezhnev came into power, its persistence in the economic strategy of giving priority to the development of heavy industry has been used merely as an important pillar in pursuing the social-imperialist military expansionist policy.

We should make clear the completely different social nature of this policy. The persistence in this economic strategy has already thrown the Soviet Union into a predicament of serious imbalance in its economy.

Priority for the Growth of Means of Production. Does this deny the law of priority given to the growth of means of production? Does the economic development target of increasing the production of final consumer goods contradict the law of giving priority to the growth of means of production? Evidently, it should not be understood that way because, firstly, what does priority to the growth of means of production mean? In Lenin's words, "the production of means of production increases faster than the production of means of consumption." (Lenin, *Collected Works*, Vol. I, p. 88, "On the So-called Market Questions". Moscow: Foreign Languages Publishing House, 1960). Speaking separately, "Growth in the production of means of production as means of production is the most rapid, then comes the production of means of production as means of consumption, and the lowest rate of growth is in the production of means of consumption." (*Ibid.*, p. 87).

But an increase of production of final consumer goods as the target of economic development requires the production of primary and intermediate products to serve the production of final consumer goods. It also requires the production of heavy industry that mainly supplies means of production to serve the production of agriculture, light industry and communications, which in turn mainly supply consumer goods. Both offer different implications.

Sticking to the latter does not necessarily lead to the negation of the former. In other words, given the prerequisite of increasing production of final consumer goods as the target of economic development, it is still possible to give priority to growth in the means of production. The question is whether the purpose of the development of heavy industry is to serve its own growth or to serve mainly the production of consumer goods. Furthermore, why should priority be given to the growth of the means of production? It is because under certain conditions of technological progress, the demand of society in expanded reproduction for additional means of production is faster than the demand for additional labour (and for additional means of consumption).

Lenin made the point very clear when he said: "The proposition that means of production grows faster is merely a paraphrase of this law [the law of the tendency of constant capital growing faster than variable capital — *translator's note*] as applied to social production as a whole." (Lenin, *Collected Works*, "On the So-called Market Questions", p. 87. Moscow: Foreign Languages Publishing House, 1960). However, faster growth of the production of means of production and of manufacturing means of consumption stemmed precisely from expanded reproduction in the sectors producing means of consumption under certain conditions of technological progress. Although faster growth in the production of means of production as means of production resulted directly from the production of means of production as means of consumption, in the final analysis it came from the production of means of consumption.

As a whole, therefore, faster growth in the production of means of production results from a growing demand for the production of means of consumption. Lenin put it correctly when he said: "It goes without saying that, in the last analysis, productive consumption is always bound up with personal consumption." (Lenin, *Collected Works*, Vol. III, p. 55, "The Development of Capitalism in Russia." Moscow: Foreign Languages Publishing House, 1960). It is evident that insofar as the meaning of or the reason for giving priority to the growth of means of production is concerned, it does not necessarily contradict the increasing of the production of final consumer goods as the target of economic development.

It must be pointed out further that for a long time some people interpreted the law of giving priority to the growth of means of production in absolute terms — as if the development of modern social production must call for giving priority to the growth of means of production under any conditions. We cannot say that the prolonged undue emphasis on the development of heavy industry had nothing to do with this understanding. It is clear now that this approach to the question is by no means perfect.

Firstly, according to Marxist-Leninist theory, it is only under conditions of technological progress that expanded reproduction calls for priority to the growth of means of production, and expanded production in the absence of technological progress does not necessarily call for priority given to the growth of means of production. In his analysis of the accumulation of capital in "Das Capital" Vol. I, Marx first dealt with the accumulation of capital under the condition that the composition of capital did not change. He then dealt with the accumulation of capital on the condition that the composition of capital increased. This theoretical analysis of Marx spoke to the historical development of capitalism. Secondly, the history of technological progress in modern social production shows that certain kinds of technological progress, such as those related to biological measures in agriculture, do not necessarily call for giving priority to the growth of means of production; and that certain kinds of technological advances, such as the replacement of manual construction by modern machine-building industry, calls for giving priority to the growth of means of production. Clearly, it cannot be taken for granted that expanded reproduction under conditions of technological progress necessarily requires faster growth in means of production. Thirdly, even if technological advances called for the faster growth of means of production, the question of whether priority can be given to such growth depends on other conditions. In the early period of capitalist industrialization, rapid technological advances were made in light industry and its production also grew quickly. However, the machines used in light industry and its production also grew quickly. However, the machines used in light industry were still built by hand and as a consequence the production of means of production did not grow rapidly. The shortage of capital funds needed in the development of heavy industry was an important factor in this respect.

So far as industrial development in China is concerned, it was necessary to give priority to the development of heavy industry for a certain period in the early years following the founding of New China, when appropriate conditions also existed for such development. In semi-colonial and semi-feudal old China, light industry was fairly well-developed, but heavy industry was in a very poor state. After nationwide liberation, with the change in the ownership of the means of production, both agriculture and light industry acquired great potential for further growth. Under such conditions, heavy industry could be developed at a properly higher rate. But in later years, heavy industry was developed to an extent that it departed from the foundation of agriculture and light industry. The prolonged undue emphasis on the development of heavy industry under such conditions went over to the opposite side and led to the serious imbalance of the economic structure. Clearly, the increase of production of final consumer goods as the target of economic development does not by itself contradict the principle of giving priority to the development of means of production. But giving additional priority to the growth of light industry as a strategic principle for economic development is also compatible with the principle of giving priority to the growth of means of production.

Heavy-Type and Light-Type Structures. But now some people are saying that in the past two years priority was given to the development of light industry and light industry grew at a higher rate than heavy industry. This year, the proportion of light industry to total industrial output value has surpassed that of heavy industry. Thus, it is now time to switch priority again to the development of heavy industry. This view is supported by another theoretical proposition that the irrational "heavy-type structure" should be gradually readjusted to a "light-type structure."

By "light-type structure," it means that agriculture and light industry account for more than 60% of the total industrial and agricultural output value and heavy industry for less than 40%. By "heavy-type structure," it means that heavy industry accounts for more than 40% of the total industrial and agricultural output value, and agriculture and light industry for less than 60%. The premise for undertaking this division is to rectify the serious imbalance among agriculture, light industry and heavy industry; indeed, it may play a certain positive role in changing the existing structure of underdeveloped agriculture. In fact, however, this view inevitably leads to the conclusion that we should stop giving priority to the development of light industry, especially since in 1980 agriculture and light industry already accounted for nearly 60% of the total industrial and agricultural output value, a proportion that will probably exceed 60% in 1981. This way of division is improper not only because the division between light and heavy industries is at best relative and is becoming more and more relative, but moreover because they do not include important economic sectors such as transportation, posts and telecommunications, commerce and service trades, as well as science, education and public health.

As to the question we are discussing, the main shortcomings are:

1. There are not now nor can there be fixed standard proportions for agriculture, light industry and heavy industry in the total industrial and agricultural output value so as to indicate in which proportions they would be well-coordinated. Such proportions are determined by the development of social productive forces, changes in the economic system, population growth and other complex factors. Even under present conditions in China, it cannot be said that the above-mentioned standards for the "light-type structure" correspond to actual conditions. The proportions of agriculture and light industry in total industrial and agricultural output value have already approached these standards, but the serious imbalance among agriculture, light industry and heavy industry has not yet been changed fundamentally.

2. The method of dividing the proportions of the economic structure merely according to their quantitative output cannot reflect the quality of that structure and therefore cannot show whether the structure is balanced. Theoretically, we can make two assumptions: at a given level of development of social productive forces, heavy industry may account for more than 40% of total industrial and agricultural output value. But heavy industry is built on the basis of the development of agriculture and light industry and exists to serve the development of agriculture and light industry; therefore, its relationship to agriculture and light industry is in balance. Under the same conditions of the productive forces, heavy industry may also account for more than 40% of the total industrial and agricultural output value, although to this extent it serves only its own growth. It shows that its relations with agriculture and light industry are not balanced. At present, although heavy industry in China accounts for 40%, its proportion to the total industrial and agricultural output value is still too great and the extent to which heavy industry serves its own growth has not been changed notably. Therefore, the proportions of agriculture, light industry and heavy industry are still not balanced.

Of course, this does not deny the success achieved during the past two years in readjusting the national economy in China under the guidance of the party's policy of economic readjustment. The growth rate of light industry in the past two years has surpassed that of heavy industry; the slow development of agricultural production that had lasted for many years was notably changed; and new progress was made in the readjustment of the production of heavy industry. However, it is difficult for the prolonged serious imbalance among the proportional contributions of agriculture, light industry and heavy industry to be totally changed in one or two years. Moreover, some sectors did not implement the policy of economic readjustment effectively, and this further delayed progress of the readjustment to a certain extent. In short, in readjusting the industrial structure at present, we must not only strengthen agricultural production and continue to give priority to the development of light industry, but also readjust the service orientation of heavy industry and change the irrational self-propagation of heavy industry so as to rationalize the industrial structure step by step.

The Goal and Measures for the Readjustment of the Economic Structure

The question of the goal and measures for readjusting the economic structure is an important theoretical and practical question raised in the work of economic readjustment in China that calls for urgent solution. This question was discussed at the seminar on the theory and practice in restructuring the economic management system jointly held recently by the Industrial Economics Research Institute under the Chinese Academy of Social Sciences and the Sichuan Provincial Academy of Social Sciences. Based on the discussions at that seminar, I would like to present my tentative ideas about the goal and measures for the economic readjustment.

As a whole, the goal of the economic readjustment is to proceed from actual conditions in China and to establish an economic structure with relatively balanced proportions, relatively high economic returns and sound development.

The main components of this economic structure are:

1. A proportional relationship among the

different sectors of the national economy to the extent that the internal relationships of these sectors and the relationships among the different links of the social reproduction are roughly balanced.

2. Rational utilization of the manpower, material power and financial power of society.

3. The development of production and construction in ways closely bound up with the improvement of the people's livelihood. Once such an economic structure is established, we can achieve greater economic results and ensure that the material and cultural life of urban and rural residents can be improved as much and as steadily as possible within the limits permitted by the national power on the basis of the steady rise of national income.

The Three Stages of Readjustment. In order to reach the general goal stated above, the economic readjustment can be divided into three stages. The first stage is a stage of economic stabilization. Its main task is to strike a balance between revenues and expenditures, to stabilize prices and the economy, to make large efforts to develop the production of consumer goods, to expand commerce and service trades, to develop the collective and individual economy and to create more job opportunities for young people and to ensure that the livelihood of the people continues to be improved while maintaining present income levels. This stage will take about two years.

The second stage is a stage of further balancing the proportions of the two sectors. The main efforts will be made to readjust the proportional relationship among agriculture, light industry and heavy industry to the extent that the relationship between these two sectors of social production will be in the main coordinated and so that the livelihood of urban and rural people will continue to be improved. This stage will take about three years.

The emphasis in the third stage will be placed on solving the problem of underdevelopment of energy, transportation, posts, telecommunications and urban public utilities and on establishing relatively balanced relations among different segments of the national economy to the extent that economic returns will be markedly increased and so that the income of the people will grow faster and their livelihood will be improved markedly. This stage will take about five years.

These tentative ideas are to be tested, enriched, perfected and revised in further research.

The first two stages can be defined as periods of readjustment. When targets set for the second stage are reached, the most fundamental proportional relationships in the national economy — the relationships among agriculture, light industry and heavy industry — will in the main be balanced. Therefore, the period that takes readjustment as its focus will end. The task for readjustment in the third stage can be fulfilled in the course of future normal economic development.

II. The Reform and Rationalization of the Economic Management System

In order to break a new path in developing the socialist economy in China it is necessary not only to rationalize the economic structure but also to rationalize the economic management system.

Why Must the Economic Management System Be Reformed?

The present economic management system in China is a system with a high degree of centralism, using administrative management as its main content. This system, in its basic form, was copied from the Soviet Union. That is, it is similar to the system adopted in the Soviet Union in the late years of Stalin.

China's practical experience in the past 30 years has shown that this system has many shortcomings. They can be summed up into four points:

1. The enterprises are regarded as appendages to administrative organs at various levels and their relative independence is denied. Our enterprises are treated like beads in the abacus which are pushed up and down by the central ministries and local industrial departments and bureaus while they themselves have no initiative. This is not because they do not want to possess initiative, but rather because our present system has hampered that initiative.

2. The economy is run according to the administrative networks and administrative regions; each forms an independent system, resulting in severance of the internal relations of the economy. For example, the Chinese enterprises are controlled by the central or local authorities in charge of them. Their interrelationships are mainly vertical — from top to bottom; they do not have horizontal relationships. This has given rise to many irrational phenomena.

3. There are too many directive plan quotas set by the high authorities for the enterprises and

their production has been too tightly controlled. Producers and consumers can never meet each other directly and relationships between those producing and those marketing and between the producers and the consumers are disjointed. Therefore, on the one hand, many products are overstocked in large quantities, while many others are in short supply.

4. As revenues and expenditures are controlled by the central government, the economic departments and enterprises all take "iron rice bowls" to "share food from the same pot." This means that they do not assume fiscal responsibility and pay no attention to economic returns that are the result of egalitarianism. Owing to these shortcomings, the present economic system inevitably deters the encouragement of initative and creativity on the part of enterprises and their workers and staff members, and is detrimental to the effective control of economic life by the state and to the success of the four modernizations.

This economic system does not conform with the objective law of development of the socialist economy. It does not fit the requirements of the development of commodity economy, nor does it fit the constantly growing and changing needs of the people. This system, under which everything — from planning to distribution of commodities and from employment to state revenues and expenditures — is controlled by the state, inevitably leads to highly centralized management using mainly administrative rather than economic means to run the economy. This management system and its methods make it impossible for the socialist commodity economy to grow rapidly. An inactive economy with poor returns has much to do with the shortcomings of the present economic system.

The prolonged practice of this management system originates from our understanding of the character of the socialist economy. In concrete terms, it is because in the past we did not regard the socialist economy as a planned commodity economy, but a semi-natural economy. Today, when we are restructuring the economic system, we must have a correct understanding of the nature of the socialist economy in our country. This is a prerequisite for correctly solving the problems of orientation, principle, policy and ways of restructuring the economic system.

The Present Nature of the Socialist Economy in China. How should one understand the nature of the socialist economy in our country at the present stage? There still exist a variety of views on this question. The majority hold the view that the socialist economy in China at the present stage is a planned socialist commodity economy with the public ownership of the means of production holding the dominant position. Of course, some people disagree. The main point at issue is whether or not commodities are defined as the means of production under the socialist system, and therefore whether or not the socialist economy is a commodity economy. This view once held the dominant position in China and some people still hold it today.

My personal view is that our economy at present is a planned socialist commodity economy with the public ownership of the means of production holding the dominant position. Of course, our commodity economy is different in nature from the commodity economy in a capitalist society. The capitalist commodity economy is built on the basis of capitalist private ownership and is unplanned. Our socialist commodity economy is built on the basis of public ownership of the means of production and is a planned commodity economy. They are different in nature.

To recognize the socialist economy as a commodity economy is a great advance in theory, a leap forward. We know that the question of socialist commodity production has been a question under discussion for the last century. There has been a debate among the Marxists. Comrades have all read Marx's "Critique of the Gotha Programme," written in 1875. In this book, Marx said that socialism is the primary stage of communism, under which there still exist the birthmarks of the old society. The birthmarks of the old society referred mainly to the principle of distribution to each according to his work. The socialism he pictured at that time would be built on the basis of highly-developed capitalism; no commodity-money relations would exist. Marx did not predict that countries whose capitalism was moderately developed — or even countries like ours where capitalism was only at the primary stage of development and natural economy was still predominant — could achieve socialist revolution and build socialism. Nor did he predict that countries like ours, with an underdeveloped economy, would have to make full use of the commodity and money categories in socialist construction. In other words, that the socialist economy must be a planned commodity economy.

There is another question for discussion: Can the highly developed capitalist countries abolish commodity production and money immediately after the working class wins political power and then build a socialist system? This question is now being considered by many Marxists. In recent years, I had opportunities to study in Japan, the United States and some other developed capitalist countries in Western Europe. A common view among members of our study group was that these countries are no longer the same as what Marx described in his time. Marx did not foresee the great development of capitalism one hundred years later. From the time when Marx published his "Critique of the Gotha Programme" 105 years ago, productive forces in the developed capitalist countries have multiplied several dozens of times. But even at the present level of economic development, can these countries abolish commodity economy and money immediately after the proletariat win political power without hindering economic development and creating social disorder? Evidently not. If the name of money at that time is changed to labour certificates — whose function remains the same as that of money — what's the point of doing it? If money is really abolished, that means the commodity economy is also abolished, and that will give rise to a host of problems.

We saw a department store in Tokyo, called the Mitsukoshi Department Store. Although not as large as stores such as Macy's in New York, it sells more than 500,000 commodity items. The largest department store in China, the Shanghai No. 1 Department Store on Nanjing Road, sells more than 40,000 commodity items. The Wangfujing Department Store in Beijing handles only 24,000 items. We saw a supermarket near San Francisco in the United States, in a small town with a population of 200,000. It deals in foodstuffs and handles more than 14,000 items. If commodity money is abolished, how will these goods be distributed effectively? It was only after tens of thousands of years following the birth of mankind and by repeated practice in life that money was invented. It has played a tremendous role in promoting the economic development of mankind. If it should be abolished now, something more rational must be found to replace it. This is not a simple matter. Evidently, the above-mentioned view of Marx's can only be regarded as a presumption which has to be tested through practice in the future generations. As long as social productive forces are not yet highly developed and as long as labour has not yet become the prime want of the people in their lives, it will not be practical to abolish the commodity economy and money.

In his book "The State and Revolution", written prior to the October Revolution, Lenin quoted Marx's words and expounded his views as dealt with in the "Critique of the Gotha Programme" and stood for the abolition of the commodity economy and money under socialism. After the victory of the October Revolution, the Soviet Union adopted the wartime communist economic system. Wartime communism was practised mainly because of imperialist intervention and the civil war, but it had also something to do with the theory of the abolition of the commodity economy and money. The subsequent attempt to abolish the commodity economy and money during the wartime communist period failed. Lenin summed up the experience and put forth the new economic policy in line with the existence of five economic sectors, particularly the existence of a small commodity economy and of small-scale production in large quantities in the Soviet Union.

The new economic policy sought to use the commodity/money relationship as a means of developing commerce and promoting the restoration and development of the socialist economy. Unfortunately, Lenin died soon after that writing and did not witness the completion of the socialist transformation. After the socialist transformation was completed, the five economic sectors no longer co-existed and there was only one single socialist economic sector. Should a commodity economy exist under such circumstances? Lenin did not give an answer.

The question was put before Stalin. The socialist transformation in the Soviet Union was completed under the leadership of Stalin. After the completion of agricultural collectivization, Stalin said that since two modes of public ownership co-existed, namely the ownership by the whole people and the collective ownership, there must be two classes of workers and peasants and there must be exchange. However, Stalin did not clearly explain or confirm for a long time following agricultural collectivization in the Soviet Union whether the exchange between the two public ownerships would be commodity exchange, and whether the law of value would still operate. Therefore, the question remained under dispute in the Soviet Union during that period.

It was only in his later years, that is in 1952, that Stalin recognized the existence of commodity production and commodity exchange between the two modes of public ownership. This came in his book, "Economic Problems Of Socialism in the U.S.S.R.," in which he said that the law of value must be utilized. The conclusion was made in the Soviet Union after 20 years of dispute. During the previous 20 years, they did not make good use of the commodity/money relationship and the law of value in handling the relations between the two public ownerships.

Commodity/Money Relationships. In his "Economic Problems of Socialism in U.S.S.R.," Stalin admitted that commodity/money relationships existed between the two public ownerships, but he still held the view that the law of value did not operate as a regulator in the production of raw materials in agriculture. He once more stressed the necessity of restricting commodity production and the function of the law of value. Therefore we can say that Stalin had never regarded the socialist economy completely as a commodity economy, but rather as a semi-natural economy. Based on this theory and understanding, the economic management system designed and practiced during the Stalin era was not instituted to suit the requirements of the commodity economy, but rather to suit the requirements of the semi-natural economy. It did not regard products as commodities for exchange at equal value but adopted the unitary directive plan, totally rejecting regulation through the market. It adopted highly-centralized administrative methods of management. The unitary directive plan treated the whole national economy as a factory. Indeed, Lenin spoke of all of society as a factory.

But, today, we find this question very complicated. If we take the whole society as a factory, many problems crop up. The highly centralized economic management sytem we adopted denied the enterprises their relative independence and also addressed the whole society as a factory. Are there not many problems when we do things this way? A leading comrade of the State Council said recently we have actually treated the whole country as a big enterprise in which the Ministry of Finance looks like its financial section and the other ministries and bureaus also function like their equivalent sections. It is impossible to run the national economy well in such a way. The experience of China and other countries shows that it is certainly impossible to run the economy well if the whole society is run as a factory.

Stalin's theory and practice exerted tremendous influence on socialist construction in our country. The economic management system model designed and adopted under his leadership also had a great influence on us. The economic management system which has been adopted and is still being adopted in our country is basically the Stalin model. Of course, some changes have been made. State control of planning, distribution, employment and budgeting forms the primary content of the Stalin model. To change this model, we must first of all remove the theoretical foundation for this model — that is to say, break down erroneous or outmoded conventions. If this is not done, it will be impossible for us to break down the old model that hinders economic development or to create a new model that promotes economic development.

Now we have broken down the model theoretically. We should say that this is an important result of emancipating our minds. Without the theoretical breakthrough, there would be no tentative ideas and practices for the reform now being made in the system. We have learnt to understand that under the socialist system not only the means of subsistence are commodities, but the means of production are also commodities, and not only the exchange between the ownership by the whole people and the collective ownership is commodity exchange, but the exchange among the state-owned enterprises is also commodity exchange. Of course, other scholars hold to a different view and have had their articles published in the press. This is also a good thing, because the truth is clarified through debate. We should carry forward the spirit of letting different schools of thought contend.

Thanks to progress on the theoretical level, not only means of subsistence but also means of production are now sold at market. For example, the Anshan Iron and Steel Company has opened a retail shop selling its steel products — something which never happened before. Today, machines are also sold at market. In 1979, machines and electrical products sold through the market accounted for 20% of the total output value of the machine-building industry; that percentage was expected to go up in 1980. Some factories will sell as much as 70—80% of their products through the market. Some people object to this, but practical experience has shown that this trend has played a positive role in promoting economic development. The experience also demonstrates that the economic system must be changed.

Orientation in the Structuring of the Economic System

In restructuring the economic system, we must adhere to a correct orientation. In light of the theory that the socialist economy is a commodity economy, some tentative ideas exist for the orientation of the reform: change the monopoly control by the central authorities and hand down the decision-making power in microeconomy to the enterprises; change the unitary practice of regulating production through plan and give play, under the guidance of state plans, to the function of the market in production regulation; and change the practice of sole reliance on administrative means to run the economy, combine economic means with administrative intervention and use mainly economic levers and economic laws and regulations to manage the economy.

In line with the general orientation for the reform, we have formed a general picture of the reform: gradually separate the power of the party and government from that of the enterprise; hand down some of that power; expand the decision-making power of the enterprises and the power of the workers in democratic management; encourage the establishment of all forms of economic combination; establish industrial organizations and reorganize the enterprises in a rational way; change the closed, single-outlet and multi-link commodity distribution system and establish a multi-outlet, minimal–link and open commodity distribution system; establish a wide variety of economic centers with the large and medium-sized cities as their backdrop and organize rational economic networks.

A number of reforms have to be made in planning, finance, taxation, pricing, banking, commerce, supply, foreign trade, labour and wages to supplement the restructuring of the economic management system. Obviously, the orientation and content of the restructuring must conform with the requirements of development of socialist commodity production and large-scale social production.

Recent Achievements in Restructuring Economic Management. A number of achievements have been made in the past two years in restructuring the economic management systems. We have extended the decision-making power of some factories; practiced the regulation of production through the market under the guidance of the state plans; promoted various forms of economic integration and coordination between urban and rural areas and among the different localities, industries and enterprises under guidance of the principle of making the best use of one's advantages while protecting competition and promoting integration; introduced the experiment of replacing government allocations by bank loans for investments in capital construction, technical innovations and technical transformation; combined industry with trade in promoting export business; and allowed multiple economic sectors and multiple modes of business operations to exist under the condition that public ownership of the means of production is absolutely predominant. Moreover, the experimental work of restructuring the industrial management system at the county level has been started. The experimental work of replacing profits with taxes and assuming sole responsibility for profits and losses as well as the experimental work of reforming the leadership system were also introduced in a limited number of enterprises.

Practical experience shows that the orientation for the reform in the past two years has been correct, marked achievements have been made, and the reform has played a positive role in inspiring the initiative of the people in all walks of life, in invigorating the economy and in increasing economic returns.

Some problems have also cropped up in the course of the reform, including the construction of unnecessary projects, the plan-less production of unwanted goods and the overissuance of bonuses and subsidies. These problems can all be solved only if macroeconomic guidance is strengthened rather than inhibited.

Two Views to Be Discussed on the Question of the Orientation for the Reform in the Economic Management System

One view to be discussed is whether it is appropriate for state-owned enterprises based on manual labour and with limited organic composition to assume sole responsibility for profits and losses while it is inappropriate for those enterprises with a higher level of productive forces and greater organic composition to assume responsibilities for profits and losses — with the state assuming responsibility for their profits and losses.

There is no doubt that small state-owned enterprises based on manual labour and with smaller organic composition should assume responsibility for their profits and losses. Even their workers can contract to run these enterprises on the basis of assuming full responsibility for profits and losses. However, it is not correct to think that other state-owned enterprises do not have to assume the responsibility for their profits and losses. The essence of the question is whether or not the state-owned enterprises are to be considered as relatively independent commodity producers. If this point is accepted, it must be acknowledged in principle that all state-owned enterprises must assume the responsibility for their profits and losses. This is so because the assumption of this responsibility by enterprises for their profits and losses under the guidance of the state plans is a relatively good economic management system and one that reflects the economic status of the enterprises as relatively independent commodity producers. If this principle is negated, the economic status of the enterprises is in fact negated. Because in actual economic life, the economic status of the enterprises is manifested in the form of assuming responsibility for their profits and losses. This point is made quite clear by the explanation that the socialist economy is a planned commodity economy, and there is no need to say more on it.

Application of Marx's Socialist Nationalization to China. What does demand a detailed discussion is the following point of view:

As stated above, there are many shortcomings in the present economic management system in

China and an urgent reform is needed. But the point is to reform the concrete method of managing ownership in a socialist country, namely, under the present economic management system; the point is not to negate totally socialist state ownership proper. However, some people hold the view that the root cause for the shortcomings in our economic life is that the development of productive forces in China has not yet reached the level of practicing socialist state ownership. This view states that the way out is to reform state ownership itself and to retreat back to collective ownership.

Obviously, this view is not compatible with the Marxist theory of socialist nationalization, nor with the actual conditions in our country.

On what was the Marxist theory of socialist nationalization based? It was put forth in the light of the contradiction between social production and capitalist private ownership of the means of production in capitalist production, and was meant to solve this basic contradiction. This brilliant thesis was clearly dealt with by the founders of Marxism in the "Manifesto of the Communist Party," which marked the birth of scientific socialism. Later, Engels expounded it in his huge scientific work, "Anti-Duhring."

The present question is whether this Marxist principle applies to China. In semi-colonial and semi-feudal old China, the degree of development of capitalism was far behind that in Western capitalist countries. However, "China's modern industry, although the value of its output amounts to only about 10% of the total value of output of the national economy, is extremely concentrated; the largest and most important part of the capital is concentrated in the hands of the imperialists and their lackeys, the Chinese bureaucrat-capitalists." (*Selected Works of Mao Tse-tung*, Vol. IV, p. 369, "Report to the Second Plenary Session of the Seventh Central Committee of the C.P.C." Beijing: Foreign Languages Press, 1969). The basic contradictions of capitalism stood out sharply here. There is no doubt that after the state was established under the dictatorship of the proletariat, the socialist nationalization of these capitalist enterprises ought to be achieved through confiscation. In the national capitalist economy, the degree of social production was lower, but the basic capitalist contradictions existed. The proletarian state must, through peaceful transformation, change it into a socialist state-owned economy. In short, the Marxist theory about socialist nationalization applies to China in principle. Of course, because capitalism was not well developed in old China, the scope of socialist nationalization was narrower than it would be in the capitalist countries after the proletariat in those countries win political power. But this is a question of the scope of socialist nationalization, not a question of inability to achieve socialist nationalization.

It should be pointed out further that since the founding of New China its economic development has met with serious setbacks under the influence of prolonged "Left" mistakes, especially owing to the counter-revolutionary disruption by Lin Biao, Jiang Qing and their ilk. However, the socialist industry has greatly developed and the degree of socialization of production as a whole has risen. How under such circumstances can socialist state ownership retreat back to collective ownership against the requirement of socialization of production? Of course, under the influence of "Left" mistakes there had emerged the erroneous tendency of overzealousness in bringing about the so-called "transition" from collective ownership to socialist state ownership (namely the ownership by the whole people) by turning large numbers of collectively-owned industrial enterprises in the urban areas into enterprises under quasi-ownership by the whole people and turning a number of small enterprises that, based on hand labour, should have become collectively owned into state-owned enterprises. Turning back enterprises that function under quasi-ownership by the whole people into truly collectively owned enterprises in the light of their productive forces seems superficially to be a "retreat," but in fact is a correction of the mistake. But this should be treated as a local question and not as an overall question. In other words, the issue is not that socialist nationalization should not be practiced, or that all socialist state-owned enterprises should be turned back into collectively-owned enterprises.

If, as some people propose, all of the socialist state-owned enterprises are changed into collective enterprises, how then shall the planned development of the national economy be ensured and the anarchy of social production be avoided? If socialist state ownership no longer existed, would it be possible for collective ownership to be consolidated and developed forever or could the state under the dictatorship of the proletariat be firmly built forever on the basis of the economy under the collective ownership? All these questions have to be treated earnestly and seriously.

III. On Readjustment, Restructuring, Consolidation and Improvement; Industrial Reorganization; and the Rationalization of Enterprise Organization

To achieve industrial reorganization and rationalize the organization of enterprises, the primary and fundamental link is the reorganization of industry and the establishment of various forms of economic complexes for integrating enterprises on the principle of specialization, coordination and economic rationality.

Establish Various Forms of Economic Complexes for the Integration of Enterprises

The integration of enterprises is an objective requirement of the development of the productive forces of modern society, an objective requirement of technological progress. In the light of the experience in the development of capitalist production towards the end of the 19th century, Lenin pointed out: "Technical progress must entail the specialization of different parts of production, their socialization." (Lenin, *Collected Works*, Vol. I, 'On the So-called Market Questions', p. 101. Moscow: Foreign Languages Publishing House, 1960). Current technological progress has greatly pushed forward the specialization of products, of parts, of technologies, of production, of raw materials and of auxiliary production. This is one aspect of the matter. On the other hand, since social production as a whole is an organic whole, different sectors and different enterprises become more and more interdependent as a result of the increasing specialization. This calls for integration on a broad scale to suit the requirements of specialization and coordination. Lenin said that "A very important feature of capitalism in its highest stage of development is so-called combination of production, that is to say, the grouping in a single enterprise of different branches of industry." (Lenin, *Selected Works*, Vol. I, Part II, p. 445, "Imperialism, the Highest Stage of Capitalism." Moscow: Foreign Languages Publishing House, 1952). The growth of this combination, on the one hand, was the result of the development of modern capitalist relations of production and, on the other, of the development of modern social productive forces. In a general sense, this system of combination also applies to a socialist society.

Comparisons with Japan and the United States. The reality in China is that after 30 years of socialist construction, industrial production and technology have developed greatly as compared with the underdeveloped industry of semi-colonial and semi-feudal old China. This development called for the wide-scale expansion of specialization and coordination. The serious problem of establishing big and small all-embracing production systems is found widely throughout industrial organizations; their level of specialization and coordination is very low. According to a 1978 investigation made by the First Ministry of Machine-Building Industry, only 162 of the 6,057 enterprises under the ministry were specialized cast-iron plants, producing only 18% of the total output; there were only 52 plants specialized in the production of forgings, producing only 9% of the total output of forgings. The cast-iron production of specialized plants in Japan accounts for more than 60% of total output and that of the forgings, 84%. About 70% of all engineering products made in the United States are produced by specialized factories in terms of the total value of sales; 1.2% of the factories produce castings and forgings for themselves and 4.46% have special equipment for heat treatment. Many of the large machine-building plants in Japan and the United States produce only the principal parts of the machinery; almost all of their raw materials, blanks and spare parts are produced by a wide production network established through economic integration. It is true that the level of productive forces in our country is still relatively low and it is impossible for the level of specialized production to reach the height of the United States and Japan, but the problem of the incompatibility of the low degree of specialization in our country with the needs of development of production has to be solved. The all-embracing production systems in many industrial enterprises is an important factor in the low productivity and poor returns in industry. Obviously, to modernize China's industry it will be essential to reorganize industrial production and to achieve the integration of enterprises on the principle of specialization and coordination.

Reorganization and Integration. The reorganization of industry and integration of enterprises is called for by the readjustment of the national economy. At present, the national economy in China is totally out of balance. Some of the departments and enterprises have excessive productive capacity while others are short of productive capacity. Experience shows that the integration of enterprises greatly helps to reduce overproduction of unwanted goods and to expand production of wanted goods. In this sense, it can well be said that integration means readjustment. Readjustment not only entails the integration of enterprises, but also the consolidation of enterprises resulting from readjustment, including the closing down, suspension, merging or transfer of part of the enterprises. In turn, this provides favourable conditions for the integration of enterprises, raising the management level and increasing economic returns.

The reorganization of industry and integration of enterprises is also called for by restructuring the economic management system. The characteristics of the existing economic management system are high centralism and administrative control. Highly centralized leadership in fact means leadership of the economic departments at the central and provincial, municipal and autonomous regional levels. This kind of administrative control has severed economic ties among the different industries and localities. This is incompatible with the requirement of the development of the socialist commodity economy. The integration of enterprises, especially those in different industries and localities, helps break down barriers among different sectors and localities in a way that suits the needs of the development of socialist commodity production. In this sense, it can also be said that integration means reform. However, this reform not only calls for the integration of enterprises, but also promotes competition among the enterprises as a result of the extension of the decision-making powers of the enterprises and of regulation through the market under the guidance of the state plans. This, in turn, promotes the integration of enterprises.

In short, the reorganization of industry and integration of enterprises are requirements of expanding socialist construction in China and of implementing the principle of economic readjustment.

However, reorganization and integration must be in conformity with reality and may take different forms. To sum up, there are the following forms:

1. Combinations of producing, marketing and transporting enterprises.

2. Combinations of capital funds, technologies, manpower and materials.

3. Joint exploitation of resources, joint production and joint marketing, and agricultural-industrial-commercial complexes.

4. Mother-and-son companies — combinations of several factories and communes or their subdivisions through the pooling of capital funds, or combinations of several factories for joint production and marketing.

5. Combinations of state-owned enterprises, of state-owned enterprises and collective enterprises, of collective enterprises and of urban and rural enterprises.

How to Reorganize Industry and Integrate Enterprises. Shall this be done entirely by order from the higher authorities? Or entirely through "free love"? The practical experience in recent years has shown that the correct way to achieve this is to observe objective economic laws, and combine consultation from bottom to top with necessary administrative intervention on the basis of the principle of voluntariness and mutual benefit. Especially at a time when administrative control by ministries and local authorities is still gravely hindering the industrial reorganization and integration of enterprises, it is all the more necessary for the state to use its authority to break down these restrictions and open the way for reorganization and integration. The industrial reorganization and integration of enterprises must suit local conditions and should not follow just one model. At the initial stage, the integration of enterprises should be started on a smaller scale; the number of items for joint production should be fewer; the degree of integration should be lower; and the units joining the integrated corporations should be near to each other. Of course, there are exceptions. For example, some enterprises already have a higher degree of socialization in production and more experience in management; it is both possible and necessary for them to form large national or regional economic combinations with unified supply, production and marketing systems. In short, the problems should be solved in a down-to-earth manner.

Whether in a capitalist or a socialist society, the development of modern productive forces gives rise to the tendency of integration of enterprises. But integration processes in the two societies are totally different in their social economic nature:

1. The combination and monopoly of capitalist enterprises proceeded on the basis of capitalist private ownership of the means of production. Therefore, after such combinations and monopolies are formed, they could restrict free competition but could not eliminate competition. The competition among monopoly enterprises, especially between the monopoly enterprises and other enterprises, would become even more acute. Dwelling on this point, Lenin said: "Here we no longer have competition between small and large, technically developed and backward enterprises. We see here the monopolists throttling those which do not submit to them, to their yoke, to their dictation." (Lenin, *Selected Works*, Vol. I, Part 2, 'Imperialism, the Highest Stage of Capitalism,' p. 455). The integration of socialist enterprises proceeds on the basis of public ownership of the means of production. Relationships among integrated enterprises or between the integrated and the unintegrated are relationships between the socialist enterprises. There is also competition

among them, but it is based on the identity of their fundamental interest and the difference of their local interests. Relationships between capitalist monopoly enterprises as the oppressors and non-monopoly enterprises as the oppressed no longer exist.

2. The integration and monopoly of capitalist enterprises was the result of the spontaneous action of capitalist economic laws. Once the combinations and monopolies were formed, it was still impossible to eliminate totally the anarchy of social production. Since World War II, the capitalist countries have strengthened their control over the combination and production of enterprises. But this control has not been able to affect spontaneous economic behaviour and therefore economic crises have broken out one after another. The integration of socialist enterprises is the result of the action of socialist economic laws and is developed under the guidance of state plans and in ways to accord with the requirements of the planned and proportionate development of the national economy. Therefore, the integration of enterprises should promote the balanced development of the national economy.

3. The development of the combination of capitalist enterprises is related to capitalist ownership only in form and is suited to the requirements of socialization in production to a certain extent. In essence, however, more and more capital is concentrated in the hands of a few capitalists and the basic contradictions of capitalism have become more and more acute.

Under the socialist system, the integration of enterprises is a requirement of the development of social production as well as a means to promote the socialization of production. The socialization of production coincides with the nature of socialist public ownership; that is, it lays the material foundation for the consolidation and strengthening of the socialist system. All of this demonstrates the superiority of socialist relations of production over capitalist relations of production.

Establish Industrial Associations for the Integration of Different Industries

To establish industrial associations for the integration of different industries is also an important part of the rationalization of industrial organizations.

China's present system of management over the enterprises is a system of administrative management by different industrial ministries set up on the basis of the division among the large industries. The essential shortcomings in this management system are:

1. The enterprises are treated as appendages to the state administrative organs. This does not suit the requirement of the economic status of the enterprises as relatively independent commodity producers. Therefore, it gravely hampers the initiative of the enterprises.

2. Absolute control by different ministries has cut off horizontal economic ties among the enterprises. This is incompatible with the requirements of modern social production and commodity economy.

3. With the socialization of production, the division of labour is even more developed. The ministerial control of enterprises is increasingly incompatible with the requirements of development of industrial modernization.

4. Under the present industrial management system, a central industrial ministry can control only the enterprises directly under it but not the enterprises in the same industry or under other ministries and localities. It is responsible for the production of products made by enterprises under it, but not for the multiple use of natural resources. In fact, however, the production of any product by any industry is not the product of one industry, but a product of two or more industries. Therefore, the main problem in the present management system is not only that it has controlled what it should not but, even more important, it has not controlled what it should have. To change this, it is necessary to establish industrial associations for the integration of different industries in ways other than handing over the microeconomic decision-making power to the enterprises and integrating enterprises under the guidance of the state.

The nature and task of an industrial association can be described thus: It is a coordinating organ formed by enterprises in the same industry on a voluntary basis. It is an integration of management; namely, management under a council democratically elected by the enterprises joining the association. The association can define due rights and obligations for its member enterprises. The special feature of such an association is that it is not a state administrative organ but a semi-official or non-official organization under state guidance and endowed with certain administrative power. Although it is not an economic combination, it has certain economic functions. It operates as a bridge between the state and the enterprises or between enterprises. To the government, it represents the industries; to the enterprises, it represents the government in democratic consultation.

The functions of an industrial association are:

1. To draft plans for the development of that industry in accordance with state policies and plans; coordinate the activities of the enterprises in the same industry; provide liaison, guidance, services and consultation.

2. Develop the specifications and technical standards for the products produced by the industry.

3. Organize cooperation among the enterprises concerned.

4. Organize exchange of technical information among the enterprises of the same industry.

5. Provide assistance in the training of managerial and technical personnel.

To establish industrial associations for the integration of industries helps to implement state policies and plans; to meet the requirements of the readjustment of the national economy; to readjust the production of unwanted and wanted goods; to avoid construction of unnecessary plants and production of overstocked goods; to reorganize industry on the principle of specialization and coordination and to promote the integration of enterprises; and to break down absolute control by the ministries and blockades by the localities.

In these ways, the associations can replace the government for some functions in running the economy. All this shows that to establish industrial associations for the integration of industries is both a requirement of the readjustment and reform as well as an important way of achieving their objectives.

As an historical phenomenon, industrial associations or guilds were born as early as in feudal society when a commodity economy began to develop. In the developed capitalist countries of the present day, industrial associations have been widely developed. But the industrial associations which China is going to establish and develop are totally different in nature from guilds in feudal society or from industrial associations in capitalist countries. Guilds in feudal society were based on simple commodity production and were economic organizations of a feudal character; the purpose of guild activities were to serve the interests of those who joined them. Industrial associations in capitalist society are based on capitalist commodity production and are capitalist economic organizations; their purpose is to coordinate contradictions among the capitalists and to serve the interests of the capitalists in increasing exploitation of the working class for greater profits. Industrial associations in socialist society are socialist organizations based on socialist commodity production; the purpose of their activities is to better develop socialist production and to improve the material and cultural life of the people on the basis of the development of production.

Establish Economic Centres for Integration of Regions

The establishment of economic centres for the integration of regions plays an important part in the rationalization of economic organizations.

As a whole, the economic centres are centres for social economic activities in a given sphere (or activities of social reproduction), namely, activities that include production, exchange, distribution and consumption. They operate within the setting of cities of considerable size and are products of the development of the commodity economy to a given stage. Economic centres appeared with the rise and growth of cities and with the growth of the commodity economy of the slave society and the feudal society. But the large economic centres, especially the national economic centres, took form along with the growth of the capitalist commodity economy. Obviously, the formation of the national economic centres was bound up with the formation of unified national markets; but the formation of unified national markets was the product of the development of capitalist commodity production. However, the development of economic centres in the modern sense is the outcome of the development of modern capitalist commodity production as well as of the development of modern industry and modern science and technology.

Socialist economic centres also depend on cities and are also products of the development of the commodity economy. They are totally different in social-economic character from preceding economic centres. That is to say, they are based not on the commodity economy under the private ownership of the means of production but on the commodity economy under ownership by the whole people. Therefore their formation and development, unlike that of the previous centres, were not products of the spontaneous development of the commodity economy but was achieved under the guidance of state plans. Relationships between the economic centres and the non-economic areas connected with the economic centres are not those of antagonistic interests as under the private ownership of means of production, but are relationships with an identity of fundamental interests and differences in their local interests.

The economic centres can be set up in this way: integration of regions with cities of considerable size as their centres. These are not economic complexes, although there will exist coordinating committees for the economic centres elected on a democratic basis by various economic organizations (such as enterprises, economic complexes of all forms and industrial associations) and these will take part in the activities of the economic centres. Such committees will coordinate the activities of the economic organizations under the guidance of state policies and plans. They are not administrative organs of the state, but they can gradually take up part of the functions of the state in running the economy under the guidance of the state.

In this way, the economic centres will become an important part of the whole socialist commodity economic system and an important factor for promoting the planned development of the commodity economy under the conditions of socialism. At present, the establishment of economic centres helps to promote the development of economic readjustment and to break down the absolute control by the ministries and localities, and therefore forms an important part of readjustment and reform.

Here we can see that under the socialist system the functions of the economic centres are totally different from previous economic centres. This is to say, they do not serve the exploiting classes but serve the purpose of developing the socialist commodity economy and, in the final analysis, the purpose of improving the material and cultural life of the people.

Learning from Some of the Experiences of Capitalist Countries. We have underlined the fundamental differences between the socialist and capitalist combinations of enterprises, industrial organizations and economic centres. But this does not mean that some of the concrete experiences in these respects in capitalist countries are useless to us. The point is that the socialist economic system is totally different from the capitalist one, although the combinations of enterprises, industrial organizations and economic centres under both social economic systems are the products of the development of the commodity economy with modern social production as its material basis. In this respect, they have something in common, and therefore we can also learn from some of the experiences of the capitalist countries. For example, the combination of modern capitalist enterprises is characterized by the tendency to form monopolies. However, capitalist countries as representatives of the interests of capital also pay attention to upholding the interests of competition. Therefore, in the combination of enterprises, capitalist society also gives attention to opposing the tendency of monopoly. In view of this, when we are organizing united corporations we must not allow monopoly control or the elimination of competition. The capitalist combinations of enterprises also oppose the centralization of power among themselves. This also tells us that in organizing the corporations we must correctly handle relations between centralization and decentralization of power in the organization of the corporations at different levels. Moreover, we must correctly handle the relations of material interests among them.

Earmarks of a Rational Economic Organization

Based on the analyses made above, I think the earmarks of a rationalization of economic organization are as follows:

1. Gradual separation of government power from enterprise management so that the enterprises will become relatively independent commodity producers.

2. Organization of economic complexes of various forms on the principle of specialization, coordination and economic rationality.

3. Establishment of industrial organizations as an important link between the government and the enterprises.

4. Establishment of a number of economic centres with industrially concentrated cities as their settings to organize economic integration on a nationwide or regional basis and exercise some managerial functions.

5. Tightening of state control of the macroeconomy while breaking down the multi-departmental and multi-level administrative management system.

When all this is achieved, China's socialist commodity economic organizations can be integrated into a network. At the same time, some of the managerial functions of the administrative organs of the state will be exercised by economic organizations under the guidance of the state plans. In this way, the separation of administrative power from enterprise management – to make the enterprises relatively independent commodity producers – will materialize.

In short, as long as we unswervingly follow

the line adopted at the Third Plenary Session of the 11th Central Committee of the Chinese Communist Party, and implement the principle of economic readjustment in all economic fields and gradually rationalize the economic structure, economic system and economic organizations, the future is bright for the great cause of socialist modernization in our country. And we should be confident of this!

3. CHINA'S ECONOMIC READJUSTMENT AND REORIENTATION
By Fang Weizhong

It has been more than two years since China started its economic readjustment. It is necessary now to clearly explain the reasons for the economic readjustment and to assess the work of the past two years, future tasks and prospects for the readjustment. The following discussion therefore attempts to present to our readers an outline of all these aspects.

I. The Dual Significance of Economic Readjustment

The policy of readjusting, restructuring, consolidating and improving the national economy was adopted on the basis of intensive studies and discussions by the Central Committee of the Communist Party of China and the State Council in March 1979. The Second Session of the Fifth National People's Congress, held in June of that year, discussed and approved the Report on the Work of the Government and decided to shift the emphasis in the work of the whole nation to the orbit of socialist construction and socialist modernization. It defined the implementation of the policy of readjusting, restructuring, consolidating and improving the national economy as the "first battle" for the four modernizations following the shift of the focus of our work. The formulation of this policy meant a new start for a down-to-earth approach to our economic work.

The fundamental cause for the readjustment of the national economy was a serious imbalance in economic growth, mainly manifested by three aspects:

1. *Over-extended capital construction and an excessively high rate of accumulation affected improvement of the people's livelihood and the balance of financial and material resources.*

This tendency was discernable in 1970, when total investment in capital construction in that year shot up to 29,500 million yuan from 17,100 million yuan in 1965 and 18,600 million yuan in 1969; it then made another climb to about 36,000 million yuan in 1976. Of the total investment in 1976, the portion covered by the national budget — excluding the investment put up by various enterprises, localities and departments — was 29,400 million yuan, as against a range of 15,400 million to 16,600 million yuan during the years 1965 to 1969, and as against 25,500 million yuan in 1970. With the growth of investment in capital construction and excessive expansion of liquid assets, the rate of accumulation in the national income grew rapidly. The accumulation rate was 27.1% in 1965, and has remained above 30% since 1970.

Due to the interference and sabotage by Lin Biao and the Gang of Four, coupled with the excessive magnitude of capital construction and an excessively high rate of accumulation, little improvement was made in the people's livelihood during the period 1966 to 1976; in some areas, in fact, living standards fell. For peasants in the vast rural areas, per capita income from the collective economy averaged 62.8 yuan in 1976 as against 52.3 yuan in 1965, an increase of only 10.5 yuan over the entire 11 years. Thus, the annual increase of per capita income averaged less than 1 yuan. Because of inadequate supplies of food grain and very small amounts of cash payments — in some areas, even no cash payment — life was still very hard indeed for the peasants in many people's communes and production teams.

So far as the workers and staff in urban areas are concerned, the total wage bill somewhat increased due to the increase in the number of workers and staff. However, since the standard wage system had not been adjusted for a long period, the average per capita wage of the workers and staff somewhat decreased. The wages of workers and staff members in units owned by the whole people averaged 652 yuan in 1965, and declined to 605 yuan in 1976. Insufficient appropriations for urban construction led to acute housing shortages and other problems of people's livelihood. Yearly per capita consumption, both rural and urban, as calculated from consumption funds, was 161 yuan in 1976, as compared with 125 yuan in 1965, with an increase of only 2.2% a year if price factors are excluded. The growth of consumption levels in rural areas was slower than that in urban areas. Thus, improvement of the people's livelihood was not only a strong desire of the people, but also a serious political challenge.

Efforts to Restore the Disrupted Economy. After smashing the Gang of Four, the party and government made arduous efforts to restore and develop the disrupted national economy. That approach was absolutely correct. And remarkable achievements were made. The people also benefited from the restoration and development of production. However, because of our lack of careful analysis of the economic situation and our inadequate understanding of the serious disproportions between consumption and accumulation, as well as our impetuosity in the modernization drive, a Ten-

Year Plan with high production targets and an excessive range of capital construction was drafted.

This resulted in a further expansion of investment in capital construction and a rise of the proportion of accumulation in the national income, instead of proportionately reducing the scope of capital construction and rehabilitating the people's livelihood. Total investment in capital construction in 1978 reached 48,000 million yuan, of which state investment accounted for 39,600 million yuan, an increase of 10,200 million yuan over 1976. With an increase of accumulation in other areas, the accumulation rate reached 36.5% in 1978, a level rarely seen in the past. Owing to excessive expansion of capital construction and over-centralization of state finances, state revenues in 1978 accounted for 37.2% of national income, which was abnormally high. Yet, state revenues and expenditures were still difficult to balance. More than 8 million tons of rolled steel were imported in 1978, an increase of more than 60% over the previous year. However, steel was still in short supply. Thus, capital construction was over-expanded at the expense of consumption and markets, and this seriously affected the raising of people's living standards.

Furthermore, had the Ten-Year Plan not been called off, a great number of projects, including those built with imported equipment, would have to have been placed under construction, giving rise to further large increases in accumulation and appropriations for capital construction set aside both in national income and state revenue, thus leading to an even more serious imbalance between revenues and expenditures, and between supplies of and demands for materials. Under these circumstances, the people's standard of living would have been worsened instead of stabilized. This would eventually dampen the enthusiasm of the masses and bring great losses to the socialist modernization, albeit quickening its pace. That was an important reason for readjusting our national economy.

2. *Too rapid growth of heavy industry and slow development of agriculture and light industry led to an irrational industrial structure.*

Old China was extremely weak in heavy industry. In order to meet the demands for consumer goods and for national defence, it is definitely necessary to attach importance to heavy industry, the means of production. However, due to over-emphasis on heavy industry and corresponding neglect of agriculture and light industry, the ratio of agriculture and light industry to the gross output value of industry and agriculture declined rapidly. Calculated in constant prices, the proportion of agricultural output value to the gross output value of industry and agriculture was trending down to 25.6% in 1978 — from 43.5% in 1957, 29.8% in 1965 and 28.8% in 1976. Meanwhile, the ratio of the output value of light industry to the total output value of industry declined to 42.7% in 1978 from 51.7% in 1957, 50.4% in 1965 and 43.7% in 1976. The slow development of agriculture and light industry thus slackened the pace to improve the people's livelihood.

In the pursuit of high-speed development of heavy industry, great efforts had to be made by heavy industry to supply its own needs. Particularly, in order to develop the iron and steel industry, the policy of "taking steel as the key link" was long over-emphasized. This policy required not only large funds to be set aside for the construction of the steel industry itself, but also for the construction of related industries such as fuel and power, chemicals and heavy machine-building. As a result, a huge amount of iron and steel was consumed in these respects. Therefore, despite the rapid growth of heavy industry and a considerable rise in iron and steel output, agriculture and light industry still could not get enough fuel and power, raw materials, machinery and equipment. Even the demand for rolled steel in making small farm tools was not adequately met. A variety of rolled steel products needed for light industry had to be imported.

Most of the targets in the Ten-Year Plan drafted in 1978 were set too high. For example, the plan called for 60 million tons of steel to be produced annually by 1985. In order to fulfill this target, tremendous financial and material resources would be allocated to the construction of heavy industry and to the iron and steel industry in particular. This would lead to further imbalances between agriculture, light industry and heavy industry. Here was another reason for economic readjustment.

3. *Within heavy industry itself, fuel- and power-consuming industries and particularly processing industries developed far beyond the capacity for energy supply. On the other hand, a serious imbalance between extraction, tunnelling and recoverable reserves emerged in the fuel and power industries, and mainly in the petroleum and coal industries because of a long period of over-extraction. All this required readjusting the arrangements for production and construction.*

In general, China's energy development has not been slow. Coal output increased to 618 million tons in 1978 as against 70 million tons in 1953; crude oil reached 104.05 million tons in 1978 as against 1.46 million tons in 1958. The total output of primary energy topped 600 million tons of standard coal, which was quite considerable. During this period, however, industrial enterprises which consumed excessive energy mushroomed across the nation. Coupled with heavy waste in the utilization of energy, this led to a serious energy shortage. As a result, many enterprises were under-utilized, some of them constantly suffering from partial or total shut-downs. In addition, several newly completed projects could not go into production because of insufficient fuel and power supplies.

The output of crude oil increased 4.8 times during the nine years from 1970 to 1978, averaging an increase of 9.15 million tons or 19% a year. Yet the growth of recoverable oil reserves lagged far behind that of production. Many oilfields found it difficult to continuously increase their output, and they faced the danger of destroying the wells by continued exploitation. Coal output increased 2.3 times in these nine years, realizing an average increase of 39 million tons or 9.8% per year. But due to backward techniques in extraction and tunnelling, a number of coal mines found it difficult to go on expanding their production, and some even ceased extraction entirely. Therefore it was necessary to readjust the national economy so as to bring about a harmonious proportion between extraction and recoverable reserves and between extraction and tunnelling in the petroleum and coal industries, and to bring the development of other sectors of the national economy into proportion with that of energy.

From the above-mentioned three aspects, it is apparent that the policy of readjusting the national economy put forward by the Central Committee of the Party and the State Council is absolutely necessary and completely correct. The immediate significance of the economic readjustment is to alter the serious imbalance in the national economy so as to surmount the difficulties before us. Otherwise, our socialist modernization programme cannot advance smoothly.

It should be noted that readjustment of the national economy is not only designed to solve current problems. It is of more profound significance for us to rectify our thinking in guiding economic work, to change our guiding principles and policies for economic development and to blaze a new trail suited to actual conditions in China for the growth of the national economy, and thereby bringing socialist modernization into an orbit of coordinated, steady and healthy development.

Past Achievements and Mistakes. Since Liberation in 1949, the Chinese people have, under the leadership of the party and the government, exerted every effort in large-scale socialist construction and made remarkable achievements. Following the completion of socialist transformation, the system of exploitation was abolished and socialist public ownership has since held a dominant position in the economy as a whole. An independent and comparatively comprehensive system of industry and national economy has been established on the basis of the extremely backward economy of old China. Much progress has been made in science, education and culture. A series of new branches in science and technology has been established from scratch. Remarkable improvements have been made in the people's livelihood in both rural and urban areas as compared with the situation before Liberation. However, China is a big country with a backward economy and with varied conditions. Due to lack of experience in socialist construction and over-eagerness to change poverty and backwardness, we paid too much attention to the needs of economic development and neglected its possibilities. Coupled with many defects and mistakes in our guiding work, especially the "Left" mistakes of seeking hasty successes, our national economy suffered several major setbacks. Had we not managed our economy in this way, we would have achieved more.

In the past 31 years, we did a fairly good job during the Rehabilitation period (1950-1952) and the First Five-Year Plan period (1953-1957). Not only had the targets for recovering and developing the national economy been fulfilled on time, but the relationship between the growth of production, the improvement of the people's livelihood and the economy as a whole had been handled in a comparatively coordinated way.

During the 1958-1960 period, our economy became seriously imbalanced because of setting "high targets," stirring up a "communist wind" and being over-anxious to make achievements. This brought great difficulties to both production and construction and to the people's livelihood as well. In the latter half of 1960, the Party Central Committee and the State Council put forward the policy of readjusting, restructuring, consolidating and raising standards. Tremendous efforts were made and the national economy recovered and developed rapidly.

During the ten-year "cultural revolution" (1966-1976), the masses and the great majority of cadres, despite counter-revolutionary sabotage by Lin Biao and the Gang of Four, did their utmost to maintain and even develop production under extremely difficult circumstances. After 1970, however, we still sought after high quotas in guiding our economic work, and overextended the scope of capital construction. Coupled with the disrupted economic order, our national economy became seriously imbalanced once again. After smashing the Gang of Four, everybody wanted to make up for lost time as quickly as possible. However, we underestimated the serious ravages of the previous ten years. Moreover, we did not fully sum up the positive and negative lessons and experiences in economic construction since the founding of New China. We were still over-eager to make greater achievements and put forward some excessively high and unrealistic targets, thus further expanding the scope of capital construction which had already been overextended. We correctly adopted the policy of using foreign funds and importing new technologies but, due to lack of experience, the magnitude of imported plants and equipment exceeded our capacity. This mistake of impetuosity and rash advance intensified economic disproportions, aggravated financial and economic difficulties and bred new danger in our economy.

The experience of the past 31 years proves that our party and government were working whole-heartedly for the well-being of the people and that they attained wide-ranging achievements. The reasons why we were anxious to make achievements in the past was that, in the main, we wished to make our country prosperous and powerful as soon as possible so that fundamental improvements could be made in the people's livelihood. However, the lack of intensive study of national conditions and the failure to carefully calculate the actual possibilities and effects resulted in "more haste, less speed." Therefore, in the current readjustment of the national economy, we must learn from the lessons and experiences gained in the past so that we can shake off the yoke of "Left" ideas and practices in our economic work. We must proceed from the fact that China has a population of nearly 1,000 million, 80% being peasants. We must run various undertakings according to our ability, proceed sequentially and advance systematically, and pay attention to actual results. Our great cause of socialist modernization should be closely integrated with gradual improvement of the people's livelihood. Our goal should be reached steadily. Major twists and turns in future economic construction should be avoided as far as possible. In this sense, the current readjustment of the national economy is not only an important step which will protect against possible difficulties. It is also the most far-reaching and fundamental reorientation in our economic reconstruction since the founding of New China.

II. Achievements and Problems in the First Stage of Economic Readjustment

Two years have elapsed since the beginning of economic readjustment. This two-year period (1979-1980) can be seen as the first stage in economic readjustment.

During the past two years, economic readjustment was mainly undertaken in the following three aspects:

1. *Readjustment of the ratio between accumulation and consumption and raising the people's income in both rural and urban areas.*

With respect to the peasants, readjustment has come about mainly through an increase in purchasing prices of major farm and sideline products and through reducing or exempting from taxes the poorer communes and production teams. In 1977, the state raised the purchasing prices of such major farm and sideline products as grain, cotton, oil-bearing crops, sugarcane, sugarbeets, hogs, beef cattle, sheep, eggs, aquatic products and silkworm cocoons; and, in 1980, increases in the purchasing prices of some farm and sideline products such as cotton, sheep and goat skins, jute and ambary hemp, timber, raw lacquer and tung oil. As a result, the overall index of the purchasing prices of farm and sideline products increased by 22.1% in 1979, and by a further 7.1% in 1980. Thanks to the growth of agricultural production and to large increases in the purchasing prices of farm and sideline products, the sales of these products brought the peasants an additional 25,800 million yuan of income over two years. They further benefited by about 4,500 million yuan from the reduction and remission of agricultural taxes and taxes on industries run by the communes and production brigades. Altogether, the peasants gained 30,000 million yuan.

As for urban inhabitants, the major measures were to provide more jobs, to raise wages and salaries of part of the workers and staff, and to universally institute the bonus system. In 1979, 9.03 million jobs were provided in towns and cities throughout the country; an additional 9.05 million jobs were provided in 1980. Therefore, 18.08 million jobs were provided over these two years. In 1977, the average number of persons supported by a worker was 2.06 persons (including himself); this figure declined to 1.8 persons in 1980. Forty percent of the workers and staff received wage increases, and wage categories were adjusted in 1979. Coupled with the adoption of piece-work pay on a wider scale and the universal institution of a reward system as well as subsidies for price rises in non-staple foods, the total wage bill of workers and staff went up to 77,300 million yuan in 1980, as against 56,900 million yuan in 1978, an increase of 20,400 million yuan over two years, or a 13.6% increase for 1979 and a 19.5% increase for 1980, respectively. The annual per capita income of workers and staff in units owned by the whole people also increased from 644 yuan in 1978 to

803 yuan in 1980, an increase of 159 yuan in two years, or a 7.6% increase in 1979 and a 6% increase in 1980 if the factor of rising prices is deducted.

With the growth of people's income in both rural and urban areas, there was a considerable increase in the level of consumption. The nation's average level of per capita consumption increased to 224 yuan in 1980 from 174 yuan in 1978, an increase of 50 yuan in two years, or an increase of 25 yuan per annum — as against only 3 yuan for the entire period of 20 years from 1957 to 1977. Even if price increases in these two years are deducted, the increase of the nation's level of consumption was still much higher than that over the previous 20 years. Therefore, the achievements were significant.

In order to ensure an increase in the level of consumption in our country, the state reduced the amount of investment in capital construction in the state budget. Total budgeted investment in capital construction was slashed to 28,100 million yuan in 1980, down from 39,600 million yuan in 1978 and from 39,500 million yuan in 1979. In capital construction, expenditures on productive construction were reduced while the share of non-productive construction to meet the demands of the people's material and cultural life was increased from 17.4% in 1978, to 27% in 1979 and to 33.7% in 1980. Total floor space of urban residential buildings completed was less than 30 million square metres annually before 1977. It shot up to 62.56 million square metres in 1979, and made another climb to 82.30 million square metres in 1980.

As a result of these readjustments, accumulation funds of the national income increased by about 10,000 million yuan during the 1979-1980 period, while consumption funds soared to 58,000 million yuan. This led to a change in the ratio between accumulation and consumption.

	Share of Accumulation (%)	Share of Consumption (%)
1978	36.5	63.5
1979	34.6	65.4
1980	32.4	67.6

2. Readjustments in the proportions between agriculture, light industry and heavy industry, and accelerating the development of agriculture and light industry.

In developing agriculture, the state mainly adopted three important policies:

(1) To ensure the decision-making power of the people's communes, production brigades and teams in production, management and distribution, and to carry out and gradually institute and perfect various systems of responsibility linking output with payment;

(2) To diversify the rural economy according to actual conditions and to encourage commune members to engage in household sideline occupations on the basis of the development of collective economy;

(3) To raise the purchasing prices for farm and sideline products by large margins and to open village fairs in a orderly manner.

All of these measures triggered the enthusiasm of the rural cadres and commune members for production. In 1979, China's agriculture witnessed a bumper harvest rarely seen since the founding of New China. Grain output reached an all-time high. We reaped another comparatively good harvest in 1980, despite serious drought in the north and serious flooding in the south, both of which were unprecedented in severity for several decades. The production of industrial crops, which had been stagnant for many years, also increased. Cotton output, which had declined to 2.17 million tons in 1978 from 2.34 million tons in 1966, increased to a record level of 2.707 million tons in 1980. The output of oil-bearing crops, which had been fluctuating for 20 years within a range of from 5.09 million tons in 1956 to 4.02 million tons in 1977, registered a considerable increase in 1980 to 7.691 million tons. The production of such industrial crops as sugar, jute and ambary hemp, silkworm cocoons and tea all showed increases to varying degrees. A diversified economy in the people's communes, production brigades and teams as well as in household sideline occupations developed quite rapidly. A long sought-after situation, in which the rural economy is prosperous and the peasants are in high spirits, began to emerge at last in the vast countryside.

As for light industry, the state in its national planning gave priority to its development, allocated more loans to its construction and supplied more raw materials, fuel and power for its production. New channels were provided for the production of light industry and handicrafts. As a result, the growth rate of light industry surpassed that of heavy industry. In 1979, the growth rate of heavy industry was 7.7%, and light industry, 9.6%; in 1980, heavy industry grew by 1.4%, and light industry by 18.4%. Although the rate of growth of heavy industry slackened, new progress was made in readjusting the orientation of its products, in better serving agriculture and light industry, in increasing the variety of its products and improving their quality, and in reducing material consumption. Apart from the policy of readjusting the national economy, the reform of the system of management, which was just begun on an experimental basis, also played a great role in the development of light and heavy industries.

Due to the more rapid development of light industry than of heavy industry, a change took place in the proportional shares of light and heavy industries in the gross output value of industry (calculated at 1970 constant prices):

	Light Industry (%)	Heavy Industry (%)
1978	42.7	57.3
1979	43.1	56.9
1980	46.9	53.1

On the basis of increased production of agriculture and light industry, the amount of commodities supplied for both rural and urban areas rose markedly. The total volume of retail sales increased by 6,800 million yuan per annum in the 1965-1978 period. It increased by 24,100 million yuan, or 12.4%, in 1979; by 3,400 million yuan, or 12.2%, in 1980 (in constant prices), exceeding growth rates during the preceding 20 years.

3. Readjustment of the production of crude oil and coal, speeding up geological exploration of crude oil and tunnelling in coal mines, and striving to conserve energy.

In order to improve the imbalance between extraction and reserves and between extraction and tunnelling, we stabilized or reduced the output of crude oil and coal in a planned way during the past two years. The output of crude oil almost levelled off, with 104.05 million tons produced in 1978, 106.15 million tons in 1979 and 105.95 million tons in 1980. Coal output declined to 620 million tons in 1980 from 635 million tons in 1979.

Measures were taken to increase oil reserves:

(1) Continuing geological exploration in the Northeast, North China and East China;

(2) Conducting geophysical surveys in cooperation with foreign oil companies over a area of 410,000 square kilometres in the South China Sea and the southern Yellow Sea, and preparing to start bidding for joint exploration and development in the immediate future; signing contracts with foreign oil companies to carry out exploration and development in parts of the Bohai Sea and Beibu Gulf, where progress was made in exploration;

(3) Conducting exploration in the continental sedimentary basins of Jungar, Qaidam, Tarim, Shaanxi-Gansu-Ningxia and Sichuan in the western and southwestern parts of China. Although these reserves will remain inaccessible in the near future, exploration was underway on a wide scale, and turned out good indications for hopeful prospects.

In the exploitation of coal, the following measures were taken:

(1) Speeding up tunnelling and stripping of existing coal pits, and endeavouring to help those coal pits where extraction and tunnelling were out of balance in order to make up for thier unfulfilled quotas;

(2) Taking measures to reduce the intensity of labour of the workers and staff in coal mines, and paying more attention to labour protection and safety facilities;

(3) Increasing expenditures for the maintenance of simple reproduction, and speeding up the tapping of potential of existing coal mines;

(4) Maintaining a certain level of capital construction in coal mines by budget appropriations, bank loans and foreign funds.

State Energy Policy. Concerning energy policy, the state laid equal stress on exploitation and economy. In the near future, priority will be given to energy conservation so as to maintain a certain growth rate of industrial production. The specific measures were:

(1) Gradually transforming the energy-consuming tendency of the industrial structure and product mix into a energy-saving one;

(2) Strengthening energy management, endeavouring to strike a balance in power and heat supply, and reducing energy consumption per unit of product;

(3) Speeding-up technological transformation of out-of-date equipment and backward technologies characterized by high energy consumption, introducing centralized supply of heating, and integrating power generation and heat supply;

(4) Gradually updating motorized machines and tools which consume too much energy;

(5) Placing rigid control over the use of oil as fuel, and actively promoting the use of coal in place of oil.

All these measures showed initial results. Total industrial output value in 1979 increased by 8.5% while energy production went up by only 3%. In 1980, although energy production dropped by 1.3%, the gross output value of industry increased by 8.7%. Today, the waste of energy is still enormous, so the potential for saving energy remains huge. The fact that we could guarantee a given growth rate for industrial production under conditions of small increases or even slight declines in energy production in 1979 and 1980 has enhanced our confidence in increasing production by practicing economy.

I have touched upon three aspects of the readjustment of the national economy. Of course, they are not all-inclusive. Nevertheless, these facts show that much progress was made and great results attained in 1979 and 1980. The current excellent situation, which has not been seen during the past 20 years or so, finds full expression in the obvious improvement in living standards of the great majority of our nearly 1,000 million people; in the stability of social order in rural areas where 800 million live, in the great enthusiasm and initiative of the peasants for production, and in the vistas of prosperity and vitality in agriculture, which is the foundation of the national economy; in the initial changes in the industrial structure, a structure that has long been irrational, and in the gradual rise in economic efficiency and closer integration of industrial growth with the interests of the enterprises, the workers and staff. These facts also prove that the series of principles and policies adopted since the Third Plenary Session of the 11th Party Central Committee, as well as the policy of readjusting, restructuring, consolidating and improving the national economy, are correct.

Budget Deficits and Over-Issuance of Currency. Some new conditions and problems also emerged during the readjustment period. These were mainly budget deficits, over-issuance of currency and increases in market prices. In 1979, state finances were 17,000 million yuan in the red and, in 1980, 12,100 million yuan in deficit. Owing to the rise in financial deficits and to increased overdrafts from the People's Bank, an additional 2,600 million yuan of bank-notes beyond the plan were issued by the bank in 1979, and another 4,600 million yuan in 1980. The increase of paper money in circulation and the failure to increase consumer goods correspondingly led to an increase in the average index of retail prices by 1.9% in 1979 over that of 1978. The year 1980 saw another increase of 6% over the previous year, which reflected a rise of 8.1% in the cities and of 4.4% in the rural areas.

Why did this take place? Two major reasons may be cited:

1. While consumption expenditures for the improvement of the people's livelihood were greatly increased and the state revenues were decreased, appropriations for capital construction were not scaled down accordingly. What is more, other expenditures continued to grow. This led to a situation in which the sum of investments in capital construction and all kinds of consumption expenditures covered by the state budget exceeded state revenues.

State financial resources set aside for raising the purchasing prices of farm and sideline products as well as for increasing wages and bonuses for workers and staff went up by 18,500 million yuan in 1979 over the previous year; there was another increase of 16,900 million yuan in 1980 over 1979. However, factors causing decreases in state revenues prevailed over those that increased state revenues during these two years. This led to a net decrease of 5,200 million yuan in state revenues (excluding foreign loans) in 1979 as compared with 1978, and in 1980, to another decrease of 3,200 million yuan as compared with 1979.

Investments in capital construction by the state totalled 36,000 million yuan in the readjusted national plan for 1979, a decrease of 3,500 million yuan from the previous year. Although these investments were already large, actual investments in capital construction completed in 1979 reached 39,500 million yuan. Total investments in capital construction in the 1980 national plan were 24,100 million yuan, yet actual investments completed in 1980 were 28,100 million yuan. That is to say, the actual scope of capital construction in 1979 was not scaled down, and it was not reduced sufficiently in 1980. In particular, owing to a big increase in capital construction funds raised by the localities and by departments and enterprises, the total investment jumped to 53,900 million yuan in 1980, a 7.8% increase over the previous year. The large increase of capital construction investment outside the state budget adversely affected the balance of state finances to a certain extent.

The total sum of expenditure on national defence, administrative expenses of the state organs and establishments and allocations for science, culture, education and health work increased by 8,900 million yuan in these two years. Of the total sum, some of the increases were necessary, while some were not.

Given the better performance of production during the past two years, we really did not expect such a large budget deficit. We were not firm enough in implementing the readjustment policy in some aspects, especially in reducing the scope of capital construction. Furthermore, certain additional expenditures were made during the implementation of the national plan which should not have been made at all. Many units also passed out bonuses in an indiscriminate way. All these actions exacerbated the imbalance between state revenues and expenditures.

2. Although we energetically speeded up the growth of agriculture and light industry and increased the supply of consumer goods, the supply of commodities still could not keep pace with the large increase in social purchasing power in both urban and rural areas. This circumstance was due to the constraints of objective conditions and to inadequate work.

As mentioned above, the total volume of retail sales increased by 58,000 million yuan during the 1979-1980 period, a level of increase that had never been experienced in the past. However, in the same period the level of social purchasing power increased by 67,600 million yuan, surpassing the supply of commodities. It is known to all that with more money in hand and with commodities in short supply, prices cannot be stabilized and will eventually go up.

It should be noted that there were some other abnormal factors behind these price increases besides the two basic ones — increase of money supply and inadequate supply of consumer goods. Some enterprises, both industrial and commercial as well as services, raised commodity prices at will in order to receive more bonuses. Some raised prices openly, while some did so in disguised forms. The scope of commodities selling at negotiated prices was for a time too broad because there were no stipulations about the variety of such commodities or about price ceilings. As a result, some commodities were sold at negotiated prices when they should not have been. Moreover, negotiated prices were much higher than list prices, a factor that also contributed to the rise in prices.

In 1979 and 1980, considerable financial deficits, over-issuance of currency and price hikes affected the livelihood of both urban and rural dwellers, especially those workers and staff members who received no bonuses. In these two years, a total of about 16,000 million yuan of people's income was thus offset by higher prices. And a danger looms that if no prompt and firm measures are taken to further readjust the national economy, state finances in 1981 will again experience a comparatively large deficit, the bank would continue to issue a large amount of banknotes and commodity prices would, no doubt, continue to shoot up. If so, not only the workers and staff but the peasants as well would gradually lose the economic benefits gained in the past two years. The consequences would be that it would not only be hard to stabilize the economy, but political stability would also be affected.

To sum up, remarkable results were achieved in the course of economic readjustment in both 1979 and 1980.

On the other hand, some new problems came up. They are not the result of the readjustment; rather, they came to the fore simply because readjustment is still underway (it is, after all, impossible to complete economic readjustment within two years), and because certain readjustment jobs have not been done very well. It was absolutely necessary to increase the share of consumption funds in the past two years. Otherwise, it would not have been possible to realize such a good economic situation as is prevailing now. Nevertheless, in the same period the scope of capital construction was not resolutely scaled down by a large enough margin and expenditures were not resolutely cut down as they should have been. This shows that the influence of "Left" ideas in economic work has not been cleared up, nor has a real comprehensive balance been achieved, nor has the principle of acting according to our ability been earnestly pursued.

Latent Dangers Prior to Readjustment. Can it be said that there would be no financial deficits, inflation, price hikes and hidden dangers if we had not readjusted the national economy? As a matter of fact, there had been a latent danger long before. Just as mentioned in the first part of this article, the ten-year upheaval of the "cultural revolution" created a serious imbalance among the sectors of the national economy. The impetuosity and rash advance in 1978 resulted in immediate enlargement of the scope of capital construction, further aggravated the imbalance of economic relationships and intensified financial difficulties. A new economic danger thus lay hidden. In fact, there was a financial deficit in 1978. Although the state budget had a surplus of 1,000 million yuan in that year, the central government's finances had already registered a deficit of 4,500 million yuan due to excessive added investments in capital construction. And the state had to resort to overdrafts from the bank to make ends meet. In so doing, the imbalance of bank credits in 1979 was intensified and more bank notes had to be issued by the bank. Meanwhile, in order to link the targets put forward in the 1979 national plan which was worked out in 1978 with the declared targets set for 1985, some production targets were set too high and the scope of capital construction was too broad; furthermore, there was a large gap in the supply of material resources. Planned state revenues also included unrealistic and impractical factors. Therefore, even if the ratio between accumulation and consumption was not readjusted, the implementation of the original plan would bring about considerable deficits in state budgets and the bank would still be compelled to issue more banknotes. If we stuck to the originally drafted Ten-Year Plan, our national economy would have become even more seriously imbalanced, budget deficits would have been more serious, and commodity prices would have risen more abruptly. If so, great losses rather than improvements would be brought about in the people's livelihood during these two years. It is thanks to the implementation of the readjustment policy since 1979 that such a trend was reversed and a possible outbreak of crises avoided. However, these long-nurtured adverse consequences and problems accumulated from the past could not be dealt with in a straightforward manner within the short span of two years. Therefore, it is safe to say that the current hidden dangers were in place a long time ago. Due to readjustment, the danger has been moderated. In the meantime, the good results gained through readjustment have provided favourable conditions for removing such dangers.

III. Tasks, Policies and Principles for the Second Stage of Economic Readjustment

Inasmuch as the current latent dangers consist of inflation and price rises caused by budget deficits and inadequate supplies of consumer goods, the tasks for the second stage of economic readjustment should be to stabilize the economy, readjust the structure, tap the potential and achieve better economic results.

1. Stabilize the economy. By stabilizing the economy we mean to strike a balance between state revenues and expenditures so as to wipe out budget deficits and, on this basis, to balance credits and debts. Further, market prices must be stabilized so that people's livelihood will not suffer any loss.

In order to strike a balance between state revenues and expenditures, financial income should, first and foremost, be increased. The proportionate share of state revenue to national income somewhat declined in the past two years. It accounted, generally speaking, for about one-third of the total in the previous 20 years, but declined to 28.7% in 1980, and could go down to 26.6% in 1981. It is necessary to reduce this proportion adequately so as to overcome the over centralization of national finances. Nevertheless, it declined a little too much during the past two years, mainly due to a failure to collect profits and taxes that should have been collected and due to the decentralization of parts of state revenues that should not have been decentralized. In particular, business management in some enterprises was quite chaotic. And there existed many kinds of financial "leaks" and "loopholes." Such a state of affairs was not only harmful to the overall interests of the country, but gave the green light to extravagance and waste and provided chances to gain advantages through profiteering and trickery. Therefore, it was necessary to take active measures to tap financial resources, to plug loopholes and to increase state revenues so as to strike a financial balance, support economic development and overcome financial difficulties. Meanwhile, spending on capital construction and on all kinds of administrative expenses should be reduced and consumption put under proper control.

The State Council has decided that total investment in capital construction in 1981, including all the funds raised by central authorities, localities and enterprises and all projects built with loans — both foreign and domestic — should be slashed to 30,000 million yuan from 53,900 million yuan in the previous year. Of the total sum, investments covered by the state budget should be cut to 17,000 million yuan from 28,100 million yuan in the previous year. The construction of non-feasible projects and of redundant projects which compete for raw materials, fuel and power with existing enterprises should be stopped. In so doing, some equipment will have to be stock-piled, and some construction projects will have to be held up. Losses, to a certain extent, have to be borne. Yet, such losses would be much smaller than those that might be caused by a long "war of attrition," and would be much preferable to having the national economy dragged to collapse by overextended economic burdens. Moreover, such a change would be favourable for concentrating investment on those projects and auxiliary facilities which are badly needed for current production and can be promptly put into production after their completion. It would also favour the construction of living quarters and urban public utilities, thus yielding economic results as quickly as possible. Not only in 1981 but also during the entire period of the Sixth Five-Year Plan, the scope of capital construction should be rigidly controlled. It should never happen again that the scope of capital construction should be so rigidly controlled. It should never occur again that the scope of capital construction expands rapidly whenever the national economy begins to take a turn for the better. With regard to expenditures on national defence and administration as well as on all other kinds of undertakings, the State Council has followed the same policy of contraction so that these expenditures can be brought into conformity as far as possible with the nation's capabilities.

To raise the level of the people's consumption is an important starting point in the readjustment of the national economy. In the past two years, we took big steps in raising the purchasing prices of farm and sideline products and in readjusting the wages of the workers and staff members. Great efforts have been made by the party and the government and remarkable results have been attained. Currently, we are carrying out a further readjustment of the national economy to wipe out budget deficits and to stabilize commodity prices, so that the economic benefits gained by the people in the past two years will not be offset and so that the material conditions for further improvement of the people's livelihood can be created. In order to stabilize the economy, proper control should be placed over expenditures of consumption along with a reduction of investment in capital construction and all kinds of administrative spending. Without proper control, expenditures might exceed the nation's financial and material resources. That eventuality would intensify inflation, thereby doing harm rather than good to the people. We must not lose sight of the fact that ours is a country with a huge population, our economy had a weak foundation to start with, and the problems of living conditions of the people that have accumulated for many years can only be dealt with gradually on the basis of increased production. It is unrealistic to talk about the improvement of people's livelihood without taking the development of production into consideration. Nor can one be achieved without the other. Capital construction must be carried on according to the nation's strength. This principle also applies to consumption.

2. **Readjust Economic Structure.** It is necessary to readjust economic structure and to realize rationality of economic structure so as to overcome the inadequate supply of consumer goods as well as fuel and power.

First of all, due emphasis must be put on the development of agriculture. Agriculture is the foundation of our national economy and its development is vital to the growth of the national economy. We must further implement rural economic policies, continue to perfect various systems of responsibility in production and strive to achieve comparatively large growth in agriculture. In developing agriculture, we must continue to do a good job in grain production and never relax our efforts to bring about effective measures for the expansion of grain production. However, we must also actively diversify the rural economy so that a rational structure covering farming, forestry, animal husbandry, fishing and sideline occupations, covering the production of grain and cash crops and can be achieved. If so, our agriculture can supply more products and raw materials for the people's livelihood, industry and exports, thus accelerating the flourishing of our national economy.

Secondly, we must speed up the development of light industry and make further changes in the ratio between heavy and light industries. With less capital, light industry can still yield quick returns and greater accumulation. A speedy development of light industry can help increase state revenues, withdraw excess currency from circulation, boost the market and stabilize commodity prices. At the same time, as light industry develops in vigorous strides, the state can support agriculture with increased financial resources and exchange, with the peasants using a more adequate supply of commodities, thus promoting the development of agriculture. In the immediate future, light industry should develop at a faster pace than heavy industry, so as to bring the supply of commodities into correspondence with purchasing power.

Thirdly, we must continue to do a good job in energy conservation and in energy exploitation. The growth rate of heavy industry during the period of the Sixth Five-Year Plan depends, to a great extent, on the development of energy production. We must continue to take more rigid and effective measures and strive to obtain greater results in energy conservation. However, attention to energy exploration and its exploitation must not be relaxed. While continuing to do a good job in oil exploration, priority must be given to the development of coal mines, especially to the development of mines in Shanxi and Guizhou provinces. Existing production capacity should be brought into fuller play and more efforts should be concentrated on expanding and updating some small and medium-sized coal pits. In so doing, not only more capital can be saved to avoid excessive additional burdens on state finances, but better results can be achieved in a comparatively quicker way. This will provide the energy conditions necessary for the quicker development of the national economy in the latter half of the 1980's.

Fourthly, the internal structure of heavy industry should be changed. In the past, owing to the lengthy pursuit of "taking steel as the key link," heavy industry developed lop-sidedly, with much of its produce serving the industry itself. The machine-building industry mainly served capital construction and suffered from excessive redundancy, duplication and disproportionate production capacities. Now that investment in capital construction has been greatly reduced, in order not to shrink the production of heavy industry — especially that of machine-building industry — it is necessary to readjust the internal structure of heavy industry so as to conform with the structural readjustment of the economy as a whole. Sectors of heavy industry such as metallurgy, chemicals and machine-building must be reoriented to the production of consumer goods, and be made to supply needed raw and semi-finished materials, machinery and equipment for the production of consumer goods. In the machine-building industry, we must mainly convert its service to the technical transformation of the national economy, the domestic market, the expansion of exports and the modernization of national defence. Those enterprises which are operating below capacity and which have no future for development can be merged with enterprises in light industry and shifted to the manufacture of consumer goods, coordinate their production with other light industrial enterprises. Those enterprises which have turned out high-cost and low-quality goods or have long operated at a loss must be shut down, must suspend operations, or must be amalgamated or switched over to the manufacture of other products.

Last, but not least, new channels must be explored for employment, thus changing the structure of the labour force. Due to the reduction of investment in capital construction, we must, apart from the development of labour-intensive trades, depend on the development of various service trades, including commerce, services, banking, telecommunications, urban public utilities, entertainment, tourism, etc., so as to increase employment. All of these trades cannot only absorb a huge amount of labour power, but can promote the development of production and bring conveniences to the life of the people. On the other hand, since the income of many of these trades is in the nature of redistribution of wages, their expanded income does not require the expansion of state expenditures nor does it increase pressures on purchasing power. At present, many people are waiting for jobs and some of them are just idling along; on the other hand, the service trades are least developed and much can be done in this area. There should be significant development in this field in the expansion of various forms of collective and individual businesses.

3. Tap the potential. What will production depend on when the scope of capital construction is reduced? The answer lies in bringing the existing enterprises into fuller play and in tapping their potential.

After more than 30 years of socialist construction, China's industry has acquired a certain foundation. There are a total of 400,000 enterprises in industry and communications across the nation, with 50 million workers and staff and some 600,000 million yuan of fixed and liquid assets. Annual output of energy is equivalent to above 600 million tons of standard coal. At present, production capacity is far from being fully exploited and its potential is great. Henceforth, we must do our utmost to operate existing enterprises well, especially the several thousand key enterprises, so that they can play a greater role in production.

The first measure is to do a good job of consolidating existing enterprises. We must earnestly attend to basic work in the management of enterprises, institute a strict system of technical responsibility in production, do a good job of economic accounting, implement the principle of "to each according to his work" and establish normal production procedures and rigid labour discipline. At present, business management is still in disarray in many enterprises where the system of responsibility in production has yet to be established, and huge waste has been incurred. Enterprise management must be put on the right track after consolidation. And this measure can, without any investment, increase production and income.

The second measure is to go on with the reorganization of the enterprises. All enterprises must be rationally reorganized according to the principle of specialization and coordination as well as of economic rationality. There are a great number of departments. Departments and administrative regions enforce rigid control over their own units independently and in their own way. Not only has a large amount of financial and material resources been wasted, but technological progress has been hindered. Doing a good job in inter-enterprise coalition and coordination is the only way to tap the potential of existing enterprises. Getting organized means tapping potential as well as increasing production capacity and speed.

The third measure is to update equipment in existing enterprises and carry out technological transformation in a planned way. With out-of-date equipment and backward technologies, many enterprises are still manufacturing products of low quality and at high cost. The initiative of the workers, technicians and cadres must be mobilized to carry out technical innovations from which new products, extra manpower and raw materials can be obtained. In the course of technological innovation and transformation, special attention must be given to energy conservation.

In order to tap the potential of existing enterprises, a system of education for the workers and staff must also be established, so that all of them can attend training courses to raise their political, cultural, technical and managerial levels. During the readjustment period, we must seize the opportunity to have the workers and staff trained in those enterprises which are operating below capacity. Even in enterprises that are running at full capacity, this must also be done whenever possible.

4. Achieve better economic results. The current financial difficulty lies, in the final analysis, in

poor economic results. If remarkable achievements can be made in raising economic results, we will be in a better position to surmount this difficulty.

A big defect in economic work is that for many years we did economic work without considering its results. Whenever we talked about the development of production, it meant the launching of new projects in capital construction. Moreover, we rushed into the construction of new projects before feasibility studies had been made, before geological conditions had been earnestly explored and their locations studiously selected. Further, we did not take into account the rational deployment of productive forces, the conditions for their construction and conditions for production after their completion. During construction, we did not pay enough attention to strengthening management. It took such a long period of construction to complete a project that some of new projects could not be put into operation for a long time. Even if some of them did start production, they could not run at full capacity, due either to lack of proper coordination of production capacity or to the inadequate supply of raw materials, fuel and power. All of these shortcomings led to tremendous losses. As for the enterprises completed, we often did not do our best to run and manage them well, nor to attach sufficient importance to the maintenance and updating of the equipment, nor to personnel training and improvement of their technical levels, nor to the management and utilization of funds. As a result, our production technology has long been stagnant, and even regressive in certain instances. With high costs and poor quality, waste was staggering. In production, undue emphasis on output value and output quotas, as well as neglect of market demands, led to a situation in which many products were not wanted on the market and production was divorced from marketing. Coupled with excessive links in the circulation of commodities and with ineffectiveness in the turnover of funds, large quantities of products had to be stockpiled in the course of distribution, thus causing great waste. This being the case in the three fields of production, construction and circulation, China's national economy was inevitably in a state of high accumulation, heavy waste, low results and low consumption. We paid a high price, yet got low results, and our people did not derive much benefit. We cannot and must not act in such a way any longer.

To increase economic results should be seen as an important target in our future economic work. Leading bodies at all levels and all economic units should shift their attention to economic accounting and economic results. By changing the guiding principles, consolidating and reorganizing the enterprises, carrying out technical transformation, changing the industrial structure and restructuring the economic system, a new trail will be blazed along which our national economy will develop steadily on the basis of increased economic results. After these goals are accomplished, the economic situation in China will surely be greatly changed.

During the course of further readjustment of the national economy, some comrades are anxious that reductions in the scope of capital construction and the contraction of expenditures will, when coupled with the shortage of energy, bring about long-term shrinkage in production and financial imbalance, and that such readjustments would fail to steadily and gradually improve the people's livelihood. It should be recognized that there are in fact two possibilities ahead. Given the conditions that neither energy production nor the scope of capital construction will be expanded, if we still follow the old track and old methods, production would possibly decline, state revenues would go down and budget deficits go up. As a result, the people's living would not be stabilized and the economy as a whole would suffer from a vicious cycle. However, if we take to a new path and new methods — namely, the path of raising economic results — it is most likely that we can, working with less energy supplies and investment, maintain a steady growth of production and ensure a steady increase of state revenue. In this way, the people's living standards cannot only be gradually raised rather than lowered, but the economy as a whole will enter into a sound cycle. In order to realize the latter possibility, we should resort not only to economic readjustment but also to the reform of the economic system, integrating readjustment with reform in an organic way.

Integrating Our Efforts. To sum up, the above-mentioned four tasks, namely, stabilizing the economy, readjusting the economic structure, tapping potential and increasing the results, are closely interrelated. If our economy is not sufficiently stabilized and if we do not retreat enough in the areas where we should have retreated — especially in reducing investments in capital construction and all expenditures to within the scope of our nation's strength — neither inflation can be put under control nor can work in other fields be successfully undertaken. However, if we do not firmly press on in the areas where we should have pressed on and do not energetically yet prudently readjust the economic structure, tap the potential of existing enterprises and raise economic results, the problem of economic imbalance will not be solved, production will decline, and the economy as a whole will not be stabilized. Therefore, fulfilment of above tasks does not mean we can slacken our efforts. On the contrary, it requires that we should do our work more creatively, more conscientiously and more actively. Raising economic results means, first of all, raising the efficiency of our work. We must continuously adhere to the principle of empancipating our minds, using our brains, seeking truth from facts and carrying forward the revolutionary spirit of plain living and hard struggle and working hard for the prosperity of the country. With several years of arduous efforts, we will cause our national economy to achieve remarkable improvements in levels of organization, business management and production technology. This is necessary to our modernization drive. This is where we place our hope.

During the readjustment period, the scope of importing equipment will be properly reduced owing to the reduction of investment in capital construction. Yet this does not mean a change in our foreign policy. Economic and technical cooperation and interchange between China and other countries will develop on the basis of equality and mutual benefit. This is our firm and unswerving principle. While mainly relying on our own efforts, we will continue to use funds from abroad, import new technologies which are beneficial and suitable to China's conditions, and apply them to the development of energy, communications and transportation, and to the transformation of existing enterprises. Meanwhile, we must endeavour to integrate both the use of foreign funds and the import of technologies with the domestic capacity for providing auxiliary equipment, the ability for repayment and for incorporation, so that real benefits can be reaped. With the progress of readjustment and the development of the national economy, economic cooperation and exchanges between China and foreign countries will be increasingly expanded. Therefore, doing a good job in the economy as a whole and raising the efficiency in our work are conducive to the expansion of our economic cooperation and technical interflow with foreign countries.

All these are the tasks we must fulfill during the second stage of economic readjustment.

Overcoming Sectoral Imbalances. As mentioned above, the fundamental task for economic readjustment is to overcome the imbalance among different sectors of our national economy. Because various kinds of problems were interwoven, it is difficult to put it right straight away, and time is needed. At the same time, it inevitably requires a process of thought to effect a fundamental change in the guidance of our economic work, to see that economic readjustment does not mean restoring the old order but blazing a new trail of development. Therefore, it should take more time to complete economic readjustment than the period of three years as originally planned.

When Will the Readjustment Be Completed? When will the economic readjustment be completed? It depends on the progress of our work and on the extent of the results we will achieve. Anyway, as soon as we fulfill the tasks assigned for the second stage, stabilize the economy, gradually achieve rationality of economic structure and put the national economy on a sound cycle during the period of the Sixth Five-Year Plan, then we can say the tasks of readjustment of the national economy have, in the main, been fulfilled. In the long run, of course, economic structure will not remain unchanged. After fulfilling the tasks of the current readjustment, there will, however, be other tasks in the future, which are different from our present tasks of readjusting the serious imbalance in the national economy.

All in all, following the readjustment of the past two years, the overall economic situation is good. The series of policies and measures adopted by the party and the government enjoy the wide support of the masses across the nation and visible achievements have been made. So long as we resolutely carry the readjustment policy through to the end, we will be able to get rid of the latent danger and further develop the excellent situation, thus bringing our national economy onto a healthy and steady track. Our future is full of promise.

4. ON THE QUESTION OF THE RESTRUCTURING OF CHINA'S ECONOMIC SYSTEM
By Liao Jili

The socialist revolution and socialist construction in China has been carried out not on the basis of a very high level of development of the social productive forces or of a well-developed commodity economy, but rather on the basis of a very low level of development of socialist productive forces and an underdeveloped commodity economy. The kind of economic system that should be established in the world is also a question of the kind of socialist economy that should be developed across the Chinese land. This is a question of great national importance, a question to which not only the whole people of China have paid great attention, but which has also drawn wide attention outside of the country. To help our readers understand this question, I would offer some of my personal views.

I. Why Should the Economic System in China Be Restructured in All-Around Way?

Over the more than 30 years past, we have built independent and fairly comprehensive industrial and national economic systems. A fairly solid material foundation has been laid for the national economy and there exists great potential. We have made great achievements and it is entirely wrong to ignore these. However, our achievements are still insufficient when compared with the hard work performed by the people of the whole country and when compared with the superiority the socialist system should have demonstrated. As compared with the developed capitalist countries, economic and technical levels in China are still underdeveloped. Our country is still poor and the living standards of the people are still low. There are many causes for this, but an important cause is that we have adopted an economic system that is not suited to basic conditions in China.

China's economic system, which was established as early as in the First Five-Year Plan period, was based on the experience of the Soviet Union during the historical conditions that prevailed between the 1930's and 1950's. It is an economic system with a high degree of centralism and one that mainly uses administrative means to run the economy. It must be admitted that at a time when the national economy was seriously damaged, China had been divided by prolonged feudal separatist rule. Economic and technical levels were low and the economic structure was simple. The new system did play an important role in concentrating material, financial and technical forces in China to ensure quick rehabilitation of the national economy. Successful fulfilment of targets in economic construction centered on 156 projects, and these efforts were rewarded with satisfactory results.

But the premise of this system lay in the restriction of commodity production and of the distribution of commodities. It rejected the law of value and restricted the function of the law of value. It was only because of the co-existence of several economic sectors that we were able to make use of the function of the market. Following the completion of the socialist transformation, we treated the socialist economy — a vast and complicated entity which is both close-knit and divided into multiple branches — merely as a big factory or a big machine: Greater emphasis was laid on centralism; the function of the market was rejected; undue attention was paid to administrative means; and state control over the economy became tighter and tighter. It was believed that only in this way could the machine operate and this was the only path of a socialist planned economy.

But circumstances proved just the opposite of this thinking. This system did not help to inspire the initiative and ingenuity of the enterprises and working people. Nor did it help the central government to maintain effective control over economic life. Rather, this system gravely obstructed economic development in our country. The defects of the system became more and more apparent to the people as time went by.

The Record of Previous Reforms. In the past 20 years, reforms of this economic system were attempted several times, but these were conducted within the limits of administrative management. The problem was never understood and solved once and for all. Especially under the influence of Lin Biao and the Gang of Four, the system became all the more rigid and incompatible with the development of productive forces.

The defects in this system are as follows:

1. The enterprises are treated as appendages to the administrative organs existing at different levels, and are not regarded as relatively independent commodity producers. This approach is incompatible with requirements for development of the socialist commodity economy.

2. The economy is controlled by the ministerial systems and administrative regions, with the effect of cutting off internal or natural relations among the industries and regions themselves, and between the ministries and administrative regions. This is incompatible with the requirement of modern socialist production.

3. Production is controlled too tightly and too rigidly by mandatory targets and fails to meet the actual needs of the market. This is incompatible with the complex and varying demands of society.

4. As all revenues and expenditures are controlled by the state, all localities and enterprises "share porridge from the same pot" and don't care about their own economic returns. This is incompatible with the requirement of using minimum labour to obtain maximum economic returns. This economic system has been accompanied by the setting up of more and more central ministries and regional departments, each controlling a number of enterprises and dividing their own spheres of influence. The multiple levels of administration, complicated formalities, sluggishness in handling matters and slow response have given rise to bureaucracy.

This economic system has been developed under the guidance of "Left" ideology, runs counter to the level of development of the productive forces at the present stage of socialism and is therefore also divorced from the corresponding relations of production. In some aspects, it has skipped over the present level of development of productive forces; in other aspects, it still falls behind the present level of development of productive forces. To a great extent, it has hampered the realization of the superiority of the socialist system.

The Onset of Socialist Modernization. After the Gang of Four was smashed, especially after the convening of the Third Plenary Session of the 11th Central Committee of the Communist Party of China, the focus of work was shifted to socialist modernization, calling for scientific management of the economy. This focus requires urgent restructuring of the economic system in an overall way.

On the other hand, there also exists a possibility for restructuring and perfecting the socialist economic system and for simultaneously placing on the agenda within this context the overall reform of the economic system. This possibility exists, firstly, because the mental shackles that used to restrict the people's thinking have been destroyed. Thus, it is possible for us to sum up the experience of the past 30 years through both positive and negative examples in a realistic way and to restudy the objective laws of socialist society. Secondly, the seemingly endless succession of political movements have come to an end and political stability and unity has come to stay. This has made it possible for us to concentrate our strength on the restructuring of the economic system. Thirdly, as the national economy is being readjusted, the serious imbalance in the national economy has drawn the attention of the whole party and the people throughout the country. Effective measures are being taken to solve the problem and industrial and agricultural production is growing steadily. This has created conditions for the smooth restructuring of the economic system. Fourthly, as the closed-door policy has been changed, we can learn from the foreign experience in management and make use of it. These facts indicate that it will possible to adapt the national economic system gradually to socialist modernization within a matter of ten years or so.

II. In What Direction Shall the Economic System Be Restructured?

As economic and social conditions vary from country to country, so will economic systems vary as well. Even in the different countries existing under the socialist system or within different periods in the same country, economic systems may also vary. There is not nor should there be a mechanical model. There have been no examples of success from merely copying foreign experiences mechanically.

The direction for the restructuring of the economic system in China should be determined on the basis of the present level of development of social productive forces in China and the characteristics of its socialist economy; it should be directed at the main problems in the existing system. Our direction for advance can only be determined on the basis of earnestly learning from experence at home and abroad.

China is a developing socialist country. It is a big country with a large population but a poor economic foundation. The degree of socialization of production is not high. Economic and technological development is not evenly balanced. Communications and telecommunications are still poor and the commodity economy is underdeveloped. When New China was founded, modern industry accounted for only 10% of economic output, while agriculture and handicrafts made up 90% of the total; nearly 90% of the population lived in the countryside. This situation inevitably gave rise to the co-existence of multiple economic sectors. After 30 years of socialist construction, modern industry has grown considerably. With the infusion of some advanced technical equipment, it has formed an industrial system and a national economic system of considerable size. However, manual labour and self-supporting production still constitute a great part of agricultural production. A considerable part of the production in industry is also performed by hand or is semi-mechanized. The degree of socialization of production is not high; commodity production is not yet developed; the different regions have not developed evenly; and technological levels vary greatly from industry to industry and from enterprise to enterprise. In other words, social productive forces in China are still at a very low stage of development and therefore still exist as the productive forces of multiple layers.

This situation demonstrates that the socialist economy in China at the present stage ought to become a commodity economy, with public ownership of the means of production holding the dominant position. The economic system in China must be a system of multiple levels — that is, a system under which the state, the economic units and the working people jointly make decisions. It must be a system in which regulation by plan plays the main role and regulation by market is secondary. It must be a system that mainly depends on the economic organizations and upon economic means to run the economy. It must be a system that truly gives due consideration to the material interests of the state, the collective and individuals.

Guidelines for the New Reform. In line with this direction, our general ideas about the reform are:

1. *To extend the power of the enterprises and free them from the rigid control of the ministries and local governments.* In this way, they will become relatively independent economic units which, having paid all taxes, expenses and loans with interest, can then take maximum advantage of their own special abilities, actively develop their production and distribution, independently determine the activities of their management and business operations and adopt a system of independent accounting and responsibility for profits and losses on the condition that they do not violate the state plans and decrees. After paying income taxes, the enterprises can establish production development funds, welfare funds, bonus funds and reserve funds. While ensuring the fulfilment of the quotas set by the state, the enterprises can plan their own production and business activities according to the needs of society. They can themselves purchase the materials they require and sell what they produce. They also have the power to decide forms of wages, employ workers and dismiss surplus workers.

2. *To organize national, regional and/or cross-provincial economic complexes according to the principles of specialization, coordination and economic rationality as well as the principle of mutual benefit under a unified plan.* Thus, we can alter the conditions of random allignment and mutual independence existing among the enterprises. The complexes should be organized both from top to bottom and from bottom to top and should take various forms. For example, complexes can be organized for the joint production of a well-known brand of commodity by merging factories that possess similar technical processes; some can be organized for the multiple use of raw materials and fuels; and some for integrating the elements of production, such as raw materials, labour power, capital funds and techniques. The complexes should adopt unified management and maintain unified accounting; but some may keep separate accounting, some may be structured as regional complexes and some as trans-provincial complexes.

3. *To open more outlets for the circulation of commodities and to establish unified commodity markets.* Both the means of production and the means of subsistence should be treated as commodities. Except for a few commodities that are vital to the national economy and to the people's livelihood and for which rationing should be used, all other commodities should be allowed to be sold or bought freely. More outlets should be opened for the distribution of commodities, intermediate links should be reduced, regional administrative barriers should be removed and distribution should be organized according to economic regionalization so as to establish systematically a wide variety of trade centres.

4. *To establish a variety of economic and trade centres based upon natural economic relationships for the purpose of strengthening these inter-relationships according to the needs of large-scale social production and to replace the existing organization of economic activities that is controlled solely by the ministries and localities.* A number of economic centres can be built in different parts of the country with industrially and commercially developed cities as their supports. Each large economic centre can be surrounded by a number of medium-sized or small economic centres with medium-sized and small cities as their main points of connection to other cities and towns and to the rural areas. The activities of each economic centre can be interwoven. But they should not be restric-

ted by administrative regionalization so as to impede their forming a flexible, organic economic network.

5. *To turn the planning system of setting mandatory quotas from top to bottom into a planning system of setting production quotas from bottom to top, combining both government guidance and directives.* The state gives guidance to the development of the national economy mainly through long-term and medium-term plans, which should cover the direction for the development of the national economy, the major ratios, the scale of capital construction, investment and major construction projects, and the range of improvements in the people's livelihood. As an executive plan, the annual plans should cover the balance between revenues and expenditures and between credit receipts and payments as well as the balance in supplies and the balance between foreign exchange receipts and payments. A mandatory planning system will be adopted only for a limited number of major enterprises that are vital to the national economy and for the people's livelihood, for the production and purchase of major industrial and agricultural products, for commercial and wholesale centres and for some major construction projects. A system of state guidance will be adopted for all other enterprises. The government will use mainly economic means to guide the business operations of the enterprises according to plan.

6. *To use prices, taxes, credit and other economic means to regulate economic activities and to replace the former practice of sole reliance on administrative measures to run the economy.* General product prices should be fixed on the basis of product cost and average profit rate, and readjusted periodically to keep up with the changes in product cost and in supply and demand. Price controls should be flexible and price forms should vary. Unified fixed prices should be adopted for major agricultural and sideline products, for raw materials, for fuels and for major consumer goods; floating prices should apply to certain agricultural and sideline products, to raw materials, to most processed goods and to consumer goods; market prices should be adopted for all other industrial and agricultural products. The present system of turning over profits should be changed to the system of paying taxes, and various taxes and tax rates should be adopted to regulate the profits of the enterprises. The banking system should make fullest use of its function to regulate and control capital funds. It is responsible for handling the settlements of accounts of the enterprises and public undertakings, absorbing idle capital and issuing both circulating funds and capital construction loans. Apart from using economic means, the government can also use administrative means to intervene in economic activities according to law when necessary.

7. *Laws and disciplines must be observed strictly. Economic legislation, jurisdiction and supervision over economic work must be strengthened.* The state must enact civil laws, financial laws, banking laws, accounting laws, tax laws and price laws so that all economic activities can be governed by law. Economic tribunals should be established to try economic cases. At the same time, an economic supervision system should be set up at all levels and full play should be given to supervision by the statistical, financial, taxation, banking, price, industrial and commercial administrative departments.

8. *All party organizations and government departments at different levels should free themselves from trifling matters of economic management, and pay attention to principles and policies and to ideological and organizational work.* Concrete economic affairs should be handed over to the economic organizations existing at all levels, thus bringing an end to the situation in which the party and government meddled too much with concrete economic affairs.

9. *To change the overconcentration of power over economic work at the central level and to extend the power of local authorities in economic management through policy, planning and supervision.* Local governments should promote urban construction and service trades as well as cultural, educational and health work.

10. *To establish and perfect the system of workers' congresses under the leadership of the party committees, to give play to the role of the workers and staff members as masters of their enterprises; and to strengthen the democratic management of the enterprises while practicing the system of personal responsibility of factory directors under leadership of the party committees.*

The above points are interrelated, forming an organic whole. Implementation of these points in an all-around way will enable China's economic system to bring forth the advantages of the socialist planned economy and to give full play to the role of the market mechanism. As a result, our economy will benefit both from unified leadership and from flexible practices. There will be overall control without rigidity, and flexibility without chaos. This economic system will function in genuine harmony both with the level of development of productive forces in China at the present stage and with the demands for expanding China's socialist commodity economy and its modernized mass production.

The total reform of the economic system is an important and complex job involving the readjustment of economic interests and the shifting of administrative authority in all quarters. It is in this sense a profound revolution in the economic base and superstructure. Experience in China and other countries shows that we must undertake full preparation in guidelines, planning, work methods and similar areas and that the necessary material conditions be created so that this reform can be carried out systematically. It is absolutely essential to guard against impetuosity, rashness and hasty mass action. Our two previous major reforms of the economic system — in 1958 and again in 1970 — fell through because we failed to undertake thoroughgoing deliberations, lacked circumspect planning and preparation, rushed the pace of decentralization, and hastily abandoned old practices while failing to introduce new ones to take their place. Past experience shows that, while cementing our determination to carry out the reform, we should choose the right direction, take steady strides, coordinate the efforts of all quarters, and proceed in an orderly and systematic way and, all the while, try to accelerate the pace of the reform.

III. Progress in Restructuring the Economic System Over the Last Two Years

Restructuring has been going on for two years in various localities and departments in line with the instructions of the Chinese Communist Party Central Committee and the State Council and on the basis of extensive investigations and study. On the whole, the measures that have been taken are experimental. The following are the major aspects of this reform:

1. *Experiments have been carried out in extending the decision-making power of enterprises in the areas of operation and management.* The 6,600 industrial enterprises chosen to carry out these experiments together account for 60% of the total production value and 70% of the profits of all state-owned industrial enterprises in China. These experimental enterprises — which now enjoy certain economic benefits, some powers of decision-making in production, supply of raw materials and sale of products, and certain economic conditions for self-expansion — have now become economic units with a degree of self-determination. This transition has lent tremendous impetus to arousing the enthusiasm of workers and staff, expansion of production and improvement of operations and management. Preliminary statistics from 28 provinces, municipalities and autonomous regions show that 5,777 experimental enterprises registered a total value of industrial production of 165.3 billion yuan in 1980, which was 10.5 billion yuan, or 6.8%, more than in 1979. They realized a combined profit of 33.3 billion yuan, an increase of 3.5 billion yuan, or 11.8%, over 1979, and turned over to the state 2.9 billion yuan, an increase of 2 billion yuan, or 7.4%, over 1979.

2. *Market regulation has been practiced under the guidance of planning.* Capital goods have gradually entered the market as commodities, and many new sales outlets have been opened for consumer goods. Previously, however, all capital goods were produced and allocated according to plan; now such goods can be produced and sold by the enterprises themselves after they have met state quotas.

Last year, iron and steel enterprises sold on the market 2.91 million tons of rolled steel, which accounted for 11% of total national sales of rolled steel. Industrial enterprises under the First Ministry of Machine-Building sold on the open market 16 billion yuan's worth of products, accounting for 46% of the national total.

Most products controlled by the central ministries were produced according to plans drafted by the enterprises on the basis of orders received. Preliminary statistics show that 224 of the 256 categories of materials previously allocated by the state are now in ample supply on the open market. More than 600 companies and 60 exchange centres handling capital goods have been established in various places, and commission services in purchasing, marketing, processing and materials marketed by industrial enterprises themselves in 1980 came to a total value of 4.2 billion yuan. The production and marketing of consumer goods proceeded at an even brisker pace. Goods accounting for over 30% of total national retail sales last year were produced by enterprises on their own and in line with market demands.

3. *The financial system of "dividing revenues and expenditures between the central and local authorities and holding each responsible for its surplus and deficits" has been put into practice.* This two-tier system of financial management — plus the practice of allocating to the enterprises a share of excess (after quota) profits, allowing those who earn more to spend more, permitting all enterprises to retain their own savings and integrating rights and obligations — has inspired the enthusiasm and initiative of local authorities and enterprises to seek increased revenues and to

economize on operational expenses.

Local financial revenues in the country reached 77.6 billion yuan in 1980, an increase of 3.5% over 1979; local expenditures came to 56.4 billion yuan, down by 11%. A number of enterprises which had for long operated at a loss were ordered by local authorities to cease production or to switch to other lines, and to improve their financial management. These actions also help the economic readjustment.

4. *A number of enterprises have begun to organize themselves into specialized business companies, complexes or various other combinations.* A number of specialized companies and integrated enterprises have been established in some provinces and municipalities on the principle of co-operation along special lines and in conjunction with the readjustment of industry.

Statistics from 28 provinces, municipalities and autonomous regions show that 1,900 specialized companies and complexes had been formed by the end of 1980. Some 30% of the enterprises in the three municipalities of Beijing, Tianjin and Shanghai have now been merged into complexes or companies. In some cases, combinations of joint operations, joint ventures and compensation trade have been established between different localities, between state-owned and collective enterprises, or between urban enterprises and those run by rural communes or their subdivisions. These new establishments have improved economic performance since their structure enables the participating partners to turn their strong points to good account. In 1979, Shanghai's handicrafts industry established six complexes to produce athletic shoes, electric irons and other items. With different special lines working in cooperation, these complexes have increased production of athletic shoes by well over 50% and electric irons by 34%. More than 100 state farms in different parts of China have established joint enterprises involving farming, industry and commerce.

5. *Experiments have been carried out in changing the method for funding capital construction projects from state allocations to bank loans.* Over 550 construction projects in light industry, textiles, coal, electric power, petroleum, communications, building materials, distribution, tourism and other trades and industries have been selected for these experiments. The trades in light industry, textiles, railways, communications and other sectors have raised short and medium-term bank loans for the purpose of acquiring new equipment and tapping production potential, renovating and transforming enterprises. By the end of November 1980, these experimental units had signed contracts to finance 690 construction projects through loans totalling 3.35 billion yuan. Under previous practice, funds for capital construction projects were all earmarked by the state and neither the construction units nor the project-owning departments shouldered any economic responsibilities. Various departments and local authorities often vied with one another for funds and projects but made scarcely any careful checking into the use of funds or their economic returns. The change-over to the uee of bank loans has strengthened the sense of economic responsibility of these units, fully utilized the role of banks and improved economic results in general.

A good example is provided by the construction of a copper strip workshop with an annual capacity of 10,000 tons in Shanghai's nonferrous metal rolling mill. The original plan called for purchase of a set of rolling equipment with an annual capacity of 40,000 tons through an appropriation of 6.85 million yuan. However, the capacity of the rolling equipment was four times that of the actual need. After the method of funding was changed, the management of the mill gave it second thought and began to worry that they might not be able to repay the loans. So they gave up the plan and decided to adopt technical measures to tap the mill's existing potential. In the end, they raised a loan of about 2 million yuan and succeeded in satisfying market demands.

6. *Diversified forms of operation are encouraged, and expanded and varying sectors of the economy are permitted to exist simultaneously.* More flexible policies have been implemented in many rural areas in light of their specific conditions, and the system of job responsibility with reference to production quotas has been generally adopted. Some production teams have taken on the practice of fixing farm output quotas for each subgroup (or even for each household in backward mountain areas). Individual economic activity is permitted. A number of collectively-run enterprises in handicrafts, retail sales, catering, repair, transport and construction have reappeared.

As a result, large numbers of jobless people have found employment and the market has been enlivened to the benefit of the people. Of the 9 million people who found jobs in 1979, 4 million, or 44% of the total, were recruited by collective enterprises. The comparable figures for 1980 were 7 million, 2 million and 32%, respectively. There were 8.8 million self-employed workers in the early days of the People's Republic. The figure was cut to 2 million by 1966, and further reduced to 150,000 by the end of 1978. It rose to 320,000 in 1979 and again in 1980 to between 800,000 and 900,000.

In short, these preliminary measures to restructure the economic system, which represent only a small beginning, are breaking through the bounds of the present economic system and stimulating the enthusiasm and initiative of local authorities, enterprises and workers for improving management, increasing production and economizing. Very good results have been obtained, the economy as a whole has been invigorated and an abundance of experience has been accumulated for the future all-round restructuring of the economic system. The direction is correct and the success is notable.

IV. Requirements for Reform of the Economic System During the Period of Readjustment

In order to tackle more thoroughly the country's long-standing and serious economic dislocation and the new problems arising from ineffective readjustment and the faults and errors in our economic work during the last two years, the Party Central Committee and the State Council have set forth the task of further readjusting the national economy. Generally speaking, our strategies for readjustment and reform are interrelated and they should support each other both for the present and in the long run. In some cases, they cannot be separated from each other; in others, measures for readjustment can be effective only if they are accompanied by corresponding measures for reform. On the other hand, we must also take note of contradictions between the two just as we do in the case of other matters.

During the course of the readjustment, our economic resources will remain very limited in capacity; we do not have adequate financial and material resources for carrying out an all-round reform of the economic system. Neither is it possible for the leaders of the country to devote their energies equally to the readjustment and to the reform at the same time. Both are giantic tasks. This is why we must place the readjustment at the focal point, subordinate the reform to the readjustment, and make it serve the purposes of the readjustment.

To put it in more specific terms, we should actively carry out the reform in areas which help change the irrational structure in production; which help enliven production and distribution while ensuring the fulfilment of state plans; which help correctly handle relations between the state, the collective and the individual; and which inspire the enthusiasm of production and business units and of the workers. The reform must be slowed down in those aspects that may be rational in the long run but contradict the readjustment at present. In my view, the reform can be carried out in the following respects during the period of the readjustment:

1. *Consolidating and improving the restructuring of the system of enterprise management that has already been started.*

An important aspect of the current reform is to coordinate as far as possible into an integral whole those preliminary steps that have already been taken. Our experiments in broadening the decision-making power of the enterprises have mainly focused on the sharing of above-quota profits. Now we should take steps to raise the managerial level of the experimental enterprises and grant them the necessary authority in making decisions for expanding lateral links between enterprises. At the same time, we should strive to carry out the reorganization and merger of existing enterprises, particularly in the machine-building industry, in conjunction with the economic readjustment.

On the other hand, we should continue encouraging collective and individual trades and services in areas such as handicrafts, commerce, catering and repair. We should also continue expanding outlets for distribution and adopt a variety of forms of distribution in the light of the importance of different commodities and their supply and demand, thus invigorating the market.

2. *Making conscious use of the regulatory role of economic levers.*

We should adopt appropriate measures to carry out systematically a small-scale readjustment of prices between different products and trades so as to resolve the problem of drastic differences in the sharing of above-quota profits arising from irrational pricing. We should ensure that this new practice will truly benefit market supplies and competition between enterprises. We should also undertake the necessary experiments in taxation by systematically changing the practice of collecting profits from state-owned enterprises to the collecting of income taxes. This practice will ensure that all enterprises can derive average levels of profits from their capital funds under normal production and reasonable operations and ensure further that national and local authorities will continue to receive regular financial revenues.

In the use of funds, we should in a planned way undertake a transition from state budgetary appropriations (including capital construction investments and circulating funds) to bank loans. The banks should charge interest on these loans as a reflection of their regulatory role. As for employment, we should combine recommendations by labour departments with the practice of jobseekers organizing themselves for employment or finding jobs on their own. Enterprises may also recruit workers through open examinations according to their own personnel plans.

3. *Strengthening the guiding role of planning.*

With the development of lateral economic links, the state must greatly strengthen the guiding role of planning so as to meet the needs of socialized mass production, ensure the proportionate growth of the national economy, and avoid blindness in production and construction. But the state should devote its main energies to maintaining an overall balance by taking satisfactory measures to accommodate the major objectives of economic development, of establishing key ratios of the people's livelihood, of the scale of capital construction and of major construction projects. Only in this way is it possible to demonstrate the guiding role of planning. While maintaining a balance of finances, credits, material supplies and foreign exchange, the state should enable the enterprises to draft their annual plans in line with the requirements of the national plans and of the contracts they have signed.

Plans should be formulated from bottom to top and go through the process of coordinating and balancing at each level, so that the requirements of the higher and lower levels can be integrated and so that the role of regulation by means of planning and by means of regulation through the market can be turned to full account.

4. *At the same time, comprehensive economic departments should be established systematically at various levels; information and prediction systems should be set up accordingly; and controlling organizations for planning, statistics, banking, taxation and prices should be improved and strengthened.*

Further steps should be taken to promulgate appropriate economic laws and regulations and to establish corresponding supervisory organs. A variety of measures should be adopted to improve workers' education and efforts should be made to train large numbers of specialists in economic construction.

In short, readjustment and restructuring are inseparable from each other. The better they are coordinated, the more favourable it will be for the steady and harmonious development of our national economy. This is why we should actively carry on with those aspects of the reform which are effective and conducive to the readjustment, all the while taking the readjustment as the centre of our work. We must not give up the reform halfway. Still less, we must not turn back to the old state of affairs in which flexibility meant chaos and overall control led to stagnation. It is my view that the orientation of the restructuring of our economic system is correct and the experiments have produced signal successes. So long as we carry on our theoretical study and make constant improvements in practice, surely we will be able to develop a Chinese economic system that is different from either the Soviet model or from the model of any other country.

5. THE ADVANCEMENT OF INDUSTRIAL ENTERPRISES AMIDST CONSOLIDATION
By Yuan Baohua

Consolidation of enterprises is important for China's industry. While marked successes in restructuring enterprises have been reported in recent years, continued efforts to consolidate our enterprises in accordance with the requirements of socialist modernization will surely play a bigger role in implementing the Party Central Committee's policy of further readjustment of the economy and achievment of greater political stability.

1. How Did the Question Arise?

After the smashing of the Gang of Four, the Chinese Communist Party Central Committee launched a policy of consolidating China's industrial enterprises, aimed at exposing and criticizing Lin Biao and the Gang of Four, setting things right, and restoring and establishing normal production order. At the end of 1978, the Third Plenary Session of the 11th Party Central Committee made a historic decision to shift the focus of the party's work to socialist modernization. Soon after, the Central Committee introduced a policy of readjusting, restructuring, consolidating and improving the national economy (the Eight-Character Policy), ushering in a new period for the consolidation of industrial enterprises in our country.

Consolidation means to improve management, raise economic output, tap the potential of the enterprises and, especially, shake up those enterprises where management is in chaos. It is an important component for carrying out the "Eight-Character Policy." In the past three decades or so, China has built more than 370,000 industrial enterprises, including over 4,000 better-equipped big and medium-sized key enterprises. Our four modernizations must rely resolutely on the existing enterprises. But the potential of the enterprises cannot be fully realized owing to China's irrational economic structure, management system, organization of enterprises, and backward management. Waste is common and serious, economic output is low.

To change such a condition in a fundamental way, readjustment and restructuring are necessary. We can surely blaze a new trail for economic development if we go all out to readjust the grave disproportions, reform the unreasonable economic structure and management system, rationally organize present enterprises, and gradually realize rationalization of economic structure, management systems and enterprise organization. To achieve this, we should make unremitting efforts to shake up the enterprises.

Consolidation is the foundation. Without successful consolidation, there will be no reliable base for readjustment and restructuring, and improving economic results will be out of the question. In brief, the aim of readjustment, restructuring and consolidation is to liberate the productive forces and raise production levels, technical levels and management levels, so as better to meet the increasing material and cultural needs of the people. The four aspects of the "Eight-Character Policy" are interrelated and support each other. At present, the most important and urgent task before us is to shake up our enterprises, causing a readjustment which will tap their potential and seek better economic results through improved management.

2. A Review of History

We have been engaged in socialist construction and modern enterprise management for over 30 years. After Liberation, we confiscated bureaucrat-capitalist firms and turned them into socialist enterprises owned by the whole people. In these enterprises, we launched democratic reform and production improvement campaigns, eradicated the reactionary relations of production which exploited and enslaved the workers, and correspondingly established socialist enterprise management organs and systems, thus restoring and developing production rapidly. In 1952, our country victoriously accomplished the task of economic rehabilitation.

During the First Five-Year Plan period, the state concentrated efforts on building a number of key projects. At that time, we mainly gained experience from the Soviet Union and began to pay attention to employing scientific management systems and methods suitable for modern large-scale production. Through state plans, we integrated the production, technical and financial activities of enterprises in accordance with the demands for developing a socialist economy. Within the enterprises, we stressed the quality of products, business accounting, and intensified enterprise management. By so doing, industrial enterprise management in our country basically stepped onto the track of scientific management, and we obtained experience in managing socialist enterprises, trained large numbers of cadres, pushed production forward, and guaranteed the victorious advance of large-scale economic construction.

In learning from Soviet experience in enterprise management, there was the problem of mechanically copying their practices in total disregard of our own concrete conditions — such as sole reliance on administrative orders to the neglect of democratic management, one-sided stress on material incentives to the neglect of ideological work, etc. In 1956, Comrade Mao Zedong, in his speech "On The Ten Major Relationships," criticized the wrong attitude of blindly copying and learning from others. After that, we began to explore and evaluate our own system and methods of managing modern industrial enterprises, and gained some more experience.

But owing to "Left" mistakes in economic work, harmful trends appeared in the 1958 "Great Leap Forward," such as not paying attention to objective laws, arbitrarily abrogating rules and regulations, pursuing high targets without paying proper attention to quality and economic results.

In 1960, Comrade Mao Zedong summed up our country's experience in industrial enterprise management. In a report on the situation of the Anshan Iron and Steel Company, he presented important instructions and put forward the principles for modern enterprises (called the Charter of the Anshan Iron and Steel Company), stressing the importance of:
a) Keeping policies firmly in command;
b) Strengthening party leadership;
c) Launching vigorous mass movements;
d) Instituting the system of cadre participation in productive labour and worker participation in management, of reform of irrational and outdated rules and regulations, and of close cooperation among cadres, workers and technicians; and
e) Launching the technical revolution.

In 1961, in order to implement the policy of readjustment, consolidation, developing and raising standards as directed against the prevailing problems of enterprises at that time, the Party Central Committee formulated Regulations Concerning the Work in the State-Run Industrial Enterprises (Draft) (called "70-Point Document in Industry" for short). After several years of hard work, the party adopted a series of consolidation measures to change the chaotic management in many enterprises. As a result, economic results in enterprises improved markedly. The profit obtained per 100 yuan of investment in state-run enterprises rose from 8.5 yuan in 1962 to 24.2 yuan in 1966; labour productivity rose from 4,797 yuan in 1962 to 10,115 yuan in 1966, recording the highest level in history. During this period, the Daqing oilfield came to the limelight as an example of being self-reliant, hard-working and following our own road of developing industry.

Answering Comrade Mao Zedong's call "in industry, learn from Daqing," and after further practice, the people on the industrial front gradually established a set of management systems and methods which integrated our country's revolutionary traditions with scientific management in modern large-scale production, thus promoting the development of socialist economic construction. At that time, our country's industrial enterprise management was basically suited to the growth of the productive forces. The basic content of this set of management systems and methods can be summarized as follows:

— —To enforce the system of the factory director assuming responsibility under the leadership of the party committee, combining collective leadership with division of labour and individual responsibility, in accordance with the principle of democratic centralism;

— —To set up the system of a workers' congress under the leadership of the party committee, ensuring that the workers and staff can practice their democratic rights of participating in the management and supervising the cadres, thus combining centralized leadership with democratic management;

— —To institute the system of cadre participation in productive labour and worker participation in management, of reform of irrational and outdated rules and regulations, and of close cooperation among cadres, workers and technicians, so that they may jointly study and solve problems in production and management. This is an important system in following the mass line in enterprise management, correctly handling contradictions among the people and bringing into full play the initiative of the masses;

— —To launch the mass movement of technical innovations and creating rational proposals, so as to bring into full play the workers' socialist enthusiasm, wisdom and creativeness;

— —To set up various management systems with the job responsibility system as the centre, so that each worker has someone to look after, a special responsibility and a standard to follow, so that labour has a production quota. Special stress is put on establishing and perfecting the system of special responsibility in production techniques of the managerial personnel;

— —To adhere to the principle of considering ideological work to be of prime importance, combining political-ideological education with material reward; this principle is the basic guarantee to mobilize the socialist enthusiasm of the masses to do better work in enterprises;

— —To persist in the principle of running enterprises industriously and thriftily, to establish the system of business accounting, and to unfold economic activities analyses and all kinds of mass activities to practice economy.

3. Two Stages of Enterprise Consolidation and Their Achievements

After the smashing of the Gang of Four, the consolidation of China's industrial enterprises in light of the contents and special features may be divided into two stages:

The first referred to the two years prior to the Third Plenary Session of the 11th Party Central Committee. In this period, consolidation was basically in the nature of rehabilitation, with the main targets of solving the chaotic situation caused by the disruption and sabotage by Lin Biao and the Gang of Four, restoring control over the leadership of some enterprises which had been usurped by the Gang's followers, and speedily resuming production.

The second stage referred to the period after the Third Plenary Session. Along with the shift of the focus of work of the whole country and in order to meet the needs of the four modernizations, the party put forward new requirements for enterprise consolidation.

The consolidation of a rehabilitative nature was meant to heal the wounds of the ten year upheaval. During the "cultural revolution," Lin Biao and the Gang of Four savagely pushed the ultra-"Left" line to stir up anarchism and negate enterprise manaement. They criticized the so-called "theory of productive forces," "profit in command," "material incentives," "control, check, oppression," etc., thus doing away with a set of regulations and methods in enterprise management which had taken shape through long years of practice, and causing confusion in theory, thinking and management. As a result, many enterprises were forced to cease all work and production. They incited bourgeois factionalism, split the ranks of the proletariat, created a "full-scale civil war," causing real losses to production and construction.

After the downfall of the Gang of Four, in accordance with the six standards of enterprise consolidation put forward in the Decisions on Some Questions Concerning the Acceleration of Industrial Development (Draft) (Called "30-Point Document," for short) issued by the Party Central Committee, we, in the mass movement of learning from Daqing in industry, consolidated the leading bodies of the enterprises, vigorously strengthened the ranks of workers and staff, resumed and established necessary rules and regulations, and shook up the enterprises group by group in a planned way. After these shake-ups, the enterprises took on a new look, and outstanding results were made in enterprise management and production. Up to the end of 1979, 85% of the enterprises at the county level and above and 90% of the big and medium-sized enterprises had been consolidated. Taking the country as a whole, the task of consolidation of a rehabilitative nature was basically completed.

The Third Plenary Session of the 11th Party Central Committee pointed out: "Carrying out the four modernizations requires great growth in the productive forces, which in turn requires diverse changes in those aspects of the relations of production and the superstructure not in harmony with the growth of the productive forces, and requires changes in all methods of management, actions and thinking which stand in the way of such growth. Socialist modernization is therefore a profound and extensive revolution." The industrial departments conscientiously implemented the spirit of the Third Plenary Session, firmly carried out the principle of readjusting, restructuring, consolidating and improving the national economy.

From then on, the enterprise consolidation entered a second stage. Consolidation was carried out with production as the centre and the increase of economic results as the focus in an effort to raise the enterprises' levels of production, technology and management. While continuing enterprise consolidation, various areas and departments chose over 6,000 enterprises to experiment with in expanding decision-making power.

After the smashing of the Gang of Four, enterprise consolidation achieved the following remarkable successes:

— —Leading enterprise bodies were readjusted and strengthened and the composition of leading enterprise cadres initially improved. According to incomplete statistics in Beijing, Tianjin, Shanghai, Liaoning, Sichuan and Hubei, the number of leading cadres in key enterprises who have a grasp of technique and are familiar with management increased from one-third to one-half; their average age was lowered, the percentage of middle-aged and young cadres increased; the power of the leading bodies was enhanced.

— —Vigorous efforts were made to build up the ranks of workers and staff, thus increasing the workers' political consciousness and technical and professional level. Through political and ideological education, bourgeois factionalism was eradicated and proletarian ideological style was restored and carried forward. At the same time, in-service training was conducted. More than 328,000 leading cadres in the enterprises at the county level or above participated in training in rotation; 50% of the big and medium-sized enterprises ran their own schools, with about 20% of the workers and staff attending.

— — Basic work was strengthened. Many enterprises consolidated and strengthened the basic work of keeping original records, statistics, calculations, blueprints, technology, overhauls and technical standards. The enterprises under the First Ministry of Machine-Building Industry in the last few years persisted in strengthening the basic work in accordance with the 12 standards formulated by the ministry. By the end of 1980, 564 of the 597 key enterprises proved up to standards, accounting for 94.5% of the total.

— — Overall business accounting and total quality control were implemented. Many enterprises, the experimental units in particular, introduced the accounting system at the three levels of factory, workshop and team; some tried out the internal system of settling accounts in accordance with the principle of combining rights, responsibilities and interests, therefore bringing into full play the enthusiasm of the workers and staff and achieving outstanding results. Total quality control was gradually spread across the nation from key units to areas. By the end of 1980, the number of experimental units grew to over 4,400, energetically promoting the improvement of the quality of products.

— — Attention was being paid to enterprise operations. Many enterprises, under the guidance of state plans, made extensive use of the market, developed various forms of selling activities, attached importance to market investigations and forecasts, strengthened the sense of operations, marketing, competition and service, integrated production with demand and further linked up industrial production with the needs of the society. According to statistics, 46% of the 1980 total output value of the first Ministry of Machine-Building Industry was obtained through sales on the market.

— — The economic results of enterprises were raised. In 1980, while energy production dropped by 1.3%, industrial production increased by 8.7% over the 1979 level. The variety and number of specific industrial products increased and their quality improved. A total of 255 civil industrial products won gold or silver medals awarded by the state. Consumption of raw materials, fuel and power dropped. Labour productivity in industrial enterprises owned by the whole people reached 12,031 yuan, increasing by one-third over the 9,134 yuan in 1976 and surpassing the best level in history. Profits per 100 yuan of funding was 15.6 yuan, an increase of 27% over the 11.4 yuan of 1976. But other technical and economic targets did not reach the highest standard in history. The phenomenon of high consumption and big waste is still quite serious. This shows that our enterprises have great potential and that further consolidation and improvement are needed.

4. **Basic Tasks of Enterprise Consolidation**

Enterprise consolidation involves many aspects, so we must grasp the key points and concentrate our efforts on the outstanding weak links. At the same time, we must, in the light of the requirements of socialist modernization, make an overall plan, carry out constant shake-ups and make steady improvements. Judging from the practices in enterprise consolidation, we must pay attention to the following aspects:

1. *To do a good job in the consolidation and building of the leading bodies of the enterprises.*

This is the key to enterprise consolidation, and also the organizational guarantee for accomplishing the four modernizations. In the first stage of consolidation, around the work of exposing and criticizing Lin Biao and the Gang of Four, we put stress on solving the main problems in the leading bodies: to ferret out the factionalist set-up of Lin Biao and the Gang of Four in organization, to liquidate their pernicious influence, especially bourgeois factionalism, in ideology and style of work, to solve the problem of "weakness, laziness and aversion to discipline." By so doing, the majority of the enterprises each had a united and militant leading body.

The requirements for the second stage were to form a leading body that adhered to the four basic principles, resolutely carried out the party's line, principles and policies, and was capable of leading the workers to engage in the four modernizations with one heart and one mind; to solve in a planned way the problem of making the leading bodies "revolutionary, young, and with general and specialized knowledge." In order to open all avenues to recruiting people of talent, many areas and departments adopted the method of mass recommendations, examination by the higher authorities and coordination between higher and lower levels to choose and appoint capable persons. This method has gained good results.

2. *In order to establish and perfect the scientific management system, attention must be paid to all basic work, to restoring and establishing the system of job responsibility and to tightening labour discipline.*

After the first stage of consolidation, the

chaotic situation in management changed for the better, but the basic work was not done in a down-to-earth way.

So new measures have been taken during the past two years. For example, in taking concrete measures to ensure the fulfilment of the system of job responsibility, we reaffirmed the identity of rights, responsibility and interests, combined the three aspects — the system of job responsibility, the system of examination and the system of awards and penalties — establishing a direct link between the performance of the enterprise and the contribution of the individuals and material interests, thus bringing the initiative of the workers and staff into full play. In enterprise consolidation, we instituted total quality control and all-around business accounting and launched the nationwide movements of "high quality month," "safety month" and "energy conservation month," so that the basic work was further improved and advanced one step further towards the modernization of management.

3. *To strengthen democratic management is an important link in enterprise consolidation.*

The basic feature of socialist enterprise management is that the workers are masters of the enterprise and democratic management must be instituted; with progress in readjustment and restructuring, the workers become more and more concerned with the performance of the enterprise. In the experimental units for expanding decision-making power, workers can run their own affairs, enjoy more rights in democratic management and display greater socialist enthusiasm. After a few years of consolidation, we have restored and established various forms and systems of democratic management which had been undermined by Lin Biao and the Gang of Four, and set up and improved the system of workers' congresses which provides organizational and system guarantees for the workers' rights to participate in enterprise management and to supervise the cadres. Socialist democracy is further applied in the enterprises.

4. *To take positive measures to improve operation and performance is important in enlivening the enterprises and the economy.*

To carry out market regulation under the guidance of the state plan, it is necessary to put an end to the situation of paying attention only to production while neglecting sales, of grasping only management while ignoring business, to change from the method of stressing management inside the enterprise to the method of all-around management of integrating production and sales and initiatives both inside and outside the enterprise. Many enterprises have come to know that the key to improving operations lies in decisions, while the foundation to making correct business decisions lies in market investigations and forecasts. Therefore we must gradually establish a set of management systems sensitive in mirroring the market situation, and put the basis of running enterprises onto the track of serving the consumers. This is a new direction for industrial enterprise management in China.

5. *Implementation of the principle of distribution according to work, and restoration and establishment of a rational reward system are two effective measures to bring the enthusiasm of the workers and staff into full play and promote production.*

In order to ensure that bonuses really play the role of rewarding labour performed above quota and encouraging the advanced, the departments concerned are trying to find out and perfect the method of distributing bonuses so that the results of production and business can be closely integrated with workers' contributions. On the basis of readjusting production quotas and strengthening management, we generally adopt the method of giving awards according to work points, while some enterprises may give awards on the basis of piece-work for collectives surpassing production quotas, or practice the piece-rate wage system. In implementing the award system, we attach importance to aspects of collective welfare, such as housing, canteens, nurseries, etc.

6. *To devote major efforts to strengthening ideological and political work is an important guarantee for running an enterprise and for developing the economy.*

One of our party's good traditions is to strengthen ideological and political work. But, for a time, some comrades slackened ideological and political work, and wrongly thought that ideological and political work was no longer important since the emphasis of our work was on material interests. After criticizing the fallacy of Lin Biao and the Gang of Four that "spirit is all powerful," some enterprises went from one extreme to the other, one-sidedly stressing material interests, and distributing bonuses indiscriminately. The Party Central Committee in good time corrected this wrong trend, and now things have changed. From practice we have come to know that after the shift of the focus of our work, ideological and political work is still the life-line of economic work. Only by combining political and ideological education with concern for workers' material interests can the initiative of the masses be brought into full play.

7. *To do a good job in workers' training is an important task in developing the intellect to suit modernization.*

In these years, we have restored training in the basic technical and professional skills among the workers, opened all kinds of schools and training centres, employed different forms of study, trained in turn leading cadres of the enterprises, specialized managerial personnel and workers by means of releasing them from work for study or on-the-job training. A systematic educational system and regulations for workers have gradually come into being so that the work of workers' training has entered a new stage.

Resolutely implementing the principles and policies adopted since the Third Plenary Session of the 11th Party Central Committee, continuously working around the demands of improving management and raising economic results, our country's industrial enterprises are advancing victoriously on the course of consolidation. Our enterprises should operate in accord with the readjustment of the national economic structure and thus readjust product mix and service orientation under the guidance of state plans. It is necessary to reform various management systems within the enterprises in accordance with the demands of the reform of the economic system. The enterprises should be rationally organized in the light of the principle of cooperation between specialized units and rational economy. Thus we can manage our enterprises in a more scientific and modern way and make a greater contribution to the four modernizations.

6. WHAT TO DO AFTER WE HAVE DECIDED ON THE REFORM
By Yu Guangyuan

The economic structure must be reformed — this is a conclusion drawn from historical experiences and from lessons in China and other socialist countries. The Party Central Committee and the State Council are resolved to effect such a reform, and economic circles in China are identical in their views on the necessity of reform. The cadres and the masses, too, share the desire for reform. Of course, there are still some people who do not understand this necessity. That is why we have to elaborate and publicize it in detail. However, I am not going into that in this article. I'm going to discuss what should be done after we have resolved to effect a reform.

In my opinion, three problems should be solved properly, namely: 1. To clarify the orientation of the reform; 2. To create an overall design for the new economic structure; 3. To map out steps to enforce the reforms.

In clarifying the orientation, to my mind, our work has reached a stage where almost all questions to be considered have already been raised. Specifically, these are:

1. *The forms of socialist ownership that should be established and the rational structure of socialist ownership in China.*

This is the foundation of the socialist economic system. By socialist economic system, I mean the concrete form of the basic socialist economic system in a country.

2. *Policies towards the non-socialist economic sectors.*

At present, the socialist sector should not be the sole sector in our national economy. While some non-socialist economic sectors are not permitted to exist, some others — mainly the non-socialist individual economic sectors — should be allowed to exist and to properly expand on the condition that the socialist sector is predominant. The adoption of different policies towards different non-socialist economic sectors is a matter closely related to the socialist economic system, although it is not within the framework of the system itself.

3. *The economic function of the state and the means it employs to manage the national economy through planning.*

The economic function of the state comes within the framework of socialist ownership. What I am referring to is the role of the state only in managing the national economy. The questions concerning the means used by the state in its planned management of the national economy include: Which means are the chief ones — administrative or economic? What is the significance and role of administrative and legislative means if the economic means become the main ones to apply? What is the relationship between economic means and administrative and legislative means? Etc.

4. *The commodity nature of the products of the socialist economy and the role of the market in regulating production and consumption.*

The problems involved are: Whether or not the means of production should be considered as a commodity? To what extent and within what framework should the means of production of merchandized? What are the nature and characteristics of the socialist market? All these warrant study.

5. *The distribution of power among the enterprises and local and central administrative organs.*

The present formulation is to enlarge the decision-making power of the enterprises, remove restrictions between the administrative regions and trades, and promote integration of the enterprises in accordance with economic principles. The formulation of enlarging the enterprises' decision-making power should be applied only when the enterprises have been given too little of such power. It cannot be taken as a long-term policy since some day the enterprises will have enough power, in which case it should not be expanded further. But the distribution of power among enterprises and local and central administrative organs and the removal of barriers between regions and trades with a view to promoting combination of enterprises are long-term policies.

6. *The status of labourers as masters of economic units.*

It will take a fairly long time for labourers to go through the transition from participating in the management of an economic unit to fully becoming its masters. We should take a positive attitude towards labourers becoming masters of economic units. It is necessary to study the concrete conditions of a given enterprise. A number of systems should be established in economic units to support and facilitate this reform and to create conditions for the gradual progress from labourers' participation in management to management on their own.

7. *Various forms of socialist economic units, including grassroots economic units, joint economic units, economic units of different trades, and economic units combining producers with consumers.*

What should be their forms, status and roles?

8. *The roles played by various social organizations — the party, the trade unions and other social organizations — in socialist economic management and socialist economic development.*

In what manner should they do their work and carry out their activities?

There may still be other questions of orientation that have not been raised. But I think they are few.

To my mind, to put forward the abovementioned questions is in itself an achievement in our work to reform the economic system. It has enlivened the people's thinking and has paved the way for reform.

On the question of the orientation of the reform, our weak points are that not much theoretical work has been done, that the fundamental issues concerning this reform have not been fully discussed, that more attention has been paid to a few problems while others have been barely touched upon. If my judgment is correct, what should be done in this respect is to devote ourselves to further study of the theoretical basis for the reform of China's economic system. This study is indispensable to clarifying and ensuring the orientation of the reform, to educating the cadres and the masses and to persuading those who are still sceptical about the reform.

Preparing a Blueprint for the New Structure. As for the designing of the new economic structure, if we have a blueprint of the new structure our understanding of the orientation will become more distinct. Here I purposely apply the concept of engineering the design to the socialist economic structure, with a view to making people realize that before the reform is made, they must solve not only the question of orientation and principle but also many concrete problems. This will ensure that the proposed new economic structure is viable, that contradictions arising from the reform are foreseen, that methods to settle them are all at the ready, and that the new economic structure is a harmonious, integral one.

We all know that the various aspects of social economy — production, distribution, exchange and consumption — are closely interrelated as links in a chain. The direct production process is a process in which many departments are closely linked one after another by variety, quantity, direction and time. On the other hand, socialist economic organization as a whole is the summation of numerous grassroots units, departments, local administrative organs and other economic bodies. Therefore, the proposed reform of the economic system must link up the parts to form the whole and an overall plan is needed to make the new economic structure viable. Of course, this does not mean that a separate part of the reform cannot be carried out entirely. What I mean is that a particular reform can be made only if it is a part of the overall reform and is coupled with the other reforms. Otherwise, we shall encounter insurmountable difficulties.

What stage have we reached in this respect? It seems that only some reforms have been initially designed. As for the overall structural reform, we are still in the stage of investigation and experimentation aimed at gathering data. It is vital for us to act in conformity with the law of the development of things. We still need some time before we can work out an overall plan. But in terms of engineering design, of course, such an overall plan still cannot extend to the blueprint stage. It can only reach the draft stage. Even in the draft stage, such preparations as collecting data, hard thinking and drawing sketches may not have been completed.

So the design of a new economic structure is not an easy task. It cannot be accomplished by a few persons in an office. One should not raise the unrealistic demand for quick results. To advance bit by bit is permissible. Yet, we must have a plan for the overall design. Since we lack both experience and qualified persons in designing a new economic structure in a planned and systematic way, we must ponder over what kind of knowledge those persons engaged in this job should acquire and how they can as soon as possible make up for any deficiencies.

Any design must be examined. As far as an engineering design is concerned, the designers and the examiners should work independently of each other. The examiners, of course, should also have the required knowledge. Unfortunately, our intellectual institutions are far too weak. It is imperative to strengthen them substantially.

With regard to the third problem — the mapping out of steps to enforce the reform — we can say that if the second problem is how to draw up a blueprint for the new economic structure (a structure which is the ultimate result of the reform), then the third problem is how to work out a timetable for those measures to be taken one after another in order to establish the new economic structure.

Our definite aim is to effect an all-around and deep-going reform. We will not be content with partial or limited reforms. However, as the existing economic structure has seriously hindered the development of China's economy, we should take actions immediately rather than wait for the completion of the design of the new economic structure by economic theoreticians and practical workers.

From now on, we should get down to business and advance step by step. Unlike Hungary, which has a population of a little over 10 million, China, with a population of more than 900 million, faces a much more complicated situation. It has far more difficulties than Hungary has in carrying out reforms. It is therefore necessary to make some experiments and to first carry out reforms in some local areas so as to gain the experience needed for a comprehensive reform. What is more, the ten-year "cultural revolution" caused serious damage to China's economic construction. So every effort must be made to avoid losses that may be caused by possible dislocations in the course of the reform and to ensure that every reform measure can promote production. For these reasons, the problem of working out steps and measures for the reform is of particular importance. If they are taken properly, the reform may go smoothly and even quickly. If they are not properly chosen, the result will be the opposite: We will encounter difficulties that ought to be avoided, or even suffer setbacks.

Examination of Conditions Before Implementation. To enforce a reform measure requires certain conditions. In essence, the study of the steps of reform means a careful examination of all the conditions required for each measure. If we fail to get a clear idea of these conditions, we can hardly take appropriate steps. We cannot achieve the expected results if we insist on making a reform in the absence of the required conditions. On the other hand, if we fail to make a reform when the conditions are ripe, we will lose the opportunity.

In pressing forward a reform measure, the economic situation is a condition that must be taken into consideration. For instance, there exists a close link between readjustment of the national economy and economic reform. It is very difficult to carry out a comprehensive reform of the economic structure under circumstances where there are serious disproportions between various sectors of the national economy and when the industrial structure is grossly irrational. The readjustment will not only affect the overall reform but also certain individual reforms. Under the present situation in China, to do a good job in the readjustment of the national economy is a more pressing task than to carry out reforms, for the former will create a favourable condition for the latter.

Raising the Level of Organizational Work. To effect reforms, it is also necessary to raise the level of organizational work. We can take the rationalization of prices as an example. It is known to all that if the prices of products, raw materials and fuels are irrational, the net income and the profit rate can only reflect the ups-and-downs of the management level of an enterprise rather than the different levels of management of different trades. Consequently, the reform of enterprise production (e.g., to introduce planned management) by these economic means will be adversely affected. To effect such a reform measure, the improvement in our pricing work will become a prerequisite. Hungary took the establishment of a well-organized and dynamic pricing bureau as an important step in reforming the economic structure (of course, well-organized statistical work is also needed in this respect). As prices are very irrational and pricing work is poorly carried out in China, the adoption of the above-mentioned reform measures will meet many obstacles.

The Conditions for Reform. Some conditions required for taking a reform measure are not within the framework of reform. The economic situation and the organizational work mentioned above are two examples. However, some other reform measures themselves can serve as conditions for those reform measures which we are to study. That is why some reform measures should be carried out first, some should be enforced later and some should be adopted simultaneously.

We should also appreciate that some conditions required for taking a reform measure are quite complicated. For instance, as we plan to take net income and profit rates as means for introducing planned management of enterprises, whether or not the prices are rational becomes a criterion. But tax policy and credit policy may come up as a condition for employing these economic means. By way of reducing their taxes and extending credits to them at low interest rates, we can increase net incomes and raise the profit rates of those enterprises whose product prices are relatively low and whose costs are relatively high. As to those enterprises whose product prices are relatively high and costs relatively low, our approach may be just the opposite. This shows that pricing policy, tax policy and credit policy are complementary to each other. As a result, the "measure-condition" problem presents a greater complication.

The study of the stages of reform requires us not only to analyze the economic situation in

China and to follow its changes, but also to deepen our understanding of the law governing the economic movement. The two requirements can be taken as the first aspect. The second aspect is to sum up the experience in the course of reform. In the past few years we have, among other things, conducted experiments on expanding the decision-making power of enterprises. This measure has proved appropriate. It has promoted production and has by practice changed the minds of those who were sceptical about the reform. Such experiments as promoting integration of enterprises are also of significance. Good work should be done in summing up the experience gained in taking measures of an experimental nature. In summing up experence, the study of the conditions for effecting a certain measure is one of the most important functions.

7. SOCIALIST ECONOMIC DEMOCRACY — THE ESSENCE OF RESTRUCTURING ECONOMIC MANAGEMENT
By Jiang Yiwei

I. What Is the Essence of Restructuring Economic Management?

A leading member of the central authorities said recently that the way out for China's economy lies in the improvement of economic performance. What are the ways to improve economic performance?

One is readjustment and the other is restructuring. "We should, by way of readjustment and restructuring, achieve step by step the rationalization of the economic structure, the rationalization of the system of management and the rationalization of the organization of enterprises so as to explore a new road for developing our economy." As I understand, the three rationalizations are interrelated. The rationalization of the economic structure is the central point of readjustment, the rationalization of the system of management is the central point of restructuring, while the rationalization of the organization of enterprises involves both readjustment and restructuring.

Both readjustment and restructuring have their short-, medium- and long-range objectives. I am going to discuss the ultimate objective of restructuring or, in other words, the criterion or principle for rationalization of the system of economic management. In my view, this ultimate objective, this criterion or principle, is the achievement of socialist economic democracy; or, in other words, the establishment of a socialist system of economic management on the principle of democratic centralism.

Drawbacks of the Present System. We all know that the present system of economic management in our country has many drawbacks. The ultimate objective of our restructuring of the system of management is to provide a solution to problems such as: In what form can the activity of the national economy be rationally organized? Along what lines shall enterprises organize themselves? Along what lines shall relations between enterprises be organized? How can the state exercise centralized leadership so as to bring the relations of production into harmony with the demands of the growing productive forces?

What will be the model of the future system of management after the restructuring is completed? This is a question we are all concerned about. Quite a few comrades are worrying that restructuring might lead to capitalism. Some scholars and specialists abroad also view our restructuring in this light. As I see it, the restructuring we are now firmly carrying out is by no means oriented to capitalism. On the contrary, it is firmly oriented to socialism. What, after all, is the model for the system of management after this restructuring?

The tentative idea about combinations proposed by Marx and Engels in their early years provides a very good answer to this question. They said that an enterprise should be a combination of free and equal producers; the social economy should be a great alliance of all such combinations; and members of society should consciously engage in social labour in accordance with a common, rational plan. This tentative idea embodies both the democracy and the centralism as well as the unity of a socialist economy. Lenin also said that democratic centralism should be applied to the realm of the economy. I think it is in conformity with the four basic principles (adherence to the socialist road, Communist Party leadership, the dictatorship of the proletariat, and Marxism-Leninism-Mao Zedong Thought) to take these concepts as the guidelines as well as the objectives of our restructuring.

The achievement of socialist economic democracy is an inevitable demand raised by the development of the socialist economy. Economists in other countries define the Soviet Union's economic system as a model of the centralized type and that of Yugoslavia as a model of the decentralized type. The relationship between centralization and decentralization is essentially a relationship between democracy and centralism. It is a historical imperative, following the victory in socialist revolution, to transform the capitalist free economy into a unified socialist economy and to adopt the system of centralization for a certain period of time.

Lessons of the Soviet Union and Yugoslavia. China also adopted the Soviet model of centralization following the victory of the revolution. The development of the economy, however, laid bare the weaknesses of a system that stresses only centralization and thereby deprives the socialist economy of its vitality. Yugoslavia was the first country to tear itself away from this system and to strike out on its own path. But, in so doing, Yugoslavia's economy lapsed into over-decentralization, which also has shortcomings.

Drawing on the experience and lessons of both extremes, we should be able to blaze a new path by correctly handling the relationship between democracy and centralism and by practicing centralism on a foundation of democracy.

Viewed on a broader horizon, the issue of socialist democracy is also a fundamental problem in the current international Communist movement. Unless this problem is resolved, it will be very difficult to give full play to the superiority of the socialist system. Nor will it be possible to win ultimate victory over capitalism. Economic democracy constitutes the basis of political democracy; democratic reform of the economic system and the correct application of democratic centralism in the realm of the economy are objective demands raised by the development of socialism.

In view of the drawbacks of overcentralization, our restructuring must proceed from democracy, must take the enterprise as the basic unit, and must free it from present shackles. This emancipation, carried out on the basis of collectivism, is a historic action of great importance, while the establishment of a new socialist economic system based on democratic centralism is the essence of this restructuring.

II. The Enterprise Is a Combination of Free and Equal Producers

China's economy at the present stage is of necessity marked by the coexistence of various economic sectors. But the individual economy is not the principal component. The principal economic entities are the collectively operated enterprises. Despite distinctions in ownership, enterprises owned by the whole people and those run by collectives are all operations run by free and equal labourers collectively and all are basic units of the socialist economy.

To practice socialist economic democracy, it is essential first of all to emancipate the enterprises and recognize them as relatively independent commodity producers with relatively independent economic rights and interests. This is where our restructuring should and must start from. But our enterprises are, after all, different from capitalist enterprises in that there are no capitalists who own the means of production. This is why they ought to be regarded as combinations of free and equal producers. While capitalist economic democracy is based on individualist private ownership, socialist economic democracy is based on collectivist public ownership.

The Enterprises as Independent Commodity Producers. We can truly give full play to the superiority of the socialist system only if we recognize the enterprises as relatively independent commodity producers. Under the present system, what we mean by the integration of the labourers and the means of production in enterprises owned by the whole people is viewed from the angle of taking the labouring class as a whole. When it comes to an individual enterprise, the labourers do not have the feeling that they are the owners of the means of production and may even feel that they are not much different from hired labourers. Herein lies the reason why the enthusiasm of the workers in enterprises owned by the whole people, which are more advanced in terms of the relations of production, is not so high as in collectively run enterprises.

Our recognition of enterprises as relatively independent commodity producers possessing the right to use the means of production and a certain amount of power to allocate their fruits of labour will help resolve this problem. I don't think it is necessary for enterprises owned by the whole people to backslide to collective ownership. It is equally possible to fuse the labourers with the means of production in enterprises owned by the whole people through the practice of collective operation and collective responsibility for the results of operation, all the while maintaining the system of ownership by the whole people. Ownership by the whole people of the means of production has tremendous advantages because it favours the state's exercise of unified leadership over the national economy.

So there are two systems of ownership existing side by side: One is ownership by the whole people with operation by the collective; which means the state entrusts the enterprise, a combination of free and equal producers, with the responsibility of joint operation and management. The other is ownership and operation by the collective. Although both are operated collectively, there will still be differences between these two types of enterprises owing to their different systems of ownership. These differences are primarily manifested in their responsibility for profits and losses. Collective enterprises should be completely responsible for their own profits and losses, whereas the enterprises owned by the whole people should share profits and losses with the state.

Now there arises one question worth studying: Should a limit be set for the amount of capital goods in enterprises owned by the whole people, by collectives and by individuals — so as to prevent them from enjoying all the differential earnings yielded by the means of production?

"Rights" and "Interests" of the Enterprises. The relative independence of enterprises is mainly reflected in their possession of relatively independent rights and interests. What we call the power of decision, in effect, consists of two parts — "rights" and "interests." The issue of "rights" is the primary one. From the perspective of the entire social economy, the enterprises should be taken as the basic units and the state's centralized leadership should be built on the basis of democracy. As for the enterprise, it should likewise be organized on the principle of democratic centralism, with the entire staff exercising the enterprise's power of decision. We must not reform our system of management along the lines of the Soviet system of one-man leadership — by broadening the scope of the manager's authority only. This is why the reform of our system of management, while broadening the enterprise's power of decision, must further resolve the problem of democratic centralism within the enterprise. In reforming its system of management, the enterprise should take the workers' congress as the supreme organ of power and practice genuine democratic management, while enabling the director to give centralized guidance, so that a system of democratic centralism can be established by combining the two.

The second issue is that of "interests." The principle of material benefits should be implemented in an all-around way. First of all, the profits and losses of the enterprise should be shared rationally between the state and the enterprise, so that the enterprise receives benefits commensurate with contributions made in the form of labour by the enterprise as a whole. This, in essence, constitutes a distribution to the enterprise as a whole according to its work, and then this amount is again distributed among the small collectives and individuals in the enterprise according to their work. In this way, the workers' personal material interests will be linked up with the results of the enterprise's operation and management. The rational distribution of benefits among the state, the enterprise and the individual is an expression of the principle of democratic centralism in economic interests. Only in this way is it possible fully to arouse the enthusiasm of the labourers.

III. Combination of Enterprises and Great Alliances of Combinations

The social economy as a whole should move toward a democratic alliance with the enterprises as the basic units. Combination is an inevitable demand raised by the socialization of production. The question that needs to be studied in this connection is on what principle and in what form such combination should be achieved. To my mind, such combination should be formed on the principle of democratic centralism.

1. Combination of enterprises.

The growth of the productive forces requires the organization of economic activities on the principle of cooperation between different specialized lines. In this sense, the reform of our system of management is directly linked with the restructuring of industry.

The organizational principle for the combination of enterprises should be democratic centralism. Combination under capitalism develops spontaneously through competition and by way of annexation. Socialism, on the other hand, is able to promote combination in conformity with objective laws. The experiences of 1979 and 1980 tell us that neither sole reliance on administrative orders nor sole reliance on voluntary participation in forming such combination will suffice. It is necessary to integrate the two: relying on administrative authority to promote combination while forming such combination in line with objective economic laws. Administrative intervention is necessary in forming such combination, but the main task of administrative intervention is to break the bounds of different departments and localities, otherwise it would be impossible to achieve such combination.

Combination should be formed on the basis of voluntary participation and mutual benefit and, at the same time, administrative authority should be used to promote it. This is a manifestation of the principle of democratic centralism. The same principle should also be applied within the combination. A loosely knit combination or joint company may adopt the system whereby the manager shoulders full responsibility under the leadership of the board of directors or the joint committee.

Such combination may take a variety of forms. The differences between several concepts should be made clear. Cooperation between different specialized lines is one thing and combination of different enterprises is another. Such cooperation does not have to take the form of a combination; a combination does not have to take the form of a company, still less of a highly centralized corporation such as a trust. The combination may be loosely or closely knit but, whichever form it takes, it should be in harmony with the level of development of the productive forces and should help to improve economic performance. Uniform rules should not be applied indiscriminately.

What we refer to as an "enterprise" means an economic entity which operates independently and has independent business accounting. A participant in a loosely knit combination remains an enterprise and retains its own independent status. When a combination develops into an integrated company, it will do its business accounting independently and thus become an enterprise, and the subordinate factories will become its branches and cease to be independent enterprises. The company's organ of democratic management is the board of directors or management committee, and the organ of democratic management in a subordinate factory is the workers' congress. But a large company may also adopt the practice of exercising management at different levels. These are all applications of the principle of democratic centralism.

2. Combination of a whole trade.

To my mind, the combination of a whole trade is a kind of combination in management. This kind of organization is not an economic entity, be it called association or guild. It should be a democratic management body composed of the members and president of a council elected by the participating enterprises. The participants have both rights and obligations and should keep themselves within the confines of the rules and regulations of the trade. This body can take over part of the administrative power from the top on down and this helps break the bounds of different localities and departments. Each enterprise is free to join in or withdraw from an association of the trade, and may participate in one or several relevant associations at the same time.

An association plays the part of a bridge or link between different enterprises and between the enterprises on the one hand and the government on the other. Its functions are to draw up development programmes for the whole trade, make proposals to the administrative department in charge, stipulate through consultation the standards and prices of products and other common rules and regulations for the whole trade; organize inter-factory cooperation and hold consultations on economic benefits between different enterprises; arrange exchanges of technology and information and provide consulting services; and undertake cooperation in training personnel and introducing technologies.

There is a view that regards the administrative body of a trade as an economic entity which has the right to retain a share of the above-quota profits of the whole trade. This is open to question. If the body can regulate the earnings of its subordinate units, it becomes, in effect, a sort of company and ceases to be an organization of the above-mentioned character.

3. Economic centres — a regional combination.

An economic centre is a regional combination formed around a city (or town) and covering different trades. Different from either an administrative division or a local administrative organ, it is yet another form of combination in management which should be established on the basis of combinations existing within various trades. It could take the form of a democratically elected economic committee with the participation of various trade associations. The congregation of different trade associations will naturally give rise to economic centres, each with its special characteristics and advantages. The functions of such centres are to handle common economic issues and coordinate relations among various economic combinations and among various trade associations. By handling common problems, these centres will be able to take over a still bigger part of the functions of the present administrative organs at various levels. They may also be a kind of semi-official organ for democratic management in the economic field.

Proceeding from the combination of enterprises and the combination of trades to the establishment of economic centres, we are able to form a network of economic organizations or, in other words, to weld all of the combinations into a great alliance. Founded on a democratic basis, this great alliance will embody the essence of socialist economic democracy.

With the establishment of trade associations and economic centres, the government can greatly simplify its organs of economic management and systematically separate administration from enterprise.

IV. The State's Unified Leadership Over the Socialist Economy

The achievement of socialist economic democracy does not mean sole concentration on democracy to the neglect of centralism; it means the establishment of the state's unified leadership over the socialist economy on the basis of democracy. This means strengthening control over the macro-economy while enlivening the micro-economy. The present reform of the system of management is only preliminary and control over the macro-economy has failed to keep pace with this reform. It is therefore no wonder that certain problems have emerged. What we should do is to study ways of bringing such control abreast of the reform. We should not retreat to old methods in the face of new problems.

Quite a few people see control over the macro-economy as regulation through planning and see this control as opposition to regulation through the market. Others equate regulation through planning with the issuance of command plans. It follows that strengthening control over the macro-economy would seem to mean strengthening regulation through planning, and that strengthening regulation through planning would be equivalent to issuing command plans. These views are open to question. In my opinion, control over the macro-economy does not mean regulation through planning, still less the issuance of command plans. The content of control involves the whole process of the socialist economy and methods of control include those of an administrative and economic nature or a combination of both. So a single plan will be unable to solve all the problems.

The socialist economy is a planned economy. Management of the national economy through planning is a characteristic of the socialist economy. What we describe as management through planning consists of two functions: namely, planning and control. A plan is the objective of action; it is a tentative idea proposed in accordance with the objective economic laws. While a plan should be founded on scientific estimates, it is, after all, subjective. It follows that a plan, in its original sense, can only be a form of guideline. But it is entirely necessary for the state to act on behalf of all the labourers and to exercise unified leadership over the socialist economy; the state must draw up, after considering overall balance, a plan that accords more or less with the requirement for proportionate economic development as a unified objective for all labourers to work conscientiously to achieve.

As the expression of the will of the collective, a plan cannot materialize spontaneously. Its fulfilment or near fulfilment must depend on a requisite degree of regulation and control exercised by the state over the process of economic activities. But the drawing up of a plan and control over the macro-economy under the guidance of planning are two different matters. Such control should be exercised in a variety of ways and in many areas; it cannot be exercised merely by means of a plan. The command plan now being discussed is in essence a means of control through the management of material supplies. It is only one of a variety of control measures, although a very important one, and this measure alone cannot ensure the all-around fulfilment of the planned targets.

Control over the macro-economy should, at the very least, be instituted and systematized in the following respects:

1. **Administration.**

What we call separation of administration from enterprise does not mean that the government will no longer take care of the economy or that administration is no longer necessary; it means that the government will no longer issue direct orders concerning the economic activities of enterprises. On the contrary, administration is an important measure in exercising control over the macro-economy. It at least contains the following elements:

A. *Registration of enterprises:* The establishment of new enterprises and major changes in the business lines of old ones should be submitted to the relevant department for examination and approval and then registered with the department in charge of industrial and commercial administration. This is an important link to ensure proportionate development of the economy.

B. *Formulation of special rules and regulations:* These include specific rules and regulations — for environmental protection, safety in production, labour protection, standardization, patent rights and market management — which are to be followed by all enterprises.

C. *Organizational administration:* There should be government departments in charge of trade associations, economic centres and other organizations of democratic management. These departments need to exercise control over such matters as examination of the opening of new enterprises and their business scopes, examination and authorization of plans for major technical renovation and expansion, pooling of plans and statistics, appointment of managers (or directors) and examination of their qualifications.

2. **Legal control.**

While the state needs to formulate various economic policies and carry them out via the administration, a number of long-range principles and policies need to be institutionalized in legal form so that legal control can be exercised. These include laws concerning enterprises, environmental protection, safety in production, taxation, and legal sanction against embezzlement, bribery, major accidents and serious cases of waste.

3. **Key projects.**

Key construction projects should not only be carried out according to plan but should be directly organized by the state and turned over upon completion to the workers who will be responsible for operating the enterprises.

4. **Control of material supplies.**

In order to ensure the fulfilment of the planned targets, it is necessary for the state to exercise direct control over the manufacture and distribution of certain products. But the practice of the state in placing orders for goods should be adopted to replace the issue of so-called command plans. This practice is different from issuing command plans in that placing orders for goods is an economic activity in which the supply unit or commercial department, on behalf of the state, signs contracts with enterprises to define the economic responsibilities of either side in explicit terms. From the standpoint of the enterprises, fulfilling government and non-government orders and marketing their products directly or indirectly are all undertaken for the purpose of meeting market demands. The only difference is that government orders provide the most stable market and that giving priority to the fulfilment of government orders is the obligation of all socialist enterprises.

5. Control of capital.

All the capital of an enterprise owned by the whole people belongs to the whole people. It is illogical to say that the enterprise should have capital of its own. To strengthen unified control of capital and facilitate the separation of administration from enterprise, such capital may take the form of credits controlled by the state bank; the use of capital may be regulated by means of interest.

Here I would mention in passing the problem of handling certain categories of funds in an enterprise after the adoption of the practices of giving the enterprise a share of the above-quota profits and of the state collecting taxes instead of profits from the enterprise.

It is inappropriate to regard all those categories of funds of which the enterprise may keep a share for its own use as income belonging to the enterprise. These funds should be distinguished from one another according to their character and should be controlled by different methods.

Funds for expanding production have two different uses: one is for carrying out specific projects for better utilizing potential, for renovating or transforming the enterprise technologically, and for financing projects of scientific research and trial manufacture of new products. This portion of funds should be entered under production costs and does not have to be included under funds for expanding production. If necessary, such funds can be obtained from the bank in the form of a short-term loan. The other is for undertaking major technical transformation and expansion of the enterprise. This portion of funding is in the character of a state allocation of construction funds — funding which the enterprise has the right to use but does not own. If this portion of funding is not in use for the moment, it may be deposited in the Construction Bank. It may also be used in advance and obtained from the bank in the form of a loan, to be repaid with shares of above-quota earnings at a later stage. This part of funds should be retermed as "funds for production and construction." Plans for using them need to go through the process of examination and approval. Upon their completion and commission, such projects will become fixed assets of the enterprise and thus belong to the whole people. In order to give enterprises greater flexibility, the standards for the value of fixed assets may be raised appropriately.

Funds for collective welfare amenities also fall into two categories. One is for direct consumption by the workers, such as various kinds of subsidies and odd expenditures on welfare. This portion of the funds should rather be defrayed out of bonus funds to be discussed later on. The other portion is for constructing housing, hospitals and other such welfare facilities. This part is in the nature of a state allocation of social welfare funds, which the enterprise is entitled to use but does not own, and methods for repayment should be worked out. This kind of funding should be retermed as "funds for construction of welfare facilities" so that they can be differentiated from welfare expenditures in general.

Funds for awards should be renamed "bonus funds." Further reform may place this kind of funding within the wage fund category as part of collective payment for labour in the enterprise. This kind of funding can be used for two purposes. One is to be distributed directly among the workers; the other is to cover expenditures of welfare facilities such as hospitals and nurseries. This item of funding constitutes the real earning of the enterprise and it belongs to the entire staff.

Only by clearly defining the nature of each of the above items of funding is it possible for the state to exercise control over accumulation and consumption in the enterprises at the grassroots level. The profits or losses of an enterprise are mainly reflected in the increases or decreases of its bonus funds or rebates at a given ratio, and the enterprise has to hold back part of such funds as reserves.

6. Control of labour.

The regulation of labour power is also one of the chief means for macro-economic control. It is necessary to establish labour companies and give full play to their role so that they become economic entities for the recruiting, supplying and training of the labour force. The staff of an enterprise may be divided into three categories: regular workers, contract workers, and temporary workers. The second and third categories are to be provided by labour companies. After observation and testing over a given period of time, the enterprise may choose regular workers from among the contract and temporary workers. If and when the state is in a position to provide unemployment subsidies in the future, they may also be placed under the control of labour companies.

There are many other means of macroeconomic control, such as price control and regulation through taxes, both of which are important methods. In content, they represent economic levers and, in form, they constitute administrative control via the price and tax authorities.

In short, the state plan represents the goal of economic development which is to be fulfilled or approximately fulfilled by way of the abovementioned methods of control. The plan is an all-around programme, covering both production and circulation of materials directly under state control and those not directly under such control. In the distribution of the national income, it covers both the portion directly under state control and the portion which the enterprise is entitled to allocate or to utilize directly. Likewise, this kind of control through planning embodies the principle under which there exists both centralism and democracy, both discipline and freedom. This is why the essence or ultimate objective of restructuring the system of management can be regarded as the achievement of socialist economic democracy or, in other words, is how the principle of democratic centralism is to be applied to the realm of economics. This new system of economic management, which fully embodies the principles of socialism, can be established only under the system of socialist public ownership.

8. REFORM OF THE INDUSTRIAL MANAGEMENT SYSTEM IN SICHUAN PROVINCE

By Lin Ling

Vice-President, Academy of Social Sciences, Sichuan Province

The 11th Central Committee of the Chinese Communist Party at its Third Plenary Session set forth the policy and task of restructuring China's economic management system. In line with this policy, experimental reforms have been extensively carried out in various economic sectors in Sichuan Province — in industry, agriculture, supplies, commerce, planning, finance, banking, etc. The experiment, which began in the last quarter of 1978, has caught the attention of many people at home and abroad. This article is meant to provide a preliminary examination of the successes as well as of the experiences and lessons gained from the Sichuan experiment as carried out during the past two or more years within the industrial sector of the province.

Overcoming Two Defects: Over-Concentration of Power and Stifling Initiative

There are two serious defects in the industrial management system in our country. One is over-concentration of power; the other is "all eating from the same pot with no regard for merit." Under the latter system, enterprises have become appendages of government organs, with all of their initiative bound in fetters. Therefore, any positive reform must start with an extension of their decision-making power so as to bring their initiative into full play. The same is true of the situation in Sichuan. Beginning with trial enlargement of decision-making power in six industrial enterprises, the reform in Sichuan Province has expanded steadily both in magnitude and in the variety of forms it takes. To date, the number of enterprises at provincial, prefectural and municipal levels involved in the experiment has increased to 417, accounting for 70% of the total output value of local industry, 80% of its profits and 90% of the profits turned over to the state. These figures indicate that success or failure of the movement is of pivotal importance for the future of industry in the province. In addition, the experimental extension of decision-making power has also been introduced in a number of enterprises operated in the province by various ministries and in most of the enterprises at the county level as well.

The aim of extending the autonomous power of enterprises is to free them from the fetters of the existing management system and to transform them into true commodity producers enjoying relative independence. This objective can, however, by no means be achieved overnight but only through a process consisting of several stages.

The following is our scheme for Sichuan: At first, the enterprises involved will be allowed to retain a portion of their profits for themselves and be given correspondingly extended power over planning, marketing and expanded production; they will be allowed to keep separate accounts, contributing to the state by paying income tax instead of turning over their profits as previously, and assuming responsibility for profits and losses; finally, on the basis of thoroughgoing reforms in the financial and tax systems, the traditional departmental and regional affiliations of enterprises will be severed so as to make them still freer to the extent that they may manage their businesses independently, albeit under the guidence of the state plan.

At present, most of the enterprises involved in Sichuan are still in the first stage of the experiment and only ten are experimenting with the assumption of responsibility for profit and loss. Provided our plan is feasible, there will still be a long way to go before the enterprises can become veritable commodity producers enjoying relative independence.

Five Questions for the Reform

No sooner had the extension of decision-making power been attempted than a series of questions arose. These occurred mainly in five areas:

1. Should an enterprise be given certain powers over planning and, specifically, be allowed to organize production according to market needs under the guidance of the state plan?

2. Should an enterprise be given certain powers over marketing, and be allowed to market part of its products, including capital goods?

3. Should it be given certain economic interests of its own, and be allowed to retain as the enterprise fund a portion of its profits on its merits?

4. Should it be given certain powers over expanded production, and be allowed to use its own funds to engage in expanded production, tapping

its potential and undertaking innovation and transformation projects?

5. Should it be given certain power over personnel affairs, and be allowed, among other things, to promote managerial staff and to recruit or lay off employees?

Under the existing system, resolution of these problems by means of reforms will inevitably affect the powers presently enjoyed by the planning, financial, supplies, commercial, labour, personnel and other governmental branches — powers that in turn are governed by the policies, rules and regulations enforced by concerned departments of the central government. Hence, greater decision-making power for the enterprises is possible only when a change is made in the existing economic management system as a whole. Reforms must thus provide for the delegation of power to enterprises by the economic administrative departments concerned. In this sense, extension of the power of enterprises will add impetus from below to the introduction of reforms in the economic management system, and will objectively provide certain guidelines for the adoption of correct reforms.

During the past two years of experimentation in Sichuan, a series of important reforms have been introduced.

Under the former planning system, enterprises were required to adhere absolutely to production targets set for them by the state, which took the effect of commands. Today they are allowed to engage in extra production to satisfy market needs. They are also in a position to modify the state assignment with regard to the variety and specifications of the products to be turned out — in case they are found to be not well suited to market needs. Needless to say, this constitutes a major reform in the planning regime.

In the supplies field, the theory that capital goods are not to be regarded as commodities has been overturned. Exceptions exist for a limited number of items that bear upon the national economy and the people's livelihood, those that are in short supply, and dangerous articles such as explosives — the purchase and distribution of which still comes under unified state control. However, a greater part of capital goods are now allowed to enter into circulation. Such goods are made available either through supply contracts signed directly between enterprises, bypassing supplies departments, or through direct purchases on the market.

Commercially, diversified forms of purchasing and marketing (unified, selective, negotiated, etc.) and a variety of channels of distribution involving different forms of ownership (state, collective, individual and mixed) have replaced the conventional system of unified purchases, unified marketing and monopoly operations. Enterprises are now allowed to market part of their products through their own outlets. Large stores may receive deliveries direct from factories without having to go through wholesale channels.

Financially, there is a break-away from the conventional system of unified collection of revenues and unified expenditures by the state under which "all eat from the same pot with no regard for merit." The relatively separate economic interests of individual enterprises are recognized, while priority is given to the interests of the state as usual. They are now allowed to retain a portion of their profits. The precise amount hinges on their merits. Such funds may be used for tapping the enterprise's potential and for undertaking innovation and expansion projects, for providing increased collective welfare to workers and staff members, and for increasing bonuses.

In the labour system, enterprises are now empowered to promote middle-level cadres and to approve overtime work. However, two rights that have been granted — the right to recruitment based on skill and proficiency, and to dismissal — are actually not being exercised in view of the current government policy to maximize job opportunities.

In short, through the above-mentioned reforms, enterprises now enjoy varying degrees of power to conduct part of their own planning, to market part of their own products, to retain a portion of their profits, to engage in expanded reproduction with their own funds, and manage portions of their own labour and personnel affairs. Those enterprises experimenting with the assumption of financial responsibility enjoy greater power than others and are held responsible for their losses. As a result, they are undergoing a profound change: They have ceased to be passive instruments, like an abacus waiting to be operated by higher authorities. Rather, they have become like an organic body which possesses exhuberant vitality and dynamism and is able to propagate itself. This change in the nature of enterprises is of profound, far-reaching significance as it promises to enliven the entire economy.

Reform of the Management System

Our experience in Sichuan has shown that reform of the management system must be a multi-pronged operation. This is because in enlarging the decision-making powr of enterprises, additional power must be delegated to them at the same time in a number of areas which are inseparably related to one another. For instance, at the same time an enterprise is given greater power over its finances, it should also be granted greater power over its planning, marketing and expanded reproduction. Moreover, the management system of the national economy is an integral network composed of many lesser systems; what happens to the components is bound to affect the network as a whole. So reform of the financial system must be accompanied by corresponding reform of the planning, supplies, commercial, labour and other systems. Without orchestration, no band can possibly produce good music.

Here in Sichuan, reform is carried out through coordinated measures, although this is still at a low level. Further reforms will call for coordinated moves on a larger scale and at higher levels. It is beyond any doubt that when in future, overall reform of the management system of the national economy is undertaken, there has to be a comprehensive programme for coordination of work at high and low levels. In our view, those reforms aimed at extending the decision-making power of enterprises should call for coordinated moves on a small scale. Reforms such as those introduced in pricing and tax systems and in the removal of departmental and regional affiliations of enterprises to pave the way for their assuming of responsibility for profits and losses and for their embarking on a course of reorganization and integration — these should call for coordinated measures on a medium scale. The reform of the structure and leadership system of the national economy should call for coordinated moves on a large scale. This arrangement is made solely according to our tentative ideas, and practice is most likely to confront us with a situation much more complex than we think it is going to be. But one thing is certain: in a country as big as China, and in one with so uneven an economic development throughout its territory, no reform of the economic management system will succeed without the adoption of coordinated, synchronized measures within different spheres. But one should not refrain from an early start just because all of the required coordinative measures have not yet been organized.

The Regulatory Role of the Market

In the course of the experiment in Sichuan, an element which has always been considered as incompatible with the socialist economy — regulation through the market — has made its way into our economic life and has become a strong force in activating the economy.

The regulatory role of the market is notably visible in the following respects:

One long-standing theory has it that the law of value plays no regulatory role in the sphere of production in our country. Now that by means of the reform enterprises are empowered to engage in production outside the state plan, changes in supply and demand begin to a certain extent to regulate the production and the use of funds in these enterprises, making them also work for meeting market needs instead of operating solely for fulfilling the state plan. This constitutes a radical change in the functioning of the enterprises and greatly eases the long-standing problem of inadequate linkage between production and needs. It speaks to the fact that the sphere of production is not supposed to be separate from market regulation.

The same theory, while recognizing the regulatory role of the law of value in the sphere of distribution, confines it to the distribution of consumer goods exclusive of capital goods. In fact, under the influence of this theory, even consumer goods were being distributed in a planned way. All this had led to a serious state of disconnection between supply and demand. At present, the reform also subjects a greater proportion of capital goods to market mechanisms, thereby giving fuller play to the regulatory role of the market in the sphere of distribution. As a result, the gap between supply and demand has been narrowed substantially.

In the final analysis, market regulation is a question of price. Although we have not attempted any reforms in our pricing structure, which remains basically a unitary system of planned pricing, this structure has in fact disintegrated under the impact of market regulation. The new price pattern in effect today is composed of:

1. *Fixed prices* — those involving basic means of production and livelihood as well as a considerably large portion of commodities still exchanged at prices fixed by the state.

2. *Floating prices* — those mainly involving capital goods in excessive supply — such as electrical and mechanical equipment — whose prices are allowed to flat with their state-fixed prices as ceilings.

3. *Negotiated prices* — those mainly involving commodities in short supply, including both consumer and capital goods whose prices are fixed through negotiations between buyers and sellers.

4. *Free prices* — those prices offered at local market fairs which are automatically regulated by changes in supply and demand. This change in the pricing structure, while having resulted in price increases for a number of commodities, has helped reduce some of the more serious disparities between price and value and has paved the way for us to use price levers to promote production and to introduce additional reforms in the pricing structure.

Competition and Its Effects. The regulatory role of the market is having its most potent effects on those economic interests of enterprises which have begun to be determined by the competitiveness of their products on the market. As things stand today, the more competitive the products of an enterprise, the greater its economic gains; the less competitive its products, the smaller its economic gains. Thus, what has once been considered as one of the unique characteristics of capitalism — competition — has crept in among enterprises engaged in the same trade, apparently without being noticed. Market competition, like an invisible but powerful propeller, is driving our enterprises to exert their utmost to turn out fine, readily saleable products at low cost and to provide good services to customers in order to attain the best possible interests for themselves. Competition is constantly urging those lagging behind to catch up with the more advanced by improving their technical proficiency and management skills. Sichuan is one of the areas in China where industry is less developed. Its industrial products are far inferior in quality and variety to those produced in coastal areas. In the past, a protectionist policy was enforced in the interest of Sichuan's own industry to limit the entry of coastal products. The end result, however, was just the opposite, since it was backwardness that was being shielded.

Now, as protectionism has given way to competition and as large quantities of coastal goods are streaming in, people begin worrying again that local industry might be defeated in the keen competition. However, facts show that while on the one hand, competition does pose a serious threat to local industry, on the other it provides an impetus more vigorous than any administrative means can promote. It urges enterprises in the province to go all out to increase their technical proficiency and to improve their management. Today, more and more Sichuan products have found themselves to be in a good competitive position nationwide.

The emergence of competition among socialist enterprises owned by the whole people and the economic results it has yielded shows that even in the socialist mode of production there are objective conditions for the existence of competition. Where there is commodity economy, there is competition — with the only possible difference being in its character. Hence, socialism is not exclusive of competition but should "protect" it. The State Council decision on "protection of competition" is a breakthrough both in theory and in practice and will certainly have far-reaching effects on the development of our economy.

The four aspects mentioned above all testify to the regulatory role of the market. How then can one best combine regulation through planning with regulation through the market? It must be admitted that this is a problem still awaiting proper solution in Sichuan. But it is equally true that the macro-economy has not gotten out of hand because of the presence of market regulation. The state has not ceased handing down mandatory production plans. Production based on market trends accounted for only 20% of total output in terms of value in 1980. This shows that production according to plan has remained dominant. In the same year, retail sales bypassing state channels accounted for only 17% of the total, with industrial goods marketed by enterprises themselves occupying only 6%. This shows state commerce has remained the main channel in the distribution of commodities. As for prices, those of principal capital goods, daily necessities, and of most other commodities remained under the control of the state plan. It is true that because of inadequate guidance by the state plan, there were instances of confusion in pricing. But they did not represent the main trend of development in the coexistence of regulation through planning and competition.

Cooperation and Integration. By enjoying greater decision-making power and by engaging in competition, enterprises begin to break through the confines of trade, region and ownership. Direct horizontal links have now been established between industrial enterprises, between industrial enterprises on the one hand and supplies and commercial enterprises on the other, between industrial and agricultural enterprises, and between industrial enterprises and scientific research institutes. A variety of new forms of cooperation and integration along specialized lines have developed at appropriate moments. There are associations of producers mainly devoted to the manufacture of the same product, associations of marketing, associations for producing complete sets of equipment through mutually complementary operations and production-research associations for developing new products and new technologies, as well as agriculture-industry, agriculture-commerce, and agriculture-industry-commerce complexes. At the end of 1980, there were 45 specialized companies, 8 combinations and 150 associates of all descriptions encompassing a total of 988 enterprises.

As specialized companies and economic associations came into being, a process of concentration of means of production and funds took place, resulting in the development of additional productive forces. For instance, the Zhongqing Clock and Watch Industrial Co., which acquired a yearly production capacity of 700,000 alarm clocks and 300,000 wristwatches with 17 million yuan of investment over 12 years, has boosted its output of alarm clocks by 43% to 1 million and that of wristwatches by 66% to 500,000 within one year. The story is that since last year, when it assumed responsibility for its own profits and losses, the company has entered into partnership with 20 other enterprises.

Judging from the experience in Sichuan Province, the development of cooperation and integration along specialized lines is not at all an artificial process but one evolving from the intrinsic need of the enterprises in competition to acquire larger production capacities and to achieve better economic results. For this reason, to do a good job of extending the decision-making power of enterprises and to encourage competition among them will be of great importance in promoting such cooperation and integration. Any such cooperation and partnership must be based on the principle of equality and mutual benefit. One-sided emphasis on rationality in the division and coordination of work without paying due attention to the economic interests of the parties concerned would make integration impossible. In other words, a partnership will succeed only when it protects and advances the economic interests of all. The regional or departmental affiliation of enterprises constitutes the biggest barrier to their cooperation and integration, and must be removed in order to make them relatively independent. This means that other reforms must be introduced as well, including one by which enterprises contribute to the state by paying income tax instead of turning over profits as before.

Ours is a socialist planned economy. Cooperation and integration along specialized lines must be programmed as a whole from the higher levels so that it will be organized rationally and carried out in a systematic and planned way. To ensure plain sailing, the present "free combination" at the grassroots level must be lent a hand by state organs acting as promoters, organizers, coordinators and intercessors.

Formulas for the Distribution of Profits

In this experiment, our province, basing itself on the recognition that enterprises should have relatively separate interests of their own, has worked out and tried five formulas for the distribution of profits between the state and the enterprises and three formulas for the distribution of profits between the enterprise and individuals.

The five formulas are:
1. A sharing of the basic profits plus a sharing of the output.
2. A sharing of the whole of the profit.
3. The enterprise assumes chief responsibility for its profit and loss.
4. The enterprise is held financially responsible only in case of losses or small surpluses.
5. A 4:3:3 (or 4:4:2) profit sharing ratio for enterprises at the county level.

All the five formulas are effective but with some defects.

The first provides reliability and security in revenue for both the state and the enterprise. But since the basic profit defined for each year is to be calculated on the basis of the previous year's actual profit, it tends to dampen the enthusiasm of the enterprise for tapping its potential in a big way.

The second one is easily applicable. But an improper ratio for the share-out would, to a certain degree, adversely affect the revenue of the state.

The third formula, under which the revenue of the state is guaranteed and the enterprise has some risk to run, proves markedly effective in bringing about better economic results. But as an income tax rate has thereby to be fixed for each enterprise, it is not easy to apply this formula extensively.

The fourth proves to be effectual as well. The Zhongqing Metallurgical Industry Bureau applied the formula on a trade-wide basis and achieved even better results.

The fifth is meant for small county-run enterprises, which, however, can be expected to attain still better economic results if switched to the system of bearing responsibility for profits and losses and of contributing to the state in income tax instead of turning over its profits.

Our experience in Sichuan shows that in distributing profits (after industrial and commercial taxes) between the state and the enterprise, a proper ratio must be set and a clear division must be made between expenses to be assumed by the state and those taken by the enterprise itself. Thus, the interests of the state, which should always come first, are ensured and those of the enterprise are kept up rationally. Any improper treatment would result in disputes between industrial and financial departments, or between the enterprise and financial departments concerned, and even lead to divergent appraisals of the reform itself.

The objective criterion for a proper approach is that the enterprise be made responsible for meeting expenses to be incurred in undertaking expanded reproduction (an undertaking closely linked to simple reproduction), for providing collective welfare for its workers and staff and for paying their wages and bonuses — since the enterprise as a more or less independent commodity producer held responsible for its profits and losses, it now enjoys economic power in these three areas. Given that this criterion is correct, the proper ratio for the division of profit between the state and the enterprise should, as the experiment in Sichuan has identified, stand at 80% : 20%.

But the economic power delegated to the enterprise to make it into a relatively independent commodity producer is not the only factor to be taken into account in determining a proper ratio. The fiscal situation of the state also counts considerably. In view of the economic situation in recent months, the share of the profit to be retailed by the enterprise should be limited to an amount which is potentially recoverable by the treasury from future growth in the enterprise's profits. This is because reform of the economic management system can go on healthily only when there is a steady growth in the state's financial revenues. If no increase is possible, then there should at least be a reduction in expenditures. Judging from the experience in Sichuan over the past two years, we believe 10% to be the proper rate for profit retention.

The three formulas for the distribution of profits between the enterprise and its workers and staff are:

1. When the division of profits between the state and the enterprise is based on a sharing of the basic profit plus a sharing of the output, the basic wages of the workers and staff, the officially prescribed bonus rates (equivalent to 12% of standard wages) and the collective welfare fund (equivalent to 11% of the total wage outlay) should both be handled as usual according to relevant state stipulations, but an additional sum should be appropriated from the retained profits for defraying collective welfare expenditures and new bonuses for individuals.

2. Where a sharing of the entire profit is practiced, basic wages should be handled as usual according to state stipulations, but all funds for collective welfare and for bonuses should be defrayed from the retained profits.

3. In an enterprise held responsible for profits and losses, basic wages, bonuses and collective welfare funds should all be appropriated from its after-tax profits.

These three formulas make enterprises different in their relationships to the economic interests of their workers and staff members. An enterprise adopting the third formula is closest to its employees while one using the second formula comes next. An enterprise operating under the first formula is believed to be least close to its employees. But even so, it is a formula much preferred to "eating from the same pot with no regard for merit." It is my view that the third formula should be applied wherever possible so as to place the enterprise and its workers and staff all in the same boat. Before taking up that formula, it is advisable to take the first two formulas as the stepping stones.

The Question of Leadership in the Enterprises

By the time an enterprise has come to enjoy greater power in running its business, the question of who is to decide on important matters arises. Ours are socialist enterprises which theoretically are mastered by the workers. But as there was little decision-making power for the enterprises before. The workers, although nominally entitled to taking part in the management, found themselves in a position of being able only to fulfil tasks assigned to them from above, without being able to participate in the making of decisions on important matters.

Now that the enterprise enjoys powers of self-management, one of the most important things to do is to define the proper relationship between the director and the workers. In some socialist countries, the relationship between the director and the workers in an enterprise has turned out to be one of subordination of the latter to the former. Consequently, success or failure of the management depends largely on the decisions made by the director. In Yugoslavia, where a system of autonomy of the workers has been in effect for years, the director of a plant is responsible to the workers' committee. Under conditions existing in China, it is necessary to convert gradually the workers' congress into organs of power of the enterprises. The director, charged with the management of the enterprise as the representative of the workers and staff, should be elected by the workers' congress and be held responsible to it.

In the meantime, under the system of state ownership, the director is in charge of management as the representative of the state and should therefore be appointed by and held responsible to the state. All important matters concerning the enterprise should be decided by the workers' congress. The director should take part in the making of decisions from beginning to end and should execute the resolutions of the congress. In case of a resolution running counter to the interests or policies of the state, the director is entitled to request its reconsideration, to stay its execution and to report to higher authorities for an examination and ruling. Such a procedure of decision-making appears to better suit actual conditions in our country.

The reforms in Sichuan as cited above have enlivened its industry and agriculture to a degree unheard of before. In the first year of the experiment, the total output value of the 84 enterprises involved rose by 14.9%, their profits by 33%, and their turned-over profits by 24.2%, as compared with the preceding year. All of these growth rates surpassed those achieved by comparable enterprises not involved in the experiment. In the second year, five enterprises experimenting with the assumption of responsibility for profit and loss manifested their newly acquired vitality with a 41.7% increase in total output value, an 80.7% rise in their profits and a 49.1% hike in their turned-over profits, as compared with 1979. Enterprises experimenting with the system of profit retention registered a lower rate of output growth than in 1979 because of serious below-capacity operations in those heavy industrial enterprises beset with energy shortages. Nevertheless, they made remarkable progress in achieving better economic results and in better meeting the needs of society by changing their product line-up and improving the quality and variety of their products and the serviceability of the enterprises. Collective welfare services in these enterprises, especially housing projects, improved in unprecedented proportions. The income of the workers increased considerably. Moreover, the effects of the reforms were felt far beyond the economic sphere. They have extended to the superstructure of the society, including the ideology of the people, in that the reforms have helped to remold some of the people's old conceptions and alter their cultural life. The reforms have opened the eyes of the people to where the hope of China's economic development lies, making them more confident in carrying forward the four modernizations. All this is of greater importance than mere economic gains.

New Problems Encountered in Course of the Reforms

On the other hand, the reform of the industrial management system in Sichuan has run up against some new problems. While trying to enliven the micro-economy, we did not provide adequate guidance for and exercise enough control over the macro-economy. We thereby experienced cases of failure to observe the state plan, of excessive and willful issuance of bonuses, and of unauthorized prolongation of the list of items for sale through an enterprise's own outlets. While giving scope to the regulatory role of the market, we failed to exercise adequate control and supervision over the market accordingly and to subject violations of law and discipline to timely sanctions and penalties. Some measures of reform did not prove appropriate enough, thereby affecting the correct handling of the mutual interests of the state, the enterprise and the individual, and of those interests between the enterprises. Nevertheless, these are problems that have cropped up along the way of advance and we are capable of solving them by summing up our experience from time to time while carrying on with our reforms.

With regard to the reform now underway, there are questions on which views differ, and discussions are therefore needed:

1. *Criterion for Assessing the Results of the Reform*

A scientific criterion must be set up for assessing the results of the reform of the industrial system or of the economic system. In Sichuan, the rates of growth in output value, profit and turned-over profit are employed as yardsticks. This suggests that the higher the rates, the better the results of the reform; the lower the rates, the lesser the results. If the rates are down, the reform is believed to have gone wrong. In 1979, when growth rates achieved in the three areas were impressive, people generally applauded the reform as indispensable. In 1980, however, when rates were not so impressive and when some of the enterprises even experienced declines instead of growths, some people began to question the reform. The question is then whether or not the three indices should constitute the only scientific indicators of the success of a reform. The answer offered by our practice is — "not quite."

In 1979, thanks to an extension of decision-making power, the Chengdu Measuring and Cutting Tools Plant, as compared with the preceding year, scored an increase of 28.97% in output value, a rise of 25.97% in profit and a growth of 15.7% in the profit turned over to the state. But blindness in production in the same year resulted in stockpiles amounting to 14 million yuan, or 25% of total output. The following year the state assignment for the plant was two-thirds less than in 1979, with many of the items on the list being virtually unmarketable. Remembering the lesson of the preceding year, the plant coped with the situation by turning to market needs. It changed its product line-up and developed a number of new products on a trial basis; it succeeded in adding operations for mining, tanning, railway transport and other trades, apart from serving its traditional customer — the machine-building industry. It thereby greatly broadened its markets and enriched its technological resources. The result was that all of the products turned out by the plant in that year proved readily saleable. But viewed against the three indices, the plant declined by 16.82% in output value, by 11.23% in profit and by 8.27% in the turned-over profit as compared with 1979.

The same was true of the situation in the Chengdu Seamless Steel Tube Plant, the Ningjiang Machine Tool Plant and the Zigong Hard Alloy Smelter.

A question is then put to us: As far as social and economic results are concerned, shall we prefer to have high growth rates in the three indices together with huge stockpiles, or lesser or even negative growth rates accompanied by a high marketability of products? Needless to say, it would be best to achieve both high growth rates and high marketability at the same time. But if one has to choose between the two, the latter is more preferable because it means more social wealth has been created and people can benefit more from it, and this is the very objective we want to attain in readjusting our national economy and launching the reform of the economic management system.

Hence our conclusion: proper assessment of the results of a reform of the industrial system should in the main be based on how well social needs are met subsequently and not just based on the mere growth rates in output value, profits and turned-over profits. (By the way, evaluation based on the three indices is in itself not scientific enough during a period of overall economic readjustment, when the external conditions of an enterprise could be so changeable that many items are simply incomparable with what they were a year ago.)

2. *Expanded Reproduction in an Enterprise With its Own Funds*

Leaders of the State Council recently pointed out that from now on we must not develop our national economy chiefly by increasing capital construction projects but by giving fuller play to the role of our existing enterprises. This is a decision of paramount importance which will help us to get rid of the inveterate obsession for undertaking capital construction projects and establishing new enterprises. It will help us blaze a new trail towards steady development based on improved economic results of the existing enterprises. But how to do it remains a problem. Some economists are of the view that in giving fuller play to the role of the existing enterprises, the primary thing to do is to scrap the existing depreciation rate for fixed assets and return the depreciation funds almost in their entirety to the original enterprises for use in equipment renewal in consonance with scientific and technological progress. And expanded reproduction in the existing enterprises should be financed by new state investments.

In Sichuan, however, a different view and a new approach have developed through practices over the past two years or more. That is, in addition to being left with the major part of the depreciation funds for use in equipment renewal at its own discretion, the enterprise should be encouraged to engage in expanded reproduction, which is closely linked with simple reproduction, with its own funds and, when necessary, with loans from banks. The most distinct advantage of this formula is that it relates the transformation directly to the economic interests of the enterprise, thereby giving strong stimulus to the initiative of the enterprise and the workers. Under this formula, expansion projects will be carried out with careful calculation in the use of funds, materials, equipment and manpower and will take the shortest possible time to complete. In a word, this is a way to achieve greater, faster, better and more economical results than could possibly be achieved if the state were acting as the investor in an expansion project. It is estimated that in the past two years, expansion projects undertaken by the enterprises themselves cost almost 25% less than they would have if the state had been in charge.

Would dependence on enterprises or banks for funds in expansion projects lead to cases of overlapping in capital construction and production and result in too big a scope in capital construction? It is possible. But this situation can be averted if greater control is exercised on the macro-economy for an overall balance and if such expansion projects are made subject to authorization by government organs. As a matter of fact, whether or not a major project of expansion can come to fruition often depends on the availability of the required raw materials, energy supplies, equipment and semi-finished products and transportation means. Such elements are beyond the control of an individual enterprise and can be made available only through balance-conscious planning departments.

At present, since the serious disproportions in our national economy have not yet been corrected, enterprises should be given limited power over investment for expansion purposes and tighter control should be exercised over the macro-economy. But once the economy returns to a state of proportional balance, greater power can then be delegated so as to give fuller play to the initiative and the investment potential of the enterprises.

3. *Activation and Control*

Activating our economy is one of the objectives of our reform, a goal that is to be attained by extending the decision-making power of enterprises over planning, marketing, pricing, use of retained profits, expanded reproduction, etc. While the economy is livening up, disorder and even speculation and other violations of law and discipline may be expected to take place concomitantly. Our reform is based on the premise that ours is a socialist planned commodity economy, and is aimed at giving full play to the regulatory role of the market and to greatly promoting commodity production and commodity exchange under the guidance of the state plan. Hence we must tackle those ills and defects typical of the commodity economy that have stemmed from our reforms. That is to say, while we try hard to enliven the micro-economy, we must put an end to disorder and violations of law and discipline by stepping up the work of planning, guidance and regulation of the macro-economy. This includes the use of sanctions where necessary. Efforts on these two tracks can be complementary and should go hand-in-hand.

Because of lax control, the reforms in Sichuan did give rise to a certain amount of disorder. Some people — without bothering to make specific analyses — blamed the disorder entirely on our effort to enliven the economy and advocated a return to rigid control over the economy. In truth, exercise of rigid control is one thing we are capable of and is an easy task to perform since we have a lots of administrative organs around. And it did happen that for a time in some places in Sichuan, while disorder was being brought under control, the economy lost its liveliness. Today more and more people have come to realize that the long-standing alternating state of disorder and inertia within the economy — caused by a stress on activation at one point and on rigid control at another — must be discontinued at any rate. Our policy should be one that ensures both liveliness and order. To activate our economy is the fundamental goal, and one for which support must be given. To bring an end to disorder is also necessary. But one must first correctly distinguish disorder from liveliness and then proceed to tackle those real problems by steering things into the right course with combined economic, administrative and legal means. As long as there is a commodity economy, there will be some sort of disorder. Hence, the assurance of both liveliness and order will be our task for a long time to come.

4. Protection of the Vested Interests of the Enterprises

Enterprises owned by the whole people should have relatively distinct interests of their own. This is what Sichuan has achieved through the reform of its industrial system. Once an enterprise has acquired economic interests of its own, it also gains an internal motivating force to actively manage its own economy. The question now, and one that Sichuan has not solved properly thus far, is how to correctly integrate the interests of the enterprises with those of the state, and how to make the interests of individual enterprises more or less identical with one another. The most controversial issue involved is whether or not the vested interests of an enterprise should be preserved. In view of the changeableness of policy in the past, enterprises endowed with extended decision-making power now strongly demand that their interest be protected from possible equalitarian action at their expense or from any reversal of the present situation. This is only just. To deprive enterprises of their gains will only spell failure for the reform. So, whether or not the interests of enterprises should be protected is a matter of principle that affects whether or not the reform should be carried forward at all. Nevertheless, while many of the gains of the enterprises have been legitimate, others have not been. Legitimate gains are those derived from improved management, from higher labour productivity and from the better economic results yielded. Illegitimate gains are those derived from some excessive high prices fixed by the state, from advanced installations and equipment in place prior to the reform, and from ease of access to various resources. Only legitimate interests should be effectively protected. The illegitimate ones should be subject to readjustment and regulation in accordance with new policies to be worked out. In 1979, a very generalized sologan with no regard for legitimacy — "safeguard the vested interests of enterprises" — was followed in Sichuan. As a result, a number of enterprises were able to achieve part of their gains at the expense of the state; moreover, the imbalance of interests caused by the special advantages or handicaps of individual enterprises was allowed to persist. This should be taken as a lesson. But the solution to these problems must be approached gradually and should be based on reforms in the pricing and tax systems. Haste will only lend to new problems.

5. Assumption of Financial Responsibility by Enterprises Owned by the Whole People

Whether or not enterprises owned by the whole people can or should be allowed to assume responsibility for profits and losses remains a controversial issue among many theoreticians and within various administrative departments. Initial practice in Sichuan shows that an enterprise of such ownership should not always come under the scheme of profit retention within the reform if the goal is to have it become a relatively independent commodity producer. Although it remains true that an enterprise practicing the system of profit retention is better off than one in which the state is responsible for all its income and spending, such an enterprise will still find itself falling into the category in which "all eat from the same pot." Only in bearing the responsibility for its profits and losses can the role of an enterprise as a commodity producer be brought into full play. However, it must be pointed out that for state-owned enterprises, such a responsibility is assumed while the state remains in full control of its means of production, its production plans and the distribution of its profits. So it remains limited in its scope to a certain degree and is therefore responsible for profits and losses only in a relative sense. This is different from the system in practice within a capitalist enterprise in both character and dimension; it might therefore be called partial responsibility for profits and losses.

The five enterprises experimenting with the assumption of financial responsibility in this regard are both large and medium-sized and have generally achieved a fairly high level of socialization. Some of them had their capacities assigned to them by the state with their supply of the required raw and semi-finished materials and energy fully ensured and with the products planned for production readily marketable. Others, however, found themselves in a much less favourable condition inasmuch as state assignments placed only 17% to 40% of their capacities in operation. But all five succeeded in achieving good results, thanks to three measures that had the effect of holding them financially responsible and making their leadership and workers active in ensuring profits and averting losses.

These measures were:

1. The enterprise retains the whole of its after-tax profits;

2. All of its development funds, wage funds, reward funds, collective welfare funds and reserve funds are defrayed from the retained profits and the state grants no additional appropriations for these funds;

3. In case of a loss, the enterprise receives no state compensation and, when there is no adequate reserve fund to make up for the loss, it has to cut back the wages of its employees to offset the deficit.

Based on our experience, we are able to conclude that assumption of the responsibility for profit and loss is a logical development of the system of retaining a portion of the profits by the enterprise. But this is not to say this system is applicable without having to depend on certain conditions. A basically ensured supply of raw and semi-finished materials and basic marketability of the products are two fundamental conditions.

On the other hand, one should not refrain from starting until such point as all required conditions are in place. To assume responsibility for profits and losses implies that one has some risks to run. But it is those very risks that urge one to go all out. So it is simply meaningless for one to wait so as to undertake the responsibility in the most favourable conditions and then to proceed in ease and comfort. At present, it is desirable to introduce this system gradually in enterprises such as consumer-goods manufacturers which are required to develop in this period of economic readjustment. Here, two types of enterprises are recommended. For those enterprises that are important enough to affect the national economy and the people's livelihood and are of a high level in socialization, assumption of partial responsibility for profit and loss is preferable; the other type are those smaller ones with a low level of socialization, whereby assumption of full responsibility is preferable and whereunder the operating collectives are held fully responsible for profits and losses, with their enterprises continuing to be owned by the whole people.

Conclusion

Now that our country is in a period of economic readjustment, the focus of our work should naturally be on the readjustment. But the reform should in no way be discontinued in those instances where it can serve the interests of the readjustment. Otherwise, we shall fall short of the objective of the readjustment. During the past two years, the reform work in Sichuan was primarily aimed at enlivening the micro-economy. While we are continuing our work in this respect, we must also improve the planning and guidance of the macro-economy. Only by coordinating our work on both tracks can we attain what we are aiming at through the reform. Improvement in the guidance of the macro-economy must be viewed in a broad perspective. It should include better guidance through mandatory and instructive plans, through economic levers and through economic information, economic legislation and economic supervision. In addition, administrative intervention is implied when necessary. The work to enliven the micro-economy should be primarily devoted to consolidating the gains already made through the extension of decision-making powers. Meanwhile, it is desirable to work out trade-wide programmes for readjusting the interests among the enterprises of the same trade, for tapping their potential, and for undertaking innovations and transformation projects within the enterprises. This is necessary because it will help correct the existing imbalance of interests among the enterprises and help overcome the defect of overlapping in capital construction. At the same time, it will help pave the way for industrial reorganization and integration.

Promotion of industrial reorganization and integration with the stress on key cities and on developing consumer goods production is the focus of this year's work of readjustment and restructuring. Going hand in hand with it will be experimental reform of the tax system, without which it would be difficult to break the enterprises' regional or departmental affiliations — links which stand in the way of industrial reorganization and integration. We should blaze a new trail in our economic construction, one which gives fuller play to the role of our existing enterprises and yields better economic results. Hence, it is imperative to streamline and reform the management system of our existing enterprises, especially at a time when energy is in short supply.

The restructuring of our economic management is where the hope of our four modernizations lies. Our experiments in Sichuan in this field shall continue to proceed firmly and steadily.

9. THE SYSTEM OF RESPONSIBILITY IN AGRICULTURAL PRODUCTION IN ANHUI PROVINCE

By Zhou Yueli

Deputy Director, Anhui Provincial Agricultural Commission

Changes Conforming to Actual Conditions

A system of responsibility in production was introduced to the rural areas of Anhui Province during the winter of 1977 on the basis of the implementation of the rural economic policy. At that time, a new Provincial Party Committee headed by Comrade Wan Li was set up on the instructions of the Central Committee of the Communist Party of China, and Regulations Concerning Some Questions on Present Rural Economic Policy were formulated. This gave great impetus to implementing the new rural economic policy and to stabilizing the situation in the rural areas by giving full play to the initiative of commune members — an initiative that had been suppressed as a result of sabotage of rural economic policy by Lin Biao and the Gang of Four.

In 1978, a terrible drought struck Anhui Province. Most parts of the province received no saturating rain for a ten-month period. Even during the normally rainy summer season, reservoirs were empty and rivers ran dry in quite a few areas. The Huaihe River, one of the five largest rivers in China, had a small flow of only 0.5 cubic metres per second. More than 60 million *mu* of cultivated land were heavily affected by the calamity, while an area with a population of 4 million fell short of water for its inhabitants as well as for its livestock. When the sowing season came in autumn, it was impossible to plant wheat and rape seeds, because there was insufficient moisture in the soil. Attending to the actual conditions, the Provincial Party Committee decided rather than to let the land lie waste, to lend those plots which the collective could not sow to commune members to grow wheat or rape individually. As a result, the enthusiasm of the commune members for production was raised, the autumn sowing was speeded up and seeding acreage was expanded. Specifically, additional acreage of more than two million *mu* was seeded with wheat in the hilly areas along the Huaihe and Changjiang rivers.

At that time, a nationwide discussion on the criteria of truth was going on. Encouraged by this excellent situation, the practice of fixing farm output quotas on the basis of groups was introduced in some localities. In a few communes, production brigades and production teams, output quotas were fixed on a household basis on the initiative of the commune members themselves.

The Only Objective Criterion is Social Practice. Cadres at various levels held differing attitudes towards such new forms of management created by the masses. Some kept silent for fear of taking risks since practices such as fixing output quotas on the basis of groups or households or giving material incentives had been criticized in the past and many comrades had suffered as a result. But there were those comrades who stood for letting the facts speak for themselves and for using practice as the criterion for showing what is right and what is wrong. They held that the party's correct lines, principles, policies and measures all come from practice, and the readjustment of agricultural policies is no exception.

For the sake of strengthening the management of the people's communes and boosting agricultural production, we collected the different opinions and reported them to Comrade Wan Li. He pointed out that these opinions were a reflection of two ideological lines on agriculture. He asked us to undertake a serious, comprehensive investigation and study of the problem and then hand in a written report. In so doing, Comrade Wan Li said that it was necessary to make concrete analysis of what had been criticized. Criticism is a subjective means of understanding things and should not be taken as the objective criterion for testing truth. It might be right and it might be wrong. The only objective criterion is social practice.

The Provincial Party Committee organized groups of cadres to cooperate with the Chuxian and Liu'an Prefectural Party Committees to investigate the various forms of the system of responsibility for production. These included the method of fixing work-points (units indicating the quantity and quality of labour performed and the amount of payment earned) according to the output and on the basis of production groups — as practiced in the Weiying Production Team of Lai'an County; the method of fixing output quotas in cotton cultivation on a household basis, with extra pay for above-quota output — as practiced in Mahu Commune of Fengyang County and in Xinjie Commune of Tianchang County; the method of fixing output quotas for field crops on a household basis, with the households retaining any resultant surplus and paying for any resultant losses as might occur — as practiced in the Shannan District of Feixi County; and methods of rewarding leaders of production brigades and production teams for good management and penalizing them for failure in fulfilling the planned targets — as practiced in Guangda Commune of Lai'an County.

These methods combined the gains of collective production with the personal material benefit of the labourers and, at the same time, eliminated careless and slipshod work in production and equalitarianism in distribution of profits. As a result, production developed enormously in these areas.

After studying these reports, Comrade Wan Li, basing himself on the doctrine that practice is the only criterion for testing truth, agreed to conduct experiments with these methods in various areas of the province. He said that even the method of fixing output quotas on a household basis as practiced in the Shannan District of Feixi County might be tried out; he felt that these methods should not be adopted rashly but should be introduced systematically after experiences had been summed up in the experiments.

In accordance with the instructions of leading comrades of the Provincial Party Committee, places were selected for the experiments. Experiences were then summed up by the Chuxian and Liu'an Prefectural Party Committees and by the Fengyang, Jiashan, Lai'an, Feixi and Xuancheng County Party Committees. In less than three months, following their examples, over 41,000 production teams, or 15.2% of the total number in the province, had adopted the system of responsibility of taking output into account. Even some communes and production teams that were not selected as experimental units began to practice this system on their own accord.

Affirming the System of Fixing Output Quotas on the Basis of Production Groups. In the spring of 1979, when the system of responsibility of taking output into account was being spread from the experimental units to the vast rural areas in the province, two documents on agriculture adopted by the Third Plenary Session of the 11th Central Committee of the Chinese Communist Party were published. The documents affirmed the system of responsibility of fixing output quotas on the basis of production groups, with remuneration given according to output and rewards provided for overfulfilment of planned targets. Those comrades with apprehensions were put at ease. Those in favour of it took an active role in popularizing the system, and the commune members were elated. The responsibility system of taking output into account spread quickly, with various forms introduced extensively in different parts of the province. These included the method of fixing output quotas on the basis of production groups; the method of giving work-points according to output; the method of full responsibility for all farm work; the method of fixing output quotas for one or more selected crops on a household basis; and the delimitation of "plots to grow ration grain." In areas where the system had not yet been adopted, measures of fixed-quota management and allotment of work-points through appraisal of the work done were implemented through discussions by commune members. Contracts for fixed output quotas on a household basis were adopted in some remote mountainous areas where transport connections are inconvenient and in areas where the production level is low and the people's life difficult. Different forms of the system of responsibility were adopted simultaneously within one county, one commune, one production brigade, or even within the same production team in order to demonstrate the relative superiority and vitality of one method over the other.

Affirming the System of Responsibility in Production of Taking Output into Account. In early 1980, the Provincial Party Committee convened a conference on agriculture to sum up and exchange experiences in practising the different forms of the system of responsibility in production. After repeated discussions and comparisons, the conference affirmed the system of responsibility in production of taking output into account. In particular, the conference recognized the method of fixing output quotas on a household basis as a form of the responsibility system because of that method's remarkable success in transforming poor and backward areas. It was clearly pointed out at the conference that no matter what forms of the responsibility system were adopted, they must be based on respect for the wishes of commune members and in accordance with actual local conditions. The party committees at various levels should give positive guidance to whatever forms were introduced so as to help improve them.

By the end of 1980, 29.5% of the production teams in Anhui Province had adopted a responsibility system that did not take output into account; meanwhile, fully 69.9% of the province's teams had begun to practice the system of responsibility of taking output into account. Of these, 53.9% adopted the system of fixing output quotas on a household basis. At present, 86.3% of all production teams in the province follow the system of responsibility of taking output into account; of these, more than 70% practice the method of fixing output quotas on a household basis. Indeed, this method has become the main form of responsibility system in agricultural production currently in use in Anhui Province.

The extensive and rapid application of the system of responsibility in production of taking output into account and the form of fixing output quotas on a household basis in particular is determined by specific economic conditions or levels of development of productive forces in the rural areas of Anhui Province. Since 1955, when the cooperative transformation of agriculture was completed, agricultural production in the province has made significant advances in improving farming conditions and technical facilities. Up to 1977, the total capacity of agricultural machinery in the province reached 6,025,000 hp; the acreage irrigated by electric and mechanical facilities occupied 65.9% of total effectively irrigated land (which accounted for 51.6% of all farmland in the province, thanks to the construction of water conservancy projects); 27.3% of all cultivated land was ploughed by tractor; processing of farm products was in the main mechanized or semi-mechanized; engine-drawn transportation facilities took up 36% of the total transport work in agriculture; the average application of chemical fertilizers per *mu* was 16 kg. and every peasant maintained an average of 0.32 *mu* of land giving stable and high yields. However, agricultural production in the province still remained at a very low level because the peasants' enthusiasm for production was seriously dampened by mistakes and shortcomings in management measures, such as arbitrary directives, careless and slipshod farm work and equalitarianism in distribution.

In such circumstances, water conservancy and irrigation projects, agricultural machines and other production facilities could not be used effectively, the ability to resist natural disasters was weak, and most of farm work was done by hand or with animal power. Some areas of the province were acutely short of draught animals. During the period of the agricultural cooperatives, the province had 2,720,000 head of draught animals. But by 1977, the number was reduced to 2,020,000, a drop of 25.7%. In areas north of the Huaihe River, some commune members had to plough and harrow the fields by manual labour. Agricultural natural resources were far from being sufficiently utilized, with forestry, animal husbandry, sideline production and fisheries placed in a subordinate position. The labour force in the villages was thus mainly engaged in grain production. Therefore, the scope of management was narrow and both labour productivity and the commodity rate of production were at a very low level. The income of the peasants was low and in many places the peasants were inadequately fed or clothed.

In 1979, following two years of rehabilitation that came after the downfall of the Gang of Four, this backward situation was still not much improved. The dislocation in agriculture remained quite serious. The output value of forestry, animal husbandry, sideline production and fisheries occupied only 23.4% of the total output value of agriculture — a proportion lower than both the national average and those of Anhui's six neighbouring provinces. Each person engaged in agricultural production produced an average of only 942 kg. of grain, only 80.5 kg. more than that produced in 1957, and representing an average annual increase of only 0.42%. The average per capita gain of major agricultural and sideline products (with the exceptions of grain and edible oil) were all below the national average. Per capita income from collective distribution was only about 70 yuan. The commune members in 33.7% of the production teams received an average per capita income of less than 50 yuan, while those in 47.1% of the production teams received 50-100 yuan. This means that both production levels and living conditions among most of production teams were difficult or comparatively difficult. Therefore, the present system of responsibility in production of taking output into account — particularly the form of fixing output quotas on a household basis — is beneficial to the development of production in most communes, production brigades and production teams.

A System Welcomed by the Commune Members

There are various forms of the system of responsibility in the rural areas of Anhui Province. However, they may be divided into two general types — those that take output into account and those that do not take output into account. The overwhelming majority of communes, production brigades and teams have adopted the first kind, inasmuch as its economic results are better than those of the latter, and as it closely links the labour of commune members with its ultimate fruit — output. Only a small number of communes, production brigades and teams now practice the latter form.

At present, the system of responsibility that does not take output into account mainly follows two forms:

1. Individuals or groups undertaking to fulfil certain norms in farm work; and

2. Allocating work-points by evaluating the work done. The form of allocating work-points by evaluating the work done can only reflect the working ability of a labourer, or his latent labour

power rather than the whole process of labour and the final result of labour. Therefore, it cannot exert influence on careless or sloppy habits in production, nor can it eliminate equalitarianism in remuneration for the work done. It cannot embody the principle of "to each according to his work." Commune members do not actually recognize it as a form of responsibility, and hence it was gradually being replaced by other forms.

The form of committing to fulfil certain norms in farm work is more advanced as it requires an allotment of labour norms that take into account the quantity and quality of certain forms of farm work that a normal labourer can fulfil in a set time. Reasonable standards for the amount of work-points to be allocated are worked out on the basis of fixed norms and according to requirements of skill, the intensity of labour the work demands and its importance within the overall process of production. Then the production team divides all of its labourers into a number of temporary or stable groups according to the requirements of different types of farm work. The team signs temporary, seasonal or annual contracts with these groups that specify fixed tasks, time limits, quality of work and work-points to be allocated. The production team checks the fulfilment of the contracts by the groups or individuals according to the requirements of the work undertaken, and on that basis determines the remuneration — the amount of work-points as stipulated in the contracts — along with rewards for overfulfilment and penalties for failure.

Compared with the form of allocating work-points by evaluating the work done, this method enhances the efficient organization of labour since it fixes norms for farm work and makes it easy to inspect the process of labour of the commune members. However, it still cannot guarantee the quality of farm work as it fails to link production with output. This, in addition to its complex methodology, adds to the difficulty of achieving satisfactory results.

In a talk in Handan in September 1961, Comrade Mao Zedong said that there were "37 processes, 49 percentages and 1,128 accounts" in financial matters. Similarly, this method requires a high level of management from the cadres. During the past two years, such methods have been practiced only in those communes, production brigades and teams in Anhui Province where conditions of production have been relatively good, where income is high, where the collective economy is relatively consolidated and where the cadres are competent in administration. However, there are still some aspects to be improved in practicing this type of responsibility system. For instance, an unnecessary amount of administrative restrictions should not get in the way of giving commune members certain decision-making powers in production or of enabling them to engage in household sideline occupations and attend to their private plots, as long as they continue to do a good job in collective production. In particular, the implementation of the principle of "to each according to his work" within production groups should be dealt with satisfactorily.

Differences with the System of "The Fixed Quotas and One Reward." The system of responsibility of taking output into account that emerged after the Third Plenary Session of the 11th Central Committee of the Communist Party of China that is to be developed on the basis of the system of responsibility that does not take output into account is also a breakthrough in the latter respect. At the beginning, it took the form of fixing output quotas on the basis of groups. It then gradually developed to the point of fixing quotas on a household basis and further to fixing quotas on the basis of specialized groups, with remuneration paid according to output. Fixing quotas on the basis of groups is similar to the system of "three fixed quotas and one reward" practiced in the advanced agricultural producers' cooperatives. The only difference is that in the latter system the contract was drawn between the production brigade and the production team; now, it is between the production team and the groups.

The system of fixing output quotas on the basis of groups is generally practiced as follows: under unified accounting and distribution by the production team, the labourers are divided into a number of stable groups that are assigned fixed plots of land, draught animals and farm tools for their own use. Ownership, however, remains with the production team and, in some places, draught animals and farm tools remain under the unified control of the production team. The team signs contracts with groups for fixed quotas of output and for a fixed amounts of work-points and expenditures, stipulating rewards for above-quota output and penalties for losses. The groups hand over to the production team their products in exchange for their work-points and receive remuneration from the team under unified distribution. In some places where this system is practiced, the production groups conduct distribution according to the unified distribution programme of the production team after delivering fixed amounts of agricultural and sideline products to the state and the collective. This system reduces the scope of labour organization and more directly links output to the economic benefits of commune members. Therefore, commune members have both a greater sense of responsibility and greater enthusiasm for production. They pay attention both to the quantity and quality of their work, as well as to both work-points and output. As the phenomena of drifting along and poor organization in labour are reduced and as equalitarianism is to a certain extent overcome, this system can give great impetus to agricultural production.

The unprecedented bumper harvest reaped in Anhui Province in 1979 was directly related to the implementation of this responsibility system. However, problems still exist in this system, such as determining whether the allotment of work-points and quotas of work in the production groups are reasonable. Equalitarianism within the production team may be overcome but equalitarianism may still exist within the groups, since the distribution of products is conducted mainly according to the amount of work-points. That is why a number of production teams have instead adopted the system of fixing output quotas on a household basis.

Fixing Output Quotas on a Household Basis. The system of fixing output quotas on a household basis is developed from the system used on a production-group basis. It retains the collective ownership of the means of production and collective economy, with the production team as its mainstay and the principle of "to each according to his work." At the same time, it overcomes various contradictions in practicing the system of responsibility on the basis of groups, particularly those that occur in the collective labour of the production team.

This system is generally practiced as follows: the production team concludes contracts with households — according to the number of people and the size of the labour force in each family — to undertake the farm work in certain plots of land set aside for them to manage individually. The contract stipulates fixed output quotas, the amount of work-points and expenditure, rewards for over-quota output and penalties for losses. Meanwhile, the team retains the power to make unified production plans, unified distribution and control of water sources, irrigation projects, draught animals, farm tools and other means of production owned by the collective. The team also retains the authority to operate the industries and sideline occupations of the production team. However, the complicated management of this form of the responsibility system is inconvenient both to the cadres and commune members. Moreover, factors of equalitarianism continue to prevail in distribution. Therefore, only a small number of teams have adopted this type.

In most places, the peasants opt for the system in which individual households assume full responsibility for most of the farm work. This method is similar to the above-mentioned type in the utilization of land and in the control of the draught animals, farm tools and other means of production and ways of management. The difference lies in that while the former method provides for the handing over of products to the production team so that it may receive its stipulated amount of work-points and distribution from the team in a unified way, the latter method calls for distribution according to the economic contracts, thus changing the method of distribution solely according to the amount of work-points.

The economic contracts concluded between the production team and the individual households in this type of responsibility system clearly stipulate the output quotas (value) of different crops; the amount of farm and sideline products to be delivered to the state and the amount to be delivered to the collective for public accumulation; the means of production handed over at discount prices to the groups or individual households by the production team; the period of their use; the amount of depreciation charges; and rewards for overfulfilment of work quotas and penalties for failure, and other necessary provisions. The main advantage of this type of responsibility system is that it takes into consideration the interests of the state, the collective and the individual. It does away with the equalitarianism of unified distribution by the production team and dispenses with complicated management, particularly in financial control. It suits the cadres' level of management and at the same time is easily accepted by commune members to the extent that it is the best possible way to implement the principle of "from each according to his ability, to each according to his work" and "more work more pay." At present, more than half of the communes and production brigades and teams in Anhui Province which implement the system of responsibility in production of taking output into account adopt this simple and easily practicable method.

The Contract for Fixed Quotas. A promising form of the system of responsibility that takes output into account is the contract for fixed quotas (value) with remuneration given according to the output of specialized groups, households or individuals. This system provides that under the production team's unified leadership, a number of specialized groups, households or individuals are organized according to their special skills and techniques and according to requirements in farm work, forestry, animal husbandry, sideline production and fishing, and then enter into contracts and receive remuneration according to productive output (value). The main advantage of this form is that it brings into full play the superiority of unified management and of sharing out the work. By coordinating units with one another, it stabilizes the collective economy, making the production team its mainstay by giving scope to the enthusiasm of commune members. It develops a diversified economy that can utilize fully the capability of labourers, land and resources. This form, however, requires certain material conditions as well as a high level of management. In Anhui Province, this form is adopted mainly by those communes, production brigades and teams that possess adequate conditions for specialization in production, and those that have developed diversified economies and competent cadres in management. With the development of agricultural productivity, the growth of a more diversified economy and the raising of the cadres' administrative level, such a form is bound to be adopted by more and more communes, production brigades and teams and will contribute to the promotion of China's agricultural production to higher stages of socialization and specialization. In those communes, production brigades and teams where conditions for adopting this form are not yet ripe, conditions should be created in a positive way so as to enable the gradual adoption of this form.

Besides the above-mentioned main forms of responsibility systems that take output into account, there are also other forms such as the method of responsibility in field management and remuneration according to output, with crops reaped by the production team in a unified manner and with the method of individual households assuming responsibility for producing a part of the crops on the basis of fixed quotas.

A Major Reform in China's Collective Agriculture. The emergence of various forms of the system of responsibility in production that take output into account marks a major reform in the management of China's collective agriculture. These forms link the remuneration of the commune members not only with the quantity and quality of their labour but also with their output — the final result of labour. The practice of these forms enables us to switch gradually from administrative to economic methods in the management of agriculture. Since the introduction of this system in Anhui Province, quite a few "Left" patterns that work against objective laws in the management of the agricultural economy have been broken through.

For example, the organization of labour by concentrating scores or even hundreds of labourers together is by this means replaced with a decentralized method of sharing out the work and with a system of coordination under unified planning in production by means of which only a dozen or fewer labourers work together or even individual households are assigned to fulfil certain work.

This method results in a higher sense of responsibility on the part of labourers and in a higher quality of production. It effectively overcomes carelessness and sloppiness in labour. Arbitrary decisions by the production team leader in the management of production through administrative directives is replaced by the arrangement of production by commune members themselves according to the actual conditions and under the production team's unified leadership; this method guarantees the commune members' decision-making power in production. The method of allocating workpoints by evaulating the work done is replaced by a system of remuneration according to output; this makes commune members more concerned about output then about the amount of work-points, and overcomes the tendency of caring only about the quantity of work done and the amount of work-points while paying little attention to the quality of work and output. The distribution of remuneration solely according to the amount of work-points is replaced by remuneration determined by the contracts for fixed output quotas; this results in the implementation of the principle of "from each according to his ability, to each according to his work — more work, more pay" by completely eradicating equalitarianism in the distribution of products.

The practice of the various forms of the system of responsibility has brought about a series of major changes in the management of agricultural production and has ushered in an excellent situation in which the people in the vast rural areas have ease of mind, in which the economy is thriving and in which the market is brisk.

Notable Successes Following Introduction of the System of Responsibility

Implementation of the system of responsibility in agricultural production during the past two years shows that things are better with the practice of this system than without it; the form of the system of taking output into account is better than a system that does not take output into account; and, in some areas which long remained poor and backward, the form of fixing output quotas on a household basis is more effective than other forms in improving the economy.

By integrating more closely the results of collective production with the material benefits of individual commune members, the form that takes output into account embodies more directly the principle of "more work, more pay" in distrition. Agricultural output increased markedly as commune members brought into full play their long-suppressed enthusiasm for production and showed concern for each production measure and for the overall quality of farm work.

In 1978, Anhui Province was hit by the worst drought in a century. Yet, total grain output of the province reached 14,800,000 tons, approaching that of a normal year. A bumper harvest was reaped in 1979 with a total output of 16,100,000 tons, an 8% increase over the previous year. The output in 5 prefectures and 31 counties surpassed the highest records in history for these areas. The province as a whole delivered 4 million tons of grains to the state, with a 23% commodity ratio. Even in the ten counties of Sixian, Wuhe, Lingbi, Guzhen in the plain north of the Huaihe River; in Dingyuan, Fengyang and Jiashan in the hilly areas along the Changjiang and Huaihe rivers; and in Xuancheng, Langxi and Guangde south of the Changjiang River — the three well-known backward regions of the province — grain output was increased by 32.9% and rapeseed by 59% compared with the previous year. This was thanks to the practice of various forms of the system of responsibility that took output into account in 58.4% of their production teams. Many of the production teams that used to depend on state relief for food grain, production and livelihood increased production and income and made greater contributions to the state.

In 1980, Anhui Province once again suffered heavy natural calamities in the form of floods, cold temperatures, unbroken spells of rainy weather, plant diseases and insect pests — all exceeded in severity only by those of 1954. A total of 32,050,000 mu of cultivated land was affected, with 21,560,000 mu adversely affected by the disasters and 3,940,000 mu left barren of any harvest. Total grain output decreased by 9.6% in 1980. Aside from natural calamities, another important factor in these losses was the failure in some areas of practicing the system of responsibility in production. Facts testify to the power of the form of fixing output quotas on a household basis in overcoming serious natural calamities. An annual report in 1980 shows that the proportion of production teams that adopted the form of fixing output quotas on a household basis was very high in those 20 counties of the province where output of grain increased. Outstanding among them were the seven counties in Chuxian Prefecture, where the method of fixing output quotas on a household basis was introduced earlier than in other areas and formed the largest proportion among the production teams. Combined output of grain in these seven counties, each of which increased production, registered a 13.6% increase

over the record output year of 1979. In the 13 counties where grain output decreased by large margins, the proportion of production teams adopting this form was very small. Even in the counties where output decreased, the few production teams implementing this form generally raised their output or at least greatly reduced the level of losses suffered by other teams working under the same conditions of natural calamity.

Increased Effectiveness in Combatting Poverty. The system of responsibility in production for fixed output quotas on a household basis has been shown to be more effective in areas badly in need of getting rid of their poverty, backwardness and decrease in farm output.

Take Fengyang County, for example. This county used to suffer from famine 9 years out of 10. In 1979, it introduced the system of fixing output quotas on the basis of groups in 70% of its production teams. It reaped a good harvest that year — 19.9% higher than its previous high. The amount of grain purchased by the state reached 43,500 tons for the first time and over 25,000 tons were delivered to supply other places; the latter amount surpassed the total amount delivered in the 26 years since the state monopoly purchasing and marketing began in 1953. Per capita income was 91 yuan, or 17 yuan higher than the previous best. In 1980, 95% of all production teams in the county began to adopt the method of contracts for fixed quotas on a household basis. Total output of grain that year once again saw a 14.2% increase over that of the previous year, with a per capita grain output of 534.5 kg. The state's purchase of grain amounted to 55,000 tons, which was higher than the total annual output of the early years of Liberation or of the three difficult years (1959-61). Per capita income was 114 yuan, an increase of 23 yuan over the previous year. A number of impoverished production teams and households managed to become well off within one year or even within one season.

Statistics show that the number of teams in Anhui Province with per capita income of more than 300 yuan grew from 1 production brigade and 13 teams in 1979 to 15 brigades and 212 teams in 1980, an increase of more than 10 fold. A survey of 510 households in different areas shows that only 4 households — or 0.78% of the total — had a per capita income above 300 yuan in 1978; the figure increased to 30 households, or 5.9% in 1979; and 46 households, or 9% in 1980.

Diversification of the economy and individual household sideline production took place at a faster pace in parallel with the popularization of the system of responsibility that takes output (value) into account. Take Fuyang Prefecture on the plain north of the Huaihe River, for instance. With no mountains or rivers in the area, the pefecture had little in the way of natural resources for the development of a diversified economy. Poor natural resources and the hard life of its people made it difficult to raise adequate funds. However, the prefecture was able to achieve notable development of a diversified economy, together with a continuous increase in grain output only within two years after the system of responsibility that takes output (value) into account was introduced. Statistics show that income from the development of a diversified economy throughout the prefecture reached 784.8 million yuan in 1980, an increase of over 30% over 1979 and accounting for 43.9% of the total output value of agriculture. The output of rapeseed and peanuts and production of poultry and rabbits surpassed all previous records. State purchases of cotton, tobacco, hemp, honey, silkworm cocoons, aquatic products, products for foreign trade, livestock and other local agricultural and sideline products all increased by a wide margin over the previous year. The increase of 200,000 head of draught animals set the highest annual record since Liberation Out of the net income of the rural commune members in the province, the proportion from household sideline production underwent the most rapid increase. A survey of 510 households in different areas showed that they received 24% of their net income from household sideline production in 1978. That percentage rose to 42% in 1979 and to 45.1% in 1980.

Thanks to the advance in production and to increases in personal income, the lives of commune members have improved greatly. In 1980, per capita expenditure for living costs of the above-mentioned 510 households was 162.9 yuan, an increase of 18.1 yuan or 12.5% over the previous year. In their daily food consumption in 1980, the intake of meat grew by 29.3%, eggs 21.5% and fish 32.2% over the previous year. In 1980, every ten households had an average of 1.56 bicycles, a 2.2% increase over previous year; 1.5 sewing machines, a 55.4% increase; 3.94 radio sets, a 64.9% increase; 3.8 clocks or watches, a 28.4% increase (2.5 of which were watches, an increase of 37.6%). The improvement of material life has also brought an upswing in cultural life. The commune members in some places have by joint efforts built simple cinemas, theatres and cultural centres for multi-purpose use.

Changes in Relationships Among the People. The practice of the various forms of the system of responsibility in production that takes output into account, particularly fixing output quotas on a household basis, has brought about a change in relationships among the people. The phenomena of disputes — over the assignment of jobs, evaluation of the work done in allocating work-points and the distribution of money and grain that often occurred between the cadres and the commune members in the past — have disappeared. Cadres at the grassroots levels are universally of the opinion that work is now performed more easily. Free from the arduous work of urging people to undertake the ploughing, sowing, and delivering of grain to the state, they are now able to take an active part in productive labour as other commune members do. Commune members no longer have to accept the coercive, arbitrary and impractical direction in production that had existed in varying degrees for a long time. Overdrawn accounts and arrears, arbitrary transfers of resources, extravagance and the wanton borrowing that remained difficult problems for years in management have been completely solved. Unreasonable measures and unhealthy tendencies in management and administration in the communes have been done away with. Commune members are delighted over the excellent situation. Women are even more satisfied and happy with the contracts for fixed quotas on a household basis as now they can more freely arrange their time for both farm work and household chores and can also pay occasional visits to their relatives. No wonder they have the feeling of "emancipation for the second time."

New Divisions of Labour and New Integrated Economic Complexes. Apart from the use of contracts for fixed quotas on a household basis, one of the most encouraging new changes is the emergence of new forms of division of labour and of large numbers of new integrated economic complexes in the rural areas. Thanks to rising labour productivity, some commune members have become rich by virtue of ample grain, money and more surplus labour power which in turn result in a rapid development of household sideline production, a diversified economy and industries run by the communes, production brigades and teams. And there have also appeared large numbers of households engaged in both farm work and sideline and industrial production. In Liu'an and Chuxian prefectures, where contracts for fixed quotas on a household basis were practiced earlier than in other areas; large numbers of newly integrated economic complexes have emerged. Some of them are engaged in coordination of production centered on specialized skills and techniques such as growing tobacco; some, in the use of farm machinery, such as setting up tractor stations through the acquisition of tractors with joint funds; some, in the coordination of production by exploiting certain natural resources such as afforestation, fishing, quarrying and supplying sand for construction sites; some, in cooperating to meet the needs of certain production projects such as building small water conservancy works, roads and bridges; some, in coordination to render services to certain links of production such as collective elimination of plant pests and insects and nurturing of seedlings. These complexes are organized and managed according to the principle of voluntary participation and mutual benefit, breaking past the barriers of the production teams, brigades or communes that the partners may belong to. Their management is directly linked to the personal benefits of the participants — who are both producers and managers at the same time. Therefore, they are all run efficiently and democratically and with satisfactory economic results.

The emergence of such newly integrated economic complexes has not only given impetus to production and rendered convenience to the people, but has also brought about extensive changes in the distribution of the rural labour force, the structure of production and the composition of the income of commune members. Since the introduction of the use of contracts for fixed quotas on a household basis in Bingzi Commune, Feixi County, 52.4% of its households, or 32.6% of its labour force, have become engaged in both contracted farm work and sideline and industrial production; they now earn 40.2% of their income from the latter. In the new development of rural areas, we can observe the embryo of specialization and socialization that agricultural production is gradually advancing to. China's socialist agriculture is bound to advance more rapidly so long as the correct line, principles and policies are adhered to along with a scrupulous observance of the natural laws governing the economy.

SECTION IV:

GENERAL SURVEY OF CHINA'S ECONOMY

SECTION IV:

GENERAL SURVEY OF CHINA'S ECONOMY

1. CHINA'S ECONOMY IN 1980
By Wei Liqun

The History of Economic Development in New China

After the founding of New China in 1949, the Chinese people of all nationalities, under the leadership of the Communist Party of China and the People's Government, carried out extensive and thorough socialist transformation and large-scale economic construction on the ruins of semi-colonial and semi-feudal old China. In spite of repeated serious setbacks, we have accomplished tremendous gains never achieved in old China, and have brought about great changes in China's economy. We have eliminated the exploitation system, established the absolute predominance of socialist public ownership over the entire national economy, transformed a backward agricultural country into a fairly well-developed industrial — agricultural country, and built an independent and all-embracing industrial system and a national economic system, thus laying a material and technical foundation of considerable size for the great cause of socialist modernization in China.

The following are the major achievements in China's economic construction over the past 31 years:

1. We have established an economy of public ownership.

Both the economy of ownership by the whole people [i.e. "state" ownership — Ed.] and the economy of collective ownership have grown tremendously. The economy of ownership by the whole people has held a firm leading position in the national economy and has controlled the life-lines of the national economy. The proportion of output value of industry under ownership by the whole people to total industrial output value rose from 26% in 1949 to 79% in 1980; and the proportion of retail sales of the state-owned commercial establishments to the total volume of retail sales in China rose from 6.9% in 1950 to 85.4% in 1980. Industrial output value of the collective enterprises accounted for 20.6% of China's total industrial output value in 1980.

Collective agriculture has become the main component of agricultural production. In 1980, China had 54,000 people's communes, with a population of 810 million of whom 320 million were labourers. At present, given the condition that the economy of socialist public ownership has absolute predominance, some individual economy is allowed to exist and develop as an indispensable supplement to the socialist economy.

2. Economic growth has been fairly rapid.

Between 1949 and 1980, China's total industrial and agricultural output value rose from 46,000 million yuan to 661,900 million yuan, a 16.1-fold increase (calculated at comparable or constant prices), yielding an average annual increase of 9.4%. Total agricultural output value rose from 32,600 million yuan to 162,700 million yuan, a 3.8-fold increase, or an average annual increase of 4.4%. Total industrial output value rose from 14,000 million yuan to 499,200 million yuan, a 46.2-fold increase or an annual average increase of 13.2%.

National income (the net output value of the material producing departments including industry, agriculture, construction, communications and transport, and commerce) rose from 35,800 million yuan to 363,000 million yuan, an 8.8-fold increase, or an average annual increase of 7.3%. National revenues increased from 6,520 million yuan in 1950 to 106,610 million yuan in 1980, a 16.4-fold increase, or an average annual increase of 9.8%.

3. Considerable progress has been made in material production capacity and in technological development.

When China was liberated in 1949, national fixed industrial assets were estimated at about 12,800 million yuan. This was all that was left over from old China. After 31 years of construction, China now has nearly 400,000 industrial and transport enterprises. By the end of 1980, the fixed assets of state-owned enterprises in China amounted to more than 500,000 million yuan, including 370,000 million yuan of fixed industrial assets. In addition, there were about 330,000 million yuan of circulating funds.

China's industry has begun to make inroads in its technical backwardness and uneven development and has established an all-embracing and rationally distributed production system. New industries have sprung up having begun from scratch. Both productive and technical levels of old and new industries have been raised and a great number of new materials, new processes, new equipment and new technologies have been developed. Farmland and water conservancy construction has been carried out on a huge scale in the rural areas. In the past 31 years, the water supply in 17.3 million hectares of low-lying land formerly subject to water-logging has been brought under control; 13.3 million hectares of saline land and hill-side land have been transformed; and 86,000 reservoirs, with a total capacity of more than 400,000 million cubic metres, have been built. Total irrigated farmland has been extended from 15.3 million hectares in 1950 to 44.6 million hectares in 1980, and now accounts for 45% of the country's total farmland.

Progress has also been made in agricultural mechanization. Before 1949, there was virtually no farm machinery in the Chinese countryside. By the end of 1980, China had 745,000 large and medium-sized tractors together with drainage and irrigation equipment with accumulated 74,650,000 horsepower. Tractor-ploughed land now accounts for 41.3% of total farmland. Almost no electricity was used in the rural areas before 1949. In 1980, 32,100 million kilowatt-hours of electricity were consumed in the countryside, about 7.5 times the annual rate during the early post-Liberation period.

4. *Both domestic and foreign trade have grown considerably.*

The total value of commodities purchased by commercial departments rose from 17,500 million yuan in 1952 to 226,300 million yuan in 1980, an increase of 12.9 times. The total value of retail sales (calculated at current prices) rose from 27,700 million yuan in 1952 to 214,000 million yuan in 1980, an increase of 7.7 times.

In foreign trade, total import and export value increased from 4,150 million yuan in 1952 to 56,300 million yuan in 1980, a rise of 13.6 times.

5. *The livelihood of urban and rural people has improved fairly well.*

Per capita consumption levels rose from 76 yuan in 1952 to 197 yuan in 1979, an increase of 160% (or an actual increase of 85%, after deducting price rises). The per capita consumption level of peasants rose from 62 yuan in 1952 to 152 yuan in 1979, an actual increase of 65.2%; and that of the wage-earners from 148 yuan to 406 yuan, an actual increase of 114.5%. Free medical service has been introduced for the personnel of enterprises under ownership by the whole people, of government departments and of public undertakings, as well as for students in institutions of higher learning. Public health centres have been set up in all people's communes and cooperative medical services have been introduced in the production brigades (subdivisions of the people's communes). Owing to improvements in medical services and living conditions, the average life expectancy of the Chinese people has nearly doubled and the mortality rate has dropped from 1.8 in 1950 to 0.62 in 1979.

6. *A large contingent of workers and scienti-*

fic and technical personnel has been trained, and scientific and educational work has expanded considerably.

By the end of 1980, the number of workers employed in state-owned and collective enterprises rose to 104,440,000. A great number of competent technicians and managerial personnel have been brought up through the ranks. In the past 31 years, 3.18 million students have been graduated from universities and colleges. The number of natural scientists and technicians working in units under ownership by the whole people totalled 5.3 million, 12 times the 1952 figure; the number of scientific research personnel in 1980 totalled more than 300,000, 40 times the 1952 figure. We have established a number of new divisions in science and technology. Successful nuclear testing, the launching and accurate recovery of a man-made earth satellite and test flights of carrier rockets in the Pacific Ocean conducted during the first half of 1980 all marked the relatively high level of China's scientific and technological achievements.

All these achievements spoke to the hard work done by the people of various nationalities in China. They also demonstrated powerfully that the socialist road is the only road that will enable China to eliminate poverty and backwardness and to gradually build a prosperous and strong country.

Of course, New China has had twists and turns in its economic development. The national economy grew rapidly and steadily in certain periods while in other periods, owing to mistakes, it suffered serious setbacks. The impetuous advance that began in 1958 led to a grave economic imbalance. As a result, we had to embark on a five-year period of readjustment in 1961. During the "cultural revolution" that began in 1966, there was another serious disruption to the national economy caused by the sabotage by Lin Biao and the Gang of Four and by the "Left" deviationist mistakes committed in economic construction. The national economy began to revive and grow after the Gang of Four was smashed in October 1976. However, we did not conduct a complete appraisal of the consequences of the ten-year disorder, nor did we do away with the mistakes of the impetuous advance in guiding thought over economic work. Instead, we were overeager to achieve success and raised a number of impractical slogans and targets, creating new difficulties in continued development of the national economy. In as much as "Left" deviationist mistakes in economic construction went uncorrected for a long period and because of the political turmoil that lasted for many years and the defects in the economic system, the proportional contribution of different branches of the national economy were thrown seriously out of balance, while management of the enterprises and the people's communes and their subdivisions was disrupted and the rate of economic achievement decreased. All of these factors created tremendous waste in the national economy and hindered its realization of goals that otherwise could have been reached. Improvements in the people's livelihood also failed to reach levels that should have been attained.

In 1979, following the Third Plenary Session of the 11th Central Committee of the Chinese Communist Party, the party's Central Committee and the State Council adopted the policy of readjusting, restructuring, consolidating and improving the national economy in light of the development of China's national economy and of existing problems with a view to overcoming serious economic difficulties resulting from the "cultural revolution" and to correcting mistakes in economic work between 1977 and 1978.

Readjustment. Readjustment means to consciously readjust proportional relations in the economy that had for so long been dislocated; thus, all branches of the national economy can develop in a relatively coordinated manner and a rational ratio can be maintained between accumulation and consumption.

Restructuring. Restructuring means to restructure, both systematically and comprehensively, aspects of the existing economic management system that hamper the development of productive forces, with the result that the superiority of the socialist system can be fully brought out.

Consolidation. Consolidation means to consolidate and better run existing enterprises, especially those whose management was once disrupted, so that they will advance along the correct road and play a full part in China's modernization.

Improvement. Improvement means to significantly raise production levels, technical levels and management levels.

The adoption and implementation of this policy marks a fundamental change in the ideology guiding China's economic work. It shows that China's economic construction has begun to shake off the yoke of "Left" deviationist ideas and practices; it has begun to adhere to the principles of proceeding from actual conditions, of acting according to one's ability and of doing things step by step and seeking practical results; and has begun to develop along a road of steady and healthy development.

The Economic Situation in 1980

The year 1980 was the second year China had followed the policy of readjustment, restructuring, consolidating and improving the national economy. New progress was made in economic work through the strenuous efforts of the people of all nationalities throughout the country.

I. Economic Readjustment

Economic readjustment continued in 1980 in accordance with the policies, tasks and requirements of readjusting the national economy and, as a result, major proportional relations became more balanced.

Agriculture. Firstly, agricultural production was further improved and the situation in China's rural areas — which have a population of more than 800 million — became better and better. By implementing those documents of the Party Central Committee concerning agricultural development and by continuing to eradicate influences of "Left" deviationist mistakes in the rural areas, the government adopted the following policies and measures to aid agricultural production:

Earnestly ensure the power of rural communes and their subdivisions in the management of production and the distribution of income.

Conscientiously adhere to the distribution principle of "to each according to one's work" through the adoption of job responsibility systems in various forms.

Readjust the structure of the agricultural economy and encourage the development of diversified economies wherever local conditions permit.

Raise the purchasing prices of cotton, tung oil, resin and selected other farm and sideline products in 1980 (following the large increases in purchasing prices of 18 major agricultural and sideline products in 1979).

Encourage peasants to cultivate private plots and to plant private trees for the development of household sideline production, on the condition that the collective economy is well developed.

Open rural markets under the appropriate supervision.

All of these policies and measures further inspired the enthusiasm and initiative of rural cadres and peasants engaged in agricultural production. At the same time, communes and their subdivisions in many areas underwent consolidation.

Despite floods in the south and drought conditions in the north that were often the most severe in several decades, a relatively good harvest was produced. Although total grain output for

1980 fell 14 million tons short of the total in 1979, it still surpassed that of 1978 and was the second best harvest in 31 years.

Changes also took place in the structure of agricultural production. The one-sided emphasis on grain production was altered somewhat and the total area under industrial crops was expanded. The output of many industrial crops was increased considerably. The total output of cotton, oil-bearing crops, sugarcane, sugar beets, tea, jute and ambary hemp all set new records. New achievements were also made in forestry, animal husbandry, sideline production and fisheries. In short, agricultural production grew steadily and the rural economy improved.

Light Industry and Textiles. Secondly, the growth rate of light industry continued to exceed that of heavy industry and the industrial structure became more rational. In 1980, the Chinese government continued to follow policies and measures that encouraged the development of light industry. Planning departments at all levels gave priority to the production needs of light industry and textiles by granting increased loans for the construction of new projects and for supplies of raw materials, fuels and electricity and it opened more channels for the development of light and textile industries as well as handicrafts.

The total annual output value of light industry in 1980 came to 234,400 million yuan, 18.4% more than in 1979. The proportion of output value of light industry to total industrial output value rose from 43.1% in 1979 to 46.9% in 1980.

Mining and Heavy Industry. Although the growth rate of heavy industry slowed, its internal structure began to change for the better. The proportional share of mining and tunnelling within the mining industry were somewhat readjusted. For many years, the proportion of mining and tunnelling and the proportional shares of mining and stripping were seriously out of balance, while safety measures lagged far behind requirements. In 1980, tunnelling and stripping work in the coal mines and prospecting work for oil resources were strengthened.

The production of iron, steel, machines and chemicals was brought under control and the production of chemical fertilizers, plastics, cement and household electrical appliances was stepped up. The output of small-size shaped steel products, steel wires, sheet steel and welded tubes was 28.5% greater than in 1979; the proportion of these items to the total output of rolled steel rose from 44% in 1979 to 57% in 1980. The output of large-size shaped steel, medium-size and thick plates, seamless tubes and high-quality shaped steels dropped by 13.7% as compared with 1979. The output of mining equipment, metallurgical equipment, power generating equipment and hand tractors dropped, while the production of engineering products required in the people's daily lives increased considerably.

Sectors producing building materials and chemicals also increased their production of products and raw materials so urgently needed by the country. Incomplete statistics show that in 1979 enterprises under the First Ministry of Machine-Building Industry produced only 23 products for light industry, with a total value of 650 million yuan. In 1980, they produced 93 items for light industry, with a total value of 4,000 million yuan. The value of products for civilian use manufactured by defence industries accounted for about 30% of the total output value of the defence industry in 1980, as against 20% in 1979. Statistics show that the output value of consumer goods produced by industries other than the light and textile industries were equivalent to 31% of the total output value of the country's light industry.

Consumption and Income Levels. Thirdly, the ratio between accumulation and consumption began to improve and the consumption level of the urban and rural populations was raised. In the past 20 years, the rate of accumulation in the distribution of national income was too high, thus holding down the consumption level. A focal point of the economic readjustment is to improve the ratio between accumulation and consumption and raise the consumption level of urban and rural people. In 1980, the government coordinated the proportional relationships between accumulation and consumption through controls over capital investments in the state budget, by reducing circulating funds and by increasing consumption funds. The proportion of accumulation funds to the national income dropped from 36.5% in 1978 to 32% in 1980; the proportion of consumption funds rose from 63.5% in 1978 to 68% in 1980.

State investments for capital construction in 1980 totalled 28,100 million yuan, or 11,400 million yuan less than in 1979. By the end of 1980, the number of large and medium-sized projects under construction dropped from 1,187 to 904. A greater part of investments in 1980 were made in light industry, energy production and development, communications and transport and other weak links in the national economy. The proportion of investment in industrial construction to total investment dropped from 51.4% in 1979 to 50.8% in 1980. The proportion of investment in light and textile industries to total investment rose from 6.4% in 1979 to 9.2% in 1980.

The proportion of investment in heavy industry to total investment dropped from 45% in 1979 to 41.6% in 1980. The proportions of investment in the chemical, machine-building and defence industries all dropped notably. The proportion of investment in workers' housing construction, cultural, educational and health work, and urban public utilities was raised from 17.4% in 1978 to 27% in 1979 and again to 33.7% in 1980. The investment in housing construction in 1980 increased by 3,400 million yuan as compared to 1979 and its proportion of the total investment rose from 14.8% in 1979 to 20% in 1980. Readjustment in the proportions of investment in capital construction will play an important role in systematically reducing the rate of accumulation to a level suited to current actual conditions in China and in further improving the production and distribution structure of the national economy.

The Chinese government made great efforts to raise the consumption level of the population, while the livelihood of most of the people in urban and rural areas continued to improve. Owing to good harvests and to increases in the purchasing prices of farm products, most peasant households increased their incomes. In 1980, Chinese peasants were able to increase their income from sales of farm products and from labour services by about 13,000 million yuan; average per capita income earned from the collective was 85.9 yuan, an increase of 2.5 yuan over 1979 and 11.9 yuan over 1978. This two-year increase greatly surpassed the accumulated increase of the 11-year period from 1965 to 1976. Individual incomes of peasant families also increased considerably.

Housing. The party and government also adopted forceful measures to support housing construction in rural areas. Beginning in 1980, planning departments in China at all levels incorporated into state plans the supply of building materials to rural areas. According to statistics, about 25 million peasant families built new houses or rebuilt their homes during the three years between 1978 and 1980; this group accounted for 14% of all peasant households in China.

Employment. In 1980, jobs were provided to 9 million people, including graduates from universities, colleges and secondary technical schools. A total of 28 million people in urban areas received jobs during the four-year period between 1977 and 1980. A number of conditions — including the enlarged workforce, the fact that 40% of all workers and staff members received increased wages as of November 1979, the readjustment of wage categories in some regions, the implementation of piece-work pay for workers, an increased number of adoptions of the bonus system among enterprises and public undertakings, and the provision of subsidies for price increases of non-staple foods — the total wage bill for workers and staff members of units under ownership of the whole people and under collective ownership was 19.5% greater than in 1979, while average wages in these categories also increased notably. Wages of workers and staff members in units owned by the whole people averaged 803 yuan in 1980, 13.9% more than in 1979, or an actual increase of 6% after deducting the rise in the cost-of-living index.

As a result of growth in industrial and agricultural production and increased income of workers and peasants, social purchasing power rose greatly. Total purchasing power was 32,000 million yuan higher in 1979 than in 1978 and was 35,000 million yuan higher again in 1980 than in 1979. This was more than five times the average annual increase of 6,500 million yuan in the ten years leading up to 1977.

Intellectual Resources. Fourthly, attention began to be paid to the development of intellectual resources and readjustments were made in the relationships between economic construction and the development of scientific, cultural and educational work. In 1980, the financial strength of the government was not great and expenditures were greatly reduced in other fields. Nevertheless, not only was the proportion of capital investments in scientific, cultural and educational work to total state investment increased by a substantial margin, but operating expenses in these fields were also increased. This was done in order to accelerate the development of intellectual resources and gradually change the imbalance between economic construction and the development of scientific, cultural and educational work. Proportional relations among these departments were also readjusted.

In 1980, more than 2,600 major discoveries were made in scientific research, and 107 of them were acknowledged by the state as inventions. The dissemination of scientific knowledge was also strengthened. New facilities and other amenities were provided to the universities and colleges.

In 1980, school buildings with a total floor space of 3.2 million square metres were completed at universities and colleges throughout China, the highest rate since 1949. The number of students now in universities and colleges totalled 1.14 million, or 12.2% more than in 1979.

The educational level of primary and middle schools as well as that of universities and colleges was raised. Some changes were made in the structure of secondary education and more secondary technical schools were reopened. The use of television, correspondence and night classes in higher education was expanded.

Medical Services. Medical and health institutions were being readjusted in ways to strengthen their scientific management and operation. The prevention and treatment of diseases were strengthened, and the quality of services in hospitals was improved. Literature, drama, cinema, ballet and fine arts began to prosper. Sports, broadcasting, television, publications and archaeology were also developed.

II. Restructuring of the Economic System

In 1980, experimental work to restructure the present economic system continued in line with the principle of taking a positive but prudent attitude while bringing about the economic readjustment. This work has invigorated the entire national economy.

1. *Experimental work to expand the power of the enterprises in self-management was extended.*

After the State Council issued relevant documents on restructuring the management system of the state-owned industrial enterprises in July 1979, experiments to expand the power of enterprises began one by one in different parts of the country. By the end of 1979, more than 4,000 enterprises had entered the experiment. In 1980, experimental work developed in depth and breadth. Except for the Tibet Autonomous Region, more than 6,000 industrial enterprises in 28 Chinese provinces, municipalities and autonomous regions on the mainland took up the experimental work. These enterprises make up 15% of the total number of industrial enterprises that contribute to the state budget; they produce 60% of goods in terms of output value and earn 70% of the total profits of industrial enterprises.

The content of the experiment also expanded. In 1979, enterprises that began the experiment had authority to retain only part of the profits they earned. But in 1980, they acquired authority in varying degrees to plan production, to purchase raw materials, to sell products, to develop new products, to use operating funds, to issue bonuses, to reduce or expand administrative structures, and to appoint or dismiss cadres at the middle level. Moreover, a limited number of enterprises were selected to pay taxes instead of turning over their profits to the state, to keep independent accounts and to assume responsibility for their own gains and losses. By the end of 1980, the city of Liuzhou in Guangxi, the Light Industry Machinery Corporation of Shanghai, and 80 other enterprises joined in this experiment, bringing the total number of enterprises that had begun the experiment at this level to more than 200.

Effects of the Reform on Economic Growth. The reform of expanding the power of enterprises in self-management produced a profound effect on economic growth in China. To a certain extent, this reform integrated in an organic way the economic responsibilities, economic results and economic interests of the enterprises. With more power over self-management, the economic interests of the enterprises and their workers and staff members are directly linked to the effectiveness of their operation. This enhanced the sense of responsibility on the part of workers and staff members as masters of their own enterprises, inspired their initiative and creativity in production and increased their awareness of business operations, markets, services and competition. The new spirit played a helpful role in invigorating the economy, improving management, tapping potential, and increasing production and income.

Preliminary figures from 5,777 enterprises (not including the 200 enterprises that started the experiment of paying taxes rather than turning over profits) showed that they produced 165,350 million yuan in value of output in 1980, which was 10,550 million yuan or 6.8% more than in 1979; they earned 33,360 million yuan in profits, or 3,520 million yuan (11.8%) more than in 1979; and they turned over 29,000 million yuan in profits to the state, 2,000 million yuan (7.4%) more than in 1979. In the distribution of the profits they earned, the interests of the state, the enterprise and its individual workers were all taken into consideration. In 1980, these 5,777 enterprises turned over 87% of their profits to the state and retained 10% of the profits for their own disposal. The remaining 3% was used to repay bank loans or relevant subsidies. In the case of a small number of enterprises that began the experiment, the results were not satisfactory as both the value of their output and profits declined. This was due to added factors placing pressure on profits, to overpayment of bank loans and to poor management and operations.

2. *Preliminary reforms were made in the planning, supply and commercial systems.*

The reforms that took place in conventional systems — under which all production quotas were set by higher authorities, capital goods were prohibited from entering the markets and all commodities were purchased by state purchasing agencies — began with experimentally expanding the power of these enterprises in self-management and with limited use of the market as a means of regulating production under the guidance of planned economy. The main changes in this respect were:

A. Enterprises were allowed to produce more goods that were required by the market and consumers as long as they could assure fulfilment of targets set in the state plans and contracts they signed with customers. For example, the volume of goods produced on their own initiative to meet market demands by enterprises under the First Ministry of Machine-Building Industry accounted for 13.9% of the total output value of those enterprises in 1979, and for 46% in 1980. B. More and more commodities were supplied without limits or marketed freely. Of the 210 major items of capital goods distributed by the central government in 1980, 146, or 69%, were supplied without limitation. In the distribution of consumer goods, only 13 commodity items were controlled by state purchasing agencies. As to other commodities, enterprises were permitted to sell a portion of products produced in excess of quotas set in state plans and under contracts. C. More outlets were opened for the distribution of commodities. Departments of supply, commerce and foreign trade entered the purchasing and marketing businesses on a commission basis. The volume of these kinds of transactions amounted to 3,500 million yuan in 1979 and to 5,000 million yuan in 1980. More shops, stores and other commercial establishments were opened throughout the country. More than 600 capital goods service corporations were set up in 1980 and capital goods trade fairs were opened in 60 or more cities. More than 16,000 sales departments were set up by industrial and transport enterprises and some of these factories, communes and farms opened shops in cities or towns. More than 2,900 free markets selling agricultural produce were opened in Chinese cities and the number of rural fairs increased to 37,000. Many departments and localities held sales exhibitions and goods exchange fairs in various forms. The adoption of these systems and policies greatly helped to increase the supply of commodities. According to estimates, about 35% of retail sales were regulated through the market in 1979; during the first half of 1980, more than 30% of goods sold at retail were marketed in this way. Preliminary reforms in the planning, supply and commercial sectors aided economic readjustment and promoted production and construction.

3. *Initial steps were made in changing the organizational structure of the economy.*

In 1979, while implementing the policy of readjusting, restructuring, consolidating and improving the national economy, some provinces, municipalities and autonomous regions, as well as industrial and transport ministries under the State Council, started the experimental work of reorganizing and readjusting industrial enterprises on the principle of specialization, coordination and economic rationality. They established a number of special corporations and general works and technical cooperation centers. In the first half of 1980, the central government put forth the policy of "making the best use of the advantages, protecting competition and promoting integration;" joint production, joint ventures and compensation trade were launched among various enterprises and localities, and between urban and rural areas. According to statistics from 28 provinces, municipalities and autonomous regions on the mainland (not including Tibet), 1,973 special corporations and general works centres had been set up by the end of 1980. These embraced 19,173 enterprises, or 5.38% of the total number of enterprises in these provinces, municipalities and autonomous regions. The three municipalities of Beijing, Shanghai and Tianjin had set up 278 special corporations and general works centres, embracing 4,548 enterprises, or 31% of all enterprises in those cities. The 28 provinces, municipalities and autonomous regions also formed more than 3,400 economic complexes. Some ministries also set up experimentally a limited number of joint operations between national corporations and localities. More than 570 state farms set up 194 agriculture-industry-commerce complexes. These included shops and factories processing farm produce and shops selling processed goods not derived from farming. They accounted for 28% of the farms under the Ministry of State Farms and Land Reclamation.

Initial progress was recorded in industrial reorganization and integration. This was manifested in the following ways:

A. *They accelerated the readjustment.* Through integration, a factory that produced the same goods or had similar processes, or factories which operated over or under capacity, were reorganized into special corporations, general works centres or economic entities. In this way, their production was placed under a unified plan so as to restrict the production of unwanted goods and to expand the production of textiles and other consumer goods that were marketable both at home and abroad.

B. *They promoted specialization and coordination among localities and enterprises.* Through reorganization and integration, some localities and enterprises began to change the circumstances under which many enterprises were producing the same goods, and began to reorganize production along specialized lines.

C. *They saved capital investment and focused the use of previously scattered manpower, material power and financial power.*

D. *They promoted increases in production and technological levels as well as technological transformation.*

E. *They began to break through the existing management system and promoted economic integration among different localities and different industries, opening a road for further reforms in the economic system.*

4. *A multi-sector economy and multiple forms of business were restored and developed.*

In the latter part of the 1950's, under the guidance of "Left" deviationist thinking and policies, the superiority of ownership by the whole people was made absolute; there was overemphasis on transition from collective ownership to ownership by the whole people, there was stress on the transition from small collective units to large collective untis and on "cutting off the tails of capitalism" such as private plots; moreover, household sideline production, rural fairs and the rural individual economy were greatly restricted. In the urban areas, the individual economy was eliminated and the collective economy was reduced. Especially during the "cultural revolution," under the ultra-"Left" line pushed by Lin Biao and the Gang of Four, rural ownership by the production team as the basic unit in the communes was changed to the ownership by the production brigade or even by the commune, and both the diversified and individual economies were repudiated as "capitalist elements."

In the cities and towns, many service items which serve the needs of the masses were banned and the colorful styles and methods of business operations were simplified. As a result, diversified economy was constrained, growth of the collective economy slowed down and the individual economy was almost eliminated. As an example, there were 9 million self-employed labourers in urban areas in 1953, but the figure dropped to 1.56 million in 1966 and to 150,000 by the end of 1978. The number of commercial and service establishments was greatly reduced. Statistics showed that in the early 1950's there were about 100 cities with a ratio of 50 restaurant establishments for each 10,000 families; by 1980, however, only a few cities had 5 eating or drinking establishments for every 10,000 families.

The Growth of Economic Diversity. For the past two years, multiple ownership and a multi-sector economy have been allowed to coexist and to grow (on the condition that public ownership is predominant), so as to keep pace with the present level of development of productive forces. In rural areas, uniformity is no longer imposed on farm production and the authority of production teams in management has begun to be respected. The practice of interfering with and restricting farm production has been altered and self-employed labourers are now permitted. In the cities and towns, a large number of collectively owned industries, transport services, construction enterprises, retail shops, catering and service units and repair stations have been set up and a number of self-employed labourers have been allowed to produce handicrafts, open restaurants and engage in repairs, mending and peddling. In 1979, the number of collective commercial establishments in the county towns and cities grew to 128,000, or 83% more than 1978. Last year, the number shot up to more than 1.3 million. The volume of retail sales by collective units accounted for 10% of the total volume of retail sales in China in 1980, as against 5% a year ago. By the end of 1980, there were 810,000 self-employed labourers in Chinese cities and towns, 490,000 more than in 1979. There were from 10,000 to 20,000 individuals or families doing business or running workshops on their own in cities such as Shanghai and Tianjin and in the provinces of Liaoning, Anhui and Jilin.

The restoration and expansion of the multi-sector economy and these multiple forms of doing business have promoted China's economic construction:

A. *They have invigorated the economy, made things convenient for people and increased the wealth of society.* In rural areas, the new policies have promoted the growth of the diversified economy and production. In the cities, most of the new economic units were set up in order to redress omissions and deficiencies. For this reason, they have become supplements to economic life. Apart from providing better services, they also produce goods badly needed in the market and some even make high-quality export items that increase national foreign-exchange earnings.

B. *They make the best use of idle funds and of those idle people with good skills and local resources in order to expand production of farm produce and handicraft items.*

C. *They provide more jobs for jobless people in the cities and for surplus manpower in the countryside.* In 1979, jobs were given to 9 million people in the cities and towns, of which about 4 million were in collective units. In addition, 7 million people found jobs in urban areas in 1980, of whom 4 million were in units under ownership by the whole people and 2.6 million in collective units; 400,000 people were self-employed.

D. *It helped competition, urged enterprises to improve their management and benefitted the restructuring of the economic system.* Different economic forms have different forms of business operations and different management systems. The coexistence of the multiple economic sectors encouraged state-owned enterprises to change their conventional notions of doing business, to reassess the present practice of "sharing porridge from the same pot" and to overcome bureaucratic methods and styles. In short, the coexistence and development of different forms of economic activities and multiple economic sectors provides a good way of making the best use of labour power, materials and capital funds for the development of social productive forces.

5. *The start of a reform in the management system for capital construction.*

The State Council decided to gradually replace government allocations for capital investment with loans from the Construction Bank in August 1979. This represented a major reform in the management system for capital construction. For many years, capital investment was provided to units requiring construction in the form of government allocations, and for use without compensation. This system affected returns from the investment. On the principle of permitting capital investment to take the form of compensated bank loans, enterprises requiring construction must sign contracts with the Construction Bank for loans on specified terms; they are required to pay back the loans with interest and according to schedule. Those which pay back their loans ahead of schedule are to be rewarded and those which delay repayment shall be fined. This experimental reform was begun in eight projects in Shanghai, Jilin and Henan in 1979 and was extended to 4,400 projects in 1980. These projects belonged to more than a dozen industries covering power generation, light industry, coal mining, petroleum, communications and transport, construction materials, metallurgy, chemical engineering and commerce; they were located in all parts of China. The loans totalled 2,600 million yuan.

The Construction Bank and its offices at various levels also used bank deposits earmarked for capital construction to issue capital construction loans to 4,700 units requiring construction projects with a total value of 1,360 million yuan. Experimental work in the past year showed that the change from government allocations to bank loans had played a positive role in strengthening the management for capital construction and increasing returns from investment by integrating economic responsibilities, economic rights and interests of the enterprises and by bringing into full play the functioning of economic organization and economic means under guidance of the state plan.

6. *A major reform was made in the financial and credit system.*

In the past, the purpose of China's financial management was to exercise absolute control by the central government over the revenues and expenditures. In order to meet the requirements of restructuring the economic management system and of modernization, the State Council decided to adopt new measures starting in 1980 on the basis of reforms made in the financial system in previous years. The basic principle is to specify the rights and responsibilities of the authorities at different levels while consolidating the unified leadership and unified planning of the central government and ensuring the necessary expenditures of the central government so that governments at all levels share the rights and responsibilities and so that the initiative of both central and local governments are brought into full play.

The main practices were as follows: A special system of fixed quotas was adopted for Guangdong and Fujian provinces; subsidies from the central government to the five autonomous regions of Xinjiang, Ningxia, Inner Mongolia, Tibet and Guangxi and to the three provinces of Yunnan, Guizhou and Qinghai would increase at an annual rate of 10%, while all previous special treatment for these regions and provinces were to be preserved; all other provinces and the three municipalities of Beijing, Tianjin and Shanghai would adopt the system of "dividing revenues and expenditures at different levels and holding the authorities responsible at each level for their own balances. This means that local governments can spend more if they have more revenues and can spend less if they have less revenues so as to balance their own budgets. The new measures prompted the initiative of local governments in handling their own financial matters. Consequently, local governments at all levels tried in every way to open more avenues for increased production, to find more sources of revenue and to reduce expenditures.

Reforms in Banking and Credit. The banking and credit systems was also reformed. The basic principle was to maximize the role of the banks in economic development under the guidance of state planning. The present credit system was formulated in the early 1950's on the basis of the Soviet experience. Its basic function is to issue only short-term loans to industrial and commercial enterprises — in effect, to issue annual loans to cover operating expenses. This practice undoubtedly limits the functioning of bank credit as an economic lever. In 1980, the People's Bank of China began to issue short and medium-term loans (3-10 years) for purchasing new equipment; the loans so issued totalled 4,130 million yuan, including 1,500 million yuan for light industries and textiles. The credit system of the Agricultural Bank was also reformed in 1980. In rural areas, a new credit management system was introduced under unified planning, unified policy and a unified system. The system was also introduced in one or two provinces on a trial basis in 1980 for state-owned agricultural enterprises. Beginning in 1980, local banks can retain 75% of newly increased portions of workers' savings deposits from state-owned agricultural enterprises as a fund for credit loans to these enterprises. These measures helped local authorities to take the initiative in pooling local funds, as well as to manage and use them in a proper way.

7. *Changes were also made in the foreign trade system.*

For more than 20 years, all foreign trade in China was controlled by the Ministry of Foreign Trade. Under this monopoly system, industry had nothing to do with trade and producers never knew who the buyers of their products were, thus hampering the initiative of both industry and producers. In the second half of 1979, China began to make some changes in its foreign trade system. The main changes that took place were as follows:

A. *Export commodities were controlled at different levels and local foreign trade departments were allowed to handle more commodity items.*

B. *The power of local authorities in foreign trade was expanded.* All provinces, municipalities and autonomous regions had the right to set up their own special trade corporations to handle the export of local commodities or of certain special commodities and to control import business within their own localities. Ministries under the State Council were permitted to set up export corporations to handle the export of commodities produced by enterprises under their jurisdiction. By the end of 1980, the central government had approved the right of Shanghai, Tianjin, Beijing, Liaoning, Sichuan, Shandong and 18 ministries under the State Council to set up foreign trade corporations.

C. *The power of industrial enterprises in foreign trade was also expanded.* A limited number of qualified industrial enterprises took a direct part in international trade activities or trade talks with foreign businessmen to obtain first-hand information so that they could arrange production according to the requirements and needs of their customers.

D. *A system was adopted of allowing local governments and enterprises to retain part of the foreign exchange earned from their exports.* Preferential customs duties were levied on goods imported for the manufacture of exports so as to encourage the expansion of export business.

E. *Special policies and flexible measures were adopted in 1980 for Guangdong and Fujian provinces in economic activities with foreign countries and regions.* With the approval of the Standing Committee of the National People's Congress and the State Council, parts of Shenzhen, Zhuhai and Shantou in Guangdong Province and Xiamen in Fujian Province were designated as special economic zones so as to foster better economic cooperation and technical exchange with other countries and regions.

For the past two years, China has also begun to pay attention to economic legislation. For many years past, the absence of economic laws, and especially the wanton sabotage of the socialist legal system by the Lin Biao and Jiang Qing counter-revolutionary cliques, caused unwarranted losses to China's economic work. In the course of strengthening the work of the socialist legal system, governments at all levels have paid close attention to economic legislation and have formulated or have begun to formulate a number of economic laws and regulations. Preliminary statistics showed that as of the end of October 1980, the Standing Committee of the National People's Congress, the State Council and the ministries had promulgated 210 economic laws, regulations and decrees during the period from 1977 to 1980, of which 86 were issued in 1980 alone.

Moreover, economic judicial work was also strengthened. Procuratorial work, supervision and arbitration systems were established in many parts of China. According to statistics from 28 provinces, municipalities and autonomous regions, more than 1,000 economic tribunals were set up and more than 6,000 economic cases handled in China in 1980. China in its economic life had begun to resort to law, to enforce laws strictly and to take legal action against violators of laws.

To summarize, all of these reforms were preliminary and some were made on a trial basis. However, China began to break away from the conventional system of overconcentration, regulating production only through plan and using mere administrative means to manage the economy. It took a welcomed step forward in managing the economy according to the requirements of economic laws, thus accumulating experience for overall reform of the economic management system.

III. Improvement of Economic Performance

While readjusting the ratio among the different branches of the national economy and restructuring the economic system, progress was also made in the consolidation of existing enterprises. Many localities readjusted and strengthened the leadership of the enterprises, selected and promoted to leading posts a number of young cadres who were politically and ideologically sound, as well as vocationally and technically competent, and who knew how to manage enterprises; they relieved those cadres who had not demonstrated competence in leading positions. The practice of training cadres and workers was restored and developed. In 1979 and 1980, more than 1.19 million cadres were trained, including 330,000 leading cadres of enterprises run at the county level and above. Workers' schools and training classes of all types were established. By the end of 1980, about 50% of all large and medium-sized enterprises in China had set up spare-time, part-time or full-time schools and training courses, enrolling about 20% of all workers and staff members. On the basis of consolidation of enterprises, more than 4,400 enterprises adopted the "Thorough Quality Control" system and strengthened their economic accounting. The level of managerial work of many enterprises was improved.

Steady progress was made throughout the national economy in 1980 as a result of the effective work done. New achievements were scored in industrial and agricultural production, communications and transport, capital and technological development and culture and education; the targets set in the state plan for these fields were all reached satisfactorily. Total national industrial and agricultural output value surpassed the annual target by 3.2%, and exceeded the 1979 figure by 7.2%. Total industrial output value surpassed the annual target by 3.1% and exceeded the 1979 figure by 8.7%. And total agricultural output value surpassed the annual target by 3.3%, and improved on the 1979 figure by 2.7%. It must be stressed that economic performance in all fields improved to varying degrees.

Achievements in Energy Conservation. Further achievements were made in saving energy.

In 1980, the party and government decided on the policy of giving equal stress to the development of energy resources, and to energy conservation and to giving priority to saving energy consumption in the next few years, while at the same time focusing major efforts on the technological transformation of existing equipment and changes in energy composition as a means of saving energy. All industrial departments and enterprises worked hard to save energy and, as a result, overfulfilled the annual national targets of saving 3% of electricity, 5% of coal and 10% of oil — thus, for example, the equivalent of 35 million tons of standard coal was gained. The drop in energy consumption greatly helped to ease the short supply of energy and to ensure fulfillment of the annual industrial production plan. In 1980, national primary output of coal and petroleum dropped by 1.3% as compared with 1979, while industrial production rose by 8.7%.

Upgrading Quality and Expanding Variety. The quality of products in all industries as a whole was improved and the variety of products was also increased. Statistics from major enterprises in metallurgy, coal mining, petrochemicals, building materials, light industry and textiles showed that the quality of 57 of 66 major products had improved over previous year.

Of 74 quotas for the consumption of raw materials, 50 could be reduced. Many industrial departments and enterprises adopted positive measures to increase the production of new varieties and new products. Light industrial enterprises in China developed more than 7,000 new products and more than 100,000 new patterns and styles, and about half of these were put into serial production. The textile industry put more than 30,000 new products into production in 1980.

The machine-building industry also developed more and more new products as well as new specifications. Enterprises under the First Ministry of Machine-Building Industry alone trial-produced 730 new products; about 98.7% of their major products were up to prescribed standards, the best performance in recent years.

The consumption of raw materials and energy was also reduced. The utilization rate of rolled steel rose by 3.3% as compared with 1979 and the amount of operating funds used in producing every hundred yuan of value dropped by 5.5 yuan. In 1980, the per capita labour productivity of industrial enterprises under ownership of the whole people was 12,031 yuan, or 2% higher than in 1979. The amount of circulating funds possessed by state-owned industrial and commercial enterprises also dropped.

Productivity and Profits in Agriculture. For many years past, the disregard of economic results and of labour costs in agricultural production and construction resulted in unwarranted increases in the cost of agricultural production. While production increased in many places, income remained the same or even fell. During the past two years, this situation has been changed somewhat. The proportion of agricultural production costs to total agricultural income dropped from 32.3% in 1978 to 31.9% in 1980. Instead of suffering great losses as they had done for years running, state land reclamation enterprises earned 520 million yuan in profits in 1979 and profits of 400 million yuan in 1980, this despite increased pay for some of their workers as well as subsidies to all of their workers and for nonstaple foodstuffs totalling more than 600 million yuan. These profits also came about despite serious floods and droughts in many areas. Actual profits increased by 52.7% over 1979.

Outstanding Problems and Trends in Development

China's economic development in 1980 gave added proof that it is absolutely necessary and entirely correct for the party and government to adopt the policy of readjusting, restructuring, consolidating and improving the national economy as well as a series of other new economic policies. These policies have instilled new vigor in the Chinese economy and have already played and continue to play a tremendous and positive role in promoting the healthy development of the entire national economy. However, because it was impossible to alter the serious imbalance in the national economy in one or two years and because some measures for economic readjustment taken during the past two years were not as effective, potential dangers lurked within this excellent situation.

There were still many problems and difficulties in China's economic life, as manifested in the following respects:

1. *The scale of capital construction continued to be overextended.*

Capital investment included in the state budget in 1980 was reduced, but not enough, and those investments not included in the state budget increased considerably: a. Capital funds pooled by local governments and enterprises came to 16,400 million yuan, or 5,900 million yuan more than in 1979, and surpassing the state-controlled figure of 8,000 million yuan by over 100%. b. Investments made through borrowing from other countries amounted to 5,400 million yuan, or 2,600 million yuan more than in 1979. Investment made by means of domestic borrowing amounted to 4,100 million yuan, or 3,600 million yuan more than in 1979. As a result, the total investment for capital construction was not reduced but expanded.

In 1980, 904 large and medium-sized projects were still under construction. The unfinished portions of these projects will require an additional expenditure of more than 100,000 million yuan from 1981 onwards, and will take five or six more years to complete at the 1980 level of investment — even if not a single new project is started during the period. It is obvious that the present scale of capital construction is not compatible with the present national capacity and this has become an important factor in economic instability.

2. *The battle line of industrial production was over-extended and progress in industrial reorganization and consolidation was not as quick as expected.*

In 1980, thousands of enterprises were closed, suspended, merged or shifted over to the production of other goods, while more than 20,000 new enterprises were built or put into operation. As a result of these developments, the total number of industrial enterprises by the end of 1980 was 22,000 more than had existed at the beginning of the year. Most of the new factories were small processing enterprises built without the supervision of the state plan. This resulted in the overproduction of unwanted goods and aggravated the contradictions between fuel, power and raw materials industries on the one hand and the processing industries on the other. The contradiction between the production of energy and raw materials and the demand for them became even more acute. Because of slow progress in industrial organization and consolidation, the economic results in industrial production and construction were not satisfactory. For example, the quality of 43% of the products made by industrial enterprises owned by the whole people and the unit consumption of 56% of these products failed to reach the previous best standards. About 23.3% of the enterprises still suffered losses of varying degrees and overstocking of some goods remained a serious problem. By the end of 1980, 19.54 million tons of rolled steel were stocked in warehouses, or 3.2% more than in the previous year.

3. *Large deficits continued to appear in the state budget and currency was overissued.*

Another budget deficit totalling 12,100 million yuan, approved in 1980, followed the 1979 deficit of 17,000 million yuan. The 1980 imbalance resulted from the overextended scale of capital construction and from increases in administrative and other expenses that exceeded state revenues. The central government was compelled to take an overdraft from the bank, leading to an over-issuance of currency. The bank had originally planned to issue 3,000 million yuan throughout the year, but it actually had to issue 7,800 million yuan, or 4,800 million yuan above the quota.

4. *The price rise covered a considerably wide range of commodity items.*

Prices of many commodities rose because more market money was in circulation; the production and supply of consumer goods, restricted by objective conditions and because of insufficient subjective efforts, were not able to meet the needs of the fast-growing purchasing power among urban and rural people; some enterprises arbitrarily raised the prices of their products for the sake of giving more bonuses to their workers; the range of commodity items sold at negotiated prices were too broad and market control was not tight.

In 1980, the total price index for retail sales throughout China (including official prices, negotiated prices and market prices) was 6% greater than in 1979 — 8.1% greater in the cities and 4.4% greater in rural areas. The index of official prices of state-owned shops rose by 4.4%, and food by 7.4% (nonstaple food, 13.8%). The price rise affected, to a certain extent, the livelihood of urban people, especially those workers and staff members who received no bonuses.

Post-1980 Readjustments. These facts showed that the serious imbalance in China's national economy had as yet to be totally righted and that the passive state of economic work had as yet to be changed. In view of this situation, the Party Central Committee and the State Council decided at the end of 1980 to further readjust the national economy on the basis of the readjustment made in the two previous years. The main target was, first of all, to strike a balance between revenues and expenditures in the course of readjusting the proportions of different branches of the national economy and, on this basis, to strike a balance between credit receipts and payments, to stop the issuance of currency solely for financial reasons and to stabilize market prices. In the course of the readjustment, those that should retreat must retreat; capital investment, spending on national defence and war preparedness, and administrative expenses must be reduced to the extent allowed by the national interest; and enterprises that consume far more fuel and raw materials than they need, those that produce low-quality products and those that suffer great losses must be closed, suspended, merged or changed over to the production of other goods.

At the same time, those which should be developed must be developed: Production and construction tasks that are needed by society, allowed by objective conditions and that can be fulfilled through effort must all be fulfilled. During the next few years, readjustment of the economic structure should proceed in a planned and deep-going way so as to make the economic structure more rational. Great efforts must be made to develop the production of consumer goods so as to increase revenues, improve the livelihood of the people and allow the national economy to develop healthily and in a coordinated way. Achievements already made in the restructuring of the economic system must be consolidated and reforms that are beneficial to the readjustment will be actively continued. Industrial reorganization and consolidation will be developed in a down-to-earth manner so as to make the economic organizational set-up more rational and so as to raise the managerial level of the enterprises. At the same time, equipment in existing enterprises will be renewed systematically so as to raise technological and production levels in those enterprises.

We are confident that after these measures are adopted, difficulties confronted in the development of China's national economy will be gradually overcome and that China's socialist modernization will gradually take the road of steady development in accord with China's actual conditions.

2. CHINA'S AGRICULTURE IN 1980

By Zhang Siqian
Institute of Agricultural Economics
Chinese Academy of Social Sciences

I. The Development of Agriculture Since the Founding of New China

Agriculture in China before the founding of the People's Republic of China consisted of small-scale production, with feudalist ownership of land occupying the dominant position. Not long after the founding of New China, land reform was carried out and the goal of "land to the tiller" was realized. Soon afterwards, socialist transformation of agriculture was carried out and socialist collective ownership and ownership by the whole people were set up. As a result, there was large-scale development in production; this played an important role in the development of industry as well as throughout the national economy.

Generally speaking, socialist collective ownership was manifested in the form of mutual-aid teams in agricultural production, elementary agricultural producers' cooperatives, advanced agricultural producers' cooperatives and the people's communes. By the end of 1956, when China was at the high tide of agricultural collectivization, the transition from the peasant individual ownership to socialist collective ownership had been basically completed. And at the end of 1958, a further transformation from agricultural producers' co-operatives to people's communes took place. At present, the people's communes employ a system of integrating government administration with commune management. It consists of a three-level system of ownership of the means of production, with ownership by the production teams as the basic form. At the end of 1980, there were in the countryside 54,000 people's commune, 710,000 production brigades and 5.66 million production teams. There were 170 million rural households with a population of over 800 million, over 300 million labour personnel resided in the rural people's communes. People's communes are the main units of agricultural production in our country. The vast preponderance of principle agricultural products — such as grain, cotton, oil-bearing crops and so on — purchased by the state are from the people's communes.

Agriculture under ownership by the entire people in China [i.e., "State" ownership – Ed.] consists of various state-owned farms, forest farms, livestock farms and fish farms. The first lot of such farms were set up as early as 1947. These were of two types: one were agricultural enterprises with economic accounting systems, whose main task was to set up a variety of commodity bases to develop agricultural production and to provide the state with marketable agricultural products and by-products; the other type consisted of undertakings whose main task was to pursue scientific experiments, to breed improved varieties of crops and livestocks and to popularize advanced techniques. In 1980, there were 2,093 state farms with 4.92 million staff members and workers under the Ministry of State Farms and Reclamation. These farms covered an area of 66.82 million *mu* of cultivated land accounting for 4.5% of the country's total cultivated area. Although the state farms did not occupy a large proportion of agriculture, they achieved relatively high rates of labour productivity and commodity production. Commodity ratios accounted for by this sector in 1980 were as follows: grain, 39.8%; cotton, 89.8%; and oil-bearing crops, 49.6%.

China's agricultural sector provides for individual sideline occupations of commune members. This activity is attached to the socialist collective economy. It plays an important part in the development of the agricultural economy, in improvement of the lives of commune members, in food supply in cities and towns and in the development of economic construction of the country. In 1980, the output value of individual sideline occupations accounted for about 18.9% of the total agricultural output. Most pigs, poultry, eggs and other animal by-products purchased by the state, as well as most agricultural by-products in the rural markets, came from the individual sideline occupations of commune members.

During the last 30 years there has been a great improvement in the technical conditions of agricultural production, and various levels of increases in principal agricultural by-products. From 1979 to 1952, the utilization of chemical fertilizers was extended from 300,000 tons to 54.28 million tons, combined horsepower of agricultural machinery power grew from 250,000 hp to 181.91 million hp, electricity used in rural areas was extended from 50 million kwh to 28,300 million kwh and effective irrigated acreage of cultivated land was extended from 300 million *mu* to 670 million *mu*. The output of major products increased as follows: grain output doubled, cotton increased by 69% and vegetable oils increased by 53%. The output of sugar crops in 1979 was 3.2 times that of 1952, the output of meat was 3.1 times that of 1952 and the output of aquatic products was 2.6 times that of 1952. This was the result of hard work of millions of peasants under the leadership of the Communist Party of China and the Chinese government.

It has to be pointed out that the superiority of the socialist system has not been brought into full play as a result of "leftist" guiding thought. During the "cultural revolution" in particular, agriculture suffered great losses because of disruption and damage caused by the Gang of Four. After the smashing of the Gang of Four in October 1976, the "cultural revolution" came to an end. The Third Plenary Session of the 11th Party Congress, which was of great historical significance, was held in December 1978. The principles of emancipating one's mind, using one's brains, seeking truth from facts and of uniting as one to look ahead were put forth. Under such conditions, the confusion created by the Gang of Four began to be quickly cleared up. Some principles and policies which were not in accord with reality were changed or readjusted. That enabled our agriculture to advance again along the path of healthy development.

II. Agricultural Production and Peasant Life in 1980

The year 1980 witnessed a good harvest in our country despite severe natural calamities. The north suffered from extensive droughts, while the south suffered from serious flooding. Neither problem had been experienced to such a profound extent during the past dozens of years. The areas affected were large and some were at the centre of major grain-growing regions. The maximum extent of the drought during the hot season amounted to more than 200 million *mu*. Some regions in North China had rarely experienced such drought conditions in the past hundred years. Water dried up in many rivers, reservoirs and ponds. Seedlings died of drought over large areas. In vast areas of the south, there were continuous low temperatures and rainy weather with little sunshine continuing from spring to summer. During the summer, the rainy season in the middle and lower reaches of the Changjiang River was long and there were frequent storms. Extremely heavy floods occurred, exceeded only by those of 1954 and 1931. Great efforts were made to combat the flooding. Nevertheless, over 130 million *mu* of farm land suffered from water-logging. Even so, except for grain output, other main agricultural products enjoyed large increases. Total grain output amounted to 318.22 million tons; although this was less than 1979, it was still the second highest yield since the founding of the People's Republic of China. Out of the 29 provinces, municipalities and autonomous regions, 13 increased their output. Of these, six had previously achieved high production levels: Sichuan, Guangdong, Guangxi, Fujian, Liaoning and Beijing; the remaining seven — Gansu, Ningxia, Qinghai, Yunan, Guizhou, Henan and Tibet — were among those that frequently suffered from calamities and low output and were consistently short of grain, but in 1980 had actually scored better harvests. Nine suffered rather large-scale declines: Hebei, Shaanxi, Shanxi and Inner Mongolia in the north; Hubei, Jiangsu, Zhejiang, Anhui and Shanghai in the south. Seven retained the same level of output or experienced a slight reduction in crops: Heilongjiang, Jilin, Shandong, Xinjiang, Jiangxi, Hunan and Tianjin.

Industrial crops realized extremely good harvests. The total output of cotton was 2,707,000 tons, an increase of 22.7% over 1979. Of the 15 major cotton-growing provinces, municipalities and autonomous regions, 9 increased their output; of these, Shandong was outstanding. The cotton output increased from 167,000 tons in 1979 to 537,500 tons in 1980, representing a 3.2-fold increase. Hebei and Henan doubled that of the previous year. But those provinces and municipalities along the middle and lower reaches of the Changjiang River which used to have a high yield of cotton all suffered a decrease in production as a result of low temperatures and rainy weather. Oil-bearing crops in 1980 had an increase of 19.5% following a good harvest in 1979. Sugar crops scored a good harvest as well. Total output of these crops went up by 18.3% over the previous year. Heilongjiang and Jilin, the major regions for growing sugar beets, had striking increases of more than double those of the previous year. The output in Inner Mongolia increased by 65.7%.

Mulberry-feeding silk-worms increased by 20% and tea increased by 9.7%. The output of jute had a slight increase in production. Cured tobacco, fruits and vegetables underwent slight declines compared with 1979.

Afforested acreage throughout the country covered 4,552,000 hectares, an increase of 1.4% over the previous year. The output of rubber increased by 4.3% over 1979, walnuts by 31.7% and chestnuts by 41.8%. The output of raw lacquer and rapeseeds declined.

The output of animal husbandry continued to increase based on significant growth experienced in 1979. The total output of pork, beef and mutton amounted to 12,055,000 tons, an increase of 13.5% over the previous year. Within this total, pork increased by 13.3%, beef by 17% and mutton by 17.1%. At the end of 1980, the population of draught animals increased by 0.7% and sheep by 2.3%. The pig population decreased by 4.5%, although the amount of pigs available for sale and slaughtering increased by 5.8%.

The output of aquatic products in 1980 was 4,497,000 tons, an increase of 4.5% over 1979. Among these, freshwater products increased by 11.1% and marine products by 2.1%.

The fine situation in agricultural production was also reflected strikingly in the rural markets. Activity in over 37,000 rural markets all over the country was very brisk. The quantity of agricultural products on the markets had risen by a large margin, with increased varieties and more stable prices. Some prices even went down a bit. According to statistics for 206 rural markets all over the country as provided by the Industrial and Commercial Administration Bureau, the value of agricultural and sideline products sold by peasants in 1980 at rural fairs amounted to 574.46 million yuan, representing an increase of 37.4% over the previous year. Compared with the same period in 1979, the combined level of commodity prices at the rural markets decreased by 1.6% as of the end of September, and by 1.8% as at the end of December. The gap between market prices and official prices set by the government was reduced by 3% as compared with 1979. Of the prices of ten major commodities, seven of them went down: those for rice, wheat, maize, edible oil, pork, Chinese cabbage and piglets. Three increased somewhat: tobacco, eggs and firewood.

The increase in production and brisk markets ensured increases in peasants' income and raising of consumer levels. The average monthly income each peasant received from basic collective accounting units was 85.9 yuan, or 2.5 yuan more than in 1979. The total income of rural commune members experienced a relatively sharp increase over the previous year owing to the fairly rapid developemnt of individual sideline occupations and to state increases in the purchase prices of some agricultural products.

Purchasing power in rural area and consumption rates of the peasants were also undergoing change. Retail quantities of consumer goods throughout the rural areas increased by 27.7% over 1979. Moreover, retail quantities of agricultural means of production purchased by production teams and commune members increased by 6.8% over the previous year. Judging by the sale of consumer goods in the villages, there was a remarkable increase in the sale of clothing and other commodities of daily use. The demand for television sets, radios, bicycles, sewing machines and watches also increased rapidly. More and more new houses were built by the peasants. Some 5 million farm households rebuilt their houses or constructed new ones throughout the country in 1980. The total area amounted to over 300 million square metres, including offices built by communes and production teams. Newly built houses in the rural areas of Jilin Province alone covered an area of 5,910,000 square metres. Some 100,000 peasant households moved into new houses there. Newly built houses in the rural areas of Liaoning Province covered an area of 14,960,000 square metres. Over 280,000 households of commune members moved into new houses. In the rural areas of Zhejiang Province, there were even more new houses, amounting to 37 million square metres and accommodating 570,000 households.

Savings deposits in rural areas also showed a rapid increase. Deposits in rural areas for the entire year were about 14,800 million yuan, an increase of more than 49% over the previous year. Deposits by peasants totalled about 12,060 million yuan, an increase of 53.8% over 1979. There were record increases in deposits throughout the rural areas in 1980, with deposits throughout the rural areas The pattern of sudden rises and falls in deposits that had prevailed in past years had clearly been changed.

It must be pointed out particularly that substantial changes occurred in many communes and production teams which had been poor and economically backward for many years. There were 43 poor counties which comprised over half the counties in Guizhou Province which had been described this way in the past: "No place has any level ground and no person has even a small amount of money." But in 1980, 32 of these counties increased both their production and income. According to the investigations conducted by the Statistical Bureau of the province, in 390 farm households in 13 counties the cash income of commune members belonging to poor production teams during the first quarter of 1980 increased by 39.1% over the corresponding period in 1979. Their growth rate was 12% higher than that of commune members in more prosperous teams. The ratio of poor production teams in Heilongjiang Province fell from 22.4% in 1979 to 13.3% in 1980. Some 6,753 poor production teams had begun to take on a new look. The income of commune members also increased as compared with 1979. In nearly 3,000 poor production teams, the average income per person had surpassed 90 yuan. In Liaoning district of Shandong Province, one of the poorest regions in the country, the average income per person in 1978 was 46 yuan; in

1979, the income went up to 54.8 yuan and in 1980, it went up further to 126 yuan which was 2.3 times as much as the previous year. The situation of "production relying on loans, grain rations relying on resold grain, and life relying on relief" had changed in many poor communes and production teams throughout the country. Both collective and individual incomes were much higher in 1980 than in the past.

III. Agricultural Reform and Readjustment in 1980

There were five main elements in the agricultural reform and readjustment of 1980:

1. *The reform of the system of agricultural administration by the state.*

The principal aspects were reform of the agricultural planning system, changes in the statistical targets of agricultural plans and popularization of the contract system.

A. *Reform of the agricultural planning system.*

Under the old agricultural planning system, all kinds of specific instructions, including crop varieties, output, areas planted to main products and numbers of livestock were usually issued from upper levels to lower ones. Production teams had to comply. In some places, it was not the production teams but higher authorities who fixed the plots, planting schedules and methods of sewing, manuring, irrigation and harvest. These procedures greatly restricted the decision-making power of the production teams. Some production teams had no power to make decisions at all. As a result, several absurd situations developed. For example, activities suited to local conditions that yielded high outputs and good economic results were not able to develop. In other cases, activities that were not suited to local conditions and that produced low outputs and poor economic results were forced to be taken on. Thus, maximum economic success could not be realized. Under the reformed agricultural planning system, production planning targets worked out by higher authorities were no longer issued to the lower levels in the form of commands, but rather as proposals made for their reference. However, targets for purchasing and allocating agricultural products as set by the state still took the nature of directives and production units were expected to meet them. The process of the reform varied according to local conditions.

In early 1980, the Sichuan provincial government stipulated that agricultural plans could be worked out with the production team taken as the basic unit, with negotiations to take place between upper and lower-level authorities. Planned targets for planting were no longer set by the higher authorities, although targets for production were still set by them. In mid-1980, the Qinghai provincial government also stipulated that upper-level authorities would no longer give directives on the production plan to production teams; rather, they would set forth marketable targets for grain, edible oil and major animal products. In November of the same year, it was decided in Zhejiang Province that targets for crop acreage and output would not be issued by the upper authorities as directives. By the end of 1980, virtually no directives on targets for crop acreage were being issued by upper-level authorities anywhere in the country.

B. *Changes in statistical targets of the agricultural plan.*

In 1980, the State Planning Commission, the State Agricultural Commission, the Ministry of Agriculture and the State Statistical Bureau jointly issued a document which stated that in planning and statistical work "the per-*mu* output of farm land" and "the amount of livestock on hand at the end of a year" would no longer be regarded as targets for measuring the achievements of agricultural production. In future, whether or not grain production was high or low would be judged mainly by total output, by the volume of marketable products, by whether or not average output and consumption per person increased, by whether or not the cost of production decreased and by whether or not the income of farmers increased. Animal husbandry output would be judged by the quantity of animal products and production costs and by increases in the incomes of farmers and herdsmen. Targets for animal products varied according to the different uses of different animals. That was an important change.

There were a host of shortcomings in the two old methods for evaluating gains in the production of grain and livestock. Owing to the pressure exerted by higher authorities and to a quest for noteriety, some communes and production teams resorted to trickery — such as under-reporting areas under cultivation — and the practice of fraud was encouraged. Some production teams paid no attention to speeding up the turnover of livestock and the rate of selling and slaughtering domestic animals, focusing rather on increases of the amount of livestock on hand at the end of a year. Thus, the practical economic benefits of animal husbandry were reduced. These practices were quite disadvantageous to the development of agriculture. After the reform, the old targets were kept in the form of statistics so as to provide reference data for the study of livestock production and land utilization.

C. *Popularization of the contract system.*

The system of developing economic relations between purchasing, supply and marketing departments and production units was tried out through implementation of the contract system in some places prior to initiating the reform of the agricultural planning system. For example, the system was tried out as early as in the winter of 1978 in Jin Xian County, Hebei Province. It was afterwards tried and popularized in many other places during 1980. Contracts varied in nature from comprehensive to simple. In Nantong district of Jiangsu Province, a major cotton growing region, a comprehensive contract that covered principal production jobs, purchasing, supplies and marketing began to be disseminated in 1980. The concrete method was: that departments of grain, supplies marketing, commerce and agriculture in the districts, counties and communes took the initiative to sign contracts separately with counties, communes and production teams (we shall call the former "Party B" and the latter "Party A"). The commitments of Party A were to fulfil the tasks of production and sales of grain, oil and pigs as set in the contract for a normal harvest year. The commitments of Party B were to ensure the supply of marketable grain, chemical fertilizers, agricultural chemicals and other means of production; to correctly carry out the price policy and the policy of compensation for sales. Contracts were made in some places only for purchasing and marketing of a single product — pigs, sugar-cane or oil-bearing crops. Quantity, quality and delivery dates were stipulated in the contract as responsibilities of the production unit. Moreover, the quantity, quality and supply dates for the means of production provided by the purchasing and marketing units and the means of providing compensation were stipulated in the contract. In many places, the method used prior to the "cultural revolution" for purchasing agricultural and sideline products of the third category by means of contract was restored and the practice adopted during the "cultural revolution" of giving directives for purchasing targets was abolished.

The above-mentioned reforms played an important part in protecting the right of production teams to act on their own. They also helped in the development of agricultural production through measures worked out to suit local conditions.

2. *To continue the restoration and development of the job-responsibility system in agricultural production.*

As early as the 1950's, the period of the agricultural cooperatives, a job responsibility system for production and output, including the fixing of work and farm output quotas for each group, was already in use throughout the collective sector of the economy. The widely used practice of the time was referred to as "three contracts and one reward," and had been adopted in people's communes prior to the onset of the "cultural revolution." Moreover, in some places this method for fixing the farm output quotas for individual households was also in use although it was labelled as a manifestation of "capitalism and revisionism" and was severely criticized. So, after several ups and downs, there was no chance to put it into general practice. During the "cultural revolution," the method of fixing farm output quotas for each household was criticized again as were measures for fixing work quotas and farm output quotas for each group. Nearly all of the communes and production teams stopped enforcing the rule of job-responsibility. Only a few communes and teams maintained the rule on and off, but did so secretly. Because of the abolishment of the job responsibility system, production was often chaotic and the principle of distribution according to work was impossible to carry out. The result was that the enthusiasm of hundreds of millions of peasants was dampened.

Following the "cultural revolution," especially after the Third Plenary Session of the 11th Party Congress in 1978, the system of job responsibility in agricultural production was restored and began to develop progressively.

The first element to be restored was the system of fixing work for each group. The usual way of implementing the system was for the basic economic accounting unit — usually the production team, but in some cases the production brigade — to determine the amount of work to be done in a fixed period of time, as well as quality, quantity and the compensation for completing a given task while meeting the required level of quality. Work was fixed for each working group. The production team had the right to determine rewards or penalties for the contractor according to how the work was done. The system of fixing work was restored at a relatively rapid pace prior to 1980. Compared with the system of "working together and receiving equal payments," the job responsibility system was undoubtedly a great improvement and was welcomed by the majority of the peasants. By the end of 1980, some two-fifths of the production teams in the country had implemented the system of fixing work for each group.

The second element to be restored was the system of fixing farm output quotas for each group. The usual way of implementing the system was for the production team to fix certain production tasks for each working group responsible for output (or production value). The distribution of products was carried out by the production team. The working group, having fulfilled the production task, could receive their pay according to the agreement. Reward was offered for the overfulfilment of the task, and penalties were given for reduced output that resulted from poor management. In addition, another measure was to fix the amount purchased by the state and the amount of accumulation funds and public welfare funds which the production team was due to receive, as well as those funds to be delivered to upper-level authorities. The remaining amount was distributed among members in the working group. Products turned out by the working group were not handed over to the production team for unified distribution. Owing to the "Left" influences, even after the Third Plenary Session of the Party Congress, the system of output responsibility was considered to be in conflict with socialism in some places. The system of fixing farm output quotas for each group, once thought to be a heresy, was restored only slowly. But by the summer of 1980, things began to take a turn for the better.

The reinstitution of the job responsibility system in agricultural production during 1980 represented a clear confirmation of measures to fix farm output quotas for each household and for each labour unit — measures which had never been allowed to take root since the transformation of the agricultural cooperative. Furthermore, the method of fixing payments for defined projects and of organizing production according to specialized professions was now widely encouraged.

The similarity between fixing farm output quotas for each household and fixing farm output for each group is as follows: Contractors are responsible for output (or production value). The difference between the two approaches is that the contractor of the former is a household and that of the latter is a working group. The basic characteristics of the household method are:

(1) The main means of production — which include land, irrigation facilities made or bought by the production team, draught animals, farm tools and machines — belong to the production team; while those suitable for decentralized management can be turned over to individual commune members to keep and use.

(2) The production team carries on unified management; and the commune members work with their own families.

(3) The output of products is counted by households. The output fixed for each household is distributed to commune members by the production team and extra output is given as a reward to the contracted commune members or is divided between the production team and the contractor according to a fixed ratio. As the production teams differ from each other, so too does the range of fixing output quotas. Some teams fix only a part of the work for each household.

Another form is to divide up the work and assign a portion of it to each household.[1] The differences between this and fixing farm output quotas for each household are as follows: In the production of products, the production team only sets requirements for that portion which will be purchased by the state; commune members have the right to decide themselves what they will grow and how much they will grow to fill out the remainder of production. In the distribution of products, the commune members are responsible only for fulfilment of the state purchasing quota and for accumulation, public welfare and other funds that are to be handed over to the production team. Extra income belongs to the commune members and is for their use as well.

Fixing output quotas for each labour unit is similar to fixing quotas for each household. The difference is that the contractor of the former is a labour unit and that of the latter is a household.

In 1979, the system of fixing output quotas for each household and for each labour unit had already been carried out in some production teams; it had been carried out even earlier in some communes and production teams. Although the situation then was different from the one during the "cultural revolution" — when this method was criticized for being part of the "capitalist" and "revisionist" road, it was still seen as a means of "going it alone" or "a disguised form of going it alone" or "sliding onto the road of going it alone." In the end, it would lead to extremes and would harm agricultural production. In practice, results proved just the opposite. In places where fixing output quotas for each household and for each labour unit were carried out, the situation in agricultural production was extremely good. In the backward places in particular, production developed even faster, the collective economy stabilized and the lives of commune members were improved greatly. It held out a great appeal to those production teams that had similar productive conditions. In 1980, there was a substantial increase in the number of communes and production teams that carried out the system of fixing output quotas for each household or for each

---

[1] Strictly speaking, the way of dividing up the work and assigning a part to each household is not a form of job responsibility. Yet, it is widely used in some places and is playing an important part in the restoration and development of agriculture. It is introduced here because it has some similarities with the method of fixing output quotas for each household.

labour unit. In the latter half of the year, the Central Committee of the Party issued a document on the further strengthening and improvement of the system of job responsibility for agricultural production. Various job responsibility systems in agricultural production were reaffirmed and emphasis was placed on working in accord with reality and on trying to avoid being limited to only one method. Thus, fixing output quotas for each household or for each unit of labour power had acquired full legitimacy as did the system of assigning the work to each household.

The system of job responsibility in compensating for work and production according to use of specialized professional work is one form in the system of fixing output. It differs from the fixing of multiple production jobs in that the contractor is responsible for only one product. For example, some may make contracts on grain production, some on planting fruit trees, some on raising pigs and cows. Owing to varying conditions, the method of fixing output for each group can be used in some places, while the method of fixing output quotas for each household can be adopted in other places; and the method of fixing output quotas for each labour unit can be adopted in yet other places. Besides the advantages shared by other forms of fixing work, the system of responsibility of payment for fixing output and production according to specialized profession has some other advantages. It not only can be applied to presently backward areas, but can also be used to promote levels of agriculture specialization by raising productivity. In the past, very few communes and production teams adopted this method. It was not until the latter part of 1980 that these measures were encouraged to any large extent.

The restoration and development of various forms of job responsibility in agricultural production has been very important to the development of agriculture in our country. During the past 20 years, socialist superiority in agriculture had not been fully realized. One main reason was that we had for many years failed to adopt an effective method of management and had failed to apply various forms of the job responsibility system with methods that adhered to local conditions. In fact, these forms are consistent with the socialist road and incorporate methods of management that suit the requirements of the peasants. As a result, the enthusiasm of hundreds and millions of peasants has been brought into full play and the development of agricultural production has been promoted.

3. *Encourage and support individual sideline production by commune members.*

Under "Left" influences, the individual sideline production of peasants had not been stressed for over 20 years. During the "cultural revolution," such production was criticized and abolished as the "tail of capitalism." In some places, it was completely banned and the production of some farm products fell sharply. The subsequent great decrease in the variety and quantity of goods had seriously affected the lives of the people both in urban and rural areas and hindered the country's socialist economic construction.

After the "cultural revolution," the party and government began to correct the past mistake of abolishing individual sideline production. It was decided that peasants could retain small private plots and engage in individual sideline production as long as the collective economy was assured to be in absolute predominance. This decision gave a big push to the restoration and development of individual sideline production. A new stipulation was made in the Decision on Several Questions Concerning the Acceleration of Agricultural Development, worked out at the Third Plenary Session of the 11th Party Congress. It provided that individual sideline production of the peasants should be encouraged and supported so long as the strengthening and development of the collective economy was assured. This stipulation, which is in accord with reality in our rural areas has given great impetus to the restoration and development of individual sideline production of the peasants.

In 1980, especially in the second half of the year, restrictions were further relaxed to varying degrees. Many unreasonable restrictions on individual sideline production of the peasants were abolished and the practice was encouraged and supported in the following respects:

A. *To expand private plots and forage plots.* According to old regulations, the acreage of private plots of the peasants was limited to a range of 5–7% of the total farmland of the production team. According to the local conditions in Sichuan Province, 3 million *mu* of farm land was given to commune members by the production teams to expand private plots and forage plots; by this means, the acreage of private plots of the peasants exceeded 10% of the total farmland. In Ningxia, the acreage of private plots was set at a maximum area of 12% of the total farmland. In Shaanxi, about one *mu* of forage plot was allotted in some places to a peasant who raised one draught animal; in addition, part of the collective wasteland could be given to the peasants for planting trees and grass. In southern Xingjiang, forage plots were allotted to peasants who raised cattle. In Guangdong, it was decided that production teams, where possible, could give a certain amount of land to the commune members as forage plots. In Heilongjiang and some other places, similar measures were adopted.

B. *To allot private hillsides to commune members.* In Jiangxi, it was decided to give to commune members a portion of waste hills and waste hillsides which the collective had not sufficient labour to cultivate or was not able to cultivate. Commune members were encouraged to plant trees there. Both the trees and all income from them belonged to those who had planted them. Experiments were made in some places to be systematically introduced on a wider scale. In Shaanxi, similar decisions were made. In Sichuan, it was decided that private hills allotted to commune members in the past would continue to belong to them. In addition, private hills could be allotted, if conditions permitted, by those communes which had never given any to their commune members.

C. *To abolish the unreasonable restrictions on the range of individual sideline production by commune members.*

In the past, it had been decided in some places that private plots must be used mainly for the production of grain and vegetables and for subsistence products, but not for commodity production. There were strict restrictions on the quantity and variety of livestock and poultry. In agricultural regions, sows and draught animals could not be raised, only pigs and sheep. In livestock regions, dairy cows could be raised, but not beef cattle. In some other places, it was even decided that income from individual sideline production of commune members could not exceed 30% of their total income. Before 1980, these restrictions had been abolished in Gansu Province and in a few other provinces. In 1980, new decisions were made in Heilongjiang, Shaanxi, Sichuan, Qinghai, Guangdong and some other provinces, municipalities and autonomous regions. The general idea was that commune members were free to grow, plant and do business in order to provide more products and raise income, so long as they took an active part in collective production and refrained from exploiting others or damaging state-owned resources.

D. *To support individual sideline production of commune members with materials and technology.*

Both the needs of the collective economy and the needs of individual sideline production were given unified consideration when the production team worked out its plans for production. Manure was given to commune members in proportion to these balanced needs. Some communes and production teams even provided commune members with chemical fertilizer, seeds and water for irrigation in order to improve the production conditions of private plots. Aids were given to commune members who raised domestic animals and poultry. The usual measure adopted in Heilongjiang was that young animals were supplied to commune members for raising and production teams helped them with the breeding of cattle and sheep raised by them. Equal epidemic prevention treatment was given to domestic animals and poultry raised by the collective and by commune members themselves. Fairs to propagate domestic animals were held to facilitate the exchange of livestock among commune members who either had spare domestic animals or were short of them. Pasture areas were set aside for commune members to use for grazing; in other cases, a certain amount of fodder grass was allotted to commune members by the production teams. Similar measures were adopted in other regions.

E. *To facilitate the raising of adequate funds by commune members for the management of individual sideline production.*

In Shaanxi, it was decided that the state should give financial support to both the collectives and individuals who had difficulties in raising draught animals, pigs and sheep. In some counties of Jiangxi, interest-free loans were provided for individual planting and stock raising by commune members. In some communes in Heilongjiang, the four restrictions on providing loans (no loans for household sideline production; for raising oxen or donkeys; for raising hens, ducks, geese and rabbits; or for small-scale industry) were abolished. Many counties, communes and production brigades supplied funds for individual sideline production of the commune members.

F. *To readjust the channels of distribution, prices and taxes.*

In order to ensure the sale of individual sideline products of commune members, the departments of commerce, supply and marketing and foreign trade signed contracts for production and marketing with commune members through their communes and production teams. Thus, the sale of all products could be ensured. In some places, it was also stipulated that peasants could sell either locally or at long distance their individual sideline products as allowed by the state once they had fulfilled their task of selling to the state. In some provinces, municipalities and autonomous regions, prices and taxes were readjusted according to local conditions. In Xinjiang, it was decided that commune members could sell, tax-free, those oxen, horses, mules, donkeys, camels, pigs and sheep which were raised by themselves. Neither had they to pay taxes if they slaughtered domestic animals for their own consumption. In Yili district, it was stipulated that the purchasing price of beef cattle raised by individuals could be 50% higher than the normal purchasing price.

4. *Progressively readjust the structure and distribution of agricultural production in a planned way.*

In China's agriculture, a big problem which has existed for many years has been the irrational structure and distribution of agricultural production. It found concentrated expression in the single-product economy which was becoming more and more predominant. In this case, the structure of production went against the principle of overall development. The production of industrial crops, forestry, animal husbandry, fishing and sideline production had been given far less attention than the production of grain had. In the production of grain crops, we grew more rice and corn than other food grains. The distribution of production went against the principle of working out measures suited to local conditions. The key link was grain, whether in forest regions, pastoral regions or fishery regions. In order to grow grain, people in many places blindly destroyed forests and grass lands so as to open up wasted land; and built dykes to reclaim land from lakes. Natural resources were seriously damaged and ecological distribution become unbalanced. The outcome was that conditions for the production of forestry products, animal husbandry, sideline products, fish and industrial crops were worsened; the function of helping each other progress in the various sectors of agriculture was not given full play; and grain production itself was unable to develop very quickly.

After the "cultural revolution," the party and government began to show great concern for the readjustment of the irrational structure and distribution of agricultural production. The recovery and development of agriculture was rated as an important matter. In the Decisions on Some Questions Concerning the Acceleration of Agricultural Development, the Central Committee of the Communist Party of China pointed out: "The present agricultural structure and food composition of the people must be readjusted progressively and in a planned way. The present situation of paying attention only to grain production but not to industrial crops, forestry, animal husbandry, sideline production and fishing must be changed." In 1980, the Central Committee further put forth the strategic policy of giving full play to favourable conditions and fostering strength and circumventing weaknesses. These policies all made clear how we should readjust our country's structure and distribution with regard to agricultural production. The principal tasks of readjustment of the structure and distribution of agricultural production were as follows:

A. *To further carry out the principle of working out measures suited to local conditions and readjust the proportion of the production of grain and industrial crops.*

In 1980, the acreage under grain was 1,747.09 million *mu*, which was 41.85 million *mu*, or 2.4% less than in 1979. The acreage under industrial crops was 238.82 million *mu*, which was 17.31 million *mu* or 7.8% more than in 1979. The distribution of crops was tending towards consolidation. In Hunan, the production task of 300,000 *mu* of cotton fields scattered all over the western and southern parts of the province had been assigned to two other districts — Changde and Yueyang. Some readjustment had been made for cotton growing in other regions, making it possible for cotton-growing regions to expand by about 500,000 *mu*. In Jiangxi Province, more than 50 counties had in the past been requested to grow cotton, but now the task was given to 20 counties for the purpose of consolidation. The three districts in the Hexi corridor of Gansu Province was one of the main sugar-beet growing regions in China. In 1980, the acreage under sugar beets was extended to 70,000 *mu* or 48.9% more than that of the previous year. In 1980, some provinces decided to further readjust planting acreages and distribution. It was decided in Shaanxi to let Dali, Lintong and three other cotton-growing counties (municipalities) take over the production task of 290,000 *mu* of cotton fields in 13 other counties which were not fit for cotton growing and to increase the acreage under cotton in the five counties. The production of rape was concentrated to the counties in Baoji municipality and Hanzhong basin. There had been an increase of 300,000 *mu* of the acreage under rape in these areas.

B. *Resources of production for forestry, animal husbandry, sideline production and fisheries should be protected and rationally utilized.*

Different regions should develop according to local conditions. Those suited to farming should develop agriculture. Those suited to animal husbandry should develop husbandry and those suited to fishing should develop fisheries. The principles of making full use of local advantages and of giving full play to favourable conditions and superiority were accepted by increasing numbers of people. Instances of destroying forests and grasslands so as to open up waste land had been greatly reduced. In places where conditions permitted, land had been returned to forestry and animal husbandry.

For example, in Qinghai Province, 3 million *mu* of cultivated land had been returned to use as grassland. In Hunan Province, 560,000 *mu* of land was returned last spring for the growing of forests. But in quite a few places, the grave situation of destructive felling of forests still existed. To put up dykes to reclaim land from lakes was no longer encouraged in the provinces. Freshwater fish culture improved over the previous year. Over 80 counties in 11 provinces all over the country built 320,000 *mu* of fishing ground as bases suited to fish culture. Protection of resources had been given enough attention in offshore fishing. In the Yellow Sea and Bohai Sea waters, a fishing off-season was strictly implemented. The number of fishing boats was strictly controlled during the autumn shrimps-catching season. In the East China Sea waters, the off-season fishing period was extended from three to four months. The use of drift nets, purse seines, small hooks and other measures were adopted once again.

C. *New centres for agricultural and sideline products should be set up and old ones consolidated and developed.*

The State Council decided that agricultural mechanization should be promoted in the northeast. Centres for the production of marketable grain and beans are to be set up rapidly as one of the important projects of the state plan. This decision was beneficial to the speeding up of the building of centres for producing marketable grain and beans; to an increase in total output and commodity rates of grain and beans; to the support of the regions for industrial crops, tree farms, livestock farms and fishing farms in order to enable them to make full use of their favourable conditions; and to the readjustment of the structure and distribution of agricultural production of the country. The State Council further decided that Hainan Island should develop on a large-scale the production of tropical crops such as rubber, coconuts, coffee, cocoa, pepper, and aromatics, which were of high economic value, as well as commercial forests. An ecologically balanced environment and a new structure of agricultural production suited to Hainan Island would be built up progressively and Hainan Island would become one of China's production centres for tropical industrial crops and valuable tropical forests.

D. *In other regions, centres of various agricultural and sideline products must be set up and strengthened.*

In some regions, there has been a clearer direction in this development. Apart from centres for grain production, the building of centres for industrial crops, forestry, animal husbandry, sideline production and fisheries had been given adequate attention in these regions. For example, 58 centres for industrial crops had been built up in Fujian by 1980. Out these, there were 13 sugarcane centres with a yearly output of over 10,000 tons, 5 tea centres with a yearly output of 2,500 tons, and 8 tea bases with a yearly output of 500 tons. Besides, there were 21 centres for fruit, 3 for jute and bluish dogbane and 2 each for cured tobacco, mulberry-feeding silkworms, rubber, sisal hemp. It was decided that oil-bearing-crop centres should be built up in three counties, such as Changling in the west of Jilin; sugar-beet centres should be established among some communes in 16 counties such as Nongan. It was also decided that centres for sunflower and castor-oil plants should be established in Baiquan and 10 other counties in Heilongjiang. Another 24 counties such as Anda should become sugarbeet centres. Guanzhong Plain in Shanxi should become a cotton growing centre. Most parts of the farmland in Qinghai was grassland. In the past, animal husbandry was not given enough attention because of a blind search for self-sufficiency in grain. It was decided in 1980 that Qinghai should be an animal husbandry base. Shaanxi also decided to transform the northern part of the province into a centre for forestry and animal husbandry. Animal husbandry centres all over the country were also developing. The Ministry of Agriculture had set up marketable beef cattle centres in 200 counties. Progress had been made in the fields of improved breeding, livestock raising and grassland improvement. One hundred and forty of these centres were put into production in 1980. Beef cattle purchased by the state were mainly provided by these centres. There were 157 counties which had centres for raising goats. Those centres had been jointly set up by the departments of supply and marketing, agriculture and foreign trade. Goat skins provided by these centres made up 60% of total purchases by the state. In addition, a great number of other production centres for fruits, dry fruits, edible fungus, *mao* bamboo, raw lacquer, day lily, palm reed and dozens of other native products had been set up.

Grain supply must be guaranteed during the course of the readjustment of structure and distribution. The State Council decided that the central government and Guangdong Province should provide Hainan Island with 500 million *jin* of grain during a period of five years beginning in 1981 in order to reduce the pressure of grain production and to promote the production of tropical industrial crops. The state would provide Shaanxi with 320 *jin* of grain every year from 1980 to 1985 to help cotton production there. The state has provided Fujian with 200 million *jin* of grain every year in recent years to solve the problem of low grain rations for sugarcane growers. In Hunan Province, from 1979 to 1980, out of 800 million *jin* of grain allocated by the provincial government, over 400 million *jin* went to cotton-growing regions, over 200 million *jin* to forestry regions, and over 100 million *jin* to support the production of other industrial crops and animal husbandry. Some regions had adopted the policy of selling industrial crops and animal products instead of selling grain. In some major sugar-beet planting regions in Gansu, Inner Mongolia and Heilongjiang, it was stipulated that sugar beets could be sold to the state in place of the state purchasing quota for grain. In Gansu, one *jin* of grain could be replaced by 10 *jin* of sugar beets. In Inner Mongolia, one *jin* of grain could be replaced by 8 *jin* of sugar beets. As alternatives, the state could sell grain to the communes according to the same exchange rate or the state could reduce or exempt its grain-purchasing requirement. Shanxi Province provided that those communes and production teams burdened with production of forestry products, animal husbandry and oil-bearing products, could sell the products of those activities to the state in place of grain. A measure for exchanging those products and cotton for grain was adopted. Grain could be sold as a bonus to those communes who sold cotton or oil according to the proportion set by the government. In Jilin Province, it was stipulated that the amount of grain purchased by the state from forestry, animal husbandry and industrial-crop centres could be reduced. This regulation was to remain unchanged for a few years. It was stipulated for nearly all provinces that those communes and production teams which grew industrial crops, engaged in forestry or raised animals, should have grain rations not less than those in nearby grain-producing regions. Some regions had also adopted the measure of exchanging products. In Guanghan County, Sichuan Province, one *jin* of rapeseed oil could be exchanged for 7 *jin* of corn from other regions. Huaxian Farm in Guangdong Province exchanged 60,000 *jin* of peanut oil with Zhujian Farm for 700,000 *jin* of cereals. This method not only gave full play to favourable local conditions within regions, but also solved the grain problem.

E. *To provide funds for the readjustment of structure and distribution in agriculture.*

Both central and local governments gave help to many production projects and regions in matters of finance, credit and prices. In Fujian Province, the central and provincial governments invested over 7 million yuan to back the production of industrial crops from 1978 to 1980. In order to give full play to favourable conditions in mountainous regions, the transportation bureau in Anhui Province gave 8.63 million yuan in subsidies for road repairs. Funds were also allocated by the forestry departments of the province, districts and counties for afforestation. Leading bodies in the province decided to increase subsidies for planting trees for use in construction, trees with economic value and trees for afforestation. For instance, subsidies for planting China fir were raised from 6 yuan per *mu* to 10 yuan per *mu*. Banks and credit cooperatives in many places offered loans to help diversify the economy. For example, supply and marketing co-ops in many places set up funds for the development of native products and provided communes with interest-free loans. As of November 1980, such funds had come to 730 million yuan. It was stipulated in some provinces that local governments should offer a certain amount of subsidies towards the purchase of certain products in addition to the increased purchasing price set by the state. Inner Mongolia's purchasing price for sugar beets was set at 75 yuan per ton as stipulated by the state, in addition to a subsidy of 15 yuan by the government of the autonomous region. In Heilongjiang, the subsidy was an additional 10 yuan. It was provided in the Shantou region of Guangdong Province that in addition to the purchasing prices per ton of sugar cane and jute as fixed by the state, a further allocation of funds in the form of subsidies was made out of local revenue and from the profits of rural processing factories and from supply and marketing and commercial departments. It was stipulated in Guangdong Province that beginning from the new sugar-cane pressing season in 1980, a part of the profits of the sugar factories would be given to sugar-cane planting communes. Similar decisions were made in Jilin Province in the form of sugar beets delivered to sugar refineries for processing by the communes. In Zhejiang Province, it was stipulated that the amount of tea purchased by the state in 1978 was to be taken as the base amount; and if more was delivered by the communes to the state-owned tea factories for pressing, 70% of the profits obtained were to be given back to the communes.

In addition, much work had been done in the supply of materials, technical guidance, cooperation between producing and marketing, communications, storing, processing and selling. This gave impetus to the production of industrial crops, forestry products, animal husbandry, sideline occupations and fishing.

5. *Actively try out the policy of economic integration with the participation of the rural communes.*

The collective economy of the rural people's communes in our country was organized according to administrative divisions and different administrative levels. Economic cooperation beyond this limitation was not allowed. Plans for future development were to extend step by step, according to administrative divisions and levels. In other words, the basic accounting unit on the level of the production team could pass on to the level of the production brigade through integration. Then these brigades could undergo further transition to those basic accounting units on the level of the commune through further integration. In these two years, especially since 1980, the old method of transition through combination of levels one at a time has begun to be broken through. Cooperation among various levels of the economy has been under experiment. The main forms are:

A. *Economic cooperation among the production teams within the same communes.*

In September 1979, Xiangyang Commune in Guanghan County of Sichuan Province tried to launch joint enterprises using the investment of production teams and achieved remarkable results. These experiments were widely popularized throughout Guanghan County in 1980. The principle was that the teams participating in these joint enterprises were free to join or to withdraw. The management committee of the enterprises was set up by means of elections at a congress of the share-holders. The congress of share-holders or the management committee made decisions on the direction of operations, plans for production, financial expenditures, personnel arrangements and penalty and reward measures. The profits of the enterprise were divided according to the shares after deducting a portion for the expansion of production. Thus, the past system of commune-run enterprises set up with labour power and funds from the production teams was changed into one of joint enterprises run by share-holding production teams.

B. *The integration of communes and production teams in different communes and regions.*

Lili Commune in Wujian County of Jiangsu Province and Linghu Commune, known as "native place of water chestnuts," in Wuxing County, Zhejiang Province jointly managed the production of freshwater chestnuts. Lili Commune provided 20,000 *mu* of paddy fields and was responsible for management; Lingju Commune provided water chestnut seeds and was responsible for planting. Some communes and production teams in Wujian County and Huxing Commune in Jiading County, Shanghai worked together in the production of yellow grass (a kind of grass used by craftsmen) Shanghai provided seeds and manure and sent technicians to give instructions on planting; Wujian County provided land and labour power. Some production teams in Jiading County provided ponds and worked together to cultivate pearls with the Yingbing Production Brigade, well-known for its pearl-cultivation, in Huangdi commune of Wuxian County, Jiangsu Province. The income gained by these joint enterprises was divided according to the shares. Contracts had been signed among the communes and production teams in Peng Xian County of Sichuan Province to provide each other with products and to create conditions for production. The communes and production teams in mountainous regions provided communes and production teams on flat lands with the seeds of potatoes, the rhizomes of *chuanxiong* and other crops. In return, the communes and production teams on flat lands provided rice seedlings and sweet-potato seedlings to the mountainous communes and brigades. Farm cattle and labour power were shared among them. In addition, they jointly opened up mines of asbestos and coal in mountainous regions and divided income according to their shares.

C. *Rural communes undertook economic cooperation with state farms or more often with joint enterprises in agriculture, industry and commerce under the system of the state farms.*

Cooperation between suburban communes in Chongqing, Sichuan Province and joint enterprises in agriculture, industry and commerce in the city of Changjiang was made up of 26 state farms, livestock farms and fish farms and had a representative character. In 1979, 50 production teams joined the cooperative venture and, in 1980, there were over 800 production teams involved in this cooperative effort. The main forms of joint enterprises were:

1. *The joint enterprises processed and sold products on behalf of the production teams.* Having fulfilled the task of selling products to the state, production teams sent their extra tea and oranges to the joint enterprises for processing and sales. A part of the profits were returned to the production teams.

2. *Production teams provided services or processed products to the joint enterprises which paid a certain amount of the expenses and offered some elements of support for production.* For example, the Changshou Lake fish farm, in a joint enterprise, left its weanling milk cows to the care of nearby production teams; the teams would take care of them for one year and earn 200 yuan per head. Condensed fodder and medical expenses for the young milk cows were provided by the enterprises.

3. *Both the joint enterprises and the production teams provided the conditions needed for production and ran the business together.* For example, the Changshou Lake fish farm provided ponds, fish fry and fish nets and sent technicians; while five nearby production teams provided labour power and bait. All participants jointly ran the business. Thirty percent of production went to the production teams, with 70% to be sold by the fish farm. Eighty percent of the profits in the business went to the production teams, while 20% went to the fish farm.

4. *Funds were collected and counted as shares, with the business run jointly.* For instance, in the orange management department, with the Baxian branch of the joint enterprise as the core, production, processing and sales of oranges were made into a coordinated process. Any production team with a yearly output of over 10,000 *jin* of oranges could apply for membership in the management department. Each share was valued at 200 yuan and the amount of shares was not limited. One portion of the profits of the department went to expansion, with the remainder divided among the production teams according to the amount and the quality of oranges each production team had provided. Even those teams with no shares could take part in the profits if they sold oranges to the department. Another portion of profits was divided according to the number of shares held. In addition, commercial departments and service centres maintained joint funds. This form of joint enterprise was also tried out in full or in part in Zhejiang, Hubei, Shenshi, Jilin and other provinces, municipalities and autonomous regions. Some other forms had come into being as well.

D. *The economic union between production teams and state-owned industry.*

For example, after fulfilling the task of selling to the state, those production teams could send their surplus rural products to the state-owned factories for processing. In 1980, over 1,000 production teams in Yushu County, Jilin Province, sold surplus grain to the state-owned brewery. Profits were divided according to the shares held. The same method was adopted between tea-growing communes and state-owned tea factories in Zhejiang, and between sugarcane-planting communes and state-owned sugar refineries in Guangdong Province. Moreover, some production teams undertook processing for state-owned industries. Factories were jointly run and profits were divided according to the shares.

E *Economic union between rural communes and commercial departments.*

In 1980, there were about 700 such joint enterprises, including joint enterprises for production, processing and marketing in Foshan area, Guangdong Province. In Kaiping County of Foshan district, 1,600 commodity bases for oranges and tangerines, cows, sheep and rabbits were set up one after another through the use of joint enterprises. Because of the situation in the market, supply and marketing co-ops in Zhongshan County played an important role in helping the communes market some of their products. Profits of the joint enterprises were divided according to the proportion of the investment and products were divided according to a percentage agreed upon by all.

Rural communes now take part in various forms of economic cooperation, thus promoting the development of the national economy. They have activated the rural economy and have helped to increase the income of communes and production teams. They are beneficial to the state, to the collective and to commune members. This is a good way to develop the rural economy.

Some Existing Problems and Trends for Future Development

In 1980, there was great development in our country's agriculture. But backwardness left over by the old society had not been completely transformed and there were still many difficulties and problems in agriculture. The main problems were:

1. *The "Left" ideological influence which had been shaped over a long period was far from being eliminated.* In the leading administrative organs and rural communes and production teams, there was great unevenness in carrying out the lines, principles and policies worked out at the Third Plenary Session of the 11th Party Congress and afterwards. The peasants' enthusiasm in some parts of the regions, communes and production teams had not been fully aroused.

2. *The material and technical conditions for agricultural production were still relatively backwards.* In all of China, there was only an area of 340 million *mu* of land which gave stable, high yields irrespective of drought or water-logging. One-third of the cultivated land still consisted of unimproved saline-alkaline land, water-logged low-lying land, acid soil, cold water paddy fields (in mountainous regions, paddy fields are irrigated with mountain springs), poorly drained paddy fields, farmland on slopes which suffered serious water loss and soil erosion. There were not enough farm machines, their quality was not up to stan-

dard or they did not exist in complete sets. In some places, even the need for draught animals, animal-drawn farm implements and manually operated farm implements could not be fully met.

3. *Low public accumulation and shortages of production funds in communes and production teams.* The fixed assets of production teams throughout the country were on the average only somewhat over 100 yuan per capita in the rural areas. Many production teams found it difficult to ensure both an increase in fixed assets as well as the need for circulating funds. According to statistics from 3,602,000 production teams in 26 provinces, municipalities and autonomous regions, average circulating funds owned by the production teams themselves only covered about 15% of their actual needs.

4. *Levels of culture, technology and management in the field of agriculture were all very low.* Only 30% of all youngsters and middle-aged people in rural areas had an educational level above junior middle school; 40% of them had a primary-school level of education. In fact, there were only 250,000 people who were engaged in the work of science, technology and education in the field of agriculture. On the average, there was only one agro-technician for every six thousand *mu* of cultivated land (with a rural population of 3,200 people). According to investigations in some places, only one-third of cadres in rural area had some knowledge of management and administration; another one-third had little knowledge; the other one-third had no working experience in rural areas nor any knowledge of agricultural management.

5. *The proportional dislocation of the national economy had caused difficulties in the development of agriculture.* The supply of agricultural means of production was inadequate to meet the needs. Equipment for transportation, processing and storing of agricultural products was insufficient. Distribution channels were sometimes blocked.

Under such conditions, the level of agricultural production was low and unstable. As compared with some of the developed countries, there were large gaps in per-unit-area yield of agricultural crops, in the ratio of livestock for selling and slaughtering and in rural labour productivity. The average output of agricultural products per capita was even lower because of the rapid growth in population. In some areas, average per capita output was even lower than in 1957. The peasants' life in some regions was still relatively difficult. Persistant, hard efforts had to be made to completely put an end to the backwardness of agriculture in China. But since the economy in our country had always been somewhat backward and because our state finances at present are undergoing substantial difficulties, the economic power of rural communes and production teams remains quite weak. Therefore, for a period of time to come, a large increase in investments cannot be looked to as a means of changing the condition of agricultural production. In order to achieve rapid development in agriculture and good results, the following principal measures should be adopted in order to make the best of the potential:

1. *To persistently carry out the spirit of the Third Plenary Session of the 11th Party Congress; to go on eliminating "Left" ideological influences; to ensure the implementation of a series of principles and policies worked out by the party and government; in particular, to work out measures suited to local conditions for carrying out various forms of the system of job responsibility for agricultural production; to further bring the enthusiasm of 800 million peasants into full play.*

These are the fundamental principles and preconditions for putting other measures into effect. Judged by the situation in 1980, development in this field in various parts of the country was quite uneven. A quick change of this situation will give great impetus to agricultural production.

2. *To proceed from the real situation in our rural areas, an economic structure with socialist collective ownership as the mainstay, with simultaneous existence of various sorts of economic components and with multiple levels of administration must be established after further readjustment and restructuring.*

The system of integrating government administraion with commune management in the rural people's communes must be actively and stabily reformed. Different forms of economic cooperation must be consolidated and developed. It goes without saying that the above-mentioned reforms will play an important part in promoting the development of the rural economy.

3. *To make full use of labour and natural resources in rural areas and to continue the readjustment of the rural production structure in order to make possible the large-scale development of a diversified economy in agriculture, together with good control of grain production.*

This will be beneficial to the full development of the functions of mutual reliance and mutual promotion among all rural departments, to increasing public accumulations of the communes and production teams and peasants' income and to improving conditions for expanding agricultural production.

4. *To popularize in a significant way scientific and technical measures suited to the situation in our country and to combine traditional methods which are still effective with modern science and technology.* For example, improved seeds must be cultivated and popularized and manuring, irrigation, cultivating methods, etc. must be improved. These measures will achieve good results with less investment and have bright prospects. To further implement a series of principles and policies of the party and government will greatly inspire the initiative of millions of peasants to study and make use of science. The important role these measures will play in the development of agriculture should not be underestimated.

5. *To achieve better economic results from agricultural investment.* Although the state will not be able to make large increases in the amount of agricultural investments in the near future, good results can be achieved by making rational use of the investments that are available. Terrible waste in the use of agricultural investments in the past was a big problem. In water conservancy construction, for example, there were severe losses and a great deal of abandoned projects and equipment. This was very often due to the fact that production installations and technical devices supplied were incomplete, or that the principal components of the projects and field drainage and irrigation systems were also incomplete so that those elements that had been put into operation lost much of their effect. In the field of agricultural mechanization, agricultural machines were of poor quality, were high in price and were also supplied in incomplete form. At the same time, they were not kept in good condition and their utilization ratio was quite low. Mechanized equipment was scattered extensively, which also reduced the effect of the investment. A better solution to existing problems and an increase in the economic results of investment will have the effect of an increase in investment.

3. CHINA'S STATE FARM AND LAND RECLAMATION SECTOR

By Guo Chunhua
National Institute of Agricultural Economy

I. Historical Department of the State Farm and Land Reclamation Sector

China's state farm and land reclamation programmes have had a history of more than 30 years since their establishment. As early as 1947, base areas in the Northeast and some inside Shanhaiguan (a pass of the Great Wall at its easternmost starting point) experimented with a system of local state farms whose main task then was to mass-produce and disseminate fine crop strains, to popularize advanced farming techniques, in the prevention and elimination of diseases and pests, in the collection and application of manure and in guidance of the peasants in improving farming techniques. The founding of the People's Republic of China prompted an acceleration in the development of state farms.

In December 1949, Comrade Mao Zedong approved for issuance the 1950 Directive on the Army's Participation in Production and Construction.

At the National Work Conference on Agriculture held by the Ministry of Agriculture in that year, it was pointed out: "We must take the People's Liberation Army as a great force in the country's production and construction, and enthusiastically help them to go in for production." A proposal for "experimental state farms and the cultivation of 3 million *mu* of land in 1950" was advanced.

A large number of PLA officers and soldiers were transferred to take part in agricultural production. A group of state farms was set up in Heilongjiang, Xinjiang, Jiangsu, Ninxia and Shandong provinces and autonomous regions. In 1952, rubber plantations were set up in Guangdong, Guangxi, Yunnan and Fujian. A host of local state-owned agricultural and pastoral farms or farms of indigenous products were established in succession on lakesides, hillsides and coastal areas in other provinces and autonomous regions and on the outskirts of municipalities.

The main task of the state farms as laid down by the state were: first, to produce large quantities of marketable grain, raw materials for industry and animal products for the state; second, to set an example for peasants with profitable economic results of high-yield and low-cost; third, to promote agricultural production by aiding peasants with fine strains, breeding stock, farm machinery and advanced agricultural expertise; fourth, to demonstrate the superiority of mass collective production so that peasants would be prompted to become organized and take the road of collectivization. The state farms, at that time, did not only have the economic task of increasing production but also an important political mission in promoting agricultural collectivization.

The Production and Construction Corps of the Xinjiang Military Command was founded in July 1954. In August, the first group of officers and men of the railway corps went to Hulin Prefecture, Heilongjiang Province to reclaim land for the establishment of state farms. In June 1956, the Land Reclamation Administration of the Mishan Railway Corps was set up and at the end of the year, 10,000 demobilized officers and men of the railway corps marched into the Great Northern Wilderness. With these troops stationed to garrison the frontier and to open up wasteland, the state farms could shoulder the major military and political tasks of exploiting, constructing and safeguarding the border areas and of helping fraternal nationalities in their socialist construction.

Establishment of a Ministry. To meet the needs of the development of the state farms, the central authorities decided in 1956 to set up a Ministry of State Farms and Land Reclamation. Provinces, municipalities and autonomous regions correspondingly established managerial organizations for the state farms to strengthen their leadership in land cultivation.

A large number of former military men trooped into the Great Northern Wildness in March 1958, and the large-scale reclamation of the Sanjiang Plain was underway. At the same time, a high tide of "going up mountains and going down to the countryside to open up waste-land" emerged in various places throughout the country. Fifty thousand cadres in Jiangxi set up some 80 state-owned agricultural and forestry farms in mountainous areas. One hundred thousand people in Hunan went out to develop mountainous areas. An upsurge of vigorous reclamation of wasteland was brought about in Hubei and Gansu. State farms throughout the country witnessed great development under this situation. A total of 10,450,000 *mu* of wasteland was cultivated in 1958, approximately equal to the total of the previous eight years since the founding of the PRC.

Development of Rubber. China's natural rubber also continued to develop during that period. In 1955, China's second natural rubber plantation centre was set up in Xishuanbanna and other places in Yunnan. After 1958, natural rubber centres based in Guangdong increased their cultivated land for rubber plantations. They summed up their relatively positive experiences as "taking hills and forests as the base" and "tree networks, terraced fields, fine strains and plant cover." These efforts made China the only country at that time to succeed in planting rubber trees on a large acreage north of 17°N.

Start farms took on a steady development after the implementation of the 1962 policy of "readjustment, consolidation, filling out and raising standards" for the national economy. By 1966, there were 1,940 state farms with an output of 8,090 million *jin* of grain (including soya beans) from a cultivated area of 47.84 million *mu*. They handed in to the state 2,820 million *jin* of grain and 775,000 tons of cotton. In 1966, they realized profits of 165 million yuan from an accumulated total of 2.5 million *mu* of rubber trees.

During the time of the "cultural revolution," state farms and land reclamation were seriously undermined by Lin Biao and the Gang of Four. In 1969, the Ministry of State Farms and Land Reclamation was abolished and most of its administrative units in various provinces, municipalities and autonomous regions were shut down. Some state farms were turned into people's communes. They suffered losses for years on end because the managerial system was turned upside down. No one was in charge of production and economic results were neglected.

Post-1977 Changes. After the smashing of the Gang of Four, the confusion was put right and the pernicious influence of Lin Biao and the Gang of Four was gradually wiped out. From late 1977 to early 1978, the State Council held a national state farms working conference. The conference recommended the consolidation of state farms and demanded that state farms be built into bases for marketable grain and industrial raw materials; that they became groceries for urban consumption and exportation; and that they play an exemplary leading role in agricultural modernization. In February 1978, the State Council approved the Minutes of the National Working Conference on State Farms, and decided to establish the General Bureau for Land Reclamation so as to strengthen the leadership and management of state farms throughout the country. It also decided that four reclamation areas in Heilongjiang, Xinjiang, Guangdong and Yunan be placed under the dual leadership of central and local authorities, with the provinces and autonomous regions as the mainstay. It demanded that authoritative and powerful administrative organizations be established in other provinces, municipalities and autonomous regions. The conference was followed by a readjustment of leading bodies, working forces, and management and by the restoration of necessary rules and regulations. These steps progressively restored production, improved management and cut down losses.

To further strengthen the leadership over state farms, the Central Committee decided, in 1979, to re-establish the Ministry of State Farms and Land Reclamation. State farms witnessed relatively good harvests in agricultural and pastoral production that year and changed the pattern of long-time losses.

1980 Statistical Summary. China's state farms and land reclamation have been developed and constructed over a wide scope during the past 30-odd years. By the end of 1980, there were a total of 2,093 state farms and 6,072 industrial enterprises (including farm-run workshops), with a population of 11,360,000 people and 4,920,000 workers. The farms held 66,820,000 *mu* of land under cultivation; 4,830,000 *mu* in rubber plantations; more than 1,600,000 *mu* in orchards, mulberry fields and tea plantations; 90 million *mu* in usable pastures and a population of 13 million domestic animals. The total horsepower of agricultural machinery was 8,790,000, with 54,600 large and medium-sized tractors, 16,200 combines, 21,600 trucks and 31,000 machines for irrigation and drainage.

For the past three decades, the state farms have initially established a network of centres for marketable grain, industrial crops, urban-oriented foodstuffs and commodities for export. These centres have supplied to the state large quantities of grain, soya-beans, cotton, rubber, oilseeds, sugar, meat, fur, tea, fruit, milk, and ginseng and antler, as well as small quantities of tropical cash crops such as sisal hemp, oil palm, coffee beans, spices, pepper, etc.

The development of the state farms and land reclamation has made an important contribution to the exploitation, construction and defence of the frontier, to the thriving of economy and culture in the border areas and to the enhancement of national unity. It has been an example for collective agriculture and has given it due support in areas of farming techniques, production, popularization of fine breeds and farm machinery. It has helped solve employment problems for demobilized officers and men, cadres going to the countryside for manual labour, educated youths and migrants. A vast number of cadres and workers have acquired, through long practice, experience in managing and running agricultural enterprises and production, and have thus formed a mighty fighting force in developing the range and quality of production.

II. Development of State Farms in 1980

In 1980, state farms throughout the country conscientiously implemented the two documents concerning agricultural development issued by the Party Central Committee after its Third Plenum and carried out a series of policies, such as readjustment of the economy and enterprises, the practice of allotting financial responsibility, expansion of enterprises' decision-making power, the practice of personal responsibility for production, the upgrading and increase of wages and the increase of workers' income. Good results were achieved in production, construction, management and administration. This was due to the fact that the enthusiasm of workers and technicians was brought into play in popularizing advanced experiences and scientific research and through the application of science and technology to forestry, agricultural and pastoral production, and through the state farms' experiments with agricultural-industrial-commercial integrated enterprises and other forms of economic integration.

1. *Agricultural Production.* Although China's grain output decreased in 1980 because of serious natural disasters, the state farms in that year set records in fulfilling quotas. Thanks to arduous efforts on the part of the vast number of workers, the state farms — particularly those in Heilongjiang and Xinjiang which had increased production by large margins — surpassed the highest previous records for the five main categories of general-output quotas: per-*mu* yield, marketable grain sold to the state, value of industrial and agricultural output and profits. The state farms reaped an all-around increase in the production of grain, cotton, edible oils, sugar, tea, rubber, etc.

The total output of grain was 75,330 million *jin*, the highest level record in history and a 4.7% increase over that of 1979. A total of 6,100 million *jin* of grain was sold the state, 21.8% more than in 1979. The total output of cotton was 93,000 tons, an increase of 11.2% over 1979. The total output of oilseeds was 115,500 tons, 4.1% more than that in 1979.

The total output of sugarcane and sugar beets was 1,460,750 tons, a 28.7% increase over 1979.

As for animal husbandry, there were 200,000 head of cattle on state farms by the end of the year and the year's total output of milk was 650 million *jin*, an increase of 8.7% over 1979. There were 6,995,000 sheep in the pens, an increase of 0.03% over 1979; 3,987,000 pigs in the pigsties, 18.4% less than that of 1979. Meat sold to the state totaled 274 million *jin*, or 21.8% more than that sold in 1979.

In the past few years, farms in various places gave stress to afforestation by increasing investments in forestry, organizing professional forestry units, systematically developing nurseries and implementing policies on afforestation. All state farms planted trees on a total of 890,000 *mu* of land, 300,000 *mu* more than in 1979.

The output of rubber was 103,000 tons, 3.6% more than in 1979. Guangdong's rubber plantations overfulfilled the plan even though two typhoons broke off or uprooted 9.6% of their tapped trees.

The main reasons for the rapid development of agriculture, forestry and animal husbandry in the past three years are as follows:

1. *Comparatively good economic results were achieved through the implementation of the readjustment policy and good overall arrangements to bring into play natural and economic advantages.* In Xinjiang, under the prerequisite of continuing increases in total grain output and fulfillment of the sale of marketable grain to the state, state farms managed their crops in a planned way by properly enlarging areas sown to cash crops such as cotton, oilseeds, sugar beets and hops. Some farms in northwest and north China planted sunflowers, rape and flax on arid and alkaline land not suited to grain. Some farms in the south planted tea and tangerines on hilly land. When typhoons and cold waves struck rubber plantations in Guangdong and Guangxi, many planted tea, sisal hemp and tropical cash crops. After the readjustment, the approach to production tended to be more rational and realized quite favourable economic results.

2. *The popularization of advanced technology helped to raise levels in scientific farming, animal husbandry and rubber-tree cultivation.* With regard to scientific farming, work has been carried out mainly in the following areas:

A. Great efforts have been made to stress production of specialized strains, mechanization in processing, standardization of quality and distribution of crops according to regional conditions. The establishment of regional centres focusing on specialized strains and the application of more than 1,000 seed selectors have generally improved the quality of plant varieties used in production.

Many regions have made use of general surveys and appraisals of seed varieties to resolve problems of multiple, confused or mixed varieties of seeds. This has created conditions for a more appropriate distribution of crop varieties in agricultural areas. As to the utilization of superior hybrids, in addition to the fact that crossbred maize and kaoling are commonly used in state farms, the use of hybrid rice has ranged from the south's indica rice to the north's japonica rice.

B. The application of fertilizer has been increased and techniques improved. The quantity of chemical fertilizer applied in the field jumped from 24 *jin* per *mu* in 1977 to 38 *jin* per *mu* in 1980. The technique of deep-spreading and side-spreading chemical fertilizer was widely adopted; moreover, the use of fertilizers was increasingly based on soil surveys, with importance attached to coordination of the three essential elements of fertilizers and to the rate of their utilization.

C. The adoption of chemical herbicides in combination with machine weeding has effectively prevented weeds from over-growing crops and has raised the level of field management. In 1980, China's state farms used herbicides on a combined area of more than 19,650,000 million *mu*, or about one-third of the total area under their cultivation.

D. The quality of machine operation has been improved to meet agricultural demands.

E. Advanced science and technology has been adopted, such as the development of sprinkling, aircraft operation, popularization of biological prevention and elimination of pests, the application of cycocel, the application of calcium chloride in seed-dressing, the spraying of ethylene in cotton fields for early ripening, etc. These techniques have produced notable results in increasing production in cases where proper measures were taken.

With regard to scientific animal husbandry, work has been carried out mainly in the following areas:

A. In order to upgrade the raising of cattle, endeavours were made to improve the breeding of dairy cows and cattle. These efforts met with impressive results.

B. The technique of using frozen semen for artificial insemination was stressed. As a result, the utilizaton of frozen semen accounted for over 95% of breeding activities in suburban dairy farms and for more than 30% among cattle-breeding stations.

C. Pastural areas placed emphasis on the production and preservation of fodder while state farms in suburbs stressed the expansion of cultivated land for producing cattle fodder.

D. Some pastural farms in Inner Mongolia, Xinjiang and Heilongjiang popularized the technique of fattening lambs to reduce the death rate and to raise the production rate for mutton; their more frugal use of fodder brought improved results.

With regard to scientific rubber plantations, the stress was placed mainly on rubber plantation management techniques such as using grass coverings along forest belts, green dressing and fertilizer spreading. Some farms pruned saplings and undertook transplanting and bud-grafting on a large scale in order to transform underdeveloped forests. They took conscientious action to coordinate management, planting and tapping so as to achieve the dual function of increasing both production and tree planting.

3. *Construction of water conservancy projects for farmlands was intensified, and efforts were made to acquire complete complements of agricultural machinery so as to improve conditions for production.*

Many water conservancy projects on state farms in Xinjiang which had not been maintained for years and whose irrigation networks had not been completed did not have an adequate soil-water balance. This condition affected the development of agricultural production. The goal of constructing water conservancy projects for farmland was firmly undertaken between 1978 and 1980. The reinforcement and maintenance of reservoirs, the prevention of seepage in canals, the completion of wells, the transformation of diversion works and the levelling of land — all of these measures created favourable conditions for the resumption and development of production.

Farms in Jiangsu have taken highly effective measures in pursuing water conservancy during the past few years. Some of the disaster-struck farms with low yields in northern Jiangsu realized great improvements in production. The Panjin farms in Liaoning and the coastal farms in Hebei all undertook water conservancy projects so as to ensure stable and high yields even in circumstances of drought or excessive rainfall.

The supply of a more complete range of farm machinery also helped to improve production conditions. The supply of urgently-needed combines, large-scale sprayers, seed selectors and transport vehicles played a dramatic role in guaranteeing timely fulfilment of tasks while maintaining high quality, increasing output and reducing loss and waste.

2. Industrial Production. Industrial activity on state farms was first set up in border areas to meet needs for agricultural machinery repairs and maintenance and for the processing of farm produce. Along with the development of the farms and their production, industry that had the aim of serving agriculture and workers' daily life has been developed gradually. Suburban and inland farms have also developed industries that serve larger industry, supply cities and increase exports. Industries on state farms have developed through the year a certain foundation and scale. Up to 1980, the state farms had 6,072 factories with a total output value of 3,820 million yuan. Industrial activity was distributed as follows (in terms of output value for some main industries): food processing accounted for 30.2% of the total; textile industries, 13.1%; chemical industries, 8.2%; machinery industries, 17.5%; construction materials, 7%; petrochemicals and petroleum, 5.8%; paper-making, 2.9%; and coal, 2.1%. Industries on state farms produced over 1,000 categories of products.

Those state farm industries that were guided by the state plan and adjusted by the market made great headway in 1980. The value of industrial products in that year was 3,820 million yuan, comprising 44.4% of total industrial and agricultural output. This was an increase of 8.3% over 1979 (calculated at constant prices). A total of 98 major products were supplied to the state in 1980. These included coal, 4.14 million tons; generated energy, 498 million kwh; cotton cloth, 116 million metres; chemical fertilizers, 98,000 tons; farm chemicals, 900 tons; cement, 490,000 tons; bricks and tiles, 4,350 million units; paper, 77,000 tons; sugar, 153,000 tons; spirits, 54,000 tons; vegetable cooking oils, 43,600 tons; dairy products, 21,000 tons; tea, 14,300 tons; and farm tools and machinery, 5.3 million units. Quality was improved and varieties increased. A number of products were selected for their particularly fine quality. In 1980, departments at various levels took hold of the following principles for industry:

1. Readjustment in Industry:

A. *They placed emphasis in industrial development on processing and on those light and textile industries whose raw materials came from cultivation.* The proportional size of light and textile industries within total state farm industry increased overall. Take Shanhai and Xinjiang for example: Shanghai's light industry made up 64.7% of the total, while Xinjiang's made up 70.4%.

B. *Factories which turned out low-quality products at high cost and with poor sales results, or which were without sources of raw materials or which had suffered losses over a long period of time were closed down, suspended, integrated or shifted over to the production of other products.* According to statistics of Heilongjiang, Xinjiang, Hebei, Shaanxi, Liaoning, Jilin, Hubei and Jiangsu provinces and autonomous regions, a total of 120 enterprises were either closed down, suspended, integrated or transformed; in Heilongjiang, 13 were closed down or suspended, thus saving losses of more than 3 million yuan.

C. *The relationships between industry and agriculture in the distribution of profits were adjusted.* Quite a few factories returned part of their profits to the production units that supplied them with raw materials. This ensured an adequate supply of needed raw materials and gave impetus to the suppliers. Second, the "Report on the Intensification of the Management of Industrial Planning in State Farms," as endorsed by the State Planning Commission, State Economic Commission and State Agricultural Commission, was implemented. Concerned departments in many provinces, municipalities and autonomous regions opened accounts for industries in state farms and gave support and assistance to their plans, provided material supplies and offered business guidance. Third, administrative departments of state farms at various levels and of industrial enterprises themselves took on the following work to enliven industrial production:

Breaking paths for the sales of their products through agricultural-industrial-commercial integrated enterprises, through contract negotiations or by means of exhibitions, etc.

Adopted the practice of assumption of responsibility for production by means of "stipulations, contracts and bonuses" in industrial enterprises.

Encouraged enterprises to pursue many kinds of integration so as to use each unit's special advantages in overcoming difficulties in technology, funding and equipment. Fourth, industrial enterprises took hold of the concepts of innovation, reform and tapping potential. For example, the reform of eight small sugar mills in Hunan boosted their combined processing capacity of 2,200 tons of sugarcane per day to 4,300 tons daily, thus saving 60% of their funds for the establishment of a new plant. The chemical fertilizer plant of Baigezhuang Farm in Hebei Province lowered its per-ton consumption of coal and costs of ammonium by a large margin through reform, innovation and tapping potential. It earned profits of more than 600,000 yuan, and changed a pattern of 12 years of losses.

2. Diversified Economy. *"Taking one item of cultivation as the main thing while engaging in a diversified economy" is the central policy of business activity for state farms.*

At the initial stage, state farms engaged only in monoculture, or agriculture; this policy led to low yields, high costs and big losses. Afterwards, historical experiences were summed up, leading to the discovery of the importance of a diversified economy. the past 30 years witnessed to a certain degree the development of a diversified economy in the state farms'. This was mainly manifested in the following respects:

A. *Different kinds of farms were set up according to different business principles.*

In 1980 there were 2,093 state farms, of which 48% were mainly engaged in grain and cash-crop production; 21% in animal husbandry; 8% in rubber and tropical crops; and 14% in fruit and tea production. Ginseng and antler farms comprised 4% of the total, while 5% were engaged in other activities.

B. *These different farms developed agriculture, forestry, animal husbandry, industry, sideline occupations and fisheries according to their own characteristics.*

The total value of agricultural and industrial output for 1980 was 8,600 million yuan — 55.6% from agriculture and 44.4% from industry. Of the total value of agricultural production, crops accounted for 59%; animal husbandry, 12.6%; fisheries, 0.4%; rubber, 13.8%; forestry, 2.6%; and sideline occupations, 11%.

C. *Grain was taken as the main crop and cash crops were grown secondarily according to local conditions.*

In 1980, grain (including soyabeans) took up 76.4% of the total sown area, with soyabeans taking up 14.9%. Of the total sown area of main cash crops, 4.7% went to oil-bearing crops (including peanuts, rapeseeds and sesame); 3.6% went to cotton and jute; 1.4% to sugarcane and sugar beets; and 2.6% to vegetables.

D. *In animal husbandry and poultry, the rearing of meat-producing animals was taken as the main activity followed by animal-raising for milk, eggs and fur; and by raising as draught animals, and for special purposes and aquatic production.*

Pigs were made predominant in the raising of animals for meat followed by the raising of cattle and sheep; milk cows were stressed as the main source for milk followed by milk goats; sheep were the main fur animals followed by hares, martens and muskrats; chickens were the main egg producers followed by ducks, geese and quail; oxen, horses, donkeys and mules were the main draught animals along with a small number of camels; deer were the main animals for special purposes; fish was taken as the main aquatic product followed by prawns, crabs, tortoises and turtles, while bees were taken as the focus of major activity among other animals.

E. *In forestry, natural jungles and man-made forests were given the major stress, with orchards, mulberry and tea plantations given the minor part.*

F. *In rubber and tropical crops, rubber was taken as the major plant, followed by tropical and subropical crops such as sisal hemp, oil palm, spices, coffee, pepper and coconut trees.*

G. *In industry, 98 products were stressed, including iron, steel, coal, electricity, gasoline, diesel fuel, chemical fertilizers, farm chemicals, motor vehicles, hand tractors, combines, farm tools, cement, bricks, cotton cloth, knitting wool, paper, sugar and edible oil.*

H. *With respect to communications and transportation, most state farms are situated in border areas where conditions for communications are far from ideal. In the early years, many farms relied on themselves for building roads and bridges for transportation.* Farms on rivers and lake shores or in coastal areas purchased boats or ships. Therefore, state farms have come to possess a considerable quantity of motor vehicles, trailers, motorized junks, horse carts, wheel-barrows and other means of transportation.

I. *In construction, all but a few state farms have their own construction teams that take up construction by themselves.* After the experiment in agricultural-commercial-industrial enterprises, some units established construction companies.

J. *In trades and services, many stage farms maintained commercial networks to provide services for the daily life of their workers.* After the establishment of agricultural-industrial-commercial enterprises on a trial basis, these networks were extended and spread far and wide. Some units also set up supply and marketing companies.

3. Agricultural-Industrial-Commercial Integra-

ted Enterprises. Since fall 1978, when leading comrades of the State Council called for the experiment of agricultural-industrial-commercial integrated enterprises in China, 20 provinces, municipalities and autonomous regions have established general companies of agricultural-industrial-commercial integrated enterprises ran by state farms. By 1980, there were 209 state-farm-run integrated enterprises throughout the country. Altogether 936 state farms, 44% of the total, have joined integrated enterprises at various levels.

The organizational forms of current experimental joint enterprises fall mainly into the following four categories:

1. *Integration among state farms:*

A. Departments in charge of state farms in some provinces, municipalities and autonomous regions or in prefectures, cities and counties have set up agricultural-industrial-commercial enterprises by merging their subordinate agricultural and pastoral farms; this has taken place in Beijing, Tianjin, Shanghai, Shihezi in Xinjiang and East and West Lakes in Wuhan.

B. A single agricultural farm operates a company consisting of integrated enterprises. The state farm in the Huanghe River inundated area of Henan and the Liming Farm of Yunnan are cases in point.

C. Farms and factories have been merged. An example is the merger of sugarcane farms with sugar refineries in Guangdong.

D. Specialized companies are organized according to their products, such as milk companies in Beijing, Tianjin and Shanghai; a salt company in Jiangsu, a pearl company in Dawa Prefecture, Liaoning; and ginseng and antler companies in Jilin.

2. *Economic alliances have been set up between state-owned and state-farm-run integrated enterprises and rural communes and production teams.* For instance, 26 agricultural, forestry, pastoral farms, fisheries and tea plantations under the Changjiang Agricultural-Industrial-Commercial Integrated Enterprises Company in Chongqing jointly operate the production, processing and sale of tea, fruit and milk together with over 800 production teams in the vicinity.

3. *The trans-specialization and trans-regional economic integration of the integrated enterprises of state farms with other economic departments or localities.* For example, the Huguang Agricultural-Industrial-Commercial Integrated Enterprises Company of Zhanjiang, Guangdong jointly manages the manufacture and sale of furniture and timber production with the Changxindian Furniture Workshop in Beijing; it jointly sells its products with the Xinjiekou Street Neighbourhood Committee in Beijing.

4. The agricultural-industrial-commercial integrated enterprises of state farms have begun to undertake joint ventures with foreign firms in processing agricultural produce and in agricultural and pastoral production. As an example, the Tianjin Agricultural-Industrial-Commercial Integrated Enterprises Company and a French firm jointly operate a winery.

Since the experiment of integrated enterprises began two years ago, achievements have been realized in the following areas:

1. *The experiment has increased the production and income of enterprises on state farms and has translated losses into profits.*

The practice of agricultural-industrial-commercial integrated economy returns part of the industrial and commercial profits to those agricultural units which supply raw materials for the development of agricultural and pastoral production. In return, the units further the development of industrial and commercial production with supplies of raw materials. Enthusiasm in agriculture, industry and commerce is brought into play in this way as a means of increasing income and profits. In light of recent investigations into the economic effects of 48 integrated enterprises of state farms that have had a relatively long period of experimentation in 1980, participants realized increases of 14.9% in the total value of agricultural and industrial production as compared with 1979; this rate was 3.2% higher than the rate of increase of all state farms. Those taking part in the experiment had a 68.6% increase in tax payments over 1979. The great majority of state farms achieved large increases in profits in 1980 over 1979; the exception were a few farms whose profits were affected by reduced production caused by natural disasters.

2. *The experiment has accelerated the rate of accumulation of funds relative to the rate of expansion of reproduction.*

The processing and direct sales of portions of the produce and animal products by integrated enterprises have reduced the intermediate links, lowered the cost of products and increased the income of the enterprises. By maintaining the momentum of increases in their accumulative funds, these enterprises have been able to expand production with an emphasis on agricultural development. For an example, in 1979 the General Chang Cheng Agricultural-Industrial-Commercial Integrated Enterprises Company of Beijing, by practicing the method of partial refunds of profits, was able to set aside some funds for the development of milk production in 1980 (these funds were in addition to money obtained from the adjustment of milk prices). That year saw a 15% increase in milk production over 1979.

3. *The experiment has opened wide avenues of production, has provided surplus labour, and has improved the standard of living of the workers.*

A common and serious problem at present is that of surplus labour power in the enterprises of state farms. Joint enterprises may transfer surplus labour resources to processing, selling, servicing and construction departments within the enterprise. According to incomplete statistics by the departments of farms administration in Shanghai, Chongqing, Jiangsu, Liaoning, and Beijing, a large quantity of surplus labour-power has been placed in jobs since the onset of the experiment of integrated enterprises.

The emergence of integrated enterprises has stepped up the tempo of production and has increased their income and profits, thus in turn increasing workers' income and improving their welfare.

4. *The experiment has played a positive role in enlivening markets and in making things more convenient for the masses.*

From the inception of the experiment in agricultural-industrial-commercial integrated enterprises until October 1980, some 2,200 commercial establishments had been set up. These realized a turn-over of 270 million yuan during the first half of 1980. Because they sold their products themselves they were able to generate a ready supply of fresh products at cheap prices. As a result, purchases were more convenient for the masses and demands of the markets were met.

The agricultural-industrial-commercial integrated enterprises of all of China's state farms held a sales exhibition in Beijing in October 1980, with 5,000 products worth approximately 10 million yuan on display. Visitors to the exhibition totalled half of a million during somewhat more than a month's time. The total value of retail sales reached 10 million yuan, while the total value of all business conducted amounted to 30 million yuan. The sales exhibition had a strong impact throughout the whole country.

5. Scientific Research, Education and Public Health

1. Scientific Research Institutions and Research Achievements. In 1980, there were three scientific research institutions throughout the country for land reclamation within the state farm and land reclamation system. One of these is the South China Research Institute for Tropical Crops, a subsidiary of the Ministry of State Farms and Land Reclamation; the two others are reclamation research institute subordinate to provinces or autonomous regions. There were also 66 provincial or regional scientific research institutes and over 1,400 experimental stations. According to incomplete statistics, the number of scientific and technical personnel working in reclamation departments totals over 50,000. Of these, more than 8,000 are involved in scientific research work. One-third are assistant researchers, agronomists and engineers — the backbone of the scientific and technological contingents. Since 1978, as a result of the restoration of research institutions and their initial adjustment and development, the party's policies have been implemented, the scientific and technological contingent has been strengthened and the enthusiasm of the scientific and technical personnel has been mobilized. Thus, scientific research was carried out and propagated with relative ease. Some significant achievements were made. During the past two years, 33 major scientific and technological projects at the ministry level and 143 studies have been carried out, among which seven were classified as major national projects. According to incomplete statistics, since 1978, of those research projects that the provinces, municipalities or autonomous regions chose to take up voluntarily, more than 750 have realized positive results and more than one-third have won awards from leading departments at various levels. By the end of 1980, upon the approval of the Committee of Science and Technology of the Ministry of State Farms and Land Reclamation, 51 projects won first prizes, 22 won second prizes, and 16 won third prizes. Some research results have achieved outstanding levels at home and abroad. Some have been applied to production with positive economic results. For example, the Wen Chang Research Institute in Guangdong Province has bred a new species of rubber tree, "Hai Ken No. 1," which is wind-resistant, high-yielding and asexual. It grows well and produces a high yield in an area generally characterized by strong winds and poor soil. Therefore, this breed has become very popular. The Research Institute of the Reclamation Bureau in the Bazhou area of Xinjiang Autonomous Region has succeeded in

mastering the technology of planting "Hu Yang" trees (a kind of poplar), thus solving the long-term problem of afforestation in Xinjiang's saline-alkaline regions. In recent years, over 5,000 *mu* have been planted in "Hu Yang." In 1980, more than 70 kg of tree seeds were supplied to other provinces. Since 1973, the Shuguang Farm in Heilongjiang Province has developed a composite technology for improving white clay. For the past six years, the yield has increased annually and profits have risen with each passing year. The organic composition of the soil has increased by about 2%. This technology has been carried to other areas of the province. The Reclamation Research Institute of Hebei Province bred an improved variety of rice, "Kenfeng No. 5." The yield per *mu* averages 1,000 jin, while the maximum yield can run as high as 14,000 jin per *mu*. It has now been disseminated over one million *mu* throughout the country. In cooperation with the Virus Department of the Chinese Academy of Sciences, the Jian Hu Farm in Hupei Province has succeeded in developing and making an insecticide to counter the bollworm virus. The prevention effect is as good as or better than the highly efficient chemical insecticide used locally. This kind of insecticide increases cotton output and is safe to use.

2. Education. In 1980, state farms had 14,147 schools of various types. Of this total, five were colleges (one was a college of tropical crops in South China, attached to the ministry; four were run by provinces or autonomous regions). Of the five colleges, three were agricultural science colleges, and one a medical college. There were 25 technical secondary schools, 15 polytechnical schools, 44 vocational schools, 2,184 regular middle schools, 11,383 primary schools and 491 schools offering both primary and secondary school education.

In 1980 there were 2.84 million students at these schools; staff numbered 200,000, of whom 161,000 were teachers. Most state farms are located in border areas and are far from cities; therefore, schools are mainly run by the workers themselves. In the major reclamation areas, eight years of secondary education has been made universal.

Training of workers and staff. In 1980, cadre schools and several training classes were set up in the reclamation departments; 121,000 cadres and 197,000 workers were trained. In the course of their training, cadres and workers had the chance to attend specialized courses on a regular basis. Their scientific and technological levels were raised. This has played a role to a certain extent in promoting production and improving management and administration.

3. Public Health. In 1980, there were a total of 14,000 medical service units on state farms and in land reclamation departments; of these, 30 were hospitals run by administrative bureaus of localities, 1,631 were hospitals run by farms or factories and 13,000 were clinics run by branch farms or production teams. These medical service units had a total of 48,000 hospital beds and 65,000 medical workers and their families and in promoting birth tals have played an active role in providing medical treatment, in ensuring the good health of the workers and their families and in promoting both control.

6. Wages on State Farms

For over 30 years, the state farms have practiced various wage systems and have undertaken some wage-system reforms. Before 1952, following the war-time practice, the farms practiced the supply system. After 1952, in line with the wage system reform made throughout the country, they pursued a grade/wage system. Afterwards, workers and staff who merged into state farms from co-ops continued to receive their pay on the basis of the work-point system used by the agricultural co-operatives. In 1956, the state farms began to variously practice a piece-rate wage system, a three-contract wage system (involving a production contract, a job contract, and a cost contract) and the "three fixed, one award" wage system. But these systems were only practiced in some reclamation areas or on some farms. All were suspended shortly after the "cultural revolution" broke out. In 1973, according to instructions of the late Premier Zhou Enlai, some farms tried to change the supply/wage system and grade/wage system to the work-point wage system. (Some educated youths working in production and construction received their pay through the supply system). At present, of the 4.8 million workers and staff in reclamation enterprises, about 80% receive their pay through the grade/wage system and 20%, through the work-point wage system. The grade/wage system is something like the "iron rice bowl" along with "sharing meals from a cauldron." It is unfavourable to mobilizing the initiative of the enterprises, workers and staff. The work-point system requires recording the work-points earned by workers and calculating their pay according to quantity. Since the quantity and quality of work in agricultural production are more difficult to estimate than they are in industry, this wage system also has some weak points.

For the past two years, many state farms have begun reforms and improvements to overcome weaknesses in the existing wage system. Since 1980, the Party Central Committee has called on the people to implement the system of job responsibility in production. Many farms have combined the system of personal production responsibility with salaries and rewards. They have practiced the wage system in which workers and staff receive their pay and bonuses on the basis of how well and how much they have done. This system takes different forms: Some farms which pursue the grade/wage system divide their pay into two parts. Part of the wage is calculated according to the grade; the other part is calculated according to how much a person has worked, thus resulting in a system of grade-plus-output. For farms which pursue the work-point wage system, some may distribute pay according to net profit. Workers receive bonuses by getting a share of the profits they have produced. Some receive their bonuses by dividing up all profits made (that is, where there is profit, there is a bonus). So far, there are no unified regulations as to which wage or reward system should be pursued at present.

7. Profits and Losses of State Farm Operations

In the early 1950's, losses were incurred on many farms due to lack of experience, the practice of unitary agriculture and the existence of wide gaps between industrial and agricultural products. From 1953 to 1960, because the art of managing farms had been improved and economic accounting implemented, profits were realized in all years but one. In reclamation units such as the Xinjiang Production and Construction Corps, industrial enterprises and commercial service centers were set up to make up losses incurred in agriculture. They were able to realize profits for 12 years running — from 1955 to 1966 — averaging 84.17 million yuan per year. State farms all over the country were making profits before 1966, except during the period 1961-1963, when losses were incurred as a result of natural disasters which lasted for three years. For an overall period of 18 years (1949-1966), state farms made profits for 11 of those years and incurred losses for 7 years. Profits balanced losses, yielding a net profit of 700 million yuan for the period.

During the "cultural revolution," great losses were incurred by the state farms. From 1967 to 1976, losses totalled 3,196 million yuan, or an average of 320 million yuan per year.

After the downfall of the Gang of Four, state farms were reorganized and their management strengthened. Losses began to decrease yearly, falling from over 400 million yuan in 1977 to 93 million yuan in 1978. In 1979, a radical change occurred. Heavy losses that had previously been incurred for a number of years were turned into profits of 390 million yuan. In 1980, profits of over 600 million yuan were realized even though natural calamities had occurred in many areas and expenditures had been increased by about 600 million yuan for pay raises, non-staple food subsidies and so on.

III. Major Current Problems and Trends for Future Development

In light of the principle established by the Central Committee of implementing further readjustments in the economy and bringing about stability in politics, the main problem in the reclamation departments is how to make adjustments so that agricultural production and a diversified economy will be further developed, so that skills of management will be improved, and so that productivity and commodity rates will develop in an all-around way.

1. Readjusting Operation Principles. At present there are still some state farms whose principles of operation are either not clearly defined or are in a great state of flux. Principles should be established in accord with local natural conditions, economic conditions and natural resources. Formerly unreasonable principles must be regulated and crop distribution readjusted at the same time in order to lay a solid foundation for building a rational economic structure.

2. Regulating the Economic Structure and Developing a Diversified Economy. "Taking one trade as the principal line and developing a diversified economy" is the guiding principle for state farms. At present, their economic structure is quite irrational. The problem is mainly that forestry, animal husbandry, sideline occupations and fisheries take up a small proportion consisting of one-third of total agricultural output value. State farms are rich in national resources. They possess fertile land, vast grasslands, forests and water resources which have not been fully utilized. A diversified economy that includes forestry, animal husbandry and fisheries should be developed in accord with local conditions. Course grains and oil crops can be grown on hilly land in order that natural resources will be fully and rationally exploited and used, and an ecological environment should be developed in ways that will benefit human life.

3. Developing a Stratified Economic Struc-

ture. The ownership of state farms is primarily ownership by the people. Since the people's communes were set up, some communes and production brigades have merged into the farms. In 1980, there were 44 communes, 777 production brigades and 3,712 production teams included in the state farms. The ownership of these units remains collective ownership. From the point of view of developing a diversified economy, so long as state farms occupy a dominant position in socialist public ownership, the workers are allowed to develop family sideline occupations and their family members can organize to develop collective production and service trades. In a word, three types of ownership (ownership by the whole people, collective ownership and private ownership) should be allowed to exist side by side, a situation that will help speed up development of the reclamation economy.

4. **Paying Close Attention to Grain Production and Developing Cash Crops.** Farms may develop cash crops in line with natural local conditions and on the premise that grain output will continue to increase and the task of turning over grain to the higher authorities can be fulfilled. Cultivated land not suitable for grain should be approved for growing other crops. In the south, tea and fruit can be grown on hilly land. In the rubber-producing reclamation areas, so long as rubber production is guaranteed, tropical or subtropical crops may be grown on land where rubber trees cannot be grown.

5. **Causing Production to Become Specialized and Socialized in a Step-by-Step Way.** At present, the production systems of state farms are basically "large and comprehensive" or "small and comprehensive." As the agricultural economic structure is readjusted, these systems should be changed, with production systematically becoming specialized and socialized.

Specialization of production teams should be carried out first according to geographic sections within state farms; afterwards, the specialization of the farms themselves should take place. Finally, specialized farm complexes or a number of specialized production areas should be established within a large reclamation area. At the same time, socialization in services should also be considered.

6. **Active, Steady Development of Agricultural-Industrial-Commercial Integrated Enterprises.** State farms should implement farming-industry-commerce joint management and administration and should progressively develop into enterprise complexes. It is an important strategic measure to speed up agricultural modernization and to narrow down the three differences (differences between town and country, between physical labour and mental work and between workers and peasants). Enterprise complexes are now in the trial stage. They should be positively developed, gradually and in a planned way. After consolidation, strengthening, improvement and summing up of experiences, all state farms should be turned into enterprise complexes.

7. **Developing Reclamation Industry in the Course of Readjustment.** State farms should mainly develop processing industries which use their own agricultural and animal products as raw materials. Textile and construction industries, along with other labour-intensive industries, should be developed as long as there is no duplication in the building of factories and no competition for raw materials with larger factories. However, such development should keep to the principles of mutual cooperation, national distribution and overall planning.

8. **Speeding Up the Modernization of State Farms.** Reclamation enterprises should employ modern scientific techniques and be allocated modern equipment. In this respect, it is very important to strengthen capital construction of fields and to progressively bring about agricultural mechanization. It is also very important to adopt advanced scientific techniques and to run reclamation enterprises with modern management in order to raise land and labour productivity and commodity rates, and to attain a higher level of fund accumulation for the country as a whole.

9. **Strengthening Education in Scientific Research, Exploiting Mental Resources and Fostering Talented Persons.** Scientific research should be conducted in accord with the characteristics of reclamation enterprises and should be centred on grain production and a diversified economy that includes cash crops, animal husbandry and local products. Research should be carried out in the problem areas of technological economy and modernized management — two areas which are in dire need of improvement. We should pay attention to the effective operation of reclamation colleges, popularizing secondary education and improving its structure, strengthening the training of cadres and workers, and raising the levels of both scientific and general knowledge of farm cadres, workers and their families in order to meet the needs of the four modernizations.

10. **Improving the Material and Cultural Life of Workers.** On the basis of developing production, we should improve the material and cultural life of

the workers. On state farms, residential communities gradually will be built into modern, small towns, providing conditions exist.

The general objective is to build state farms into agricultural-industrial-commercial integrated enterprises which take one trade as the principal line, practice diversified economy and combine modern agriculture with labour-intensive industry that possesses the characteristics of high utilization of natural resources, high yields, high labour productivity and high commodity rates — all at less expenditure, with low costs and good economic effects.

[*Author's note:* The percentage figures of 1980, when compared with those of 1979, are worked out according to the comparable figures for 1979.]

4. CHINA'S WATER CONSERVANCY
By the Editorial Office of "Water Conservancy in China"

Water conservancy in China entered a new stage in 1980. During that year, a majority of water conservancy workers analysed the characteristics of water resources in China and studied China's history of floods and droughts. They drew lessons and conclusions from the experience of New China's water conservancy work. They also looked into the role water conservation could play in the program of the four modernizations. They set tasks and made proposals for the further improvement of water conservancy work during the period of national economic readjustment. Under the unified national plan, great progress has been made in water conservancy.

I. General Introduction to China's Water Resources

China is a vast country with numerous rivers. The total length of all large and small rivers in the country is about 420,000 kilometres (km.) There are more than 5,000 rivers which have a drainage area of over 100 square kilometres (sq. km.) each. Of these, 1,500 have a drainage area of over 1,000 sq. km. There are, in addition, more than 2,000 large and small lakes, of which 130 have an area greater than 100 sq. km.

Main Features of China's Water Resources.

1. *Although China has a plentiful supply of water, per capita supply is low.* China's yearly precipitation averages 630 millimetres (mm.). Total yearly precipitation amounts to 6,000,000 million cubic metres (cu. m.), which is about 5% of the total that falls on the land surface of the entire earth. The average yearly runoff of the rivers in China amounts to 2,700,000 million cu. m., which is 5.5% of the world's total (47,000,000 million cu. m.) China's surface water (total runoff) is less than that of Brazil, the Soviet Union, Canada and the United States, and therefore ranks fifth in the world. The water available on a per capita basis, however, is only 2,700 cu. m., which is one-fourth of the world's per capita total and lower than the per capita amount in most countries of the world. This is approximately the same as the 1975 per capita water consumption level of the United States (2,528 cu. m.).

2. *Uneven geographic distribution of water resources.*

About half of China has insufficient rainfall. The southern part of China has an abundance of water while the north is scarce of it. Along the southeast coast, the normal yearly rainfall is over 1,600 mm., while in the region south of the Qinling Mountains and the Huaihe River, it is more than 800 mm. However, in most parts of northern China, the normal yearly rainfall is only 400 to 800 mm., while in the vast northwestern region it is less than 250 mm. About half of China's land area is short of rainfall. Eighty percent of China's total runoff comes from the Changjiang (Yangtze River) Valley and the areas south of the river, yet less than 5% of the national total comes from rivers north of the Changjiang — the Haihe, the Huaihe and the Huanghe (Yellow River). Nevertheless, the north has over one-third of the total cultivated land of the whole country. Although there is an average of 2,643 cu. m. of water available for each *mu* of cultivated land in the Changjiang River basin, there is only 188 cu. m. in the Haihe River basin, 214 cu. m. in the Liaohe River basin, 281 cu. m. in the Huaihe River basin and 286 cu. m. in the Huanghe River basin. China's hydro-electric power potential is estimated to be 680 million kilowatts (kw), of which 70% is in the southwest and 30% is scattered over the rest of the country.

3. *Seasonal and annual precipitation varies greatly.* Most parts of China have less rainfall in winter and spring, and more in summer and autumn. In the high water season, the rainfall is so concentrated that there is flooding, while in the other seasons water shortages occur constantly. Rainfall during the flood season in the north is 70–80% of annual precipitation, while in the south it constitutes 50–60% of the yearly total. Annual precipitation also differs greatly between wet and dry years.

4. *Rainfall in China is heavily influenced by the monsoons.* China has so many mountains and hills with so few plains that, whenever rain storms occur, there are high floods in the middle and lower reaches of the rivers.

These features explain why water conservation in China is bound to be a difficult, complex and protracted undertaking.

China is a country where the disasters of flood and drought occur frequently. According to incomplete statistics there were 1,092 major floods and 1,056 major droughts during the period from 206 B.C. to 1949 A.D., or an average of almost one major flood or drought in every year.

The Huanghe (Yellow River). During the past 2,000 years and more, dykes along the lower section of the Huanghe were breached 1,500 times and its main course changed 26 times. Roughly speaking, that means the dykes were breached twice every three years and the river changed its course once every hundred years. Areas affected totalled 250,000 sq. km. and stretched from the city of Tianjin in the north to the areas between the Changjiang and Huaihe rivers in the south. In the year 1117 (the 7th year of the Zhenghe Period, under the rule of the Emperor Huizong, Song Dynasty), a breach of the dyke resulted in more than one million casualties. In 1642 (the 15th year under the Emperor Chongzhen, Ming Dynasty), the bursting of the dyke flooded Kaifeng City, drowning 340,000 of its 370,000 inhabitants. In 1933, the main dyke along the lower reaches broke at 54 places. As a result, 3,600,000 people in 67 counties in Henan, Hebei, Shandong and Jiangsu provinces were affected and 18,000 died.

The Changjiang. Over 200 floods have occurred in the more than 1,300 years since the Tang Dynasty. The great flood of 1931, at its peak, reached a flow of 63,000 cu. m. per second (at Yichang). All of the cities along the Changjiang from Shashi down to Shanghai were flooded. Over 50 million *mu* of farmland and more than 28,550,000 people were affected by the disaster, in which 145,000 people died. During the 1935 Hanjiang flood, 22,640,000 *mu* of farmland, including portions of the Changjiang basin, were flooded. The flood affected 10,030,000 persons, of whom 142,000 drowned.

The Huaihe. During the past 500 years, following the time when the Huanghe changed its own course into the Huaihe, the Huaihe has flooded 350 times. In 1921 and 1931, two extraordinary floods occurred covering the entire river basin. In 1931, the Changjiang and the Huaihe flooded simultaneously, sending water into Bengbu City and inundating the Tianjin-Pukou Railway. Seventy-seven million *mu* of farmland were flooded, and 75,000 people were drowned. In the Lixiahe River area of northern Jiangsu Province, more than 10 counties were inundated.

The Haihe. During the 580 years before Liberation, 387 floods occurred. In 1917, 6,350,000 people suffered when the waters of the Haihe flowed over 25 million *mu* of farmland, reaching Tianjian City. In 1939, 50 million *mu* of farmland were inundated, 8 million people became victims, 160 km. of railway were damaged and Tianjian City was again flooded.

The Zhujiang. In 1915, the Beijiang and Xijiang tributaries of the Zhujiang flooded simultaneously. The dykes were breached, the city of Guangzhou was flooded for seven days and boats had to be used for transportation within the city. The Zhujiang River Delta became one vast sea, with 4.5 million *mu* of farmland under water and 3 million people affected.

The Songhuajiang. The major flood in 1932 submerged not only large areas of farmland along the river but also the city of Harbin. There were 380,000 people in the city, of whom 240,000 were affected, including 120,000 who were left homeless.

The four worst droughts in modern Chinese history occured in 1920, 1921, 1928 and 1934. The 1928 drought affected 13 provinces in north, northwest and southwest China. Hundreds of miles of scorched land were strewn with the corpses of starved people. Victims totalled 120 million.

History tells us that flood and drought have been serious threats to the existence and development of the Chinese nation. Thus, due to both natural and social conditions, water conservancy work has always held a very special position in Chinese history. It has become and will continue to be an essential factor in the future development of the country as a whole, and in the further improvement of the people's living standards in particular.

II. Water Conservancy Work During the Past 30 Years

In the very early years after the founding of New China, the Central Committee of the Communist Party of China, led by Chairman Mao Zedong and Premier Zhou Enlai, gave great stress to water conservancy work as they summed up the historical experience of the country. Since then, a lot has been accomplished through efforts made by party committees and government organizations at all levels, as well as by the masses. In the course of the past 30 years, the state has invested 49,000 million yuan in water conservation work, with an additional 29,000 million applied as operating expenses. In addition, an estimated 58,000 million yuan was contributed by communes and brigades in cash and labour. The grand total came to 136,000 million yuan.

Through these investments, China built and equipped many large flood control and irrigation systems, power generating stations, water drainage projects, etc. Specifically, 165,000 km. of dykes, protective embankments in lakeside areas and seawalls were repaired or built. Drainage channels were dredged and renovated, and flood diversion canals were dug for the Hai and Huai rivers. Two hundred and forty-one large sluices and more than 86,000 reservoirs of various sizes were built. An additional 6.4 million smaller water-retaining dykes for creating ponds and pools were built. (There were only 23 big and medium-sized reservoirs and 10 to 15 sluices in the whole country before Liberation.) All this provided a total water storage capacity of 400,000 million cu. m. More than 5,200 irrigated districts with an irrigated area of over 10,000 *mu* each were completed.

The total capacity of mechanically and electrically-operated pumping facilities increased from something over 90,000 hp just after Liberation to more than 74 million hp. Starting from scratch, we developed 2,090,000 mechanical and power-operated wells. Generating units installed for producing electricity had a total capacity of 9 million kw, of which over 6.3 million kw were in small hydroelectric stations. The projects and facilities mentioned above represent 100,000 million yuan in fixed assets, of which over 40,000 million yuan is managed by the state.

The benefits resulting from these projects are evident:

A. With the initial control of floods and water-logging, development of industrial and agricultural production and the safety of the cities and the countryside have been assured. With respect to river control, 31 years of tranquility has been won on the Huanghe. Rivers like the Changjiang, Huaihe, Haihe, Liaohe, Songhuajiang and Zhujiang have also been preliminarily stabilized.

B. The development of irrigation, the elimination of water-logging and the control of saline-alkaline soil have provided favourable conditions for increasing agricultural production. China's total irrigated area has increased from something over 200 million *mu* in the early post-Liberation years to the present level of 670 million *mu*. Out of 340 million *mu* of farmland formerly subject to water-logging, initial progress has been made in controlling 260 million *mu* (76% of the total). Initial gains have also been achieved on 62 million *mu* (56%) of the country's 110 million *mu* of saline-alkaline land.

C. Cities and industries have been provided with sufficient water supplies. Important industrial cities like Beijing, Tianjin, Changchun, Shenyang and Fushun now receive an average annual supply of some 10,000 million cu. m. At the same time, in remote mountainous areas where there were endemic water shortages, drinking water has been provided to over 40 million people and 20 million head of livestock.

D. Comprehensive utilization of water resources has provided a great deal of electricity. In addition to large and medium-sized hydroelectric stations, small hydroelectric power stations all over the country generated 12,700 million kwh of electricity in 1980, accounting for one-third of the nation's power consumption in rural areas. There are currently 720 counties which in the main depend on small hydroelectric stations for electricity. These stations have become an important source of electricity in the countryside. They have played a remarkable role in transforming mountainous areas and in developing local industry and enterprises run by communes and brigades as well as in improving the material and cultural life of the people. Moreover, 19 million *mu* of 30 million *mu* of reservoir water surface has been utilized for fish culture.

It should be pointed out that the nation's population has nearly doubled in the past 30 years. Total grain output increased from more than 110,000 million kg. to over 330,000 million kg. This represents an increase in per capita grain production from 253 kg. to 408 kg. for the rural population. Water conservation played an important role in making these increases possible.

As for the water conservation work itself over the past 30 years, there were tremendous achievements, rich experiences and profound lessons. The most fundamental lesson is that it is important to respect science, to act in accordance with both natural and economic laws, to think carefully so as to achieve maximum economic results at minimum cost and, when making plans, to prevent any forseeable negative effects. Lessons and experiences can be summed up as follows:

1. *We should be strictly scientific; we should constantly develop the understanding of natural law; and we should try in every way possible to avoid being subjective and giving arbitrary and impractical directions.*

Water conservancy work is a struggle waged by human beings to change nature. The natural world is complex with dialectical relationships. What is harmful can be developed into something beneficial, and vice versa. This change is crucial to water control work where, at any one time, it is necessary to see not only the favourable but also the unfavourable aspects.

Experience of the past 30 years in areas of work such as hydrology, geology, overall planning, design and scientific research, has shown that whenever a strictly scientific attitude was stressed and used there were remarkable results.

2. *We should constantly study the laws of socialist economic construction and attach great importance to the economic results of our work.*

In any project undertaken, in addition to studying the scientific nature of the relevant techniques, it is also necessary to study whether the project is economically feasible. We must not build any project without taking account of its economic returns.

3. *In water conservancy we should work according to our ability and not be overanxious for quick results.*

In making plans and deciding what projects to undertake, the work will be expedited if consideration is given to the actual conditions (including manpower, financial resources, available materials and technical capability) and if leeway for adjustment is provided.

If, conversely, consideration is given only to what is needed with no regard to practical conditions, the result is bound to be "haste makes waste."

4. *We should promote democracy in technical work and let engineers, technicians and professional departments play a full role.*

It is true that during the last 30 years much has been accomplished in water conservancy work due to the special attention paid by party committees and government organizations at all levels as well as the personal participation and backing of many leading comrades. Nevertheless, correct decisions can only be made by developing democracy in technical work, by fully utilizing the abilities of the professionals, by making comparisons and by pooling the wisdom of the masses.

5. *We should have well-publicized policies, well-defined systems of procedures and a reasonable body of laws.*

In carrying out water conservation work, not only must relationships between the state, the collective and individuals be handled properly, but so must relationships between the present and the future and between the whole and the parts. Therefore, laws, policies and systems are needed to coordinate activities.

6. *We should strengthen the management of water conservation facilities, since only then can these facilities be fully utilized.*

7. *We should strengthen the technical and professional education of water conservancy personnel, raising their scientific level to meet the needs of the four modernizations.*

At present, improvements are needed in the scientific and technical levels of staff, in basic work such as surveying, geological investigation, planning and engineering, and in education and training work in water conservancy. In order to reduce and avoid losses, waste and errors in water work, it is necessary to pay more attention to education and research work and to spend more money in these areas.

III. The Role of Water Conservancy in the Four Modernizations

In the course of modernization, we should be prepared strategically for two things: to deal with war and to cope with natural disasters, especially large-scale flooding. Water is a crucial element in both strategies.

During the last 30 years, natural disasters occurred quite a few times in China. According to available statistics, an average of about 400 million *mu* farmland were affected by floods and/or droughts every year, out of which some 100 million *mu* were treated as disaster areas. Floods, droughts and water-logging are great threats to the Chinese people. In the process of modernization, not only the development and prosperity of agriculture, but also the development of the national economy require reliable water conservation work. Both goals require a dependable flood control system, an adequate supply of clean water, a good scientific system for coordinating water conservancy work and a sensible and comprehensive plan for the proper use of water. As time passes, modernization will demand more and more from water conservation workers. If water conservancy work is unprepared to meet these requirements, the result will be to impede the four modernizations.

1. *China's capacity for flood control is still very low.*

Besides the seven big rivers — the Changjiang, Huanghe, Huaihe, Haihe, Zhujiang, Songhuajiang and the Liaohe — there are many medium-size and small rivers which have not been brought under complete control. On most large rivers in particular, existing flood control systems still cannot withstand large-scale floods such as those that have occurred since Liberation. In China, areas threatened by floods tend to be densely populated and economically well-developed. Flood control is a prerequisite for ensuring the welfare of society and the orderly implementation of the four modernizations. We must not treat it lightly.

2. *It is especially important to develop water conservancy projects and increase the capacity to resist natural disasters.*

Agriculture is the foundation of the national economy of China. It is necessary to speed up the development of agriculture in order to stabilize the present economic situation and to carry out the four modernizations. Without effective water conservation work, it will not only be difficult to modernize agriculture but impossible even to carry on regular agricultural production.

At present, the nation's irrigated area totals only a little more than 670 million *mu* and more than half of the farmland still has no irrigation facilities. Even in areas that have irrigation facilities, the efficiency level of irrigation is not very high. Areas where some amount of irrigation is assured total only 500 million *mu*, while areas where crops can be assured regardless of drought or water-logging total just over 300 million *mu*. Every year China loses some 5,000 million kg. of grain because of natural disasters, so there is an urgent need to raise the capability of combatting natural calamities.

3. *Water conservation is the lifeline of not only agriculture but also of industry.*

As the four modernizations proceed, the tasks undertaken by water conservation will become more numerous and more difficult with respect to protecting industry, cities and railways, and to providing water for industrial and domestic use.

At present, China has more than 160,000 km. of embankments and 80,000 large, medium-size and small reservoirs. These projects protect not only 400 million *mu* of farmland and vast stretches of rural areas, but also several dozen key cities and many small and medium-sized towns, mines, industrial enterprises, railways and highways. At the same time, water is supplied to urban mines, industrial enterprises and populations.

4. *Out of the 3,400 million* mu *of usable grassland, only somewhat over 5 million* mu *are irrigated.*

Yet, due to inadequate rainfall and water supply, the pastures have been deteriorating and grazing capacity is low. If animal husbandry is to be developed seriously, something must be done about water conservation on the grasslands with the aim of solving the problem of drinking water for people and animals and developing the places where little or no water is now available.

5. *Water conservancy is needed in order to develop the forest industry.*

It is especially necessary in the arid northwest area where annual precipitation is less than 200—300 mm. and in some areas is even below 100 mm. Obviously, trees have to be planted in such areas. Since water is scarce, the survival rate is low. Even with many trees planted every year, they never grow into forests. On the other hand, where water is plentiful there are forests, trees grow and crops flourish. This shows that forestry and water conservation complement each other.

6. *Building hydroelectric stations requires centralized planning that takes into consideration multipurpose utilization and all-around benefits.*

Hydroelectric construction is just one part of water conservation work. In river control work, plans should be made in such a way that minimum investments will yield maximum economic results. We should build more projects which can simultaneously serve flood control, irrigation, navigation and power generation. We should avoid building single-purpose projects.

IV. Principles and Tasks for Water Conservation Work During the Period of Readjustment

At present, one of the most favourable conditions in the field of water conservancy stens from the fact that many major projects have been completed. During the readjustment period, the main tasks in water conservation are to improve the management performance of existing projects and to make sound preparations for future development by doing good basic work, particularly in planning. The guidelines for water conservancy work during the readjustment period, as set forth in October 1980, are: to continue the construction of existing projects and their adjuncts; to strengthen management and seek practical results; to lay all the necessary groundwork and to raise scientific levels to prepare for future development.

The main work which needs to be done is as follows: to improve the management and the performance of the existings facilities; strive to get through the flood season safely at reservoirs and on major rivers so as to ensure normal production in industry and agriculture; to work out plans and do the work well in the pre-planning stages; to make readjustments and reduce the scope of capital construction and to make every effort to get immediate results from each project; to complete the auxiliary work to ensure increases in agricultural production; to build more small water conservation projects suited to local conditions and to carry out farmland construction; to strengthen the work in preventing loss of water and soil erosion; to continue to build more small hydroelectric stations; to protect water resources; to develop the science and technology of water conservancy and promote education; to ensure a good supply of materials for water conservation work; and to formulate laws and regulations concerning water conservancy.

Another important task in water conservancy during the period of readjustment is reorganization. At present, careful studies should be made and pilot projects conducted in the following areas:

1. *In river control, it is necessary to break down the old geopolitical administrative limits and shift to a management system with authority over an entire river basin.*

Water conservation agencies of this kind have been established on the Changjiang, Huanghe, Haihe, Huaihe, Zhujiang and other rivers. Active preparations should be made to set up such water conservancy commissions on the Liaohe and Songhuajiang rivers. These commissions should have effective administrative organs to handle the overall planning and day-to-day management of the entire river basin under their jurisdiction. Major tributaries and projects which involve two or more provinces, cities or prefectures should be placed under the direct control of these commissions. Each province, prefecture and county should act in this spirit and manage and regulate the rivers in their areas.

2. *Management of capital funds should be improved so as to achieve the greatest possible gains from the investments made in water conservancy.*

The deployment of water conservation funds for investment should be decided at the central and provincial levels of government and not at lower levels. The provincial government should control local funds for water conservancy, and these funds should be designated for specific purposes and not used for other things. Decisions regarding funding should be jointly studied and made known by the State Planning Commission, the Ministry of Finance and the Ministry of Water Conservancy.

3. *The wage scale for labourers engaged in water conservancy work should be studied and restructured.*

Strict distinctions should be made between wages for people who come from areas which will benefit from the given project and those who do not. Differences in wages should be set in accord with the degree of benefit received, so that no financial loss (either in cash or in grain) will be borne by communes or brigades which provide labourers but do not benefit from that specific project.

4. *Policies for resettlement necessitated by construction of reservoirs should be studied and improved.*

5. *Policies regarding fees charged for water supply should be studied and improved.*

V. Progress in Water Conservancy During 1980

During the past year, the cadres and workers engaged in the water conservancy work — implementing the party's line, principles and policies set forth since the Third Plenary Session of the 11th Party Central Committee — did a great deal of work and achieved new successes.

1. *Affirming achievements and defining the orientation.*

As a result of the discussions held among water conservancy workers and cadres at the National Water Conservancy Conference, an official paper has been prepared on the basic experience in water conservancy over the past 30 years and suggestions for future work. The report received a good response from all over the country. Most provinces summed up their experiences in water conservancy in a similar manner.

2. *Ensuring victory in the struggle against flood and drought.*

During 1980, droughts occurred in the north and floods in the south. These conditions put China's water conservancy projects to the test. The flood peak recorded at Hankou Hydrological Station on the Changjiang was slightly smaller than those of 1954 or 1931. Nevertheless there were no breaches of the main dykes and protection embankments, and thus this work had ensured the safety of the cities and plains along the river. During the flood period, the discharge capacity of the pumping facilities in Hubei Province came to more than 3,000 cu. m. per second, and the volume of water pumped into the river totalled over 16,000 million cu. m. Although more than 19 million *mu* of land were flooded, only 6.4 million *mu* were declared a disaster area thanks to the presence of effective drainage facilities. In the area of the Dongting Lake and the lower reaches of four tributaries of the Changjiang in Hunan

Province, the water-logged area totalled 4.24 million *mu*, but the disaster area was reduced to 1.01 million *mu*. 950,000 tons of grain were harvested thanks to the timely draining of water by the pumping stations. In Jiangxi Province, 770,000 *mu* of land along the Yangtze River and in the Boyang Lake area were water-logged, although only some 300,000 *mu* were seriously affected; in Anhui Province, out of 9 million *mu* of flooded area, 1.96 million *mu* of land suffered from crop failures; and 1.36 million *mu* were flooded, with 600,000 *mu* seriously affected in Suzhou and the Taihu Lake area of Jiangsu Province. The decrease in the flood-stricken area clearly illustrated the enormous role of pumping facilities and projects along the river. The economic returns were thus remarkable.

In 1980, the Danjiangkou water control project successfully held back the peak-flow of more than 10,000 cu. m. per second six times, ensuring safety along the downstream areas of the Hanjiang River. The project thus prevented damage from flood-diversion. It lightened the burden of the Changjiang in flood-control by retaining a water volume of 17,400 million cu. m. Moreover, it gave rise to conditions for power generation and irrigation during the winter and spring of 1981.

Comparatively large floods also occured on the upper and middle reaches of the Huaihe River. There, the existing five large reservoirs of Anhui Province played a remarkable role in flood control during 1980.

In the nine provinces, municipalities and autonomous regions hit by serious drought in northern China, the role of water conservancy was plainly obvious in the struggle against drought. Were they not able to draw water from the Guanting and Miyun reservoirs during the severe drought of 1980, Beijing and Tianjin would have suffered unimaginable effects on their populations and on their industrial production.

3. *Closing the main channel of the Changjiang at the site of the Gezhouba project and construction of other major projects.*

In July 1979, the Ministry of Water Conservancy held a meeting on reviewing the design of closure work of the Gezhouba project, and decided to carry out this project during the dry season of 1980 — one year ahead of the planned schedule. After a period of intensive construction work and preparation for closure, a ceremony for the intermediate approval of the first stage of the project was held by the State Capital Construction Commission; the construction schedule of the closure was approved by the State Council in October 1980. The upper and lower openings to be closed were reached respectively on November 27 and December 14 of 1980. In accordance with the hydrological features and diversion conditions, the upper cofferdam began to advance forward at 7:30 a.m. on January 3, 1981. The closure, taking 36 hours and 23 minutes in all, was successfully completed at 19:53 on January 4, 1981. The total advanced distance of closure work was 203 m. and the total volume of dumped rubble and other materials came to 106,000 cu. m., with daily intensity of 72,000 cu. m. at an average rate of 3,000 cu. m./hour. The observed discharge was 4,400—4,800 cu. m. The maximim velocity of flow during the closure was more than 7 m./second. It was an unparalleled feat in the history of Chinese water conservancy and hydroelectric construction.

In October 1980, at the same time the Gezhouba project was progressing smoothly, the Guxian reservoir project on Luohe River dammed up the cofferdam; the first generating unit was installed at Panjiakou project; and rock-plug blasting was successfully carried out at the spill tunnel for the Miyun reservoir. Construction work for diverting water from the Luanhe River as well as the supplementary works on the Miyun and Yuecheng reservoirs were under way. The total capacity of small hydroelectric power stations completed this year came to 800,000 kw. A meeting to exchange experiences on provincial capital construction and management was held at Biliuhe Reservoir.

4. *The legal system was improved.*

Official papers were issued on Temporary Rules and Regulations on Diverting Water for Irrigation from the Lower Reaches of the Yellow River; Some Rules and Regulations Regarding Safety on Farmland Construction Works; Management of Small Hydroelectric Power Generation; Temporary Regulations on Management of Construction Equipment; Estimated Costs for the Design of Water Conservancy and Hydroelectric Power Projects; Trial Implementation of Bonuses for Outstanding Results in Research on Water Conservancy; and Management of Materials and Products for the Ministry of Water Conservancy. In addition, a number of laws, regulations, rules and specifications were drafted and revised.

5. *A corporation for diversified operation and management of water conservancy projects was founded to improve the management and administration of these projects.*

Due to the strengthening of financial management, annual profits exceeded the planned figure by 176%, while the cost of capital construction decreased by 8.7% over 1979. Some 52,219 staff members in the water conservancy field were promoted.

6. *Basic work was strengthened.*

Meetings on overall planning for the Haihe, Changjiang and Zhujiang rivers were held. A national zoning grid for water conservancy was drawn up, water resources were appraised and a compilation of flood investigations was made. Scientific research organizations in the field were strengthened. New techniques, such as remote sensing with aircraft on the Yellow, Haihe and Zhujiang rivers, were adopted. Professional books on 96 subjects within the field of water conservancy, totalling more than 2 million copies, were published.

7. *The training of staff members was strengthened.*

During 1980, more than 4,000 cadres were trained. Persons trained in the capital construction field came to 20,000.

8. *International technical-exchange activities were intensified.*

An International Symposium on River Sedimentation was held in Beijing in March 1980. An International Flood Control Workshop was held in Zhengzhou in October 1980; and a UNIDO Workshop/Study Tour on MHG Technology Transfer was held in Hangzhou in October 1980.

The Hydraulic Engineering Corporation of China was founded for the purpose of extending water conservancy services abroad. Up to 1980, 23 projects in 14 countries have been undertaken by the ministry and its affiliated organizations. In addition, many delegations were sent abroad in 1980 for the purpose of studying other experiences in water conservancy.

The construction of water conservancy projects that will relieve China from the ravages of floods, that will benefit current and future generations and that will create a favourable ecological environment for mankind and all other creatures — these are protected and arduous tasks. Natural conditions impel us to pursue water conservancy. By working under the leadership of the Communist Party of China and the people's government and by relying on the joint efforts of the Chinese people and the hard struggle of the water conservancy workers, steady progress will be made in water conservancy.

5. CHINA'S FORESTRY IN 1980

By the Propaganda Bureau, Ministry of Forestry

I. General Survey of China's Forestry Sector

China has a vast expanse of land. With its southern provinces located in the tropical and subtropical zones and its northern provinces near to the frigid zone, China is well-situated geographically, with natural conditions suitable for the growth of trees of all kinds. China's 9.6 million square kilometres of land include extensive stretches of barren hills and wastelands fit for afforestation. Moreover, tree-planting is carried out in a major way around homes and villages and along roads and ditches. Thus, land availability is relatively adequate for the development of forestry.

Principal Species. At present there are more than 2,800 varieties of arbor species. Those native to China include Metasequoia glyptostroboides, Cathaya argyronhylla, Pseudolarix amabilis, Glyptostrobus pensilis, Taiwania cryptomerioides, Fokienia hodginsii, Keteleeria fortuei and Cunninghamia lanceolata. Important economic tree species include Aleurities fordii, Camellia oleifera, Sapium sobiferum, Rhus vernififlua, Heveabrasiliensis and Eucommia ulmoides, while valuable industrial species include Fraxinus mandshurics, Juglans mandshurica, Cinnamomum camphora, Fhoebe bournei and Swietenia mahogani.

Afforestation. Since the founding of the People's Republic of China in 1949, the Communist Party of China and the people's government have placed great stress on forestry development, drawing up a series of principles, policies and laws to this end. During the last 30 years, areas set aside for afforestation throughout the country amount to more than 400 million *mu*. More than 3,900 state forest farms and over 200,000 commune- and brigade-run forest farms have been set up. Today, there are more than 119.78 million hectares of forests in China covering 12.57% of its total land area and constituting a forest volume of 9,350 million cubic metres.

Forest Industry. Forest industries have undergone a parallel development. Since 1949, 186 large and medium-sized enterprises for tree-felling and timber transportation along with more than 2,200 commune-and brigade-run afforestation enterprises have been established. Over 10,000 km. of railways and nearly 100,000 km. of highways have been built in the forest areas. Timber output has been raised from 5.67 million cubic metres annually during the early years following Liberation to 53.59 million cubic metres at present; sawn timber production has increased from 3.44 million cubic metres to 13.69 million cubic metres. At present there are 209 timber processing factories, 244 "three-board" (fibre-board, plywood and particleboard) enterprises and 259 resin factories; annual production of the "three boards" is 690,000 cubic metres and that of resin, 290,000 tons.

The development of forestry plays an important role in improving natural resources in China, in enhancing the production of agriculture and animal husbandry and in raising the living standards of the people. Furthermore, it has created and tempered an army of more than 2 million forest workers while accumulating experience in production and administration, raising scientific and technological levels and laying an impressive foundation for capital construction, mechanization and scientific education and research.

Impediments to Forestry Development. Despite China's achievements in the expansion of forestry, forestry development continues to move at a slow pace; afforestation is lacking in quality and sharp contradictions exist between supply and demand. Indiscriminate felling has become a serious problem due to erratic changes in policy, overlapping leadership, chaotic administration and structure, and insufficient funds for the management of forests. At present, the national per capita forest area is less than 2 *mu*, and per capita forest volume less than 10 cubic metres. As far as the per capita forest coverage is concerned, China ranks 120th among the 160 countries in the world. Thus, there remains a long and arduous task ahead in protecting forests, in developing forestry, and in transforming the situation of not enough forests and insufficient timber.

II. Progress Amidst Readjustment

The year 1980 was the second year of implementation of the principle of readjustment, restructuring, consolidation and improvement in the national economy in China. The Communist Party Central Committee and the State Council have taken a series of measures to strengthen leadership over the forestry construction. On March 3, 1980, the Central Committee of the CPC and the State Council issued the Directive on Afforestation, in which the goal for developing forestry was put forward in a major way, and the principles and policies for forestry construction during the period of readjustment were worked out. The directive emphasized that agriculture, forestry and animal husbandry were dependent upon one another and should be placed on an equal footing; it was requested that party committees and people's governments at various levels place forestry construction on their agendas, mobilizing people of all nationalities throughout the country to pursue afforestation in a major way.

On December 5, the State Council again issued an Urgent Notice on Banning Indiscriminate Felling of Trees in which it was decided that protective measures should be taken for the existing forests and that centralized and unified administration should be implemented with regard to timber and bamboo phyllostachys pubescens. This series of important decisions provided vital guarantees for the forestry development in China.

In order to mobilize people from all walks of life, the broad masses of the people and youngsters to answer the call of the party and government, to take part in the afforestation campaign, and to install throughout society the habit of loving and protecting trees, the Ministry of Forestry, the State Administration of Urban Construction, the General Political Department of the People's Liberation Army, the Central Committee of the Communist Youth League and the Beijing Municipal People's Government on March 10 jointly held a Mobilization Meeting on Afforestation. Based on thorough investigations and research, the Ministry of Forestry held a succession of special meetings throughout the collectively-owned forest areas in southern China, in state-owned forest areas and among the scientific research and education community at which concrete plans for readjustment were put forward. In accordance with the demands for readjustment, cadres and workers on the forest front increased production, practiced economy, and accomplished all assigned tasks in afforestation, commercial forestry and capital construction. Their achievements in forestry development included the following:

1. Continuous Progress and Steady Development in Afforestation Work. During 1980, the policy formulated by the Central Committee and the State Council of relying mainly on the communes and brigades to build forests, of vigorously expanding the number of state-owned forests and of encouraging commune members to grow trees was adhered to throughout the whole country. With the economic interests of the masses taken into consideration, an encouraging situation was brought about wherein the state, the collectives and individuals joined forces in the promotion of forestry.

In 1980, 68.28 million *mu* of land were afforested, registering an increase of 1.4% over the previous year. In that year, earnest efforts were also made to eliminate the ideological influence of "Left" mistakes in previous afforestation work. A great number of specific programmes were undertaken in the implementation of forest policies, yielding marked results:

A. In those brigades with large areas of barren hills and wasteland, the policy was implemented of giving a certain amount of such land to commune members for their own private use. Whoever plants trees will be entitled to own them. This policy will earn people's trust and encourage them further to plant trees.

B. In the state-owned and commune-and brigade-run forest farms, the responsibility system in forest production was popularized, with tree planting and tending carried out on a contract basis. Contracts would be signed and compensation paid according to survival rates and timber-production rates, thus using economic means to encourage the masses to plant trees and protect forests.

C. In state-owned forest areas, local people should be accepted for participation in regenerating, cutting and protecting the forests of the state farms, and in maintaining roads and performing other productive activities. They would be paid directly by the forest departments concerned or share out profits according to their contract. The development of mountainous areas and fulfilling the immediate interest of the masses should be linked together; i.e., to rely on, to cultivate and to earn a livelihood from the mountains and, likewise, to rely on, to protect and to gain profits from the forests.

D. Joint afforestation was to be attempted in sectors such as railways, communications, coal mining and light industry. Efforts were to be made to encourage people of all trades and professions to engage in forestry in different ways and means.

These methods have effectively mobilized the enthusiasm of the broad masses of the people in planting trees and served as a motivating force in the accomplishment of the tasks of afforestation in 1980.

In 1980, important achievements were also recorded in key programmes such as state construction of shelterbelts in northwest, north and northeast China, the planting of farmland shelterbelts on the plains; the construction of fast-growing industrial timber sites in the south; and the regeneration of overcut areas in the Northeast. In planting soil and water conservation shelterbelts, windbreaks and sandbreaks in northwest, north and northeast China, a mixed planting of trees, bushes and grass was employed. In 1980, a total of 7.78 million *mu* of farmland shelterbelts, soil and water conservation shelterbelts, windbreaks and sandbreaks and pasture shelterbelts were afforested.

In the course of planting trees, the people in various places gave heed to the laws of nature, advocated scientific afforestation and took care to apply their own special skills to afforestation. They made it a point that timber forests, economic forests, firewood forests and shelterbelts should be arranged in a unified way so that the layout is rational. And efforts were made to ensure that the right trees were planted in the right places and at the right times, utilizing proper densities and conscientious tending so as to improve the survival rate. In 1980, the forestry departments of various localities, together with parks administration bureaus, advocated the planting of trees, flowers and grass in large and medium-sized cities and taught young people and urban residents to take up the habit of loving trees, flowers and grass.

2. **Certain Achievements Have Been Made in the Selection of Superior Tree Species and in the Nursing of Seedlings.** In the spring of 1980, the Central Committee and the State Council advanced the suggestion that superior tree species be selected, sturdy seedlings be nursed, and seed-producing sites be set up. These steps would help achieve the goals of specialization, of seed standardization, of quality and of dissemination of superior tree species. In accordance with these requirements, most provinces, municipalities and autonomous regions have restored or established corresponding administrative bodies and have held special meetings to strengthen their organizations, to rectify administration of seedling nurseries and to establish and strengthen various regulations and methodologies.

Measures were taken in various places to support the nursing of seedlings by communes and production brigades and lend support to state tree nurseries. Individual commune members and people of all trades and professions were encouraged to devise their own means for nursing seedlings. Special funds to support communes and brigades in the nursing of seedlings were obtained from state afforestation subsidies or from local finances; chemical fertilizers and subsidy grains were set aside for this purpose. Communes and brigades were helped in funding, materials and technical support so as to help them efficiently operate their key seedling nurseries and to develop small-sized seedling nurseries.

In 1980, conditions at 357 sites for planting superior tree species were adjusted or completed, and seedling gardens with a total area of 130,000 *mu* and seed-bearing forests of 650,000 *mu* were established. In the 15 provinces, municipalities and autonomous regions of north China, mechanized nursing of seedlings was tried out and ten low-temperature seeds storage stations were set up with a combined area of over 5,400 square metres. By the last quarter of 1980, there were 1,946 state seedling nurseries throughout the country with a total area of more than 1.6 million *mu*. Owing to the mutual cooperation and development of the commune- and brigade-run seedling nurseries and the state seedling nurseries, the total seedling nursing area reached 5.89 million *mu*, basically meeting the needs of national afforestation.

3. **To Control Felling, Strengthen Regeneration of Overcut Areas, and Readjust Imbalanced Relationships Within Forestry.** Timber production quotas set by the state plan in 1980 were reduced to about 51 million cubic metres from some 54 million cubic metres in 1979 – a cut of 7.6%. This measure enabled forestry bureaus that had suffered from excess felling to undertake rehabilitation.

National forestry industrial enterprises and the commune- and brigade-run forest farms earnestly implemented the principle of "taking forestry as the leading factor in pursuing a diversified economy, and developing those trees which yield quick profits alongside those which yield slow profits so that the quick-profiting could support the slow-profiting." These units did a good job in economic accounting, tried their best to develop their resources while regulating exploitation and utilization, and steadily improved management. The above-mentioned measures effectively raised economic results in forestry industry production. In 1980, national profits from forestry industries registered an increase of 30% over the level of 1978, thus making a good beginning for national readjustment work in forestry.

We should develop comprehensive utilization of timber and try our best to increase the utility of timber. In order to pursue comprehensive use of timber and diversification in the forest areas, the national forestry industries, beginning from 1980, tried to alter the product structure by manufacturing articles according to the size of the timber being used, and thus increasing the variety of products. In addition, they pursued reforms in the use of fuels as a further means of conserving timber. Efforts were made to increase the quantity of and to improve the quality of the "three boards." In the meantime, efforts were made to develop the production of articles made from small-sized timber, and to develop the production of by-products such as mushrooms, fungi, honey and herbal medicines, thus achieving simultaneous development of timber, the "three boards" and forest by-products.

4. Strengthening of Forest Protection. In 1980, indiscriminate felling still occurred in a number of places, further damaging forest resources. To protect forest resources, the State Council on December 5, 1980 issued an Urgent Notice on Banning Indiscriminate Felling of Forests. And the party committees and people's governments in the provinces, municipalities and autonomous regions rapidly took measures to propagate and implement the spirit of this notice. In 13 provinces and autonomous regions including Fujian, Jiangxi and Sichuan, unified purchasing and selling was adopted for timber and bamboo so as to strengthen control over the felling and transportation of timber within the forest areas. This step succeeded in freezing indiscriminate and wanton purchases and sales of timber.

Timber inspection stations were set up in the forest areas in various places; markets trading in timber and bamboo were closed; forest protection organizations and networks were set up and strengthened; local police stations and procuratorates were set up and forest police brigades were formed to clear up accumulated cases of damaging forests and thus cracking down on a batch of criminals. Today, indiscriminate felling throughout the country has been mainly stopped. Normal procedures have been restored throughout the vast forest areas and there now exists a situation of security and stability.

Forest-Fire Prevention. In 1980, all departments in the forest areas drew earnestly from the serious lesson of forest fires during the ten years of chaos [i.e., the "cultural revolution"] and took the prevention of forest fires as a matter of major importance. They conducted frequent publicity campaigns, timely inspections and programmes for long-term prevention; they established and strengthened the responsibility system in the prevention of forest fires and formulated regulations for rewards and penalties. In the principal forest areas, aeronautical forest protection was practiced, air-borne fire brigades were set up and anti-fire roads were constructed. According to incomplete statistics, the outbreaks of forest fires in 1980 were cut down by 40% as compared with 1979 and the extent of ravaged areas fell by 60%. During the fall season of the fire-prevention period, virtually no major fires broke out in the forests.

The work of detection and control of forest pests and diseases was also carried out widely in various provinces, municipalities and autonomous regions. Prevention areas covered 32% of all infected forests. In order to strengthen the protection of the wild flora and fauna, the forestry departments, in collaboration with the related organs, strengthened the management and construction of natural preserves. By the end of 1980, China had 75 natural preserves covering a total area of 1.7 million *mu*.

In 1980, a considerable amount of work was done in research and education on the forest front, including the conducting of scientific and technological research, publicising scientific and technological achievements, improving educational levels in forestry colleges and schools and strengthening the training of cadres and workers in forestry departments. Considerable achievements have been recorded in this regard. In 1980, more than 100 scientific and technological achievements were reported in the forestry field; 27 of these came from the State Scientific Commission and the Ministry of Forestry. These research achievements attained high standards and have proved to be of great practical value. In 1980, 1,323 cadres and 1,956 technicians were trained in forestry methods.

III. 1980 Prospects for Speeding Up Forestry Development in China

1. Stabilizing Ownership of the Mountains and Forests. If ownership is clearly established, an ownership certificate for the forest should be issued to guarantee that status. If ownership is under dispute, the relevant government bureau should seek resolution by consulting the parties concerned.

2. Further Implementing the Responsibility System in Production. On state forest farms, commune- and brigade-run forest farms and afforestation farms, the job responsibility system should be practiced earnestly in light of the characteristics of forest production; responsibility and pay, as well as collective interests and individual interests, should be closely linked. In collectively owned forest enterprises such as commune- and brigade-run farms, special contracts and payments according to production should be popularized. Such methods may also be practiced on a basis of teams, households or individuals.

3. Practicing Centralized and Unified Control over Timber. In accordance with the principle that the consumption rate of timber should be lower than its growth rate, it is imperative to continue to place felling under strict control. Timber assigned

by the state, locally used timber and timber used by state forestry units and other departments should be consolidated into unified cutting plans. There should be only "one account" throughout the entire country.

4. **Increasing State Economic Assistance to Forestry.** It is essential for all localities to try their utmost to earmark part of their local financial funds for the support of forestry. It is necessary also to set up a state forestry fund system.

5. **Developing in a Major Way the Comprehensive Use of Timber and Economical Substitutes.** Timber processing and comprehensive uses for timber should be developed systematically in the forest areas. Emphasis should be on tapping potential, innovation and reform of existing timber mills and factories so as to raise productivity and improve product quality. At the same time, means for conserving timber and the development of wood substitutes should be pursued actively.

6. **Adhering to the Policy of Relying Mainly on the Communes and Brigades for Planting Forests, Vigorously Expanding State-Owned Forests and Encouraging Commune Members to Grow Trees.** It is necessary to mobilize the broad masses of the people from all walks of life in the cities as well as in the countryside to plant trees with an enthusiastic spirit, to quickly work and put into practice a five-year plan for planting trees and expanding forest coverage and to put forward 10 and 20-year targets to speed up the afforestation of the motherland.

To develop forestry and to afforest the motherland — these are great causes suited to the present period and beneficial to future generations. As long as we earnestly implement the lines, principles and policies laid down by the party since the Third Plenum of the 11th Central Committee, and work in a down-to-earth spirit, forestry in China will have a bright future and the grand goal of afforesting the motherland will certainly be attained.

6. CHINA'S FISHERIES
By Jin Shui
State Administration of Aquatic Products

The fishing industry forms an important component of agriculture. Its development plays a key role in providing variety in the domestic market and in helping to meet the daily needs of the people as well as in increasing exports. It helps towards diversifying the agricultural structure and promoting the overall economic development of the countryside. It provides a useful channel for promoting rapid prosperity for the fishermen and peasants. China's fisheries in 1980 made progress in line with the implementation of the national economic readjustment according to the spirit of the Third Plenary Session of the 11th Central Committee of the Communist Party of China.

I. Recent Achievements and Development

In February 1979, the State Administration of Aquatic Products, a division under the State Council, held a nationwide work forum on aquatic products. Summarizing lessons learned from past experience, the forum studied adjustments in aquaculture work. Policies laid down for the near future included the following provisions: protection of resources, development of breeding, readjustments to inshore fishing, opening up deep-sea fishing grounds, incorporating modern technology, strengthening scientific management, raising product quality and improving market supplies.

Accordingly, three key areas for readjustment were underscored: 1. Protection and reasonable use of resources, with emphasis on limiting inshore fishing so as to prevent overfishing and to allow resources to restock. 2. Making better and fuller use of water surfaces and actively developing aquaculture; the aim is to strive to make use of all existing freshwater surface areas and at least half of the available sea surface area during the decade of the 1980's. These developments are to form the main sources of increased yields in the near future. 3. The provision of equipment to maintain fish at optimum freshness for processing and solving the problem of obsolete methods in this work. This will provide better quality fish.

Readjustments during the past two years have brought about preliminary results which became evident in all aspects of fishery work during 1980. In that year, the total output of aquatic products was 4,497,000 tons, an increase of 4.5% over 1979.

Output of Freshwater Fish. There was still a sharp increase in the output of freshwater products despite heavy flooding of the Changjiang River, spring frosts in the Zhujiang River delta and drought in the northern provinces. The freshwater figure of 1,240,000 tons broke the 1959 record of 1,230,000 tons. An important factor in increasing output was the establishment of supply centres for freshwater fishing, set up with state support. In 1980, more than 80 counties in 11 provinces had established concentrated and integrated centres of this type, creating an area of 320,000 *mu* suitable for intensive aquaculture. Of this area, 250,000 *mu* began producing fish in 1980. The 15,000 tons in output equalled the accumulated 20-year total of annual increases in the breeding of freshwater fish. Of the 1980 total, 5,000 tons were supplied to the state, double the amount in 1979.

Fishing policies have been relaxed, the right to use water surfaces for fishing has been assured and various responsibility systems have been set up. As a result, there was considerable growth in the number of communes and production teams taking up fish farming. In addition, many commune members' families have made fish breeding into a sideline occupation. Record fish outputs were achieved by communes and production teams in Jiangsu, Zhejiang, Hubei, Sichuan, Guizhou, Shaanxi, Shanxi, Hunan, Guangdong, Fujian, Jiangxi, Liaoning, Shanghai, Tianjin and Beijing. The situation has not been as good since the cooperative movement of the 1950's and well illustrates the momentum of the party's policies.

Output of Marine Aquaculture. In 1980, readjustments in marine aquaculture were mainly made in variety. Different districts developed varieties according to local conditions. There was a 4.5% increase of water surface utilized in 1980 as compared to 1979. The area devoted to the cultivation of clams, razor clams, scallops, fish, prawns and laver increased. In 1980, output of marine products increased by 6.8% over 1979. The total volume of 444,000 tons consisted of 250,000 tons of kelp, or 56%; 60 tons of mussels, or 13.5%; and 57,000 tons of razor clams, or 12.8%. Output of prawns increased at the fastest rate during the last two years, doubling its yield each year.

By the end of 1980, 43 commercial sea farms had been established or were being set up, with a combined area of about 200,000 *mu*. At the same time, six new centres were set up for producing marine delicacies: three for abalone and three for trepang and scallops.

Output of Deep-Sea Fishing. In 1980, work on deep-sea fishing was centred on the protection of marine resources and adjustments in work in that field. In coastal waters off the Yellow Sea and the Bohai Gulf, the use of fixed nets during the off season was forbidden. There were strict limits on the number of boats under licence allowed out during the prawn-fishing season. In the East China Sea, an off season for fish was declared for the four-month period of July through October. Steps were taken to restore fishing by use of dragnets, encircling nets and small hooks and lines. During 1980, the problem of dwindling resources for hairtail fish in the East China Sea took a turn for the better, and the proportion of large and medium-size fish increased.

Progress in Research. Scientific work in aquaculture registered over 60 achievements. Most important were improved breeding methods for freshwater products, improved varieties of crossbred carp and popularization of a variety of methods, including use of high-yield fish in pond farming, fish rearing in paddy fields, and artificial breeding of prawns and scallop larvae. Other important achievements were the popularization and use of insulated holds in motor and sail-powered fishing boats. Six million African crucian carp (tilapia mossambica) were reproduced during the year, and these fish are now being bred in more than a dozen provinces. These fish can reach weights of 450-600 grams in four months and are ready for marketing within one year. More than 1.2 million pond shrimps are now being propagated and experiments are being made in Guangxi and Shanghai to breed them productively. Three different species of carp have been cross-bred, Heyuan carp, Yü carp and Furong carp; these have been introduced to 13 provinces and municipalities. Progress has also been made in the artificial rearing of prawn and scallop larvae and good production results have been achieved. In 1980, 800 motorized and sail-powered fishing boats belonging to collective fish farms had installed insulated holds. This meant that fish could be held at temperatures of 3-4°C lower and that boats could stay at sea 2-3 days longer.

Research into the country's natural fish resources and into the division of work in the fishing areas have resulted in pilot projects being started in key bodies of water and regions; scientific collaboration groups were set up to study resources in continental shelf waters and in important inland water systems; six of these groups were set up for the Yellow Sea, East China Sea, South China Sea, Heilongjiang River system, Zhujiang River and Huanghe River systems. Each group has drawn up study plans and all are starting to carry out their tasks. Some provinces and municipalities have also started to carry out research work.

Improved Processing Methods. In the area of ensuring fresh processing and improving quality, efforts have been concentrated on retaining freshness at the initial point — at sea. Past measures which have proved effective have been restored, including washing, sorting, packing in boxes and adding ice. Now about half the catch is packed in boxes. Of the 1980 hauls made at sea, about 1.3 million tons of fish were chilled fresh, 500,000 tons frozen and 200,000 tons made into fish meal, canned fish and other processed products. Quite a large proportion is salted and dried. Fish-processing factories in Shanghai use black scraper fish for canning, fish sausages, fish cakes and fish-liver oil for veterinary use; they are finding growing markets for their products.

Improved Management. Improved management has cut down losses and increased profits. In 1980, profits reached 28.65 million yuan. For many years, the country's marine and freshwater fishery enterprises had been run at a loss, a trend that was reversed for the first time in 1980.

More channels were opened up for supply and marketing, producers were able to contact consumers, restrictions on country fairs were removed so that sales of aquatic products livened up considerably. Statistics show that in 1980 about 635,000 tons of marine and freshwater products went on sale in urban and rural markets throughout the country. This did much towards balancing the supply of aquatic products between urban and rural outlets. Furthermore, increasing foreign revenues have been earned from exports of aquatic products. This total rose from US$160 million in 1977, to US$250 million in 1978, to US$340 million in 1979 and to US$356 in 1980.

Progress made in readjustment and in carrying out economic policies resulted in more accumulation and income for most fishing communes and brigades. Figures from 17 provinces and municipalities showed an increase in accumulation in 1979 of 16% over 1978; and an average per capita increase of 35%, or from 93 to 126 yuan. These increases continued in 1980.

II. Resources and Problems

China has rich aquatic resources. It has a

coastline of 18,000 km. on the south and east. Its continental shelf consists of 430,000 square miles of 200-metre-deep fishing grounds. About 1,500 different kinds of fish are found in China's waters, of which about a dozen have great economic importance. The coastal shore is wide and provides an area of 7,400,000 *mu* suitable for raising seafoods such as molluscs, sea algae, fish and prawns, as well as delicacies like abalone and trepang. Inland rivers, lakes, ponds and reservoirs provide 75 million *mu* of water surface suitable for fish-breeding. The wide latitudes pass through frigid, temperate and tropical zones and provide suitable conditions for developing the aquatic products industry.

Historical Development of the Aquatic Products Industry. China has been active in the aquatic products industry for thousands of years and has generations of valuable experience. The world's first book on fish culture, written by Fan Li, appeared in 460 B.C. Summarizing experiences of that time, the "Canon on Fish Culture" pointed out that aquaculture was one of the five methods of culture. China is in the world's front ranks in fish-breeding techniques and has always led in freshwater fish farming. In recent years China has trained 140 experts in fish farming for the United Nations — an activity that has earned the appreciation of participant countries.

In the 30 years since the founding of the People's Republic of China, yields in aquatic products have risen from 910,000 tons in 1950 to 4.3 million tons by 1979, taking third place in the world behind Japan and the USSR. Aquatic products account for 1.4% of the total value of agricultural output.

Developments in China's aquatic products industry can be divided into four stages:

1. From 1949 to 1957. Because of lingering disruption left from the war years, this period was mainly one of rehabilitation and development. At that time, natural resources were very rich so, with the liberation of productive forces by democratic and socialist reform, yields rose steadily. During these eight years production rose from 450,000 tons to 3.12 million tons — a seven-fold increase. Quality was also good.

2. From 1958 to 1969. During this period, aquaculture came under the influence of the "Left" ideology — first, the wind of communization; then, the wind of exaggeration in reporting yield figures; and finally, the wind of blind direction that swept the whole country, culminating in the "cultural revolution," when aquaculture suffered from sabotage by Lin Biao and the Gang of Four. Thus, despite the fact that many deep-sea fishing boats were added during this period, yields were uneven and there was no significant increase.

3. From 1970 to 1978. During this period, the number of motorized fishing boats were increased rashly and yields were the highest ever recorded — reaching 4.7 million tons in 1977. Overfishing did not give natural resources the chance to replenish themselves. Immature fish, low-value fish, molluscs and algae accounted for more than 50% of the catch. The damage done caused catches and quality to decline drastically.

4. Since 1979. Since 1979, agriculture has been brought into line with readjustments in the national economy. Under the policy of readjustment, restructuring, consolidation and improvement, the aquatic products industry started to improve.

The experiences of the past 30 years have taught us much. We now recognize that in order to develop the aquatic products industry, scientific and objective laws must be observed. Proceeding from actual conditions, we must keep within our capabilities and strive for solid economic results. It was because these laws were ignored for so long in the past that the aquatic products industry found itself mired in difficulties from which it could not readily break free. The most serious of these were as follows:

1. Damage to Resources. For a long time in the past, we were influenced by "Left" ideology and did not realize the importance of protecting and making rational use of aquatic resources. In this respect, we lacked basic scientific knowledge and pressed forward subjectively with no thought for natural laws governing the replenishing of resources. It was erroneously believed that where there was water there must be fish; we had only to increase our fishing fleet to make bigger catches — the immense stretches of sea providing limitless resources. So we blindly added boats and nets, with the result that we overfished our natural resources. In fact, the fishermen were encouraged to get a good haul during the slack season and to do even better during the peak season. We did our best to double our catches, fishing for big as well as small fish and never giving nature a chance to recoup. The painful consequences were that commercial fish (apart from prawns and shrimps) have mostly disappeared from the seas around the Bohai Gulf. There was no longer any fishing season for hairtail fish and small yellow croaker in the Yellow Sea. The damage done to the big yellow croaker off the coast of the East China Sea was

just as bad. The fish caught off the coast in the South China Sea were mostly the young fry of commercial fish. Catches for big yellow croaker dropped from the record figure of 190,000 tons to only 80,000-90,000 tons a year. Catches for small yellow croaker dropped from 160,000 tons to 20,000-30,000 tons a year. The catch for hairtail fish, which had once peaked at 570,000 tons, dropped to 470,000 tons a year.

The damage done to inland freshwater resources was even worse. Blindly filling in lakes to create more farmland and building barriers and dams not only greatly reduced the water surface but also did great harm to spawning grounds by cutting access to them by the fish. Environmental pollution helped to wipe out natural resources too. Since the end of the 1950's, catches from freshwater lakes and ponds have been dropping sharply. The yearly figure of 500,000 tons fell to 400,000 tons annually during the 1960's and to 300,000 tons in the 1970's. All of this was the result of "Left" ideology.

2. **Advantages of the Breeding Industry Have Not Been Fully Utilized.** For many years, the policy of overall development of agriculture, forestry, animal husbandry and fisheries has not been conscientiously carried out. At all levels throughout the country there was a one-sided emphasis on grain as the key link. Because of this, every idle *mu* of land had to be accounted for. Meanwhile, no one cast so much as a glance at unused water areas even though these totalled tens of thousands of *mu*. The situation was exacerbated by the fishery departments, which tended to pay more attention to the size of catches than to the need for replenishing stocks. With the economic policy not being carried out and no scientific measures being taken, the excellent advantages existing for fish rearing were not fully utilized. Today, only slightly more than half of China's water surface is utilized and unit-area yields are highly uneven. The national average yield per *mu* is only 40 catties, with high yields reaching 400-500 catties and sometimes 1,000 catties. Most of the shallow waters around the coastal areas are still not fully used. We have not solved the problem of building processing facilities for products such as kelp and mussels, in which we are specialized. Transportation and marketing difficulties still exist. Many economic policies are unreasonable and dampen the enthusiasm of the fishermen and peasants in fish breeding. Fish-raising, like pig-raising, requires feed, but right up to the present there is no clear policy about the supply of feed; this severely restricts the growth of the aquaculture industry.

3. **Problems of Few Varieties, Low Quality and Losses Through Waste.** The aquatic products industry embodies industry and agriculture, it is an agricultural side-line which is also multi-faceted. Another special feature is that the products of this industry are most fresh when alive, yet spoil easily. China ranks third among the world's fishing nations, yet per capita fish consumption is recorded as less than 9.2 catties — one-forth the world average of 34 catties per capita, putting China well below 100th place in world per capita consumption of fish.

Because we did not give special attention to these facts and did not fully acknowledge the situation, the quality of fish was bad and the wastage rate was high. This was caused by poor management and irrational pricing, together with too much bureaucracy and backward processing and storage facilities. Apart from about one million tons of fish salted and dried every year, much of the remaining catch became spoiled because of delayed processing and transportation difficulties, so that it could be used only as animal feed or fertilizer. For this reason, the actual consumption of fish per capita fell even lower.

III. Policies and Measures for Readjustment

In accordance with the spirit of the Party Central Committee that we should break free of our mental shackles, relax policies and enliven the economy, steps were taken in 1980 to revise plans for the aquatic products industry. However, the many difficulties accumulated over the years were firmly entrenched and hard to eradicate with one stroke. For instance, the coastal population had increased, which meant that as time passed there were more people coming onto the labour market for whom jobs had to be planned. But this contradicted the necessity to protect resources by limiting fishing. The resources protection issue had already been an urgent one many years back, but because the fishermen needed to fish for their livelihood, a quick solution was impossible. Also, the people wanted to eat fish and public opinion pressed for increased market supplies at the same time the fishing industry was faced with the choice to reduce its catches. Revisions in fishery plans had to take the whole situation into account and make plans from a practical point of view to be carried out over an extended period of time.

In 1980, the following measures were taken with a view to reviving the aquatic products industry:

1. *Legislation, arbitration and coordination were used to carry out scientific management in fishing.*

Restricted fishing in offshore waters and rational use of resources have been implemented for two years, but because legislation is as yet incomplete and supervisory measures are inadequate, the results have not been great and work is progressing very slowly. Some forward steps include coordination in arranging fishing grounds, regulations for fishing licences, for prohibited fishing grounds and for off seasons, as well as work to study the proportion of immature fish. Regulations have also been worked out to require the issuance of permits before new fishing boats can be built or imported. At present, work is underway for formulating fishery regulations.

2. *Different techniques have been adopted to speed up the time required for rearing fish.*

In order to make the most of different conditions in different places, we have advocated the relaxing of regulations and used various means to mobilize enthusiasm everywhere to bring in everyone — from the state, collectives and individuals — to increase speed. Apart from establishing supply centres and encouraging suburban fish farming, we are encouraging communes and production teams to raise fish wherever conditions are favourable and have solved problems on the policy level of fish feed, purchasing of products, pricing, etc.

For instance, Guangdong Province has laid down the policy that fish raising bases have their tasks, purchases and allocations to the state fixed for three years; for areas not specializing in fishing no assignments are made — communes and brigades are allowed to sell their produce at country fairs; the allowance of bonus feed grain has been increased: an equal weight of fish can be exchanged for an equal weight of grain. Diversified forms of fixing yield outputs and award systems encourage fish farming by commune families. This policy is getting good results.

In aquaculture we have also encouraged joint associations such as those between the state and provinces, localities or counties; province and province; county and county; production area and sales area; the state and collectives; and between aquaculture and other industries. These different methods can all be tried.

3. *We should open up more means of production and change the habit of practicing monoculture or a single-product economy.*

While carrying out fishing as its main occupation, a fishing brigade can pursue other occupations and other forms of production. To the extent permitted by local conditions, they can create conditions for the development of processing and integrated industries. They can also engage in agriculture, livestock, transportation and other sideline activities. Areas with suitable conditions can start pilot projects and gradually develop in the direction of fishing, industrial and trade complexes.

4. *The relaxation of economic policies has mobilized the enthusiasm of producers.*

The two key areas are easing the policy for products processing and adjusting the relationship between the state and the collective. In the past, the state set most of the assignments and quotas; management by individuals was controlled too rigidly. Furthermore, as far as prices and materials were concerned, there could not be exchange at equal value. Thus, by reducing the planned quotas for sale to the state, by lowering the proportion going to the state and by allowing for reasonable price fluctuation, the fishermen obtained more say in handling their products. State purchasing quotas should be established as much as possible by taking into consideration the relationship between fish and other market products and by basing contracts on exchange at equal values. This policy should be strictly enforced. Some assigned quotas should remain fixed for several years, and some areas should be given a free hand with their produce, with only certain products being sold to the state under the state plan. Purchases of products under the state plan are mainly intended for the supply of large cities, key mining and forest regions and troops stationed in border regions.

As for the policy regarding planned state purchases, apart from stipulating a reasonable amount for commodity bases established or newly established with state aid, other areas should not be obliged to sell their produce to the state once they have met their agreed quotas for state purchase plans. They should be allowed to dispose of the surplus themselves whether they be collectively owned units or state-managed units. This policy should extend to processing, transport and marketing of produce in the cities. Units should be free to make direct contact with factories, mines, hotels and restaurants; to enter cooperative arrangements with them; or to sell to them at mutually agreed prices. When Guangzhou city carried out a policy of fixed quotas at relatively low prices, the production brigades had no encouragement to raise fish yields. Thus, the market was always short of fish, despite the fact that the state encouraged suburban fish farming and despite many meetings and the granting of material incentives.

However, when policies were relaxed in 1980, a good response came in the form of a 17% increase in yields of pond fish, providing a better market supply. Another effective policy was giving the basic accounting unit more responsibility for fixing quotas and awards, so that the people received more real benefits from the policy of distribution according to work. Because there are more risks in deep-sea fishing and because more capital is needed, the economic accounting unit for this activity should not be too small. In distribution it should be recognized that there are differences in the work of different units and suitable arrangements should be made. Fish breeding could be assigned to a special production team, unit, family or group of workers within the planned scope of the collective and compensation based on production results. More remotely situated fish ponds not easily managed by the collective can be assigned to individual commune members to manage by themselves.

5. *Livening up supply and marketing.*

It is necessary to correct the past practice of unified purchasing and sales by the state. This practice has led to high costs, poor results and frequent wastage due to fish spoilage and has placed greater burdens on the consumer. From now onward fish for villages and small towns should be supplied locally through increased production. Important provincial, municipal and autonomous region markets should have their supply problems resolved through provincial planning. The needs of a few cities like Beijing and those of some mining and forest regions and of border-based military forces as well as of other special places should be met by direct arrangements with production areas under a uniform plan and by using various methods.

Supply and marketing enterprises should make more use of economic measures to promote production and stabilize market supplies in the service of consumers. Special stress should be placed on collaboration between producers and marketing stations, on arranging sales and marketing agents and on processing, freezing, warehousing and other services. Support should be given to trial fishery-industry-commerce joint ventures.

6. *More education in science and technology and the training of large numbers of skilled personnel.*

We must rely on the correct policies and scientific methods if production is to increase. During 1980, studies of resources and regional plans were undertaken. Scientific achievements were popularized. All this has served to improve production practices. It has also brought excellent results in the protection of our natural resources and in promoting the breeding and production of marine and freshwater products.

A Tang Dynasty poet, Liu Yuxi, wrote: "By the sunken wreck a thousand sails pass; Beside the withered tree countless saplings mass." This period of readjustment shows there is a great future for the development of China's fisheries.

7. CHINA'S ANIMAL HUSBANDRY
By Zheng Xingjie
State Bureau of Animal Husbandry, Ministry of Agriculture

I. Developments Since the Founding of New China

Although animal husbandry has undergone ups and downs since the founding of the People's Republic of China, generally speaking it has undergone substantial development. The total population of domestic animals increased 3.7-fold, from 160 million in 1949 to 588 million in 1980. Pig-raising developed the fastest with the total jumping from 57 million to 305 million, an increase of more than 5-fold; sheep went from 42 million to 187 million, also increasing 5-fold; draught animals increased from 60 million to 95 million, a growth of 1.6-fold.

In recent years, owing to steady development in animal husbandry, China has come to account for a considerable proportion of the world's livestock total and meat output. Pig-breeding is an important family stock-breeding activity among Chinese peasants. Nearly every peasant household breeds pigs. Pork accounts for over 90% of China's total meat output. During the past few years, China has ranked first in the world in both number of pigs and pork output, as well as in numbers and output for horses, mules, goats and rabbits. In 1979, the total number of pigs, cattle and sheep in China constituted one-seventh of world totals; the total amount of pork, beef and mutton produced in China surpassed 10 million tons, making up 10% of the world's total output of 107,284 million tons.

Thanks to the steady development of China's livestock breeding, prevailing meat and egg shortages during the last decade have recently began to decline. Except for a few areas, state-run stores in urban areas throughout the country are able to supply adequate quantities of pork and fresh eggs during peak periods. The amount of meat on sale in markets and the turnover of meat in rural trade fairs have been increasing yearly. Market sales of pork and eggs during the first half of 1980 increased by 52% and 24%, respectively, compared with the same period in 1979.

Owing to well-stocked supplies on the domestic market, labour productivity and capacity utilization rates in related light and textile industries have been raised to new levels. Woolen textiles, pigskin and meat processing industries are growing rapidly.

II. Achievements in 1980

China's animal husbandry in 1980 continued to advance in stride with 1979's rapid growth rates. In 1980, party committees and people's governments at all levels — further implementing the spirit of the Third Plenary Session of the 11th Party Central Committee — readjusted various economic policies concerning the development of livestock breeding in rural and pastoral areas, and abolished stipulations forbidding or restricting commune members from raising and butchering livestock.

During March 1980, the State Council successively approved the Ministry of Agriculture's Report on Speedy Development of Animal Husbandry and a report submitted jointly by the ministries of agriculture, commerce and food — An Emergency Report on the Current Conditions of Pig Production. In the process of carrying out these policies, several provinces, municipalities and autonomous regions set forth concrete policies suitable to local conditions. The road of development in animal husbandry grows wider and wider.

Combatting Natural Disasters. With the further mobilization of positive factors on every front, the peasants and herdsmen in 1980 effectively combatted the most serious drought of the past three decades in the northern pastoral areas. Despite this and other natural calamities such as extended low temperatures in agricultural areas, water-logging in the south and declining forage yields, animal husbandry has developed steadily.

Increasing Pig Output. In 1980, the number of marketable pigs increased by a large margin. In most areas, pork is in unlimited supply. In order to protect the peasants' initiative in pig breeding, the Central Committee and the State Council propitiously drew up the policy of reducing prices to promote sales, providing financial subsidies and stabilizing pig breeding. This policy has achieved tangible results. By the end of 1980, the number of pigs put up for sale was about 200 million, increasing by 10 million over 1979. The number of pigs purchased by the state in that year was 133 million, an increase of 3 million over 1979; and the number of pigs sold was 131 million, an increase of 9.8 million.

Draught Animals. In addition, the number of draught animals had a slight increase, thus putting an end to three years of wavering. The number of sheep and goats was 187 million, reaching the highest record in history.

Apiculture and Poultry. The output of honey in 1979 was 110,000 tons. It fell to 96,000 tons in 1980, although this quantity, accounting for one-seventh of total world output, ranked China first in the world, surpassing the United States for the first time. With the emergence of full-time households engaged in domestic fowl farming, the production of poultry also advanced.

Breeding Herbivorous Animals. In order to speed up further development of livestock breeding, it is necessary to take effective measures to solve livestock problems in pastoral areas, where the pattern has often been "well-fed in summer, fat in autumn, lean in winter and dead in spring." We must take full account of the advantages offered by mountainous and hilly districts to breed herbivorous animals. We must continue to eliminate "Left" influences so as to prevent the reappearance of such practices as forbidding or restricting peasants and herdsmen to raise and butcher livestock on their own. It is necessary to clear distribution channels for live animals and animal products so as to facilitate production and consumption.

The following are key aspects of the development of China's animal husbandry sector in 1980:

1. *Positive measures were taken to readjust the internal structure of animal husbandry.*

There were notable changes in the internal structure of animal husbandry in 1980. Improvements were realized in livestock variety, breeding and in age and sex proportions within livestock herds. These achievements fully proved the correctness of the line, principles and policies formulated since the Third Plenary Session of the 11th Party Central Committee. They have inspired peasants and herdsmen to speed up the development of livestock breeding and to lay stress on quality and scientific breeding. Today, peasants in some areas place stress on good breeds and the use of proper proportions of pig feed in pig-breeding. The sales rate for pigs in 1980 was raised to 62%, putting an end to unreasonable livestock herd structures.

On the question of livestock variety, while the Third Plenary Session's resolution on the development of agriculture did much to stabilize pig raising during the past year, much attention was also paid to increasing the number of herbivorous animals — cattle, sheep, rabbits and bees. The breeding of more herbivorous animals has a great future. It allows making full use of China's numerous hilly districts and large grassland areas. This has become one of the focal points in speeding up China's livestock breeding. Many provinces, municipalities and autonomous regions have issued announcements to encourage commune members and collective units to breed more herbivorous animals such as cattle, sheep, rabbits and bees. The proportion of herbivorous animals within the overall livestock population has increased. Of the total number of livestock in 1980, the percentage of draught animals and sheep was 48%, an increase from 46.4% in 1979. According to the 1980 growth rate, it is estimated that by the end of 1982, herbivorous animals will make up 50% of the total livestock population. This is a good beginning in gradually changing the present state of affairs wherein grain is the staple food and pork is the principal meat.

Several regions in 1980 worked to improve livestock herd structure and increase the proportion of lambs. To increase output from herd livestock, pastoral areas in Xinjiang, Inner Mongolia, Gangsu and Sichuan have carried out the method of fattening and slaughtering lambs during their first year; and fattening and slaughtering veal calves at 18 months.

This measure has already achieved initial results. Over one million lambs have been put on the market. Notable results were achieved when big-tail lambs in Xinjiang were fattened and slaughtered in the year they were born: the number of lambs slaughtered in Xinjiang in 1977 was 75,000; the figure rose to 100,000 in 1978; to 170,000 in 1979; and to 300,000 in 1980. This method was also applied to fine-wool Xinjiang sheep, of which 340,000 were fattened and slaughtered last year. The proportion of ewes of slaughtering age has increased from 56% in 1956 to 65% in 1980.

In summer and autumn, forage grass grows quickly, making these seasons suitable for breeding and fattening livestock. To make full use of these characteristics, new methods have been found to economically and effectively utilize our country's rich grassland and livestock herd resources.

2. *The construction of livestock breeding centres in 1980.*

The construction of livestock breeding centres is a reliable means of raising the output and commodity quantities of livestock products. The building of grass-feeder centres began in 1978. After two-three years of effort, centres for breeding commodity cattle, milk goats and lambs have begun to take shape and to supply commodities to the market.

In the last two years or more, 140 commodity-cattle centres in 22 provinces, municipalities and autonomous regions have begun to supply the market with meat, milk and skins. Production capacities have been established as the result of a variety of measures such as improving mating techniques, clearing pasture land and altering modes of production. In 1980, the total number of breeding cattle surpassed one million, increasing by one-third over the 1979 total of 680,000; cross-bred cattle in stock were 1.4 million.

Raising milk goats has become an increasingly important livestock activity in China. The establishment of centres for raising milk goats has gone on in Shaanxi, Shandong, Henan, Hebei, Shanxi, Zhejiang, Jiangsu, Jiangxi, Sichuan and other provinces. Fuping County of Shaanxi Province was the first county centre for milk goats in China. Milk goats and milk-goat products have developed at a high speed. At the end of 1975, the number of milk goats in the country was 74,000 and output of dairy products was 455 tons; in 1979, the population had risen to 100,000 with output of dairy products at 1,000 tons — 50% more than the total national output of dairy products during the early years of the People's Republic.

Experience gained in many base counties has shown that in raising one milk goat with an annual yield of 500 kg. of milk, if one invests 1 yuan, then one may recover 4 yuan in that same year. The method generally practiced is for each household to raise one milk goat; it's yearly income of 100 yuan will suffice the family's purchases of daily necessities and clothing, as well as pay tuition fees. Further, the sale of the milk from one milk goat to a dairy products processing factory can provide the state with 68 yuan in taxes and profits per year. Cadres and masses in milk-goat base counties consider the development of milk goats to be a livestock breeding activity of small investment and great benefit to the people, the state and the collective. Milk-goat centres have expanded steadily. There are now over 2 million milk goats, double the total at the end of 1978.

3. *Experiments in modernization of livestock breeding have achieved results.*

During the past two years, in order to gain experience in modernizing livestock breeding the feeding of herbivorous animals in pastoral and mountain areas, the Ministry of Agriculture, in collaboration with 8 provinces and regions, has carried out three types of experiments in 17 counties with different types of grazing conditions: (1) modernization of grasslands; (2) comprehensive experiments in the modernization of livestock breeding (including grasslands construction, scientific breeding of livestock, mechanization of animal husbandry and prevention and cure of animal diseases); (3) experiments in integrated complexes that combine animal husbandry, industry and commerce.

These experiments involved 710 key communes, farms and production brigades. At present, most of these experimental projects have taken shape, have established a certain production capacity, have begun to play a part in production and have set examples for dissemination of results of the experiment. By 1980, a total of 4 million *mu* of grassland were enclosed with fencing; about 300,000 *mu* were seeded by aircraft; and 600,000 *mu* were planted with seeds of prime forage grass. In 1980, 615 million kg. of grass were in stock, an increase of 60% over 1977 (before the experiment).

Following its reorganization, the integrated complex of animal husbandry, industry and commerce of Ruoergai County, Aba Tibetan Autonomous Prefecture, Sichuan Province, bred more cattle and sheep, contributed more to commerce, received more dividends, accumulated more for the collective and earned more income for its commune members. The per capita income in 1980 was 200 yuan, an increase of 58 yuan compared with that prior to the experiment. The four categories of animal products under state plan have all overfulfilled the state-set allocation target. The prefecture committee set an allocation plan of 500,000 kg. of wool in 1980, and the integrated complexes supplied the five major wool-product factories in Sichuan with 590,000 kg. of wool. The output of beef, mutton, cowhide and sheepskin have all surpassed the state-fixed plans, a result that was gratifying to the state, management units and individuals.

4. *Initial work on grassland protection, utilization and construction.*

China is rich in natural grazing grounds. The total area of grasslands and grassy shoreline is 5,300 million *mu*, making up one-third of the country's total territory. Of this, 4,300 million *mu* consist of grasslands in pastoral areas; 1,000 million *mu* are grassy hills and slopes in agricultural areas; 40 million *mu* are sea beach grasslands. About 4,000 million *mu* of the grassland total can be utilized for animal husbandry.

After Liberation, feudalist ownership was abolished, mutual-aid and co-operative movements were carried out, and the policy of "protecting grasslands to develop stock-raising" was implemented. As a result, stock-raising in pastoral areas lept forward. During recent decades, however, due to an enormous increase in livestock numbers, a falling off in grassland management and construction, and disruption and sabotage by Lin Piao and the Gang of Four, we have experienced the phenomena of fertile pasturelands degenerating into wasteland and of alkaline content in soil becoming increasingly serious. Pastureland yields have been reduced by 30-50% and stock-raising for long suffered from slow growth, low quality and instability.

Since the Third Plenary Session of the 11th Party Central Committee, the party and government have stressed grassland management and construction; combining the protection and rational utilization of natural grazing grounds with the construction of large-scale man-made grasslands; putting equal stress on enclosing, building and managing lands for livestock breeding; and taking suitable measures to fit the local conditions. The party and government have placed emphasis on rotation grazing and the adequate storage of forage grass to tide over livestock during seasonal winter and spring shortages. They have systematically established forage grass centres to bring about stability, good quality and high output in animal husbandry. Up to the end of 1980, a total of 70 million *mu* of grassland had been enclosed, playing a positive role in fighting natural calamities and protecting domestic animals. At the same time, a survey of grassland resources was begun. Experimental stations for introducing and breeding superior varieties of forage grass were set up. In order to improve management of grasslands, the state started formulating a "grassland law."

Artificial grass planting has grown rapidly in recent years. In the northern provinces there are large areas under forage grass; their varieties have steadily increased and their quality has improved. Acreage in the region has increased from 5.2 million *mu* in 1976 to 6.4 million *mu* in 1977, 8.9 million *mu* in 1978 and 12 million *mu* in 1979; the average annual increase over the four years was more than 22%. According to incomplete statistics, total acreage under forage grass was about 13 million *mu* in 1980.

In 1979 and 1980, China sought to open up new channels to large-scale transformation of grassland by carrying out experiments in aerial seeding. Initial results were recorded in 14 counties (or banners) in eight provinces and autonomous regions: Inner Mongolia, Ningxia, Xinjiang, Guangxi, Hunan, Guizhou, Jilin, Shaanxi and in Beijing. In 1979, about 192,000 *mu* were seeded by plane, with the cost per *mu* coming to 0.23 yuan. The acreage under full stands of seedlings was 61,000 *mu*, making up 31.8% of the total area seeded by this method. In 1980, about 370,000 *mu* were seeded by plane. The average per-*mu* charge was 0.24 yuan. The acreage under full stands of seedlings was 156,000 *mu*, making up 42.1% of the total area seeded by plane.

5. *Improvement of forage grass seeds.*

The establishment of a system for breeding good strains of forage grass seed is an important aspect of capital investment in livestock breeding. Before 1977, wild forage grass seed collected by individuals and collectives made up the greatest proportion, while artificially cultivated grass seed only accounted for a small amount. Beginning in 1978, about 30 forage grass seed centres were set up in Inner Mongolia, Qinghai, Xinjiang, Heilongjiang, Jilin, Shaanxi, Gansu, Hebei and Henan to plant forage grasses. In 1980, while consolidating these centres, additional new seed centres were built to assist livestock breeding in the southern mountainous areas of Hunan, Hubei, Guangxi, Jiangxi, Fujian, Sichuan, Yunnan, Guizhou, Zhejiang and Jiangsu. Up to the end of 1980, state-run forage grass seed farms planted 290,000 *mu* and turned out 4 million kg. of grass seed. The total annual yield of forage grass seed was 15 million kg., not including seeds collected by individuals and collectives.

Since 1979, the State Bureau of Animal Husbandry of the Ministry of Agriculture has organized 14 agricultural and stock-raising research institutes and units to study and domesticate local and foreign grass breeds. Successful results have been achieved in some categories.

In November 1980, the State Bureau of Animal Husbandry convened a meeting on the work of growing forage grass seeds. The meeting summed up production experiences in this field and issued several documents: the National Forage Grass Seed Regional Plan (trial draft); Forage Grass Seeds Check-Up Regulations (draft); Standard for Grading Forage Grass Seeds (trial method); and Trial Prices for Several Kinds of Major Forage Grass Seeds. The meeting put forward future tasks for the planting of forage grass seeds: to consolidate and raise the level of existing work, to develop and intensify research work and to perform tasks in accord with local conditions. Such tasks would lead to the establishment of a first-rate forage grass seed breeding system that would satisfy the needs of our country's stock raising.

III. Survey of Experiences in Livestock Breeding During the Last Three Decades

Under the leadership of the Communist Party and the People's Government, the Chinese people have removed the three mountainous burdens on the heads of the Chinese peasants. In pastoral areas, they carried out policies beneficial both to herdsmen and herd owners, they implemented economic rehabilitation in both the countryside and pastoral areas; and they brought every positive factor into play in the development of livestock breeding. Cattle plague, which had prevailed in old China for many years, was eliminated in 1955, while other prevailing animal epidemics were brought under control. The first positive stage in the development of livestock rearing was completed in September 1957 with the culmination of China's First Five-Year Plan. In 1956, the sheep population had surpassed that of pigs. During the three years of recovery (1949 to 1951), the numbers of pigs, sheep and draught animals increased at annual average rates of 15.8%, 8.4% and 13.4%, respectively. During the period of the First Five-Year Plan, the average rates were 10.2%, 1.9% and 9.8%, respectively. In 1956, the State Council adopted a pig-raising policy of "private ownership and breeding with public assistance," and raised by 15% the purchasing price of live pigs. Within 1956, peasants bred an additional 60 million pigs, an increase of 70%. Thus, in 1956 the number of live pigs increased at the highest rate recorded in the three decades of New China.

During 1963-1966, the country carried out the policy of "readjustment, consolidation, filling out and raising standards," and issued a Revised Draft on People's Communes in the Rural Areas. The state took measures to stop the rash advance in agriculture and animal husbandry, implemented the pig-raising policy of "collective and individual pig-breeding, with stress on the latter." The central government adopted the "Resolution on Developing Draught Animals" and implemented the policy of rewards for hardworking stockmen. In some areas, if stockmen propogated livestock in excess of the set quota, they would receive extra payments as rewards in addition to their earned work-points. In 1965, thanks to the rapid development of animal husbandry, eggs and meat piled up in the markets. People's lives were improved by a large margin, and the physical well-being of the younger generation was enhanced. The average baby's birth-weight in Beijing increased from 2.6 kg. in 1951 to 3.1 kg. in 1965. This constituted the second period of accomplishment.

At the end of the 1970's, following the smashing of the Gang of Four and especially after the Third Plenary Session of the 11th Party Central Committee, livestock breeding lept forward as a result of correct policies that relaxed restrictions in the countryside and pastoral areas and shook off "Left" ideological trammels. Thus there emerged an excellent situation in livestock breeding which had not been known since the founding of the People's Republic.

We should sum up these experiences in order to draw useful lessions.

IV. Development Trends and Policies in Animal Husbandry

1. *To increase households, groups, and brigades engaged in specialized breeding and to provide them with superior breeds and advanced techniques.*

At present, 90% of the meat and eggs available in the market are supplied by peasant families. The conditions of household livestock breeding directly determine both supply conditions in the market and the production situation in animal husbandry. There is great potential here for further development. A good procedure is to transform household sideline production into livestock raising by special households. At present, there are over 30,000 households in Shenyang raising pigs, accounting for one-15th of the peasant population but supplying one-third of the city's total live-pig requirements.

At present, general problems in livestock breeding include large expenses, high costs and poor economic results. These problems should be addressed by attending to existing conditions, by focusing on management and by taking a long-range view. The ideal circumstance should be the simultaneous development of small, medium-sized and large enterprises, with emphasis on the smaller ones. In means of production, the emphasis should be on a combination of mechanization, semimechanization and manual operation, with primary stress on manual operation. On the system of responsibility in production, methods should be many and varied, with priority given to "specialized households." Since "specialized households" will probably, in the long run, become basic production units in livestock breeding, the state should take appropriate measures to set up comprehensive service companies. These should provide high-quality breeds, fodders mixed for different needs, measures for prevention of epidemics and other techniques. The centres can in this way encourage "specialized households" to join hands so as to bring about socialization in livestock breeding and to steadily increase social productivity.

The above measures have already been carried out in Lanzhou, Shenyang, Tianjin and other large cities. It is expected that this approach will bring about an increase in the volume of animal products supplied by the specialized households.

2. *To develop herbivorous animals, especially cattle, sheep, rabbits and bees.*

Furs of herbivorous animals are in short supply in the market. Woolen goods were often sold in the domestic market during 1980. In that year, the wool textile industry in China turned out 100 million metres of woolen goods, of which 80% were supplied to the home market. In addition, 100 million metres of chemical fibres were imported. Nevertheless, these quantities were far from adequate in meeting the people's demands. If each metre of cloth is estimated to sell at 20 yuan, then the state could recover 4,000 million yuan from the increased sales volume. Recently, the Ministry of Textiles decided to cease construction projects for cotton textiles and to concentrate on the expansion of woolen textiles. The goal is to double woolen textile production capacity by 1985. There are also increased needs for hides and skin by-products. This makes it imperative to increase the population of those herbivorous animals that supply raw materials for textiles and light industries.

3. *Livestock breeding can reap huge export profits.*

Rabbit fur and bird feathers are two large foreign exchange earners. Due to temporary shortages, we have occasionally been unable to meet orders from foreign traders. This situation is certain to stimulate growth in rabbits, sheep and feather-producing poultry.

It can be concluded that the rapid development of animal husbandry depends mainly on correct policies, scientific methods and flexible management. We should stick to set policies that are beneficial to the development of animal husbandry. We should at the appropriate time readjust the low prices for some animal products. In the management of livestock products, we should open up more channels and reduce unnecessary bureaucracy so as to enhance production and consumption.

Integration among agriculture, forestry and animal husbandry is the correct road to agricultural modernization in keeping with conditions in China. By following this road, all three sectors can help one another, develop together and achieve common prosperity.

8. CHINA'S INDUSTRY IN 1980
By Wang Haibo and Wu Jiajun

*Institute of Industrial Economics,
Chinese Academy of Social Sciences*

The place of modern industry in the national economy was very small in old China. Under the rule of the imperialists, feudalists and bureaucrat-capitalists, industrial techniques and enterprise management fell far behind levels elsewhere in the world. After the founding of socialist New China and through 30 years of arduous struggle, the extremely backward industrial outlook that had characterized the economy of old China was fundamentally changed.

After the founding of the People's Republic, bureaucrat-capitalist industries were confiscated and industries of national capitalists and individuals were transformed. Thus, socialist industry came to occupy a dominant position. China's industrial construction achieved great progress on the basis of socialist public ownership. Industrial investments during the 1952–79 period totaled 384,450 million yuan, while newly added industrial fixed assets totalled 251,111 million yuan.

With the development of industrial construction, industrial production also developed rapidly. In 1979, the total output value (calculated at 1970 constant prices) of China's industry registered 459,100 million yuan, an increase of 42.5 times compared with 1949. In the course of improving old industries, many new and developing industrial sectors — such as petrochemicals, electronics, atomic energy and space navigation — have been or are in the process of being established. The application of science and technology in the most advanced branches of China's industry — such as electronics, atomic energy, automation and lasers — has already begun. Successful experiments in nuclear detonation and in the launching and recovery of man-made earth satellites are clear indications of our attainments of new levels in science and technology. In short, during the past 30 years of construction, China has built up an independent and fairly comprehensive industrial system with relatively complete categories, considerable production capacity and a certain level of technology.

Along with the growth of industry, the number of industrial workers increased from 12.46 million in 1952 to 53.40 million in 1979. The number of workers and staff employed in industries owned by the whole people [i.e., state-owned — Ed.] increased from 5.1 million to 31.09 million, while engineers and technicians increased from 164,000 to 166,690. The rate of fixed assets per worker was 2,101.9 yuan in 1952 and 10,577.3 yuan in 1979, an increase of more than 400%. Overall labour productivity (calculated according to 1970 constant prices) was 3,004 yuan in 1949 and 11,790 yuan in 1979, an increase of 292.5%.

On the basis of developing industrial production, the wage earnings of workers have risen remarkably. The average annual wage of workers and staff members in industries owned by the whole people was 515 yuan in 1952; this figure rose to 758 yuan in 1979, an increase of 47.2%. During the same period, the general cost-of-living index for workers and staff had increased by only 22.9%. Therefore, even when deducting factors of price increases, the average wages of workers and staff still increased. The increased earnings of workers and staff is further manifested in the rise in welfare funds for labour protection and in different kinds of allowances. Welfare funds for labour protection in units owned by the whole people totalled 952 million yuan in 1952, comprising 14.1% of total wages. These funds rose to 6,691 million yuan in 1978, corresponding to 15.7% of total wages. According to calculations by relevant departments, welfare funds and various types of state allowances received by workers and staff in enterprises owned by the whole people averaged 526.7 yuan per capita in 1978, corresponding to 81.71% of the average wage paid in that year. All of these figures indicate that the livelihood of China's industrial workers and staff has improved considerably when compared with the early period after Liberation.

The development of China's industry and improvements in the livelihood of its workers and staff as indicated above clearly demonstrates the superiority of the socialist system.

I. Problems Facing China's Industrial Development in 1980

The development of China's industry in 1980 proceeded on the basis of the great successes that had been achieved during the 30 years since the founding of the People's Republic. China's industrial development in 1980, however, also faced a number of problems.

First, an irrational structure in production was

manifested by several instances of serious disproportion:

1. *The development of industry and agriculture is not well-coordinated, with agriculture seriously lagging behind industry, a fact hindering development of the national economy.*

During 1950-79, the total output value of industry increased by an annual average of 13.3%, while the total output value of agriculture increased only by 4.5% yearly.

2. *The growth of heavy industry was too fast, while light industry seriously lagged behind and was unable to satisfy the necessities of people's lives.*

During 1950-79, the output value of heavy industry increased by a yearly average of 16.5%, while the output value of light industry increased only by 11%; the proportion of output value of heavy industry in total industrial output value rose from 29.3% to 56.3%, while the proportion of output value of light industry decreased from 70.7% to 43.7%.

3. *Industries producing fuel, power and raw and semi-finished materials fell behind, while processing industries developed too quickly; as a result, the former could not satisfy the demands of economic development, while the latter's productive capacity was excessive.*

During 1953-79, the output value of excavating industries and raw and semi-finished materials industries increased by a yearly average of 10.4% and 12.4%, respectively, while the growth rate in output value of manufacturing industries reached 15%. In 1952, the share of the former two industries in the total output value of heavy industry accounted for 15.3% and 42.8%, respectively, while the output value of manufacturing took up 41.9%. By 1979, the proportion of the former two had dropped to 11.5% and 36.9%, respectively, while the latter went up to 51.6%.

During 1953-79, China's total industrial output value increased by a yearly average of 11.1%, while energy output only increased by 10%; this factor, plus serious wastage in energy consumption, caused energy to become a serious problem in the present-day economy. Today, China's capacity for producing machine tools is 3-4 times higher than the supply of steel products. Moreover, despite the existence of a large quantity of machine tools, the proportion of machine tools with capacities for rough machining is very high compared to the number of machine tools for finish machining — a condition ill-suited to demands for technological reforms of the national economy.

4. *The backwardness of the building materials industry is not suited to the needs of economic development.*

During 1953-79, the building materials industry grew by a yearly average of 11.6%, a rate just slightly higher than industry, which increased by 11.1% yearly during the same period. However, the building materials rate was lower than that of heavy industry, which grew by 13.4%.

5. *Heavy industry mainly served its own development, and not that of light industry and agriculture.*

Although the proportion occupied by steel used for agriculture and agricultural machinery within the consumption pattern for steel production increased from 6.7% in 1953 to 15% in 1979 (this proportion is not large considering the fact that China's agricultural population is enormous and the proportion of agriculture in the national economy is fairly big), steel consumption by light industry dropped from 22.5% to 12%, while that of machinery manufacturing increased from 24.6% to 29.3%. Moreover, although the proportion of electricity consumed by rural areas within overall electricity consumption of all sectors increased from 0.5% in 1952 to 11.8% in 1979 (this proportion is not large either), while the proportion of electricity used by light industry fell from 28% to 12.8%, and while the share of urban consumers dropped from 14.6% to 5.3%, the share of electricity used by heavy industry increased from 35.6% to 54%. In addition, utter discord prevailed in the ratios among various departments within heavy industry (such as the relationships between extraction and tunnelling in the oil and coal industries and between mining and smelting as well as smelting and steel rolling) and in the ratios between "bone" and "flesh" in industrial construction.

Second, the conditions of "big and all-embracing" or "small but all-embracing" were relatively prevalent in the organization of industrial production in China, while the level of specialized cooperation was very low. According to studies by the First Ministry of Machine-Building in 1978, of its 6,057 enterprises, those factories that specialized in cast iron numbered only 162; the value of cast iron was only 18% of total iron output (as compared to more than 60% in Japan). Factories specialized in forging numbered only 52, with the value of forgings comprising only 9% of total output (84% in Japan).

Third, the technical level of industrial products was very low. Referring again to the initial analysis by the First Ministry of Machine-Building of the technical levels of its machinery and electrical products, more than 60% of present products were at the technical level of the 1940's and 1950's; more than 30% were at the level of the 1960's; and less than 5% were at the level of the 1970's.

Fourth, the cultural, technical and management level of workers and staff was low, while the proportion of technical personnel was too small. According to a survey of 20 million workers and staff at the end of 1979, 80% did not reach the cultural level of junior middle school; 7.8% of them were illiterate or semi-literates. Moreover, the technical level of workers was low, with most of their technical grades below the third grade. The majority of management personnel lacked management knowledge of modern enterprises. Technical personnel in industrial departments made up only 2.8% of the total number of workers and staff, many of them never having received higher education.

Fifth, the economic results of industrial construction and production were very poor. The amount of investment required for every yuan added to the national income during the period of the First Five-Year Plan was 1.68 yuan; during the period of the Fourth Five-Year Plan it was 3.76 yuan, an increase of more than 100%. The profits realized for every 100 yuan of expenditures by state-owned industries and enterprises with independent accounting during the period of the First Five-Year Plan were 22.86 yuan; in the period of the Fourth Five-Year Plan, the proportion was 16.12 yuan, a decrease of nearly 30%.

The causes for the problems mentioned above were:

1. The "Left" error long prevailing in the guidance of economic work, mainly manifested in the blind pursuit of high targets in production, unusually high targets in heavy industry, and especially high targets in the steel industry. This relegated to second place the sectors of agriculture, light industry, urban construction, scientific research and education, while heavy industry was reduced to serving its own development. This sort of error had taken place in 1958 and again in 1970; and in 1978, inasmuch as "Left" guiding thought had not yet been eradicated, the same error took place once again.

2. China's economic management system is marked by a high degree of centralization of state power. This system gives priority to administrative management, under which enterprises become the accessories of state administrative organs, thus seriously hampering the initiative of the enterprises.

3. China's enterprise-management level, which was in any case low, was seriously sabotaged by Lin Biao and the Gang of Four during the "cultural revolution" period. Therefore, the management of many enterprises became mired in a state of chaos.

In accordance with the situations described above, the Party Central Committee after its Third Plenary Session put forward the guiding principle of readjustment, restructuring, consolidation and improvement with readjustment as the central link. Thus it was on the aforementioned industrial basis and under the guidance of this central principle that industry in 1980 developed.

II. Achievements of China's Industrial Development in 1980

1. Some Characteristics of Industrial Production and Construction in 1980. Under the guiding principle and on the basis of achievements made in 1979, China achieved notable successes in industrial development during 1980. In 1980, China's total value of industrial output was 499,200 million yuan, fulfilling 103.1% of the state plan, and representing an increase of 8.7% over the previous year.

The important characteristics of industrial development in 1980 were:

1. *The growth rate of light industry far exceeded that of heavy industry.* The output value of light industry was 234,400 million yuan, an increase of 18.4% over the previous year, while the output value of heavy industry was 264,800 million yuan, an increase of 1.4%. After 1979, the proportion of output value of light industry in the total industrial output value rose even further, increasing from 43.1% in 1979 to 46.9% in 1980.

2. *Energy conservation achieved remarkable success.* Although the total output of the three kinds of energy — coal, oil and electricity — increased by only 1.9% in 1980, the value of industrial output increased by 8.7%. That meant that a large portion of the energy that would have been required for the growth of industrial production was compensated for through conservation.

3. *Housing units completed and under construction during 1980 reached an all-time high.* Overall housing under construction totalled 156 million sq. m. of floor space, an increase of 25.8% over 1979. Of this total, completed units accounted for 82.30 million sq.m., an increase of 31.6% over the previous year and exceeding the

three-year total for completed housing from 1974 to 1976. The rate of housing completions was 52.7%, registering another increase over the 1979 rate of 50.4%.

All of these figures indicate that China's industrial front achieved remarkable success again in 1980.

2. *The Readjustment of Industry in 1980.* The foremost achievements of industry in 1980 consisted of the positive results yielded by the readjustment of both industry and the entire national economy.

There were two main aspects of the readjustment: one was the readjustment of industrial structure; the other was the readjustment of distribution structure. The first readjustment mainly focused on ratios and relationships among agriculture, light industry and heavy industry:

1. *Following the Third Plenary Session of the 11th Central Committee of the Communist Party of China, a series of measures to boost agricultural development were adopted by the state.*

These included implementation of a series of economic policies of the party in rural areas; the state strengthened financial support to agriculture; the purchase prices of farm and sideline products were raised by a relatively large margin; and portions of rural taxation were reduced or remitted, thus fostering rehabilitation in the rural areas. These measures greatly aroused the enthusiasm of the peasants. And, once funding had been provided, agricultural production began to develop at a relatively rapid pace. The fairly quick development of agriculture provided conditions for faster development of industry and especially light industry related to grain, non-staple foods and raw and semi-finished materials. In 1980, the total value of farm and sideline products purchased by commercial units amounted to 67,700 million yuan, an increase of 15.4% over 1979 (or about 9% if adjusted for price-increase factors), a year in which such purchases also registered a large increase. In 1980, the amount of cotton purchased reached a record 2.6 million tons, an increase of 25.8% over the previous year.

2. *The Party Central Committee and the State Council had stated at the Second Session of the Fifth National People's Congress that for the years of readjustment, one of the major aims is "to achieve a growth rate for the light and textile industries equal to or slightly greater than that of the heavy industry."*

In order to give priority to the development of the light and textile industries, the State Council decided to enforce the principle of "six priorities" for textiles and light industry in 1980, giving priority to the supply of raw and semi-finished materials, fuels and electricity; to measures for tapping potential, renovation and transformation; to capital construction; to bank loans; to foreign exchange and imports of technology; and to transport and communications services. In 1980, raw and semi-finished materials used for production by textiles and light industry for the most part enjoyed a remarkable increase over the previous year. For example, timber for the papermaking industry increased by 7%; cast iron for sewing-machine production by 25%; supplies of copper, aluminum, zinc for light industries were to increase by a range of 8.7% to 43.3%; and soda and caustic soda for the textile industry were to increase by 7.2% and 18.8%, respectively. Imports of industrial raw materials for textiles and light industry amounted to U.S.$2,375 million in 1980, an increase of 83% over 1979; the proportion of these imports to the gross total of imported commodities increased from 8.4% in 1979 to 12.8% in 1980.

Investments in textiles and light industry in 1980 amounted to 4,360 million yuan, an increase of 1,330 million yuan over the previous year; their proportion of total investments increased from 6.1% in 1979 to 8.1% in 1980. In addition, the state extended foreign-exchange loans of over 200 million yuan to units in light industry and affiliated organizations for the purpose of importing advanced foreign technology and equipment. All of these measures enabled light industry to develop at a faster pace than heavy industry during 1979 and 1980.

3. *In order to readjust the serious disproportions among agriculture and light and heavy industries, the growth rate of heavy industry was further reduced over the previous year.*

Despite the growth-rate decline, the variety and range of specifications of heavy industrial products were somewhat increased and quality somewhat improved. Divisions within heavy industry, including steel, machinery, chemicals and military production, had made progress in readjusting their product allignments so as to better serve agriculture, light industry and foreign and domestic markets.

Readjustments in distribution structure sought mainly to strike a balance between accumulation and consumption.

For many years, China's accumulation and consumption had also been in a state of serious disproportion. The rate of accumulation was too high. Within the total accumulation fund, the proportion of productive accumulation was too large, while non-productive accumulation was too small; within the productive accumulation, the proportion of heavy industry was too large, while that of agriculture and light industry was too small.

This state of serious disproportion began to change somewhat in 1979 when the rate of accumulation decreased from 36.5% to 33.6%. In 1980, the rate further declined to about 32%. Following the drop of the rate of accumulation, the consumption funds of the people in towns and villages increased. In 1980, the average wage of workers and staff in enterprises owned by the whole people was estimated at 803 yuan, an increase of 13.9% over 1979; the average wage of workers and staff of collective enterprises in cities and towns was estimated at 624 yuan, an increase of 15.1% over the previous year. Even when accounting for the fact that the general index of retail prices across the country in 1980 rose by 6% over 1979, the growth in the average wage of workers and staff was still relatively large.

Of total investments in capital construction in 1979, the proportion of investments in productive construction decreased from 82.6% in 1978 to 73%, while that of nonproductive construction increased from 17.4% to 27%. Within the latter category, investments in housing construction increased from 7.8% to 14.8%. In 1980, investments in productive construction were 5,700 million yuan; their share in total investments declined to 66.3% from 73% in 1979. Investments in nonproductive construction were 18,200 million yuan, the proportion in total investments rising to 33.7% from 27% 1979; within this category, investments in housing construction were 10,800 million yuan, their proportion of total investments increasing from 14.8% in the previous year to 20% in 1980, reaching a record high in terms of both investments in housing construction and their proportion of total investments.

In 1979, the share of industrial construction investment in capital construction investments decreased to 56.4% from 61.4% in 1978. Industrial construction investment in 1980 showed a slight increase over 1979, but its share in total capital construction investment decreased from 56.4% in 1979 to 54.1%. In 1980, investments in capital construction for heavy industry totalled 24,800 million yuan, about 300 million yuan less than in 1979; their share of the total investment went down to 46.1% from 50.3% in 1979. The investment proportion of chemicals, machinery and defence industries all fell dramatically as compared with 1979. Investments in textiles and light industry amounted to 4,360 million yuan, topping the previous year's figure by 1,330 million yuan; their share of total investments rose from 6.1% in 1979 to 8.1% in 1980.

These readjustments in the structure of production and distribution assured the development of China's industry, particularly the more rapid development of light industry in the fields of raw materials, energy, equipment and funds. Moreover, it provided conditions for improving the livelihood of workers and staff (including housing levels) in commodity supply and monetary income, thus boosting the working incentive of workers and staff and expediting the development of China's industry.

3. Reform of the Industrial Management System in 1980. Reform in the economic management system also gave an important impetus to industrial development in 1980:

1. *Carrying out of experiments on enlarging the decision-making power of enterprises.*

In the past two years, experiments in enlarging the decision-making power of enterprises at selected sites had made successive advances and had attained a certain magnitude. In 1980, more than 6,000 state-owned industrial enterprises of various provinces, municipalities and autonomous regions (excluding Tibet), participated in the experiment, comprising 15% of the 42,000 industrial enterprises operating under the state plan and accounting for 60% of total industrial output value and 70% of total profits. These enterprises enjoyed varying degrees of decision-making authority in matters of retaining certain portions of profits, production plans, sales of products, trial production of new products, use of funds, reward methods and organizational set-ups and personnel. Since 1980, a few enterprises had been selected by some provinces, municipalities and autonomous regions as experimental units to practice the substitution of taxes for profits, independent accounting and assumption of sole responsibility for their own profits and losses under the guidance of state plans. According to incomplete statistics, through the end of 1980, units engaging in this experiment included a city (Liuzhou), a corporation (the Shanghai Light Industry Machinery Corporation) and more than 80 individual enterprises.

Following their achievements in 1979, enterprises with enlarged powers continued to register remarkable economic results in 1980. During that year, some enterprises with widened powers worked below capacity and had to cope with unfavourable factors such as rising prices of raw and semi-finished materials and shortages of energy. These factors posed certain difficulties for these enterprises in their quest to fulfil production and financial income plans. However, their wider authority to a certain extent helped bring about integration of the strengths, the responsibilities and profits of the enterprises; it linked the enterprises' economic interests with results gained from their management of production; and it fused interests of the state with those of the enterprises. As a result, the enterprises gained in inner resolve. With the unfolding of competition, the enterprises were placed under external pressure. Therefore, the enterprises' initiative was brought into full play, enabling the vast majority of them to achieve increased production and increased income.

According to preliminary statistics from 5,777 experimental enterprises (not including those units experimenting in assuming sole responsibility for their profits and losses) belonging to local industries of 28 provinces, municipalities and autonomous regions, total industrial output value came to 165,350 million yuan, an increase of 6.8% over the previous year; profits realized were 33,360 million yuan, an increase of 11.8%; profits turned over to the state were 29,000 million yuan, an increase of 7.4%. On the basis of increased production and increased income, the integration of the interest of the state and that of the enterprise was realized. Of the profits of 33,360 million yuan realized by afore-mentioned enterprises, 29,000 million yuan were turned over to the state, occupying 87% of their total profits; 3,330 million yuan were kept by the enterprises, occuying 10% of their profits; the remaining 3% went to repayment of loans and subsidies. Whereas enterprises outside of the experiment during 1980 had resorted to the method of drawing down on enterprise funds, enterprises in the experiment actually earned excess funds of 1,240 million yuan, occupying 35.2% of their increased profits of 3,520 million yuan; moreover, a large portion of these increased profits went to the state. This indicates that expanding enterprises' decision-making powers had brought about increased production and increased income, with the income of both the state and the enterprises enhanced.

2. Implementation of market regulation under guidance of the state plan.

In the past two years, reforms were carried out in the management systems for planning, materials and commerce, and market regulation was put into effect under guidance of the state plan. The main purpose was to gradually reduce the planned targets in production, permitting the enterprises to work out their supplementary production plans after fulfilling the state plan in accordance with market needs and their own conditions, thus bringing about a preliminary change of the situation in which state-owned departments of materials and commerce held a monopoly over management, allotment of materials and purchases and marketing of products. The new reforms permitted free purchasing and marketing of a certain segment of materials and commodities. This played a positive role in impelling the enterprises to broaden the avenues of production, to compensate for deficiencies, to readjust the orientation of products, to transform the structure of products, to readjust the relationship between production and demand, to promote the readjustment and to activate the economy. The reforms also played a role in spurring the enterprises to strengthen management, improve the quality of products, increase the variety of products, decrease the cost of production, raise labour productivity, improve the style of management and provide good technical service. Finally, it helped to broaden the channels of distribution, reduce the links in distribution, tighten the relationship between purchasing and marketing, and invigorate the market. As indicated above, one clear sign of the serious disproportion in China's national economy was surplus production in the machinery industry. The implementation of market regulation under the guidance of the state plan played a beneficial role in changing this situation. For example, Changchun, as a municipality chiefly engaged in the machinery industry, has had to confront a situation of a serious reduction in its production tasks. However, the Changchun machinery industry was able to compensate for this fall-off by adopting a series of measures for taking the initiative and contracting for processing, increasing the variety of their products, improving their performance, raising quality and enlarging their own role in marketing their products. Thus, they not only developed production but also raised labour productivity. From January to November 1980, labour productivity across the municipality increased by 5.6% over the same period in 1979 (the machinery industry increased by 6.9%). All of these results were inseparable from the introduction of market regulation under guidance of the state plan.

3. Implementation of the reorganization and integration of industries and enterprises.

For the last two years, experiments have been undertaken to reorganize industries according to the principle of coordination among specialized departments. In this vein, a group of specialized corporations, general plants and technological coordination centres were established. According to recent statistics from 28 provinces, municipalities and autonomous regions (except Tibet), 1,973 specialized corporations and general plants (including 225 experimental enterprise-type corporations) had been established; in addition, 19,173 enterprises had been organized, constituting 5.38% of the total number of enterprises in these 28 administrative divisions. Within these totals, the three big municipalities of Beijing, Tianjin and Shanghai had already established 278 corporations and general plants, with 4,548 enterprises participating — making up 31% of the total enterprises in the three municipalities. Moreover, some localities broke down the limitations of ownership by regions, departments and trades and organized more than 3,300 economic integrated bodies of different forms such as cooperation in operation, joint operation and domestic "compensatory trade," with 8,000 enterprises participating.

The reorganization and integration of industrial enterprises began to alter the organization of industrial production and to break through the presently dissected economic management system, thus promoting the development of coordination among specialized departments, strengthening the economic links among departments and localities. This played a beneficial role role in raising the level of coordination among the specialized departments, taking advantage of their assets, tapping production potential, accelerating the technological transformation of enterprises, improving the quality of products, raising labour productivity and lowering the cost of production. It also played a supportive role in reducing production capacity for unwanted products, enhancing production capacity of products in short supply and readjusting the structure of industries and products.

In 1952, there were 25,878 factories of all types in Shanghai with a total labour productivity of 6,288 yuan; profits and tax receipts created for the state by workers and staff for the year averaged 1,200 yuan per capita. Since then, Shanghai has established certain key new industries on the one hand and, on the other, has carried out, on four successive occasions, fairly large-scale reorganization schemes among existing enterprises. By the end of 1980, factories throughout the city were merged and reorganized into 6,770 units, a reduction in number of nearly 75% over 1952. During the same period, however, total labour productivity rose by 370%, with profits and tax receipts created by workers and staff per capita increasing by an average of 650%.

4. *Carrying out experiments to reform the industrial management systems of county-level enterprises.*

According to incomplete statistics, current experiments to reform the industrial management systems of county-level enterprises are underway in 125 counties (or cities) of 25 provinces (or municipalities). The experimental work of Qingyuan County of Guangdong Province had taken a fairly early start, and gained some experience in this regard. In the past, this county had only 17 state-owned industrial enterprises, with 6,000 workers and staff; they functioned under the administration of eight bureaus. The economic commission and bureaus were in charge of production but were not in charge of personnel, finance and materials, while other multiple departments with responsibility for personnel, finance and materials were not in charge of production. An industrial management system with so many administrative levels seriously handicaps the initiative of enterprises. In 1979, Qingyuan County took steps to restructure this system. The restructuring resulted in the abolition of the bureaus. Personnel, finance, materials, production, supplies and marketing activities of the enterprises, which had formerly been subordinated under different bureaus, were shifted to the direct management of the county's economic commission. Tasks for enterprises by upper level departments were now exclusively set by the economic commission, which transferred a part of its power to the enterprises. The enterprises now had the right to draw and retain a portion of profits, to liquidate fixed assets, to set production tasks outside the plan, to sell products exceeding quotas, to select a bonus system and reward measures and to recruit, penalize and dismiss workers; they also had the right to establish new organizations and to administer their personnel affairs. Although this sort of restructuring was preliminary, it achieved good results. In 1979, profits realized by local state-owned industrial enterprises across the county came to 4.25 million yuan, three times the figure of 1978. In 1980, under conditions of rising prices for raw and semi-finished materials and fuels, insufficient production tasks in portions of enterprises and energy shortages, profits realized still came to 5.424 million yuan, a 26.7% increase over 1979. In 1979, the nationwide profit rate of output value was 9.3 yuan, an increase of 170% over 1978; it reached 11.14 yuan in 1980, an increase of 19.7% over 1979.

For a long time, under the guidance of "Left" thinking, collectively-owned industries were too quickly "escalated" to the category of state ownership, thus seriously handicapping the development of collectively owned industries. Collective ownership was in fact not only the dominant economic practice in rural areas, but also had great potential for development in the cities. After the Third Plenary Session of the 11th Central Committee of the Communist Party of China, such "Left" errors began to be put right, and the recovery and development of collectively owned industries achieved remarkable progress. In 1979, the number of workers employed by collectively owned industries in the cities and towns came to 22,735,000, an increase of 2,255,000, or 11%, over 1978. In 1980, the figure soared to 24,250,000 an increase of 1,515,000, or 6.7%, over the previous year. The development of the collectively owned economy has played an important role in promoting China's industrial development. In 1980, China's total industrial output value reached 499,300 million yuan, an increase of 40,100 million yuan over 1979; of the 1980 figure, industries owned by the whole people occupied about 60% and collectively owned industries, around 40%. It should be pointed out that at present in the industrial output value of China's second light industry system, collectively owned industries account for more than 90%, while in the industrial output value of the light industry system, the industrial output value of the second light industry system accounts for more than 50%. The development of collectively owned industries, therefore, is of special significance to the development of China's light industry.

4. The Consolidation and Improvement of Industries in 1980. The growth of industry in 1980 was also due to the consolidation of enterprises. In the consolidation of enterprises, new successes were achieved in 1980. These included:

1. *A further step was taken to readjust and strengthen administration in the enterprises.*

A number of cadres who were well versed in political ideology, familiar with their field of work and techniques, knew how to manage the business at hand and were in the prime of life were promoted to leading positions; some cadres who were incompetent were removed; and the structure of cadre contingents underwent preliminary improvement. According to incomplete results from Beijing, Tianjin, Shanghai, Liaoning, Sichuan and Hubei, leading cadres proficient in technology and management now comprised about half of the membership of the leading groups in key enterprises; their average age, 53, was somewhat lower than the mean; their average culturel levels were raised somewhat, with about one-third of the cadres having received college or secondary professional school educations.

2. *A strict system of responsibility began to be established.*

The system of responsibility with the factory director responsible for the entire enterprise as the core was strengthened. The factory director was now to take full charge of organizing and directing the production of the enterprise; the general engineer was to take charge of the technical work of production; and the general accountant was to take charge of financial work. Each link at every level as well as every position and every process was to acquire a clear measure of responsibility. The situation prevailing in many enterprises in the past, in which only collective leadership was advocated with no assignment of personal responsiblity, began to be changed.

3. *The basic work of enterprise management was consolidated and strengthened.*

About 4,000 enterprises practiced overall quality control — that is, the control of quality throughout the process, from design, trial manufacture and production through to utilization.

4. *The enterprises generally strengthened their economic accounting.*

Some enterprises systematically conducted an overall economic accounting for the entire factory, reviewing the entire production process with the participation of all workers and staff members. As a result, they accumulated some useful experience:
A. They established and strengthened the three-tier accounting system comprising the factory, workshops and teams and groups; B. They strengthened cost management and financial management; C. They practiced the delineation of norms — the major norms for technical economy in the enterprise were divided among relevant administrative offices, workshops and teams and groups down to the level of machines and individuals; D. They checked and confirmed distribution fund quotas and the amounts of fixed funds needed by related workshops and administrative offices within the enterprise as well as those of the enterprise itself, and assessed the state of fund holdings; E. They established a periodic analysis system for economic activities of the factory, the workshops and the teams and groups; F. They gradually established a system wherein an enterprise settled its account internally. Some enterprises adopted internal methods for calculating profits and losses on their own and drew up economic contracts within the enterprise.

5. *Training work for all workers and staff was enhanced.*

Leading cadres of enterprises above the county level who were trained in rotation numbered 328,000; 50% of all large and medium-sized enterprises operated schools and some 20% of their workers and staff participated in the training.

6. *Many enterprises — especially those experimental units with widened powers — began to stress the broadening of the scope of management work.*

The previous state of affairs in which attention was paid only to production but not to marketing and only to administration but not to management began to change. Some positive results achieved in this respect have been:

A. The strengthening of marketing organizations, identifying marketing as the key link in management work, and integrating production plans with marketing plans. B. Launching timely market investigations and forecasts so as to become apprised of new conditions, changes and trends taking place in domestic and foreign markets; and thus increasing products suitable for marketing, enhancing the gains for both production and marketing. C. Strengthening the impact of scientific research, design and trial manufacture and taking full account of market information and its "feedback" to improve the design of products and their quality; and to energetically develop new products, apply new techniques and new crafts, thus reducing costs so as to achieve high quality, new varieties and low prices. D. Effectively publicizing products and actively launching various activities to serve consumers, in particular improving technical services. E. Fulfilling economic contracts with respect to requirements for quality, quantity and schedule, stressing credit for the enterprise. F. The factory director should be personally in charge of management, paying attention to information, grasping opportunities and determining management policies promptly and opportunely.

In short, the enterprise should organize production and determine management policy based on both the state plan and market demands; it should systematically establish corresponding structures and systems of management; and it should launch wide-ranging management activities that link up production with marketing.

7. *Democratic administration of enterprises has begun to be strengthened and workers and staff have begun to exercise their democratic rights as masters of their own affairs.*

According to incomplete statistics, the enterprises which have established the system of workers' congresses now number 36,200.

Consolidation of China's industrial enterprises has raised their management levels and has upgraded major standards in economic techniques. From January to November, 1980, the 60 principal norms for product quality in the ten industrial divisions averaged an 80% improvement over the corresponding period in 1979. Of the 74 major norms for material consumption, 68% showed a decline compared with the same period of the previous year. Moreover, the average labour productivity of workers and staff in state-owned industrial enterprises was valued at 12,031 yuan, a 2% increase over the previous year.

III. Challenges and Prospects for Future Work in Readjustment

In 1980, conspicuous successes had been achieved in implementing the party's guiding principle and in developing industry and the entire national economy. Nevertheless, some latent crises emerged: Since 1980, some fairly large financial deficits have appeared, leading to the over-issuance of bank notes and price increases for a large number of commodities. If no remedies had been taken, large financial deficits would have again emerged in 1981, and the entire economic situation would deteriorate further. Such an occurance would influence political stability.

Fundamentally, these problems were due to the long-term influence of "Left" thinking in economic work, a tendency that had brought about serious disproportions in the national economy. Since the party's Third Plenary Session, the Central Committee and the State Council have determined to carry out the guiding principle for the national economy that takes readjustment as the core. This ought to bring about a basic turning point in China's economic development. However, this guiding principle was not effectively implemented, as evidenced by the fact that the general scale of capital construction was not in any way reduced; construction work on some of the 22 large imported projects which should have been stopped was in fact not stopped; and localities and enterprises continued to be blindly engaged in a large number of redundant construction activities.

In 1980, the total investment in capital construction throughout the country came to 53,900 million yuan, an increase of 7.8% over 1979. The level of duplicated construction, however, was quite serious. For example, China's machine-building industry had already reached a stage of serious over capacity, with the rate of utilization of machine tools in 1979 reaching only 52.1%. But according to statistics from 20 provinces, municipalities and autonomous regions, 2,018 new machinery industry enterprises were established during the first ten months of 1980. In China's textile industry, production capacity was already well above levels required by supply levels of domestic raw materials. Nevertheless, there was a further increase of 1.02 million spindles in 1979, bringing the total to 16.63 million spindles. In 1980, there was a further increase of 800,000 spindles (including 400,000 spindles added for technical reasons).

On the industrial production front, there were also serious problems of over-extension and duplication. Despite the fact that in 1979 some 3,600 enterprises either closed down, suspended operations, merged or switched to other kinds of manufacture, by the end of that year the total number of enterprises across the country registered an increase of 6,566. According to incomplete statistics from 20 provinces, municipalities and autonomous regions, during the first ten months of 1980, 4,110 enterprises ceased operation, while 13,611 enterprises were newly constructed and entered operation. Adding other factors of growth or cutbacks, the net increase in the number of enterprises by the end of October as compared with January 1980 was 7,331. In terms of the ownership of the new enterprises, those run by rural communes numbered 8,272, accounting for 60.8% of the total. In terms of their activity, most of the new enterprises were engaged in textiles and industry, using farm and sideline products as raw materials; enterprises in this category numbered 9,378, accounting for 69% of the total. The majority of those newly-constructed were small enterprises which were brought into being haphazardly and which duplicated production. They had the effect of squeezing the larger and more advanced enterprises, thus aggravating the difficulties of readjustemnt work.

Another important problem in the readjustment of industrial production was that it proved virtually impossible to cut down on products in excessive supply — especially output levels of iron and steel products with high energy consumption. The iron and steel industry is a sector marked by a huge concentration of funds and by high levels of energy consumption. Gross funds of the nation's iron and steel industry in 1979 came to 41,450 million yuan, accounting for 10.5% of total gross industrial funds; energy consumption (in terms of units of standard coal) for the year was 72.69 million tons, or 18.5% of the nation's industrial energy consumption. In other words, funds for the iron and steel industry were equal to one-half of those for light industry, while its energy consumption was one-third more than that of light industry. The planned output of steel was 33 million tons, a reduction of 1.48 million tons compared with actual output in 1979. This cut-back was designed to economize on energy and to make greater use of steel product inventories. But actual output reached 37.03 million tons, of which 5.85 million tons was derived from small and medium-sized steel mills. The latters' comprehensive energy consumption per ton was 5.02 tons, a rate 180% higher than that of the major steel factories. Thus, if the output of small and medium-sized steel factories could be reduced by 4 million tons, the equivalent of 20 million tons of standard coal could be saved in one year. The same situation prevailed in chemical fertilizers, especially in the small-scale production of synthetic ammonia.

This situation indicates that up to now, the serious disproportions long existing in our national economy had not basically changed and that this state of affairs must have taken its effect on economic results. From the perspective of state-owned industrial enterprises within the state budget, profits realized for the output value of each 100 yuan in 1980 were 16.7 yuan, an increase of 3.2 yuan over the 1976 level of 13.5 yuan; but this represented an increase of only 0.1 yuan as compared with the 16.6 yuan ratio of 1979 and was 8 yuan lower than the 24.7 yuan ratio achieved in 1957. The profits realized from sales income for each 100 yuan worth of products were 17.3 yuan, an increase of 3.1 yuan over the 14.3 yuan ratio of 1976; but this was an increase of only 0.1 yuan as compared with the 17.2 yuan ratio of 1979, and a reduction of 5.8 yuan as compared with the 23.1 yuan level of 1957. Circulating funds for each 100 yuan of output value came to 31.2 yuan in 1980, a reduction of 7.3 yuan from the 38.5 yuan level of 1976; but this was a reduction of only 0.8 yuan as compared with the 32 yuan ratio of 1979, and an increase of only 3.8 yuan as compared with the 27.4 yuan level of 1957. According to our calculations, if tax revenues and profits realized for each 100 yuan of funds in state-owned industrial enterprises were raised to the average level of 31.8 yuan achieved during the period of the First Five-Year Plan, then tax revenues and profits could realize additional increases of 20,000 million yuan; if circulating funds for each 100 yuan of output value could be reduced to the average level of 19.6 yuan of the First Five-Year Plan period, then tens of billions of yuan in circulating funds could be saved.

In order to further implement the readjustment policy for industry, great efforts must be made in the following respects in future:

1. *To further compress investments in capital construction.*

Construction projects (including imported projects) not already provided with construction means or that have not yet entered the construction stage must be suspended resolutely; in addition, duplicated construction projects that compete with existing enterprises for raw materials, fuel and power must also be suspended. Investments should be concentrated on construction projects of immediate necessity that are already in production; on construction projects that have been supplied with all components and that can be rapidly completed and put into operation; on construction of housing for workers and staff; and of municipal public utilities, etc. In the meantime, enterprises which turn out low-quality, high-cost, unwanted goods and that show large deficits and, especially, small, backward enterprises that compete with advanced enterprises for raw materials, fuel, power and transportation, must close down, cease operation, be amalgamated, or change over to other products — with emphasis placed on amalgamation and change-over. The state should resort to administrative intervention and to economic measures as means of accelerating this work.

2. *To ensure the large-scale growth of production in light industry this year.*

This is a critical factor in increasing financial revenues and foreign-exchange income and in stabilizing commodity prices. Therefore, the "six-priorities" principle is to be applied constantly to light industrial production this year, with the following four points to be put into effect at the same time:

A. In addition to a sizeable increase in the quantity of products, light industry must strive to improve quality, to expand variety, to transform the array of products and to enlarge the proportion of high- and middle-quality goods. B. Integrated coordination is to be organized for large-scale production centred on famous-brand goods and on goods in short supply. C. Regulating the supply of raw materials needed by light industry. For raw materials from agriculture, sideline production and animal husbandry needed by light industry — and especially those needed by large cities like Shanghai, Tianjin and Beijing — localities must guarantee supplies according to the state allotment plan. D. Industrial enterprises under collective ownership in towns are characterized by their flexibility, diversification and strong adaptability, as well as being able to absorb additional workers. Their characteristics must be fully taken advantage of, and handicrafts and other labour-intensive products should be actively developed in this sphere.

3. *Heavy industry must genuinely turn to the path of serving agriculture and light industry and, in the last analysis, of meeting people's daily needs so as to achieve healthy development for itself.*

The machinery industry, which at present mainly manufactures equipment for capital construction items, must turn to serve the technological transformation of enterprises in different trades, focusing on the conservation of energy and electricity; moreover, its production of durable consumer goods must be increased as much as possible. Similarly, the metallurgical industry, which at present mainly serves capital construction, must also revert to serving the technological transformation of the national economy, and supply various kinds of high-standard semi-finished materials for the production of durable consumer goods. The chemical industry must not deal solely with fertilizers; it should make great efforts to increase the production of different kinds of raw and semi-finished materials needed by light and textile industries. The energy industry should continue to implement the policy of laying equal stress on increasing production and practicing economy, with increasing stress on the latter during the near future. The consumption of energy must be greatly reduced through readjustment of industry and products structures and through technological transformations that save energy and electricity; a greater quantity of goods that have enjoyed good sales are to be produced with existing levels of energy. To accomplish these tasks, existing generating units that use oil must be converted to coal as soon as possible; thus, needed oil will be freed up to alleviate the serious under-capacity output of petrochemical works. In the meantime, a portion of petroleum output must be set aside for export so as to obtain foreign exchange. These revenues are to be specially used as circulating funds for the conversion of generating units.

Further readjustments in the economy in the near future will mainly seek to establish a fundamental balance in financial revenues and expenditures, to stabilize the economy and to avoid the potential crisis that has not yet emerged. But more important, through readjustment, a new path for developing our economy should be found — that is, a path that uses more limited investments to achieve better results. Of course, the pursuit of this path through sole reliance on readjustment is not enough. Even during the present period of readjustment, any restructuring that serves or enhances readjustment is to be implemented. Specifically with regard to industry, restructuring should take the following forms:

A. Those 6,000-odd enterprises that have already experimented with broadened powers of decision-making must strive to continue their experimental work and to sum up their experiences earnestly so as to perfect the various measures undertaken. The scope for this sort of experimentation will not be enlarged during 1981. For those enterprises which have not joined the experiment, the enterprise fund system is to be enforced as usual; meanwhile, they may apply the method of assuming responsibility for a given task until it is completed. Enterprises and cities which have experimented with "substituting taxation for profit, with independent accounting and assuming sole responsibility for their profits and losses" must continue carrying on with the experiment to gain experience from it. C. Market regulation must be carried on under the guidance of the state plan. The departments in charge should strengthen the work of market forecasting and use necessary administrative intervention so as to avoid acting blindly. D. This is the opportune moment to take advantage of the success of readjustment in actively carrying out the reorganization and integration of enterprises. Various forms of economic integration are to be organized according to the principle of coordination among specialized departments and of economy and rationality, through integration from the bottom up and through leadership and coordination from the upper authorities, and by means of combining economic measures with requisite administrative interventions. E. Experimental work in restructuring the leadership system of some enterprises should be carried out earnestly in order to obtain experience. But all enterprises should stabilize their leadership systems in cases of those where the director of a factory still takes responsibility for production under the leadership of the party committee. Party leadership in such factories must be improved and strengthened conscientiously; the factory director is to take full responsibility for the administrative work of the enterprise, with the principle of democratic management properly taken into account. F. Experiments in restructuring the industrial management system should be carried out on the county level.

If the above-mentioned course is to be attained, the consolidation and management of the several hundred thousand existing enterprises must be carried out, especially in the case of the several thousand large and medium-sized enterprises. For the present, the following tasks should be carried out in due course: A. Continue to consolidate and build the leadership body. B. Earnestly consolidate the basic work and actively practice overall economic accounting and overall quality control. C. Energetically comprehend the tasks of management. D. A rational award system is to be implemented; awards should be assessed by means of points registered on the basis of responsibility and examination systems as well as by strengthening quota controls and should be calculated according to the principle of "to each according to his work." Rewards paid to workers and staff must be strictly commensurate with the results of production and management and with overfulfilment of labour quotas by the workers and staff; and egalitarianism must be resolutely avoided. E. Great efforts should be made to provide training to all workers and staff. F. Strengthen and improve ideological and political work. G. Earnestly launch activities to emulate Shanghai and its progress. H. Lastly, equipment renewal and technological transformation of existing enterprises — especially equipment for conserving energy — must be carried out methodically and systematically.

We believe that if the path put forward by the Central Committee of the Communist Party and the State Council is followed and provided that the guiding principle for the national economy centered on readjustment is implemented resolutely, not only can the existing potential crisis be completely overcome, but also the long-surviving errors of "Left" tendencies can be fundamentally eradicated — with the result that we can march forward on the healthy track of economic development. China's socialist modernization has a very bright future.

9. CHINA'S LIGHT INDUSTRY
By the Policy Research Office,
Ministry of Light Industry

Light industry in China mainly provides consumer goods for daily use. It is closely linked to the provision of clothing, food, daily necessities, housing and communications to hundred of millions of people in China. China's light industry is an important sector of the national economy, with a great number of divisions, enterprises, workers and staff members. The development of light industry plays an active role in improving people's livelihood, bringing forth flourishing markets, withdrawal of currency from circulation, expanding exports, increasing financial revenues and foreign exchange, as well in promoting sound development of the entire national economy.

I. Contrasts Between Present and Past Conditions in Light Industry

Early Contributions. China has a long history and is the home of one of the world's earliest civilizations. The history of many light industrial products can be traced back several hundred to several thousand years ago. China's art of painted earthenware and the technique of making salt from sea water both began in the neolithic age. In the Shang Dynasty of 3,000 years ago, handicrafts such as bronze ware were relatively well-developed. The invention of paper, porcelain and lacquerware in China made outstanding contributions to disseminating culture and enriching people's lives throughout the world.

Pre-Liberation Conditions. As a result of its long-term suffering from feudal rule and due to imperialist invasion, brutal exploitation and oppression in the mid-19th century, old China's modern light industry developed very slowly. By 1949, the total national output value of light industry amounted to only 4,380 million yuan (calculated at 1970 constant prices, excluding handicrafts, textiles), yielding only 8.9 yuan per capita.

At that time, the varieties of light industrial products were few and outputs low. Even the highest pre-Liberation output was very limited. For example, raw salt had reached 3,918,000 tons (1943); sugar, 414,000 tons (1936); machine-made paper and paperboard, 165,000 tons (1943); and cigarettes, 2,363,000 cases (1947). By 1949, the output of light industrial products had been reduced by one-third to one-half compared with previous record outputs.

Developments Since the Founding of New China. After the founding of the People's Republic of China, under the leadership of the Communist Party of China and the people's government, workers and staff members of light industry worked hard and diligently to resume production. By 1952, the output of major light industrial products surpassed the previous highest levels in history. During the Five-Year Year Plan, the party's policy was carried out in socialist transformation of capitalist industry, commerce and handicrafts; in the realization of joint state-private operation of entire trades; and in the cooperative transformation of the handirafts industry. As a result, the country's productive potential was liberated from the yoke of the old relationships of production. At the same time, capital construction was carried out in a planned way; productive capacity was expanded; and light industry underwent great changes. Output increased at an average annual rate of 14.3% during these five years.

During the Second Five-Year Plan, due to the influences of arbitrary and impracticable directives and to boasting and exaggeration, as well as to the "tendency to bring about the transition to communism prematurely," production suffered a serious setback. In 1962, the total output value of light industry was 3% below that of 1957. Later the policy of readjustment, consolidation, filling out and raising standards was implemented. Light industrial production again picked up rapidly. From 1963 through 1965, output increased at an average rate of 13.1% per year.

During the ten years of the "cultural revolution," light industrial production again suffered a very serious setback. The management of enterprises was chaotic, the quality of products declined, their variety was reduced, labour productivity fell, production costs were raised and the deficits of enterprises grew as never before. The time needed for construction projects was long, the rate of putting them into operation was low, and the economic results very poor.

After the Gang of Four was smashed in 1976, and particularly after the Third Plenary Session of the 11th Central Committee of the Communist Party of China, production underwent a steady increase at a relatively high speed. Variety and quality showed marked improvement and economic results gained.

Present Product Lines and Status of Light Industry. At present, 43 trades function under the administration of the Ministry of Light Industry. These include: paper-making, salt-making, sugar refining, cigarettes, bicycles, sewing machines, clocks and watches, enamelware for daily use and ceramics, glassware for daily use, electric bulbs, photosensitive materials, dry batteries, three types of glue (bone glue, hide glue and gelatin), articles for cleaning, essences and perfumes, toothpaste, matches, printing ink, typewriters, pens, alcoholic beverages, canned foods, dairy products, foodstuffs, gourmet powders, plastic products, leather, furs and fur products, arts and crafts products, carpets, toys, hardware for daily use, tools and hardware for construction, electric household appliances, weighing apparatus, clothing, shoes and hats, stationery, sporting goods, furniture, bamboo products, rattan and palm fibres, miscellaneous goods for daily use, special daily necessities for national minorities and machinery for light industry.

According to 1980 statistics, there were 69,000 light industrial enterprises in China with 11.18 million workers and staff members. Total output value was 96,100 million yuan.

Key Growth Indices Since 1949. Since the founding of the People's Republic, the path that light industry has taken has been tortuous. Nevertheless, it has achieved remarkable success and has undergone relatively enormous changes.

The speed of development of New China's light industry has by far exceeded that in old China. Total output value in 1980 reached 96,100 million yuan, nearly 21.9 times that of 1949, and yielding an average annual increase of 10.5%. The 1980 total was 9.6 times that of 1952's output of 9,960 million yuan, and since then has had an average rate of increase of 8.4%. This rate of increase not only far exceeded that of old China, but also surpassed that of many other countries. The output of all major light industrial products increased by wide margins. According to the statistics for 37 kinds of products, 23 varieties increased at an average rate of more than 10% every year during the past 30 years. The number of bicycles manufactured in 1980 totalled 13,024,000 and sewing machines came to 7,678,000 — both totals ranking first in the world.

Geographic Distribution. In China's coastal and interior cities, light industry has undergone significant changes. Shanghai has become an important centre for production, exporting and scientific research in light industry. Shanghai's total output value in light industry amounted to 12,380 million yuan in 1980, accounting for 12.9% of the national total and ranking first in China. Provinces ranked after Shanghai were Guangdong, Shandong, Jiangsu, Liaoning, Zhejiang and Sichuan; in each, the total value of light industrial output exceeded 5,000 million yuan. There was also notable progress in the hinterlands and remote border provinces which previously had weak foundations in this sector. During the past 30 years, for example, output of light industry in Guangxi Zhuang Autonomous Region increased at an average annual rate of 11.1%, higher than the national growth rate. At present, Guangxi's output of refined sugar accounts for about one-sixth of total national output and ranks second in the country. Its canned products account for one-tenth of the national total and occupy fourth place in the country.

Owing to the inland development of light industry, production areas have been enlarged nationwide. During the early years after Liberation, only three or four provinces manufactured bicycles, sewing machines and clocks; toothpaste, thermos bottles and fountain pens were produced only in five or six provinces. Now, the production of most of these products, which are planned by the state and by the ministry concerned, has been extended to 27 or 28 provinces, municipalities and autonomous regions.

Growth in Variety and Product Diversity. The basic categories of light industry in New China are now complete, whereas in old China these were very few. Before Liberation, not only were the categories of light industry very few, but even the spare parts for some products and materials, as well as equipment for special purposes, had to be imported. Scientific research and professional training were almost non-existent.

Since the birth of New China, the structure of light industry has gradually been perfected, trades are relatively complete, and complete arrays of products and lines exist within the trades. Education, scientific research and machine manufacture in service of light industry have been initiated. New manufacturing sectors for watches, photosensitive materials, essences and perfumes, synthetic detergents, fatty acid, household electrical appliances, etc. have been successively developed or set up, while old trades have also developed with higher technical levels or new products. For instance, the paper industry has evolved a good assortment of papers for technical use and can produce basically all kinds of paper for domestic needs. The salt industry has developed a salt chemical industry. The dry battery industry has developed silver and zinc cells. The electric light and lighting industry has developed fluorescent lamps and a variety of special lamps. Industries producing hardware for daily use and musical instruments have developed electronic products. The productive capacity of materials, semi-finished products and spare parts for special purposes has been augmented within all trades and the creation of comprehensive production lines has been strengthened.

Take the clock and watch industry, for example: a comprehensive production capacity has been established — from the basic materials, spare parts (gem bearings, shockproofing, hairsprings and mainsprings) of watches and clocks to complete movements and machine tools for special purposes, as well as scientific research. A complete production line for the electric light and lighting industry has also been built up — including tungsten and molybdenum materials, lamp holders and fluorescent powder. Photographic gelatin, base paper and most of the film base of the sensitive-materials industry are self-supplied.

Education and Research. Educational programs, scientific research units and machine manufacturing that serve production and construction in light industry have been built from scratch. Higher and medium levels of training at institutes and schools of light industry, as well as training of workers and staff members, have been gradually developed. There are now 13 colleges of light industry, 10 comprehensive engineering institutions of higher learning with courses specializing in light industry, and over 70 secondary technical schools. Since the founding of the People's Republic, more than 17,000 university graduates and 29,000 technical secondary school graduates have been trained for light industry. There are now 341 scientific and technological research institutes within the system of light industry throughout the country; these have more than 27,000 workers and staff members. There are also a number of professional researchers engaged within large and medium enterprises. Quite a number of exceptional technical innovators have emerged.

Technological Development. In the early period after Liberation, the annual output of light industrial machinery only aggregated several hundred tons; today, however, various kinds of equipment for special purposes can be produced. Output aggregated 130,000 tons in 1980.

The technical level of production in New China's light industry has registered continuous growth, while that in old China was extremely backward. Apart from the handicrafts field (including art handicrafts) — which had attained a higher technological level, production techniques of light industry in old China were very low, poor in quality and limited in variety. In New China, innovations in light industrial production technology have increased steadily, the quality of products has improved, the variety of goods has increased, and a large number of products of famous brands and fine quality are now welcomed by consumers.

According to incomplete statistics, nearly 2,000 research projects have achieved important scientific results since the birth of New China; 201 items received awards at the National Science Conference convened in 1978. These achievements have played an important role in raising the level of science and technology in all fields of light industry. Some trades which were mainly characterized by manual operation have now markedly raised their levels of mechanization. For example, about 40% of sea-salt production has been mechanized or semi-mechanized, while 80% of well-ore salt production has adopted the method of vacuum evaporation. Through innovation, those trades which had been basically mechanized have since strikingly altered their production technology. The degree of mechanization in large-scale sugar plants has been raised from 50% to 90%, while single-machine automatic control has been achieved for portions of working procedures.

The Guangzhou General Flashlight Factory, which accounts for half of national output, has installed semi-automatic and automatic production in 40% of its processes. In addition, automatic production lines for glass bottles, table-tennis balls and plastic drawing-pins have also come into being. New technologies in electronics, microwaves, lasers, infra-red rays, electrodialysis and silicon-controlled rectifiers are also being applied and popularized in some fields.

Revenue Contributions and Profits. Light industry in New China is an important contributor to the state's financial revenues and is a significant source of foreign exchange. In contrast, in old China, several light industrial products had to be imported with large sums of foreign exchange. Since the founding of the People's Republic, along with supplying the domestic market, light industrial export products have increased continuously, producing a large quantity of construction funds and foreign exchange for the state. In 1980, 21,600 million yuan in profits and taxes were provided to the state by national sectors of light industry.

Since 1949, the total accumulation of profits and taxes turned over to the state totalled 261,900 million yuan. The proportion of profits and taxes from light industry in state financial revenues has been going up steadily. During the period of rehabilitation, it accounted for 5.1% and during the First Five-Year Plan, 7.7%; it accounted for 13% during the Second Five-Year Plan, and from 1963 to 1965, it made up 14.8%; the share was 15.9% in the Third Five-Year Plan; 17.5% in the Fourth Five-Year Plan; and stood at 20% in 1980.

Exports and Foreign-Exchange Earnings. Exports of light industrial products have expanded steadily. There were only 50 kinds of products for export in 1953; these have since increased to more than 700 items sold to over 150 countries and regions. By 1980, light industrial goods worth U.S.$4,000 million were exported, accounting for 24.7% of the total sum of China's foreign exchange earned from foreign trade.

Since the birth of New China, accumulated foreign exchange from light industry totalled U.S.$24,400 million. The proportion of light industrial products in the total amount of export foreign exchange has also grown continuously. During the period of rehabilitation, it accounted for 5.1%; during the First Five-Year Plan, 8.7%; during the Second Five-Year Plan, 16.6%; and from 1963-65, 19.2%; it accounted for 20.5% during the Third Five-Year Plan; for 20.7% during the Fourth Five-Year Plan; and for 26.4% in 1977, an all-time high.

Supplies to the Domestic Consumer Market. In order to meet the needs of the people's livelihood, New China's light industry has sought to provide inexpensive products of good quality, while in old China many light industrial goods were priced beyond the means of the broad masses. Since 1949, the production of light industrial goods has been greatly increased; quite a number of products are low-priced and of fine quality and have made important contributions to improving people's livelihoods and to establishing flourishing urban and rural markets.

In 1979, retail sales of products manufactured by enterprises under the Ministry of Light Industry totalled 51,180 million yuan, accounting for 35.8% of national retail sales of consumer goods. Consumer expenditures for light industrial products have demonstrably increased in comparison with the early post-Liberation period.

According to statistics from 20 major light industrial products, the average consumption volume per capita of sewing machines, watches, clocks, bicycles and aluminium pots was raised from 17 to 32 times in 1980 over 1952; consumption of electric bulbs, pencils, thermos bottles, enamel wash basins, batteries and leather and cloth shoes increased from 5 to 11 times; fountain pens, sugar, soap, enamel drinking bottles, flashlights, iron pots, cigarettes and liquor increased from 2.6 to 4 times.

In rural areas, a large quantity of sewing machines, bicycles and watches have been sold. Furthermore, goods owned by consumers have increased markedly. A bicycle was formerly called "foreign horse" in the countryside, but today in North China the peasants call it "the little donkey which does not eat grass." By the end of 1980, there were 90 million bicycles in China — one for every 11.3 persons; 43 million sewing machines — one for every 4.3 households; and 130 million watches — one for every 7.5 persons. Price discrepancies between light industrial products and farm products have been steadily minimized. The maximum retail price for salt is 0.15 yuan per catty — the days of exchanging a catty of salt for an entire decalitre of rice in the remote border areas of old China has gone forever.

II. Current Readjustments and the Speeding-Up of Development

In New China, light industry has made progress without parallel in old China. This is obvious to all.

However, for a long period the guiding policy for economic construction placed undue emphasis on the development of heavy industry, taking "steel as the key link." As a result, the development of light industry fell far short of meeting demands to improve the livelihood of the people. From 1949 to 1978, heavy industry increased 91.5-fold, while light industry increased only 20.7-fold. The proportion between light and heavy industry fell seriously out of balance.

For many years past, the supply of several industrial products for daily use fell short of demand. Most of the 66 major industrial products as listed in the national plan and by relevant departments failed to meet demands. Production technology in quite a number of light industrial enterprises is still lagging. Labour productivity is low. Some light industrial goods are poor in quality, variety and design, sometimes using out-of-date patterns that have been passed down for dozens of years.

Tasks for the Current Readjustment. In 1979, the Central Committee of the Communist Party and the State Council set forth the policy of readjustment, restructuring, consolidation and improvement. In readjusting the economy, primary attention will be given to the coordination of the proportional relationship between agriculture, light industry and heavy industry — to speed up the development of agriculture and light industry. In the past two years, in compliance with the state plan, the speed of development of heavy industry was decelerated and a series of measures adopted for the active development of light industry. Priority was given to the supply of raw materials, fuel and electricity, and measures were taken to encourage tapping potential, innovation and reform of techniques; for the provision of labour for capital construction; for granting bank loans; for expending foreign exchange and importing new technology; and for communications and transportation.

During the past two years, light industry has gradually aroused attention and obtained support from all sides and a great deal of work has been done by light industrial divisions in readjustment and restructuring. A new situation of speeding up the development of light industry has emerged throughout the country.

The total output value of light industrial production in 1979 increased by 6.8% over 1978; in 1980, it increased by 14.3%. There were large increases in the output of major products. The output of 6 of 17 major light industrial products increased by more than 20% in 1980 over 1979; and 9 products increased by 10-20%.

The output of bicycles, sewing machines, clocks and watches, cigarettes, leather and cloth shoes, clothing, glassware for daily use and electrical household appliances increased in 1980 by more than 16% over 1979, some even doubling in production. Some consumer goods, such as paper for printed materials, cleaning articles, electric bulbs, iron pots and powdered milk, have been in sufficient supply in the domestic market. The export of light industrial products also increased rapidly, registering a 18.3% rise in 1980 over 1979. While increasing production in the past two years, the divisions of light industry have given increased attention to the following:

1. *The focal point of work has shifted from the quantity and value of output to quality and variety.*

At the Third Plenary Session of the Party's 11th Central Committee emphasis was placed on shifting the focus of our work to modernization of socialist construction. By taking account of actual conditions in light industry, the Ministry of Light Industry urged departments and enterprises at all levels to raise the quality and variety of their products. Variety and quality serve as key links in developing light industry, and a relatively sound job was done. After a serious study of present conditions in quality and market demands at home and abroad, a general plan was mapped out for raising the quality of products, finding substitutes for present products and defining the objectives and measures to be adopted.

An exhibition to compare domestic and foreign products was sponsored and circulated in Beijing, Shanghai, Wuhan, Chengdu and other places. Workers and staff members of light industrial enterprises in nearby provinces or districts visited this exhibition to learn from advanced products and broaden their outlook.

Quality Control. Enterprises generally enhanced the basic work of technology and established and broadened systems of quality control. Overall quality control tests were conducted at more than 1,000 enterprises, and over 46,000 quality control units were set up.

Some major trades established quality inspection centres. In 1980, a number of national inspection centres and 26 district inspection stations were set up for quality control of 17 different products. In 1979 and 1980, the Ministry of Light Industry conducted contests to compare and assess the quality of 70 and 89 categories of products produced by comparable divisions throughout the country. The more advanced versions were praised and the less advanced were criticized.

Stress on Brand-Name Products. The production of formerly popular brands has resumed and new products created. Of 2,000 types of products of fine quality submitted from various parts of China, 28 won national gold medals, 70 won silver medals, and 815 were given certificates of merit by the Ministry of Light Industry. Products winning gold and silver medals included traditionally popular brands such as Maotai liquor from Guizhou, Wuliangye liquor from Sichuan, blue-and-white and powder-enamel porcelain from Jingdezhen in Jiangxi, under-glazed tableware and tea sets from Liling in Hunan, Xuan paper from Anhui, fine powdered ink sticks from Anhui, Zhang Xiaoquan scissors from Hangzhou, Pock-Marked Wang scissors from Beijing, and Fengchuan woolen carpets from Tianjin. Newer product brands that won awards included 28-inch PA 22-type Flying Pigeon bicycles, produced in Tianjin; 28-inch PA 13-type Forever bicycles, made in Shanghai; JA 1-1-type Butterfly household sewing machines, of Shanghai; 100-type Hero fountain pens, of Shanghai; Double Crane electronic computer paper from Shandong; Jingjiang No. 5 thermos bottles from Hubei; Hong Mei sweet condensed milk from Heilongjiang; Yilan Brand eucalyptus oil from Yunnan; pig suede leather for garments from Zhejiang; Gold Cup footballs from Tianjin; White Pigeon porous plastic slippers from Fujian; Nanhai rattan articles from Guangdong; drawnwork table cloths from Changshu in Jiangsu; Triangle stainless steel tableware from Tianjin; Three Circle padlocks from Shandong; Tiantan men's shirts from Beijing; Hailuo men's shirts from Shanghai; Red Double Happiness table-tennis balls from Shanghai; and Xiamen photographic paper from Fujian. According to preliminary appraisals, about 60 of the above-mentioned products have reached or approached international levels in quality.

New Products. More than 10,000 new products have been successfully trial-produced within two years. A number of new products, patterns, varieties and packaging designs have been supplied for the market and are being well-received by consumers. Through practice, light industrial enterprises have come to realize that it is in their vital interest to serve the people by maintaining quality and increasing variety. There will be a bright future for these enterprises if they give high priority to the improvement of products by raising their level of quality, expanding variety and finding substitutes. Otherwise, they will lose their competitiveness and fall behind.

2. *Altering the structure of products by adjusting the output of products that exceed demand so as to increase those in short supply, and by expanding output of products that fit the needs of the market.*

In keeping with the policy of readjusting the national economy, light industry departments placed emphasis on readjusting the structure of products. Because market demands are great, most products are in short supply. Production capacity is insufficient and raw materials are limited. However, a small portion of products enjoy adequate production capacity with output to spare as a result of changes in the market. The timely readjustment of the structure of products, a reduction in overstocked products and increases in goods in great demand will aid light industry's ability to meet market demands. For example, in accord with changes in market demand at home and abroad, the Shanghai Light Industry Administration drew on the products whose supply exceeded demand to offset those whose supply was short of demand; it cut down low-grade products and increased high-grade ones. It also developed the product lines of popular brands.

In 1980, 106 products with ready markets were produced, resulting in a net increase of 210 million yuan in output value for those products as compared to 1979. Of these, bicycles increased by 10% (with high-quality bicycles increasing by 42.9% and their proportion of the total rising from 28.2% to 36.67%); sewing machines increased by 6.04% (high-grade machines increased by 10.19% and their proportion rose from 48.62% to 50.54%); watches increased by 17% (output of calendar watches approximately doubled and lady's watches increased by 64.7%).

During the past two years, the Shanghai Handicrafts Administration readjusted the production orientation of 47 enterprises, expanded the production capacity of products in great demand and concentrated its efforts on the production of 100 products in great demand. The administration registered an increase of 32% in 1979 as compared with 1978, thus achieving an increase of 200 million yuan in output value. In 1980, output value increased by 300 million yuan, an increase of 37% over 1979. Through the readjustment of the structure of their products, exports from these two administrations registered a relatively large increase. The net increase of exports within these two years was 820 million yuan, an average annual increase of 18.4%.

Apart from the readjustment of the structure of products, readjustment of the structure of enterprises and trades was also carried out in some concentrated light industrial areas, while specialized coordination and economic combination was developed and the latent potential of production was tapped; some readjusted the structure of productive techniques, integrating the readjustment of the structure of products with the popularization of new technology and advances, thus raising the rate of production in labour and the technical level of production; some other areas adjusted the structure of raw materials to better suit the needs of production development.

3. *In the course of readjustment of enterprises, experimental units should be given more power of self-management and should make efforts to improve the management of enterprises.*

During the "cultural revolution," the management of light industrial enterprises was thrown into confusion as a result of disruption and sabotage by Lin Biao and the Gang of Four. After the downfall of the Gang of Four and especially since 1979, close attention has been paid to the readjustment of enterprises.

By the end of 1980, more than 500 large and medium-sized light industrial enterprises had been fundamentally readjusted. Most enterprises under the administration of provinces and districts were also readjusted, although the readjustment of widely dispersed enterprises at the county level developed disproportionately. While some readjustments were done well, others were poorly handled. Generally speaking, however, the readjustment achieved remarkable success. Through readjustment, the structure of the leading groups of many enterprises began to change after they were joined by a number of cadres who were young and were skilled in technology or management.

The System of Personal Responsibility. To increase production, practice economy, increase revenues and to cut down expenses, a variety of rules and regulations were further established and amplified with the system of personal responsibility as the core; work on original production records, statistics and measurements was strengthened and management of production quotas and oversight of raw materials, energy and utilization of man-hours were strictly carried out. Thus, economic accounting was developed day by day.

In order to improve economic results, 133 light industrial enterprises in Liaoning Province carried out measures such as the "method of selling on commission" inside the factory, the system of economic contracts and various forms of accounting including proportional profit allocation and allocation of bonuses by the hundred-mark method. Through readjustment, many enterprises raised their level of enterprise management and a good situation of parity, safety and high-level production has emerged.

Granting enterprises more power of self-management is an important aspect of the reform of the economic management system. Experiments have proved that this has played a stimulating role in mobilizing the enthusiasm of enterprises, workers and staff members in production development and has increased output and income.

Extending Rights of Self-Management. The practice of giving experimental units of light industrial enterprises more rights of self-management began in Sichuan Province in September 1978. Up to the end of 1980, there were a total of 861 such experimental units operating in Sichuan, Shanghai, Beijing, Tianjin and 15 other provinces and cities. In the past, the production achievements of enterprises and business management had nothing to do with the vital interests of workers and staff members, no matter what results they achieved. Furthermore, the phenomenon of turning a blind eye to squander and extravagance in spending money persisted despite all efforts. But from the time an enterprise has been given extended authority in self-management, profit-allocation — which is directly related to the interests of the workers and staff members — became available. People acted as their own masters in conducting financial transactions.

They undertook careful calculations and strict budgeting and practiced thrift in all areas.

Many enterprises improved their analysis of economic activity in the manufacturing process, from raw materials to finished products. Targets for reducing expenses were broken down into small components which were handed down to groups or individuals for the purpose of working out accounts at all levels of the factory. In the past, enterprises organized production in accordance with plans assigned by higher authorities, no matter whether the products in question were fit for sale or not. Now, production is organized according to what the market needs in an attempt to increase sales. Formerly, authority was concentrated in the hands of higher administrative bureaus. When enterprises met with difficulties in areas such as assignment of production tasks or supplies of raw materials, they often had to wait for the higher authorities to address these problems. Once an enterprise is given more power in making its own decisions, it acquires an independent economic interest and will shoulder more economic responsibility, taking the initiative to overcome difficulties and to seek out every means for increases in production and income.

In 1980, the total output value of the Chongqing First Light Industry Bureau of Sichuan Province increased by 12.8% over 1979 and profits increased by 25%. The total output value of 32 enterprises which had been given more power of self-management rose by 18.9% and their profits increased by 30.5%. The Chongqing Watch Industry Company, which is experimenting in "substitute taxation for profits," increased its total output value by 68% and its profits by 224%, achieving remarkable economic results.

Owing to the fact that enterprises that are given more power to manage their own affairs have retained a certain amount of profits, the proportion of deducted or retained depreciation funds for fixed assets has also been raised; now that enterprises have the economic capacity for developing production, they are speeding up the expansion of reproduction. The collective welfare of workers and staff members has also been initially improved.

In 1980, the Tianjin No. 3 Plastic Plant withdrew 906,000 yuan from its retained funds, or more than one-third of state investments during the past ten years. Of this amount, 421,000 yuan was spent on expanding reproduction and purchasing equipment such as an hydraulic press, a kneading machine and a punch press. In addition, a new product — foam slippers — was manufactured. This novel style of slippers has now been marketed in more than ten countries and regions.

4. *Under the guidance of the state plan, market regulation is being carried out and some products are being sold through channels of the enterprises themselves.*

The production and sale of light industrial products had for a long period been managed separately by industrial and commercial departments. Products were monopolized for purchase and exclusive selling by commercial departments. This unitary distribution channel was not only prone to becoming blocked up, but production also failed to meet the needs of the masses. Products were sometimes either out of stock or overstocked. Under these circumstances, the situation was unfavourable both to production and consumption.

Since 1979, the departments and enterprises of light industry in many areas, while strengthening their links with the commercial sectors and improving production, have put into effect the principle of market regulation under the guidance of the state plan and as put forward by the Third Plenary Session of the 11th Party Central Committee. By means of seriously investigating the market situation, they have actively developed sales through their own channels, thus enlivening industrial production.

Instituting Direct Sales by the Enterprises. In the past two years, sales of light industrial products through the channels of the enterprises themselves have developed step by step. According to incomplete statistics, by the end of 1979 the bureaus, companies and enterprises of light industry sectors from 21 provinces, municipalities and autonomous regions had set up 3,788 direct-sales retail departments. These bureaus and companies also established a number of management departments for supplies, marketing and service, handling both retail and wholesale transactions. More sales outlets were added in 1980. Methods for self-sale are flexible and various. Besides retail and wholesale activities, many other forms of endeavour have evolved through practice. These include participation in various kinds of exhibitions for the exchange of experience in goods supply; visiting other provinces or cities in order to sell products and at the same time conduct market research; sponsoring sales and supplying fairs; inviting commercial departments to judge samples and place orders; bringing factories and commercial stores into direct touch with each other; setting up trial sales sections for new products in the stores; and appointing large stores as wholesale agents.

In September 1979, the National Exhibition of Light Industrial Products was held in Beijing by the Ministry of Light Industry. Light industry sectors from 28 provinces, municipalities and autonomous regions took part. More than 4,000 kinds of products were on display. The exhibition lasted for one month. It was attended by 800,000 visitors, and the turnover of sales amounted to 31,260,000 yuan.

This was the first large-scale fair to produce great results in promoting direct sales through industry's own channels. Products within the scope of direct sale by industry include above-quota products, surpluses after planned selection by commercial departments, portions deducted from planned purchases by commercial departments, new products, portions of products made from self-derived raw materials, products that commercial departments do not purchase or manage and traditional direct-sale products.

The volume of direct sales and the proportion occupied by them have both increased. According to incomplete statistics from light industry departments of 21 provinces, municipalities and autonomous regions, the total of direct sales in 1979 amounted to 2,880 million yuan, accounting for 5.1% of total output value. Of this amount, the total of the first light industry sector accounted for 4% and the total of the second light industry sector for 10%. According to statistics from the second light industry departments of 26 medium-sized cities, the total of direct sales from January through September 1980 reached 1,390 million yuan, accounting for 38.8% of total sales.

Production Gains from Direct Sales and Regulation Through the Market. The implementation of market regulation under the guidance of the state plan and the evolution of direct sales by industry have promoted the development of production. First of all, they have played a positive role in assuring implementation of the state plan. After direct sales by industry was put into practice in 1979, the departments concerned handled the sale of products themselves. These were products that commercial sectors did not need, so that unmarketable goods became goods which sold well. This rapidly put an end to overstocking and to the resultant setting aside of part of productive capacity. It also halted decreases in production. In the latter half of 1979, production increased at a rapid rate, paying overdue bills and ensuring the implementation of the annual plan. In 1980, direct sales by industry developed further, since the integration of production and sales is an important factor in greatly increasing production.

Secondly, market regulation enhanced the goal of serving consumers and promoted the raising of quality and the variety of products. New products and new varieties developed. In the past, the Dandong Watch Factory produced only one variety and three designs of bad quality, resulting in a large quantity of overstock in commercial departments. Since 1979, by visiting stores and consumers and listening to opinions for raising quality, this factory has manufactured large quantities of new watches, increasing its output to 5 varieties and 58 designs. They have exchanged 450,000 old watches for new watches distributed by selling agents all over the country. Their watches are not only in great demand on the domestic market, but are also exported to Hong Kong.

Thirdly, it facilitated timely investigation into changes in market demand in order to guide production and make products that would satisfy the needs of the customers. At present, direct sales by industry have become an indispensable supplement to the distribution of commodities. Commercial purchases and direct sales by industry complemented each other. Their mutual promotion is also beneficial to making the market more active.

5. *Making good use of capital investment and loans in raising economic results.*

In the field of capital construction in the past two years, light industry departments have carried out projects conscientiously and have strengthened the organization, management and inspection of construction projects, devoting major energy to gaining full advantage from these investments. Therefore, the erroneous tendency of ignoring whether or not the application of investment is rational or whether its results are good has begun to change. In 1979, actual investments from the state budget for national capital construction in light industry totalled 950 million yuan; the total for 1980 was 698 million yuan. Both overfulfilled the state plan.

The rate of forming fixed assets was raised steadily, reaching 77% and 78.3%, respectively, in the two years. During that period, 32 large and medium-sized projects went into operation and 29 large and medium-sized projects were partially put into operation. Paper, sugar, salt, beer, bicycles, sewing machines, watches, leather, synthetic detergents, electric bulbs, products of high-quality aluminium, pottery and porcelain for daily use have increased in production capacity.

At the same time, the share of housing construction in investments has been increased; 4.3 million square metres of floor space were completed in the two years. Figures for the completion of the capital construction plan and for buildings being put into use in 1979 and 1980 were the best in recent years.

In capital construction, we have begun the reform of moving from state appropriations to bank credits. By using loans, enterprises will bear explicit economic responsibility. When an enterprise decides upon the construction of an item, it selects those items that will have good sales, good construction conditions and can easily repay loans. When loans are in hand, attention is given to careful calculation and strict budgeting. Enterprises will strive to put new items into operation sooner and to achieve desired results earlier, thus repaying loans earlier. By taking this approach, the economic gains in most undertakings have been evident. In 1980, light industry used 700 million yuan in short-term bank loans, and production capacity increased in that year: bicycles increased by 1.5 million; sewing machines by 900,000; clocks, 550,000; watches, 2 million; beer, 25,000 tons; high-quality liquor, 21,000 tons; pigskin, 8 million pieces; leather shoes, 2.97 million pairs; and furniture made of steel and wood, 2.7 million pieces.

6. *Enhance work in scientific research and education and strengthen these weak key links in light industry.*

Owing to using limited funds mainly for expanding production capacity, scientific research and education in light industry have always been weak. During the past two years, the leading groups in scientific research institutes, colleges and secondary schools as well as the ranks of scientific research personnel and teachers have been strengthened. Investments for capital construction and using foreign exchange have been appropriately increased and equipment urgently needed for scientific research and teaching aids purchased, so that the conditions for scientific research and teaching have been improved. Scientific research institutes in light industry throughout the country have increased from 253 in 1978 to 341 in 1980, while research personnel have increased by more than 3,000. While developing organizations for scientific research, research work within the enterprises has also been strengthened. For example, 85 enterprises of the first Light Industry Bureau of Shandong Province have set up scientific research institutes or departments.

Scientific and technological advances have been achieved all over the country. Applications for awards for 1,331 items of scientific and technological results produced during 1978-80 were made by light industry departments; of these, 671 items received awards from the Ministry of Light Industry and 279 of those have since been put into operation. These items have solved some technical problems that had existed in the light industry sector and have achieved marked technological and economic results. A high-speed laser-beam drilling machine that was successfully manufactured in Shanghai and Suzhou can be used for drilling watch jewels at rates of 10-16 particles per second, reaching international standards.

Activities in Education. Students enrolled in colleges of light industry and in science and engineering schools affiliated with light industry increased to over 13,000 in 1980; students in technical secondary schools numbered over 16,400 — increases of 50% and 72%, respectively, over 1978. At the same time, education for workers and staff members has been developing gradually. In addition to spare-time study classes sponsored by the enterprises for elementary education and for learning technology and management, students enrolled in all types of higher educational institutions for workers and staff members numbered more than 16,000; those in technical secondary schools for workers and staff numbered more than 8,000. Technical schools have grown to 250, with over 28,000 students. The quality of teaching has been raised.

Bright Prospects for the Future

During the past two years, light industry has achieved a great deal of success. However, China has for a long period placed stress on the development of means of production, ignoring means of consumption, so that agriculture, light industry and heavy industry have developed well out of proportion. This situation cannot be rectified within a short period of time. At present, technical equipment is rather backward, factory buildings are rather crowded, technical strength is weak, production capacity is insufficient, production management is relatively backward and low in economic results, while increases in production fail to keep pace with increases in social purchasing power, and some light industrial products are still short in supply on the market. But these weaknesses are also potentialities. Once light industry is developed adequately, we can supply more consumer goods for the market, accumulate more funds, earn more foreign exchange, absorb more social labour forces, consume less energy and, as the period for construction is short, we can achieve quick returns. This is vital for improving market supplies, withdrawing currency from circulation, balancing financial revenues and expenditures and consolidating and developing the desirable situation of stability and unity. Proper handling of the production of light industry is a problem of major importance to the entire question. The government has decided to place the production of consumer goods in a strategic position, urging all sectors to support light industry and to increase the production of consumer goods.

The current situation is extremely favourable to light industry. In 1981 and the coming five years, light industry will continue to develop at a comparatively high speed. Advances will occur amidst readjustment. In the course of readjusting the relations between light industry and other sectors of the national economy, the structure within light industry should also be properly readjusted so as to lay a good foundation. Progress must be made from the present foundation, applying the limited funds that exist to technological reforms. Efforts should be made to increase production and practice economy. The acceleration of production should be promoted along with raising quality, reducing attrition, increasing products that satisfy the needs of customers and striving for economic results to better meet the needs of people's livelihood.

In 1981, the structure of products must be readjusted, special attention must be given to the production of items such as bicycles, sewing machines, clocks and watches, paper, salt, plastic products, articles for cleaning, cigarettes, sugar, beer, leather and its products, furniture, electrical household appliances, clothing and arts and crafts. In particular, Shanghai, Tianjin, Beijing and other key cities in light industry have to increase the production of famous-brand goods. Products of the best quality should be developed. Apart from continuing the promotion of light industrial products of excellent quality throughout the country, "hundred-flower contests" in arts and crafts should also be conducted. We must bring the role of existing enterprises into full play, enhance coordination between industry and commerce, enact the reforms well, and improve business management.

10. CHINA'S TEXTILE INDUSTRY
By the Research Office,
Ministry of Textile Industry

The textile industry is an industrial sector of China's national economy which underwent a relatively early development and has a relatively good foundation. Socialist transformation and socialist construction carried out since the founding of New China have transformed the industry into an industrial sector that is quite comprehensive in nature, self-sufficient in raw materials and equipment and in possession of fairly advanced production technology.

There are now more than 11,900 enterprises and 4.29 million workers and staff members in China's textile industry. An annual output of more than 1,000 million metres (m.) of fabrics made from cotton, wool, flax, ramie, silk and chemical fibres has made it possible for the textile industry to supply China's urban and rural markets with a wide variety of textile products and to contribute its share in the accumulation of capital construction investment and to the development of foreign trade as well.

I. Thirty Years in Retrospect

China's modern textile industry was founded in the 1880's and thus has a history of 100 years. The development of the textile industry in old China is, in effect, the history of the gradual disintegration of the handicraft textile industry and of the difficult struggle of national capital under the oppression of the "three big mountains" (*viz.* imperialism, feudalism and bureaucrat-capitalism — which weighed like mountains on the backs of the Chinese people before Liberation). In contrast, the 30 years of New China's modern textile industry bespeaks the history of the Chinese people advancing along the socialist road under the leadership of the Communist Party of China and the people's government, relying on their own efforts, working hard for the prosperity of the country and continuously moving from strength to strength.

Cotton. The cotton industry has the largest production capacity and the best foundation in China's textile sector. In 1979, China ranked first in the world by producing 2.63 million tons of cotton yarn and blended cotton-synthetic yarn and 1,215 million m. of cotton fabric.

Wool. Considerable progress has also been made in the wool industry. During the 70-year period from China's first woolen mill (known as the Gansu General Bureau of Woolen Piece Goods) — set up in 1876 by Zuo Zhongtang in Lanzhou, Gansu Province — up to 1949, there were only 130,000 spindles in China. The total number of wool spindles installed during the 30 years of construction since the founding of New China is equivalent to over three times the number installed during the 70 years prior to Liberation. In 1979, 90.17 million m. of wool piece goods and over 40,000 tons of hand-knitting yarn were produced.

Silk. China was the first country to produce silk fabrics. As early as 2,000 years ago, exquisite silks were shipped along the renowned Silk Road to countries in the west and became highly regarded all over the world.

Since the 20th century, however, China's silk industry suffered from the plunder and destruction by reactionary forces at home and abroad, and a gradual decline took place. On the eve of Liberation, output of silk fabrics was only one-fourth of the previous peak record.

After Liberation, silkworm breeding and mulberry cultivation were encouraged by the state, bringing about a gradual restoration of the silk industry. Now, China's mulberry silk reels are approximately 10 times those of 1949. In 1979, 29,749 tons of silk and 663,450 m. of silk fabrics were produced. Exquisite silk fabrics still comprise one of the important export commodities in foreign trade.

Jute, Flax and Ramie. A significant change has also come over the jute, flax and ramie industries, represented by a rapid growth of the jute industry and the construction of a number of linen and ramie textile mills. At present, China's aggregate number of spindles in these industries is 5.9 times that of 1949. In 1979, 344 million jute bags, 20.81 million m. of linen fabrics and 15 million m. of ramie fabrics were produced.

Key Aspects of Post-1949 Development. The development of the textile industry over the past 30 years is demonstrated not only by an increase in production capacity, but also by the following achievements:

1. *Significant improvement in regional distribution of the industry.*

The textile industry of old China was concentrated mainly along the coastal regions. Cotton spindles in Shanghai, Qingdao and Tianjin accounted for approximately 70% of the country's total and wool spindles in Shanghai alone accounted for 75% of the national total.

In the early 1950's, New China plunged into large-scale economic construction. Under the direction of state planning, new textile bases were set up in Hebei, Henan and Shaanxi provinces — all raw-material producing areas. At present, cotton spindles installed in cotton-producing areas account for two-thirds of the country's total, while wool spindles installed in wool-producing areas account for one-half of the country's total. Textile mills of various sizes were also constructed in border areas and autonomous regions such as Inner Mongolia, Xinjiang, Qinghai, Ningxia and Yunnan.

2. *Increased production of natural fibres and great efforts in the development of chemical fibres.*

Old China was not self-sufficient in raw materials for the textile industry. In 1946, imported cotton accounted for 50% of the total amount of cotton consumed by spinning mills throughout the country. The majority of wool was also imported.

After Liberation, a set of economic policies and measures with respect to the restoration and development of agriculture and animal husbandry was put into effect, resulting in inciting the initiative of the peasants and herdsmen. From 1952 to 1979, the amount of cotton purchased by the state increased by nearly 100%, that of sheep wool by over 300% and that of mulberry silk cocoons by approximately 300%. As to other textile materials, such as ramie, goat hair, tussah silk and rabbit hair, further developments and rational utilization were effected.

Along with the development of natural fibres, vigorous measures were taken to start from scratch construction of a chemical fibre industry. In the early 1950's, the Baoding Viscose Rayon Plant and the Beijing Synthetic Fibre Experimental Plant were established. Subsequently, in the mid-1960's, a vinyon plant and an acrylic fibre plant were built. After the 1970's, capital expenditure by the state for the construction of the chemical fibre industry was increased and new petrochemical technology was imported from abroad. Large-sized modern chemical fibre complexes using either petroleum or natural gas as raw materials underwent construction in Jinshan County of Shanghai, Liaoyang city of Liaoning Province, Changshou County of Sichuan Province and Tianjin, lending great impetus to the development of the chemical fibre industry. At present, chemical fibres account for 12% of the overall textile materials consumed in China.

3. *Manufacture of textile machinery through self-reliance.*

The growth of the textile industry over the 30 years following the establishment of New China was made possible by the effort to manufacture textile machinery through self-reliance. Before Liberation, China's textile machinery plants could not even manufacture a complete machine; they could only carry out repairs on textile machinery. After Liberation, machinery repair plants were reorganized and amalgamated according to their specialization and coordinated on a nationwide basis, thus bringing about the initial establishment of a textile machinery manufacturing system. With 30 years of experience in construction, China can now build more than 1,200 types of machinery for integrated production lines. These are for use by 13 different textiles sectors, including cotton, wool, linen, silk, chemical fibres, knitting, printing, dyeing and finishing. For the cotton industry alone, more than 15 million spindles and 500,000 looms have been manufactured. As a result, not only were the domestic needs of construction in the textile industry satisfied, but complete sets of machinery for over 1.8 million spindles were manufactured for export to foreign countries.

4. *Continuous improvement in product quality.*

For many years in the past, China's textile industry has always attached great importance to correctly handling the relationship between quantity and quality; in this respect, it has given priority to tasks concerned with improving the quality of products and increasing product variety. Recently, many enterprises have strengthened their basic technical management and some enterprises have initiated a total quality control programme, resulting in a significant improvement in product quality. China's cotton fabrics and cotton textile products enjoy a relatively high reputation both at home and abroad.

The quality of raw silk and silk fabrics have been improved. Double-A-grade raw silk, considered to be the highest quality in the early 1950's, is now regarded as a medium-quality product owing to the fact that many enterprises can currently produce 5-A grade or even 6-A grade superior quality raw silk. Silk fabrics with traditional Chinese motifs produced in Hangzhou and Suzhou, printed silks from Shanghai with contemporary motifs, Beijing's Iceberg Brand fine-count cotton-polyester fabrics and Changzhou's

Watermoon Brand cotton khaki are in great demand on both foreign and domestic markets because of their excellent quality and extensive range of product variety.

5. *New levels in textile science and technology and in textile education.*

At present, China has 14 textile technology colleges with an aggregate enrollment of more than 10,000 students. The number of engineers and technicians working in the industry has increased from 7,000 in pre-Liberation days to over 50,000 today. This growth has played an important role in pushing China's textile science and technology to a higher level. China's production rate per spindle ranks among the highest in the world. Important results have been achieved in research into new spinning processes, such as open-end spinning, self-twist spinning and electrostatic spinning; new weaving processes using air-jet looms, rapier looms and gripper-projectile looms; and new dyeing, printing and finishing processes, such as rotary screen printing and transfer printing.

In the wake of these developments in production and construction in the textile industry, the technical qualifications of vast numbers of workers and staff have been substantially raised through participation in actual production and training in spare-time colleges and trade schools. As of today, China has formidable technical contingents in engineering, construction, assembly and production management.

6. *Rapid increase in textile exports.*

Textile exports in 1950 amounted to only U.S.$26 million; by 1979, the figure had reached U.S.$2.9 billion, 100 times that of 1950. China's export of grey goods ranks first in the world, while its exports of filature silk account for three-fourths of the total volume of world trade in that commodity. China's textile products are sold in over 130 countries and regions abroad and are in great demand on the international market.

After the fall of the Gang of Four and especially after the Third Plenary Session of the 11th Party Central Committee and the implementation of policies in shifting the focus of work to the modernization of socialist construction and to the policy of readjustment, restructuring, consolidating and improving the economy, the development of China's textile industry reached a new stage. The principle of "six priorities" (priority in the supply of materials, fuel and power; priority in measures concerning technical innovation, tapping potential and reformation; priority in capital construction; priority in bank loans; priority in foreign exchange and importation of new technology; priority in communications and transportation) put forward by the State Council for application to light industry and textiles has given powerful impetus to the development of the textile industry.

Over the last few years, the share of textile industry in the national economy has increased, its output value accounting for 12% of the country's total industrial output value. Profits turned over to the state account for 10% of state revenues. Sales on the domestic market account for 20% of the country's total volume of retail sales in consumer goods, while foreign-exchange earnings from textile exports account for approximately 20% of the country's total foreign-exchange earnings from exports.

II. New Advances Under the Readjustment Plan

The year 1980 was the second year of readjustment in the national economy. In light of China's actual conditions, a readjustment of the relationship between agriculture, light industry and heavy industry has been carried out over the past two years. As a result, the textile industry has developed at a speed surpassing that of heavy industry and now has the highest growth rate among China's industrial sectors.

1. *Output increased and new target levels reached.*

With the support of other sectors, the textile industry sought out every possible means to broaden its sources of raw materials and to effect measures for increasing output. In this respect, every effort was made to obtain more imported raw materials and to undertake the processing of imported raw materials and raw materials supplied by foreign companies. With a view to expanding production, many enterprises exerted great efforts to open up new avenues for obtaining raw materials.

A rotary four-shift system has been put into practice as a reform of the old labour system in the cotton industry and in parts of the wool and jute industries. This system calls for three shifts on duty and one off duty every day. Like the Chinese saying "Let the rider be knocked off and keep the horse going," textile mills work around-the-clock in three shifts, fully utilizing machinery capability.

An intensive movement for mutual aid and mutual learning in the various areas has effectively narrowed the gap in production levels between inland and coastal enterprises. In areas and enterprises where such movements were adequately launched, product quality improved, product variety increased, management strengthened, and production costs fell, all of which gave rise to growth in production and earnings.

In 1980, the output value of the textile industry was 1,355 million yuan, an increase of 24% over 1979. Output of all major textile items overfulfiled state production targets. Chemical fibre output was 450,000 tons (an increase of 38% over 1979), including 314,000 tons of synthetic fibres (an increase of 46.7% over 1979). Production of cotton yarn was 16.286 million bales (or 2.93 million tons) and cotton fabrics, 13,470 million linear metres (or 12,800 million sq. m.) – increases of 11.4% and 10.9% (or 12%), respectively, over 1979. Wool fabrics amounted to 101 million m. and hand-knitting yarn, 57,000 tons – increases of 12.2% and 29%, respectively, over 1979. Production of filature silk was 35,400 tons and silk goods, 759 million m. – increases of 19.2% and 14.5%, respectively, over 1979. A total of 433 million jute bags were produced, representing an increase of 25.9% over 1979. Annual taxes and profits paid to the state in 1980 increased by 24.8% over 1979 and all major technical and economic targets reached all-time highs.

2. *New developments in product quality and variety.*

With a view to bringing about further improvements in product quality, vigorous attempts were made in 1980 to strengthen basic technical management of the enterprises. A series of technical seminars on topics which were considered to be weak points in production technology were organized throughout the country. Aiming at raising operating techniques, many areas organized textile workers to give demonstrations of their working methods. Some areas launched comprehensive quality-control programmes, bringing about good initial results.

In 1980, 15 quality indices of 9 major categories of textile products examined by the state overfulfiled their targets and surpassed 1979 levels.

Good results were obtained from activities to establish famous brands and high-quality textile products. During 1980, over 30,000 textile products with variations in materials, weaves, patterns and colors were designed and produced. By the end of 1980, the industry had 1,714 high-quality products, 328 famous-brand products and 80 products that won medals of quality from the state.

As to popular consumer textiles such as wool-type chemical fibre fabrics (polyester and viscose staple fibre-blended fabrics), polyester filament knitwear, silk quilt covers and upholstery fabrics, which are well-received by people in all walks of life, not only was output raised, but achievements were gained in product type, design and color. At present, there are over 30 types of wool-type chemical fibre fabrics with more than 80 kinds of patterns and colors.

3. *Returns of capital investments realized by vigorous efforts to expedite completion and commissioning of construction projects.*

In 1980, the state allocation of capital construction investments to the textile industry was increased slightly. Meanwhile, there were substantial increases in allocations to the textile industry in the form of funds raised by local governments and through bank loans. Local authorities responsible for capital construction have focused their efforts on faster completion and commissioning of construction projects so that better economic results could be achieved. Thirty-four large and medium-sized projects under state planning with a total value of 1,100 million yuan in capital investments (110% of the target value) were completed. Of this total, 807 million yuan in investments came under the state budget, accounting for 124% of the annual plan. Of 13 projects to be completed in 1980, 12 were wholly or partially put on stream.

Most of the key chemical fibre projects have already reached the stage of completion and commissioning. The Sichuan Vinlon Plant, China's first large-scale chemical fibre plant using natural gas as the basic raw material, was put into operation and has already produced certified products. Some production units in the two petrochemical fibre complexes in Liaoyang and Tianjin underwent test runs, while other units were put into operation. Construction of two spinning plants in Acheng and Dandong, which form an integral part of the Liaoyang Complex, was completed.

The Shanghai General Petrochemical Works completed the first phase of its construction, which has been inspected and accepted. Up to the end of 1980, synthetic fibres produced by this plant totalled 280,000 tons; aggregate output value amounted to 4,770 million yuan; and profits and taxes turned over to the state totalled 1,810 million yuan – equivalent to 82% of total capital investment for the first phase of construction. Construction of the second phase has already started. In addition to this, excellent progress has been made in the construction of textile processing projects.

4. *The programme of tapping potential, technical innovation and reform for existing plants continued, while the clearing of bottlenecks strengthened.*

In addition to vigorous measures to get more

projects completed and put into operation, a campaign for tapping potential, technical innovation and reform, and for making up for what is lacking, was launched in key enterprises. Fruitful results were achieved in upgrading product quality and boosting production of products which had fallen short of market demand. In 1980, the Ministry of Textile Industry allocated special loans to 478 projects to carry out plans on tapping potential, technical innovation and reform.

By the end of 1980, 143 projects were completed, accounting for 30% of the total. Most of the work on projects such as printing and dyeing of polyester-cotton blends, spinning of wool-type acrylic fibres and technology for production of silk fabrics — all of which commenced in 1978 — were completed by the end of 1980. In this way, the long-term contradiction of insufficient production capacity and growing demands of the market were somewhat alleviated. In addition to increasing production capacity by adopting measures for tapping potential, work was also carried out by local governments to renovate buildings which were classified as dangerous and liable to collapse and to put up new warehouses, apartment buildings and facilities for waste-water treatment.

Construction of new plants and tapping the potential of existing plants brought about the following increases in annual production capacities of the different sectors: 60,000 tons of chemical fibres; 880,000 cotton spindles (including 761,000 new spindles from capital construction); 70,000 wool spindles and facilities for dyeing, printing and finishing; 900 million metres of cotton fabrics and polyester-cotton blends.

5. *Strengthening of scientific and technological work.*

Following the National Science Congress held in 1977, relatively significant developments took place in the scientific and technological work of the textile industry. Textile research institutes of the ministry and of provinces and cities directly under provincial administration increased from 48 to 83, while the number of research workers increased by 89%. With the gradual implementation of the party's policies on intellectuals, the initiative of scientific and technical personnel was greatly aroused, with a consequent quickening in the pace of scientific research. Fruitful results were achieved in long-standing research projects which for years could not make breakthroughs at critical points; some of these were eventually popularized and applied in the industry. Breakthroughs in spinning and weaving technologies — such as open-end spinning, self-twist spinning, air-jet looms, rapier looms and tufted blanket looms — made it possible for these technologies to be initially applied to the industry. A number of scientific and technical achievements have been successfully used in the technical innovation of existing production facilities in the textile industry. Batch production of new types of chemical fibres — such as profile fibres, conjugated fibres, polypropylene split filaments and mass-dyed polyester fibres — was begun. Several research projects on energy conservation were near completion. At the end of 1980, the Convention for Scientific Research Achievements in Textiles was held by the Ministry of Textile Industry; awards were given to 340 research projects, 193 of which were applied in the industry.

6. *Export targets for textiles well-fulfilled.*

Given the recession in textile markets in the capitalist world which occurred in 1980, China's textile organizations and enterprises used their best efforts to increase export volumes and foreign-exchange earnings.

Priority was given to increasing exports of textile products which would bring greater foreign-exchange earnings. Earnings from exports of worsted and woolen fabrics, woolen blankets, wool knitwear and garments were up by 24-28% over 1979. In the category of cotton fabrics, the proportion of printed, dyed and yarn-dyed fabrics rose to some extent. The Shanghai No. 1 Knitting Mill produced a variety of high-quality, high-fashion knitwear by improving workmanship, edging garments with rims, inlaying threads and piecing together material of different colours. In this way, the mill was able to realize a considerable increase in output value. The average output value per garment in 1980 increased by 24.7% over 1979. The Tianjin Wool and Jute Corporation expanded production of famous-brand products such as pure wool worsted flannel and pure wool gabardine. As a result, the average purchasing price per metre of worsted and woolen fabrics exported by this corporation in 1980 rose by 19.4% over 1979.

More and more export products came up to high quality standards and fulfilment of export contracts showed an improvement. All corporations under the management of the Tianjin Bureau of Textile Industries either set up new systems or improved on existing systems for the execution of export contracts. In these systems, an account of each export contract was kept so that monthly analyses and quarterly check-ups could be performed and corporations would be in a position either to redistribute the work or assist those enterprises which had difficulties in fulfilling the export contract. The fulfilment rate of contracts reached 95.7% in 1980, an all-time high. Shanghai was generally able to deliver all categories of textile exports on schedule.

Textile exports in 1980 jumped to U.S.$3,250 million, an increase of 11.4% over 1979.

7. *Market research and product development was boosted.*

With a view to making textile products sell well and to increasing their competitiveness, textile organizations of various localities held sales exhibitions and carried out market investigations and research. Never before were sales exhibitions so enlivening. In Beijing alone, more than ten sales exhibitions of textile products from over ten localities were held in various department stores and markets. Beijing, Jiangsu and Hubei provinces, together with several foreign-trade organizations, held sales exhibitions in Hong Kong and the United States, and carried out market investigation and research. Furthermore, retail stores selling new textile products were established throughout the country by provinces, cities and autonomous regions; others were set up by perfectures and counties and still others by factories and industrial organizations. There also emerged a small number of retail stores jointly run by the industry and the commercial organizations themselves. These stores took up different forms, some handling general commodities and others specialized commodities.

Many cities and provinces set up factories and retail stores under a system whereby textile products were distributed directly to retail stores, resulting in a closer link between industry and commerce. During the past two years, the Bureau of Textile Industries in Liaoning Province held meetings twice a year for product selection and production quotas. These meetings were also attended by representatives from industry and commerce. After product selection, contracts were signed providing for allocations of raw materials, organization of production and purchases of products. During the past two years, the number of enterprises attending these meetings steadily increased to over 300. Product types, designs and styles exhibited at the meetings doubled, now totalling 7,400. New products shown at each meeting reached 50% and fulfilment of production-marketing contracts exceeded 95%.

Sales exhibitions, trial-sale stores and meetings for product selection and production quotas all served to link production closely with market demand, to promote quicker development of new products, to enliven the industry and to enrich market supply.

8. *Preliminary achievements in the reform of economic management.*

During 1980, the textile industry carried out experiments in granting extended decision-making power to 60% of its enterprises. These experiments stimulated the enterprises and produced positive results. Under the policy of granting individual enterprises the right to reserve part of the profits, enterprises were able to use the money to develop production and increase welfare benefits of workers and staff. According to incomplete statistics, construction of 2,670,000 sq.m. of floor space of residential housing for workers and staff was started in 1980 and 750,000 sq. m. were completed, representing a record high. At present, a portion of profits can be retained by the participating bureau, corporation or even the enterprise itself. Despite the variety of approaches used, significant results were achieved. However, problems do exist and a careful summing up of experiences is required to resolve them.

In 1980, the Shanghai Bureau of Textile Industries initiated experiments in granting extended decision-making power by retaining a portion of profit for all enterprises under its management. The bureau held itself responsible to the state for three guarantees:1. The guarantee to fulfil the annual growth rate in output value; 2. The guarantee to pay to the state the aggregate amount of profits for five years; 3. The guarantee to reach the target for foreign-exchange earnings.

Under the condition that the above-mentioned guarantees would be fulfilled, 90.5% of the total profits made by the Shanghai Bureau of Textile Industries would be turned over to the state and 9.5% would be retained by the enterprises as their share of the profit.

As a result of this experiment, significant economic results have been achieved over the past year. In camparison with 1979, the year 1980 showed an increase of 11.6% in total output value, an increase of 17.8% in profits (from which a portion was deducted to pay back loans, leaving a net increase of 16.6% in profits turned over to the state) and an increase of 13.2% in foreign-exchange earnings from textile exports. Such growth rates represented all-time highs.

Some cities and provinces set up regional textile corporations while others conducted experiments in establishing organizations with joint participation of industry, commerce and foreign trade. Shaanxi Province set up a Textile Industries Corporation in October 1979. The corporation exercised centralized leadership and centralized management over all enterprises directly under its control, in matters of production, administration, financing and work between the party and the masses. The resulting elimination of superfluous administrative levels raised work efficiency.

III. Major Problems at Present

Despite the many achievements in the textile industry, several problems exist at present, including:

1. *Developments in production have been unable to meet the requirements for improved livelihood of the people.*

Particularly in the past two years, the purchasing power for commodities has rapidly increased. With the raising of the people's living standards, a change has taken place in the structure of consumer goods whereby the proportion of garments in the total volume of retail sales of consumer goods has been increasing steadily. At present, the textile market is on the whole thriving, but there are still some products which fall short of market demand.

2. *Existence of some weak links in major sectors of the industry.*

In sectors such as wool spinning, chemical fibre production, knitting, dyeing, printing and finishing, plant capacity cannot meet the needs of the market. A relatively wide disparity exists among different localities and among different enterprises. In some old textile centres and existing enterprises, many buildings are classified as dangerous and liable to collapse; a large quantity of waste-water from dyeing and printing houses is in need of treatment; and there is a general shortage of housing for workers and staff, as well as of warehouse space.

3. *A tendency towards decentralization and lack of planning in capital construction.*

In some localities, small-scale textile mills have cropped up. These mills produce poor quality products and consume added raw materials, thus affecting the normal flow of adequate raw materials to the large mills.

In order to produce more textile products of better quality to meet the demands of the urban and rural people, to accumulate funds for national capital construction and to increase foreign exchange earnings, the textile industry will have to make greater efforts to implement the readjustment policy by curtailing capital construction, developing science and technology, strengthening management and administration, increasing production, improving quality, widening product range and raising economic efficiency.

11. CHINA'S HANDICRAFTS INDUSTRY
By the Policy Research Office,
Ministry of Light Industry

I. 30 Years of Development and Change

China is a country with an ancient civilization and its handicrafts industry has a long history. Through the ages, China's handicraft labourers had become known throughout the world for their intelligence and wisdom as well as for their assiduousness and deligence.

In *The Chinese Revolution and the Chinese Communist Party,* Comrade Mao Zedong said: "Throughout the history of Chinese civilization, its agriculture and handicrafts have been renowned for their high level of development ... The compass was invented in China very long ago. The art of paper-making was discovered as early as 1,800 years ago. Block-printing was invented 1,300 years ago, and movable type 800 years ago. The use of gunpowder was known to the Chinese before the Europeans." All of these early discoveries made brilliant and lasting contributions to world civilization.

Setbacks Under Imperialism and the Kuomintang. However, China's handicraft production developed slowly as the result of brutal exploitation and oppression by the ruling class of past dynasties. Particularly during the 100 years or so since the Opium War, the handicrafts industry could not develop smoothly along the path of modern, large-scale industry. It suffered from severe attacks and devastation stemming from imperialist aggression and the dumping in China of large quantities of imported goods. During the reactionary rule of the Kuomintang, handicraft production was damaged even further. A great number of craftsmen were forced to leave home and wander about. Some traditional handicraft techniques were on the verge of becoming extinct. It is only in New China that genuine prosperity in handicrafts production and thorough emancipation of the handicrafts industry have been realized.

Early Progress Under the People's Republic. Since the founding of the People's Republic of China, in accordance with the principles of Marxism-Leninism and Mao Zedong Thought, the Communist Party of China and the people's government have led craftsmen to advance towards the road of collectivization and modernization. Generally speaking, they have achieved great success and have enriched their experiences despite some setbacks met in the course of the advance. The total output value of the handicrafts industry in 1949 was 3,240 million yuan, an amount that increased to 7,310 million yuan by 1952. According to a survey taken in 1954, about 18,910,000 people were then engaged in handicrafts, of whom some 7,700,000 were individual craftsmen and 10,000,000 were peasants who had taken up the commercial production of handicrafts on a part-time basis.

There were numerous sectors and product varieties in the handicrafts industry, including metal and wood processing; cotton; textiles and knitted goods; fabrics of wool, flax, hemp and silk; foodstuffs, paper-making, pottery and porcelain; leather products, stationery and sporting goods; products of bamboo, rattan and palm fibre; arts and crafts; building materials; iron smelting; non-metallic ore mining; and chemical processing. There were also several hundred kinds of natural trades and tens of thousands of handicrafts products.

Distribution of handicrafts was on a wide scale and had an extensive base among the broad masses. According to statistics in 1952, 36.5% of craftsmen throughout the country lived in urban areas and 63.5% in the countryside; 46% were in coastal cities and 54% in the hinterland. An estimated 400,000 to 800,000 people were engaged in handicrafts in the provinces of Jiangsu, Zhejiang, Shandong, Sichuan, Guangdong, Hebei, Henan and Hunan, where handicrafts were comparatively well-developed. In 1952, the gross output value of handicrafts accounted for 8.8% of the output value of industry and agriculture, and for 21.3% of the total output value of industry.

The Cooperative Movement. Following the fundamental principles of Marxism-Leninism and combining these with China's actual conditions, the Communist Party of China and the people's government drew up a series of policies, measures and means for transforming individual handicrafts; at the same time, special bureaus in charge of handicrafts cooperative undertakings were set up at all levels one after another. By 1956, under the guiding light of the general line for the transitional period and through the three developmental stages of model example, universal dissemination and cooperative upsurge, China's handicraft industry, in 1956, basically accomplished the socialist transformation of the ownership of means of production of individually produced handicrafts, thus bringing about a fundamental transformation from the individual to the collective and from private to public ownership. Six million craftsmen joined the socialist collectivization. Although during the co-operative movement some shortcomings emerged — such as developing too fast, blindly setting up big cooperatives, merging service establishments and too much concentration — it may be nevertheless concluded that productive forces had been extensively emancipated, giving an impetus to the rapid development of production.

In 1957, the gross output value of the nationwide handicrafts industry reached 13,370 million yuan, a more than four-fold increase over 1949, and a 77% increase over output in 1936, the peak period for handicrafts production prior to Liberation. Productivity per capita in 1957 reached 2,190 yuan, a 55.8% increase over 1952. With the development of production, the living standards of craftsmen and staff members was greatly improved.

Setbacks in 1958. But China's handicrafts industry has not developed smoothly and has gone through repeated twists and turns. Following the cooperative movement in handicrafts, new relations of production were established. At that point, steps should have been taken to consolidate and improve the cooperative organization of handicrafts, perfecting it systematically so as to promote the further development of productive forces. However, under the influence of erroneous "Left" thinking in 1958, policies such as "transition in a rush" and "transfer of production and change of orientation" were carried out. Of the more than 100,000 handicraft cooperatives (or groups) with more than 5 million members then in existence, 85% were transferred to other factories or trades; 48% were shifted over to local state-owned factories, while a considerable portion of the sector was converted to cooperative factories. As a result, the production of manufactured goods for daily use decreased, while the varieties and types of handicrafts products declined. This caused great harm to people's livelihoods.

The Restoration of 1959-1961. During the period from 1959 to 1961, measures were adopted by the Central Committee of the Communist Party of China. These included Instructions on Rapid Restoration and Development of Handicrafts and Provisions on Some Questions Concerning the Policy of Handicrafts in the Urban and Rural Areas (Draft). These two measures were promulgated, with the result that integrated organizations were restored at all levels of the cooperative handicrafts sector. This development played an important role in adjusting ownership and restoring and developing production of handicrafts, as well as in consolidating the collective economy. It achieved marked results.

By 1965, handicrafts enterprises had reached 100,000, with 6 million workers and staff members. In that year, the No. 2 Ministry of Light Industry was established and placed in charge of several trades including enterprises under collective ownership and those owned by the whole people [i.e., state-owned — Ed.].

Administrations in charge of handicrafts were also set up by local governments at all levels and correspondingly improved, and both leadership and management were further strengthened.

Sabotage Under the "Cultural Revolution." During the ten years of turmoil of the "cultural revolution," the handicrafts industry was severely sabotaged. Institutions were withdrawn and amalgamated, enterprises were merged, equalitarianism and indiscriminate transfer of resources was practiced and workers and staff members were transferred to lower levels — all causing great losses to production and seriously dampening the socialist enthusiasm of the workers and staff members.

Post-1978 Reforms. After the smashing of the "Gang of Four," and particularly after the Third Plenary Session of the 11th Central Committee of the Communist Party of China, a good situation of thriving handicrafts emerged with the implementation of the policy of readjustment, restructuring, consolidation and improvement. In many provinces, municipalities and autonomous regions, energetic measures have been taken to recover and develop the second sector of light industry [i.e., the sector formerly known as the handicrafts industry — Ed.], especially handicrafts enterprises with collective ownership in the towns. In light of concrete local conditions, new policies have been formulated and economic regulations have been relaxed; the proportionate distribution among enterprises has been readjusted; added power of self-management has been granted; combined regulation though planning and market forces has been practiced; the scope of enterprise-sold products has been expanded; market forecasting has been strengthened; the structure of products has been rationally readjusted and specialization coordination enhanced; and economic integration was carried out — all these measure provided the handicrafts industry with new impetus for development.

Survey of the Handicrafts Industry in 1980. According to the 1980 statistics, there were 58,000 enterprises within the second national sector of light industry; these had 6,970,000 workers and staff members. Gross output value amounted to 49,330 million yuan, a 15.6% increase over 1979; realization of profits and taxation accounted for 5,650 million yuan, a 12% increase as compared with 1979. Products in urgent need by the market were greatly increased in 1980. For example, clothing output was increased by 33.3%, arts and crafts by 12.7%, leather by 35%, pigskin shoes by 29.4%, leather shoes by 38.7%, cloth shoes by 36.6%, washing machines by 130%, electric fans by 260% and furniture by 6.3%.

With the emphasis of the party's work shifted to socialist construction, handicraft production has further developed soundly. Attention was paid to arranging production in accordance with market demand, the tendency of stressing output value and yield and neglecting quality and variety was corrected, and priority was given to improving quality, variety and design. The control of quality was strengthened and quality competitions held. Thus, the quality of handicraft articles was markedly improved and traditionally known products were restored and developed. In 1980, 19 kinds of handicraft articles won national gold and silver medals and 169 products were designated as "fine quality" by the Ministry of Light Industry. Several trades and enterprises also trial-manufactured new products, designs and varieties.

Systems of Ownership. Through years of evolution, China's handicrafts industry has taken on diversified ownership, with collective ownership predominating. This situation suits the present level of development of productive forces.

Collective Ownership. Enterprises of collective ownership are the major components of the handicrafts sector. Among these are handicrafts cooperative organizations which were formed in 1956 on the basis of socialist transformation of individual handicrafts. Included are neighbourhood factories organized by socially idle productive forces consisting mainly of housewives; "May 7" factories sponsored by many state-owned industrial enterprises in the early 1970's; and producers' service cooperatives recently established by urban youths who are waiting for jobs. The collective economy of the handicrafts industry has a strong vitality. However, under the influence of erroneous "Left" ideology, it was limited and cut back on several occasions in the past 20 years. Nevertheless, it broke through all obstacles time and again, and grew in strength.

This demonstrates that the superiority of collective economy cannot be repressed. Firstly, collective economy can effectively integrate the interests of the state, the collective and the individual; it can link the economic interests of the individual with the economic results of the enterprise, thus better mobilizing the enthusiasm of workers and staff members. Secondly, enterprises which are carrying out independent accounting and which assume sole responsibility for their profits and losses can divert production in directions closer to the demands of society; they possess greater authority for self-management in business matters than do enterprises owned by the whole people; and under the guidance of the state plan, they may take full advantage of regulation through the market. Thirdly, a great number of handicrafts enterprises are characterized by small size and flexibility; they can readily make use of local materials, extensively utilize social resources, arrange production according to local conditions and the need of the masses in different areas. Fourthly, given the elastic and diversified modes of handicraft management, they can adapt to the diverse, complex and ever-changing needs of society. Fifth, the handicrafts industry has a fine tradition of industrious and thrifty management, paying attention to careful calculation and strict budgeting, to diligence and frugality and particularly to economic results.

Ownership by the Whole People. Handicrafts enterprises under ownership by the whole people have in the main been transformed from handicraft enterprises of collective ownership. In national terms, economic sectors owned by the whole people are the economic foundation of China's socialism. Within the scope of handicrafts, although the proportion of enterprises owned by the whole people is very small, this segment plays an important role in the production of industrial goods for daily use.

According to 1979 statistics from the second sector of light industry [i.e., comprising handicrafts enterprises — Ed.], there were a total of 2,100 enterprises owned by the whole people, making up 3.8% of all enterprises within the second sector of light industry. Despite this small proportion in number, their output value accounted for 22% of the total. Generally speaking, these enterprises are large-scale units with good technological equipment and comparatively high productivity. They have provided experience and served as an example to other enterprises capable of large-scale production and suited to development in mechanization and specialization. Collectively owned enterprises and enterprises owned by the whole people can learn from and help each other, each drawing on the other's advantages to enhance their contribution to developing the production of industrial consumer goods and artistic handicrafts, thus satisfying people's diversified needs.

Individually produced handicrafts, under the leadership of the socialist economy, are a necessary supplement to socialist economy. Individually produced handicrafts represent a type of ownership that is characterized by individual labour and that occupies a part of the means of production on its own. In the course of the past 20 years, individualized handicrafts were regarded as a feature of capitalism, and the phenomenon was almost eliminated. Since the Third Plenary Session of the Central Committee of the Communist Party of China, with the readjustment of the national economy and relaxation of economic regulations, and under the conditions of an economy dominated by systems of ownership by the whole people and collective ownership, individualized handicrafts marked a new stage of development. In the present period, individualized handicrafts are a form of ownership subordinant to the socialist state-owned economy and the collective economy.

Jointly Operated Handicrafts Sector. This is a new form of ownership. Since the Third Plenary Session of the Central Committee of the Communist Party of China, in the course of carrying through the policies of readjustment, restructuring, consolidation and improvement and "seeking out excellence, competition and integration," various kinds of economic associations have emerged, systematically forming jointly operated handicrafts enterprises. Associated handicrafts enterprises were first organized by the Shanghai Handicrafts Administration. The state of the handicrafts industry there had been characterized by numerous trades, a wide variety of goods and a broad range of services — some products exceeding demand, while others fell short; some enterprises had heavy tasks, while others had light or insufficient tasks; some were lacking in funds, factory buildings and equipment, while others had assets, buildings and equipment that were lying idle. In 1979, in order to rapidly step-up production of industrial products for daily use — and in line with the demands for tapping the latent potential of enterprises, raising economic results, increasing products in short supply and organizing specialized coordination — the Shanghai Handicrafts Administration organized various forms of economic association among different trades, enterprises of different ownership and different sectors. Since 1980, additional attempts have been made to organize joint operation of handicraft enterprises. The superiority of this approach has begun to become evident and good economic results have been achieved.

After 30 years of development, China's handicrafts industry has undergone tremendous changes. Few handicrafts enterprises still resemble the original "family stores" or workshops, and few remain under completely manual operation; a considerable number of enterprises now have considerable size and are mechanized to a certain degree. As such, these enterprises now form a component part of light industry, often referred to as the second sector of light industry. Although this is still sometimes called the handicrafts industry, that term is habitual and no longer conforms to reality.

II. The Role of the Handicrafts Industry in Socialist Modernization

Handicrafts are an important component of China's national economy and play an active role in socialist modernization. Handicrafts fall into the category of labour-intensive work, and are therefore able to engage a large workforce and use more flexible management techniques. Handicrafts enterprises are adaptable, convenient for the masses, require less investment, produce quick results, and consume low quantities of energy. To achieve modernization, the handicrafts sector must gradually adopt modern science and technology and must make efforts to change its backward aspects. However, the positive role of the handicrafts industry in achieving modernization must not be underestimated.

China is a populous large country with a rich reserve of labour. But China has a weak foundation, its technology is backward and its economy undeveloped. To enable the handicrafts sector to reach its full potential, we must fully utilize all kinds of resources, open up all avenues of production and increase production of industrial consumer goods and arts and crafts. All this is of profound significance to improving people's livelihoods, to enlivening urban and rural markets, to increasing accumulation, to expanding exports and to satisfying employment goals, among other things. Some important aspects of the role of handicrafts in promoting modernization are as to follows:

1. Handicrafts are an important force for developing industrial goods for daily use.

Devoting major efforts to developing the production of consumer goods is a matter of vital importance to the national economy as a whole. It is also an important component in the readjustment of the structure of the national economy. Stepping up the production of consumer goods is at the crux of enlivening the national economy. Most handicrafts items are consumer goods. They are daily necessities for everyone and are closely linked to the people's livelihood. The main categories of products include hardware, plastic goods, leather, fur and fur products, clothing, shoes and hats, stationery, sporting articles, wooden furniture, sundry goods for daily use, bamboo products, rattan and palm-fibre goods and arts and crafts. There are tens of thousands of varieties. Some small commodities for daily use include buttons, thimbles, nipples for feeding bottles, hair pins, collar hooks, shoe eyes, needles, washboards, rolling pins, knives, scissors, locks, pots, bowls, wooden dippers and spoons. Although these products are small, they have a great impact. Shortages in these commodities would cause great inconvenience to the broad masses. Items such as washing machines, electric fans, electric irons, refrigerators, ready-made furniture, high-quality leather shoes and clothing, as well as mass-produced arts and crafts managed by handicrafts enterprises and departments of the second sector of light industry are required in ever-growing quantities as living standards of the people are constantly raised.

2. *Handicrafts are an important source for state accumulation of construction funds.*

Handicrafts enterprises are not large, and most of their products are small items with low profits. However, the handicrafts sector embraces numerous enterprises which manufacture a large quantity of products; the profits of these tens of thousands of products, if added together, would amount to a fairly sizeable figure. Industrial goods for daily use and manually-produced arts and crafts funds occupy a very large proportion of product output. Inasmuch as the fixed capital of these enterprises is rather low, it is possible to achieve greater results with less money and bring about fast results with less investment. According to statistics, recovery of investments in heavy industry takes an average of 5 years and 7 months, but in light industry it takes an average of only 1 year and 7 months. The recovery rate of investments in handicrafts is even faster. In arts and crafts, for example, from 1973 through 1979, state investments totalled 86.1 million yuan; productive capacity in terms of output value increased from 1,000 million to 4,000 million yuan; and total output value increased in real terms from 1,600 million yuan to 3,700 million yuan. For each yuan of investment, output value can be increased by 5—7 yuan, investments can begin to yield returns within the same year.

During this period, industrial, commercial and income taxes paid to the state amounted to 1,920 million yuan, yielding a ratio to state investments of 1:22.

3. *Handicrafts can create wealth for society by fully utilizing a variety of resources.*

Many approaches can be taken in the development of handicrafts production. As to raw materials, with the exception of imported materials, materials controlled by the state and those being distributed according to a unified plan — certain products can make use of local materials. Craftsmen who live on mountains can live off the mountain, those who live near the sea can live off the sea. In this way, waste can be converted into useful materials. Examples include feathers, shells, wicker, bark, weeds, palm leaves, maize husks, wheat stalks, bamboo shoots and leaves, all of which are useful for woven and carved products. Products made of bamboo, rattan, palm fibre and palm leaves have been developed into a wide category of arts and crafts employing 30 kinds of raw materials. With the exception of a small quantity of rattan, which has to be imported, all other materials are either agricultural sideline products or natural raw materials.

There are over 66,000 workers and staff members now engaged in these trades, with those working part-time totalling more than one million. The gross output value of these products in 1979 was 650 million yuan, with foreign-exchange earnings from exports amounting to U.S.$190 million.

China's handicrafts products are in great demand in western and northern Europe, Japan, Hong Kong, Southeast Asia and other countries and regions, and account for approximately 40% of the capacity of the international market. The arts and crafts straw-weaving factory of Linhai County in Zhejiang Province utilizes natural raw materials such as leaves from bamboo shoots, stalks, maize husks and ornamental grasses such as eulaliopsis to produce 200 kinds of straw-plaited hanging baskets, candy boxes and planters, which are exported to more than 30 countries and regions. There were only ten workers and staff members when the factory was established in 1971. By 1979, it increased its workers and staff members to 156 persons, with 25,000 persons outside the factory engaged in processing work for the factory; its annual output value reached 5.52 million yuan, with profits of 470,000 yuan. During the past nine years, the annual increase of output value was 56%. Total exports for the period earned U.S.$12,420,000 and profits reached 2.04 million yuan. Payments for processing work performed in rural areas amounted to 9.84 million yuan. With the growth of production, both peasants' income and exports have increased.

4. *Relatively fewer raw materials but more labour is used in handicrafts production, resulting in low levels of energy consumption.*

Much handicrafts production has now got rid of the slow pace and intensive manual labour of the past. Many processes have been mechanized or semi-mechanized. In some cases traditional craftsmanship has been combined with modern science and technology and thus greatly enhancing productivity. However, generally speaking, the share of input from manual labour is still relatively large. Engraving, weaving, drawnwork, embroidery and other work are mainly done by hand, and consumption of energy is relatively low. But in arts and crafts trades, consumption of coal and electricity has been even lower; the average amount of coal consumption for 10,000, yuan of output value was 0.96 tons, and electricity consumption, 540 kwh. According to statistics from Shanghai, in 1979 the average value of taxes and profits produced by 10,000 tons of energy (expressed in standard coal units) throughout Shanghai's industry enterprises was 7 million yuan; the average value produced by the Handicrafts Bureau was 22.02 million yuan — more than three times the aggregate level for the city.

For example, some peasants dramatically demonstrated the productive efficiency of drawnwork and embroidery; production requires a hosiery needle — which costs only 0.30 yuan, a string and two hands, and yet it is able to meet the demands of domestic and foreign markets. It will increase income and gain foreign exchange for the state, and it is a factory without smoke. This shows how the development of industrial goods for daily use and the production of arts and crafts will play a very important role in saving energy and in supporting the four modernizations.

5. *The larger the proportion of handicrafts exports, the greater the income from foreign exchange.*

Many manufactured consumer goods, especially arts and crafts, have a long tradition of superb techniques and fine quality. They enjoy a good reputation on the international market and are welcomed by customers abroad, thus earning a high rate of foreign exchange. Generally speaking, some of the products of the intensive labour type are not being manufactured in capitalist countries, where there is a shortage of labour forces and the wages are high. Giving full play to the superiority of the large number of labourers and low wages, we should develop these kinds of products. According to statistics, the export value of handicrafts and of products from the second sector of light industry reached U.S.$3,110 million in 1980, an increase of 25.6% over 1979; among these products, arts and crafts accounted for U.S.$1,200 million, an increase of 13.2% over 1979; hardware for daily use, U.S.$195 million, up 25%; hardware for use as tools and in construction, U.S.$198 million, up 44%; leather and fur products accounted for U.S.$386 million, an increase of 27.4%. Exports of clothing and of products made of feathers and velvet have expanded with particular speed in recent years, increasing by more than three times from 1977 to 1979; exports of these products reached U.S.$814 million in 1980, an increase of 41.4% over 1979. It should be noted, however, that many of our export products still occupy a very small proportion in international trade, and a great potential for expansion still exists. Exports to the United States and Europe in particular are relatively small. China's arts and crafts exports to the United States account for only 0.54% of the total trade volume of these products in the U.S. market.

6. *Handicrafts are able to accommodate a larger labour force and can thus expand social employment.*

China has a large population. An important means of solving the employment problem is to develop consumer industrial products and arts and crafts, especially those products that require intensive labour. According to statistics, the numbers of employees in heavy industry for each 1,000,000 yuan of fixed assets was 94 persons, while in light industry and textiles, the number was 257. In the four trades of arts and crafts, clothing, hardware for daily use and leather, however, the average number of employees for each 1,000,000 yuan of fixed assets was 800 persons, or 8.5 times the ratio in heavy industry and 3.1 times that of the overall average for light industry and textiles. Employment numbers would be even larger if people engaged in processing work outside of the factories were included. For example, regular workers and staff members in drawnwork and embroidery factories total 60,000, while those engaged in processing outside of the factories numbered 3,780,000. The drawnwork and decorative fringe factory at Changshu, Jiangsu Province, has more than 200 workers and staff members, while processing workers outside of the factory numbered 150,000.

In view of the above points the importance of China's handicrafts industry should not be underestimated. We want to accomplish a Chinese type of socialist modernization under which automated, mechanized and semi-mechanized production as well as various kinds of manual labour can be developed in coordination and so that the range and quality of production can be developed.

III. Measures for Further Development of the Handicrafts Industry

The party and government have decided to further carry out readjustment of the national economy beginning in 1981. This major policy decision followed an overall analysis of China's economic situation. Since the founding of the People's Republic, China's handicrafts have greatly developed and have achieved tremendous successes. However, there still exist quite a number of problems and the industry is still not able to meet objective demands. Some problems must be solved in the course of readjustment of the national economy. Possible solutions should be studied carefully in order to systematically develop and improve handicrafts.

Eliminating "Left" Influences. To lay the ideological foundation for the further development and improvement of handicrafts, the influence of "Left" thinking should be eliminated. In tackling problems in handicrafts, the main manifestations of "Left" thinking were: 1. Disregard for the objective law that relations of production must be suited to the nature of productive forces, thus advocating a too rapid and premature transition to ownership by the whole people. 2. Infringing on the proprietary right of collective-ownership enterprises, using various forms to indiscriminately transfer resources and divert funds, property and labour force of the collective economy. 3. Disrespect for the right of self-management in production and operations in enterprises of collective ownership and excessive interference in the internal affairs of enterprises; running collective ownership enterprises according to the models of enterprises owned by the whole people, thus discarding a host of fine traditions. 4. Lack of unified planning and due consideration for the full range of commodities concerned; lack of rational management of small commodities; planning without accounts and having no targets for material supply, with the result that for a long time production of small commodities was unstable. This abnormal production and reduction in the number of designs and varieties affected people's livelihood. 5. The administrative organs of handicrafts and combined organization of collective economy of mass character were abolished or amalgamated on several occasions. Effective systems and methods that had been formed over many years were undermined. This shows that considerable harm was done to handicrafts by the mistakes of "Left" tendencies. If this influence is not eliminated, the continued development and improvement of the handicrafts industry will be hindered.

Therefore, the influence of "Left" ideology must be eliminated in order to correctly handle the relationships between the goals of modernization and development of handicrafts and to establish the policy for a long-term rigorous development of handicrafts, and to correct some wrong views and practices as regards handicrafts; not only do enterprises owned by the whole people and those of collective economy have to be developed, individualized handicrafts also have to be developed properly.

Aspects of the Current Readjustment. In the course of its development the handicrafts industry has accumulated a wealth of positive and negative experiences. In view of the demands of the present new situation, it is extremely important to further emancipate thinking and rationally readjust all economic policies in handicrafts. Many collective handicrafts enterprises have been converted from small to large collective enterprises; enterprises that took sole responsibility for their own profits and losses have been converted to enterprises for which cities (or counties) are assuming unified responsibility for profits and losses; and from running a cooperative democratically to granting final say to administrative officials, effectively transforming enterprises into government organs.

The management of some enterprises has become like that of state-owned enterprises and this has encouraged workers and staff members to think in terms of the "iron rice bowl" and of "eating from the same pot." This situation must be steadfastly altered. Handicrafts enterprises under collective ownership should acquire the following attributes: with the aid of the state, working people should associate with each other voluntarily, raise funds by themselves, take part in manual labour, control the means of production together, carry out independent accounting, assume sole responsibility for profits or losses and practice distribution according to work; in other words, they should become collective economic organizations of a mass character. In compliance with the above mentioned, "government-run" enterprises should be transformed into enterprises "run by the people" — that is, enterprises of collective ownership that are worthy of the name.

In regard to the supply of raw materials, sales, exports, taxes, prices, wages and welfare facilities, old policies of utilization, restriction and transformation that applied to capitalist industry and commerce were followed. These imposed more restrictions but gave less assitance, required more effort, but helped solve only a few problems. This obstructed the development of handicrafts. As for those policies, measures and regulations which hamper the development of handicrafts production and dampen the enthuusiasm of workers and staff members, they must be reviewed seriously and reformed thoroughly. For instance, the supply of raw materials should be carried out through normal channels, and materials for unified distribution should be brought under state and local plans so as to assure continuous supply.

In the past, the major characteristics of handicrafts were: small but flexible; strong in adaptability and diversified in management; carrying out mass production and repair services; accepting manufacturing from raw materials and repairs as well as turning old materials into new ones; maintaining service branches and mobile services in support of both concentrated and diffuse production, both of which can be beneficial to productivity and convenient for people's livelihoods. Today, these traditional forms of management have for the most part been discarded, causing great inconvenience to people's livelihoods and arousing dissatisfaction among the masses. In the large and medium-sized cities, people say that it is difficult to buy or make clothing, to have something repaired or to buy furniture.

There are subjective reasons for this situation. Some enterprises prefer to manufacture goods instead of carrying out repair services; they prefer to engage in mass production rather than processing services; they prefer to produce goods that earn more profits rather than small, inexpensive commodities with low profits. This state of affairs has its causes. For example, the prices of small commodities, as well as the charges for processing and repairs are low, as are the profits, and this undoubtedly affects development of the enterprises and the welfare of workers and staff members. Moreover, they had failed to acquire materials through normal channels. All these issues should be resolved.

Improving Methods of Management. In order to bring into play the active role of the handicrafts industry, to make things convenient for the masses and to suit social needs in all aspects, the methods of management must be improved.

Firstly, organizational forms in handicrafts must be diversified and some large-scale enterprises should produce products in great demand by society. The scale of enterprises that produce small commodities which are manufactured and sold locally should not be too large for the purposes of changing designs or varieties at any time in accordance with social demand. If a number of small plants are merged into large factories, in terms of adaptation to market demands, they would not be as flexible as when they were functioning as scattered, small factories.

Secondly, the handicrafts processing that uses raw materials should be restored and developed. Some trades, such as clothing, shoes and hats, wooden articles, furniture and hardware should increase their service branches, expand processing with raw materials and accept orders for processing according to samples, turning old materials into new ones and so on.

Thirdly, the role of market regulation should be brought into greater play and factories should be more directly linked to the stores. Sales of most small commodities for daily use should be carried out by giving priority to the stores, thus cutting down on distribution and reducing expenses. Some products can be sold by the factories themselves, with the prices of products allowed to float to a certain degree to suit the situation of supply and demand in the market.

12. COMMUNE-AND-BRIGADE-RUN INDUSTRY IN CHINA'S RURAL AREAS

By Qi Zong

Bureau of Commune-Run Enterprises, Ministry of Agriculture

China has a population of 1 billion, 80% of which lives in rural areas. The collective economy has but a poor foundation and the living standard of the peasants is still rather low. In 1952, the labour force in rural areas numbered about 180 million and the various kinds of agricultural machinery had an aggregate horsepower of only about 250,000. But in 1979, total motorized power increased by 180 million hp while the labour force in the countryside, instead of shrinking, gained 130 million people since the period of the early 1950's. In 1952, each peasant worked 9 *mu* of cultivated land, but in 1979, each peasant had responsibility for only 4.8 *mu*. Thus, the increase in usage of machinery in farming has created a surplus labour force.

In order to alter the state of poverty and gradually provide work for surplus labourers in the countryside, the Central Committee of the Communist Party of China pointed out in the Decision on Some Questions Concerning the Acceleration of Agricultural Development that "it is not possible or necessary for all of the surplus labour force to find jobs in the existing large and middle-sized cities of the country, while it is also not possible or necessary for planned industrial and construction projects to be built in these cities." The solutions to these problems are: 1. Exploitation, utilization and development of resources should be undertaken in order to promote a diversified economy; 2. The individual economy of commune members should be allowed to expand; 3. Commune-and-brigade-run enterprises should be actively developed in market towns in the rural areas.

Through the general development of agriculture, forestry, animal husbandary, sideline occupations and fishing as well as the comprehensive management of agriculture, industry and commerce, the raising of labour productivity and the increase of the commodity exchange, the rural areas of China will be built into a rich and prosperous socialist countryside. The maintenance and development of commune industry is not only part of an inevitable trend but is also urgently needed by the majority of Chinese peasants.

I. Development of Commune-and-Brigade-Run Industry

China's commune-run industry came into existence in 1958, and has continued to develop and expand for over 20 years. The industry has long been underdeveloped and the rural areas had a "natural" economy for a long period of time. Initially because of the needs of the peasants, the handicrafts industry, the "five kinds of artisans" (the carpenter, bricklayer, blacksmith, mason and bamboo stripknitter) and the "four kinds of mills" (the power mill, bean-noodle mill, oil mill and bean-curd mill) were predominant at that time. Then, due to the socialist transformation of the handicrafts industry and to the state monopoly over the purchasing and marketing of grain, cotton and oil, many handicrafts mills were merged. The "four kinds of mills" were forced to cease operations due to a shortage of raw materials. These changes caused the peasants much inconvenience in their daily lives at home and at work. Enthusiastic endorsement for industry in the communes was prevalent after the people's communes were set up throughout the country in 1958. In order to develop commune-run enterprises, the property of the agricultural producers' cooperatives and their members was requisitioned without compensation. By the end of 1958, the labour force in the commune-run enterprises had reached 18 million and the gross output value of these enterprises was over 6,000 million yuan. This kind of "Left" adventurism seriously dampened the enthusiasm of the masses, causing a drop in agricultural production in 1960.

In order to correct the mistake of depriving the peasants of their property and to regain their confidence, slogans such as "return what one has unlawfully taken or pay compensation for it" and "going bankrupt for repaying debts" were promoted. Therefore, the commune-run enterprises were closed one after another. By 1961, the gross output value of commune-run industry throughout the country had been reduced to 1,980 million yuan. In 1962, the state also stipulated that "as a rule, the communes and production brigades are not to set up enterprises." Thus, by 1963, the gross output value of commune-run industry was reduced to 410 million yuan. There were 120,000 commune-run enterprises in Shandong province in 1958, but only 138 several years later.

In 1966, the Party Central Committee decided that "it is necessary for the communes to run some small factories." In response to this decision commune-and-brigade-run industry once again began to develop. By 1971, the gross output value of the commune-and-brigade-run industry reached 7,790 million yuan.

Following the Conference on Agriculture for North China in 1970, because of the prevalent ultra-"Left" notion of "learning from Dazhai in agriculture," commune-run industry was often criticized and compared to capitalist industry. But these enterprises had a strong appeal and inspired a great vitality among the people, so they continued to develop despite the criticism. In 1976, the gross output value of commune-and-brigade-run industry reached over 24,300 million yuan, of which 12,390 million yuan was attributed to commune-run industries, and 1,196 million yuan to brigade-run industries.

Since the downfall of the Lin Biao and Jiang Qing cliques, commune-and-brigade-run enterprises have won legitimacy. In 1978, the Third Plenary Session of the 11th Central Committee of the Communist Party of China pointed out in its "Decisions on Some Questions Concerning the Acceleration of Agricultural Development" that "under the principles of reason and economy, all agricultural and sideline products well-suited to being processed in rural areas should be increasingly produced by commune-and-brigade-run enterprises. Factories in the cities should, in a planned way, turn over those products or parts which can be processed in rural areas for processing by the commune-and-brigade-run enterprises, as well as lend support in equipment and guidance in technology." It was also stated that "the commune-and-brigade-run enterprises are entitled to a tax cut or tax exemptions." In 1979, the State Council promulgated the Resolutions on Some Questions Concerning the Development of Commune-and-Brigade-Run Enterprises (Draft for Trial Implemention). Since then, commune-and-brigade-run industry has been developing healthily. In 1977, the gross output value of the commune-and-brigade-run enterprises reached 32,270 million yuan and increased by 63.6% to 52,800 million yuan in 1980.

II. The State of the Commune-and-Brigade-Run Industry in 1980

The commune-and-brigade-run industry consists of enterprises run collectively by the communes, production brigades and market towns in rural areas. These enterprises include metallurgical, power, coal and coking, petroleum, chemical, engineering, building materials, forest, food, textile, sewing and leather, paper-making and stationery industries as well as arts and handicrafts such as knitting and embroidery.

There were 767,000 commune-and-brigade-run enterprises in 1980 employing over 19.91 million commune members. The gross output value of these enterprises reached 52,800 million yuan, of which the commune-run enterprises shared 28,700 million yuan or 54.3% of the total. The brigade-run enterprises shared 22,730 million yuan, or 42.1%, while the collective enterprises belonging to the commune-run industry in towns and cities shared 1,860 million yuan or 3.5%. The gross output value of commune-and-brigade-run enterprises in 1980 was 18,300 million yuan more than that of all industry in China in 1953.

The gross output value of the commune-and-brigade-run enterprises of different provinces, municipalities and autonomous regions, arranged in descending order, is as follows: the output value of Jiangsu Province reached 10,000 million yuan, accounting for 21.2% of the total in the country; the output value of Shandong, Guangdong and Zhejiang between 3,100 and 5,000 million yuan each, accounting for 24.4%; the output value of Hebei, Henan, Liaoning, Sichuan and Shanghai between 2,100 and 3,000 million yuan each, accounting for 26.3%; the output value of Hunan, Hubei and Shanxi between 1,100 and 2,000 million yuan each, accounting for 10.1%; the output value of Beijing, Tianjin, Jilin, Heilongjiang, Fujian, Jiangxi, Anhui and Shaanxi between 600 million and 1,000 million yuan, accounting for 14.3% each; the output value of Guangxi, Inner Mongolia, Yunnan, Guizhou, Gansu and Xinjiang between 100 million and 500 million yuan each, accounting for 3.5%; and the output value of Qinghai and Ningxia less than 100 million yuan each, accounting for 0.2%.

By examining the increase in output value of commune-and-brigade-run industry, it can be seen that output value in Shanghai, Jiangsu, Zhejiang and Guangdong increased by more than 31% in 1980 over the previous year; output value in Qinghai, Xinjiang and Fujian increased by between 21 and 30%; Liaoning, Beijing, Yunnan, Tianjin, Shaanxi and Hubei increased by between 11 and 20%; Jiangxi, Shandong, Shanxi, Jilin, Heilongjiang, Anhui, Henan and Hunan increased between 1 and 10%; and Hebei, Guangxi, Gansu, Inner Mongolia and Guizhou showed no increase in output value.

Light industry took up 43% of the total gross output value of the commune-and brigade-run industry and heavy industry accounted for 57%, of which the excavation industry took up 22.3%; raw materials industry, 14.3%; and manufacturing industry, 63.4%.

The commune-and-brigade-run industry has several distinguishing features. It has a collective-ownership economy of "independent accounting" and "assumes sole responsibility for its profits and losses." Only 20% of the industry's production, supply and marketing were directly or indirectly brought into the state plan; the rest was regulated by the market economy. Most of commune-and-brigade-run enterprises are small, each having an average of 20 workers and 19,000 yuan of fixed assets. Most of the enterprises are labour-intensive — every 10,000 yuan of fixed assets can provide for 10 workers and each worker turns out an output value of 2,624 yuan annually.

In order to take advantage of local conditions, to assure a rational distribution of industry and to avoid unnecessary redundancy in the construction of factories, the boundaries of different regions, communes and production brigades have been broken up. Under the principle of independent accounting, over 20,000 integrated economic complexes of various forms with each assuming responsibility for its own profits and losses have come into being, and over 1,100 specialized companies have been set up throughout the country.

To find a new way to speed up rural economic development, an experiment in setting up combined agricultural, industrial and commercial enterprises was carried out in 20 provinces, municipalities and autonomous regions in 1979. There were two kinds of experimental units for the rural collective economy: one was a state farm comprising collective units; the other was a combined organization within the collective unit. The experimental units were run by counties, people's communes, or production brigades. At present, the 16 county-run experimental units are well-developed. The include Yushu, Nongan and Huaide counties in Jilin Province; Anda and Keshan in Heilongjiang; Haicheng in Liaoning; the southern suburb of Taiyuan, Shanxi; Changan in Shaanxi; Fuyun in Xinjiang; Ruoergai in Sichuan; Puqi in Hubei, Kaiping and Gaoyao in Guangdong; Gaoan in Jiangxi; Jiading in Shanghai; and Taicang in Jiangsu. All of these experimental units have shown the superiority and great vitality of this new form of enterprise.

To clear the supply and marketing channels of the commune-and-brigade-run enterprises, supply and marketing corporations with a combined total of 30,000 staff members have been set up in over 95% of the counties in the country. These corporations had a turnover of 2,500 million yuan in 1980.

III. The Role of Commune-and-Brigade-Run Enterprises

China's commune-and-brigade-run enterprises can be divided into five categories: commune-and-brigade-run industry; agricultural and breeding farms; communications and transportation; building; and commercial services. Proportional distribution among the five sectors is as follows:

1. *The proportion of the number of enterprises:* commercial services, 9.3%; building, 3.3%; communications and transportation, 5.6%; plantations and breeding farms, 30%; industry, 51.8%.

2. *The proportion of workers in the enterprises:* commercial services, 5%; building, 10.3%; communications and transportation, 4%; plantations and breeding farms, 18.2%; industry, 62.5%.

3. *The proportion of income of the enterprises:* commercial services, 5.6%; building, 7.5%; communications and transportation, 4.1%; plantations and breeding farms, 6.5%; industry, 76.3%.

The commune-and-brigade-run enterprises have manifested ten areas of contribution to our country's national and rural economies:

1. *Commune-and-brigade-run enterprises have already played quite an important role in the national economy.*

In 1980, the total output value of commune-and-brigade-run industry amounted to 52,800 million yuan. The building materials produced by commune-and-brigade-run enterprises (brick, tile, lime, sand and stone) made up 80% of the total national output. Commune-and-brigade-run enterprises turned out 30% of the gold, 17% of the coal, 15% of the silk and 11% of the salt produced in China. Most arts and crafts products, such as knitting and embroidery, are made or processed by the commune-and-brigade-run enterprises and commune members. In 1980, commune-and-brigade-run enterprises provided 2,270 million yuan worth of export products for foreign trade, and supplied the home market with large quantities of goods, accounting for 10% of the output value of the country's light industrial products.

2. *Commune-and-brigade-run enterprises constitute an important part of the rural collective economy.*

The total income of these enterprises in 1980 was 61,400 million yuan, making up 34% of the total income of the rural economy; fixed assets were 32,600 million yuan, accounting for 35% of total rural fixed assets.

3. *Commune-and-brigade-run enterprises have helped the agricultural economic structure to develop from a single-management system, which cultivated only a limited variety of products, to a*

multiple-management system of agriculture, whose domain includes many aspects of farming, forestry, animal husbandry, sideline occupations and fishing.

In 1980, agriculture accounted for 54.2% of output in the six rural vocations of farming, forestry, animal husbandry, sideline occupations, fishing and industry. Of the 54.2% earned from agriculture, commune-and-brigade-run enterprises made up 28%; and forestry, animal husbandry, sideline occupations and fisheries, 17.8%. Tree farms, orchards and vegetable gardens run by communes and brigades covered 110 million *mu* of land. Cultivated forests occupied 19% of the total; fruit groves, 30%; tea, 33%; and silkworm cocoons, 10%.

4. *Commune-and-brigade-run enterprises have increased the country's revenue.*

In 1980, they paid 2,560 million yuan in state an agricultural taxes.

5. *Commune-and-brigade-run enterprises have helped the development of agricultural production.*

In 1980, they spent 2,260 million yuan of their profits to help agriculture.

6. *Commune-and-brigade-run enterprises have increased the incomes of commune members.*

In 1980, they paid a total of 1,190 million yuan in workers' wages. This means that each commune member added an average of 15 yuan to his income, accounting for 18% of the collective labour distribution of the commune member's income.

7. *In their supporting role, the commune-and-brigade-run enterprises have served the cities' big industries well.*

As big industry specializes in its production of a greater variety of products, it needs more small-sized factories to supply raw materials, semi-finished products, spare parts and fittings, and to make use of waste gas, liquids and residues, turning harmful wastes into less dangerous and even useful forms.

8. *Commune-and-brigade-run enterprises have served the interests of scientific research and development.*

Due to limitations in installations, capital and raw materials, some scientific research units met with much difficulty in experimental and small-batch production. Owing to a series of technological problems, many big factories have been unwilling to undertake the responsibility for scientific research. Commune-and-brigade-run factories, on the other hand, have given much priority to undertaking experimental scientific research work *gratis*, to acquiring new techniques to trial-produce new products, and to filling in gaps in the fields of science and technology for localities and the state.

For instance, in 1980, commune-and-brigade-run factories in Wuxi and Wujin counties of Jiangsu Province cooperated and signed contracts with over 100 science and teaching units. With assistance from scientific research units, the commune-and-brigade-run enterprises in Suzhou Region trial-produced over 100 new products.

9. *Commune-and-brigade-run enterprises have played an important role in the construction of market towns in the countryside.*

The industrial output value of market towns in the Chinese countryside in 1980 was 30,570 million yuan, an average of 560,000 yuan per town. In addition, the communes and brigades have operated service and repair trades in market towns. They are also important sources of construction capital in market towns. According to a survey of 35 towns in Wuxi County, Jiangsu Province, the total construction fund was 150 million yuan, 70% of which came from commune-and-brigade-run enterprises.

10. *Commune-and-brigade-run enterprises have opened a new means for absorbing surplus labour forces in the countryside.*

At present, commune-and-brigade-run enterprises have provided work for 29 million surplus labourers. As these enterprises grow, more of the surplus labour force will be absorbed.

IV. Existing Problems and the Direction for Future Development

The concept of commune-and-brigade-run enterprise, although relatively new, is of extreme importance for the Chinese peasants. Due to a lack of experience, and influenced by erroneous "Left" thinkers, who were over-anxious for the transition of ownership without a concrete programme, and due to the side-effects of sole reliance on market regulation, commune-and-brigade-run enterprises have developed on an uneven course. Most of the enterprises' profits have been used for expansion and the vital interests of the masses have been neglected. In addition, administration and financial management have not developed as well as could be desired. All of these problems must be settled in the course of the readjustment of our national economy.

From a long-term point of view, commune-and-brigade-run industry has a bright future. Along with the readjustment of economic policies for the countryside, this industry will surely break through the limitations of communes and production brigades, and combine into various forms of industries run by the brigades, by commune members jointly, by peasant individuals, as well as into handicrafts workshops run by each commune member-household.

The development of the commune-and-brigade-run industry should focus on the county as its basic unit. On the basis of investigation, exploitation and full use of local resources, the industry should be integrated with the development of rural market towns. Through unified planning and the rational distribution of local, state, urban and rural collective enterprises, and the handicraft workshops of commune members, commune-and-brigade-run enterprises will develop in the direction of combined specialized production and multiple-level management of industry, agriculture and commerce.

The task at hand is to gradually change the present system of commune-and-brigade-run enterprises, so that it may be built on the basis of joint-management by brigade and commune members.

After readjustment, consolidation and reform, the commune-and-brigade-run enterprises will surely develop more vigorously, and play an ever greater role in our country's socialist construction.

13. CHINA'S PETROLEUM INDUSTRY
By the Research Office,
Ministry of Petroleum Industry

The petroleum industry is one of the important energy industries in our country. During 1980, China's crude oil production reached 105.95 million tons (excluding Taiwan, as below), ranking sixth in the world, while natural gas production was 14,270 million cubic metres (cu.m.), placing China 13th. By supplying 26.8% of China's total primary energy production, petroleum and natural gas occupy an important position in the country's energy balance. The development of China's petroleum industry has been a significant achievement in our socialist construction.

I. Petroleum Development in China Since 1949

In 1949, when New China was founded, there were only three oil fields: Laojunmiao (also known in the West as Yumen) in Gansu Province, Dushanzi in Xinjiang and Yanchang in Shaanxi Province; there were two gas fields: Shengdengshan and Shiyougou, both in Sichuan Province; and there were two shale-oil plants, both in Liaoning Province. Annual production of crude oil was only 120,000 tons. At that time, China had only a few rigs for drilling medium-deep wells. With an annual drilling footage of only 4,500 metres (m.), the foundation of the petroleum industry was very weak.

Progress in Exploration and Output. After Liberation, the Ministry of Geology conducted massive geological prospecting work to develop China's petroleum industry. During the period of rehabilitation (1950-1952) and the First Five-Year Plan (1953-1957), production from the original oil fields was restored and expanded; exploration and exploitation of oil resources in the northwest were carried out, and the Karamay oil field in Xinjiang and the Lenghu oil field in Qinghai were successively discovered and developed.

During the First Five-Year Plan, the average annual growth rate for oil production was 27.1%. Oil production increased to 1.46 million tons in 1957 and natural gas production rose to 70 million cu.m. During the period of the Second Five-Year Plan (1958-1962), regional exploration was conducted in several large basins in the northeast, southwest and northern sectors of the country. Crude oil production was increased by a large margin during this period.

In 1959, the first commercial oil flows from the Songliao Basin in Northeast China confirmed the reserves of the Daqing oil field. In 1960, the battle for Daqing was organized and in only a few years exploitation of the new oil field had begun. In 1963, China's crude oil production rose to 6.48 million tons.

In December of the same year, at the Fourth Session of the Second National People's Congress, Premier Zhou Enlai solemnly declared that China has become basically self-sufficient in petroleum. The days when the Chinese people had to rely on imported oil had passed forever. Exploration and exploitation of the Daqing oil field not only removed the "oil-poor" label from China, but also provided much experience, such as in the application of dialectical materialism to the analysis and study of various contradictions in underground conditions in the oil fields, to the formulation of general and specific programmes for exploitation, and to the solution of technological problems in geology and development. Daqing also contributed to the fostering of the style of the "three honests and four stricts" (i.e., be honest in thought, word and deed; set strict standards for work, organization, attitude and observance of discipline) and to adoption of the system of personal responsibility, etc.

Starting in 1964, the stress of exploration was shifted to the Bohai Gulf basin. The Shengli oil field in Shangdong Province, Dagang oil field in Tianjin, Liaohe oil field in Liaoning Province, Jizhong oil field in Hebei Province were discovered and exploited one after another. Meanwhile, a large number of new oil fields were discovered in Jiangsu, Henan, Hubei and in the Shaanxi — Gansu — Ningxia area. In 1978, China's crude oil output reached 104.05 million tons, rising to 106.15 million tons in 1979. By then, China had become one of the major oil producing countries in the world.

Current Output. China can now meet its own needs in crude oil production, with a small surplus available for export. During the 30-year period from 1950 to 1979, the average annual growth rate for petroleum output was 25.3%, a relatively high rate. By the end of 1979, oil and gas fields had been discovered in 19 provinces, municipalities and autonomous regions. Of these, 122 fields were put into production. In addition, a total of 15 oil and gas production centres were established in Daqing, Jilin, Liaohe, Jizhong, Dagang, Shengli, Henan, Jianghan, Jiangsu, Xinjiang, Qinghai, Yumen, Changqing, Yanchang and Sichuan. The current state of development of several major oil and gas producing areas is described as follows:

Daqing. The Daqing oil region is located in the central part of the Songnen Plain in Heilongjiang Province. Daqing is an anticlinal structural oil reservoir of Cretaceous sediments. Exploitation of Daqing began in May 1960. At present, three oil fields are in operation, covering 1,022.4 sq.m. By the end of 1980, a total of 7,000 oil and water wells had been drilled, and a stable annual oil output of 50 million tons has been registered successively in the five years since 1976. As the oilfield was developed, water injection was initiated at an early stage to maintain the reservoir's pressure.

Daqing's crude oil is a paraffin-base light oil, with a wax content of 20-30%; its melting point is 25-30°C; viscosity is 10-11 centipoise; and sulfur content is below 0.1%. With a fairly complete array of production, scientific research, education and public service facilities, Daqing has become the largest oil producing base in China, as well as one of the giant oil fields of the world.

Shengli. The Shengli oil region lies in the Lubei Plain, adjacent to the seacoast near the mouth of the Huanghe River in the Bohai Gulf. Shengli, in operation since 1965, now comprises 23 producing oil fields, including Chunhua, Pingfangwang, Shangdian, Binnan, Linpan, Shanghe, Kenli, Kenxi, Bonan, Yihezhuang, Yibei, Yidong, Lijin, Wenliu, Shengtuo, Gudao, Dongxin, Chengdong, Yongan, Haojia, Xianhezhuang, Guangli and Wangjiagang. In 1980, total crude oil production reached 17.58 million tons.

The major productive formations in Shengli oil district are of Tertiary sandstone, mainly in the form of anticlinal structural reservoirs and fault-block reservoirs.

Jizhong. The Jizhong oil region is situated in the northern part of the Huabei Plain. The major productive formation is a Sinain Carbonate reservoir overlying a buried-hill type basement. Jizhong has been in production since 1976. Today, 14 oil fields covering 114.8 sq.m. are on stream. These include: Renqiu, Yanling, Longhuzhuang, Liulubei, Liulizhuang, Nanmeng, Hejian, Balizhuang, Xuezhuang, Balizhuangxi, Bieguzhuang, Zhongchikou, Yongqing and Mozhoudong. Crude production in 1980 reached 16.026 million tons. The discovery of Jizhong's buried-hill reservoirs has opened a new sphere of oil exploration for our country.

Liaohe. The Liaohe oil region is located in the northeastern part of the Liaodong Gulf. The major productive formations are Tertiary sandstone, mainly anticlinal structural reservoirs and fault-block reservoirs. Since the start of the high-production oil flow from the first well in the middle part of the Xinglongtai faulted structure zone in July 1969, nine oil fields were discovered and exploited in succession, including the Xinglongtai, Shuguang, Huanxiling, Gaosheng, Huangjindai, Yulou, Rehetai, Fahaniu and Damingtun fields. These oil fields, covering 174.5 sq.m., produced 5.09 million tons of oil in 1980.

Liaohe also contains oil and gas reservoirs of various types and the distribution of oil, gas and water is rather complex. In recent years, some comprehensive measures have been taken in line with the characteristics of Liaohe's oil fields and conditions for exploitation have been improved.

Dagang. The Dagang oil region lies at the mouth of the Haihe River, south of Tianjin. In late 1965, the Beidagang oil field was discovered in the Tertiary. Thereafter, another nine oil fields were discovered and exploited, with a total area of 150.5 sq.m. These include Yangsanmu, Yangerzhuang, Banqiao, Zhouqingzhuang, Wangxuzhuang, Kongdian, Zaoyuan and Wangguantun. Most of these oil fields were created by faulting. Some produce thick oil of high viscosity, and sand up vigorously. Oil production in 1980 totalled 2.908 million tons.

Xinjiang. The Xinjiang oil region — with the discovery of the Karamay oil field in 1955 — now has three oil fields on stream; these include Karamay, Dushanzi and Baikouquan. The productive formation is Tertiary sand-conglomerate, consisting of a stratigraphic oil accumulation formed by monocline and faults. By adopting the techniques of water injection at an early stage and seperate-layers injection, output has risen steadily, reaching 3.905 million tons in 1980.

Sichuan. The Sichuan oil and gas region includes Sichuan Province and part of western Hubei. It covers 230,000 sq.km. of sedimentary basins. Drilling here began in 1953. Up to now, a total of 59 gas fields and 11 oil fields have been discovered. Of these, 53 gas fields have been put into operation, with a flow of 6,300 million cu.m. in 1980. The Sichuan basin contains ten oil and gas bearing formations dating from the Sinian to the Jurassic; the reservoirs are mainly fractured. In recent years, stimulation measures have included the drilling of deep exploratory wells, seismic exploration and large-scale acid fracturing treatment, all adopted with good results.

The Continental Shelf. In addition to the above fields, the Ministry of Petroleum Industry and the Ministry of Geology have carried out geophysical exploration and exploratory drilling on the continental shelf. In the Bohai Gulf, 95 exploratory wells have been drilled successively, of which 22 have resulted in commercial oil flows with three production platforms constructed. In the South China Sea, in Beibu Gulf, Yinggehai and outside the Zhujiang River estuary, 17 exploratory wells have been drilled, 8 of which have produced oil. Exploratory work has also been carried out in the East China sea.

Developments in Refining. With the continuous growth of crude oil production, the refining industry of our country has also developed considerably. When the People's Republic of China was founded, there were only a few small refineries in Gansu and Liaoning provinces, with a total annual crude distillation capacity of only 116,000 tons. At that time, the country was dependent mainly on imported petroleum products. After Liberation, these refineries were rapidly restored and put back into operation. After reconstruction and expansion, their capacity was greatly increased. However, they could then produce only 38 varieties of petroleum products, such as gasoline, kerosine, diesel fuel and small quantities of lubricating oils.

The Lanzhou Refinery. In 1958, China's first large refinery, at Lanzhou, had its test run. In 1963, the Daqing refinery, the first to be designed, equipped and constructed by China, went into operation. During the 1960's, some of the most advanced petroleum refining processes of that time — such as catalytic cracking, catalytic reforming, delayed coking, and manufacture of catalysts and additives — were mastered by China's refiners, resulting in a wider variety and better quality of products. Thus, we achieved our goal to rely basically on domestic petroleum products, and our country became basically self-sufficient in this area. In the 1970's, new processing technologies were developed successively; for example, riser catalytic cracking, multimetallic catalytic reforming, hydro-treating and molecular sieve dewaxing. At the same time, great progress has been made in refinery construction. Today, refineries are distributed over 21 provinces, municipalities and autonomous regions. Refineries with annual capacities of over 500,000 tons now total 33. They can produce 687 kinds of products. The capacity of China's refineries, as well as the variety, quality and quantity of their products, can now basically satisfy the requirements of socialist construction in our country. In addition, China's petroleum products have begun to enter the international market. A description of some of China's major refineries is given below:

The Lanzhou Refinery was completed and placed into operation in 1958. Its original designed capacity was 1 million tons per year; now the capacity is 3 million tons per annum. This refinery has become a petroleum processing complex, including production of fuels and lubricating oils, as well as the manufacture of catalysts, additives, petroleum equipment and instruments. The refinery consists of 52 processing units. It produced 109 kinds of petroleum and petrochemical products and in 1980 was chosen as an advanced organization in product quality and energy conservation.

The Changling Refinery. The Changling Refinery went into production in 1970. Its designed capacity was 2.5 million tons per year, now expanded to 3.5 million tons annually. The refinery is of fuel-catalyst type, possessing nine process units. In 1980, it produced 25 kinds of petroleum products and chemicals and was selected as an advanced refinery in energy conservation, product quality, environmental protection and personnel training.

The Shanghai Refinery. The Shanghai Refinery had been a storage terminal prior to 1949. At present, its crude capacity is 4.3 million tons per annum. This refinery is a fuel-lubricating oil refinery, with 22 processing units. In 1980, it produced 79 kinds of petroleum products, and has been singled out as an advanced refinery in energy conservation and product quality, as well as in enterprise management.

The Daqing Petrochemical Complex. The Daqing Petrochemical Complex went into operation in 1963. Its designed annual capacity was 1 million tons, now increased to 4.8 million tons. The complex consists of a fuel–lubricating oil refinery, a chemical plant and a fertilizer plant. In 1980, it produced 38 kinds of petrochemical products, and was selected as an advanced organization in product quality.

The Dalian No. 7 Petroleum Refinery. The Dalian No. 7 Petroleum Refinery had a crude capacity of only 49,000 tons annually in 1950; by 1980, its annual capacity stood at over 5 million tons. It is now a fuel-lubricating oil refinery. In 1980, this refinery produced 84 kinds of petroleum products, and is one of China's major exporting refineries. It has been closen as an advanced enterprise in energy conservation.

The Dongfanghong Refinery. The Beijing Yenshan Petrochemical Industry Corporation's Dongfanghong Refinery went into operation in 1969. Its original designed capacity was 2.5 million tons per year. By 1980, its capacity stood at 7.5 million tons per year. The refinery is a fuel-lubricant type, and possesses 15 refining units. In 1980, it produced 40 kinds of oil products, and was elected as an advanced refinery in environmental protection.

Pipeline Construction. With the development of the petroleum industry, the construction of long-distance oil and gas pipelines has been carried out vigorously. Up to the end of 1979, a total of 9,746 km. of long-distance pipeline were built, and a crude oil pipeline network was initially set up in northeastern and northern China. Crude oil from major oil fields such as Daqing, Jizhong, Dangang, Shengli and Liaohe can be transported directly to ports and refineries through the pipelines. The oil pipeline volume in 1979 accounted for 61.2% of China's total domestic crude oil transportation.

Technological Progress. Through 30 years' efforts, great advances have been made in petroleum science technology:

Geological Exploration. In the field of geological exploration, a complete range of comprehensive exploratory methods for oil and gas has been established and mastered. Moreover, the geological theories of lake basin deposit facies, oil and gas field formation, and oil generation in sedimentary basins of continental origin have been enriched.

Also, important achievements have been made in research into the mechanism of buried-hill type formations and fault-block reservoirs. Comprehensive geophysical prospecting techniques — including gravity, magnetic, electric and seismic surveys — have been promoted. Digital seismic instruments have been introduced, hence significantly improving the technique and precision of seismic exploration. Seismo-stratigraphy geology has been applied to the study of strata, rock character and facies.

A large quantity of field geophysical logging instruments have been successively manufactured. Logging series and log interpretation methods for sand-shale have been established; a digital processing technique has been preliminarily developed and is being advanced with the aim of achieving a complete range of logging series and digitalization.

Drilling Technology. In drilling, as the techniques of jet drilling, high-efficiency bits and high-quality mud have been popularized, drilling speed and quality have been raised. Deep-drilling techniques for depths of more than 3,000 m. have been skillfully applied, and eight ultra-deep wells of 6,000-7,000 m. have been tentatively put into operation. In oil field development, the production techniques of water injection for pressure maintenance and separate-layer production have received wide-scale application and expanded development; reservoir engineering methods and production techniques suitable to the specific conditions of China's oil fields and aimed at higher productivity and long-term stable oil production, have been initially created.

Refining Technology. Daqing, in particular, has become more advanced in the study of exploitation geology and production technology. Based on its mastery of 1960's refining technologies, Daqing has developed refining techniques suited to the characteristics of China's crude oil, as well as to the needs of the national economy; a number of oil products have been especially developed for sophisticated defence purposes and for use in imported equipment; a large quantity of high-efficiency refining machinery and equipment have been put into use; production processes controlled by computers have been tested on some atmospheric-vacuum units; and a group of in-line analyzers have been developed.

In some refineries, storage and transport systems have been computerized and are automatically operated with remote metering, controls and signalling. Also, some new technologies and techniques have been applied to oil sewage treatment and to noise-pollution control.

Research Capabilities. In the course of scientific research and production, a corps of scientists and technicians has been built up, who are capable of tackling key problems independently. At present, we have set up a number of scientific research organizations of considerable size and advancement; these comprise a relatively complete range of specialties. There are a total of 29 key scientific research institutes and 6 experimental centres possessing comparatively advanced scientific research facilities, including a number of pilot plants, model test engines and test rigs.

Education. Great achievements have been gained in educational work in the petroleum industry. Before Liberation, there were no petroleum educational institutions in our country. Petroleum specialties were established in the institutions of higher learning only after the foundation of New China. As a result of 30 years' construction, five petroleum institutions have been set up — Huadong, Xinan, Daqing, Jianghan and Fushun. They offer a total of 36 programmes of specialization, with a combined enrollment of 7,383 students; graduates of these programmes number 23,734. There are 25 secondary technical schools in the petroleum industry, with a total of 122 specialities and an enrollment of 14,943; accumulated graduates number 87,290. Petroleum enterprises have themselves established 18 colleges for their own workers and staff members; they also operate 92 complete college-level television courses with more than 5,800 students enrolled.

After 30 years' construction, Chinese petroleum industry has attained relatively high levels and a fairly high volume of exploration, exploitation, crude-oil processing, machinery manufacture, oil field facilities and pipeline construction, as well as in scientific research and design. Large numbers of petroleum workers and staff members with a relatively complete range of specialties have been developed. Over the past 30 years, the petroleum industry's accumulated volume of profits and taxes turned into the state tripled the value of total investments in capital construction. In 1979, the profit ratio per 100 yuan of investment funds was 60 yuan; circulating funds per 100 yuan in output value was 16.8 yuan.

II. Petroleum Industry Development in 1980

In implementation of the guiding principle of readjustment of the national economy, the production and construction situation in the Chinese petroleum industry progressed fairly well in 1980.

Readjustments and Output in 1980. In oil field development, the exploitation of new regions was carried out conscientiously in each oil field, the construction of newly exploited areas proceeded normally and their oil output was fairly stable. Comprehensive readjustment, including measures to increase oil production and to retard depletion rates, was carried out in 22 sectors of existing oil fields such as those at Daqing, Jizhong, Dagang, Liaohe and Karamay. Crude oil production totalled 105.95 million tons in 1980, or 100.3% of planned state targets for the whole year; the production of natural gas totalled 14,270 million cu.m., or 104.2% of the annual target. More than 13.309 million tons of crude oil was exported, while exports of petroleum products totalled 4.2 million tons.

Exploration Activities in 1980. Exploration for oil and gas has been carried out in the eastern part of the country with searches for geologically

CHINA'S CRUDE OIL AND NATURAL GAS PRODUCTION

Period	Average Annual Production		Annual Crude Processing Volume (million tons)	Number of Products
	Oil (million tons)	Gas (million cu.m.)		
Rehabilitation Period (1950-52)	.32	6	.38	38
First 5-Year Plan (1953-57)	1	28	1.24	140
Second 5-Year Plan (1958-62)	4.45	824	4.28	416
Readjustment Period (1963-65)	8.76	1,060	8.34	494
Third 5-Year Plan (1966-70)	19.36	1,806	17.6	577
Forth 5-Year Plan (1971-75)	56.12	6,188	41.76	636
1976	87.16	10,100	57.71	642
1977	93.64	12,123	63.10	648
1978	104.05	13,734	70.70	656
1979	106.15	14,515	71.46	668
1980	105.95	14,276	75.38	687

FINANCIAL STATISTICS FOR THE PETROLEUM INDUSTRY

Period	Output Value (million yuan)	Investment in Capital Construction (million yuan)	Profits (million yuan)	Taxes (million yuan)
Rehabilitation Period (1950-52)	336.69	156.1	63.93	6.09
First 5-Year Plan (1953-57)	2,259.15	1,954.73	673.58	232.22
Second 5-Year Plan (1958-62)	7,874.1	3,739.31	2,644.62	959.60
Readjustment Period (1963-65)	8,702.51	1,701.01	3,123.96	1,223.23
Third 5-Year Plan (1966-70)	30,112.78	4,007.64	12,839.50	3,281.40
Forth 5-Year Plan (1971-75)	70,591.56	9,213.60	30,646.98	8,817.34
1976	19,660.03	2,250.15	8,734.58	2,190.13
1977	21,456.65	2,321.62	9,409.11	2,390.19
1978	24,412.91	4,389.00	10,419.11	2,707.98
1979	15,727.09	3,404.91	10,520.81	2,909.42
1980	26,559.12	3,576.60	10,615.91	3,030.82
Totals	237,692.59	36,714.67	99,692.09	28,288.42

complicated reservoirs. At the same time, regional exploration (mainly seismic surveys) was strengthened in several large basins in the west. Commercial flows of oil and gas were begun in more than 400 exploratory wells in the east; hence, a number of oil-bearing regions and sectors were discovered and proved. In offshore exploration, agreements with foreign oil companies were signed, and geophysical surveys were conducted over an area of 430,000 sq.km. in the South China sea and southern Yellow Sea; 110,000 km. of seismic lines were finished; and four contracts were signed with Japanese and French oil companies to carry out joint exploration and exploitation of oil and gas in parts of the Bohai Sea and Beibu Gulf.

Readjustments in Refining. In adapting to the demands of the national economy, all refineries readjusted their processing schemes, placing stress on raising yields, improving quality and conserving energy. Production plans were fulfilled in all respects. Outputs of gasoline, lubricating oils, commercial fuel oil, petrochemical naphtha, paraffin and asphalt increased by large margins over 1979. Of these, production of petrochemical naphtha increased by 41.5%. The overall commodity yield of petroleum products reached 91.8%, while the volume increase in petroleum products came to 950,000 tons. Among the oil products of major refineries, world-level quality requirements were approached or attained for 88 kinds of products, including jet fuel, lamp kerosene, motor gasoline, refined white paraffin, universal diesel oil, asphalt and portions of naphtha output. National gold and silver medals were awarded to ten oil products.

Efforts in Energy Conservation. All petroleum enterprises made great efforts to reduce energy consumption as well as to raise output. By introducing measures such as oil transportation without heating, recovery of light hydrocarbons, treatment of oily sewage, and converting oil-burning boilers to coal, cumulative energy consumption of all oil fields fell by 0.6% as compared with 1979. Hence, commodity yields of crude distributed by state monopolies reached 95.1%, with crude supplies surpassing the state plan by more than 1 million tons. Refining enterprises carried out energy-saving transformation on 16 units and implemented energy-saving measures such as recovery of waste heat, renovation of heating furnaces, improvement of boiler efficiency, regulation of machines and pumps, readjustment of heating networks and heat exchange flow; these efforts resulted in lowering cumulative energy consumption by 10.58% over the previous year. As a result, even though refining volume increased by 5% in 1980, overall energy consumption fell by 6%.

In long-distance pipeline transportation, measures were taken to reform oil transportation procedures, to rationalize operating conditions and to transport oil without raising or lowering temperatures; as a result, the energy consumed by pipeline transportation fell by 4%. In 1980, all petroleum enterprises saved a total of 960,000 tons of crude and fuel oils, 300 million kwh of electricity and 26,000 tons of oil products.

Achievements in Research. With regard to scientific research in petroleum, the management of scientific planning and the achievement of results was strengthened. A total of 46 scientific and technological research projects were completed. Many of these were badly needed for current production and yielded significant techno-economical results after being put into practice. For example, a foam-plastic pipe-line cleaner prepared by the Pipeline Transportation Bureau of the Ministry of Petroleum Industry solved the problem of pipeline deformation and difficulties caused by paraffin. After being put into use in the northeast, the annual pipeline flow volume increased from 37 million tons to 40.3 million tons. An atmospheric residue catalytic cracking and metal deactivator, developed by the Petroleum and Chemical Engineering Scientific Research Institute, showed good results in reducing the requirement for feed-stock in catalytic cracking and in increasing the yield of light products by 6%; a total of 2 million yuan was saved on a pilot unit with an annual capacity of 120,000 tons. By popularizing CO combustion supporters, more than 80,000 tons of diesel oil was saved and an accumulated annual increase of more than 19 million yuan in income was achieved in refineries such as Changling, Daqing and Shanghai.

In 1980, the Ministry of Petroleum conducted an appraisal of 64 scientific and technological research results: 12 were presented with national invention awards and four each won second, third and fourth grade awards.

Reforms in Management. In 1980, all petroleum enterprises further improved their operational management, vigorously pursued either increased production with efforts to economize or increased revenues and reduced expenditures, and good results were obtained. A total of 15 refineries and 3 machinery building factories gained experience in methods of increasing their decision-making powers. Based on the principles of "fixing tasks and costs, retaining a portion of surpluses and savings and offering rewards according to *fen* (a unit of grade mark)," all oil fields further improved and perfected their managerial methods; good economic results were also obtained from establishing internal cost-accounting; vigorously enforcing economic responsibilities and improving the system of rewards. In 1980, gross output value for the petroleum industry registered an increase of 3.2% over 1979; profits turned into the state for 1980 were 10,610 million yuan; and taxes totalled 3,030 million yuan.

Current Problems. Currently, the main problems facing China's petroleum industry are: deficiencies in proven reserves, disproportions in reserves-to-production ratios, depletion of old oil fields, and difficulties in maintaining current production levels. These problems owe mainly to three factors: the decade of turmoil (the "cultural revolution"), when growth of crude production exceeded that of reserves; after 1976, insufficient regional exploration was carried out and no important breakthroughs were gained; the load on old oil fields had to be increased in order to maintain production growth.

According to the guiding principles of readjustment of the national economy and to national energy policy, during the period of readjustment, an appropriate readjustment in crude production should be made and exploration should be enhanced so as to increase crude reserves, to improve the reserves-to-production ratio and to prepare for future development.

Future Prospects. Thirty years' practice in petroleum exploration and exploitation, as well as the current situation in the petroleum industry have shown that targets for readjustment of the petroleum industry can be realized and that the prospect for future development is fairly good. Throughout China's land area, widely dispersed sedimentary rocks are favourable for oil and gas accumulation and generation. The land area covers 4.2 million sq.km., while the area of offshore continental shelf (with a water depth of 200 m.) is 1.3 million sq.km.; average thickness of sedimentary rocks is 4,000 m., hence the total volume is about 22 million cu.km.

The eastern region, including the Songliao Basin, Bohai Gulf Basin, Erlian Basin and Nanyang Basin, covers 940,000 sq.km. Hundreds of oil and gas fields have been discovered, among which is one giant oil field as large as Daqing and an oil field with production as high as Jizhong. Although the region has been extensively explored, new discoveries have occurred continuously by drilling in the deeper formations; and additional new reserves have been enlarged by quite a number of newly discovered oil-bearing structures and blocks after further exploration; also, new oil-bearing areas may be discovered in the less explored basins and depressions.

The western region, including the sedimentary basins of Junggar, Tarim, Qaidam, Ordos and the Hexi Corridor, covers 1.18 million sq.km. Apart from the known oil fields at Yumen, Karamay, Lenghu and Changqing, throughout this widespread region only a small amount of general investigation and drilling work has been carried out in local areas. Hence, this is an important area for increasing crude reserves.

China's continental shelf extends for 1.3 million km., while the area of main sedimentary basins covers 950,000 sq.km. Based on the preliminary analysis of current data, 400 structures were discovered in portions of the sea areas of Nanhai, Huanghai and Bohai and oil flows were established in 30 wells over the sea area of Bohai and Nanhai. The prospect for locating oil and gas reserves is fairly favourable — the continental shelf is an important area for solving the problem of expanding known crude reserves.

The marine carboneous sediment area in southern China — occuring in Dian, Qian, Gui, Jiangzhe and Xiange — covers 2 million sq.km. and has been subject to only minimal investigation.

In Sichuan, sedimentary deposits cover 230,000 sq.km. and are rich in natural gas resources.

Throughout the above-mentioned widespread sedimentary regions there exist many oil-bearing formations; commercial oil and gas flows have been discovered in sediments from the Sinian and Cambrian levels of Paleozoic to Tertiary of Cenozoic. During the past 30 years, however, exploratory work has been conducted mainly in shallow formations above 3,000 metres. Most are known as structural oil pools; hence, some important spheres for oil exploration have yet to be broken through. The prospecting potential for oil and gas resources is fairly high.

Accordingly, in the period of readjustment, maintenance of current levels of crude production will rely mainly on the eastern region, while further increases in reserves and production will depend on activities in the western region and offshore.

For the eastern region, efforts will be made to improve and perfect the development of the old oil fields, as well as to increase recovery rates; to prolong stable crude production and to retard depletion; to adopt technically advanced and economically appropriate measures to exploit those portions of proven reserves which are relatively difficult to develop; and to enhance exploration so that more reserves can be found and stable production be maintained.

In the western region, selecting favourable areas with good geology and surface conditions, seismic investigation could be carried out to a wide extent; if exploratory drilling can be increased steadily according to the progress of exploration and to resources of the state, then new oil fields might soon be discovered. At the same time, cooperation with foreign oil companies should be continued; utilization of foreign capital and technology are pursued vigorously and conscientiously, exploration and exploitation of offshore oil resources can be accelerated. And, if after several years' efforts, reserves-to-production ratio may be improved, then favourable conditions for the further development of the petroleum industry may be formulated.

For the future development of the petroleum industry, advanced technology, larger investments and greater amounts of work are needed. By implementing the guiding principle of readjustment of the national economy, drawing up feasible techno-economical policies, reforming operational management, reinforcing scientific research, enhancing technical training and doing all work in a down-to-earth manner, the readjustment targets of the petroleum industry can ultimately be realized.

14. CHINA'S COAL INDUSTRY
By the Research Division, General Office,
Ministry of Coal Industry

I. Development of China's Coal Industry

Coal is the principal energy resource of China. Since the establishment of the People's Republic in 1949, coal has supplied approximately 70% of the country's energy consumption needs. The coal industry has thus become one of China's major industrial sectors.

China is rich in coal resources and has all types of coal deposits. Proven reserves exceed 600,000 million tons. Of China's 2,000 or more counties (municipalities), more than half have coal deposits. Shanxi Province alone has proven reserves of well over 200,000 million tons.

The party and the government have attached great importance to the growth of China's coal industry. Total capital investment in the coal industry has amounted to 44,930 million yuan since the founding of New China. The capacity of mines brought into production each year has averaged 11,087 million tons. Meanwhile, as a result of the further tapping of the existing potential, of technical innovations and of selected reconstruction of existing mines — along with the vigorous growth of small, locally run mines — coal production has been increasing rapidly.

Growth in Output Since 1949. In 1949, the total output of raw coal was only 32.43 million tons. By 1957, following three years of economic rehabilitation beginning in 1950 and after completion of China's First Five-Year Plan, coal output increased to 13,073 million tons. Although the coal industry had by then gone through some tortuous roads on the way to advance, the rate of development has been relatively fast. In 1977, after the overthrow in 1976 of the Gang of Four, annual coal production reached 500 million tons, and maintained a level above 600 million tons during the period from 1978 to 1980. Thus, during the period from 1949 to 1980, China's coal output increased at an average annual rate of 10%.

Through 31 years of reconstruction since 1949, China's coal industry has become an industrial sector of considerable scale. There are now 2,200 coal mines operated above the county level. Total employment is 4,190,000. Of the total number of mines, 580 are under the jurisdiction of the Ministry of Coal Industry; these have a combined annual designated capacity of 290 million tons. Coal mines operated by the provinces, prefectures and counties total 1,634, with an annual designated capacity of over 180 million tons. The number of coal mining centres with an annual production of more than 50 million tons has expanded to 20, of which 10 have production capacities exceeding 10 million tons. Annual production in the Kailuan and Datong coal mining centres has reached more than 20 million tons each.

Improvements in Processing. Significant improvements have also been made in coal processing. A total of 176 treatment plants have been built or expanded. At present, processed raw coal in China totals 100 million tons annually. Additional new coal mining centres, mines and treatment plants are now under construction.

Technological Development. With development both in production and construction, a great many changes have also taken place in technological levels of the Chinese coal industry. Coal mining in China has virtually done away with the backward methods of human postage and hauling by draught animals as practised in the old society, and fully mechanized and semi-mechanized operations have been installed. At present, China has more than 1,200 single-drum shearers of domestic manufacture, and 223 installations of fully mechanized equipment supplied both by domestic and overseas manufacturers. Similarly, coal production methods in China's coal mines have been improving, advanced mining technology has been progressively popularized, plans for mining development are following rational procedures and technical know-how in equipping the mines is increasing steadily. Today, single longwall mining is extensively used for dip and flat-dip and thin and medium-thick seams, while double-unit face longwall and inclined longwall methods have been used successfully in some mines. In most flat-dip and dip thick seams, inclined slice and slice-with-water sand stowing are in general use. In steep seams, mining methods such as horizontal slicing with artificial roofs, overhead step systems, small steps and coal winning with shields are all widely used methods. In addition, hydraulic mining has also been developed to a considerable extent. At present, in mines under jurisdiction of the state coal industry, the longwall method of mining accounts for 86.74% of the coal produced, while the methods of horizontal slicing, coal winning with shields and the overhead step system for steep seams as well as hydraulic mining account for 4.58% of the total.

Technical and equipment capabilities in capital mine construction are improving and the construction work force has become rich in skills. Techniques of shaft construction are improving rapidly. A production line for shaft sinking mechanization has begun to be adopted in common shaft sinking, while other special sinking methods have achieved varying results. Since the country's liberation in 1949, more than 300 shafts have been successively sunk using techniques of freezing, bore-holes, the curtain method and drop-shaft sinking; 21 shafts have been sunk with shaft-sinking machines: these have a maximum diameter of 7.9 mm. and depths up to 308 metres. A number of grabbing, hoisting, loading and hauling machines for sinking and tunneling have been developed, and a small quantity of complete sets of equipment have been imported. The mechanization level for underground heading and loading has reached 80%.

In order to keep pace with the development of the coal industry, educational units and special research organizations pursuing geological engineering and scientific subjects have been established.

Exploration, Planning and Research. There are now 24 coal geology companies and 125 geological exploration teams at work throughout the coal industry. Borehole and geophysical surveys are the major methods for geological exploration at present. In areas with good conditions, a combination of geophysical and borehole methods is adopted. Meanwhile, the development of up-to-date exploration techniques, the manufacture of digital seismographs and modernization of drilling equipment is underway.

Up to the present, 30 coal-mining engineering and planning institutes have been set up, of which eight are main institutes under the Ministry of Coal Industry. These institutes can undertake design and planning work for mines and processing plants of various capacities. New computer technologies have begun to be employed in design and planning.

There are now 31 coal science research institutes and laboratories engaged in a range of research work in areas such as coal geology and exploration, coal extraction, mine construction, mining safety, coal processing, mining machinery and coal chemistry.

There are at present 12 colleges, 36 technical schools and 102 vocational schools training personnel for the coal industry. The number of graduates since 1949 has totalled 120,000.

The fact of the development of China's coal industry eloquently proves the superiority of the socialist system. It is clear that we could have accomplished still greater achievements and a faster development rate had it not been for the setbacks caused by the ten-year calamity of the "cultural revolution" and the influence of erroneous "Left" thinking.

II. The Consolidation and Advance of China's Coal Industry in the Midst of the 1980 National Economic Readjustment.

Because of long-term interference and sabotage by Lin Biao and the Gang of Four during the "cultural revolution" and the influence of "Left" thinking in our economic work, serious imbalances occurred in the coal industry. The serious imbalance between extraction and development in some mines, caused by improper coordination in the production chain and poor application of safety measures and compounded by problems of insufficient housing for workers, brought about great difficulties in the development of the coal industry.

In 1980, China's coal industry adhered the policy of taking readjustment as the key link and embraced the spirit of ensuring the necessary supply of coal during the national economic readjustment, while at the same time pursuing the readjustment within the coal industry itself. The readjustment work proceeded apace, and various tasks in coal mine production and construction were satisfactorily fulfilled. The coal industry has been able to achieve both consolidation and advancement in the course of the readjustment:

1. Coal output: *Coal production was maintained at 600 million tons while readjustment work in the mines progressed.*

China's raw coal output in 1980 was 620.13 million tons, representing a 7.9% increase over the state plan requirements. This accomplishment was both essential and advantageous to readjusting proportionate relationships within the coal industry. Although coal output in 1980 was 2.4% less than the 1979 total, the average annual production level of 600 million tons, a high level of production, was maintained.

Of the 1980 total, 344.39 million tons were produced by state-owned mines, exceeding the state plan by 0.7%, although falling below 1979's total by 3.7%. Coal output from small, locally run mines was 275.74 million tons, over-fulfilling the state plan by 8.2%, and 0.7% below 1979. Of the above total, output from small mines run by provinces, prefectures and counties was 162.12

million tons, or 9.33 million tons less than in 1979. Output from small mines run by communes and brigades was 113.62 million tons, representing an increase of 7.31 million tons over 1979.

Output of washed coal in 1980 was 58.66 million tons, of which output from state-owned mines accounted for 50.75 million tons. Treated raw coal in 1980 accounted for 34.7% of total production, a higher total than 1979. Output in 1980 of large-sized coal from state-owned mines was 33.53 million tons, of which anthracite accounted for 7.87 million tons; bituminous coal, 23.63 million tons; and brown coal, 2.03 million tons.

Raw coal production from state-owned mines in 1980, classified according to type, was as follows: anthracite, 39.5 million tons; brown coal, 11.99 million tons; and bituminous coal, 292.9 million tons, of which coking coal (including coking coal, fat coal, gas coal and non-flammable coal) made up 213.24 million tons.

Effects of the Readjustment. As to the readjustment situation in China's coal industry during 1980, due to clear projections and effective application of taking readjustment as the key link, good results were achieved throughout the coal industry.

In order to adjust the relationships between extraction and tunneling in mines, great efforts were made both in underground mine development and in removing overburdens in open-cast mines. The development schedule for state-owned mines in 1980 was 840,000 metres, with 946,000 metres actually fulfilled in that year. According to statistics released for 96 mines with problems in balancing extraction and development, 898,000 metres were left incompleted prior to the readjustments. Eventually, however, 167,000 metres and 253,000 metres respectively were completed during 1979 and 1980. Thus, 36 mines were restored to a normal balance in their extraction and development activities (among which six had undergone this adjustment in 1979). For five open-cast mines with imbalance problems between extraction and development, there were 63.6 million cubic metres of over-burden left undone, with 14.3 million cubic metres removed in 1980.

The readjustment programme was preliminarily worked out following an investigation into the current state of imbalance problems in the extraction of thin and thick seams. As a result, output from thin coal seams in 33 coal-mining administrations (including Kailuan, Fengfeng, Zaozhuang and Jiaozuo) increased substantially over 1979.

Qualitative Improvements. New breakthroughs were also made in improving the quality of coal and in increasing coal washing capacity. The ash content of salable coal from state-owned mines reached an average of 21.58%, or 1.27% lower than the planned index of 22.85%. Waste content averaged 0.51%, or 0.24% lower than the index of 0.75% and thus breaking the best ratio ever of 0.62%. A total of 114 provinces and 49 coal-mining administrations had gained record results in reducing waste content during 1980. Ash content for washed coal was 10.27% on the average, or 0.08% lower than the index of 10.35%. This was the best result to be achieved since 1973.

The quality of the products in 24 coal treatment plants was improved, while 43 treatment plants transformed their product patterns and attained multi-product outputs. The level of water content in washed coal achieved the best record since 1971, with an average content of 12.03%. There were 116 new coal treatment projects underway in 1980, of which 73 were completed in that year. As a result, the amount of raw coal processed increased by 8.1 million tons while screening capacity increased by 3.75 million tons.

Improving Safety Standards. Meanwhile, strict attention was paid in all mines to strengthening basic work standards. Owing to efforts made in work safety and to preventive maintenance overhauls, there was a considerable reduction in the fatal accident rate, in mechanical and electrical equipment shutdowns and in the proportion of road-ways that were out of repair. Great changes took place in safety. A total of 39 state-owned mines were able to raise their standards of safety production.

Rectifying Imbalances. During 1980, a number of mines succeeded both in rectifying the imbalance between extraction and development and in increasing production. For example, the Hegang Coal Mining Administration of Heilongjiang Province seriously implemented the policies of the readjustment, beginning by strengthening its basic work standards. Its imbalance problem was progressively corrected and its coal production steadily increased. Its raw coal output in 1980 was 12.73 million tons, overfulfilling its plan by 1.13 million tons and placing Hegang first among the coal mining administrations in the surpassing of production targets. The Coal Mining Administration of Henan Province had serious problems of imbalance between extraction and development. As a result of taking readjustment work as the key link and, at the same time, seeking every opportunity to increase production, Pingdingshan not only achieved a rapid pace in readjustment, but also maintained a production level of more than 13.6 million tons. After two years of hard work, the Xieyi Coal Mine of the Huainan Coal Mining Administration in Anhui Province succeeded in overcoming the imbalance problem, and raw coal production in 1980 reached 1.55 million tons, an increase of 240,000 tons and 150,000 tons, respectively, as compared with 1978 and 1979. Above all, good achievements were also gained in coal mining administrations such as Huaibei in Anhui Province, Datong in Shanxi Province and Zibe in Shangdong Province.

[For detailed information on technical-economic norms fulfilled by state-owned mines, please see tables 1, 2, 3, and 4 below.]

2. Work Safety: *Work safety in mines was improved and a new approach was taken to mining safety.*

Coal in China is extracted mainly by underground methods. The geological structure of most mines is complex and natural calamaties occur quite readily.

Table 1: The Structure of Output in State-Owned Mines in 1980

Category		Percentage (%) of total output
Seam thickness	up to 1.3 m.	12.60
	1.3 – 1.5 m.	44.21
	over 3.5 m.	43.19
Dip of the coal seams	< 12°	47.87
	12° – 25°	36.29
	25° – 45°	10.59
	> 45°	5.25

Table 2: Partial Production Figures for Working Faces of State-Owned Mines in 1980

Item	Unit	Quantity
face		2,167
Working length face (average)	m./face	95
advance/month	m.	39.3
output/month	ton/month	11,032
Production capacity of the coal seams	ton/m²	2.95
Total output	10,000 tons	28,687

Table 3: Partial Index for Prepared Face of State-Owned Mines in 1980

Face prepared	Average number	Advance/month (average) (m./face/month)
Total	5,269	107.9
Coal heading	1,744	154.6
Alternate heading	1,381	121.9
Rock heading	2,144	60.9

Table 4: Selected Technical-Economic Index of State-Owned Mines in 1980

Item		Unit	Index
Productivity	total	ton/manshift	0.912
	face worker	ton/manshift	4.129
	heading worker	m./manshift	0.125
Quality of coal	salable ash	%	21.58
	coal waste	%	0.51
	washed recovery	%	56.16
	coal ash	%	10.27
	water	%	12.03

In 1980, China's coal industry persisted in the policy of "safety first." Moreover, by paying special attention to readjustment and management, improved results were gained in safety. The accident fatality rate dropped by 20.58% from the previous year; within that figure, the rate of decline in state-owned mines and capital construction units fell by 32.31% and 20%, respectively. The fatal accident rate per million tons of coal extracted reached the lowest level in the past 7-8 years. Compared with 1979, 81% of all coal mining administrations (coal mines) under the jurisdiction of the Ministry of Coal Industry achieved some level of reduction in fatal accidents and 52 coal mines achieved a record of no fatal accidents for the entire year.

Similarly, reductions were achieved in all types of accidents throughout the coal industry: roof accidents dropped by 23.2%; haulage accidents by 13.0%; methane accidents by 31.8%; and mechanical and electrical accidents by 12.7%.

Mining safety readjustments and work-safety standards were taken into consideration at various levels in the coal industry in 1980:

The idea of safety first was repeatedly inculcated, with leading cadres taking full responsibility for safety and for conducting a programme of safety meetings as laid down by the Ministry of Coal Industry and by provincial coal bureaus.

Regulations for Coal Mining Safety were issued by the Ministry of Coal Industry in February 1980. Classes for studying these regulations were held from the ministry level down to the coal mining administrations and coal mines themselves where more than 158,000 workers and staff members attended. Meanwhile, investigations and safety measures were undertaken by various organs in accordance with the regulations. Thus, safety at work was assured and safety management was strengthened.

There were 332 safety readjustment projects throughout the coal industry, involving a total investment of 43.65 million yuan, of which 165 were fulfilled by the end of the year. After further reorganization and readjustment, safety standards in mines run by provinces, municipalities and autonomous regions were substantially improved.

"May Safety Month" campaigns and "100 Days of Safe Production" (i.e., no fatal accidents) competitions were launched and, during the fall, thoroughgoing safety examinations were carried out. The goal of "100 Days of Safe Production" was realized in 175 state-owned mines, of which 71 mines realized "100 Days of Safe Production" three times in succession. The Linxi Coal Mine of the Kailuan Coal Mining Administration achieved a record of no accidents for 400 days running. In August and September of 1980, advanced-experience propaganda teams were organized by the Ministry of Coal Industry and by coal mining unions to promulgate experiences among the coal mines.

In strengthening organizations safety through supervising and enthusiastically introducing safety supervision work, coal mining safety-supervision administrations were authorized for 11 provinces and autonomous regions. Safety-supervising divisions had already been set up in 41 state-owned coal mining administrations. At the same time, for the purpose of readjusting the existing structure, some leading cadres were assigned to safety supervision at various levels.

3. Improvements in Mechanization:

Total output from mechanized methods in state-owned mines was 106.3 million tons in 1980, an increase of 9.98 million tons over 1979.

The mechanization level (the ratio of the mechanized output to total production) reached 37.06% in 1980, an increase of 4% over 1979.

Coal-mining mechanization in China consists of three categories:

A. *Coal mining by general mechanization.* These mainly are Type 80 single-ranging drum shearers of domestic manufacture; there are at present more than 1,200 such pieces of equipment in China. The average number in utilization in 1980 was 453; their output totalled 63,003 million tons, which accounted for 21.97% of total production.

B. *Coal mining by full mechanization.* China has 223 installations of fully mechanized equipment (56 made in China and 171 imported). The average utilization number in 1980 was 93; their output was 37.73 million tons, which accounted for 13.16% of total production. The 1980 figure was twice the output of 1979.

C. *Hydraulic mining.* Output from hydraulic mining in 1980 totalled 5,534,000 tons, or 1.93% of total production.

Various technical-economic indexes of fully mechanized mining had been further improved in 1980. Coal output increased by 18.79 million tons compared to 1979. The output of working faces per month reached 33,600 tons, or an increase of 1.6 tons compared to 1979. One hundred newly imported installations of fully mechanized equipment from overseas were all received by the end of 1980; of these, 76 were installed underground and 66 were put into production. The average monthly output from these faces reached 42,800 tons, with an O.M.S. of 12.3 tons.

A number of coal mines have emerged with high-level mechanization and advanced mechanized mining. The mechanization level in the coal mining administrations of Luan, Jixi, Shuangyiashan, Yiangquan and Jincheng and of 55 coal mines, including Shigejie and Pangzhuang, exceeded 70%. Thirty-three fully mechanized mining teams and 177 general mechanized teams had come up to the standard team level set by the Ministry of Coal Industry in which the annual output of the No. 1 Fully Mechanized Mining Team of the Tongjialiang Coal Mine, Datong Coal Mining Administration, reached 920,000 tons, with O.M.S. up to 34 tons.

D. *Tunnelling mechanization:* There were 6,670 scraper-type rock loaders, scoop-type rock loaders and coal loaders in state-owned mines in 1980; 2,850 heading faces were so equipped. Loading mechanization in terms of drivage (e.g., boring by rock and electrical coal drills and loading by machines) was 37.49%, or an increase of 1.9% as compared to 1979. Within this category, loading mechanization for rock headings came to 63.78%; alternate headings, 42.32%; and coal headings, 21.74%.

Investigations and studies were carried out

with regard to the production chain of drivage mechanization work lines, and an equipment schedule for rock headings was worked out. A number of heading faces began work towards the goal of mechanization work lines — consisting of heading machines with extensible and suspended belt conveyors or heavy-type flight-bar conveyors — were preliminarily set up. In 1980, 82,900 metres were completed, accounting for 1.21% of the total drifting footage of all state-owned mines. Meanwhile, main stress was laid on ten mechanization work lines in coal mining administrations such as Datong, Kailuan and Xuzhou. The annual drifting footage was 6,926 metres for mechanization work lines in the Dangzhuang Coal Mine, Xuzhou Coal Mining Administration, with a monthly footage of 577 metres; drifting footage reached 1,125 metres in April alone.

E. *Coal Mining Machinery Manufacturing and Repairing*: Most coal mining equipment used in China today was made domestically. There are now 173 enterprises engaged in the manufacture of coal-mining machinery and equipment, of which 34 are major manufacturers under the Ministry of Coal Industry.

For the above 34 manufacturers, total employment is 63,000; they have a combined total of 7,290 metal-cutting machines, 1,482 units of forging equipment; and 730 million yuan worth of fixed assets. Their main products include shearers, coal loaders, flight-bar conveyors, coal-mining safety instruments and metal roof supporting facilities.

Insufficient production tasks that occurred during the readjustment were compensated by vigorous measures taken by these manufacturers to improve the quality and increase the range of their products, as well as in the carrying out of technical services to users. Finished products were the equivalent of 142,000 tons.

Readjustment and transformation among coal mining machinery manufacturers according to the principle of reasonable economy and coordination among specialized departments is now underway, and reorganizations are being carried out. The China General Specialized Coal Mining Equipment Service Corporation and the China Coal Mining Safety Equipment Industrial Corporation, both set up in 1980, have already begun operations.

There are 99 coal mining machinery repair workshops in the state-owned mines and in the coal mines run by various provinces, with total employment of over 91,000. These workshops are responsible for repairing mining machinery and for manufacturing spare parts for different mining areas.

4. Coal Mine Construction: *Proposed projects and the scale of coal mining capital construction were readjusted and great attention was paid to the economic results.*

Readjustment was carried out among ongoing projects in 1980, and stress was placed on speeding up construction, improving engineering quality, reducing costs and increasing returns on investments. In this way, certain results were achieved:

A. *Capital construction investment for the coal industry totalled 3,610 million yuan in 1980.* Of this amount, 1,352 million yuan was used for the construction of new mines and 422 million yuan for tapping the potential of and expanding existing mines.

B. *There were 31 coal mines set up and put into operation in 1980 with a combined annual production capacity of 8.29 million tons.* Of these, 24 were newly constructed mines, with a combined annual production capacity of 5.93 million tons; and 7 were expanded mines with a total annual production capacity of 2.36 million tons. Of the 31 mines, 13 belonged to large and medium-sized projects with a combined annual production capacity of 5.25 million tons. There already were four newly opened mines in 1980, with a total annual designed capacity of 4.8 million tons.

C. *A thorough examination of on-going projects was carried out, following which development was halted on 22 mines with an annual designed capacity of more than 30,000 tons each.* In addition, a number of pending mine construction projects and production chains for coal mining areas were suspended. Investments could thus be better concentrated and more reasonably distributed.

Thanks to the implementation of the policy of economic readjustment, the construction scale for coal mines with an annual designed capacity of more than 30,000 tons was reduced to 140.22 million tons in 1980 from 114.43 million tons in 1979. Those ongoing new mining centres with an annual designed capacity of more than 10 million tons include Gujiao in Shanxi Province, Yianzhou in Shandong Province, Huainan and Huaibei in Anhui Province and Handan in Hebei Province. Ongoing new mining centres with an annual production capacity of 500,000 tons include Tiefa and Shenbei in Liaoning Province, Zaoteng in Shandong Province and Datun in Jiangsu Province.

Shanxi Province, which commands one-third of China's proven reserves, has made further use of its rich coal reserves and has accelerated its coal exploitation. The production capacity of ongoing projects in Shanxi Province reached 18.14 million tons in 1980; Yianzishan in Datong and Xiqu in Gujiao are among the largest mines, with an annual designed capacity of more than 3 million tons each. Preparations were also made in the pre-exploitation of large mines such as Guishigou in Jiangquan and Chengzhendi in Gujiao. The three large mines of Xinglongdian, Baodian and Dongtan in the Yianzhou coal mining centre of Shandong Province are now under construction, with a combined annual designed production capacity of 10 million tons. The Xinglongdian Coal Mine, which has an annual production of 3 million tons, was to be put into operation in 1981.

Preliminary results in coal mining capital construction in 1980 centred on accelerating production rates, increasing efficiency, improving quality costs and readjusting management. The annual drifting footage for the newly constructed mines overfulfilled the schedule by 1%. The percentage of first-line projects in mine construction, civil engineering and installation engineering increased to 38%, 67% and 76%, respectively. Efficiency levels in the drivage of shafts, rock headings and inclined headings all increased to some extent compared to 1979.

Geological Exploration: In 1980, geological exploration by China's coal industry was conducted according to capabilities. The overall approach in geological exploration was regulated and the scale of exploration was reduced in areas south of the Chiangjiang River and in some provinces and autonomous regions with relatively low reserves. On the other hand, great efforts were made and exploration was accelerated in the major coal mining areas such as Shanxi, Henan, Heilongjiang, Anhui and Shandong.

Planning and Design: In coal mine planning and design work carried out during 1980, few new projects were undertaken in the midst of the economic readjustment. Rather, meticulous preparations were made for future mine construction. Seven full-scale design projects were completed in 1980, with a combined capacity of 88.85 million tons; preliminary coal mine designs totalled 20, with a total capacity of 16.44 million tons; processing plant designs totalled 11, with a capacity of 18.4 million tons. Standardization, serialization and interchangeability work was carried out in design, including interchangeable designs completed for five types of large mines with capacities of 900,000–3,000,000 tons; for coal treatment plants with capacities of 600,000–1,800,000 tons; and for repair workshops in four or five categories of coal mining centres.

5. Scientific Research: *scientific research and education in china's coal industry are progressing.*

A total of 152 projects were taken up under the research and development programme of the coal industry in 1980; of these, 39 were major state projects. More than 70% of the projects were carried out in accordance with the programme, and 51 scientific research achievements were recorded, including the following notable results:

A. The development of NDZ-18 self-contained hydraulic prop and DZ-18 hydraulic prop, providing needed accessories for the development of high-level general mechanized mining.

B. The development of BM-100 thin seam shearers suitable for coal seams of 0.8–1.3m.

C. The development of a SMY 540/1500–61 pressure filter and a GUD-30 single-chamber belt filter which reduces the solid content in filtration liquids to below state disposal standards, thus providing new capabilities for reducing the loss of coal slurry and for preventing environmental pollution.

D. The technology of recovering sulphur iron ore from coal waste was preliminarily developed.

E. The development of an AZL–40 filtration self-rescuer has increased effective protection time from 40 to 70 minutes.

Of the 50 advanced technical findings which were to be disseminated in early 1980, 17 produced positive results.

Education and Training: In 1980, 2,922 students and 36 postgraduate students were enrolled in 11 colleges of coal mining under the jurisdiction of the Ministry of Coal Industry. Correspondence courses were resumed and set up in eight mining institutes with 680 students enrolled. Following readjustment and augmentation, 24 worker's colleges in mining areas were officially approved as institutions of higher learning for workers and staff members; these have an enrollment of more than 2,000 students. Administrative units of higher educational institutions under the jurisdiction of the Ministry of Coal Industry were adjusted and consolidated. Among the new administrators, 46 newly assigned leaders, professors and associate professors account for nearly one-third of the total.

Coal-mining technical schools have been expanding rapidly. For the 100 technical schools in

1980, graduates totalled 11,200; 20,000 full-time students were enrolled; 45,000 students were attached to the schools; and teachers and staff members totalled 8,000.

Stress was placed on the training of workers and staff members at their posts: According to statistics provided by 45 units, of the total of 1.7 million workers and staff members in 1980, training for 320,000 was planned, and 350,000 were actually trained; of these, 82,000 attended full-time training courses.

Fully mechanized mining requires more rigorous training of workers. In 1980, 3,400 workers were released from work to attend training courses, and 250 coal-mining administration directors, managers and engineers in charge of mechanized mining operations underwent training.

Work in the training of cadres has been strengthened. A training programme for the 1982-1990 period has been worked out, while 25 training schools which can receive 5,600 cadres at a time have been restored or established.

III. Major Problems and Trends for Future Development of China's Coal Industry

The situation in China's coal industry is excellent, but difficulties and problems still exist. The readjustment of existing mines is an arduous task. The size of recently constructed new mines is relatively small and cannot meet requirements for the development of the national economy. The rational utilization of coal resources, the limited range of coal products, the small proportion of processed coal and low overall quality are all factors that are unfavourable to coal.

Above all, there are still huge gaps in technical equipment and management levels as compared with major coal-producing countries. The mechanization level in China's coal industry is not high. The status of safety in coal mines has not been essentially changed and there are still quite a few accidents.

The Communist Party of China and the people's government have attached great importance to the coal industry. They have established coal as China's main energy resource and have given priority to its development. Proceeding from the actual conditions in our country, the vital policies of laying equal stress on both development and conservation of energy resources and giving priority to saving energy in the near future have been worked out. The prospects of the Chinese coal industry are splendid.

In order to meet the requirements of national economic readjustment and to stabilize the life of the people, the coal industry should not only carry out good readjustment work within its own confines, but should also maintain certain production levels and continue the pursuit of progress. Therefore, "two speed-ups" should be grasped:

1. *Speeding up the readjustment and consolidation of coal mines and maintaining the production level of 600 million tons.* Tapping potential, promoting innovation and reconstructing selected existing mines should be carried out continuously so as to ensure increases in production. In order to stabilize present production levels, supportive measures for small, locally-run mines should be taken. Consolidation of management and administration should be vigorously pursued so as to increase economic results. In addition, those enterprises engaged in the manufacture and repair of mining machinery will be readjusted and reorganized; coal science research and education will be expanded and the physical well-being of miners will be improved steadily.

2. *Speeding up the construction of the new mines will be expanded and accelerated.* In exploiting coal reserves, the old mining bases should be fully made use of. Expansion and reconstruction of those existing mines with suitable conditions will be carried out. New mines will be opened up in the old mining areas so as to increase coal production. Meanwhile, coal fields in areas with rich reserves and convenient transportation facilities will be selected for systematic development and new mining centres will be opened up. Shanxi, East China, the Northeast region (including three eastern administrative divisions of the Inner Mongolia Autonomous Region), and Henan will become the main coal-producing areas.

Furthermore, great attention will be paid to the development of open-cast mines. A number of small and medium-sized mines requiring less investment and promising immediate results will enter construction during the readjustment period. In order to speed up coal-mine development, co-operation with various friendly countries and enterprises will continue to expand and all foreign investments will be welcome.

3. *The structure of coal products will be changed so as to create conditions for consumer energy conservation.*

Coal processing will be increased on a large scale; coal quality will be improved; and coal products will be variegated so as to meet the needs of various sectors. Coal chemistry, gasification and liquifaction will be studied and pursued, as will the comprehensive utilization of coal.

4. *Coal-mining mechanization will be increased and safety in mines will be improved.*

In light of actual conditions in our country, not only will the full mechanization of mining be increased, but hydraulic mining, general mechanization and small-scale mechanized equipment will also be developed. With coal mining mechanization as the centre, mechanization levels in geological exploration, shaft sinking, civil engineering, coal preparation, safety and transportation activities will also be stepped up. The technical equipment level of China's coal industry will be improved in an all-around way.

5. *Scientific research and education in China's coal industry will be strengthened.*

The training of cadres and workers will be expanded. Mine management will be consolidated. And the coal industry will march forward towards the great goal of modernization.

15. CHINA'S ELECTRIC POWER INDUSTRY
By Chen Zengqing
Ministry of Power Industry

I. The Development of China's Electric Power Industry

Before Liberation, the electric power industry in China was very backward. In 1949, when the People's Republic of China was founded, total electric energy generation was only about 4,300 million kwh, ranking China 25th in the world. Total installed generating capacity was only 1,850 mw., and most of the power stations were located in a few big cities in the coastal regions; there was very little electricity supply in the vast expanse of China's interior provinces. As for transmission lines, there were only a few 154-kv (kilovolt) lines and only one 220-kv line in the northeastern region, while there were neither extra-high-voltage transmission lines nor extra-high-voltage power grids at all in other parts of the country.

After three decades of national construction under the leadership of the Communist Party of China and the government, by the end of 1979 the country's total electric energy generation amounted to 282,000 million kwh, representing an increase of 65.6 times over that of 1949 and ranking China seventh in the world. The average annual growth rate of energy generation from 1949 to 1979 was 15%.

At the end of 1979, installed generating capacity of the entire country showed an increase of 34 times over that of 1949, with an average annual growth rate from 1949 of 12.5%. Energy generation and installed capacity of hydroelectric power amounted to 17.8% and 30.3%, respectively, of the national total.

In the past 30 years, we built a great many hydroelectric and thermal power stations and power grids, and the distribution of the power industry had been greatly changed. The irrational placement of most power stations in coastal regions no longer existed.

By the end of 1979, there were 2,860 hydroelectric and thermal power stations above 500 kw. (1,524 hydro and 1,336 thermal), of which 70 large power stations had capacities above 250 mw.; aggregate capacity was 30,520 mw. A total of 32 power grids had been built in the country with installed generating capacity above 100 mw., of which 12 were in excess of 1,000 mw. The length of 330-kv transmission lines in the country was 801 kw., while 220-kv lines and 110-kv lines totalled 25,000 km. and 61,000 km. respectively. Total capacities of power transformers on 330-kv, 220-kv and 110-kv lines were 1,900 mva, 63,000 mva and 72,320 mva, respectively.

Technological Advances. Along with the development of science and technology, we have used on a rather large scale some modern techniques and innovations in power stations and power grids, and have gained certain experiences in construction and operation. The maximum capacity of hydroelectric power units has ben raised to 300 mw.; the highest water head of reservoirs is 629 metres, and the lowest is 6 metres; all of these hydro power units are of domestic manufacture.

The largest thermal power units, both domestic and imported, are 300 mw. and 320 mw., respectively, and a large number of 200-mw. thermal units have already been placed in operation. Among thermal power stations above 500 kw., high-temperature and high-pressure units, medium-pressure condensing units and cogeneration units make up 62%, 29% and 10%, respectively, of the total thermal units.

Automatic monitoring equipment for ensuring reliable operation — such as scanning and measuring equipment for steam parameters, steam turbine metal expansions, vibrations, axial displacements, oil systems; and automatic monitoring and control equipment for steam, water, draft and fuel systems of boilers — have been used in the large thermal stations. In some power stations, partial monitoring and control with computers have been in trial operation.

Several technical methods of improving the stability of power system operations — such as fast single-phase automatic reclosers and series capacitive compensations on transmission lines; quick response excitations, automatic load shedding and electric breaking on generators; and various kinds of communication facilities, such as power line carriers, microwave, extra-high frequency communication equipment, etc. — have been widely used in many power grids. Systemized modern protective relays on generators, power transformers and transmission lines, and telesignals, telemeters, CRT displays and digital computers for off-line calculations in the large system dispatch centres have contributed a great deal to reliable and economical system operations.

Fuel Consumption. In general, however, the development of technology in our power industry is still lagging, and the main consumption indexes are comparatively high. The average unit fuel rate of all thermal units above 6,000-kw. was 456 grams of standard coal per kwh on bus bar in 1979 (422 grams of standard coal per kwh on generator). In 1979, total fuel consumed by both thermal and cogeneration units amounted to 125 million tons of raw coal and 19.83 million tons of oil. Both the coal and oil consumed were equivalent to 111.65 million tons of standard coal, accounting for 21.5% of total fuel consumption in the country. The average rate of power stationhouse use and line loss were 6.54% (0.195% in hydro power stations, 7.63% in thermal power stations) and 9.24%, respectively. The average of annual utilization hours for all generating units was 5,175 (3,112 for hydro power units, 5,956 for thermal power units). At present, the average electricity rate in the country is about 0.065 yuan per kwh, a figure that has been kept almost unchanged for the past 30 years.

Energy Use by Sector. An analysis of the structure of electric energy consumption shows that industries took a very large share, rural consumption grew rapidly and used a larger and larger share, while the portions of transportation and of municipal and residential consumption were rather small. The structure of electric energy consumption in each sector in 1979 was as follows: house consumption of power stations together with line losses, 15.1% of total generation; industrial sector, 65.4% (10.1% for light industry, 55.3% for heavy industry); agricultural sector, 13.6%; transportation sector, no more than 0.5%; municipal and residential sectors, only 5.4%.

With a population of nearly 1,000 million, electricity generation per capita in 1979 was only 290 kwh (it was a meagre 8 kwh in 1949). Indeed, this figure is quite low, and about one-half of rural families, mainly in mountainous and border districts, are still without any electricity supply.

The Bottleneck. In the past 30 years, although our electric power industry had developed quite rapidly, disproportionate relationships emerged in our national economy because of mistakes in the economic work, particularly in the 10-year period of upheaval. As a result, the power shortage in the country lasted even more than 10 years. The development of industry, agriculture and people's daily lives were adversely affected by the power deficiency, and the electric power industry became a bottleneck in our national economy.

II. Production and Construction in the Electric Power Industry in 1980

Our electric power industry proceeded in 1980 under the guidance of the principle of readjustment of the national economy. In the readjustment period, the guiding principles of production and construction in the power industry seek primarily to manage and effectively utilize existing power facilities and to carry out necessary technical innovations so as to bring them into full play and to reduce energy consumption. Secondly, the plan calls for great efforts to construct new power stations and to exploit new electric energy sources, in order to gradually change the unfavourable power shortage.

In the 1980 plan, aggregate electricity generation was targeted at 290,000 million kwh; actually, 300,600 million kwh were generated, an increase of 6.6% over the previous year. Hydroelectric generation accounted for 58,200 million kwh of the 1980 total, an increase of 16.1% over 1979. The aggregate heat supply from congeneration stations was 73.40×10^{12} Kcal, an 1.8% increase over the previous year.

In 1980, 28 generating units were commissioned, of which 13 were hydro power units and 15 were thermal power units. In addition, a large number of small power stations up to 500 kw were built in the rural areas. We also built 5,812-km. transmission lines of 110 kv and over, as well as 5,840 mva sub-station equipment.

In accordance with the guideline of "safety first," power system operations proved to be more reliable in most utilities as a result of the readjustment and consolidation of technical management. Following the reduction of accidents to some extent in the previous two years, accidents were further reduced by 23.8% in 1980 compared with 1979, and severe accidents were reduced by 21%. Furthermore, improvement work on power plant and power grid facilities continued.

Consumption and Conservation. As a result of the strengthening of technical management and economical dispatch, the main consumption indexes improved in 1980. The share of high-temperature and high-pressure thermal units in total generation increased. The average coal consumption per kwh (calculated on bus bar) for all thermal generating units of 6,000 kw. and above in 1980 was 448 grams, an equivalent savings of 2.9 million tons of raw coal. As a result of the economical utilization of water resources in existing hydro power stations, water consumption per kw. in 26 major hydro power stations was reduced in 1980. Consequently, more than 1,600 million kwh of electricity could be generated, equivalent to a savings of 1 million tons of raw coal.

With respect to electric energy conservation, routine activities and some technical measures succeeded in reducing the average rate of house consumption of power stations of 6,000 kw. and above to 6.44% (0.19% in hydro stations, 7.65% in thermal stations) in 1980, and as a result 260 million kwh of electricity were saved. The average rate of line loss was cut to 8.93%, and 770 million kwh of electricity were saved. In addition, 7,000 million kwh of electricity were saved in all sectors of our society. A programme of oil conservation has also made progress.

Power Supply. With an increase of 18,600 million kwh of electricity generation in 1980, and owing to the readjustment of national industrial structure and the implementation of load management (including priority supply to customers of advanced industries), the electric power demands of agriculture, light and textile industries, and residents in cities and towns were basically met. The critical situation of power supply in a number of interior provinces (municipalities) was alleviated, but the power supply in the industrial bases of the coastal regions, such as power grids in Northeast China, Beijing-Tianjin-Tangshan, East China and some other provinces, remained critical. The average value of annual utilization hours of all generating units in 1980 was 5,078 (3,293 for hydro power units, 5,775 for thermal power units). Although a little lower than 1979, the figure was still very high.

Because of the readjustment of the national economy, the structure of power consumption changed somewhat in 1980. An analysis of the share of power consumption in each sector (compared with 1979) shows that energy for agricultural use increased 0.7%, which was the highest among all sectors, while industrial use decreased 0.1% (light industry use increased 0.5%, heavy industry use decreased 0.6%). The share of transportation use remained unchanged, and municipal and residential use increased 0.1%.

Management. In 1980, we also augmented the centralization of power system management and extended the power grids. As a result, we were able to establish the Northwest China Electric Power Administrative Bureau and the North China Electric Power Administrative Bureau. Meanwhile, we experimented on enlarging the decision-making powers in some operations and construction enterprises, which yielded certain positive results.

Other Achievements. In the field of capital construction, following the re-establishment of both the Hydroelectric Power Construction Administration and the Electric Power Construction Administration in 1979, we opened some survey and design institutes in 1980. As a result, the preliminary work of power industry projects was strengthened to some extent, and progress was speeded up for some projects under construction. Based on the consolidation of engineering management, we initiated a system of total quality control and quota management, which improved the quality of engineering work.

Some scientific research achievements and technical innovations were made in the power industry in 1980. Management and administration were also improved somewhat. Much work was done to ensure the fulfilment of state revenue quotas and to receive sufficient funds for our enterprises, as well as supplying enough materials to both production and construction projects. In addition, work on finance, auditing of assets, and material and inventory management yielded relatively good results.

Some progress has been made in the consolidation of organizations and in personnel training sytems. A system of training our cadres and workers has been initiated; on-the-job training programmes for workers and staff have also been established. Training organizations have been set up, and cadres and teachers solely responsible for on-the-job training have been augmented in 21 training schools. Correspondence courses for higher education, television education, on-the-job polytechnic training and general-knowledge courses have been conducted in electric power enterprises. The leading cadres at different levels have been trained, and some two-year programmes of off-job training for young and middle-aged leading cadres have also been conducted. In 1980, 217,000 workers and staff, representing 29.5% of the total, were trained in all enterprises under the Ministry of Power Industry.

The living standard of workers and staff in the power industry has been raised to some degree. In accordance with state stipulations, the wages of about 40% of the workers and staff were increased. Moreover, the bonus system was expanded. In addition to the regular bonus system in each enterprise, rewards were given in utility enterprises for encouraging energy conservation (particularly fuel conservation and reduction of line losses), and in construction enterprises for encouraging the saving of materials, such as steel, cement, wood, etc. In addition, we built many living quarters for our workers and staff. The total floor space of living quarters now under construction in the power industry is about 3.8 million square metres.

Remaining Problems. Although the power industry made definite progress in 1980, because of power deficits accumulated over many years, problems of serious dislocation between the power industry and the national economy still have not been thoroughly resolved. Moreover, within the power industry, disproportionate relationships between generation, transmission and distribution still exist in varying degress within each power grid. As for power production and construction, we are facing many problems concerning reliable operation, quality of construction, economic accounting and cost-effectiveness.

III. Trends in Power Industry Development

The power industry is an important part of the energy industry. Whether during the period of readjustment or in the long term, the power industry should make great efforts to increase the power supply capability. At present, the electric power supply cannot meet demands, and therefore the government has attached tremendous importance to the power industry. At a time of further readjustment of our national economy as a whole and reduction of the scale of national capital construction, capital investment in the power industry in 1981 has been somewhat reduced compared with 1980. However, its share in national capital investment, the number of projects and the scope of construction all have increased in comparison with 1980.

Future Goals. In the years to come, the principle of readjustment, restructuring, consolidation and improvement of the national economy should be implemented continually in the power industry. In the readjustment period, in order to generate and supply electric energy reliably and economically, we must first of all consolidate existing generating facilities and power grids, reinforce the management of the power industry and focus on the policy of "safety first." The national plan of power generation should be achieved with high quality and in sufficient quantity as well.

Energy conservation is a long-term policy in our national economy, and it should be strictly implemented in the power industry. We must carry on the load management, encourage the rational use of electric energy by consumers, supply electric power to advanced industrial units with priority, and further convert oil-fired thermal power units into coal-fired ones.

Water Power Development. Based on the reality of our energy resources, the policy of the power industry in the long run can only be the development of both water power and thermal power according to local conditions in different parts of the country. Although at present thermal power exceeds hydro power in quantity, we must concentrate our efforts on increasing the proportion of hydro power generation to 25%-30% within this century.

Water power resources in our country are abundant: the theoretical potential of waterpower amounts to about 680,000 mw, and the exploitable potential of water totals, 370,000 mw (1.9×10^6 million kwh of annual electricity generation), of which not more than 5% has been exploited in both large and small hydro power stations. In the exploitation of waterpower, we should place emphasis from a long-term point of view on the southwest, south-central and northwest regions. However, some medium-sized hydroelectric power stations should also be built in the east, north and south-central regions.

New Construction. Another strategy of our energy industry will be to expedite the construction of combined coal mining and electric power generation facilities. We shall build a number of thermal power stations in areas such as Shanxi, Inner Mongolia, Shaanxi, Ningxia, Henan and Anhui, where coal deposits are abundant. Meanwhile, we shall also build some load centre and estuary power stations in locations where land and sea transportation is convenient and loads are relatively concentrated.

In order to gain experience, we shall build a few nuclear power stations, initially in the regions where natural energy resources are comparatively scarce. In addition, some geothermal, wind, tidal, solar and bio-gas energy resources shall be utilized according to local conditions.

We must take vigorous measures to develop large-capacity generating units that will be manufactured by our own factories. In view of the vast territory and great dispersive loads of our country, thermal generating units of 200, 300 and 600 mw. capacity will be widely installed.

Power Grids. To bring the advantages of large power grids into full play and to attain optimum economic results, the development of power grids must be based on the practical distribution of loads and energy resources instead of on administrative borders. Modern techniques and advanced technical equipment must be adopted in power grids to improve the quality of electric energy and to raise the reliability of power system operations. Rural electrification relies mainly upon the supply from power grids. Meanwhile, the development of small hydroelectric and thermal power stations and small power grids is also necessary.

We must fully exploit scientific research and survey and engineering design, which are of vital importance to the preliminary stages of all construction work in the electric power industry. Environmental protection is also important, and we must strive to take effective measures to prevent power stations from polluting the water and air.

16. CHINA'S CHEMICAL INDUSTRY
By the Research Office,
Ministry of Chemical Industry

China's chemical industry is developing at a relatively fast pace. Before Liberation, the foundation of the chemical industry of China was rather weak. Only eight chemical factories of significant size and some manually operated shops existed in coastal cities such as Shanghai, Nanjing, Tianjin, Qingdao and Dalian. Production of sulphuric acid in 1949 was 40,000 tons, caustic soda 88,000 tons and chemical fertilizer 6,000 tons. Other production consisted of rubber articles and medicinal preparations processed in small volume; organic chemicals were nonexistent.

Since the founding of the People's Republic of China, the chemical industry has made great progress under the leadership of the Communist Party and the government adhering to the policy of independence and self-reliance. The annual average rate of growth of China's chemical industry from 1950 to 1978 was 17.7%, higher than that of industry as a whole. The following table shows the rate of increase of the chemical industry compared with that of all of industry in different periods.

Table 1. Growth Rate of China's Chemical Industry

Year	Rate of increase of all industry (%)	Rate of increase of chemical industry (%)
Recovery Period (1950-52)	34.8	63.6
First 5-Year-Plan Period (1953-57)	18.0	31.2
Second 5-Year-Plan Period (1958-62)	3.8	14.3
Readjustment Period (1963-65)	17.9	23.9
Third 5-Year-Plan Period (1966-70)	11.7	17.3
Fourth 5-Year-Plan Period (1971-75)	9.1	10.4
1953-78	11.2	17.7

From 1952 to 1979, state-owned chemical enterprises (including pharmaceuticals in and prior to 1978) contributed a total amount of profits and taxes equal to 2.5 times capital investments for the same period, thus increasing significantly the accumulation of the state.

Expansion of the Industry. The chemical industry of China has now been placed on a relatively solid foundation. By the end of 1979, the fixed assets owned by state chemical enterprises with independent business accounting amounted to 10.5% of the national total; output value accounted for 12.8% of the whole; and the sum of profits and taxes accounted for 12% of industrial taxes collected by the government. There are many major divisions of the chemical industry, including chemical ores, chemical fertilizers, acids and alkalis, inorganic salts, synthetic rubber, synthetic fibres, synthetic resins and plastics, organic raw materials, pesticides, dyestuffs, coatings, photosensitive substances, rubber products, solvents and additives and catalysts — altogether producing more than 20,000 varieties of products of relatively complete categories. Most main commodity chemicals are produced on a large scale.

Currently there are 5,880 state-owned chemical enterprises with independent business accounting in China, of which 302 are priority enterprises. A rational distribution of the industry is underway. In addition to coastal enterprises, including both newly constructed large-scale plants and old ones that have developed considerably through technical transformation, many new enterprises have been established in the interior; and some chemical factories have been constructed in border regions such as Yunnan, Guizhou, Qinghai, Xinjiang, Ningxia, Inner Mongolia and Tibet.

The output value of the chemical industries in Shanghai, Beijing, Tianjin, Qingdao, Dalian and Shenyang accounts for 30% of the total, and these cities have become major centres of centralized chemical production. The chemical industries in Guangzhou, Nanjing, Chongqing, Changzhou, Wuhan, Xian, Harbin and Taiyuan are also developing at a comparatively rapid pace, with their output value accounting for 10% of the total.

After the completion of large-scale chemical complexes in Jilin, Lanzhou and Taiyuan in the 1950's, more than 10 petrochemical complexes and large-scale fertilizer plants have been built one after another in Yanshan (Beijing), Qilu (Zibo, Shandong), Daqing, Guangzhou, Anqing, Yueyang, Jintang and Luzhou, with their output value accounting for 17.5% of the total.

The number of production and non-production workers and staff in state-owned chemical enterprises has reached a total of 2,800,000.

Research and Education. Scientific research and engineering design institutions, with relatively complete lines of specialities, are being gradually established. Currently there are 180 chemical research units in China, of which 23 research institutes belong directly to the Ministry of Chemical Industry and 8 are operated by large-scale complexes. In addition, 146 research institutes (or laboratories) are maintained by large enterprises. Colleges of chemistry also have their own facilities that conduct research in the fields of organic and inorganic chemistry, petrochemicals, rubber processing, mining of chemical ores and chemical equipment and machinery. There are 17 major chemical engineering design units in China, of which 13 belong to the Ministry of Chemical Industry. Large-scale complexes also have their own design units. Provinces and cities with relatively large numbers of chemical enterprises usually have their own research and design units.

Education for the chemical industry is being developed continuously. There are now 40 chemical colleges and colleges with chemical specialities (five led by the Ministry of Chemical Industry), with 29,000 students enrolled. There are also 34 technical middle schools, 133 technician schools and 1 cadre school.

Characteristics of the Industry

The chemical industry of China, at its present stage of development, is characterized by the following features:

1. *The industry is composed mainly of medium-sized and small enterprises.*

For 30 years, the central and local governments have placed much emphasis on chemical production and construction with increasing investment. Local investment, including investment by enterprises themselves, accounted for a considerable part of the capital outlay. State and local investment in the chemical industry during different periods are shown in Table 2.

Practically all local investment and a portion of state investment were for the development of medium-sized and small enterprises. Consequently, these enterprises have experienced comparatively rapid expansion and have become the major forces in the chemical industry.

In 1979, the production of main products by small enterprises, except for a few chemicals such as soda ash and synthetic rubber, accounted for a considerable portion of the total. This was particularly true in the case of chemical fertilizers and synthetic ammonia, more than half of which was manufactured by small enterprises.

2. *The amount of chemical products for agriculture, light and textile industries accounted for a large part of total production.*

An analysis of the composition of capital investment shows that investment in chemicals for agriculture constituted 57% of the total, that for light and textile industries 20%, and that for other sectors only 23%. The output value of chemicals serving agriculture and light and textile industries in 1978 amounted to 72% of the total value, while in 1979 the value of chemicals for these purposes rose to 77.5%. Gains were especially strong in chemical fertilizers. As the main products support-

Table 2. Investment in China's Chemical Industry

Year	Total Investment	Source of Chemical Investment				Chemical Investment of Total Industrial Investment (%)
		State Investment (%)	Local Investment (%)	State (%)	Local (%)	
1949	220	220	—	100	—	—
Recovery Period	10,210	9,300	870	91.5	8.5	3.2 in 1952
First 5-Year Plan Period	138,900	109,100	29,800	91.4	8.6	4.8
Second 5-Year-Plan Period	529,792	340,500	189,300	77.5	22.5	7.3
Readjustment Period	247,569	222,600	25,000	89.9	10.1	11.4
Third 5-Year-Plan Period	616,288	340,092	276,196	82.6	17.4	11.1
Fourth 5-Year-Plan Period	1,274,376	816,200	458,200	65.5	4.5	12.5
Fifth 5-Year Plan (First 4 Years)	1,236,900	883,400	353,500	69.4	30.6	12.4

ing agricultural production, chemical fertilizers usually occupy a leading position in the development of the chemical industry, with their output increasing year by year. Table 3 shows the yearly production of chemical fertilizers from 1950 to 1979.

Tables 6 and 7 show the production of synthetic materials and some major organic chemicals in different periods.

4. *New breakthroughs in scientific research and design have been made continually.*

Table 3. Annual Output of Chemical Fertilizers

	Total	Large & medium-size	% large & medium-size of total	Small	% Small of total
Type of enterprises:	7,362	328	4.5	7034	95.5
Output value (100 million)	407.1	213.0	53.3	194.1	47.7
Output of main products (10,000 tons):					
Pyrite ore	633.7	334.1	52.7	299.6	47.3
Phosphate ore	851.7	444.0	52.2	407.7	47.8
Sulphuric acid	699.7	388.7	55.6	311.0	44.4
Soda ash	148.5	137.7	92.8	10.8	7.2
Caustic soda	182.5	146.7	80.4	35.8	19.6
Ammonia	1,348.1	619.7	46.0	728.4	54.0
Fertilizers	1,065.3	426.7	40.1	638.6	59.9
Pesticides	53.6	40.0	74.6	13.6	25.4
Plastics	79.3	57.6	72.6	21.7	27.4
Dyestuffs	7.2	3.4	47.0	3.8	53.0
Paint	42.6	9.8	22.9	32.9	77.1
Calcium carbide	140.7	61.7	44.0	79.0	56.0
Synthetic rubber	12.1	12.1	100.0	—	—
Tires	1,168.8	608.0	52.0	560.8	48.0

In addition to engineering plastics for use in industry and agriculture and films for farming use, the plastics industry provided the consumer market with a considerable quantity of plastic sandals, raincoats and articles for daily use. In recent years, the dyestuff industry has annually placed on stream more than 10 varieties of disperse, vat and cation dyestuffs, thus greatly improving the coloration of textile fabrics.

3. *The chemical raw material industry has developed at a comparatively rapid rate.*

The foundation of the chemical raw material industry left by old China was very small, and there was no production of organic chemicals. Practically the entire industry was established and developed after the liberation of China. A comparison of the raw materials industry and the processing industry in different periods is shown in Table 5.

The relative portion of chemical raw material industry in whole chemical industry was increasing year by year. Organic chemicals and the "three synthetic materials" started in the 1960's, and along with the construction of large-scale petrochemical complexes, the speed of development accelerated in the 1970's.

In the middle 1960's, the development of small and medium-sized plants in the nitrogenous fertilizer industry was greatly advanced by the application of the carbonization-synthetic ammonia process for the manufacture of ammonium bicarbonate and the three new catalytic technologies of desulphuration by zinc oxide, low-temperature conversion and methanation, applied to the 50,000-ton/year synthetic ammonia units.

Table 4. Chemical Fertilizer Production

	Chemical fertilizers (on 100% basis)	
Year	Output (in 10,000 tons)	% increase over previous year
1950	1.5	—
1965	172.6	—
1976	524.4	—
1977	723.8	38.0
1978	869.3	20.1
1979	1,065.4	22.6

Annual average rate of increase from 1977 to 1979 = 26.87%.

Table 5. Raw Materials and Processing Industries

Year	Raw materials industry (%)	Processing industry (%)
1st Five-Year Plan Period	24.59	75.41
2nd Five-Year-Plan Period	19.98	80.02
3-Year Recovery Period	42.81	57.19
1974	49.00	51.00
1975	52.20	47.80
1979	48.70[1]	51.20
1980	56.40[2]	45.60

[1] Including pharmaceuticals, comparable with previous years.
[2] Not including pharmaceuticals, not comparable with previous years.

Table 6. Production of Synthetic Materials (in 10,000 tons)

Year	Ethylene	Plastics	Synthetic rubber
1965	0.30	9.70	1.59
1975	6.50	33.00	5.67
1979	43.50	79.30	12.06
% increase in 1979 over 1975	69.2	240.30	212.70
Avg. % increase (1975-79)	60.8	24.5	20.8

Since the production of synthetic ammonia by the 300,000-ton/year units in recent years, eight kinds of new catalysts, which are indispensable to the operation, have been successfully tried, and a considerable portion of spares and components for the ammonia units can now be fabricated domestically.

In other lines of the industry, the following achievements should be mentioned: the dual process for production of soda ash, the manufacturing technology for cis-butadiene rubber, industrialization of the metallic anode-diaphragm process for manufacture of chlor-alkali, preliminary achievement on beneficiation technology for collophane, the heavy water production installation at a certain level of technology, the successful production of various chemicals and materials for missiles and atomic bombs, and the mastering of production technology for colour films by using oil-soluble colour couplers and technicolour. All these achievements testify to the high level of science and technology reached by the chemical industry of China.

Problems of the Chemical Industry

Although it has made great progress in the past 31 years, the chemical industry of China is still quite behind those of developed countries, and cannot keep pace with the demands of national economic development. Its shortcomings are indicated by the following:

1. *Sectors inside the chemical industry are not well-coordinated and not in proportion to each other.*

The raw material industry and the processing industry still do not relate well to each other. Since the 1970's, major organic chemicals have experienced comparatively rapid progress. However, because of weakness in the foundation, the development is still insufficient and not well-balanced. The exploration, mining and ore dressing of chemical mines are lagging behind; the development of sulphuric acid and alkalis are slow; and the production of basic raw materials, major chemicals, various intermediates, additives, solvents and catalysts are not meeting requirements. All these result in a surplus of processing capacity. Among the different kinds of fertilizers, the ratios of nitrogen, phosphorus and potassium are much out of proportion, and the ratio of phosphorus and potassium to nitrogen even declines year after year.

2. *The structure of products is not rational.*

Nitrogenous fertilizer accounts for the largest part of the fertilizer industry. Ordinary and lower-grade products are manufactured in much larger quantities, while fine chemicals, particularly those necessary for the production of high-grade and durable products by the light and textile industries, are not well-developed. These chemicals are few in variety and are being manufactured in small batches at a high price.

3. *There are too many small enterprises, and most of them are not well-organized.*

A great majority of the small enterprises are "small but complete," with high material and energy consumption and low product quality, and thus have relatively poor economic effects. The number of small enterprises accounts for 95.5% of the total, while their profits account for only 13.1%. The labour productivity of the small enterprises is only about half that of the large enterprises.

4. *Insufficient attention has been paid to the*

reconstruction and upgrading of existing enterprises.

More funds have been invested for newly constructed enterprises, whereas little in used for renewal of equipment, technical innovation and improvement of product quality. Furthermore, much remains to be done in pollution treatment, warehousing and residential construction. Because of a deficiency of fuel and raw materials and the unfitness of supplementary construction the productivity of some enterprises cannot be sufficiently utilized, and others are at a relatively low level of production, technology and management.

5. *Logistics services, such as scientific research, design and education, were weakened by the 10-year "cultural revolution."*

The interrelationship of basic theory study, technical development and applied research is not quite satisfactory. The period between research and application of the results is usually too long. Technical development and applied research are not well-coordinated with each other, thus adversely affecting the application of new products and the upgrading of old ones. In the field of education, not enough attention is given to the training of economic management personnel. The number of technical schools is decreasing to some extent. The ratio of students in secondary technical schools to those in colleges and universities has declined from 3:1 to 1:1. Storage and transportation facilities are also lagging far behind, affecting the turnaround of products and exports.

6. *In importing equipment and technology from abroad, more equipment is purchased than patents and technical information, and less importance is attached to the use of the advanced technology introduced.*

In 1978, in a case where feasibility studies had not been well-conducted and the provision of raw material and funds not assured, four sets of ethylene plants and four sets of fertilizer plants were imported, without considering the actual financial and material effects on the country.

All these problems testify to the fact that the adjustment of the chemical industry is a rather difficult task. However, it is evident that only through adjustments and reforms can the chemical industry of China be developed to meet the requirements of the national economy.

Achievements of China's Chemical Industry in 1980

In 1980 the chemical industry, while carrying out the policy of "readjustment, restructuring, consolidation and improvement" raised by the Central Committee of the Communist Party, adjusted its capital construction by halting or delaying some large and medium-sized projects. At the same time, many small enterprises, because of high consumption, low quality and poor sales, were closed, merged or transformed to manufacture other products. For factories located at random with products manufactured in duplication, adequate concentration and redivision of production were effected. The manufacture of products that were in surplus was restricted or changed to others, while the production of those needed by the textile and light industries and the consumer market was increased through rational reorganization.

Applied research work was strengthened in the areas of energy conservation, lowering of raw material consumption, upgrading of product quality and treatment of pollution. The development of new products and the expansion of applications of old products were actively undertaken. Under the guidance of the national plan, market regulation was conducted to further enlarge product sales.

In a number of places, the assignment to each line of the industry of full responsibility for gains and losses and the granting of more power of operation were tried out; and different forms of economically united organizations, such as general factories and specialized corporations, were established. In certain localities, some loosely united, trans-trade organizations were formed. The chemical industry, in the process of adjustment, was advancing steadily, and recorded good results in 1980 both in production and construction.

Production Gains. The output of 19 major products of the chemical industry surpassed the amount specified by the national plan. Gains were especially strong in products serving agriculture, light and textile industries or directly placed on the market. For instance, the production of soda ash, caustic soda and sulphuric acid increased 8.5%, 5.3% and 9.2%, respectively, over the previous year. The volume of fertilizers reached 12.32 million tons, 15.7% more than that of 1979 and the output of ready-sale products, such as paints, rubber shoes and plastics, was also greater than in the previous year.

There are now over 700 varieties of rubber shoes being placed on the market by enterprises of the chemical industry. Plastic flooring and furniture have also been supplied to the market. The figured candles manufactured by the Yanshan General Petro-Chemical Corporation not only increase the pleasant atmosphere of festive occasions for the Chinese people, but also are being marketed in Hong Kong, Macao and Southeast Asia.

Forty-nine new varieties of medium and high-grade dyes were produced in 1980 alone, which further enriched the colour pattern of fabrics. The production of chemicals needed by the light and textile industries and those made directly for the market in large cities such as Beijing, Tianjin and Shanghai was increasing with comparatively great speed. The production of main chemical products and their rate of increase in 1980 are shown in Table 8.

in 1980 increased 6%, production costs were lowered 0.8%, profits submitted to the government increased 8%, and total labour productivity rose 4.6%. Losses sustained by small enterprises for each ton of ammonia produced was 65 yuan in 1979, and dropped to 10 yuan in 1980. Consequently, the total deficit by small nitrogenous fertilizer plants declined from 410 million yuan in 1979 to 85 million yuan in 1980. An economic profile of the chemical industry in recent years is shown in Table 10.

Exports of chemical products in 1980 were

Table 7. Production of Selected Organic Chemicals (in 10,000 tons)

	1965	1975	1979	% increase in 1979 over 1975	Avg. % increase (1975-79)
Methanol	4.40	13.70	24.7	180	12.4
Acetic acid	2.07	6.69	11.5	172	11.4
Phenol	2.08	4.13	7.0	170	11.2
Pure benzene	11.80	21.20	33.9	159	9.7
Acetone	0.73	2.19	3.2	150	8.5
Naphthalene (technical)	0.53	4.61	6.3	147	8.0
Butanol	1.44	3.19	3.9	122	4.0

Awards. The quality of chemical products has been further improved. In 1980 national gold and silver awards were won by 17 products, including Red Triangle Brand soda ash, Yanshan Brand cis-polybutadiene rubber, Friendship Brand 729 inward-grained rubber for ping-pong bats and Warrior Brand high basketball shoes. A total of 237 products were recognized as being of high quality by the Ministry of Chemical Industry; 39 products, including Double Coin Brand 900-20 automobile tires, Heaven Brand technical sulphuric acid, Ship Brand white alkyd enamel and Panda Brand light rubber shoes, won national gold prizes or silver prizes; and 222 products won certificates for quality issued by the Ministry of Chemical Industry.

Conservation. Energy consumption in the industry decreased by a wide margin. Consumption by priority enterprises in the production of caustic soda, calcium carbide, synthetic ammonia and oil refining decreased 8% in 1980, as compared with 1979, with a total energy saving for the year equivalent to 3.3 million tons of standard coal. Conservation was particularly notable in small enterprises. Table 9 shows energy consumption per ton of synthetic ammonia.

Economic Data. Economic efficiency was improved to some extent. Compared with the previous year, the total value of industrial production

Table 8. Output of Major Chemical Products in 1980 (in 10,000 tons)

Product	Output	% increase (decrease) from previous year
Pyrite	578.3	− 8.7
Phosphate rock	1,072.6	25.9
Sulphuric acid (100%)	764.2	9.2
Concen. nitric acid (100%)	22.8	−19.1
Soda ash	161.3	8.5
Caustic soda (100%)	192.2	5.3
Synthetic ammonia	1,497.5	11.1
Chemical fertilizer	1,232.7	15.7
Plastics	89.7	13.1
Polyvinyl chloride	37.8	13.9
Polyethylene	30.2	14.8
Polypropylene	9.5	26.7
Synthetic rubber	12.3	1.7
Pesticides	53.2	− 0.9
Calcium carbide	151.9	8.0
Refined methanol	29.8	20.2
Pure benzene	35.99	6.2
Glacial acetic acid	12.5	7.8
Dyestuff	6.5	−10.0
Paint	48.0	12.6
Ethylene	48.99	12.6
Tyres (10,000 sets)	1,145	− 1.2

Table 9. Rate of Energy Consumption
(per ton ammonia)

Year	Coal consumption (kg.)	Electricity consumption (kwh.)
1977	3,766	2,005
1978	3,257	1,765
1979	2,740	1,590
1980	2,393	1,508
% decrease in 1980 from 1979	12.7	5.2

the best ever. In the early 1950's, less than 10 varieties and about 20,000 tons of chemical products were exported; and by the end of the 1970's, 40 varieties and 150,000 tons were exported. in 1980, exports were valued at 1,100 million yuan, 58% more than in 1979.

Table 10. Economic Performance by the Chemical Industry, 1976-80

	1976	1977	1978	1979	1980
Profits submitted (100 m. yuan)	17.02	18.85	39.00	43.50	47.00
Production cost reduction (%) by priority enterprises	−2.63	4.84	5.75	1.99	0.80
Labour productivity (yuan)	11,344	13,049	13,072	15,231	15,930
Deficit by small fertilizer plants (100 m. yuan)		9.10	5.90	4.15	0.85
% deficit decrease compared with previous year			35.16	29.66	79.50

Development Trends

According to the demands of the national economic readjustment, for a period of time the development of the chemical industry will focus on the needs for clothing, food, shelter, transportation and daily necessities. Emphasis will also be placed on the provision of raw materials and chemicals needed by the light, textile, electronics and construction industries, and on production of chemical fertilizers and pesticides for agricultural use. At the same time, some chemical end-products will be provided directly to the market, supplying the daily living requirements of 800 million peasants and the urban population. Thus, improvement of product structure, reorganization of lines of industry and reconstruction of existing enterprises should be carried out step by step, so that the chemical industry can progress continuously and steadily.

1. *In accordance with the demands of national economic development, we should readjust the proportional relationships of various sectors within the chemical industry.*

We should further readjust the ratio between the raw material industry and the processing industry by giving top priority to the production of raw materials and chemicals. We should increase the output of basic chemicals, such as acids and alkalis and major organic chemicals, and accordingly develop the production of various intermediates, additives, solvents and catalysts; in this way the relation between the "bone" and the "flesh" can exist in a much more normal and harmonious way.

We should devote major efforts to the production of phosphate fertilizers, study and develop potassium resources, expand the production of complex fertilizers, and increase the output of trace element fertilizers. Thus, the disproportionate relation among nitrogen, phosphorus and potassium fertilizers can be corrected gradually. We should develop the petrochemical industry and increase the output of organic chemicals according to our own conditions. At the same time, we should strengthen technical logistics in the course of the readjustment to make it suit the development of production and construction.

2. *We should gradually change the structure of products.*

There should be substantial development of chemicals necessary for the production of the light, textile, electronics and construction industries, especially synthetic materials, such as plastics and chemical fibres. We should make every effort to increase the production of ready-sale, high-grade products, such as high-grade dyestuffs, synthetic paints, additives and other fine chemicals. Efforts should be made to have a considerable part of the main chemicals used in production of ready-sale, durable consumer goods supplied domestically in the not too distant future.

There is also the problem of readjustment concerning the constitution of varieties for each line of industry. For instance, readjustment of the pesticide industry seeks primarily to increase new varieties and formulations of highly effective pesticides with low toxicity, to develop adequately some fungicides and herbicides, and to guide their application for best results. The chemical enterprises could manufacture some end-products to be placed directly on the market, and could also provide light industrial enterprises with processing technology and guidance in application.

3. *We should reorganize the lines of industry and carry out overall planning by trade, step by step according to schedule.*

In compliance with the principle of specialized coordination and economic rationality, general factories or corporations are to be established by regions of dispersely located enterprises producing the same category of products. The production of raw materials is to be centralized, while the processing plants could be more or less dispersed. Trans-trade or trans-region unions could also be formed where conditions permit. In that case, the first step is to form a loosely coordinated organization, laying emphasis on the coordination, directing, servicing and consulting. The large-scale complexes should continue to apply comprehensive management more efficiently. Effective policies are to be formulated to control the uncontrolled growth of small enterprises.

4. *Full use should be made of existing enterprises, and the levels of production, technology and management should be raised.*

In the reconstruction of old enterprises, emphasis is to be placed on energy conservation, treatment of pollution and environmental protection. Through renewal of equipment and technical renovation, production could be continuously increased, the quality of products upgraded, new varieties of products developed and accumulation increased. Investment in the chemical industry will hereafter be focused on innovation, reconstruction and tapping the production potential of old enterprises.

5. *Developing the task of scientific research and education.*

In the next few years, we should continue to strengthen the work of scientific research. Emphasis is to be placed on research and development of new products and reconstruction of old enterprises. Units of scientific research and production should be organized in closer cooperation, through contract or other form; some can even be united economically. In the field of education, aside from improving higher education, emphasis will be placed on the development of secondary technical schools and technician schools. Economic management specialities will be established in some colleges and secondary technical schools to train management personnel.

6. *Exerting more effort on international exchange.*

The approach to importing foreign equipment and technology will be shifted away from complete sets of equipment into individual machines and technical know-how and patents where conditions permit. Technical exchange and technical cooperation should be positively developed. Furthermore, it is important to understand international market conditions so that the export of chemical products can increase step by step.

17. CHINA'S FIRST MACHINE-BUILDING INDUSTRY
By Yan Qiushi
*Policy Research Office,
First Ministry of Machine-Building*

As an important equipment supply sector of the national economy, the industry under the First Ministry of Machine-Building has played an essential role in socialist construction since the founding of the People's Republic.

Without any foundation to speak of, the machinery industry of old China was dispersed throughout several coastal cities, such as Shanghai, Tianjin, Shenyang and Dalian, where a number of small and medium-sized machine shops were engaged in the manufacture and repair of such simple machines as small motors and belt-drive machine tools, using primitive methods and equipment. It was on this dilapidated foundation left over from semi-feudal and semi-colonial China that we started to construct a new machine-building industry.

Since the birth of People's Republic, steps have been taken — in accordance with the policy of self-reliance and hard struggle — to develop a sizeable machine-building industry composed of nearly 100 branches, including machine-tools, power generators, metallurgical plants, mining equipment, general machinery, autos and bearings.

Achievement of the Industry

This new machine-building industry now yields some 26,000 types of products. Its annual output value in 1980 was more than 50 times that of 1952. Under the management of the Ministry, the industry, in the course of the past 30 years, has furnished a large amount of machinery (including complete sets of technologically advanced plants) to more than 3,000 large or medium-sized industrial projects in the country.

Notable Examples. A few outstanding examples are the complete plant for an iron and steel combine with an annual capacity of 1.5 million tons of steel, which has been running smoothly since its completion; a 30,000-ton die-forging press; a 2,800-mm. aluminium-plate rolling mill; a 12,500-ton aluminium extruder; and a railroad wheel and tire rolling mill — all of which have proved satisfactory in their operation.

Other examples are the complete plant for a 2.5 million-ton-per-year colliery shaft and a 3 million-ton-per-year washery; a complete set of drilling, pumping, storing and transferring equipment for oil fields; a 2.5 million-ton-per-year crude refinery; 100-, 125-, and 200 mw. steam power plants; a 225 mw. mixed flow hydroturbine; and 330 kv. power transmission equipment. A 170 mw. Kaplan hydroturbine has been produced on a trial basis.

For the development of our chemical industry, the machine-building industry has successfully produced a complete 300,000 ton-per-year synthetic ammonia plant and a 240,000 ton-per-year urea plant. Both plants are turning out satisfactory products in Shanghai's Wujin Chemical Factory.

In addition to this heavy equipment, our machine-building industry has also produced much state-of-the-art equipment, including some 110 kinds of high-precision machine tools. Examples include the T42200 jig-borer with raster-measurement and digital display manufactured by the Kunming Machine Tools Factory, which has a 2m. × 3m.-long worker table and a positioning accuracy up to 0.01 mm., and the S7450 and the SG7432 thread grinders made by the Shanghai Machine Tools Factory, which can work, respectively, on 5m.-long or 0-class leadscrews.

An outstanding achievement for the machine-building industry was gained by the No. 2 Motor Factory, in which most of the operating equipment for machining, including several dozens of transfer lines and numerous highly efficient specialized machine tools, is made in China.

Exports. In the course of its development, the industry has exported 137 kinds of products to 97 countries and regions. These have included machine tools, metal-forming equipment, refrigeration plants, electric motors, bearings, measuring tools and cutters. Moreover, we have undertaken the construction of more than 50 projects for foreign countries as part of technical or economic aid programme of China. These have included a heavy machinery complex, cable factories, bearing factories and fastener factories.

Shortcomings. In spite of its many achievements, much remains to be improved in the structure of the industry and the First Ministry of Machine-Building. This is reflected in the lack or short supply of certain equipment needed by agriculture, as well as our light and textile industries and the service sectors for equipment renewal in the facilities of the various branches of the national economy.

This shortcoming is partly due to the lapse in technological progress during a certain period and the lagging of research and development, and partly due to the lack of an effective management system. What we need is better-organized specialization in production.

Progress in 1980

However, as a result of implementing the policy of "readjustment, restructuring, consolidation and improvement," the industry under the First Ministry of Machine-Building made considerable progress in 1980.

First of all, we have improved, to a certain extent, the structure of the industry so that it is now more correctly oriented and in a better position to meet not only the needs of heavy industry but also of the light and textile industries, urban construction, equipment replacement in existing factories, the export trade and the people's demand for consumer goods.

By 1980, our industry had supplied 93 kinds of light industry equipment or durable consumer goods, with their output value three times that of 1979. This included equipment used in the plastic knitting, jute carding, shoe making, animal slaughter and herb-medicine processing industries. Much specialized equipment and automated processing lines have also been provided for the bicycle, motorcycle, sewing machine and watch-making industries to facilitate their technical renovation.

Due to the expanding scope of service, the industry attained an output value in 1980 approximately equal to that of 1979, in spite of the decrease in capital investment under the economic readjustment. The volume of exports of machinery products in 1980, however, registered an increase of 60.6% over the preceding year. The output of major machine products in 1980 was as follows:

Machine tools	134,000 sets
Forging equipment	48,000 sets
Power generation plants	4,193 mw.
AC motors	25,700 mw.
Automobiles	222,000 units
Bearings	227,550,000 sets

Ten Positive Trends. Pursuant to the reform in management systems and the adoption of market regulation as a complement to the planned economy, many of our industrial enterprises have gained fresh motivation and have begun to show new signs of progress. These may be summed up in the following 10 points.

1. Industrial enterprises are shifting away from serving mainly heavy industry to actively catering to the needs of agriculture, the light and textile industries, people's daily consumption, urban construction and the export trade.

2. They are turning from meeting chiefly the demands of capital construction to actively satisfying the demands of technical renovation of the various branches of the national economy.

3. They are turning gradually from production merely for the fulfilment of high production targets to production for satisfying the demands of the users.

4. They are turning from placing more emphasis on quantity than on quality to trying to win in competition through improving quality.

5. They are turning from producing limited specific types of products to extending their range to achieve much greater variety.

6. They are turning from supplying mainly the principal equipment to providing complete plants, spare parts and accessories.

7. They are turning from placing more emphasis on production to actively undertaking services such as equipment maintenance, installation, adjustment and personnel training.

8. They are turning from a relative negligence of economic results to intensive economic accounting and raising economic benefits.

9. They are turning from subjecting contracts to pre-set production plans and producing in disregard of demand to arranging their production according to the users' demands on the basis of optimum profitability.

10. They are turning from placing emphasis only on domestic markets to also penetrating into foreign markets and seeking to expand exports.

These favourable developments indicate a gradual improvement in our economic management and operation.

Integration. In the meantime, steps have been taken by our industrial enterprises to increase the production of certain badly needed items by pooling their efforts. Such joint efforts have brought about progress in the specialization of production among different enterprises. On the basis of mutual benefit, such integration of enterprises takes various forms, according to existing circumstances. There is integration in the manufacture, sales or export, product development and the providing of complete plants through joint efforts.

Many associations, formed for the purpose of meeting the demand of a product which is in short supply on the market, have achieved favourable results in the quality, variety, cost-reduction and growth of production through tapping the potential resources of existing enterprises and organizing specialized production.

The Ningbo Water Meter Works played an active role in organizing an association involving 19 factories, each of which is charged with the mass production of certain special parts. Their output and turnover have doubled for three consecutive years.

Meanwhile, the First Ministry of Machine-Building has undertaken to develop, step by step, the industrial integration of the casting, forging, heat-treating and electric-plating processes in 33 industrial cities, with a view to saving energy, protecting the environment and improving productivity.

Quality Gains. The improvement of enterprise management has resulted in higher quality and economic gains. Some enterprises have now moved ahead from merely being concerned with the proportion of sub-quality products to trying to upgrade quality standards and earn a good reputation for their products. Some have advanced their quality control systems from merely final inspection and rejection to stressing quality control in every step of the operation, from design, manufacture, examination, sale, and service to market research.

Some enterprises have gone forward gradually from paying attention only to the physical accuracy of a product to improving the intrinsic quality — namely, the accuracy, durability, service life and reliability — of a product. Still others have changed their quality standards from factory inspection requirements to meeting the users' own requirements.

Evidence of such improvement in quality are the 1,756 production groups and 162 kinds of products that won the "Reliable Quality" awards of 1980. The most outstanding 29 items to win the State Quality Awards include the T42100 double-column jig-borer produced by the Kunming Machine Tools Factory, the Z3040x16 radial drilling machine produced by the Shashi No. 1 Machine Tools Factory and the Sino-Czechoslovak People's Friendship Factory, the "Shanchuan" 3BA, 4BA and 6BA single-stage centrifugal pumps produced by the Boshan Pump Factory, the 12,500 ton horizontal non-ferrous metal extruder produced by the Shenyang Heavy Machinery Factory, the "Yunfeng" 100 mw. hydropower generator produced by the Harbin Electric Generator Factory, the "Leidian" 4114 auto engine spark plug produced by the Nanjing Porcelain Insulator Factory, the "Diamond" 400 mm. AC desk fan produced by the Guangzhou Far Eastern Electric Fan Factory and the "Shield" ½-inch and 5/8-inch roller chains produced by the Hangzhou Chain Factory.

New Products. Another achievement of the industry under the First Ministry of Machine-Building in 1980 was attained in the development of new products, processes and techniques. This is reflected in the fruition of some 600 research projects and the development of 937 new products.

Twenty-four items are considered to have reached a high level of technology. Among them are the double-cone seal for 2m. and 3m. diameter high-pressure containers, the model study of low- and high-pressure centrifugal fans, the 150 mm. band reduce-rolling mill, the trackless underground mining machinery powered by an internal combustion engine, the brushless revolving transformer, the silicon-controlled hand-operated arc welder and the Y-series three-phase asynchronous meters.

In addition to these 24 advanced items, we have achieved 131 research projects that reached the higher level set by our national standards and 50 other projects that pioneered new fields in our domestic production.

Additionally, progress also has been made in the design and production of a number of new products to serve the purposes of energy conservation and environmental protection. Included in this category are some 18 different kinds of waste-heat boilers in 12 series, as well as many different types of air-purification, sewage or acid-gas disposal and dust-removal equipment that have proved satisfactory to their users.

With the readjustment of the national economy as the central pivot of our work, we shall concentrate on the restructuring and reorganization of the machine-building industry and the reform of our industrial enterprises, in order to raise the industry under the First Ministry of Machine-Building to a new and higher level.

18. CHINA'S SHIPBUILDING INDUSTRY
By Hong Lun
*Policy Research Office,
Sixth Ministry of Machine-Building*

China's centuries-old shipbuilding industry once was one of the most advanced in the world. But the industry developed very slowly because of the long-term bondage under imperialism, feudalism and bureaucrat-capitalism. In the period before Liberation in 1949, only ship-repairing could be done. Even if ships were built, all material and equipment had to be brought from abroad. There was no capability for manufacturing marine equipment and for scientific research and design. The Chinese shipbuilding industry lagged further and further behind those of the developed countries. On the eve of Liberation, most of the shipyards were destroyed and production came to a standstill.

Development of the Modern Industry

Since the foundation of New China under the leadership of the Communist Party and the People's Government, however, the industry has developed rapidly, becoming a multiple industry. Today it not only builds ships but also produces diesel engines, marine auxiliary machinery and instruments, and has played an important role in the buildup of the national economy and national defence.

Since Liberation, the shipbuilding industry has gone through a transformation from ship-repairing to shipbuilding, from transfer and copying to self-design and self-manufacture and from small shipbuilding to the building of warships, oceangoing merchant ships and various kinds of engineering vessels.

Government Steps. At the beginning of Liberation, the People's Government confiscated the shipbuilding enterprises owned by the bureaucrat-comprador capitalists and took over some shipyards owned by foreign capitalists. The government also turned some privately owned factories into state-privately owned enterprises. At the start of the Five-Year Plan, the state reconstructed and expanded the major ship-repairing yards in Shanghai, Guangzhou, Dalian, Wuhan and Tianjin, gradually turning them into shipbuilding bases. Dozens of small and medium-sized shipyards were built and expanded in the main water transportation and fishing areas, resulting in the development of capacities for building river boats and small and medium-sized coastal ships. At the same time, one shipyard after another introduced an important innovation — welding in hull construction in place of riveting.

During this period the state proceeded to establish ship research and design organizations (the first was the Ship Design Institute) and began building several kinds of warships, as well as 10,000-dwt-class oceangoing cargo vessel on the basis of foreign designs, foreign materials and foreign equipment. In 1958 the 10,000-ton vessel *Dongfeng* was designed and built with domestic material and equipment.

In the 1960's, the industry's scientific research capacity was strengthened and a fairly comprehensive ship research and design system, with the ability to design various types of vessels, was established. At the same time, priority was given to the building of marine equipment facilities, such as diesel engine works and navigational instrument factories. As a result, the production of marine equipment was increased to suit the shipbuilding capability. Since then, the shipbuilding industry has been developing continuously.

Ministry Operations. At present, China's shipbuilding industry is managed by the Sixth Ministry of Machine-Building, the Ministry of Communication and the State Administration of Aquatic Products, as well as by the provinces, municipalities and autonomous regions concerned.

The Sixth Ministry of Machine-Building operates more than 100 enterprises and institutions, with more than 70 building berths, including 10 berths for vessels over 10,000 tons, and 9 dry docks, including 3 docks for vessels over 10,000 tons. Major shipyards are located in Jiangnan, Dalian, Hudong, Guangzhou, Zhonghua and Wuchang. The Henan Diesel Engine Works, Shaanxi Diesel Engine Works, Wuhan Marine Machinery Works, Wuhan Forging Works, Hanguang Machinery Plant and Nanjing Marine Auxiliaries Plant are major factories among the marine diesel engine works, auxiliary machinery works and instrument plants.

The Sixth Ministry of Machine-Building manages a certain number of shipbuilding, marine equipment research and design organizations. Among them are the Marine Design and Research Institute of China, which has strong ship design capabilities; the China Ship Science Research Centre, China's largest ship performance research organization; and various research institutes specializing in marine diesel engines, auxiliaries, electrical equipment and materials. The Ministry also runs the Shanghai Shipbuilding Technology Research Institute, which is a pioneer in the development of new shipbuilding technology; the Jiujiang Precision Instrument Technology Research Institute, which deals mainly wtih design for high-accuracy and sophisticated technological equipment and elements; and the Shanghai Shipbuilding Engineering Design Institute, which is engaged in design for factories. In addition, the Sixth Ministry of Machine-Building operates three institutions of higher learning, the Shanghai Jiaotong University, the Harbin Shipbuilding and Engineering Institute and the Zhenjiang Shipbuilding Institute, as well as two secondary technical schools. Shipbuilding departments are also maintained in some of the universities.

By the end of 1980, with the coordination of different sectors of the national economy, the Sixth Ministry of Machine-Building had built 14,700 vessels of 500 different types. These include large and medium-sized merchant vessels, such as 50,000-dwt tankers, 25,000-dwt bulk carriers, 24,000-dwt tankers, 15,000-dwt tankers, 16,000-dwt coal-ore carriers, 13,000-dwt cargo ships and 7,500-dwt passenger-cargo ships, as well as various engineering vessels for special purposes, such as oceangoing instrumentation ships, oceanographic research ships, large dredgers, powerful tugboats and self-elevating drilling rigs. The Ministry also had submitted various types of warships and auxiliary ships to the People's Navy. In addition to marine products, the Ministry also manufactured non-marine products; the first set of 12,000 T hydraulic presses in China was made by the Jiangnan Shipyard in 1958.

In 1980 various enterprises controlled by the Sixth Ministry of Machine-Building fulfilled the State Plan. Total output value increased by 20% and commodity value by 18%; the actual profit exceeded the target set in the state plan by 65%. More than 1,800 vessels, with a total tonnage of 484,000, were built during this time.

Rocket Tests. In May 1980, when China carried out long-range carrier rocket tests in the Pacific Ocean, an oceangoing fleet was assembled, consisting of multi-purpose instrumentation vessels, oceanographic research ships, salvage vessels, oil-water supply ships, oceangoing tugboats and escorts. All of these vessels were developed, designed and built by China. The fleet fulfilled triumphantly the tasks of survey, salvage and escort, and its performance demonstrated a new level of the Chinese shipbuilding industry in the scientific and technical field.

Achievements in 1980

The Sixth Ministry of Machine-Building and its affiliated factories and departments conscientiously carried out the policy of readjustment, restructuring, consolidation and improvement in 1980, achieving the following successes:

1. *Readjusting service orientation; rationalizing production structure.*
The ministry readjusted its service orientation and production structure according to demands in domestic and foreign markets. It made great efforts in expanding the scope of business and provided more services for users. Production capacity for merchant ships was increased, while the production plan of military products was fulfilled; products were manufactured not only for domestic markets, but for foreign markets. Besides ships, consumer goods and other non-marine equipment were also produced; statitics gathered from marine equipment manufacturers show that in 1980 the output value of non-marine products amounted to 32% of their total output value. Expansion in the production capacity of offshore oil exploitation equipment (drilling and production platforms) is a new facet in the development of China's shipbuilding industry.

2. *Reforming the financial system; implementing the policy of allowing the enterprises concerned to keep the remaining profits after delivering taxes and a predetermined amount of profit to the state.*
This is a fairly important reformation. The new policy adopted in 1980 replaced the planned profit system previously used in the shipbuilding industry. In line with the new policy, the Ministry allowed most of its affiliated enterprises to practice the new measure and worked out means to allow the other enterprises to earn more profits. Thus all enterprises were able to reap more economic benefits so long as they overfulfilled their profit quotas, thereby encouraging them to increase their production.

In order to raise their profits, all enterprises have geared their products to the needs of the market, expanded their business scope, increased production, cut down expenses and practiced economy for better financial results. Although the Ministry did not obtain enough production tasks for the factories from the state in 1980, the total amount of profits earned by its enterprises, nevertheless, exceeded that of the previous year by a considerable margin and set a new historical record. In this the new policy played an important role.

3. *Readjusting investment ratio; sorting out capital construction projects.*

The focus in investment has shifted from construction of new factories to technical transformation of existing factories, scientific research and education. The amount of investment for these projects has gone up. While the shipbuilding industry obtained less investment from the state, the priorities for using the investment have been given to the construction of a 100,000-dwt building berth in the Dalian Shipyard and reconstruction of a 50,000-dwt dock in the Jiangnan Shipyard, in order to increase their capacity for 50,000–100,000-dwt class ships. In the field of scientific research, advance work has been strengthened; expenditures for advanced applied research and basic theory research reached at least 30% of total expenditures.

4. *Proceeding to reform the management system.*

Under the guidance of instructions issued by the State Council, eight factories in the Shanghai area have been chosen as experimental units. They are gradually being given more power of self-management and are being freed from the limitations of the system of unified management with its over-concentration of power. This has further stimulated the initiative of the enterprises, as well as workers and staff. Furthermore, the Guangdong Shipbuilding Corporation and the Shanghai Marine Power Station Equipment Corporation were founded in 1980 on the principle of economic integration.

5. *Further strengthening foundational work in various aspects; improving business management and upgrading technical levels.*

Several business management training courses, mainly for leading cadres in charge of factories, were conducted for the purpose of raising management competence. More attention was paid to the education and training of workers and staff at their posts. A training programme for all people on the job was unfolded. About 80,000 people – 30% of all employees in the industry – studied in short-term training courses, part-time and television universities, etc. Nearly 50,000 people participated in the basic study of total quality control, which has continued to be popularized in the industry and has improved the management of factories and the quality of products.

National quality awards, three gold and nine silver, were given to 12 kinds of products, including a small ship propeller and underway oil and water transfer system of the Dalian Shipyard and an oceangoing instrumentation ship of the Jiangnan Shipyard. A quality-control group for a cast-steel anchor chain in the Dalian Shipyard won the honour of national high quality group. Because of total quality control, the elongation percentage of anchor chain made by this group increased from 14% to 22% or better, and has been brought up to international standards.

6. *In 1980 the Sixth Ministry of Machine-Building made great strides in adapting to foreign market demands, and as a result achieved a breakthrough in ship exports.*

This development has promoted readjustment of the shipbuilding industry, given great impetus to its growth and is of considerable significance in the history of New China's shipbuilding industry. In the past, products manufactured by the Chinese shipbuilding industry were mainly for domestic users. Not until 1977 did the industry export its first vessel, a 3,700 dwt freighter. Since then, China has received additional export orders.

Functions of the CCSI

In order to develop ship exports, the state restructured the import/export management system for the shipbuilding industry. The China Corporation of Shipbuilding Industry (CCSI) was founded in 1978. In March 1980, the government approved the corporation as an independent import/export corporate body integrating industry and trading. It has been allowed to negotiate and sign contracts directly with foreign companies.

Range of Activities. The business lines of the new corporation are as follows: export of various vessels and offshore oil exploitation equipment; repair of various ships; export and import of marine engines and equipment; introduction of advanced technology, licence trade, joint design, cooperative production, compensation trade, processing or assembling of given materials or parts, and joint ventures; hydrodynamics and structural mechanics research and test service; ship design and consultant service; shipyard, marine engine works and instrument factory design and consultant service; acting as an agency or jointly running maintenance and service stations for foreign marine engines and equipment of all kinds and other non-marine products.

In addition, the corporation also offers qualified technical personnel and a skilled labour force for research, design and construction of ships. The factories and research institutes affiliated with CCSI may also negotiate and sign agreements directly or indirectly with foreign companies for product export and repair service. CCSI has branches and offices in Shanghai, Guangzhou, Wuhan, Jiujiang and Shenzhen for export business.

The China Corporation of Shipbuilding Industry has been making every effort to meet the requirements in foreign trade, with quality products. It has the ability to meet contract delivery dates, equip ships with marine machinery up to international standards and provide technical services. CCSI's policies in dealing with overseas companies are highly flexible, allowing shipowners to select equipment commonly used throughout the world and to choose Classification Societies for their ships. By the end of 1980, the Shipping Register Bureau of the People's Republic of China had signed technical cooperation agreements with 11 foreign Classification Societies, from France, Britain, West Germany, Italy, Norway, Japan, Romania, Yugoslavia, Poland, the Democratic Republic of Korea and the USSR. Both sides may mutually act as an agency for ship inspection.

To broaden mutual understanding, CCSI participated in the maritime exhibition "Expo-Ship Far East 80," held in Hongkong in November and organized by the Seatrade Publication (Far East) Ltd of England. This was the first international non-governmental trading exhibition in which CCSI participated. Visitors from all over the world expressed great interest in China's exhibits.

Integration. Integrating industry with trading is one of the major reforms in the shipbuilding industry. Under the integration system, industrial organizations engage in import and export trade, and manufacturers may enter into direct contact with clients, thus reducing the role of the middle man. They take responsibility both for the technical and economic aspects of their trade, so that the new system brings into play the initiative of the industrial departments and enterprises.

CCSI has made rapid strides in business since dealing directly in foreign trade. In May 1980 the corporation concluded a contract with the Regent Shipping Company of Hong Kong for a 27,000-dwt bulk carrier. By the end of the year, total tonnage of export orders received by CCSI reached more than 300,000 tons, including 27,000-dwt and 36,000-dwt bulk carriers and numerous barges. The corporation is expecting to export more vessels, especially drilling rigs, pleasure boats and various kinds of small and medium-sized ships of up to 5,000 dwt, such as cargo vessels, perishable-goods ships, lumber carriers, etc. CCSI also has signed contracts on assembly work using the buyer's materials or on compensation trade for containers, deck cranes, cement spreaders for highway-building, radios and cassette tape recorders. In one of these agreements, a container plant was built within 14 months as a subsidiary of the Guangzhou Shipyard, and went into operation in September 1980. The containers made in this plant have met the requirements of Bureau Veritas of France.

Licencing Agreements. In the light of demands of foreign markets, CCSI has upgraded the industry in a short time. Eight well-known licences were purchased in 1980 — including those for B&W heavy-duty, low-speed marine diesel engines, deck cranes, hatch covers, marine diesel generating sets and hydraulic deck machinery — from Denmark, West Germany, Japan and other nations. With the 4 licences acquired previously, the corporation now has a total of 12 foreign licences. Several kinds of prototype machines have been turned out under licence.

CCSI also has signed three agreements with foreign companies for technical transformation of shipyards and engine works. Furthermore, several factories have established technical cooperation relations or friendly enterprise relations with overseas enterprises, enabling them to utilize their partner's advanced technology and management techniques to implement the reformation of their production management system as well as technical transformation.

Problems and Prospects

Tremendous progress has been made in China's shipbuilding industry over the past 31 years. However, the following problems remains to be solved: the organization lacks interdepartmental coordination; the industry is still behind advanced countries in management systems; technical exchange with foreign countries is not widespread enough; and some marine equipment made in China has not been up to international standards. All of these have to be resolved in the course of the readjustment of the national economy and the shipbuilding industry.

China is a vast country with 18,000 km. of coastline and 108,000 km. of inland waterways, and it has many deepwater and ice-free harbours. The shipbuilding industry has benefited from these favourable natural conditions. In recent years China's shipbuilding industry has laid a fairly strong foundation, developed international contacts and made a good beginning in ship exporting. It certainly can be expected that China's shipbuilding industry will make important contributions to national defence, communications and transportation, exports, oceanographic exploitation, agriculture and consumer goods production in the course of further readjustment of the national economy.

19. CHINA'S AGRICULTURAL MACHINERY INDUSTRY AND AGRICULTURAL MECHANIZATION

By Long Jiyan

Ministry of Agricultural Machinery

China is a nation with a population of about one thousand million people, of which eight hundred million are peasants. It has a vast expanse of territory and wide differences in natural conditions and economic development. In such a country, therefore, it is an arduous task to carry out agricultural mechanization, to replace manual labour with power farming and increase the output of agricultural production by raising both land and labour productivity, to gradually change the backwardness of China's rural areas and to lift the peasants out of the poverty which they have endured for thousands of years. Agricultural mechanization, however, is of vital importance to the development of the entire national economy of China.

Since the establishment of New China, our government has paid great attention to the development of the agricultural machinery industry and agricultural mechanization, and has put forward a series of guiding principles, policies and specific measures. Despite errors and setbacks during the course of development, China has made, nevertheless, great progress in the agricultural machinery industry and attained brilliant achievements in agricultural mechanization. For most sections of China, agricultural machinery now has become an indispensable element in agricultural production and rural economic life. By summing up both the positive and negative experiences in the development of the agricultural machinery industry and agricultural mechanization in the past 30 years, we will undoubtedly break a new path to farm mechanization that accords with the realities of China.

I. Growth of the Industry and Mechanization

The development of China's agricultural machinery industry and agricultural mechanization began only after the establishment of New China. Before 1949, there was hardly any substantial industry in China, to say nothing of an agricultural machinery industry. All that could be produced for farm use at that time were traditional hand tools, such as hoes and sickles, which the peasants had been using for a thousand years in agricultural production. On the eve of Liberation, the country had only 300 to 400 tractors and a limited number of irrigation and drainage units that had been imported from abroad at different times.

Early Developments. After the founding of New China, as part of the restoration and development of the national economy, animal-drawn implements such as improved ploughs, portable steam engines and horse-drawn harvesters, began to make their appearance to meet the urgent needs in agriculture. In 1953 we started the preparatory work for the construction of the Luoyang No. 1 Tractor Plant, the largest tractor manufacturer in China. By 1957, after the fulfilment of the First Five-Year Plan, the number of animal-drawn implements introduced into China's rural areas amounted to over 4.6 million.

During that period, 352 tractor stations and 710 state farms were set up. Tractors in use approximated 25,000 standard units (one standard unit = 15 drawbar hp). The area of power-cultivated land amounted to 39 million *mu*, about 2.2% of all land under cultivation. The combined capacity of irrigation and drainage equipment was 560,000 hp, and the area under mechanical irrigation amounted to 18 million *mu*, accounting for about 1% of the total cultivated area.

In 1959, the Luoyang No. 1 Tractor Plant was completed and went into production, thus beginning the mass production of tractors in China. Around that time a number of manufacturers of combines, diesel engines and some other attached implements were built up or rebuilt. In the same year, a new government department — the Ministry of Agricultural Machinery — was established to administer the work of the agricultural machinery industry and agricultural mechanization in China. Since then, China has been capable of producing not only animal-drawn, semi-mechanized implements but also tractors, diesel engines, and their accessories in quantity.

In the meantime, relevant research work on farm machinery began to develop. By the end of 1961, three national research institutes of agricultural machinery — the Chinese Academy of Agricultural Mechanization Science, the Luoyang Tractor Research Institute and the Shanghai Research Institute of Internal Combustion Engines — and a large number of research centres of provinces, prefectures and counties were established. As a result, China came to have its own ranks of research workers in agricultural machinery engineering science.

The State of the Industry in 1979. By 1979 the agricultural machinery industry and agricultural mechanization in China had developed to a considerable degree. The total output value of the agricultural machinery manufacturing industry amounted to 10,910 million yuan, 161 times that of 1952. By the end of 1979, China had more than 1,900 agricultural machinery factories above the county level and 2,400 county manufacturing and repair factories, with 189,000 machines for metal-cutting and 24,000 machines for forging and pressing, and a total number of workers and staff of 1.45 million.

China is now able to mass-product 75-hp and 100-hp crawler tractors and bulldozers; engines ranging from 0.5-hp petrol engines to 10,000-hp diesel engines (for ships), as well as a variety of internal combustion engine electric generating sets below 500 kw.; various wheel tractors ranging from 20 to 55 hp suitable for both paddy fields and dry land; self-propelled or trailed grain combines and head-feed rice combines; irrigation and drainage equipment, including deep well pumps, electrosubmersible pumps and large-sized automatically adjusted axial flow pumps with diameters of 1.6 m., 2.8 m., 3.1 m. and 4 m.; sprinkling equipment, including large-sized centre pivot sprinklers; various types of power-driven rice transplanters, boat tractors and rice windrowers; and other agricultural machinery and implements. In short, China can now basically produce by itself all the kinds of agricultural machinery it needs.

In addition, the county farm machine manufacturing and repair factories possess 73,500 metal-cutting machines, 11,600 forging and pressing machines and 15,700 sets of repairing and testing equipment. In 1979, they repaired 217,800 large and medium-sized tractors, 362,900 small-sized tractors and 483,000 internal combustion engines.

Technical Achievements. China has trained a contingent of relatively proficient research workers and engineers of agricultural machinery. By the end of 1979, trained personnel numbered over 100,000; they were able to design and construct various types of agricultural machine-making and assembling factories on different levels and to provide them with complete equipment. They could also develop all kinds of agricultural machinery to suit for the specific features of China's agricultural production and natural conditions.

China also has made appreciable progress in higher education for the field of agricultural machinery. By 1979 there were 11 colleges of agricultural machinery and a number of agricultural machinery departments set up in agricultural or engineering colleges, with a total enrolment of 23,000. The teaching staff of the seven agricultural machinery colleges directly under the leadership of the Ministry of Agricultural Machinery numbered 3,400, including 180 professors and associate professors and 1,600 lecturers. Graduates from these colleges during the 1953-79 period totalled about 40,000.

Machinery and Mechanization. By the end of 1979, the amount of agricultural machinery held by peasants and the relevant level of mechanization were as follows:

1. *Equipment for irrigation and drainage.* There were over 5 million units, with a combined capacity of 71 million hp. Power-irrigated areas amounted to 379.81 million *mu*, accounting for 56.3% of the effective irrigated area.

2. *Machinery for processing grain, cotton and oil-bearing seeds.* There were over 3 million units in all, with a combined capacity of over 20 million hp, averaging 5 units per production brigade. Except in some remote regions, wheat and rice processing had been basically mechanized in most of China's rural areas.

3. *Equipment for crop protection.* There were 230,000 power-operated units and 20 million hand-operated units. Almost every production brigade used some of this equipment.

4. *Equipment for agricultural transportation.* Trailers pulled by large and medium-sized tractors amounted to 460,000 units; trailers pulled by small-sized tractors, 1.29 million units; animal-drawn, rubber-tyred carts, 2.47 million units; wheel barrows, 32 million units; power-driven boats, over 84,000 units; and trucks for agricultural use, 100,000 units, most of which were on state farms.

5. *Harvesting machinery.* Grain combines amounted to 20,000 units, windrowers 70,000 units. Post-harvest machinery, including threshers and grain throwers, totaled 2 million units, with a combined capacity of about 10 million hp.

6. *Tractors and implements.* Large and medium-sized tractors amounted to 670,000 units, small-sized tractors 1.67 million units, with a combined capacity of 48 million hp. In addition, there were 1.3 million large and medium-sized tractor-drawn implements, including 180,000 seeders. A total of 90,000 power-driven rice transplanters, 430,000 hand-operated rice trans-

planters, and 96,000 boat tractors were employed in the paddy areas.

7. *Equipment for animal husbandry.* Feed-milling machines amounted to 1.39 million, with a capacity of about 10 million hp; forage harvesting and processing machines, 11,000; power-driven clippers, 2,000; and power-driven milkers, 1,300.

8. *Equipment for forestry and fishery.* There were 5,900 skidding tractors, with a combined capacity of 258,000 hp. Fishing vessels and motorized junks numbered over 50,000.

The total power capacity for agricultural machinery was estimated at 180 million hp.

The average amount of equipment for every 10,000 *mu* of cultivated land in China was: 4.5 large and medium-sized tractors, 11.2 small-sized tractors, irrigation and drainage units of 477.2 hp and 0.7 agricultural truck; total average power capacity amounted to 1,218 hp.

The power-ploughed area in China totalled 630 million *mu*, accounting for 42% of the total cultivated land; power-sown area, 230 million *mu*, 13% of dry crop land; power-harvested area, 57 million mu, 2.6% of China's grain crop area.

China's agricultural machinery consists mainly of medium-and small-sized models. Priority has always been given to the development of irrigation and drainage equipment, crop protection equipment and semi-mechanized implements. Large cultivating machines, combines and agricultural trucks account for only a small proportion of the total, which is in keeping with China's realities and the practical needs of the rural areas.

Benefits of Mechanization. Widespread use of agricultural machinery and the development of agricultural mechanization has played an increasingly important role in promoting agricultural production and bringing about economic prosperity in rural China. The grain output in China has been increased from 100 million tons per year in the early years after Liberation to 300 million tons per year at the present time, thus enabling China to feed 20% of the world's population, which inhabits only 7% of the world's land. This would have been impossible without the contribution of agricultural mechanization.

In the first place, the use of agricultural machinery has strengthened the ability to fight against natural calamities. Because China has a vast territory with a great variety of climates, a very large area could be stricken by natural calamities each year. During the past 30 years the area hit by calamities averaged 420 million *mu* annually. With the steady expansion of water conservation installations and the widespread use of irrigation and drainage equipment and crop protection equipment, the ability to cope with natural calamities has been increasingly improved, leading to a gradual reduction of disaster areas year after year.

In 1978, when 11 provinces in China's east and central-south regions suffered from serious drought, we used diesel engines with a combined capacity of 21 million hp and electric motors with a combined capacity of 10 million kw. to pump over 170,000 million cubic metres of water — the equivalent of three and a half years' discharge of the Huanghe River. This enabled China to reap a bumper harvest, with an output of 20 million tons over that of 1977.

The benefits realized by the large-scale use of equipment to protect crops from pests and of grain dryers to reduce grain loss from mildew have been widely recognized.

Secondly, the use of agricultural machinery has helped the peasants do their farm work faster, resulting in a rise in land productivity and an increase in agricultural production. In China, farmland per capita is comparatively small, and the land available for reclamation is also limited. Therefore, the chief means of increasing output is to raise both worker and land productivity. Farmland under power ploughing can yield much higher harvests, because tractor-pulled ploughs till the soil deeper and loosen it more effectively than animal-drawn ploughs. This makes the root mass of the plant well-developed and increases soil fertility.

Seasonal shortages in manpower and animal-power commonly occur all over China, whether in the north or the south, especially during the period of "double rushes" (rush harvesting and rush planting) in South China, or the periods of "three summer jobs" (harvesting, planting and field management) and "three autumn jobs" (harvesting, ploughing and sowing) in the Huanghe River and Huihe River Valley. Racing against time to get these farm jobs done often causes either a decrease in crop production or an increase in production but no increase in harvests because there is no labour to get the crop in. With the widespread introduction of agricultural machinery in these areas, however, this problem has basically been settled.

North China has a comparatively large area of farmland and a low population density. As the frost-free period there is short, an early frost often threatens crop production due to untimely sowing and harvesting. With the development of agricultural machinery, sowing and harvesting can be done in a shorter time, enabling a growing number of communes and brigades to show a steady increase in output.

Thirdly, the introduction of agricultural machinery has raised labour productivity and helped to develop a diversified economy and commune and brigade-run enterprises, thus bringing about a prosperous rural economy and higher scientific and cultural levels in rural areas. As a whole, China has abundant labour resources but a scarity of farmland. Moreover, the population of China is not evenly distributed. In border provinces such as Heilongjiang, Xinjiang and Inner Mongolia, there are large areas of farmland and small populations. Labour shortages cause extensive cultivation of land, resulting in low per-unit yield and unsteady total output. If forestry and animal husbandry are to be developed, the labour shortage will be even more serious. Naturally, peasants in those areas have an urgent need for agricultural mechanization.

Example of One Brigade. In the densely populated lower reaches of the Changjiang River, mechanization can also play an important role in agriculture when conditions mature. The No. 1 Production Brigade of Yuexi Commune in Wuxian County, Jiangsu Province, is a typical case in point. That brigade started with mechanization of irrigation and drainage, followed by the mechanization of tillage (the most labour-consuming job) through the use of walking tractors. In order to relieve the peasants from "back-breaking" operations of rice transplanting and harvesting, rice transplanters and rice harvesters were used, and at the same time seedlings were nursed in workshops instead of in the fields. Then came the gradual mechanization of grain and feed processing and water transportation. Later, some sprinklers were installed in part of the paddy fields.

As a result of mechanization, 70% of the brigade's labour force was saved. The surplus labour was channeled to intensive and meticulous cultivation and sideline occupations, with pig-raising the main job. The brigade cultivated various water plants, such as water peanut, water cabbage and water hyacinth, to feed pigs, sheep and poultry, whose manure, in turn, helped bring about three crops a year (one crop of wheat and two of rice). It also set up a farm machinery-repair and spare-parts factory and an electronic parts workshop.

By 1979, the brigade's labour force engaged in agricultural production had been reduced from 90% of the total in 1970 to 50%. The total output value of agriculture, industry and sideline occupations amounted to 1.2 million yuan, 16 times that of 1970; of that total, industry and sidelines accounted for 750,000 yuan, or 62.5%. The output value per capita (in terms of agricultural population) averaged 751 yuan. This production brigade, with farmland averaging only 1.2 *mu* per capita, had a high commodity grain production rate, accounting for 43% of the total grain output. Including the consumption of concentrated feed for pigs, fish and poultry bred for sale, the actual production rate of commodity grain reached 55.8% of total output. Some agricultural economists both at home and abroad believe that the road this brigade was taking to agricultural mechanization is the road toward the modernization of China's agriculture.

The development of agricultural mechanization in China has created millions of new-type peasants with a fairly good knowledge of science and technology, and this undoubtedly has had a significant effect on the raising of scientific and cultural levels in China's rural areas.

Remaining Problems. In the course of development of China's agricultural machinery industry and agricultural mechanization over the past 30 years, we have long suffered the influence of "Left" thinking and especially serious interference and sabotage by Lin Biao and the Gang of Four in the 10 years of "cultural revolution." As a result, there are errors, setbacks and quite a number of problems to be solved.

The main problems are: lack of thorough investigation and understanding of China's realities; underestimation of the difficulties for agricultural mechanization owing to ignorance of the differences in social and economic conditions in China's rural areas and the diversity of China's crop varieties, cultivation methods, and cropping systems and lack of a real understanding of the complexity, difficulty, and specifics of carrying out farm mechanization. Errors and mistakes in our guiding work included an impatience for success, which resulted in seeking the same speed of development for different areas; reaching for too rapid development of agricultural mechanization, which was out of step with the development of the national economy; neglecting the actual needs of agricultural production and other wishes of the peasants, resulting in the erroneous tendency to bring about agricultural mechanization by administrative orders and running everything by ourselves to the exclusion of the peasants; and, in particular, ignoring the actual economic results of agricultural mechanization (that is, seeking to attain agricultural mechanization only for its own sake).

In developing agricultural machinery products, there used to be an erroneous tendency to lay stress on crop production machinery at the expense of machinery for animal husbandry, and to emphasize grain crop machinery at the expense of machinery for cash crops. The agricultural machinery industry itself also had the shortcomings of overlapping projects and production, unreasonable structure and disproportionate development; furthermore, our agricultural machinery enterprises remained at low levels of technology, productivity and management. Compared with the products of developed countries, ours display some superior features and qualities such as small and medium sizes, lower prices, and good adaptability and durability; but as a whole our products are comparatively backward in performance, lacking in variety and unsatisfactory in quality.

II. Major Achievements in 1980

In keeping with the policy of "readjustment, restructuring, consolidation and improvement" of our national economy in 1980, the agricultural machinery industry and agricultural mechanization were also being readjusted by continuously eliminating the pernicious influence of "Left" thinking. In order to meet the new demand for agricultural machinery as a result of continual implementation of rural economic policies and the institution of various systems of responsibility in agricultural production, the departments responsible for agricultural machinery scored inspiring achievements in developing production and in improving both the quality and varieties of products.

The following are some of the successes achieved in 1980:

1. *Output of principal agricultural machinery products:*

Large and medium-sized tractors	98,000
Small-sized tractors	218,000
Internal combustion engines (aggregate million hp)	25.39
Combines	5,979
Large and medium-sized tractor-operated implements (including ploughs, harrows and seeders)	106,000
Large and medium-sized farm trucks	73,000
Power-driven machines for crop protection	64,000
Agricultural pumps	706,000

2. *A marked improvement in the quality of principal agricultural machinery products.* The Ministry of Agricultural Machinery made selective checks on 67 principal products from 50 agricultural machinery enterprises, 65.7% of which reached the standard of first-rate products and high-class products, compared with 48% in 1979.

In the appraisal of "high-quality products" under the direction of the State Economic Commission, seven products were awarded state silver medals in 1979; in 1980 another seven products were awarded state silver medals and two products awarded state gold medals. In addition, 52 products from 55 enterprises were awarded certificates for high-quality products by the Ministry of Agricultural Machinery.

Products awarded the state gold medal and/or the state silver medal were as follows: Models S195 diesel engine by the Changzhou Diesel Engine Works (silver medal in 1979 and gold medal in 1980); Model 495A diesel engine by the Shanghai Internal Combustion Engine Works (gold medal); Model S195 diesel engine by the Wuxi County Diesel Engine Works (silver medal); Model Dongfeng-12 walking tractor by the Changzhou Tractor Factory and the Wuxi County Tractor Factory, respectively (silver medal); Model 518-12 walking tractor by the Shenyang Small Tractor Factory (silver medal); Model 261P Turbocharger by the Wuxi Power Machinery Factory (Silver medal); Crankshaft for Model Dongfanghong-75 tractor by the Chengde Crankshaft & Connecting Rod Factory (silver medal); Model L-5-35 heavy-duty 5-furrow plough by the Heilongjiang Agricultural Machinery Factory (silver medal); 24-row applicator-planter by the Xian Agricultural Machinery Factory (silver medal); Model ZF40 gearbox for ships by the Hangzhou Gearbox Factory (silver medal); "Torch" Brand spark plug by the Zhuzhou Spark Plug Factory (silver medal); Model 1100 thresher by the Jiamusi Combine Factory (silver medal); Model 40 mixed-flow pump by the Wuxi Pump Factory (silver medal): Model 6135C diesel engine by the Shanghai Diesel Engine Factory and the Guizhou Diesel Engine Factory, respectively (silver medal); Model X195 diesel engine by the Gold Horse Diesel Engine Factory, Yunnan Province (Silver medal).

3. *Progress in modifying outdated products and developing new products.* The most impressive achievements are the marked modification of the large-sized combines by the Siping Combine Factory, the Jiamusi Combine Factory and the Kaifeng Combine Factory, respectively; develop-

ments of new varieties of the Model Tieniu-55 wheeled tractor, Model Dongfanghong-28 wheeled tractor, Model Hongqi 100A crawler tractor and Model Dongfeng-12 small tractor, in addition to structural modifications; the advanced-structured four-wheel drive tractor with 60 hp being developed by the Luoyang no. 1 Tractor Plant and displaying satisfactory performance after 2,000 hours of field tests; another four-wheel drive tractor with 150 hp under development; and two gas engines with 1,000 hp and 1,200 hp, respectively, being developed by the Hongyan Diesel Engine Factory so as to conserve petroleum and to make use of a variety of energy sources for agricultural machinery.

The year 1980 also saw inspiring progress in the development of machinery for animal husbandry. We succeeded in building complete sets of large, medium- and small-sized feed-processing equipment, mechanized equipment for chicken-raising, and equipment for hay-harvesting, including a variety of mowing machines, raking machines, self-propelled windrowers, square balers, round balers and hay stackers. In addition, other machinery for animal husbandry, such as hay resowers, silage combines and livestock and hay trucks, were also developed.

4. *The start of readjustment in the agricultural machinery industry.* Measures taken included a reduction of capital construction projects; a reduction of overlapping enterprises that compete with existing enterprises for raw materials, fuel and energy; and an increase in production capacity of products in short supply. In 1980 there were only 38 tractor factories, 34 walking tractor factories and 199 internal combustion engine works whose production quotas were assigned directly by the Ministry of Agricultural Machinery.

Compared with 1978, the year 1980 saw a 75% increase in production capacity of large and medium-sized grain combines. New facilities included 12 more factories for manufacturing machinery for animal husbandry (added to the original 12 factories in 1979); 2 factories for manufacturing complete sets of equipment for chicken raising and 2 factories for manufacturing complete sets of equipment for silage processing; 8 manufacturers of seed separators; 12 grain-dryer factories with 8 relatively mature products; and 3 factories for manufacturing large-sized sprinklers. Moreoover, the output of the above products in short supply was greatly increased.

5. *An increase in exports of agricultural machinery products and extension of technical cooperation with other countries.* Our agricultural machinery products are simple in construction, easy to operate, and low in price, making them suitable for Third World countries. In 1980 we exported over 100 agricultural machinery products to 68 countries and regions, the export volume rising by 46% over 1979. Up to the present we have established technical cooperation agreements with 34 countries and regions.

In 1980, the United Nations Industrial Development Organization (UNIDO) organized in Beijing the Meeting on Exchange of Experiences and Cooperation among Developing Countries in the Development of Agricultural Machinery Industry, which was attended by representatives of over 30 countries. During the meeting the representatives visited the Exhibition of China's Agricultural Machinery and showed great interest in a variety of medium- and small-sized agricultural machinery displayed. The meeting passed a resolution to set up an agricultural machinery research center for developing countries in Beijing.

6. *Implementation of various systems of responsibility in agricultural production throughout China's rural areas.* This action brought into full play the enthusiasm of the peasants for production, leading to an all-around development of agricultural production, an increase in the peasants' income and a steady improvement in the standard of living. At the same time, it promoted the development of agricultural mechanization. In formerly poverty-stricken Guizhou Province, commune and brigade collectives, as well as commune members, purchased in 1980 agricultural machinery valued at 34.8 million yuan, of which 30 million yuan were funded by communes and brigades and commune members themselves — over three times the average annual self-raised funds for the purchase of agricultural machinery in the three previous years.

In Chuxian Prefecture of Anhui Province, which had long suffered from natural disasters and therefore yielded low harvests, productivity was low and the life of the people was poor. Since the implementation of the systems of responsibility in agricultural production, great changes have taken place. According to preliminary statistics, the commune members of the prefecture purchased 126 large and medium-sized tractors, 1,933 small tractors, 1,926 produce-processing machines and 18 agricultural trucks with their own funds in 1980.

It was not a novelty for commune members to purchase tractors with their own funds and operate a tractor station to plough land for the peasants, who were practicing the system that fixes output for each peasant household and for individual peasants and pays according to the output. The system brought about changes in the management of agricultural machinery. The implementation of the party's economic policies, the changes in methods of management, the development of production and the competition among peasants to purchase agricultural machinery were the most impressive developments in the rural areas. These developments activated the rural economy, brought about a better standard of living, and stimulated the peasants' enthusiasm for agricultural mechanization.

7. *Preliminary reforms in the management of agricultural machinery products.* Previously, the state had a monopoly on the purchase and marketing of agricultural machinery products, which were then distributed by administrative departments at each level without direct contact between producing and marketing departments. This system gave rise to a series of abuses, such as lack of communication between producing and marketing departments and insurmountable barriers between one economic department and the other. In 1980 a preliminary reform was carried out in the state monopoly for purchase and marketing of products, opening up a market for agricultural machinery under the guidance of state unified planning. The monopoly was lifted on the supply of most products, and customers were free to choose and purchase. Enterprises were allowed to market their own products after they had sold to the state the amount specified by the state plan, giving rise to competition under socialist conditions, which had a positive effect on raising the quality of products, reducing costs, developing new products, better service for customers, and improving management.

III. Industry Goals During Readjustment Period

In the ongoing readjustment of the national economy, efforts have been made to speed up agricultural development. At present, the fundamental principle for developing agriculture is centred on "implementation of specific policies and application of scientific knowledge." "Implementation of specific policies" implies continuing to break away from the fetters of "Left" thinking, and strengthening and perfecting various practicable systems of responsibility in agriculture suitable for the local level of development of the productive forces, so as to bring into full play the initiative of the peasants. Practice has proved this is the prerequisite for the development of agricultural mechanization. "Application of scientific knowledge" implies efficiently extending and applying to agricultural production achievements in science and technology, whose application is, in turn, inseparable from advanced production tools including various agricultural machinery.

The development of the agricultural machinery industry and agricultural mechanization, therefore, should accord with the development of the national economy. In view of the country's current conditions and the actual needs of agricultural production, our principle is to act according to our capability and to lay stress on increasing economic results. The requirements of the continuing readjustment of the national economy and state of the agricultural machinery industry necessitate further readjustment in the agricultural machinery industry and the programme of agricultural mechanization.

Principal Requirements. The main tasks of the readjustment of the agricultural machinery industry are: (1) readjustment of the orientation of services of the agricultural machinery enterprises and the disproportionate relationships within the agricultural machinery industry; (2) restructuring the agricultural machinery industry, i.e., organizing existing agricultural machinery enterprises into integrated economic complexes of all forms; (3) carrying out technical transformation of agricultural machinery enterprises so as to raise the quality of products, increase vareities and enlarge the export volume and; (4) reform of the system of enterprise management, supply and marketing, scientific research and management of agricultural mechanization. It is imperative that the levels of management technology, production and services be raised in order to lay a good foundation for the future development of enterprises.

1. *Readjustment of the orientation of structures of products, and expansion of the scope of services.* Five kinds of "catering" are to be put into effect, i.e., catering to the needs of agriculture, forestry, animal husbandry, sideline occupations and fisheries; catering to the needs of commune- and brigade-run enterprises; catering to the needs of urban and rural construction and to the people's livelihood; catering to the needs of increasing exports; and catering to the needs of technical transformation of various departments of the national economy.

In the light of the development of agriculture and the demands of the market, agricultural machinery enterprises should increase the varieties of products in short supply; expand the production capacity for urgently needed products; eliminate systematically outdated products that are of poor quality and do not sell well on the market, or which have a high consumption rate of energy and materials; and develop new products that sell well on the market.

Moreover, according to the actual needs of implementation of various systems of responsibility in agricultural production we should expand the production of small, semi-mechanized implements and hand tools. We should utilize fully the production capacity of the agricultural machinery industry, strive to develop light industrial and electromechanical products for the people's livelihood that sell well on the market, and help fill in the gaps by completing sets of equipment for other branches, such as engineering, construction, transportation, communications and so on.

2. *Restructuring the agricultural machinery industry according to the principle of economy and rationalization, and specialized cooperation.* Overlapping production has to be reduced, and scattered and backward small-scale production has to be converted into specialized production. It is imperative to readjust and restructure trades, one by one, under the leadership of the National Commission of Engineering Industry. The key agricultural machinery enterprises whose products are marketed throughout the country should be integrated so as to connect various regions and trades. Local agricultural machinery enterprises may be readjusted and restructured according to local needs by the local administration. As for agricultural machinery manufacturing and repairing factories at the county level and commune- and brigade-run manufacturing and repair units, apart from undertaking the tasks of manufacturing and repairing agricultural machinery, they are to be readjusted (in light of the principle of serving local needs) by the local administration to become general machine manufacturing and repair factories that mainly serve agricultural production and concurrently manufacture some other products for the market. During the period of readjustment we must select a group of agricultural machinery enterprises that have good facilities but inadequate tasks, and require them to produce light industrial produce whose processing technology is similar to that of the agricultural machines they are producing and whose supply falls short of people's demands.

3. *On the basis of readjustment and restructuring, we must carry out technical transformation of key enterprises step by step in a planned way, and strive to raise the quality of products and labour productivity by relying mainly on our technical strength and with appropriate introduction of new technologies from abroad.*

4. *Corresponding readjustment and restructuring of scientific research and educational work in the field of agricultural machinery.* It is necessary to reorganize the technical and research personnel of scientific research institutes, institutions of higher learning and key agricultural machinery enterprises; to make a rational division of work, giving full play to their professional knowledge; to stress the key programme and the application of research work to production; and gradually to change the present dispersion of technical personnel and overlapping of research programme so as to spur the development of the agricultural machinery industry and agricultural mechanization.

5. *Gradual restructuring, during the period of readjustment, of the system of management, supply and marketing, as well as scientific research and educational work of the agricultural machinery industry and agricultural mechanization.* Restructuring must be subordinate to and benefit readjustment, and must be carried out steadily.

The Country's Realities. During the period of readjustment, it is necessary to make a thorough study of China's realities on the basis of historical expreriences, going further into the orientation, road and steps of China's development of agricultural mechanization. From the point of view of agricultural mechanization, special attention should be paid to the following basic realities of the country:

1. *A very large population and limited farmland.* China has a territory of 9.6 million sq. km. but the average resources per capita are not great. Farmland per capita is about one-fourth that of the entire world, one-eighth that of the United States, one-seventh that of the Soviet-Union, one-third that of France, and two-fifths that of India. Forest per capita is about 12% that of the world, and grassland per capita is less than 50% that of the world. Moreoover, the distribution of the population and agricultural resources is unequal from place to place. 90% of the population lives on only 10% of the land. Even so, a large part of the land and resources have not been exploited and utilized. The emphasis of agricultural mechanization, therefore, should be placed on cultivated land, which is, however, not enough. From a long-term point of view, we must give our attention to 4,000 million *mu* of grassland, 1,000 million *mu* of grass hill, approximately 2,000 million *mu* of forest, 250 million *mu* of inlsnad water and one million square nautical miles of sea areas.

2. *Variations in natural conditions, crop varieties and farming systems, and the high multiple crop index, which lead to the complexity and difficulty of our mechanization of agriculture.*

China's plains account for only one-fourth of the total territory, while the mountain areas, hilly land and plateau regions cover three-fourths of the land. Annual rainfall varies from dozens of mm. to over 1,000 mm., and frost-free periods range from 100 days to 300 days or more, resulting in one, two or three crops a year. The farming system of interplanting and intercropping multiplies the difficulties for agricultural mechanization. Any subjective or metaphysical way of specifying the same speed of development for all places will not succeed.

3. *A great disparity in economic development from place to place.* There are highly developed coastal areas whose per-capita GNP exceeds US$1,000, while in remote border mountain areas people are still practicing slash-and-burn cultivation. In view of the diversity of natural conditions as well as the great disparity in levels of economic and cultural development from one place to another, we should not specify the same speed for developing agricultural mechanization throughout the country. We must establish our priorities in line with local conditions, with an appropriate array of measures and methods.

4. *An underdeveloped commodity economy in the rural areas.* At the present time, the commodity economy is not well-developed in China's rural areas, where the principal commodity for exchange is a small amount of "surplus grain." For a production brigade to realize mechanization, there must be a variety of agricultural machinery; however, the utilization of such machines is very limited because of the variety of crops raised. This is one of the chief reasons why some areas have quite a few machines and equipment but have still not achieved a high level of mechanization or improved economic results. In order to correct this situation we must raise agricultural productivity, give full play to commodity production, move step by step toward a relatively concentrated distribution of crops and specialized agriculture, which is a very long process. The speed of development of agricultural mechanization must correspond with these considerations.

5. *Surplus manpower and its proper arrangement.* Surplus manpower as a result of agricultural mechanization should be absorbed wherever it exists, and should not be allowed to overflow into the cities. This is an important difference between China and other countries. The agricultural mechanization of the country will take a relatively long time. It is a process involving the gradual transfer of manpower from grain production to a range of economic activities including industry and sideline occupations and commune- and brigade-run enterprises. Such a transition requires a considerable period of time, and it cannot absorb manpower as quickly as large-scale industry does. The speed of development of agricultural mechanization, therefore, must accord with the realities. Otherwise, it will give rise to an excess of manpower, adversely affecting the economic benefits of mechanization.

6. *Simultaneous industrial development and agricultural mechanization.* China's agricultural mechanization experience is different from that of developed countries, where industrialization preceded agricultural mechanization; it is proceeding simultaneously with industrialization. As a result, we have to cope with difficulties in obtaining enough iron and steel, rubber, oil, electricity and transport facilities necessary for the realization of agricultural mechanization. In the case of transport, for example, some mountain areas are lacking highways, thus preventing machinery and equipment, if any, from being sent there. The pressing problem for these areas is to build highways. Furthermore, agricultural mechanization requires considerable investment, which is impossible and inappropriate for the state to offer in a short time.

In view of these realities, agricultural mechanization should by no means develop at too fast nor on too large a scale. For a fairly long time to come we will have to follow the principle of developing mechanization and semi-mechanization simultaneously, using a combination of manual power, draught animals and machinery.

20. CHINA'S ELECTRONICS INDUSTRY
By the Policy Research Office,
Fourth Ministry of Machine Building

I. Establishment and Development of China's Electronics Industry

Just after the Liberation of China in 1949, relying on the forces for assembling and repairing radio stations in the areas liberated earlier, we managed to take over 10 or more very small wire and wireless telecommunications factories, scattered in Tianjin, Nanjing, Shanghai, Chongqing, Wuhan, etc., from the hands of the Kuomintang reactionaries. At that time, we had only 4,106 empolyees in this field and could assemble and repair only a small quantity of radio sets and radio stations with components and parts bought from abroad. The total output value was 4.95 million yuan, representing a mere 0.05% of total national industrial output value. That marked the beginning of China's electronics industry. Despite its weak basis, the electronics industry, owing to the great concern shown by our party and government and the efforts of our workers and staff members, overcame numerous difficulties and succeeded in developing rapidly from assembling and repairing to manufacturing and from copying products to designing its own.

The Present Scale. After more than 30 years of development, China's efforts in the electronics field have produced a fair-sized industry. According to 1980 statistics, the Fourth Ministry of Machine Building has 3,137 directly run and locally run electronics enterprises with 1,355,000 employees and more than 7,800 million yuan of fixed assets. The output value of the industry in 1980 was 20,100,000 yuan, accounting for 4% of total national industrial value. That represents an increase of 4,000 times over 1949, and a 30.7% average annual growth rate. Up to 1979, the profit and tax handed over to the state by the electronics industry amounted to 3.2 times the state's investments in capital construction in the electronics field during the same period.

In addition to the ministry's directly run electronics enterprises and the locally run ones, there are fair-sized electronics research and manufacturing facilities operated by the Ministry of Posts and Communications, the Ministry of Railways, other ministries of machine building, the Chinese Academy of Sciences and various universities and colleges.

Distribution of the Industry. Before Liberation, the 10 or more radio industry enterprises of China were concentrated mostly in such large coastal cities as Shanghai, Nanjing, and Tianjin. After the founding of New China, the State successively set up a number of primary electronics factories in major cities and inland areas. At the same time, various provinces, municipalities and autonomous regions set up their own electronics factories, greatly promoting the development of both the coastal and inland industries. At present, our 29 provinces, municipalities and autonomous regions all have established their electronics enterprises. The electronics operations of Shanghai, Jiangsu, Beijing, Liaoning, Shandong, Tianjin, Sichuan, Hubei, Shaanxi, Guangdong, Guizhou and Jiangxi are particularly concentrated and are growing rapidly, thus forming the basis of China's electronics industry. The previous irrational distribution of the electronics industry has been basically corrected, and a solid foundation has been formed through the linking of central and local, coastal and inland enterprises.

Main Products and Technical Capabilities. China's electronics industry, though a nascent industry, has developed so far as to be able to manufacture a fairly wide range of specialized products for both military and civilian uses. The industry can produce good used in production or by consumers, for scientific and cultural purposes, for use by society, both military and civilians, as well as for general military-civilian use.

The main product categories are the following:

1. Radar, fire control systems and associated products.

2. Communication and navigation equipment used for cable communication, HF communication, microwave communication, troposphere-scatter communication, satellite communication and different types of mini-radio stations. Some of these products have reached an advanced level.

3. Computers. The industry can now produce Series 100 and Series 200 computers in volume. The IC computer with 5 million calculations/second was successfully developed in 1979. The production capacity for large and medium-sized computers is more than 400 units per year.

4. Radio and television broadcast products. The industry can now turn out black-and-white TV sets, radios and recorders in large quantities, and colour TV sets in small batches. The annual production of radio sets amounts to 30 million units; the assembling capacity of TV sets is 4 million per year, and that of recorders is 600,000 per year. The production of videorecorders has already begun. The production of radio and TV broadcast equipment can basically meet the requirements in this field. The industry can also produce more than 730 varieties of electronic products for the national economy, science and culture, as well as for society; more than 700 types of electron tubes; more than 600 types of discrete semiconductor devices; more than 400 types of ICs; 2,000 kinds of electronic parts; 500 kinds of electronic measuring instruments; and special-purpose radio equipment as well as special-purpose materials for the electronics industry.

The development of these specialized categories enables us to provide electronic products for the national defence industry, the national economy, and the requirements of the material and cultural life of the people. A certain number of the products are available for export.

Science, technology and education. China's electronics industry is served by a strong contingent of scientific and technical research personnel. At present, the engineers and technicians in the industry number more than 10,000 and more than 10,000 students are now majoring in electronics science and technology at institutions of higher learning and secondary technical schools. During the past 30 years, the large number of achievements of research and development personnel have made a significant contribution to the electronics industry.

In the early 1950's, a 1,000-kw. MW radio broadcasting transmitter was designed and manufactured on our own. Though scientific research suffered a setback during the turmoil of the "cultural revolution," our scientific workers nonetheless designed and manufactured a set of satellite earth stations, successfully developed colour TV broadcasting equipment, explored laser infrared technology, developed and manufactured such technologically advanced communications equipment as a 300-channel small-diameter coaxial cable carrier system, a tropospheric-scatter communications system, a high-powered SW transmitter, etc. Since the smashing of the Gang of Four, the 5 million calculations/second computer, Model 210, 220-1 and 260 computers, the 960-channel small-diameter coaxial cable carrier system, the 1 million-x radio telescope, the 4096-bit memory chip, etc., have been successfully developed one after another, and a number of other scientific research projects have reached high levels and passed official evaluations.

In 1979, 218 items among the scientific and technological achievements in the electronics industry won the national significant technology improvement achievement prizes, 247 items won the top-level science and technology achievement prizes and 3 items won the national invention prizes. With the application of scientific research to production, the quality of electronics products has been improved and a number of well-known brand products have emerged, 3 of which won gold medals and 11 won silver medals in a national competition.

II. The Electronics Industry in 1980

In early 1980, at a meeting of leading cadres of the electronics industry, the principle of "readjusting actively and doing a good job of the change" was put forward in accordance with the guiding principle of readjustment, restructuring, consolidation and improvement and in conformity with the actual situation in the electronics industry. The meeting stressed the need for readjustment in five major areas — military and civilian products, scientific research work and production, equipment and bases, capital construction and enterprise organization.

A new approach must be taken in each of these five areas. Scientific research work should be changed to strengthen basic research in the technological sciences, applied research, research and development of new-generation products of great significance, and advanced research for the long-term development of the electronics industry. The production of military products should be changed to permit a rational composition of the industry that will accommodate both military and civilian needs. The expanded reproduction should be changed to carry out coordination among specialized units and technological transformation. Business management should be changed to combine economic methods with administrative measures. Training of personnel and cadres should be changed to meet the new requirements of modernization.

Important steps. One year's experience has shown that it was both necessary and timely to set forth the principles of readjustment and transformation in these five areas. Good results have been obtained and advances have been made in different areas of work because of the implementation of the above principles. Major examples of this progress are as follows:

1. *Production has been further increased, particularly of civilian products, and the product composition of the electronics industry is already beginning to orient itself more rationally.* Readjustment of the product composition of the electronics industry has been under way for a year. While the production of military products has been guaranteed, the production of urgently wanted but scarce products such as TV sets, radios, recorders, phonographs, etc., as well as major associated parts, components and accessories, has been increased.

The total output value of the electronics industry in 1980 was 21,000 million yuan, an amount 22.5% greater than that of 1979. The output value of civilian products of the national electronics industry accounted for more than 80% of total output value. The number of TV sets produced by the enterprises affiliated with the Fourth Ministry of Machine Building increased 87% compared with 1979; radios, 80%; recorders, 500%; phonographs, more than 100%; electronic calculators, 600%; TV transmitters, 267%; and retransmitters, 37%.

2. *Considerable progress has been made in research and development and in trial-production, and scientific research has been accelerated.* The industry supplied electronics systems for the experimental launching of carrier rockets over the Pacific Ocean. These systems proved to be stable, reliable and accurate, and accomplished their assignments quite satisfactorily.

Design work has been completed for microcomputer models 051 and 061 and the computer 100/132, which adopted Chinese-made LSI's. A prototype of computer Model 153, with its sophisticated software, has been developed. The floppy disc unit is already in use. The 30-m.-high Oersted permanent magnetic material of rare earth cobalt has been finalized and is up to world standards. The 4096-bit RAM and monolithic microprocessor circuits have passed the evaluation of final design stage. Prototypes of decimetre-wave TV transmitters and retransmitters, 2/3-inch small-sized colour pickup cameras, low-lights level TVs and X-ray medical TVs have been produced.

Progress also has been made in the trial-production of single-tube colour projection-type TVs and colour videorecorders. Design institutes affiliated with factories have made great and continuous efforts to increase the designs and varieties of their products. New models of radios, radio/recorders, radio/recorder/photographs and decimetre-wave TV sets have been produced on a trial basis. Some of these units, which are small, attractive, and perform well, have been mass-produced and placed on the market.

3. *The quality of electronic products has been improved, and the acceptance inspection of quality rectification and the practice of overall quality control have brought good results.* In 1980, the Fourth Ministry of Machine Building practiced acceptance inspection of quality rectification in a certain number of its affiliated enterprises and some local enterprises, while implementing a trial practice of all-around quality control in some other enterprises. Concurrently, an extensive effort was made to produce high-quality products.

In addition, some related units and departments jointly held a forum on overall quality control of TV and radio sets, at which a tentative method for managing reliability tests of some components and devices was proposed, emphasizing the need to improve the reliability, stability and uniformity of components, devices and raw and processed materials. This plan also demands that certain districts set up two major quality control feedback systems — one consisting of the industry, commerce and user, and the other involving equipment, components and devices — so that an in-trade and trans-trade all-around quality control can be carried out.

The Shanghai Instrument Bureau and several specialized corporations have organized a large quality feedback network involving 11 equipment plants and more than 70 components and devices plants. The Electronics Bureau of Jiangsu Province has formed "a dragon" (or coordination chain) system for conducting series quality control of products ranging from equipment to components and devices. Preliminary reports on the results of these efforts show that the reliability of equipment, components and devices has been improved to varying degrees.

In 1980, 3 electronic products were awarded the state national gold medals and 14 received silver medals. In addition, many electronic products won a high reputation for quality in the provinces and municipalities. The MTBF (Mean Time Between Failure) of TV sets made from discrete components and ICs has reached 1,500 and 2,000 hours, respectively. The main specifications for certain brands of recorders have neared or reached the advanced level of foreign-made recorders of the same grades.

A great amount of work has been done in improving the reliability of electronic components and devices. The Fourth Ministry of Machine Building successfully selected 70 plants producing components and devices and organized 82 "experimental lines of 7-special-item quality control," resulting in the production of more than 400 varieties of components and devices of greater reliability. The availability of component products for major projects was raised from the original

20% to 95%. The life time of Chinese-made B/W tubes exceeded 5,000 hours.

4. *The state plan for investment in capital construction has been fairly implemented.* The scale of capital construction has been greatly reduced. In 1980, 104.9% of the state investment plan was implemented by the electronics industry, and newly increased fixed assets accounted for 76.7% of fulfilled investment. Major capital construction projects undertaken by ministry-related enterprises included: the Xianyang Colour Tube Plant, the IC production line in the Jiangnan Radio Appliances Factory of Wuxi and the line-cutting machine of the Chengdu Hongguang Electron Tube Plant. The colour TV assembly line of the Tianjin Radio Factory was built and put into trial-production. The local electronics industry also made great strides: among other achievements, assembly lines for 16/12-inch B/W tubes in the Shanghai Electron Tube Factory and the Shijiazhuang Tube Plant were built and entered into production. In 1980, 520,000 sq. m. of housing was built for ministry-affiliated enterprises and institutions, the largest amount of construction ever completed in one year by the electronics industry. This construction helped to alleviate crowded living conditions for workers and staff.

5. *Progress has been made in our experiment conducted at selected points, to enlarge enterprises' decision-making powers and to promote their integration.* The reform of the economic management system in the electronics industry has begun. The experiment to enlarge self-decision powers was carried out at some ministry-affiliated enterprises, research institutes and local enterprises, while a single-item profit package system was practiced in some other ministry-affiliated enterprises. All these enterprises succeeded in expanding their production capacity and increasing profits. Of these enterprises, the ministry-affiliated ones overfulfilled the year's planned profit quota by 21.2%. Good results also were obtained at those research institutes that conducted the experiment of enlarging self-decision powers.

As for the promotion of integration, the year of 1980 witnessed the establishment of the China Nanjing Radio Company and preparation for organizing joint corporations in Shanghai, Tianjin, Guangzhou, Chongqing, Chengdu, and other cities. The establishment of the China General Company of Electronic Components and Devices served as a guide to learning how to run nationwide specialized corporations. In addition to the corporations that were established a few years earlier and were being perfected, some new corporations and economic complexes of various forms were set up, and the organized management of enterprises was raised to a higher level. The establishment of these corporations and economic complexes play an active part in the development of the electronics industry.

Since its founding, the Nanjing Radio Company, has overfulfilled its production plan every month, and its 37 affiliated enterprises have succeeded in turning over much greater profits to the state. The readjustment of product composition within the company was already under way, and some new products were developed. The enterprises affiliated with the China General Company of Electronic Components and Devices overfulfilled the planned total output value by 45%; the output of kinescopes exceeded the plan by 24%, and the profit total by 32%.

In some provinces and municipalities where electronics corporations were founded, management and technical capabilities were more concentrated and enterprises shared in the work and cooperated with one another, so that the production potential of these enterprises was in a better position to be utilized fully. For example, with the establishment of the Shanghai TV Industry Company, 10 TV set assembly lines came into being through transformation and reorganization of existing production facilities, and the production of certain associated parts was automated to varying degrees on the single-machine basis. As a result, production capacity increased several times and the profit for one month equalled the total investment in the transformation of the 10 production lines.

The Dandong Municipal Electronics Company of Liaoning Province reorganized its 21 enterprises into 13 and readjusted the varieties of products from 201 to 101. With the realization of large-scale specialized production, the annual production capacity of tuners reached one million, which is one-fourth of the total capacity of the country. The profits it made in 1980 accounted for one-third of the total profits realized by the entire electronics industry of the province in that year. This is a good example of the advantages of integration and reorganization.

6. *Business with foreign countries has increased, and a good beginning has been achieved in the reform of the foreign trade system.* In May 1980, the China Electronics Import and Export Corporation, a combined industry and trade outfit with branches in Tianjin, Guangzhou and Shanghai, was established. As a first step, a team of foreign trade experts within the electronics industry was formed. The corporation vigorously pushed import and export business and signed three contracts for importing the Solar computer, fixed-

head magnetic disc drive and controlled printer; its export business is now up to US$25 million. According to incomplete statistics, more than 300 contracts for the processing and assembly of imported materials and components, valued at US$27 million, have been signed by various provinces, municipalities and autonomous regions.

7. *Management and administration have shown some improvement, and good results have been obtained in the drive to vitalize the economy and increase economic efficiency.* Various regions and enterprises strengthened their marketing methods and began to investigate market conditions. The Radio Appliances Corporation and its various branches have turned from centralized distribution, purchasing and selling, and the manufacture of complete sets of equipment — its dominant business in the past — to concentrate on selling, adjusting to market conditions and organizing department shows and sales, commissioned sales outlets and trial sales. The corporation also enlarged the range of supply services. The total volume of supply was 25% more than that of the previous year. The quota for savings on major goods and materials, such as steel, gold, silver and lumber, have been overfulfilled, and more than 42% of the surplus, as well as long-kept goods and materials in stock that were discovered through a warehouse inventory, have been put to use. Joint ventures were initiated with the local goods and materials departments of the electronics industry in Anhui, Jiangxi and Fujian provinces, and better results were achieved.

Various enterprises have strengthened their accounting and put into practice various economic responsibility systems, thus succeeding in reducing production costs of their products, particularly of the so-called "four kinds of machines" (TV sets, radios, tape recorders and phonographs). Among these, the costs of various TV sets were reduced by from 3.8% to 32%, and the average cost reduction of radios ranged from 4.4% to 8.6%. The market for tape recorders was opened up through the positive cooperation between assembly plants and various component-manufacturing plants, enhancing the quality, developing new products and reducing costs (although it was affected twice by a reduction in prices of imported products), and thus both production and income were increased.

Some plants that produce special parts and accessories for assembly plants reduced selling prices on the basis of increasing yields and lower production costs, creating favourable conditions for further reducing the costs of complete sets. In 1980 the "four kinds of machines" alone accounted for sales of about 2,100 million yuan, and turned over to the state 33% more profits and taxes than in 1979.

To promote the development of the electronics industry, the role of technical services was strengthened. In addition to the former Communication Engineering Corporation were established the China Computer Technical Service Corporation, Radio and TV Broadcasting Service Corporation and Instrument Joint Service Department. Businesses that contract for engineering projects, design machine rooms, install, align and service electronic equipment, train operators for the users, and organize department shows and sales of electronic products were expanded.

At the same time, various types of technical services were offered in provinces, municipalities and enterprises. It was reported that more than a quarter of the total number of TV manufacturing plants in China began to provide services at customers' homes during the guarantee period of the purchased products. Some of these plants made considerable efforts to set up service networks or points in urban and rural areas or to offer service-on-wheels (mobile service) to meet the customer's needs. All these services were warmly welcomed by users.

8. *Considerable progress was made in education and cadres' work.* The education of qualified personnel and the assignment of cadres began to adapt to the new requirements of modernization. Two secondary technical schools in Guilin and Hangzhou now have been formally upgraded to colleges, and some college branches for training computer software personnel were established. Emphasis was placed on renovation of college facilities, thus improving school conditions and expanding enrollment capacity. Through consolidation, 20 colleges for staff members and workers run by factories managed to raise their education quality basically up to the requirements of the state.

The training of leading cadres and staff and workers of the enterprises also was strongly emphasized. Training classes for leading cadres have been given 15 times, and 771 cadres trained. Leading groups of some ministry-affiliated enterprises have been readjusted. A total of 115 young and middle-aged cadres who had good professional qualifications have been promoted to positions of leadership. The proportion of leading members of enterprises with university, college and senior middle school educations is already as high as 40.7%. The party's policy towards intellectuals has been further implemented. The enthusiasm of technical personnel in general has been mobilized by the widespread adherence to previous stipulations which promoted technicians to the rank of professionals.

III. Main Tasks of Further Readjustment

The general state of the electronics industry in 1980 was favourable. Good results were achieved, and some development was attained. But the passive position of the industry caused by the "Left" errors and mistakes in the past has not been fundamentally changed. Imbalance within the industry and unreasonable structures are still relatively serious problems. The main problems at present are as follows:

Wide differences exist between the changing of product composition and rational economic requirements. Professional reorganization and technical reform have not made great progress, and the organization of enterprises is a long way from meeting the requirements of mass production. Scientific research work is still weak and has not yet succeeded in "moving ahead of production," and the technical levels of products and production cannot meet the needs of development. The composition of cadres and of staff and workers has not yet fundamentally changed to accord with the development of the electronics industry. The management of enterprises is relatively backward, and quite a few enterprises still suffer from high consumption and waste and poor economic results. All of these problems demonstrate that the further readjustment and reform of the electronics industry is still a rather difficult task.

Five Structures. During the period of further economic readjustment, the main task of the electronics industry is to quicken the readjustment and to promote changes that will enable the industry to proceed on a coordinated, steady and sound path. The electronics industry must establish five reasonable structures through readjustment, reorganization, combination and relevant reforms:

1. *Establish reasonable product composition to serve the Four Modernizations and the needs of both domestic and overseas markets.* The general requirement is that the electronics industry must serve various social needs. This means that military electronic products have to be guaranteed; durable consumer electronic products must be increased; the electronic products used for production, scientific research and educational and cultural purposes, as well as social management, must be developed; and electronic products for export must be expanded. To meet this requirement, basic products and complete sets must be developed in a coordinated manner. For the so-called five major items (TV, radio, tape recorder, phonograph and calculator), we must achieve mass production, high quality, low cost, expanding grades and increasing varieties so as to accommodate the purchasing power of various social strata. As for electronic clocks, watches and household utensils, close attention must be paid to relevant research and development, as well as to reduce costs in preparation for mass production.

Those electronic products that are needed by various sectors of the national economy — especially by light industry, textiles, transportation and energy, all of which are engaged in technical reforms — must be positively developed. The electronic computer, in particular, is a tremendous potential need. Investigations must be made to determine actual market conditions and to make technological preparations for new production while present production is going on.

The current position in electronic products for export must be expanded and consolidated. The amount of high-grade products for export will be gradually increased. Special workshops and plants producing goods for export, as well as export bases, will be established so as to open up new markets and increase foreign exchange earnings. The ratio between the production of basic products and that of complete sets, and the proportional relations between various kinds of basic products, must be reasonably readjusted. Special attention must be paid to adopting effective measures to deal with such weak links as LSI's, B/W picture tubes, high-reliability components and devices and critical parts for assembly of complete CTV sets.

2. *Realize a rational composition of science and technology so as to meet the needs of product renewal and change of product generations and to speed the development of electronics science and technology.* In developing products, it is essential to improve one generation while developing another and preparing for the development of still another. The method of "three generations at the same time" must be implemented effectively so as to achieve a balance between applied scientific research, pre-research, major products study, technological research and reliability study. As for production technology, it is essential for us to accommodate modern mass production, strengthen the study of manufacturing processes, implement technical reforms and renew manufacturing equipment and combine advanced technology with applied technology and manual work. Therefore, readjustment in three areas, i.e., orientation of scientific research, scientific organizations and items and subjects of scientific research, should be made. In particular, the readjustment of scientific organizations must be carried out firmly and effectively with a view to bringing about the unification of ministry and research institutes and

the unification of factory and research centres. The tight integration of scientific research and production will clarify the direction and task, rationalize the organizational structure and make scientific research projects and subjects suit the development of the electronics industry. This readjustment will enable us to achieve more highly valuable results, and at a faster pace.

3. *Establish rational organizational structures for enterprises so as to suit the needs of mass production.* Existing enterprises must be reorganized in a planned and sound way according to the principles of professional cooperation and economic rationality. This will promote the establishment of various economic complexes and raise the organized management of enterprises to a higher level, resulting in a more rational organization of production capabilities of the electronics industry. First of all, enterprises manufacturing components and devices must be thoroughly readjusted, reorganized and integrated. On the basis of reorganization and integration, technical reforms and the renewal of technology and equipment will be achieved in a planned way.

In order to establish the rational organizational structures for enterprises, the integration of ministry-affiliated enterprises and local enterprises must be promoted in various ways. In large and medium-sized cities, provinces and districts where ministry-affiliated enterprises and local enterprises are more densely concentrated, some sort of loose integration must be carried out when conditions permit. Those that are already integrated should explore ways to become economic complexes.

4. *Establish sound management structures so as to obtain good results from invigorating the economy and increasing economic efficiency.* The main points are as follows:

1. The management system should be rationalized. It is necessary to organize economic activities according to the principles of social mass production and economic rationality.

2. Management methods should be improved so as to combine administrative management with economic management, making the latter the dominant factor and introducing administrative methods, as needed. The work of economic legislation should be strengthened with a view to combining economic efficiency, economic profit and economic responsibility.

3. Investigations of the market should be carried out through organizational construction and actual studies so as to make technically based forecasts of both domestic and foreign markets and bring the role of market adjustment under the guidance of planning work.

4. The powers of self-decision granted to the enterprises should be further expanded, giving them more vitality.

5. Marketing centres and sales networks of the electronics industry should be established. Electronic appliances corporations located in various districts will shift their focus to selling products and gradually become marketing centres. Our target is to set up sales networks and points of sale in all large and medium-sized cities throughout the country in two or three years.

6. Technical services will be greatly strengthened, and various technical service corporations and service stations will be established so as to develop such services as product popularization, equipment installation and adjustment and training of technical personnel.

5. *Set up a rational system of ranking cadres and workers to meet the requirements of the Four Modernizations.* First of all, education work must be readjusted and strengthened in order to allot a suitable proportion of education in colleges and universities for training senior and middle class personnel and basic workers. School conditions must be improved to allow key universities to enroll students according to their capacity and the building of more key technical secondary schools. And it is necessary to realize the potential of setting up factory-run technical schools and of converting factories that have suspended operation, but have the proper facilities, into schools.

Secondly, specialities should be properly adjusted and the ones that are lacking should be made up. Special attention should be paid to the training of qualified personnel in the fields of computer software, economic management, machinery, information and foreign trade, with a view to ensuring that experts of various specialities are available.

Thirdly, a relatively regular educational system for staff personnel and workers should be established to raise their political and ideological levels, develop their competence in science, culture, the professions and economic management through various channels, thus creating a larger pool of people who know well their own professions and work and who are familiar with the modern economy, modern science and technology and modern management. The proportion of young and healthy leading cadres, specialists and skilled workers who understand technology and management must be increased year by year. The ranks of cadres must gradually be filled with younger people familiar with the professions and knowledgeable about various specialities. The cultural and technical levels of staff and workers must be raised.

21. CHINA'S METALLURGICAL INDUSTRY
By Chen Lei and Zhang Xinchuan
*Research Institute of Metallurgical Economy,
Ministry of Metallurgical Industry*

I. History of the Metallurgical Industry

China is rich in coal, iron, non-ferrous metal and hydropower resources. Its proven iron ore reserves amount to over 40,000 million tons. In addition to the four big mining areas — Anshan and Benxi, Jidong (East Hebei Province), Panzhihua and Xichang, Ma'anshan and Nanjing — many provinces and autonomous regions also have numerous iron mines. Its reserves of tungsten, antimony, tin and rare-earth metals are the largest in the world. Reserves of zinc, lead, copper, aluminium, nickel, molydenum, manganese, tantalum, niobium, mercury and titanite, as well as gold and silver, are among the second and third largest in the world. These vast mineral deposits are one of the basic factors in the development of the metallurgical industry in China.

Ancient Period. China's metallurgical industry has had a long and brilliant history. From vast quantities of unearthed bronze utensils and excavations of metal-smelting and casting sites, we know that that the smelting and casting of bronze utensils began early in the Shang Dynasty, about 3,100 to 3,700 years ago. Among these objects, "Simuwu," a large, square tripod unearthed from the Yin Dynasty ruins in Anyang, weighed 875 kg. Many of these utensils have fine patterns and distinctive characters, showing that the smelting and casting techniques of the Shang Dynasty were very advanced.

At the old mining and smelting site of Daye and Tonglushan (from the Spring and Autumn and the Warring States periods until the Song Dynasty), a mine pit more than 50 m. deep has been found. The site contained various kinds of copper-smelting shaft furnaces and underground furnaces and over 400,000 tons of dregs. It is estimated that nearly 100,000 tons of copper had been produced there. This discovery clearly demonstrates that copper-smelting in ancient China was carried out on a large scale and employed sophisticated techniques.

Iron-smelting came into existence 2,500 years ago, during the transition between the Spring and Autumn Period and the Warring States Period. By the Han Dynasty, the smelting and casting techniques of pig iron and of steel-smelting had developed rapidly. The Han iron-smelting site in Guying County, Zhengzhou, has an area of over 60,000 sq. m.; the surface area of the hearths of two iron-smelting furnaces measured 8.5 sq. m., and the reserved iron in the furnace hearth weighed more than 20 tons.

By the Han Dynasty, even the technique known as "iron tempered one-hundred times" had appeared. A sword "tempered thirty times," 111.5 cm. in length, was unearthed in 1974 in Cangshan, located in Linyi Prefecture, Shandong. According to chemical and physical tests, its steel structure was rather homogeneous, containing a moderate amount of carbon, with a cutting edge of little inclusions (impurities) after being quenched. Engraved inscriptions on this sword record that it was made in 112 A.D., showing that, early in the Eastern Han Dynasty, we already practiced very sophisticated iron- and steel-smelting and forging techniques.

Our ancestors were already using gold and silver several thousand years ago. Even before the Shang Dynasty, there were gold utensils. Gold disks had been used as currency in the kingdom of Chu. The "gold-embroidered jade dresses" found in the Western Han Dynasty tomb of Prince Liu Sheng and his wife, the Princess Zhong Shan Jing Wang, were made of pieces of jade strung together by gold strands 0.14 mm. in diameter. The two dresses contained 1,800 g. of gold thread. The use of so much gold and the delicacy of the workmanship were both noteworthy at that time. Liu Yuxi, a Tang Dynasty poet, even wrote a poem in Guizhou, which read:

> Sunshine over Chengzhou clears up river fog, gold diggers — girl partners over the riverside crowd; all beauty decorations and lords' signets come from the depths of waves and sands.

This famous poem vividly recorded the scene of Chinese workers in ancient times washing out gold on a large scale.

Slow Development. After the Opium War, China's metallurgical industry stagnated during the period of semi-feudal and semi-colonial rule. To provide materials for building railroads, the Hanyang Iron Plant (later reorganized as the Hanyang-Daye-Pingxiang Co.), the first modern iron and steel plant in China, was set up in 1890 by Chang Zhidong, the Governor-General of Hubei and Hunan. But due to various policy errors with regard to mineral analyses, site location and selection of equipment, the period of construction was too long, the technique inapplicable, and the economic effects even worse.

From the 1890's to 1948, about half a century, the cumulative steel output was less than 7 million tons. The highest yearly output (in 1943) was only 923,000 tons. The output of copper, tungsten, antimony, tin, mercury and other minerals was also small. Moreover, the refining industry had not been created. At the time of the founding of the People's Republic of China in 1949, the country ranked 26th in the world in output of steel, with only 158,000 tons. At that time, the total output of copper, lead, zinc, tin, antimony and other non-ferrous metals was very small, and, there was no indigenous production of aluminium, nickel and many other important non-ferrous metals.

Growth Since 1949. Despite this poor heritage, the country's metallurgical industry, under the leadership of the Chinese Communist Party, and relying on the efforts of hard-working people, has established an extensive integrated network of large, medium and small enterprises. The tremendous achievements we have made, unimaginable in old China, fully testify the superiority of socialism. The following are some major features of this development:

1. *Substantial rate of growth.* Between 1949 and 1979, iron production totalled 430 million tons, steel 397 million tons and rolled steel 278 million tons. In 1979, steel output reached 34.48 million tons, ranking fifth in the world. Compared with the 1.35 million tons produced in 1952, the average growth rate per year was 12.8%. During the same period, average growth rate per year in output of 10 non-ferrous metals reached 10.6.

2. *Considerable improvement in industrial distribution.* While developing the metallurgical industry in the coastal areas, we simultaneously developed the inland metallurgical industry. While building big key enterprises, we simultaneously built medium-sized and small ones. The annual steel production potential of the large iron and steel enterprises in the coastal areas is currently as follows: the Anshan Iron and Steel Company, about 7 million tons; Shanghai, 5 million tons; the Capital Iron and Steel Company, the Tangshan Steel Plant, the Tianjin Steel Plant and the Benxi Iron and Steel Company, each more than 1 million tons. The inland iron and steel enterprises — such as the Wuhan Iron and Steel Company, the Baotou Iron and Steel Company, the Taiyuan Iron and Steel Company and the Panzhihua Iron and Steel Company — each produced from 1 to 3 million tons. In all, we established more than 10 major new and enlarged iron and steel enterprises, more than 10 special steel plants, dozens of medium-sized plants and nearly 100 small iron and steel plants throughout the country.

The development of non-ferrous metals follows the same general pattern. Take the aluminium industry for example. We have built not only large new aluminium oxide plants and electrolytic aluminium plants, but also several large new aluminium processing plants. These large aluminium plants are located in Liaoning, Heilongjiang, Shandong, Inner Mongolia, Henan, Guizhou, Sichuan, Gansu, Ningxia and other places. In addition, many provinces, municipalities and autonomous regions have established their own small aluminium plants.

3. *Considerable improvements were made in the variety and quality of products.* Old China could produce only 100 kinds of common carbon steel; but now we can smelt more than 1,000 kinds, including high-temperature alloy steel for aeronautical use and pure iron for use in high-energy particle accelerators as well as precision alloys. Based on the special features of our own resources, we have set up a regime of alloy steels containing silicon, manganese, nickel, tungsten, molybdenum, vanadium, titanium, niobium, boron and rare-earth metals. In 1953 only about 400 specifications of steel materials could be rolled; now more than 20,000 specifications can be rolled.

Not only have we solved for the first time the problem of supplying a wide variety of and different qualities of many metal materials needed in the production of railroads, automobiles, airplanes, ships, agricultural machinery, heavy machinery, power stations, large factory buildings and light industry products, but we also have made many breakthroughs in the field of research and development of materials for sophisticated equipment. The materials needed to make atomic bombs, hydrogen bombs, missiles, artificial satellites and nuclear submarines can basically be produced by the domestic industry.

4. *The level of technical equipment in the metallurgical industry has been greatly advanced.* From 1950 to 1979, the total amount of state investment for basic construction in the metallurgical industry was 73,000 million yuan (including 55,700 million yuan for the iron and steel industry). By the end of 1979, the gross value of fixed assets of the metallurgical industry was 55,110 million yuan, and the net value was 39,450 million yuan. The total weight of equipment in the

industry reached 6.52 million tons.

Although some of the equipment is old and backward, dating to the 1950's and 1960's, the general metallurgical technical equipment level has been greatly improved. In mineral mining, we now have large rotary drills, large electric shovels and electric-drive wheel trucks. For making iron, we have a 2,580-cubic-metre blast furnace at the Anshan Iron and Steel Company, and a No. 2 blast furnace, with such advanced techniques as bell-less top and top combustion stove, at the Capital Iron and Steel Company. In steel-making, our largest basic oxygen converter reaches a maximum of 150 nominal tons; open hearth furnaces, 500 nominal tons; electric furnaces, 50 nominal tons; and our oxygen-making machines generate 35,000 cubic metres per hour. In steel-rolling, the highly automatic 1,700-mm. cold and hot continuous rolling mill of the 1970's has been introduced by the Wuhan Iron and Steel Company. At the same time, the Benxi Iron and Steel Company has installed a 1,700-mm. continuous rolling mill designed and made in this country.

5. *A huge corps of workers and cadres has been established.* By the end of 1979, China had a total of 3,107 metallurgical enterprises and business units: 2,313 productive enterprises, 219 basic construction units, 66 scientific research institutions and branches and 61 metallurgical colleges and universities. The total number of workers and staff in the metallurgical industry increased from 380,000 (at the end of 1952) to 3,810,000 (at the end of 1979). That figure includes: industrial production staff, 2,960,000; construction and installation staff, 480,000; geological survey staff, 112,000; survey project personnel, 35,000; scientific research staff, 39,000; and personnel in colleges, universities and technical schools, 36,000. Of the 3,810,000, 600,000 were cadres, of which 190,000 were engineers and technicians (including 110,000 university graduates).

While we have realized the achievements enumerated above in the past 30 years, we have also experienced an uneven road. Owing to sabotage by Lin Biao and the Gang of Four, and to the mistakes committed in our work, our metallurgical industry has been interested repeatedly and has suffered great damage. Otherwise, our achievements would undoubtedly have been even greater.

II. Forging Ahead in Readjustment and Restructuring

The correct line formulated at the Third Plenary Session of the 11th Party Central Committee and the policy of readjustment, restructuring, consolidation and improvement for the national economy put forth later by the Party Central Committee, pointed the way of advance for the metallurgical industry. For quite a long period of time, influenced by the guiding ideology of impetuosity and too-rapid advances, there existed in the metallurgical industry, particularly in steel, a number of problems. These included too much emphasis on the importance of basic construction while overlooking current production; achieving higher and quicker indexes but neglecting better and more economic results; focusing on smelting and mining while paying little attention to mineral mines; and stressing ore mining but overlooking driving in (stripping), etc.

It follows naturally that we have not attached adequate importance to economic gains, workers' livelihood, production security and environmental protection. In 1977 and 1978 some unduly large projects and high targets beyond the national ability were initiated. We rushed into construction of the Baoshan Iron and Steel Complex with indiscriminate purchases of imported equipment. All these undertakings were in violation of the principle of "acting according to one's capability," thereby aggravating the imbalance within and without the metallurgical industry.

It is urgent that we correct this state of affairs. The economic management system of "sharing alike without taking account of different contributions" has to be gradually reformed. The still very backward enterprise management, sabotaged during the 10 years of turmoil, needs even more vigorous consolidation and improvement. The metallurgical industry is confronted with an arduous task of readjustment and restructuring.

III. Major Achievements of 1980

Under the correct leadership of the Party Central Committee and the State Council, with the efforts made by all the workers and staff in the metallurgical industry and with assistance from various fronts, new achievements were made in the metallurgical industry. Some encouraging changes marking a significant turning point appeared in 1980. In that year, the metallurgical industry forged ahead in readjustment and restructuring. Following are some of the major achievements in 1980:

1. *Major branches of metallurgical production attained peak economic targets, with some attaining the best results ever achieved.*

2. *Product structure of the industry began to*

change, shifting gradually to production of consumer goods. In the past, as undue stress was placed on the development of heavy industry in the national economy, many enterprises did not grasp the idea of shifting metallurgical production to serving agriculture, light industry, the civil construction industry and the market; nor did they attach sufficient importance to producing metallurgical products of high quality and reasonable price so as to meet the needs of different sectors of the national economy. As a result, some products badly needed by the state and the people fell short of demands in their variety, quantity and quality. For example, the supply of steel strips for making bicycles, tin plate for cans and wire for housing fell short of demand, with the result that portions or even most of the supply had to be made up from imports. On the other hand, heavy rail, steel for railway wheels and tires, and large-sized sections and plates which were unsaleable at the moment became goods whose supply exceeded demands.

In 1980, some encouraging changes began to take place in the metallurgical industry. These included readjusting product structure, increasing products in short supply, cutting down products that exceeded demands, raising product quality and fostering the idea of serving customers. In the case of rolled steel, for example, in 1980 27.16 million tons, or 2.19 million tons more than in 1979, were turned out. Of this quantity, the output of the four main kinds of products that had fallen short of demand — wire, small bars, sheets and welded tubes — went up from 12.08 million tons in 1979 to 15.51 million tons in 1980, representing an increase of 3.43 million tons, or 28.4% over the previous year. In 1978, the output of these four kinds of products accounted for only 44% of the total output of rolled steel, while increasing to 57% in 1980. In the meantime, the total output of three kinds of rolled steels whose production had exceeded demands — i.e., heavy rails, large-sized sections and plates — dropped to 4.23 million tons, a decrease of 560,000 tons or 11.7% compared with the previous year. The product orientation in the industry began to shift in 1980 to suit the market, with the following goals:

(1) To gear the products to demands, especially those of light industry and the market. For instance, the Shanghai No. 1 Steel Plant, No. 3 Steel Plant and No. 10 Steel Plant have increased production of 19 manganese steel strip by several thousand tons for the manufacture of high-grade and medium-grade bicycles; the Shanghai No. 5 Steel Plant raised the output of steel springs for clocks and watches to meet the needs of clock and watch manufacturing industries throughout the country; and the Shanghai Iron and Steel Research Institute succeeded in producing in large amounts a degasifying agent that prolongs the life of Chinese-made TV sets from 2,000 to 8,000 hours.

Table 1. 1980 Production of Some Key Metals

Items	Actual output in 1980 (in thousands of tons)	Compared with previous year	Historical comparison
Rolled steel	27,160	+8.8%	Best historical level
Crude steel	37,120	+7.7%	Best historical level
Of which:			
LD steel	15,090 (40.7% of total output)		
Open hearth steel	11,890 (32.0% of total output)		
Electric furnace steel	7,110 (19.1% of total output)		
Miscellaneous	3,030 (8.2% of total output)		
Pig iron	38,020	+3.5%	Best historical level
Total value of metallurgical industry output	43,027 million yuan	+4.9%	Best historical level

In the first year that the 1,700-mm. rolling mill at the Wuhan Iron and Steel Company came into commission, the hot rolling plant produced 880,000 tons of hot-rolled sheets, the cold-rolling plant produced 260,000 tons of cold-rolled sheets and the silicon steel plant produced 48,000 tons of steel sheet. Included in this production were products badly needed in light industry such as galvanized sheets (70,000 tons), tin plates (20,000 tons), enamel sheets (10,000 tons), steel strips for bicycles (44,000 tons), silicon steel sheet (13,000 tons), ship-building plates (45,000 tons) and plates for automobiles (150,000 tons). Besides supplying more than 1,000 customers inside China, nearly 50,000 tons of these products were exported. Although the new mill's production capacity is far from being fully utilized, its management level still rather low, and its product quality not up to customers' demands, it undoubtedly has great potential for shifting rolled steel to consumer goods production and serving the technical transformation of the national economy.

In the past, stainless steel sheets for making guide-rollers and winches used in enterprises under the Ministry of Textile Industry were all imported. However, after interviewing customers, the Fushun Steel Plant has trial-produced and tested such sheets successfully, and customers have begun to order the domestic product. Non-ferrous metal materials, which were used mainly in heavy industry and in production of military hardware in the past, have found new uses in the light and textile industries since 1980. For example, production of eight kinds of materials badly short of demand in light industry, such as aluminium foil, extra-thin aluminium sheets and copper antenna casings, increased by 42% in 1980 over the previous year. The Northeast Light Alloy Processing Plant, the Southwest Aluminium Processing Plant and some other plants also successfully trial-produced a wide variety of new civilian products, such as aluminium bicycles, aluminium doors and windows, aluminium sections for building and aluminium pipelines for agricultural irrigation sprinkling systems.

(2) To improve product quality continuously according to customers' needs. In 1980, 17 kinds of metallurgical products were awarded quality prizes by the government, and 158 kinds of products were chosen as high-quality products by the Ministry of Metallurgical Industry. Some of the gold-medal products — such as the "Yan" (Swallow) Brand super-surface aluminium sheet produced by the Southwest Aluminium Processing Plant and the shipbuilding plates and bars made by The Shanghai No. 1 Steel Plant, the Wuhan Iron and Steel Company and the Anshan Iron and Steel Company — won favourable comment from customers abroad. In 1980, more than 90 key task teams were set up in the Anshan Iron and Steel Company to tackle problems relating to product quality. They concentrated on six common failings — i.e., impure steel, inferior properties, inaccurate dimensions, dim surface, indistinct markings and bad packaging. The quality of rolled steel was universally raised through the adoption of such measures as second refining and on-line testing. All of the workers and staff of the Northeast Light Alloy Processing Plant were mobilized to tackle quality problems associated with 227 kinds of products; in just one year, problems associated with 210 of them were solved. The three main problems — the oxidized film on forged pieces, the properties of magnesium alloy thin-walled shapings, and the surface corrosion of shaping material after more than 10 years — were all solved. The number of products honoured for high quality increased from 16 in 1979 to 55 in 1980. One such product, the heavy, deep-drawing 08 rolled steel plates for automobiles was awarded a gold medal by the government. The extra-fine aluminium powder was awarded a silver medal. Nevertheless, judging from the overall situation, the quality of many of our metallurgical products is still not as high as that of similar products produced by the advanced nations and there remains much room for improvement.

(3) To visit consumers and to make market surveys and economic forecasts aimed at serving consumers. In 1980 the Ministry of Metallurgical Industry arranged an investigation and forecast on the supply of and demand for rolled steels. A group led by a vice-minister and directors of the departments in charge of the specified work visited customers in the textile industry and other light industries. Sales or market survey departments were set up in key enterprises and under the bureaus of metallurgy of the provinces, municipalities and autonomous regions, and many visits to consumers, surveys, forecasts and customer services were organized.

For example, a sales section staffed by engineers and technicians who specialize in market surveys and customer service was set up in the Shanghai Smeltery in 1980. During the year they edited more than 20 issues of a market information newsletter and solved a great number of problems put forward by customers. On learning that powder of aluminium-clad nickel could not yet be produced in China and had to be imported, the team earnestly went about studying and experimenting, and finally succeeded in turning out the material in quality up to world standards and supplying 52 customers throughout the country.

The Fushun Steel Plant set up a technical service section, under the leadship of its director, especially geared to the needs of customers and staffed by a number of engineers and career experts. It offered such technical services as: advising customers on how to select desirable materials, helping customers make technological innovations, solving problems concerning product quality, meeting customers' specific needs and undertaking product finishing for customers. By doing all this, the plant closely integrated production technology with demand, gained respect and opened up new markets.

3. *Energy consumption was further reduced, and the industry strived for new growth by saving energy in metallurgical enterprises.* The metallurgical industry, especially steel, is a major consumer of energy. In 1979 the amount of energy consumption in the industry totalled 83.26 million tons of standard coal (of which the steel industry consumed 72.69 million tons), representing 14.2% and 12.4%, respectively, of the total energy consumption of the entire country. The overall energy consumption per ton of steel was as high as 2.28 tons, almost double the amount consumed in production of steel by advanced methods abroad. The average overall energy consumption per ton of steel in key enterprises was as high as 1.57 tons.

Such high consumption was something the country could hardly afford. It was detrimental not only to the development of light industry and the national economy as a whole but also to the development of the metallurgical industry itself. Only by steadily reducing energy consumption can the metallurgical industry make further progress.

In 1980 most of the metallurgical enterprises made great efforts to save energy. Energy management was enhanced, technical reforms and structural reconstruction were initially centred on energy-saving, and a preferential energy supply policy was put into practice. As a result, while steel output in 1980 increased by 2.64 million tons over 1979, total energy consumption (70.9 million tons) decreased by 1.79 million tons of standard coal. An increase in output was thus achieved with less energy consumed.

In 1980 the average overall energy consumption per ton of steel in key enterprises dropped to 1.47 tons, and the charging coke ratio per ton of iron decreased from 553 kg. in 1979 to 539 kg. in 1980. Among the large integrated iron and steel works, the Anshan Iron and Steel Company did better than others. Its overall energy consumption per ton of steel dropped to 1.225 tons of standard coal and its comparable energy consumption to 1.014 tons of standard coal. The Hangzhou Iron and Steel Plant was the best among the medium-sized integrated iron and steel works. Its overall energy consumption per ton of steel declined to 1.433 tons of standard coal and its comparable energy consumption to 1.101 tons of standard coal. Both plants succeeded in saving energy while increasing output.

In the non-ferrous industry, a total of 400,000 tons of standard coal was saved in 1980 as compared with the previous year. The electrical energy consumption per ton of aluminium in key aluminium plants was reduced from 15,820 kwh in 1979 to 15,432 kwh in 1980, the lowest level ever attained. The electrical energy consumption per ton of aluminium in the Fushun Aluminium Plant, the Zhengzhou Aluminium Plant and the Baotou Aluminium Plant even fell below 15,000 kwh.

4. *The economic viewpoint was strengthened, and much importance was attached to economic results in the metallurgical industry.* For a long time there has been considerable waste and undesirable economic results in the metallurgical industry. From 1950 to 1979, total capital investment of 73,100 million yuan was granted by the state to this industry, while total profit and tax revenues of the industry amounted to merely 90,700 million yuan. In other words, the amount of profits and taxes for each yuan invested averaged only 1.24 yuan (only 1.1 yuan for the iron and steel industry). This was less than half of the average return (2.8 yuan) achieved by all industrial sectors of the country during the same period. Calculated by profit and tax rate of capital —

$$\frac{\text{profit}}{\text{net value of fixed assets} + \text{holding amount of circulating capital}} \times 100\%$$

— the figure for the metallurgical industry was only 11% in 1979 against 16.5% for all industrial sectors of the country. This wide gap was due mainly to inadequate attention to economic results in the past.

In 1980, the economic point of view was universally strengthened and great efforts were made to increase income and reduce expenditures. Remarkable economic results were achieved. The net profit of the entire metallurgical industry was 6,825 million yuan in 1980, increasing by 17.7% over 1979 and exceeding the growth rate of output value (4.9%) for the same period by a large margin. It was also higher than the growth rate of the output of steel (7.7%), of 10 kinds of non-ferrous metals (8.9%), and of gold (15.9%) for the same period.

Enterprises that achieved a large increase in output value (annual growth rate over 20%) included the Benxi Iron and Steel Company, Xiangtan Iron and Steel Company, Baotou Iron and Steel Company, Wuhan Iron and Steel Company, Capital Iron and Steel Company, Chongqing Iron and Steel Company, Hebei Provincial Metallurgical Bureau, Kunming Steel Plant, Hangzhou Steel Plant, Anyang Steel Plant, Yunnan Smeltery, Baotou Aluminium Plant, Shaoguan Smeltery, Daye Non-ferrous Metals Company, Southwest Aluminium Processing Plant and Zhuzhou Smeltery.

The Hangzhou Steel Plant incurred long-term losses in the past, and by the end of 1977 its net losses totalled 86.06 million yuan. It then began to make up deficits and increase surpluses and realized a profit of 19.31 million yuan in 1978, 33.81 million yuan in 1979 and 47.52 million yuan in1980 (up by 41% over 1979). In 1980, the profit margin of capital for the Hangzhou Steel Plant was 27.3%, showing that all the capital investment can be returned in three years and eight months.

In 1980, because some small and medium-sized local iron and steel enterprises with poor economic results stopped production, closed down, merged with other enterprises or shifted to make other products, and because management and administration were improved, the long-term losses of the past were reversed. The net loss of 292 million yuan in 1979 changed to a net profit of 474 million yuan in 1980, marking a fundamental turning point. For the metallurgical industry as a whole, both the profit and tax rate of capital and the profit margin of 100 yuan output value rose in 1980 as compared with the previous year, while the holding amount of 100 yuan circulating capital decreased. In the same year, seeking to make gainful use of idle hours, some capital construction teams ("seeking rice for cooking"), contracted projects valued at 520 million yuan from other sectors, thus making a contribution to the national economy.

It is worth noting that economic research organizations were set up in 1980 by the Ministry of Metallurgical industry, by provincial bureaus and by metallurgical enterprises. The Research Institute of Metallurgical Economy was founded under the ministry at the end of 1979. Economic research institutes were set up in the Anshan Iron and Steel Company, Benxi Iron and Steel Company, Taiyuan Iron and Steel Company, Wuhan Iron and Steel Company, Baotou Iron and Steel Company, Shenyang Smeltery and Fushun Aluminium Plant. Economic research offices were set up by the Chongqing Iron and Steel Company, Qiqihar Steel Plant, Fushun Steel Plant, Xinfu Steel Plant, Kunming Steel Plant, Chengdu Seamless Steel Tube Plant, Changzhi Steel Plant, Lianyuan Steel Plant and Shenyang Metallurgical Machinery Plant. The Huludao Zinc Plant organized an economic research group. Economic research offices or groups were also set up under the Shanghai Municipal Metallurgical Bureau and the metallurgical bureaus of Hebei and Jilin provinces. By integrating various professional groups with the broad masses and focusing on achieving better results in the industry and in enterprises, these economic research organizations combined theory with practice, implemented readjustment policy as the heart of their work and carried out investigations aimed at meeting specific needs. As a result of these steps, they began to play a definite role in providing reference information to leading cadres for decision-making and to those who are in direct charge of economic work.

5. *Initial reforms of systems and structures in the metallurgical industries were carried out to continue expanding decision-making powers in some enterprises on a trial basis and to stimulate the enterprises.* By the end of 1980, 277 metallurgical enterprises had been given expanded powers of self-management on a trial basis. Although they represented only 12% of all existing metallurgical enterprises, their output value accounted for over 70% and their total profit more than 80%. Experience to date shows that the reforms were correct in orientation, the results were remarkable and the economy and management of these enterprises were enlivened.

First of all, the reforms stirred the enthusiasm and initiative of workers and staff members of the enterprises. By assigning more financial power to enterprises and by linking power, duty and profit on an economic basis, the state gets more revenue, the enterprises receive a greater share of profits, and the workers and staff members earn more. The above-mentioned enterprises whose profit growth was over 20% in 1980 were all enterprises that undertook self-management on a trial basis. This policy resulted in increasing income and reducing expenditure.

For instance, by implementing the rule of sharing the increased profits among all its enterprises and factories, the Shanghai Metallurgical Bureau yielded a profit of 1,345 million yuan in 1979, a 20% increase over 1978. In 1980 this bureau showed a profit of 1,470 million yuan, 31.2% over that for 1978. During these two years, a total profit of 2,580 million yuan was turned over to the state (340 million yuan more was collected by the state). Consequently, the Shanghai Bureau will no longer ask the state or local authorities for capital investment, funds for renewal of equipment and funds for trial-production.

Secondly, we discarded the dictum that "means of production are not commercial goods."

As a result of implementing the policy of combining regulation by planning with market regulation, some enterprises have been encouraged to sell their own products under the guidance of central plans. Some large enterprises, such as the Chongqing Iron and Steel Company, the Taiyuan Iron and Steel Company, the Southwest Aluminium Processing Plant and the Chengdu Seamless Steel-pipe Factory were all languishing because orders from the state amounted to only 40%–60% of their production capacity. The policy that producers could sell their own products not only saved the above enterprises from having to cut down production but also increased the variety of products, promoted quality, improved service and raised the level of management.

In 1980, key state-owned steel enterprises were able to sell 2.5 million tons of steel products on their own in addition to fulfilling the production quotas set by the state. Their independent sales accounted for 14% of total sales. The 2.5 million tons, together with 8.57 million tons produced by local medium- and small-sized enterprises (whose products are distributed by local authorities instead of the state), amounted to 11.07 million tons, about 40.8% of total steel products. Likewise, sales of non-ferrous metal products by the producers in 1980 was about 42% of total output, and that of rare metal products, 80% of the total.

Thirdly, the Ministry of Metallurgical Industry established the China Metallurgical Import and Export Corporation (CMIEC) in April 1980. Under the guidance of the unified foreign trade policy, the enterprises and companies can engage in foreign trade. By the end of 1980, CMIEC signed more than 300 contracts for exporting various metallurgical products. With total sales of over US$200 million, it received US$62 million in foreign exchange. Products exported included pig iron, rolled steel, ferro-alloys, iron castings, steel castings, various non-ferrous metal and rare metal products, bauxite and graphite electrodes. CMIEC has done business with over 120 customers in 16 countries.

The high quality of certain export products, such as pig iron, sponge titanium, titanium ingot, Swallow Brand aluminium sheet with superior surface, etc., has been recognized by some foreign traders who honour these products as "creditable" products. This foreign trade system, which brings producers into direct contact with trade circles and brings together production with needs, was well-accepted by foreign businessmen for the convenience that both buyers and sellers were familiar with production techniques.

The above reforms are but preliminary steps. Because of a lack of experience, some shortcomings and faults could be found in the past. However, we have taken the right way forward, as indicated by the achievements and results. As long as the reforms are advantageous to readjustment in the future, we will keep on making them and build on our experiences for further improvement.

6. *The metallurgical industry made further efforts to enhance gradually the tasks in ore mines, improved the management of enterprises and raised the level of science and technology.* In 1980 the industry also carried out the training of personnel in whole establishments, attached more importance to safety measures and environmental protection, as well as gradually raising the level of the workers' material and cultural well-being. It was a year in which achievements were made in all sectors of the metallurgical industry.

IV. Outlook for the Industry

Over the past 31 years, the metallurgical industry has had a history of twists and turns, with positive and negative experiences. One lesson is clear, we must proceed from China's actual realities and capabilities and strive for real and practical results. In the past we took a route not in keeping with our national strength, anxious to gain success, blindly seeking to fulfil quantitative targets, regardless of the need for scientific integrated balance, and paying no attention to the variety, quality and economic effect of products. This approach led to heavy investment, wasteful consumption, high costs, poor quality, low efficiency and little profit.

Experience has proved that this approach was impractical and should be avoided. From now on, we should adopt a new approach that sets targets and speed within our reach. The variety of products should be suitable (in terms of serving the consumer, the technical improvement of the national economy and national defence); their quality should be reasonably better; consumption (especially energy consumption) should be relatively lower; efficiency should be higher; and the economic results much larger and less costly.

Weakness in the Industry. The iron and steel industry and the non-ferrous metals industry fall into the category of industrial raw materials, essential to the national economy and the people's livelihood. They are crucial to the development of the national economy and the realization of the Four Modernizations. Our current metallurgical industrial products, with respect to their variety, quality and quantity, are not suited to the development of the national economy.

From 1949 to 1980, imports of all types of steel materials totalled about 70 million tons, approximately equal to 23% of the country's output during that period. Imported copper and aluminium were approximately equal to 48.7% of the output of this country during that period. These figures indicate that our self-sufficiency in metallurgical products is still very low.

In keeping with the changes in the national economic structure, demands for iron and steel may be lower than in the past, but the requirements in the range of variety and quality will be much stricter and higher. Therefore, as national strength permits, it is still very important to pay adequate attention to developing the iron and steel industry and the non-ferrous metals industry, especially with regard to the range of variety and quality. But, for the purpose of reducing the burden on our country's financial, material and energy resources, we must first consolidate the present foundation and realize its full potential.

Readjustment Goals. The readjustment of the metallurgical industry is a very difficult task, impossible to accomplish in one or two years. We must do our utmost to complete the readjustment during the Sixth Five-Year Plan. With regard to the metallurgical industry itself, in addition to the cutbacks in basic construction in 1981, the main points of readjustment should be the following: (1) the weakest link, the condition of mines, must be readjusted and improved; (2) the range of products and product quality must be improved; (3) energy sources must be further conserved; (4) the non-ferrous metal industry must be emphasized; (5) the level of management must be raised; (6) scientific and technological work must be strengthened considerably; (7) training and education of personnel must be energetically addressed; and (8) we should raise the standard of living of workers and cadres, see to safety in production and environmental protection.

When readjustment is completed, by 1985, the metallurgical industry is expected to have a much more solid material foundation, especially in terms of mines, the variety and quality of products and energy savings, and great progress should have been made in technical levels and enterprise management. By that time, the output of non-ferrous metals and rolled steel should also have been raised.

22. CHINA'S CAPITAL CONSTRUCTION IN 1980
By Kang Zhixin
Institute of Economic Research,
State Capital Construction Commission

Capital construction is an important means of expanding reproduction in socialist society. Its present task is to expand the existing scope of fixed assets and form new fixed assets through the economic activities of construction, expansion, reconstruction, restoration and purchase. Thus, it is an important component of socialist accumulation. Capital construction not only provides new productive capacity and advanced equipment and technologies to various material-producing departments — including industry, agriculture, communications, posts and telecommunications, construction and commerce — but also affects the industrial structure and the rational distribution of the productive forces in different parts of the country. At the same time, capital construction furnishes a material basis for social development and improvement in the living conditions of the people.

I. The Effects of Large-Scale Capital Construction

Since the founding of New China, the county has successfully engaged in capital construction on a large scale and has played an important role in the development of the national economy. Between 1950 and 1979, China invested 651,700 million yuan in capital construction and added new fixed assets amounting to 454,100 million yuan. Hundreds of thousands of factories, mines, railways, harbours, highways, post and telecommunication facilities, water conservation projects, and commercial, scientific research, cultural, educational and medical establishments have been put into operation or service. There are now 400,000 industrial and transport enterprises owned by the whole people or collectively owned, more than treble the number in 1949.

Broad Achievements and Changes. Large-scale capital construction has increased the productive capacity of China's modern industry. The new fixed assets of industry in the 30 years ending in 1979 were 21 times those accumulated in old China for neary 100 years. By 1979, steel-making capacity had increased 35 times, ranking fifth in the world; coal mining capacity had increased 10 times, ranking third in the world; power generating capacity had increased 29 times; and the number of cotton yarn spindles had increased more than 3 times. Gone are the days of old China, when the output value of modern industry accounted for only 10% of the total industrial and agricultural output value.

China's economic structure has been changed by large-scale capital construction. Many industries or trades that had not existed or had been backward in old China were built or expanded, and an independent and all-embracing national economic system began to take shape. The metallurgical, machine-building, chemical, petroleum, power and coal industries grew rapidly, putting an end to old China's dependence on other countries for many heavy industrial products. The light and textile industries also expanded considerably. Many new industries, such as motor vehicles, tractors, airplanes and electronic computers, were established.

The total length of new railways and highways rose 2.3 times and 11 times, respectively, since 1950. Water conservation projects were built on a large scale. Progress was made in efforts to bring the Haihe and Huaihe rivers under control. China built 164,000 kilometres of dikes and dams and 82,000 water reservoirs that can hold more than 40 million cubic metres of water and irrigate 45 million hectares of farmland, or 45.2% of the country's total farmland.

Large numbers of scientific, cultural, educational and medical establishments, urban public utilities and housing estates sprang up. Total floor space of new housing built in the urban areas in the 30 years was 594,280,000 square metres; newly laid running water pipes totalled 27,000 kilometres; and urban roads totalled 18,000 kilometres. All this contributed to the development of social undertakings and to the improvement of the material and cultural life of the people.

Large-scale capital construction changed the geographical distribution of China's industry. In the past 30 years, about 40% of China's capital investment went into the construction of projects in the hinterland and in areas inhabited by minority people. Investment in the hinterland accounted for 54% of total investment in 1979, compared with 39% in 1952. The number of factories and mines operating in northwest and southwest China increased from 300 in 1952 to 80,000 in 1979.

Compared with 1952, the proportion of the

fixed assets of state-owned industrial enterprises to the national total rose from 27.1% to 53.6%, the proportion of steel increased from 14.2% to 34.4%, coal from 52% to 63.9%, electric power from 35.7% to 45.3% and cotton yarn from 17.5% to 37.2%. The growth of industry in the hinterland that began almost from scratch introduced a change in the exceptionally irrational geographical distribution of industry left over from old China.

The programme of large-scale capital construction has tempered and expanded the ranks of workers and technicians. In 1979, workers and staff members employed in the state-owned construction enterprises throughout the country totalled 4.63 million, of which 268,000 were surveyors and designers. The two figures were 5 times and 11.6 times, respectively, as large as in 1952. These employees have undertaken the design, construction and assembly of hundreds of thousands of projects, as well as many major overseas projects. The 156 large and medium-sized projects built during the First Five-Year Plan period (1953-1957), the Panzhihua Iron and Steel Complex built in the 1960's, the dozen imported chemical fertilizer and fibre plants built in the 1970's and the Gezhouba Hydroelectric Station (the first key water-control project on the Yangtze River, now under construction) all reached fairly high levels of speed and quality. Construction workers and technicians have become one of the important props for the development of China's national economy.

Major Problems. However, there also were major setbacks in capital construction under the influence of "Left" deviationist mistakes.

The outstanding problems in that period were:

(1) The scale of investment was overextended. For many years the scale of capital construction squeezed national economic capabilities, resulting in a high rate of accumulation. There were financial deficits in a number of years. Not only did this strategy aggravate the imbalance among agriculture, light industry and heavy industry, but it also seriously hampered the improvement of the people's livelihood.

(2) The investment was not properly distributed. Of the total investment in the past 30 years, investment in agriculture accounted for 11.2%, light industry 5.9% and heavy industry 50.9%. This resulted in a lopsided development of the national economy. Within the heavy industry sector, the proportions of investment between the metallurgical, machine-building and chemical industries and the fuels, power, building materials and communications industries were not properly balanced. Industries in the coastal areas were not fully utilized and developed, while the development of new industries in the hinterland was overemphasized. As a result, a large number of projects failed to operate at full capacity.

(3) The returns from investment declined. The proportion of newly added fixed assets to investment fell from 83.7% during the First Five-Year Plan period to about 70% in recent years, and the average period of construction rose from six years to ten years or even longer.

In short, we overemphasized capital construction and gave inadequate attention to production, high accumulation rate and low efficiency in the more than 20 years after 1958. The problems did not receive any attention until the Third Plenary Session of the 11th Central Committee of the Chinese Communist Party adopted the policy of readjusting the national economy and initialled measures to solve them.

II. Implementing the New Policy

The focal point of capital construction in 1980 was to implement the policy of readjustment, restructuring, consolidation and improvement of the national economy. Total investment amounted to 53,900 million yuan, and the newly added fixed assets totalled 42,700 million yuan, of which 79.2% was put to use. New projects completed included 82 large and medium-sized multi-item projects and 216 large and medium-sized single-item projects. The new capacity for major products included: 8.29 million tons of coal, 5.75 million tons of petroleum, 2.87 million kilowatts of electric power, 2.74 million tons of iron ore, 3.38 million tons of rolled steel, 60,000 tons of chemical fibres, 1,008 kilometres of railways, 8.14 million tons of handling capacity at harbours and 807,000 cubic metres of petroleum tanks for commercial departments.

Major projects that began operation in 1980 included: the Maotiaohe Hydroelectric Station in Guizhou; the Tianshenggang Power Plant in Jiangsu; the Yaomeng Power Plant in the Pingdingshan coal mines in Henan; the Lanzhou Vinylon Plant; the Dandong Chemical Fibre Plant; the railroad between Changping, north of Beijing, and Tongliao in Inner Mongolia; two coal mines, each producing 600,000 tons per year, in Shanxi and Henan; part of the installations at the Liaoyang Chemical Fibre Plant and the Sichuan Vinylon Plant; and sections of the Xiangfan-Chongqing, Shijiazhuang-Taiyuan and Longhai railroads now being electified. These new projects have helped to ease the shortage of energy, consumer goods and transport capacity.

Important Steps Taken. In 1980 the projects under construction were reexamined, the scale of investment within the framework of the state budget was reduced and the proportions of investment among the different branches of the national economy were readjusted. In 1979, 295 large and medium-sized projects and 1,600 small projects were halted or postponed, and 584 projects were partially halted or postponed. The reduction of investment in these unfinished projects amounted to 11,500 million yuan.

In 1980 another 120 large and medium-sized projects and 839 small projects were halted or postponed, and 406 projects were partially halted or postponed. The investment reduction in these projects amounted to 9,800 million yuan. By the end of 1980 the number of large and medium-sized projects under construction had dropped to 904, from 1,187 at the end of 1979.

At the same time, some of the provinces, municipalities and autonomous regions also halted some of their local projects that had been arranged as technical measures to increase the current year's production but actually had the character of capital construction. Some departments and local governments invited technical and economic specialists to discuss the feasibility of some vital projects from the standpoint of thir impact on the overall development of the national economy and society, as well as of their impact on construction and production conditions in specific sectors and locales.

Preliminary readjustments were made in 1980 to the disproportionate distribution of investment among the different departments, industries and localities, which had been a long-standing problem. The proportions of investment for the light, textile and energy industries, communications and non-production projects were raised, and priority was given to investment in projects in the weak branches of the national economy and projects that directly concern the people's livelihood.

The proportion of investment in the light and textile industries rose from 6.4% in 1979 to 9.1% in 1980, and that in heavy industry dropped from 45% to 42.7%. Within heavy industry, the proportions of investment in the national defence, chemical and machine-building industries also declined markedly. The proportion of investment in productive projects dropped by 6.7% as compared with 1979, while that in non-productive projects rose from 27% to 33.7%. Investment in housing projects increased from 14.8% in 1979 to 20%, and the total floor space completed was 82.3 million square metres, 31.6% more than in 1979 and a new record since 1949. Investment in cultural, educational, medical and scientific work also increased. The floor space of new buildings for universities and colleges totalled 2.83 million square metres, basically enough to meet the needs of new students enrolled in 1980. A number of professors and other college teachers moved into new homes.

Urban public utilities and urban construction also grew rapidly. The shortages of water, power, urban transport, commercial establishments and warehouses were eased in some cities. Moreoever, the government strengthened its leadership over the construction of housing in the rural areas and supplied more construction materials and housing designs to the peasants. About 5 million peasant families built new homes or rebuilt their homes in 1980, with a total floor space of 300 million square metres. The readjustment of the capital construction programme greatly helped the government to reach the goal of readjusting the national economy.

Management Changes. Progress was made in restructuring the management system for capital construction in 1980 by building on past experience and improving the experimental work. During the year the experiment of replacing government allocations with bank loans in capital investment was introduced in 28 municipalities, provinces and autonomous regions and in more than a dozen industries covering power, textiles, coal and petroleum. The number of projects financed with bank loans increased to 4,414, with a total value of 2,650 million yuan.

In the past, capital investment was made in the form of government allocations without compensation, and the economic liabilities, results and interests were not directly linked. As a result, the units that needed new construction were very energetic in applying for investment, but showed less interest in increasing returns from that investment.

In 1979 the State Council decided to introduce a new method of issuing bank loans in capital investment for state-owned enterprises. The Bank of Construction issues loans to enterprises that have the ability to pay back, and the enterprises are required to repay the loans with interest from the shares of profits they retain or from other revenues under contracts they sign with the Bank of Construction after the projects begin operation. After the new method was introduced, all units requiring construction had to select their best construction plans and watch their spending. This helped to put an end to the construction of unnecessary projects and to careless spending of investment funds without regarding to economic returns.

The experiment of expanding the power of management was begun in construction enterprises in all provinces, municipalities and autonomous regions and in some industrial ministries. The earning of legal profits by the construction industry, which had been cancelled for many years, was restored. The construction enterprises in Liaoning and Shanghai introduced the practice of sharing part of the profits in excess of specified amounts to be turned over to the state. The bureaus of construction industry in some provinces, municipalities and autonomous regions were changed to bureaus of enterprises. Commercialization of construction products began in housing construction in some cities.

These preliminary steps improved the management of the construction enterprises, providing them with the incentive to run production more efficiently, and laid the foundation for gradually turning the construction industry into a genuinely independent material-producing department of the national economy.

Ninety survey and design units began to organize their work along business lines. Units that received more assignments greatly increased their output, and those that were given fewer assignments gained the initiative to contract for more projects to balance their revenues and expenditures or to have a small surplus. By charging for what they design, the design units have enhanced their sense of responsibility and at the same time retained part of their profits for buying new instruments and equipment and improving the livelihood of their workers and staff.

Other Reforms Undertaken. The reform in the system of capital construction involves a number of other reforms in economic management, such as the state planning system, the financial system and the supply system. The situation is complex, however, and new experience has to be absorbed and more experimental work done in a planned way.

Great efforts were made in the reorganization and consolidation of the construction ranks and enterprises. A nationwide survey of construction enterprises, the most extensive since the founding of New China, was conducted in 1980. Most of the provinces, municipalities and autonomous regions issued licences to the qualified enterprises. Work is now being done to survey, register and check the survey and design units and issue them certificates.

Many localities and departments have strengthened the leadership of enterprises in the construction industry, reassessing the professional competency of engineers and technicians, giving them titles and promotions and thus upgrading the technical management system. Many professionally competent engineers and technicians were promoted to leading positions at different levels. Technical training was provided in many localities and departments, and a large number of leadership of construction departments and enterprises attended advanced study courses. The training of specialized personnel will help raise the management level of the construction industry in China.

An incentive drive aimed at building top-quality projects was started in some of the construction enterprises, greatly helping to improve enterprise management and the practice of economy. In some parts of the country, the enterprises were given more management authority and began to introduce a contract system.

Total construction and assembly by the construction enterprises throughout China in 1980 was valued at 36,700 million yuan, up 10.6% over 1979. The total floor space finished in 1980 was 145 million square metres, 20.8% more than in 1979. The per-capita labour productivity of the state-owned enterprises was 4,240 yuan, 6.2% more than in 1979. At the same time, all construction enterprises strengthened the education and training of their staff and workers to lay an even better foundation for a new construction boom.

III. Problems Caused by Over Extension

Progress was made in capital construction in 1980, but as a whole economic returns on the investment in capital construction did not increase much, and in some instances even declined. Only 8.3% of the large and medium-sized projects under construction were put into operation, compared with 9.7% in 1979. Annual targets for new capacity were reached in only 18 of the 34 major projects. The productive capacity of 27 projects was less than in the preceding year.

The principal factor affecting economic results was the over-extended scale of capital construction. This was manifested in the fact that while investment in the state budget was cut by 24.9% as compared with 1979, investment not included in the state budget — namely, capital funds pooled by the local governments, ministries and enterprises in various forms — increased by 56.2%. The actual annual investment totalled 53,900 million yuan, 7.8% more than in the peak year of 1979.

Roots of the Problem. The three main causes of the over-extended scale of capital construction in 1980 are as follows:

(1) Some of the major projects that should have been halted or postponed were not halted early enough. While the number of large and medium-sized projects under construction was reduced by 283, the scale of large and medium-sized projects started was so great that the overall capital construction programme was by no means reduced. An additional investment of 130,000 million yuan would be needed to complete all the large and medium-sized projects still under construction at the end of 1980. Assuming an annual investment of 21,800 million yuan, it would require six more years to finish all these projects. As a matter of fact, total investment in the coming years will be cut greatly, and therefore even more years would be needed.

(2) As the policy of maximizing advantages was not correctly understood in some areas, construction of unnecessary projects became a serious problem in the absence of guidance and overall balance in state planning. For example, by the end of 1979, there were 16.6 million cotton yarn spindles, but if all those were put into operation there would be a shortage of one million tons of cotton to supply them. Despite this excess capacity, new cotton mills with 2.6 million spindles were built or were being built in 1980.

The problem was even more serious in the wasteful construction of small tobacco factories, small wineries, small silk mills and other small enterprises. Statistics showed that more than 6,100 small projects, each with an investment of 100,000 yuan, were started in 1980. This not only directly extended the scale of capital construction, but led to competition with large and old factories for raw materials and electric power. The small factories replaced the large ones and backward processes replaced advanced ones, affecting the economic returns of the existing enterprises.

(3) Because funds not included in the state budget for capital construction could be obtained through more and more channels and no proper measures were taken to achieve an overall balance, the scale of capital construction not covered by the state plan got out of control. It was estimated that more than 40% of the funds set aside for technical innovation and revamping of outmoded equipment, as well as medium-term and short-term bank loans for replacing old equipment, were used to build new projects. In some cases, circulating funds and major overhaul funds were used for capital construction, thus disrupting existing production process. Not only was simple reproduction affected, but expanded reproduction became virtually impossible.

Because the scale of capital construction exceeded the capacity of the nation's financial and material resources, and because of other problems, the rate of accumulation remained as high as 32% in 1980. Even more serious, a large financial deficit had to be maintained to keep capital construction going, thus aggravating imbalances in the state budget, credits, supplies and foreign exchange reserves. The bank issued more currency for financial reasons and money in circulation exceeded the supply of commodities leading to a price rise and potential danger to China's economy. If this situation were to continue, the benefits gained by the workers and peasants would be lost again.

The Road Ahead. It is essential, therefore, to eradicate vigorously the influences of the "Left" deviationist mistakes in capital construction by taking practical and effective measures to reduce the scale of capital construction to a level suited to the nation's current capabilities and by halting a large number of projects. At the same time, it is also necessary to deal properly with problems arising from the cessation of the projects, reducing the losses to a minimum, and using the capital funds mainly for speeding the construction of projects that are vital to the national economy and to the people's livelihood. This is a task of paramount importance for capital construction in China.

At the end of 1980, the party and government decided to readjust the national economy further. It was made clear that the scale of capital construction would be further reduced in the course of economic readjustment. Looking ahead, we are confident that, as long as we draw lessons from the economic work over the past 30 years and firmly adhere to the policy of readjustment, restructuring, consolidation and improvement of the national economy, we will find a new road in capital construction based on the new foundation, a road that requires less investment but yields greater returns, so as to make further contributions to the steady improvement of the material and cultural life of the people.

23. CHINA'S BUILDING MATERIALS INDUSTRY
By Zhong Jianwen
Research Office,
Ministry of Building Materials Industry

I. Development of the Building Materials Industry in Modern China

China has a long history in the production and use of building materials. However, up to the time of Liberation, the building materials industry was underdeveloped — there being only a few enterprises, all of whose equipment was out of date and mostly operated by manual labour — characterized by low productivity, poor product variety and quality. The building materials used for foreign style multi-storied buildings before Liberation were almost entirely imported. In 1949, there were only some 40 small enterprises turning out cement, sheet glass and ceramic sanitary wares. Output of cement was only 660,000 tons; sheet glass, 1.07 million standard crates (10 sq. m. of glass with a thickness of 2 mm. is counted as one standard crate); and the total value of building materials in the entire country was only a little more than 50 million yuan (statistics given above do not include Taiwan).

Since the founding of New China, the building materials industry has developed greatly in line with progress throughout the national economy. Between 1952 and 1980, national investment in building materials totalled 8,000 million yuan. In this period, more than 100 large and medium-sized new factories were set up, 40 large and medium-sized old factories were expanded, and construction was underway on dozens of new plants. In addition to the enterprises built with state investment, many smaller enterprises were set up with investments from local governments and people's communes.

Today, there are 46,000 plants of all sizes turning out building materials in China; they employ a total of 3,800,000 workers and staff. Of the 46,000 plants, 5,300 are owned by the whole people — i.e., state-owned — employing 1,600,000 workers and staff, and 40,000 are collectively owned, with 2,200,000 workers and staff. In 1980, the output of cement was 79.86 million tons, a total increase of 121 times over 1949, or an average increase of 16.7%. The output of plate glass was 27.71 million standard crates, a total increase of 25.7 times over 1949, or an average annual increase of 11%. The total value of building materials in the entire country in 1980 was 18,180 million yuan, an increase of 361 times over 1949.

Not only the output but also the variety of building materials and non-metallic mineral products has increased remarkably. New lightweight building materials have been developed and successfully produced. The geographical distribution of factories has been rationalized to a great extent. Scientific and technological levels in the industry have risen significantly. Today, the building materials industry occupies an important place in the raw materials industry within the national economy; it plays a vital role by providing materials for industrial and agricultural construction, for residential buildings in rural and urban areas and a range of non-metallic products and new inorganic materials for use by various sectors of the national economy.

The Post-1978 Readjustment. Since the Third Plenary Session of the 11th Central Committee of the Party held in 1978, the building materials industry has undergone readjustment in accordance with various principles and policies, and has yielded excellent results. In 1978 and 1979, production increased steadily. The total value of the building materials industry in 1979 increased by 8.7% over 1978, and in 1980 it increased by 5.5% over 1979. The output of principal products exceeded the quotas set by the national plan.

Cement output in 1979 increased by 13.3% over 1978, and by 8.1% in 1980 over 1979. The quality of products has been improved on the whole. High-grade plate glass accounted for 77.8% of the total output of plate glass, an increase of 4.92% over 1979. In the last two years, the state has awarded prizes for high quality to 21 building materials plants; 3 received gold medals and 16 received silver medals.

In 1980 about 2.5 million tons of standard coal were conserved throughout the country. In large and medium-sized cement enterprises, the rate of consumption of standard coal per ton of clinker produced dropped by 0.62 kg. from the 1979 rate. Consumption of coal per crate of plate glass produced in 1980 was 1.54 kg. less than that in 1979.

The efficiency of converting losses into profits was evident. In 1980, profits earned by enterprises under the management of the Ministry of Building Materials Industry were 23.2% higher than those of 1979. The percentage of enterprises operating at a loss dropped from 27.2% to 19.5% in 1980, while the volume of losses decreased by 45%. The plan for capital construction investment was overfulfilled in both 1979 and 1980. Some new plants were constructed and put into production. The newly added production capacity of large and medium-sized cement plants was 1.4 million tons. In 1979 the volume of exports of 10 categories of building materials products increased by 8.6% over the previous year; in 1980, it increased by 12% over 1979.

II. Increase in Variety of Products Since 1949

Since the establishment of New China 31 years ago, the building materials industry has developed into a multi-branch, multi-variety industry, turning out 500 different types of products under the management of the Ministry of Building Materials Industry. These products may be divided into the three following categories:

1. *Building and construction materials (excluding timber and steel)*. In this category are: cement, plate glass, ceramic sanitary ware, bricks and tiles, sand, stone, building blocks, waterproofing and heat-insulation materials, gypsum board, aerated concrete, plastics for building use, wallpaper and wall cloth and various types of new lightweight building materials.

2. *Non-metallic minerals and their processed products*. In this group are: asbestos, mica, graphite, gypsum, diamonds, limestone, quartz sand, marble and granite.

3. *New non-metallic minerals and products processed or made using materials from Groups 1 and 2 as raw materials*. These include: fibreglass, graphite fibre, fibreglass reinforced plastics, special technical glass and ceramics, quartz glass, cast stone, cement boats, cement railroad sleepers and cement electricity poles.

All the materials and products in Group 1 are used for building and construction, while only a portion of those in Groups 2 and 3 are used for this purpose. Most of the materials and products in the two latter groups constitute important raw materials for the metallurgical, chemical, electronic, aviation and national defence industries. Materials in Group 3 have been developed since the late 1950's and have made positive contributions to the advancement of China's industry, science and technology.

Following are historical surveys of the development of the cement, plate glass and non-metallic minerals industries.

The Cement Industry

Prior to Liberation, China's cement industry was characterized by its poor foundation, slow rate of development, low output, limited variety and highly irrational geographical distribution of cement plants. In the 43-year period from the establishment of China's first cement plant at Tangshan in 1906 to the founding of New China in 1949, only 35 small cement plants were set up in the entire country (excluding Taiwan). These plants were concentrated in the coastal areas of north-eastern China, and the highest annual output of that period was 2.29 million tons. Cement output in 1949 was only 660,000 tons.

Post-Liberation Expansion. During the first three years after the founding of New China, the main task for the cement industry was to repair and rehabilitate plants that had been destroyed or closed down. In 1953, the cement industry began to develop on a large scale according to state plans. By the end of 1980, more than 4,200 cement plants had been constructed and put into production. They employed more than 700,000 workers and staff and turned out 79.86 million tons of cement per year. Of these 4,200 plants, 50 were large and medium-sized enterprises with a combined output of 25.59 million tons and employing about 100,000 workers and staff. The 4,533 small-sized plants had a combined output of 54.27 million tons. The large and medium-sized plants were built with investment from the central government, and their products were sold under the management of the central government. The small plants were set up with investments from local authorities and collectively owned units and these plants sold their own products.

The geographic distribution of cement plants in the country has been improved. All provinces, municipalities and autonomous regions — except for Tibet, Ningxia and Tianjin — now have large and medium-sized plants, while small plants are scattered over 80% of the counties throughout the country.

The varieties of cement produced have expanded from a single silicate system to a system of phosphate and alumina. China now produces five major categories of cement — silicate cement, slag cement, common cement, pozzolanic cement and fly-ash cement and several dozen other categories. Production of special cements, such as oil-well cement, dam cement, quick-hardening cement and coloured cement, is now adequate to satisfy domestic demand.

Advances in Technology. The scientific and technological levels of cement production have been raised. In the 1950's, most of the key equipment installed was imported. Plants which used small- and medium-diameter kilns for wet processing and semi-dry processing, as well as plants that used different types of mechanical shaft kilns, were equipped with products made in China. In the mid-1950's, China experimented with a cyclone preheater; from the 1960's on, cement production lines using multi-stage cyclone preheaters and shaft-preheaters were set up successively in four cement works.

During the early 1970's, studies were conducted on the new pre-calcining process, and experimental production lines using the pre-calcining process with coal and oil as fuels were set up. In 1977, a production line using the pre-calcining process and with an output of 4,000 tons per day was imported and assembled.

Small-Scale Cement Plants. The development of small-scale cement works equipped with shaft kilns is of special significance. In its initial stages of development, the small-scale cement industry had to meet the demands of capital construction for agricultural purposes and of restoration of residential dwellings in the countryside. The industry has greatly expanded with the aid of local investment and through self-reliance and hard work. The small-scale cement industry has not only played an important role in the development of the country's agriculture, but has also made considerable contributions to the development of local industry, transport and communications, as well as to important national projects.

In 1980, there were 4,533 small-scale cement plants in the country, with a combined output of 54.27 million tons, or about two-thirds of the country's total output for that year. Of the 54.27 million tons, 47 million were turned out by state-owned enterprises above the county level and 7 million were turned out by enterprises owned collectively by the communes and brigades.

In the beginning, small-scale cement enterprises were plagued with problems such as poor product quality and high costs. These problems were due to poor equipment, weak technical capabilities and ineffective management. The situation has improved enormously as a result of readjustment, personnel training and technical guidance over many years. Since 1979, in particular, management at various levels of building materials plants has seriously implemented the policy of "readjustment, restructuring, consolidation and improvement" and has made great efforts to improve quality, reduce costs, elevate technical and management levels and increase economic efficiency.

As a result, conditions have changed for the better. According to a survey of 2,186 small-scale cement works, the quality of finished products has greatly improved. In 1980, the percentage of quality cement produced by all factories was 85%, an increase of 12% over 1978. Of the quality products, No. 400 cement and grades above it accounted for 95% of total output; production of No. 500 cement increased from 2.64 million tons to 8.80 million tons.

Industry profits increased and losses declined. From 1979 to 1980, the proportion of factories above the county level operating at a loss declined from 42% to 23%, while the number of provinces, municipalities and autonomous regions that increased their profits rose from 14 to 28. In 1979 and in 1980, annual cement output increased by an average of 6 million tons, an annual rate of increase of 11.3%. Output in each of the eight provinces of Jiangsu, Shandong, Hebei, Henan, Hunan, Liaoning, Sichuan and Guangdong exceeded 3 million tons.

China has a vast territory and a large population, but a weak scientific and technological foundation and backward economy. While it needs more large and medium-sized cement works to serve as the backbone of the building materials industry and to meet the demands of major projects, it also needs more small-scale cement works which make use of rich local limestone resources. Future development must be done in ways that take account of local conditions, meet the demands of agriculture and make up for the inadequate supply of cement from large and medium-sized works.

The development of small-scale cement works in conjunction with large and medium-sized ones has brought about prosperity characterized by the joint development of enterprises run by both central and local governments. The results show that this is the correct path and one eminently suited to China's unique conditions.

The Plate-Glass Industry

Early Development. The first sheet-glass factories in China, the Qinhuangdao Glass Works and the Yaohua Glass Company Ltd., were constructed in 1922 and began production in 1924 with outputs of 400-500 standard crates daily. By 1949, prior to Liberation, there were three sheet-glass factories with a combined output of 1.08 million standard crates per year. Since Liberation, nine plate-glass factories have been set up and three old factories have been expanded with state investment. Now there are 12 large and medium-sized factories in all, employing over 30,000 workers and staff.

Because of the serious shortage of plate glass during the last two years, some factories in other industrial sectors have been converted to produce plate glass following the readjustment of the national economy. Thus, the number of small-sized glass works has increased to 100, double the previous number.

In 1980, the output of plate glass was 27.71 million standard crates, an increase of 18.9% over 1979. Of this amount, 17.66 million standard crates were produced by the large and medium-sized works, while 10.06 million were produced by small-sized works. The varieties of plate glass have increased and their uses have been expanded. Prior to Liberation, China could produce only ordinary window glass, frosted glass and sandblasted glass and in small quantities at that. Today, in addition to window glass of various thicknesses, China can produce several dozen kinds of plate glass — such as ground glass, laminated glass, wired glass, figured glass, tempered glass, safety glass, heat-absorbent glass, electricity-conducting glass and bullet-proof glass. These products are used widely in light industry as well as in the motor vehicle, aviation, chemical and instrument and meter industries, and also in agriculture.

At present most glass works use the Fourcault process; their productivity is more or less equal to that of glass works in foreign countries. In 1971, China set up its first production line for float glass on an experimental basis. Today, some large and medium-sized works using the float process are under construction.

The Non-Metallic Minerals Industry

Non-metallic minerals have been known and used for a long time and are still widely used throughout the world. China has proven reserves of 80 kinds of non-metallic minerals. Its deposits of iron pyrite, gypsm and barytes rank first in the world, while its deposits of asbestos, fluorspar and bentonite rank second in the world. Deposits of phosphorus, talc, pyrohyllite, graphite, kaolin, magnesite, salt, perlite, limestone and mica are nearly as significant. Prior to Liberation, however, China had only a few sulphurous iron and phosphorus mines and turned out only small quantities of asbestos, gypsum and talc. At that time, the non-metallic minerals industry was virtually non-existent.

Non-metallic minerals with special properties such as resistance to high temperatures, to acid, oxidation, and X-rays, and with qualities such as high strength, extreme hardness, heat insulation, sound-proofing and lubrication, are indispensable raw materials for modern industry, national defence, modern science and technology.

Since the founding of New China, the Chinese government has attached great importance to the mining and processing of seven key non-metallic minerals: asbestos, gypsum, graphite, kaolin, talc, mica and diamonds. During the 31 years since Liberation, China has set up 281 state-owned non-metallic mineral enterprises; they are above the county level and employ 124,000 workers and staff. Of these, 50 are large and medium-sized enterprises employing a total of 74,000 workers and staff. Output of non-metallic minerals has increased greatly. In 1980, China's output of asbestos, gypsum, graphite and talc was 131,700 tons, 3,348,000 tons, 160,000 tons and 915,000 tons, respectively. These amounts represented increases of 219 times, 341 times, 178 times and 398 times, respectively, over amounts produced in 1949.

III. Current Problems and Future Prospects

Demands Still Exceed Supplies. In the past 31 tears, China's building materials industry has made significant progress in development of quality, quantity, variety, productive technology and research, thereby making positive contributions to the development of the national economy and raising the people's standards of living. However, the rate of development is still not great enough to meet the needs of the national economy and the needs of the people's livelihood. A big gap still exists between supply and demand.

The principle problems are out-of-date technical equipment, relatively low efficiency and the poor quality of scientific research, design and equipment manufacture.

The average rate of growth of the building materials industry during 1952-1978 was 11.5%, a rate lower than that of heavy industry. The rates of increase of some major products, such as cement and plate glass, were notably lower than the average rate of increase of the industry as a whole, except during the First Five Year Plan period and during 1962-1964. Except for a few products such as mica, fibreglass and quartz glass, all main products of the building materials industry are in short supply. The supply of cement turned out by large cement works for the use of major capital construction projects and urban maintenance work is several million tons short of requirements. More serious is the situation with plate glass. Current output of plate glass can only meet about 40% of the needs of capital construction and urban use; very little of it is supplied to the countryside. Output of ceramic sanitary ware can only meet one-third of the demand; asbestos can meet only 70% or so of demand; and long-fibre asbestos only 30% of demand.

The blame for this situation can be traced to the mistakes of "Left" deviations in the guiding ideology for developing the national economy. There was insufficient appreciation of the importance of the position and role of the building materials industry. As a result, the rate of development of the building materials industry did not match that of the national economy. During the 27-year period from 1952 to 1978, investments in the industry accounted for only 1.7% of total state investment in capital construction — a much smaller percentage than the investment in other sectors of heavy industry. Hence, the building materials industry has long been a weak link in the national economy.

The Course for Future Development. Since the Third Plenary Session of the 11th Central Committee of the Communist Party, held in 1978, the Central Committee and the State Council have attached major importance to the development of the building materials industry, pointing out that this industry, like the coal, electric power, oil, transport and communications industries, is a pioneer industry in the national economy. They also stressed that research in this industry should be carried out with due account being taken of the needs of China's 1,000 million people. Since building materials are in short supply, the industry must accelerate its pace of development in line with the readjustment of the national economy. So, in accordance with the instructions of the Party Central Committee, the building materials industry should carry out further the policy of readjustment and take active measures to raise production so as to keep pace with the development of the national economy and with the needs of housing construction in both urban and rural areas.

The major points to be stressed for future development are as follows:

1. *We should run existing enterprises well.* Today there are more than 46,000 enterprises in the building materials industry, providing a solid foundation for further development. In order for the industry to achieve steady and significant progress, we must readjust the existing enterprises, carry out technical transformation and renewal of equipment, adopt new technologies, raise technical and management levels, fully tap potential and improve economic efficiency. We must improve the quality and increase the variety of products, reduce costs, and try to develop products needed by the market. We should also cut down on energy consumption, pay attention to the needs of environmental protection and ensure safety in production.

We should attach importance to the readjustment and consolidation of small-sized enterprises. In small-sized enterprises that enjoy favourable resource and production conditions, we must carry out technical improvements and raise efficiency in a systematic way. Small-sized enterprises that lack adequate supplies of raw materials and fuel and those that have incurred losses for years and have turned out poor quality products at high cost should be merged with other enterprises or converted to production of other materials.

2. *Great efforts should be made to produce primary building materials products such as cement and plate glass.* Given China's actual conditions, it will be a considerably long time before large quantities of timber and steel will become available for use in building and construction. Although clay bricks and tiles have long been used — and are still widely used — for construction purposes, the use of these materials for building walls and roofs is costly and consumes a great deal of energy. Furthermore, the large-scale use of clay for the manufacture of bricks and tiles destroys farmland. So we should shift from producing clay bricks and tiles to production of cement, reinforced concrete, plate glass and ceramic sanitary ware, supplemented by new lightweight building materials. In addition, we should step up the search for energy-saving substitutes, which China has in abundance. While China's total cement output is high, its annual per capita consumption of cement is only 80 kg., considerably lower than the world average of 230 kg. and figure of over 700 kg. for Japan. To speed up the production of cement and plate glass, we must stress technical transformation and expansion of old plants, while setting up of new plants should be moderate.

3. *We must produce and supply more building materials to fulfil the needs of the countryside.* In the past few years, economic conditions in the countryside have improved overall and the income of peasants has risen. The current surge of housing construction in rural areas has not been matched since the early years of New China. In 1980, 5 million farm households either renovated their dwellings or added new buildings. The floor space of new buildings was over 300 million sq. m. For a long time, whenever we drew up and balanced the plan for building materials, we considered chiefly the needs of capital construction and gave little consideration to the need for building materials in rural areas. This oversight has led to an acute shortage of building materials in the countryside. In 1980, the state, the provinces, municipalities and autonomous regions supplied rural areas with about 100,000 tons of steel for making reinforced concrete and 900,000 standards crates of plate

glass. These were enthusiastically received by the peasants. From now on, it is expected that the state will supply increasing quantities of steel and plate glass to the countryside.

The scale of housing construction will become larger and larger hereafter, and more materials will be needed. As China is a vast territory, conditions of climate, geography, resources and customs vary widely from place to place, while levels of economic development are uneven. Thus, we must proceed from the realities, stick to the principle of using local materials, making good use of such resources as river mud, earth mounds, minicement, bamboo, stone, etc., and use industrial wastes to manufacture bricks, tiles and small building blocks. We must no longer make bricks and tiles using clay taken from fields under cultivation.

4. *We must energetically develop new lightweight building materials.* Since the early 1960's we have undertaken research in the production of lightweight building materials and have set up several aerating plants. Since 1975, we have carried out extensive systematic research and production of new building materials. From 1976 to 1980, new lightweight building materials were used in the construction of 500,000 sq. m. of office buildings and dwellings in 23 cities. By 1980, 38 new production lines were set up, and 36 kinds of new materials were in mass production; in addition, two small production centres were established and seven large and medium-sized centres were under construction.

The advantages of constructing buildings with new materials are evident. The dead weight is less; the function of integration is better; construction time is shorter (since all the components can be prefabricated and erected *in situ*); less intensive labour is required and labour efficiency is higher, as compared with construction using traditional methods and traditional materials. Another advantage is that the new lightweight building materials can be manufactured from industrial wastes.

The development of new lightweight materials is essential to the future development of the building materials industry. However, the technology and technical equipment required for producing such materials is relatively complicated. Thus, our policy is first to select some large and medium cities as experimental sites for the construction of dwelling complexes, then make technical-economic analysis and comparisons and, finally, disseminate the new methods systematically. At the same time, we must strengthen research and trial-production in order to solve the difficult technical problems that we face in applying new methods and materials.

24. CHINA'S BUILDING INDUSTRY
By the Research Office,
General Administration of Building Construction

During the 31 years since the founding of the People's Republic, great developments have been made in the building industry. A total of 1,880 million sq. m. of industrial and civil construction has been completed in the whole country at a cost of 421,800 million yuan, of which 95,000 million yuan was spent on 666 million sq. m. of buildings executed by enterprises of the construction industry. The large masses of workers and staff members working in this field have laboured diligently in the rehabilitation and development of the national economy, making great contributions to the country's socialist construction.

In 1980, movements to increase production and to improve the economy were launched in construction enterprises in many different localities, centring on an emulation drive to construct buildings of good quality. Administration and management were strengthened to obtain better economic results. State-owned construction enterprises had a workforce numbering 1.7 million and collectively-owned enterprises above the county level had a workforce of 1.3 million. The total building area completed by the former in 1980 increased by 12.5% over that of the previous year. The amount of labour expended in 1980 increased by 18% and 7.3%, respectively, over that of 1979. Labour productivity per capita in state-owned enterprises amounted to 5,013 yuan (an increase of 8.9%) and in collectively-owned enterprises to 3,965 yuan (an increase of 6.8%).

The duration of construction projects has been shortened. A great number of large and medium-sized projects were completed on schedule. The Lanzhou Vinylon Fibre Plant, the Jiaxing Woollen Mill, the Dandong Chemical Fibre Plant, the expansion of the Shizhuishan Power Plant, the Sichuan Chemical Works, the Xiangxiang Cement Plant in Hunan and the Harbin Cold Storage have gone into operation. Some factory buildings with imported equipment, e.g. the Shaanxi Tricolor TV Tube Factory, the Pingdingshan Cord Fabric Factory, the Shanghai Petro-Chemical Works, the Yantai Leatherette Factory, and the Zhejiang Chemical Fertilizer Plant, are in the finishing stage, with installations under test run, while others are under construction. The speed at which civil buildings are being constructed has also been increased. According to statistics obtained from a number of provinces and municipalities, the time required for constructing a single project of 2,500 sq. m. has been shortened by 28 days, 10% less than that of the previous year.

A high quality of workmanship has been obtained in building construction. The percentage of construction appraised as being of good quality has reached 61.4% of all projects carried out by the state-owned construction enterprises and 80-90% of all projects carried out by the municipal enterprises of Beijing, Tianjin and Shanghai. To meet the demands of the population as far as possible, emphasis has been placed not only on the quality of structural work, but also on decorative work; not only on structural design, but also on functional design. When projects were handed over, they were ready for immediate use by consumers, with everything cleaned and in order, including interior finishings, installations, the surrounding areas and roads. Some of the construction enterprises have even set up a system of return visits and one-year repair service free of charge.

I. Emulation Drive for Excellent Workmanship

An emulation drive for excellent workmanship between construction enterprises of Beijing, Tianjin and Tangshan started in 1978. In 1980, the area of completed buildings appraised as having excellent workmanship increased, reaching 1.77 million sq. m. in Beijing, 1.01 million sq. m. in Tianjin and 940,000 sq. m. in Tangshan. The percentage of increase over that of the previous year was 51%, 135% and 570%, respectively. Emulation drives were also conducted between Shanghai, Nanjing and Hangzhou, as well as between construction enterprises in other provinces, municipalities and districts. Building construction bureaus in 29 provinces, municipalities and autonomous regions and six building construction bureaus directly under the General Administration of Building Construction altogether executed more than 12 million sq. m. of construction of excellent workmanship, amounting to 27% of the total. Municipal and provincial building bureaus in Beijing, Tianjin, Shanghai, Liaoning, Jilin and Yunnan all achieved percentages above 40%. In many localities model projects have been set up.

II. Housing Development

In the readjustment of investment in capital

construction, priority has been given to housing. The enthusiasm of local authorities and enterprises as well as individuals for housing construction has been encouraged. In 1980, the total amount of housing completed in all cities and towns reached 82.3 million sq. m., a record-breaking figure. Of that amount, Beijing had accounted for 3.36 million sq. m., an increase of 870,000 sq. m., or 34.9%, over the previous year. The ratio of completed housing construction to the total amount of construction in the city increased from 61% in 1979 to 68.8% in 1980.

Unified planning, investment, design and construction of large-scale housing developments has been adopted in many cities. In some large cities, simultaneous development of utility services such as gas, water, sewage, electricity and roads, as well as public buildings such as schools, kindergartens, shops and post offices, have been carried out. In the construction of two housing estates, Jinsong and Tuanjiehu in Beijing, attention was paid to complete sets of utility services so that the buildings were ready for habitation shortly after completion. By the end of 1980, 420,000 sq. m. of the two estates had been completed and put in use. Dalian paid attention to the design and construction of complete sets of utility services so that 710,000 sq. m. of building area out of the 780,000 sq. m. construction (90.7%) were ready for use right after completion.

The percentage of high-rise apartment buildings has increased. In 1980, 400,000 sq. m. high-rises were built. The Lixin Zhonglu Housing Estate, the first large-scale rehabilitation project in Guangzhou, occupies an area of 96,000 sq. m.; the first stage of construction work has been completed.

The state has given encouragement and support to individuals and overseas Chinese to build housing. Private houses built during 1980 amounted to some 1.8 million sq. m., of which 400,000 sq. m. was in Guangdong Province. Construction projects started in 1980 included the Yinhai Housing Estate in Zhuhai, Guangdong, a group of garden houses jointly invested in by the municipal authority of Zhuhai and businessmen of Hong Kong and Macao; and the Overseas Housing Estate in Shantou, Guangdong, jointly invested in by the municipal authority of Shantou and Hong Kong businessmen.

III. Reconstruction Work in Tangshan

Reconstruction work in Tangshan, following the earthquake, has been proceeding rapidly, spurred by the deep concern of the party and the State Council. Preparation for reconstruction started in 1978 and comprehensive large-scale construction was carried out in 1979. By the end of 1980, 7.69 million sq. m. had been completed, with 4.11 million sq. m. of residential buildings, constituting 53.4% of the total residential building area, still to be reconstructed. More than 500,000 families in the city have moved into their new homes. In 1980, the emphasis was placed on residential buildings and public facilities. Total building area completed in that year amounted to 2.6 million sq. m., of which 1.95 million were residential buildings.

Reconstruction work in Tangshan has been energetically supported by local authorities throughout the country. To assist the people of Tangshan in rebuilding their new homes and resuming production, large contingents of builders were sent from Hebei, Liaoning, Jilin, Heilongjiang, Shanghai, Shaanxi and the Second Construction Bureau of the General Administration of Building Construction.

In the reconstruction of Tangshan, attention was given to constructing public buildings, service facilities and municipal works as well as residential buildings.

IV. Hotels and Buildings for Tourists

A total of 890,000 sq. m. of hotels, facilities for tourists, cinemas, gymnasiums and exhibition halls were constructed in 1980. Hotels have been built at scenic spots and in cities with historic ruins to meet the demands of the growing tourist trade. These hotels are designed to function efficiently, and to have a beautiful appearance and modern equipment.

Among the hotels completed in 1980 is the 22-storey Yanjing Hotel in Beijing, the tallest building in the city. It is 66.7m. high and covers a total area of 40,000 sq. m. Large amounts of marble, glazed tiles, plastic flooring and plastic wallpaper were used in the interior and vinyl-ethylene paint was used on the exterior. Construction of the hotel took 15 months.

The Tourist Centre at the Zhongshan Hot Springs in Guangdong Province, jointly invested in by the Zhongshan Branch of the China Travel Service and the Chinese-Australian Construction Investment Company, occupies a plot of 130,000 sq. m. and has a total building area of 30,000 sq. m. Built in a combination of traditional Chinese style and local style, it comprises five hotels and ten villas, with a total of 200 rooms and 400 beds. Hot spring bathhouses and other tourist facilities are provided. Construction was started in November 1979 and completed at the end of 1980.

Other hotels completed in 1980 were the Dunhuang Hotel in Gansu and the Taishan Hotel in Shandong. Among hotels currently under construction are the Xiangshan Hotel, the Huaqiao Hotel, the Jianguo Hotel and the Great Wall Hotel, all in Beijing. Together, they will have 10,000 rooms and a total area of over 800,000 sq. m. The 28-storey White Swan Hotel under construction in Guangzhou, using foreign investment and modern equipment and management, has a total area of approximately 80,000 sq. m. The 37-storey Jinling Hotel which is being built in Nanjing with investment from overseas Chinese will be the tallest building in the country. Its top floor will feature a revolving tearoom from which one can enjoy a panoramic view of the city.

V. Buildings for Education, Scientific Research and Health Services

Educational Buildings. Construction of educational facilities in China broke all records in 1980. A total of 3.25 million sq. m. was constructed: 280,000 sq. m. in Sichuan; 260,000 sq. m. each in Shandong and Jiangsu; 220,000 sq. m. in Liaoning and 110,000 sq. m. in Inner Mongolia. In 1980, 38 institutions of higher learning directly under the Ministry of Education added 600,000 sq. m. of lecture halls, dormitories and buildings for research and athletics to meet the urgent need for improved education. Large numbers of middle and primary schools were also built in many cities.

Scientific Research Buildings. In 1980, 1.62 million sq. m. of buildings to house scientific research activities were completed. The Beijing Meteorological Centre accounted for 14,000 sq. m. and the Shanxi Broadcasting and Television Technical Centre accounted for 20,000 sq. m. Among other recently completed buildings are research facilities for the State Seismological Bureau, the Guangxi Institute of Pharmacology and the Plateau Atmosphere Research Institute.

Buildings for Health Services. A total of 2.46 million sq. m. of buildings for health services were completed in 1980. These included the out-patient department of the No. 1 Hospital at Beijing Medical College, in-patient buildings for the Beijing Traditional Medicine Research Institute, the No. 2 Hospital in Tianjin and the People's Hospital in Dalian.

VI. Experimental Centres for Industrialization

In order to transform outdated modes of production and to adopt socialized mass production, experimental centres were set up in Changzhou (Jiangsu Province) and Nanning (Guangxi Autonomous Region) in 1978. Initial results obtained in these two cities show that construction capacity in Changzhou increased from 180,000 sq. m. in 1977 to 400,000 sq. m. in 1980, while in Nanning it increased from 350,000 sq. m. in 1977 to 650,000 sq. m. in 1980.

Ten production lines have been set up in Changzhou for mass production of wall panels, floor slabs, roof slabs, building blocks, premixed concrete, steel windows, etc., increasing China's construction capacity by 280,000 sq. m. within three years. Of the 700,000 sq. m. of residential buildings constructed within those three years, 33% were constructed by this mechanized process.

The most conspicuous improvements brought about by the industrialization of building construction were the speeding up of construction and the realization of quick returns on investment. It now takes only three months to construct panel apartment houses of 2,000 sq. m., four months to construct apartment building blocks and less than one year to construct factory buildings of 10,000 sq. m. or residential complexes of 100,000 sq. m. Garden Village, a new residential complex in Changzhou, took ten months to complete — only one-half the time formerly required for a similar job.

The major technical-economic indices in the cities of Changzhou and Nanning have risen significantly since industrialization, as shown in the following table:

City	Labour Productivity (in yuan per capita)	Increase of Labour Productivity (%)	Increase of Building Area Completed as Compared with 1977 (%)	Area Completed Per Capita (sq. m.)
Changzhou	7,219	31	79	63
Nanning	4,158	62	58	42

The results show that building industrialization not only speeds up the process of construction and increases the amount constructed in a given period, but also produces buildings of better quality. Industrialization is the most effective approach to the reform and development of the building industry.

VII. Architectural Design and Research

After the criticism of "Left" errors committed in the past, Chinese architects have produced more and better architectural designs. From 33 design institutes above the provincial level, construction drawings for projects covering 27.85 million sq. m. were completed in 1980, 1% more than were produced the previous year. To meet the demand for building industrialization, 1.96 million copies of "National Unified Building Design Drawings" were distributed during the year.

All of the design institutes have raised the quality of their design. Now 90% of their work is considered of "good quality." And some designs have reached a new level of excellence in structural design, functional arrangement and architectural treatment. Designs for residential buildings prepared in Beijing and Tianjin show improvement in plan arrangement, lowering of storey height and enlargement of usable space. In the design of the Chengdu Gymnasium prepared by the Southwest Building Design Institute, suspension cables without tension rings, lightweight roofing, cantilevered platform slabs and inclined frames combine to produce a satisfactory functional arrangement that is pleasing in appearance and relatively low in construction costs.

In the field of building research, emphasis has been placed on applied technique. Techniques that are already practiced and proven satisfactory include: attaching silicate wall panels with fly-ash as adhesive; fly-ash admixtures; seasoning wood with far-infrared rays; curing concrete with solar energy, erecting prefabricated wall panels *in situ;* standardized steel forms; various admixtures; and equipment for diaphragm walls.

The number of buildings of modern design increased significantly, reaching a total area of 22.54 million sq. m. in 1980 (an increase of 55% over the previous year). Of that total, 9.83 million sq. m., representing 22%, was begun in 1980. Buildings constructed with large forms were the most popular, accounting for 3.15 million sq. m. (an increase of 1.17 million sq. m. over the previous year) and 32% of all buildings of modern structural design. Prefabricated panel buildings also became more popular, accounting for 2.31 million sq. m. or 23% of total construction. This technique, integrating design and construction, has been systematized in Beijing, where 58% of the buildings constructed with forms had brick exterior walls and *in situ* cast interior walls. The average cost of such construction is 127 yuan per sq. m., which is about the same as that of mixed construction.

Construction using prefabricated panels has proven to be even more popular in Guangxi, Yunnan and other regions. In Guangxi, hollow panel construction accounted for 68% of all buildings of modern structural design in that region. This technique calls for less labour and less consumption of wood, cement and steel. The unit cost of such construction is nearly the same as that of construction using brick and concrete.

Industrialized construction of single-storey factory buildings, which offers the advantage of arranging standardized components in flexible combinations, has been adopted in some cities.

VIII. Contracts for Construction in Foreign Countries

Since its establishment in 1979, the China Construction Engineering Corporation (CCEC) has negotiated construction contracts with more than 120 firms in 22 countries. By 1980, it had signed 15 agreements of intention and 88 contracts covering design, construction or labour with the governments or independent firms of Iraq, North Yemen, Kuwait, Sudan, Italy, France, the United States, West Germany, Japan and Hong Kong. Eighteen projects, including hospitals, residences, hotels, restaurants, etc., have been completed in North Yemen and other countries.

CCEC, a large enterprise, which contracts for construction jobs in foreign countries, has its own staff for exploration and design and more than 100,000 workers involved in construction and installation. It also has a number of well-known architects serving as its technical staff or advisors. In addition to its branches in 19 provinces, municipalities and autonomous regions, CCEC maintains overseas branches in Hong Kong, North Yemen, Iraq, Kuwait, Thailand and Macao, as well as branches which specialize in building metallurgy and landscape architecture. Cooperative firms jointly established by CCEC and foreign construction enterprises include: Companhia de Construcau e Fomento Predial Hwashan, Lda; China-Tai Construction & Engineering Co. Ltd.; Yemeni-China Construction & Engineering Co. Ltd.; Gulf Realty Construction, Inc.; Carino Realty Company Limited; and Watson Architectural, Engineering & Design Consultant.

Projects constructed by CCEC have been completed on or ahead of schedule and have won praise from clients and relevant parties.

IX. Problems and Trends

Since the founding of the People's Republic, innumerable buildings of various types have been constructed and hundreds of cities and towns have been renovated and expanded. This has provided an important basis for establishing an independent and integrated national economy, a solid national defence and a better standard of living for the people. However, many problems still plague the building industry, owing in part to the interference and sabotage of Lin Biao and the Gang of Four and in part to the limitations of the current system of economic management.

The main problems are as follows:

1. *Decentralized management and multi-headed leadership.* The present organization and management of construction enterprises according to the administrative system not only leads to blindness in development, but also to a lack of communication between building departments and local authorities and between the different enterprises themselves. The net result is a great waste of productive energy.

2. *Irrational supply system of building materials.* The present system allocates building materials to clients, according to the system of investment, rather than to the constructors, according to the specific project. Constructors have to request materials from their clients in batches. Materials cannot be centrally controlled and regulated, seriously hindering effective organization of production on the part of constructors.

3. *Productive activities of construction enterprises are not listed in the state plan.* The building industry is not considered an independent productive sector in the national economic plan and in national economic statistics. Construction is not assigned a planned value of output nor a planned amount of output. Articles like watches, cigarettes and bicycles are all assigned plans for projected output. However, there has never been a plan for housing. In balancing the state economic plan and local plans, the items to be balanced include personnel, finances, materials, production, supply and marketing. However, the same items in the building field have never been considered. The building industry is, nevertheless, one of the productive sectors of the economy. Thus, its output value and major products (housing, schools, hospitals, etc.) should be included and balanced in the state economic plan.

The development of the building industry is closely related to the prosperity of the national economy. The task of developing it is a difficult one. In a country of 1,000 million people, a large and strong building industry is indispensable for modernization. The building industry needs readjustment as well as transformation. In addition to resolving the three problems mentioned above, efforts must be made in years to come to change the present practice of small-scale production in building construction. Construction should be undertaken in groups and blocks with unified planning, so that buildings become commodities to be sold or rented by the unit. Efforts should also be made to organize development companies to handle real estate, site levelling, municipal facilities and building construction. A unified management is needed to run overall development and construction. SACE and the Construction Bank have jointly organized the China Building Construction and Development Corporation, which will undertake some experimental projects in order to find a way to rapidly construct more buildings of good quality with less capital and materials.

25. CHINA'S PHARMACEUTICAL INDUSTRY
By Jin Tongzhen and Ma Ding
State Pharmaceutical Administration

The pharmaceutical industry in China comprises both the production and distribution of traditional and Western drugs and of medical instruments. It is involved in commercial management as well as in industrial, agricultural and various other types of production. Financially, the industry contributes to our socialist economy; socially, it serves the health and welfare needs of the people. Throughout history, the development of the pharmaceutical industry has made contributions to the propagation of our peoples and to the prosperity of our country; it continues to play an important role in ensuring public health during the current period of socialist construction and modernization.

I. A Brief History of the Industry

Since the founding of the People's Republic, the pharmaceutical industry, under the leadership of the Chinese Communist Party and the people's governments, and by relying on the efforts of workers and staff members in this field, has expanded tremendously. It has produced medicines in quantities sufficient not only to meet the needs of the people, but with surpluses for export. Prices of pharmaceuticals have been lowered by significant amounts several times to lighten the financial burden on the people, thus making important contributions to health care, family planning and general well-being.

Traditional Chinese medicine, which has a history of several thousand years, is one of the valuable legacies of our motherland. The production and use of traditional medicines is an art unique to China, one which has enjoyed great fame throughout the world. However, under the reactionary government of old China, this art was on the verge of extinction prior to Liberation. Since the founding of the People's Republic, the party and the people's government have paid great attention to the production of traditional medicines.

At present, there are more than 5,000 kinds of traditional drugs in use. Five million *mu* of arable and non-arable land were allocated by the state for growing medicinal herbs. With established farms being continually improved and new farms under development, about 150 commonly used varieties of drugs are now being produced. Drugs derived from wild plants and animals have been gathered in a planned way so as to preserve the environment and natural resources. Moreover, experiments have been carried out to cultivate the roughly 800 drugs most frequently used in China. For example, Tianma (*Rhizoma gastrodiae*) and some 50 other drugs have been successfully cultivated. Certain valuable drugs, such as Renshen (*Radix ginseng*), Sanqi (*Radix notoginseng*) and Lurong (*Cornu cervi pentotrichum*) are produced in sufficient quantities to meet health service needs.

The "southern drugs" — called thus because they were, in the past, imported from countries that were our sole source of supply — are now successfully cultivated in our country. Among the 20 kinds cultivated, Muxiang (*Radix aucklandiae*) and Bingpian (*Borneolum*) are produced in sufficient quantities for our own use as well as for export.

In the years immediately after Liberation, traditional Chinese remedies were still prepared by hand in crude workshops. These workshops were later transformed into mechanized and semi-mechanized factories. Today, there are about 800 such factories employing a total of 66,000 workers and staff and producing more than 3,000 different drug categories and prescriptions. Traditional medicines are available in various forms, ranging from pills, powders, plasters and pellets to more modern dosage forms such as injections, tablets, mixtures and aerosol sprays. Traditional Chinese preparations and drugs are not only used in China, but are also sold to more than 70 countries and regions throughout the world, where they have received an enthusiastic welcome.

Under the semi-feudal and semi-colonial rule of old China, the pharmaceutical chemical industry was relatively backward. Nearly all bulk pharmaceuticals were then imported. Since Liberation, the pharmaceutical industry has been developed in a careful and systematic way. We have given priority to the production of the most extensively used pharmaceuticals, such as antibiotics and sulfa drugs, and to those remedies indispensable for the treatment of common and frequently occurring endemic diseases. We have made significant progress on this score. The output of bulk pharmaceuticals in 1957 was more than ten times greater than that of the early years after Liberation.

Since 1958, we have not only steadily increased the output of pharmaceuticals, but also expanded the range of products. We have produced successively different kinds of vitamins, steroid hormones and biological products. Now we are capable of producing approximately 1,000 different kinds of bulk pharmaceuticals in annual quantities of 40,000 tons (excluding glucose) and more than 3,000 standard preparations. In other words, we are able to produce most of the standard pharmaceuticals we need. We have also created effective new drugs for the treatment of cancer, cardiovascular diseases, bronchitis and malaria. Our pharmaceutical industry now comprises more than 1,500 pharmaceutical and chemical factories of different sizes employing a total of 250,000 people — a nationwide production network of considerable scope.

In the early years after Liberation, we produced virtually no medical instruments. Most of our medical instruments were imported. From the old regime we had inherited only a few workshops that repaired and made copies of imported hospital equipment. In the last 30 years we have progressed from repairing to manufacturing such equipment, advancing from simple to more and more sophisticated models. In the process, we have developed a new, versatile and comprehensive branch of industry. At present, China has more than 300 factories, with a total workforce of over 50,000, engaged in the manufacture of medical instruments. These factories produce more than 1,500 items with 5,000 specifications — items ranging from conventional apparatuses to specialized precision instruments.

Production techniques have advanced from manual labour to mechanized and semi-automatic operation. Production lines for the more commonly used products have been set up to turn out packages of these products for supply to thousands of medical units at the grassroots level. The quality of some of our products is now up to advanced world standards. For example, we are now capable of producing electronic equipment for nuclear medicine and laser treatment, as well as for monitoring purposes.

Along with the development of production, we have made great strides in distribution. There are now more than 2,600 wholesale units in the country operating at three levels, and a nationwide retail network; together they constitute an integrated system for distribution of pharmaceuticals in both urban and rural areas. The total workforce engaged in procurement, storage, transportation and marketing of pharmaceuticals now exceeds 300,000. As compared with 1955, procurement of all medical commodities has increased nine-fold in value; domestic sales, seven-fold; and exports, more than 20-fold. Since Liberation, prices of pharmaceutical products have been significantly reduced eight times. The current retail prices of pharmaceuticals average only one-fifth of the prices prevailing at Liberation. Traditional drugs retail for about two-thirds of their former prices. Prices for medical instruments have also been reduced repeatedly. Birth-control pills and devices are provided free of charge, as are drugs for some endemic diseases, thus lessening the financial burden on the masses and improving the country's general health standards. In contrast to the old days, when there was a popular saying, "Medicine is more valuable than gold," and when workers were left to suffer from disease and pestilence, the superiority of the socialist system cannot be disputed.

For a period of ten years, however, the production and distribution of pharmaceutical products were severely disrupted by the actions of Lin Biao and the Gang of Four and by the influence of "Left" policies. At that time, we blindly pursued quantity goals and overlooked the importance of quality and variety in production, resulting in woeful neglect of the people's needs for treatment and health care. Over-anxious to achieve quick results, we set ourselves impossibly high and totally unrealistic production targets; we overlooked the unique features of the socialist commodity economy and the effects of the law of value, paying little attention to economic results, management and administration. We downgraded the positive role of science, technology and intellectuals and ignored the training and rational placement of technical personnel. Chaos existed in the administration, management and production of pharmaceuticals. Factories were set up at random and pharmaceuticals were produced without government approval. Valuable drugs that were in short supply became commodities for speculation and quacks took the opportunity to make and sell sham remedies. The balance between production and distribution was upset, with shortages of items in some places while huge stocks existed in others. Science and education were held back, with the result that production technology could not advance. All of these actions not only brought economic loss to the country but, most importantly, undermined the health of the people.

II. Establishment of a Unified Pharmaceutical Administration and Other Improvements

After the Third Plenary Session of the 11th Party Central Committee, the State Council, in an effort to bring order out of chaos and to eliminate the influence of "Left" policies, created a single department to replace the multitude of leadership groups involved in the administration of the pharmaceutical industry. The State Pharmaceutical Administration thus formed was empowered to supervise the national production and distribution of pharmaceuticals and medical instruments, related activities with foreign countries, research and development, education and the dissemination of scientific information.

In the past two years, pharmaceutical organizations at all levels have, in accordance with the party's ideological, political and organizational line, implemented the policy of readjustment, restructuring, consolidation and improvement and made remarkable achievements in every aspect of their work. In 1980, production, sales and exports of pharmaceuticals increased; stocks of pharmaceutical goods became more balanced; coordination between production and sales improved; and, as a result, various targets were surpassed. The output value of pharamceuticals (including traditional drugs and preparations and medical instruments) in 1980 rose to 7,830 million yuan, representing a 7.5% increase over that of the previous year. After measures were taken in accordance with the principle of "cutting surpluses to make up shortage," the total output of 12 principal categories of pharmaceutical chemicals — including antibiotics, sulfa drugs, antipyretics, vitamins, etc. — increased to 39,400 tons, exceeding the original target by 6.5%. The output of traditional drugs and preparations alone rose to 76,400 tons, exceeding the original target by 9.4%. In 1980, total sales of pharmaceuticals and medical instruments amounted to 7,800 million yuan, with exports yielding US$545 million — increases of 5.15% and 18.35%, respectively, over 1979 sales.

In implementing the policy of readjustment in 1980 we have given special attention to the following five aspects of our work:

1. *Vigorously adopting measures to consolidate pharmaceutical factories.* To fulfil the needs of the people and to end the chaos of setting up factories at random and producing drugs indiscriminately, we have required that all production of pharmaceuticals be carried out in strict accordance with the conditions specified in the (tentative) "Rules for Pharmaceutical Administration." All pharmaceutical products had to comply with the Pharmacopoeia and other official standards; otherwise, their production, sale, procurement and use were not allowed. Toward this end, we have undertaken extensive investigations and consolidation measures in all existing factories, while local authorities have jointly organized special task forces. For example, leading cadres in public health and pharmaceutical administration departments in Guangdong, Henan and Heilongjiang, among other places, have worked with local authorities to establish effective guidelines for carrying out consolidation. At the end of 1980, consolidation had taken effect nationwide, except in certain outlying districts.

According to reports from 20 provinces, municipalities and autonomous regions, 317 unlicenced factories that lacked satisfactory production facilities have already been ordered to suspend operation, merge with others, or shift to another type of production. Some provinces and municipalities have already taken resolute steps to ban those units which unlawfully produce and sell drugs. For example, 196 so-called factories in Anyang District and 49 in Xuchang County, both in Henan Province, and 54 units in Juacheng County, Shandong Province, have been banned. Bureaus of public health, pharmaceutical administration, public security and industry and commerce in 15 provinces, municipalities and autonomous regions, such as Sichuan, Shandong, Guizhou, Zhejiang, Henan and Inner Mongolia, have acted in close coordination to issue public information on the importance of pharmaceutical administration and to check the illegal production and sale of drugs, as well as false advertizing.

Licences have been granted to factories that have good management and have passed inspection by the authorities. Eighteen of the provinces, municipalities and autonomous regions have organized discussions to review the clinical efficacy of locally produced drugs and have made preliminary suggestions to eliminate certain items. In other localities, the chemical composition of pharmaceutical products have been circulated to members of the medical profession for analysis and approval.

2. *Improving the quality of pharmaceutical products.* Since pharmaceutical products directly affect the life or death of patients, they must be made perfectly safe. A "quality month/year" campaign has been launched to encourage factories to give priority to quality control, strengthen management and tighten inspection procedures so as to bring out "best quality" products that are up to advanced world standards. In 1980, a total of 135,000 workers and staff joined in the training programme for quality control. At the same time, 1,600 quality monitoring groups were organized in more than 400 enterprises and statistical analyses were applied to rationalize management of production.

The quality of most pharmaceutical products has improved during the past two years. Thirty traditional and Western drugs and medical instruments have won national quality prizes. These award-winning products included "Lishizhen" Brand Angong-Nuihuang-Wuan (pills); "Camellia" Brand Yunnan-Baiyao, Liushen-Wuan (pills) produced by the Shanghai No. 1 Traditional Chinese Pharmaceutical Factory and the Suzhou Leiyunshang Drug Store; tetracycline hydrocloride made by the Shanghai No. 3 Pharmaceutical Works; sodium penicillin G manufactured by the North China Pharmaceutical Industry; Rigampicin made by the Sichuan Pharmaceutical Factory; "Huatao" Brand acupuncture needles; and "Crane" Brand slit-lamp microscopes. Hundreds of products have been judged "best quality" products by the State Pharmaceutical Administration and the authorities of provinces, municipalities and autonomous regions. The bulk pharmaceuticals produced have all met and surpassed the requirements of the Chinese Pharmacopoeia.

3. *Emphasis placed on "production according to need, supply according to demand" and the practice of economy*. The surplus production of pharmaceutical products was cut back while production of pharmaceuticals in short supply was encouraged. Thus, output targets for ten pharmaceutical chemicals with a production surplus have been reduced by 22.8%; while those for seven bulk pharmaceuticals produced for export have been increased by 25.7%. Owing to the change in the kinds of pharmaceuticals produced, the annual output of pharmaceutical chemicals in 1980 increased in value by over 7%, though it dropped in weight by 5.1% compared with the previous year.

As regards traditional drugs, the area under cultivation for 30 state-controlled drugs in short supply increased by 9.3% over the previous year, while procurement increased by 4.7%. With increased production, the number of items previously in short supply has dropped from about 100 to 80. Meanwhile, the area allocated to cultivation of state-controlled items that were in surplus has been reduced by 48% from the previous year and the procurement of these items decreased by 50.2%.

Owing to the readjustment of production and sales, stocks of pharmaceutical products dropped by 7% in 1980, while their turnover obviously accelerated.

4. *Improving the marketing of pharmaceutical products to ensure adequate and steady supplies.* As the living conditions of the people, especially the peasants, improved and purchasing power increased, the demands for pharmaceutical products rose steadily. In 1980, the major increase in the sales of all pharmaceutical products occurred primarily in the countryside. Below the county level, sales increased by 10.88%; at levels above the county, there was no notable change in sales. Sales of traditional drugs in their various forms set an even better record, increasing by 15.89% over 1979.

An unexpected development in the pharmaceutical market has been the constantly increasing interest of the masses in healthful and nutritious medications. This trend was particularly noticeable in the countryside of Beijing, Shanghai, Guangxi, Hunan, Zhejiang, Anhui, Fujian, Jiangsu, Jiangxi, Guangdong and Hubei. For example, sales of Renshen and Lurong in Shanghai increased by 53% over 1979. In Shaoxing County, Zhejiang Province, the sales of Renshen extract, Royal Jelly preparations, medicinal liquors and other traditional tonics in the first eight months of 1980 exceeded sales during the same period in 1979 by 48.7%; during the peak month of October, sales of Renshen and Baimuer (*Tremela*) showed a further increase of 54.4% over the previous month. In Jiangxi Province, sales of expensive items such as Tianqi, Lurong, Royal Jelly preparations, *Tremela* and Renshen exceeded sales during the same period in 1979 by 50%.

Traditional Chinese dietotherapy, which has a history of more than 2,000 years, has been enjoying a revival in recent years. Health drinks, wholesome food and nutritious candies were reportedly in great demand in Guangxi, Beijing, Tianjin, Shanghai and Chengdu.

5. *Greater attention was paid to research and development.* A number of new drugs, new preparations and medical instruments, as well as new production technologies, have been developed through the joint efforts of research institutes, medical units and production concerns. During 1980, 40 new pharmaceutical items and 30 types of medical instruments were approved for use. Chemical syntheses of homoharringtonin, amidarone and phosphonomycin, and production technologies for the optical fibre gastroscope and the artificial kidney dializer have been successfully developed.

In the domain of crude drug cultivation, the sexual propagation of Pingbeimu (*Bulbu fritillariae ussuruensis*), the artificial breeding of ground beetles (*Eupolyphaga sinensis Walk.* or *Steleophaga plancyi Bol.*) and improvement in the production of Chenxiang (*Lignum aquilariae resinatum*) have been successful.

At present, pharmaceutical organizations at all levels are continuing to carry out the policies adopted by the party at the Third Plenary Session of the 11th Central Committee, taking into account specific local conditions. In this way, the organizations are moving closer to their goal of further economic readjustment and the realization of political stability. They are making efforts not only to eradicate the problems resulting from the impact of "Left" policies, but also to correct the imbalance in the industry by combatting disorder and strengthening the country's unified pharmaceutical administration.

III. Goals for Future Improvement of the Pharmaceutical Industry

We have gained much experience during the development of our pharmaceutical undertakings. The evaluation and analysis of this experience will be of enormous value to the further modernization of the industry as well as to the larger economic readjustment of the country.

1. *It is of utmost importance to improve the quality and guarantee the safety and efficacy of pharmaceutical products and medical instruments.* Pharmaceuticals and medical instruments are vital for the treatment and prevention of disease. They differ fundamentally from common household commodities in that they can save lives if they are safe, effective and exact, or take lives if they do not have those qualities.

Mindful of the health of the people, the Party's Central Committee and the State Council have always paid great attention to the quality of pharmaceutical products. However, there have been two periods after Liberation when this concern was not in evidence. One was in the early 1960's, when pharmaceutical factories were set up at random and pharmaceuticals and medical instruments were indiscriminately produced in many districts. Therapeutic accidents caused by bad quality drugs occurred frequently in that period. In 1964, an exclusive National Corporation was created to provide management for the pharmaceutical industry. Standardization of medical instruments was enhanced and models, specifications, raw-material requirements and methods of testing were unified. At that time, the Ministry of Public Health and the Ministry of Commerce jointly devised standards and grading specifications for 54 varieties of traditional drugs. The quality of pharmaceutical products improved and stabilized.

The second deviation occurred during the "cultural revolution," when quality control departments at all levels were disbanded, technical personnel were sent away to perform manual labour, and regulations that had proved effective for quality control were ignored. As a consequence, the quality of pharmaceutical products declined a second time. It was only after the smashing of the Gang of Four that quality control of pharmaceutical products was restored. At present, departments of pharmaceutical administration and health authorities at all levels are doing their utmost to improve the quality of pharmaceutical products, to introduce well-known brands of certain products to foreign countries and to provide the people with the highest quality health care.

2. *Our pharmaceutical administration system should be characterized by unified leadership, multi-level management and better collaboration between production and sales.* The administration of pharmaceutical production and sales has undergone many transformations since Liberation. In the early years, production and sales of Western drugs and medical instruments were supervised by the Ministry of Public Health, while those of traditional Chinese drugs were handled first by the Ministry of Trade, then by the Ministry of Light Industry, and then by the Ministry of Commerce. In 1956, the Ministry of Chemical Industry took over the production of bulk pharmaceuticals and their dosage forms; the First Ministry of Machine Building assumed responsibility for the production of medical instruments; the Ministry of Commerce took charge of controlled sales of pharmaceutical products; and the Federation of Supply and Marketing Cooperatives took charge of procurement, processing and sales of traditional drugs. The latter two functions were later transferred to the Ministry of Health. Thus, there were five central departments involved in the administration of the pharmaceutical industry.

At that time, the country's economic foundations were relatively weak, and dispersed management allowed opportunities for development according to individual situations. Nevertheless, shortcomings in the system of multiple leadership and the lack of overall planning handicapped harmonization among the different departments. When the National Corporation was formed in 1964 as an experiment in industrial management, centralization was strengthened. Closer coordination was realized as a result of unification of pharmaceutical production throughout the country. But there was little flexibility in this arrangement, and the initiative of local authorities was not given full play.

By contrast, during the "cultural revolution" in the 1960's, when overall management was disrupted and the various sectors of the industry were run locally, lack of unified planning resulted in discrepancies in production and sales. Because quality control was slackened, profiteering and smuggling in pharmaceutical products occurred and fake remedies proliferated.

From experience, we may conclude that inflexibility and over-centralization are equally inimical to the development of the pharmaceutical industry. The ideal system should be characterized by unified leadership, multi-level management and close coordination between production and sales. In June 1978, the State Council decided to set up the State Pharmaceutical Administration at the national level. Together with local administrations in all provinces, municipalities and autonomous regions, it supervises production, supply and use of all pharmaceuticals, drugs and medical instruments throughout the country. This major improvement in the administration of the pharmaceutical industry was made on the basis of past experience. In two years, the system has already demonstrated its value in terms of promoting production, supply and research work in the pharmaceutical field. With continuing improvement, this system is expected to demonstrate its superiority even further.

3. *The accelerated development of the pharmaceutical industry requires overall planning, the reasonable distribution of production sites and full utilization, renovation and reform of existing enterprises.* Pharmaceutical products must serve all the needs of medical practice. Owing to the diversity in demands for the prevention, diagnosis and treatment of diseases, as well as the exigencies of emergencies, the variety of pharmaceutical products in stock at any one time has to be large. However, some indispensable products may be needed only in small quantities; others may have a limited shelf-life; and still others may require special preparation techniques. It is both impossible and unnecessary, therefore, for every locality to be self-sufficient in all kinds of products. Furthermore, owing to variations in the extent to which epidemics, catastrophes and emergencies related to national defence may occur, it is common for annual requirements to fluctuate. Consequently, production targets cannot be set arbitrarily, solely with the aim of achieving "high speed." Comprehensive planning and overall balance in production and supply must be considered in order to have well-balanced development with a reasonable distribution of production sites. Specialization, collaboration and coordination will have to be emphasized to ensure a free flow of supply. From experience, we should have learned that defective planning, repeated bad investments and production practices and profiteering result in heavy losses to the state.

As mentioned above, there are altogether about 2,700 factories in China manufacturing pharmaceuticals, traditional drugs and medical instruments. In order to develop faster, better, more economically and more comprehensively, emphasis must be placed on full utilization, renovation and reform of existing facilities. The potential for development is immense. Take the North China Pharmaceutical Industries, for example. Since its establishment, it has realized a 20-fold increase in production of antibiotics mainly through efforts made in strain selection and innovative technology, which raised the yields both in fermentation and extraction. The quality of its products was upgraded as well. The net profit and tax it paid to the state over the years was equivalent to 24 times the total investment.

The Northeastern General Pharmaceutical Works may serve as another example of successful development according to the principles of full utilization, renovation and reform. The enterprise was established some 40 years ago. Since 1969, with few additions in personnel and equipment, it has increased annual production six-fold in volume and four-fold in variety. Net profits turned over to the state by the enterprise increased eight-fold simply as a result of stressing better industrial management, adopting new technology and developing new product lines. Although it is an old operation, it is continuously making new contributions. These examples demonstrate that, along with the improvements made in the administrative system and the enlargement of self-management powers, the principle of full utilization, renovation and reform of existing facilities can give further impetus to the development of pharmaceutical undertakings.

4. *Adopting and pursuing appropriate economic policies according to the law of value will ensure a planned and well-balanced development of pharmaceutical production.* Production and supply of pharmaceutical products, especially of traditional crude drugs, which are diverse in variety, complicated in nature and scattered in origin, require selective application of economic policies. Traditional drugs are closely associated with agriculture, forestry, animal husbandry and fishing and are closely concerned with the interests of collectives as well as of individuals. Experience has proved that whenever justifiable policies were practiced, production thrived, whenever unreasonable policies were practiced, production declined. In the early 1960's, the production of herbal medicines dropped precipitously as a result of national turmoil. Later, when the state implemented appropriate pricing policies and adopted measures to encourage productivity, production recovered quickly. At that point, the state required that the income peasants derived from production of her-

bal medicines be no less than that obtained from sideline occupations in which they might otherwise be engaged. Indeed, the peasants should be allowed to derive slightly more profit from the production of certain drugs which call for more demanding techniques or more restrictive seasonal requirements. As regards the production of items in short supply, awards were given in the form of supplementary quotas of grains, fabrics, and fertilizers. To encourage the production of new varieties, losses incurred during the experimental stage were partially compensated by the organizations concerned with procurement. In this way, communes and brigades were motivated and production increased.

During the "cultural revolution," when emphasis was placed exclusively on the production of staple foodstuffs, the cultivation and collection of drugs were prohibited as activities that "fostered capitalism." Production was hampered to such an extent that crude drugs were out of stock even in the localities of origin. Not only did the peasants incur a loss, but the practice of traditional medicine also suffered seriously because prescriptions could not be filled.

After the Third Plenary Session of the 11th Central Committee, proper economic policies regarding rural areas were fully enforced. Under state guidance, brigades and peasant families were organized to take part in the cultivation and collection of drugs. The production of traditional drugs has prospered ever since.

It is also important to adopt appropriate pricing policies in the procurement and marketing of other pharmaceuticals and medical instruments. During the early years of the People's Republic, the state supported the newly developed pharmaceutical industry by providing subsidies so as to hold down the prices of domestically produced drugs. Imported drugs were procured in bulk by the state and turned into dosage forms at a low profit. The principle at that time was "let marketing shoulder the loss of procurement." However, along with the progress in production technology and the lowering of costs, prices were adjusted accordingly. As regards pricing, we insisted on "planning according to demand, overriding costs." We adhered to the principle of serving the interests of the people and approaching the goal of marginal profits. Rational adjustments in prices were made from time to time and, in exceptional cases, losses were tolerated by the state.

However, discrepancies are inevitable whenever the law of value is not properly observed, whenever prices are not reasonably set and corrections are not made in time because of the inflexibility inherent in an over-centralized system. Under these circumstances, production of items with a surplus may not give way to production of items in short supply, and obsolete factories may not give way to modernized facilities. This kind of anomaly could last for some time. Higher profit ratings set on prescription drugs as compared with bulk pharmaceuticals induced haphazard production of dosage forms; lower profit ratios set on marketing as compared with production reduced the incentive of distribution organizations. All of these problems will be resolved step-by-step during the readjustment period.

5. *Intensified efforts in scientific research, development and education are keys to future progress.* Looking back over the past 30 years of development, we can conclude that whenever research and development were emphasized, pharmaceutical undertakings flourished; whenever they were neglected, pharmaceutical undertakings floundered. In the first years after Liberation, the party and government provided general support for research departments of pharmaceutical industries, allowing them to devote their efforts first to the work of development, thereby stimulating production. Thus, a vast amount of experimental data was collected on the technology of manufacturing antibiotics, sulfa drugs, vitamins, steroid hormones, etc.

This data served as the basis for projection, design, and manufacturing activities in the years that followed. For example, the Hunan Institute of Pharmaceutical Research, formerly the Beijing Institute of Pharmaceutical Research, which was disbanded during the "cultural revolution," completed more than 200 research and development programmes from the time it was established in the early 1950's. Among those programmes, about 40 were considered competitive with then prevailing practices. They were only part of the research and development contributions that paved the way for rapid advances in the production of pharmaceuticals and medical instruments.

Industrial development provided material for further study, as for example in pharmacology and in medicinal chemistry. So far, encouraging results have been obtained in analyzing and improving traditional formulas, as well as in the preparation of new herbal remedies and dosage forms. In searching for new drugs, some very interesting structural varieties were found to possess characteristics that had hitherto gone undetected.

On reflection, our pharmaceutical activities, except in the domain of new drug research, were not far below advanced world standards in 1966. Then, the ten years of disaster under the Gang of Four set back our pharmaceutical research by at least 20 years. It is especially dismaying to realize that even in the field of traditional Chinese medicine our studies lagged behind those of Western countries. Bitter experience has taught us that research and development is the key and education the foundation for further development. What we must do now is strengthen the work of research and development and education. By adhering to the principle of "serving the interests of the masses," by combining Western and traditional Chinese medicine, by associating pharmaceutical research more closely with clinical practices and manufacturing processes, we may begin to bring our pharmaceutical industry up to the advanced standards of the West.

6. *The principal objective of pharmaceutical supply is to meet the needs of the people.* The practice of medicine and the supply of pharmaceutical products have always been closely intertwined. Both are essential in the struggle to conquer disease. In China today more than 80% of pharmaceutical supplies are dispensed on a prescription basis. So it is natural for medical practitioners and pharmaceutical suppliers to collaborate closely in the common interest of serving the people's health needs. In localities where this collaboration is successful, medical departments give advance notice of their needs to the distribution units so as to facilitate the flow of supplies. Distribution units, for their part, organize physicians, nurses and pharmacists with the support of the medical departments, to discuss and evaluate pharmaceutical products. They also take the opportunity to inform the medical departments of the composition, the characteristics and the supply situation of new products. The distribution units also organize training courses for health care personnel at the grassroots level, enabling them to identify and gather herbal drugs, supplying them with seeds and seedlings and coordinating them in support of the cooperative medical system.

The supply of pharmaceutical products allows for no waste of time. In certain circumstances, time means life. There should always be a ready supply of pharmaceuticals for people who need them. In the past, supplies of pharmaceuticals and medical instruments have met needs in time. Experience has shown that we should always maintain, in addition to regular stocks, emergency supplies for serious accidents, epidemics, natural disasters or outbreaks of war. To do so, wholesalers at all levels should strengthen collaboration by allowing for free distribution of commodities according to needs, reducing costs of distribution and thus speeding up the distribution process. The problem of inadequate storage facilities and retail outlets should also be attended to.

In addition to seeing that domestic needs are satisfied, we must be concerned with developing production of pharmaceutical products for export. We should seek to increase the proportion of export commodities that bring in high foreign exchange earnings, such as traditional Chinese drugs and preparations and other pharmaceuticals in dosage forms. In order to render our products more competitive on the international market, we must improve the quality of production and packaging and advertize the effectiveness of our products more widely.

We live in a socialist country. Our task is to serve the interests of one billion people by providing them with good quality pharmaceuticals at a price within their means, thus promoting their health. We must resolutely institute the policy of readjustment, restructuring, consolidation and improvement, taking into account the current limitations of the pharmaceutical industry and the needs of the Chinese people. Factories will have to be consolidated and unsatisfactory products eliminated. The standards of all pharmaceuticals and medical instruments will have to be raised. The relationship between the production and supply of pharmaceuticals will have to be coordinated according to the principle of "cutting surplus to make up shortages" and overall planning will have to be improved. Unified systems of administration to supervise personnel training programmes, research and development and education in the field of pharmaceuticals will have to be developed. The style of leadership and working methods will have to be modified. And development of political thought must continue.

With readjustment, we will advance and overcome the chaotic states of industrial management and pharmaceutical administration within three to five years. Then, we shall be able to set an even faster pace in the modernization of our socialist country.

26. CHINA'S COMMUNICATIONS AND TRANSPORT
By the Institute of Comprehensive Transportation,
State Economic Commission

Transportation is an important part of the national economy, a tie connecting social production, distribution, exchange and consumption, as well as a key link between town and country, industry and agriculture, one region and another, China and other countries. Since the founding of the People's Republic of China, there has been a great development in transportation under the leadership of the Chinese Communist Party and the government. Over a period of 31 years (1949-1980), passenger traffic volume increased 25 times, freight traffic 15 times, transportation facilities developed steadily and the distribution of transportation was considerably improved. All of this made great contributions to the development of production, ensuring socialist construction, strengthening national defence and improving the life of the people.

I. Growth of the Transport Network

By the end of 1980, the total length of the national transport network had increased consider-

of navigable inland waterways was not very high, the maximum extent achieved having been 172,000 km. in 1961. In fact, the total length has been greatly lessened because the policy of comprehensive river utilization was not well carried out, some ill-designed water dams and gates hindered navigation and there was a lack of dredging and maintenance of the waterways. The length of pipelines exceeded 8,000 km., including 5,438 km. of crude oil pipeline, 560 km. of refined oil pipeline and about 2,662 km. of natural gas pipeline. The routes of civil aviation lines expanded rapidly, including 159 domestic lines, 110,400 km.; and 18 international and 3 regional lines, 81,200 km.

II. Distribution of Transportation

Before Liberation, the vast southwest and northwest areas of China were hard to reach and backward in production. Since Liberation, however, the conditions of transportation have greatly improved. Railway mileage in these areas increased from 5.5% of the total national mileage in 1949 to 24.8% in 1979. All the provinces, municipalities

Table 1. Growth of Various Means of Transport (in 1,000 km.)

Mode of Transport	1949	1980	Increase Multiple (compared with 1949)
Railways	22.0	51.9	2.36
Highways	80.7	875.8	10.85
Inland waterways	73.6	107.8	1.46
Civil aviation	11.4 (1950)	191.7	16.82
Pipelines	...	8.6	...
Local railways	...	3.4	...

ably as against 1949 (see Table 1). Of the 51,900 km. of railways opened to traffic, over 8,000 km. were double-tracked. Of the 875,800 km. of highways, there were 110,000 km. of national trunk lines, more than 130,000 km. of inter-provincial and provincial lines and 630,000 km. of county-commune lines. Roads of high-quality and medium-quality road surface totalled about 151,000 km., 17.2% of total highway distance. The growth rate

and autonomous regions except Tibet are now accessible by railway. These lines pass through high mountain ridges, deep rivers and narrow canyons, and construction conditions are extremely difficult.

Highway mileage in the southwest and northwest areas also increased, from 24.2% of the national total in 1950 to 31.9% in 1979. All the counties except Maituo County in Tibet and

Derong County in Sichuan Province have highways, and 90% of the rural communes are accessible by bus and truck service. As for inland navigation, great efforts have been made to dredge the waterways in Sichuan Province and other major rivers. The improvement of transportation has played an important role in speeding up the development of the inland economy.

The northeast and coastal areas have always been the primary regions of industry and transportation. Over the past 30 years, the railway and highway networks were further expanded. Coastal and river navigation of these areas also was developed. On some railway trunk lines with heavy traffic, technical reconstruction was carried out.

In the development of civil aviation, priority has been given to setting up airline networks in distant and remote areas. In the early 1950's the Tianjin-Chongqing line was opened, and in the early 1960's the Beijing-Lhasa line was opened. At present, scheduled flights connect 80 large and medium-sized cities, including some border areas in Yunnan, Xinjiang and Tibet. Air service plays an active role in the development of the border areas.

Pipelines offer unique advantages, such as larger traffic volume, lower cost, less loss, smaller area of land used and economy of investment. In 1979, crude oil transported by pipeline accounted for 61.27% of the total crude oil traffic volume, thus saving nearly 4,000 tank wagon loads per day. This reversed the situation in which crude oil transport mainly depended on railways, thus reducing the burden on the rail lines.

With the increase of international exchanges and the growth of foreign trade, China's ocean shipping transport also has developed substantially, To date, China has established business relations with 101 countries and regions and 427 ports.

In summary, during the past 30 years the rational distribution of transportation in China played an important part in developing the economic superiority of the northeast and coastal areas, in exploiting inland areas, in comprehensively utilizing the five modes of transportation (railway, highway, waterway, air and pipeline) to form a nationwide unified transport network, in strengthening national defence and in linking China with the rest of the world.

III. Transport Facilities

The number of locomotives and railway carriages in 1979 were 2.5 times and 5.6 times, respectively, those in 1949. China has designed and built fairly large locomotives and carriages on its own. At present, locomotives of 2,200 tons and over make up 60% of the total number, and large carriages of over 50 tons account for 81.4% of the total. Railway lines laid with ties of over 50 kg. cover 42.4% of the total length of railways, and 91.7% of railway lines have automatic and semi-automatic block systems. An initial renovation was carried out in traction power, with diesel and electric locomotives now accounting for 22.2% of the total. Mechanization of loading and unloading equipment reached more than 40% of the total.

In water transport, the horsepower of river towboats increased 9.7 times during the period 1950-1980, and the loading capacity of barges and self-propelled vessels increased 42.4 times. The proportion of self-propelled vessels in total water traffic volume increased from 68% to 88%. The number of coastal vessels in 1980 increased by 19.5 times over that of 1949. The large and medium-sized ports were basically mechanized for loading and unloading. In highway transport, automobiles for civilian use in 1980 were 46 times greater than the number in the early days of Liberation. The mileage of all-weather roads increased from 42% of the total in the early days of Liberation to 67.5% in 1979.

Table 2. Passenger Traffic Volume (in millions of persons)

Year	TOTAL	Railways[1]	Highways	Water	Air
1949	137	103	18	16	...
1979	2,897	864	1,786	244	2.98
1980	3,418	922	2,228	264	3.43
Increase multiple from 1949 to 1980	24.94	8.95	123.78	16.5	...
Average annual growth rate, 1949-80	10.9%	7.3%	16.8%	9.5%	...

[1] Includes local railways.

Table 3. Freight Traffic Volume (in 1,000 tons)

Year	TOTAL	Railways[1]	Highways	Water	Pipelines	Air
1949	160,970	55,890	79,630	25,430	...	20
1979	2,480,280	1,118,930	815,560	432,290	113,420	80
1980	2,405,060	1,112,790	760,170	426,760	105,250	88.9
Increase multiple from 1949 to 1980	14.94	19.91	9.55	16.78	...	4.45
Average annual growth rate, 1949-80	9.1%	10.1%	7.5%	9.5%	...	4.9%

[1] Includes local railways.

IV. Passenger and Freight Traffic

Since 1949, the volume of both passenger and goods traffic has increased substantially. By 1980, the volume of passenger traffic had grown by 25 times, and that of freight traffic, 15 times.

In 1980, the heavy volume of passenger traffic reached a total of 3,418 million persons, an increase of 18% over 1979. An average of 9.36 million passengers were carried each day (7.94 million passengers per day in 1979). The growth of passenger traffic was due principally to the economic readjustment that created a very brisk market, an increase in peddlers, purchasing agents and salesmen, an increase in passengers visiting relatives and friends, a considerable income rise for workers and peasants and the rapid development of tourist services.

Compared with 1979, the volume of freight traffic was reduced by 3% in 1980. This was because of the continuous reduction in capital construction and in traffic volume related to heavy industry during the readjustment.

Turnover Volume. Compared with 1949, the passenger turnover volume in 1980 increased 15 times and freight turnover, 45 times.

Table 4. Passenger Turnover (in millions of passenger-km.)

Year	TOTAL	Railways	Highways	Water	Air
1949	15,500	13,000	800	1,500	200
1979	196 800	121,600	60,300	11,400	3,500
1980	228,060	138,300	72,900	12,900	3,960
Increase multiple from 1949 to 1980	14.71	10.64	91.13	8.60	19.8
Average annual growth rate 1949-80	9.1%	7.9%	15.6%	7.2%	...

Table 5. Freight Turnover (in millions of ton-km.)

Year	TOTAL	Railways	Highways	Water	Pipelines	Air
1949	25,547	18,400	814	6,312	...	21
1979	1,090,772	559,803	26,826	456,420	47,600	123
1980	1,151,744	571,721	25,506	505,276	49,100	141
Increase multiple from 1949 to 1980	45.08	31.07	31.33	80.05	...	6.71
Average annual growth rate, 1949-80	13.1%	11.7%	11.8%	15.2%	...	6.3%

Table 6. Average Passenger Haulage (in kilometres)

Year	TOTAL	Railways	Highways	Water	Air
1949	113	126	44	97	685
1979	68	142	34	47	1,174
1980	67	151	33	49	1 153

Table 7. Average Freight Haulage (in kilometres)

Year	TOTAL	Railways	Highways	Water*	Pipelines	Air
1949	159	329	10	248	...	848
1979	440	500	33	1,056	420	1,538
1980	479	514	34	1,184	467	1,586

*Note: The tremendously rapid increase of average water haulage was due to the development of ocean transport in recent years, average oceanshipping freight haulage being as much as 8,246 km.

Average Haulage. The average passenger haulage distance travelled was the highest in 1949 but has been reduced every year since. By contrast, the average haulage of freight has increased in distance by 10.3 km. per year.

Changes in Proportions of Travel Modes. Over the past 31 years, the major changes in proportion were as follows:

(1) *Passenger traffic*. Highway passenger traffic volume increased quite rapidly, reaching about two-thirds of total traffic volume; railway and water traffic volume decreased to a certain extent, totalling about one-third. The share of passenger turnover of highway traffic also registered a rapid increase, accounting for 30% or more of the total, whereas that of railways remained at 60% because of the large number of long-distance passengers.

(2) *Freight traffic*. Railway traffic volume increased steadily, amounting to 46% of national traffic volume, while its turnover volume was half of the national turnover. The proportion of inland water traffic volume was reduced, but the water turnover volume increased to 43.9% of the national turnover because of the abrupt rise of ocean-shipping transport.

Table 8. Changes in Proportions of Different Modes of Transport (in %)

	Passenger Traffic Volume					Passenger Turnover Volume				
Year	TOTAL	Rail	Road	Water	Air	TOTAL	Rail	Road	Water	Air
1949	100	75.2	13.2	11.4	0.2	100	83.9	5.1	9.8	1.2
1979	100	29.8	61.7	8.4	0.1	100	61.8	30.6	5.8	1.8
1980	100	27.0	65.2	7.7	0.1	100	60.6	32.0	5.7	1.7

	Freight Traffic Volume						Freight Turnover Volume				
Year	TOTAL	Rail	Road	Water	Pipeline	Air	Total	Rail	Road	Water	Pipeline	Air
1949	100	34.7	49.5	15.8	...	...	100	72.0	3.2	24.7	...	0.1
1979	100	45.1	32.9	17.4	4.6	...	100	51.3	2.5	41.8	4.4	...
1980	100	46.3	31.6	17.7	4.4	...	100	49.6	2.2	43.9	4.3	...

If the result of conversion of passenger and freight traffic is taken into account, the proportions of different modes of transport in the total converted turnover volume are as follows:

in the east, the northeast and the central-south areas has to be conveyed from the north, the northwest and the southwest, involving a great deal of traffic volume over long distances.

Year	Total Turnover	Rail	Road	Water	Pipeline	Air
1949	100	76.5	3.9	19.1	...	0
1979	100	52.9	6.8	36.3	3.7	0
1980	100	51.46	7.13	37.55	3.56	0

Composition of Freight Traffic. China's freight traffic has consisted mainly of energy fuel materials, followed by capital construction materials and mineral and metallurgical materials. The proportion of agricultural products is smaller.

In 1979, the fuel traffic volume accounted for about 40% of the national total. Coal and oil accounted for 43% of railroad traffic volume and 52% of water traffic volume undertaken by the various enterprises directly under the Ministry of Communications.

The reason that energy transport represents such a great share is due to the uneven distribution of energy resources in China. Coal and oil are concentrated in the west and the north. In the ten provinces south of the Changjiang River, only 17.7% of China's coal and 1.4% of its total industrial output value is produced. As a result, coal in the north is shipped to the south, while the coal in the west is shipped to the east; oil in the north is shipped to the south. In other words, coal needed

Port Capacity. The freight-handling capacity of ports also increased rapidly. The capacity of coastal and Changjiang River ports in 1950 was 13.84 million tons (including 8.29 million tons for sea ports and 5.55 million tons for Changjiang River ports). In 1980, the volume handled increased to 306.86 million tons (including 217.31 million tons for sea ports and 89.55 million tons for Changjiang River ports), representing an increase of 22.2 times over 1950. Of the total volume handled, coal, oil and minerals accounted for two-thirds. Of the volume handled by sea ports, materials and products accounted for by foreign trade made up one-third.

V. Transportation Efficiency and Main Economic Indices

A comparison between transport efficiency indices in 1979 and 1980 and those in 1950 is illustrated below as follows:

Indices	Unit	1950	1979	1980
Railway freight-car turnover time	days	3.34	3.00	3.02
Freight-train locomotive, daily output (gross ton-km. per locomotive per day)	10,000 ton-km.	43.4 (1952)	72.3	72.3
Yearly output per ton-ship of shipping enterprises directly under the Ministry of Communications.	ton-km.	29,066 (1952)	39,447	41,401
Ship layover time at major coastal ports	days	3.0 (3.1 in 1957)		2.9
Layover time at major coastal ports for foreign vessels	days	4.0	8.2	7.7
Yearly trucking output of highway transport enterprises (per ton-car)	ton-km.	6,424	43,600	39,382

In 1980, all transport departments stressed improvements in operations and management. Railways placed emphasis on organizing rail operations strictly according to the train working diagramme, on strengthening planned and smooth flow of transport, on improving transport priorities and on securing transport safety. The average speed of freight trains rose to 28.7 km./hr., somewhat higher than in 1979. The average layover time for a single freight operation came to 13.1 hours, or 0.2 hours less than in 1979. The punctuality rate of passenger and freight trains reached 94.2% and 91.7%, respectively, an increase of 1.3% and 2.3% over 1979.

Ship layover time at major coastal ports in 1980 was 2.9 days, 0.2 days less than in 1979; the average layover time for foreign vessels was 7.7 days, or 0.5 days less than in 1979.

Due to the great demand for vehicles by various enterprises and institutions not normally involved in mass transport, the transport departments are short of materials. Consequently, the yearly road transport output (ton-km./ton-car) in 1980 was reduced by 9.7% from 1979.

VI. Coordinated Transport and Container Traffic

Shortly after the founding of New China, some transport agencies and shipping offices were established to handle goods consignments, transfers and deliveries for clients. In recent years, with the development of the national economy, coordinated transport has improved significantly. In 1980, more than 48 million tons of materials and products were brought into the national railway-waterway coordinated transport plan, involving roughly 4% of total rail traffic volume and 40% of total water transport volume undertaken by the transport enterprises directly under the Ministry of Communications. Most railway stations handled the railway-waterway trunk line coordinated transport services. A total of 97 ports handled land-water coordinated transport services, and 227 ports handled river-sea coordinated transport services.

In April 1980, the government ratified the Yangquan-Qingdao-Shanghai water-land coordinated transport programme for coal, which was carried out quite well. In recent years, various types of coordinated transport lines have been opened within and between various provinces and cities. Some of the provinces or cities have even promulgated rules and regulations for coordinated transport. The Shanghai-Dalian-Northeast land-water coordinated transport line for general merchandise and foodstuffs has been operating for more than 10 years, saving 46 million yuan of distribution costs for the commercial departments. Coordinated transport services for passengers, which is mainly booked through tickets, developed to some extent in 1980.

There was some development in container transport in 1980, when 78,700 containers were available throughout the country, an increase of 25% over 1979. A total of 178 railway stations, as well as major ports on the seacoast and along the Changjiang River, were equipped to handle container transport. The container traffic volume in 1980 was 2.03 million tons, an increase of 108% over 1979. Domestic waterway container transport volume amounted to 22,500 tons, an increase of 180%. International container traffic (handled in the five major ports of Shanghai, Tianjin, Qingdao, Huangpu and Dalian) totalled 64,286 containers, a 96% increase. The trucking departments handled 1.05 million containers of "door-to-door" conveyance. In air transport, a small-sized container of 1.5 tons was put on trial use for domestic and international air routes.

VII. Urban Transport

A key problem in urban transport concerns passenger traffic. Among China's 216 cities, 202 are now provided with public transport facilities. The public transport routes total 52,000 km.; 32,000 vehicles, including 26,000 buses, are in use. Since the 1960's there has been a rapid growth of trolley buses, now totalling 3,300 in 24 large and medium-sized cities. Trams (streetcars) are being gradually eliminated, and at present only 310 trams are operating in four cities in the northeast. Some cities located along rivers provide ferry passenger transport services. Thirty-two cities have organized taxi services. In 1980, urban public, transport enterprises handled a traffic volume of 17,800 million passengers.

In addition to the development of public transport, there has been rapid growth in other motorized vehicles. For example, Beijing now has 170,000 vehicles for civilian use (including trucks and buses). In addition, the number of bicycles has increased sharply; there are more than 3 million in Beijing and 2 million in Tianjin.

With the rapid development of socialist construction since Liberation, and the lax control of population growth, the urban population has expanded sharply. At present, urban transport has become a critical problem in urban construction and management for two reasons: (1) existing buses and cars are unable to cope with the increasing demand due to the rapid growth of passenger traffic, so that the buses are generally overcrowded and seriously overloaded, thus affecting the transport order especially during rush hours; and (2) most of the existing urban roads, except a few that were newly built according to a planned design, are narrow and in poor condition. Except for a few in Beijing, the roads are intersected by grade crossings. All this results in low traffic capacity, slow speed and frequent accidents. This problem can be solved only through the coordination of all departments concerned and an integrated plan. It will be necessary to redesign urban trunk roads, improve road surface quality, widen the old roads, reconstruct the road crossings, strengthen transport management and improve the traffic control system.

China has built its first subway in Beijing. The first phase of the project is 23 km. long, passing through 17 stations. The whole line is provided with automatic signal and centralized traffic control systems. The trains travel at 80 km./hr., and the minimum interval between trains is 1.5 minutes at peak hours. The completed section was officially opened to traffic in 1973. In 1980, subway passenger volume reached 53.2 million. The second phase of the project — the first round-the-city subway line — is now under construction.

VIII. Three Outstanding Problems

Although China has achieved great successes in transportation in the past 31 years, transport facilities are still inadequate to meet the demands of the national economy. This is a major weakness, clearly manifested in the following three problems:

(1) *Insufficient transport capacity in major railway sections.* In the last 31 years, railway goods traffic turnover volume increased 31 times, but railway mileage increased only 2.36 times, locomotives 2.5 times and railway cars 5.7 times. Thus, the growth of transport capacity lags far behind that of traffic volume. On the major trunk lines at present, more than 10 "limited sections" have been formed, with a carrying capacity capable of meeting only 50-70% of total demand.

The shortage of railway capacity resulted principally from inadequate investment for a certain period of time and the less than rational distribution of existing investments. Too much emphasis was put on the construction of new inland lines to the neglect of the reconstruction of old lines in coastal areas. The population in the northeast and coastal areas represents 77% of China's total population, and the railway goods traffic volume in those areas amounts to 80% of the national total. Investment in these old lines, however, accounted for only 20.2% of total investment in 1950-1978 (reduced to 10% in the past ten years or so), which caused the old coastal lines to become even more insufficient than before. Furthermore, the economic results of the investment were far from satisfactory. The construction costs of new railways increased from 500,000-600,000 yuan per km. in the 1950's to 2 million yuan. Construction management in the 1980's was inadequate, with considerable waste.

The insufficiency of transport capacity is strikingly evident in coal transportation. Railways are the principal means of transporting coal, moving 67% of the country's total coal output. In recent years the supply of coal has been insufficient, particularly in the east, northeast and central-south areas, thus hampering, to a certain extent, the development of production.

In 1980, the main effort in railroad construction was focused on the reconstruction of some heavy traffic sections of existing lines; the investment ratio of the old lines to the newly built lines was 1.6:1. New double-track lines increased by 151.6 km., and electrified lines by 642 km., helping to speed up coal transportation. In 1980, the coal traffic volume in Shanxi Province was more than 70 million tons, 10 million tons higher than in 1979, yet still falling short of demand. The gap in 1981 was still larger. In the near future, railway construction will continue to stress coal transport by strengthening renovation of the "limited sections" — i.e., building double-track lines, electrifying existing lines, etc. At the same time, more locomotives and railway cars must be built and the organization of transportation must be improved.

2. *Shortage of berths in major coastal ports.* The overstocking of cargoes and the length of ship detention in harbours are serious problems, resulting mainly from the fact that China has long remained a "closed-door" country, ignoring harbour construction and suffering from careless planning and poor management. Over the past 31 years, the handling capacity of the ports increased 26.2 times, but the number of coastal wharves only doubled while deep-water berths increased by about 4 times. At present, the handling capacity per berth in China's major ports is the largest in the world, and total volume handled by the 15 major ports exceeds the approved handling capacity by 16%. However, port-handling is still slow. In 1979, the layover time for foreign ships in Chinese ports was as long as 8.2 days, and in 1980, 7.7 days. In the port of Shanghai there are often nearly 100 foreign ships waiting for berths, sometimes for weeks. In 1980, the ship demurrage losses for all the major ports were estimated to be as high as U.S.$200 million.

3. *Inadequacy in passenger carrying capacity.* In the past 31 years, China's passenger traffic volume increased 25 times and passenger turnover volume, 15 times. Especially since the second half of 1980, both water and land traffic volume throughout the country has increased rapidly. However, the number of railway passenger coaches has increased only about 4 times, ship passenger seats and berths only about 3 times and highway buses only 13 times, obviously far short of current needs. The results have been severe crowding in buses and ships, overcrowding in harbours and stations, great disorder and problems in booking tickets, getting on board, dining and lodging, public hygiene and security.

The capacity of the 41 major railway stations throughout the country has already been saturated, and it is too difficult for the 25 trunk lines to add more passenger trains. In 1980, the number of railroad passenger coaches increased by 1,000 and highway buses by 4,000, but the expanded capacity is still too small to alleviate the problem. Although a number of emergency measures have been taken, such as using boxcars for makeshift passenger cars, refitting some ships for passengers and scheduling extra buses and night-shift buses, the growing demand has not been met.

IX. Problems and Prospects

During the readjustment of the national economy, transportation remains a weak link, requiring rapid development so that it can catch up with the pace of development of the overall economy. Meanwhile, it is necessary to regulate various proportional relationships between different modes of transportation, as well as between different departments within each mode of transportation, and to form an efficient and mutually coordinated comprehensive transport system. Such a system would be capable of not only meeting current transport demands but also maintaining enough reserve capacity to place transportation in the vanguard of the national economy. The following are important steps that should be taken to strengthen transportation in China:

1. *Speed up construction to expand transport capacity.* China's railway freight traffic volume reached 11.99 million tons in 1980, ranking second in the world. The average handling volume of each berth at coastal harbours was the highest in the world. Therefore, tapping the potential of existing facilities will not be enough; the way to solve the above-mentioned problem is to create new capacity.

The construction period for new railways and ports is quite long. Construction of new lines, old lines and berth buildings often requires 3-5 years. Consequently, such projects should be undertaken as early as possible under a unified plan.

The key investments in the near future will be directed to strengthening the technical renovation of railway "limited sections" and to constructing more port berths and passenger traffic facilities. In view of China's limited financial and material capabilities, it is not advisable to proceed on a very large scale; investments should be focused on places where the need is urgent. Efficiency in construction should be strongly emphasized; unnecessary or duplicate construction should be avoided at all costs. Attention must be paid to integrating the construction of land, water, air and pipeline transport, as well as that of vehicles, vessels, harbours and stations so as to achieve a unified, comprehensive productive force.

2. *Readjust the structure of transportation and exploit the advantages of different modes of transportation to allow more comprehensive utilization.* For medium- and long-distance transport of domestic goods in large amounts within China, railways are most advantageous because of their relatively low cost, low energy consumption and high speed. However, the building of railways involves sizeable investments, long construction periods and great difficulties.

China has over 5,800 natural rivers, with a total length of more than 430,000 km., and more than 18,000 km. of coastline. It is thus in a good position to make use of water transportation. Water transportation is low in cost and energy consumption. But for various reasons, the superiority of China's water transportation has not been brought into full play; on the contrary, the navigable distance on inland rivers in 1979 was a third less than in 1962. At present, the density of freight traffic on China's inland rivers is far less than that in the developed countries. There is a considerable potential to be tapped.

Urgently needed at the moment are measures that will exploit the advantages of the Changjiang River, the Zhujiang River, the Grand Canal and offshore waters. In general, all goods suitable for water transport should be transported by water as often as possible. For example, part of the freight flow of the Beijing-Guangzhou and the Tianjin-Shanghai railway lines could be diverted to sea transport; the Huaihe River and the Grand Canal are able to bear part of the coal transport from Yanzhou in Shandong Province and Xuzhou in Jiangsu Province; and the Xinjiang River can be dredged to open a new channel for coal transport from Guangdong and Guangxi provinces.

At present, the short-distance freight traffic volume borne by railways is too large. According to statistics, freight traffic volume with hauls shorter than 100 km. accounts for 23% of the total, and with hauls shorter than 50 km., 14%. Such short-distance traffic greatly increases the burden on various railways and station operations and raises transport costs.

In order to achieve comprehensive utilization, part of the short-distance freight traffic should be transferred to waterways and highways. Both highways and local waterways now have surplus transport capacity. If a rational division of labour can be ensured between railways, on the one hand, and highways and waterways, on the other, both types of transport will benefit. For this purpose, it is necessary to draw up a unified plan, readjust a number of policies, improve highway and local waterway transport conditions and, in particular, make some necessary changes in freight traffic.

At present, the short-distance freight rate on railways is 1/17 as much as on highways, lower than the actual cost. Provided that the difference between the two freight rates can be reduced, and that highway transport can provide convenient door-to-door service (generally, transhipment has to be done at railway terminals), the highways can surely absorb part of the flow of railway freight.

Local railways — those that are built, managed and used by local authorities — also play an important role. Local railways began operating in 1958, and their total operating trackage at present is 3,381 km. The construction cost of local railways is one-sixth that of national railroads, their average transport cost being 0.065-0.07 yuan per ton-km. More flexible than the national railways, local railways can make use of old rails and other equipment discarded by the national railways. If conditions permit, it is advisable to build more local railways.

Pipeline transportation has quite a bright future. Besides extending crude oil pipelines, we must make certain that refined oil pipelines also grow appropriately.

Civil aviation, too, must steadily expand so as to handle more long-distance passenger traffic.

3. *Improve management and tap the potential of existing facilities*. The state-run transport enterprises which are the mainstay for fulfillment of current transport tasks, now possess fixed assets of 80,000 million yuan. In order to use and manage these enterprises more effectively, it is necessary to strengthen our political and ideological work, study scientific methods of production management and research proper technical policies. Problems in the existing management system have to be solved step by step during the readjustment of the national economy.

The country has a number of other transport enterprises — e.g., automobile, animal-drawn cart and wooden sailing-boat enterprises — as well as loading and unloading organizations. All these enterprises and organizations are collectively owned. These collectively owned transport enterprises must be effectively utilized and made to operate as a supplementary force of the national transport enterprises. The collectively owned transport enterprises will require assistance in such problems as obtaining funds and fuel supplies.

27. CHINA'S RAILWAY TRANSPORTATION
By the General Office,
Ministry of Railways

Since the founding of the People's Republic, China's railway transportation has developed considerably. Features of old China's railways, such as inadequate stocks of poor-quality, outdated technical equipment and uneven distribution of rolling stock, have begun to change.

From 1949 to 1979, the country's railway routes increased from 22,000 km. to over 51,000 km., an increase of 2.4 times. In old China, there were no railways in six provinces — Tibet, Xinjiang, Qinghai, Ningxia, Sichuan and Fujian. Now, with the exception of Tibet, all provinces and autonomous regions are linked by railways.

The layout of the railway network has also changed. In 1950, railway lines west of the Beijing-Guangzhou Railway made up 19.5% of the total lines in the country. In 1979, that figure rose to 45.3%. Thus, the earlier concentration of railways in the northeast and eastern coastal areas has undergone a change. Railway technical equipment has also been improved. Double tracks have been expanded from 866 km. to 8,221 km., an increase of 9.5 times. The construction of electrified lines, starting from scratch, reached 1,301 km. by 1979. Lines equipped with automatic block systems increased from over 100 km. to nearly 6,000 km. Between 1949 and 1979, the number of locomotives increased by 2.5 times, while passenger cars and wagons increased by 3.4 times and 5.7 times, respectively.

Since 1949, the railway industry has developed from a system that was capable only of repairs to one basically equipped with complete facilities capable of repairing and manufacturing in all phases. Today, the railway industry is able not only to manufacture steam locomotives, general passenger cars, wagons and special railway equipment, but also to mass-produce diesel locomotives, electric locomotives, large freight cars and luxury passenger cars for domestic use as well as for export.

Both passenger traffic and freight traffic have increased continuously. Passenger traffic rose from 102.97 million per-passenger/trips in 1949 to 856.11 million in 1979, an increase of over 8 times. Freight traffic rose from 55.89 million tons in 1949 to 1,090 million tons in 1979, an increase of 19.7 times. Railways handle more passenger and freight traffic than any other means of transportation in the country. They have made significant contributions to economic construction, national defence and the enhancement of the people's livelihood.

In 1980, the railways made remarkable achievements in increasing transport, industrial production and capital construction through im-

Table 1. Development of Railway Transportation in China, 1949-79

Item	Unit	1949	1979	% Increase, 1949-79
Route length	km.	21,989	51,500	134.3
Passengers carried	100,000 passengers	10,297	85,611	731.4
Passenger-km.	100,000,000 passenger-km.	130	1,214	833.9
Goods transported	10,000 tons	5,589	109,495	1,859.1
Freight turnover	100,000,000 ton-km.	184	5,588	2,937.0
Average number of standard gauge cars loaded per day	freight car	5,762	62,789	989.7

plementing the policy of readjustment, restructuring, consolidation and improvement.

I. Transport of Passengers and Freight

In 1980, railway passenger traffic throughout the country exceeded 910 million per-passenger/trips, 56.35 million more than in 1979. The rate of increase was 6.6%, the highest on record. Passenger-kilometres totalled 138,300 million, an increase of 13.7% over 1979. Because of the increased passenger flow, railway departments raised the capacity of passenger traffic as much as possible by running more trains and putting more cars on each run.

To accommodate the large increases in passenger flow during holidays and festivals — especially during Spring Festival — regular trains are supplemented by special passenger trains. Around Spring Festival time, over 300 special passenger trains are placed in operation throughout the country each day.

At present, Beijing is connected by train to all provinces, municipalities directly under the central government and autonomous regions, except for Tibet. Many passenger trains run by or through such large cities as Shanghai, Tianjin, Guangzhou, Shenyang, Harbin, Wuhan and Zhengzhou every day, forming a nationwide passenger traffic network with Beijing as the centre. The network serves the domestic population as well as the development of tourism.

With the large increase in passengers, the passenger traffic staff has continuously upgraded its services. Services such as booking tickets by telephone, advance booking and door-to-door service are now provided at railways stations in all China's large cities. Furthermore, improvements have been made in food service, in the procedures for checking luggage and parcels and in sanitation.

At present, diesel or electric locomotives are used to haul passenger trains running on trunk lines from Beijing to Guangzhou, Beijing to Shanghai, Beijing to Shenyang, Harbin to Dalian, Shanghai to Hangzhou and Baoji to Chengdu. This modern equipment has made train travel more comfortable, shortened travel time and speeded up the turnaround of cars. Express trains run between Beijing and Shanghai in 18 hours, 58 minutes — an average speed of 77 km./hr. Express trains running between Beijing and Shenyang have shortened the travel time to 8 hours, 55 minutes — an average speed of 94 km./hr. (the highest speed in the whole system). Some trains running between Guangzhou and Shenzhen and between Beijing and Shanghai have been equipped with air conditioning.

Freight Traffic. In 1980, railway freight traffic reached 1,080 million tons, a decrease of 0.8% compared with the all-time record of 1979. The decline was mainly due to the reduction of capital construction, lower consumption of energy and raw materials and changes in the composition of freight traffic following the readjustment in the national economy. The volume of ores and mineral construction materials transported in 1980 was less than that in 1979, but coal transport set a record, increasing by 0.4% over 1979. As a result of improved conditions for coal transport, the railways can handle the entire annual production of many mines as well as over 800,000 tons of backlog.

The volumes of cement and timber transported in 1980 increased by 8.1% and 7.2%, respectively, compared with 1979. In line with the readjustment of the national economy, railway departments have given priority to all phases of shipment of light industrial products, textiles and agricultural products. The total traffic volume in 1980 increased by 7.8% compared with that in 1979. In 1980, because of the increase in the proportion of long-distance freight traffic, the overall volume of freight traffic declined; but the number of freight ton-kilometres increased by 2.1% over 1979, reaching a total of 571,000 million.

In 1980, there were 4,630 stations and 11,264 pieces of loading and unloading equipment in the railway system. Of the 4,630 stations, 59% had freight sidings and ramps and 70% had warehouses. Mechanized loading and unloading accounted for 46% of the annual volume. Container traffic has also developed. In 1980, over 75,000 containers were handled by 178 stations. Container traffic in that year exceeded 2.035 million tons — twice as much as that of 1979 and 10% of the total part-load traffic.

Indexes Fulfilled. With the change in composition in freight traffic, long-distance hauls of goods increased and the work of coordinating stations over some districts also increased. Although the change brought more difficulties, the majority of employees in the railway departments made every effort to increase efficiency. They fulfilled not only various indexes of quantity for the year but also various technical and economic indexes with better results.

The turnaround time of freight cars was 3.02 days, meeting the planned requirement. Average time of detention of local cars in one operation was 13.1 hours, 0.2 hours less than that in 1979. Average transit time per car was 3.6 hours, the same as in 1979. The average speed of freight trains reached 28.7 km./hr., 0.1 km./hr. faster than that in 1979. Freight locomotive-kilometres

Table 2. Main Goods Transported by Rail in 1980

Item	1980 (10,000 tons)	% of plan	% Increase/Decrease over 1979
Total volume	108,584	106.5	− 0.8
Coal	41,478	102.7	+ 0.4
Petroleum	5,563	105.0	− 6.2
Smelting materials	19,357	103.0	− 3.4
Mineral construction materials	15,843	108.8	− 4.9
Cement	2,363	110.9	+ 1.1
Timber	4,241	114.6	+ 7.2
Textiles & light industrial products supporting agriculture	13,466		+ 7.8
Chemical industrial products	3,321		+ 10.1
Industrial machinery	541		− 17.0

per locomotive day reached 415 km., 3 km. more than in 1979. Daily locomotive output reached 723,000 ton-kilometres. Punctuality of departing passenger trains was 99.3%, and of running trains, 94.2% — an increase of 0.2% and 1.3%, respectively, over 1979. Punctuality of departing freight trains was 93.6%, and of running freight trains, 91.7% — an increase of 0.8% and 2.3%, respectively, over 1979.

Safety in the whole system was further improved in 1980. Serious and major accidents were reduced by 38.6% compared with 1979. The number of accidents during the year was at the lowest since 1965. Accidents involving freight traffic were reduced by 19.3% compared with 1979. Compensation for every 10,000 yuan of freight traffic revenue was reduced by 50.9% compared with 1979.

Fuel Savings. In 1980, employees in locomotives departments saw to it that trains ran safely and on schedule, hauling more and running faster. They also further reduced the consumption of coal and fuel in locomotives. The consumption of coal in steam locomotives for every 10,000 ton-km. was 106.4 kg. in 1980, 3.1 kg. less than in 1979. Coal conservation was carried out in 80% of the steam locomotives throughout the system.

The consumption of fuel in diesel locomotives for every 10,000 ton-km. was 35 kg., 0.7 kg. less than in 1979. Fuel conservation was achieved in 40 diesel locomotive depots throughout the system. The consumption of power in electric locomotives for every 10,000 ton-km. was 129.8 kwh., 12.2 kwh. lower than targeted in the plan. Total savings of power in the year exceeded 20 million kwh. Power conservation was practiced in all electric locomotive depots.

Maintenance. In 1980, 2,581 km. of rails were replaced, marking a new high in rail replacement. Intermediate maintenance of track covered 3,175 km. Replacement of reinforced concrete sleepers totalled 3.9 million. Since Chinese railways started to produce and lay concrete sleepers in 1956, 50 million sleepers have been produced and laid (including concrete sleepers with prestressed wire Model 69, produced by the Fengtai Bridge Factory, which received a silver medal from the state in 1980). In 1980, 749 km. of jointless track were laid, 111 km. more than in 1979. Since Chinese railways laid the first jointless track in 1957, a total of 7,900 km. has been installed so far.

Major maintenance and technical reforms were carried out in 1980 on automatic block systems in the districts — namely, Zhumadian-Guangshui, Zhengzhou-Anyang, Jinzhou-Masanjia and Harbin-Suihua — and on electric centralized interlocking systems in 20 stations such as Fengtai Western, Tangshan and Nanxiang, as well as in three districts, including Xi'an-Baoji. A total of 658 km. of long-distance cable was laid and 657 km. of overhead open lines were given major maintenance.

In 1980, cab signals and automatic alarm devices were installed on 1,288 locomotives, 44 of which were also equipped with automatic stop devices. In addition, 974 stations received ground equipment for alarm devices.

Table 3. Main Indexes of Railway Transport in 1980

Item	Unit	1980	% of plan fulfilled	Increase/Decrease over 1979
Passengers carried	100,000 persons	91,246	108.6	+ 6.6
Passenger-km.	100 million passenger-km.	1,380		+ 13.7
Goods transported	10,000 tons	108,584	106.5	− 0.8
Freight turnover	100 million ton-km.	5,707		+ 2.1
Average daily car loading	freight car	61,298	104.2	− 2.4
Wagon static load	ton	48.0	102.1	+ 1.3
Turnaround time of wagon	day	3.02	100.0	+ 0.02 day
Travel speed	km./hr.	28.7		+ 0.1 km.
Locomotive-km. per locomotive day	km.	415	101.7	+ 0.7
Punctuality of departing passenger trains	%	99.3		+ 0.2
Punctuality of running passenger trains	%	94.2		+ 1.3
Punctuality of departing freight trains	%	93.6		+ 0.8
Punctuality of running freight trains	%	91.7		+ 2.3

II. Railway Capital Construction

The focus of railway capital construction in 1980 was on the technical transformation of existing railway lines; investment for technical transformation was over 40% of total investment in railway capital construction. A total of 24 large and medium-sized projects required technical transformation during the year. The main object of technical transformation was to facilitate transport of coal out of Shanxi Province and to increase the passenger carrying capacity of trains serving the coastal areas, harbours, and the southwest and northwest regions. New double tracks were constructed in the eastern section of the Lianyungang-Lanzhou Railway, the Jinan-Qingdao Railway, the Shijiazhuang-Dezhou Railway, the Tainjin-Nanjing Railway, the western section of the Beijing-Baotou Railway and the southern section of the Beijing-Guangzhou Railway. Electrification was carried out on the Shijiazhuang-Taiyuan Railway, the Xiangfan-Chongqing Railway, the western section of the Lianyungang-Lanzhou Railway and the eastern section of the Beijing-Baotou Railway. Also in 1980, the Beijing and Zhengzhou junction terminals were expanded, and 10 projects involving technical renovation of existing operating lines were completely or individually begun, accounting for 41.7% of the projects under construction. Investments made in 1980 achieved better results than at any time in the recent past.

The amount of capital construction work done in 1980 included: 33.08 million cu. m. of earth and stone work on subgrade; 17,000 m. of tunnels; 17,000 m. of major and medium-sized bridges; 277 km. of track laid on newly constructed lines; 386 km. of newly built double track; 502 km. of sidings in stations; and 3.45

million sq. m. of floor space in buildings. Placed in operation were 1,007.9 km. of new new lines, 158.4 km. of double tracks and 642.6 km. of electrified railway. The electrified lines placed in operation were as follows::

(1) *The Xiangfan-Ankang (eastern) section of the Xiangfan-Chongqing Railway.* The third line to be electrified in China, it has a total length of 372 km. Construction began in 1975 and was completed in October 1980. The terrain over which the line is laid is complicated; nearly half of the line runs through tunnels or over bridges. The carrying capacity of the line was greatly increased after electrification.

(2) *The Shijiazhuang-Yangquan section of the Shijiazhuang-Taiyuan Railway.* The first electrified double-track line in China, it has a total length of 119 km. Electrification, begun in 1974 and completed in September 1980, more than doubled the line's carrying capacity, increasing its capacity for transporting coal out of Shanxi Province.

(3) *The Baoji-Tianshui section of the Lianyungang-Lanzhou Railway.* Electrification of this key, 151.6-km. section began in January 1977 and was completed in December 1980.

Double-track construction in 1980 included: the 187.5 km. Zhengzhou-Xuzhou section of the Lianyungang-Lanzhou Railway (now in operation); a 123.8 km. stretch of the Datong-Baotou (northern) section of the Beijing-Baotou Railway; part of the Shijiazhuang-Dezhou line (126.5 km. of double tracks laid, of which 100.8 km. have been placed in operation); and 74.9 km. of the Jinan-Qingdao Railway.

Also in 1980, preparation for construction of bridges and tunnels on the southern double-track section of the Beijing-Guangzhou Railway was underway. In addition, parts of the renovation projects at the Zhengzhou, Beijing and Jinan junction terminals were completed and put into operation.

III. Locomotive and Rolling Stock Repair and Manufacturing

In 1980, factories of the railway locomotive and rolling stock industry repaired and manufactured more locomotives, passenger cars, freight cars and cranes than were called for in the plan, thus amply meeting the needs of railway transport. The output of new steam locomotives, passenger cars and the output of repaired freight cars increased by 10%, 17.1% and 3%, respectively, in comparison with 1979, while the output of new electric locomotives remained the same as that of 1979. The gross industrial output value in 1980 was 1,600 million yuan. Above and beyond their fulfillment of the state plan, all factories undertook to repair and manufacture locomotives and rolling stock for enterprises other than the railways. The quality of products in 1980 was higher than in 1979 while production costs were lower.

The 25.5-m. air-conditioned coaches with soft reclining seats produced by the Sifang Rolling Stock Factory have been used on express passenger trains running between Guangzhou and Kowloon and between Beijing and Shanghai. The coach is safe, comfortable and attractive and has a maximum speed of 160 km./hr. Inside are 68 revolving seats with backs that can be inclined to three different positions. Temperature inside the coach is maintained at 24°C to 28°C in summer and 18°C in winter.

The Wuchang Rolling Stock Factory began mass production of B19 mechanical refrigerator units in 1980. Each refrigerated train set is composed of five cars, of which four are for freight and one is for power generation and for the train crew. The tare weight of each freight car is 39 tons, and the loading capacity is 40 tons. Each car performs five functions: refrigerating, heating, thawing frost, maintaining constant temperature and ventilating. The cars can be controlled centrally or individually. When the outside temperature is 40°C, the temperature inside an empty car can be brought as low as −18°C. When the outside temperature is −45°C, the temperature inside the car can, with the help of an electric heater, be maintained at 15°C.

Among the high-quality products turned out by the factories are: the exciter manufactured by the Yongji Factory, the 500 A heavy-duty silicon cells produced by the Dalian Factory, the hydraulic torque converter produced by the Sifang Factory and the 25.5-m. dining car produced by the Puzhen Factory.

IV. Railway Science and Technology

With the implementation of the party's policy on intellectuals, the country's scientific and technical personnel have been reactivated and scientific and technical work related to the railways has speeded up. In 1980, the Ministry of Railways appraised 43 important scientific and technical achievements and awarded prizes for excellence to 32 of them. Two other achievements received the state's 1980 award for outstanding inventions.

Table 4. Repair and Manufacture of Locomotives and Rolling Stock in 1980

	Item	Units produced in 1980	% of plan
Repair	Steam locomotives	2948	101.7
	Diesel locomotives	290	105.1
	Coaches	2425	100.4
	Freight cars	42951	101.0
	Cranes	347	103.3
Manufacture	Steam locomotives	342	105.2
	Diesel locomotives	130	108.3
	Electric locomotives	40	100.0
	Coaches	1002	100.2
	Freight cars	10571	105.7
	Cranes	57	114.0

Major achievements in scientific research in 1980 were as follows:

(1) Heavy duty test bench for diesel locomotive jointly developed by the Dalian Diesel Locomotive Research Department, the Dalian Rolling Stock Factory, the Beijing February 7th Locomotive Factory and the Zhuzhou Electric Locomotive Factory. Inspection, measuring and data processing are done by computers. The automation is quite high and the functions are relatively complete. The adoption of computers for inspecting, measuring and data processing enables the device to test mechanical, thermomechanical and braking capacities of various diesel locomotives between 1,000 and 1,670 mm. track gauge at speeds of 0 to 200 km./hr. and to simulate their performances. It has provided an important means of testing for improved performance and quality of diesel locomotives in China, and was awarded second prize for scientific research results by the ministry.

(2) The Qiqihar Rolling Stock Factory succeeded in developing the QNY1002 diesel rail crane with a lifting capacity of 100 tons. Its advantage is that it can start faster than steam cranes, an important factor in rescue operations. It is highly regarded by users.

(3) Spring fastenings for concrete sleepers and prestressed concrete switch sleepers were developed and trial-produced by the bridge and sleeper factories and related design and scientific research departments, and then were appraised and placed in mass production.

(4) The Communication and Signalling Company studied the command system of subway train operations and the automatic control system for train operations. The Scientific Research Institute of the Ministry of Railways and other departments studied the JP2 approach continuous cab signal, the ZTL-1 locomotive automatic stop device and the DY-1 remote-controlled signal for large stations.

All of this equipment played a role in improving transport organization, raising transport efficiency, ensuring the safety of train operations and improving working conditions.

V. Railway Organization

By the end of 1980, the whole railway system was divided into 20 railway administrations, namely: Qiqihar, Harbin, Jilin, Shenyang, Jinzhou, Beijing, Huhehot, Taiyuan, Zhengzhou, Wuhan, Jinan, Shanghai, Nanchang, Guangzhou, Liuzhou, Chengdu, Xi'an, Lanzhou, Urumqi and Kunming. Under each railway administration, railway sub-administrations or offices have been established according to the volume of transport and track conditions. There are a total of 60 railway sub-adminsitrations and 3 offices throughout the system. Each railway administration has established several professional districts or depots in accordance with the requirements of transport. By the end of 1980 there were 167 locomotive depots, 116 vehicle depots, 235 engineering districts, 176 signalling and communications districts and 65 train crew districts.

The following are other main areas of railway organization:

(1) *Industry.* There are 68 factories directly subordinated to the railway system, including 33 locomotive, rolling stock, machinery and electric machinery factories; 10 bridge and sleeper factories, 4 engineering and freight-handling machinery factories; 9 signalling, communication and electrical apparatus factories; 8 timber preservation factories; and 4 permanent route materials and spare parts factories. All these factories undertake the repair and manufacturing of locomotives, rolling stock and various equipment for the entire railway system.

(2) *Capital construction.* There are nine engineering and construction bureaus: the First, Second, Third, Fourth and Fifth Construction Bureaus, the Plant Engineering Bureau, the Electrification and Automation Engineering Bureau, the Tunnelling Bureau and the Major Bridge Engineering Bureau. In addition, there are five design institutes: the First, Second, Third and Fourth Survey and Design Institutes and the Specialized Design Institute. These engineering and construction bureaus and design institutes undertake the design and construction of railways. Seven material procurement and supply divisions are in charge of supplying materials for transport, industry and construction.

(3) *Research work.* There are eight research/planning institutes or departments: the Scientific Research Institute of the Ministry of Railways, the Railway Planning Institute, the Dalian Diesel Locomotive Research Department, the Sifang Rolling Stock Research Department, the Qishuyan Locomotive and Rolling Stock Technology Research Department, the Zhuzhou Electric Locomotive Research Department, the Labour Hygiene Research Department and the Wuhan Engineering Machines Research Department.

(4) *Education.* There are eight universities or institutes: Northern Jiaotong University, Southwest Jiaotong University, the Shanghai Railway Institute, the Dalian Railway Institute, the Lanzhou Railway Institute, the Changsha Railway Institute, the Nanjing Railway Medical Institute and the Shanghai Railway Medical Institute. Eastern China Jiaotong University, Suzhou Railway Teachers' College and Xi'an Railway Teachers' College are under construction.

There are also 41 secondary technical schools, 32 professional workers' schools and 1,527 railway middle and primary schools subordinated to the railways.

VI. Challenges Facing China's Railways

China has a vast territory and rich resources. But because the distribution of resources is uneven, the distribution of factories is also uneven, most factories being located in the coastal areas. The extraction industries are usually far away from the processing industries. Civil aviation and highway transport are comparatively weak. For these reasons, passenger traffic and long-distance transport of bulk goods are undertaken mainly by railway. Therefore, railway transport is in the vanguard of the socialist modernization of China. At present, railway lines in China are still few in number, and technical equipment is backward and unevenly distributed. In order to meet the requirements for the Four Modernizations, railways in China must develop substantially.

The carrying capacity of existing rail lines in areas along the coast is strained, and the main trunk lines are overloaded. This is the main problem in railway transport. In the future, most of railway freight traffic will continue to be concentrated in areas along the coast and in the northeast region. Hence, efforts must be focused on improving existing lines and the appropriate construction of new lines.

Expansion of Capacity. In the short term, the expansion of carrying capacity depends primarily on tapping potential and upgrading efficiency. In the long term, the basic way to increase carrying capacity is to build new lines and strengthen technical transformation of existing lines. This requires funds and time. Therefore, to ease the current shortages in transport, we need to mobilize the masses, tap the potential of existing lines and raise the carrying capacity.

We also need to strengthen the organization of transport, implement transport schedules and increase the proportion of night operations. In remote areas and districts, it is imperative that we exploit existing capacities to the full so as to meet the transport requirements of various fields. We must make use of existing railways such as the Shacheng-Tongliao, Xindian-Tai'an, Jiaozuo-Zhicheng, Zhicheng-Liuzhou, Zhuzhou-Guiyang, Goubangzi-Haicheng and Beijing-Yuanping lines and organize traffic patterns so as to ease the strain on the Beijing-Guangzhou, Tianjin-Nanjing, Beijing-Shenyang, Jinan-Qingdao and Lianyungang-Lanzhou lines.

As for railway tractive power in China, steam locomotives are, and will be for a comparatively long period, the main force of transport. While we tap the full potential of steam locomotives, we must also vigorously develop electric and diesel locomotives.

In the area of railway technical equipment, it is imperative to modernize gradually such equipment as coaches, freight cars, track, bridges, communications and signalling, to mechanize loading, unloading, track maintenance and rolling stock repair and construction, and to develop automation in train control and operations management. Expanding carrying capacity, ensuring safety and improving working conditions should be considered primary goals in the current phase of railway development.

Necessary Steps. At present, passenger traffic is growing continuously. Many passenger trains are overloaded. It is necessary to achieve a balance between passenger and freight traffic, increase the number of passenger trains as much as possible in districts with heavy traffic, increase investments accordingly, build more passenger cars and improve passenger traffic facilities. In order to improve and expand passenger service, it is equally necessary to develop commuter transport in large cities.

Responsible transport should be strengthened, loading, unloading and management of freight yards improved and container traffic positively developed. Through trains and freight-car groups should be utilized as much as possible for the transport of bulk goods (such as coal, iron, steel, mineral construction materials, timber, petroleum, etc.) and wagons with special features should be developed for the transport of toxic materials, chemicals, grain, cement, livestock and fresh produce, so as to ensure safety in transport and reduce damage and loss of goods enroute.

28. CHINA'S HIGHWAY TRANSPORTATION
By Cheng Yinghua
Highway Administrative Bureau, Ministry of Communications

Before the founding of the People's Republic of China, highway transportation was extremely backward. In 1949 the 80,000 km. of highways open to traffic were mostly concentrated on the plains and rolling countryside in the inland and coastal regions. The mountains and border regions that cover over two-thirds of the country's total area, and inhabited mostly by the national minorities, had scarcely any roads at all.

I. Development of the Highway System in New China

After Liberation, highway construction developed fairly rapidly. By the end of 1980, the routes open to traffic totalled about 870,000 km., nearly 11 times that of 1949. At present, almost all the counties and more than 90% of the people's communes have been brought into the highway network. Even many of the mountainous border regions, inaccessible in the past, now have roads.

A beginning has been made in forming a nationwide network of highways, with Beijing at its centre, linking up the provinces, municipalities, autonomous regions, large and medium-sized cities, major ports and railway junctions.

After Liberation, countless miles of highways were built over the Qinghai-Tibet Plateau, known as the "roof of the world." The most well-known of the highways is the Sichuan-Tibet Highway, built in 1950-1954. It runs more than 2,400 km. at an average elevation of 3,000 m. above sea level from Chengdu in Sichuan Province to Lhasa, the capital of the Tibet Autonomous Region. The highway passes through such towns as Ya'an, Ganzi and Maniganggo, climbs high mountains such as the Erlangshan, Zheduoshan and Qiaoershan and crosses swift-running rivers such as the Dadu, the Jinsha, the Langcang and Nujian. The high elevation, low atmospheric pressure, very changeable weather and difficult topographic and geological conditions made the building of the highway one of the most arduous engineering feats in China's history of highway construction, rarely equalled even in world records.

Higher Quality. As the distances of roads increased, their quality and engineering techniques greatly improved. In the early days after Liberation, most of the highways did not rate even in the lowest class because they were low-lying, had narrow subgrades and lacked bridges and drainage culverts. Moreover, their poor alignment produced sharp curves and steep grades. Today, almost all highways in the country meet the requirements of different classes specified by national standards, and about 73% of these highways are paved.

By the end of 1980 there were 151,000 km. of asphalt roads, compared with only 315 in 1949. In the construction of first-class highways, priority has been given to access roads of large and medium-sized cities and to connecting roads. Some examples are: the Beijing-Miyun Highway, with a total length of 71.3 km. (39.1 km. of which feature a centre separation strip), subgrade width of 25-28 m., surface width of 21-25 m.; the six-lane Shenyang-Fushun Highway, total length 27 km., subgrade width of 29 m., surface width of 25 m.; and the Nanjing-Liuhe Highway, total length 24.7 km., subgrade width of 23 m., centre separation strip of 1.5 m., with a surface width of 10 m. on either side.

Bridge Construction. Following Liberation, highway bridges were also built at a high rate. In old China, bridges were largely timber or stone structures with small spans, and ferries were usually needed to cross large rivers. At present, there are more than 120,000 bridges with a total length of over 3 million linear metres; 92% of the bridges are permanent.

Several bridges now straddle the once impassable chasm of the mighty Changjiang River, which is over 5,000 km. long. The Changjiang River Highway Bridge in Chongqing, opened in July 1979, is a pre-stressed concrete, T-shaped, rigid-frame bridge, with an overall length of 1,121 m., main span length of 174 m. and deck width of 21 m. The Huanghe River is now crossed by more than 30 bridges, one of which is the longest highway bridge ever built in China — the Luoyang Huanghe River Highway Bridge, in Henan Province — with an overall length of 3,400 m. Both the construction scale and the techniques of design and construction of these bridges are relatively advanced.

Maintenance. In 1980 the highway engineering departments improved the maintenance work on existing highways, stressed technical improvements for the trunk roads and built some new roads at key points. In that year, with better maintenance work, trunk roads in good technical condition increased by 6%. A number of trunk roads have been brought up to second-class standard, e.g., the Huhehot-Wuyuan Highway, passing through Baotou in Inner Mongolia; the Taiyuan-Yuanping Highway, passing through Xinxian County in Shanxi Province; the section of the Beijing-Fuzhou National Highway in Zhejiang Province; the Fuzhou-Xiamen (Amoy) Highway in Fujian Province; and access roads to many large cities.

Other New Construction. Two new trunk roads have been built and opened to traffic. One is the Qinghai-Xinjiang Highway, east from Chaka, Qinghai Province, to Hetian, in the Xinjiang Uygur Autonomous Region; the other is the highway from Guanghua to Fangxian in Hubei Province. Major highway bridges have also been built, including the Hanjiang River Bridge at Guanghua in Hubei Province, a T-shaped, pre-stressed concrete, rigid-frame bridge with an overall length of 2,000 m. and main span of 90 m.; the Fujiang River Bridge at Santai, Sichuan Province, a pre-stressed concrete, cable-stayed bridge with an overall length of 560 m. and main span of 128 m; and the Dongjiang River Bridge at Huiyang, Guangdong Province, a reinforced concrete box arch bridge with an overall length of 805 m. and main span of 75 m. About 20,000 km. of county and commune highways were also built in 1980.

Growth of Road Transport

As the length of highways open to traffic increases steadily and the motor vehicle and petroleum industries develop, road transport is growing at an even faster pace. In 1949 there were only 50,000 motor vehicles; by the end of 1980 there were 1,700,000 in civilian use (including 1,300,000 freight trucks, 110,000 buses and 140,000 freight trailers), about 35.6 times that in 1949. The number of motor vehicles under government transport departments totalled 199,000 (including 159,000 freight trucks and 40,000 buses), about 11% of the total number of vehicles in civilian use. Almost every county now has its own motor transport service, accommodating more than 90% of the people's communes. Container transportation has started, and a certain amount of carrying capacity for extra-large freight has been provided, with a maximum single load capacity of 600 tons. The greatest length of freight carried has reached 70 m.

In 1980 highway transportation handled a volume of freight amounting to 760 million tons and a volume of cargo of 76,400 million ton-km., and carried 2,230 million passengers (about 6 million passengers daily). Of those vehicles under government transport departments, the percentage of freight trucks maintained in good condition was 86.5%; ratio utilized, 73.1%; average distance per vehicle daily, 172 km.; and percentage of utilized loading capacity, 61.5%. The volume of truck and trailer combinations averaged more than 39,000 ton-km. per truck-ton annually, and the volume of cargo reached 255 million ton-km. All these figures were higher than those of previous years.

Although highway construction and motor transport have greatly developed, they remain unable to meet the needs of the developing national economy in which they are still a weak link. At present, in the course of carrying out the policy of readjustment and restructuring, the task of speeding up highway construction and expanding motor transport capacity continues to be of great importance.

29. CHINA'S WATER TRANSPORTATION
By Sui Qiren
Bureau of Water Transport, Ministry of Communications

China has very favourable natural conditions for water transportation, with a long coastline of over 18,000 km., thousands of offshore islands and more than 900 large and small inland lakes. Most of the ocean bays and rivers are ice-free year-round and suitable for building ports. In China, there are many rivers, abundant in water, with a total length of 430,000 km. A general survey of inland waterways conducted recently shows that the navigable distances of these rivers is 108,000 km. The Changjiang River, which is the longest in China and the third longest in the world, is more than 6,300 km. long. Its main stream of 2,958 km. is navigable year-round, and its trunk stream and tributaries of 18,000 km. are navigable for steamers.

In the 31 years since Liberation, China's coastal waterways, inland waterways and ocean transport have been developing rapidly. At the same time, much progress has been made in building ports and wharves, dredging waterways, erecting navigational markings and manufacturing cargo-handling machinery, as well as in communications, navigation, and rescue and salvage.

I. Coastal and Inland Water Transport

The coastal waters of China are divided into two shipping areas: one, under the charge of the Shanghai Coastal Shipping Administration, is called the Northern Shipping Area and extends from Xiamen in Fujian Province to the mouth of the Yalu River in the north; the other, which covers the coastal waters from Xiamen to the mouth of the Beilun River, is the Southern Shipping Area, administered by the Guangzhou Coastal Shipping Administration. The Changjiang River Shipping Administration is responsible for trunk line transport on the Changjiang from Shanghai to Chongqing. In addition, provinces and autonomous regions situated along the coast or with navigable rivers all maintain their own coastal or river shipping authorities, engaging in local transportation and collecting and distributing cargoes from and to the main shipping lines.

The hub of Chinese coastal water transport is Shanghai, from which vessels can sail to all ports along the Chinese coast. Ships of 10,000 tons can directly enter the mouth of the Changjiang River and moor there. A water transport network linking both rivers and sea, and consisting of trunk lines and branch lines that are interconnected, is gradually taking shape.

Progress Since Liberation. Just after Liberation, there were only 23 coastal freighters totalling 34,000 tons and 61 deep-water berths in all the Chinese ports and harbours, and cargo handling was mainly done manually. At that time, boats and ships plying the Changjiang River totalled no more than 200,000 tons; ports on the river were uncared for; and many of the vessels used in inland navigation were old, poorly maintained junks.

Since the founding of New China, however, important progress has been made in marine and inland water transport. The number of coastal ships has increased rapidly, and more and more large and special-purpose freighters have been put into use. In recent years, shipyards in China have supplied the coastal shipping fleet with a number of 25,000-ton bulk cargo ships and 24,000-ton oil tankers. The average carrying capacity of the ships owned by the Shanghai Coastal Shipping Administration increased from 2,000 tons in the initial post-Liberation days to more than 9,000 tons at present.

Great changes also have taken place in inland water transport. In 1949, 70% of inland water traffic volume was handled by sailing boats, which were rowed or towed manually. Now, the number of steamers and barges on inland rivers has increased over 10 times from that of the early post-Liberation period. Motor barges can handle 88% of the traffic volume, while the largest tug-barge flotilla steaming in the lower reaches of the Changjiang River is able to carry nearly 10,000 tons of cargo.

In the past, a round-trip between Wuhan and Shanghai by passenger ship took 12 days, but now it takes only 7 days (if by fast liner, only 5 days). Just after Liberation, along the Changjiang River there were only 17 ports and 72 wharves, without a single piece of cargo-handling machinery in use. Now there are 25 port authorities, over 200 shipping stations, more than 400 wharves and over 3,000 pieces of loading and unloading machinery. Generally speaking, mechanization and semi-mechanization have been realized for cargo handling.

New Procedures. In recent years, advanced transport techniques, i.e., an integrated barge and towing system, have been popularized on a large scale for inland water transport on the Changjiang, the Heilongjiang and other large rivers. The aggregate tonnage of all the section barges in China is over 300,000 tons, with the carrying capacity of a barge ranging from 200 tons to 1,000 tons. The largest pushing boat we now have, with an engine output of 4,000 hp, is able to move 12,000 to 15,000 tons of cargo. In organizing transport, bulk cargo and cargo requiring long-distance shipment are moved in special liners on rivers and along coastal waters. In addition, container transport is in wide use, thus speeding up the shipment and improving the quality of freight transport.

The Changjiang River Shipping Administration has opened more than 30 special routes for a new method of shipment, known as the "five fixednesses" — fixed ships, fixed shipping periods, fixed berths, fixed loads and fixed kinds of cargo. In this way, the administration has increased total traffic volume by over 60%. In order to ensure the transport of general cargo from Shanghai to the three provinces in Northeast China by way of Dalian, a coordinated transport process has been operated since 1965 by the Shipping Administration, the port authorities, the commercial departments and the railway bureaus concerned. In so doing, the Shipping Administration and the port authorities are responsible for maintaining ships, berths, loads and shipping schedules while the railway departments arrange train wagons. This system has brought excellent results during the last 10 years or so.

Advances in 1980. A number of new passenger ships with over 9,000 places were added to the fleet in 1980; cargo ships increased by 1,124 (totalling nearly 400,000 tons); and five 10,000-ton berths, two 5,000-ton berths and the Dalian Passenger Shipping Station were built to augment coastal and inland water transport capacity. In that year, 350 million tons of cargo and 260 million passengers were transported by river and sea, an increase of 0.2% and 9.1%, respectively, over 1979. Priority was given to the shipment of farm produce, light industrial products and textiles, coal, oil and other key materials.

In 1980, further advances were made in coastal water transport and in shipping on the Changjiang River, with more and more container ships coming into use. Consequently, an international container traffic business was begun in the five ports of Tianjin, Shanghai, Qingdao, Dalian and Huangpu, handling over 60,000 containers totalling 380,000 tons of cargo — an increase of 96% and 133%, respectively, over 1979.

In the 1960's, in coastal waters and on the Changjiang River, "inter-port unitized transport" was introduced. Since then, 59 shipping routes have been designated for that kind of transport, and 5 million tons of cargo have been handled that way. Because internal transport was running smoothly, several coastal freighters, with a carrying capacity of 500,000 tons, could be transferred to foreign trade shipping. Also in 1980, shipping services for foreign trade were started in the seven ports of Nanjing, Nantung, Jiujiang, Wuhu, Wuhan, Huangshi and Chongqing, which handled over 200,000 tons of cargo. At home, two "fixednesses" special routes were opened to ship general cargo from Shanghai to Fuzhou and Wenzhou.

II. Ocean Transport

Before Liberation, China had virtually no ocean transport of its own. The few foreign shipping companies operating in Shanghai and Tianjin had long monopolized all foreign shipments.

After the founding of New China, China and Poland jointly set up the Sino-Polish Shipping Company in 1951, the first step in developing China's own ocean transport service. In the 1950's, China shipped its foreign trade materials mainly by chartered vessels. In the early 1960's, however, China, on the basis of self-reliance, began to build and then to expand its own ocean maritime sector systematically and in a planned way. Accordingly, the China Ocean Shipping Company (COSCO) was set up in 1961. In April of that year, the first ocean-going passenger ship, the *Guanghua*, made her maiden voyage to Indonesia. After that, two Chinese-built freighters, *Peace* and *Friendship*, sailed to Burma, Sri Lanka and Guinea in West Africa.

When it was formed in 1961, the ocean-going merchant fleet owned only 20 vessels with a combined dead-weight capacity of 190,000 tons. But the number of ships has increased year by year, especially in the 1970's. By the end of 1980, China's ocean-going merchant fleet had 431 ships with a total dead-weight capacity of 7.92 million tons, an increase of approximately 40 times in 20 years. Now, merchant vessels flying China's five-starred red flag sail to more than 400 harbours in over 100 countries and regions, constituting the mainstay of China's ocean transport.

In 1980, 33.9 million tons of cargo were shipped and 14,300 million ton-miles handled. The merchant fleet also entered the international shipping market and began to transport cargo for third parties. In so doing, it made positive contributions to the development of China's foreign trade, socialist economic construction and friendly relations with other countries.

With headquarters in Beijing, COSCO has shipping companies in Shanghai, Guangzhou, Tianjin, Qingdao, Dalian and elsewhere. In addition, shipping companies jointly owned by China and other countries have been set up, such as the Sino-Polish Shipping Company, the Sino-Tanzanian Joint Shipping Company and the Sino-Sri Lanka Joint Shipping Route. In Hong Kong, we have the China Merchants Steam Navigation Co., Ltd. In 1980, the China Ocean Shipping Company, together with the local authorities in Jiangsu, Zhejiang, Hebei and some other provinces, established joint ocean shipping companies.

The Chinese merchant fleet owns not only general cargo vessels of various types and classes, but also a considerable number of bulk cargo ships and oil tankers. In recent years, additions to the fleet have included some newly built and technically sophisticated roll-on/roll-off ships, container ships and multi-purpose ships, some of which are equipped with automatic control systems for unattended engine rooms.

China began to engage in container shipping in 1973. At that time, the container ships used were merely ordinary cargo liners loaded from Xinggang and Shanghai, carrying no more than 100 containers and used only for freight forwarding. In 1978, the sea route between China and Australia was opened up, with two semi-container ships carrying over 200 containers each sailing monthly between Shanghai, Xinggang, Sydney and Melbourne. Since January 1980, two roll-on/roll-off ships have replaced the semi-container ships and sail this route four times a month by way of Hong Kong, where more cargo is taken on. In June of 1980, a shipping route between Huangpu and Europe was opened for container vessels sailing twice a month, also by way of Hong Kong where more cargo is loaded. In November, a regular line between Shanghai and ports along the coast of West Africa went into operation, with Chinese cargo liners sailing once a month via Hong Kong.

With the rapid development of ocean transportation, China has made much headway in recent years in enhancing friendly ties with other countries and promoting international economic cooperation. The China Ocean Shipping Company has set up the Transoceanic Shipping Agency in Amsterdam, the Consfur Shipping Agency Co. Nv in Antwerp and the Five Star Shipping and Agency Co. PTY Ltd., with ship brokers or shipping agents of the Netherlands, Belgium and Australia, respectively. In addition, it has started the Chung Ling Marine Service Company, Ltd. with Japan and the Yuan Tung Marine Service Company, Ltd. with the Netherlands to provide each vessel with essential ship supplies.

III. Waterway and Harbour Construction

When the People's Republic of China was founded in 1949, navigable inland waterways extended for only 73,600 km. Of the total, only 24,200 km. were fit for steamers, and most rivers were in a poor natural state. Along the coast, only six major ports and harbours with a total of 119 berths were operational.

Since the founding of New China, there has been a fairly rapid development both in waterway dredging and harbour construction. By 1961, the navigable length of inland waterways had been increased to 172,000 km., 2.3 times that in the early days after Liberation. Then, because of construction of locks and dams, the length was reduced considerably in the last decade. As a result, only 108,000 km. of waterways remained, but this is still 47% more than in the early days after Liberation.

Waterways. In the opening up and dredging of waterways, China has experienced both positive and negative results. From 1958 to 1960, the policy of "unified planning, comprehensive utilization and construction by stages" led to great achievements. For example, the Grand Canal, navigable for 404 km. in northern Jiangsu and fit for a barge fleet with a carrying capacity of 2,000 tons, was dredged in only three years. In addition, 10 sluices and other water conservation facilities were built successively. Thus, navigation in that region has been greatly improved; the capacity of passage has been raised by 11 times, and the total quantity of cargo shipped has reached 20 to 25 million tons. This has helped reduce the load on rail transport in the southern section of the Tianjin-Pukou Railway and has supported irrigation, flood-prevention and drainage, contributing greatly to the development of agriculture and industry in the area.

The Lianjiang River in Guangdong Province, which flows 262 km. through a mountainous region, could serve as another example. It has numerous shoals and zigzags, a sharp gradient and very swift waterflow. From 1959 to 1975, however, canalization was realized, with 10 cascades built in the section from Lianzhou to Hanguang and rubble dams constructed downstream. Chuanjiang, 660 km. long, a section of the Changjiang River between Chongqing and Yichang that runs through hilly areas with many high mountains and steep gorges (including the well-known Three Gorges), has 128 dangerous shoals with turbulent currents. From 1953 to 1978, 101 shoals were ameliorated, and the former 2.1 × 33 × 440 m.

shipping lane, suitable only for seasonal navigation, was expanded to 2.9 × 60 × 750 m., permitting day and night navigation for a barge fleet of 1,000-ton carrying capacity.

Since the 1960's, greater importance has been attached to the maintenance and construction of waterways and to comprehensive water conservation. With more than 2,000 sluices and locks built, many sections of the navigational lanes were blocked by silting, resulting in a 2.5% annual decrease in navigable distance. By 1970, a total of 63,000 km. had been lost. A typical example is the Peijiang River in Sichuan Province: with the setting up of 10 hydroelectric power stations, the former 500-km. shipping lane was no longer navigable.

Harbours. In the area of coastal harbour construction, China devoted its main efforts in the 1950's to the recovery and reconstruction of the old ports and harbours of Shanghai, Tianjin and Qinhuangdao, as well as the construction of a number of deep-sea berths in a few harbours such as Zhanjiang. Since 1960, with the immense growth of foreign trade, the shortage of wharves in coastal harbours has become a critical weak link in the development of the national economy.

In 1973, China decided to raise port handling capacity by expanding port construction. In a few years, a great number of terminals for bulk cargo, general cargo, petroleum and passengers, as well as numerous port facilities for water and bunker supply, were built. Now, there are more than 300 wharves, 139 with deep water for berthing ships up to 10,000 tons.

In the past, China had only one oil terminal of the 20,000-ton class — in Dalian. Now there are quite a number of oil terminals of the 100,000-ton class, 50,000-ton class and 20,000-ton class in four ports, with a yearly oil delivery capacity of 41 million tons. The handling capacity of coal and general cargo terminals has also been raised considerably. In addition, container terminals are being built in the ports of Shanghai, Tianjin and Huangpu, and will soon be placed in operation.

IV. Water Transport Industry

In the early years after Liberation, the water transport industry in China was very weak. The total output value of all water transport enterprises under the Ministry of Communications in 1950 was only 10.9 million yuan. There were merely 450 metal-cutting machine tools and six small dry docks, permitting only simple repairs and the building of a limited number of barges. As for the local water transport industry, it had only a few shipyards that were barely capable of building junks. All cargo-handling machinery was imported.

In 30 years, the water transport industry has made great progress in such fields as ship repair and shipbuilding and the manufacture of cargo-handling machinery, spare parts and complete sets of equipment. In 1980, water transport industry enterprises under the Ministry of Communications had more than 8,300 metal-cutting machine tools, 24 repair docks of over 3,000-ton class (15 dry docks, 9 floating docks), among which 15 are of over 10,000-ton class, the largest being of the 50,000-ton class. There were 61 shipways and slipways of varying sizes. The total output value in 1980 was 613 million yuan, which is 56 times the total in the early years after Liberation. Most local water transport industry enterprises are now able to build steel ships, and some of them can construct cargo ships of 3,000 to 5,000 tons.

Importance of Ship Repair. The ship repair and building industry follows the policy of "repair and build, taking repair as the main task." The ship repair industry is being developed in a planned way and in concert with the development of water transportation. There are ship repair yards in every major port and harbour along China's coast and the Changjiang River to ensure the timely and convenient repair of ships when they arrive. In order to shorten repair time in the yards, improve quality, reduce costs and render better service, the yards have been improving management in recent years, thus enhancing both repair efficiency and quality.

Meanwhile, advanced repair technology and equipment have been introduced, e.g., removing rust with water jetting, ship-side crawling magnetic rust-removing, airless paint spraying, shipside electric hanging scaffolds, laser measurement and chemical washing. In the field of mechanization of bench work and pipe processing, hydraulic and pneumatic tools have been employed, and flame pipe-bending machines and medium-frequency pipe-bending machines have been successfully developed in a number of yards. The mechanization of pipe processing has been basically realized.

As regards the organization of ship repair, the arrangement of production according to workers' trades, which has been practiced for years, is being successfully reformed. The aim is to organize production in conformity with technological processes and to establish a system in which each worker will know several trades.

Shipbuilding Capability. In shipbuilding, China can now design and build its own ocean-going cargo ships of the 10,000-ton class, tugs of 4,000 h.p, passenger-cargo ships of various kinds navigating in the Changjiang and along the coast and barges of the 5,000-ton class. In September 1978, the Shanghai Shipyard built the first ship for export, a 14,000-ton oceangoing cargo ship named *Shaoxing,* for the Sino-Polish Joint Shipping Company. The main engine, a low-speed diesel engine Model 6ESDZ 76/160, with a continuous output of 9,000 hp, was built in the Shanghai Shipyard. The hull, power machinery, navigation aids and communication facilities were all in compliance with China's steel ship construction rules and regulations and the requirements of international conventions. In sea trials, the ship proved worthy and its performance won praise from the user.

In 1980, water transport enterprises under the Ministry of Communications repaired 1,128 Chinese ships and 20 foreign ships and built ships totally 183,000 deadweight tons, including four tugs of 900 hp for Romania, 10 barges of 1,000 tons each for Hong Kong shipowners and a 5,000-ton passenger-cargo vessel named *Tianhu* for trading on the Bohai Sea.

Cargo-Handling Machinery. The cargo-handling industry was set up in 1960. Now, after 20 years' development, a complete system is taking shape. At present, there are eight factories in which various mobile machines, such as wheeled cranes, fork lifts, tractors, single-bucket loaders and two-way bulldozers, can be designed and built. Also being manufactured are various rubber-tyred transferring cranes, bulk-loading machines, grain-sucking machines, container lifts, container tractors, derricks and rotary floating cranes, bulk grab buckets, electro-magnetic loading devices, etc.

In recent years, the cargo-handling machinery built in these factories, besides meeting the needs of China's harbours and enterprises, is beginning to be exported. Among the equipment shipped abroad are 1-cu. m. single-bucket loaders, buckets of various kinds and 30-ton, 40-ton, 63-ton and 150-ton shore cranes.

V. Rescue, Salvage and Towage

Rescue and salvage in China was initiated and developed only after Liberation. The People's Salvage Company was established in 1951 with only one tug of 150 hp and 37 divers. Since 1975, the China Salvage Company, China Towing Company and China Ocean Engineering Services were formed, operating on a joint basis and with offices in Beijing, Guangzhou, Shanghai and Yantai. These companies have entrusted Wah Tak Marine Engineering Co., Ltd. in Hong Kong to act as their agent and have signed cooperative arrangements with salvage companies in seven other countries, including Japan and the United Kingdom.

By the end of 1980, China's rescue and salvage organizations comprised 600 divers, 800 technical personnel and 121 ships of various types, including the largest tug (20,800 hp), a floating crane with a lifting capacity of 2,500 tons, and a self-propelled engineering ship of 3,200 GRT and several deck barges of 5,000 tons. In addition, there were numerous diving and salvage facilities and equipment of different types. With personnel and equipment, these companies now have enormous capabilities in rescue, salvage and towage operations, as well as in rendering ocean engineering services.

The China Salvage Company has conscientiously fulfilled its international obligations in sea rescue by setting up 11 permanent rescue stations and a number of seasonal ones along China's coast, where round-the-clock service is available and immediate dispatch of rescue ships and personnel can be made at any time. In the past 30 years, the companies rescued more than 4,800 persons and 730 ships, of which 106 were from over 20 foreign countries.

Some Notable Successes. In 1979, the Guangzhou Salvage Company rescued — under extraordinarily severe weather and sea conditions and in a particularly difficult sea area called the Langhua Reefs in the Xisha Islands — the U.S. cargo vessel *American Sioux,* which had run aground. The successful operation won high appreciation and wide admiration in international salvage circles.

In recent years, wreck removing techniques have been raised to new levels. The method of refloating a ship by pumping out oil in holds to use their inherent buoyancy succeeded in 1976 in the case of the 10,000-ton *Nan Yan* oil tanker. In 1977, the salvage operation of a Japanese cargo ship, the *Awa Maru,* which sank during World War II, was a highpoint in the history of salvage in China. The work was initiated in order to clear the fishing grounds off Niushan (Ox Mountain) in Fujian Province. The operation took 400 arduous days and proceeded in the face of tremendous difficulties, such as great sea depth, strong monsoons, rough gales and turbulent currents. It was successfully completed with the raising of the ship's fore part. More than 5,000 tons of cargo were salvaged, and the remains of over 300 Japanese seamen were recovered and turned over to the Japanese government. The operation was significant not only in the tempering of salvage personnel but also in the strengthening of friendship between the Chinese and Japanese peoples.

In 1979, experience was gained in salvaging a complete section of a broken ship by means of pontoons in an operation involving the 15,000-ton cargo vessel *Han Yin* in the Bohai Sea. With some 910 ships of different sizes salvaged in the past 30 years, the China Salvage Company has made an impressive contribution to waterway clearance and navigational safety.

With the use of high-powered tugs, the China Towing Company undertakes both domestic and international towing operations. A total of 419 towing operations involving drilling rigs, VLCC, cargo vessels, barges, engineering ships, floating cranes, floating docks and heavy equipment on deck barges have been performed between Singapore, Japan, India and China in recent years. On one occasion, a 3,600-hp tug was manned and sailed by the company all the way from Japan to Mauritania. The company has been commended time and again by clients for its safe, reliable and on-schedule service.

Engineering Achievements. Ocean engineering services have been expanded continuously along with the development of offshore oil exploration. Since 1979, the China Ocean Engineering Service has towed giant jack-up and semi-submersible rigs 14 times between Japan, Singapore and China; contracted to tow, transport and inspect offshore rigs for the BP Oil Company and China's Ministry of Petroleum Industry and Ministry of Geology in the Yellow Sea, China Sea and South China Sea; undertaken salvage of sunken objects dropped from rigs in water as deep as 76 m.; and engaged in inspection work on rig supports. In addition, the China Ocean Engineering Service has been involved in diving operations and cable- and pipe-laying in harbours and bays, reservoirs, mine wells and hydraulic power plants.

Equipment and Research. The manufacturing of diving equipment has been growing rapidly in the course of the development in salvage and towage operations and ocean engineering services. Equipment for scuba, helmet-type diving and heliox helmet-type diving, facilities for underwater cutting, welding and illumination, as well as working tools produced in the Shanghai and Wuhu diving equipment works not only meet domestic needs but are also exported.

Scientific research in connection with salvage has been well advanced. Experience in air diving has been gained; a simulated test of heliox diving at a depth of 156 m. succeeded in 1975; and practical work at around 100-m. depths is currently being performed. Meanwhile, new techniques of underwater welding, cutting, directionary blasting, grabbing and magnetic lifting have been fully utilized.

In 1980, in line with the policy of "salvage and towage, taking salvage as the main concern," 60 ships were rescued, 50 ships salvaged and 85 towing operations completed. As the country's shipping and offshore industries continue to grow, it is expected that salvage, towage and ocean engineering services will also develop at a fairly rapid pace.

30. CHINA'S CIVIL AVIATION
By Wu Erer
General Administration of Civil Aviation of China

I. Thirty Years of Development

Civil aviation is a modern branch of transportation. Characterized by speed, manoeuvrability, versatility and efficiency, civil aviation is also a means of production, serving directly the needs of industry and agriculture. In old China, civil aviation grew very slowly, and was far from being well established. Air service in China first began in 1929, but up to 1949 the volume of traffic transported by air totalled only 200 million ton-km. The Civil Aviation Administration of China (CAAC) was established in 1949 and began scheduled flights and aerial work activities in 1950 and 1951, respectively. In 1962, CAAC was expanded and reorganized into the General Administration of Civil Aviation of China. The General Administration has under its jurisdiction six regional administrations – Beijing, Shenyang, Shanghai, Guangzhou, Chengdu and Lanzhou – which in turn control their respective sub-regional administrations in the provinces, municipalities and autonomous regions and at airports.

Comprehensive Growth. Civil aviation in China made rapid progress after the founding of the People's Republic. Air transportation has increased at an average rate of 20% per year. The volume of traffic transported each year is now up to 430 million ton-km., which is 2.1 times as much as the total volume of traffic carried in the 20 years before Liberation. Aerial work has increased at an average rate of 15% per year, and actual flying time has reached 43,000 hours per year. Through 30 years of growth, our civil aviation has laid a solid foundation and is playing an increasingly important role in improving national economic construction and the well-being of our people.

CAAC now operates 182 routes, which, measured without duplication, total 210,000 km. Of these routes, 159 are domestic, with a total length of more than 110,000 km., while the rest include 23 international routes and some regional routes, with a total length of more than 90,000 km.

Our domestic air routes now link more than 80 cities. With Beijing as the centre, a domestic network connecting different provincial and regional capitals and important cities has been basically formed. The ratio of air transportation to all forms of transportation has increased from year to year. All the benefits of air transportation, such as safety, speed, comfort and economy, have been increasingly appreciated by the people. The government has attached great importance to the development of air services in the regions populated by minority nationalities and the border areas. CAAC flights have now become an important mode of transportation to Tibet and Xinjiang. There are direct scheduled flights from Chengdu, Xi'an and Lanzhou to Lhasa. The direct flight from Beijing to Urumqi takes only three hours, thus greatly shortening the distance between the coast and the interior. Ten air terminals in the Xinjiang Uygur Autonomous region form a regional network in that area.

International Air Service. Along with the rise of China's international standing and the development of its economy and tourism, the international services of CAAC also have experienced rapid growth. There is now an international network of air services linking China with 21 cities in 18 countries in four continents – namely, Pyongyang in the Democratic People's Republic of Korea, Rangoon in Burma, Moscow in the Soviet Union, Tokyo, Osaka and Nagasaki in Japan, Karachi in Pakistan, Paris in France, Tehran in Iran, Bucharest in Romania, Frankfurt in the Federal Republic of Germany, Addis Ababa in Ethiopia, Belgrade in Yugoslavia, Zurich in Switzerland, Sharjah in the United Arab Emirates, Baghdad in Iraq, London in Great Britain, Manila in the Philippines, Bangkok in Thailand, and New York and San Francisco in the United States.

CAAC has concluded aviation agreements with more than 40 countries and has set up agency relations with airlines in 180 countries and regions. In November 1971, the 74th Council of the International Civil Aviation Organization (ICAO) passed a resolution to reinstate China as a member of that organization. In September 1974, at the 21st Congress of the ICAO, China was elected a Council member of ICAO and, accordingly, it has set up a Permanent Representative's Office at ICAO. China is also party to the Hague Convention (for the suppression of unlawful seizure of aircraft) and the Montreal Convention (for the suppression of unlawful acts against the safety of civil aviation).

Aerial Work Services. CAAC has set up a fairly comprehensive aerial work system. Aerial work services started with insecticide spraying, and have since expanded to include aerial photography, aerial prospecting, aerial survey, offshore operation and rescue services, aerial sowing, top dressing of fertilizer, weeding, pest and plant disease control, forest sowing, forest patrol and fire fighting, forage grass sowing, artificial rainfall, etc.

The work areas of our aerial services now extend to all provinces, municipalities and autonomous regions (with the exception of Taiwan), and the flying time for these services has increased 44 times since the early years of the People's Republic. In these 30 years flying time for aerial prospecting and aerial photography totalled 200,000 hours, and the serviced areas for pest control and forest seeding totalled over 500 million *mu* and 160 million *mu*, respectively. In some areas, the seeds sown by CAAC planes years ago have now grown into full-sized trees and have begun to provide the people with timber.

Airports. Over the years, the government has built, expanded and reconstructed more than 80 airports. Among them, Capital Airport in Beijing, Hongqiao Airport in Shanghai, Baiyun Airport in Guangzhou, Diwopu Airport in Urumqi, Jianqiao Airport in Hangzhou, Zhangguizhuang Airport in Tianjin, Luogang Airport in Hefei and Yanjiagang Airport in Harbin can all handle take-offs and landings of large jet aircraft under difficult meteorological conditions.

Adequate communications, air navigation and meteorological services have been provided at all airports and on all air routes. At major airports with comparatively high densities of scheduled flights, enroute surveillance radar and landing-aid radar are used to guide plane movements in coordination with the control towers for high-, medium- and low-altitude flights. Reliable weather forecasts are also furnished by meteorological observatories at the airports. In recent years, CAAC has strengthened the planning and construction of its air route network and provided air route services for more than 10 foreign airlines.

Variety of Aircraft. CAAC now operates a mixed fleet of more than 20 types of aircraft. Boeing-747s, Boeing-727s, Il-62s, Tridents and Il-18s are mainly used for international and domestic route flights, while AN-24s, AN-12s, Viscounts are used for medium- and short-distance flights and Yun-5s, Li-2s, Il-14s, Skylarks, An-30s, Twin Ottors and Bell-212s are used for aerial work flights.

Maintenance. CAAC has its own maintenance system. The maintenance base in Beijing and the repairs works in Shanghai and Chengdu, with their up-to-date maintenance equipment and well-qualified engineers and technicians, are capable of performing airframe and engine overhauls for such types of aircraft as Il-18s, An-24s, Il-14s, Li-2s and Yun-5s. At airports under regional administrations and provincial, municipal and autonomous sub-regional administrations, there are maintenance crews for repair plants handling line maintenance or ground checks for transit aircraft on both international and domestic flights.

Training, Research and Safety. CAAC attaches great importance to the educational and training of its personnel and to scientific research work. The Chengdu Flight Training School and the CAAC Tianjin Professional Training School conduct education and training programmes for air crews and ground personnel (in navigational control, telecommunications, meteorology, transportation services, maintenance, management and administration) to meet the needs of civil aviation organizations and other production, operational and technical departments all over the country. The six regional administrations of CAAC in Beijing, Shanghai, Guangzhou, Chengdu, Lanzhou and Shenyang all have their own training bases and schools for technicians and workers, chiefly responsible for the training of skilled maintenance workers and for the short-term training of various kinds of technical and operational personnel.

The airport design and research organization of CAAC is now competent to design on its own a large, modern airport. For example, Capital Airport in Beijing and Hongqiao Airport in Shanghai were both designed by CAAC personnel. The scientific research work of CAAC has made valuable contributions to the cause of civil aviation in our country, and the State Science and Technology Commission of the People's Republic of China and the Science and Technology Commission for National Defence of the Chinese People's Liberation Army have honoured CAAC for its development and manufacture of instrument-landing equipment and UHF ADF items, respectively.

CAAC has conscientiously carried out the late Premier Zhou Enlai's directive — "Ensure safety first, improve passenger services, and strive for flight regularity" — and has educated its staff and workers to devote their primary attention to flight safety and to always give it top priority. CAAC has a work force of well-trained air crews and a set of strict rules and regulations for flight control and the execution of other duties, and its achievement in flight safety is already well known throughout the world.

Flight Group I of the Beijing Regional Administration, in charge of international and main domestic flights, has flown large numbers of scheduled flights and important special missions and chartered flights to more than 180 cities in more than 90 countries all over the world, and has maintained its flight safety record for 24 consecutive years. With more and more large, modern aircraft and advanced communications and navigational equipment coming into use, the flight regularity of scheduled services in our country has been improved correspondingly. CAAC always gives great attention to the improvement of its passenger services, and therefore has been steadily increasing its service facilities, enlarging the scope of its services, and sharpening the professional skills of its personnel.

II. Readjustment and Reform in 1980

In 1980, CAAC conscientiously implemented the policy of readjustment, restructuring, consolidation and improvement of the national economy. It vigorously and steadily carried out its readjustment and reform according to the state's requirement that civil aviation is to develop into an enterprise. Beginning in March 1980, CAAC was placed under the direct control of the State Council, with all its subordinate organizations — the regional administrations, the sub-regional administrations in the provinces, municipalities and autonomous regions, and the airports under their respective jurisdictions — under the dual control of the CAAC system and the local governments concerned. The management system and organizational structure mainly under CAAC's vertical control were consolidated in line with the requirements for enterprises.

To comply with the demands set on administrative executives by the state, young and energetic persons with better understanding of ideology and policy, as well as technical know-how and experience in business management, were promoted to strengthen the managing bodies of the different units. The units, economic accounting and business management structures were also consolidated. The regional administrations began to operate independently on a profit-making basis, and, in time, the sub-regional administrations will also become responsible for economic accounting. All these changes greatly raised the morale of executives at different levels, promoted the development of production and enhanced the economic results. The entire civil aviation system exceeded the state's production plan and made the greatest gains since the founding of the People's Republic.

Production Targets Exceeded. The total volume of traffic in 1980 reached 430 million ton-km. or 107% of the annual plan, an increase of 14% over 1979. The total number of passengers carried was 3.3 million, 118% of the annual plan, an increase of 12% over 1979. The total volume of cargo and mail transported amounted to 83,000 tons, 117% of the yearly plan, and 8% in excess of 1979. The number of hours flown by the aerial work service reached 42,792, or 143% of the annual plan, and an increase of 8% over 1979.

Operating revenues in 1980 amounted to 440 million yuan or 114% of the annual plan, and 16% more than in 1979. Net profit realized in 1980 was 62.4 million yuan, of which 37 million or 12% of the state target, was turned over to the Treasury. Foreign exchange revenues for the year netted US$144 million. The average rate of labour productivity was 14,500 yuan per capita, 12% higher than in 1979.

International Traffic. In 1980, CAAC opened up five international routes: Beijing-Sharjah-Baghdad, Beijing-Karachi-Baghdad, Beijing-Guangzhou-Bangkok, Beijing-Frankfurt-London and Shanghai-Osaka. In addition, three more regional routes were opened: Beijing-Hong Kong, Guangzhou-Hong Kong and Hangzhou-Hong Kong. During the year, international flights carried 297,000 passengers and 15,000 tons of cargo and mail, an increase of 101% and 57%, respectively, over 1979. The number of charter flights for passengers and cargo doubled since 1979.

Beginning in April 1980, three Boeing-747s were placed in service. This wide-bodied aircraft can carry 291 passengers and is equipped with such advanced devices as an automatic braking system, colour weather radar, proximity warning, all-range auto throttle and over-rotation takeoff warning, and flight manoeuvrability is power-controlled. The 747s have an average speed of 950 km. per hour and can fly 15 hours without stopping for refuelling.

Extension of Aerial Work. The year 1980 saw the aerial work service adopting new equipment and new technology, as well as extending its experiment of new service items. All of this was done with good results. For instance, remote sensing was used in searching for subterranean hot water, and general investigations were made on environmental pollution and soil planning. An advanced ultra-low-volume spraying technique was adopted for the prevention and control of plant diseases and the elimination of pests. The area covered by each flight increased from 300-500 *mu* in routine operations to 8,000-10,000 *mu*, and the amount sprayed on each *mu* was reduced from a constant amount of 4 *jin* to below 0.66 *jin*. Foliage dressing and spraying of plant hormones such as PIPA and petroleum stimulant, together with the prevention of tropical cyclones and the development of strains of wheat with resistance to low-temperatures, made agricultural production increase over large areas.

In 1980, the area serviced by CAAC's farming-forestry flights reached over 37 million *mu*, of which forest sowing accounted for 10.76 million *mu*; rice sowing more than 0.1 million *mu*; forage grass sowing, 0.31 million *mu*; prevention and control of plant diseases and elimination of pests, 18.84 million *mu*; fertilizing agricultural crops, 4.13 million *mu*; and weeding, 1.59 million *mu*. The quality of all these operations was improved.

New Airfields and Auxiliary Facilities. Expansion of Beijing's Capital Airport began in 1974 and the main engineering work was completed after seven years. The new facility opened on January 1, 1980. The new west runway is 3,200 m. long, 50 m. wide and 38 cm. thick. It can support a weight of 350 tons, and is capable of accommodating the largest aircraft in the world, such as the Boeing-747, the DC-10 and the Concorde. Lengthening of the old east runway was due to be completed in 1981. This runway will be 3,800 m. long, 60 m. wide and 42 cm. thick. It will bear a weight of 500 tons and will be able to accommodate the landing and takeoff of the world's largest transport planes, which weigh up to 150 tons more than the largest planes flying today.

The new terminal, capable of accommodating 1,500 passengers at peak hours, has an overall area of 59,500 sq. m. The east and west wings of the main buildings are connected to two "satellite" waiting halls by an automatic walkway 100 m. in length. These waiting halls are, in turn, connected to the aircraft by an automatic passenger bridge. Around each "satellite" waiting hall, there are eight parking spaces for large and medium-sized aircraft. Inside the waiting halls are the most advanced passenger service facilities, including telegraph, telephones, post offices, banks, taxi service and electronic screens for flight information, as well as advanced installations for traffic control, such as closed-circuit TV, teletypewriters, etc.

Capital Airport is the largest operational centre in the country. In 1980, it recorded a turnover of 1,088,000 passengers and 38,000 tons of cargo and mail. The modern ATC Centre, in the Flight Control Building, was due to begin operations by the end of 1981.

Aircraft Maintenance. In 1980, the aircraft repair works and the aircraft maintenance departments at different levels strengthened both their quality control and technology control. The three repair works repaired and released 97 different types of aircraft and 448 aircraft engines, and finished the modification and special repair for 11 large and medium-sized aircraft, such as the Boeing-707, Il-62, An-12 and An-30, with an output value of 32 million yuan. To tap the full potential of existing equipment and technical capability, the organization of aviation maintenance was reformed. The maintenance department of Capital Airport was merged with the Beijing Aircraft Repair Works to form the Beijing Maintenance Base, which will serve as the maintenance centre for large and medium-sized civilian aircraft in China.

To meet the growing demands of civil aviation in China, The China Aviation Supplies Corporation was formed with the approval of the government on October 1, 1980. The functions of the firm are to place purchase orders at home and abroad for various kinds of aviation supplies and ground equipment, including aircraft and aircraft engines, and to sell and dispose of domestically manufactured aviation supplies, as well as surplus materials. It also acts as an agent for buying and selling aviation supplies. The corporation has six regional offices — for the North, East, Central-South, Northwest and Northeast. These were formed to organize and carry out in their respective regions the work of placing orders and procuring and furnishing aviation supplies, thus greatly expediting operations.

Educational Work and Technical Training. In 1980, the CAAC Chengdu Flight Training School graduated 120 flying cadets out of an initial enrollment of 200. The CAAC Tianjin Professional Training School opened 28 classes with an enrollment of 900 students. Another 1,000 candidates were enrolled at six technical schools. These institutions turned out a total of 15 Boeing-747 flying teams, ensuring that the new aircraft will begin operations on time.

Of CAAC's total flight personnel, more than 700 were either promoted to the position of captain for different types of aircraft, transferred to different instrument ratings and the position of right-seat instructor or passed for solo flight. The different organizations attached major importance to the in-service training of staff members. A total of 114 short courses were given, with 2,300 trainees enrolled, thus effectively enhancing the staff members' technical and professional competence.

Flight Safety and Service Quality. In 1980, CAAC launched successively the "Safety Month," "100-Day Emulation" and "Quality Month" drives, each of which placed top priority on safety. To implement the directive of the Central Committee of the Party and the State Council, namely, "ensure the safety of all types of aircraft" CAAC adopted 10 forceful measures, including orders on flight safety and service quality, flying regulations, flight control working rules, flying accident investigation regulations, air navigation regulations, etc. CAAC also re-established the system of coordination — which had been abolished during the 10 years of turmoil — whereby dispatching is centralized under the direction of the senior officer on duty; thus, flight safety was once again ensured both organizationally and institutionally.

Meanwhile, flight planning and its execution was strengthened as was the professional training of flight personnel. The functional role of the captains was brought into full play, and the flight crews' ability to cope with any situation under extraordinary circumstances was enhanced. Of the 24 flying groups in the system, 21 had no fatal flying accident during the year. The Boeing-747 Flying Group under the Beijing Regional Administration achieved a good safety and faultless performance record for 400 consecutive days.

In 1980, CAAC operated in all 26,243 scheduled flights, 78 special flights and 3,403 charter flights. The punctuality of scheduled flights and the turnaround time of planes at airports both improved over 1979. The monthly on-time rate of international scheduled services reached an all-time high of 99.3%.

CAAC has repeatedly instructed its staff members to serve whole-heartedly both domestic and foreign passengers and cargo owners. In 1980, an "If I Were A Passenger" drive was launched among CAAC flight attendants and other service personnel to underscore and improve their professional training. CAAC also sent employees abroad to observe and learn the service operations of foreign airlines. It also modified its service work, and thus upgraded service quality.

As approved by the government, duty-free shops were set up at the international airports in Beijing, Shanghai and Guangzhou. In these shops, a variety of domestic products and handicrafts of distinctive national character are sold for foreign currencies. The shops are a great convenience for foreign passengers and compatriots from Hong Kong, Macao and Taiwan.

The Beijing Aviation Food Company, a joint venture between CAAC's Beijing Regional Administration and Hong Kong Aviation Catering, Ltd. opened for business in May 1980. With advanced equipment and efficient management, the company can prepare food not only for all the international and domestic flights originating from Beijing, but also provide high-quality meals for the 10 foreign airlines that make regular flights to China's airports.

III. Challenges of the Future

China's civil aviation has made considerable progress in the 30 years since the founding of the People's Republic. But compared with the air transport industry in the developed countries, we still lag far behind both in the volume of traffic carried and in carrying capacity. In our country, the proportion of the volume of traffic carried by air transport to the total volume of traffic of all modes of transportation is very small. Many small and medium-sized cities and tourist sites are still in want of scheduled air services. CAAC's system of management, labour and wage systems, etc. also cannot meet the requirements of a state enterprise, and further readjustment, restructuring, consolidation and improvement remain to be done.

Higher Economic Targets. The Four Modernizations and growth of tourism have imposed new and greater demands on civil aviation. The government's policy to develop civil aviation in the course of the readjustment of the national economy is entirely sound and correct. Accordingly, the various economic targets of civil aviation for several years to come will be raised to new levels. CAAC, as a state enterprise, is required to attain an overall balance in its management. It must reform its system of administration and the style and method of management.

As of 1981, CAAC adopted the following targets: a fixed amount of financial contributions to be raised; a fixed amount of profit to be turned over to the government; excess profit to be shared proportionally between the government and the enterprise; and no subsidy or compensation for deficits. In an effort to strengthen the enterprises' internal cooperation and coordination, to raise the load factor of scheduled flights and improve economic results, the principal regional administrations are required to operate jointly on domestic route flights. The labour system also has to be reformed; and existing temporary employment system for a few categories of employees will be changed to regular employment so as to stabilize the workforce. We shall expand further our international air routes and readjust our domestic air routes.

To meet the needs of tourism growth, we shall also build, expand and reconstruct a number of airports, open new air routes and increase the frequency of scheduled flights. The expansion of Guilin Airfield was completed in May 1980, and the airfield is now capable of handling large types of aircraft. Other airfields under expansion include Fuzhou Airfield and Tunxi Airfield. Changsha Airport, Dalian Airport and Nanchang Airport will also be reconstructed. New airports, airfields or new stations are planned for Dunhuang, Datong, Qingdao, Quanzhou, Lushan, Sanya and all major tourist sites.

Further Measures. We must give special attention to the fostering of talented personnel and their training in technical skills. We must strengthen the work of our institutions of higher learning and scientific research. We shall seek the approval of the State Council for changing the status of the Tianjin Professional Technical School to that of a college. We shall also make every effort to establish a centre for advanced training of CAAC technical and operational personnel during the period of the Sixth Five-Year Plan.

We shall continue to do our utmost to ensure flight safety, to enhance flight regularity and to improve passenger service. In this way, we shall further strengthen the competitive position of our civil aviation to service the Four Modernizations.

31. CHINA'S POSTS AND TELECOMMUNICATIONS
By the Research Office,
Ministry of Posts and Telecommunications

I. History of Post and Telecommunications Services in New China

In the early days after Liberation, there were some 26,000 post and telecommunications offices and about 400 old mail trucks in the entire country. The telecommunications network was in a state of total confusion. Under the leadership of the Chinese Communist Party and the People's Government, however, postal and telecommunications workers took up the task of rehabilitation and, within a very short time, constructed a postal and telecommunications network that radiated from Beijing to connect cities and rural areas throughout the country. The guiding principle was to serve the needs of the people and national defence, both politically and economically, and to coordinate various crucial tasks. The financial target of balancing expenditures with revenues, leaving some reserve, was realized. What had been formerly a bureaucratic structure was reorganized into a socialist undertaking to serve the people.

During the First Five-Year Plan period, post and telecommunications authorities started working on the technological transformation and expansion of telecommunications services. Key centres with modern equipment were built, e.g., the Beijing Telegraph Building, the No. 1 Radio Transmitting Station in Beijing, the International Radio Station in Xinjiang and a number of other installations. Rural communications were reorganized and strengthened, and the foundation of a socialist communications system was essentially established.

A Series of Setbacks. In the years after 1958, posts and telecommunications networks were further expanded and the sphere of services further enlarged. The industry for manufacture of telecommunications equipment was started as well. But some of the projects were too ambitious and impractical to provide real benefits. Thus, from 1961 to 1963, some readjustments were made to enable post and telecommunications undertakings to grow in a more stable and sure manner. During the "cultural revolution," posts and telecommunications work suffered severe interference from Lin Biao and the Gang of Four, but the ranks of postal and telecommunications workers stood firm, assuring that services remained normal at all times and even producing some new advanced equipment.

Mail Services. In the past 30 years, with the growing pace of socialist construction, much has been accomplished through post and telecommunications undertakings. At the end of 1979, the total length of mail routes reached more than 4 million km., which was 6.8 times that of 1949. The number of service offices increased overall by 88.6%; the growth was even more significant in rural and remote border areas where mail service, under old China, had been extremely backward.

The railroad mail routes, which are the main carriers of mail, have increased eight times in total length since 1949, and directly operated motor truck mail routes have increased 32 times. New equipment and devices for handling mail have been put into use. There are 34 offices in the larger cities and towns where parcel sorting is done with mechanized equipment; lift trucks and traction cars are used at the more important mail transfer centres along rail lines. The volume of mail has increased greatly since 1949; letters have increased by more than 6 times, parcels by 26.5 times and postal money orders by 28.4 times. The volume of newspapers and periodicals distributed increased by 55.8 times between 1950 and 1980.

Telecommunications. The basis of a national telecommunications network has been established with open-wire and shortwave radio as the chief means of transmission, supplemented by cable and microwave systems. With the growth in telecommunications, responsibility systems have been set up and improved for equipment maintenance, operations and administrative duties. Construction of the first 1,800-channel medium coaxial cable carrier system was begun in October 1973 and was completed and put into operation in March 1976. This achievement is significant in that it provided the technical basis for construction of national trunk lines. Microwave routes now connect 26 provinces, municipalities and autonomous regions, using the 960- and 600-channel systems. Total capacity of urban exchanges has increased more than seven times over that of 1949. Telegraph circuits are now three times those of the period just after Liberation, and long-distance toll circuits are seven times greater.

In international communications, three earth

satellites in Beijing and Shanghai are now handling international traffic via the Intelsat satellites over the Pacific and Indian oceans. The jointly operated China-Japan submarine cable began operating in October 1976. At present, China has direct telecommunications circuits with 46 countries and regions and direct postal relations with 111 countries and regions.

Equipment and Training. Post and telecommunications equipment manufacturing, technological research and personnel training also have made steady progress in the past 30 years. The equipment-manufacturing industry, which started from scratch, developed from the manufacture of parts and assembly to the production of complete modern systems. In research and development, there are two scientific research institutes of posts and telecommunications and 38 research laboratories, with a number of auxiliary workshops.

For personnel training and education, there are four college-level institutes of posts and telecommunications and two polytechnical schools in addition to the departments in various universities which offer courses in telecommunications engineering. Post and telecommunications administrations in provinces, municipalities and autonomous regions also sponsor vocational schools for the training of their staff. College correspondence courses, various training classes and televised teaching programs are also available for the in-service training of personnel.

Technical Advances. The technological level of post and telecommunications plants and installations is being upgraded continuously. In postal services, the motorized transport of mail rose from a ratio of 13.5% in 1949 to 33.4% in 1979. In telecommunications, carrier systems advanced from the single, 3-channel and 12-channel open-wire and the 60-channel balanced cable systems to the 1,800-channel transistorized coaxial cable system. Radio equipment has evolved from the 60- and 600-channel electron tube microwave systems to the 960-channel microwave system using transisitorized equipment. Crossbar and semi-electronic local exchanges, coded crossbar exchanges for automatic switching of toll calls, facsimile transmission systems, low- and high-speed telegraph and low- and medium-speed data transmission systems are all being used efficiently, and our factories are capable of producing this equipment.

Compared with advanced world levels and the objective needs of the country, China's post and telecommunications services are, at present, still quite backward. However, as a result of development and construction efforts during the past 30 years, post and telecommunications networks now extend in all directions from Beijing to all the provinces and districts, and service offices are located throughout the country. As a vital part of the national economy and as an important element of social productivity, post and telecommunications services are playing a larger and larger role in socialist construction and in the life of the people.

II. Growth and Development of Posts and Telecommunications in 1980

The provision of good-quality communications services was the principal task of the post and telecommunications departments in 1980, with special importance placed on readjustment. During the year, enormous efforts were made in the following areas: enhancing communications capabilities, improving quality, expanding services, increasing revenues, cutting expenditures and readjusting enterprises. All these steps contributed to the satisfactory achievement of national economic tasks.

Total revenues from communications services in 1980 were 1,330 million yuan. Traffic volume included 3,310 million letters, 71.53 million parcels, 135 million postal money orders (giro), 160 million issues of publications, 17,098 million copies of newspapers and periodicals, 140 million telegrams and 210 million outgoing toll-call bills. By the end of the year, there were 1.34 million urban telephone subscribers and 799,000 telephone subscribers in rural areas.

Gains in Capacity and Service. Readjustment significantly enhanced communications capabilities. In 1980, the capacity of automatic telephone exchanges in large and medium-sized cities increased by 65,000 lines, toll circuits increased by 1,700 lines and productive floor space in metropolitan areas increased by more than 20,000 sq. m. The microwave transmission network is now being used for domestic telephone services, with a gain of 259 additional long-distance voice circuits. On some circuits connecting Beijing with 19 cities, automatic or semi-automatic toll dialling systems have been installed.

Service quality has been improved through a variety of means. In the past year or two, the post and telecommunications authorities reactivated and/or expanded several types of postal services. These included: (1) acceptance of commercial parcels, retail sales of publications, stamp collection services, express delivery of parcels and postal money orders; (2) urban telephones, public telephones, private-line telephone service and international service; (3) data communications, recorded-image communications, telex, subscriber facsimile services, international express mail, intracity mailing of confidential correspondence, advertizing agency services and purchases on subscribers' behalf (on a trial basis). All these services are beneficial to the development of the national economy and are of great convenience to the public.

In 1980, telegraph circuits provided by the post and telecommunications administrations completed the linkup of the State Planning Commission's computer centre with a number of the country's principal iron and steel enterprises and 28 provincial planning commissions. The inauguration of the State Planning Commission Data Network produced time-saving and labour-saving results and promoted management efficiency. An experimental recorded-image communications service has been utilized by relevant departments for broadcasting nationwide programmes of sports, news, on-site athletic competitions, lectures and discussions on various professional topics. All of these services were welcomed by subscribers.

Finances Strengthened. By vigorously carrying out the policy of raising production and practicing economy, the post and telecommunications enterprises have greatly improved their financial condition. The Ministry of Posts and Telecommunications demanded that, as of 1980, all provincial administrations implement the policy of reconciling income with expenditures, bearing full responsibility for their deficits and sharing their surpluses. This policy gave incentives to offices at all levels. On the basis of developing advantages, opening various channels and expanding services, the rank and file made every effort to increase income and reduce expenditures. As a result, gross income for 1980 was 17.2% above that of 1979 and gross profit was three times the 1979 figure.

Readjustment. Most of the nearly 3,000 post and telecommunications enterprises were reorganized to varying degrees. The number of advanced enterprises rose, while the number of backward ones decreased. According to statistics from 22 provinces, municipalities and autonomous regions, in the first half of 1980, 220 post and telecommunications enterprises were nominated as advanced enterprises. Chief engineers were appointed in 20 district post and telecommunications administrations and in 27 provincial centres and key-point offices. The leading groups of most of the enterprises were either reshuffled or reinforced. As a result, management was strengthened and service quality was improved.

Postal Code (Zip Code) System. With the goal of mechanizing and automating mail sorting to shorten the letter-processing time cycle, the ministry introduced a six-digit postal code system (on a trial basis) throughout the country on July 1, 1980. In the course of implementing the system, the post and telecommunications authorities received many complaints from the public. After reviewing the criticisms, the authorities decided not to refuse or return mail that was not coded. The ministry called for continued efforts to familiarize the public with the system, teaching letter-writers first to learn their own zip code and then those of the addressees. Obviously, coded and uncoded mail will co-exist for some time to come.

New Issues. The issue of new stamps and services for stamp-collecting expanded considerably. In 1980, there were 11 commemorative issues (totalling 27 stamps) and 13 special issues (totalling 66 stamps). In all, 790 million new stamps were produced, while ordinary stamps totalled 1,300 million. The stamp-collecting service experienced a significant growth, earning US$3 million in foreign currency during the year. The magazine, *Stamp Collection,* which had suspended publication for 14 years, resumed publication in January 1980. Judging from the circulation, the magazine ranked first among all philatelic publications in the world. In 1980, stamp-trading branch offices and stamp-collecting retail departments were established in 49 cities. In addition, branch offices in six cities, including Beijing and Shanghai, opened mail order services for stamp collectors.

III. Major Problems Confronting Services

Despite the fact that the post and telecommunications enterprises have made significant progress in the past 30 years, their level of service still lags behind the needs of the national economy. Means of communication are backward, capacity is insufficient and the gap between demand and supply is very wide. Post and telecommunications services should be logically in the forefront of the national economy, but in fact they are a particularly weak link, as shown in the following observations:

(1) *The insufficiency of telephones in urban areas, especially in large and medium-sized cities, is conspicuous.* There are only 3.4 telephones per thousand people at present. A great number of requests for telephone installations are denied because of insufficient capacity; currently, there are 300,000 applicants on the waiting list.

(2) *The lack of toll circuits causes serious traffic congestion.* The existing trunk commission network consists mainly of open wires, which are noted for their limited capacity, inferior quality, low connectivity and long waiting time. However, because the local telephone network is growing slowly, the ratio between toll and local junction lines is disproportionate, which has a direct impact on the connectivity rate of both toll traffic and international traffic.

(3) *Post office work areas are overcrowded and services for mail transport and delivery are understaffed and time-consuming.* Since Liberation, the volume of various kinds of mail has increased by several dozen times. The annual volume of newspapers and periodicals sent through the mail has reached 17,000 million copies, while the number of post offices has increased by a mere 3.2 times.

In many major cities, municipal construction planning took no account of post and telecommunications offices, resulting in very limited serving points. Postal operation sites and publication issuing sites are highly congested; all staff have to work in the open air, with trucks parking on roadsides and parcels piling up at train stations. Steamer and vehicle route lengths account for only one-third of the total mail route length in the country. Because the capabilities of postal transport on the main routes are far from sufficient, mail is often stacked up. Both urban and rural postal delivery forces are deficient, and the level of service is low.

(4) *Communications technology and equipment are backward.* In the rest of the world, communications technology has been developing rapidly: long-distance communications mainly utilize underground cables, microwaves and satellites, and the use of optical fibre techniques is spreading. In China, by contrast, open wires are still the principal transmission media, and the potentialities of existing microwave and cable systems have not yet been fully exploited. In many countries, long-distance direct dialling and automatic telegraph switching have long been in operation, but we are still using manual switching. Stored-programme controlled exchanges have been used extensively in international telephone switching systems, but in China we still have a large percentage of manual-switching telephones, and most of the automatic telephone switching equipment dates from the 1920's and 1930's.

Postal techniques are even more backward. Mail processing is done largely by manual labour. Moreover, with regard to management efficiency, communications quality, economic results, etc., there remain a host of outstanding problems that have to be dealt with in the near future.

Measures Needed. In view of the fact that the post and telecommunications services are a weak link in the national economy, post and telecommunications enterprises will take some steps forward and other steps backward during the course of further readjustment. On the whole, however, there will be progress, with upgrading of services to meet the needs of all sectors of the economy.

First, with communications as the centre, we must carry out basic construction, tap potential, introduce innovation and reform, strengthen weak links and enhance communications capabilities. Second, it is necessary to continue the policy of increasing production and practicing economy, further developing advantages, opening various channels, expanding services, increasing revenues, improving operations and management and stressing economic results. Third, we must emphasize the reorganization of supervisory groups and branch offices, continue to readjust enterprises, strengthen basic-level office work and upgrade management. Fourth, we must continue to study and experiment, working out economical post and telecommunications systems and testing methods. Fifth, we must carry out staff training programmes, emphasizing on-the-job training that will raise technical and managerial proficiency.

32. CHINA'S COMMERCE IN 1980
By the Commerce Research Institute,
Ministry of Commerce

In 1980, China continued to readjust prices and expand commodity distribution channels by implementing its policy of readjustment, restructuring, consolidation and improvement and by developing industrial and agricultural production. Urban and rural markets in China were expanded continuously and improvements were made in the management and administration of commercial departments and their faculties throughout the country.

I. Large Increases in Commodity Distribution and Retail Sales

In 1980, China's agriculture suffered from serious natural calamities, but the losses were minimized by the party and government's implementation of a series of correct agricultural policies and by their encouragement to rural cadres and communes to increase production. Output of many industrial crops, such as cotton, edible oils, sugar beets and sugar cane, as well as sideline products increased considerably, although output of grains decreased slightly. Also in 1980, the total value of textiles and other light industries increased by 18.4% over the previous year. It was on this basis that China's commercial departments developed their methods of buying and selling with a view to expanding the distribution of goods.

Value of Purchases. In 1980, the total value of goods purchased by state-run commercial departments amounted to 226,300 million yuan, a 13.6% increase over 1979. This rate of increase was higher than the average annual rate of increase of 9.4% between 1953 and 1979. Purchases of farm crops and sideline products amounted to 67,700 million yuan, a 15.4% increase over 1979 — the real rate of increase was 7.7%, taking account of price rises.

Farm Crops. Purchases of principal farm crops and sideline products in 1980 were larger than those of 1979. Purchases of cotton in the production year from September 1980 to April 1981 totalled 2.65 million tons, an increase of 24% over the previous production year and up 14.6% from the record 1973 production year. Purchases of edible oils during the production year from April 1980 to March 1981 totalled 1.89 million tons, an increase of 27.3% over the previous production year and up 24% over the record 1955 production year.

Livestock. The number of pigs sold in 1980 totalled 133.93 million, which was 3.89 million more than in the record year of 1979. The average gross weight per animal was 177.3 catties, up 10.3 catties from the previous year. The total increase in gross weight was equivalent to an additional purchase of 8.26 million pigs.

Purchases of mulberry cocoons, tussah cocoons, tea, goatskins, kidskins, Zhejiang lambskins, sheep wool, feathers, bristles, oranges, straw mats, etc. set records and purchases of ramie, cattle hides, sheepskins and dates also increased.

Industrial Goods. The purchases of industrial goods amounted to 156,760 million yuan in 1980, an increase of 12.8% over 1979. Purchases of consumer goods increased by 17.3% while those of producers' goods increased by 3.1%. Purchases of consumer goods manufactured with industrial products as raw materials amounted to 64,890 million yuan, an increase of 20.2%, while purchases of industrial consumer goods manufactured with farm produce and sideline products as raw materials amounted to 47,190 million yuan, an increase of 13.5%. Among 42 kinds of principal industrial goods, purchases of 34 such kinds increased by comparison with the previous year. Purchases of another eight kinds of goods increased, while purchases of still another eight kinds decreased.

Purchase of cotton cloth went up 17.9% over 1979, while purchase of polyester fibre cloth, woollen fabrics and satins went up 30-96%. In terms of clothing, undershirts and sleeveless undershirts, cotton jerseys and trousers, rubber footwear and other items went up 14-54%. Purchases of articles of everyday use, such as matches, detergent, thermos bottles, wristwatches, etc., went up 3-34%; of TV sets, 40%; and of radios, 87%.

Purchases of some goods previously in short supply increased once the enterprises producing them developed their potential and increased their output. For example, purchases of soap, bicycles and sewing machines went up 11%-28%. Meanwhile, purchases of some miscellaneous manufactured goods also increased at a higher rate. Purchases of some goods that were produced in ample quantities decreased somewhat after their output was readjusted. For instance, purchases of hardware appliances, various kinds of switches and so forth went down 40-65% and table tennis equipment went down 74% from the previous year.

With respect to agricultural producers' goods, purchases of chemical fertilizer went up 9.2%, while those of pesticides and apparatus for their application went up 34.8%.

The total value of retail sales reached 214,000 million yuan, an increase of 3,400 million yuan or 18.9% over 1979. The real rate of increase was 12.2%, taking account of price rises. Such a growth in the value of retail sales has not been witnessed since the founding of New China.

Retail sales of all consumer goods went up 21.5%, while those of agricultural producers' goods went up 6.8%. Rural retail sales went up 20.8% and urban retail sales increased by 16.6%. Of total retail sales, the value of sales to consumers went up 22.6% while the value of sales to units and groups went up by 13.2%.

Retail sales of important consumer goods — including food, clothing, articles of everyday use and fuel — showed an overall increase over those of 1979. Retail sales of food supplies increased by 20.8%. Of these, grain increased by 10%; edible vegetable oils increased by 20%; pork increased by 5.3% (supplied sufficiently throughout the country); sugar, confectionery, cakes, cigarettes and tea increased by 7.8-9.2%. Retail sales of clothing increased by 22% and the variety, design and quality of clothing have all improved. Retail sales of cotton cloth increased by 7.6%; chemical fibre cloth, polyester cloth, woollen fabrics, silks and satins increased by 25-34.4%; polyamide socks and stockings, cotton jerseys and trousers, mattresses and sheets, wool knitting yarn and so forth increased by 12.5-29.8%; rubber shoes increased by 14.7%; leather shoes increased by 34%; retail sales of some garments of new design, colour and cut doubled and then doubled again. Retail sales of articles of everyday use increased by 22.9% overall. Among these articles, watches, soap, detergent, thermos bottles, enamel basins and so on increased by 10%; sewing machines, bicycles, and watches increased by 23-30%. Retail sales of commodities for cultural and recreational use increased by 32.7%. Of these, radios increased by 66%; TV sets by 50%; cassette recorders by 300%. Sales of publications, newspapers and magazines increased by 40.9%. Retail sales of traditional Chinese medicines, western medicines, medical apparatus and instruments increased by 12.5%; traditional Chinese medicines and traditional Chinese pills increased by 32.4%. Retail sales of fuels increased by 15.1%; of these, coal and kerosene increased by 16.4%.

With the growth in volume of commodity purchases and sales, stocks of commodities increased correspondingly. Between the end of 1979 and the end of 1980, total commodity stocks held by state-owned commercial departments went up 9.2%. During the same period, enterprises under the Ministry of Commerce increased their stocks by 18.3%, while those under the Federation of Supply and Marketing Cooperatives and the Ministry of Food increased their stocks by 11.8% and 8.1%, respectively.

II. Channels of Commodity Distribution Expanded, Leading to Brisk Urban and Rural Markets

In the early years of New China, the country's commerce was organized into five economic sectors; socialist state-run commerce; collective commerce; state capitalist commerce; private capitalist commerce; and individual commerce. When the socialist transformation of the country was basically completed in 1956, there were still four economic sectors and multiple channels of commodity distribution. Later, under the influence of "Left" ideology, and especially in 1958 and during the "cultural revolution," there was an impatient drive to achieve high-speed development. During this period, the collective commerce sector was weakened and the individual commerce sector and trade fairs were restricted. By 1975, there were 6.27 million workers in the state-run commercial departments; the value of their retail sales accounted for 92.1% of the total value of retail sales. In the cooperative stores and cooperative groups, there were only 1.46 million workers, and the value of their retail sales accounted for 7.8% of the total. In the individual commerce sector, there were only 80,000 traders, and the value of their retail sales accounted for a mere 0.1% of the total value. As a result of these changes, channels of commodity distribution were narrowed and obstructed, production was hindered, the variety of commodities reduced and many characteristics of business disappeared.

Since the smashing of the Gang of Four and especially since the Third Plenary Session of the 11th Party Central Committee, channels of commodity distribution have increased rapidly with the restoration of country-fair trade, the opening of city markets for farm produce and sideline products, the active expansion of collective commerce and the development of individual commerce. By the end of 1979, 33,302 country fairs were restored; 2,226 city markets for farm produce and sideline products were opened; 700 trade warehouses were restored or established in towns and cities; the number of establishments of collective commerce, catering trade and service trade went up to 676,000, employing 28.81 million workers; and the number of traders in individual commerce up to nearly 300,000.

In 1980 commodity distribution expanded further through various channels and urban and rural markets perked up as a result of the following developments: the abolition of exclusive selling for a large number of industrial goods by state-run commercial departments; the experimentation with a state monopoly for purchase and marketing, planned purchases, order or choice purchases; the implementation of rural economic policies step by step; and the state's encouragement of collective commerce and individual traders by deferring or reducing their taxes, offering loans, or making available supplies of goods.

1. *Collective and individual commerce were quickly restored and developed.* By the end of 1980, there were 763,000 establishments engaged in urban and rural collective commerce, catering trade and service trade — an increase of 13.9% over the previous year — employing 3,334 million workers — an increase of 15.7%. There were 686,000 shops and 897,000 traders in individual commerce, a threefold increase over the previous year. The share contributed by retail sales of urban and rural commerce and catering trade to the total value of retail sales went up from 8.9% in 1979 to 12.6% in 1980.

2. *Direct sales by industrial departments increased greatly.* According to statistics from the Ministry of Commerce, there were more than 11,000 direct selling establishments throughout the country, up 3.7 times, and nearly 80,000 workers, a fourfold increase. The total value of direct sales amounted to 16,500 million yuan, an increase of 59.3% over the previous year. The share in the total value of retail sales increased from 5.8% in 1979 to 7.7% in 1980.

3. *Markets for farm produce and sideline products enjoyed unprecedented activity.* At the end of 1980, there were 40,809 trade fairs, 10,806 more than in 1979, representing a 36% increase. The volume of business amounted to 23,800 million yuan, an increase of 29.4% over the previous year. If calculated in terms of state listed prices, the increase would be equivalent to 8.4% of the total value of retail sales. The increase was 0.7% above the 7.7% of 1979. A breakdown of the trade fairs held showed that there were 37,890 rural fairs whose volume of business totalled 21,200 million yuan, an increase of 24% over the previous year. (This figure surpassed the volume of business done in 1965 before the "cultural revolution.") There were 2,919 city markets for farm produce and sideline products doing a volume of business of 2,600 million yuan, an increase of 100% over 1979. In 1980, trade fair dates were restored throughout the country and morning fairs, evening fairs, temple fairs, mule and horse fairs, meetings for internal exchange of goods and other forms of exchange were resumed.

4. *Increase in number of trade warehouses.* According to incomplete statistics, there were 1,900 trade warehouses in the urban and rural supply and marketing cooperatives at the end of 1980. Their volume of business amounted to 2,500 million yuan. There were 100 trade warehouses for the pharmaceutical departments; 490 for trust companies under the Ministry of Commerce (actually, the number would be 580 if warehouses run by the collective commerce sector were included); 3,300 warehouses for grain and oil (including centres for exchange and neighbourhood service centres) — an increase of 43% over the previous year.

Wholesale markets for small commodities, wholesale-retail shops, as well as stores associated with a variety of departments and economic sectors were also restored and developed.

III. Unreasonable Prices Readjusted in a Planned Way with a View to Developing Production

For 30 years since the founding of The People's Republic, the general level of prices in China has been stable on the whole. In 1979, the total index of retail prices went up 24% over that of 1952, an annual rate of increase of only 0.7%. However, disparities between prices for farm produce and prices for industrial goods have persisted for a long time. In 1979, in the spirit of the Third Plenary Session of the 11th Party Central Committee, the government sharply raised the state purchasing price of major farm produce and sideline products throughout the country, and in 1980, it again raised the prices of cotton, sheepskin and goatskin, jute and ambary hemp, timber, raw lacquer and tung oil. In addition, the state purchased more farm produce at negotiated prices, and paid higher prices for quantities above the purchase quota. As a result, the total purchasing price index for farm produce and sideline products went up 7.1% over the previous year's, which was 22.1% above that of 1978. In 1979 and 1980, the state raised the mine price, ex-factory price and purchasing price of coal, gold, silver, iron, tin, etc. Appropriate increases in prices for farm produce and mineral products play an important role in promoting the development of agricultural production and of raw material industries.

Retail Prices. Starting in November 1979, the state raised the retail prices of the principal non-staple foodstuffs, such as meat, eggs, poultry, milk, and aquatic products, but it also subsidized purchases of these products. In 1980, the state readjusted the listed retail prices for a number of retail goods in a planned way.

In foodstuffs, the prices of kelp, gourmet powder, Chinese prickly ash, honey, etc. were lowered, while the prices of fresh vegetables, salted vegetables, bean products, some cigarettes, wine, tea, cakes, confectionery, fresh and dried fruits, etc. were raised. In clothing and footwear, the prices of some silks and satins, cotton and polyester khaki, elasticized polyamide socks, blend fabrics, etc. were lowered, while the prices of woollen fabrics, garbardine, cotton clothing, woollen sweaters, leather shoes, etc. were raised. Among articles of everyday use, the prices of aluminium pots, imitation leather bags, fluorescent lamps, plastic film, imported electronic wristwatches, imported black-and-white TV sets, etc. were lowered, while the prices of manufactured goods, wooden furniture, items of porcelain, fountain pens, ink, diaries, etc. were raised.

Because more prices were raised than lowered, the 1980 list prices for retail consumer goods sold by state-run commercial departments went up 5.2% over 1979, thus causing the general level of retail prices in 1980 to register an average 4.4% increase over 1979. If account is taken of the expansion of the sphere of negotiated prices and of rises in trade fair prices, then the general level of retail prices in 1980 registered an annual average of 6% increase. The average was obtained from the 8.1% increase in cities, the 4.4% increase in rural areas, the 7.1% increase in consumer goods prices and the 1% increase in the prices of means of production for rural use. Among consumer goods, prices of clothing remained the same and prices of foodstuffs remained stable, while prices of non-staple foodstuffs rose 13.8%, prices of articles of everyday use rose 1.2%, prices of commodities for cultural and recreational activities rose 0.7%, prices of pharmaceuticals rose 0.9% and prices of fuels went up 0.7%. To prevent indiscriminate price rises and to stabilize the livelihood of the people, the state has taken measures to maintain retail prices at the level prevailing on December 7, 1980.

IV. Improvement of Enterprise Management and Administration Through Reform and Consolidation

The initial reform of the commercial system, including the development of various economic sectors and the transformation of the different forms of purchasing and marketing, has played a positive role in promoting the improvement of management and administration of commercial departments. Through such measures as increasing production and reducing waste, expanding buying and selling, organizing properly the transportation of commodities, reducing the stages in their distribution, as well as publicly acknowledging the "best shops" and rewarding sales workers for "excellence," we have achieved continuous improvement in the management and administration of all state commercial departments.

Losses incurred by departments under the Ministry of Food in 1980 were no greater than they were in 1979 even though inventories increased and total wages went up. Profits realized by the pharmaceutical departments in 1980 increased by 15.7% over 1979 profits while expenditures rose by 0.78% and losses of the deficit enterprises dropped by 53%. Compared with 1979 figures, profits made by enterprises under the Ministry of Commerce in 1980 increased by 6.74%, the largest increase since the founding of New China, while profits made by the Federation of Supply and Marketing Cooperatives increased by 13.27%, the largest annual increase since 1956. Expenditures of the departments under the Ministry of Commerce and the Federation of Supply and Marketing Cooperatives rose by 7.79% and 9.87%, respectively, the smallest increases since the founding of New China. In 1980, the annual turnover rate of circulating funds of departments under the Ministry of Commerce was 2.18 times, the fastest turnover rate since 1957, while in the Federation of Supply and Marketing Cooperatives it was 2.33 times, the fastest turnover rate since 1966. Losses of the deficit enterprises under the Ministry and the Federation decreased by 21% and 17%, respectively.

The experiment to broaden managerial powers, initiated by the state commercial departments in 1979, continued in 1980. According to incomplete statistics of the Ministry of Commerce, the All-China Federation of Supply and Marketing Cooperatives and Ministry of Food, the experiment was extended to 9,000 enterprises (including wholesale, retail, catering and service establishments, as well as industries run by the state commercial departments), making up 7% of all accounting units. Overall, these enterprises achieved good economic results. Total sales of the 3,900 enterprises taking part in this experiment increased by 15.1% over the previous year — 2.3% higher than the average general rate of increases, while expenditures decreased by 0.43% — 0.15% lower than the average general rate of decrease.

To hasten the consolidation of commercial activities, enterprises under the Ministry of Commerce implemented on a trial basis the "Regulations Governing the Management of the State's Three-Level Wholesale Enterprises," the "Regulations Governing the Management of the State Retail Enterprises" and the "Regulations Governing the State Catering and Service Enterprises," while the Federation of Supply and Marketing Cooperatives changed its method of profit distribution in the interest of the local cooperatives. The results in both instances have been excellent.

V. Develop the State Commerce Sector in Keeping with the Scale of Commodity Distribution

The development of state commerce must keep up with the enlargement of the scale of commodity circulation so as to achieve a free flow of goods and promote the development of production. For a long time, however, under the influence of "Left" ideology, the importance of production was emphasized while that of distribution was ignored. Thus, the imbalance between the development of commerce and that of purchase and sale of commodities has become a major aspect of the imbalance in the national economy. Thus, state commerce must be developed step by step.

According to statistics provided by the departments of commerce, food, and supply and marketing, total investment in capital construction in 1980 increased by 51.9% over the previous year. New production capacity and additional floor space in new buildings are as follows: 148 cold storage facilities with 1,189,000 tons of refrigeration capacity; 56 oil storage facilities with a capacity of 807,000 cubic metres; storage capacity for 1,820 million catties of grain; 934,000 square metres of storage capacity for other commodities; 2,624,000 square metres of living quarters for workers and staff; 490,000 square metres for schools and industries run by the state commercial departments. The speed of construction of cold storage and the total capacity added are without precedent.

In 1980, the number of state commercial establishments (including rural purchasing and marketing agencies) increased to 1.1 million, an increase of 4.4% over the previous year; their workers and staff increased to 6.98 million, an increase of 5.9% over 1979.

Commercial education has developed quickly. In 1980, the number of schools and colleges run by commercial departments, cooperatives, food and pharmaceutical departments reached 362 (9 universities and colleges, 198 vocational schools, 155 technical schools), an increase of 43 schools over the previous year. The enrollment was 86,000 more than that before the "cultural revolution." The training of cadres was intensified. According to incomplete statistics, there were 1,000 cadre schools and established training classes in which 25% of cadres of all levels were trained. Spare-time schools for workers numbered 4,890, with 30% of all workers and staff enrolled.

The principal problems with China's commerce in 1980 are: the huge gap between the supply of retail commodities and social purchasing power; shortages of various commodities; and random price increases under various guises in some units and localities. Although channels of commodity distribution were restored and considerably developed some enterprises still lack guidance from the state plan because of the slow pace of administrative work. Although the number of workers in urban areas has greatly increased, there is still a shortage of retail personnel in shops. The scarcity of restaurants, stores, and tailoring services is another problem that needs to be solved.

33. HOW CHINA MANAGES ITS SUPPLIES
By Li Kaixin
State Bureau of Supplies

The management of supplies encompasses the distribution of those industrial products classified as means of production or producer goods. This work has followed a tortuous path during the advance of China's socialist construction in the past 31 years.

I. History of Supply Management

During the period of economic rehabilitation between 1949 and 1952, supply management was placed under the unified control of the Financial and Economic Commission of the Administrative Council. In 1950, eight major materials including rolled steel, timber, coal and cement were allocated directly by the central government or administrative regions, each consisting of a number of provinces. The number of major materials was increased to 55 in 1952 and the state controlled the supply and marketing of all major raw materials and fuels in order to curb speculation and profiteering, thus providing the means for putting an end to old China's runaway inflation and rocketing prices, and for bringing about a normal economic order and for developing production.

Material Categories. In the first five-year plan (1953-1957), the State Planning Commission extended the list of materials under unified allocation. Producer goods fell into three categories: those under unified state allocation, those allocated by different industrial ministries and those allocated by local authorities. Goods in the first and second categories were mainly products of enterprises run by the state at a level not lower than the provincial government or some large-scale, state-private joint enterprises, products of private enterprises entirely purchased and marketed by the state or products produced on state orders, and materials imported by the state. Such materials accounted for 70% to 90% of all producer goods in the country. The rest was allocated by provincial, municipal and autonomous regional authorities.

Products in the first and second categories were not allowed to be marketed by the enterprises themselves. They were to be supplied through a combination of direct planning (planned allocation) and indirect planning (supply through market). The enterprises directly under the central ministries, large and medium-sized local state enterprises and state-private joint enterprises obtained materials they needed at allocation prices according to state allocation plans. The state earmarked part of the materials under its control and supplied them at market prices to some small local state enterprises, state-private joint enterprises and private enterprises, handicraft shops and collective farming units through the channel of the commercial departments.

By 1957, the types of materials under the first and second categories had grown to number 532. The enterprises received almost all their supplies from their central or local authorities. The goods of the third category were always distributed freely through market channels. Thanks to the great attention given to overall planning aimed at a balanced development of the national economy, the supply of materials was generally in conformity with the demands of production. This assured that both industrial production and construction of major projects would attain sustained growth proportionate to the national economy at a high speed.

Supply Channels. The main problem at the time was that under the influence of the theory that the means of production exchanged between the socialist enterprises owned by the whole people was essentially not a commodity, the supply channels to the market were becoming narrower and narrower. The control of materials was so rigid that it fettered the initiative of local authorities and enterprises. The documents of the Eighth National Congress of the Communist Party of China and Comrade Mao Zedong's "On Ten Major Relationships" had already pointed out the need for correctly handling the relations between the central and local authorities and between the state and enterprises, as well as the means for properly tackling problems arising from the distribution and exchange of the means of production. Unfortunately, these policies were not properly implemented in the succeeding years.

Between 1958 and 1960, there was a serious shortage of materials, chaotic management and frightening waste, all of which caused great difficulties for major production units and construction projects directly under the control of the central authority. This predicament came about because the production targets of industry — heavy industry in particular — were set so high as to be beyond the capability of the country's economy. To make matters worse, control over allocation and distribution of many kinds of materials in the first and second categories were given over to the local authorities. In 1961, the Party Central Committee and the State Council decided to adopt policies of readjustment, consolidation, expansion and raising standards for the national economy. While reducing the scope of capital construction and readjusting industrial production, the state strengthened its unified control of materials. The number of the materials in the first and second categories increased to about 500.

Controls. Between 1962 and 1965, the question of controlling the supply of materials was discussed on many occasions by the Party Central Committee and the State Council; decisions for work improvements were made. An emphasis was put on giving adequate leeway to authorities for controlling distribution of materials, while strengthening supervision over the implementation of contracts for material supplies. All this helped to bring about gradually a balance between supply and demand.

On controlling the circulation of goods, Comrade Liu Shaoqi's concept of setting up a system of "second commerce" was put into practice. This included establishment of institutions in charge of materials management, i.e., specialized material supply corporations and stations; organizing service teams to keep regular contacts with user enterprises at the grassroots level; setting up many factories and shops for processing materials according to fixed models — shops for repair and remoulding and for recycling waste materials and rental of equipment and tools. A whole set of methods for supplying producer goods was introduced: making direct deliveries of goods from producers to large user enterprises, purchasing in large quantities and supplying in small quantities to small user enterprises and regulating supplies in fixed quantities from producing units to enterprises requiring regular amounts of certain goods; and setting up in major cities supply companies of producer goods and initiating trust service. As a result, there was a marked improvement in the supply of materials.

Disruption. During the ten years of turmoil between 1966 and 1976, however, the supply of producer goods was seriously disrupted. The ministry in charge of that supply was "smashed." Such state institutions in 24 provinces and autonomous regions were suspended and most of the special goods supply companies, service companies and supply stations were either dissolved or merged. In addition, service teams were disbanded and all colleges and schools which trained personnel specializing in material supply were closed down. Consequently, state control of the allocation and distribution of producer goods was greatly weakened.

During the period of economic readjustment in 1975, particularly after the downfall of the Gang of Four, the institutions in charge of material supply gradually resumed work and some regulations for the management of goods which had proved effective during the 1960's were reinstated. There has been a strengthening of state control for the allocation and distribution of producer goods. Most of the goods in the first category have been placed once again under control of the state organizations in charge of material supplies and they are to supply materials in a uniform way. And there has been an improvement in the methods of supply and service. Meanwhile, local authorities have been enjoying greater power in the control of goods. The goods in the first category under the control of local authorities in 1978 accounted for the following percentages of the national total: coal, 46%, rolled steel, 42%, copper, aluminium, lead and zinc, 36%, timber, 18%, and cement, 71%. In view of the reappearance of adventurism in the country's economic construction as a result of underestimating the serious consequences of the ten years of turmoil, the work of the management of material supply must be closely supervised.

New Policies. After the Third Plenary Session of the 11th Central Committee of the Chinese Communist Party, people began to emancipate their minds, seek truth through practice and overcome "Left" errors. The policy of readjustment, restructuring, consolidation and improvement of the national economy has been implemented. As a result of reducing the scope of capital construction and changing the proportion between light and heavy industries, there has been a gradual easing in the distribution of goods. A breakthrough has occurred in the conventional idea that producer goods exchanged between socialist enterprises owned by the whole people are in essence not commodities and are not allowed to be circulated freely. So, under the guidance of the state plans, part of the goods of the first category are regulated by the market. The distribution of goods has become more lively and there has been initial improvement in the management of material supply.

II. Supply of Consumer Goods in 1980

The year 1980 saw a tremendous improvement in the work of material supply. Positive results were made. The artificial tension that had lasted for many years when supply constantly fell short of demand abated. The vicious circle of stockpiling in face of a shortage of goods — and the stockpiling of more goods the greater the shortage — was virtually broken. Never has the circulation of goods been so lively and the economic results so high in the past dozen years or so.

Balanced Distribution of Producer Goods

To meet the needs of readjusting the national economy, efforts have been made to improve distribution of producer goods and the structure for such distributions, namely, to make arrangements in the order of people's livelihood before production and of production before capital construction. A better balance has been achieved and the structure of distribution has improved markedly. Although the sources of major goods of the first category were drastically reduced as a result of the readjustment of the economy and the extension of decision-making power to enterprises, there was still an increase in 1980 in the supply of materials to light industry for repairs and technical innovations, and to agriculture and the fuel, transport and communications industries. For example, the amount of rolled steel under the first category for distribution (including domestically produced, imported and stockpiled) decreased by 8.8% in 1980 as compared with 1979, but the supply of rolled steel for the production of light industrial goods and to commercial departments to be processed into products rose by 8.3%. The maintenance of equipment in production enterprises rose by 11.7%; for technical innovations and transformation of existing enterprises, by 38.6%; for agricultural production and rural house building, by 6.6%. And correspondingly, allocations to the machine-building industry and capital construction decreased by 23.6% and 28.1% respectively in the same period. Major allocations of rolled steel in 1980 as compared with 1979 (in terms of percentages of the total amount distributed by the state) were as follows: light industry, 11.2% (from 9.4% in 1979); maintenance of equipment in production enterprises, 16.4% (from 13.4%); technical innovations and transformation of existing enterprises, 4.2% (from 2.7%); machine-building, 17.4% (from 20.8%), and capital construction, 17% (from 21.5%). This change in patterns of distribution for producer goods was also apparent in the distribution of timber, cement, coal and major non-ferrous metals. The distribution of lorries to most departments decreased in 1980 as compared with 1979, but it increased 86.3% and 68% for agriculture and specialized transportation departments respectively. Ten thousand lorries were sold to rural people's communes and their sub-divisions according to plan in important commodity grain and industrial crop-producing regions and in major stockbreeding areas. The communes bought the lorries with their own collective funds. Such a scale of distribution of lorries to the rural districts was without parallel in the history of the People's Republic.

Changing the order of priorities was not limited to distribution of producer goods. Priority was also given to textiles and other light industries, the fuel industry and the transport and communications departments in matters such as accepting orders, day-to-day dispatching of goods and marketing of products by producing enterprises. State orders on the supply of producer goods were implemented better than in the past. By the end of 1980, these orders for the supply of rolled steel, timber, pig iron, seven non-ferrous metals, caustic soda, pure soda and rubber to the ministries of textile and light industries had been fulfilled or nearly fulfilled. The actual amounts supplied showed marked increases over that of 1979; among them, pig iron was up 70.4%, caustic soda up 31%, pure soda up 19%, rolled steel up 16% and coal up 1.1%.

Patterns of Distribution of Producer Goods

In compliance with the requirements of the readjustment of the national economy and the reform of the economic system, the circulation of producer goods in 1980 was diversified from the original single form of planned allocation into a number of forms of distribution. The following are their main forms:

(1) *The few important types of producer goods which were in short supply continued to be distributed and allocated by the state according to plan.* The sources of such goods were put under strict control but their method of supply was made as flexible as possible. Take coal for example. In mining areas where coal was placed under unified state distribution schemes, the dispatching departments were asked to increase their supervisory role to ensure that all supplies were allocated strictly in accordance with state plans and contracts. On the other hand, in areas where coal was being used, assistance was given to the users to strengthen their control in the use of coal, to check actual needs, to get supplies of quality coal and to reduce consumption.

As for the supply of non-ferrous metals, sources of supplies were strictly controlled to ensure unified distribution, supplies were organized in such a way as to allow users to place orders to mines located as close as possible within the same administrative regions and "supply coupons" were issued to small users so that they could get their supplies at any time. This arrangement guaranteed timely supplies and thus helped cut back stockpiling. In 1979 and 1980, coupons representing 289,000 tons of copper, aluminium, lead, zinc, and products of copper, aluminium and lead were issued but the users bought only 4,173 tons. And in 1980, 166,000 tons were used from the users' stockpiles.

(2) *Some of the producer goods ceased to be distributed and allocated under a unified state plan but were supplied freely by material-supply departments in accordance with state policies.* In 1980, of the 256 kinds of producer goods originally under unified distribuion by the State Planning Commission and the State General Administration of Allocation of Materials, 78 semi-finished metal products, two chemicals and 144 machinery products and electrical machinery units were freed from restrictions. Meanwhile, enterprises handling the supplies of producer goods were given priority to place orders or were encouraged to act as wholesale dealers.

(3) *After fulfilling plans for deliveries of goods to be distributed by the state, enterprises were permitted to market their own products.* In 1980, machine-building plants marketed 22.37 billion yuan worth, or 33.3% of the total value of their products. Metallurgical plants sold by themselves 2.91 million tons of rolled steel, accounting for 11% of their total rolled steel. These products were sold either directly by the producers to users or through material-supply enterprises such as wholesale dealers or agents. Both the unrestricted supply through marketing and sales by producer enterprises themselves help to break up the restrictions of "departmental ownership" and "regional ownership" and enable producers and users to exercise a certain amount of decision-making power in purchasing and marketing producer goods, and enhance economic ties between different enterprises.

(4) *There was some development of the trust business in the supply of producer goods.* Business done by the means of production service companies in various localities in purchasing, marketing and processing such goods in 1980 totalled 4,260 million yuan, or 21.7% more than the previous year. Barter trade of producer goods organized by the departments in charge of material supply was valued at 3 billion yuan. Compensation trade in producer goods also grew.

(5) *Trading centres for producer goods were set up in large cities to provide organized and flexible marketplaces for free trade in such goods.* There were 68 trade centres of this type set up by the departments in charge of the distribution of producer goods in 1980. Such marketplaces in Shanghai alone did 310 million yuan of business in 1980, or 34% more than in 1979. Within two years such marketplaces have developed from spot transactions into both spot and future trading places which were supplemented by regular trust business, thus forming metropolitan trade centres. A more flexible form and a wider scope in the distribution of goods proved to be useful to spur both production and the distribution of goods.

The diversification of the forms of supply distribution is in fact the trial implementation of what Comrade Chen Yun proposed many years ago, namely, the establishment of a unified socialist market in keeping with the actual conditions of the country and the interests of the people. Such a market will have planned production as its backbone, supplemented by free production, and will have a planned market economy as the mainstay, supplemented by a free market.

Materials Management and Supply Services

As channels for distribution of materials increase, socialist competition emerges among producer enterprises, material-supply enterprises and between the former and the latter. This forces supply departments to change their working style of "bureaucratic commerce" and to improve their management and service. In 1980, material-supply departments in most provinces, municipalities and autonomous regions expanded their business network, adding counters to warehouses in urban and rural areas. Over 470 supply units were set up in Liaoning Province alone, increasing the total number by one quarter. Many material-supply enterprises cooperated with commercial enterprises in starting joint managements or appointing agents for marketing goods. The material-supply departments in Shanghai alone established a marketing network of 1,083 agents in state-run and collective-run commercial enterprises.

Supply Activities. The supply departments in many places reinforced their staff and sent representatives to solicit criticisms and suggestions from factories and rural areas. They supplied metals and cable cut to order, sold glass, rubber and asbestos plates fashioned as economically as possible, retailed chemicals by pounds and ounces and expanded their rental business in industrial equipment and tools. They provided warehouses for clients to store rolled steel and timber and also provided such materials on a temporary basis. They supplied goods via mail and cable orders. They registered customers' needs for certain goods which were out of stock and supplied them at the earliest possible date. They supplied consumers with galvanized steel tubes, small-sized rolled steel, plastic and wooden products and plexiglass. They gave priority to the supply of glass, bricks and tiles, cement and concrete parts for building rural houses and materials for building marsh-gas pits, greenhouses and fishing boats.

Innovations. Progress was made in 1980 in technical service and in processing. The experience of the Hangzhou Timber Company in timber processing helped to popularize the supply method of furnishing both semi-finished and finished products in accordance with the needs of clients. In coal supply, the Shanghai Fuel Corporation helps consumers to control coal consumption, to train stokers, to remodel boilers and to supply mixed or patterned coal in order to raise the heat efficiency of boilers. In supplying machinery, including electrical machinery, some innovative enterprises provided services such as installing, maintaining and repairing the equipment and allowed clients to defer payment until after trial use. These methods have helped to boost sales.

Some material-supply departments introduced a system of comprehensive supply. They organized specialized material-supply corporations to supply whole sets of machinery, electrical equipment and other materials to enterprises for their technical innovation and transformation. Some supply firms made deliveries to users in accordance with the users' production, maintenance and construction schedules. In managing materials, the old backward practice of buying, selling and stocking materials in bulk was changed in some enterprises. They started to replenish their stockpiles in view of sales according to specifications and requirements and supplied materials as needed by users. The new practice has demonstrated its ability to supply complete sets of materials, to meet the needs of users, to make timely deliveries and to help users and supply enterprises to raise work efficiency and reduce costs.

On the basis of fair competition, joint management has started between material-supply enterprises and between supply and production enterprises by merging their administrative systems to establish cooperation within the same trade or between different trades. The enterprises exchanged market information, improved market forecasting and geared their purchasing and marketing according to market demand. This has led to a smoother flow of materials. Some provinces, municipalities and autonomous regions have begun to organize the supply of materials according to a system of economic zones. This rationalizes the transport of materials and cuts distribution costs by reducing the transport of the same kinds of materials moving in opposite directions because of the boundaries of administrative units.

Improvements. Many material-supply departments cancelled business transactions in early 1980 because they could not adapt themselves to the new situation. However, with improvement in management and service, both supply and demand have picked up. According to statistics from material-supply departments in the 29 provinces, municipalities and autonomous regions, total sales of all kinds of materials in 1980 were 12.2% higher than in 1979, while the total value of materials in stock was 8.3% lower. The turnover of circulating capital was 13 days faster and the distribution cost of materials was 0.07% lower. All this shows that trade in producer goods could grow rapidly under present economic conditions. The development of this trade, however, is contingent upon replacing the monopoly of "bureaucratic commerce" by good management and better service for users.

Changes in Stock of Materials

For many years, the stock of machinery, electrical equipment and rolled steel had been growing far more rapidly than the amount required for normal distribution. These stocks took up a large part of China's accumulation fund and squeezed out the stock of consumer goods, creating a grave problem for the economy.

Recent Trends. This trend was arrested in 1980. The stock of machinery and electrical equipment registered an average annual increase in value of 5.8 billion yuan between 1977 and 1979. The stock was drawn down in 1980, the first decline since statistics on stocks of such materials were made available in 1975. The stock of rolled steel, which had increased by 2.9 million tons in 1978 and 3.43 million tons in 1979, increased only by 670,000 tons in 1980. It has remained stable since the beginning of 1981.

There was also a change in the structure of

stockpiled materials throughout the country. Among the national stock of rolled steel, users' stock dropped from 77.9% in 1979 to 76.7% in 1980, while that of material-supply departments and steel mills rose from 22.1% in 1979 to 23.3% in 1980. Among the national stock of machinery and electrical machinery, the percentage of users' stock fell from 75.4% to 74%, while that of material-supply departments and producers rose from 24.6% to 26%. Although the change was only a modest beginning, it helped material-distribution departments to play a more effective role in regulating supply and demand and helped users to accelerate the turnover of materials and funds, thus improving the national economy.

The changes in stocks of rolled steel and machinery, including electrical machinery, has been a result of the preliminary readjustment of the national economy and market regulation under the guidance of state planning. It was also due to the measures taken by all departments and enterprises to check their inventories, to set quotas of permissible inventories for distribution and to send surplus materials to other units for use. According to statistics from 59,800 enterprises and undertakings in 28 provinces, municipalities and autonomous regions and 34 central departments, there was a total of 9.61 million tons of rolled steel in stock at the end of June 1980. The permitted quota of stock for normal distribution was 7.291 million tons. Surplus stock totalled 3.185 million tons and accounted for 33.1% of the total stock. In machinery and electrical machinery, the total value of the stock was 31.69 billion yuan; the permitted quota for normal distribution was 21.49 billion yuan; and surplus stock was 13.46 billion yuan, or 42.5% of the total.

Among the surplus of rolled steel, 1.28 million tons, or 40.1% of the total, were used in 1980, fulfilling the target of using 30-40% of the overstock. The target of using 20-30% of machinery and electrical machinery was also basically fulfilled; 3.35 billion yuan worth of products, or 24.9% of the stockpile, were used. Including the use of surplus rolled steel stock in 1979, a total of 2.6 million tons of steel from the stockpile was used, accounting for 81.6% of the total. The total value of machinery and electrical machinery which were put into use in 1979 and 1980 from overstocked supplies was 7.17 billion yuan, or 53.2% of the total.

The rate of use of overstocked materials was even higher in some provinces and departments. For instance, Sichuan Province used 98.6% of its surplus stock of rolled steel and 83.8% of its surplus stock of machinery and electrical machinery. The Ministry of Railways used 96.1% of the surplus stock of rolled steel and 85% of the surplus stock of machinery and electrical machinery. The rate for Yunnan Province and for the Ministry of the Petroleum Industry was 80.4% and 96.4% respectively for surplus stock of rolled steel and 73.8% and 58.8% respectively for surplus stock of machinery and electrical machinery. The surplus stock of rolled steel and of machinery and electrical machinery would have been much less in 1980 if there had not been additions to surplus stock resulting from the non reduction of capital construction and the fact that goods were returned because some factories blindly produced unnecessary products simply to achieve higher targets for output value.

Saving, Substituting, Recovering and Recycling Materials

Efforts to economize fuel and timber by using their substitutes and efforts to recover and recycle scrap iron and steel produced excellent results in 1980.

Coal and Fuel Oil. In 1980, a total of 23 million tons of coal and 2.17 million tons of fuel oil were saved because industrial fuel consumption decreased, yet industrial production rose in most parts of the country. The state allocated over 400 million yuan in 1980 to subsidize the technical transformation needed to utilize exhaust heat for power generation and other purposes and for improving boilers and processing mixed coal. The state also allocated 130,000 tons of rolled steel needed to implement measures for conserving fuel oil and coal, for multiple use of gangue and for converting oil-burning boilers into coal-burning boilers.

The supply of coal was controlled in 1980 as was the supply of grain. A rationing system was put into effect to conserve coal supplies. All enterprises run by counties and administrative units above the county level in most provinces, municipalities and autonomous regions were allotted fixed quotas of coal consumption; they established a system for drawing down and using coal and gas, storing coal and recovering cinder, and awarding bonuses for saving coal. Over 15,000 people were trained in thermal techniques, and the regulation of heat has begun in 500 enterprises, each consuming annually at least 5,000 tons of coal or 3,000 tons of oil. Forums were held to exchange information on how to save coal in boilers and furnaces and on methods of using exhaust heat.

An emulation drive was launched among fuel-supply corporations in 111 cities in saving fuel and improving service. As a result, four million tons of coal, 400,000 tons of fuel oil and 80,000 tons of coke were saved. To substitute coal for oil, furnaces consuming annually a total of 2.57 million tons of oil were converted to use coal as fuel.

Substitute Materials. Progress was also made in saving timber and using its substitutes. Through the joint efforts of planning, production, design, consumer and material-supply departments, six million cubic metres of timber were saved in 1980. Of that amount, 3.69 million cubic metres were saved through the use of substitute materials, 101% more than in 1979. The rest was saved through various other ways and was 1% more than the amount saved in 1979. Among the substitutes for timber, steel accounted for 55% of the total. Steel replaced timber in the manufacture of props, mould plates, window frames and furniture. Cement accounted for 42% of total substitutes and was used for making electric poles, railway sleepers and other products. Calcium plastics and small tree branches accounted for 3% of total substitute materials.

Timber. In saving timber, the experience of the Hangzhou Timber Corporation was taken as the model. The corporation raised its timber utilization rate by processing timber in bulk to supply finished and semi-finished products and to allow for multiple-use of the remnants. It raised the wood recovery rate by putting stricter controls on use of timber in packing and in the building industry and reduced the spoilage of wood during the process of unpacking and dismantling mould plates. It also began to rent mould plates, scaffolds and other implements used in construction. The conservation of timber through the use of substitutes played an important role in reducing the high demand for timber to meet production needs.

Scrap Iron and Steel. In 1980, 17.08 million tons of scrap iron and steel were recovered, overfulfilling the annual target by 12.6%, or 1.3% higher than in 1979. A record 3.31 million tons of scrap iron and steel were handed over to material-supply departments, overfulfilling the target by 43.5%, or 20.1% higher than in 1979. The quality of products manufactured with recovered scrap iron and steel was better than in the past and 85% of the total was of first-grade quality, which was from 5-10% higher than in 1979.

III. Current Problems of Supply

Although China's management of materials supply has improved continuously, it is still backward in many respects. Overstocking and sluggish distribution of materials are still serious problems, with adverse effects on the economy. The main tasks in economic readjustment and restructuring are as follows:

(1) *Achieve an overall balance in important materials.* Experience shows that any plan which causes an imbalance in the supply of materials is not a reliable guide. When the supply of materials is very tight, distribution cannot be smooth no matter what system is used and regardless of measures taken. Therefore, a balance in the supply of materials, similar to the balance in finances and credits, must be one of the basic aspects of the overall balance of the national economy. In achieving a balance, the guiding principle should be that the balance must serve to promote the production of consumer goods to realize the readjustment of the economic structure, so that the structure of a balanced distribution of materials conforms to changes in the industrial structure and in the structure of products.

The method of achieving a balance is to begin by assessing resources of energy and raw materials in short supply, then strike an overall balance between production and consumption of all important materials, taking account of our capabilities and leaving some margin for adjustments. For those important materials vital to the national economy and the people's livelihood, a balance should be achieved not only between supply and demand of the resources under unified state control, but also between supply and demand of all resources in the country. Conditions should be created to solve gradually the problem of drawing up plans too late and making too many changes in the original plans. Meanwhile, reasonable and practical quotas should be worked out for the consumption of materials, stockpiling and the compilation of statistics on materials, market surveys and forecasts.

(2) *Under the guidance of state planning, efforts should be made to improve the supply of materials.* Reform of materials distribution has been correct in orientation and has registered initial successes. However, some new problems have cropped up due to lack of experience. Some products in short supply were sold on the market by producers themselves, thereby disrupting the state allocation plan. The pricing of some materials has gone out of control. The high market price of timber, for instance, has led to the indiscriminate felling of trees. Speculation and profiteering have increased. Appropriate measures should be taken to solve these problems so that regulation through market forces will develop properly under the guidance of state planning.

First, supervision and inspection must be strengthened under the state plan for allocation of materials to ensure an all-around fulfillment of the state allocation plan and contracts for the supply of goods. The enterprises which are allocated materials must be assured they will receive them when they order and the products must satisfy their needs. Producing enterprises must deem the fulfillment of the state plan for the supply of products as their primary task and the selling of their products in the marketplace must be placed under strict state control.

Second, it is necessary to change the situation in which all kinds of materials needed can be obtained only through the application and allocation by the various levels of regional and departmental administrations, regardless of their supply sources, use and quantity. The kinds of materials which are supplied without limitation should be expanded; some kinds of materials should be supplied after check ups and others supplied only upon presentation of coupons. Measures should be flexible so that materials flow smoothly. The procedure should be simple and convenient and the service considerate.

Material-supply departments should strive to organize the market for trading producer goods and to consult and cooperate with industrial departments in order to establish a closer relationship between industry and commerce. They should support and assist producer enterprises in promoting sales of products in demand and should actively support various forms of joint management with industrial departments and producer enterprises. They should also promote coordination among various provinces, municipalities and autonomous regions in the supply of materials. Without disturbing the basic stability of market prices, it is necessary to readjust prices of some industrial producer goods and improve methods of price control so as to bring into play the regulating role of prices.

Third, it is necessary to improve the legal system, enforce state financial discipline and tighten market control so that the distribution of materials will be controlled — but not too rigidly, so that it will be flexible but not chaotic.

(3) *Strengthen the material-supply departments.* A network of nearly 10,000 shops in cities and less than 20,000 shops in rural areas has been formed. This network falls far short of the needs for the proper growth of industrial and agricultural production. Statistics on materials and transportation and storage facilities are inadequate and technical facilities for the distribution and processing of materials are insufficient. Management personnel have not received adequate political scientific and professional training. Under the leadership of the party and the government, material-supply departments at all levels must take effective measures to bring an end to this backwardness. They must make certain that management of materials meets the need for vigorous growth of the socialist economy and assures the steady growth of the national economy.

34. GROWTH OF CHINA'S FOREIGN TRADE
By Zhang Peiji
Research Institute of International Trade,
Ministry of Foreign Trade

I. China's Foreign Trade Since Liberation

Foreign trade is an important component of our national economy. Its task is to conduct economic exchanges between China and other countries and to serve socialist modernization.

In China, a country with 1,000 million people, socialist modernization must be achieved through self-reliance. That is to say, we should carry out economic construction mainly by relying on the labour and wisdom of our own people and by making full use of our own natural resources on the economic foundations we have already established. But self-reliance in no way means self-sufficiency or autarchy.

Trade Policies. Our basic policy is to develop trade relations with other countries and facilitate economic exchange according to the principles of "equality, mutual benefit and making up what the other lacks." With the development of production, our exports will expand. In the meantime, according to actual needs and the ability of our economic system, we shall continue to import certain useful and advanced technology and key equipment, as well as some important materials needed for production and consumption so as to promote economic development, stimulate the domestic market and strengthen our capability of self-reliance.

Foreign trade is an important aspect of our external relations. A variety of business contacts helps to expand friendly cooperation and to enhance mutual understanding and friendship between the peoples of the world. Foreign trade also plays an important role in opposing hegemonism and safeguarding world peace.

Ups and Downs. With the development of the national economy since Liberation, China's foreign trade has grown rapidly — at a higher rate than overall economic growth. The total value of imports and exports in 1979 was 85 times that in 1949, equivalent to an annual average growth rate of 16%, or 12.8% after allowing for price changes. In the same period, total output value (in real terms) of industry and agriculture increased at an annual rate of 9%. But China's foreign trade, like its national economy, has had ups and downs. Complications happened mainly in two periods: the first was during the "Great Leap Forward" when China's foreign trade declined successively from 1960 to 1962; the second was during the "cultural revolution" when the ultra-"Left" line of Lin Biao and the Gang of Four caused havoc in our foreign trade for several years. Although the causes of the two setbacks were different in nature, they both adversely affected the development of our foreign trade.

Since the downfall of the Gang of Four, foreign trade has made rapid gains. From 1977 to 1979, the total value of our imports and exports almost doubled, representing an average annual growth rate of 17% (in real terms).

Composition of Foreign Trade. Over the past 30 years, the composition of commodities in foreign trade has changed profoundly. In old China, imports consisted mainly of consumer goods, and exports mainly of agricultural and sideline products. Since the founding of New China, priority has been given to the import of means of production or producer goods. With the exception of a few years, capital goods accounted for about 80% of the total value of imports. In export trade, apart from increasing exports of traditional agricultural and sideline products, China has made vigorous efforts to export manufactured goods, with textiles and light industrial products showing marked increases. In 1973, China began to export crude oil and expand exports of heavy industrial products. Between 1953 and 1979, the percentages of different categories of exports changed as follows: agricultural and sideline products fell from 55.7% to 23.1%; textiles and light industrial products rose from 26.9% to 45%; and heavy industrial products increased from 17.4% to 31.9%.

Expanding Trade Relations. Based on the principles of "equality, mutual benefit and making up what the other lacks," China's economic and trade relations with various countries and regions have developed enormously. As of 1980, we have established trade relations with more than 170 countries and regions, of which over 80 have signed bilateral government trade agreements or protocols with us.

Despite the rapid growth in the volume of foreign trade, the total value of foreign trade is still comparatively low — lower not only than that of the industrialized nations, but also than that of some developing countries and regions. In 1979, the total value of China's exports accounted for only 0.8% of world exports. This situation is incompatible with the requirements of China's socialist modernization, with the rapid expansion of foreign trade contacts and with the development of foreign relations. Vigorous measures are now being taken to boost our foreign trade.

II. China's Foreign Trade in 1980

Acting on the resolution passed by the Third Plenary Session of the 11th Central Committee of the Communist Party of China, the emphasis of our work has been shifted to socialist modernization. In June 1979, the Second Session of the Fifth National People's Congress decided to readjust, restructure, consolidate and improve the national economy in order to bring about systematic, sustained and balanced development.

In line with the national economic readjustment, China's foreign trade has undergone further expansion. In 1980, the state plan for foreign trade was carried out satisfactorily, with the total value of two-way trade reaching 56,300 million yuan, 23.6% higher than in 1979. Exports amounted to 27,200 million yuan, an increase of 28.7% over 1979. The value of imports reached 29,100 million yuan, 19.2% above that of 1979.

The main features of the development of China's foreign trade in 1980 are as follows:

(1) *Steady development in our foreign trade.* The growth rate of exports in 1980 was larger than that of imports. The trade deficit was thus reduced significantly.

(2) *As a result of the readjustment of the national economy, imports of raw materials for heavy industry and machinery were reduced and imports of food grains, cooking oils and materials for agricultural use as well as raw materials for textiles and light industries increased.* In 1980, imports of grains, animal fats and vegetable oils, cotton, synthetic fibres, chemical fertilizers, industrial chemicals and woodpulp were 51% higher than in 1979. Their combined share in the total value of imports rose from 41.7% in 1979 to 52.8% in 1980. Imports of steel, non-ferrous metals and machinery and instruments decreased by 3.5% from 1979 and together accounted for only 47.2% of the total value of imports, down from 58.3% in 1979.

(3) *Further changes in the composition of exports.* The proportion of exports of heavy industrial products went up, while that of agricultural and sideline products as well as of textiles and light industrial products declined. In 1980, the percentages of different categories of exports changed, as compared to 1979. Agricultural and sideline products fell from 23.1% to 18.8%; textiles and light industrial products fell from 45% to 41.8%; and heavy industrial products (including crude oil and refined oils) rose from 31.9% to 39.4%. The value of exports of machinery and transport equipment increased by 44.6% over 1979.

The satisfactory fulfilment of the 1980 plan for foreign trade was made possible by the following measures:

(1) *The implementation of the principle of economic readjustment and various economic policies.* Local production was expanded and so was the supply of certain items for export.

(2) *Opening all avenues of doing business and tapping the potential of enterprises.* We further developed the manufacture of goods using processed imported materials and thus promoted the production and export of commodities that are welcomed by the international market.

(3) *Aiding comprehensive export production bases, special factories and workshops to develop their production and exports and to improve the quality of their products.*

(4) *Adopting various flexible ways of doing business in order to increase export transactions.* In 1980, more trade missions were sent abroad to promote sales and more trade fairs and shows were held at home. The national import and export corporations held 28 mini-fairs for various export commodities in 10 provinces and municipalities while continuing to run the biannual Guangzhou (Canton) Trade Fair.

Some reforms were introduced in 1980 to our foreign trade system. The major ones were: devising special policies and more flexible procedures for Guangdong and Fujian provinces and granting them more freedom in handling foreign trade; transferring responsibility for making business transactions in certain commodities to the provinces and other departments; establishing in some industrial departments and provinces and municipalities in China import and export corporations with the authority to handle foreign transactions in certain commodities. This was an experiment in promoting cooperation between industry and trade. These reforms helped to bring into full play the initiative of localities and other departments in promoting foreign trade by increasing production and expanding exports and in improving management and administration.

Because of our lack of experience and inadequate administrative measures, new problems have emerged in our import and export work. But these are being solved by the departments concerned.

III. Foreign Trade During the Readjustment of the National Economy

During the period of readjustment, the central task of China's foreign trade is to serve the goals of economic readjustment and assure the stability of the national economy. Foreign trade can serve the goals of readjustment in the following ways:

(1) *Promote production and increase the supply of export goods that meet market requirements.* As production is the material foundation for the development of foreign trade, we must speed up the production of export commodities and steadily increase the supply of goods sought by foreign markets.

For many years, the main problems encountered in developing our exports were that we did not produce sufficiently those goods that were wanted abroad and that the quality and styles of our products, as well as their packing and packaging, failed to satisfy foreign customers.

Economic readjustment will surely create more favourable conditions for the development of agricultural and industrial production and the expansion of production capacity. We shall step up our efforts to expand production of export goods, paying special attention to improving the quality of products and their appeal for foreign markets. The government and responsible departments should take effective measures to develop and promote the production of export goods and to encourage people in all fields of work to expand production so as to raise the quality and the supply of export commodities.

(2) *Ensure the smooth progress of the readjustment by securing imports of the most needed materials for our economic stability, enhancing import management and reducing trade deficits.* During the period of economic readjustment, imports of agricultural and industrial materials needed for maintaining economic stability and developing the textile and light industries must be timely and orderly. Imports of technology and equipment needed for upgrading existing industries, expanding energy production, communications and transportation facilities and for advancing science, education and culture must be organized in a planned way. Only in this way can imports serve the goals of economic readjustment.

This does not mean that we shall import everything. In drawing up foreign trade plans, we must take into consideration not only the need for imports, but also our actual export capabilities. Today we are still running a deficit in our international trade balance. Foreign exchange is not easy to earn. From the short-term as well as the long-term point of view, import controls will be necessary. In economic construction, we shall hold to the basic principle of relying mainly on our own efforts and only secondarily on external assistance.

We shall not import those items that can be produced domestically in sufficient quantity and with satisfactory quality. Items that we can make at home but are still importing now will eventually be supplied mainly by domestic production. In this way, we can save our limited foreign exchange for the most essential items and make the composition of our imports more reasonable.

(3) *Make further changes in the composition of our export commodities.* The percentage of manufactured goods — especially machinery and electrical products — in our total exports will gradually increase.

Currently, our major export items are primary products — raw materials, agricultural and sideline products — and textiles and light industrial products of low or medium-grade quality, which are obviously not competitive in the international market. This kind of export structure cannot meet the requirements of the country's economic development.

Following the gradual expansion of production in the readjustment period, our export structure should improve. In order to earn more foreign exchange, China must increase exports of more valuable manufactured goods. Further development of agriculture and textiles and light industries, made possible through readjustment, will make larger supplies of goods available for export. It is expected that while exports of agricultural products, native produce, animal by-products and foodstuffs will increase in volume, they will constitute a smaller percentage of the total value of exports. Exports of certain products might show little increase or even decrease due to the growing demands of the domestic market. Exports of textiles and light industrial products will increase, but we are more concerned about upgrading their quality than seeking large increases in quantity.

China is rich in labour resources, an advantage in the development of processing industries, i.e., industries that process imported materials for incorporation into manufactures destined for export. There is great potential for developing the export of labour-intensive products.

Crude oil is one of our important export

items. There can be no increase in the export of oil in the next few years unless we solve the problems of exploration and exploitation of oil, which will take a fairly long time. From a long-term point of view, the export of coal holds brighter prospects, although coal also presents problems in exploration and transportation.

However, we shall energetically increase exports of mineral and chemical products on the basis of increased production. We have already set up a fairly good foundation for the machine-building industry. In the readjustment period, production will certainly be expanded and techniques improved through the technological reform of existing enterprises. There is much room for improvement in our exports of machinery and electrical products.

(4) *Continue to learn from our experience and reform our foreign trade system step by step in order to promote foreign trade.* Changes in China's foreign trade system constitute part of the reform of the overall economic system, which itself is a long-term task.

Reforms must be subordinated to economic readjustment and must be beneficial to it. Owing to our lack of experience, changes must be continually studied and tested against China's actual conditions; in this way we will gradually perfect our foreign trade system.

(5) *Further improve the management and administration of foreign trade.* We must firmly reduce inventories so as to cut the costs of management and speed up capital turnover. All enterprises related to foreign trade must pay attention to business accounting, improve their research, marketing and purchasing, acquire a thorough understanding of import and export prices and utilize their potential fully in order to reduce deficits and increase surpluses.

The readjustment of the national economy will undoubtedly bring about a healthy growth in foreign trade because economic readjustment will make the relationships between various sectors of the national economy more balanced and rational, thus giving new impetus to production, to improvement of quality and to expansion of exports. Increased exports will enable China to spend more on imports of advanced technologies and of key equipment needed for further economic readjustment, as well as of important materials and goods for the domestic market, thereby strengthening the weak branches of its economy.

35. CHINA'S IMPORTATION OF TECHNOLOGY
By the Research Department,
State Administrative Commission on Export and Import Affairs

China is a developing socialist country. In the current phase of its modernization, China's long-term strategic policy is to learn diligently about the advanced technologies available in foreign countries and to import in a planned, selective way the practical advanced technologies it urgently needs.

I. History of Imported Technologies

During the 30 years from 1949 to 1979, China imported a total of 851 items of technology and plants with a combined value of US$16,500 million. In the 1950's, the economic blockade imposed by imperialist powers forced China to import technology and plants mainly from the Soviet Union and East European countries. These technologies and plants, with 156 construction projects as the core, cost about US$2,700 million; they formed the backbone of China's industrial construction at that time and laid the preliminary foundation for socialist industrialization.

Filling the Gap. In the early 1960's, the Soviet leadership caused tremendous difficulties for the Chinese people, cancelling contracts and withdrawing Soviet technicians. With a view to filling the technological gap, China turned to Japan and Western Europe for sorely needed technology and equipment in the petroleum, chemical, metallurgical, electronic and precision machine industries. On the whole, these imported technologies produced good results. Imports during that period cost US$280 million. However, from 1966 to the early 1970's, due to the disruptive influence of Lin Biao and the Gang of Four during the "cultural revolution," the importation of technology was in the main suspended.

In the early 1970's, significant changes took place in the international situation and China's diplomatic relations entered a new phase. Braving the interference and disruption of the Gang of Four, the People's Government signed a large number of contracts to import technology and plants from more than a dozen countries, including Japan, West Germany and the United States. By the end of 1977, the volume of transactions totalled US$3,960 million, covering 26 projects — including 13 chemical fertilizer plants, 4 synthetic fibres plants, 2 petrochemical works, a 1.7-metre rolling mill for the Wuhan Iron and Steel Complex and 43 sets of automatic coal mining equipment. Items that were intended to boost agricultural output and production in textiles and light industries accounted for 51% of China's total foreign-exchange spending.

Large Scale Imports. After crushing the Gang of Four, China was determined to speed up the Four Modernizations and import more urgently needed technology and equipment. However, the influence of "Left" ideology on our economic work, the lack of overall balance, the failure to act on the principle of "acting according to one's capability" and the rashness of starting projects without careful analysis led to the error of importing on an excessively large scale. In 1978, contracts signed with foreign countries amounted to US$7,800 million, almost double that of the five preceding years, and were mostly paid for in free foreign exchange. This sum far exceeded China's means of payment and exacted a heavy toll on the national economy. As a result, some projects had to be halted or postponed.

In 1979, drawing a lesson from its experience with the import of technology in the previous year, China began to control the general scale of importation, adjust its priorities and change the practice of importing complete plants on a large scale. The new approach began with investigations into the problems arising from acquisition of technology that was incompatible with China's actual conditions and with the requirements of economic readjustment. In 1979, the total value of imported technology dropped to US$1,800 million and only four new plants were bought, of which two were power stations.

II. Guidelines for Importation of Technology in 1980

The National Conference on Imports and Exports, convened at the end of 1979, reviewed the experience and lessons learned about China's acquisition of technology and formulated guidelines for future acquisitions. The principal guidelines were as follows: coordinate the acquisition of technology with the readjustment of the national economy and subject it to the requirements of economic readjustment; focus on consolidating agriculture, the textile industry and the weak links in the national economy; combine the acquisition of technology with the development of energy resources, communications and transportation, the development of basic industries and full utilization, renovation and transformation of existing factories and enterprises, while starting fewer new projects; combine the acquisition of technology with the increase in the capacity of the machine-building industry; reduce the importation of complete plants and import more specialized manufacturing technologies, taking into account the capacity of domestic manufacturing plants and China's general capabilities; strike an overall balance in imported technologies and carry out feasibility studies of these technologies.

Following these guidelines, China radically altered the scale and the methods of its importation of technology in 1980, from the selection of technologies to actual trade negotiations.

Total imports of technology and equipment in 1980 were valued at US$2,600 million. They differed from imports in previous years in the following ways:

(1) *The importation of big plants was basically controlled.* For a long time, imported plants made up a large proportion of total imports of technology. The proportion had been smaller in the 1950's when subcontracted parts produced in China generally accounted for 40-50% (and in some years, over 60%) of the plants. But from 1973 to 1978, complete plants accounted for more than 80% of the US$11,700 million in signed contracts. In 1978, only a few single machines were produced under subcontract by domestic machine-building plants.

In 1979, the number of imported plants decreased sharply. In 1980, the total value of imported plants (excluding the Baoshan Iron and Steel complex) was only US$120 million, or 4.8% of the total value of US$2,600 million transacted that year.

(2) *The proportion of single-item technologies showed a large increase.* In the past, money spent for the acquisition of technology accounted, on the average, for 3% of the total value of all imports. In certain years, it accounted for only about 1% or even less. The imported items were exclusively equipment, and most of the imported equipment consisted of plants. But in 1980, the situation changed; imported technologies made up 50% of the volume of foreign transactions. The total spent on single-item technology was US$231 million, or 8.8% of the volume of business transacted.

(3) *The number of duplicated items was reduced.* One of the main problems with regard to imports was the duplication of imported items, causing great waste. We started to correct this tendency in 1979. Duplication of items among imports of equipment by some ministries was largely eliminated in 1980, although it continued to be a problem in imports by local governments and departments.

In 1980, a good deal of work was done in digesting and absorbing the imported technology, in raising the level of negotiations and in training professional personnel. In addition, temporary regulations and policies or measures governing the acquisition of technology and equipment were drafted. Also in 1980, progress was made in the acquisition of technology and equipment through compensatory trade and cooperative management. Three large projects of compensatory trade, valued at US$101.42 million, were approved.

III. Policies for the Future

In the years ahead, guided by the principle of relying mainly on one's own efforts and by the lesson learned in 1978 about the disadvantages of reckless large-scale importation of plants, China will import in a steady and moderate way the advanced technologies and managerial expertise suitable to its domestic conditions. It will formulate plans for the acquisition of technology with a view to maintaining overall balance and in conformity with its long-term plan for the development of the national economy, science and technology.

China will undertake serious investigations of conditions at home and abroad and make a feasibility study of each project; it will consider the need for supplementary items and will compare and choose among available technologies to ensure good economic results. We are determined to avoid duplication of imports and will switch over from the import of plants to that of technology. Even if some plants are imported, the proportion of subcontracted parts will be larger.

Imported technology will serve to upgrade production techniques, perfect and transform production processes, lower consumption of energy and raw materials, raise productivity and help modernize existing enterprises. In accordance with the overall reorganization of the country's economic and industrial structure, the proportion of imported technology for energy production, transportation, agriculture, textile and light industry and the chemical and building materials industries will be enlarged.

To achieve greater self-reliance, we must strive to master, digest and utilize those imported technologies that have the greatest potential for promotion of economic development and innovation.

36. CHINA'S ABSORPTION OF FOREIGN INVESTMENT
By the Research Department,
Foreign Investment Commission

Guided by the principle of relying mainly on our own efforts while seeking external assistance and taking account of conditions in China, the Chinese Government is using foreign investment in a positive and steady way to speed up socialist construction. This is long-term strategic policy.

China is a vast country with rich natural resources, huge population and enormous market potential. Politically stable and united, it is determined to carry out the Four Modernizations. China thus offers great attraction for foreign investment and broad prospects for foreign industrial and commercial investors.

I. History of Foreign Investments in China

The absorption of foreign investment started shortly after the founding of the People's Republic of China in 1949. In the face of extremely difficult conditions caused by the economic blockade imposed on New China by imperialist powers, the liberated Chinese people undertook the construction of their country on a grand scale.

Soviet Loan. In February 1950, the Chinese Government and the Soviet Union, then headed by Stalin, signed an agreement under which the USSR would provide China with a long-term loan of 7,400 million old rubles (equivalent to US$1,900 million) at a 2.5% interest rate. This loan was mainly used for major projects in China's First Five-Year Plan and played a part in establishing China's socialist industrial base. In the early 1960's, however, Soviet Premier Khruschev's government tore up the contracts, causing severe difficulties for the Chinese economy. But by 1965, the China had paid off the principal and interest of the loan.

Foreign Investments. Beginning in the early 1960's, China turned to Japan and some Western European countries for technology and equipment and adopted the common international practice of deferred payment. According to statistics, this form of payment accounted for about 40% of the total value of imported plants between 1973 and 1977. During this period, the government used foreign exchange deposits at the Bank of China to enable the transportation departments to buy ships for an oceangoing merchant fleet. Meanwhile, small loans of foreign exchange were granted to other departments and localities in the country.

However, due to the 10 years of turmoil caused by the counter-revolutionary clique of Lin Biao and the Gang of Four, as well as to the influence of "Left" ideology on economic work, China's absorption of foreign investment was confined to two forms in the 1960's and 1970's. After the smashing of the Gang of Four and after the Third Plenary Session of the 11th CPC Central Committee had adopted the open-door economic policy, a new phase began in China's absorption of foreign investment. On July 30, 1979, the 10th Session of the Standing Committee of the Fifth National People's Congress established the Foreign Investment Control Commission. The main task of this body is to work out, in consultation with various relevant departments, the policy and law on the absorption of foreign investment, to formulate regulations on joint ventures, to organize departments to examine and approve the agreements, contracts and rules governing joint ventures and to coordinate the use of foreign funds by various departments and localities.

II. Current Uses of Foreign Investment

In recent years, progress has been made in various aspects of China's absorption of foreign investment.

Absorption of Foreign Loans. By the end of 1979, foreign loan agreements signed between the Bank of China and foreign countries totalled US$27,586 million, of which US$11,845 million were in the form of export credits extended by Britain, France, Italy, Canada, Sweden, Australia and Belgium. Only US$2,986 million were actually used. In 1980, the Bank of China signed an export credit agreement valued at US$100 million with a Norwegian bank, another one valued at US$300 million with an Argentine bank and a third, valued at 500 million marks (US$250 million), with a West German bank. These export credits totalled over US$12,400 million. China, however, did not make much use of them because it was undergoing economic readjustment and imported only a few plants.

The long-term, low-interest loans offered by foreign governments or international financial institutions were given priority in China's absorption of foreign investment. In 1980, China reached agreement on loans with the governments of Japan and Belgium. Under the agreements, the Japanese Overseas Economic Cooperation Fund would offer loan to finance six projects: Shijiusuo port construction, Yanzhou-Shijiusuo railway construction, Beijing-Qinhuangdao railway extension, Qinhuangdao port expansion, Guangzhou-Hengyang railway extension and Wuqiangxi hydropower station. The amount of credit would be determined each year by the two parties concerned in light of the projects' progress. The loan effected for the fiscal year 1979-80 was 106,000 million yen (US$400 million), at an interest rate of 3%; repayment would begin in the 11th year and the credit would be paid off in 20 years.

The Japanese Export and Import Bank's US$2,000 million loan, signed in 1979, is for developing energy resources. In 1980, the Japanese paid US$435 million, mainly to build coal mines and to develop oil fields. The interest rate was 6.25%; the loan is to be repaid in instalments over a period of 15 years after each project comes into operation.

The Belgium government's interest-free loan of US$31.5 million, to be repaid in 30 years, is earmarked mainly for the purchase of power generating equipment.

With its representation in the International Monetary Fund and the World Bank restored in 1980, China has developed increasingly closer relations with both agencies and has made an investigation in preparation for borrowing funds.

Establishment of Joint Ventures. In July 1979, the Second Session of the Fifth National People's Congress approved and promulgated the "Law of the People's Republic of China Concerning Joint Ventures Using Chinese and Foreign Investment." China welcomes investments by compatriots in Hong Kong and Macao and joint ventures with these and other investors. Since the promulgation of the law, many foreign investors have come to China to consult and negotiate with departments about actual investment projects. At the end of 1979, there were some 100 projects under discussion.

By the end of 1980, 20 joint-venture enterprises have been approved by the Chinese Government; their total investments amounted to US$210 million, with more than US$170 million coming from overseas investors. These joint venture projects included 13 industrial enterprises, 3 hotels, 1 catering company, 2 service enterprises and 1 pig farm. The partners in the joint ventures are from Hong Kong, Switzerland, France, the United States and Japan.

In 1980, 12 such enterprises went into formal operation. They included the Beijing Airline Catering Ltd., a joint venture of the Beijing Administration of the Civil Aviation Administration of China and China Air Catering Ltd. in Hong Kong; the China-Schindler Elevator Co. Ltd., a joint venture of the China Construction Machinery Corporation, the Schindler Holding A.G. of Switzerland and the Jardine Schindler (Far East) Holdings S.A. in Hong Kong; the Guangming Overseas Chinese Electronics Industry Corporation Ltd., a joint venture of the Overseas Chinese Enterprise Corporation Ltd. in Guangdong Province and the Electronic Enterprise Corporation Ltd. in Hong Kong; the West Lake Rattan Furniture Corporation Ltd., a joint venture of the Furniture and Fixtures Industry Corporation in Zhejiang Province and the New Arts (Xin Yi) Corporation in Hong Kong; the Yanhua Standard Battery Factory Ltd., a joint venture of the Shijiazhuang No. 3 Radio Factory in Hebei Province and the Standard Battery Factory Ltd. in Hong Kong; the Sino-French Winery, a joint venture of the municipality of Tianjin and the French Remy-Martin Company; the Guangming Pig Farm in Guangdong Province, a joint venture of Overseas Chinese Enterprise Corporation Ltd. in Guangdong Province and the Philippines Overseas United Corporation Ltd.; the Jinhua Watch Dial and Watch Hand Corporation Ltd., a joint venture of the Wrist Watch Industry Corporation in Tianjin and the Wahing Watch Dial Factory Ltd. in Hong Kong.

The technology used by these enterprises has brought about good economic results. For instance, from May 1980 (when the enterprise went into operation) to the end of December 1980, the Beijing Airline Catering Ltd. increased the number of meals it served per day from 600 to 2,100; its monthly sales rose from 370,000 yuan to 540,000 yuan and its net profit was 280,000 yuan. Another example was the Shanghai Elevator Works (one of the partners in the China-Schindler Elevator Co. Ltd. venture). In the second half of 1980 (one year after it began joint operations), the company's production and output values rose by 10% compared with the same period in 1979. The quality of all its products was first-rate. Production for export increased by 200% and profits went up by 60%.

In 1980, China entered into more than 30 joint ventures with businessmen in Hong Kong, Macao and other foreign countries. Their total investment exceeded US$80 million, half of which was foreign capital. Of these 30 enterprises, 19 have already gone into operation.

Joint Exploration and Exploitation of Off-Shore Oil. In the period 1978-79, the departments concerned with oil exploration and exploitation carried out investigations and research on the prospects of cooperation in developing offshore oil. They decided to prospect and exploit offshore oil in cooperation with foreign firms under risk-bearing contracts. There would be two phases — first, a survey by geophysical methods; then, prospecting and exploitation.

In 1980, China signed nine agreements for maritime geophysical surveys in the South China Sea, the southern Yellow Sea and Bohai Bay with more than 40 oil companies from the United States, Britain, France and Italy. The contractors went to work between May 25 and late November and all but one finished the processing and interpretation of seismic data and produced reports and maps showing results of the geologic surveys. The costs were borne by foreign investors. On the basis of the surveys, we entered the phase of cooperative prospecting and exploitation of offshore oil. By the end of 1980, four contracts had been signed by the China Petroleum Company with Japanese and French oil companies for joint prospecting and exploitation of oil in Bohai Bay and Beibu Gulf in the South China Sea. Under discussion between the China Petroleum Company and a number of American oil companies was a project for joint prospecting and exploitation of oil in the Yinggehai basin of the South China Sea; invitations to tender were being prepared.

Establishment of Special Economic Zones. In July 1979, the government decided to implement a special policy and flexible measures in Guangdong and Fujian provinces and to designate Shenzhen, Zhuhai and Shantou in Guangdong Province and Xiamen in Fujian Province as special economic zones (SEZ). In these zones, foreign enterprises and individuals, overseas Chinese and compatriots in Hong Kong and Macao are encouraged to invest or establish joint-venture enterprises in the fields of industry, agriculture, commerce, tourism, housing construction and other services.

In 1980, preparations began for the construction of the special economic zones. On August 26, the Standing Committee of the Fifth National People's Congress approved and promulgated the "Regulations on Special Economic Zones in Guangdong Province." A Special Zone Administration was established and economic activities were started. Infrastructure construction — such as land-levelling, water and power supplies, drainage systems, roads, wharves, communications, storage facilities and other public utilities — financed by foreign investment, has been underway in Shenzhen and Zhuhai. According to statistics, the number of joint-venture projects in the Zhuhai SEZ at the end of 1980 totalled more than 70. The total value of foreign investment in the zone was over US$80 million; foreign exchange revenues were US$37 million and revenues from exports were over US$10 million. Employment was provided for 3,700 persons.

In the Shenzhen SEZ, joint-venture projects that had been agreed to numbered 580, of which 400 have since gone into operation. Foreign investment in the zone totalled over HK$1,600 million.

Among the projects financed by foreign investors, industry accounts for 68%, agriculture, sideline products and fishing 24%, tourism 2.6%, commercial services about 2.4%, communications and transportation, as well as land and real estate, about 1.2% each. There are 360 projects involving processing and assembling with imported materials, nearly 200 co-production projects, 6 joint ventures, 4 compensatory trade projects and 6 projects with exclusively foreign capital.

Absorption of Foreign Investment by the China International Trust and Investment Corporation. In October 1979, the China International Trust and Investment Corporation (CITIC) was set up to channel, absorb and use foreign capital, to import advanced technology and equipment and to run joint ventures with foreign firms. It was to carry out these tasks under the commission of various regions and departments and in accordance with the "Law of the People's Republic of China Concerning Joint Ventures Using Chinese and Foreign Investment."

By the end of 1980, projects financed by CITIC with foreign capital were the Xiaosigou Molybdenum and Copper Mine, the Zhongyuan Molybdenum Corporation, the Jinning Phosphorus Mine and the Hefei Carbon Factory. The total investment in these four projects was over US$16 million. CITIC and the Oriental Leasing Company Ltd. of Japan have jointly set up the China Oriental Leasing Company, which is just getting underway. Trust and investment corporations and similar companies have been set up in Guangdong, Sichuan, Liaoning, Hubei, Fujian, Zhejiang, Shanghai, Beijing, Guangzhou, Shanxi, Henan and Tianjin.

Utilization of Foreign Investment in Compensatory Trade and Cooperative Management. As early as July 1978, the government decided to develop external compensatory trade, processing with imported materials and assembling with imported parts. In September 1979, the State Council formally promulgated the "Regulations on External Processing and Assembling and Small and Medium-Sized Compensatory Trade."

The above-mentioned flexible forms of trade

are exempt from tariffs and industrial and commercial taxes. Encouraged by this policy, our small and medium-sized compensatory trade has been booming. According to incomplete statistics, by the end of 1979, 157 small and medium-sized compensatory trade items had been transacted in Beijing, Shanghai, Tianjin, Guangdong, Guangxi, Fujian, Jiangsu, Zhejiang, Shandong, Hebei, Henan, Hunan, Shaanxi, Sichuan and Heilongjiang — altogether, 14 provinces and municipalities and one autonomous region. The imported equipment cost US$117 million. In 1979, their sellback products yielded US$24.64 million worth of revenues.

In 1980, 205 compensatory trade items in all were transacted. The imported technology and equipment cost US$137 million. Sellback products yielded over US$30 million.

By the end of 1980, China has approved 300 cooperative management projects (contractual joint ventures), involving over US$500 million, mainly for service trades such as tourism, housing and taxi service. For these projects, no ratio of investment was defined. The profits would not be divided according to capital equity; the parties concerned would share profits and risks as provided in the contracts. (With regard to some contracts, China does not bear the risk.)

In order to meet the demands of the absorption of foreign capital, China has made some progress in its legislation on foreign trade. In 1980, a number of laws were promulgated, including the "Income Tax Law on Joint Ventures with Chinese and Foreign Investment," the "Personal Income Tax Law" — and the detailed rules and regulations for implementation of the two laws, "Regulations on the Registration of Joint Ventures Using Chinese and Foreign Investment," "Regulations and Labour Management in Joint Ventures Using Chinese and Foreign Investment," and the "Provisional Regulations of the State Council of the People's Republic of China Concerning the Control of Resident Offices of Foreign Enterprises."

III. Prospects in the Absorption of Foreign Capital

We have been readjusting our national economy over the past two years and a long-term economic plan has yet to be outlined. We have only started to accept foreign capital and we still lack experience, but we have made a good start. In the present period of economic readjustment, as well as in the course of future economic development, we will continue to pursue an open-door policy and will positively and cautiously absorb foreign capital.

We welcome all investments by foreign friends, overseas Chinese and compatriots in Hong Kong and Macao. We will give foreign investors equal opportunities and treatment. We will abide by the principle of equality and mutual benefit, ensure the mutual rights and interests of both sides and strengthen our legislation on foreign trade. In 1980, our government signed an investment insurance and guarantee agreement with the US Government, negotiated investment protection agreements with the governments of West Germany and other countries and began to negotiate and conclude tax credit agreements.

At present, various forms of absorption of foreign capital must be subordinated to the economic readjustment which will correct the imbalance in the national economy and rationalize economic structures. We must act according to our capabilities.

Priorities. During the early 1980's, we will give priority to use of foreign funds in the following sectors: (1) development of crude oil, coal and electricity; (2) construction of railways, harbours, telecommunications and infrastructure in urban areas and industrial zones; (3) small and medium-sized projects (which require small investments, yield rapid economic results and help expand exports) in textile and light industries, building-materials, chemical, metallurgical, machine-building and electronic industries and tourism; and (4) technical transformation of existing enterprises.

By 1985, we expect to have carried out economic reorganization and technical transformation of existing enterprises according to the principles of specialization and coordination so as to tap their full potential. The methods and directions of China's utilization of foreign capital must help to realize this goal.

37. CHINA'S AID IN DEVELOPMENT PROJECTS TO OTHER COUNTRIES

By Wei Jing

Ministry of Economic Relations with Foreign Countries

Provision of economic and technical aid to other countries constitutes an integral part of China's foreign relations. Since the founding of New China, the Chinese People's Government, adhering to the principles of proletarian internationalism, has provided friendly Third World countries with economic and technical assistance. This has played a positive role in helping the recipient countries to resist foreign aggression and to develop their national economies and in strengthening the unity and friendship between the Chinese people and the peoples of the recipient countries.

I. History of China's Foreign Aid Ventures

China has gradually increased its aid to other countries as it has developed its external relations. In the 1950's, China established economic aid relations with 15 countries. In the 1960's, following Premier Zhou Enlai's visits to a number of Asian and African countries during which he declared the Eight Principles Governing China's Aid to Other Countries, the number of countries that China assisted economically increased to more than 30. Beginning in the 1970's, China further expanded its economic aid to other countries as its external relations developed rapidly. To date, China has provided economic and technical aid to more than 70 countries.

China's foreign aid is provided under the guidance of the Eight Principles. Having successfully carried out its own socialist revolution, China deems it a duty to support the struggles of oppressed nations and peoples the world over. China, therefore, assists those Third World countries that have already won their independence to develop their national economies, to consolidate their political independence and to oppose the aggression, subversion, control and interference of nations practicing imperialism, colonialism and hegemonism.

Aid with Principles. The aim of Chinese aid is to help recipient countries become economically self-reliant. Strictly respecting the sovereign rights of recipient countries, the Chinese Government attaches no strings to the aid it provides nor asks for any privileges. China is firmly opposed to the use of foreign "aid" as a means to control and plunder recipient countries.

Most loans provided by China are interest-free and the period of use, as well as that of repayment, are generally long. China makes every effort to ensure that its aid is used for projects which require a relatively small investment but bring high returns — projects that enable the recipient countries to increase their national income and accumulate capital for national construction. China supplies recipient countries with the best-quality equipment and materials of its own manufacture at international market prices.

In giving technical assistance, China sees to it that the personnel of the recipient countries fully master the necessary technical skills. The personnel dispatched by the Chinese Government to assist recipient countries have the same standard of living as the technical personnel of those countries. In observing the Eight Principles governing its foreign aid, China has won the deep appreciation of friendly Third World countries.

Complete Projects. Supplying complete projects in its foreign assistance. Over the past 30 years, China has constructed more than 950 complete projects for other countries. In order to promote the development of their national economies, China has gradually increased the proportion of complete projects in its foreign assistance. Over the past 30 years, China has constructued more than 950 complete projects for other countries. Some of the projects are large but most are small and medium-sized ones. These projects cover agriculture, forestry, water conservation, light industry, textiles, foodstuffs, electricity, machinery, metallurgy, chemicals, construction materials, transportation and communications, culture and education, health, posts and telecommunications, broadcasting, geological surveys and public works, etc. Between 1977 and 1980, after the downfall of the Gang of Four, China committed itself to 141 new complete projects, began 173 such projects and completed 181 others.

Aid Personnel. Since 1963, China has sent medical teams to 38 countries; the number of medical personnel dispatched totalled over 5,400. Over 900 Chinese medical people are now serving in 76 medical units in 31 countries.

The number of professionals, engineering and

technical personnel dispatched by China over the past 30 years to render assistance abroad amounted to more than 400,000. They have made useful contributions to the cause of internationalism and the promotion of friendship between peoples.

II. Current Development Projects in Other Countries

The construction of complete projects is a complex and demanding task which requires heavy administration and detailed organization. The Chinese Government and its engineering and technical personnel take their work for recipient countries to heart and regard the national construction of the recipient countries as their own. Before undertaking a development project, they consider carefully the recipient country's development needs and attach importance to feasibility studies to determine whether the proposed project, when completed, will be beneficial to improving the material and cultural life of the people. China is active in undertaking those projects which will benefit recipient countries and which are within China's own capabilities, and it makes great efforts to do them well. As for those projects which are not feasible or are beyond its capabilities, China presents the facts as they are to the recipient countries and advises them not to build such projects or to postpone their construction.

Procedures. Once a particular project is approved, Chinese personnel seriously organize the collection of basic data and information, carry out surveys and produce designs in light of local conditions, select the project site, develop a rational production programme, suggest a reasonable production capacity, determine the appropriate technology and the right specifications of equipment, take care to balance "supply, production and marketing" with the availability of energy supplies, transportation facilities and other conditions, and work out the various economic and technical targets. In short, they try their best to ensure that the project will achieve good economic results after its completion.

In the course of construction, the Chinese team follows the requirements set out in the design and the agreement reached between the two sides by actively organizing the construction or by providing effective technical guidance in order to ensure the quality of the construction and to complete the work and installation of equipment as scheduled. After completion, it organizes trial production and conducts the inspection for acceptability before handing over the project to the recipient country. Chinese personnel may also continue technical cooperation with the recipient country.

Agricultural Projects. Most of the complete projects supplied by China to other countries are for industrial and agricultural production. With respect to agricultural development, China has followed the principles of "adopting measures suited to local conditions" and of "developing a diversified economy" in assisting African countries to establish farms and agricultural technical stations, to reclaim wasteland and to construct irrigation systems. At the same time, China has also provided recipient countries with necessary agricultural machinery and pesticides and helped them to build plants for manufacturing farm implements and tools and agricultural machinery workshops. All this is conducive to raising agricultural production and the technical proficiency of recipient countries. So far, China has undertaken 45 agricultural projects in Africa, involving about 37,300 hectares (89,520 acres) of land which was either reclaimed with Chinese help or worked under Chinese guidance to popularize agricultural techniques.

Some completed projects have already achieved considerably good economic results. For example, the Mbarali Farm in Tanzania, which consists of 3,200 hectares (7,680 acres) of cultivated land, was set up with assistance from China. In 1980, 2,400 hectares (5,760 acres) were sown with paddy rice and the crop yield totalled over 17,500 tons. It was reported in local newspapers that the output of this farm made up one-fourth of the total rice yield of Tanzania, thus, contributing to the country's effort to ease its food shortage. In Upper Volta, where paddy rice had been grown on a very limited scale in the past, projects developed with China assistance have helped to increase the production of paddy rice. In 1980, the land sown with paddy rice totalled 1,600 hectares (3,840 acres) and accounted for 84% of the total irrigated area in Upper Volta. This means the country will produce about 7,000 tons of husked rice every year. Most of the farmers in the reclamation area have increased their income and improved their livelihood on the basis of this higher production.

Light Industries. China has assisted friendly countries in constructing a number of light industrial projects and projects for processing agricultural produce by utilizing local resources. These include textile mills, garment and knitwear factories, tanneries and leather shoes factories, sugar mills, grain and oil processing factories, cigarette factories, match factories, ceramics factories and brick works. In the past, recipient countries depended on imports for many of these items, but since these projects went into operation, they have been producing such items in quantities sufficient to meet the demands of home markets and, in some cases, with a surplus for export, thus increasing their income. The cigarette and match factory in Somalia, built with China's aid, has ended the country's total dependency on imports for cigarettes and matches. The factory had recovered all of its investment in capital construction within one year after it went into operation. The raw materials for making matches, i.e. quartz powder and gypsum powder, are both available locally.

Water and Power. China has helped some African countries to sink wells and construct water-supply projects in dry areas in order to end serious water shortages which had plagued the people for generations. When a new well is sunk and the local people have taken their first drink of clear water, they jump with joy and excitement, and call it "Chinese water" or "water of friendship."

The small power stations constructed with China's aid have provided illumination to towns and villages which had never had power supply, and they facilitated greatly the production and livelihood of the local people.

Infrastructure. The railways, roads, bridges and harbours built with Chinese help have contributed to the expansion of transportation and communications in the recipient countries and have stimulated the exploitation of resources and exchange of goods between towns and rural areas. Some well-known projects include the Tanzania-Zambia Railway, the Belet Huen-Burao Highway in Somalia and the dry dock in Malta. The completion of the Tanzania-Zambia Railway was hailed as an epoch-making event in the annals of unity between China and Africa, Extending 1,800 km. in total length, this railway is a magnificent tie linking two friendly, neighbouring countries, Tanzania and Zambia. It provides Zambia with an important passage to the sea and improves communications between Tanzania's inaccessible hinterland with its capital Dar-es-Salaam.

China has also helped some developing countries to construct buildings for civil use, with a total floor space of 650,000 sq. m. Some tall standard buildings, such as the Hall for International Conferences in Sri Lanka, the Friendship Hall in the Sudan and the People's Palace in Zaire, have attracted world-wide attention for their impressive designs and good equipment.

Medical Teams. The medical teams China has dispatched to African countries have worked untiringly for the health of African people, healing the wounded and rescuing the dying in the spirit of revolutionary humanitarianism. Many teams successfully performed a large number of operations under difficult conditions caused by the simple equipment available and insufficient medicine supply. Some were major operations which had never — or had rarely — been attempted in these countries, such as skull operations, resection of liver tumours, removal of spinal cord tumours and reattachment of severed limbs. Some medical personnel penetrated into remote mountainous areas and villages to help wipe out infectious diseases or to undertake emergency missions to save patients in critical condition. The teams, while performing their medical work, have enthusiastically trained local medical personnel, thus helping to develop and consolidate the medical and health work in the recipient countries.

Transmission of Expertise. The achievement of the best possible economic results by completed industrial and agricultural projects depends on good management and the skilful command of production know-how by the personnel of the recipient countries. With respect to non-productive projects, regular maintenance of equipment and buildings is required for their normal operation and long lifespan. With a high sense of responsibility, the Chinese Government undertakes to pass on all of its technical and managerial expertise to the personnel of the recipient countries. In order that local personnel will play a full role in production, the Chinese engineering and technical personnel begin to give them on-job training in the course of project construction by means of verbal instruction as well as demonstration.

For some complicated types of work, the recipient countries may dispatch their nationals to be trained in similar enterprises in China. When a project is completed, an agreement on technical cooperation will be signed betweeen the appropriate Chinese department and that of the recipient country in order to help the recipient country to further raise its technical and managerial level. In 1980, China undertook 52 technical cooperation projects of this type, all of which proceeded as planned.

The Chinese personnel dispatched to work abroad, whether they are senior experts approaching advanced age or young and middle-aged technical workers, fight on the frontline of production and construction throughout the year, fearing no hardships and braving intense heat. They work alongside local personnel, treat them equally, learn from them and serve wholeheartedly the people of the recipient countries.

During the past 30 years, more than 500 Chinese personnel assigned to work abroad have died at their posts for the cause of internationalism. Their remains were buried in the recipient countries and their names have not been forgotten by the local people.

China has been accorded active cooperation and support in its foreign aid work by the governments and peoples of the recipient countries. Chinese personnel serving in foreign countries have received warm care and attention from the leaders and the people. The completion of every project or the success of every major surgical operation is the result of the friendly cooperation between the Chinese Government and the host government and of the joint efforts of the Chinese technical personnel and their counterparts in that country. Recipient countries speak highly of China's foreign aid. A leader of one friendly country commented: "China is a true friend, a reliable friend in the time of difficulties, and an 'all-weather' friend." The leader of another country said: "Only Chinese aid is most economical, most effective, and suits our conditions best. Cooperation with China is most assuring." The Chinese personnel working abroad have won high appreciation from the recipient countries for their good skills, fine working style and plain life. Some foreign friends said: "We never have the sense of inferiority or feel the difference of colour when we are working with the Chinese experts. We have learned from the Chinese technical personnel not only techniques and skills but also the hard-working spirit. We see a glorious image of socialist China in the Chinese technical personnel." These comments are certainly encouraging to the Chinese technical personnel.

The Chinese Government has consistently held that assistance is always mutual. China's socialist revolution and construction and its just stand in the international struggle have constantly won sympathy and support from the peoples of various countries. Such valuable support has always served, and will continue to serve in the future, as a source of immense strength inspiring the Chinese people in their revolution and construction — and in developing their friendship with peoples throughout the world.

III. China's Contribution to Third World Countries

The Chinese Government consistently upholds proletarian internationalism and supports Third World countries in opposing imperialism, colonialism and hegemonism, and in maintaining their national independence and developing their national economies. China will continue to follow the Eight Principles governing its foreign aid and to provide friendly countries with certain amounts of aid, depending on its economic capabilities at any given time. China is a developing socialist country and its present economic capacity is limited; therefore, its aid to other countries is also limited. Consistent with the growth of our economy, we are willing to make contributions in various forms to the national development of Third World countries.

Forms of Cooperation. Since attaining independence, Third World countries have developed their national economies to a considerable extent through many years of efforts. Many of these countries are endowed with rich natural resources and considerable financial capabilities. Recently, quite a number of countries have proposed closer economic and technical cooperation with China in a variety of forms, with funds that they themselves will raise. In accordance with international practice and in response to the requests of friendly countries, China has opened up new ways of cooperation, which mainly include: contracting for projects, providing technical services, conducting joint production operations and expanding multilateral economic and technical cooperation. These forms of cooperation have obtained initial good results and are expected to be developed steadily in the future.

Project Quality. The quality of all complete projects constructed by China as aid projects or on a contract basis in other countries is good or fairly good. Only a very few completed projects have met with some problems in production and management because of complex reasons. In some cases, things went well at first but problems developed later. These problems either have been solved or are being solved, thanks to the joint efforts of the Chinese government and the countries concerned. China has always monitored with interest the practical benefits a project brings to the recipient country. It not only tries its best to build the projects successfully but also actively gives technical guidance in production, helps to improve project management, and assists in maintaining and updating equipment, as well as ordering replacements and spare parts, so as to ensure that the projects have significant impact on the development of Third World countries.

Along with progress in its friendly relations with other Third World countries, China will extend its scope of cooperation with them in economic and technical fields — and such cooperation should bear ever richer and more varied fruit in the future.

38. CHINA'S CUSTOMS SERVICE
By the General Office,
Customs General Administration

Guarding China's economic gates, the Chinese Customs Service, an organ of the state, exercises powers of supervision and control at the country's ports. Acting in accordance with the Provisional Customs Law of the People's Republic of China, the Customs Service is responsible for the supervision and control of import and export cargoes, currencies, bullion, postal matter, passengers' luggage, means of conveyance and articles carried by their crew; the collection of customs duties, taxes, fees and other charges levied by the Customs Service according to the law, as well as for the prevention of smuggling and the performance of other customs work. In brief, supervision and control, collection of customs revenue and prevention of smuggling are the three basic functions which enable the Customs Service to implement effectively government policies, laws and other enactments on imports and exports, to guard against foreign political and economic infiltration and to prevent smuggling and illicit operations. All these actions contribute to the protection of domestic production, the stabilization of the market, the promotion of foreign economic and trade activities on the basis of equality and mutual benefit and to the enhancement of friendly relations between our people and those of foreign countries.

I. History of the Customs Service

Since 1949, the year when the Chinese people, under the leadership of the Communist Party of China, won the great victory of the New Democratic Revolution, and simultaneously wrested from the hands of the imperialists and Kuomintang reactionaries the Customs Service's administrative rights and tariff autonomy, the key to China's economic gate has been returned to the hands of the Chinese people. This put an end to the long history of humiliation extended over a period of more than 100 years during which Chinese customs had been an instrument of imperialistic exploitation. Under the leadership of the People's Government, the General Customs Administration of the People's Republic of China was set up. It took over the old Customs Service and thoroughly reformed it by abolishing all harmful practices. The new, completely independent Customs Service devotes itself entirely to the task of protecting the socialist economic construction of our country.

In the 31 years since the founding of the People's Republic, the new Customs Service has made positive contributions to the safeguarding and promotion of socialist economic construction, as well as to the consolidation of the democratic dictatorship of the people.

During the ten years of turmoil, the interference and sabotage of Lin Biao and the Gang of Four severely damaged the work of the Customs Service. It disrupted customs procedures, weakened customs supervision and control over import and export cargoes and interrupted the compilation of Customs Statistical Returns. All this greatly weakened the function and role of the Customs Service.

Since the smashing of the Gang of Four, however, and under the leadership of the State Council, the Customs Service emphatically eradicated the harmful effects of "Left" ideology, gradually restored and improved the system of customs work and consequently strengthened the organization and development of customs working procedures. At a meeting of customs workers from all parts of China held in April 1979, the guiding principle of customs work in light of the general tasks for China's new epoch was formulated: "To safeguard and promote the four modernizations by making full use of the customs' power of supervision and control to collect customs duties, to facilitate the passage of lawful inward and outward traffic and to prevent smuggling and contraband." The guiding principle clarified the correct orientation, tasks and requirements of customs work and has directed and given impetus to that work in the past two years.

II. An Era of Reform

The year 1980 was one in which customs work underwent the greatest reform since the founding of the People's Republic. Under the leadership of the State Council, reforms were made in the administration of the customs system, with emphasis placed on the centralization of customs leadership. Certain customs working procedures were restored and improved, bringing the Customs Service's function of supervision and control into fuller play.

During 1980, the Customs Service performed

635

its work fairly well: the total volume of import and export cargoes passing through customs was around 89.93 million tons; the number of inward and outward passengers totalled about 12.97 million; the volume of postal matter was about 3.34 million pieces; and revenue collection was fulfilled. The number of cases of seizure involving smuggling totalled more than 36,000.

All these achievements were obtained simultaneously with progress in the readjustment and reform of our national economy and therefore contributed to the safeguarding and promotion of the socialist modernization of our country.

The following reforms were accomplished in 1980:

(1) *Reform of the customs administration with a view to strengthening and centralizing customs leadership.* Since the founding of the People's Republic, the Customs Service's administrative system has undergone several changes. In the early years after Liberation, the General Customs Administration, being under the direct leadership of the State Council, exercised unified control over customs establishments throughout the country. In 1960, because of the changed situation in the country and because of other reasons, the control of customs work was transferred to the authorities at the level of the province, municipality or autonomous region, and the General Customs Administration was made a department in charge of customs affairs under the Ministry of Foreign Trade.

Practice showed that the transfer of staff control to local authorities was not compatible with the nature and tasks of the Customs Service. It affected adversely the correct implementation of relevant government polices and laws and also hampered the carrying out of the functions of supervision and control. It was not good for the training of the professional working staff and staff operations, nor for the customs organization as a whole. The problem became especially acute when the government began to adopt an open-door policy and to introduce reforms in the country's system of economic management.

With a view to remedying this situation, the State Council, on February 9, 1980, decided to reform the customs administrative sytem by returning the staff to the control of the central government and to restore the General Customs Administration which, being under the direct leadership of the State Council, is empowered to exercise unified control over custom houses throughout the country, together with their staff and operations. According to this decision, all custom houses throughout China are directly supervised by the General Customs Administration and provincial authorities exercise supervision and guidance only over custom houses established within their area of jurisdiction. The essence of the State Council's decision is to strengthen the centralized and unified leadership of customs work and to give full play to the customs functions of supervision and control so as to give more effective protection to the socialist modernization of our country.

In the past year, customs establishments throughout China have devoted themselves wholeheartedly to the implementation of the decision of the State Council and, with the support of local authorities, have accomplished to a great extent the task of reforming the Customs Service's administrative system. The General Customs Administration has resumed control over the authorized quota of customs staff for the whole country, set up the Guangdong sub-office as an agency of the General Customs Administration, strengthened its leadership of all customs establishments in Guangdong Province and has begun to adjust the composition of the leading groups of various customs establishments and to readjust their internal structures.

The former Shanghai Customs School was replaced by the Shanghai Customs College. And, as part of the effort to provide professional training for customs staff, a training class for leading cadres has been opened in Tianjin.

The reform of the administrative system has not only enhanced the status and role of the Customs Service, but also strengthened centralized and unified leadership, thus pushing forward constructive customs work and ushering in a new phase of development for the Customs Service. The past year's practice has proved that the State Council made the right decision when it reformed the customs administrative system at the very beginning of the readjustment and reform of our national economy.

(2) *Strengthen customs supervision and control over import and export cargoes in order to ensure the effective implementation of relevant government policies, laws and decrees.* In accordance with the provisions of the Provisional Customs Law, import cargo from the time of its entry until release, export cargo from the time of its customs declaration until departure, cargoes in transit or transhipment through our territory from the time of their entry until departure, as well as the import and export of articles for exhibition, advertizement and demonstration are all subject to the Customs Service's supervision and control. Without its permission, cargoes under its supervision and control are not allowed to be loaded or unloaded, to be delivered or to be taken delivery

of, to be unpacked, to be repacked, to be substituted or to be recovered. All import and export cargoes must be declared to the Customs Service and are subject to examination. After examination, customs will only release those cargoes which are found to be in conformity with government policies, laws and decrees on imports and exports. The documents, on the strength of which customs exercises its powers of supervision and control, are the import or export licences or other papers issued by legal bodies having the right of issuance according to the law. Cargoes which according to the law are liable to commodity inspection (including those required by contract), to animal or vegetable quarantine, or to control or restriction are only to be released on the production of relevant documents issued by the offices concerned.

Import cargo is permitted to enter into, and export cargo to leave from our country only after being examined and released by the Customs Service. Hence, the customs' role of supervision and control over cargo traffic is one of the important means by which the People's Government realizes its administrative control over imports and exports. Therefore, the importance of customs in ensuring the effective implementation of government policies, laws and decrees must be emphasized.

In recent years, following the reform of our foreign trade system and the adoption of the policies of absorbing foreign capital and technology and of expanding exports, the enthusiasm of enterprises in various localities has been brought into full play and foreign trade has grown considerably. But a series of new problems has cropped up. Smuggling and illicit activities in imports and exports are on the increase. Especially through the channel of compensatory trade or under the cloak of importing materials and parts for processing and assembly, some persons have sought to evade the payment of customs duties.

Should such unlawful activities not be curbed in time, the readjustment and stabilization of our national economy will be jeopardized. Meanwhile, as more and more business firms have been set up to engage in foreign trade, it is important to centralize administrative control over import and export trade. This further enhances the importance of the Customs Service in supervising and controlling imports and exports and in making our tasks all the more arduous.

III. Customs Work in 1980

In 1980, the General Customs Administration accomplished the following tasks:

(1) *Along with our efforts to simplify customs formalities, to expedite examination and facilitate import and export cargo traffic, we also paid special attention to the lawful entry into and exit from China of cargoes, putting into practice a unified foreign trade policy, a unified plan and a unified principle in dealing with foreigners.* When we say that cargo is lawful in entry and departure, we mean that all documents declared to customs must be complete and correct and also must meet the requirements of related government policies, laws and other decrees. The name, quality, specifications, quantity (or weight), value, country (or region) of origin or destination of cargo declared to customs must be in full agreement with the particulars given in the covering documents. Any discrepancy discovered by customs will be handled according to law and will be dealt with as a case of smuggling or violation of regulations or whatever it may be, depending on the nature of the offence. For the past year, in the sphere of supervision and control of cargo traffic, the Customs Service has drawn up and put into force a unified customs declaration form, with special emphasis on verification of the cargo with its accompanying documents, its examination and the "check-off," thus keeping the entry or exit of imports and exports in full accordance with government policies, laws and other decrees.

To counter new problems arising in recent years, customs has tightened its supervision and control over those import and export cargoes classified as compensation or other flexible forms of trade, chiefly through the examination of relevant business contracts and the checking-off of imported materials and parts against contracts. The examination of business contracts enables customs to ascertain the nature of the trade so as to determine whether the cargo is liable to or exempt from duty treatment, and to prevent illegal importation or exportation and evasion of payment of customs duties under the pretense of processing and assembling cargoes for compensation trade. The amount of materials, parts or components to be supplied by the buyer as stipulated in the contract must be in reasonable quantity required for processing and assembly.

Imports of materials and parts exceeding the amount stipulated in the contract or not required for processing work, as well as the deliberate increase in the percentage of the defective products' allowance, are in contravention to relevant government regulations and will be handled by customs according to the relevant regulations depending on the nature and seriousness of the offence.

Imports for compensatory trade are confined to "technology, equipment" and "necessary materials" required by the compensation trade items concerned. Export of domestic products to foreign clients in exchange for equal value of equipment, raw materials and component parts, or the import of goods not directly connected with any particular item of compensatory trade, irrespective of their repayment in whatever products, shall not be regarded in the nature of compensatory trade and therefore will be treated as ordinary imports.

Materials or parts used in processing or assembly are in fact temporary duty-unpaid imports of a bonded nature and are subject to customs supervision and control from the time of import until the time of re-export, after which they are finally made into products and can be checked off from the records. This is necessary to guard against materials being diverted for other use, transferred for sale on the domestic market without authorization or otherwise used for unlawful purposes. Within one month after the completion of processing or assembly, the enterprises and firms concerned should apply to customs for checking off the materials against the records; failure to comply before expiration of the time limit will be dealt with according to relevant laws or regulations.

According to prevailing regulations, all products thus processed or assembled are to be re-exported to the supplier of the materials and parts. In case the materials or parts imported for processing or assembling, or the products processed or assembled therefrom, are transferred for domestic consumption for valid reasons, application for completion of import formalities should be immediately made to the Customs Service. On the strength of the import licence or similar document approving the import that is issued by the foreign trade control body, customs will collect the required import duty and other levies and will check off the records concerned.

(2) *Perform our duty conscientiously in the supervision and control of trade with Taiwan.* With the aim of enforcing the basic guiding principle for the return of Taiwan Province to China and the realization of the reunification of our motherland as promulgated by the National People's Congress, the General Customs Administration, under the State Council, in April 1980, established concrete provisions governing customs control of trade, mail and navigation matters between Taiwan and the mainland. Since Taiwan is a province of our country, trade between Taiwan and the mainland is by its nature an interregional flow of goods.

Under present circumstances and with a view to facilitating trade between the mainland and Taiwan, cargoes shipped to and from Taiwan may be declared to customs through the filing of a declaration form by the trading companies on the mainland. Customs will accept as valid such documents issued by the Taiwan authorities and their subordinate organs. Taiwanese products purchased directly from factories and enterprises in Taiwan or from their branch offices in Hong Kong, Macao or other foreign cities and shipped directly from Taiwan, or transhipped in original packing through Hong Kong, Macao or other foreign ports, will not be liable to import duties. Since Taiwanese products purchased from overseas Chinese, Hong Kong or Macao merchants, or foreign traders who have imported them from Taiwan, are by nature re-imports of domestic products, they are liable to payment of import duties. Shipments of commodities exported directly from the mainland to Taiwan will be exempt from export duties.

Ships belonging to owners of Taiwan public or private enterprises will be accorded by customs the same treatment as ships of our own nationality sailing overseas and therefore are entitled to the exemption of payment of tonnage duties. These duties also will not be levied on foreign ships holding the Certificate of Tonnage Dues issued by Taiwan authorities within the period of validity of the certificate. On its expiration, however, tonnage duties will be levied accordingly.

In 1980, Chinese customs has played a positive role in implementing the government's guiding principles, policies, laws and regulations on foreign trade and in maintaining a unified policy, unified planning and a unified principle in dealing with foreigners by facilitating import and export cargo traffic and promoting trade between the mainland and Taiwan. At the same time it has adhered to the principle of conducting supervision and control of cargo traffic in accordance with the laws and by strictly enforcing them and by seriously tackling unlawful imports and exports, evasion of customs duties, cases of smuggling and illicit outflow or fraudulent purchase of government-controlled foreign exchange, as well as other law-breaking activities.

Moreover, 1980 also witnessed the resumption of compilation of customs statistical returns after a disruption of ten years. The returns are a part of Chinese national statistics and serve as an important basis for the study and formulation of the guiding principles, policies and plans of China's foreign trade. They are also helpful to a certain extent in the examination and formulation of national economic plans. During the past year, the Customs Service overcame all kinds of difficulties arising from the shortage of staff and unfamiliarity with statistical work; established a working system for compilation, giving particular attention to verification and cross-checking of statistical copies of customs declarations for imports and exports; and successfully accomplished the first year's task of collecting and checking statistical data.

(3) *Strengthen the supervision and control over importation and exportation of noncommercial articles, facilitate normal contacts and curb unlawful profiteering.* The supervision and control of noncommercial articles refers mainly to the supervision and control over luggage and articles carried by incoming and outgoing passengers, and to the importation and exportation of personal mail and printed matter.

According to provisions of the Provisional Customs Law and other enactments, incoming and outgoing passengers, together with their luggage, should pass through entrances where there are customs establishments. Luggage of persons entering or leaving China, whether being carried in person or consigned for shipment, must be declared accurately to customs and are not allowed to be taken delivery of or loaded without being first examined and released by customs officials. The importation and exportation of personal postal parcels or printed matter are usually passed on to customs for examination by the post office. Postal parcels mailed at places where there are no customs offices should be declared by the sender directly to the customs officer stationed in the post office for examination and completion of all customs formalities for export. All incoming and outgoing postal parcels and printed matter may be delivered or mailed by the post office only after being examined by customs and after customs duties have been paid.

The purpose of supervising and controlling noncommercial articles is to prevent the perpetration of unlawful trade and other illegal activities under the cloak of passengers' luggage and postal matter so as to safeguard the effective implementation of the laws and regulations concerning government control of foreign trade and foreign exchange. Meanwhile, the Customs Service must give due consideration to the reasonable requirements of the senders and recipients of postal matter as well as that of incoming and outgoing passengers' luggage, by simplifying customs formalities and expediting customs examination and release, so as to facilitate normal social contacts among the people of different countries.

Under the influence of "Left" ideology, the Customs Service once manifested a tendency of being too strict and too severe in its supervision and control of imported and exported noncommercial articles and put too much stress on restrictions while neglecting the necessity of giving due consideration to reasonable needs and of facilitating normal social intercourse. The rigid manner and working style of our customs staff has left an unfortunate impression both at home and abroad.

In recent years, the Customs Service has gradually rectified its "Left" ideological inclinations in its supervision and control of noncommercial articles for import and export. It has been made clear that the Customs Service must adhere to the following guiding principle: "Strictly uphold the criterion of personal use; give due consideration to reasonable needs; guard against smuggling and evasion of customs duties; and expedite examination and release." By the "criterion of personal use," it is meant that the articles in question should be confined to those intended for one's personal or family use and do not include those items intended to be sold or brought in for others. By "giving due consideration to reasonable needs," we mean that while setting limits to the quantity and value of goods and fixing duty treatment for different articles allowed to be examined and released by customs officials according to various categories of passengers or of senders or recipients of postal matter, and under the criterion of personal use, the normal and reasonable needs of people should be taken into consideration. Meanwhile, under the prerequisite of preventing smuggling and evasion of customs duties, customs officials are to simplify and expedite the procedures for examination and release so as to facilitate normal social intercourse among people of different countries. In accordance with this guiding principle, the Customs Service has been making amendments to existing procedures governing examination and release of noncommercial articles by relaxing the limitations on quantity, value and duty treatment of certain articles and by simplifying and improving procedures of examination and release, as well as the deportment and working style of the customs staff. For the convenience of incoming and outgoing passengers from Hong Kong or Macao, separate duty-free and dutiable passageways have been set up in Jiulong and Gongbei customs houses.

While strictly implementing the party's guiding policies on the ideological and cultural front, the Customs Service has made adjustments in the supervision and control of printed matter of noncommercial nature. With the exception of reactionary or obscene literature, and of printed matter impairing the stability and unity of our country, every possible facility will be given to the release of printed matter in order to promote normal cultural, scientific and technological interchanges with other countries.

The adjustment of regulations governing customs examinations and the release of noncommercial articles has proved to be helpful in the promotion of social intercourse with foreigners, the interflow of science and technology and the development of tourism.

There have been cases of incoming and outgoing passengers, as well as of senders and recipients of postal matter, who have taken advantage of the favourable treatment accorded to home-coming compatriots by customs officials and have resorted to such contrivances as undertaking frequent incoming and outgoing trips, assuming other names or using false names and mailing goods in scattered lots. They have perpetrated speculative and profiteering activities by bringing in and out unusually large quantities of goods having large price differentials on home and foreign markets. Such fraudulent practices have considerably weakened our domestic market control, disrupted our socialist economic order, slowed down customs examinations and release of articles, and therefore have impeded the normal interchange of visits and mail. In 1980, appropriate measures were progressively taken by customs to strengthen its supervision and control and to block smuggling and profiteering. This is not only essential to safeguard national interests and to effectively enforce government rules and regulations regarding control of foreign trade and foreign exchange, but it also is necessary to provide convenience to law-abiding passengers on their incoming and outgoing trips as well as to the normal interflow of postal materials.

With a view to implementing our basic policy of returning Taiwan to the motherland and realizing the sacred cause of reunification of our country, as well as to promote visits between compatriots in Taiwan and their friends and family members on the mainland, the General Customs Administration formulated, in April 1980, the Regulations Governing the Control of Luggage Carried by Incoming and Outgoing Taiwan Compatriots and Personal Postal Parcels Mailed from Taiwan. The visits between people in Taiwan and those on the mainland are normal comings and goings between fellow countrymen.

Under present conditions, articles and luggage carried by Taiwan compatriots coming to the mainland to visit their relatives will be released after examination by customs, insofar as they are brought in for personal use and in reasonable quantities. Incoming and outgoing Taiwan compatriots residing abroad, in Hong Kong or in Macao will, on the presentation of their papers, be entitled to the same treatment as that accorded to overseas Chinese or to Chinese from Hong Kong and Macao and will be released by customs accordingly. Personal parcels mailed from Taiwan, including those remailed in transit through Hong Kong or a foreign port, will be released leniently insofar as they are kept for personal use and are in reasonable quantities.

(4) *Implement the tariff policy and bring the role of customs tariffs in the protection and regulation of the national economy into full play.* In accordance with the provisions of the Provisional Customs Law of the People's Republic of China, customs import and export tariffs, as well as the rules governing the levy of import duties on articles and luggage of incoming passengers and personal postal parcels, the Customs Service collects duties on import and export cargoes, postal matter and passengers' luggage.

Our customs tariff policy in force is one of protective tariffs. As pointed out by the former Administrative Council of the central government in the Resolution on Customs Tariff Policy and Customs Work, passed in 1950, our "Customs tariffs should give protection to our domestic production and protect the domestic products against the competition of foreign commodities." The principles governing the drafting of Chinese customs tariffs were also formulated to the effect that the import duty rates of those goods, similar to home-made products needing protection, shall be fixed higher than the difference in costs between foreign goods and those of domestic make; that still higher duty-rates shall be fixed for import of luxury items and of non-necessities; that for the import of those daily necessities or goods which cannot be produced or can only be produced domestically in limited quantities, low duty rates or duty-free treatment shall be provided and that very low export duty rates or duty-free treatment shall be fixed for exports. Meanwhile, it was also provided that the preferential tariff system (i.e., minimum tariff rates) and the general tariff system shall be enforced.

Customs duties serve not only as a source of national revenues but also as a weapon for protecting our domestic production. They are also a lever in regulating the volume of imports and exports in our economic relations with other countries and in foreign trade. The levy of customs duties is therefore an aid by means of which the effective implementation of the policy and laws for the control of our foreign trade is ensured. The levy of, reduction in or exemption from customs duties are stipulated and put in force in the form of laws and decrees and must therefore be strictly enforced.

Consequent upon the development of our foreign trade and the readjustment and reform of our national economy, the role of customs duties has grown in importance. In recent years, in accordance with the national policy of encouraging the import of advanced technology, expansion of export trade and development of tourism in order to realize the four modernizations, the Customs Service, acting in accordance with relevant laws and regulations, has granted reduction in or exemption from import duties to those articles imported under medium and small-sized compensatory trade contracts for processing and assembly, to materials imported for processing into finished products for re-export, and to those items imported for building hotels for tourists. For a more effective implementation of the customs tariff policy, the customs tariff of the People's Republic of China was revised in 1980 with the approval of the State Council. This revision, which was the 19th since its enforcement in 1951, reduced the rates of duty on 68 tariff imports and cancelled those of four tariff exports.

In 1980, custom houses throughout China, in their performance of the task of collecting customs duties, conscientiously carried out the customs tariff policy and acted strictly in accordance with the provisions of the customs tariff and its relevant laws; upheld the principle of centralization and unification of the powers to approve of duty reduction or exemption; established and simplified a number of relevant rules and regulations; levied customs duties according to tariff rates and granted duty exemptions and reductions according to law. They thus brought the role of the customs tariff policy in protection and regulation into full play and consequently helped to enforce the national policy of control over trade, imports and exports. Meanwhile, tariff revenue collection also contributed to capital accumulation for the socialist modernization of our country.

(5) *Deal severe blows to smuggling and illicit activities infringing on government laws and decrees.* In accordance with the provisions of the Provisional Customs Law of the People's Republic of China and other relevant laws and decrees, cases of unlawful transport, carriage or mailing of goods, bullion, currencies, negotiable securities, etc. into or out of Chinese territory; evasion of customs supervision and control; illicit outflow and/or fraudulent purchase of foreign exchange; and the evasion of customs duties are acts of smuggling. Economically, acts of smuggling undermine state control over foreign trade and the domestic market, and impair the economic interests and the industrial and agricultural production of our country. Politically, they endanger public security and disrupt social order. Ideologically, they corrupt public morals and degenerate the general environment of our society. Furthermore, smuggling of sham or inferior medicines presents a direct threat to the people's health.

Smuggling is the product of the great disparity in prices of certain commodities on the external and domestic markets and brings enormous profits to the smugglers. As Karl Marx quoted from T.J. Dunning, the British labour activist: "With adequate profit, capital is very bold. A certain 10% will ensure its employment anywhere; 20% certainly will produce eagerness; 50% will make it ready to trample on all human laws; 300%, and there is not a crime at which it will scruple, nor a risk it will not run, even to the chance of its owner being hanged . . . . Smuggling and slave trade have amply proved all that is here stated." Since the founding of the People's Republic, smuggling has gone up and down, but it never ceases to exist and will continue to exist for many years to come. In the past 31 years, the Customs Service, relying on the leadership of local government, with the support of the masses and working in close collaboration with the government departments concerned, has dealt severe blows to smuggling and illicit activities, thus ensuring the implementation of government policies, laws and regulations governing the control of imports and exports. Customs supervision and control and the collection of customs duties have contributed to a certain degree to the consolidation of the democratic dictatorship of the people and to the stabilization of socialist economic order.

In recent years, smuggling activities have been especially rampant along the coast of southeastern China. Gangs of smugglers and other lawless elements in Hong Kong and Macao have attempted to evade customs supervision and control at open ports by concealing, falsely declaring, and masking contraband articles, as well as taking advantage of the flexible patterns of trade, or under the false declaration of "gifts," "donations," etc. They have even organized ships specially built for smuggling to sail along the coast of Guangdong, Fujian and Zhejiang provinces. Smuggling across the frontier of the border regions, especially in Yunnan and Tibet, has also been a serious problem.

Large consignments of industrial consumer goods, because of large price disparities on foreign and domestic markets, have flooded in, while large quantities of gold, silver, jewellery, antiques, and precious Chinese drugs have flowed out. Such a state of affairs has not only gravely undermined state control of foreign trade and foreign exchange, affected government revenues, disturbed public order and upset market controls, while inflicting tremendous economic loss upon our country, but it has also corrupted the minds of some government cadres and workers, exerted adverse influence on social morale, disrupted our industrial, agricultural and fishing activities, and directly endangered the political stability and the unity of our country.

The causes of stepped-up smuggling activities are manifold. Aside from the economic factor of gaining huge profits in smuggling, a main cause is that, following the adoption of an open-door policy by our government which has given rise to a sudden increase in the volume of import and export traffic and in the number of passengers, the necessary controlling measures have failed to cope with the situation, especially in certain regions where border control and supervision of domestic markets still leave many loopholes to be plugged. During the ten years of turmoil, unhealthy tendencies have developed both in the party and among the people and the conscienciousness of discipline also has flagged. Certain members within the ranks of government cadres and employees have tolerated and even participated in the unlawful activities of smuggling and disposal of contraband.

In 1980, the seriousness of increased smuggling and its accompanying evil consequences have gradually been understood by government leaders at various levels and by the people. Under the unified leadership of the State Council and following the concrete measures taken by local government authorities, a nationwide anti-smuggling campaign is being waged. Customs houses in various localities have been most conscientious in performing anti-smuggling duties, have readjusted and strengthened their anti-smuggling forces and have intensified the search for smugglers and the investigation of special cases. Meanwhile, in regions along the coast and frontier, where smuggling activities have become rampant, the Customs Service, in close coordination with the departments concerned and under the leadership of the local government authorities, has embarked on joint operations against smuggling with remarkable success.

In conclusion, we have to point out that under the leadership of the State Council, with the support of local government authorities and departments concerned, and through the joint efforts of the whole customs staff, customs houses throughout the country have fulfilled their task satisfactorily and have made definite contributions to the guarding of China's economic gate and to safeguarding and promoting the four modernizations of our country. But there is still room for improvement. For example, customs laws and regulations, as well as certain decrees of an economic nature formulated by the departments concerned, need to be perfected; the supervision and control of articles imported under flexible patterns of trade are not sufficiently strict; and the blows dealt to smuggling and illicit activities are not heavy enough, etc.

Today, the rapid development in our economic and trade relations with foreign countries sets higher demands on the work of our Customs Service. Hereafter, we should conscientiously carry out the important guiding principle of further readjusting the national economy and achieving political stability, bring the customs' role of supervision and control into fuller play, guard with greater care China's economic gates and wage a relentless and effective struggle against all kinds of unlawful activities which sabotage our economic readjustment and undermine our stability and unity. On the other hand, we must facilitate the passage of law-abiding inbound and outbound traffic so as to promote friendly relations between the Chinese people and people of other countries and to better serve the socialist modernization of our country.

39. CHINA'S FINANCIAL SYSTEM
By Shen Jingnang and Chen Baosen
Finance Research Institute, Ministry of Finance

China's financial system has grown tremendously since the founding of the People's Republic. In 1950, the first budget year, revenues were only 6,500 million yuan while expenditures totalled 6,800 million yuan. In 1980, state revenues amounted to 106,000 million yuan, more than 16 times that in 1950, and state expenditures were 118,700 million yuan, or about 17 times what they were 30 years ago. This growth of revenues and expenditures is an indication of the rapid development of China's national economy and remarkable growth of its economic strength.

A powerful lever of distribution controlled by the socialist state, the financial system has played a major role in changing the relations of production and developing productive forces.

Initial Tax Policy. During the period of the socialist transformation of agriculture, the state enforced a programme of progressive taxation and rational tax reduction and exemption to promote agricultural cooperation. It also made allocations in the form of cooperative funds to help poor peasants overcome difficulties in starting cooperatives. Even after people's communes were set up, the state continued to appropriate huge sums to help poor communes and brigades to consolidate their new-born collective economy.

To facilitate the socialist transformation of the handicrafts industry and small tradesmen and peddlers, the state provided funds and granted tax cuts. Taxes on cooperative shops and groups, on account of the nature of their business operations, were kept relatively low so that these groups could raise their living standards and become more enthusiastic about production and commerce.

As capitalist industry and commerce were undergoing socialist transformation, the state followed a tax policy that was helpful to their transformation. Rates of taxation on different industries were graduated according to each industry's usefulness to the national economy and to the people's livelihood. The profits of industry and commerce were apportioned into income tax going to the state, accumulation funds for enterprises, welfare funds and bonuses for workers and dividends for capital. This was what we called "four horses sharing the forage." The former owners of capitalist enterprises received a fixed amount of interest for their capital in 1956 when joint state-private enterprises were set up.

With the completion of the socialist transformation of the society, China's financial system began to base itself on two types of ownership for its source of revenue. It also began to display its power in laying the material and technical foundations of socialism.

Capital Construction. In the past 31 years, the state has allocated a total of 650,000 million yuan for capital construction. The fixed assets of state-owned enterprises totalled more than 400,000 million yuan. From 1952 through 1980, the state appropriated huge sums, totalling 188,000 million yuan, to support agriculture. This brought about a considerable development in farmland improvement projects, water conservation, meteorology and all branches of agronomy — thus laying a solid foundation for the country's modernization programme.

Financial Setbacks. But over the past 31 years, it was not plain sailing for the development of China's finances, just as it was not for the national economy as a whole. Generally speaking, the First Five-Year Plan succeeded brilliantly, with state revenues growing year by year and economic results improving. Our financial work suffered its first setback during the three years of the "Great Leap Forward" — whose consequences became apparent only in 1961 — and did not recover until after the subsequent three years of economic readjustment. The second setback came during the ten years of turmoil from 1966 to 1976. The two setbacks resulted in a drastic drop in revenue and the poorest economic performance in 30 years. During the First Five-Year Plan period, 35 yuan out of every 100 yuan of national income was saved, but the rate dropped to 26.16 yuan per 100 yuan by the time of the Third and Fourth Five-Year Plan periods.

The root cause of these setbacks was the influence of "Left" ideology, which manifested itself in the overanxiousness to achieve quick results in disregard of objective laws. Funds were allocated wrongly or excessively. Since the Third Plenary Session of the 11th Central Committee of the Chinese Communist Party, these "Left" errors have progressively been overcome and the country has followed a policy of readjustment, restructuring, consolidation and improvement.

Recent Reforms. Economic reforms have been carried out, bringing about industrial and agricultural growth, improvements in the people's living standards and a thriving domestic economy. However, rashness was not totally eliminated; we still lacked a matter-of-fact attitude and carried out capital construction and other undertakings beyond our actual capabilities — so much so that we ran huge deficits in 1979 and 1980.

The Party Central Committee and the State Council detected the latent dangers in the situation in good time and decided to make further readjustments in the national economy beginning in 1981. They resolved to reduce the scope of capital construction and to cut back defence and administrative spending in an effort to balance the state's debits and credits and to stabilize prices. This policy decision removed the hidden danger and created favourable conditions for the healthy development of the national economy.

II. The 1980 State Budget and the Necessity and Possibility of Balancing the Budget

The 1980 state budget approved by the Third Session of the Fifth National People's Congress set revenues at 106,290 million yuan and expenditures at 114,290 million yuan, leaving a deficit of 8,000 million yuan. The actual budget performance, however, resulted in revenues of 106,610 million yuan (320 million yuan more than projected) and expenditures of 118,720 million yuan (443 million yuan more than planned), leaving a deficit of 12,100 million yuan.

The revenue target for 1980 was met and targets for various taxes were all exceeded. The industrial, transport and commercial enterprises all achieved their revenue targets, but the food departments suffered great losses because of the readjustment made in the base price for state purchases, while the foreign trade departments also suffered losses because of changes in the variety of commodities and of price increases in the international market.

The large deficit showed that there was still much to be done in economic readjustment. In 1979 and 1980, following the policy of economic readjustment, we raised the prices of farm and sideline products by a large margin, extended employment, raised the wages of factory and office workers and introduced the bonus system. Three measures played an important part in firing the enthusiasm of the workers and peasants and in boosting the country's industrial and agricultural production.

But when expenditures for the improvement of the people's livelihood increased by a large margin and state revenues declined, the budget allocation for capital construction was not adequately reduced. Various administrative expenses, including defence spending and operating expenses of the state organs and undertakings, continued to rise. Consequently, total spending for capital construction and various other expenditures exceeded state revenues.

China is a developing country. What is more, she went through ten years of great turmoil. Many things need to be done immediately to satisfy the needs of the people. However, it is beyond the capability of the country to do all these things at once. China can only do what is within her power. This reality was not given due consideration when the 1980 national economic plan and state budget were planned and carried out — an indication that "Left" influence has not been eliminated from the country's financial work.

The large deficits in 1979 and 1980 and the consequent growth of the money supply played a large part in pushing up prices of various commodities, with detrimental effects for the national economy and political stability.

Late in 1980, the State Council studied the financial and economic situation and decided to take measures to achieve a rough budget balance and a credit balance. Can we achieve this goal? We argue that it is both necessary and possible for us to do so, if we only recall our financial work in the past three decades and understand how we time and again overcame financial difficulties.

Basic Budget Policy. China's basic budget policy is to maintain an annual balance between revenues and expenditures with a little surplus. This policy is aimed at ensuring a continuous and steady growth of the national economy and a real improvement in the people's livelihood under a stable economy.

We do not condone budget deficits because China's social system is different from that of Western countries. Unlike Western countries, China does not have economic recessions caused by overproduction and insufficient investment, so there is no need to use a budget deficit to stimulate the growth of China's economy.

Under our social system, a budget deficit shows that the distribution of national income exceeds the production of national income and that development programmes exceed the country's financial capabilities. The inevitable result is inflation, price fluctuations and a drop in the real income of the workers.

Although we do not condone budget deficits, it does not mean that we have never had financial deficits. Deficits have occurred several times. There have been two kinds of budget deficits. One kind was the objective result of wars and natural disasters; the 1950 deficit was of this kind. The other kind was due to subjective errors — in particular, rashness; the deficits that occurred after 1956 were of the second kind.

In 1956, carried away with the tremendous successes we had achieved in socialist transformation and construction, we quickened the speed of construction. That year, our investments in capital construction increased by more than 50% and our expenditures and agriculutral loans exceeded their planned levels. As a result, we incurred a budget deficit of 1,800 million yuan and a deficit in bank credit. These deficits resulted in shortages of both producer and consumer goods, which led to barter trade and profiteering. At that time, our style of working was practical and realistic, so we lost no time in discovering our problems and reviewing our experience.

We recognized theoretically that the scale of construction should conform to our capabilities and that we should maintain an overall balance in the budget, in credit and in the supply of materials. Meanwhile, we took practical measures to increase production and practice economy, to cut back capital construction investment and to control social purchasing power in a planned way. By 1957, we were able to achieve a balance between revenues and expenditures and between credits and debits. Shortages of raw materials and consumer goods were eased, the market stabilized and economic order was restored.

The 1958-60 Debate. During the three years of the "Great Leap Forward," the distribution of national income was again carried to excess. During 1958-60, erroneous tendencies, such as setting overly high production targets, boasting about exaggerated output and enforcing communism, cropped up under the influence of "Left" ideology. In the 1958 budget, the revenue target was more than double that of 1957. Actual revenues in that year totalled 38,760 million yuan, a mere 25% increase over the 1957 figure. Capital construction investment in 1958 was nearly double that of 1957, while payroll expenses escalated out of control. This state of affairs continued until 1960.

The impact of the 1958-60 financial deficits on China's economy was rapid and strong. The over-expenditure of funds and the resultant imbalance between industry and agriculture caused by erroneous economic policies led to severe shortages of raw materials and consumer goods. Speculation ran wild, prices rocketed and even the credibility of the currency was endangered, causing a decline in bank savings. The people's standard of living dropped. In view of the dangers, people simmered down.

Readjustment. In 1960, China set out to readjust its national economy. Major decisions during the readjustment were to cut back capital construction investment, control payroll expenditures and restore the balance between revenues and expenditures. Capital construction investment was reduced from 38,400 million yuan in 1960 to 12,300 million yuan in 1961 — and again to 6,700 million yuan in 1962.

Meanwhile, 20 million people were mobilized to resettle in the countryside so as to help cut consumer expenditure and increase the supply of grain. Efforts were made to strengthen enterprises — a large number of enterprises running at a deficit were either closed, merged with other enterprises or switched to other types of production. This readjustment helped to balance revenues and expenditures, credit receipts and payments and purchasing power and the supply of commodities. The money supply was reduced and prices stabilized. The chaos in economic life was eliminated and production went up rapidly. Economic results in 1965-66 achieved an all-time high.

Consequences of "Left" Errors. "Left" thinking reached its zenith in the ten years of turmoil between 1966 and 1976. During that period, the view that an overall balance is necessary was criticized by Lin Biao and the Gang of Four as "right deviationist conservative thinking," and once again high targets, high rates of accumulation and expanded capital construction exceeded actual capabilities. In agriculture, the policy of "poverty transition" (forced transition from a lower level to a higher level of collective ownership even when people became poorer) was advocated. In industry, workers were urged to stop production. These measures led to financial deficits for three consecutive years (1974-76) and brought the national economy to the verge of collapse.

Even after the downfall of the Gang of Four, we still did not truly understand the damage that "Left" ideas had done to our economic work. In 1977 and 1978, when we had achieved a measure of success in our economic work, we again became impatient and wanted to "quicken our pace" in construction. In 1978, the scope of capital construction was expanded, various expenditures were increased and the accumulation rate went up to 36.5%, second only to that in 1959. Capital construction investment reached an all-time high of 47,960 million yuan in 1978, a 31.6% increase over the 1977 figure. This rate of increase was not only higher than that of total industrial and agricultural output value and that of the national income, but also higher than that of national revenues. The impetuous advance aggravated the imbalance of the national economy and caused deficits in the following years.

The history of the past three decades shows that "Left" errors were the root cause of China's deficits. Impatience for success led to the over-distribution of funds, giving rise to inflation and price increases. Experience shows that, under socialism, it is not difficult to maintain a balanced budget, a credit balance and a balance between supply and demand, provided we do not exceed our capabilities. As the distribution of revenues is mainly controlled by the state, we can cut back high expenditures, just as long as we adhere to the principle of living within our means. Only by doing so, can we ensure a continuous and steady growth of the national economy.

III. Financial Readjustment and the National Economy

China's state budget covers the greater part of the nation's net social income, so the distribution of funds is important to the establishment of the ratio between accumulation and consumption. The budget has a decisive impact on the proportion of distribution between productive accumulation and nonproductive accumulation and on the proportion of funds distributed among the various departments of the national economy in productive accumulation. It is an important function of our financial work to effect the rationalization of the national economic structure through a rational distribution system.

Accumulation Rates. How can the distribution system be made rational? To understand this question, we must look at the many detours China has taken in the past three decades. On the question of the proportion between accumulation and consumption, since the late 1950's we have laid undue stress on productive accumulation, in the belief that a high rate of accumulation would ensure rapid development. Consequently, the accumulation rate during the Second and Fourth Five-Year Plan periods (1958-62 and 1971-75) exceeded 30%. In 1977 and 1978, after the downfall of the Gang of Four, the rates were 32.3% and 36.5%, respectively.

The facts show that high capital accumulation did not bring good results. In the late 1950's, when the accumulation rate was the highest, 100 yuan of accumulation funds only yielded one yuan of national income, whereas in the First Five-Year Plan period (1953-1957), when the rate was low (24%), and during the economic readjustment of 1963-65, when the rate was 22%, 100 yuan of accumulation funds yielded 35 and 57 yuan of national income, respectively.

To avoid an unduly high rate of accumulation, we must use finance as a regulatory valve. On the one hand, we must transfer the over-accumulation of national income to workers and peasants, using prices and wages as levers. On the other hand, we must reduce the scope of capital construction to achieve a balanced budget.

Distribution of Investment. As for the proper distribution of investment among economic departments, Chairman Mao, in his "On the Ten Major Relationships," had advanced the thesis that in the long run the greater development of agriculture and light industry will lead to a greater and more rapid development of heavy industry. History proved that this thesis is correct. Between 1952 and 1978, every yuan of investment in China's light industry yielded 10 yuan of profit and tax, while every yuan invested in heavy industry yielded only about 1.2 yuan of profit and tax. In this 27-year period, light industry, which received only one-tenth of the total investment in heavy industry, produced as much in profit and tax as was produced by the total investment in heavy industry. In other words, if we had devoted one-tenth of the investment in heavy industry to develop light industry, we would have accumulated enough funds to double the productivity of heavy industry.

In the late 1950's, we placed undue emphasis on development of heavy industry, especially on development of iron and steel. The investment in heavy industry between 1958 and 1960 accounted for 85.5% of the total investment in China's industry, but the performance of heavy industry was very poor and there was almost no increase in revenues. After 1965, large amounts of investment were spent on building the backward areas of remote and border regions, still laying undue stress on heavy industry. In the decade from 1966 to 1975, capital investment in heavy industry accounted for 91.8% of the total capital investment in industry. But between 1966 and 1970, every 100 yuan of capital investment produced only 21 yuan of profit and tax; and in the 1971-75 period, every 100 yuan of investment produced only 9 yuan of profit and tax. This illustrates the decisive impact of the national economic structure on revenues. To change the irrational structure of the national economy, we must first change the structure of distribution of funds.

As for the relationship between material production departments and nonmaterial production departments, it is what we call a "bone and flesh" relationship, with "bone" referring to production and "flesh" referring to those departments that serve production — such as urban construction, commerce, service trades, science, education, culture, public health and housing construction. The departments of material production and non-material production are interdependent, just like bone and flesh.

For a fairly long time, however, we took a one-sided approach to the non-material production departments, regarding them as having nothing to do with production. We paid little attention to them and invested too little in them. We paid dearly for this neglect: a host of problems in production, a lower living standard, the backwardness of China's science and education and tremendous obstacles in the way of the modernization of the national economy. These problems arose because we did not understand properly the relationship between material and nonmaterial production, which led to errors in the orientation of investment. To solve these problems, we first had to readjust the distribution structuue of investment.

Readjustment Ratios. Since the Party Central Committee and the State Council adopted the policy of readjustment, restructuring, consolidation and improvement of the national economy, much has been done by the financial departments in readjusting the ratio between accumulation and consumption, in balancing the relationship among the various departments of the national economy and in developing energy production, communications and transport and the building industry. Progress has been made in readjusting the ratio between accumulation and consumption, although some problems have not yet been thoroughly solved and some capital construction projects which should have been cut have not been cut.

In readjusting the ratio between accumulation and consumption, we have raised the consumption level of workers and peasants through various channels. In 1979, we raised the state purchasing price of farm and sideline products by a large margin and reduced the agricultural tax in some low-yielding areas so that rural China might recuperate and rebuild its strength. Beginning in the summer of 1979, the state raised the prices it paid for 18 major farm and sideline products, including grains, cotton, edible oils, jute, sugarcane, sugar beets, pigs, cattle, sheep, fish, eggs and silk cocoons. The state paid farmers higher prices for quantities of grains, cotton and edible oils produced beyond the required quota. In 1979, state subsidies for this purpose totalled 10,000 million yuan; in 1980, the figure was even higher.

Also in 1979, the state raised the level of yield subject to agricultural tax in low-yielding and grain-deficient areas. Areas where the per hectare yield was below the new minimum were exempted from tax altogether. In all, taxes were reduced or waived for 2,350 million tons. Furthermore, the state raised by a proportionate amount the level of yield subject to industrial and commercial income taxes for enterprises run by rural people's communes and their subdivisions, as well as extended the period of tax reduction and exemption for new enterprises. Regulations were worked out to exempt from industrial and commercial taxes for a period of five years those enterprises located in counties in national autonomous regions and border regions.

Income and Jobs. Thanks to the growth of farm production and the rise in the state purchasing price of major farm products and sideline products, China's peasants received from the collective in 1979 an average per capita income of 83.4 yuan, or 9.44 yuan more than in 1978. The average per capita income figure in 1980 was 85.9 yuan, or 2.5 yuan more than in 1979.

In 1979, various jobs were given to 9,030 million urban people, including jobless city residents and the 1979 graduates of colleges and technical schools. About 40% of factory and office workers were given wage increases and the wage scales in some areas were readjusted. A bonus system was introduced in state-owned enterprises and subsidies were issued to all workers to compensate for price increases introduced for non-staple foods.

The average annual pay of workers in state-owned enterprises in 1979 was 705 yuan, or 61 yuan more than in 1978. In 1979, 7,500 million yuan from the state budget was allocated for these purposes. In 1980, jobs were given to 9 million people and the average 1980 pay of workers in state-owned enterprises amounted to 803 yuan, or 98 yuan more than the 1979 figure.

Special Allowances. Price allowances and various other allowances have been made to ensure that the people's standard of living would not decline. State allowances for basic consumer goods in 1980, such as grain, cotton, edible oils, meat, eggs, vegetables and coal for home use, totalled 12,000 million yuan. Subsidies for purchases of farm produce (after the state raised the price for farm products produced in excess of the quota) exceeded 5,000 million yuan. Allowances for products classified as agricultural means of production and as aids to agriculture which were sold at preferential prices totalled more than 3,000 million yuan. These allowances reduced national revenues; but under present conditions, these allowances play a valuable role in ensuring the steady improvement of the people's livelihood.

In readjusting the relationship between production accumulation and nonproduction accumulation, special funds were drawn out of capital investment and, together with the funds of localities and enterprises, were used to expand housing construction for factory and office workers. In 1979, a total of 62,560 million sq.m. of housing floor space was constructed in cities, towns and industrial and mining districts, representing a 66% increase over the 1978 figure. The 1980 figure was 82,000 million sq.m. These were the two years when housing construction was the highest in terms of floor space since the founding of New China.

Flexible Funds. To give localities and enterprises greater financial power, the state allowed them to increase their flexible funds. This was beneficial to stimulating the national economy, promoting production, increasing income and correcting the serious imbalance between the "bone" and the "flesh." In 1979, the state stipulated that 49 large and medium-sized cities might retain 5% of their industrial and commercial profits as funds for urban construction, and that localities might take out a certain proportion of income from industrial enterprises run by the counties to use for their own flexible funds, which thus increased by 2,000 million yuan.

Meanwhile, a system of drawing funds has been introduced to state-owned enterprises and profit-sharing has been carried out on a trial basis in more than 4,000 industrial enterprises, commercial departments and affiliated organizations. Thus the enterprises received 4,000 million yuan of flexible funds. In 1980, this experiment was extended to more than 6,000 state-owned enterprises and their flexible funds were greater than the 1979 figure.

State Aid. In readjusting investment proportions among agriculture, light industry and heavy industry, more funds were allocated to develop agriculture and light industry. In 1979, 9,010 million yuan was earmarked as operating expenses for rural people's communes and various agricultural undertakings. Meanwhile, 1,500 million yuan was given to the light and textile industries to carry out technical innovations and transformation, in addition to 2,300 million yuan which had been given to them for capital construction. Priority was given to them for supplies of fuel, power and raw materials. In 1979, the growth rate of light and textile industries was 9.6%, while that of heavy industry was 7.7%.

Large increases were registered in output of major manufactured goods that are in urgent demand, including cotton cloth, chemicals, textiles, paper, bicycles, sewing machines, wristwatches, television sets, synthetic detergents and household electrical appliances. In 1980, the state continued its generous financial aid to agriculture and to light and textile industries. Aid to rural people's communes amounted to 8,367 million yuan in 1980 for investment and operating funds. And the 1980 growth rate of China's light and textile industries reached 18.4%. In both 1979 and 1980, the state also made a point to help boost energy production and transport.

IV. Restructuring the Financial and Managerial System

In a vast, unified socialist country like China whose economy is dominated by ownership of land and the means of production by the whole people, the proper handling of the relationship between central and local authorities and between the state and enterprises on the question of how power should be divided among them is a matter of great importance to bringing into full play the initiative of the masses and upholding the centralized and unified leadership of the country. Too much centralization, without giving local authorities and enterprises the necessary decision-making power, would hamper their initiative, inflate the bureaucracy and dampen the enthusiasm of grassroots organizations. Whereas too much decentralization would prevent the state from making overall arrangements for the national economy in the interests of the whole country, cause anarchy among localities and enterprises and make it difficult for the state to concentrate its power and to effect an overall balance for planned economy. For a long period of time, centralization was the main trend.

To overcome it, China undertook to restructure its economy through the decentralization of power, in 1957 and again in 1970. Meanwhile, there was also a certain measure of decentralization in budget control and financial management of enterprises. However, the work did not yield anticipated results because it did not solve the question of achieving an overall balance in a macroscopic sense, nor did it bring into full play the initiative of enterprises in the microscopic sense.

After the overthrow of the Gang of Four, the country decided to break with conventional practice and seek to restructure the economy in conformity with the reality of the country. The following measures hae been taken to restructure the financial system:

1. *In budget control, a system of "delimiting revenues and expenditures at different levels" was instituted in 15 provinces in 1980.* This system is characterized as delimiting revenues and expenditures.

The revenues of the central authorities consist of: (1) fixed income, which includes the income of enterprises and undertakings directly under the control of the central authorities, customs duties, industrial and commercial taxes on imported goods, industrial and commercial taxes paid by railway departments, foreign loans, repayments of loans by foreign countries, and other income; (2) the portion of local fixed income to be handed over to the central authorities; (3) the portion of redistributary income (industrial and commercial taxes) to be transferred to the central authorities; and (4) the portion of basic depreciation funds of local enterprises which is stipulated to be granted to the central authorities by the local authorities.

The revenues of the localities consist of: (1) fixed income of the local governments, including the income of locally run enterprises and undertakings, salt tax, agricultural tax, industrial and commercial taxes (such as the animal slaughtering tax, car and ship license-plate taxes, real estate tax, livestock trade tax, and rural trade fair tax), income from delayed payment of taxes and fines on delays in tax payment, and other local incomes; (2) a fixed proportion (20%) of the income of centrally run enterprises; (3) the portion of redistributary income (industrial and commercial taxes) as stipulated to be given to the local authorities; (4) fixed subsidies given by the central authorities to certain localities; and (5) the basic depreciation fund as stipulated to be handed over to the central authorities.

Expenditures are delimited in a similar way. Expenditures to be paid by the central authorities consist of: (1) allocations and loans for capital construction to be made by the central authorities; (2) additional circulating funds for centrally run enterprises; (3) additional bank credit loans; (4) funds for technical innovations; (5) expenses for developing new products; (6) expenses for geological prospecting; (7) national defence expenditures; (8) aid to foreign countries; (9) expenditures for state reserves of supplies; (10) expenses for national cultural, educational, scientific and public health undertakings; (11) operational expenses in industry, transport and commerce; (12) expenditures to aid agriculture; and (13) other expenses by the central government.

Local expenditures consist of: (1) funds or loans for capital construction undertaken by local governments; (2) additional circulating funds for local enterprises; (3) funds for technical innovations by local enterprises; (4) funds for developing new products by local enterprises; (5) local aid-to-agriculture funds; (6) operational expenses in agriculture, forestry, water conservation and meteorological service; (7) operational expenses in industrial, transport and commercial undertakings; (8) expenditure on urban maintenance; (9) expenses on aid-raid shelters; (10) expenses for resettling urban residents in the countryside; (11) expenses in local cultural, educational, scientific and public health undertakings; (12) social relief and pensions for the disabled and families of the deceased; (13) administrative expenses; and (14) other expenses.

The state makes expedient allocations for disaster relief, flood and drought control and other emergencies.

Determining the limits of revenues and expenditures is accomplished in accordance with the method of delimitation described below. The revenues and expenditures of a certain province over a definite period of time are determined; using these figures as a base, calculations are made to find out the proportion of local income to be handed over to the state, the proportion of local income to be retained by the province or the amount of subsidies to be given by the central government to the province. Once determined, such fixed proportions and amounts of subsidies are valid for five years. This system of "delimiting revenues and expenditures at different levels" was originally meant to be introduced to the provinces, but some provinces have applied it to their counties.

Since its introduction in 1980, the system has yielded some positive results:

(1) it has helped bring into play the initiative of local governments in financial management;

(2) it has helped local governments make overall arrangements and perform their economic tasks in a flexible way;

(3) it has helped to promote the country's economic readjustment;

(4) it has helped to increase income and cut expenditures so as to overcome current financial difficulties; and

(5) it has helped to strengthen financial management.

Some problems have cropped up in the course of implementing this system. The main one is the tendency toward unnecessary duplication of production and capital construction. Another is that, whereas local governments are supposed to use their surplus income and make up for deficits on their own, some localities still turn to the central government for subsidies when they run a deficit, thus weakening the central government's efforts to balance the state budget.

A "fixed quota system" was instituted for Guangdong and Fujian provinces in 1980. Under this system, the amount to be handed over to the central authorities and subsidies made to them by the central government are fixed for five consecutive years. During these five years, the local government will retain all the increased revenue resulting from economic growth. Under this system the local government gets greater benefits than under the system of "delimiting revenues and expenditures at different levels," by which the local government has to hand over a fixed proportion of increased revenue to the central government. The fixed quota system was designed to give Guangdong and Fujian greater flexibility in implementing special policies. With greater decision-making power in financial matters, the two provinces are able to fully exploit their advantages for more rapid economic growth.

The regions inhabited by national minorities, which are economically underdeveloped, have been granted special preferential treatment. Their budget deficits are subsidized by the central government. In addition, the national autonomous regions enjoy preferential treatment in the following three ways:

(1) The national autonomous regions are entitled to a higher percentage of reserve funds than other regions. The reserve funds for ordinary provinces and municipalities account for 3% of their budgetary expenditure, whereas autonomous regions are entitled to 5%, the autonomous *zhou* (equivalent to a prefecture embracing several counties) to 4% and the autonomous counties to 3%, as against 2% for ordinary counties.

(2) The state sets aside special funds to help national autonomous regions meet their special needs in production, the people's livelihood, culture, education and public health services.

(3) The state sets aside funds for national minorities in autonomous regions to help develop their culture. These funds are equivalent to 5% of all operational expenses of the locality.

In 1980, the financial control of national autonomous regions was brought into line with the principle of "delimiting revenues and exenditures at different levels." This allowed national autonomous regions to keep all revenues derived from industrial and commercial taxes. Other regions, however, only got to keep part of their revenues from industrial and commercial taxes. Not only were autonomous regions allowed to keep all their extra revenue, but the subsidies given to them by the central government from the state treasury were to be increased by 10% each year. Also in 1980, the state set up an economic development fund to aid underdeveloped areas of the country, in which national autonomous regions were included.

2. *The financial management of enterprises constitutes an important aspect of the country's financial management system, which is a feature of the socialist system.* While it is important to reform the budget control system, it is even more important, in a sense, to restructure the system of financial management. The reason is that workers in the enterprises are the real creators of material wealth, and reforms of the superstucture will not promote economic growth unless they are aimed at bringing into full play the initiative of enterprises and their workers.

The financial management of an enterprise is supposed to solve the following major problems:

(1) How can the state, through a proper distribution of funds, ensure that enterprises enjoy optimum conditions for maintaining simple reproduction and a certain measure of expanded reproduction?

(2) What kind of distribution should an enterprise employ to protect the proper interests of the state, the collective and individuals?

(3) What obligatons should an enterprise have for using state funds to undertake production?

In short, in order to enable enterprises to undertake reproduction under optimum conditions and to expand reproduction in light of society's needs and objective possibilities, it is necessary to allow enterprises to have the necessary funds and financial power to run their operations. Furthermore, in order that enterprises and their workers care about the results of their management of material interests, they should be entitled to share the economic returns of their enterprises. To this end, a system of enterprise funds was introduced on an experimental basis in 1978. Under this system, an enterprise, after fulfilling its annual planned targets, was entitled to draw on an enterprise fund equivalent to 5% of its total annual payroll. However, because the enterprise fund was related only to the total payroll and was proportionate to the number of workers employed in the enterprise, it did not stimulate the enterprise to improve its performance, although this was the intended effect. There was no link between the material interests of the enterprise and those of its workers with the actual performance of the management.

In July 1979, the State Council issued "Regulations Concerning State-Owned Enterprises Retaining Part of Their Profits." On an experimental basis, some enterprises were allowed to retain a fixed proportion of their profits for the purpose of establishing a reserve fund. With the reserve fund, enterprises could set up three other funds — a product development fund, a workers' welfare fund and a bonus fund. Since the reserve fund would grow with the growth of profits, enterprises would be encouraged to cut costs, increase output and improve product quality, thereby accumulating more funds for the state.

The experience of the enterprises that took part in this experiment showed that whereas enterprises which used to have low profits, more manpower and greater potential for increasing their income enjoyed a higher ratio of reserves and more benefits, those enterprises which used to perform well, earned greater profits and employed fewer workers obtained a lower ratio of reserves and less benefits. This was clearly not fair.

To solve this problem and to encourage enterprises to increase their production and income, some changes were made in the system in 1980. Accordingly, an enterprise's reserve fund should be drawn in proportion to both its base profit and increased profit. In other words, when an enterprise's profits in the current year are higher than those in the previous year, only that portion equivalent to the profit of the previous year, in accordance with the verified ratio of the base profit, will go into the reserve fund. Of the increase in profits, only that amount determined in accordance with the ratio stipulated by the state for increased profit will go into the reserve fund. When an enterprise's profits in the current year are lower than those in the previous year, the reserve fund should be made up of the actual profit on the basis of the verified ratio for drawing the reserve fund from the base profit. As a result of this revision, all enterprises, regardless of how much profit they earn, should benefit from profit increases in a more reasonable way.

Along with the profit-retaining practice, experiments were carried out in making payments for the use of fixed capital in enterprises which retained part of their profits in 1980. Payments for the use of capital vary with the rates of proft, which differ in various trades. The monthly rate for the use of capital ranges from 0.2% to 0.8%. Furthermore, beginning October 1, 1980, all enterprises which had completed an all-round check of their assets began to pay fees for the use of circulating funds at the monthly rate of 0.21%. The two fees are paid out of the enterprise's turnover to the state treasury as part of state revenues.

Profit retaining is an important step in restructuring the financial management system of enterprises. But there is still room for improvement, mainly in the following two aspects: (1) the well-run enterprises will get a lower retaining ratio based on the original funds than poorly run enterprises, and since they have less potential for increased production, they will have greater difficulty drawing reserve funds from increased profits — this is hardly encouragement for well-run enterprises; and (2) grassroots enterprises lack sufficient guidance from departments above them in planning how to use their reserve funds — in certain cases, funds have not been used to full advantage.

In addition, experiments in making enterprises "perform independent accounting, pay taxes to the state and bear sole responsibility for profit or loss" have been carried out in a few enterprises in Shanghai, Sichuan and Guangxi. These pilot enterprises now pay the state taxes instead of profits; whatever is left after paying taxes is at the disposal of the enterprises, to be used with guidance from the state plan. Enterprises which operate well and reap high profits may retain more for their own use. This is a relatively recent experiment in giving enterprises a larger share of decision-making power.

With respect to financial management in capital construction, state allocation was replaced by state loans in 1980.

The restructuring of the financial management system in recent years has proved correct in orientation and has yielded positive results. It has played a valuable role in improving economic performance and in mobilizing forces to overcome financial difficulties. At present, what we should do is to sum up our experiences and consolidate what we have already achieved.

China decided to further readjust its national economy at the end of 1980. This is an important policy decision. To ensure that this primary task is carried out smoothly, the reform of the economic structure must be subordinated to and beneficial to the task of readjustment.

V. Tax Reform and Taxation in the New Historical Period

The state obtains its revenues mainly through

taxes and profits. During the past 31 years, taxation as a control lever of distribution in the hands of the proletarian state has played an important role in accumulating funds for construction, in regulating the incomes of various economic sectors and in developing the national economy in order to promote productive forces.

Taxation in a socialist country is part of the socialist superstructure. It embodies the will of the people and governs the relationship between the state and the taxpayers. It serves as an instrument for consolidating the country's economic base. In the past 31 years, the tax system has reflected changes in the economic base and in the political and economic tasks of the state at different periods.

The main features of these changes are as follows:

1. *During the economic rehabilitation period, we adopted the plural taxation system and levied several categories of tax simultaneously at different points in the production and sales of industrial and comercial enterprises, including an excise tax, a business tax and a stamp tax.* Some of these taxes were levied several times. Such a taxation system was called for by the conditions that then existed. At that time, multiple economic sectors coexisted. There were large numbers of private industrial and commercial enterprises; they varied in forms of management and often evaded taxes. The plural system of taxation helped to implement the policy of utilizing, restricting and transforming capitalist industry and commerce.

2. *China enforces taxation mainly in the fields of production and distribution.* The principal tax category is the industrial and commercial tax, which ranks first in revenue among all other taxes and accounts for at least three-fourths of total tax revenues. The object of such taxation is the turnover.

China levies virtually no income tax on individual property. The income of urban and rural residents is low, so it is not advisable to increase the burdens of the people by levying an income tax. Moreover, in a socialist country like China, personal income is fairly equitable and there is no need yet to regulate the incomes of different strata by levying an income tax.

Only during the period of socialist transformation did we adopt the "four horses sharing the forage" system — dividing revenues from the industrial and commercial income tax on enterprise profits among the state (34.5%), the welfare funds for workers (15%), the accumulation funds (30%) and the dividends for capital (20.5%). That system constituted part of the policy of utilizing, restricting and transforming capitalist industry and commerce.

3. *After the completion of the three socialist transformation movements, reforms were made to simplify the tax system.* The simplification of the tax system was certainly necessary, but our thinking on this question tended to be one-sided. We thought that because our country was moving in the direction of a system of unitary ownership, the simpler the taxation system, the better. As a result, the categories of tax were reduced and some taxes which ought to have been levied separately were merged with others. While this reform did simplify the tax system, it greatly weakened the role of taxation as a lever for control of distribution.

After the Gang of Four was overthrown, and especially after the Third Plenary Session of the 11th Party Central Committee, China entered a new historical period in which socialist construction has become the central task. The "Left" ideological line that was prevalent during the ten years of upheaval was criticised, confused theories were cleared up and policies were cleansed of the "Left" influence. This brought about profound changes in the economy which, in turn, brought further reform of the tax system.

Between 1979 and 1980, the following reforms were carried out in the system of taxation.

1. *In 1980, the Ministry of Finance selected the city of Liuzhou in the Guangxi Zhuang Autonomous Region for an experiment in tax reform and reform of the financial system of enterprises.* Enterprises in Liuzhou are required to pay four categories of tax and two kinds of fees instead of delivering their profits to the state. Those taxes are:

(1) Value-added tax, levied on products such as machines, equipment and farm machinery and implements. The original tax on the sales of such products has been changed to a tax on what is left after the enterprise deducts the cost of materials.

(2) Resources tax, levied on crude oil, natural gas, coal, metals and non-metallic minerals.

(3) Excess-profits tax, levied according to the amount of profits on sales. When the profit rate of sales is under 15%, no tax is levied; when the profit rate exceeds 15%, 0.6% of tax is levied for every 1% over 15%.

(4) Income tax on state-owned enterprises, levied at a flat rate of 50% on the income of state-owned enterprises. The taxable income of an enterprise is the total income from the sale of

products after deduction of costs, non-operating expenditure, industrial and commercial taxes and the excess-profits tax. Of the total tax, 50% is delivered to the state and the other 50% is retained by the enterprise.

Fees for possessing fixed funds and circulating funds are replaced by the fund dividends method, which retains after-tax profits at a rate ranging from 25% to 60%.

Apart from Liuzhou, small-scale tax experiments are being carried out in Sichuan, Hubei and Shanghai. The guiding principle is essentially the same, but there are minor differences. We shall sum up the experiences of these pilot districts and try to find the best system.

2. *The income tax law concerning joint ventures with Chinese and foreign investment was formulated and promulgated.* In order to expand international cooperation and technical exchange, China encourages foreign firms, enterprises and other economic organizations and individuals to run joint ventures in China with Chinese companies and other economic organizations on the basis of equality and mutual benefit.

The first problem in running joint ventures with Chinese and foreign investment is how to handle the relationship of rights and interests between the state and such enterprises. With a view to defining this relationship, the Third Session of the Fifth National People's Congress adopted in September 1979 the "Income Tax Law of the People's Republic of China Concerning Joint Ventures with Chinese and Foreign Investment."

The range of taxation mainly covers joint ventures with Chinese and foreign investment within China's territory. But in view of future development, the law stipulates that the income tax on the income derived from production, business and other sources by branches within or outside the territory of China of such joint ventures shall be paid by their head offices. It also stipulates that income tax paid abroad by their branch offices may be credited against the assessed income tax of the head office as foreign tax credit. Where agreements on avoidance of double taxation have been concluded between the Chinese government and the government of another country, income tax credits shall be handled in accordance with the provisions of the relevant agreements.

Income from joint ventures is taxed at a flat rate of 30%. In addition, a local surtax of 10% of the assessed income tax shall be levied. The tax rate is lower than those in developed countries and in many developing countries, where rates are 50% and 35-40%, respectively.

The income tax rates on joint ventures exploiting petroleum, natural gas and other resources shall be stipulated separately. This is so because joint ventures exploiting petroleum and other resources are more complicated than general joint ventures and because such taxation in other countries is generally very high. Some countries even levy a petroleum income tax or a special tax. China is working out such tax rates and tax regulations as best suits its actual conditions.

To encourage foreign investors to reinvest in China their share of profit, the income tax law stipulates that in the case of a foreign participant in a joint venture remitting its share of profit from China, an income tax of 10% shall be levied on the remitted amount and no tax will be levied on the unremitted amount of profit.

The tax law lays down the following preferential treatment toward joint ventures:

— A newly established joint venture scheduled to operate for a period of 10 years or more may be exempted from income tax in the first profit-making year and allowed a 50% reduction in the second and third years.

— Joint ventures engaged in such low-profit operations as farming and forestry or which are located in remote, economically underdeveloped outlying areas may be allowed a 15-30% reduction in income tax for a period of 10 years, in addition to tax exemption and reduction in the first three years.

— A participant in a joint venture which reinvests its share of profit in China for a period of not less than five years may obtain a refund of 40% of the income tax paid on the reinvested amount.

— In addition, two methods shall be adopted to compute the taxable income of a joint venture. One is that in computing depreciation of fixed assets, apart from the prescribed useful life, exceptional useful life may be set in cases where the fixed assets of a joint venture need to accelerate depreciation. This is laid down in the detailed regulations for the implementation of the income tax law. The other method is that losses incurred by a joint venture in a tax year may be carried over to the next tax year, and should the income in the subsequent tax year be insufficient to make up for the said losses, the balance may be made up with further deductions against income annually for a period not exceeding five years.

VI. Enforcement of the Individual Income Tax Law

The main regulations concerning the implementation of the national tax rules, promulgated in 1950, included the provision about taxation on wages and salaries and on service compensation. But in view of China's low wage system and low individual income, the income tax was not levied.

With the development of the economy, the number of people with high earnings will gradually increase and it is a matter of course that they should contribute more to the state. Moreoever, as China expands its economic exchanges with other countries, the number of foreign personnel who derive their income in China will increase gradually and there will be an increasing number of Chinese personnel engaged in economic activities or services in other countries who will have to pay income tax in the countries where they work. In order to protect national economic interests, China has enacted the individual income tax law in the spirit of equality and mutual benefit and in the light of China's actual circumstances. This law was adopted in September 1980 at the Third Session of the Fifth National People's Congress.

The individual income tax law stipulates that individual income tax shall be levied on incomes earned within or outside China by any individual residing for one year or more in China. For individuals residing in China for less than one year, individual income tax shall be levied only on that income gained within China.

Taxable and Nontaxable Categories. The new tax law lists the following categories of incomes to be taxed: wages and salaries; compensation for personal services; royalties; interest, dividends and bonuses; income from lease of property; and other kinds of income specified as taxable by the Ministry of Finance of the People's Republic of China.

It also lists the following categories of income that are to be exempted from individual income tax: prizes and awards for scientific, technological or cultural achievements; interest on savings deposits in state banks and credit cooperatives of the People's Republic of China; welfare benefits, survivor's pensions and relief payments; insurance indemnities; military serverance pay, decommission or demobilization pay for cadres and soliders in the armed forces; severance pay or retirement pay for cadres, staff members and workers; salaries of diplomatic officials of foreign embassies and consulates in China; tax-free incomes as stipulated in international conventions to which China is a party or as stipulated in agreements China has signed; and incomes approved as tax-free by the Ministry of Finance of the People's Republic of China.

Income Tax Rates. The tax law has set two individual income tax rates. One is for wages and salaries in excess of specific amounts; these are taxed monthly at progressive rates of seven scales ranging from 5% to 45%. The other is for income from compensation for personal services, royalties, interest, dividends, bonuses and the lease of property and other kinds of income, taxed at a flat rate of 20%.

For the sake of simplicity and convenience, taxable income is computed according to fixed amounts of monthly income, at fixed rates and with certain deductions. For income from wages or salaries, a monthly deduction of 800 yuan is allowed as daily expenses for the wage earner and his relatives and for other necessary expenses. Only that part in excess of 800 yuan is taxed. After this deduction, the number of people in China who need to pay income tax is very small — and the taxable amount is very small too.

For income from compensation for personal services, royalties or lease of property, the taxable amount is computed by deducting a fixed percentage of 20%. But in view of the fact that the amount of income from compensation and lease of property may vary widely and because the deduction of a fixed percentage might make the range of taxation too extensive, the tax law provides that if the amount in a single payment is less than 4,000 yuan, a deduction of 800 yuan is allowed. This has narrowed the range of taxation and benefits for taxpayers with smaller incomes.

For interest, dividends, bonuses or other kinds of income, the tax law provides that they shall be taxed on the full amount of each payment.

Tax Controls. In regard to taxation control, we mainly adopted the method of controlling tax sources, that is, making the paying units the agents responsible for withholding taxes due and making out payments. Taxpayers not covered by withholding are required to file their own declarations of income and to pay the tax themselves. Any taxpayer who earns income outside China is required to pay the tax due at the end of each year.

The tax law also stipulates that the tax authorities have the right to conduct investigations concerning the payment of tax and, acting at their discretion, may impose fines on those who have concealed income or have evaded or refused to pay tax. Penalties imposed will depend on the seriousness of the offence and may involve bringing the cases before the local people's courts.

40. CHINA'S TAXATION IN 1980
By Liu Zhicheng
General Taxation Bureau, Ministry of Finance

Tremendous achievements were made in China's taxation in 1980 under the guidance of the principles and policies adopted at the Third Plenary Session of the 11th Central Committee of the Chinese Communist Party. This was done with the support of party committees and people's governments at all levels and by conscientiously implementing the policy of readjusting, restructuring, consolidating and improving the national economy.

I. New Taxation Policies

In 1980, as the policy of readjusting the national economy was implemented on all fronts, great changes were made in the sources of taxation. Although many measures were taken to reduce or exempt some enterprises from taxes and many contradictions and difficulties arose in taxation, the taxation departments overfulled their 1980 target by displaying the revolutionary spirit of hard struggle. They worked whole-heartedly to implement tax policies correctly, to promote the development of production and to strengthen the control of taxation.

National revenues from industrial and commercial taxes and the salt tax exceeded the 1980 target by 2,200 million yuan, or 5.8% more than in 1979. Most provinces, municipalities and autonomous regions exceeded their quotas. For instance, Shanghai, Beijing, Hubei, Zhejiang, Jiangsu, Guangdong, Liaoning and Henan all exceeded their quotas by 100 million yuan or more each.

In carrying out the policy of readjusting, restructuring, consolidating and improving the national economy, many readjustments and improvements were made in the stipulations of existing tax policies in 1980 to suit the needs of the new economic situation. In order to help young people in the cities to find jobs and to stabilize the social order, the period of tax exemption was extended for new collective enterprises run by students who had left school in the cities. Enterprises which had difficulties in paying taxes on the goods they produced had their taxes reduced or were exempted from taxes.

In line with the policy of allowing the private economy to grow while encouraging the collective economy, taxes were levied only on that part of the income of cooperative shops in excess of specified amounts at eighth-grade progressive rates — such as in the case of collectively owned handicraft enterprises in urban areas, instead of at the previous ninth-grade progressive rates. Rural cooperative catering, service and repair units which had difficulties in paying taxes had their taxes reduced or were exempted from taxation. It was clearly stated that the system of taxing the whole income at 14th-grade progressive rates would not be imposed on the private economy for the time being and only that part of income in excess of specified amounts would be taxed at eighth-grade progressive rates for collective enterprises in the cities. This was intended to lighten the tax burden on cooperative shops and the private economy. Industrial and commercial taxes levied on matches and tinned foods were properly reduced to encourage increased production of these items after the prices of raw materials were raised.

Industrial and commercial taxes were also reduced or exempted during periods when commercial departments reduced the selling prices of pork in order to keep down the overstocking of meat in cold storage.

Those readjustments in tax policies gave full play to the function of taxation as an economic lever in regulating production and consumption.

II. Reform of the Tax System

Progress was made in reforming the industrial and commercial tax system as part of the effort to restructure the economic management system. Many investigations were made in various parts of China and good initial results were achieved in the experimental work done in some areas. Taxation work received great attention from the leadership at the central, provincial, municipal and regional levels and was widely supported by economists. A brief report was made to the Central Financial and Economic Leading Group on the taxation work in August 1980. Both Premier Zhao Ziyang and Vice-Premier Wan Li gave important instructions on the purpose, requirements, principles, policies and implementing measures in the reform of the tax system. In September, Wang Bingqian, Minister of Finance, also spoke of the reform in his report which was endorsed at the Third Session of the Fifth National People's Congress. Gratifying progress was made in the reform during 1980.

A value-added tax was introduced in 345 enterprises in Shanghai, Xiangfan, Changsha, Zhuzhou and Liuzhou on an experimental basis. It had positive significance in balancing the tax burdens between enterprises producing everything from raw materials to finished products, and those enterprises with more limited production. The tax benefited industrial reorganization and supported the development of production along specialized lines.

An important change in the relations of distribution of income between the state and enterprises was the replacement of the system of turning over profits to the state by state-owned enterprises with the new system of collecting income tax. Efforts were made in 1980 to begin the experiment, which is now being tried out in more than 200 enterprises in different parts of the country. These include 40 enterprises under the Shanghai Municipal Light Industry Machinery Corporation, 74 enterprises in Liuzhou city and 15 enterprises under the Guanghua County government in Hubei Province, as well as some enterprises in Sichuan Province. The experimental work in 1980 showed that the reform closely integrated the economic rights, responsibilities and interests of enterprises and gave further play to their initiative in management, thus promoting the development of production.

New Income Tax Law. In order to encourage overseas businessmen to invest in China, we undertook serious study and investigation and formulated the Income Tax Law Concerning Joint Ventures with Chinese and Foreign Investors and the individual income tax law. These laws called for light taxes, preferential treatment and simple procedures in the light of international practices. The two laws, adopted at the Third Session of the Fifth National People's Congress, were promulgated and went into effect in 1980. Detailed rules for the implementation of the two laws were issued by the Ministry of Finance with the approval of the State Council. These laws are very important to the safeguarding of China's national rights and interests and to the promotion of international economic exchanges on the basis of equality and mutual interest.

Staff Training. In 1980, the number of tax officials was increased and their special knowledge was broadened. Guangdong, Shaanxi, Shanxi, Liaoning and Tibet reported an increase of 12,500 new workers in taxation offices. The total number of taxation officials throughout the country reached 170,000. Special training was provided in many places to broaden their vocational knowledge. Two training courses were given at the national level for nearly 200 officials who were equal to or above county taxation bureau directors in rank. Training courses were also offered in the provinces, municipalities and autonomous regions to provide training in taxation, accounting and inspection for section or division leaders.

Many prefectural and county taxation bureaus used different methods to train their staffs. A course in international taxation was held in Dalian, Liaoning Province, where lectures were given by specialists from Harvard University and other American universities. The lectures were attended by 100 people from all parts of the country. In order to train personnel in the methods of collecting taxes from foreigners, a foreign language course was given at the Dalian Foreign Language Institute for selected staff members from the taxation departments of provinces, municipalities and autonomous regions. More and more people working in taxation departments in various parts of China are studying foreign languages in their spare time.

In addition, theoretical research and propagation of taxation policies are under way.

41. CHINA'S BANKING SYSTEM
By the Research Institute of Finance and Banking,
The People's Bank of China

I. Development of China's Banking System

The People's Bank of China was founded on December 1, 1948, on the eve of the country's liberation. The founding of the bank and the issuance of legal tender — Renminbi — marked the beginning of a unified monetary and credit system for New China. Thereupon, the people's government banned the circulation of gold, silver and foreign currencies and started taking out of circulation the old currency issued by the Kuomintang government, exchanging the old currencies in liberated areas for Renminbi. It established thus an independent and unified socialist monetary system.

After Liberation, the People's Bank of China, acting on behalf of the people's government, took over credit institutions which were entirely constituted by bureaucrat-capital, confiscated the shares of the "big four" families in jointly operated state-private banks, and set up numerous branch offices in the cities and countryside, thus forming an extensive banking network across the country.

Over the past 31 years, China has established a more or less integrated banking system, consisting of the People's Bank of China, the Agricultural Bank of China and the agricultural credit co-operatives, the Bank of China and the State General Administration of Exchange Control, and the People's Construction Bank of China.

The People's Bank of China is the central bank, authorised by the state to formulate monetary policies, guidelines, rules and regulations for the whole country; to regulate the issuance of notes, cash flows, trading in gold and silver; and to control the wage fund. At the same time, by means of bank credits and interest rates, the bank mobilizes domestic funds to finance economic construction, to promote and control all economic activities and to regulate and coordinate the activities of economic units. As the hub of all economic entities and the link among different economic sectors, the bank is the nation's centre for clearance and collection and for loans and payments.

The Agricultural Bank of China exercises control over funds serving the needs of agriculture. It grants agricultural loans, supervises agricultural credit cooperatives and promotes bank services in rural areas. Agricultural credit cooperatives are simultaneously collective credit institutions and the grassroots units of the Agricultural Bank of China; they engage in banking activites in the countryside.

The Bank of China and the State General Administration of Exchange Control specialize in international banking. They exercise unified control over foreign exchange and are responsible for maintaining a balance in China's international payments.

The People's Construction Bank of China specializes in allocating government funds and granting loans for capital construction. It also holds short-time deposits from units engaged in capital construction and grants the units short-term loans.

Since the founding of New China, the People's Bank of China has done a great deal to promote production and marketing and to regulate the nation's economic life. Notably, the readjustment of the national economy in the early 1960's was made considerably easier because the bank took such measures as stressing the centralization of banking operations, strictly regulating bank credit and cash flows, maintaining discipline in settling payments when they became due, drawing a line between government allocations and bank credit and prohibiting the diversion of bank credit to capital expenditure.

Due to the interference and disruption by the ultra-"Left" line pursued by Lin Biao and the Gang of Four during the "cultural revolution," the concept of relying on money, credit and interest rates for economic leverage was rejected. Consequently, the role of the People's Bank in the national economy was considerably weakened. But events took a fundamental turn for the better after the downfall of the Gang of Four. The bank has gained increasing importance in the national economy and has been able to use its powers fully and positively. Its development has been increasingly significant for the readjustment and development of the national economy.

In 1980, China's banking activities were in full swing. In implementation of the policy of readjustment, restructuring, consolidation and improvement of the national economy, the various departments of the banking system engaged in activities aimed at stabilizing price levels and maintaining monetary stability by observing economic laws and by adopting scientific methods. Their efforts have helped greatly to revitalize both production and marketing, as well as to facilitate the readjustment of the national economy.

II. Significant Banking Reforms in 1980

Prior to 1980, there were a number of shortcomings and drawbacks in the economic system. The major problems were: (1) industrial and commercial enterprises relied mainly on government grants and very little on bank credit, thus circumscribing the role that the banks could have played; and (2) the bank had little decision-making power and was, in effect, administering a system of "funds allocation." Confronted with these problems, the People's Bank of China undertook some significant reforms in 1980.

The primary purpose of the reforms was to utilize the bank's powers to regulate the national economy in conformity with economic laws; to enable the bank, under the guidance of state plans and in line with established credit policies, to mobilize idle funds in the county and channel them to where they were most needed for the ongoing readjstment of the national economy.

1. *The People's Construction Bank provided loans to enterprises for capital expenditures to replace part of previous government loans.* This reform not only helped to improve economic performance, but also reined in the over-extended scale of capital construction in the interest of readjusting the economy.

The People's Bank began to extend two kinds of loans — short- and medium-term loans for purchases of equipment and loans for specified purposes — primarily to the textile and other light industries. Priority was given to enterprises that would use the funds to tap production potential, renovate obsolete plants and equipment and bring in quicker and larger returns, both at home and in markets abroad, in proportion to the money invested.

According to 1980 statistics, the People's Bank granted a total of 3,980 million yuan in short- and medium-term equipment loans to finance more than 15,000 projects for tapping production potential and for renovations. Over 5,600 of the projects were completed and put into full or partial operation in 1980. The total output value of these projects reached 4,650 million yuan. Loans to textile and other light industries accounted for 58% of total loans; these industries achieved the best results by producing 73% of the total production value of 4,650 million yuan. They not only increased their production of commodities demanded by the market — 690,000 bicycles, 730,000 watches and 440,000 sewing machines — but also improved the quality and variety of their products and lowered the cost of production. The enterprises thus speeded up the turnover of working capital.

The People's Bank also extended short- and medium-term equipment loans totalling 180 million yuan to finance commercial enterprises in the food industries, such as processing mills for cereals and oils, delicatessens, restaurants and pastry shops, and loans totalling 240 million yuan to finance 530 hydroelectric projects. These loans also achieved good results.

The facts show that the kinds of loans granted by the People's Bank played an active part in readjusting the relationship between light and heavy industries, enlarging the supply of commodities, promoting foreign trade and supporting the technical renovation of enterprises. Bank loans to finance hydroelectric projects contributed to the development of energy resources, the supply of electricity to the countryside and the increase of agricultural production.

Formerly, the bank had granted loans only to industrial and commercial enterprises for working capital, while loans to other sectors had been much restricted. After new regulations were introduced in 1980, the bank could grant loans to cultural and scientific organisations, public utilities and the tourist industry, as well as to collective and individual enterprises run by young people in the cities — so long as their activities conform to government policies and they are able to pay off the loans. By assisting these economic sectors to prosper, the bank helped to meet market demands and to create employment opportunities. By removing restrictions on bank loans, the new regulations enabled the bank to provide more flexible services.

2. *Exercising its decision-making powers, the People's Bank adopted the principle of differentiating among borrowers and giving priority to enterprises that perform well.* Loans were to be made according to the government's credit policy, with particular reference to the purposes for which the loans were to be used and provided that the sum total of loans did not exceed the credit ceiling set by the government. The bank, however, had the freedom to select the borrower and to decide on the amount and term of the loan.

By exercising its decision-making powers, the bank was able to establish priorities of loans in the interest of readjusting the national economy. Priority was given to industries such as textiles, energy, transport and construction materials — which had trailed behind other industries — and to well-managed enterprises within these industries. The bank scaled down loans to poorly managed enterprises producing goods of inferior quality in an effort to spur these enterprises to improve their management and their product quality. In the interest of national economic readjustment, the bank restricted loans to some enterprises so as to induce them to change their lines of production or even to close down.

In 1980, the People's Bank granted loans primarily to textile and other light industries to help them improve the quality and variety of their products and to increase production of goods in short supply. By the end of 1980, total loans to industrial enterprises had increased by 6,500 million yuan over the beginning of the year. Loans to the textile and other light industries totalled 2,987 million yuan, an increase of 33.53% over 1979, whereas loans to heavy industries rose by only 11.17%. Industrial loans to the collective enterprises in the cities increased by 2,835 million yuan, or 48.91% over 1979.

In 1980, the bank also provided commercial enterprises with working capital to finance the stocking of farm and sideline products, as well as of manufactured goods currently in demand. The bank encouraged a marketing scheme whereby the commercial enterprises dealt directly with suppliers and had as few intermediaries as possible, stocked shops with goods promptly and speeded up sales. According to estimates, the value of manufactured goods purchased directly from suppliers by shops and stores in 1980 was up by about 50% from the year before. As a result, the stores were well stocked and business was brisk.

3. *The reform in the bank's internal administration spurred local banks to raise and utilize loanable funds.* In 1980, the People's Bank put into effect on a nationwide trial basis a new scheme of "multilevel management under a unified plan, linking up loans with deposits and controlling the differential between them." According to this scheme, any branch bank that overfulfilled the norm of the differential between deposits and loans set by the head office was at liberty to grant additional loans to the extent of the additional deposits it had taken in. This scheme aimed to make each branch accountable for its own profit and loss. Hitherto, branch banks had simply passed on their credits and debits to the head office and had not bothered about whether their accounts balanced — which is figuratively called "sharing porridge from one big pot."

The new scheme has given branch banks an incentive to collect more deposits, accelerate turnover and make the most of loanable funds. Moreover, a system of cost accounting was introduced in the internal management of the People's Bank to link the material welfare of the branch banks' staff with their economic responsibility and business efficiency. As a result, staff members began to show more interest in the profitability of banking operations and in the resources and employment of loanable funds. They took measures to improve the management and administration of the bank by speeding up the turnover of bank funds, raising efficiency and cutting back on expenditure. Thus, the turnover of bank funds was accelerated by 10% in the first half of 1980 as compared with the corresponding period in 1979; work efficiency was increased by 12.3% and cashiers' errors were reduced by 17.4%.

4. *Emphasis was placed on the interest rate as an economic lever.* Enterprises were given more decision-making power and more funds at their disposal. The incomes of urban workers and rural commune members also increased because of wage increases for some workers, the introduction of the bonus plan and increases in the prices the state paid for farm and sideline products. To take advantage of this new situation, the People's Bank again raised interest rates on savings deposits and enlarged the range of interest-bearing deposits to mop up surplus funds in the hands of the public, using interest rates as leverage.

Penalty rates were introduced on loans to industrial and commercial enterprises. The normal rate was to be raised by 20% for overdue loans, 30% for loans tied up in inventories and 50% for diversion of funds to unauthorized uses. The introduction of penalty rates encouraged enterprises to be more concerned about the results of their operations by improving business management. It was very effective in inducing enterprises to speed up the turnover of working capital, to reduce overstocking and to cut down on the amount of money that was tied up.

Individual savings grew very rapidly and the sum total of savings deposits increased substantially in 1980, largely due to increases in the incomes of farmers and city workers. But the increase in interest rates on savings deposits gave them additional incentive to make more deposits. Savings deposits in cities increased by 7,600 million — a record annual increase. By the end of 1980, the outstanding balance of savings deposits of city residents amounted to 27,900 million yuan, up 37% from 1979. There were 180 million savings accounts in 1980, of which 81% were fixed deposits; long-term deposits for 3-5 years accounted for 40% of these fixed deposits. By the end of 1980, savings deposits of rural commune members had risen by 4,200 million yuan to 12,060 million yuan, up 53.8% from 1979. The steady increase of savings deposits in the city and countryside was of great help to withdrawing currency from circulation, raising loanable funds, relieving pressure on the market that could not keep up with the gorwing demand and promoting the readjustment and restructuring of the economy. (See Appendix: Current Interest Rates on Savings Deposits.)

III. Flexible and Diversified Banking Services

To keep up with economic progress, traditional forms of bank services formerly provided in China or generally provided by banks in other countries were restored, giving more flexibility and diversity — and hence more vitality — to banking activities.

1. *The domestic insurance business was resumed.* The People's Insurance Company of China is the sole state-owned insurance institution in China. After the national conference on insurance was held in November 1979, and in line with the policy of promoting production and serving the masses, the domestic insurance business resumed in 1980. The company set up more than 300 branch offices throughout the country and increased its staff by about 5,000 workers. Domestic insurance, mainly business property insurance, was resumed in large and medium-sized cities, as well as in counties where industry and commerce were concentrated. Insurance covering merchandise shipments, family property, automobiles, third-party liability, ships, etc. was underwritten in some cities.

The value of insured assets in China amounted to over 130,000 million yuan in 1980. Insurance premiums totalled more than 10 million yuan in nine provinces and muncipalities. Total premiums for the country added up to 280 million yuan.

More than 1,300 indemnity cases were settled in 1980. The insurance business expanded at a rate much faster than had been expected. The company put emphasis on the prevention of disaster or attenuation of damage by promulgating various forms of propaganda and by conducting inspection tours of workshops, warehouses, docks and railway stations and by making suggestions. It also helped the insured to salvage property in order to minimize losses to state-owned property. Premiums collected by the company became a source of funds loanable by banks, thus contributing to the withdrawal of currency from circulation.

Progress was made by the company in the foreign insurance business in 1980. Premiums from import and export shipment insurance and other foreign insurance coverage amounted to some 216 million yuan, up 25% from 1979. The number and tonnage of ships insured also increased considerably. To meet the requirements of international business relations as far as possible, insurance coverage was extended to new fields: insurance covering all risks of construction and installations, package insurance on the processing of materials supplied by foreign traders, insurance on compensation trade, insurance on offshore oil exploitation, surety insurance, insurance on foreign responsibilities and obligations and insurance against political risks (including war, legal seizure or requisition and changes in government decrees). More than 300 vessel or cargo surveyors were appointed in over 100 countries and regions to appraise damage on the spot for the purpose of settling insurance claims.

The People's Insurance Company of China gives a substantial share of its insurance to foreign insurance companies for reinsurance and it accepts reinsurance from foreign insurance companies. It has established reinsurance relations with more than 960 insurance companies in 120 countries, from which it collected reinsurance premiums of US$150 million in 1980, or 20% more than in 1979.

2. *The Agricultural Bank of China was restored to improve rural banking services.* (See Chapter 42: China's Rural Banking.)

3. *The People's Bank of China in some large and medium-sized cities began to handle trust and investment business on an experimental basis and lifted restrictions on some commercial loans.* Within a year of its establishment in October 1979, the China International Trust and Investment Corporation received more than 4,000 visitors from some 40 countries and regions. The corporation negotiated over 100 co-production ventures with foreign firms, of which a dozen contracts have been or are to be signed, and agreements and letters of intent for over 60 joint projects which also have been signed. It has also concluded with a dozen foreign banks and financial institutions special credit arrangements, some of which are already operative.

4. *The People's Bank of China, with the authorization of the State Council, issued four series of commemorative coins in 1980.* These exquisite coins were minted by the China Mint Company and were well received by domestic and foreign collectors. (See Appendix: Varieties and Specifications of Commemorative Coins.)

To add variety to the currency in circulation, the People's Bank, with the authorization of the State Council, has issued since April 15, 1980, metallic coins in denominations of 10, 20 and 50 fen and of one yuan. These are in circulation on a par with banknotes of the same denominations. The four metallic coins were issued mainly to add variety, not to replace paper currency in circulation. (See Appendix: Descriptions of Metallic Coins Issued in 1980.)

The People's Bank of China raised the official purchase prices of gold, silver and platinum as of March 1, 1980, and the quantities of those precious metals purchased have increased considerably. By the end of September 1980, purchases of gold and silver amounted to 3.4 times and 1.5 times, respectively, the quantities bought a year ago. (See Appendix: Old and New Purchase Prices for Gold, Silver and Platinum.)

5. *In line with the development of tourism and of economic and cultural exchanges with foreign countries, the Bank of China, with the authorization of the State Council, issued foreign exchange certificates as of April 1, 1980, in order to facilitate payments by foreign visitors, overseas Chinese and compatriots from Hong Kong and Macao, to tighten exchange controls, to ban circulation of foreign currency in the country and to preserve the integrity of Renminbi.* Like travellers' cheques issued by the Bank of China and like the special Renminbi cheque, the foreign exchange certificate is a kind of payment instrument issued by the bank, not a currency. It is to be used for shopping at designated places for defraying expenses that must be paid in foreign currency. Exchange of foreign currency for the certificates is handled mainly by the Bank of China and a few branches of the People's Bank designated by the Bank of China. Foreign exchange certificates are in denominations of 1, 5, 10, 50 and 100 yuan and of 10 and 50 fen. When giving change for a value lower than 10 fen, Renminbi coins are to be used.

6. *The People's Bank of China also made progress in other fields of activities.* To date, 22 universities and colleges have begun to offer banking as a subject of specialization to over 2,900 students. There are also 22 banking schools below the college level with an enrollment of 8,000 students. In 1980, a national conference was held to chart the course for higher education in banking. Arrangments have since been made for teachers to write textbooks on banking for colleges and banking schools. Bank branches at all levels trained 70,000 staff members of different ranks; these accounted for about 30% of the total number to be trained.

Research on banking theory has been upgraded. By the end of 1980, research departments had been established in virtually all bank branches. Banking societies were set up in 20 provinces, muncipalities and autonomous regions. A veritable army of researchers in banking has emerged. Special studies have been undertaken on such subjects as currency in circulation and the reform of the banking system. Research on banking has contributed significantly to the emancipation of people's thinking, banking reforms, the training of staff members, improved efficiency and better management of economic development.

IV. Current Tasks of the People's Bank

(1) The People's Bank of China should focus its work on the strict control of note issuance, active support for national economic readjustment and maintenance of price stability. Budget deficits over the recent years coupled with over-issuance of bank notes have led to substantial growth in the money supply and, hence, to rising prices. The bank must make greater efforts to collect deposits and mop up excess money in circulation through control of bank credits, the mechanism of settling payments, regulation of cash flows, inducements to save and the stepping up of the insurance business. The bank must further tap the resources of savings deposits, mobilize idle funds as much as possible and exercise strict control of bank loans. Emphasis should also be placed on accelerating the turnover of loanable funds and using them to the best advantage.

(2) Versatility in banking is essential to the emergence of a flourishing economy. Bank loans should be granted to efficient enterprises in the interest of readjusting the economy. Emphasis must be put on the economic effectiveness of loans. Loans should enable borrowers to diversify production, as well as to increase the supply of goods to the market so as to provide the public with the incentive to withdraw money from circulation. The bank should give priority to financing the following sectors:

— textiles and other light industries, for the purpose of boosting production of textiles and other manufactured goods in short supply or of daily necessities;

— projects that tie up little money but bring large returns, thus creating greater wealth for the nation;

— other lines of production essential to the people's livelihood, such as cultural activities, tourism, service industries; and

— heavy industries that shift to the production of consumer goods, so as to increase market supplies and to enrich the economic and cultural life of the people.

(3) In the interest of readjusting the economy, the bank should continue to improve its work. Progress has been made in 1979 and 1980. For instance, the bank has adopted the principle of giving priority to well managed enterprises in granting loans. It has provided a wider range of services to a large number of clients with different needs and has supported cultural activities and service industries. It has provided working capital to collective enterprises run by young people in the cities and to private businesses. It has lifted restrictions on some commercial credit and has experimented with the trust and investment business. Experience has shown that such improvements in banking are beneficial to the overall economic readjustment.

However, bank services should keep up with new developments. Further improvements to be made should primarily serve the interests of readjusting the national economy.

(4) The People's Bank should perform the function of the central bank. In line with the development of the national economy, the banking system should develop into one in which various specialized banks share the work and cooperate with one another under the overall planning and coordination of the central bank. There should be a basic division of labour among specialized banks, although some overlapping is unavoidable.

The head office of the People's Bank of China should carefully examine and determine the ceilings of bank loans for specialized banks. The specialized banks may work out their own plans for bank loans, but their loans are not to exceed the ceilings set by the People's Bank of China. This requirement is necessary for the purpose of maintaining credit and cash balance so as to realize the withdrawal of money from circulation.

APPENDIX:

Current Interest Rates on Savings Deposits

Description		Interest rate per month (%)	Interest rate per annum (%)
Personal	1. Demand deposits	2.4	2.88
savings	2. Fixed deposits by instalments	3.6	4.32
deposits	for 6 months	3.6	4.32
of urban	for 1 year	4.5	5.40
and rural	for 3 years	5.1	6.12
residents	for 5 years	5.7	6.84
Overseas	Fixed deposits		
Chinese	for 1 year	4.8	5.76
Renminbi	for 3 years	5.4	6.48
deposits	for 5 years	6.0	7.20

Descriptions of Metallic Coins Issued in 1980

Denomination	Metal	Diameter (mm.)	Weight (grams)	Thickness of rim (mm)
10 fen	copper & zinc alloy	20	2.62	1.3
20 fen	”	23	4.18	1.5
50 fen	”	26	6.02	1.7
RMB ¥1	copper & nickel alloy	30	9.32	1.9

Current Interest Rates on Deposits and Loans

Description	Interest rate per month (%)	Interest rate per annum (%)
1. Deposits of state-owned industrial, commercial and agricultural enterprises, and collective enterprises operated by agricultural communes and brigades	1.5	1.80
2. Interbank deposits of credit cooperatives	2.7	3.24
1. Loans to state-owned industrial and commercial enterprises and to urban collective enterprises	4.2	5.04
2. Loans to industrial and commercial enterprises to cover accounts receivable in the course of collection; short- and medium-term loans for purchasing equipment	4.2	5.04
3. Loans to the grain trade	2.1	2.52
4. Loans for making down-payments on the purchase of farm and sideline products	3.6	4.32
5. Loans to state farms, agricultural communes and brigades to meet production costs and to provide working capital to enterprises run by communes and brigades	3.6	4.32
6. Loans to communes and brigades for buying production equipment or for constructing hydroelectric power stations	1.8	2.16
7. Loans to credit cooperatives	1.8	2.16

Varieties and Specifications of Commemorative Coins

Title	Face Value (in RMB ¥)	Fineness (%)	Diameter (mm.)	Weight (grams)
International Children's Year				
gold coin	450	90	27	17.17
China Olympic Committee				
gold coin	300	91.6	23	10
silver coin	30	80	32	15
silver coin	30	80	32	15
silver coin	20	80	28	10
copper coin	1	copper & zinc	23	5.8
copper coin	1	copper & zinc	28	8.8
copper coin	1	copper & zinc	32	11.9
copper coin	1	copper & zinc	32	11.9
Winter Olympics				
gold coin	250	91.6	23	8
silver coin	30	80	33	15
copper coin	1	copper & zinc	33	12
copper coin	1	copper & zinc	33	12
copper coin	1	copper & zinc	33	12
copper coin	1	copper & zinc	33	12
Year of the Cock (1981)				
gold coin	250	91.6	23	8
silver coin	30	85	33	15

Old and New Purchase Prices for Gold, Silver and Platinum*
(Effective March 1, 1980)

Description	Old prices (RMB ¥)	New prices (RMB ¥)
Purchase price at the bank counter:		
gold (per gram)	3.04	13.00
silver (per gram)	0.10	0.20
silver dollar (per piece)	2.50	5.00
platinum (per gram)	9.12	25.00

*Note: All purchase prices are based on net weight.

42. CHINA'S RURAL BANKING
By Cao Jiren
Agricultural Bank of China

In the three decades since the founding of New China, the Communist Party and the people's government have attached great importance to agricultural banking.

History of the Agricultural Bank. To improve agricultural banking and promote agricultural production, the Agricultural Bank of China was reorganized several times. As early as 1949, when Beijing was liberated, the government took the old Farmers' Bank and the cooperative treasury and merged them into the Cooperative Bank of Agriculture. But shortly after that, the Cooperative Bank of Agriculture was merged into the People's Bank of China. On three separate occasions — in 1951, 1955 and 1963 — the Agricultural Bank of China was established, but it was closed down each time for the purpose of streamlining the administrative structure.

On February 25, 1979, the State Council issued a decision reestablishing the Agricultural Bank of China. It is now a specialized bank responsible for agricultural banking in the country and a organization directly under the State Council. Its main tasks are to manage funds for financing agriculture, to grant rural loans, to supervise agricultural credit cooperatives and to develop agricultural banking in the interest of agricultural modernization.

The Agricultural Bank of China has a four-level administrative structure: a head office in Beijing, branch offices in the provinces, municipalities and autonomous regions, central sub-branch offices in prefectures and cities and sub-branch offices in counties.

Under the guidance of the Agricultural Bank, the people's communes have established credit cooperatives, which are at once collective financial entities and grassroots units of the Agricultural Bank. In most production brigades there are credit centres which form an integral part of the credit cooperatives.

Restoration of the Agricultural Bank at all levels has been completed. By the end of 1980, the agricultural banking network, comprising 27,228 offices of the Agricultural Bank and 59,500 credit cooperatives, was distributed throughout China's vast countryside.

Current Tasks of the Agricultural Bank. To enhance agricltural banking, the first national conference of bank managers was convened in October 1979, following the reestablishment of the bank. At the conference, the managers gained a deeper understanding of party policy by criticizing "Left" thinking, by reviewing the lessons learned from experience and by distinguishing between the right and wrong of our political lines. At the same time, these main tasks were set forth: to foster agricultural banking, to mobilize lending funds, to manage them well and employ them in the best possible way, and to promote the rapid development and modernization of agriculture.

In May 1980, a meeting was convened to exchange experiences in "how to support the production of marketable farm products to stimulate the economy." At the meeting it was declared that the guiding principle of agricultural banking was to support the production of marketable farm products by taking measures suited to local conditions, with emphasis on practical performance, so as to stimulate the rural economy. A separate forum for branch managers was held from June to July 1980 to discuss ways in which to reform the banking system, to reformulate credit policy, to enlarge the range of loans, to provide more flexible services by the bank and credit cooperatives and to achieve greater progress in rural banking.

China has a rural population of 800 million, over 2,000 counties, 50,000 communes, 710,000 production brigades, 5 million production teams, 170 million farm families and 1.5 million enterprises operated by communes and brigades, plus a multitude of state-owned farms and ranches. We see great potential for the expansion of agricultural credit.

Rural Banking Achievements in 1980. With the growth of agricultural credit and the rural economy, progress was made in rural banking in the following five areas:

(1) The Agricultural Bank placed top priority on the mobilization of lending funds and rural deposits grew rapidly. By the end of 1980, deposits with the Agricultural Bank and credit cooperatives totalled 41,800 million yuan, up 9,600 million from the previous year, or an increase of 30%. Of the total, 14,800 million yuan were in savings deposits in the countryside — an increase of 4,900 million yuan, or 49%, over 1979 and the highest annual increase since the founding of the People's Republic.

(2) The Agricultural Bank granted loans with

a quicker turnover and produced the desired results. By the end of 1980, loans granted by the Agricultural Bank and credit cooperatives totalled 31,000 million yuan, or 11,600 million more than the previous year, representing an increase of 59.6%. Repayments amounted to 24,400 million yuan, up 7,400 million from the year before, or an increase of 43.4%. A larger share of the loans were used to encourage the production of marketable farm products by communes, brigades and individuals, and a smaller share for relief or for covering deficits. Loans for rural trade increased by 5,400 million from the year before, an increase of 19.7%. The loans have increased sales in the rural areas and have stimulated trade between the cities and the countryside.

(3) The Agricultural Bank made a preliminary reform of credit control by instituting a scheme whereby branch offices might make more loans with the additional deposits they have collected. This gave the branch offices a material incentive to collect more deposits, to make the most of lending funds and to speed up their turnover.

(4) The Agricultural Bank achieved good results in unifying its control of lending funds, in supervising government allocations to the agricultural sector, in training accountants for the communes and production brigades and in giving them advice on how to use their funds to the best advantage.

(5) The Agricultural Bank did much work in setting up and staffing branch offices, training staff members, experimenting with cost accounting and procedures and instituting or upgrading some regulatory systems.

43. THE DEVELOPMENT OF CHINA'S INTERNATIONAL BANKING
By the Research Department,
Bank of China

Since the founding of the People's Republic, China's international banking has played an important role in rehabilitating and developing its national economy and in advancing socialist construction.

I. Principles and Policies

China has adhered to the following principles and policies in its international banking:

(1) *Maintain the Bank of China's independence and its centralized and unified management of international banking.* Until Liberation, the financial market in China had been dominatd by foreign banks and by Chinese bureaucratic capitalists, landlords and compradors. China's international payments and banking had been manipulated by foreign banks in China.

After the founding of New China, the government took over the Kuomintang's financial institutions and transformed the banks and money shops that were under private ownership into enterprises under joint state-private ownership. The Bank of China was designated by the state as a specialized bank for international banking. Control over the financial market was tightened. The government liquidated foreign banks in China, stripped them of special privileges and put foreign exchange under its centralized control and unified management.

Renminbi was declared the legal tender. Its exchange rates against foreign currencies were officially quoted by the Bank of China. Holders of foreign currencies were required to sell them to the bank within a given time. Renminbi was not allowed to be taken out of China and the free inflow of foreign currencies and foreign capital was banned.

Organizations and individuals are prohibited from dealing in foreign exchange or transferring abroad their funds, property or interests in China without authorization. Unless otherwise authorized, their foreign exchange incomes must be sold to the Bank of China. If they should have need of foreign exchange, they may purchase it from the Bank of China according to official regulations and with the approval of the government.

Individuals are allowed to possess gold and silver, but trading in these metals without authorization is prohibited. The People's Bank of China is the institution which handles such transactions in China and the Bank of China is the institution in charge of such transactions abroad.

Before 1968, foreign currencies had been used exclusively to settle trade payments. In that year, Renminbi was adopted for trade payments on a trial basis between China and Hong Kong and Macao. Payment in Renminbi was extended to countries in Europe such as the United Kingdom, France, Switzerland and West Germany in 1970, thus bringing to an end the era in which trade payments were made exclusively in foreign currencies.

(2) *Mutual benefit and equality guide China's international banking.* In the old days, our international payments were manipulated by foreign banks in China and discriminatory payment methods were imposed on Chinese banks and traders. For instance, Chinese banks could only issue the authority to purchase – instead of letters of credit – to settle payments for imports and had to make 100% down-payments to the negotiating bank when the authority to purchase was issued. Foreign correspondent banks, on the other hand, could open letters of credit to cover their import payments and they made payment only on receipt of the shipping documents.

Since the founding of New China, such discriminatory practices have gradually been eliminated. Upholding the principle of mutual benefit and equality, we improved the terms of payment and speeded up the receipt of export proceeds. In settling payments with Third World countries, we deal as far as possible with their native banks so as to encourage the development of their banking industries.

(3) *Respect contracts and commitments and safeguard the country's credit standing.* It has always been our policy to respect contracts and commitments in international banking. In the 1960's, the Soviet Union reneged on its contracts with China and withdrew its experts, causing a period of economic distress. Notwithstanding these difficulties, we paid off our loans to the Soviet Union ahead of schedule.

The Bank of China is always prompt in settling international payments. It repays the principal

667

and interest on interbank deposits and on loans when due. The Bank of China is highly regarded in the international money market and it prides itself on safeguarding the nation's international credit standing.

For a long time, the Bank of China had not done as much as it should have done in pooling, investing and accumulating foreign exchange funds. Not until the end of the 1960's did it expand interbank deposits with foreign banks and grant loans to domestic enterprises for the import of essential equipment to advance our socialist economy. Such loans were granted, as an exception, to the transport department for the purchase of freighters from abroad to build up China's ocean-going fleet. But due to "Left" guidelines in economic construction and, in particular, to the disruption caused by Lin Biao and the Gang of Four, foreign capital was used on a limited scale.

II. Recent Developments in China's International Banking

After the smashing of the Gang of Four, China embarked on an ambitious programme to turn itself into a strong, modern socialist country. Because of the shortage of funds and lack of expertise in advanced technology and business administration, China has had to pursue an open-door economic policy based on the principles of self-reliance, mutual benefit and equality. As a result, it has made substantial progress in international banking.

(1) *Upgrading of governmental powers and responsibilities and restructuring of government organizations.* With a view to overseeing the import-export trade and the utilization of foreign capital, the State Council of the People's Republic of China established in 1979 the State Administrative Commission on Import and Export Affairs and the Foreign Investment Commission. It also set up the State General Administration of Exchange Control (SGAEC) and the China International Trust and Investment Corporation (CITIC) in March and October, respectively, of that year and placed these two organizations under its direct leadership.

To give full scope to the role of the Bank of China, the State Council approved the restructuring of the bank's organization and placed the bank under its direct control. Furthermore, in September 1980, the State Council approved the bank's revised Articles of Association, which determined its status as a socialist state-owned enterprise. The bank's capital was also increased from 400 million yuan to 1,000 million yuan.

In line with the expansion of China's economic, trade and financial ties with foreign countries, the Bank of China had broadened its domestic network to 114 branch offices by the end of 1980. Its overseas offices had multiplied to 206, of which 196 are in the Hong Kong and Macao region, 6 in Singapore, 3 in the United Kingdom and one in Luxembourg. The bank established a representative office in Tokyo and preparations are underway for setting up a branch office in New York and a representative office in Paris.

(2) *Discretionary use of foreign capital and the strengthening of financial cooperation with other countries.* To speed up its modernization, China has been prudently absorbing foreign capital and selectively importing the advanced technology and equipment it urgently needs. China's external financial policy is that "self-reliance comes first, to be supplemented by assistance from abroad." Apart from increasing the deposits of the Bank of China, the government signed credit agreements in 1978 with the United Kingdom, France, Japan, Italy, West Germany, Sweden, Canada, Australia, Belgium and Argentina. So far, very little of the credits has been used. The relations of the Bank of China with the United States are growing fast.

By the end of 1980, China had made use of the following forms of foreign credit: low-interest loans from foreign governments; buyer's and seller's credits; interbank loans; compensation trade; joint ventures; cooperative production; leasing; and processing and assembling raw materials or parts supplied by foreign buyers.

Apart from its undertaking to complete formalities with foreign financial instutions for credit arrangements, the Bank of China has stood surety for Chinese enterprises engaged in various joint ventures with foreign firms. In 1980, two financial corporations were set up in Hong Kong, one jointly run by the banks of the People's Republic of China, the United States and Japan (CCIC Finance Ltd.) and the other by the banks of China and Japan (the Kincheng-Tokyo Finance Company). The Hong Kong and London branches of the Bank of China have taken part in international loan consortia. What is more, the head office of the Bank of China, established in October 1980 a trust department which signed reciprocal arrangements with many foreign banks and leasing companies, and so did the trust departments of more than 10 Bank of China branches.

To suit China's present financial conditions, we mainly make use of low-interest or interest-free loans from foreign governments or international financial organizations and some buyer's credits. On the basis of mutual benefit and equality and without detriment to our national sovereignty, we use foreign capital in various forms customary to international practice. In utilizing foreign capital, the primary consideration is the economic performance the loan will provide. We first study whether the project is feasible and then synchronize its financing, technological requirements and business administration. We accept foreign loans according to our ability to repay and respect international contracts and commitments.

(3) *Resumption of China's representation in the International Monetary Fund and the World Bank and extension of cooperation with the world financial community.* China is one of the founding members of the International Monetary Fund (IMF) and the World Bank, but it was unable to exercise its representation in those organizations for 31 years. Through negotiations with the two organizations in March and April 1980, and with the friendly support of many countries, China's representation in the Fund and the Bank was restored respectively on April 17 and May 15, 1980.

Li Baohua, President of the People's Bank of China, was appointed China's Governor in the IMF and Wang Weicai, Vice-President of the Bank of China, was named Deputy Governor. Finance Minister Wang Bingqian and Vice-Minister Li Peng were appointed, respectively, China's Governor and Deputy Governor in the World Bank.

On September 3 and 26, 1980, respectively, the two organizations passed resolutions increasing China's quota in the IMF and its subscription to the World Bank. We assigned our executive directors and deputy executive directors to the organizations after additional seats were made available to us. In September 1980, the delegation of the People's Republic of China attended the annual meeting of the IMF and the World Bank for the first time. China will exercise its rights and fulfil its obligations according to the charters of the IMF and the World Bank.

The Bank of China has established correspondent relationships with 1,003 banks of 144 countries and regions, including their 2,735 branches. The China International Trust and Investment Corporation has business ties with financial institutions in many countries.

Two foreign banks – the Standard Chartered Bank and the Hong Kong and Shanghai Banking Corporation – and two overseas Chinese banks – the Bank of East Asia, Ltd. and the Overseas-Chinese Banking Corporation – which had operated in China in the old days still remain in business for historical reasons. In 1980, eight foreign banks and three insurance companies received approval to establish representative offices in Beijing. These banks and companies represent Japan, the United States, France, Italy and the United Kingdom.

Business contacts between Chinese and world banking circles have also increased. China received 156 delegations of foreign bankers in 1980 alone and the range of business discussion was widened. During these visits, we had the opportunity to organize a number of seminars and forums on international financial problems. In 1980 the Bank of China sent 14 delegations to visit the banking communities of the United States, Japan, Canada, Korea, the Philippines, Singapore and Thailand and to attend some international forums on the world economy and China's economy. The Bank of China also sent staff members as trainees to banks in the United States, Japan and the United Kingdom to study international finance.

(4) *Enacting economic legislation to protect China's interests and the legitimate interests and rights of foreign investors.* With the expansion of China's economic, trade and financial relations with foreign countries, it has become a matter of increasing urgency to enact laws that will provide a code of conduct for the Chinese and their foreign partners in joint ventures and to protect their mutual interests.

In July 1979, the Law Concerning Joint Ventures with Chinese and Foreign Investment was promulgated to protect the interests of foreign investors in statutory form. A series of regulations were issued in 1980. The Provisional Regulations for Exchange Control were promulgated in December 1980 and went into effect on March 1, 1981. Supplementary provisions related to these regulations will be made known.

In respect to exchange controls, we will continue to follow the policy of centralized control and unified management. The limited foreign exchange in the hands of the government will be used according to plan and where it is most needed for the improvement of the people's livelihood and for the country's socialist construction.

With the development of our national economy, increased external economic activities and the restructuring of organizations, exchange controls have been extended to new fields. For instance, to encourage foreign investments in China, joint ventures with Chinese and foreign ownership are given some leeway in foreign exchange transfers, provided these are related to normal business activities and are subject to the supervision of the Bank of China. In addition, local governments, government departments and enterprises that have been given larger decision-making powers also have been given permission to retain a portion of the foreign exchange they earn – to be used at their discretion, but in accordance with the plan and subject to the supervision of the Bank of China. Private individuals are allowed to retain a certain percentage of the foreign exchange they own. The details governing extended exchange controls will be set forth in supplementary regulations.

In the last two years, the open-door economic policy has increased the amount of business handled by the Bank of China. The bank's balance sheet for 1980 showed a rapid increase in business volume: deposits went up 46% from the previous year; remittances increased by 60%; guarantees, trusts and collections grew by more than 28%; and lending rose by over 50% (an increase of 96% if interbank deposits are excluded). The bank's net profits more than doubled.

China is in the midst of readjusting its national economy, and its international banking activities must be coordinated with overall economic activities. There is no change in our policy of making use of foreign capital, but foreign capital must be used mainly to support the readjustment of the national economy, the production of goods in short supply, the growth of export-oriented industries, the efforts of tapping production potential and renovating old factories, and the improvement of the people's livelihood.

We are confident that through this readjustment, China's economy will develop on a sounder basis. China holds out bright prospects for its economic construction and for still closer economic, trade and financial ties with other countries.

44. PRICES IN CHINA
By Duan Jianke
State Administration Bureau for Commodity Prices

Since the founding of the People's Republic of China, we have adopted the policy of stabilizing prices so as to improve the people's standard of living and to carry out smoothly the country's socialist construction.

I. History of Price Controls

In the early years after the founding of the People's Republic, the government consolidated its control of the nation's finances and the economy by deflating the currency, regulating taxes and strengthening market controls. By controlling the group purchasing power of state-owned enterprises, organizations and army units, the amount of money in circulation was significantly reduced.

At the same time, the government stocked such major commodities as grain, cotton cloth, coal, salt, etc. and sold them at fixed prices in the country's major cities, thus dealing a heavy blow to the speculative activities of the capitalists who were endangering the national economy. This put an end to the chaos of inflation and brought us a decisive victory in the struggle to stabilize market prices. By 1952, price stability was further consolidated with the recovery and development of the national economy.

First Five-Year Plan Period. During the First Five-Year Plan period (1953-1957), the policy of placing state orders for processing materials and manufacturing goods with private enterprises was begun in order to achieve the socialist transformation of agriculture, handicrafts and capitalist industry and commerce. This policy gave the state the monopoly of the purchase and marketing of such basic commodities as grain, cotton, oil crops and pigs, and of the proper application of the law of value. In the exchange of industrial goods for agricultural products, we adopted a policy of exchanging goods of equal or near-equal values. For industrial goods, we also implemented the policy of seeking small profits but rapid returns. For some agricultural products, such as grain, oil, pigs, we raised the state's purchasing price while keeping market retail prices stable. In this way we were able to narrow the price differential between industrial and agricultural products that was the legacy of the old society.

Comparing 1957 with 1952, the purchasing prices of agricultural products increased by 20.2% while retail prices of industrial products in rural areas increased by only 2.2%. The price differential between industrial and agricultural products was thus narrowed by 15%, which meant that peasants could obtain 17.6% more industrial products in exchange for the same amount of agricultural products.

The Difficult Years. During the difficult years from 1959 to 1961, serious natural calamities and our own errors caused industrial and agricultural production to drop by a large margin. Many major consumer goods were in short supply as purchasing power outstripped the supply of commodities. In 1960, the supply of consumer goods was only 87.9% of total purchasing power. Prices at rural fairs went up sharply during this period, averaging three times as much as the list prices in state-owned shops.

Tight Controls. To tighten control over prices, the State Commodity Prices Commission issued on February 25, 1963 a list of 18 commodities considered as daily necessities and stipulated that the prices of these commodities, which accounted for about 60% of the living expenses of staff members and workers, must be maintained at the stipulated level, with no fluctuation permitted. Any losses suffered by enterprises as a result of the stipulations would be subsidized by the state. This was an extremely important government measure to guarantee the standard of living of staff members and workers.

At the same time, in order to make up the losses incurred by enterprises and to narrow the gap between purchasing power and the supply of commodities, the state raised the prices of more than ten kinds of secondary consumer goods. Through the sales of these higher-priced items, several thousand million dollars of purchasing power were absorbed.

During the three years of economic difficulties, market prices rose to a level unprecedented since the founding of the People's Republic. Comparing 1962 with 1957, the general index of retail prices in the country increased by 25.8%, and in 1961 alone an increase of 16.2% was registered over 1960. In 1963-64, the overall economic situation improved, prices at rural fairs dropped significantly and market prices as a whole returned to normal.

Market Price Problems. By 1965, the readjustment of the national economy was basically achieved and market prices had returned to normal. The prices of the 18 daily necessities had remained stable and the ratio between prices at rural fairs and prices at state-operated shops had also returned to normal. Most high-priced commodities were selling at parity prices, while other high-priced item had their prices considerably lowered. Nevertheless, there were some outstanding problems with market prices:

(1) The unified selling price of grain in cities and towns was not only lower than the unified selling price of grain in rural areas, but also lower than the unified purchasing price of grain. This resulted in the irrational situation in which people in urban areas could buy grain at lower prices than the peasants.

(2) In northern and northeastern China, where much of the coal is mined, the selling price of coal was low and, as a result, losses were incurred in commercial sales of coal.

(3) The price of cotton cloth had remained unchanged for many years and was incompatible with the new situation. Prices for low-grade cloth were low, so that profits were low and losses were even incurred in sales of some items, thus affecting production and supply. On the other hand, prices for high-grade cloth were high and allowed a large profit to be made, but the prices affected their marketing.

Price Readjustments. The Central Committee of the Communist Party of China and the State Council jointly issued the "Resolution on the Readjustment of Present Market Prices" on January 19, 1965. Its main provisions were as follows:

(1) The unified selling price of grains in cities and towns should be raised on a par with the unified purchasing price of grain. To alleviate the difficulties this would cause to the majority of staff members and workers in the cities, those staff members and workers with low incomes should be subsidized according to the increase in the price of grain, so as to guarantee their standard of living.

(2) The market price of coal should be raised

Table 1. General Price Index for 1979

Index	National retail price	Purchasing price of farm by-products	Retail price of industrial products in rural areas	Composite price parities between industrial and agricultural commodities	
				$\frac{(3)}{(2)} \times 100$	$\frac{(2)}{(3)} \times 100$
	(1)	(2)	(3)	(4)	(5)
Average 1950 prices = 100	138.6	265.5	109.9	41.4	241.6
Average 1952 prices = 100	124.0	218.3	100.2	45.9	217.9
Average 1965 prices = 100	114.3	181.6	98.0	54.0	185.3
Average 1957 prices = 100	102.0	141.3	92.9	65.7	152.1
Average 1975 prices = 100	105.1	127.2	100.3	78.9	126.8
Average 1978 prices = 100	102.0	122.1	100.1	82.0	122.0

Note: In this table, the general price index includes the list price, the negotiated price; the increased price for quantity supplied in excess of purchasing quota and the market price.

by an appropriate amount where losses have been incurred in the commercial sale of coal.

(3) While the general selling price of cotton cloth should remain basically unchanged, the prices of certain low-grade cloth should be raised and the prices of certain high-grade cloth should be lowered; at the same time, regional price differentials and differentials between wholesale and retail prices should be readjusted.

(4) In order to raise the low incomes of grain-growing peasants and to promote the production of grain, a reward system would be set up whereby production teams supplying commodity grain in excess of the quota set by the state would receive higher prices for their grain. Furthermore, the prices of agricultural means of production would continue to go down and the prices of certain manufactured goods for which prices were high but which were supplied in sufficient quantity, would be lowered.

Compared with 1962, the general retail price index for the nation in 1965 dropped by 4.7% and prices at rural fairs went down by 46%.

During the ten years of the "cultural revolution," chaos reigned in politics and in the economy. In order to maintain price stability, the party's Central Committee and the State Council jointly issued the "Provisions Concerning Stricter Economy in Making Revolution, Control of the Social Purchasing Power and Enhanced Control of Funds, Materials and Price," with the intention of freezing prices. But, due to the interference and sabotage of Lin Biao and the Gang of Four, price organizations were practically abolished in 1969, their personnel were transferred to other posts and no readjustments in prices were made. As a result, the unreasonable price parities between industrial and agricultural products, between raw materials and manufactured goods and between new and old products were not corrected for a long time and problems piled up. Compared with 1965, the nation's general retail price index in 1976 showed a drop of 2.2%. Because price discipline was slack during the 10-year period, prices were increased at will and price rises in disguised forms were very common. In 1976, prices at rural fairs were up by 40% over those in 1965, seriously affecting the stability of market prices and the people's standard of living.

II. Recent Developments in Achieving Price Stability

Since the smashing of the Gang of Four, price organizations at all levels have been restored or established, the number of people working in them has increased and unreasonable prices have gradually been readjusted. In December 1978, the Third Plenary Session of the 11th Party Central Committee, with a view to narrowing the price differentials between industrial and agricultural products, suggested that the State Council take the following decisions: raise the unified purchase price of grains by 20% beginning in 1979, when the summer grain crops reach the market; raise by a further 50% the purchase price of grains supplied in excess of state purchasing quotas; and raise gradually — and by amounts corresponding to different conditions of production — the purchase prices of sideline products, such as cotton, oil crops, sugarcane and beets, animal products, aquatic products, forestry products and so on.

The Third Plenary Session of the Party Central Committee noted, however, that after the increases in the purchase prices of agricultural products, the state should ensure that there is no reduction in the living standard of staff members and workers in the cities and that, therefore, retail grain prices should in no case be raised, while prices of other farm products, constituting the daily necessities of the masses, would also be stabilized. For certain items whose prices must be raised, the recommendation was that appropriate allowances be given to consumers.

Purchasing Prices. It was in this spirit that the purchasing prices of 18 major farm products were raised by a large margin in April 1979. While the general index of purchasing prices of farm products rose by 22% over the previous year, the producer price of plastic film for farm use in some areas, as well as the maximum price for farm diesel oil in remote areas, were lowered. These adjustments played an important role in promoting agricultural production and in improving the living standard of the peasants.

The producer price of coal was raised as of May 1, 1979, so as to end the losses incurred by many coal mines due to the unreasonably low prices that had prevailed for a long time. In addition, the prices of certain non-ferrous metals and mineral products were also raised, while the prices of certain engineering and electronic products were lowered.

The rise in the purchasing prices of farm products and in the producer prices of certain industrial products, such as coal, helped to raise production, enlarge the distribution of commodities, stabilize the market and adjust relations among producers, commercial departments and consumers.

Selling Prices. In September 1979, the State

Council made the following decisions pertaining to selling prices of consumer goods under different conditions:

(1) The selling prices of daily necessities, such as food grains, edible oils, cotton cloth, sugar and coal, would remain unchanged, with the state subsidizing any deficit that might be incurred as a result.

(2) The selling prices of eight nonstaple foods — pork, beef, mutton, poultry, eggs, aquatic products, vegetables and milk — would be raised as of November 1, 1979. In order not to lower the living standards of staff members and workers as a result of these price rises, subsidies for nonstaple foods would be granted at the same time, simultaneous with wage increases and the raising of wage scales in certain regions. After price rises in these eight nonstaple foods, changes in the prices of related products and in charges for repairs and services woud be strictly controlled, unnecessary links cut out, large price differentials narrowed, profits on the high side lowered, and the quality of products guaranteed, with any covert price rises forbidden.

(3) The selling prices of other consumer goods in general should not be raised if they could be maintained at the old level. Price rises that must be made should be balanced by the simultaneous lowering of other prices.

With a view to stimulating the production and distribution of small consumer goods and to satisfy market demand, the State Council further stipulated that the law of value should be fully utilized in respect to the small volume of farm by-products and special local products. The function of market regulation should be brought into play gradually to return to the method practiced before 1957: namely, prices can go up and down, products can be purchased and sold at negotiated prices, such that high prices in can be offset by high prices out, and low prices in can be matched by low prices out. The necessary measures of control should be taken in order to avoid serious price fluctuations.

Retail Prices. After the increase in prices of eight major nonstaple foods and of their related products in November 1979, the general index of national retail prices for the month of December — including list prices and negotiated prices — increased by 5.9% compared with that for the corresponding period in the previous year. The list prices of state-operated shops increased by 5.3%, or 1.9% if compiled on an annual basis.

Over the past 30 years, market retail prices in the cities and countryside have been basically stable. The purchasing prices of farm produce have been raised gradually, while the prices of the agricultural means of production have been lowered, and price differentials between industrial and agricultural products have been narrowed step by step. Comparing 1979 with 1950, the nation's general retail price level — including list prices, negotiated prices and market prices — increased by 38.6%; the purchasing prices of agricultural products rose by 165.5%; and retail prices of industrial products in the countryside were up by only 9.9%, thus narrowing the price differentials between industrial and agricultural products by 58.6%. Peasants now obtain twice as many industrial goods against the same amount of agricultural products.

Curbing Prices. To ensure the stability of market prices and the people's standard of living, the Party Central Committee and the State Council issued on April 8, 1980, the "Circular to Tighten the Control of Prices and to Curb Resolutely Unrestrained and Disguised Price Rises." By this means, the party and government prohibited unauthorized rises in commodity prices under the state plan and unauthorized increases in collection items. Also prohibited were disguised price rises, such as making up deficits, adding to surpluses and increasing bonus funds. Poor-quality products which are the result of shoddy workmanship or inferior materials must be improved within a given time. If quality fails to improve within the given time, the price of the products should be revised, i.e., reduced, accordingly.

In respect to agricultural products, the higher prices paid for supplies in excess of the state purchasing quota and price subsidies should be granted in conformity with the stipulations of the State Council. Not all localities and departments are allowed to increase the assortment of purchases or to enlarge the range of price increases and subsidies.

Commodities whose prices are subject to negotiated purchase and sale are limited to the third category of agricultural products and to small industrial consumer products and to the first and second categories of agricultural products which are allowed to be put on the market after their purchasing quotas have been fulfilled. Negotiated purchase and sale of manufactured goods for daily use in the first and second categories is equally prohibited. The assortment of commodities subject to negotiated purchase and sale is to be specified by the provinces, municipalities and autonomous regions. The price level for negotiated purchase and sale should be set so as to help promote the development of production, to increase the supply of commodities, to activate markets in cities and rural areas and to keep down prices at rural fairs — thus taking into consideration the interests of the state, the producers and the consumers.

After the "Circular" was issued, different localities, departments, enterprises and institutions organized teams to monitor prices.

In the second half of 1980, the national economy was still sluggish. Revenues and expenditures did not balance; the gap between the purchasing power of social groups and the supply of commodities remained large and the prices of many commodities went up. Multi-outlet business operations were encouraged to play an active role in stimulating city and rural markets. However, their activity was not immediately followed by proper measures of control; it set off another round of price fluctuations.

To implement the "Circular" issued by the Party's Central Committee and the State Council and to stabilize the economy and the people's livelihood so as to guarantee the smooth progress of socialist construction, the State Council issued its "Circular Concerning the Tight Control of Prices and the Rectification of Negotiated Prices." The stipulations in this document stressed that the retail prices of industrial and agricultural commodities listed by the state must be held steady, without exception, and prohibited their increase. The retail price of commodities sold at negotiated prices in all cities, industrial and mining districts, county towns and villages must not rise above the level of December 7, 1980. These prices are permitted to go down, but not to rise.

Negotiated purchase and sale of commodities must be carried out according to the principles laid down by the State Council and within the range specified by the governments of the provinces, municipalities and autonomous regions. Means of production allocated by the state plan, including that portion in excess of production quotas and the portion which individuals may sell, as well as the first and second categories of manufactured goods for daily use, must be sold at the prices fixed by the state. The first and second categories of agricultural by-products are not allowed to be marketed at negotiated prices or sold at rural fairs before fulfilment of the state purchase quotas. Also, products produced by collectives are not allowed to be distributed to individuals for resale.

Units which make purchases in areas where production of agricultural by-products in the third category is concentrated must submit to unified control and supply of goods, and the mutual driving up of prices is strictly forbidden. The top limit of negotiated prices should be determined by the people's governments of the provinces, municipalities and autonomous regions and these prices should be made public. Resale of goods for profit by any organization, team, army unit or institution is strictly prohibited. Control of rural fairs must be enhanced according to state policy so as to give full scope to its positive role.

Price Investigations. After the second "Circular" of the State Council was promulgated, the State Administration Bureau for Commodity Prices together with a number of related departments jointly organized 14 price inspection and investigation teams to go into different localities throughout the country. The task of these teams was to assist in the implementation of various measures set forth in the "Circular," to correct any violations of the price policy and to study the new situation and new problems.

The initial report of the investigation teams indicated that all localities paid attention to the "Circular" and earnestly carried out the required steps. The prices of commodities managed by state-operated shops and by supply and marketing cooperatives were put under control. Some of the commodities which had to comply with the stipulations relating to negotiated prices were no longer sold at negotiated prices. The level of prices at rural fairs remained stable or even went down a little.

Retail Price Index. Compared with 1979, the general index of national retail prices, including the list price, negotiated price and market price, increased by 6% in 1980. This accounted for increases of 8.1% in cities and of 4.4% in rural areas. The prices of consumer goods rose by 7.1% and the cost of agricultural means of production by 1%.

Implementing Price Controls. In order to further implement the principle of readjusting the economy and to achieve political stability, we must first of all put into effect the State Council's "Circular Concerning the Tight Control of Prices and the Rectification of Negotiated Prices." We must make a great effort to readjust the range and level of negotiated prices of agricultural products. Prices of the means of production allocated under the state plan must be strictly controlled according to state stipulations. Price inspections must be made continually in order to maintain the stability of market prices and of prices for light industrial products.

Following the implementation of the principle of readjustment, restructuring, consolidation and improvement of the national economy, the price system as well as the management of prices should undergo a comprehensive readjustment and restructuring on the basis of increased production and a stable economy to the extent permitted by the financial and material resources of the country.

Table 2. Classified Index of Retail Prices in China in 1980 (1979 = 100)

	General Index	List price index of state-operated commerce
General index of retail prices	106.0	104.4
1. Index of prices of consumer goods	107.1	105.2
A. Foods	110.5	107.4
Grains	103.5	100.3
Nonstaple foods	119.0	113.8
Tobacco, liquor, tea	100.5	100.5
Other foods	106.4	105.5
B. Clothing	100.0	100.0
C. Articles of everyday use	101.2	101.0
D. Articles for cultural and entertainment use	100.7	100.7
E. Medicine	100.9	100.9
F. Fuels	100.7	100.2
2. Price index of the agriculutral means of production	101.0	101.0

Note: In this table the general index includes the list price, negotiated price and market price.

45. RAPID DEVELOPMENT OF TOURISM
By the General Office,
General Administration of Travel and Tourism of China

China's tourism grew rapidly in 1980. The volume of foreign tourists, the total number of tourists in all categories and income in foreign currency were the highest in history.

Statistical Summary

In 1980, China's tourist departments and other relevant divisions received 5.7 million visitors. These comprised foreigners, compatriots from Hong Kong, Macao and Taiwan and overseas Chinese who came to China as tour members, on visits, on vacation or on survey trips, or to engage in trade, sports activities and scientific and cultural exchanges. The 1980 figure represented an increase of 1,499,100, or 35.6% over 1979.

Among the visitors in 1980, 529,000, or 9.3% of the total, were foreigners, an increase of 46% over 1979; 34,000, or 0.6%, were overseas Chinese, an increase of 64.6%; 5,139,000, or 90.2%, were compatriots from Hong Kong, Macao and Taiwan, an increase of 34.5%. Over 90% of the total number of visitors who entered China last year were compatriots from Hong Kong, Macao and Taiwan on home visits.

The China International Travel Service received 218,700 foreign tourists, an increase of 33.9% over 1979. The China Travel Service (the Overseas Chinese Travel Service) received 694,700 overseas Chinese, compatriots from Hong Kong, Macao and Taiwan and foreign nationals of Chinese origin, a decrease of 13.8%.

The All-China Federation of Trade Unions, All-China Youth Federation and the State Commission of Physical Culture and Sports received over 20,000 compatriots from Hong Kong, Macao and Taiwan, overseas Chinese and foreign visitors.

In 1980, foreign currency income from tourism rose to U.S.$617 million, an increase of U.S.$167 million, or 37.1%, over 1979. Of this total, 36%, or U.S.$222 million, came from the sales of commodities (the rate in Shanghai was 40%). The average spending rate for commodities was U.S.$108.1 per person. However, foreign tourists had a higher consumption level, with tourist groups from Europe, America and Oceanea averaging about U.S.$1,000 per person.

The foreign tourists visiting China in 1980 came from 110 countries and regions. Japanese made up 32% of the total; U.S. visitors were second, with 19.2%.

Tourist Cities and Areas

In 1980, 220 cities and areas were open to foreign tourists. They included:

Beijing; Tianjin (including Dagang and Yangcun);
Hebei Province: Shijiazhuang, Tangshan, Zunhua, Shashiyu, Handan, Qinhuangdao, Chengde, the Zhaozhou Bridge, Xibaipo village, the Gangnan Reservoir, Beidaihe and Zuoxian County;
Shanxi Province: Taiyuan, Dazhai, Yangquan and Datong;
Inner Mongolian Autonomous Region: Hohhot, Baotou and Xilinhot;
Liaoning Province: Anshan, Dalian and Fushun;
Jilin Province: Changchun and Jilin;
Heilongjiang Province: Harbin and Daqing; Shanghai;
Jiangsu Province: Nanjing, Suzhou, Wuxi, Yangzhou, Zhenjiang, Changzhou, Huai'an, Yixing, Lianyun Port and Xuzhou;
Anhui Province: Hefei, Wuhu, Ma'anshan, Huangshan Mountain and Qingyang (Mt. Jiuhua);
Zhejiang Province: Hangzhou, Shaoxing, Ningbo, Wenzhou, Leqing (Yandang Mountain) and Mt. Mogan;
Fujian Province: Fuzhou, Xiamen, Zhangzhou and Quanzhou;
Jiangxi Province: Nanchang, the Jinggang Mountains, Mt. Lushan (including Jiujiang and Xingzi County) and Jingdezhen;
Shandong Province: Jinan, Qingdao, Shengli Oilfield, Tai'an (Mt. Taishan), Zibo, Yantai, Changwei (Weifang, Anqiu, Linqu) and Qufu;
Henan Province: Zhengzhou, Luoyang, Anyang, Linxian County, Kaifeng, Xinxiang, Huixian County, Gongxian County, Sanmen Gorge, Xinyang (Mount Jigong) and Yuxian County;
Hubei Province: Wuhan, Shashi, Xiangfan, Danjiang and Xianning;
Hunan Province: Changsha, Shaoshan, Xiangtan, Hengyang and Yueyang (Lake Dongting);
Guangdong Province: Guangzhou, Zhaoqing, Conghua, Foshan and Hainan Island (Haikou);

Guangxi Zhuang Autonomous Region: Nanning, Guilin, Liuzhou, Wuming, Guiping, Yangshuo and Binyang;
Sichuan Province: Chengdu, Chongqing, Wanxian County, Leshan and Mt. Emei;
Yunnan Province: Kunming, Lunan (Stone Forest) and Jinghong (Xishuangbanna);
Shaanxi Province: Xi'an and Yan'an;
Gansu Province: Lanzhou, Jiuquan, Jiayu Pass and Dunhuang;
Xinjiang Uygur Autonomous Region: Urumqi (Heaven Lake), Shihezi and Turpan.

Also included was the section of the Changjiang River between Chongqing and Shanghai; and the coast line extending from Shanghai to Qingdao, Yantai, Dalian and Tianjin.

Some areas not included on the above list may receive tourists by special permission. Examples are Lhasa of Tibet and Dazhu of Sichuan.

Beijing, Shanghai, Guangzhou, Hangzhou, Xi'an, Guilin, Nanjing, Suzhou and Wuxi were the most frequented cities. Some 80% of all tourists visited Beijing. In addition to being the national capital, Beijing is a place of scenic beauty; major sites include the Great Wall, the former Imperial Palace, the Ming Tombs and the Summer Palace. Other cities have a similar appeal for tourists.

Development of Tourist Facilities

Hotels. By 1980, China had a total of 39,000 hotel beds for foreign guests.

More than 20 tourist hotels were built or expanded in 1980, and 4,300 beds were added. Eight hotels were built with foreign investment — in Guilin, Nanjing, Suzhou, Wuxi and Zhenjiang — each with 110 rooms. The Yanxiang Hotel in Beijing, with 144 rooms, was also built with the participation of foreign capital. The 250-room Yongzhou Hotel in Nanning was built with state investment. The Huagang Hotel and Zhejiang Guest House of Hangzhou were expanded.

Construction of several large hotels began in 1980 — the Yanjing (515 rooms), Jianguo (528 rooms) and Xiangshan (320 rooms) in Beijing; the Jinling (804 rooms) in Nanjing; and the Baietan (996 rooms) in Guangzhou.

Hotels in traditional Chinese style were built or refurbished in Zhuoxian County and Jixian County, and were well received by foreign tourists.

In 1980, many places of interest were restored following damage during the "cultural revolution." For instance, in Beijing the Tanzhe Monastery, Dazhong Monastery, Dagoba Monastery and Fayuan Monastery were open to Chinese and foreign tourists. The Leshan area of Sichuan has been restored to its former beauty. The home of Confucius in Qufu, Shandong Province, including his temple, residence and tomb, which are precious parts of the Chinese culture, were restored following serious damage under the rule of Lin Biao and the Gang of Four. Restoration work began a few years ago and was basically completed by 1980. Qufu was opened to visitors in the same year.

Construction was also under way at some famous sites. Work began at Mt. Taishan to install a cableway to the mountain top. This will be of great help to old or infirm visitors and will greatly reduce the time required for climbing. Roads were repaired on Huangshan Mountain, with hotels, restaurants and shops added there.

A few years ago, some famous tourist areas suffered from serious pollution. In 1980, initial successes were gained in pollution control in Guilin and Suzhou. In Jinan, factories consuming large quantities of water were moved out of the city and a number of wells were filled. As a result, the Baotu Spring and Daming Lake were saved. Moreover, the volume of water was increased and its quality improved.

Varied Itineraries for Tourism

With the development of tourism, many new forms have been adopted. Usual activities for a foreign tourist group had mainly consisted of visits to historic places of interest, scenic spots, factories and schools. They went sightseeing from one city to another. This routine often proved dull and monotonous. New varieties were adopted in 1980. Fishing trips were organized on Lake Taihu in Wuxi, Jiangsu Province. The Suzhou tourist service provided facilities for Japanese tourists to visit the Hanshan Monastery on the eve of the lunar new year and to strike the large bronze bell there. Nanjing organized 20 members of the Amagasaki Cyclists Association of Hyogo Prefecture, Japan, to bicycle from Nanjing to Yangzhou and from Wuxi to Suzhou. These activities were much appreciated by the participants. In addition, Chinese shadow-boxing tours, Chinese language learning tours and Grand Canal tours were offered in east China. On-ice tours held in Harbin in winter were mainly composed of compatriots from Hong Kong and Macao. They viewed the ice sculptures and took part with great delight in various activities.

Day Trips. One-day tours were conducted in the Shenzhen and Zhongshan areas. These were mainly organized for foreign tourists and compatriots from Hong Kong and Macao. The Xili Reservoir, 32 km. north of Shenzhen, was opened for use as a weekend campsite. In the midst of rolling hills and luxuriant vegetation, holiday-makers may enjoy swimming, angling, boating, shooting, riding and cycling. Camp fires are built in the evening and people picnic by their light. Hundreds of people flock to Xili from Hong Kong every weekend.

To accomodate one-day visitors from Macao, Zhongshan County has built a 130,000 sq. m. hot-springs health resort at Yongmo Village, 20 km. from Macao; investment was provided by the China-Macao Construction Investment Corporation. Zhongshan has a guest house with 400 beds, 20 hot-spring baths, a shop, restaurant, music hall, swimming pool and other recreational facilities. The hotel is set in the cool shade of trees and bamboo groves. Rare flowers abound. A fountain spurts high above the rockeries. After taking a hot-spring bath, guests can take a 30-km. excursion to the hometown of Dr. Sun Yat-sen, at Cuiheng Village, and to the scenic area of Shiqi.

Cruises on the Yangtze. A new tourist route leading through the world-famous Three Gorges on the Changjiang River was officially opened in 1980. The *Kunlun,* a luxurious yacht, began plying the river between Chongqing and Nanjing and between Chongqing and Wuhan, and was often fully booked by foreign passengers. It also calls at Jiujiang and Wanxian, and passengers have time to sightsee at Mt. Lushan and Shibaozhai. Last year, the ship made more than 20 round-trips, with this new route becoming one of the most famous tourist excursions in China.

Mountaineering. China began to organize mountaineering trips in 1980. The State Commission of Physical Culture and Sports received 40 teams comprising a total of 228 climbers. Eight peaks have been opened to foreign mountaineers. These are: Qomolangma ["Mt. Everest"] (8,848m.) and Xixabangma (8,012 m.) in Tibet; Muztagata (7,546 m.), Kongur (7,719 m.), Kongur Jiubie (7,595 m.) and Bogda (5,445 m.) in Xinjiang; Gongga (7,590 m.) in Sichuan; and Anyemaqen (7,160 m.) in Qinghai.

In 1980, the head office of the China International Travel Service and the Beidaihe Tourist Corporation jointly provided services at the coastal resort of Beidaihe for the first international symposium on mine planning and development techniques, thus opening a new field for China's tourism. A total of 310 foreign specialists and their wives, representing foreign firms that took part in the accompanying exhibition, plus members of the working staff, were in attendance. The meeting lasted for five days. The foreign guests visited Beijing and some other places before and after the meeting.

The head office of the China International Travel Service provided services for an international tourist conference, "China — 1980," sponsored by British Travel Promotions Ltd. and other organizations.

Improved Services

International Tourism. Measures were taken in 1980 to improve service quality. These efforts met with a favourable response from tourists. The General Administration of Travel and Tourism of China convened a conference of hotel managers to exchange experiences in management and approved "Basic Requirements for Tourist Hotels." The conference played an active part in improving service quality. The Dongfang Guest House in Guangzhou and the Friendship Guest House in Luoyang have led in this respect.

New measures have been taken by the Beijing branch of the China International Travel Service. These are: coaches serving air-conditioned cold drinks in summer; frequent arrangements for tourists to dine in famous restaurants; a schedule of activities to be provided to tourists upon arrival. Guides were instructed to provide weather forecasts and news headlines at the beginning of the day's activities and to promptly answer questions raised by foreign tourists in the course of the tour.

Efforts were also made to improve service offered by CAAC, China's airline. New flights were put into in operation between Beijing and London and Beijing and Hong Kong via Hangzhou. Domestic flights have also been expanded and readjusted, especially those linking tourist cities. Starting in 1980, CAAC gave favourable discounts to tourists coming to China — a 20% discount for off-travel and a 15% discount for CAAC international passengers when travelling domestically in China.

The production and sale of goods for tourists also grew quickly last year. According to incomplete statistics, there are 2,000 factories and 3,000 shops catering to the needs of tourists. The variety of commodities also increased. For instance, 27 new shops were commissioned in Guilin in 1980, selling shell carvings, feather pictures, bamboo carvings, embroidery and other handicrafts products in more than 1,000 varieties. An exemplary bamboo carving, *Liu Sanjie on a Spring Excursion,* is a clever blend of beautiful scenery with popular folk lore. The design is elegant and the figures are vivid. It is always in demand.

Tourists like to purchase low- and medium-priced commodities. However, there are still many who wish to buy high-grade articles of artistic merit. For instance, in October 1980, the embroidery, *Spring Outing,* modelled after an ancient painting, was sold to an American couple at the shop of the Zhongzhou Guest House, Zhengzhou. The price of this exquisite piece of art was 50,000 yuan.

Progress in Promoting Tourism

Education and Research. Five new journals for tourists appeared in 1980: *Traveller* (China Youth Publishing House), *Tourism* (Beijing Publishing House), *Tourism* (Guangdong People's Publishing House), *Tourist World* (Shanghai Cultural Publishing House) and *Tourist Land* (Sichuan People's Publishing House). Beijing's *Tourism* had the largest circulation — in 1980, each issue was printed in 400,000 copies. The China Tourist Publishing House put out in the same year more than 40 books, brochures, maps and postcards in 3.3 million copies. Among them is the *Travel Guide,* co-published with a foreign firm. Distribution of its English and Japanese editions began last year. This was the first of its kind edited by Chinese staff. The China Tourist Publishing House is putting out a *China Tourism Series.* The first volume, *A Trip to West Lake,* came out in 1980. Many provincial publishing houses and tourist departments have put out publications introducing individual cities and scenic areas. The *Wonders of West Lake,* published by the Zhejiang People's Publishing House, has been received favourably.

Film and television studios produced a number of scenic films in 1980 which have helped in the expansion of tourism. Statistics show that 30 TV films and 11 films on tourist cities and areas were made during the year.

Education. Tourism education was enhanced in 1980. Tourism economics courses were begun at Hangzhou University. A Japanese tour guide department was established in Dalian Foreign Languages Institute. In addition to Shanghai and Jiangsu, tourism schools for training medium-level service personnel were set up in Sichuan and Hubei provinces. Other personnel will be trained in vocational schools and in short-term courses run in Beijing, Tianjin, Zhejiang, Guangdong, Shaanxi and Jiangxi. Establishment of a national tourist institute is under way.

Research. Research on tourism became active in 1980. The first national forum on tourist economics was held from December 4 to 10. The conference received 40 theses, reports and pieces of reference material. Some of them were read out to the participants. Articles on promotion of tourism were published in the newspaper. For instance, the journal *Architect* has carried articles entitled "On the Layout of Scenic Cities and Protection of Scenic Spots," "On the Establishment of Scenic and Cultural Relic Preserves" and "On the Development of Construction in Scenic Areas of Famous Mountains." *On Tourism,* a book published by the China Tourist Publishing House, discusses methods for development of China's tourism.

Domestic Tourism

With the development of political unity and stability, the people's livelihood has been improving. This has brought about rapid progress in domestic tourism. According to incomplete statistics, Beidaihe's beaches received 780,000 tourists during the summer. The figure for the peak day was 45,000. Mt. Lushan received 1,310,000 visitors between May and August. Although Huangshan Mountain is far away from main communication lines, over 400,000 people climbed to its summit. The daily record was 6,000. This volume of visitors is unprecedented in history.

Trade and communication departments all over the country also played their part in tourism. A meeting convened by the Ministry of Commerce in Hangzhou urged that commercial departments in various places set up travel services for domestic tours. It is stated that service bureaus in over 40 cities are now engaged in domestic tourism.

Domestic tourism has been well developed in Shanghai, Beijing. Nanjing, Hangzhou, Chengdu and Kunming.

The Shanghai Travel Service runs some 30 tourist routes — short-distance, medium-distance and long-distance. Short-distance trips include Suzhou, Wuxi and Hangzhou. Medium-distance trips involve 3-7 days, with itineraries inclusive of Zhenjiang and Nanjing in Jiangsu Province; Tiantai Mountain, West Tianmu Mountain, Mogan Mountain and Shaoxing in Zhejiang Province; Wuyi Mountain in Fujian Province; and Huangshan Mountain in Anhui Province. Long-distance trips take 7-30 days. They are for special participants only, and take in destinations such as Qingdao, Mt. Lushan, Yandang Mountain, Guilin, Hainan Island, Xiamen, Beidaihe, Beijing, Kunming, Chengdu, Chongqing and Wuhan. Trips organized in Beijing by the Taxi Company and the Long-Distance Bus Company include scenic spots on the city's outskirts, as well as Chengde and Beidaihe. The service company affiliated with the Nanjing Second Bureau of Commerce runs six trips — three (of 1-day duration) within Jiangsu Province (Yixing, Zhenjiang and Yangzhou); the other three are to Huangshan Mountain (5 days), Hangzhou (4 days) and Mount Langya and Zuiweng Pavilion (1 day).

The company handled 16,000 tourists between May (when these trips began) and the end of the year.

Tourist itineraries operated by the Kunming Service Company, apart from visits to the nearby Stone Forest and West Hills, include Kunming-Suzhou-Hangzhou-Shanghai, Kunming-Guilin and Kunming-Emei Mountain-Chengdu.

Most domestic tourists in 1980 were teachers, staff members and students of colleges and middle schools. According to figures obtained from Beijing University and seven other institutes of higher learning, 20,000 students spent their summer vacations at Beidaihe, Chengde, Dalian, Qingdao, Mt. Taishan, the Summer Palace and the Miyun Reservoir. Many others were retired cadres, staff members and workers. Statistics show that in Hangzhou, half of the tourists received were retired workers; in Shanghai, 25% were pensioners, 35% workers and staff members, 16% teachers, 13% technical personnel and professors and 9% students. In some rural areas, owing to the realization of the party's policies, both output and personal income increased. Some peasants could make trips to visit scenic places. For example, the Xiazhuang Brigade, Wulong Commune, Zibo, Shandong Province, pays two yuan for one work-day. With the cash available, the brigade was able to organize a trip for its members to Mt. Taishan.

The mode of travel for domestic tours varies. Some people travel by bike, some on foot. Some make sightseeing trips, some honeymoon trips. Honeymoon trips are encouraged since they enable the couple to see more of the country rather than spending a lot of money on giving feasts. This represents a change in social traditions. Special rooms are provided at a discount to newlyweds at Beidaihe and other places. More and more young people are now taking part in such trips.

Review of China's Tourism

The Beijing Overseas Chinese Travel Service was established in 1953 to receive overseas Chinese on home visits or on tours. Its head office was established in 1963. In 1973, it was renamed the Head Office of the China Overseas Chinese Travel Service. Another organization, China Travel Service, was set up in 1974 to take care of compatriots from Hong Kong, Macao and Taiwan and foreign nationals of Chinese origin coming on home visits or on tours.

International travel services in China began in 1954 when the China International Travel Service was established. Then, its main function was to receive tourists from the Soviet Union, Eastern Europe, Korea, Vietnam and some other countries. Beginning in the early 1960's, tourists from Western countries were received. The Bureau of Travel and Tourism was officially set up in 1964. However, up to the outbreak of the "cultural revolution," tourist departments received only a limited number of guests. There were only 4,500 in 1966, providing an income of U.S.$2 million. During the "cultural revolution," tourism came to a standstill owing to disruption wrought by Lin Biao and the Gang of Four.

China's tourism developed only after the downfall of the Gang of Four and by virtue of the concern of the party. In 1978, the bureau was renamed the General Administration of Travel and Tourism of China. Documents were issued by the central government calling on departments concerned to energetically develop tourism. The China International Travel Service received 124,000 foreign tourists in that year, greater than the total number of tourists received in the more than 20 years prior to the smashing of the Gang of Four.

To improve facilities, new hotels have been built and old ones expanded and renovated during the past three years. In addition, some luxurious guest houses have been turned over to tourist departments. For instance, some of the buildings in the State Guest House at Diaoyutai in Beijing are now used for tourists.

During the three years between 1978 and 1980, tourism progressed rapidly, as did the growth rate of revenues in foreign currency. Tourism income was U.S.$260 million in 1978, U.S.$440 million in 1979 and U.S.$610 million in 1980.

Emphasis used to be placed on the political side, that is, to make new friends through tourism, so that China would be better understood by the world. The economic role of tourism was neglected. During the past few years, tourism was initially looked upon as an economic undertaking. It was, at the same time, considered an extension of foreign relations. Efforts have been made to ensure good results both economically and politically.

However, problems have come along with this rapid development. The main problem is the large number of people who wish to come to China. But owing to the limited facilities, it is impossible to receive all of them within two or three years. The slow increase in the capacity for receiving guests is holding back the capability of the whole country with regard to tourism.

Problems have remained despite improvements in service quality — bad manners on the part of some hotel attendants, poor service and poor environmental sanitation; and unqualified guides and interpreters who are unable to answer questions posed by tourists. Owing to bad management, rooms were often not provided promptly upon arrival of tourists during the busy season; and schedules were often changed because of failure to obtain plane tickets. Unreasonable charges were made at some places. All this aroused discontent among tourists. Further improvements are needed in these areas.

More tourist areas have to be set up. During the busy season, some famous sites are much too overcrowded. Examples are Beijing's Great Wall at Badaling and the Underground Palace at the Ming Tombs; Suzhou's gardens; and Shanghai's Yuyuan Garden. People jostle each other, sometimes blocking the traffc. During the summer of 1980, rooms and food were hard to come by on the famous mountains — Taishan, Lushan, Huangshan and Emei. This state of affairs has to be changed. Otherwise, more tourists will feel disappointed and the landscape and cultural relics will be destroyed or polluted by poor planning. This will also have a bad effect on the development of international tourism. To cope with the rapid development of domestic tourism, the major cities should divert domestic tourists to new tourist spots. At the same time, effective measures should be taken to control the number of tourists visiting famous places.

46. THE SCIENCES IN CHINA
By the Policy Research Office,
Chinese Academy of Sciences

The victory of the Chinese Revolution in 1949 paved the way for the development of science in the country. In the early post-Liberation period, the Chinese Academy of Sciences was established as the country's highest scientific institution, embracing a number of research institutes. Afterwards, various academies of specialized sciences were set up, such as the Academy of Agricultural Sciences, the Academy of Medical Sciences, the Academy of Geological Research and the Academy of Railway Research.

The "Common Programme of the Chinese People's Political Consultative Conference," adopted on the eve of the founding of the People's Republic, stated explicitly: "Efforts shall be made to develop the natural sciences in the service of industrial, agricultural and national defence construction. Scientific discoveries and inventions shall be encouraged and rewarded and scientific knowledge shall be disseminated." This idea was developed in China's Constitution of 1954.

I. The History of Scientific Research in the Last 30 Years

In 1955 and 1956, at a time when the Central Committee of the Communist Party of China and the people's government issued a call to develop the sciences, the Chinese Academy of Sciences established awards for natural sciences, institutionalized a system of post-graduate studies with conferral of academic degrees, set up the Scientific Council of the Chinese Academy of Sciences and drafted the "Outline Programme of Scientific and Technological Development, 1956-1967." At the conference called by the Central Committee of the CPC to deal with the question of intellectuals, a correct policy was formulated and effective measures for improving the working conditions of intellectuals were put forward. The result was the mobilization and organization of scientific and technical personnel and the return to China of many Chinese scientists who had been residing abroad to take part in socialist construction. Within a fairly short time, a number of gaps in the sciences were closed and weak links were strengthened. The study of some newly emerging areas of technology was begun, opening up a new era in scientific research.

The development of science after 1957 met with twists and turns, but the general trend was still one of progress. The temporary economic difficulties in the three-year period beginning in 1960, though they resulted in a reduction in the number of scientific undertakings, enhanced the determination of scientific and technical personnel to regenerate the country through self-reliance and hard struggle. During this period, China's scientific and technical personnel pressed forward, conducing research on atomic energy and man-made satellites, artificial synthesis of insulin and other highly specialized subjects.

Setbacks and Milestones. The "cultural revolution" which began in 1966 subjected to ruthless persecution large numbers of diligent and accomplished scientists who had made outstanding contributions. It nearly brought scientific research to a standstill and resulted in the loss of a generation of scientific talent. The gap in science and technology between China and the advanced, developed countries, which had been narrowing, widened greatly again. This state of affairs continued until the downfall of the Gang of Four, whereupon scientific undertakings were given a new lease on life and were gradually restored to their former conditions.

The National Science Congress convened by the Central Committee of the CPC in March 1978 marked a milestone in the annals of scientific development in China. At that congress, leaders of the central government adopted the "Draft National Outline Programme for Scientific and Technological Development, 1978-1985" and commended a large number of outstanding scientific and technical personnel. At the congress, science and technology were formally acknowledged as having played a crucial role in China's modernization and scientific and technical personnel were hailed as an important segment of China's working class. Thus began another "springtime of science."

The year 1980 saw continued progress and good results in the restoration and consolidation of China's scientific undertakings. People from various walks of life paid greater attention to the role of science and technology in social and economic development; more and better results were obtained in scientific research; academic exchange grew considerably, as did the popularization of science; and cooperation and exchanges with scientific institutions in other countries continued to expand.

II. Involvement of Scientific and Technical Personnel in Various Levels of Decision-Making

Along with the development of the country's socialist construction, leaders at various levels became increasingly aware of the role of science and technology in social and economic development. On the eve of the 1980 Spring Festival, central government leaders invited a number of scientists to a discussion at which they encouraged scientists to put forward proposals and contribute to the country's modernization. At similar meetings in Jiangsu, Liaoning and other localities, party and government leaders discussed with local scientists ways to advance scientific and technological development.

Policies for Scientific Development. At the Second Congress of the China Association for Science and Technology, held in March 1980, Hu Yaobang, the Secretary-General of the party's Central Committee, made an important speech on behalf of the Central Committee. He pointed out that science was a tremendous motive force pushing history forward and that modernization would be impossible without advanced science and technology. He also put forward the following three measures for developing the sciences: (1) China should build up a contingent of cadres with specialized knowledge and abilities who are capable of adhering to the socialist road; (2) China should start a large-scale programme to build up a reserve force of trained scientific and technical personnel; and (3) the party should give full support to scientists by giving free scope to their talents.

The Secretariat of the party's Central Committee asked the Chinese Academy of Sciences to arrange for distinguished scientists to give lectures to leading members of the Central Committee and the State Council. Accordingly, on July 24, 1980, Professor Qian Sanqiang gave a lecture entitled, "A Brief Introduction to the Development of Science and Technology." Subsequent lectures were given by Professors Wu Zhonghua, Wang Ganchang, Guo Musun and Bao Hansen on the question of energy, and by Professors Tu Guangchi and Ye Lianjun on resources and their rational utilization. The specialized knowledge and proposals provided by these scientists will exert positive influence on party and state leaders in policy-making.

Apart from giving lectures, scientists and many other scientific workers acted as advisors to leaders at the national and local levels by putting forward proposals, offering their services as consultants, or organizing "brain trusts" or technical service companies. For example, the Chinese Society of Agronomy and two other societies sponsored a symposium on agricultural mechanization in northwestern China, with participants coming from nine provinces and autonomous regions; and the Chinese societies of agronomy, forestry, water conservancy and ecology jointly sponsored a symposium on the development of ecological equilibrium in tropical and subtropical mountainous and hilly areas, with participants drawn from 11 other societies and 15 provinces. These symposia yielded many important proposals concerning the development of the loess highlands and of tropical and subtropical mountainous areas.

Water conservancy specialists in Shanxi Province made public the irrationality of a project which was designed to divert water from a river to Xiyang county, and the project was stopped after this appraisal caught the attention of the leadership. Botanist Hou Xueyu's "broader concept of agriculture" and his proposals have attracted attention and they are expected to have an important bearing on China's policies for agricultural production and developing food resources. Natural scientists and social scientists cooperated in forecasting the population growth trend, which will play an important role in the country's effort to formulate demographic and social policies.

Many scientific workers served as consultants to local leaders at various levels. For example, in 1980, scientific workers in Shanghai put forward a total of 42 major proposals, 25 of which have been adopted. The Scientific and Technological Commission of Liaoning Province set up 22 groups to serve as advisory bodies for the provincial leadership. The "brain trust" of Zhuzhou city in Hunan Province submitted to the city authorities more than 50 proposals which proved very useful. In Yichun County, Jiangxi Province, a scientific and technical service company was set up.

At the same time, scientific and technical personnel were recruited into leading bodies at various levels. In addition to Professor Wang Jinling, who was made vice-governor of Heilongjiang Province, and Professor Yang Jike, who became vice-governor of Anhui Province, many scientific and technical personnel were elected or appointed in 1980 to leading posts in the government and in various departments. One of them was Associate Professor Zheng Shouyi, who became vice-mayor of Qingdao. Many counties also sought scientific and technical personnel for their leading organizations. A case in point was Gaomi County in Shandong Province, which appointed a number of scientists to leading posts after overcoming the prejudice against intellectuals.

The participation of scientific and technical personnel in the policy-making process and the selection of such personnel for leading posts have promoted scientific standards in policy-making and greatly improved the quality of leadership.

III. Results of Scientific Research

Scientific research, which has enjoyed stable conditions in the years following the downfall of the Gang of Four, made important advances in 1980. Some research results attained high standards. The government has adopted the policy of encouraging and rewarding excellence in research and of actively promoting the popularization and application of research results.

In May 1980, China successfully launched a carrier rocket over the Pacific Ocean. This achievement was significant for the further development of China's science and technology and the acceleration of its modernization programme.

Chinese scientists and technicians completed 2,600 major research projects in 1980. Of the 1,576 projects completed under the aegis of the Chinese Academy of Sciences, 329 were of great importance. Institutions of higher learning in China also made remarkable progress during the year.

Many research results were of vital importance to industrial and agricultural production. In research on large-scale integrated circuits, the successful development of a 4K MOS memory computer was followed by that of several other models. The 16K MOS memory computer, in particular, was as advanced and performed as well as similar models produced in other countries. This breakthrough paved the way for the development and production of large-scale integrated circuits in China.

The electric-spark seismic source which China developed for seismic prospecting of offshore oil had its own unique features and performed well. Progress was made, too, in the study of many scientific and technological problems related to the reclamation of marsh land through well-drainage and irrigation or to the construction of the hydroelectric power station at Ertan, as well as to the application of remote sensing techniques, to research on rare-earth permanent magnetic materials, and to the improvement of the properties of polypropylene fibres.

The research institutes for national defence undertook research projects for civilian purposes while fulfilling with flying colours the research tasks in their own specific fields.

Basic Research. The institutes under the Chinese Academy of Sciences and the various institutions of higher learning continued to press forward with basic research. In medical sciences, basic research was started in areas such as molecular disease, cancer and immunological engineering with good initial results. A survey of 24 major research projects showed that 8 approached or had attained advanced international levels.

Awards. Various government departments, provinces, municipalities and autonomous regions became more aware of the need to give due recognition to research results. Beginning in 1980, the State Scientific and Technological Commission gave out awards for discoveries and inventions; it has approved three lists of inventions, or 107 in all.

A number of important research results won acclaim from various government departments. For example, the Ministry of Agriculture announced in January 1980 its second list of awards to 56 research projects in agricultural and animal husbandry sciences and technologies.

At a ceremony in February 1980, Beijing Municipality presented awards for 535 research projects, 13 of which won first prizes. In March, Shanghai Municipality awarded 10 first prizes to major research projects. Shaanxi, Sichuan, Heilongjiang, Guizhou, Inner Mongolia, Zhejiang, Henan and other provinces, municipalities and autonomous regions followed suit.

In accordance with the "Regulations of the People's Republic of China Concerning Awards for Natural Science," which was promulgated by the State Council on November 21, 1979, the State Scientific and Technological Commission formed the Awards Committee for Natural Sciences and adopted its "Provisional Constitution." The committee's appraisal of deserving research projects was going forward in 1980.

Research Applications. Various departments paid greater attention to the application and popularization of research results. The Ministry of Agriculture recommended the results of 19 agricultural research projects and demonstrated them at selected points thought the country in an effort to popularize them. The products of these research projects are technically sound, economical and rational; they require small investment and show rapid and good results, and are therefore widely welcomed. They included: two improved strains of rice, Zhongdan No. 1 and No. 2, and all-octoploid triticale; the technique of deep application of chemical fertilizers and pellet fertilizers; the method of selecting types of small-scale bio-gas digesters and sealing techniques; new cooking stoves with high heat efficiency; and new insecticides.

In 1980, hybrid rice was sown on over 5.3 million hectares in an effort to popularize this improved strain throughout the country; the increase in yield was 3.5 million tons of rice, for an average increase of approximately 0.75 tons per hectare. Zhejiang Province popularized a Xian-type hybrid rice, which showed potential for increasing output by 0.75 to 1.125 tons per hectare. Lumian No. 1 cotton was grown on large tracts of land in Shandong Province in 1980 and showed a potential for increasing output by 25%. Hubei Province popularized the nitrogen-fixing blue-green algae on 47,000 to 53,000 hectares of farmland.

IV. Management of Scientific Institutions and of Scientific Research

By the end of 1979, China boasted 4,600 scientific institutions that operated independently at or above the prefectural level. Of this number, 116 were under the Chinese Academy of Sciences. The total number of such scientific institutions did not increase significantly in 1980. Attention was focused on consolidation, expansion and raising standards.

Industrial Research Institutes. There was considerable growth, however, in the number of research institutes attached to industrial and mining enterprises. In the past, such research institutes were rare, which was an important reason for the backwardness of production techniques and for the long interval between two generations of products. In recent years, especially in 1980, with the beginning of reforms in the economic system, enterprises were given greater powers and responsibilities. This gave them incentive to improve their products in order to be more competitive. Hence, factories and mines set up their own research institutions. For example, the number of research institutes and laboratories run by the factories and mines in Liaoning Province expanded to more than 800, with 13,000 full-time staff members, while the 15 specialized research institutes already existing in the industrial sector employed 7,000 professional research personnel.

Research institutes attached to factories and mines are geared closely to production and are capable of quickly training people with specialized knowledge. The growth of such institutes will have a far-reaching influence on scientific and technological development and on the country's social and economic development.

Experiments in Self-Management. In accordance with the party's policy of "readjustment. restructuring, consolidation and improvement," scientific institutions at various levels experimented in 1980 with restructuring the management of scientific research. An important aspect of restructuring the system of management of scientific research is the expansion of the research institutes' authority to run their own affairs. Such experiments, which started in Sichuan, were inspired and influenced by those carried out in the economics field. The essence of the experiment was that scientific institutions were given more authority to plan their research projects and to undertake tasks assigned to them by units to which they were not affiliated or to transfer research results to such units — on condition that they first fulfilled assignments from the organizations directly above them. Scientific institutions were allowed to acquire and dipose of financial resources other than the funds allocated to them by the government and other higher bodies.

As a result of their expanded self-management powers, some institutions eagerly undertook new and promising projects through closer links with production units; in some localities, organizations combining scientific and production units were set up on a trial basis. This new system made it possible to undertake a number of projects aimed at application, shortened the time required before application of research results begins and allowed scientific and technical personnel greater scope for initiative.

In line with the reform in the management of scientific research, a number of localities introduced the practice of signing contracts between a scientific institution and a production unit. At present, there are contracts for undertakings commissioning scientific research projects (designing and testing), for transfers of research results, technical services, technological consultations, training of personnel on behalf of the production units and for the development of new products. Both research and production have benefited from this practice. Thus, the Combinational Machines Research Institute of Dalian, which had been operating below capacity, had the best record for research results in 1980 and increased its income by 600,000 yuan as a result of its cooperation with factories in Changzhou and Wuhan. And the enterprises in question are each expected to benefit from such cooperation by several million yuan in 1980 as well as in 1981. Shanghai Municipality tried out in 1980 the practice of having higher organizations sign contracts with the organizations under them, while the Ministry of Public Health experimented with inviting tenders for research projects.

The question of scientific research management received attention from leaders at various levels. The State Bureau of Scientific and Technological Personnel and the Chinese Academy of Sciences conducted courses for training administrators. A national symposium on the administration of science was also held in 1980.

V. Scientific Research Personnel

The ranks of scientific and technical personnel working in China's scientific institutions have grown considerably in recent years. At the end of 1979, independent scientific institutions at or above the prefectural level employed 751,000 people in all, of whom about 263,000 were scientific and technical personnel. Women accounted for 27.3% of all scientific and technical personel.

Because of the interruption of scientific research and teaching during the "cultural revolution," the average age of China's scientific and technical personnel is relatively high. In the Chinese Academy of Sciences, for example, the average age of the personnel is approximately 40; only one-fourth of the personnel are under 35 years of age. This is a critical problem at present.

Improved Living and Working Conditions. Continued efforts were made to improve the living and working conditions of scientific and technical personnel, to raise the level of basic theoretical knowledge, experimental skills and foreign language ability, and to transfer those persons who could not put their specialized knowledge to use in their assigned jobs to more appropriate jobs. Great efforts were also made to build up reserves of scientific and technical personnel.

In 1980, over 50% of all scientific and technical personnel received pay raises. At the same time, a large number of scientific and technical personnel with outstanding achievements were given senior academic or technical titles appropriate to their level of expertize. Moreover, the government allocated special funds, totalling 100 million yuan, for housing projects for senior scientific, technical and educational personnel working under the Chinese Academy of Sciences, the Ministry of Education, the Ministry of Public Health, the Ministry of Culture and the State Commission of Physical Culture and Sports.

Various localities concentrated on the problem of scientific and technical personnel who had been assigned to the wrong kind of work. According to statistics for the first half of 1980, Zhejiang Province reassigned 6,000 people and Liaoning Province transferred more than 10,000 people. Attention was also given to bringing back into service those formerly trained scientific and technical personnel who had not been employed. In various localities efforts were made to give such personnel professional jobs again and, as a result, some people with useful experience and skills were rediscovered.

Education and Training. Scientific and technical administrative organs at various levels and scientific institutions throughout the country did much work in selecting and training promising personnel. At a special meeting called by the State Bureau of Scientific and Technological Personnel, it was stressed that the selection and training of scientific and technical personnel and the rational use of their talents were the pressing tasks at the present time.

Following the suggestion put forth by scientists themselves that scientific institutions be allowed to select and use promising people, a number of scientific institutions experimented with recruiting promising individuals for research work. The Xinjiang Branch of the Chinese Academy and several other organizations placed great emphasis on the training of scientific and technical personnel from among the minority peoples.

Within scientific institutions, young people who had showed proficiency and had served as the mainstay of research projects were promoted to leading posts. This greatly improved the quality of leadership and the organization and management of scientific research work.

Various scientific institutions and institutions of higher learning strengthened the training of post-graduate students. In 1980, the number of post-graduate students in the natural sciences and applied sciences totalled 21,600. On February 12, 1980, the Standing Committee of the Fifth National People's Congress promulgated the "Regulations of the People's Republic of China Concerning Academic Degrees." In December, the Committee on Academic Degrees held its first plenary meeting, at which the "Measures for Implementing the Regulations of the People's Republic of China Concerning Academic Degrees" was adopted. Those measures were later approved by the State Council.

VI. Funding for Scientific Research

The party and the government have attached great importance to the development of scientific research and have created conditions as favourable as possible for their rapid growth. Science and technology figured prominently at the Third Session of the Fifth National People's Congress, which took place in August 1980. The allocations for cultural, educational, public health and scientific undertakings in the national budget for 1980 totalled 14,830 million yuan, up 1,620 million yuan over 1979 — a huge increase considering the reduction of expenditures necessitated by the overall readjustment of the national economy.

Although funding for scientific research has

increased in recent years, the ratio between funds for scientific research and the gross national product has not yet been restored to the previous highest level because of the damage inflicted during the "cultural revolution."

VII. Activities of Academic Societies

National academic societies were extremely active in 1980. They sponsored a total of 760 symposia during the year, considerably more than in 1979.

At the second national congress of the China Association for Science and Technology held on March 15, 1980, representatives from various fields of science and technology gathered to discuss ways of developing scientific research and contributing to the country's modernization. Following the national congress, 15 provinces and autonomous regions held their own congresses. Of the country's 2,757 administrative units at the county level, 1,758 had science and technology associations, and over 1,000 communes, factories and units set up such associations on a trial basis.

In 1980, 10 new national academic societies were founded, bringing the total to 105. There are academic societies as well for a number of important specialized fields in science and technology. For instance, the nation's nuclear scientists and scientists engaged in radiation protection held their own first congresses in 1980, while societies for biophysics, space science and other important sciences were established.

Science and technology associations were active in disseminating scientific knowledge, training personnel and organizing technical exchanges. The China Association for Science and Technology organized an exhibition of fine art works for the popularization of science and sponsored a meeting at which artists working in this field could exchange experiences. At a meeting of the Association of Popular Science Writers, guidelines were formulated for the future work of its members. The association also put together a selection of "Popular Science Works for the New Long March" and called a meeting to discuss the promotion of scientific and technical activities among youngsters. Local science and technology associations also participated actively in the popularization of scientific knowledge.

VIII. Scientific Publications and Information Services

Remarkable progress was made in the publication of scientific and technical books and periodicals in 1980. Incomplete statistics show that 5,715 scientific and technical books were published in 1980, as against 4,199 in 1979, an increase of 36%. A total of 1,384 scientific periodicals were issued in 1980, an increase of 42% over the 978 published in 1979.

The readership of scientific books, periodicals and newspapers also expanded greatly. In 1980, China's 85 national and provincial popular science magazines had a total circulation exceeding 16 million. The magazines *Radio*, *Science Pictorial* and *Science and Life* each had a circulation of over one million. During the year, the Popular Science Publishing House issued 105 books. Various provinces, municipalities and autonomous regions published more than 30 scientific and technical newspapers; their total circulation was about 4.5 million. Also in 1980, 48 popular science books and 58 articles written between 1977 and 1979 were re-issued. The thriving situation of publication work mirrored the advances made in science and technology, as well as the public's growing interest in scientific knowledge.

Information Services. In July 1980, the State Scientific and Technological Commission called the Fifth National Conference on the Work of Scientific and Technical Information. At this conference, past activities were evaluated and the direction and tasks of current work were charted. Since the compilation of scientific and technical information was began in 1956, various departments under the State Council and various provinces, municipalities and autonomous regions have set up a total of 72 institutes for scientific and technical information. Scientific and technical information services have contributed to the formulation of scientific and technological policies and plans, to the importation of technologies and to scientific research and designing work.

Library services also have made headway in recent years. Apart from the specialized libraries catering to science and technology, there are national and local general libraries that offer a wide range of scientific and technical services. In addition to performing their cultural and educational functions, general libraries have begun to play an important part in the scientific and technical information system.

Archives. In July 1980, the State Economic Commission, the State Capital Construction Commission, the State Scientific and Technological Commission and the State Archives Bureau jointly held a conference on scientific and technical archival work. The conference called on various economic departments and scientific research institutions to restore order to the country's scientific and technical archives as quickly as possible and to expand, organize, store and use such archives effectively in the service of socialist modernization. A report submitted by the conference was subsequently circulated in a State Council document. The State Council approved the "Regulations Concerning the Work of Scientific and Technical Archives."

IX. International Scientific Cooperation and Exchanges

There was considerable growth in 1980 in the exchange of visits by scholars and scientists. The China Association for Science and Technology, for example, played host to 21 foreign delegations with 132 people and received over 300 scientists who came to China as tourists. The association also sent abroad 22 delegations with a total of 130 people. Also in 1980, the number of Chinese academic societies that had joined international academic organizations increased by 12, to reach a total of 60.

Various central ministries and commissions, institutions of higher learning and the Chinese Academy of Sciences also engaged in scientific exchanges. The Chinese Academy of Sciences sent 950 people abroad as members of delegations and study tours or as participants in international conferences, and it received 1,760 foreign scientists — almost a 50% increase over 1979. In addition, the Chinese Academy of Sciences sent 674 people abroad for post-graduate studies and advanced training or as visiting scholars.

Nine international conferences were held in China in 1980, including the International Conference on Particle Physics in Guangzhou, the Second International Symposium on the Role of RNA in Development and Reproduction, the Symposium on the Qinghai-Tibetan Plateau, the International Laser Conference and the International Symposium on Paddy Soil.

Honours for Scientists. A number of famous Chinese scientists received titles of honour from other countries. Among them were Guo Kexin, who was appointed a foreign member of the Swedish Royal Academy of Engineering Sciences, and Zhang Xiaotong, who received the Threshold Award.

Chinese academic bodies and scientific institutions conferred titles of honour on a number of foreign scientists or invited them to serve as part-time consultants or professors. For example, the Systems Science Institute under the Chinese Academy of Sciences invited professors Shing Shen Chern and P.D. Lax, members of the National Academy of Sciences in the United States, to become honorary research professors and members of its academic committee; and the Mathematics Institute invited Professor Shing Tung Yan of Princeton University and Associate Professor S.Y. Cheng of the University of California at Los Angeles to serve as members of its academic committee.

International Cooperation. China's scientists cooperated with their foreign counterparts on a number of joint expeditions or research projects during 1980, such as the Sino-French joint expedition to study the geological structure of the Himalayas. Also in 1980, the Chinese-language editions of two U.S. publications, *Scientific American* and the *Encyclopaedia of Science and Technology,* were published in China.

X. Current Scientific Policies

Along with progress in scientific research, there was much lively discussion of scientific policies and many related issues that merit further study. The main issues brought up for discussion were:

(1) *The relationship between science and technology and social and economic development.* As science and technology penetrate daily into ever wider fields of the society and economy, they become increasingly important factors in the country's overall development. It is imperative that science and technology be taken into consideration when social and economic development planning is done. In turn, science and technology should make greater and more effective contributions to social and economic development. To place economic work more solidly on the basis of science and technology and to give full scope to the role of science and technology, scientific grounds for major decisions relating to economic and social development should be proven before such decisions are taken. At the same time, planning departments must draw up plans that unify and coordinate the development of science, technology, economy and society.

(2) *Guidelines concerning the development of science and technology.* In 1980, there was animated discussion about the guidelines China should adopt for developing science and technology in light of the successes and failures of other countries. It was agreed that science and technology should be developed in harmony with

the economy and the society, and that the primary task of their development should be the promotion of economic deveopment. Other recommendations included: placing emphasis in research on production techniques; the correct selection of technologies within a national framework; strengthening technical exploitation and extension work at industrial and mining enterprises; ensuring the steady development of basic research; and making the study, digestion and assimilation of scientific and technological achievements from other countries an important part of China's scientific and technological development.

These and other views received careful attention from leading organizations. The Chinese Academy of Sciences, the country's leading research centre in the natural sciences, focused its discussions on how to use science and technology to better serve the country's modernization programme while upholding the principles of placing emphasis on basic sciences and of raising standards of research.

(3) *Readjustment of scientific and technological work.* The implementation of the policy of "readjustment, restructuring, consolidation and improvement of the national economy" entails the readjustment of scientific and technological work. China aims to strengthen its scientific, educational, health and cultural undertakings while cutting capital investments and administrative expenses and readjusting production plans in certain sectors of heavy industry.

Scientific organizations themselves have called for the readjustment of their internal structure, notably to correct the imbalance between the various branches of science, between various kinds of research projects and between various kinds of personnel. Other problems that must be solved include the dispersion of efforts, overlapping of projects and some outdated projects. These problems must be resolved through readjustment, consolidaton and restructuring.

In 1980, the initial exploration and discussion of these problems, as well as the carrying out of selective experiments and preliminary reforms were all underway. As the policy of "readjustment, restructuring, consolidation and improvement" is further implemented still greater progress is expected of scientific research in 1981.

47. STANDARDIZATION IN CHINA
By Huang Weijian
State Administration of Standards

The work of standardization in China began only after the founding of New China and has grown gradually with the development of the national economy. Since the Third Plenary Session of the 11th Party Central Committee, the work of standardization has grown rapidly and comprehensively. It has played a positive role in improving the quality of products, utilizing resources in a rational way, saving raw materials and energy, organizing specialized production, developing new varieties of products and raising the level of enterprise management.

I. The History of Standardization

Old China was a semi-feudal and semi-colonial country with a backward economy, and foreign capitalists controlled most of its industrial enterprises. There were a limited number of national industrial enterprises, but they operated at a low level of efficiency and depended on foreign capital economically and technically to a considerable extent. There were almost no independent standards in old China. Although the Kuomintang government had set up a bureau of standards and the China Standards and Specifications Committee, these agencies did not do any real work in standardization.

Enterprises entirely operated by foreigners adopted foreign standards, and most national industrial enterprises also adopted the standards of the countries with which they had economic or technical relations. For example, most enterprises in northeastern China adopted Japanese standards and most enterprises in Jiangsu, Zhejiang, Shanghai and other coastal cities relied on British or US standards, while a number of enterprises used German or French standards. An outstanding example of the semi-feudal and semi-colonial character of the economy of old China in respect to standardization was pre-Liberation Shanghai, where two voltage standards were in use — 220 v. and 110 v.

Establishing Standards. After the founding of New China, the party and the government turned to the work of establishing China's own standards. During the period of economic rehabilitation, the Financial and Economic Affairs Commission of the then Administrative Council created a special department to take charge of the work. Standardization was started in the railway, iron, steel, cement and textile industries in 1950.

Other industries and departments began to work out their own standards to keep pace with the development of economic construction during the First Five-Year Plan period. One after another, the industrial ministries set up departments to work out standards at the ministerial level. By the end of 1957, the metallurgical industry, for example, had issued 205 ministerial standards and produced standard product samples.

In 1953, the then Ministry of Fuels Industry called the first conference on standards in national petroleum products and set up a national committee to examine specifications for petroleum products. During the period of the First Five-Year Plan, standardization was started in the machine-building, chemical, electronics, shipbuilding, coal and other industries. In all, more than 100 standards were established between 1953 and 1957.

Control Measures. Before 1957, each industrial ministry conducted its own work in standardization. In 1957, however, a bureau of standards was attached to the former State Scientific and Technological Commission. Progress in standardization continued, but it was not as satisfactory as was expected owing to the influence of "Left" deviationist mistakes in our economic work. By 1960, only 33 national standards for industrial and agricultural products had been established and some of them presented problems when they were applied.

To overcome the consequences of "Left" deviationist mistakes in our economic work, the Party Central Committee put forward in 1961 the policy of readjustment, consolidation, development and improvement of standards. As a result, the work of standardization was considerably strengthened. In 1962 the State Council approved and promulgated the "Measures to Control the Technical Standards for Industrial and Agricultural Products and Construction Projects." The measures drew on our experience in standardization work since the founding of the People's Republic, formulated guiding principles for establishing standards and proposed concrete methods. Among the points made in the "Measures" were that scientific research departments, production units and users should work together, that investigations and experiments should be conducted before standards are established and that the standards must be suitable to China's actual conditions and reflect the principles of economy and rationality.

In 1963 the First National Standardization Conference was called to draft a 10-year plan for the development of standardization. Following this conference, the ministries under the State Council held separate working meetings to prepare documents for the implementation of the "Measures," to establish or strengthen their own standardizing organs and to formulate plans for the development of their standardization work. In addition, a number of representative scientific research and designing units and industrial enterprises were appointed to revise existing national and ministerial standards and to establish new ones.

All these steps helped to accelerate the establishment and revision of national and ministerial standards for the country, as well as to raise the level of standards — some of which were already approaching the international standards of that time.

Obstacles. During the "cultural revolution," the work of standardization was criticized, standardizing organs were abolished and their personnel transferred to other jobs, records and files were damaged, regulations and systems were abrogated and the work of standardization was seriously undermined. In 1972, the State Bureau of Standardization and Metrology was set up with the approval of the State Council to ensure product quality. As a result, the work of standardization gradually resumed, but there were still many obstacles and progress was slow.

Only after the Gang of Four was smashed, and especially after the Third Plenary Session of the 11th Party Central Committee, was the work of standardization fully restored. It has made substantial progress since then. In May 1978, the State Council set up the State Bureau of Standards to supervise standardization work throughout the country. This provided strong leadership for our standardization work and solved the long-standing problem of organizational separation between standardization and production.

New Regulations. In March 1979, the State Administration of Standards called the Second National Work Conference to review both the positive and negative experiences in standardization work since the founding of the People's Republic. The conference defined the policy of "strengthening management, consolidating the work and laying a good foundation for positive development," drew up a series of specific guiding policies and set the targets to be achieved during the period of economic readjustment.

In July 1979, the State Council promulgated the "Regulations to Control the Standards in the People's Republic of China" — an extension and improved version of the earlier "Measures to Control the Technical Standards for Industrial and Agricultural Products and Construction Projects" which had been issued by the State Council in 1962. The new regulations clearly defined the principles, policies, scope of work and functions of the standardizing departments. After the second conference, the ministries concerned and the provinces, municipalities and autonomous regions held further meetings, established or strengthened their standardizing organs, worked out the details for implementing the regulations and planned their own work. Comprehensive progress has been made in China's standardization work in the two years since the second national conference.

Practical experience in the past 30 years has shown that standardization is an important part of economic management. The development of the national economy requires the appropriate development of standardization work which, in turn, promotes the development of the national economy. Therefore, the healthy development of the national economy is the primary requisite for ensuring the development of standardization work. In accordance with the readjustment and development of the national economy since the Third Plenary Session of the 11th Party Central Committee, the party and the government have paid great attention to standardization work.

In 1979 and 1980, 986 national standards were worked out for industrial and agricultural products, accounting for more than 42% of all national standards established in the past 20 years. China is now eliminating the influences of "Left" deviationist mistakes in the national economy and standardization work is sure to grow in a comprehensive and sustained way.

II. Principles and Methods of Standardization

China is a socialist country and its standardization work is controlled by the government. The State Administration of Standards is the functional department under the State Council in charge of standardization work throughout the country. Its responsibilities include: defining principles and policies concerning standardization, drawing up and executing national standardization work programmes and plans, monitoring standards and supervising and inspecting the quality of products. The divisions of standards under the scientific and technical bureaus of various ministries are in charge of standardization work in the respective ministries. At present, 23 provinces, municipalities and autonomous regions have set up bureaux of standards, while six others have set up standardizing organs. Some industrial cities, prefectures and a limited number of counties have also set up bureaux, divisions or sections.

The State Administration of Standards has a multi-branch research institute of standardization which is responsible for studying the principles and methods of standardization and for working out basic standards. Thirteen ministries have departments responsible for research in standardization and for the establishment and revision of national standards and ministerial standards. The standards library under the Scientific and Technical Information Research Institute of China is the centre for information on standards in China. Reference centres on standards have been set up in 17 provinces. There are about 300 industrial standardizing organs responsible for creating or revising national standards and ministerial standards. With a view to improving the establishment and revision of standards, China has, in 1979 and 1980, set up 19 industrial standards technical committees composed of representatives from ministries, enterprises, scientific research institutes, colleges and users.

Diagram of the Organizational Structure in Charge of Standardization in China

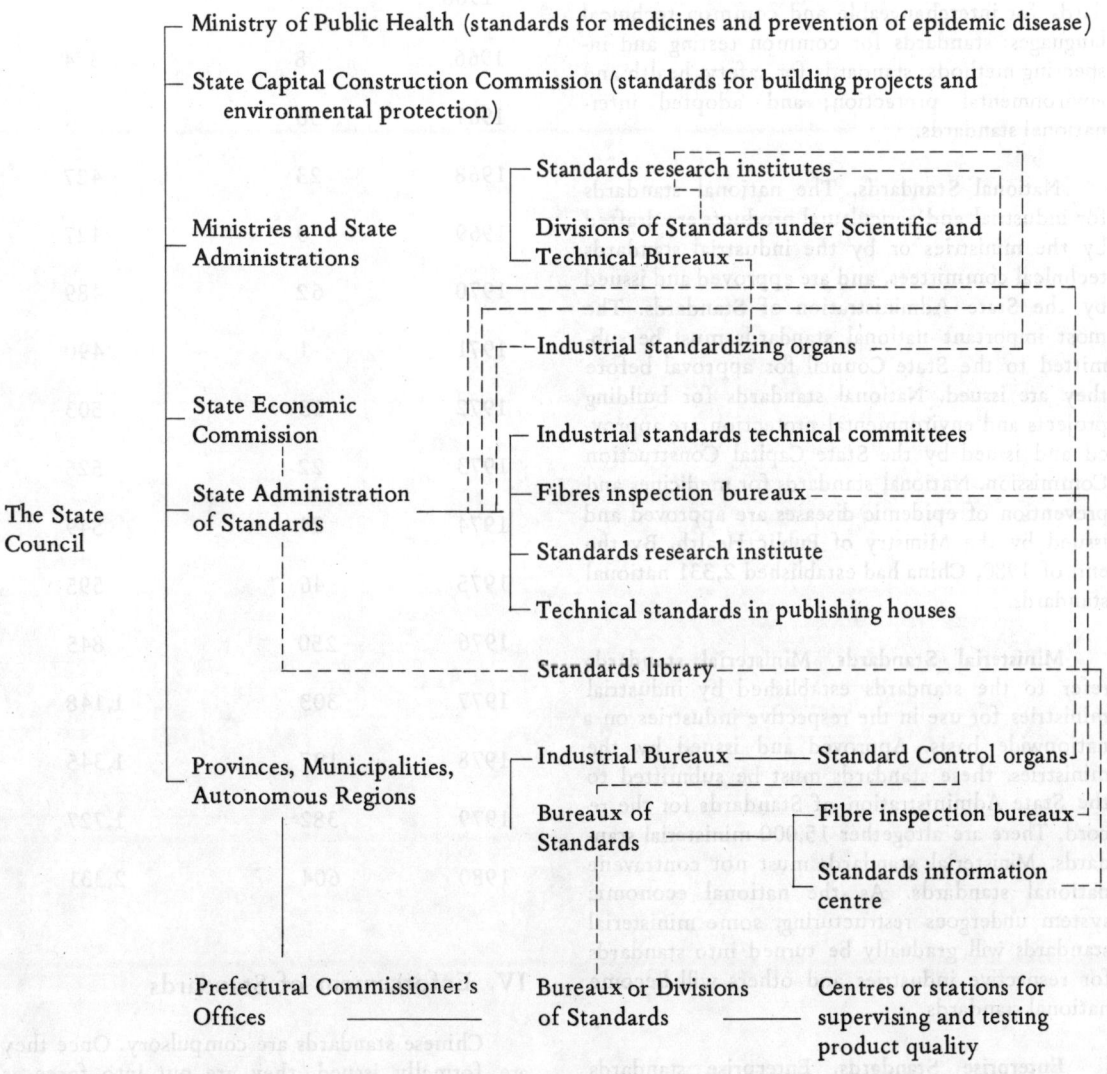

Note: ——— indicating relations of leadership
 - - - - indicating relations of technical guidance

III. The Organizational Structure in Charge of Standardization in China

The standards in China are divided into three categories: national standards, ministerial standards and enterprise standards. National standards (coded GB) are those of vital importance to economic and technological development and must be followed by all enterprises in the country. They include standards for basic raw materials and semifinished materials; standards for important industrial and agricultural products which are essential to the people's livelihood, or are produced in large quantities or are made by two or more different enterprises; standards for interchangeable parts, accessories, components, appliances, structural parts, tools and measuring instruments; standards for interchangeable and common technical languages; standards for common testing and inspecting methods; standards for safety, health and environmental protection; and adopted international standards.

National Standards. The national standards for industrial and agricultural products are drafted by the ministries or by the industrial standards technical committees, and are approved and issued by the State Administration of Standards. The most important national standards must be submitted to the State Council for approval before they are issued. National standards for building projects and environmental protection are approved and issued by the State Capital Construction Commission. National standards for medicines and prevention of epidemic diseases are approved and issued by the Ministry of Public Health. By the end of 1980, China had established 2,331 national standards.

Ministerial Standards. Ministerial standards refer to the standards established by industrial ministries for use in the respective industries on a nationwide basis. Approved and issued by the ministries, these standards must be submitted to the State Administration of Standards for the record. There are altogether 15,000 ministerial standards. Ministerial standards must not contravene national standards. As the national economic system undergoes restructuring, some ministerial standards will gradually be turned into standards for respective industries and others will become national standards.

Enterprise Standards. Enterprise standards must be worked out for products for which no national standards or ministerial standards exist. They must not contravene national standards or ministerial standards. In order to improve the quality of products, enterprises are encouraged to create standards more advanced than national or ministerial ones as well as those to be controlled by the enterprises themselves. Enterprise standards can be established by one enterprise for its own use or for use by other enterprises.

Table 1. Numbers of National Standards for Industrial and Agricultural Products Before and After 1966

Year	Number of New National Standards	Total Number
Before 1966	—	366
1966	8	374
1967	30	404
1968	23	427
1969	0	427
1970	62	489
1971	1	490
1972	13	503
1973	22	525
1974	24	549
1975	46	595
1976	250	845
1977	303	1,148
1978	197	1,345
1979	382	1,727
1980	604	2,331

IV. Enforcement of Standards

Chinese standards are compulsory. Once they are formally issued, they are put into force as technical decrees which all production, construction, scientific research, designing and management departments, as well as enterprises and undertakings must strictly follow. Proper actions or even legal actions will be taken against those who violate the standards and cause great losses, depending on their severity. Those who have difficulties in following the standards must explain their reasons and submit their requests to higher authorities for consent and to the departments issuing the standards for approval. All industrial enterprises must follow the established standards in testing raw materials, semifinished products and finished products. To ensure that the standards are correctly followed, the departments in charge of standards shall examine the standards to be adopted before new products are designed and put into production.

Product Quality. The quality of products can be reliably guaranteed only when the standards are strictly followed in production or in the supervision and testing of products. Supervision and testing are the indispensable means to put the standards into effect and to organize production on modern lines, and they are an important part of standardization work. The State Administration of Standards and the local bureaux of standards are in charge of supervising and testing the quality of products at the national or local levels.

Local bureaux of standards and quality supervising organs have appointed a number of competent research institutes and large enterprises to serve as stations for testing the quality of products and, at the same time, to restore and set up product inspection stations so as to gradually build a local network of supervision and inspection centres. In addition, the Fourth Ministry of Machine-Building Industry and the ministries of Building Materials, Light Industry and Chemical Industry have set up their own inspection centres. There are now more than 50 industrial inspecting centres under various ministries, more than 40 quality supervision and inspection centres for local products and more than 500 testing stations.

International Standards. The China Association for Standardization (CAS) joined the International Organization for Standardization (ISO) in September 1978. As an active member of the ISO, China has participated in the organization's 51 technical committees, 127 subtechnical committees and two advisory committees. The CAS sent 273 representatives to 176 international standardization technical meetings in 1979 and 1980. China joined the International Electrotechnical Commission (IEC) in 1957 and sent 130 people to 69 International Electrotechnical Committee meetings in 1979 and 1980. China has signed agreements with Britain, France, the United States and West Germany for long-term cooperation in standardization and has established channels for exchange of information and data on standards with 38 countries and standardizing groups.

IV. The Advantages of Standardization

China's practical experience in standardization over the past 30 years — since 1978, in particular — has fully demonstrated that standardization is an important means of promoting the development of the national economy and of achieving the best economic results.

(1) *Standardization helps to improve the quality of products.* During the "cultural revolution," the quality of products made in China became an outstanding problem. After 1977, however, the quality of products has been gradually restored or improved and the standardizing departments at various levels have done a great deal of work to improve the quality of products. Since September 1978, when the first nationwide "quality month" was launched, the standardizing departments of ministries and local governments have conducted a nationwide investigation of existing standards to find out where and why no standards have been adopted or existing standards have not been followed. They have mobilized all available forces to create enterprise standards and to follow existing standards so that no enterprise will produce goods without standards, lower existing standards or produce goods without following present standards.

Many enterprises have developed new enterprise standards after reaching existing national or ministerial standards, with a view to producing goods that are equal to or even better than the famous brands of their counterparts abroad. From 1979 on, many enterprises have adopted unpublished control standards for the quality of raw materials, semifinished products and finished products; for technological requirements, processes, means of testing and measuring; for production, technical and equipment management; and for the work of production workers doing different jobs. This has greatly improved the quality of their products. For example, the Ministry of Metallurgical Industry has adopted unpublished control standards for the entire processes of 67 quality products.

In the "Supplementary Rules for the Implementation of the 'Regulations on Awards to Quality Products in the People's Republic of China,'" the State Economic Commission listed the development and observance of unpublished control standards which are higher than existing technical standards as one of the qualifications for state quality product awards.

(2) *Standardization helps to make rational use of resources and to reduce consumption of raw materials.* Extensive research shows that correct determination of parameters for product standards can help to utilize resources in a rational way and to reduce consumption of raw materials. For example, the revised standards for cement allow the content of magnesium chloride to increase from 4.5% to 5%, which will greatly extend the period of limestone mining by cement plants. After standards were adopted for cement boats using steel mesh, Jiangsu Province reduced the consumption of steel by 37% for the five-ton cement boats it builds.

When the standards for China's No. 2 aviation oil were adopted, the freezing point for Chinese oils was tried out by temperature measurements at high altitudes and by actual test flights. This not only helps to make full use of China's oil resources, but also increases the production of fuels for jet planes.

The existing standards for Chinese matches were developed on the basis of extensive investigations and according to the principle of optimization, so that the size of matchsticks was reduced to the permissible extent in order to save 90,000 cubic meters of timber each year on the basis of present output.

(3) *Standardization is an important guarantee for energy saving.* Standardization for energy consumption is an important part of standardization work. By working out and following standards for energy consumption and for energy-saving products, the control of energy can be tightened, energy can be utilized scientifically and rationally, and energy consumption can be reduced. For example, the city of Dalian in 1980 worked out fuel consumption standards for all types of boilers; industrial furnaces, brick kilns and cement kilns; standards for oil consumption by all types of motor vehicles; standards for power consumption by small fertilizer plants, electric arc furnaces, cement plants and chemical works; and standards for water consumption by boilers and industries. These standards cover 60% of the total energy consumption in Dalian. When all these standards are followed, about 15% of current energy requirements can be saved.

The adoption of standards for energy consumption by industrial boilers alone can save 130,000 tons of standard coal. The development of standards for energy-saving products has just begun in China. Standards are being developed in various parts of China for efficient engineering and electrical products, low-resistance electric conduction materials, well-insulated construction and heat-preserving materials and other materials that can conserve energy.

(4) *Standardization is the prerequisite for organizing specialized production.* To organize production along specialized lines, the variety of products must be simplified, regular parts and spare parts must be made interchangeable and goods must be produced in uniform quantities. Therefore, specialized production requires the standardization of products, regular parts and spare parts. The higher the degree of standardization, the better are the economic results in specialized production. For example, there were originally more than 700 specifications for fasteners produced by different factories, but after standards were adopted and revised, the number of specifications was reduced to 200. This has resulted in a higher degree of standardization, increased production of the same item, improved processes and better economic performance in specialized production.

Table 2. Comparisons of Economic Performance for Fasteners in Shanghai in Selected Years

Item	1956	1962	1974	Comparisons between 1974 and 1956
Employment (persons)	11,156	8,487	7,917	−29%
Output (pieces)	1,092 million	2,117 million	9,992 million	915%
Annual labour productivity (yuan/worker/year)	2,514	7,383	28,240	1,156%
Utilization rate of materials	40%	60%	80%	100%
Profits turned over to the state (in 1,000 yuan)	2,560	28,450	85,790	3,350%

(5) *Standardization is an effective measure for developing new varieties in a rational way.* The designing of products according to the principle of standardization and the development of product variations from base-model products are beneficial to the rational development of new varieties for different needs.

For example, when a radial drilling machine is designed according to the principle of standardization, it can easily be modified or adapted for different uses or types of drilling by adding or replacing some parts. When the standard mechanism for alarm clocks was developed, the variations in shapes and sizes of clocks increased from 20 to 100, making it possible to meet the different needs of different consumers at home and abroad. Thus, standardization helps to promote China's foreign trade and the sales of Chinese products in other countries. Moreover, standardization is essential to the improvement of public health and safety and to environmental protection.

Standardization is an important means of achieving better results in the development of the national economy with less investment. If better economic results are to be achieved in the future development of the national economy, attention must be paid to improving product quality, reducing energy and raw material consumption, cutting production costs, producing more goods that are wanted by consumers and increasing exports. But these measures cannot be accomplished without standards. Therefore, we must further raise the level of our work of standardization during the period of economic readjustment.

48. EMPLOYMENT, WAGES, WORKERS' WELFARE AND LABOUR PROTECTION IN CHINA
By Zheng Ji
Policy Research Department, State Bureau of Labour

Before Liberation, China's economy was in very poor condition. Vast numbers of unemployed had long existed, and the people lived in destitution. Since the founding of New China, however, fundamental changes have taken place. With the development of the national economy, there has been an unprecedented increase in the number of workers and staff members in China. Their working conditions have been improved, and their wages, labour insurance and welfare benefits significantly increased.

Since the smashing of the Gang of Four in 1976, the Communist Party and the People's Government, with a view to making up for the losses suffered in the 10 years of turmoil, have made great efforts to increase employment. The authorities have emphasized the need of follow the principle "from each according to his ability, to each according to his work," gradually improved the living standards of workers and staff members on the basis of developing production, devoted much attention to safety in production and encouraged the initiative of workers and staff members. In this way, the national economy and other fields of work have been restored and developed at a fairly rapid pace.

I. Employment and Vocational Training

With the development of the national economy since the founding of New China, the increase in the number of workers and staff members has been unprecedented. In 1949 there were 8,090,000 workers and staff members throughout the country. In addition, there were 7,240,000 self-employed in cities and towns. By the end of 1980, the total work force was 104,440,000 with 80,190,000 working in state-owned enterprises and 24,250,000 in enterprises under collective ownership. In other words, the work force increased by nearly 11.9 times within 31 years.

There was not simply an increase in numbers, but a rise in ideological and political consciousness and cultural and technical levels as well. Many workers with a wide range of skills and millions of specialized people have emerged. The proportion of technical personnel in the total work force with degrees from secondary technical schools and colleges rose from 2.7% in 1952 to 6.1% in 1979. The number of graduates from institutions of higher learning between 1949 and 1979 totalled 3,030,000 – more than 16 times the 185,000 who graduated between 1928 and 1947 prior to Liberation. And in the same 30-year period, graduates from secondary technical schools totalled 5,390,000, while those trained in the 16 years from 1931 to 1946 totalled only 546,700. These workers and staff members trained since the founding of New China constitute a mighty force in building socialism.

Reorganizing the Labour Force. In the early years after Liberation, the number of unemployed left over from the old society was more than four million. In an effort to solve the problem, the People's Government adopted a policy of "retaining" all workers and other employees in bureaucratic-capitalist enterprises and all personnel in Kuomintang military and administrative institutions. Government policy towards private industrial and commercial enterprises was to give them necessary support to prevent them from closing down and dismissing their workers and other employees.

While employing workers wherever they were needed in production, the government made considerable efforts to help the unemployed find work by means of "self-help through labour," "providing odd jobs instead of giving relief," "retraining in preparation for new jobs," etc. With cooperation from all sides, production developed rapidly and unemployment was wiped out by the end of 1958.

In the meantime, a system of unified recruitment and regulation of the labour force was gradually set up. Labour departments exercised unified control over recruitment and distribution when state or private industrial and commercial enterprises were short of manpower; and surplus labour was transferred or shifted to other enterprises by the competent authorities or labour departments. In this way, a system characterized by an overwhelming majority of regular workers gradually came into force.

Under that system, management was not permitted to dismiss regular workers, no matter what changes were effected in the operation of an enterprise. Only in the case of odd jobs and seasonal work were temporary or seasonal workers employed by signing labour contracts. The system played a positive role in permitting enterprises to operate smoothly and in holding unemployment steady. However, the universal and indiscriminate application of this system was not conducive to simplifying the administrative structure and improving labour organization. Moreover, some workers could not fully utilize their skills or expertise because they were assigned unsuitable jobs, while other workers did not observe labour discipline since they were paid the same whether they worked well or not. Therefore, when the First Five-Year period was nearing completion, reform of the labour system was placed on the agenda. Under consideration were different schemes for regular workers, temporary workers and seasonal workers, so as to achieve a more flexible system of labour.

Vocational Training. During this period, vocational training was developed. The competent authorities in charge of our national economy, the labour departments and some large factories and mines systematically set up many vocational training schools. Between 1949 and 1980, 1,430,000 students were trained in these schools. At the same time, the state established a new apprenticeship system that absorbed the good points of the old system while dispensing with its outmoded conventions and customs. The majority of New China's skilled workers received their training under this new system.

Developments After 1976. After the fall of the Gang of Four in 1976, and especially since the Third Plenary Session of the 11th Central Committee of the Communist Party, China has adopted quite a number of measures in the administration of the labour force and vocational training. They include:

1. *Making great efforts to solve the problem of unemployment.* The 10 years of turmoil created by Lin Biao and the Gang of Four disrupted production and construction as well as education. As a result, large numbers of middle school graduates and other young people were unable to find jobs, creating a serious social problem.

Since the smashing of the Gang of Four, however, the party and the government have paid considerable attention to this problem. They have instructued the governments at all levels and various departments to provide more jobs by vigorously developing light and textile industries, handicrafts, repair services, commerce, service trades, catering, animal husbandry and other breeding industries, tourism, public utilities, gardening, afforestation, etc., wherever necessary and whenever conditions permit.

In addition, the authorities have encouraged job-seekers to set up workshops and cooperatives themselves, i.e., develop individual and collective undertakings within a prescribed range. Meanwhile, the state has allocated funds to establish labour service companies in large and medium-size cities throughout the country to provide job-seekers with vocational training or casual work.

In August 1980, the Party Central Committee convened a national conference on employment to review the experience, both positive and negative, in New China. This conference officially adopted the policy that the problem of unemployment should be solved under the unified planning and guidance of the state through a combination of labour departments providing work for job-seekers, and job-seekers participating voluntarily in cooperative enterprises and self-employment. At the same time, the conference underlined the need for governments at all levels to support and establish all kinds of collective enterprises, to encourage young job-seekers to set up cooperatives, to develop agricultural, forestry and stockbreeding farms as well as agricultural-industrial-commercial enterprises that absorb mainly school graduates, to encourage self-employment and to establish and run labour service companies. In the four years from 1977 to 1980, more than 28,000,000 people were given jobs.

2. *Restoring and developing vocational training.* To raise the technical level of rank-and-file workers, the government has devoted great attention to the vocational training of the reserve skilled workers and on-the-job workers.

Vocational training schools are an important means of training reserve skilled workers in our country. After the smashing of the Gang of Four, these schools were restored and developed. In 1980, a total of 680,000 students were enrolled in such schools.

The fundamental task of vocational schools is to train and provide various sectors of the national economy with average skilled workers who have acquired socialist consciousness and have mastered modern production skills. The students spend half of their time in school workshops or in productive enterprises to receive on-the-job training and the other half in classes for general and technical education.

Apprenticeship is China's traditional way of training large numbers of reserve skilled workers. In recent years, more than one million apprentices have been enrolled each year in industrial enterprises owned by the state. The duration of apprenticeship varies from trade to trade and from profession to profession. In general, it lasts three years; at a minimum, no less than two years.

An apprentice is expected to acquire the skill and know-how of a second-grade skilled worker within two or three years; that is, he or she should reach the technical standard set by the relevant ministries, acquire sufficient basic and theoretical knowledge pertaining to his or her trade, and have a full grasp of basic skills and multi-purpose operational techniques. At the end of the apprenticeship, an apprentice is required to take an exam before becoming a qualified worker.

Vocational training of on-the-job workers is mainly provided by the enterprises, which will draw up plans and train workers systematically in accordance with their own production needs and with the workers' technical competence. Enterprises generally set up a special office to deal with this matter. On-the-job training is provided in various forms. Different forms are used for different trades and workers, and training may be full-time, part-time or spare-time. Workers are paid basic wages during the period of training, and receive rewards for exemplary results.

3. *Carrying out research and experiments in the reform of the system of labour.* Since 1979, various places have adopted a method of recruiting workers and staff members which takes account of the applicants' moral, intellectual and physical qualifications. Wherever this system has been applied, the workers and staff members have been qualified for the operational skills in the enterprises concerned, and their professional knowledge has been better utilized.

In the textile industry since 1980, a system of "four groups of workers rotating on three shifts" has been tried out in all cotton mills with more than 30,000 spindles and in half of the woollen and flax mills. This system not only provides a large number of jobs, but also allows workers a longer rest period. (According to the new system, each worker enjoys two days off after every six working days.) As a result, workers are better rested and more energetic on the job, the utilization rate of equipment is higher and production is enhanced. According to a Chinese saying, it is a case in which "the rider changes while the horse keeps on running." With a view to protecting workers' health, shorter working hours and job-rotation at regular intervals are also being tried out in some chemical plants and mines.

II. Wages, Labour Insurance and Workers' Welfare

Since the founding of the People's Republic, we have reformed step by step, in accordance with the principle "to each according to his work," the irrational wage systems left over by the old society. With a view to protecting the health of workers and staff members, helping them overcome the difficulties in their livelihood, and providing the disabled and invalids with material assistance or social security, we have also established a system of labour insurance that covers their welfare benefits.

Wage Level and the Time-Rate Wage System. With the development of the national economy, the wage level of workers and staff members as a whole has been raised considerably. In 1980, the average annual wage in state-owned enterprises was 803 yuan, an increase of 80% over the 446 yuan in 1952 and of 32.7% over the 605 yuan in 1976. However, there were both increases and decreases throughout the years. The most significant rises in the wage level occurred during the period of the First Five-Year Plan and during the four years after the fall of the Gang of Four. In the last year (1957) of the plan, the average wage was 637 yuan, i.e., 42.8% higher than in 1952, for an average annual growth of 7.4%.

After the downfall of the Gang of Four, in spite of numerous difficulties, the government made strenuous efforts to raise the wage levels of the workers and staff members, while at the same time increasing the incomes of the peasants and production brigades and communes in the vast rural areas. On three occasions in the last four years, we readjusted the wages of the workers and staff members, 83% of whom received pay raises. The average annual increase was 7.3%, about the same as during the period of the First Five-Year Plan. From 1963 to 1965, China underwent a period of readjustment, but even then about 40% of the workers and staff members had their wages increased with an average annual growth of 3.3%. Declines in wage levels occurred during the following two periods: in the Second Five-Year Plan, when the annual decrease was 1.5%; and in the 10 years of the "cultural revolution," when the annual drop was 0.5%.

We have pursued a policy of "lower wages and more jobs," which is not only in the interest of expanding employment, but also enables families with more than one member at work to increase their income. Because of the continuous growth of the number of employed workers and the strict enforcement of family planning in recent years, the dependent members of workers' families have gradually decreased in number, thus reducing their economic burden.

The Time-Rate System. Quite diverse wage

systems existed in our country in the early years after Liberation. In some liberated areas the "supply system" prevailed, in others it was the "supply system" plus a partial wage system, and in still others a monetary wage system was in force with wages calculated on the basis of a number of commodities. In newly liberated areas, the old wage system was preserved in most cases, while in a few other places the "supply system" was applied. During the period of the First Five-Year Plan, we carried out reforms on the wage system several times. Our current wage system basically came into force following a total reform in 1956.

Since then, the majority of enterprise workers have been paid according to an eight-grade wage system, in which the highest grade receives approximately three times as much as the lowest.

For cadres, a hierarchical system based on their ranks or posts has been introduced. For government functionaries, there is a 24-grade salary system, with the highest grade receiving 12 times as much salary as the lower grade. For engineers and technical personnel, a 17-grade salary system has been implemented, the maximum rate being 9 times the minimum. The scientific, research, cultural, educational, health and physical culture sectors have their own pay scales.

Although the government has not laid down rules and regulations dealing with promotion, it nevertheless decided on different occasions to adjust wages upwards in accordance with the development of the national economy. In general, the wage or salary earner is moved to a higher grade in the wage system to which he or she belongs. On some occasions, we adopted the principle of ensuring a minimum amount of increase while at the same time limiting the maximum amount. Promotions are usually based on the attitude toward work, proficiency, contribution, seniority and, at times, political behaviour.

The Piece-Rate System and the System of Premiums. Generally speaking, the piece-rate system is a direct reflection of the principle of "more work, more pay and less work, less pay," whereas the system of premiums is a necessary supplement to this principle. In fact, when the principle of "to each according to his work" was observed, the two systems were implemented; otherwise they were not.

The percentage of production workers in state-owned enterprises covered by the piece-rate system changed quite often. It was 32.5% in 1952, 42% in 1957, (the peak year), below 5% in 1960 and 19.9% in 1963. After 1966, the piece-rate system almost ceased to exist.

The system of premiums followed a similar pattern. In the period of the First Five-Year Plan, the various sectors of the national economy introduced a uniform system of premiums. In general, such premiums were linked to the results of production, e.g., over-fulfilling, effecting economies, achieving better quality and developing new products.

Management and technical personnel received premiums when state production plans were fulfilled or over-fulfilled. During the period of the Second Five-Year Plan, the premium for over-fulfilment of production and other premiums were combined and changed into a unified premium plus a "leap-forward" premium. During the "cultural revoluton," the piece-rate system ceased to exist and the premiums were converted into an "additional wage" paid every month. It was only after the collapse of the Gang of Four that the piece-rate system and the system of premiums were gradually restored.

On April 1, 1980, the State Planning Commission, the State Economic Commission and the State Bureau of Labour promulgated the "Provisional Regulations Concerning the Piece-Rate Wages in State-owned Enterprises," which stipulated that piece-rates could be applied to all workers whenever conditions permit or wherever this system is more applicable. The ways of application may be divided into group-piece-rate and individual-piece-rate. On condition that rational and advanced production norms be maintained, there is no limit to the extra amount of wages a worker may receive under the piece-rate system.

On May 7, 1978, the State Council issued the "Circular on Introducing the Premium Payment and Piece-Rate Payment Systems." The premiums are generally drawn from the total payroll of all workers and staff members in the enterprises concerned and are included in the cost of production; they amount to 10%-20% of the total payroll of all workers covered under the system.

In 1979, with a view to restructuring the system of economic management, the government decided to start the experiment of extending the decision-making power of some state-owned enterprises. In these enterprises, the premiums were derived mainly from that part of profit retained by the enterprises. The first group of enterprises that started this experiment were allowed to retain part of the profit, at a percentage calculated on the basis of the full profit they made and, according to the percentages approved by the government, another part of the profit for expanding production, workers' welfare and payment of premiums. Since 1980, most of the enterprises have adopted a method of sharing the excess profits. Premiums in enterprises are usually paid every month in addition to a year-end bonus. The total amount of premiums should not exceed 1.5 to 2 months' standard wages, but a small number of enterprises have overstepped this limit.

Allowances and Subsidies. In order to encourage workers and staff members to go and work in areas or at posts where the living and working conditions are harsh but where extra people are urgently needed, the central and local governments have decided to provide various kinds of allowances or subsidies. These are given to such workers as underground miners, construction workers, forestry workers, field workers, workers exposed to excessive heat, workers at certain meteorological stations, ship crews, truck drivers, train crews, postmen on outdoor duties, scientific researchers, school teachers giving extra lessons, head instructors in primary and middle schools, group leaders in workshops, outstanding athletes and sportsmen, etc. These allowances and subsidies are meant to encourage people to take up jobs which others are unwilling to do, or to encourage people to achieve outstanding results.

Labour Insurance. There are two basic systems of labour insurance. One is for workers and staff members in state-owned enterprises who are covered by the "Labour Insurance Regulations of the People's Republic of China" promulgated by the Government Administration Council in February 1951. A 1953 revision increased the benefits. For instance, work-injury benefits were increased from 5%-20% of the wages of the injured to 10%-30%; the old-age pension rose from 35%-60% of the wages of the insured to 50%-70%, the minimum up by 15% and the maximum by 10%; and sick benefits during the first six months were raised from 50%-100% of the wages to 60%-100%, the minimum up by 10%. Other benefits — such as funeral grants or allowances and pensions and preferential treatment to lineal dependents of the deceased for death sustained at work or not at work — were also increased in different degrees.

The main features of our labour insurance system are as follows: (1) the insurance fund is borne in full by the enterprises, and the workers and staff members do not make any contribution to it; (2) the payment of insurance benefits is based on a worker's remuneration (i.e., wages), and adequate consideration is given to his or her seniority of service; and (3) insurance benefits cover childbirth, old age, sickness, death, injury and disability. For example, women workers are granted a 56-day maternity leave with full pay; sick, injured or disabled workers enjoy free medical care, food allowances and invalid pensions during the period of hospitalization; retired workers and staff members receive old-age pensions; funeral grants or funeral allowances and pensions may be given when a worker or his or her lineal dependent dies.

Labour insurance is jointly administered by the labour departments and trade unions, each having their own sphere of activity. Generally, the labour departments explain laws and decrees, while the unions supervise, control and implement the regulations at the grassroots level.

As for state organs, institutions and people's organizations, there is another system of labour insurance that is similar in some respects to the above system but different in others. Comparatively speaking, the benefits for sickness and death are higher than those in enterprises, but the lineal dependents do not enjoy free medical care.

In February 1958, the State Council promulgated the "Provisional Regulations Concerning the Retirement of Workers and Staff Members" and the "Provisional Regulations Concerning the Resignation of Workers and Staff Members." The two regulations are applicable to both state-owned enterprises and state organs, institutions and people's organizations, thus combining the two different systems into one.

Two improvements were made over the previous regulations. First, the qualifications for retirement benefits were relaxed, e.g., men at age 50 and women at age 45 may retire when in poor health or disabled if they have worked for 15 years, including 5 years of continuous service, and if they are confirmed by doctors or by the labour qualification committee to be disabled; or, regardless of his or her age, or he or she has worked for 25 years, including 5 years of continuous service, and if confirmed to be disabled; or if he or she has worked for the revolutionary cause for 20 years but is unable to continue service due to poor health. Second, terms and allowances are provided for those who want to resign before the age of retirement (maximum grant not exceeding 30 months' wages).

In May 1978, after approval by the Standing Committee of the National People's Congress, the State Council promulgated the "Provisional Regulations on Proper Treatment for the Aged, Weak, Sick and Disabled Cadres" and the "Provisional Regulations Concerning the Retirement and Resignation of Workers" for experimental application in enterprises and government institutions.

In comparison with the previous regulations, the main changes are as follows: First, new provisions are introduced to give veteran cadres honourable duties or retirement with full pay and all welfare benefits. Second, retirement benefits were improved. For example, those who joined the revolution during the War of Resistance against

Japanese aggression or during the War of Liberation may enjoy an old-age pension equivalent to 90% and 80% of their wages, respectively, if they are qualified for retirement. This is 10%-20% higher than the pension provided in the 1958 regulations that was equivalent to 70% of wages to those who had worked for the revolution for over 20 years.

Ordinary workers and staff members receive retirement pensions equivalent to 60%-75% of their wages, the minimum being up 10% and the maximum up 5% from 1958.

Third, a new rule provides retired workers with a guaranteed minimum pension of 25 yuan per month to ensure their livelihood. Fourth, a retired worker is entitled to have one of his or her children receive a job from the labour departments if the child meets the requirements for recruitment.

Workers' Welfare. Since the founding of the People's Republic, workers' welfare has been improved considerably, especially in new housing, welfare facilities and government subsidies. In 1952, new housing with a total of 7.5 million sq.m. of floor space was built for the workers. In the period of the First Five-Year Plan, another 94 million sq.m. were completed. In some regions and enterprises, many workers built their own houses with the help of the government. Since the downfall of the Gang of Four, the party and government have devoted much attention to housing construction and have made considerable achievements in this respect.

In 1952, there were 1,345 hospitals with 121,000 beds and 270 sanatoriums in urban areas. Many enterprises and institutions set up their own community canteens, kindergartens and day nurseries. During the period of the First Five-Year Plan, collective welfare facilities for workers and staff members rapidly increased. In 1957, there were 1,656 hospitals with 221,000 beds and 835 sanatoriums in urban areas. After the fall of the Gang of Four, workers' welfare facilities developed even faster. By 1978, the government had spent 6,691 million yuan on labour insurance and welfare benefits in the state-owned enterprises. Welfare benefits included allowances for home-heating and transportation, and travel subsidies for workers to visit their families. In addition, workers pay very low rent. In Beijing, for example, the rent per sq.m. of floor space is only about 0.20 yuan, which is not even enough to meet the cost of repairs. Thus the government must allocate large sums in the form of housing allowances.

In order to solve the problem of shortages of agricultural and sideline products, various enterprises, state organs, military units and schools far from cities have engaged in agricultural and sideline production, carrying forward the revolutionary tradition of the Great Production Campaigns in time of war. The total land now under cultivation is 7 million *mu,* with an annual output of 1,000 million *jin* of grain and 3,000 million *jin* of vegetables, and a large quantity of oil, meat and fruits. All this has effectively improved the livelihood of the workers and staff members and has created favourable conditions for the employment of the workers' children.

III. Labour Protection

A major policy in China is to ensure the safety and health of the workers engaged in production. In the 31 years since the founding of the People's Republic, we have achieved significant results in labour protection.

Building a Foundation. The 17 years prior to the "cultural revolution" constituted a period of initiation and development of labour protection work in China. This period may be summarized by the following principal developments:

(1) The guiding principle for safety in production was defined in the light of Chairman Mao's directive: "While efforts are being made to increase production and practise economy, attention must also be paid to the safety, health and the indispensable welfare amenities of the workers and other employees; if attention is paid only to the one while the other is forgotten or neglected even to a small extent, this is a mistake."

(2) A whole series of laws, rules and regulations on labour protection were established. During the First Five-Year Plan period, the state promulgated 15 laws and regulations, such as "Regulations on Factory Safety and Sanitation." "Regulations Governing Safe Working Conditions for Construction and Installation Projects" and "Regulations on the Reporting of Accidents Resulting in Injury or Death of Workers and Other Employees." In addition, various ministries and bureaus at the national level and corresponding departments at local levels promulgated altogether more than 300 rules and regulations.

(3) Labour protection organs were set up and cadres trained. After the establishment of the People's Republic, labour departments, competent industrial authorities and the trade unions successively set up administrative organs for labour protection and trained a large number of cadres. According to 1953 statistics, 200,000 activists in

different enterprises were doing labour protection work after having received specialized training.

(4) Scientific research and teaching institutions were established. An Institute of Labour Protection, the preparation of which had started in 1955, came into being in 1957. Moreover, courses in safety measures were opened in the science and engineering departments of institutes of higher learning. For instance, a Labour Protection Department was formed in the Peking Labour College (now called the Beijing Institute of Economics).

(5) Working conditions were improved. Matters relating to working hours of the workers and staff members and protection of special interests of young workers and women workers are explicitly stipulated in our Constitution and other important laws. Funds earmarked by the government for labour protection increased year by year. According to the statistics of eight ministries — Metallurgy, Coal, the First Machine-Building, Railways, Communications, Textiles, Chemical Works and Forestry — the government had directly allocated by the end of 1957 a total of 490 million yuan for the purpose of improving working conditions. As a result, many important pieces of equipment to ensure safety and industrial sanitation were installed, such as installations for ventilation and drainage in mines, devices to protect workers against high temperature, devices to protect workers from toxic gases or silica dust, equipment to relieve workers of heavy manual labour and safety devices against electric shock.

According to incomplete statistics from 21 provinces and 3 municipalities, in the three years from 1954 to 1956 over 81,000 major pieces of equipment were systematically installed to ensure safety and sanitation. The enterprises and workers were mobilized on a large scale to carry out seasonal and specialized inspections on safety and sanitation; in other words, the enterprises, workers and staff members relied on themselves to improve their working conditions.

Furthermore, the Chinese government has since 1955 set up special organs to inspect boilers, pressure vessels and other special equipment in all stages of design, manufacture, installation, operation and repair. In the past two decades and more, achievements have been made in legislation, training of personnel, inspection, summarizing and popularizing experience. Statistics show that the accident rate fell from 39 per 10,000 boilers in the 1960's to 5.9 in the 1970's.

Recent Accomplishments. Since 1979, in order to rectify the erroneous tendency of "concentrating on increased output without regard to safety" and to implement the policy of safety in production, we have done work in the following areas to ensure labour protection.

1. *Additional legislative measures.* In 1979, we reaffirmed the implementation of the "Regulations on Factory Safety and Sanitation," "Regulations Governing Safe Working Conditions in Construction and Installation Projects," "Regulations on the Reporting of Accidents Resulting in Injuries or Death of Workers and Other Employees" and other regulations, and set out to draft new laws and regulations.

2. *Nationwide "Safety Month."* This was sponsored by the State Economic Commission and nine other ministries. With the approval of the State Council, a televised rally to observe "Safety Month" was held in April 1980 in Beijing.

All over the country, radio braodcasts, pictures, slides, films, art performances and exhibitions have been used to educate the people in safety. In the coal industry, widespread activities have been organized to study the regulations on safety in coal mines. Statistics from 84 bureaus and mines show that more than 700,000 workers and staff members have received training in safety, including about 57,000 cadres.

Through the "Safety Month" campaign, a considerable number of hidden dangers and possible accidents were avoided. According to statistics provided by Heilongjiang, Jiangsu, Shaanxi and 18 other provinces, muncipalities and autonomous regions, during "Safety Month," more than 2,050,000 possible hazards were discovered, and measures have already been taken to eliminate 1,280,000 of them.

3. *Publicity, education and the training of cadres.* In the past year or more, the State Bureau of Labour has conducted five courses to train 500 cadres for labour protection work. Extensive teaching materials on labour protection (more than one million words) have been compiled, and a series of books and reference materials published. Special rooms for education in labour protection have been built in 40 enterprises, and eight films (both feature and documentary) on safe production have been shown.

4. *Funds for labour protection measures and development of scientific research.* According to statistics, good results have been achieved in more than 200 labour protection projects in more than 20 industries. The content of dust and toxic particles in the air in these factories and mines has, in the main, been reduced to the hygiene standard

set by the government. In 1980, the state and local authorities, as well as various ministries, allocated a total of more than 300 million yuan for labour protection measures to improve working conditions.

In the field of scientific research, another 11 institutes of labour protection are under preparation or being established.

5. *Dealing with major accidents.* Special personnel were sent to investigate and handle such recent major accidents as the gas explosion in a coal mine at Songshuzhen, Jilin Province, and the capsizing of the Bohai No. 2 oil rig. In particular, the decision of the State Council on August 25, 1980, on the Bohai No. 2 accident was widely supported by the broad masses of workers and staff members. Various local authorities and central ministries held a series of meetings to draw useful lessons from the Bohai No. 2 accident and to make a comprehensive check-up in their own fields. As they learned about the serious consequences of the accident, many departments and enterprises perfected their own rules and regulations and took measures to remove hidden dangers.

Some units, in line with the State Council's directive to strengthen education in legislation governing industrial and communications enterprises, and to deal with injuries and fatal accidents strictly by law, have enforced a system of "three not-let-slip-away's" (do not let accidents slip away before their causes are analysed and determined; do not let accidents slip away before those responsible and the working masses have learned their lessons; and do not let accidents slip away before preventive measures are worked out).

Gains in Safety and Health. Because of our efforts in recent years, and in 1980 in particular, the number of injuries and deaths resulting from accidents has begun to drop. According to incomplete statistics, the number of fatal accidents (including accidents to non-employees) fell by 11.2% in 1980 as compared with the previous year, and the number of serious injuries by 7.2%. The rate of deaths in state-owned enterprises dropped by 14.7% and the rate of serious injuries by 9.5%.

Owing to the attention paid by the party and the government and the efforts made by various enterprises in every industry and trade in the past 31 years, there are now numerous exemplary units with outstanding records in the implementation of the policy of safety in production and in the protection of the safety and health of workers and staff members. In the Xialong Tungsten Mine for example, the content of silicon dioxide in the ore is high as 58% to 97%. Since 1958, however, X-rays have been given annually to workers and staff members in contact with silica dust, and for 22 years no worker has ever been found to be suffering from silicosis. The Zhangjialing Coal Mine in Shaodong County, Hunan Province, is not only a highly gaseous mine but also a commune-run enterprise with crude and simple equipment. Nevertheless, in the 20 years since 1960, there have been no serious injuries or deaths due to accidents, and the figure for minor injuries has dropped year after year.

The Beijing Refractory Materials Factory makes use of funds provided by the state for labour protection and raises funds itself to improve factory management, to rebuild equipment and to take measures to reduce dust. As a result, the dust content in 96.62% of the work places was brought within acceptable limits in 1979, while in none of them was it below permissible levels in 1973. In the Electrochemical Works in Wuxi County, Jiangsu Province, the leakage rate of pipes has decreased to within 5 per 10,000; the air there is fresh, and the plant is known as a "garden factory" full of beautiful flowers and green grass. The Water Pump Factory in Shijiazhuang, Hebei Province, has not had a single case of death due to accidents for 30 consecutive years and no serious injuries in the last five years.

IV. Remaining Problems

China has made outstanding achievements in the broad labour field since the founding of the People's Republic. However, because of the lack of a comprehensive appreciation of the importance of labour protection and mistakes in our work — and particularly the disruption caused by Lin Biao and the Gang of Four from 1966 to 1976 — many problems do exist, and some of them are quite serious.

Weaknesses in Education. For a long time, we have paid attention only to providing employment, but in one way or another neglected intellectual development. Both general and vocational education in China are lagging behind the advanced countries, and our vocational education is especially backward. At present, the levels of general and technical education of large numbers of workers and staff members are rather low, and are unable to meet the requirements for the realization of the four modernizations.

Difficulties Cited. In providing employment, we often do not pay attention to economic results and labour efficiency. This state of affairs is also due to poor management, which finds expression in lack of discipline, disregard of rules and regulations, inefficiency, and overstaffing. Due to the slow economic growth and the existing economic structure and ownership system, which are unfavourable both to economic development and to expanding employment, the avenues for employment are becoming ever narrower.

With the government having to retain all workers and other employees on the job while young people wait for the government to assign them jobs — mainly in units owned by the state or in collective enterprises — the employment structure has become most irrational. As a result, productivity and efficiency in many units have declined, and many people have seen a drop in their standard of living. No significant change has been made in a situation in which "there are people without work, and there is work without proper people."

Housing Shortage. Because China is a populous yet poor country, and because in the course of economic construction we have placed undue emphasis on capital accumulation to the detriment of consumption, the standard of living of our workers and staff members is still low. Some workers' families find it difficult to make ends meet, particularly those who receive no premiums.

The most serious problem is the acute shortage of housing. Due to the vigorous efforts of the state, the construction of average floor space per capita increased from 3.61 sq.m. in 1978 to 3.74 sq.m. in 1979 and to 3.9 sq.m. in 1980, showing an average annual increase of 2.6% in the three years. Nevertheless, housing remains a serious problem.

Steps to be Taken. With regard to safety in production and the health of workers and staff members, apart from financial and material deficiencies, many problems have risen because of mismanagement or insufficient education. Some 70%-80% of the accidents are due to the neglect of existing rules and regulations by either the management or the workers.

In order to make our labour arrangements suit the needs of the four modernizations, greater efforts should be made to reform the employment structure, achieve better labour administration in enterprises, implement the principle "to each according to his work," and improve safety measures, the system of labour administration and existing legislation. Meanwhile, through the growth of production and the increase in labour productivity, we will endeavour to solve step by step the problems related to the standard of living of our workers and staff members.

49. CHINA'S TRADE UNIONS
By the Research Office,
All-China Federation of Trade Unions

I. Growth of the Trade Unions After Liberation

The Chinese trade unions are the mass organizations of the working class of China. The founding of the People's Republic in 1949 ushered in a new era in Chinese history and brought about a fundamental change in the status of the Chinese working class and trade unions. Since then, Chinese workers have been transformed from an oppressed, exploited and ruled class to the leading class of the country and masters of the new society.

After having won political power, the historical mission of the working class has shifted from one of destroying and overthrowing the old political power of the Kuomintang to one of strengthening and consolidating the new political power of the peoples' democratic dictatorship, led by the working class and based on the alliance of workers and peasants. The mission also includes rehabilitating and developing the national economy and building up the new life of socialism. As a pillar of the state's power, the trade unions have been unremitting in their efforts to mobilize and organize the masses of workers and staff members to strive for the accomplishment of their own historical mission.

Restoration of ACFTU. A year before the founding of the Peoples' Republic, the Sixth National Labour Congress was held in Harbin in August 1948. In this way, the All-China Federation of Trade Unions (ACFTU) was restored, and the unity of the working class of the whole country was achieved. In July 1949, ACFTU held a national conference on trade union work in Beijing. Soon afterwards, workers and staff members throughout the country were organized into trade union organizations at various levels. In June 1950, the national people's government promulgated the "Trade Union Law of the People's Republic of China" which laid down the rights and duties of the trade unions. Thereafter, the workers' movement developed rapidly on a nationwide scale.

Early Activities. During the period of rehabilitation of the national economy after the founding of New China, the people's government, with the assistance of the trade union organizations, took over the bureaucratic-capitalist enterprises, turned them into socialist enterprises and restored production immediately. In privately owned enterprises, trade unions mobilized workers and staff to carry out the principle of "developing production, promoting economic prosperity, giving consideration to both public and private interests and benefiting both labour and capital." In this way, those enterprises beneficial to the national economy and people's livelihood were given a new life.

Meanwhile, trade unions educated workers and staff members in historical materialism, the Communist Party and communism, thus helping to raise their consciousness, foster a new attitude towards labour and bringing about an upsurge of enthusiasm in labour.

In July 1950, the National Conference of Labour Heroes of Workers, Peasants and Soldiers was held. In August 1950, the Government Administration Council of the central people's government (which was replaced in 1954 by the State Council) issued the "Decision on Rewarding Inventions, Technical Innovations and Rationalization Proposals with Regard to Production." The Government Administration Council also promulgated the Labour Insurance Regulations in 1951.

All these activities further aroused the enthusiasm and initiative of the workers and staff members of the whole country. After the masses of workers and staff in Northeast China launched the campaign to set new production records, workers and staff members in other parts of China followed suit. The campaign became a national movement for rationalization proposals.

Wartime Contributions. After the outbreak of the War to Resist U.S. Aggression and Aid Korea (1950-1953), Chinese trade unions educated the broad masses of workers and staff in patriotism and internationalism. Tens of thousands of workers and staff members volunteered to fight at the front and the others worked heroically and dauntlessly in the rear. The trade unions at various levels organized workers and staff in a patriotic emulation drive to increase production and practice economy, popularizing the experiences of the Ma Hen-chang Group in the machine-building industry and Hao Jianxiu's spinning method in the textile industry. All these greatly raised labour productivity, accelerated the rehabilitation of the national economy and effectively supported the front.

During the period of rehabilitation of the national economy and the War to Resist U.S. Aggression and Aid Korea, the Chinese trade unions mobilized the broad masses of workers and staff to participate actively in a series of major campaigns on a nationwide scale. These were aimed at suppressing revolutionaries and achieving democratic reforms in the enterprises (abolition of feudal "gangmaster" and "labour contractor" systems and establishment of a democratic management system). San Fan and Wu Fan movements were launched to fight attacks by the bourgeoisie in order to consolidate the people's democratic dictatorship. The San Fan movement (1951-1952) was directed against the "three evils" (corruption, waste and bureaucracy within the party, government, army and mass organizations). The Wu Fan movement, begun in 1952, fought against the "five evils" (bribery, tax evasion, theft of state property, cheating on government contracts and the stealing of economic information, as practiced by owners of private industrial and commercial enterprises).

Planned Economic Growth. Beginning in 1953, our country entered a period of planned economic construction. In May of that year, the Seventh National Congress of Chinese Trade Unions was held. The fundamental tasks for trade union organizations as formulated by the Congress were: (1) to keep in close contact with and to educate the masses of workers, and (2) to raise the level of consciousness and organization of the working masses under the leadership of the Chinese Communist Party, so as to strive for the fulfilment of the plan of national industrial construction.

To fulfill and exceed the First Five-Year Plan for developing the national economy, the trade unions mobilized the masses of workers and staff to broaden and deepen socialist labour emulation. One of the prominent features of the emulation was the combining of labour emulation with technical innovation and mass proposals for rationalization. Wang Chinglun, a worker in the General Machinery Plant of the Anshan Iron and Steel Company, was an outstanding example. Using technical innovations, he fulfilled the production quota of four years in one single year of 1953.

In 1954 and 1955, socialist emulation drives to raise technical levels, improve skills and study and master new techniques were launched in various parts of China. This resulted in stimulating the work of evaluating and popularizing advanced experience, as well as organizing rationalization proposals. In 1956, the movement of advanced workers spread throughout the country. All these efforts stepped up the pace of socialist construction.

In private enterprises, the trade unions, in line with the Communist Party's policy of utilization, restriction and transformation of capitalist industry and commerce, mobilized workers and staff to exercise supervision over management. In the latter half of 1955 and the first half of 1956, along with the upsurge in the establishment of agricultural and handicraft cooperatives, the trade unions extensively mobilized workers and staff to assist the government in encouraging owners of private industry and commerce to accept the principle of joint state-private ownership of enterprises. This ensured smooth progress in the socialist transformation of capitalist industry and commerce, and the rapid development of production in enterprises of joint ownership.

We abolished the system of exploitation of man by man, transformed the system of ownership by small producers and established the comprehensive socialist public ownership of the means of production, thus making possible for the Chinese people, who account for more than one-fifth of the world population, to enter socialist society. This was the greatest and most profound change in the history of our country.

The Five-Year Plans. Until December 1957, when the Eighth National Congress of Chinese Trade Unions was held, the First Five-Year Plan had been fulfilled and overfulfilled. In the report of the Eighth Congress of Trade Unions, it was stated: "Proceeding from the present basis, our task is to strive to develop industry, actively support agriculture and concentrate all efforts on implementing the forthcoming Second Five-Year Plan." After the beginning of the Second Five-Year Plan for national economic construction in 1958, the trade unions mobilized and organized workers and staff to participate actively in the implementation of the plan and to contribute their wisdom and efforts to the building of socialist industry and agriculture.

During the three difficult years in the early 1960's, the trade unions mobilized and organized workers and staff to carry out labour emulation for increasing production and practicing economy, and to implement the party's policy of readjusting, consolidating, filling out and raising standards of the national economy, thus facilitating the rehabilitation of the economy. During this period, the trade unions paid special attention to the workers' livelihood and vigorously engaged in agricultural and sideline production in places where conditions permitted. These efforts played an important role in helping workers and staff to overcome the difficulties.

The Catastrophe. In the 17 years before the

"cultural revolution," the Chinese trade unions scored tremendous successes in their work. However, they also suffered some setbacks. They were wrongly charged with committing errors of "syndicalism" and "economism," and for a certain period there was a great deal of talk about the "withering away of trade unions." Even worse, during the period of the "cultural revolution," the trade unions suffered a catastrophe as a result of sabotage by the counter-revolutionary cliques of Lin Biao and Jiang Qing. Many trade union cadres, labour heroes and trade union activists were persecuted, and the All-China Federation of Trade Unions was forced to suspend its work for 11 long years.

II. Restoration and Development After 1976

In October 1976, under the leadership of the Party's Central Committee, the Chinese people smashed the Gang of Four in a great, historic victory. Since then, China's trade unions have been restored and developed as a result of efforts to consolidate them ideologically and organizationally.

The Ninth National Congress of Chinese Trade Unions, which was held in October 1978, set forth the basic principles and tasks for the workers' movement and trade union work in the new period, adopting the new "Constitution of the Trade Unions of the People's Republic of China" and electing the Ninth Executive Committee of the All-China Federation of Trade Unions. The national leading body of the Chinese trade unions, whose activities had been suspended for 11 years, resumed its function.

A New Beginning. The Ninth National Congress of Chinese Trade Unions marked a new starting point for the workers' movement in China. The congress laid down the following principle: Under the leadership of the Chinese Communist Party, the trade unions should unite, educate and encourage the workers and staff to raise continuously their level of political consciousness, master modern science and technology, take an active part in enterprise management, extensively promote socialist labour emulation, raise labour productivity and gradually improve the material and cultural life of the workers and staff on the basis of production growth. In this way, the trade unions will strive to fulfil the general task in the new period.

Historic Meeting. The Third Plenary Session of the 11th Party Central Committee, which was convened in December 1978, proved to be of great historic significance. The decision was made to shift the focus of party work to socialist construction. It is the historical mission of the Chinese trade unions to mobilize and organize the working class to provide the main force in the building of a modern and powerful nation.

The Party's Central Committee has attached great importance to trade union activities, emphasizing time and again the importance of strengthening the work and issuing a number of important instructions. In his speech to the Ninth National Congress of Chinese Trade Unions, Comrade Deng Xiaoping expressed the hope that trade unions will indeed become the workers' own "organizations which are trustworthy, speak up on their behalf and work in their interests." In his speech at the celebration of the 30th anniversary of the founding of the People's Republic of China, Comrade Ye Jianying asked the trade unions to act as "an important representative of the masses"; in addition to "safeguarding the interests of the state and collective, the trade unions should resolutely safeguard the interests of the masses they represent."

In October 1979, Comrade Hu Yaobang pointed out in his speech at the national working conference of the educational workers' trade unions that the trade unions at present should resolutely protect the right of the working class to be masters of the state, show earnest concern for the masses' well-being, bring the socialist initiative of the working class into full play and continuously raise the communist consciousness of the masses of workers. These important instructions on trade union work, given by the leading comrades of the Party's Central Committee, reflect the great concern of our party for trade union work.

Committee Sessions. Trade unions at all levels have made unremitting efforts to implement the principles and policies formulated since the Third Plenary Session of the 11th Party Central Committee as well as the party's instructions concerning trade union work, bringing their role into full play and making certain that they really represent the workers and staff. In February 1979, the Second Enlarged Session of the Standing Committee of the Ninth Executive Committee of the ACFTU discussed how trade union work could effectively support the socialist modernization programme. It adopted a resolution on "Strengthening Stability and Unity and Launching a Campaign to Increase Production and Practice Economy in an Extensive and Thorough Way."

In October and November 1979, the Third Enlarged Session of the Ninth Executive Committee of the ACFTU was held. The participants studied carefully Comrade Deng Xiaoping's speech at the Ninth National Congress of Chinese Trade Unions, as well as Comrade Ye Jianying's speech at the meeting in celebration of our National Day. They also corrected the mistake of the national trade union conference on the rectification movement held in 1958, and discussed and formulated specific tasks for the trade unions in achieving the readjustment of our national economy.

The Fourth Enlarged Session of the Standing Committee of the Ninth Executive Committee of ACFTU, convened in April 1980, adopted a resolution on "Mobilizing the Workers and Staff to Contribute to the Four Modernizations and Launching the Campaign to Increase Production and Practice Economy in a Thorough Way in Preparation for the 12th National Party Congress." Acting in accordance with the above-mentioned resolutions, the trade unions at all levels have taken many measures and have done a great deal of work, thus gradually resuming and stepping up their activities.

III. Major Accomplishments of the Trade Unions

Trade unions have played an active role in rapidly rehabilitating and developing the national economy after 10 years of chaos (1966-1976) by mobilizing and organizing the workers and staff to carry out socialist labour emulation, with emphasis on increasing production and practicing economy. The unions launched a campaign to make contributions to the Four Modernizations and encouraged the advanced collectives and persons on the economic fronts.

Emulation Drives. In recent years, groups, teams and individuals in a number of enterprises have participated in emulation drives to achieve higher scores in fulfilling the fixed norms based on their enterprises' economic indexes according to the state plan. Bonuses are worked out on the basis of how well these norms are fulfilled. These drives link the economic responsibility of an enterprise with its economic results and interests, on the one hand, and consider the interests of the state, the collective and the individuals, on the other, thus mobilizing the initiative of the workers and staff and boosting the growth of production.

For example, the power industry, which was the first to introduce such a drive in 1979, produced 3,900 million more kwh of electricity in excess of the state plan and saved 4.35 million tons of coal and 1,840 million kwh of electricity. In the first half of 1980, the output of electricity reached 50.7% of the annual plan. From January to May, 1.5 million tons of coal were saved. Such emulation drives spur the enterprises to improve steadily their managerial work and encourage the workers and staff to study and adopt new techniques to improve their technological level.

Some industries launch labour emulation drives, such as the emulation of "weaving 10,000 metres of cloth without any fault" carried out in the textile industry; "safe operation without any accident in 100 days" among railway workers; and "all-excellent projects" for the building industry: An "all-excellent project" must meet these six criteria: (1) the project must be of high quality; (2) the project must be completed on time; (3) its labour efficiency must exceed state norms; (4) it must consume less raw material than the original plan; (5) it must be accomplished without major accidents causing serious injuries or deaths; and (6) it must have strict operation management, a tidy and clean construction site and the finished work must meet design requirements.

This particular emulation was initiated by No. 1 Division of Beijing No. 6 Building Company. By the end of 1978, the All-China Federation of Trade Unions, the State Capital Construction Commission and the State Bureau of Labour jointly called a meeting to popularize the experience. The emulation was quickly adopted by building enterprises in different places, and good results have been achieved. According to initial statistics from building enterprises in 18 provinces and municipalities, such as Beijing, Tianjin, Shanghai and Liaoning, 1,793 "all-excellent projects" with a total floor space of over 3,390,000 sq. m. were created in the first half of 1980, exceeding that of 1979.

Some industries are organizing inter-factory emulations, such as the emulation between bicycle factories in light industries and that between TV set manufacturing factories in the electronics industry. These emulations enable factories to support and learn from each other and to exchange techniques, thus helping the growth and technical improvement of the entire industry.

The TV set manufacturing industry suffered a loss of 10.62 million yuan for the first half of 1979. However, as a result of introducing inter-factory emulations in July 1979, it got out of the red. Taking 1979 as a whole, it gained a net profit of 960,000 yuan, and in 1980 its profits amounted to 80 million yuan. The output increased by 68% as compared with 1979, and the quality improved remarkably. In addition, trade unions at various places organized workers and staff in the same trade or doing the same type of work to emulate each other, and also organized contests between individuals and groups. All these activities also produced good economic results.

Four Modernizations. In 1980, a drive "to make contributions to the Four Modernizations" was launched in many provinces and municipalities. It closely integrated economic production and other activities of the various units with the effort to realize the Four Modernizations. The campaign gave great inspiration to the workers and staff members and won wide support. It has played a significant role in improving enterprise management, boosting production and mobilizing the initiative of the workers and staff.

In recent years, through extensive socialist labour emulations and the drive to make contributions to the Four Modernizations, the trade unions have achieved marked results in organizing the workers and staff to make rationalization proposals and carry out technical cooperation. According to statistics for the first half of 1980, 2.08 million workers and staff made more than 1,283,000 million proposals either individually or jointly, and more than 688,000 were adopted. Of those proposals adopted, 275,000 represented total annual savings of more than 1,900 million yuan.

According to incomplete statistics from 27 provinces, municipalities and autonomous regions for the first half of 1980, there were 2,000 organizations for technical cooperation and 186 technical exchange stations at the city and county levels and 22,000 organizations of technical cooperation at the grassroots enterprise level. In the first half of 1980 alone, 3,242 technical demonstrations were held and 7,947 lectures were organized by the technical exchange stations run by trade unions at or above the county level. More than 851,000 attended the activities of inspecting and learning from each other's work. A total of 3,329 new techniques were popularized through these activities. There were more than 15,000 activities designed to help agriculture. The technical exchange stations and teams for popularizing professional knowledge organized by trade unions at or above the county level helped solve more than 3,000 key technical problems.

Model and Advanced Workers. In the extensive socialist emulation drives and activities contributing to the Four Modernizations, a great number of model workers and advanced workers emerged. They are outstanding representatives of the advanced productive force. Award ceremonies were held by the State Council in September and December 1979 to commend the national advanced enterprises and national model workers in industry, transport and communications and capital construction, as well as the national advanced units and national model workers in agriculture, finance and trade, education, health and scientific research.

In 1980, 61 million workers and staff members in 264,000 basic units elected among themselves 1.23 million advanced collectives, including 920,000 advanced teams and groups, and 11.15 million advanced workers, which was 1.83 million more than in 1979, 7.95 million more than in 1963 and 10.95 million more than the total number between 1949, the year when New China was founded, and 1952.

Moreover, the trade unions at various levels rehabilitated veteran model workers who were persecuted during the "cultural revolution" and made certain that the policies of the party were well-implemented in their cases. The trade unions also publicized the advanced ideas and deeds of the model workers of all trades and professions and lauded their exemplary role. All these activities helped to promote the growth of the social productive forces.

The Workers' Congresses. Experience was gained and good results were achieved in the trade unions' unremitting efforts to restore and develop the system of workers' congresses and carry out experiments with the democratic election of leading cadres at the basic level. It has always been an important task for the trade unions to organize workers and staff to take part in the democratic management of enterprises and safeguard the democratic rights due them as masters of the enterprises.

As far back as 1948, it was decided at the Sixth National Congress of Labour to set up workers' conferences and factory management committees in industrial enterprises, these conferences and committees to be composed of factory directors, engineers, cadres in charge of production, trade union representatives and some of the delegates elected by the workers' general meeting. In May 1949, the Workers' Conference of North China adopted a resolution on the establishment of management committees and workers' conferences in factories and worked out regulations for its implementation. These regulations were promulgated and put into force by the People's Government of North China.

In an editorial in the *People's Daily* on February 7, 1950, entitled "Learn How to Manage An Enterprise," it was pointed out that "to learn to master managerial work and transform bureaucratic-capitalist enterprises into socialist ones should become a predominant slogan for the Chinese working class." A specific directive issued by the Party Central Committee called for taking this editorial as a guideline for running enterprises and boosting production at that time.

Subsequently, the Financial and Economic Commission of the Government Administration

Council issued a "Directive on the Establishment of Management Committees in the State-Owned and Public-Owned Factories." In the early years of the founding of the People's Republic, such a system was introduced in most of the state-owned and public-owned enterprises throughout the country. The Eighth National Party Congress held in 1956 declared that the system of workers' congresses under the leadership of the Party Central Committee should be adopted, while the system of factory directors bearing responsibility under the leadership of the Party Central Committee is enforced. In March 1957, the character, function and terms of reference of the workers' congresses were defined by the Party Central Committee, and thus the workers' conference, an advisory body, developed into the workers' congress, an organ of power.

In the "Draft Regulations Regarding Functions of State-Owned Industrial Enterprises" worked out in 1961, there is a chapter on workers' congresses. Trade unions have done a great deal to safeguard the democratic rights that are due workers and staff as masters of the enterprises and in supporting and helping them to take part in the management of the enterprises. In this they have gained considerable experience, even though there have been forward and backward steps.

After the downfall of the Gang of Four, the Party Central Committee and the State Council attached great importance to the rights of workers to be the masters of their enterprises. They reiterated that democratic management should be consolidated and the system of workers' congresses under the leadership of the Party Central Committee should be practiced by all enterprises without exception. Trade unions at all levels have made great efforts to restore and carry out this system.

Practice over a number of years shows that the system of workers' congresses under the leadership of the Party committee is fundamental to our socialist enterprise. The workers' congress is a basic form of democratic management of enterprise and an organ of power in which the workers and staff manage the enterprise and supervise the cadres. Under the guidance of the state plan and within the limits of the power of self-management of enterprise laid down by law, it has the right to make decisions on important issues concerning production, management and working conditions, wages, rewards and welfare. It has the right to elect and dismiss leading personnel of the enterprise and to recommend them to higher authorities for appointment or removal. It also has the right to examine and supervise the work of the leading personnel and ascertain that they carry out the resolutions adopted by the workers' congress.

As a working body of the workers' congress, the trade unions exercise the following main functions and powers: (1) to organize the election of the workers' representatives to the congress; (2) to solicit opinions from among the masses; (3) to prepare the convening of the congress; (4) to supervise and check up on the implementation of the resolutions adopted by the congress; (5) to organize and guide the regular activities of the workers' representatives; (6) to handle the complaints of the workers and staff members; and (7) to deal with other matters referred to by the congress.

Gratifying progress has been achieved in introducing the system of workers' congresses in China's enterprises over the last few years. By the end of June 1980, the system of workers' congresses was restored and established in more than 36,000 basic units, among which about 33,000 are industrial and mining enterprises and over 2,400 are cultural, health and educational institutions. A number of enterprises and undertakings carried out on a trial basis the democratic election of leading personnel at the grassroots level. This was a major development in the democratic management of enterprises.

Statistics show that in the first half of 1980, group and section chiefs of 33,225 basic units, workshop heads of 11,186 basic units and directors or managers of 965 enterprises were elected. In the country as a whole, however, the system of workers' congresses developed in an uneven way, with the large and medium-sized enterprises in industrial cities having always set up the congress.

The system of workers' congresses has yielded good results and played a remarkable role whenever it has been practiced properly. In bringing workers and staff together to discuss the important issues relating to production and management, the workers' congress has greatly enhanced their sense of responsibility and effectively boosted production. It has strengthened the ties between the cadres and the masses and consolidated unity and stability. It has also helped the leadership to solve the day-to-day problems of great concern to workers, which had remained unsolved for a long time, such as the allocation of housing, the employment of workers' grown-up children, etc. Some enterprises refer these problems to the workers' congress for discussion and a decision, and as a rule they are solved satisfactorily.

Labour Protection. The trade unions have improved their work in labour protection and the protection of women workers in order to reduce accidents, guarantee the health and safety of the workers and staff and promote safety in production. For years, the trade unions at all levels, under the leadership of the party and in coordination with the departments concerned, have done much to implement the party's policies and the government's laws and decrees in regard to labour protection, and all this has played a positive role in urging the enterprises to ensure labour safety and safety in production. By 1957, the unsafe and unhealthy situation left over by the old society was fundamentally changed, and accidents causing injuries and death were reduced to the lowest level in the history of China. As a result, production made much headway.

Because labour protection was completely ignored during the "cultural revolution," safety in production suffered a great setback and accidents rose sharply year after year during that period. After the downfall of the Gang of Four, and in the course of restoration and development of production, the party and the government have time and again emphasized the importance of safety in production.

The Third National Trade Union Conference on Labour Protection, which was convened by the ACFTU in June 1980, decided to further implement the important directives of the Party Central Committee and the State Council on labour protection. The conference urged that trade union work in regard to labour protection of the masses be improved, and that the unions help and supervise the management of enterprises, in coordination with related departments, in taking effective measures to sharply reduce accidents and eliminate hazards caused by dust and toxic pollutants. These measures will ensure safety in production and further the smooth advance of the Four Modernizations.

After the Bohai No. 2 oil rig (operated by the Oceanic Petroleum Exploration Bureau of the Ministry of Petroleum Industry) capsized because of violations of safety rules, the ACFTU and other departments concerned formed a joint investigation group to study the case and report its conclusion to the Party Central Committee and the State Council. The State Council's findings on the accident were made public on August 25, 1980. Those directly responsible for the disaster were punished according to the criminal law and given administrative penalties. Since the decision of the State Council on the accident was implemented, serious accidents leading to injuries and deaths have been notably reduced, and safety in production and labour protection for the masses have made remarkable progress.

In 1980, the number of deaths and injuries due to industrial accidents dropped by 11% and 7.2%, respectively, compared with 1979. In the coal industry, the number of deaths dropped by 21.4% from 1979 and was the lowest since the founding of the People's Republic. Encouraging results — ideological, organizational and professional — have been obtained in the labour protection work carried on by the trade unions. At present, trade union councils in 18 provinces, municipalities and autonomous regions and in 40 cities directly under the provincial governments have restored and established labour protection working committees; and some 500,000 labour protection inspectors are working in production groups. The restoration and development of labour protection for the masses has played a large role in reducing accidents and improving labour and working conditions.

Women Workers. The trade unions at all levels also have strengthened the protection of women workers. Departments of women workers of the trade unions throughout the country, in coordination with the departments concerned, made a study of the labour protection of women workers in 1980 and put forward positive suggestions to the governments at different levels. With the approval of the provincial and municipal governments, measures and regulations for the protection of women workers have been implemented in the basic units.

For the protection of women workers, some enterprises have adopted measures as shorter working hours, regular rotation on different jobs, transfer of pregnant or breast-feeding workers to other jobs and transfer of women workers from jobs that involve excessively heavy manual labour. Rapid progress has been made in the work of providing more facilities for protecting women workers at various localities. According to incomplete statistics from Hubei, Liaoning, Jilin, Beijing, Shanghai and Tianjin, 1,513 clinics for women workers were established or restored in 1980. With the help and support of the trade unions, the health protection departments conduct regular examinations for gynaecological diseases and provide prompt treatment. All these measures have improved the health of women workers and won their approbation.

Workers' Well-Being. The trade unions look after the well-being of the workers and staff so as to help them with their personal and family problems. After the fall of the Gang of Four, the party and government took a series of measures to improve the well-being of the workers and staff. Apart from wage increases for more than 75% of the workers and staff throughout the country, the bonus system has been introduced and more people have been employed. As a result, there has been a notable increase — of nearly 80 yuan in 1980 as compared with 1979 — in the annual income of the workers and staff in the state-owned enterprises.

Nine million people in cities and towns were given jobs in 1979, and another seven million were employed in 1980. Housing with a total floor space of more than 78 million sq. m. was completed in cities and towns in 1980, an increase of more than 25% over 1979. Trade union organizations also help the workers and staff build houses with their own money or with state subsidies. In 1979, 1,580 households of workers, staff and residents in Fuzhou, Fujian Province, built their own houses (totalling 87,870 sq. m. of floor space) with state subsidies.

While helping the workers and staff to understand the difficulties of the government and to realize that their livelihood can be improved only gradually on the basis of expanded production, the trade unions urged and helped management to improve the living conditions of the workers and staff. They opposed the bureaucrats' indifference to the well-being of the masses and their infringement upon the immediate interests of the workers and staff.

Trade union organizations at all levels have spared no effort to help improve the education of teenagers and children and to see that junior middle schools, primary schools, nurseries, breast-feeding rooms and other welfare facilities are well managed. In June 1980, there were 112,863 kindergartens, nurseries and breast-feeding rooms operated by industrial enterprises, with a total enrollment of 3,250,000 — an increase of 350,000 over 1979, 2,350,000 over 1964 and 3,200,000 over 1952. At present, in most parts of the country, more than 60% of babies are cared for in nurseries; in Shanghai, Jiangxi Province and Gansu Province the figure is no less than 70%.

The trade unions are in charge of labour insurance in the enterprises and the sanatoriums for the workers and staff, and they have paid great attention to administering this work well. The sanatoriums run by the trade unions have been gradually restored in recent years. In June 1980, the local trade unions operated a total of 157 sanatoriums and rest homes, with more than 24,000 beds. In addition, factories, mines and other basic units operated 634 sanatoriums and rest homes with 20,668 beds.

Mobilizing the masses and pooling their resources to solve some of their living problems has been a fine tradition and successful experience of our trade unions. By June 1980, no less than 255,000 units at the grassroots level had set up mutual-aid savings funds with a total membership of more than 35,132,000 workers and staff. Total deposits amounted to 960 million yuan, and more than 32,800,000 people received loans for them.

Labour mutual-aid activity has made much headway among the masses. Mutual aid among the workers and staff in many places has become a common practice in such activities as building and repairing houses, moving homes, helping with domestic chores, holding wedding parties, making funeral arrangements, nursing the sick, looking after orphans and mediating disputes.

Education. The trade unions have stepped up the ideological, political, cultural and technical education among the workers and staff for the purpose of raising their political consciousness and cultural and technical levels so that they can contribute to the Four Modernizations.

There were nearly 50 million workers and staff in 1965, and the number surpassed 100 million in 1980. The veteran workers who entered factories before Liberation or in the early years after Liberation are not many and few of them are in the vanguard of production. The majority of workers today started working in the 1970's. The advantage of this change in the composition of workers and staff is that today's contingent is young and has more education, but the disadvantage is that the younger workers lack strict training.

A survey of 20 million workers and staff at the end of 1979 showed that 80% of them had an educational level below that of a junior middle school graduate, and 7.8% of them were either illiterate or semi-literate. Half of the workers and staff in the country started to work after the "cultural revolution" began, and their educational level is generally below that required by formal schooling. Most of the workers are below Grade 3, and most of the managerial personnel are lacking in knowledge of modern enterprise management. It is highly important, therefore, that we strengthen the educational work among the workers and staff in general, and the young in particular.

The trade unions consider the ideological and political education of the workers and staff to be an important task. Workers are taught to realize that they are the masters of the state and the enterprises and to understand that the interests of the state, the enterprises and the individuals coincide, as do the long-term and immediate interests of the working class.

Ideological and political education consists of education on the current situation and tasks, on the fine tradition of the working class, on revolutionary ideals, on morality and on the communist outlook on life. Since the Third Plenary Session of the 11th Central Committee of the Communist Party, the trade unions have in various ways and through different channels propagated and publicized the principles and policies of the party, especially the significance of upholding socialism, the dictatorship of the proletariat, the leadership of the Communist Party and Marxism-Leninism-Mao Zedong Thought. This has raised the political consciousness of the workers and staff, strengthened their confidence in the socialist road and further stirred their enthusiasm to contribute to the Four Modernizations.

In carrying out the ideological and political work, many trade union organizations have commended good people and good deeds; fostered the spirit of uprightness and resisted unhealthy practices and noxious tendencies; and conducted thorough and painstaking ideological work among veteran, as well as young workers, women workers and intellectuals in light of their particular characteristics. The trade unions mobilized and organized their cadres and activists to make home visits and to have confidential talks with workers to help solve their personal problems. At present, emphasis is being placed on the ideological education among young workers — to help the advanced make further progress and the less advanced to become advanced.

Recreation and Sports. Trade unions at various levels make full use of all available facilities to draw the workers and staff into recreational and sports activities so as to enrich their leisure-time life and education. Trade unions at various levels have restored some of the workers' cultural palaces and clubs and constructed some new ones. In 1950, there were only 16 cultural palaces in the country. By the end of June 1980, 1,505 cultural palaces and clubs were restored and set up by county and municipal trade union councils and industrial unions, 179 more than in 1979. In 1950 there were only 773 cultural clubs. In 1980, there were more than 13,200 clubs run by industrial enterprises, an increase of about 2,000 over 1979.

In addition, county and municipal trade union councils and industrial unions have set up 2,898 libraries, 678 more than in 1963. Their collections total 13 million volumes. More than 105,000 libraries, with more than 211 million volumes, are run by the grassroots trade unions, representing an increase of 39,000 libraries over 1979 and 64,000 over 1963. In 1950, there were only 360 libraries run by the basic units and trade unions. A total of 1,446 film projection teams are run by county and municipal trade union councils and industrial unions below the provincial level, while another 18,500 are run by grassroots trade unions. At present, there are more than 15,700 workers' amateur troupes and groups, with 330,000 participants, and more than 8,800 workers' literary and artistic creation groups, with 53,300 members.

The basic units have more than 3,600 gymnasiums or stadiums and have established 8,800 sports associations and 208,000 sports teams with 2,196,000 workers taking part. In the first half of 1980, more than 70,000 basic units held 298,000 sports events, with 6,524,000 people participating. The county and municipal trade union councils and industrial unions below the provincial level set up 213 gymnasiums and stadiums and organized more than 10,000 spare-time sports teams with 107,000 athletes, and held over 20,000 competitions in which 1,100,000 people took part.

Spare-Time Education. In order to meet the needs of the Four Modernizations and the demands of the workers and staff, trade unions at all levels, in cooperation with the departments concerned, have made great efforts to restore and develop spare-time education. At the end of June 1980, more than 72,200 spare-time schools for workers and staff members had been organized throughout the country, an increase of 9,300 as compared with 1979. Of these, over 68,000 schools are run by basic units, an increase of 7,000 over 1979, and 1,887 are spare-time colleges including 310 run either by the municipal and county trade union councils or by the industrial trade unions below the provincial level.

More than 8,334,000 workers and staff members attended spare-time schools at different levels, and 4,954,000 attended short-term technical training classes of various kinds. Thus, total enrollment amounted to some 13,299,000 — 3,000,000 more than in 1979 and 9,000,000 more than in 1965. In 1949, the year of the founding of the People's Republic, only 276,000 workers and staff attended spare-time courses throughout the country. A large number of skilled workers and qualified technicians have since been trained by these schools.

Organizational Development. With the restoration and development of trade union activities, the reconstruction of trade union organizations is gradually being stepped up. By the end of 1980, there were 18 national industrial trade unions: the Metallurgical Workers' Trade Union, the Machine-Building Workers' Trade Union, the Chemical Workers' Trade Union, the Coal Miners' Trade Union, the Petroleum Workers' Trade Union, the Water Conservancy and Electricity Workers' Trade Union, the Textile Workers' Trade Union, the Light Industry Workers' Trade Union, the Railway Workers' Trade Union, the Road Transport Workers' Trade Union, the Seamen's Trade Union, the Postal and Telecommunications Workers' Trade Union, the Building Workers' Trade Union, the Geological Workers' Trade Union, the Agricultural and Forestry Workers' Trade Union, the Financial and Commercial Workers' Trade Union, the Educational Workers' Trade Union and the National Defence Industry Workers' Trade Union. The banks and the ministries of machine-building have separate trade union organizations. All the trade union councils in 29 provinces (except Taiwan Province), autonomous regions and municipalities directly under the central government have been restored.

Both primary trade union organizations and union membership have increased. In June 1980, there were more than 376,000 primary trade union organizations across the country — an increase of over 46,000 as compared with that of a year earlier, 190,000 more than in 1964 and 169,000 more than in 1952. There were 449,000 trade union organizations at the workshop level, an increase of 8,000 over 1979; and more than 4,541,000 trade union groups, an increase of 701,000 over 1979.

In the basic units where trade union organizations are established there are in all 61,160,000 union members out of 74,480,000 workers and staff, i.e., 82.1% of the workers and staff members are organized. The membership rose by 9,690,000 over June 1979, an 18.8% increase and nearly three times the number in 1964. In 1949, union membership was only 2,374,000 in the whole country.

The number of trade union cadres has also increased. In June 1980, there were 243,000 full-time trade union cadres throughout the country, an increase of 22,000 over 1979 and nearly three times the number in 1964. They included 190,000 cadres of primary trade unions, 26,100 cadres in county trade union councils or in councils at higher levels, over 15,100 cadres in the industrial (bureau) trade unions and more than 11,700 cadres in trade unions at the company level.

The number of trade union activists has grown considerably. At the end of June 1980, the number of activists in primary trade union organizations throughout the country reached 7,700,000, an increase of 1,730,000 or 28.9% over the number a year earlier and 3,420,000 more than in 1964. In 1952, there were only 1,696,000 trade union activists.

The training of trade union cadres is also being improved. Throughout the country, 31 trade union cadres' schools have been restored or set up by provincial and municipal trade union councils, and more than 12,000 trade union cadres were trained in the first half of 1980. In addition, 27,000 trade union organizations all over the country held various kinds of short-term training classes on trade union work in which 1,234,000 trade union cadres and activists were trained.

Shortly before the Ninth National Congress of Chinese Trade Unions, the All-China Federation of Trade Unions resumed the publication of the *Workers' Daily*. Its circulation increased sharply: 977,000 copies in early 1979, 1,391,000 copies in early 1980 and 1,768,000 copies in early 1981, more than five times that on the eve of the "cultural revolution."

International Ties. Chinese trade unions have resumed and expanded friendly ties with trade union organizations in 86 countries on all continents. The international liaison work of trade unions serves the development and expansion of the international united front to help the fight against hegemonism and for the needs of the Four Modernizations.

The Task Ahead. Although trade union activities in our country have gradually resumed and have made progress in recent years, trade union work still falls behind the requirements of the party and the needs of the workers and staff members. We should sum up our experience, add to the achievements, overcome shortcomings and organize and mobilize the working class throughout the country to build China into a democratic and civilized modern socialist nation.

50. CHINA'S CULTURAL ACHIEVEMENTS IN 1980
By Cui Yongsheng
Policy Research Department, Ministry of Culture

In accordance with the requirements for the readjustment, restructuring, consolidation and improvement of the national economy, following the directive that literature and art should serve the people and socialism and in implementation of the principles of "let a hundred flowers blossom and a hundred schools of thought contend," "make the past serve the present and foreign things serve China," "weed out the old to bring forth the new," China has in 1980 achieved considerable success in promoting and developing literary and artistic production, in training professionals in culture and art and in reorganizing various cultural establishments. All this has been done with a view to meeting the needs of the people and modernizing the country.

To show the progress that has been made in cultural work in 1980, as compared with that of the past 30 years, it is necessary to review briefly the development of cultural establishments since the founding of New China.

I. Laying New Foundations for Cultural Development

China has an ancient civilisation and a rich cultural legacy. In modern times, however, especially in the semi-feudal and semi-colonial conditions of old China, cultural establishments were few and extremely backward. Before 1949, there were very few film studios, professional cultural and art organizations, colleges and schools of art, public libraries, theatres or cinemas. Traditional art was not supported by the government. Traditional opera, which had occupied a major place in the cultural life of the people, was in a state of decline. The artists of traditional opera had no secure means of livelihood and enjoyed a very low social status. The culture and art of the minority nationalities was in an even worse state, near to extinction. The cultural life of the masses, especially those living in the countryside and mountainous regions, and in the regions inhabited by the minority nationalities, was extremely poor.

In the years after the "May Fourth Movement," there was a surge of revolutionary and progressive literature and art under the leadership of the Communist Party of China, but it could not be sustained because of Kuomintang suppression. In the revolutionary bases and liberated areas, cultural activities were hampered by wartime conditions; the only professional cultural activities that could be carried on took the form of song-and-dance ensembles or teams.

With the founding of New China in 1949, culture and the arts entered a new historical period of development under the leadership of the Communist Party of China and the People's Government and received the support of leading comrades in the Party Central Committee and State Council.

After the three years of rehabilitation and development of the national economy immediately after Liberation, China adopted its First Five-Year Plan. During the period from 1953 to 1957, a large number of cultural establishments were set up. By the end of 1957, there were a total of 11 film studios — 6 of them producing feature films and the rest producing science and educational films, animated cartoons and newsreels. Film projection units in 1957 numbered 9,965, more than four times the number in 1952. Most of the new units consisted of film clubs in factories and mines and mobile film projection teams in the countryside. Film clubs had increased from 426 in late 1952 to 2,243 in 1957, while mobile projection teams had increased from 1,113 to 6,692 in the same period. Newly organised professional troupes performing traditional operas, modern dramas and operas, folk songs and folk dances, acrobatics, shadow plays, puppet shows, ballets and symphonies totaled 2,884, about 800 more than in 1952. The number of theatres increased from 823 in 1952 to 2,372 in 1957. Art education developed rapidly with the establishment of 17 colleges of art.

With the development of popular culture, the country had 400 public libraries, 39 art galleries (engaged mainly in collecting and selectively introducing folk art and in directing the recreational activities of the masses), 2,748 cultural centres and 2,417 cultural stations which engaged mainly in popularizing culture, art and science in localities below the county level and in organizing spare-time cultural and artistic activities for the masses. At mines and factories throughout the country, spare-time clubs and reading rooms were opened. And in the minority nationality regions, professional organizations of art and culture, performing troupes and facilities were set up.

With the cooperation of the departments of machine-building, chemistry and electrical engineering, production of art and film equipment became possible. In addition, factories for the manufacture of film and film machinery, dye-transforming factories, scenery equipment factories and factories for making stage settings were constructed.

Following the guidelines put forward by Comrade Mao Zedong in his speech at the Yan'an Forum on Literature and Art, and in accordance with the principles of "let a hundred flowers blossom and a hundred schools of thought contend" and "weed out the old to bring forth the new," literature and art flourished. Writers and artists produced many excellent works which attempted to depict the new era and the new life and struggle of the people. The traditional arts of the minority nationalities began to thrive as they had never done before. Performing troupes for all types of opera and drama were set up. Through rewriting and restructuring, thousands of operas and plays discarded the dross of feudalism and incorporated the essence of democracy. The folktales, folk art, folk songs and dances of the minority nationalities were collected and promoted. The social status and the standard of living of writers and artists were greatly improved and older writers, artists and artisans were accorded the respect due them.

The achievements made in the first eight years after Liberation, and especially during the period of the First Five-Year Plan, laid a solid foundation for the development of cultural work in our socialist country.

During the Second Five-Year Plan, which started in 1958, the mistakes of the "Great Leap Forward" followed by three years of natural disasters put a brake on this work. With the exception of art education and film projection units, there was relatively little development of cultural facilities.

However, the quality of various works of literature and art produced for the 10th anniversary of the founding of New China in 1959 showed vast improvement. In that year, 82 feature films were presented and traditional opera troupes put on many performaces of operas dealing with modern social life as well as of newly written historical plays.

With the year-by-year improvement of the economic situation after 1962, there came a new growth of cultural establishments. By late 1965 there were 3,564 threatrical troupes of various kinds, 16 film studios, 20,263 film projection units, 22 colleges of art, 59 secondary art schools and over 1,000 art students. In the whole country there were 577 public libraries, 62 art galleries, 2,621 cultural centres, 2,087 cultural stations, 2,524 theatres and 2,528 cinemas. A network of film studios, colleges and schools of art and professional theatrical troupes of all kinds was basically in place.

Unfortunately, just as these cultural establishments were ready to develop further, the "cultural revolution" began. From the summer of 1966 to the autumn of 1976, the country's cultural establishments were severely damaged by the counter-revolutionary cliques of Lin Biao and Jiang Qing. Fabricating charges of "a sinister line of literature and art" and "revisionism," they attempted to write off at one stroke all the cultural achievements of the 17 years after Liberation.

During these years, writers and artists were cruelly persecuted, all the fine works of ancient and modern and Chinese and foreign writers and artists were banned and most theatrical troupes were disbanded. Colleges and schools of art, public art galleries and research institutes in the arts were closed down. Many theatres throughout the country were deserted. Numerous local cultural organs, such as cultural centres, cultural stations and libraries, saw their work disrupted; some ceased to exist except in name. As a result, socialist culture and art in China suffered a severe setback.

The perverse acts of the Lin Biao and Jiang Qing counter-revolutionary cliques in the political, economic and cultural spheres ultimately led to their own downfall. In October 1976, the Central Committee of the Chinese Communist Party, acting on the wishes of the people, smashed the Jing Qing counter-revolutionary clique. Correct party policies with respect to literature and art and artists were gradually restored and implemented.

Cultural establishments of various kinds soon reopened and resumed their work. In late 1978, the Third Plenary Session of the 11th Central Committee of the Chinese Communist Party decided to shift the focus of the work of the party and the country to the building of a modern socialist country. Starting in 1979, China embarked on a new period of socialist modernization. The same was true of literature and art.

II. The Achievements of 1980

By 1980, cultural activity had not only resumed its pre-"cultural revolution" level but had also extended to new fields. In 1980 the country boasted 17 film studios (11 of which were producing feature films), 125,000 film projection units (over six times the 1965 figure or twice as many as in 1976); 3,533 theatrical troupes of all kinds (68 more than in 1965); over 2,500 indoor theatres and clubs open to the public, 109 schools of art (of which 26 were colleges of art and 83 were secondary art schools, with a total enrollment of over 21,000), an increase of 28 over 1965. Art schools revised their teaching plans and programmes for various subjects and courses, compiled new teaching materials, established a stable teaching schedule, livened up the atmosphere of academic discussion and improved the quality of teaching. There were 1,732 public libraries in the whole country, three times as many as in 1965.

Culture for the Masses. There were also new developments in the cultural activities for the masses. To modernize agriculture in an all-around way it is very important and highly necessary to raise the level of cultural work in the countryside, to develop cultural establishments and to liven up the cultural life of China's 800 million peasants. In 1980, professional theatrical troupes of all kinds toured the countryside to give over 500,000 performances. Cultural organizations serving the countryside included 13 slide-producing centres, 218 public art galleries, 2,912 cultural centres and more than 25,000 commune-run cultural stations. 76,000 commune-run film projection teams and over 90,000 amateur theatrical troupes.

In 1980, in accordance with the instructions of the Party Central Committee to build up the small towns of the country into political, economic and cultural centres, a number of communes and towns strengthened their cultural offerings with the help of the collective economy. In these localities there were already some cultural organizations and facilities, such as cinemas, theatres, cultural centres, libraries and reading rooms. They served as multiple-purpose centres: educating peasants in socialist ideology and morality, popularizing knowledge of agricultural science and technology, organizing cultural and theatrical activities of all kinds and raising the general cultural level of the countryside. Cultural activities in the countryside became quite lively and were much appreciated by the peasants, especially by the young.

To encourage literary and artistic activities among the masses, many literary and art magazines were published; these publications promoted the exchange of ideas about the organization of cultural activities and made accessible to the masses a variety of short, vivid and popular writings on literature and art.

Professional Training. The training of professional writers, artists and artisans was improved and expanded. In 1980, there were in all 800,000 people working in various areas of culture and art. During the 10 catastrophic years of the "cultural revolution," writers and artists were forced to abandon their professions and were deprived of the right to work. Some young people who were chosen from among the ranks of educated youth for cultural work never received formal training and lacked professional knowledge and fundamental skills. They must be given professional training if we are to improve artistic quality and raise levels of artistic creativity and performance.

Since the beginning of 1981, cultural organizations at all levels, federations of literature, art circles, art schools and theatrical troupes have begun to offer short training courses, classes and professional seminars in various forms of artistic creation, such as art collecting, conducting, performing, the construction of Chinese musical instruments, scenery design and so forth. In addition, some leading comrades in charge of cultural work were sent to study in party schools. Cultural departments in many provinces, municipalities and autonomous regions have reinstated schools for educating cadres in culture and art and have trained, by turns, a number of professional workers and cadres from theatrical troupes, art galleries, cultural centres and film projection teams and organized them for professional study. Some organizations, such as film studios and theatrical companies, sponsored seminars and research groups to broaden their members' knowledge and to encourage them to learn from each other for common progress. Some colleges and schools of art also held special classes to provide the minorities with professional training in the arts.

A Cultural Renaissance. Literary and artistic work in China is now thriving as it has never done before. The guidelines adopted by the Third Plenary Session of the 11th Central Committee of the Party and the discussions on "practice as the only criteria for examining truth" gave great impetus to ideological emancipation in the cultural field and to the implementation of the principle of "let a hundred flowers blossom and a hundred schools of thought contend." The result has been a renaissance of the arts.

In 1980, over 90 novels were published, three times the number published in 1959, which held the previous record for the number of novels produced. Incomplete statistics compiled by more than 40 leading publishing houses at central and provincial levels show that over 130 novelettes and 2,400 short stories were published in 1980, far more than in any previous year. The number of films produced in 1980 was 82, including feature films and stage art films. Both the quality and the quantity of animated cartoons, documentaries and newsreels were remarkably by comparison with other years.

The 30th anniversary of the founding of the People's Republic in 1979 was marked by unparalleled achievements in the creation and performance of modern operas, traditional operas, dramas, songs and dances. A number of new modern operas added excitement to the field of drama, while traditional opera was infused with new vitality. Some excellent modern plays were created and staged following the restoration of the principle "develop the three dramas simultaneously" — the three being traditional drama, newly compiled historical drama and modern drama.

In 1980, the leading magazines on literature and art published by central and local governments carried selections from 43 new, revised or rearranged scripts; of these, 19 were modern dramas, 8 were newly compiled historical dramas and 16 were revised traditional dramas. More than 20 of these plays were widely staged by local theatrical troupes. Some provinces, municipalities and autonomous regions jointly organized performances of modern dramas.

In music, the number of compositions increased and the quality improved. There was also progress in the field of dance. At the First National Dance Competition held in Dalian in 1980, 46 works (including solo dances and dances for two and for three people) received prizes for choreography and performance, 26 won prizes for music composition and 72 dancers were awarded prizes for artistry.

Painting and drawing also flourished. Since the beginning of 1980, 32 major exhibitions — not including exhibitions of works by artists who are no longer alive — have been sponsored by the National Art Gallery. The works on exhibit totalled over 10,000.

Problems and Shortcomings. There were some shortcomings in the new works of literature and art. For example, the range of subjects treated was narrow; writers tended to descend "like a swarm of bees" on the same few subjects. The forms of artistic expression were nearly all the same and the themes of some dramas were not satisfactory.

On the whole, however, the new works tried to restore and continue the realistic tradition of socialist literature, to widen the scope and improve the content of dramatic works, to express the aspirations, concerns and wishes of the masses, to raise and answer timely questions about actual life and to explore new forms of artistic expression.

Arts of the Minority Nationalities. The year 1980 also saw important progress in the literature and art of China's minorities. In 1979, the State Council had approved the establishment of a number of film studios in the autonomous regions of Inner Mongolia, Xinjiang and Guangxi. These began to produce films in 1980. In the regions inhabited by minority nationalities, there were 18,556 film projection units (of which 17,872 were mobile teams) and 603 professional theatrical troupes of various kinds. Some excellent operas by the minority nationalities, which had not been seen for years, were presented. These included traditional operas of the Tibetan, Bai, Dai and Uygur nationalities. A number of minority nationalities, such as the Mongolians, the Hui, the Tibetans and the Tu, staged new dance dramas and song-and-dance dramas based on their own traditions. The wealth of new dramas produced in 1980 demonstrated that the artistic creativity of our minority nationalities is expanding and that the level of professional skill has risen markedly.

The highlight of the celebration of the 31st anniversary of the founding of the People's Republic in 1980 was a national drama festival which was hailed as one of the most significant cultural events since the Jiang Qing counter-revolutionary clique was smashed. A total of 1,196 professional and amateur artists from 55 minority nationalities took part in this month-long festival, which included 21 programmes comprising 473 song-and-dance numbers, popular entertainment acts and folk operas. The entire festival was recorded and videotaped and some of the programmes were filmed. The largest festival organized since 1949, it demonstrated vividly the recent achievements made in restoring and developing the cultural traditions of the minority nationalities.

Research in the Arts. The research institutes specializing in the theory of literature and art have been restored; there are now more than 30 such bodies in the whole country. The China National Research Academy of Art (under the Ministry of Culture) completed a number of works and theses dealing with the history of Chinese literature and art and art documentation. The Research Institute of Traditional Opera recorded and videotaped 238 operas, representing 45 different types of local operas. Local research organizations also produced dozens of special works and theses on the history of literature; some have been published and others will soon be published.

For the National Conference on Science and Technology, cultural workers made some contributions to the research on scientific and technological subjects. Among the 39 projects that received awards were the "Direct Current Outdoor Scenery Lamp with Dysprosium-Holmium Filament," "New Technique of Dye Transfer Process

— Sound Track Produced with Silverless Dyestuff," and "HF — A Silver-Extracting Technique." These inventions and techniques helped to preserve traditional musical instruments and to reduce health hazards for actors. Progress was also made in simplifying stage scenery, lighting and props so as to make it easier for travelling theatrical troupes to give performances in the countryside and mountainous regions. Some of these modifications have already been introduced with gratifying artistic and economic results.

III. Current Policies and Problems

The cultural achievements of 1980 were made possible by many factors. The major factors were:

1. *The Party Central Committee improved and strengthened its leadership role in literature and the arts and gave more effective ideological guidance in these areas.* Deng Xiaoping's congratulatory speech at the Fourth National Congress of Literature and Art, held in early 1980, was followed by a long and important speech by Hu Yaobang, then a member of the Political Bureau of the Party Central Committee and Head of the Central Committee's Propaganda Department. Comrade Hu's speech dealt with the creation of dramatic works. He gave a lengthy exposition on the current state of literature and the arts and the fundamental problems concerning literary and artistic creation. The congress not only provided ideological guidance but also improved and strengthened the party's leadership in literature and the arts. It was followed by a meeting of the heads of the provincial cultural departments at which the guidelines of the Third Plenary Session of the 11th Central Committee of the CPC and the congratulatory speech of Comrade Deng Xiaoping, as well as the main points of Comrade Hu Yaobang's speech, were studied and arrangements were made to implement the principles of readjustment, restructuring, consolidation and improvement in cultural institutions.

Later, other meetings were held: the National Working Conference of Compilers of Literary Magazines, the Forum on Music Work, the Working Conference on Repertoires of Traditional Operas, the Forum on Literary Creation for Minority Nationalities and on Music and Dance. These conferences and forums were actually continuations of the 1980 forum on literature and art.

2. *The system governing examination and approval of film and play scripts was reformed.* The power to examine and approve artistic productions was handed over to those who produce art. This aroused the enthusiasm, creativity and initiative of writers and artists and further emancipated the productive forces of art.

Unresolved Problems. To develop into a modern, powerful, socialist country, we must not only attain a high level of material well-being, but also high socialist, intellectual standards. At present there is still a large gap between the quality and scope of our cultural achievements and the requirements of the era and of the people. Many problems remain to be solved.

The quality and quantity of artistic creation still fails to meet the growing need of the people for a richer cultural life. The range of subjects of theatrical works is narrow and there are not enough works reflecting the construction of a modern socialist country and describing the experience of workers, peasants, soliders and children. Cultural facilities in general fall short of what the people need for a rich cultural life; they are even less adequate in vast areas of the countryside, in the border regions and the regions inhabited by minority peoples.

Because we failed to follow standard practices for art production and cultural activities, many problems appeared in the operation and management of cultural organizations. Some of the problems are: (1) inadequate rules and regulations in management; (2) overlapping units of artistic production; (3) irrational staff size, with some organizations overstaffed. Because of these problems, the enthusiasm and creativity of the workers in literature and art cannot be brought into full play. These problems must be solved through further readjustment.

At present, the magnificent cause of building a modern socialist country is attracting and inspiring a large number of writers and artists. Guided by the correct ideological, political and organizational line adopted at the Third Plenary Session of the 11th Central Committee of the party and by the party's principles and policies on literature and art, China's new culture and art will surely develop more fully in the course of building a modern socialist country.

51. PUBLISHING IN CHINA
By the Editorial Department,
Chinese Publications Yearbook

China is the country where paper-making and the art of printing were invented. Thanks to the early start of printing and publishing, our splendid ancient culture has been preserved, making a great contribution to human civilization. However, the development of publishing in China was very slow, due to the long centuries of feudal rule. Later, during the semi-feudal and semi-colonial period, China's publishing activities still lagged behind those of some developed capitalist countries. It was only the great victory of the new democratic revolution and the founding of New China that opened up broad prospects for the development of our publishing industry.

I. Development of Publishing Since 1949

After the establishment of the People's Republic of China in 1949, the Central People's Government set up a state organ to direct and manage the work of publication and began to establish a network of publishing enterprises of a new socialist nature throughout the country.

In the past 31 years — except for the disastrous 10-year period during which the country as a whole suffered a historical retrogression — but particularly in the four years since the smashing of the Gang of Four, the publishing industry has advanced steadily in the direction of serving the people and serving socialism. For the purpose of reviewing the development of publishing in New China, we may divide the 31 years into the following stages:

1949-1952. In this period, publishing developed rapidly and achieved significant successes. In the early days after Liberation, the party and the government took a series of important measures for the development of publishing: (1) the lawful confiscation of the publishing industry of the reactionary Kuomintang government and bureaucrat-capitalists; (2) the unification of the Xinhua Bookstores, until then under decentralized management, into a national state-run publishing enterprise; (3) the establishment of the Central People's Publishing House and various provincial and municipal people's publishing houses, with all publishing work under the management of Xinhua Bookstores; (4) the setting up of Xinhua Printing Houses in various locales, with all printing work under the management of Xinhua Bookstores; and (5) the creation of a number of specialized publishing organizations.

When the task of rehabilitation of the national economy was completed at the end of 1952, there had already been considerable development in the publishing industry. In 1952, we published 13,692 titles, a 45% increase over the books published in 1936, the pre-Liberation year in which the largest number of books were published. The total number of copies published in 1952 was 785.66 million, an increase of 341% over 1936.

1953-1957. After the First Five-Year Plan was adopted in 1953, the following tasks were carried out: (1) the state-run publishing enterprises were developed and a great number of scientific and technical publishing houses were set up to meet the need of national economic construction; (2) the socialist transformation of the private publishing industry was in the main completed; (3) planning of publications was improved; (4) a series of unified rules and regulations were worked out for the publishing industry; (5) a network of book distribution centres in cities and rural areas was formed; and (6) the printing of books and periodicals was improved. The First Five-Year Plan called for a 54.2% increase in the number of books published as compared with 1952. This target was exceeded by a large margin in 1956. In fact, 28,773 books with a total of 1,784.37 million copies were published, representing an increase of 110% in numbers of books and a 127% increase in numbers of copies over the figures in 1952. Sales of books in 1956 came to 301.89 million yuan, 126.23% over sales in 1952. At the end of the First Five-Year Plan in 1957, the amount of paper used for printing books came to 4.13 million reams, as against 67,000 reams in 1950.

During 1953-57, the growth of publishing was demonstrated not only in the large number of books printed, but also in the increasing variety of titles and the improved quality of book production. In that period, 241 titles by Marx, Engels, Lenin and Stalin were published. The publication of the *Collected Works of Lenin* and the *Collected Works of Marx and Engels* was started in 1955 and 1956, respectively. Also published were the *Selected Works of Mao Zedong,* in three volumes. The large numbers of scholarly works and books on literature and art that were published reflected the lively academic activity and flourishing literary and artistic creativity which characterized this period. Other publications included the annotated *Collected Works of Lu Xun,* multi-volume editions of writings by Guo Moruo and Mao Dun and a good many new works all well-received by readers. In 1956, books on philosophy and the social sciences numbered 3,727; on literature and the arts, 9.372 — increases of 171% and 87%, respectively, over 1952.

Also published in 1956 were 8,698 scientific and technical books and 2,391 popular books, increases of 181% and 30.8%, respectively, over the books published in 1952. The publication of some Chinese classics and the translation and publication of foreign works saw remarkable success in those years, as did the publication of books for young people and children and books in minority nationality languages or foreign languages. In 1956, 484 different periodicals were printed, a increase of 36.7% over 1952.

1957-1965. During this period, the publication of works by Marx and Lenin was extensive. By 1959, all 39 volumes of the *Selected Works of Lenin* and the 19 volumes of the *Collected Works of Marx and Engels* had been published. In 1960 a new edition of the *Selected Works of Lenin* in four volumes was published, and in 1965 the four volumes of the *Selected Works of Marx and Engels* were printed. After publishing the fourth volume of the *Selected Works of Mao Zedong,* we published editions A and B of selections from his works. In 1958, the publication of the 10-volume annotated edition of the *Collected Works of Lu Xun* was completed.

This period also saw the publication of many good novels such as *Song of Youth, Red Cliff, Keep the Flag Flying* and *Builders of a New Life.* Before 1960, large numbers of academic writings were also published. For example, we published many selections, specialized articles and reference books on such subjects as the research methodology in the history of Chinese philosophy, problems of aesthetics and problems of formal logic. All of these works were widely discussed in academic circles at that time. We also published many teaching materials for liberal arts colleges and reading materials on common knowledge. In this period, the publication of periodicals also developed very rapidly. In 1964 alone, 856 different periodicals were printed, an increase of 76.86% over 1956.

During this period, publishing suffered severe setbacks as a result of the growing "Left" ideological trend. In the 1957 anti-rightist campaign, a large number of comrades who had offered well-meaning criticisms and positive proposals in regard to our work in publishing were, without any justification, labelled rightists. This campaign seriously dampened the enthusiasm of writers and workers in publishing. The attempt to effect a premature transition to communism during the period of the Great Leap Forward also carried over into publishing. We published a great number of pamhplets to publicize the "Three Red Banners," but these pamphlets were discarded as useless soon afterwards. Moreover, some effective regulations and procedures in the publishing industry were disrupted. As a result, the quality of books published then was far inferior to that of earlier books. In the campaign against "Right Opportunism" in 1959 and 1960, a number of worthy literary and artistic works and academic works were unjustly criticized, as were many writers and editors.

Because of the disturbances produced by the "Left" ideological trend, the policy of "let a hundred flowers blossom and a hundred schools of thought contend" (also known as the "Double Hundred" policy) could not be implemented. Academic works decreased and the trend toward "formulaism" and generalization in works of literature and art became ever more serious. The decline was reflected in the smaller number of new books printed. In 1965, we published only 20,143 new titles, 30% less than in 1965.

1966-1976. During the 10 years of turmoil of the "cultural revolution," Lin Biao and the Gang of Four attacked the work achieved in publishing during the first 17 years after Liberation. The industry was accused of being "the dictatorship of counter-revolutionaries" and the people working in publishing were labelled "basically bourgeois elements." Many publishing houses were disbanded and large numbers of splendid books were reviled as "feudalist, capitalist and revisionist poisonous weeds."

The decline in publishing may be seen in the following statistics: the number of new books dropped from 20,143 in 1965 to 11,055 at the beginning of the "cultural revolution" in 1966 and dropped further to 2,925 in 1967 (a mere 10% of the new books published in 1956). In subsequent years, a total of about 4,000 new books were published. It was only as a result of Comrade Zhou Enlai's exhortation in 1971 to publish more good books that the number of new books began to rise again. However, the pace was very slow because of sabotage by the Gang of Four. Between 1966 and 1976, the average number of new books published each year was 6,340, about 44% of the number published between 1950 and 1965.

Besides, a great number of the books published in the years 1966-1976 were really "poisonous weeds"; they served as vehicles for the

Gang of Four to manipulate public opinion and to unsurp supreme party leadership and state power. Moreover, some books were shoddy, published only "to suit the needs of the struggle" at that time. The publication of conspiratorial writings on literature and art and books with historical allusions ran rampant while worthy academic works and cultural and artistic creations were rarely seen. Books dealing with advanced science and technology and trends in contemporary academic thinking and the schools of thought in literature were almost non-existent.

Many books published in the 10 years of catastrophe not only exerted a pernicious political influence, but also confused right and wrong theories, thereby bringing about heavy economic losses. After the smashing of the Gang of Four in 1976, the sale of these books was stopped because of their erroneous content; they represented more than 200 million yuan worth of books, about one-third of the total sales of the "Xinhua Bookstore" in 1976.

II. A New Era in Publishing

In the period from 1977 to 1980, our publication work entered a new stage with the guideline of serving the people and serving socialsim.

Reformulation of Guidelines and Policies. The national forum on publishing held at the end of 1977 repudiated the two counter-revolutionary evaluations of workers in publishing imposed by the Gang of Four, and removed their spiritual shackles. After the Third Plenary Session of the Party's 11th Central Commttee, the workers continued to emancipate their thinking and criticize the pernicious influence of the ultra-"Left" line.

A national forum on publication work, held in Changsha at the end of 1979, further defined the fundamental tasks of publishing in the new stage. These tasks include: 1) to mobilize and organize writers and translators to create, edit and translate more works; 2) to publish books needed by the country and the people; 3) to propagate Marxism-Leninism and Mao Zedong Thought; 4) to disseminate and compile scientific and technical knowledge and achievements; 5) to enrich the people's cultural life and contribute to raising the scientific and cultural levels of the entire Chinese nation and to the realization for the Four Socialist Modernizations.

The 1980 national forum on publishing reviewed the publication work in the past few years and reaffirmed the necessity of upholding the principles and tasks defined of adhering to the guideline of "serving the people and serving socialism" and the "Double Hundred" policy as well as to the principle of "quality first." These forums held under the direct leadership of the Propaganda Department of the Party's Central Committee summed up ideological achievements and the lessons, both positive and negative, drawn from our work in the past 30 years and were tremendously important to the development of socialist publication work.

III. Publishing Activities in 1980

Expanded Facilities. The number of publishing, printing and distribution organizations has grown as a result of our efforts. By the end of 1980, there were 193 publishing houses (101 at the central level and 92 at the local level) with a total of 15,000 workers and staff members; 179 printing houses (for books exclusively) with a total of 120,000 workers and staff members. The annual capacity for printing books and periodicals has increased by 30 times as compared with that in the early years of Liberation. According to incomplete statistics, these printing houses increased their productivity over 1979 by the following measures: typesetting, 115.78%; stereotype printing, 111.45%; offset printing, 116.62%; bookbinding, 116.01%.

Distribution and Sales. By the end of 1980, there were 7,884 state-run bookstores throughout the country, employing a total of 58,945 workers and staff members. In addition, there were nearly 60,000 bookselling agents commissioned by the state-run commercial enterprises or by supply and marketing cooperatives; of this figure, 25,000 were located in the countryside. Total book sales in 1980 exceeded 1,500 million yuan, an increase of 22% over 1979 and of 96.33% over 1977 — the year following the end of the "cultural revolution."

From Table 1, we can see that the number of titles published in 1980 increased by 67.9% over 1977, and by 178.23% over 1971. The number of copies printed in 1980 hit an all-time high in our history of publishing, increasing by over 138.84% over the 1977 figure and 189.7% over the 1971 figure. It shows that publishing was restored and developed very rapidly after the smashing of the Gang of Four.

Major Categories. Of the 21,621 titles published in 1980, 15,669 were general works (an increase of 112.5% over 1977 and 318% over 1971); 3,440 were textbooks (an increase of 11.6% over 1977 and 79.5% over 1971); and 2,512 were illustrated books (an increase of 3.37% over 1977 and 19.76% over 1971).

Table 1. Volume of Books Published, 1971-80

Year	Titles	Copies (in millions)
1971	7,771	2,421.08
1977	12,886	3,308.04
1980	21,621	4,592.98

From Table 2 it would appear that the rate of increase of books on philosophy and the social sciences was not very high — new titles published in this category in 1980 were up only 13.2% as compared with 1971. However, the rate of increase registered for 1980 would certainly have been much higher if we had not had to publish those pamphlets to serve the political movements during the "cultural revolution."

The number of new books on literature and the arts in 1980 was 165.1% more than the number published in 1977 and 8.2 times that in 1971. This shows that after the smashing of the Gang of Four, literary and artistic creation flourished under the guidance of the party's "Double Hundred" policy. In 1980 we published 109 new novels or novelettes — a new record since the founding of the People's Republic. The rate of increase in books on literature and the arts showed that our readers eagerly welcomed the publication of Chinese and foreign literary masterpieces.

Books on the natural sciences and technology published in 1980 increased by 100% compared with 1977 and by 6.3 times compared with 1971. In the same year, books on culture and education increased by 360.4% over 1977 and by 17 times over 1971. These figures show that as the party shifted the emphasis of its work to the Four Modernizations after the smashing of the Gang of Four, we needed large numbers of books on science and technology and on culture and education to meet the demand for progress in those fields. They also show that our writers, translators and employees in publishing have worked extremely hard to produce so many books.

In 1980, we published 2,446 new children's books with a total of 554.96 million copies. The number was 40.82% greater than in 1979 and the number of copies constituted 29% of the total number of copies of general books printed in that year.

Also in 1980, we published 1,921 new books in various minority nationality languages, with a total number of 34.27 million copies. The increases in titles and copies were 24.4% and 26.6%, respectively, over 1979.

Of the 3,440 textbooks published in 1980, 1,599 were for universities, colleges and technical secondary schools, 1,207 were for primary and middle schools and 634 were for spare-time education and other teaching purposes. The total number of copies was 1,895 million, an increase of 63.84% over 1977 and of 160% over 1971. Now, the primary and middle schools in most parts of the country can get enough textbooks before the opening of the new school year. This has contributed to the development of primary and middle school education.

Supplying books for China's 800 million peasants is a primary task of publishing. In the past few years, employees in publishing and distribution have made great efforts in this respect. About 900 million out of the 1,500 million yuan of total sales in 1980 came from the county towns and the countryside (460 million of the 900 million came from the countryside, representing an increase of 31.5% over 1979). With the growth of economic prosperity in the countryside, cultural needs have grown. However, sales of books in the countryside, while they have gone up rapidly, are still lagging behind demand. Thus, we urgently need to step up the publication and distribution of books for the countryside.

The nature of publishing has changed remarkably in the past few years in that it no longer serves as a tool for political movements. With the shift of emphasis in the party's work and the restoration of political stability and unity, the

Table 2. Categories of Books Published, 1971-80

Year	Philosophy and Social Sciences	Literature and the Arts	Natural Science and Technology	Culture and Education
1971	1,847	404	911	121
1977	2,057	1,253	2,857	455
1980	2,091	3,322	5,715	2,095

publishing industry has been able to pay attention to the working out of a long-term plan and especially to the publication of major books which require many years to complete.

Reference Books. Preparations for the publication of the first large encyclopaedia of New China began in 1978 and the first volume, "Astronomy," was published in 1980. Also published in 1980 was the *Chinese Medical Encyclopaedia, Otolaryngology*. The compilation of the *Chinese Agricultural Encyclopaedia* has begun. The new edition of the annotated *Collected Works of Lu Xun* is being set and will come off the press on the centenary of his birth in 1981. A new one-volume edition of *Ci Hai* (Lexicology) and the first two volumes of *Ci Yuan* (Etymology) have been published. The revision of these texts had been going on for many years. A comprehensive dictionary of Chinese phrases and a comprehensive dictionary of Chinese characters are being compiled. The bound volume of *Jiaquwen* in 13 fascicles, mainly compiled by Guo Moruo during his lifetime, is coming off the press. ("Jiaguwen" are Shang Dynasty inscriptions on bone or tortoise shell). In 1980, we also published the *Chinese History Yearbook,* the *Yearbook of World Economy* and the *Chinese Publications Yearbook* as well as other large reference books.

Academic and scientific works by prominent Chinese scholars have also been published. These works include Xue Muqiao's *China's Socialist Economy* and *Current Problems of China's Economy;* Xu Dixin's *On Socialist Production, Circulation and Distribution;* Zhu Guangqian's *A History of Western Aesthetics;* Li Siguang's *An Introduction to Geomechanics;* Qian Xuesen's *Engineering Cybernetics;* and Qian Weichang's *Calculus of Variations and Finite Elements.* In the past few years, we have translated and published many foreign classics and literary works, including *The Complete Works of Shakespeare, Gespräche mit Goethe,* Kant's *Prolegomena Zu Einer Jeden Künftigen Metaphysik die Als Wissenschaft Wird Auftreten Können* and Hegel's *Aesthetics.*

Periodicals. The publication of periodicals has flourished in recent years. In 1980, 2,191 different periodicals were registered with the publishing administrative organizations, representing an increase of 156% over the 856 periodicals published in 1964. Among the 2,191 periodicals, 1,384 (63% of the total) dealt with the natural sciences and technology; 265 dealt with literature and art; 210 were devoted to the social sciences; and the remaining 332 covered a variety of other subjects. The publication of so many periodicals reflects the desire for further development in the sciences and technology, as well as the growing enthusiasm of the writers. A good number of these periodicals, however, are of poor quality and should be improved.

IV. Future Tasks of Publishing

Since the smashing of the Gang of Four, our publication work has achieved great success. However, to achieve the Four Modernizations and to meet the people's increasing need for books, we still have a long way to go. Although the number of titles published in 1980 (21,621) greatly exceeded that in the period of the "cultural revolution," it was only 75% of that in 1965. And the total number of all titles published in 1980 was only 61.6% of the total in 1965.

The gap is particularly large in books on literature and art. This showed how seriously the influence of "Left" thought over a long period, and especially the denial of the "Double Hundred Policy" during the 10 years of turmoil, had damaged our scientific research, literature and the arts. In order to make our publications rich and varied, it is necessary for writers, translators and employees in publishing to do a lot of hard work. In the past we have published books of poor quality and too many copies of unnecessary books. In addition, some units that had nothing to do with publishing, published many books at random. At present, our printing facilities are inadequate

Table 3. Decline in Publishing Between 1956 and 1980

Year	Philosophy and Social Sciences	Literature and the Arts	Natural Science and Technology	Culture and Education
1956	3,727	9,375	8,698	2,391
1980	2,091	3,322	5,715	2,095
1980:1956	56.1%	35.4%	65.7%	87.6%

— typesetting and bookbinding are particularly weak. Both in the quality of printing and in the techniques of printing, our standards are far below those of the advanced countries.

As regards the distribution of books, we are currently short of sales agents in the cities as well as in the countryside, and the management of bookstores at the basic level needs much improvement. The number of editors and other staff members in the publishing, printing and distribution units should be increased and their professional levels raised. The organization of the publishing industry also needs restructuring. The workers in publishing, under the leadership of the party and the government, are studying ways of gradually overcoming these shortcomings and difficulties so as to develop the publishing industry and make it prosper.

52. CHINA'S JOURNALISM IN 1980
By the Press Research Institute,
Chinese Academy of Social Sciences

China is now undergoing a great historical period of transition. As a link between the Chinese Communist Party and the masses, journalism is also experiencing development and rapid change. Guided by the spirit of the Third, Fourth and Fifth Plenary Sessions of the 11th Central Committee of the Chinese Communist Party, journalism in China was marked by reform and healthy development in 1980.

Press reform has improved all areas of journalistic work — from theory to practice, from content to form, from style of writing to coverage, from quality to quantity. Meanwhile, lively academic activities in the field of journalism have started. These changes have forged closer links between the party and the masses, restored and promoted the fine traditions of the press and raised the prestige of journalism.

I. The Development and Restoration of China's Journalism

In the early years after the founding of the People's Republic, journalism took on a completely new image in the eyes of the public. But its scale was far from adequate to satisfy the needs of the 400 million people in China.

By 1952, through the attentive care of the party and the people's government, radio stations had been established at the national, provincial, municipal and autonomous regional levels. There were 129 newspapers published by organs above the provincial level, with a total circulation of 1,384 million copies. In 1958, broadcasting stations were established in districts, towns and counties throughout the country, and 220 newspapers were published with a total circulation of 2,893 million copies. By 1965, prior to the "cultural revolution," the national broadcasting network had been extended to every people's commune, production brigade and production team, and everyone could listen to central and local broadcasting programmes.

A Time of Havoc. During the 10 years of turmoil, Lin Biao and the Gang of Four kept a tight control over the mass media in the country. They made special efforts to control the national newspapers and magazines, creating havoc in the entire field of journalism. Large numbers of journalists were persecuted and many publications were closed down. They wantonly revised the nature and tasks of the press, using newspapers, radio and television as their tools to usurp the leadership of the party and state power. In news reporting, idealism spread unchecked, metaphysics ran wild, and there was an endless assortment of lies, empty talk, boasting, extreme expressions and clichés — all of which served to confuse the people, sabotage national economic construction and undermine the party's fine tradition.

Lin Biao and the Gang of Four also fostered fascist cultural despotism on a massive scale, forbidding the publication and presentation of outstanding works of literature and art — ancient and modern, Chinese and foreign — in the press, radio and television. Their perverse acts gravely impaired the prestige of journalism among the masses, causing a great retrogression in the history of journalism. From 1966 to 1970, the number of newspapers in the country went down to 49.

Emancipation. After the Gang of Four was smashed and conditions were set aright, a large number of veteran journalists were rehabilitated and the people regained control of people's journalism. By repudiating the reactionary Lin Biao and Jiang Qing cliques, by acting in accordance with the guidelines of the Third, Fourth and Fifth Plenary Sessions of the Party's 11th Central Committee and by carrying out discussions on the principle "practice is the only criterion for testing truth," journalists further emancipated their minds, the press underwent significant changes and journalism was gradually restored. By 1979, there were 69 newspapers above the provincial level with a total circulation of 13,082 million copies.

II. Rapid Advances in Journalism in 1980

Journalism in China continued to enjoy rapid growth in 1980. In that year there were 188 newspapers above the provincial level with a total circulation of 14,042 million copies. During 1980, *Chinese Peasants* and *China's Legal System*, as well as the English-language *China Daily*, began trial publication. Professional papers, regional, town and county papers, as well as evening papers such as the *Guangzhou Evening News* and *Beijing Evening News* also resumed or started publication.

Radio and Television. The country now has 106 radio stations, 484 transmitting and relay stations, 2,560 radio diffusion centres and more than 100 million loudspeakers. The Central People's Broadcasting Station beams two comprehensive radio programmes to the whole nation, one programme to the minority nationalities, one programme to Taiwan and one special frequency modulation musical programme. Broadcasting stations in various provinces, municipalities and autonomous regions produce 130 radio programmes.

Radio broadcasting to foreign countries began in 1950. At present, the international broadcasting station is offering 38 language programmes, as well as programmes in standard Chinese and four dialects for overseas Chinese and foreign nationals of Chinese origin.

Television broadcasting was initiated in 1958, and television stations now have been set up in 29 provinces, municipalities and autonomous regions (one is under construction in Tibet). The Central TV Station and more and more local TV stations are showing colour programmes. The nation has 38 TV stations, 246 transmitting and relay stations, each with a power of 1,000 watts, and 2,000 TV translator stations with a power of less than 50 watts. In order to train more people for national construction in the shortest possible time, TV stations and the Ministry of Education have jointly initiated a TV broadcasting university, which has an enrollment of 324,000 students and represents the first stage in the development of a TV university education network.

News Agencies. The Xinhua News Agency has 29 local branch offices in China, with 700 reporters, and 85 branch offices in foreign countries, with 150 resident correspondents. Every day the domestic branch offices send news stories from their reporters to the head office in Beijing via telex, telegram or telephone to be handled by the Home News Department of the head office.

The Xinhua branch offices abroad send news dispatches home in English, French, Spanish and other languages, sometimes in the Chinese phonetic alphabet or in Chinese code. The dispatches are sent by telex or telegram to transmitting centres set up by Xinhua in foreign countries, which relay them back to the head office in Beijing.

In addition to providing home service, Xinhua News Agency also operates foreign services in five languages – English, French, Spanish, Arabic and Russian. The foreign services include an English service to the whole world and special line services to different regions of the world in English, French, Spanish, Arabic or Russian, broadcasting a total of 150,000 words in five languages daily.

The Xinhua News Agency publishes news bulletins in six languages – Chinese, English, French, Spanish, Arabic and Russian, and "News from Foreign Agencies and Press" in three languages – Chinese, English and French.

The China News Agency, established in 1952, has resumed operations and has expanded. Its head office is in Beijing, and it has branch offices in Guangdong, Shanghai and Fujian and correspondent centres in Guangxi and Yunnan. It also has an office in Hong Kong, which sends dispatches, general news, feature stories and pictures to Chinese-language newspapers abroad and newspapers in Hong Kong and Macao. It also releases films abroad introducing China's beautiful scenery, cultural relics, construction projects and local dramas.

Research and Training. Twelve universities in the country provide special training in journalism, including five departments of journalism and two specialized courses in journalism, with a total enrollment of 1,106 students. In 1980, institutes for research in journalism were also set up in Beijing and elsewhere.

The All-China Journalists Association has resumed its activities. Branch associations were restored or set up in Yunnan, Anhui, Hubei, Hebei, Liaoning, Jilin, Heilongjiang, Fujian and Tianjin.

The Beijing Journalists' Society, composed mainly of journalist units in the capital, was founded on February 6, 1980, with Hu Qiaomu as honorary president, Hu Jiwei as president and a number of veteran journalists as advisers. Journalists' societies were also set up in Hebei, Anhui, Jiangsu, Hubei and Tianjin.

After the founding of the Press Research Institute of the Chinese Academy of Social Sciences in 1978, journalism research institutes were set up in Heilongjiang, Jilin and Shanxi. Journalism research departments or offices have also been established by the Xinhua News Agency, the *Liberation Army Daily*, the Beijing Social Sciences Research Institute, Fudan University in Shanghai and the Beijing Broadcasting Institute, as well as by some provincial newspapers, such as the *Dazhong Daily, Sichuan Daily, Chongqing Daily, Fujian Daily, Hunan Daily, Ningxia Daily, Hubei Daily, Guangxi Daily* and *Tianjin Daily*.

The *People's Daily* established a spare-time self-study journalism school to train journalists on the job. It stresses research in journalism theory and press reform. The All-China Journalists' Association and the Chinese People's University jointly set up an evening school for training journalists who work in Beijing.

In 1980, academic activities in the field of journalism were many and varied; a number of publications dealing with basic theoretical problems in the areas of legislation governing the press, news writing, news reform and photo journalism came off the press.

Competition. Sponsored by the monthly *News Front* and the Beijing Journalists' Society, a nationwide campaign to honour good news writing — the first since the founding of the People's Republic — was launched in 1979. Included for consideration were all news articles published in newspapers or news stories broadcast over the radio in that year. The aim of the campaign was to stimulate press reform and encourage journalists to write more, better and more concise stories to serve the Four Modernizations. A total of 31 news items and stories were selected, 6 for first prize and 25 for second prize. The campaign was conducted again in 1981 on a large scale. The book *Good News* was published by the Beijing Journalists' Society and the editorial department of *News Front*.

Press Publications. A number of publications for the profession specialize in the dissemination of research on journalistic theory and experiences of journalists. These publications are on sale to the public. The monthly, *News Front,* founded by the *People's Daily,* resumed publication in 1979. New publications in 1980 included: *Data on Journalistic Research,* a quarterly published by the Press Research Institute of the Chinese Academy of Social Sciences; the quarterly *Press Research,* published by the *Shanxi Daily;* the monthly *Press Study,* published by the *Hubei Daily; Journalistic Theory and Practice,* put out by the *Gansu Daily; International Press Circles,* a publication of the Journalism Department of the Chinese People's University; and *Broadcasting Journal,* by the Beijing Broadcasting Institute.

Forums and Meetings. The Press Research Institute of the Chinese Academy of Social Sciences, in April, September and December of 1980, invited specialists, scholars and leading members of the press to separate forums to discuss such topics as compiling the history of journalism and the basic problems of journalistic theory.

The Beijing Journalists' Society sponsored a dozen academic reports and forums on press reform, the basic problems of journalistic theory, including legislation governing the press, the value of news and news writing, economic reporting and the use of media to air criticisms.

The five dailies in North China (in Beijing, Tianjin, Hebei, Shanxi and Inner Mongolia) held meetings in April and August of 1980 in Shijiazhuang and Beidaihe, respectively, at which participants exchanged experiences on how to make the newspapers ideological centres of stability and unity and how to make economic reports lively.

In May 1980, representatives of more than 40 press units from 18 provinces and cities held a symposium sponsored by the five dailies in Northwest China (in Shaanxi, Gansu, Qinghai, Ningxia and Xinjiang). This symposium, held in Lanzhou, discussed the nature, task and role of newspapers, as well as the objective laws of journalism and other issues affecting the press.

Newspapers in the three provinces of Northeast China held a meeting in Shenyang in June 1980 to deliberate on the questions of how to continue to emancipate the mind and how to criticise the influence of the "Left" line in reporting industrial news.

Six provinces in East China and Shanghai Municipality jointly held a forum in Shanghai in August, attended by leading members of eight dailies (Dazhong, Anhui, Xinhua, Zhejiang, Jiangxi, Fujian, the *Wenhui Daily* and the *Liberation Daily*). They exchanged experiences on publicizing economic work in the new situation and reviewed the problem of how to make economic reporting lively.

A national meeting of all city newspapers was held in Hangzhou in November to exchange experiences on how to run city papers and how to expand the role of the press. Ways and means for improvement were also discussed.

Reform and Improvement. Journalistic research in 1980 promoted press reform; improved news content, writing style and newspaper layout; and gave further play to the guiding role and militancy of proletarian journalism.

At the beginning of 1980, the *People's Daily* revised its layout, expanding the paper from six to eight pages, giving more space to economic news and encouraging shorter, more substantial and informative reports. Articles criticizing certain people and events have won the approval of the paper's readers.

With timely reporting on the profound changes in every area of national life, the Xinhua News Agency, in accordance with objective reality, improved its work in all respects. It placed emphasis on the readjustment of the organizational structure in the head office, on the training and education of the staff and on the renewal and improvement of press equipment.

The Central People's Broadcasting Station greatly reformed and expanded its news programming. At present, there are 22 newscasts a day, with a total of 30,000 words, accounting for 335 minutes or 15% of the total broadcasting time.

Both national and local newspapers undertook reforms and achieved tangible results.

In 1980, after a series of studies and reforms,

the press in China gradually regained its fine tradition of seeking truth from the facts, gave prominence to major developments, stressed truthfulness in reporting, broke away from conventional ideas and practices and extended news coverage.

Economics Reporting. Many newspapers gave priority to reports on the economy. The *Wenhui Daily* in Shanghai, for example, increased the proportion of economic news on the front page month by month in 1980 — 13% in August, 20% in September, 42% in October and 47% in November. Besides giving priority to economic news, the *People's Daily* and other newspapers, as well as radio stations, also initiated special columns on economic news: "Men of Action" in the *People's Daily*, "Trades" in the *Workers' Daily*, "Economy and Management" in the *Guangming Daily*, "Contributions to the Four Modernizations" in the *Beijing Daily* and "Market Information" in the *Wenhui Daily*. All these special columns reflecting economic life were warmly welcomed by the readers.

Criticism Restored. Critical reporting regained its proper place in the newspapers, ending the former practice of reporting only the good. It has restored and brought into full play the Chinese Communist Party's three important styles of work — integrating theory with practice, forging close links with the masses and practicing self-criticism — and reflects the spirit of socialist democracy in China.

An example of such open critical reporting was seen at the time of the Bohai No. 2 drilling rig accident. The articles, which drew praise from readers at home and abroad, not only broke away from the past restrictions that "major accidents are not allowed to appear in newspapers," but also resulted in a demerit for one vice-premier, the removal of the minister of the petroleum industry from office, and the sentencing of some leading members of the Oceanic Oil Exploration Bureau.

Other examples included reporting that exposed an ill-advised project to divert a river from west to east and uncovered the false reports by Xiyang County on its grain yields. All these reports had a tremendous influence on the readers.

Other Advances. Coverage of important meetings also changed for the better. When the Third Plenary Session of the Fifth National People's Congress was going on, the *People's Daily* published excerpts of the delegates' speeches. The Xinhua News Agency divided the session's working reports into subject areas and reported on them separately. These changes produced timely and lively reporting.

The contents of literature supplements and art and literature columns became more varied — to the delight of readers who were eager to have an opportunity to study the excellent Chinese and foreign literary works that had been banned for a long time.

At present, newspapers in China display the following common characteristics: original layout, numerous special columns, illustrated feature articles and lively and interesting subjects. Newspapers in Beijing alone have added about 50 special columns. News stories contain interesting sidelights, articles carry subheads and feature stories are accompanied by photos. All these improvements have been welcomed by the masses.

The transformation and development of journalism is continuing unabated. Further reform will require arduous efforts by the profession to sum up the experience and the lessons of the past and to improve news coverage in all branches of the media.

53. CHINA'S FILM INDUSTRY
By Ji Hong
Film Bureau, Ministry of Culture

Since the founding of New China 30 years ago, enormous progress has been made in China's film industry. In the 17 years prior to the "cultural revolution," the industry reached a high level of production and proficiency. By 1965 there were seven feature film studios, one animated film studio, one newsreel and documentary film studio and three studios specializing in scientific and educational films. Between 1949 and 1965, they produced a total of 603 feature, stage art and opera films, 279 reels of animated films, 8,342 newsreels and documentaries and 1,980 reels of scientific and educational films.

During the 10 years of calamity caused by Lin Biao and the Gang of Four, the Chinese film industry — like other industries — was disrupted and seriously damaged. The vast majority of film workers were attacked and persecuted. In the period from 1966 to 1975, only 69 feature films, 36 reels of animated films, 1,473 newsreels and documentaries and 731 reels of scientific and educational films were produced. In the years 1967 to 1969, with the exception of a few documentaries, all film studios suspended production. All films made prior to the "cultural revolution" were regarded as "poisonous weeds" and banned. China's film industry was on the verge of being destroyed.

I. Recovery of the Film Industry

After the smashing of the Gang of Four, however, the film industry began to revive. Films banned during the "cultural revolution" were again shown to the public, and the warm welcome they received greatly inspired the film workers. New productions were gradually resumed. It was at this time that the Hunan Film Studio was founded. Three feature film studios also were established in the Xinjiang, Guangxi and Inner Mongolia autonomous regions in order to strengthen the cultural development of minority nationality regions. By the end of 1980, China had 11 feature film studios. The animated film studio, newsreel and documentary film studios and scientific and educational film studios also were revived and strengthened.

Following restoration and consolidation, and adhering to the political and ideological line laid down by the Third Plenary Session of the 11th Party Central Committee, the workers in the film industry have upheld the principle that literature and art should serve the workers, peasants and soldiers, as well as socialism. In this way, they have implemented the policy of "letting a hundred flowers blossom and a hundred schools of thought contend," thus bringing about the prosperity of the film industry.

In 1979, the release of films presented in honour of New China's 30th anniversary marked the beginning of a favourable turn in the film industry. Produced during the year were 65 feature and stage art films, 25 reels of animated films, 375 newsreels and documentaries and 349 reels of scientific and educational films. Especially heartening was the emergence of a number of films that were of high intellectual and artistic quality and were well-received by the audiences. Among them were 22 feature films, including *From Slave to General, Ji Hongchang, Xiao Hua, Anxious to Return, The Cradle, Twins Come in Pairs* and *What a Family;* 8 stage art films, including *Romance of an Iron Bow;* 8 documentaries, including *The Premier of the People* and *Counterattack in Self-Defence;* 7 newsreels, including *China's New Look (No. 1)* and *China Today (No. 1);* and 15 scientific and educational films, including *Biological Evolution, The Movement of the Earth's Crust, Lace Wing* and *Grotto Art in Dunhuang.* All of these films received awards from the Ministry of Culture in 1979.

II. Continued Progress in 1980

In 1980, further progress was made by building on the foundations laid in the previous year. A total of 82 feature films were produced — 75 by the 11 feature film studios and the remaining by the Central Newsreel and Documentary Film Studio and other studios. In addition, 32 reels of animated films, 365 newsreels and documentary films and 337 reels of scientific and educational films were produced. Some of the films showed marked improvement in both content and form. Among the films honoured by the Ministry of Culture in 1980 were the feature films

Evening Rain, Legend of Tianyun Mountain, In and Out of Court, A Young Hero, The Tenth Bullet Scar, Unmelted Snow, The Young Teacher and *The Man Who Deals with Devils;* the stage art film *The White Snake;* the animated films *Three Monks* and *Snow Boy;* six newsreel and documentary films, including *Eternal Glory to Comrade Liu Shaoqi* and *Huangshan Mountain;* and seven scientific and educational films, including *Life and Protein — Synthetic Crystalline Insulin* and *Remote Sensing.*

The important achievements of China's film industry in 1979 and 1980 also included the broadening of the ranks of creative workers. Among the 65 feature and stage art films produced by the feature film studios in 1979, 15 were directed by young artists. Among the feature and stage art films produced in 1980, over 30 were directed by young artists. Middle-aged and young artists also directed various films in other departments and units. Many of these films were of good quality. The talent of these young directors added a freshness and sparkle to China's screen. The Beijing Film Institute, one of the major centres for training film workers, was revived after the smashing of the Gang of Four.

Audiences Broadened. When the People's Republic was established, there were only 596 cinemas in the whole country. The vast majority of these cinemas were concentrated in a few major cities. People in the countryside and in the smaller towns had very little opportunity to see films. In order that the masses might have access to movies, the party and government made great efforts to develop film projection facilities outside the large cities while expanding film production. By the end of 1980, there were 125,000 film projection units, one-third of them in the cities and two-thirds in the countryside. Because of the large population and the backwardness of the economy, however, the number of film projection units remains inadequate and their quality is mediocre.

Only a few of the film projection units in the large cities are in actual cinemas; most operate in theatres, in auditoriums of societies, factories and mines and in clubs; or else they travel from place to place. About half of the projection units located in the countryside are equipped to show 16 mm. films, the other half to show 8.75 mm. films. Most units in the countryside are mobile projection teams which show films in the open air.

In recent years, following the implementation of the party's policy on agricultural economy, the development of agricultural production and the reactivation of the rural economy, many towns in the rural ares have established regular showing facilities. According to incomplete statistics, there are about 2,000 of these crude cinemas in small towns, thus expanding the viewing opportunities for the peasant audiences. The establishment of more crude cinemas will make an important contribution to the cultural development of China's small towns.

Organization and Training. The China Film Distribution and Exhibition Corporation is responsible for the distribution of all films in the country. It also handles film import and export. In addition to the central office, there are more than 3,300 branch organizations reaching to every province, municipality, autonomous region, prefecture and even county. In the communes, there are film administrative stations. All films shown in the cinemas and clubs and by projection teams are handled by these corporations and stations.

The China Film Equipment Corporation was established to organize the production and supply of film equipment and parts. It handles the import and export of film equipment. The central office, together with its 180 branches, is responsible for supplying and maintaining equipment in each province, municipality and autonomous region.

Personnel for film distribution and projection are trained in 14 film technical schools and training organizations throughout the country. In addition, some film corporations hold classes for their employees from time to time. At present, about 400,000 people are working in the areas of distribution, projection, equipment supply and maintenance.

III. Contributions to Culture and Education

The film industry in China is considered an important component of culture and education. For this reason, admission and film rental fees are kept low; rural projection teams receive support for their 16-mm. and 8.75-mm. film showings by sharing part of the income earned by 35-mm. film showings in the cities; and film screenings in the national minority areas are subsidized or even free of charge. These measures are aimed at speeding up the development of film showing capabilities and at making films more available to the countryside, mountainous areas, remote inland and national minority areas.

International Exchanges. With the development of political, economic and cultural contacts between China and other countries, film exchanges have increased rapidly. At present, China's film industry has relations with 180 film companies in 63 different countries and regions. Between 1976 and 1980, we sold a total of 1,848 "film rights" (one film can be sold a number of times) for both long and short films, and imported 158 films. In 1979 and 1980, we held film festivals featuring productions from Korea, Romania, Yugoslavia, Japan, France, Egypt, Australia and many other countries. Some of these countries, in turn, held festivals of Chinese films.

The China Film Co-Production Corporation, established in 1979, facilitates co-production with foreign countries and provides assistance to companies interested in making films in China. It was founded on the principle of mutual benefit and friendship. Since its establishment, it has held talks with companies from more than 30 countries and regions. A number of agreements were reached, leading to 18 completed films at the end of 1980. These included the feature films *Beyond Forbearance* and *Roof of Tile;* the documentary *Film and Television in China;* and the scientific-educational film *Medicine and the Japanese.* A number of other films are under production. These exchanges have promoted mutual understanding and friendship between the Chinese people and the people and film workers of other countries.

Self-Reliance. In order to develop our film industry on the basis of independence and self-reliance, we started to build up our film equipment and film stock industries shortly after Liberation. Previously we had relied completely on imported equipment and film stock. The necessary material conditions for the development of the Chinese film industry have gradually been attained. Large-scale film equipment factories have been established in Nanjing, Shanghai, Harbin, Beijing and Gansu Province. In addition, there are more than 50 equipment factories of various sizes in other localities and numerous repair and spare-parts centres. Some equipment still has to be imported, but basically we are self-sufficient. Besides the large No. 1 and No. 2 Film Stock factories, there are also some smaller film stock factories. At present we can manufacture black-and-white positive, colour positive and black-and-white negative stock — all of which are used in large quantities. However, we still have to rely on imported colour negative and inter-negative film, in which there remain quality-control problems. There are two major film-processing laboratories, in Shanghai and Beijing; in addition, every film studio and some film stock factories have their own processing facilities. Altogether there are more than 40 laboratories to handle the needs of more than 100,000 exhibition units.

Remaining Tasks. We have been greatly encouraged by the revival and development of the film industry since the downfall of the Gang of Four. At the same time we are very aware of the many remaining problems. First of all, films are not always compatible with the demands of the new historical period. The range of subjects is not broad enough; especially lacking are films about the lives and struggles of China's 800 million peasants and films about children. There are few works depicting the psychological aspects of the current great historical period. The ideological and artistic quality of our films also needs to be raised.

Shortcomings also exist in the industry itself. Manpower and equipment are not being developed and used to their full potential. We have more than enough equipment, film stock and processing laboratories but our technical skill and forces are scattered. Also, the quality of the equipment manufactured is not high enough, obliging us to import colour negative and inter-negative film, as well as some equipment. We have a large number of film exhibition units, but many are of low quality and do not meet the needs of the masses. All these problems must be solved through adjustment, correction and improvement. We believe that under the correct leadership of the party and the government, our film industry will be raised to new heights.

Appendix:

CATALOGUE OF FEATURE AND STAGE-ART FILMS OF 1980

Studio	Title of Film	Colour	Reels	Screenplay	Director	Photography	Principal Players
Peking Film Studio	Marriage of Li Tianbao	Colour	12	Min Bin, Feng Po	Chen Fangqian, Duan Jishun	Wen Zhixian	He Quanzhi, Ma Lan, Chen Jing, Li Jinying, Li Qi

Studio	Title of Film	Colour	Reels	Screenplay	Director	Photography	Principal Players
Peking Film Studio	Zhuge Liang in Mourning	Colour	11		Chen Huai'ai	Nie Jing	Shen Fengmei, He Quanzhi, Tian Fagen, Chen Jing, Mu Baicheng
" "	They Are In Love	Colour	10	Yang Lingyan, Wang Qi	Qian Jiang, Zhao Yuan	Sun Changyi	Zhang Ping, Da Shichang, Xiao Xiong, Guo Xuxin, Xu Yushun
" "	Song of Loyalty	Colour	11	Su Shuyang	Xie Tian, Zheng Guoquan	Huang Xinyi	Zheng Rong, Yu Shizhi, Hu Zongwen, Xiu Zongdi, Zhang Ping
" "	A Hand-Cuffed Passenger	Colour	11	Ji Ming, Ma Lin	Yu Yang	Zhang Qinghua	Yu Yang, Shao Wanlin, Ge Cunzhuang, Zhao Ziyue, Ma Shuchao
" "	Death of the Marshal	Colour	10	He Xingtong, Yu Li	Shi Yifu, Que Wen	Xu Xiaoxian, Tu Jiakuan	Li Rentang, Zhao Na, Zhu Yanping, Zhang Xian
" "	The Young Teacher	Colour	9	Yan Tingting, Kang Liwen	Wang Junzheng	Zheng Yuyuan, Zhou Jinxiang	Li Ling, Wang Jianing, Xu Huan, Guan Qiang, Zhu Yurong
" "	The Second Handshake	Colour	12	Cao Shuolong, Dong Kena	Dong Kena	Zhang Shicheng	Xie Fang, Kang Tai, Yuan Mu, Shi Yu
" "	Mysterious Buddha	Colour	10	Xie Hong, Zhang Huaxun, Zhu Hongsheng	Zhang Huaxun	Chen Guoliang, Liang Ziyong	Zhang Shunsheng, Liu Xiaoqing, Guan Zongxiang, Ge Cunzhuang
" "	Sleeping Tiger Ridge	Colour	12	Ding Yisan, Wu Zhaoti	Wu Zhaoti	Wang Zhaolin	Feng Chunchao, Bai Zhidi, Hu Peng, Bao Gang, Xiao Xiong
" "	Effendi	Colour	10	Wang Yuhu, Xiao Lang	Xiao Lang	Wu Shenghan, Li Yuebin	Tuyikun, Abulmid, Abak
Shanghai Film Studio	Murder in Room 405	Black & white	10	Yu Benzheng, Shen Yaoting	Shen Yaoting	Zhang Guifu, Zhao Junhong	Zhong Xinghuo, Xu Min, Yan Xiang, Shi Jiufeng

Studio	Title of Film	Colour	Reels	Screenplay	Director	Photography	Principal Players
Shanghai Film Studio	When the Leaves Turn Red	Colour	10	Gao Xing, Luo Zhiming	Tang Huada, Yu Benzheng	Shen Xilin	Wu Haiyan, Ding Jiayuan, He Lin, Gao Ying, Ma Guanying
" "	Our Little Kitten	Colour	4	Wang Tianyun, Zhang Yuqiang, Wang Runsheng, Wu Yigong	Wu Yigong, Zhang Yuqiang	Weng Shijie, Sun Guoliang	Bai Mu, Zhao Shuying, Chen Wenjie
" "	A Circus Dog	Colour	4	Shao Hongda, Yu Jie	Yu Jie	Tang Shibao, Wu Dewei	Gu Yelu, Wei Langhui, Qi Yong, Liu Tielei, Tielei, Zheng Dasheng
" "	The Torn Picture	Colour	4	Script collectively written, edited by Tang Junhua	Sha Jie	Jiang Shuzhen, Wu Liekang	Lu Qing, Chen Ye, Yu Zhenhuan, Wang Yi, Yuan Ling
" "	A Gift of Greeting	Colour	4	Zhao Fujian, Li Tianji, Zhang Huijun, Chen Chan	Zhang Huijun, Chen Chan	Li Kui, Wang Tingshi	Han Fei, Shun Jinglu, Cheng Zhi, Zhang Wenrong
" "	Death Ray on Coral Island	Colour	9	Tong Enzheng, Shen Ji	Zhang Hongmei	Luo Zhengsheng Sun Hualin	Qiao Qi, Ling Zhihao, Qiao Zhen, Ma Junqin, Qiu Yufeng
" "	The Story of Four Fellows	Colour	10	Li Yunliang, Yang Shiwen, Wang Lian	Zhao Huanzhang	Zhu Yongde, Cheng Shiyu	Mao Yongming, Ma Xiaowei, Wang Guojing, Meng Jun, Hong Xueming, Zhao Jing
" "	Child Violinist	Colour	9	Zhao Danian	Fan Lai	Li Chongjun, Wang Yi	Xiang Mei, Wu Cihua, Gao Xiaoyang, Ding Yi, Mao Weiyu
" "	Romance on Lushan Mountain	Colour	9	Bi Bicheng	Huang Zumo	Shan Lianguo, Zheng Xuan	Zhang Yu, Guo Kaiming, Wen Xiying, Zhi Shiming, Wu Hao, Gao Cui
" "	Evening Rain	Colour	9	Ye Nan	Wu Yonggang, Wu Yigong	Cao Weiye	Li Zhiyu, Zhang Yu, Qiang Ming, Zhong Xinhuo, Ouyang Ruqiu

Studio	Title of Film	Colour	Reels	Screenplay	Directors	Photography	Principal Players
Shanghai Film Studio	Come Home Swallow	Colour	10	Shi Yong, Meng Senhui, Shi Minshan	Fu Jinggong	Qiu Yiren, Zhou Zaiyuan	Gao Ying, Da Shichang, Yang Rong, Yuan Yue, Zhang Xiaolei
" "	The Story of a Football Team	Colour	9	Zhou Kangyu, Da Shibiao, Lu Ren	Lu Ren	Zhang Yuanmin, Ji Hongsheng	Sun Bin, Ma Guanying, Zhao Jing, Tan Pengfei, Jia Deying
" "	Legend of the Tianyun Mountain	Colour	12	Lu Yanghou	Xie Jin	Xu Qi	Shi Weijian, Wang Fuli, Shi Jianlan, Zhong Xinghuo, Hong Xueming
" "	The Blue File	Colour	10	Hua Yongzheng, Meng Senhui, Shi Yong	Liang Tingduo	Chen Lin, Cai Guangen	Xiang Mei, Liang Boluo, Tang Ke, Li Wei, Shen Guangwei
" "	The White Snake	Colour	15	Original script by Tian Han; edited by Zhao Laijin, Li Zhongcheng	Fu Chaowu	Huang Shaofen, Yu Shishan	Li Bingshu, Fang Xiaoya, Lu Boping, Su Shengyi
" "	What Is Love	Colour	10	Li Tianji	Yan Bili	Ma Linfa	Wang Weiping, Yan Zhengan, Ye Linlang, Lu Yukun
" "	Sweet Sorrow	Colour	10	Ye Dan, Huang Jinjie	Song Chong	Lu Jinfu	Gong Xue, Guo Kaimin, Gao Bo, Gao Cui, Yuan Yue
" "	The White Lotus	Colour	11	Xie Hong, Zhang Huaxun	Zhongshu Huang, Sun Yongping	Ying Fukang, Zheng Hong	Wu Haiyan, Gong Xibin, Xu Fu, Wang Hui, Yu Guichun
Changchun Film Studio	The Story of a Woman Volleyball Player	Colour	9	Lu Jianhua	Lu Jianhua	Fang Weice, Jia Shouxin	Guo Zhenqing, Huang Daliang, Cui Muyan, Guo Min, Pan Yuehua
" "	North Star (part two)	Colour	9	Hu Su	Zhou Yu	Yan Xuzhong, Duan Zhenjiang	Huang Zhongqiu, Li Yuanhua, Wang Runshen, Du Defu, Yuan Zhiguang

Studio	Title of Film	Colour	Reels	Screenplay	Directors	Photography	Principal Players
Changchun Film Studio	Cross the Dadu River	Colour	12	Lu Qi	Lin Nong, Wang Yabiao	Wang Qimin	Han Shi, Zhao Shenqiu, Liu Huaizheng, Fu Xuecheng, Cheng Baoguo
″ ″	Wedding On the Execution Grounds	Colour	12	Zhang Yisheng, Cai Yuanyuan, Zhao Yurong	Quangbu Daorji, Cai Yuanyuan	Li Huailu, Zhang Xiaoqiu	Song Xiaoying, Li Qimin, Zhao Yamin, Kuang Ping
″ ″	Red Peony	Colour	10	Yan Fengle	Xue Yandong, Zhang Yuan	Meng Xiandi	Jiang Lili, Sun Shulin, Gao Baocheng, Zhao Fengxia, Guo Shugen
″ ″	Be Proud, Mama	Colour	10	Zhang Tianmin	Li Guanghui, Bai Dezhang	Li Guanghui, Li Fengming	Wang Baosheng, Gong Xibin, Gong Jianhua, Zhang Baishuang
″ ″	The Last Eight Soldiers	Colour	11	Xu Zhiheng, Zhao Wanjie	Yu Yanfu	Xu Shouzeng	Luo Guoliang, Hou Guanqun, Qu Xuanhe, Zhao Yamin, Xu Changxi
″ ″	Fang Zhimin	Colour	11	Fang Lan, Zhou Yiru, Sun Bo	Yin Yiqing	Dansennima, Sun Hui	Wei Xin, Zhao Wenyu, Chen Guojun, Zhao Hengduo, Li Ning
″ ″	Through No Fault of Their Own	Colour	12	Li Dong, Chang Yan, Wang Yungao	Chang Yan	Chang Yan, Gao Hongbao	Xia Zongxue, Wu Xiqian, Zhang Ning, Liang Tongyu, Zhang Xiaomin
″ ″	The Flashing Arrow	Black & white	10	Jiang Junfeng, Wang Zhewei	Wang Feng	Tang Yunsheng	Chai Yunqing, Wang Xiangle, Wang Feng, Tang Ke
″ ″	The Peacock Embroidery	Colour	11	Wang Yiping	Liu Wenyu	Zhong Wenming	Chen Ye, Shi Zhongqi, Gu Wei, Pu Ke
″ ″	Wake Up, Spring!	Colour	11	Zhang Xiaotian	Su Li	An Zhiguo	Tian Chengren, Pu Ke, Li Xiaofen, Wang Runsheng
″ ″	Huang Yinggu — A Heroine	Colour	11	Chen Lide	Jin Jie, Shu Xiaoyan	Shu Xiaoyan	Zhang Jinling, Wu Lusheng, Li Chengbin, Chen Rubin

China's Film Industry

Studio	Title of Film	Colour	Reels	Screenplay	Directors	Photography	Principal Players
Changchun Film Studio	Where the Guests Come	Colour	11	Guo Weiqiang	Guangbu Daoerji	Zhang Xiaoqiu	Du Xiongwen, Xue Li, Kai Ti, Xu Guangming
" "	Fallen Blossoms	Colour	9	Xiao Yinxian, Sun Yu	Han Dongxia	Han Dongxia	Lin Qiang, Zhao Fengxia, Xu Meina, Wei Bingzhe, Zheng Hua
" "	Unmelted Snow	Colour	10	Huo Zhuang, Huang Jianzhong, Xu Xiaoxing	Jiang Shusen	Chen Changan	Li Yan, Siqin Gaova, Xu Zhan, Yao Xiangli
Pearl River Film Studio	An American Pilot	Colour	9	Fan Ruoyou	Wang Weiyi, Wang Yi	Lu Dongqing	Zhang Qindao, Liu Zhengguo, Wu Jing, Wang Xiaozhong
" "	The Man Who Deals With Devils	Colour	11	Liu Shizheng	Lin Lan	Liu Jingtang	Guo Yongtai, Chu Min, Zhu Manfang, Fang Hua, Lu Shuren, Wang Zhigang
" "	Plum Blossom Embroidery	Colour	11	Wang Jingzhu, Zhang Liang	Zhang Liang	Li Zhexian	Wang Qingbao, Zhang Jie, Qi Mengshi, Huang Wansu
" "	Misty Capital	Colour	10	Kuang Haowen	Zhang Bo, Wang Jin	Wei Duo	Yan Shikui, Pang Min, Shi Jin, Wu Jing, Qian Yongfu
" "	Morning After After a Nightmare	Colour	9	Wang Pei	Wang Ti	Shi Fengqi, Xia Lixing	Yu Ping, Ma Yi
" "	Meeting by Flowered Wall	Colour	11	Script written by Tianmian Opera Troupe	Chen Gang, Zhou Shaofeng	Liu Jintang, Ma Liguo	Hu Xiangying, Hu Xinzhong, Wen Xiaopei, Shao Shizhong
" "	Who Does He Love?	Colour	9	Bi Bicheng	Xian Biying	Liang Xiongwei, Bai Yunshen	Pan Zhiyuan, Che Xiuqing
Xi'an Film Studio	The Black Masks	Colour	10	Zhao Donghui, Wu Shuang	Zhang Jinglong, Shi Daqian	Chen Wancai, Niu Han	Liu Jia, Jin Di, Wei Ke
" "	Love or Legacy?	Colour	10	Li Yunliang	Yan Xueshu	Zhang Faliang	Zhang Yuyu, Zhou Jintang, Mao Yanhua, Yuan Zhongfu, Han Yueqiao

Studio	Title of Film	Colour	Reels	Screenplay	Directors	Photography	Principal Players
Xi'an Film Studio	The Tenth Bullet Scar	Colour	11	Chong Weixi, Ai Shui	Ai Shui	Cao Jinshan	Cao Huiqu, Bao Xun, Cao Jingyang, Chen Lizhong, Yang Tong
" "	Traitor	Colour	9	Ji Xing, Ji Rao	Zhang Qichang	Niu Nan	Ma Jingwu, Yu Ping, Na Renhua, Shen Guanchu
" "	Butcher Scholar	Colour	12	Liu Anmin and others	Lin Feng	Xu Deyun, Wang Hui	Wang Guangmin, He Lin, Duan Linju, Li Xiaoliu
" "	Longing for Reunion	Colour	10	Guo Qilong	Wu Tianming, Teng Wenji	Zhu Dinyu, Liu Changxi	Liu Dong, Xu Min, Li Weixin, Liu Yu
Emei Film Studio	Not for Love	Colour	10	Yang Tao, Cui Changwu	Ying Xianglin	Li Dagui	Li Shixi, Nicoletta Bewwlen, Liu Dong, Pel Lan
" "	Butterflies Bring Reunion	Colour	10	Zhao Danian, Fan Jihua	Zhang Fengxiang, Yang Gaisen	Zhang Shicheng, Gao Lixian	Wang Danfeng, Xiang Kun
" "	Bamboo	Colour	9	Wang Suihan, Shitu Zhaodun	Wang Suihan, Shitu Zhaodun	Liao Jiaxiang, Yu Defu	Cui Xinqin, Li Lan, Liu Zhongyuan, Zhao Chunming, Liu Yulong
" "	Maple Leaves	Colour	10	Zheng Yi	Zhang Yi	Li Erkang, Wang Wenxiang	Xu Feng, Er Li, Tu Zhongru
" "	In and Out of Court	Colour	9	Song Rixun, Chen Dunde	Chong Lianwen, Lu Xiaoya	Feng Shilin	Tian Hua, Zhou Chu, Lin Moyu
" "	Spring Comes Late	Colour	9	Rao Qu, Tan Su	Ma Shaohui, Tai Gang	Mai Shuhuan	Zhang Jiatian, Xiang Hong
" "	Zhou Enlai in Chongqing	Colour	9	Yan Yi	Qian Qianli	Hong Wenyuan	Wu Gang, Xiang Kun
August First Film Studio	The Spy	Colour	11	Lin Yu, Chong Sheng, Liu Shuichang	Hao Guang	Wei Linyu	Du Yulu, Tang Tangmin, Qiu Yingshan, Pan Xiaozhi
" "	The Three Lost Soldiers	Colour	10	Li Jing, Yan Jizhou	Yan Jizhou	Xu Boqing, Bai Fujin	Long Yishun, Yi Bo, Yu Shaokang, Sun Yuzhen

China's Film Industry

Studio	Title of Film	Colour	Reels	Screenplay	Directors	Photography	Principal Players
August First Film Studio	The Stars Are Bright Tonight	Colour	10	Bai Hua	Xie Tieli	Cai Jiwei, Xu Lianqing	Li Xiuming, Tang Guoqiang, Zhao Fuyu, Huang Xiaolei
" "	A Young Hero	Colour	10	Lu Zhuguo, Bao Mengmei	Jing Mukui	Yang Guangyuan	Bao Xun, Mu Huaihu, Yuan Xia
" "	Tank No. 008	Colour	9	Jin Jingmai and others	Hua Chun, Ren Pengyuan	Wang Menyuan, Ding Shanfa	Li Shixi, Li Lan, Li Po
Guangxi Film Studio	It Is Not an Easy Life	Black & white	9	Zhou Minzhen, Wu Yingxun	Wu Yingxun, Gao Bu	Meng Xiaogqiang, Liao Fan	Wang Xiangpu, Lu Shuren, Liu Guiqing, Tang Xuefang
" "	Ten Days	Colour	13	Bai Chen and others	Bai Chen	Yang Yuming	Zhu Xinyun, Han Fei, Cheng Zhi, Fang Hua
" "	Mist Over Fairy Peak	Colour	10	Hu Bing	Guo Baochang	Yang Yuming	Zhang Guomin, Zhao Songkai, He Ling, Hou Keming
Xiaoxiang Film Studio	Spectre	Colour	10	Chen Zhaoming, Zhang Jinbiao	Chen Fangqian	Yun Wenyue	Shao Huifang, Yu Shaokang, Ren Dao, Wang Mingsheng
" "	Light Through the Clouds	Colour	9	Liu Cheng	Ouyang Shanzun	Shen Miaorong	Liang Yuru, Pan Hong, Hua Jianchang, Song Yining
Tianshan Film Studio	Gunshots over the Grasslands	Colour	10	Sheng Kai, Xia Zhixin	Meng Qingpeng, Song Jie	Liu Yongsi	Azhati, Fatiha, Halunbake Mutlif
Central Newsreel & Documentary Film Studio	The Blood-Stained Portrait of a Beauty	Colour	11		Sha Dan	Yang Yongsong, Xu Zhaode	Li Shujun, Bai Shilin
Agricultural Film Studio	Peasant Dances	Colour	8	Tang Yingchao and others	Tang Yingchao and others	Liu Huizhong and others	— — —
Zhejiang Film Studio	Yanzhi	Colour	10	Wei E, Shuang Ge	Wu Peirong, Jin Sha	Zhou Rongzhen	Zhu Biyun, Xia Jiangnan, Zhang Zhiming, Ping Fan
Henan Film Studio	Judge Bao Zheng	Colour	12	Wang Jixiao	Li Tie	Sun Lun and others	Zhang Baoying and others

Studio	Title of Film	Colour	Reels	Screenplay	Directors	Photography	Principal Players
Yunnan Film Studio	Yao Qi	Colour	9	–	Ma Changshu	Wen Yuzhang	Qiu Shirong, Ma Kaihuai, Yu Cun
" "	The Stolen Imperial Horse	Colour	5	–	Ma Changshu	Wen Yuzhang	Qiu Shirong
Others	Misfortunes Never Come Singly	Colour	9	Collectively written; edited by Zhang Lei	Zhang Shouguang	Yang Shijiang	Wang Zhitao, Chen Lianzhong and others

54. EDUCATION IN CHINA
By Ji Hua
Ministry of Education

Owing to the long rule of feudalism and, in particular, to aggression at the hands of imperialist powers, old China was a semi-feudal and semi-colonial country with corrupt politics, a depressed economy and an extremely backward cultural and educational system. The broad masses of the working people were deprived of the right to education. On the eve of the founding of New China, over 80% of the population were illiterate or semi-literate and only about 20% of school-age children attended school. The total enrollment in institutions of higher learning was only 155,000, while that in middle schools was 1,879,000.

The distribution of schools was extremely uneven. Universities and colleges were concentrated in a few large cities and coastal provinces. Middle schools and primary schools were concentrated in cities and towns, with a very small number scattered in the countryside. In border regions and national minority regions, schools were virtually non-existent.

I. Development of Education Since 1949

After the founding of New China, under the leadership of the Chinese Communist Party and the people's government, and with the efforts of China's own teaching and administrative staff, as well as those of people of all nationalities, the party's correct line was carried out most of the time on the educational front. Educational institutions left over from old China were systematically transformed and remarkable successes in education were achieved along with the successful development of the national economy.

School Enrollment. In 1979, the nationwide enrollment of students in institutes of higher learning, middle schools and primary schools was 207,940,000, or an eight-fold increase over that of the early post-Liberation years. In 30 years, college enrollment had increased 8.7-fold; middle school enrollment, 47.5-fold; and primary school enrollment, 6-fold.

Spare-time education at all levels, including preschool education and education for the blind and other handicapped, also increased. The education of women received much attention from the party and the government, with the result that girls now make up 45% of all primary school pupils, 41% of middle school students and about 24% of college students. The situation in the national minority regions also changed drastically. In 1979, the enrolment of national minority students in schools at all levels throughout the country reached 9,546,000, for a rate of increase well above the national average rate of increase over the past 30 years.

The past 30 years also saw a steady growth in the number of teachers and school administrators. In 1979, the total number of teachers and administrators in all types of schools reached 11,120,000, or an increase of 10.8 times over 1949. The teaching and administrative staff in state-run schools numbered 6,100,000, or a seven-fold increase over 1949.

During the past 30 years, a total of 3,030,000 competent people with professional training graduated from institutes of higher learning and 5,390,000 people received training in technical secondary schools. These people — particularly those who were trained and graduated in the 1950's and 1960's — constitute an important segment of China's intellectuals. With 10 to 20 years of working experience behind them, the graduates of the 1950's and 1960's represent the main force for carrying out the country's Four Modernizations.

Over the past 30 years, 46,000,000 have graduated from senior middle schools; 147,000,000 from junior middle schools; and 305,000,000 from primary schools. In addition, agricultural middle schools, vocational middle schools and regular primary and middle schools together have trained several million people to provide reserve forces of labour, and thereby have assured the development of various undertakings in our country.

Organizational Changes. The development of New China's education has been marked by socialist construction, profound reforms and constant improvements. In the early years after Liberation, we took over all public and private schools from the Kuomintang and transformed and merged them with missionary schools that had been financed by foreign subsidies, abolished the reactionary educational system of old China and established party leadership over all schools. Party and Youth League organizations were formed in schools, the system of ideological and political work was established and courses on Marxism-Leninism were conducted. An ideological remoulding movement was started among teachers so as to unite all patriotic intellectuals to serve the people in education.

After 1952, the institutes of higher learning and their departments were reorganized, teaching reforms were introduced and the unified college enrollment system and system of assigning college graduates were adopted. In this way, higher education was brought under the control of state planning. On the basis of the experience gained in educational work in the former liberated areas and of the experiences of other countries in the sphere of education, Chinese schools at all levels formulated for each subject matter a set of teaching plans, a syllabus and textbooks — all of them geared basically to actual conditions in China.

Policies and Rules. After 1957, all schools made an effort to carry out the policy put forward by Chairman Mao, namely: education must serve proletarian politics and must be combined with productive labour, and everyone who receives an education should be enabled to develop morally, intellectually and physically and should become a worker with socialist consciousness and culture. All schools actively experimented with teaching reforms in the effort to establish a socialist educational system with Chinese characteristics and further developed the experiece of running various types of schools according to the principle of "walking on two legs." In so doing, however, some "Left" errors were made.

In 1961, on the basis of our experience in educational work during the 12 years after the founding of New China, we worked out three sets of basic rules for schools: the "Draft Provisional Regulations Concerning the Work in Institutes of Higher Learning Directly under the Ministry of Education" (which became the "Sixty Regulations for Institutes of Higher Learning"); the "Draft Provisional Regulations Concerning the Work in Full-time Middle Schools" (which became the "Fifty Regulations for Middle Schools"); and the "Draft Provisional Regulations Concerning the work in Full-time Primary Schools" (which became the "Fifty Regulations for Primary Schools"). These regulations put our educational work on the road of healthy development, and led to the establishment of a stable teaching order, a rise in the professional level of teachers and striking improvements in teaching quality and scientific research.

Advances and Achievements. In the 17 years prior to the 10 years of turmoil, the number of educational institutions of various types and at all levels increased rapidly. During those years, regular colleges and universities turned out 1,550,000 graduates — approximately 9.4 times the number of college graduates in the 20 years prior to Liberation, and 16,000 persons received postgraduate training.

During the same period, 200,000 people graduated from spare-time colleges and correspondence colleges and 2,960,000 people graduated from professional secondary schools. Today, most of these graduates serve as key members in various fields.

In 1965, the total enrollment in institutes of higher learning throughout the country was 674,000, or 5.8 times as many as in 1949. Students in middle schools totalled 14,320,000, or 11.3 times as many as in 1949; and pupils in primary schools totalled 116,210,000, or 4.8 times the number in 1949. The number of teachers and administrative staff members in all types of schools at all levels reached 5,6743,000, or 5.5 times the number in 1949, and the political consciousness and professional level of those working in education rose steadily.

Schools at all levels possessed buildings and basic teaching facilities. This was especially true of institutes of higher learning and technical secondary schools; they undertook extensive construction, acquired large quantities of books, reference materials and instruments and, thus, met the material requirements for both teaching and scientific research. Institutes of higher learning conducted scientific research on a large scale and produced a number of significant results, thus narrowing the gap between China and the advanced developed countries. Party leadership in schools at all levels was constantly strengthened during the period in question and basic experience in how to exercise party leadership in education was gained. In the 17 years before the 10 years of turmoil, we carried out on the whole a Marxist line. In spite of our lack of experience, which led to some errors and shortcomings, our achievements were outstanding.

Setbacks and Problems. Education in China was seriously undermined by Lin Biao and the Gang of Four during the 10 years of turmoil. The quality of teaching dropped drastically, affecting an entire generation of China's youth. The result has been a temporary, yet severe, shortage of competent people to succeed the older generation on every front of endeavour. Although vast numbers of those who were engaged in educational work laboured diligently at their posts under the most difficult circumstances and waged a protracted struggle against the fascist cultural despotism of the Gang of Four, they were unable to turn the tide because of certain conditions at the time.

In the four years since the smashing of the Gang of Four, order has returned to education, thanks to thorough reform, restoration and consolidation carried out under the leadership of the party. The prospects for education have definitely improved. Nevertheless, old wounds have not completely healed, vigour has not been fully regained and a number of problems have yet to be solved.

II. Lessons Learned from Our Experiences in Education

The facts show that we have followed a correct line in education for most of the past 30 years, that our achievements have been substantial and that, having learned both positive and negative lessons, we have laid a solid foundation for further development. The principal lessons learned from our experiences in the past 30 years are:

1. *Socialist education must be well coordinated with economic construction; that is, it must be developed in a planned and proportionate manner.* To maintain a proper and relatively stable balance between education and economic construction, education must be suited to the development of the national economy. At the same time, the material prerequisites for expanding educational facilities must be guaranteed and given priority in overall planning. The view that educational institutions are purely units of consumption and therefore nonessential must be thoroughly refuted. It is equally important to refute the view that quantity can be obtained without consideration of the existing conditions and quality.

2. *Socialist schools must stick to the principle of training students to be red and expert by stressing their all-around development.* Everyone who receives an education should be enabled to develop morally, intellectually and physically and should become a worker with socialist consciousness and culture for the purpose of attaining socialist modernization. Schools at all levels must concentrate on teaching and must steadily improve the quality of education.

3. *It is imperative to carry out correctly the party's policy toward intellectuals.* Intellectuals are a part of the working class and also a force that the party can rely on. Party organizations at all levels must trust them, care about them and help them. Their working and living conditions should be gradually improved. While encouraging intellectuals to bring their role into full play, party organizations should help them to acquire a communist world outlook and to advance in the direction of being both red and expert.

4. *It is essential to strengthen the party's leadership in education and to adhere to the four fundamental principles.* Any statements and actions that weaken the party's leadership are harmful and must be corrected.

III. The Current Situation in Education

As in all other areas of endeavour, the current situation in China's education is excellent. Since the smashing of the Gang of Four and particularly since the Third Plenary Session of the 11th Party Central Committee, fundamental changes have taken place and remarkable achievements have been obtained in education.

1. *The Party Central Committee has attached great importance to education.* The Fifth Plenary Session of the 11th Party Central Committee decided that no time should be lost in establishing an educational programme and system that are suited to the development of our national economy. The Party Central Committee and the State Council have discussed the educational work several times and have made decisions and issued instructions on important questions calling for urgent settlement. Under the leadership of party organizations at various levels, the teaching and administrative staff and students have gradually liquidated, through the "exposure-criticism-investigation" movement, the pernicious influence in ideology and theory of the "ultra-Left" line pursued by Lin Biao and the Gang of Four.

The Central Committee has annulled the "Summary of the National Conference on Educational Work in 1971" as well as other erroneous documents. It has thoroughly repudiated the Gang of Four's reactionary "two appraisials" and has broken the mental shackles that had been fastened on educational workers. Cases of people being unjustly, falsely and wrongly charged or sentenced have been redressed. The party's policies towards intellectuals and cadres have been further implemented. The leading groups of various types and at all levels have been reestablished through readjustment and consolidation. All students have been taught to adhere to the four fundamental principles: the socialist road, the dictatorship of the proletariat, the leadership of the party and Marxism-Leninism-Mao Zedong Thought.

The students also have been taught to love their motherland, the people, labour and science and to take good care of public property. They have been guided to acquire lofty revolutionary ideals and a communist outlook on life, to uphold patriotism and the spirit of plain living and hard struggle, to observe discipline and public morality and to follow the orientation of being both red and expert. The tendency to neglect politics — which had appeared among some students — has been put right. Erroneous ideas concerning the four fundamental principles have been criticised.

2. *Institutes of higher learning have revived and developed.* In 1977, institutes of higher learning resumed the practice of holding entrance examinations. This has aroused the enthusiasm of students, improved the quality of entering students and brought study back into vogue. In recent years, both the number of institutes of higher learning and the enrollment of college students have grown. In 1980, there were 675 colleges and universities in China. Of that number, 316 admitted 2,964 post-graduate students, thereby increasing the total number of post-graduates in school to 17,728, or 14.1% more than in 1979. In 1980, institutes of higher learning admitted 281,200 undergraduates in regular programmes and special programmes and turned out 146,600 graduates. Thus, the number of students in school totalled 1,143,700, or a 12.1% increase over 1979. In accordance with the state plan, 273,800 students were enrolled, 143,500 graduates matriculated, and the total number of students in school was 1,030,900, up 13.4% over 1979. According to each local plan, 7,400 students were admitted and 3,100 were graduated. Thus, the total number of students in school was 112,800, or an increase of 1.4% over 1979.

In 1980, the number of teachers and administrative staff members in colleges and universities totalled 631,900, of which 246,900 were full-time teachers. There were altogether 4,212 professors, 13,788 associate professors and 119,102 lecturers.

In order to meet the needs of national construction, more students have been channelled into those fields and specialties which need strengthening — e.g., finance and economics, political science and law. As a result, the distribution of students among the various fields and specialties in institutes of higher learning has changed. The percentage of students in finance and economics increased from 1.2% in 1976 to 3.2% in 1980. In the same period, the percentage of students in political science and law went from 0.1% to 0.5% and that of students trained as teachers, from 19.4% to 29.6%.

Institutions for scientific research at colleges and universities have all been restored and a number of new scientific research institutes have been established. Progress has been made in scientific research and a number of achievements with relatively high scientific standards and important economic consequences have been registered. All these measures have helped to develop China's science and technology and have contributed to the fulfilment of the Four Modernizations.

3. *Training of competent people in secondary professional skills has been strengthened.* Socialist modernization in China needs not only a large number of competent people with advanced professional skills, but also a large number of competent people with secondary professional skills. To suit the needs of socialist construction in the 1980's and to promote such construction, the National Conference on Secondary Professional Education was held in 1980. The participants affirmed that secondary technical schools, characterized by less investment, rapid construction and a shorter training period, are an important means for training more competent people in secondary professional skills in a faster, better and more economical way. The conference also decided policies and requirements for running these schools in the future.

Appropriate adjustments were made in the length of schooling in secondary technical schools. For schools enrolling junior middle school graduates, the length of schooling is generally four years, varying to five years for a few schools and to three years for some specialties. The length of schooling in schools which enrol senior middle school graduates is generally two years, extending to two-and-a-half or three years for some specialties.

Approved by the State Council, academic titles for teachers in secondary technical schools are: associate professor, lecturer, assistant and probationary teacher. The "Provisional Rules Concerning the Designation of Academic Titles and Promotion for Teachers in Secondary Professional Schools" will first be tried out in a few schools and then implemented in all such schools by stages and in groups.

In 1980, there were 3,069 secondary technical schools; they admitted 467,000 students, graduated 410,300 students and had a total enrollment of 1,243,000 students — a 3.7% increase over 1979. Among these schools were 2,052 secondary worker-training schools, which took in 252,900 students, turned out 201,200 graduates and had an enrollment of 761,300 students, for an increase of 6.6% over 1979. There were 1,017 secondary teachers' schools, which admitted 214,700 students, graduated 209,100 students and had 482,100 students enrolled – representing a 0.5% drop from 1979. The number of teachers and administrative staff members in all secondary technical schools was 298,400, of which 128,600 were full-time teachers. Compared with 1979, the total number of teachers and administrative staff members increased by 35,900, and that of full-time teachers, by 15,800.

4. *The overall arrangement of middle schools has been readjusted and technical education has developed in a positive way.* During the ten years of difficulties, the concept of "two educational systems" was wrongly criticized and all technical schools and agricultural middle schools were closed. On the other hand, unscrupulous actions were taken to develop senior middle schools. First-year senior middle school classes were attached to junior middle schools and first-year middle school classes were attached to primary schools. Key teachers at each level were transferred to higher-level schools. All this had an adverse impact on primary schools and lowered the quality of middle schools as well. In the past two years, the overall arrangement of middle schools began to be readjusted in every region and the enrolment for senior middle schools was brought under control. Middle schools that were unable to remain open in the absence of necessary conditions were either closed down or merged with or turned into primary schools.

In 1980, China had 118,400 regular middle schools with a total enrollment of 55,081,000 students. Compared with 1979, the number of schools declined by 23,700 and the number of students in school dropped by 3,734,000. The total number of teachers and administrative staff members in the general middle schools was 3,897,100, of whom 3,019,700 were full-time teachers.

Based on the "Report on the Reform of Structure of Secondary Education" issued by the Ministry of Education and the State Bureau of Labour, and approved by the State Council, local authorities at all levels, after first conducting experiments, have set up vocational schools, agricultural middle schools and vocational training classes, and have been opened vocational courses in some middle schools. In 1980, there were 3,314 vocational schools and agricultural middle schools throughout the country. These schools took in 307,200 students, bringing the number of students in school to 453,600 – an increase of 93.1% over 1979. The number of vocational schools increased from 31 in 1979 to 390 in 1980. Enrolling 121,800 students in 1980, these schools had a total number of 133,600 students, or 15.9 times that of 1979. There were 2,924 agricultural middle schools, which admitted 185,400 students and enrolled 320,000 for an increase of 41% over 1979. The number of teachers and administrative staff members of vocational schools and agricultural middle schools in China totalled 40,800, of whom 23,200 were full-time teachers.

5. *Achievements in the popularization of primary education were consolidated.* At present, 93% of China's school-age children attend school, although only about 60% will finish the five-year courses. In order to solve problems in the popularization of primary education, the Party Central Committee and the State Council issued in 1980 the "Decision on Some Problems Concerning the Popularization of Primary Education," which called on the whole party to give close attention to primary education and to work for its popularization. The popularization of primary education throughout the country in the 1980's has been designated as an historical task. Programmes for universal primary education are being mapped out in every locality, based on local economic, cultural and other conditions, so that primary education will be made universal by stages and in groups.

In recent years, in order to help universalize primary education, the overall distribution of primary schools in the countryside has been readjusted on the principles of letting children attend nearby schools and of sparing manpower and material resources. While efforts are made to operate efficiently full-time primary schools, other types of primary schools have been set up, e.g., part-time primary schools, primary schools which are open every other day and mobile primary classes or groups. All these efforts have produced more opportunities for school-age children.

The local authorities of provinces, cities and autonomous regions have given close attention to rural primary education and some have taken earnest measures to increase the pay of primary school teachers in the countryside and to solve their living problems. In some places, part of the local revenues has been used for school building maintenance. In 1980, there were 917,300 primary schools; 29,423,400 pupils were admitted, 20,532,700 pupils finished the five-year schooling, and the number of pupils in school totalled 146,270,000, which was 359,800 less than that in 1979. The number of teachers and administrative staff members of all primary schools was 6,054,100, representing an increase of 179,400 over 1979, and 5,499,400 of them were full-time teachers, which was an increase of 117,600 over 1979.

6. *Preschool education, education for the blind and deaf-mute, and education on a work-study basis have received attention from people in all walks of life.* "The Regulations Concerning the Work of Kindergartens in Cities," drawn up in 1979, redefined the task and training purpose of kindergartens. At present, preschool educational institutions are run on a large scale by all departments of education, government organizations and mass organizations, army units, industrial enterprises and communes and production teams all over the country.

In 1980, there were 170,000 kindergartens throughout the country. The number of children in kindergartens totalled 11,507,700, which was an increase of 30.9% over 1979. In 1980, there were 292 schools for the blind and deaf-mute. These schools took in 5,900 students, turned out 3,700 graduates and thus had a total enrollment of 33,100 students. In 1979 and 1980, 112 work-study schools were set up in 23 provinces, municipalities and autonomous regions, with a total enrollment of 7,200 students.

With support from people in all walks of life and thanks to the hard work of both cadres and teachers in these schools, remarkable results have been achieved in educating and rehabilitating youngsters who have taken a wrong step in life. In October 1980, a national forum on work-study schools was held, at which experiences in running these schools were exchanged and a document on how to run work-study schools was prepared.

7. *Great importance was attached to education for national minorities.* Education for the national minorities in China has gradually revived and developed in the last four years as a result of the implementation of the party's policy toward national minorities. The provinces and autonomous regions concerned have adopted a series of concrete measures. In planning secondary and primary education for national minorities, first consideration has been given to the actual conditions of each nationality, with emphasis on quality and actual results.

Efforts have been concentrated on operating efficiently a group of state-run middle and primary schools and on restoring or setting up a number of middle and primary boarding schools. Expenses are guaranteed for these schools, more competent teachers are provided and priority is given to building or renovating school premises and purchasing facilities. It has been stressed that the content of courses and teaching methods should suit the characteristics of the national minorities. For national minorities that have written languages of their own, those languages should be used in teaching. Students are required to learn the language of their own nationality while learning Chinese.

In order to accelerate the training of competent people for construction in the minority nationality areas, courses on minority nationalities were offered in four key universities and colleges in 1980. Some institutes of higher learning in areas where national minorities live also offered such courses. The decision has been taken to operate colleges and schools for national minorities in every autonomous region or province where national minorities are relatively numerous in order to train more qualified teachers for minority nationalities.

In 1980, national minority students in schools at all levels numbered 9,656,000, of which 42,900 were college students, 84,000 secondary techical school students, 2,007,500 middle school students and 7,522,200 primary school pupils.

8. *Education for adults has developed considerably.* Both in 1979 and in 1980, the Ministry of Education convened national conferences on education for ministry staff members and workers, education for peasants, correspondence universities and evening universities run by institutes of higher learning and other forums. At these conferences and forums, past experience was summed up and tasks for future work were clearly defined. All this has given great impetus to education for adults. In 1980, television colleges had an enrollment of 324,400 students. Preparations are now being made to offer liberal arts courses.

Beginning in 1979, all universities for staff members and workers and for peasants who meet the standard for higher education were given formal recognition by local authorities of provinces, municipalities and autonomous regions, or by the ministries, commissions and general bureaus under the State Council. This was carried out according to the docment of the Ministry of Education approved by the State Council — "Temporary Regulations for Procedures of Approval Concerning the Running of Institutes of Higher Learning for Staff and Workers and Peasants."

In the "Proposals Concerning Large-scale Development of Correspondence Education and Evening Universities," approved by the State Council, it was affirmed that correspondence education and evening universities, both sponsored by colleges and universities, play an important part in developing higher education in our country. The "Proposals" stipulate that those who enroll in undergraduate courses or special college courses given by correspondence or in evening universities should be given college diplomas by the colleges or universities they attend upon their completion of the required courses and their passing formal examinations. And the best students should also be granted degrees in accordance with the set requirements. In 1980, worker-peasant students receiving higher education of this type numbered 1,554,100; those receiving secondary education, 8,044,700; and those receiving primary education, 16,461,000. In 1980, 5,388,000 illiterates in the country learned to read and write.

9. *Chinese students were sent to study abroad, foreign students came to study in China and international academic exchanges were organized.* Since 1978, China has sent a total of 5,609 students to 46 countries to pursue further studies and has accepted 1,276 foreign students from 79 countries in exchange. China has also invited a large number of foreign experts and scholars to give lectures at Chinese institutions. Many delegations of Chinese educators and researchers have been sent abroad to study, or to attend important international academic conferences.

Since it joined UNESCO, China has done some work to promote mutual understanding with other countries and to strengthen international unity and friendship. In 1980, China sent abroad 2,124 students, thereby increasing the number of Chinese students in foreign countries to 4,654. In 1980, foreign students studying in China numbered 1,382; of these, 569 were accepted in 1980.

10. *Trial implementation of temporary work regulations for colleges and universities, middle schools and primary schools has resumed.* Regulations for middle school students and primary school pupils have been reformulated. After being revised and implemented, these regulations have helped all schools to restore teaching order. In the future these regulations should be further revised and perfected. Our country's first regulations concerning academic degrees have been ratified by the Standing Committee of the National People's Congress for trial implementation. These regulations are bound to exert a far-reaching influence on the development of education and the sciences in China. The Central Research Institute of Education has been restored and research work in education has begun. Societies of education have been set up in all localities and problems in the theory of education have been discussed.

11. *Much work has been done to compile teaching materials and to construct school buildings and laboratories.* Trial editions of standardized teaching materials for the 10 years of basic schooling in all primary and middle schools have been published (with a few exceptions). The results obtained in using these teaching materials is being summed up in preparation for the publication of official textbooks. A large quantity of new teaching materials for liberal arts, science and engineering, agriculture and medicine in institutes of higher learning have been published. Among them, 523 kinds of new teaching materials for basic courses in science and engineering and in technology were compiled under the direct supervision of the Ministry of Education; these were published by the end of 1980. Teaching materials for most courses in secondary technical schools have already been compiled; teaching materials for the rest of the courses are being compiled.

The state budget allocates a guaranteed amount each year for construction and maintenance of educational institutions. In addition, some provinces, municipalities and autonomous regions have taken sums out of local financial reserves, various extra charges, city maintenance expenditures and funds for aiding underdevelopd areas, or they have raised funds specifically to subsidize educational institutions. With the help of the departments in charge of capital construction and units doing actual construction, investment in capital construction for educational institutions was increased in 1980.

Special consideration was also given to construction of school buildings and supply of building materials. In 1980, capital construction completed for institutes of higher learning totalled 3,250,000 sq. m. of floor space — an amount unprecedented in the past 30 years. As a result, rooms for college students enrolled in 1980 were ensured and housing conditions for some teaching and administrative staff were improved. There has been a significant increase in the quantities of instruments and other equipment and of books and reference materials in schools at all levels. Quite a number of laboratories for basic science and technology courses in colleges and universities have been put into operation. Some key universities and colleges have begun to use audio-visual teaching aids, while some middle and primary schools have begun to use lantern slides in their teaching.

12. *The teaching faculties in schools of various types and at all levels have been strengthened.* In addition to reopening previously existing advanced and secondary teachers' schools and setting up new ones, provincial, prefectural and county authorities have set up in-service teachers' schools and colleges for advanced studies. Self-study, off-the-job training and research activities have been organized for the in-service teachers, helping to raise the level of their political culture and professional knowledge. In 1980,

774,400 in-service teachers of middle schools attended teachers' colleges (or schools) for advanced studies and comprised 25.6% of the total number of middle-school teachers. In-service teachers of primary schools who attended teachers' schools for advanced studies numbered 1,531,200 and accounted for 27.8% of the total number of primary school teachers.

In June 1980, the Fourth National Conference on the Work Concerning Normal Education was convened. At the conference, it was reaffirmed that normal education performs the work of a "machine tool" in the system of education as a whole. It was stressed that the basic task for teachers' schools at all levels is to turn out qualified teachers for the people. New requirements for all teachers were proposed at the conference. Teachers are required to work hard at acquiring a relatively broad and profound store of knowledge, to study earnestly in order to master the science of education so as to grasp the rules of education, and to have a high moral character and noble ideals. In short, teachers are required to be worthy of the name of teacher.

To guarantee the quality of candidates in teachers' training schools, it was decided that, beginning in 1980, one key normal university or teachers' college in each province, municipality and autonomous region would be given the same privilege as the nation's key colleges and universities in selecting entering students. In 1980, the number of teaching and administrative staff members of normal schools of various types and at all levels throughout the country totalled 11,540,000, of whom 9,333,300 were full-time teachers. In state-run normal schools, the total number of teaching and administrative staff members was 6,619,700, of whom 4,718,900 were full-time teachers. In normal schools not financed by the government, the total number of teaching and administrative staff members was 4,920,300, of whom 4,614,000 were full-time teachers.

Current Problems. The above-mentioned facts show that immense changes have taken place in China's education and that our work on the educational front has gradually moved onto the right path, thus creating favourable conditions for the future development of education. Nevertheless, the current state of affairs in education falls far short of satisfying the needs of the country's Four Modernizations. The main problems are as follows:

(1) Higher education and secondary technical education have developed slowly. There is a severe shortage of competent, professionally trained people, especially at advanced levels. Our ability to train competent people is limited and the quality of training provided is not high. What is more, most of the people trained so far are in a limited number of fields, while there are none in other fields.

(2) In secondary education, efforts have been concentrated on the development of general education. Vocational education has just recently been revived. The gap between secondary education and economic construction has not yet been closed. Primary education has not been made universal and the number of young illiterate people is growing.

(3) Education for workers and peasants has not been carried out satisfactorily. The educational and technical level of workers is very low. According to incomplete statistics in 1979, the level of education of 80% of workers and administrative personnel is below that of junior middle school. In the case of workers and administrative personnel who began working during and immediately after the 10 years of turmoil the actual level of education is generally below the level indicated by their record of schooling.

The operating conditions of schools at all levels are still far from satisfactory. Expenditures for education and capital investment for educational institutions are far from sufficient. School facilities are overcrowded. Teaching equipment and scientific research are inadequate and outdated. There is a shortage of teachers and the quality of existing teachers is substandard. The social status of teachers and teachers' living conditions are unduly low. During the 10 years of turmoil, the quality of education declined significantly. First-year classes at higher levels were attached to schools at lower levels, while key members at lower-level schools were transferred to jobs at higher-level institutions. This looked impressive, but had no real benefit because the quality of education offered by schools at all levels was lowered. The consequences of those years are still being felt.

IV. Education and Our Readjustment Policy

At present, all economic departments are continuing to carry out the policy of readjustment, restructuring, consolidation and improvement, with readjustment as the key. The work in education should be carried out in line with this policy, even though education has its specific problems. It is essential to eliminate the "Left" ideological influence and to adhere to the correct guiding ideology in educational work. Many expressions of the "Left" ideological influence are still to be found in education. For instance, the inherent link between economic construction and cultural construction was ignored for many years and education was not given due consideration in the overall state economic plan, with the result that education failed to develop in step with economic construction.

In the past, class struggle was stressed as the key link and successive political movements were launched. People who studied diligently were criticised for "following the road to becoming specialists without socialist consciousness." This kind of thinking adversely affected teacher training in all schools and discouraged competent people from becoming both red and expert in order to serve socialist construction. There was an ultra-"Left" deviation in carrying out the policy against intellectuals which downplayed the important role of intellectuals in socialist construction.

Teachers had low social status and received unreasonably low pay. Thee was little understanding of the need and the importance for cadres to acquire both general and scientific knowledge. Consequently, a good number of cadres were content to stay with what they knew and a whole generation of cadres were hindered from developing in all-around manner. In developing educational institutions, high targets were set without due consideration for the country's capability, thus causing many ups and downs in educational work. As a result, student enrollment dropped and, more importantly, the quality of education declined.

Strengthening the Weak Link. Education is currently a weak link in our national construction and it urgently needs to be strengthened. During the readjustment of the national economy, education should be regarded as an important aspect of overall readjustment. It is just as essential to strike the proper balance between education and the economy as it is to strike the right balance between different sectors of the economy. More attention must be given to the development of "manpower resources." In both the long-term programme and the annual economic plan, priority should be given to investment in education, so as to ensure the necessary conditions for operating schools. Unless these conditions are improved and outstanding problems are solved, it is impossible to increase the number of people receiving an education or to improve the quality of education. Another important task in the readjustment of education is to correct the disproportion between various types of educational institutions at different levels, to enable us to achieve systematically the planned and balanced development of socialist education.

The nature and purpose of education should be further clarified, so that it can better meet the various needs of society and better serve the construction of a modern, powerful socialist country. In the course of readjustment, necessary reforms must include a reform of the structure of education and of its rules and regulations. The system of education should be gradually combined with the organization of labour and of cadres. Records of formal schooling and actual educational ability should be required in recruiting workers and selecting cadres, so that trained personnel can apply what they have learned and fully utilize their skills.

In the past, the readjustment policy was not fully understood and the serious consequences of the actions of Lin Biao and the Gang of Four were underestimated. For this reason, the readjustment policy was not accompanied by effective measures. Now, however, it is imperative to carry out the policy thoroughly and resolutely and to work harder for the success of readjustment in education. The whole party should be engaged in educational work. Party committees and people's governments at all levels must put educational work on their agenda and tackle the important problems in education while there is still time. In the course of readjustment, particular emphasis should be placed on improving the quality of education at all levels. We must avoid the temptation to make worthless things appear impressive. Weak educational institutions must be truly strengthened, as must be leadership at all levels. Ideological and political work must be undertaken in earnest and the position of Marxism in schools must be consolidated to enable us to carry out better the policy of enabling everyone who receives an education to develop morally, intellectually and physically. Primary education must be made universal as soon as is feasible. Effective measures will be taken to ensure that primary school pupils will complete the five-year programme and will reach the proper educational level by the time they finish school.

Reform Measures. We will work vigorously for the restructuring of secondary education. Various types of secondary technical education will be offered according to plan. In the course of operating and developing higher and secondary professional education, close attention will be paid to the training of competent people in such fields as economics and law, science, engineering, agriculture and medicine. Education for national minorities will be taken seriously and strengthened. Continued efforts will be made to develop adult education, preschool education and education for the blind and other handicapped. We will also redouble our efforts to train more competent teachers, compile more and better teaching materials and supply schools with more instruments and other equipment. We will carry out the correct policy toward intellectuals and, while consolidating the nation's contingent of teachers, we will further raise their social status, their living standards and their political and professional expertise.

Effective measures will be adopted to improve the operating conditions of schools at all levels, with emphasis on the major colleges and universities, major middle and primary schools and major schools of other types. Construction of laboratories and the acquisition of books and reference materials will be strengthened in a systematic fashion, and the use of audio-visual teaching aids will be popularized gradually. In the course of readjustment, the leading organs and administrative systems will undergo readjustment, as will the system of schooling, educational rules and regulations and teaching. However, these reforms must be accomplished on the basis of our past experience and in accordance with actual conditions. They must be tested first before being popularized, systematically and in a planned way.

Furthermore, it is imperative to draw on the relevant experience of foreign countries and to continue our scientific, cultural and educational exchange with friendly countries all over the world.

In short, in accordance with the requirements of the Four Modernizations, we must constantly review our experience, adhere to our correct guiding ideology, analyze the new conditions and tackle new problems in order to make our educational system a success. We will strive to make education flourish and turn China into a powerful, modern, socialist country.

55. CHINA'S HEALTH SERVICES
By Wei Zhi
Ministry of Public Health

In the 31 years since the founding of New China, under the leadership of the Chinese Communist Party and the people's government, the health services have undergone fundamental changes and made remarkable achievements.

Before Liberation, the masses lived in extreme poverty, epidemic diseases were rampant and health facilities were scarce. The people's health standard were very low. Since Liberation, the working people have been freed from exploitation and oppression. Their material and cultural life has greatly improved.

Owing to the efforts made by the government in developing mass health service, the health standards of the people have been raised considerably. The mortality rate, which was about 25% before Liberation, has fallen to 6.2%. Incomplete statistics show that in 31 years the average life span has increased from 35 years to 68 years.

I. The Fight Against Disease

As a result of the nationwide, patriotic movement for health and for preventive and curative measures, such infectious diseases as plague, smallpox, venereal diseases, kala-azar, recurrent fever, typhus, etc., have been successively eradicated or basically controlled. Schistosomiasis once was prevalent in 347 counties of 12 provinces and one autonomous region in the southern part of China; more than 10 million people suffered from this disease in an area of 13,000 square miles infested with snails. In the past 31 years, however, snails have been wiped out in two-thirds of the affected area and two-thirds of the sufferers have been cured. Schistosomiasis has been wiped out completely in Guangdong, Guangxi, Fujian, and Jiangsu provinces and in Shanghai Muncipality. In more than 200 counties the disease has been basically eliminated.

Before Liberation there were more than 30 million people afflicted with malaria. Now, through intensive control, the number of malaria patients has dropped to some 3.3 million and the mortality rate of malaria in 862 counties has dropped to below 0.5%. Also, nearly 10 million patients with endemic goiter have been cured, and new cases of goiter have been controlled in more than 100 counties.

Keshan disease, Kaschin-Beck disease, and endemic fluorosis have been controlled to a certain extent. The incidence of acute infectious diseases, such as poliomyelitis, measles, diphtheria, pertussis and tetanus in new-born infants, has decreased considerably. Statistics on the causes of death among inhabitants in some localities show that mortality caused by respiratory diseases, digestive diseases and acute infectious diseases has dropped, and that heart disease, cerebrovascular disease and malignant tumours have emerged as the main causes of death for the population.

Preventive Measures. Much has been done with regard to environmental, industrial, food, and school hygiene, as well as health protection from radiation. Since 1971, systematic tests and surveys have been carried out on the water quality of five big water systems, including 177 rivers, five lakes and six bays, and on the air quality in 75 cities, producing 730,000 items of scientific data. We have organized several nationwide campaigns for screening and treating occupational diseases. In the three years from 1974 to 1976, more than 2,900,000 workers doing jobs in dusty air were examined; at the same time those with detected silicosis were hospitalized for treatment and then transferred to other jobs. For the prevention of food contamination, data from nearly 100 million tests were collected, analysed and scientifically tested preparatory to the establishment of 54 national hygiene standards that were implemented on a trial basis for 14 items, including food grains, oil, meat, eggs and aquatic products.

Medical and Health Facilities. Before Liberation, China had very few medical institutions or workers' health facilities, and those few were concentrated in cities and coastal regions, leaving the vast countryside and remote regions without medical care and drugs. After Liberation, we trained a large number of medical workers, built many medical and health institutions and established an urban-rural medical care network composed of various kinds of institutions staffed with professional medical and health workers.

In the past 31 years, 406,000 students have graduated from higher medical colleges throughout the country, or 42.7 times as many as in the 20 years prior to Liberation, and 354,000 students have graduated from middle medical schools, or 20.6 times the pre-Liberation figure. From 1949

753

to 1980, the number of medical and health institutions rose from 3,600 to 181,000, an increase of 49.2 times; hospital beds from 80,000 to 1,982,000, an increase of 24.8 times; and professional medical and health workers from 541,000 to 3,535,000, an increase of 6.5 times. Among the latter, health technicians increased from 505,000 to 2,798,000, an increase of 5.5 times; and physicians from 360,000 to 1,153,000, an increase of 3.2 times. From 1949 to 1980, based on the average number for every thousand persons, hospital beds increased from 0.15 to 2.02, health technicians from 0.93 to 2.85, and physicians from 0.67 to 1.17.

Rural Health Services. Since 80% of China's population lives in the countryside, priority in medical and health care is given to rural areas. In the past 31 years, the developments in rural health services have been especially remarkable. In 1980, there were 2,337 general hospitals at the county level, 2,093 anti-epidemic stations, 1,885 maternal and child health stations and 1,165 postgraduate health schools throughout the country. In some counties, hospitals of traditional Chinese medicine, institutes for drug control and specialized institutions for preventive and curative services have been established.

There were 55,413 public health centres in 50,000 and more communes, and cooperative medical care stations or health stations generally in every one of the 600,000 and more production brigades throughout the country, with the cooperative medical care system operating in 68.8% of the production brigades. China has a total of 1,214,000 hospital beds, 1,485,000 professional medical and health workers, 1,463,000 "barefoot" doctors, and 2,992,000 rural health workers and midwives. The growing number of "barefoot" doctors and the development of the cooperative medical care system have played important roles in putting an end to the scarcity of medical care in rural areas.

Medical Research. Before Liberation, research work in medical science had been very backward, with only four research institutes and no more than 300 researchers. At present, a comprehensive medical research system has been established on a preliminary basis. There are 282 independent research institutes and 18,000 professional research workers, and more than 300 research institutes affiliated with higher medical colleges which employ several thousand research workers.

In the past 31 years, 4,576 medical and health research achievements at the provincial and national levels have been obtained, among which 353 items were given state awards. 802 items were awarded prizes by the Ministry of Public Health and seven inventions were recognized. Some items such as the treatment of deep burns over a large area, reattachment of severed limbs, acupuncture, anaesthesia, and the treatment of acute abdominal and bone joint damage, anal/rectal disorders, etc., etc., combined with Chinese traditional and Western medicines, have attained or nearly reached international standards. The advances in completing a series of research projects on basic, preventive, clinical and traditional medicines have given an impetus to the development of medical and health sciences in China.

II. Medical Advances and Achievements in 1980

In 1980, the policy of readjustment, restructuring, consolidation and improvement was implemented in health services in accordance with actual conditions under the guidelines put forward by the Third Plenary Session of the 11th Party Central Committee. At the National Conference of Health Bureau Directors held early in 1980, eight health tasks were proposed and arrangements were made for carrying them out in the course of the year. After the conference, health authorities at various levels succeeded in overcoming "Left" influences and began to readjust some policies, as well as establish, supplement and renovate certain systems, thereby strengthening the preventive and curative health services. Among the achievements of 1980 were:

1. *Development in the construction of rural health services.* Based on past experience and lessons learned from the actual conditions of the country, a portion of the available manpower and resources was concentrated on the consolidation and improvement of the medical and health establishments at the county level. These establishments were gradually to become direction and education centres for medical, health and family planning services in the counties, and would thus contribute to the constant improvement of the medical techniques of the rural medical network as a whole. Health services should be improved, and within a given period of time — beginning in one-third of the counties. This plan was integrated into the local agriculture production development programme in different localities and carried out according to local conditions.

The Ministry of Public Health issued the "Opinions on the Improvement of Reconstruction of Health Services in One-Third of the Prefectures" and "Opinions on the Enhancement of

Country Hospital Work" and obtained information and experience in the pilot counties. In the first one-third of pilot counties, problems chiefly concerning the improvement of administrative ability and technical knowledge of leading authorities were solved during the year. Attention was paid to the establishment of leading groups, of ranks of technical personnel and of rules and regulations. In some counties, attention was also given to the reconstruction of medical and health centres of several major communes. Training courses for hospital directors, station leaders and institute chiefs, as well as special courses in medicine, surgery, genetics, pediatrics, nursing and laboratory work, were successively conducted in one-third of the counties. Effective results were obtained in training the staff and raising their professional techniques to a higher level.

Persistence in the improvement of the cooperative medical service and the consolidation and improvement of the work of "barefoot" doctors were instrumental in strengthening the construction of rural health services. In 1980, different methods of operating cooperative medical services and of collecting funds and reimbursing medical expenditures were used, depending on the economic conditions of different places. In the better-off brigades which had relatively more funds, the scope and proportion of reimbursement were greater, while in the poorer brigades they were smaller. For those not in a position to reimburse expenses for the time being, drugs were sold at cost. In those brigades where conditions are not appropriate for the formation of cooperative medical services, health centres that collect charges or medical units which operate in other ways can be organized. The methods to be used depend on the opinions of the masses and the brigade has the right to make decisions. The training and re-education of "barefoot" doctors will continue. About one-third of them have attained the technical level of middle health school graduates.

2. *Health authorities at various levels continued to implement the policy of stressing preventive medicine, to launch anti-epidemic and patriotic health movements and to strengthen the preventive and curative services.* In 1980, emphasis was placed on the prevention and treatment of parasitic, endemic and communicable diseases such as schistosomiasis, malaria, filariasis, endemic goiter, hepatitis, pulmonary tuberculosis, etc. and on planned immunization. The "practice of vaccination" was adopted. Teams of investigators were dispatched to several provinces in northeastern China and to the south to obtain information on the development of planned immunization. The investigation and examination of malaria were carried out in focal malaria districts, and five provinces (Jiangsu, Shandong, Henan, Hubei and Anhui) held a joint conference on malaria prevention in Shandong in 1980 to exchange experiences. To promote anti-malaria work, 328 anti-malaria training courses with 14,093 persons attending were conducted in the same five provinces. Some 995 microscopic examination stations and 69 monitoring stations for malaria were established. Eradication of mosquito breeding grounds and drug treatments during the quiescent stage were carried out in combination with the urban and rural patriotic health movement, improvement of city surroundings and farmland construction. Epidemics in large areas were fundamentally controlled during the year.

Quarantine at seaports and airports was intensified and arrangements for "monitoring infectious diseases at border ports" were promulgated; quarantine stations were set up at Kunming, Nanning, Hangzhou, Urumqi, Shenyang, and five ports on the Changjiang River. The "Provisional Regulations Governing Port Service" were issued jointly by the Ministry of Communications, Ministry of Foreign Trade and the Customs General Administration.

The Ministry of Health issued "Opinions on the Strengthening of the County Anti-epidemic Stations" and gave attention to the establishment of training bases for anti-epidemic health workers in Heilongjiang, Jiangsu, and Hubei provinces. It formulated "Food Hygiene Criteria" (draft), convened a conference on food hygiene criteria and issued "Rules for Health Control on Imported Food" jointly with the Ministry of Foreign Trade and the Ministry of Food.

After the issuance of the "Provisional Regulations on Middle and Primary School Health Service," the "Provisional Regulations on Health Service in Institutes of Higher Learning" was issued together with the Ministry of Education. Twenty-two provinces, cities and autonomous regions were organized to carry out eye examinations of 250,000 students in 500 schools.

With a view to popularizing medical and pharmaceutical knowledge among the masses, much has been done by the national and local newspapers, radio and television broadcasting stations, publishing houses and the health propagation and education centres of some provinces, cities and districts. The Health Publishing House of the Ministry of Health is publishing 340,000 copies of *Health* per issue.

3. *To implement the party's policy on traditional Chinese medicine and to promote the integration of Chinese traditional and Western medicine, a national conference was held in March at*

Beijing. The conference proposed the policy of simultaneous development and long-term coexistence of three forces — traditional Chinese medicine, Western medicine and combined traditional-Western medicine. Colleges or schools of traditional Chinese medicine and drugs should be improved for the training of traditional doctors and druggists; training of apprentices by masters should be advocated; on-the-job training and education for traditional doctors and druggists, as well as postgraduate training, should be actively enforced; Western-trained doctors should be encouraged to learn traditional Chinese medicine so that there will be a corps of senior physicians with both Western and traditional medical knowledge; Tibetan, Mongolian and Uygur medicines should be developed; therapeutic, educational and scientific research institutions of traditional Chinese medicine should be established and improved; and the theory of traditional Chinese medicine and the means of modern medicine should be thoroughly studied.

Experts on Chinese or Western medicine or drugs who have made outstanding contributions to the research of traditional Chinese medicine or to the integration of Chinese traditional and Western medicines will be promoted and honoured, according to the conditions specified. This will give impetus to the development of Chinese traditional medical service. With the approval of the State Council, the "Report on the Work of Combining Traditional Chinese Medicine and Western Medicines" was issued; and on the basis of investigation some new regulations and arrangements were provided.

The Chinese Traditional Medical Association conducted nationwide scientific activities and conferences, such as the National Conference of the General Secretaries of the Chinese Traditional Medical Associations, held at Shanghai; the Symposium on Anal-Rectal Disorders in the Theory of Traditional Chinese Medicine, held at Fuzhou; the Symposium on the Scientific Research on "Qigong" (energy), held at Hangzhou; the Symposium on the Treatment of "Three Deficiencies," held at Harbin; and the Symposium on the Theoretical Research on Traditional Chinese Medicine, held at Kunming.

With the approval of the State Council, provisions allowing doctors to practise individually was issued. This enables the traditional and Western-trained doctors who are not working for the state or for collective medical units to utilize their professional knowledge and provides them with the opportunity to serve the masses in preventing and treating diseases.

4. *New achievements in medical research.* In 1980, medical research gave priority to tumors, cardiovascular diseases, paracholera, malaria, hepatitis, epidemics, schistosomiasis, the prevention and treatment of occupational diseases, basic medicine, microsurgery, biomedical engineering, molecular biology, immunology and such new techniques and new disciplines as organ transplantation.

In order to improve the management of scientific research, measures such as the monitoring of specifications, graded responsibilities, assessment by colleagues and signing of contracts have been adopted systematically. After adoption of the contract system, the sense of responsibility on the part of research units and researchers has grown stronger and has accelerated their research. Most projects were carried out according to the contracts and some have completed the research in advance or have obtained promising results. With a view to utilizing the limited investment to do as much work as possible, encouraging the enthusiasm and creativity of scientific and technical personnel, accelerating the process of scientific research, activating scientific thought and protecting academic competition, the "competitive contract" in the form of a "bid" has been introduced.

Assessment of major scientific achievements and inventions in 1978-1979 was carried out. Of the 1,145 items, 104 were selected as achievements attaining the ministerial level and among these, 40 were selected as first-class and 64 as second-class achievements. Among the first-class achievements was the research on the law and principle of acupuncture analgesia by the Shanghai No. 1 Medical College, which demonstrated through human and animal experimentation that acupuncture analgesia was different from "stress analgesia," thus solving an important problem in the laws of acupuncture analgesia and providing an experimental basis for its clinical use. A certificate of honour and 2,500 yuan were awarded for each first-class achievement.

At the request of the National Scientific Council, the Ministry of Public Health and the National Medicine and Drug Administration jointly set up the Committee to Assess Medical and Pharmaceutical Inventions. The Committee assessed 78 inventions and reported to the National Scientific and Technical Commission that seven of the inventions had been approved. The "sexual reproduction of *Gastrodia elata*," successfully developed by the Institute of Materia Medica and others of the Chinese Academy of Medical Sciences, and the "Artemisinine" developed by the Academy of Traditional Chinese Medicine and others, have played important roles in practical use. The success of sexual reproduction of

Gastrodia elata has shortened its maturation period, solved the problem of regression, increased the output and expanded the area for plantation. Other major achievements were: the "sterilization by injection into *vasa deferens*" by the Chongqing No. 1 Workers' Hospital; the "omentum roller skin flap" by the Beijing Jisuitan Hospital; the new anti-leptospirosis drug — Imidazole-4(5)-carboxylic acid ethyl ester — developed by the Institute of Epidemiology and others of the Chinese Academy of Medical Sciences; the "hemostatic powder No. 10" developed by the Institute of Blood under the Chinese Academy of Medical Sciences; and the "screening test for serum and blood glutamic pyruvic transaminase activity" developed by the Beijing Medical College.

5. *Further enhancement of high- and middle-level medical education and staff training.* In 1980, on the basis of the rectification and restoration of medical education in 1978 and 1979, emphasis was placed on the improvement of teaching quality. National conferences on higher and middle medical education were successively convened. These conferences summed up both the positive and negative experiences and lessons of the past 30 years. In the implementation of the policy of enabling the student to develop morally, intellecturally and physically, the conference on student's ideological work was held to analyse the thinking of students, to exchange experiences in developing ideological work and to discuss concrete methods of strengthening such work. The health conditions of students in colleges and schools were inspected and experiences were exchanged.

In 1980, many measures were taken to improve teaching quality. Various colleges were encouraged to take full advantage of their special features. Colleges were given more independence in teaching and were allowed a certain flexibility in matters of curriculum, teaching schedules and the selection of teaching materials. Some colleges offered special subjects and lectures. In about a dozen colleges, medical courses taught in foreign languages were organized to help students improve their foreign language proficiency. In these courses, foreign language textbooks were used and most of the lectures were given in a foreign language. After two years, the preliminary results have been good. All medical schools took practical measures to upgrade training in foreign languages, the fundamentals and self-teaching. Emphasis was placed on practical training and experimentation and on the use of audiovisual aids in teaching.

In regard to the development of staff education, the authorities in medical education at various levels investigated the conditions of health service personnel. A national conference on the education of health workers was held to exchange experiences and to define the direction, tasks and methods of staff education over the long term. One result was the formulation of a 10-year training programme. It is estimated that more than 110,000 professional and technical personnel have already participated in the training programme on a full-time or a part-time basis.

Training courses for directors of health bureaus and medical colleges of provinces, cities and autonomous regions were also conducted. A number of provinces, cities and autonomous regions conducted training courses for health service administrators at various levels. Furthermore, the Ministry of Public Health charged health bureaus and medical colleges of certain provinces and cities to conduct national training courses for the key personnel in various branches of medicine. In 1980, 270 such courses were conducted, with 4,400 persons participating — more than double the number in 1979. Also in 1980, provinces, prefectures and counties drew on existing teaching bases to conduct local training programmes for large numbers of non-professional health workers, thus making a head start in the improvement of the technical level and management of medical and health units and services.

In 1980, selected post-graduate students were sent abroad for further training under the auspices of the World Health Organization or through bilateral arrangements, and foreign medical experts were invited to lecture in China. About 1,200 persons have been trained in this way and some advanced techniques suitable for China's current conditions have been introduced.

6. *Technical direction of family planning and health care for mothers and children.* Development of family planning has always been an important routine task of the Ministry of Public Health. The medical and pharmaceutical units at various levels have made great contributions in this effort and achieved excellent results in the improvement of sterilizing procedures and the development of more effective and more easily practicable contraceptive methods, drugs and devices.

In the field of maternal and child care, more than 860,000 patients with uterine prolapse and urine fistula have been cured. In 1980, the Ministry of Public Health issued the "Regulations for Maternal and Child Health Service" (draft for trial implementation), the "Regulations for City Nurseries" (draft) and the "Regulations for City Nursery and Kindergarten Health Service Systems" (draft). A symposium on nursery service was held to discuss the problems of early education before three years of age and it led to the formulation of a "Programme for the Cultivation and Education of Children Below Three Years of Age" (draft). Discussions were held on teaching projects for nursery directors, health workers, child-care workers and cooks, and on the standards for model and experimental nurseries.

7. *Improvements carried out in drug factories and on drugs in 24 provinces, municipalities and autonomous regions led to better quality drugs and instruments, a large number of category specifications and more effective methods of production.* This development enabled the production and supply of drugs and instruments to better serve the prevention and treatment of disease and the protection of people's health. Drug standards were tightened through the enforced ratification of drug categories, the development of effective drugs, the absolute elimination of ineffective drugs and a strict ban on the manufacture and sale of false and substandard drugs. The State Council approved and promulgated the "Report on the Tightening of Drug Control and Ban on the Manufacture and Sale of False and Substandard Drugs" in 1980. It also issued the "Rules for Drug Standard Control" and the "Regulations for the Drug Code Committee."

8. *The scientific control and financial control of health services were strengthened.* Various medical and health service units made certain changes in technical and financial control and revised or established more than 50 kinds of medical and health regulations, systems and control measures. The results were improved hospital order and a better attitude toward patients, stricter ward control and an increase in number of outpatients and inpatients.

The tightening of financial control in observance of economic laws was a major change in the administration of health services. Beginning in 1979, we have been popularizing the reforms in drug control and the ways of increasing revenue and reducing expenditures. At the same time, we have tried to implement in some of the hospitals at or above the county level a new financial system. The system would allow hospitals to exercise some independence in their financial arrangements, yet integrate the interests of the state, the collectives and individuals by making hospital cadres and staff conscious of the need to maximise revenues and reduce expenditures — i.e., do things more economically.

The financial control of commune health centres was organized according to each commune's particular conditions, and was introduced first in selected centres. The "comprehensive budget" arrangement, introduced by the Ministry of Finance, and the "contract system" for scientific research projects were adopted on a trial basis at anti-epidemic stations, maternal and child care stations, institutes for drug control and scientific research and education units. By the end of June 1980, about 50% of the hospitals at or above the county level and about 20% of the commune health centres throughout the country were on this system of financial control.

In implementing stricter financial controls, many provinces and cities investigated hospital costs and suggested ways of reducing the deficits in hospital operating costs. To carry financial control even further, some units practised "fixed-amount" control, undertook to raise funds for schools, made warehouse inventories and audits. Attention was given to the coordination of financial and technical control and of administrative and ideological work, with serious implementation of the related government principles, policies, decrees and provisions for more effective operation of the socialist welfare service and for better quality medical care for the masses. It was prohibited, however, to seek more income by lowering the quality of medical care or by imposing unreasonable costs on the patients.

III. Principal Tasks of the Health Service

At present we are readjusting the national economy. The health service is an important component of our socialist system; it is vital to the people's health, the country's growth and the continuation of the nation. Hence, the government has decided that the development of the health service must be pushed forward as much as possible during the period of readjustment. Emphasis will be placed on the readjustment, restructuring, consolidation and improvement of existing establishments, on the full utilization of existing medical and health units. In this way, we will raise the standards of medical science and techniques, administrative capability, the quality and efficiency of our work, as well as arouse the enthusiasm of the masses of health workers for the prevention and treatment of disease, thereby serving the people's needs and the needs of modernization.

The realization of modernization in China's medicine and medical service is in keeping with the World Health Organization's target of "Health for All by the Year 2000." We are striving for more rapid development of our medical sciences and techniques, for the popularization of knowledge about health, for a marked improvement in urban and rural hygiene and in the general health of the people.

With a view to attaining this ambitious target, the current guidelines and main tasks of our medical and health service are as follows:

1. *Give priority to the improvement of medical service in the countryside, in factories, mines and cities.* Over 80% of China's population live in the countryside, where numerous endemic infections and parasitic diseases proliferate and where medical and health services are still relatively scarce. Therefore, the principal challenge remains the prevention and treatment of disease among the country's 800 million peasants. However, the relationship between the countryside and the cities should be correctly handled; we cannot provide more and better services to the countryside until health services in urban areas have been improved. The organization of basic health services for both urban and rural areas will be strengthened and the health centres in rural communes and the health stations in urban communities should be consolidated and improved.

The training and advancement of "barefoot" doctors will continue. Those "barefoot" doctors who have attained the level of middle medical school graduates and have passed a qualifying examination will be certified as "rural physicians." To increase the ranks of "barefoot"doctors, we will grant them reasonable living stipends. The current cooperative medical service in the countryside is an ideal system for providing medical care to peasants, so it should be consolidated and developed. However, other ways of organizing medical and health services that would entail payment for treatment will be allowed.

Preventive and curative services for the masses can only be secured after the basic health establishments in urban and rural areas have been well organized. In the meantime, county medical and health institutions will be grouped, by stages, into technical direction centres and training bases for primary medical and health workers in the areas of epidemic prevention, maternal and child care and family planning.

2. *Continue the policy of stressing preventive medicine.* Because China's population is large and there are many diseases, the fundamental goals of health services must be to mobilize the masses to take care of their health, to prevent diseases, to advocate clean living, to transform certain social habits and to improve the environment. We must strengthen anti-epidemic work, launch patriotic health movements, actively prevent and treat debilitating diseases and enhance the general health of the people.

3. *Adhere to the policy of developing and integrating the three forces – traditional Chinese medicine, Western medicine and the combination of traditional and Western medicine.* The integration of Chinese traditional medicine and Western medicine should be strengthened in order that we may evolve a medical science with distinctive Chinese characteristics. Priority in medical research will be given to the study of major technical problems and to the basic theories of those diseases that are severely debilitating.

4. *Adopt various forms and methods of operating medical services.* The urban and rural medical and health institutions are run by the state, the enterprises, the collectives and a small number of individuals who have acceptable medical skills and are qualified to practise medicine in our country. The forms and methods of operating medical systems should vary with the conditions in their location.

5. *Support for family planning and strong technical guidance should be a major responsibility of the health service.* In the effort to limit China's population to under 1,200 million, the party and the government have called upon the people to have only one child per couple. This is an important measure which wil affect the progress and future of China's modernization, the health an welfare of our descendants and the long-term and immediate interests of the nation. The health service should provide technical guidance for family planning, stress the policy of contraception, strengthen the training of technical personnel and improve contraceptive techniques, while advocating eugenics, strengthening maternal and child care service, improving pre-natal health care, protecting the health and safety of children and improving nursery organizations in cooperation with other departments involved.

6. *Coordinate steps in medicine and pharmacy and combine medicine with pharmacy more closely.* Active support should be given to the readjustment of medical and pharmaceutical services and the improvement of pharmaceutical plans and products. Drug administration and control should be strengthened so that the production, supply, quality, quantity, categories and standards of drugs, biological products, medical intruments and contraceptive devices may more adequately meet the needs of preventive and curative health services and of family planning.

7. *Improve the training of technical and managerial personnel in the health service.* This affects not only the immediate needs of the health service, but also its modernization in the long run.

The higher and middle medical schools should be run well and the quality of teaching should be raised. Special attention should be paid to developing various forms and methods of staff training with a view to forming a pool of skilled personnel who possess modern scientific and technical knowledge, as well as scientific management ability.

8. *Strengthen the financial, scientific and administrative control of the health service.* In improving the medical service, consideration should be given to economic returns, that is, raising quality while cutting expenses. Medical service is closely linked to economic construction. The improvement of medical service depends on existing economic conditions and, in turn, promotes the development of economic construction. Therefore, the readjustment of the medical service in a systematic fashion is crucial to the normal development of the national health service. If we carry out our task by following closely the correct policies and principles laid down by the Party Central Committee, we will surely overcome difficulties and achieve with success the central task of adjustment, improve the people's health and contribute to the modernization of our country.

56. FAMILY PLANNING IN CHINA
By the Policy Research Section,
Family Planning Office of the State Council

Family planning in China has been a lengthy process. Initially, we did not grasp the importance of this work and lacked practical experience. Now, family planning work has been brought within the scope of the national economic plan and is proceeding smoothly in coordination with the growth of the national economy.

I. Thirty Years of Stops and Starts

Human reproduction is decided by a social mechanism. There is a close relationship between material production and human reproduction. China's experience has proved that family planning has a direct bearing on the speed of a country's economic development, on the improvement of the people's livelihood and on the welfare of the nation as a whole. It took China as long as 30 years to understand this issue clearly and to give it serious attention.

Early Efforts. Family planning in China has been consistently advocated and implemented under the leadership of the people's government. The issue was publicized as early as the 1950's, soon after the founding of New China. In August 1953, the Government Administration Council directed the Ministry of Health to help the people carry out family planning. In 1956, Comrade Mao Zedong presided over the drafting of the "National Programme for Agricultural Development," in which is stipulated: "Other than in areas inhabited by national minorities, birth control should be publicized and popularized in all densely populated areas and family planning advocated, so that the family can avoid being overburdened and the children can have better education and chances of full employment."

In September 1956, Comrade Zhou Enlai, in his report on the "Proposals on the Second Five-Year Plan for the Development of the National Economy," advocated an appropriate birth control policy in the interest of protecting women and children, of educating our descendants and of ensuring the health and prosperity of the nation. He called on the health departments to take effective measures for this purpose.

In 1957, Comrade Mao Zedong indicated at the 11th Supreme State Conference and at the Third Plenary Session of the Eighth Party Central Committee that mankind should exercise control over nature and grow in a planned way. He said there should be a 10-year plan for family planning with some years allowed for testing, publicizing and popularizing the measure. Some Chinese economists likewise advised controlled population growth in China.

However, these views and proposals were never given effect due to the "Left" influence on the country's guiding ideology. In 1958, a scholar doing research in population theory who was an advocate of family planning was unjustly criticized. After that, population theory became almost a forbidden subject, and the work in family planning was greatly hampered.

During the three years of great economic difficulties due to natural disasters (1959-61), the natural growth rate of the Chinese population declined. In 1962, following the recovery of the national economy, there was a tendency towards rapid increase in population growth. In view of this trend, the Party Central Committee and the State Council issued the timely directive to carry out family planning work conscientiously so as not to jeopardize the nation's economic growth. This became an established policy for China's socialist construction.

On numerous occasions, Comrade Zhou Enlai had dealt with the importance of late marriage and birth control and had proposed certain concrete measures. In 1964, the Office of Family Planning was established under the State Council and made a good beginning in population control. When the "cultural revolution" began in 1966, this good beginning was frustrated by Lin Biao and the Gang of Four. Family planning organizations were suspended, the personnel in this field were attacked and the work once again fell into a state of neglect.

In 1971, Comrade Zhou Enlai again took a personal initiative in establishing family planning work. A leading group for family planning was set up under the State Council in August 1973. Family planning was brought into the Fourth and Fifth Five-Year plans for the development of the national economy.

In spite of many explicit directives and correct proposals from the party and the government for work in family planning, the majority of the people did not understand sufficiently for a long period of time that population growth should be coordinated with the growth of the national economy; instead most of us clung to the notion that the more people, the better. Although we advocated family planning work, we did not devise specific measures to implement it. For a time, therefore, population growth went unchecked, and the resulting high birth rate coupled with a low mortality rate added up to an extraordinarily high rate of natural population growth. In the 30 years from 1949 to 1979, China's population grew by more than 430 million — from 540 million in 1949 to 970 million in 1979.

Population Growth. The last 30 years have been characterized by the imbalance between population growth and economic growth. China's grain output in 1979 was over 660,000 million catties (330,000 million kg.), nearly treble the 1949 output, but the average amount of grain per capita in 1979 had risen only 135 kg. over the amount of 1949. The imbalance has greatly hampered the improvement of the people's livelihood, both materially and culturally.

During the first 20 years after Liberation, poor family planning led to an annual 2% increase in population. From the early 1970's on, after the government included family planning in the plans for national economic development and attached importance to this work, the population growth rate dropped. In 1970, the birth rate was 33.6 per thousand population; in 1979 it dropped to 17.9 per thousand. The natural population growth rate of 26 per thousand population in 1970 dropped to 11.7 in 1979.

Because human reproduction takes place in relatively long cycles, the current birth rate is influenced by what happened 20 years ago, just as the birth rate today will influence the future 20 years hence. The experience of the past 30 years has taught us that population growth should be conducted in a planned way, in keeping with material production. The national economy must be developed while population growth must be reduced to achieve a better balance.

Since 1978, with the return of political stability and unity and the readjustment of the national economic plan, the guidelines and policies of the party and the government relating to family planning have become more explicit and work in this field has proceeded with satisfactory results.

II. Family Planning Developments in 1980

The heartening achievements in family planning obtained in 1980 can hardly be separated from the basic work done in the previous years. Since the Third Plenary Session of the 11th Party Central Committee, a correct ideological line has been established together with correct political and organizational lines and a series of correct policies have been promulgated. In 1979, stability and unity returned and the national economy developed according to the guidelines of readjustment, restructuring, consolidation and improvement.

Flexible economic policies in rural areas brought about improvements in the people's livelihood. To coordinate population growth with economic development in China, the government strengthened its guidance over family planning work. Leaders at all levels attached importance to this work and all the departments concerned coordinated their tasks. Much attention was given to propaganda and educational work, as well as to research in population theory. Posts in family planning units and departments were filled and arrangements were made to assign to every people's commune, town and neighbourhood one person specifically in charge of this work. Provinces, municipalities and autonomous regions promulgated provisional rules and regulations on family planning that came with awards and penalties. All these measures contributed to the advance of family planning work in 1980.

The "One Couple, One Child" Policy. In light of China's actual conditions, the central government has called for even stricter controls on population growth with the slogan "one couple, one child." The report on the work of the government at the Second Session of the Fifth National People's Congress called for practical measures to reward couples who agree to have only one child. This is a new development in China's family planning policy — and a well-founded one.

Thanks to years of effort in this field, the Chinese people are beginning to realize the importance of family planning and more and more couples have decided to have only one child. The planned birth rate has risen but the rate of second and third births has dropped. A number of units have distinguished themselves in family planning work. Sichuan, for example, is China's most densely populated province. Its natural growth rate was as high as 29 per thousand population in 1971, but in 1979 it dropped to 6.7. A number of advanced counties achieved outstanding results, reducing their natural growth rate by a big margin.

All this clearly demonstrates that effective family planning depends on propaganda and practical measures. If the work is done well, the plan for one-child families will be carried out smoothly. It is most important for the masses and cadres to realize that population growth must be made compatible with economic development and that the success of the current policy is in the interest of the individual, the collective and the whole nation from both the long-term and the immediate point of view.

The Importance of Family Planning. In 1980, family planning was placed on the agenda for discussion by the party and the people's government at all levels. In June 1980, the Secretariat of the CPC Central Committee called a meeting specifically to discuss control of population growth and family planning. At the meeting, it was pointed out that family planning is a strategic issue for the nation, and that the proper handling of this issue is a long-term task with major policy implications. The meeting also called on party committees at all levels to strengthen the leadership over this work and to make efforts to grasp the importance of family planning for the development of material production and to place it on the long-term programme for national economic development.

On September 25, 1980, the Central Committee of the CPC issued an open letter calling on Communist Party and Youth League members to take the lead in limiting population growth to one child per couple. This letter spelled out the general target and the policies of population control in China. Each province, municipality, autonomous region, prefecture, county and commune appointed one leading comrade — sometimes even the top leader — to take responsibility for family planning work. The work was to be put often on the agenda for discussion and review, so that problems in connection with the implementation of family planning could be solved promptly.

The idea of raising the national economic growth rate and reducing the birth rate has been accepted by more and more people. The planning, review and supervision of population growth and national economic growth have been coordinated in practice with the cooperation of all departments concerned.

The effective control of the birth rate in 1980 was ensured by the following measures:

(1) *We launched a popular educational campaign via mass media to provide information about family planning and to encourage couples of child-bearing age to volunteer to practice birth control.* Activities in making comparisons between unplanned and planned population growth were widely carried out in 1980 in provinces, municipalities, prefectures, counties and towns, and down to the communes, production brigades, production teams and individual households. Everyone participated in calculating population growth rates during the past 30 years, changes in farmland and grain consumption per capita. People came to realize that if population growth continued unchecked, per capita acreage would decrease because the total farmland area remained a constant. Although grain output had doubled since the early years after Liberation, grain consumption per capita had not increased much. Given the reality of the present, people were asked to think about the future and future generations.

Great advances were made in the study of population theory. Twenty-nine research institutes and research departments have been set up in the provinces, municipalities and autonomous regions. Subjects included: study of the population theory under the guideline of Marxism; ideological approaches to both material production and population growth; China's current population policies; population forecasting; control of urban and rural population growth; and family planning for national minorities.

(2) *We practised family planning by implementing economic measures.* In 1980, economic rewards and penalties were introduced. Rewards were given to those units and individuals who had done good work on family planning. Those couples who volunteered to have only one child received regular child care allowances. Economic penalties were levied on the few who, after patient ideological education, still paid no attention to family planning and the very few individuals who undermined this work were punished. Rules and regulations regarding rewards and penalties have been formulated in various localities and good results have been achieved in promoting family planning work and population control.

(3) *We used models in family planning.* Cadres at all levels and the broad masses of party and Youth League members conscientiously took the lead in having only one child. Parents who had passed child-bearing age persuaded their married children to have only one child. This had a good effect on popularizing family planning and got the broad masses of people to follow their lead. The open letter of the CPC Central Committee calling on party and Youth League members to take the lead in having one-child families in the interest of the whole nation strengthened the people's confidence in the work. By the end of 1980, statistics from 25 provinces, municipalities and autonomous regions showed that there were 19.51 million couples with only one child and that 11 million couples received certificates for pledging to have only one child.

(4) *We stressed knowledge about eugenics.* The basic guideline for family planning is to con-

trol the population and improve the health of the offspring by encouraging fewer but healthier births. In 1980, publicity on eugenics was emphasized. Investigation and study on hereditary diseases were started and consultant clinics on eugenics were set up in some medical and health units where conditions permitted. Forecasting the health of the foetus was begun.

It is stipulated in China's marriage law (Chapter II, Article 6) that marriage is not permitted in circumstances where the man and woman are lineal blood relatives or collateral blood relatives up to the third degree of relationship. Neither is marriage permitted where one party is suffering from any disease which is regarded by medical science as rendering a person unfit for marriage.

(5) *We paid attention to the study of new trends and to the solution of new problems.* The restructuring of China's economic system, the relaxation of agricultural economic policies and the implementation of various forms of payment in the countryside brought about an unprecedented affluence in the rural economy and new challenges in family planning work. Accordingly, certain effective new measures had to be formulated for population control. These included contracts for late marriage and one birth and other measures which are under review for trial implementation.

(6) *We have intensified our cooperation with other countries in family planning work.* Following the development of family planning work in China, we have cooperated and exchanged experience with world organizations on population and family planning and with family planning departments of other countries. We have cooperated in the programmes organized by the United Nations Fund for Population Activities and have sent abroad various study groups and individuals to conduct scientific research on family planning. In June 1980, China set up the Family Planning Society, which has collaborated on projects with a Japanese nongovernmental organization – the Japanese International Cooperative Financial Group of Family Planning. In our work with foreign countries, we have learned advanced scientific technology and gained broad experience in family planning work and have made use of foreign funds and equipment to advance family planning work in China in light of the country's actual conditions.

In summary, family planning work achieved good results in 1980, mainly through renewed ideological education supplemented by appropriate and necessary economic measures. However, there are still problems to be tackled, such as: the uneven development of the work; relatively more multiple births in remote and mountainous regions; the shortage of technical personnel; bad management and primitive, coercive working methods; the shortage of contraceptives and their poor quality; and inadequate implementation of the "one couple, one child" policy.

III. Excellent Prospects for the Future

We are conducting the work of family planning in a developing country with nearly 1,000 million people, of whom about 800 million are peasants. The country is not rich and its science, culture, education and public health are comparatively backward. What is more, vestiges of feudalism remain and influence the people's thinking. All these factors make population control difficult. However, in family planning work, as in the work being done in other fields, difficulties are being surmounted and progress is being made. We have every reason to expect that our progress in the future will be excellent.

(1) *We have legal guarantees.* The Constitution adopted at the Fifth National People's Congress in 1978 stipulates in Article 53: "The State advocates and encourages family planning." Article 12 of the marriage law adopted at the Third Session of the Fifth National People's Congress in 1980 stipulates: "Husband and wife are duty bound to practice family planning." Is it the legal obligation of every Chinese citizen to abide by the law and practice family planning, including the practice of late marriage and birth control.

(2) *Family planning organizations have been set up from the topmost level down to the grassroots, with responsible party and government members taking a leading role.* Even at the level of the commune and the street neighbourhood, there are people specially assigned to take charge of family planning work. They receive support from a strong network of activists in family planning. Authorities at the national and the local level have drawn up plans for population control on the basis of local conditions and the opinions of the masses.

(3) *The principle in family planning is to persuade people to practice birth control voluntarily under the guidance of the state and to use comprehensive methods of contraception.* In cities as well as in rural areas, contraceptives are distributed free of charge by women cadres, medical workers, women production team leaders, family planning counsellors and pharmacy shop-assistants. Sterilization procedures are performed free of charge and recuperation leave is granted with full

pay. Where conditions permit, some factories and communes also give food allowances and other subsidies to couples who practice family planning.

(4) *Health services for mothers and children are being improved.* A network of health services for women and children is gradually being set up in China. There are health clinics for mothers and children, hospitals of gynaecology, obstetrics and pediatrics in the provinces, municipalities and autonomous regions. There are health centres in prefectures and counties, county doctors and midwives at the commune and production brigade levels and all kinds of nurseries and kindergartens in cities and in the countryside. There are also clinics for periodic check-ups and outpatient services especially for one-child families. Vaccinations and injections are given free of charge to prevent the spread of infectious diseases and to ensure the healthy growth of children.

In urban areas, workers and staff members, upon retirement, receive pensions which ensure their living expenses. In the countryside, each village has its own arrangements for the care of old people without children to support them.

(5) *A sizeable detachment of scientific and technical personnel for family planning is gradually taking shape.* Researchers in population theory and workers in the natural sciences, as well as in the social sciences, are concerned with the work of controlling population growth. All departments are working together and mapping out plans according to the Party Central Committee directive to implement the policy of the one-child family. Fundamental to this work and favouring its success is the leadership given by the Chinese Communist Party and the superiority of the socialist system, which can bring all the advantages into full play and create news ones. Now that family planning has been brought within the scope of the national economic programme, administrative measures can be used to promote this work. The Chinese people are highly intelligent and have a strong sense of discipline, so they will understand the importance of practicing family planning in the interest of the health and prosperity of the whole nation and that of the welfare of future generations.

We have now recognized the objective law governing the control of population growth. We have found the solution to the issue which was raised over 20 years ago. Proceeding from China's present-day reality, in keeping with the objective law governing the control of population growth and through the concerted efforts of the people, we are confident that we can maintain our population growth at an ideal level.

57. ENVIRONMENTAL PROTECTION IN CHINA
By the Research Section,
Office of the Environmental Protection Leading Group
of the State Council

China's environmental protection work began in the early 1970's. At the first National Conference on Environmental Protection, held in 1973, the "Regulations Concerning Protection and Improvement of the Environment" (draft for trial implementation) were adopted. In 1974, the State Council set up a leading group with an office under it to direct environmental protection work and issued or authorized the circulation of the following rules and reports: the "Provisional Regulations for Preventing Contamination of the Sea," the "Report on Preventing Food Contamination," the "Sanitary Standards for Designing of Industrial Enterprises" and the "Provisional Emission Control Standards for Industrial Waste Gas, Water and Residues."

Since that time, various areas and departments have done a great deal of work to prevent and treat pollution and have achieved quite a few successes. However, because of the turmoil during the years 1966-76, and the influence of erroneous "Left" ideas on our economic work, the principles, policies and measures concerning environmental protection have not been fully implemented. Pollution of the environment, destruction of natural resources and disturbance of the ecological balance have not been effectively controlled.

In the winter of 1978, the Third Plenary Session of the 11th Central Committee of the Chinese Communist Party took a decision of historic significance, namely, to shift the focus of the party's work to modernization. At the end of that year, the Central Committee authorized the circulation of the "Main Points of the Report on Environmental Protection" prepared by the environmental protection leading group of the State Council, and issued important instructions for stepping up the work in this area. The report of the leading group explicitly pointed out that environmental protection is essential to economic construction and the realization of the Four Modernizations, and that environmental pollution problems must be tackled while construction is going on.

The leading group convened a national conference on environmental protection in March 1979 in Chengdu. The participants conscientiously studied the Central Committee's instructions, reviewed the work that had been done in the interim and called for improved management of the environment. In September 1979, the Standing Committee of the National People's Congress adopted and promulgated the "Environmental Protection Law of the People's Republic of China" (for trial implementation), thus initiating a new stage in China's environmental protection work.

I. Principal Achievements in Environmental Protection in 1979-80

In the past two years, in accordance with the principles and policies adopted since the Third Plenary Session of the 11th Party Central Committee, various areas and departments have carried out the Environmental Protection Law and the Central Committee's relevant instructions, introduced and exercised better management of the environment and accelerated the progress in this work.

Environmental Protection in Urban Areas

China's 216 large and medium-sized cities all suffer to varying degrees from air, water and noise pollution. Over the past few years, the cities have vigorously tackled the most urgent local environmental pollution problems. Thanks to the efforts made by various departments in Beijing, Shanghai, Tianjin, Shenyang, Lanzhou, Guilin, Hangzhou and Suzhou — cities designated by the state as major targets for environmental protection — pollution in these cities has been more or less reduced or controlled.

Beijing. In the past two years, and particularly in 1980, environmental protection in the capital has been stepped up. Some achievements were made after the Secretariat of the Party Central Committee put forward four suggestions concerning guidelines for construction in Beijing. These suggestions included: "Transform the environment of Beijing, improve afforestation and sanitation and, by taking advantage of the hills, waters, cultural and historic sites, turn the capital into a first-rate, beautiful, clean and modern city."

Beijing's water supply comes from the Guanting, Miyun and Huairou reservoirs. With improved environmental protection, the water from these reservoirs now meets drinking water standards laid down by the state. The Changhe, Tonghui, Lianhua and four other rivers used to be contaminated by effluents from 401 major sources of pollution. Over the past few years, and especially during the past two years, treatment of 324 of the sources has significantly reduced the discharge of toxic substances into these rivers. Comparing the figures for 1980 with those for 1974, it can be seen that discharges of phenol have been reduced by 88%, cyanogen by 80%, cadmium by 85%, arsenic by 87% and chlorine by 45%.

To control smoke and soot pollution, 86% of the 5,095 furnaces in Beijing proper have been renovated, resulting in a reduction of such discharges. At the same time, emissions of sulphur dioxide have been reduced by using less coal. As a result, except during the central heating season, the air quality in Beijing basically meets the standards that the state has set for the city.

To reduce noise pollution in residential areas of Beijing, 31 factories that were considered serious sources of noise pollution were either merged with other factories or relocated, and 53 machines for making honeycomb coal briquettes were renovated in 1980. In some areas of the city, trees were planted to upgrade the environment.

Shanghai. Since 1977, the Shanghai Municipal People's Government has invested nearly 200 million yuan for treatment of pollution and has constructed a number of facilities for the treatment of waste water and gas. In 1980 alone, the government invested 78,480,000 yuan and completed 2,290 treatment facilities with the capacity for treating 155,000 tons of waste water a day, 321 cu. m. of waste gas per hour and 576,000 tons of residues per year. The dust level in the city proper has been reduced and the discharge of major pollutants such as mercury, cyanogen and cadmium has by and large been brought under control.

To check the spread of industrial pollution, the departments in charge of protecting Shanghai's environment have exercised strict supervision over capital construction. Since 1978, more than 92% of the construction projects achieved in the city have been carried out with close attention to the regulations concerning environmental management. Environmental protection measures were also adopted during the process of factory construction.

The Municipal People's Government has also set up a special organization to bring together experts to draw up plans for the treatment of the serious pollution of the Huangpu River.

Tianjin. The Haihe River is the chief source of Tianjin's water supply. During the dry season each year, backwash from the sea brings in saline water. Between April and July 1977, there were 80 days when the chloride content of the water was over 500 mg./litre, and sometimes as high as 1,855 mg./litre, resulting in an increase of sulphates and general mineral content. Hence, protection of the Haihe River's water quality became an urgent matter. In recent years, to block the backwash from the sea a dam was built across the lower reaches of the river, an air curtain was used to operate the lock gate and all sewage outlets along the river were sealed. In 1980, the chloride content was maintained at below 200 mg./litre and oxygen consumption below 5 mg./litre, while other major pollutants such as phenol, cyanogen, mercury, chlorine and arsenic were all kept within the limits set by the state. The water quality was 90-95% up to standard. To improve the management of the Haihe River, the Standing Committee of the Tianjin Municipal People's Government recently adopted the "Provisional Regulations for Protecting the Section of the Haihe River System Inside Tianjin."

A good deal of work has been done to eliminate smoke and soot discharged from industrial and other furnaces. More than half of the 5,800 or more furnaces in the city have been remodelled. However, control of industrial waste gas is inefficient and the amounts of sulphur dioxide and nitrogen oxides in the air still exceed the limits set by the state.

Shenyang. In 1979, the Shenyang Municipal People's Government drew up a "Programme for Environmental Protection, 1980-1985," which made control of air pollution its chief target, and began city-wide all-around prevention and treatment of pollution. In accordance with the requirements of the programme, construction of a gasification station and a heat-supply unit in the Tiexi Power Plant was stepped up to supply the city with gas and heat. In 1980, the city invested over 50 million yuan in pollution control projects, of which 300 have been completed. Furnaces and kilns were remodelled to eliminate smoke and soot, and waste gas was conducted to adjacent areas for heating use. Consequently, air pollution has been brought under initial control; dust levels and the content of sulphur dioxide in the air have dropped.

The Hunhe River, an important source of Shenyang's ground water supply, is contaminated by phenol and other toxic substances. The city is simultaneously trying to save water and to treat waste water. In 1980, the supply of water to 131 factories whose daily consumption of water exceeded 10,000 tons was regulated, with the result that water consumption was 6.7% less than in 1979. The use of recycled water in industrial plants reached 44.3%, an increase of 13.4% over 1979, while waste water treatment capacity increased by 21 million tons a year. These measures led to a 5,532-ton reduction of such pollutants as phenol and arsenic, thereby lessening the pollution of the Hunhe River.

The greening of Shenyang is part of the environmental protection programme. In 1980, 210,000 trees were planted, 2,000 *mu* of land were afforested and an area of 288,000 sq. m. was covered with new lawns.

Lanzhou. Owing to its location in a river valley, Lanzhou was subject to temperature inversions in winter and heavy smog throughout the year. The air pollution problem used to be very serious. Over the past three years, however, 71% of the boilers in the city, 43% of the industrial furnaces and kilns and 67% of the boilers for drinking water have been remodelled to eliminate smoke and soot. Industrial waste heat was circulated to heat homes in densely populated residential areas covering 650,000 sq. m., and more than 200,000 tons of anthracite of low sulphur content and volatility were brought in from other provinces for home heating. At the same time, emission of industrial waste gas was kept within certain bounds and a time limit set for its treatment.

In 1980, 235 pollution treatment projects went into operation, considerably improving the air quality in Lanzhou. In the winter of 1980, the sulphur dioxide content in the air was 0.152 mg./cu. m., 75% less than in 1977, bringing it almost into compliance with state standards. The floating dust content was 1.41 mg./cu. m., 42% lower than in 1977, but still higher than state standards. Heavy smog has basically been eliminated.

Guilin. For some time, Guilin's beautiful Lijiang River had been contaminated by industrial pollutants. To protect the scenery of Guilin and the Lijiang River, the State Council issued special instructions and allocated funds for the treatment of the river. The Guangxi Zhuang Autonomous Region and the Guilin Municipal People's Government restored and reconstructed scienic spots and achieved initial success in putting a stop to the destruction of the area's famous karst landscape. To control industrial pollution, 13 of the city's factories were ordered to suspend production or close down, and a number of factories that polluted the environment with waste water and gas were instructed to install pollution control devices. Today, the water quality of the Lijiang River has improved and the scenic beauty of Guilin has basically been restored.

Suzhou. Suzhou is a beautiful city of gardens and trees. But, because no attention was paid in the past to protecting the landscape, more than 400 factories were allowed to be built in the city, and the rivers and air became seriously polluted. In recent years, the Suzhou Municipal People's Government has adopted certain guidelines with regard to the expansion of the city and has ordered the construction of facilities for the treatment of industrial waste water. This has reduced the emission of toxic substances. In 1979, it was found that 68% of the water from the Grand Canal was contaminated with phenol, cyanogen, arsenic, chromium and mercury; the levels of these pollutants exceeded by 31% the permissible limits. In 1980, only 41% of the water was contaminated and the level of toxic substances had dropped to 14% above the permissible limit. The famous Hanshan Temple in Suzhou was once subject to contamination by waste water and residue discharged by the Huasheng Paper Mill. After the mill was renovated, the discharge of waste water was reduced by 42% and that of residue by 72%.

In line with industrial readjustment, certain factories that had high noise and vibration levels, were serious polluters, or produced combustibles or explosives have been moved out of the city.

Hangzhou. The Hangzhou Municipal People's Government has all along attached importance to the protection of the environment of West Lake. In recent years, the Yuewang Temple and other well-known sites have been repaired and the areas surrounding the lake have been cleaned up. Repairs were made over 20 km. of the embankment and a revetment built. To prevent offices and institutions located along the banks and local residents from discharging sewage into the lake, a sewage conduit, 9.4 km. in length, was laid around the lake and eight sewage pumping stations built. Fifty-six diesel engine boats working on the lake were converted into storage battery boats to prevent contamination from oil leaks. In 1980, the lake was dredged and 60,000 cu. m. of sludge removed.

To control the noise level in Hangzhou, trucks were not permitted in the vicinity of the lake and 280 diesel engine vehicles were banned from entering the city limits. To keep the air in the scenic area clean, 55 furnaces belonging to offices and to other buildings located along the banks were renovated to eliminate smoke and soot, and most of the furnaces belonging to teahouses in the area switched to using liquified petroleum gas. Four factories that spoiled the view were moved out of the vicinity of the lake.

In 1980, the Hangzhou Society for the Study of Environmental Science was established to evaluate the environmental quality of the lake and to study anti-pollution measures.

Prevention and Treatment of Water Pollution

In China, the average annual surface water runoff amounts to 2,600,000 million cu. m. and that of groundwater runoff to 700,000 million cu. m. The country ranks third in the world in terms of total storage of water. But the average annual surface water per capita is no more than 2,700 cu. m., about one-fourth of the per capita average in the world. China is not rich in water resources. Moreover, 15 of its 37 large rivers are seriously contaminated. The Party Central Committee and the State Council have attached great importance to the prevention and treatment of water pollution, and have obtained initial successes in this respect.

The Bohai and Huanghai Seas. Two of China's important bodies of water, the Bohai and the Huanghai seas, border on the provinces of Liaoning, Shandong, Hebei and Jiangsu and on the city of Tianjin. Large quantities of untreated effluent from factories, harbours and oil fields along the coast, as well as from ships and vessels that sail on the two seas, contaminate the waters with petroleum and heavy metals. The pollution in the Bohai Sea is particularly serious because the Bohai is a semi-closed inland sea.

In 1977, the State Council called a conference and set up a leading group with an office under it to take charge of planning 195 treatment projects. By the end of 1980, 142 of the projects were completed. The Petroleum Administration of the Dagang, Shengli and Liaohe oil fields and the Offshore Petroleum Bureau built eight sewage treatment stations which have the capacity to treat 92% of the oil effluent in the Bohai. At the same time, a number of chemical factories and metallurgical plants along the coast changed their production techniques and began to treat pollutants, thereby reducing the emission of heavy metals. Oil pollution in the Bohai and Huanghai seas is now basically under control. The waters of Bohai Bay and Laizhou Bay have met the quality standard set for surface water and are approaching the standard set for fisheries. Except in a few areas near the coast, where the pollution from heavy metals slightly exceeds the acceptable standard for fisheries, the levels of toxic substances such as cadmium, lead, chromium and copper are within the acceptable limits set by the state.

To further combat pollution of the seas, 16 environmental protection stations have been set up along the coast, with 145 monitoring posts under them. A monitoring network has been set up under the National Research Centre for Maritime Environmental Studies to conduct day-to-day monitoring.

Songhua River. The Songhua River and its tributaries supply Jilin and Heilongjiang with most of their water. However, these rivers are heavily polluted. In 1978, a leading group was set up to study the problem and initiate the construction of water treatment projects. By the end of 1980, 68 of 141 planned projects, representing a total investment of 85 million yuan, were completed on schedule. Construction of the country's largest pollution treatment project was begun in 1979 to deal with the pollution from the Jilin Chemical Industrial Complex — once the principal sources of pollution of the Songhua River. The project includes a 65-km.-long sewage pipe, a monitoring station, a neutralization station, a residential sewage treatment station, sludge incinerators and three other components. When it is completed, the project will have a treatment capacity of 8,000 tons per hour. At the end of 1980, only the first stage of the project had been completed. The state's investment in this project is 40 million yuan.

The Changchun No. 1 Motor Vehicle Plant, the Changchun Pharmaceutical Factory, the Northeast Low Alloy Processing Plant, the Harbin Oil Refinery, the Mudanjiang Paper Mill and some other enterprises located along the Songhua River have basically completed their treatment projects on schedule, so that the amounts of organic substances and heavy metals discharged into the river system have been reduced.

Ya'er Lake. Situated in eastern Hubei Province, between the middle and lower reaches of the Changjiang River, Ya'er Lake is a shallow body of water rich in organic substances. The lake is replenished chiefly by surface water, runoff which is abundant and of excellent quality, and is ideal for breeding fish. In the 1950's, the lake's annual output of fish was over 500,000 kg. After the Wuhan Gedian Chemical Factory went into production, the lake became contaminated by large amounts of toxic industrial effluent; agriculture and fishing in the area were adversely affected and the people's health was endangered. The State Council thereupon gave special attention to the treatment of pollution in Ya'er Lake. In 1973, construction began on a treatment project with 6,530,000 yuan of state investment. Completed in August 1976, the project includes a tertiary lagoon with an area of 6,200 *mu,* a 5,500-m. embankment, a 38-km. flood discharge, a 5,600-m. pipeline, 12 bridges, 16 culvert sluice-gates and an electric drainage station. The project has played a significant role in reducing the contamination of the lake. The annual output of fish that meets the state's food standards is 250,000 kg. With pollution under control, the areas sorrounding the lake have once again become suitable for agriculture.

Key Water Areas. While paying close attention to treating water contamination, the state has strengthened management of key water areas, conducted monitoring, assessment and scientific surveys of these areas, studied the changes in water quality and mapped out comprehensive plans and programmes for pollution control.

The Changjiang River is extremely long and its water, in its natural condition, is of excellent quality and of such abundance that it has a tremendous diluting and self-purification capability against pollutants. By the end of 1980, 172 monitoring stations had been set up, forming a preliminary network for protecting the water quality of the Changjiang. In the same year, a "Report on the Investigation of the Pollution Load in the Main Stream of the Changjiang River" was prepared, and research was conducted on the laws governing the dilution of pollutants and self-purification in typical sections of the main stream, as well as on the river's carrying capacity. The investigation showed that its absolute pollution load is remarkable; it also showed that the river was contaminated in sections where it passed big cities and industrial areas. But in terms of amount of water in the river as averaged over a number of years, the ratio between natural water and contaminated effluent discharged into the main stream is estimated at 200:1; so the average amount of pollutants in the river itself is not high and water quality as a whole is good.

The Huanghe (Yellow River) is the second longest river in China. In recent years, industrial waste water discharged into the river every day reached three million tons. To protect the river, 18 monitoring projects, constituting part of a larger network, monitored 127 sections of the river. By the end of 1980, one had a clear idea of the state of contamination of the river as a whole. In addition, investigations and research on protection of the Lanzhou section of the Huanghe River, the biological assessment of water contamination in the middle and upper reaches of the river and the study of the self-purification capability against BOD in the Xianyang-Xi'an section of the Weihe River and of the impact of the Sanmenxia Reservoir on ecology have provided a scientific basis for comprehensive prevention of pollution.

The average annual amount of flow in the Zhujiang River (Pearl River) is 341,000 million cu. m., second only to the Changjiang River and also second in the whole country. Analyses made on the basis of research and monitoring data collected between 1971 and 1981 showed that water contamination of the river system was either minute or slight. In recent years, contamination in the lower reaches of the Xijiang River and the Dongjiang River has been reduced from slight to minute, whereas in 15% of the Beijiang River's sections, contamination has increased from slight to moderate. Guangzhou was found to be the biggest source of contamination of the Zhujiang River. Contamination in the Guangzhou section had reached serious proportions in 1975. However, owing to pollution treatment over the past few years, contamination in this section has been significantly reduced.

Treatment of Industrial Pollution

Pollution and destruction of the environment in China are caused mainly by the discharge of industrial wastes. In the past two years, various areas and departments have integrated the work of eliminating pollution with that of tapping the potential of industry, renovating industry, promoting comprehensive utilization and strengthening production management.

Petroleum Industry. The departments and units concerned with petroleum production have vigorously popularized the new technology of "sewage recycling reinjection," thus reducing the emission of waste material. By the end of 1980, 78 sewage disposal stations had been built in oil fields throughout the country. These stations dispose of over 290,000 tons of sewage every day. The rate of comprehensive treatment reaches 92% and that of sewage recycling reinjection, 76.4%. The Daqing Oil Field is able basically to dispose of its own sewage water and use it in place of clear water for recycling. This has prevented environmental pollution, controlled the tendency of the water table to drop each year, and helped increase production. The oil refining industry has treated environmental protection as part of production management. It has actively devised means for recovering and utilizing waste gas and sewage water.

Every year, several hundred thousand tons of crude oil are recovered. In 1980, the amount of water consumed in refining one ton of oil was reduced to 6.7 tons, 50% less than in 1979. The Changling Oil Refinery in Hunan Province was once a source of serious pollution. After many years of effort, it now sets an excellent example in environmental protection to the entire oil refining industry. The refinery built its own advanced waste water treatment equipment which can handle 600 tons of effluent per hour. It was the first such unit designed by our own country. The treated water is basically of the same quality as surface water. In the past, the No. 5 Oil Refinery in Jinzhou, Liaoning Province caused several fires when it discharged industrial pollutants into the river. In recent years, it has paid close attention to the treatment of contaminated water. In 1980, 97.3% of contaminated water was so treated, reducing the emission of oil into the water to 660 tons and thus cutting down on the pollution of rivers and bays. In the process of treatment, 25,041 tons of oil were recovered from the effluent.

Metallurgical Industry. The departments and units of the metallurgical industry are placing emphasis on the multi-purpose utilization of resources and energy. According to statistics, the output value of products recovered through multi-purpose utilization in 1980 was over 800 million yuan, double that of 1976. Many wastes that pollute the environment have been turned into raw materials. In the case of non-ferrous, precious and rare metals, over 50,000 tons are recovered every year. The non-ferrous metal smelteries now recover and utilize highly concentrated sulphur dioxide gas to produce more than 800,000 tons of sulphuric acid annually, an increase of 300,000 tons over 1972. In the steelworks, 71% of the blast furnace slag is re-used. Over half of the cement enterprises in the whole country make use of water sediment as cementite.

In the field of waste heat utilization, certain successes have also been achieved. The utilization rate of combustible gases in the key steel works increases yearly. In 1980, the utilization rate of blast furnace coal gas reached 90% and that of coke oven coal gas, 96%. These two items alone amounted to a saving of more than 10 million tons of standard coal. The Shenyang Smelting Plant was once an exceptionally serious polluter. Over the past three years, the enterprise has made the elimination of pollution a major target of its technical transformation and has introduced technical innovations and comprehensive utilization for this purpose. In 1980, it produced 113,000 tons of sulphuric acid from waste gas, and its re-utilization rate of water reached 75%, thus saving over 25,000 tons of water every day. It also achieved a notable reduction in the emission of heavy metals. The Shenyang Smelting Plant invested 18,550,000 yuan in environmental protection. However, just by increasing the output of sulphuric acid, recovering all kinds of metals and saving water, it has saved the equivalent of 17,290,000 yuan.

Chemical Industry. In 1980, nine big chemical enterprises, including those in Jilin and Lanzhou, completed a total of 105 pollution control projects. With the environmental protection installations that were built in the past, there are now altogether 307 installation units. This has served not only to conserve resources and reduce pollution, but also to create savings of 9,430,000 yuan each year.

The Lanzhou Chemical Company has completed an installation for the disposal of nitric acid tail gas and a project for the recovery of flare gas. The amount of nitrogen oxide emitted in nitric acid tail gas decreased from 970 kg. to 160 kg. per hour, meeting state emission control standards. Most of the 500 kg. of flare gas emitted per hour is recovered and used as fuel for boilers. This has led to a significant reduction of flare gas emissions and basically solved the pollution problem caused by the "yellow smoke dragon" and the "red smoke dragon" — a particularly severe problem in the Xigu district of Lanzhou.

Of the 121 chemical plants under the Shanghai Municipal Chemical Bureau which emit chlorine, hydrogen chloride, nitrogen oxide and sulphur dioxide, 80 have now brought pollution under initial control.

Building Materials Industry. The cement industry is focusing on dust elimination in its environmental protection work. By the end of 1980, 137 kilns in 49 large and medium-sized cement works all over the country were equipped with 121 electrostatic precipitators and large numbers of bag collectors. These devices enabled the cement works to recover altogether one million tons of powdered dust, which converts into a value of about 20 million yuan and constitutes 9.2% of their profits. In the past, the Dukou Cement Plant was almost hidden in clouds of cement dust. After several years of treatment, the dust emission level has dropped from 10% of the cement output per year in the past to 0.4% of the present output. The environment of the plant has undergone marked improvement.

Light Industry. In recent years, the paper-making industry has vigorously engaged in the recovery of alkali and the popularization of the ammonium sulphite process, the ammonia process and the use of semi-chemical pulp. The leather industry has introduced a new process of tanning by dehairing hides with enzymes. The synthetic fatty acid and detergent industries have begun the recovery of mirabilite and the comprehensive utilization of waste hydrochloric acid. The battery producing industry is popularizing non-mercuric cells, while the food industry, including the industries engaged in sugar and wine production, is making efforts to make full use of raw materials. Successes have been achieved in all these areas.

In 1980, 190,000 tons of caustic soda were recovered by paper mills, 60,000 tons more than in 1973. The Jilin Paper Mill recovers 30,000 tons of caustic soda annually and uses waste pulp to manufacture over ten kinds of products, totalling more than 1,000 tons. Its annual output value from comprehensive utilization is over 13 million yuan. The output value of the Hefei Leather Mill as a result of comprehensive utilization is over 1 million yuan, with a profit of over 200,000 yuan every year. About 20% of the factories under the Shanghai Bureau of Handicraft Industries have brought waste water under control and over 60% of the boilers and industrial kilns have been equipped with smoke-eliminating and dust-reducing devices. Some of the factories have also brought noise, vibration and dust under control and recovered many resources at the same time.

Power Industry. The power industry has increased the use of fine coal ash. According to statistics, the country's coal-burning thermal power plants discharge a total of about 26 million tons of ash every year. About 9% of this ash residue is used for various purposes. In recent years, many departments have extended the uses of fine coal ash beyond that of manufacturing building materials such as bricks and tiles. The Zhuzhou Power Plant in Hunan Province uses fine coal ash to manufacture No. 400 cement, a type of cement with little chamotte. Shanghai uses fine coal ash to pave the load-bearing layer of road surfaces. Power plants in Yantai, Qingdao and Chongqing separate dressed iron ore from fine coal ash, thus reducing the harmfulness of pollution from coal ash.

Coal Industry. The coal industry is making multiple uses of gangue. According to incomplete statistics, 60 or 70 million tons of gangue are discharged throughout the country every year. Now, over 10 million tons, or about 20%, may be reutilized. Shandong Province has made use of over 2,700,000 tons of gangue, about one-third of the amount discharged, thus saving more than 300,000 tons of coal. In recent years, many coal-washing plants have built installations with a closed system for the treatment of coal sludge, thus reducing pollution caused by coal sludge.

Communications Departments. The communications departments have strengthened harbour environment management. Sewage treatment installations and installations for recycling garbage have been constructed in Dalian, Qinhuangdao, Qingdao and Zhanjiang. In 1980, these installations handled 5,880,000 tons of sewage containing oil discharge from ships and boats and recovered over 33,400 tons of waste oil. This has brought them an income of 8,290,000 yuan. Harbour pollution has been controlled to some extent.

Cultural Departments. Over the past three years, the 10 film-processing factories under the Ministry of Culture have recovered more than 20,000 kg. of silver from waste water discharged in the course of film processing.

In accordance with the policy of industrial readjustment, reorganization and integration, many areas and departments have dealt with serious polluters and irrationally-distributed factories so as to reduce damage from pollution. The Jinan Municipal Chemical Bureau of Shandong Province has called upon seven chemical plants, located on the windward side of the urban district and upstream from water sources, to shift to other types of production, and thus solve the pollution problem caused by these chemical enterprises. The Jinan Municipal Light Industrial Bureau has integrated factories which can make mutual use of their industrial wastes to turn the wastes into useful materials. For example, a printing and dyeing mill supplies a nearby paper mill with waste alkali effluent as a substitute for caustic soda. This not only reduces the pollution caused by waste water containing alkali discharged from the printing and dyeing mill, but also saves coal and electricity valued at 150,000 yuan a year.

The steel casting and forging, heat treatment, electroplating and printing plate industries have factories scattered far and wide, where most of the work is done by hand. The noise and dust pollution and the emission of toxic or other harmful substances is considerable. It is costly for a factory to engage single-handedly in the treatment of pollution and some factories do not have the facilities to do so. In accordance with the policy of industrial readjustment, cities such as Tianjin, Jinzhou, Lanzhou, Jinan and Qingdao have amalgamated these factories to carry out specialized production, thus raising labour productivity and facilitating the treatment of pollution.

Protection of the Natural Environment

The protection of the natural environment — land, water, forests, grasslands, wild animals and plants — is of far greater strategic significance than the sole prevention and control of pollution. Since the Third Plenary Session of the 11th Central Committee of the Party, the Central Committee and the State Council have issued the "Decision on Some Questions Concerning the Acceleration of

Agricultural Development" and the "Directive on the Vigorous Development of Afforestation," both of which have played important roles in protecting and improving the natural environment of our country.

National Investigation of Natural Resources and Regionalization of Agriculture. In 1979, the State Council set up the Committee for the National Investigation of Natural Resources and Regionalization of Agriculture. The committee, in turn, set up nine specialized groups to study land resources, water resources, rural energy resources, agricultural mechanization, extensive use of chemical fertilizers and other farm chemicals, natural reserves, rural housing, rural economy and comprehensive regionalization of agriculture. Investigation of natural resources and regionalization of agriculture are strategic measures of overall importance for the reasonable exploitation, use and protection of natural resources, the planning and guiding of agricultural production in line with local conditions, and the achievement of socialist modernization of agriculture in our country.

In the past two years, 28 provinces, municipalities and autonomous regions have carried out regionalization of agriculture at the provincial level and 243 counties have proposed regionalization at the county level — regionalization is now being carried out in 695 counties. Many areas have readjusted the structure and distribution of agricultural production on the basis of investigation and regionalization, gradually restoring and improving the ecological balance where it has been disturbed.

Construction of Shelter Belts. The Huanghe River basin is the cradle of our civilization. The areas along its middle and upper reaches were once covered with dense forests and luxuriant grass. Over hundreds and thousands of years, the natural environment has been destroyed and the areas of forest vegetation have dwindled, causing severe ecological imbalance, with some areas becoming barren desert land. Since Liberation, the party and the government have done a great deal to improve the natural environment and great successes have been won. However, the problem remains quite serious.

The shelter belt system affects 324 counties and banners in the 11 provinces and autonomous regions of Xinjiang, Qinghai, Ningxia, Gansu, Shaanxi, Inner Mongolia, Shanxi, Hebei, Liaoning, Jilin and Heilongjiang. The area covered has a rural population of 44 million people, 290 million *mu* of cultivated land, over 800 million *mu* of pastureland and 81 million *mu* of forest. Only 2.1% of the area is forested. According to the plan, the goal of the first phase of the project is to afforest 80 million *mu*, while carefully protecting the existing forest vegetation. This will expand the current 4% of forest-covered agricultural and pastoral land in the windy and sandy regions (not including the Gobi Desert) to 10%. It will also increase the current 5% of forest-covered of land in the heavily eroded areas around the middle reaches of the Huanghe River to 18%. And, it will mean an initial improvement in the natural environment and the life of the people in this area.

The State Council has set up a leading group to guide the construction of shelter belts and has also established, within the Ministry of Forestry, a bureau for the construction of shelter belts in the north, northwest and northeast. Since 1979, a contingent of over 8,100 professionals has been organized to carry out surveying and planning work. The 11 provinces and regions have drawn up a general plan, taking the county and banner as the basic unit, and are collecting seeds and raising seedlings. By 1980, more than 39.20 million *mu* of trees had already been planted in these areas.

Afforestation of the Plains. Afforestation of the plains is a significant measure for the improvement of the natural environment and agricultural ecology of our country. Because the State Council has attached importance to this project, the work has developed fairly fast. Over the past three years, a network of 100 million *mu* of farmland and forest shelters has been created. 15 million *mu* of cultivated land were planted with farm crops, sectioned off by belts of paulownia and planted with 3,200 million trees. The area of afforested land is approaching the sum total for the previous 27 years. Since the Party Central Committee and the State Council issued the directive on the vigorous development of afforestation in 1980, over 100 counties out of 400 on the North China Plain have built networks of tree-sheltered farmland. In addition, a number of advanced counties in south China have carried out afforestation work.

Nature Reserves. The creation of nature reserves is another important measure for the protection of the natural environment. In 1979, while regionalization of agriculture was underway, scientific surveys and designations of nationwide nature reserves were also being carried out. The tentative plan is to create over 300 nature reserves of various ecological types in different parts of the country, comprising 1% of the total territory. In 1980, another 17 new nature reserves were designated while the existing ones were consolidated and their administration strengthened.

The nature reserves that have been approved

by the State Council include: the Laotieshan Mountain and Snake Island areas located in Liaoning Province, where the emphasis is placed on the protection of snakes and migratory birds; the Sacsaoul area in the Inner Mongolia Autonomous Region, where the target of protection is the area's sandy vegetation; the Nangunhe River area in Yunnan Province, where the principal targets of protection are the tropical rain forests, rare animals and elephants; and the Xinjiang Poplar Conservation Zone, where the targets of protection are the diverse-leaved poplars of desert areas.

By August 1980, 75 nature reserves had been established with a total area of 2,100,000 hectares, constituting 0.22% of the entire country.

II. Environmental Management in 1979-80

Legislation and Standards. In 1979, the Standing Committee of the Fifth National People's Congress approved and promulgated China's Environmental Protection Law (for trial implementation) and China's Forestry Law (for trial implementation). Later, the state also promulgated the Regulations for the Protection of Aquatic Resources of the People's Republic of China, the Standards of Water Quality for Farmland Irrigation, the Standards of Water Quality for Fisheries and the Standards for Safety in the Use of Insecticides. The enforcement of these laws and standards is an important indication that China has made new headway in environmental protection.

The Environmental Protection Law, being the basic law of environmental protection, proceeds from the actual conditions of the country. The purpose of the law is to enforce the rational use of the natural environment, the control of environmental pollution and the prevention of damage to ecosystems in the course of building a socialist modernized country. The law aims to create a clean, healthy and pleasant environment in which the people can live, work and carry out economic development.

The scope of the environment to be protected is specified in the Environmental Protection Law: the air, water, land, mineral resources, forests, grassland, wildlife, wild plants, aquatic plants and animals, historic sites, scenic spots for tourists, hot springs, nature reserves, residential districts and so forth. The chapter on the natural environment deals with soil, water and aquatic flora and fauna, mineral resources, forests, grassland and the resources of wild life and wild plants. The chapter on the prevention and elimination of pollution and other hazards to the public specifies nine kinds of pollutants to be dealt with: waste gas, waste water, residues, dust, garbage, radioactive material, noise, vibration and bad odours.

In 1980, the people's congresses and people's governments of the provinces, municipalities and autonomous regions adopted a number of regulations for the enforcement of the Environmental Protection Law.

Economic Measures. In the last few years, China has begun to use economic measures in environmental management. The principal measures adopted are:

(1) *The inclusion of investments for environmental protection purposes in the state's capital construction plan.* Such investments ensure that enterprises under construction adhere to specifications for environmental protection and supplement efforts to control pollution in existing enterprises. In 1980, supplementary investments amounted to 107,680,000 yuan, accounting for 0.2% of the total investments in capital construction.

In order to control pollution, a number of important industrial departments have set aside funds for environmental protection in their capital construction plans and plans for technical innovation. According to incomplete statistics of eight departments — including those of the metallurgical, chemical and petroleum industries — a total of 489,710,000 yuan was spent on technological transformation and on the construction or installation of devices to reduce the discharge of pollutants and to dispose safely of industrial wastes.

(2) *The adoption of economic penalties.* The Environmental Protection Law stipulates: "In cases where release of pollutants goes beyond the limits of the specified national standards, a fee shall be charged according to the quantities and concentrations of the pollutants, as specified."

In 1980, the Standing Committees of the people's congresses of Shanxi, Heilongjiang, Liaoning, Shandong, Jiangsu, Yunnan and Guizhou provinces, and the people's governments of Hebei, Zhejiang, Anhui, Hubei, Sichuan, Gansu, Xinjiang and Shanghai formulated relevant regulations and measures and charged fees to 8,700 enterprises for the discharge of pollutants. The fees thus charged are generally a little higher than the expenses needed for the proper disposal of pollutants, and the fees were included in the enterprises' production costs and paid out of the profits at their disposal. Out of consideration of their own economic benefits, the enterprises have shown interest in protecting the environment, thereby facilitating the control of pollution.

(3) *The adoption of economic incentives.*

The production of pollutants by industrial enterprises is tantamount to a waste of resources and energy. Therefore, the state encourages the multipurpose utilization of resources and energy. It is stipulated in the Environmental Protection Law that "the state will grant tax reductions or exemptions on, and apply a preferential pricing policy to products manufactured by using waste gas, waste water and waste residues as main material, and the profits thus derived need not be turned over to the state but will be used by the manufacturers concerned to control pollution and improve the environment." To implement this stipulation, the Ministry of Finance and the Environmental Protection Leading Group of the State Council have worked out specific measures. In 1979, enterprises were allowed a total of 81,000,000 yuan out of their profits for use in developing their capacity for utilizing waste water, gas and residues and the elimination of pollution. In 1980, multi-purpose utilization and utilization through recovery of waste materials registered considerable success. The various light industrial enterprises in Shanghai alone recovered 17.5 kg. of platinum, 280 kg. of gold, 34,450 kg. of silver and 28.89 kg. of palladium from waste water and residues.

Administrative Measures. The principal administrative measures that China has adopted for environmental management are as follows:

(1) *Urban planning.* In 1979, Shenyang and Suzhou worked out urban environmental plans. Their example was followed in 1980 by such large cities as Beijing, Tianjin, Shanghai, Guilin, Guangzhou, Lanzhou, Wuhan, Baotou, Changchun, Luoyang and Qingdao.

The principal measures taken by Shenyang in designing its urban environment were:

— The building of a plant with a gas-producing capacity of 540,000 cu. m. to increase the percentage of gas-using homes from 44% to 92%. Construction of the plant began in 1980.

— The expansion of facilities to supply central heating. Work has started on enlarging the heat-supplying equipment of the Tiexi Power Plant, to replace the large number of small boilers in the city's industrial section, and also supply heat for the central heating system of a number if the workers' homes.

— The use of waste hot water from power plants for domestic heating purposes. In 1980, waste heat was used for central heating in houses with a total floor space of 800,000. sq. m.

(2) *Strengthening environmental management of capital construction projects.* With regard to new construction, reconstruction and extension projects, the state requires that measures for environmental protection shall be designed, built and put into operation at the same time as the main project, so as to control new sources of pollution. In 1980, the State Planning Commission, the State Capital Construction Commission, the State Economic Commission and the Environmental Protection Leading Group of the State Council jointly issued a circular requiring that all enterprises contemplating a large or medium-sized capital construction project compile a report on the potential environmental effects. In 1980, 53% of all capital construction projects fulfilled the above requirement, whereas only 39% did so in 1979.

(3) *Setting a time limit for enterprises with serious pollution problems to control the pollution.* In October 1978, the State Planning Commission, the State Economic Commission and the Environmental Protection Leading Group of the State Council ruled that 261 sources of pollution in 167 industrial and mining enterprises would have to be completely controlled before 1982. Later the number of pollution sources was changed to 267 and the number of enterprises affected to 164. By the end of 1980, 143 or 53.5% of the pollution sources had been put under control.

Environmental Science Research

There are about 6,000 people engaged in environmental science research in China. Specialized research organizations at the provincial or ministerial level include: The Chinese Research Academy of Environmental Sciences, the Institute of Environmental Chemistry of the Chinese Academy of Sciences, the institutes of environmental protection of 27 provinces, municipalities and autonomous regions, and 7 institutes of environmental protection of the ministries of chemical, metallurgical and light industries. In 1979 the Chinese Society of Environmental Science was set up.

China has made great headway in environmental science research.

In the study of environmental social science research has begun on the level of fees to be charged when the discharge of pollutants exceeds the limits specified by the government, and on the basic theory and policies of the environmental management system, environmental economics, environmental law and the science of environmental management.

In the study of environmental quality, pollution surveys and environmental quality assessments have been made for many bodies of water such as the Guanting River system, certain sections of the Huanghe River and of the Changjiang River, the Second Songhua River, the Jiyun, Xiangjiang and Lijiang Rivers, Taihu Lake, the Yellow and Bohai seas, Hangzhou Bay and the mouth of the Zhujiang River. Surveys and assessments have also been made for cities such as Beijing (western and southeastern suburbs), Shenyang, Lanzhou, Nanjing, Panzhihua, Xi'an and Maoming. In some cases, charts of environmental quality have been drawn. Investigations and studies have been made of the pollution sources of over 3,000 large and medium-sized enterprises as well as of nearly 10,000 small ones. In some areas, files of pollution sources have been established. Research has been conducted on samples of ice, snow, soil and on animals and plants of the Changbai Mountains and Mount Qomolangma, and on the soil background values of certain cities and districts. Progress has been made in the study of the index system of environmental quality assessment, and of the modes of transformation and transport of pollutants.

In addition, Chinese environmentalists have advanced new concepts, such as "pollution degree," "pollution fields" and "ecological factors" — which have helped them formulate theories and methods of conducting environmental quality assessment under the conditions particular to China.

In the study of pollution control techniques, a tremendous amount of research on the treatment of various kinds of sewage has been carried out in combination with research on production technology. Achievements have been made in the treatment and purification of waste water containing alkali-chlorine and heavy metals; of waste water from electroplating, petroleum-refining, leather-processing, charring and film developing; and on the disposal of organic sewage and sewage with high acid content.

In the field of air pollution control, dust-collecting equipment such as scrubbers with Venturi high-voltage wide-spaced electrostatic precipitators and scrubbers with water film inclined pipes have been successfully produced, and research has been made on the recovery of high-density sulphur dioxide. Progress has also been made in the multi-purpose utilization of industrial waste residues, such as pulverized coal ash, red mud from aluminium plants, gangue and steel slag.

In the fields of environmental chemistry, environmental biology, environmental medicine and environmental acoustics, studies have been conducted on the laws of degradation and transformation of such pollutants as heavy metals, pesticides, phenol and cyanogen in soil and bodies of water; on the ecological effects of such pollutants on farmland and on water; and on the laws of their accumulation and metabolism in plants and animals. Attempts have been made to study the harmful mechanism of trichloro-acetaldehyde on wheat and the degradation mechanism of pesticides by symbiotic algal bacteria, as well as the effects of microbial activity on the speed at which sediment in bodies of water release methl mercury. All these studies have provided useful data for the elimination of pesticide contamination and the control of mercury contamination in water. Through experiments, a number of plants that are resistant or sensitive to SO_2, HF or Cl_2 have been screened. Colour plates of symptoms of affected plants have been compiled.

In the study of the effects of environmental pollution on people's health, epidemiological surveys of and research on the rapid screening of carcinogenic contaminants have been made. Investigations have been conducted in 22 cities and in Xuanwei Prefecture, Yunnan Province, into the interrelationship between air pollution and lung cancer. Research on the effects of heavy metal pollution of the Bohai and Yellow seas on human health, the effects of mercury pollution of the Songhua River on the health of fishermen, and the effects of minute quantities of organo-chlorine in drinking water on human health. The double-region theory of carcinogenic activity of polycyclic aromatic hydrocarbons has been advanced.

In the study of the elements of life and health, research has been conducted with positive results into the causes of Keshan and Kaschin-Beck diseases.

In the field of noise control, surveys of transport noise have been made in Beijing and Tianjin and other large cities. China has set environmental noise standards and testing norms, and industrial noise standards. Research has also begun into sound absorption, sound insulation, sound resistance and vibration absorption, as well as into the control of air flow noise.

Environmental Monitoring

Environmental monitoring is the basis of environmental management and research and provides important data for the formulation of policies, laws and regulations on environmental protection.

Since the founding of the People's Republic, we have steadily carried out monitoring work with regard to public health, weather, surface water and ground water. After the First National Environmental Protection Conference was held in 1973, work on environmental monitoring began; it has developed considerably in the last two years. By the end of 1980, there were 312 environmental monitoring stations throughout the country, with a total staff of 5,200. If the environmental science research institutes and their staff were included, the total would come to 354 units and 6,800 persons. Specialized monitoring units have also been set up in departments of industry, communications, public health, agriculture and forestry, water conservation, foreign trade, commerce, fishing, oceanography and meterology, as well as in many large and medium-sized enterprises. In some areas, environmental monitoring networks are taking shape.

In accordance with the provision laid down in the Environmental Protection Law that environmental protection organizations at all levels should "organize environmental monitoring in a unified way," the Office of the Environmental Protection Leading Group of the State Council saw to it that standard monitoring methods were used by the various monitoring organizations, and that the organizations were supplied with standard monitoring instruments, equipment, reference materials and reagents. This office also supervised the drafting of the "Method of Analysis of Environmental Monitoring Standards." In addition, it made preparations for the establishment of a general environmental monitoring station for the nation, while equipping 64 provincial stations and stations of provincial capitals and other key cities.

Up-to-date technology, such as remote sensing and telemetering, laser techniques and electron-activated techniques, has been applied, though on a limited scale. Automatic atmospheric pollution monitoring vehicles and water quality pollution monitoring boats have been manufactured and put to use on a trial basis. The monitoring of air and water quality, noise and the discharge of industrial waste water, waste gas and waste residues has been strengthened to varying degrees.

To further improve environmental monitoring work, a national conference was held in December 1980. At the conference, the orientation, tasks and aims of monitoring work were clarified. The regulations on environmental monitoring work throughout the country and detailed rules for their implementation were revised. The conference decided that the system of filing environmental quality reports would begin in 1981, first in 38 provinces and cities — with Liaoning Province and Chongqing as the pioneers who would set the example for the whole country.

Education and Publicity Concerning the Environment

Education on environmental issues is of strategic importance for environmental protection. At present, such education takes the form of school education, social education and the training of in-office cadres.

The aim of education on environmental issues in schools is to train specialists and popularize environmental knowledge among children and young people. Experiments were conducted in 1980 in some kindergartens and primary schools. Teaching materials on environmental issues have been compiled for middle schools, to be tried out in the key cities. In the whole country, 21 institutes of higher learning have started 25 departments and selective sections in environmental studies to train personnel for environmental management, research and monitoring. In Changsha and Guangzhou, two secondary technical schools specializing in environmental protection have been set up. The state has also sent a number of scientific and technical personel abroad for advanced study in the field.

The purpose of educating the society at large about environmental issues is to help the Chinese people realize the importance of environmental protection, to popularize knowledge and techniques of environmental protection, so as to cultivate an awareness among the citizens of their responsibility to protect the environment.

Of crucial importance is the training of the personnel of environmental protection departments and the large number of cadres transferred only recently from other posts to become administrative personnel in environment protection. At the present time, this is the focus of our efforts in education about environmental issues. In 1979 and 1980, the Office of the Environmental Protection Leading Group conducted four study courses to train 635 environmental protection cadres for local people's governments, ministries under the State Council and key enterprises. It also conducted three courses on prediction assessment of air quality and other subjects attended by 294 people. In addition, 21 provinces, municipalities and autonomous regions, 11 ministries under the State Council and the Office of Environmental Protection of the People's Liberation Army have in recent years run a total of 202 training courses for 9,067 technical personnel on water quality analysis, air monitoring, urban noise monitoring, environmental statistics, assessment of environmental quality, sewage disposal, new technology electroplating, and smoke prevention and dust control for industrial furnaces. At present, the Office of Environmental Protection Leading Group of the State Council is preparing to establish an environmental protection cadre school in Qinhuangdao, Hebei Province.

Since environmental protection is a new undertaking, it is essential to publicize its importance and popularize general knowledge about environmental science. In March 1980, a month-long campaign to publicize environmental protection was launched throughout the country. Remarkable results were obtained as a result of the concerted efforts of the propaganda department, the press, the departments of industry, transport and communications, public health and environmental protection, the Chinese Science and Technology Association, the trade unions, the Communist Youth League and the women's association. Incomplete statistics show that over 2,000 editorials, commentaries, news reports and articles were published during the month. A dozen or so films, including *Protection of Water Sources,* were shown in various places. Tens of thousands of pamphlets were printed and distributed, and forums on environmental protection were broadcast over the radio. Everywhere, lectures, workshops and forums were held. Shanghai alone reported 3,400 such gatherings, with 890,000 participants. In most provinces, cities and autonomous regions, the leading officials spoke to the masses about the importance of environmental protection. The chairmen of the standing committees of the people's congresses in Shandong and Hubei provinces went to grassroots units to investigate the environmental problems and to explain to the people the importance of pollution control.

Environmental Management Organizations

The Environmental Protection Leading Group of the State Council was set up in 1974. Composed of officials of the relevant ministries and commissions of the State Council, the group is now headed by Gu Mu, who is concurrently Vice-Premier of the State Council. The functions of the group are: (1) to implement and supervise the carrying out of national guidelines, policies, laws and decrees relating to environmental protection; (2) to draft regulations, rules, standards, economic and technical policies relating to environmental protection in conjunction with relevant departments; (3) to draw up long-term programmes and annual plans for the protection of the environment in conjunction with relevant departments, and to supervise their implementation; (4) to make unified plans for organizing the monitoring of the environment, investigate and keep under review the environmental conditions and trends of development throughout the country and recommend improvement measures; (5) to organize and coordinate environmental science research and environmental education in conjunction with relevant departments, and actively promote advanced experience and techniques — foreign as well as domestic — in the field of environmental protection; (6) to direct the environmental protection work of all the departments under the State Council, and of the provinces, autonomous regions and municipalities directly under the central authorities, and; (7) to organize and coordinate international cooperation and exchanges in the field of environmental protection.

The Office of the Environmental Protection Leading Group of the State Council attends to the day-to-day work of the leading group. Directly subordinate to it are the Chinese Academy of Environmental Science, the General Environmental Monitoring Station of China, the China Environmental Science Publishing House, and the Environmental Protection Cadre School. Environmental protection bureaus, offices and subsidiary units have been set up in other relevant departments of the State Council which are in charge of the chemical, metallurgical, petroleum, power, textile and other industries, as well as those in charge of the communications, railways, agriculture, forestry, public health, education, oceanography and national defence industries.

Environmental protection bureaus have been set up under the people's governments of 22 provinces, municipalities and autonomous regions. Environmental protection offices have been set up in the rest of the provinces and autonomous regions. All large and medium-sized cities, most of the prefectures and small cities, and some counties now have environmental protection institutions. The local government departments in charge of enterprises, and the large and medium-sized industrial enterprises generally have offices or personnel in charge of environmental protection.

In the drainage basins of the Changjiang (Yangtze), Huanghe (Yellow), Songhua, Huaihe and Zhujiang rivers, and in the areas of Bohai and Yellow seas, Taihu Lake and Guanting Reservoir there are organizations in charge of the protection of water sources. The local environmental protection organizations are under the direct leadership of the people's governments at the corresponding level, and in professional affairs they accept the guidance of the environmental protection organizations at the higher level. Their main tasks are: (1) to supervise and monitor the implementation of the state's guidelines, policies, laws and decrees relating to environmental protection by the departments and other units in their respective areas; (2) to draft specific environmental protection standards and norms for their areas; (3) to organize environmental monitoring and review the environmental situation and trends of development in their respective areas; (4) to draw up, in conjunction with relevant departments, long-term programmes and annual plans for the protection of the environment in their areas and to supervise their implementation; (5) to organize, in conjunction with relevant departments, research and educational programmes in environmental science in their areas; and (6) to actively promote advanced experiences and techniques, foreign as well as domestic, in the field of environmental protection.

Environmental Protection and International Cooperation and Exchanges

In the past two years, China has further expanded its international cooperation and exchanges in environmental protection. In 1979, 40 people were sent abroad to attend international environmental protection meetings, engage in academic exchanges or investigate environmental protection practices; and 152 foreigners were invited to China for academic exchanges. China attended a workshop in Stockholm sponsored by the United Nations to discuss resources, environment and population and their interrelationships. It ran a methane training course on behalf of the U.N. Environment Programme and discussed with this body the possibility of cooperating in building a methane training centre and a desert control training centre. Discussions were also held in Beijing between China and the Intercontinental Engineering Company of Canada concerning the techniques of controlling atmospheric pollution.

In 1980, 57 persons were sent abroad and 111 foreigners visited China in connection with environmental protection. China also took part in numerous conferences, such as the conference of specialists on soil protection, called by the U.N. Environment Programme; a conference to discuss the relationship between the wider use of coal and the environment; a conference to compare and assess the effects of different kinds of energy on the environment; an conference on environmental statistics of the Pacific region; the second conference to discuss an agreement concerning the use of motor vehicles; a conference on air quality and water quality techniques; and a conference on the recovery and disposal of waste materials. The Workshop on Environmental Management, jointly sponsored by China and the East-West Centre's Environment and Policy Institute, was held in Beijing. Through these technical exchanges, we acquired a new understanding of the situation of environmental protection in other parts of the world and foreign achievements in this field.

China also became a signatory to the International Union for the Conservation of Nature and Natural Resources, the Convention on International Trade in Engendered Species of Wild Fauna and Flora, the International Convention for the Regulation of Whaling, and the International Whaling Commission. The Protocol for Scientific and Technical Cooperation in the Field of Environmental Protection was signed by the United States' Environmental Protection Agency and China's Office of the Environmental Protection Leading Group of the State Council. China also signed with the World Wildlife Fund the Protocol for the Establishment of a Research and Conservation Centre for the Giant Panda and an "Action Plan."

III. The Outlook for 1981

In the last two years China has had varying degrees of success in different fields of environmental protection. There are however, quite a few problems. Generally speaking, we have not been able to control the pollution of the environment and the destruction of natural resources. In fact, environmental quality in many places is deteriorating. This is a problem which can only be solved gradually as our national economy develops.

The future of environmental protection in China is bright. Both the party and the government attach great importance to this problem. On February 24, 1981, the State Council issued the "Decision on Strengthening the Work of Environmental Protection During the Period of Readjustment of the National Economy." This is another historic document which will serve as a guide to our future work in environmental protection. This decision attaches new significance to environmental protection, regarding it as a matter of principle and referring to it as a fundamental task in the modernization of the country. It specifies the guiding principles and tasks for environmental protection in the period of the readjustment of the national economy and puts forward a series of policies and measures to that end. This document has provided us with guidance in our work on environmental protection in the forthcoming period.

Readjustment and Environmental Protection. The ongoing readjustment of the national economy has also created many favourable conditions for environmental protection. For example, the various policies and measures adopted in accordance with the economic readjustment (reduction of the scale of capital construction; inclusion of all capital construction projects in the state plan; strict observance of the procedures for capital construction; consolidation, reorganization and amalgamation of industrial enterprises; conservation of energy resources; tapping the potential of productive resources; reforms and renovations in older enterprises; improvement of city planning, and filling in the gaps in municipal construction) have all benefited to no small degree the work of environmental protection. If environmental protection is carried out in coordination with the various tasks of economic readjustment, both the economy and the environment stand to benefit.

Indeed, the State Council has pointed out explicitly in the above-mentioned decision: "The state shall give better planned guidance to environmental protection" and gradually "work out plans for improving, developing and utilizing the land of the country." Leading comrades of the State Council in charge of such work have repeatedly stressed that land use, planning and city planning are actually environmental planning. China has a total area of 9,600,000 sq. km. Such a huge area cannot be managed well without a unified plan and unified control. A fundamental plan for environmental protection is also needed in the cities. We must stop the indiscriminate development of cities, undertake city planning, study population control and urban development policies, rationalize the distribution of industries and enforce pollution control. In order to do good job of protecting the general environment, we must consider the orientation and tasks of environmental protection in a socialist country from a macroscopic point of view. This will help to define more clearly the future prospects of our work.

We expect that in 1981 environmental control in China will see further progress. We shall promulgate a whole series of laws and regulations concerning environmental control for nationwide and local application. We shall work out the necessary technical and economic policies that will benenit socialist construction as well as environmental protection. We shall try to solve a number of outstanding environmental problems in a planned and systematic fashion and in accordance with the resources at our disposal during the period of readjustment, so that the environmental quality of key cities and regions will be further improved. We shall attach even greater importance to the work of recycling waste water, waste gas and waste residues into useful resources, improve production techniques, carry out multi-purpose utilization of materials, and recover harmful substances and turn them into useful materials.

From a macroscopic point of view, we shall continue to study ways of improving the lands and land use throughout the country, the relationship between the consumption of natural resources and the renewal and supply of such resources and the relationship between exploitation of resources and ecological balance. We shall improve overall planning and work hard to create a decent environment for living and for the development of our industry, agriculture, forestry, animal husbandry, fishing and other occupations.

58. ECONOMIC DEVELOPMENT IN ANHUI PROVINCE
By the Economic Research Institute,
Anhui Provincial Planning Commission

Geography and Population

Anhui Province lies in the southeastern part of China, extending across the middle and lower reaches of the Changjiang and Huaihe rivers. It covers an area of 139,000 sq. km. and has a population of 48,920,000 (urban inhabitants, 6,631,000; peasantry, 42,290,000). The province has 66,690,000 *mu* of cultivated land; 18,000,000 *mu* of water surface and 53,660,000 *mu* of forest land. It is rich in mineral resources. Over 40 types of mineral deposits have been verified, including coal, iron, copper, manganese, molybdenum, lead, zinc, pyrite, iron, phosphorus, alunite, gypsum, limestone and halite. Reserves of coal, iron, copper alunite and pyrite have national significance. Anhui's climate and abundant rainfall are suitable for a variety of crops. Rice and wheat are chief among the grain crops, followed by beans, corn, sorghum and sweet potatos. Principal industrial crops are cotton, tobacco, peanuts, rapeseed, tea, jute, ambary and silkworm cocoons.

Pre-Liberation Economy

Before Liberation, owing to the exploitation of the labouring people by the reactionary ruling class and to plunder by the imperialists, the economy in Anhui had long been stagant. Irrigation and water conservancy facilities were in long disrepair, resulting in frequent floods and droughts. There was a folk saying along the banks of Huaihe: "We have famines nine out of ten years." In times of famine, people fled their villages and went begging, leaving farm lands unattended. The level of agriculture was very low. In 1949, the total value of agricultural output was only 1,728 million yuan; grain output was 12,784 million catties; cotton, 34,700,000 catties; and oil-bearing crops, 2,986,000 catties. Anhui's industrial foundation was also extremely backward. No heavy industry existed except for the Huainan Coal Mine run by the compradorebourgeoisie. There were only about 60 small fragmentary mines and mills and a few industrial handicrafts shops. The total value of industrial output in 1949 was only 340 million yuan. Transport and communications were undeveloped, with only 719 km. of railway lines and 2,088 km. of highways. Science, education, culture and public health were also in a backward state. In 1949, the ratio of university undergraduates per 10,000 population was 0.4; middle school students, 11; and primary school pupils, 238. The ratio of medical workers was even less, averaging only 0.1 per each 10,000.

After Liberation, under the leadership of the Communist Party of China and the government, the people of Anhui, having finished the task left over by democratic revolution, embarked on socialist economic construction in a planned and systematic way. Because of the hard work and arduous struggle of people throughout the province, great achievements have been made in socialist construction. Since the Third Plenary Session of the 11th Central Committee of the Party, all fields of work have been moving forward along the right track as a result of following the correct line, general and specific policies, and the policy of readjusting, restructuring, consolidating and improving the national economy.

Agriculture

Agriculture in Anhui Province occupies an important position in China. Both the party and the government attach great importance to agriculture. Since Liberation, the state has invested 4,430 million yuan in farmland improvement and water conservation work in Anhui.

Some 390 rivers, extending over a total of 8,200 km., have been harnessed; 4,089 reservoirs have been built with a combined storage capacity of 22,500 million cu.m. Among these are ten large reservoirs with a storage capacity of over 100 million cu.m. each, including Fuziling, Meishan, Xianghongdian, Mozitan, Chencun, and Hualiangting. The large Pishihang Irrigation Project has been completed, and some new man-made rivers excavated, such as Ci Huai, and Xin Bian. Within the province, effectively irrigated area amounts to 36,570,000 *mu,* of which 22,750,000 *mu* can ensure stable yields despite drought or waterlogging, an increase of 3 and 14.8 times, respectively, over post-Liberation conditions. Agricultural machinery has increased gradually. By 1980, there were over 17,000 tractors, 116,000 walking tractors and 4,287 trucks. Power-driven irrigation and drainage machinery total 4,980,000 aggregate hp. Mechanized farm machinery aggregates 9,038,000 hp. while the areas now ploughed by tractor amounts to 29.4% of all cultivated land. The amount of chemical fertilizer applied averages 73.66 catties per *mu*. Power consumption in agriculture totals 1,060 million kwh. The adoption of a series of correct policies for agriculture by the party and the government and the gradual improvement of production conditions have boosted agricultural production. Over the 31 years since Liberation, the total value of agricultural output has increased 2.43 times at comparable prices, or at an average annual rate of 2.9%; grain output has increased by 2.3 times; cotton 7 times; and oil-bearing crops, 3.3 times. The number of hogs and the output of other industrial crops have all multiplied substantially.

Agricultural Output in 1980. In 1980, further implementation of the party's economic policies for agriculture along with the strengthening and perfecting of all kinds of systems of responsibility in production have mobilized the enthusiasum of cadres and commune members for increasing production. As a result, good harvests were achieved despite severe flooding. Industrial crops, forestry, animal husbandry, sideline production and fisheries all registered increases, with grain the only exception. The output of grain was 29,078 million catties, down 9.7% from the previous year; cotton output was 244 million catties, an increase of 25.4%; oil-bearing crops, 996 million catties, an increase of 11.53%; tobacco, 48.3 million catties, an increase of 13%; silkworm cocoons, 8.98 million catties, an increase of 22.3%; jute and ambary, 326.2 million catties, an increase of 5.4%; and tea, 64 million catties, an increase of 6.8%.

The total output value of forestry, animal husbandry, sideline production and fisheries increased by 8.3%, and their combined percentage in the total output value of agriculture increased from 23.4% in 1979 to 25.2% in 1980. Afforested area totalled 1,560,000 *mu*, an increase of 34%. By the end of 1980, draught animals numbered 2,915,100 head, having increased by 10.2%; the total output of pork, beef and mutton was up to 518,000 tons, an increase of 1.76%. Aquatic products amounted to 72,800 tons, increasing by 30.5%.

In Chuxian Prefecture, where the system of responsibility in agricultural production had earlier been put into effect, output of grain and oil-bearing crops registered greater increases than in other prefectures. Chuxian's grain output increased by 13.6% over 1979, averaging more than 1,000 catties per person. The output of oil-bearing crops increased by 52.9% over 1979. A good example is offered by Fengyang County, one of the poorest counties in China. In 1980, 10.5% of the peasant households in this county produced 10,000 catties of grain each.

Industry

Since the founding of the People's Republic, great changes have taken place in industry in Anhui Province. Today, sizeable industries have been set up, including coal mining, electricity, metallurgy, chemicals, machine-building, electronics, building materials, forestry, food, textiles and paper-making. There are 140,000 industrial enterprises with a total work force of 1,418,000. Among these units, 2,795 were owned by the whole people with fixed assets of 9,140 million yuan and 959,000 workers and staff. Over 12,000 were enterprises under collective ownership, having 459,000 workers and staff. The province has 97 large and medium-sized industrial enterprises. Their output value accounted for 35.2% of the province's total growth rate. Over the past 31 years, the total value of industrial output in Anhui increased 35.9 times, with an average growth of 12.2% per year.

Readjustment in 1980. In line with the policy of readjusting, restructuring, consolidating and improving the economy, some essential measures were adopted for the development of industry in Anhui in 1980: 1. Priority was given to light industry and textiles for the supply of fuel, power, local materials, funds and imported raw materials. The sum of capital construction investment, technical development funds and other loans spent on these industries increased by 40% over the year before. 2. Work began to reform the economic system, and the regulatory rule of the market was brought into play under the guidance of national planning. The number of enterprises given greater decision-making power on an experimental basis increased from 87 to 174. 3. Resolute support was given to the development of the collective economy, and new avenues of production were tapped. 4. Some beneficial attempts were made to give free rein to superiority, protection of competition, and promotion of integration. As a result, in spite of critically inadequate investments in the machinery industry, total industrial output value still reached 12,170 million yuan, increasing by 6.9% over 1979. Of this total, light industry grew by 16.6%, exceeding the rate of heavy industry. The proportion of light industry within the entire industrial sector rose from 47.9% in 1979 to 52.2%. Plans for the production of over 40 main industrial products such as steel, rolled steel, pig iron, coal, timber, cement, plate glass, synthetic ammonia, chemical fertilizers, chemical fibres, cotton yarn and cotton cloth, were fulfilled or overfulfilled. Products such as watches, bicycles, radios, TV sets and sewing machines all increased greatly, by 2.1, 3.3, 3, 2.5 times and 66.4% over the previous year, respectively. Textiles and light industries also strove to improve quality and increase their variety of patterns and designs. According to incomplete statistics, 2,300 new patterns and designs were brought out, and 110 products were designated as "High-Quality Product" either by the province or the ministry.

Transport, Posts and Telecommunications

Progress was also made in transport, posts and telecommunications. Railway lines were completed, linking Wuhu and Tongling, Qinglongshan and Fuyang; and the lines between Wuhu and Jingdezhen in Jiangxi, Fuyang and Huainan were under construction. Anhui's rail lines open to traffic totalled 1,501.2 km. (including 320.4 km. of double track), 110% the length during the early post-Liberation period. In 1980, the volume of passenger traffic reached 4 million passenger-km; freight volume was 18,145.3 million ton-km., increases of 16% and 2%, respectively, over the previous year. Highway mileage reached 24,262 km., an increase of 11.6 times over that during the years immediately after Liberation. Civilian vehicles numbered 50,000 in 1980, of which 7,030 were in the possession of the transport departments, an increase of 17.8 times over the early post-Liberation period. In 1980, the volume of passenger traffic and highway freight reached 3,850 million passenger-km. and 1,090 million ton-km., respectively, increasing by 19.2% and 5.5% over the preceding year. Transportation capacity of inland rivers such as the Changjiang River also increased. Civil aviation has grown up from nothing. Airports have been built in Hefei, Anqing, Tunxi and Fuyang. Regular air services connecting Hefei to Beijing, Shanghai, Jinan and Wuhan have been opened.

Postal and telecommunication services have made considerable progress, and the total length of postal routes has increased by 5.3 times; long-distance telephone calls, by 9.5 times; telegraphic services, 3.2 times; and the capacity of telephone exchanges within cities, by 32.7 times. The output value of postal and telecommunication services amounted to 38,498,000 yuan in 1980, an increase of 14.7 times over 1950 and 5.1% over 1979; in 1980, mail service output increased by 8.07% and telegraphic services by 5.6%.

Capital Construction

Large-scale capital construction has been undertaken throughout the province with the aim of putting an end to the backwardness of Anhui's economy, scientific endeavours, education, culture and public health services. From 1952 to 1980, cumulative funds in this sector amounted to 18,789 million yuan, of which productive construction accounted for 84.6% and non-productive construction for 15.4%. Newly increased fixed assets amounted to 12,419 million yuan; the rate of utilization was 66%. In 1980, Anhui's total investments were 1,456 million yuan, a 5.5% increase over 1979. Of this, investment within the state budget was 840 million yuan, dropping by 27.1% compared with the previous year. Funds raised by the province reached 290 million yuan, increasing by 34.9%. Domestic loans for investment purposes exceeded 100 million yuan. In 1980, newly increased fixed assets amounted to 870 million yuan.

Great gains have been made in readjusting investments in capital construction and in accelerating the construction of major projects. Compared with 1979, the amount of investment fulfilled in heavy industry increased by 1% in 1980; light industry, 62%; coal industry, 13%; power industry, 22.5%; building-materials industry, 27.9%; and housing, culture, public health and urban construction, 10.7% (of which the investment in housing increased by 17%, with 1,820,000 sq.m. of floor space completed; and the investment in the construction of college buildings grew by more than 100%, with 152,000 sq.m. completed. More than 20 major projects were basically completed). Conversely, 41 projects were halted or postponed, saving investments of more than 250 million yuan. By the end of 1980, 594 individual engineering projects had been halted or postponed, cutting investments by 86 million yuan.

Domestic and Foreign Commerce and Tourism

With the growth achieved in industry and agriculture, the purchase and sales of commodities have increased steadily and the ranks of workers in commercial departments have been expanded. By 1980, the total volume of retail sales had increased by 16.2 times over 1949. Purchases of domestic commodities increased by 16 times over 1952, and sales by 19.1 times. During the 30-year period from 1949 to 1979, the profits of state-owned commerce turned over to the state amounted to 3,450 million yuan, and taxes from these sources totalled 1,470 million yuan. In 1980, as a result of initial reforms in the management system, along with the institution of multiple channels of distribution and multiple forms of operation, the combined volume of commodity buying and selling registered remarkable increases. Net purchases of domestic merchandise amounted to 6,990 million yuan, increasing by 8.9%. Of this total, industrial products came to 3,770 million yuan, increasing by 8.9%; and agricultural products to 3,180 million yuan, increasing by 9%. Retail sales amounted to 7,530 million yuan, an increase of 15.2%. Net sales volume of major consumer items all increased to varying degrees: pigs and pork, 0.6%; sugar, 19.3%; synthetic and polyester/cotton cloth, by 38.7% and 34.8%, respectively; knitted underwear, 30%; bicycles, 9%; sewing machines, 17.7%; watches, 35.7%; and TV sets, 65.2%. By the end of 1980, the total value of goods in stock amounted to 4,560 million yuan, a 2.4% increase over one year before. In 1980, the index of retail prices went up by 3.4% over 1979. The index of list prices in state-run commerce rose by 3.6%, that of negotiated prices in state-run commerce by 12.4%, and that of prices in country markets by 0.2%.

Foreign Trade Activity. In recent years, foreign trade in Anhui Province has increased greatly. In 1978, the total foreign-trade purchases had increased by 16.4% over 1977; and in 1979, by 32.1% over 1978. In 1980, these purchases amounted to 710 million yuan, an all-time high and representing an increase of 96 times over 1950 and 12.1% over 1979. Direct exports and imports both grew considerably. In 1980, the volume of direct exports was U.S.$39 million, an increase of 42.4% over 1979. The categories of such exports increased to 57 and included items such as frozen pork, fresh eggs, aquatic products, pears, candied dates, cans, rabbit hair, feathers and feather products, goat skins, fur pelts, tung slabs, calcium, citric acid, coal, cement, towels, writing paper, thermoses and chinaware for everyday use. Good sales were made to Hong Kong, Macao, Japan, the Soviet Union, the United States, Federal Republic of Germany, Italy, France and Spain. At the same time, direct imports were tried and contracts signed with 74 firms in 16 countries or regions. Anhui imported 65 categories of goods, chiefly raw materials to supply chemical, textiles and other light industries. In 1980, a commercial port was opened at Wuhu, thus creating favourable conditions for the further development of foreign trade.

The tourist trade underwent even greater development: Three cities — Hefei, Wuhu and Ma'anshan, and two scenic spots — Huangshan Mountain and Jiuhuashan Mountain, were opened to foreign visitors. In 1980, Chinese compatriots from Hong Kong and Macao, overseas Chinese, and foreign guests coming to Anhui on tour or on business together totalled more than 15,000, an increase of 56.3% over 1979. Income from the tourist trade increased by 267% over 1979. Overseas Chinese and compatriots from Hong Kong and Macao also made contributions to the construction of their home towns.

Science, Education, Culture and Public Health

Since the founding of the People's Republic, great achievements have been made in science, education, culture and health services. At present, there are 91 independent research organizations in natural science with a staff of 5,839, of which 2,578 are professional researchers. There are 79 non-independent research institutes in the natural sciences with a staff of 1,456, of which 770 are professionals. The number of universities and colleges has increased from 2 to 21; technical secondary schools, from 24 to 105; middle schools, from 143 to 4,420; primary schools, from 12,000 to 45,000. Compared with 1949, the number of students attending these four categories of schools increased by 35.8, 8.5, 81 and 12 times. respectively. Anhui now has more than 20 opera companies, 137 performing arts troupes and ensembles, 123 cinemas, 108 theatres and over 1,800 cultural centres. In 1980, 110 million books in 399 titles were published.

Health services in both Anhui's cities and rural areas have improved, with hospitals and health centres now totalling more than 6,600. The total number of hospital beds is 86,000, 457 times that in 1949. Medical personnel number 105,000, 338 times more than in 1949. A network of medical services has taken shape. In line with developments in education, health services and cultural establishments, both the physical and cultural level of the people has improved.

Living Standards

Since Liberation, the national and cultural life of the people both in town and country has improved gradually on the basis of increased production. In the first place, employment has increased rapidly. The total number of workers and staff in state-owned units increased by 7.4 times at the end of 1980 over that at the end of 1952. The workforce in units under collective ownership nearly doubled between 1964 and 1980. Due to the opening of new avenues for employment since 1978, 460,000 people have been added to the workforce. Of these, 217,000 received jobs in 1980 alone. As a result of increasing employment and pay raises, the total wage bill has increased greatly. For the 29 years since 1952, the total wage outlay for workers and staff in state-owned units has increased by 19 times. The wage bill for 1980 reached 2,267 million yuan, increasing by 21% over 1979. The annual wage per worker increased from 598 yuan in 1979 to 684 yuan in 1980, a rise of 14.38%. The average wage per year of a worker in state-owned units was 739 yuan, an increase of 15.4%; and that of workers in urban collective units was 541 yuan, an increase of 11.7%. All this resulted from increased payments for 40% of workers and staff, raises in wage scales, the institution of rewards in factories and mines, and subsidies for urban workers and staff due to increases in food prices. In order to improve living conditions in the cities and towns, an average annual increase of over 700,000 sq.m. of floor space has been added over the 31 years since the founding of New China. Even greater improvements were achieved during the last three years, with the addition of 1,600,000 sq.m.

Living Standards in Rural Areas. Peasants' lives have improved significantly thanks to the abolition of exploitation. In 1980, due to the development of agricultural production and increases in purchasing prices by the state for portions of farm and sideline-produce, the income of the overwhelming majority of the peasants increased to varying degrees. According to incomplete statistics, 15 production brigades and 212 production teams had average incomes from their collectives that reached 300 yuan or more per person; there were 8 brigades and over 40 teams whose per capita income, including earnings from domestic sideline production, averaged around 400 yuan.

Problems and Prospects for Future Growth

To sum up, since the founding of New China, economic construction in Anhui Province has been a demonstrated success. However, Anhui has suffered from a poor foundation left over from old China and from the failure to bring into full play the superority of the socialist system. This was due to the long prevailing influence of "Left" guiding thought in economic construction, and especially to the serious interference and sabotage by Lin Biao and the Gang of Four. As a result, average income per capita in Anhui is below that of the whole country. The main problem is that the national economy continues to be out of balance, a situation that has as yet to be completely rectified. Thus, the overall economic situation remains relatively poor. To be specific, as over-extended capital construction goes beyond the availability of financial and material resources, the effectiveness of investment declines. With poor management in many enterprises, their production capacity has not yet been put to full use and their economical and technical targets have not attained optimum levels. Losses have been incurred to varying degrees in 17.6% of state-owned enterprises engaged in independent accounting.

In farming, Anhui's ability to offset disasters is still weak and per-unit yields are low. Even more serious has been a continuing inadequacy in adapting methods to local conditions, in developing a diversified economy and in taking full advantage of economic assets. These approaches had long been ignored in the past, and this situation has not totally changed today. Historically, Anhui Province has been a major producer of "Qi Hong" (a variety of black tea) and "Tun Lu" (a variety of green tea), both highly regarded at home and abroad. However, slow development has failed to meet the requirements of domestic and overseas markets. Freshwater fish-breeding has not developed fully despite the fact that Anhui's inland water surface ranks first in China. The output of some industrial crops cannot meet the requirements of local textile and light industries.

An irrational internal structure in industry and blind development in the machine-building industry have led to overproduction of general-purpose machine tools with the result that quite a few enterprises are operating below capacity. On the other hand, the development of textile and light industries has lagged behind the needs of the people. Anhui is self-sufficient in only 70% of the industrial products needed for daily use. Demand greatly exceeds supply. The proportion between the "bone" and the "flesh" is not coordinated. A lot has to be done to improve the people's livelihood and great difficulties have to be overcome to achieve full employment. Therefore, in the future, the principle of readjusting the national economy should be further carried out, and the influence of "Left" ideology completely eliminated. The reform of various management systems to benefit economic readjustment should be continuously implemented so as to tap the potential of existing enterprises. Economic results will be further improved by gradually readjusting the structure of industrial product mix and the organizational structure within enterprises.

At present, the general need is to cut capital construction, increase production, reduce expenses, achieve a balance between revenues and expenditures, stabilize prices and stimulate the market. This means that capital construction should be resolutely curtailed to suit the province's financial, material and energy resources.

Those enterprises which produce in an unplanned way with poor economic results should be shut down, combined with others or shifted to other lines of production. Expenditures should be trimmed to balance the budget, while production output should be increased. Agriculture, textiles and light industries should speed up production so that increases in agricultural and sideline production can gradually catch up to the needs of light industry and so that the development of light industry can meet increasing demands for consumer goods. Energy, transport, building materials, education, science and technology, culture, hygiene, public health, urban construction, environmental protection and tourism should continuously develop, and the work of family planning must be carried out successfully. All of these steps are certain to raise the living standards of the people both in urban and rural areas.

59. ECONOMIC DEVELOPMENT IN BEIJING
By the Research Office,
Beijing Municipal People's Government

Survey of Economic Development Since 1949

Beijing has made rapid progress in economic construction in the 31 years since the founding of the People's Republic. Remarkable changes are evident in the city's industry, agriculture, domestic and foreign trade, housing construction and public utilities. Today, Beijing is more than the political and cultural centre of China — the city also plays an essential role in China's economy.

The capital of several feudal dynasties, Beijing has always had a strong political and cultural tradition, but its economy has long been relatively backward. In 1949, the city's total industrial output was valued at 170 million yuan; its agricultural output, 130 million yuan; and its volume of retail sales, 280 million yuan. The total value of its export commodities in 1950 was US$2,420,000. By 1980, however, the total value of industrial output had grown to 23,200 million yuan, a 210-fold increase over 1949; that of agricultural output, 1,390 million yuan, an 8.75-fold increase; that of retail sales, 6,100 million yuan, a 21.7-fold increase; and that of exports, US$590 million, a 245-fold increase. The volume of construction — including buildings, roads and public utilities such as water supply, sewers, gas, heating, public transport and telecommunications — has increased 10 to 20 times in the past 31 years. Specific examples of the principal aspects of Beijing's economic construction are given below.

Industry. In 1949, only a handful of factories in Beijing employed more than 100 people. At that time, the city's annual production was meagre: approximately 20,000 tons of pig iron, 1,000,000 tons of coal, 30,000 tons of cement, 12 million metres of cotton cloth, 7,000 metres of woollen fabric, 2,000 tons of paper and 150 million kwh. of electricity. Neither steel nor machine tools were made, and consumer articles such as toothpaste, scented soaps and even iron nails had to be brought in from other cities. The industrial work force of Beijing then numbered only 83,000 and the city's total fixed assets were worth just 80 million yuan.

Industry grew rapidly after Liberation. During the First Five-Year Plan period (1953-57), 41 new factories were built and 329 plants were renovated or extended. By 1957, the city's total industrial output value had increased to 2,140 million yuan.

Industry saw even greater expansion in 1958-60, and by 1960 the total value of industrial output had soared to 9,330 million yuan. The output value dropped to 4,360 million yuan in 1963 as a result of the economic readjustment between 1961 and 1963. But in 1964-65, sound progress was made and the total value of industrial output in 1965 was up to 5,910 million yuan.

By 1970, after the Yanshan Petrochemical Complex went into production and after the expansion of the motor vehicle and internal combustion engine plants, the city's industrial output value totaled 12,920 million yuan. By 1976, it had reached 15,500 million yuan, and at the end of 1979 it was 21,150 million yuan. In the past 31 years, Beijing's industrial output value had grown at an annual rate of 18.8%.

Of the 3,725 industrial enterprises located in Beijing today, 1,098 are state-owned while the other 2,627 (not including those run by production brigades in the suburbs) are collectively owned by those who work in the producing units. Beijing now boasts an industrial work force of 1.35 million people, constituting 43% of the city's working population. The city's fixed assets are now valued at 14,300 million yuan (at their original value).

Production figures for the city's major industrial products in 1980 were as follows: 290 million metres of cotton cloth, 11 million metres of woollen piece goods, 1.52 million watches, 450,000 sewing machines, 58,000 washing machines, 25,000 refrigerators, 50 million garments, 7 million pairs of leather shoes, 55,000 tons of beer, 31,500 tons of candy and confectionery, 280,000 television sets, 1,910,000 transistor radios, 7,000 metal-cutting machines, 28,000 jeeps and light trucks, internal-combustion engines with a total capacity of 3.9 million hp., electric motors with a total capacity of 1.4 million kw., 2.17 million tons of cement, 2,900 million bricks, 240,000 tons of ethylene, 160,000 tons of high-pressure polyethylene, 150,000 tons of synthetic ammonia, 3 million tons of pig iron, 2 million tons of steel, 1.52 million tons of rolled steel, 7.8 million tons of coal, and 10,650 million kwh. of electricity.

Among China's major cities, Beijing ranks second only to Shanghai in industrial output value. Of the products made in Beijing, 37 have won the state's gold or silver medals for good quality and another 137 have come first in national quality competitions.

Agriculture. At present, there are 6,380,000 *mu* of cultivated land and a rural population of 3,750,000 around Beijing. Beijing's agricultural production, like its industry, was fairly backward in 1949. In that year, the total grain output was 830 million catties, averaging 128 catties per *mu*; the output of vegetables was 210 million catties, averaging 3,000 catties per *mu*. This meant an annual agricultural output value of 58 yuan per capita for the city's rural population.

Since Liberation, enormous efforts have been made by the government to develop agriculture. There has been significant progress in mechanized farming and in the construction of irrigation and drainage facilities. Chemical fertilizers are now applied in quantity, and electricity is available in almost all villages.

Since Liberation, Beijing has constructed 82 water reservoirs of varying size, sunk 37,000 motor-pumped wells for irrigation and built over 6,000 pumping stations. This has increased the area under irrigation from 373,000 *mu* in 1952 to 5,100,000 *mu* in 1980, which constitutes 80% of the total area under cultivation.

In 1952, the farms near Beijing had only seven tractors. By 1957, the number was a mere 299; and existing agricultural machinery had a combined total of 30,000 hp. By 1980, however, there were 7,665 large and medium-sized tractors, 24,912 walking tractors, 4,581 trucks and 535 combines. Together, these machines totalled 3,190,000 hp., representing a 106-fold increase over 1957.

In 1952, a total of 432 tons of chemical fertilizers and 510,000 kwh. of electricity were used for agriculture in Beijing. By 1980, the figures had jumped to 588,000 tons for chemical fertilizers, averaging 184 catties per *mu*, and 76,753 million kwh. for electricity, averaging 120 kwh. per *mu*.

In addition, great headway has been made in soil amelioration, the popularization of better seed strains and improvement of cropping programmes and plant protection. Although the area of cultivated land was reduced in 1980 by 2.5 million *mu* (representing 35% of the total), grain output in that year still reached 3,720 million catties, a 4.5-fold increase over the output of 1949. The average per-*mu* yield in 1980 was 747 catties, or 5.8 times the 1949 figure of 128 catties.

Progress has also been made in vegetable production, forestry, animal husbandry, sideline occupations and fishing. In 1980, the output of vegetables reached 3,519 million catties, almost 17 times that of 1949; output of dried and fresh fruits reached 310 million catties, a 3.5-fold increase over that of 1949; the number of pigs sold to the state was 2.28 million, a 19-fold increase over the 1949 figure; production of milk was 136 million catties, or 18 times the output of 1952; and production of aquatic products totalled 8,074,000 catties, 14 times the figure for 1957. Earnings from commune-run industries and sideline production reached 1,210 million yuan, 3.5 times more than in 1975.

These developments brought the per capita output value for Beijing's rural population in 1980 to 372 yuan, which was 5.4 times that of 1949. Each person received 182 yuan from the collective in 1980, or 3.3 times more than the sum for 1958.

Commerce and Service Trades. There has been a tremendous increase in Beijing's commercial transactions since 1949. The total value of goods purchased by commercial departments in 1949 was 280 million yuan. By 1980, this figure had risen to 12,220 million yuan, representing a 43.6-fold increase. Whereas 85,000 people employed in the retail business in 1949 and the volume of retail sales in that year came to just 280 million yuan, by 1980 the number of people employed in the retail business had increased to 79,000 and the retail sales volume had risen to 6,100 million yuan.

There were similar developments in the catering and repair trades. In 1980, 97,000 persons were working in these trades in the city proper and in the suburbs, whereas in 1949 there were only 28,000.

Foreign trade and tourism have also expanded over the last few years. The amount of foreign currency earned by exporting goods in 1980 was 9.1 times that of 1970. Beijing accommodated 286,000 foreign tourists in 1980.

Architecture and Urban Construction. At the time of Liberation, there were few modern buildings in Beijing. Old and shabby houses could be seen everywhere in the city and suburbs. However, large-scale capital construction has been going on non-stop since then and an average of 2.6 million sq. m. of floor space has been added every year. Floor space in Beijing has expanded four-fold since 1949.

Of the 80 million sq. m. of floor space added since 1949, 37.56 million sq. m. have been used for factories and office buildings, nearly an 8-fold increase over the 1949 figure of 4.77 million sq. m., while 44.35 million sq. m. have been used for residences and service facilities, a three-fold increase over the 1949 figure of 15.78 million sq. m. Large buildings now surround Tian An Men Square and line East and West Chang'an boulevards. Clusters of factories, apartments and embassies have risen in the eastern suburbs, while the western suburbs house many government offices. Universities and colleges are clustered in the northern suburbs. All this construction has changed the appearance of the capital city.

Public utilities in Beijing were extremely scarce and of poor quality in the early years after Liberation. In 1949, there were only 215 km. of paved roads and 86,000 tons of running water available daily. There were only 221 km. of sewage pipes. The city had 14,000 telephones and 164 trams and buses. Gas was unavailable. Only 772 hectares of land were planted with trees and grass.

Great improvements have been made in extending public utilities over the years. By 1980, 1,185 km. of roads had been paved, or 10 times the pre-Liberation mileage, and the daily running water supply had risen to 1.34 million tons, or 15.6 times the amount in 1959. The sewage system had been extended to 1,423 km., 6.4 times the 1949 figure. The city had installed 210,000 telephones, a 14.3-fold increase over 1949. Buses and trolley buses serving the city numbered 3,000, an 18.3-fold increase. A total of 2,693 hectares of land had been planted with trees and grass, 3.5 times the area in 1949. There were 802,000 households using gas for cooking, representing 62.5% of all households in urban Beijing. New apartments had central heating. A 24-km. subway was constructed in 1969, and a ring road with nine flyovers was completed in 1980.

Current Problems and Goals for Future Development

The last 31 years have seen great progress in Beijing's economic construction. However, owing to "Left" mistakes in our economic work, a number of serious problems remain to be solved.

(1) *Imbalance between heavy and light industries.* The tendency over the years has been to build an all-inclusive, self-contained industrial system in Beijing, making it one of the industrial centres of the country. The one-sided emphasis on the development of heavy industry has resulted in a steady decrease in the proportion of light industry. In 1957, the proportion of light industry in Beijing was 58%, but by 1971, it had been reduced to 28%. The result was that heavy industrial products piled up and machines lay idle while the rising demand for consumer goods — food, clothing and other daily necessities — was left unsatisfied.

The water and mineral resources in Beijing are limited. There is no big river nearby and the sea is far from the city, thus the city lacks the means of water transportation. Large-scale expansion of industry in Beijing has not only aggravated the shortage of water and power supplies and the availability of transportation, but has also adversely affected the environment.

(2) *Uneven development in city construction.* While a great many factories and office buildings have been erected in the past 31 years, construction of housing, public utilities and service establishments has been limited. Living quarters for the residents of Beijing are becoming increasingly crowded. In 1949, the per capita housing space in the city proper was 4.75 sq. m.; in 1972, it was 4.29 sq. m. In the past 31 years, the city's urban population has grown 3.1 times, the number of motor vehicles, 44 times and the number of bicycles, 21 times. However, the total road mileage has increased only 10-fold and the total road surface area only 12-fold. The volume of sewage has increased 29 times, but there has been only a 5.9-fold increase in the total mileage of sewage pipes. The peak demand for tap water on any day is 1.4 million tons, but the actual supply cannot exceed 1.34 million tons. The volume of passenger traffic has increased 81 times, but the number of buses and trolley buses in service has increased only 18 times. All this causes considerable strain on traffic control, public transportation, and water supply and sewage disposal systems. The construction of public facilities such as hospitals, nurseries, sports grounds and parks has also failed to match the growth of the urban population, causing great inconvenience to the residents of the city.

(3) *The inadequate development of agriculture, forestry, animal husbandry, fishing and sideline occupations in the city's rural sectors.* For many years, efforts have been limited to growing grains and vegetables, and there has been insufficient emphasis on other fields of production to ensure an all-round development. Premature transformation of the relations of production in the city's outer suburbs prevented the full exploitation of the production potential. Although mountains account for 62% of the total area of greater Beijing, commercial forests developed very slowly over the years. The output of dried fruits and nuts, including chestnuts and walnuts, was 9,225 tons in 1952. In 1961, the output dropped to 4,435 tons. In 1976 it climbed back, but only to 9,490 tons. The number of draught animals for the years between 1952 and 1979 fluctuated around 300,000, and that of goats and sheep was approximately 500,000 between 1960 and 1979. Peasants in the rural districts have not prospered as rapidly as they should have over the past 31 years.

(4) *Imbalance between sales and service trades and other trades.* In contrast to the enormous expansion of the urban area and the rapid growth of population, the number of stores and service units has decreased. At the time of Liberation, there were 72,000 shops and service units in the city and suburbs for a population of 1.76 million — which means that, on average, each shop catered to 24 customers. In 1957, when the city's population stood at 3.42 million, the number of shops and service units had been reduced to 31,000 — as a result of placing commercial and service units under joint state-private management, many shops and service units became integrated into larger units while others closed down. The ratio of service outlets to customers changed to 1:107. After 1958, quite a number of stores were reorganized into factories. During the "cultural revolution," which began in 1966, a great number of collectively owned and privately owned commercial establishments and service units went out of existence. In 1979, when Beijing's population reached 8,706,000, with 4.41 million living in the city proper, there were only 9,400 stores and service units left, each catering to an average of 469 persons. This inevitably meant poor service for the consumers. At present, food stores, tailor shops, restaurants, hairdressers and repair shops are all badly overburdened.

Recent Improvements. Following the removal of the Gang of Four from power in 1976 and especially after the convening of the Third Plenary Session of the 11th Party Central Committee in 1978, China gradually freed herself from the influence of the "Left" guidelines that had previously controlled her economic construction. Measures were taken to restore order and to right wrongs so that the country could be set on the right track. As the nation's capital, Beijing is China's political, scientific and educational centre as well as the centre of international exchanges. To give full play to these roles, the Secretariat of the Party Central Committee put forward in 1980 a four-point proposal to tackle the problems in city construction. Gratifying changes have taken place in the last two years:

(1) *Priority has been given to the food, textile, household electronic and electrical appliances, printing and other light industries.* Branches of heavy industry which used to manufacture products mainly for their own use are now beginning to serve the textile and light industries. The output value of light industry in 1979 showed a 13.1% increase over 1978, and another 22.2% increase was registered in 1980. The output value of heavy industry in 1970 increased by a mere 9% and in 1980 by only 4%. In 1980, light industry accounted for 39.5% of the city's overall industrial capacity. Progress has also been made in solving environmental pollution and problems caused by industrial development.

(2) *Priority has been given to construction of housing projects and public facilities.* In 1979 and 1980, the city completed 7.02 million sq. m. of floor space for housing, an amount surpassing the total floor space constructed during the entire 10-year period between 1966 and 1976. In these last two years, 796 million yuan has been spent on the construction of roads, water supply, sewage, gas and thermal power supply systems, and on tree-planting and landscaping projects. This amount was 2.3 times that spent during the period 1966-76.

(3) *Emphasis has been laid on developing forestry, animal husbandry, fishing and sideline production, while grain and vegetable production is still encouraged.* In the last two years, trees have been planted on 600,000 *mu* of land in the suburbs of Beijing, three times the annual rate of afforestation during the period 1966-76. Today, not only state farms raise pigs and chickens, but peasant families and production teams are also encouraged to do so. In 1980, the supply of pork increased by 15% over 1979 and that of eggs by 8.4%. Sideline production undertaken by rural collectives and individuals has also made great progress in the past two years.

(4) *Commerce and service trades have been emphasized.* New stores and service units have been established and some old ones have been reopened. By giving more support to the collectively owned and individually owned stores and services, organizing village fairs and opening farm-produce markets in the city, the incoveniences formerly experienced by the population have been mitigated to some extent. The number of stores and service units in 1980 increased by 3,600 over 1979 and that of service staff by 32,000. Foreign trade and tourism have also increased substantially.

Continued efforts will be made to implement the party's four-point proposal and the policy of economic readjustment. It is expected that Beijing will undergo great changes in the next 10 to 15 years and become a clean, beautiful and prosperous city.

60. ECONOMIC DEVELOPMENT IN FUJIAN PROVINCE
By the General Office,
Fujian Provincial People's Government

Geography and Population

Location. Fujian Province is located on the southeast coast of China to the north of the island of Taiwan. It is bordered by the province of Zhejiang to the north, Jiangxi to the west, Guangdong to the southeast, the South China Sea to the south and the Taiwan Straits to the east.

Population and Administrative Divisions. The province has a population of 25.18 million. The Han ethnic group makes up 99% of the population, while She, Hui, Miao, Manchu and other ethnic groups account for only 1%. In addition, there are several million Fujianese residing in more than 90 different countries and regions of the world. The province is subdivided into seven prefectures (or secondary administrative units) and two municipalities. These subprovincial areas are again subdivided into 62 counties (including Jinmen to be returned to the embrace of the motherland) and four county-level municipalities. Fuzhou, the capital of the province, is also the centre of politics, economy and culture.

Geographic Characteristics. The province has an area of more than 120,000 sq.km. About 95% of Fujian is mountainous, with one half of it at elevations between 200 and 500 metres. The province is characterised by mountain ridges of steep gradients with a chain of low hills undulating between river valleys and basins. The main mountain ranges are Wuyi, Shanlin, Boping and Daiyun. The major rivers are the Minjiang, Jiulongjiang and Tingjiang.

Climate. The province, facing the sea and with mountains behind, lies just the north of the Tropic of Cancer in the subtropical zone. The climate is temperate and humid. The mean temperature in Fujian is between 17.8 and 21.5°C. The frost-free period within the year lasts from 240 to 330 days. Rainfall averages between 900 and 2,000 mm.

Natural Resources and Agriculture. The province is abundant in natural resources. The most prevalent resource is timber. Forests cover about 39.46% of Fujian. The main species of timber are: Masson pine, cedar, cypress, *cryptomeria fortunci,* camphor, phoebe nanmu, sassafras, castanopsis, evergreen chinquapin, banyan, oil tea camellia, tung tree (*Paulownia*), bamboo and other rare timber like Metasequoia, *Taxus Chinensis, Pseudolarix Amabilis* and gingko.

The shoreline is extremely irregular, with a total length of 3,324 km., providing many excellent natural harbours and extensive fishing areas. Some 600 different species of fish are caught in Fujian waters.

The six major fruits of Fujian are orange, longan, lichee, banana, loquat and pineapples.

The province is also rich in tea, dry bamboo shoots, mushrooms, fungus, resin and medicinal herbs. In addition, Fujian has considerable mineral wealth, including estimated coal deposits of over 800 million tons, 500 million tons of iron ore and various amounts of tungsten, copper, molybdenum, lead and zinc.

Survey of Economic Development Since 1949

Fujian's economic development stagnated prior to Liberation. The total area of cultivated land was about 21,750,000 *mu* which provided for an output of 284,000 tons of grain. At that time, Fujian's industry consisted only of some small printing presses, food processing and match factories, thermal power stations, machine maintenance workshops and handicraft workshops. The total number of workers employed was less than 3,000. Even a nail had to be imported from other provinces. The problems posed by Fujian's difficult terrain to the development of internal communication and transport had not been tackled, which left the province very isolated. There were no railways in the province at all; roads existed only in 44 counties, and in 28 of them the roads were not serviceable. In addition, the impervious terrain of the inland rivers meant that navigable waterways were limited in number.

Capital Construction. After Liberation, the party and the government instituted land reform and organized the peasants to take the road of socialist collectivization and to undertake land-leveling, water conservancy and soil improvement projects. Over 600 large, medium-sized and small reservoirs and 100,000 small water conservancy works have been built, and electric irrigation equipment of 100,000 hp. has been installed. A number of breakwater and tidal protection dykes, with a total length of 5,000 km., have been constructed. Shelter belts have also been put up along the uncultivated coastal areas. Scientific farming has been widely adopted.

These developments have improved immensely the economic situation in Fujian. The total area of cropped land is now approximately 19,000,000 *mu*. In 1980, it yielded about 802,000 tons of grain, 3.8 times the amount in 1949, or an average annual growth rate of 3.3%. Agriculture has also been further diversified and developed.

Industry. Fujian now has a relatively adequate industrial foundation with many branches of industry, including: metallurgy, power, coal, chemical, machinery, building-materials, forestry, light industry, electronics, drugs and pharmaceuticals. A defence industry has also been established. To date, there are more than 16,000 factories and enterprises, of which more than 2,600 are state-owned, having a work force of 1,670,000; and more than 7,900 are collectively owned factories, employing 630,000 workers.

The total value of industrial output in 1980 was 7,550 million yuan. The average annual growth rate of industrial output has been 12.4% since Liberation. The output of steel in 1980 was 240,000 tons; pig iron, 320,000 tons; rolled steel 200,000 tons; coal, 4,630,000 tons; chemical fertilizer, 240,000 tons; and electricity, 5,000 million kwh. "Narcissus" Brand canned food and some other handicraft products are exported to more than 50 countries and regions. Shaushan stone carvings, Fuzhou lacquerware, cork carvings and Dehua porcelain are products equally well-known both at home and abroad.

Transportation. The province is now served by two major railway lines — one connecting Yintan with Xiamen, the other running from Waiyang to Fuzhou. Both play a very important role in the economic development and the distribution of commodities in the province. In addition to these two trunk lines there is the Zhanglung Line, the Zhangfu Line, the Fuma Line — altogether totalling over 1,000 km. Road construction has been intense. A total of 30,000 km. of road now link all the counties, with Fuzhou, Xiamen, Quanzhou, Nanping, and Yongan as major junctions. The Xiamen Causeway was constructed in 1956 to connect the island with the mainland. The Wulungjiang Highway Bridge was completed and put to use in 1971, greatly facilitating south-north highway transportation. Navigation on inland waterways has greatly improved after dredging operations were performed in over 100 locations. Xiamen, Mawei in Fuzhou, Quanzhou, and Sanduao in Ningde are Fujian's major ports. At present, there are regular civil air services between the provincial capital, Fuzhou, and Beijing, Tianjin, Shanghai, Hangzhou, Nanchang and Guangzhou.

Education. Fujian has 114 research institutes, 2,994 professional and technical people, 16 universities and colleges attended by more than 38,000 students, 1 television university, 82 secondary technical schools with 38,000 students, 1,148 middle schools with 1,090,000 students and 28,000 primary schools with 3,760,000 pupils.

Review of 1980

Fujian's economy has continued to move ahead during the implementation of national economic readjustment policies. The total value of industrial and agricultural output was 11,681 million yuan, 10.49% higher than the previous year. Industrial output rose 11.9% to reach 7,550 million yuan while agricultural output was 4,130 million yuan, an increase of 5.7%. The total volume of retail sales was 5,180 million yuan, an increase of 15.8%. The total export value was U.S.$360 million, an increase of 47.5%. The total revenue of the provincial budget was 1,530 million yuan. With total expenditures of 1,508 million yuan, the province was able to reach almost a balanced budget with a small surplus.

Agriculture. In 1980, Fujian Province suffered a number of natural disasters including low temperatures, drought and typhoons. The afflicted area amounted to 11,560,000 *mu*, representing 37% of the total area under crops. However, the implementation of the agricultural policies of the party and the State Council, the further development and improvement of the system of responsibility, and the restructuring of the internal composition of agriculture in a planned way helped to make full use of local advantages, emphasised scientific farming mobilised financial aid and material supplies, fired the enthusiasm of the commune members and thus overcame the natural disasters.

In the wake of the third bumper harvest year came a fourth. Grain output increased to 130,000 tons, a 1.7% increase over the previous year. The major cash crops — apart from peanuts, tobacco and hemp, which experienced a small decline in output — all registered increased yields. The policy of providing grain subsidies as incentives for sugar cane production resulted in a bumper sugarcane crop despite two typhoons. The total yield of sugarcane was 3,512,000 tons, an increase of 7.9%

over the previous year. The total yield of rapeseeds was 20,000 tons, an increase of 30.5%. The output of fruit was 126,600 tons, a 2.2% increase over the previous year, registering an all-time high since 1958. The orange crop reached 33,500 tons while the output of dry longan was the highest in the country. Narcissus was cultivated over 940 *mu*. Fujian is one of the major tea producers in China and its total output of tea in 1980 reached 25,850 tons, an increase of 13.5% over the previous year. Wuyi tea is one of the well-known species of China tea, combining the light flavour of green tea and the sweet fragrance of black tea. The yield of Wuyi tea was about 125 tons in 1980. The output of Jasmine tea and Iron Buddha tea — varieties well known at home and abroad — came to 7,500 tons and 200 tons, respectively.

The province is one of the six major forest regions in China. The total forest land is 98,710,000 *mu*. The total area of replanting was 2,627,000 *mu* in 1980; of seedling 37,000 *mu*; of nursing sapling 5,880,000 *mu*. Output of roundwood was 3,407,000 cu.m. in 1980, that of sawn timber 541,000 cu.m. and artificial board 38,000 cu.m. The total output value of forestry industry was 316 million yuan in 1980.

Industry. The industrial output value increased by 16.99% in 1980, a relatively big increase for the fourth year in succession. Some of the major products like sugar, chemical fibre, chemical fertiliser, cement, paper, steel etc. all overfulfilled their plan targets. Some daily necessities of good marketability like woollen yarn, TV sets, plate glass, sewing machines, bicycles and photofilms also had considerable increases.

The "Xin-lo-quan" Brand red wine manufactured by Longyan Brewery was awarded a gold medal for the national best quality products. "Xiamen" Brand photo paper by Xiamen Photochemical Factory, "Heron" Brand Six-flavour Glutinous Rehmannia Pills by the Xiamen Medicinal Herb Factory, and the "Sailing Boat" Brand resin by the Wuping Forestry Chemical Factory received silver medals of a similar nature. The consumption of raw material and energy was further reduced, so that the cost came down and the profit went up in most factories and enterprises. Some 300,000 tons of coal, 130 million kwh. of electricity and 20,000 tons of petroleum were saved. The state-owned enterprises, at the county level and above, netted 20.8% more profit than in the previous year — bringing about increases both in production and profit.

Light industry achieved a quicker development. There were over 227 improvements conducive to tapping the potential of existing equipment while some 110,000,000 yuan was newly invested. Consequently, production capacities of sugar, paper, textile and food-processing factories have been enhanced. The output of paper and cardboard was 224,000 tons in 1980, an increase of 1.6% over the previous year; sugar 371,000 tons, an increase of 14.3%; chemical fibres 13,500 tons, increasing by 19.1%; cotton yarn 24,000 tons, increasing by 20.7%; cotton cloth 130,000,000 m., up 6.8%; bicycles 27,000, up 71.1%; sewing machines 130,000, up 73.7%. The total output value of light industry registered an increase of 14.3% over the previous year, surpassing that of heavy industry, at 6.3%. The output value of light industry, which accounted for 59.6% of the total output of industry in 1979, increased to 61.3% in 1980. The textile industry alone increased by 22% over the previous year in output value.

Transportation. The weak links in transportation were also strengthened. The modification of the Ying-Xia and Waifu railway lines has already started, involving a cost of 24,000,000 yuan. The total volume of freight transported will be enhanced by 30%, when the modification is completed in 1982. The Zhang-Quan Railway Line has a designed length of 252 km. of which 57 km. of rails had already been laid down. The Fude-Jiándou section, the most difficult part of the line, has been finished. After inspection, it was put into operation on May 1, 1981. In line with the demand for the development of foreign trade, the ports of Hondu in Quanzhou, Gongko in Shaoan County, Zhuyukou in Pingtan, Dongao and Xiazhai in Zhangpu county have all been opened for shipping export commodities. The freighter *Gushan* made her maiden voyage to Singapore in November 1979, which marked the first step to the opening up of an ocean shipping line. In addition, the Fujian and Guangdong transportation companies jointly run coach lines between Fuzhou and Guangzhou, Quanzhou and Shenzhen, greatly facilitating the travel between Hong Kong, Macao and Fujian.

Foreign Trade. In 1980, Fujian continued to carry out the special policies of the central government coupled with flexible measures and energetically developed its external economic activities. Accordingly it established new economic units and restructured existing ones. The Fujian Investment and Enterprise Corporation (called "Hua Fu" for short) officially sanctioned by the State Council, was set up in January 1979 for the purpose of channelling, absorbing and utilizing foreign funds, advanced technology and equipment into Fujian. It subsequently established branch offices in some of the major cities and key areas. In addition, the General Corporation of Foreign Trade, the Industry Trading Company, the Agricultural Trading Company and Hua Min Company (H.K.) Ltd. — the general agent for all the Fujian units involving external economic activities, were opened. Many districts within the province have assumed a positive attitude to initial two-way trade following the changes in foreign trade apparatus.

The province has granted local governments some autonomy. The Fujian Investment and Enterprises Corporation, in cooperation with relevant departments, has received over 1,300 foreign businessmen from 31 countries and regions and held talks and discussions on trading, economic activities and technical exchanges. Extensively applying international practices, we have actively conducted business in the form of processing with raw materials supplied, assembling products from premanufactured parts, or participating in joint ventures, to bring in advanced technology and equipment. So far, more than 700 contracts in light industry — chemicals, forestry, metallurgical, construction materials, electronics, transportation, food-processing, livestock- and marine products-processing, farm cultivation and fish cultivation — have been signed. The finalization of these contracts will contribute to the economic development of the province. The value of purchasing export goods in 1980 scored an increase of 43.1% over the previous year; the total export value for the same period scored an increase of 47.4% over the previous year; while that of imports was 95.3%. The total foreign exchange earnings for the same year recorded an increase of 37%.

In October 1980, the State Council approved the setting up of a Special Economic Zone in Xiamen. An area of about 2.5 sq. km. has been delineated in Huli for this purpose. The Administration Committee of the Special Economic Zone has already started to function. The first phase of its construction is underway. In the zone, top priority will be given to such branches of industry as electronics, light industry, textiles, instruments and meters, arts and crafts, precision instruments and, at the same time, to further develop resident construction and tourism. The authorities have invited compatriots in Hong Kong and Macao, overseas Chinese and foreign businessmen to invest or set up their own enterprises in that area. Due to the favourable conditions of the zone, much keen interest and response has been expressed from overseas.

In March 1980, Fuzhou, Xiamen, Quanzhou and Zhangzhou were opened to foreigners. Leaders of many countries such as the Democratic People's Republic of Korea, Romania, Japan, Australia, New Zealand and Singapore as well as delegations from other foreign countries have visited Fujian since then. In April 1980, Premier Doug Lowe of Tasmania, Australia, visited Fujian, initiating the establishment of friendly state and province relations between Tasmania and Fujian to assist the development of economic and cultural exchanges. The trip was crowned with success. In November the same year, Fuzhou and Nagasaki in Japan became sister cities. The tourist industry also showed a marked development. The influx of tourists reached more than 130,000 (including repeats) and hard currency earnings registered an increase of 37% over the previous year.

Current Problems and Goals for Future Development

The major problem in the economic development of Fujian Province is disproportionate growth. We overreached ourselves in the field of capital construction, overtaxing the province's financial and material resources, as a consequence of which some of the weaker links such as transportation, communications and energy development have not been able to be duly strengthened.

Transportation. The transportation system is strained as the handling capacity has practically reached its peak. As for shipping transportation, the silting of river mouths poses some problems; some harbours and wharves are outdated; the delays in loading and unloading are serious. The civil air service is also not able to cope with the demands of economic development of the province.

Agriculture. Agricultural produce falls short of the demands of economic development and the needs of the people. Grain consumption per capita is still less than that of the best record of the past. Some other cash crops like peanut, hemp, cured tobacco, lichee and longan are still well under the all time high record reached in the past. The income of commune members is rather low. The development of animal husbandry and fishing is stagnant. In forestry, more trees are being felled than replanted, not only overtaxing the timber resources but also eroding the balance in the ecological environment, thus representing a direct threat to agricultural production.

Industry. Many industrial enterprises need to upgrade their business management because of poor economic efficiency. Some factories are simply pursuing a high quantity of output, but do not attach much importance to quality or diversity. Sometimes they even manufacture blindly.

The result is a substantial surplus of inventories, a waste of energy and ineffective utilization of funds. The overlapping of building factories of a similar nature is quite outstanding. As a consequence, although industrial output registered quite a big margin of increase, it failed to represent the actual growth of effective social wealth. In addition, the gap between the amount of social purchasing power and supplies of commodities is widening year after year. Within enterprises, business management has failed to catch up with the new status following the release of market forces and the resumption of multi-channel marketing, causing instability of the market and commodity prices. The development of science and technology, education and culture and medical and public health services are far from adequate to keep pace with economic development.

With the above-mentioned problems in view, the basic requirement in the economic development of the province is that Fujian will continue, in the present period of national economic readjustment, to pursue the decision of the central government to implement special policies and flexible measures. The province will strive to balance the ratio between consumption and accumulation, enhancing this ratio to better the standard of living; proportioning the development of agriculture, light industry and heavy industry in overall economic development by giving top priority to agriculture and light industry; readjusting the relation between production and capital construction, between the tapping of the potential of existing enterprises and the setting up of new ones, proceeding from the present groundwork and assuring ongoing production; readjusting the inter-relationship among different branches of industry; strengthening the weak links in communications, transport and energy development; resolving the relationship between production, construction, science, technology, education and culture; arranging appropriately for the market to stabilize commodity prices; and expanding foreign trade. We must lay the foundation for a coordinated, well-balanced development of the economy. At the same time, we will fully take advantage of the power granted by the central government to implement special policies and flexible measures, bring the strong points and favourable conditions of the province into full play, actively utilize the funds provided by overseas Chinese and foreign entrepreneurs to import advanced technology to expedite the development of economy and technology as well as bring up more people with knowledge and skill to alter the economic backwardness of the province and improve the life of the people.

The ten key points in the economic development plan are as follows:

1. *Develop agriculture significantly.* While stressing grain production, efforts should be made to establish base areas of forestry, animal husbandry, fishing and cash crops (mainly oil-bearing crops, sugarcane, tea and fruit).

2. *Protect forest resources.* Conduct comprehensive utilization and stablize the production of timber in the next few years, identify the ownership of the forest areas and the forests themselves; implement the policy of forestry in a down-to-earth way; intensify refforestation and the comprehensive utility of timber; enhance the production of forestry by-products.

3. *Develop the farming and cultivation of marine products.* Combining with the development of oceanic fishing, fully make use of the shallow coasts and inland waterways to develop sea water and freshwater fish farms.

4. *Bring about a breakthrough in the area of light industry.* Bigger strides are to be expected in the production of some major products including sugar, paper, canned food, electronics products, lacquer ware and arts and crafts, to greatly enhance the production of consumer goods and expand processing agreements with materials supplied and compensation trade, so as to expand production, increase income and provide more jobs.

5. *Modify the industrial structure.* Make better use of the existing production force to manufacture all kinds of daily commodities and durables and provide the advanced machinery and equipment for the technical renovation of every branch of industry.

6. *Explore and mine mineral deposits with particular emphasis on non-metallic deposits.* Intensify the exploration of metallic reserves. Build up the Qinlin Tungsten Mine. Extensively develop the exploration and mining of river sand, kaolin, granite, limestone, barite and raw salt and other non-metallic deposits.

7. *Do a good job of electricity generation.* Build hydro- and thermal power stations, but particularly hydroelectric stations. A circular power grid will be formed in 1985.

8. *Change the backward status of transport and communications.* Emphasis should be laid on the completion and modification of Dongdu Port

in Xiamen; the dredging and modification of Mawei Port in Fuzhou; the first phase of modification of the Yingxia and Waifu railway lines; the modification and extension of the Fuzhou and Xiamen air terminals; and the installation of the 10,000-line telephone switcher in Fuzhou and Xiamen.

9. *Develop tourism.* Emphasis is to be placed on setting up tourism centres in Fuzhou, Xiamen, Wuyi Mountain and other scenic spots in anticipation of increased foreign currency earnings from tourism.

10. *Develop science and technology, culture and education, and public health.* In the following years more funds are to be squeezed out to maintain a greater share of investment in this aspect of the economy. Stress must be placed on popularizing primary education, restructuring secondary education and running the key high schools and tertiary education units better, so as to nurture and educate more people with better knowledge and skills.

61. ECONOMIC DEVELOPMENT IN GANSU PROVINCE
By the General Office,
People's Government of Gansu Province

Geography and Population

Location, Geographic Characteristics and Climate. The province of Gansu, situated in the northwestern part of China, covers an area of 45,000 sq. km. Its distance from southeast to northwest is 1,655 km.; the longest distance from north to south is 530 km. and the shortest is only 25 km. The land area of the province averages 1,000-3,000 m. above sea level and gradually descends southeastward. Mountain ranges crisscross the province in a complex pattern. Its water system includes the Huanghe, Changjiang and Inland rivers. Gansu has a dry climate which varies greatly in temperature; it enjoys adequate sunshine but has little rainfall. Natural diasters — drought being the worst of all — frequent the area during most parts of the year.

Population and Administrative Divisions. Gansu has under its jurisdiction 13 prefectures, cities and *zhou* (including 2 autonomous *zhou* and 3 provincial cities); 81 counties, towns and districts (including 7 autonomous counties, two county-level towns and 6 county-level districts). The land is inhabited by 19.18 million people distributed among 14 nationalities, including Han, Hui, Mongolians, Tibetans, Uygurs, Tu and Dongxiang. Minorities total 1.44 million people and comprise 7.6% of the population of the province.

Natural Resources and Agriculture. Total cropland in 1979 was 53.32 million *mu*. More than 20 grain crops are grown, including wheat, corn, millet and highland barley. Cash crops include cotton, rapeseed, fruit, melons and medicinal herbs. The province's grassland totals 200 million *mu*. The major livestock are pigs, cattle, horses, donkeys and camels. More than 50 million *mu* of land is covered with forests which contain timber trees such as dragon spruces, Chinese pines and poplars.

Gansu is relatively rich in mineral and hydraulic resources. It has a potential capacity of 14.24 million kw. of hydroelectric power. The combined flow volume of all rivers is 52,900 million cu.m. per year. There are 61 verified minerals, including nickel, copper, lead and zinc. Gansu is among the major producers of these minerals in China. Apart from the large quantities of fuel provided by two oil fields, Yumen and Changqing, there are 5,950 million tons of coal reserves.

Survey of Economic Development Since 1949

In the past 30 years or so since the founding of New China, Gansu has made great achievements in socialist construction. Compared with pre-Liberation days, the economy of Gansu has gone through tremendous changes. The industrial and agricultural output value of 1979 was 10,458 million yuan, 10.9 times that of 1949, and has risen at an average rate of 8.3% a year.

Agriculture. In the period immediately following Liberation, farming conditions were extremely backward: farm machinery and chemical fertilizers had never been introduced or applied; and irrigated land never exceeded 2.3 million *mu*. Annual grain output was only 4,000 million catties in 1979. Total farmland was 53.32 million *mu*, of which 12.69 million *mu* was effectively irrigated, while 9.67 million *mu* had ready access to irrigation. The former made up 23.8% of total farmland and the latter, 18.6% — or 5.2 times the area of the early post-Liberation period. There were in the rural areas 16,000 large or medium-sized tractors and 52,000 walking tractors. As a result, machine-ploughed fields reached 12.6 million *mu*, 24% of total farmland. In 1979, there were 2,375 agricultural trucks, 670,000 tons of chemical fertilizers applied and 700 million kwh. of electricity consumed in the countryside. The total output of grain in 1979 was 9,230 million catties and total agricultural output value was 2,180 million yuan; both figures were 2.2 times the totals of 1949.

Industry. Shortly after Liberation, industry in Gansu was almost nil. What we did have were 1,100 small factories, mines and handicrafts workshops, which together employed 7,000 workers. Industrial output value was 120 million yuan. The total amount of electricity generated each year was 5.3 million kwh. The Yumen Oil Field, then already well-known throughout the country, produced merely 69,000 tons of oil a year.

In 1979, the number of industrial enterprises

reached 4,710; total industrial output value was 8,279 million yuan, 65 times that of 1949, of which 7,782 million yuan, or 94%, was derived from state-owned enterprises. Industrial production capacity in 1979 was: 9.35 million tons of iron, 195,000 tons of steel, 4.2 million tons of oil, 48,000 tons of electrolyzed copper, 320,000 tons of chemical fertilizers, 2.82 million kw. of electricity, 5.95 million tons of coal, 80,000 tons of synthetic fibres and 28,000 wool spindles. The output of major industrial products in 1979 was: 54,000 tons of pig iron, 17,000 tons of steel, 68,000 tons of rolled steel, 1.1 million tons of crude oil, 2.91 million tons of processed oil, 158,000 tons of chemical fertilizers, 57,000 tons of methanol, 41,000 tons of rubber, 49,000 tons of oil equipment and 4.36 million m. of woollen fabrics, Gansu had already become one of China's important bases for nonferrous metals, hydroelectric power, petroleum chemicals and oil equipment.

Transport. In 1949, Gansu's railways were only 50 m. long, while in 1979 they amounted to 2,245 km. Lanzhou, the capital of the province, has become an important railway hub. The province in 1979 had 31,188 km. of highways, while in 1949 it had only 3,700 km. An extensive network of bus services links more than 97% of the communes and 70% of the production brigades. Air services linked Lanzhou with Beijing, Shanghai, Guangzhou, Shengyang and Urumqi. There were two air routes operating in the province: one between Lanzhou and Qinyang, the other between Lanzhou and Jiuquang.

Review of 1980

In 1980, economic readjustment began to yield marked results owing to the further implementation of the policy of readjustment, restructing, consolidation and improvement.

Agriculture Development. In agricultural production, 1980 was the best in recent years. The rural economy clearly changed for the better. Efforts had been made to further implement flexible rural policies. Varying forms of the system of responsibility were adopted; the system of fixing output quotas or assigning work to each household was practiced by 71.8% of all production teams. Thanks to the implementation of the policy of taking agriculture as the key factor; of developing agriculture and animal husbandry simultaneously; of promoting agriculture, forestry, animal husbandry, sideline production and fishing in an all-around way; of suiting measures to local conditions and placing different emphasis on them; and also owing to financial and material aid provided by the state, the majority of cadres and peasants were highly enthusiastic in running agriculture. The total output value in 1980 was 2,380 million yuan, a 9.3% increase over the previous year. Output of the major agricultural products included grain, 9,850 million catties, an increase of 6.8% over 1979; oil-bearing crops, 27,900 million catties, an increase of 64.9%; cotton, 5,360,000 catties, an increase of 32.3%; and beets, 12,600 million catties, an increase of 42.8%.

In 1980, the total area of afforestation reached 855,600 *mu*, an increase of 6.6% and an all-time record. The year also saw great progress in animal husbandry. The number of large livestock at the end of 1980 amounted to 3,923,000 head, an increase of 5.3% over 1979 and reaching an all-time high. The number of sheep and goats in stock was 11,800,000 head, showing an increase of 6.7% over 1979. The numbers of pigs, cattle and sheep slaughtered or sold all showed increases over the year before.

Industrial Development. Industrial production yielded good economic results and the structure of industry was gradually being rationalized. In accordance with the eight-point formula for economic readjustment, we set about restructuring the production of industrial products, reducing products in over-supply and promoting those in short supply. Based on the principle of economic rationalization, some enterprises which had incurred losses were shut down, suspended, combined or shifted to production of other items. Experiments were conducted in 51 enterprises to enlarge their decision-making authority. The method of sharing out profits from over-fulfilment of production plans or increases was adopted in enterprises affiliated with provincial industrial bureaus. These changes had the effect of arousing the enthusiasm of the enterprises and their workers and staff and improving their management. Meanwhile, efforts were made to restructure industry in the province. A proportionate relationship developed among various industries that was advantageous to the development of the provincial economy and to the improvement of the people's livelihood. Heavy industrial output value was reduced to 6,476 million yuan, a decrease of 4.8%, caused by poor markets, the untimely supply or drying up of mineral resources, the lack of raw materials, great demands on railway transport and general shortcomings in our work. Although light industrial output value reached 1,610 million yuan, an increase of 8.9% over 1979, the increase in light industry could not make up for the decrease in heavy industry. As a result, total industrial output value amounted to only 8,086 million yuan, representing a 2.3% decrease from the year before. Economic results improved, however, as can be seen from the following: budgeted profits turned over to the state reached 720 million yuan, overfulfilling the plan by 17.5%; losses incurred by enterprises were 33.68 million yuan less than 1979, or a decrease of 29.5%; the share of light industry in total industrial output value increased to 19.9%, as against 17.9% in 1979; there was an increase in the designs and variety of products, and an improvement in their quality. A total of 338 new products were manufactured or trial manufactured. Of 140 major products assessed, 122, or 87.1%, met required quality standards; 97, or 77.6%, were improved or retained their 1979 land. Forty-five products from Gansu ranked first, second or third in nationwide contests.

Marketing and Sales. Markets were brisk in 1980; there was a marked increase in purchases, sales, allocations and storage of products. Along with progress in industry and agriculture, the transformation of management and methods in running industry also improved. The value of purchases totalled 2,440 million yuan, up by 9.12%. Of this total, 1,560 million yuan was used to purchase industrial goods from outside the province, a decrease of 1.5%; 680 million yuan went for agricultural and sideline products, an increase of 21.4%. Owing to the growing purchasing power and to relatively ample supplies of goods, the total volume of retail sales reached 2,960 million yuan, rising by 8.9%. Of this total, 2,560 million yuan was accounted for by consumer goods, up 15.5%; 394 million yuan was for agricultural means of production, a decrease of 20.6%. The total volume of retail sales of industrial products jumped to 196.75 million yuan, or 86% above 1979; their proportion in the total volume of retail sales of the province rose from 3.8% in 1979 to 6.6% in 1980. The trade volume of urban and rural fairs amounted to 258 million yuan, an increase of 23.8%. The total value of commodities in stock rose by 4.2%. Moreover, the year witnessed new developments in foreign trade. Thanks to harminious cooperation among various departments in manufacturing, supply, marketing and foreign trade, the variety of export goods grew from dozens of items to over 170. Total purchases of export commodities reached 194 million yuan, rising by 26.5% over 1979 and including a 2.2% increase in the value of local and animal by-products, cereals, oils and foodstuffs; a 31.4% increase in the value of textiles and light industrial products; and a 43.7% increase in the value of chemical fibres and machinery. The total volume of direct exports amounted to U.S.$37.89 million.

Capital Construction and Investment. The scope of capital construction was reduced in 1980. The total amount of investments in capital construction was 840.86 million yuan, a decrease of 55.69 million yuan from 1979. Of this total, budgeted capital was reduced to 512.71 million yuan, a decrease of 207.3 million yuan from the previous year, while non-budgeted capital reached 328.15 million yuan, an increase of 151.16 million yuan. The increase was the result of more funds collected by various departments after they had enlarged their decision-making powers. Invested capital was mainly used for projects in science, culture, education, public health and people's livelihood. Compared with the amount of work done the year before, a 42.97% increase was registered in science; a 12.45% increase in culture, education and public health; and a 39.55% increase in housing. The total floor space of housing under construction was 263 million sq.m. Of this, 1,432 million sq.m. were completed in 1980, representing an increase of 335,000 sq.m. over 1979. Thus, 1980 was the peak year in housing construction. The quality of construction also improved gradually. The number of projects rated as good quality increased from 872 in 1979 to 997 in 1980, showing a 14% increase. The ratio of highly rated projects reached 56%. In construction planning, stress was placed on guaranteeing the completion of 39 major projects. These were required to be wholly or partly completed within the same year. By the end of 1980, 12 projects, including the Lanzhou Vinlon Plant and the Dunhuang Hotel, had been put into use; 17 projects, including expanded school buildings at Lanzhou Normal University, had been partly completed. Invested capital produced better results than in 1979.

Finance and Commerce. In finance, revenues and expenditures were balanced and there was a small surplus. Local revenues of the province in 1980 totalled 1,489.12 million yuan, or 5.7% more than budgeted revenues. Local expenditures were 1,250.83 million yuan, or 89.68% of budgeted expenditures; this was a decrease of 6.5% from the year before, resulting in a net surplus of 143.92 million yuan. Bank savings by the end of the year amounted to 3,128 million yuan, an increase of 109 million yuan over 1979. The total amount of currency put into circulation in the whole year amounted to 165 million yuan, an increase of 5.43 million yuan.

Income and Livelihood. The livelihood of the

people in Gansu was improved. The majority of peasants, workers and staff increased their income. According to incomplete statistics, all peasants in the province increased their income — except those living in Pingliang and Qingyang prefectures where agricultural production went down due to the year's natural disasters, thus reducing the income of commune members. The total wage bill for workers and staff in state-owned enterprises and departments was 1,346 million yuan, an increase of 14.8% over 1979. The annuage wage for each worker averaged 890 yuan, an increase of 98 yuan over the previous year. By the end of 1980, an additional 105,500 persons had been given jobs. The betterment of the people's livelihood was also demonstrated by the large increases in bank savings. At the end of 1980, total savings deposits of urban and rural residents reached 479 million yuan, of which 107 million yuan were deposits held by the commune members. Urban savings rose by 33.4% and those in the countryside by 34.2%.

Current Problems and Goals for Future Development

The facts mentioned above show that Gansu's economic situation is good. There are, however, many problems. The major ones are that no fundamental changes have been brought about in farming conditions: grain output is low and unstable; the province is not yet self-sufficient in cereals; the rate of marketable grain is low; the province can only supply itself with 1,000 million catties of grain out of total requirements of 2,200 million catties; and the output of cash crops such as oil-bearing crops, cotton, sugar beets and tobacco is limited and cannot hope to supply light industry with more raw materials within the next future. Furthermore, the structure of agriculture is irrational: forestry output value makes up only 2.16% of the total agricultural output value; that of animal husbandry occupies 10.08%. Major sectors of the economy are seriously out of proportion. Over the 30 years since the founding of New China, investments in industry and agriculture were 15,130 million yuan, or 77.6% of total investments of 1,950 million yuan. Of that total, 9.9% went to agriculture, 3.2% to light industry and 64.5% to heavy industry. This trend obviously produced a much greater proportion in heavy industry. In 1980, heavy industrial output value made up 80.1% of the total industrial output value. Thus, overall industrial production has fluctuated due to large decreases in heavy industrial production caused by the on-going economic readjustment. The year 1981 will see a further decline of 4-7% in industrial production. More than 85% of Gansu's revenue comes from industrial taxes. Fluctuation in industry will seriously affect its revenues as well as the development of agriculture, culture and education. Revenues have shown a steady decline in recent years: from 1,530 million yuan in 1979 to 1,840 million yuan in 1980.

Unemployment is also a serious problem. Because of reduction of the scope of capital construction, as well as some enterprises being shut down, temporarily suspended, combined into bigger ones, or switched to producing other items, about 100,000 workers and staff now must work either part time or else have nothing to do at all. Moreover, at the end of 1980, 100,000 people in the province were still jobless. The fact that there are too many workers from state-owned enterprises, and that the collective and individual economis have developed very slowly, has made it more difficult to solve this problem. These existing problems show fully the correctness of the decisions made at the working meeting of the Party Central Committee to further readjust the national economy and to achieve further political stability. In line with conditions in the province, economic readjustment is therefore a task that brooks no delay.

To extricate ourselves from this stagnant situation and to remove potential dangers, we must accomplish the following:

1. *Do all we can to achieve a good harvest, focusing our attention on the production of grain and the development of forestry, animal husbandry and a diversified economy in line with local conditions.*

2. *Do well in industrial readjustment and transformation and try to increase production of most-needed commodities.*

3. *Promote the circulation of currency, improve market supply, continue to stabilize prices, and solve the unemployment problem.*

4. *Try to increase revenues and cut expenditures so as to bring about a balanced badget.*

Apart from increasing production and revenues, efforts must also be made to cut down expenditures and lower production costs. At the same time, we must reduce the scope of capital construction and achieve good economic results from invested capital.

From a long-term point of view, in order to ensure rapid growth in Gansu's economy, we must blaze a new path in line with concrete conditions in the province. In the first place, in industry we must make full use of existing economic, material and technical conditions, adopt effective measures and tap the potential of enterprises so as to increase production. In other areas such as agriculture, finance and trade there is also great potential which needs to be tapped through vigorous efforts. We should gradually restructure the province's economy; try to set up an agricultural structure that suits the conditions of our province and that combines farming, forestry and animal husbandry; and restore and rebuild the ecological balance so as to free agriculture from vicious cycles. Industrial readjustment must be carried out actively and in a planned and systematic way. Light industry must be developed on a large scale. Priorities for heavy industrial products must be readjusted, and products that are in demand and fit for sale should be increased. We should develop on a large scale the collective economy in cities and small towns so as to better solve the problem of unemployment. Finally, we should continue to look into experiences in transforming the systems of economic and enterprise management, including further perfecting methods of expanding the rights of enterprises in making their own decisions, improving labour, wage and incentive systems, enhancing market regulation as guided by the state plan, and implementing reforms in the leadership system of enterprises. A set of practical methods for reform should be put forward to speed economic readjustment.

62. ECONOMIC DEVELOPMENT IN GUANGDONG PROVINCE
By the Geography and Population
Investigation and Research Division, General Office,
Guangdong Provincial People's Government

Guangdong Province is the southernmost province in China. It is located in both the tropical and subtropical zones, so its natural environment is relatively favourable. Guangdong has a total area of 212,000 sq. km., with a cultivated area covering 47.95 million *mu*. The population in 1980 was 57.8 million, including 50.47 million rural inhabitants. Within 30 years since Liberation, economic development in the province has achieved great success, establishing a leading position in the national economy and laying a primary material and technological foundation. The industrial sectors, with comprehensive and diversified divisions, has achieved a fairly large scale of mechanization, and the production has reached a relatively high level. Light industry in particular has developed quite rapidly. As for agricultural production, conditions have been improved dramatically and the ability to cope with natural calamities has been enhanced. As a result, agricultural output continues to grow steadily. Today, the population's material and cultural life has improved and tremendous changes have taken place both in urban and rural areas.

Review of Economic Development Since 1949

Agriculture. Over the past 30 years, agricultural production has improved greatly due to more effective irrigation of farmland; the total irrigated area has increased more than 7-fold to 32.23 million *mu*. The quantity of agricultural machinery and the use of chemical fertilisers and electricity have continued to increase. In 1979, the total aggregate of agricultural machinery reached 8,289,000 hp., and agricultural irrigation equipment reached 2,360,000 hp. Cultivated land under mechanization now accounts for 38.6% of Guangdong's total cultivated land. In 1980, an average of 14.2 kg. of chemical fertilizer was used on each *mu* of farmland, and 1,190 million kwh. of electricity were consumed. The seeds of many rural crops, including rice, have improved greatly, giving rise to many improved varieties of rice characterized by high yield, fine quality, the ability to withstand natural calamities, early ripening and short stalks.

Production has developed rapidly with the improvement of working conditions. By 1979, the total output value of agriculture had reached 8,115 million yuan and accounted for 28.9% of the total output value of industry and agriculture, increasing 3.2 times over the 1949 figure with an average annual growth rate of 3.7%. The total output of grain reached 34,760 million catties, an increase of 2.4 times over 1949 — with an average increase rate of 2.9% per year. There have been increases to varying degrees for other agricultural products; sugarcane, 11.3-fold; peanuts, 6-fold; and jute and ambary, 27-fold. Some 90,000 tons of dry rubber was produced in 1979. There have also been large gains in forestry, animal husbandry, sideline production and fishing. The number of hogs increased by 5.3 times over 1949, while aquatic products increased 3.2 times.

Industry. Many industries have developed from virtual non-existence to high levels of production; from few to large numbers. By 1979, there were 22,000 industrial enterprises in Guangdong, an increase of 14,000 over the 1949 figure. The original value of fixed assets came to 12,910 million yuan, 32 times the total of the early years after Liberation. The total industrial output value in 1979 was 21,040 million yuan, an increase of 32 times over 1949, with an average annual increase of 12.3%. Before Liberation, industry in Guangdong consisted mainly of light industry and handicrafts. After Liberation, a large number of industrial enterprises were built to cover a vast range within light industry. The output value of light industry in 1979 was 11,975 million yuan, ranking fourth in the country; the output of more than 20 kinds of products now rank among the nation's top five. Refined cane sugar is one of the main light industrial products of Guangdong. Sugar output in 1979 ws 980,000 tons, an increase of 13 times over 1949, and accounting for 39.2% of the country's total production. Heavy industries such as metallurgy, petrochemicals and machine-building, have been established since Liberation. The machine-building industry consists mainly of light industrial and agricultural machinery, as well as machine tools, chemical equipment, precision instruments and household electrical appliances.

Communications and Transport. There has been great development in transport, posts and telecommunications. In 1979, there were 31,000 km. of highways open to traffic, an increase of 18 times over 1949. A provincial highway network, with Guangzhou as its centre, has been initially formed. The volume of shipping has increased. The tonnage of local ships in 1979 increased by 25% over 1950. State-run shipping enterprises have developed gradually, and water transportation in particular has reached a high level. Railway transportation has gradually improved. Civil aviation has also been expanding day by day. Transport capacity has been gradually raised along with the development of the national economy. The total freight volume of the province in 1979 was 52 million tons, which showed an increase of 28 times over 1950. With Guangzhou as its centre, postal and telecommunication services have formed a provincial network. Postal and telecommunication offices exist throughout the province. All the counties and communes are connected by long-distance telephone exchanges, and telecommunications equipment has gradually improved. The total value of post and communication services in 1979 increased 8.86 times over 1950.

Commerce and Foreign Trade. The commerce economy of Guangdong Province has been flourishing. After Liberation, the exchange of goods and materials between cities and towns has been increasing. The total volume of retail sales increases annually, having grown by 9.4 times from 1949 to 1979 and now ranking fourth among all provinces in China. In the last ten years the retail prices of agricultural produce and industrial goods have dropped steadily, while the costs of several agricultural products have increased. The ratio of industrial to agricultural products has narrowed. Purchasing power has uninterruptedly risen with the development of production. Sales of major commodities have increased substantially. As has been the case for many years, however, production is still unable to meet growing consumer demands.

Foreign Trade. There has been a relatively rapid increase in foreign trade. The total purchase value of foreign trade in 1979 was 3,040 million yuan, or 11.4 times as much as in 1955. The total export value from Guangdong ports was U.S.$1,700 million, an increase of 15.5 times over 1950. At present, several thousand commodities are produced for export to 124 countries and regions. Guangdong's exports now account for 10.8% of the national total, ranking second in the country behind Shanghai. Foreign-exchange income from port activity now accounts for 13.9% of the nation's total, ranking third after Shanghai and Liaoning. Guangdong has become a major foreign trade port in South China and the main point of supply to Hong Kong and Macao. In 1979, the Party Central Committee approved Guangdong's adoption of special policies and more flexible measures in its economic activities with foreign countries. Since then, foreign trade has become more active and exchanges with foreign countries have become more frequent. People going in and out of China through Guangdong totaled over 8.53 million in 1979.

Science, Culture and Health. Significant achievements have been made in scientific and technical fields. By 1979, there were 432 independent research organizations with 230,000 scientists and technicians. Among these units, more than 1,700 were at advanced levels, while over 20,000 were at the middle level. In 30 years, they have completed 1,332 research projects of great significance, of which 414 received awards at the National Science Conference.

Education has developed greatly and a large number of people have been trained in the means of socialist construction. Within 30 years, 199,000 university and college graduates, including spare-time university gradutes, have been trained, as well as 269,000 graduates from the secondary technical schools and 12,558,200 graduates from junior and senior middle schools (including the agricultural schools), and 18,599,700 graduates from primary schools. The number of students attending various schools in 1979 reached 11,400,000, or 7 times the total of 1950. Today, Guangdong has 29 universities and colleges, 242 secondary technical and teacher-training schools, 2,957 middle schools and 30,000 primary schools.

After Liberation, a patriotic hygiene campaign was launched energetically and the spread of pestilence was basically stopped. Public health organizations were set up systematically, and health personnel were recruited. In 1979, Guangdong had 2,442 hospitals of various types, an increase of 13.3 times over 1950. Hospital beds increased 10.2 times. Technical personnel in public health increased 4.3 times. Conditions existing in the old society — when there were neither doctors nor medicine — have been greatly changed.

Income and Livelihood. There has been a clear improvement in people's livelihood. In rural people's communes in 1979, the income per capita from collective sources was 88.3 yuan, or double the 1957 figure. The average grain ratio per capita was 491 catties, an improvement over 1957. The average annual wage of workers and staff in state-owned enterprises was 702 yuan, 2.78 times that of 1952 (the average wage of all workers and staff was 676 yuan).

Economic Development in 1980

In 1980, the province continued to implement the spirit of the Third Plenary Session of the 11th Central Committee of the Chinese Communist Party and carried on the policy of readjustment, restructuring, consolidation and improvement of the national economy. In accordance with the instructions of carrying out special policies and flexible measures in Guangdong Province and of bringing favourable local conditions and advantages into full play, we initially reformed economic management, readjusted the economy, strengthened agriculture, readjusted industry and developed light industry in a big way. We tried our best to enlarge our activities for foreign trade and new trails were blazed in introducing a special economic zone and in moving every undertaking steadily forward in the course of readjustment.

Agricultural Development. Agriculture achieved an all-around bumper harvest and industry grew continuously. We initially readjusted the internal structure of agriculture and tried our best to raise the yield per *mu* and to enlarge the areas planted to cash crops. Both grain and cash crops achieved bumper harvests. In 1980, the area planted to grain decreased. Although part of the early crops suffered from natural calamities, the yield per *mu* and the total output of grain and oil-bearing crops both exceeded the highest levels in history. The total output of grain was 36,200 million catties, an increase of more than 1,400 million catties, or 4%, over 1979, and 2,000 million catties more than the bumper year, 1977 (or an increase of 7.1%). The total output of peanuts was 1,039 million catties, an increase of 182 million catties, or 21.2%, over 1979. The total output of edible vegetable oils was 164.60 million catties, an increase of 6.6%. The total output of soybeans was 236.39 million catties, an increase of 38.4 million catties, or 19.38%, over 1979. Other cash crops such as sugarcane, mulberry, tea and fruits all increased to varying degrees over 1979. Their agricultural output value was 8,810 million yuan, an increase of 6.23% over 1979. The sideline production of the communes and brigades and commune members increased greatly. The total income of commune and brigade enterprises was 4,165 million yuan, an increase of 24.7% over 1979.

Industrial Development. The readjustment of industry achieved excellent results. In 1980, a number of enterprises either closed down, ceased production, amalgamated with other enterprises or converted to other products. These enterprises had high consumption, large losses and irrational layouts, and could not find markets for their products. But then textiles and light industries were strengthened so as to increase their industrial production and income. Increases in light industry were especially significant. In 1980, the total output value of industry was 22,292 million yuan, an increase of 9% over 1979. The total output of light industry was 13,851 million yuan, 15.7% more than 1979. On the other hand, the total output of heavy industry in 1980 was 8,441 million yuan, a decline of 0.4%. The proportion of light industrial output value to the total for all industry increased from 58.57% in 1979 to 62.1% in 1980. The long-prevailing irrational proportion of light industry to heavy industry began to shift. In 1980, the output value of industry under collective ownership — chiefly that belonging to the Second Light Industry Bureau — reached 6,600 million yuan, rising by 17.8% over 1979 and exceeding the growth rate for state-run industry by more than 4-fold. Heavy industry adjusted its products orientation and increased the commodities supplied to agriculture and light industry and for the people's livelihood.

There was a sharp increase in the output of marketable commodities and the quality of these products improved. In 1980, ten products made in Guangdong won state prizes for fine quality, 47 products won the titles of "fine quality," "brand-name," and "reliability" as granted by various ministries, and 118 were appraised as fine quality products at the provincial level. Twelve products won first prizes in quality appraisals. Light and textile industries trial-produced more than 5,000 new products and varieties. Thanks to the attention paid to economic results and to improved operation and management, various economic and technical targets were over-fulfilled. Profits provided by state-run industrial enterprises increased by 20.2% over 1979, a growth rate far in excess of the increase in output value.

Passenger traffic increased by 17.9% over 1979. The volume of goods transported via the professional transport system slightly decreased because of a large increase in self-transporting capacity.

Revenues and Expenditures. A financial balance was achieved between revenues and expenditures, the market became more active and the people's livelihood improved. Financial revenues from production increased by 11.03% over 1979, while expenditures were reduced by 9.52% (final accounts), yielding a balance with a slight surplus.

Finance and Commerce. Due to production increases in agriculture and light industry, and to lively channels of distribution, purchases and sales, market supplies were notably improved. In 1980, domestic net purchases, net sales and retail sales increased by 17.8%, 15.8% and 21.3%, respectively, over 1979. Supplies of meat to large and medium-sized cities and to some towns were increased as were supplies of vegetables. Many industrial daily necessities that used to be in short supply can now be supplied without restriction. And there was a large increase in high- and middle-grade products. Agricultural and sideline products in the market were in much greater supply, and the volume of business increased by 8.48 times over 1979.

Income and Livelihood. Due to adjustments in wages, the paying out of bonuses, cost-of-living bonuses and the opening of major new avenues for jobs, the income of workers and staff and of urban dwellers all increased. The average wage of the workers and staff increased from 676 yuan in 1979 to 776 yuan in 1980. Housing conditions of city dwellers improved, with a record 5.12 million sq.m. of floor space added throughout the province, an increase of 50.6% over 1979. Jobs were offered to 457,000 people in cities and towns. Bumper harvests markedly increased peasants' income. The total income of the rural collective economy in 1980 increased by 14.6% over 1979. The average per capita income for commune members was 105 yuan, an increase of 18 yuan over 1979 and the highest level in 31 years. Household sideline incomes of commune members increased greatly. By the end of 1980, the combined savings deposits of commune members increased by 515 million yuan, or 58.65%, over the year before.

Foreign Trade. Economic relations with foreign countries were pursued more actively. With reduced supplies of goods from other provinces, the total purchase value of foreign trade and the total value of exports still exceeded the highest record in history. The total purchasing value increased by 27.4% over 1979, while the total U.S. dollar value of exports increased by 24.9%. Of this, the value of exports originating in Guangdong itself increased by 35.1%. Exports to Hong Kong and Macao increased by 31.3%. There were ever greater achievements in processing and assembling of foreign products, medium-sized and small compensation trade, cooperative production and joint ventures. The province earned U.S.$2,500 million for the country, an increase by 23.5% over 1979.

Tourism. There was growth in the tourist trade as well. 35 new tourist installations were added. In 1980, Chinese and foreign passengers coming in and out of Guangdong port reached 11,578,000, an increase of 46.4% over 1979. The foreign- currency earnings from tourism and the sale of tourist articles increased 1.7 times over 1979.

Special Economic Zones. Preliminary blueprints were prepared for the construction of three special zones in Shenzhen, Zhuhai and Shantou. The first-phase of the Shenzhen Special Zone Project is focused on a 0.8-sq.-km. area that stretches from Eastern Luohu Station to the north of Wenjin Ferry and to the south of the old city area. This area will be used as a commercial service district. The Shangbu Industrial District is to be set up in an area of 3 sq.km. Water and power supplies, as well as land levelling for roads have been carried out and some big projects are under construction. For Shekou industrial district (which began construction earlier), about 700,000 sq.m. have been levelled. Some factory buildings and a residential quarter for workers and staff are under construction. Construction has begun on huge buildings such as Yinhai New Village and Gongbei Hotel in Zhuhai Special Zone. Preparations are being made for the construction of a wharf open to navigation with Hong Kong as well as for the Shuiwantou Seashore Village. A 2-km. avenue connecting Shantou Special Zone and its old town has been built. The project for supplying water and electricity has just started.

Science, Culture and Health. New progress was registered in culture, science and technology and public health. In 1980, more than 400 achievements in scientific research were recorded, of which 64 were major achievements in science and technology. Educational quality was improved. There were 11,329,800 students attending school in the province. In public health, major efforts were made to prevent epidemics and to provide better drinking water to segments of the rural population. Hospital beds and medical personnel were added.

Current Problems and Goals for Future Development

At present, the economic situation in Guangdong is in general very good. But passive attitudes towards economic work have not changed fundamentally. Serious disproportions still exist in the economy. The development of agriculture does not yet meet either the needs of the people's livelihood or of industrial development. Energy resources are in short supply. Traffic volume is dense, while coal, oil and electricity remain grossly insufficient. The supply of many materials in Guangdong Province depends mainly on other provinces. However, the capacity for trains passing through the short section of the Beijing – Guangzhou Railway is not adequate for these needs. This comprises an obstacle to the economic development of our province.

For 1981, it is necessary resolutely to implement the policy of effecting further readjustment in the economy and realizing further political stability as put forward by the Party Central Committee, and to continue to develop the good situation so as to promote modernization steadily. Economically, subject to state centralization and unification, we will take readjustment as the core and continue special policies and flexible measures, exploit Guangdong's favourable conditions, activate the overall economy, further develop production, significantly raise economic results, harmonize ratios for the national economy, balance revenues and expenditures, stabilize prices, invigorate the market and improve people's livelihoods. In order to attain these goals, we must strive to do the following work in the future:

1. *Continue to readjust the internal structure of agriculture.* At the same time, we must ensure that grain production will increase year by year. We must actively develop a diversified economy and raise the proportion of forestry, animal husbandry, sideline occupations and fisheries within the farming sector so as to make agriculture develop in a major way in the course of readjustment.

2. *Further readjustment of industry.* We must continue to close down some enterprises, stop their production, amalgamate them with other enterprises or convert them to other products. With fewer enterprises closing down and more enterprises amalgamating or converting. We must adjust the ratio of light industry to heavy industry and speed the development of both. We must give energetic aid to light industry and strive to increase the production of those light industrial and textile products that have been found to be marketable. We must pay attention to the balance of energy sources as well as to their rational development and utilization. We must do a good job of reforming the structure of industry and promote technological innovations focused on saving energy. We must implement a variety of effective policies and measures for conserving energy sources. We must strengthen communications and transport. We must actively expand shipping between the south and north and develop coastal and inland water transportation. We must give energetic aid to collectively owned transportation.

3. *Reduce investments in capital construction and strictly control the scale of construction.* We must insist upon the principle of production first and capital construction second; innovation, reforming and tapping the production potential first, and enlarging construction or starting new construction second. We must adjust the direction for investments. All capital should be used for tapping industrial potential, innovation, transformation and developing products which are out of supply, as well as for energy resources and communications, and on education, science and technology, housing and public facilities that serve the livelihood of the broad masses. We must earnestly obey the needs of national and overall readjustment and the province's key readjustments.

4. *Strengthen activities concerning economic relations with foreign countries, strive to expand exports and increase foreign-currency earnings.* We must continue to engage in the processing and assembly of foreign products, while carrying out compensation trade, cooperative production and joint ventures and organizing the export of labour services. We must actively make use of foreign capital and the capital from overseas Chinese and introduce new technology so as to serve the readjustment of the national economy. We must strengthen the construction of the special economic zones and properly enlarge their rights.

5. *Stabilize commodity prices and enliven the market so as to make market commerce brisk.* We must do a good job of market regulation, promote the development of industrial and agricultural production and enlarge material exchange between the cities and the countryside, and within and outside the province. We must actively purchase materials, expand sales and reduce the amount of currency in circulation.

6. *Make a sustained effort to increase production and practice economy, increase revenues and economize on expenditures.* We must strictly obey financial regulations and principles so as to increase revenues. We must decrease expenditures, strengthen the management of credit and control the issuance of currency so as to guarantee the balance of payments. We must earnestly carry out the principle of distribution according to labour, increase the income of the people and raise the people's livelihood on the basis of production development.

7. *Develop educational undertakings, strengthen the work of science and technology, and raise the level of the people's science and culture. Do a good job of family planning and strictly control the growth of the population.*

63. ECONOMIC DEVELOPMENT IN GUANGXI ZHUANG AUTONOMOUS REGION
By the Institute of Economic Research,
Planning Commission of Guangxi Zhuang Autonomous Region

Geography and Population

Located in southern China, the Guangxi Zhuang Autonomous Region faces the Beibu Gulf to the south and borders on Vietnam in the southwest. It covers an area of 236,000 sq. km. At the end of 1980, it had a population of 35,380,000. There are 12 nationalities living in the autonomous region, including Zhuang, Han, Yao, Miao, Dong, Mulao, Hui, Maonan, Jing, Shui and Gelao. The people of the Zhuang nationality number 11,830,000 — about one-third of the population; Hans total 22,030,000. The population in 1950 stood at 18,750,000 and has grown at an annual rate of 2.14% over the past 31 years. The natural growth rate in 1980 was 1.647%.

Guangxi has a complex terrain. Mountains account for 63.9% of its total land area; rolling country, 10.9%; and tableland, 8%. Plains, which account for 14.4%, are generally small and widely scattered; the largest is the Xunjiang Plain, covering only 62,700 hectares. Karst is well-developed throughout the region, accounting for 51% of the total area; about 41% of it emerges above the ground surface, forming world-famous scenery such as that at Guilin. Their beauty notwithstanding, karst areas have more rocks than soil and are vulnerable to both drought and flooding. They are not favourable for agricultural production. The Beibu Gulf offers good prospects for the development of marine fisheries.

Climate. Situated in the subtropical monsoon zone, Guangxi has abundant solar radiation and heat, and abounds in aquatic animals and plants. Annual sunshine totals 1,600–1,800 hours in most parts of the region and the mean annual temperature increases from 17°C in the north to 22°C in the south. The frost-free period in the northern and central parts of the region lasts 10-11 months and almost no frost occurs in the south. A small area south of 24°N falls within the northern tropical zone. Annual rainfall is between 1,250 and 1,750 mm., but it is concentrated in spring and summer. The annual surface runoff is 184,000 million cu.m., accounting for 7.1% of the national total. Rain and heat occur in the same seasons and therefore benefit agricultural production.

Economic Development Since 1949

At the end of 1980, Guangxi had 2,636,000 hectares of farmland. About 1,650,000 hectares are paddy fields and the rest dry fields. Forests cover 23% of the total area.

Guangxi contains known reserves of 96 of the 160 usable minerals that exist in the world at present. Quantified reserves of 81 minerals have been verified. These include tin, aluminium, tungsten, antimony, lead and zinc. Deposits of manganese, limestone for cement, barite and talc rank high within China.

Although natural and climatic conditions in Guangxi are favourable, both industrial and agricultural production were backward before the founding of New China in 1949. Soils are mainly mountain yellow and red soil, and are infertile. Low-yield fields make up 30% of total farmland. Rice is the leading crop, followed by maize. Sugarcane, jute, ambary and subtropical fruits grow in abundance.

Under the leadership of the Chinese Communist Party and the people's government, the people in Guangxi, together with the rest of the Chinese people, have been active in socialist construction and have made tremendous achievements in the past 31 years.

Agriculture. In the area of water conservancy, the autonomous region has built 98,500 reservoirs and ponds with a total storage capacity of 20,800 million cu.m.; pumping stations with a total capacity of 947,000 hp.; and 2,385 km. of sea and river dykes. It now has 22,000 large and medium-sized tractors and 104,000 mechanized hand tractors. About 1.83 million tons of chemical fertilizers were used in 1980, an average of nearly 700 kg. per hectare. Grain output rose from 4,324,500 tons in 1950 to 11,904,500 tons in 1980, increasing at an average annual rate of 3.4%. Sugarcane output rose from 427,500 tons in 1950 to 4,019,200 tons in 1980, yielding an average annual growth rate of 9.74%. Jute and ambary hemp output rose from 3,800 tons to 102,500 tons — an average annual increase of 23.3%. High growth was also recorded in the production of tobacco, tea, silk-worm cocoons and fruit. The total agricultural output value was 5,016 million yuan in 1980, representing an average annual growth rate of 4.2%.

Industry. Metallurgy, power, coal, chemicals, machine-building, electronics, light industrial products, textiles, timber, building materials and defence industries, as well as modern communications networks, have begun to take shape. Total industrial output value in 1980 amounted to 7,758 million yuan, representing an annual growth rate of 13.1%.

Output of major industrial products in 1980 were: steel, 208,000 tons; pig iron, 180,000 tons; manganese ore, 849,000 tons; aluminium, 2,900 tons; tin, 3,000 tons; coal, 5.9 million tons (representing an average annual increase of 17% over 31 years); electricity, 5,360 million kwh. (an average annual increase of 20.2%); sugar, 416,000 tons (an average annual increase of 9.1%); cigarettes, 506,000 cases (an average annual increase of 16.2%); and gunny bags, 24 million. The output of logs also showed a major increase.

Transport and Communications. Railway lines in operation now total 1,710 km. (including local railways, 308.6 km.), and annual rail freight carried amounts to 20.34 million tons. Highways in operation total 31,673 km., with annual road freight 21.43 million tons. Motor traffic now extends to 96% of the rural communes. Navigable inland waterways total 4,663 km., moving 13.33 million tons of freight a year. Ships and boats sail to 56 of Guangxi's 86 counties and cities.

Capital Investments. Total investment in 1980 amounted to 1,030 million yuan. Investment in agriculture accounted for 27.2%; light industry, 12.2%; and heavy industry, 60.5%.

Culture, Education and Health Services. With the growth of the economy, cultural, educational and health work in Guangxi have also expanded. There are now 18 institutions of higher learning with a total enrollment of 25,500 students; 227 secondary technical schools with a total enrollment of 23,700 students; and 16,000 middle and primary schools with a total enrollment of 6.58 million students. There are 5,359 medical establishments with a total of 53,000 hospital beds and medical staff numbering 66,667 persons. The number of film projection units is now 5,113.

Employment and Livelihood. Workers in state-owned and collective enterprises and undertakings and in government departments have increased in line with the development of production. Workers and staff members employed in state-owned units numbered 2,085,500 at the end of 1980; average annual pay per worker was 736 yuan. Per capita labour productivity of state-owned industrial enterprises was 8,664 yuan. Revenues and expenditures were balanced. The total volume of retail sales amounted to 5,049 million yuan in 1980; the average annual growth rate has been 9.43% over 31 years. The region sold 421,000 watches, 143,000 sewing machines and 440,500 bicycles last year.

Economic Conditions in 1980

In 1980, the people of Guangxi made gratifying achievements in all fields through concerted efforts and by carrying out the policy of readjusting, restructuring, consolidating and improving the national economy as adopted at the Third Plenary Session of the 11th Central Committee of the Communist Party of China. Total industrial and agricultural output value was 12,774 million yuan, an increase of 5.73% over 1979. The livelihood of the people was also improved.

Agriculture in 1980. In agriculture, the job responsibility system was further implemented and the authority of production teams in managing farm production was respected in accordance with the principles and policies of the Central Committee of the Party concerning the development of agricultural production. At the same time, natural laws were observed, guidance over production through planning was strengthened and preliminary readjustments were made in agricultural structure and distribution on the principle of attending to local conditions and making the most of advantageous factors. In 1978 and 1979, 152 communes were designated as sugarcane growing bases and 35 counties as cattle breeding centres; last year, 150 communes were designated as commodity grain producing bases and 28 counties as bases for the development of forestry, animal husbandry and special local products.

Despite unfavourable natural conditions, Guangxi gathered a good harvest in 1980. Total agricultural output value rose by 4% over 1979. Grain production achieved a new local record, increasing by 150,000 tons over 1979 and by 900,000 tons over 1978. More grain than ever before was sold to the state.

Diversification within the economy also increased. Sugarcane output increased by 2.3%, a new record achieved despite the fact that area sown to the crop decreased by 15,300 hectares. Guangxi produced 209,000 tons of oranges, tangerines, bananas, pineapples and other fruits — 34.3% more than in 1979. Mulberry silkworm cocoons increased by 7.7%; medicinal herbs, 12.5%; dried fungus, 11%; and dried mushrooms, 125%. Output of marine fish rose by 22%, and fresh-water fish by 2.4%. The total income of enterprises run by communes and production brigades rose by 2.5%.

Industry in 1980. In industry, new progress was made in the work of readjustment and restructuring. Through integration and transfer, the region reorganized 448 enterprises that were irrationally distributed, had no ensured supply of raw materials, consumed more raw materials and fuels than necessary, produced unwanted goods or suffered bad losses for many years running. The number of enterprises that were given more power in self-management increased from 86 in 1979 to 146 in 1980, accounting for 9.7% of the total number of industrial enterprises in the autonomous region. The output value of this group was 12.3% higher than in 1979 and they accounted for 39% of Guangxi's total industrial output value. The profits they earned increased by 10.96% as compared with 1979 and they accounted for 80.5% of the total budgeted amount of profits from all industrial enterprises in the region. The profits they turned over to the state increased by 2.7% over 1979, which was above the budgeted rate of increase for all industrial enterprises in the region.

Under the guidance of state planning, regulation by the market was brought into play, enabling some enterprises to improve management, find new outlets for their products and reduce or eliminate losses. The new financial system of "apportioning local revenues and expenditures among different levels and holding each responsible for balancing its own budget" helped many enterprises to increase incomes and reduce expenditures and to fulfil their financial targets.

These changes were rewarded. Industrial production grew despite the short supply of electric power and raw materials. Total industrial output value in 1980 was 7.4% greater than 1979; that of light industry, 15.17% greater; and that of heavy industry, 2% less. The proportion of light industrial output value to total industrial output value rose from 54.7% in 1979 to 58.7% in 1980. Of the 78 major products made in Guangxi, the output of 44 was greater than in the previous year. The output of television and radio sets was more than doubled, while the output of chemical fibres, bicycles and watches increased by more than 30%.

The quality of 35 products — including refined tin, hand tractors and calcium-magnesium-phosphate fertilizer — was improved. Three products won state silver medals and eight were recommended as top-quality products by relevant ministries or state bureaux. More than 2,000 new varieties, designs and styles were added and 47 of them won Guangxi's "Hundred-Flowers Prize." New progress was made in saving energy: annual energy consumption was 4.3% less than in 1979. The amount of profits earned by the industrial enterprises within the budget increased by 15% as compared with 1979, while the amount of losses fell by 9.4%.

Good results were also achieved in communications, postal services and telecommunications, and geological work.

Capital Construction and Investments in 1980. The scale of capital construction was reduced and a number of projects were halted. Planned total investment in 1979 was reduced by 13.8% as compared with 1978 and that for 1980 was further cut by 13.7% over 1979. Most of the 61 projects that were halted were heavy industrial projects. The proportion of investment in housing, scientific, cultural, educational, health work, and urban construction rose from 19% in 1979 to 28.5% in 1980. Eighteen of the 19 projects included in the construction plan were completed.

Revenues and expenditures in the autonomous region were balanced with a small surplus. The market was brisk, with more commodities purchased and sold. Total purchases of commodities were 12.6% greater than in 1979 and the total volume of retail sales was 11.5% greater. Transactions made at the rural fairs increased by 25%. The purchase of commodities for export and the total volume of exports increased by 25.5% and 27%, respectively.

There were new achievements in education, scientific research, health work, cultural work, the press, publishing, broadcasting, sports and tourism.

People's Livelihood in 1980. The livelihood of the people was further improved. The peasants received more income from collective production and they earned even more from household sideline occupations. Most of peasants had more food grain to eat and their purchasing power was raised. Most of workers in enterprises and offices increased their income as a result of increased pay for some workers, the issuing of bonuses and expanded employment. Bank savings deposits in urban and rural areas throughout the region rose by 42% over 1979. The total floor space of housing estates for workers completed in 1980 was 2.86 million sq.m., 54% more than in 1979.

Problems and Goals for Future Development

On the whole, economic work in 1980 was successful and the situation was excellent. However, some problems remain to be solved:

1. *The scale of capital construction is still overextended and materials for capital construction were in short supply.* There is also a shortage of capital funds for a portion of the projects under construction. As a result of the

overissuance of currency, social purchasing power surpasses the actual supply of commodities and the price of some commodities has gone up.

2. *The economic structure is not yet rational and the special advantages of Guangxi were not yet being exploited.* The inner structure of agriculture is not rational and the advantages of the mountainous areas were not being fully utilized. The share of light industry in the economy is relatively small and the growth rate of consumer goods production lags behind the growth rate of social purchasing power. Electricity is in short supply. Mineral resources for nonferrous metal and cement have yet to be developed.

3. *Economic results were not satisfactory.* Fixed assets formed through capital construction in Guangxi over the past 31 years account for 66.9% of total capital investment. The average amount of taxes and profits turned over by state-owned industrial enterprises per 100 yuan of funds is only 17.47 yuan.

It is necessary to continue to eradicate the ideological influence of "Left" deviations and to further readjust the economic structure; reform the management system; speed up the development of agriculture, light industry, hydroelectric industry, cement industry and nonferrous metal industry; increase economic results; and give full play to the advantages of the autonomous region in light of existing geographic conditions, resources and economic and technical conditions, and on the basis of reducing capital investments and production funds and reducing spending so as to strike a balance between revenues and expenditures and between credit payments and receipts, and to keep prices stable.

Goals for future development should focus in the following areas:

Sugarcane. Natural conditions in Guangxi are suitable for growing sugarcane. Twelve and a half tons of sugar can be produced from each 100 tons of cane. Cane is grown over 111,000 hectares; 4,019,000 tons of cane and 416,000 tons of sugar were produced in 1980. About 287,000 tons of sugar were supplied to other parts of China. In the future, major efforts will be made to raise the per-hectare cane yield.

Hydroelectric Resources. Hydroelectric resources in Guangxi are abundant and concentrated. The conditions for the development of these resources are favourable, and development of water power resources along the Hongshui River is important.

Nonferrous Metals. Guangxi has many kinds of nonferrous minerals of rich content and these large reserves occupy an important place nationally. Conditions exist in the region for the development of tin and aluminium resources and for construction of major nonferrous metal producers.

Forestry and Local Products. There are many species of trees in Guangxi that grow fast. Pines and China firs mature for use as timber in 20-30 years, while commercial forests can produce fruit in 3 or 4 years. Some trees provide hardwood, including *Burretiodendron hsienmu* and *Garcinia pancinervis*. There are still barren hills, rocky hills and rolling country suitable for afforestation. Native and special products include anise, tung oil, fennel oil, mushrooms, fungus and Luohan fruit. Prospects exist for the development of subtropical fruits such as pineapple, banana, longan and lichee.

Guangxi has abundant limestone resources of good quality, providing good conditions for developing cement production.

The landscape and scenery at Guilin are beautiful and fascinating in all seasons, drawing large crowds of visitors from inside and outside of China and providing superb conditions for expanding the tourism industry.

An important task for economic work in Guangxi is to make surveys of local economic conditions, to make full use of the local resources, to ensure rational distribution within the economy and to establish a rational economic structure.

64. ECONOMIC DEVELOPMENT IN GUIZHOU PROVINCE
By Jin Yanshi

Geographical Setting

Situated in southwest China, Guizhou Province covers an area of more than 170,000 sq.km. The population in 1980 was 27,770,000, of whom 25,190,000 lived in rural areas and 2,580,000 in cities and towns. Guizhou is a multi-national province. Apart from the Hans, there are Miao, Bouyei, Dong, Yi, Shui, Hui, Gelao, Zhuang, Yao and other nationalities who make up one-fourth of the population.

Guizhou is located on a vast ladder-shaped slope on the eastern part of the Yunnan-Guizhou Plateau, with the western part at a higher altitude than the eastern part and lying at an average altitude of 1,000 m. above sea level. Of the total area, 87% is mountainous, 10% hilly and 3% intermontane basins. The climate is subtropical, with an average temperature of 15°C or above for most of the province. Annual rainfall is about 1,100 mm.

Guizhou is rich in natural resources. There are 984 rivers which extend over 10 km. each. The potential capacity for water power is about 18,769,000 kw. There are 28,580,000 *mu* of cultivated land, or 11% of the total area; more than 38,000,000 *mu* of forests, or 14.5% of the total; 42,000,000 *mu* of grazing land, or 16.1% of the total area, and 120,000,000 *mu* of sparsely wooded areas and barren hills and slopes. There is a broad prospect for all-around development of agriculture, forestry and animal husbandry. Among grain crops, rice and corn are the main crops. Among industrial crops, forest products and animal husbandry, cured tobacco, rapeseed, bast fibres, tung oil, raw lacquer, tussah silk, tea, tallow tree, *gastrodia elata, Eucommia ulmoides,* China fir and cattle are dominant locally and occupy an important place in the country as well. Among mineral deposits, reserves of mercury are the highest in China; phosphorous, coal and aluminium deposits are also significant in the nation. There are also considerable deposits of manganese, antimony, zinc, rare earth minerals and limestone, all of which exist in exploitable quantities.

Economic Development Since Liberation

During the anti-Japanese war period, there was a short-lived development in industry and commerce in Guizhou due to the shift of some industrialists and businessmen from southeast coastal areas and the lower reaches of the Changjiang River. Breweries, cigarette making, pottery and porcelain, chemicals, machinery, mining, metallurgy and other industries sprang up successively. Their production was mainly performed by manual labour. However, adversely affected by the imperialists and beauracrat-capitalists, most of these enterprises declined rapidly and closed down after the victorious conclusion of the anti-Japanese war. By 1949, both industry and commerce in Guizhou were on the verge of extinction. On the eve of Liberation, there was only individual and subsistence agriculture in Guizhou. There was virtually no modern industry and the province was inaccessible via modern communications and backwards economically.

After the founding of New China, the people of all nationalities, under the leadership of the Communist Party of China and the people's government, fundamentally transformed this backwardness. They achieved great success in economic reconstruction through their hard efforts during the past 30 years. By 1979, the output value of industry and agriculture reached 7,334.24 million yuan, 14.8 times the total of 1949 and growing at an average annual rate of 5.4%

Agricultural Development. Before Liberation, there was only a one-crop economy in Guizhou's agriculture. The production level was low, with widespread practice of slash-and-burn techniques and widely scattered cultivation. Improvements have been made in the conditions of production and reforms have been introduced in methods of cultivation during the past 30 years. Hence, agriculture production has been strengthened. The total output value of agriculture in 1979 amounted to 2,859.42 million yuan, which was 2.07 times that of 1949, yielding an average annual increase rate of 2.5%. The grain yield went up to 12,460 million catties, which was 3.1 times that of 1949, and with an annual rate of increase of 2.5%. Cured tobacco increased 16 times; rapeseed, 3.6 times; and the number of pigs in stock, 3 times. Electricity is available to 43% of the production teams, thus bringing an end to the situation where pine resin was used for lighting and when people had to husk rice with mortar and pestle late into the evening.

Industrial Development. During the past 30

years, industry in Guizhou Province started from scratch and developed through three stages: the period before 1957, when the main task was to reform existing enterprises; the period from 1958 to 1965, when a number of local industries and enterprises were set up; and the period after 1966, when large-scale construction was carried out in China's interior, enabling Guizhou's industry to develop rapidly. Metallurgy, coal mining, phosphate mining, electricity, machine-building, chemicals, electronics, building materials and textiles and light industries have been set up successively. There are altogether more than 7,200 industrial enterprises with 6,980,000 employees and net fixed assets valued at 5,640 million yuan. Moreover, Guizhou now has more than 47,000 metal-cutting machine tools. The considerable production capacity has made it possible to exploit and utilize Guizhou's rich resources.

A great variety of modern industrial products in great demand for national construction as well as for people's livelihoods can now be manufactured. In 1979, the total output value of industry increased to 4,470 million yuan, 31 times that of 1949 and representing an annual growth of 12.1%. The share of industrial output value of combined agricultural and industrial outout value rose from 14.8% in 1949 to 61% in 1979. The formerly backward economic structure in Guizhou has thus been transformed, and an important material and technological foundation for the four modernizations has been laid.

Development in Transport and Communications. There was a saying in the past that "there was not even three *li* of flat ground" in Guizhou Province. Communications were truly difficult then. In 1949, there were only 150 km. of poorly maintained railways and 1,950 km. of highways actually open to traffic. There was no bus service for half of the county towns. Most links among cities and towns were provided by "post routes" built during the Ming and Qing dynasties. In the vast rural areas, especially in the areas inhabited by minority peoples, there were only meandering footpaths. By 1979, after the founding of New China, highway mileage came to 27,367 km., or 14 times that of 1949. This was thanks to the large investment put into the development of communications and transport services by the state. Four railway lines — Guizhou—Guangxi, Sichuan—Guizhou, Guiyang—Kunming and Hunan—Guizhou — were built in succession together with provincial branch lines. The railway mileage open to traffic in 1980 was over 1,391 km., 9 times that of 1949. A communications and transport network has been established, with Guiyang as its centre, linking up Sichuan, Yunnan, Hunan, Guangxi and various points within the province. Now, all county towns, 99.7% of the districts and 80% of the communnes are accessible by automobile. The former situation of inaccessibility and backwardness when "birds could not even fly through" has been changed. Suffering from "sore shoulders and bleeding feet" because of portage through the mountain areas of Guizhou has been greatly reduced.

Development of Minority Areas. After Liberation, the party and people's government have given tremendous support and help to the economic development in the minority areas. In Guizhou's two autonomous prefectures and nine autonomous counties, grain yields increased by 2.16 times in 1979 over 1949 and the output value of industry increased 28 times. Before Liberation, there were only a few manually operated workshops and mills in Kaili, capital of the Qiandongnan Autonomous Prefecture of the Miao and Dong nationalities and in Duyun, capital of the Qiannan Autonomous Prefecture of the Bouyei and Miao nationalities. Now, both towns have become new industrial cities with important industries in cement, electronics, machine tools, bridge construction, metallurgy, paper-making, tanning, chemical fertilizers and textiles.

"Miasma" (the source of malignant malaria), which used to pose a serious threat to people's lives in minority areas, has been wiped out. Today, people have extricated themselves from the hard times before Liberation when they wore clothing made of palm leaves, used straw and stalks as quilts and lived in caves.

Research, Education and Health. For 30 years, science and technology, education and public health have continuously developed. In 1979, there were 207 natural science research institutes with combined staffs of 1,800. At the 1978 National Science Conference, some 148 scientific research projects won awards. In 1979, the province had a total of 39,824 schools, including universities and colleges, middle and primary schools; these had a total of 234,000 teachers and an enrollment of 5,415,000 students, 49.3 times, 34.1 times and 43.3 times more than the totals of 1950. In 1979, there were 14 universities and colleges, an increase of 5.7 times over 1950; these had 3,350 teachers — an increase of 14.8 times, and 17,800 students — an increase of 17.6 times.

In 1979, the province had 6,200 medical and health centres with 60,600 professional personnel and 42,800 hospital beds — representing increases of 75.5 times, 92.2 times and 46.8 times, respectively, over 1950. There was also some progress in rural medical care where problems in lack of medical care and medications were greatly improved.

Improvements in People's Livelihood. People's lives in Guizhou have improved greatly since the early post-Liberation years as the result of developments in the economy. In 1979, there were 1,423,200 employees in enterprises owned by the whole people, an increase of 44 times over 1949. The average annual wages of employees increased by 3.47 times over 1950; the average net income of peasants increased by 4.06 times. The purchasing power of people in cities and rural areas was 7.5 times more than in 1950, and the situation of "nobody has three pieces of silver" has become a thing of the past.

Problems in Development. Guizhou's national economy has achieved great progress during the 30 years since the founding of New China. However, there were serious mistakes and setbacks in economic construction because of the influence of "Left" errors and incorrect guiding thought after 1958. The three years of the Great Leap Forward and the ten-year disorder of the "cultural revolution" brought serious difficulties to the economy and caused imbalances between accumulation and consumption; in the proportion between agriculture, light and heavy industries; in the ratio of production to capital construction and to economic construction; and in science, culture, education and population growth. The economic structure was unreasonable and economic results were very poor, as best reflected by the fact that the rate of population growth was greater than the means of subsistence. The average grain yield per capita in 1979 was 181 catties less than in 1957. The agricultural foundation was fairly weak and heavy industry developed beyond the ability of agriculture; light industry developed rather slowly and Guizhou was self-sufficient in only about one-third of its requirements for daily industrial products; science and education lagged behind; housing space for employees and the public service facilities lagged far behind planned targets; technology and management levels were very low; and major technological and financial quotas in the province were in the main lower than average levels in the country. The economic situation began to improve during the first two years following the downfall of the Gang of Four. But serious proportional imbalances in the economy were not given enough attention and further mistakes were made during the economic reconstruction, with the result that the situation of imbalance was intensified in some respects. At present, the economy of Guizhou Province is still among the worst in China. Since the Third Plenary Session of the 11th Party Central Committee, the economic situation began to change. Economic construction has begun a new turning point with the implementation of the principle of readjusting restructuring, consolidating and improving the national economy.

Economic Development in 1980

The year 1980 saw new improvements in the national economy in the province over 1979 with the further rectification of the "Left" errors in economic construction and the continued implementation of the principle of readjusting the national economy.

Agriculture in 1980. In agriculture, the passive situation began to come to an end and the national economy obtained stability with the relaxation of agricultural policies and the establishment of various responsibility systems in agricultural production. Commune members in mountainous areas were widely dispersed and the actual levels of economy and management in these areas were very low. Thus, the overwhelming majority had long cried for transition to centralized management. Thus, in 1980, various responsibility systems in production were fundamentally established in the rural areas, and more than 70% of the production brigades voluntarily chose the method of fixing farm output quotas and tasks on the basis of households. Therefore, the problem of some aspects of production relations not matching the level of productive forces was primarily solved; peasants' initiative for production was effectively mobilized; and the agricultural production was promoted. Grain output amounted to 12,970 million catties in 1980, an increase of 4.1% over the year before. As for cash crops, rapeseed output was 269.1 million catties, a 51.9% increase over 1979 and the highest level ever recorded. There were increases to varying degrees of ramie, jute, ambary and tea.

Animal husbandry has developed continuously. The number of pigs in stock at the end of 1980 was 8,957,000, 2.4% more than in 1979; the number of cattle rose to 3,795,000, increasing by 2.9% — both represented the highest figures in history. There were relatively large achievements in economic diversification and in household sideline occupations, which effectively utilized natural resources in agriculture along with surplus labour force, and expanded the base of commodity production. Thus, rural economic activities became increasingly active. Total agricultural output value reached 2,930 million yuan, an increase of 2.4% over the year before, and its proportion in total combined industrial and agricultural output value rose from 39% in 1979 to 40% in 1980.

During the past two years there were some improvements in proportional divisions within agriculture because of the implementation of the principle of developing agricultural production by "paying attention to farming, animal husbandry and forestry; by developing farming, sideline occupations and industry together." The proportion of farming output value in the total value of agriculture declined from 66.11% in 1978 to 63.81% in 1980, while the proportion of output value of forestry, animal husbandry, sideline occupations and fisheries in the total output value of agriculture increased from 33.9% to 39.19%. The rural areas displayed good signs that had not appeared in many years. For example, production brigades that had once been reliant on loans for production, had spent money on relief and bought grain back from the state have taken on a new look. The quantity of resold grain declined rapidly. Trading markets for agricultural goods are flourishing and prices for grain, oil and meat have shown a stable downward trend.

The lives of commune members have been greatly improved. According to a typical survey of 690 peasant families in 23 counties, the average income per capita in 1980 was 189.5 yuan, an increase of 21.79% over 1979. The number of well-off families increased 2.5 times, while needy ones were reduced by two-thirds. The spending power of commune members was 139.2 yuan per head, up 19.7%. The number of families which built new houses increased; residential space by the end of 1980 increased by 4.1% over that of the year before. There was a total of about 72,330,000 yuan in bank deposits by commune members, an increase of 53.7% over the year before. Thus, the problems of basic livelihood for most peasants have been fundamentally solved.

Industry in 1980. In industry, plans called for textiles and light industries to develop faster, while production tasks for heavy industry were reduced. Thus, the internal structure of industry began to change. The year 1980 saw an increase of 10.6% in textiles and light industries and a decrease of 7.5% in heavy industry. In the total industrial output value, the proportion of light and textile industries increased from 32.3% in 1979 to 36.3% in 1980 and the proportion of heavy industry was reduced accordingly. There were large increases in quantities of main products of textiles and light industries and of household electrical appliances. Traditional local products were increasing, cigarettes reached 439,700 cases, an increase of 28.1%; soft drinks came to 43,600 tons, up 13.8%; and production of world-famous Mao Tai liquor increased by 5%. Quality was improved and new styles and designs were developed for many products.

Heavy industry geared its production according to demands, expanded those products that could realize the quickest returns; and reduced those products which had not been well received. The principle of closing down, stopping production, merging and diversifying was carried out in those enterprises which had a high rate of national and full consumption, poor quality in their products, which failed to meet demands and had long suffered losses. As a result, many enterprises now enterprises which had a high rate of material and fuel consumption, poor quality in their products, Output of electricity was 4,517 million kwh. increasing by 0.6%; chemical fertilizers for agricultural use reached 303,400 tons, an increase of 38.3%.

The economic reforms brought many enterprises back to life. In 1980, 50 industrial enterprises which were experimental units for enlarged decision-making power accomplished 115% of their industrial output value quotas and 119% of their profit plans, up 7% and 10%, respectively, over the year before and higher than the average rates of other enterprises. Many enterprises took the initiative in their own hands and practiced more flexible management in line with market regulation and under the guidance of the national plan. Output value achieved through market regulation comprised about one-third of total industrial output value. Average energy consumption (of standard fuel) per 10,000 yuan in industrial enterprises owned by the whole people was reduced by 1.21 tons. Losses by local industrial enterprises were 22% less than in 1979. Net profits after deducting losses were about 90,410,000 yuan, an increase of 5.9% over 1979. Five products won state gold or silver medals and 126 products were designated as high-quality or good products by the province.

Capital Construction in 1980. The proportion of grants from the national budget for capital construction in Guizhou was markedly decreased. In 1980, investments in the province's budget totalled 646,000,000 yuan, or 14.2% less than the year before. Adjustments were made in areas earmarked for investment. The proportion of investments in science, culture, education, public health, housing and urban construction in the local comprehensive plan was 28%, an increase of 2.6% over the year before. Housing space under construction totalled 2,310,000 sq.m., and completed space was 1,300,000 sq.m., or 230,000 sq.m. more than in 1979 and the highest rate in Guizhou since the founding of New China. Investments achieved much better results. The completion rate for construction during 1980 was 48.4%, a small gain over the year before.

Transport and Communications in 1980. In transportation, the volume of freight carried by rail reached 11,920,000 tons, or 110.3% of the planned target and an increase of 5.3% over 1979. But rail transport was still a weak link in the national economy. Because of insufficient orders, freight transported by truck totalled only 7,240,000 tons, 29% less than in 1979.

Commerce in 1980. In commerce, markets in cities and rural areas were active and purchases and sales flourished. Total purchase value was 1,770 million yuan, an increase of 11.1% over the year before. Total retail sales came to 2,790 million yuan, an increase of 9.3% over 1979. There was a large increase in purchases for foreign trade and exports. The market supply was further improved, with more styles and designs and more high-quality commodities. Recently, the growth of industrial and commercial enterprises under collective ownership in cities and rural areas was encouraged and more than 10,000 families engaged in private commerce and services were given licences. The realm of commodity distribution began to take on an active, positive situation — a variety of economic sectors, channels of distribution and forms of management existed together, and city and rural markets flourished. The quantity and variety of agricultural products and native produce were both large, and turnover increased greatly. All of these factors were of great convenience to the people.

Finance and Budget in 1980. In finance, the system of fixing responsibilities at various levels and setting quotas for revenues and expenditures was carried out in 1980, bringing into play the initiative of various departments in increasing production and practicing economy and in increasing revenues and cutting down on expenses. Local financial revenues totalled about 583.8 million yuan, 13.46% above the plan and 3.48% more than in 1979. Financial expenditures (including subsides from the central government and special grants) came to about 1,210.36 million yuan, comprising 74.85% of the fiscal year budget and a slight decrease from 1979.

Employment and Livelihood. While developing industrial and agricultural production, many channels were opened up for exploiting the potential for employment, and thus the lives of most of the masses continued to improve. In 1980, an additional 123,500 people were employed in Guizhou. According to a survey, the average number of persons to be provided for by each urban worker in 1980 was 2.3, as compared to 2.5 in 1979. The average income per capita in workers' families reached 316 yuan, or 50 yuan more than in 1979. The average annual wage per capita in enterprises owned by the whole people reached 797 yuan, an increase of 15.2% over 1979. A survey conducted in Guiyang and Zunyi cities and in Kaili and Meitan counties showed that the average housing space per capita in 1980 was 0.5% more than in 1979. There was some increase in the construction budget for minority regions in 1980. The province built and rebuilt highways in those regions, as well as about 26,000 sq.m. of space for housing, schools and clinics. Conditions for transportation, schooling, medical care and drinking water in these regions all improved.

Generally speaking, the economic situation in Guizhou Province in 1980 was good, but there were still many difficulties and problems. Grants in the capital construction budget were reduced, but investments outside the budget increased and the scale of capital construction was even larger than in 1979. Some industrial products did not meet quantity standards and total industrial output value did not reach the planned target. There was a large decrease in the output of tobacco, which had a bad influence on the tobacco industry and its financial revenues. Popular consumer goods developed too slowly. And the scale of losses in industrial enterprises expanded while profits submitted to the state decreased. Thus, levels of local financial revenues and expenditures were quite low, too much money was issued, the gap between supply and demand for goods widened and prices went up. All these developments showed that the national economy needed further readjustment.

Problems and Prospects for Future Development

The problems and difficulties the economy of Guizhou Province is now facing in its forward progress are inheritances of a long period of poor economic work. After the Third Plenary Session of the Party Central Committee, the situation in the province clearly changed significantly. The rectification of the internal structure of agriculture began to achieve good results. Nevertheless, the entire national economy did not fundamentally reverse the tide of passiveness. The tasks facing the national economy in the province remain to rectify "Left" mistakes continuously, to take a correct attitude in guiding economic work and to further adjust the national economy in its particular application to Guizhou. At present, measures are being taken to continue to reduce the scale of capital construction and to decrease financial expenditures; at the same time, the province must go all out to develop its agriculture, textiles and light industries in order to meet the people's needs for consumer goods and services; it must reduce the money in circulation, increase financial revenues and stabilize prices and the economy. The main task for readjustment is to gradually change the situation of serious imbalances in the national economy and the economic structure.

First, the economic structure must be adjusted to meet both the demands of the people for clothing, food, housing, transportation and services and the demands of the country from the province. Agriculture, textiles and light industries must be fully developed and the orientation of heavy industry — especially the machinery industry, which formerly mainly served capital construction and itself — must be turned to the service of agriculture, textiles and light industry as well as markets, exports and technical innovations.

Second, well-received products must be developed and the product mix must be adjusted. The province must go all out to develop its important products like cigarettes, spirits and textiles and must produce more products such as leather goods, garments, furniture, household electrical appliances, sewing machines, washing machines, bamboo and straw ware, motorcycles, oil presses, trucks and building materials — for which the province has adequate raw materials, markets and processing abilities. Guizhou should strive to increase coal output in order to meet the demand of other provinces and of exports. At the same time, it must continuously speed up production of traditional products, increase styles and designs of its products and enhance their quality.

Third, barriers between regions and departments must be broken down and consolidations and reforms focusing on products in given industries must be carried out. It is necessary to do a good job of closing down, stopping production, merging and diversifying enterprises and readjusting the structure of industry. On this basis, the province should do a good job of innovation within enterprises and tapping potential, of restructuring enterprises and bringing the role of existing enterprises into full play so as to enhance economic results. Through readjustment, a reasonable regional economic structure should be set up in the province's national economy suiting the socialist aims of production and realizing its superiority. Thus, the national economy of Guizhou Province will proceed gradually along a road of less investment, better results and harmonious development.

65. ECONOMIC DEVELOPMENT IN HEBEI PROVINCE
By the Hebei Provincial Planning Commission

Geography and Population

Location. Hebei Province is situated from 36°5' to 42°37' N. longitude, and from 113°11' to 119°45' E. latitude, on the northern part of the North China Plain along the lower reaches of the Huanghe (Yellow) River. The province faces Bohai Gulf to the east, and is bounded by the Taihang Mountain range and Shanxi Province on the west. Hebei's northwest, north and northeast sections border on the Inner Mongolia Autonomous Region and Liaoning Province. Its southeast and southern sections border on Shandong and Henan provinces, respectively. Beijing and Tianjin, both centrally governed, are set in the midst of Hebei.

Geographic Characteristics. Hebei covers an area of 185,000 sq. km., with the mountain chains of Taihang and Yanshan accounting for 35% of its territory; low-lying plateaus cover 12%; and plains, hills and river basins, 50%, with most level ground concentrated in the Haihe River Valley and Luanhe River Valley. The remaining area consists of lakes and lowlands. The province has a coastline of about 500 km.

Climate. Hebei has a monsoon climate. The average annual temperature range is 1-13°C., with vast contrasts between north and south. Frost-free periods last from 120-220 days. The range of average annual rainfall is 300-1,000 mm., with most precipitation occuring from June through August. Hebei is prone to drought during spring and autumn.

Population and Administrative Divisions. At the end of 1980, Hebei's population stood at 51.68 million, with 91% living in rural areas. The province has 10 prefectures (Handan, Xintai, Shijiazhuang, Baoding, Zhangjiakou, Chengde, Tangshan, Langfang, Changzhou and Hengshui), 2 municipalities under the direct jurisdiction of the provincial government (Shijiazhuang and Tangshan), 7 cities and 139 counties. The provincial capital is Shijiazhuang.

Survey of Economic Development Since 1949

Since the founding of the People's Republic, Hebei's economy has developed rapidly. In 1979, the value of its industrial and agricultural output totalled 29,797 million yuan — 10.2 times the figure for 1949 and yielding an average annual growth rate of 8%. Of the 1979 total, the value of agricultural output was 9,346 million yuan, a 3.8-fold increase, with an average annual growth rate of 4.5% since 1949; light industry accounted for 8,409 million yuan, a 27-fold increase, with an annual growth rate of 11.6% since 1949; and heavy industry was 12,042 million yuan, an 87-fold increase, with an average annual growth rate of 16.1% since 1949.

During this period, there were dramatic changes in the relationships to gross output value of agriculture, light industry and heavy industry. The proportional contribution of agriculture to total output value dropped from 76.9% in 1949 to 31.4% in 1979, while light industry grew from 17.1% to 28.2%, and heavy industry rose from 6% to 40.4%. The province's gross income for 1979 stood at 16,183 million yuan, yielding a per capita gross income of 318.5 yuan.

During the past 30 years, total investment in capital construction reached 28,300 million yuan, of which 18,460 million yuan, or 65.2%, went for fixed assets. These funds have laid a solid material basis for the province's on-going economic development.

Agriculture. Hebei Province has a long farming history. One of the first areas in China to take up settled agriculture, Hebei's farming plays an important role within China's national economy. Hebei's total cultivated area is approximately 100 million *mu*, which works out to 1.96 *mu* per capita. During the past 30 years, Hebei's agricultural sector has undertaken land reform, cooperative transformation and the establishment of people's communes. The Haihe River has been harnessed and capital construction in agriculture has taken place. Each of these developments has greatly improved farming conditions.

The province now has 48 large and medium-sized reservoirs with a total storage capacity of 8,728 million cu.m. Some 573,000 pump wells are in operation. Paddy fields and irrigated land total 55,060 million *mu*. Agricultural machinery came to an aggregate 16.4 million hp.; some 59.79 million *mu*, or 60%, of Hebei's farmland is now under mechanized farming. Chemical fertilizers were applied at an average rate of 75 catties per *mu*. Field crops comprise by far the largest agricultural sector. Extensive development has also occured in forestry, animal husbandry, sideline occupations and fishing. Field crops account for 60% of the total agricultural output value. Grain and cotton occupied 80% of the area planted to crops. Hebei is now one of China's major wheat and cotton producers.

Principal Crops. In 1979, Hebei's grain output reached 35,590 million catties, averaging 473 catties per *mu*, and surpassing by about 380% and 440%, respectively, the figures for the early post-Liberation period. Per capita grain share increased from 304 catties in 1949 to 697 catties in 1979, a rise of 130%. Cotton output was 231 million catties, an average of 27.7 catties per *mu*; and oil-bearing crops, 640 million catties, an average of 111.6 catties per *mu*. All registered increases over the early post-Liberation years.

Animal Husbandry. Hogs in stock were 13.52 million head, a 3.9-fold increase over the early post-Liberation period; draught animals, 3,469,000 head, a 15.7% increase; sheep and goats, 7,288,000 head, a 4.3-fold increase; aquatic products rose to 95,000 tons, up by 89.2%; forests amounted to 41,884,000 *mu*, increasing 50 times. Hebei's afforested area rose from 3.4% of its total area in the early post-Liberation period to 15% by 1979. Output of fresh and dried fruits was 1,650 million catties, an increase of 240%.

Minerals and Mining. Hebei is endowed with 80 kinds of minerals of which 50 are known to exist in significant quantities. Coal, iron and petroleum are abundant, and there are large reserves of copper, lead and zinc.

Industry. Hebei was industrially backward at the time of Liberation. The value of industrial output in 1949 totalled only 554 million yuan. Main commodities were steel, 3,700 tons; coal, 4,950,000 tons; and electricity, 260 million kwh. Production of pig iron, oil and chemical fertilizers was non-existent. Textiles were confined to 20,000 spindles for cotton yarn. Machine-building and light industries were operated entirely by manual labour. After 30 years of planned socialist construction, the province has acquired a healthy array of industries. In 1979, there were 14,000 industrial and mining enterprises in Hebei, including 183 large and medium-sized key units such as Kailuan Coal Mine, Fengfeng Coal Mine, North China Pharmaceutical Plant, Yaohua Glass Factory, Qixin Cement Plant, Changzhou Chemical Fertilizer Plant, and Shijiazhuang No. 2 Cotton Mill. The workforce in industry reached 2,535,800. Fixed assets in this sector came to 17,074 million yuan.

Compared with 1949, steel-making capacity has risen 500-fold. In 1979, 1,675,800 tons of steel were produced. Pig-iron output reached 2,348,400 tons. Coal extraction capacity increased eight times, with output reaching 58.41 million tons in 1979; power-generating capacity increased 31 times, with 1979's output at 19,051 million kwh. Cement output rose 51 times to 5,153,700 tons; plate glass stood at 3,990,000 cases; and chemical fertilizers at 904,000 tons. There was a 23-fold increase in the number of spindles, which turned out 195,000 tons of cotton yarn in 1979. Looms increased 40-fold and produced 858 million metres of cloth. Paper-making capacity rose by 536-fold, with 256,000 tons of machine-made paper and paperboard produced in 1979; porcelain ware for daily use came to 267 million pieces. Starting from scratch, the province is now able to produce in commercial quantities products such as motor vehicles, tractors, bicycles, sewing machines, wristwatches and TV and radio sets.

Communications and Transport. Communications and transport also registered rapid expansion. Several trunk railways such as the Beijing-Guangzhou, Beijing-Shanghai, Beijing-Shanhaiguan and Beijing-Baotou lines traverse the province. There are now 2,558.1 km. of trunk rail lines operated by the central government within the province and the 1979 volume of freight transport came to 111 million ton-km.; in addition, province-run railways total 569.4 km., and carried 4,473,000 ton-km. of freight in 1979. A total length of 39,000 km. of highways link all of the counties. Ice-free Qinghuangdao harbour, with 17 berths, now handles 24.08 million tons of cargo annually. With growth in production and construction, commerce, foreign trade, science, education, culture and public health have also been able to expand.

Review of 1980

In 1980, the people of Hebei conscientiously carried out the national policy of readjusting, restructuring, consolidating and improving the economy. Initial successes were achieved. The total value of industrial and agricultural output came to 29,950 million yuan, with revenues reaching 17,970 million yuan. Both totals exceeded figures for the previous year.

Agricultural Development. Marked changes have taken place in the composition of agriculture, with rapid expansion in cash crops such as cotton and oil-bearing plants. In 1980, severe drought, spring frosts, wind and hail storms affected 40.82

million *mu*, or 30%, of Hebei's total sown area. There was a shortfall of at least 30% on 29.47 million *mu*, representing 22% of the total sown area. Thanks to the implementation of new policies in agriculture and to the adoption of the job-responsibility system in production — which triggered the enthusiasm of the peasants for farm production and for fighting against natural disasters — total grain output nevertheless reached 30,449 million catties, the second highest yield since 1949.

Cash crops also achieved good harvests. Cotton output rose to 494 million catties, more than double the 1979 yield and reaching an average of 60 catties per *mu* the highest in Hebei's history; and oil-bearing crops totalled 900 million catties, 40.5% higher than in 1979 and topping all previous records. Meat production also increased substantially. Some 2,788,500 *mu* of land in Hebei was afforested during 1980, bringing the total afforested area in Hebei to 42,429 million *mu*, a 1.3% increase over 1979. The total annual agricultural output value was 8,025 million yuan, a 6.6% decrease compared with 1979 — a decline mainly due to the drop in grain output caused by bad weather.

Industrial Development. In industry, the principles of technological competance, economic efficiency and coordination between specialized units were stressed. As a result, 617 enterprises that had produced high-cost, poor-quality or unmarketable goods, or which operated at a loss, were closed down, merged or switched over to other product lines; 199 integrated economic complexes were set up; and 76 enterprises were experimentally given greater authority to make their own decisions. A more rational balance between light and heavy industry began to take shape, and light industry grew at a faster pace than heavy industry.

The province's total industrial output value in 1980 reached 21.22 million yuan, 3.8% more than in 1979. Of this, light industry contributed 9,620 million yuan, a 14.4% increase; and heavy industry, 11,600 million yuan, a 3.6% decrease. The proportion of output value of light industry to total industrial output value rose from 41.1% in 1979 to 45.3% in 1980, while the share of heavy industry fell from 58.9% to 54.7%. Production targets were reached ahead of schedule or were surpassed for 75 of 94 major products. Steel output reached 1,903,900 tons; pig iron, 2,515,700 tons; rolled steel, 1,258,800 tons; coal, 53.51 million tons; crude oil, 16.027 million tons; electricity, 19,630 million kwh.; cement, 5,498,000 tons; plate glass, 3,896,000 cases; chemical fertilizer for agriculture, 499,500 tons (counted on the basis of 100% effectiveness); and pesticides, 11,100 tons. Hebei also produced 2,212 tractors and internal combustion engines aggregating 369,000 hp.

Textile and light industrial production in 1980 rose by a large margin. Major increases included: 552,000 radios, up 140% over 1979; 334,000 bicycles, up 93.4%; 133,000 sewing machines, up 60%; 41,000 TV sets, up 15.8%; 317 million pieces of porcelainware for daily use, up 18.7%; 36,650,000 light bulbs, up 12.5%; 23,400 tons of soap, up 13%; 523,600 cases of cigarettes, up 9.7%; 5.38 million thermos flasks and glass liners, up 61.7%; 13.72 million metres of silk piece goods, up 40.1%; and 9,901 tons of chemical fibres, up 7%.

To meet the domestic market's needs, both the variety and specifications of industrial products increased and quality of products improved, resulting in improved economic results. A survey of 60 kinds of products showed that 76.7% of them improved their performance over 1979 in per-unit consumption of energy and raw materials; 73.5% of them surpassed the highest previous levels.

Profits from industrial enterprises covered by the provincial budget totalled 1,545 million yuan, a 10.13% increment over 1979. The profit ratio for output value per 100 yuan rose by 7.9% over 1979. Labour productivity in state-owned enterprises responsible for their own profits and losses increased by 0.8%.

Capital Construction and Investment. The scale of capital construction was reduced, with actual investments totalling 1,860 million yuan (excluding the investment alloted for Tangshan's rehabilitation) — a drop of 210 million yuan, or 10.4% as compared with 1979. Some 556 projects were cancelled or suspended in 1980, saving 151 million yuan in investment outlays. The proportional distribution of investments was also changed. Investments for expansion of productivity fell by 13.5%, with the proportional share of this category in total investments decreasing from 66% in 1979 to 59% in 1980; investments in non-productive items increased by 17.8%, with the proportion of total investments rising from 34% to 41%. Investments in housing construction totalled 353 million yuan, a 21.9% increase over 1979; work began on 5,606,000 sq. m. of new floor space, 4.038 million sq. m. more than in 1979, or an increase of 75.7%; 3,370,000 sq. m. of housing were completed, 497,000 sq. m. more than in 1979, or an increase of 17.3%. Investment efficiency improved. Labour productivity in state-owned construction units performing independent accounting was 4,650 yuan, an increase of 12.9% over 1979; the proportion of total floor space completed rose from 52.2% in 1979 to 57.1%; 1,926 million yuan's worth of fixed assets were added through capital construction in 1980.

Tangshan City. Tangshan city has made good progress in reconstruction following the devastating earthquake of July 28, 1976. Industrial and agricultural production in 1980 reached or surpassed pre-quake levels. Total investment in capital construction for the city was 930 million yuan, exceeding the previous year by 17.3%. The city gained an additional 600 million yuan worth of fixed assets through capital construction in 1980, an increase of 180% over 1979. The rate of availability of such assets rose from 24.1% in 1979 to 65.1%. Of the work begun on 3,764,000 sq. m. of total floor space of housing, 2,218,000 sq. m. were completed, representing an increase of 10.2% and 34.8%, respectively, over the previous year.

Finance and Commerce. In finance and trade, revenues for 1980 reached 3,512 million yuan, an increase of 0.6% over 1979; of this total, revenues from industrial enterprises accounted for 33.2%; receipts from various duties and taxes made up 64.3%; and other income accounted for 2.5%. Expenditures amounted to 28.47 million yuan, a decrease of 16.8% over 1979.

Urban and rural markets were brisk. The total value of commodities purchased by the province was 8,640 million yuan, an increase of 11.6% over 1979; retail sales came to 10,240 million yuan, an increase of 10.8%; urban sales rose by 13.4% and rural sales by 4.8%.

Foreign Trade. Hebei's foreign trade has expanded steadily. In recent years, the province has established economic trade relations with 115 countries and regions. Principle commodities for export include coal, plate glass, pottery and porcelain, cotton yarn, cotton cloth, leather and fur products, woven and plaited products, chestnuts, walnuts, jujubes, pears, red beans and canned goods. Local products include Qianxi's chestnuts, Shexian's walnuts, Changzhou's jujubes, Hebei Ya pears, Zhangbei's furs and leather, and Ahuxian's gold interwoven tapestries, all of which have a long-standing reputation at home and abroad. The total value of ready-for-export commodities purchased by the province in 1980 reached 1,319 million yuan, a 29.9% rise compared with 1979. Export value totalled over U.S.$607 million, a 45.1% increase over 1979.

Science, Education and Health. Science, education, culture and health work developed vigorously. The province now has a total of 162 research institutes. The number of people engaged in scientific and technological work at all levels came to 300,000 in 1980. One hundred research projects were completed during the year and some have already been applied to production with good results. The province had 28 institutions of higher learning in 1980. Their total floor space, including dormitories, was 958,000 sq. m., of which 11,000 sq. m. were added in 1980. Student enrollment totalled 41,400 in 1980, 34.5% over the previous year. The province also set up TV, broadcasting, correspondence and spare-time colleges and other higher education classes for adults. The total number of people attending these classes exceeded 290,000. The 120 secondary technical schools had an enrollment of 60,000. The 10,000 regular middle schools had a student body of 3,250,000. To reform the structure of secondary education, a number of agricultural and vocational schools were added recently, enrolling 25,600 students.

Primary education is now universal. In 1980, 97% of school-age children were at school. In 1980, there were 4,336 hospitals and clinics with 87,000 hospital beds; professional medical workers came to 152,000. Some 65% of all production brigades in rural areas took part in cooperative medical services, employing a total of 111,400 "barefoot" doctors.

The natural population growth rate stood at 9.2 per one thousand; one-child families made up 61.5% of the total, while 78.65% of newly married couples have offered commitments to bear just one child.

Income and Livelihood. Readjustment of the economy brought improvements in the livelihood of the people. Pay increases for 40% of the workers and staff, coupled with increased wage grades in some areas and the institution of a bonus system, brought significant increases in the income of workers and staff in cities and towns. The average annual wage of workers and staff members employed in units owned by the whole people was 753 yuan in 1980, or 98 yuan more than in 1979; the average annual wage of workers and staff in collectively owned units was 591 yuan, or 72 yuan above the 1979 figure. The total income of the majority of rural commune members increased substantially over 1979. Per capita income derived from the collective in rural people's communes rose from 98.2 yuan in 1979 to 105 yuan in 1980.

Savings. At the end of 1980, individual savings deposits of the urban and rural population totalled 2,106 million yuan, an increase of 671 million yuan or 46.8% over the 1979 figure. Of this sum, urban savings deposits came to 1,246 million yuan, an increase of 41.4%, and rural savings deposits to 860 million yuan, an increase of 55.2%.

Current Problems and Goals for Future Development

Although economic readjustment has made remarkable achievements in Hebei in 1980, long-established disproportions in the national economy cannot be substantially resolved within a short period. Agricultural production is not yet stable; the ability to overcome natural calamities is weak; and the development of forestry, animal husbandry and fisheries has been slow. The internal structure of industry remains irrational, with excess emphasis on heavy industry. Moreover, heavy industry tends to disproportionately serve its own interests rather than those of agriculture and light industry. Light industry is a distinctly weak link within the national economy. Capital construction is still over-extended and beyond the country's financial and material resources. Science, education, culture and public health are backward. Levels of management and technology are low and economic results are not satisfactory. All these problems have yet to be resolved.

Hebei will continue economic readjustment in 1981. The province plans to further scale down capital construction. Total investment in capital construction within the province's budget in 1981 will be 40% less than that in 1980, with more cuts in heavy industry; meanwhile, the sum alloted for science, education, culture and public health is to go up 28.5%. There will be appropriate controls over the production of heavy industrial commodities that consume too much energy or which are in over-supply. Efforts will be made to increase the production of light industrial and textile goods and other urgently needed commodities such as bicycles, sewing machines, wristwatches, TV sets, chemical fibres and garments. In agriculture, while assuring increased grain output, efforts will continue to readjust the internal structure, to develop cash crops and diversify the economy in accordance with local conditions.

66. ECONOMIC DEVELOPMENT IN HEILONGJIANG PROVINCE
By Zhong He
Heilongjiang Provincial People's Government

Geographical Setting

Heilongjiang Province is situated in the northernmost border region of northeast China. It has an area of more than 460,000 sq.km. — 5% of the total area of China. Heilongjiang has 130 million *mu* of farmland and 50 million *mu* of reclaimable land. Forests make up 49% of the province's area, with stands of 1,760 million cu.m. There are five large rivers in the province, namely, the Heilongjiang, Songhuajiang, Wusulijiang, Nenjiang and Suifen rivers. In addition, there are 1,741 relatively large rivers and streams, with a total length of 4,900 km. The fresh-water surface area totals 30 million *mu*. Prairies and grasslands come to 75 million *mu*, placing the province among the ten leading stock-raising regions in the country.

The province is rich in minerals. Apart from coal and petroleum, deposits of gold, copper, aluminium, lead, zinc and other nonferrous and rare metals also occupy an important place in the country. Heilongjiang is not only an important base for commodity grain but is also one of China's main centres for coal, petroleum, timber and machine-building industries.

Economic Development Since Liberation

Since the founding of New China, great changes have taken place in the economy of the province under unified state planning. During the period of the First Five-Year Plan, Heilongjiang was one of the country's high-priority construction provinces. Twenty-two major projects were built in the province, and some 20 large and medium-sized enterprises were transferred in from other parts of the country. This, plus the development of forests in the Daxingan Mountains and the construction of the Daqing Oilfield in the early 1960's, combined to lay a solid technical and material foundation for the development of industry. In the meantime, the state set up a cluster of state farms in the province. Heilongjiang now has 872 state farms with an aggregate cultivated area of 30 million *mu*, accounting for 23.2% of the province's cultivated land, or 40% of the area of all state farms throughout the country.

Agriculture. In agriculture, total output value in 1979 was 3.4 times that of 1949, with an average annual growth of 4.2%. Grain output in 1949 was 11,500 million *jin*; it topped 20,000 million *jin* in 1966; and stayed above 29,000 million *jin* each year between 1978 and 1980, a rate 2.6 times that of 1949. During the past 30 years, the average annual growth rate for grain output was 3.1%, and the average commodity rate for grain and soybeans was 40%.

The use of farm machinery has developed rapidly. The province now has 56,000 farming tractors which plough an area of 90 million *mu*, 69% of the province's total farmland.

Animal husbandry has also expanded in the past 30 years. The number of pigs in stock in 1979 was 7,983,000, an increase of 4.4 times over the 1949 total.

Industry. By 1979, the province had 14,000 industrial enterprises, 2.6 times those of 1949; fixed industrial assets amounted to 22,600 million yuan, 17.2 times that of 1952; total output value of industry reached 21,100 million yuan, 32.3 times more than in 1952, with average annual growth of 12.3%. Of this total, heavy industrial output was valued at 14,750 million yuan, a 40.7-fold increase over 1949, or an average annual growth rate of 13.1%; light industry stood at 6,300 million yuan, 21.8 times that of 1949, or an average annual increment of 10.8%.

Transport and Communications. Transportation and communications have developed rapidly along with increased production in agriculture and industry. The mileage of railways open to traffic in 1979 was 5,048 km., some 1,100 km. more than the 1949 figure; highway mileage was 42,000 km., more than 7 times the 1949 figure; and civil aviation and inland waterways navigation also increased considerably.

The development of production has resulted in higher living standards and expanded purchasing power in both urban and rural areas. The volume of retail sales in 1979 registered an increase of 20 times over 1949, while the average consumption of consumer goods per capita went up 6-fold. Urban housing projects investment during the period from 1953 to 1979 amounted to 3,000 million yuan, or 9.5% of the province's total investment. In 1979, 40 million sq.m. of housing were completed, and 0.8 million workers' families moved into new houses.

Education and Health. Progress was also made in education and culture, science and technology, the press and broadcasting, and public health and publishing. The number of institutes of higher learning increased from 5 in 1949 to 27 in 1979, with the student body growing some eight times. That of professional secondary schools (including skilled workers' schools) increased from 11 to 272, with the student body increasing 25 times. The number of secondary school students increased 112 times, and primary school pupils, 5.5 times. The number of scientific and technical personnel in natural sciences amounted to 280,000. There are about 400 scientific institutions in the province. The number of medical and health establishments grew from 213 in 1949 to 8,372 in 1979; hospital beds increased from 2,800 to 10,000; and medical personnel went from 2,300 to 120,000.

During the past 30 years, although the economic development in the province encountered some detours due to the influence of "Left" thinking and the construction speed was delayed because of grave sabotage by Lin Biao and the Gang of Four. Nevertheless, the people of the province under the leadership of the Communist Party, working in the spirit of plain living, hard struggle and self-reliance, managed to transform this once poor and backward "Great Northern Wilderness" into a prosperous "Great Northern Granary."

Economic Developments in 1980

As a result of the implementation of the policy of readjustment, restructuring, consolidation and improvement in 1980, the province's economic structure tended to become more rational, with improved proportions and better economic results. The entire economy of the province has begun to develop in a coordinated way.

Agriculture in 1980. Successive bumper harvests were achieved in agriculture, and the internal structure of agriculture was improved. Farming, forestry, animal husbandry, sideline occupations and fisheries developed in coordination. Although in 1980 Heilongjiang Province suffered from a series of severe natural calamities including low temperatures, windstorms, insect infestations and summer droughts, a good harvest was brought in because party committees and people's governments at all levels earnestly implemented the party's economic policies for rural areas and strengthened and improved the system of production responsibility, thus arousing the enthusiasm of the peasants for production and enabling them to overcome disasters. Total output of grain in 1980 reached to 29,250 million *jin,* exceeding the 29,000 million *jin* mark for the third time in local history. Of this total, wheat output came to 7,890 million *jin,* 18.5% above the previous year and also a record yield for the province. The province overfulfilled the state purchase quota of grain by 20%. The total value of agricultural output amounted to 6,449 million yuan, an increase of 8.1% over the previous year.

Cash crops developed considerably as a result of the readjustment of the internal structure of agriculture. The area sown to cash crops in 1980 was 102,050 million *mu,* 68% more than the previous year. The output of main cash crops such as oil-bearing seeds, cast fibres and sugarbeets, broke previous records. Oil-bearing crops yielded 263,350 tons, increasing by 3.9 times. The output of cast fibres was 190,200 tons, an increase of 66.3%, of which the output of flax reached 174,900 tons, a 78.6% increase; sugar beets yielded 3.16 million tons, 2.5 times the output of the previous year.

Moreover, significant progress was also made in the fields of forestry, animal husbandry, sideline occupations and fisheries. In 1980, the actual afforested area amounted to 3.45 million *mu,* an increase of 9% compared to 1979. The readjustment in animal husbandry promoted the development of livestock breeding. The number of dairy cattle increased by 21.9% over the previous year; and sheep and goats, by 23.3%, setting a record. As a result of the overall development made in farming, forestry, animal husbandry, sideline occupations and fisheries, the income of commune members increased and their living standards improved. Thus, the collective economy was further consolidated. Per capita income from the collective economy in 1980 increased to 115 yuan, a 5% increase over the previous year, and a record high as well. A total of 6,753 production brigades began to change their backward outlook; 3,000 of these raised per capita income to 90 yuan or more. The proportion of poor brigades in the province dropped from 22.4% in 1979 to 13.3% in 1980.

Industry in 1980. Industrial production developed steadily, with textiles and light industries growing faster than heavy industry and with new changes taking place in the structure of industry. In 1980, Heilongjiang carried out the policy of readjusting the national economy. Enterprises with poor management, high consumption, low product quality and big deficits were closed down, amalgamated with other enterprises or converted to produce other products. Defence and machine-building enterprises operating at below capacity were reoriented to produce ready-to-sell products. Readjustment has brought about better economic results, a marked increase in the variety of products, and notable changes in the speed of development and in the proportion between light and heavy industries and in the structure of industry and the composition of products, all to better meet social needs. The total industrial output value of Heilongjiang increased by 5.2% over the previous year, of which the output value of light industry was 16.3% more than in 1979. The proportion of light industry to the whole of industry increased to 33.2% as against 30% in the previous year.

The quality of products was improved and their variety increased as a result of better economic management. Of the 759 major products examined by the provincial authorities, 210 were classified as high-quality products, constituting 27.7% of the total. In the nationwide quality contest, Heilongjiang won 12 silver medals as against 6 in the previous year. Incomplete statistics from the cities of Harbin, Qiqihar, Mudanjiang and Jiamusi indicated that more than 600 new varieties of products with 3,000 designs had been manufactured. The readjustment boosted revenues because of increased profits from industry. Profits turned over by industrial enterprises within the budget were 39.3% higher than in 1979, exceeding the initial plan by 27.6%. The number of enterprises operating at a loss was reduced, with deficits falling by 12.7%.

Capital Construction in 1980. In capital construction, investments financed by the state showed a decrease while those provided by the province itself increased. A new record was set in housing construction. In 1980, the investment in housing construction amounted to 610 million yuan, 56.5% more than the previous year. Work was begun on a total floor space of 6.03 million sq.m., constituting 52.3% of all construction work undertaken by the province. Housing completed in 1980 covered an area of 3.58 million sq.m., or 59.4% of all houses under construction, also a record in Heilongjiang unmatched since 1949.

Commerce in 1980. Market purchases and sales were brisk and the people's livelihood improved considerably. Total retail sales in 1980 amounted to 9,270 million yuan, 15.6% more than 1979. Sales of bicycles came to 566,000, 9.7% more than the previous year or 38 times the figure of 1953; 117 million watches were sold, a 38.3% increase over the previous year or 13 times more than in 1953; 132,000 TV sets were sold, 3.6 times more than the previous year; and pork sold was 229,000 tons, 31% more than sales in 1979. Total purchases by commercial departments amounted to 9,020 million yuan, 9.9% more than 1979; and the total value of stocks increased by 9.1%. In addition, 163 million yuan worth of goods were sold at 400 peasant fairs, 26.8% more than the previous year.

Provincial revenues and expenditures were in balance with a small surplus. Revenues totalled 17.4% more than the previous year. Savings deposits of the urban and rural population increased by 48%, also a record.

Commodities purchased for foreign trade in 1980 were valued at 1,770 million yuan, 8.7% more than the previous year. The tourism industry also underwent new development. In 1980, in Harbin alone, 6,346 overseas Chinese, compatriots from Hong Kong and Macao, foreign nationals of Chinese descent and foreigners visited the city, 58.4% more than in 1979. Earnings from tourism amounted to 907,000 yuan, or 2.2 times the figure in the previous year.

Education and Health Work in 1980. Developments were seen in the fields of culture, education, science and technology, public health and physical culture. Students at institutes of higher learning numbered 41,800 in 1980, an increase of 10.6% over 1979. There were 91,900 students in professional secondary schools (including skilled-workers' schools), an increase of 4.4% over 1979. In addition, there were also 23,000 students taking courses at 133 spare-time colleges. In scientific research, 442 projects attained national or provincial advanced levels and achieved effective results in application to production and construction. Medical conditions and health work improved steadily. The province had 133,000 medical personnel and 104,000 hospital beds, an increase of 5.6% and 3%, respectively. In sports activities, Heilongjiang won 25 gold medals in national competitions and broke a world record in model airplane flying in 1980.

Problems and Prospects for Future Development

During the past 30 years, great achievements

have been made in the development of Heilongjiang's economy. However, problems still exist, chiefly the proportions among different sectors of the economy and irrational economic structure. First, agriculture remained unable to meet the needs of the state and the province due to unstable yields and low rates of growth. Agriculture in Heilongjiang still lags behind the average national rate of growth in both total output value and grain output. The share of forestry, animal husbandry, sideline occupations and fisheries in the total value of agricultural output has continued to decline yearly. Forest resources have been seriously depleted because timbering has far exceeded afforestation. Forest stocking has decreased by 30.4% as compared with the 1950's. Within animal husbandry, priority has been given only to the development of pigs, to the neglect of herbivorous animals such as cattle, sheep and rabbits. Second, the light industry remains the "shorter leg." Even though its proportion has increased to 33.2% following the readjustment, this is still below the average national level of 43%. Heavy industry is also disproportionate within its own structure. There is a great strain on transportation and a serious shortage of fuel and power. Third, social welfare facilities cannot keep up with the needs of people's lives. Heilongjiang is still far from self-sufficient in consumer goods for daily use. Culture, education, public health and urban construction lag behind population growth. All these problems must be solved in the course of economic readjustment.

In line with the province's economic basis, its present conditions and natural resources, a tentative plan has been mapped out for development during the 1981-90 period. The plan is designed to bring our strong points and superiority into full play, to continue to boost the production of raw materials and basic industries and to speed up development of secondary and tertiary processing of agricultural and forestry products, animal byproducts and minerals. The purpose is to change the situation in which there is an over-abundance of primary products being supplied to processing industries. It is necessary to establish centres for animal by-products, sugar and paper-making, while continuing to strengthen the existing centres of grain, timber, coal, petroleum and machine-building industries. The level of the provincial economy is to be doubled on the basis of higher technology and labour productivity. To this end, it is imperative to control strictly the growth of population and to accelerate the development of industry, to readjust the economic structure and to speed up rural construction and the development of culture, education and scientific research.

As regards the population, the rate of natural growth will gradually be reduced to 0.6% by 1985 and thereafter to 0.5%. By 1990, the population of the province must be kept to below 35 million. Gross output value of agriculture and industry should increase by an average annual rate of 6.1% during the period 1981-85, and by an annual rate of 7.1-8.2% during 1986-90. Over the next ten years, economic structure must be properly readjusted with stress on speedier development of rural construction, coordination between agriculture, industry and commerce, and increases in the income of peasants so as to avoid an influx of rural population into the cities. Industries owned by communes and production brigades should be developed on a large scale on the basis of expanding agriculture and diversification. It is envisaged that per capita income of the rural population derived from the collective will reach 150 yuan by 1985 and 200 yuan by 1990. Efforts should be made to expand culture, education and scientific research and train more qualified personnel to cope with the growing needs of economic development and the four modernizations.

These are arduous tasks in view of the actual conditions in Heilongjiang Province. However, the tentative plan for the next decade can eventually be realized through the hard work of the entire people of the province.

67. ECONOMIC DEVELOPMENT IN HENAN PROVINCE
By the Financial and Economic Department,
General Office of the Henan Provincial People's Government

Henan Province is situated in the central plains of China. It has a population of 72,000,000, covering a area of 167,000 sq.km. Henan is relatively rich in natural resources. Before Liberation, under the dark rule of the Kuomintang reactionaries, the people of Henan were oppressed by "the three big mountains" of imperialism, bureaucrat-capitalism and feudalism, and they were constantly harassed by the four evils — floods, drought, locusts and the Kuomintang warlord Tang Enbo. Thus the economy was exceedingly backward. The province had only one coal mine and a few small power plants, textile mills, oil-pressing mills, cigarette factories and egg products plants. In 1949, the population of Henan came to 7.7% of the national total, whereas total output value of industry and agriculture was only 4.5% that of the whole country. Per capita income derived from industrial and agricultural production averaged 50.4 yuan. This was 58.5% of the level of the whole country. Because the economy was backward, the people lived in extreme poverty.

Review of Economic Development Since 1949

After Liberation, under the leadership of Communist Party of China, the people of Henan rapadily healed the wounds of war, restored the economy and initiated socialist economic construction on a large scale. Having overcome many difficulties, they have made quite rapid progress in industry, agriculture and in the entire national economy through 30 years of hard work, although they encountered setbacks along the way.

Agriculture. Great changes have taken place in agricultural conditions and the level of agricultural production has been greatly incrased. By the end of 1979, the province had 613,000 power-operated wells and more than 2,400 reservoirs. These brought over 54,000,000 *mu* of farmland under irrigation; there were over 52,000 large and medium-sized tractors for agricultural use, over 100,000 hand tractors and more than 780,000 drainage and irrigation machines. The area of machine-ploughed land comprised 47% of total farmland. Electricity for agricultural use and chemical fertilizers have also increased. The improvement of conditions has significantly promoted the development of agricultural production. In 1979, total agricultural output value reached 10,300 million yuan, nearly 4 times that of 1949; total grain output reached 42,690 million catties, which was 2.9 times the amount of the early post-Liberation years; the per-*mu* output of grain reached 518 catties, 3.8 times that of those days. Forestry, animal husbandry, sideline occupations and fisheries also showed great increases.

Industry. Starting from scratch and then growing from small to large, provincial industries have advanced with great strides. In Zhengzhou, Luoyang, Kaifeng, Pingdingshan, Xinxiang, Anyang, Jiaozuo and Hebi, a number of large, modern enterprises have been set up, including tractor, bearing, mining machinery, iron and steel, aluminothermy, textile and chemical plants. In 1979, the province had 14,959 industrial enterprises, with more than 4,400,000 workers and staff members. Industrial output value reached 16,990 million yuan, 75 times that of 1949.

Transport and Communications. With the upsurge of economic construction, communications and transport, of which land routes are the backbone, have sped up. The Beijing-Guangzhou and Longhai railways, two important trunk lines, crisscross the province. The Jiao-Zhi and Xin-Jiao branch railway lines were newly added. Local railways have sprung up from scratch and are developing quickly. New narrow-gauge rail lines extend over 1,200 km. Highways, totalling more than 36,000 km., lead out in all directions, with all-weather surfaces coming to over 19,000 km. These roads form a highway network, with Zhengzhou, Luoyang, Kaifeng, Xuchang, Nanyang and Xinyang as the hubs. Paved roads link up all counties and communes in Henan. There are regular bus services between most communes and towns. The volume of freight transported throughout the province in

1979 was more than 170 million tons, or 51 times that of 1949. There was also further development in posts and telecommunications in 1979. Newly-added postal routes totalled more than 160,000 km. The volume of employment in this sector was 38 times higher than in 1949.

Financial revenues and the supply of commodities have grown year by year. In 1979, total provincial revenues were 3,280 million yuan, 12 times higher than in 1950, and representing an annual growth rate of 9%. Retail sales increased from 480 million yuan in 1949 to 10,290 million yuan in 1979, a 21-fold increase. The total value of purchases was 9,190 million yuan, a 12-fold increase.

Economic Developments in 1980

In line with the policy of readjusting, restructuring, consolidating and improving the national economy as set by the Central Committee of the Party, much work was done in 1980 to readjust Henan's economy on the basis of 1979's encouraging achievements, and this brought about definite results.

Agriculture in 1980. Agricultural production went up by a fairly large margin. In 1980, in the countryside and throughout the province, the party's rural economic policies were implemented. About 400,000 production teams, in accordance with local conditions, introduced the system of responsibility in production. All this greatly stimulated the peasants' enthusiasm for production and promoted the overall development of agricultural production. Although the province suffered from natural disasters in 1980 (droughts, floods, hailstorms, insects, etc.), the harvest was a fairly good one. Total agricultural output value amounted to 11,080 million yuan, representing an increase of 7.5% over the previous year. Total output of grain reached 42,970 million catties, or 280 million catties more than in 1979, which was also a good year.

While keeping to the principle of placing grain production in the dominant position, we readjusted the internal agricultural structure and the proportion of various crops in accordance with concrete local conditions. As a result, cash crops did unprecedentedly well. Total output of cotton reached 8,120 million catties, more than double the figure of 1979. Total output of oil-bearing crops was 9,240 million catties, 24.5% more than in 1979. Total output of roasted tobacco was 3,740 million catties, 5.1% more than in 1979. Total output value of commune- and brigade-run industries and sideline occupations reached 3,500 million yuan, 15.5% higher than in the previous year. Owing to the development of agricultural production and to substantial increases in state purchasing prices for major farm and sideline products, peasants' incomes increased remarkably and their average per capita income was some 20 yuan higher than in 1979. There were considerable increases in incomes of both collectives and individuals.

Industry in 1980. Industrial structure advanced in a rational and coordinated way. Industrial production grew continuously in the course of readjustment. In carrying out the principle of readjustment in Henan Province, special attention was paid to the proportion between heavy and light industries and the development of textiles and light industries was placed in a prominent position: one-third more investments were made in these sectors than in 1979, and over 81 million yuan in loans were provided to transform and renew these industries. Moreover, they were given priority in the supply of raw materials, fuel, power and the means of transport. All this accelerated the development of textiles and light industries. Their total output value in 1980 came to 9,400 million yuan, 18.2% more than in 1979. The rate of increase greatly surpassed that of heavy industry (which grew by 0.1%). The ratio of textiles and light industries to total industrial output value rose from the previous year's 46.9% to 51% in 1980. Output of key products such as cigarettes, bicycles, sewing machines, watches, electronic products, domestic electrical appliances, high-grade cotton cloth, woollen fabrics, silk and chemical fibres, famous wines, building materials, leather, clothing, earthenware and chinaware for daily use each increased by at least 23% over 1979.

At the same time, the quality of products was gradually improved and varieties increased. In heavy industry, products in over-supply were cut back while marketable goods in high demand increased. Steps were taken against some small steel and iron works, ammonia plants and machinery plants which were known for their high consumption of materials and fuel and for low quality, and whose operations had resulted in waste and losses for a long period and had competed with large enterprises for raw materials. These units were either closed down, suspended, combined or transformed. By so doing, higher overall efficiency was achieved.

Commerce and Finance in 1980. On the

financial and commercial fronts, inspiring achievements were recorded. On the premise of keeping the state-owned economy as the dominant sector, collective trade has been developed actively and private trade is being developed appropriately so as to open up and broaden various channels of distribution. At the same time, methods of management have been improved, promoting purchases and sales and creating brisk urban and rural markets. In 1980, net purchases amounted to 11,090 million yuan, 20.6% higher than in 1979; net sales reached 12,380 million yuan, 12.5% higher; retail sales amounted to 11,850 million yuan, 15% higher. Trade at village fairs was even more prosperous, with transactions amounting to 1,900 million yuan. This kind of trade is playing an active role in augmenting the state-owned and collective economies.

Foreign Trade in 1980. Foreign trade has developed remarkably, with purchases of exports increasing by 31% over 1979 and total export value increasing by 49%. Revenues and expenditures were roughly in balance, and in fact showed a slight surplus. Financial revenues came to 3,180 million yuan, or 7.8% more than in 1979.

Capital Construction in 1980. Investments budgeted for capital construction were drastically reduced, leading to improved results. In 1980, 26 capital construction projects in Henan, each of which had been planned to absorb more than 1 million yuan in investment, were halted or postponed, bringing the total number of curtailed projects since 1979 to 116. The allotment of investments has been drastically readjusted, with more appropriated for agriculture, textiles and light industries, education, housing and municipal construction.

Readjustment Policy in 1980. Reform of the economic system achieved initial success. Guided by the readjustment policy, 336 enterprises in Henan are engaged in an experiment to enlarge their decision-making powers; these make up 15.5% of all budgeted enterprises in the province. Their output value comprised 53% of the province's total and their profits, 90% of the total. Facts have shown that the expansion of decision-making powers is playing an active role in enhancing the enthusiasm of enterprises and corresponding individuals in enlivening the economy, improving management, raising production and income, and pushing ahead reforms across the entire economic system. According to statistics for 170 such enterprises, their output value in 1980 increased by 14.73% over the previous year; profits turned over to the state increased by 6.91%.

The Anyang Iron and Steel Works has strengthened its economic accounting and has unfolded a drive to increase production and to practice economy on the one hand and to increase income and cut expenditures on the other. As a result, the enterprise realized 35.76 million yuan in profits in 1980, 3.19 times that of 1979. This is the highest level since the establishment of the Anyang works.

In the course of industrial readjustment, many enterprises have taken the road of integration to develop production according to the principle of economic rationality and specialization. In Henan, 971 enterprises have been integrated into 110 profit-making companies or combined factories. In order to turn out competitive products in a united effort, they have broken with the restrictions of different systems, regions and ownerships, and have demonstrated the superiority of professional coordination and cooperation, as well as the superiority of integrated production.

Owing to the readjustment, economic results improved in various areas in 1980. Energy consumption fell by about 6%, while industrial output increased by 8.2%; the proportion of industrial enterprises suffering losses dropped from 32% in 1979 to 30.7% in 1980, and overall losses went down by 39.4% compared with the previous year. Meanwhile, the cost of comparable products fell by 2.29%.

Problems and Prospects for Future Development

Although further progress was made in economic readjustment in Henan in 1980, quite a few problems remain. Owing to the fact that "Left" mistakes in economic construction have not been rectified for a long time, the proportions among various sectors of the national economy are out of balance; furthermore, the consequences of the ten-year destruction (of the "cultural revolution") were underestimated during the first two years following the downfall of the Gang of Four, and "Left" mistakes in directing economic work were not sorted out. As a result, imbalanced relations in the national economy have not been fundamentally reversed, and the task of readjustment will thus be arduous.

In agriculture, backward working conditions have not been fundamentally changed, and agricultural production is still badly affected by natural conditions. The economic structure in agriculture is not yet sufficiently rational. Proportional distribution of areas sown to different crops are basically appropriate, although these areas are still somewhat dispersed. Forestry and animal husbandry are backward and sideline occupations are still too few. The combined value of the above three sectors only occupies 30% of the total output value of agriculture.

Nor is Hebei's industrial structure rational enough. Quotas and tasks for the machinery industry are drastically insufficient; although textile and light industries have plenty to do, their production capacities are low. Because of undue emphasis on the development of heavy industry and on "taking steel as the key link," capital construction projects were undertaken at random; iron and steel and machine-building enterprises were aimlessly set up and often overlapped one another. Hebei has more than 370 machine-building enterprises (at or above the county level), mostly "big and all-embracing" or "small but all-embracing" types.

It follows from this situation that economic results are poor. Because insufficient investments are made in textiles and light industries, they are unable to produce enough to meet the needs of the market; along with the growth of industrial and agricultural production, purchasing power is increasing rapidly. That is why the contradiction between supply and demand is becoming sharper.

Enterprises under collective ownership have been restrained for too long, and rash demands were imposed on them, thus inhibiting the growth of collective enterprises. Prodution techniques and management levels, on the whole, are low, giving rise to poor efficiency. The products of quite a few enterprises are of high cost, consume excessive energy and do not meet the needs of consumers; in short, they are not competitive. In 1980, 112 yuan of output value was obtained from each 100 yuan worth of fixed assets in Henan — a rate 16.6% below the best record in history; 9.2 yuan in profits were obtained from each 100 yuan of output value, 40.1% below the previous record; every 100 yuan of output value required 39.51 yuan in working capital — 6.75 yuan more than the best previous record or 12.9 yuan more than the national average. The capacity of spinning and weaving equipment in Henan ranks sixth nationally, although its output value and profits rank only ninth in the country, while the amount of profit for each 100 yuan of output value ranks only 15th. The amount of currency in circulation is enormous, and there is a big gap between social purchasing power and the supply of commodities. If effective measures are not taken to develop the production of consumer goods, the contradiction between supply and demand would sharpen, and that would affect political stability and unity.

In order to change the above-mentioned backwardness as soon as possible, further adjustment is necessary for the national economy of Henan. The "heavy structure" (in which heavy industry is placed in the dominant position) should give way to the "light structure" — that is, agriculture should be developed on a large scale and textiles and light industries should be placed in the dominant position; energy resources, communications, transportation and those branches of heavy industry that serve agriculture and light industry should be correspondingly developed. In agriculture, grain production should be strengthened and great attention paid to the development of diverse economic undertakings. Under the prerequisite of guaranteeing increases in grain yield, cash crops are to be developed actively so as to reap good harvests of both grain and cash crops. In industry, conscientious readjustment is to be carried out, the development of textiles and light industries is to be accelerated, more consumer goods are to be produced and production within various divisions of heavy industry is to be reorganized so as to suit the production of consumer commodities and to change the situation of too much heavy industry and too little light industry.

Priority is to be given to cities such as Zhengzhou, Luoyang, Kaifeng, Anyang and Xinxiang, since they are more crucial to the development of Henan's national economy. Great attention is to be paid to such products as textiles, cigarettes, liquor, watches, bicycles, sewing machines, garments, furniture, plastics and building materials. At the same time, concern is to be shown for the production of small articles of daily use. Through readjustment, the economic structure is expected to be rationalized and present conditions of poor efficiency and huge waste are to be changed so as to pave a new road in economic development where more is gained with less investment.

68. ECONOMIC DEVELOPMENT IN HUBEI PROVINCE
By the Research Department of the General Office,
Hubei Provincial People's Government

Geographical Setting

Hubei Province is in China's central plain. It has a total area of over 180,000 sq. km., with a population of 46,840,000. The Changjiang (Yangtze) River flows through the province from west to east. The Beijing-Guangzhou Railroad traverses from north to south. Highways also extend in all directions. Thus, Hubei is the hub of inland waterway and land communications in China.

The Jianghan Plain is situated in the central part of the province. The Wushan and Daba mountains are in the west; the Tongbai Mountains are located in the north; the Dabie Mountains found in the east; and the Mufu Mountains are in the south. There are many rivers and lakes within Hubei, and its soil is fertile. It has a temperate climate and is rich in rice, wheat, cotton and oil-bearing crops. Freshwater fishing and aquatic breeding flourish: Hubei is known as "a province of a thousand lakes and a land of fish and rice."

Raw lacquer, tung oil, tea, ramie, citrus fruit and white fungus are well-known native products. Hubei abounds in mineral resources, especially iron, copper, phosphorus, gypsum, barite and rock salt. The output of gypsum ranks first in China. The province's white fibre gypsum is of the highest quality and is sold both at home and in foreign markets. Large quantities of high-grade iron ore are widely found in Hubei. The Daye Iron Mine is well known throughout China. Hubei is also rich in water resources.

Wuhan, the capital of Hubei, is situated at the confluence of the Changjiang and Hanshui rivers. Wuhan's urban district consists of three towns — Wuchang, Hankou, and Hanyang, each one separated from the others by the rivers. Wuhan is the political, economic and cultural centre of Hubei, as well as one of the largest cities in China with a population of 4,007,000.

Economic Development Since Liberation

Hubei has undertaken intensive socialist construction and has achieved great successes in all fields since Liberation over 30 years ago. The province's investment in capital construction ranks third in the country, valued at 37,560 million yuan. There are 285 large and medium-sized projects in operation including such famous ones as the Jing-Jiang Flood Diversion Project, Wuhan Iron and Steel Company, Wuhan Changjiang Bridge, Danjiang Key Water Conservatory Project, Han-Dan Railroad, Xiang-Yu Railroad, Jiao-Zhi Railroad (Hubei section), No. 2 Motor Vehicle Plant, Hubei Chemical Fertilizer Plant, Jingsha Cotton Mill and the first stage of the Gezhouba Water Control Project.

Industry. Over the past 30 years, Hubei has built up an industrial system with a wide variety of physical equipment and technical capabilities. The province's 1979 total output from industry and agriculture reached 28,539 million yuan. This figure yields an average annual growth rate of 8.6% over the past three decades. Pig iron output in 1979 ranked second in the country; steel and rolled steel ranked third; cotton yarn ranked fifth; cotton cloth and printed and dyed cloth ranked fourth; the generating capacity of hydroelectric power was 1.56 million kw. for generated energy of 4,000 million kwh., ranking Hubei fourth in that category; output of automobiles and hand-tractors ranked third and fourth, respectively.

Agriculture. There has been significant growth in agriculture through constant improvement of production conditions. There are now 6,200 reservoirs, either completed and near completion, in the province, with a designed storage capacity of 47,200 million cu. m. About 62.68% of the cultivated land is effectively irrigated. The aggregate power of agricultural machinery is 9,757,100 hp. Some 34.3% of all cultivated land is worked by machine. Agricultural output value in 1979 reached 9,417 million yuan, 3.78 times that of 1949; grain output was 36,990 million catties, 3.2 times that of 1949. Cotton output was 8,951 million catties, 7.8 times that of 1949. The output of oil-bearing crops was 6,409 million catties, 2.4 times that of 1949.

With the development of the national economy, education, science, technology, and public health in the province have also achieved remarkable progress. National income has been increasing steadily, and living standards of the people have been rising progressively.

The year 1980 was one in which the people of Hubei continued to march forward under the guidance of the Third Plenary Session of the 11th

Central Committee of the Communist Party of China. People all over the province conscientiously carried out the policy of readjusting, restructuring, consolidating and improving the national economy. The readjustment of the national economy has made some progress. Relationships among major sectors of the economy have moved towards balance.

The 1980 Flood. Meanwhile, we won the battle against a great flood and stabilized the situation in the countryside. It rained heavily in Hubei from May to August, 1980, and we suffered from severe flooding. The peak flood water at Wuhanguan was 27.76 m., which was 3 to 4 m. higher than the elevation of central Wuhan. Since Liberation, the water level reached a higher level only once — in 1954. Flooded area in Hubei was 19.5 million *mu,* or 34.6% of the province's total farmland. Out of the flooded area, there were either no harvests or poor ones on 5.9 million *mu.* Thanks to the concern of the Party Central Committee and the State Council, the people in Hubei struggled hard against the flood and made full use of a series of flood control installations built since the founding of the People's Republic to drain flooded fields. As a result, they saved the main dyke of the Changjiang River and protected industrial cities such as Wuhan, Huangshi and Shashi. The damage suffered from the flood was reduced. Compared to 1979, the total output of grain, cotton and oil-bearing crops decreased by 16.9%, 29.3% and 35.8%, respectively.

Rural Reforms. As rural economic policies and the system of job responsibility were implemented, some readjustment were made in the infrastructure of the agricultural system. Diversified production– including forestry, animal husbandry, sideline occupations and fisheries — has developed. Gross output value from commune- and production brigade-run enterprises was 10% higher than in 1979. Average per capita income from the collective economy was less than the previous year, but commune members' income from household sideline production increased. So there was a small net increase in real income over 1979.

Capital Construction. The use of investments for capital construction and the ratio of investments were readjusted. The proportion of investments used for productive construction was reduced from 74.5% in 1979 to 67% in 1980, and the proportion of investments used in nonproductive construction rose from 25.5% to 33%. This included a 28% investment increase for science, culture, education and public health, and a 46% investment increase in housing. In industry, the proportion of heavy industry decreased as the proportion of light industry went up.

Industry in 1980. As industrial output went up, income also increased. The gross output value of light industry topped 10,000 million yuan for the first time ever. In 1980, enterprises in industry and transportation throughout the province launched a movement to increase production and practice economy with a focus on saving energy and improving quality. The gross output value of industry grew substantially for three years running, reaching 22,410 million yuan in 1980 or 17.2% more than in 1979. This figure had doubled in the four years beginning in 1977. Total profits from industrial enterprises which keep separate accounts increased by 22.9% over 1979. Productivity rates rose by 12%, reaching 12,716 yuan and surpassing previous levels in history. The quality of products was improved further during 1980.

The quality of more than 20 products ranked first in comparison with comparable products all over the country. Winners of state gold and silver medals were: Type Z3040 x 16 Radial Drilling Machine, made by Shashi No. 1 Machine Tool Plant; Heaven Goose Feather Brand 28/28 Big Flowers Venetian Cloth, produced by the Wuhan Printing and Dyeing Mill; East Lake Brand Printed and Dyed Coloured Sheets, produced by the Wuhan Textile Mill; Ginjang–5 thermos bottles, produced by the Thermos Factory of Shashi; Silver Sparrow Brand 17g. Carbon Paper, produced by the Hanyang Paper Mill; Ginseng Brand Bi Yan Pian, produced by the Wuhan Zhonglian Drug Factory; Wuhan Brand Benzoic Sodium Acid, produced by the Wuhan Organic Synthetic Chemical Factory; 55-SMNVB Double Channel and Single Surface Steel Spring Plate, produced by Daye Steel Works; Wuhan Brand Compressed Vacuum Gauge, produced by the Glass and Instrument Plant of Hubei Province; Peasant-Worker Brand JT-815 Trailer, produced by the Truck Plant of the Transport Department of Hubei Province.

Factories in light industry are being developed rapidly and are producing varieties of products to meet the needs of society. Output value of light industry in 1980 was 10,700 million yuan, an increase of 23.3% over 1979. The share of the textile industry in gross industrial output value increased from 45.4% in 1979 to 47.4% in 1980. Most products increased to varying degrees, with high-grade and middle-grade goods increasing more rapidly; radios increased by 95.5% as compared with the previous year; TV sets, 75.8%; bicycles, 62.2%; watches, 57%; and sewing machines,

82.6%. We have clearly changed the situation in which too much attention was paid to the development of heavy industry without realizing the importance of developing light industry.

Experiments in Self-Management. We made achievements in some areas where we had been experimenting with economic reforms. In 1980, while concentrating on the work of economic readjustment in our province, we actively promoted the experimental work of extending enterprises' powers of self-management. As many as 290 experimental units in industry and transport extended their self-management. Prospects for these units changed greatly because of improvements in their management and strengthening of the responsibility of personnel in charge of production. The total output value of these units increased by 29% over the previous year, while profits increased by 30%. The economic results are obvious.

By adhering to the principle of exploiting advantages and avoiding shortcomings and on the basis of voluntary participation and mutual benefit, 212 economically associated enterprises of various forms were set up in Hubei. Shashi, the famous light industry city, transformed 50 enterprises into 7 companies and 5 general factories without changing either the ownership of the enterprises, the worker's original relationships or the relationships of their financial affairs. As a result of these mergers, the motivation of existing enterprises was brought into full play. In the past, several electronic instruments plants, electrical appliances factories and instruments and, meter plants decentralized their management and thereby "used their neighbour's field as a drain," shifting their own troubles to others. New production was also unable to move forward. As a result, a new instruments and meter company was founded. Electric instrument production rose from 30,000 units per annum to 200,000.

In 1980, the output value and profits of 11 out of 12 economically integrated enterprises in the city increased by 27.75%, and 29.4%, respectively, over the year before. This great alliance brought about substantial growth and a new life to many enterprises which originally had difficulties in supply, production and marketing. These alliances improved enterprises seeking to merge and reformed various enterprises that were in the process of readjustment. Further, collectively run enterprises throughout the province have been growing rapidly with the implementation of the policies for the collective economy. Annual gross output value from the collectives in 1980 totalled 4,130 million yuan, 21% higher than in the previous year. Moreover, more collective commercial units, individual traders and merchants have been recruited to help those people waiting for job assignments.

Family Planning. A new achievement in family planning was made. In 1980, Hubei strengthened the leadership in family planning and firmly coordinated the growth of economic construction with the population programme. In 1980, the province's population grew by 1.1% over 1979. Some 4,780,000 couples of child-bearing age wisely used birth-control measures. The success rate of the birth-control programme increased from the previous year's 78% to 83.5% in 1980. The 384,000 couples of child-bearing age with only one child had certificates for their single offspring.

Environmental Protection. Environmental protection has also improved. In 1980, a monthly public information programme, "Environmental Protection," reached all residents. Moreover, the provincial People's Congress, the provincial government and the provincial People's Political Consultative Conference organized an inspection team. The team laid special stress on examining large factories and mines in six cities with concentrated industries. The provincial people's government published temporary provisions for collecting fees from the enterprises for work in draining polluted water, stopping gas pollution, and disposing of garbage and dangerous chemicals. Hubei conscientiously managed programmes and installations which counteracted environmental pollution and at the same time we required projects of new construction, rebuilt construction and extension construction to carry out the above measures. We strictly observed environmental design guidelines, construction demands and production mandates across the board.

As information efforts were combined with economic measures, the problem of pollution from factories near residential areas, natural water sources and tourist spots decreased. About 65% of the boilers in Huangshi, a city with severe air pollution, were changed with the aim of eliminating smoke and dust. These boiler conversions radically decreased air pollution.

Finance and Commerce. Finance and trade registered remarkable increases, and the people's living standards progressively improved. Revenues of the province in 1980 were 3,382 million yuan, 12.5% higher than in 1979. Operating expenditures decreased. Income was 719 million yuan more than overall expenditures. Commodities for purchase, sale and storage in the province increased. The total volume of retail sales for the whole year (not including sales by peasants to non-agricultural residents) was 9,710 million yuan, 16.7% higher than in 1979. The total value of commodities purchased for foreign trade increased by 33% over the preceding year. The total value of exports increased by 11.3%.

People's Livelihood. With the development of the economy, the people's living standards improved steadily. The total outlay for wages in the province was 3,500 million yuan, an increase of 15.1% over the previous year (after deducting price adjustments). The income of most workers increased. A total of 308,000 people were given jobs in the cities and towns. Some 5,350,000 sq. m. of floor space for workers and staff housing in units owned by the whole people were constructed, a 30.5% increase over 1979.

Research and Education. Science and education also made progress. There were 255,000 scientific and technical workers in the province. There were 580 scientific research institutions at the county level and above, with 15,000 scientific research personnel. There were 57 institutions of higher learning, with 73,000 students; 1,356 postgraduates and 16,842 faculty members (including 1,957 professors and associate professors, 7,238 lecturers and 7,647 assistants). Wuhan University, Central China Engineering Institute, Wuhan Cartographical Institute, Wuhan Institute of Water Conservation and Power, Wuhan Institute of Building Materials, Wuhan Geological Institute, and Central China Agricultural College are Hubei's key institutions of higher learning.

Problems and Prospects for Future Development

For more than 30 years since the founding of the People's Republic of China, Hubei's economy has witnessed great development. Problems still exist, however, stemming from disproportions in the national economy resulting from doing things against objective economic laws. Such problems include the following: the scale of capital construction is over-extended and its scope is too wide, while the proportion for non-productive construction investment is too small; plant construction has been redundant and not clearly directed. Further, the production of the means of consumption lags behind that of the mean of production, while agriculture lags behind industry. Also, the structure of both industry and agriculture is out of proportion. The quantity and quality of light industrial products cannot meet market needs. And business management remains at a low level.

Within a certain period, the focus of attention in readjusting the national economy in Hubei Province should be to balance the relationship between the two major sectors of the national economy. This will cause social production to adapt to the demands of social consumption and will help all branches of the province's national economy to progress toward a more coordinated development programme.

The scale of capital construction should be reduced and controlled according to the dictates of the national plan. The direction of investment should be adjusted so as to produce better results. In accordance with the need to rationally readjust the structure of agriculture, light industry and heavy industry, investments in industry should first be assured, after which agricultural investments should be appropriately increased; at the same time, expenditures for education and science should be increased. The investment method formerly used neglected agriculture to the advantage of industry, thereby squeezing light industry to the benefit of heavy industry. This approach paid more attention to capital construction than to production, leading to high accumulation and low efficiency. This tendency must be changed. In using investment funds, the demand for equipment renovation and technical transformation should be assured, so as to operate existing enterprises in a more satisfactory way.

So as to develop agriculture in an all-around way, we must continue to implement rural economic policies, perfect those systems of responsibility and management which are suited to the level of development of agricultural productive forces, actively spread the results of research in agricultural science, and strive to use scientific methods to enhance the level of planting. Further, we must insist that large and medium-sized cities link up with mining operations and other enterprises for the purpose of boosting agriculture; we must fortify ourselves to fight natural calamities so as to achieve a good harvest in 1981. We must increase research and education, proceeding from natural conditions in the whole province, and in this way do a good job of planning for agricultural districts; adjust measures to local conditions so that they are managed according to classifications; and rationally transform the structure of agricultural production.

We should do an especially good job in construction of rice/cotton bases on the Jianghan Plain and other bases for industrial crops. We should strive to change gradually the long-established heavy industry—light industry—agriculture priority structure in Hubei into a new structure that emphasizes agriculture as the base with a well-coordinated structure of agriculture, light industry and heavy industry.

We should strive to speed up the development of light industry. As an important province for cotton production, Hubei normally accounts for 20% of the country's total cotton output. Hubei has ideal conditions for textile industry development and has a wealth of resources suited to the development of light industry. Moreover, it has clear superiority in metallurgy industry, machinery and power. All of these factors offer good conditions for the development of light industry.

We must persist in implementing the policy of developing light industry, tapping the potential, renovating and transforming existing enterprises, adjusting the structure of production and increasing marketable products, improving production management, practicing economy and pursuing good economic results, and promoting industrial organization and consolidation. It should then be entirely possible to raise the proportional value of light industrial output within the total value of industrial output in Hubei from last year's 47.7% to 50% in 1981.

Under the premise of facilitating adjustment and enlivening the economy, we should speed up the pace of industrial reorganization and consolidation in light of the principles of specialization and cooperation. We should overcome the ideas of "big and all-embracing" and "small but all-embracing," break the boundaries of different branches, areas and ownerships; and fully utilize economic measures and necessary administrative intervention to create conditions for accelerating industrial reorganization and consolidation.

In line with the national programme, we must gradually consolidate and improve the coordinated activities of enterprises. Proceeding from actual conditions, we must first form loose combinations in order to increase production of light industrial products, daily necessities, and scarce items required by society. Then we must gradually consolidate and strengthen these combinations. Industrial reorganization and consolidation should be stressed in six cities: Shiyan, Huangshi, Shashi, Xiangyang, Yichang and, particularly, Wuhan. Through industrial reorganization and consolidation, we will be able to make full use of the resources of our province, and further mobilize Hubei's more than 20,000 existing enterprises to make greater contributions to socialist modernization.

69. ECONOMIC DEVELOPMENT IN HUNAN PROVINCE
By the Research Division, General Office,
Hunan Provincial People's Government

Geography, Population and Resources

Population and Administrative Divisions. Hunan Province covers an area of 204,300 sq. km. with a population of 52.31 million, of whom 4.49 million live in cities and towns and 47.82 million are rural inhabitants. The province is subdivided into ten prefectures, one autonomous prefecture, five municipalities under the direct jurisdiction of the provincial government and 99 cities.

Geography and Climate. Hunan enjoys favourable conditions for economic development. Located south of the Changjiang River and north of the Wuling Mountains, the province benefits from a subtropical climate with plenty of rain, a long frost-free period, an annual mean temperature of 16°–18°C., an annual mean precipitation of 1,300 to 1,700 mm. and 1,300 to 1,900 hours of sunshine a year. Its terrain is composed of 13.3 million hectares of mountains, 3.44 million hectares of farmland and 1.33 million hectares of water surface. Both water and land transportation are well developed: the Xiangjiang, Zishui, Yuanjiang and Lishui rivers flow north into Dongting Lake; the Beijing-Guangzhou, Zhijiang-Liuzhou and Changsha-Guiyang railway lines crisscross the province; and a network of highways extends to every nook and corner.

Agriculture and Natural Resources. Richly endowed in natural resources, Hunan has long been known as a "land of rice and fish" and a "centre of nonferrous metals." Sizeable reserves of 70 minerals have been verified. Hunan's deposits of tungsten, bismuth, antimony, realgar and fluorite are the largest in China, and those of lead, zinc, manganese, molybdenum, beryllium, mercury, sulphur, phosphorus, kaolin and diamonds are also quite significant. The more than 4,000 rivers and streams in Hunan have a total power-generating capacity of 13 million kw. Timber reserves are estimated at 180 million cu. m. and bamboo reserves at 890 million sticks. There are some 5,000 species of plants, including 2,000 kinds of trees. The main farm crops and sideline products include rice, cotton, tea, ramie, tobacco, citrus fruit, oil-bearing seeds, hogs and aquatic products. There are also plenty of wild animals and plants. Among the best-known local products are Hunan embroidery, ceramics, fireworks and firecrackers, leather, bamboo carvings, feather and down products, tung oil and lotus seeds.

Survey of Economic Development Since 1949

Hunan was economically backward before it was liberated in 1949. At that time, the total value of industrial and agricultural production stood at only 1,902 million yuan, of which 1,584 million yuan came from agriculture and 318 million yuan came from industry. Farming conditions were poor and yields were extremely low. There were neither farm machines, nor large reservoirs, and the province was constantly pestered by flood, drought, insects and plant diseases. Total grain output reached only 6.4 million tons, averaging 1,940 kg. per hectare. Total cotton output came to only 7,000 tons, averaging 120 kg. per hectare. Production and average yield of the other crops were also very low.

There was little industry to speak of in 1949. The province had only 24 state-owned and joint state-private enterprises. All other production took place in 1,376 poorly equipped private workshops and 193,000 households of individual handicraftsmen. Transport, postal and telecommunications services were also quite underdeveloped. Thirty-seven counties had no motor roads and there were no telephones in the countryside.

Following Hunan's liberation in August 1949, land reform was initiated, the new democratic revolution was completed and industrial and agricultural production revived under the leadership of the Communist Party and the People's Government. This was followed by the systematic socialist transformation of the system of ownership of the means of production and tremendous efforts to expand production and construction. There was considerable economic progress despite momentary diversions and setbacks. Important successes were achieved in capital construction, farming conditions were greatly improved and a definite industrial infrastructure was laid.

Capital Construction. The province spent altogether 20,840 million yuan on capital construction between 1950 and 1979, increasing the value of fixed assets by 13,370 million yuan. Its reserve funds were used primarily to develop agriculture and those branches of industry serving agriculture. A great deal of work was done to dredge Dongting Lake, build reservoirs in mountainous and hilly areas, develop electrically powered irrigation and drainage facilities in lake areas, and construct small water conservation and hydropower projects in hilly areas, greatly improving irrigation, drainage and power supply in the countryside.

By the end of 1979, Hunan had completed 20,175 water conservation projects, 317 of which were large or medium-sized. The total generating capacity of small hydropower stations was 640,000 kw. The total volume of water stored, channelled and pumped rose from 2,100 million cu. m. in 1949 to 29,800 million cu. m., and the area of irrigated land grew from 1,358,600 hectares in 1949 to 2,416,000 hectares, or 71.1% of the farmland in the province. Farmland with stable yields despite drought or excessive rain increased from 268,000 hectares in 1949 to 2,220,000 hectares, or 65% of total farmland. By 1979 some 60,000 hectares were irrigated by sprinklers.

Farm machinery in the province had a combined capacity of 6.87 million hp. in 1979, and irrigation, drainage, threshing, plant protection and the processing of farm and sideline produce were for the most part mechanized or semi-mechanized. The amount of chemical fertilizers used totalled 3.25 million tons a year, averaging 945 kg. per hectare.

Industry. In industry, a number of new branches and key projects were established. At the end of 1979, the province boasted 20,198 industrial enterprises, with a combined staff of 1.68 million and total fixed assets worth 13,800 million yuan. Of these enterprises, 3,576 were state-owned, with a combined staff of 1.184 million. Major industrial products included metals, coal, electric power, basic chemicals, building materials, heavy machinery, tractors, electronic instruments and meters, cotton yarn and cloth, chemical fibres, cotton knitwear, soap, cigarettes, salt, pesticides and plastic sheets for farm use. Hunan's non-ferrous metals, cement, chemical fertilizer, paper, ceramics and linen textile industries occupied an important place in the national economy.

Transportation and Communications. Rapid growth also occurred in transport, posts and telecommunications. The total length of railways in operation in the province grew from 950 km. in 1949 to 2,255 km. in 1979, while highway mileage increased from 3,142 km. to 59,541 km. In the 30-year period, the total volume of freight carried by water and land increased about 20 times. By 1979, telephone services were available in 99.9% of the commune offices and 80.8% of the production brigades.

Industrial and Agricultural Production. The province's total agricultural output value in 1979 reached 9,416 million yuan, which was 3.87 times the 1949 figure and represented an average annual rate of increase of 4.6%. Total grain production increased 3.46 times to reach 22.18 million tons, for a 4.2% annual rate of increase. Total cotton output increased 13.4 times to reach 93,500 tons, for a 9% annual rate of increase. The number of live pigs sold increased 8.55 times to reach 16.25 million, for a 7.4% annual rate of increase. Output of vegetable oils, bast fibers, cured tobacco, tea, citrus fruit and aquatic products all went up by a wide margin. Commune-run enterprises earned a total of 2,897 million yuan, accounting for one-quarter of the revenues of the communes and their subdivisions. Hunan's total industrial output value in 1979 amounted to 15,306 million yuan, which was 56 times what it was in 1949 and represented an average annual growth rate of 14.4%. Of this total, light industry production came to 5,948 million yuan, an increase of 26.3 times, representing an annual growth rate of 11.5%; and heavy industry production accounted for 9,359 million yuan, an increase of 203.5 times, for an annual growth rate of 19.4%.

Over the last 30 years, the province's industrial enterprises have contributed altogether 20,000 million yuan to the nation's total accumulation, of which more than 8,000 million yuan was net income after deduction of state investment.

Finance and Commerce. With the rapid growth of revenues, domestic and foreign trade have expanded steadily. The province's total revenues in 1979 reached 2,863 million yuan, which was 7.03 times the 1952 figure and represented an annual growth rate of 7.2%. Total revenues over the last 30 years came to 35,290 million yuan, of which 7,528 million yuan was turned over to the state treasury and the rest used to cover the province's own expenditures. Total purchases of commodities in 1979 equalled 7,740 million yuan, which was 11.2 times the 1952 figure and represented an annual growth rate of 9%. Retail sales amounted to 7,780 million yuan, 8.2 times the 1952 figure, for an annual growth rate of 7.7%. The total value of exports reached US$223 million, 7.7 times the 1952 figure, for an annual growth rate of 7%. The varieties of export commodities increased from a dozen to 323, and the number of countries and regions buying from Hunan increased from 10 to 86.

Science and Technology. Considerable progress was made in science and technology as well, with the establishment of a number of new scientific and technological departments. Statistics at the end of 1979 showed that the province had 565 research institutions at or above the county level and a total of 216,700 scientific and technical personnel, including 9,800 professional research workers. During that year, the province issued awards for 265 scientific and technological achievements, including the cross-breeding of rice and theoretical studies in mechanics.

Income and Livelihood. The people's standard of living was improved. Hunan's state-owned enterprises had a combined staff of 2,993,600 at the end of 1979, or 5.95 times the number in 1952. The workers' annual wages averaged 644 yuan per capita, 2.06 times the 1952 figure. The state has invested a total of 1,186 million yuan in housing construction for workers in the last 30 years, and the houses built had a total floor space of 20.95 million sq. m. The peasants' annual per capita spending increased 2.26 times, from 64.4 yuan in 1952 to 145.7 yuan in 1979. Average grain consumption per capita rose from some 150 kg. in the early post-Liberation years to 287 kg. in 1979. The average commune members' net income was 92.3 yuan in 1979. All this was a sharp contrast to the peasants' miserable plight before Liberation.

Review of Economic Developments in 1980

Hunan scored new successes in economic construction in 1980 by continuing to carry out the policy of readjustment, restructuring, consolidation and improvement of the economy and by adopting flexible measures to stimulate the economy. The province's total industrial and agricultural output value stood at 26,154 million yuan, a 4.6% increase over 1979.

Agriculture. The rural communes reaped a good harvest after overcoming serious natural adversities. The province was plagued with abnormal weather conditions in 1980 — low temperatures and excessive rain in the spring, floods in the north and drought in the south during the summer, and frequent windstorms and hailstorms. Natural calamities affected 1.33 million hectares of farmland, resulting in a complete loss of crops on 270,000 hectares. The damage, however, was greatly reduced as a result of the implementation of the Communist Party's new policies for the rural economy: including greater decision-making power to the production teams and the introduction of various systems of responsibility in production, which fired the commune members' enthusiasm. Total grain output in 1980 came to 21.24 million tons, the second highest yield since the founding of the People's Republic. Although somewhat smaller than the 1979 harvest, the 1980 harvest was 369,000 tons more than that of 1978, which was also a good year.

A notable development in agriculture was the emphasis given to crop diversification, an encouraging step toward changing the age-old one-crop farming economy. The distribution of cash crops was readjusted and a number of centres producing cotton, oil-bearing crops, bast fibres, tea, citrus and sugarcane were established. The provincial government appropriated 200,000 tons of food grain to aid the peasants in these centres, earmarked 15 million yuan for the construction of sprinkler irrigation and other such facilities, and raised proportionately the purchasing prices of certain farm and sideline products.

These measures boosted the production of cash crops. Now, 1.4 million hectares of forest land in Hunan have been cultivated to produce tea-oil, tungoil, citrus fruits and tea, while another 586,000 hectares of farmland have been sown with various cash crops. Total earnings from the diversified economy in 1980 exceeded those of the previous year by 122 million yuan. All cash crops showed increases, except for oil-bearing crops, fruits, tobacco, jute and ambary, which were seriously damaged by natural calamities. Cotton output reached 96,245 tons, up 2.7%; tea, 60,835 tons, up 6%; sugarcane, 733,800 tons, up 10.6%; and silkworm cocoons, 2,110 tons, up 30.6%. In 1980, there was also considerable growth in forestry, animal husbandry, sideline occupations and fishing. An additional 245,000 hectares of barren land were planted with trees, 4% more than in 1979.

Animal Husbandry. The number of pigs raised in 1980 was 38 million, an increase of 1.7% over 1979. Of this number, 17.78 million live pigs were sold, an increase of 9.4%. The number of sheep raised went up by 44,100; the number of domestic fowls rose by 3.69 million; and output of aquatic products reached 159,000 tons, up 14.5% from 1979 and 6% from the previous peak year of 1959.

Industry. Industrial production continued to grow, with rapid progress especially in the light and textile industries. Despite the tight energy situation and the serious shortage of work and raw materials for a number of enterprises, Hunan's industry managed to meet its targets by enlarging the enterprises' decision-making power, organizing their cooperation and integration, extending their scope of production, applying market regulation, improving product quality and business management, and encouraging contributions to the modernization programme. The total industrial production of the province in 1980 was 16,840 million yuan, an 8% increase over 1979. Economic performance was also improved, and the locally-administered state industrial enterprises turned in 1,237 million yuan of profits, 8.15% more than the previous year.

Emphasis was placed on the expansion of the light and textile industries, which were provided with more raw materials, fuel, power and funds. The central and provincial authorities invested a total of 220 million yuan, 46% more than in 1979, or the greatest single annual outlay since 1949. The provincial authorities spent US$13 million out of their foreign exchange reserves for imports of raw materials badly needed by the light and textile industries. Machinery and defence industry plants began to change their lines of production to serve the needs of agriculture and the light and textile industries, as well as to turn out durable consumer goods. Total output value of the province's light and textile industries in 1980 came to 7,075 million yuan, an increase of 18.3% over 1979, greatly exceeding the growth rate of heavy industry. The proportion of light and textile industries in total industrial production rose from 38.3% in 1979 to 42%. All light industrial and textile products except detergents and electronic products for civilian use exceeded their targets, and both their quality and variety showed improvement.

Heavy industry cut down on items that were overproduced and expanded those in short supply, with a slight increase in total output. Communications and transport met by and large the needs of industry and agriculture as well as the personal needs of the people. New progress was also made in the postal and telecommunications services, geological prospecting, surveying and mapping.

Capital Construction. The scale of capital construction was curtailed and efforts were made to tap the potential of existing enterprises, to update and renovate their techniques and facilities. Appropriations for capital construction were 31.7% less than in 1979. Seventy-eight projects, each requiring an investment of 100,000 yuan or more, were either cancelled or deferred, saving a total of 230 million yuan.

Available financial and material resources were used in a relatively concentrated way to accelerate the construction of major projects. Eight key industrial projects were completed and put into operation and 810 enterprises underwent technical renovation or transformation, thereby increasing the province's total industrial production capacity by 1,200 million yuan. The new projects included two pairs of coal shafts with a combined production capacity of 120,000 tons a year, power-generating units with a total capacity of 178,000 kw. and 358 kw. of transmission lines of 110 kilovolts or higher. Transmission lines connecting Hengyang and Zhuzhou were completed and the power grids in southern and northcentral Hunan were linked up.

Finance and Commerce. Revenues and expenditures balanced with a small surplus, and new increases were gained in home and foreign trade. The new system of "apportioning local revenues and expenditures between the central and local authorities and holding each responsible for its own profit and loss" aroused enthusiasm at all levels for improving finance and promoted the movement to increase revenues and cut back expenditures. Total revenues in 1980 amounted to 2,986 million yuan, topping the annual target and exceeding the 1979 figure by 4.3%. Total expenditures came to 2,344 million yuan, 6.9% less than in 1979. Savings deposits in town and country totalled 1,020 million yuan toward the end of 1980, an increase of 326 million. Total purchases of commodities reached 8,748 million yuan, up 13% and total retail sales, 9,232 million yuan, for a 17.3% rise. Total purchases of export commodities were 1,139 million yuan, up 25% from 1979. Thanks to the expansion of export business handled by the province itself, total exports equalled US$314 million, a 41% increase over the previous year. Foreign exchange earnings from processing imported materials, compensation trade and tourism also increased.

The collective economy grew rapidly in both town and country, and the individual economy began to revive and develop. Policies were formulated for expanding collective enterprises in industry, commerce and service trades, and the government provided assistance in the form of investments, loans, tax benefits, supplies of raw materials and purchases of products. This promoted the rapid growth of collectively run industrial, commercial, repair and service establishments. By the end of 1980, well over 100,000 collective enterprises had been established in cities and towns across the province.

The distribution of commodities was greatly accelerated as a result of the coexistence of enterprises belonging to different systems of ownership and forms of business. Collective commercial and service units in the province numbered 7,419, with a combined staff of 53,496. More than 10,000 individual peddlers, repairmen and service workers were licensed in cities and towns. The 190 farm produce markets in 14 cities increased their transactions by 73.8%, while the 1,984 village fairs increased theirs by 34%. Rural household sideline occupations, such as raising cattle, sheep and rabbits, and bee-keeping, weaving and embroidery also developed extensively.

Science and Technology. New achievements were reported in science and technology, with an impressive growth in research institutions and technical personnel. Twenty-seven research institutions (16 of them independent ones) were established at the provincial or prefectural (city) levels, and 720 professional research workers added. Altogether, there were 268,000 scientific and technical workers in the province, including both professionals and non-professionals. More than 2,400 people were promoted to the position of engineer or chief engineer, and some 7,100 scientific and technical workers and college graduates who had not been properly employed were given jobs in research units. The province produced 440 major scientific and technological results in 1980.

Standard of Living. Great efforts were made to improve the people's standard of living. To help the people in areas stricken by natural calamities, the central and provincial authorities earmarked 72.8 million yuan for relief work, issued 10 million yuan of interest-free loans, allocated 14,000 cu. m. of timber, 350,000 sticks of bamboo and large amounts of grain, cooking oil, sugar, cotton, cloth and other daily necessities and building materials, and reduced or remitted some of the purchase and taxation quotas in the stricken areas. Commune members' income from collective sources decreased slightly because of the natural calamities, but their income from domestic sideline occupations increased markedly. Investigations of 327 households in 26 counties revealed that commune members' income from domestic sideline production averaged 88.4 yuan per capita, 29.3 yuan more than in 1979. The standard of living of urban inhabitants also improved. A total of 208,400 jobless people were employed in the province. The total wage bill increased by 20.7%. Most workers and city dwellers increased their income as a result of either pay raises for some of the workers, the increase of employment and the issuance of bonuses. The central and local authorities and enterprises spent a total of 404 million yuan on housing construction, and new houses with 4.1 million sq. m. of floor space were completed. The provincial government also appropriated 2.4 million yuan and 1,400 hectares of land for building suburban vegetable centres.

Current Problems and Goals for Future Development

Hunan's economy continues to be plagued by a number of problems of long standing which have not yet been satisfactorily resolved. The main problems to be tackled are as follows: (1) the deep-rooted influence of "Left" thinking, which has not been eliminated and which is hampering the implementation of the policy of readjustment; (2) the imbalance between various sectors of the economy which has not been corrected — agriculture, the light and textile industries and energy remain the weak links — and the irrational structure of industry, as well as of the composition of products and the organization of enterprises; (3) the lack of production tasks for 20% of the enterprises, mainly those in the machine-building and defence industries; (4) the low standards and inefficiency of management in industrial production and capital construction, which has resulted in a slackening of the system of control through planning and centralized leadership (e.g., certain localities have inappropriately expanded industries for processing farm and sideline produce, giving rise to the situation in which small and less-developed enterprises are squeezing out the large and technologically advanced ones); and (5) many problems related to the people's livelihood, such as the inadequate supply of vegetables to cities and towns, shortages in housing and transport, environmental hazards, unemployment and inadequate educational facilities. All of these problems call for immediate solution.

The overriding task for Hunan's economy in the immediate future is to continue to concentrate on readjustment. Hence, it is imperative to eliminate the "Left" influence and draw up the province's sixth five-year plan and ten-year programme with an eye on the actual conditions in Hunan. Emphasis should be laid on restructuring the irrational economic set-up and further strengthening the weaker elements, such as agriculture and the light, textile, electronics, building materials and energy industries, communications and transport. While continued efforts are needed to increase grain production, steps must also be taken to make full use of the province's mountainous areas and water surfaces for the expansion of forestry, animal husbandry, sideline occupations and the fishing industry, giving attention to the improvement of production conditions and raising the average yield. Reorganization and integration in industry should be carried out with a view to expanding the production of consumer goods, turning existing fixed assets to better account and tapping the potential of existing enterprises. Scientific research should serve the economic readjustment by developing and designing important products and products currently in short supply, and by popularizing new technologies, processes and materials. Continued steps should be taken to readjust the ratio between accumulation and consumption, and efforts should be made to resolve the problems relating to the people's standard of living wherever possible.

70. ECONOMIC DEVELOPMENT IN THE INNER MONGOLIA AUTONOMOUS REGION
By the General Office,
Inner Mongolia Autonomous Region People's Government

Geography and Population

Population and Administrative Divisions. Founded on May 1, 1947, the Inner Mongolia Autonomous Region was the first region to be granted national autonomy under the People's Republic of China. According to the 1980 census, the region had a total population of 18.765 million, of whom 2.09 million were Mongolian, and the rest were divided between Hans — who made up the majority — and several other minority nationalities. The total area of the region is 1.183 million sq. km. The region now administers nine leagues (administrative divisions of the region) and three municipalities, which are subdivided into 99 banners (administrative divisions at the county level), counties, cities and districts. The capital of the region is Hohhot.

Location. The Inner Mongolia Autonomous Region is situated on China's northern border, in the shape of a long narrow strip extending from northeast to southwest. It is bounded on the east by the provinces of Heilongjiang, Jilin and Liaoning, on the west by Gansu Province and the Ningxia Hui Autonomous Region, on the south by the provinces of Hebei, Shanxi and Shaanxi, and on the north by Mongolia and the Soviet Union.

Geographic Characteristics. The entire region is on a plateau with an elevation ranging from 1,000 m. to 1,500 m. above sea level. In its eastern part stand the Daxingan Mountains covered with dense woods; traversing the central part from east to west are the Yinshan Hills, the great bend of the Huanghe River and the Tumd Plain; in the south lie the Ordos Highlands, and in the west is the vast expanse of the Tengger Desert.

Climate. The whole region is under a continental monsoon climate of the temperate zone, with a long winter and short summer. The mean annual precipitation is 300 mm. and the frost-free period in a year is 150 days.

Agriculture and Natural Resources. The Inner Mongolia Autonomous Region is richly endowed with resources. As one of China's main bases for animal husbandry, it has 88 million hectares of grassland which account for 30% of the country's total pastureland. Grasslands such as Hulun Boir, Xilin Gol, Ulanqab, Ordos and Horqin, are all famous natural grazing grounds. Sheep, cattle, horses and camels are the main animals being bred. The "Sanhe horse," "Sanhe cattle," "Inner Mongolia fine wool sheep," "Ujumqin cattle" and "Ujumqin sheep" are all well-known within and outside the region. The cultivated area of the region is 5,252,000 hectares.

The Hetao (Great Bend of the Huanghe River) Plain, with vast expanses of fertile land and a crisscross network of irrigation channels, is an important grain producer for China. Other important grain producers are the Horqin Plain of the Liaohe River valley, the Tumd Plain of the Huanghe River valley, the Yinshan Hills and the areas east and south of the Daxingan Mountains. The main varieties of grain are wheat, naked oats, millet, sorghum, maize and potato. Industrial crops are soybeans, linseed plant, rapeseeds, sunflower seeds and beets. The region offers a wide range of native and special produce, such as mushrooms, hedgehog hydnum, black moss, hoantchy, licorice root, fennel, black melon seeds, Hetao honeydew melon, goat's blood, Chinese ephedra and Herba boschniakiae, all enjoying a good reputan within China and abroad.

The region is also rich in forest and mineral resources. The Daxingan Mountains have more than 13 million hectares of natural forests, their timber reserves accounting for one-sixth of the national total. Over 60 types of minerals have been located in the region, distributed in more than 500 deposits. The reserves of rare earth minerals in the region rank first in the world, and the deposits of niobium and natural soda are the biggest in China. The coal reserves rank second in the country with four coal fields each having a deposit exceeding 10,000 million tons. The deposits of gold, mica, asbestos, chromium, iron, copper, zinc, lead, salt and mirabilite are all important for the country's livelihood.

The major rivers within or running through the region are the Huanghe, the Xiliaohe, the Ergunhe and the Nenjiang with a combined length within the region of 3,472 km., draining an area of 614,700 sq. km. Their combined average annual flow is 66,700 million cu. m. In addition, there are lakes such as Dalai Nur, Daihai, Ulansuhai Nur, Qagan Nur and Lamawan. These lakes, with a total area of approximately 357,000 hectares, teem with many varieties of fish.

Survey of Economic Development Since 1949

The Inner Mongolia Autonomous Region has been an inalienable part of China's territory since ancient times, when Chinese minority nationalities — Xiongnu, Linhu, Loufan, Donghu, Wuhuan, Xianbei, Rouran, Tujue, Huihe, Khitans, Nuzhen, Tanguts, Mongols — and the Hans began to labour and live in this part of the motherland. However, in the disaster-ridden old society, the people of the various nationalities, the Mongolians in particular, lived in misery under the class and national oppression imposed by the ruling classes of the successive dynasties. The rich natural resources could not be exploited and utilized. After the Opium War, the imperialist powers, in collaboration with the traitorous warlord government and the traitors from the Han and Mongolian peoples, stretched their tentacles into Inner Mongolia and greedily plundered the natural resources of the province and the property of its people. In an area where once "Vast was the sky, boundless the wilds and cattle and sheep were everywhere in sight when grass inclined in a breeze," the pastures deteriorated and livestock died in large numbers. The economy and culture of the region remained extremely underdeveloped. Diseases of all kinds ran rampant, reducing the population of the Mongolian and other minority peoples year by year. When the Inner Mongolia Autonomous Region was founded, the combined output value of industry and agriculture was only 525 million yuan, of which agriculture accounted for 90%, light industry 8.3% and heavy industry 1.7%.

After the establishment of the Inner Mongolia Autonomous Region, and particularly after the founding of the People's Republic of China, the people of the various nationalities in the region united to work together with one heart under the leadership of the Communist Party and the people's government and with the guidance of the party's policies for nationalities. Following the smooth accomplishment of democratic reform in the pastoral areas and land reform in the farming areas, they carried through the socialist transformation of capitalist industry and commerce, and of handicrafts and agriculture in 1956, thus establishing a new, socialist organization of production in town and country. This promoted a rapid and vigorous development of economic and cultural construction. Inner Mongolia, once poor, backward and ravaged, is now a socialist region of national autonomy with growing prosperity.

Agriculture. Agricultural production which includes farming, forestry, animal husbandry, sideline occupations and fishing, is of primary importance to the region's economy. According to 1979 statistics, the total output value of agriculture, which made up 35% of the combined output value of industry and agriculture, was 2,850 million yuan, 3.29 times that of 1949. Grain output was 5.1 million tons, 2.76 times that of 1949. The total number of livestock was 39.02 million head, four times that of 1949 or an average increase of 4.2% a year, and the percentage of the total output value of animal husbandry as compared to the gross output value of agriculture grew from 20.3% in 1949 to 29.3% in 1979. There was also a marked improvement in the quality of the animals. Improved breeds of sheep accounted for 49.4% of the total. In a 31-year period, the region delivered to the state 423,000 tons of meat, 270,690 tons of wool, 58.54 million furs and pelts, and 2,343,000 draught animals, totalling 3,750 million yuan in value, thus making a contribution to the economic construction of the motherland. In addition, fairly rapid advances were also made in forestry, production of oil-bearing crops and beets, and fishing.

Over the past 30 years, the conditions for agricultural production have been greatly improved. In 1979, the region had 5,466 million hp. in machinery for agricultural and stock-raising use and 1.28 million hp. in drainage and irrigation machinery for rural use — 55 times that of 1959. The number of major tractor-drawn farm implements totalled 42,000, 13.5 times that of 1959. At present, every production brigade owns an average of 2.6 large and medium-sized tractors. One-third of the region's farmland is ploughed by machinery. Grain processing and fodder crushing have been basically mechanized.

As a significant improvement of the transport and communications facilities, carrying of loads on human backs, on horseback and with barrows is giving way to the use of horse-drawn rubber-wheeled carts, tractors and lorries. The numbers of lorries and rubber-tired carts were 44.8 times and 10.2 times, respectively, those of 1959.

In the expansion of water conservation works, effective irrigation was extended to an area of 1.18 million hectares by 1979, 4.5 times that of 1947. The consumption of electricity and chemical fertilizers in the farming and grazing areas increased greatly. Good progress was made in the development of hailstorm dispersion and cloud seeding techniques. All of this effectively promoted agricultural production.

Agricultural production in the Inner Mongolia Autonomous Region has the following features:

(1) With a long winter and short summer, a large amount of sunshine, a high annual cumulative temperature and a wide temperature range between day and night, the region is suitable for the growing of grain crops with a relatively short growing period and industrial crops such as linseed plants and beets.

(2) The vast territory of the region has diverse natural and economic conditions, requiring that farming, animal husbandry and forestry should be developed in a manner suitable to local conditions. Most areas in the region are suitable for growing trees and grass. This should be considered as the fundamental way to improve the natural conditions for agricultural production and to ensure a steady growth of agricultural output in the region.

(3) The vast expanses of natural pastureland provide exceptional advantages for developing animal husbandry. Even in farming and semi-farming areas, favourable conditions are also present for developing animal husbandry. Efforts should be stepped up to improve the grasslands, increasing their capacity to support animals and to produce animals for market, so as to supply more raw materials to light industry and increase the share of animal husbandry in the combined output value of industry and agriculture. This will ensure a greater role to animal husbandry in the national economic construction.

(4) Native and special products and rare birds and animals command a considerable share of the region's exports. Products such as licorice root, Chinese ephedra, black moss, honeydew melon and hoantchy, all sell well on foreign markets. Production of such products should be encouraged through better management, proper utilization of all resources and by giving full play to those areas not able to produce these products. This policy will not only bring life to the economy in the farming, pastoral and forest areas, and improve the welfare of the people there, but also promote foreign trade.

Industry. The Inner Mongolia Autonomous Region has built industry to its present size almost from scratch. In the early period following the establishment of the autonomous region, the industry was limited to power plants for lighting, coal mines for home fuel, and grain processing and fur processing workshops. The fixed assets of industry at that time were only a little over 20 million yuan. After 31 years of efforts, the region has established such large and modernized enterprises as the Baotou Iron and Steel Company and many nonferrous metals enterprises as well as small and medium-sized iron and steel plants. Coal, electrical power, forest, machine-building, chemical, electronics, building materials, light, textiles and defence industries have all been added and developed rapidly. Rapid progress has also been made in the modernized production of woollen textiles, dairy products, processed meat and leather and felt goods. As compared with 1947, the output of coal increased 65 times to 22.75 million tons in 1979; electricity, 339 times to 4,400 million kwh.; timber, 62 times; salt, 7.5 times; and leather, 13.8 times. The output of dairy products in 1979 was 3,776 tons, 64 times that of 1950 when the dairy industry was started; and output of woollen fabrics was 2.991 million m., 1,495 times that of 1952 when the production was in its initial stages; sugar output (machine-made) was 45,668 tons, 5.5 times that in the initial stages in 1955. The region began to produce steel, iron, cement and chemical fertilizer for agriculture in 1958. By 1979, its output of steel had reached 1.21 million tons, an increase of 173 times; of pig iron, 1.21 million tons, an increase of 24 times; cement, 1.03 million tons, an increase of 3,452 times; and chemical fertilizer for agricultural use showed an increase of 235 times. Statistics show that the total number of industrial enterprises in the region in 1979 was more than 7,000, almost 11 times the 1947 figure; the total workforce in the industrial branch was 681,000, up 70 times; the total output value of industry reached 5,290 million yuan, up 116 times from 1947; and the original value of fixed assets was more than 9,000 million yuan.

The major characteristics of industrial production in the Inner Mongolia Autonomous Region are:

(1) Industry has advanced by leaps and bounds as a result of both the hard-working spirit of the local people who have started the various industries almost from scratch and of the energetic support from the state. The cumulative investment up to 1979 of the state in capital construction for the industrial branch exceeded 8,000 million yuan. The output of various industrial products has thus increased by between ten and a hundred times. This fully testifies to the superiority of the socialist system.

(2) Products with natural and local characteristics have a promising future for development. The woollen textile industry is a good example. Since the 1950's when this industry started, the output of knitting wool, woollen fabrics and woollen blankets has increased a great deal. Their

quality has also improved steadily and the variety of products has expanded. Of the products selected by the autonomous region as being of exceptionally fine quality in 1980, light industrial and textile products made up 70%. Some of the products were also appraised by the state as being of fine quality and have become brand-name products, with a ready market at home and abroad.

(3) The region has a large number of small and medium-sized enterprises and enterprises under collective ownership. By the end of 1979, small and medium-sized enterprises accounted for 99.7% of the total industrial enterprises in the region, and their output value made up 76.4% of the region's industrial output total; enterprises under collective ownership accounted for 73% of the region's total enterprises, and their output value made up 19.5% of the total.

(4) Quite a few enterprises located in the region are affiliated to ministries of the central government. These enterprises are well equipped, have strong technical capabilities and can be counted on to help the region better utilize its industrial potential.

(5) The region has a large number of newly-established enterprises, with great potential to be tapped further through technical innovation and transformation. In addition, these enterprises have fairly strong technical capabilities.

The development of industrial production has played an important role in transforming the autonomous region. The proportion of industrial output value to the combined output value of industry and agriculture increased from 10.1% in 1947 to 65% in 1979. The proportion of taxes from industry to the region's total taxes increased from 19.4% in 1949 to 68.6% in 1979. The cumulative taxes industrial enterprises have paid in the past 30 years and more amount to 4,600 million yuan.

Communications and Transport. Before Liberation, there were only three railways in Inner Mongolia, with a total length of 1,577 km. Trains were few and far between and operated at low speeds. After Liberation, communications and transport services developed by leaps and bounds. By 1979, the main railway lines in the region had all been connected with Beijing, the capital of the country, the Northeast, Taiyuan, and the important cities in the Northwest — Lanzhou and Yinchuan. These, plus the Jining-Erlian line for international train service, and feeder railways and sidings for the Baotou Iron and Steel Company and forest zones, have facilitated economic exchanges within the region and between the region and other parts of the country. The total mileage for train service has increased 2.4 times and the volume of goods transported 11 times.

By 1979, there were more than 23,700 km. of highways, 12 times more than in 1947. All-weather highways, which had been non-existent, totalled 6,900 km. The volume of goods transported by highways had increased over 20,000 times and the number of motor vehicles for civilian use had increased 444 times. A network of roads now link up towns and reach farming and pastoral areas of the region.

Between 1952 and 1979, the number of postal and telecommunications offices went up 13.2 times, the overall length of postal routes increased 5.3 times, the length of long-distance telecommunication lines 2.1 times, and the number of telephones in towns 474 times. Farming and pastoral areas, which knew nothing of telephones in the past, are now serviced by 80,000 km. of telephone lines. According to the 1979 statistics, 96.9% of the communes and 89.4% of the production brigades could be reached by telephone. As a result of more than 30 years of construction, a postal and telecommunications network has been established in the region, radiating from its capital, Hohhot, to industrial enterprises, mines, various organizations and offices, farming and pastoral production brigades in all parts of the region and hooked up with the national network.

Civil aviation service was inaugurated in the region in 1958. At present six air routes for civil use are in operation, connecting the main cities of the region with Beijing, Lanzhou and Yinchuan as well with each other. The total mileage of air services has more than trebled.

Finance and Commerce. Before the establishment of the autonomous region, commercial activities in Inner Mongolia involved mainly the collecting and marketing of wools, hides, grains, various small merchandise and medicinal herbs. Rich merchants and tradesmen travelling between Inner Mongolia and other parts of the country offered cigarettes, alcoholic beverages, tea, cloth and sugar in exchange for cattle, horses, camels and sheep at an extremely unfair ratio, making exhorbitant profits. Now, a unified socialist market has been set up, linking up the towns with the rural areas, and the workers with the peasants and herdsmen. The total value of goods purchased by the commercial departments has increased significantly. The net total value of goods purchased for domestic trade in 1978 exceeded 2,300 million yuan, 67.5 times more than in 1949. The value of industrial goods purchased increased more than 2,000 times and that of farm and sideline produce grew 27 times. The volume of retail sales came to 3,915 million yuan, 38 times more than in 1949. In the purchase of livestock and by-products, the volume of sheep meat purchased in 1979 was three times that of 1953; that of eggs, twice that of 1953; the volume of cattle hides increased 3.2 times; sheep skins, 5.4 times; and wool, 5.7 times. Foreign trade has steadily developed from nothing. The value of export-oriented purchases totalled 250 million yuan in 1979 and the export volume was US$12.62 million.

Since the establishment of the autonomous region, the difference between the prices of industrial and agricultural products has been greatly reduced. In 1947, a sheep with 18 kg. of net meat could only be exchanged for 3.68 kg. of refined sugar, less than 2.8 m. of plain white cloth, or 1.25 pieces of brick tea. In 1979, it was worth 20 kg. of refined sugar, or 33 m. of plain white cloth, or 11 pieces of brick tea. After the purchasing prices for farm and sideline produce were raised in 1979, the region's comprehensive index of rates of exchange between farm produce and animal by-products on the one hand and industrial products on the other was reduced by 15% as compared with 1978. In an effort to serve the rural and pastoral areas, the commercial departments supplied more than 5,000 million yuan worth of means of production for farming and animal husbandry to people's communes and commune members in such areas between 1952 and 1979.

Education, Science and Technology. Before the autonomous region was founded, there were only 30 middle schools and 3,700 primary schools in Inner Mongolia, and 90% of the population was illiterate. In 1979, by contrast, the region had 15 colleges and universities with a total enrollment of 15,000, 25.4 times more than in 1952. Inner Mongolia University is one of China's major universities. As compared with 1947, the number of students in secondary technical schools in 1979 was up 19.2 times, the number in middle schools was up 355 times and enrollment in primary schools was up 13.7 times.

Education for minority nationalities has rapidly developed. In 1979, about 4,000 minority nationality students were studying in institutions of higher learning, of whom more than 3,000 were Mongolian. Some colleges and universities have added courses on the Mongolian language and classes in which teaching is conducted in the Mongolian language. In 1979, there were 501 secondary schools for minority nationalities, 167 times more than in 1947; and more than 4,000 primary schools for minority nationalities, 11 times more than in 1947. In 1979, close to 6,000 Mongolian students were studying in 12 secondary technical schools run specially for them; 150,000 students were studying in 203 middle schools of the same nature; and likewise, 330,000 children of Mongolian extraction were studying in 3,167 special primary schools. The number of students in these three types of schools represented an increase of 420 times, 329 times and 15.8 times, respectively, as compared to 1947. The advancement of education has augmented the supply of managerial, technical and research personnel for economic construction and scientific and technological undertakings throughout the region.

Scientific and technological undertakings, which were started only after the establishment of the autonomous region, have been steadily expanded and increased. In 1979, there were altogether 252 scientific research institutions operating independently at or above the level of banners (counties), indicating an increase of 28 times over 1956. They were staffed by 2,453 scientific personnel, an increase of 7.5 times over 1956. Following the establishment of the Academy of Social Sciences of the Inner Mongolia Autonomous Region, the region's Academy of Animal Husbandry Science, Academy of Agricultural Sciences and Academy of Forestry Sciences were set up simultaneously. Encouraging results have been achieved in particular in the study of animal husbandry and grasslands, and of the comprehensive utilization of iron ores and rare metals. The region has reached an advanced level in the application of potato seedlings in production; the breeding of the Aohan fine wool sheep; the study of the three-axle sliding, the common gear mechanism; the theory of elementary particles and high-energy astrophysics; and haemoglobin. One hundred and fifty-one items of research were commended at the National Science Congress. The advancement of science and technology has played a positive role in developing the province's productive forces.

Standard of Living. On the basis of a steady growth of industry, agriculture and animal husbandry, the living standards of the people have improved. Between 1952 and 1979, the number of workers employed in the state-owned enterprises increased 11.4 times and the total amount of wages, 20.1 times. The average annual wage per staff/worker increased from 454 yuan to 750 yuan. There was also a big increase in the number of workers and staff of minority nationalities. The number of workers and staff of Mongolian extraction was only 7,000 in 1947, but went up 22.4 times to 157,000 in 1979. During the same period, the number of workers and staff of other minority nationalities increased 57 times from 1,000 to 57,000. Because of the rapid increases in employment rates, the growth rate of real income for families of workers and staff greatly surpassed the growth rate of average wages. The income of peasants and herdsmen also increased greatly. In 1979, the average income for each herdsman and peasant derived from the collective was 127 yuan and 72.56 yuan respectively, increasing by 8.3% and 33.1% over 1959. The purchasing power of the workers and staff and commune members grew along with their incomes. Between 1952 and 1979, the average purchasing power of peasants and herdsmen for consumer goods increased 2.59 times, that of city residents increased 2.64 times. The urban and rural savings deposits increased 111 times.

Housing. There has been marked improvement in the housing conditions for urban people. Take Hohhot and Baotou for example. By 1979, the cumulative floor space of housing projects completed was 2.34 million sq. m. and 4.31 million sq. m. respectively. Each resident lived on an average of 4.75 sq. m. in Hohhot and 4.9 sq. m. in Baotou.

Health Care. Health work has developed rapidly. Around the time of the establishment of the autonomous region, diseases ran rampant in towns and throughout the countryside, endangering the lives of the people. After Liberation, the people's government made great efforts to develop health undertakings. The number of hospitals and sanitoriums in the region increased 67 times from 26 in 1947 to 1,743 in 1979; the number of hospital beds went up 94 times to more than 40,000 in 1979; and the number of professional medical workers rose 11 times to more than 60,000. Commune clinics have been set up extensively in rural and pastoral areas, and the cooperative medical service has been introduced to 63% of the production brigades. And a three-tier medical network covering banners (counties), communes and brigades has been formed to meet the needs of the region.

Economic Develpments in 1980

The economic growth in the Inner Mongolia Autonomous Region has been fast and achievements have been remarkable. However, there have been difficulties. Different periods and years varied greatly in speed of growth and economic results. Things had been going well before 1957, but the ensuing years saw drastic rises and falls, resulting in a serious imbalance among the sectors of the national economy. New changes have taken place in the region through its initial effort to implement the policy put forward by the Central Committee of the Party to "readjust, consolidate, restructure and improve" the national economy.

Initial readjustment of the region's economy alleviated the existing imbalances and a good, stable economy has emerged.

Agriculture and Animal Husbandry. More flexible policies for agriculture and animal husbandry have heightened the people's enthusiasm for production. In the course of implementing the two documents of the Central Committee of the Party which deal with work in the rural areas, the region has, taking into account its actual conditions, formulated the guideline: "Lay emphasis on animal husbandry, combine farming, animal husbandry and forestry and allow various localities to give particular attention to certain areas of production in light of their specific conditions to ensure a diversified economy and all-around development." The region also advanced a series of specific economic policies and regulations concerning rural and pastoral areas, causing the enthusiasm of the peasants and herdsmen to be greatly enhanced. In 1980, an extremely serious drought hit over 50% of the areas cultivated with grain, reducing the yield by 20%. However, thanks to the implementation of various economic policies, such as the introduction of the production responsibility system in a variety of different forms, the decision to allow the peasants and herdsmen to have an appropriately greater amount of farm plots, cattle and trees for private use, the exemption of animal husbandry taxes and exemption of agricultural taxes for those communes and brigades that had been hard hit by the drought, etc., the income of the peasants and herdsmen increased from the previous year and a sense of security prevailed in the rural and pastoral areas. By the end of June 1980 (animal husbandry production year), the total number of animals in the region registered 40.58 million head, a net increase of 4% over the corresponding period of 1979, approaching the best record in local history. Good harvests of beets and oil-bearing crops hit an all-time high. The output of beets in 1980 was 811,500 tons, an increase of 60% over the previous year, satisfying the needs of the local sugar refining industry for the first time in many years. The output of oil-bearing crops was 250,000 tons, over 30% more than in 1979. About 323,000 hectares were harvested, 8.2% above the yearly plan. The number of enterprises at the commune and brigade levels increased by 10%, and their profits rose by more than 15%.

Industry. Major relationships among industrial branches are moving in the direction of harmony. In spite of the fact that a considerable number of enterprises operated under capacity in 1980, the region registered a total industrial output value of 5,483 million yuan, which was 1.04% more than in 1979, 7.59% more than in 1978, and 21.96% more than in 1977. Of this total, 2,326 million yuan came from light industry, 10.88% more than in 1979, and 3,023 million yuan from heavy industry, a drop of 5.41% from 1979. There was a significant change in the ratio between light and heavy industry: the share of light industry in the total industrial output value increased from 39.6% in 1979 to 43.5% in 1980. Among the 45 kinds of light industrial products covered in a statistical survey for 1980, 36 products increased their output significantly. The balance of products also changed markedly, with 338 new products in 1,190 designs and styles entering the market. High-grade commodities in urgent demand, such as bicycles, sewing machines, pure wool dress suits and woollen fabrics with silver strips were produced in greater quantity. A number of products received silver medals for fine-quality and brand-name certificates from the state, and sold well on the domestic and foreign markets. The uniform woollen fabric produced by the Inner Mongolia No. 3 Woollen Mill is exported to Japan, United States and other countries, with profits in 1980 being 72 times more than in 1979.

Capital Construction and Investment. The scope of capital construction has been reduced to improve the balance between the "bones" and the "flesh." The actual investment for capital construction in 1980 was 1,312 million yuan, a drop of 143 million yuan or 10.3% from 1979. After two years of efforts, 273 projects, each requiring an investment of 50,000 yuan and more, have been stopped or postponed, trimming 355 million yuan off the original investment plan. As regards the orientation of investment, priority is now given to agriculture, animal husbandry, light and textile industries, and at the same time greater sums have been spent on education, health, housing, and municipal construction, so that the proportions between the "bones," essentially meaning heavy industry, and the "flesh," essentially meaning production of consumer goods and undertakings that are closely linked with people's livelihood, have been relatively harmonized.

In 1980, the actual investment in agriculture was 152 million yuan, accounting for 11.59% of the total actual investment; that in light industry was 96.07 million yuan, or 7.32% of the total; and that in heavy industry was more than 400 million yuan, or 37.23% of the total. Of the money spent on heavy industry, 56.92% went to the energy industry. The ratio of agriculture to light industry and to heavy industry in 1980 was 1 : 0.63 : 3.21, almost the same as the ratio during the period of the First Five-Year Plan.

Investment in capital construction of productive projects in 1980 accounted for 60.5% of the total investment, 7.8% less than in 1979; investment in capital construction of non-productive projects accounted for 39.5% of the total, 7.8% more than in 1979; the ratio of investments in productive projects to non-productive projects was 1.53 : 1. Of the investment in non-productive projects, the share of science, technology, culture, education and housing increased considerably. The share of investment for scientific research as compared to the total investment spent in 1980 increased from 0.56% in 1979 to 1.21% in 1980; that for cultural, educational and health undertakings rose from 6.75% to 8.35%. School buildings with a total floor space of 259,000 sq. m. were constructed in 1980, providing 72.94 million additional places for students. Investment in housing projects increased by 21.87%, and housing projects with a total floor space of 1.81 million sq. m. were completed, the highest yearly increase since 1949.

Finance and Trade. 1980 saw a brisk market throughout the region. The net purchases by the commercial department for domestic supply totalled 2,560 million yuan in value, 8.7% more than in 1979. In spite of bad weather, the total value of agricultural and sideline products purchased in 1980 increased by 15.4% to 1,030 million yuan. Local industrial goods purchased totalled 1,510 million yuan in value, an increase of 5.2% over 1979. Net sales by the commercial departments on the home market reached 4,680 million yuan, 6.8% more than in 1979; retail sales amounted to 4,310 million yuan, 10.2% more than in 1979. Flexible economic policies boosted the turnover of rural and urban trade fairs by 40.5% to 190 million yuan in 1980. The total purchase value of export-oriented commodities in 1980 increased by 18.47% and the total value of exports more than doubled. The total value of imports increased by 58.97%, of which the share of light industrial goods and textiles made up 71.62%. In 1980, Inner Mongolia traded with 22 countries and regions, as against 10 in the past.

In 1980, the Inner Mongolia Autonomous Region maintained a balance between revenues and expenditures with some surplus. It overfulfilled the plan for local revenues in the revised budget by 5.7% and cut the expenditures by 10.6%.

Many new changes have resulted from the restructuring of the economic system. In 1979 and 1980, experiments were carried out in 49 enterprises in expanding the power to make decisions, including the system of allowing them to keep a certain percentage of profits. The experiments showed good results. The 24 enterprises included in the experimental programme of 1979 registered an output value of 430 million yuan, 4.4% more than in 1978, and turned over 32% more profits to the state than planned. In 1980, 49 enterprises were involved and they combined to produce 1,128 million yuan in value, 2.9% more than in 1979. They turned over 109 million yuan of profits to the state, 13.1% more than in 1979, and their growth rate of output value and profits was better than that of other enterprises. Meanwhile, under the guidance of state planning, enterprises were allowed to adjust their production to the needs of the market. This gave a new life to those enterprises that used to operate under capacity. Such enterprises were thus able to find new orders for themselves, and some of them even had more orders than they could fill.

Education. Education in the region expanded rapidly after Liberation. During the "cultural revolution," grave damage was done to educational projects. The schools for the Mongolians and other minority nationalities were particularly hard-hit. After the downfall of the Gang of Four, educational projects were given new life and made new progress. In 1980, there were 14 colleges and universities in the region, with a student body of close to 20,000, of whom 4,049 were of Mongolian extraction. Secondary technical schools (including secondary teachers' training schools) numbered 72, with a total number of 30,000 students, of whom 6,842 were of Mongolian extraction. Middle schools numbered 2,870, of which 253 were for the Mongolian nationality, with a total number of 1.35 million students, of whom 140,000 students were of Mongolian extraction. Primary schools numbered 20,000, of which 2,880 were for the Mongolian nationality, with a total number of 2,898,579 pupils, of whom more than 330,000 were of Mongolian extraction. A television university was started in 1979 and is now attended by 5,078.

The quality of teaching on the whole has also improved. In addition to the large number of teachers giving lessons in the Mongolian language in primary and secondary schools, colleges and universities have professors and associate professors specializing in this language, some of whom have begun to offer post-graduate courses.

Standard of Living. After the smashing of the Gang of Four and particularly after the Third Plenary Session of the 11th Central Committee of the Chinese Communist Party, the party and the state took a series of steps to raise the wages of the staff and workers and to improve their standard of living. In 1980, the average annual wages for workers and staff members in units owned by the whole people was 88 yuan more than in 1979, with the region paying 283 million yuan more in wages. According to a survey of economic conditions among 460 peasant families and 80 herdsmen families which were chosen as being representative of the population, the net income per capita for commune members in the farming areas was 186 yuan in 1980, 26 yuan more than in 1979, while the net income per capita for commune members in the pastoral areas was 265 yuan, 29 yuan more than in 1979.

Between 1979 and 1980, 416,000 people were provided with jobs throughout the region. This was six times greater than the total number of new jobs provided in the previous two years, 1977 and 1978.

Remarkable progress was made in family planning. In 1980, the natural population growth rate was 11.53%, a drop of 1.67% from 1979; the natural growth rate of urban population was 8.5%, a drop of 0.1%.

The higher average income resulted in the rapid growth of social purchasing power. The social purchasing power of the whole region in 1980 was 4,720 million yuan, 12.7% more than in 1979. Savings deposits in cities and towns increased by 48% to 465 million yuan at the end of 1980, with each resident depositing an average of 37 yuan. 1980 was the best year for the region in the growth of bank deposits.

Current Problems and Goals for Future Development

Though serious economic imbalances were significantly improved after two years of readjustment, there were too many problems to be resolved in a short time. The main problems awaiting solution are as follows:

(1) For years, the region has been spending more than it can pay, with the combined amount of accumulation and consumption funds budgeted greatly surpassing the output value. Therefore the central government has had to subsidize the region to cover the deficit.

(2) Economic results are generally poor, management is not adequate and the economy has sustained big losses. Though industrial production has been developed on a considerable scale, the output value and income of enterprises have not increased accordingly. The main reasons are the drop in labour productivity, the low utilization rate of equipment and enormous losses

and waste. In 1980, the state-owned enterprises which operated as independent accounting units showed a drop of 0.6% in labour productivity from 1979, or a drop of 28.3% from 1966. The rate of output value realized for every 100 yuan of fixed assets in 1980 decreased by 20.2% as compared with 1965 and the rate of profit realized for every 100 yuan of output value decreased by 42.6%.

Capital construction has been overextended as a result of poor investment and there have been considerable losses and waste. A large number of enterprises have suffered serious losses and are poorly managed. They have failed to fulfill the eight economic and technical targets set down by the state, turning out substandard products at high costs or products that do not sell, and tying down circulating funds. In addition, too many intermediate links in the distribution network impede the flow of goods and result in serious overstocking.

(3) The population growth rate has far exceeded the increase of grain output. In particular, too fast a growth of the urban population buying food grain from the state has created a big gap between the population's needs and the amount of locally available grain. For a long time, the region has remained deficient in its supply of grain. In a period of 30 years, the output of gran only doubled, while the population more than trebled. Thus the per capita supply of local grain has dropped sharply.

(4) There are many problems concerning the standard of living. For the last ten years or so, the development of industry and agriculture has slowed down, and the tendency to seek too high a rate of accumulation has reduced the proportion of funds for consumption. As a result, problems concerning the standard of living have begun to accumulate. The increase in the average income has been slow and the real living standard has not significantly improved. The small proportion of investment in nonproductive projects has resulted in an inadequate development of cultural, educational and health projects, a serious urban housing shortage, inadequate public transport services, serious environmental pollution, reduction of labour productivity and a rather high rate of unemployment. These problems cry out for solutions.

To address these problems, the Inner Mongolia Autonomous Region will develop its economy according to the following guidelines:

a) The region will firmly implement the party's policies and principles concerning agriculture and animal husbandry. It will continue to act upon the guidelines formulated by the Party Committee of the Inner Mongolia Autonomous Region, namely, to "lay emphasis on animal husbandry, combine farming and forestry and allow various localities to give particular attention to certain areas of production in the light of their specific conditions to ensure diversified economy and development in all areas." The region will further put into practice and improve the various systems of production responsibility in a manner suitable to local conditions, so as to bring the relationship between all levels of production into harmony with the development of the productive forces.

On the basis of a steady and continuous increase in the total grain output, efforts will be made to develop industrial crops. In animal husbandry, great attention will be paid to the protection and rational utilization of grasslands by encouraging the construction of enclosed pastures on the basis of groups or families. At the same time, attention should be paid to the increase of the quality and the amount of livestock for supply and the share of furs, pelts, hides and meat to be used as commodities.

The vast expanses of Inner Mongolia are frequented by strong sandstorms and serious droughts. Therefore, planting of trees and grass will be energetically promoted to improve vegetation and reach a new ecological balance. This is a plan of vital strategic importance.

b) Light and textile industries have bright prospects for development. The region already has a considerably production capacity and an abundant supply of raw materials. To fulfill the targets set by the state, the region will devote great efforts to speeding up the growth of light and textile industries, bringing into play the advantageous conditions that the region affords these industries. Heavy industry will be geared to the needs of agriculture, animal husbandry, light and textile industries as well as to the individual's needs.

The Inner Mongolia Autonomous Region is very rich in energy resources but its transport capacity is limited. Thus, the energy industry does have broad prospects for development. This, plus the availability of soda and salt in large quantities, promises a large-scale development of a multiple-chemical producing industry in the future.

c) There is a great potential for making those enterprises running at a loss yield profits and for increasing the revenues and reducing expenditures of all enterprises. This is one of the keys to overcoming the financial difficulties of the region. In 1980, the enterprises in the fields of industry, communications, finance and trade throughout the region, after balancing their profits and losses, including losses entailed by policy-related subsidies, showed deficits instead of contributing to the local treasury. The regional authorities had to subsidize them with income gained from taxation. Therefore, it is an important, long-term task to improve management and economic results. The overstocking of commodities equivalent to 900 million yuan calls for determined efforts to make an inventory of warehouses and put the materials and goods to use again after necessary remodelling or reprocessing. This is certain speed up the flow of funds.

d) Home and foreign trade will be promoted energetically. The Inner Mongolia Autonomous Region has a huge market but the supply of goods, particularly daily necessities, still falls far behind the local demand. The improvement of the standard of living raises new demands on production of commodities. Inner Mongolia, with its rich resources and many special products native to the region, should strengthen the management, utilization and processing of such resources, improve the quantity and quality of traditional products for export and further develop more varieties of products. The region must investigate all possible avenues for increasing income and enlivening the economy.

e) Scientific and educational projects will enjoy further development and attention will be paid to the development of intellectual resources. In this way, the various branches of the economy will be supplied with trained personnel and can keep up with the needs of the Inner Mongolia Autonomous Region in its efforts to realize its modernization programme.

71. ECONOMIC DEVELOPMENT IN JIANGSU PROVINCE
By Mao Junyi
Jiangsu Provincial Statistical Bureau

Geography and Population

With a dense population, mild climate, moderate rainfall, rich resources and a rather good foundation for industrial and agricultural production, Jiangsu province has one of the better developed economies and cultures in China. The province covers an area of 102,600 sq. km. and has a population of 59,380,000 with a density of 579 people per sq. km. Within the province are 7 prefectures, 11 municipalities under the jurisdiction of the provincial or prefectural governments and 64 counties.

Survey of Economic Development Since 1949

Under the rule of the Kuomintang, before Liberation, the people of Jiangsu lived in misery with a bankrupt economy and soaring inflation. After the birth of the New China, the people of Jiangsu, under the leadership of the Chinese Communist Party, strove to revive and develop the economy rapidly. In the 30 years of socialist economic construction, the province has attained remarkable achievements in spite of some setbacks.

In 1979, the total value of industrial and agricultural output in the province amounted to 52,526 million yuan, ranking second in China. This was an increase of 12.2 times as compared with 4,317 million yuan in 1949. Of this total, the output value of agriculture rose 4.6 times, light industry 16 times and heavy industry 242.6 times. There has been a significant change in the proportions between agriculture, light industry and heavy industry. The proportion of agriculture fell from 69.9% in 1949 to 26.6%, while that of light industry rose from 28.3% to 37.4%, and heavy industry from 1.8% to 36%.

In the last 30 years, there has also been a marked increase in the national income. The national income in 1979 amounted to 24,796 million yuan (421 yuan per capita), growing 4.4 times over 3,563 million yuan in 1952 (95 yuan per capita).

Agricultural Production. In 1979, the province's grain yield ranked second in China, totalling 25.14 million tons, an increase of 3.4 times over 1949. Although Jiangsu's population grew by 67.8% during the same period, the growth of the grain yield actually exceeded that of the population. Its cotton yield ranked first in China, totalling 531,700 tons, an increase of 18.9 times over 1949. The output of oil-bearing crops increased 2.4 times. The number of pigs in stock went up 5.7 times.

Industrial Production. The output of steel was up to 621,900 tons in 1979, as compared to 1,000 tons in 1949. Coal output was 17,257,000 tons, an increase of 21.2 times over 1949. Total electricity generated in 1979 reached 14,700 million kwh., up 74.2 times over 1949. Chemical fertilizers for rural use amounted to 914,000 tons (counted on the basis of 100% effectiveness), up 228.6 times. Cotton yarn totalled 318,000 tons, an increase of 7.4 times. And output of cotton cloth amounted to 1,568 million m., up 6.8 times. Many products, such as pig iron, rolled steel, crude oil, insecticides, tractors, motor vehicles, plate glass, chemical fibres, electronics, sewing machines, bicycles and wrist-watches have been developed from scratch. The output of machinery, cement, machine-made paper, salt and soap has increased up to one hundred times.

Transport and Communications. In 1979, the volume of passenger traffic carried by the local transportation system and that of freight increased by 23.4 and 23.1 times, respectively, over 1949. The total amount of chargeable postal and telecommunications services rose 11.7 times.

Capital Construction and Investment. In the past 30 years, a total investment of 19,640 million yuan has been put into capital construction: 2,980 million yuan, or 15.2%, for water conservation projects; and 11,318 million yuan, or 57.6%, for industrial construction. The major projects which have been undertaken include: the Main Irrigation Canal in Northern Jiangsu; the waterway from the Huaihe River to the Changjiang River; the key water control project at Jiangdu through which the Huaihe River has been brought under permanent control; the Nanjing Iron and Steel Works; the Nanjing Oil Refinery; the Xuzhou Coal Mine; large thermal power stations at Xuzhou, Jianbi and

Nanjing; the Lianyungang Harbour Project; the extension of the Nanjing Chemical Industry Corporation; the China Cement Works; and a large number of other chemical, light industrial, textile and building-material enterprises. Through the self-reliance of the Chinese people, the Nanjing Changjiang River Bridge — a highway-railway bridge, built in 1968 to link up the north and the south — and hundreds of large and medium-sized capital construction projects were completed and put into operation.

Other Developments. Since 1957, the province's annual coal-mining capacity has risen by 13.25 million tons and its power-generating capacity by 2.22 million kwh. These are important factors underlying the rapid growth of industrial and agricultural production and other undertakings. These factors provide an essential base from which the modernization programme can develop.

Income and Livelihood. In 1979, the number of workers and staff in state-run and collectively owned enterprises in cities and towns totalled 6,038,000. The number of people employed in the state-run enterprises totalled 3,739,000, an increase of 7.8 times over 1949. The total volume of retail sales reached 12,440 million yuan in 1979, an increase of 16 times over 1949. According to a survey of rural families, the annual net per capita income of peasants in 1979 averaged 200.2 yuan, or 2.3 times the 1954 figure. A survey of urban workers and their families conducted in the first quarter of 1980 showed that the monthly per capita living expenses of these families averaged 30.91 yuan, an increase of 58.4% over 1957. The standard of living of people in both urban and rural areas has improved markedly.

In addition, there was also fairly rapid development in education, culture, public health, municipal construction and housing. In 1979, the number of students in all levels of schools increased 4.6 times as compared to 1953. There were 13.7 times as many hospital beds as there were in 1952. And between 1951 and 1979, the province built housing with a total floor space of 19.31 million sq. m., of which 7,457,200 sq. m. were erected between 1977 and 1979, thus improving the living conditions of workers and their families.

Survey of Jiangsu's Economy in 1980

In 1980, the total output value of industrial and agricultural production in Jiangsu Province amounted to 60,440 million yuan, an increase of 15.1% over the previous year. Agriculture accounted for 14,692 million yuan of this total, up 5.2%; light industry accounted for 24,988 million yuan, up 27.2%; and heavy industry was responsible for 20,757 million yuan, up 9.7%. A change also took place in the balance between agriculture, light industry and heavy industry in the province's economy. The proportions of agriculture and heavy industry fell from 26.6% and 36% in 1979 to 24.3% and 34.3%, respectively, whereas that of light industry rose from 37.4% to 41.3% during the same period.

Agriculture. In 1980, due to the considerable development of brigade-run enterprises regarded as sideline occupations, the total output value of agriculture increased somewhat despite a drop in the output of major crops, such as grain, cotton, oil-bearing seeds and cast fibres, as a result of natural calamities.

In 1980, total grain yield was 23.57 million tons, a decrease of 6.2% from the previous year, but still the third best harvest since 1949. The cotton yield was 420,000 tons, a drop of 21.5%. The yield of oil-bearing seeds was 386,300 tons, a drop of 10.9%, and the cast fibres harvest was 38,830 tons, a decrease of 34.9%. The number of pigs in stock at the end of the year was 20.89 million, a drop of 11.3% from the previous year.

The output value of the brigade-run enterprises increased to 4,343 million yuan, a rise of 48.3% over the previous year. The yields of silkworm cocoons, tea and aquatic products showed increases of 18.2%, 10.5% and 9.7%, respectively. However the number of draught animals and goats dropped by 6.8% and 11.4%. And the output of sugar crops and tobacco decreased by 17% and 57.3%, respectively. Approximately 427,000 *mu* of land was afforested.

There was a further change in the balance of agricultural production. The proportion of farming fell from 63.5% in 1979 to 55.4% in 1980, while that of sideline occupations rose from 21.5% to 29.9%, of which the proportion of brigade-run enterprises increased from 21% to 29.6%.

In 1980, the total power of farm machinery reached 15.15 million hp. with 16,000 large and medium-sized tractors, 256,000 hand tractors and irrigation and drainage equipment totalling 6.02 million hp. A total of 1.181 million tons of chemical fertilizer (counted on the basis of 100% effectiveness) were used, and the average amount applied per *mu* increased by 3 kg. over the previous year. Some 544 million more kwh. of power were consumed in rural areas as compared to 1979. And meteorological observatories were more accurate in their weather forecasts.

Industry, Communications and Transport. In 1980, the total output value of industry amounted to 45.74 million yuan, an increase of 18.6% over the previous year. The output value of state-run industries rose by 10.8% while the collectively-owned industries, including the commune-run enterprises, showed an increase of 30.4%. A further readjustment was effected in the proportions within industry. The proportion of light industry rose from 50.9% in 1979 to 54.6% in 1980 while that of collectively-owned industry rose from 34% to 37.3%.

The production targets for 94 of the 110 products included in the economic plan were fulfilled. The output of 37 of the 39 products of light and textile industries included in the plan increased. And the output of marketable consumer products which were highly in demand rose considerably. Among them, the output of radios, television sets, cameras and tape recorders more than doubled. The output of chemical fibre products, sewing machines, bicycles, wrist-watches, knitting wool, gunny bags and leather rose by more than 30%. The output of cotton yarn, cotton cloth, printed and dyed cloth, woolen piece goods, silk, silk fabrics, cigarettes, bulbs, soap, battery cells and beverages rose by more than 10%.

The output of some of the equipment used in agricultural production increased while some decreased. The growth rates for producers of chemical fertilizers and insecticides were 22.2% and 12.8%, respectively, while the growth rates for manufacturers of machine-driven threshers, machine-driven rice transplanters, hand-dusters and hand-sprayers, fishing boats and plastic film for farm use ranged from 105 to over 110%. There were decreases in the production of tractors, farm pumps and rubber-tired handcarts. The output of five metallurgical products increased, while that of pig iron, coking coal and ferro-alloys dropped. The output of cement, plate glass, glass fibre and artificial boards all increased. Among 19 chemical products, the output of 15 increased. The machine-building industry, which is one of the main departments which requires readjustment, registered a drop in output in 18 of its 32 products.

In 1980, 22 gold and silver medals were awarded to civil industrial products made in Jiangsu.

As a result of the initial readjustment of the light and heavy industrial structure, bringing under control the production of products which consume much energy and improving business management, some progress has been made as regards energy-saving. Although power generation increased by only 6.3% and the output of coal dropped by 2.1% the amount of standard coal used per 10 million yuan of output value decreased by 15% as compared with the previous year, thus bringing about a large increase in the total industrial output value. This shows a healthy trend in industrial readjustment.

In 1980, the volume of passenger traffic carried by local transport systems increased by 16.2% and the volume of freight traffic increased by 14%. The total amount of postal and telecommunications services rose by 11.4%.

In 1980, labour productivity, calculated in terms of the total workforce in the state-owned independent accounting industries, went up to 15,755 yuan, an increase of 4.2% over the previous year.

Capital Construction and Investment. In 1980, the total capital construction investment fulfilled by state-owned enterprises amounted to 2,610 million yuan, an increase of 18.6% over the previous year. Of this total, state-budgeted investments accounted for 1,470 million yuan, 30 million yuan or 16.4% less than last year, while the investments fulfilled by localities and enterprises climbed to 1,141 million yuan, an increase of 71.1 million yuan or 160% over the previous year due to the relaxation of controls on investments outside the budget.

In 1980, the fixed assets brought into use for the state-run capital construction projects were 2,330 million yuan, an increase of 38%. The rate of fixed assets brought into use accounted for 89%, an increase of 12.5% over the preceeding year. A total floor space of 8,342,000 sq. m. was completed, an increase of 35.2%. Of this, the floor space of residential housing came to 4,619,000 sq. m., an increase of 41.4%.

Two large-scale projects and 15 individual projects were completed and put into operation in 1980, four more than during the previous year. The production capacity increase, due to the completion of construction projects, accounted for 950,000 tons of coal, generating sets totalling 451,000 kwh., 323.7 km. of power transmission lines, 250,000 television sets, 165,000 bicycles, 164,000 sewing machines and 510,000 wrist-watches.

Of the total capital construction investments undertaken by the state in 1980, the proportion used for non-productive sectors, such as housing for workers and staff, urban public utilities, scientific, educational and public health establishments, rose from 25.1% in 1979 to 34.5%. Results of the readjustment of capital construction investment policy are already becoming evident.

Finance and Commerce. In 1980, the total volume of commodities purchased by commercial departments amounted to 20,760 million yuan, an increase of 14.7% over the previous year. Of this total, industrial products accounted for 14,490 million yuan, an increase of 20.3%. Agricultural and sideline products accounted for 6,160 million yuan, an increase of 3.5% (but a small decrease as compared with last year if the increase in the state's purchasing prices of major agricultural and sideline products is not taken into account). The total volume of retail sales reached 14,970 million yuan, an increase of 20.3% over the preceeding year or an actual increase of 16.4% if the price hikes are not taken into account. This is the highest rate of growth since the founding of New China. This also shows a notable rise in the living standards and purchasing power of the people. In 1980, the volume of sales of major consumer goods, such as foodstuffs, clothes, fuel, and other daily necessities, increased significantly: 15.3–25% for grain, vegetable oil, pork and sugar; 10–50% for chemical fibre cloth, polyester fibre cloth, silks and satins, woollen goods, knitting wool, leather shoes and cotton jerseys and trousers; 20–100% for wristwatches, bicycles, sewing machines, television sets, radios and electric fans; and 410% for tape recorders. The total volume of goods in stock at the end of the year increased by 7.5% as compared with the same period of the previous year.

Of the total volume of commodities purchased, 3,450 million yuan was purchased for foreign trade, an increase of 24.8%. The total volume of exports handled by the localities themselves in 1980 rose to U.S.$850 million, an increase of 37.2% over the previous year.

In 1980, the number of compatriots from Hong Kong and Macao, overseas Chinese and foreign nationals who came to Jiangsu to visit friends and relatives, on sightseeing tours or on business, totalled 238,000, which was 56,000 more than the previous year.

Science, Culture and Health. By the end of 1980, the number of scientists and technicians in state-owned enterprises and establishments totalled 189,800. They had accomplished 938 scientific research projects during the year.

In 1980 there were 43 institutions of higher learning in Jiangsu, seven more than during the previous year. The enrollment increased by 8,600 to a total of 82,500 students. 17,700 of these students were admitted during the year, an increase of 1,800 more than were admitted during the previous year. In addition, there were 25,500 students in broadcasting and television colleges, an increase of 7,700; 15,300 at the technical schools, an increase of 2,300; 61,000 at secondary vocational schools, an increase of 9,000; 3,205,000 students at the middle schools, a drop of 274,000; 8,369,000 pupils at the primary schools; and 1,237,000 children in the kindergartens.

New progress was also made in culture, broadcasting and publishing during 1980.

There were 127,500 beds in public health establishments in 1980, of which hospital beds accounted for 116,000, an increase of 2,224 over the previous year. The number of professional medical personnel totalled 150,000, an increase of more than 4,000.

Jiangsu's athletes also enjoyed a considerable measure of success in 1980. They won honours for the country by taking 77 gold medals in competitions at home and abroad.

Income and Livelihood. In 1980, the standard of living for the majority of the urban and rural population was improved. Despite a drop in agricultural production as a result of natural calamities, the actual total income of commune members increased because of significant developments in brigade-run enterprises, the diversification of the economy, the further rise of the purchasing prices of agricultural and sideline products, the expansion of household sideline production and the increased yields on private plots of land. Data on rural and urban families shows that the annual net per capita income of the peasants averaged 217.91 yuan in 1980, 17.8 yuan more than the previous year. The monthly per capita living expenses of the workers' families averaged 33.47 yuan in the fourth quarter of 1980, an increase of 8.3% over that in the first quarter.

In 1980, jobs were provided for 388,000 people in cities and towns of Jiangsu, including graduates from colleges and secondary vocational schools who were assigned jobs under a unified state plan. The numbers of workers and staff in the province exceeded 6,400,000, an increase of 370,000 over the previous year. Of this total, 3,980,000 were employed by state-run enterprises and establishments, an increase of 248,000 over the previous year, while 2,420,000 were working in collectively-owned enterprises and establishments, an increase of 120,000.

Owing to the increased number of workers and staff, plus the pay rise for 40% of the workforce, the readjustment in wage scales, the institution of a bonus system and the monthly subsidy to offset the increased prices of nonstaple foodstuffs to all workers and staff, the total wage bill for 1980 reached 4,140 million yuan, an increase of 24.9% over the previous year. Of this, the payroll for workers and staff in establishments owned by the whole people totalled 2,727 million yuan, an increase of 23.4%.

In 1980, the average annual per capita wage of workers and staff in establishments owned by the whole people went up to 720 yuan, an increase of 102 yuan or 16.5% over 1979.

Current Problems and Goals for Future Development

Over the past 30 years, the economic development of Jiangsu Province has been uneven, handicapped by disproportions in the economy on several occasions. The causes leading to these disproportions were complex. According to a quantity analysis, "high speed," "high accumulation rates" and "high targets" were the essential causes. Because of several rash economic policies after 1958, the accumulation rate was as high as 30%. At that time, the economy seemed to be developing rapidly. But serious disproportions were brought about and it was necessary to make retrenchments. The over-extension of the scope of capital construction, the emphasis on the expansion of production capabilities and the failure to allocate investment for capital construction according to our capabilities led to the lack of coordination between the basically irrational economic, industrial and production structures and to poor economic results. There was also the waste of a considerable amount of manpower, material and financial resources. This affected the consumption of products, the completion of municipal construction projects and the development of scientific, cultural, educational and public health establishments. Even if we had been able to issue more banknotes, we could not have maintained stable prices, and the living standards of the people could not have been raised significantly.

The major steps that must be taken for future economic development in Jiangsu Province are as follows:

(1) *We must continue to propagate and study the principles and policies formulated by the Third Plenary Session of the 11th Party Central Committee, to rectify the influence of "Left" ideology and to clarify political, ideological and organizational policies.* As regards the study of economics, it is essential to improve the collection, sorting, analysis and study of economic information in order to carry out economic calculations and forecasts. Great efforts must be made to achieve an overall balance in the local economy. Effective measures should be adopted to prevent possible "Left" mistakes, both in ideology and methods of work, so that the national economy can develop in a healthy way.

(2) *We must use every possible means to develop all aspects of agricultural production.* The rural population of Jiangsu Province is 50 million, making up nearly 85% of the total population. From a strategic point of view, agriculture is the lifeline and foundation of Jiangsu's economy. During the past 30 years we have gained the valuable knowledge that a prosperous agriculture will enliven the province's economy as a whole. We must develop agricultural production through scientific and technological research. Because Jiangsu Province is characterized by a large population but a small area of cultivatable land, it is necessary to organize and utilize rural labour power and use the land to its fullest.

Rural areas should strive to diversify their economy while raising the output of grain. Readjustment and consolidation should be undertaken in the industries run by the people's communes, production brigades and production teams. Suitable measures should be taken, depending upon local conditions, to institute various systems of organizational responsibility in agricultural production so as to arouse the enthusiasm of the rural cadres and commune members for production and to stabilize the rural labour force. In addition, efforts should be made to popularize agricultural science and technology; maintain and develop the fine tradition of intensive cultivation; strengthen management and administration over production; significantly increase crop yields and income to contribute to the nation's economy; undertake careful calculations and strict budgeting; reduce the cost of agricultural production; raise the commodity rate of farm and sideline products; increase the earnings of the people's communes, production brigades and production teams; improve the standard of living of commune members; and continue to progress in the modernization of our agriculture.

(3) *We must move towards consolidation of various enterprises and, in certain cases, shift production to other items.* It may be necessary to close or suspend the operation of various enterprises. Economization of energy consumption is of great importance. This may be achieved by the innovative readjustment, transformation and reorganization of the more than 32,000 existing industrial enterprises run at or above the people's commune level in Jiangsu. In particular, stress must be laid on the readjustment and reorganization of the machinery and textile industries. In addition, it is essential to promote increased production and, by relying on the abundant labour force, develop the light and handicraft industries and the production of arts and crafts. These enterprises are labour-intensive; they turn out high-quality products that sell well on the market, have low energy consumption and can be produced at a low cost.

Thus, such enterprises are more competitive on the domestic and international markets.

(4) *We must continue to reduce the scope of capital construction and control the flow of funds raised for capital construction purposes.* A reasonable allocation of construction expenditures should be made for integration and combination of enterprises, shifting of production to other items, technical innovation and transformation, urban public utilities, housing, scientific, cultural, educational and public health establishments and environmental protection. The proportion of construction investment between the productive and non-productive sectors should be readjusted.

(5) *Reform of the economic system is fundamental to economic construction.* At present, such reform is under way. Only by an overhaul of the economic system can the realization of socialist modernization be ensured.

(6) *It is to our advantage to develop our intellectual resources to their fullest capabilities.* This can be achieved by the specialization and intellectualization of the cadre contingent, the enhancement of the quality of teaching at schools of all levels and the popularization of education and scientific and technological research. Moral, intellectual and physical education should be enforced not only in schools, but also throughout the population, so that a healthy population can develop their intellectual capabilities to help promote the socialist modernization.

(7) *We must promote good family planning.* According to an analysis of age groups of the population in Jiangsu Province, there will be two peak periods of child-bearing before the year 2000. The first one is beginning this year. Strenuous efforts will be required to maintain the population growth rate at 6.25%, the 1980 level.

72. ECONOMIC DEVELOPMENT IN JIANGXI PROVINCE
By Zhen Yanchu

Geography and Population

Geographic Characteristics and Climate. The province of Jiangxi lies south of the Changjiang River. It has a total area of 166,600 sq. km. (64.5% mountains, 15.2% arable land and 10% water). The terrain varies greatly, the southern part lying at a higher altitude than the northern part. It is mountainous on three sides, with the northern border being made up of numerous rivers and lakes. The climate is subtropical, generally warm and humid, with an average temperature during the year of 16.3–19.7°C and an annual rainfall of 1,350 to 1,910 mm.

Population. At the time of Liberation in 1949, the population was 13,140,000. In the past 30 years since Liberation, the population increased at an annual rate of 3% to 32,280,000 in 1979. By 1980, the total population of the entire province was more than 32,700,000, of which 27,620,000 lived in rural areas.

Natural Resources and Agriculture. Jiangxi is rich in natural resources. Among the mineral products which can be found are tungsten, copper, silver, tin, lead, zinc, manganese, molybdenum, coal, iron, salt, phosphate rock, dolomite, serpentine, kaolin and other rare metals and rare earth minerals.

Animals and agricultural resources are abundant in the six nature conservation areas of Jinggangshan, Lushan, Jiulianshan, Wuyishan, Guanshan and Taohungling. There are many species of wild life, some of which are unique and valuable and have been given special protection. More than 5,000 species of plants can be found in the province. The mountainous areas are covered with trees, bamboo, oil-bearing plants, amylum and fabric plants and herbs, which are of high economic value. The Poyanghu Plain in northern Jiangxi, the Jitai Basin in central Jiangxi and the hilly land in southern, central and western Jiangxi are rich in rice, cotton, oil, sugarcane, hemp, tobacco, fruit and tea. Nearly 100 kinds of fish and various aquatic plants and animals can be found in the province's rivers and lakes, which cover more than 20 million *mu*. By the time of the Han Dynasty, Jiangxi's land had already been cultivated. Even then it was known as a land of fish and rice.

Survey of Economic Development Since 1949

Before Liberation, owing to the reactionary rule of the Kuomintang, the province's population decreased sharply. The rural economy nearly went bankrupt because of the damage done to forests, the neglect of the water conservancy system and the abandonment of cultivated land which was allowed to go barren and wild. Industry was extremely underdeveloped. Apart from a few small power, textile and machinery repair plants and grain processing factories, there were literally no modern industries. The rich deposits of tungsten and coal could only be extracted by manual labour. The province's world-famous china, locally produced paper and linen were also made by hand.

In the last 30 years since the founding of New China, the economy of Jiangxi has made great strides under the leadership of the Communist Party and the people's government. New industries have been set up and developed. Industrial enterprises such as steel works, rolling mills and coking plants and industries for nonferrous metal products, crude oil processing, both organic and inorganic chemical industries, tractors and trucks, machine tools, electrical machinery and other machinery-building, cement, salt, electronics, synthetic fibre, refined sugar, paper, daily necessities and other manufactured items have come into being. The total value of agricultural and industrial output increased 7.7 times from 1949 to 1979, at an annual rate of 7.1%. Industry increased 41 times, at an annual rate of 13.1%, while agricultural output increased 3.5 times, at an average annual rate of 4.2%. The total yield of grain alone increased 3.3 times. And revenue increased 10 times.

However, there have been twists and turns in the economic development of Jiangxi during the past 30 years. During the three-year period of economic recovery and the First Five-Year Plan period, industrial production in the province developed fairly rapidly. From 1950 to 1957 the total value of industrial and agricultural output increased at an average annual rate of 10.8%. And a number of industrial enterprises were set up in the province during the first two years of the Second Five-Year Plan, thus paving the way for economic development. But owing to the influence of the erroneous "Left" ideology, the total value of output only increased at an annual rate of 0.7% from 1958 to 1962, resulting in a disproportionate development of the economy. After the readjustment of the economy from 1963 to 1965, industrial and agricultural production in Jiangxi gained new momentum. The total output of industry and agriculture in 1965 increased by 41% over 1962, representing an annual rate of 12.2%. But it was followed by ten years of turmoil during which the economy in Jiangxi suffered a tremendous setback. From 1967 to 1976, the total output value of industry and agriculture only increased at an annual rate of 3.8%. In particular, the agricultural output increased by only 1.7% which was below the growth rate for the last 30 years.

Review of Jiangxi's Economy in 1980

In 1980, the Party Committee and the people's government of Jiangxi Province further implemented the policies and guiding principles of the Third Plenum of the Central Committee, so that the provincial economy could make new headway in the process of readjustment. Good harvests were achieved, even during years of natural disasters. There was also a big increase in the light and textile industries. Markets thrived and buying and selling were brisk, while the income of the people in both urban and rural areas increased considerably. The total output value of industry increased by 8.2% in 1980 over 1979, light industry showing an increase of 19.3% and heavy industry decreasing by 0.3%. The total investment in capital construction increased by 10.2%. The total volume of retail sales increased by 14.1%. There was an 8.2% increase in revenue and a 7.9% decrease in expenditure. And the national income increased by 6.4%.

Agricultural Development. In agriculture, attention has been paid to the flexibility of policies, the improvement of management, the introduction of measures specifically suited to local conditions, the development of production and the implementation and improvement of various systems of production responsibility. Despite some serious natural disasters in 1980 which affected quite a few areas in the province, a moderately good harvest was still achieved and the grain yield was still the second highest since the founding of New China — all due to the party's policies being put into effect, the great efforts of the cadres and commune members and the success of the system defining responsibilities in production. The harvest of industrial crops, apart from cotton, oil-bearing crops and tobacco which dropped in production, increased in output by varying degrees.

Progress was made in the diversification of the agricultural economy, in industry run by the communes and in commune families' sideline production. The proportion of the output value of forestry, animal husbandry, sideline activities and fishing to the total value of agricultural production increased from 28.6% in 1979 to 32%. In the two years of 1979 and 1980, both the average growth rate of the total agricultural output value and of the total grain yield for the whole province were greater than the average growth rates for the province since Liberation. The state purchasing quota for grain has been overfulfilled for many years running, while marketable grain purchased by the state according to the set quota and grain purchased at a negotiated price hit an all-time high. In addition, great changes have taken place in some communes and brigades that used to be fairly poor. Much improvement has been made in the standard of living of the peasants. A sign of this is the fact that the savings deposits in rural areas increased by 74.9% from 1979 to 1980, the highest annual increase since the founding of New China.

Industrial Development. Benefitting from the readjustment, industrial production has been developing steadily. The total output value in 1980 increased by 8.2% over 1979, profits turned over to the state from enterprises registered an 8% increase over 1979, while labour productivity increased by 5.8%.

Priority has been given to the light and textile industries. Consequentially, the growth rate of light industry is greater than that of heavy industry. The output value of light industry in the province increased by 19.3% over 1979. In particular, the output value of the textile industry increased by 31.3%, with a profit increase of 60%. That is to say, a profit of 15.96 yuan was made out of every 100 yuan in output value, a rate which ranks seventh in the nation in terms of profit making. The province's textile output increased by 27% and the output value of the textile machinery industry increased by 48.2%. As for other light industrial products, the output of high and medium-grade durable commodities have greatly increased. The output of watches increased by 81%, sewing machines by 5.8 times and bicycles 3.3 times. Also, electronic products both for industrial and civilian use have seen a fairly rapid development. Production of TV sets increased 3.2 times and radios 3.6 times. Of the 43 primary light and industrial chemical products, the output of 22 items exceeded the highest record in history.

The output value of heavy industry decreased by 0.3% compared with 1979. As compared to the total value of industrial output, the proportion of light industry increased by 43.4% in 1979 to 47.8%, while the proportion of heavy industry was reduced from 56.6% to 52.2%. Formerly, heavy industry had dominated the province's industrial economy. Now, the internal structure of the province's industry has begun to incline towards light industry.

Although the growth rate of heavy industry is slowing down, products and specifications have become more diversified and their quality improved. The output of electricity in the province has been increasing year by year. The quota for coal production last year was fulfilled and timber production also met its quota. Production in the electronics industry has increased considerably, and there has been an increased diversification of production in the iron and steel and machinery industries. Products are geared to the needs of agriculture, light industry and the markets. Railway freight volume has increased and local communications and passenger transport is now better than the transport of goods and freight.

In 1980, Jiangxi Province actively and consistently undertook preliminary steps towards reform. The experimental units in industry and enterprises where autonomy of economic management was expanded increased from 34 in 1979 to 103. These enterprises have been further reorganized in the experimental process, bringing about satisfactory changes. As a result of this, the output value and rate-of-profit increase in those enterprises with expanded autonomy are higher than the average levels of those still running on the old models in the province.

Finance and Commerce. The marketing rate of agricultural and sideline products has gone up considerably thanks to the flexibility in the rural economic policy, especially now that family plots of land are rationally allocated, that the development of family sideline production is permitted and encouraged and that country fairs are opened. The total amount of agricultural and sideline products purchased by the state in 1980 increased by 16.3% over 1979, setting a record for the province.

The total amount of commodities purchased by the province increased by 16.7% over 1979. The commercial departments have reorganized wholesale departments of certain areas and begun to plan commodity circulation according to economic areas. So the rate of expenditure on commodity circulation was somewhat reduced in both the province's commercial establishments and in supply and marketing units from 9.03% and 12.83% in 1979 to 8.11% and 10.46% respectively.

The market is brisk. Compared with 1979, there was a 14.1% increase in 1980 in retail sales, of which consumer goods bought by local inhabitants increased by 17.9%, and capital goods purchased by production teams and commune members increased by 7.6%. More and more commodities are available now because of the increased quantity of goods purchased by the state and resold to the people.

As regards local industrial products, the commercial departments have changed the practice of state-guaranteed purchase and marketing into state monopoly of purchasing and marketing, purchase according to plan and purchase by order and by choice, thus contributing to the development of rational sales of needed commodities. Improvements have also been made where goods in high demand and high-grade commodities were in short supply. In 1980, the amount of local products purchased by the province's commercial departments constituted 31.3% of the total amount of goods purchased in the province, a 16.2% increase over 1979. Purchases of export commodities rose by 19.6%.

With the present state of the economy, where state commerce still predominates and state planning plays a leading role, tolerance of many diverse forms of enterprise, distribution channels and different ways of running business is shown, thus enlivening the economy as a whole. Collective or individual businesses in cities and towns of the province increased to more than 20,000 in 1980. Also in that year, the total amount of commodities sold wholesale by commercial establishments and supply and marketing units to collective businesses or individual traders constituted 5.8% of the total amount of the province's commodity supply, increasing by 84.8% over 1979. The number of open markets in the urban and rural areas of the province was restored to over 1,400. Both the variety of commodities marketed and the volume of business increased. The volume of business in 1980 had a 40% increase over that of 1979.

Standard of Living. Because of the development of production, the standard of living continued to improve. The per capita income both from commune and family sideline production increased by 7.5% in 1980 over 1979. The average level of consumption in the countryside increased by 5.4%. The per capita income of staff and workers (including those employed in both state and collective enterprises) increased at an average rate of 17.7%, while the average level of consumption in cities and towns increased by 10.7%. By the end of 1980, the savings deposits of city residents had increased by 46.1%, while those of commune members had grown by 44.8%.

The housing conditions of city residents and commune members have also improved to a certain extent. In 1980, the province built new residential housing in towns and cities totalling 1,924,800 sq. m., which was a 43.9% increase over that of 1979. The average per capita housing space for city residents is 3.5 sq. m. About 29,000 households of staff and workers in cities have now moved into new houses, while more than 10% of the commune members in the countryside have built their own new homes.

Current Problems and Goals for Future Development

Since the Third Plenum of the Party Central Committee, vast numbers of cadres and people at all levels in Jiangxi Province have achieved remarkable success in carrying out the policy of readjustment, restructuring, consolidation and improvement under the leadership of the party and the government. However, there are still some problems: capital construction is overextended in scope, being far beyond the financial and material means of the province. The investment in capital construction has been reduced by the state budget in the last two years, but the money spent on construction coming from different channels other than the state budget has increased. And much of the construction that is carried out is redundant and useless. Not enough attention has been paid to doing things according to capacity and to balancing revenues and expenditures. The result has been too much spending. The economic structure is not rational, managerial skill still remains low and the economic performance is inefficient. As far as agricultural production is concerned, the diversified economy is still not satisfactory: the development of industrial crops, forestry, animal husbandry, sideline activities and fishing has been slow, as a result of which the light and textile industries in the province have been affected by a short supply of raw materials, and the profit rate of the industrial enterprises has remained rather low.

After the Working Conference of the Central Committee of the party in December 1980, the party committee and the people's government of Jiangxi Province, in keeping with the party's policy for further readjustment of the economy and for further political stability, have made specific arrangements for the economic readjustment of the province in 1981, proposing measures suitable to the specific economic situation in Jiangxi. In order to carry out the readjustment, it has been determined in the 1981 economic plan of Jiangxi Province that the total value of agricultural and industrial production will increase by 4% over 1980. This means that the total value of agricultural production will increase by 5.6% and that of industrial production by 3%; the general scale of capital construction will go down by 34.5%; revenues will increase by 5.6% and expenditures will be reduced by 30% as compared with the final accounts for 1980; and the total amount of retail sales will increase by over 3.1%. It has also been decided that the province's limited capital should be carefully used only for important projects: to improve the standard of living; to develop agriculture, especially industrial crops, and a diversified economy; and to develop the light and textile industries as well as the energy industry. It is expected that with these readjustments, the economy of Jiangxi will develop even more steadily in the future, and the standard of living will accordingly be improved to a considerable extent.

73. ECONOMIC DEVELOPMENT IN JILIN PROVINCE
By the General Office,
Jilin Provincial People's Government

Geography. Situated in the central part of Northeast China, Jilin Province is a beautiful place with fertile land and rich natural resources. It covers an area of more than 180,000 sq. km. and has a population of 22,098,000. Its mountainous eastern part is covered with dense forests of high economic value. It has a wide distribution of mineral deposits. The central plains, with fertile land and a mild climate, have a great potential for agricultural development. The vast grasslands in the west are suitable grazing grounds for developing animal husbandry.

Survey of Economic Development Since 1949

However, these rich natural resources lay unexploited and unutilized before Liberation. Agricultural production in the province was very backward and the industrial foundation very weak. The working people lived in dire poverty.

After the founding of the People's Republic of China, the people of various nationalities in the province, under the correct leadership of the Chinese Communist Party, carried out socialist transformation with regard to the ownership of the means of production and large-scale economic construction. The national economy developed in an all-around way, registering great advances in all fields.

Economic Changes. Starting from scratch and proceeding from a small scale to a big scale, the province has built a large number of industrial and mining enterprises. Among them are the Changchun No. 1 Motor Vehicle Plant, the Changchun Coach Plant, the Changchun Rolling Stock Plant, the Changchun Tractor Plant, the Jilin Chemical Company, the Fuyu Oilfield, the Yunfeng Hydroelectric Power Station, the Tonghua Iron and Steel Plant, the Jilin Paper Mill, the New China Sugar Refinery, the Changchun Textile Mill, the Changchun Sewing Machine Plant and the Changchun Bicycle Factory.

At the same time, vast efforts have been made in farmland capital construction and the level of farm mechanization and electrification has been greatly raised. Much has been done also in applying chemical fertilizers and in bringing irrigation to farmland. The development of industrial and agricultural production has been accompanied by growth in communications and transport, and in scientific, technological, cultural, educational and health undertakings. Jilin Province has effected a fundamental change in its economic structure. This is a sizeable material foundation for the province to realize the Four Modernizations.

Ups and Downs. The economic development in Jilin Province, as in other parts of the country, suffered ups and downs over the years, especially during the disastrous decade when Lin Biao and the Gang of Four were in power. As a result, there was a serious imbalance among agriculture, light industry and heavy industry and grave damage was done to economic construction. However, with the downfall of the Gang of Four, especially with the convocation of the Third Plenary Session of the 11th Central Committee of the Chinese Communist Party, the province quickly brought an end to economic stagnation and backsliding by earnestly implementing the principles and policies put forward by the Party Central Committee. It was able to restore the economy and to make new advances in a matter of two or three years.

Economic Growth. In economic construction in 1980, Jilin Province acted upon the eight-character policy centering around readjustment; devoted its main attention to agricultural and light industrial production and to arrangements for the people's livelihood; and carried out experiments on restructuring the management system in selected areas. The economy continued to grow in the course of readjustment. The industrial and agricultural output value totalled 16,950 million yuan in 1980, 5.5% more than in 1979 or 127.6 times more than in 1949. The share of industrial output value in total industrial and agricultural output value rose to 77.6% in 1980 from 28.7% in 1949.

Agriculture. A fairly good harvest was gathered in spite of very bad weather. In 1980, the province, acting on actual conditions, readjusted and relaxed agricultural policies, introduced the system of responsibility in production and new measures to restructure the management system. This stimulated the enthusiasm of the peasants and resulted in the development of production. Although bad weather seriously affected crops in an area of 1.44 million hectares, the output of grain and soybeans totalled 8,585,000 tons in 1980 — the fourth best year since Liberation. Output of industrial crops increased by a big margin and beets amounted to 1,176,625 tons, more than double the 1979 figure. Production of oil-bearing crops came to 266,045 tons, or 87.1% more than in 1979. Both surpassed the best years in history.

There was also new growth in forestry, animal husbandry, sideline production and fishing. The province afforested 170,000 hectares, or 12,200 hectares more than in 1979. A total of 5,929,000 pigs were raised, which was on a par with the province's best record. The number of sheep aggregated 1,707,000 head, 14.4% more than 1979, and this set a new record in local history. Collective and household sideline production showed considerable growth. The output of ginseng and deer antlers — known as "treasures of the Northeast" — amounted to 2,170,000 kilograms and 27,715 kilograms, respectively, or 14.5% and 30.6% more than in 1979, respectively.

Total output value of commune-operated and brigade-run enterprises was 880 million yuan, a 17.4% increase over 1979. The output of industrial crops rose by a large margin thanks to the readjustment of the agricultural structure, while a fairly balanced development of farming, forestry, animal husbandry, sideline occupations and fisheries was ensured. This broke the past pattern of a drop in grain production resulting in a simultaneous drop in total agricultural output value. Although the province produced 450,000 tons less grain than in 1979, total agricultural output value increased by 3.8%. This was an outstanding feature of agricultural production in 1980.

The conditions for agricultural production in the province have been greatly improved. By the end of 1980, the province had built 81 large and medium-sized reservoirs and 6,200 km. of river dykes, and had sunk 53,387 pump wells. These facilities ensured effective irrigation for 730,000 hectares. About 457,000 hectares of farmland had been improved to ensure high and stable yields. As 1980 ended, the province had 65,470 powered irrigation and drainage machines for rural use and 25,961 tractors, 25,873 hand-tractors and 59,199 large and medium-sized tractor-drawn farm implements. At present, one-third of the province's farmland is plowed by machine.

The amount of chemical fertilizers applied in a year totalled 1,201,000 tons (calculated on the basis of 100% effectiveness) and averaged 304.5 kilograms per hectare. Electricity is available in 99.4% of the communes, 97.5% of the production brigades and 95.4% of the production teams.

In accordance with a decision of the State Council to build marketable grain-producing bases in Northeast China, Jilin in 1980 designated 14 more counties as such bases, bringing the total to 23 in the province. With 3,298,000 hectares of farmland, or 81.6% of the province's total, these counties combined to produce 7,115 million tons of grain and soybeans in 1980, making up 82.9% of total output in the province. They sold 2.5 million tons of grain to the state, accounting for 86% of the total amount of grain the province sold to the state in the year. The marketable grain from these counties averaged 215 kg. per capita for the rural population, or 40.5 kg. more than the average for the province. This is of major significance to the province in its efforts to make the best use of its favourable conditions in order to promote grain production and speed up agricultural modernization.

Industry. Industry continued to advance in the course of readjustment, with light industry showing greater expansion. In 1980, the light and textile industries grew at a fast pace. With regard to heavy industry, the province readjusted its internal structure and product mix by closing, merging or retooling for alternate production a number of enterprises which had turned out substandard products, consumed much material and fuel or operated at a loss for a long time. Efforts were intensified to improve the management of enterprises. Experiments in expanding the authority of enterprises to decide their own affairs were conducted at selected places. The regulating role of the market was given greater scope under the guidance of planning and economic policies were further implemented. The result was that the workers and staff members were able to bring their enthusiasm into full play.

The province achieved fairly good economic results and increased both production and revenues. In 1980, total industrial output value was 13,160 million yuan, a 5.8% increase over 1979. The output value of heavy industry came to 7,980 million yuan, increasing by 1.7% over 1979. Production of light industry amounted to 5,180 million yuan, an increase of 13.3%. Light industries surpassed heavy industries in growth rate. The share of light industry in total industrial output value rose from 36.8% in 1979 to 39.3% in 1980. The enterprises covered by the province's budget met the target of profits one month ahead of time. The amount of profit realized from every 100 yuan of output value rose from 7.85 yuan in 1979 to 8.75 yuan in 1980, a 9.2% increase.

The work to put enterprises in order resulted in better management, higher quality of products and a great variety, and lower consumption of raw materials and fuel. The light and textile industries alone added 136 new varieties, 222 new products and 2,439 new styles. Twenty-two industrial products manufactured by the province won first prizes in the national trade-wide quality appraisals. Five products were awarded state medals for good quality. "Lujin" Brand plywood won the state gold medal and the state silver medals winners included "Peony" Brand H acid, "Changbaishan" Brand potash prussiate and "Shenhua" Brand An Nao Niu Huang Pian.

Jilin Province produced an excellent situation in the light and textile industries by giving them priority in the supply of raw materials, energy and other things. Foodstuffs, clothing and other light industrial goods for daily use increased by big margins. In the early post-Liberation days, the province did not produce such high-grade goods as bicycles, sewing machines, radios and wristwatches. In the period 1957-1962 of the second five-year plan, the province retained an annual capacity of producing about 5,000 bicycles, roughly the same number of sewing machines and 8,000 radios. In 1980, however, the province turned out 170,000 bicycles, 135,000 sewing machines, 700,000 radios and 310,000 wrist-watches. It also began to manufacture TV sets and washing machines. In an effort to supply the people with more clothing, the province produced 11,750 tons of chemical fibres in 1980, as against something over 5,000 tons in 1966, thus expanding production 2.4 times during this period.

Transportation and Communications. There was also a big development in communications and transport. Targets for both passenger traffic and freight by rail and road for 1980 were over-fulfilled. Total volume of freight amounted to 78,670,000 tons and the number of passengers totalled 132,370,000. The total railway mileage within the province stood at more than 3,400 km., or 46% more than in 1949. Highway mileage was more than 23,000 km., or 6.9 times more than in 1949. All the people's communes and 60% of the production brigades are now accessible by motor road. The management of transport enterprises was improved in 1980 and the number of traffic accidents dropped by 4% from the previous year.

Capital Construction and Investment. By readjusting the areas of investment, capital construction achieved better results. In 1980, state-budgeted investment in the province and funds raised by the province itself shrank from the 1979 total, but the province invested 2.2 times more money than in 1971 in the light and textile industries and 25.1% more in housing. Construction of key projects progressed at a faster pace. The 13 projects designated by the state as key items over-fulfilled the plan for the year by 10.2%. Three key projects were completed as scheduled. The results of investment were markedly improved.

The province maintained a balance between revenues and expenditures and had a slight surplus. In 1980, a financial system was introduced by which each administrative level was entitled to keep a portion of the surplus after fulfilling the quota set by the next higher authority. Thus, departments at various levels became more eager to increase production and revenues and to cut costs and expenses. The province increased the revenues and over-fulfilled the annual financial plan. Urban and rural savings deposits increased considerably to a total of 1,060 million yuan at the end of 1980 — five times the 1962 figure and 2.6 times the figure for 1976.

Commerce. Trade was brisk in urban and rural markets during 1980. A commercial system embracing multi-economic sectors, with units under public ownership as the predominant sector and having multichannels of distribution and multiforms of operation, began to take shape. This was made possible by introducing market regulation under the guidance of state planning, opening all possible avenues for production and restructuring channels for commodity flow to reduce intermediate links. Market supplies were significantly improved. The supply of sugar, cigarettes, liquors and candies were ample and the shortage of certain industrial goods was eased. The network of restaurants, snack shops and service units was expanded and their range of business and services was extended so that the volume of trade increased.

In 1980, retail sales totalled 5,800 million yuan, or 15.6% more than in 1979. This range of increase was unprecedented in the province since the founding of the People's Republic. Compared with 1976, the supply of pork, eggs and sugar all increased by more than 30%, and that of wristwatches and bicycles increased by at least 60%. The supply of TV sets and tape recorders rose by 140% and 270%, respectively, over 1979.

Foreign Trade. The year 1980 was also the best for the province in the purchase of export-oriented commodities and in export volume. The volume of such purchases was valued at 470 million yuan, a 50% increase over 1979 and the highest since Liberation. The volume of exports handled by the province itself amounted to 93 million yuan, which was 53.5% more than planned and an increase of 111% over 1979.

Science, Culture and Health. Scientific, technological, cultural and educational undertakings continued to develop. In 1980, there were 440 institutions of natural sciences run at various levels throughout the province. Their professional staff from assistant researchers on up numbered 3,780 and accounted for 33% of the total personnel working in the field of science and technology. The year also saw the largest number of scientific research items completed. Of the 158 research projects, 47 were verified and 14 were up to advanced levels in the country. Industrial and mining enterprises made headway in conducting research projects geared to production as part of the effort to make scientific research serve production directly.

The teaching quality of primary and secondary schools and of institutions of higher learning was raised markedly. The cut in the number of middle schools and a great expansion of vocational (technical) schools of various forms both in towns and rural areas brought a change in the structure of secondary education. The province enrolled 10,515 college students in 1980, or 1,035 more than in 1979. In addition, united, spare-time, television and correspondence universities and universities for day students were founded.

Health and medical work also progressed. A total of 2,829 beds were added to hospitals throughout the province in 1980. More than 537,000 patients suffering from any of five endemic diseases received free medical treatment.

The province also showed good results in physical culture. The provincial women's basketball team won the national championship. Seventy-four athletes placed first in eight national contests, including speed skating, track and field, weightlifting and cycling. Mass sports activities were also developed. And new successes were scored in the fields of culture, arts, broadcasting, television, the press and publishing.

Income and Livelihood. The people's livelihood was also improved in 1980. As production developed and the state readjusted the ratio between the accumulation fund and the fund for consumption, the income of the urban and rural populations generally increased. After two pay raises, the average annual wages for workers and staff members in the province in 1980 rose to 810 yuan, or 130 yuan more than in 1979 and an annual increase of 32.5 yuan. In the last two years, thanks to the implementation of the party's policies, higher state purchasing prices for farm and sideline products and the expansion of peasant household sideline production, the overwhelming majority of the peasants in the province earned more income. The net income per peasant in 1956 averaged 85 yuan (based on a survey of 432 typical peasant households) and it increased to 244 yuan in 1980 (based on a survey of 360 households), a rise of 159 yuan. The purchasing power per urban resident in 1980 was 205.6 yuan, or 14.2% more than in 1979. As urban employment increased, the number of dependents that a worker supported decreased. A survey of 13,643 families in early 1980 revealed that each family had an average of 2.37 wage earners, one more than in the corresponding period of 1965, while each wage earner had to support an average of 1.97 dependents, 1.7 less than in 1965.

In 1980, housing projects under construction in towns and rural areas totalled 3.56 million square metres of floor space, an increase of 15% over 1979, and 1.91 million square metres of floor space were completed, an increase of 23.2% over 1979. More than 5.91 million square metres of housing were built in the countryside in 1980 and 100,000 peasant families moved into new homes.

Current Problems and Goals for Economic Development

Jilin's economy made certain progress in 1980, but the results were still far from satisfactory in readjusting the proportions among agriculture, light industry and heavy industry and in the ratio between accumulation and consumption. The scale of capital construction is still larger than appropriate, a fact compounded by overlapping or ill-conceived projects. The problem of inferior products, high prices and lack of competitiveness has not been fundamentally solved. There was no marked improvement with regard to the low level of enterprise management, substandard technical levels and poor economic results. Further economic readjustment is necessary in view of these problems. The general requirements are: a sufficient retreat in capital construction, a balance between revenues and expenditures, stable prices, signficant growth of agriculture, expansion of light industry, readjustment of heavy industry, and steady and moderate development of scientific, technological, cultural, educational and health undertakings.

Agricultural Growth. The province envisages the vast development of agriculture. While grain production is ensured, vigorous efforts will be made to diversify the economy in the light of actual conditions. In order to increase production in an all-around way, the province will further implement the two documents of the Party Central Committee concerning agriculture, eliminate the influence of "Left" mistakes, make serious efforts to correct past erroneous practices, and stabilize and implement the rural economic policies. It will continue to readjust the distribution of crops and the pattern of production, strengthen the construction of the bases for marketable grain, forestry, animal husbandry and oil-bearing crops, carry out a series of measures to increase production, such as farm mechanization and farmland capital construction, and raise the level of scientific farming.

Industrial Readjustment. Industrial readjustment is one of the focal points of the economic readjustment in the province. In view of the fact that the province's industrial structure is on the "heavy" side, the province plans to readjust heavy industry and speed up the growth of light industry in order to promote the restructuring of industry as a whole and gradually establish an industrial structure tipped to the "light" side. Through readjustment, the output value of light industry will further increase and so will its share of total industrial output value. In accordance with people's needs and along the lines of specialization and cooperation, the province will carry out industrial reorganization and integration in nine cities in 1981, centering around the enterprises producing brand-name items or goods in short supply.

Enterprises that produce inferior products, consume too much materials and fuel or operate at a loss for a long time will be closed down, suspended, merged or switched to other lines of production, with emphasis on merging and switching over. In view of the fact that local energy supplies are not likely to increase significantly in the near future, the province will concentrate on increasing production through saving energy and will try to do a good job in the comprehensive utilization of energy resources.

Capital Construction and Investment. The scale of capital construction will be further curtailed. Efforts will be made to improve the results of investment. In 1981, the main areas of investment will be projects producing goods in short supply and those that have long been neglected, such as agriculture, light industry, science and technology, education, housing and municipal public utilities. To ensure timely completion of the key projects, centralized management will be enforced over capital construction projects, with strict control over the number of new projects. Effective measures will be taken to look after projects to be stopped or deferred.

Finance and Commerce. In financial and commercial work, stress will be put on the effort to achieve a balance between revenues and expenditures — with a slight surplus — by increasing revenues and cutting expenditures. The main steps to be taken are: make vigorous efforts to open more sources of finance and to reduce expenditures and promote production, in order to achieve the two-fold target of higher output and greater revenues; help those enterprises running at a loss to eliminate deficits and yield profits; tighten financial regulations and discipline; continue to enforce the financial system of letting each administrative level retain part of the profits above the set target; strictly control expenditures and cut spending for nonproductive purposes. In order to ensure a lively market and a thriving economy, commodity distribution will be further improved, while resolute measures will be taken to stabilize prices and to control price hikes.

Science, Education and Culture. The scientific, technological, cultural and educational undertakings in the province will continue to progress amidst readjustment. The focus of scientific research will be on those sectors of the economy which will grow in the course of readjustment, such as agriculture, light industry, energy sources and communications, and on the development of new products which are in demand on the market. Further readjustment will be conducted with regard to scientific institutions and efforts will be made to quickly apply the results of research in production. The internal structure of education will be further readjusted to ensure the harmonious development of all types of schools. The restructuring of secondary education will continue so as to expand vocational and technical education by taking vigorous and appropriate steps. Cultural and health undertakings will develop correspondingly in the course of readjustment.

Under the correct leadership of the Party Central Committee and the State Council, Jilin Province will, by making full use of favourable conditions and by mobilizing all people to work with one heart and mind, achieve a stable development of its economy through readjustment, and it will create favourable conditions for its long-term development in the future.

74. ECONOMIC DEVELOPMENT IN LIAONING PROVINCE
By the Liaoning Provincial Statistical Bureau

Geography and Resources

Location. Situated in the southern part of Northeast China, Liaoning Province borders Hebei and Inner Mongolia on the west, adjoins Jilin on the northeast, faces the Democratic People's Republic of Korea across the Yalu River to the southeast, and reaches the Yellow and Bohai seas in the south.

Geography. The province covers an area of 140,000 sq. km., of which 62% is mountainous, 30% flat and 8% water surface. Of this total, 3.76 million hectares or 26% is farmland, 39.4% forest and 3.6% pasture.

Climate. Lying in the north temperate zone, Liaoning benefits from a mild climate with much sunshine and rain, which is salubrious for farm crops.

Population and Administration Divisions. Liaoning has a population of 34,869,000, of whom 94% are of the Han nationality. Among the minority nationalities in the province, the Manchus number 1,147,000 and account for 45% of the total Manchu population in the country. Urban residents make up 31.8% of the total population and rural inhabitants 68.2%. There are altogether 7,615,000 wage earners, 71% of whom work in state-owned units, and 6.78 million able-bodied farm workers, or 30% of the rural population. The province consists of 12 municipalities and prefectures, 45 counties, 2 cities under the administration of prefectures, 42 districts (28 of which are urban districts) and 1,149 people's communes.

Transportation. Liaoning is linked with other parts of the country and the neighbouring Democratic People's Republic of Korea by rail. It has such important sea ports as Dalian, Yingkou and Dandong. Thus, Liaoning is a major foreign trade outlet for Northeast China.

Minerals. Being an area with abundant mineral resources, Liaoning boasts a quarter of China's total iron deposits and leads the country in magnesite and borax reserves. It also has rich resources of coal and oil. Deposits of a variety of rare metals which can be used for the atomic energy and space industries have been discovered in recent years.

Principal Crops. The main cereal crops include rice, maize, sorghum and soybeans and cash crops are cotton, tobacco, peanuts and sunflowers. The province also produces tussah silk, ginseng, apples, prawns and other seafoods. Liaoning's tussah silk output accounts for 75% of the national total and apple exports are about the same percentage.

Water Resources. With well over 360 rivers, both big and small, Liaoning has abundant water power resources. Apart from the boundary river, the Yalu, the main inland waterways in the province include the Liaohe, Taizi, Hunhe and Daling rivers, which have a total flow of 46,500 million cu. m. per year. Liaoning's coastline extends for 2,187 kilometres and provides excellent conditions for developing aquatic products. The province ranks among the five major sea salt producers in China.

Survey of Economic Development Since 1949

Despite its favourable natural conditions and rich resources, Liaoning was not sufficiently developed in the pre-Liberation years as a result of the prolonged rule and plunder by the Japanese imperialists and Kuomintang reactionaries. Since Liberation, the local people have worked hard under the leadership of the Chinese Communist Party and people's government and have won tremendous successes in socialist revolution and construction, with substantial assistance from other parts of the country.

Liaoning has now become an industrial centre with the steel and machine-building industries as the main producers. The province's industrial enterprises numbered 16,000 at the end of 1980, and their position among the provinces in the national economy was: combined fixed assets, first; total industrial output value, third; heavy industrial output, first; light industrial output, fourth; and financial revenues, second.

Impressive progress has been made in Liaoning's industry, agriculture, transport and commerce over the past 30 years. A breakdown shows that provincial income has gone up by an annual average of 9.1%; industrial production, 13.7% (heavy industry, 16.5%; light industry, 10.4%); farm production, 4.5% (grain output, 3.7%); and retail sales, 9.8% (per capita sales of consumer goods, 6.8%).

With the growth of the economy, the standards of the people's livelihood, cultural life and medical conditions of both the urban and rural population in Liaoning Province have improved too.

Review of Liaoning's Economy in 1980

In accordance with the policies formulated by the Third Plenary Session of the Chinese Communist Party Central Committee held in December 1978, Liaoning Province made considerable progress in economic readjustment in 1980, as evidenced by the new achievements of various departments.

1. *Preliminary readjustment of the economy was made in the course of development.* In agriculture, the peasants' socialist enthusiasm rose tremendously thanks to the implementation of the two documents of the Party Central Committee on agricultural development and the party's various economic policies, the establishment of the responsibility system in production, and increases in the purchasing prices of farm and sideline products. Good harvests were reaped despite serious natural adversities.

The province's grain output in 1980 totalled 12.215 million tons, an all-time high. Considerable increases were also registered in cash crops: the output of oil-bearing crops exceeding the 1979 mark by 64% and the per hectare yield of cotton rising by 27.6%. The output of tussah silkworm cocoons topped the 50,000-ton mark, surpassing the previous year's output by 32.5%. All these items hit their highest levels since the founding of the People's Republic. Initial restructuring was carried out in agriculture, with progress made in forestry, animal husbandry, sideline occupations and fisheries as well. Total output value of the commune-run industry also showed a fairly large increase. The rural economy began to take on a new look.

In industry, notable changes were made in the industrial structure and a great impetus was given to the growth of light industry by taking full advantage of the concentration of heavy industry and the abundance of raw material industries in the province, by breaking the barriers of different departments, localities and systems of ownership and forming combines or encouraging cooperation between specialized units, and by carrying out the principle of giving priority to certain industries.

Liaoning's industrial production for 1980 totalled 45,600 million yuan, an 8.4% increase over 1979. Of this, light industry rose by 28% while heavy industry was up 0.9%. The proportion of light industry in total industrial production rose from 27.7% in 1979 to 32.4% in 1980. Collectively run enterprises also made great progress, scoring a 19.2% growth in total output — as compared with 3.9% chalked up by state-owned enterprises.

Some 550 enterprises which had long been running at a loss because of substandard products and high consumption of materials and energy, were either closed down, stopped, merged with other enterprises or switched to different lines of production. This made it possible to divert the limited supplies of energy and materials to those enterprises whose products are of good quality and have a ready market and whose energy consumption is low and profits are high. Satisfactory economic results were gained as a result.

Preliminary success was also made in ameliorating the serious dislocation between stripping and extraction in the major coal mines in the province. All of them overfulfilled the 1980 targets for tunnelling, development opening and stripping and made up for some of the previous losses. The recoverable amount of coal in a shaft during the three stages of development opening, preparation and extraction was greater than in the same period of the previous year.

The steel, machine-building and other heavy industries strengthened their own readjustment, broadened their scope of service and tried in many ways to produce goods in short supply which were needed by agriculture, light industry and the market. While meeting their own production targets, defense industry enterprises also took active steps to produce goods for civilian use.

The scale of capital construction was further reduced and changes were made in the use of funds. Projects involving a total investment of 3,380 million yuan were completed in 1980, an increase of 20.5% over 1979. Of this total, 1,440 million yuan was spent on nonproductive projects, or 53.3% more than the previous year, and its proportion rose from 33.5% of total investment to 42.6%. The investment in housing was up 55.1%, with its proportion of total investment growing from 25.6% to 31.8%. Appropriations for the cultural, educational, health, scientific research, municipal construction and other departments were also larger than in 1979. Improvement was made in the quality of the projects built and in the results of investment.

2. *Active steps were taken to restructure economic management.* The province's 262 industrial enterprises which had been chosen to experiment in broadening the powers of decision increased their total output value by 6.4%, turned over 9.5% more profits, or 330 million yuan, to the state and received an additional 66 million

yuan as their share of profits. While the state and the enterprises themselves increased revenues, the workers also earned more. The same experiment was carried out in a number of financial, trade and scientific research units.

In the spirit of taking full advantage of the strong points of enterprises, protecting competition and promoting combination, Liaoning Province established 173 specialized companies (comprising 1,900 enterprises), 507 economic integrations and nearly 500 joint industrial-agricultural-commercial enterprises in 1980 to give fresh momentum to the growth of industry and agriculture.

Financial departments in the province adopted the new system of "apportioning the revenues and expenditures among different levels and holding each to account for its profits and losses" — which fired the enthusiasm of all units for increasing revenues and economizing on expenses. The restructuring of the banking, credit and taxation systems also produced fairly good results.

3. *The regulating role of the market was given full play under the guidance of unified planning.*

The machine-building industry sought orders from all possible quarters and thus began to overcome the difficulties arising from a serious shortage of production tasks. Total production of the enterprises under the provincial machine-building bureau in 1980 amounted to 4,370 million yuan, maintaining the 1979 level. The commercial departments encouraged the simultaneous development of various economic sectors, channels of distribution and forms of business, increased the number of distributive and catering facilities, and thus greatly promoted the growth of commerce and service trades.

In 1980, Liaoning established 6,401 collectively run distributive, catering and service units, which accounted for 27.1% of the total number of such units in the province. Some 60,000 people were licensed to run private units of this nature, more than four times the number in 1979. More trading warehouses were built, the number of urban and rural trade fairs rose to 963, an increase of 147, and they did 600 million yuan's worth of business, which was 62.2% more than the previous year. Government departments of supplies discarded the outdated concept that means of production is not a commodity, overcame the drawback of overstrict control, adopted the practice of procuring materials through a multitude of channels and encouraging multilateral cooperation, and thus enlivened the supply of materials and benefited production as a result.

4. *Great efforts were expended to increase production and practice economy, thereby improving economic performance as a whole.* While striving to increase production, industrial enterprises tried in every way to improve product quality, lower the consumption of raw materials and fuel, eliminate deficits and increase profits, raise income and cut expenses — and these efforts yielded satisfactory results. The average coke consumption for each ton of pig iron stood at 508 kg. in 1980, or 7 kg. less than in 1979; the average coal consumption for each kwh. of electricity was 385 grams, or 6 grams less; and the average coke consumption for each ton of synthetic ammonia was 1,503 kg., or 137 kg. less.

Twenty-five products in Liaoning won gold or silver medals issued by the state in 1980, and 174 others were given certificates for superior quality by the ministries in charge. Fifteen products of the first light industry and 14 of the second light industry won first prizes in a nationwide competition. The textile industry had 12 products selected as outstanding brands and 60 others as superior quality goods. Of the 65 products of the machine-building industry subjected to state examination, 25 were rated as first grade. State-owned industrial enterprises which practiced independent accounting turned in 6% more profit tax in 1980 than in 1979; the amount of profit yielded by each 100 yuan's worth of products increased by 2%; and the amount of circulating funds tied down by each 100 yuans' worth of products decreased by 2.55%. Statistics of 1,081 light industrial enterprises showed that their production costs decreased by 1.43%.

5. *The people's livelihood improved with the growth of production.* A total of 708,000 urban residents got jobs in 1980 as various localities and departments enlarged employment opportunities by a variety of ways. Some 40% of the workers were upgraded and 350,000 received a pay raise through an upward revision of their wage rates. The province's total wage bill grew by 21.5%.

Investigations of 960 workers' families in six cities revealed that the average monthly income per capita in the fourth quarter of 1980 reached 36.37 yuan, a 57.9% increase over the 1977 average. The rate of increase in the average income of workers' families during the three years after the fall of the Gang of Four exceeded the figure for the 12 years between 1965 and 1977. Statistics toward the end of 1980 showed that there were, on the average, 123 bicycles, 68 sewing machines, 93 radio sets, 240 wrist-watches and 31 TV sets for every 100 workers' homes. The peasants' average per capita annual income derived from the collective was 122.5 yuan, 7.5 yuan more than in 1979.

Investigations of 500 peasant families distributed in 50 different communes in 18 counties revealed that the net income per capita in 1980 totalled 273 yuan, an increase of 16.2% over 1979. Of this, 152 yuan was furnished by the collective, growing by 4 yuan, and 84 yuan came from household sideline occupations, up 19.3 yuan. There were, on the average, 67.8 bicycles, 55.9 sewing machines, 62.9 radio sets and 174 watches and clocks for every 100 peasant homes.

Liaoning's total retail sales in 1980 were valued at 11,600 million yuan, or 20.7% more than in 1979. Increases were registered in all consumer goods — foodstuffs, garments and everyday articles. Pork, soda, electric bulbs, soap, detergent and other such items which had long been rationed were now in ample supply. Sales of high-grade and durable goods such as TV sets, tape recorders, radios, sewing machines, bicycles, wrist-watches and woollen fabrics rose by a big margin.

New housing with a total area of 5.36 million square metres of floor space was completed and turned over for use in 1980 — more than four times the amount built in 1976. The average living space for each urban worker increased from 2.94 sq. m. in 1976 to 3.41 sq. m. The peasants' living conditions also improved with the construction of new houses comprising a total of 770,000 rooms. Total savings deposits in both town and country aggregated 2,420 million yuan, an increase of 44.3% over 1979.

6. *Progress was made in scientific, educational, medical and cultural undertakings.* Research institutions in Liaoning produced more than 2,000 new results in 1980, some of which reached or approached advanced national or international standards. Their application in industry and agriculture yielded satisfactory economic results. The principle of "walking on two legs" by running different types of schools was carried out in the field of education. The institutions of higher learning in the province had a total enrollment of 63,000, which was an all-time high. Radio, television, correspondence, workers' and evening colleges grew rapidly and enrolled a total of 88,000 students. The restructuring of secondary education got under way following experiments at selected spots and a number of secondary technical, vocational and skilled workers' schools were established. Medical institutions were reorganized, with improvement resulting in the quality of medical service. Effective measures were taken to popularize family planning and to encourage each family to have only one child.

Current Problems and Goals for Economic Development

As a result of the influence of "Left" mistakes in economic construction over the years, and especially of the serious disruption caused by Lin Biao and the Gang of Four counter-revolutionary clique, Liaoning Province suffered from a serious imbalance in its economy, a weak agricultural foundation, a shortage of consumer goods and an acute dearth of energy. A great deal of work was yet to be done to improve the people's livelihood. This state of affairs began to take a turn for the better following the fall of the Gang of Four, but the serious dislocation of the basic proportional relations in the economy has not yet been fundamentally reversed. Liaoning still faces arduous tasks in readjusting, restructuring, consolidating and improving its economy. To make matters worse, while consumption grew in 1980, the rate of accumulation was not reduced. This resulted in inflation and price hikes and added to the difficulties for the future tasks of economic readjustment. To cope with this situation, it is imperative to solve the following problems:

1. *Expand agriculture and light industry and increase the production of consumer goods.* Liaoning's agriculture is weak and incapable of meeting the needs of the present industrial and urban population. Over the 30 years since the founding of the People's Republic, Liaoning's total industrial production has grown 47 times, heavy industry 97 times and light industry 20 times, whereas total farm production has risen only 3.76 times and grain 2.9 times. Despite the improvement in agricultural production in 1979 and 1980, the weakness of local agriculture has not been fundamentally changed. Agriculture still accounts for only a tiny fraction of total industrial-agricultural production and Liaoning remains the province whose proportion of agriculture in the entire economy is the smallest in China. A large portion of the food grain, cooking oil, meat, eggs and raw materials it needs for light industry still has to be shipped in from other provinces. The backwardness of agriculture also hampers the growth of those branches of light industry which use farm and sideline produce as raw materials. As a result, Liaoning's light industry is a shorter leg than its heavy industry.

Although light industry has developed somewhat in the past two years, its production still constitutes only 32.4% of total industrial production — far below the national average of 46%. Many kinds of consumer goods fall short of the growing demands of the urban and rural population in terms of quantity, variety, specification and design. To increase the production of consumer goods, it is essential to turn the advantages of Liaoning's industry to good account while tapping the potential of agriculture and light industry to the fullest possible extent.

During the present restructuring of industry, steps should be taken to increase products for farm use, including chemical fertilizers, insecticides, certain types of rolled steel and farm machinery best suited to farming in the province. Steps need also to be taken to make use of the advantages of Liaoning's heavy industry and to provide better service for light industry. The metallurgical industry should strive to produce more rolled steel of lighter types and smaller sizes and other items in short supply which are needed for the light and textile industries, the people's livelihood and city construction. The machine-building and defense industries should make use of their favourable conditions and spare equipment to produce goods for light industry and civilian use. The chemical industry should carry out multiple utilization and produce more chemical fibres as raw materials for the textile industry. Besides, it is necessary to break the bounds of different departments, localities and systems of ownership in the course of industrial organization so as to increase the production of consumer goods through combination of and cooperation between specialized lines.

2. *Take firm steps to curtail the scope of capital construction.* Curtailment of the over-extended scope of capital construction is the central link in economic readjustment. In 1980, Liaoning spent 3,380 million yuan on capital construction — the highest level of investment in history. This magnitude of construction overstepped the limits of the province's financial and material resources, resulting in a tremendous strain on material supplies, an increase in unfinished projects and poor returns on the investment. There were 3,329 state-owned projects, each calling for an investment of at least 100,000 yuan, under construction in 1980, which represented an all-time record, comprising 616 more projects than in 1979. Projects left unfinished by the end of the year numbered 2,043, also a record. The huge investment in 1980 was mainly occasioned by spendings outside the budget.

During the readjustment, it is essential to make circumspect arrangements and to strengthen guidance through planning. It is imperative to tighten control over the scale of construction started by local authorities and enterprises with funds collected by themselves and over their use of such funds. Every possible effort should be made to use the limited financial and material resources to strengthen energy, transport and other weak links such as light industry, urban construction and housing — all of which are closely associated with the people's livelihood. Resolute steps must be taken to stop those projects which lack the necessary conditions for construction or which, even when completed, will lack the necessary conditions for going into production. This also applies to those duplicate projects which will contend with existing enterprises for raw materials, fuel and power supplies. All this is aimed at matching the scope of capital construction with the country's financial and material capabilities.

3. *Carry out the movement to increase production and practice economy, strengthen management of enterprises and improve their economic performance.* There has been serious chaos over the years in the areas of production, construction and distribution, and especially in the management of certain enterprises — a consequence of errors in the principles guiding the economy and drawbacks of the economic management system. A fairly large number of enterprises still fall short of their own previous peaks or that of their own trades in terms of product quality and consumption of raw materials and fuel. Quite a few enterprises have produced large amounts of goods which find no ready market, and this has resulted in over-stocking products, lowering the rate of profit, increasing circulating funds needed and raising production costs. Some enterprises to this day are running at a loss because of very poor economic performance. The scope of capital construction is over-extended, resulting in poor returns on investment and striking losses and waste. There are too many links in the distribution of commodities and capital turnover is slow.

Firm steps must be taken during the readjustment to change the practice of stressing capital construction to the neglect of production and stressing the value and quantity of production at the expense of quality, consumption and management. Liaoning will have to rely mainly on tapping the potential of existing enterprises to enable them to expand production by their own efforts if the province is to develop its economy in the foreseeable future. To achieve this objective, it is necessary to carry out technical transformation rationally. Efforts should be made to raise product quality, increase variety, cut down the consumption of raw materials and fuel, reduce expenses on distribution and all other items, improve management, expand the movement to increase production and practice economy, try in every way to increase revenues and curtail expenditures, and fulfill the province's financial targets. In order to meet these targets, it is imperative to resolve the shortage of energy while strengthening management and achieving an all-round improvement of economic performance.

The shortage of energy has seriously hampered Liaoning's economic and financial growth in recent years. To tackle this problem, the coal industry should speed up its readjustment and the construction of new shafts to boost coal production, the oil industry should strengthen exploration and increase the production of crude oil and natural gas, and the power plants should improve the maintenance of existing power-generating units, carry out technical transformation and strive to increase power output under normal operations. At the same time, great efforts are required to conserve energy and raise the utilization rate of heat so that the energy saved can be used to increase production.

4. *Improve market supplies, stabilize prices and raise the people's living standards.* With the growth of industrial and agricultural production and the introduction of market regulation under the guidance of planning, commodity supplies have increased and retail sales have gone up considerably in the last two years. In spite of this, ready cash and savings deposits in the hands of urban and rural inhabitants have likewise increased by a wide margin, because the amount of money put into circulation has grown at a faster rate than the retail sales of commodities. In view of this, efforts should be expended to increase the production of consumer goods, appropriately reduce the stocks held by the commercial, supply and marketing and foreign trade departments and augment market supplies. Resolute and effective measures should be adopted to increase revenues and retrench expenditures, stop the indiscriminate handing out of bonuses, strictly control the issue of banknotes, strengthen price control and further stabilize the market and the economy as a whole.

Work should be done to make a good arrangement for the people's livelihood on the basis of expanded production. It is now necessary to expand employment opportunities for jobless people in cities and towns. More workers' housing should be built where the necessary funds and materials are available. On the other hand, firm and effective measures should be taken to improve family planning and control the growth of population.

75. ECONOMIC DEVELOPMENT IN NINGXIA HUI AUTONOMOUS REGION
By the Research Division,
General Office of the Ningxia Hui Autonomous Region People's Government

Geography, Population and History

Location. Ningxia Hui Autonomous Region is situated in the northwestern part of China. It lies in the middle and upper reaches of the Huanghe River and borders on Inner Mongolia Autonomous Region in the north, Shaanxi Province in the east and Gansu Province in the west and south.

Geography and Population. The region has a total area of 66,400 square kilometres and can be divided into two geographical districts: the southern loess highland formed by ranges of the Liupan Mountains and others; and the northern alluvial Yinchuan Plain around the Huanghe River. The total population of Ningxia is 3.737 million, among whom there are 1.167 million Huis as well as Manchu, Mongolian, Tibetan, Miao, Dongxiang, Uygur, Zhuang, and Korean nationalities.

History. Ningxia has a long history. As early as the Spring and Autumn Period, it was inhabited by Qiang people. From the Qin and Han dynasties, administrative organs under the central government were set up in this region and it became a place where army troops camped. At the end of the Tang Dynasty and beginning of the Yuan Dynasty, a kingdom named Western Xia was founded here. Later it was destroyed by Yuan and the region was called Ningxia Lu (at the provincial level). During the Ming Dynasty it was called Ningxia Wei (at the provincial level), and in the Qing Dynasty, Ningxia Fu. During these dynasties, immigrants came from Shanxi, Jiangsu and Anhui. At the beginning of the Republic of China, the name was changed to Suo Fang Dao, meaning "northern district." Not until 1929 was Ningxia Province established.

In 1935, Chairman Mao and the Central Committee of the Communist Party of China led the Red Army on the Long March across Mt. Luipan and through several counties in Ningxia (Longde, Xiji, Guyuan, Haiyuan, Tongxin and Yanchi) to Northern Shaanxi. Red regimes were set up in Yanchi and Yuhai counties as part of the Shaanxi-Gansu-Ningxia Border Region. After Liberation, according to the party's policy for national regional autonomy, Guyuan and Wuzhong autonomous prefectures and Jingyuan Autonomous County were founded. The Ningxia Hui Autonomous Region was established in 1958.

Before Liberation, the region's economy and culture were backward. In 1949, this province had a population of only 1.19 million people, but Ma Hongkui, the ruler of the region, enrolled 100,000 soldiers to support his reactionary rule. He colluded with despotic landlords and reactionary religious leaders to force people into his army and extorted taxes and levies. In particular, the Hui nationality was cruelly exploited. In those days, all business languished and prices kept rising. The people were struggling for places in the hunger line.

In September 1949, Ningxia was liberated. Then the grain output was only 642 million catties, the total value of agricultural output was 94.03 million yuan and industrial output was only 12.15 million yuan. As for industrial enterprises, there were only some handicrafts, an electric company with a 20-kw. generator (once used in the Empress Dowager Ci Xi's court) and a machine repair shop. Transport was provided by cattle, donkeys, camels and a few wooden boats and sheepskin rafts. The conditions of education and health were even worse. There were only 9 middle schools, 639 primary schools, and 3 makeshift hospitals with a total of 40 beds.

Survey of Economic Development Since 1949

After Liberation, especially after the establishment of the Ningxia Hui Autonomous Region, the regional economy was developed rapidly with the help of the state and the energetic efforts of various nationalities. Great changes have taken place in agriculture. On the basis of reconstructing some famous canals dug in ancient Ningxia, such as the Qin Canal, Han Canal, Tanglai Canal and Huinong Canal, the Qingtongxia Water Conservancy Project was built. Later, some main canals were dug: the No. 1 and No. 2 Farm Canals, West Main Canal, East Main Canal, Yuejin Canal and Dongxin Pumping Project. The irrigated area has been enlarged from 1.93 million *mu* in the early years after Liberation to 3.577 million *mu*. Farm machinery was developed from practically nothing. By the end of 1980, there were 5,811 big and medium-sized tractors and 16,404 walking tractors; the motive power for farming and irrigating machinery was 188,000 hp.; and the total motive power of farm machinery was 1,145,000 hp. Over 65% of the farmland can be cultivated by machine. In the plains, 90% of the communes and brigades have electric power, and so have 40% of the communes in the mountainous area. The level of scientific farming is up to par. Grain output was 3.75 times that in the post-Liberation period and the total value of agricultural output had increased by 470%.

Industrial Development. Industrial production developed rapidly. The number of industrial enterprises has increased from 293 handicrafts plants before Liberation to 1,097 and newly built enterprises numbered more than 700, of which 29 were large and medium-sized enterprises. Now a primary industrial system has been formed that consists of coal, petroleum, electricity, nonferrous metallurgy, machinery, electronics, instruments, chemicals, building materials, paper-making, foodstuff-processing, tanning and wool and cotton textile industries. At the end of 1980, there were 11,332 machine tools and 2,539 pieces of forging equipment. The total value of industrial output in 1980 was 112 times that at the time of Liberation.

Transportation and Communication. Great changes have taken place in transport and communications. The railway from Baotou through the Huanghe River irrigationed areas to Lanzhou is a major artery in Northwest China. It links the Beijing-Baotou line in the east with the Lanzhou-Xinjiang line in the west. Our region has a total of 421 kilometres of railroads. The highway network, with Yinchuan as the centre, extends to every country, city and industrial base and also goes through Ningxia to Xi'an and Lanzhou. The main roads total 6,848 kilometres in this region. There are also airline flights from Yinchuan to Beijing, Baotou and Lanzhou.

Mineral Reserves. Initial achievement has been made in geological work. The reserves of coal have been verified to be 8,490 million tons and gypsum reserves are 1,270 million tons. Other minerals such as glass sand and limestone are also abundant.

Science and Education. Achievements have been made in science, culture, education and public health. Now there is one scientific academy, 39 research institutes and 46 academic societies. All together, there are 2,398 scientific personnel. Ningxia has 5 universities and colleges with 4,156 students; one TV university, 5,150 students; 20 secondary technical schools, 8,174 students; 508 middle schools, 223,700 students; and 5,107 primary schools, 583,700 pupils. There are 14 libraries at the county level and above with collections totalling 1,853,000 volumes. There are 20 cultural centres. Some 60 hospitals have 7,866 beds and 12,709 medical workers.

Survey of Economic Development in 1980

In 1980, under the leadership of the Regional Committee of the Communist Party of China and the people's government, the people of all nationalities conscientiously carried out the party's policy of readjusting, restructuring, consolidating and improving the national economy that was adopted at the Third Plenum of the 11th Party Central Committee to make up for the loss incurred during the ten-year "cultural revolution," and Ningxia made initial achievements so that the economic situation became better than ever.

Agriculture. A bumper harvest was reaped in 1980. In the rural areas, governments at various levels carried out the provisions of the documents on agriculture issued by the Party Central Committee, readjusted economic policies, implemented the party's economic policy and instituted various production responsibility systems. The people's government of Ningxia Hui Autonomous Region reduced or exempted the state grain-purchasing quotas for the communes and brigades in mountainous areas and fixed the state grain-purchasing quotas for the brigades and communes on the plains. After readjusting the agricultural structure, peasants became more active in production, and they worked very hard to make themselves richer.

Thanks to good weather conditions in 1980, a harvest was yielded in agriculture, forestry and animal husbandry in the region, except for some mountainous areas which suffered from natural disasters. The grain output totalled 2,400 million catties, or 13.4% more than in 1979, and an all-time high. The output of oil-bearing crops reached 71.964 million catties, or 65.1% more than in 1979. Sugar beet production amounted to 125 million catties, or 3.75 times what it was in 1979. The output of the fruit of Chinese wolfberry was 836,000 catties, a 12% increase over 1979.

Despite a drought on the grasslands, the number of livestock and sheep increased by 3.5% and 0.9%, respectively. The commodity rate of sheep and hogs was up. Livestock and poultry bred privately by peasants also grew remarkably in number. Some 265,000 *mu* of land were afforested in 1980.

The total value of agricultural production was 534 million yuan in 1980, or 15.7% more than in 1979. Now the countryside presents a new look.

Industry. Through readjustment, industrial production was marching forward. The industrial departments of Ningxia reduced the output of some products which were not competitive because of poor quality and high prices and of those products already in stock. Some enterprises with high consumption, poor quality and long-time deficits were stopped, closed down or merged or converted to producing other items. On the other hand, stress was put on existing enterprises carrying out the industrial production plan practically, so that industrial growth remained constant.

The value of industrial output was 1,367 million yuan in 1980, 5% less than in 1979. Of this total, the output value of light industry reached 367 million yuan, an increase of 7.8% over 1979, and that of heavy industry was 1,000 million yuan, a decrease of 9%. The imbalance between light and heavy industries was improved during the year. The proportion of light industrial output value to total industrial output value increased from 23.6% in 1979 to 26.8% in 1980. The quality of products was much improved. Of the 35 indexes listed for quality examination, 20 met the planned requirement and accounted for 57.1% of the total. In contests, 20 high-quality products were chosen from the region, among which 6502-Type Jacquard Woollen Blanket and 40T Carrier with Scrapers were awarded state silver medals.

Some work was done in reforming the economic system and the reorganization and amalgamation of industry got off to a good start. Under the guidance of planning regulations, market regulation was brought into play. The industrial departments steadily did experiments in giving more authority to some enterprises. These measures played an active part in improving the management of enterprises, boosting production and raising economic efficiency. The collectively owned industry and individual handicrafts in cities also were developed to a certain extent.

Investment and Finance. The investment in capital construction was reduced so as to modify the conditions of wide coverage, multiple items and less efficiency. In 1979 and 1980, 75 projects — each with investments exceeding 50,000 yuan — were suspended or cancelled so that 750 million yuan was saved. The stress on invested items was shifted: in agriculture, the investment was raised from 13% in 1978 to 16.4% in 1980 and in light and textile industries, from 1.9% to 6.1%; but in heavy industry it decreased from 70.9% to 33.4%. For the last three years, the average annual investment in culture, education, public health and housing was five times the average annual amount of what has been invested since the founding of New China.

The initiative of the local authorities was aroused by the financial system of apportioning revenues and expenditures among different levels and by holding each responsible for profits and losses. Due to decreased incomes of the enterprises in the course of industrial readjustment, our region's revenue in 1980 was 194.57 million yuan, a drop of 22.5% compared with the previous year; expenditure was 584.16 million yuan, 8.2% less than the year before.

Commerce. With the bumper harvest, the increase of light industrial products and the relaxing of some policies, the market supply was much improved. Some major commodities which are closely related to people's daily lives are in ample supply and more varieties and colours are available. The situation of a market slump and deficient goods resulting from the ten years' havoc has initially changed. A great number of traditional items and farm and sideline products which had not been seen for many years running, have appeared again on the market. Even some goods in short supply in past years, such as eggs and sugar, are now available without limit.

The total purchasing value of farm and sideline products in 1980 was 157.23 million yuan, up 39.3% over 1979; and retail sales came to 784.95 million yuan, a 9.7% increase. At the time when state-run commercial units expanded their purchasing and improved their service, many enterprises under collective and individual ownership sprang up and developed, such as the shopping, catering, servicing, and repair businesses. As the number of shops was increased, the distribution of commodities appeared more active.

Science and Technology. Science and technology showed fresh growth. In 1980, 149 achievements in scientific research were approved; some of them were up to advanced domestic standards. The W-I 1500KG Pendulum Impact Tester paved a new path for the development of high-energy impact testing machines; some technical performances of Magnetic Power Clutch of DGF-2.5 type and DGF-5 type surpassed those of imported models; No. 204 Alkaline Protease opened a new source of fermenting for our tanning industry; the 864 Needles Electronic Jacquard Blanket Loom filled a gap in our textile industry; and the Laser Velocity Meter ushered in a new field in the development of instruments and tools. Some experts and units put forward proposals on how to rationalize the structure of agriculture, forestry and animal husbandry in the Huanghe River irrigated areas and how to bring about scientific farming, which formed an important scientific basis for agricultural modernization in the Ningxia irrigated area. In addition, much progress was made in the fields of education, culture, public health and physical culture.

Income and Livelihood. The people's life showed some actual improvement. The income per person from collectives in the countryside was 77 yuan in 1980, up 12.4% over 1979; the grain ration per person was 449 catties, or 67 catties more than in 1979. Having money in hand and grain in store, the peasants were in high spirits to build new houses and purchase clothing and medium and high-grade consumer goods. Based on typical investigations, the average housing space enjoyed by each peasant in our region in 1980 was 8.8 square metres, an increase of 0.5 square metre over 1979. Every 100 peasant families on the average possessed 90.5 bicycles, 25 sewing machines, 24 radios and 52 wrist-watches. Some peasant families even began to buy TV sets. The average savings deposit per peasant was 16.3 yuan in 1980, up 40.5% over 1979. As life becomes better, people live longer than before, and the number of people aged 70 to 90 is growing fast in the rural areas. In 1980, 37,516 persons obtained employment, including casual labourers and contract workers.

More than 40% of the workers and staff members had their wages raised. A bonus system was widely carried out in enterprises. The annual average wage of workers and staff members in units owned by the whole people was up 10% compared with 1979. The increased income for most families lightened living burdens. The space of new houses totalled 470,000 sq. m., which meant an average of 0.46 sq. m. for every urban resident. According to a survey of urban families, every 100 families had 209 wrist-watches, 26 TV sets, 130 bicycles and 56 sewing machines. Some families had record players and tape recorders.

Facts prove that the economic situation in Ningxia is excellent indeed. The line and policies adopted since the Third Plenary Session are correct and have won the support of the masses. The people of all nationalities in Ningxia are confidently marching along the socialist road.

Current Problems and Goals for Future Development

In the past 30 years since Liberation, Ningxia has been marching forward rapidly with many achievements in socialist construction. But certain problems still exist because of the "Left" mistakes in the guiding ideology of our economic construction They are:

(1) Owing to incorrect estimation and vague understanding about our own economic foundation and ability, and regardless of our poor condition and backward economy and culture, we always intended to go faster and blindly pursued distant targets at high speed and with an exaggerated degree of self-sufficiency, so we were led into an alley of much accumulation and less consumption for quite a long time. To deal with a great number of problems, we put forward some slogans so divorced from reality that we were unable to fulfill them.

(2) In capital construction, we went in for grandiose projects and hoped to achieve quick results. Therefore, our battle line was overextended, economic structure was out of proportion and light industry lagged behind for a long time. Our investment did not produce much effect and was generally wasted.

(3) The way of attaching importance to accumulation, not consumption, and to production, not people's living, created an imbalanced ratio between the "bone" and the "flesh." As a result, cultural and educational undertakings and the people's livelihood were badly affected.

(4) In our economic work, we copied some things from other provinces mechanically. And subjectivism and formalism still exist in our work.

(5) On the question of ownership, premature transition was practiced and our people's communes were still too large in size. In spite of the actual limitations of our productive forces, we once confiscated private plots in some rural areas and forbade country trade fairs, because the slogan urged us "to cut off the tail of capitalism." In urban areas, we did not take the collective economy into full consideration but put a ban on individual economy so that the path for the unemployed to get jobs became narrower and narrower.

Influenced by the above-mentioned "Left" thinking, the economic construction of the whole region suffered a great deal. From this we must learn a profound lesson.

In line with the guiding principle laid down by the Party Central Committee and the State Council for further readjustment of the national economy, our main task in the next few years is to pursue readjustment resolutely, to concentrate our efforts on promoting agricultural production, and to correct the relations between agriculture, forestry and animal husbandry. This will turn the

Huanghe River irrigated areas into a farm produce base as soon as possible and should quicken the development of forestry and animal husbandry in the mountainous areas to enable farming, forestry, sideline production and fishing to progress in a coordinated manner.

We are going to make the most of Ningxia's coal resources and devote major efforts to develop the energy industry. With the development of animal husbandry, forestry and cash crops, light and textile industries will be going on at a greatly accelerated pace, as will the tanning, woollen textile and food industries — including meat packing, dairy production, sugar refining and wine making. The structure of heavy industry will be well adjusted so as to raise the production level. We will enhance the construction of communications facilities to ensure that transport will be the vanguard of the national economy. In capital construction, we must act according to our capability.

And we must stabilize prices and rearrange the market in order to increase financial income and to give more persons employment so as to enable the people to live a happy life and to permit our region to advance steadily in the course of economic readjustment.

76. ECONOMIC DEVELOPMENT IN QINGHAI PROVINCE
By the Economic Research Office, Qinghai Provincial Planning Commission

Geography and Population

Location. Situated on the Qinghai-Tibet Plateau, Qinghai Province covers an area of 720,000 sq. km. and has a continental plateau climate. Most of the province consists of pastoral areas intermingled with small farming plots, except for the northeastern part which has 14 towns and counties in the Huangshui and Huanghe river valleys and whose agricultural area accounts for 5% of the total area of the province.

Population. Qinghai Province is inhabited by seven nationalities, namely: the Han, Tibetan, Hui, Tu, Salay, Mongolian and Kazakh. At the end of 1980, the population was 3,770,000, of whom 1,430,000 or 38% were minority peoples.

Survey of Economic Development Since 1949

Before Liberation, Qinghai had long been subjected to the shackles of semi-feudalism and semi-colonialism, with pastoral areas still in the grip of the slave system. Locked in an inland area, lacking means of communication and with a backward economy and culture, the people lived in utter poverty. After Liberation, democratic reform and socialist transformation and construction were carried out under the leadership of the Chinese Communist Party, giving Qinghai a new look. The major economic achievements may be summed up as follows:

Industry. Before Liberation, there were only eight handicraft workshops and a 223-kilowatt water turbine generator in the entire province. Since Liberation, however, such modern industrial departments as light industry, textiles, metallurgy, coal, power, petroleum, chemicals, machine-building, electronics, building materials and timber processing have been set up. By the end of 1979, enterprises in the province totalled 1,310, of which 38 were large or medium-sized undertakings. Enterprises owned by the whole people with independent accounting had 2.3 million yuan's worth of fixed assets and employed 187,000 workers and staff members. The variety of products increased to more than 400 from under 20 before Liberation.

Total industrial output value grew from 18.9 million yuan in 1949 to 1,390 million yuan in 1980 (at constant 1970 prices). The provincial capital, Xining, has become a new-rising city of more than 500,000 people. With the development of industry, the unitary agricultural and stock-raising economic structure has been initially changed. The proportion of industrial output value in the total of industrial and agricultural output value shot up to 68.3% in 1979 from 12.3% in 1949. The light and textile industries with 9,100 spindles for wool spinning and the machine-building industry with 16,500 machine tools accounted for about 30% each of the gross industrial output value.

Major industrial products included plush, knitting wool, woollen blankets, leather products, furs, salt, potassium chloride, asbestos, gypsum, copper concentrate, rolled steel, machine tools, tractors and heavy-duty lorry and mining machinery. But generally speaking, Qinghai is an economically underdeveloped area and industry is still in its initial stage of development.

Animal Husbandry. Animal husbandry is a major component part of the provincial economy. In 1949, the number of draught animals, sheep and goats in stock was 7,480,000 head and output of wool was over 2,500 tons. Since Liberation, the party and government have energetically helped and supported livestock breeding in the form of finance, credit, supplies and technology. The purchasing price of animal by-products has been markedly raised three times. Livestock breeding and veterinary stations have been widely set up at various places for the prevention and cure of animal diseases. Movements have been unleashed to wipe out insect pests and rats in the grasslands and to improve the breeds of sheep. All this has brought about a rapid development of livestock breeding. By the end of 1979, animals, sheep and goats in stock numbered 21.53 million head, an increase of 2.87 times over that of 1949.

Agriculture. Qinghai Province has a dry climate. Since Liberation, the people of various nationalities, under the leadership of the party and government, have devoted major efforts to building irrigation projects on a large scale. 69 irrigated zones with at least 10,000 *mu* of land each have been built. The effective irrigated area has risen to 2,340,000 *mu* from 750,000 *mu* before Liberation. Meanwhile, the opening up of wasteland in the Qaidam Basin and other areas suitable for farming has brought the farmland of the whole province up to 8.7 million *mu*. Though grave natural calamities occurred in 1979, grain output still totalled 820 million kg. and production of oil-bearing crops was 58.5 million kg., rising 2.77 and 7 times, respectively, as compared with 1949; and average per-*mu* yield jumped respectively from 64.5 kg. and 25.5 kg. to 130 kg. and 53 kg. Growth was also registered in other industrial crops and sideline products.

Transport and Communications. There was no railway or airline in Qinghai Province before Liberation and there were only 472 kilometres of make-shift highways. After Liberation, a highway network around Xining was built and roads to other provinces were opened. Highways within the province totalled 15,495 kilometres, of which all-weather highways reached 11,349 kilometres. The Xining-Lanzhou railway was completed in 1959 and construction of the Qinghai-Tibet railway started a few years ago. Railway tracks have been laid to Golmud in the first stage of a construction project. Civil aviation also has begun to move forward. Thus, the state of inaccessibility in the province has been changed drastically.

Science, Education, Culture and Public Health. Before Liberation, there was no institution of higher learning or of scientific research in the province. The people of all nationalities had long been shackled in superstition and ignorance and illiterates were seen everywhere, while epidemic diseases spread widely. Since Liberation, great efforts have been made by the party and government to develop science, education, culture and public health. Now, there are 30,000 scientists and technicians of natural science and 31 independent institutions of scientific research. These institutions achieved success in selecting and breeding improved seed strains and spreading advanced cultivation techniques for spring wheat, potato and rape. They have improved animal breeds and have prevented and cured animal diseases. Scientists are selecting and cultivating forage seeds, surveying plateau biological resources, exploring and utilizing the resources in salt lakes and studying petroleum deposits and geological structures.

There are now six institutions of higher learning with 3,736 students, and 614 middle schools and 6,000 primary schools with a total enrollment of 820,000, a 19.6-fold increase over that before Liberation. There are 1,029 hospitals and other health institutions, with the number of hospital beds increasing to 11,621 from 100 before Liberation. A number of epidemic and endemic diseases that gravely endanger people's health have been basically eliminated or brought under control. Population mortality has dropped by a big margin. Culture, arts, the press, publishing, broadcasting, sports and other public undertakings have been rapidly forging ahead.

The great changes in the national economy and social look of Qinghai Province during the past 30 years fully proves that the leadership of the Chinese Communist Party and the socialist system is the fundamental guarantee for the people of all nationalities to rid themselves of poverty and advance along the road to common prosperity. On the other hand, under the influence of "Left" thinking in the past 20 years, economic construction in Qinghai suffered from major blunders and met with serious setbacks. The "big leap forward" in 1958-1960 and the calamitous ten-year "cultural revolution" in particular incurred heavy losses for the national economy and caused serious difficulties for the people's livelihood. Since the crushing of the Gang of Four, the national economy has taken on a new look as a result of the readjustment which began in 1979.

Economic Readjustment in 1980

The economic readjustment in Qinghai actually began in the second half of 1979 and had achieved initial success by the end of 1980.

(1) *Rational readjustment was made in the structure of agriculture and animal husbandry*. In the last two years, agricultural policies of the party and government were carried out conscientiously. All forms of the job responsibility system were instituted and improved, and purchasing prices of agricultural and sideline products were raised by a large margin. Some taxes on poor production brigades and communes were reduced or remitted. Thus, initiative in production by peasants and herdsmen was brought into play. At the same time, the proportions between and within agriculture and animal husbandry were readjusted to an appropriate rate.

In 1979, some farmlands in the stock-raising areas were turned back into pastureland. Further measures were taken to preserve and build up the grasslands. Readjustment of the composition of animal groups was started by increasing the ratio of female animals. Instead of the common practice of seeking one-sidedly high stock quotas at the end of the year, much attention was attached to raising the survival rate, marketing rate and commodity rate. The total growth rate of livestock was about 15% in 1980, or 2% higher than the previous year. The total number of cattle, horses and sheep in stock at the end of the year was 21.66 million head. Meat output (including pork) was 84,855 tons and wool output totalled 16,660 tons, up 18.4% and 7.6%, respectively, over the previous year. The number of livestock also rose markedly in agricultural areas where commune members were given fodder-land, and unreasonable restrictions on livestock breeding for personal needs were lifted.

Within agriculture, the distribution of crops was readjusted in line with local conditions. The natural advantages for growing rape were brought into full play in areas where the frost-free period was short, while in mountainous areas the acreage of drought-resistant crops was appropriately enlarged and proper rotation of crops was carried out. Thanks to plentiful rainfall and proper temperatures in the summer and autumn of 1980, a bumper harvest was gathered. Output of grain totalled 955 million kg. and of oil-bearing crops 70.5 million kg., up 16.5% and 20.5%, respectively, over the previous year. Both topped the previous highest levels.

Much attention was paid to forestry. Afforested areas in 1980 increased by 7,333 hectares — a record high in the past 20 years.

New developments were also made in collective and household sideline production in rural and pastoral areas. Income from collective sideline production in 1980 was 79.78 million yuan.

(2) *The readjustment of industry got under way.* Measures were taken in 1980 to speed up the development of light and textile industries; quotas of certain heavy industrial products were lowered; regulation by the market under the guidance of the state plan was brought into play; and production of commodities which were in great need in the market was increased. In the last two years, 43 enterprises which had insufficient raw material supply and outlets for their products and had suffered losses for a long time were either closed, stopped or transferred to produce other products. After initial readjustment, changes took place in the industrial structure.

Total industrial output value of the province reached 1,390 million yuan (at constant 1970 prices) in 1980 and stood at the same level as the previous year. The output value of light industry was 470 million yuan, up 9.4%, and that of heavy industry was 920 million yuan, down 6.4%. The proportion of the output value of light industry to that of industry as a whole rose to 33.9% in 1980 from 30.8% in the previous year.

There are favourable conditions in the province for the development of a number of products which are needed in the market and for export — such as plush, coarse woollen fabrics, knitting wool, woollen blankets, carpets, leather goods, furs, milk powder, minimotors, cream separators, salt and potassium chloride. Output of these products generally increased by 10%. Production of goods for minority nationalities was also developed and their varieties were increased and quality improved. Plush and insecticide powder No. 2 for oats were awarded the nation's high-quality silver medals. Twenty-one of the province's high-quality products were chosen. Comparable costs of products dropped by 2% as compared with the previous year.

The priorities of capital construction investments were rearranged in a proper way and 61 projects were stopped or postponed. Reasonable investments were earmarked for light industry, salt, nonferrous metals and other industrial departments.

(3) *Markets tended to be brisk.* The commercial departments paid attention to arranging commodity interchange between different economic areas, enhancing the supply network, properly developing collective businesses and the trade of individual pedlars, opening more country fairs, encouraging purchases and sales at negotiated prices — and thus promoting the interchange of goods between cities and countryside. The total volume of retail sales in the province in 1980 was 900 million yuan, up 9% over the previous year. If the factor of price hikes is deducted, there was still an increase of 5.6%. Retail sales of collective and individual businesses rose by 54.9% and 33% respectively. Trade between nationalities was restored and promoted. Special goods for minority nationalities increased from 400 to more than 600 varieties.

In foreign trade, the total purchasing value of export goods in 1980 stood at 75.43 million yuan (at 1974 planned prices), up 33.5% over that of the previous year, of which industrial and mineral products rose by 47.5%.

(4) *Local finances improved.* Since Liberation, the central government has paid much attention to economic development in Qinghai and has given it special treatment as an autonomous nationality region. Some 400 million yuan of financial subsidies and 86 million yuan of development funds for economically underdeveloped areas, as well as other special allocations, constituted the main components of Qinghai's financial sources in 1980. Local financial income totalled 164.93 million yuan and expenditure were 588.51 million yuan, accounting respectively for 115.6% and 79.1% of the budget. Reserve funds of local governments increased slightly.

(5) *New growth was achieved in education.* The energetic promotion of education is one of the important tasks of the readjustment. Investment in capital construction for education in 1980 was 128% more than that of 1978. Allocations for operating expenses in education also increased. During the last two years, newly constructed school buildings had a total floor space of 146,000 sq. m., with newly added seats for 45,000 students in primary and middle schools. The serious shortage of classrooms in middle schools was somewhat eased.

As specific measures were taken in the past two years to push nationality education forward, boarding primary schools have been set up in some production brigades and most communes in pastoral areas. There are middle schools for minority nationalities in most counties, and teachers' training schools for minority nationalities and secondary medical schools in all autonomous prefectures. The Qinghai Institute for Minority Nationalities was enlarged and it opened preparatory courses. Enrolled pupils and students from minority nationalities throughout the province totalled 186,000, doubling the 1966 figure. Generally speaking, however, education in the province is still underdeveloped; there are insufficient teachers and the quality of education is relatively low.

(6) *The people's livelihood was improved.* Despite a bumper harvest and improved livestock breeding in 1980, the purchasing prices of agricultural and sideline products were raised in the last two years. Some taxes on poor communes and production brigades in rural and pastoral areas were reduced or remitted, while state purchase quotas of grain were also reduced. Therefore, the livelihood of peasants and herdsmen was improved.

Grain rations for peasants were 24% more than the previous year. Meat and dairy products for herdsmen also increased. Per capita income that peasants and herdsmen received from the collective in 1980 was 86.4 yuan and 189.4 yuan, respectively, up 13.7% and 6%, respectively, from the previous year. Commune members' income from household sideline production increased markedly. The livelihood of the people living in the cities also improved. The income of workers and staff members showed an increase. Newly built housing for workers and staff members in 1980 came to 550,000 sq.m., a record high since Liberation. However, the income of peasants and herdsmen is still rather low and they are living a difficult life in some areas. The livelihood of workers and staff members is still rather hard.

Family planning made headway. The natural population growth rate in 1980 was lower than the previous year. The people of minority nationalities in pastoral areas have demanded family planning.

Current Economic Problems and Goals for Future Development

During the past 20 years, the economic construction in Qinghai was greatly influenced by "Left" thinking. Those in charge of the construction work paid little attention to local realities, were overanxious for quick results, ignored economic results and acted blindly. Therefore, an irrational economic structure was formed. Since inadequate care was given to the development of livestock breeding, forage grass is the most urgent problem today. Gross output in the pastureland is low and only a small quantity of animal by-products can be provided to the market.

The superiority of resources has not been brought into full play in developing industry. Too much importance has been attached to capital construction, while little attention has been paid to management. Most enterprises are operating under poor management and at low technical levels. Their products are of poor quality and are not competitive. Capital construction requires a long building time and high costs. Investment results are not up to standard. Cultural and educational levels are low. Scientific, technological and managerial personnel are in short supply. All this is a far cry from meeting the needs of economic development. Population growth is too fast and has led to serious problems. These problems should be studied seriously and settled systematically in the economic readjustment.

Under the guidance of the unified state plan, the national economy of Qinghai should raise its economic results and make greater contributions to the state by proceeding from reality, readjusting structures on the existing basis, reforming the system, tapping full potential and renovating equipment. The following measures are to be taken to achieve these ends:

(1) *We must bring about a great advance in livestock breeding.* Qinghai has 500 million *mu* of pastureland, but its capacity to support animals is low. In the coming years, we should step up pastureland construction. At present, we should put emphasis on preservation and rational utilization, improve and rejuvenate natural pastures and build artificial grazing ground in places where conditions permit, so as to raise the production capacity. At the same time, we should continue to

restructure the composition of animal groups, heighten livestock quality, raise more young animals, butcher more meat animals in the fall and provide more market stock and animal by-products.

(2) *We should develop a diversified economy while increasing grain production in agricultural areas.* Since the area of arable land is limited, intensive and scientific farming is the main way to raise per-unit output. Much attention should be paid to animal husbandry, forestry and sideline production and to the all-around development of farming, animal husbandry, forestry, sideline occupations and fisheries. A diversified economy should also be developed in pastoral areas.

(3) *We must continue to readjust the industrial structure and bring into full play the superiority of our resources.* We should develop in a planned way the light and textile industries with animal by-products as raw materials; exploit and utilize the resources of water and salt lakes and of nonferrous metal ores and asbestos; readjust the product mix of the machinery industries and reorganize them in line with the principle of coordination among specialized departments; rely on old factories, tap their potential and carry out their renovation and transformation; strive to raise management and technological levels; and increase the competitive power of products and their economic effects.

(4) *We must energetically develop science and education.* We should train qualified personnel for science, technology and management; continue to take measures to speed up the development of education for minority nationalities; and make great efforts to heighten the quality of education.

(5) *We should control the speed of population growth by lowering the natural population growth rate.* We should advocate family planning among minority nationalities in the pastoral areas.

77. ECONOMIC DEVELOPMENT IN SHAANXI PROVINCE
By the General Office,
Shaanxi Provincial People's Government

Geography and Resources

Location. Shaanxi Province occupies a large part of the Huanghe River basin and adjoins Shanxi, Henan, Hubei, Sichuan and Gansu provinces and the Ningxia Hui and Inner Mongolia autonomous regions. It is an important passage linking East China with the Northwest and Southwest. It has an area of more than 190,000 sq. km. and a population of 28,310,000.

Land and Climate. Shaanxi has three natural regions: the northern part falls in to the loess plateau and the climate is temporate; the central part, the Guanzhong Basin, is historically known as the "Qin Valley 800-*li* long", and with a warm-temperate climate it is a notable production area for wheat and cotton; and the southern part, in the Qin-Ba mountainous region, is in the subtropic zone and is a rice producer.

Principal Products. Shaanxi's principal agricultural products include: raw lacquer, tung oil, tea, mulberry and silkworm cocoons, fungus, gastrodia, cotton, rapeseed, walnuts, apples, dates, chestnuts and oranges. In output of raw lacquer, Shaanxi ranks first in China; in persimmons, second; in dates and apples, fifth; in tung-oil seeds, sixth; and in silkworm cocoons and chestnuts, eighth.

Minerals. The province is rich in mineral resources, both metallic and nonmetallic. Nearly 100 kinds of minerals have already been found, and deposits of 57 kinds have been verified. Metals such as iron, manganese, molybdenum, chromium, aluminium, copper, cobalt, vanadium, lead, mercury, nickel and gold are found mainly in the prefectures of Hanzhong and Shangluo. Shaanxi's deposits of molybdenum, aluminium, vanadium, mercury and nickel are among the largest in the whole country. Nonmetallic minerals include coal, phosphorus, barite, fluorite, dolomite, limestone, clay and building stones. The province's coal reserves are estimated at 200,000 to 220,000 million tons, of which about 21,270 million tons have been proven; these reserves are located mainly in northern Weinan and the northern part of the province.

Hydropower. Shaanxi's water resources include 587 rivers, the smallest of which has a drainage area of 100 sq. km. The province's potential hydropower reserves total 12,740,000 kw. At 322 selected dam sites, power-generating units producing up to 5,500,000 kwh. can be installed.

Survey of Economic Development Since 1949

Prior to Liberation, Shaanxi's economy was extremely poor. Grain output in 1949 barely reached 6,620 million catties, with a per-*mu* yield of 119.7 catties. Cotton output totalled 87,400,000 catties, with an average per-*mu* yield of only 27.8 catties. The industrial base was quite weak, with a total output value of only 277 million yuan, or 18.4% of the total output value from industry and agriculture. The annual output of coal amounted to a meagre 610,000 tons. Power-generating capacity was 130,000 kw. and the annual output of electricity was less than 30 million kwh. There were a few small, poorly equipped factories located in Xi'an and Baoji which used manual labour to turn out a dozen or so light industrial products, such as cotton yarn, matches, textiles, and some flour-processing mills and distilleries.

Agriculture. Since the founding of the People's Republic, Shaanxi's economy has made great progress despite some difficulties and setbacks. The conditions of agricultural production have improved greatly, the composition of crops and farming methods have undergone enormous changes and levels of production have risen considerably. By the end of 1980, the province had over 1,500 reservoirs and 150,000 pump wells. In the past 31 years, the increase in areas under irrigation amounted to 15,410,000 *mu,* or 3.5 times the total irrigated land just after Liberation, for a total effective irrigated area of 18,720,000 *mu.* The total power of farm machinery amounted to 6,410,000 hp., including 20,400 large and medium-sized tractors and 68,900 walking tractors. The amount of agricultural chemical fertilizers applied in 1980 totalled 296,000 tons. The total amount of electric power for rural consumption was 1,210 million kwh.

The total output value of agriculture in 1980 amounted to 3,556 million yuan, three times what it was in 1949. Grain output reached 15,140 million catties, an increase of 130% over 1949. Cotton output was 161,690,000 catties, or a net increase of 85%. Forestry, animal husbandry, sideline production, and commune- and brigade-run enterprises all registered considerable growth. Bast fibre plants, sugar-bearing crops, tobacco and industrial crops, the staple products of mountainous areas and special local products all showed big increases.

Industry. Shaanxi's industries have developed rapidly. The older coal, oil, electric power, engineering, and textile industries have grown at a good pace, while new industries, which started from scratch in 1949, have also developed quickly. Shaanxi's fuel, power, manufacturing and electronics industries play a particularly important role in the national economy.

The coal industry has established as its bases in Tongchuan, Hangcheng and other counties of northern Weinan four mines with an annual output of 15 million tons. In 1980, coal output in the province amounted to 17,920,000 tons, or 29.4 times the output in 1949. A huge power network has been set up, with Xi'an as its centre, extending to Baoji in the west, Yan'an in the north, Hanzhong in the south, and Huayin in the east; the total capacity of 1,678,000 kw. is 127.3 times the power output in 1949. In 1980, Shaanxi's output of electricity totalled 7,914 million kwh., or 264 times the output in 1949.

The engineering industry of Shaanxi is one of the most important bases in the whole country. In 1980, the output value of the engineering industry reached 3,730 million yuan, an increase of 341 times over that of 1949, and accounted for 34.8% of the province's total industrial output value. Other products of Shaanxi that occupy an important place in their respective fields of production include: high-tension transmission and transforming installations, precision machine tools, cutting tools, industrial automatic meters, heavy-duty forging equipment, metallurgical equipment, oil industry installations, coal mining equipment, textile machinery and farm machinery.

The textile and light industries have developed rapidly as the key industries in recent years. Guanzhong Prefecture, famous for its cotton, has been built up as one of the up-to-date bases for the textile industry in China, with a total of 887,000 spindles and 22,000 looms. In 1980, its total output of cotton yarn was 150,000 tons, and that of cotton cloth, 558 million metres. The textile industry in Shaanxi also produces wool yarn, printed and dyed silk, knitwear and needlework. The variety of products is great, and many of the best-quality products have made inroads into the market for textiles in dozens of countries and regions. There is also large-scale production of enamelware, watches, sewing machines, bicycles, bulbs, paper, detergent and large special-use weighing apparatus. Shaanxi's "Camel" Brand enamelware, "Yan'an" Brand watches and "Standard" Brand sewing machines are among the best-selling items on the domestic market.

Transportation. Transportation in Shaanxi has grown rapidly since the founding of the People's Republic. The railways within the province, the Longhai, Baocheng, Xiantong, Xihan, Yangan and Xiangyu, have a total track length of 1,855 km., or 4.27 times more than that in the period right after Liberation. Of this total, 830.7 km. have been electrified, accounting for 49.8% of the nation's total electrified lines. The total mileage of highways in the province has extended to 33,600 km. In recent years, 5,860 km. of highways have been built in the mountainous regions. By the end of 1980, 98% of the communes in the province had been linked by highways. The improvement of transport played an important role in the exchange of goods between the cities and rural areas, greatly promoting economic growth. Now a highway network has been formed which runs through counties and communes in all directions, with Xi'an as it centre.

With the development of the economy and transportation, trade and commerce are also flourishing in Shaanxi Province. Xi'an, the provincial capital, is one of the eight major cities of China and the commercial centre of the province. Baoji and Xianyang are now the important trade centres in the west on the Longhai Railway. In 1980, the total volume of retail sales in the province reached 4,960 million yuan — 14.7 times the figure in 1950 — of which 3,010 million yuan of goods were sold to urban consumers and 860 million to rural commune members. Foreign trade, which started on an insignificant scale, grew rapidly to a considerable magnitude. The value of commodities purchased for export in 1980 came to 514 million yuan, or 386 times the figure soon after Liberation. "Qin" pepper, textiles, raw lacquer, walnuts, sheepskins, rare medicinal herbs, and other products from Shaanxi are all welcomed in world markets.

Education and Culture. After Liberation, there was great development in education, science and culture in Shaanxi Province. By the end of 1980, there were 34 institutes of higher education — 30 more than in 1949 — enrolling 53,200 students or 23.4 times as many as in 1949. The number of college students for every 10,000 people was 18.9, ranking Shaanxi fourth in the country. The province had one TV university with

14,000 students; 79 secondary vocational schools with 45,200 students, or 10.7 times as many as in 1949; 181,000 natural science and technology workers; 3 academies of science and 143 scientific research institutes; 1,600 natural science and technology personnel; and 206 professors, 814 associate professors and 6,352 lecturers, who made up 57.9% of the teaching staffs at institutions of higher learning. In 1980, 409 achievements were registered in scientific research and technology, of which 282 were applied techniques. There were 118 cultural centres, 33 museums and memorial halls and 15 libraries housing over 4.82 million volumes.

Tourism. Shaanxi Province is one of the birthplaces of the Chinese nation. Thirteen dynasties, including the Zhou, Qin, Han, Sui and Tang, had made Shaanxi the site of their capital. It therefore is rich in cultural relics and is now one of the important places under special protection and preservation; 20 cultural sites are state-protected and 28 are sites of the revolution. The Qin Dynasty tomb figures, the ruins of ancient Banpo Village, Huaqing Pool, the Forest of Steles, the Dayan and Xiaoyan pagodas, and the Qian and Zhao tombs are all well-known to the world. Shaanxi is also famous for its scenery. The Huashan, Lishan and Taibai mountains and the Foping Preserve — one of the 10 major panda reserves under state protection — are among the most famous. Xi'an, which is being developed as one of China's six major tourist regions, attracted a total of 32,000 foreign tourists in 1980.

Review of Economic Developments in 1980

In 1980, Shaanxi Province continued to carry out the policy of readjustment, restructuring, consolidation and improvement of the national economy, and some progress was made in various areas of economic work.

Agricultural Readjustment. In agriculture, readjustment of the structure of agriculture and the distribution of production was begun in 1979. The guiding principle of agricultural production followed the principle of adapting economic measures to local conditions and of giving full play to special regional features. Accordingly, central Shaanxi will be developed into a major producer of grain, cotton and oil-bearing plants. Southern Shaanxi will develop a diversified economy based on special local products, forestry and animal husbandry and will strive to be become self-sufficient in grain. Northern Shaanxi will focus on developing forestry and animal husbandry, while trying to achieve self-sufficiency in grain production.

In 1980, the proportion of forestry, animal husbandry, sideline production and fishing in the total output value of agriculture rose to 30.5% from 25.89% in 1978. The distribution of crops began to be readjusted according to plan. The 390,000 *mu* of low-yield cotton fields not suitable for cotton-growing was allocated for different purposes to Dali, Weinan, Lintong and Juaxian counties and to Xianyang City. In Baoji, Hanzhong and Ankang prefectures, where growing conditions favour rapeseed and the local people are experienced in its cultivation, the land under cultivation was increased and the per-*mu* yield was raised, thus making the area a base for the production of rapeseed. Proper readjustment was also made for other crops and the distribution of crops was made more proportionate.

In the spring and summer of 1980, central Shaanxi and Yulin Prefecture were exceedingly dry, while in southern Shaanxi there were natural calamities such as floods, excessive rain and low temperatures. Forty-one counties were severely affected by natural calamities; the calamity-stricken areas totalled 32,700,000 *mu*, representing 46% of the land under crops. This brought about great difficulty for both agricultural production and the people's livelihood. With the support of the Party Central Committee and the State Council, the provincial party and administrative organizations at different levels sent large numbers of cadres to the calamity-stricken areas to organize the masses. Relying as much as possible on the original capital construction in agriculture, the workers brought an additional 300,000 *mu* of land under irrigation. The various policies of the Party Central Committee concerning the rural areas were warmly and earnestly propagated and carried out. Some 91% of the production brigades in the province adopted various methods of the system of job responsibility and succeeded in stimulating the peasants' enthusiasm for production. The losses caused by natural calamities were greatly lessened.

Although the output of grain and cotton in the province dropped by 16.8% and 21.1%, respectively, as compared with 1979 — a year of bumper harvests — the output of oil-bearing crops was the highest in history, amounting to 2,194,000 catties, or a net increase of 14.3% over the previous year. The afforested area amounted to 4,760,000 *mu*, over one million *mu* more than planned. The number of draught animals, pigs, sheep and goats also increased. The income of the commune- and brigade-run enterprises reached 930,000,000 yuan — 19.5% more than that of the previous year. Progress was also made in other agricultural and sideline productions as well as in the commune members' household sideline production.

Industrial Advances. In 1980, the total value of Shaanxi's industrial output amounted to 10,717 million yuan, up 2.4% from 1979. In capital construction investment, emphasis was placed on agriculture, light industry, science and education, as well as the people's livelihood. In the readjustment of industry, attention was paid to tapping potential production, to innovation and transformation, to the problems of raw materials, power, communications, transport and capital construction. As a result, the textile and light industries advanced rapidly in 1980.

The output value of light industry in 1980 was 5,189 million yuan, 14.3% higher than that of the previous year. The proportion of the output value of textile and light industries to total industrial output value increased to 48.42%, as against 43.4% in the previous year — approximating the proportion of heavy industry and restoring it nearly to the 1965 level. The quality of the main industrial products for civilian use was restored to the highest level in history. Of the textile products, 8 were honoured with state awards and 37 were acclaimed as excellent products. Nearly 300 kinds of new products were manufactured and over 8,000 styles and designs were added in the textile and light industries.

The output of industrial products for daily use increased by a big margin. Some 167,000 bicycles were produced, 4.1 times higher than in the previous year; 123,000 radio sets, 11 times higher; 40,500 TV sets, 3.5 times; 453,000 sewing machines, up 20%; 1,023,000 watches, up 25.2%; and increases in the output of chemical fibre cloth, silk products, shoes and furniture ranged from 18% to 30%. All this played an active part in keeping the market brisk, increasing state revenues and meeting the daily needs of the people.

Some experimental units were chosen where the reform of the economic system was carried out steadily and actively. In consequence, the enthusiasm of the enterprise and its working staff was aroused and production and distribution were facilitated. In 1980, 119 industrial enterprises were granted more decision-making power, accounting for 9.16% of the total number of locally administered state enterprises covered by the provincial budget, but their output value accounted for 55.55%, and their profit amounted to 82.19%. The experimental enterprises earned 3,113 million yuan, an increase of 9.36% as compared with that of the previous year; and their profits handed over to the state amounted to 469,700,00 yuan, an increase of 9.15%. In 94 experimental enterprises in the departments of commerce, food, supply and marketing, where more initiative was given to run the business, general improvement in management and administration was achieved and remarkable economic results were realized.

In 1980, 473 enterprises were merged into 51 economic organizations in accordance with the principles of economic rationalization and cooperation between specialized trades, totally regardless of the department, region, subordination and ownership to which they belong. Of the 51 enterprises, 32 belong to the textile and light industries group. Such reorganized enterprises played a very active part in promoting production, tapping full potential, improving product quality and reducing production cost.

Commerce. Experiments were also made in the administrative systems of commerce, finance, credit and capital construction. Collective and individual economy in towns were restored to some extent. In 1980, commercial service shops run by collectives in the towns and cities numbered 6,100, with 54,100 employees. Individual commercial services in towns and cities involved 10,680 households, employing 12,600 people. With the preliminary reform of the economic system, under the guidance of state planning, a combination of planning and marketing regulation was put into effect. This brought about a new situation in which a number of economic sectors began to grow, various channels were opened and several forms of purchasing and marketing began to coexist, thus making the market more brisk, the economy more prosperous and improving the production and distribution of commodities.

Through readjustment, the ratio between accumulation and consumption in the province in 1980 was improved, i.e., the accumulation ratio was reduced to 32.1% as against 36% in 1978. In the state budget's allocation of investment for capital construction, the proportion of agriculture increased by 1.39% as compared with the previous year; that of textile and light industries increased by 0.57%; and that of culture, health and education, by 1.77%; while the proportion of investment for heavy industry was reduced by 29%. Housing with a total floor space of 2,286,000 sq. m. was built in 1980, an increase of 29.6% over 1979 — the largest increase since the founding of the People's Republic. The economic structure and the composition of commodities began to develop more evenly.

Current Problems and Goals for Future Development

Although rapid progress has been made and proper proportions of the economic sectors improved in Shaanxi Province, the tasks of readjustment are still quite arduous. The chief problems may be summed up as follows:

(1) *Agriculture is still not strong enough to overcome natural disasters.* The main agricultural products produced in the province, such as grain, oil and cotton, are not as yet self-sufficient. Agriculture still remains a weak link in the whole chain of the national economy. Particularly owing to natural disasters in 1980, the crop output dropped and exerted an unfavourable influence on the people's welfare as well as on the work of readjustment.

(2) *The industrial technical level is not high and equipment capacity has not been fully tapped.* The variety of products is still limited and the management and administration of enterprises are relatively backward. Within the industrial sectors, the development of light industry lags behind that of heavy industry. In 1957, the output value of light industry made up 72% of total industrial value. In 1979 it dropped to 43.4% and in 1980 it was raised to 48.2%. Of all light industrial branches, the textile industry has a fairly good foundation, but its production level and rate of profits are lower than those in Shanghai and other municipalities and provinces. The food industry and secondary light industries are too backward to meet the needs of the people.

(3) *The output value of the machine-building industry is as high as 34.8% of the total industrial output value, and 75% of its production is essential to the country.* Owing to the readjustment of the national economy and the reduction in the scale of capital construction, some enterprises cannot obtain their full quota of machines to carry out production, leading to the overstocking of materials and parts.

(4) *Capital construction projects are not well arranged and the channels of financial resources are too numerous.* It is thus impossible to exercise unified administration and achieve an overall balance, hence the scale of capital construction cannot be effectively controlled and tends to become over-extended.

In order to develop the national economy, the policy of readjustment, restructuring, consolidation and improvement must be pursued, with readjustment as the key. Priority should be given to the development of agricultural production and workers should strive for a bumper harvest all around. Readjustment of industry should be further implemented and the textile and other light industries should be developed at a rapid pace. Management should establish a plan and an overall balance. Strict measures should be taken to curb capital construction, to increase revenues and reduce expenditures, and to achieve a balance between income and expenditure on the basis of increased production and a higher standard of living for the people.

78. ECONOMIC DEVELOPMENT IN SHANDONG PROVINCE
By the Economic Research Centre,
Shandong Provincial Planning Commission

Geography and Population

Location. A coastal province in eastern China, Shandong is located in the lower reaches of the Yellow River between 34°30′–38°15′N. and 114°50′–122°50′E. The province is made up of two parts, the peninsula and the interior. Jutting out between the Bohai Sea and the Yellow Sea, the Shandong Peninsula faces the Liaodong Peninsula to the north across the Bohai Strait. The interior borders on the four provinces of Jiangsu, Anhui, Henan and Hebei. Shandong has a total area of more than 150,000 sq. km. and a coastline of more than 3,000 km.

Climate. Shandong lies in the warm-temperate zone and its climate is influenced by monsoons. There are four distinct seasons. Summers are hot and rainy, winters are cold and dry. Annual rainfall ranges from 600 mm. to 900 mm. The frost-free period lasts 180–220 days and sunshine is plentiful.

Population and Administrative Divisions. Shandong has a population of over 72 million, averaging 477 persons per sq. km. It ranks second in the country both in absolute number and density of population. Administratively, Shandong consists of four municipalities under the direct jurisdiction of the provincial government – Jinan, Qingdao, Zibo and Zaozhuang; and nine prefectures – Yantai, Changwei, Linyi, Tai'an, Jining, Dezhou, Heze, Huimin and Liaocheng. Under the prefectures are five cities – Yantai, Weifang, Jining, Dezhou and Weihai; and 106 counties.

Minerals. Shandong's complex geological structure yields abundant mineral resources. So far, more than 90 varieties of minerals have been found or are being mined. They include coal, petroleum, natural gas, iron, gold, copper, aluminium, diamonds, graphite, gypsum, magnesite, barite and amargosite.

Agriculture and Industry. The province's major agricultural products include: grain, cotton, edible oils, tobacco, bast fibres, fruits, aquatic products and animal by-products. Major industries and industrial products include: coal, petroleum and petroleum products, electricity, rolled steel, pig iron, machine tools, motor vehicles, cement, synthetic ammonia, tractors, cotton yarn, cotton cloth, salt, cigarettes, clocks, wrist-watches and bicycles.

Survey of Economic Development Since 1949

After the founding of the people's republic in 1949, Shandong carried out land reform and the socialist transformation of agriculture, handicrafts and capitalist industry and commerce. Placing the economy on the basis of public ownership of the means of production has propelled the development of productive forces and has brought about profound economic changes throughout the province. In 1979, Shandong's total industrial and agricultural output value reached 42,150 million yuan, or 12.8 times the figure for 1949, representing an average annual increase of 8.9%. Total income was 20,680 million yuan, or eight times that in 1949.

Agriculture. Shandong has a rural population of 67.1 million and 108,980,000 mu of farmland. Construction of water conservation and farm improvement projects has proceeded on a large scale since 1949. So far the province has built 175 large and medium-sized reservoirs and more than 5,400 smaller ones. It has dredged or otherwise improved 31 big and medium-sized river courses and freed over 70% of low-lying areas from the threat of floods. It now has more than 700 irrigation zones, each benefiting at least 10,000 mu of farmland, and 423,000 pump wells. The irrigated area has expanded from 3.7 million mu in the early post-Liberation years to 66 million mu today.

In the same period, the area under forest has increased from 4.5 million mu to 20.87 million mu. Forest belts, previously nonexistent, now protect 30.5 million mu of farmland. Serious soil erosion has in the main been brought under control.

Farm mechanization has been upgraded. The province now has large numbers of farm machines, totalling 17 million hp. There are 194,000 tractors and 236,000 tractor-drawn implements. About 64.8 million mu of farmland is ploughed by tractors.

Improvement in farming conditions and the

application of advanced farming techniques have made the peasants less dependent on the vagaries of the climate for food. Shandong Province has set up 184 agricultural research institutes and a network of stations to disseminate farming techniques extending from the provincial to the prefectural, county and commune levels. This network has effectively promoted the popularization of advanced science and technology in agriculture, animal husbandry, forestry, fruit growing, fishing, water conservation and farm mechanization. For instance, four generations of fine-strain wheat and maize have been popularized. Lu Mian No. 1 cotton, a strain of high and stable yield, has been grown on an increasing scale since 1977. Early ripening and midway ripening varieties of peanuts have been popularized. Chemical fertilizers and insecticides have become important factors in increasing farm yields.

All this has increased the amount of marketable farm products and improved the structure of agriculture. In the early years of the People's Republic, crop planting accounted for 80% of Shandong's total agricultural output value, while the combined output of forestry, animal husbandry, sideline occupations and fishing accounted for 20%. The proportion of the latter grew to 28.2% in 1979, when the total output value of agriculture was 12,370 million yuan, representing an average annual increase of 4.5% over three decades. Compared with 1949, the output of grain was up 2.8 times, that of cotton and peanuts doubled, and cured tobacco, pigs, aquatic products and fruits all showed a seven-fold increase. The growth of agricultural production has prepared the foundation for all-around economic development.

Industry. Shandong's industry has developed rapidly under unified state planning. In the early days of the People's Republic, the province had only a few textile mills, food-processing factories, coal mines, machine shops and light industry plants. Starting almost from scratch, it has set up a fairly complete industrial system in the past 30 years. Now it manufactures both producer and consumer goods. Among its products are: iron and steel, petroleum, chemical fertilizers, motor vehicles, tractors, chemical fibres, woollen textiles, plastics, detergents and wrist-watches. The coal, power, chemical, building materials and electronics industries have grown remarkably. Shandong's fuel, power, major raw and semiprocessed materials and agriculture-oriented industries have attained sizeable proportions. A good foundation has been laid for its light and textile industries.

All counties in Shandong now have their own light and heavy industries. In 1979, there were more than 18,000 industrial enterprises at or above the commune level, with 20,200 million yuan worth of fixed assets and a workforce of 2,396,000. A network of industrial bases, including Jinan, Qingdao, Zibo, Zaozhuang, Yantai and Weifang, has been formed and a number of new small cities and towns have sprung up.

With improved quality and increased variety, Shandong's industrial goods are entering the world market at a fairly rapid pace. In 1950, industrial goods — some textiles and other consumer goods — accounted for only 2% of the province's exports, but the proportion shot up to 53.8% in 1979, when the province exported not only consumer goods but metals, minerals, chemicals and machines.

Shandong's total industrial output value has been rising at an average annual rate of 12.9% in the past 30 years. Industrial output value now makes up more than 70% of the province's combined industrial and agricultural output value, as against 29% in the early post-Liberation years. Industrial expansion has laid the foundations for the technical transformation of Shandong's economy and for the consolidation of the alliance between workers and peasants.

Transportation and Communications. Railway lines open to traffic have increased by 56% since 1949. Trains now reach all the prefectures and municipalities in the province with the exception of Linyi and Liaocheng prefectures. In 30 years, the total length of highways has increased 11-fold to link up the communes in rural areas. Almost all of Shandong's counties are connected by all-weather roads. Sea transportation has increased, too, due to the improvement of Qingdao and Yantai harbours and a number of smaller ports along the coast. Jinan, the provincial capital, now has air links with Beijing and Shanghai. Compared with 1949, the volume of freight has increased 41-fold and passenger traffic, 11-fold. The development of transportation has effectively promoted rural and urban economic growth, foreign trade, domestic and international economic and cultural exchanges, as well as tourism. More than 22,000 foreign tourists visited Qingdao, Jinan, Qufu, Tai'an and other places of interest in Shandong in 1979.

Culture, Education, Science and Public Health. Great progress also has been achieved in these fields. The province now has more than 95,000 full-time primary and middle schools and colleges, with a total enrollment of 14.73 million. Thus, the number of people in school represents 20.3% of the province's population, as against 4.4% in 1949. Every village has its own primary school and all the communes have middle schools.

Over 95% of school-age children are enrolled. Shandong has 38 universities and colleges, with an enrollment of 44,700. Preschool education, schools for the blind and deaf-mutes and spare-time education have also expanded.

All the counties now have hospitals and disease prevention centres, all communes have clinics and production brigades have health centres, in sharp contrast to the old days when the rural areas lacked both medicine and health facilities. The death rate has dropped to 6.7 per thousand, as against 25 per thousand before Liberation.

In the cultural field, all counties have theatrical companies, cinemas and cultural centres and all communes have film projection teams. Sports, the press, publishing, radio broadcasting and television have all developed.

In science and technology, a contingent of scientists and technicians has come into being through cooperation between specialists and the masses. In 1979, Shandong had 510 industrial, agricultural, medical and other specialized research institutes, more than 780 factory-run research centres and laboratories and 120 academic societies. There were also more than 200,000 peasant groups engaged in scientific experiments and over 11,000 workers' technical innovation groups.

Income and Livelihood. Living standards have been going up with the development of production. The problem of large-scale urban unemployment left over from old China has in the main been solved. More than 4.85 million people in the cities and towns are employed in state-owned and collective enterprises and their average annual wages have increased from 276 yuan to 631 yuan in the past 30 years. An average family now has more wage-earners but fewer dependents to support than in the past. This has brought about a general improvement in living conditions. Retail sales have been rising at an average annual rate of 8.5%. In both urban and rural areas, the people's purchasing power has more than trebled in the past three decades.

Enormous Achievements. Although Shandong's economic development has known setbacks because of interference by "Left" errors, it has scored enormous achievements. The facts show that the socialist system, which represents the common interests of the people, is able to speed up the development of productive forces.

Since the Third Plenary Session of the 11th Central Committee of the Communist Party, Shandong has reviewed its experience and lessons in economic construction in the past 30 years and has thoroughly analyzed its economic situation.

Shandong's rich material and human resources, relatively strong economic base and flourishing agriculture and industry are considered favourable conditions. Calculated on a per-capita basis, however, the area of farmland and the amount of goods produced and consumed are small, and the province's cultural, educational, scientific and medical resources are insufficiently developed. These are the unfavourable conditions. Since agriculture is a major factor in Shandong's economy and 93% of the population live in rural areas, the conditions of the peasants are decisive to the overall economic situation. In the 1980's, Shandong will proceed from these realities, take full advantage of the favourable conditions and rectify the unfavourable conditions, so as to achieve better results in its economic development.

Economic Developments in 1980

Rural policies were readjusted to give the production teams a free hand in managing their own affairs. A system of job responsibility, varying in form but each linking remuneration to output, was adopted to ensure the implementation of the principle "to each according to his work." This has stimulated the peasants' initiative. Making the best use of local conditions, they actively developed a diversified economy while ensuring grain production, and were rewarded with an all-around good harvest.

Agricultural Development. Though summer crops were affected by natural calamities, total grain output was 23.84 million tons — the second best harvest since 1949. The output of cotton shot up to 537,300 tons and that of peanuts to 1,404,300 tons — both all-time highs. Other production statistics were: cured tobacco, 157,000 tons; silkworm cocoons, 16,900 tons; bast fibres, 163,700 tons; fruits, 1,525,500 tons; pigs, 22.12 million head; and sheep and goats, 10.41 million head. With the exception of fruits and bast fibres, they all surpassed the 1979 output.

The agricultural structure improved in 1980. Cash crops, such as cotton, edible oils, tobacco and bast fibres, accounted for 26% of Shandong's total farm output in 1980, as against 14.4% in 1979. Total output of forestry, animal husbandry, sideline occupations and fishing increased by 13% over the previous year. Total agricultural output value reached 13,470 million yuan, an increase of 8.9% over 1979. The commodity rate went up and so did the peasants' income. Conditions in the rural economy were the best in many years.

Industrial Development. Industrial readjustment continued during the year. Stress was placed on accelerating the development of light industry to ensure a rapid increase of consumer goods. Output value of light industry was 16,450 million yuan, an 18.3% increase over 1979. In 1980, Shandong produced 1,902,000 radios, 92,000 television sets, 459,000 sewing machines, 1,163,000 bicycles, 1,364,000 wrist-watches and large quantities of chemical fibres, soap and thermos flasks. The increases ranged from 25% to more than 100% compared with 1979. The output of cigarettes totalled 1,728,000 boxes; cotton yarn, 233,000 tons; and cotton cloth, 1,090 million metres. Production of silk and woollen fabrics and knitwear also increased.

The energy industry was strengthened. It produced 42,905,000 tons of coal, 18,318,000 tons of crude oil and 1,420 million cu. m. of natural gas. The machine-building, chemical, metallurgical and defence industries underwent readjustment and reorganization so that they could better serve agriculture, light industry and the market. More than 370 heavy industrial enterprises whose products were not in demand switched to the production of consumer goods and electronic products to accord with market demands. The output of heavy industrial products was kept within certain limits. In 1980, the province produced 1,415,000 tons of pig iron, 901,000 tons of steel, 11,000 motor vehicles, 13,000 tractors of 20 or more hp., 7,800 machine tools and 1,445,000 tons of synthetic ammonia.

Industrial management was improved and market regulation was introduced under the guidance of state plans. Thus the enterprises geared their production to better serve market demands while fulfilling state plans. Competition and various forms of joint operation were encouraged, resulting in better quality goods and a greater variety to choose from. More than 3,000 kinds of new products and 20,000 new designs and styles were added in one year, bringing industrial production closer to meeting the needs of society. Total industrial output value was 32,290 million yuan, up 8.4% from the previous year. During the economic readjustment in 1979 and 1980, light industry grew faster than heavy industry, and in 1980 it made up 50.9% of Shandong's total industrial output value, as against 45.1% in 1978.

Commerce. Trade was brisk in both town and country, thanks to the opening of different economic sectors, new ways of management and more channels for the distribution of commodities. Total purchases of commodities reached 16,890 million yuan, while retail sales amounted to 14,350 million yuan, up 20.1% and 21%, respectively, over the previous year. The number of collectively owned shops increased by 28,000 and that of individually owned shops by 38,000. Rural fairs exceeded 3,750, including 99 in the cities, with a total turnover of 2,100 million yuan. The fairs played an important part in stimulating the exchange of goods between town and country, invigorating the rural and urban economies and providing much needed services for the convenience of the masses.

Education and Science. Education and science served economic construction in a better way. Preliminary reforms were carried out in the structure of secondary education as required by the situation in employment and the modernization programme. A number of regular middle schools in the rural areas were turned into secondary agricultural or agrotechnical schools, with special courses in agronomy, farm machinery, forestry, pomiculture, water conservation, animal husbandry, veterinary medicine and rural economic management.

In 1980, there were 280 senior secondary agricultural schools, with an enrollment of 26,500. A number of regular middle schools in the cities were turned into vocational schools, and 22 middle schools also offered 35 vocational classes to a student body of 1,900 specializing in light industrial machinery, textiles, semiconductor elements, motor vehicle maintenance, survey and cartography, fine arts and book-keeping. College enrollment increased by 6,300 and new buildings totalling 269,000 sq. m. of floor space were added to the campuses.

Scientific research institutes were readjusted and their management was improved. Encouraging results were achieved in trying out a contract system with some research projects and in giving research institutes greater power in making decisions. The number of factory-run research organizations exceeded 1,200. More than a million people took part in agricultural science experimentation. In 1980, Shandong completed 868 major research projects and popularized 84 major research results, which promoted industrial and agricultural production.

Income and Livelihood. The income of workers grew considerably on the basis of increased production. Total employment in the cities and towns increased by 252,000 in 1980. Average annual wages rose to 745 yuan per worker, an 18% increase over 1979. The annual income for workers in state-owned enterprises was 774 yuan and for those in collective enterprises, 654 yuan. In rural areas, commune members received 29% more income from the collective in 1980 than in 1979 — thanks to good harvests, reduced production costs and a lower rate of accumulation. The increased purchasing power of commune members greatly boosted the sales of higher-grade goods.

Compared with 1979, sales of TV sets and radios doubled; those of chemical fibres, cloth, bicycles, sewing machines and wrist-watches increased from 30 to 60%; and sales of household electrical appliances, furniture, clothing and leather shoes also rose. A selective survey of 380 families in six cities showed that for every 100 families, there were 151 bicycles, 74 sewing machines, 223 wrist-watches, 93 radios, 28 TV sets, 5 tape recorders and 9 electric fans. Rural and urban bank deposits at the end of 1980 were up 42.2% from the year before. Housing conditions continued to improve with the completion in 1980 of 3,848,000 sq. m. of new housing in the cities and in industrial and mining districts. About 80,000 workers' families moved into new homes. In the rural areas, about 10-15% of the peasant families built new houses.

Shandong's economic development in 1980 proved the correctness of the policy of readjusting, restructuring, consolidating and improving the national economy.

Current Problems in Economic Development

A major problem is that the economic results are not yet satisfactory. The reason lies with the "Left" influence which persisted for many years. In the macro-economy, it led to a failure to handle correctly the relations between accumulation and consumption, between production and livelihood, and between economic construction and the development of science and culture, and by a one-sided pursuit of a high accumulation rate and high-speed growth; in the micro-economy, it led to enormous waste and low productivity in the course of production, construction and distribution. Too much money was put aside for accumulation, thus slowing down the improvement of people's living standards.

Another problem is the gap between different regions in economic development. Yantai and Changwei prefectures on the Shandong Peninsula have more highly developed industry and agriculture, while the northwestern part of Shandong, where nearly one-third of the province's population live, has for years lagged behind. There is a big gap between the advanced and the backward units. For instance, the highest yield of ginned cotton is 125 kg. per *mu*, or nearly treble the provincial average. For peanuts, the provincial average is 150 kg. per *mu*, while the figure for Zhaoyuan County is 234.5 kg. — and for the best production team, over 500 kg. This implies a great potential to be tapped.

A third problem is the dispersal of authority in industrial administration. The industrial enterprises are controlled by different regions and departments without proper stratified organization, specialization and coordination. Insufficient attention is paid to the role of the major cities.

Under the guidance of unified state planning and according to the principle of readjustment to achieve rational distribution and overall balance, Shandong Province will strive to achieve better economic results and to make greater contributions to China's socialist modernization by making full use of its rich human and material resources and its existing economic base.

79. ECONOMIC DEVELOPMENT IN SHANGHAI
By He Gaosheng
Municipal General Office, Shanghai Economic Research Centre

Geography and Population

Shanghai is one of the largest industrial cities in China. It covers an area of over 6,100 sq. km. and has a population of more than 11.4 million (of which over 5.8 million live in the 141-sq.-km. city centre). There are over 7,100 factories, 20,000 stores and 205 rural people's communes. Workers and staff engaged in the various economic sectors number more than 4.4 million–in addition to a suburban rural labour force of over 2.7 million. In 1980, Shanghai's industrial output value reached 62.6 million yuan, its seaport turnover exceeded 84 million tons and its local revenue was over 17.2 million yuan, comprising about 13%, 39% and 16%, respectively, of the national total.

Under the leadership of the Central Committee of the Communist Party of China and the State Council and with the support of the people, the city has taken advantage of its economic and technical superiority to contribute to the socialist modernization of the country.

Survey of Economic Development Since 1949

Shanghai was liberated in May 1949. Old Shanghai was a semi-colonial and semi-feudal city, with a lopsided economic structure, undeveloped industrial production and low technical capabilities. Total industrial output value in 1949 was less than half of the present-day monthly average. At that time, the strongest sectors of the economy were the light and textile industries, accounting for 86.4% of the total industrial output value, while only 13.6% could be attributed to heavy industry. The manufacture of metals and chemicals was particularly insignificant. The city relied heavily on imports of primary equipment, raw materials and many industrial products needed for daily use, because it could not produce them itself. Now, after 30 years of socialist transformation and construction, with a system of socialist public ownership predominating, Shanghai has become a socialist industrial city with high industrial and agricultural production levels, advanced science and technology and developed domestic and foreign trade.

Industrial Development. Industrial production has expanded significantly. The city's total output value in 1979 rose 24 times as compared with 1949, representing an annual growth rate of 11.2%. Shanghai has renovated or expanded many key factories and developed a number of new industries. The original value of industrial fixed assets is nearly seven times as much as that of the early post-Liberation period. The variety of products has increased, with high and medium grade products occupying an increasingly larger proportion of the total. The city's production of chemical fibres, bicycles, sewing machines, watches and TV sets all have a relatively significant share in the national total.

Agricultural Development. The suburban counties have a non-staple food base, catering to the urban population. Shanghai is nearly self-sufficient in its supply of cooking oils and vegetables. And the city supplies 50% to 60% of the pigs, poultry, eggs and fish that it needs. Per-unit yields of grain, cotton and oil-bearing seeds rank among the highest in the country.

Science, Technology and Education. Science, technology and education have expanded rapidly. In 1979 there were 246 independent scientific research institutes, employing more than 60,000, as compared with only 12 research institutes and about 200 researchers in the early post-Liberation days. The number of scientists and technicians increased in the same period from 30,000 to 240,000, comprising 5.7% of the city's total workforce. There are over 10,000 schools of all levels with an enrollment of more than 2.4 million. Of these schools, 48 are universities and colleges with 70,000 undergraduates.

Other Developments. Foreign trade has grown substantially: business relations have been established with over 150 countries and regions, and the total value of exports has grown at an annual rate of 13.1%. The amount of daily necessity industrial products that the city ships to other parts of the country has risen at an annual rate of 6.9%, and the city's retail sales have increased annually at about 5.8%. Public utilities have witnessed rapid growth too, and the look of the city has changed enormously. Before Liberation, due to the disintegration of the imperialist concessions, Shanghai's public utilities were in a state of divided and decentralized management, which resulted in an extremely irrational distribution, with few public facilities in the working people's quarters, rendering their living conditions unacceptable. Now the utilities have long been under unified management, and the supply of power, water and gas as well as the public transportation system have all improved substantially. For instance, there were over 610,000 gas-supplied households in 1979 as contrasted with 17,000 shortly after Liberation. Since Liberation, housing with a total floor space of over 15 million sq. m. has been constructed in the city proper, constituting more than one-third of the city's total housing space.

In keeping pace with the transformation of the city proper, more than ten industrial areas and satellite towns have emerged in the suburbs, and a number of key factories and important scientific research institutes have been moved to or built in these areas. The employment rate has grown steadily every year. Approximately 60% of the urban population are wage earners. The number of family members supported by each employee has decreased from an average of 2.97 (including himself) in the early post-Liberation period to 1.67 in 1979. As production expands, workers' wages and peasants' income have risen gradually, so that the standard of living of both the urban and rural population has improved considerably.

In the past 30 years, the citizens of Shanghai have manifested pioneering revolutionary spirit through arduous efforts and have achieved great success. Were it not for the mistakes we made and for the sabotage of Lin Biao and the Gang of Four, Shanghai would undoubtedly have fared even better. For a long time, however, under the guidance of "Left" ideas, there existed a tendency to go after things beyond our capabilities and to be overanxious to make achievements in all fields of work. For example, there were attempts to set up an all-inclusive industrial complex, plans for enormous increases and quick results and indifference to the need for improving the working conditions of the existing enterprises. Industrial construction far outshadowed construction of urban dwellings, public utilities and other necessary facilities occupied a great deal of land, thus worsening the city's growing pains and aggravating the lack of harmony between economic growth and urban construction. The long-accumulating disproportions in the city's economy have reduced the city's role as an industrial base. The rational readjustment of its economic structure by learning from past experience and proceeding from actual conditions in both Shanghai and China has thus become an important task for Shanghai's future economic and social development.

Review of Economic Developments in 1980

In 1980, all of the sectors of Shanghai's population vigorously implemented the guidelines, principles and policies formulated since the Third Plenary Session of the 11th Party Central Committee. Freeing their minds to see the truth of the matter, they rectified the "Left" mistakes, consolidated and developed political stability and unity, systematically readjusted the economy and thus furthered Shanghai's development. Shanghai's economy advanced steadily in its course of readjustment.

Industrial Development. In 1980, by rigorously increasing the production of daily-needed consumer goods in the light, textile, handicraft and civilian electronic industries, and by gearing the metallurgical, chemical and machine-building industries to the needs of the market and to serve the technical transformation of the light and textile industries and old factories, the city's industrial output value rose by another 6.1% on the basis of an average annual growth rate of 9.4% between 1977 and 1979. Light industry rose by 11.9%, far exceeding the 0.3% increase registered by heavy industry. Its share in the city's total industrial output value advanced to 52.6% from 49.9% in the previous year. The textile industry strove hard to develop high and middle-grade products and its output value grew by 11% as compared with the previous year. Output of the "big three" in light industry (bicycles, sewing machines and watches and clocks) and the "big three" in the electronics industry (TV sets, radios and tape recorders) grew substantially. A total of 2,300 new products and nearly 30,000 new varieties, styles and specifications were developed in 1980. A great number of products improved in quality. In the inter-industry competitions of 596 products sponsored by various ministries of the State Council, Shanghai won 270 first prizes, about 45.3% of the total. A resource-saving drive achieved good results too. In particular, the technical transformation which centered around energy saving helped to realize the goal of increasing production without incurring additional consumption of energy. In consequence, the drive for increasing production and saving resources brought about in 1980 a 6.4% increase in local budgeted revenue as compared with the previous year.

Agricultural Development. In 1980, the weather in the Shanghai area was quite abnormal, bringing about serious waterlogging and resulting in a 20% decrease in the output of grain, cotton, oil-bearing seeds and vegetables. Owing to the implementation of the principle of readjustment and consolidation, and with the stress on planning well the raising of animals, the market supply of pigs reached 3.47 million, surpassing the planned target by 5.3%. The purchasing targets for eggs and poultry were 1.3% and 15% higher, respectively, than the previous year. There were 6.6% more cows in stock than in the previous year. The catch of fish and seafood was 35% higher than planned. Commune-run industries and sideline production grew steadily. Total agricultural output value, including that of commune-run industries and sideline production, stood at 2.47 million yuan, 5.3% higher than 1979.

Finance and Commerce. In 1980, shipments of daily needed industrial products to other parts of China totalled 10,600 million yuan, an increment of 5.8% over the previous year. The outflow volume of most commodities increased to varying degrees. Owing to the expanded production of light industrial and textile products and the inflow of agricultural and sideline products from other areas, the city's retail sales reached 8,700 million yuan, some 1,190 million or 15.7% higher than the previous year. Accompanying the rise of the average level of consumption, the consumption structure has undergone certain changes. The retail sale of consumer goods recorded a substantial growth: that of clothing rose by 22.9%, of articles for daily use by 19.5% and of edible products by 12.3% (of which about 6% was due to price hikes). Within the categories of clothing and articles for daily use, consumers tended more and more to purchase medium and high-grade products: sales of watches, bicycles, woollen garments, silks and satins grew by about 20%: woollen fabrics increased by more than 30%; TV sets and cameras went up by more than 50%; desk electric fans were up by 120%; production of tape recorders, washing machines and refrigerators was also on the rise; and orders for metal decorations, cosmetics, high-grade confectioneries, winter nutritional items and holiday feasts grew in some cases by nearly 100%.

As for exports, the export value of Shanghai Port in 1980 exceeded the previous year's figure by 16.1%, an unprecedented record due to the vigorous implementation of the import-for-export policy, the improvement of management, the exploitation of multiple trade channels, the employment of internationally prevailing means of transaction and the enforcement of the measure of retaining a portion of foreign exchange. As regards export commodities, heavy industrial products rose by 48.2% as compared with the previous year, light industrial and textile products by 11.5% and agricultural and sideline products by 8.3%. Shanghai's foreign trade departments and manufacturers all worked to expand export supplies. Hence, the purchases of export commodities rose by 16.8% over 1979, of which those procured in the city rose by 25.7%.

Tourism has developed rapidly. In 1980, more than 310,000 foreigners, tourists, merchants, overseas Chinese and compatriots from Hong Kong and Macao visited Shanghai, a rise of 46% over 1979. While the economic and cultural flow between urban and rural areas and between the city and foreign countries increased and tourism expanded, the turnover of Shanghai Port as well as the volume of freight moved by rail, water and land all overfulfilled their targets, exceeding, for the most part, the previous year's levels.

Capital Construction and Investment. Since the implementation of the principle of readjustment in Shanghai, 339 construction projects and 324 technical undertakings have been cancelled, suspended or postponed, thereby reducing investments by a total of more than 2,000 million yuan. While the scope of capital construction was curtailed, further efforts were made to readjust the orientation of investment, with emphasis laid on the construction of residential housing, environmental protection facilities and public utilities. In 1980, 397 projects were wholly or partially completed. The planned target for housing was 2.5 million sq. m. of floor space. But by adhering to the principle of integrating state-financed construction with locally financed construction, thus bringing into play individual initiative, a total of some 3.04 million sq. m. of floor space were completed, 40.9% more than in the previous year. In the same year, work continued on 252 waste control projects, of which 146 were completed. These projects have begun to show beneficial effects, one after another. In the meantime, by introducing such economic measures as charging industries for the use of water and fining them for discharge of polluted water, water pollution has been reduced to some extent. The precipitating density of floating dust in the air has also declined as compared with the previous year. As regards public utilities, an additional daily water supply capacity of 270,000 tons and gas supply capacity of 80,000 cu. m. were added. Progress also occurred in the construction and improvement of roads, bridges and parking lots.

Science, Technology, Culture and Education. In 1980, by further integrating science and technology with economic construction, Shanghai produced more than 600 significant technological achievements, improving agricultural production, developing new products in the light and textile industries, exploring new basic materials and saving energy. Many of these achievements have already been put into effective use. For instance, the ultra-red drying catalyser made by certain research units, when applied in the manufacturing process of paint finish, coating-fluids and carbon-inks in a dozen factories, showed good results in shortening drying time by 20% to 50%, saving electricity by 20% to 40% and increasing productivity.

The quality of education at all levels has improved. Primary and middle schools have restored the 12-year schooling system. As regards higher education, some branch universities and specialized institutes were readjusted, and colleges enrolling day students who could cover their own expenses were opened on an experimental basis. In 1980, Shanghai's universities and colleges enrolled over 20,000 freshmen, secondary technical schools nearly 10,000 students, professional schools over 2,500 and technical schools 29,000. In addition, the urban and rural spare-time schools enrolled 823,000 students. Much progress was also made in the fields of culture, physical training and public health. Family planning reported new successes.

Income and Livelihood. In 1980, nearly 2 million employees received wage increases and 230,000 job-seeking youths were employed. Wage increases together with enlarged employment and the introduction of bonuses raised the city's total payroll by 16.3% over 1979. The average monthly pay for workers in publicly owned units reached 76 yuan, or 12.3% more than the previous year. Suburban commune members' annual income derived from the collective maintained the previous year's level of 278 yuan. Although prices rose a little, the real living standards of most urban and rural labourers improved in varying degrees. According to a survey of 500 families, holdings of durable consumer goods increased significantly. At the end of 1980, every 100 families had 99 radios, 250 watches, 79 sewing machines, 64 bicycles, 58 TV sets and 44 electric desk fans. For many suburban commune members, there were five major improvements: namely, new housing was completed, more furniture and more high-quality clothing was purchased, more surplus food grain was accumulated, and more savings were deposited. By the end of the year, total savings deposits for both urban and rural residents exceeded 3,000 million yuan, a rise of 22.8% over the previous year.

In 1980, Shanghai's economy continued to improve due to a thorough implementation of the policy of readjustment, restructuring, consolidation and improvement. With economic readjustment in progress, initial experiments were made to restructure the economic system, to consolidate enterprises and to improve the technical and managerial levels. By the end of 1980, 1,284 locally administered, state-owned industrial enterprises, 53.7% of the total, had been given greater autonomy. The metallurgical and textile industrial bureaus and the bicycle, sewing machine and 26 other industrial corporations also experimented with various degrees of managerial autonomy. The Light Industrial Machinery Corporation, the Shanghai Diesel Engine Plant and the Pangpu Machinery Factory began to keep independent business accounts, to pay taxes rather than hand over profits to the state and to assume responsibility for their own profits and losses. The combination of economic rights, economic responsibilities, economic results and economic interests has enhanced the vitality of these enterprises and increased their economic gains. The growth rates of their production and profits in 1980 were 7.1% and 7.2% higher, respectively, than the previous year and well above the city's overall average. Enterprises under the auspices of the construction, supplies, commercial and foreign trade bureaus and state farms also increased their autonomy by retaining part of their profits or by holding each unit responsible for profits and losses.

Under the guidance of national planning, all economic departments vigorously strove to enliven the economy. By the end of 1980, there were more than 500 industrial sales shops and business and service stores, over 60 farmers' markets and a number of capital goods exchange centres and agricultural and sideline product trade warehouses. 1980 also saw a great variety of exhibitions, fairs and contract negotiating meetings. Various business practices, such as factory-shop links, industry-commerce united sales, compensation trade, trust purchases and sales, negotiated purchases and sales and the planned control and supply of commodities on demand were also introduced, activating the markets and boosting production.

Furthermore, some departments and enterprises, in order to increase production, found it to be to their advantage to coordinate their efforts with one another. They broke many of the barriers between the various regional and departmental systems of ownership, and established, on an experimental basis, 300 economic "combinations" of various types, such as parent factories, joint operation of state and collective enterprises, united industrial and agricultural operations, operations transcending provincial and municipal barriers, combined industrial and trade businesses, combined industrial and commercial businesses and joint ventures with Chinese and foreign investment. The successful combination of the reorganization of enterprises with the restructuring of the economic management system yielded excellent results.

Current Problems and Goals for Future Development

In 1980, Shanghai's economy fared quite well.

However, the economic readjustment was and still is in a preliminary stage. Disproportions in the economy still remain, and there will, no doubt, be problems and difficulties on the road to readjustment. The industrial structure is still irrational; basic facilities such as power and gas supply, dockyards and railway stations still cannot keep pace with the development of industry; the trade and service networks are far from adequate; and some enterprises operate under capacity while others find it hard to cope with their production targets. Problems also remain regarding employment, housing, public utilities, disposal of industrial wastes and industrial distribution. These problems are to be settled in a planned and orderly manner in future economic readjustment.

For the year of 1981, following the policy defined by the Party Central Committee and the State Council of "carrying economic readjustment further and achieving political stability" and pursuing the general goals of the national readjustment plan, Shanghai must continue to readjust the investment orientation in capital construction within the limits set down in the national plan, guarantee the construction of residential units and corresponding public utility facilities and persist in improving the relationship between "bone" and "flesh." Shanghai must go even further to restructure its industry, to enforce the reorganization and technical transformation of enterprises in order to satisfy the demands of the market and to vigorously improve the production of consumer goods in the light, textile, handicraft and civilian electronics industries. Heavy industry must be geared to serve light industry, to facilitate the technical transformation of old enterprises, to energetically manufacture marketable commodities and to expand exports. A city-wide drive for readjustment in order to increase economic gains, promote production, practice economy, expand revenues and economize on expenditures is necessary if we are to fulfill the state quotas. The city must also give full play to the role of market regulation while relying in principle on the implementation of national plans to boost production and distribution. Efforts should be made to stabilize prices and to contribute to the realization of a balance in national finances, credits, materials and foreign exchange, as well as to the stabilization of the economy. All of these will prepare us for a sustained, coordinated and steady development of the national economy in the future.

The disproportions in Shanghai's economy have come into being over many years, and it will take years of strenuous efforts to rationalize the economic structure. What kind of city will Shanghai develop into in the long run? This is a strategic question calling for in-depth study and careful planning. Shanghai, with its limited area, huge population and few natural resources, is a city of processing industries, dependent on support from the rest of the country. It has a better manufacturing foundation, higher technological capabilities and established and extensive foreign economic relations. In the years to come, we must base our development on Shanghai's actual specific conditions, comply with the demands of the national construction plan and make the most of the merits, avoid the faults and bring into full play the advantages enjoyed by the existing enterprises. It is necessary to combine reorganization of enterprises, technical innovation and system restructuring, to combine technical progress, exploitation of human resources and research facilities and economic development and to combine the expansion of foreign trade, technical transformation and aid to the interior.

Shanghai will proceed along the road to realizing better economic results with less human, natural and financial resources, and push ahead the economic and social construction in a well-organized manner. In the upcoming years, great efforts must be made to improve considerably the irrational organization of the different sectors, the industrial structure, the types of products produced and the organization of enterprises in order to achieve progress in such areas as employment, housing construction, city communications, urban environmental protection, etc. It is imperative to prevent the current urban "growing pains" from getting worse and to make necessary preparations for an effective cure, so as to build Shanghai into an industrially advanced, scientifically well-developed, economically prosperous, administratively well-coordinated, clean and civilized city. In this way we can make greater contributions to the Four Modernizations of our country.

80. ECONOMIC DEVELOPMENT IN SHANXI PROVINCE
By the Shanxi Provincial Planning Commission

Geography and Population

Location. One of the places of origin of the Chinese nation, Shanxi Province has a very long history, excellent cultural legacies and glorious revolutionary traditions. It lies to the west of the Taihang Mountains and in the middle valley of the Yellow River. On the east, it borders on Hebei Province, with the Taihang Mountains as the boundary; on the west, it borders on Shaanxi Province, with the Yellow River as a line of boundary; on the north, it has the Inner Mongolia Autonomous Region as its neighbour across the Great Wall; and on the south, it borders on Henan Province across the Maling Mountains and the Yellow River.

Geographical Characteristics. The total area of Shanxi Province is more than 150,000 sq. km., and 67.5% of the land is mountainous. The width of the province is 290 km. from east to west and 550 km. from north to south.

The topography of the province is relatively high, with most of its districts more than 1,000 metres above sea level. It has the Taihang Mountains in the east, the Luliang Mountains in the west, the Hengshan and Wutai mountains in the north and the Zhongtiao Mountains in the south.

The Fenhe River traverses the province from north to south; the Hutuo River encircles the Wutai Mountains; the Sanggan River washes the Datong Basin; and the Qinhe and Zhanghe rivers flow through the southeastern districts. There are many basins among the mountains, including the Datong, Xinding, Taiyuan, Changzhi, Linfen and Yuncheng.

Climate. The climate of the province is continental. Temperature ranges are wide during the year and between day and night. Rainfall and snow are concentrated in a few months of the year and in some parts of the province. The average annual temperature is 4°C-14°C. The lowest temperature on record is −44.8°C (on Mount Wutai), and the highest ever recorded was 42.7°C. The average annual rainfall is 400-600 mm. The frost-free period is about 200 days in the south of the province and 90-120 days in the north.

Population. By the end of 1980, Shanxi had a population of 24.76 million, including the Han, Hui, Mongolian and Manchu nationalities. Of these, 3.37 million people lived in the cities and 21.39 million in the countryside.

Survey of Economic Development Since 1949

Before Liberation, the people of Shanxi were subjected to savage oppression and exploitation by imperialism, feudalism and bureaucrat capitalism. After the 1911 Revolution, Kuomintang warlord Yan Xishan controlled the region for a long period. The Japanese imperialists' aggression seriously destroyed Shanxi's economy and hampered its growth. The province's total industrial and agricultural output value in 1949 was merely 1,340 million yuan, of which agriculture contributed 1,140 million yuan and industry 190 million yuan. Output of principal products included grain, 5,190 million catties; cotton, 40 million catties; oil-bearing crops, 70 million catties; steel, 12,000 tons; coal, 2.67 million tons; cement, 14,000 tons; and electricity, 40 million kwh.

After Liberation in 1949, the Chinese Communist Party and the People's Government led the country in a profound socialist transformation and large-scale economic construction. Great changes took place in the economic situation, the system of exploitation was destroyed, major developments took place in the industrial and agricultural fields, and a heavy industrial base centred on the coal industry was formed. Since the Third Plenary Session of the 11th Central Committee of the Chinese Communist Party, we have executed the policy of readjustment, restructuring, consolidation and improvement, and our national economy has embarked on a road of rational and healthy development.

Agriculture. In 1980 there was 58.822 million *mu* of cultivated land in the province. Through capital construction projects on the farmland, the course of the main rivers in the province were regulated and some 900 reservoirs were built, each with a storage capacity of one million cu. m. of water. The total capacity of these reservoirs reached 4,200 million cu. m. Other projects included the digging of 103,000 pump wells and the establishment of 19,000 power-driven drainage and irrigation stations, which can irrigate 16.727 million *mu* of farmland.

Some 1,804 communes in the province now

can utilize electric power. The total volume of consumption of electricity in 1980 was 1,360 million kwh. Total power of the farm machinery was 7.375 million hp., of which irrigation machinery accounted for 2.475 million hp. There were 33,000 large and medium-sized tractors and 31,000 walking tractors, 6,655 trucks and 303,000 tons of chemical fertilizer for agriculture.

The development of agricultural production was promoted by the improvement of conditions. Though drought hit 66 counties and 8 prefectures and cities in 1980, we still achieved a good harvest of grain crops and a large increase in cash crops by executing the Party Central Committee's two documents on speeding up the development of agriculture, by enhancing the responsibility system and by reorganizing planting plans according to soil conditions.

Total grain output in 1980 was 13,710 million catties, the fourth bumper harvest in this province. Cotton production totalled 160 million catties, an increase of 7.7% over the preceding year. The output of oil-bearing crops was 267 million catties, up 61.5%; bast fibres, 11.6 million catties, up 7%; and beets, 230 million catties, up 19.7%. Production of tobacco was 2 million catties, and beef and mutton, 350 million catties. The total value of agricultural output amounted to 3,870 million yuan, 3.3 times over that in 1952.

Industry. In 1980, there were 9,553 industrial enterprises in the province, and the total value of industrial output was 11,000 million yuan — 1.9% more than in the preceding year, or 6.6 times over 1952. The ratio of industrial production to the total value of industrial and agricultural output rose to 74% from 24.7% in 1952.

The output of main industrial products compared with 1952 was as follows: coal, 120 million tons, up 12.2 times; cast iron, 1.714 million tons, up 8.6 times; steel, 1.494 million tons, up 16.2 times; rolled steel, 975,000 tons, up 10.5 times; coke, 1.609 million tons, up 3.8 times; electricity, 12,000 million kwh., up 78.4 times; cement, 2.879 million tons, up 29.7 times; gypsum, 604,000 tons, up 13.2 times; caustic soda, 43,000 tons, up 86 times; mirabilite, 325,000 tons, up 15.4 times; metal-cutting machine tools, 1,345, up 11 times, cotton yarn, 84,000 tons, up 10.2 times; printed cloth, 184 million metres, up 34.9 times; knitting wool, 775 tons, up 28.9 times; machine-made paper, 115,000 tons, up 35.9 times; and cigarettes, 186,000 boxes, up 5.8 times.

The manufacture of many other important productions has been recently developed. These include electrolytic copper, electrolytic aluminium, sulphuric acid, sodium carbonate, pesticides, synthetic ammonia, chemical fertilizer, plastics, pharmaceuticals, synthetic rubber, mining machinery, metallurgical machinery, cranes, industrial boilers, tractors, chemical fibres, detergent, thermos bottles, electric bulbs, etc.

Of the total value of industrial output, the value of heavy industrial products was 7,560 million yuan, which accounted for 68.7%; the value of light industrial products was 3,440 million yuan, or 31.1%. Because the output of light industrial products could not meet the needs of the market, about 40% of these products were shipped in from other provinces. In the course of the readjustment of the national economy in 1980, we enhanced the development of light industry. The capital invested in the light and textile industries, as well as for renewal and transformation of equipment, amounted to 160 million yuan — an increase of 58 million, or 112.3% over the previous year, the greatest investment since Liberation. The value of light industrial products increased by 13.3% over 1979.

The growth rate of light industry exceeded that of heavy industry by a substantial margin. The output of many important commodities greatly increased over that of 1979: radios, 150%; bicycles, 100%; TV sets, 94%; sewing machines, 71%; leather shoes, 40%; knitting wool, 27.4%; woollen pieces goods, 14.7%; beverages, 28%; sugar, 17.5%; and furniture, 15.1%.

Minerals and Mining. Shanxi Province is rich in mineral resources, including iron, copper, lead, zinc, molybdenum, cobalt, gold, coal, phosphorus, pyrite, mirabilite, gypsum, graphite, bauxite, feldspar, mica, glass sand and refractory clay. Its coal reserves are especially large. The province is an ideal energy source for the modernization of our country.

The coal industry affords the greatest opportunity for development. The output of mineral coal in the province represents one-sixth of the country's total. Profits from the coal industry amounted to more than 50% of profits from all industrial production and communications services in the province. About one-third of the technicians and workers were employed in the industry.

The prospects for further developing the coal industry are bright because the coal reserves are very rich. All types of coal can be found in the province; the quality is superior; the underground deposits are very shallow; and the layer is thick and continuous, so that investment in exploitation is economical and can achieve early results.

At the national coal industrial meeting held in Benxi in July 1980, it was decided to fully exploit coal resources in Shanxi Province before the end of this century. *People's Daily* published an editorial urging that the province be turned into an energy resource base, and the provincial people's government submitted a report to this effect to the State Council.

Although investment in heavy industry has been cut drastically, the coal industry in 1981 will still gain a larger investment than in 1980. Simultaneously, in order to encourage enthusiasm in all departments for developing the coal industry, many new management methods are being used. In recent years, the average annual increase in coal output has been more than 10 million tons. In 1980, the output of coal totalled 120 million tons, half of which came from the mines managed by the local authorities, communes and brigades.

Transport, Posts and Telecommunications. Railways open to traffic in the province totalled 2,129 kilometres at the end of 1980. The main trunks were the Jing-Yuan and Shi-Tai lines linking Beijing and Taiyuan, the Jing-Bao line through Datong and the Tong-Pu and Tai-Jiao lines through the province from north to south. New railways under construction are the Han-Chang and Tai-Gu-Lan lines. The total capacity of railway freight was about 110 million tons. The number of travellers in 1980 was 25.22 million, 4.4 times that of 1952.

Highways open to traffic totalled 27,000 kilometres, 11.6 times the number in 1952. Of these, 8,509 kilometres are serviceable in all weather conditions, 21 times over 1952. The volume of goods transported was 70.04 million tons, and the turnover of goods was 1,570 million ton-kilometres. The number of highway travellers was 33.42 million.

Air services were available from Taiyuan to Beijing, Tianjin, Xi'an, Yan'an, Lanzhou, Xining, Chendu and Chongqing. There were also flight facilities within the province between Taiyuan and Changzhi, and Taiyuan and Datong.

Postal routes in the province covered 142,000 kilometres.

Finance. In 1980, financial revenue was greater than expenditure in the province. Total revenue amounted to 2,094 million yuan, an increase of 3.43% over that of the previous year. Expenditure was 1,656 million yuan, 81% of the budget and 5.5% less than the previous year.

Of the 1980 revenue, 44.6% was derived from enterprise profits, 48.5% from industrial and commercial taxes, 3% from the agricultural tax and 7% from other sources. Expenditures comprised 18.5% for capital construction, 15% for agriculture, 23.9% for culture, education, science and technology, 11.6% for administration and 31% for other purposes.

The systems of finance and financial affairs were reformed preliminarily in 1980. From the beginning of the year, a new sytem was instituted to "apportion revenue and expenditure at different levels and hold each responsible for profits and losses." As part of a trial programme to enlarge the decision-making power in selected places, the factories and enterprises further executed a number of measures, such as retention of profit according to certain proportions, responsibility for the budget and other financial affairs, independent accounting, assumption of sole responsibility for profits and losses and fixing the amount of revenue and expenditure. These measures encouraged the activities of the administrative departments and units at all levels, enabling them to achieve more effective results in increasing production and realizing economies.

Of the 116 factories and enterprises that tried to enlarge the decision-making power, the total output value and the profits of 30 units increased 9.6% and 30.2%, respectively, over the previous year. Many factories and enterprises were carrying out the policy of combining the regulation through planning with market regulation, and were handling sales themselves.

Investment in capital construction in the province totalled 1,729 million yuan, which, in addition to the fund allocated from the province, included the national fund, internal loans, foreign capital and funds raised by administrative departments, prefectures, cities, counties and factories and enterprises. The distribution of funds was as follows: productive investment, 69% of the total, or 9.2% less than in 1979; and unproductive investment, 31%, or 9.2% more than in 1979. Investment in housing increased by 58.7% over the preceding year and represented 15.3% of total investment, an all-time high.

Commercial Activity. Owing to the policy of combining regulation through planning with market regulation in economic work, as well as the opening of more outlets and improved distribution, sales in the town and country markets were brisk. The supply of commercial products was better, and the purchasing, selling and storing of products all increased considerably in 1980.

The total value of goods purchased in the province in 1980 was 6,100 million yuan, a 5.3% increase over the previous year. Of this, net purchases within the province accounted for 62.8%, and those from the other provinces 37.2%. The total volume of retail sales was 5,090 million yuan, 9.1% more than 1979. Of the total, sales of consumer goods increased by 15.1%, the largest increase in several years. The total value of goods in stock of state-run commerce was 3,350 million yuan, an increase of 4.2% over 1979.

Markets in the town and country fairs were busy in 1980. The number of country fairs rose to 597, or 130 more than in 1979. The volume of business reached 260 million yuan, 48.4% more than in the previous year.

The value of exports was 600 million yuan, an increase of 51.4% over 1979. The sum of purchases in the province was 470 million yuan, up 41.4% over 1979. Of this, purchases of industrial and mineral products increased by 51%, and purchases of agricultural and sideline products and local and special products rose 13.2%.

In 1980, the general level of retail prices in the province increased 3.5% over the previous year (5.7% in the cities and towns, and 1.4% in the rural areas). The real prices of state-run commerce and the negotiated prices went up 3.3%. The government adopted certain measures to stabilize prices in November 1980, and market prices were kept basically under control.

Education, Health and Science. The province has 171 scientific research institutes, with 4,400 research workers; 16 colleges and universities, with 33,000 students, including 218 post-graduates; and 2,422 professors, associate professors and lecturers. There is also a TV college attended by more than 8,000 students. There are 67 spare-time colleges for workers and cadres, enrolling 11,000 students; and 90 secondary technical schools, with 46,000 students. The 9,895 middle schools enrolled 1.79 million students, with 100,000 teachers, and the 38,000 primary schools had 3.84 million pupils and 148,000 teachers.

In 1980, the province had 702 hospitals of all kinds, 69,000 beds and 105,000 doctors and nurses. The number of "barefoot" doctors in the countryside was 58,000.

Many achievements were made in 1980 in the scientific and technological fields; 194 research projects won government prizes. They were being used and applied.

Tourism. Prospects for the gorwth of tourism in Shanxi Province are good. "Ding-Village Man," which was dug up in Xiangfen County, a site of the ancient cultural remains of the middle period of the Stone Age, has proved that human beings began to live on this land more than 100,000 years ago. It is said that Pingyang was the capital of Yao, Puban was the capital of Shun and Anyi was the capital of Yu — all of which are in Shanxi Province. Of the 541 scenic spots and historical sites in the province, 14 are designated as important cultural antiquities protected by the government. They include the Yungang Grottoes in Datong; Shanhua Temple, Huayan Temple, Sakyamuni Tower in Yinxian County; Mount Wutai, Nanchan Temple, Foguang Temple, Jin Temple in Taiyuan; Yonle Palace in Ruicheng County; Guangsheng Temple in Hongtong County; Ding Village site in Xiangfen County; and the site of ancient "Jin" in Huoma. Some of these places are not yet open to the public. In 1980, 17,000 tourists visited the province, 88% more than in the preceding year.

Employment and Income. The life of the people improved as a result of the development of production. By the end of 1980, the number of workers and staff was 2,899,000. In 1979-80, 440,000 more people were employed, of whom 365,000 were educated youth.

In 1980, average yearly income for the workers and staff in units owned by the whole people [i.e., "state" ownership – Ed.] was 795 yuan, an increase of 36.2% over 1956. In the units under collective ownership the figure was 581 yuan. Average income from the collective for each peasant was 49 yuan in 1956, 63 yuan in 1976 and 82 yuan in 1980. In 1976, the peasants had 190 million yuan in savings deposits; by 1980 the amount had grown to 510 million yuan.

Problems. Through 31 years of socialist construction since the founding of the People's Republic of China, the economy in Shanxi Province has developed greatly. But it suffered much during the 10 years of chaos at the hands of the Gang of Four. Since the smashing of the Gang, under the guidance of the correct line of the Party Central Committee, our provincial economic situation has been much improved. However, the serious disproportions among different branches of the national economy cannot be changed in a short period of time, and we still face many difficulties.

Agriculture, for example, cannot meet the ever-increasing demands of the people. A large portion of commodities must still be purchased from other provinces. The scale of capital construction is overextended. The economic results of some enterprises have yet to be improved. In addition, there are still problems concerning housing, medical and health work, culture and education, public utilities, environmental protection, etc. These will be resolved gradually in the course of economic readjustment.

81. ECONOMIC DEVELOPMENT IN SICHUAN PROVINCE
By the Institute of Economics,
Academy of Social Sciences, Sichuan Province
and the Institute of Economics,
Sichuan Provincial Planning Commission

Geography and Population

Situated in Southwest China, Sichuan Province has a population of more than 98 million and an area of 570,000 sq. km. There are 14 nationalities in the province.

Natural Resources. With a mild climate, plentiful rainfall, fertile soil, rich natural resources and abundant agricultural products, the province, especially the western region, is world-renowned as "the land of abundance." The nearly 100 million *mu* of cultivated land, 110 million *mu* of forested land, large areas of grassland and plentiful water supplies provide good conditions for the overall development of farming, forestry, animal husbandry, sideline occupations and fisheries. More than 70 types of minerals are found in the province, and there are relatively large deposits of titanium, vanadium, nickel, halite, iron, mica and asbestos. Thus, Sichuan has the natural resources for substantial industrial development. The province is rich in water resources and deposits of coal and natural gas, which afford the necessary energy requirements for economic development.

Survey of Economic Development Since 1949

Before Liberation, the province was very backward economically because of the reactionary rule of the Kuomintang. Since Liberation, millions of industrious people have engaged in large-scale economic reconstruction with their own hands under the leadership of the Chinese Communist Party. Although these hard-working people have gone through many reversals, they have achieved tremendous progress and brought about profound changes in the province.

Agriculture. In the past, agriculture in the province consisted mainly of subsistence farming, and productivity was rather low. In 1949, total agricultural output value was only 3,620 million yuan; grain output, 29,890 million catties; cotton, 30.7 million catties; oilseeds, 472 million catties; sugarcane and sugar beets, 1,138 million catties; and pigs, 10.19 million head.

Over the past 30 years, agricultural production has increased greatly. By 1979, total agricultural output value had reached 13,205 million yuan, an increase of 156%; grain output, 64,020 million catties, a 114% increase; cotton output, 222.5 million catties, a remarkable 625% increase; oilseeds output, 130.45 million catties, a 176% increase; sugarcane and sugar beets output, 4,249 million catties, a 273% increase; and pigs, 50.92 million head, an increase of 400%. Now, miraculously, this province can feed 10% of China's population with only one-fifteenth of the total arable land of the country.

After 30 years of reconstruction, the conditions for agricultural production in the province improved significantly. In the western region, for example, the irrigated area before Liberation was reduced from 3 million *mu* to only 2 million *mu* because the famous Dujiangyan irrigation system had long been out of repair. After Liberation, the party and the government organized the people in this area to rebuild the system on a large scale, to intensify planning and management and to make rational use of water. In this way, the ancient weir has been brought back to life.

The irrigated areas have been expanded to more than 11 million *mu* and the grain output in this area has risen from only 400 catties per *mu* before Liberation to over 1,000 catties. With water conservation projects in other regions completed by 1979, the actual irrigated land in the province had expanded to about 44.58 million *mu*, about 45% of the province's farmland.

Power consumption in the countryside is 1,280 million kwh. The average consumption per *mu* is about 12.88 kwh. The consumption of fertilizer is 1,095,000 tons, with the average consumption per *mu* about 22 catties.

The allocation of agricultural production has been gradually established. In addition to the 23 marketable grain bases that already have been determined, the province has preliminarily formed a number of cash crop bases, which are comparatively large in area and output. They include the cotton base covering Jianyang, Renshou, Nanbu and 14 other counties; the oil-bearing crop base covering Guanghan, Shifang, Xindu and 22 other counties; the sugarcane and sugar beet base covering Neijiang, Zizhong, Fushun and 21 other counties; the ramie base covering Dazhu, Daxian, Quxian and 5 other counties; and the tobacco base covering Yibin, Leshan, and Neijiang prefectures. The formation of these bases provides a better opportunity for the development of light and textile industries in the province.

Industry. The industrial foundation in Sichuan Province before Liberation was very weak. In 1949, total industrial output value was merely 731 million yuan; steel output was 9,000 tons; coal, 2,010,000 tons; natural gas, 11 million cu. m.; electricity, 147 million kwh.; cotton yarn, 6,630,000 bales; and cloth, 99,720,000 m.

Sichuan's industry has developed tremendously during the past 30 years. In 1979, total industrial output value of the province amounted to 24,617 million yuan, nearly 33 times that of 1949. In 1979, steel output was up to 2,929,000 tons, an increase of 325 times; coal, 38,380,000 tons, up 19 times; natural gas, 6,468 million cu. m., up 588 times; electricity, 15,639 million kwh., up 106 times; cotton yarn, 111,400 tons, up 9.4 times; and cloth, 566,770,000 m., an increase of 5.7 times.

Currently, Sichuan's industry is of a considerable size, and its status in the province's economy has changed greatly. By 1979, the portion of the industrial output value in the province's total agricultural and industrial output value had increased from 16.8% in 1949 to 65.1%. At the end of 1979, the province had more than 6,000 state-owned enterprises and more than 37,000 enterprises under collective ownership. It has preliminarily established industrial bases centred around Chongqing, Chengdu, Zigong and Dukou, each with its own features. The bases have played an important role in the development of the country's industry.

Transportation. In earlier times, transportation to and within Sichuan Province was difficult. "Tortuous paths in Sichuan Province were very difficult to walk on, more difficult than going to Heaven." This saying by the famous ancient poet Li Bai gives an idea of travel conditions in the province at the time. At the beginning of this century, local gentry with capitalist ideas proposed to build a railroad from Chengdu to Chongqing and tried to finance it by levying taxes on farmland. After several attempts, however, they were unable to succeed because of the obstacles set by the imperialists and the feudal powers.

In 1949, immediately after Liberation, the construction of this railroad was begun under the leadership of the party and the government. In 1952, the railway for which the people of Sichuan had yearned for 40 years was realized. Soon after that, rail arteries and feeder lines were also constructed from Baoji to Chengdu, from Sichuan to Guizhou, from Chengdu to Kunming and from Xingfan to Chongqing. Now, the railways open to traffic total 2,639 km.

In 1949, there were only 4,846 km. of highways in the province. By 1979, the province had 59,775 km. of highways open to traffic, up 12.3 times. Air transport is also expanding in all directions. At present, a communications and transport network of railways, highways and waterways centred on Chengdu and Chongqing is virtually completed and the "tortuous paths in Sichuan" no longer exist. All these improvements have laid a foundation for the steady development of Sichuan's economy for the future.

Reconstruction of the Economy in 1980

In 1980, economic reconstruction in Sichuan Province was marching on victoriously with the implementation of the policy of readjustment, restructuring, consolidation and improvement of the national economy. After initial adjustments, the problem of a serious imbalance in the province's economy began to change, and a more rational economic structure has begun to develop. Since Liberation, the preliminary reform of the province's economic management system has brought a new life to the economy, and the province is now a scene of prosperity.

Changes in Agriculture and Industry. In agriculture, the party and the government carried out correct policies for the rural areas and handled affairs according to objective economic and natural laws. Systems of responsibility in production in various forms were instituted. All this fired the peasants to greater enthusiasm. Farming, forestry, animal husbandry, sideline occupations and fisheries began to develop in line with local conditions, as a result of readjustments made in the existing agricultural structure.

In 1980, the province again reaped a good harvest on the basis of large increases in production in the previous three years. Total grain output was about 65,280 million catties, a 2% increase over the previous year. Oil seeds output was up 10.2%; silkworm cocoons, up 23.5%; the number of pigs purchased, up 14.3%; and oranges, up 77.4%. Although there was some decrease in cotton, sugarcane and tobacco output as compared with 1979, agricultural production still kept rising at a regular rate. Total agricultural output value amounted to 13,860 million yuan, a 5% increase over 1979. In industry, the implementation of the principle of economic readjustment somewhat changed the proportion between light and heavy industry, as well as their internal structures. The proportion of light industry in the total industrial output value reached 45.7%, up from 41.5% in 1979. Faster-growing products in light industry were durable goods and high-grade consumer goods. For example, the production of TV sets increased 2.35 times, radios 3.73 times, sewing machines 69.64%, bicycles 15.4 times and wrist-watches 73%. In light industry, the proportion of output value for those products using agricultural and domestic products as raw materials decreased to 76.6% from 78% in 1979. In heavy industry, products meeting the needs of consumers and serving the light industrial market also increased.

Management Reforms. The experimental reform of the economic management system that started in the last quarter of 1978 continued to make progress in 1980. The number of the province's local industrial enterprises involved in the trial enlargement of decision-making power grew from 84 in 1979 to 417. Their output value accounted for 70% of the province's total local industrial output value, and their profits made up about 80% of the total. With the placing of responsibility in local hands, economic relations among the state, the enterprises and the workers have been preliminarily readjusted, and the interests of these three sectors have been combined. Thus, the enterprises' and the workers' socialist enthusiasm as masters of their own destiny has been mobilized to the full.

The extension of power in enterprises and the readjustment of markets carried out under the guidance of planning have given enterprises an internal impetus while placing external economic pressure on them. In this way, enterprises are being pushed to increase the variety of styles and designs, enhance the quality of their products, produce according to demands, improve management, intensify productivity, do a better job of economic accounting, reduce costs, make every effort to improve their services, create a better image, try by every means to serve end-users and customers, actively do a better job in tapping potentialities, and gradually realize technical innnovation and self-development. Planning, materials, commerce, banking, financing, capital construction and other aspects of the managerial system also have undergone reform under the impetus of the enterprises' extension of power. All these factors have played a positive role in the development of the whole economy.

In 1980, the industrial output value obtained by these experimental enterprises increased by 9.7% over the previous year; profits rose by 7.9%. The growth rate was generally larger than that of the other units. Five enterprises tried out the practice of "independent accounting, paying taxes instead of turning over profits to the state, and assuming sole responsibility for their own profits and losses." The total output value they achieved was 42.7% more than in the year before, their profits increased by 80.7%, and the tax on industry and commerce, income tax and tax on fixed assets that they paid the state increased by 49.1%.

Taking the province as a whole, although there were difficulties such as insufficient energy supply, insufficient work in machinery industry, insuffiient supply of certain raw materials, price increases on some raw materials, and price decreases on many manufactured goods, industrial production still kept rising. The total industrial output value of the province showed a 6.78% increase over 1979. Moreover, the quality of industrial products also improved markedly. In 1980, 109 products in the province gained the distinction of high-quality products, and 15 of them were awarded a gold or silver medal by the state. The province also trial-manufactured and developed 2,077 new products and new varieties.

New Investment. After the readjustment, the province changed the direction of capital construction investment, increasing the proportion of investment in areas not directly related to production. In 1979, of the total investment completed in the province's capital construction, the ratio of investment in productive construction to investment in areas not directly related to production was 2.3:1; in 1980, the ratio was 1.7:1. The increase of investment in areas not directly related to production was mainly reflected by the proportion of investment in housing construction, which rose to 25.4% in 1980 from 16.4% in 1979. In 1980, floor space of new housing completed was 6,010,000 sq. m., a one-third increase over 1979, and the largest increase since Liberation. As for investment in productive construction, the proportion of light and textile industries rose from 9.9% in 1979 to 10.9%.

Commercial Gains. Economic readjustment and system reform promoted production and brought prosperity to the market. The number of commercial enterprises involved in extended decision-making power in the province rose from 40 in 1979 to 238 in 1980. The commercial enterprises under both collective and individual ownership also developed rapidly. Their growth rate of retail sales in 1980 was higher than the 8.6% increase of the state-owned commercial enterprises. Collective commercial enterprises up were up

57.3%, and individual commercial enterprises were up 128.9%. Thus, the monopoly of the state-operated commercial enterprises was broken.

On the basis of increased supply of goods and increased purchasing power, the retail sales of commodities in cities and rural areas of the province grew by 20.1% over 1979. The increase amounted to 11.1% if the factor of price hikes was excluded. The commercial department had overall expansion in purchasing, marketing, and transferring and stocking of goods. Total purchases for 1980 showed a 12.9% increase over 1979, of which the purchases of industrial goods rose by 12% and those of agricultural and sideline produce increased by 14.2%. In order to keep pace with the purchasing power that was growing rapidly both in cities and rural areas, the province transferred and transported a large volume of commodities from other provinces. This increase accounted for a 30.7% rise over 1979. The amount of stocking by the end of the year was 10.4% more than in 1979. Because of the obvious improvement in people's lives, there were sizeable increases in the sale of high-grade durables and other consumer goods. For instance, the sale of polyester blended cloth increased by 75.8%; silks and satins, 66%; woollen piece goods, 66.9%; and consumer goods such as radios, TV sets, bicycles, sewing machines and watches registered another increase of 75.8% on top of the 43.5% increase in 1979.

Progress in Other Areas. The province made further developments in science, culture, education and public health, and the people's living standards improved. In 1980, there were 46 universities and colleges in the province, 4 more than one year before. And the number of students in school increased by 14.2% over 1979, or 8.2% more than in 1960 — the previous peak.

The life of the overwhelming majority of peasants improved markedly as a result of continued development in farming and sideline occupations and the increase of purchase prices. According to a survey of 2,181 peasant families, the average net income per capita in 1980 was 20.4% more than in 1979, and the income from enterprises run by communes or brigades was 8.4% higher. Workers in industrial and mining enterprises also gained increased wages because of the expansion of employment, readjustment of some workers' wages and wage categories, and distribution of bonuses and subsidies for nonstaple foods.

The total amount of workers' annual wages in enterprises owned by the whole people was 4,310 million yuan, an increase of 720 million yuan over 1979. The workers' annual wage in enterprises under collective ownership in cities and towns was 950 million yuan, about 170 million yuan more than the year before. The average annual wage of a worker was 743 yuan, a 16.3% increase over 1979. The actual increase was 6.3% after deducting the rise in the cost of living.

Remaining Problems. Economic development in Sichuan Province has been enormous, but there are still many problems, two of which have a great bearing on the whole economy. The first concerns the economic structure. The huge industrial and agricultural potentialities have not been expoited to the full because of the serious imbalance among the various departments of the national economy. Therefore, readjustment must be carried out further in order to rationalize the economy gradually.

The other problem involves the economic management system. Despite initial reforms, the old system still remains intact and poses a main obstacle to economic development. Thus, readjustment and reform must be closely linked. Reform that fosters readjustment must be actively carried out, and changes should be promoted through reform. At present, millions of people in Sichuan Province, under the leadership of the party and the government, are summing up their experience and lessons, eliminating the influence of "Left" mistakes, striving to handle affairs strictly according to natural and economic laws, overcoming all difficulties, trying to achieve greater victories in the year to come, and enabling the economy of Sichuan to develop in a healthy manner.

Note: Output value for 1949 is calculated at the constant price of 1952. Output value for 1979 is calculated at the constant price of 1970.

82. ECONOMIC DEVELOPMENT IN TIANJIN
By the Institute of Economics, Tianjin Academy of Social Sciences

Population and Administrative Divisions. Tianjin is one of China's largest cities and the municipality is a famous industrial and commercial centre. At present, it has a population of 7.51 million and an area of 11,305 square kilometres. Administratively, the municipality consists of nine urban districts, four suburban districts and five suburban counties. The Tianjin New Port is the biggest in North China.

Communications and Transportation. Situated on the eastern edge of the North China plain and facing the Bohai Sea, the city is the gateway to the sea for China's capital, Beijing. Its land and water transportation is highly developed. For overseas shipping, the New Port handles shipping with many foreign countries. For inland navigation, it connects with the Ziya, Yongding and Daqing Rivers and the Grand Canal at the confluence of the Haihe River. Economically, Tianjin is closely linked with the vast region of North China. The Tianjin-Pukou Railway runs south to provinces in Southeast China and the Beijin-Harbin Railway goes north through Shanhaiguan to provinces in Northeast China. The city has a network of highways extending in all directions and linking the broad hinterland provinces. Tianjin Airport will be able to receive large jet airliners and cargo planes after expansion. At present, CAAC airliners fly from Tianjin to all the major cities in the country.

Natural Resources. Tianjin is comparatively rich in natural resources such as salt, oil and natural gas. The famous Changlu Salt Field has an annual output of 4.5 million tons. With over 96% sodium chloride content, this good-quality salt provides an ideal raw material for the chemical industry. For oil, in addition to the Dagang Oil Field, which has been developed since the mid-1960's, joint exploration of offshore oil deposits in Bohai Bay with France and Japan is well under way.

As it is only about 120 kilometres away from the nation's capital, Beijing, Tianjin therefore has several advantages for developing its economy, urban construction, science and technology and its tourist industry by receiving help from the capital.

History. Tianjin has a long history. In 1419, the Ming Dynasty made Beijing the imperial capital, and the following year Tianjin became a garrison town for Beijing. After that, the city's handicraft industry and commerce began to develop. During the Ming and Qing dynasties, to encourage water transport of grain to the imperial capital, native and special products were allowed into the city free of tax. Thus, Tianjin became at the same time a junction for water transport and a distributing centre for goods, which in turn enabled the city to flourish. In 1860, Tianjin was made a trading port under the so-called Treaty of Beijing, and imperialist powers immediately rushed in one after another to make use of the rich natural resources in and around Tianjin and to take advantage of its cheap labour force. Those activities gave a spur to the development of Tianjin's trade, finance and processing industries. Factories and banks were set up; ports, railways and highways were constructed; and the city moved further towards a capitalist commodity economy.

During World War I (1914-1918), when the imperialist powers were deadlocked in fighting against one another, Tianjin was able to develop its industry and commerce rapidly. Such trades and industries as textiles, salt, alkalies, flour, matches and edible oil, together with their corresponding machine-manufacturing and repairing industries, also developed, and gradually Tianjin became one of North China's most important industrial bases and a centre for domestic and foreign trade.

However, during the Kuomintang period, imperialism, feudalism and bureaucrat capitalism monopolized most of the city's large enterprises and seriously hindered the development of industry and commerce. According to statistics, the city, with an urban population of nearly 1.8 million in 1948, had an industrial output value totalling 500 million yuan, of which 61% was owned by foreign firms and bureaucrat capitalist enterprises, which practically controlled all the railways, ports, navigation, telecommunications, banks, foreign trade and customs. At that time, Tianjin's financing and foreign trade ranked second in the country after Shanghai, and Tianjin was the country's second largest city in economic importance.

Nevertheless, Tianjin was a lop-sided industrial and commercial city. Of the total industrial output value, the textile industry accounted for 64.1% and the food industry for 13.2%, while heavy industry accounted for only 10%. The engineering industry could only make repairs and supply replacements. All this shows that Tianjin was a colonial and semi-colonial city.

Survey of Economic Development Since 1949

After Liberation in 1949, Tianjin, under the leadership of the Communist Party, confiscated bureaucrat capital, abolished imperialist privileges and carried out land reform, thus completing the new democratic revolution. Ever since then, the city has concentrated on socialist transformation and socialist construction, and great changes have taken place. In spite of twists and turns, the city has made tremendous achievements in developing its economy. The main achievements are as follows:

Industry. Since Liberation, great progress has been made in developing the city's industry, which is of primary importance to the national economy. In 1980, the city's industrial output value totalled 19,400 million yuan, which was 30 times the value in 1949. There are now 4,071 industrial enterprises with 1.3 million workers and staff members. Their fixed assets total 10,000 million yuan.

Tianjin's industry has changed from a lopsided one before Liberation to a comprehensive one today. In heavy industry, such new branches as power, metallurgy, chemicals, oil, electronics and engineering have been established. In light industry, an all-around development has been realized by gradually changing the irrationally high proportion of the textile and food industries. The proportion of those branches of light industry using agricultural and sideline products as main raw materials was reduced from 88.2% in 1949 to 59.9% in 1978. The proportion of those branches of light industry with industrial products as main raw materials went up from 11.8% to 40.1%.

Tianjin's industry has these features:

(1) Industry is characterized by its comprehensiveness, with a large number of closely packed small and medium-sized enterprises and collective cooperatives. Of the nation's 164 branches of industry, Tianjin shares 153. Its small and medium-sized enterprises compose 99% of the city's total of 4,071 enterprises and account for 76% of the total output value, while the collective cooperatives make up 71% of the city's enterprises and 16.7% of total output value.

(2) The city has a number of "backbone" trades and fast-selling products. There are 41 backbone trades, each with an annual output value of 200 million yuan. They combine to make up 77% of the city's industrial output value and hold a considerable position in the country. There are a great number of fast-selling products, 54 kinds of which are each valued at more than 50 million yuan. These products are well received both at home and abroad — for example, cotton textiles, woollen articles, carpets, bicycles, watches, garments, tableware and metal products.

(3) There is a strong industrial technical force of high professional competence in Tianjin: 320,000 veteran workers and about 10,000 scientific and technical personnel in the research institutions and offices of various industrial bureaus. A number of scientific accomplishments have been made. The machine-building sector now has such heavy forging equipment as a 6,000-ton hydraulic presses and 5-ton pneumatic hammers. High-speed centrifugal spindles have replaced plane spindles throughout the textile industry, automatic looms have taken over from hand looms, and such new techniques as air-jet looms, arrow-shaft looms and yarn-weaving have already been partially adopted.

(4) The industrial structure of Tianjin is based on the processing of light industrial products. In the early post-Liberation years, light industry made up 88.5% of the city's total industry, but in recent years the heavy and light industries are by and large equally proportioned. In heavy industry itself, the processing industry accounts for 77% of total output value.

The growth of industry has changed the lopsidedness of Tianjin's economy, which is playing an increasingly important role in socialist construction. The share of industrial tax in the city's taxes increased from 47% in 1952 to 78.6% in 1978. The industrial accumulations of 1978 accounted for 8.12% of the city's total financial income. Over the past 30 years, the industry of Tianjin has contributed more than 52,700 million yuan in profit and taxes to the state, or 6.8 times as much as the total investment in capital construction during the same period. Industry also has submitted 39,100 million yuan in central finance to the state. From 1953 to 1978, it sent to all parts of the country industrial products worth 64,700 million yuan. In addition, it has supplied 13 provinces and autonomous regions with its technical forces, technology and equipment.

Trade and Commerce. The ports of Tanggu and Xingong (the New Port) underwent large-scale repairs and reconstruction after Liberation, and in 1979 the two ports owned 27 docks and berths, including 12 10,000-ton berths with an annual handling capacity of 12,770,000 tons, or 41 times that in pre-Liberation days. The size of the ports and their handling capacity rank third and fifth, respectively, in the country. Since the crushing of the Gang of Four, the city has made rapid progress in its foreign trade and now has trade and economic relations with more than 150 countries and regions. In 1979, the ports of Tianjin handled U.S.$1,220 million worth of exports and ranked fourth in the country. If the exports from Beijing and Hebei province via Tianjin were included, the total worth of exports would be over U.S.$2,000 million. The city's total purchasing volume of exports for 1979 reached 1,530 million yuan, 11 times that of 1953, and ranked sixth in the country. The ports of Tianjin have a promising future, with railroads connecting with highways and sea and river transportation closely linked. The ports are advantageously situated, with a big city and a vast area of hinterland at the rear. If their advantages are tapped to the full, this will further promote Tianjin's economy.

Before Liberation, Tianjin was a gathering and distributing centre for goods from all over northern China. In 1953, Tianjin handled 30,000 million yuan's worth of commodities, or 11.3% of the total volume of sales for the country. There were at that time 689 import and export trade companies. Later, the commerce of Tianjin developed somewhat, but its position was weakened due to the imperialist blockade and other factors. In 1979, there were 313,000 commercial workers in Tianjin including those in the departments of foreign trade and supplies, or nearly four times as many as in 1949.

The city's commercial facilities are relatively comprehensive, with 11 first-grade commercial stations, 14 import and export branch corporations and 47 governmental supply and sales offices stationed in Tianjin. The total purchasing and sales volume of goods for 1978 came to 63,400 million yuan, with 43.6% devoted to the city itself and the remaining 56.4% exported to other places in China and abroad. In 1979, Tianjin transferred 5,400 million yuan's worth of commodities to Northern China, which amounted to 19% of the total volume of goods received from outside. Tianjin has a sound base for both foreign trade and commerce. The city's economy will make further development, once domestic and foreign trade, industry and commerce are combined to promote a socialist commodity economy.

Agriculture. The total area of the cultivated land in Tianjin is now 7 million *mu*. According to 1979 statistics, total agricultural output value reached 13,500 million yuan, 9.1 times more than that in 1949. Its total grain output amounted to 27,700 million catties, six times more than that in 1949. Farming, forestry, animal husbandry and fishery contributed 600 million yuan, making up 45% of total agricultural output value, while sideline occupations provided 750 million yuan, covering 55% of the total — thus forming an agricultural economic structure based on half agriculture and half industry. The agricultural mechanization of Tianjin is high, with over 70% of ploughing, harrowing and transportation done by machine. The average annual income peasants get from the collective is 145 yuan per head — 74% higher than the national average of 83.4 yuan per head.

Tianjin's agriculture has the following features:

1. Since the land is low-lying and much of it is subject to floods, the soil is salinated and output is relatively low. However, years of experience have proved to the peasants that rice-growing, reed-planting and fish-raising yield a high output, thus turning the disadvantage into an advantage.

2. As the suburban counties adjoin a big city, they enjoy the advantage of close relations with industry and commerce, since farming provides the city with agricultural products and native produce while industry supplies farming equipment and a technical force in return.

3. There has been a tradition of exporting agricultural products and native produce. Tianjin's red beans, rice, oil-bearing crops, marten furs and rabbit skins are well received abroad and therefore are big foreign exchange earners. In addition, the advantage of having agricultural products close to ports is important in achieving a flexible agricultural economy.

Agriculture must allow for local conditions and ensure an all-around development so as to further diversify the economy in line with national policies and scientifc developments.

Science and Technology. The scientific and technological personnel of Tianjin have high professional competence. In 1979, the city had such 120,000 such personnel and 184 scientific research institutions, including the Tianjin Academy of Sciences and the Tianjin Academy of Social Sciences. There are approximately 12,000 people engaged in science and research work, among whom 10,000 people or more in 140 research units are devoted to work related to industry. More than 300,000 workers are of the fourth technical grade or higher. There are 18 unvesities and colleges in Tianjin.

Tianjin has been fairly quick at adopting new science and technology and is actively developing its own scientific and technological force. Over the past 30 years, Tianjin has accomplished 2,043 important scientific and technological achievements, among which 349 items were credited at the National Science Conference. To name just a few, industrial items include a mobile offshore drilling rig, a 500-ton floating crane and an 11,000-watt water turbo generator. Agricultural items include the Red Flag-16 rice strain, which is capable of resisting Xanthomonas Oryzae. Thanks to the improvement of science and technology, the quality of many industrial products is up to advanced domestic standards.

Current Economic Problems

Years of implementing a policy of emphasizing capital construction at the expense of production and pursuing high accumulation while ignoring low efficiency have led to serious disportions in the economy. Two years of readjustment have brought some improvements but have not solved the problem radically. The main problems are:

1. *There is a discoordinated industrial structure and an imbalance between industrial production and social demand.* The balance between light industry and heavy industry has been upset. Over the past 30 years, while heavy industry has grown too quickly, the light and textile industries have developed at a snail's pace, thus failing to give full rein to the latter. Furthermore, heavy industry has not been clearly oriented because there is too large a proportion of self-service. Statistics show that heavy industry in 1978, compared with 1957, increased 8 times, as against only 2.9 times for light industry. While 71.1% of total heavy industrial products were produced for use by heavy industry itself, only 29% were produced for agriculture and textile and light industries. The processing industry has developed too fast, with supplies of raw materials lagging far behind — chemical raw materials in particular. As a result, not only has the development of heavy industry been adversely affected, but also that of other national economic departments. The mining industry is comparatively weak in exploration. Consequently, the technical force has not been fully tapped in some processing trades. And it is commonplace in all trades that products do not meet the market demand. More striking is that the machine-building industry is operating well under capacity, the overstocking of products is serious and the waste is appalling.

The machine-building industry has yet to change from mainly serving heavy industry and capital construction to contributing to agriculture, light industry, exports and the improvement of old enterprises.

2. *Undesirable economic effects remain a serious problem for the economy.* Prevailing in many enterprises is the fact that they pursue output value only and ignore market demands. As a result, production and sales are dislocated and the overstocking of products is serious, thus affecting the rapid development of Tianjin's industry. Poor management and the failure to replace old equipment and improve production methods have caused many enterprises to remain in a backward state, resulting in high consumption, low quality and poor performance of their products. As far as capital construction is concerned, neglect of preparatory work, failure to observe construction procedures and indifference to economic effects have brought about such grave results as prolonged cyclical periods, high cost, low efficiency, great consumption and poor performance. This is the consequence of implementing the erroneous "Left" policy of emphasizing capital construction at the expense of production and of pursuing high accumulation while ignoring low efficiency.

3. *The serious disproportion between, so to speak, the "bone" and "flesh" in urban construction leaves much to be desired.* Over the past 31 years the total investment in the capital construction of Tianjin has amounted to approximately 14,900 million yuan, among which investment in production projects makes up 80%, while that in non-production projects accounts for only 20%. The proportion of the latter experienced a gradual decrease in the last 20 years from 40% in the First Five-Year Plan period to 23% in the Second Five-Year Plan period; and the "cultural revolution" caused a further decrease to 13%. As a result, improvement in this arrrea has come to a standstill and leaves much to be desired as far as the housing situation and urban facilities are concerned. To make things worse, the violent earthquake of 1976 brought great destruction to the city and caused a more tense housing situation, heavily loaded traffic, serious pollution, a water shortage and a lack of shopping centres. All these problems cry out for solution.

Review of Tianjin's Economy in 1980

Ever since the Third Plenary Session of the 11th Party Central Committee, the city's participation in the national economy has shown improvement. On every front, advances were made in the readjustment of the national economy during 1980.

1. *Changes in the ratio of light and heavy industries.* The proportion of investment in light industry rose from 35.4% of the total investment in 1978 to 49.5% in 1979 and 55.1% in 1980. The industrial output value of Tianjin in 1980 totalled 19,399 million yuan, of which 10,316 million yuan was accounted for by light industry, an increase of 19.2% over 1979, while heavy industrial output value amounted to 9,083 million yuan, a rise of only 2.6%. The speed of development of light industry greatly surpassed that of heavy industry. The ratio between the two underwent a change from 49.4: 50.6 in 1979 to 53.2: 46.8 in 1980. A change also occurred in product mix. For example, bicycles, watches, woollen piece goods and dyestuffs developed not only in scope but increased in the quality of high- and middle-grade goods. Heavy industry, which used to serve itself and capital construction, began to turn to serving agriculture and light industry.

Production of the Iron Ox Type-55 tractor increased in output from 6,020 in 1978 to about 9,000 in 1980, showing an output capacity of 10,000. In the steel industry, the proportion of steel, wire and welded tubes or pipes required by light industry rose from 50.7% to 59.9%. The not easily saleable medium-gauge plates decreased by a wide margin.

There was a rapid development in the production of export commodities. The output value of direct exports in 1980 was double that of 1978.

2. *Changes in the ratio of foreign trade and domestic trade volume.* In 1980 the commercial departments prospered in purchases and sales. The market was brisk and supplies of commodities grew. The purchase value for the domestic trade totalled 6,070 million yuan, a 6% increase over 1979. Tianjin's purchasing value for foreign trade increased from 1,100 million yuan in 1978 to 2,122 million yuan in 1980. It had almost doubled within two years.

The commodities purchased for export effected a structural change. Grain, edible oil, foodstuffs, and other agricultural and sideline products rose from 8.2% to 9.4%. Heavy industrial products such as minerals and metals, chemical products and machinery increased from 20% to 25.2%. The proportion of general light industrial products dropped from 71.8% to 65.4%. The above figures show that over 90% of Tianjin's exports were industrial products. This is essentially different from pre-Liberation Tianjin, which exported mainly agricultural and sideline products, and indicates the improved level of development of the national economy in Tianjin.

3. *Changes in the agricultural structure.* After the Third Plenary Session of the 11th Party Central Committee, Tianjin implemented the decision for the acceleration of agricultural development to bring the initiative of the peasants into full play. As a result, the situation in the rural areas of Tianjin has been prosperous for the past two years. There was a bumper harvest in agriculture in 1979: grain yield topped 2,770 million catties — a record high for Tianjin. In spite of the fact that 1980 was a year of serious drought in Tianjin, its grain yield was still near the 1979 level. Output of cash crops increased by a big margin. An improvement in the internal agricultural structure also occurred. There was a reversal in the declining tendency in the ratio of forestry and animal husbandry, which began to move upwards. In these two years the local financial departments and district banks gave substantial support to agriculture and the amount of investment and loans increased each year — all of which helped to promote Tianjin's agriculture.

The public revenue of Tianjin was valued at 4,094 million yuan in 1980, overfulfilling the yearly plan by 107% and surpassing that of 1979 by 10.8%. Expenditures came to 1,467 million yuan, which was 420 million yuan under the budget figure and 3.6% less compared with 1979. Cash deposits in banks exceeded outgoing withdrawals and thus the withdrawal of currency from circulation in 1980 amounted to 88 million yuan, an increase of 55 million yuan over the previous year.

4. *Readjustment of the ratio between the "bone" and the "flesh."* In order to coordinate the relationship between the "bone" and the "flesh" and to speed up the reconstruction of disaster-ridden areas, Tianjin reduced capital construction investment and suspended 74 projects that were under construction (amounting to over 500 million yuan). The nonproductive investment rose from 17.9% in 1978 to 39.3% in 1980. During these two years new residential housing space totalled 4.4 million square metres. The floor space of new housing construction equalled the total housing area that had been completed from 1971 to 1978. The investment in education, culture and public health also showed an increase, rising from 1.7% of the total investment in 1978 to 3.9% in 1980. These two years saw the addition of 40,000 seats in middle and primary schools and of 1,330 beds in hospital wards.

5. *Improvements in economic results.* The quality of industrial products improved. Of the 419 products under the charge of Tianjin's muni-

cipal bureaus, 97.9% either reached or outstripped the quality criteria of the 1979 level. In the nationwide appraisal of the quality of different products held in November 1980, 283 kinds of products came in first, second and third or won the title of "famous product" or "quality product," accounting for 55.2% of the total number of products entered in the appraisal. Labour productivity was enhanced. The labour productivity of state-owned industry in 1980 was 19,085 yuan, a 13.9% increase over 1978. The labour productivity of the units in charge of capital construction under way rose from 5,185 yuan in 1978 to 5,933 yuan in 1980, showing a 14% increase. The quality of civil engineering was augmented considerably. The quality rate reckoned in terms of square metres rose from 37% in 1978 to 59% in 1979 and 69% in 1980. The construction cycle of housing construction was shortened.

6. *Preliminary reform of the economic system.* Beginning in 1979, 495 locally administered state enterprises have been set aside consecutively in Tianjin as pilot projects for practising the maintenance of a certain percentage of profit for the enterprises themselves and extending power to make decisions. In 1979, these enterprises registered an increase of 13.1% in their output value as compared with that of 1978 and an increase of 12.9% in the profits turned over to the state. In the first half of 1980, they registered an increase of 15.2% in output value and an increase of 23.6% in turned-in profits. Both grew at a higher speed than the other enterprises. These pilot enterprises achieved three things at the same time: more income for the state; more profit for the enterprises; and more personal gain distributed among their staff members and workers.

Under the guidance of the state plans, planning regulation and market regulation were put into practice simultaneously. As a result, a new situation has appeared in which all economic elements, distribution channels and purchasing and marketing forms are put to use at the same time. They have brought about a brisk market and a prosperous economy, facilitating the interflow of goods between countryside and city, strengthening economic connections between provinces and cities, and stimulating production and distribution of commodities.

7. *Improved standard of living.* In 1980, the average wages of the workers and staff members of state-owned units reached 872 yuan, an increase of 24.4% compared with 1978. The average income of the peasants increased greatly in the past two years: the per capita income from collectives and from household sideline occupations and private plots averaged 155.8 yuan and 48 yuan, respectively, showing increases of 7% and 60%, respectively, over 1979.

In 1979 and 1980 alone, 400,000 people were given jobs. The number of employed people in the city in 1980 was 2,260,000. As employment expanded, fewer people were dependent on wage earners for support. Every worker now supports an average of one dependent, compared with two in the early post-Liberation days.

8. *Restoration and readjustment of education.* Tianjin's educational undertakings suffered great setbacks during the "cultural revolution," notably due to sabotage by the Gang of Four and the damaged caused by the 1976 earthquake. During the period, teaching staffs were disbanded, school buildings were wrecked and teaching equipment was damaged. The number of institutions of higher learning in the city was reduced from 16 in 1965 to 11 in 1976 and the number of students fell from 28,000 to 17,000. After the downfall of the Gang of Four, and expecially since the Third Plenary Session of the 11th Party Central Committee, Tianjin's educational undertakings have been undergoing gradual recovery and readjustment.

In 1980, there were 18 institutions of higher learning and 10 branch institutions with 30,000 students, of whom 590 were postgraduates. At present, these institutions have a teaching staff of 8,312, including about 574 professors and associate professors and 3,350 lectures. In addition, there are 29 foreign experts and teachers working in these institutions and 41 foreign students. The institutions offer 188 specialized courses and have 13 scientific research institutes and 36 discipline research offices, with a library collection of 4.85 million books.

With their long history and good teaching staffs, both Nankai and Tianjin universities are key institutions of nationwide importance where the party's policy toward the intellectuals is better implemented.

The city has 999 middle schools with 528,000 students and 3,399 primary schools with 789,000 pupils. In the last few years, the level of education in middle and primary schools — particularly in the key middle and primary schools — has been greatly raised.

The city's adult education, which takes the form of in-service training, spare-time training and broadcasting and TV correspondence universities, has made much progress over the years. In 1980, 30% of the 2.19 million workers and staff members participated in the adult education programme, which was an increase of 10% over 1979. Under the leadership of the city's council for Worker-Peasant Education, adult education has been comprehensively organized at elementary, intermediary and advanced levels. This complements the regular education programme and therefore contributes much to the economic construction of the city.

9. *Recovery and development of medical and health work.* Like education, Tianjin's medical and health work also suffered serious setbacks during the ten years of turmoil, when the medical structure was disrupted, medical instruments were damaged and medical personnel were sent away to all parts of the country. Much progress has been made in this field since the downfall of the Gang of Four. In 1980, the city had 3,535 medical establishments, including 332 hospitals. There were 20,911 hospital beds, an average of 2.8 beds per thousand, and 5,066 medical and health personnel, an average of 6.76 qualified persons per thousand. In 1980, 32,743 million persons sought diagnosis. Tianjin Medical College and the College of Traditional Chinese Medicine have famous specialists and doctors in their medical, surgical, obstetrics and gynaecology departments, as well as in paediatrics and other departments. In 1980, progress in the health service was highlighted by a higher rate of bed utilization from 84.2% in 1979 (11th in the country) to a record 93.3% in 1980 (first in the country), and an increase in the number of in-patients to an all-time high of 250,000 in 1980, representing an increase of 28,000 over the previous year. With the development and popularization of the city's medical and health work, there has been a higher life expectancy. In 1980, Tianjin's average life expectancy was 70.6 for males and 72.49 for females, ranking it third in the country after Beijing and Shanghai.

10. *Development of the tourist industry.* Over the years, Tianjin has made great efforts to develop its tourist industry. Founded in 1979, the Tianjin International Travel Bureau received 17,770 tourists from 54 foreign countries and regions in 1980, or 2.4 times the number in 1978. Direct revenue from the tourist industry totalled U.S.$5 million. Of course, this marked only the beginning of the tourist industry in the city.

Though not rivalling Beijing in charm and entertainment, Tianjin's scenic spots and historical sites have their own distinctive features. The Tiancheng and Dule temples and Cuiping Lake in suburban Jixian County are famous both for their picturesque landscape and for such cultural antiquities as the colour modelling of the Liao Dynasty and the fresco of the Ming Dynasty. The beautiful scenery of the "Park on the Water" can be compared favourably with that of the Summer Palace in Beijing. Many other cultural relics which were damaged during the 1976 earthquake are being repaired and will be open to the public in the future.

Tianjin's Goals for Future Development

The development of Tianjin's economy continues to be centred on the principle of readjustment. Innovation in the economic system must be made only when it is favourable to and in conformity with the work of readjustment. We shall continue to march forward on all fronts in our work.

1. *In industry, stress is to be laid on readjustment, and frugality in the use of water and power is our key work.* To raise the level of economic efficiency is our aim. Our enterprises must be chiefly engaged in tapping their full potential and making innovations and transformations. The functions played by existing enterprises must be further developed to the full, with incessant improvement in product quality and repeated raising of labour productivity, so that we can develop, in the spirit of cooperation between specialized lines, production on a grand scale.

Industry ought to display its special capabilities according to its own characteristics. First, it has to develop the light and textile industries, laying special stress on those products that enjoy popularity and command ready sales on the competitive world market. It is necessary to expedite the development of light and textile industries at a higher speed than heavy industry. Second, it is required to make the inner structure of heavy industry further resemble that of light industry. Heavy industry must be put on the track of being serviceable to agriculture and the light and textile industries. Third, from strategic and long-term points of view, it is desirable to develop the favourable trend of Tianjin's oceanic chemical engineering as well as petroleum chemical engineering. It is also recommended that we combine the two branches of enginering organically so as to push the advancement of the national economy, and especially of industry.

2. *We shall develop greatly our domestic trade and foreign trade – with special attention to foreign trade – in order to take advantage of the favourable nature of the port city of Tianjin.* We have to combine production with transportation, revive every channel of communication and vitalize progress in production. At the same time, we have to make investigations of the world market, to chiefly produce such commodities as are suitable for that market and to accomplish innovation in our foreign trade pattern. The purpose is to

revitalize our foreign trade. Meanwhile, we have to make our domestic trade serviceable to the interflow of the internal economy and to produce such articles as are badly needed by our fellow cities and fellow provinces so as to combine domestic trade and foreign trade into a united effort in activating the national economy. Simultaneously, we have to modernize our harbour with modern equipment for the means of transport, posts and communications.

3. *In agriculture it is necessary to realize our party's rural policy and to make full-fledged development as far as local conditions permit.* Attention must be paid to ecological balance and also to the fact that agriculture should cater to the needs of the city, industry and export trade. This means that we must develop tremendously our socialist commodity economy.

4. *We have to develop scientific work and education enthusiastically.* In educational work, stress must be laid on the betterment of teaching quality and on the training of teachers. We have to continue to improve our work on key schools — with special regard to key universities — in order to meet the needs for economic construction on the road of the Four Modernizations. The purpose is to provide personnel not only for our city but also for the whole country, and to combine education with scientific research work and scientific research work with production for the purpose of developing Tianjin's national economy. Care, likewise, must be taken of cadres' and workers' education in Tianjin.

5. *Concerning city construction, it is a pity that we are heavily in debt and that city construction can only be done by giving priority to the most urgent requirements.* For the present, we must concentrate on clearing the city of houses damaged by the 1976 earthquake. The problem of sheltering the people is by far the most urgent problem to be settled, for then the problems of pollution, water supply, etc. will be solved according to well-planned and well-arranged projects so as to bring about conspicuous changes in the appearance of Tianjin. Efforts will be made to make Tianjin a highly civilized, beautiful and modernized socialist city.

83. ECONOMIC DEVELOPMENT IN TIBET AUTONOMOUS REGION
By the General Office of the People's Government,
Tibet Autonomous Region

Geographical and Historical Setting

The Tibet Autonomous Region is located on China's southwestern border. On the northwest, it is bounded by the Xinjiang Uygur Autonomous Region, with the Kunlun Mountains separating Xinjiang from Tibet. On the northeast, Tibet is connected to Qinghai Province by the Tanggula Range. On the east, it is contiguous to Sichuan Province; and on the southeast, to Yunnan Province. On the south, Tibet is bordered by Nepal, Sikkim, Bhutan, India and Burma.

The region covers an area of 1,200,000 sq. km., about one-eighth of the total area of China. With an average elevation exceeding 4,000 m. above sea level, Tibet encompasses the largest and highest plateau in the world and is known as the "roof of the world."

Tibet has a population of more than 1.8 million people. Tibetans are the main nationality, making up about 93% of the population. Other nationalities include Hui, Loba, Monba, Naxi, Nu and Han.

Tibet is an inalienable part of China's territory. Exchanges between the various nationalities in Tibet and those in other parts of the country can be traced far back in history. In the seventh century A.D., during the early years of the Tang Dynasty, these exchanges underwent significant growth.

During the decade of the 1240's, Tibet was officially incorporated into Chinese territory, and became an administrative region under the direct jurisdiction of the central government of the Yuan Dynasty.

Along with closer political relations, economic and cultural exchanges between the Han and Tibetan nationalities also grew stronger, promoting the development of Tibet's agriculture and handicrafts and a culture of its own identity. Tibetans and the other nationalities living in Tibet, such as the Monba and Loba, are fine members of the big family of the great motherland. They are industrious, honest, intelligent and courageous; they love the motherland and firmly oppose foreign aggression; and, like the people of other brotherly nationalities, they have made outstanding contributions to the creation and development of our great motherland.

Agriculture and Animal Husbandry. Tibet is rich in natural resources. It can be roughly divided into four natural zones according to its topographical features. These are: Northern Tibet Plateau, the Ngari area, Southern Tibetan Valley, and the Hengduan Mountain Ravine in eastern Tibet. Both the Northern Tibetan Plateau and the Ngari area have extensive natural pasturelands and are the chief pastoral areas in Tibet. The main animals raised here are yak, sheep, goats and horses. The Southern Tibetan Valley is an agricultural area.

The main crops are highland barley, wheat, rape, broad beans, peas and buckwheat. Highland barley, with a short growing period, is the staple grain of the Tibetan people. A small part of Nyingchi and Minling and most parts of Bomi, Medo and Zayu of the Southern Tibetan Valley have average elevations below 3,000 m. Here, there are dense forests and the warm climate and fertile soils are suitable for growing subtropical crops. The Eastern Tibetan Ravine is semi-agricultural and semi-pastoral, in addition to being a timber producer.

Mineral Deposits. Tibet abounds in mineral resources. According to incomplete figures, the region is known to have more than 40 kinds of minerals, including boron, chromium, copper, iron, coal, mica, natural sulphur, lead, zinc, arsenic, cobalt, molybdenum, barite and salt. Tibet ranks first in China in reserves of boron sand and chromium and third in copper.

Water Resources. An adequate rainfall and torrential rivers provide the region with inexhaustible water resources. It is estimated that potential hydroelectric power resources of the region is about 200.56 million kw., or about 29.3% of the nation's total hydroelectric power potential and ranking Tibet first in the country in this resource. The region also has abundant geothermal and solar energy resources.

Forests. Tibet is one of the important forest areas in China, with 3.1 million hectares under timber. Tibet's natural forests have a timber reserve of 610 million cu. m., ranking it fifth in the country. Surveys indicate that there are more than 4,500 species of plants, including evergreen *pinus yunnanensis,* dragon spruce and hemlock — among the most precious species in the world.

Fauna. More than 100 kinds of indigenous animals, including quite a few rare varieties, are to be found in Tibet, including bison, wild ass, Tibetan antelope, Mongolian gazelle, blue sheep, bear, wolf, tiger, leopard, roe-deer, deer, lynx, otter, snow hog, stoat, fox, lesser panda, Tibetan takin, blue-eared pheasant and golden monkey. Lesser panda, blue-eared pheasant and Tibetan takin are on the state list of rare animals for special protection.

There are about 100 varieties of medicinal herbs and other medicinal materials, such as cordiceps, fritillary bulb, rhizome of wind-weed, tuber of elevated gastrodia, Tibet calamus, angelica root, rhubar, rhizome of Chinese goldthread, aucklandia lappa, Chinese ephedra and dried peppermint herb. These native products are important items for shipment to other parts of the country and for export.

These natural resources provide favourable condition for Tibet's economic development, and their exploitation and utilization also help China's construction as a whole.

Economic Achievements Since Liberation

Under feudal serfdom, the Tibet of former days was extremely backward economically, politically and culturally. With the peaceful liberation of Tibet on May 23, 1951, imperialist forces of aggression were driven out and the Tibetan people returned to the embrace of the great motherland. After Liberation, Tibet went through democratic reform, socialist revolution and socialist construction. With the productive forces freed from their fetters, Tibet's economy made rapid headway and scored great successes. The following is a brief account of the main achievements the Tibet Autonomous Region has made in various economic sectors:

Agriculture and Animal Husbandry. Farming and animal husbandry are predominant in Tibet, wth their combined output value making up more than 70% of Tibet's gross output value. However, these sectors were very backward before Liberation. At that time, the normal yield of grain crops was only 750 kg. per hectare. Animal husbandry remained at the stage of natural grazing, and maintained a very low breeding rate. Today, with changes in the social system, the region has started to place emphasis on scientific cultivation and grazing and has made rapid growth in both agricultural production and animal husbandry. Total grain output in 1980 was 505,000 tons — 3.1 times that of 1959 when the democratic reform was carried out. The region raised more than 23 million head of animals, 2.1 times that of 1958, the year before the democratic reform. The total output value of agriculture and animal husbandry in 1980 reached 451 million yuan, of which agriculture accounted for 164 million yuan, or 36.3% of the total; animal husbandry output was valued at 250 million yuan, or 55.4% of the total; sideline production came to 37 million yuan, or 8.3% of the total. Agriculture in Tibet has the following special features:

1. *The region, being extensive in area and with extremely diverse natural conditions, promises a great potential for the development of agriculture, provided crops are grown rationally and suited to local conditions.*

2. *A mixture of farming and animal husbandry is the main aspect of its economic structure.* However, only some parts are suitable for farming and forestry while the region as a whole is suitable for animal husbandry. Hence, it enjoys particularly good conditions for developing animal husbandry.

3. *Abundant wild life and plants provide good conditions for developing a diversified economy.* Many native and special products, such as pilose antler, musk, cordiceps, fritillary bulbs and animal pelts, enjoy popularity on domestic and foreign markets.

Industry. Old Tibet knew nothing of modern industry. Even its handicrafts were underdeveloped. Industry underwent large-scale development following Liberation and now makes up an important element in the economy. Its 1980 output value was 150 million yuan, accounting for 25.3% of Tibet's total output value. The region has medium-sized and small enterprises for power generation, chromium and coal mining, chemicals, building materials, machine-building, forestry, industry, woollen textiles, matches, paper, printing, tanning and food processing. It produces 52 major products. The original value of fixed assets was 153 million yuan.

Handicrafts. The handicrafts sector engaged in making traditional Tibetan goods has a long history but suffered great damage during the decade of turmoil (the "cultural revolution"). After the Third Plenum of the 11th Party Central Committee, the party's policy was implemented and traditional handicrafts were restored and developed. In 1980, there were 64 handicrafts workshops, turning out phrue (a kind of tweed), woollen cushions and mattresses, Tibetan quilts, traditional aprons, Tibetan shoes, knives, wooden bowls and churns for making butter. Their total output value was 6 million yuan.

Transport and Communications. Highways were non-existent in Tibet in the old days. After Liberation, five trunk roads were built: the Sichuan-Tibet, Qinghai-Tibet, Xinjiang-Tibet, Yunnan-Tibet and Sino-Nepalese highways. Fundamental changes have thus taken place in communications facilities. Today, total road length is 21,000 km. More than 400 bridges, permanent and semi-permanent, have been erected, totalling 13,000 m. in length. A network of highways now radiates out from Lhasa. Lhasa is also linked with Chengdu and Xi'an by direct, scheduled air connections. The development of communications and transport facilities has promoted economic and cultural exchange between Tibet and the interior part of the motherland as well as within the region, and has helped bring prosperity and well-being to the Tibetan people.

Postal and telecommunications services have also seen significant growth. Post offices are to be found in all the counties as well as all localities with a concentration of industrial or mining enterprises. International postal services are available in Lhasa, Xigaze, Yadong and Zham.

Commerce and Foreign Trade. Commerce before Liberation was in a sorry state. But it grew quickly after Liberation, thanks to the attention by the Communist Party and the government. A socialist market has been fundamentally established, with state-owned commerce as the main element catering to the minority nationalities and incorporating multiple economic sectors. In 1980, the number of workers engaged in commerce was 12,000. The whole region was served by 2,600 shops, of which 378 were owned by the state. Since the democratic reform, purchases, sales, transfers and stocks have continually increased. In 1980, total purchases of commodities in Tibet exceeded 40 million yuan, eight times the total of 1959. Goods transferred from other parts of the country were valued at 180 million yuan, 4.8 times more than in 1959. Total retail sales reached 344 million yuan, 19.2 times more than in 1959.

In 1980, Tibet's foreign trade amounted to U.S.$10 million. All this played an active role in promoting Tibet's farming and animal husbandry, in enlivening the market and in providing a secure life for the people.

Science, Culture, Education and Health Work. Before Liberation, there were only seven primary schools for children of nobles and one Tibetan hospital. Since Liberation, Tibet has made great advances in these fields. There were four institutions of higher learning in 1980, with a combined student body of 1,400; 23 secondary technical schools, with 3,500 students; and 6,000 primary schools, with 240,000 pupils. Most gratifying is the fact that Tibet now has a contingent of more than 6,000 teachers of Tibetan and other nationalities. The people of Monba and Loba nationalities, who recorded events in the old days by tying knots, now have their own college graduates. By 1979, the region had set up a number of scientific research institutes with a combined staff of 14,000. They achieved gratifying results in research projects in animal husbandry, industry, communications, architecture, medicine and meteorology.

In 1980, the region had 800 hospitals and clinics, with 3,700 beds and 6,000 medical personnel. Tibetan medicine and pharmacology are being promoted and developed. Music, dancing, literature, drama, sculpture and painting, rich in national styles, were all revived and took on new splendour.

Living Standards. In old Tibet, the three categories of manorial lords (officials, clergy and the nobility) — who made up approximately 5% of the population — lived in extragance and waste, while the serfs and slaves — making up more than 95% of the population — laboured all day long and yet could not get enough to eat. After Liberation, the party and the state did much work and appropriated large sums of money to help the Tibetan people develop production and solve their difficulties of livelihood. Between 1951 and 1980, the state allocated over 83 million yuan for social relief; state loans to assist the needy totalled over 97 million yuan; and the state issued 108 million yuan in funds to help cooperatives and people's communes. In the 29 years following Tibet's liberation, the state granted Tibet more than 5,000 million yuan to subsidize local finances. A total of 300,000 tons of grain were brought into Tibet during the 22 years following 1959.

In 1980, in particular, the Party Central Committee issued important directives concerning Tibet and adopted special and flexible economic policies. This speeded up local economic development and brought improvement in the people's livelihood. In 1980, each peasant or herdsman received an average of 150 yuan from his collective. At the end of 1980, total bank savings of peasants and herdsmen came close to 14 million yuan; those of the urban residents reached 60 million yuan. The wages of workers and staff employed in enterprises under ownership by the whole people averaged 673.7 yuan per person, over 90 yuan more than the 1979 rate because of wage increases and bonuses.

Population Growth. Better living standards and health facilities have resulted in a large growth in population. According to historical records, during the reign of Emperor Qianlong of the Qing Dynasty (1736-96), the Tibet region (excluding Qamdo) had a population of 2 million. In the ensuing 100 years and more, it was reduced by more than 1 million as a result of the rule of feudal serfdom. At the time of the democratic reform, the population had shrunk to 870,000 (excluding Qamdo). By 1980, the population of the Tibetan nationality in Tibet had grown by 60% compared with 30 years ago. The demographic change testifies to the reactionary nature of the old system and to the superiority of the socialist system.

Problems in Present Economic Work and Tentative Ideas for Future Development

Long years of "Left" influence created many problems in various aspects of the economy in Tibet. Problems yet awaiting solution include: serious imbalances in the relationships among industry, agriculture and animal husbandry and also within the various branches of agriculture; a long-entrenched approach to economic work which did not heed actual conditions in Tibet, and ignored economic accounting and results; and backward conditions in science, technology, culture and education.

In order to make its economic work conform to the needs of the Four Modernizations, Tibet should in the future concentrate on readjusting the economy so as to bring its damaged economic structure back to the previous condition in which a mixture of farming and animal husbandry formed the economic core, and so as to restore the traditional handicrafts industry and household sideline occupations within three to five years. The aim is to bring about a proportionate and planned development of the economy and to effect a marked improvement in people's living standards throughout the region and in their cultural and scientific level. To this end, the following aspects of work should be grasped well:

Agriculture. Tibet has an economic structure based on a combination of farming and animal husbandry. In this, animal husbandry takes up a large proportion and is closely linked with people's clothing, food, shelter, transportation and other articles for daily use. Therefore, whether in the farming, pastoral, semi-farming or semi-pastoral areas, animal husbandry should be developed. While developing animal husbandry, a real effort should be made to successfully develop grain production, afforestation and a diversified economy, thus achieving simultaneous and harmonious progress in farming, forestry, animal husbandry, sideline occupations and fisheries.

Industry. Vigorous efforts should be made to restore and develop the traditional handicrafts industry, especially the production of light industrial products and special products for minority nationalities that use animal products as raw materials. We must carry out technical transformation of handicrafts, systematically introducing mechanization and semi-mechanization. Those enterprises which depend on the interior of China for their materials, which have not passed the grade technically, which incur big wastes, which turn out inferior products or which operated at a loss for a long time should be closed, suspended, merged or retooled for alternate production as each case merits. Existing enterprises should be put in order and should be managed well. Efforts should be made to tap their existing potential through technological innovation and transformation so as to lower production costs, raise productivity and fulfil this year's production plans.

Power Resources. Tibet suffers serious fuel and power shortages due to small coal reserves. This has seriously affected economic construction and people's livelihood. The most effective measure for solving this problem is to utilize Tibet's very rich water resources for hydroelectric power generation, chiefly through the construction of small power stations. The next step is to make full use of geothermal resources and solar energy, so as to lay a good foundation in energy for the exploitation of Tibet's rich resources in the future.

Transport and Communications. Being vast in territory, road transportation must serve as Tibet's main artery in the region's economic development. Highway and bridge construction should be strengthened and transport conditions improved. Efforts must be made to establish a thorough network of communications throughout the region during the period of the Sixth Five-Year Plan.

Traditional Trade. Local commerce should be vigorously encouraged to cater to the needs of the people of the minority nationalities. Commercial activity should lend vigorous support to production. Efforts should be made to expand purchases, strengthen the shipment of goods from the interior, encourage sales, enliven the market, withdraw currency from circulation and basically stabilize prices. At the same time, foreign trade should be actively expanded.

Livelihood. We should develop the economy and raise the level of the people's material lives, as well as their scientific and cultural levels. While adhering to socialist principles, we should adopt more flexible economic policies in Tibet so as to rapidly realize the region's wealthy potential. Capital construction must be curtailed, financial expenditures kept within the budget and state investments put to use in developing agriculture and animal husbandry and in the production of badly needed goods. We shall strive to primarily alter Tibet's poor and backward state within two or three years. Culture, education, science and technology should be adapted to suit the special conditions of Tibet, and they should advance through readjustment.

Stress in education should be placed on the Tibetan nationality, on middle and primary education, and on public schools. More efforts should be made to collect, sort out, study and pass on Tibet's traditional cultural heritage, including fields of astronomy, Tibetan medicine, Tibetan opera, music, dancing, painting and sculpture, and to develop socialist Tibetan culture. It is necessary to step up the training of personnel, particularly from among the minority people, for the general task of developing the region into a united, prosperous and socialist new Tibet.

84. ECONOMIC DEVELOPMENT IN XINJIANG UYGUR AUTONOMOUS REGION
By the Office of Research and Investigation,
People's Government of Xinjiang Uygur Autonomous Region

Geography. The Xinjiang Uygur Autonomous Region lies on the northwest border of the country and has an area of over 1.6 million sq. km., making up one-sixth of the country's total area. Xinjiang is a vast region with rich and varied natural resources. In the fertile regions on both sides of Tianshan Mountains live 13 nationalities; the Uygurs are the main ethnic group.

Survey of Economic Development Since 1949

Before Liberation, under various reactionary rules, the economic development of this rich land was negligible. The whole region's industry consisted of only ten very small, poorly equipped factories. Even daily necessities such as nails and matches had to be transported from other parts of the country. Agriculture and animal husbandry were even more backward. A considerable part of the region was still at the primitive stage of production. Communication and transport, finance, commerce, science, culture, education and public health were very backward. The people of all nationalities were living in dire poverty.

In 1949, the heroic People's Liberation Army entered Xinjiang and from then on the people were their own masters. Under the leadership of the Party Central Committee, the army and the people of all nationalities united to undertake economic construction in various fields which started from scratch and grew rapidly. The economic situation has changed tremendously.

Major Economic Advances. For 30 years, the region's industrial and agricultural output value increased by an average annual rate of 7.7%. Agriculture and animal husbandry increased 4.3 times in value, from 490 million yuan in 1949 to 2,142 million yuan in 1979. At present, the area of cultivated land is over 48 million *mu*, or triple that in the early days after Liberation. The output of grain reached 7,780 million catties in 1979, or 4.5 times that in 1949. There was 750 million *mu* of pastures with 25.85 million head of livestock in 1979, or 2.5 times what it was 30 years earlier.

Industry, communications and transport have also undergone tremendous changes. Iron and steel, nonferrous metals, electric power, coal, petroleum, chemical, cement, automobile, tractor, electronics, motor, farm machinery, cotton and wool textile, paper-making, sugar refining, cigarette, salt, and defence industries have been established. Now there are altogether 4,000 industrial enterprises, with an annual output of 3,140 million yuan as against 80 million yuan in 1949, an increase of nearly 39 times. A foundation for socialist industry has been laid. Railway mileage is over 1,100 km. and highways total more than 21,000 km., seven times that in 1949. Civil aviation has also developed considerably.

With the development in industry and agriculture, the region's revenue in 1979 was 31 times what it was at the time of Liberation. The commercial network extends throughout the region and two-thirds of it is in agricultural and pastoral areas. With the continuous rise of the people's living standard, retail sales reached 2,470 million yuan in 1979 — 11 times that of 1950 — thus satisfying the needs of and providing convenience to the people of different nationalities.

Principal Scientific and Cultural Achievements. In the past 30 years, the region's science, culture, education, public health, publishing, press, broadcasting and sports have also greatly developed. In 1951 the whole region's sole scientific organization was staffed by only 55 workers. In 1979, research organizations numbered 191, with 3,591 workers. As for education, the number of universities and colleges rose from 1 to 12; vocational schools, by 9.2 times; secondary schools, 221 times; and primary schools, 7.8 times. By 1979, the region had trained 26,000 university graduates and 91,000 vocational school graduates. The number of health organizations, hospitals, hospital beds, and medical workers has increased 51, 20, 86 and 131 times, respectively, since 1949. The shortage of doctors and medicine in the vast agricultural and pastoral areas has been tremendously alleviated.

Progress Despite Setbacks. For 30 years the achievements in Xinjiang's economic construction were gigantic. However, due to the long-term disturbance of "Left" ideology, especially that of the ten-year catastrophe caused by Lin Biao and the Gang of Four, economic construction suffered serious damage and the speed of economic development was slowed down.

After the collapse of the Gang of Four and

under the correct line and policy of the Third Plenum of the 11th Party Central Committee, our region's national economy has speedily revived and developed due to the carrying out of the national economic readjustment policy, the rectification of guiding thought in economic construction and criticism of a whole string of "Left" mistakes. With the steady rise in industrial, agricultural and livestock production, the living standard of the people has continued to improve, the national economy has been revitalized, and along the Tianshan Mountains the whole picture is a cheering and heartening one.

Economic Development in 1980

The correct implementation of the Party Central Committee's two documents concerning agriculture and the region's policies for agriculture and livestock breeding, the institution of many forms of responsibility systems and of the principle of "to each according to his work," and the reorganization of the agricultural structure have all served to arouse the peasants' and herdmen's zeal for production, thus further developing agriculture and animal husbandry.

Agriculture. The total output value of agriculture in 1980 was 2,330 million yuan, an increase of 8.8% over that of the previous year. Despite a decrease of 1,279,000 *mu* of land sown to grain, the total output nevertheless reached 7,723 million catties. Even though the output was 65 million catties less than the previous year, the per-*mu* yield was 7 catties more, reaching a record 238 catties. In particular, the region's cash crops showed sharp increases. In comparison with the previus year, cotton, oil-bearing crops and beets increased by 49.4%, 24.3% and 29.9%, respectively — the best records since 1966. The yield of grapes, melons, other fruits and vegetables surpassed that of the previous year.

In view of the fact that in the three prefectures in southern Xinjiang — Kashi, Hotan and Kergez — production developed sluggishly for the past 10 years or so and the people there are still in difficulty, the region's party committee decided to speed up their economic development with financial aid. In 1980, they were appropriated 36.1 million yuan and granted a loan of 73.1 million yuan for agricultural use. They were also given special consideration in the allocation of merchandise. That year the Kashi and Hotan prefectures reaped a bumper harvest in agriculture and significant growth in numbers of livestock. Grain yield increased by 5.3% over the previous year, the yield of cotton and oil-bearing crops surpassed former records and livestock achieved a net increase of 500,000 head.

All this played an active part in the acceleration of the region's agriculture and animal husbandry. In line with the policy of all-around development of agriculture, forestry, animal husbandry, sideline production and fishing also showed considerable development in 1980; 380,000 *mu* of trees were planted — the region's highest annual record. Some changes have also taken place within agriculture; the increased rate of output value of ture; the increase rate of the output value of livestock breeding and sideline production began to surpass that of farming itself. The collective economy and household sideline production are most active, presenting a picture of prosperity for the urban-rural economy.

What is most gratifying is the changes in the state farms, which have an important place in the region's agricultural economy. In 1980, their main products such as grain, cotton, oil-bearing crops, beets and livestock attained or surpassed their previous records. Great strides were also made in improving management and turning deficit to profit.

Livestock breeding has an important position in the region's economy. Since the party's Third Plenum, the people's governments at all levels have reinforced the leadership over animal husbandry. The tendency of paying too much attention to agriculture and too little to animal husbandry is being overcome. In accordance with the principle of raising livestock, where it is most suitable, readjustments have been made. A group of semi-agricultural, semi-pastoral counties and communes have been officially changed to full pastoral counties and communes. In the management of livestock economy, an overall policy of assigning herds to specific groups, families and herdsmen and a system of payment according to results have been advocated. The policy concerning private livestock and their unlimited number has been further stressed. With the advance of scientific research and popularization of technical skills, the construction of pastures in pastoral areas has been given major importance. In 1980, the region's investment in construction of pastoral areas totalled 13.8 million yuan. A total of 325 pump wells have been dug in the region and over 900 ponds and 7,490 permanent corrals have been built. The zeal of the herdsmen is very high. By the end of 1980, the total number of livestock reached 26.726 million head, increasing by 3.4% over the previous year — the best record since 1966. The output of meat totalled 127,000 tons, or 12,000 tons more than that of the previous year. The output of wool was 34,000 tons, surpassing that of the previous year. Commune members had a total of 7.53

million head of private livestock. On the whole, the situation in animal husbandry is most encouraging.

Industry. Industry pressed forward amid readjustment. In 1980, industrial enterprises were resolute in tapping their full potential, making inovations and transformations and increasing income and cutting down expenditure. As a result, industrial production climbed steadily. The region's total output of industrial products reached 3,489 million yuan, or 10.9% more than in 1979. The development of light industry was given special attention. Under the principle of giving priority to raw material, fuel, power, capital construction, bank loans, foreign currency and transportation, 51% of the funds for tapping potential, innovations and transformations, technological improvement loans and portions of short-term facility loans were used for light and textile industries, which resulted in a 13.1% growth in output value. This surpassed the speed of growth in heavy industry and caused a change in the proportion of light to heavy industry.

The output of main products showed increases in comparison with the previous year. Woollen piece goods, knitting wool, sugar, cigarettes, paper and cardboard, tractors, rolled steel, coal, crude oil, cement, steel and timber all set new production records. The quality of industrial products also improved. In a November 1980 survey of 47 items on the quality index of main enterprises, 31 items surpassed the previous year's level and 18 reached or surpassed the previous best levels — an increase of 4 items compared with the previous year's survey. No. 18 refrigeration motor oil and Tianshan Brand cement were awarded national silver medals. A total of 1,200 new styles, designs and varieties were added to the list of industrial products.

A mass movement of increasing industrial production and income and cutting back expenditures and material was under way. The years 1979 and 1980 saw the overfulfillment of the 150 million yuan target set by the plan for increasing production and practicing economy. In economizing on the use of energy, favourable results were achieved.

Communications and Transport. There were also new achievements in the area of communications and transportation. In 1980, railway passenger transport over fulfilled the year's plan by 45.1%, an increase of 10.6% over that of the previous year. Merchandise transportation overfulfilled the year's plan by 2.7%. Transportation belonging to enterprises directly subordinate to the region's Bureau of Communications overfulfilled the annual target of merchandise distribution by 10.9%. The tension resulting from problems in highway transportation was evidently relaxed.

After investigation and study by the communications departments, 96 enterprises were closed down or suspended, drastic adjustments were made to 269 other enterprises and favourable results were achieved. Through consolidation, the leadership of these enterprises was strengthened, their management improved, their economic accounting reinforced, their product quality elevated, their production increased and their technical level raised.

Capital Investment. The investment in capital construction yielded favourable results. The region's 1980 capital construction investment proportion was appropriately readjusted and the proportion for agriculture, light industry, textile industry, education and culture was raised. At the same time, funds were added for the construction of housing, public utilities and other non-productive projects. Of the region's construction projects involving at least 1 million yuan each, 102 were postponed for two years and the total investment of 710 million yuan was cut down. The quality of construction improved and more projects were completed and put into operation, adding 812 million yuan in fixed assets.

Commerce and Trade. Finance and commerce also achieved favourable results. Along with the region's development of industry, bumper harvests and improvements in animal husbandry and sideline products, many attempts were made to activate the urban-rural economy. The further development of country markets, opening up city markets for farm products and increasing merchandise distribution channels created a prosperous climate in sales. In 1980, purchases in commercial operation reached 2,650 million yuan, increasing by 25.6% over that of the previous year. Retail sales totalled 3,050 million yuan, increasing by 23.5% — the best record since the founding of the People's Republic. With the market livening up, difficulties in the supply of merchandise were overcome and some merchandise in short demand for a long time is now in ample supply. The open supply of merchandise has played an active part in reassuring the masses and increasing the withdrawal of currency from circulation.

Foreign trade was actively developed in the light of local conditions. In 1980, the region's purchases for export were valued at 176 million yuan, 5% more than the preceding year. Export commodities included 65 kinds of products, an increase of 29. Among them, special local products such as pilose antlers, deer horns, sheared and fine wool, hops, safflower seeds, allium, honeydew melons and fresh grapes all showed large increases.

Science and Culture. There were also new developments during 1980 in the fields of science and technology, education, culture, public health and sports. The status of science and technology was further reinforced. Thousands of scientific and technical personnel who had been misplaced in their jobs were returned to their own specialized fields and created over 300 items of value in scientific research, of which more tham 50 reached advanced national standards.

In education, teaching order was rectified, teaching quality raised, funds and construction investment for schools added, educational courses on radio and television and sparetime university education developed. Vocational schools also were developed, their enrollment enlarged and the ratio of enrollment for national minority students increased. In 1980, the number of students studying in universities, colleges, vocational schools and middle schools increased by 25.6%, 5.38% and 8.95%, respectively. Further developments were made in press and publishing. Family planning also witnessed new developments.

Living Standards. The living standard of the people in the region was greatly raised. In 1979 and 1980, 800 million yuan were spent in increasing the people's income to improve their living conditions. In agricultural and pastoral areas, commune members have increased their income by 40% on the average in the past four years. In 1980, the average increase in income per capita was 5 yuan. The average increase in grain was 15 catties per capita, reaching 400 catties annually. Household sideline production totalled 110 million yuan; grain yield from private plots was 430 million catties; private livestock, 7.53 million head; and urban and rural savings, 1,070 million yuan, an increase of 200 million yuan over the previous year. At the same time, for production brigades with a per capita income lower than 40 yuan, primary school textbooks were provided free of charge, as was medical care given for favus of the scalp and brucellosis, thus lightening the peasants' and herdsmen's financial burden. As for workers and staff members, besides receiving raises in salary and wages according to the national rules, they were granted subsidies in food, awards and bonuses in enterprises and other considerations peculiar to local conditions, such as subsidies for heating in winter; better terms on home leave; border region health subsidies; and readjustments on subsidies for those sent on special missions. All this thereby increased their actual incomes by quite a margin.

In 1980, the average increase in annual income was about 120 yuan, and after deducting the rise in actual expenses, the average income netted a 10.2% increase over the previous year. In 1980, newly built residential areas totalled 2,370,000 sq. m., the highest figure since the founding of the People's Republic. In cities and towns, new channels in production were opened, giving employment to 110,000 people.

Current Problems and Goals for Future Development

The year 1980 witnessed certain favourable results in the region's economic construction and the current situation, on the whole, is heartening. But there are still vestiges of disturbance left over from the "Left" line of the past. In the development of the national economy there are still serious problems and shoals. They are evidenced by the annual decreases of revenue, the increasing expenditure, the growing circulation of currency that adversely influences the stability of market prices and the people's livelihood, and capital construction scale becoming too large. The progress in closing down, suspending, merging or switching industrial enterprises is too slow and our products are too high in price and too low in quality, thus making them noncompetitive. Besides, the readjustment in industry is far from adequate for the needs of readjustment of the national economy. Financial results are poor and losses and wastage are serious. These conditions reflect the fact that our technical skills in production and management are still very much behind the times and our passive position in economics has not undergone a decisive change.

According to the Party Central Committee's policy of further readjustment of the economy and further political stability, 1981 is a crucial year in the region's economic readjustment. The main task of the region is to firmly and resolutely carry out the directives of the Party Central Committee and the State Council concerning the work in minority areas and to earnestly apply the spirit of the Third Session of the Fifth National People's Congress and the Working Conference of the Party Central Committee. The national autonomy policy, unity between peoples and further readjustment of the national economy should be strengthened. We shall continue to preserve stability, resolutely cut down the scale of capital construction, fully develop agriculture and livestock breeding, speed up the development of light and textile industries, appropriately develop science, culture and education, strive to increase revenue and cut spending, earnestly solve the burning question of providing more food, meat and spending money for the people — and in general push forward our region's socialist construction.

85. ECONOMIC DEVELOPMENT IN YUNNAN PROVINCE
By the General Office,
Yunnan Provincial People's Government

Geography and Resources

Yunnan Province is located on the southwestern border of China and is bounded by Vietnam, Laos and Burma. Its total area is more than 390,000 sq. km. The province has a population of 31.74 million; 22 minority nationalities account for about one-third of the population.

Yunnan Province is vast in area and rich in natural resources. Its forest reserves rank fourth among China's provinces and water resources are third. Its deposits of nonferrous metals and phosphorous rank first. Yunnan's varied climate is suitable for developing forestry, animal husbandry and a diversified economy.

Survey of Economic Development Since 1949

The national economy of Yunnan Province has developed very rapidly in the past 30 years. The major achievements are summarized as follows:

Agriculture. Agriculture has embarked on the path of collectivization and has greatly developed through land reform, the cooperative movement and the people's commune system. Total grain output in 1979 doubled that in 1949 and the annual average increase was 2.35%. The output of sugarcane in 1979 was 6.6 times that of 1949; cured tobacco, 48 times; tea, 6 times; and oil-bearing crops have almost doubled. The area of rubber plantations increased to 700,000 mu. The number of pigs has increased 4.8 times; draught animals have almost doubled; and sheep have risen 3.4 times. More than 50,000 irrigation works have been built, with a total storage capacity of 5,700 million cubic metres. The effective irrigated area amounted to 13.56 million mu, which accounted for 33% of cultivated land. The number of tractors increased 21 times over that in 1962. The quantity of chemical fertilizer applied increased 26 times and consumption of electric power 33 times.

Industry. Before Liberation, Yunnan's industry was very backward. There was a small quantity of industry and handicrafts only in cities such as Kunming and Geji. After Liberation, the following light and heavy industries were established in the province: ferrous metal, steel, machinery, coal, electric power, forestry, chemicals, textiles, foods, daily necessities, etc. Now Yunnan has more than 7,000 industrial enterprises and 8,000 million yuan's worth of fixed assets. Total industrial output value in 1979 was 32.3 times that in 1949, accounting for 61% of total industrial and agricultural output value, as against 16.7% before Liberation. The output of major products has increased greatly. Steel output increased 1,157 times; eight ferrous metals, 71.3 times; electricity, 108 times; coal, 57 times; timber, 133.4 times; cigarettes, 26.2 times; sugar, 7.2 times; and cloth 4.5 times. Machine-building, optics and chemical industries all have increased to a certain degree. A firm foundation was laid for electronics, textiles, paper-making, printing, pharmaceuticals, pottery and porcelain, and glassware trades.

Transportation. Before Liberation, transportation in Yunnan was very backward, especially in the mountainous and border areas where transportation mainly depended on man and horse. The railroads in the whole province were narrow-gauge rail: from Kumming to Hekou, from Kumming to Zhanyi, from Gejiu to Bisechai to Shiping. Highways aggregated only 2,700 kilometres and two-thirds of the counties had no motor traffic. After the founding of the People's Republic, traffic and transportation have greatly developed. The railroad from Kunming to Hekou (metre gauge) has been restored and railroads from Guiyang to Kunming and from Chengdu to Kunming (standard gauge) have been built, greatly strengthening Yunnan's connection with various inland provinces. By 1979, the railway mileage had increased 3.6 times over 1949. Highways had increased 9.3 times to more than 44,000 kilometres. Motor traffic was available for all counties. Civil aviation has also developed rapidly with services by many new air routes both inside and outside the province.

On the basis of the continuous growth of production in industry and agriculture, finance and trade have also developed to a great degree. Retail sales of commodities in 1979 increased 8.1 times over 1952, purchases of export commodities increased 3.1 times and financial income increased 5.6 times.

Education, Science and Culture. With the development of economic construction, education, science, culture and public health made great progress. In 1979 there were more than 64,000 universities, middle and primary schools in the province — a 5.5-fold increase over 1950. The total number of students in schools was 5.415 million, increasing 9.3 times. There were 263,000 teachers and workers in various schools, an increase of 15.3 times. There are 1.32 million minority nationality students in school, accounting for 24% of the total number of students. In the past 30 years, the universities and colleges have trained 49,800 graduates for the country and the secondary professional schools, 140,000 graduates.

At present, there are 154 independent scientific research organizations at the county level and above. And there are 125,600 technical personnel in the natural sciences, of whom 121,700 are in state-owned units — an increase of 18 times over 1952. The province has 238 cultural halls or centres and 59 professional ensembles, 95 professional art troupes, 155 cinemas and 66 libraries with more than 10,000 volumes of books each.

Public health institutions in the whole province have increased from 96 units in 1949 to 579 today. Medical professionals have increased in number from 571 to 68,262 and hospital beds have increased from 615 to 64,623, averaging 2.06 beds per 1,000 people as against 0.04 beds before. There are now 2.18 medical professionals per 1,000 people as against 0.4 professionals per 1,000 population in 1949.

Income and Livelihood. People's lives have improved gradually. The average consumption level of the peasants increased from 44.7 yuan in 1952 to 131 yuan today, and the average consumption level of workers and staff members rose from 109.1 yuan to 411.2 yuan. During the past 30 years, a total of 1,192.38 million yuan has been invested for housing construction and in 1979 and 1980 alone the completed housing space was more than 3.74 million square metres. This helped to lessen housing pressures which had caused tensions for a long time. Savings accounts in urban and rural areas totalled 782.19 million yuan, increasing 8 times over 1957.

Review of Economic Developments in 1980

Agriculture had an all-around good harvest in 1980 and the situation in the countryside was excellent. Due to the implementation of several important documents issued by the Party Central Committee concerning agriculture and of various economic policies stipulated by the committee and provincial people's government, the enthusiasm of cadres and commune members was fired and the development of agricultural production accelerated. Total grain output in 1980 reached 17,311 million catties, the highest level in history. Output of main cash crops increased in varying degrees: oil-bearing crops by 52.2%, spices by 50%, tea by 20.1% and sugarcane by 1.6%. Thanks to the good harvest and the practice of giving extra bonuses for excess production or profit return, in addition to price increases for some agricultural and sideline products, the commune members' annual income averaged 147.7 yuan per head — an increase of 22.5 yuan over the previous year.

Industrial Advances. Industrial readjustment made progress in 1980 as both industry and transportation marched forward steadily. Some 125 enterprises, because of poor markets, inferior product quality, higher prices and serious financial losses, were shut down, amalgamated or switched to another line of production. According to market needs, the defence and machinery industries readjusted the composition of their products and service orientation and started to produce light industrial products for daily use. Various measures were taken to speed up the development of the light and textile industries. And there was a big increase in the production of light industrial goods needed in the market. The variety, designs and styles of products increased by more than 1,600 items.

The experiment of enlarging decision-making power was carried out in 195 units in the province. Some units adopted the method of sharing out profits and being responsible for profits and losses. Adjustments in the market were made and economic integrations were organized. Therefore, industrial production was promoted and the enthusiasm of managers and producers aroused. The total industrial output value was 6,138 million yuan, an increase of 3.4% over 1979. The economic results increased to some extent. The total output value of industrial enterprises in the provincial budget increased by 1.3% over 1979, their profits increased by 5.6%; energy consumption was reduced by 9% and comparable costs decreased by 0.2%. The total loss incurred in the enterprises decreased by 12.8%. The quality of products was improved to some extent.

Capital Investment. The scale of capital construction was reduced. A number of capital construction projects were stopped or postponed. The investment for capital construction in the whole year was 1,401.2 million yuan, a reduction of 5% from 1979. At the same time, efforts were concentrated on speeding up the key projects. The number of projects wholly or partially put into operation in 1980 made up 51% of all projects under construction. Newly added fixed assets were valued at about 1,000 million yuan. The direction of investment for capital construction was readjusted. The percentage of investment in nonproductive construction increased by 8.5% over the previous year and the absolute value increased by 39.3%.

Markets. Purchasing and selling operations in the whole province improved and the market was brisk. Retail sales amounted to 4,120 million yuan, an increase of 9.6%. Compared with 1979, the sale of pork increased by 12%; fresh eggs, 13.6%; tea, 25.8%; polyester-cotton cloth, 41%; woollen fabrics, 22%; silks and satins, 35%; TV sets, 69%; wrist-watches, 22%; bicycles, 15.6%; and semi-conductor radios, 14.1%. The village fairs flourished and registered a 35% increase in transactions over 1979. The difference of market prices was reduced by 12.1% and the general level of prices dropped by 11.2%.

Main Problems and Future Plans

The economy and culture of Yunnan Province have developed greatly during more than 30 years of socialist construction. But Yunnan Province is a border province with many nationalities and its economic development is faced with many problems for historical and geographical reasons. The main problems are as follows:

(1) *The present irrational economic structure.* The grain production level is low and the development of forestry, animal husbandry and cash crops cannot meet the needs of the market and light industry. Light industry is weak in its foundation and its pace of development has been slow. Some products are inferior in quality and high in price. The variety is less than it should be and designs and styles are simple. The whole economic structure is inclined to heavy industry. Of the total output value of industry and agriculture, industry makes up 61%, and agriculture 39%. Of the total output value of industry, heavy industry accounts for 57.9% and light industry for 42.1%. The agricultural structure is one-sided. Of the total output value of agriculture, farming accounts for 63.6%; forestry, 6.5%; animal husbandry, 16.9%; sideline production, 12.7%; and fishing, 0.2%. The ratio among different branches of the national economy is not coordinated.

(2) *The commodity economy is underdeveloped.* The regional and closed characteristics of Yunnan's economy are quite obvious. All districts except those with better communications and an early history of development have self-supporting natural economies. In a few areas inhabited by minorities the economy is still in a primitive stage. The production rate is very low. The development of the national economy is seriously influenced by the backward mode of production of the natural economy and its habitual tendency for small-scale production.

(3) *Traffic and communications are inconvenient.* The railways open to traffic within the whole province total only 1,700 kilometres, running through 20 counties and concentrated in the northeastern corner of the province. Basically, there is no river transport. Communications and transport mainly depend on highways but they are few and average only 14.9 kilometres per square kilometre in the province. Also, the standard is low; only 56% of existing highways are all-weather roads and they are irrationally located, poorly connected, easily damaged by natural disasters, comprise indirect routes and are costly to maintain.

(4) *Culture, education, science and technology are still backward.* In the province the illiterate make up almost a quarter of the population. Primary schools are attended by only about 50% of eligible pupils. Universities and secondary technical schools are small and their training capacity is limited. The personnel engaged in science and technology are small in number; engineers and technicians account for only 2% of the total number of workers and staff members. There are only 3.9 agro-technicians per 10,000 agricultural population. Among the scientists and technicians, graduates from universities, colleges and secondary technical schools make up only 32% of the total. High and middle-ranking personnel in science and technology make up only 6.84%, which is lower than the national average. There are especially few scientists and technicians among the minority nationalities — 15 persons for every 10,000 in minority nationality areas, which is much lower than the provincial level of 49 persons for every 10,000 people.

The future plans for Yunnan's economic development are as follows:

(1), *We must readjust the irrational economic structure and advance agriculture and light industry.* We plan to speed up the development of agriculture and light industry and to raise their proportion in the national economy. We must try our best to readjust the economic structure and to make it more balanced and rational. Agriculture will continue to implement and carry out the provision of important documents and relevant policies issued by the Party Central Committee concerning agricultural development and will try to perfect various forms of production responsibility. Forestry, animal husbandry and a diversified economy will be developed in a big way while ensuring the production of grain. The development of light industry mainly depends on regrouping and reforming existing industrial enterprises, strengthening their operational management, implementing technical innovations and improving the economic results.

(2) *We will give full play to the superiority of the local economy and develop the commodity economy in a big way.* Since the natural resources of Yunnan Province are especially rich, the successful readjustment of the national economy will actively create favourable conditions and give full play to the superiority of the resources in various places. We will develop such local products as cigarettes, tea, sugarcane, animal by-products, spices, medicinal herbs, ferrous metal products, forestry products, rubber products, phosphorous products, hardware and other local specialities. We will strive to produce many competitive first-rate products and brand-name products.

(3) *We will vigorously develop transport and communications and strengthen exchanges inside and outside the province.* In the near future we must develop highway transport and raise the capacity of existing highways. At the same time, we should pave interrupted highways and keep highways open to collection and distribution areas for agricultural and sideline products. We should give priority to the construction of mountain-area highways having economic value and post roads. We should vigorously develop transportation run by the local people. Transport should be oriented towards heavy-duty and diesel vehicles so as to raise transport efficiency and lower costs.

(4) *We will firmly grasp education and speed up the training of qualified personnel.* We should stick to the policy of "walking on two legs" and bring the initiative of various quarters into play to undertake various forms of schooling. According to the circumstances, we will run primary schools well and make education universal. We should actively reform the secondary education structure and properly convert ordinary middle schools into various secondary technical schools while developing agricultural middle schools and part-work and part-study schools. Teachers' universities and schools should be well run in order to raise the level of teachers, as should higher education and secondary technical schools so as to provide more qualified personnel. We must pay attention to and give aid to cultural and educational undertakings by operating free lodging middle or primary schools, by vigorously training intellectuals and special professionals of minority nationalities, by developing spare-time education for adults and by running broadcasting and TV universities, night universities and correspondence universities well. We will gradually establish a spare-time educational system from the lowest level to higher education. We should do a good job of training workers and staff members and raise the scientific, technological and cultural levels of workers and staff. In the countryside especially we should make strenuous efforts to wipe out illiteracy and improve education so as to stress agricultural techniques.

86. ECONOMIC DEVELOPMENT IN ZHEJIANG PROVINCE
By Ji Wei and Zhong He
Synthesizing Office, Zhejiang Provincial Planning Commission

Population, History and Resources

Population. Zhejiang is one of China's small but densely populated provinces. It has an area of more than 100,000 sq. km. At the end of 1980, the population was 38.27 million, averaging 376 persons per sq. km. About 34.36 million people live in rural areas.

History. The province has a long history behind it. During the Spring and Autumn Period (770 B.C.–476 B.C.), it was part of the state of Yue, which had its capital at present-day Shaoxing. After the unification of China under the Qin Dynasty (221 B.C.–207 B.C.), it was divided between Huiji and Minzhong prefectures. During the Sui Dynasty (581 A.D.–618 A.D.), a canal was dug from Gongchengqiao in Hangzhou in the south to connect with the Grand Canal north of the Changjiang River. This waterway became an artery between the north and south in ancient China. Hangzhou was then the seat of a prefecture.

With the development of maritime trade in the Tang Dynasty (618–907), Mingzhou (present-day Ningbo) and Wenzhou became major sea ports. Later, during the Five Dynasties and Ten States Period (907–960), Hangzhou became the capital of the state of Wuyue. It was also the capital of the Southern Song Dynasty (1127-1279), but it was then called Lin'an and was known as the principal city in southeast China. Zhejiang became a province during the Yuan Dynasty (1271–1368).

Natural Resources. Zhejiang is known as the "home of fish, rice and silk." The Hangzhou-Jiangxing-Huzhou and Ningbo-Shaoxing plains abound in rice and natural silk. Hills and mountains cover 70% of Zhejiang, supporting the growth of timber trees, bamboo, tea and citrus fruits. The province borders a vast stretch of sea and faces the Zhoushan Islands, one of China's major fishing grounds. Along the extensive coastline there are fine harbours such as Ningbo, Wenzhou, Haimen, Dinghai and Zhapu.

The province has enormous easy-to-work reserves of non-metallic minerals such as fluorspar, alumstone, limestone, amargosite and arenaceous hyaline-quartz. Verified coal and iron ore deposits are small.

Transportation. Water transport is convenient in the lower reaches of large rivers and along a labyrinth of small rivers and canals which criss-cross the plains. Hangzhou is a railway hub from which one can reach all parts of China through the Shanghai-Hangzhou, Zhejiang-Jiangxi, Xiaoshan-Ningbo and Hangzhou-Changxing trunk lines and the branch line between Xinanjiang and Jinhua. Hangzhou is also a road transport centre from which highways branch out to all parts of the province and to adjacent provinces and Shanghai Municipality.

Economy. Zhejiang's economy is dominated by agriculture and light industry, although a foundation has been laid for heavy industry. Thanks to the fine natural conditions, the province has become a comprehensive agricultural economic zone with farming, forestry, animal husbandry, fishing, sideline occupations and various other undertakings. The silk, paper, woollen textile, linen, food and ceramics industries, as well as other light and handicraft industries, have fairly solid bases. Zhejiang's foreign trade began quite early and the province now accounts for an important share of China's exports. Zhejiang is also known for its picturesque landscape and cultural and historical relics. Hangzhou is one of China's tourist centres.

Survey of Economic Development Since 1949

Zhejiang's economy has made tremendous progress since 1949, although there have been ups and downs. Large-scale farm improvement projects have been built on the basis of agricultural collectivization. As a result, farming conditions have improved continuously and productivity has increased steadily.

Agriculture. More than 80% of the farmland is irrigated, either mechanically (three-fourths, or 17.1 million *mu*) or electrically. Average consumption of electricity now exceeds 60 kwh. per *mu* of farmland and that of chemical fertilizer about 20 kg. (counting only the effective content). With the improvement in agricultural techniques, unit yields have gone up steadily. Although farmland averages only 0.72 *mu* per capita, the province has been able to meet the basic needs of its population, provide light industry with more and more raw materials and increase exports of farm and farm-related products.

Industry. In the early 1950's, Zhejiang's light industry consisted mainly of handicraft workshops. There were few modern factories. Since then, a large number of key enterprises have been built and the old enterprises have been renovated and expanded. This has greatly increased the production capacity of the silk, cotton, textile, paper, food and ceramics industries. The new industries that have sprung up make such goods as woollen fabrics, linen, chemical fibres, plastics, sewing machines, bicycles, clocks and wrist-watches to fill the gaps in the supply of consumer goods. Industry as a whole has been updated technically in a systematic fashion.

With regard to heavy industry, Zhejiang had nothing more than a few small power plants and iron works in the early post-Liberation period. Starting with the construction of the Xinanjiang Hydroelectric Power Station in the First Five-Year Plan period, a series of new heavy industrial divisions have been set up. They include the metallurgical, heavy machinery, electronic meters, building materials, basic chemicals, chemical fertilizer and insecticides industries.

Transportation and Communications. Progress has also been made in transport and communications. Compared with the early post-Liberation period, the total length of railways open to traffic has doubled, that of highways has increased 9.9-fold and that of waterways open to modern shipping rose 8.8-fold. Civil aviation, posts and telecommunications also have developed rapidly.

Economic Structure. Development of production and construction has brought about a radical change in Zhejiang's economic structure and a noticeable improvement in the people's livelihood. In 1949, Zhejiang's total industrial and agricultural output value was 2,474 million yuan. Of this sum, 1,814 million yuan came from agriculture and 660 million yuan from industry, while heavy industry accounted for only 37 million yuan of the total. In 1979, the province's total industrial and agricultural output value reached 23,145 million yuan or 9.4 times the 1949 figure, averaging an annual increase of 7.7% over 30 years. To this total, agriculture contributed 8,200 million yuan, an increase of 4.5-fold over 1949, and industry 14,940 million yuan, an increase of 22.6-fold. The output value of heavy industry in 1979 was 6,110 million yuan, 165 times the 1949 figure. Of the total 1949 output value, agriculture accounted for 73.3%, light industry 25.2% and heavy industry 1.5%, but the figures for 1979 were 35.5%, 38.1% and 26.4% respectively. National income for the province averaged 66 yuan per capita in 1949 and it rose to 370 yuan in 1979 (at 1970 constant prices).

Since 1979, Zhejiang has carried out the principle of readjustment, restructuring, consolidation and improvement of the national economy in accordance with the principles and policies of the Third Plenary Session of the 11th Party Central Committee. In view of Zhejiang's actual conditions, emphasis was put on giving full scope to the strong points of the province's diversified rural economy, light and textile industries and tourism so as to improve the economic structure step by step. Considerable progress has been made in the course of readjustment.

Review of Economic Developments in 1980

Agricultural Development. Agricultural production in 1980 was marked by a fairly good harvest and structural improvements, though it suffered from one of the worst natural calamities in several decades. Total agricultural output value reached 8,500 million yuan, an increase of 3.6% over 1979 and 17.6% over 1978. Grain output was 14,355,000 tons, which was less than the 1979 output but about the same as the good 1978 harvest.

Output of most industrial crops increased as follows:

Crop	1980 Output	Percentage increase over 1979
Cotton	82,900 tons	19.1
Rapeseeds	272,100 tons	7.0
Jute and ambary	149,700 tons	− 3.8
Silkworm cocoons	65,000 tons	12.6
Tea	75,400 tons	15.2

Output of pork, beef and mutton in 1980 totalled 698,000 tons, or 22.7% more than in 1979. Sales of hogs were up 12% while the number in stock at the end of 1980 was down 9.4% compared with 1979.

Total output of aquatic products in 1980 was 817,000 tons, or 0.7% over 1979. Marine products made up 91.8% of the total. Fishing operations were readjusted and the total haul was limited in order to protect ocean fisheries.

Substantial financial and material aid has been given to forestry during the readjustment in the past two years. Grain purchase and sales quotas for mountainous areas have been readjusted. In 1980, trees were planted on 137,400 hectares of land, an area 10.5% larger than in the previous year. But excessive cutting over the years has reduced the proportion of full-grown trees in forest reserves. It is therefore necessary to limit the volume of cutting.

Sideline occupations and industries run by production brigades and teams accounted for 22.4% of the total agricultural output value in 1980, as against 16.4% in 1979. Commune-run industries also made impressive progress.

Industrial Development. Zhejiang's industry has developed steadily in the course of economic readjustment. The total industrial output value in 1980 was 19,040 million yuan, 27.5% more than in 1979. Output of major industrial products was as follows:

Product	1980 Output	Percentage increase over 1979
Steel	393,500 tons	44.6
Pig iron	322,600 tons	3.9
Coal	1.43 million tons	– 15.2
Electricity	8,146 million kwh.	43.1
Shipped timber	581,500 cu. m.	– 5.9
Cement	2.28 million tons	10.0
Plate glass	1,117,000 standard cases	18.5
Chemical fertilizer (counting only the effective content)	494,300 tons	19.8
Plastics	22,700 tons	14.1
Power generating equipment	176,600 kw. (aggregate)	15.5
TV sets	74,695	191.1
Radio sets	1,715,600	182.5
Silk	8,099 tons	29.3
Silk piece goods	171 million m.	28.6
Cotton yarn	94,200 tons	13.1
Cotton cloth	476 million sq. m.	22.7
Machine-made paper and paperboard	221,200 tons	18.2
Bicycles	137,200	71.5
Sewing machines	264,900	31.9

In 1980, the volume of freight carried by all means of transport totalled 6,489 million ton-km., an 8.69% increase over 1979. Of this total, the volume of freight carried by road was 825 million ton-km., 8.4% more than in 1979; that carried by inland shipping was 3,390 million ton-km., 12% more than in 1979; and that carried by coastal shipping was 2,280 million ton-km., 4.2% more than in 1979. The Zhejiang branch of the China Ocean Shipping Corporation, set up in 1980, inaugurated freighter services from Ningbo and Wenzhou to Hong Kong and began to carry cargo to and from Korea and Japan.

Zhejiang's industrial development in 1980 had three salient features:

(1) The structure of industry was better co-ordinated, with light industry growing faster than heavy industry. The total output value of light industry in 1980 was 11,510 million yuan, an increase of 30.4% over 1979. Its proportion of the province's total industrial output value rose from 59.1% in 1979 to 60.5% in 1980.

(2) Collectively owned enterprises grew faster than state-owned enterprises; the total output value of the former in 1980 was 7,380 million yuan, a 39.6% increase over 1979, accounting for 38.8% of Zhejiang's total industrial output value in 1980.

(3) The system of economic management underwent preliminary reform. The management in a number of enterprises was given greater decision-making power. Market regulation was introduced under the guidance of the state plan. Various forms of joint ventures were adopted. All this stimulated the enthusiasm of the enterprises and workers for production, strengthened the system of economic responsibility and improved economic results.

For most industrial products, quality was improved, variety increased and consumption of raw materials was reduced. Locally administered state industrial enterprises reduced the costs of comparable products and turned over 14.7% more profits to the state in 1980 than in 1979. About one-fourth of the enterprises that had been losing money began to turn a profit, cutting the total losses of locally administered state industrial enterprises by 31.5% as compared with 1979.

The major problems in industrial production were that the readjustment and reorganization of industrial enterprises and the improvement of their techniques and management did not proceed fast enough, and that some products were not made in line with market demands.

Capital Construction and Investment. In capital construction, the investment structure was improved and work on key projects was accelerated. More than 820 million yuan worth of fixed assets were added through the completion of new projects in 1980. Among them were power-generating sets with an aggregate capacity of 133,000 kw., 5,000 spindles for woollen mills, 30,000 spindles for cotton mills, facilities for the dyeing and printing of 20 million metres of terylene fabrics and 10 million metres of silk fabrics, and waterworks with a daily capacity of 75,000 tons. New buildings for colleges completed in 1980 totalled

100,000 sq. m. of floor space — a record in the past 30 years. New tourist facilities were built with a total floor space of 15,000 sq. m. and 454 beds. The Zhejiang and Huagang hotels, as well as the Jingshan Hotel in Wenzhou, were completed on schedule.

Investment in capital construction was reoriented in 1980. More money went to science and technology, education, public health, urban construction and housing than in the past. Nonproductive projects accounted for 32.2% of the total investment in 1980, as against 21.7% in 1979.

The main problem in capital construction was still overextension. The scale of capital construction exceeded financial and material capabilities. As a result, the ratio of projects completed to the total number under construction dropped.

Finance and Commerce. With increased production, business was brisk in both urban and rural markets and government revenue increased. The total value of commodities purchased by the commercial departments in 1980 reached 10,590 million yuan, or 18.7% more than in 1979. Retail sales totalled 8,940 million yuan, an increase of 14.9% (after deducting the rise in prices) over 1979. Compared with 1979, sales of pork went up 19.2%; fresh eggs, 13.5%; sugar, 20.6%; cotton cloth, 14.7%; chemical fibre cloth, 29.2%; mixed polyester fabrics, 40.8%; woollen fabrics, 76.8%; silk fabrics, 49.1%; bicycles, 37.6%; sewing machines, 25.1%; wrist-watches, 40.4%; transistor radio sets, 59%; TV sets, 126.1% and electric bulbs 28.2%.

Total revenues collected by the province in 1980 reached 3,080 million yuan, an increase of 20.2% over 1979. Of this amount, local revenues accounted for 1,730 million yuan, a 26.9% increase over 1979. Local expenditures during the year totalled 1,740 million yuan, an increase of 0.9% over 1979. Spending to tap the full potential of enterprises and to renovate enterprises rose by 45.1%, while expenditures on science, education, culture and public health went up 22%. However, allocations for local capital construction projects declined by 27.5%.

Foreign Trade and Tourism. In 1980, total purchases of goods for export totalled 1,920 million yuan, an increase of 27.2% over 1979. Of this, silk and other textiles accounted for 555 million yuan, or 13.8% more than in 1979. Purchases of metals, minerals, chemicals, medicine, machinery and equipment rose by 68.9% over the previous year, and their proportion of total purchases increased from 12.8% in 1979 to 17% in 1980.

The number of visitors to Zhejiang has increased enormously in recent years. They included foreign nationals, overseas Chinese and Chinese compatriots from Hong Kong and Macao who took tours, visited relatives or came for other purposes. To cope with this situation, repairs were begun on scenic spots around the West Lake in Hangzhou and other tourist centres. These included Fuchun River, Mogan Mountain, the tomb of Yu (the reputed founder of the Xia Dynasty, circa 21st—16th century B.C.) and Lanting (Orchid Pavilion) in Shaoxing; the Tiantong and Yuwang monasteries in Ningbo; Putuo Mountain in Zhoushan; the Guoqing Temple in Tiantai; and Yandang Mountain in southern Zhejiang. Tourist facilities were improved.

Science, Culture and Health. In 1980, Zhejiang had 95 independent scientific research institutes staffed by 3,789 scientists and technicians, and 67 affiliated scientific research institutes staffed by 1,155 scientisits and technicians. New results were achieved in applied sciences relating to the increase of farm yields, the breeding of aquatic products, energy saving, and the improvement of quality and increase in the variety of goods produced by the silk, paper, ceramics and other light industries.

Total enrollment in the province's 22 institutions of higher learning in 1980 was more than 37,000, an increase of 16.6% over 1979. In addition, over 11,000 students were enrolled in the Television University. Enrollment in the 89 vocational secondary schools was 31,000; in regular middle schools, 1.7 million; and primary schools, 4.82 million. Nearly all school-age children were enrolled.

Progress was also made in the development of culture, public health, sports, broadcasting and publishing. In 1980, there were 69,000 hospital beds, an increase of 5.4% over 1979. The incidence of some diseases dropped.

Population and Employment. At the end of the year, Zhejiang's population exceeded 38.26 million, surpassing the 1979 figure by more than 340,000.

During the year, jobs were found for 227,000 urban inhabitants, including educated young people who returned from the countryside after the "cutlural revolution." This brought the total number of newly employed persons in the period 1978-80 to 808,000. Most cities and counties in Zhejiang have basically solved the problem of unemployment left over from past years.

Income and Livelihood. The people's livelihood improved significantly in 1979 and continued to improve in 1980. Increased farm output and state purchasing prices added 1,100 million yuan to the peasants' income from sales of farm and sideline products in 1979, compared with the preceding year, and a further increase of 330 million yuan was recorded in 1980. A commune member's income from the collective averaged 116 yuan in 1980, which was 13.3% more than the 102.4 yuan of 1978. The actual increase was even bigger, because the above-mentioned figures did not include the pay rises that commune members working in industry received directly from the enterprises run by communes and their subdivisions, nor did they include the peasants' rising income from sideline production.

Urban workers earned more in 1980 than before as a result of the November 1979 pay raise and the significant increases in bonuses and subsidies. Annual wages in state-owned enterprises averaged 772 yuan per worker in 1980. This was 19.3% more than 1979 (647 yuan) and 29.3% more than 1978 (597 yuan). In this case, too, the actual increase was larger, when the increase in employment is taken into consideration. The total floor space of new housing for workers completed in 1979 was 1.36 million sq. m.; and in 1980, 2.32 million sq. m. Construction in the two years put together exceeded one-third of the total housing constructed in the preceding 30 years.

Current Problems and Future Prospects

Under the influence of "Left" ideologies, there was for a long time an overemphasis on the development of heavy industry and disregard for the potentialities of Zhejiang's natural resources. Instead of making full use of the province's advantages in agriculture and light industry, considerable manpower, financial and material resources were devoted to the development of the coal and iron industries. This failed to produce the expected results because the resources were limited.

During the "cultural revolution" in particular, the economy became seriously imbalanced as a result of the policies of Lin Biao and the Gang of Four. The readjustment undertaken in the past two years or so has corrected the imbalance to a certain extent. However, the economic structure is still far from satisfactory.

The main problems are as follows:

(1) *Agriculture is not sufficiently strong and its internal structure still needs improvement.* Zhejiang is usually described as a province comprising "70% mountains, 10% water surface and 20% farmland." But forestry makes up only 2.6% and fishing only 3.7% of the province's total agricultural output value. Some mountain regions are underdeveloped and the conditions of production are poor. In some places, forest resources have been wantonly destroyed, and this has had an adverse effect on the ecological balance.

(2) *The development of light industry has lagged behind market demands.* Though Zhejiang's light industry started relatively early, for many years it did not receive sufficient investment and hence did not grow fast enough. In 1950-78, its total output value averaged an annual increase of 9%, less than the national average of 11% in the same period. The rate of increase has accelerated in the past two years. However, because investments were insufficient and because not enough attention was paid to renovating old enterprises, quite a number of enterprises at present are not adequately equipped and their technological processes are rather backward and ill-coordinated. Consequently, the products of these enterprises cannot satisfy international market demands in terms of quality, variety, design or packaging, nor can they meet the growing demands of the home market.

(3) *The processing industries have developed faster than the supply of raw and semi-processed materials and of energy.* Heavy industry still consumes too much energy and some enterprises in this sector are operating below capacity. Some light industrial projects are redundant and for some branches of the industry the processing capacity has exceeded the available supply of raw and semi-processed materials. One of Zhejiang's main tasks in readjusting and developing its industry is to improve the technological level and the product mix of its industries so as to save energy and raw and semi-processed materials.

(4) *Transport and communications, electric power and water supply are not sufficiently developed, nor are some undertakings required by the development of society.* Science, technology, culture and education, all of which suffered a great deal during the 10 years of turmoil, cannot keep pace with economic construction. Urban reconstruction and the building of public utilities in Hangzhou, Shaoxing and other tourist centres have lagged behind the development of tourism. Environmetnal protection should be strengthened.

Economic Goals. In carrying out economic construction under the guidance of unified state planning, Zhejiang will henceforth proceed on the basis of local resources and socio-economic conditions, so as to maximize its advantages and minimize its disadvantages. It will carry on the readjustment of the economy, continue to strengthen the agricultural and light industrial sectors, strive for better economic results, speed up the development of tourism and foreign trade and continuously raise the people's standard of living on the basis of increased production.

In agriculture, emphasis will be placed on intensive farming, cultivation of crops suited to local growing conditions, raising the land utilization rate and increasing grain output, while increasing the production of commodities that will yield not only nonstaple foods, but also raw materials for the textile and light industries. Efforts will be made to renovate existing light industrial and textile enterprises, improve the product mix, increase the intensity and accuracy of processing operations and develop labour-intensive products.

Foreign trade will be expanded through the development of such businesses as processing imported or supplied materials and various forms of compensatory trade, and production of market-oriented products will be increased to meet the demands of home and international markets.

Heavy industry will be readjusted and reorganized so that it will gear itself mainly to the needs of the technical transformation of agriculture, light industry and existing enterprises. At the same time, transport, communications, power and other basic industries will be strengthened.

Investment in science, technology and education will be increased to speed up the training of specialists and to improve the technical level and management of the economy as a whole.

Addenda:

A. SURVEY OF ECONOMIC DEVELOPMENT IN TAIWAN PROVINCE
By Gao Lingzhen

Geographic and Economic Setting

Taiwan, a beautiful and richly endowed island, has since ancient times formed an inalienable part of the sacred territory of our great motherland. The compatriots there are kith and kin of the big family of the Chinese nation. Making China independent, unified and prosperous is the unanimous aspiration and common responsibility of the people on the mainland and on Taiwan Island.

Lying on the edge of the continental shelf of the East China Sea, Taiwan is separated from the mainland in the west by the 100-km. broad Taiwan Strait. It borders on the Pacific Ocean in the east and faces the Philippines in the south and Japan across the sea to the north.

Taiwan province consists of 80 islands, including Taiwan Island and the Penghu Islands. The province covers an area of 36,000 sq.km., accounting for 0.4% of the total area of China. Its population stands at 17.8 million, averaging 494 persons per sq.km., making Taiwan the most densely populated province in the country.

Han and Gaoshan nationalities are the principal inhabitants of the island. With a warm climate, abundant rainfall, diversified topography and 55% forest coverage, Taiwan is richly endowed by nature. It enjoys abundant outputs of rice, sugarcane, tea and various fruits such as pineapples, bananas and tangerines, which are famous at home and abroad. Camphor is one of its special products. Cattle and pigs are raised widely. It has very rich offshore fishery resources and is one of the principal sea-salt producing areas of our country. A quantity of minerals and plenty of hydroelectric and geothermal resources are also found on Taiwan.

1980: A Difficult Year. The Gross National Product of Taiwan Province in 1980 stood at 1,449,300 million New Taiwan dollars (NT$), the equivalent of U.S.$40,200 million. Its annual growth rate was 6.66%, compared with 8.1% in 1979, and failed to meet the planned goal of 8%. The 1980 growth rate was the lowest since 1975. Per capita income was registered at U.S.$2,281, a 4.6% increase over the previous year. The growth rate of industrial output value was 8.3%, of which mining was 4.3%; manufacturing 7.2% (including increases of 9.4% in heavy industry, 4.4% in light industry, and 7.5% in utilities); and housing construction 20.5%. Agricultural output value fell by 1%, of which agricultural products dropped by 1.8% and forest products by 5.9%; animal by-products rose by 0.3%, and fisheries increased by 1.2%. The total volume of foreign trade stood at U.S.$39,400 million, of which imports accounted for U.S.$19,733 million and exports, U.S.$19,810 million, yielding an favourable balance of U.S.$77.5 million — a sharp decline from the 1970 total of U.S.$1,350 million, a peak not seen since 1974. Wholesale prices increased by 21.6% over 1979. Urban consumer prices were 19% higher. The money supply reached NT$305,400 million, up 19.9%. Savings deposits reached NT$649,200 million, a rise of 23%. The bank discount rate stood at 11%, while loan interest rates ranged from 13.5% to 16.2%. Total employment in 1980 was 6,547,00. The unemployment rate rose to 2.05%, up from 1.88% in 1979. The average monthly per capita wage of employed workers averaged U.S.$210. Nominal wages could not catch up with price increases, resulting in a decline of real wages.

The direct causes of the slow-down in Taiwan's economic growth in 1980 were:

1. *The impact of the petroleum crisis.* Oil consumption in Taiwan shot up from 5.59 million tons in 1973 to 20.26 million tons in 1980, of which 20 million tons, or 99.1%, were imported at a cost of U.S.$4,100 million, an 88.7% rise over the U.S.$2,175 million of 1979. Oil import expenditures accounted for 21% of all import costs. Due to skyrocketing oil prices in the international market, oil prices in Taiwan rose twice between July and September 1980; including a readjustment in 1979, the accumulated increase came to 88.4%. The cost of electricity rose by 77%; railway cost increases ranged from 41% to 86%; and prices for industrial products were 20% higher. Thus, the oil impact brought about tremendous adverse effects and almost insurmountable difficulties for Taiwan's economy and for the lives of its people.

2. *Aggravated inflation.* Imports accounted for over 50% of the gross domestic product in 1980. Supplies of oil, raw materials, grain and machinery equipment required for the development of production largely depend on foreign countries. Marked price hikes for imported goods heightened production costs, in turn resulting in the skyrocketing of commodity prices. In order to stimulate the economy and deal with the oil impact, financial expenditures in 1980 were in-

creased to NT$20,500 million, boosting the budget deficit from NT$24,629 million to NT$45,129 million. Due to the reckless issuance of banknotes in an attempt to make up the financial deficit, the money supply increased by nearly 20%. Rising prices and the over-issuance of banknotes forced a devaluation of the currency. The 100-dollar banknote was no longer in circulation; instead, banknotes of 500- and 1,000-dollar denominations were issued in late February, aggravating the already serious inflationary trend. Although the bank discount rate and the savings interest rate were raised and other measures taken to encourage savings, tighten the money market and curb inflation, these efforts produced no marked effect, and were in fact detrimental to investment stimulation.

3. *Productivity declined.* With prices skyrocketing, wages in term of money rose slightly; however, productivity grew to a lesser extent and even declined in some instances. Wages in the manufacturing sector in 1980 stood at 89% above the 1976 level, while productivity grew by only 41%. Therefore, labour costs had increased by 34%. The 2.5% decline in agricultural productivity pushed up the prices of export products, weakening their competitive power on the international market. The competitive power of exports could not be restored, even though the Taiwan dollar had been devalued by 5% against the U.S. dollar.

4. *Exports were stagnant.* The favourable trade balance was reduced. Taiwan's exports in 1980 grew normally by 22%, although their actual rise was only 7%, below the growth rate of the previous few years. Moreover, an unfavourable trade balance was registered for half the year. Among the 27 major export products, 7 were below the 1979 level, 19 maintained the same level and only 11 grew slightly. Public opinion in Taiwan was of the view that "1980 was a hard year for Taiwan's economy."

Changes Over the Past Three Decades

The economy of Taiwan Province has grown considerably during the past 30 years. The GNP growth rate averaged 9.1% a year. A rate of 6.9% prevailed during the period from 1953 to 1962; 10.1% for the period 1963-72; and 8% for the period 1973-78. GNP grew most rapidly in the 1960's, and slowed in the 1970's. The grow rate varied greatly from year to year. It fell sharply from 11.9% in 1973 to 0.6% in 1974. In that year, the industrial growth rate dropped to −1.5%, the manufacturing growth rate fell to −2.7%, and the trade deficit shot up to U.S.$1,327 million. The economy began to pick up in 1976 and climbed up to a record growth rate of 12.8% in 1978. But it went down again to 8.1% in 1979 and to 6.66% in 1980. In the 1970's, Taiwan's economy developed in a highly unstable manner with two upward and two downward surges.

Taiwan's economic structure has also changed, evolving from dominance by agriculture to dominance by industry. However, economic development in Taiwan was not based on economic independence and initiative, but relied rather on the demands of the international market. Beginning in the 1960's, the export processing industry expanded rapidly, producing inbalances between industry and agriculture and between raw materials and primary industries and the processing industry. Consequently, a lop-sided industrial structure was formed.

Changes in Taiwan's Economic Structure

Year	Agricultural Sector (farming, forestry, animal husbandry, fishery)		Industrial Sector (mining, manufacturing, construction, public utilities)		Service Sector (communications, commerce, banking, services)	
	Output Value	Employment	Output Value	Employment	Output Value	Employment
1952	35.8	51.4	17.7	20.4	46.5	28.2
1960	32.6	46.5	24.2	22.4	43.2	31.1
1970	17.7	36.7	33.8	28.3	48.5	35.0
1977	10.4	21.5	45	41.8	44.7	36.7

Industry. Under the colonial policy of "industry — Japan, agriculture — Taiwan" as practiced in Taiwan during the period of Japanese occupation, agricultural products were plundered by Japan and industrial products were dumped in Taiwan. During the Second World War, Taiwan did not suffer serious destruction as did the mainland. On the eve of the liberation of the mainland, large quantities of capital and equipment were transferred to Taiwan. Taiwan's light and textile industries developed in the 1950's with the assistance of the United States and by stimulation from the War of Aggression in Korea. The 1960's, the post-war "golden age" for economic development in the capitalist world, provided a favourable environment for the development of Taiwan's economy and industry in particular. During this period, developed capitalist countries transferred some of their labour-intensive and seriously polluting industries to underdeveloped areas. Under these circumstances, Taiwan's export processing industry made rapid progress. In the 1970's, Taiwan began to develop such energy-intensive heavy and chemical industries as iron and steel, shipbuilding and petrochemicals.

From 1953 to 1978, the annual industrial growth rate averaged 14.8%, with industrial output value increasing from NT$5,600 million to NT$994,900 million. The output of principal industrial products grew rapidly.

Industry has occupied an increasingly important position in the economy of the province. The proportion of light and heavy industries within the manufacturing sector has greatly changed with light industry dropping to a share of 43% in 1980, down from 75.2% in 1952, and

Output of Taiwan's Principal Industrial Products, 1952 to 1978

Product	Unit	1952	1980
Coal	million tons	2.28	2.57
Crude oil	kilolitres	2,900	211,000
Natural gas	million cu. m.	173	1,700
Electricity	megawatt-nours	1,400	40,800
Steel	thousand tons	16	3,310
Cement	thousand tons	440	14,030
Granulated sugar	thousand tons	620	728
Cotton yarn	thousand tons	13.6	341
Cotton cloth	million metres	85.42	8,072.65
Aluminium ingots	tons	3,856	63,549
Refined oil	kilolitres	—	202,600
Petrochemicals	thousand tons	—	1,310
Chemical fibres	thousand tons	—	1,450
Plastics and rubber	thousand tons	—	450
TV sets	thousand units	—	57,435
Automobiles	single units	—	132,580
Housing units	thousand cu.m.	—	35,280

heavy industry rising to 57% from 24.8%. Taiwan's industry at present is still based on labour-intensive activities using simple techniques; highly mechanized industries only account for 24% of the total manufacturing output value.

The Role of Foreign Investment. Taiwan's economy has developed with the assistance of U.S. and Japanese monopoly capitalists. From 1951 to 1978, Taiwan received U.S.$1,500 million in "economic aid" from the United States, U.S.$7,478 million in loans from foreign countries, U.S.$1,250 million in local-currency loans from branches of foreign banks in Taiwan, and U.S.$1,329 million in private direct foreign investment. The amount of U.S. aid to Taiwan from 1952 to 1960 was equivalent to 58.8% of the composition of total fixed capital in this period. In the middle and late 1960's, huge sums of overseas capital flowed into Taiwan. The number of enterprises funded by overseas capital totalled about 2,500 in 1978; these had nearly 300,000 employees, accounting for 15% of total employment in the province in that year. Exports from these enterprises came to 29% of the total export volume of Taiwan. By 1980, overseas capital had amounted to more than U.S.$2,700,000 million.

For a long period, the wages of Taiwan workers were very low. The average wage in the 1950's only came to about 5% of the average wage in the industrialized capitalist countries. Since the 1960's, the wage of a Taiwan worker equalled only one-fourth to one-third of that of a Japanese worker. In export processing areas, poorly paid women and child workers still comprise up to 80% of the workforce in some units. Low pay has increased the competitive power of export products, enabling foreign capital to score staggering profits. Japan extracted U.S.$6,100 million in profits with less than U.S.$200 million in investments during the 1965-75 period. One U.S. company raked in profits totalling 22 times its investments during a period of 3-4 years. In 1980 alone, foreign capital earned U.S.$21,000 million in profits from export processing activities.

Most of the raw materials and energy required by Taiwan's industry relies on imports. For instance, all raw cotton needed by the textile industry was imported from the United States, while all fuel oil and raw materials needed by the power, oil refining, chemical fibres, plastics and rubber industries relied on imported petroleum. About 80% of Taiwan's manufactured goods were sold abroad. Thus, Taiwan's economy and development of industrial production cannot but be severely affected by fluctuations on international markets. The two ups and downs of Taiwan's economy and industry stemming from the two recent world economic crises and oil shortages clearly show the vulnerability of Taiwan's economy.

The Role of Public Capital. "Public capital" occupies a dominant position in Taiwan's economy and industry. Production in the sectors such as power, petroleum, natural gas, aluminium, chemical fertilizers, salt, sugar, cigarettes, wine, and in undertakings such as railways, posts and telecommunications and water supply, were all operated by "public capital." Moreover, basic materials for the petrochemical industry, steel and shipbuilding were largely in the grip of "public capital." Thirteen out of the 16 banks in Taiwan are owned by bureaucrat-capital. The three others also have shares of bureaucrat-capital. A 1979 industrial and business survey conducted in Taiwan showed that although publicly-owned enterprises accounted for only 0.24% of all industrial and commercial enterprises, their fixed capital accounted for 45.7%, and total value of their assets accounted for 57%. "Private capital" operates mostly medium-sized or small enterprises with relatively backward equipment and techniques. Their level of productivity and the competitive power of their products are rather low. As the international economic environment gradually deteriorates, these medium and small enterprises tend either to go bankrupt or to be annexed or else they are forced to turn into joint operations. Therefore, along with the development of its economy and industry, Taiwan's socio-economic and class contradictions are also growing and deepening.

Agriculture. Of the total agricultural output value, farm products account for 50%, fishery products 20% and animal by-products 30%. The province has 816,000 hectares of farmland. Output of main products in 1980 included rice, 2.32 million tons; sugarcane, 8.91 million tons; pineapples, 225,000 tons; bananas, 195,000 tons; fish, 940,000 tons; beef, 6,175 tons; and pork, 667,000 tons. The rate of agricultural mechanization averages 60-70%. The area ploughed by tractor now approaches 90%. Rice shoots transplanted by machine account for 30% of the total; crops reaped by machine stand at 40%; and grains dried by machine amount to 36%.

In the last 30 years, Taiwan's agriculture has achieved certain progress, although its growth rate has fallen behind that of industry. The average growth rate during the period from 1953 to 1971 was 4% a year, with a 0.7% decline (with farm products dropping by 4%) registered in 1969. The growth rate from 1972 to 1979 averaged 2.8%, with a 2% decline registered in 1975 and a 1.8% drop in 1978. The year 1980 also witnessed a decline. Taiwan used to be a grain exporting province of China. Now, except for rice, which has a small surplus, grain can only meet 40-60% of demand. The proportion of agricultural output value in the national economy has continuously declined, amounting to only 7.7% in 1980.

Ownership in Agriculture. According to a 1975 survey of Taiwan's agriculture, 676,000 among the 880,000 peasant households throughout the province were peasant-owned, comprising 554,000 hectares of farmland and making up 67.79% of the total area of farmland. Of the owner-peasants, 2.3% were rich peasants owning more than three hectares of land each and holding 11.8% of the total farmland; middle-income and rich peasants engaged in small-scale production made up 53.5%, working on 73% of the farmland; and small farmers with farmland below 0.5 hectares made up 44.2%, holding 15.3% of the farmland. Apart from the owner-peasants, there were 189,000 households of semi-owner peasants and tenants, holding 212,200 hectares of farmland.

Capitalist relations in agriculture have developed step by step. In 1975, there were 1,263 large capitalist farms. Some 5% of farm households participated in various forms of "joint management" in the supply, transport and sale of their agricultural products. In recent years, on the basis of joint management, they formed agricultural "specialized areas," such as Chinese olive and tea specialized areas. "Commission management" is currently in vogue in Taiwan. Those peasant households with small plots of land and those short of labour and incapable of buying machines on their own have partly or totally entrusted specialized agricultural service teams to manage their farmlands.

Productivity and Income. Agricultural productivity in Taiwan is much lower than that of industry. In the period from 1954 to 1978, the average annual productivity growth rate was 5.12%, with industry at 8.04% and agriculture at 3.98%. Taiwan's farmers shoulder heavy taxes and levies. For instance, each peasant household pays on the average of NT$2,607 in taxes and other levies, making up 26.13% of its annual income. Taiwan has always pursued a low grain-price policy so as to maintain low wages and low costs for industrial goods, and to promote industrial production and industrial exports. During the 1950-59 period, the price index for agricultural products was only 70% of the general price index; the price index of rice in the period of 1950-59 was 60%; in 1960, 84%; and in 1969, 71%. With the constantly increasing costs of agricultural production, the disparity between the income of peasants and that of people in other trades has increasingly widened. The average per capita income of peasant households in 1966 was NT$4,509, while non-peasant households earned NT$6,464. The differentials were NT$1,955 in 1966, NT$3,801 in 1972, and NT$7,011 in 1975. Taiwan peasants can not make a living by merely doing farming and must engage in other work. In 1975, specialized peasant households in the province totalled 160,000, making up 18% of all peasant households. The number of specialized peasant households was reduced by 59%, or 220,000, between 1960 and 1975. During the same period, peasant households engaging in other occupations numbered 730,000, accounting for 82% of the total. This figure represented a growth of 72%, or 300,000 households, from 1960 to 1975. Of this total, 260,000 peasants left home to engage in other work — the equivalent of 1 person per 34 households; 890,000 peasants stayed at home to do other jobs concurrently, amounting to 1 person in each family. Altogether 50% of the labour force in the countryside had other occupations. One-third of part-time peasants

Product Composition of Taiwan's Foreign Trade

Year	Exports				Imports	
	Agricultural Products	Processed Agricultural Products	Manufactured Goods	Machinery Equipment	Raw Materials for Industry and Agriculture	Consumer Goods
1952	22.1%	69.8%	8.1%	16.5%	72.0%	11.5%
1969-72	8.2%	12.6%	79.2%	32.5%	62.4%	5.1%
1979	4.4%	5.2%	90.4%	24.6%	69.0%	6.4%

made a living by selling their labour. They comprised proletarians or semi-proletarians.

Foreign Trade. Foreign trade is a "pillar" of Taiwan's economy. The total combined import and export value in 1952 was U.S.$303 million; in 1979, the amount rose to U.S.$30,874 million. The proportion of commodity and labour imports and exports in the gross domestic product increased from 14.18% in 1953 to 56.43% in 1980. The average growth rate was 15.8%. Starting from 1971, an unfavourable balance of trade that had lasted for 18 successive years was reversed. In 1978, the total value of foreign trade surpassed the total output value of industry and agriculture. The trade surplus in 1978 was valued at U.S.$1,700 million, a record figure in Taiwan's foreign trade. The structure of foreign trade has also changed. The proportionate value of manufactured goods increased from 8.1% in 1952 to 90.4% in 1979; the share of agricultural products and other processed goods dropped from 22.1% and 69.8% in 1952 to 4.4% and 5.2%, respectively, in 1979.

Among Taiwan's exports, textile goods ranked first in 1980, making up 21.2% of total export value. Electronics and electrical equipment accounted for 18.4% of the total. Imported fuels and raw materials amounted to 67.3% of the total. Crude oil ranked first, making up 20.8%, while machinery and metal products took up 19.2%.

Taiwan's foreign trade was mainly directed to the United States, Japan and countries of the Middle East. The volume of trade with the U.S. in 1980 was U.S.$11,419 million, making up 28.92% of Taiwan's trade total; trade with Japan totalled U.S.$7,411 million, accounting for 19% of the total.

The growth of foreign trade has given impetus to the development of Taiwan's economy, but has also brought about a state of grave dependency and instability.

Prospects for the Future

The state of affairs in the first four months of 1981 indicated that Taiwan was still in a very difficult situation. The general index of industrial production from January to March 1981 increased by 2.8%, with manufacturing industry up by 0.9% (heavy industry increased by 2.7%, while light industry fell by 1.5%). An unfavourable balance of payments prevailed for three months running, amounting to U.S.$483 million. From January to April, overseas investments fell sharply: the total was U.S.$74.6 million, dropping by 50% compared with that of the same period last year. Taiwan public opinion considers 1981 to be "an unhappy year."

Authoritative sources in Taiwan acknowledge that in the past three decades Taiwan has advanced amidst difficulties. The same pattern can be projected for Taiwan's future. In the 1980's, with the economy of the capitalist world in recession and continuing shortages of energy, oil prices will rise and competition in world markets will become fiercer. Taiwan's labour-intensive industrial structure has changed from a motivating force to an obstruction to economic development. Taiwan has to turn to the development of high-technology industry in order to raise labour productivity and to reduce pressure on energy resources and manpower. But it will also rely more on developed capitalist countries for capital, precision equipment and sophisticated technology. Deepening social and class contradictions, a lop-sided economic structure and heavy reliance on other countries are chronic maladies in Taiwan's economy. If the Taiwan authorities go against the will of the people and against historical trends and if they refuse to resume contacts with the mainland, economic conditions cannot improve fundamentally and Taiwan will be unable to rid itself of its dependence on others. In the difficult international situation, Taiwan can only drift with the tide and can never manage to be master of its own destiny. Only by returning to the embrace of the motherland at the earliest possible time and by integrating with the mainland into one unified country can Taiwan's economy look to a bright future.

B. ECONOMIC DEVELOPMENT IN HONG KONG
By Gu Nianlong and Yuan Shibang

Geographic and Economic Setting

The total area of Hong Kong Island, including nearby Tsing Chiu Island, Ap Lei Chau (Aberdeen) Island and other small offshore islands, is 75.6 sq. m. Kowloon is 11.1 sq. m. Together, the two occupy 86.7 sq. km. Hong Kong was ceded to Britain by the government of the Qing Dynasty which signed the "Treaty of Nanking" in 1842 and the "Treaty of Peking" in 1860. The New Territories, consisting of a mainland area adjoining Kowloon and 235 adjacent islands, were leased to Britain under a 99-year lease under the Second Convention of Peking in 1898. Thus, the total area under the administration of the Hong Kong British authorities is 1,046.3 sq. km.

Hong Kong is the transportation hub of Southeast Asia, possessing the region's finest natural harbour. With these favourable natural conditions, following Hong Kong's establishment as a free port, the territory gradually became a centre for entrepot trade — a port for taking in and sending out large quantities of goods for China's southern areas, and a bridge of trade with foreign countries, the Southeast Asian countries in particular. During the 100 years following its establishment as a free port, Hong Kong's economy has in general relied on entrepot trade, lacking a solid industrial base.

After the liberation of China's mainland, owing to a variety of complex factors, large amounts of capital — including foreign capital and manpower — flowed into Hong Kong to seek an outlet, thus creating favourable conditions for industrial development. During the war to resist U.S. aggression and aid Korea, Hong Kong's British authorities carried out a policy of "embargo," dealing heavy blows to the traditional entrepot trade on which Hong Kong depended for its existence. This forced Hong Kong's economy to find a new way out — the development of industry.

Economic Development Since the 1950's

Due to its lack of natural resources and its limited internal markets, objective factors gave rise to Hong Kong's development as an entrepot trade port during the initial 100 years, focusing on activities such as international communications, transportation, finance and banking, telecommunications equipment and commerce. Thus, Hong Kong's economy and industry from the very beginning was geared to the needs of exporting. Some scholars have described Hong Kong's economy before 1955 as the period of entrepot trade; the period from 1955 to 1970 is regarded as the first industrial revolution.

During the latter period, abundant supplies of manpower and low wages favoured production for exports. A series of labour-intensive industries entered a period of rapid development; these included textiles, garments, plastics and rubber products, clocks and watches, electronics and metal-processing trades. By the end of the 1960's, Hong Kong's industry had established a foundation, and the port was transformed into an industrial city. Manufactured exports from Hong Kong began to occupy a prominent place among exports from the world's developing countries and regions. At the same time, exports of Hong Kong goods began to face fierce competition from South Korea, Singapore and China's Taiwan Province; on the other hand, owing to the needs of local economic development, Hong Kong's economy began to develop in the direction of finance and banking, and step by step the port became a regional financial and banking centre.

From the early 1950's to the beginning of the 1970's, Hong Kong's population had risen from 1 million to over 4 million. The economic growth rate surpassed that of the population. Per capita output value in 1970 was H.K.$4,716. The total value of exports was H.K.$15,100 million, among which the value of re-exports was H.K.$2,800 million. The total value of imports was H.K.$17,600 million. Textiles and garments ranked first among exports, comprising 45% of total export value. Workers engaged in these trades accounted for 40% of the total workforce of 570,000. Plastic and rubber toys ranked second among exports, amounting to 25% of the total. In 1970, Hong Kong's banking density was 1.01 banking offices for every 10,000 people. The average per capita bank deposit at the end of 1970 was H.K.$2,650.27. The issuance value of Hong Kong currency at the end of 1970 totalled H.K.$2,578 million. Banknotes in circulation were H.K.$6,548 million.

Generally speaking, the 1970's were the most prosperous years in Hong Kong's history. Apart from signal progress in trade, manufacturing and tourism, the growth of real estate construction and finance and banking was all the more striking. This growth pattern both reflected the features of Hong Kong's economy and illustrated its problems.

Hong Kong's Economy in 1980

Hong Kong's population in 1980 reached

5,148,000. Average per capita output value surpassed H.K.$15,000. The total export value was H.K.$98,242 million, 6.5 times the total of 1970. Exports of Hong Kong-made products totalled H.K.$68,171 million; re-exports were valued at H.K.$30,072 million. Total value of imports was H.K.$111,651 million, 6.6 times higher than in 1970.

Industry and Exports. In 1980, employees in textiles, clothing manufacturing, electronics equipment, plastic and rubber products, toys, and watch and clock industries made up 67% of the total Hong Kong industrial labour force of 892,100.

In that year, the total export value of textiles and garments was H.K.$27,793 million; output of cotton yarn, 160 million kg.; output of synthetic and blended fibre yarns, 46 million kg.;and output of worsted wool yarn, 4.7 million kg. A total of 28,784 machines in the textile industry turned out 748 million sq. m. of fibre and blended fabrics in 1980. The clothing industry employed 275,000 workers, making up 31% of the labour force in Hong Kong industry. The total value of garment exports in 1980 reached H.K.$23,258 million.

The electronics industry ranked second among Hong Kong's export industries. In 1980, 88,000 workers in 1,197 electronics factories produced H.K.$8,306 million in electronics exports.

The 86,314 workers in 4,816 plastic and rubber products factories produced H.K.$5,397 million worth of exports. Toys predominated among plastic and rubber products, with Hong Kong's toy exports ranking first in the world.

The clock and watch industry mainly turned to electronic products. The 40,628 workers in 1,054 factories produced a total export value of H.K.$6,576 million.

Hong Kong's 5,148,000 people relied on imports for their consumption and raw materials, and for components and semi-finished products needed by virtually all industries. Processing activities comprised the main source of income for various industrial trades and supplied the bulk of wages for all sectors of Hong Kong's population.

Imports. In 1980, the value of imports of raw materials and semi-finished products was H.K.$46,489 million, accounting for 42% of the total import value. The main items were synthetic fabrics, valued at H.K.$4,430 million; plastic and rubber dies and materials, H.K.$2,605 million; watch and clock elements, H.K.$3,688 million; iron and steel, H.K.$3,426 million; cotton cloth, H.K.$2,641 million; electrical appliances, components, diodes, semiconductors and integrated circuits, H.K.$1,927 million.

The value of imported consumer goods was H.K.$29,469 million, making up 26% of the total import value. Main items were: diamonds, H.K.$4,178 million; garments and clothing accessories, H.K.$3,461 million; radios, TV's, record players, records and tape recorders, H.K.$2,744 million; watches, H.K.$2,137 million; jade, gems, ivory, jewellery, gold objects, and silverware, H.K.$1,502 million.

Imports of industrial production installations and machinery reached H.K.$16,055 million, amounting to 14% of the total. These included electronic components, H.K.$2,823 million; transport equipment, H.K.$3,079 million; electric machinery, H.K.$1,669 million; textile machinery, H.K.$765 million; machinery for other industries, H.K.$788 million; and office equipment, H.K.$731 million.

The value of imported foodstuffs was H.K.$12,065 million, making up 11% of the total. Main items were fish and fish products, H.K.$1,750 million; fruits, H.K.$1,614 million; meat and meat products, H.K.$1,475 million; live pigs, H.K.$1,170 million; and vegetables, H.K.$1,231 million. Imports of petroleum and oil products were worth H.K.$7,573 million.

Apart from the above-mentioned geographical and historical conditions that led to the growth of trade and manufacturing in Hong Kong in the 1970's, one cannot ignore the role of various measures taken by the Hong Kong British authorities in implementing the policy of free trade and in actively developing international trade.

Banking and Finance. In the wake of an upsurge of trade and manufacturing industry, the banking business has been developing rapidly. It has increasingly evolved into an important force in giving impetus to the growth of Hong Kong's economy inasmuch as Hong Kong has become a major centre of trade, shipping, finance, banking and investment in the Asian-Pacific region. This is one of the important characteristics of the modern Hong Kong economy that is drawing increasing public attention.

At the end of 1980, there were 113 registered banks; 1,146 bank offices; 108 branches or representatives of foreign commercial banks; and 302 companies engaged in foreign financial business. At the end of 1980, Hong Kong's deposit-taking banks and companies absorbed H.K.$131,206 million in domestic deposits and H.K.$167,333 million in overseas deposits. Their deposits in banks outside Hong Kong amounted to H.K.$119,786 million, while overseas loans totalled H.K.$59,665 million and domestic loans, H.K.$124,287 million. In 1980, Hong Kong issued H.K.$10,464 million in banknotes, more than four times the amount in 1970. The M1 money supply was H.K.$24,124 million (M1 represents the narrow definition of money, comprising the total value of banknotes and coins in circulation together with bank deposits on current account); M2 money supply was H.K.$96,862 million (M2 represents the sum of M1 and current, demand, time and savings deposits); the M3 money supply was H.K.$139,578 million (M3 represents M2 plus deposit holdings of all financial institutions).

Hong Kong has few restrictions on foreign capital and businessmen can move their capital in and out freely. This policy has led to rapid expansion of credit, to excessive supply of capital and to increased import prices, all of which have led to a continuous increase of prices in Hong Kong. The inflation rate in Hong Kong was 16% in 1980.

Tourism is an important source of invisible trade income in Hong Kong, providing an important means of compensation for the unfavourable trade balance and increasing opportunities for employment. In 1980, 2,300,000 tourists come to Hong Kong, producing earnings of H.K.$6,595 million in foreign exchange.

Real Estate. Owing to its relatively scarce land and to the policy of Hong Kong authorities in maintaining high land prices, the cost of housing property in Hong Kong is very high. Hong Kong's real estate market absorbs a tremendous volume of investments. The total area of housing, buildings and factories completed in 1980 was 2,077,000 sq. m., built at a cost of H.K.$4,674 million. Among various real estate transactions in 1980, those involving entire estates totalled H.K.$7,288 million; purchases and sales of floors of buildings were valued at H.K.$19,853 million; and real estate mortgages were valued at H.K.$32,563 million, making up 23% of total bank loans. Policies promoting high land prices and speculation in real estate enable speculators to gain enormous profits, with related sectors such as banking and the construction industry also reaping substantial gains.

The auction of land owned by the authorities has become an important income source in the financial budget of the Hong Kong British authorities. Such income not only made up for the budget deficit but also contributed much to Hong Kong's enormous financial surpluses in recent years. Ordinary industrial and commercial enterprises — the small and medium-sized ones in particular — are keenly aware of the heavy burden of unbearably high land prices and housing rentals which make it difficult for them to engage in business. The broad masses of inhabitants constantly complain about this situation, which has become a grave obstacle to the further growth of Hong Kong's economy.

Future Development. Economic recession in Western countries, the growth of world-wide protectionism and increasingly fierce competition among neighbouring countries and regions, together with restrictions from internal conditions, have made Hong Kong's industrialists and businessmen feel increasingly hard pressed in running their factories and firms. At the beginning of the 1980's, noted figures in Hong Kong's industrial, commercial and academic circles put forth the view that Hong Kong's economy was facing another structural change. Some took the view that Hong Kong was in the second stage of its industrial revolution. Apparently, the Hong Kong British authorities had premonitions of this change. In December 1979, they issued a report from a 1979 advisory committee on the multiple economy of Hong Kong which reviewed the history of Hong Kong's economic development and proposed a number of suggestions on goals and directions for further economic growth. The contents, both wide-ranging and general, have given rise to widespread comments in Hong Kong's academic circles.

C. ECONOMIC DEVELOPMENT IN MACAO
By Huang Weiliang

Geography and History

Macao, with a total area of 15.52 sq. km., is a peninsula located southwest of the mouth of the Zhujiang (Pearl) River. Its northern boundary is the Barrier Gate. It contains three main segments: Macao Peninsula, 5.42 sq. km.; Taipa Island, 3.48 sq. km.; and Coloane Island, 6.61 sq. km.

Macao has been China's territory since time immemorial. In 1535, the Portuguese entered Macao under the pretext of finding a place to dry goods in the sun. In 1557, they "leased" Macao from local Chinese officials. They occupied Taipa Island in 1851 and Coloane Island in 1864. On December 1, 1887, the Portuguese and the government of the Qing Dynasty formally signed the "54 Clauses Between China and Portugal," confirming stipulations of the "Sino-Portugal Trade Protocol" signed on March 26, 1887 to the effect that "China resolutely approves Portugal's permanent administration over Macao and its dependencies without any difference from other places under the jurisdiction of Portugal." In 1928, however, China proclaimed the abrogation of this protocol.

Economic Setting. Under rule by the Portuguese authorities, Macao is a "free port." But due to its shallow water and antiquated dock equipment, sea transportation has been subject to limitations. Thus, over the last 400 years, Macao's economy has been in a state of underdevelopment. In the past, the only industries were handicrafts such as firecrackers, matches, joss sticks and candles. Since the 1960's, the Portuguese authorities in Macao have adopted the policy of "attracting foreign capital to promote economic prosperity in Macao"; from then on, Hong Kong's Chinese capital financial groups have begun businesses in Macao, investing in gambling houses, tourism, shipping, gold trading and real estate; at the same time, foreign capital from the United States, Britain, Japan and Portugal has entered Macao in succession to invest in finance and banking, as well as in industrial and commercial enterprises. Thus, Macao's economic structure has undergone great changes in recent decades. At present, tourism, import and export trade, building and industry are the main pillars of Macao's economy.

Owing to lack of resources, Macao's economy is mainly dependent on other places. Consumer products and industrial raw materials are both reliant on imports. Thus, Macao's industry in general focuses on processing and assembly. Macao's foreign trade relies mainly on the European Common Market, the United States, Japan and former Portuguese colonies. In addition, it serves as a transit point for goods from Hong Kong. Macao's economy has its own specific characteristics and flexible nature: its economic structure is simple, the scale of industry is not large and wage levels are low. Provided there is a small quantity of orders from abroad, production can be maintained and, in face of economic difficulties, it is usually easy to find a way out.

Macao's Economy in 1980

The current population of Macao is 500,000, of whom 97% are Chinese. Macao borders on the mainland and has good land and water transport services. Supplies of rice, non-staple foods, fresh fruits and vegetables and fresh aquatic foods all rely on imports from the mainland. The West European Common Market lists Macao as an area still awaiting exploitation, so restrictions on Macao's exports are lax, a situation beneficial to the development of Macao's economy.

Tourism. Tourism, one of the pillars of Macao's economy, experienced a boom in the 1970's, but slowed in its rate of development in 1980. Tourists from Hong Kong in 1980 totalled 3,362,000, an increase of 3.55% over 1979; the rate of increase, however, had dropped sharply. Actual expenditures of tourists were also on the decline. Tourists from Hong Kong and foreign countries spent 2,000 million patacas (the unit of currency used in Macao) in 1980, an increase of 12% over 1979. Real expenditures fell by 7% as against those of 1979 when factored with the local 20% inflation rate. The number of foreign tourists visiting China via Macao has been on the rise, totalling 36,741 in 1980. The local tourist industry viewed the vigorous development of China's tourism as a clear boost to Macao's tourism.

Improved conditions in Macao's hotel and communications sectors have to some degree reduced obstacles to the growth of Macao's tourism that have been caused by shortages in hotel space and in transport facilities connecting Macao with Hong Kong. Water craft travelling between Hong Kong and Macao now carry 9,360 passengers daily. In view of busy passenger traffic between Hong Kong and Macao, many Hong Kong and Macao enterprises have applied for permission to build docks in Macao. They have also taken positive measures to improve links between Macao and docks in China's Zhuhai City to meet growth needs for passenger transport.

Foreign Trade. Macao's export trade in the last decade grew rapidly. Since 1976, the rate of increase has increased and the structure of goods and foreign-trade markets has undergone great changes. The average annual growth rate for Macao's exports was 3.8% during the 1950's. In 1979, the value of Macao exports was 2,014 million patacas, or 14.6 times higher than the total of 138 million patacas in 1966. In the 1950's, exports consisted mainly of marine products and traditional handicrafts such as joss sticks, candles, firecrackers and matches. Since the 1960's, the textile industry has grown rapidly. Textiles exports, making up 51.5% of total exports in 1965, increased to 87.13% of the total by 1979. Products include knitted garments, handkerchiefs, gloves and wool yarn. In addition to textiles, electronics have developed rapidly in recent years, including radios, tape recorders, transistor radios, and electronic and photo-controlled toys.

Export markets have expanded beyond the traditional destinations of Portugal, Portuguese colonies and Hong Kong that were dominant in the 1960's to the European Common Market and the United States in the 1970's. In 1979, export markets for Macao goods had spread to over 70 countries and regions. The United States took first place in Macao's export goods in 1979, followed by West Germany, France, Hong Kong and Britain. Since 1976, Macao began to reverse its long-existing pattern of foreign trade deficits. Trade surpluses reached 169 million patacas in 1976, 119 million patacas in 1977, and 196 million patacas in 1979.

Housing and Construction. In the construction field, land prices for commercial buildings and housing are comparatively lower than in Hong Kong. However, with large amounts of foreign capital filtering into Macao for real estate investment, and with the artificial driving-up of prices, the cost of real estate has skyrocketed. During the first half of 1980, activities of speculators had been restrained somewhat by high interest rates, although the price of housing did not come down.

From late May to the end of July, 1980, there were four successive drops in interest rates; the total decline was over 20%. Owing to this trend, together with the influence of rising real estate prices and stocks in Hong Kong, the real estate market in Macao became brisk again and prices subsequently began to rise at an increased rate. By the end of 1980, prices of industrial buildings had increased by 40% over rates at the beginning of the year; low- and medium-income residential buildings had gone up by 20%; high-income residences, 30%; and commercial buildings, 40%. In November 1980, bank interest rates went up three times in a row, reaching the highest level in history, and the real estate market again fell into stagnation. In terms of building construction, 1980 was the most prosperous of recent years. The total of construction sites was 420, 10% higher than 1979; 288 blueprints were approved, an increase of 23% over the previous year; and total floor space of completed housing was 224,559 sq. m., rising by 10.93%.

Industry. In the past two decades, together with growth in the economy, Macao's processing industries developed to a new stage, now including scores of trades and several hundred products including clothing manufactured goods, weaving, woollen textiles, printing and dyeing, hats and shoes, procelain, plastics, rubber products, silk flowers, gloves, umbrellas, handbags, electronics, toys, hardware, furniture, food and optical instruments. Most of these commodities are produced for export. By the end of 1980 there were 1,332 large and small factories under industrial licence, employing 33,600 workers. By February 1981, ten new factories entered production, including two glove factories and firms turning out sewing machine thread, feather products, leatherette suitcases and bags, rayon flowers, electric-fan parts, machine-embroidery, iron grill work and toys.

Prospects for Future Development

It is projected that despite all kinds of difficulties, Macao's economy will continue to grow to a certain extent. The main premises for this view are:

1. *On the basis of continuing growth in good relations between China and Portugal, the Portuguese Macao authorities have adopted positive measures to improve Macao's economy such as simplifying procedures in foreign trade and increasing public expenditures.* In 1981, the authorities planned to allocate 125 million patacas for capital construction, twice the amount of 1980. Preparations are being made to streamline entry formalities for foreign tourists and to set up new factories. All these measures will be beneficial to the development of Macao's economy.

2. *Most of Macao's factories are small and medium-sized and are easily adaptable to changing market circumstances.* For purposes of future development, they have devoted themselves to improving the quality of products and to opening new markets. Stocks of textile goods in the European countries and North America are low at present. Once the economic situation changes for the better, local businessmen in these markets will import more goods. Moreover, inasmuch as European countries and the United States have less restrictions on imports from Macao, textile exports can look to relative stability in the future.

3. *Thanks to the growth of tourism in the Asian-Pacific region and to its geographical proximity to Zhuhai City and Zhongshan County,* Macao has become a new centre for attracting tourists. It is estimated that tourism in Macao will continue to grow. The same is true for the real estate market and for construction, which will play an important role in supporting Macao's economy.

SECTION V:

CHINESE ECONOMIC THEORY

THEORETICAL STUDIES BY CHINESE ECONOMIC CIRCLES IN RECENT YEARS: PROGRESS AND FUTURE TRENDS

By Zhao Renwei and Xiang Qiyuan

*Institute of Economics,
Chinese Academy of Social Sciences*

With the downfall of the Gang of Four, China put an end to years of turmoil and instability and entered a new period of development. Breaking through the gloomy atmosphere which had existed for many years, the Chinese economics profession also come into a period of unprecedented activity. The four years following the downfall of the Gang of Four may be described as the most fruitful period of the past three decades, a period in which Chinese economists discussed the largest number of questions and gained the greatest successes.

The first two years were largely devoted to criticizing the Gang of Four's economic theories, wiping out their vicious influence and sweeping away obstacles. In the next two years, to cope with the needs of shifting the focus of work, economists concentrated on discussing and exploring theoretical questions concerning the programme of socialist modernization and the readjustment and restructuring of the national economy. The discussion covered a very wide area and extended to many branches of economics; here, we will describe briefly only the most representative questions and mainly from the viewpoint of socialist political economy.

I. Concerning the Basic Economic Law of Socialism

There have been several occasions in the last three decades when the economic law of socialism came up for discussion in Chinese economic circles. One such occasion took place around 1955, and dealt with economic laws in the transition period. One of the central issues under discussion at that time was whether and how the basic economic law of socialism could play its leading role while various economic sectors co-existed during the transition period. Another discussion took place during the readjustment of the national economy in 1962-65. The background to that discussion was the "big leap forward," which violated both objective laws and socialist economy. People wanted to review that experience and take from it theoretical lessons that would enable them to better apply economic laws. The latest discussion occurred following the downfall of the Gang of Four. By vigorously preaching subjective idealism and completely negating the existence of economic laws, Lin Biao and the Gang of Four created confusion in both thinking and theory. On the one hand, the discussion helped to clear up the confusion. On the other hand, the in-depth examination of erroneous "Left" ideas in socialist construction made people increasingly aware that the correct or incorrect application of economic laws would determine the success or failure of socialism. Hence, the discussion of the basic economic laws of socialism once more drew wide attention.

The Third Plenary Session of the 11th Party Central Committee was followed by an in-depth discussion of making practice the only criterion for testing truth.

Many economists pointed out that a major shortcoming in our economic work had been our relative neglect of the purposes of socialist production in our socialist construction. Some suggested that in the process of criticizing the Gang of Four we should restore the primacy of the basic economic law of socialism as elaborated by Stalin. At that time, an editorial in the *People's Daily,* entitled "Seek A Clear Understanding of the Purpose of Socialist Production," drew widespread attention.

For a time, people working in the field of economics concentrated on discussing the purpose of socialist production. Compared with previous discussions, this one integrated more closely the theory with the practice of socialist construction and showed greater emancipation of thinking. Many excellent views were put forward. It was generally agreed that the orientation of socialist economic development, the structure of the economy and the overall balance in the national economic plan hinged on our correct understanding and conscious implementation of the purpose of socialist production.

During China's First Five-Year Plan (1953-57), targets were better fulfilled, both production and construction advanced at a fairly rapid pace and the people's living standard also showed relatively fast improvement. One of the major reasons was the prudent ideology guiding our socialist construction and our conscious understanding of the purpose of socialist production. In the 20 years after 1958, we blindly followed a policy of seeking to develop at an unrealistically "high speed" and of "production for production's sake." This led to a high rate of accumulation, imbalance in the national economy, lop-sided development of the economic structure and a huge gap between state construction and the people's well-being. In that period, the ideology guiding socialist construction deviated in a certain degree from the purpose of socialist production.

The purpose of socialist production clearly plays a decisive role in socialist production as a whole. It should become one of the major guiding principles in the readjustment of the national economy and the reform of the economic management system. In mapping out the strategy of the country's long-term economic development, we must first give consideration to improving the welfare of the people and meeting social needs. In so doing, we will enhance people's understanding of the basic economic law of socialism.

The discussion concerning the purpose of socialist production has just concluded. It has prompted economists to propose many new topics for study, such as the final products of socialist production, the economic mechanism for realizing the purpose of socialist production and the relationship between the purpose of social production and that of enterprise production. This signifies that the discussion will be on-going.

For a long time there have been different views about the basic economic law of socialism. Some views put forward in the discussion over the last few years are noteworthy.

A number of economists deny the existence of the basic economic law of socialism. One of their main arguments is that the purpose of socialist production belongs to the category of subjective will, and not to that of objective economics. Most of the people studying economic theory and doing economic work do not agree with this view. They argue that the purpose of social production is decided by the nature of the ownership of the means of production and embodies the vital material interests of the class, group or social members who own the major means of production. Various economic formations of society have different systems of ownership of the means of production and different purposes of social production. Under capitalism, production aims at increasing surplus value; under socialism, it aims at satisfying the material and cultural needs of the whole society. These aims are independent of man's will. Therefore, the purpose of social production belongs to the category of objective economics.

Among those who affirm the existence of the basic economic law of socialism, the content of that law, as set forth by Stalin, is generally accepted. However, some consider that Stalin's formulation is not perfect and insufficiently specific and that it should be extended and enriched by new content drawn from empirical experience. As to the satisfaction of social needs mentioned by Stalin, apart from personal living needs, there are different views with regard to whether the needs for expanded production and for national defence and foreign aid should also be included. Some people say that the purpose of social production has its objective nature, but they doubt whether the means to achieve this purpose mentioned by Stalin reflect the essence of the socialist relations of production and share their objective nature.

One school of economists disagree with Stalin's basic economic law of socialism. They argue that the study of basic economic law should proceed from the contradiction between productive forces and the relations of production and the basic economic contradictions to which it gives rise. Others hold that the basic economic law of socialism is the concrete manifestation of the law of correspondence between the relations of production and productive forces.

II. Concerning Ownership of the Means of Production

It is known that, as early as 1956, China carried out, in the main, the socialist transformation of the ownership of the means of production, and that socialist public ownership became predominant in both town and country. Some 20 years later, the notion that the economy owned by the people as a whole is unconditionally superior to the collective economy and that individual economy engenders capitalism still prevailed among the economics profession. Therefore, as far as ownership was concerned, the remaining questions were how to bring about the rapid transition of the collective economy to an economy owned by all the people and how to eliminate the individual economy, the vestige of capitalism.

Because few people gave serious thought to the question of the ownership of the means of production in the 20 years after 1956, a series of mistakes were made in practice. There were two outstanding mistakes. One was the attempt to realize the transition to the socialist economy owned by all the people and even to the communist economy at a time when the rural collective economy was still weak. It was argued that the transition would be difficult once units of the collective economy became rich and differences between their respective living standards increased. The transition method adopted encroached upon the right of the rural basic accounting units to make their own decisions, ignored their economic interests and essentially appropriated the peasants' interests without compensation. It led a number of units of the collective economy to kill their draught animals, fell trees and distribute all savings among their members, thereby damaging the productive forces and suppressing the peasants' incentives to produce.

The same mistake was made in dealing with the urban collective economy. Handicraft cooperatives and other collective industries in the urban areas such as the "May 7th" factories set up by family members of workers and staff were universally forced to undergo transition. Collectives at the elementary level were raised to a higher level, and collectives at the higher level were actually transformed into units owned by all the people. The urban collective economy remained only in name and this transition meant, in essence, expropriation of the handicraftsmen and other working people without compensation.

Another mistake was to eliminate the small plots for peasants' personal use and peasants' household sideline activities and wantonly reduce the number of artisans, peddlers and people in the service trades working on their own in the urban areas. In 1953, there were nine million individual workers in cities and towns, accounting for one-third of the people employed at that time. After the socialist transformation was more or less completed, there were still one million of them. During the ten ensuing years of turmoil, their number dwindled to 150,000. This measure enormously reduced the retail, service and repair shops and greatly inconvenienced the public.

In the last few years, the economics profession has thoroughly reviewed these mistakes and learned from them. They have come to understand that the basic reason for these mistakes was the violation of the law of correspondence between the relations of production and productive forces. Therefore, to improve the relations of ownership of the means of production in China we must take into account the existence of various levels of productive forces, ranging from the very backward to the modern, and preserve some non-socialist economic elements and flexible forms of management.

In order to promote the development of productive forces, it is necessary, first, to preserve and develop the individual economy to a certain degree. In both urban and rural areas there generally exist manual labour and small trading activities that are run in a decentralized fashion and are suited to management in the form of individual ownership. Particularly in the tailoring, catering and repair trades, individual management can offer consumers the advantages of flexible and better service. The individual economy plays an important supplementary role to the socialist public economy and helps create more jobs.

Many economists also argue that the nature of the individual economy should be examined in the context of the economic system as a whole. With the socialist public economy in a dominant position, individual handicrafts and trades can be assimilated into the society's production and distribution system by allowing them to make sales, process raw materials supplied by state enterprises and get commodities from state wholesale shops. This will turn these individuals into assistants and dependents of the socialist public economy and prevent them from developing along the capitalist line. In recent years the individual economy in China's urban areas and countryside has been restored and developed and small plots for personal use of rural commune members and household sidelines activities have been encouraged.

Secondly, the collective economy has to be consolidated and expanded and made truly collective in nature. Under the influence of the above-mentioned concept and practice of "poor transition," the units of China's rural collective economy usually lack even rudimentary decision-making power. Production management, distribution of income and the members' standard of living are all decided by organs of political power at the higher level. The department in charge of the units of collective economy in an urban area usually assumes overall responsibility for the profits and losses of local units, thus turning them into its appendages.

Much of the discussion on consolidating and expanding the collective economy in recent years has focused on the question of how to respect the decision-making power of the production teams and basic accounting units, and how to let units of the urban collective economy assume responsibility for their own profits and losses so as to enhance the features and advantages of the collective economy. More than a few economists have pointed out that the urban and rural collective economy at present has great vitality and will co-exist with the economy owned by the whole people for a long time. Setting things right theoretically has heralded the adoption of flexible economic policies, and promising changes in this respect have appeared in actual economic life over the past few years.

Thirdly, the economy owned by the people as a whole also needs to undergo a process of gradual improvement. This point has been recognized by a growing number of economists. In the past, Chinese economists always identified socialist ownership by the people as a whole with state ownership. In the course of discussing the reform of the economic management system in recent years, some economists hold that many drawbacks in the internal economic management of units owned by the people as a whole, such as bureaucracy and the use of purely administrative orders, are often connected with the form of state ownership, and that the essence of reforming the economic management system lies in changing the form of state ownership adopted by units owned by the people as a whole. Some other economists adhere to the traditional concept that ownership by the people as a whole can only adopt the form of state ownership and that the reform of the economic management system should only be carried out within this scope. However, a greater number of economists are of the opinion that state ownership is not the perfect form of the socialist ownership by the people as a whole and one differs from the other. As conditions for the elimination of state ownership do not exist at present in China, the reform of the economic management system can only be carried out within the scope of state ownership. But the majority of economists agree that efforts should be made to develop state ownership to the perfect form of ownership by the people as a whole.

III. Concerning the Use of the Market Mechanism in a Planned Socialist Economy

For a long time Chinese economists have discussed the nature of commodity production and the law of value under the socialist system. The discussion in recent years on how to make use of the market mechanism in the planned socialist economy may be taken as a continuation of the above-mentioned discussion. It may also be taken as a new development because it went much farther than previous discussions.

Take the question of the role of the market mechanism in the economy owned by the people as a whole. In the past, Chinese economists generally denied the existence of commodity relations within the economy owned by the people as a whole; they held that the economy owned by the people as a whole had to maintain the cover of commodity relations only because of its coexistence with the collective economy. In other words, costs, prices and other terms of value were only tools of calculation in the units owned by the people as a whole and were not objective economic mechanisms; among enterprises there was only the relationship of allocating goods, not that of buying and selling commodities.

There were both theoretical reasons and practical considerations for the prolonged domination of this view in the Chinese economics profession. This view was propounded by Stalin, and it is common knowledge that Chinese economic thinkers were profoundly influenced by Stalin's socialist economic theories. Moreover, the discussions among Chinese economists concerning commodity production and the law of value, especially those held after the universal establishment of people's communes, were undertaken with the practical consideration of upholding the autonomy of units of the collective economy in their capacity as commodity producers. The major questions to be solved at that time were the relations between the two types of public ownership and the economic management system in the people's communes. Hence, emphasis was given to the analysis of the commodity-money relations between the two types of public ownership and among the various economic units under collective ownership.

The discussions in the last few years, however, focused on the role of economic management in the entire socialist economy. Since the founding of the People's Republic of China, the economic management system has been plagued by problems such as irrational, excessive concentration and rigidity in the planned management of the national economy; overall management of incomes and expenditures in financial affairs; unified allocation in the management of materials and exclusive purchases and sales in the relations between industry and commerce; unilateral emphasis on administrative means and neglect of economic means; one-sided stress on the state; overall and long-term interests with little attention given to the interests of enterprises and individuals and immediate interests. In fact, all these problems are directly related to the view that exchanges among state enterprises are not commodity exchanges and to disregard of the law of value. Practical considerations demand that we explore and explain questions of why commodity relations exist among units owned by the people as a whole and how to use the market mechanism.

Chinese economists now give different explanations for the existence of commodity relations among units owned by the people as a whole and the market mechanism. Some hold that the exchange of equal values is necessary to solve economic contradictions and conflicts of interests among individuals and between workers' collectives, even though their fundamental economic interests are identical. Some say that, owing to the immaturity of socialist ownership by the people as a whole, that is, the existence of collective ownership, exchange among state enterprises still involves a transfer of ownership in a certain sense. Others attribute the existence of commodity relations to the fact that there is still individual or partial individual ownership of labour power today, such that labour is still not direct social labour. They generally recognize the existence, in essence, of commodity relations within the units owned by the whole people and agree with the viewpoint that the means of production circulated between enterprises owned by the people as a whole are also commodities.

This theoretical breakthrough is of great significance in recognizing enterprises as relatively independent commodity producers, enlarging their decision-making power, overcoming the use of purely administrative means and adopting more economic means, and giving value-related economic levers (prices, credit, tax and wages) a role to play. It also provides an important theoretical basis for reforming the internal economic management system of units owned by the people as a whole.

Another question concerns the role played by the law of value in the socialist economy. Chinese economists had long accepted Stalin's view that the law of value exercises only marginal influence on socialist production and does not play a regulatory role. This view has been negated by the practice of socialist construction since the founding of the People's Republic of China. After a few years of discussion, it is generally agreed that as the law of value is the fundamental law governing the commodity economy, its role cannot be excluded where commodity production and commodity exchange exist. Therefore, if we accept the general existence of commodity relations in the development of the socialist economy, we must accept the regulatory role of the law of value in the whole process of socialist production.

Other discussions focused on the relationship between the law of value and the law of planned, proportionate development of the national economy. Chinese economists hold fairly divergent views with regard to this question. One view denies the objective existence of the law of planned development of the national economy. The present socialist economy is still a commodity economy based on public ownership, so the law of value is the only regulator of socialist reproduction. Marx said a long time ago that in a commodity economy the law of value regulated the proportionate distribution of total social labour-time. Now we should give full play to the objective regulatory role of the law of value and consciously incorporate the law of value in working out the national economic plan.

Another view holds that the fundamental feature of the socialist economy is planned economy and not commodity economy. The law of planned development of the national economy is the main regulator of the socialist economy and the law of value only plays a secondary regulatory role. In working out the national economic plan, therefore, we should take the former law as the basis but we should also take into consideration the requirements of the law of value.

A large number of economists regard the socialist economy we have at present as both a planned economy and a commodity economy, but they differ in the degree of emphasis they place on the two aspects. Economists who emphasize the commodity nature of the socialist economy call it a planned commodity economy; those who stress the planning aspects of the socialist economy call it a planned economy under the conditions of commodity economy. Both groups agree that the law of planned development and the law of value function in basically the same direction, and that their functions interweave to regulate the national economy. Therefore, the national economic plan has to be worked out simultaneously on the basis of the two laws regulating the economy.

There is still no unanimous opinion on the relationship between the law of value and the law of planned development. However, compared with the situation which existed for a long time before the downfall of the Gang of Four, the question is being discussed on a higher level and in greater depth, and we have made a step forward in understanding the role of the law of value in the socialist stage.

As to the relationship between planning and the market, the prevailing opinion in the past was that planning and the market conflicted with each other and were mutually exclusive. Wherever planning was operative, the market ceased to play its role; and vice versa. In recent years many economists have cast aside this view; they now hold that planning and the market are integrated, with the former playing the main role. As to how they are integrated, some economists deem that they are not put together like plates but by mutual infiltration. Some economists consider that integration of planning and the market must proceed from platelike integration to the stage of mutual infiltration. Other economists have analysed the integration of planning and the market at the macro-economic and micro-economic levels. Although opinions differ on this question and deeper and specific discussions are called for, the change from the view that planning and the market are mutually exclusive to the view that they are integrated certainly represents a great advance in theory.

As to the question of competition in the socialist economy, its existence has long been denied by the Chinese economics profession. However, as a result of discussions in recent years, Chinese economists now generally accept the concept that competition is an integral part of the commodity economy and that wherever commodity production and exchange exist there is competition. As long as the relationship between commodity production and the market persist in the socialist economy, there will be competition. Furthermore, production, supply and marketing according to market needs, allocation of investments according to their results and recruitment of personnel according to the principle of choosing the best qualified persons are all inseparable from competition. Under the conditions of the socialist planned economy, limited competition plays a positive role in encouraging the advanced, spurring the backward, improving the quality of products and raising management efficiency.

Apart from affirming the necessity of socialist competition, Chinese economists have also studied and discussed the difference between socialist and capitalist competition and between socialist competition and socialist emulation, and the question of how to foster competition while simultaneously strengthening guidance.

IV. Concerning Economic Structure

China's present economic structure was gradually formed over the last 30 years. What are its features? What are its problems? Although economists have conducted different analyses, their basic conclusions are more or less the same. These may be roughly summed up in two main points.

1. *The economic structure is, in many respects, unbalanced or lop-sided.*

There is imbalance between agriculture, light industry and heavy industry. The last has been intensively developed while the development of the first two has been neglected. Between 1949 and 1978, agriculture increased 3.4-fold and agricultural industry 39.2-fold; but during the same years, light industry rose 20.8-fold and heavy industry 91.6-fold. In agriculture, there was undue emphasis on farming at the expense of animal husbandry, fishing and forestry. In industry the fast growth of processing industries outstripped the development of materials and energy industries.

The rate of accumulation was greater than that of consumption, and stayed high for many years starting from the Second Five-Year Plan (1958-62). In 1958, 1959 and 1960, it was respectively 33.9%, 43.8% and 39.6% of the national income. Though the accumulation rate dropped to 22.7% in the readjustment period of the early 1960's, it rose to 26.3% and 33%, respectively, during the Third Five-Year Plan (1966-70) and Fourth Five-Year Plan (1971-75). It jumped to 36.9% in 1978, then dropped to 33.6% in 1979, but it was still relatively high.

The too-rapid increase of the Chinese population, as some economists have pointed out, has caused an imbalance between material growth and population growth for a long period. It is also one of the principal causes of the imbalance in the national economy.

2. *The economic structure is of a closed type bent on self-sufficiency.*

Its closed character is expressed in the two following aspects: In China's external economic relations the closed-door tendency finds expression in the small proportion of foreign trade in the national economy, weak ability to import and export and the lack of competitive commodities on the international market. In China's internal economic relations there is the tendency towards autarchy in the various departments, regions and production units. Farm production has long been self-sufficient to a great extent and a high proportion of the heavy industry serves itself; despite unfavourable local conditions and features, many areas strive to build their own integrated economic systems; a large number of enterprises have become all-embracing and self-supporting units or societies.

To overcome the above-mentioned shortcomings and rationalize the economic structure, Chinese economists have put forward the following suggestions:

1. *It is necessary to overcome the policy of blindly seeking high speed and to strive instead for overall balance in the national economy.*

Many economists point out that seeking to develop at excessively high speed is one of the major reasons for the serious imbalance in the national economy. Practices such as setting unrealistically high targets, regarding comprehensive balance with reserves as a "negative balance," and praising plans with unbridged gaps as a "positive balance" will not spur the economy forward but will only result in serious imbalance in the national economy. Therefore, on the basis of past experience and the lessons derived from that experience, we should not seek high-speed economic growth at the price of skewing the plan and we must maintain a good overall balance especially among the four major fields of finance, credit, materials and foreign exchange.

2. *It is imperative to discontinue the one-sided development of heavy industry so as to ensure concerted growth of the various branches of the national economy.*

Although Chinese economists hold different

views with regard to the prior growth of the means of production under socialism, they are almost unanimous in their support for the view that, in the period of readjustment, the rate of growth of heavy industry must be slowed down and that of the light industry and agriculture speeded up.

The current economic readjustment is proceeding in this direction. It is noteworthy that we have vigorously developed labour-intensive industries while developing capital-intensive industries in the last few years. According to statistics, the average number of workers employed for every million yuan of fixed assets in China is 94 in heavy industry, 257 in light industry and 800 in such labour-intensive trades as arts and crafts, production of clothing, metal wares for daily use and leather goods. Vigorous development of labour-intensive industries is certainly conducive to the rationalization of China's economic structure. Moreover, it helps solve the employment problem in a populous country like ours.

3. *It is necessary to moderate the single-minded drive of raising the rate of accumulation and take into consideration the relationship between production and livelihood.*

In view of the relatively high rate of accumulation over a long period, Chinese economists have recently stressed the need to study the ratio between accumulation and consumption. Many of them point out that the rate of accumulation varies from country to country and according to the specific conditions at different periods of development and cannot be set uniformly. A 30–40% rate of accumulation is obviously high and will severely reduce consumption as China's per capita national income is very low. Under ordinary conditions, it is inadvisable to undertake production and construction by holding down the people's standard of living.

Of course, to handle better the relations between state construction and people's livelihood, it is not enough to lower the rate of accumulation; one must also examine the uses to which the accumulation fund is put. China not only has the problem of a fairly high rate of accumulation but also the problem of bad results in how the accumulation fund is used. In dealing with these problems, the latter should not be dwarfed by the former. Some economists suggest that, given better results in the use of the accumulation fund, the rate of accumulation should preferably be set around 25% under China's present conditions.

4. *The economic management system must be reformed to promote the rationalization of the economic structure.*

Many economists hold that the highly centralized economic management system is one of the causes for the imbalance among the various branches of the national economy and for the tendency towards self-sufficiency in the various departments, areas and enterprises. Therefore, the readjustment of the economic structure and the reform of the economic management system, which is a manifestation of the relationship between readjustment and reform, are inseparable.

Readjustment is the basis of reform, but the further rationalization of the economic structure needs to be promoted by the reform of the economic management system. Many reform measures, such as the use of the market mechanism, the enlargement of decision-making power of enterprises, the strengthening of horizontal links in economic life, the growth of competition and integration, advances in specialization and coordination, are conducive to bringing about a balance in the national economy and overcoming the tendency towards self-sufficiency.

V. Concerning Material Interests and Distribution According to Work

The question of material interests under the socialist system is one of the major theoretical principles distorted and tampered with by the Gang of Four. The Gang condemned material interests, particularly personal material interests, as being diametrically opposed to Marxism and absolutely inconsistent with the socialist economic system. Whoever stressed material interests was accused of spreading revisionism. In the process of criticizing the Gang of Four, this theoretical taboo was set aside and heated discussions were held on this question.

The consensus among Chinese economists is that economic relations between people are mainly those of material interests and that in striving for the realization of the socialist ideal, the proletariat, in the final analysis, aims at protecting the material interests of all workers. These are basic principles of Marxism. At the present stage of development, we should pay full attention to the basic material interests of the state, the collectives and individuals, but we cannot neglect the material interests of the workers as individuals and the socialist enterprises as collectives. One of the basic principles of socialist economic management is to integrate properly the interests of the state, the productive units and the workers.

Setting theoretical things right on the question of material interests helps us enormously in understanding commodity production and commodity exchange under socialism, in respecting the legitimate rights of enterprises as relatively independent commodity producers, and in carrying out resolutely the principle of distribution according to work.

The question of distribution according to work had been discussed repeatedly by Chinese economists for a long time. However, under the influence of "Left" guiding ideas, the principle of distribution according to work had not been earnestly carried out. The Gang had frequently alleged that the principle of distribution according to work was the bourgeois standard of distribution. They cited passages about the bourgeoisie from the works of Marx and Lenin. The Gang even went so far as to portray the distribution according to work as a relation of exploitation. This caused tremendous losses to the socialist economy.

After the downfall of the Gang of Four, this question attracted widespread attention and four national discussions were devoted to it in 1977 and 1978.

These discussions first dispelled the confusion and reaffirmed the socialist nature of distribution according to work. In order to set things right and restore the honour of distribution according to work, many economists had to address the questions of whether distribution according to work is a socialist principle of distribution and whether it may become the economic basis engendering new bourgeois elements.

An outstanding feature in the discussions over the last few years was to criticize and overcome the tendency towards equalitarianism. In the past 20 years or so, the principle of distribution according to work came under frequent attack and the piece-work wage system, bonus system and eight-grade wage system were also criticized on many occasions. As a result, the rewards for the labour of workers and staff members were increasingly separated from their contributions. Equalitarian distribution led to a situation where it made little difference whether one worked more or less, whether one did a good or bad job and even whether one worked or not. The practice of equalitarian distribution seriously affected the enthusiasm of workers and staff members and discouraged production efficiency. Low production efficiency, in turn, aggravated equalitarian distribution.

In the 20 years between 1957 and 1976, there was only one relatively general wage rise, in 1963. Not only did original workers and staff members not receive higher pay corresponding to their contributions, but equalitarianism became even more strictly enforced in the wages for workers and staff members newly recruited in this period. Although these workers and staff members in their 30's or 40's were the backbone of the workforce, their wages were generally the lowest. Clearly, in the relations between efficiency and equality, the experience of the past 20 years showed that the equalitarian tendency retarded the rise of efficiency.

Many economists have pointed out that, to overcome equalitarianism, we must overcome the situation in which differences between existing incomes do not reflect the existing contributions of labour. Of course, we must also admit that, because China is undertaking socialist construction on the basis of a fairly low level of the productive forces, there will come a stage of development in which the differences between both people's labour contributions and their resultant incomes will be enlarged. Consequently the policy of letting a section of the working people get rich first has its objective basis: in the short run it may widen the differences in incomes among the working people but it is beneficial to raising production efficiency; in the long run the policy will speed up the realization of general prosperity for all working people. Allowing differences in incomes and a time sequence for people to get rich is the inevitable road for the general prosperity of the entire workforce and conforms to the socialist principle.

In the discussions over the past few years the question of closely linking the material interests of individual workers and staff members with the management of their enterprises was put forward. In China today, where commodity-money relations generally exist, workers and staff members getting the same amount of bonus and equal income despite profits or losses of their enterprises is an expression of equalitarianism which dampens the masses' enthusiasm for socialism. Economists differ in their theoretical analyses of how the income of workers and staff members is linked with the management of their enterprises (some say it follows the law of distribution according to work; some say it follows the law of value; and others say it follows both laws), but they have all given attention to this question. During the reform of the economic management system, many enterprises experimenting with enlarged power of management have adopted measures to effect this link and obtained good results.

To link closely the rewards for labour with the fruits of labour, Chinese economists also studied and discussed various forms of rewards for labour. Among the forms of rewards proposed are integrated basic and flexible wages for workers and staff members and rewards on the basis of output in the rural people's communes.

VI. On Comparing and Choosing Different Socialist Economic Models

This is a comprehensive question which is

closely linked to the above-mentioned questions, particularly that concerning the relationship between planning and the market. However, Chinese economists are beginning to study and discuss this question as an independent one. Breaking with the narrow concept that the socialist economy can have only one model, we have come to understand that, as long as socialist public ownership holds the predominant position and there is no exploitation of man by man, the socialist economy is completely free to adopt various models. Different socialist countries may, according to their specific conditions, choose their own arrangements to link planning with the market and centralization with decentralization, and choose the best model on the basis of comparing the conditions of decision-making, information and motivation.

In the discussions, the two following points have attracted special attention:

1. *What was China's original economic model?*

The prevailing explanation is that China's original economic management system was copied from the Soviet Union in the early 1950's and conformed to the centralized model, or Stalinist model. Further analysis led some economists to point out that this model showed some variations in China. In the period after 1958, in particular, decisions became more centralized, more mobilization was used, economic relations tended to be embodied more in goods, greater stress was given to self-sufficiency and more factors of war communism appeared. According to some economists, these features were clearly related to the traditional domination of small-scale production in China and the country's relatively isolation in the international community during the 1960's. Thus, a study of China's original economic model is of significance in understanding and analysing the starting point of the reforms of the economic management system.

2. *What kind of economic model should China adopt?*

It has been generally agreed that China should not copy any of the existing models in foreign countries but should work out a model suited to its domestic conditions in light of its own features as well as the experiences of other countries. The opinion of Chinese economists in recent years is that both the highly centralized model and the highly decentralized model are inappropriate. The former did play a positive role in the past, but it has many drawbacks and must be changed.

In the relationship between centralization and decentralization, recent reforms tend to enlarge the scope of the latter; in the relationship between planning and the market, they tend to let the latter play a more significant role; in the relationship between administrative and economic means, they tend to make greater use of the latter in managing the economy.

However, this does not mean that the more power is decentralized and the bigger the role played by the market, the better the result. Nor does it mean the complete rejection of using administrative means. The focus of recent discussions is where the line should be drawn in the various sets of relations. Centralized decision-making for macro-economic activities and decentralized decision-making for micro-economic activities seems to be the overall guideline, but many specific lines have to be studied and worked out.

As long as we follow the principle of seeking truth from the facts, we will surely work out a model of a planned socialist economy suited to our conditions, thereby providing a theoretical basis for reform of the economic management system and a strategy for economic development.

VII. Future Trends in Chinese Economic Circles

We have briefly described some theoretical questions which preoccupied Chinese economists in the past few years. From the questions discussed and the academic activities of economists, including those of economic theorists, we can discern the following noteworthy trends in Chinese economic circles.

First, the study of economic theory has become more closely integrated with economic construction. During the period when the line of the ultra-"Left" prevailed, economists were generally prohibited from expressing their empirically derived views on major economic questions. As a result, the study of economic theory often became superficial. In recent years, however, discussions of traditional questions as well as some new questions are all closely related to the lessons and experiences gained from 30 years of economic construction, to the readjustment and restructuring of the national economy and to the long-term goal of realizing the Four Modernizations. Many valuable suggestions have since been put forward.

This trend is obviously inseparable from the shift of focus of party and government work which was first raised by the Third Plenary Session of the 11th Party Central Committee in December 1978. For a long time prior to 1978, economics was somewhat esteemed only because of its service to ideological struggles and it was expected only to explain certain phenomena of class struggle. With the shift of focus in our work economics has become highly esteemed as a science in the service of economic construction and is asked to seek scientific answers to many urgent problems in economic construction. Apart from the questions mentioned above, economists have addressed many other questions, such as the stages of development of socialism, economic results, population and vestiges of feudalism in the economy.

This new trend will certainly revitalize Chinese economic circles.

Second, the isolated state of Chinese economic studies has begun to be breached and academic exchanges with foreign countries strengthened. For a long time, in connection with the tendency towards self-sufficiency in economic construction, the closed-door tendency also existed in the Chinese economics profession. This was particularly so with regard to economists specializing in socialist economic problems who knew even less about the outside world.

Remarkable changes have taken place in this respect in the last few years. The numbers of Chinese economists going abroad and foreign economists coming to China have increased enormously and there is considerable exchange of academic views. Our previous attitude towards Western economics was one of complete negativism. In recent years an increasing number of economists hold that our attitude towards Western economics should be one of factual analysis: throwing away its dross, drawing on its essence and critically absorbing the parts which may be useful to China's economic construction and theoretical studies of economics.

The discussions of the questions mentioned above, especially those concerning the comparison and choice of economic models, the relationship between planning and the market and the forms of ownership by the people as a whole, obviously not only drew on China's own experiences but also on certain academic achievements of foreign economists who were inspired by those experiences. This exchange, of course, is still in an early stage, but it is indicative of a healthy trend.

Third, Chinese economists have begun to integrate quantity analysis with quality analysis. For a long time, China stressed solely quality analysis and seriously neglected quantity analysis in economic studies. The lack of statistics and their inaccuracy further aggravated this one-sidedness. This situation has begun to change in the last few years. Not only is econometrics now regarded as an independent field of study, but attention has been paid to strengthening quantity analysis in the study of many theoretical and practical questions, such as calculation of investment results, determination of accumulation rates and population forecasts.

Take the accumulation rate for instance. Many economists are of the opinion that the aforementioned rate of 25%, a relatively proper one, is derived only from experience, and is not a scientific forecast reached after analysing the quantitative relations of various factors which determine the accumulation rate. Efforts to integrate quantitative analysis with qualitative analysis are clearly conducive to the development of China's economics.

SECTION VI:

CHINA'S ECONOMIC STATISTICAL DATA

1. SELECTED ECONOMIC STATISTICAL DATA

Compiled by the State Statistical Bureau of the People's Republic of China

Explanatory Notes:

1. These statistical data are provided by the State Statistical Bureau. For the data published previously, some statistics have been verified and others revised due to the changes in measuring units and statistical coverages.
2. Figures for Taiwan Province are not included, except in total surface area.
3. In order to facilitate comparison of data for different periods, 1949-57 data of state-owned and collectively owned enterprises include joint state-private enterprises, privately owned enterprises and handicraft units at that time.
4. Annual average increase rate is calculated on the basis of geometric mean method.

Distribution of Population and Natural Resources

Item	Unit	End of 1979
Population	10 thousand	97,092.00
Of which: urban	”	12,862.00
rural	”	84,230.00
Labour force employed in national economy	”	40,580.00
Of which: agriculture	”	29,934.00
industry	”	5,340.00
Total surface area	10 thousand km.^{2}	approx. 960.00
Cultivated land[1]	10 thousand hectares	9,950.00
Plains	”	5,473.00
Hilly and mountain areas	”	4,477.00
Of which: horizontal terraced fields	”	800.00
Forestry area[2]	”	25,509.00
Of which: forest area	”	11,978.00
forest thinning area	”	1,563.00
bush area	”	2,957.00
young growth forest and young plants	”	472.00
Rate of forest-covered area	%	12.50
Forest growing stock	100 million m.^{3}	93.50
Prairie area	10 thousand hectares	31,908.00
Freshwater area	”	1,664.00
Hydropower resources	100 million kw.	6.76
Length of inland rivers	10 thousand km.	43.00
Marine fishing area	10 thousand square nautical miles	81.80
Coastline[3]	km.	18,000.00

Notes:

1. The figure of cultivated land is under-estimated and remains to be verified.
2. The figures of forestry area and forest growing stock are from statistical data of 1973-76. The figure of fresh water area refers to 1974.
3. Coastline excludes the coastline of islands.

Population
(in 10 thousands)

Year	Population (year-end figure)	By sex		By residence	
		Male	Female	Urban	Rural
1949	54,167	— —	— —	5,765	48,402
1952	57,482	— —	— —	7,163	50,319
1957	64,653	33,469	31,184	9,949	54,704
1965	72,538	37,128	35,410	10,170	62,368
1975	91,970	47,126	44,844	11,171	80,799
1979	97,092	49,754	47,338	12,862	84,230

Note: The figures for Taiwan Province, Hong Kong and Macao are not included in this table.

Main Indicators of China's National Economy
(absolute figures)

Item	Unit	1949	1952	1957	1965	1975	1979
1. Population	10 thousand	54,167	57,482	64,653	72,538	91,970	97,092
2. Labour force employed in national economy	"	— —	20,729	23,771	28,670	38,168	40,581
Of which: staff and workers	"	— —	1,603	3,101	4,965	8,778	9,967
3. Gross industrial and agricultural output value	100 million yuan	466	827	1,241	1,984	4,504	6,175
Gross agricultural output value	"	326	484	537	590	1,285	1,584
Gross industrial output value	"	140	343	704	1,394	3,219	4,591
Light industry	"	103	221	374	703	1,393	1,980
Heavy industry	"	37	122	330	691	1,826	2,611
4. National income	"	358	589	908	1,387	2,505	3,350
5. Revenue	"	65.2*	183.7	310.2	473.3	815.6	1,103.3
Expenditure	"	68.1*	176.0	304.2	466.3	820.9	1,273.9
6. Investment in capital construction	"	11.3*	43.6	138.3	170.9	391.9	499.9
7. Volume of freight transport	100 million ton-km.	255.4	762.3	1,809.6	3,461.3	7,285.9	10,897.7
8. Retail sales of commodities	100 million yuan	140.5	276.8	474.2	670.3	1,271.1	1,800.0
9. Total value of imports and exports (Renminbi)	"	41.5*	64.6	104.5	118.4	290.4	455.6
Imports	"	21.3*	37.5	50.0	55.3	147.4	243.9
Exports	"	20.2*	27.1	54.5	63.1	143.0	211.7
10. Output of major industrial and agricultural products							
Coal	100 million tons	0.32	0.66	1.31	2.32	4.82	6.35
Electricity	100 million kwh.	43.0	73.0	193.0	676.0	1,958.0	2,820.0
Crude oil	10 thousand tons	12.0	44.0	146.0	1,131.0	7,706.0	10,615.0
Steel	"	15.8	135.0	535.0	1,223.0	2,390.0	3,448.0
Cotton cloth	100 million m.	18.9	38.3	50.5	62.8	94.0	121.5
Sugar	10 thousand tons	20.0	45.0	86.0	146.0	174.0	250.0
Bicycles	10 thousand	1.4	8.0	80.6	183.8	623.2	1,009.5
Sewing machines	"		6.6	27.8	123.8	356.7	586.8
Wrist-watches	"			0.04	100.8	782.2	1,707.0
Grain	10 thousand tons	11,320.0	16,390.0	19,505.0	19,455.0	28,450.0	33,212.0
Cotton	"	44.5	130.4	164.0	209.8	238.1	220.7
Oil-bearing crops	"	256.4	419.3	419.6	362.6	452.1	643.5
Pork, beef and mutton	"		338.5	398.5	551.0	797.0	1,062.4
Aquatic products	"	45.0	167.0	312.0	298.0	441.0	431.0

Notes: 1. 1949 and 1952 figures of gross industrial and agricultural output value are calculated at constant prices of 1952; figures of 1957 and 1965 at constant prices; and figures of 1975 and 1979 at constant prices of 1970. Other indicators in value terms are calculated at current prices.
2. National income refers to the net output value of five material production sectors including industry, agriculture, construction, communications and transport, and commerce.
3. Asterisked figures(*) denote 1950 data.
4. Retail sales of commodities include the retail sales by peasants to non-agricultural residents.

Main Indicators of China's National Economy
(Rate of Increase)

Item	Index numbers (1952 = 100)			Average annual % increase rate	
	1957	1965	1979	1953-79	1950-79
1. Population	112.5	126.2	168.9	2.0	2.0
2. Labour force employed in national economy	114.7	138.3	195.8	2.5	—
Of which: staff and workers	193.5	309.7	621.8	7.0	—
3. Gross industrial and agricultural output value	167.8	268.3	845.2	8.2	9.4
Gross agricultural output value	124.8	137.1	249.4	3.4	4.5
Gross industrial output value	228.6	452.6	1,734.0	11.1	13.3
Heavy industry	183.2	344.5	1,061.0	9.1	11.0
Light industry	310.7	650.6	2,991.2	13.4	16.5
4. National income	153.0	197.5	484.9	6.0	7.3
5. Revenue	168.9	257.7	600.6	6.9	10.2*
Expenditure	172.8	264.9	723.8	7.6	10.6*
6. Investment in capital construction	317.2	392.0	1,146.8	9.5	13.9*
7. Volume of freight transport	237.5	454.2	1,429.6	10.4	13.3
8. Retail sales of commodities	171.3	242.2	650.3	7.2	8.9
9. Total value of imports and exports	161.8	183.3	705.3	7.5	8.6*
Imports	133.3	147.5	650.4	7.2	8.8*
Exports	201.1	232.8	781.2	7.9	8.1*
10. Output of major industrial and agricultural products					
Coal	198.5	351.5	962.1	8.8	10.5
Electricity	264.4	926.0	3,863.0	14.5	15.0
Crude oil	331.8	8,527.3	24,134.6	22.5	25.4
Steel	396.3	905.9	2,553.8	12.8	19.7
Cotton cloth	131.9	164.0	317.2	4.4	6.4
Sugar	191.1	324.4	555.6	6.6	8.8
Bicycles	1,008.2	2,299.5	12,629.2	19.6	24.5
Sewing machines	421.0	1,874.0	8,882.3	18.1	—
Grain	119.0	118.7	202.6	2.6	3.7
Cotton	125.8	160.9	169.2	2.0	5.5
Oil-bearing crops	100.1	86.5	153.5	1.6	3.1
Pork, beef and mutton	117.7	162.8	313.9	4.3	—
Aquatic products	186.8	178.4	258.1	3.6	7.8

Notes: 1. Increase rates of gross industrial and agricultural output value and national income are calculated at comparable prices.
2. Asterisked figures (*) refer to the average annual increase rates of 1951-79.

Average Daily Figures for Selected Main Indicators

Item	Unit	1949	1952	1957	1965	1979
1. Output of main industrial products						
Coal	10 thousand tons	8.8	18.1	35.9	63.6	174.0
Electricity	10 thousand kwh.	1,178.0	2,000.0	5,288.0	18,521.0	77,260.0
Crude oil	tons	329.0	1,205.0	4,000.0	30,986.0	290,822.0
Steel	”	433.0	3,699.0	14,658.0	33,507.0	94,466.0
Chemical fertilizers	”	16.4	107.0	414.0	4,729.0	29,189.0
Cement	”	1,808.0	7,836.0	18,795.0	44,767.0	202,466.0
Cotton cloth	10 thousand m.	518.0	1,049.0	1,384.0	1,721.0	3,329.0
Bicycles		38.4	219.0	2,208.0	5,036.0	27,658.0
Sewing machines		—	181.0	762.0	3,392.0	16,077.0
Wrist-watches		—	—	1.1	2,762.0	46,767.0
Television sets		—	—	—	12.0	3,641.0
Sugar	tons	548.0	1,233.0	3,356.0	4,000.0	6,849.0
Machine-made paper and paper board	”	301.0	1,014.0	2,493.0	4,740.0	13,507.0
2. Railway transport						
Volume of freight transport	100 million ton-km.	0.50	1.65	3.69	7.39	15.31
Volume of passenger transport	100 million passenger-km.	0.36	0.55	0.99	1.31	3.33
3. Completed floor space of dwelling houses	10 thousand m^2	—	—	7.72	4.73	17.14
4. Total value of retail sales	10 thousand yuan	3,849.0	7,584.0	12,992.0	18,364.0	49,315.0
5. Publication of books	10 thousand copies	28.8	215.3	349.4	594.9	1,115.6
Magazines	”	5.5	56.0	86.3	120.7	324.3
Newspapers	”	112.9	440.8	669.2	1,298.9	3,584.2

Birth, Death and Natural Growth Rates
(per thousand)

Year	Nation			Municipalities			Rural Counties		
	Birth rate	Death rate	Natural rate growth	Birth rate	Death rate	Natural rate growth	Birth rate	Death rate	Natural growth rate
1949	36.0	20.0	16.0	—	—	—	—	—	—
1952	37.0	17.0	20.0	—	—	—	—	—	—
1957	34.0	10.8	23.2	44.5	8.5	36.0	32.8	11.1	21.7
1965	38.1	9.6	28.5	27.6	5.9	21.7	39.5	10.0	29.5
1975	23.1	7.3	15.8	15.2	5.6	9.6	24.2	7.6	16.6
1979	17.9	6.2	11.7	13.9	5.1	8.8	18.5	6.4	12.1

Note: Increase rates in this table are calculated on an annual mean population basis.

National Labour Force Employment
(year-end data; in 10 thousands)

Year	Labour Force Employed in National Economy		Staff and workers in state-owned and collectively owned enterprises in cities and towns	Self-employed labourers in cities and towns	Labour force employed in rural people's communes
	Total	Percentage of total population			
1952	20,729	36.1	1,603	883	18,243
1957	23,771	36.8	3,101	104	20,566
1965	28,670	39.5	4,965	171	23,534
1975	38,168	41.5	8,198	24	29,946
1979	40,581	41.8	9,967	32	30,582

Employment in State-Owned Sectors, by Sectors of the National Economy
(year-end data; in 10 thousands)

Item	1952	1957	1965	1975	1979
Total	1,580	2,451	3,738	6,426	7,693
Industry	510.0	748.0	1,238.0	2,691.0	3,109.0
Construction	104.8	271.4	383.0	558.5	671.2
Agriculture, forestry, water conservancy and meteorology	23.9	112.3	422.0	723.3	810.4
Transport, posts and telecommunications	112.9	166.5	245.0	399.5	463.9
Commerce, catering and service trades	292.3	488.7	550.0	829.5	1,027.8
Science, education, culture and health	239.2	327.3	533.0	755.1	998.1
Civic public utilities	4.1	21.8	44.0	74.7	110.9
Finance	34.4	36.2	36.0	36.6	50.4
Governmental and public organizations	258.5	278.9	287.0	357.6	451.0

Wages and Employment in State-Owned Sectors, by Sectors of National Economy
(year-end data; in 10 thousands)

Item	1952	1957	1965	1975	1979
Total	68	156	235	386	529
Industry	24.6	50.7	86.4	169.1	230.2
Construction	5.9	21.7	24.9	39.0	54.2
Agriculture, forestry, water-conservancy and meteorology	0.9	5.4	18.1	32.8	44.5
Transport, posts and telecommunications	6.2	12.4	18.8	27.0	37.0
Commerce, catering and service trades	9.5	26.5	31.3	46.3	63.5
Science, education, culture and health	9.2	18.3	31.1	42.1	59.9
Civic public utilities	0.3	1.4	3.1	4.7	7.3
Finance	1.4	2.2	2.3	2.3	3.1
Governmental and public organizations	9.5	17.8	19.3	22.8	29.7

Wages and Employment in Collectively Owned Sectors in Cities and Towns

Item	1965	1977	1978	1979
1. Number of staff and workers at end of year (in 10 thousands)	1,226.6	1,916.4	2,048.0	2,273.5
Industry	505.4	1,142.0	1,215.0	1,327.7
Construction	93.5	157.0	174.5	219.1
Farming, forestry, animal husbandry, sideline occupations and fishing	72.3	51.4	59.2	51.6
Transport	172.6	188.9	204.3	218.6
Commerce, catering and service trades	200.3	203.1	211.3	259.4
Education, culture and health	117.8	123.0	128.4	132.9
Management bodies	6.3	14.0	14.2	17.0
Others	58.4	37.0	41.1	47.2
2. Total wage bill (100 million yuan)	—	89.0	100.2	117.2

Fixed Assets of State-Owned Enterprises (Original Value[1])
(in 100 million yuan)

Item	1952	1957	1965	1975	1979
Total at end of year	240.6	522.9	1,445.8	3,414.3	4,892.5
Of which: industry	107.2	272.2	961.0	2,290.3	3,253.2
agriculture	—	—	—	90.8	146.8
construction	1.7	21.7	22.9	47.5	80.4
transport, posts and telecommunications	115.2	182.7	337.9	672.0	890.2
commerce, catering and service trades	11.5	33.9	91.1	209.6	358.7
supply and marketing of means of production	0.1	1.8	8.8	23.9	41.6
civic public utilities	4.9	10.6	24.1	37.6	59.1
science, education, culture and health	—	—	—	17.0	25.9

Notes: 1. Original value of fixed assets refers to payments by independently accounting enterprises for the purchase and construction of various fixed assets.
2. Data in this table are classified by management systems instead of by sectors of national economy.

Use of Quota Circulating Funds by State-Owned Enterprises
(in 100 million yuan)

Item	1952	1957	1965	1975	1979
Total at end of year	171.7	401.8	915.9	2,298.6	3,087.5
Of which: industry	33.0	62.9	230.4	770.8	1,026.5
agriculture				47.0	129.8
construction	3.7	19.5	18.0	30.8	41.0
transport, posts and telecommunications	7.1	9.5	20.7	61.9	75.8
commerce, catering and service trades	123.2	290.1	493.4	1,061.0	1,421.5
supply and marketing of means of production	4.3	19.4	152.3	299.3	354.3
civic public utilities	0.4	0.4	1.1	3.4	5.1

Note: Data in this table are classified by management systems instead of by sectors of national economy.

National Income, Consumption and Accumulation

Item	Unit	1952	1957	1965	1965	1979
National income[1]	100 million yuan	589	908	1,387	2,503	3,350
Index numbers (1952 = 100)	%	100	153.0	197.5	384.7	484.9
National income per capita	yuan/person	104	142	194	274	347
Available national income[2]	100 million yuan	607	935	1,347	2,451	3,356
Consumption	"	477	702	982	1,621	2,195
Accumulation	"	130	233	365	830	1,161
Accumulation ratio	%	21.4	24.9	27.1	33.9	34.6

Notes: 1. All indicators are calculated at current prices except the index numbers of national income, which are calculated at comparable prices.
2. Available national income is not equal to total national income because of the difference between imports and exports and of the statistical discrepancy.

People's Communes in Rural Areas

Year	People's communes	Production brigades (10,000)	Production teams (10,000)	Households joining communes (10,000)	Persons joining communes (10,000)	Average number of production brigades per commune	Average number of production teams per production brigade	Average number of persons per production team
1958	23,630	—	—	12,861	56,017	—	—	—
1966	74,755	64.8	541.2	13,527	59,112	8.7	8.3	109
1975	52,615	67.7	482.6	16,448	77,712	12.9	7.1	161
1979	53,348	69.9	515.4	17,491	80,739	13.1	7.4	157

Area of Cultivated Land

		Of which:		% of total cultivated land	
Year	Area of cultivated land (10,000 hectares)	Paddy field (10,000 hectares)	Irrigated land (10,000 hectares)	Paddy field	Irrigated land
1949	9,788	2,282	323	23.3	3.3
1952	10,792	2,585	489	24.0	4.5
1957	11,183	2,753	1,068	24.6	9.6
1965	10,359	2,496	1,011	24.1	9.8
1975	9,971	2,553	2,068	25.6	20.7
1979	9,950	2,542	2,230	25.5	22.4

Note: The figures of cultivated land are underestimated and remain to be verified.

Gross Agricultural Output Value

Year	1952 = 100	Previous year = 100	Year	1952 = 100	Previous year = 100
1949	67.3	—	1965	137.1	108.3
1950	79.2	117.8	1966	148.9	108.6
1951	86.6	109.4	1967	151.3	101.6
1952	100	115.2	1968	147.5	97.5
1953	103.1	103.1	1969	149.2	101.1
1954	106.6	103.4	1970	166.4	111.5
1955	114.8	107.6	1971	171.4	103.1
1956	120.4	105.0	1972	171.1	99.8
1957	124.8	103.6	1973	185.5	108.4
1958	127.8	102.4	1974	193.2	104.2
1959	110.4	86.4	1975	202.1	104.6
1960	96.4	87.4	1976	207.1	102.5
1961	94.0	97.6	1977	210.6	101.7
1962	100.0	106.2	1978	229.6	109.0
1963	111.6	111.6	1979	249.4	108.6
1964	126.7	113.5			

Note: Constant prices of gross agricultural output value have been changed 3 times, and the index numbers presented are calculated at comparable prices. Growth rates of the agricultural output of different years can be calculated by using these index numbers.

Gross Output Value of Farm Products, Forestry, Animal Husbandry, Sideline Occupations and Fisheries

Year	Farm products	Forestry	Animal husbandry	Sideline Occupations Total	Of which: brigade-owned enterprises	Fisheries
1. Absolute figures (100 million yuan)						
1949	224.3	1.6	33.7	11.6	—	0.6
1952	346.6	2.9	47.9	18.3	—	1.3
1957	432.6	9.3	69.0	22.9	—	2.9
1965	446.8	12.0	82.7	38.0	—	10.1
1975	932.4	37.1	179.4	117.0	82.6	19.1
1979	1,059.6	45.0	221.2	238.9	198.0	19.6
2. % of gross agricultural output value						
1949	82.5	0.6	12.4	4.3	—	0.2
1952	83.1	0.7	11.5	4.4	—	0.3
1957	80.6	1.7	12.9	4.3	—	0.5
1965	75.8	2.0	14.0	6.5	—	1.7
1975	72.5	2.9	14.0	9.1	6.4	1.5
1979	66.9	2.8	14.0	15.1	12.5	1.2

Output of Major Farm Products, Aquatic Products and Forest Products
(in 10,000 tons)

Item	1949	1952	1957	1965	1975	1979
Grain crops	11,320.0	16,390.0	19,505.0	19,455.0	28,450.0	33,212.0
Cotton	44.5	130.4	164.0	209.8	238.1	220.7
Oil-bearing crops	256.4	419.3	419.6	362.6	452.1	643.5
Of which: peanuts	126.8	231.6	257.1	192.8	227.1	282.2
rapeseed	73.4	93.2	88.8	108.9	153.6	240.2
seasame	32.6	48.1	31.3	25.6	20.8	41.7
Jute, ambary hemp	3.7	30.6	30.1	27.9	70.0	108.9
Mulberry silkworm cocoons	3.1	6.2	6.8	6.7	15.3	21.3
Tussah silkworm cocoons	1.2	6.1	4.5	3.9	4.2	5.7
Tea	4.1	8.3	11.2	10.1	21.1	27.7
Sugarcane	264.2	711.6	1,039.3	1,339.2	1,666.7	2,150.8
Sugar beets	19.1	47.9	150.1	198.5	247.7	310.6
Roasted tobacco	4.3	22.2	25.6	37.2	70.1	80.6
Fruits	120.0	244.3	324.8	324.0	538.1	701.5
Aquatic products	45.0	167.0	312.0	298.0	441.0	431.0
Marine water	—	106.0	194.0	201.0	335.0	319.0
Freshwater	—	61.0	118.0	97.0	106.0	112.0
Rubber	—	—	0.02	1.66	6.86	10.83
Tung oil seed	—	43.5	51.8	—	37.0	32.5
Tea oil seed	—	24.9	49.4	33.2	42.5	61.7

Output Index of Farm Products, Aquatic Products and Forest Products
(1952 = 100)

Item	1957	1965	1975	1979
Grain crops	119.0	118.7	173.6	202.6
Cotton	125.8	160.9	182.6	169.2
Oil-bearing crops	100.1	86.5	107.8	153.5
Of which: peanuts	111.0	83.2	98.1	121.8
rapeseed	95.3	116.8	164.8	257.7
sesame	65.1	53.2	43.2	86.7
Jute, ambary hemp	98.4	91.2	228.8	355.9
Mulberry silkworm cocoons	109.7	108.1	246.2	343.5
Tussah silkworm cocoons	73.8	63.9	68.8	93.4
Tea	134.9	121.7	254.8	333.7
Sugarcane	146.1	188.2	234.2	302.2
Sugar beets	113.4	414.4	517.1	648.4
Roasted tobacco	115.3	167.6	315.8	363.1
Fruits	133.0	132.6	220.3	287.1
Aquatic products	186.8	178.4	264.1	258.1
Marine water	183.0	189.6	316.0	300.9
Freshwater	193.4	159.0	173.8	183.6
Forestry products	—	—	—	—
Tung oil seed	119.1	—	85.1	74.7
Tea oil seed	198.4	133.3	170.7	247.8

Hogs, Sheep and Goats and Meat Production

Year	Number of slaughtered fattening hogs (10,000)	Number of hogs at the end of the year (10,000)	Production of pork, beef and mutton (10,000 tons)	Number of sheep and goats at end of year (in 10 thousands)		
				Total	Goats	Sheep
1. Absolute figures						
1952	6,545	8,977	338.5	6,178	2,490	3,688
1957	7,131	14,590	398.5	9,858	4,515	5,343
1965	12,167	16,693	551.0	13,903	6,077	7,826
1975	16,230	28,117	797.0	16,337	6,804	9,533
1979	18,768	31,971	1,062.4	18,314	8,057	10,257
2. Index numbers (1952 = 100)						
1957	109.0	162.5	117.7	159.6	181.3	144.9
1965	185.9	186.0	162.8	225.0	244.1	212.2
1975	248.0	313.2	235.5	264.4	273.3	258.5
1979	286.8	356.1	313.9	296.4	323.6	278.1

Note: "Slaughtered fattening hogs" refers to the sum of fattening hogs which were purchased by the state and slaughtered by collectives, commune members, state farms and other units.

Major Farm Products, Average Output per Hectare
(sown area; Kg./hectare)

Item	1949	1952	1957	1965	1975	1979
Grain crops	1,030	1,322	1,460	1,626	2,350	2,785
Of which: Rice	1,892	2,411	2,692	2,942	3,514	4,244
Wheat	642	732	858	1,021	1,638	2,137
Corn		1,341	1,435	1,510	2,539	2,983
Soybeans	612	815	788	715	1,034	1,029
Tuber crops	1,405	1,879	2,090	1,776	2,604	2,599
Cotton	161	234	284	420	480	489
Peanuts	1,014	1,287	1,012	1,042	1,208	1,363
Rapeseed	486	501	384	598	665	870
Sesame	394	455	332	386	390	495
Jute, ambary hemp	1,276	1,937	2,105	2,469	2,357	3,008
Sugarcane	24,463	38,885	38,925	38,154	31,868	42,008
Sugar beets	11,938	13,686	9,440	11,608	8,175	9,557
Roasted tobacco	705	1,194	721	1,145	1,524	1,583

Per Capita Output of Grain, Cotton, Oil-Bearing Crops, Hogs and Aquatic Products

Year	Grain (kg.)	Cotton (kg.)	Oil-bearing crops (kg.)	Flattening hogs (head)	Pork, beef and mutton (kg.)	Aquatic products (kg.)
1949	209	0.82	4.73	—	—	0.9
1952	288	2.29	7.37	0.12	5.95	2.9
1957	306	2.57	6.58	0.11	6.25	4.9
1965	272	2.93	5.07	0.17	7.70	4.2
1975	312	2.61	4.96	0.18	8.74	4.8
1979	344	2.29	6.67	0.21	11.0	4.5

Large Animal Population

	Year	Total	Of which: draught animals	Cattle, buffaloes	Horses	Asses	Mules	Camels
1.	Absolute figures (10,000 head)							
	1949	6,002	—	4,393.6	487.5	949.4	147.1	24.7
	1952	7,646	5,142	5,660.0	613.0	1,180.6	163.7	28.5
	1957	8,382	5,368	6,361.2	730.2	1,086.4	167.9	36.5
	1965	8,421	4,322	6,695.1	792.1	743.8	144.7	44.8
	1975	9,686	5,122	7,354.7	1,129.9	812.7	335.4	53.5
	1979	9,459	5,029	7,134.6	1,114.5	747.3	402.3	60.4
2.	Index numbers (1952 = 100)							
	1957	109.6	104.4	112.4	119.1	92.0	102.6	128.1
	1965	110.1	84.1	118.3	129.2	63.0	88.4	157.2
	1975	126.7	99.6	129.9	184.3	68.8	204.9	187.7
	1979	123.7	97.8	126.1	181.8	63.3	245.8	211.9

Major Agricultural Machinery
(Year-end data)

Item	Multiple	1957	1957	1965	1975	1979
Total horsepower of agricultural machinery	10,000 hp.	25	165	1,494	10,168	18,191
Large and medium-sized tractors	10,000	1,307	14,674	72,599	344,518	666,823
Hand tractors	10,000			0.4	59.9	167.1
Large and medium-sized tractor-driven agricultural tools	10,000			25.8	90.8	131.3
Combine harvesters		284	1,789	6,704	12,551	23,026
Motor-driven threshers	10,000			11.4	155.3	232.8
Power-driven drainage and irrigation machines	10,000 hp.	12.8	56.4	907.4	4,866.6	7,122.1
Rice mills, wheat mills	10,000				217.7	291.2
Cotton gins	"				30.2	26.7
Oil presses	"				16.7	21.6
Trucks			4,084	11,063	39,585	97,105
Rubber-tired animal-drawn carts	10,000			133.5	245.5	247.7
Rubber-tired hand carts	"			875.7	2,361.1	3,262.4
Motor-driven fishing boats	10,000 hp.		10.3	64.0	213.6	312.9

Agricultural Modernization

Item	Unit	1952	1957	1965	1975	1979
Actual tractor-ploughed area	10 thousand hectares	13.6	263.6	1,577.9	3,320.3	4,221.9
Tractor-ploughed land as % of total cultivated land	%	0.1	2.4	15.0	33.3	42.4
Irrigated area	10 thousand hectares	1,995.9	2,733.9	3,305.5	4,328.4	4,500.3
Irrigated area as % of total cultivated area	%	18.5	24.4	31.9	43.4	45.2
Power irrigated area	10 thousand hectares	31.7	120.2	809.3	2,288.9	2,532.1
Power irrigated area as % of total irrigated area	%	1.6	4.4	24.5	52.9	56.3
Consumption of chemical fertilizer[1]	10 thousand tons	7.8	37.3	194.2	536.9	1,086.3
Chemical fertilizer consumption per hectare of cultivated land	kg.	0.7	3.3	18.7	53.8	109.2
Small-sized hydroelectric stations in rural areas		98	544		68,158	83,224
Generating capacity	10 thousand kw.	0.8	2.0		144.4	276.3
Electricity consumed in rural areas[2]	100 million kwh.	0.5	1.4	37.1	183.1	282.7
Electricity consumed per hectare of cultivated land	kwh.		1.3	35.8	183.6	284.1

Notes: 1. Consumption of chemical fertilizer is calculated on the basis of 100% effectiveness.
2. Electricity consumed in rural areas refers to electricity consumed for production and daily use by the communes, brigades and teams in rural areas, excluding electricity consumed by state-owned units in rural areas.

Index of Gross Output Value of Heavy and Light Industry

Year	1952 = 100			Previous year = 100		
	Total	Light industry	Heavy industry	Total	Light industry	Heavy industry
1949	40.8	46.6	30.3			
1950	55.7	60.6	46.7	136.4	130.1	154.1
1951	77.0	81.0	69.7	138.2	133.6	149.1
1952	100	100	100	129.9	123.5	143.5
1953	130.3	126.7	136.9	130.3	126.7	136.9
1954	151.6	144.8	163.9	116.3	114.3	119.8
1955	160.1	144.8	187.7	105.6	100.0	114.5
1956	204.7	173.3	262.3	128.1	119.7	139.7
1957	228.6	183.2	310.7	111.5	105.7	118.4
1958	353.8	245.0	555.5	154.8	133.7	178.8
1959	481.8	299.0	822.7	136.1	122.0	148.1
1960	535.7	269.5	1,035.5	111.2	90.2	125.9
1961	330.7	211.1	553.6	61.8	78.4	53.5
1962	275.9	193.5	428.4	83.4	91.6	77.4
1963	299.4	198.1	487.8	108.5	102.3	113.8
1964	358.3	233.4	590.3	119.6	117.8	121.0
1965	452.6	344.5	650.6	126.4	147.7	110.2
1966	547.4	394.3	829.2	120.9	114.5	127.5
1967	471.8	366.4	663.6	86.2	92.9	80.0
1968	448.0	348.3	629.8	95.0	95.1	94.9
1969	601.6	436.1	906.6	134.3	125.2	143.9
1970	786.0	514.9	1,289.9	130.7	118.1	142.3
1971	903.3	548.2	1,565.5	114.9	106.5	121.4
1972	962.9	582.2	1,675.1	106.6	106.2	107.0
1973	1,054.2	643.6	1,820.7	109.5	110.6	108.7
1974	1,056.9	660.6	1,790.9	100.3	102.7	98.4
1975	1,216.4	746.4	2,091.8	115.1	113.0	116.8
1976	1,232.2	766.4	2,102.2	101.3	102.4	100.5
1977	1,408.4	873.7	2,402.9	114.3	114.3	114.3
1978	1,598.6	968.1	2,777.7	113.5	110.8	115.6
1979	1,734.4	1,061.0	2,991.6	108.5	109.6	107.7

Note: Constant prices of gross industrial output value have been changed 3 times, and the index numbers presented are calculated at comparable prices.

Gross Industrial Output Value, by Major Sector

Industrial sectors	1952	1957	1965	1975	1979
Total (100 million yuan)	343.3	784.0	1,393.9	3,218.8	4,590.7
Of which: Metallurgical industry	20.2	60.0	149.5	288.3	410.3
Electric power industry	4.3	11.7	43.1	124.7	176.7
Coal industry	8.3	20.6	36.0	90.0	118.1
Petroleum industry	1.8	8.0	45.1	179.8	249.6
Chemical industry	16.6	48.2	179.4	364.5	561.8
Of which: Chemical fertilizers and insecticides	0.37	1.63	26.2	61.4	106.9
Machine building industry	39.0	119.0	310.2	890.5	1,244.8
Of which: agricultural machinery	0.87	2.81	14.3	82.3	109.1
Building materials industry	10.3	22.7	39.6	99.95	167.3
Forest industry	22.3	40.6	39.9	61.1	84.8
Food industry	82.8	138.4	175.5	386.1	518.7
Textile industry	94.3	143.6	220.7	396.1	593.1
Paper-making industry	7.6	15.4	24.5	41.4	60.3
Percentage of total	100.0	100.0	100.0	100.0	100.0
Metallurgical industry	5.9	8.5	10.7	9.0	8.9
Electric power industry	1.3	1.7	3.1	3.9	3.8
Coal industry	2.4	2.9	2.6	2.8	2.6
Petroleum industry	0.5	1.1	3.2	5.6	5.4
Chemical industry	4.8	6.8	12.9	11.3	12.2
Of which: Chemical fertilizers and insecticides	0.1	0.2	1.9	1.9	2.3
Machine building industry	11.4	16.9	22.3	27.7	27.1
Of which: Agricultural machinery	0.3	0.4	1.0	2.6	2.4
Building materials ind.	3.0	3.2	2.8	3.1	3.6
Forest industry	6.5	5.8	2.9	1.9	1.9
Food industry	24.1	19.7	12.6	12.0	11.3
Textile industry	27.5	20.4	15.8	12.3	12.9
Paper-making industry	2.2	2.2	1.8	1.3	1.3

Note: 1952 figures are calculated at constant prices of 1952; 1957, 1965 and 1970 figures are calculated at constant prices of 1957; 1975 and 1979 figures are calculated at constant prices of 1970.

Index of Gross Industrial Output Value, by Major Sector
(1952 = 100)

Industrial sectors	1957	1965	1975	1979
Total	228.6	452.6	1,216.4	1,734.4
Of which: Metallurgical industry	359.4	895.6	1,768.5	2,516.9
Electric power industry	253.5	934.0	2,699.1	3,824.6
Coal industry	220.5	385.2	762.5	1,000.6
Petroleum industry	411.1	2,317.8	10,703.1	16,342.5
Chemical industry	389.2	1,449.0	5,294.8	7,782.4
Of which: Chemical fertilizers and insecticides	632.4	10,164.4	33,306.7	57,988.5
Machine building industry	366.7	955.9	3,783.0	5,288.2
Of which: Agricultural machinery	434.5	2,211.4	17,420.7	23,093.5
Building materials ind.	248.5	433.3	1,170.4	1,959.0
Forest industry	190.1	186.9	243.5	337.9
Food industry	185.5	235.4	397.3	533.8
Textile industry	151.1	232.2	419.3	627.8
Paper-making industry	239.5	381.0	611.7	891.1

Note: The figures in this table are calculated at comparable prices.

Output Index of Major Industrial Products
(1952 = 100)

Item	1957	1965	1975	1979
Coal	198.5	351.5	730.3	962.1
Crude oil	331.8	2,570.5	17,513.6	24,125.0
Electricity	264.4	926.0	2,682.2	3,863.0
Of which: hydropower	369.2	800.0	3,661.5	3,853.8
Rolled steel	391.5	831.1	1,530.2	2,355.7
Steel	396.3	905.9	1,770.4	2,554.1
Pig iron	307.8	558.0	1,268.9	1,903.1
Machine-made coke	250.0	541.9	1,233.3	1,510.8
Timber	248.8	355.2	413.0	485.6
Cement	239.9	571.3	1,617.5	2,583.9
Plate glass	216.9	322.5	682.2	1,093.9
Sulphuric acid	332.6	1,231.6	2,551.1	3,683.2
Soda ash	263.5	459.4	647.4	774.0
Caustic soda	250.6	703.8	1,631.6	2,311.4
Synthetic ammonia	402.6	3,905.3	15,992.1	35,478.9
Chemical fertilizers for agricultural use	387.2	4,425.6	13,453.8	27,317.9
Of which: nitrogenous fertilizers	330.8	2,659.0	9,510.3	22,617.9
Chemical insecticides	3,250.0	9,650.0	21,100.0	26,850.0
Plastics	650.0	4,852.0	16,500.0	39,650.0
Outer rubber tires	209.5	552.4	1,666.7	2,783.3
Mining equipment	2,938.9	2,222.2	10,894.4	14,650.0
Metallurgical equipment	6,900.0	8,700.0	41,050.0	36,450.0
Chemical industry equipment	720.0	3,420.0	7,590.0	6,640.0
Power-generating equipment	3,300.0	11,383.3	82,750.0	103,533.3
Alternating-current motors	228.1	682.8	4,373.4	5,567.2
Transformers	359.0	699.1	3,501.7	4,976.9
Pumps	364.3	1,107.1	8,485.7	8,971.4
Metal-cutting machines	204.4	289.1	1,276.6	1,019.0
Forging and pressing machines	263.6	681.8	4,063.6	3,272.7
Rolling bearings	898.3	2,610.2	13,790.7	18,235.6
Internal combustion engines	1,725.0	6,975.0	58,700.0	72,700.0
Locomotives	835.0	730.0	2,630.0	2,865.0
Freight railway cars	125.9	50.0	270.7	275.9
Passenger railway cars	7,566.7	2,666.7	13,400.0	14,266.7
Steel ships for civilian use	769.0	615.5	1,910.7	3,298.8
Cotton yarn	128.7	198.2	321.3	401.7
Cotton cloth	131.9	1,640.4	245.4	317.2
Towels	164.3	193.8	342.4	486.6
Hoses	162.4	120.9	164.9	227.6
Knitting wool	285.0	550.0	1,330.0	2,220.0
Woollen piece goods	429.6	1,002.4	1,641.4	2,131.7
Blankets	120.2	337.5	715.5	962.3
Gunny bags	123.9	186.6	285.1	513.4
Silk	176.8	162.5	412.5	530.4
Silk textiles	223.1	526.2	698.5	1,020.0
Bulbs	265.4	738.5	2,000.0	3,269.2
Soap	271.1	324.7	629.9	776.3
Matches	113.7	132.5	179.7	207.7
Crude salt	167.3	231.7	299.2	298.4
Sugar	191.1	324.4	386.7	555.6
Cigarettes	168.3	180.4	374.3	491.7
Canned food	494.4	974.4	2,807.2	4,010.4
Leather	289.7	216.1	744.5	934.2
Leather shoes	210.8	150.7	553.8	967.3
Rubber shoes	216.7	416.7	600.0	600.0
Machine-made paper and paperboard	245.9	467.6	921.6	1,332.4
Radio sets	2,070.6	4,794.1	55,035.3	81,217.6

Output of Major Industrial Products

Item	Unit	1949	1952	1957	1965	1975	1979
Coal	100 million tons	0.32	0.66	1.31	2.32	4.82	6.35
Crude oil	10 thousand tons	12.00	44.00	146.00	1,131.00	7,706.00	10,615.00
Natural gas	100 million m.³	0.07	0.08	0.70	11.00	88.50	145.10
Electricity	100 million kwh.	43.00	73.00	193.00	676.00	1,958.00	2,820.00
Of which: Hydropower	"	7.00	13.00	48.00	104.00	476.00	501.00
Rolled steel	10 thousand tons	13.00	106.00	415.00	881.00	1,622.00	2,497.00
Steel	"	15.80	135.00	535.00	1,223.00	2,390.00	3,448.00
Pig iron	"	25.00	193.00	594.00	1,077.00	2,449.00	3,673.00
Machine-made coke	"	43.00	222.00	555.00	1,203.00	2,738.00	3,354.00
Timber[1]	10 thousand m.³	567.00	1,120.00	2,787.00	3,978.00	4,626.00	5,439.00
Cement	10 thousand tons	66.00	286.00	686.00	1,634.00	4,626.00	7,390.00
Plate glass	10 thousand standard crates	108.00	213.00	462.00	687.00	1,453.00	2,330.00
Sulphuric acid	10 thousand tons	4.00	19.00	63.20	234.00	484.70	699.80
Soda ash	"	8.80	19.20	50.60	88.20	124.30	148.60
Caustic soda	"	1.50	7.90	19.80	55.60	128.90	182.60
Synthetic ammonia	"	0.50	3.80	15.30	148.40	607.70	1,348.20
Chemical fertilizers for agricultural use[2]	"	0.60	3.90	15.10	172.60	524.70	1,065.40
Of which: Nitrogenous fertilizer	"	0.60	3.90	12.90	103.70	370.90	882.10
Phosphate fertilizer	"	—	—	2.20	68.80	153.10	181.70
Chemical insecticides	"	—	0.20	6.50	19.30	42.20	53.70
Plastics	"	—	0.20	1.30	9.70	33.00	79.30
Outer rubber tires	10 thousand	3.00	42.00	88.00	232.00	700.00	1,169.00
Chemical pharmaceuticals	10 thousand tons	0.01	0.22	1.05	2.73	4.17	
Mining equipment	"	0.07	0.18	5.29	4.00	19.61	26.37
Metallurgical equipment	"	—	0.02	1.38	1.74	8.21	7.29
Petroleum equipment	"	—	—	0.59	1.29	6.32	9.30
Chemical industry equipment	"	0.02	0.10	0.72	3.42	7.59	6.64
Power generating equipment[3]	10 thousand kw.	—	0.60	19.80	68.30	495.50	621.20
Alternating-current motors	"	—	64.00	146.00	405.00	2,799.00	3,563.00
Transformers	10 thousand kva.	12.00	117.00	420.00	818.00	4,097.00	5,823.00
Pumps	10 thousand	0.30	1.40	5.10	15.50	118.80	125.60
Metal-cutting machine tools	"	0.16	1.37	2.80	3.96	17.49	13.96
Forging and pressing machines	"	0.03	0.11	0.29	0.75	4.47	3.60
Motor vehicles	"	—	—	0.79	4.06	13.98	18.57
Of which: Trucks	"	—	—	0.62	2.65	7.76	11.67
Rolling bearings	10 thousand sets	14.00	118.00	1,060.00	3,080.00	16,273.00	21,518.00
Tractors	10 thousand	—	—	—	0.96	7.84	12.56
Hand tractors	"	—	—	—	0.36	20.94	31.75
Combines	"	—	—	124.00	655.00	2,484.00	4,587.00

Continued next page

Output of Major Industrial Output (Cont'd)

Item	Unit	1949	1952	1957	1965	1975	1979
Internal combustion engines	10 thousand hp.	1.00	4.00	69.00	279.00	2,348.00	2,908.00
Of which: for drainage and irrigation		—	—	26.50	66.30	1,028.20	654.20
Locomotives		—	20.00	167.00	146.00	526.00	573.00
Freight railway cars	10 thousand	0.14	0.58	0.73	0.29	1.57	1.60
Passenger railway cars		23.00	6.00	454.00	160.00	804.00	856.00
Steel ships for civilian use		—	84.00	646.00	517.00	1,605.00	2,771.00
Chemical fibres	10 thousand tons	—	—	0.02	5.01	15.48	32.63
Cotton yarn[4]	"	32.70	65.60	84.40	130.00	210.80	263.50
Cotton cloth[5]	100 million m.	18.90	38.30	50.50	62.80	94.00	121.50
Towels	100 million	—	2.24	3.68	4.34	7.67	10.90
Hose	100 million pairs	—	3.59	5.83	4.34	5.92	8.17
Knitting wool	10 thousand tons	0.18	0.20	0.57	1.10	2.66	4.44
Woollen piece goods	10 thousand m.	544.00	423.00	1,817.00	4,240.00	6,943.00	9,017.00
Blankets	10 thousand	22.20	71.70	86.20	242.00	513.00	690.00
Gunny bags[6]	100 million	0.10	0.67	0.83	1.25	1.91	3.44
Silk[7]	10 thousand tons	0.18	0.56	0.99	0.91	2.31	2.97
Silk textiles	100 million m.	0.50	0.65	1.45	3.42	4.54	6.63
Bulbs	100 million	0.13	0.26	0.69	1.92	5.20	8.50
Synthetic detergents	10 thousand tons	—	—	—	3.00	22.30	39.70
Synthetic fatty acid for soap-making	tons	—	—	—	8,671.00	47,064.00	58,422.00
Soap	10 thousand tons	—	9.70	26.30	31.50	61.10	75.30
Matches	10 thousand cases	672.00	911.00	1,036.00	1,207.00	1,637.00	1,892.00
Crude salt	10 thousand tons	299.00	495.00	828.00	1,147.00	1,481.00	1,477.00
Sugar	"	20.00	45.00	86.00	146.00	174.00	250.00
Cigarettes	10 thousand cases	160.00	265.00	446.00	478.00	992.00	1,303.00
Canned food	10 thousand tons	—	1.25	6.18	12.18	35.09	50.13
Leather	10 thousand pieces	—	330.00	956.00	713.00	2,457.00	3,083.00
Leather shoes	10 thousand pairs	—	1,200.00	2,529.00	1,808.00	6,646.00	11,608.00
Rubber shoes	100 million pairs	0.30	0.60	1.30	2.50	3.60	3.60
Clothing	100 million pieces	—	—	—	3.85	6.73	7.44
Machine-made paper and paperboard	10 thousand tons	11.00	37.00	91.00	173.00	341.00	493.00
Radio sets	10 thousand	0.44	1.70	35.20	81.50	935.60	1,380.70
Recorders	"	—	—	—	—	—	16.50
Television sets	"	—	—	—	0.43	17.78	132.85
Cameras	"	—	—	0.01	1.72	18.49	28.81
Bicycles	"	1.40	8.00	80.60	183.80	623.20	1,009.50
Sewing machines	"	—	6.60	27.80	123.80	356.70	586.80
Wrist-watches	"	—	—	0.04	100.80	782.20	1,707.00

Notes:
1. Timber refers to amount shipped.
2. Chemical fertilizers for agricultural use are calculated on the basis of 100% effectiveness.
3. Power generating equipment refers to water turbogenerators, turbogenerators and gas turbines with generating capacity of 500 kw. and over. Alternating current motors refer to those with power capacity of 0.5 kw. and over.
4. Cotton yarn includes pure and cotton blend yarn and pure chemical fibre yarn; it excludes cotton thread, substitute fibre yarn and hand-made yarn.
5. Cotton cloth includes pure and cotton blend cloth, pure chemical fibre cloth and canvas; it excludes substitute fibre cloth, handwoven cloth and cord fabric.
6. Gunny bags include pure gunny and blend gunny bags and bags made of pure chemical and substitute fibres; it excludes handmade and regenerated gunny bags.
7. Silk does not include hand-made silk.

Overall Labour Productivity of State-Owned Industrial Enterprises Using Independent Accounting

(at constant prices of 1970)

Year	Overall labour productivity (yuan/person/year)	Index numbers (1952 = 100)
1952	4,167	100
1957	6,336	152.1
1965	8,943	214.6
1975	9,994	239.8
1979	11,790	282.9

Main Financial Indicators for State-Owned Industrial Enterprises Using Independent Accounting.

Item	Unit	1952	1957	1965	1975	1979
Original value of fixed assets	100 million yuan	149.2	336.6	1,040.0	2,428.3	3,466.7
Total value of funds	”	147.1	331.8	1,037.3	2,569.0	3,487.6
Net value of fixed assets	”	101.1	241.3	777.2	1,716.3	2,378.6
Quota circulating funds	”	46.0	90.5	260.1	852.7	1,109.0
Profits and taxes	”	37.4	115.1	309.2	582.7	864.4
Profits	”	28.3	79.5	217.0	363.4	562.4
Taxes	”	9.1	35.6	92.2	219.3	301.6
Ratio of profit to fixed assets (original value)	yuan	19.0	23.6	20.9	15.0	16.2
Ratio of profit to funds	”	19.2	24.0	20.9	14.1	16.1
Ratio of profit and tax to funds	”	25.4	34.7	29.8	22.7	24.8
Ratio of profit to gross industrial output value	”	14.2	17.1	21.3	14.2	15.8
Ratio of gross output value to fixed assets (original value)	”	134.0	138.0	98.0	105.0	103.0
Ratio of circulating funds to gross output value	”	23.1	19.4	25.5	33.4	31.0

Postal and Telecommunications Transactions

Year	Total transactions (10,000 yuan)	Letters (10,000)	Circulation of newspapers and magazines (10,000)	Telegrams (10,000)	Long-distance telephone calls (10,000)	City telephones (10,000 subscribers)	Rural telephones (10,000 subscribers)
1949	9,717	59,874	—	1,129	902	21.77	—
1952	16,434	80,894	1,363	1,204	1,628	29.53	5.84
1957	29,368	164,054	3,264	1,533	2,090	46.45	20.00
1965	62,826	217,571	5,621	5,277	8,869	77.11	49.22
1975	95,757	273,379	7,823	11,234	15,151	103.28	65.92
1979	125,546	307,980	12,680	13,495	20,587	127.02	76.28

Transportation Routes

(in 10,000 km.)

Year	Railway lines			Highways open to traffic	Navigable inland waterways	Civil aviation routes		Petroleum and gas pipelines
	In operation	Open to traffic	Total track length			Total	Of which: international routes	
1949	2.18	2.20	3.00	8.07	7.36	—	—	—
1952	2.29	2.45	3.51	12.67	9.50	1.31	0.51	—
1957	2.67	2.99	4.31	25.46	14.41	2.64	0.43	—
1965	3.64	3.74	5.89	51.45	15.77	3.94	0.45	—
1975	4.60	4.84	7.91	78.36	13.56	8.42	3.71	0.53
1979	4.98	5.15	8.68	87.58*	10.78*	16.00	5.13	0.91

Note: Asterisked figures (*) refer to figures as of end of October 1979.

Volume of Freight Transport

Year	Total	Railways	Highways	Waterways		Petroleum and gas transported by pipeline	Air freight
				Total	By ocean-going freighters		

1. Freight transport (10 thousand tons)

Year	Total	Railways	Highways	Total	By ocean-going freighters	Pipeline	Air
1949	16,097.4	5,589	7,963	2,543	—	—	2.4
1952	31,516.2	13,217	13,158	5,141	14	—	0.2
1957	80,364.8	27,421	37,505	15,438	60	—	0.8
1965	120,340.7	48,358	48,987	22,993	246	—	2.7
1975	200,268.7	86,746	72,499	34,987	2,424	6,032	4.7
1979	245,630.0	109,495	81,556	43,229	4,249	11,342	8.0

2. Volume of freight transport (100 million ton/km.)

Year	Total	Railways	Highways	Total	By ocean-going freighters	Pipeline	Air
1949	255.4	184	8.1	63.1	—	—	0.2
1952	762.3	602	14.5	145.8	28	—	—
1957	1,809.6	1,346	48.0	415.5	77	—	0.1
1965	3,461.3	2,696	95.1	670.2	237	—	0.3
1975	7,285.9	4,246	202.6	2,574.7	1,757	262	0.6
1979	10,897.7	5,581	268.3	4,564.2	3,174	476	1.2

Note: Indicators of highway transportation hereafter refer only to that handled by specialized transportation departments at various levels. Railway transportation does not include local railways, and the coverage is smaller than the relevant indicators in "Communique of Fulfilment of 1980 National Economic Plan."

Volume of Passenger Transport

	Passenger transport (10,000 persons)			Volume of Passenger transport (100 million person-km.)		
Year	Railways	Highways	Waterways	Railways	Highways	Waterways
1949	10,297	1,809	1,562	130	8.0	15.2
1952	16,352	4,559	3,605	201	22.6	24.5
1957	31,262	23,772	8,780	361	88.1	46.4
1965	40,708	43,693	11,369	478	168.2	47.4
1975	69,648	101,350	21,015	953	374.5	90.6
1979	85,611	178,618	24,360	1,214	603.3	114.0

Freight and Passenger Transport
(1952 = 100)

	Volume of freight transport			Volume of passenger transport		
Year	Railways	Highways	Waterways	Railways	Highways	Waterways
1952	100	100	100	100	100	100
1957	223.6	331.0	285.0	179.6	389.8	189.4
1965	447.8	655.9	459.7	237.8	744.2	193.5
1975	705.3	1,397.2	1,765.9	474.1	1,657.1	369.8
1979	928.2	1,850.3	3,130.5	604.0	2,669.5	465.3

Main Indicators of Capital Construction for State-Owned Units

Item	Unit	1950	1952	1957	1965	1975	1979
1. Newly increased fixed assets	100 million yuan	10.09	31.14	129.22	159.93	250.53	418.27
2. Total investment of capital construction	"	11.34	43.56	138.29	170.89	391.86	499.88
a) By sources of funds:							
National budget	"	10.41	37.11	126.45	154.37	318.12	394.97
Self-raised funds of local authorities and enterprises	"	0.93	6.45	11.84	16.52	73.74	104.91
b) By uses of investment:							
Construction and installment works	"	8.59	28.40	85.06	103.88	218.98	328.30
Purchase of equipment, tools and implements	"	2.21	11.07	45.85	55.07	144.63	137.17
Other investment	"	0.54	4.09	7.38	11.94	28.25	34.41
c) By purposes of construction:							
Productive construction	"	7.37	29.14	105.09	144.74	335.88	365.14
Non-productive construction	"	3.97	14.42	33.20	26.15	55.98	134.74
Of which: dwelling units	"	1.25	4.48	12.82	9.43	22.94	73.79
d) By sectors of national economy:							
Industry	"	—	16.89	72.40	88.96	231.03	256.85
Light industry	"	—	4.06	11.04	7.01	23.13	30.60
Heavy industry	"	—	12.83	61.36	81.95	207.90	226.25
Construction	"	—	0.89	4.62	4.11	6.89	11.47
Transport, posts and telecommunications	"	—	7.61	20.69	30.51	68.67	64.09
Agriculture, forestry, water conservancy and meteology	"	—	5.83	11.87	24.97	38.40	57.92
Commerce, catering and service trades	"	—	1.20	3.72	4.63	12.01	20.57
Science, culture, education and public health	"	—	3.34	10.50	9.12	15.12	33.47
Civic public utilities	"	—	1.64	3.82	4.45	8.25	29.91
Geological exploration	"	—	0.68	3.02	0.74	2.06	7.40
Others	"	—	5.48	7.65	3.40	9.43	18.20
3. Number of large and medium-sized projects							
Projects under construction		—	516*	992	1,261	1,539	1,610
Projects completed and put into operation		—	38*	262	289	167	128
4. Housing floor space completed	10 thousand m^2	—	3,639*	6,802	4,704	7,751	12,000
Of which: dwelling units	"	—	1,342*	2,816	1,728	2,791	6,256

Notes: 1. Investment for technical innovation and reconstruction funds outside of plan are excluded.
2. Asterisked figures (*) refer to data for 1953.

Retail Sales
(in 100 million yuan)

Item	1952	1957	1965	1975	1979
Value of retail sales	265.0	461.0	657.3	1,246.1	1,752.5
Urban area	113.8	225.2	325.9	581.9	767.7
Rural area	151.2	235.8	331.4	664.2	984.8
1. Retail sales of consumer goods	250.9	428.4	577.1	1,021.4	1,428.5
a) By urban and rural areas					
Urban area	113.8	225.2	325.9	581.9	767.7
Rural area	137.1	203.2	251.2	439.5	660.8
b) By types of consumers					
Retails sales to residents	226.1	382.1	524.1	897.8	1,264.2
Retail sales to social organizations	24.8	46.3	53.0	123.6	164.3
c) By commodity categories					
Food	136.5	227.8	314.5	530.8	717.5
Clothing	50.8	82.6	112.5	219.4	339.2
Daily necessities	39.5	65.3	68.6	126.5	185.0
Cultural and educational articles	6.7	12.7	17.3	29.3	55.4
Books, newspapers and magazines	2.0	4.9	6.4	9.8	16.4
Chinese and Western medicine and medical equipment	6.8	16.7	27.8	57.1	58.5
Fuels	8.6	18.4	30.0	48.5	56.5
2. Retail sales of means of agricultural production	14.1	32.6	80.2	224.7	324.0

Note: Retail sales by peasants to non-agricultural residents are excluded in this and following tables.

Index of Retail Sales Value

Item	(1952 = 100)				Average annual increase rate (1953-79)
	1957	1965	1965	1979	
Value of retail sales	174.0	248.0	470.2	661.3	7.2
Urban area	197.9	286.4	511.3	674.6	7.3
Rural area	156.0	219.2	439.3	651.3	7.2
1. Retail sales of consumer goods	170.7	230.0	407.1	569.4	6.7
a) By urban and rural areas					
Urban area	197.9	286.4	511.3	674.6	7.3
Rural area	148.2	183.2	320.6	482.0	6.0
b) By types of consumers					
Retails sales to residents	169.0	231.8	397.1	559.1	6.6
Retail sales to social organizations	186.7	213.7	498.4	662.5	7.3
c) By commodity categories					
Food	166.9	230.4	388.9	525.6	6.3
Clothing	162.6	221.5	431.9	667.7	7.3
Daily necessities	165.3	173.7	320.3	468.4	5.9
Cultural and educational articles	189.6	258.2	437.3	826.9	8.1
Books, newspapers and magazines	245.0	320.0	490.0	820.0	8.1
Chinese and Western medicine and medical equipment	245.6	408.8	839.7	860.3	8.3
Fuels	214.0	348.8	564.0	657.0	7.2
2. Retail sales of means of agricultural production	231.2	568.8	1,593.6	2,297.9	12.3

Retail Sales of Consumer Goods

Item	Unit	1952	1957	1965	1975	1979
Grain	10,000 tons	2,961.0	3,723.5	3,682.0	4,196.5	4,650.0
Edible vegetable oil[1]	,,	76.5	103.0	74.0	83.0	100.0
Pork[2]	,,	170.4	176.5	277.7	425.9	573.1
Eggs	,,	13.2	25.9	33.9	29.9	60.9
Aquatic products	,,	77.9	142.4	137.5	187.1	168.5
Sugar	,,	47.1	87.9	112.2	199.4	333.0
Wine and spirits	,,	64.6	86.7	93.7	199.5	289.2
Tea	,,	3.7	6.1	4.3	9.6	13.9
Cloth[3]	100 million m.	32.4	43.4	44.4	69.9	86.8
Woollen piece goods	10,000 m.	362.6	709.4	2,444.0	5,679.0	10,599.0
Silk and satin	,,	3,092.3	7,090.8	9,666.0	22,516.0	35,321.0
Knitted underwear	10,000 pieces	2,900.4	20,253.6	23,199.6	60,283.7	90,928.0
Leather shoes	10,000 pairs	1,356.7	1,942.1	1,422.0	5,916.0	12,628.0
Rubber shoes	,,	6,465.1	11,673.7	18,136.0	34,619.0	36,208.0
Matches	10,000 boxes	816.0	1,100.0	1,266.0	1,631.5	1,937.6
Soap	10,000 boxes	630.0	1,165.0	1,357.0	3,224.1	3,676.0
Thermos bottles	10,000 pieces	840.0	2,770.8	3,277.0	4,594.6	9,112.0
Sewing machines	,,	10.0	25.1	89.7	302.7	540.0
Wrist-watches	,,	38.5	107.6	189.1	819.9	1,944.4
Bicycles	,,	33.5	84.7	176.2	561.4	954.5
Radio sets	,,	2.0	26.4	83.6	714.4	1,639.5
Machine-made paper	10,000 tons	21.9	33.4	24.1	37.2	46.2
Kerosene	,,	19.3	47.5	69.8	102.2	95.0
Coal	,,	2,361.1	5,413.4	7,500.0	9,350.0	10,600.0

Notes: 1. Edible vegetable oil includes both edible oil and oil equivalent of oil-bearing crops for other uses.
2. Pork includes fresh and frozen pork and pork products.
3. Cloth includes chemical fibre cloth and cotton polyester cloth.

Index of Consumer Goods Retail Sales
(1952 = 100)

Item	1957	1965	1975	1979
Grain	125.8	124.3	141.7	157.0
Edible vegetable oil	134.6	96.7	108.5	130.7
Pork	103.6	163.0	249.9	336.3
Eggs	196.2	256.8	226.5	461.4
Aquatic products	182.8	176.5	240.2	216.3
Sugar	186.6	238.2	423.4	707.0
Wine and spirits	134.2	145.0	308.8	447.7
Tea	164.9	116.2	259.5	375.7
Cloth	134.0	137.0	215.7	267.9
Woollen piece goods	195.6	674.0	1,566.2	2,923.1
Silk and satin	229.3	312.6	728.1	1,142.4
Knitted underwear	698.3	799.9	2,078.5	3,135.0
Leather shoes	143.1	104.8	436.1	930.8
Rubber shoes	180.6	280.5	535.5	560.1
Matches	134.8	155.1	199.9	237.5
Soap	184.9	215.4	511.8	583.5
Thermos bottles	329.9	390.1	547.0	1,084.8
Sewing machines	251.0	897.0	3,027.0	5,400.0
Wrist-watches	279.5	491.2	2,129.6	5,050.4
Bicycles	252.8	526.0	1,675.8	2,849.3
Radio sets	1,320.0	4,180.0	35,720.0	81,975.0
Machine-made paper	152.5	110.0	169.9	211.0
Kerosene	246.1	361.7	529.5	492.2
Coal	229.3	317.6	396.0	448.9

Imports and Exports (Value)

Year	Absolute figures (100 million yuan)			Index numbers (1952 = 100)		
	Total import and export value	Exports	Imports	Total import and export value	Exports	Imports
1952	64.6	27.1	37.5	100.0	100.0	100.0
1957	104.5	54.5	50.0	161.8	201.1	133.3
1965	118.4	63.1	55.3	183.3	232.8	147.5
1975	290.4	143.0	147.4	449.5	527.7	393.1
1979	455.6	211.7	243.9	705.3	781.2	650.4

Note: Conversion from U.S. dollars to Renminbi is calculated on the official exchange rate established by People's Bank of China.

Imports and Exports (Commodity Composition)

Year	Value of exported commodities (total = 100)			Value of imported commodities (total = 100)	
	Industrial and mineral products	Processed farm and sideline products	Farm and sideline products	Means of production	Means of subsistence
1952	17.9	22.8	59.3	89.4	10.6
1957	28.4	31.5	40.1	92.0	8.0
1965	30.9	36.0	33.1	66.5	33.5
1975	39.3	31.1	29.6	85.4	14.6
1979	44.0	39.9	23.1	81.3	18.7

General Price Index
(1950 = 100)

Year	Retail price indexes	Price indexes of living cost for workers and staff members	List purchasing price indexes of farm and sideline products	Retail price indexes of industrial products in rural areas	Parity price ratio of industrial and agriculural products	
					Purchasing list price indexes and sideline products	Retail industrial price indexes of products in rural areas
1952	111.8	115.5	121.6	109.7	90.2	110.8
1957	121.3	126.6	146.2	112.1	76.7	130.4
1965	134.6	139.0	187.9	118.4	63.0	158.7
1975	131.9	139.5	208.7	109.6	52.5	190.4
1979	138.6	147.4	265.5	109.9	41.4	241.6

Price Indexes (at state list prices)
(1950 = 100)

Year	Indexes of retail list prices			Price indexes of living cost for workers and staff members at list prices	List purchasing price indexes of farm and sideline products	Parity price ratio of agricultural and industrial products		
	Nationwide	In urban areas	In rural areas			Retail price indexes of industrial products in rural areas	Purchasing list price indexes of farm and sideline products	Retail price indexes of industrial products in rural area
1952	112.1	114.2	110.4	115.3	121.6	109.7	90.3	110.8
1957	121.4	124.1	118.9	126.1	146.2	112.1	76.7	130.4
1965	132.3	134.5	130.5	134.7	185.1	118.4	64.0	156.3
1975	128.4	133.7	125.1	133.3	201.3	109.6	54.4	189.7
1979	130.9	136.4	127.4	135.5	242.7	109.9	45.3	220.8

Price Index for State Retail List (by Commodity Groups)
(1950 = 100)

Item	1952	1957	1965	1975	1979
General indexes	112.1	121.4	132.3	128.4	130.9
1. Consumer goods	112.3	122.2	134.1	132.6	135.1
a) Food	110.9	128.8	148.6	153.7	158.4
Grain	112.1	120.4	131.2	145.0	147.2
Fresh vegetables	116.7	149.4	136.7	173.9	188.5
Non-staple foods	110.3	138.8	168.4	167.6	175.0
Tobacco, wine, spirits and tea	111.8	127.0	152.3	151.3	152.5
Others	111.9	114.5	126.4	125.5	131.0
b) Clothing	111.9	111.7	113.6	112.7	112.3
c) Daily necessities	118.2	116.2	130.4	126.2	127.1
d) Cultural and educational articles	117.1	96.2	97.6	88.5	92.1
e) Medicine and medical equipment	122.9	114.8	99.3	63.5	65.4
f) Fuels	135.9	150.3	160.1	154.0	154.4
2. Means of agricultural production	108.2	110.8	114.7	100.0	100.5

Price Index for State Purchasing List of Farm and Sideline Products (by Commodities)
(1950 = 100)

Item	1952	1957	1965	1975	1979
General indexes	121.6	146.2	185.1	201.3	242.7
1. Grain	121.4	141.4	190.9	222.8	271.3
2. Industrial crops	113.0	126.4	152.8	165.1	200.4
a) Oil-bearing crops	108.2	167.9	246.7	307.8	398.1
b) Cotton	113.3	111.1	122.9	126.9	162.4
c) Jute, ambary hemp	131.0	139.9	170.3	184.3	197.0
d) Tobacco	116.5	124.0	174.0	175.7	177.1
e) Sugar crops	87.2	102.9	135.3	151.3	184.7
f) Tea	154.7	241.6	304.1	323.6	365.1
3. Products of animal husbandry	105.7	145.5	192.1	200.6	247.4
a) Livestock and meat production	102.7	142.9	193.2	199.4	248.6
b) Poultry and eggs	104.7	152.5	188.5	213.6	261.5
c) Hides and skins	136.8	150.2	163.1	179.5	204.0
d) Bristle	136.5	143.1	168.3	183.2	202.8
4. Other farm and sideline products	160.6	210.2	251.4	267.0	302.5
a) Timber	115.1	105.9	141.7	171.0	199.3
b) Paint for industrial purposes	103.9	132.1	214.9	249.9	288.9
c) Silkworm cocoons and silk	115.9	122.0	163.8	176.4	214.0
d) Dry and fresh fruits	130.7	160.2	183.1	184.8	209.6
e) Dry and fresh vegetables and condiments	179.0	237.2	235.0	251.5	282.9
f) Crude drugs	136.7	222.3	297.2	263.1	276.1
g) Native products	177.4	234.3	306.0	328.7	362.3
h) Aquatic products	105.0	145.0	175.2	178.3	214.6

State Public Finance Revenues and Expenditures

Year	Amount (100 million yuan)			Index numbers (1952 = 100)	
	Revenues	Expenditures	Balance of revenues and expenditures	Revenues	Expenditures
1952	183.72	175.99	7.73	100	100
1957	310.19	304.21	5.98	168.8	172.9
1965	473.32	466.33	6.99	257.6	265.0
1975	815.61	820.88	−5.27	443.9	466.4
1979	1,103.27	1,273.94	−170.67	600.5	723.9

Savings Deposits in Urban and Rural Areas

Year	Total (100 million yuan)	Savings in urban areas (100 million yuan)		Savings of rural commune members (100 million yuan)	Savings deposits per capita		
		Total	Of which: fixed deposit		Total	Urban areas	Rural areas
1952	8.6	8.6	4.8		1.5	12.0	
1957	35.2	27.9	19.6	7.3	5.4	28.0	1.3
1965	65.2	52.3	43.4	12.9	9.0	51.4	2.1
1975	149.6	114.6	94.5	35.0	16.3	102.6	4.3
1979	281.0	202.6	166.4	78.4	28.9	157.5	9.3

Annual Consumption Per Capita

Year	Consumption (at current prices)			Index numbers (at comparable prices, 1952 = 100)		
	Urban and rural population	Peasants	Non-agricultural residents	Urban and rural population	Peasants	Non-agricultural residents
1952	76	62	148	100	100	100
1957	102	79	205	122.9	117.1	126.3
1965	125	100	237	126.4	116.0	136.5
1975	158	124	324	156.9	143.1	181.1
1979	197	152	406	184.9	165.2	214.5

Note: This table is calculated by dividing private consumption expenditure (excluding services) from available national income by mean population of the year.

Basic Condition of Families of Workers and Staff Members

Item	1957	1964	1980 (4th quarter)
Number of persons per household	4.37	5.30	4.30
Number of employed persons per household	1.33	1.56	2.35
Number of persons supported by each employed person	3.29	3.40	1.83
Monthly per capita earnings (in yuan)	21.13	20.29	42.80
Monthly per capita earnings available (in yuan)	19.62	18.92	37.70

Note: Figures of 1957 are based on a household survey of more than 5,900 families of workers and staff members in state-owned industrial units in 27 large and medium-sized cities in the first half of the year · of more than 4,800 families of the same type in 32 large and medium-sized cities in the second half of the year.

Per Capita Consumption of Households in Rural People's Communes

Item	Unit	Absolute figures		Comparison between 1978 and 1979	
		1978	1979	Absolute figures	%
Grain (unprocessed)	kg.	248	257	9	3.6
Vegetables	”	137	131	− 6	− 4.4
Edible oil	”	2.05	2.38	0.33	16.1
Meat	”	5.91	6.51	0.60	10.2
Poultry	”	0.25	0.32	0.07	28.0
Eggs	”	0.81	0.90	0.09	11.1
Fish, shrimp and prawns	”	0.71	0.70	− 0.01	−1.4
Sugar	”	0.73	0.80	0.07	9.6
Wine and spirits	”	1.22	1.42	0.20	16.4
Cotton cloth (including ready-made clothing)	m.	5.63	5.20	− 0.43	−7.6
Cotton	kg.	0.40	0.45	0.05	12.5
Chemical fibres	m.	0.41	0.73	0.32	78.0
Woollen piece goods	m./100 persons	2.33	5.67	3.34	143.3
Silk and satin	”	2.00	5.00	3.00	150.0
Knitting wool and sweaters	kg./100 persons	1.33	2.33	1.00	75.2
Gym shoes and rubber shoes	pair	0.32	0.44	0.12	37.5

Note: Data are based on a household survey of about 10,000 commune-member households in 23 provinces, municipalities and autonomous regions.

Number of Enrolled Students in Schools at Various Levels

Year	Total	Institutions of higher learning	Ordinary middle schools	Secondary technical schools	Industrial and agricultural middle schools and vocational middle schools	Primary schools
1949	2,577.6	11.7	103.9	22.9	—	2,439.1
1952	5,443.6	19.1	249.0	63.6	1.9	5,110.0
1957	7,180.5	44.1	628.1	77.8	2.2	6,428.3
1965	13,120.1	67.4	933.8	54.7	443.3	11,620.9
1975	19,681.0	50.1	4,466.1	70.7	—	15,094.1
1979	20,789.8	102.0	5,905.5	119.9	—	14,662.9

Note: Worker's training schools are not included in the figures of secondary schools.

Teacher-Student Ratios in Schools at Various Levels

Year	Institutions of higher learning		Secondary schools		Primary schools	
	Teachers (10,000)	Number of students per teacher	Teachers (10,000)	Number of students per teacher	Teachers (10,000)	Number of students per teacher
1952	2.7	7.1	13.0	24.2	143.5	35.6
1957	7.0	6.3	29.3	24.2	188.4	34.1
1965	13.8	4.9	70.9	20.2	385.7	30.1
1975	15.6	3.2	216.5	21.0	520.3	29.0
1979	23.7	4.3	319.1	18.9	538.2	27.2

Health Institutions and Hospital Beds

Year	Health Institutions		Hospital beds (10 thousands)			
	Total	Of which: hospitals	Total	Of which: hospital beds in rural areas	% of hospital beds in rural areas of the total	Number of hospital beds per 1,000 people
1949	3,670	2,600	8.0	2.0	25.2	0.15
1952	38,987	3,540	16.0	3.9	24.3	0.28
1957	122,954	4,179	29.5	7.4	25.1	0.46
1965	224,266	42,711	76.6	30.8	40.2	1.06
1975	151,733	62,425	159.8	96.1	60.1	1.74
1979	176,793	65,009	193.2	119.2	61.7	1.99

Growth Indicators for Culture, Radio and Television Broadcasting

Item	1949	1957	1965	1975	1979
Feature films produced	6	40	52	27	65
Feature films dubbed in Chinese	3	79	15	30	43
Film projection units (10,000)	0.06	1.00	2.04	6.97	12.2
Art troupes	1,000	2,884	3,465	2,836	3,482
Cultural halls	896	2,748	2,621	2,589	2,892
Public libraries	55	400	577	629	1,651
Museums	21	72	214	242	344
Broadcasting stations	49	61	87	88	99
Wire-broadcasting stations in rural areas and cities	11	1,698	2,365	2,481	2,560
Wire-broadcasting loudspeakers (10,000)	0.09	94	873	10,818	10,772
Television centres	—	—	12	32	38
Television transmitting and relay stations with transmitters of 1 kw. or more	—	—	—	—	238

2. COMMUNIQUE OF THE STATE STATISTICAL BUREAU OF THE PEOPLE'S REPUBLIC OF CHINA ON FULFILMENT OF CHINA'S 1980 NATIONAL ECONOMIC PLAN

(April 29, 1981)

Under the leadership of the Communist Party of China and the People's Government, the Chinese people of all nationalities conscientiously carried out the policy of readjusting, restructuring, consolidating and improving the national economy, and made new achievements through energetic efforts in 1980. The total annual value of industrial and agricultural output, calculated at constant prices of 1970, was 661,900 million yuan, 3.2% above the plan and 7.2% over the previous year. The preliminary figure for the national income was 363,000 million yuan, which, calculated at constant prices of 1970, was 6.9% above the previous year (the national income for 1979 was readjusted from 337,000 million yuan to 335,000 million yuan). The livelihood of the people continued to improve on the basis of increased production. The main problems were that there was another relatively large financial deficit, considerably more currency was issued, and the prices of many commodities rose.

Fulfilment of plans by the various sectors of the national economy was as follows:

1. Industry

In 1980, there was a sustained increase in industrial production, and the proportional distribution among industries gradually became more rational and appropriate. Total annual industrial output value, calculated at constant prices of 1970, was 499,200 million yuan, 3.1% above the plan and 8.7% over 1979. Output value of light industry was 234,400 million yuan, an 18.4% increase over 1979, and that of heavy industry, 264,800 million yuan, a 1.4% increase. The proportion of the output value of light industry to total industrial output value increased from 43.1% in 1979 to 46.9% in 1980. Targets were reached or surpassed for the output of 93 of 100 major products, including coal, crude oil, electricity, steel, pig iron, rolled steel, cement, plate glass, sulphuric acid, soda ash, caustic soda, chemical fertilizers, motor vehicles, locomotives, chemical fibres, paper, sugar, television sets, bicycles, sewing machines and wrist-watches. Targets for detergents and six other products were not fulfilled.

The initiative of the enterprises and their workers and staff members was brought into greater play and the management of enterprises was strengthened in 1980 as a result of continuing the experiments in expanding the power of enterprises in self-management and introducing market regulation over the production and supply of a number of products. Although energy production dropped 1.3%, industrial production continued to achieve a fairly rapid growth rate, the number of varieties and specifications of industrial products increased, the quality of products improved, and consumption of raw materials and fuels fell. State gold and silver medals were awarded to 255 industrial products for civilian use. The output value of industrial enterprises owned by the whole people was 12,031 yuan per worker, 2% higher than in the previous year.

However, the economic results of industrial enterprises as a whole were not yet satisfactory. The indices for quality and per-unit consumption for many of the products did not reach the best historical levels. About 23.3% of state-owned industrial enterprises still suffered losses to varying degrees, thus affecting the increase of state revenues. A considerable amount of rolled steel, machinery and power equipment was overstocked by the end of 1980.

Industrial Output in 1980

Item	Output	% Increase over 1979
Coal	620 million tons	− 2.4
Crude oil	105.95 million tons	− 0.2
Natural gas	14,270 million cubic metres	− 1.7
Electricity	300,600 million kwh.	6.6
Rolled steel	27.16 million tons	8.8

Continued next page

Note: Figures for Taiwan Province are not included in the communique.

Industrial Output (Cont.)

Item	1980 Output	% Increase over 1979
Pig iron	38.02 million tons	3.5
Steel	37.12 million tons	7.7
Coke (machine-made)	34.05 million tons	1.5
Timber	53.59 million cubic metres	− 1.5
Cement	79.86 million tons	8.1
Plate glass	27.71 million standard cases	18.9
Sulphuric acid	7.64 million tons	9.1
Soda ash	1,613,000 tons	8.5
Caustic soda	1,923,000 tons	5.3
Chemical fertilizers	12.32 million tons	15.7
Of which:		
Nitrogenous fertilizers	9.99 million tons	13.3
Phosphate fertilizers	2.31 million tons	26.9
Potash fertilizers	20,000 tons	25.0
Chemical insecticides	537,000 tons	0
Ethylene	490,000 tons	12.6
Plastics	898,000 tons	13.2
Pharmaceuticals (chemical)	40,100 tons	− 3.8
Calcium carbide	1.52 million tons	8.0
Rubber tyres	11.46 million	− 2.0
Mining equipment	163,000 tons	−38.3
Power generating equipment	4,193,000 kw	−32.5
Machine tools	134,000	− 4.3
Motor vehicles	222,000	19.4
Tractors	98,000	−22.2
Hand tractors	218,000	−31.4
Internal combustion engines (sold as commodities)	25.39 million hp.	−12.7
Locomotives	512	−10.6
Railway passenger coaches	1,002	17.1
Railway freight cars	10,571	−34.1
Steel ships for civilian use	818,000 tons	1.1
Television sets	2,492,000	87.5
Radio sets	30.04 million	117.5
Cameras	373,000	56.7
Chemical fibres	450,000 tons	38.0
Of which:		
Synthetic fibres	314,000 tons	46.7
Cotton yarn	2.93 million tons	11.4
Cotton cloth	13,470 million metres	10.9
	(or 12,800 million square metres)	12.0
Woollen piece goods	101 million metres	12.2
Silk	35,400 tons	19.2
Silk textiles	759 million metres	14.5
Gunny bags	433 million	25.9
Machine-made paper and paperboard	5.35 million tons	8.5
Sugar	2.57 million tons	2.8
Cigarettes	15.2 million cases	16.7
Beer	688,000 tons	33.3
Salt	17.28 million tons	17.0
Detergents	393,000 tons	− 1.0
Bicycles	13.02 million	29.0
Sewing machines	7.68 million	30.8
Watches	22.16 million	29.8
Light bulbs	950 million	11.8

2. Agriculture

In 1980 many parts of the country suffered from natural calamities seldom seen in many years. However, correct policies of the party and the government were carried out, which triggered the enthusiasm of rural cadres and peasants for production so that most areas achieved fairly good harvests. A few, including Hubei and Hebei had considerable decreases in grain output. The total value of agricultural output, caculated at 1970 prices, was 162,700 million yuan, 3.3% above the plan and 2.7% more than in 1979. Except for grain, targets were met or surpassed for all seven other major agricultural products — cotton, oil-bearing crops, sugar-cane, sugar beet, jute and ambary hemp, silkworm cocoons and tea. The diversified economy of the rural communes and their subdivisions and household sideline production grew fairly quickly.

Some 4,552,000 hectares of land in China were afforested in 1980, 1.4% more than in 1979. Output of some forest products increased sharply: that of rubber was 4.3% higher than 1979; walnuts, 31.7% higher and chestnuts, 41.8% higher. Output of raw lacquer and tea-oil seeds was below 1979. Trees were felled at random in many areas.

Output of major animal products increased in 1980. Except for hogs, animals in stock at the end of the year grew in number.

Output of aquatic products was 4,497,000 tons, up 4.5% over the previous year. Output of fresh-water products increased by 11.1%, and marine products, 2.1%.

State farms achieved all-around growth in

Agricultural Output in 1980

Item	Output	% Increase over 1979
Grain	318,220,000 tons	− 4.2
Of which:		
Paddy	139,255,000 tons	− 3.1
Wheat	54,155,000 tons	−13.7
Tubers (counted on the basis of 5 kg. of tubers equals 1 kg. of grain)	27,845,000 tons	− 2.2
Soybeans	7,880,000 tons	5.6
Cotton	2,707,000 tons	22.7
Oil-bearing crops	7,691,000 tons	19.5
Of which:		
Peanuts	3,600,000 tons	27.6
Rapeseed	2,384,000 tons	− 0.7
Sesame	259,000 tons	−37.9
Sugarcane	22,807,000 tons	6.0
Sugar beets	6,305,000 tons	103.0
Jute, ambary hemp	1,098,000 tons	0.8
Silkworm cocoons	326,000 tons	20.3
Tea	304,000 tons	9.7
Pork, beef and mutton	12,055,000 tons	13.5
Of which:		
Pork	11,341,000 tons	13.3
Beef	269,000 tons	17.0
Mutton	445,000 tons	17.1
Milk	1,141,000 tons	6.6
Sheep wool	176,000 tons	15.0
Hogs slaughtered	198,607,000 head	5.8
Hogs (end 1980)	305,431,000 head	− 4.5
Large animals (end 1980)	95,246,000 head	0.7
Sheep and goats (end 1980)	187,311,000 head	2.3

production. In 1980, grain output by state farms under the land reclamation departments was 4.7% higher than in 1979; cotton, 11.2% higher; oil-bearing crops, 4.1% higher; sugarcane and sugar beets, 28.6% higher; and milk, 8.7% higher. The total accounts of all state farms under the land reclamation departments showed a 52.7% increase in profits, but 40% of the farms still suffered losses to varying degrees.

Attention was paid during the year to the development of farm machinery suited to local conditions. By the end of the year, China had 745,000 large and medium-sized tractors, 78,000 more than in 1979; 1,874,000 small and hand tractors, 203,000 more than in 1979; power-driven drainage and irrigation equipment for rural use with an aggregate of 74,645,000 hp., an increase of 3,424,000 hp.; and 135,000 farm trucks, 38,000 more than in 1979. Tractor-ploughed farmland came to 40,991,000 hectares, accounting for 41.3% of all farmland. A total of 12,694,000 tons of chemical fertilizer were applied, averaging 127.8 kg. per hectare, a 17% increase over 1979. Total electricity used in the rural areas came to 32,100 million kwh., 13.5% more than in 1979.

By the end of 1980, China had 86,000 reservoirs of all sizes and 2.09 million diesel and electric pump wells. Improved management of water conservancy facilities helped raise resistance to drought and ability to drain off excessive water.

The meteorological departments last year improved their service, giving prompt forecasts and warnings for droughts, water-logging, typhoons and frost, thus raising the effectiveness of the struggles against these natural calamities.

3. Capital Construction

All over China, units owned by the whole people had an additional 42,700 million yuan worth of fixed assets through capital construction in 1980, a 2.2% increase over 1979. The rate of availability of such assets reached 79.2%, a 4.5% decrease compared with 1979. Total floor space of housing completed for the whole year came to 145 million square metres, an increase of 20.8% over 1979.

Annual added production capacity from capital construction in 1980 consisted mainly of facilities for producing 8.29 million tons of coal, 5.75 million tons of crude oil, 880 million cu. m. of natural gas, power-generating capacity of 2.87 million kw., 2.74 million tons of iron ore, 710,000 tons of steel, 279,000 tons of chemical fertilizer, 60,000 tons of chemical fibres, 2.88 million tons of cement and 113,000 tons of sugar. Also added were 761,000 cotton spindles. New railway lines totalling 1,008 km. were put into service. The cargo handling capacity at newly built or expanded ports was enlarged by 8.13 million tons.

Total investment in capital construction in units owned by the whole people all over China in 1980 was 53,900 million yuan, a .78% increase over 1979. Investment covered by the national budget was 28,100 million yuan, a decrease of 24.9% compared with 1979. Of the total investment, the proportion for costs of non-productive use to meet the needs of the people's material and cultural life rose from 27% in 1979 to 33.7% in 1980, investments, in housing construction went up from 14.8% in 1979 to 20% while those in light industry increased from 6.4% in 1979 to 9.1%.

A number of projects were cancelled or suspended in 1980. The number of large and medium-sized projects under construction was 904 by the end of the year, 283 less than in 1979. However, owing to the large scale of some newly built projects, the national construction scale was not curtailed. Eighty-two large and medium-sized projects were completed and put into operation in the whole year, 46 less than in 1979. Two hundred and sixteen single-item projects attached to big and medium-sized projects were completed and put into operation, 124 less than the year before. The rate of large and medium-sized projects that went into operation to the total number under construction dropped from 9.7% in 1979 to 8.3%. Of the newly added production capacity for 34 major products listed in the state plan, the capacities of 16 products failed to meet the planned targets. The results for investment were insufficient.

New reserves of iron ore, coal, phosphorus, pyrites and 17 other major minerals which were verified in 1980 met or surpassed the state targets. Known deposits of iron ore increased by 2,140 million tons, and coal by 24,840 million tons. In addition, more reserves were also proven for 40 kinds of minerals, including niobium, tantalum, cobalt, blue asbestos, gypsum, graphite, ceramic clay and mica. Total drilling footage for geological prospecting completed in 1980 was 12.49 million metres. A number of new oil and gas fields were discovered and appraised, as were more than 100 metallic and non-metallic mineral sites. But the work of fundamental geology, general surveying of mineral resources and mining geology remains poor and the economic results of geological prospecting still needs to be improved.

4. Transport, Posts and Telecommunications

In 1980, the volume of freight carried by all

means of transport totalled 1,202,600 million ton-km., a 5.6% increase over 1979. The volume of railway freight transport was 571,700 million ton-km., a 2.1% increase over 1979. The volume of waterway cargo transported was 505,300 million ton-km., a 10.7% increase. The volume of road freight transported was 76,400 million ton-km., an increase of 2.6%. The volume of air freight shipment was 140.6 million ton-km., an increase of 13.9%. The volume of oil and gas carried through pipelines was 49,100 million ton-km., a 3.2% increase. The volume of cargo handled at major sea ports was 217.31 million tons, 2.2% more than the previous year.

The volume of passenger transport by all means of transport totalled 228,100 million passenger-km. in 1980, a 15.8% increase over 1979. The volume of railway passenger transport was 138,300 million passenger-km., an increase of 13.7%. The volume of waterway passenger transport was 12,900 million passenger-km., 13.2% higher. The volume of road passenger transport was 72,900 million passenger-km., a 20.9% increase. The volume of passenger transport by air was 4,000 million passenger-km., a 14.3% increase.

Post and telecommunication transactions for the whole country amounted to 1,334 million yuan in 1980, surpassing 1979 by 6.3%. Among this was a 7.56% increase in letters, a 29.6% increase in the distribution of newspapers and magazines, an 8.7% increase in telegrams, and a 4% increase in long-distance calls.

In 1980, fuel consumed per steam locomotive and per diesel locomotive for each 10,000 ton-km. dropped by 2.8% and 2%, respectively.

In the same year, the railway departments made new achievements in technical transformation of the existing lines. Electrification of the Baoji–Tianshui section of the Longhai Railway, the Shijiazhuang–Yangquan section of the Shijiazhuang–Taiyuan line and the Xiangfan–Ankang section of the Xiangfan–Chongqing line raised transport capacity. However, transport is still over-burdened and certain sections of trunk railways have a relatively small carrying capacity. The handling capacity at some sea ports also cannot meet the growing needs of foreign trade. And trucks show great waste in empty runs as a result of lack of coordination in management.

5. Domestic Trade

The total value of commodities purchased by commercial departments owned by the whole people reached 226,300 million yuan in 1980, topping that of the previous year by 13.6%. This included 156,760 million yuan worth of manufactured goods, an increase of 12.8% over 1979: and 67,700 million yuan worth of farm products and sideline products, an increase of 15.4%. Purchases of most manufactured goods and farm produce surpassed those of 1979. Among them, the purchase of cotton cloth rose by 17.9% over 1979; chemical fibre cloth, 71.3%; leather shoes, 43.5%; wrist-watches, sewing machines, bicycles and television sets, 24 to 40%; radio sets and cassette recorders, 85%; cotton, 25.8%; edible vegetable oil, 26.7%; and hogs, 3%. The purchase of grain, which suffered a loss due to natural disasters, was slightly below the previous year.

The 1980 total value of retail sales was 214,000 million yuan, an 18.9% increase over 1979, or a 12.2% increase if the rise in retail prices is excluded. (The 1980 total value of retail sales included 6,900 million yuan from retail sales by peasants to the nonagricultural population. The 1979 total value of retail sales is correspondingly readjusted to 180,000 million yuan from the original 175,250 million yuan.) Retail sales of consumer goods were marked by an overall increase, and the growth of sales of durable consumer goods was even more rapid.

Compared with the 1979 retail sales of main consumer goods, the sale of edible vegetable oil went up by 20%; pork, 15.3%; sugar, 9.2%; cotton cloth, 7.6%; chemical fibre cloth, 32.5%; woollen textiles, 34.2%; silk fabrics, 25%; leather shoes, 34%; sewing machines, bicycles, radio sets and wrist-watches, from 23 to 66%; and television sets and cassette recorders, 100% and 240%, respectively.

By the end of 1980, commercial departments owned by the whole people kept 9.2% more goods in stock than in 1979.

Although there was a greater supply of market commodities in 1980, supplies still could not meet the growth in social purchasing power. Some industrial consumer goods fell short of demand. The supply of some consumer goods and building materials for rural needs was not sufficient. Some commodities in stock did not satisfy consumer demands.

The government again raised the state purchasing prices for some farm produce in 1980, including cotton, sheep and goat skins, jute and ambary hemp, timber, raw lacquer and tung oil. In addition, more farm produce was purchased at negotiated prices, and at higher prices for that part above the purchase quota. As a result, the total purchasing price index for farm produce and sideline products went up by 7.1% over the previous year, which was 22.1% above 1979. Starting in November 1979, the state raised the retail price for principal nonstaple foodstuffs, and in 1980 many places readjusted the retail prices for a small number of manufactured goods, thus causing the annual average level of retail prices of the nation (including state listed prices, negotiated prices and prices on the rural market) to register a 6% increase over 1979. (The general level of retail prices is calculated according to the average prices of the year. It shows a 2.2% rise if December 1980 is compared with the corresponding 1979 period.) Among these was an 8.1% increase in cities and a 4.4% increase in rural areas; a 7.1% increase in consumer goods prices and a 1% increase in the price of means of production for rural use.

Among price fluctuations for consumer goods, the price of clothing remained the same; food rose by 10.5% (of which state list price of non-staple food rose by 13.8%); daily necessities, 1.2%; commodities for cultural and recreational activities, 0.7%; pharmaceuticals, 0.9%; and fuel, 0.7%.

6. Foreign Trade and Tourism

The total value of imports and exports came to 56,300 million yuan in 1980, a 23.6% increase compared with 1979. Export value totalled 27,200 million yuan, exceeding 1979 by 28.7%, and imports were valued at 29,100 million yuan, a rise of 19.2%. Import value outstripped export value by 1,900 million yuan.

The proportion of heavy industrial products and mineral products among exported commodities rose from 44% in 1979 to 51.8% in 1980. Coal, oil products, machine tools and bearings experienced relatively large export growth.

Of imported commodities, complete sets of equipment showed a 103.9% increase over 1979, accounting for 12.9% of total import value as against 7.6% in 1979. Imports of raw materials for textile and light industries, such as cotton, chemical fibres and paper pulp, shot up by 68.6% over 1979, and their proportion of the total import value rose to 24.3% as against 17.2% in the year before. The import of consumer goods, including grain, fats, vegetable oils, wrist-watches, television sets and cassette recorders, went up by 35.6% over 1979, accounting for 21.2% of the total import value as against 18.6% in 1979. Imports of chemical fertilizer and other means of production for rural use rose by 48.4% over the previous year, and their proportion of the total import value rose from 5.9% in 1979 to 7.3% in 1980. Imports of single-item equipment, rolled steel and pig iron were cut back considerably.

In 1980, the total number of foreigners, overseas Chinese and Chinese compatriots from Hong Kong and Macao coming on tours and visits and for trade, sports and scientific and cultural exchanges reached 5.7 million, 1,499,000 more than in the previous year, or a 35.6% increase. Among them, tourists from 164 countries and regions totalled 529,000, a 46% rise. Annual foreign exchange income from visitors was 920 million yuan, 32% more than 1979.

7. Science and Technology, Education, Culture

At the end of 1980, there were 5,296,000 personnel in the natural sciences and technological units owned by the whole people. Good results were achieved in more than 2,600 major scientific and technological research items in 1980. Among these were 107 innovations and inventions ratified by the state.

The number of institutions of higher learning in 1980 reached 675, or 42 more than the figure in the preceding year. The student body came to 1,144,000, an increase of 124,000 over 1979. This included 281,000 newly enrolled (including locally enlarged enrollments), 6,000 more than the previous year's figure. There were 324,000 people enrolled in TV colleges, an increase of 44,000 over the preceding year. In addition, 455,000 people were enrolled in factory-run or spare-time colleges. Secondary technical schools had an enrollment of 1,243,000, 44,000 more than in 1979. Reform in the structure of secondary education continued. There were 55,081,000 regular middle-school students, a decline of 3,734,000 compared with the previous year. There were 454,000 students in agricultural and other vocational schools at the secondary education level. Workers' training schools had a total enrollment of 680,000. There were 146.27 million primary school pupils and 11.51 million children in kindergartens. With a view to training specialists, 2,124 students were sent abroad to study by educational departments in 1980. Many departments, localities and units organized various types of courses for workers, staff members, peasants and job-waiting youths to study and improve their general knowledge or vocational skills.

Literature, drama, films, ballad-singing, music, dance and fine arts flourished in 1980. Eighty-two feature films were produced in the year, and altogether 116 new full-length films of various types were distributed. More than 1,000 theatrical productions were staged in 1980, including items on modern themes, new versions of historical themes and traditional items. There were 125,000 film-projection units, 3,553 performing arts troupes, 2,912 cultural centres, 1,732 public libraries, and 365 museums in China. The number of broadcasting stations reached 106, with 484 transmitting and relay stations. There were 38 TV centres and 246 TV transmitting and relay stations, each equipped with transmitters of 1,000 watts or more. The annual output of national and provincial newspapers was 10,040 million copies. An aggregate of 1,120 million copies of magazines and 4,500 million copies of books were published.

In science and technology, education and culture, problems remain: insufficient scientists and technicians; insufficient school buildings, and backward equipment; irrational structure of secondary education; and improper use of persons with special knowledge.

8. Health Work and Sports

Efforts continued in 1980 to readjust health departments at various levels, consolidate medical and health work organizations and strengthen scientific management. The national total of hospital beds reached 1,982,000, or 2.6% more than the previous year. There were 2,798,000 professional medical workers, representing a 5.9% increase over the preceding year. They included 262,000 doctors in traditional Chinese medicine, 447,000 senior and 444,000 junior doctors of Western medicine, and 466,000 nurses. Health departments at various levels strengthened in-service training of medical workers, launched patriotic health campaigns and conducted work to prevent and treat diseases on a wide scale.

The year 1980 saw Chinese athletes chalk up world records in seven sports: weight-lifting, shooting, model-airplane flying, parachuting and model boats, as well as equal three other world records. China won three world championships in table tennis and gymnastics. One hundred and twenty national records and 46 junior national records were broken. Some 23,000 sports meets were held at the county level and above. An additional 8.56 million people attained the standards set by the National Physical Training Programme, representing a 37% increase over the preceding year.

9. People's Livelihood

Continued improvements were made in the livelihood of most of the urban and rural population in 1980. The per capita income in rural people's communes derived from the basic ac- counting units of the collective economy was 85.9 yuan, an increase of 2.5 yuan over 1979. Owing to a fairly rapid development of household sideline occupations, coupled with a rise in the state purchasing prices of some farm produce and other factors, the total income of members of rural people's communes increased substantially over that of the previous year.

Nine million people were provided with jobs in 1980. They included young people waiting for jobs and other people in cities and towns throughout China, and graduates of universities, colleges and secondary technical schools in 1980 who were assigned jobs under the unified state plan. The total number of workers and staff members employed in units owned by the whole people and collectively owned units came to 104.44 million at the end of 1980, 4.77 million more than a year before. They included 80.19 million in units owned by the whole people, an increase of 3.26 million over the 1979 figure; and 24.25 million in collectively owned units in cities and towns, an increase of 1.51 million over the number in 1979. In addition, more than 810,000 people operated individual businesses in cities and towns, representing an increase of 500,000 over 1979.

Owning to the increase in the number of workers and staff members, pay rises for workers and staff members, the adoption of piece work pay on a wider scale, the implementation of a reward system and subsidies for price rises in nonstaple foods, the total 1980 wage bill reached 77,300 million yuan, exceeding the previous year by 19.5%. The wage bill for workers and staff members employed in units owned by the whole people amounted to 62,800 million yuan, an increase of 18.5% over 1979. The wage bill for workers and staff members in collectively owned units in cities and towns totalled 14,500 million yuan, an increase of 23.9%.

Wages of workers and staff members throughout the country averaged 762 yuan in 1980, a 14.1% increment over the previous year, or a real increase of 6.1% after deducting the 7.5% rise in the cost of living index. The average wage of workers and staff members employed in units owned by the whole people was 803 yuan in 1980, representing a 13.9% increase over 1979, or a real gain of 6%. The average wage of workers and staff members in collectively owned units in cities and towns was 624 yuan, representing a 15.1% increase over 1979, or a real gain of 7.1%.

At the end of 1980, the savings deposits of the urban and rural population totalled 39,900 million yuan, topping the 1979 figure by 41.9%.

Some 82.3 million sq. m. of housing were built in 1980 for workers and staff members in units owned by the whole people using investment for capital construction, a 31.6% increase over 1979.

Some problems remain in people's livelihood: Life is still rather hard for the peasants in some areas affected by natural calamities; price hikes affect the living standards of workers and staff members who receive no bonuses; jobs have yet to be given to some people in cities and towns; some units pass out bonuses and subsidies indiscriminately and in violation of state regulations; and quite a few units raise prices at will or in disguised forms.

10. Population

At the end of 1980, China had a population of 982.55 million, an increase of 11.63 million, or 12%, over the 1979 figure of 970.92 million.

3. CHINA'S 1980 MONETARY STATISTICS

Receipts and Payments of State Credit Funds
(in 100 million yuan)

Item	End of 1979	End of 1980
Deposits	1,340.04	1,658.64
Deposits by enterprises	468.91	573.09
Deposits by the treasury	148.68	162.02
Capital construction funds	131.30	171.75
Deposits by government departments and organizations	184.88	229.45
Savings deposits in cities and towns	202.56	282.49
Deposits in rural areas	203.71	239.84
Deposits by international monetary institutions		34.27
Currency in circulation	267.71	346.20
Bank working funds	427.88	477.33
Bank surplus	49.45	27.19
Others	77.52	80.63
Total credit funds	**2,162.60**	**2,624.26**
Loans	2,039.63	2,414.30
To industrial production enterprises	363.09	431.58
To industrial supply and marketing enterprises and materials supply departments	242.12	236.03
Commercial loans	1,232.25	1,437.02
Short-and medium-term loans for buying equipment	7.92	55.50
Industrial and commercial loans to urban collective and individual enterprises	57.51	78.29
For earned money	6.98	7.88
To state farms	6.86	9.40
To rural communes and production brigades	122.90	158.60
Gold purchases	12.16	12.16
Foreign exchange purchases	20.58	−8.47
Balances with the International Monetary Fund		36.04
Money advanced to the Ministry of Finance	90.23	170.23
Total credit funds used	**2,162.60**	**2,624.26**

Deposits and Loans by Rural Credit Co-operatives
(in 100 million yuan)

Item	End of 1979	End of 1980
Total deposits	**215.88**	**272.34**
Deposits by communes and production brigades	98.33	105.48
Deposits by commune- and brigade-run enterprises	21.93	29.47
Deposits by commune members	78.43	117.03
Others	17.19	20.36
Total loans	**47.54**	**81.64**
Agricultural loans to communes and production brigades	22.54	34.54
Loans to commune- and brigade-run enterprises	14.15	31.11
Loans to individual commune members	10.85	15.99

Exchange Rates, Foreign Exchange and Gold Reserves

Item	1979	1980
Exchange rates:		
Renminbi exchange rate for one SDR (year-end rate)	1.9710	1.9517
Renminbi exchange rate for one US dollar (year-end rate)	1.4962	1.5303
Renminbi exchange rate for one US dollar (average rate for the year)	1.5549	1.4984
Gold and foreign exchange reserves:		
Foreign exchange (1.00 million US dollars)	21.54	22.62
Gold (10 thousand troy ounces)	1,280	1,280

SECTION VII:

CHRONOLOGY OF MAJOR ECONOMIC EVENTS IN CHINA

CHRONOLOGY OF MAJOR ECONOMIC EVENTS IN CHINA

December 1978 — December 1980

Prepared by the Library,
Institute of Industrial Economics, Chinese Academy of Social Sciences

1978

December

December 10 to 20. The Ministry of Metallurgical Industry held a national meeting of outstanding units and workers on the metallurgical front in Beijing to celebrate a breakthrough in China's steel output, which topped 30 million tons.

The State Council approved and circulated the Regulations on the Trial Use of Enterprise Funds in State Enterprises laid down by the Ministry of Finance.

The Xinhua News Agency reported that the Wuhan Iron and Steel Works had basically completed construction of a 1.7-m. rolling mill. Construction began on our first large, modern iron and steel production centre — the Baoshan Iron and Steel Complex in Shanghai. The Zhicheng-Liuzhou Railway was completed and opened to traffic. It is 885 km. long and is the second major north-south railway line in China.

December 18 to 22. The Third Plenary Session of the 11th Central Committee of the Communist Party of China was held in Beijing. It was decided at the Plenary session that, beginning from 1979, the focus of the party's work should be shifted to socialist modernization. The session discussed and adopted in principle the arrangements set forth in the national economic plans for 1979 and 1980. It discussed agricultural problems in a thoroughgoing way and agreed to distribute the Decisions of the Central Committee of the Communist Party of China on Some Questions Concerning the Acceleration of Agricultural Development (Draft) and the Regulations on the Work in the Rural People's Communes (Draft for Trial Implementation) to the provinces, municipalities and autonomous regions for discussion and trial implementation.

1979

January

January 15. The State Council issued a notice on protecting forests and forbidding the unplanned and uncontrolled felling of trees. Ten measures were put forward in the notice.

The Xinhua News Agency reported that another large modern chemical fertilizer plant in our country — the Chishui Natural Gas and Chemical Fertilizer Plant, in Guizhou Province — was completed and went into production.

February

February 4 to March 12. A national conference of heads of the administrative bureaus for industry and commerce was convened in Beijing. The conference defined the guiding principle of supporting industrial and agricultural production, promoting the interchange of commodities, enlivening markets and aiding consumers.

February 5 to 28. The People's Bank of China held a national conference of presidents of bank branches in Beijing to discuss how to bring the role of banks into greater play and thus promote the readjustment, consolidation and rapid development of the national economy.

A national conference of heads of light industry bureaus was held in Shanghai. The conference set tasks and worked out concrete plans for turning out more light industrial products of higher quality and newer design.

A national conference of heads of administrative bureaus for industry and commerce was held in Beijing. It discussed questions on encouraging open markets in large and medium-sized cities.

A national conference of heads of geological bureaus decided to reform the management system and management methods through a division of labour according to fields of specialization.

February 5 to March 1. The State Bureau of Aquatic Products held a national aquatic products working conference. The conference decided to strengthen the breeding and protection of aquatic resources, to energetically expand reproduction and to conscientiously carry out fishery policies.

February 10. The State Council promulgated the Regulations for Breeding and Protection of aquatic resources.

The 870-km. Beijing-Tongliao Railway was completed and opened to traffic. It is the second main trunk line linking up north China to the northeast.

The State Council decided to revive the operations of the Agricultural Bank of China.

February 17 to 23. The Sixth Session of the Standing Committee of the Fifth National People's Congress was held in Beijing. It adopted in principle the Forest Law of the People's Republic of China (Draft for Trial Implementation) and decided to designate March 20 as National Tree-Planting Day. The session approved the establishment of the State Agricultural Commission, the Ministry of Forestry and the Ministry of Agricultural Machinery. It also approved the renaming of the Ministry of Agriculture and Forestry as the Ministry of Agriculture and the separation of the Ministry of Water Conservancy and Power into the Ministry of Power Industry and the Ministry of Water Conservancy.

Chinese frontier troops launched a counter-attack against the Vietnamese aggressors.

The Ministry of Finance decided to further reduce taxes on the rural people's communes, brigades and production teams beginning from 1979 and specified methods for implementation.

March

March 3. The Chinese Association of Enterprise Management was set up in Beijing. Yuan Baohua is the president.

A national standardization working conference was held. The conference discussed the Regulations of the People's Republic of China on the Management of Standardization Work (Draft).

The State Capital Construction Commission convened a national working conference in Beijing to discuss capital construction. The conference suggested that the major task on the capital construction front at present is to do a good job in the readjustment, consolidation and restructuring of capital construction work.

Beginning in March, the State Council successively raised state purchase prices for 18 major farm products by an average of 24.8%.

The Xinhua News Agency reported that another railway linking up China's north and south-central region — the Taiyuan-Jiaozuo Railway — was opened to traffic. It also reported that the Gongzui Power Station, with a generating capacity of 750,000 kw., was completed and had begun generating electricity. The station is situated in Leshan County, Sichuan Province. It is at present the largest hydroelectric power station in southwest China.

April

April 1. With the approval of the State Council, the People's Bank of China raised the interest rate on time deposits in Renminbi (RMB) made by urban and rural inhabitants and by overseas Chinese.

A national conference of heads of statistical bureaus in various provinces, municipalities and autonomous regions was held. The conference suggested improving statistical work in six critical areas.

April 3 to 7. The State Agricultural Commission, the State Scientific and Technological Commission, the Ministry of Agriculture and the Chinese Academy of Sciences jointly held a national conference in Beijing to discuss investigation of natural agricultural resources and regional planning. The conference declared the formal establishment of the National Commission for Investigating Natural Agricultural Resources and Regional Planning.

March 20 to April 23. A national postal and telecommunications working conference was held in Beijing. The conference held that it must conscientiously implement the principle of readjustment, restructuring, consolidation and improvement, and transform the backwardness of postal and telecommunications work as speedily as possible.

The State General Administration of Exchange Control was set up.

May

The Ministry of Agricultural Machinery convened in Beijing a national conference of heads of agricultural machinery bureaus in various provinces, municipalities and autonomous regions. The conference called for a conscientious readjustment of the agricultural machine-building industry.

A national working conference on customs work was held in Beijing. The conference held that customs workers must "levy taxes in accordance with the law, facilitate the lawful traffic of people and goods, prohibit smuggling and illegal activities, and defend and promote the Four Modernizations."

May 16. The State Economic Commission set up a telephone conference in Beijing to mobilize the workers, cadres and technicians on the industrial and communications front throughout the country to rapidly bring about an upsurge in the mass movement to increase production and practice economy.

The State Economic Commission issued a circular specially demanding that various areas and relevant departments give priority to textiles and other industries in supplying fuel, power and raw materials.

May 28 to June 4. In Beijing, the State Economic Commission, the State Scientific and Technological Commission, the State Agricultural Commission and the Ministry of Agriculture jointly convened a national conference of heads of offices for promoting the use of methane gas. The conference summed up the experience of recent years in rural production of methane gas and laid down concrete steps to energetically promote the use of methane gas in rural areas.

June

June 18 to July 1. The Second Session of the Fifth National People's Congress was held in Beijing. Premier Hua Guofeng delivered the report on the work of the government. The session approved the national economic plan for 1979 and the budget for 1978.

The State Agricultural Commission and the State Scientific and Technological Commission called a national forum in Wuxi County, Jiangsu Province to discuss setting up centres for scientific experiments in agricultural modernization.

The Ministry of Finance held a national taxation working conference in Chengdu. The conference stressed making full use of taxation as an economic lever.

The Ministry of Agricultural Machinery held a national forum in Yueyang, Hunan Province, on the regionalization of agricultural mechanization. The forum called for doing a good job in this field in accordance with natural and economic laws.

June 28 to July 4. The Chinese Standardization Association held its first national representative assembly in Hangzhou.

June 30. The State Council promulgated the Regulations of the People's Republic of China on Rewards for Quality Products.

The State Planning Commission, the State Economic Commission and the State Bureau of Labour jointly issued a circular requiring the various areas, departments and units throughout the country to earnestly implement the labour defence laws and regulations issued by the State Council.

The first phase in the construction of the Shanghai Petrochemical Works — a large, modern petrochemical fibre complex — was succcessfully completed, examined and accepted for operation.

July

July 1. The Standing Committee of the Fifth National People's Congress convened its Ninth Session. The session decided to set up the Financial and Economic Commission under the State Council and appointed Chen Yun as a vice-premier of the State Council and concurrently as chairman of the commission. The Tenth Session, held on July 30, decided to set up the Foreign Investment Commission and the Administrative Commission on Import and Export Affairs. Vice-Premier Gu Mu was appointed chairman of both commissions.

The Financial and Economic Commission under the State Council called a conference of leading cadres of relevant financial departments under the Party Central Committee and the State Council and comrades in economic circles in order to undertake extensive investigations and research into economic problems related to national economic readjustment and to thorough economic restructuring.

The All-China Federation of Supply and Marketing Cooperatives held a national working conference in Beijing on rural catering and service trades. The conference decided to speed up the development of catering and service trades.

The Ministry of Water Conservancy held a national water conservancy conference which summed up experiences in water conservancy work over past 30 years and put forward the major tasks in this field for the three-year period of national economic readjustment.

July 3. The State Council promulgated the Regulations on Some Questions Concerning the Development of Commune- and Brigade-Run Enterprises (Draft for Trial Implementation) and urged that the various provinces, municipalities, autonomous regions and institutions under the State Council immediately discuss and implement these regulations on a trial basis.

July 6 to 11. The Central Committee of the Communist Party of China and the State Council convened a national conference in Beijing on farmland capital construction. Comrade Hua Guofeng attended the conference and made a speech calling on the country to make earnest efforts to shift the focus of work and concentrate on improving the national economy. The speech stressed that farmland capital construction should be carried out in accordance with local conditions and in a diligent manner.

In Dong'an County, Hubei Province, the Ministry of Agriculture convened a national conference of counties where experiments were being conducted in the specialization of seed production, mechanization of seed processing, standardization of seed quality and regionalization of seed varieties, and where seeds were being systematically supplied to counties which are taken as basic units.

July 8 to 26. The Ministry of Commerce held a national forum of heads of commercial bureaus in Beijing. In line with the tasks of national economic readjustment, the conference made further arrangements for work in the field of commerce.

July 10 to 23. The State Council convened a national working conference in Chendgu on increasing production and practicing economy in industry and communications.

A national conference of heads of supply bureaus was also held in Chengdu. The conference decided that the present task was to maintain a balance between supplies and needs, to practice economy resolutely, to clear out warehouse stocks to make room for new goods and to enliven supply work.

The Ministry of Agriculture convened a national on-the-spot meeting on development of the grasslands in livestock-raising areas in the Bairin Right Banner of Iu Uc League, Inner Mongolia Autonomous Region. The meeting summed up the popularized advanced experiences in grassland development.

July 13. The State Council officially issued the following five documents: Some Regulations on Enlarging the Management and Administrative Decision-Making Powers of State-Owned Industrial Enterprises, Regulations on the Retention of a Portion of Profits by the State Enterprises, Provisional Regulations on Increasing the Depreciation Rate of Fixed Assets and Improvement of Depreciation Provisions of State-Owned Industrial Enterprises, Provincial Regulations on Imposing Fixed Assets Taxes on State-Owned Industrial Enterprises, and Provincial Regulations on Instituting Complete Reliance on Bank Credit for Working Capital in State-Owned Industrial Enterprises. The State Council also issued a circular requiring various areas and relevant departments under the State Council to select a number of enterprises under the industrial and communications departments as experimental units.

July 31. The Regulations of the People's Republic of China on Standardization Management were promulgated.

August

A national working conference to discuss problems concerning provision of complete sets of equipment was held in Beijing. The conference required that proper arrangements be made regarding complete sets of equipment immediately required for key projects undertaken by the state.

August 8 to 16. The Ministry of Light Industry convened in Beijing a national assembly of representatives of artists and designers in the industrial arts and crafts.

The Ministry of Agriculture, the Ministry of Light Industry and the Ministry of Commerce jointly called a national conference in Linhai County, Zhejiang Province, of counties that are milk-goat centres. The conference summed up experiences and put forward relevant measures to speed up the breeding and raising of milk goats.

The State Economic Commission held a national assembly of representatives of quality control groups in Beijing. The conference decided to invoke mass supervision of product quality.

The State Council approved a report suggesting that investment in capital construction should take the form of loans instead of allocation of funds and also approved and circulated the Draft Regulations on Capital Construction Loans laid down by the State Planning Commission, the State Capital Construction Commission and the Ministry of Finance. It demanded that the various areas and departments conscientiously organize experimental units.

August 22 to September 12. A national conference of heads of supply and marketing cooperatives from various provinces, municipalities and autonomous regions was held in Beijing. The conference decided to promote the purchase and sale of rural products so as to bring about faster agricultural economic expansion.

August 25. The State Council approved promulgation by the Ministry of Communications of the Regulations of the People's Republic of China on Control of Foreign Ships.

The Xinhua News Agency reported that another large chemical fertilizer plant using imported equipment – the Dongting Nitrogen Fertilizer Plant – had been basically completed. It also reported that track-laying for the Southern Xinjiang Railway (the Turpan-Korla line) had been completed.

September

September 1 to 19. A national working conference on tourism was held in Beidaihe. The conference put forward the plan of receiving 3,500,000 tourists by 1985.

The Xinhua News Agency reported that more than 140 kinds of minerals had been found in our country, making China one of the few countries in the world known to possess a relatively comprehensive assortment of minerals. The Nanyang oil field, another new high- and stable-yield oilfield in China, was constructed and went into operation.

Construction of the new passenger terminal and ancillary buildings of the Beijing International Airport was successfully completed. It is the largest modern airport in China.

A huge meeting in celebration of the second Quality Month was held in Beijing on September 8 and broadcast live through the nationwide broadcasting and television network. The State Council presented 51 gold medals and 121 silver medals for products of outstanding quality.

The State Planning Commission, the State Economic Commission and the State Bureau of Supplies jointly held a second national meeting on reducing oil consumption and economizing on oil.

The Ministry of Commerce held a national forum on catering and service work. The conference called for further development of catering and service networks and centres and for efforts to restore good management and traditional varieties.

September 11 to 13. The Standing Committee of the Fifth National People's Congress convened its 11th session. The session adopted in principle The Environmental Protection Law of the People's Republic of China (for Trial Implementation).

September 25 to 28. The Fourth Plenary Session of the 11th Central Committee of the Communist Party of China was held in Beijing. The session adopted The Decision of the Central Committee of the Communist Party of China on Some Questions Concerning the Acceleration of Agricultural Development.

September 27 to October 17. A national meeting of presidents of branches of the Agricultural Bank was held in Beijing. The meeting resolved to develop credit in the rural areas, to promote the rapid development of agriculture and to realize the modernization of agriculture.

September 28. The State Council held a grand prize award ceremony in Beijing to honour advanced enterprises and model workers on the industrial, communications and capital construction fronts. Represnetatives of 118 advanced enterprises and 222 model workers accepted the highest awards conferred by the state.

September 29. The Central Committee of the Communist Party of China, the Standing Committee of the National People's Congress and the State Council held a grand rally in celebration of the 30th anniversary of the founding of the People's Republic of China. Comrade Ye Jianying made an important speech at the rally.

October

October 4. The Board of Directors of the China International Trust and Investment Corporation was formally established. Rong Yiren was appointed chairman of the board and president of the corporation.

October 6 to 14. The Ministry of Finance conducted a national working conference in Beijing on agricultural finance. The conference discussed and studied how to raise more funds for the acceleration of agricultural development and how to make better use of funds allocated to agriculture.

The General Administration for Industry and Commerce held a national working conference in Hangzhou to discuss trademarks. The conference decided to do better in the unified registration of trademarks and in strengthening trademark control.

A national sales exhibition of light industrial products was held in Beijing. During the exhibition, the Ministry of Light Industry called a national forum on work in light industry, at which a study was made of ways to do a good job in designing and turning out new light industrial products.

The Central Committee of the Communist Party of China and the State Council issued a circular announcing their decision to raise the prices of eight major non-staple foods, i.e., pork, beef, mutton, poultry, eggs, vegetables, aquatic products and milk, beginning from November 1 and, at the same time, to grant workers and staff members a subsidy for purchasing non-staple foods. The circular also announced the decision to give job promotions to 40% of China's workers and staff members and to increase their wages starting from November 1979.

The National Broadcasting and Television Station broadcast live a meeting held in Beijing marking "Energy-Saving Month." The meeting urged the various areas, trades and professions to mobilize immediately to reduce energy consumption and to conserve energy.

November

November 5. The State Council issued a

circular demanding that various areas carry out a well-publicized, extensive survey of market prices.

The Ministry of Agriculture convened a national meeting in Chengbu Miao Autonomous County, Hunan Province, to discuss animal husbandry in the rural areas, the utilization and development of grass-covered mountains and the breeding and raising of herbivorous livestock.

The National Defence Industries Office held a working conference in Beijing at which it was decided that military industry enterprises should turn out products for both military and civilian use.

November 19 to 27. A national insurance meeting was held in Beijing. The meeting made practicable arrangements for the domestic insurance business, which the State Council had agreed to resume in 1980.

The State Planning Commission, the State Economic Commission and the State Bureau of Supplies jointly held a national working conference on questions relating to timber to promote the experience of the Hangzhou Timber Corporation in making multiple use of timber and in improving utilization rates.

The Ministry of Agricultural Reclamation and State Farms held a national meeting in Wuhan on state farm administration and management. The meeting declared that agricultural reclamation enterprises throughout the country were no longer operating at a deficit as they had been over the last 13 years. The meeting also formulated the Regulations on Some Questions Concerning the Better Administration and Management of State Farms (Draft for Trial Implementation).

The State Council held a national grain meeting in Beijing. The meeting emphasized that, to solve the grain problem, it was necessary to implement resolutely the principle of "basing ourselves on domestic supply, being self-reliant, promoting production and practicing strict economy" as put forward by the Party Central Committee and the State Council.

The People's Construction Bank of China held a working conference in Beijing. The meeting decided to implement on a trial basis in 1980 the Draft Regulations on Capital Construction Loans, as approved by the State Council, with application to textiles and light industries and to tourism in Beijing, Shanghai and Guangdong Province.

The Ministry of Agricultural Machinery held a national working conference at which it was decided to make readjustments in the farm machine-building industry. Ten measures in that regard were put forward at the conference.

December

The State Council held its second awards ceremony in Beijing to honour the nation's advanced units and model workers in the fields of agriculture, finance, commerce, education, public health and scientific research.

Beginning in December, China began trial implementation of the Standards for Farmland Irrigation Water and the Standards for Fishing Waters that were jointly approved and promulgated as national standards by the Environment Protection Leading Group under the State Council, the State Planning Commission, the State Economic Commission, the Ministry of Agriculture and the State Bureau of Aquatic Resources.

December 2 to 9. The State Capital Construction Commission and other units jointly held a national working conference in Qingdao on rural housing. The conference urged various areas to treat rural housing construction as a priority.

The Ministry of Agriculture and three other units jointly called a national meeting in Beijing to discuss silkworm cocoon production. The meeting summed up the situation in silkworm cocoon production during the past few years.

The Ministry of Water Conservancy, the Ministry of Finance and the State Bureau of Aquatic Resources jointly held a meeting in Dongguan County, Guangdong Province, to exchange experiences in fish breeding in reservoirs and in the use of reservoirs for other purposes. The meeting urged water conservancy project departments to promote fish breeding and to utilize reservoirs for other productive activities.

December 5 to January 8. A national forum on the work of trade unions at grassroots levels was held in Beijing. The forum pointed out that trade unions should do a good job of ideological and political work among workers and staff while focusing on economic readjustment.

December 15 to 20. A national conference of heads of family-planning offices in various provinces, municipalities, autonomous regions, and in the army was held in Chengdu. The conference drew up detailed population plans for 1980-81 in line with the 1980 national economic plan.

The State Scientific and Technological Commission and the Ministry of Building-Materials Industry held a meeting in Suzhou to exchange experiences in manufacturing new types of building materials and in experimental construction techniques.

December 15 to 21. The State Council held a national meeting on cotton production in Beijing. The meeting stated that the central task of cotton producing centres for the coming two years is to promote cotton production.

The Xinhua News Agency reported that the Sichuan Vinlon Plant, the largest in China, was virtually completed. Since 1979, 24 large and medium-sized light industrial projects were completed and put into operation, while eight large and medium-sized projects in the textile industry entered service.

1980

January

January 1. The National Committee of the People's Political Consulative Conference held a New Year's Tea Party. Chairman Deng Xiaoping pointed out in his speech at the party that the 1980's are crucial to the realization of the Four Modernizations, that the most important task, domestically, is to do a good job in economic construction and that leadership by the Communist Party is the cardinal rule of the four basic principles.

Renmin Ribao (People's Daily) published an editorial "Usher in a New Period of Great Achievements."

The State Council approved of a trial method whereby the People's Bank of China would grant medium- or short-terms special loans to light industries and textiles. According to the principle of "six priorities," the bank would issue 2,000 million yuan of medium- or short-term special credits and U.S.$300 million in foreign-exchange credits to buyers so as to extend the productive capacity of light industries and textiles.

The First Ministry of Machine-Building instituted floating prices for 16 types of mechanical and electrical engineering products.

Beginning from 1980, cultural, educational and scientific research institutions and administrative establishments were tentatively made responsible for their own budgets.

The first set of amino-hexaphosphate manufacturing equipment in China was put into production at the Jiande Organic Chemical Plant, Zhejiang Province. The first bank gangue-burning power station was built in Jixi, Heilongjiang Province. It was reported that at the end of 1979, the first installation for alkene production was designed, built and outfitted by China and a sand cracking stove was put into production by the Lanzhou Chemical Industrial Corporation.

January 2. Renmin Ribao published a commentary entitled "Carrying Out the Spirit of Plain Living and Hard Struggle," which pointed out that the goal of socialist production is to ensure that the increasing material and cultural demands of the whole society are met to the maximum.

January 3. The State Council approved and circulated a report of the Ministry of Agricultural Machinery on the vigorous development of wheat harvesting machinery and pointed out that appreciation of the importance of wheat harvesting mechanization is an important step in realizing overall agricultural mechanization.

The State Bureau of Metrology held a national working conference in Beijing, summing up experiences and drawing up work plans.

January 4 to 18. A national conference of heads of geological bureaus was held in Beijing. The conference decided to readjust plans for mineral exploration so as to meet the needs of the Four Modernizations.

January 4 to 23. A national meeting to discuss commodity prices was held in Beijing. The meeting laid down principles and tasks for 1980: proceeding from the desire for stability and unity, to keep prices relatively stable, to make earnest efforts to strengthen price controls and to continue to monitor prices.

January 5. The All-China Federation of Trade Unions held a working conference of women workers and staff members in Beijing. The conference discussed current tasks and called for the mobilization of women workers and staff members to make greater contributions to the Four Modernizations.

January 5 to 12. A national symposium on economic theories of collective ownership in cities and towns was held in Shenyang.

January 6. The Chinese Financial Society and the Chinese Society of Accountants were officially founded at a meeting in Foshan, Guangdong Province.

January 7. The state decided to institute the principle of "six priorities" in light industries and textiles to guarantee rapid development of light industry, textiles and handicrafts.

The Ministry of Agriculture held a forum in Changsha on administration and management of commune- and brigade-run enterprises. The forum proposed to strengthen work in this field in five respects.

January 7 to 23. A national working conference on metallurgy was held in Beijing. The conference decided that, in view of the overall situation and practical considerations, the departments of the metallurgical industry should adhere to the principle of making way for other industries, while going all out to increase production, thus promoting comprehensive development.

January 11. The People's Insurance Company of China offered two new types of insurance — business liability insurance (insurance against contractual breaches) and insurance against political risk.

The Xinhua News Agency reported that since 1977, three high-yield petroleum and natural gas wells had been drilled in the Tarim Basin in the southern part of the Xinjiang-Uygur Autonomous Region.

January 12. The Ministry of Coal Industry held a national coal mining telephone conference to call for a movement of "100 days safe production without accidents."

January 13. The first 500,000-volt power transformer in China was successfully trial-manufactured by the Shenyang Transformer Plant. This marked a new level in the transformer manufacturing industry of our country.

January 14 to 31. A national meeting of heads of chemical industry bureaus was held in Beijing. The meeting called for competition that was broader in range and more extensive in content. The meeting required the leading cadres of the chemical industry bureaus and enterprises in various provinces, municipalities and autonomous regions to become personally familiar with sales work, to allow scope for the regulatory role of the market and to promote chemical industrial production.

The State Economic Commission, the State Agricultural Commission and the General Administration for Industry and Commerce jointly issued a circular which demanded the immediate investigation and registration of industrial enterprises.

January 15. The Xinhua News Agency reported that a huge coal field — the Yunlian Coal Field — was discovered in Sichuan Province. Proven coal deposits were over 2,400 million tons.

January 17. The Ministry of Water Conservancy and other units jointly held a national on-the-spot meeting in Chengdu regarding small hydroelectric power stations to address the problem of how to strengthen the "construction, management, supply and utilization" of small hydroelectric stations.

January 19. The first high-dam hydroelectric power station in China — the Wujiangdu Power Station, in Guizhou Province — began generating electricity.

A basic protocol for Sino-Japanese cooperation in developing the Sanjiang wasteland in Heilongjiang Province was signed in Beijing.

January 20. The Jining-Heze Railway was opened to traffic. It is 108 km. long.

January 21. The National Defence Industries Office of the State Council held a meeting in Beijing to discuss the livelihood of workers and staff members in national defence industries. The meeting emphasized the necessity of plain living and hard struggle and of proper management of collective welfare.

The State Council issued an emergency circular to prohibit the distribution of year-end bonuses during this year's Spring Festival.

January 22. The State Council approved and circulated the Trial Policy of Allowing the State-Owned Industrial Enterprises to Keep a Portion of Their Profits, as laid down by the State Economic Commission and the Ministry of Finance; and it informed those enterprises conducting experimental restructuring that they should begin implementation of the new policy in 1980.

Shaanxi Province ascertained that coal reserves of the Binxian County Coal Field exceed 4,000 million tons and that the area of the coal field is 1,170 sq. km.

January 22 to February 6. A national working conference on electric power supplies was held in Beijing. At the conference it was decided — on the basis of fulfilling state plans in an all-around way — to strive to generate an extra 10,000 million kw. of electricity and to install power generators with an extra capacity of 1 million kw. above the targets set in the plans for 1980.

January 23 to February 2. A national meeting of heads of textile industry bureaus was held in Beijing. The meeting decided that the focal point of work for the year was to carry out internal readjustment and to go all out to promote chemical fibre production. The meeting declared that it was necessary to tap potential and make progress in regard to the quality and variety of products.

January 24. The Central Committee of the Communist Party of China and the State Council issued a circular demanding that the various areas and units throughout the country strictly reduce nonproductive spending and combat waste.

The State Economic Commission called a special meeting to draw up energy-saving plans for 1980. The meeting urged various departments to adopt effective measures to significantly cut down energy consumption.

January 26. It was reported that the State Council recently approved the Bank of China's Report on Protecting the Renminbi (RMB), Centralizing Markets and Prohibiting the Circulation of Foreign Currencies in Internal Markets and demanded its implementation by the various localities and departments.

January 28. Another large oil and natural gas field in our country, the Liaohe oil field, was reported to have begun production. It was reported that at present, the annual output of crude oil is 5 million tons and that of natural gas, 1,700 million cu.m.

January 28 to February 8. A national conference of leading cadres of the electronics industry was held in Beijing. The conference emphasized studying questions concerning readjustment and consolidation in the electronics industry and drew up plans for work in 1980. The conference proposed that a change should be made in the present situation in which there are too many factories and strength is scattered; thus, readjustment should be carried out well and the role of local electronics industries should be brought into full play.

January 29. A working conference of financial supervisors was held in Beijing. The conference demanded that the financial supervisory departments in various places combat activities that violate financial and economic regulations.

January 30 to February 8. A meeting of heads of machine-building industry departments and bureaus of various provinces, municipalities and autonomous regions was held in Beijing. The meeting resolved that during the present period of readjustment the machine-building industry should tap new sources to achieve development.

February

February 1. The State Council promulgated the Provisional Regulations on Instituting a Division of Revenues and Expenditures Between Central and Local Authorities, While Holding the Latter Responsible for Their Own Surpluses and Deficits.

With the approval of the State Council, the Chinese Modern Building Materials Corporation was founded in Beijing.

The Ministry of Foreign Affairs of the People's Republic of China and the Embassy of the United States in China exchanged notes in Beijing, whereupon the agreement on Sino-U.S. trade relations came into force.

February 4. The *People's Daily* published a commentary entitled "Tapping New Sources of Production," stating that this was an important measure in readjusting the national economy and in implementing the principle of promoting production and practicing economy; it said that this was a major issue in economic work for 1980.

February 11. A new industrial zone went under construction in the Shekou area of Shenzhen, Guangdong Province, to facilitate investment and factory building in China by firms from Hong Kong, Macao and foreign countries.

February 12. The 13th Session of the Standing Committee of the Fifth National People's Congress was held in Beijing. Yuan Baohua, Vice-Chairman of the State Economic Commission, gave a report on the situation in industry and communications in 1979 and on planned tasks for 1980. He set forth five tasks and ten projects for 1980 which would receive special attention. In order to consolidate unified leadership in the machine-building industry, the session decided to establish a machine-building industrial commission under the State Council. Vice-Premier Bo Yibo is concurrently chairman of the commission.

February 13. The State Council issued the "Circular on Drawing Up Long-Term Plans," which enunciated the decision to begin drawing up a ten-year programme (1981-90) for national economic development.

February 15. The State Council decided to set up the General Administration of Customs of the People's Republic of China.

February 19. The Ministry of Agriculture held a national conference of heads of bureaus (departments) of agriculture and animal husbandry in Beijing; it stressed an overall increase in agricultural production in 1980.

The State Economic Commission put forward three proposals for doing a good job in trying to enhance the decision-making powers of enterprises. Over 3,000 industrial enterprises — or 7% of all major state-run industrial enterprises, accounting for more than 30% of gross output value — were experimenting with added decision-making powers.

February 21. The State Economic Commission decided to stress work in five fields in 1980 and to successfully carry out enterprise readjustments according to the requirements of modernization.

A large coal field was discovered in the Inner Mongolia Autonomous Region. It has proven coal reserves of 14,600 million tons, with estimated reserves exceeding 36 billion tons.

February 22. The State Council approved and distributed a report on strenghthening energy-saving efforts submitted by the State Economic Commission and the State Planning Commission. It pointed out that in order to realize the Four Modernizations the energy question should be handled well.

February 23 to 29. The Fifth Plenary Session of the 11th Central Committee of the Communist Party of China was convened in Beijing. A Secretariat of the Central Committee was established; Comrade Hu Yaobang was elected General Secretary of the Secretariat.

February 25. The Xinhua News Agency reported that by the end of 1979, China's proven coal deposits exceeded 600 billion tons.

February 25 to March 10. A national working conference on coal mining was held in Beijing. The conference decided to take readjustment as the central task in drawing up work plans for 1980. It also decided that the coal industry should successfully carry out readjustment while promoting production and practicing economy.

February 27. The State Economic Commission held a production control meeting which decided to close the Production Control Bureau under the State Economic Commission and issued the Circular on Bringing into Play the Role of Production Control by Various Departments and Localities.

The State Administration of Urban Construction issued a circular on going all out to plant trees in cities.

February 28 to March 9. The Chinese Enterprise Management Society held its first annual meeting in Beijing.

The State Planning Committee and four other units jointly held the third national forum on controlling group purchases in Beijing. The forum urged that, in 1980, close attention be paid to controlling purchases by social groups and that this work be done well.

March

March 1. The Environmental Protection Leading Group under the State Council inaugurated a National Environmental Protection Propaganda Month, for March.

March 1 to 14. A national conference of heads of light industry departments and bureaus was held in Beijing. The conference summed up and exchanged experiences in speeding up the development of light industry and demanded that party committees at all levels consolidate and improve leadership in light industry. To this end, the *People's Daily* published an editorial entitled The Whole Party Attaches Importance to Light Industry.

March 3. It was reported that China's proven iron ore deposits stood at 44,000 million tons.

March 5. The Central Committee of the Communist Party of China and the State Council issued a directive on going all out to plant trees and pointed out that planting trees was a major strategic task.

March 8. The All-China Federation of Trade Unions promulgated the Regulations Concerning Selection of Model Workers.

March 11 to 18. The national working conference of the building materials industry was held in Beijing. The conference decided to increase production in the building materials industry in 1980 and, during the readjustment, to bring the role of existing enterprises into full play and make the building materials industry a truly leading industry.

The State Economic Commission promulgated the Tentative Rules for Exercising Total Quality Control in Industrial Enterprises.

March 13. The Ministry of Agricultural Machinery held a national working conference on agricultural machinery management. The conference put forward the task of raising the level of agricultural machinery management to a new stage in 1980 and worked out six concrete measures in this regard.

A wind-driven electric power generator with an 18-kw. capacity, the largest of this type in China, began generating electricity on Sijiao Island, Zhejiang Province.

March 15. Annex I to the Protocol Between the Chinese and U.S. Governments on Cooperation in Hydroelectric Power, Generation and Related Use of Water Resources was signed in Beijing.

March 15 to 23. The second national congress of the Chinese Scientific and Technical Association was held in Beijing.

March 16. It was announced that a national working conference on housing property and construction was held recently. It agreed to strive for the construction of more housing in 1980 than 1979.

March 19. The China Construction Machinery Corporation, the Schindler Holding Ag (a Swiss firm) and the Jardine Schindler (Far East) Holdings, S.A., (a Hong Kong firm), signed an agreement in Beijing for establishment of a joint-venture elevator company in China.

In order to strengthen foreign-exchange controls, the State Council authorized the Bank of China to issue foreign-exchange certificates beginning April 1.

March 21. A contract to establish a joint-venture company for joint management of shipping business was signed in Beijing between the China National Ship-Building Industry Corporation, the China National Ship-Chartering Corporation, the Hong Kong Shipping Group and World International Finance Limited.

March 21 to April 14. A national working conference to discuss capital construction was held in Beijing. The conference held discussions on continuing the policy of readjustment, curtailing capital construction and reforming the managerial system. It held that the most important task in capital construction readjustment was to curtail and limit the scope of capital construction.

March 22. The State Council approved and distributed the Report on Speeding Up the Development of Animal Husbandry made by the Ministry of Agriculture and pointed out that animal husbandry was a very weak link in China's agriculture and that it was important to speed up the development of animal husbandry, to increase the proportion of livestock breeding in agriculture, and to increase the proportion of pork, egg and dairy products in the national diet.

March 24 to 30. A national working conference was held on exporting electronic industrial products.

A large coal field was discovered in Huating County, Gansu Province. Its proven area is over 100 sq. km. with known coal reserves of 3,300 million tons.

March 25. A national forum of heads of commercial bureaus was held in Beijing. The forum put forward eight measures to ensure the basic stability of market prices in 1980.

March 26. A national working conference to discuss economic relations with foreign countries was held in Beijing. The tasks put forward by the conference were to work earnestly for good economic relations with foreign countries and to strengthen international economic and technical cooperation.

March 29. The Xinhua News Agency reported that in 1979 the crude oil output of the Renqiu Oilfield in north China exceeded 10 million tons, comprising over 10% of the national output of crude oil.

March 31. The national conference of heads of administrative bureaus for industry and commerce held it closing session. The conference decided that the main tasks for 1980 were to support production, promote distribution, increase co-ordination, enhance the welfare of the masses, protect legal operations and prohibit illegal activities.

April

April 1. The State Planning Commission, the State Economic Commission and the State Bureau of Labour jointly issued a circular calling for the trial implementation of the Provisional Rules Concerning the Piece-Work System in State Enterprises (Draft).

Beginning today, with the approval of the State Council, the People's Bank of China again increased the interest rates on urban and rural savings deposits of individuals, as well as on deposits in Renminbi (RMB) made by overseas Chinese.

Foreign Minister Huang Hua and Vice Foreign Minister Han Nianlong sent telegrams to the International Monetary Fund and World Bank, respectively, demanding restoration of China's legitimate seats in those two international financial organizations.

April 2. The spokesman for our General Administration of Customs discussed problems concerning customs formalities and tax collection in trade between Taiwan and the mainland and made it clear that trade between Taiwan and the mainland is an exchange of goods between localities.

The State Economic Commission, the State Scientific and Technological Commission and the State Planning Commission jointly held a forum on developing new products and adopting new techniques. The meeting called for the application to production of new ideas gained from scientific research and new technologies developed at home and abroad, so as to change the backwardness of our industrial products and production technology as quickly as possible and to meet the demands of international and domestic markets.

April 3. The State Council approved and distributed the report of the Agricultural Bank of China on the meeting of the heads of its branch banks and pointed out that resumption of the operations of the bank was an important measure for accelerating the development of agriculture and that funds for agricultural loans should be well managed and used so as to derive their maximum returns.

April 4. The *People's Daily* issued an editorial, entitled "The Guiding Ideology of Doing Things Within the Limits of Our Capability Is Very Important." On June 9, 12, 16 and 26, the newspaper carried four editorials in succession, entitled "It Is An Important Principle to Do Things Within the Limits of Our Capabilities in Capital Construction," "More Haste, Less Speed," "Leaving No Loopholes Is a Very Important Principle in Planning Work" and "What to Uphold and What to Oppose in Our Economic Work." All four editorials expounded on the guiding ideology of doing things within the limits of China's capabilities.

April 4 to 15. A national working conference on transport and communications was held in Beijing. The meeting called for strengthening weak links, adjusting ratios and making great efforts to improve transportation and communications.

The People's Bank of China issued Renminbi currency coinage in four new denominations: 10 cents, 20 cents, 50 cents and 1 yuan.

April 5. The State Capital Construction Commission, the All-China Federation of Trade Unions and three other units jointly held a meeting to commend and present awards to capital construction enterprises in Beijing, Tianjin and Tangshan in the drive for high-quality work.

The meeting of the heads of the branch banks of the People's Bank of China was held in Beijing. The meeting stated that work should continue to be done in accordance with economic laws so as to revitalize bank work.

April 6 to 21. A national meeting of the heads of material supply bureaus was held in Nanjing, at which it was decided to further implement the principle of combining regulation through planning with regulation through the market and to make the distribution of means of production more flexible.

April 7. The State Council approved and circulated the Report on Strengthening Education in the Legal System in Industrial and Communications Enterprises and Adhering Strictly to the Law in Dealing with Worker and Staff Injuries and Deaths. The report was submitted by the State Economic Commission, the State Bureau of Labour and the All-China Federation of Trade Unions. It pointed out that those who neglected their duties, acted irresponsibly, disregarded safety regulations, broke operational rules, resorted to coercion and commandism and issued arbitrary orders and, as a result, were responsible for major injuries and deaths, should be punished.

The Ministry of Textile Industry and the State Bureau of Labour jointly issued a circular enunciating their decision to introduce the system of "four groups with three at work and one at rest" in 54 woolen textile and 24 linen textile enterprises.

April 8. Li Renjun, the vice-minister in charge of the State Planning Commission, gave a report on the implementation of the 1979 National Economic Plan and on arrangements for the national economic plan for 1980 to the 14th Session of the Standing Committee of the Fifth National People's Congress.

The Central Committee of the Communist Party of China and the State Council issued a circular concerning strengthening price controls and strictly forbidding arbitrary price increases or concealed measures of inflation. They required all localities and units to strengthen price controls and to basically ensure stable market prices.

A national meeting of the heads of China's customs houses ended. The meeting pointed out that the central task in customs work is the exercise of its supervision and control functions.

April 9 to 19. The State Council held a national working conference in Nanjing on increasing production, practicing economy, boosting revenues and cutting down expenditures in industry and communications. At the conference, five major policies concerning enterprise management were discussed.

April 10. The Xinhua News Agency reported that up to now, 3,358 industrial enterprises, or 8% of all enterprises under the state budget, had experimented with added decision-making powers. Their output value accounted for one-third of the total output value of all industrial enterprises and their profits accounted for 40% of total profits.

April 10 to 14. A meeting to make commendations and issue awards in the geological field was held in Beijing. Units and individuals with outstanding achievements in geological and mineral exploration over the past 30 years were commended and rewarded.

April 14. The State Council approved the setting up of a "Safety Month" programme for stepping up our efforts in labour safety protection in industrial and mining enterprises. The State Economic Commission and nine other units jointly issued a circular instituting "Safety Months."

April 14 to 18. The China Technical Economy Research Society and China Management Modernization Research Society jointly held a symposium on economic reforms in Beijing.

April 17. The International Monetary Fund and the Executive Board of the World Bank, respectively adopted resolutions on the restoration of China's legitimate seats in the two organizations.

April 20. A national conference to discuss recomputation of enterprise assets, making up deficits, increasing surpluses, and economic accounting ended in Nanjing. The conference called on all enterprises to do what they could to discover additional sources of revenue, to increase revenues, and to strictly control and economize on expenditures.

April 21 to 28. The China World Economic Society held its inaugural meeting in Shanghai.

April 22. The Central Committee of the Communist Party of China and the State Council jointly issued a circular announcing the decision to combine the National Conference of Model Workers and the National Conference of Model Agricultural Workers into one conference, namely, the National Conference of Model Workers, and to postpone its first session until around May 1, 1981.

April 30. The State Statistical Bureau issued a communique on the fulfilment of China's 1979 national economic plan. According to the communique, total industrial and agricultural output value in 1979 was 617,500 million yuan, an 8.5% increase over 1978. National income totalled 337,000 million yuan.

May

May 1. The second major trunk railway from Beijing to Northeast China — the Beijing-Tongliao Railway — was opened to traffic. It is 806 km. long.

The Xinhua News Agency reported that the output of the Daqing oil field reached 50 million tons for four years running.

May 2. The All-China Federation of Trade Unions held the fourth (enlarged) session of its Ninth Standing Committee. A resolution was adopted to mobilize workers and staff to make contributions to the Four Modernizations and to thoroughly implement the policy of increasing production and practicing economy.

May 3. A national conference of leading cadres in charge of railway services was held in Beijing. It was decided at the conference to speed up the work of renovating old railway lines and to further strengthen weak links in transportation and communications.

May 4. The State Capital Construction Commission and four other units jointly issued the Provisional Rules Concerning Expansion of Managerial and Administrative Decision-Making Powers in State-Owned Construction Enterprises.

May 5 to 17. A national conference of heads of architectural engineering bureaus was held in Beijing. The conference urged that construction quality be improved, that the time required to complete a project be reduced and that a positive attitude be taken in promoting building products as commodities.

May 6. The Secretariat of the Central Committee of the Communist Party of China issued four suggestions regarding the work of the Beijing Municipal Government.

May 8. The State Council approved promulgation of Provisional Rules Concerning Professional Titles for Agro-Technicians as worked out by the State Agricultural Commission, the

Ministry of Agriculture, the Ministry of Agricultural Reclamation and State Farms and the Bureau of Scientific and Technical Personnel under the State Council.

The State Council circulated a Summary of the Meeting of Leading Groups in Charge of Building Shelterbelts in the Northwest, the Northern Part of North China and the Western Part of the Northeast, calling on provinces and autonomous regions in these parts of China and relevant departments to strengthen leadership, combine efforts and build a good shelterbelt system.

May 9. A national working conference to discuss product quality supervision and examination was held in Wuhan. It urged that efforts be stepped up to establish a network for supervision and examination of product quality.

May 11. A national working conference dealing with inventions was held in Beijing, at which some of the details involved in the implementing of the Regulations Concerning Awards for Inventions were discussed.

May 11 to 19. A national conference on purchases of summer grain and oil by the state was held in Beijing.

May 12. With the approval of the State Council, the Ministry of Geology and seven other ministries jointly issued the Measures for Rewarding People Who Report Mineral Deposit Discoveries.

May 13. A ceremony to celebrate the 20th anniversary of Daqing's great battle for oil and the march towards modernization on the national oil front was held in Daqing. Medals were awarded to those who had made great contributions to opening up the building of the Daqing oil field. Souvenir badges were presented to all workers and staff.

The Xinhua News Agency reported that in the 20 years since the Daqing oil field was opened, it has produced 490 million tons of crude oil and turned over 50,000 million yuan in profits and taxes to the state, an amount 17.8 times the total state investment in the oil field.

May 16. The State Council approved distribution of the Provisional Rules Concerning Professional Titles for Statisticians drawn up by the State Statistical Bureau.

The Jiangxia Experimental Tidal Power Station began generating electricity. It is the first two-way tidal-power generating station in China.

May 21 to June 4. A national meeting of heads of medicine and drug administrations was held in Beijing. The meeting called for the consolidation and development of a unified system controlling the production, sale and use of medicines and drugs.

May 22. Entrusted by the Party's Central Committee, Hu Yaobang, General Secretary of the Central Committee of the Communist Party of China and Wan Li, member of the Secretariat of the Party and Vice-Premier of the State Council, made an inspection tour of Tibet. They discussed with local cadres and masses vital questions concerning the improvement of the material and cultural well-being of the Tibetan people as quickly as possible and proposed six major programmes in this regard.

The Xinhua News Agency reported that China's first 500-kv. transformer and transmission line was erected in northeast China. It was designed by Chinese personnel and built with domestically manufactured equipment.

May 23. The Ministry of Power Industry announced that China's hydroelectric resources have a total potential capacity of 680 million kw., nearly 100 million kw. more than the total from a survey during the 1950's. Of the current total, 370 million kw. is suitable for exploitation.

The Committee for Management of Worker and Staff Education was set up in Beijing, with Yuan Baohua as its director and personnel from the All-China Federation of Trade Unions, the Ministry of Education and 12 other units making up its membership.

The *People's Daily* carried a commentary calling for integration of enterprises in the further development of light industry.

May 26. The Central Committee of the Communist Party of China circulated the Summary of the Forum on Our Work in Tibet. The Central Committee set forth the central task in building Tibet, its goals and eight specific policies in that regard.

The Ministry of Commerce, the Ministry of Finance and the State Administration of Commodity Prices jointly issued a circular which required that the purchase price of pigs remain stabilized and that policies conducive to pig-raising be unchanged.

May 28. The government named the President of the People's Bank of China, Li Baohua, and the Minister of Finance, Wu Bo (later replaced by Wang Bingqian), as the directors representing China in the International Monetary Fund and World Bank; Vice-President of the Bank of China, Wang Weicai, and Vice-Minister of the Ministry of

Finance, Li Peng were appointed as vice-directors in these two organizations.

May 29. The China Petroleum Company and two French oil companies signed a contract to carry out joint exploration and exploitation of oil in portions of the Bohai Gulf.

China and Japan signed their first long-term contract to carry out joint exploration and exploitation of oil.

May 31. On November 23, 1979, owing to orders given contrary to regulations, a gas explosion occurred in the No. 2 coal pit of the Songshuzhen Coal Mines under the Tonghua Coal Mining Administration in Jilin Province. It was an accident involving serious criminal liability. The People's Court of Hunjiang municipality sentenced the persons responsible for the acccident according to the law.

June

June 2. Comrade Hua Guofeng inspected the Baoshan Iron and Steel Complex, encouraging the workers to do a good job of building this large modern iron and steel enterprise.

June 3. A meeting held by the Third Ministry of Machine Building to discuss production of goods for civilian use ruled that the aviation industry should also turn out products for civilian use.

The State Administrative Commission on Import and Export Affairs and the Ministry of Foreign Trade issued the Provisional Measures Concerning Export Permits so as to strengthen control over exports and to facilitate a uniform approach in international trade.

June 13. A forum was held by persons in economic circles, during which it was pointed out that considerations for economic results should take priority in all economic work and that the idea of seeking quick results should be discarded.

The China National Electric Devices Industrial Corporation was set up in Beijing. This is the first entrepreneurial industrial corporation operated by China's electronics industry; the corporation was set up on a trial basis.

June 15. Shaanxi Province decided to suspend a project to divert water from the west to the east in Xiyang County. The *People's Daily* published a relevant editorial, entitled "Let's Have No More of This Kind of Folly."

June 18. The State Economic Commission, the State Bureau of Supplies and two other units jointly issued the Measures for Reducing the Stockpile of Rolled Steel, requiring that 4 million tons of overstocked rolled steel be put on nearby markets.

June 19. The third national trade union conference on labour protection ended in Beijing. The meeting called on trade unions at all levels to improve labour protection and to ensure production safety.

June 20. The People's Government of the Tibet Autonomous Region issued a notice announcing a series of new economic policies to speed up economic development and to overcome the current backwardness in Tibet as quickly as possible.

The *People's Daily* carried an editorial, entitled "In Developing Heavy Industry, Emphasis Should Be Put on Tapping the Potential of Existing Enterprises." The editorial pointed out that China had had some problems in understanding and putting into effect the slogan "Give priority to the development of heavy industry" and that, henceforth, the emphasis of most industrial departments would be placed on tapping the potential of existing enterprises and renovating and transforming them.

June 21. The State Council approved and circulated the Temporary Measures for Strengthening the Work of Tapping the Potential of Existing Enterprises and of Renovating and Transforming Them in Industry and Communications. These measures were formulated by the State Economic Commission, the State Planning Commission and the Ministry of Finance.

The State Economic Commission, the State Scientific and Technological Commission and the State Bureau of Metrology jointly published the Measures for Implementing Control of Weights and Measures in Factories, Mines and Other Enterprises.

June 25. Li Chaobo, head of the Environmental Protection Office under the State Council, announced in Geneva that China had decided to join the International Federation for the Protection of Nature and Natural Resources and the International Endangered Wildlife and Plant Species Trade Accord.

June 28. The State Bureau of Labour announced that in the past three years nearly 20 million people had been given jobs by the state.

The State Economic Commission issued a circular calling for the start of the second "Energy-Saving Month."

June 30. The *People's Daily* issued an editorial entitled "Giving Full Play to Advantages." It pointed out that taking actual conditions into full account, making the best possible use of favourable conditions and avoiding unfavourable ones and giving full play to advantages while avoiding shortcomings should be primary considerations in our drive for Chinese-style modernization, upon which the success or failure of our modernization drive hinges.

The State Commodity Inspection Bureau was set up.

The State Council issued a circular on earnest implementation of the policy on unified state purchasing and marketing of cotton yarn, cloth and knitted and cotton goods.

July

July 1. A meeting of the Standing Committee of the State Council adopted the Provisional Regulations Concerning the Promotion of Economic Intergration. It was pointed out in the regulations that the pursuit of integration and the development of various forms of economic integration was necessary for readjustment of our national economy and for further restructuring of the economic managerial system, and also that this was the inexorable trend of China's economic development.

The Standing Committee of the Party Committee of the Inner Mongolian Autonomous Region held a forum during which the Party Central Committee's instruction on work in Tibet were studied. It was held that good work should be done with respect to five aspects, that more flexible policies should be introduced in the economic sphere, and that the production policy of "taking livestock raising as the key link" should be resolutely put into effect.

A postal code system was instituted in China.

The Chongqing-Changjiang River Bridge, the first large highway bridge spanning the Changjiang River on its upper reaches, was opened to traffic.

July 2. The State Council approved and distributed Several Provisions Concerning Supervision of Financial Affairs and issued a circular calling on all financial supervisory organs to exercise their functions and to struggle against acts in violation of the financial system.

July 3. The Ministry of Finance sponsored a national working conference in Kaifeng, Henan Province, to discuss agricultural tax questions. The meeting required all localities to use the money from the reduction and remission of agricultural taxes for the benefit of the communes, production brigades and production teams in impoverished areas.

July 4. The Party Committee of the Ningxia Hui Autonomous Region held a meeting of secretaries of prefectures, municipalities and counties, at which they studied the instructions given by the Party Central Committee concerning work in Tibet and the important suggestions of the Secretariat of the Party Central Committee concerning work in Ningxia, and made five decisions regarding relaxation of economic policies.

July 6. The Xinhua News Agency reported that the former leader of Xiyang County, Shaanxi Province had resorted to deception and had falsely exaggerated county grain output by 270 million catties during the period from 1973 to 1977.

July 7. The members of the Standing Committee of the Party Committee of the Guangxi Zhuang Autonomous Region and the secretaries of the region's countics and prefectures studied the instructions given by the Party Central Committee concerning work in Tibet and held a working conference in Nanning attended by comrades from eight minority nationality autonomous counties. The conference held that it was imperative to relax economic policies in rural areas and to give play to the advantages of each autonomous county so as to quicken the pace of economic construction.

July 8. A project to divert water from the west to the east in Xiyang County was completely halted.

July 12. The Nanjing Radio Company was set up. It is the first entrepreneurial company in our electronics industry to be formed jointly by enterprises under ministries and local enterprises.

July 14. The State Council decided to devote major efforts to developing farm mechanization in northeast China and to speed up the construction of centres for the production of commodity grain and soybeans.

In accordance with instructions given by the Party Central Committee, and the State Council, the Ministry of Coal Industry decided to gradually introduce a "four-shift, six-hour day" system for underground workers in coal mines under its direct administration.

July 15 to 26. A national forum to discuss the question of carrying out ideological and political work among workers and staff was held by the

All-China Federation of Trade Unions in Dalian.

The State Council approved and circulated a summary of a meeting on reforming the managerial system in the railway bureaus of Beijing and Taiyuan where experiments in managerial reform had been conducted.

July 18. The 18th national working conference on postal and telecommunications work was held in Beijing. The conference called for integration of enterprises so as to speed up the growth of postal and telecommunications services.

July 21. The Xinhua News Agency reported that the number of state-owned industrial enterprises given greater decision-making powers had increased to 6,600 by the end of June. They now constitute 16% of the total number of state-owned industrial enterprises and their output value and profits account for about 60% and 70%, respectively, of the total. In most cases, both revenues and production have increased.

July 21 to 28. The Ministry of Finance held a national conference in Beijing to exchange experiences in rural financial management. The conference discussed how to better manage funds for agriculture, put them to better use and achieve better results.

In accordance with the instructions of the State Council, the Ministry of Light Industry decided to vigorously develop labour-intensive products.

July 23. The Research Association for Studying Capital Construction Economics in China was established in Beijing.

July 23 to 30. The second national meeting on the investigation of natural resources and regional planning was held in Beijing. The meeting put stress on good performance in resource surveys so as to provide scientific data for making adjustments both in the internal structure of agriculture and over-all regionalization of crops.

July 24. The State Council approved and circulated a summary of the forum on the problem of Hainan Island, deciding to take measures to develop it step by step into a production centre for tropical cash crops and valuable woods.

In his speech on energy policy delivered at the national coal industry conference held at Benxi, Vice-Premier Yu Qiuli declared that the energy policy decided upon by the Party Central Committee and the State Council had placed equal stress on exploiting energy and economizing on energy consumption but that, for the present, priority would be given to saving energy and making every endeavour to carry out technical transformation and structural reform.

The Xinhua News Agency reported that the average annual per capita income in 1,622 production brigades of rural people's communes exceeded 300 yuan in 1979, with some topping 1,000 yuan.

The State Council and the Central Military Commission approved and distributed a report by the Administrative Bureau for Industry and Commerce and other departments on strengthening controls in regard to goods brought into China by overseas Chinese, compatriots in Taiwan, Hong Kong and Macao, and on the struggle against smuggling, speculation and profiteering. They called for earnest implementation of the demands raised in the report.

July 25 to 31. The Ministry of Commerce convened a forum on trust trade attended by comrades from eight cities including Beijing and Shanghai. It was maintained that trust trade offers an important channel for the distribution of commodities in socialist countries and is also an important way to encourage market regulation and commodity distribution.

The State Council published the Measures for Registration and Control of Joint Ventures with Chinese and Foreign Investment and the Rules Concerning Labour Management in Joint Ventures with Chinese and Foreign Investment.

July 27. It was announced that the State Council had recently issued a circular calling for the earnest examination of the problem of enterprises which had suffered losses over a long period and for the suspension of those enterprises which have been turning out high-cost, low-quality products, have long been operating at a loss and where management was in a state of confusion, so that they can undergo readjustment.

August

August 2 to 7. The Party Central Committee held a national conference on employment in Beijing. The conference pointed out that the way to solve the problem of employment was to emancipate thinking, adopt more flexible policies, promote production, open up new avenues of employment and combine employment on the recommendation of state labour departments with employment through mutual-help teams and self-help.

August 3 to 13. The second national symposium on economic theory in animal husbandry was held in Xining. It probed into questions concerning readjustment of the economic structure in animal husbandry, ownership, the system of responsibility in production and commodity distribution.

August 8. The Defence Industries Office under the State Council held an on-the-spot meeting in Shenyang, at which it was stressed that defence industry enterprises should switch quickly from turning out products only for military use to turning out products for both civilian and military use.

August 9. The Central Discipline Inspection Commission issued a notice concerning deterioration of goods as a result of the serious overstocking in a Shanghai wool and jute company and silk company. The notice emphasized that it was imperative to strengthen party discipline and inspection in economic matters. Bureaucrats who act irresponsibly and neglect their duties shall be held responsible and be dealt with strictly.

August 11 to 30. A national mechanical and electrical engineering products trade fair was held in Changsha. The volume of business was 2,000 million yuan.

August 19. The State Economic Commission issued a circular calling on all provinces, municipalities and autonomous regions to select one or two state-owned industrial enterprises for experimentation in economic management reform. The chosen enterprises were to carry out independent accounting, pay taxes to the state, and assume responsibility for their own profits and losses.

August 25. The State Council made a decision on the "Bohai No. 2" drilling rig accident. The Minister of Petroleum Industry, Song Zhenming, was relieved of his post and Vice-Premier Kang Shien, who was in charge of the petroleum industry, was issued a demerit of the first degree.

August 25 to 27. An emergency meeting of leading cadres of all oil enterprises was held by the petroleum industry in Beijing. The meeting concentrated on summing up the lessons from the capsizing of the "Bohai No. 2" oil rig.

August 26. The 15th Session of the Standing Committee of the Fifth National People's Congress approved the Regulations Concerning the Guangdong Province Special Economic Zones and decided to establish the State Energy Commission with Vice-Premier Yu Qiuli as its director.

In order to lighten the burden on the peasants, to support agricultural production and to change conditions of impoverishment in poor areas, the State Council approved and distributed the Report on the Implementation of the Policy of Setting a Level Below Which Agricultural Tax Is to Be Remitted, issued by the Ministry of Finance; the council called for implementation of the policy of stabilizing agricultural taxes and increasing production without increasing taxes.

August 28. It was reported that a national meeting on the work of former seed reproduction farms had been convened in Beijing. The meeting called for a good job to be done in reproducing and popularizing improved varieties and regarded this work as an important measure for the modernization of agriculture.

August 29. The second national meeting of the representatives of the group for quality control cited 70 groups which have done excellent work in total quality control.

August 30. The State Council approved and distributed the Bank of China Measures Concerning Short-Term Foreign Exchange Loans and the report submitted by the Bank of China for instructions on these measures. The State Council required governments at all levels to give full play to the functioning of the Bank of China.

The Ministry of Coal Industry held a national coal mining telephone conference in Beijing, mobilizing cadres at all levels to carry out the decision made by the State Council on the capsizing of the "Bohai No. 2" oil rig to draw lessons from it, and to pay attention to safety in production. The Minister of Coal Industry, Gao Yangwen, criticized himself for responsibility in the gas explosion in the Songshuzhen Coal Mine and other major accidents.

August 30 to September 10. The Third Session of the Fifth National People's Congress was held in Beijing. The session heard an important report delivered by Comrade Hua Guofeng; appointed Zhao Ziyang Premier of the State Council; adopted resolutions on Arrangements for the National Economic Plans for 1980 and 1981, the Final State Accounts for 1979, the Draft State Budget for 1980 and Financial Estimates for 1981, the Income Tax Law of the People's Republic of China Concerning Joint Ventures with Chinese and Foreign Investment, and the Individual Income Tax Law of the People's Republic of China. The delegates raised questions concerning the construction of the Baoshan Iron and Steel Complex and the overstocking of certain goods.

September

September 1. The third national "quality month" meeting was held in Beijing and was broadcast and televised live throughout the country. The State Council awarded gold and silver medals for 293 high-quality products.

September 2. The State Council approved and distributed the Report on Experimentation with Added Decision-Making Powers in Enterprises and Opinions for Future Work submitted by the State Economic Commission. The State Council approved expansion of decision-making powers in all state-owned enterprises.

The Economic Tribunal of the Tianjin Intermediate People's Court publicly tried those who were directly responsible for the "Bohai No. 2" oil rig accident and sentenced them according to law.

September 4. The China Supply and Marketing Corporation for Enterprises Run by the People's Communes was set up.

September 5. The State Economic Commission, the State Bureau of Labour and the All-China Federation of Trade Unions jointly held a meeting on production safety. The meeting set forth four measures for improving safety in production to be implemented by all factories, mines and bureaus of transport and communications.

September 9. The double-track electrified section of the Shijiazhuang-Taiyuan Railway, from Shijiazhuang to Yangguan, was opened to traffic. This is China's first double-track electrified line.

September 16 to 22. The first national conference on regional planning of natural environmental protection zones was held in Chengdu. Protection zones would increase from 72 to 300.

September 17 to 22. Sponsored by the Ministry of Finance, a national working conference on financial management in cultural and educational departments and administrative establishments was held in Beijing. The conference emphasized that comprehensive extension of the system under which cultural and educational departments and administrative establishments take responsibility for their own budget surpluses and deficits is a key reform in financial management.

September 18. It was reported that the China Society for the Study of Forestry Economics had been established in Beijing.

September 20. The China Production Cost Research Society was set up in Beijing.

September 29. A Chinese delegation attended the joint annual meeting of the International Monetary Fund and the World Bank held in Washington. It was the first occasion that a delegation from China had attended this meeting.

October

October 1. The branch bank of the People's Bank of China in the Tibet Autonomous Region decided to implement a policy of offering interest-free loans for agriculture, animal husbandry, and handicrafts industries for a period of three years starting from October 1.

October 5. The first national exhibition of goods produced by state-run integrated agricultural-industrial-commercial complexes opened in Beijing.

A meeting of heads of water conservancy bureaus was held recently in Beijing. The meeting earnestly summed up the experience and lessons of the past 30 years and set forth the principles for water conservancy work during period of readjustment.

October 5 to 15. Sponsored by the State Capital Construction Commission, a national conference on urban planning was held in Beijing. The conference stressed that it was imperative to eradicate the pernicious influence of ultra-"Left" ideology and to work out a feasible urban planning programme.

October 8 to 22. A national conference of heads of farm machinery bureaus was held in Beijing. The meeting made concrete suggestions for reforming the managerial system in farm machinery production and marketing.

October 10 to 24. An inter-regional symposium on cement-making techniques sponsored by the U.N. Industrial Development Organization and China was held in Beijing.

The State Planning Commission, the State Agricultural Commission, the Ministry of Agriculture and the State Statistical Bureau jointly issued a circular pointing out that "the number of animals in stock at the end of the year" and "the per-*mu* yield of grain on cultivated land" were no longer targets to be used in assessment of achievements in agricultural production.

October 11. With the approval of the State Council, the Ministry of Finance decided to take measures to reduce the income tax on cooperative trades and individual economy.

October 11 to 21. A meeting of state-run integrated agricultural-industrial-commercial complexes was held in Beijing. The meeting urged all state farms to move as quickly as possible towards becoming integrated agricultural-industrial-commercial complexes.

October 15 to 21. A national meeting to exchange experiences in economizing on market coal was held in Beijing. The meeting set forth seven measures and called for trying to conserve 4 million tons of coal this year.

October 17. A meeting of the Standing Committee of the State Council adopted temporary regulations on expanding and protecting socialist competition and expressed hope that it would be carried out earnestly in all localities and departments according to actual conditions.

October 17 to 27. The Ministry of Finance sponsored a national forum attended by heads of financial departments and bureaus in Beijing. It was decided at the forum to make vigorous efforts to promote production, increase revenues, control expenditures and reduce deficits.

October 20. The State Council approved and distributed the Report on Foods for Infants and Children submitted by the Ministry of Light Industry, the Ministry of Commerce, and the Ministry of Food, calling for study and implementation of suggestions in the report.

October 20 to 24. A meeting sponsored by the U.N. Industrial Development Organization and the Chinese government to exchange experience and to promote cooperation in expanding the farm machinery industry in developing countries was held in Beijing.

October 20 to 28. The first phase of meetings of the second international symposium on the application and development of hydroelectric techniques for small-scale projects was held in Hangzhou.

October 23 to November 9. The State General Supply and Marketing Cooperative held a meeting of heads of supply and marketing cooperatives of the provinces, municipalities and autonomous regions in Beijing. The meeting discussed and laid down plans for readjustment and restructuring in supply and marketing cooperatives and affiliated organizations.

October 27. The State Council issued instructions on cutting down the use of all kinds of oil-burning boilers and industrial kilns and furnaces, calling for strict implementation of the plan for utilizing oil and of a check-up and approval system.

October 27 to November 20. A working conference of the People's Construction Bank of China was held in Beijing. The conference decided that the task at present was to control and reduce the scope of capital construction according to the state plan.

October 29 to November 3. A national meeting to exchange experience in energy-saving was held in Beijing. The meeting demanded that technical innovations and structural reforms focusing on energy-saving be carried out to ensure that the energy equivalent of 20 million tons of standard coal can be saved each year during the period of the Sixth Five-Year Plan.

October 30. The State Council published the Provisional Regulations for the Administration of Foreign Enterprises Agencies in China.

October 31. The first national sales exhibition of goods turned out by commune- and brigade-run enterprises ended in Chengdu.

November

November 1. The State Planning Commission, the State Capital Construction Commission, the State Economic Commission and the Environmental Protection Leading Group under the State Council jointly issued a circular on strictly implementing the policy of simultaneous planning, construction, and operation of environmental protection facilities within new capital construction and technological projects.

The Xinhua News Agency reported that 4,300 sites containing non-metallic ore deposits had been discovered and that reserves of 8,000 non-metallic ore deposits had been proven. Among these, reserves of iron sulphide, gypsum, magnesite, boron, phosphorus, arsenic, asbestos, fluorite, alunite and rock salt stood in the front ranks of the world.

November 4. The State Council issued the Circular on Paying Close Attention to Revenues and Expenditures in the Last Two Months of the Year and on Controlling Financial Deficits and Increases in the Money Supply.

November 7. The first session of the commercial cooperation conference of five provinces and autonomous regions in northwest China was held in Xi'an. The session decided, through consultation, to break down provincial barriers and to organize the distribution of goods according to economic zones and traditional practices.

The Zhujiang River Water Conservancy Commission under the Ministry of Water Conservancy held its first meeting in Foshan on planning and cooperation among five provinces and one autonomous region in the Zhujiang River basin. It was decided at the meeting to unify planning for comprehensive control and exploitation of the Zhujiang River basin.

November 11. It was reported that the State Scientific and Technological Commission, the State Planning Commission and the State Energy Commission recently held a forum on nuclear energy in Beijing. The forum suggested that the state regard vigorous development of nuclear energy as a long-range policy and first build nuclear power stations in east China and in Guangdong and Liaoning provinces.

The Ministry of Finance sponsored a national working conference of accountants and an annual meeting of the Accountants Society in Beijing.

November 13. A conference to exchange experience in rice production in south China was held in Jiaxing County, Zhejiang Province. At the conference, the Ministry of Agriculture proposed to give full play to favourable conditions in the south for producing rice, so as to increase paddy output.

November 14. The State Bureau of Aquatic Products held a national meeting in Wujin County, Jiangsu Province, for the exchange of experiences in fish-rearing on the part of communes and brigades.

November 17. Early this month, the Ministry of Forestry held a national conference in Xianning Prefecture, Hubei Province to exchange experiences in growing tree seedlings.

November 18. The State Council approved and distributed a Report on Providing Loans Instead of Allocating Funds for Capital Construction, jointly submitted by the State Planning Commission, the State Capital Construction Commission, the Ministry of Finance and the People's Construction Bank of China; and a Circular on the Decision to Provide Loans Instead of Allocating Funds to Enterprises Practicing Independent Business Accounting and Having the Ability to Repay Loans, Beginning from 1981.

November 21. The State Economic Commission, the Ministry of Finance and the People's Construction Bank of China announced that as of 1981 the funds for tapping potential (in production) through innovation and transformation arranged by the State Economic Commission and the Ministry of Finance will be provided in the form of loans from the People's Construction Bank of China, instead of in the form of allocations by the state.

The Chinese Research Association of Water Conservancy Economics was founded in Danjiangkou, Hubei Province.

November 25. A contract between the China International Trust and Investment Corporation, the Beijing Machinery and Electrical Equipment Corporation and the Oriental Leasing Company, Ltd. (of Japan) on establishing the China Oriental Leasing Company was signed in Beijing. This was the first joint venture leasing company in New China.

November 29. The Xinhua News Agency reported that over 1,000 large production centres for local products and by-products were established in China. Some 60% of local products and by-products purchased by the state come from these centres.

November 30. In 1980, over 100 million sq. m. of urban housing was under construction. By the end of November, total floor space of over 40 million sq.m. had been completed. The living conditions of urban dwellers has thus been improved to some extent.

December

December 2. The *People's Daily* carried an editorial entitled, "Completely and Resolutely Implement the Policy of Readjustment."

The China Coal Mining Equipment Service Corporation was set up in Beijing.

December 3. It was reported that a national working conference on the export of mechanical and electrical products was held in Beijing. The meeting called for tapping potential in the machine-building industry and increasing the export of mechanical and electrical products.

A national meeting for the examination and approval of food hygiene standards and for exchanging experiences ended. The meeting examined and adopted China's first set of food hygiene standards.

December 4 to 10. A symposium on the purpose of socialist production was held in Beijing.

It was declared that a clear understanding of the purpose of socialist production was of vital importance to the readjustment of the national economy and to the reform of economic management; that in guiding our production we must conform to the demands of the essential nature of socialism; that we should make new arrangements for production in accordance with the needs of the market; and that we should formulate a complete set of policies and principles for guiding production and serving the interests of the people on the basis of Marxist political economy.

December 5. The State Council issued an urgent circular to all localities and departments resolutely forbidding the reckless felling of trees.

An integrated electrical equipment company formed by six large electrical equipment producing factories was set up in Beijing.

December 7. The State Council issued a circular entitled Strictly Control Prices and Consolidate Negotiated Prices to all provinces, municipalities, autonomous regions, the ministries and commissions under them and organs directly under the State Council.

December 7 to 23. A national conference on prices was held in Beijing. The conference decided that the central task for the present was to implement suggestions made in the circular entitled Strictly Control Prices and Consolidate Negotiated Prices issued by the State Council so as to keep prices stable.

December 8. The General Administration for Industry and Commerce issued a circular on the registration of agencies of foreign enterprises in China.

A national meeting to exchange experience in highway passenger transportation was held in Changsha, at which the experience of Suzhou and other places in joint highway passenger transportation services was popularized.

The State Bureau of Prices, the Ministry of Commerce, the All-China Federation of Supply and Marketing Cooperatives, the Ministry of Food, the General Administration for Industry and Commerce, the Ministry of Light Industry, the State Bureau of Metrology and the State Bureau of Aquatic Products issued a circular to various places and relevant departments at all levels on December 8, 9, 10, 12 and 13, respectively, calling for the study and implementation of the circular entitled Strictly Control Prices and Consolidate Negotiated Prices.

December 10. The State Council officially approved the establishment of the Xiamen Special Economic Zone.

December 14. With the approval of the State Council on December 10, the Ministry of Finance promulgated the Detailed Regulations for the Implementation of the Income Tax Law of the People's Republic of China Concerning Joint Ventures with Chinese and Foreign Investment and the Detailed Regulations for the Implementation of the Individual Income Tax Law of the People's Republic of China.

A national meeting to exchange experience in synthetic fibre production ended in Shanghai. The meeting called for further promoting synthetic fibre production so as to solve the problem of clothing for China's 1,000 million people.

December 18. The State Council published the Provisional Regulations of the People's Republic of China on the Control of Foreign Exchange.

December 19. A national customs conference on supervision and control of freight transport was held in Beijing, calling for still better supervision and control of imported and exported goods.

A national meeting of the heads of aquatic products departments and bureaus ended in Beijing. The meeting concentrated on the study of policies concerning readjustment in the production of aquatic products.

December 20. A meeting of heads of bureaus in charge of the inspection of commodities ended in Beijing. It called for improvements in the inspection and control of import and export commodities.

December 27. With the approval of the State Council, the State Economic Commission and three other units promulgated the Regulations Concerning Science and Technology Archives.

December 29. A national working conference on imports and exports closed in Beijing. The conference discussed how import and export work could serve the readjustment of the national economy well, along with relevant policies and measures.

December 30. The Xinhua News Agency reported that the State Statistical Bureau had made a survey of the living conditions of over 80,000 families in 44 cities. The investigation found that the number of families of workers and staff members with an average monthly income exceeding 25 yuan per person had risen to 76.5%.

APPENDIX

APPENDIX

1. DIRECTORY OF CHINA'S NATIONAL FOREIGN TRADE CORPORATIONS: HEAD OFFICES, BRANCHES AND MAJOR COMMODITIES TRADED

China National Cereals, Oils and Foodstuffs Import and Export Corporation

Major Import and Export Items:
   Rice, wheat, flour, other grains, seeds;
   Soya beans, peanuts and peanut products, peanut oil, cottonseed oil, teaseed oil, edible vegetable oil and vegetable oils for industrial use, animal fats; salt;
   Livestock, live poultry, frozen poultry, frozen rabbit meat, meat and meat products, eggs and egg products;
   Fresh fruits, fruit products and quick-frozen fruits; fresh and dried vegetables, quick-frozen vegetables, salted and preserved vegetables;
   Prawns, fish, shellfish, algae and shells, jellyfish;
   Sugar, confections, biscuits, cakes and pastries, wines and liquors, beverages, dairy products, rice and wheat flour products, seasonings;
   Canned goods.

HEAD OFFICE

Address: 82 Donganmen Street, Beijing
Cables: CEROILFOOD BEIJING
Telex:
   22281 CEROF CN, 22111 CEROF CN
Telephone: 555180

BEIJING BRANCH
Address:
   No. 1 Building, Fuwai Street, Beijing
Cables: CIFCPB BEIJING
Telephone: 895104

TIANJIN CEREALS AND OILS BRANCH
Address: 126 Chifeng Road, Tianjin
Cables: CEROIL TIANJIN
Telex: 22502 TJCER CN
Telephone: 24280

TIANJIN FOODSTUFFS BRANCH
Address: 134 Chifeng Road, Tianjin
Cables: FOODCO TIANJIN
Telex: 22503 TJFDS CN
Telephone: 20497

HEBEI BRANCH
Address: 52 Beima Road, Shijiazhuang
Cables: CEROILFOOD SHIJIAZHUANG
Telephone: 2907

SHANXI BRANCH
Address:
   Finance and Foreign Trade Building, Yingze Street, Taiyuan
Telephone: 23890

INNER MONGOLIA BRANCH
Address: 24 Zhongshan Road W., Hohhot
Cables: CEROILFOOD HOHHOT
Telephone: 2837

LIAONING CEREALS AND OILS BRANCH
Address: 145 Stalin Road, Dalian
Cables: DALCEROIL DALIAN
Telephone: 27289

LIAONING FOODSTUFFS BRANCH
Address: 145 Stalin Road, Dalian
Cables: DALFOOD DALIAN
Telex: 86159 DACOF CN
Telephone: 27940

JILIN BRANCH
Address: 81 Stalin Street, Changchun
Cables: CEROILFOOD CHANGCHUN
Telephone: 36208

HEILONGJIANG BRANCH
Address: 55 Heping Road, Harbin
Cables: CEROILFOOD HARBIN
Telephone: 52721

SHANGHAI CEREALS AND OILS BRANCH
Address: 11 Hankou Road, Shanghai
Cables: CHINAFAT SHANGHAI
Telephone: 219760

SHANGHAI FOODSTUFFS BRANCH
Address: 26 Zhonghsan Road E. 1, Shanghai
Cables: FOODSTUFFS SHANGHAI
Telex: 33070 FOODS CN
Telephone: 216233

JIANGSU BRANCH
Address: 50 Zhonghua Road, Nanjing
Cables: CEROILFOOD NANJING
Telephone: 23153

ZHEJIANG BRANCH
Address: 29 Xiangyang Road, Hangzhou
Cables: CEROILFOOD HANGZHOU

Telex: 35102 CEROF CN
Telephone: 22701

ANHUI BRANCH
Address: 135 Hongxing Road, Hefei
Cables: CEROILFOOD HEFEI
Telephone: 3475, 5508

FUJIAN BRANCH
Address: Foreign Trade Building, Fuzhou
Cables: FOODCO FUZHOU
Telephone: 33552

JIANGXI BRANCH
Address: 25 Zhenqian Road, Nanchang
Cables: 1120 Nanchang
Telephone: 64707

SHANDONG CEREALS AND OILS BRANCH
Address: 29 Wusong Road, Qingdao
Cables: NACEROIL QINGDAO
Telephone: 28063

SHANDONG FOODSTUFFS BRANCH
Address: 70 Zhongshan Road, Qingdao
Cables: FOODSTUFFS QINGDAO
Telephone: 28603

HENAN BRANCH
Address: 6 Wenhua Road, Zhengzhou
Cables: YUFOOD ZHENGZHOU
Telephone: 4656

HUBEI BRANCH
Address: 319 Zhaojiatiao, Hankou
Cables: CEROILFOOD HANKOU
Telephone: 21353

HUNAN BRANCH
Address: 103 Wuyi Road E., Changsha
Cables: REDEAST CHANGSHA
Telephone: 25697

GUANGDONG CEREALS AND OILS BRANCH
Address: 48 Xiti Road 2, Guangzhou
Cables: FOODCO GUANGZHOU
Telephone: 35840

GUANGXI BRANCH
Address: Hongxing Road, Nanning
Cables: CEROILFOOD NANNING
Telephone: 3519

SICHUAN BRANCH
Address: 15 Renmin Road C., Chengdu
Cables: CEROILFOOD CHENGDU
Telephone: 7048

GUIZHOU BRANCH
Address: 13 Beijing Road, Guiyang
Cables: CEROILFOOD GUIYANG

YUNNAN BRANCH
Address: 113 Huashan Road S., Kunming
Cables: CEROILFOOD KUNMING
Telephone: 4434

SHAANXI BRANCH
Address: 210 Xiyi Road, Xi'an
Cables: TUHSU XIAN

QINGHAI BRANCH
Address: 55-17 Railway Station, Plaza, Xining
Cables: 3111 XINING

XINJIANG BRANCH
Address: 10 Tuanjie Road, Urumqi
Cables: CEROF URUMQI
Telephone: 3619

Hong Kong and Macao Agents

NG FUNG HONG
Address:
115-119 Queen's Road West, Hong Kong
Cables: NGFUNG HONGKONG
Telex: 74054 NGFUN HX
Telephone: 5-404021

NAM KWONG TRADING CO.
Address:
Nan Tung Bank Building, Rua da Praia Grande, 65-A, Macao
Cables: NAMKWONG MACAO
Telephone: 84255

China National Native Products and Animal By-Products Import and Export Corporation

Major Import and Export Items:
1. *Native produce* — Industrial raw materials, tobacco and tobacco products, bast fibre and bast fibre products, resin, feed, fire-crackers, fireworks, spices, essential oils, dried fruits, dried vegetables, bamboo and wood articles, and sundries;

2. *Animal by-products* — bristle, bristle brushes, casings, hides and skins, leather and leather products, fur and fur products, rugs and carpets, sheep wool, goat wool, cashmere, camel hair, rabbit hair, feather and down products;

3. *Tea* — black tea, green tea, jasmine tea, oolong tea, white tea, compressed tea, coffee and cocoa;

4. *Traditional Chinese medicines* — various herbal medicines, patent medicines and tonics, medicated liquors and beverages.

HEAD OFFICE

Address: 82 Donganmen Street, Beijing
Cables: CHINATUHSU BEIJING
Telex: 22283 TUHSU CN
Telephone: 554142, 553808

BEIJING BRANCH
Address: 52 Xijiaominxiang, Beijing
Cables: TUHSUBRAN BEIJING
Telephone: 334998

TIANJIN NATIVE PRODUCE BRANCH
Address: 33 Harbin Road, Tianjin
Cables: NCNPC or DRUGS TIANJIN
Telex: 22505 TJNPC CN
Telephone: 34276

TIANJIN ANIMAL BY-PRODUCTS BRANCH
Address: 66 Yantai Road, Tianjin
Cables: BY-PRODUCTS TIANJIN
Telex: 22504 TJBYP CN
Telephone: 36309

TIANJIN CARPETS BRANCH
Address: 43 Baoding Road, Tianjin
Cables: JUNCOCARPET TIANJIN
Telex: 22514 TJCAR CN
Telephone: 33551

HEBEI BRANCH
Address: 8 Jichang Road, Shijiazhuang
Cables: CHINATEX SHIJIAZHUANG
Telephone: 1646

SHANXI BRANCH
Address:
   Foreign Trade Building, Xinjian Road, Taiyuan
Cables: 3964 TAIYUAN
Telephone: 23274

INNER MONGOLIA BRANCH
Address: 24 Zhongshan Road, Hohhot
Cables: 0427 HOHHOT

LIAONING NATIVE PRODUCE BRANCH
Address: 139 Stalin Road, Dalian
Cables: PRODAIREN DALIAN

LIAONING ANIMAL BY-PRODUCTS BRANCH
Address: 139 Stalin Road, Dalian
Cables: BYPRODUCTS DALIAN

JILIN BRANCH
Address: 81 Stalin Street, Changchun
Cables: PROKIRIN CHANGCHUN
Telephone: 27156, 26054

HEILONGJIANG BRANCH
Address: 55 Heping Road, Harbin
Cables: HNAIEC HARBIN
Telephone: 52956

SHANGHAI TEA BRANCH
Address: 74 Dianchi Road, Shanghai
Cables: NATIONTEA SHANGHAI
Telex: 33068 SHETA CN
Telephone: 216896

SHANGHAI NATIVE PRODUCE BRANCH
Address: 18 Dianchi Road, Shanghai
Cables: CHINAPROCO SHANGHAI
Telex: 33060 CNPCS CN
Telephone: 215680, 216126

SHANGHAI ANIMAL BY-PRODUCTS BRANCH
Address:
   23 Zhongshan Road E. 1, Shanghai
Cables: BYPRODUCTS SHANGHAI
Telex: 33065 ANIBY CN
Telephone: 212327

JIANGSU BRANCH
Address: 50 Zhonghua Road, Nanjing
Cables: CHINATEA NANJING
Telephone: 23696

ZHEJIANG BRANCH
Address: Miahexiang, Hangzhou
Cables: CHINATUHSU HANGZHOU
Telex: 35103 TUNSU CN
Telephone: 5101

ZHEJIANG TEA BRANCH
Address: Weinin Road, Hangzhou
Cables: NATIONTEA HANGZHOU

ANHUI BRANCH
Address: 135 Hongxing Road, Hefei
Cables: ANHUITUHSU HEFEI

FUJIAN BRANCH
Address: Foreign Trade Building, Fuzhou
Cables:
   PROFUKIEN or BYPRODUCTS FUZHOU
Telephone: 33787

FUJIAN TEA BRANCH
Address: Foreign Trade Building, Fuzhou
Cables: NATIONTEA FUZHOU

JIANGXI BRANCH
Address: Foreign Trade Building, Nanchang
Cables: 5420 Nanchang

SHANDONG NATIVE PRODUCE BRANCH
Address: 16 Baoding Road, Qingdao
Cables: CUSNP QINGDAO
Telephone: 24506

SHANDONG ANIMAL BY-PRODUCTS BRANCH
Address: 24 Hubei Road, Qingdao
Cables: BY-PRODUCTS QINGDAO
Telephone: 28739

HENAN NATIVE PRODUCE BRANCH
Address: 6 Wenhua Road, Zhengzhou
Cables: 5509 Zhengzhou

HENAN ANIMAL BY-PRODUCTS BRANCH
Address: 6 Wenhua Road, Zhengzhou
Cables: BY PRODUCTS ZHENGZHOU

HUBEI NATIVE PRODUCE BRANCH
Address: 766 Zhongshan Street, Hankou
Cables: PROWUHAN HANKOU

HEBEI ANIMAL BY-PRODUCTS BRANCH
Address: 56 Dongting Street, Hankou

HUBEI TOBACCO, RAMIE AND TEA BRANCH
Address: 79 Yanjiang Street, Hankou
Cables: TORAMTEA HANKOU

HUNAN BRANCH
Address: 103 Wuyi Road E., Changsha
Cables: TUHSU CHANGSHA
Telephone: 23349

HUNAN TEA BRANCH
Address: 103 Wuyi Road E., Changsha
Cables: HUNANTEA CHANGSHA
Telephone: 24276

GUANGDONG NATIVE PRODUCE BRANCH
Address: 486 Liu'ersan Road, Guangzhou
Cables: PROGANTION GUANGZHOU
Telex: 44072 KINB CN
Telephones: 86745, 86866

GUANGDONG ANIMAL BY-PRODUCTS BRANCH
Address: 48 Shamian Street S., Guangzhou
Cables: BYPRODUCTS GUANGZHOU
Telex: 44073 KABB CN
Telephone: 85576

GUANGDONG TEA BRANCH
Address: 486 Liu'ersan Road, Guangzhou
Cables: NATIONTEA GUANGZHOU
Telex: 44072 KINB CN
Telephone: 87848, 87986

GUANGXI BRANCH
Address: Hongxing Road, Nanning
Cables: PRONANNING NANNING
Telephone: 3653

SICHUAN NATIVE PRODUCE BRANCH
Address: 305 Jiefang Road C., Chengdu
Cables: NATIVE CHENGDU
Telephone: 8024, 5863

SICHUAN ANIMAL BY-PRODUCTS BRANCH
Address: 15 Renmin Road C., Chengdu
Cables: BYPRODUCTS CHENGDU
Telephone: 5864, 5347

SICHUAN TEA BRANCH
Address: 305 Jiefang Road C., Chengdu
Cables: 0674 CHENGDU

GUIZHOU BRANCH
Address: 13 Beijing Road, Guiyang
Cables: 3964 GUIYANG

YUNNAN NATIVE PRODUCE BRANCH
Address: 113 Huashan Road S., Kunming
Cables: PROEXCORP KUNMING
Telephone: 4339

YUNNAN ANIMAL BY-PRODUCTS BRANCH
Address: 113 Huashan Road S., Kunming
Cables: BYPRODUCTS KUNMING

YUNNAN TEA BRANCH
Address: 113 Huashan Road S., Kunming
Cables: TEAEXCORP KUNMING
Telephone: 3286

SHAANXI BRANCH
Address: 210 Xiyi Road, Xi'an
Cables: TUHSU XIAN

GANSU BRANCH
Address: 28 Dingxu Road, Lanzhou
Cables: CHINAPROCO LANZHOU

QINGHAI BRANCH
Address: 65 Dazhong Street, Xining
Cables: 3964 XINING

NINGXIA BRANCH
Address: 8 Funing Street, Yinchuan
Cables: 1120 YINCHUAN
Telephone: 4048

XINJIANG NATIVE PRODUCE BRANCH
Address: 10 Tuanjie Road, Urumqi
Cables: 2496 URUMQI

XINJIANG ANIMAL BY-PRODUCTS BRANCH
Address: 10 Tuanjie Road, Urumqi
Cables: BYPRODUCTS URUMQI

Hong Kong and Macao Agents

TECK SOON HONG LTD.
Address:
  37-39 Connaught Road W., Hong Kong
Cables: STILLON HONGKONG
Telephone: 5-456041

NAM KWONG TRADING CO.
Address:
  Nan Tung Bank Building, Rua da Praia Grande 65-A, Macao
Cables: NAMKWONG MACAO
Telephone: 84255

China National Textiles Import and Export Corporation

Major Import and Export Items:
  Raw silk, spun silk, tussah silk, tussah spun silk;
  Ginned cotton, cotton yarn;
  Raw wool, woollen yarn, blended woollen yarn;
  Synthetic fibres, spun rayon yarn;
  Grey, bleached, dyed, printed and yarn-dyed piece goods;
  Linen, blended fabrics, velvets;
  Worsted and woollen piece goods, plush, camelwood interlining, blankets;
  Silk piece goods, tussh silk pongee, synthetic fibre piece goods, mixed silk-rayon piece goods, dyed, printed, yarn-dyed and jacquard silk piece goods, ready-made silk goods, silk embroidery, damask;
  Knitwear in pure silk,, cotton, wool, synthetic and blended fibres;
  Garments for men, women and children, infants sets;
  Other textile goods of every-day use.

HEAD OFFICE

Address: 82 Donganmen Street, Beijing
Cables: CHINATEX BEIJING
Telex: 22280 CNTEX CN
Telephone: 553793

BEIJING BRANCH
Address:
  No. 1 Building, Fuwai Street, Beijing
Cables: PEKITEX BEIJING
Telex: 22148 PETEX CN
Telephone: 893203

TIANJIN BRANCH
Address: 114 Dagu Road C., Tianjin
Cables: CHINATEX TIANJIN
Telex: 22508 TJTEX CN
Telephone: 30707

HEBEI BRANCH
Address: 8 Jichang Road, Shijiazhuang
Cables: CHINATEX SHIJIAZHUANG
Telephone: 553793

LIAONING BRANCH
Address: 139 Stalin Road, Dalian
Cables: CHINATEX DALIAN
Telephone: 26100

LIAONING GARMENTS BRANCH
Address: 139 Stalin Road, Dalian
Cables: GARMENTS DALIAN
Telex: 86154 LDTEX CN

SHANGHAI BRANCH
Address:
  27 Zhongshan Road E. 1, Shanghai
Cables: TEXTILE SHANGHAI
Telex: 33055 SHTEX CN
Telephone: 218400

SHANGHAI GARMENTS BRANCH
Address:
  27 Zhongshan Road E. 1, Shanghai
Cables: GARMENTS SHANGHAI
Telex: 33056 GAREX CN
Telephone: 218500

SHANGHAI SILK BRANCH
Address: 17 Zhongshan E. 1, Shanghai
Cables: CHISICORP SHANGHAI
Telex: 33059 CTSSB CN
Telephone: 215770

JIANGSU BRANCH
Address: 50 Zhonghua Road, Nanjing
Cables: CHINATEX NANJING
Telephone: 44841

JIANGSU GARMENTS BRANCH
Address: 1 Baixia Road, Nanjing
Cables: GARMENTS NANJING
Telephone: 44583

JIANGSU SILK BRANCH
Address: 1 Baixia Road, Nanjing
Cables: CHISICORP NANJING

FUJIAN BRANCH
Address: Foreign Trade Building, Fuzhou
Cables: CHINATEX FUZHOU
Telephone: 33957

SHANDONG BRANCH
Address: 78 Zhongshan Road, Qingdao
Cables: CHINATEX QINGDAO
Telephone: 24058

HENAN BRANCH
Address: 6 Wenhua Road, Zhengzhou
Cables: TEXTILE ZHENGZHOU
Telephone: 6450 or 3356

HUBEI BRANCH
Address: 32 Huangpi Road, Wuhan
Cables: TEXTILE WUHAN

HUNAN BRANCH
Address: 103 Wuyi Road E., Changsha
Cables: HNTEXS CHANGSHA

GUANGDONG BRANCH
Address: 255 Yenan Road 2, Guangzhou
Cable: CANTEX GUANGZHOU
Telex: 44071 KITTEX CN
Telephone: 31750

GUANGDONG SILK BRANCH
Address: 255 Yenan Road 2, Guangzhou

Hong Kong and Macao Agents

CHINA RESOURCES COMPANY
Address:
 Causeway Centre, Gloucester Road, Hong Kong
Cables: CIREXP HONGKONG
Telephone: 5-7569111

NAM KWONG TRADING CO.
Address:
 Nan Tung Bank Building, Rua da Praia Grande, 65-A, Macao
Cables: NAMKWONG MACAO
Telephone: 84255

China National Light Industrial Products Imports and Export Corporation

Major Import and Export items:
 General merchandise;
 Paper, paper board and pulp;
 Glazed porcelain ware and wall tiles;
 Electric appliances;
 Radio sets, TV sets;
 Photographic and cinematographic equipment and supplies;
 Stationery, musical instruments and sports goods;
 Toys;
 Leather shoes and other leather products.

HEAD OFFICE

Address: 82 Donganmen Street, Beijing
Cables: INDUSTRY BEIJING
Telex: 22282 LIGHT CN
Telephone: 556749

BEIJING BRANCH
Address: 76 Changan Street W., Beijing
Cables: INDUSPK BEIJING
Telex: 22142 LITPK CN
Telephone: 335906

TIANJIN BRANCH
Address: 172 Liaoning Road, Tianjin
Cables: INDUSTRY TIANJIN
Telex: 22506 TJLIP CN
Telephone: 23882

TIANJIN STATIONERY AND SPORTING GOODS BRANCH
Address: 172 Liaoning Road, Tianjin
Cables: STASPORT TIANJIN
Telex: 22506 TJLIP CN
Telephone: 30732

HEBEI BRANCH
Address: 52 Beima Road, Shijiazhuang
Cables: INDUSTRY SHIJIAZHUANG
Telephone: 1645

INNER MONGOLIA BRANCH
Address: Hohhot
Cables: 4349 HOHHOT
Telephone: 3585

LIAONING BRANCH
Address: 110 Stalin Road, Dalian
Cables: INDUSTRY DALIAN
Telephone: 24441

JILIN BRANCH
Address: 81 Stalin Street, Changchun
Cables: INDUSTRY CHANGCHUN
Telephone: 27011-350

HEILONGJIANG BRANCH
Address: 53 Heping Road, Harbin
Cables: 6110 HARBIN
Telephone: 52539

SHANGHAI BRANCH
Address: 128 Huqiu Road, Shanghai
Cables: INDUSTRY SHANGHAI
Telex: 33054 INDUS CN
Telephone: 216858

SHANGHAI TOYS IMPORT AND EXPORT CORPORATION
Address: 165 Puan Road, Shanghai
Cables: CHINATOYS SHANGHAI
Telex: 33037 TOYS CN
Telephone: 288640

JIANGSU BRANCH
Address: 50 Zhonghua Road, Nanjing
Cables: INDUSTRY NANJING
Telex: 34105 INDNK CN
Telephone: 44447

ZHEJIANG BRANCH
Address: 190 Baochu Road, Hangzhou
Cables: INDUSTRY HANGZHOU
Telephone: 25396

ANHUI BRANCH
Address: 135 Hongxing Road, Hefei
Cables: 0756 Hefei

FUJIAN BRANCH
Address: Foreign Trade Building, Fuzhou
Cables: INDUSTRY FUZHOU
Telephone: 31305

SHANDONG BRANCH
Address: 8 Tianjin Road, Qingdao
Cables: INDUSTRY QINGDAO
Telephone: 27251

HENAN BRANCH
Address: 6 Wenhua Road, Zhengzhou
Cables: INDUSTRY ZHENGZHOU
Telephone: 4463

HUBEI BRANCH
Address: 75 Shengli Street, Hankou
Cables: INDUSTRY HANKOU
Telephone: 25419

HUNAN BRANCH
Address: 103 Wuyi Road E., Changsha
Cables: INDUSTRY CHANGSHA
Telephone: 22510

GUANGZHOU GENERAL MERCHANDISE EXPORT DEPARTMENT
Address: Foreign Trade Centre, Guangzhou
Cables: LIED GUANGZHOU
Telephone: 30849-688

GUANGDONG BRANCH
Address: 2 Qiaoguang Road, Guangzhou
Cables: INDUKT GUANGZHOU
Telex: 44078 LECKB CN
Telephone: 31237

GUANGXI BRANCH
Address: Hongxing Road, Nanning
Cables: INDUSTRY NANNING
Telephone: 4914

SICHUAN BRANCH
Address: 15 Renmin Road C., Chengdu
Cables: INDUSTRY CHENGDU
Telephone: 5738

SHAANXI BRANCH
Address: 210 Xiyi Road, Xi'an
Cables: INDUSTRY XIAN
Telephone: 23044

XINJIANG BRANCH
Address: 17 Tianchi Road, Urumqi
Cables: INDUSTRY URUMQI
Telephone: 2366

Hong Kong and Macao Agents

HUA YUAN CO.
Address:
    8-12 Stewart Road, Wanchai, Hong Kong
Cables: HYCOMP HONGKONG
Telephone: 5-7569540

NAM KWONG TRADING CO.
Address:
    Nan Tung Bank Building, Rua da Praia Grande, 65-A, Macao
Cables: NAMKWONG MACAO
Telephone: 84255

China National Arts and Crafts Import and Export Corporation

Major Export Items:
   Porcelain and pottery; jewellery; drawnwork and embroidery; ivory and jade carvings; lacquerware; cloisonne; paintings; calligraphy; curios and replicas; straw, wicker, bamboo and rattan woven articles; furniture and other handicrafts.

Major Import Items:
Elephant tusks, precious stones, jade and jadeite, rosewood, teak, sandalwood, mahogany, glass beads, rattan canes, nylon straps, organdy, crash linen, cotton batiste, etc.

HEAD OFFICE

Address: 82 Donganmen Street, Beijing
Cables: ARTCHINA BEIJING
Telex: 22155 CNART CN
Telephone: 552187

BEIJING BRANCH
Address: 1 Xijiaominxiang Beijing
Cables: PEKARTCO BEIJING
Telephone: 754189
Telex: 22334 BJART ON

BEIJING JEWELLERY BRANCH
Address:
No. 1 Building, Fuwai Street, Beijing
Cables: PEKJEWECO BEIJING
Telex: 22188 PEKJW CN
Telephone: 891315

BEIJING DRAWNWORK BRANCH
Address: 22 Fuwai Street, Beijing
Cables: PEKEMP BEIJING
Telex: 22495 BJEMB CN
Telephone: 892838

TIANJIN BRANCH
Address: 135 Tangshan Road, Tianjin
Cables: ARTS TIANJIN
Telex: 23507 TJART CN
Telephone: 31539

HEBEI BRANCH
Address: 8 Jichang Road, Shijiazhuang
Cables: CRAFTS SHIJIAZHUANG
Telephone: 1638

INNER MONGOLIA BRANCH
Address: 84 Zhongshan Road W., Hohhot
Cables: 4349
Telephone: 3585

LIAONING BRANCH
Address: 2 Hongyuan Street, Dalian
Cables: ARTS DALIAN
Telephone: 35407

JILIN BRANCH
Address: 81 Stalin Street, Changchun
Cables: 7177 CHANGCHUN
Telephone: 22225

HEILONGJIANG BRANCH
Address: 53 Heping Road, Harbin
Cables: 6120 HARBIN
Telephone: 52362 or 52539

SHANGHAI BRANCH
Address: 16 Zhongshan Road E. 1, Shanghai
Cables: ARTSCRAFTS SHANGHAI
Telex: 33053 ARTEX CN
Telephone: 212100 or 218357

JIANGSU BRANCH
Address: 50 Zhonghua Road, Nanjing
Cables: ARTS NANJING
Telephone: 44959

ZHEJIANG BRANCH
Address: Zhejiang Hotel, Hangzhou
Cables: ZJARTS HANGZHOU
Telephone: 43277

ANHUI BRANCH
Address: 135 Hongxing Road, Hefei
Cables: 0756 HEFEI
Telephone: 2323

FUJIAN BRANCH
Address: Foreign Trade Building, Fuzhou
Cables: ARTCRAFT FUZHOU
Telephone: 31632

FUJIAN DRAWNWORK BRANCH
Address: Foreign Trade Building, Fuzhou
Cables: ARTCRAFT FUZHOU

JIANGXI BRANCH
Address: 401 Zhongshan Road, Jingdezhen
Cables: POTTERY JINGDEZHEN

SHANDONG BRANCH
Address: 14 Baoding Road, Qingdao
Cables: CRAFT QINGDAO
Telephone: 24060

HENAN BRANCH
Address: 6 Wenhua Road, Zhenghou
Cables: POTTERY ZHENGZHOU
Telephone: 4463

HUBEI BRANCH
Address: 75 Shengli Street, Hankou
Cables: HPCRAFTS HANKOU
Telephone: 25419

HUNAN BRANCH
Address: 103 Wuyi Road E., Changsha
Cables: HNARTS CHANGSHA
Telephone: 24976

GUANGDONG BRANCH
Address: 2 Qiaoguang Road, Guangzhou
Cables: ARTCANTON GUANGZHOU
Telex: 44029 KCACB CN
Telephone: 34208

GUANGZHOU PORCELAIN EXPORT DEPARTMENT
Address: Foreign Trade Centre, Guangzhou
Cables: POTTERY GUANGZHOU
Telephone: 30849-691

GUANGZHOU ARTS AND CRAFTS EXPORT DEPARTMENT
Address: Foreign Trade Centre, Guangzhou
Cables: 5050 GUANGZHOU
Telephone: 22318-349

GUANGXI BRANCH
Address: Hongxing Road, Nanning
Cables: ARTCRAFT NANNING
Telephone: 4909

YUNNAN BRANCH
Address: 148 Huashan Road S., Kunming
Cables: YUNAPRO KUNMING
Telephone: 5105

Hong Kong and Macao Agents

CHINESE ARTS & CRAFTS (H.K.) LTD.
Address:
233-239, Nathan Road, Garley Building, Kowloon, Hong Kong
Cables: CACAGENT HONGKONG
Telephone: 3-670061

NAM KWONG TRADING CO.
Address:
Nan Tung Bank Building, Rua da Praia Grande, 65-A, Macao
Telephone: 84255

China National Chemicals Import and Export Corporation

Major Import and Export Items:
Petroleum and petroleum products;
Industrial chemicals;
Rubber, rubber tires, rubber and latex products;
Chemical fertilizers, agricultural pesticides;
Pharmaceuticals, medicines, medical instruments and supplies, surgical dressings;
Chemical reagents;
Dyestuffs and pigments;
Paints and printing ink,

HEAD OFFICE

Address: Erligou, Xijiao, Beijing
Cables: SINOCHEM BEIJING
Telex: 22243 CHEMI CN
Telephone: 891289

BEIJING BRANCH
Address:
190 Chaoyangmennei Street, Beijing
Cables: SINOCHEMIP BEIJING
Telephone: 552126

TIANJIN BRANCH
Address: 171 Jianshe Road, Tianjin
Cables: SINOCHEM or NICIPHARM TIANJIN
Telex: 22510 TJCHM CN
Telephone: 30463

HEBEI BRANCH
Address: 8 Jichang Road, Shijiazhuang
Cables: SINOCHEM SHIJIAZHUANG
Telephone: 1608

LIAONING PETROLEUM BRANCH
Address: 135 Stalin Road, Dalian
Cables: SINOCHEMIR DALIAN
Telephone: 27379

LIAONING CHEMICALS AND PHARMACEUTICALS BRANCH
Address: 135 Stalin Road, Dalian
Cables: SINOCHEMIR DALIAN
Telephone: 26717 or 24689

SHANGHAI BRANCH
Address: 27 Zhongshan Road E. 1, Shanghai
Cables: SINOCHEMIS SHANGHAI
Telex: 33044 CCIEE CN
Telephone: 210894

JIANGSU BRANCH
Address: 50 Zhonghua Road, Nanjing
Cables: SINOCHEM NANJING
Telex: 34105 INDNK CN
Telephone: 24813

ZHEJIANG BRANCH
Address: 22 Baochu Road, Hangzhou
Cables: SINOCHEMIS HANGZHOU
Telephone: 27782

FUJIAN BRANCH
Address: 1 Jianbing Road, Fuzhou
Cables: SINICHEM FUZHOU
Telephone: 34177

SHANDONG BRANCH
Address: 82 Zhongshan Road, Qingdao
Cables: SINOCHEMAO QINGDAO
Telephone: 26816

GUANGDONG BRANCH
Address: 61 Yanjiang Road 1, Guangzhou
Cables: SINOCHEMIC GUANGZHOU
Telex: 44076 HAGON CN
Telephone: 85531

Hong Kong and Macao Agents

CHINA RESOURCES COMPANY
Address:
   Causeway Centre, Gloucester Road, Hong Kong
Cables: CIRECHEM HONGKONG
Telephone: 5-7569111

NAM KWONG TRADING COMPANY
Address:
   Nan Tung Bank Building, Rua da Praia Grande, 65-A, Macao
Cables: NAMKWONG MACAO
Telephone: 84255

China National Metals and Minerals Import and Export Corporation

Major Import and Export Items:
   Rolled steels, steel pipe, steel wire, steel wire ropes, steel cable, steel scrap, pig iron, iron ore;
   Non-ferrous metals, extruded and finished products, high-purity metals, precious and rare metals, non-ferrous metal ores;
   Coal, coke;
   Cement, building stone, bricks and tiles, other building materials, stone articles;
   Non-metallic ores and minerals, mineral ores and powders, aluminia, all kinds of clays, bentonite, etc;
   Refractory materials;
   Hardware for building, fasteners;
   Cast iron products and other metal products.

HEAD OFFICE

Address:
   Erligou, Xijiao, Beijing
Cables: MINMETALS BEIJING
Telex: 22241 MINET CN
Telephone: 892376

BEIJING BRANCH
Address:
   190 Chaoyangmen Street, Beijing
Cables: MINMET BEIJING
Telephone: 551454

TIANJIN BRANCH
Address: 319 Heping Road, Tianjin
Cables: MINMETALS TIANJIN
Telephone: 22370

HEBEI BRANCH
Address: 52 Beima Road, Shijiazhuang
Cables: MINMENTALS SHIJIAZHUANG
Telephone: 8510

LIAONINC METALS BRANCH
Address: 143 Stalin Road, Dalian
Cables: MINMETALS DALIAN
Telephone: 23981

LIAONING MINERALS BRANCH
Address: 143 Stalin Road, Dalian
Cables: MINMETALS DALIAN
Telephone: 23981

SHANGHAI BRANCH
Address: 27 Zhongshan Road E.1, Shanghai
Cables: MINMETALS SHANGHAI
Telephone: 219242

JIANGSU BRANCH
Address: 50 Zhonghua Road, Nanjing
Cables: MINMETALS NANJING
Telephone: 23937

ZHEJIANG BRANCH
Address: 221 Baochu Road, Hangzhou
Cables: MINMETALS HANGZHOU
Telephone: 27787

FUJIAN BRANCH
Address: Foreign Trade Building, Fuzhou
Cables: MINMETALS FUZHOU
Telephone: 34535

SHANDONG BRANCH
Address: 9 Tangyi Road, Qingdao
Cables: MINMETALS QINGDAO
Telephone: 24430

HUNAN BRANCH
Address: 103 Wuyi Road E., Changsha
Cables: MINMETALS CHANGSHA

GUANGDONG BRANCH
Address: 61 Yanjiang Road 1, Guangzhou
Cables: MINMETALS GUANGZHOU
Telex: 44077 WUJIN CN
Telephone: 85647

GUANGXI BRANCH
Address: Hongxing Road, Nanning
Cables: MINMETALS NANNING
Telephone: 2668

YUNNAN BRANCH
Address: 148 Huashan Road S., Kunming
Telex: 0674 KUNMING
Telephone: 2983 or 4669

Hong Kong and Macao Agents

CHINA RESOURCES COMPANY
Address:
  Causeway Centre, Gloucester Road, Hong Kong
Cables: MINERALS HONGKONG
Telephone: 5-7569111

NAM KWONG TRADING COMPANY
Address:
  Nan Tung Bank Building, Rua da Praia Grande, 65-A, Macao
Telephone: 84255

China National Machinery Import and Export Corporation

Major Import Items:
  Metallurgical machinery;
  Mining equipment;
  Petrochemical equipment;
  Transportation equipment and vehicles;
  Building machinery;
  Hoisting equipment;
  Agricultural machinery;
  Machinery for light industry.

Major Export Items:
  Vessels, marine diesel engines, equipment for ships;
  Rolling stock;
  Complete plants and technology;
  Textile machinery and accessories;
  Building machinery, lifts and excavators;
  Cereals, oils and foodstuffs processing equipment, farm and forestry products processing equipment, farm machinery;
  Rubber-making machinery;
  Hand tools, agricultural implements;
  Instruments and meters.

HEAD OFFICE

Address: Erligou, Xijiao, Beijing
Cables: MACHIMPEX BEIJING
Telex: 22242 CMIEC CN
Telephone: 891974

BEIJING BRANCH
Address:
  190 Chaoyangmennei Street, Beijing
Cables: MACHBRANCH BEIJING
Telephone: 553504

TIANJIN BRANCH
Address: 14 Zhangde Road, Tianjin
Cables: MACHIMPEX TIANJIN
Telex: 22509 TJMAC CN
Telephone: 30283 or 32641

HEBEI BRANCH
Address: 52 Beima Road, Shijiazhuang
Cables: MACHIMPEX SHIJIAZHUANG
Telephone: 1608

SHANGHAI BRANCH
Address:
  27 Zhongshan Road E. 1, Shanghai
Cables: MACHIMPEX SHANGHAI
Telex: 33066 SHCMC CN
Telephone: 215066

JIANGSU BRANCH
Address: 50 Zhonghua Road, Nanjing
Cables: MACHIMPEX NANJING
Telephone: 25922

ZHEJIANG BRANCH
Address: 221 Baochu Road, Huangzhou
Cables: MACHIMPEX HANGZHOU
Telex: 35014 MACHI CN
Telephone: 21764

FUJIAN BRANCH
Address: 1 Jianbing Road, Fuzhou
Cables: MACHIMPEX FUZHOU
Telephone: 34088 or 34471

SHANDONG BRANCH
Address: 82 Zhongshan Road, Qingdao
Cables: MACHIMPEX QINGDAO
Telephone: 27385

HUBEI BRANCH
Address: 75 Shengli Street, Hankou
Cables: MACHIMPEX HANKOU
Telephone: 22201

GUANGDONG BRANCH
Address: 61 Yanjiang Road 1, Guangzhou
Cables: MACHIMPEX GUANGZHOU
Telex: 44076 HAGON CN
Telephone: 85531

Hong Kong and Macao Agents

CHINA RESOURCES COMPANY
Address:
   Causeway Centre, Gloucester Road, Hong Kong
Cables: CIRECO HONGKONG
Telephone: 5-7569111

NAM KWONG TRADING COMPANY
Address:
   Nan Tung Bank Building, Rua da Praia Grande, 65-A, Macao
Cables: NAMKWONG MACAO
Telephone: 84255

China National Instruments Import and Export Corporation

The China National Instruments Import and Export Corporation was set up in February 1979 to meet the requirements of socialist modernization, especially the development of science and technology. It handles imports only for the time being.

Major Import Items:
   Telecommunications equipment;
   Electronic computers;
   TV transmitting equipment;
   Radio broadcasting equipment;
   Radio positioning and ranging equipment;
   Electronic components;
   Nuclear instruments;
   Electric instruments;
   Physical-optical instruments;
   Electronic-optical instruments;
   Optical metrological instruments;
   Geodesic and aerophotogrammetric surveying instruments;
   Electronic-magnetic analysis instruments;
   Material testing machines and equipment;
   Geophysical surveying instruments;
   Pollution testing equipment;
   Laboratory instruments and appliances;
   Industrial control instruments;

Address: Erligou, Xijiao, Beijing
Cables: INSTRIMPEX BEIJING
Telex: 22304 CHEC CN
Telephone: 890931

China National Technical Import Corporation

The China National Technical Import Corporation specializes in the import of complete plants and, according to state plans, government trade agreements, loan agreements and market needs, importing new techniques (including technological processes, equipment manufacture and the transfer of technology); purchasing all kinds of complete plants, production lines, main equipment, parts and supplies, as well as machine tools, instruments and meters, experimental installations, electronic computers, and raw materials and accessories for imported projects; contracting with foreign businesses for engineering design, technical consultation and plant transformation; undertaking Chinese and foreign compensatory trade, co-production and joint ventures; engaging foreign technicians for imported projects and sending training personnel abroad. The corporation also assists in the export of Chinese scientific techniques.

This corporation undertakes the above import and export activities under the commission of all departments and companies at home, and also acts as agent for foreign enterprises in China.

Address: Erligou, Xijiao, Beijing
Cables: TECHIMPORT BEIJING
Telex: 22244 CNTIC CN
Telephone: 890931

China National Foreign Trade Transportation Corporation

The National Foreign Trade Transportation Corporation (CNFTTC) is a state-owned enterprise under the Ministry of Foreign Trade. It shares the work of the China National Foreign Trade Import and Export Corporations and also deals with orders from them. It undertakes the transport of China's imports and exports. CNFTTC has branch offices at ports and border stations throughout the country. These branches oversee the delivery of import cargo to end-users and export cargo to the receivers abroad.

Its scope of business is:
To organize the transportation of imports and exports by sea, land, air and mail;
To charter vessels and bulk space;
To arrange the handing over or taking delivery of cargo and documents at China's ports and border stations;
To accept orders from principals in China for storage and to dispatch to end-users cargo imported by sea;
To accept or deliver, distribute or dispatch imports and exports by air, except perishable goods;
To arrange international through transportation of imports and exports in transit via China;

To arrange the work for trucks exclusively carrying foreign-trade cargo;

To make arrangements for transportation within China of foreign exhibits to be shown in China.

Address: Erligou, Xijiao, Beijing
Cables: SINOTRANS BEIJING
Telex:
  22153 TRANS CN
  22154 TRANS CN
  22265 TRANS CN

China National Chartering Corporation

The China National Chartering Corporation is a state-owned enterprise which handles the chartering of vessels and booking of shipping space. It is entrusted by the China National Foreign Trade Transportation Corporation to charter vessels on the international market, and operate and sublet them on behalf of the charterers.

The China National Chartering Corporation also negotiates the booking of shipping space on behalf of the China National Foreign Trade Transportation Corporation. It has therefore entered into agreements with many shipping companies to dispatch vessels regularly to our ports or foreign ports to carry China's import and export cargo.

This corporation also acts as agent for foreign charterers wishing to charter vessels or book shipping space.

Address: Erligou, Xijiao, Beijing
Cables: ISINOCHART BEIJING
Telex:
  22153 TRANS CN
  22154 TRANS CN
  22265 TRANS CN

China National Packaging Import and Export Corporation

This corporation's original name was "China National Export Commodities Packaging Corporation." It was changed to the present name in August 1980 and is under the Ministry of Foreign Trade.

It mainly handles the import and export of packaging materials, containers, machinery and tools.

Packaging Materials: Corrugated medium, kraft paper, white board with grey back, white board with white back, sack kraft paper, white card-board, stencil steel board, aluminium-foil laminated paper, decorative paper for packaging; all kinds of plastic film, metallized film, laminated material; ink, coating, adhesives, bronze powder and jute cloth.

Packaging Containers: paper, plastic and metal containers.

Packaging Machines and Tools: Corrugators, die cutting machines, paper-bag makers, crate nailing machine, can makers, metal drum makers, glass bottle manufacturing machines, closure and cap makers, moulds; printing machines, plate making equipment; blow moulding machines, injection moulding machines, plastic foaming machines, blow and cast extruders, laminating machines, plastic bag makers; vacuum packers, shrink wrap, blister pack, forming, filling, sealing, casing, cartoning, strapping, labelling, marking and weighing machines; testing instruments and equipment for packaging materials and containers.

The corporation also undertakes agency business as entrusted by foreign clients, and contracts for the processing and converting of packaging machines and materials with raw materials supplied by foreign clients and by joint ventures with foreign interests to produce packaging machines and materials.

Address: 2 Changan Street E., Beijing
Cables: CHINAPACK BEIJING
Telex: 22168 METPK CN
Telephone: 557610

China Foreign Trade Consultation and Technical Service Corporation

Address: 2 Changan Street, E., Beijing
Cables: CONSULTEC BEIJING
Telephone: 553031, ext. 561

China National Machinery and Equipment Import and Export Corporation

The China National Machinery and Equipment Import and Export Corporation is a state foreign trade enterprise under the First Ministry of Machine Building.

Major Export and Import Items:
  Complete plants;
  Machine tools, forging and casting equipment;
  Heavy-duty machinery, mining machinery;
  Power-generating machinery;
  Electricity generating sets, electric motors, welding machines, electric appliances, cables, porcelain insulators, switches, electric instruments and meters;
  Motor vehicles and parts;

Pumps, pneumatic tools, air compressors, valves;
Printing machinery, refrigerating equipment, wood-working machinery;
Laboratory instruments, surveying instruments, optical instruments, educational apparatus, industrial electric furnaces, photographic and cinematographic equipment;
Bearings, cutting tools, measuring tools, grinding tools, electric tools.

HEAD OFFICE

Address:
12 Fuxingmenwai Street, Beijing
Cables: EQUIPEX BEIJING
Telex: 22186 EQUIP CN
Telephone: 866462

BEIJING BRANCH
Address:
190 Chaoyangmennei Street, Beijing
Cables: EQUIBRANCH BEIJING
Telephone: 556229

TIANJIN BRANCH
Address: 14 Zhangde Road, Tianjin
Cables: EQUIPEX TIANJIN
Telex: 22509 TJMAC CN
Telephone: 30283 or 34559

HEBEI BRANCH
Address: 9 Hezu Road, Shijiazhuang
Cables: EQUIMPEX SHIJIAZHUANG
Telephone: 9763

LIAONING BRANCH
Address: 145 Stalin Road, Dalian
Cables: EQUIMPEX DALIAN
Telephone: 23824

SHANGHAI BRANCH
Address:
958 Beijing Road W., Shanghai
Cables: EQUIMPEX SHANGHAI
Telephone: 537338

JIANGSU BRANCH
Address: 50 Zhonghua Road, Nanjing
Cables: EQUIMPEX NANJING
Telephone: 25922

ZHEJIANG BRANCH
Address:
67 Tianmushan Road, Hangzhou
Cables: EQUIMPEX HANGZHOU
Telephone: 25072 or 23883

ANHUI BRANCH
Address: 216 Changjiang Road, Hefei
Cables: EQUIMPEX HEFEI

FUJIAN BRANCH
Address: 1 Shengfu Road, Fuzhou
Cables: EQUIMPEX FUZHOU
Telephone: 33902 or 31490

JIANGXI BRANCH
Address: 4th Jiaotong Road, Nanchang
Cables: EQUIMPEX NANCHENG

SHANDONG BRANCH
Address: 127 Guanxian Road, Qingdao
Cables: EQUIMPEX QINGDAO
Telephone: 24172

HUBEI BRANCH
Address: Dongdi Street, Changsha
Cables: EQUIMPEX CHANGSHA

GUANGDONG BRANCH
Address:
51 Liuhuaxincun, Xincun Highway, Guangzhou
Cables: EQUIMPEX GUANGZHOU
Telephone: 30446

GUANGXI BRANCH
Address: Minzhu Road, Nanning
Cables: EQUIMPEX NANNING
Telephone: 2943

SICHUAN BRANCH
Address: Renmin Road C., Chengdu
Cables: EQUIMPEX CHENGDU

Hong Kong and Macao Agents

CHINA RESOURCES COMPANY
Address:
Causeway Centre, Gloucester Road, Hong Kong
Cables: CIRIMP HONGKONG
Telephone: 5-756911

NAM KWONG TRADING COMPANY
Address:
Nan Tung Bank Building, Rua da Praia-Grande 65-A, Macao
Cables: NAMKWONG MACAO
Telephone: 84255

China National Aero-Technology Import and Export Corporation

The China National Aero-Technology Import

and Export Corporation is under the Third Ministry of Machine Building; it is a state enterprise which handles import and export business in aviation technology and products.

Its business scope is:

Managing the export of aero-products of various companies, including aircraft, aero-engines, meters and instruments, accessories, electrical devices as well as other machinery, meters and instruments;

Handling investment in joint ventures, co-production, processing and assembling with materials and parts supplied, and accepting orders according to customers' samples and designs;

Contracting to design and construct complete aircraft factories, repairing bases, air fields, aviation testing facilities and civil buildings, offering services of engineering and technical personnel and the manual labour of skilled and qualified workers;

Undertaking the translation of technical materials, books, periodicals on aero-products;

Introducing to China advanced aviation technology and complete sets of equipment and importing aviation electronic devices, precision parts and components and test instruments from abroad.

Address: 67 Jiaonan Street, Beijing
Cables: CAID BEIJING
Telex: 22318 AEROT CN
Telephone: 442444

China National Electronic Technology Import and Export Corporation

The China National Electronic Technology Import and Export Corporation has been set up under the Fourth Ministry of Machine Building. Its scope of business is:

Handling the import and export of electronic products, technology, equipment, parts and materials;

Processing and assembling electronic products with materials and parts supplied;

Entering into joint ventures and handling compensatory trade;

Providing technical services and labour abroad;

Acting as agents for importing needed electronic equipment for other Chinese departments.

HEAD OFFICE

Address: 49 Fuxing Road, Beijing
Cables: DZJSJCK BEIJING
Telex: 22383 FMMB CN
Telephone: 811888 or 810731-964

TIANJIN BRANCH

Address: 197 Heping Road, Tianjin
Cables: 0455 TIANJIN
Telephone: 23322

SHANGHAI BRANCH

Address: 170 Jiangxi Road C., Shanghai
Cables: 1116 SHANGHAI
Telephone: 218215

GUANGZHOU BRANCH

Address: 24 Huanghua Xincun, Guangzhou
Cables: 0263 GUANGZHOU
Telephone: 78743

SHENZHEN BRANCH

Address: P.O. Box 020, Shenzhen (Shumchun)
Cables: 5478 SHENZHEN
Telephone: 2197

China National Metallurgical Products Import and Export Corporation

The China National Metallurgical Products Import and Export Corporation is under the Ministry of Metallurgical industry. Its scope of business is:

Export of metallurgical products including mineral products, pig iron, steel, rare metals and rare-earth metals, ferro-alloys, metallurgical coking products, refractory materials, resistor rods, alumina, fluorite and magnesia;

Service of foreign compensatory trade and joint investment;

Import and export of metallurgical technology;

Import of metallurgical equipment, parts and supplies, instruments and meters;

Co-production of metallurgical (including mining) equipment and processing parts and metallurgical products with supplies materials.

HEAD OFFICE

Address: 46 Dongsi Street W., Beijing
Cables: 2250 BEIJING
Telex: 22461 MIEC CN
Telephone: 550197 or 557431-780

GUANGDONG BRANCH

Address: 48 Zhongshan Road 2, Guangzhou
Cables: 1105 GUANGZHOU
Telex: 44119 MIECG CN
Telephone: 77291-245 or 246

WUHAN BRANCH

Address: Qingshan District, Wuhan
Telephone: 62471

China Precision Machinery Import and Export Corporation

The China Precision Machinery Import and Export Corporation has been set up under the China Precision Machinery Corporation, which is a state-owned enterprise handling complete sets of precision machinery for aerospace, aircraft-building, ship-building industries, as well as general-purpose machinery. Its scope of business includes:

The import and export of precision and general-purpose machinery;

The import and export of related technologies;

Joint ventures and co-production with foreign firms;

Compensatory trade, processing and assembling with materials and parts supplied;

Services on commission.

Main Exports:

Autopilots, control instruments, radar equipment, telemetering equipment, navigation equipment, fusing devices, as well as various testing equipment, instruments and meters;

Infrared, laser and optical machinery and parts, 800,000x electron-microscopes;

Mini-motors, current converters, charges, relays, signal sources, switches, plugs and sockets;

Electronic computers, facsimile equipment, television relay vans, wire broadcasting equipment, stereo recorders;

Chemical batteries (silver-zinc batteries, acid batteries, thermo-electric batteries and watch batteries), Freon, synthetic ammonia, and various gases for industrial use;

General-purpose machinery, engineering machinery, transport machinery, light industrial machinery, agricultural machinery, medical appliances and tools, standard fasteners, and compound fixtures.

Address: 2 Yuetan Beixiaojie, Beijing
Cables: CPMIEC BEIJING
Telephone: 895012

North China Industrial Corporation

The North China Industrial Corporation is a comprehensive enterprise for industrial production and foreign trade. It handles business of processing and assembling with materials and parts supplied, compensatory trade, joint ventures, and contracting engineering designs at home and abroad.

Its imports and exports include:

Diesel engines, presses, hydraulic presses, engineering machines;

Light and heavy vehicles;

Precision machines, tools;

Optical glass, optical instruments, photographic and cinematographic equipment, testing instruments;

Chemicals, high polymer materials, paints and coatings, chemical industrial equipment;

Detonating equipment, protectors;

Special technical equipment.

Address: 47 Yuetan Street S., Beijing
Cables: NORINCO BEIJING
Telex: 22339 CNIC CN
Telephone: 862254 or 862072

China Shipbuilding Industry Corporation

This is a state corporation under the Sixth Ministry of Machine Building, whose main business is to handle the import and export of ships and marine equipment. Its business scope includes:

The export of ships up to 100,000 tons, including general cargo ships, passenger ships, tugs, engineering vessels, pleasure boats and oil drilling platforms, main and auxiliary ships' engines, deck machinery, navigation and communications equipment;

Importing equipment for building ships, ships' engines and marine instruments as well as shipbuilding technology from abroad;

Cooperation with foreign firms through joint-venture enterprises, compensation trade, co-production; ship repair, collaboration with foreign firms to set up joint ship maintenance and repair yards;

Designing for ships, shipyards and engine yards as well as technical consultation, technical services and labour for foreign shipbuilding industries.

Address: 10 Yuetan Beixiaojie, Beijing
Cables: CCSI BEIJING
Telex: 22335 CCSI CN
Telephone: 895947

China Great Wall Industrial Corporation

The China Great Wall Industrial Corporation is a comprehensive enterprise engaged in research, design and manufacture of various special-purpose precision machinery, electronic instruments, as well as vacuum, cryogenic and automatic control techniques. With several research institutions and factories attached to it, the corporation handles direct export business of its own products; deals in joint ventures with foreign firms, compensatory trade, processing and assembling with materials and parts supplied by customers; undertakes maintenance services for imported goods on commission basis; contracts for technical and civil engineering designs for overseas projects; and provides technical services.

Main Exports:

Precision machinery, such as gyroscopes, servo-actuators, hydraulic motors, pumps, valves, actuating cylinders;

Special-purpose machines, cutting tools, moulds, fuelling lorries, lane excavators, semi-trailers, truck-mounted cranes, ultra-sonic precision gas-cutting machines, high-pressure air flasks, metal hoses, corrugated tubes, stainless steel welding rods;

Electronic computers and peripherals, analog computers, radar equipment, satellite navigation equipment, telemetry and remote-control equipment, electrostatic printers, magnetic recorders, screen display and terminals.

Integrated circuits, transducers, amplifiers, accelerometers, strain gauges, crystals, relays and sockets;

Testing instruments and meters;

Medical appliances;

Vacuum and cryogenic devices;

Magnetic tapes, heads, discs and equipment for the manufacture of magnetic tapes;

Automatic candy packers, automatic-count tablet packers, duplicators, etc.

Address: P.O. Box 847, Beijing
Cables: CWIC BEIJING
Telephone: 893155

Oriental Scientific Instruments Import and Export Corporation

The Oriental Scientific Instruments Import and Export Corporation is under the Chinese Academy of Sciences. The scope of its business includes:

Exporting new materials, agents, components, devices, advanced techniques and technologies produced or developed by units under the academy;

Co-producing scientific instruments and equipment with foreign firms, processing with materials supplied, and rendering technical services;

Business of international cooperation in publication work.

Address: Sanlihe, Beijing
Cables: 2233 ASCHI CN
Telex: 22474 ASCHI

China National New Building Materials Corporation

This is an enterprise under the Ministry of Building Materials Industry. It manufactures and sells new-type building materials. It also undertakes design and work on construction using new-type building materials, and handles the import and export of new building materials and related technology and complete equipment.

Address: Zizhuyan Road, Beijing
Cables: 4554 BEIJING
Telephone: 891260

China National Seed Corporation

The China National Seed Corporation is engaged in the import and export of crop seeds, saplings, roots, bulbs, cuttings and sprouts.

Address: 16 Donghuan Road N., Beijing
Cables: 4429 BEIJING
Telephone: 593619

China National Breeding Stock Import and Export Corporation

China National Breeding Stock Import and Export Corporation is the sole concern engaged in import and export business for stud animals including cattle, sheep, goats, swine, horses, donkeys, camels, rabbits, dogs, poultry, bees and seeds of forage crops.

Address: Hepingli, Beijing
Cables: CNABSIEC BEIJING
Telephone: 464344

Tianjin Foreign Trade Corporation

The Tianjin Foreign Trade Corporation exercises unified control over the import-export trade, foreign trade transportation, chartering, export commodity packaging, and advertizing business of the Tianjin Municipality.

Address: 57 Hubei Road, Tianjin
Telephone: 34872

Shanghai Foreign Trade Corporation

The Shanghai Foreign Trade Corporation exercises unified control over the import-export trade, foreign trade transportation, chartering, export commodity packaging, storage and advertizing business of the Shanghai Municipality.

In addition to the already established foreign trade branches, an import department and the Shanghai Toys Import and Export Corporation have been set up.

Address: 27 Zhongshan Road E. 1, Shanghai
Cables: SHANTRA SHANGHAI
Telex: 33034 SIMEX CN
Telephone: 213257

Fujian Foreign Trade Corporation

Address: 1 Shanghai Road, Fuzhou
Cables: FUJIANTRACO

Guangdong Foreign Trade Corporation

Address: 2 Qiaoguang Road, Guangzhou
Cables: GDFTC GUANGZHOU
Telex: 44088 GDFTC CN

The Chinese Export Commodities Fair

GENERAL INTRODUCTION

The Chinese Export Commodities Fair is held binannually in Guangzhou during spring (April 15 — May 15) and autumn (October 15 — November 15).

The Chinese Export Commodities Fair focuses on exports. Combining trade negotiations with sample showing, the Fair is but one of China's trade activities. The Fair helps business people from all over the world make selections against samples during on-the-spot talks. Meanwhile, import negotiations for China's needed goods are carried out between Chinese importers and their foreign counterparts.

ORGANIZATION AND BUSINESS NEGOTIATION METHOD

The Fair is directed by a leading committee, consisting of a chairman and several vice-chairmen, a secretary-general and several deputy secretaries-general, and a number of committee members.

At the Fair, China's foreign trade corporations are represented by ten trade delegations dealing respectively in cereals, oils and foodstuffs; native produce and animal by-products; textiles; light industrial products; arts and crafts; metals and minerals; chemicals; instruments; machinery; and machinery and equipment. These ten trade delegations work under the leading committee.

There is a head, several deputy heads, a secretary-general and several deputy secretaries-general for each trade delegation. Commodity divisions and groups are set up to be in charge of business talks with clients at the Fair.

Contracts signed at the Fair are executed afterwards by the Chinese foreign trade corporation concerned. In case of problems arising in implementation of the contract, the pertinent Chinese foreign trade corporation will consult with the clients for clarification.

PROCEDURES FOR ATTENDING THE FAIR

Invitations are issued by the Fair or by the commercial counsellors' offices of the embassies of the People's Republic of China a month or two prior to the opening of the spring and autumn fairs to businessmen of the world to attend and negotiate import and export business.

Businessmen who wish to attend the Fair are requested to write to the relevant Chinese foreign trade corporation and specify clearly their respective firms, addresses, names of the executive members of their firms, lines of business and credit information. In case the Chinese foreign trade corporation concerned finds it necessary to conduct on-the-spot business talks, invitations to the Fair are extended.

Representatives sent by the firms invited to the Fair should apply for entry visas to Guangzhou at the Embassy or Consulate of the People's Republic of China in the country where the invited firm is located, by producing the invitation extended by the Fair and the invited firm's Letter of Recommendation certifying the representatives' status. If the applicant, for personal reasons, is unable to apply for an entry visa at the Chinese embassy or consulate in his own country, he is requested to inform in good time the Chinese embassy or consulate there of the reasons and designate the place where he wishes to have the visa to be issued, so that the Chinese embassy or consulate will be able to relay the request to the embassy or consulate concerned.

In case the People's Republic of China is not yet represented in the country or region where the invited firm is located, the applicant may apply for a visa to Guangzhou at the diplomatic representative's office in a neighbouring country by presenting the invitation extended by the Fair and his firm's letter of recommendation, or may write to China Travel Service (H.K.) Ltd. for help.

FACILITIES AT THE FAIR

At the Fair, there is an information booth handling inquiries about the Fair.

Facilities for customers' entry, banking, insurance, transportation, post and telecommunications, as well as typing and copying services, are provided.

Restaurants, retail stores and a bookstore are also available in the Fair building.

China International Trust and Investment Corporation

The China International Trust and Investment Corporation is a state-owned socialist enterprise operating under the direct leadership of the State Council of the People's Republic of China.

The function of the corporation is to introduce, absorb and apply foreign investment and advanced technology, to import advanced equipment and to bring in advanced technology for purposes of China's national construction and promoting the socialist modernization of our country pursuant to the provisions of the Law of the People's Republic of China on Joint Ventures Using Chinese and Foreign Investment and other relevant laws and regulations.

The scope of business: joint ventures using Chinese and foreign investment; compensatory trade; technical cooperation; international trust deposits and investments; real estate business; undertaking commission and acting as agents; leasing business and consulting business.

Address: 2 Qianmen Street E., Beijing
Cables: 0207 CITIC BEIJING
Telex: 22305 CITIC CN
Telephone: 753600

China Foreign Turnkey Contract Corporations

In order to meet the need of international economic cooperation, many foreign turnkey contract corporations have been set up in China.

China National Complete Plant Export Corporation

The China National Complete Plant Export Corporation undertakes turnkey jobs on complete industrial and agricultural plants in foreign countries as well as providing guidance in production techniques; this corporation also deals in the export of single items of equipment, the supply of spare parts and the training of administrative personnel. Technicians and skilled workers will be also provided for projects undertaken by this corporation.

Address: Andingmenwai, Beijing
Cables: COMPLAINT BEIJING
Telephone: 445678 or 440325

There are five special branches under the China National Complete Plant Export Corporation. They are:

Electricity Branch: Undertakes turnkey jobs on hydro-power stations, thermo-power stations, transmission lines, transforming lines, transformer sub-stations, tube and pump stations; provides guidance in production techniques; exports complete power plants; processes and assembles with materials and parts supplied; operates joint ventures and compensatory trade; provides other technical services and labour.

Address: Baiguang Road, Beijing
Cables: 7193 BEIJING
Telex: 22466 CHMEP CN
Telephone: 338601

Building Materials Industry Branch: Undertakes turnkey contracts for building materials industry; provides guidance in production techniques; exports building equipment and building materials; undertakes joint investment and compensatory trade; provides other technical services and labour.

Address: Baiwanzhuang, Beijing
Cables: CPECB BEIJING
Telephone: 8992942

Coal Branch: Undertakes turnkey jobs on coal mining projects and engineering and provides guidance in production techniques; handles export of complete mining equipment, single-item equipment, materials and parts; maintenance and servicing and the training of administrative personnel, technicians and skilled workers will also be provided; undertakes technical services and labour.

Address: Hepingli, Beijing
Cables: CNCDC BEIJING
Telex: 22494 CNCDC CN
Telephone: 463759

Chemical Branch: Undertakes turnkey contracts for the chemical industry; provides guidance in production techniques; handles exports of complete chemical industry equipment and single equipment; provides technical services, labour and technology transfers.

Address: Hepingli, Beijing
Cables: CNCIC BEIJING
Telex: 22492 CNCCC CN
Telephone: 462923

Textile Branch: Undertakes turnkey jobs for textile printing and dyeing projects; provides guidance in five production techniques; handles export of complete textile equipment, single-equipment, and parts; supplies trained administrative personnel, technicians and skilled workers; provides technical services and labour.

Address: 12 Changan Street E., Beijing
Cables: 4791 BEIJING
Telephone: 550702

China Construction Engineering Corporation

The China Construction Engineering Corporation is a state-run enterprise. It contracts for all kinds of civil and public construction projects and provides technical services and labour.

Address: Baiwanzhuang, Beijing
Cables: 22477 CCEC CN
Telephone: 8992046 or 8992445, 8992249

China Road and Bridge Engineering Company

The China Road and Bridge Engineering Company undertakes turnkey contracts on highways and bridges, provides technical services and labour.

Address: 10 Fuxing Road, Beijing
Cables: CRBECO BEIJING
Telex: 22462 COMCT CN
Telephone: 8643464 or 8643514

China Civil Engineering Construction Corporation

The China Civil Engineering Construction Corporation contracts for all kinds of railway projects and other civil engineering projects; it provides technical services and labour.

Address: 10 Fuxing Road, Beijing
Cables: CHICICON BEIJING
Telephone: 8642714 or 8643034

China Marine Industry Corporation

The China Marine Industry Corporation undertakes:
To build and repair various transport ships, dredgers, work ships, salvage vessels, tugs, harbour vessels and other auxiliary vessels;
To build fibreglass yachts;
To manufacture and supply marine diesel engines and spare parts;
To manufacture and supply anchor chains, deck machinery, pumps and other machinery for ship's use;
To provide technical and labour services.

Address: 10 Fuxing Road, Beijing
Cables: CHINAHEC BEIJING
Telex: 22462 COMCT
Telephone: 864367

China National Hydraulic Engineering Corporation

The China National Hydraulic Engineering Corporation undertakes survey and design work and installations for projects utilizing water resources; drainage planning; hydraulic and hydro-power engineering; and exports complete small hydro-power stations. Technical services and labour can also be supplied.

Address: Baiguang Road, Beijing
Cables: 3068 BEIJING
Telex: 22485 WATER CN
Telephone: 363314

China National Oil Engineering Construction Corporation

The China National Oil Engineering Construction Corporation is ready to contract projects in oil-field construction, petroleum pipelines, oil refineries, petro-chemical plants and oil depots. The corporation also provides technical and labour services.

Address: P.O. Box 766, Beijing
Cables: 3112 BEIJING
Telex: 22312 PCPRC CN
Telephone: 461854

China National Machinery Foreign Economic Technical Co-operation

The corporation undertakes turnkey contracts and engineering designs related to the products made by the First Ministry of Machinery-Building; it handles joint investment, co-production, compensation trade, technical exports and provides technical and labour services.

Address: Sanlihe Road, Beijing
Cables: MACHINTERCORP BEIJING
Telex: 22341 CMIC CN
Telephone: 867524 or 867890

China National Light Industry Foreign Engineering Corporation

The corporation undertakes turnkey contracts in light industry; provides guidance in production techniques; undertakes technical cooperation in light industry production; exchanges complete plants and single-item equipment with foreign countries and joins them in providing complete plants to third countries; jointly develops and exchanges parts, and provides technical and labour services.

Address: 12 Changan Street E., Beijing
Cables: LIGHTING BEIJING
Telephone: 554718 or 551246

Sichuan International Economic and Technical Co-operation Corporation

The corporation undertakes turnkey contracts on civil and industrial construction; highway, bridge and municipal engineering; handles exports of complete plants and parts; undertakes processing with materials supplied.

Address: 243 Shengli Road W., Chengdu
Cables: 2266 CHENGDU
Telephone: 6765 or 6760

Jiangsu International Economic and Technical Co-operation of China

The corporation undertakes turnkey contracts in industry, communications, public buildings, agriculture and forestry, water conservancy, gardens, culture and education, sports and health, commercial services; handles exports of technical equipment, and provides technical and labour services.

Address: 70 Beijing Road W., Nanjing
Cables: CJIETCC
Telephone: 32354

2. LISTING OF CHINA'S MAJOR ECONOMIC RESEARCH INSTITUTES
Compiled by the Library of the Institute of Industrial Economics,
Chinese Academy of Social Sciences

The Institute of Economics, Chinese Academy of Social Sciences

Director: Xu Dixin
Deputy Directors:
Yan Zhongping, Xu Shengwu, Dong Fureng, Sun Shangqing, Liu Guoguang
Address:
2 Yuetan Beixiaojie, Fuchengmenwai, Beijing, China
Tel: 895323
Subjects of Research:
1. Political Economy, 2. Quantitative Economy; 3. The History of Economic Thought; 4. The History of Chinese Economy; 5. Theory of Population; 6. Economics of Ecology; 7. The Economy of Hong Kong and Macao.

The Institute of Industrial Economy, Chinese Academy of Social Sciences

Director: Ma Hong
Deputy Directors:
Xue Boading, Lu Feiwen, Jiang Yiwei, Chang Xuansan, Zhou Sulian, Wu Jiajun
Address:
2 Yuetan Beixiaojie, Fuchengmenwai, Beijing, China
Tel: 891013
Subjects of Research:
1. The Industrial Economics Department: Industrial Economics, Economics of Labour, Environmental Economics, the History of Industrial Economy and Management; 2. Business Management Department: Business Management, Research in Industrial Organization and Management Systems, Research in Political and Ideological Work and Behavioural Science; 3. Modern Management Department: Modern Management, Economic Systems Analysis.

The Institute of Agricultural Economy, Chinese Academy of Social Sciences

Director: Zhan Wu
Deputy Director: Wang Gengjin
Address:
2 Yuetan Beixiaojie, Fuchengmenwai, Beijing, China
Tel: 894187

Subjects of Research:
1. Agricultural Economy; 2. Forestry Economy; 3. Animal Husbandry Economy; 4. Fisheries Economy.

The Institute of Finance, Trade and Materials Economics, Chinese Academy of Social Sciences

Director: Liu Mingfu
Deputy Directors:
Jiang Junchen, Li Gengxing, Zhou Ziming, Fang Ming, Liu Jing
Address:
2 Yuetan Beixiaojie, Fuchengmenwai, Beijing, China
Subjects of Research:
1. Domestic Commerce; 2. Foreign Trade; 3. Tourism; 4. Costs; 5. Prices; 6. Finance; 7. Banking; 8. Materials; 9. Urban Economy; 10. Economy of Overseas Chinese; 11. Accounting; 12. Services.

The Institute of World Economy, Chinese Academy of Social Sciences

Director: Qian Junrui
Deputy Directors:
Qiu Qihua, Luo Yuanzheng, Li Zong, Wan Shouhai
Address:
15 Sha Tan St. (N), Beijing, China
Tel: 443551
Subjects of Research:
1. Fundamental Theory of the World Economy; 2. Economy of the Developed Capitalist Countries; 3. Economy of the Soviet Union and East-European Countries; 4. Economy of Developing Countries; 5. International Economic Relations; 6. Statistics of the World Economy.

The Institute of Technological Economics, Chinese Academy of Social Sciences

Director: Yu Guangyuan
Deputy Directors: Li Deren, Xu Shoubo

Address:
A1 Erhuai Rd (W), Chegongzhuang, Fuchengmenwai, Beijing, China
Tel: 895531-228
Subjects of Research:
1. Theory and Method of Technological Economics; 2. Technological Economics of Energy; 3. Technological Economics of Industry; 4. Technological Economics of Agriculture; 5. Technological Economics of Transport; 6. Technological Economics of Distribution of Productive Forces; 7. Application of the Computer in Technological Economy; 8. Quantitative Economy.

The Institute of Comprehensive Transport, State Economic Commission

Director: Chang Siqi
Deputy Director: Wang Weigong
Address:
23 Shijinhuayuan, North of Dongshi, Beijing, China
Tel: 441771
Subjects of Research:
1. Comprehensive Use and Overall Development of Transport by Railway, Highway, Waterway, Civil Aviation, Pipelines, etc.; 2. Research of Technological Policies and Technological Economics of Transport.

The Economics Institute of the State Planning Commission

Director: Xue Muqiao
Deputy Directors:
Wang Xiangsheng, Sun Deshan, Lu Zhongduo, He Jianzhang, Tian Fang, Liu Suinian
Address:
2 Yuetan Beixiaojie, Fuchengmenwai, Beijing, China
Subjects of Research:
1. Theory and Method of the National Economic Plan; 2. Effects of Technological Economy and Effects of Macroeconomics; 3. World Economy; 4. The Economic History of New China.

The Economics Institute of the State Capital Construction Commission

Director: Xue Baoding
Deputy Directors:
Yang Shusheng, Bai Yulong, Lin Sanmo

Address:
State Capital Construction Commission Building, Baiwanzhuang, Western Suburbs, Beijing, China
Tel: 89922061
Subjects of Research:
1. Economics of Capital Construction; 2. Architectural Economics; 3. Technical Economics; 4. Engineering Economics; 5. Distribution of Productive Forces.

The Institute of Financial Science, Ministry of Finance

Director: Xu Yi
Deputy Directors:
Shen Jingnong, Wu Jing, Liu Zhengyan, Ge Zida, Xing Guang
Address:
Sanlihe, Fuxingmenwai, Beijing, China
Tel: 866044
Subjects of Research:
1. Distribution and Redistribution of the General Social Product and National Income; 2. The Basic Theory of Finance, State Budgets and Taxes; 3. Finance of Enterprises, Finance of Capital Construction, Finance of Administration, Culture and Education; 4. Foreign Finance and Economy; 5. The History of Finance and Economy; 6. Laws of Financial Taxation, etc.

The Institute of Banking, General Office of the People's Bank of China

Director: Sun Jimin
Deputy Directors:
Cui Qiyi, Yang Beixin, Zhang Zicun, Chen Jian
Address:
Sanlihe, Fuxingmenwai, Beijing, China
Tel: 868451
Subjects of Research:
1. China's Money and Credit; 2. The History of China's Banking; 3. International Banking.

The Research Department, General Office of the Bank of China

General Director: Lin Jixin
Deputy General Directors:
Guan Yingfu, Yao Yunfang
Address:
17 Xinjiaominxiang, Beijing, China
Tel: 330776, 332762

Subjects of Research:
1. World Economy; 2. International Finance, Money and Banking; 3. International Economic and Banking Relations.

The Rural Banking Institute, General Office of the Agricultural Bank of China

Director: Lu Hanchuan
Deputy Director: Zhou Qi
Address:
27 and 62 Xijiaominxiang, Beijing, China
Tel: 331849
Subjects of Research:
1. Research in Agricultural Banking Sciences; 2. Theoretical Research of Agricultural Economy, Rural Industrial Economy and Rural Commerce Related to Rural Banking; 3. Summing-Up of the Historical Experience of Rural Banking and Studying the Experience of Foreign Rural Banking; 4. Research on Currency Circulation and Free Lending in Rural Areas; 5. Gradual Establishment of an Information System on Rural Banking, Development of Work in Economic Information and Consultancy Services.

The International Trade Institute, Ministry of Foreign Trade

Director: Su Ziching
Deputy Directors:
Fu Daling, Liu Jicai, Meng Qingyu, Chang Peiqi, Song Weibin
Address:
2 Changan St. (E), Beijing, China
Tel: 555416
Subjects of Research:
1. International Economy; 2. International Trade; 3. International Banking; 4. International Commodity Markets.

The Institute of Commercial Economy, Ministry of Commerce

Director: Xiao Fan
Deputy Directors:
Chen Dagu, Wan Dianwu, Yang Deying, Yang Chunxu, Zhao Yiguang
Address:
Ministry of Commerce Building, Xidan, Beijing, China
Tel: 668581-2459
Subjects of Research:
Problems Related to the Theory and Policy of Commercial Economy.

The Metallurgical Economy Institute, Ministry of Metallurgical Industry

Leading Cadres:
Chen Lei, Chang Xinchuan, Du Ang
Address:
Room 348, Ministry of Metallurgical Industry Building, Beijing, China
Tel: 557431-348
Subjects of Research:
1. Metallurgical Industrial Economy and Its Relationship to Macroeconomics; 2. Economy of Technology of the Metallurgical Industry; 3. Modern Management Science of Metallurgical Industry and Enterprises; 4. History of the Metallurgical Industry.

Institute of Agricultural Economy, Chinese Academy of Agricultural Sciences

Leading Cadre: Liu Zhicheng
Address:
30 Baishiqiao Road, Western Suburbs, Beijing, China
Tel: 890851-301
Subjects of Research:
1. Economics of Agricultural Technology; 2. Animal Husbandry Economics; 3. Distribution and Structure of Agricultural Production; 4. Agricultural Economic Management; 5. Foreign Agricultural Economy (including Production Economy and Management).

The Institute of Forestry Economics, Ministry of Forestry

Director: Wang Changfu
Deputy Director: Li Guojie
Address:
Shengguzhuang, Heping St. (W), Beijing, China
Tel: 464616
Subjects of Research:
1. Economic Problems in Production, Exchange and Distribution in Forestry Development; 2. Advanced Experience and Existing Problems in Foreign Forestry Management.

The Institute of Economics, Tianjin Academy of Social Sciences

Director: Li Gan
Deputy Directors:
Wang Qiang, Fu Tao, Zheng Ning, Guan Mi
Address:
32 Machangdao, Heping District, Tianjin, China
Tel: 34926

Subjects of Research:
1. Industrial Economy; 2. Urban Economy; 3. Population.

The Economic Institute, Taiyuan Iron and Steel Company

Director: Li Yanhuai
Deputy Director: Tian Jialian
Address:
Jiancaoping, Taiyuan, Shanxi Province, China
Tel: 217656, 212131
Subjects of Research:
1. Technological Economics and the Modernization of Management; 2. Economic Management; 3. Enterprise Management.

The Economic Institute, Inner Mongolia Autonomous Region Academy of Social Sciences

Director: Chen Liangbi
Deputy Directors: Bayinmeng, Wang Lu
Address:
4 Zhongshan Rd. (E), Hohhot, Inner Mongolia, China
Subjects of Research:
1. Economics of Agriculture and Animal Husbandry; 2. Industrial Economy; 3. Economics of Finance and Trade; 4. Political Economy.

The Institute of Economics, Liaoning Academy of Social Sciences

Director: Chang Zhen
Deputy Directors:
Lin Hongqiao, Fang Bingzhe, Luo Shengzhi
Address:
3 Section II, Sanhao St., Heping District, Shenyang, Liaoning Province, China
Tel: 82560
Subjects of Research:
1. Socialist Economic Theory; 2. Industrial Economy; 3. Agricultural Economy; 4. Urban Economy; 5. Economics of Finance and Trade.

The Economic Institute, Liaoning Provincial Planning Commission

Director: Yu Yan
Deputy Directors:
Wang Shouyi, Lu Guozhi, Qu Shilu
Address:
Provincial Government Compound, Beilingdajie, Shenyang, Liaoning Province, China
Tel: 63788
Subjects of Research:
1. Important Problems in the National Economy and Planning Work of Liaoning Province, Economic Laws and the Party's Line, Guiding Principles and Policies; 2. Various Important Ratios Among the National Economic Departments and Related Principles and Policies of National Economic Planning; 3. Technological Economics.

The Economic Institute, Anshan City

Deputy Directors: Ma Hangen, Wang Ji'an
Address:
Room 225, 2nd Floor, Building of the People's Government of Anshan City, Liaoning Province, China
Tel: 2140
Subjects of Research:
1. The Economic History of Anshan City; 2. Economic Problems Concerning Agriculture, Industry, Finance and Trade of Anshan City.

The Economic Institute, Anshan Iron and Steel Company

Director: Cui Huajing
Deputy Directors: Chen Jiong, Yang Guang
Address:
108 Dongfeng St., Tiedong District, Anshan, Liaoning Province, China
Tel: 95150
Subjects of Research:
1. Enterprise Management; 2. Technological Economics; 3. World Metallurgical Economics.

The Economic Institute, Benxi Iron and Steel Company

Director: Gao Ming
Deputy Director: He Youguang
Address:
Benxi, Liaoning Province, China
Tel: 73195
Subjects of Research:
1. Enterprise Management; 2. Technological Economics of Enterprise Production; 3. Applications of Behavioural Science in Enterprise Management; 4. Modernization of Enterprise Management.

The Economic Institute, Dalian Municipal Planning Commission

Leading Cadre: Pan Xiyu
Address:
  1 Stalin Square, Xigang District, Dalian City, Liaoning, China
  Tel: 32003
Subjects of Research:
  1. Planned Economy; 2. Industrial Economy; 3. Agricultural Economy; 4. Finance and Banking; 5. Enterprise Management; 6. Distribution of Materials; 7. Economic Information.

The Economic Institute, Jilin Provincial Academy of Social Sciences

Director: Pan Xiyu
Deputy Director: Liu Zhuangfei
Address:
  16 Jianshe St., Changchun City, Jilin Province, China
  Tel: 23612
Subjects of Research:
  1. Fundamental Theory of Political Economy; 2. The History of Economic Thought; 3. Industrial Economics (including Industrial Enterprise Management); 4. Agricultural Economics; 5. Forestry Economics; 6. Economics of Animal Husbandry; 7. Commercial Economics.

The Economic Institute, Heilongjiang Provincial Academy of Social Sciences

Director: Pan Xiyu
Deputy Directors:
  Wang Shaoshun, Yang Yuchun
Address:
  124 Huayuan St., Nangan District, Harbin, Heilongjiang Province, China
  Tel: 34004, 32747
Subjects of Research:
  1. Political Economy; 2. Economic Management; 3. Agricultural Economy; 4. The History of World Economy.

The Economic Institute, Daqing Petroleum Administration

Director: Li Yugeng
Deputy Directors:
  Chang Lizhong, Cui Yishou
Address:
  Daqing City, Heilongjiang Province, China
  Tel: 2341

Subject of Research:
  Enterprise Management.

The Economic Institute, Shaanxi Provincial Academy of Social Sciences

Leading Cadres: Yan Xiao, Jia Chunfu
Address:
  23 Xiaozhai Rd., Xi'an City, Shaanxi Province, China
  Tel: 51542
Subjects of Research:
  1. Theory of Political Economy; 2. Sectoral Economics, including Industrial Economics, Agricultural Economics, Commercial Economy.

The Economic Institute, Xinjiang Uygur Autonomous Region Academy of Social Sciences

Leading Cadre: Zhou Zhiqun
Address:
  Beijing Road, Urumqi, Xinjiang Uygur Autonomous Region, China
  Tel: 8372
Subjects of Research:
  1. Economics of Agriculture and Animal Husbandry; 2. Economics of Capital Construction, Industry and Communications; 3. Comprehensive Economics.

The Economic Institute, Shanghai Academy of Social Sciences

Director: Sun Huairen
Address:
  7 Lane, 662 Huaihai Road (C), Shanghai, China
  Tel: 284170-104
Subjects of Research:
  1. Socialist Aspects of Political Economy; 2. The History of Chinese Economic Thought; 3. The History of the Chinese Economy.

The Institute of Departmental Economics, Shanghai Academy of Social Sciences

Director: Cai Beihua
Deputy Directors:
  Chen Minzhi, Xu Zhihe
Address:
  7 Lane, 662 Huaihai Road (C), Shanghai, China
  Tel: 284170

Subjects of Research:
1. Industrial Economic Management; 2. Finance and Taxation; 3. Agricultural Economy; 4. Urban Economy; 5. Accounting Theory and Accounting Systems of Various Trades; 6. Population Theory, Vital Statistics, Problems and Policies of Population; 7. Principles of Statistics; 8. Overall Balance of the National Economy; 9. Economics of Tourism.

The Institute of World Economy, Shanghai Academy of Social Sciences

Deputy Director: Qin Benli
Address:
7 Lane, 662 Huaihai Road (C), Shanghai, China
Tel: 284170-103
Subjects of Research:
1. Economy of North America; 2. Banking Economics; 3. Comprehensive Economics.

The Economic Institute of Jiangxi Province

Deputy Director: Fu Wenyi
Address:
Nanchang City, Jiangxi Province, China
Tel: 64681-332
Subjects of Research:
1. Industrial Economics; 2. Agricultural Economics; 3. Economics of Finance and Trade.

The Economic Institute, Planning Commission of Henan Province

Leading Cadres: Li Qiwen, Sun Zhenshan
Address:
No. 3 Building, Administrative District, Zhengzhou City, Henan Province, China
Tel: 7336
Subject of Research:
Planned Economy.

The Economic Institute, Hubei Provincial Academy of Social Sciences

Director: Zhu Jiannong
Deputy Director: Liu Muxiang
Address:
50 Building, Donghu Road, Wuchang City, Hubei, China
Tel: 73871

Subjects of Research:
1. Fundamental Economic Theories: Problems of Socialist Ownership and the Theory of Balance of Socialist Planned Economy with Stress on the Macroeconomic Point of View; 2. Industrial Economics, Especially the Characteristics of Socialist Enterprise Management with Stress on the Microeconomic Point of View; 3. Agricultural Economics with Stress on the Relations of Production of Socialist Agriculture, Theory of Management and the Marxist Theory of Rent; 4. Finance and Trade Economics with Stress on the Theory of National Finance and Taxation, and the Theory of Forecast for Socialist Economy; 5. The Local Economy of Hubei Province.

The Economic Institute, Guangxi Academy of Social Sciences

Director: Chen Jiaxuan
Deputy Director: Liang Yunhao
Address:
Kanglu St., Nanning, Guangxi, China
Tel: 3808, 3635
Subjects of Research:
1. Industrial Economy; 2. Agricultural Economy; 3. Economics of Finance and Trade; 4. Economics of Tourism; 5. Political Economy.

The Economic Institute of the Sichuan Provincial Academy of Social Sciences

Deputy Directors:
Lin Ling, Gu Zongcheng, Zheng Qing, Tang Hongqian, Chen Changrong
Address:
Shiye St., Chengdu, Sichuan Province, China
Tel: 5364
Subjects of Research:
1. Industrial Economy; 2. Agricultural Economy; 3. Economics of Finance, Trade and Materials; 4. Economy of the Soviet Union and East European Countries.

The Economic Institute, Guizhou Provincial Academy of Social Sciences

Deputy Director: Sun Guoxi
Address:
Kexue Road, Guiyang, Guizhou Province, China
Tel: 23594

Subject of Research:
Economic Problems of Guizhou Concerning Industry and Agriculture.

The Economic Institute, Yunnan Provincial Academy of Social Sciences

Director: Li Qiaonian
Deputy Directors:
Liu Long, Chang Huaiyu, Zhao Chongling, Duan Jialing
Address:
Dongfeng Rd. (E), Kunming, Yunnan Province, China
Tel: 6296
Subjects of Research:
1. Agricultural Economy; 2. Industrial Economy; 3. The Economics of Finance, Trade, Materials and Banking; 4. National Economy (including Technological Economics, Economics of National Lands, Quantitative Economics, Management Modernization); 5. The Economic History of Yunnan; 6. Political Economy.

The Economic Institute of Kunming City

Deputy Director: Yang Shuqun
Address:
City Government Complex, Dongfeng Rd. (E), Kunming, Yunnan Province, China
Tel: 4058
Subject of Research:
The Applied Economy of Industrial, Agricultural, Commercial and Urban Economics.

The Institute of Foreign Economic Management, People's University of China

Director: Wang Jiamo
Deputy Director: Fang Qun
Address:
Haidian District, Beijing, China
Tel: 284076
Subjects of Research:
1. Foreign Economic Management Systems (mainly in the Soviet Union and East European Countries); 2. Foreign Agricultural Policies and Management Systems (mainly in the United States and the Soviet Union); 3. Application of Systems Engineering Theory in Foreign Enterprise Management; 4. The Theory and Method of Economic Analysis in the Policy Making of Foreign Enterprises.

The Labour Economics Institute, People's University of China

Leading Cadre: Zhao Lukuan
Address:
Haidian District, Beijing, China
Tel: 285431-2873
Subjects of Research:
1. The Quantity and Quality of the Labour Force; 2. Employment; 3. Labour Remuneration; 42 Labour Insurance; 5. Labour Efficiency; 6. The Making of Labour Law; 7. The Labour Movement.

The Economic Institute, Economics College of Beijing

Director: Bai Tuofang
Address:
Hong Miao, Chaoyangmenwai, Chaoyang District, Beijing, China
Tel: 593831
Subjects of Research:
1. Socialist Economic Theory and Policy; 2. Application of "Capital" in Socialist Economic Theory; 3. Theoretical and Practical Experience of Domestic Industrial Enterprise Management; 4. Theoretical and Practical Experience of Foreign Industrial Enterprise Management; 5. Chinese Economic History from the Qin and Han Dynasties to the Ming and Qing Dynasties; 6. Editing and Selecting of the Materials of Economic History of China's Past Dynasties; 7. Translation of Articles and Theses on Foreign Economic Management; 8. Translation of Articles and Theses on Foreign Enterprise Management.

The Economic Institute of Finance and Trade, Beijing College of Finance and Trade

Leading Cadres:
Li Hong, Huang Hui, Chang Shirong
Address:
68 Zaolinqian St., Beijing, China
Tel: 331919
Subjects of Research:
1. Economic Management; 2. Economic Laws; 3. Economic History.

The Economic Institute of Nankai University

Director: Teng Weizao

Deputy Directors:
  Gu Shutang, Qian Rongkun, Ding Shixum
Address:
  Balitai, Nankai District, Tianjin, China
  Tel: 264696
Subjects of Research:
  1. Economic Theory of Socialism, including Theory of Economy and Theory of Prices; 2. World Economy: Including Transnational Corporations, International Banking, Economic Theory of Capitalism, Oceanian Economy; 3. Economic Geography; 4. Economic History.

The Economic Institute, Tianjin College of Finance and Economics

Director: Yu Xinmin
Deputy Directors:
  Guo Xinchang, Guan Bai
Address:
  Huidui, Hexi District, Tianjin, China
  Tel: 82657
Subjects of Research:
  1. Industrial Management; 2. National Accounting and Input-Output Analysis; 3. The History of Chinese Banking; 4. International Banking.

The Economic Institute, Liaoning College of Finance and Economics

Director: Tong Zhehui
Deputy Directors:
  Ma Daying, Zhao Jiuxuan
Address:
  Hei Shijiao, Dalian, Liaoning Province, China
  Tel: 41101
Subjects of Research:
  1. Socialist Economic Management in China; 2. Economic Management in the Soviet Union; 3. Enterprise Management in Japan; 4. The History of Finance in China.

The Institute of World Economy, Fudan University

Director: Yu Kaixiang
Deputy Directors:
  Chen Guanlie, Jiang Zehong, Lin Shuzhong
Address:
  Fudan University, Handan Rd., Shanghai, China
  Tel: 480906-262
Subjects of Research:
  1. The European Economic Community; 2. The Economy of West Germany; 3. The Economy of France, 4. The Economy of Britain; 5. The Economy of Japan; 6. The Economy of the United States of America; 7. The Economy of the Soviet Union; 8. International Economic Relations; 9. State Monopoly Capitalism: Its Trends in Economic Development and Economic Structure.

The Economic Institute, Xiamen University

Leading Cadres:
  Yuan Zhenyue, Chang Laiyi, Xie Youquan
Address:
  Xiamen University, Xiamen, Fujian, China
Subjects of Research:
  1. "Capital"; 2. Agriculture, Industry, Commerce; 3. The Economy of Special Zones; 4. The Economic History of China.

The Economic Institute, Hubei College of Finance and Economic

Director: Liu Qifa
Deputy Director: Chen Jialing
Address:
  96 Wuluo Rd., Wuchang District, Wuhan, Hubei Province, China
  Tel: 73661
Subjects of Research:
  1. The Theory of China's Socialist Economy; 2. Economic Management; 3. Chinese History of Economic Thought.

The Economic Advisory Department, Shanghai Academy of Social Sciences

Leading Cadres:
  Huang Yifeng, Sun Huairen, Cai Beihua, Chen Minzhi, Pan Nianzhi
Address:
  7 Lane 622, Huaihai Road (C), Shanghai, China
  Tel: 284170-30
Subjects of Research:
  1. Advice on Foreign Trade; 2. Advice on Integration, Co-operation and Economic Management of Enterprises; 3. Advice on Accounting and Economic Laws; 4. Advice on Economic Information.

The Trust Department of the Bank of China

General Manager: Xu Ren
Deputy General Managers:
  Niu Yizhai, Liu Benkun, Li Shutian

Address:
17 Xi Jiaominxiang, Beijing, China
Tel: 334216

Scope of Business:
1. Make Credit Inquiries; 2. Make Price Inquiries and Surveys of Market Conditions; 3. Act as Buying and Selling Agent; 4. Joint Ventures; 5. Recommend Clients Engaged in the Leasing Business; 6. Compensation Trade; 7. Processing with Supplied Materials; 8. Assembling with Supplied Parts; 9. Co-production; 10. Recommend Importers and Exporters; 11. Act as Guarantee or Witness for Chinese Enterprises with Regard to Their Foreign Commitments.

3. LISTING OF CHINA'S COLLEGES SPECIALIZING IN FINANCE AND ECONOMICS; OTHER UNIVERSITIES AND COLLEGES WITH DEPARTMENTS AND SPECIALITIES IN FINANCE, ECONOMICS AND MANAGEMENT

I. CHINA'S 30 COLLEGES OF FINANCE AND ECONOMICS

The Central Institute of Finance and Banking Affairs
Location: Beijing
Department of Finance
 Specialities:
  Finance, Capital construction and credit
Department of Banking Affairs
 Specialities: Banking, Insurance
Department of Accounting
 Speciality: Accounting

Beijing Institute of Finance and Trade
Location: Beijing
Department of Finance and Banking Affairs
 Specialities: Finance, Banking
Department of Commercial Economics
 Speciality: Commercial economics
Department of Accounting
 Speciality: Accounting for financial affairs

Beijing College of Economics
Location: Beijing
Department of Finance and Trade
 Specialities:
  Trade economics, Accounting for industrial financial affairs, Finance
Department of Industrial Economics
 Specialities:
  Industrial enterprise management, Planning and statistics
Department of Economic Mathematics
 Speciality: Computer programming
Department of Political Economy
 Speciality: Political economy
Department of Labour Economics
 Speciality: Labour economics
Department of Labour Protection Engineering
 Specialities:
  Industrial safety technology, Industrial hygiene technology
Department of Management of Supplies
 Specialities:
  Management of machinery and electrical machinery, Management of materials, Management of supplies

Beijing College of Commerce
Location: Beijing
Department of Commercial Economics
 Specialities:
  Commercial economics, Commercial enterprise management
Department of Financial Accounting
 Speciality:
  Accounting for commercial financial affairs

Beijing Institute of Foreign Trade
Location: Beijing
Department No. 1 (English)
 Speciality: English
Department No. 2 (Other Foreign Languages)
 Specialities:
  French for foreign trade, Japanese for foreign trade, German for foreign trade, Spanish for foreign trade, Arabic for foreign trade, Russian for foreign trade, Italian for foreign trade
Department No. 3 (Foreign Trade)
 Speciality: Foreign trade
Department No. 4 (Customs)
 Speciality: Customs management

Tianjin College of Finance and Economics
Location: Tianjin
Department of Financial Accounting
 Specialities: Accounting science, Finance
Department of Banking Affairs
 Specialities:
  International banking affairs, Banking affairs
Department of Foreign Trade
 Speciality: Foreign trade
Department of Industrial Management
 Specialities: Statistics, Enterprise management
Department of Commercial Economics
 Specialities:
  Commercial economics, Accounting

Tianjin College of Commerce
Location: Tianjin
Department of Commercial Enterprise Management
 Speciality: Commercial enterprise management
Department of Refrigeration
 Speciality: Refrigeration

Hebei College of Finance and Trade
Location: Shijiazhuang, Hebei Province
Department of Financial and Banking Affairs
 Speciality: Banking affairs

Department of Commercial Economics
　　Speciality: Commercial economic management

Shanxi College of Finance and Economics
Location: Taiyuan, Shanxi Province
Department of Financial and Banking Affairs
　　Specialities:
　　　　Financial and banking affairs, Financial science
Department of Accounting Science
　　Specialities:
　　　　Accounting science, Accounting for commercial financial affairs
Department of Planning and Statistics
　　Specialities:
　　　　Planning and statistics, Commercial planning and statistics
Department of Commercial Economics
　　Speciality: Commercial economics
Department of Commodity Science
　　Speciality:
　　　　Commodity science of agricultural means of production

Inner Mongolia College of Finance and Economics
Location:
　　Hohhot, Inner Mongolia Autonomous Region
Department of Financial and Banking Affairs
　　Specialities: Finance, Banking affairs
Department of Planning and Statistics
　　Speciality: Commercial planning and statistics
Department of Industrial Economics
　　Specialities:
　　　　Industrial Economics, Accounting for industrial financial affairs
Department of Commercial Economics
　　Specialities:
　　　　Commercial economics, Trade economics

Liaoning College of Finance and Economics
Location: Dalian, Liaoning Province
Department of Finance
　　Specialities:
　　　　Finance, Banking affairs, Industrial accounting
Department of Planning and Statistics
　　Specialities: Planning, Statistics
Department of Foreign Trade
　　Speciality: Foreign trade
Department of Commercial Management of Goods and Materials
　　Specialities:
　　　　Commercial economics, Management of goods and materials
Department of Capital Construction
　　Speciality:
　　　　Financial affairs in capital construction

Jilin College of Finance and Trade
Location: Changchun, Jilin Province
Department of Financial and Banking Affairs
　　Specialities: Finance, Banking affairs
Department of Accounting and Statistics
　　Specialities: Accounting, Statistics
Department of Trade Economics
　　Specialities:
　　　　Commercial economics, Foreign trade
Department of Cereals
　　Speciality: Storage of cereals and oils

Heilongjiang College of Commerce
Location: Harbin, Heilongjiang Province
Department of Commercial Economics
　　Speciality: Commercial economics
Department of Commercial Machinery
　　Specialities:
　　　　Commercial machinery, Commercial architecture
Department of Electronic Engineering
　　Specialities:
　　　　Electronic technology, Automation of petroleum storage
Department of Refrigeration
　　Speciality: Refrigeration
Department of Chinese Herbal Medicine
　　Speciality:
　　　　Pharmacology of Chinese herbal medicine

Shanghai Institute of Finance and Economics
Location: Shanghai
Department of Financial and Banking Affairs
　　Specialities:
　　　　Finance, Banking affairs, Financial and credit affairs in capital construction
Department of Economics
　　Speciality: Political economy
Department of World Economy
　　Speciality: International banking
Department of Industrial Economy
　　Speciality: Industrial economy
Department of Trade Economics
　　Speciality: Trade economics
Department of Accounting
　　Specialities:
　　　　Industrial accounting, Commercial accounting
Department of Statistics
　　Speciality: Industrial statistics

Shanghai Institute of Foreign Trade
Location: Shanghai
Department of Foreign Trade Economics
　　Speciality: Foreign trade
Department of Foreign Languages for Foreign Trade

Specialities:
  English for foreign trade, Japanese for foreign trade, French for foreign trade

Shanghai Customs School
Location: Shanghai
  Speciality: Customs management

Shanghai Tourism School
Location: Shanghai
  Specialities:
    Accounting for financial affairs, Hotel management

Jiangsu Commercial School
Location: Nanjing, Jiangsu Province
  Speciality: Finance and economics

Hangzhou College of Commerce
Location: Hangzhou, Zhejiang Province
Department of Commercial Enterprise Management
  Specialities:
    Commercial planning and statistics, Accounting for commercial financial affairs, Commercial enterprise management
Department of Commercial Electronics
  Speciality: Commercial electronics technology
Department of Foodstuffs
  Speciality: Meat products hygiene

Zhejiang School of Metallurgical Economics
Location: Jiande County, Zhejiang Province
  Specialities:
    Accounting for industrial financial affairs, Industrial statistics

Anhui College of Finance and Trade
Location: Bengbu, Anhui Province
Department of Financial and Banking Affairs
  Specialities:
    Finance, Banking affairs, Accounting for industrial financial affairs
Department of Accounting and Statistics
  Specialities:
    Accounting for commercial financial affairs, Planning and statistics
Department of Commercial Economics
  Specialities:
    Political economy, Commercial economics
Department of Commodity Science for Farm and Sideline Products
  Speciality: Cotton processing and inspection

Jiangxi College of Finance and Economics
Location: Nanchang, Jiangxi Province
Department of Financial and Banking Affairs
  Specialities:
    Finance, Banking affairs, Financial affairs and credit for capital construction
Department of Accounting for Financial Affairs
  Specialities:
    Accounting for commercial financial affairs, Accounting for industrial financial affairs, Accounting for agricultural financial affairs
Department of Planning and Statistics
  Specialities:
    Industrial statistics, Statistics, National economic planning
Department of Trade Economics
  Specialities: Trade economics, Prices
Department of Industrial Economics
  Speciality: Industrial economics

Shandong College of Economics
Location: Jinan, Shandong Province
Department of Financial and Banking Affairs
  Speciality: Banking
Department of Accounting
  Specialities:
    Industrial accounting, Commercial accounting
Department of Planning and Statistics
  Speciality: Planning and statistics
Department of Industrial and Commercial Economics
  Specialities:
    Economics of supplies management, Foreign trade

Zhengzhou School of Management for Aviation Industry
Location: Zhengzhou, Henan Province
Department of Management of Financial Affairs
  Speciality:
    Accounting for industrial financial affairs
Department of Organizational Management
  Speciality: Management of planning
Department of Management of Goods and Materials
  Speciality:
    Management of supply of goods and materials
Department of Management of Technical Data
  Speciality:
    Management of scientific and technical data

Hubei College of Finance and Economics
Location: Wuhan, Hubei Province
Department of Financial and Banking Affairs
  Specialities: Finance, Banking
Department of Accounting for Financial Affairs

Specialities:
  Industrial accounting, Accounting for financial affairs
Department of Planning and Statistics
  Specialities:
    National economy planning, Planning of goods and materials, Statistics
Department of Financial Affairs and Credit for Capital Construction
  Speciality:
    Accounting for financial affairs and credit for capital construction
Department of Industrial Economics
  Speciality: Industrial economics
Department of Agricultural Economics
  Speciality: Agricultural economics
Department of Commercial Economics
  Specialities:
    Commercial economics, Commodity conservation
Department of Economic Information:
  Speciality: Economic information
Department of Politics:
  Specialities: Political economy, Politics
Department of Law:
  Speciality: Law

Hunan College of Finance and Economics
Location: Changsha, Hunan Province
Department of Finance
  Speciality: Finance
Department of Banking Affairs
  Specialities: Banking affairs, Rural banking
Department of Planning and Statistics
  Speciality: Statistics
Department of Trade Economics
  Speciality: Commercial economics
Department of Industrial Economics
  Specialities:
    Accounting for industrial financial affairs, Industrial enterprise management

Sichuan College of Finance and Economics
Location: Chengdu, Sichuan Province
Department of Finance
  Speciality: Finance
Department of Banking Affairs
  Speciality: Banking
Department of Accounting
  Speciality: Accounting
Department of Statistics
  Speciality: Statistics
Department of Industrial Economics
  Speciality: Industrial economics
Department of Agricultural Economics
  Speciality: Agricultural economics
Department of Political Economy
  Speciality: Political economy

Guizhou College of Finance and Economics
Location: Guiyang, Guizhou Province
Department of Financial and Banking Affairs
  Specialities:
    Finance, Financial affairs and credit for capital construction
Department of Industrial Economics
  Specialities:
    Industrial economics, Planning and statistics
Department of Trade Economics
  Speciality: Trade economics

Shaanxi College of Finance and Economics
Location: Xi'an, Shaanxi Province
Department of Finance
  Speciality: Finance
Department of Banking Affairs
  Speciality: Banking
Department of Accounting
  Speciality:
    Accounting for industrial financial affairs
Department of Statistics
  Speciality: Statistics
Department of Industrial Economics
  Speciality: Industrial economics
Department of Trade Economics
  Speciality: Commercial economics
Department of Goods and Materials
  Speciality:
    Accounting for financial affairs concerning the supply of goods and materials

Xinjiang College of Finance and Economics
Location:
  Urumqi, Xinjiang Uygur Autonomous Region
Department of Finance
  Speciality: Finance
Department of Banking Affairs
  Speciality: Banking
Department of Planning and Statistics
  Specialities:
    Planning and statistics, Enterprise financial affairs
Department of Commercial Economics
  Speciality: Trade economics

II. LISTING OF CHINA'S 27 UNIVERSITIES WITH DEPARTMENTS AND SPECIALITIES IN FINANCE, ECONOMICS AND MANAGEMENT

Beijing University
Location: Beijing
Department of Economics
  Specialities:
    Political economy, World economy, Management of the national economy

Chinese People's University
Location: Beijing
Department of Political Economy
  Specialities: Political economy, World economy
Department of Finance
  Specialities:
    Financial and banking affairs, World banking, Accounting for financial affairs
Department of Planning and Statistics
  Specialities:
    National economy planning, Statistics, Overall arrangement of production
Department of Trade Economics
  Specialities:
    Commercial economic management, Commodity science
Department of Industrial Economics
  Specialities:
    Industrial economic management, Economic management of capital construction
Department of Agricultural Economics
  Speciality: Agricultural economic management
Department of Management of Economic Information
  Speciality:
    Management of economic information

Nankai University
Location: Tianjin
Department of Political Economy
  Specialities:
    Political economy, World economy

Hebei University
Location: Baoding, Hebei Province
Department of Economics
  Specialities:
    Financial and banking affairs, Planning and statistics, Political economy, Industrial economics

Shanxi University
Location: Taiyuan, Shanxi Province
Department of Economics
  Speciality: Political economy

Inner Mongolia University
Location:
  Hohhot, Inner Mongolia Autonomous Region
Department of Economics
  Speciality: Planning and statistics

Liaoning University
Location: Shenyang, Liaoning Province
Department of Economics
  Specialities:
    Planning and statistics, International banking, Political economy, Industrial economics

Jilin University
Location: Changchun, Jilin Province
Department of Economics
  Specialities:
    Political economy, National economic planning, World economy

Heilongjiang University
Location: Harbin, Heilongjiang Province
Department of Economics
  Speciality: Political economy

Fudan University
Location: Shanghai
Department of Political Economy
  Speciality: Political economy
Department of World Economy
  Speciality: World economy

Nanjing University
Location: Nanjing, Jiangsu Province
Department of Economics
  Specialities:
    Political economy, Economic management

Hangzhou University
Location: Hangzhou, Zhejiang Province
Department of Economics
  Specialities:
    Political economy, Economics of tourism

Anhui University
Location: Hefei, Anhui Province
Department of Economics
  Specialities:
    Political economy, Planning and management of national economy, Foreign trade

Anhui Labour Academy
Location: Xuancheng County, Anhui Province
Department of Politics
  Speciality: Political economy

Xiamen University
Location: Xiamen, Fujian Province
Department of Economics
  Specialities:
    Political economy, Science of planning and statistics, Accounting for financial affairs, Financial and banking affairs, Enterprise management, Foreign trade

Jiangxi University
Location: Nanchang, Jiangxi Province
Department of Economics
  Speciality: Political economy

Shandong University
Location: Jinan, Shandong Province
Department of Political Economy
　Specialities:
　　Political economy, Economic management

Zhengzhou University
Location: Zhengzhou, Henan Province
Department of Economics
　Speciality: Political economy

Wuhan University
Location: Wuhan, Hubei Province
Department of Economics
　Speciality: Political economy

Xiangtan University
Location: Xiangtan, Hunan Province
Department of Politics
　Speciality: Political economy

Zhongshan University
Location: Guangzhou, Guangdong Province
Department of Economics
　Specialities:
　　Economics, Political economy, Commercial economics

Jinan University
Location:
　Shipai, Guangzhou, Guangdong Province
Department of Economics
　Specialities:
　　Industrial economics, Commercial economics, Accounting science, Political economy, International banking

Guangxi University
Location:
Department of Economics
　Nanning, Guangxi Zhuang Autonomous Region Speciality: Political economy

Sichuan University
Location: Chengdu, Sichuan Province
Department of Economics
　Speciality: Political economy

Yunnan University
Location: Kunming, Yunnan Province
Department of Economics
　Specialities:
　　Political economy, Enterprise management

Northwest China University
Location: Xi'an, Shaanxi Province
Department of Political Theory
　Speciality: Political economy

Lanzhou University
Location: Lanzhou, Gansu Province
Department of Economics
　Specialities:
　　Political economy, Economic management

III. LISTING OF CHINA'S 26 COLLEGES AND UNIVERSITIES OF SCIENCE AND ENGINEERING WITH DEPARTMENTS AND SPECIALITIES IN FINANCE, ECONOMICS AND MANAGEMENT

Qinghua University
Location: Beijing
Department of Economic Management Engineering
　Speciality:
　　Mathematics and computer technology in economic management.

Northern University of Communications
Location: Beijing
Department of Economics
　Specialities:
　　Railway transportation economics, Technical management of railway materials

Beijing Engineering Institute
Location: Beijing
Department of Engineering of Industrial Managerial Systems
　Speciality: Management

Beijing Institute of Posts and Telecommunications
Location: Beijing
Department of Management Engineering
　Speciality:
　　Management engineering of posts and telecommunications

Tianjin University
Location: Tianjin
Department of Industrial Management Enginering
　Speciality: Industrial management engineering

China Civil Aviation School
Location: Tianjin
Speciality:
　Planning and financial affairs of civil aviation

Hebei Geological Institute
Location: Xuanhua, Hebei Province
Department of Geological Economic Management
　Speciality: Geological economic management

Northeast China Engineering Institute
Location: Shenyang, Liaoning Province
Department of Management Engineering
  Speciality: Management engineering

Dalian Engineering Institute
Location: Dalian, Liaoning Province
Department of Management Engineering
  Speciality: Management engineering

Jilin Polytechnical Institute
Location: Changchun, Jilin Province
Department of Management Engineering
  Speciality:
    Management engineering of machine-building

Jilin Engineering Institute
Location: Changchun, Jilin Province
Department of Management Engineering
  Speciality:
    Economics and management of machine-building industry

Harbin Polytechnical Institute
Location: Harbin, Heilongjiang Province
Department of Management Engineering
  Speciality: Management engineering

Tongji University
Location: Shanghai
Department of Management Engineering
  Speciality:
    Management engineering of architecture and machinery

East China Textile Engineering Institute
Location: Shanghai
Department of Textile Engineering
  Speciality:
    Management engineering for the textile industry

Shanghai Mercantile Marine Institute
Location: Shanghai
Department of Management of Water Transport
  Specialities:
    Management of water transport, Water transport economics, Accounting for financial affairs of water transport
Department of Oceangoing Transport
  Speciality: Oceangoing transport business

Shanghai Building Material Industry School
Location: Shanghai
Department of Economic Management
  Speciality:
    Accounting for financial affairs of building-material industry

China Mining Institute
Location: Suzhou, Jiangsu Province
Department of Mining Enterprise Management
  Specialities:
    Enterprise management, Management engineering of goods and materials

Zhenjiang Agricultural Machinery Institute
Location: Zhenjiang, Jiangsu Province
  Speciality:
    Management of agricultural machinery

Zhejiang Engineering Institute
Location: Hangzhou, Zhejiang Prvoince
Department of Chemical Enginering
  Speciality:
    Industrial management engineering

Hangzhou Electronic Engineering Institute
Location: Hangzhou, Zhejiang Province
Department of Management Engineering
  Speciality:
    Enterprise management engineering for the electronics industry
Department of Industrial Economics
  Speciality:
    Accounting for financial affairs in electronic enterprises

East China Petroleum Institute
Location: Dongying, Shandong Province
Department of Petroleum Exploitation
  Speciality:
    Petroleum economics and management

Central China Engineering Institute
Location: Wuhan, Hubei Province
Department of Economic Management Engineering
  Speciality:
    Management engineering of goods and materials

Wuhan Engineering Institute
Location: Wuhan, Hubei Province
Department of Mechanical Engineering
  Speciality:
    Management engineering of machine building

Wuhan River Navigation School
Location: Wuhan, Hubei Province
  Speciality: Management of river navigation

Changsha Institute of Communications
Location: Changsha, Hunan Province
  Speciality:
    Accounting for financial affairs in engineering projects

Xi'an Highway Institute
Location: Xi'an, Shaanxi Province
Department of Management of Highway Transport
  Specialities:
    Enterprise management of motor transport, Accounting for financial affairs in motor transport

IV. LISTING OF CHINA'S 25 AGRICULTURAL AND FORESTRY COLLEGES AND UNIVERSITIES SPECIALIZING IN FINANCE, ECONOMICS AND MANAGEMENT

Beijing Agricultural University
Location: Beijing
Department of Agricultural Economics
  Speciality: Agricultural economics

Beijing Forestry Institute
Location: Beijing
Department of Forestry
  Speciality: Forestry economics

Hebei Agricultural University
Location: Baoding, Hebei Province
Department of Agricultural Economics
  Speciality: Agricultural economic management

Shanxi Agricultural University
Location: Taigu County, Shanxi Province
Department of Fundamentals
  Speciality: Agricultural economics

Shenyang Agricultural Institute
Location: Shenyang, Liaoning Province
Department of Agricultural Economics
  Speciality: Agricultural economics

Jilin Agricultural University
Location: Changchun, Jilin Province
Department of Agricultural Science
  Speciality: Agricultural economics

Jilin Agro-Technical Institute
Location: Huaide County, Jilin Province
Specialities:
  Application and management of agricultural mechanization, Economics of agricultural mechanization

Heilongjiang August 1 Institute of Land Reclamation
Location: Mishan County, Heilongjiang Province
Department of Agricultural Economics
  Speciality: Financial accounting

Northeast China Forestry Institute
Location: Harbin, Heilongjiang Province
Department of Forestry Economics
  Speciality: Forestry economics

Nanjing Agricultural Institute
Location: Nanjing, Jiangsu Province
Department of Agricultural Economics:
  Speciality: Agricultural economics

Zhejiang Agricultural University
Location: Hangzhou, Zhejiang Province
Department of Agricultural Economics
  Speciality:
    Economic management of agriculture

Anhui Agricultural Institute
Location: Hefei, Anhui Province
Department of Agricultural Economics
  Speciality:
    Economic management of agriculture

Fujian Agricultural Institute
Location: Sanming, Fujian Province
Department of Agricultural Economics
  Speciality: Agricultural economics

Shandong Agricultural Institute
Location: Tai'an County, Shandong Province
Department of Agricultural Economics
  Speciality:
    Agricultural economics and management

Central China Agricultural Institute
Location: Wuhan, Hubei Province
Department of Agricultural Economics
  Speciality:
    Economic management of agriculture

South China Agricultural Institute
Location: Guangzhou, Guangdong Province
Department of Agricultural Economics
  Speciality:
    Economic management of agriculture

Guangxi Agricultural Institute
Location:
  Nanning, Guangxi Zhuang Autonomous Region
Department of Farm Machinery
  Speciality: Agricultural economics

Southwest Agricultural Institute
Location: Chongqing, Sichuan Province
Department of Agricultural Economics
  Speciality:
    Economic management of agriculture

Sichuan Agricultural Institute
Location: Ya'an County, Sichuan Province
Department of Agronomy
  Speciality:
    Economic management of agriculture

Xichang Agricultural School
Location:
  Xichang County, Sichuan Province
  Speciality: Agricultural economics

Mianyang Agricultural School
Location: Mianyang, Sichuan Province
  Speciality: Agricultural economics

Guizhou Agricultural Institute
Location: Guiyang, Guizhou Province
Department of Agronomy
  Speciality: Agricultural economics

Northwest China Agricultural Institute
Location: Wugong County, Shaanxi Province
Department of Agricultural Economics
  Speciality:
    Agricultural management and administration

Ningxia Agricultural Institute
Location:
  Yongming County, Ningxia Hui Autonomous Region
Department of Agricultural Econmics
  Speciality:
    Economic management of agriculture

Xinjiang August 1 Agricultural Institute
Location:
  Urumqi, Xinjiang Uygur Autonomous Region
Department of Agricultural Economics
  Speciality:
    Economic management of agriculture

4. LISTING OF CHINA'S PROFESSIONAL SECONDARY SCHOOLS OF FINANCE AND ECONOMICS

Beijing (7 schools):

The Secondary Technical School Under the Ministry of Foreign Trade
Beijing Municipal Foreign Trade School
Beijing Municipal Commercial School
The Second Beijing Municipal Commercial School
Beijing Banking School
Beijing Municipal Supply and Marketing School
Beijing Municipal School of Management of Goods and Materials

Tianjin (6 schools):

Tianjin Municipal School of Finance and Trade
Tianjin Municipal School of Foreign Trade
The First Commercial School of Tianjin
Tianjin Municipal School of Supply and Marketing
Tianjin Municipal School of Management of Goods and Materials
Tianjin Municipal School of Labour Protection

Hebei Province (17 schools):

Shijiazhuang Prefectural School of Finance and Trade
   Address: Shijiazhuang, Hebei Province
Xingtai School of Finance and Trade
   Address: Xingtai, Hebei Province
Handan Prefectural School of Finance and Trade
   Address: Handan, Hebei Province
Shijiazhuang Municipal School of Finance and Trade
   Address: Shijiazhuang, Hebei Province
Zhangjiakou Prefectural School of Finance and Trade
   Address: Zhangjiakou, Hebei Province
Chengde School of Finance and Trade
   Address: Chengde, Hebei Province
Tangshan Prefectural School of Finance and Trade
   Address: Luanxian County, Hebei Province
Langfang Prefectural School of Finance and Trade
   Address: Anci County, Hebei Province
Cangzhou Prefectural School of Finance and Trade
   Address: Cangzhou, Hebei Province
Hengshui Prefectural School of Finance and Trade
   Address: Hengshui County, Hebei Province
Qinhuangdao School of Coal Finance and Economics
   Address: Qinhuangdao, Hebei Province
Hebei Banking School
   Address: Baoding, Hebei Province
Hebei Provincial School of Commerce
   Address: Shijiazhuang, Hebei Province
Boading Commercial School
   Address: Baoding, Hebei Province
Tangshan Municipal School of Commerce
   Address: Tangshan, Hebei Province
Hebei Provincial School of Supply and Marketing
   Address: Shijiazhuang, Hebei Province
Hebei School of Goods and Materials
   Address: Shijiazhuang, Hebei Province

Shanxi Province (12 schools):

Shanxi Provincial School of Finance and Trade
   Address: Taiyuan, Shanxi Province
Taiyuan Municipal School of Finance and Trade Services
   Address: Taiyuan, Shanxi Province
Shanxi Provincial Accounting School
   Address: Taiyuan, Shanxi Province
Datong Municipal Accounting School
   Address: Datong, Shanxi Province
Luliang Prefectural Accounting School
   Address: Lishi County, Shanxi Province
Yuncheng Prefectural Accounting School
   Address: Yuncheng County, Shanxi Province
Southeast Shanxi Prefectural Accounting School
   Address: Changzhi, Shanxi Province
Shanxi Provincial School of Accounting and Statistics
   Address: Taiyuan, Shanxi Province
Yanbei Prefectural School of Commerce
   Address: Datong, Shanxi Province
The Commercial School of Xinxian County of Shanxi Province
   Address: Xinxian County, Shanxi Province
Yuncheng Prefectural School of Commerce
   Address: Yuncheng County, Shanxi Province
Shanxi Provincial School of Management of Goods and Materials
   Address: Taiyuan, Shanxi Province

Inner Mongolia Autonomous Region (9 schools):

Inner Mongolia Financial School
   Address: Hohhot, Inner Mongolia Autonomous Region

Jirem School of Finance and Trade
  Address: Tongliao, Inner Mongolia Autonomous Region
Finance and Trade School of Ju Ud League
  Address: Chifeng, Inner Mongolia Autonomous Region
Finance and Trade School of Ulanqab League
  Address: Jining, Inner Mongolia Autonomous Region
Inner Mongolia Banking School
  Address: Hohhot, Inner Mongolia Autonomous Region
Inner Mongolia Commercial School
  Address: Hohhot, Inner Mongolia Autonomous Region
Commercial School of Hulun Buir League
  Address: Hailar, Inner Mongolia Autonomous Region
Inner Mongolia School of Supply and Marketing
  Address: Liangcheng County, Inner Mongolia Autonomous Region
The School of Supply and Marketing of Hulun Buir League
  Address: Hailar, Inner Mongolia Autonomous Region

Liaoning Province (16 schools):

Liaoning Provincial School of Finance and Economics
  Address: Dandong, Liaoning Province
Fuxin School of Finance and Economics of Liaoning Province
  Address: Fuxin, Liaoning Province
Shenyang Municipal School of Finance and Economics
  Address: Shenyang, Liaoning Province
Jinzhou Municipal School of Finance and Accounting
  Address: Jinzhou, Liaoning Province
Liaoning Provincial School of Foreign Trade
  Address: Dalian, Liaoning Province
Anshan Municipal School of Finance and Trade
  Address: Anshan, Liaoning Province
Liaoning Provincial Banking School
  Address: Shenyang, Liaoning Province
Liaoning Provincial School of Commerce
  Address: Jinzhou, Liaoning Province
Dalian Municipal School of Commerce
  Address: Dalian, Liaoning Province
Fushun Municipal School of Commerce
  Address: Fushun, Liaoning Province
Benxi Municipal School of Commerce
  Address: Benxi, Liaoning Province
Yingkou Municipal School of Commerce
  Address: Yingkou, Liaoning Province
Fuxin Municipal School of Commerce
  Address: Fuxin, Liaoning Province
Chaoyang Prefectural School of Commerce
  Address: Chaoyang County, Liaoning Province
Liaoning Provincial School of Supply and Marketing
  Address: Liaoyang, Liaoning Province
Liaoning Provincial School of Goods and Materials
  Address: Shenyang, Liaoning Province

Jilin Province (11 schools):

Jilin Provincial School of Finance
  Address: Changchun, Jilin Province
Tonghua School of Finance and Trade
  Address: Tonghua, Jilin Province
Yanbian School of Finance and Trade
  Address: Yanji, Jilin Province
Jilin Banking School
  Address: Changchun, Jilin Province
Jilin Provincial School of Commerce
  Address: Changchun, Jilin Province
Changchun Municipal School of Commerce
  Address: Changchun, Jilin Province
Siping Commercial School of Jilin Province
  Address: Siping, Jilin Province
Jilin Municipal School of Commerce
  Address: Jilin City, Jilin Province
Liaoyuan Commercial School of Jilin Province
  Address: Liaoyuan, Jilin Province
Jilin Provincial School of Supply and Marketing
  Address: Changchun, Jilin Province
Jilin Provincial School of Goods and Materials
  Address: Changchun, Jilin Province

Heilongjiang Province (10 schools):

Heilongjiang Provincial School of Finance
  Address: Harbin, Heilongjiang Province
Heilongjiang Provincial School of Foreign Trade
  Address: Harbin, Heilongjiang Province
Heilongjiang Banking School
  Address: Harbin, Heilongjiang Province
Harbin Municipal Accounting School
  Address: Harbin, Heilongjiang Province
Qiqihar Municipal School of Commerce
  Address: Qiqihar, Heilongjiang Province
Mudanjiang Commercial School
  Address: Mudanjiang, Heilongjiang Province
Hejiang Prefectural School of Commerce
  Address: Jiamusi, Heilongjiang Province
Heilongjiang Provincial School of Supply and Marketing
  Address: Harbin, Heilongjiang Province

Suihua School of Supply and Marketing
   Address: Suihua County, Heilongjiang Province
Harbin Municipal School of Service Trades
   Address: Harbin, Heilongjiang Province

Shanghai (4 schools):

Shanghai School of Finance and Banking
Shanghai School of Commercial Accounting
Shanghai Commercial School
Shanghai School of Goods and Materials

Jiangsu Province (16 schools):

Suzhou Municipal School of Finance and Economics
   Address: Suzhou, Jiangsu Province
Changzhou School of Finance and Economics
   Address: Changzhou, Jiangsu Province
Wuxi School of Finance and Economics
   Address: Wuxi, Jiangsu Province
Lianyungang Municipal School of Finance and Economics
   Address: Lianyungang, Jiangsu Province
Huaiyin Prefectural School of Finance and Economics
   Address: Qingjiang, Jiangsu Province
Xuzhou Municipal School of Finance and Economics
   Address: Xuzhou, Jiangsu Province
Jiangsu Provincial School of Foreign Trade
   Address: Lianyungang, Jiangsu Province
Jiangsu Provincial Banking School
   Address: Jiangpu County, Jiangsu Province
Jiangsu Provincial School of Commerce
   Address: Yangzhou, Jiangsu Province
Wuxi Commercial School
   Address: Wuxi, Jiangsu Province
Suzhou Municipal School of Commerce
   Address: Suzhou, Jiangsu Province
Yancheng Prefectural School of Commerce
   Address: Yancheng County, Jiangsu Province
Nantong School of Supply and Marketing
   Address: Nantong, Jiangsu Province
Xuzhou Prefectural School of Supply and Marketing
   Address: Xuzhou, Jiangsu Province
Huaiyin School of Supply and Marketing
   Address: Huaiyin County, Jiangsu Province
Nanjing School of Goods and Materials
   Address: Nanjing, Jiangsu Province

Zhejiang Province (10 schools):

Zhejiang School of Finance
   Address: Hangzhou, Zhejiang Province
Zhejiang Banking School
   Address: Hangzhou, Zhejiang Province
Ningbo Commercial School of Zhejiang Province
   Address: Ningbo, Zhejiang Province
Wenzhou Commercial School of Zhejiang Province
   Address: Wenzhou, Zhejiang Province
Lishui Commercial School of Zhejiang Province
   Address: Lishui County, Zheijiang Province
Zhoushan Commercial School of Zhejiang Province
   Address: Dinghai County, Zheijiang Province
Zhejiang Provincial School of Supply and Marketing
   Address: Hangzhou, Zhejiang Province
Taizhou School of Supply and Marketing of Zhejiang Province
   Address: Linhai County, Zhejiang Province
Jinhua School of Supply and Marketing
   Address: Jinhua County, Zhejiang Province
Zhejiang Provincial School of Goods and Materials
   Address: Yuhang County, Zhejiang Province

Anhui Province (6 schools):

Anhui Provincial School of Finance
   Address: Hefei, Anhui Province
Anhui Provincial Banking School
   Address: Hefei, Anhui Province
Anhui Provincial School of Commerce
   Address: Wuhu, Anhui Province
Anqing Commercial School
   Address: Anqing, Anhui Province
Hefei School of Supply and Marketing
   Address: Hefei, Anhui Province
Anhui Provincial School of Goods and Materials
   Address: Hefei, Anhui Province

Fujian Province (13 schools):

Fujian Provincial School of Finance and Economics
   Address: Xiamen, Fujian Province
Fujian School of Foreign Trade
   Address: Fuzhou, Fujian Province
Longyan School of Finance and Economics of Fujian Province
   Address: Longyan County, Fujian Province
Fujian Provincial Banking School
   Address: Fuzhou, Fujian Province
Fujian Provincial School of Commerce
   Address: Fuzhou, Fujian Province
Fuzhou Commercial School
   Address: Fuzhou, Fujian Province
Xiamen Commercial Schools
   Address: Xiamen, Fujian Province

Jianyang Prefectural School of Commerce
  Address: Jianyang County, Fujian Province
Quanzhou Commercial School of Jinjiang Prefecture
  Address: Quanzhou, Fujian Province
Fujian Provincial School of Supply and Marketing
  Address: Fuzhou, Fujian Province
Sanming Prefectural School of Supply and Marketing
  Address: Shaxian County, Fujian Province
Jinjiang Prefectural School of Supply and Marketing
  Address: Quanzhou, Fujian Province
Fujian Provincial School of Schools and Materials
  Address: Fuzhou, Fujian Province

Jiangxi Province (3 schools):

Jiangxi Provincial Banking School
  Address: Nanchang, Jiangxi Province
Jiangxi Provincial School of Accounting and Financial Affairs
  Address: Jiujiang, Jiangxi Province
Jiangxi Provincial School of Commerce
  Address: Xinjian County, Jiangxi Province

Shandong Province (17 schools):

Shandong Provincial School of Finance
  Address: Tai'an County, Shandong Province
Yantai School of Finance of Shandong Province
  Address: Yantai, Shandong Province
Shandong Provincial School of Foreign Trade
  Address: Qingdao, Shandong Province
Shandong Provincial Banking School
  Address: Jinan, Shandong Province
Shandong Provincial School of Commerce
  Address: Jinan, Shandong Province
Qingdao Commercial School of Shandong Province
  Address: Qingdao, Shandong Province
Yantai Commercial School of Shandong Province
  Address: Yantai, Shandong Province
Zibo Commercial School of Shandong Province
  Address: Zibo, Shandong Province
Changwei Commercial School of Shandong Province
  Address: Weifang, Shandong Province
Jining School of Supply and Marketing of Shandong Province
  Address: Jining, Shandong Province
Linyi Commercial School of Shandong Province
  Address: Linyi County, Shandong Province
Jinan School of Supply and Marketing
  Address: Jinan, Shandong Province
Changwei School of Supply and Marketing of Shandong Province
  Address: Weifang, Shandong Province
Dezhou School of Supply and Marketing of Shandong Province
  Address: Dezhou, Shandong Province
Jining School of Supply and Marketing of Shandong Province
  Address: Jining, Shandong Province
Hezhe School of Supply and Marketing of Shandong Province
  Address: Hezhe County, Shandong Province
Linyi School of Supply and Marketing of Shandong Province
  Address: Linyi County, Shandong Province

Henan Province (10 schools):

Henan Provincial School of Foreign Trade
  Address: Zhengzhou, Henan Province
Kaifeng Municipal School of Finance and Trade
  Address: Kaifeng, Henan Province
Anyang Municipal School of Accounting and Financial Affairs
  Address: Anyang, Henan Province
Jiaozuo School of Accounting and Financial Affairs
  Address: Jiaozuo, Henan Province
Henan Provincial Banking School
  Address: Zhengzhou, Henan Province
Henan Provincial Accounting School
  Address: Zhengzhou, Henan Province
Henan Provincial School of Commerce
  Address: Zhengzhou, Henan Province
Xuchang Prefectural School of Commerce
  Address: Xuchang, Henan Province
Shangqiu Prefectural School of Commerce
  Address: Shangqiu, Henan Province
Henan Provincial School of Supply and Marketing
  Address: Zhengzhou, Henan Province

Hubei Province (19 schools):

Wuhan Municipal School of Finance
  Address: Hankou, Hubei Province
Wuhan Municipal School of Finance and Trade
  Address: Hankou, Hubei Province
Huangshi Municipal School of Finance and Trade
  Address: Huangshi, Hubei Province
Shiyan Municipal School of Finance and Trade
  Address: Shiyan, Hubei Province
Xiangfan Municipal School of Finance and Trade
  Address: Xiangfan, Hubei Province
Huanggang Prefectural School of Finance and Trade
  Address: Huanggang County, Hubei Province
Xiaogan Prefectural School of Finance and Trade
  Address: Xiaogan County, Hubei Province

Xianning Prefectural School of Finance and Trade
Address: Xianning County, Hubei Province
Jingzhou Prefectural School of Finance and Trade
Address: Jiangling County, Hubei Province
Xiangyang Prefectural School of Finance and Trade
Address: Xiangfan, Hubei Province
Yunyang Prefectural School of Finance and Trade
Address: Shiyan, Hubei Province
Yichang Prefectural School of Finance and Trade
Address: Yichang, Hubei Privince
Enshi Prefectural School of Finance and Trade
Address: Enshi County, Hubei Province
Hubei Provincial School of Foreign Trade
Address: Wuchang, Hubei Province
Hubei Provincial Banking School
Address: Wuchang, Hubei Province
Hubei Provincial School of Commerce
Address: Wuchang, Hubei Province
Hubei Provincial School of Supply and Marketing
Address: Wuchang, Hubei Province
Hubei Provincial School of Goods and Materials
Address: Wuchang, Hubei Province
Hubei Provincial School of Trade in Farm and Sideline Products, Local Products and Specialities
Address: Suixian County, Hubei Province

Hunan Province (20 schools):

Hunan Provincial School of Finance and Accounting
Address: Changsha, Hunan Province
Zhuzhou School of Finance and Accounting
Address: Zhuzhou, Hunan Province
Xiangtan Prefectural School of Finance and Accounting
Address: Youxian County, Hunan
Hengyang Prefectural School of Finance and Economics
Address: Hengyang, Hunan Province
Hunan Provincial School of Foreign Trade
Address: Changsha, Hunan Province
Hunan Provincial Banking School
Address: Changsha, Hunan Province
Hunan Provincial School of Commerce
Address: Changsha, Hunan Province
Changsha Commercial School
Address: Changsha, Hunan Province
Xiangtan Prefectural School of Commerce
Address: Xiangtan County, Hunan Province
Chenzhou Prefectural School of Commerce
Address: Chenzhou, Hunan Province
Lingling Prefectural School of Commerce
Address: Lingling County, Hunan Province
Qianyang Prefectural School of Commerce
Address: Huaihua, Hunan Province

The Commercial School of West Hunan Autonomous Prefecture
Address: Jishou County, Hunan Province
Hunan Provincial School of Supply and Marketing
Address: Hanshou County, Hunan Province
Hengyang Prefectural School of Supply and Marketing
Address: Hengman County, Hunan Province
Shaoyang Prefectural School of Supply and Marketing
Address: Shaoyang, Hunan Province
Lianyuan Prefectural School of Supply and Marketing
Address: Lengshuijiang, Hunan Province
Changde Prefectural School of Supply and Marketing
Address: Changde, Hunan Province
Yiyang Prefectural School of Supply and Marketing
Address: Yiyang, Hunan Province
Hunan Provincial School of Goods and Materials
Address: Changsha, Hunan Province

Guangdong Province (22 schools):

Guangdong Provincial School of Finance
Address: Guangzhou, Guangdong Province
Guangzhou Municipal School of Finance
Address: Guangzhou, Guangdong Province
Foshan Prefectural School of Finance and Trade
Address: Foshan, Guangdong Province
Zhanjiang School of Finance and Trade
Address: Zhanjiang, Guangdong Province
Zhaoqing Prefectural School of finance and Trade
Address: Zhaoqing, Guangdong Province
Guangzhou Secondary School of Foreign Trade
Address: Guangzhou, Guangdong Province
Guangdong Banking School
Address: Guangzhou, Guangdong Province
Guangzhou Municipal Banking School
Address: Guangzhou, Guangdong Province
Guangdong Provincial School of Commerce
Address: Guangzhou, Guangdong Province
Guangzhou Municipal School of Supply, Marketing and Commerce
Address: Guangzhou, Guangdong Province
Guangzhou Secondary Technical School under the First Bureau of Commerce
Address: Guangzhou, Guangdong Province
Guangzhou Secondary Technical School under the Second Bureau of Commerce
Address: Guangzhou, Guangdong Province
The Commercial School of Hainan Autonomous Prefecture
Address: Tongshi Town, Hainan Island, Guangdong Province
Meixian Prefectural School of Commerce
Address: Meizhou, Guangdong Province

Shantou Prefectural School of Commerce
  Address: Shantou, Guangdong Province
Huiyang Prefectural School of Commerce
  Address: Huizhou, Guangdong Province
Guangdong Provincial School of Supply and Marketing
  Address: Nanhai County, Guangdong Province
Huiyang Prefectural School of Supply and Marketing
  Address: Huizhou, Guangdong Province
Shantou Prefectural School of Supply and Marketing
  Address: Huilai County, Guangdong Province
Hainan School of Supply and Marketing
  Address: Haikou, Guangdong Province
Guangdong Provincial School of Goods and Materials
  Address: Guangzhou, Guangdong Province
Guangzhou Secondary School of Services
  Address: Guangzhou, Guangdong Province

Guangxi Zhuang Autonomous Region (7 schools):

Guangxi School of Finance and Economics
  Address: Nanning, Guangxi Zhuang Autonomous Region
Guangxi Banking School
  Address: Nanning, Guangxi
Guangxi School of Foreign Trade
  Address: Nanning, Guangxi
Wuzhou Municipal Accounting School
  Address: Wuzhou, Guangxi Zhuang Autonomous Region
Guangxi Commercial School
  Address: Nanning, Guangxi
Guangxi School of Supply and Marketing
  Address: Nanning, Guangxi
Guangxi School of Goods and Materials
  Address: Nanning, Guangxi

Sichuan Province (26 schools):

Sichuan Provincial School of Finance
  Address: Chengdu, Sichuan Province
Sichuan Provincial School of Petroleum Finance and Economics
  Address: Nanchong, Sichuan Province
Chengdu Municipal School of Finance and Trade
  Address: Chengdu, Sichuan Province
Chongqing School of Finance and Trade
  Address: Chongqing, Sichuan Province
Zigong Municipal School of Finance and Trade
  Address: Zigong, Sichuan Province
Jiangjin Prefectural School of Finance and Trade
  Address: Yongchuan County, Sichuan Province
Fuling Prefectural School of Finance and Trade
  Address: Fuling County, Sichuan Province
Wanxian Prefectural School of Finance and Trade
  Address: Wanxian, Sichuan Province
Neijiang School of Finance and Trade
  Address: Neijiang, Sichuan Province
Luzhou School of Finance and Trade
  Address: Luzhou, Sichuan Province
Leshan School of Finance and Trade
  Address: Leshan, Sichuan Province
Wenjiang Prefectural School of Finance and Trade
  Address: Chongqing County, Sichuan Province
Mianyang School of Finance and Trade
  Address: Mianyang, Sichuan Province
Nanchong School of Finance and Trade
  Address: Nanchong, Sichuan Province
Daxian School of Finance and Trade
  Address: Daxian, Sichuan Province
Ya'an School of Finance and Trade
  Address: Ya'an County, Sichuan Province
The Finance and Trade School of Aba Autonomous Prefecture
  Address: Wenchuan County, Sichuan Province
The Finance and Trade School of Ganzi Autonomous Prefecture
  Address: Kangding County, Sichuan Province
The Finance and Trade School of Liangshan Autonomous Prefecture
  Address: Xichang, Sichuan Province
Sichuan Provincial Banking School
  Address: Chengdu, Sichuan Province
Sichuan Provincial School of Planning and Statistics
  Address: Neijiang, Sichuan Province
Chengdu Commercial School of Sichuan Province
  Address: Chengdu, Sichuan Province
Sichuan Provincial School of Supply and Marketing
  Address: Neijiang, Sichuan Province
Leshan Prefectural School of Supply and Marketing
  Address: Leshan, Sichuan Province
South Chuannan School of Industrial Management
  Address: Jiangjin County, Sichuan Province
Sichuan Provincial School of Tourism
  Address: Pixian County, Sichuan Province

Guizhou Province (16 schools):

Guizhou Provincial School of Finance
  Address: Guiyang, Guizhou Province
Guiyang Municipal School of Finance and Economics
  Address: Guiyang, Guizhou Province
Zunyi School of Finance and Trade
  Address: Zunyi, Guizhou Province
Anshun School of Finance and Trade
  Address: Anshun, Guizhou Province

Liupanshui School of Finance and Trade
   Address: Shuicheng Special District, Guizhou Province
Xingyi School of Finance and Trade
   Address: Xingyi County, Guizhou Province
Tongren School of Finance and Trade
   Address: Tongren County, Guizhou Province
Bijie School of Finance and Trade
   Address: Bijie County, Guizhou Province
Qiannan School of Finance and Trade
   Address: Duyun, Guizhou Province
Qiandongnan School of Finance and Trade
   Address: Kaili County, Guizhou Province
Guizhou Provincial School of Foreign Trade
   Address: Guiyang, Guizhou Province
Guizhou Provincial Banking School
   Address: Guiyang, Guizhou Province
Guizhou Provincial School of Commerce
   Address: Guiyang, Guizhou Province
Guizhou Provincial School of Supply and Marketing
   Address: Guiyang, Guizhou Province
Duyun School of Supply and Marketing
   Address: Duyun, Guizhou Province
Guizhou Provincial School of Goods and Materials
   Address: Guiyang, Guizhou Province

Yunnan Province (16 schools):

Yunnan Provincial School of Finance and Economics
   Address: Kunming, Yunnan Province
Yunnan Provincial School of Finance and Trade
   Address: Kunming, Yunnan Province
Kunming Municipal School of Finance and Trade
   Address: Kunming, Yunnan Province
Zhaotong School of Finance and Trade
   Address: Zhaotong County, Yunnan Province
Qujing School of Finance and Trade
   Address: Qujing County, Yunnan Province
Wenshan School of Finance and Trade
   Address: Wenshan County, Yunnan Province
Honghe School of Finance and Trade
   Address: Gejiu, Yunnan Province
Chuxiong School of Finance and Trade
   Address: Chuxiong County, Yunnan Province
Dali School of Finance and Trade
   Address: Xiaguan, Yunnan Province
Lijiang School of Finance and Trade
   Address: Lijiang County, Yunnan Province
Lincang School of Finance and Trade
   Address: Lincang County, Yunnan Province
Baoshan School of Finance and Trade
   Address: Baoshan County, Yunnan
Yuxi School of Finance and Trade
   Address: Yuxi County, Yunnan
Simao School of Finance and Trade
   Address: Pu'er County, Yunnan Province
Dehong School of Finance and Trade
   Address: Luxi County, Yunnan
Yunnan Banking School
   Address: Kunming, Yunnan

Tibet Autonomous Region (1 school):

The School of Finance and Economics of Tibet Autonomous Region
   Address: Lhasa, Tibet Autonomous Region

Shaanxi Province (8 schools):

Shaanxi Provincial School of Finance and Economics
   Address: Xi'an, Shaanxi Province
Xi'an Municipal School of Finance and Trade
   Address: Xi'an, Shaanxi Province
Shaanxi Provincial School of Foreign Trade
   Address: Xi'an, Shaanxi Province
Shaanxi Provincial Banking School
   Address: Xi'an, Shaanxi Province
Shaanxi Provincial School of Statistics
   Address: Xi'an, Shaanxi Province
Shaanxi Provincial School of Commerce
   Address: Xi'an, Shaanxi Province
Shaanxi Provincial School of Supply and Marketing
   Address: Xi'an, Shaanxi Province
Baoji School of Supply and Marketing
   Address: Baoji, Shaanxi Province

Gansu Province (3 schools):

Gansu Provincial School of Finance and Trade
   Address: Lanzhou, Gansu Province
Lanzhou Municipal School of Commerce
   Address: Lanzhou, Gansu Province
Gansu Provincial School of Supply and Marketing
   Address: Lanzhou, Gansu Province

Qinghai Province (2 schools):

Qinghai Provincial School of Finance and Economics
   Address: Xining, Qinghai Province
Qinghai Provincial School of Commerce
   Address: Xining, Qinghai Province

Ningxia Hui Autonomous Region (1 school):

Ningxia School of Finance and Economics
   Address: Yinchuan, Ningxia Hui Autonomous Region

Xinjiang Uygur Autonomous Region (11 schools):

Xinjiang Finance School
   Address: Urumqi, Xinjiang
Urumqi School of Finance and Trade
   Address: Urumqi, Xinjiang
Tacheng School of Finance and Trade
   Address: Tacheng County, Xinjiang
Ili School of Finance and Trade
   Address: Yining, Xinjiang
Bayingolin School of Finance and Trade
   Address: Korla, Xinjiang
Hotan School of Finance and Trade
   Address: Hotan County, Xinjiang
Kashi School of Finance and Trade
   Address: Kashi, Xinjiang
Aksu School of Finance and Trade
   Address: Aksu County, Xinjiang
The Banking School of the Xinjiang Uygur Autonomous Region
   Address: Changji County, Xinjiang
The Commercial School of the Xinjiang Uygur Autonomous Region
   Address: Urumqi, Xinjiang
Xinjiang Supply and Marketing School
   Address: Shihezi, Xinjiang

5. LISTING OF ECONOMIC SOCIETIES IN CHINA
Compiled by the Library of the Institute of Industrial Economy,
Chinese Academy of Social Sciences

The World Economic Society of China

President: Qian Junrui
Liaison Officer: Zhou Furen
Address:
15 North Shatan St., Beijing
Tel: 443551
Date of Establishment: April 1980

The Agricultural Economic Society of China

Leading Cadre: Cai Ziwei
Liaison Officer: Zhou Binhin
Address:
Ministry of Agriculture, Hepingli, Beijing
Tel: 594961-06
Date of Establishment: October 1978

The Financial Society of China

President: Rong Zihe
Liaison Officer: Hou Rongyao
Address:
The Institute of Financial Science of the History of Finance, Sanlihe, Beijing
Tel: 866044
Date of Establishment: January 1980

The Banking Society of China

President: Chen Xiyu
Liaison Officer: Chen Jian
Address:
The Banking Institute of the People's Bank of China, Sanlihe, Beijing
Tel: 791230
Date of Establishment: December 1979

The Society for Research on Socialist Political Economy

Leading Cadre: Feng Lanrui
Liaison Officer: Zhu Wenxin
Address:
The Political Department of the Beijing College of Economics, Beijing
Tel: 593831-321
Date of Establishment: May 1980

The Society of Labour Wages in China

Secretary General: Zhao Lukuan
Liaison Officer: Chang Peiyu
Address:
Research Department of Labour Economics, the People's University of China, Beijing
Tel: 285431-2873
Date of Establishment: October 1978

The Society of Statistics of China

Leading Cadre: Xue Muqiao
Liaison Officer: Huang Hai
Address:
State Statistical Bureau, Sanlihe, Beijing
Tel: 868521-730
Date of Establishment: November 1979

The Society for Research on Technological Economics in China

Secretary General: Xu Shoubo
Liaison Officer: Ren Yen
Address:
The Technical Economy Commission of the Chinese Association for Science and Technology, Sanlihe, Beijing
Tel: 866044
Date of Establishment: November 1978

The Society for Research on Capital Construction Economics in China

President: Han Guang
Liaison Officer: Zhou Puren
Address:
The Economics Institute of the State Capital Construction Commission, Baiwanzhuang, Beijing
Tel: 8992935
Date of Establishment: July 1980

The Society for Research on Modern Management in China

Leading Cadre: He Jianwen
Liaison Officer: Zou Hai
Address:
   The Institute of Modernized Management of China, The Chinese Association for Science and Technology, Sanlihe, Beijing
Tel: 661381
Date of Establishment: November 1978

The Society of Material Economy of China

President: Yu Xiaogu
Liaison Officer: Gao Bo
Address:
   25 North Yuetan St., Beijing
Tel: 890941-633
Date of Establishment: March 1980

The Accounting Society of China

President: Wang Bingqian
Liaison Officer: Yang Jiwan
Address:
   Accounting System Bureau, Ministry of Finance, Beijing
Tel: 868451-245
Date of Establishment: January 1980

The Society for Research on Economic Productivity in China

President: Yu Guangyuan
Liaison Officer: Wang Shengxi
Address:
   The Institute of Economics, Chinese Academy of Social Sciences, 2 Yuetan Beixiaojie, Beijing
Tel: 890651-261
Date of Establishment: November 1980

The Society of the History of Economic Thought of China

Leading Cadre: Hu Jichuang
Liaison Officer: Sun Yin
Address:
   369 North Zhongshan Rd., Shanghai
Date of Establishment: June 1980

The Society of Forestry Economics in China

Leading Cadre: Young Wentao
Liaison Officer: Chen Xiuyan
Address:
   The Institute of Forestry Economics, Ministry of Forestry, West Hepingli St., Beijing
Tel: 464616
Date of Establishment: June 1980

The Society for Research on the U.S. Economy

Secretary-General: Teng Weizao
Liaison Officer: Zheng Deguo
Address:
   The Institute of North America, Wuhan University, Wuhan, Hubei Province
Date of Establishment: October 1978

The Society for Research on International Economic Relations

President: Shi Yin
Liaison Officer: Guo Zhenyuan
Address:
   28 Donghouxiang, Andingmenwai, Beijing
Tel: 462247
Date of Establishment: July 1979

The Society for Research on China's Quantitative Economics

President: Wu Jiapei
Liaison Officer: Hu Daiguang
Address:
   The Economics Department, Beijing University, Beijing
Tel: 282471
Date of Establishment: July 1979

The Society for Research on Animal Husbandry in China

Leading Cadre: Zhan Wu
Liaison Officer: Zhu Yingke
Address:
   The Institute of Agricultural Economy, Chinese Academy of Social Sciences, 2 Yuetan Beixiao-Jie, Beijing
Tel: 890651-221
Date of Establishment: August 1978

The Society for Research on China's Territorial Economics

Leading Cadre: Yu Guangyuan
Liaison Officer: Liu Yuren
Address:
   The Scientific and Technological Commission of the People's Republic of China, Sanlihe, Beijing.
Tel: 862014
Date of Establishment: November 1980

The Society for Research on the Soviet Economy

Secretary General: Mei Wenbin
Liaison Officer: Liu Xiulian
Address:
   The Institute of World Economy, 15 North Shatan St., Beijing
Tel: 445469
Date of Establishment: 1978

The Preparatory Committee of the Society for Research on the Economy of Minority Nationalities in China

Leading Cadre: Zhang Yangwu
Liaison Officer: He Yuehua
Address:
   Office of the Institute of Minority Nationalities Economy, Central Institute for Nationalities, Beijing
Tel: 890775-302
Date of Establishment: November 1980

The Society for Research on Transportation Economics in China

Leading Cadre: Zhang Siqi
Liaison Officer: Wang Derong
Address:
   The Institute of Comprehensive Transportation, State Economic Commission, Beijing
Tel: 443594
Date of Establishment: December 1979

The Society for Research on Foreign Economic Theories

President: Chen Daisun
Liaison Officer: Li Yining
Address:
   The Economics Department, Beijing University, Beijing
Tel: 282471
Date of Establishment: September 1979

The Society for Research on the West European Economy

Leading Cadre: Yu Kaixiang
Liaison Officer: Wu Yikang
Address:
   The Institute of World Economy, Fudan University, Shanghai
Tel: 480906
Date of Establishment: December 1978

The Society for Research on the Yugoslavian Economy

Secretary General: Luo Yuanzheng
Liaison Officer: Liu Guoping
Address:
   The Institute of World Economy, 15 North Shatan St., Beijing
Tel: 444964
Date of Establishment: August 1978

The Society for Research on the Japanese Economy

Leading Cadre: Luo Yuanzheng
Liaison Officer: Sun Hanchao
Address:
   The Institute of Foreign Trade, Ministry of Foreign Trade, Beijing
Tel: 553031-722
Date of Establishment: August 1978

The Society for Research on the Romanian Economy

Secretary General: Mei Wenbin
Liaison Officer: Guo Qingyun
Address:
   The Institute of Soviet and East European Affairs, People's University of China, Beijing
Tel: 284076
Date of Establishment: 1979

The Society for Research on the Korean Economy

Secretary General: Shi Yin
Liaison Officer: Han Zhengshe
Address:
   The Institute of World Economy, 15 North Shatan St., Beijing
Tel: 444964
Date of Establishment: August 1978

The Society for Research on African Affairs

Secretary General: Zhang Tongzhu
Liaison Officer: Zhang Yaozeng
Address:
   Department of Geography, Nanjing University, Nanjing
Tel: 34651-401
Date of Establishment: July 1979

The Society for Research on China's Maritime Economy

President: Luo Yuanzheng
Liaison Officer: Ruxiang
Address:
   The Institute of Economics, Nankai University, Tianjin
Tel: 264696
Date of Establishment: April 1980

The Society for Research on Foreign Agricultural Economy

Leading Cadre: Zhan Wu
Liaison Officer: Zhu Yingke
Address:
   The Institute of Agricultural Economy, 2 Yuetan Beixiaojie, Beijing
Tel: 890651-221
Date of Establishment: August 1978

The Society for Research on Costs in China

Leading Cadre: Xu Yi
Liaison Officer: Zheng Yanxin
Address:
   The Institute of Finance and Materials Economics, Chinese Academy of Social Sciences, 2 Yuetan Beixiaojie, Beijing
Tel: 890651-204
Date of Establishment: September 1980

The Society for Research on the Economics of Agricultural Mechanization of the Society of Agricultural Mechanization

Leading Cadre: Yao Jianfu
Liaison Officer: Yao Jianfu
Address:
   P.O.B. 940, Beishatan, Deshengmenwai, Beijing
Tel: 441331-291
Date of Establishment: October 1980

The Academic Committee of Architectural Economics of the Architectural Society of China

Leading Cadre: Cheng Xi
Liaison Officer: Yao Jiaqing
Address:
   The Research Department, Chinese Academy of Architectural Science, Beijing
Tel: 8992692
Date of Establishment: July 1979

The Society for Research on the Economics of Water Conservation in China

President: Zhang Jinqing
Liaison Officer: Li Yupu
Address:
   Policy Research Department, Ministry of Water Conservation, Beijing
Tel: 365331-375
Date of Establishment: November 1980

The Society for Research on Optimum Design Administration in China

Leading Cadre: Zou Hai
Liaison Officer: Ran Yiqun
Address:
   23 Shijinhuayuan, Dongshi, Beijing
Date of Establishment: May 1980

The Society for Research on Technological Economics in China's Mining Industry

Secretary General: Zhao Xiangming
Liaison Officer: Han Guoxun
Address:
   The Design and Research Institute of Iron Mines, City Government Square, Anshan, Liaoning Province
Tel: 3184
Date of Establishment: November 1979

The Society for Research on the Economics of Fisheries in China

Leading Cadre: Zhan Wu
Liaison Officer: Zhu Yingke
Address:
   The Institute of Agricultural Economy, 2 Yuetan Beixiaojie, Beijing
Tel: 890651-221
Date of Establishment: November 1978

The Society for Research on Forestry Economics in China

Leading Cadre: Zhan Wu
Liaison Officer: Zhu Yingke
Address:
   The Institute of Agricultural Economy, 2 Yuetan Beixiaojie, Beijing
Tel: 890651-221
Date of Establishment: December 1978

The Society for Research on the Science of Economic Geography and Education in China

President: Sun Jingzhi
Liaison Officer: Yu Di
Address:
   The Finance and Trade Department, Beijing College of Economics
Tel: 893831-339
Date of Establishment: October 1980

The Society for Environmental Management Economics and Law in China

President: Chen Xiping
Liaison Officer: Chen Dongsheng
Address:
   The Institute of Industrial Economy, Chinese Academy of Social Sciences
Tel: 890651-217
Date of Establishment: February 1980

The Society for Research on Educational Economics in China (Preparatory Group)

Leading Cadre: Wang Tie
Liaison Officer: Li Jianwei
Address:
   The Research Department in Educational Theory, Central Institute of Educational Science in China, Beijing
Tel: 665931-355
Date of Establishment: September 1980

The Society for Technological Economics and Modernization of Management in the Chemical Industry

President: Wei Ruilang
Liaison Officer: Shi Zehan
Address:
   The Institute of Technological Economics, Planning Bureau, Ministry of Chemical Industry, Hepingli, Beijing
Tel: 462961-377
Date of Establishment: April 1980

The Society for Research on Optimization in Operations Research and Economics Mathematics of China

Leading Cadre: Hua Luogeng
Liaison Officer: Chen Dequan
Address:
   Entrance 19, Friendship Hotel, Beijing
Tel: 894253
Date of Establishment: April 1981

6. ANNOTATED SURVEY OF CHINA'S MAJOR ECONOMICS PERIODICALS
By Gao Liang
*Library of the Institute of Industrial Economy,
Chinese Academy of Social Science*

Economic Studies

Editor-in-Chief: Xu Dixin
Editing Organization:
  Editorial Board of *Economic Studies*
Publisher: People's Publishing House
First Year of Publication: 1955
Number of Issues Per Year: 12
Circulation: 130,000
Subscription Rate: 0.30 yuan (per copy)
Address of the Editorial Board:
  2 Yuetan Beixiaojie, Fuchengmenwai, Beijing
Readership:
  Economic researchers, students and teaching staff in economic institutes, cadres working in the economics field and amateur researchers.
Main Contents:
  A comprehensive theoretical journal, it carries articles on the study of economic problems arising in the course of China's drive for socialist modernization; basic Marxist economic theory; departmental economics, the economics of productive forces, demographic theory and mathematical economics; economic history and the history of economic thought in China and other countries; etc.

World Economy

Editor-in-Chief: Qian Junrui
Editing Organization:
  Chinese Society of World Economy and the Institute of World Economy and Politics, the Chinese Academy of Social Sciences
Publisher:
  Chinese Social Sciences Publishing House
Date of First Publication: March 1978
Number of Issues Per Year: 12
Circulation: 33,000
Subscription Rate: 0.35 yuan (per copy)
Address of the Editorial Board:
  15 Shatan St. (N), Beijing
Readership:
  Economic researchers, students and teaching staff of economics faculties and departments in colleges and universities, cadres in government economic departments, managerial staff in mines, factories and other enterprises, etc.
Main Contents:
  It deals with economic problems of major theoretical interest in the contemporary world, especially problems of economic development in capitalist, socialist and developing countries, gives full coverage to the economic growth of various countries and the important practical problems in their economic relations, and describes trends in academic studies of the world economy at home and abroad. In order to serve the needs of China's modernization programme, it makes a point of carrying articles on the approaches, methods and special features of economic modernization in various countries, on the experience and lessons to be drawn from such modernization and on future world political and economic development that will have a direct bearing on China's modernization.

China's Economic Problems

Editor-in-Chief: Yuan Zhenyue
Editing Organization:
  Editorial Board of *China's Economic Problems*
Publisher:
  Institute of Economy, Xiamen University
Date of First Publication: January 1959
Number of Issues Per Year: 6
Circulation: 30,000
Subscription Rate: 0.35 yuan (per copy)
Address of the Editorial Board:
  Institute of Economy, Xiamen University, Fujian Province
Readership:
  Theoretical workers in economics in colleges, universities and research institutes and people working in government departments and enterprises.
Main Contents:
  A comprehensive theoretical journal, it carries articles mainly on the exposition of Marxist economic theory and Comrade Mao Zedong's creative contributions to Marxist economics; exposition of the line, principles and policies laid down at the Third Plenary Session of the 11th Central Committee of the Communist Party of China and the criticism of the "Left" thinking prevailing in the economic field; discussion of new problems in China's moderniza-

tion programme by linking theory with practice; study and exposition of problems of economic theory and economic management in socialist construction; problems involving planning statistics, accounting, banking, finance and foreign trade; and the study of China's economic history and the history of Chinese economic thought.

Economic Theory and Economic Management

Editor-in-Chief: Song Tao
Editing Organization: Chinese People's University
Publisher:
   Chinese People's University Publishing House
Date of First Publication: January 1981
Number of Issues Per Year: 6
Circulation: 50,000 (estimated)
Subscription Rate: 0.40 yuan (per copy)
Address of the Editorial Board:
   Chinese People's University, Western Suburbs, Beijing
Readership:
   Researchers in economics, students and teaching staff of faculties and departments of economics and finance in colleges and universities, practical workers in economics, and cadres engaged in economic management.
Main Contents:
   A comprehensive economics journal, it attaches importance to the study of new problems in economic activiities and theories with a view to promoting China's economic construction and the growth of its economics science. It carries articles mainly about economics theory, departmental economics studies and economics management, and publishes articles and information about the study of economics classics and surveys and about the evaluation of economic theories at home and abroad.

Economic and Management Studies

Chief Editors: Liu Dekuan, Guo Daofu
Editing Organization:
   Editorial Board of *Economic and Management Studies,* Beijing College of Economics
Publisher: As above
Date of First Publication: July 1980
Number of Issues Per Year: 4
Circulation: 20,000
Subscription Rate: 0.45 yuan (per copy)
Address of the Editorial Board:
   Beijing College of Economics, Hong Miao, Chaoyangmenwai, Beijing
Readership:
   Managerial staff in enterprises, working staff in government economic departments, economic researchers and students, and teaching staff in colleges and institutes of economics.
Main Contents:
   It deals chiefly with economic theories, economic management and management of enterprises, with emphasis on the study of enterprise management and departmental and specialized economics. Main columns include lectures on management of enterprises, exchange of experience in enterprise management, a forum for managerial staff, economic data, a digest of managerial experience, and trends in management abroad.

Trends in Economic Studies

Editor-in-Chief: Xu Dixin
Editing Organization:
   Editorial Board of *Trends in Economic Studies,* Institute of Economics, Chinese Academy of Social Sciences
Publisher:
   Chinese Social Sciences Publishing House
Date of First Publication: January 1961
Number of Issues Per Year: 12
Circulation: 31,000
Subscription Rate: 0.30 yuan (per copy)
Address of the Editorial Board:
   2 Yuetan Beixiaojie, Fuchengmenwai, Beijing
Readership:
   Theoretical workers in economics and staff in government economics departments.
Main Contents:
   A learned journal dealing with economic trends and information, it carries domestic information about major academic activities in the economics field and short articles about discussions (with restricted participation) of practical economic problems and problems of basic theory in economics and departmental economics; reports on economic investigatigations (with restricted participation) and information about economic studies. Also gives information about important international symposiums on theoretical studies, research into economic theories abroad, and foreign commentaries on China's economic policies and theories. It carries briefings of Chinese scholars on their return from visits abroad and articles about the academic activities of foreign scholars in China as well as information about different schools of economics, new branches of economic studies, and economics institutions in foreign countries. It also carries brief introductions to

eminent economists at home and abroad, information about new books on economics by domestic and foreign scholars and reviews of well-known economics works.

Economic Management

Editor-in-Chief: Ma Hong
Editing Organization:
Editorial Board of *Economic Management*
Publisher: The Office of *Economic Management*
Date of First Publication: January 1979
Number of Issues Per Year: 12
Circulation: 300,000
Subscription Rate: 0.30 yuan (per copy)
Address of the Editorial Board:
2 Yuetan Beixiaojie, Fuchengmenwai, Beijing
Readership:
Leading cadres and staff in economic enterprises and operations at the grassroots.
Main Contents:
It carries articles to explain the principles and policies of the Chinese Communist Party and government, discuss the theory and practice of management, report on advanced experience in management at home and abroad, and spread basic management knowledge as widely as possible.

Pricing: Theory and Practice

Editor-in-Chief: Hu Bangding
Editing Organization:
State Bureau of Prices and Institute of Economics, Nankai University, Tianjin
Publisher:
Chinese Financial and Economic Publishing House
Date of First Publication: January 20, 1981
Number of Issues Per Year: 6
Circulation: 35,000
Subscription Rate: 0.33 yuan (per copy)
Address of the Editorial Board:
Institute of Economics, Nankai University, Tianjin
Readership:
People engaged in pricing work and researchers and teaching staff dealing with pricing theory.
Main Contents:
Articles discussing theories and laws of pricing, studies of the system of management of commodity prices, exchange of experience in pricing work, information on readjustment of prices, selected price indices and evaluations of the pricing systems of other countries.

Inquiry into Economic Problems

Editor-in-Chief: Li Qiaonian
Editing Organizations:
Economic Society of Yunnan, the Institute of Economics of Yunnan, and the Editorial Board of *Inquiry Into Economic Problems*
Publisher: People's Publishing House, Yunnan
Date of First Publication: January 1980
Number of Issues Per Year: 6
Circulation: 10,500
Subscription Rate: 0.30 yuan (per copy)
Address of the Editorial Board:
Institute of Economics of Yunnan, Dongfeng Rd. (E), Kunming, Yunnan Province
Readership:
Theoretical as well as practical workers in economics.
Main Contents:
Articles on the economic theory of Marxism-Leninism and Mao Zedong Thought, socialist economic problems, problems relating to departmental, regional and nationality economics, economic history and the history of economic thought, the analysis of contemporary capitalism and bourgeois economic theories, random economic thoughts and trends in economic studies.

Economic Science

Editor-in-Chief: Chen Daisun
Editing Organization:
Editorial Board of *Economic Science,* Faculty of Economics, Beijing University
Publisher:
Chinese Financial and Economic Publishing House
Date of First Publication: November 1979
Number of Issues Per Year: 4
Circulation: 25,000
Subscription Rate: 0.40 yuan (per copy)
Address of the Editorial Board:
The Fourth Compound of Beijing University, Haidian, Western Suburbs, Beijing
Readership:
Theoretical workers in economics, economic staff in government departments and enterprises, students and teaching staff of departments and faculties of economics in colleges and universities, and amateur researchers in economics.
Main Contents:
A learned economic journal, it carries research papers, specialized studies, book reviews, reading notes, discussions, academic materials and new developments relating to economics,

economic management, world economy, Chinese and foreign economic history and the history of economic ideas, contemporary bourgeois economics, economic statistics, etc.

Enterprise Management

Editor-in-Chief: Ma Hong
Editing Organization:
   Chinese Association of Enterprise Management
Publisher:
   Enterprise Management Publishing House
Date of First Publication: March 1980
Number of Issues Per Year: 6
Circulation: 130,000
Subscription Rate: 0.25 yuan (per copy)
Address of the Editorial Board:
   Room 801, State Economic Commission Building, Beijing
Readership:
   Cadres engaged in the management of enterprises and the economic sector and workers and staff in enterprises.
Main Contents:
   Articles expounding the party's line, principles and policies in economic work, reports on the experience and methods of enterprise management at home and abroad, discussions of theories of enterprise management and popularization of basic knowledge of the scientific management of enterprises.

Problems of Agricultural Economy

Editor-in-Chief: Wang Gengjin
Editing Organizations:
   Editorial Board of *Problems of Agricultural Economy*, Institute of Agricultural Economy, Chinese Academy of Social Sciences
Publisher:
   Chinese Social Sciences Publishing House
Date of First Publication: January 23, 1980
Number of Issues Per Year: 12
Circulation: 26,000
Subscription Rate: 0.30 yuan (per copy)
Address of the Editorial Board:
   2 Yuetan Beixiaojie, Fuchengmenwai, Beijing
Readership:
   Researchers in government agricultural economic departments, students and teaching staff in departments and faculties of agricultural economics, cadres engaged in rural work and amateur researchers in agricultural economics.
Main Contents:
   A national theoretical journal of agricultural economy, it carries articles on principles and policies for promoting China's agricultural economy and its structural reforms, approaches and methods for China's agricultural modernization, investigation of economic conditions in the rural areas, the agricultural economic situation at home and abroad, the essentials of agricultural economics, etc.

Materials Management

Editor-in-Chief: Yu Xiagu
Editing Organization:
   Research Section, State Bureau of Supplies
Publisher: Supplies Publishing House
Date of First Publication: August 1980
Number of Issues Per Year: 6
Circulation: 30,000
Subscription Rate: 0.30 yuan (per copy)
Address of the Editorial Board:
   25 Yuetan St. (N), Xicheng District, Beijing
Readership:
   Workers and staff concerned with materials and supplies management and general teaching and research staff.
Main Contents:
   A specialized journal dealing with the circulation and management of goods and materials or means of production, it expounds Marxist theory on the distribution of goods and materials, helps to promote the principles, policies, laws, decrees and regulations of the party and the state, exchanges information concerning experience, carries investigative data and research results on goods and materials management, comments on foreign trends relating to the circulation of goods and materials, and introduces related practical economic and technical knowledge and publications on this subject.

Studies of Architectural Economics

Editor-in-Chief: Wu Luoshan
Editing Organization:
   Editorial Board of *Studies of Architectural Economics*
Publisher:
   Chinese Architectural Industry Publishing House
Date of First Publication: February 15, 1980
Number of Issues Per Year: 4
Circulation: 10,000
Subscription Rate: 0.30 yuan (per copy)
Address of the Editorial Board:
   Chinese Institute of Architectural Science, 19 Chegongzhuang, Xishimenwai, Beijing

Readership:
Architects, builders and construction personnel, research and teaching staff at various levels.
Main Contents:
Basic theories of architectural economics, management and technology economics, modern management techniques in architectural economics, the trends in Chinese and foreign research into architectural economics, and lecture notes on the fundamentals of architectural economics.

Business Research

Chief Editors: Zhou Limin, Li Dianjun
Editing Organization:
Commercial College of Heilongjiang
Publisher: As above
Year of First Publication: 1958
Number of Issues Per Year: 6
Circulation: 22,000
Subscription Rate: 0.30 yuan (per copy)
Address of the Editorial Board:
50 Tongda St., Harbin, Heilongjiang Province
Readership:
Students and teaching staff in commercial colleges, business staff, and economic researchers.
Main Contents:
A comprehensive publication, it covers general information and studies about theories of commercial economics, management of businesses and enterprises, business science and techniques, business education and foreign business trends.

Business Accounting

Chief Editors:
Ministry of Commerce, Ministry of Food, and the All-China Federation of Supply and Marketing Co-operatives
Editing Organization:
Editorial Board of *Business Accounting*
Publisher: As above
Date of First Publication: January 1980
Number of Issues Per Year: 12
Circulation: 120,000
Subscription Rate: 0.20 yuan (per copy)
Address of the Editorial Board:
Ministry of Commerce Building, Xidan, Beijing
Readership:
Treasurers and accountants in the Ministry of Commerce, the Ministry of Food, the All-China Federation of Supply and Marketing Co-operatives and their subordinate organs at all levels, and students and teaching staff in colleges of finance and economics.

Main Contents:
Articles on the implementation of financial and economic policies, laws, decrees and regulations; theoretical expositions and discussions; research into business finance and accounting. It also carries lecture notes on the basic knowledge of business finance and accounting and reports experience in teaching these subjects as well as experience with regard to operation and management, improvement of output and economy, loss reduction and profit maximization, business management and accounting.

China Banking

Editor-in-Chief: Zhu Chuan
Editing Organization:
Editorial Board of *China Banking*
Publisher: China Banking Publishing House
First Year of Publication: 1952
Number of Issues Per Year: 12
Circulation: over 100,000
Subscription Rate: 0.25 yuan (per copy)
Address of the Editorial Board:
22 Xijiaominxiang, Beijing
Readership:
Cadres and staff on the banking front, students and teaching staff in colleges of finance and economics, researchers in banking theory and treasurers and accountants in government departments and enterprises.
Main Contents:
Articles explaining the party's economic and banking principles and policies, expounding banking, monetary and credit theories, exchanging experience on banking work, discussing banking theories and introducing basic knowledge of banking work.

Problems of International Trade

Chief Editor: Institute of International Trade
Editing Organization:
Editorial Board of *Problems of International Trade*
Publisher:
Chinese Financial and Economic Publishing House
First Year of Publication: 1977
Number of Issues Per Year: 24
Circulation: 10,000–15,000
Subscritpion Rate: 0.30 yuan (per copy)
Address of the Editorial Board:
Box No. 27, Beijing Institute of Foreign Trade, Xiao Guan, Andingmenwai, Beijing

Readership:
Cadres in ministries of Foreign Trade, Foreign Affairs, Commerce, Industries and Communications and people in the relevant colleges, research institutes, libraries, etc.

Main Contents:
Articles expounding Marxist-Leninist theories on international trade and world economy and China's principles and policies regarding foreign trade; basic knowledge and systematic data about world trade and China's foreign trade and reports on results and experience gained in the study of problems of China's foreign trade (import and export undertakings, foreign market surveys, availability of goods for export, storage and transport, international clearance, financial management, customs commodity inspection, packing, advertizement, trademark patents and judicial arbitration); structural reform of China's foreign trade, processing and assembly, compensation trade, joint ventures and leasing trade. It also carries theses and specialized materials dealing with economic and trade problems in the contemporary capitalist world.

Demographic Research

Editor-in-Chief: Liu Zheng
Editing Organization:
Demographic Institute, Chinese People's University
Publisher:
Chinese People's University Publishing House
First Year of Publication: 1977
Number of Issues Per Year: 4
Circulation: 40,000
Subscription Rate: 0.35 yuan (per copy)
Address of the Editorial Board:
39 Haidian Rd., Beijing
Readership:
Researchers, teaching staff and practical workers in demography-related fieldss.
Main Contents:
Articles, reports and information about demographic theories, academic trends, problems, policies and statistics, as well as the content of courses and teaching methods in demography. It also provides information about problems of demographic studies abroad.

Population and Economics

Editor-in-Chief: Sun Jingzhi

Editing Organization:
Editorial Board of *Population and Economics,* Institute of Demographic Economics, Beijing College of Economics
Circulation: 12,000
Subscription Rate: 0.35 yuan (per copy)
Address of the Editorial Board:
Hong Miao, Chaoyangmenwai, Beijing
Readership:
Researchers and teaching staff in the demographic field, workers in family planning and others engaged in demographic studies as well as the general public.
Main Contents:
A comprehensive journal of demography, it carries articles, reports, statistics, translations and materials about domestic and foreign trends in demographic theory, economics and geography, urban and national minority population, demographic statistics, sociology and ecology, and eugenics.

Finance

Chief Editors: Zuo Chuntai, Qian Duling
Editing Organization: Editorial Board of *Finance*
Publisher:
Chinese Financial and Economic Publishing House
First Year of Publication:
1956 (publication suspended in July 1966 and resumed in January 1980)
Number of Issues Per Year: 12
Circulation: 40,000
Subscription Rate: 0.20 yuan (per copy)
Address of the Editorial Board:
Ministry of Finance, Sanlihe, Fuxingmenwai, Beijing
Readership:
Cadres on the financial front, researchers in finance and economics and students and teaching staff in departments, faculties and colleges of finance and economics.
Main Contents:
Articles expounding the line, principles and policies of the party and state in financial work, unfolding discussion of financial theory and practice, exchanging experience in financial work, reporting on the achievements and developments on the financial front and providing selective information about financial work in foreign countries.

Finance and Accounting

Chief Editors: Zuo Chuntai, Qian Duling

Editing Organization:
   Editorial Board of *Finance and Accounting*
Publisher:
   Chinese Financial and Economic Publishing House
Date of First Publication: January 1979
Number of Issues Per Year: 12
Circulation: 430,000
Subscription Rate: 0.20 yuan (per copy)
Address of the Editorial Board:
   Ministry of Finance, Sanlihe, Fuxingmenwai, Beijing
Readership:
   Treasurers and accountants, researchers in finance and accounting, and students and teaching staff of departments and faculties of finance and accounting in schools and colleges, with treasurers and accountants in industrial enterprises composing the bulk of readers.
Main Contents:
   A specialized publication of finance and accounting with emphasis on the latter, it carries articles expounding the principles and policies of the party and the state on financial work, exchanging experience, discussing theoretical as well as practical problems, disseminating essential knowledge and reporting on developments in finance and accounting, and provides information about work in this field abroad.

Financial and Economic Stddies

Editor-in-Chief: Guo Senqi
Editing Organization:
   Editorial Board of *Financial and Economic Studies*, Shanghai College of Finance and Economics
Publisher:
   Scientific Research Section, Shanghai College of Finance and Economics
Date of First Publication: September 1956
Number of Issues Per Year: 4
Circulation: 5,000
Subscription Rate: 0.40 yuan (per copy)
Address of the Editorial Board:
   369 Zhongshan Rd. (N1), Shanghai
Readership:
   Students and teaching staff in colleges of finance and economics, cadres and workers on the financial and economic fronts, etc.
Main Contents:
   Articles on Marxist economic theory, industrial economics, agricultural economics, business economics, finance, banking, accounting, statistics and other financial and economic topics; experience in financial and economic work, study reports; trends in economic studies, and economic theories and related developments abroad. It also carries book reviews.

Studies of Financial and Economic Problems

Editor-in-Chief: Tong Zhehui
Editing Organization:
   Editorial Board of *Studies of Financial and Economic Problems*
Publisher:
   Institute of Economics, Liaoning College of Finance and Economics
Date of First Publication: October 1979
Number of Issues Per Year: 4
Circulation: 20,000
Subscription Rate: 0.30 yuan (per copy)
Address of the Editorial Board:
   Liaoning College of Finance and Economics, Dalian, Liaoning Province
Readership:
   Students and teaching staff in the social sciences in colleges and universities and other specialized and amateur researchers in finance and economics.
Main Contents:
   Articles and notes on various branches of financial and economic studies, such as basic economic theory, finance, banking, accounting, capital construction investment, planning, statistics, enterprise management, goods and materials management, business economics and the economics of foreign trade. Articles studying and discussing new experiences and problems arising in the course of financial and economic work and criticizing the fallacies spread by Lin Biao and the Gang of Four in financial and economic theory. Reports and translated articles on foreign economic developments.

The Journal of the Shaanxi College of Finance and Economics

Editor-in-Chief: Feng Dalin
Editing Organization:
   The Editorial Board of the Journal
Publisher: As above
Date of First Publication: July 1979
Number of Issues Per Year: 4
Circulation: 2,000
Subscription Rate: 0.30 yuan (per copy)
Address of the Editorial Board:
   Shaanxi College of Finance and Economics, Southern Suburb, Xi'an, Shaanxi Province

Readership:
Students and teaching staff in schools and colleges of finance and economics, researchers in finance and economics and staff of government financial and economic departments.
Main Contents:
A learned economic journal, it carries articles on the theory and practice of economic science, industrial economics, agricultural economics, business economics, finance, banking, management of goods and materials, accounting, statistics, etc. and attaches importance to the discussion of theoretical and practical problems arising in the course of China's drive for modernization.

The Journal of the Hubei College of Finance and Economics

Editor-in-Chief: Ren Xingchi
Editing Organization:
The Editorial Board of the Journal
Publisher:
Hubei College of Finance and Economics
Date of First Publication: May 15, 1980
Number of Issues Per Year: 4
Circulation: 6,200
Subscription Rate: 0.30 yuan (per copy)
Address of the Editorial Board:
Hubei College of Finance and Economics, Wuchang, Wuhan, Hubei Province
Readership:
Students and teaching staff of the departments and faculties of finance and economics in colleges and universities, researchers in finance and economics and cadres in government financial and economic departments.
Main Contents:
Articles expounding the line, principles and policies of the party, studies of Marxist-Leninist theory on finance and economics, discussions of theoretical and practical problems concerning economics, planning, statistics, finance, banking, industrial economics, business economics, agricultural economics, accounting, capital construction financing, etc.

Collection of Translated Articles on Economics

Editor-in-Chief: Huang Daonan
Editing Organization:
Editorial Board of the *Collection of Translated Articles on Economics,* Institute of Economics, Chinese Academy of Social Sciences
Publisher:
Chinese Social Sciences Publishing House
Date of First Publication: April 1954
Number of Issues Per Year: 12
Circulation: 11,300
Subscription Rate: 0.40 yuan (per copy)
Address of the Editorial Board:
2 Yuetan Beixiaojie, Beijing
Readership:
Researchers in economics, workers in theoretical propaganda, staff engaged in economic planning, students and teaching staff of the economics departments and faculties in universities and colleges, and amateur researchers among workers, peasants and soldiers.
Main Contents:
Translated articles relating to the economic theories of different schools abroad so as to provide China's economic researchers with materials for study, reference and criticism. Writings by Marx, Engels, Lenin and Stalin on economics which have not yet been translated into Chinese; major theoretical works as well as articles on controversial issues in socialist economics; writings on the theoretical problems of national economies, planning theory, management and reform; new disciplines and problems related to economics; and articles on different schools of bourgeois economics and their critical analyses. Also, information about the economic situation abroad, major academic activities and well-known scholars in the economic field, and book reviews, statistical data and explanations of economic terms.

Collection of Translations on World Economy

Editing Organization:
Editorial Board of the *Collection of Translations on World Economy*
Publisher:
Chinese Social Sciences Publishing House
Date of First Publication: August 1978
Number of Issues Per Year: 12
Circulation: 9,000
Subscription Rate: 0.40 yuan (per copy)
Address of the Editorial Board:
15 Shatan St. (N), Beijing
Readership:
Researchers and practical workers in world economy, researchers in economic theory, planning staff, students and teaching staff of departments and faculties of economics in colleges and universities.
Main Contents:
Translated articles on major theoretical and

practical issues in contemporary world economy, world economic developments, experience (both positive and negative) relating to modernization in foreign countries, and trends in the studies of world economy abroad.

Foreign Economic Management

Editor-in-Chief: Wang Jiamo
Editing Organization:
  Institute of *Foreign Economic Management*, Chinese People's University
Publisher:
  Chinese People's University Publishing House
Date of First Publication: April 27, 1980
Number of Issues Per Year: 6
Circulation: 25,322
Subscription Rate: 0.35 yuan (per copy)

Address of the Editorial Board:
  Chinese People's University, Western Suburbs, Beijing
Readership:
  Managerial staff in enterprises, cadres in government economic management departments, students and teaching staff of the departments and faculties of economic management and of related disciplines in colleges and universities, and researchers and data collectors in the field of economic management.
Main Contents:
  Articles on the theory, methods, experience, knowledge and developments of economic management abroad. Includes enterprise management, departmental economics, management of national economies and the theory and methods of management, with emphasis on enterprise management.

7. BIBLIOGRAPHY OF CHINA'S PUBLICATIONS IN ECONOMICS (1980)
Compiled by the Information Library, Institute of Industrial Economics
Chinese Academy of Social Sciences

I. Political Economics

New Economics Over the Past Ten Years
  By James Tobin (USA)
  Translated by Zhong Ganen
  Checked by Zhu Yang and Shou Jinwen
  The Commercial Press
  Jan. 1980 32mo* ¥0.27

On Commodity, Money and The Law of Value
  By Bao Dunjin
  Xinjiang People's Publishing House
  Jan. 1980 32mo ¥0.19

Milton Freedman and His Monetarism
  By Hu Daiguang
  The Commercial Press
  Jan. 1980 32mo ¥0.30

Socialist Distribution (Series of Basic Knowledge on Political Theory)
  By Liu Guangjie and Wu Xinmu
  Guangdong, Guangxi, Hunan and Hubei People's Publishing Houses
  Jan. 1980 32mo ¥0.19

The Law of Value, Planning, Markets and Related Subjects
  By Fujian Provincial Institute of Social Sciences and Fujian Provincial Society of Economics
  Fujian People's Publishing House
  Jan. 1980 32mo ¥0.30

Relations Between Planning and Marketing in Socialist Economy (Selected Papers on the Problems of the Law of Value in the Socialist Economy. Two Volumes)
  By the Library of the Economic Institute, Chinese Academy of Social Sciences
  China Social Science Publishing House
  Jan. 1980 32mo ¥1.70

Market Power and Economic Welfare — An Introduction
  By William G. Shepherd
  Translated by Yi Jiaxiang
  The Commercial Press
  Jan. 1980 32mo ¥1.05

Socialist Mental Work and Manual Labour
  By Wang Haibo
  Guangdong People's Publishing House
  Feb. 1980 32mo ¥0.38

The Works and Correspondence of David Ricado (4th Volume)
  By David Ricado; Sluffar, Editor-in-Chief
  Translated by Cai Shoubai
  The Commercial Press
  Feb. 1980 32mo ¥1.15

Concise Textbook on Political Economy (Capitalism: Library For Youth)
  By Li Qianheng
  Chinese Youth Publishing House
  Feb. 1980 32mo ¥0.68

Problems of Price Formation Under the Socialist System (Selected Papers on Problems of the Law of Value in the Socialist Eonomy)
  By the Library of the Economic Institute, Chinese Academy of Social Sciences
  China Social Sciences Publishing House
  Feb. 1980 32mo ¥0.64

A Study of the Daqing Experience in Political Economy
  By the Writing Group on "The Study of Daqing Experiences in Political Economy"
  Heilongjiang People's Publishing House
  Feb. 1980 32mo ¥0.92

The Foundation of Marxist Political Economics
  By Gao Ronggui
  Jilin People's Publishing House
  Apr. 1980 32mo ¥0.45

Political Economy (Capitalism)
  By Wang Ying
  Heilongjiang People's Publishing House
  Apr. 1980 32mo ¥0.52

Explanatory Notes to "The Capital" (First Volume)
  By the Teaching Staff for "The Capital," Economics Department, Beijing University
  Beijing Publishing House
  Apr. 1980 32mo ¥1.20

*"mo" is Chinese measure for book dimensions.

On Fundamental Economic Laws of Socialism
  By Ge Guangqian and Yu Taihe
  Hunan People's Publishing House
  Apr. 1980   32mo   ¥0.27

Problems of Socialist Commodity Economy
  By Wu Guanghui
  Chinese Youth Publishing House
  May 1980   32mo , ¥0.26

Various Social Economic Forms Before Capitalism
  By Xu He
  People's Publishing House
  May 1980   32mo   ¥0.29

Political Economy (Capitalism). (Trial Teaching Materials for University)
  By Writing Group from 16 Universities in South China on "Teaching Materials of Political Economy"
  Sichuan People's Publishing House
  May 1980   32mo   ¥1.90

Marx and "The Capital"
  By Hu Peizhao
  Sichuan People's Publishing House
  May 1980   32mo   ¥0.76

My Economic Theory, Philosophic Thought and Political Stand
  By Ma Yinchu
  China Financial and Economic Publishing House
  May 1980   32mo   ¥0.70

Economic Laws of Dialectical Materialism
  By Yan Beiming
  Shanghai People's Publishing House
  May 1980   32mo   ¥0.27

Collected Works on Socialist Economy
  By Su Xing
  Shanghai People's Publishing House
  May 1980   32mo   ¥0.44

Contradiction of Public Ownership in Present Socialist Practice (Series of "Reference Material for Economic Research")
  By Edvard Kardelj (Yugoslavia)
  Translated by Wang Sen
  Checked by Xu Kunming
  China Social Sciences Publishing House
  May 1980   32mo   ¥0.44

Political Economy
  By Writing Group of Hubei Province on "Political Economy"
  Hubei People's Publishing House
  June 1980   32mo   ¥1.43

Questions and Answers on Political Economy
  By the Political Economy Teaching Office, Party School of Zhejiang Province of the Communist Party of China
  Zhejiang People's Publishing House
  June 1980   32mo   ¥0.74

Science and Technology Are Parts of Productive Forces
  By Xiao Liang
  Shanxi People's Publishing Houses
  June 1980   32mo   ¥0.21

Political Economy (Imperialism)
  By the Teaching Office of World Economics, Economics Department of Chinese People's University
  Chinese People's University Publishing House
  June 1980   32mo   ¥0.45

A Brief Discussion on Socialist Economy
  By Guizhou Provincial Academy of Social Sciences
  Guizhou People's Publishing House
  June 1980   32mo   ¥0.60

The Law of Value in Commodity Production and Expanding of Enterprises' Decision-Making Power (Selected Articles on the Problems of the Law of Value in Socialist Economy)
  By the Library, Economic Institute of the Chinese Academy of Social Sciences
  China Social Sciences Publishing House
  June 1980   32mo   ¥0.86

Socialist Commodity Economy and its Laws (Series of Fundamental Political Theory)
  By Liu Zhiguang
  Hubei People's Publishing House
  July 1980   32mo   ¥0.20

Political Economy
  By the Compiling Group of Universities and Colleges in Jiangxi Province on "Political Economy"
  Jiangxi People's Publishing House
  July 1980   32   ¥1.12

Teaching Materials on Political Economy (Used for Universities and Colleges)
  By Jiang Xuemo
  Shanghai People's Publishing House
  July 1980   32mo   ¥0.87

Explanations to "The Capital" ("Das Kapital") (Third Volume)
  By Chen Zheng
  Fujian People's Publishing House
  July 1980   32mo   ¥1.05

The Reproduction Theory of Marxism
By Tian Xiangzhang
Guizhou People's Publishing House
July 1980   32mo   ¥0.26

Productive Forces and Relations of Production (Series of Fundamental Political Theory)
By Qi Li
Hunan People's Publishing House
July 1980   32mo   ¥0.26

Some Problems of Socialist Economy
By the Compiling Group of Anhui Province on "Some Problems of Socialist Economy"
Anhui People's Publishing House
July 1980   32mo   ¥0.50

Socialist Economy
By Jiang Xuemo
Guangdong People's Publishing House
July 1980   32mo   ¥0.89

Textbook on Political Economy (Socialism). (Revised)
By the Compiling Group of Jilin Province on "Textbooks on Political Economy"
Jilin People's Publishing House
July 1980   32mo   ¥0.76

Brief Textbook on Political Economy (Trial Teaching Materials for Universities and Colleges)
By the Compling Group of Guangdong Province on "Brief Textbooks on Political Economy"
Guangdong People's Publishing House
Aug. 1980   32mo   ¥0.78

An Introduction to Political Economy
By Hong Yuanming
Jiangsu People's Publishing House
Aug. 1980   32mo   ¥0.35

Socialism and Material Benefits
By Xue Yongying
Guizhou People's Publishing House
Aug. 1980   32mo   ¥0.42

Problems of Productive Forces
By Ping Xin
Joint Publishing Company
Aug. 1980   32mo   ¥1.00

Material Benefits in Socialist Society
By Xue Bingrang
Sichuan People's Publishing House
Aug. 1980   32mo   ¥0.64

A.B.C.'s of Economics (Capitalism, Political Economy). (Youth Library)
China Youth Publishing House
Aug. 1980   32mo   ¥0.52

Political Economy in Brief (Capitalism)
By Compiling Group for "Political Economy in Brief"
Henan People's Publishing House
Aug. 1980   32mo   ¥0.48

On Distribution According to Work
By Xu Chongwen
Sichuan People's Publishing House
Aug. 1980   32mo   ¥0.50

Problems of Socialist Reproduction and National Income
By Dong Fureng
Joint Publishing Company
Aug. 1980   32mo   ¥0.98

Brief Introduction to Discussions on Problems of the Law of Value Since the Founding of New China
By Economic Institute, Jilin Provincial Academy of Social Sciences
Jilin People's Publishing House
Sept. 1980   32mo   ¥0.21

Basic Knowledge on Socialist Economic Laws
By the Education Office of the Propaganda Department, Guangxi Regional Committee of the CPC
Guangxi People's Publishing House
Sept. 1980   32mo   ¥0.22

Some Problems Concerning Socialist Expanded Reproduction
By Duan Mengjue
Jilin People's Publishing House
Sept. 1980   32mo   ¥0.35

Some Problems Related to Elementary Theory of Socialist Political Economy (Economic Study Series)
By the Editorial Department of "Economic Study"
Shandong People's Publishing House
Sept. 1980   32mo   ¥1.20

On Productive Forces — Selected Articles on Problems of Productive Forces Since the Founding of the People's Republic (Volume I)
By the Editorial Department of "Economic Study"
Jilin People's Publishing House
Oct. 1980   32mo   ¥0.78

Political Economy (Capitalism)
  By the Political Economy Teaching Office, Economic Department of Beijing University
  Jilin People's Publishing House
  Oct. 1980 32mo ¥1.10

An Informal Discussion on Economic Laws
  By Tao Youzhi
  Jiangsu People's Publishing House
  Nov. 1980 32mo ¥0.23

Studying Marx's Theory on Reproduction
  By Lin Zili
  People's Publishing House and China Social Sciences Publishing House
  Nov. 1980 32mo ¥0.74
  (Large format: 32mo ¥0.91)

Natural Science Is Part of Productive Forces (Economics Series)
  By Wu Yisheng
  Beijing Publishing House
  Nov. 1980 32mo ¥0.27

Huang Songling's Posthumous Manuscripts on Problems of Socialist Economy
  By Huang Songling
  Tianjin People's Publishing House
  Dec. 1980 Large format: 32mo ¥0.85

II. Problems of China's Economy

Some Problems in Research on China's Socialist Economy
  By Su Shaozhi
  Shanghai People's Publishing House
  Feb. 1980 32mo ¥0.26

A Study on the Problems of Socialist Economy in China
  By Xu Dixin
  Beijing Publishing House
  Feb. 1980 32mo ¥0.47

Problems of Theory and Commodity Production During the Transitional Period — Symposium of Guangdong Association of Economy, 1978. (Series on Academic Studies)
  By the Editorial Department, "Academic Studies"
  Guangdong People's Publishing House
  Feb. 1980 32mo ¥0.35

A Talk About the Readjustment of the National Economy
  By Jiang Yingguang
  Guangxi People's Publishing House
  March 1980 32mo ¥0.32

Selected Economic Laws and Regulation of the People's Republic of China
  By Law Science Institute, Chinese Academy of Social Sciences
  China Financial and Economic Publishing House
  Apr. 1980 32mo ¥2.00

Communique on the Implementation of the 1979 National Economic Plan, Issued by the State Statistical Bureau of the People's Republic of China (April 30, 1980)
  China Financial and Economic Publishing House
  May 1980 32mo ¥0.15

Some Problems of Socialist Economy in China — Lectures in the USA
  By Xu Dixin
  China Social Sciences Publishing House
  May 1980 32mo ¥0.30

Selected Papers on Economic Accounting Since the Founding of the People's Republic of China
  By Zhang Wenmin
  Shanghai People's Publishing House
  May 1980 32mo ¥1.60

Some Theoretical Problems in the Reform of the National Economic Management System
  By Liu Guoguang
  China Social Sciences Publishing House
  May 1980 32mo ¥1.00

A Discussion of the Four Modernizations in China
  By Xiao Liang
  Jilin People's Publishing House
  July 1980 32mo ¥0.31

Guide to the Import of Technology
  China Foreign Translation Publishing Company
  July 1980 32mo ¥1.05

An Inquiry into the Reform of the Economic Management System in China. (Economic Research Series)
  By the Editorial Department, "Economic Studies"
  Shandong People's Publishing House
  July 1980 32mo ¥1.05

On the Guiding Ideology of "Act According to One's Capability"
  People's Daily Publishing House
  Aug. 1980 32mo ¥0.28

The Relationship Between Plan and Market in Chinese Socialist Economy
By Sun Shangqing
Jilin People's Publishing House
Sept. 1980 32mo ¥0.21

China's Economic Problems in the 1980's (A Report at the Hong Kong Seminar on China's Economic Problems in the 1980's)
By Xu Dixin
China Social Sciences Publishing House
Sept. 1980 32mo ¥0.32

A Study of Collectively Owned Industry in Shanghai
By Liu Gang
Shanghai People's Publishing House
Oct. 1980 32mo ¥0.31

Some Problems of the Current Economy in China
By Xue Muqiao
People's Publishing House
Oct. 1980 32mo ¥0.69

Imports of Technology and the Development of the Economy
By the Political Economics Teaching Office, Policy and Education Department of Jiangsu Teachers' College
Jiangsu People's Publishing House
Oct. 1980 32mo ¥0.33

Problems of Socialist Economic Construction in China
By the Editorial Department of the Publishing House of the Party School of the Central Committee of the CPC
The Party School of the Central Committee of the CPC Publishing House
Oct. 1980 32mo ¥0.40

The Economy of Taiwan
By Zhou Ren
China Financial and Economic Publishing House
Feb. 1980 32mo ¥1.40

III. Economic Planning and Management

Statistics of Industrial Enterprises
By Compiling Group, "Statistics of Industrial Enterprises"
Chinese People's University Publishing House
Jan. 1980 32mo ¥0.65

Financial Management in State-Owned Farms
By Compiling Group, "Financial Management in State-Owned Farms"
China Financial and Economic Publishing House
Jan. 1980 32mo ¥0.65

Statistical Work in Rural People's Communes
By Zhang Anyu
Guizhou People's Publishing House
Jan. 1980 32mo ¥0.54

Management of Industrial Enterprises at Daqing
By Writing Group on "Management of Industrial Enterprises at Daqing"
Heilongjiang People's Publishing House
Feb. 1980 32mo ¥0.72

Management of Industrial Enterprises
By Jing Zheng
Hunan People's Publishing House
Feb. 1980 32mo ¥0.90

Industrial Bookkeeping and Accounting
By Compiling Group on "Industrial Bookkeeping and Accounting," Economics Department, Hebei University
Hebei People's Publishing House
Feb. 1980 32mo ¥0.68

Elementary Knowledge of Management of Industrial Enterprises
By Compiling Group on "Elementary Knowledge of Management of Industrial Enterprises"
China Financial and Economic Publishing House
Feb. 1980 32mo ¥0.72

Modern Management (Series of "Knowledge of Industrial Enterprise Management")
By Zhu Rongji
Tianjin People's Publishing House
Feb. 1980 32mo ¥0.18

Statistics of Agricultural Mechanization
By Liaoning Institute of Finance and Economics
Jilin People's Publishing House
Feb. 1980 32mo ¥0.40

Industrial Accounting
By Sun Shuxun and He Shengtang
Corrected By Zhang Zhengyuan
Shandong People's Publishing House
Feb. 1980 16mo ¥1.65

Elementary Course on Statistical Collecting Programme Compiled by DJS-6 Algorithm Language
    Compiled by Economic Mathematics Department, Beijing College of Economy, and Department of Economic Information Control, Chinese People's University
    Read and Revised by the Computer Centre of the State Planning Committee
    China Financial and Economic Publishing House
    Feb. 1980 32mo ¥0.80

Theory and Problems of Quantitative Methods in Management
    By John E. Erman (USA)
    Translated by Transport Department, Shanghai Institute of Railways
    People's Railway Publishing House
    Feb. 1980 16mo ¥2.20

Elementary Knowledge for Accounting
    By Zhou Fubao
    Shanxi People's Publishing House
    Feb. 1980 32mo ¥0.75

Research on Mathematical Methods for Economics
    By Wu Jiapei
    Joint Publishing Company
    Feb. 1980 32mo ¥0.94

Maintenance of Knitting and Textile Commodities
    By Shanghai Commodities Storage and Transportation Corporation
    China Financial and Economic Publishing House
    March 1980 32mo ¥0.40

Introduction to Technical Economy
    By Xu Shoubo
    Shanghai Science and Technology Publishing House
    March 1980 32mo ¥1.00

Accounting in Administrative Units
    By the Budget Office, Financial Department of Zhejiang Province
    China Financial and Economic Publishing House
    March 1980 322mo ¥0.34

Economic Reform and Devising a Better Economic Accounting System (Collected Papers of the Conference on Economic Accounting and Economic Reform, 1979)
    By the Economic Institute of Finance and Trade Materials, Chinese Academy of Social Sciences
    China Social Sciences Publishing House
    March 1980 32mo ¥0.71

Management of Socialist State-Owned Industrial Enterprises in China (Series on Economic Management and Enterprise Management)
    By Compiling Group, "Management of Socialist State-Owned Industrial Enterprises in China"
    People's Publishing House
    March 1980 Large-size 32mo
    Vol. I: ¥1.40; Vol. II: ¥1.30

Operation and Management of Building Enterprises
    By Bai Ying
    China Building Industry Publishing House
    March 1980 Large-size 32mo ¥1.50

Specialized Coordination in Industrial Production and Industrial Companies (Series on Knowledge of Industrial Enterprise Management)
    By Han Xiulan and Liu Furong
    Tianjin People's Publishing House
    March 1980 32mo ¥0.18

Statistics of Machine-Building Industry
    By Compiling Group, "Statistics of Machine-Building Industry"
    Machine-Building Industry Publishing House
    March 1980 32mo ¥1.30

Management of Socialist Industrial Enterprises
    By Industrial Economy Teaching Office, Economics Department, Jinan University
    Guangdong People's Publishing House
    March 1980 32mo ¥0.75

Specialized Cooperation in Industry and Modernization
    By Wu Zhaoming and Lu Wangcai
    Jiangsu People's Publishing House
    Apr. 1980 32mo ¥0.26

Management of Socialist Industrial Enterprises
    By Compiling Group, "Management of Socialist Industrial Enterprises," Financial and Economic Insitute of Liaoning Province
    Liaoning People's Publishing House
    Apr. 1980 32mo ¥0.72

Management of Circulating Funds in Industrial Enterprises (Series on Elementary Knowledge of Financial Bookkeeping in Industrial Enterprises)
    By Wang Youmei and Zhang Baoshan
    China Financial and Economic Publishing House
    Apr. 1980 32mo ¥0.50

Financial Bookkeeping in Enterprises Run by Communes and Brigades
    By Taxation Department of Jiangsu Province
    China Financial and Economic Publishing House
    Apr. 1980 32mo ¥0.54

Statistics for the Rural People's Communes (Series on Management and Administration of Rural People's Communes)
   By Chen Yongbing
   Agricultural Publishing House
   Apr. 1980 32mo ¥0.44

Management and Administration of Rural People's Communes
   By Rural Work Department, Foshan Prefectural Committee of the CPC and Agricultural Economy Teaching Office, South China Institute of Agriculture
   Guangdong People's Publishing House
   32mo (undated) ¥0.23

Statistical Analysis in Basic Units
   By Ma Jiashan
   China Financial and Economics Publishing House
   May 1980 32mo ¥0.15

Problems of Improvement of Socialist Economic Management
   By L.A. Blochenikova (USSR)
   Translated by Cao Zhongda
   Tianjin People's Publishing House
   May 1980 32mo ¥0.57

Introduction to Accounting Science
   By Li Xianghui, etc.
   Chinese People's University Publishing House
   May 1980 32mo ¥0.75

Industrial Enterprise Management
   By Compiling Group of "Industrial Enterprise Management" in Nanjing
   Jiangsu People's Publishing House
   May 1980 32mo ¥0.82

Management and Administration of Agricultural Machinery Stations (Series on Agricultural Mechanization)
   By Administrative Bureau of Agricultural Machinery, Yunnan Province, and Yunnan University of Agriculture
   Yunnan People's Publishing House
   June 1980 32mo ¥0.69

Accounting for State-Owned Farms (Used for Speciality in Agricultural Economy) — Tentative Teaching Materials for National Agricultural Secondary Schools)
   By Cao Yingjian
   Agricultural Publishing House
   June 1980 32mo ¥1.20

Management and Administration of Rural People's Communes
   By Nong Gongxiao
   Jilin People's Publishing House
   May 1980 32mo ¥0.30

Economics and the Public Purpose
   By J.K. Galbraith (USA)
   Translated by Cai Shoubai
   The Commercial Press
   June 1980 32mo ¥1.00

Production Management and Electronic Computers (Linear Planning)
   By Jia Fenghe and Xie Lin
   Shaanxi Science and Technology Publishing House
   June 1980 32mo ¥1.40

Accounting for Mess Halls
   By Guangxi School of Financial Economy
   Guangxi People's Publishing House
   June 1980 32mo ¥0.23

The Secret of High Productivity (PAC — Performance Analysis and Control)
   By Kadoda Takeharu (Japan)
   Translated by the World Economic Research Group, Guangdong Institute of Philosophical Social Sciences
   Shanghai Translation Publishing House
   June 1980 32mo ¥0.53

Zero Defects
   By the Capability Ratio Society of Japan
   Translated by Sheng Jiqin
   Workers Publishing House
   July 1980 32mo ¥0.40

Managing Industrial Enterprises by Economic Means
   By Hu Shujie
   Guizhou People's Publishing House
   July 1980 32mo ¥0.34

Management of Socialist Industrial Enterprises
   By Industrial Economics Department, Shanghai Institute of Financial Economy, and Industrial Economy Research Office, Institute of Departmental Economy, Shanghai Academy of Social Sciences
   Shanghai People's Publishing House
   July 1980 32mo ¥1.25

Management of Circulating Funds in State-Owned Farms
   By Cao Feng
   Agricultural Publishing House
   July 1980 32mo ¥0.30

Accounting for Cereals and Oils Industries (Tentative Teaching Materials for Cereal Secondary Schools)
  By Compiling Group, "Accounting for Cereals and Oils Industries"
  China Financial and Economic Publishing House
  July 1980   32mo   ¥0.70

Management and Accounting of Pig Farms in Communes and Brigades. (Series on Management and Administration in Rural People's Communes)
  By Wan Zezhang and Zhou Zuyin
  Agricultural Publishing House
  July 1980   32mo   ¥0.24

Quota Management in Production Brigades
  By Wen Dezheng
  Guizhou People's Publishing House
  July 1980   32mo   ¥0.18

Management of Socialist Enterprises
  By Ma Hong and Wu Jiajun
  People's Publishing House
  Aug. 1980   32mo   ¥0.60

Economic Accounting in Industrial Enterprises
  By Kang Mingzhong
  Guizhou People's Publishing House
  Aug. 1980   32mo   ¥0.30

Fundamentals of Accounting Science (Liberal Arts Materials for Institutions of Higher Learning)
  By Ge Jiashu
  China Financial and Economic Publishing House
  Aug. 1980   32mo   ¥1.30

Brief Introduction to Economic Contracts
  By Li Changqi
  Guizhou People's Publishing House
  Aug. 1980   32mo   ¥0.20

Financial Management of Costs in Machine-Building Enterprises. (Tentative Teaching Materials for Institutions of Higher Learning)
  By Li Meichun
  Machine-Building Industry Publishing House
  Aug. 1980   16mo   ¥1.00

Management of Goods and Materials in Machine-Building Enterprises (Tentative Materials for Institutions of Higher Learning)
  By Wang Xingmin
  Machine-Building Industry Publishing House
  Aug. 1980   16mo   ¥0.96

How to Achieve Effective Accounting for Teams and Groups
  By Sun Dezhong
  Guangdong People's Publishing House
  Aug. 1980   32mo   ¥0.26

Informal Discussion on Economic Management
  By Niu Zhonghuang
  Hebei People's Publishing House
  Aug. 1980   32mo   ¥0.20

Management of Goods and Materials in the Enterprises of Communes and Brigades. (Series on Management and Administration in Rural People's Communes)
  By Yu Yulin and Li Mingzhu
  Agricultural Publishing House
  Aug. 1980   32mo   ¥0.33

Management of Socialist Industrial Enterprises
  By Industrial Economics Department, Shanghai Institute of Financial Economy
  Shanghai People's Publishing House
  Aug. 1980   32mo   ¥1.25

Importing Technology and Utilizing Foreign Capital
  By Cao Linzhang
  Shanghai People's Publishing House
  Aug. 1980   32mo   ¥0.21

Talk by Taiwan Enterpreneurs on Management and Administration of Enterprises
  Xinhua Publishing House
  Aug. 1980   32mo   ¥0.65

On Importing Technology. (Series on Knowledge of Industrial Enterprise Management)
  By Jing Wei
  Tianjin People's Publishing House
  Sept. 1980   32mo   ¥0.21

Standards of Technical Grades for Coal Industry Workers
  Formulated by the Ministry of Coal Industry
  The People's Republic of China Coal Industry Publishing House
  Sept. 1980   32 mo   Deluxe edition   ¥2.30

The Elements of Input-Output Analysis. (Series of Science on Modern Management)
  By William H. Miernyk
  Translated by Qiu Tong
  Corrected by Zhang Xuansan and Li Boxi
  China Social Sciences Publishing House
  Sept. 1980   32mo   ¥0.42

Statistics of Agricultural Mechanization
  By the Administrative Bureau, the Ministry of Agricultural Machinery
  Jilin People's Publishing House
  Sept. 1980 32mo ¥0.32

Financial Accounting for Communes and Brigades
  By the Administrative Bureau of Enterprises in People's Communes, Shanxi Province
  Shanxi People's Publishing House
  Sept. 1980 32mo ¥0.37

Management of Socialist Agricultural Economy
  By the Agricultural Economy Department, Beijing University of Agriculture
  Hebei People's Publishing House
  Sept. 1980 32mo ¥0.70

The Quality Control of Products
  By S.P. Borrishico and A.R. Kozlov (USSR)
  Translated by He Zhenhua, etc.
  Scientific and Technical Documents Publishing House
  Sept. 1980 32mo ¥0.60

Economic Accounting of Groups in Industrial Enterprises
  By Li Xingfu
  Heilongjiang People's Publishing House
  Sept. 1980 32mo ¥0.44

The Science of Management and Administration in Industrial Enterprises
  By Wu Fengshan
  Hebei People's Publishing House
  Sept. 1980 32mo ¥0.62

Elementary Knowledge of Economic Accounting in Industrial Enterprises
  By Wang Zhendao and Liu Xiongfei
  Zhejiang People's Publishing House
  Sept. 1980 32mo ¥0.26

Introduction to Industrial Economic Management
  By Sai Feng and Fang Jia
  Chinese People's University Pubishing House
  Sept. 1980 32mo ¥1.20

Management of Socialist Industrial Enterprises in China
  By the Teaching Office of Industrial Enterprises Management, Industrial Economics Department, Chinese People's University
  Chinese People's University Publishing House
  Oct. 1980 32mo ¥2.10

Elementary Knowledge of Socialist Economic Statistics
  By Zhang Changfa and Ma Zhendong
  Shanxi People's Publishing House
  Oct. 1980 32mo ¥0.61

Lectures on the Problems of Enterprise Management
  By the Theory Department of the Central People's Radio Station
  Heilongjiang People's Publishing House
  Oct. 1980 32mo ¥0.54

Management of Industrial Economy in China (Two Volumes)
  By Compiling Group, "Management of Industrial Economy in China," The Society for Research on Industrial Economic Management in China
  China Social Sciences Publishing House
  Oct. 1980 32mo ¥1.40

Elementary Knowledge of Industrial Enterprise Management
  By Du Yuelin
  Henan People's Publishing House
  Oct. 1980 32mo ¥0.65

Financial Accounting in the State-Owned Industrial Enterprises
  By the Accounting Teaching Office, Tianjin Institute of Financial Economy
  Tianjin Science and Technology Publishing House
  Oct. 1980 32mo ¥1.05

The Application of Mathematics and Physical Statistics to Quality Control
  By Yin Qicheng
  Shanxi People's Publishing House
  Oct. 1980 32mo ¥0.65

Management of Labour and Wages in Metallurgical Enterprises
  By the Labour and Wages Department, the Ministry of Metallurgical Industry
  Metallurgical Industry Publishing House
  Oct. 1980 32mo ¥0.97

Statistics of Enterprises in Communes and Brigades. (Series on Management and Administration in Rural People's Communes)
  By Xu Jingquan
  Agricultural Publishing House
  Oct. 1980 32mo ¥0.46

Accounting in the Iron and Steel Industry
   By Huang Pintang
   Metallurgical Industry Publishing House
   Oct. 1980   32mo   ¥1.25

Financial Accounting for Industries Run by Communes
   By Guo Yabin
   Heilongjiang People's Publishing House
   Oct. 1980   32mo   ¥0.51

Budget Accounting
   By Tan Tong
   Tianjin Science and Technology Publishing House
   Oct. 1980   32mo   ¥0.72

Accounting for Mess Halls
   By Qian Hongliang
   Jiangsu People's Publishing House
   Oct. 1980   32mo   ¥0.20

Elementary Knowledge of Modern Scientific Management
   By Shanghai Research Society on Technical Economy and Modern Management
   Shanghai People's Publishing House
   Nov. 1980   32mo   ¥0.59

The A.B.C.'s of Statistics
   By Weng Lixin
   Shanghai People's Publishing House
   Nov. 1980   32mo   ¥0.54

The Tapping of Potential, Innovation and Transformation in Industrial Enterprises. (Knowledge of Management in Industrial Enterprises)
   By Wu Zije and Guo Ruoxu
   Tianjin People's Publishing House
   Nov. 1980   32mo   ¥0.17

Managing Graphic Methods for Quality Control
   Edited and Translated By Gao Fenglin
   Corrected by Yang Weishi
   Science and Technology Documentary Publishing House
   Nov. 1980   16mo   ¥1.75

A Talk on Labour Management to Heads of Production Brigades
   By Zhang Liuji
   Henan People's Publishing House
   Nov. 1980   32mo   ¥0.27

Management and Administration of Rural Communes and Brigades
   By Dou Tianyu and Zhang Yue
   Jiangsu People's Publishing House
   Nov. 1980   32mo   ¥0.32

Working Manual for Labour Insurance
   By the Labour Bureau and the Trade Union Council, Hunan Province
   Hunan People's Publishing House
   Nov. 1980   64mo   ¥0.57

IV. Agricultural Economy

Selected Papers on the Experience of Agricultural Production
   By the Policy Research Office, the State Agricultural Commission
   Agricultural Publishing House
   Jan. 1980   32mo   ¥0.55

Diagrams of Accounting for State-Owned Farms
   By Cao Feng and Zheng Bangjie
   Xinjiang People's Publishing House
   Feb. 1980   16mo   ¥0.81

The Rural Economy in Old China. (Series on Knowledge on Agricultural Economy)
   By Xue Muqiao
   Agricultural Publishing House
   March 1980   32mo   ¥0.38

Cost Accounting and Analysis of Industries in Communes and Brigades. (Series on Management and Administration in Rural People's Communes)
   By Yang Meitong
   Agricultural Publishing House
   March 1980   32mo   ¥0.37

Questions and Answers on Management and Administration of the Production Teams in Rural People's Communes
   By the Agricultural and Animal Husbandry Bureau, Gansu Province
   Gansu People's Publishing House
   Apr. 1980   32mo   ¥0.29

Financial Accounting for Agricultural Machinery Stations (Teams)
   By the Agricultural Machinery Office, the Agricultural Machinery Bureau of Zhejiang Province
   Zhejiang People's Publishing House
   Apr. 1980   32mo   ¥0.40

Attaching Great Importance to the Development of Animal Husbandry
   By the Agricultural Economics Institute, Chinese Academy of Social Sciences
   China Social Sciences Publishing House
   May 1980   32mo   ¥0.90

The Special Archives on Forestry
By the Research Office of Forestry Economics, Forest Science Institute of the Forestry Academy of China
Agricultural Publishing House
May 1980   16mo   ¥0.33

Management and Accounting of Fixed Assets of Production Teams. (Series on Management and Administration in Rural People's Communes)
By Tian Jian and Zhu Haifang
Agricultural Publishing House
May 1980   32mo   ¥0.16

Agriculture Is the Foundation of the National Economy. (Series on Knowledge on Agricultural Economy)
By Zhu Jiazhen, etc.
Agricultural Publishing House
May 1980   32mo   ¥0.25

Accounting in the Basic Accounting Units of People's Communes in Pastoral Areas. (Series on Management and Administration of Rural People's Communes)
By Long Jun
Agricultural Publishing House
May 1980   32mo   ¥0.29

Elementary Introduction to Rural Economic Policy
By the Research Office on Agricultural Economy, Economic Institute of Shanghai Academy of Sciences
Shanghai People's Publishing House
May 1980   32mo   ¥0.19

Problems of Technical Economy in Agricultural Mechanization (Vol. II)
By the Economic Research Society of Agricultural Mechanization, Agricultural Mechanization Association of China
Agricultural Publishing House
May 1980   32mo   ¥0.42

Analysis of Economic Activities in State-Owned Farms
By the Compiling Group, "Analysis of Economic Activities in State-Owned Farms," Issued by the Ministry of Agricultural Reclamation and State Farms
Agricultural Publishing House
May 1980   32mo   ¥0.52

A Prosperous Road to Socialism — Selection of Materials on the Prosperous Brigades of the Communes in Liaoning Province (Rural Readings)
By the Policy Research Office, Liaoning Provincial Committee of the CPC
Liaoning People's Publishing House
May 1980   32mo   ¥0.20

Single Unit Accounting for Agricultural Machinery
By the Hebei Provincial Bureau of Agricultural Machinery Management
Agricultural Publishing House
May 1980   64mo   ¥0.14

A Collection of Reports on the Comprehensive Survey of Taoyuan
By the County Surveying Team of the Comprehensive Scientific Experimental Base of Agricultural Modernization of Hunan Province and the Chinese Academy of Sciences
Hunan Science and Technology Publishing House
May 1980   16mo   ¥4.30

Programme of Agricultural Development in the Rural People's Communes. (Series on Management and Administration of Rural People's Communes)
By Zhang Zhongwei and Zhao Donghuan
Agricultural Publishing House
May 1980   32mo   ¥0.21

Concepts and Calculating Methods of Economic Results in Agricultural Production
By Zhu Ruofeng
Agricultural Publishing House
June 1980   32mo   ¥0.50

Economic Accounting and Economic Results in Agricultural Production Communes
By Zhang Zhongwei and Yang Qiulin
Hebei People's Publishing House
June 1980   32mo   ¥0.23

A Collection of Translations on Agricultural Economy (Vol. I, 1980)
By the Editorial Department for "A Collection of Translations on Agricultural Economy"
Agricultural Publishing House
June 1980   32mo   ¥0.58

Accounting Handbook for Production Teams of Rural People's Communes
By the Gansu Provincial Bank Branch, the Agricultural Bank of China
Gansu People's Publishing House
June 1980   32mo   ¥0.36

Problems of Agricultural Modernization
By Gu Huanzhang
Jiangsu People's Publishing House
June 1980   32mo   ¥0.35

Common Knowledge for Accountants of Rural Production Teams
By the Anhui Provincial Bank Branch, the Agricultural Bank of China
Anhui People's Publishing House
June 1980   32mo   ¥0.60

Accounting in the Production Teams of Rural People's Communes
By the Shaanxi Provincial Bank Branch, the Agricultural Bank of China and the Agricultural Economics Department, Northwest Institute of Agriculture
Shaanxi People's Publishing House
June 1980 32mo ¥0.52

How to Carry Out the Agricultural Regionalization at the County Level
By Xiao Juncheng
Agricultural Publishing House
June 1980 32mo ¥0.21

Accounting for Enterprises in Communes and Brigades. (Series on Management and Administration in People's Communes)
By Wu Yongxiang
Agricultural Publishing House
June 1980 32mo ¥0.67

Managing Agricultural Reclamation Enterprises by Economic Means
By the Policy Research Office, the Ministry of Agricultural Reclamation and State Farms
Agricultural Publishing House
July 1980 32mo ¥0.36

Management and Accounting for the Funds of Production Teams. (Series on Management and Administration in People's Communes)
By Wang Xuenong and Xu Hanguang
Agricultural Publishing House
July 1980 32mo ¥0.21

Transforming Dry Land (Experience of the Hongshiling Production Brigade in Agricultural Development at High Speed)
By the Propaganda Department, Taonan County Committee of the CPC
Jilin People's Publishing House
July 1980 32mo ¥0.19

Accounting in Production Teams
By the Guangxi Regional Bank Branch, Agricultural Bank of China
Guangxi People's Publishing House
July 1980 32mo ¥0.28

Gaoxigou — A Bright Star Over the Loess Highlands
By Yu Mi
Shaanxi People's Publishing House
July 1980 32mo ¥0.21

A Guide to Rural Economic Policy
By Xie Youquan
Fujian People's Publishing House
July 1980 32mo ¥0.26

Accounting in Production Teams of Rural People's Communes (Revised)
By the Agricultural Financial Office, Beijing Bureau of Finance and Taxation
Beijing Publishing House
Aug. 1980 32mo ¥0.50

Agricultural Modernization in Major Capitalist Countries
By Liu Zhenbang
Agricultural Publishing House
Aug. 1980 32mo ¥1.10

How to Put the "Five Fixations and One Reward" System Into Effect
By Nan Zhenzhong
Shandong People's Publishing House
Aug. 1980 32mo ¥0.27

The Land's Past
By He Zhengpu
Sichuan People's Publishing House
Aug. 1980 32mo ¥0.26

A.B.C.'s of Accounting in Production Teams of Rural People's Communes
By the Liaoning Provincial Bank Branch, the Agricultural Bank of China
Liaoning People's Publishing House
Aug. 1980 32mo ¥0.62

Teaching Materials for Accountants in Production Teams of Rural People's Communes (Revised)
By the Agricultural Department of Sichuan Province and the Southwest Agricultural Institute
Sichuan People's Publishing House
Sept. 1980 32mo ¥0.35

Accounting for Enterprises in Communes and Brigades
By Yi Baoyin
Hebei People's Publishing House
Sept. 1980 32mo ¥0.25

A Manual of Economic Contracts in the System of Job Responsibility in Production Teams
By the Management and Administrative Office for People's Communes, Agricultural Department of Sichuan
Sichuan People's Publishing House
Sept. 1980 32mo ¥0.09

Accounting in the Production Teams of Rural People's Communes
By the Guangdong Provincial Bank Branch, the Agricultural Bank of China
Guangdong People's Publishing House
Oct. 1980 32mo ¥0.57

A General Outline of Agricultural Geography in China. (Series on Agricultural Geography in China)
    By the Economic Geography Research Office, Geographic Institute of the Chinese Academy of Sciences
    Sciences Publishing House
    Oct. 1980 16mo ¥7.20

V. Industrial Economy

Stipulations for the Content and Term of Years of Study for Apprentices in Water Conservancy and Hydroelectric Enterprises and Undertakings
    By the Ministry of Water Conservancy of the People's Republic of China
    Water Conservancy Publishing House
    Jan. 1980 32mo ¥0.21

Standards of Technical Grades for Workers in Water Conservancy and Hydroelectric Construction (Single-Volume Edition)
    By the Ministry of Water Conservancy of the PRC
    Water Conservancy Publishing House
    Jan. 1980 32mo ¥1.20

Standards of Technical Grades for Workers in Water Conservancy and Hydroelectric Construction (Vol. I: Machinery Operation)
    By the Ministry of Water Conservancy of the PRC
    Water Conservancy Publishing House
    Jan. 1980 32mo ¥0.25

Standards of Technical Grades for Workers in Water Conservancy and Hydroelectric Construction (Vol. II: Machinery Repair and Manufacture)
    By the Ministry of Water Conservancy of the PRC
    Water Conservancy Publishing House
    Jan. 1980 32mo ¥0.45

Standards of Technical Grades for Workers in Water Conservancy and Hydroelectric Construction (Vol. III: Power Equipment Installation)
    By the Ministry of Water Conservancy of the PRC
    Water Conservancy Publishing House
    Jan. 1980 32mo ¥0.35

Standards of Technical Grades for Workers in Water Conservancy and Hydroelectric Construction (Vol. IV: Civil Engineering and Hydrological Survey)
    By the Ministry of Water Conservancy of the PRC
    Water Conservancy Publishing House
    Jan. 1980 32mo ¥0.30

Standards of Technical Grades for Workers in Hydraulic and Electrical Construction. (Book One: Hydraulic Engineering) *(Trial Implement)*
    By the Ministry of Power Industry
    Power Industry Publishing House
    Jan. 1980 32mo ¥0.28

Standards of Technical Grades for Workers in Hydraulic and Electrical Construction (Book Two: Power Equipment Installation at Power Stations) *(Trial Implementation)*
    By the Ministry of Power Industry
    Power Industry Publishing House
    Jan. 1980 32mo ¥0.24

Standards of Technical Grades for Workers in Hydraulic and Electrical Construction (Book Three: Operation of Construction Machinery) *(Trial Implementation)*
    By the Ministry of Power Industry
    Power Industry Publishing House
    Jan. 1980 32mo ¥0.26

Standards of Technical Grades for Workers in Hydraulic and Electrical Construction (Book Four: Electro-Mechanics of Construction) *(Trial Implementation)*
    By the Ministry of Power Industry
    Power Industry Publishing House
    Jan. 1980 32mo ¥0.22

Standards of Technical Grades for Workers in Hydraulic and Electrical Construction (Book Five: Machinery Repairs) *(Trial Implementation)*
    By the Ministry of Power Industry
    Power Industry Publishing House
    Jan. 1980 32mo ¥0.26

Economic Performance in Industrial Production
    By Wu Fengshan
    Heilongjiang People's Publishing House
    Jan. 1980 32mo ¥0.45

Research in Economic Problems of Light Industry
    By Rong Wenzuo
    Hubei People's Publishing House
    Feb. 1980 32 ¥0.54

How Do Industrial Enterprises Pay Special Attention to Economic Targets?
    By Dong Jinhan and Feng Jigen
    Zhejiang People's Publishing House
    Feb. 1980 32mo ¥0.24

A New Coal City at the Old Huaihai Battlefield
    By the Propaganda Department of the Municipal Committee of Huaibei, CPC
    Anhui People's Publishing House
    Apr. 1980 32mo ¥0.22

Elementary Knowledge of Work Quotas in Industrial Enterprises
By Chen Ping
China Financial and Economic Publishing House
Apr. 1980 32mo ¥0.30

An Investigation of the Beijing No. 1 Machine Tools Factory
By the Investigating Group for the Beijing No. 1 Machine Tools Factory
China Social Sciences Publishing House
May 1980 32mo ¥0.92

Economic and Technical Targets in Industrial Enterprises (Series on Economic Management)
By Li Maohuan
Shanghai People's Publishing House
May 1980 32mo ¥0.20

Economic Accounting by Shifts and Groups
By Chen Guanyun
Zhejiang People's Publishing House
June 1980 32mo ¥0.24

Analysis of Economic Activities in Industrial Enterprises
By Xiao Yu and Chen Zhengyuan
Shandong People's Publishing House
July 1980 32mo ¥0.84

Elementary Course on Economic Appraisals of Engineering Projects
By D.H. Allen (U.K.)
Translated by Chen Yanhan
Chemical Industry Publishing House
July 1980 32mo ¥0.24

Promote Industrial Reorganization in a Positive Way
By Ji Chongwu and Rong Wenzuo
China Social Science Publishing House
Aug. 1980 32mo ¥0.19

Word List of Industrial Property (An English-Chinese and Chinese-English Bilingual Edition)
Translated by the Drafting Group for Patent Laws of the State Scientific and Technological Commission
Scientific and Technical Documents Publishing House
Aug. 1980 32mo ¥0.85

36 Sheds — The History of the Harbin Rolling Stock Plant
By Compiling Groups of the Harbin Rolling Stock Plant and the History Department, Harbin Teacher's College
Heilongjiang People's Publishing House
Sept. 1980 32mo ¥1.00

A Calculating Method for Production Targets in the Nonferrous Metallurgical Industry
By the Compiling Group of "A Calculating Method for Production Targets in the Nonferrous Metallurgical Industry"
Metallurgical Industry Publishing House
Sept. 1980 32mo ¥0.51

How to Work Out Quotas for Materialized Labour in Prospecting Engineering
By Wang Sili
Geology Publishing House
Sept. 1980 32mo ¥0.35

Accounting for Capital Construction in the Coal Industry
By the Finance Department of the Ministry of Coal Industry
Coal Industry Publishing House
Sept. 1980 32mo ¥1.65

Analysis of Economic Activities in Industrial Enterprises
By the Financial Accounting Teaching Office, Economic Department of Xiamen University
Shanghai People's Publishing House
Sept. 1980 32mo ¥0.62

Quality Control Handbook (Third Edition)
J.M. Juran, Editor-in-Chief
Dr. Frank M. Gryna, Jr., and R.S. Bingham, Jr., Associate Editors, Compiled by the Translation Group, "Quality Control Handbook"
Shanghai Scientific and Technical Documents Publishing House
Oct. 1980 16mo ¥6.00

Compilation and Analysis of Accounting Statistics Forms and Tables in Industrial Enterprises
By Du Yingbin and Yang Jichuan
Shanxi People's Publishing House
Oct. 1980 32mo ¥0.99

Costs of Plants and Stations in Building Enterprises
By Wang Sunxiong and Xie Weiyi
China Building Industry Publishing House
Oct. 1980 32mo ¥0.57

Planning, Organization and Control of Production Operations in Machine-Building Enterprises. (Knowledge of Management in Industrial Enterprises)
By the Department of Production Control, First Ministry of Machine-Building
Tianjin People's Publishing House
Dec. 1980 32mo ¥0.57

VI. The Economy of Communications and Transport

Detailed Rules and Regulations for the Implementation of the Agreement of International Through Transportation for Goods of the Organization of Railway Cooperation (ORC) *(Put into Effect from June 1979)*
People's Railway Publishing House
Jan. 1980 32mo ¥1.45

Measures for International Railway Joint Transportation (No. 1739 R.F. <79>) *(Put into Effect from Feb. 1, 1980)*
Promulgated by the Ministry of Railways
People's Railway Publishing House
Jan. 1980 32mo ¥0.43

Experience in the Management of Motor Transport Enterprises
By the Compiling Group, "Experience in the Management of Motor Transport Enterprises"
People's Communications Publishing House
Jan. 1980 32mo ¥0.47

Railway Statistics (Tentative Teaching Materials for Secondary Technical Schools)
By Long Tai and Chen Zhengzhong
People's Railway Publishing House
March 1980 16mo ¥0.95

Systems of Technical Control in Motor Transport and Repair Enterprises *(Trial Implementation)*
Promulgated by the Ministry of Communications
People's Communications Publishing House
March 1980 32mo ¥0.16

A Calculating Method for Production Targets in the Steel Industry
By Compiling Group on "A Calculating Method of Productive Targets on the Steel Industry"
Metallurgical Industry Publishing House
Apr. 1980 32mo ¥0.10

Railway Planning. *(Tentative Teaching Materials for Secondary Technical Schools)*
By Chen Fuyin
China Railway Publishing House
May 1980 16mo ¥1.00

Standards of Technical Grades for Road Maintenance Workers. *(Trial Implementation)*
Promulgated by the Ministry of Communications
People's Communications Publishing House
May 1980 64mo ¥0.06

Sketch Map for National Railway Stations
By the Department of Freight Transport, Ministry of Railways
China Railway Publishing House
May 1980 Whole Sheet ¥0.60

Budget Norms for Water Transport Engineering
Promulgated by the Ministry of Communications
People's Communications Publishing House
June 1980 32mo ¥1.20

Standards of Technical Grades for Motor Drivers. *(Trial Implementation)*
Promulgated by the Ministry of Communications
People's Communications Publishing House
June 1980 64mo ¥0.05

Ocean Transport Business
By Cao Huicheng and others
People's Communications Publishing House
June 1980 16mo ¥1.40

Income from Railway Transport
By the Financial Accounting Teaching Office, Railways Economic Department, Northern University of Communications
China Railway Publishing House
July 1980 32mo ¥0.35

Accounting for Water Transport
By Gao Yunsheng and Hao Ying
People's Communications Publishing House
July 1980 32mo ¥1.20

Accounting for Railway Capital Construction. *(Tentative Teaching Material for Secondary Technical Schools)*
By Li Yulin
China Railway Publishing House
Aug. 1980 16mo ¥0.70

Analysis of Economic Activities in Motor Transport Enterprises
By Wu Guoqing
People's Communications Publishing House
Sept. 1980 32mo ¥2.00

The National Schedule for Railway Passenger Trains (Oct. 1980 edition)
China Railway Publishing House
Oct. 1980 32mo ¥0.60

VII. Finance and Banking

State Budgets (Tentative Teaching Materials for Higher Schools of Finance)
By Compiling Group, "Teaching Materials on State Budgets"
China Financial and Economic Publishing House
Jan. 1980 32mo ¥1.15

How to Be a Good Bank Cashier. (Series on Elementary Banking Knowledge)
By Guangdong Provincial Bank Branch of the People's Bank of China
China Financial and Economic Publishing House
Feb. 1980 32mo ¥0.20

Science of Socialist Finance
By Compiling Group, "Science of Socialist Finance"
China Financial and Economic Publishing House
March 1980 32mo ¥0.85

100 Questions on Financial and Accounting Business
By Compiling Group, "100 Questions on Financial and Accounting Business," Commercial Bureau of Liaoning Province
Liaoning People's Publishing House
Apr. 1980 32mo ¥0.72

Practical Writing for Finance and Economics
By Compiling Group, "Practical Writing for Finance and Economics"
Guangxi People's Publishing House
May 1980 32m ¥0.63

The Peasants' Bank of China (Manuscripts of Materials on the History of the Republic of China)
By the Banking Research Institute, the People's Bank of China
China Financial and Economic Publishing House
May 1980 32mo ¥1.30

Accounting in the People's Bank of China (Tentative Teaching Materials for the Bank Secondary Schools)
By the Compiling Group, "Accounting in the People's Bank of China"
China Financial and Economic Publishing House
June 1980 32mo ¥0.80

Accounting for Settling Transfers in Banks. (Tentative Teaching Materials for Bank Secondary Schools)
By the Compiling Group, "Accounting for Settling Transfers in Banks"
China Financial and Economic Publishing House
June 1980 32mo ¥0.30

VIII. Trade Economics

Standards of Professional and Technical Grades for Staff and Workers in Commercial Enterprises. (Book I: Metals, Vehicles, Electrical Appliances and Chemicals)
By the Ministry of Commerce
Technical Standards Publishing House
Jan. 1980 32mo ¥0.51

Standards of Professional and Technical Grades for Staff and Workers in Commercial Enterprises. (Book III: Preservation and Transportation)
By the Ministry of Commerce
Technical Standards Publishing House
Jan. 1980 32mo ¥0.10

Standards of Professional and Technical Grades for Staff and Workers in Commercial Enterprises. (Book IV: Foodstuffs, Veterinary Medicine and Refrigeration Processing Industry)
By the Ministry of Commerce
Technical Standards Publishing House
March 1980 32mo ¥0.50

Standards of Professional and Technical Grades for Staff and Workers in Commercial Enterprises. (Book V: Sugar and Sweets, Tobacco and Cigarettes, Wines and Spirits and Vegetables)
By the Ministry of Commerce
Technical Standards Publishing House
Jan. 1980 32mo ¥0.18

Standards of Professional and Technical Grades for Staff and Workers in Commercial Enterprises. (Book VI: Foodstuffs and Beverages, Service Trades)
By the Ministry of Commerce
Technical Standards Publishing House
Jan. 1980 32mo ¥0.22

Compensation Trade
By He Xinhao
China Financial and Economic Publishing House
Jan. 1980 32mo ¥0.40

Import and Export Business. (Teaching Materials for Institutions of Higher Learning)
 By the Compiling Group, "Import And Export Business"
 China Financial and Economic Publishing House
 Jan. 1980 32mo ¥1.40

International Trade and Banking Under Capitalism. (Series on Knowledge of International Banking)
 By Wang Huaining
 China Financial and Economic Publishing House
 Jan. 1980 32mo ¥0.85

Famous Products in Zhejiang Province (Fresh and Dried Fruits, Nonstaple Foods)
 By Hu Xiongfei and Tang Shusheng
 Zhejiang People's Publishing House
 Jan. 1980 32mo ¥0.17

Knowledge of Nonstaple Foodstuffs Commodities
 By the School for Staff and Workers of the Nonstaple Foods Management Office, Dongcheng District of Beijing
 China Financial and Economic Publishing House
 Jan. 1980 32mo ¥0.60

Foreign Trade Arbitration
 By Feng Datong
 China Financial and Economic Publishing House
 March 1980 32mo ¥0.28

Inspection of Cereals and Oils. (Tentative Teaching Materials for Cereals Secondary Schools)
 By the Compiling Group, "Inspection of Cereals and Oils"
 China Financial and Economic Publishing House
 Apr. 1980 32mo ¥0.85

Commercial Statistics
 By Cui Shishuang
 Chinese People's University Publishing House
 May 1980 32mo ¥0.82

Science of Commercial Economic Management in China. (Tentative Teaching Materials for Higher Financial Institutions and Colleges)
 By Gao Guangli and Others
 Chinese People's University Publishing House
 June 1980 32mo ¥0.96

Science of Management in Chinese Commercial Enterprises. (Tentative Teaching Materials for Higher Financial Institutions and Colleges)
 By Xia Guangren
 Chinese People's University Publishing House
 June 1980 32mo ¥1.10

A Brief Discussion on Engaging in Trade with Civil Manners (Series on Commerce, Vol. I)
 China Commercial Publishing House
 June 1980 32mo ¥0.18

Brief Discussion on Modernization of Commerce
 By Hu Huojun and Wang Cainan
 Jilin People's Publishing House
 June 1980 32mo ¥0.35

Price Parities Between Industrial and Agricultural Products
 By Zhan Hongsong
 Guangxi People's Publishing House
 June 1980 32mo ¥0.13

Inspection of Aluminas
 By the Commodities Inspection Bureau of the People's Republic of China
 China Financial and Economic Publishing House
 June 1980 32mo ¥0.50

Socialist Commercial Economics (Tentative Teaching Materials for Financial and Economic Colleges)
 By Zeng Hongye
 Chinese People's University Publishing House
 July 1980 32mo ¥1.05

The International Licence Trade (Control and Laws of the Licence Trade for All Countries)
 By W. Martin, etc. (W.G.)
 Translated by Liang Huasheng
 National Defence Industry Publishing House
 Aug. 1980 32mo ¥0.85

Knowledge of Commodities – Chemical Fibre Fabrics
 By the Financial and Trade Work Department of Lanzhou Municipal Committee of the CPC and the Financial Office of Lanzhou Municipal People's Government
 Gansu People's Publishing House
 Aug. 1980 32mo ¥0.16

Socialist Commercial Economy in China
 By Liu Guoyuan and Others
 Chinese People's University Publishing House
 Sept. 1980 32mo ¥1.25

Accounting in Commercial Enterprises
By the Compiling Group, "Accounting in Commercial Enterprises," Financial Department of Chinese People's University
Chinese People's University Publishing House
Sept. 1980 32mo ¥1.00

Commercial Knowledge
By the Commercial Department of Zhejiang Province
Zhejiang People's Publishing House
Sept. 1980 32mo ¥0.63

Working Regulations for Salesmen. (Series on Foreign Commerce, Vol. 2)
China Commercial Publishing House
Oct. 1980 32mo ¥0.16

Treat Customers with Good Manners. (Series on Commerce, Vol. 3)
China Commercial Publishing House
Oct. 1980 32mo ¥0.14

How to Be a Good Shop Assistant. (Series on Commerce, Vol. 5)
By Yang Chuanxu
China Commercial Publishing House
Oct. 1980 32mo ¥0.18

Study the Science of Services. (Series on Commerce, Vol. 6)
China Commercial Publishing House
Oct. 1980 32mo ¥0.18

Handbook of Common Commodities for Telecommunications Apparatus
By the Vehicles and Electrical Apparatus Purchase and Supply Station of Shanghai, and The Shanghai Hardware, Vehicles and Electrical Apparatus Corporation
China Financial and Economic Publishing House
32mo ¥5.10

IX. Economic History

Yan Xishan and the Shanxi Provincial Bank (Manuscripts on Materials of the History of the Republic of China)
By the Modern History Institute, the Chinese Academy of Social Sciences, and the Research Office on the History of the Republic of China; Shanxi Provincial Branch of the People's Bank of China and the Compiling Group on Banking History, Financial and Economic College of Shanxi
China Social Sciences Publishing House
Jan. 1980 32mo ¥0.82

Series of Works on the History of the Chinese Economy (Two Volumes)
By Fu Zhufu
Joint Publishing Company
Jan. 1980 32mo ¥2.65

Selected Materials on the Economic History of the Society of the Ming Dynasty (Volume I). (Collected Notes on the Unofficial History of Ming Dynasty, 1)
By Xie Guozhen
Fujian People's Publishing House
March 1980 32 mo, ¥1.45

Annotations on the Economic Works of Guanzi
By Chinese People's University and the Research Group of Economic Thought on "Guanzi" Economic Institute of Beijing
Jiangxi People's Publishing House
Apr. 1980 32mo ¥1.12

Collected Works on the Economic History of Ancient China
By Gu Qiguang
Jiangxi People's Publishing House
May 1980 32mo ¥0.79

Selected Tablet Inscriptions on the Industrial and Commercial Guild Hall in Beijing From the Dynasties of Ming and Qing
By Li Hua
Cultural Relics Publishing House
June 1980 32mo ¥1.80

The History of Economic Thought in Modern China (Revised, Two Volumes). (Teaching Materials of Liberal Arts for Schools of Higher Learning)
By Zhao Jing and Yi Menghong
China Press
June 1980 32mo 1st ed. ¥0.90 2nd ed. ¥1.15

Selected Economic Works of Ancient China (Book I). (Teaching Materials for Schools of Higher Learning)
Edited by Chen Shaowen
Written by Zhou Yanbin
Shanghai People's Publishing House
July 1980 32mo ¥0.82

Brief History of Economic Thought in China (II). (Teaching Materials for Schools of Higher Learning)
By Ye Shichang
Shanghai People's Publishing House
July 1980 32mo ¥0.79

Traders and Commercial Capitals in the Dynasties of Ming and Qing
By Fu Yiling
People's Publishing House
July 1980   32mo   ¥0.56

Rural Social Economy in the Dynasties of Ming and Qing
By Fu Yiling
Joint Publishing Company
July 1980   32mo   ¥0.52

Brief History of Political Economics
By Eight Teachers' Colleges and Institutes
Hunan People's Publishing House
Aug. 1980   32mo   ¥1.36

Historical Sources on the Enterprises of the Rong Families (II)
By the Economic Research Office, Shanghai Academy of Social Sciences
Shanghai People's Publishing House
Sept. 1980   32mo   Deluxe Edition ¥3.55

Manuscript on the Economic History of the People's Republic of China
By Sun Jian
Jilin People's Publishing House
Sept. 1980   32mo   ¥0.88

Outline for the Discussions on Problems of the Chinese Economy
By Kong Jingwei
Heilongjiang People's Publishing House
Sept. 1980   32mo   ¥0.42

An Outline of Political Economic History
By Li Xiangrong
Sichuan People's Publishing House
Sept. 1980   32mo,   ¥1.48

Programme of the Economic History of China During the Last 100 Years
By Kong Jingwei
Jilin People's Publishing House
Oct. 1980   32mo   ¥0.57

The Establishment, Development and Transformation of the Dalong Machine Factory
By the Economic Institute, Shanghai Academy of Social Sciences
Shanghai People's Publishing House
Oct. 1980   32mo   ¥0.39

The Socialist Transformation of Capitalist Industries and Commerce in Shanghai
By the Economics History Research Office, Economic Institute, Shanghai Academy of Social Sciences
Shanghai People's Publishing House
Oct. 1980   32mo   ¥1.15

X. Explanation and Definitions of Economic Terms

Explanations of Political Economy Terms (Capitalism)
By the Political Economy Group of Marxism-Leninism Teaching Office, Nanjing University
Jiangsu People's Publishing House
May 1977   32mo   ¥0.23

Explanations of Political Economy Terms (Socialism)
By the Political Economy Group of Marxism-Leninism Teaching Office, Nanjing University
Jiangsu People's Publishing House
June 1977   32mo   ¥0.20

Explanations of Political Economy Terms
By the Compiling Group, "Explanations of Political Economy Terms"
Jilin People's Publishing House
July 1978   32mo   ¥0.70

Explanations of Political Economy Terms (Edition in Mongolian)
By Xu He, Etc.
Translated by the Workers' Spare-time Translating Group, Xinhua Printing House of Inner Mongolia
Nationalities Publishing House
Aug. 1978   32mo   ¥0.46

Commercial Vocabularies
By the Compiling Group of "Commercial Vocabularies," Ministry of Commerce
China Financial and Economic Publishing House
Feb. 1979   32mo   ¥1.60

Explanations of Political Economy Terms
By the Compiling Group, "Explanations of Political Economy Terms," Political Science Department of Hangzhou University
Zhejiang People's Publishing House
Oct. 1979   32mo   ¥0.46

Economy and Statistics Dictionary
By the Management Office of Social Economic Statistics Materials, Department of Commerce, U.S. Government
Translated by Dai Shiguang
Chinese People's University Publishing House
Jan. 1980   32mo   ¥0.40

Explanations of Socialist Economic Theoretical Terms
By Gao Kelin
Inner Mongolia People's Publishing House
Jan. 1980   32mo   ¥0.45

A Political Economy Dictionary
 By Xu Dixin
 People's Publishing House
 March 1980 32mo ¥1.95

A Junior Political Economy Dictionary
 By the Library, Economics Department of Jilin University
 Jilin People's Publishing House
 Apr. 1980 64mo Deluxe editionn ¥0.88

A Concise Industrial Enterprise Management Dictionary
 By the Compiling Group, "A Concise Industrial Enterprise Management Dictionary"
 Tianjin People's Publishing House
 Aug. 1980 64mo Deluxe edition ¥0.70

8. ARTICLES OF ASSOCIATION OF THE BANK OF CHINA
Including International Branches of the People's Insurance Company
(Approved by the State Council on September 22, 1980)

Chapter I: General Provisions

Article 1. The Bank of China is a state-owned socialist enterprise and is the specialized foreign exchange bank of the People's Republic of China.

Article 2. The functions of the Bank of China are: to raise, utilize, accumulate and manage foreign-exchange funds, to engage in all kinds of foreign-exchange business, and to participate in international financial activities for the purpose of rendering service to the modernization of China's socialist construction.

Article 3. The Head Office of the Bank of China shall be established in Beijing. To meet the needs of business, the Bank may set up branches, sub-branches and representative offices at places of commercial and financial importance both in China and abroad.

Chapter II: Capital

Article 4. The authorized capital of the Bank of China shall be Renminbi 1,000 million yuan.

Chapter III: Business

Article 5. The Bank of China shall engage in and handle, when entrusted, the following kinds of business:
a) International settlements in connection with foreign trade and non-trade transactions.
b) International interbank deposits and loans.
c) Overseas Chinese remittances and other international remittances.
d) Deposits and loans in foreign currencies; and, with the approval of the People's Bank of China, deposits and loans in Renminbi which relate to foreign-exchange business.
e) Buying and selling of foreign exchange (including foreign currencies).
f) Buying and selling of gold in international markets.
g) Organizing and participating in international syndicated loans.
h) Investing singly by itself or jointly with others in banking businesses, finance companies and other enterprises in foreign countries and in the Hong Kong and Macao regions.
i) Issuing bonds and securities in foreign currencies with the authorization of the state.
j) Providing trust and advisory services.
k) Engaging in other kinds of banking business approved or entrusted by the state.

Article 6. The Bank of China shall participate in international financial meetings with the authorization of the state.

Article 7. Branches and offices of the Bank of China set up in foreign countries and in the Hong Kong and Macao regions may engage in all kinds of banking business which are permitted by local laws and regulations.

Chapter IV: Organization

Article 8. The Bank of China shall have a Board of Directors consisting of an honorary chairman, a chairman, and a number of vice-chairmen, managing directors and directors, all to be appointed by the State Council.

Article 9. The functions of the Board of Directors of the Bank of China are as follows:
a) To examine and determine the business policies and plans of the Bank.
b) To receive and examine the president's reports on the work of the Bank.
c) To examine and approve the Bank's annual financial statements and proposals for the distribution of profits.
d) To appoint and remove high officials of the Bank.
e) To consider and determine the setting up and closing down of branches, sub-branches and offices of the Bank in China and abroad.
f) To consider and examine other important matters relating to the Bank.

Article 10. The Bank of China shall have a Board of Supervisors consisting of a chief supervisor and a number of supervisors all to be appointed by the State Council.

Article 11. The functions of the Board of Supervisors are as follows:
a) To supervise the Bank's implementation

of the policies, laws, and orders of the state as well as the Bank's business policies.

b) To examine the annual financial statements of the Bank.

c) To investigate matters of a serious nature and submit opinions on ways of dealing with them.

Article 12. The Bank of China shall have a president and a number of vice-presidents to be nominted by the chairman of the Board of Directors who shall, with the approval of the Board of Directors, submit his nominations to the State Council for appointment.

Article 13. The president of the Bank of China shall be responsible for the overall operation and administration of the Bank and shall submit to the Board of Directors periodic reports on the work of the Bank. The vice-presidents shall assist the president in his work.

Chapter V: Meetings

Article 14. A meeting of the Board of Directors shall be held once a year and is to be convened by the chairman. A meeting of the Board of Supervisors shall be held once a year and is to be convened by the chief supervisor. If necessary, the convocation of the aforesaid meetings may take place in advance or be postponed; and the chairman of the Board of Directors may also convene joint meetings of the directors and supervisors.

Article 15. Meetings of the Board of Directors, meetings of the Board of Supervisors, and joint meetings of the directors and supervisors shall all require a quorum of more than two-thirds of their respective members (including proxies). All resolutions, to be effective, must be passed by more than one-half of the persons attending the meetings.

Chapter VI: Addendum

Article 16. The present Articles of Association shall come into force upon the approval of the State Council. The same applies to amendments.

Board of Directors, Bank of China

Honorary Chairman:
Qiao Peixin
    Vice-President, People's Bank of China

Chairman:
Bu Ming
    Vice-President, People's Bank of China: President, Bank of China
Vice-Chairmen:
Chang Yanqing
    Vice-President, Bank of China
Chen Kedong
    Vice-President, Bank of China
Cui Yanxu
    Vice-President, Bank of China
Cui Ping
    Vice-President, Bank of China
Xiang Kefang
    Vice-President, Bank of China
Wang Weicai
    Vice-President, Bank of China
Li Pinzhou
    Inspector General, Bank of China
Managing Directors:
    (Listed in order of member of strokes of their Chinese surnames).
Ma Yinchu
    Member Standing Committee of the Chinese People's Political Consulative Conference.
Feng Tianshun
    Director, Foreign Investment Commission
Zhuang Shiping
    Delegate, National People's Congress; Chairman, Nanyang Commercial Bank, Hong Kong
Sun Xiaocun
    Member, Standing Committee of the Chinese People's Political Consulative Conference
Li Chaoying
    Vice-President, Bank of China
Sha Qianli
    Member, Standing Committee of the National People's Congress
Lin Jixin
    General Manager, Research Department, Bank of China
Jin Deqin
    General Manager, Bank of China, London
Zhao Bingde
    Vice-President, Bank of China
Rong Yiren
    Member, Standing Committee of the National People's Congress
Xu Ren
    General Manager, International Department, Bank of China
Zi Yaohua
    Chief Counsellor's Office of the People's Bank of China
Guo Dihuo
    Delegate, National People's Congress; Vice-Chairman, Chinese People's Political Consultative Conference of Guangdong Province

Cheng Muhao
   Adviser, Bank of China, Hong Kong
Jiang Wengui
   Vice-President, Bank of China
Lou Fuqing
   Member, Chinese People's Political Consultative Conference: Adviser, Bank of China
Pan Jingan
   Deputy Inspector General, Bank of China
Xue Wenlin
   General Manager, Bank of China, Singapore
Directors:
Fang Shangui
   Delegate, National People's Congress; Senior Deputy General Manager, Bank of China, Hong Kong
Niu Zhizhong
   President, Bank of China
Shi Jianzeng
   Tianjin President, Bank of China, City Branch
Liu Lixin
   Vice-President, People's Construction Bank of China
Xing Gangming
   President, Bank of China, Guangzhou
Li Yumin
   General Manager, Bank of China, Luxembourg
Chen Hong
   Delegate, Guangdong Provincial People's Congress; Senior Deputy General Manager, Bank of China, Hong Kong
Chen Boliu
   Member, Chinese People's Political Consultative Conference of Guangdong Province; Manager, Kincheng Banking Corporation, Hong Kong
Zhou Jizhi
   Adviser, Agricultural Bank of China
Zhang Jinin
   Senior Deputy General Manager, Bank of China, Singapore
Zhang Xueyao
   Rerepresentative of Bank of China in New York
He Yangxian
   Adviser, Bank of Communications, Hong Kong
Yu Mingyue
   Deputy Manager, Chung Hwa Publishing Company
Xu Guomao
   Member of the Shanghai Chinese People's Political Consultative Conference
Xu Zhanxing
   Delegate, Guangdong Provincial People's Congress; Managing Director, Sin Hua Trust, Savings & Commercial Bank Ltd.
Guo Ruiren
   Delegate, National People's Congress; Manager, Investment Company of Fujian Province

Qi Ming
   President, Bank of China, Shanghai
Zhang Wenzhong
   General Manager, Bank of China, Hong Kong
Huang Xianru
   Adviser, Bank of China, Hong Kong

Council of Supervisors, Bank of China

Head Supervisor:
Li Fei
   Vice-President, People's Bank of China
Supervisors:
Liu Jiwu
   Deputy Director, Political Department, People's Bank of China
Zhuang Mingli
   Delegate, National People's Congress
Sun Haokuan
   Professor, Institute of Foreign Trade
Li Shizhang
   Delegate, National People's Congress
Li Huizhong
   Deputy Director, Budget Department, Ministry of Finance
Shen Rixin
   Deputy Chief, Counsellor's Office, People's Bank of China
Sung Xiying
   General Manager, Administration and Secretarial Department, Bank of China
Zhang Yi
   General Manager, Personnel Department, Bank of China
Hong Zuoyao
   Member, Standing Committee of the Shanghai Chinese People's Political Consultative Conference
Pan Shilun
   Adviser, Bank of China

PEOPLE'S INSURANCE COMPANIES AND THEIR BRANCHES ENGAGING IN INTERNATIONAL BUSINESS

1. The People's Insurance Company of China

Acting General Manager: Song Guohua
Head office address:
   22 Xi Jiao Min Xiang, Beijing
Cables: 42001 Beijing
Telex: 22012 PICC CN
Telephone: 338521

PICC Liaison Office in London:
Manager: Liu Enzhen
Deputy-manager: Pan Lufu

2. The China Insurance Company Ltd.

Chairman, Board of Directors:
  Gen Dao Ming
General Manager: Song Guohua
Address:
  22 Xi Jiao Min Xiang, Beijing
Cables: CHINSURCO BEIJING
Telex: 42001 Beijing
Telephone: 338521

Hong Kong Branch
Address:
  Bank of China Bldg., No. 2A Des Voeux Road, C., Hong Kong.
Cables: CHINSURCO HONG KONG
Telephone: 5-243141

Macao Branch
Address:
  1 Avenida Almeida Ribeiro, Macao
Cables: CHINSURCO MACAO

Singapore Branch
Address:
  5th Floor, Bank of China Building, Battery Road, Singapore 0104
Cables: CHINSURCO SINGAPORE

3. The Tai Ping Insurance Co. Ltd.

Chairman, Board of Directors:
  Fen Tianshun
General Manager: Lin Zhen-feng
Address:
  22 Xi Jiao Min Xiang, Beijing
Cables: TAIPINGINC BEIJING
Telex: 42001 Beijing
Telephone: 338521

Hong Kong Branch
Address:
  13th Floor, Nanyang Commercial Bank Bldg., 151 Des Voeux Road, C., Hong Kong
Cables: TAIPINGINC HONG KONG
Telephone: 5-433261

Singapore Branch
Address:
  Four Seas Communication Bank Building, Chulia Street, Singapore 1.
Cables: TAIPINGINC SINGAPORE

9. EXCHANGE RATES OF RMB YUAN AGAINST FOREIGN CURRENCIES, 1977-1980

(Compiled by the State General Adminitration of Foreign Exchange Control).

Unit: RMB yuan

Currency	Per	1977		1978		1979		1980		
		Beginning of the period	Average of the period	Beginning of the period	Average of the period	Beginning of the period	Average of the period	Beginning of the period	End of the period	Average of the period
Australia $	100	204.73	205.76	197.71	192.76	183.14	174.17	166.72	179.47	170.72
Austria Sch	100	11.19	11.20	11.37	11.60	11.79	11.62	12.12	11.04	11.61
Belgium Fr	10000	520.62	517.57	520.41	535.22	548.09	529.98	534.17	484.27	513.92
Canada $	100	186.02	175.09	158.84	147.92	133.50	132.75	127.60	128.62	128.08
Denmark Kr	100	32.50	30.95	29.74	30.50	30.96	29.56	27.94	25.45	26.62
F.R.G. DM	100	79.57	79.75	81.68	83.80	86.18	84.84	86.37	77.94	82.67
Finland MK	100	49.54	46.27	42.49	40.88	41.78	39.93	40.16	40.69	40.42
France Fr	100	38.15	37.82	36.48	37.33	37.58	36.56	36.94	33.93	35.56
Ghana Cedi	100	165.32	162.16	155.33	113.27	59.64	56.69	54.85	56.89	54.50
Guinea Syli	100	8.84	8.81	8.58	8.52	8.39	8.17	8.02	8.12	7.97
Iran Rial	10000	269.78	263.60	252.39	240.17	232.32	211.74	210.97	223.50	211.49
Italy Lira	10000	21.51	21.04	19.93	19.80	18.95	18.69	18.45	16.59	17.55
Japan Yen	100000	642.19	690.26	722.76	805.84	813.17	713.13	622.25	749.48	663.45
Mali Fr	10000	38.38	37.92	36.85	37.27	37.06	36.55	36.94	33.93	35.47
Hollad G	100	36.14	75.57	75.12	77.77	79.90	77.55	78.32	71.68	75.57
Norway Kr	100	19.20	34.92	33.64	32.14	31.71	30.68	30.13	29.69	30.38
Pakistan Rs	100	19.20	18.84	18.04	17.13	16.57	15.76	15.24	15.80	15.14
Sierra Leone	100	157.66	161.56	162.77	160.22	152.07	147.87	143.59	143.59	143.59
Singapore $	100	77.12	76.17	73.95	73.89	72.71	71.66	69.78	73.45	69.95
Sweden Kr	100	45.53	41.51	36.79	37.20	36.80	36.22	36.09	35.05	35.51
Swiss Fr	100	77.31	77.15	85.19	94.41	97.91	93.51	93.72	85.95	89.59
Tanzania Sh	100	23.27	23.27	23.27	23.27	23.27	19.21	18.20	19.08	18.39
U.K. £	100	319.80	323.55	328.13	322.53	319.27	329.26	334.27	364.42	347.74
U.S.$	100	188.03	185.78	173.00	168.36	157.71	155.49	149.62	153.03	149.84
Hong Kong $	100	39.33	39.81	37.85	36.16	33.66	31.35	30.49	30.11	30.15

Note: The foreign exchange rates of RMB yuan quoted above are the middle rates (the average rates) between the buying and selling rates.
The foreign exchange rates of our country divide into two kinds: the buying and selling rates, the buying rate is 0.25% below the middle rate and the selling rate is 0.25% above the middle rate.

INDEX

A

Academic societies, scientific, 683, 688
Accountants, 1007, 1021
Accounting: agricultural, publications on, 1095-1098; publications on, 1090-1095
Accounts, business, 343, 451, 624; for tax purposes, 232
Accumulation-consumption ratio, 319-320, 322, 323, 382, 447, 646, 647, 953
Accumulation, national, 965t
Actors, film, 734-742
Acupuncture: ancient, 7; research on, 755
Administrative divisions, local, 59-69
Adult education, 748-749, 910-911
Aerial work services, 598-599; extension of, 600-601
Afforestation. See Forests, Forestry
Africa: agricultural projects in, 632; foreign aid to, 632-634; medical teams in, 633
Agrarian Revolutionary War, 77, 105
Agricultural Bank of China, 660, 665-666, 1012, 1062; commune-run enterprises and, 153-154; credit and, 165, 388, 666, 1005; function of, 657, 665; history of, 665; loans from, 665-666, 1012
Agricultural bases, state, 171, 401, 408, 862; for livestock, 439-440
Agricultural-industrial balance, 293-298, 301, 305-306, 320-321, 747, 952; state farms and, 411-413
Agricultural - industrial -commercial complexes, 1019, 1020; commune-run, 483
Agricultural machinery, 523-531, 970t, 992, 1007, 1019
Agricultural machinery industry, 523-531; for animal husbandry, 525, 528; benefits from, 525-526; current state of, 524, 525; equipment available from, 524-525; exports from, 528; geography and, 430-431; goals of, 529-530; labour and, 525, 526, 531; market economy and, 529; natural disasters and, 525; output of, 524, 527, 970t, 992; priorities in, 525, 529-530; problems remaining in, 526-527; quality and, 527; readjustment in, 528-530; research in, 523-524; responsibility for production and, 528-529; technology in, 524; tractors and, 523, 524; transportation and, 524
Agricultural Machinery, Ministry of, 171, 523-531, 1002, 1003, 1006, 1010-1011; colleges under, 524; duties of, 171; establishment of, 523
Agricultural management: education for, 1062-1063; publications on, 1095-1098

Agricultural output, 116, 966t, 991t
Agricultural planning, 119; aims of, 24-25; local, 372; readjustments in, 129, 395
Agricultural production: assessment of, 1019; responsibility for, 368-376, 396-398, 528-529
Agricultural production, Anhui Province: non-output oriented, 370-371; output quotas in, 168-376; standard of living in, 374-375; successes in, 373-376
Agricultural schools, 170, 415
Agricultural taxes, 647, 1016, 1018; remission of, 119, 129, 322, 1016-1018
Agriculture: aerial work in, 600-601; ancient works on, 7, 8: Anhui experiments in, 368-376; authority over, 173-174; banking and, 665-666; CPC and, 173-174; contract system in, 372, 396; diversification of, 320, 381, 400-404; education and, 170; financing of, 129, 130, 165, 402, 1005, 1007; foreign aid and, 632; geography and, 22-23; guiding principles of, 162-164, 169-174; household quotas for, 368-376, 397-398, 813; individual labour in, 50, 117-118, 162-163, 165, 323, 374-375, 379, 392, 398-399, 966t; industry and, 163, 184-185, 301-306, 320-321, 323, 447; mechanization of, 170-171, 184-185, 295, 380, 392, 404-405, 523-541, 970t, 1016; modernization of, 161-174, 417, 970t; among national minorities, 36, 38, 40; output of, 293, 379, 966t, 991t; output quotas in, 368-376; present state of, 392-406; price rises in, 129, 165-166, 322, 323, 394; primacy of, 51, 161, 162, 163, 173, 328, 610; problems remaining in, 404-406; productivity of, 24-26, 80-81; 390; profits from, 1980, 390, 416; projected output of, 1981, 121; readjustment in, 381-382, 395-404; reform of, 5, 24, 38, 82, 116, 117, 161, 323, 395-404; region, 29-33; research in, 170, 414-415, 685-686, 1046, 1048; responsibility for, 368-376, 395-404, 528-529; self-determination in, 117-118, 164, 323, 381, 395-404; setbacks to, 162, 404-406; Sichuan experiments in, 403-404; state assistance to, 164; state control of, 395-404; state farms and, 407-418; subsidies for, 129, 166, 402, 647-648; technology and, 170, 405, 406, 409-410; types of, 24-26. See also Communes and individual crops.
Agricultural, Ministry of, 171, 172, 1002; agricultural readjustment and, 395; animal husbandry and,

440; commune-run enterprises and, 159, 375-376
Air pollution: prevention of, 286-287; urban, 765-767
Airplanes: maintenance of, 599, 601; types of, 599, 600
Airports, 29, 599; Beijing, 601, 1005; design of, 599; expansion of, 602-603
Air transportation, 29, 574; development of, 598; domestic, 598; equipment for, 601; expansion of, 602-603; freight transport on, 977t; future tasks of, 602-603; international, 598, 600; passenger services and, 600, 602; readjustment in, 600-603; safety in, 599-600, 602; state of, 1980, 600, 977t; for tourists, 679; training for, 599, 601, 603
Algae, nitrogen-fixing, 686
All-China Federation of Trade Unions, 707-716, 1007, 1010, 1013, 1016-1917; restoration of, 707, 709
Alloy steel, 541
Alpine tundra vegetation, 19
Aluminium industry, 541; consumer goods and, 544
Anhui Province, 781-786; administrative divisions of, 59; agriculture in, 781-782; capital construction in, 783; commerce in, 784; conditions in, 370; economic education in, 1057, 1059, 1062, 1066; future development of, 785-786; geography of, 781; human services in, 784; industry in, 782-783; initiatives in agriculture in, 368-376; readjustment in, 783-784; standard of living in, 784-785; transportation in, 783. See also Agricultural production, Anhui Province
Animal husbandry, 399, 438-443, 814, 837, 877, 878-879, 1006; bases for, 401, 442; breeding centres for, 439-440; breeding stock imports and exports, 1041; diseases and, 442; environmental protection and, 286; exports and, 443; grassland protection and, 440-441, 880-881; individual initiative in, 399, 442; mechanization of, 525, 528; among national minorities, 34, 40; need for development of, 25, 168, 442, 1011; in North China, 29; output of, 394, 438-439, 966t; policy on, 1017-1018; priorities in, 412; readjustment in, 438, 442-443; state farm output of, 1980, 409; technology and, 410; in Tibet, 913; in Xinjiang, 919-920
Animal Husbandry, State Bureau of, grass breeding, and 441
Animals: by-products of, FTC for, 1026-1029; domestic, 25, 29, 40, 168, 438, 969t; draught, 370,

1111

375, 438, 439, 969t; herbivorous, 439, 443; Mongolian, 841, 843; priorities among, 412; rare, 34, 149, 286, 773, 843, 914; Tibetan, 914; types of, and terrain, 19
Anshan: economic institute in, 1049; industry in, 30
Anshan Iron and Steel Complex, 542; charter of, 175, 180, 193n, 341; economic institute in, 1049; production of, 27; retail sales of, 310
Anyang Iron and Steel Works, 828
Apartment buildings, 561
Appeals: of customs duties, 273-274; right to, 56
Apples, 866
Apprenticeship, 699-770
Aquaculture, 432, 1021; area suitable for, 434; encouragement of, 436; feed for, 435; freshwater, 434; history of, 434; marine, 433; research in, 433; underemphasis on, 435
Aquatic Products, State Administration of, 143-145, 432, 1001
Aquatic resources, 26, 168, 412, 432-437, 1022; commune-run enterprises and, 156; extent of, 434; improvement of, 143-144, 401, 1001; marketing of, 433, 437; output of, 394, 432, 967t, 969t; overfishing of, 434-435; protection of, 143, 286, 401, 432, 434-435; regulations on, 143-145, 168, 435-436, 774; in urban areas, 168. *See also* Fisheries
Arbitration, 126, 388; combined enterprises and, 219; on contracts, 280; joint ventures and, 257, 260; on loan contracts, 242; on taxes, 229, 231-232, 235, 238
Architecture, modern, 563, 788
Archives in science, 688-689
Area, 11, 12; of cultivated land, 965t
Artificial insemination, of cattle, 410
Arts, compensation from tax status of, 234, 236-237
Arts and crafts, 473-480
Art schools, 717, 718-719
Asbetos, 557
Asses, 969t
Assets: fixed, assessment of, 231; fixed, depreciation of, 231, 1004; fixed industrial, 444; fixed, of state-owned enterprises, 964t; intangible, 231-232; loan repayment from, 242; of production teams, 405
Associations, economic, 125, 181, 315-316; management functions of, 315-316, 353
Astronomy, ancient, 6, 7, 8
Australia-China shipping, 594
Automobiles, 574; projected output of, 1981, 121
Autonomous regions, 37-38, 50, 53; administrative divisions of, 69-71; financial administration in, 225,

387; government of, 54-55; subsidies for, 15, 212, 650; tax exemptions for, 157, 650
Autumn Harvest Uprising, 77
Aviation industry, civilian goods and, 1015
Aviation technology, FTC for, 1938-1039
Awards: to films, 732-733; for inventions, 1014; in natural science, for quality products, 194-195, 460-461, 475, 491, 518, 534, 544, 568, 1003, 1019; tax on, 236-237; in technology, 189, 464, 533, 685
Aydingkol, Lake, 12

B

Baggage, customs control of, 639-640
Bai nationality, 23; population of, 34
Bamboo, management of, 150, 430
Bank accounts: of collective enterprises, 243-244; of joint ventures, 257, 261; for resident offices, 267; in Special Economic Zones, 263
Bank of China, 667-670, 1018; articles of association of, 1106-1109; board of directors of, 1107-1108; capital of, 668; council of supervisors of, 1108; foreign banks and, 669; foreign currency and, 252-255, 661, 667, 669; foreign currency loans and, 249-251; foreign exchange certificates and, 248, 661, 1011; functions of, 657, 667-668; growth of, 678; joint ventures and, 257, 261, 668; resident offices and, 266-267; restructuring of, 668; Special Economic Zones and, 263, trust department of, 1052-1054; world finance and, 669
Banking, 657-664, 667; decision-making in, 126, 658-659; economic stability and, 661-662; education in, 667; foreign exchange and, 661; history of, 657-658; Hong Kong, 940-941; interest rates in, 659-660; international, 667-670; management reform in, 659; publications on, 1101; readjustment in, 658-663; reforms in, 1980, 658-660; research in, 661, 1047-1048; statistics on, 997
Banks, 657, 665, 667; combined enterprises and, 219; commune-run enterprises, 156; foreign, 669; foreign currency and, 252-255; funds for industrial transformation and, 216-217; Hong Kong, 940; independence of, 126, 667; international, 667-670; loan procedures of, 240-247, 249-251; new role of, 387-388, 658-661; regulatory role of, 335, 658, 661; resident offices of,

266
Banners, 841
Baoshan Iron and Steel Complex, 542, 626, 1015; questions on, 1018
"Barefoot" doctors, 753, 754; training of, 758
Bees, 412, 439, 443
Beef, output of, 394, 968t
Behaviour, of resident office members, 267
Beibu Gulf, joint oil exploration in, 324, 629
Beidaihe, domestic tourism to, 680
Beijing, 56, 787-790; administrative divisions of, 59; agriculture around, 788, 789-790; construction in, 788-789; economic development of, 787; economic education in, 1055, 1058-1059, 1060, 1062, 1064; economic institutes in, 1052; environmental protection in, 767; foreign trade corporations in, 385; improvements in, 790; industry in, 787-788, 789-790; population of, 29; problems of, 789-790; sales exhibitions in, 414; service trades in, 789, 790; special corporations in, 385; tourism and, 678, 679, 787
Beijing Agricultural University, 170
Beijing Capital Airport, 601, 1005
Belgium, loan from, 628
Benxi, industry in, 30
Benxi Iron and Steel Company, economic institute in, 1049
Berths, shipping, 519, 579, 593
Bicycles: output of, 1980, 457; projected output of, 1981, 121
Biological controls, 167
Birth control. *See* Family planning
Birth rate, 962t
Birthweight, increase in, 442
Block printing, ancient, 7
Blueprints, 207
Bohai Bay, 12, 13; joint oil exploration in, 629, 1015; oil exploration in, 324; water pollution in, 769
Bohai No. 2 Oil rig accident, 137, 142, 713; liability for, 1018; reporting of, 731; trial on, 1019
Bonuses, 119, 190-191, 293, 295, 322-323, 506, 647, 701-702, 953-954; in construction enterprises, 212; for energy conservation, 200-201, 278; funds for, 257, 259, 355, 361-362, 701-702; overissuance of, 297, 325-326; profit-sharing and, 202; quotas and, 344; taxes on, 236
Books: categories of, 724, 725t; children's, 725; "cultural revolution" and, 723-724; reference, 726; rural areas and, 725; scientific, 688; text, 725; volume published, 725t
Bookstores, 722
Border areas, 822-825, 918-922, 923-

926; state farms and, 407, 498, 411
Bottlenecks, 214; electric power industry and, 505
Bourgeoisie, 43-44, 49
Bourgeoisie, Chinese, 4; big and small, 95; redemption of, 83, 93-94
Bo Yibo, 1009
"Brain trusts," 684-685
Brand names, 460-461
Breeding stock, import and export of, 1041
Brezhnev, Leonid, 304
Bribes, 221
Bricks, 558
Bridges, highway, 590
Bronze smelting, ancient, 6, 540
Buddhism, 35
Budget Committee, Fifth NPC, report of, 140-142; recommendations in, 141-142
Budget, 1979: final account of, 128-131; deficit in, 128, 130; expenditures in, 128; readjustments in, 129-131; resolution on, 139; revenues in, 128; shortcomings of, 130-131
Budget, 1980 (draft), 131-134; budget committee on, 140; deficit in, 131-132, 644; expenditure in, 131, 644; goals of, 131; readjustment and, 131; resolution on, 139; revenues in, 131, 644
Budget, 1981 (estimated), 134-138; reforms in, 135; resolution on, 139
Budgets, 643-645; balancing of, 644; basic policy on, 644-645; central and local responsibilities for, 223-225
Building enterprises, commune-run, 483
Building industry, 560-564; "all-excellent projects" in, 710; architectural design and, 563; economic planning and, 564; experimental units in, 562-563; foreign construction and, 563-564; hotels and, 561-562; housing and, 560-561; management of, 564; quality in, 560; state of, 1980, 560; technology and, 563
Building materials: commune-run enterprises and, 483; light-weight, 559; local, 559; shortages of, 557-558; supply system of, 564; types of, 555-557, 558, 559, 1006-1007
Building materials industry, 554-559; backwardness of, 445, 558; cement, 555-556, 558; current state of, 554; emphasis on, 1010; energy conservation in, 554; exports from, 555; future of, 558-559; loss reduction in, 554-555; new materials in, 559; FTC for, 1041; non-metallic minerals in, 555, 557; plate-glass, 556-667, 558; pre-Liberation, 554; present

state of, 554; problems of, 557-558; products lines of, 555; readjustment and, 554, 558-559; whole plant exports of, 1043
Building Materials Industry, Ministry of, 554-559, 1006-1007
Bulldozers, 524
Bureaucracy, 950; rise of, 333
Buses, 578
Business Accounting (periodical), 1081
Business liability insurance, 1008
Business Research (periodical), 1081
Buyer's credits, 247, 251, 668
Buyi nationality, 23, 35; population of, 34

C

Cables, 604, 605
Cadres: in agriculture, 174, 368-376, 405; appointment to, 44; benefits for, 702-703; discipline of, 174; environmental protection and, 777-780; in industry, 177, 179, 189-190, 192, 341, 342, 451; national minority, 38; rural, 164, 169, 170, 185; in trade unions, 716; training of, 112-113, 189-190, 389, 415, 430, 451, 501, 521, 535, 751; unjust treatment of, 86
Calendars: ancient, 6, 7, 8; lunar, 6
Camels, 969
Candles, 512-513
Canton. *See* Guangdong; Guangzhou Province
Cao Jiren, 665-666
Capital: control of, 355; in joint ventures, 256; Marx on, 303, 305. *See also* Capitalism
Capital construction, 549-553; achievements of, 549-550; agricultural, 163-166; appropriations for, 1981, 132; assets/investments ratio in, 119; coal industry and, 500-501; conference on, 1002; curtailment of, 117, 122, 136, 188-189, 293-298, 299, 325, 327, 364, 453-454, 551-553, 645, 1011; electronics industry and, 535; funding of, 337-355, 644-645; future of, 553; imbalance in, 550; investment in, 117, 126, 325, 382, 448, 464, 530, 551, 552, 643; loans for, 240-242, 337, 387, 464, 551, 658, 1021; major indicators of, 979*t*; management of, 183, 552; in national minority areas, 39; 1980 economic plan and, 992; overemphasis on, 299-301, 319-320, 325, 326, 382, 390, 452, 550, 552; profits from, 552; problems remaining in, 552-553; projected, 1981, 121; projects under, 1980, 550-551; on railroads, 585-586, 588; readjustment in, 117, 122, 136, 188-189, 293-298, 299-301, 319-320, 325, 326, 382, 550-553, 1013; research on, 1047; for

social welfare, 117, 550, workers in, 550
Capitalism, 8, 302; "cultural revolution" and, 87; economic integration and, 315-317, 956; economic restructuring and, 350, 352; learning from, 317, 956; monopolies and, 314-315, 317; among peasants, 162-163; transition to socialism of, 82-83, 163, 308, 643
Cargo-handing machinery, 596
Carp, cultivation of, 433
Catalytic cracking, 488
Cattle, 168, 438, 969*t*; breeding of, 401, 410, 439-440
Cement, 1019; projected output of, 1981, 121
Cement industry, 554, 555-556; expansion of, 558; history of, 555; small plants in, 556; technology in, 555-556
Censorship, 721
Central Committee, CPC, decision on agricultural modernization, 161
Central Committee of CPC, 47; Chairman of, 47, 51-52; Political Bureau of, 47; Secretariat of, 1010; Standing Committee of, 47
Central government, 50-53; agricultural planning and, 171, 173, 395-404; economic control and, 307-318, 332-339, 353-355, 357-358, 360, 385, 455-456, 950-952; environmental protection and, 287, 777; financial difficulties, of, 225, 326; financial responsibilities of, 223, 297, 387, 649; individual aid from, 399; industrial planning and, 183-184, 446; labour and, 698-699; materials supply and, 211, 613-620; pricing policy of, 360, 610-611; profit distribution to, 361-362; recent strengthening of, 94
Centralism: historical necessary of, 350; industry and, 446; socialist democracy and, 353-354; USSR and, 307, 340-341, 350-351, 955
Central People's Broadcasting Station, 729; expansion of, 730
Central People's Publishing House, 722
Central-south economic region, 31-32
Ceramics, ancient, 6
Cereals, FTC for, 1025-1026
Chairman, Central Committee of CCP: as commander of PLA armed forces, 51; election of, 47
Chairman, Standing Committee of National People's Congress, duties and powers of, 53
Changchun, industry in, 30
Changjiang Plain, 12; agriculture in, 24, 31
Changjiang River, 393; dredging of, 594-595; floods of, 420, 424-425; navigation on, 28-29, 31,

592; pollution control on, 770; tourist cruises on, 679
Changjiang River Shipping Administration, 592; advances by, 593
Changling oil refinery, 488; pollution control at, 770-781
Changshou Lake Fish Farm, 403-404
Changzhou, construction experiments in, 461-462
Charcoal, management of, 150
"Charter of the Anshan Iron and Steel Company," 175, 180, 193n, 341
Chartering, of ships, 1037
Chemical fertilizers, annual output of, 510t
Chemical industry, 508-515; achievements of, 1980, 512-514; agriculture and, 170-171; competition in, 1008; consumer goods and, 514-515; development of, 28, 117, 508-509; energy conservation and, 513, 514t; exports and, 513-514, 515; fertilizers and, 510-511; FTC for, 1033-1034; growth rate of, 508t; imbalance in, 511; investment in, 509t; output of, 1980, 513t; plants for, 516; pollution control in, 771; present state of, 509-511; problems of, 511-512; raw materials and, 510-511; readjustment and, 512; research for, 509; tapping potential in, 515; technology and, 511-512, 515; whole plant exports of, 1043-1044; workers in, 508
Chemical Industry, Ministry of, 171, 508-515; local development and, 181-182; research and, 509
Chemicals, production of, 513t
Chengdu, industry in, 32
Chengdu Measuring and Cutting Tools Plant, 363
Cheng Yinghua, 590-591
Chen Lei, 540-548
Chen Yun, 85, 1003; on economy, 84, 297, 616
Chen Zengqing, 503-507
Chiang Kai-shek, 4, 5, 77; and US, 78
China Association for Standardization, 695
China Banking (periodical), 1081
China Civil Engineering Construction Corporation, 1044
China Construction Engineering Corporation, 563-564, 1044
China Corporation of Shipbuilding Industry, 521-522
China Electronic Import and Export Corporation, 535-536
China Film Equipment Corporation, 733
China Great Wall Industrial Corporation, 1040-1041
China International Travel Service (CITS), 677, 679, 681
China International Trust and Investment Corporation (CITIC), 629, 660, 668; establishment of, 1005
China Marine Industry Corporation, 1044
China Metallurgical Import and Export Corporation, 547
China National Hydraulic Engineering Corporation, 1044
China National Light Industry Foreign Engineering Corporation, 1045
China National Machinery Foreign Economic Technical Corporation, 1045
China National Oil Engineering Construction Corporation, 1044
China National Technical Import Corporation, 1036
China News Agency, 729
China Ocean Shipping Company, 593, 594
China Road and Bridge Engineering Company, 1044
China's Economic Problems (periodical), 1077-1078
Chinese Academy of Agricultural Science, 170
Chinese Academy of Sciences, 683-690
Chinese Academy of Social Sciences, 306, 728-731
Chinese Association of Enterprise Management, 1002
Chinese Export Commodities Fair: applications to attend; 1042; facilities at, 1043; organization of, 1042
Chinese Standardization Association, 1003
Chongqing: environmental quality reports of, 777; industry in, 32
Chongqing-Changjiang River Bridge, 1016
Chongqing Iron and Steel Company, 27
Chongqing Watch Industry Company, 462
Christianity, among national minorities, 35
Chronographs, 6
Chronology of major economic events, 1001-1022
Cinemas, 733
Cinematographers, 734-742
Circular on Reducing Non-Productive Spending and Combatting Waste, 137
Circulating funds, 137, 379, 389; capital construction and, 553; commune-run enterprises and, 158; fees for, 651; industry and, 188; of production teams, 405; saving of, 453; state-owned enterprises and, 964t; turnover rate of 1980, 611
Cities: agriculture and, 184; economic centres and, 316-317, 334-335, 353; environmental protection and, 285; housing in, 561; open to tourism, 677-678; population of, 23; by province or region, 59-71; by region, 29-33; transportation in, 578-579; workers and, 191-192. See also Municipalities
Citizens, rights and duties of, 55-56
Civil Aviation. See Air transportation
Civil Aviation Administration of China (CAAC), 598, 603; targets of 1981, 602-603; tourist service of, 679. See also General Administration of Civil Aviation of China
Class struggle, 102; as "key link," 751; in rural areas, 162-163
Climate, 11, 13-14; economic consequences of, 22-23; extremes of, 14; soil characteristics and, 17-18; summary of, 14; temperature zones and, 15t
Clock and watch industry, comprehensive nature of, 459
Coal: anthracite, 496, 1008; bituminous, 496; coking, 496; conservation of, 185, 618-619, 1020; distribution of, 26-27, 29, 30-31, 615; exploration for, 495, 500; extraction of, 496; future development of, 123, 328; pricing of, 672, 673, 674; processing of, 494; quality of, 496, 502; reserves of, 494, 1008, 1010, 1011; washed, 496
Coal industry, 496-502, 867; capital construction and, 499-500; curtailment in, 499-500; education and, 495; electric power and, 507; foreign investment in, 502; imbalance in, 476; mechanization of, 494, 498-499, 501, 502; output of, 27, 117, 320, 321, 494, 495-496, 497t; pollution control in, 772; projected output of 1981, 121; readjustment and, 324, 495-502; safety in, 496-498, 502, 1008, 1018; scientific research and, 500-501; in Shanxi Province, 897-899; technology and, 494-495; whole plant exports of, 1043; working shifts in, 1016
Coal Industry, Ministry of, 494-502; colleges under, 501; future development of, 501-502; institutes under, 495; machinery manufacturers under, 499; planning in, 506; safety regulations of, 498
Coal mines: conference on, 1010; fatalities in, 497; new policies in, 324; number of, 494; safety in, 324, 496-498, 1015; state-owned, 497t
Coastline, 11, 12-13, 592
Coaxial cable systems, 533, 604
Coins: commemorative, 660, 663t; new issues of, 660-661, 662t, 1012
Collectively owned enterprises, 351, 386, 1007; commune-run, 154,

482-483; employment in, 964t; handicrafts, 475; increase in, 450-451, 610; loans to, 243-244, 659; socialist nationalization and, 312; tax exemptions for, 655; in transport, 581; wages in, 964t
Collectivization, 351; of agriculture, 5, 24, 38, 50, 82, 83, 163, 379, 392; of handicrafts industries, 83, 474; loosening of, 93, 949
Colleges: of agriculture economics, 1062-1063; of engineering, with specialities in economics, 1060-1063; enrollment in, 746; of finance and economics, 1055-1063; reorganization of, 744; on state farms, 415; teachers', 750; technical, 458, 468
Combination, economic, 218-219, 221, 313-318, 329, 352-353, 483; extent of (1980), 337; forms of, 314; Marx and Lenin on, 350; need for, 334; in Sichuan, 360-361
Combined enterprises, 313-316, 337; administration of, 219; leadership of, 219; materials and, 218; in Sichuan, 360-361; taxes and, 219
Combines, agricultural, 523, 524; modification of, 528
Commemorative coins, 660, 663t
Commerce, 608-612; capital construction for, 612; consolidation in, 612; experiments in, 611-612; increase in, 80, 380; management of, 611-612; 1980 economic plan and, 993-994; prices and, 610-611; problems in, 612; profits and losses in, 1980, 611; research on, 1048; retail sales in, 1980, 609, 610; sectors of, 609; state purchases and, 1980, 608; trade fairs and, 610
Commerce, Ministry of, 608-612, 1004
Commissions, to withholding tax agents, 235, 237-238
Commodities, 612; competition and, 220-221; control of, 282-283; economy and, 299-318; export of, 269-270; increase in, 118, 334; inspection of, 1016, 1018, 1022; money relationship, 309-319; pricing of, 326, 335, 671-676, 1007; stocks of, 609; subsidization of, 132; supply of, 296, 326
Commodity economy: development of, 332-339; in rural areas, 531; socialist nature of, 299-318; theory on, 950-952; transition to, 334-339
Commune-run enterprises, 152-160, 163, 168, 183, 403, 481-485, 836; administration of, 159-160; combination and, 483, 485; encouragement of, 155-156, 481, 482, 1007-1008; experimentation and, 483; forum on, 1007-1008; funding for, 153-154, 160; future of, 484-485; history of, 481-482; importance of, 152; industry and, 185, 481-482; labour system on, 157, 483, 485; leadership of, 159; management of, 158-159; marketing corporation for, 1019; materials for, 155; output of, 481-482; ownership of, 154, 482-483; planning for, 154-155; pricing policy of, 156-157; products of, 1020; profits from, 158; readjustment and, 153; regulations on, 1003; scientific research and, 156, 484; state of, 1980, 482-484; taxes and, 157; types of, 151-152; urban industry and, 152, 154, 481-482, 484
Communes: in Anhui Province, 368-376; per capita consumption in, 986t; cooperation and, 402-403; culture and, 719; definition of, 50; democratic running of, 163-164, 381; employment in, 963t; enterprises run by, 152-160, 168, 403, 481-485; financial aid to, 129, 130, 133, 165; fisheries and, 432; forests and, 146-150, 431; fund shortage on, 405; grain sales of, 295; health care on, 753; income on, 119, 121-122, 129, 165, 374-375, 394-395, 484, 1017; individual labour on, 50, 117-118, 162-163, 165, 323, 374-375, 379, 392, 398-399; industry and, 184-185; integration among, 403-404; joint enterprises and, 403-404; organization of, 50; output quotas and, 368-376; ownership rights of, 164, 165, 371, 386; population of, 1980, 379, 392; private plots and, 398-399; quotas and, 368-369; 396-404; regulations on, 1001; state farms and, 417; statistics on, 965t; trucks sold to, 615
Communication equipment, 532
Communications, Ministry of, resident office applications and, 266
Communications, Ministry of, Bureau of Water Transport, 592-597
Communique on Fulfillment of 1980 National Economic Plan, 989-996
Communism, socialism and, 309-310
Communist Manifesto, 312
Communist Party of China (CPC), 8; agriculture and, 173-174; Constitution of (1977), 43-48; education and, 145; First National Congress of, 4; industry and, 175-193, 344, 347; Kuomintang and, 4, 77, 78; Mao on, 97-98; membership in, 44-46; on national minorities, 36-42; organization of, 47-48; past errors of, 86-93, 101, 108, 112; PRC and, 50, 51, 77, 79, 101, 104, 105; recent adjustments in, 94, 108-114; responsibilities of, 112; trade unions and, 707-709, 714-715
"Communist wind," 321
Communist Youth League, 47; industry and, 178, 180
Compasses, 473
Compensation, for substandard goods, 278
Compensatory trade, 629-639
Competition, economic, 220-222; in chemical industry, 1008; economic diversity and, encouragement of, 125-126, 317, 1020; materials management and, 616; in Sichuan experiment, 360; theory on, 951-952
Complete plants. See Whole plants
Computers, electronic, 532, 533, 534; emphasis on, 124, 185, 537; research for, 685
Confucius, 678; criticism of, 89
Consolidation, economic, 389; coal industry and, 502; commercial, 612; definition of, 381; extent of, 342; industrial, 181-182, 340-345, 451-452; of leading bodies of enterprises, 177-178, 342-343; pharmaceuitcal industry and, 567; stages of, 342-343; successes of, 342-343
Constitution of Communist Party of China (1977), 43-48
Constitution of People's Republic of China (1978), 49-56; amendment of, 52; enforcement of, 52, 55
Construction: costs saved in, 212; decision-making power in, 211-213; funding for, 212; guiding principles of, 213; new materials for, 125; profits from, 211-212; timber for, 150. See also Building industry
Consumer goods, 293-298; chemical industry and, 514-515; defence industry and, 1006, 1018; electronics industry and, 534; heavy industry and, 328-329, 454-455; increase in, 119, 124, 130, 141, 460; light industry and, 459, 477; market economy and, 126, 336; metallurgical industry and, 454, 543; neglect of, 299, 302; new focus on, 302-307; pricing of, 671-675, 984t; production of, 28, 30; purchases of, 608; retail sales of, 609, 981t; retail sales of, indexed, 981t; in rural areas, 394, 459; shortage of, 325, 472; subsidization of, 132, 166, 438; supply of, 1980, 614-615
Consumption: accumulation ratio, 319-320, 322, 323, 382, 447, 953; of energy, 505-506; increase in, 327-328, 382, 448, 459; Lenin on, 304-305; national,

965t; peasants', 394; per capita, 380, 984t; production and, 302-303; yearly per capita, 319, 323
Container transport, 578, 583, 593, 594
Continental shelf, 13; oil exploration on, 488, 493
Contraceptives, 764
Contracts: agricultural, 372, 396; for agricultural labour, 165; arbitration on, 280; contents of, 279; for foreign construction, 563-564; in forestry, 428; guaranteed, 279-280, 281; in industry, 182, 220; joint ventures and, 256-258, 259, 261-262; for loans, 241, 280; People's Bank and, 280; for product delivery, 207, 208; for scientific research, 686-687; supervision of, 279-281; at trade fairs, 1042; turnkey, 1043; workers, 259;
Cooperation: among communes, 403; among enterprises, Sichuan, 360-361; with Third World, 634-635
Cooperative stores, taxes on, 239
Coordination: industrial, 181-182, 385-386, 449-450; of reform efforts, 358-359; of transportation, 578
Copper smelting, ancient, 540
Corporations, Foreign Trade (FTCs), Directory of, 1025-1045
Costs: construction, 212; industrial, 188; of scientific research, 202
Cotton, 29, 323, 469, 818; cloth, pricing of, 672-673, 1016; disease prevention of, 415; export of, 470; import of, 467; Lo Mian strain, 888; production of, 25, 393, 400, 466, 1007; projected output of, 1981, 121; quality of, 467
Cotton yarn: projected output of, 1981, 121; state purchase of, 1016
Council of Supervisors, Bank of China, 1108
Counties, by province or region, 59-71
Crabs, protected, 143
Credit: to collectively-owned enterprises, 243-244; international, 667-668; local management of, 387-388
Credit policy: industrial reform and, 348; international, 668
Criminal law, 94; aquatic resources and, 145; currency speculation and, 248; on national minorities, 37
Crop index, 24
Crops, 24-26; diversification of, 381, 400-404, 412, 417, 808, 837; exchange of, 402; medicinal, 565, 568, 570-571, 914; output of, 323; priority of, 1981, 122, 167; output of, 967t; output of per capita, 969t; output of per hectare, 968t; readjustments of, 118; state purchase of, 1980, 608. See also individual crops
Cui Yongsheng, 717-721
"Cultural revolution," 86-91, 718; agriculture and, 162, 393, 396, 398, 408, 416; banking and, 657; criticism of, 88, 90; failings of, 87-88, 90, 108-109, 295, 321-322; fisheries and, 434; industry and, 342, 386; lessons of, 103-104; light industry and, 456, 474; Mao and, 86-94, 107; and national minorities, 37, 38, 103; pharmaceutical industry and, 569; prices and, 673; publishing and, 723-724; repudiation of, 92-94, 108; science and, 683; stages of, 89; trade unions and, 709
"Cultural Revolution Group," 88
Culture, 717-721; achievements in, 1980, 718-720; "cultural revolution" and, 718; education and, 719; financial aid to, 133, 383, 1019; history of, 717-718; ideological principles of, 717; importance of, 102; Mao on, 97; 1980 economic plan and, 994-995; policy on, 721; problems in, 720-721; research in, 720-721; in rural areas, 719
Culture, Ministry of, 717-721; film bureau of, 732-742
Currency: commodity relationships, 309-310; coins, 661, 662t, 1012; control of, 297; establishment of, 657; foreign, 228, 234, 247, 249-251, 252-255, 1009; income tax and, 234, 237; joint venture income tax and, 228, 232; overissuance of, 325-326, 390-391, 452, 553, 661; theory on, 309
Customs, 635-642; authority over, 635-636, 1009; conference on, 1002; control of, 1022; export licences and, 270; history of, 635; Hong Kong-Macao passengers and, 275-276, 640, 1017; import duty and, 273-274; import-export limits and, 271-272; passenger baggage and, 639-640; profiteering and, 640, 1017; resident offices and, 267; smuggling and, 636, 637, 640, 641-642, 1017; Special Economic Zones and, 264; Taiwan and, 638-639, 640, 1012, 1017; volume through, 1980, 635-636. See also Duties, customs
Customs declarations, 636-637; of foreign exchange, 255; of precious metals, 255; unified form for, 637

D

Dagang oilfield, 487
Dai nationality, 23, 35; population of, 34
Dalian, economic institute in, 1050
Dalian shipyard, 519, 521
Dance, 720
Dandong Municipal Electronics Company, 535
Dandong Watch Factory, 463
Daqing, 488; economic institute of, 1050; exemplary role of, 175, 176-177, 179, 341, 486
Daqing oilfield, 29, 486, 1013; anniversary of, 1014; pollution control and, 770
Daqing Petrochemical Complex, 488
Data-processing, standardization and, 199
Dazhai, exemplary role of, 169, 184
Death rate, 962t
Decision-making: in banking, 126, 658-659; in construction enterprises, 211-213, 220-222, 310-318, 332-339; enlargement of, 125, 134-135, 211-213, 214, 346, 357, 611, 1010, 1019; in enterprises, 310-318, 332-339, 448-449, 462; experiments in, 336, 448-449, 535, 546-547; local financial, 129-130; regulations on, 1004; scientists and, 684-685; workers' 335-336, 346-347, 351-352, 362-363
Decisions of Central Committee on agricultural development, 161-174, 482, 1001, 1005
Decisions of Central Committee on industrial development, 175-193
Defence industry: civilian production of, 1006, 1018; expenditures on, 130, 133; improvement in, 117; scientific research for, 119-120; standards and, 197; wonders in, 1008. See also National defence and Military
Deficits, budgetary, 325-326, 452, 553, 644-645; capital construction and, 645; elimination of, 131, 295-296, 297; increase in, 132, 390-391; 1979, 128, 130, 131, 140; 1980 (draft), 131-132; projected, 1981, 326; and readjustment, 130, 131, 141; types of, 644-645
Deficits, industrial, 188
Democratic management, 344-356, 452; consolidation and, 344
Democratic socialism, 44, 350-356; agriculture and, 163; centralism and, 353-354; industrial management and, 344, 351; need for, 102, 103, 111-112; workers and, 335-336, 712
Demographic Research (periodical), 1082
Deng Jingzhong, 22-33
Deng Xiaoping, 75, 85, 721; on CPC, 1007; "cultural revolution" and, 87, 88, 89; on industry, 84; Mao and, 89; support for, 89; on trade unions, 709
Department stores, 309
Depreciation, 1004; computation of,

for taxation, 231
Depreciation funds: commune-run enterprises and, 158, 159; energy conservation and, 216; loan repayment from, 241-242, 245, 251; profit-sharing and, 202
Deserts, 13, 22, 32; vegetation types in, 19
Design, architectural, 563
Design, industrial: of airports, 599; for construction, 552; examination of, 347; machine-building industry and, 518; quality control and, 205; of ships, 519
Detergents, projected output of, 1981, 121
Dialectical materialism, 164
Dictatorship of proletariat, 49, 80, 175, 177, 180
Diplomatic missions, foreign, foreign exchange and, 254
Diet: changes in, 163; of workers, 191
Diplomatic officials, tax exemption for, 234, 237
Directors, factory: responsibility of, 451; of joint ventures, 256
Directors, film, 734-742
Directory, Foreign Trade Corporations, (FTCs), 1025-1045
Disability benefits, 702
Dismissals: from work in joint ventures, 259; from work in Special Economic Zones, 264
Discipline: of cadres, 174; financial, 137, 141-142; in industry, 176, 178, 192, 364-365; party, 914; purchasing power and, 283
Disease: control of, 752, 754; prevention of, 754
Divers, 596; equipment for, 597
Diversification, economic: agricultural, 381, 400-402, 808; centres for, 401; in fisheries, 436; state farms and, 412; of tourist itineraries, 678
Dongfanghong oil refinery, 489
Dong nationality, 23, 35; population of, 34
Dongting Nitrogen Fertilizer Plant, 1004
Drainage Basins, river, 16t
Drama: national festival of (1980), 720; "three dramas" principle in, 720
Draught animals, 394, 370, 375; increase in, 439, 442; need for, 405; number of, 438
Dredging, 594-595
Drilling technology, oil, 490
Droughts, 420, 425; Anhui Province, 1978, 368, 374; 1980, 393
Drugs: distribution of, 566, 572; export of, 572; regulation of, 757, 1014; traditional, 565, 568, 570-571; types of, 565, 568
Drydocks, 519
Duan Jianke, 671-676
Duties, customs, 271-272, 273-274, 640-641; evasion of, 637, 641; exemption from, 264; Hong Kong-Macao passengers and, 275-276; on imports, schedule of, 273; reduction of, 641; resident offices and, 267
Duty-free shops, 602
Dyes, 513
Dykes, 166, 286, 401, 420, 792; construction of, 421
Dynasties, 3; chronology of (chart), 9-10; Han, 6; Ming, 8; Qin, 4, Qing, 8; Shang, 3, 6; Song, 7; Sui, 7; Tang, 7; Wei, 7; Xia, 3, 6; Yuan, 7; Zhou, 3, 6. *See also individual dynasties*

E

Earthquakes: early detection of, 6; Tangshan, 561; Tianjin, 910
East China economic region, 30-31
East China Sea, 12-13
Eastern Monsoon Zone, 20; characteristics of, 20
Economic and Management Studies, (periodical), 1078
Economic centres, regional, 316-317, 334-335, 353, 385
Economic Commissions, 184; loan approval and, 246; materials distribution and, 216
Economic contracts, supervision of, 279-281
Economic indicators, major, 363-364, 960t; average daily figures in, 962t; of capital construction, 976t; increase rate in, 961t
Economic management: central control of, 307-318, 332-339, 446; in handicrafts industry, 480; history of, 340-342; by industrial associations, 315-316; integration and, 313-318; in metallurgical industry, 546-547; ministerial, 315-316; reform of, 307-318, 329, 332-339, 462, 471, 611-612; regional, 316-317; restructuring of, 350-356, 384-391
Economic Management (periodical), 1079
Economic planning: for agriculture, 171, 372; building industry and, 564; central vs. market, 346, 353-354, 358, 385; coal industry and, 501; for commune-run enterprises, 154-156; competition and, 221; for control of purchasing power, 282-284, 297; for industry, 180-181, 182, 183-184, 192, 214-215, 315-316; for loans, 240, 246; for materials management, 613-614; publications on, 1090-1095; for quality control, 205; quotas and, 335; for readjustment, 297; for reform, 347; regulation through, 353-354; research on, 1047; state role in, 339, 353-355; theory on, 950-952; urban, 1019; for water
conservancy, 425-426
Economic Relations with Foreign Countries, Ministry of, 631-634
Economic research institutes, 1046-1054
Economic results, 329-330, 343, 384, 1015; criteria for, 363-364; industrial, 446; in metallurgical industry, 545-546; 1980, 389, 453; in textile industry, 471
Economic Science (periodical), 1079-1080
Economic Societies, 1072-1076
Economic Studies (periodical), 1077
Economic theory, 947-956; on accumulation-consumption ratio, 953; on competition, 951-952; on diversity, 955; on economic balance, 952-953; future trends in, 955-956; international exchange in, 956; law of value in, 950-952; on management, 950-951, 953; on market mechanism, 950-952; on material interests, 953-954; ownership and, 948-950; on quality analysis, 956; on self-sufficiency, 952-953; Stalin's formulation of, 948, 950, 955
Economic Theory and Economic Management (periodical), 1078
Economy: budgets for, 1979-1981, 128-138; central control over, 332-339; chemical industry and, 508-515; coal and, 494-502; combination in, 218-219, 313-318; control vs. liveliness in, 365; development of, 51, 293-298, 299-318; diversity in, 386-387; education in, 1055-1971; experiments in, 336, 343, 357, 367, 384, 413-444, 562, 1013; geographical factors in, 22-33; goals for, 306-307, 317-318, 338-339; growth in, 293; handicrafts in, 473-480; history of, 1949-1980, 379-381; ideological principals of, 50, 947-956; integration in, 313-318, 360-361, 413-414; judiciary and, 126, 136, 137, 335, 354, 388; "left" errors and, 294-295, 299-300, 301; market regulation of, 308-318, 335, 355, 359-360, 449, 529; national minorities and, 39-42; national plans for, 1980, 1981, 116-127; nature of, 307-310; oil and, 486-493; political, publications on, 1086-1087; politics and, 180, 335; post-1980 adjustments in, 391; present state of, 293-298, 308-309, 379-391; problems remaining in, 120, 130, 131, 136-138, 293-298, 329-330, 390-391; publications on, 1089-1090; purchasing power and, 282-284; reform of, 338-339, 346-349, 357-367; reporting on,

731; sectors of, 609; Sichuan experiments in, 357-367, 462; socialist nationalization and, 312; socialization of, 50, 82-86, 101-104, 321;Special Economic Zones of, 263-264; stabilization of, 326, 327; state of, 1979, 128-131; state farms and, 407-418; statistics on, 959-997; technology and, 689-690; textile industry and, 468; theoretical issues in, 947-956; USSR influence on, 298, 307, 340-341, 387-388. *See also* National Econimic Plans *and* Readjustment, economic

Education, 743-751; adult, 748-749, 910-911; aeronautical, 599, 601, 603; agricultural, 170; for agricultural machinery industry, 524; in the arts, 719; for banking, 661; for chemical industry, 509; for coal industry, 496, 501-502; commune-run enterprises and, 159; construction for, 749; in economics and finance, 1055-1071; for electronics industry, 533, 535, 538; enrollment in, 120, 121, 743, 987t; in environmental protection, 777-778; for family planning, 761; financial aid to, 133, 383; future of, 122; of handicapped, 743; for health care, 752-753, 754, 756, 758-759; history of, 743-745; increase in, 80, 380, 383; industry and, 189-190; journalistic, 729-730; "left" errors in, 745-746, 750-751; light industry and, 458, 464-465; Mao on, 744; medical, 752-753, 754, 756; among national minorities, 41, 748, 845, 848, 880, 915, 925, 926; 1980 economic plan and, 994; petroleum industry and, 490; political, 714-715, 744, 745; pre-school, 748; problems in, 750-751; in quality control, 209; for railroad industry, 588; readjustment in, 750-751; regulations on, 744; right to, 56; in rural areas, 405; in safety, 704; in science, 687, 746-747; for shipbuilding industry, 520, 521; spare-time, 715, 743, 748, 926; on state farms, 415; of tax officials, 656; of teachers, 749-750; textbooks for, 725, 749; for textile industry, 460; for tourism, 680; trade unions and, 714; of workers, 189-190, 209, 329, 342-343, 345, 389, 415, 451, 502, 698, 699-700, 750, 1014. *See also* Schools
Education, Ministry of, 743-751
Education,television, 605, 729, 748
Eggs, 392, 412, 438
Eight-Character policy. *See* Readjustment, restructuring, consolidation and improvement policy
Eighth National Congress, CPC (1956), 83-84
Eighth Route Army, 78
"Eight Principles" of foreign aid, 631
Electricity: industrial use of, 445, 505; output of, 27, 503, projected output of 1981, 121; use of, by sector, 504. *See also* Electric power industry, Hydroelectric power
Electric light industry, comprehensive nature of, 458
Electric power industry, 503-507, bottleneck in, 504; current state of, 504-506; fuel consumption and, 504-505, 506, 710; goals of, 506, 1008; history of, 503; management of, 505; nuclear power and, 506; output of, 1980, 503; power shortages and, 506; readjustment in, 504-506; safety in, 505; technology and, 503; whole plant exports of, 1043;workers in, 505
Electrification, 421; of railroads, 585-586, 1019; rural, increase in, 80, 380, 392
Electronics industry, 532-539; awards in, 533; capital construction and, 534; consumer goods and, 534, 536; decision-making in, 535; distribution of, 532; education and, 533, 536, 538; exports from, 535-536, 537, 1011; FTC for, 1039; history of, 532; integration in, 535, 538; management of, 536, 538, 1015; output of, 1980, 534; product line of, 532-533; quality in, 534-535; readjustment in, 533-539, 1009; research for, 534; service and repair and, 536; standardization in, 181, 185; state of, 1980, 532, 537; technology and, 537; weak links in, 537
Elections: of CPC central organizations, 47; of CPC primary organizations, 47; freedom of, 55; local, 54; to National People's Congress, 52; of rural cadres, 169
Elevators, 1011
Eleventh Central Committee, Third Plenary Session, CPC: on agriculture, 369, 393; economic readjustment and, 229, 318, 333, 340, 381, 438, 442, 447; "cultural revolution" and, 92-94, 293-299; open door policy of, 627
Eleventh National Congress, CPC (1977), 92
Embezzlement, 176
Emblem, PRC, 56
Embroidery, 478, 679-680
Employment, 337, 386, 963t, 964t; control of, 297; extent of, 698; handicrafts industry and, 478; individual initiative in, 338-339; policy on, 1017; provision of, 1979, 1980, 129, 322, 383, 647, 699, 1015; readjustment in, 122, 329, 383; rural, 481, 484, 531; by sector, 963t, 964t; service trades and, 329, 386. *See also* Self-employment
Emulation drives, 710
Encyclopedias: of ancient science and technology, 7, 8; modern, 726
Encyclopedia of Science and Technology, 689
Endangered species, 773, 1015
Energy conservation, 117, 119, 122, 324-325, 1009, 1010, 1015-1016; bonuses for, 200-201; building materials industry and, 554; chemical industry and, 513, 514t; coal to oil consumption, 124, 214, 324, 619; electric power industry and, 504-506, 507;goals in, 1981, 123-124, 328; handicrafts industry and, 478; industry and, 185-186, 215-216, 344, 445, 446, 453, 454, 545; materials management and, 618-619; metallurgical industry and, 545; petroleum industry and, 491-492; policy on, 1017, 1020; results of, 1980, 389; standardization and, 696; in transportation, 584
Energy policy, 185-186, 287, 324-325, 1005, 1017, 1020
Energy resources: coal 26-27, 185-186, 324, 494-503;electric power, 504-507; export of, 624; growth of, 26, 320-321; hydroelectric, 26, 421; non-polluting, 286-287, 507, 1011, 1014; nuclear, 507, 1021; oil, 26, 324, 486-493; overconsumption of, 320-321; policy on, 185-186, 287, 324-325; regional, 29-33; use of, by sector, 505;waste of, 301-302, 321, 324-325
Engineering, 883; architectural, 1013; civil, 1044; construction, 1044; hydraulic, 1044; marine, 597, 1044; oil, 1044; road and bridge, 1044; schools of, 1059-1063;standards for, 198
Engineers: promotion of, 190; responsibility of, 178
Enterprise Management (periodical), 1080
Enterprises, commune-run. *See* Commune-run enterprises
Enterprises: assets of, 1980, 379; accounting in, 343, 451; capital of, 355; central government and, 175-193, 310-318, 334, 351; circulating funds and, 137; combination of, 218-219, 314-315, 337, 350, 352-353, 360-361; competition among, 220-222; consolidation of, 340-345, 360-361, 451; construction, 211-213; contracts and, 279-281; coordination of, 181-182, 329, 334, 337;

decision-making in, 310-318, 334, 335, 346, 357, 448-449, 451, 462, 535, 546, 611; experimental, 336, 343, 357-367, 448-449, 611; financial management of, 650-651; five norms for, 180-181; foreign, 266-267; foreign trade and, 338; imbalance in, 452; independence of, 351; integration of, 313-318, 360-361, 385, 449-450, 1017; joint, 154, 314, 337, 385, 403, 628; leadership of, 177-178, 342, 343, 362-363; loans to, 243-244, 364, 659; management of, 307-317, 343-345, 350-356, 384, 451-452, 1012-1013; materials for, 613-620; ownership of, 351, 365-366, 386-387; piece-rate wages and, 277-278; politics in, 180, 344; production of, 136, 343; profits from, 125, 130, 133, 135, 343, 361-362, 365-366; reform of, 348-349, 455-456; shake-up of, 179, 340, 342; small, 553; standards and, 50, 197, 694; state-owned, 82-83, 118, 202-204, 311, 379, 404, 444, 475-478, 652-653, 963t, 964t, 976t; state role in, 354-356, 364; suspension of, 1017; tapping potential of, 214-217, 329, 364; tasks for, 180, 181-182, 188; transport, 581; vested interests of, 365; waste in, 136-137. See also Industry

Entertainment expenses, taxation of, 231

Environmental protection, 50, 766-780; afforestation and, 773; agriculture and, 166, 773; of aquatic resources, 143-145, 286; campaigns for, 1010; chemical industry and, 771; commune-run enterprises and, 156, 158; economic incentives for, 774-775; education in, 288, 777-778; of forest, 148-149, 286, 773; in Hubei, 832; industry and, 187, 285-288, 770-772; international cooperation in, 779, 1015; law on, 285-288, 766, 774; metallurgical industry and, 771; monitoring of, 776-777; nature reserves and, 773-774; organization of, 778-779; petroleum industry and, 770-771; planning for, 1020; power industry and, 507; quality reports on, 777; readjustment and, 779-780; research in, 773, 775-776; tax incentives for, 775; urban, 766-765; water pollution and, 769, 770, 774

Environmental Protection Law (trial), 285-288, 766, 774, 1005

Environmental Protection Leading Group, 766-780; functions of, 778

Environmental Protection Office, 287, 776

Environmental protection zones, 1019

Eugenics, 763-764

Europe: China's influence on, 7; exports to, 478; shipping to, 594

Everest, Mount. See Qomolangma, Mount.

Examinations: college entrance, 746; workers, 209, 259

Excess-profits tax, 652

"Exchange of equal values" principle, 168

Exchange rates, 997

Exchange students, 749

Expenditures, local, 224, 649, 1009

Expenditures, state, 224, 325, 749, 985t; 1979, 128; 1980 (draft), 131; 1981 (estimated), 134; reduction of, 295-296

Expenses, business, taxable, 231-232

Expenses, production: agricultural, 1979, 119; disallowed, in tax computation, 231

Experimental units, agricultural: in Anhui, 368-376; animal husbandry and, 440

Experimental units, economic, 336, 448, 454-455, 651; in building industry, 461; in electronics industry, 535; establishment of, 1004; in Jiangxi, 859; in metallurgical industry, 546; number of, 343, 384, 482, 1013; in Sichuan, 357-367, 903; state-owned, 1017; in Yunnan, 924

Experimentation, economic, 1018; benefits of, 413-414; financial, 651; in Hubei, 832; in Shaanxi, 885; status of, 1980, 454-455, 483, 611, 1017; in taxation, 652-653, 656; in Yunnan, 924

Exploration: aerial, 600-601; for coal, 495, 500; for oil, 324, 490-491, 492-493, 628-629, 685

Export credits, 627-728

Export licences, 269-270

Exports: of agricultural machinery, 528; of agricultural products, 168; animal husbandry and, 443; of aquatic products, 433; of building materials, 555; changes in, 621, 622, 623; of chemicals, 513-514; composition of, 982t; control of, 635-642, 1015; of documents, prohibited, 255, 276; electronics industry and, 535-536, 1015; FTCs for, 1025-1045; of handicrafts, 477-478; from Hong Kong, 940; licence needed for, 269-270; of light industrial products, 458; limits on, 271; loans in foreign currency for, 249-251; from Macao, 943; of machinery, 516; metallurgical, 547; prohibited, 276; registration for, 269; ship building industry and, 521-522; standards for, 196; from Taiwan, 934; textile, 468, 470-471; trade fair for, 1042-1043; value of, 982t; of whole plants, 1043-1044

F

Factionalism, in industry, 178, 342

Factories: energy conservation and, 201; joint ventures and, 256; management systems of, 178-179; reorganization of, 385, 411; retail sales of, 310; societies run as, 310; on state farms, 411-412

Family planning, 758, 761-765, 856; conference on, 1006; education on, 763; growth rate and, 1979, 120; history of, 761-762; in Hubei, 832; international cooperation in, 764; "left" errors and, 761; Mao on, 761; need for, 122, 763; one child families and, 762-763; projected growth rate and, 121, 169; research in, 765; rewards and penalties in, 763; state encouragement of, 56, 169; Zhou Enlai on, 761

Family Planning Office, 761-765

Fang Weizhong, 319-331

Farmland: appropriation of, 166; construction projects and, 166; distribution of, 526; improvement of, 166; irrigation of, 421; tractor-ploughed, 380; water conservancy and, 379-380

Farm Machine-Building, Ministry of, 167

Farm machinery, 167, 170, 410; local manufacture of, 152-153, 155. See also Agricultural machinery

Feathers, 443; export of, 478

Feature articles, 731

"February adverse current," 88

Fengyang County, 374, 780

Ferries, 578

Fertilizer industry, 28, 29, 510-511; imbalance in, 453; in North China, 29; projected output of, 1981, 121; in Southwest China, 32

Fertilizers, 166-167; chemical, 510-511; increased use of, 392, 410; organic, 167; research in, 685

Feudalism, 3-4, 8, 392; among national minorities, 36

Fibreglass, 555

Fibres, for textiles: natural, 466-467, 469; synthetic, 467, 469, 1008-1009, 1022

Fifth National People's Congress (1980), 1018; Budget Committee report of, 140-142; on environmental protection, 285-288; on income tax, 228-229, 234-235; on joint ventures, 256-258; on Special Economic Zones, 263-265; Wang Bingqian on budget at, 128-138; Yao Yilin on economic plans at, 116; Ye Jianying's speech to, 115

Film festivals, 734
Film industry, 732-742; achievements of, 1980, 719-720; awards in, 732-733; current state of, 732; domestic production for, 734; distribution and, 733; educational role of, 733; films produced by, 1980, 734-742; history of, 732; international exchange and, 733; quality in, 734; shortcomings in, 734; silver recovery in, 771; training for, 733; workers in, 733
Film poojection units, 717-721; in autonomous regions, 720; rural, 733
Films, 732-742; catalogue of, 1980, 734-742; distribution of, 733; on environmental protection, 776; equipment for, 734; processing of, 734; rights for, 733-734
Film studios, 717-721; in autonomous regions, 720; films produced by, 1980, 734-742; number of, 1980, 732
Finance, Ministry of, 643-654; capital construction loans and, 240-242; commodities control and, 283; on decision-making in construction, 211-213; on energy-conservation bonuses, 200-201; on financial supervision, 226-227; income taxes and, 228-229, 230-233, 238, 1002; loan approval by, 246; on profit-sharing, 202-204; on taxation of cooperative stores, 239; undeveloped areas and, 225
Finance (periodical), 1082
Finance and Accounting (periodical), 1082, 1083
Finances, 643-654; budgetary, 128-128, 644-645; commune-run enterprises and, 153-154, 158; control of, 355, 648-649; of enterprises, 650-651; industrial transformation and, 214-217; investment balance of, 646-647, 648; restructuring of, 135, 644, 645-654, 646-651; setbacks in, 643-644; state, 128-138, 643-654; taxation and, 651-654, 655-656. *See also* Taxes
Financial administration, 335, 643-654; in autonomous regions, 225; central and local responsibilities for, 223-225; culture and, 1019; discipline in, 137, 387; education in, 1055-1071; of enterprises, 650-651; for forests, 148; of health care, 757; of joint enterprises, 403-404; reform of, 134-135, 141, 659; research on, 1046, 1047; for tapping potential, 215-216, 217, 364
Financial and Economic Studies (periodical), 1082
Financial indicators, 976t
Financial Statistics, Petroleum Industry, 492t

Financial supervision, 226-227, 335, 1009, 1016, 1020; of contracts, 269-281; of enterprises, 278; of loans, 241, 246-247, 251
Financing, state, 643-654; agriculture and, 171, 399, 402; bank loans vs., 135, 212, 311, 337, 338, 387; construction and, 212; of forestry, 431; for industrial renovation, 215-216; reforms in, 387-388, 643-654; of scientific research, 687-688; supervision of, 226-227; of water conservancy, 424
Firewood, management of, 150
First Five-Year Plan, 5, 136, 294, 340, 947-948; agriculture and, 161; animal husbandry and, 442; culture and, 717-718; light industry and, 456, 458, 459; petroleum and, 486; posts and telecommunications and, 603; price control under, 671; publishing and, 722-723; standardization and, 691-692; success of, 83, 301, 708; USSR and, 627
First Front Army, 78
Fish: breeding of, 1006; overfishing of, 435; protected, 143
Fisheries: diversification in, 436; equipment for, 525; freshwater, 432; history of, 434; management of, 433, 433-435, 436-437; marine, 432-433, 434; output of, 394, 432, 966t; problems of, 434-437; processing improvements of, 433; readjustment and, 434-437; waste in, 435
Fishery Law, 168
Fishing, 30; autonomy over, 145; control of, 401, 434-435; deep-sea, 433, 434-435; environmetnal protection and, 286; forbidden zones of, 144; freshwater, 432, 435; gear and methods for, 144; marine, 432-433, 434-435. *See also* Aquatic resources *and* Fisheries
"Five kinds of artisans," 481
Five Principles of Peaceful Coexistence, 81, 103
Five-year plans, 184; First, 5, 83, 136, 161, 294, 340, 442, 446, 457, 458-459, 486, 604, 627, 671, 691, 708, 717, 718, 722-723, 947-948; Second, 457, 458, 459, 486, 708, 718; Third, 459; Fourth, 446, 459; Sixth, 134, 327, 331, 1020
Fixed assets: assessment of, 231; depreciation of, 231, 1004; industrial, 444; of state-owned enterprises, 964t; taxation of, 1004
Fixed quotas: contracts for, 372-373, 396-297; in Guangdong and Fujian, 650
Flag, PRC, 56
Flashlights, 458
Flax, 29; water pollution and, 144

Flood control, 80, 421, 422-423, 425; management of, 424; success of, 1980, 424-425
Floods, 393, 420, 425, 832
Food: inspection of, 287, 1021; standards for, 1021
Food production: distribution of, 24-25; total, 1979, 24
Foodstuffs, FTC for, 1025-1026
Forage, improved varieties ot, 441
Foreign aid, 631-634; agricultural, 632; complete projects in, 631, 632, 634; eight priinciples of, 631, 634; light industrial, 632-633; medical, 633; procedures for, 632; for transportation, 633
Foreign construction, 563
Foreign currency: control of, 252-255; exchange certificates and, 248; income in, 228, 234; loans in, 247, 249-251; retention of, 253; from tourism, 667
Foreign Economic Management (periodical), 1085
Foreign enterprises, resident offices of, 266-267
Foreign exchange: certificates of, 248; control of, 252-255, 661, 669, 1018, 1022; customs declaration of, 255; for import of technology, 217; joint ventures and, 257, 669; light industry and, 458-459; local retention of, 388, 669; purchase of, 254; rate of, 1977-1980, 110t, 1980, 997; textile industry and, 468
Foreign Exchange Certificates, 248, 1011; customs and, 272; issuance of, 661
Foreign Investment Control Commission: establishment of, 627; joint ventures and, 256, 257, 261-262
Foreign investments, 627-630; absorption of, 627-628, 668; CITIC and, 629, 668, 669; in coal, 502; credit policy on, 247, 251, 668; future course of, 630; history of, 627; income tax on, 228-229, 230-233; in oil, 628-629; protection of, 630, 669; regulation of, 669-670; resident offices of, 266-267; in Special Economic Zones, 263-265, 629; USSR and, 627. *See also* Joint ventures
Foreign nationals: foreign exchange and, 252-255; resident offices and, 266-267
Foreign participants, joint ventures, investments of, 256
Foreign policy: economic readjustment and, 331; future course of, 103; Mao on, 97
Foreign technology: agriculture and, 169; chemical industry and, 515; commune-run enterprises and, 159; control of, 626; excessive importation of, 625; funding for, 217; future of, 331, 626; import

of, 1036; industry and, 189, 447; for new products, 1012; shipbuilding industry and, 522; single-item, 162, 626; USSR and, 304, 625
Foreign trade: agriculture and, 168; compensatory, 629-630; composition of, 621, 622, 623-624; consulation service on, 1037; deficits in, 623; direct, 126; encouragement. of, 622-623; import controls in, 623; increase in, 89, 136, 380, 621-622; licences for, 269-270; loans for, 249-251; local initiative in, 118, 126, 388, 622; 1980 economic plan and, 994; organizations for, directory of, 1025-1045; policy on, 621; projected, 1981, 121; readjustment and, 622-624; research on, 1048; resident offices of, 266-267; shipbuilding industry and, 521-522; shipping services for, 593, 594; standards and, 196, 198; state of, 1980, 622; Taiwan and, 937t, 938. See also Joint ventures, Special Economic Zones
Foreign Trade Corporations (FTCs), directory of, 1025-1045
Foreign Trade, Ministry of, 266, 388; on customs, 271-272; on export licence system, 269-270
Forest fires, 148, 151; prevention of, 430
Forest Law, 1979 (trial), 146-151, 167, 286, 774, 1002
Forestry, 427-431; aerial work in, 599, 793, 810, 1001; areas suitable for, 24, 31, 32, 427; authority over, 146-147; in Central-South China, 31; commune-run enterprises and, 156; education for, management of, 1062-1063; environmental protection and, 286; equipment for, 525; industry and, 427; need for development of, 25-26, 167-168, 431; in Northeast China, 30; output of, 966t, 967t; priorities in, 412; research on, 1048; rewards and penalties in, 150-151; shelterbelts and, 146, 149, 167, 428-429, 773, 792, 1014
Forestry, 427-431; administration of, 147-148; area of, 23; by-products of, 430-431; categories of, 146; funds for, 148, 428, 439, 431; increase in, 1980, 428; management of, 146-150, 401; in national minority areas, 34-35; ownership of, 146, 428, 430; projected area of, 149; protection of, 148-149, 286, 430; utilization of, 150; vegetation types in, 19, 25-26; water conservancy and, 423
Forestry inspectors, 147
Forestry, Ministry of, 147, 151, 171, 773, 1002

Foucault process, 557
"Four fundamental principles" (of socialism), 109, 213, 299; economic restructuring and, 350; education and, 745
"Four kinds of mills," 481
Four Modernizations, 5, 130, 161, 180, 279; industry and, 189, 340, 342; trade unions and, 711; water conservancy and, 422-423
Fourth Five-Year Plan, 446, 459
Free markets, 385, 609-610, 1001
Freight traffic: average haulage of, 576t; changes in modes of, 576t; composition of, 577; containerized, 578, 589, 593, 594; highway, 591, 977t; priorities in, 593; railroad, 581, 583, 584t, 589, 977t; turnover of, 575t; volume of, 575t; 593, 594, 977t, 978t; water, 593-594, 977t
Friendship Stores, 272
Fruits, production of, 25, 30, 393
Fuels: conservation of, 200-210; forests for production of, 146
Fujian Province, 791-796; administrative divisions of, 59-60; agriculture in, 791, 792-793, 794; construction in, 791-792; development plan of, 795-796; economic education in, 1059, 1062, 1066, 1067; economic institute in, 1053; financial system in, 135, 794; foreign trade and, 793-794; FTC in, 1042; geography of, 791; grain distribution to, 401; industry in, 792, 793, 794-795; products of, 793, Special Economic Zones in, 388, 629, 794; transportation in, 792, 793, 794
Fur, 412, 443, 914; exports of, 478
Fushun, industry in, 30
Fuyang Prefecture, diversification of economy in, 374-375

G

Gang of Four, 128; agriculture and, 162, 368, 393, 408, 526; banking and, 657, 668; coal industry and, 495; "cultural revolution" and, 89-90, 108, 718; damage done by, 130, 137, 140, 176, 299, 312, 319, 332, 342, 380, 621, 645; education and, 744-745; exposure of, 176; industry and, 175, 176, 179, 180, 340-345, 386, 446, 566; journalism and, 728; Mao and, 89-90; national minorities and, 37, 38, 39; overthrow of, 89, 91-94, 108, 319, 321-322, 333, 340, 342, 343, 376, 947; tourism and, 681; trial of, 94
Gangue, 772, 1007
Gansu Province, 797-801; administrative divisions of, 60; agriculture in, 797, 798; capital construction in, 799; coal in,

1011; economic education in, 1060, 1070; finances of, 799; future tasks in, 799-800; geography of, 797; industry in, 797-798; marketing in, 799; readjustment in, 798-799; standard of living in, 799-800; transportation in, 798; unemployment in, 800
Gao Lingzhen, 933-938
Gaoshan nationality, 933; language of, 35; population of, 34
Gas, natural, 27, 32, 486-493; production of, 491t
Gasoline, 491
General Administration of Building Construction, 569-564
General Administration of Civil Aviation of China, 598-603; foundation of, 598; resident office applications and, 266; work services of, 598-599
General Administration of Customs, 274, 635-642, 1009; anti-smuggling campaign of, 642; authority of, 636-637; passenger luggage and, 639-640; reform of, 636; statistical work of, 638-639; task of, 635
General Administration for Industry and commerce: on contracts 279-281; joint ventures and, 256, 257, 261-262; resident offices and, 266, 268
General Administration of Travel and Tourism of China, 677-682
General Taxation Bureau, 233, 238, 655-656
Geography, 11-21; agricultural mechanization and, 430-431; ancient works on, 7, 8; divisions of, 19-20
Geography, economic, 22-33; agricultural, 23-24; industrial, 26-28; natural resources and, 22-23; population and, 23; regional, 29-33; transportation and, 28-29
Geology, 1001, 1007; awards in, 1013; coal and, 504; need for research in, 185; oil and, 487-488, 489-490, 492-493
Geology, Ministry of, 1014; petroleum industry and, 486
Geothermal power, 186
Gezhouba hydroelectric power station, 31, 425, 550
Giant panda, 779, 884
Glaciers, 17
Goats, 401, 438; for milk, 440, 1004; number of, 439, 968t
Gold: ancient works in, 540; reserves of, 997
Gongzui Power Station, 1002
Government, 69-71; autonomous, of national minorities; 37-38; central, structure of, 52-53; CPC and, 43-48; of communes, 50; general principles of, 50-52; local, 53-54; ministers of (1981), 57-58; municipal, 53-54, 59;

1122 INDEX

provincial, 59-69. *See also* Central government
Grade/wage system, 415
Grain: importance of, 163, 328; output of, 116, 381, 393; overemphasis on, 400, 412; per capita, 161; policy on, 1006; pricing of, 165-166, 295, 671-675; production of, 24, 29, 30, 323, 374; projected output of, 1981, 121; purchase quotas of, 166, 295; redistribution of, 401-402; state farm production of, 409
"Grain as key link" policy, 163, 400, 438
Grain rations, on communes, 165
Grand Canal, 768; dredging of, 594
Grasslands, 410, 439, 841; distribution of, 23, 24, 30, 34; enclosure of, 440, 441; modernization of, 440, 843, 1004; protection of, 286, 441; seeding of, 441; vegetation types in, 19; water conservancy and, 423
Great Britain, 939
Great Leap Forward, 84, 947; agriculture and, 161-162; culture and, 718; excesses of, 84, 294, 401, 341, 645; Mao and, 85-86; publishing and, 723
Guangdong Province, 802-806; administrative divisions of, 60-61; agriculture in, 802, 804, 806; construction in, 805, 806; economic education in, 1060, 1062, 1068-1069; financial system in, 135, 804-805; foreign trade and, 802, 805, 806; FTC in, 1042; human services in, 803, 805; industry in, 802, 804, 806; readjustment and, 806-807; Special Economic Zones in, 263-264, 388, 629, 805, 1018; standard of living in, 803-804, 805; transportation in, 803
Guangdong Provincial Administration of Special Economic Zones, 263-265
Guangxi Zhuang Autonomous Region, 31, 807-810, 1016; administrative divisions of, 69-70; agriculture in, 807, 808; construction in, 809; economic education in, 1060, 1062, 1069; forestry in 810; geography of, 807; human services in, 808; industry in, 807-808, 809; light industry in, 457; national minorities in, 34, 807; standard of living in, 808, 809; transportation in, 808
Guangzhou, trade fairs in, 1042-1043
Guangzhou Trade Fair. *See* Chinese Export Commodities Fair
Guarantees, of contracts, 279-280, 281
Guilin, environmental protection in, 768
Guizhou Province, 811-816; administrative divisions of, 61-62; agriculture in, 811, 813-814; animal husbandry in, 813-814; coal in, 328; construction in, 814-815; economic education in, 1058, 1063, 1069-1070; economic institute in, 1051-1052; geography of, 811; human services in, 812-813; industry in, 811-814; marketing in, 815; national minorities in, 811, 812; problems in, 813; readjustment in, 815-816; standard of living in, 813, 815; subsidy for, 135; transportation in, 812, 815
Gunpowder, 7, 473
Gu Mu, 778, 1003
Gu Nianlong, 939-941
Guo Chunhua, 407-418

H

Haihe River, floods on, 420
Hainan Island, 11, 12, 31, 1017; grain distribution to, 401; tropical crops in, 401, 1017
Handicapped, education for, 743, 748
Handicrafts industry, 473-480; commune-run, 158; "cultural revolution" and, 474; energy conservation and, 498; exports from, 272, 477-478; FTC for, 1031-1032; history of, 473; importance of, 185-186, 214; investments in, 477; labour and, 478; "left" errors in, 479, 949; light industry and, 476; management of, 480; Mao on, 473; maarket economy and, 480; ministry for, 474, 476; modernization of, 476-479; output of, 474; ownership in, 473-474, 475-476, 479; product line in, 477; quality in, 475; readjustment and, 474, 476, 479; sectors of, 473; taxes on, 239, 477; Tibetan, 914-915; workers in, 473, 477
Han Dynasty: Eastern, 6, 540; metallurgy in, 540; science in, 6; trade in, 6; Western, 6
Hangzhou, environmental protection in, 767
Hangzhou Steel Plant, 546
Hani nationality, 23, 34; population of, 34
Hankou Hydrological Station, 424
Han nationality, 3, 23, 34; chauvinism of, 39; economic development and, 35-36; language of, 35
Han tombs, 540
Hanyang Iron Plant, 540-541
Harbin, 30; industry in, 30
Harbour construction, 594-595; for oil shipping, 595
Haulage, average, freight, 576t; passenger, 576t
Health care, 752-759, 763; construction for, 562; education for, 753, 754, 756, 758, 759; facilities for, 562, 703, 987t; family planning and, 758; financial control of, 757, 759; future of, 122; improvement of, 81, 380, 384, 752-759; maternal, 756; among national minorities, 41, 846; 1980 economic care and, 995; personnel in, 752-753; pharmaceuticals and, 566, 572; preventive, 752, 754, 758; research in, 755-756, 774; right to, 56; rural, 753-754, 758; on state farms, 415; in Tianjin, 911; for workers, 191
Health foods, 568
Heavy industry: commune-run enterprises and, 482; consumer goods and, 328-329, 454-455; energy supply and, 320-321, 454; growth rate of, 448; investment in, 447-448; light industry balance, 293-298, 299, 301, 305-306, 320-321, 323-324, 328, 445, 446, 459, 543, 646, 658; overemphasis on, 301, 302, 306, 445, 646; output of, 971t; readjustment of, 117, 124, 293, 299-318, 328-329, 382, 447-448; USSR and, 304
"Heavy-type structure," economic, 305-306, 829
Hebei Plain, 29
Hebei Province, 817-821; administrative divisions of, 62; agriculture in, 817-818, 819; animal husbandry in, 818; construction in, 819-820; economic education in, 1055-1056, 1059, 1060, 1062, 1064; foreign trade in, 820; geography of, 817; human services in, 820; industry in, 818, 819; problems in, 821; readjustment in, 818; standard of living in, 820; transportation in, 818
He Gaosheng, 892-896
Heilongjiang Province, 822-825; administrative divisions of, 62-63; agriculture in, 822-823; commerce in, 824; construction in, 824; economic education in, 1059, 1061, 1062, 1065-1066; economic institute in, 1050; geography of, 822; human services in, 823, 824; industry in, 822, 823-824; problems in, 825; tourism in, 824; transportation in, 822-823
Henan Province, 826-829; administrative divisions of, 63; agriculture in, 826, 827; construction in, 828; economic education in, 1057, 1060, 1067; economic institute in, 1051; foreign trade in, 828; industry in, 826, 827; loan experiments in, 387; marketing in, 827-828; problems in, 828-829; production responsibility in, 827; readjustment in, 828-829; transportation in, 826-827

Highway Administrative Bureau, 590-591
Highways, 573-574, 590-591; agriculture and, 171-172; development of, 590; freight transport on, 977t; length of, 28, 574, 977t; maintenance of, 590; passenger transport on, 978t, 1022; quality of, 590
Historians, 8
History, Chinese: agricultural, 392-393; ancient, 3; Chinese Communist Party and, 4-5, 8-9; chronology of (chart), 9-10; cultural, 717-718; dynastic, 3-4; economic, 1949-1980, 379-381; imperialism and, 4, 5; industrial, 540-542; People's Republic and, 5, 80-94; pre-Liberation, 77-80, 105; publications on, 1103-1104; of publishing, 722-724; scientific, 6-9
Hoche nationality, 34
Honey, output of, 439
Hong Kong, 939-941; banking in, 940; customs rules and, 275-276, 1017; exports of, 940; foreign trade and, 939, 940; future of, 941; geography of, 939; imports to, 940; industry in, 939, 940; real estate in, 941; tourists from, 678-679
Hong Lun, 519-522
Horses, 438, 969t
Hospitals, 562, 703; beds in, 987t; costs in, 757; rural, 753; on state farms, 415
Hotels, 678; new construction of, 561-562, 678; quality of, 679; traditional style in, 678
Household quotas, for agricultural output, 368-376, 397-398, 813
Housing, 550, 560-561, 1021; allowances for, 703; increase in, 1980, 446, 551, 561, 648, 1011; investment in, 1980, 383; need for, 129, 191, 322; rural, 383, 394, 558-559, 1006; shortage of, 472, 706; workers', 119, 129, 535, 703, 714
Housing developments, 561
Hua Guofeng, 75, 1003, 1015; on economy, 1003; errors of, 92; industry and, 175, 192
Huaihe River, 368; floods on, 420, 425; harnessing of, 822; navigation on, 29; pollution control of, 770
Hua Juxian, 34-42
Huangdi clan, 3
Huanghai Sea. See Yellow Sea
Huanghe River: afforestation and, 773; floods on, 420
Huangshan Mountain, 678, 680
Huang Weijian, 691-697
Huang Weilang, 942-944
Hebei Province, 830-834; administrative divisions of, 63-64; agriculture in, 830-833; commerce in, 832-833; construction in, 831; economic education in, 1057-1058, 1060, 1061, 1062, 1067-1068; economic institutes in, 1051, 1053; education in, 833; environmental protection in, 832; family planning in, 832; future goals of, 833-834; geography of, 830; industry in, 830, 831-832; 1980 flood in, 831; nitrogen-fixing algae in, 686; products made in, 831; readjustments in, 831-834; self-management in, 832; standard of living in, 833
Hui nationality, 23, 35, 872; population of, 34
Hunan Province, 835-840; administrative divisions of, 64; agriculture in, 835-836, 837; animal husbandry in, 837; commerce in, 836, 838-839; construction in, 835-836, 838; diversification in, 837; economic education in, 1058, 1060; 1068; economic initiatives in, 838-839; geography of, 835; industry in, 836, 837-838; problems in, 839; readjustment in, 837-840; science in, 836-837; standard of living in, 837, 839; transportation in, 836
Hungary, industrial reform and, 348
Hunting, in forest zones, 149
"Hu Yang" trees, 415
Hu Yaobang: on the arts, 721; on China's future course, 108-114; on Chinese history, 105-108; election as Chairman, Central Committee, 75, 1010; on Mao, 106-107; on science, 684; speech in celebration of 60th anniversary of CPC (1981); in Tibet, 1014; on trade unions, 709
Hydraulic Engineering Corporation, 426
Hydraulic mining, coal, 499
Hydroelectric power, 26, 27, 31, 32, 33, 186, 421, 423, 425, 810, 1008; conservation in, 505; emphasis on, 507; potential of, 507, 882, 1014; small-scale, 1020; subsidies for, 212; technology and, 503; unit capacity of, 503
Hydrology, 14, 17

I

Imperialism, 4, 8, 43-44, 49
Import and Export Commission, on export licence system, 269-270
Import/export limits, 271t, 275t
Imports: change in composition of, 622, 982t; control of, 623, 635-642; duties on, 273-274; FTCs for, 1025-1045; to Hong Kong, 940; loans in foreign currency for, 249-251; prohibited, 276, 637; to Special Economic Zones, 264; of steel, 548; of technology, 625-626; value of, 982t; of whole plants, 1036
Improvement, economic, definition of, 381
Income: in Anhui Province, 374-375; categories of, taxable, 234, 236-237; from commune-run enterprises, 483, 484; on communes, 119, 121-122, 129, 165, 374-475, 394-395; control of, 293-298; definition of, for taxation, 230; distribution of, 117, 129; exempt from taxation, 234, 235-237, 654; increase in, 134, 293, 295, 322, 713; of joint ventures, 228, 653; national, 117, 379, 965t; per capita, 119, 129, 293, 319, 322, 647; projected, 1981, 121-122; rural, per capita, 119, 161, 293, 383, 394-395, 647, 1017; from tourism, 681; in undeveloped areas, 394-395
Income taxes, 157, 334, 652, 654; computation of, 230-231, 234, 235; individual, 126, 135, 234-235, 236-238, 654; on joint ventures, 126, 135, 228-229, 230-233, 257, 630, 653; rates of, 234, 235; readjustment and, 338; reduction of, 1019; in Special Economic Zones, 264; on state-owned enterprises, 652-653
Income Tax Law (1980), 234-235, 630, 654, 656, 1018; detailed rules of, 236-238, 1022
Income Tax Law (on joint ventures), 228-229, 630, 653, 656, 1018; detailed rules of, 230-233, 1022
Individual economic units, taxes on, 239
Individual labour, 50, 93, 122, 337; agricultural, 392, 398-399; encouragement of, rural, 117-118, 162-163, 165, 398-399; expansion of, 329, 610; in fishing, 432; in handicrafts, 476; "left" policy on, 385, 386, 398, 949; in medicine, 755
Industrial associations, 334; under capitalism, 316; economic management through, 315-316, 353; under socialism, 316; tasks of, 315-316
Industrial and commercial tax, 239, 242, 245, 652; exemptions for, 655
Industrial and transport enterprises, renovation of, 216
Industrial areas: base, 26, 175; development of, 26; regional, 29-33
Industrial complexes, 175, 334
Industrial design, 205, 347; of airports, 599; coal industry and, 501; for construction, 552; examination of, 347; machine-building industry and, 518; quality control and, 205; of ships, 519
Industrial Economics Research Institute, 306

Industrial management: consolidation and, 344, 455-456; democratic, 344, 456; history of, 340-342; reform of, 311-318, 448-451; restructuring of, 350-356; Sichuan experiment in, 357-367

Industrial output: by major sector, 972t; by major sector, indexed, 972t; of Taiwan, 935t

Industrial planning, 182; associations and, 316; capital construction and, 189; central vs. market, 346; five norms in, 180-181; for light industry loans, 246; state role in, 353-355; for transformation and renovation, 214-215; unified, 183-185, 215

Industrial research institutes, 686

Industry: administration of, 188, 192; agriculture and, 163, 171, 184-185, 445, 447, 646; balance in, 303, 382, 445, 447, 460, 543, 646, 952-953; cadres in, 177, 179, 189-190, 192, 341, 342, 451; capital construction and, 188-189, 448; 453-454, 549-553; chemical, 508-515; coal, 494-502; on communes, 152-160, 185, 481-482; consolidation in, 340-345, 449-450, 451-452; construction, 211-213; current problems in, 444-446; development of, 26, 80, 175-193; direct sales of, 610, 616; electronics, 532-539; energy and, 185-186, 445, 446, 453, 545; environmental protection and, 187, 285-288; experiments in, 336, 343, 448-449, 454; Gang of Four and, 175, 179; guiding principles of, 175, 192; light, 457-466; in Macao, 943; machine-building, 516-518; management of, 178-179, 182, 188; Mao on, 8-9, 175, 193n; metallurgical, 540-548; among national minorities, 41; new, 444; organization of, 181-182; output value of, 379, 446, 972t, 989-990t; petroleum, 486-493; planning for, 180-181, 182, 183-184, 192, 346; politics and, 180, 190, 213, 278, 341-342, 344; pre-Liberation, 26, 333; present aims for, 175; priorities in, 412, problems in, 444-446, 453; profits and, 202-204; production of, 444; product output of, 973t, 974t, 975t, 989-990t; publications in, 1098-1099; quality control and, 187-188, 205-210; readjustments in, 118, 181-182, 186, 214-217, 293, 301, 385-386, 447-448, 452-456; reform of, 338-339, 346-349, 448-451; by region, 29-33; renovation of, 186; research on, 1046; shipbuilding, 519-522; shortcomings in, 989; Sichuan experiments in, 357-367; socialization of, 5; standards for, 691-697; state of, 1980, 444-456, 989, 990t; on state farms, 411-414; in Taiwan, 935-936; tasks for, 180, 1011; technology and, 189-190, 445-446, 465-466; textile, 467-474; urban, and commune-run enterprises, 154; USSR model and, 298, 307, 340-341, 350-351; wages in, 190-191. See also Enterprises and individual industries

Industry and Commerce, Administration of, 243

Infant nutrition, 1020

Inflation, 130-131, 141, 295, 452, 553, 611, 671-672; China and, 296; in Hong Kong, 941; prevention of, 326-327, 611; reasons for, 325-326, 391; in Taiwan, 933-934

Inner Mongolia Autonomous Region, 30, 34, 841-850, 1016; administrative divisions of, 70, 841; agriculture in, 24, 841, 842-843, 846, 849; animal husbandry in, 841, 843, 846, 1016; coal in, 1010; commerce in, 844-845, 847-848; construction and investment in, 847; economic administration in, 1056, 1059, 1064-1065; economic institute of, 1049; education in, 845, 848; exchange transactions in, 845; finances of, 844, 847-848; geography of, 841-842; grain deficiency in, 849; health care in, 846; history of, 842; industry in, 843-844, 846-847, 849; potential of, 849-850; problems in, 848-850; science and, 845; special produce of, 841, 843; standard of living in, 845-846, 848; transportation in, 844

Inner Mongolia Plateau, 11, 29

Inquiry into Economic Problems (periodical), 1079

Inspection: of commodities, 1016, 1018, 1022; customs, 271-276, 639-640; financial, 226-227, 228-229, 232, 237; food, 287, 1021; of joint ventures, 262; for price control, 675; for purchasing power control, 283; quality, 198, 208, 461; ship, 522

Institute of Nationalities (Yan'an), 38

Instruments, technological, import of, 1036

Insulin, 683

Insurance: business, 1008; domestic, 660, 1006; international, 660; for joint ventures, 257; labour, 259, 702-703, 714; in Special Economic Zones, 263

Integration economic, 313-318, 449-450, 1017; under capitalism, 318; of communes, 403; electronics industry and, 535, 538; machine-building industry and, 518; need for, 334, 1016; in Sichuan experiment, 360-361, 403, 404; under socialism, 314-315; shipbuilding industry and, 522; among state farms, 413-414

Intellectuals, 5, 8; future role of, 102; state policy on, 683; Zhou Enlai on, 84

Interest: capital regulation and, 355; on construction loans, 241-242; on deposits and loans, 663t; increase in, 659-660, 1002, 1011; on industrial transformation loans, 216; on light industry loans, 245; on loans in foreign currency, 250; on savings 662t; tax on, 234, 236, 237

International banking, 667-670; delegations from, 669; exchange control and, 669-670; foreign capital and, 668, 669; joint ventures and, 257, 261, 668, 669-670; principles of, 667-668; world financial community and, 669

International Monetary Fund, 628, 669, 1011, 1013, 1019; appointments to, 1014-1015

International relations: current status of, 81; economic relations and, 1011; future course of, 103; PRC position on, 49; science and, 689; with Third World, 103, 113

Internatonal standards, 695

International transportation: air, 598, 600; water, 593-594

Inventions, 119; awards for, 1014; number of, 1980, 383

Investigations: of enterprises, 1008; by tax authorities, 228-229, 234, 237

Investments, foreign. See Foreign investments

Investments, local: in capital construction, 552; in chemical industry, 509t

Investments, state: in agriculture, 165, 171, 406; in building materials industry, 554; in capital construction, 117, 126, 212, 382, 448, 551; in chemical industry, 509t; in handicrafts, 477; increasing returns on, 136; in industry, 382-383, 444, 465; readjustment of, 647-648; in shipbuilding, 521; in textiles and light industry, 447, 464, 648; in water conservancy, 420-421

Iron: distribution of, 27-28, 29, 32; pig, 30; reserves of, 27, 1010; scrap, 619

Iron, electric, 337

Iron smelting, ancient, 6, 540

Iron and steel industry, 541; differential output of, 1980, 382; distribution of, 27-28, 29, 541; economic results in, 1980, 546;

energy conservation in, 545; equipment in, 542; imbalance in, 453, 542, 543; in North China, 29; in Northeast China, 30; output of, 27, 117, 118, 543, 1001; overemphasis on, 299, 300, 301, 320, 445, 453; projected output of, 1981, 121; readjustment in, 544; in Southwest China, 32; upgrading of, 124-125, 544

Irrigation, 32, 421, 781, 836; ancient, 6; equipment for, 524; increase in, 80, 379-380, 392-393; need for, 24, 166, 170, 423

Islam, 35

Itineraires, tourist, 678-679; one-day, 678-679; diversity of, 678; for domestic tourists, 680-681

J

Jade articles, ancient, 6

Japan: ancient trade with, 7; China Friendship, 596-597; China war, 5, 77, 78, 105, 300; cooperation with, 1008, 1015; economic specialization in, 313; loan from, 628; Taiwan and, 936; tourists from, 677, 678

Jiaguwen, 726

Jiangnan shipyard, 519, 521

Jiang Qing, 86, 87, 88, 89, 90, 108; downfall of, 108; Mao on, 89

Jiangsu Province, 851-856; administrative divisions of, 64-65; agriculture in, 851, 852, 855, 1003; commerce in, 853-854; construction in, 851-852, 853, 856; economic education in, 1057, 1059, 1061, 1062, 1066; family planning in, 856; finances of, 853-854; geography of, 851; handicrafts in, 855-856; industry in, 851, 853, 855-856; international technical cooperation of, 1045; problems in, 855-856; standard of living in, 852, 854-855; transportation in, 851, 853; water conservancy in, 410

Jiangxi Province, 857-860; administrative divisions of, 65; agriculture in, 857, 858; economic education in, 1057, 1059, 1067; economic experimentation in, 859; economic institute in, 1051; future goals of, 860; geography of, 857; industry in, 857-859; marketing in, 859; readjustment in, 858-869; standard of living in, 858-860

Jiang Yiwei, 350-356

Ji Hong, 732-742

Ji Hua, 743-751

Jilin Province, 861-865; administrative divisions of, 65; agriculture in, 861-862, 864-865; commerce in, 863; construction in, 863, 865; economic education in, 1056, 1059, 1061, 1062, 1065; economic institute in, 1050; foreign trade in, 863; geography of, 861; human services in, 863-864, 865; industry in, 30, 861, 862-863; loan experiments in, 387, 863; readjustments in, 864-865; standard of living in, 864; transportation in, 863

Jin Shui, 432-437

Jin Tongzhen, 565-572

Jin Yanshi, 811-816

Ji Wei, 927-932

Jizhong oil field, 487

Joint enterprises, 314, 337, 385; communes and, 154, 403; electronics industry and, 536; in handicrafts, 476

Joint ventures, 118, 628-629; in elevator construction, 1011; extent of, 1980, 628; foreign exchange and, 254-255; income tax on, 228-229, 230-233, 653; laws on, 256-258, 628, 629, 669, 1017; registration of, 228, 256, 261-262; tapping potential and, 216; taxes on, 126, 135; tax exemptions for, 228; wages in, 259; workers in, 256-257, 259-260

Joint venture leasing companies, 1021

Journal of Hubei College of Finance and Economics (periodical), 1084

Journal of Shaanxi College of Finance and Economics (periodical), 1083-1084

Journalism, 728-731; economics reporting in, 731; education for, 729-730; forums in, 730; history of, 128; honesty in, 731; news competition in, 730; publications on, 730; reform in, 730-731; state of, 1980, 728-729

Judicial system, 55, 94, 102; contracts and, 281; economic legislation and, 126, 137, 335, 354, 388; financial supervision and, 227; foreign investments and, 730; water conservancy and, 425

"Ju Gao," 6

Junggar Basin, 12; oil exploration in, 324

Jute, 393, 466

K

Kang Sheng, 86, 87, 88

Kang Zhixin, 549-553

Kaoliang, production of, 24

Kazak nationality, 23, 35; population of, 34

Kenfeng No. 5 rice, 415

Keynesian economics, 296

Khrushchev, Nikita, 304, 627

Kindergartens, 748

Korea, 866

Korean nationality, 23, 35; population of, 34

Korean War, 82; Hong Kong and, 939

Kunming, 32

Kuomintang: and CPC, 77, 78; handicrafts and, 473; and Sun Yat-sen, 4, 77; and war with Japan, 78; and War of Liberation, 78-79

L

Labour, 698-706; agricultural mechanization and, 525-526; benefits for, 702-703; on commune-run enterprises, 137-158; control of, 255-256; in handicrafts, 478; indivdual, 117-118, 337, 386, 610, 949; industrial transformation and, 216-217; insurance for, 702-703; in joint ventures, 256-257, 259-260, 1017; manual, 333, 478; material incentives for, 953-954; piece-rate payment for, 277-278; problems of, 705-706; productivity of, 136, 190-191, 389, 444, 710-711, 976t; protection of, 703-705, 713-715, 1015; quotas of, 188; in Sichuan experiment, 338; in Special Economic Zones, 264, 265; state control of, 698-699; statistics on, 963t, 964t; surplus of, rural, 481, 484, 531; training of, 698, 699-700, 705-706; wages of, 448, 647, 700-702

Labour companies, 355-356

Labour, State Bureau of, on energy-conservation bonuses, 200, 301

Laizhou Bay, 12-13

Lakes, 17, 24, 419; in national minority areas, 35

Lambs, 439

Land: cultivated, 161, 164, 166, 404-405, 965t; environmental protection of, 286; irrigated, 166; personal plots of, 165, 398-399; power-cultivated, 523, 525; in Special Economic Zones, 264; on state farms, 408; use, policies for, 166

Land reclamation, 407-418; aquatic resources and, 435; forests and, 148-149; history of, 407-408

Language: Mongolian, 845, 848; of national minorities, 35, 55, 748; reference works on, 726

Lantian Man, 3

Lanzhou, environmental protection in, 768

Lanzhou oil refinery, 488

Law of value, 674, 960-952; publications on, 1086-1089

Leaders: of combined enterprises, 219; of commune-run enterprises, 160; of enterprises, 177-178, 342, 343, 362-363, 455-456; of financial supervisory organizations, 226; of industrial transformation, 217; party, 111, 173; purchasing power control and, 283-284

Learn from Daqing Campaign, 176-177, 184, 341, 342

Learn from Dazhai Campaign, 169
Leases, tax on income from, 236
Leather, 440; emphasis on, 443
"Left" errors, 86-92, 101, 108, 299-300, 301, 312, 319, 321-322, 380, 381, 386; agriculture and, 162, 293, 373, 396-397, 398, 404, 526; banking and, 657; coal industry and, 495; communes and, 481; correction of, 294-295, 299-300; customs and, 635; education and, 745-746, 750-751; examination of, 947; in finance, 643, 645-646; fisheries and, 434-435; handicrafts industry and, 479; industry and, 333, 341, 342, 446; long-term influence of, 452; pharmaceutical industry and, 566; publishing and, 723-724
Legislation, economic, 335, 354, 388; on foreign trade, 630; on taxation, 228-238, 630, 653, 654, 656
Lenin, Nikolai: collected works of, 722-733; on economics, 309; on means of production, 304; on monopolies, 314; on technical progress, 313
Letters of credit, customs declaration of, 255
Lianjiang River, navigation on, 594
Liaodong Bay, 12
Liaohe oil field, 487
Liao Jili, 332-339
Liaoning Province, 866-867; administrative divisions of, 65-66; agriculture in, 866, 867, 869; construction in, 867, 870; economic education in, 1056, 1059, 1061; economic institutes of, 1049, 1053; environmental quality reports of, 778; foreign trade corporations in, 388; geography of, 866; industry in, 30, 462, 866, 867; national minorities in, 866; problems in, 869-870; readjustments in, 867-871; service trades in, 868; standard of living in, 868-869
Liaoyang, 30
Libraries, 719; scientific publications and, 688; trade unions and, 715
Licences: export, 269-270; foreign, in shipbuilding, 522; for joint ventures, 261-262
Life expectancy, 380; increase in, 81
Light industry, 456-465, 1010; in Central-South China, 31; collective ownership and, 451; commune-run enterprises and, 482; consumer goods and, 459; decision-making in, 462; development of, 175-193; director sales and, 463-464; in East China, 30-31; education for, 464-465; engineering corporation for, 1045; exports and, 458, 459; financing of, 130, 464, 648; foreign aid and, 632; FTC for, 1030-1031; future of, 465; growth of, 1980, 293, 457, 460; heavy industry balance, 293-298, 299, 301, 305-306, 320-321, 323-324, 328, 382, 445, 446, 447, 459, 543, 646, 658; history of, 456; investments in, 383, 448, 464; loans to, 245-247, 464, 658, 1007; machinery for, 517; market regulation of, 461, 462-464; output of, 971t; pollution control in, 772; priority given to, 116-117, 185-186, 214, 305, 323-324, 382, 447, 454, 459-460, 648; product lines in, 457-458, 460-461; projected output of, 1981, 121; quality and, 460-461; readjustment and, 459-465; research for, 458, 464; state revenues from, 458-459; total output of, 1980, 382, 446; training for, 458; workers in, 1980, 457
Light Industry, Bureau of, 245-146
Light Industry Machinery Corporation (Shanghai), economic experimentation and, 384
Light Industry, First Ministry of, 172, 246, 460, 1004, 1005; quality awards of, 461, 477; research awards of, 464
Light Industry, Second Ministry of, 474
"Light-type structure," economic, 305-306, 829
Li Kaixin, 613-620
Li nationality, 23, 35; population of, 34
Lin Biao, 86, 87, 88, 89, 90, 108; attempted coup of, 88; and national minorities, 37, 38, 39. See also Gang of Four.
Linen, production of, 466
Lin Ling, 357-367
Li Renjun, 116, 1012
Lisu nationality, 35; population of, 34
Literacy, 749, 750
Literature, 717-727; achievements in, 1980, 719; foreign, 726; journalism and, 731; publication of 722-727
Liu Shaoqi, 85; "cultural revolution" and, 87, 88, 90; on economy, 84, 614; rehabilitation of, 93
Liu Zhicheng, 655-656
Liuzhou, economic experimentation in, 384, 448, 652, 656
Livelihood. See Standard of Living
Livestock, 25; breeding of, 439-440; forests and, 149; as "key-link" policy, 1016; for personal use, 165, 399-400; state purchase of, 1980, 608; types of, 168. See also Animal husbandry and individual animals.
Li Wenyan, 22-33
Loans, 216, 355, 997; agricultural, 666, 1019; for capital construction, 240-242, 337, 387, 464, 551, 658; to collective enterprises, 243-244; in foreign currency, 249-251; for individual agriculture, 399; interst rates on, 663t; to light and textile industries, 345-247, 464, 470; penalty rates on, 659; planning for, 240, 246; policy on, 243-247, 388, 658-659, 661-662; priorities for, 661-662; review of, 246-247, 364; state appropriations vs., 135, 212, 311, 337, 338, 355, 387, 551, 651, 1004, 1021; terms of, 241-242, 245-246, 250
Loans, foreign, 627-628; payments on, 1980, 133
Local government, 53-54, 94; agriculture and, 165, 173-174, 368-376, 402; divisions of, 53-54, 59-69; environmental protection and, 287-288, 778; finanial powers of, 129-130, 135, 223-225, 387, 649-1009; 648; foreign trade and, 118, 126, 388, 621; funds of, 297, 649, 1009; industry and, 183, 335; material supply and, 211; railroad construction by, 581; standardization and, 199;
Local organizations, CPC, 47; responsibilities of, 47-48
Local people's congresses, 53-54; in autonomous regions, 54-55
Local revolutionary committees, 53-54; in autonomous regions, 54-55
Locomotives, 574, 586; testing of, 587
Loess Plateau, 11, 32
Long Jiyan, 523-531
Long March, 5, 78; new, in industry, 214-217; new, in science, 688
Longwall mining, 494-495
Loopholes, 327
Losses, 1017; commercial, 1980, 611; from curtailment of construction, 327; in joint ventures, 228, 257; responsibility for, 311, 351-352, 361-362; from state farms, 416
Luoyang No. 1 Tractor Plant, 523
Lushan, Mount, 680
Lu Xun, collected works of, 723

M

Macao, 942-944; customs rules and, 275-276, 1017; economy of, 942-943; foreign trade and, 943; future of, 943-944; geography of, 942; history of, 942; industry in, 943; real estate in, 943; tourism in, 942-943
Machine-building industry, 30, 516-518; in Central-South China, 31; development of, 28; exports of, 516; imbalance in, 516-517; integration in, 518; light industry and, 517; new products in, 518; in North China, 29; output of,

118, 516, 517; overcapacity of, 452; precision engineering in, 516; products of, 516; projected output of, 1981, 121; quality gains in, 518; readjustment in, 117, 118, 124-125, 216, 297, 328-329, 1009; research in, 518; in Southwest China, 32; standardization in, 181, 182, 185; tapping potential in, 1009; theoretical issues in, 303
Machine-Building Industry, First Ministry of, 343, 385, 516-518; light-heavy industry balance and, 382; new products and, 389, 518; on technology, 445-446
Machine-Building Industry, Fourth Ministry of, 532-539; quality control and, 534-535
Machine-Building Industry, Sixth Ministry of, 519-522
Machinery: agricultural, 523-531, 970t; cargo handling, 596; for coal industry, 499; duty-exempt, 264; FTCs for, 1035-1036, 1037-1038; Marx on, 303; metallurgical, 542; precision, FTC for, 1040; railroad, 586; retail sales of, 310; in Special Economic Zones, 264; technical cooperation, corporation for, 1045; for textile industry, 467; theory and, 303-304
Machinery repair, agricultural, 524
Ma Ding, 565-572
Magazines: scientific, 688; for tourists, 680. *See also* Periodicals
Ma Hong, 299-319
Mail. *See* Postal services
Maintenance, quality control and, 207
Maize, production of, 24
"Make the past serve the present" principle, 717
"Making best use" policy, 385
Malaria, 752, 812; control of, 654
Management: of commune-run enterprises, 158-183; contracts and, 279-281; economic, reform of, 307-318, 332-339, 450-452; of factories, 178-179; foreign loans and, 133; industrial, 178-179, 181-183; new initiatives in, 125-126, 214, 611, 832; powers of, in construction, 211-213; publications on, 1090-1095; restructuring of, 118, 125, 298, 350-356; Sichuan experiments in, 357, 367
Manchu nationality, 23, 35, 866; population of, 34
Manual labour, 334; in handicrafts, 478; in postal service, 607
Manuals, on products use, 207
Manure, 167; green, 167
Mao Junyi, 851-856
Mao Tai, 814
Mao Zedong, 8, 43-44, 49, 77, 86; agriculture and, 162; on China's future, 8-9; on CPC, 97-98; "cultural revolution" and, 86-94, 107; death of, 89; errors of, 107; on family planning, 761; Great Leap Forward and, 85-86; on handicrafts, 473; on industry, 8-9, 187, 190, 192, 193n, 312, 341; military career of, 77, 78; on new-democratic revolution, 95; personality cult of, 88, 91; primacy of, 79, 90, 94, 106, 107; on safety, 703; on social development, 84, 95-96; tragedy of, 89-90
Mao Zedong Thought, 43, 49, 50, 51, 79-80, 101, 164, 169, 174; "cultural revolution" and, 87, 92; Daqing and, 176-177; importance of, 100, 106-107; Marxism-Leninism and, 94-100, 101, 106-107, 110-111. *See also* Mao Zedong, works of
Mao Zedong, works of: on class struggle, 95; on culture, 97; on military strategy, 96-97, 300; on the party, 97-98; on policy and tactics, 97; publication of, 722-733; on socialist revolution, 96
Market economy, 334, 338-339, 343; agricultural machinery and, 529; central control vs., 308-318, 335, 355, 358, 360, 449; commune-run enterprises and, 156; competition and, 220-222, 360; consumer goods and, 126, 336; materials management and, 613-620; metallurgical industry and, 543-544; neglect of, 332, 333, 609; readjustments in, 118-119, 126; regulation of, 126, 134-135, 336; regulatory role of, 359-360, 385, 449, 454-455, 461, 462-464, 480, 547, 619, 1012; stabilization of, 296, 297; state planning vs., 346, 960-962, 955; theory on, 950-952, 955
Marketing, 385, 798; of aquatic resources, 433, 436-437; commercial, 609-610; of electronic consumer goods, 536, 538; joint ventures and, 257; as key link, 452; of pharmaceuticals, 656, 568; of producer goods, 616; reform of, 358, 452, 1020; rural, 117, 162, 165, 323, 381, 385, 394; Special Economic Zones and, 263; of textiles, 471
Market research, 343, 452, 464; electronics industry and, 338; metallurgical industry and, 544-545; textiles and, 471
Market towns, 484
Marriage: freedom of, 56; industry and, 191; medical restrictions on, 764
Marsh land, 19; reclamation of, 685; vegetation on, 19
Marx, Karl: on capital, 303, 305, 308-309; collected works of, 722-733; on machinery, 303; on production, 302; on socialism, 308
Marxism-Leninism, 4, 77, 79, 105, 164, 174; CCP constitution and, 43-44, 47, 50; on economy, 303-310, 314, 350; "cultural revolution" and, 86-87, 90-91; education in, 102; Mao on, 8; Mao Zedong Thought and, 94-100, 106-107, 110-111; and national minorities, 36-39; on production/consumption, 302-306; on socialist nationalization, 312; PRC Constitution and, 49, 50, 51
Masses, culture for, 719, 733; purchasing power control and, 382, 297
Materials management, 613-620; allocations under, 615; balance in, 615-616, 619; commune-run enterprises and, 158; competition and, 220, 616-617; construction and, 564; control over, 183, 211, 354-355, 564, 613-614; "cultural revolution" and, 614; distribution and, 216, 218, 613-620; energy conservation and, 618-619; history of, 613-614; joint ventures and, 257; for light industry, 454; marketing and, 616, 1012; priorities in, 615; for projects to be financed, 246; quality control and, 207; quotas for, 188; readjustment and, 619-620; standardization and, 696; state control of, 613-620; stockpiles and, 617-618, supply channels and, 613-614

Materials Management (periodical), 1080
Mathematics, ancient, 6, 7, 8
Maternity benefits, 702, 766
Matrilineal communes, 3
May 4th Movement, 4, 105
May 16 Circular, 87
Meadow vegetation, 19
Means of production: agricultural, 372, 405; as commodity, 346; distribution of, 613-620; free circulation of, 126, 334; growth of, 304-305; ownership of, 314-315, 351, 948-950
Meat, 412; output of, 116, 968t; state farm output of, 1980, 409
Mechanization: of agriculture, 167-174, 184-185, 380, 392; of coal industry, 494, 498-499; of light industry, 458; overemphasis on, 295
Medical benefits, 702
Medical instruments, 567, 568, 569, 757
Medical schools, 415, 752-753, 758-759; improvement of, 756
Medical treatment, 380; commune-run enterprises and, 158; for firefighters, 148; foreign aid and, 633; for joint-venture workers,

259; of women workers, 713
Medicine, 752-759; ancient, 6, 7, 8; integration of, 755; preventive, 752, 754, 758; research in, 755-756
Medicine, traditional, 753, 755; drugs for, 656, 570-571; export limit on, 275; ingredients for, 34; integration of, 754-755
Membership, CPC 44-46; application for, 45; expulsion from, 45-46; qualifications for, 44; responsibilities of, 44-45
Memory chips, 533
Merchant marine, 593-594
Metallurgical industry, 540-548; in Central-South China, 31; consumer goods and, 454, 543, 544; development of, 27, 541-542; economic results in, 545-546; energy conservation and, 545; equipment in, 542; experimental management in, 546-547; exports from, 547; FTC for, 1039; history of, 540-542; imbalance in, 543-544; independent sales of, 547; iron and steel output, 1980, 543t; loss reversal in, 546; market economy and, 543-544, 547; market research for, 544-545; outlook for, 547-548; pollution control in, 771; product line in, 541, 543, 544; quality and, 544; readjustment and, 542-548, 1008; research on, 1008; in Southwest China, 32; weaknesses in, 547-548; workers in, 542
Metallurgical Industry, Ministry of, 540-548; market research of, 544-545; research institutes under, 546
Meteorology, 992, 1007
Metrology, 1015; quality control and, 206-207
Methane gas, 119, 122, 170, 186, 779; promotion of, 1003
Miao nationality, 23, 35; population of, 34
Midwives, 753
Military, 51-52; agrarian Revolutionary War and, 77, 78; duty to serve in, 56; industry and, 186; Japan and, 78; Long March of, 78; Mao on, 95, 96-97; modernization of, 103; Northern Expedition of, 77; purchasing power and 284; spending on, 130, 133; War of Liberation and, 78-79
Military strategists, 8
Milk: goat, 440, 1004; state farm output of, 1980, 409
Millet, production of, 24
Mineral resources, 23, 540; development of, 125, 185; environmental protection and, 286; FTC for, 1033-1035; in national minority areas, 35; non-metallic, 555, 557, 1029; reporting of, 1014; variety of, 1005. *See also individual materials*

Mine shafts, 495
Ming Dynasty, science and technology in, 8
Mining: commune-run enterprises and, 156, 158, 159; development of, 185; forestry and, 147-148; longwall, 494; readjustment in, 382
Ministers of State Council (1981), 57-58
Ministries, shortcomings in management by, 315, 333, 334
Ministry standards, 197
Minority nationalities. *See* National minorities
Model workers, 711, 1005, 1010, 1013
Modernization, 108; of agriculture, 161-174, 970t; future course of, 101-102; of handicrafts, 470-479; of national defence, 103
Monetary statistics, 1980, 997
Money. *See* Currency
Mongolian nationality, 23, 841-850; population of, 34
Monopolies, 220, 314-315, 317; state purchase, 529
Monsoons, 13-14, 22, 419-420; geographic zone of, 20
Mortality rate, 380, 752
Mountaineering, 679
Mountainous areas, 12; arrangement of, 12; and coal, 29; economic significance of, 22
Moxibustion, ancient, 7
Mules, 969t
Municipalities: administrative division of, 59; economic integration in, 449-450; government of, 53, 54
Music, 720
Musical instruments, ancient, 6
Mutton, 410; output of, 394, 968t

N

Nanjing Radio Company, 535, 1016
Nanning, construction experiments in, 461-462
Nanyang oil field, 1005
Naphtha, 491
National Congresses, CPC: 8th (1956), 83-84; 9th (1969), 88; 10th (1973), 88-89; 11th (1977), 92
National defence, expenditures on, 130, 133, 391
National economic plans, 1012; building and, 564; readjustment and, 335
National Economic Plan, 1979: fulfillment of, 1013; shortcomings in, 139; success of, 139
National Economic Plan, 1980, 116; fulfillment of, 989-996; readjustments in, 116-120; resolution on, 139; results of, 120; revisions of, 132
National Economic Plan, 1981, 120-127; for agriculture, 121; main targets of, 121; new initiatives in, 123-127; readjustment and, 120-121, 123-127; resolution on, 139
National Exhibition of Light Industrial Products (Beijing, 1979), 463
National Investigation of Natural Resources and Regionalization of Agriculture, 773
Nationalities Affairs Commisssion, 38
National minorities, 3, 23, 34-42; agricultural development and, 40; air transportation and, 598; books for, 725; cadres of 38; CPC policies towards, 36-42; constitutional guarantees for, 50; culture of, 35-36, 717-718, 720; distribution of, 34-35; economic development and, 39-42; education for, 743, 748, 845, 880, 915, 925; 926; governments of, 37-38, 54-55; industry among, 26, 41; national unity and, 39; population of, 34; regional autonomy of, 37-38
National People's Congress (NPC), 47, 50, 55; composition and powers of, 52-53; on national minorities, 36-37; Standing Committee of, 52-53
National Science Congress (1978), 683
Native products, FTC for, 1026-1029
Natural disasters, 293, 368, 374, 393, 420, 438, 792; agricultural machinery and, 525; relief funds for, 224; water conservancy and, 422-423
Natural resources, 164; aquatic, 143-145; distribution of, 959t; forest, 146-150; investigation of, 171, 1002
Natural Science Awards, 289
Nature reserves, 773-774
Navigation: marine, 28; river, 29
Nets, fishing, 144, 433
"On New Democracy," 97
New-democratic revolution, 95
New products, 198, 461, 518, 527; for building, 559; development cost of, 202; emphasis on, 1012; piece prices of, 278; production of, 1980, 389; quality control of, 206; standards for, 198, 697
News agencies, 729
Newspapers, 728-731; circulation of, 976t; common characteristics of, 731; economics news in, 731; reform in, 730-731
Ningpo Water Meter Works, 518
Ningxia Hui Autonomous Region, 32-33, 872-876, 1016; administrative divisions of, 70; agriculture in, 872-873; construction in, 874; economic education in, 1063, 1071; education in, 873; geography of, 872;

history of, 872; industry in, 873, 874; marketing in, 874; national minorities in, 872; readjustment in, 875-876; science in, 874-875; standard of living in, 875; transportation in, 873
Ninth National Congress, CPC (1969), 88; "cultural revolution" and, 88
Niu Wenyuan, 11-21
Noise pollution, 287, 766; research on, 776
Non-metallic minerals, 555, 557, 1020
North China economic region, 29-30; FTC for, 1040
North China Plain, 12
Northeast China economic region, 30
Northeast Plain, 12
Northern Expedition, 77, 105
Northern Shipping Area, 592
Northwest Arid Zone, 20; characteristics of, 20-21
Northwest China economic region, 32-33
Novels, published in 1980, 719, 725
Nuclear power stations, 507, 1021
Nuclear weapons, 119, 380
Nurseries, tree, 429
Nursery schools, 748, 756

O

Occupational safety, 122, 344, 703-705, 713, 1019; in coal mines, 324, 496-498; commune-run enterprises and, 156, 158; in electric power industry, 505; gains in, 705, 713; in industry, 191, 213; in joint enterprises, 260; laws on, 703, 704, 1012; in Special Economic Zones, 264; trade unions and, 712-713; training in, 704
Ocean transport, 593-594
Oil, 23; conservation of, 124, 186, 214, 324, 618-610, 1020; crude, 27, 321, 324, 486, 487, 770; exploration for, 324, 490-491, 492-493, 628-629; export of, 454; output of, 321, 490t, 1011; production of, 27, 29, 487-488, 490t; projected output, 1981, 121; quality of, 487-488; shipping of, 595. *See also* Petroleum industry
Oil-bearing crops, 25, 31, 323; output of, 116, 393
Oil crisis, and Taiwan, 933
Oilfields, 486-488, 1009
Oil industry, engineering construction corporation for, 1044
Oil pipelines, 574; construction of, 489; energy conservation and, 492; length of, 29, 977t; volume of, 977t
Oil refineries, 27, 488-489; technology for, 489

"One couple, one child" policy, 761-762, 763
"One hundred flowers" policy, 51, 83, 717, 732
Opencast mines, coal, 502
Opera: modern, 720; traditional, 717, 720
Opium War, 4, 105, 540
Oranges, joint enterprises production of, 404
Output, agricultural, accountability for, 368-376, 396-398
Overdrafts, People's Bank of China, 128, 140, 325, 326, 391
Overseas Chinese, 56; customs and, 1017; foreign exchange and, 253-254; investments of, 561-562, 1011; remittances from, 119, 136; tourism of, 677, 681
Overtime work, 358
Ownership 220; agricultural, on Taiwan, 937; in building materials industry, 554; collective, 351, 379, 386, 392, 450-451, 474, 475, 482-483, 1007; commercial, 609-610; of commune-run enterprises, 154, 483-484; of forests, 430; in handicrafts industry, 475-476, 479; individual, 476; joint, 477; profit-loss responsibility and, 365-366; rights of, on communes, 164, 165, 371; state, 312, 346, 351, 379, 386, 475, 613; of state farms, 417; theory on, 948-950
Ownership of means production: in handicrafts, 474; state, 50, 102; transformation of, 82-83

P

Packaging materials, FTC for, 1037
Packaging standards, 196, 207
Painting, 720
Paper, 473, projected output of, 1981, 121
Paraffin, 491, 492
Parks, 149, 429
Passenger traffic: average haulage of, 576t; capacity for, 580; changes in mode of, 576t; highway, 591, 978t, 1022; railroad, 583, 978t; services by airlines, 600, 602; turnover of, 575t; volume of, 574t; water, 978t
Pastures. *See* Grasslands
Pasture Law, 168
Patrilineal communes, 3
Patrol vessels, for aquatic resources conservation, 145
Peanuts, production of, 25, 29, 31, 888, 889
Pearls, integrated production of, 403
Peasant markets. *See* Rural fairs
Peasants: banking and, 394, 659-660, 665-666, 985t; books for, 725; class struggle and, 162-163; culture for, 719, 733; enthusiasm of, 164, 323, 325; health care for, 753-754, 758; housing for, 383,

394, 1006; income of, 293, 296, 319, 322, 383, 394, 647; individual labour of, 381, 398-399; industry and, 184-185; medicinal plants and, 570-571
Peking. *See* Beijing
Peking Man, 3
Penalties: for aquatic resources violations, 144-145; for customs violations, 275-276; for environmental protection violations, 288, 774; family planning and, 763; for foreign exchange violations, 255; for forestry violations, 150-151; in industry, 178, 192, 209-210; on overdue loans, 659; for tax evasion, 229, 232, 235, 238
Peng Dehuai, 90; criticism of, 85
People's Bank of China, 657-664, 1001; accountability for, 659; coin issuance of, 660-661, 662t, 663t; on contracts, 279-281; economic stability and, 661-662; founding of, 657; function of, 657, 662; interest rates from, 659-660, 662t, 663t, 1011; loan policy of, 243-244, 245-247, 388, 658-659, 661-662, 1007; management reform in, 659; overdrafts from, 1978, 128, 140; regulatory role of, 335, 658, 661; resident offices and, 266; in Tibet, 1019; trusts and, 660
People's Construction Bank, 189; construction curtailment and, 1020; construction loans from, 212, 240-242, 355, 387, 551-552, 658, 1006, 1021; functions of, 657; technological loans and, 217
People's Daily, 729; "Advantages" editorial, 1016; economic news in, 721; "limits of capabilities" editorial, 1012; "New Period" editorial, 1007; "Plain Living" editorial, 1007; "Readjustment" editorial, 1021; restructuring of, 730; "Seek a Clear Understanding" editorial, 946; "Tapping New Sources" editorial, 1009; "Tapping Potential" editorial, 1015
People's Insurance Company, 263, 660, 1008; branches of, 1108-1109
People's Liberation Army (PLA), 47, 79; agriculture and, 163; "cultural revolution" and, 88-90; duties of, 51-52; modernization of, 103; and national minorities 40; politics and, 180; purchasing power of, 284; quality of, 81; standardization and, 199; state farms and, 407; and War of Liberation, 78. *See also* Military
People's Navy, 520
People's Republic of China (PRC): agricultural history of, 392-393; central government of, 52-53, 57-58; CPC and, 43-48, 77, 79,

101, 104, 105, 106; constitution of (1978), 49-56; cultural history of, 717-718; "cultural revolution" and, 86-91; economic history of, 379-381; economic principles of, 50; education in, 643-645; founding of, 5, 49, 79, 105; future course of, 100-104, 108-114; ideological foundation of, 49-52; local government of, 53-54, 59-69; national minorities of, 34-42, 50; objectives of, 100-104; publishing in, 722-724; rights of citizens of, 55-56; science in, 8-9; socialist transformation in, 82-86

People's University of China (Beijing), economic institutes in, 1052

Periodicals, 722-727; circulation of, 976t; economics, 1077-1985; publication of, 1980, 726

Personality cults, 103, 111; of Mao, 88, 91

Pesticides, 166-167, 410; aerial spraying of, 599, 699-601; biologic, 410-415; environmental protection and, 287

Petrochemical industry, development of, 28, 185. See also Petroleum industry

Petroleum industry, 486-493; current problems in, 492; education and, 489-490, energy conservation and, 491-492; exploration and, 490-491, 492-493; future prospects of, 492-493; history of, 486; joint exploration in, 123; management of, 492; offshore, 123, 488, 491, 493; output of, 1980, 486-487; pipelines and, 489; pollution control in, 768-769; producing areas for, 488-488; quality in, 491; readjustment in, 490-492; refineries for, 488-489, 491; statistics on, 491t; technology and, 489-490, 492

Petroleum Indutry, Ministry of, 486-493; awards from, 492

Pharmaceutical industry, 565-572; consolidation in, 567; exports from, 572; history of, 565-566; management of, 569-570; marketing and, 565, 568, 571; medical serves and, 758; output of, 1980, 567; present state of, 566; product line of, 566; quality in, 567-568, 569; readjustment in, 567-572; research and, 568-569; 571-572, 755-756; traditional drugs and, 565, 568, 570-571, 755-756

Philately, 606

Photography industry, 458, 734

Photography, journalist, 731

Physicians: "barefoot" doctors, 753; individual practice of, 755; number of, 753; training of, 752-753

Piece-rate wage system, 322, 701; regulations on, 277-278, 701, 1011

Pigs, 168; per capita output of, 969t; increased production of, 438-439, 442, 608; individual protection of, 392, 442; number of (1980), 394; production of, 25, 438, 968t; purchase price of, 1014

Pigskin, 438

Plains, 12, 22, 30, 31, 32; afforestation of, 773

Plant diseases, forestry and, 149

Plants: freshwater edible, protected, 143; medicinal, 565, 568, 570-571, 914; protection of, 286; rare, 149, 857; Tibetan,' 913-914; wild, 430. See also Vegetation

Plastics, 185; agricultural, 167; development of, 125, 511

Plate-glass industry, 554, 556-557; expansion of, 558; history of, 556; output of, 1980, 557; technology in, 557

Poland, 593

Political risk insurance, 1008

Politics: economy and, 335, education in, 744; in industry, 180, 190, 213, 278, 341-342, 344; publications on, 1086-1089; trade unions and 707

Pollution: control of, 766-772; electric power industry and, 507; prevention of, 187, 285-288; in tourist areas, 678; urban, 766-769

Polyester fabrics, 469

Population, 959t, 996; density of, 23; distribution of, 959t; of East China, 30; economy and, 952; growth rate of, 120, 962t; minority, 23, 34; of Northwest China, 32; projected growth rate of, 1981, 121; rural, 23; urban, 23, 29, 30

Population and Economics (periodical), 1082

Pork: increase in supply of, 119, 438; output of, 394, 968t; price subsidy for, 132, 438

Ports, 29, 594-595; capacity of, 577; mechanization of, 574; renovation of, 122, 595; shortage of berths in, 579, 595

Portugal, 942-944

Postal service, 604-607; backwardness of, 607; conference on, 1002; development of, 604, 605-606, 1017; 1980 economic plan and, 993; readjustment in, 606; stamps issued by, 606; state of, 1980, 605; technology and, 605; volume in, 976t; zip codes and, 606, 1016

Posts and Telecomminications, Ministry of, 604-606

Potatoes, production of, 24

Poultry, 168, 412, 439; individual production of, 392

Power grids, 507

Power industry: commune-run, 153, 170; goals for, 1981, 123; improvement in, 117; pollution control in, 771; prominence of, 185-186. See also Electric power industry

Power Industry, Ministry of, 171, 212, 1002; on hydroelectric power, 1014

Power supply, 506

Precious metals: customs declaration of, 255; prices of, 661, 664t

Precipitation: seasonal variation in, 419; yearly, 419

Precision machinery, FTC for, 1040

Prefabricated construction, 563

Prefectures, by province or region, 59-71

Preferential treatment, in Special Economic Zones, 264

Premier of State Council, 57

Prenatal diagnosis, 764

Price controls, 1022; history of, 671-673; implementation of, 675-676; reestablishment of, 673; tightening of, 674-675, 1012

Price indexes: by commodity groups, 984t; general, 983t; at state list prices, 983t; for state purchasing, 984t

Prices: agricultural, 129, 322, 381, 394, 610, 647; of commune-made products, 156-157; competition in, 221; general indexes of, 672t, 983t; increase in, 130-131, 295, 297, 322, 325, 326, 391, 671-672; indexes of, 983t, 984t; investigation of, 675; 1980 economic plan and, 993-994; of pharmaceuticals, 571; of precious metals, 661, 664t; preferential, in Special Economic Zones, 264; purchasing, 673-674; quality and, 188, 195; readjustment of, 672-673; retail, 674, 675, 676; selling, 673-674; stabilization of, 296, 327, 1011; state control of, 360, 610-611, 671-675. See also Inflation

Pricing policy, 671-676; agricultural, 381, 610, 647, 671-675; "cultural revolution" and, 673; to encourage individual initiative, 399-400; industrial reform and, 348; to regulate economy, 335, 611, 647, 671-676, 1007; in Sichuan experiment, 359

Pricing: Theory and Practice (periodical), 1079

Printed matter, customs and, 639

Printing, 724; quality of, 726-727

Priorities: in agricultural machinery, 525; in agriculture, 412; in chemical industry, 514-515; for loans, 661-662; in producer goods distribution, 615; for quality products, 195, 221; to textile industry, 447, 448, 468, 1003

Private plots, agricultural, 398-399

Problems of Agricultural Economy (periodical), 1080
Problems of International Trade (periodical), 1081-1082
Processing industries: in agricultural areas, 172; combination with producers, of, 218; fish, 432, 433; meat, 438; state farms and, 417
Producer goods, 613-620; balanced distribution of, 615; direct sales of, 616; priorities for, 615
Production: agricultural, responsibility for, 368-376; central vs. market regulation of, 308-318, 335, 355, 358, 359-360; competition in, 220-222; consumption and, 302-305; industrial, 444; management of, 211; market regulation of, 463-464; mistakes in, 299-302; potential for, 329; quality control in, 206-208; theory of, 302-306
Production-brigade-run enterprises. *See* Commune-run enterprises
Production brigades, 50, 163, 368-386, 965t; accmulation funds of, 161; Number 1, Yuexi Commune, 526; number of (1980), 392; output quotas and, 368-376
Production quotas. *See* Quotas
Production teams, 163, 965t; as basic accounting unit, 165, 386; fixed assets of, 405; joint enterprises and, 403-404, 413; number of (1980), 392; output quotas and, 368-376; ownership rights of, 371; state-owned industry and, 404
Productivity, labour, 136; in building industry, 560; campaigns for, 710-711; increase in, 119, 444, 452; per capita, 1980, 389; responsibility for Anhui, 368-386; in state-owned enterprises, 976t; on Taiwan, 934; wages and, 190-191
Productivity, land, agricultural machinery and, 525
Products, 793, 831; awards for, 194-195, 461; building materials industry and, 555-557; chemical industry and, 514-515; electronic, 532-533, 537; light industrial, 457, 460-461, 477; new, 198, 202, 206, 278, 389, 461, 518, 537, 1012; output of, 973-974t, 989-990t; output of, indexed, 975t; pharmaceuitcal, 566; quality of, 187, 194-195, 205-210, 1014; standardization of, 181, 196-199, 691-697; for tourists, 679
Profiteering, 186, 327, 569-570; customs and, 640
Profits: agricultural, 390, 411; commercial, 1980, 611; from commune-run enterprises, 158; from construction, 211-212; distribution of, experimental, 361-362, 384, 411; excess, tax on, 652; from experimental enterprises, 449; from forests, 429; illegitimate, 365; industrial, 181, 343; to investments, ratio, 341; from joint ventures, 256, 257; from metallurgical industry, 548; reinvestment of, 228, 230, 361-362; repayment of loans from, 241-242, 245, 251; responsibility for, 211, 216, 351-352, 361-362, 366; retention of, 125, 130, 133, 135, 311, 335, 347, 358, 366, 384, 471, 520-521, 552, 651, 701, 1004, 1008; from Special Economic Zones, 264; state enterprise distribution of, 361-362, 411; from state farms, 416
Profit-sharing: in Sichuan experiment, 361-362; in state-owned enterprises, 202-204
Property: ownership of, 50; state-owned, 185
Proletariat, 43-44, 49; dictatorship of, 49, 80, 175, 177, 180; international, 103, 113, Mao on, 95; victory of, 78, 80
Protected species, aquatic, 143
Protectionism, Sichuan's industry and, 360
Provinces, administrative divisions of, 59-69; government of, 53-54
Publications, 717-727; distribution of, 727; in economics (1980), 1086-1105; journalistic, 728-731; periodical, 726; reference, 726; scientific, 688-689, 726
Public health. *See* Health care
Public health centres, 380; rural, 753
Public Health, Ministry of, 752-759; health standards and, 197
Publishing: "cultural revolution" and, 723-724; decline in, 726t; of foreign classics, 726; history of, 722-724; national forum on (1979), 724; of periodicals, 726; of reference books, 726; state of, 1980, 724-725; tasks of, 724, 726-727; volume in, 725t
Purchasing power: control of, 282-284, 296, 1010; of peasants, 394, rise in, 295, 326, 383

Q

Qin Dynasty, 3-4
Qing Dynasty, science and technology in, 8
Qinghai Province, 877-881; administrative divisions of, 60; agriculture in, 877-888, 879; animal husbandry in, 877, 878-879, 880-881; economic education in, 1070; education in, 878, 880; geography of, 877; industry in, 877, 879; marketing in, 879; national minorities in, 877, 880; readjustment in, 878-881; standard of living in, 880; subsidy for, 135, 879; transportation in, 878
Qinghai-Tibet Plateau, 11, 20, 23; geographic characteristics of, 21; soil of, 17
Qingyuan County, management reform in, 450
Qi Zong, 481-485
Qomolangma, Mount, 12, 679
Quality, industrial: agricultural machinery and, 527; awards for, 194-195, 343, 460, 475, 491; 518, 527, 534, 544, 560, 1003, 1019; building industry and, 560; coal, 496; commune-run enterprises and, 158; control of, 203-210; electronics industry and, 534-535; energy conservation and, 201; film industry and, 734; of handicrafts, 475; of highways, 590; importance of, 187, 205-210; improvement in, 343, 389; machine-building industry and, 518; metallurgical industry and, 544; piece-rate system and, 278; standards for, 196-199, 695; of steel, 544; supervision of, 198, 1014; of texiltes, 467-468, 469
Quality control, 343, 344, 451, 1010, 1018; campaigns for, 1005; conference on, 1004; education, 209; guiding principles of, 205; light industry and, 460; in pharmaceutical industry, 567-568, 569; planning for, 205; in production, 206-208; rewards and penalties in, 209-210; systems of, 208-209
Quarantine, 754
Quotas, 157; for agricultural output, 368-369, 396-404; for aquatic products, 436; bonuses and, 344; central control of, 308, 335, 358; on communes, 165, 368-376; for construction expenses, 212; control of purchasing power through, 282-284; for consumption of materials, 188; for energy, 186, 200-201; flexibility in, 337; labour, 216-217; piece-rate wage system and, 277-278; revision of, 157

R

Rabbits, 168, 438, 443
Radar, 532
Radioactive materials, control of, 287
Radio Appliances Corporation, 536
Radios, 294, 533
Radio stations, 532, 604, 728-731; growth in, 988t; international, 729; number of (1980), 728-729; resident offices and, 267
Railroads, 8, 30, 32, 33, 573, 582-589, 1002, 1013; capital construction on, 585-586; development of, 582t, 589; education and, 588; efficiency of, 578;

electricifcation of, 585-586, 1019; energy conservation on, 584; equipment for, 586; facilities of, 574; freight service of, 581, 583, 584t, 977t; length of lines, 28, 977t; maintenance of, 584; management reform in, 1017; organization of, 587-588; passenger service of, 583, 589, 978t; renovation of, 1013; safety on, 584; shortage of, 579, 588; state of, 1980, 585t; technology for, 586-587
Railways, Ministry of, 582-589; awards from, 586-587
Rainfall, 13-15, 16t; distribution of, 419; economic consequences of, 22-23; geographic divisions and, 20-21; soil characteristics and, 17-18
Rainforests, 774
Ramie, 466
Rapeseed, production of, 25, 400
Rattan, 477
Raw materials: from building materials industry, 555; chemical, 510; consumption of, 389; for handicrafts, 476, for light industry, 454; textile industry and, 468
Readjustment, economic, 116-120, 123-127, 128-138, 293-298, 299-318, 319-331, 1022; agricultural, 116, 130, 167, 368-376, 381-382; in agricultural machinery industry, 528-530; animal husbandry and, 438, 442-443; assessment of, 363-367; in banking, 658-663; budgetary, 223-228; in building materials industry, 558-559; capital construction and, 117, 122, 136, 188-189, 293-298, 299-301, 319-320, 325, 326, 382, 387, 453-454, 550-553; coal industry and, 495-501; commune-run enterprises and, 153; definition of, 381; electric power industry and, 505-506; electronics industry and, 533-539; environmental protection and, 779-780; financial, 387-388, 644, 645, 646-651; financing of, 128, 131, 215-216; fisheries and, 434-437; foreign trade and, 622-624; goals of, 306-308, 317, 453-456; handicrafts and, 474, 479-480; industrial, 116-117, 124-125, 130, 214-217, 218-219, 340-345, 382, 447-448, 452-456; loans for, 240-247, 387; machine-building industry and, 517; managerial, 118, 125-126, 313-318; metallurgical industry and, 542-548; pharmaceutical industry and, 567-572; post-1980, 391; problems in, 325-326, 363-367, 390-391, 453; rationale for, 299-300; reform and, 346-356, 366-367; results of, 330-331; shipbuilding industry and, 520-521; in Sichuan Province, 356-367; socialist economy and, 299-306; stages of, 307, 342-343; success of, 363; in supply, 619-620; targets for, 1981, 120-122, 135-138; theory of, 302-306; transportation and, 214-217, 280, 600-603; water conservancy and, 423-424
Readjustment, restructuring, consolidation and improvement policy, 116-127, 128-138, 140, 220, 223, 245, 295, 299, 325, 358, 474; definition of, 381; formulation of, 319, 321, 381, 446. See also Readjustment, economic
Recreation, for workers, 191
Reform, economic, 338-339, 346, 349; assessment of, 363-367; conditions for, 348-349; overall design of, 347, 358-359; readjustment and, 366-367; in Sichuan Province, 357-367
Refrigeration, of railroad cars, 586
Regional centres, economic, 316-317, 334-335
Regions, autonomous. See Autonomous regions
Regions, economic, 29-33
Registration, of enterprises, 354, 1008; of joint ventures, 261-262, 1017; of resident offices, 266-267, 268; in Special Economic Zones, 263, 264
Registration fees, for resident offices, 268
Regulations on enterprises run by communes, 1979 (draft), 152-160, 1003
Reinsurance, 660
Relics Stores, 272
Religion: freedom of, 55, 103; among national minorities, 35
Renminbi: establishment of, 657, 667; foreign exchange and, 248, 997; protection of, 1009; rates 1110t; tax computed in, 228, 229, 234, 237
Renmin Ribao. See People's Daily
Renqiu Oilfield, 29; output of, 1011
Repair and service: of agricultural machinery, 524; of airplanes, 599, 601; of electronics equipment, 536; of locomotives, 587; of ships, 595, 596
Repayment: of construction loans, 241-242; of light industry loans, 245; of loans in foreign currency, 249, 250-251
Report of Arrangements for National Economic Plans, 1980 and 1981 (Yao Yilin), 116-127
Report on Final State Accounts for 1979, Draft State Budget for 1980, and Financial Estimates for 1981 (Wang Bingqian), 128-138
Rescue operations, marine, 596
Reserve funds, 130, 133, 651; in autonomous regions, 650; commune-run enterprises and, 153; joint ventures and, 257
Reservoirs, 521, 423, 425; fish breeding in, 1006
Residence permits, 266
Resident offices, foreign enterprises, 630; application for, 266; control of, 266-267; registration of, 266, 268; termination of, 267
Resignations, from joint ventures, 259
Resolution on Certain Questions in the History of Our Party: 1945, 78, 104; 1981, 77-104
Resources tax, 652
Responsibility: for afforestation, 428; for agricultural production, 368-376, 396-398, 528-529; in banking, 659; of factory directors, 451; in light industry, 462; personal, 451, 462; for profits and losses, 211, 216, 351-352, 361-362, 366, 416; state farms and, 416 for timber production, 430
Restaurants, number of, 386
Restraint of trade, 221
Restructuring, economic: definition of, 381; ideielogical basis of, 350; ownership and, 351; readjustment and, 332-339
Retail sales, 310, 380; of consumer goods, 981t: light industry and, 459, 463; market economy and, 336, 385; 1980 economic plan and, 993-994; price index of, 391, 674, 675, 676t; projected, 1981, 121; recent increase in, 324, 326, 386; state farrms and, 414; of textiles, 471; total, 1979, 119; volume of, 295, 379, 980t; volume of, indexed, 980t
Retail stores, 620
Retirement benefits, 702; for cadres, 702-703
Revenues, local, 224, 1009; sources of, 649
Revenues, state, 223-224, 985t; from commune-run enterprises, 484; from light industry, 458-459; 1979, 128; 1980 (draft), 131, 132, 379; 1981 (estimated), 134; sources of, 649; from taxes, 655
Revisionism, "cultural revolution" and, 87
Revolution of 1911, 4, 77, 105
Revolutionaries, 8
Revolutionary tradition, Chinese, 8
Rewards: for aquatic resource conservation, 144; economic, 129, 135, 344, 456; in family planning, 763; for forestry, 159-151; in industry, 178, 192 209
Rice: equipment for output of, 523-531; hybrid, 119, 410, 415, 685-686, 908; production of, 24, 31, 1021
"Rightists": overreaction to, 85;

rehabilitation of, 85, 93; in publishing, 723
Rivers, 14-16, 419; drainage basins of, 16t, 419; flood control on, 421, 424; navigation on, 29, 592-593, 594-595
Roads, in forest zones, 148
Rockets, carrier, 119-120, 380, 520, 685; electronics industry and, 534
Rolling stock, 586
Roman Empire, Eastern, 7
Rong Yiren, 1005
Royalties: for new technology, 126; tax on, 234, 236
Rubber; development of, 408; priority for, 412; scientific management of, 410, 414; state farm output of, 1980, 409
Rural economic policy, regulations on, 368
Rural fairs, 117, 162, 165, 323, 381; increase in, 609-610; volume at, 1980, 394, 610
Russian nationality, 34, 35
Russian Revolution, 4, 77, 105

S

Safety: flight, 599-600, 602; railroad, 584; trade unions and, 712-713; training in, 704. See also Occupational safety
Safety campaigns, 704-705, 1013; in aviation, 601-602; in coal industry, 498, 1008
Sales exhibitions: of commune-made goods, 1020; electronics industry and, 536; light industry and, 1005; textiles and, 471
Salt, 905; price-fixing of, 459; sea, production of, 29, 166, 866; tax on, 655
Salvage operations; insurance and, 660; marine, 596-597
San Fan Movement, 708
Satellite communications, 533, 604-605
Satellites, man-made, 120, 280
Savings deposits, 141, 799, 821; current interest rates on, 662t; increase in, 293; in rural areas, 394, 659, 665, 985t; total of, 1980, 659-660, 985t
Schistosomiasis, 752
Schools, 743-751; agricultural, 170; art, 718-719; construction of 1980, 562; enrollment in, 987t; health care in, 754; light industry and, 458, 464-465; medical, 752-753, 756; middle, 383, 747; nursery, 748, 756; petroleum industry and, 490; primary, 383, 747; in rural areas, 405; secondary, 383; of finance and economics, 1064-1071; on state farms, 415; vocational, 699, 747; workers', 259, 345. See also Education, Technical schools
Science, 5; academic societies in, 688; ancient, 6-8; current policies in, 689-690; economic role of, 689-690; education in, 687; films on, 733; financial aid to, 133, 687-688; international exchange in, 689; joint exploration in, 689; People's Republic and, 8-9, 51, 683-684; policy on, 684-685; projections for, 1981, 121; projects in, 685; publications in, 688-689. See also Scientific research
Science, natural, awards for, 289, 683
Scientific American (magazine), 689
Scientific archives, regulations on, 1022
Scientific research: advances in, 119-120, 685-686; on agriculture, 170, 414-415, 417, 685-686; on aquatic resources, 145, 433; in the arts, 720-721; awards for, 189, 289, 533, 685; on banking, 661; basic, 685; coal industry and, 501-502; commune-run enterprises and, 156, 484; contracts for, 686-687; costs of, 202; "cultural revolution" and, 683; in electronics, 537-538; on energy conservation, 186; on environmental protection, 288, 775-776; facilities for, 562; on forestry, 430; FTC for, 1041; funding of, 687-688; imports for, 1036; on industry, 189, 190; on light industry, 458, 464; management of, 686-687; medical, 755-756, 765; need for, 122; 1980 economic plan and, 994; on oil, 489-490, 492; on pharmaceuticals, 568-572; results of, 1980, 685-686; on safety, 704-705; on shipbuilding, 519-520; state farms and, 414-415, 417; workers in, 687
Scientific research institutions, 414-415, 890; agricultural, 888; for agricultural machinery, 523-524; in the arts, 720-721; economic, 1046-1054; industrial, 686; journalistic, 729
Scientists, 684, 687; decision-making and, 684-685; education of, 687; honours for, 689; role of, 684
Sea farms, 423-433
Seas, 12-13
Seaweeds, protected, 143
Second Five-Year Plan, 708; culture and, 718; light industry and, 456, 458, 459; petroleum and, 486
Secretariat, Central Committee CPC, 1010
Securities: foreign, 252-255; tax on income from, 236
Seeders, 524
Seed Law, 167
Seeds: grass, improved, 441; import and export of, 1041; selection and breeding of, 167, 410, 1004, 1018; tree, 429
Self-criticism: in coal industry, 1018; need for, 101, 104, 112
Self-determination: in agriculture, 173; on communes, 164; economic, 125, 129-130, 134-135; financial, 135; managerial, 125, 462, 832
Self-employment, 949, 963t; agricultural, 386; extent of, 337-338, 698, 963t
Self-sufficiency, theory on, 952-953
Sesame, production of, 25
Service trades, 329, 647, 868, 949; development of, 329, 1003, 1005; publications on, 1103
"Seventy-point document in industry," 341
Sewing machines: output of, 1980, 458; projected output of, 1981, 121
Seventh National Congress, 78
Sewage, discharge of, 287
Shaanxi Province, 882-886; administrative divisions of, 66; agriculture in, 882-883, 884, 886; coal in, 1008; commerce in, 885; economic education in, 1058, 1060, 1063, 1070; economic institute in, 1050; education in, 883-884; geography of, 882; grain distribution to, 401; grain overestimates in, 1016; industry in, 883, 885, 886; minerals in, 882; readjustment in, 884-886; textile industry in, 471, 883; tourism in, 884; transportation in, 883; water diversion in, 1015
Shandong Province, 887-891; administrative divisions of, 66-67; agriculture in, 887-888, 889; cotton output of, 393, 888; economic education in, 1057, 1060, 1061, 1062, 1067; education in, 888-889, 890; foreign trade corporation in, 388; geography of, 887; industry in, 887, 888, 889-890; marketing in, 890; problems of, 891; standard of living in, 889, 890-891; transportation in, 888
Shang Dynasty, 3; handicrafts in, 456; metal smelting in, 6, 540
Shanghai, 31, 892-896; administrative divisions of, 59; agriculture around, 892, 893-894; construction in, 894; economic education in, 1056-1057, 1059, 1061, 1066; economic experimentation in, 118, 337, 384, 450, 471, 895; economic institutes in, 1050-1051, 1053; education in, 892, 894-895; environmental protection in, 767, 894; foreign trade in, 388, 892; FTC in, 1041-1042; geography of, 892; industry in, 30, 892, 893; light industry in, 458, 462, 893; loan experiments in, 387, 895; potential of, 896; readjustment in, 893-896;

specialized companies in, 181, 385; standard of living in, 895; water transport and, 592
Shanghai Handicrafts Administration, 476
Shanghai Light Industry Machinery Corporation, experimental management of, 448, 656
Shanghai oil refinery, 488
Shantou, Special Economic Zone in, 263-265, 804
Shanxi Plateau, 29
Shanxi Province, 897-900; administrative divisions of, 67; agriculture in, 897-898; coal in, 328, 898-899; commerce in, 899-890; economic education in, 1056, 1059, 1062, 1064; finances of, 899; geography of, 897; human services in, 900; industry in, 898; minerals and mining in, 898-899; problems of, 900; standard of living in, 900; tourism in, 900; transportation in, 899
Sheep, 442, 443; number of (1980), 394, 438, 439, 968t
Shellfish: cultivation of, 432-434; protected, 143
Shelterbelts, 146, 149, 167, 428-429, 773, 792, 1014
Shelter forests. See Shelterbelts
She nationality, 35; population of, 34
Shengli oil field, 29, 487
Shenyang: environmental protection in, 766; industry in, 30
Shenzhen, Special Economic Zone in, 263, 265, 629, 804, 1009
Shifts, industrial: in coal mines, 1016; in textile industry, 468, 700, 1012
Shipbuilding industry, 519-522; capability of, 595-596; development of, 519; education in, 519-520; 521; exports from, 521-522; FTC for, 1040; integration in, 522; investment realignment in, 521; joint venture in, 1011; licence purchases in, 522; management reform in, 521; non-marine output of, 520; output of, 1980, 520; problems in, 522; profits from, 520-521; quality in, 521; readjustment and, 520-521; research in, 519; rocket tests and, 520
Shipping. See Water transportation
Shipping Register Bureau, PRC, 522
Ships, 593; chartering of, 1037; repair of, 595, 596; salvage of, 596, 597; types of, 520, 594, 595-596
Shoes, 337, 512
Shrimp: cultivation of, 433; protected, 143
Sichuan Basin, 12, 32
Sichuan experiment, 357-367, 403, 903; enterprise leadership in, 362-363; extent of, 357-358; joint enterprises in, 403-404; market as regulator in, 358-360; problems in, 363-367; profit distribution in, 361-362; success of, 363
Sichuan oil field, 487-488
Sichuan Province, 357-367, 901-904; administration divisions of, 67-68; agriculture in, 901, 902; commerce in, 903-904; economic education in, 1058, 1060, 1062-1063, 1069; economic experimentation in, 118, 357-367, 403, 656, 903; economic institute in, 1051; foreign trade corporations in, 388; geography of, 901; industry in, 902, 903; international technical cooperation corporation of, 1045; problems in, 904; readjustment in, 357-367, 902-904; standard of living in, 904; transportation in, 902
Sichuan Provincial Academy of Social Sciences, 306
Sichuan-Tibet highway, 590
Sichuan Vinlon Plant, 1007
Sideline occupations, agricultural, 50, 117-118, 162-163, 165, 323, 374-375, 379, 392, 398-399, 949, 966t
Silk: exports of, 468; production of, 25, 31, 466, 469; quality of, 467-468; tussah, 25, 866
"Silk Road," 7
Silk weaving, ancient, 6, 7
Silkworms, 393; production of, 1006
Silver: ancient works in, 540; recovery of, 772
"Simultaneous development" policy in agriculture, 163
"Six priorities" principle, 468, 1007
Sixth Five-Year Plan, 134, 327; energy conservation in, 1020
Sixth Plenary Session, Elevent Central Committee of CPC, 105; on China's future, 100-104; communique of, 75-76; on "cultural revolution," 86-91; historical review by, 77-81; on Mao, 94-100; on socialist transformation, 82-86
Sixtieth Anniversary of founding of CPC, Hu Yaobang's speech on, 105-114
Skidders, 525
Smuggling, 636, 637, 640, 641-642, 1017; causes of, 641-642
Social assistance, 56, 117; on communes, 165; investment in, 383; to workers, 191, 344
Socialism: agriculture and, 161-164, 396-297; China's future and, 100-104, 110-114; communism and, 308-309; competition and, 220, 360; constitutional requirements of, 43-44, 49-52; "cultural revolution" and, 87-88, 92; democratic, 44, 102, 103, 111-112, 163, 344, 351; economic integration under, 315-316; economic laws of, 947-956; economic restructuring and, 350, 352; economy and, publications on, 1086-1089; implementation of, 80, 84-86; Mao on, 95-96; readjustments in, 299-318; setbacks to, 85-86, 90-91; transition to, 82-84, 88, 643, 652, 948-949
Socialist modernization, 1001; of agriculture, 161-174; focus of, 333; loans for, 240-232; of handicrafts, 476-479; of industry, 175-193, 340-345; theoretical issues in, 947-956
Socialist nationalization, 312
Social practice, as criterion for truth, 368-369
Social science, 120
Soil: arable, 24; composition of, 17-18, 24; improvement of, 415; organic content of, 18; saline-alkaline, 421; weathering of, 17-18
Solar energy, 186
Somalia, foreign aid to, 633
Song Dynasty, science and technology in, 7
Songhuajiang River, floods on, 420; pollution control on, 769
South China Sea (Nanhai Sea), 12, 13, 123; joint oil exploration in, 324, 491, 629
Southern Shipping Area, 592
Southwest China economic region, 32
Soviet Union. See Union of Soviet Socialist Republics
Soybeans, production of, 24, 30
Spawning: catch restrictions on, 144; overfishing and, 435
Special Economic Zones, 388, 629, 804, 1018; administration of, 264-265; exchange control regulations for, 255; Guangdong, regulations on, 263-264; preferential treatment in, 264; registration for, 263-264
Special Economic Zones Guangdong Province, 263-265, 629
Specialization, neglect of, 445. See also Cooperation
Speculation, 221, 364
Speech, freedom of, 55, 94
Sports, 995; trade unions and, 715
Spring and Autumn Period; metallurgy in, 540; science in, 6
Stalin Josef 304, 627, 947; on socialist economics, 309-310, 948, 950, 955
Stamp Collection (magazine), 606
Stamps, 606
Standardization, 691-697, 1002; administration of, 198-199, 693, 694; authority over, 693t, 694; design and, 206; energy conservation and, 696; enforcement of, 694-695; history of, 691-692; industrial, 181; international, 695; materials management and, 696;

new products and, 697; policy on, 691-692; products under, 694t; quality and, 695; regulations on, 196-199, 692, 1002, 1004
Standard of living, 986t, 1005, 1022; in Anhui Province, 374-375; control of, 293-298; improvement of, 81, 93, 119, 129, 293-298, 322-323, 326, 380; new emphasis on, 299-318, 327-331, 391; 1980 economic plan and, 995-996; projected, 1981, 121-122; worker's, 191, 319, 444
Standards, industrial; administration of, 198-199; development of, 316; enforcement of, 694-695; enterprise, 197, 694; foreign, 691; implementation of, 197-198; international, 695; ministry, 197, 694; national, 694; numbers of, 694t; state, 196-197; for technical grades, 1098, 1100, 1101
Standing Committee of National People's Congress: chairman of, 53; composition and powers of, 52-53
State Administration for Commodity Prices, 671-676
State Administration of Standards, 194, 197-199, 691-697; responsibilities of, 692-693
State Administration of Supplies: on decision-making in construction, 211-213; on energy-conservation bonuses, 200-201; materials allocation and, 246
State Administrative Commission on Export and Import Affairs, 625-626, 668
State Agricultural Commission, 1002; agricultural readjustment and, 395
State Bureau of Building Industry, 211
State Bureau of Labour, 698-706; on decision-making in construction, 211-213; on energy-conservation bonuses, 200-201
State Bureau of Supplies, 613-620
State Capital Construction Commission, 197; on decision-making power, 211-213
State Commodity Inspection Bureau, 1016
State control: over economy, 319-331, 332-339, 610-611; of labour, 698-699; of materials, 613-620
State Council, 327, 387; on capital construction loans, 240-242; on competition, 220-222; composition and powers of, 53; customs and, 636; on economic combination, 218-219; on environmental protection, 779; on foreign exchange control, 252-255; on income tax, 236-238; industrial standards and, 194-199; on joint ventures, 259-262; on local financial management, 223-225; ministers of (1981), 57-58; on natural science awards, 289; quality awards of, 1003, 1019; on renovation of industry, 214-217; on resident offices of foreign enterprises, 266-267
State Economic Commission: on contracts, 269-181; loan approval by, 246; on profit-sharing, 202-204; quality awards of, 194-195, 527; on quality control, 205-210, 1010; on transport and communications, 573-580
State farm industrial production, 1980, 411
State farms, 407-418, 523, 822, 919; as agricultural-industrial-commercial complexes, 1020; condition of, 1980, 392, 408-416; diversification and, 412, 416, 417; education on, 415; exemplary role of, 166, 407, 408-409; experimental economics and, 413-414; future of, 417-418; health care on, 415; history of, 407-408; industry on, 411-414; integration and, 413-414, 417; military function of, 407; production of, 1980, 409; profits from, 119, 166, 408, 411, 416; readjustment and, 408-409, 411-414, 416-417; regulations on, 1006; scientific research and, 414-415, 417; tasks of, 407-408; technology and, 409-410, 414-415; wages on, 415-416
State Farms and Land Reclamation, Ministry of, 171, 172, 1006; abolition of, 408; foundation of, 470-480; integrated enterprises under, 385; resstablishment of, 408
State General Administration of Exchange Control (SGAEC), 252 255, 1002; functions of, 657, 668
State Quality Awards, 194-196
State standards, industrial: authority for, 196-197; jurisdiction of, 197; supervision of, 198
State-owned enterprises: decision-making in, 1017, 1019; employment in, 963t; financial responsibilities of, 311, 1017; fixed assets of, 964t; in handicrafts, 475, 478; labour productivity in, 976t; problems of, 949-950; production teams and, 404; profit-sharing in, 202-204; taxes on, 126, 652-653; use of circulating funds by, 964t; wages in, 963t; workers in, 444
State ownership, 50, 118, 379; agriculture and, 171, 392; commune-run enterprises and, 154; of forests, 146; of handicrafts industries, 475-476, 479; individual ownership vs., 346, 351; profits and, 125, 130, 133, 135; transition to, 82-83, 948-949
State Pharmaceutical Administration, 565-572; formation of, 567, 570
State Planning Commission: agricultural readjustment and, 395; commune-run enterprises and, 155; computer centre of, 606; on decision-making in construction, 211-213; exports and, 168; industry and, 183-184; loan approval by, 246
Statesmen, 8
State Statistical Bureau, 959-997
Statisticians, 1014
Statistics, 184, 959-997, 1002; agricultural, 395-396; industrial transformation and, 217, 384; on petroleum industry, 491t; publications on, 1090-1095; quality control and, 206; trade, 638-639
Steel; alloy, 541; imports of, 320, 548; quality of, 544; retail sales of, 336; scrap, 619; stockpiles of, 1015
"Steel as the key link" policy, 320, 328
Steel industry. See Iron and steel industry
Steel-making, ancient, 6, 7
Stockpiles, 137, 141, 363, 390, 615; reduction of, 617-618; of steel, 1015
Studies of Architectural Economics (periodical), 1080-1081
Studies of Financial and Economic Problems (periodical), 1083
Strategy, of economic development, 300-301
"Strictly Control Prices" circular, 1022
Students, 743-751; employment of, 129; foreign, 749; number of, 987t; post-graduate, 687; teachers ratio, 987t
Subsidies, 216; agricultural, 129, 166, 402, 647-648; of commodities, 132, 166; to national minority areas, 39-40, 135; for pork, 132, 438; to urban workers, 119
Substandard goods, 187-188, 197, 390; piece-rate system and, 278; in textiles, 472
Subway, 579
Sugar crops, 403, 801; beets, 25, 29, 30; cane, 25, 31, 810; output of, 1980, 393; projected output of, 1981, 121
Sui Dynasty, science and technology in, 7
Sui Qiren, 592-597
Sun Yat-sen, 4, 77, 105, 697
Supplies. See Materials management
Supply and Marketing Cooperatives, Federation of, 172
Supreme People's Court, 52, 55

Supreme People's Procuratorates, 55
Surtaxes, local, 228, 230
Suzhou, environmental protection in, 768
Sweet potatoes, production of, 24
Synthetic fibres, 467, 469, 1008-1009, 1022

T

Taiping Rebellion, 4
Taishan, Mount, 678
Taiwan Province, 11, 68, 106, 933-938; agriculture and, 934, 936-937; changes in economy of, 934t; customs and, 638-639, 640, 1012, 1017; economic difficulties of, 933-938; exports from, 934; foreign trade of, 937t, 938; geography of, 933; industry in, 935-936; inflation and, 933-934; liberation of, 49, 100, 113; oil crisis and, 933; output of, industrial, 935t; ownership in, 936, 937; products of, 937t; trade with, 638-639; U.S. aid to, 936
Taiyuan, 30
Taiyuan Iron and Steel Company, economic institute of, 1049
Tang Dynasty, science and technology in, 7; trade in, 7
Tangshan, reconstruction in, 561, 820
Tanzania, foreign aid to, 632, 633
Tape recorders, 536
Tapping potential, renovation, and transformation (of industry), 214-217, 329, 450, 1015; coal industry and, 502; example of, 337; funding of, 215-216, 470; importance of, 364; in machine-building industry, 1009, 1021; in textile industry, 469-470
Tariffs: policy on, 640-641; protective, 640
Tarim Basim, 12; oil exploration in. 324, 1008
Taxes: agricultural, 119, 129, 168, 647, 1016, 1018; business, 135; on combined enterprises, 219; on commune-made products, 157; education in, 656; experimentation in, 652-653, 656; individual income, 126, 135, 234-238, 652, 654; industrial and commercial, 239, 242, 245, 652; on joint ventures, 128-129, 228-233, 257, 653; laws on, 228-238, 630, 654, 656; from light industry, 477; local, 224; policy on, 643, 652, 1003, 1016; readjustment and, 338, 655-656; reduction of, 1019; reform of, 135, 652-653, 635-636; resident offices and, 267; revenues from, 1980, 655; socialist transformation and, 652; in Special Economic Zones, 264; value-added, 135, 652, 656
Tax evasion; individual, 235, 238; joint ventures and, 229, 232

Tax exemptions, 129, 647, 655; for commune-run enterprises, 157, 322; income qualifying for, 234, 236-237, 654; during loan repayment, 242, 245, 251; for industrial waste use, 216; for joint ventures, 228, 257, 653; for waste utilization, 216, 288, 775
Taxis, 578
Tax policy, industrial reform and, 348
Tax rate schedule, 235
Tax year, 230, 236
Tea: FTC for, 1026-1029; production of, 25, 393, 785; Wuyu, 793
Teachers, 743; education for, 749-750; materials for, 749; requirements for, 750; shortage of, 750;-students ratio, 987; in technical schools, 746
Technical cooperation, 633-634
Technical grades, standards for; in commercial enterprises, 1101; in hydraulic and electrical construction, 1098; in transport, 1100; in water conservancy, 1098
Technical schools; aeronautic, 599, 601, 603; agricultural machinery, 524, 698, 699; chemical industry and, 509; coal industry and, 495, 500-501; electronics industry and, 533, 535, 538; enrollment in, 746-747; finance and economics, 1064-1071; light industry and, 458, 464-465; petroleum industry and, 489-490; posts and telecommunications and, 605; quality control and, 209; shipbuilding industry and, 520; textile industry and, 468
Technology, 257; agricultural, 170, 405, 406, 409-410; agricultural machinery and, 524; the arts and, 721; building industry and, 563; cement industry and, 556; coal industry and, 494-495, 501; commune-run enterprises and, 159; competition and, 221; economic management and, 313; electric power and, 504; on environment, 775-776; foreign, 169, 189, 217, 266, 331, 447, 515, 522, 625-626, 1036; FTC for, 1041; glass industry and, 557; imports for, 1036; industrial, 189, 190, 217, 329, 445-446; petroleum industry and, 489-490; for pollution control, 286; for posts and telecommunications, 605; quality control and, 206-207; railroad, 587; textile industry and, 468, 470; training in, 345
Telecommunications, 604-607; backwardness of, 607; conference on, 1002; development of, 604, 605-606, 1017; 1980 economic plan and, 993; readjustment in, 606; satellite, 604-605; state of, 1980,

605; technology and, 605; telephone shortage and, 606-607; volume of, 976t
Telegrams, volume of, 976t
Telephones, 604, 605-606, 976t; shortage of, 606-607, 1002
Telescopes, 533
Television: broadcasting level, 1980, 729, 988t; educational, 605, 729, 748
Television sets, 533, 534; manufacture of, 710
Temperature zones 15t
"On the Ten Major Relationships" (Mao Zedong), 83, 341, 613, 646
"Ten needs and need nots," 176, 193n
Tenth National Congress, CPC (1973), "cultural revolution" and, 88-89
Ten-Year Plan (1978), 319-320, 326-327
Ten-Year Programmes, 184, 1009
Terrain, 11-12; animal types and, 19; economic consequences of, 22-23; macrostructure of, 12; natural divisions of, 20-21; soil characteristics and, 17-18; vegetation types and, 18-19
Textbooks, 725, 749
Textile industry, 382, 466-473; development of resources for, 467; economic experimentation in, 118; education and, 468; exports from, 468, 470-471; fibres for, 467, 469; FTC for, 1029-1030; growth rate in, 130; history of, 466; imbalance in, 452; importance of, 214; labour in, 700; loans to, 245-247, 469, 658-659, 1007; machinery for, 467, 544; management reform in, 471; marketing and, 471; in North China, 29; output of, 1980, 469; present state of, 466; priorities given to, 447, 468, 648; problems remaining in, 472; quality in, 467-468, 469; readjustment and, 468-471; redistribution of, 467; state purchases from, 1980, 608; tapping potential in, 469-470; technology for, 468, 470; whole plant exports of, 1044
Textile Industry, Ministry of, 172, 246; technical innovation and, 470, 1008-1009; wool emphasis of, 443
Theatrical troupes, 717-721; in autonomous regions, 720
Third Five-Year Plan, light industry and, 459
Third World countries; agricultural machinery industry and, 528, 1020; aid to, 631-634; banking and, 667
"Thirty-Point Document" (on industrial consolidation), 342
"Three big mountains," 8, 826
"Three honests and four stricts" policy, 192, 193n, 486

INDEX   1137

"Three-in-one combination," 215
"Three talks" policy, 176, 193n
Tian An Men Incident, 89, 92
Tianjin, 905-912; administrative divisions of, 59; agriculture around, 907, 909, 912; commerce in, 906-907; construction in, 912; economic education in, 1055, 1059, 1060, 1064; economic experimentation in, 910; economic institutes in, 1048-1049, 1053; education in, 910-911, 912; environmental protection in, 767; foreign trade in, 388, 907, 909, 911-912; FTCs in, 1041; health service in, 911; history of, 905-906; industry in, 29-30, 906, 908, 909-910, 911; problems of, 908; readjustment in, 908-912; science in, 907-908; special corporations in, 385; standard of living in, 910; tourism in, 911; transportation in, 905; Tianjin No. 3 Plastic Plant, 462
Tibetan nationality, 23, 35, 913; population of, 34
Tibet Autonomous Region, 913-917, 1014; administrative divisions of, 70-71; agriculture in, 913, 914, 916; animal husbandry in, 913, 914; bank loans in, 1019; development of, 1014, 1015; economic education in, 1070; education in, 915; flora and fauna of, 913-914; handicrafts of, 914-915; history of, 913; industry in, 914, 916; minerals in, 913; national minorities in, 34, 913; population growth in, 916; problems in, 916-917; standard of living in, 915, 917; subsidy to, 915; transportation in, 915, 916; water resources in, 913, 916
Tidal power, 1014
Timber resources, 25-26, 146, 151, 167, 427-431; comprehensive use of, 431, 1006; production quotas of, 1980, 429; projected output of, 1981, 121; regulations on, 146-150; responsibility for, 430; substitutes for, 619. See also Forests, Forestry
Tobacco, 393
"To each according to his work" principle, 50-51, 80, 157, 163, 165, 190-191, 212, 277, 371, 381, 698, 701, 954
Tonghua Coal Mining Administration, liability of, 1015
Tools, high-precision, 516
Tour guides, 679, 681
Tourism, 677-682; in Beijing, 678, 679, 788; cities open to, 677-678, construction for, 561-562; domestic, 680-681; earnings from, 119, 677; education, 680; foreign exchange certificates and, 248; hotels for, 678; improvements in, 679-680; income from, 681;

itineraries for, 678-679, 680-681; Macao and, 942-943, 944; 1980 economic plan and, 994; overcrowding and, 682; by overseas Chinese, 677, 681; plans for, 1005; problems of, 681-682; promotion of, 680; publications for, 680; research on, 680; sales to, 679; in Shaanxi, 884; in Shanxi, 900; summary of, 1980, 677; in Tianjin, 911; in Zhejiang, 930
Towering operations, marine, 596
Towns, construction of, 172
Toxic chemicals, control of, 287
Toxic wastes, 286, 766; water pollution and, 769-770
Tractors, 167, 523, 524; modification of, 527-528; number of (1979), 524-525; output of, 1980, 527t; projected output of, 1981, 121; use of, 1980, 380
Trades: ancient, 6, 7; domestic, 1980 economic plan and, 993-994; and national minorities areas, 41; with West, 6-7. See also Foreign trade
Trade deficits, 623
Trade fairs, 622; electrical engineering, 1018; Guangzhou, 1042-1043
Trademarks, 188; registration and control of, 1005; standards for, 198
Trade missions, 622
Trade unions, 707-716, 1013; cadres in, 716; committee session of, 709-710; "cultural revolution" and, 709; education and, 714-715; emulation drives of, 710; Four Modernizations and, 771; history of, 707-710; international ties of, 716; joint ventures and, 259; labour protection and, 712-714, 1015; leisure activites and, 715; membership of, 716; model workers and, 711, 1010; organization of, 715-716; political work of, 1016-1017; role of, 178, 180, 347, 1006; women and, 713; workers' congresses and, 711-712; workers' well-being and, 713-714
Traffic volume: air, 600; average haulage, 576t; freight, 575t, 977t; passenger, 574t, 978t; turnover, 575t
Transformation, industrial, 214-217
Transformers, 1008, 1014
Translated Articles on Economics (periodical), 1084
Translations on World Economy (periodical), 1084-1085
Transplanters, 524-525
Transportation, 573-580; air, 29, 598-603, 977t; averge haulage on, 576t; changes in mode of, 576t; of commune-made products, 155-156; coordination of, 578; for imports and exports, 1036-1037; publications on, 1100; research on, 1047; development of, 185;

distribution of, 573-574; efficiency of, 577t, 578; facilities for, 574; freight, 575t, 576t; growth of, 573t; highway, 28, 171-172, 573-574, 590-591; of mail, 604; in national minorities areas, 41; 1980 economic plan and, 993; passenger, 574t, 575t, 576t, 580, 978t; problems in, 579-580; projected volume of, 1981, 121; rail, 28, 573, 574, 579, 582-589, 977t; readjustment in, 214-217, 580; turnover volume of, 575t; urban, 578-579; water, 28-29, 574, 977t
Transport and industrial enterprises, renovation of, 216
Travellers checks, customs declaration of, 255
Treasury bonds, 298
Trees: felling of, 150, 167-168, 286, 428, 430, 1001, 1022; new types of, 414-415, 429; ownership of, 146; planting of, 149, 167, 286, 428-429, 431, 849, 1010; principal species of, 427, 810. See also Forests, Forestry
Trends in Economic Studies (periodical), 1078-1079
Trial production, quality control and, 205-206
Trolleys, 578
Tropical crops, 401, 791, 793, 810; priorities in, 412
Trucks, sold to communes, 613
Trust trade, 1017
Tugboats, 597
Tujie nationality, 23; population of, 34
Tunnelling mechanization, coal, 498-499
Turnkey contracts, 1043
Turnover, freight, 575t; passenger, 575t
Turtles, protected, 143
Typography, invention of, 7

U

Undeveloped areas: construction subsidies to, 212; development funds for, 133, 224-225; income in, 394-395; industrial aid to, 184; joint ventures in, 228; planning for, 169
Unemployment, 880; economic diversification and, 386-387; loans and, 243-244; prevention of, 699; rural, 482, 485, 531
"Unequal treaties," 4
UNESCO, 749
Unification, national, 80, 638, 938
Union of Soviet Socialist Republics (USSR), 44; annulment of contracts by, 162, 625, 627; economic management system of, 298, 304, 307, 340-341, 350-351, 387-388, 627, 947; economy of, 309-310; heavy industry and, 304; loan from 627; technology from, 625

United Nations, 81; environmental protection and, 779; family planning and, 764
United States, 5, 44; Chiang Kai-shek and, 78; cooperation on hydroelectric power with, 1011; economic specialization in, 313; exports to, 478; honoured scientists from, 689; investment protection agreement with, 630; Korean War and, 82; Taiwan and, 936; tourists from, 677; trade agreement with, 1009
Universities: of agricultural economics, 1062-1063; construction for, 551; economic education in, 1058-1063; enrollment in, 1080, 383, 746; engineering with specialities in economics, 1060-1063
Upper Volta, agricultural aid to, 632
Urban planning, 1019
Useful life, of fixed assets, for taxation, 231
Users, quality control and, 208
Uygur nationality, population of, 34

V

Vaccination, 754
Value-added tax, 135, 652, 656
Vegetation: agricultural, 24-25; characteristics of, 18-19; distribution of, 18t; types of, 19
Vested interests, economic, protection of, 365
Videorecorders, 534
Vietnam, 1002
Vocational training: development of, 699, 747; enrollment in, 699, 747; task of, 699. See also Technical schools

W

Wages, 953-954, 963t; 964t; average, 448, 647, 700-702; in commune-run enterprises, 157-158; in construction enterprises, 212; control of, 293-298; increases in, 129, 295, 383, 444, 647, 700; from joint ventures, 257, 259, 701-702; piece rate system of, 277-278, 1011; policy on, 190-191; in Special Economic Zones, 264; on state farms, 415-416; taxable, 234, 236; total, 1979, 119-time rate system of, 700-701
Wa nationality, 35; population of, 34
Wang Bingqian, on budget, 128-138
Wang Haibo, 444-456
Wang Hongwen, 88, 89
Wan Li, 368, 369; in Tibet, 1014
Warehouses, 183, 610
War of Liberation, 77, 78, 105, 300
Warring States Period, 6; metallurgy in, 540; science in, 6
Waste, economic, 137, 141, 327; commune-run enterprises and, 159

Waterland: cultivation of, 166, 286, 1008; overdevelopment of, 400-401; reclamation of, 407-408
Waste materials, 188; commune-run enterprises and, 155; construction use of, 559, 771; handicrafts use of, 477; metallurgical industry and, 771; reuse of, 771-772; tax exemptions for use of, 216, 288, 775
Waste treatment, 187, 286, 472; for control of water pollution, 769-770; urban, 766-769
Waterchesnuts, integrated production of, 403
Water conservancy, 379-380, 410, 419-426, 1019; ancient, 6; aquatic resources and, 144; benefits of, 421; flood control and, 421-424; hydroelectric power and, 421, 425; investment in, 420-421, 424; laws on, 425, 774; local initiative in, 166; need for, 24, 286; planning for, 425-426; politics and, 422; publications on, 1098; readjustment and, 423-424; state of, 1980, 424-426; water transport and, 595; on Zhujiang River, 1021. See also Irrigation
Water Conservancy, Ministry of, 171, 1002; conference of, 1003
Water pollution, 769-770; aquatic resources and, 144; in Bohai Sea, 769; in Huanghai Sea, 769; laws on, 774; prevention of, 286, 287, 1006; in rivers, 770; in Songhua River, 769; urban, 767-769; in Ya'er Lake, 769-770
Water resources: aquatic products from, 26, 143-145; distribution of, 22-23, 419; engineering corporation for, 1044; fees for, 424; hydroelectric power and, 507; in national minority areas, 35; natural disasters and, 420, 422; per capita, 419; standards for, 1006; in Tibet, 913
Water transportation, 574, 592-597; areas of, 592; carge-handling in, 596; chartering of, 1037; development of, 592, 595; foreign trade and, 593-594; freight volume on, 593, 977t; harbours for, 594, 595; marine, 28-29, 593-594; passengers on, 978t; present state of, 593, 595; rescue and salvage operations and, 596-597; river, 29, 31, 592-593, 594-595
Water transport industry, 595-596; ship repair and, 595
Water volume, 16t
Waters territorial, 11, 12-13; inland, 24
Weedkillers, 166-167, 410
"Weed out the old to bring forth the new" principle, 717
Wei Dynasty, science in, 7

Weights and measures, control of, 1015
Wei Jing, 631-634
Wei Liqun, 379-391
Wei Zhi, 753-760
Welfare funds, 444, 703; joint ventures, 257, 259; workers', cost of, 202, 355, 361-362
Wells, 421, foreign construction of, 633
West Germany, investment protection agreement with, 630
Whaling, 779
Wheat, 468, 818; harvesting equipment for, 1007; production of, 24, 32
Whole plants: building materials, 1043; chemical, 1043; coal, 1043; electrical, 1043; export of, 1043-1044; imports of, 625, 1036; control of, 626; textile, 1044
Wildlife, protection of, 286, 430
Wildlife preserves, 430
Wind power, 1011
Wineries, 413
Withholding tax, 234, 237; agents for, 230-235, 237, 238, 654
Women: on communes, 375; in construction enterprises, 212; education of, 743; equality of, 56, 157; mobilization of, 1007; in science, 687; trade unions and, 713; work and, 191, 702
Wool, 438, 440, 469, 843-844; exports of, 470; need for, 443; production of, 466, 847
Wool-type chemical fibres, 469
Work; conditions of, 190-192; ideological principles of, 50-51; overtime, 358; rest from, 56; right to, 56; styles of, 192
Worker-peasant alliance, 184
Workers: categories of, 355-356; on commune-run enterprises, 157-158; construction, 212, 550; decision-making and, 335-336, 346-347, 351-352, 362-363; education of, 189-190, 209, 329, 342-343, 345, 389, 458, 464-465, 501, 536, 538, 698, 699-700, 750, 1014; in electric power industry, 506; in handicrafts, 473, 477; hosuing for, 119, 129, 191, 535; income of, 119, 322-323, 383; industrial management and, 178-179; in joint ventures, 256-257, 259-260; insurance benefits for, 702-703, 714; in light industry, 457; in metallurgical industry, 542; model, 711, 1005, 1010, 1013; number employed (1980), 380, 698; projected income of, 121; quality control and, 209; safety of, 122, 156, 158, 191, 213, 260, 264, 324, 703-705, 712-714; in Special Economic Zones, 264; standard of living of, 191, 319, 444, 700; welfare funds

INDEX   1139

of, 212, 259, 355, 361-362, 444, 702-703; well-being of, 191, 344, 355, 702-704, 713-714. *See also* Labour; Peasants; Working Class
Workers' congresses, 335-336, 334, 712; functions of, 712; increasing power of, 362-363; industrial, 444; number of (1980), 452, 712
Workers' Daily, 716, 731
Working class, 191; solidarity, 178
Workmen's compensation, 702
Work points: on communes, 165, 371, 372; output and, 369, 371; on state farms, 415-416
Work-study schools, 748
World Bank, 728, 669, 1011, 1013, 1019; appointments to, 1014-1015
World Economy (periodical), 1077
World War I, 905
World Wildlife Fund, 779
Wrist-watches, 294, 463; projected output of, 1981, 121
Wu Erer, 598-603
Wu Fan movement, 708
Wuhan, 830; industry in, 31-32
Wuhan Iron and Steel Company, 31, 342
Wu Jiajun

X

Xia Dynasty, 3; science in, 6
Xiamen Special Economic Zone, 1022
Xiang Qiyuan, 947-956
Xi'an Incident, 78
Xinhua Bookstores, 722
Xinhua News Agency, 729; improvement in, 730
Xinhua printing houses, 722
Xinjiang oil fields, 487
Xinjiang Uygur Autonomous Region, 32-33, 34, 918-922; administrative divisions of, 71; agriculture in, 918-919; air terminals in, 598; animal husbandry in, 919-920; commerce in, 929-921; construction in, 920; economic education in, 1058, 1063; economic institute in, 1050; education in, 918, 921; geography of, 918; industry in, 920; local products of, 920-921; readjustment in, 921-922; standard of living in, 921; state farms in, 919; subsidy to, 919; transportation in, 920; water conservancy in, 410
Xue Muqiao, 293-298

Y

Ya'er Lake, pollution control on, 769-770
Yangtze River. *See* Changjiang River
Yanjing Hotel (Beijing), 561, 678
Yan Qiushi, 516-518
Yao nationaltiy, 23; population of, 34
Yao Yilin, 116-127; on economic progress, 116-120; on implementation of economic plans, 1980, 1981, 122-127; on main targets, 1981, 120-122; report on national economic plan, 1980, 1981, 116-127
Ye Jianying: on China's future, 93; opening speech, Third Session, Fifth NPC of PRC (1980), 115, 1005; on trade unions, 709
Yellow grass, integrated production of, 403
Yellow River. *See* Huanghe River
Yellow Sea (Huanghai Sea), 12, 13, 123; oil exploration in, 324, 491; pollution control and, 769
Yi nationality, 23, 35; population of, 34
Youth; agriculture and, 170; unemployed, loans to, 243-244
Yuan Baohua, 1002, 1014; on tasks for 1980, 1009
Yuan Dynasty, science and technology in, 7
Yuanmou Man, 3
Yuan Shibang, 939-941
Yuexi Commune, No. 1 Production Brigade, 526
Yugoslavia, as economic model, 350-351, 362
Yu Guangzuan, 346-349
Yunlian coal field, 1008
Yunnan-Guizhou Plateau, 11, 32
Yunnan Province, 923-926; administrative divisions of, 68-69; agriculture in, 923; construction in, 924-925; economic education in, 1060, 1070; economic experimentation in, 924; economic institutes of, 1052; geography of, 923; industry in, 923, 924; local specialties of, 926; marketing in, 925, 926; national minorities in, 34, problems of, 925-926; science in, 924, 925; standard of living in, 924; subsidy for, 135; transportation in, 923, 925, 926
Yu Qiuli, 1018

Z

Zambia, foreign aid to, 633
Zhang Chunqiao, 88
Zhang Peiji, 621-624
Zhang Siqian, 392-406
Zhang Xinchuan, 540-548
Zhangzhou, industrial coordination in, 181
Zhao Renwei, 947-956
Zhao Songchiao, 11-21
Zhaozhu Bridge, 7
Zhao Ziyang, 57; election as Vice Chairman, Central Committee, 75
Zhejiang Province, 927-932; administrative divisions of, 67; agriculture in, 927, 928-929, 931; construction in, 929-930; economic education in, 1057, 1059, 1061, 1062, 1066; employment in, 930; finances of, 930; history of, 927; human services in, 930; industry in, 928, 929, 931; population of, 927, 930; problems in, 931-932; readjustment in, 928-932; standard of living in, 930-931; tourism in, 930; transportation in, 927, 928, 931
Zheng Xingjie, 438-443
Zhen Yanchu, 857-860
Zhongdan hybrid rice, 685-686
Zhong He, 822-825, 927-932
Zhongqing Clock and Watch Industrial Company, 360-361
Zhongshan Hot Springs Tourist Centre, 561-562, 679
Zhou Dynasty, 3; science in, 6; Western, 3, 6
Zhou Enlai, 77, 85, 631; agriculture and, 162; on aviation, 599; on books, 723; "cultural revolution" and, 88, 89; death of, 89; employment and, 297; on family planning, 761; on intellectuals, 84; on petroleum, 486
Zhou Yueli, 368-376
Zhuang nationality, 23, 34, 35, 807; population of, 34
Zhu De, 77; on agriculture and handicrafts, 84
Zhuhai, Special Economic Zone in, 263, 804
Zhujiang River: comprehensive control of, 1021, floods on, 420; navigation on, 29; pollution control on, 770
Zhu Jiazhen, 3-10
Zip codes, 606, 1016
Zong Jianwen, 554-559

ALMANAC OF CHINA'S ECONOMY
1982
With Comprehensive Economic Survey and Statistics for 1981
SELECTED CONTENTS

Introductory Documents

1. Invitation to Members of the State Planning Commission for Discussion on Strengthening Economic Planning by Comrade Chen Yun.
2. Report on the Draft Plan for Economic and Social Development in 1982, Delivered at the 23rd Session of the Standing Committee of the Fifth National People's Congress (April 28, 1982)
   By Yao Yilin, Vice Premier, State Council; Chairman, State Planning Commission
3. Report on the Draft State Budget for 1982, Delivered at the 23rd Session of the Standing Committee of the Fifth National People's Congress (April 29, 1982).
   By Wang Bingqian, Minister of Finance
4. Resolution by the Standing Committee of the Fifth National People's Congress on Implementing the Plan for Reform of Organs of the State Council (Passed at the 23rd Session of the Standing Committee of the Fifth National People's Congress, May 4, 1982)

Section I: General Survey of China

1. Distribution of China's Minority Nationalities
2. China's Mineral Resources
3. China's Agro-Economic Geography
4. Administrative Divisions of Provinces, Autonomous Regions, Municipalities and Counties of the People's Republic of China (1982)

Section II: Economic Documents, Policies, Laws and Decrees

Major Reports

1. The Present Economic System and the Direction of Future Economic Construction
   By Zhao Ziyang
2. Report on Reform of Organs of the State Council
   by Zhao Ziyang
3. On Certain Questions Concerning Our Current Economic Work
   By Zhao Ziyang
4. Report on the Readjustment of Economic Planning in 1981 and National Revenues and Expenditures
   By Yao Yilin
5. Report on the Final State Accounts for 1980 and the Estimated Budget for 1981
   By Wang Bingqian

Agriculture

6. On Certain Questions Regarding the Strengthening and Perfecting of the Agricultural Responsibility System
7. Decisions by the Central Committee and State Council on the Question of Protecting Forests and Developing Forestry
8. Notification by the Central Committee and State Council of the Promulgation of the State Agricultural Commission's "Report on Actively Promoting a Diversified Economy in the Countryside"
9. The State Agricultural Commission's "Report on Activity Promoting a Diversified Economy in the Countryside"
10. State Council Regulations on the Implementation of Economic Readjustment by Commune- and Brigade-run Enterprises

Industry

11. State Council Regulations on Strengthening Planning and Controlling the Scale of Capital Construction
12. Supplementary Regulations on Implementing "Regulations of the People's Republic of China on Giving Awards for Top-Quality Products"
13. Regulations of the National Commission of Machinery Industry on Improving Standardization
14. Notification by the Central Committee and State Council of the Promulgation of "Provisional Regulations on Trade Union Congresses in State-Owned Industrial Enterprises"
15. Provisional Regulations on Trade Union

Congresses in State-Owned Industrial Enterprises
16. The State Economic Commission's Views on Improving the Leadership's Grasp of Consolidation of Enterprises
17. Views of the State Economic Commission and the Reform Committee of the State Council on Implementing the Economic Responsibility System in Industrial Production
18. Provisional Regulations on Implementing the Responsibility System in Industrial Production
19. Methods of Carrying Out Standardization in Industrial Enterprises (*For Trial Implementation*)
20. Local Contracts in the People's Republic of China
21. Regulations on the Practice of the Economic Responsibility System by Construction Enterprises
22. Provisional Regulations on the Work of Directors of State-Owned Factories
23. Financial Taxation
24. Notification by the Ministry of Finance on Individual Taxation of Foreign Workers in China
25. Decisions by the State Council on Balancing Financial Income and Rigidly Enforcing Financial Management
26. Provisional Regulations of the Ministry of Finance on Reducing Management Expenses in State-Owned Enterprises
27. Regulations by the State Council on Readjusting the Industrial and Commercial Tax Burden on Commune- and Brigade-Run Enterprises
28. Banking Regulations
29. State Council Decisions on Strengthening Credit Management and Controlling Loans
30. Report by the People's Bank of China on Readjusting Interest Rates on Deposits and Loans
31. Regulations on Workers' Wages
32. Decisions by the Central Committee and State Council on Improving the Education of Staff and Workers
33. Decisions by the Party Central Committee and State Council on Enlivening the Economy and Solving the Urban Unemployment Problem
34. Regulations on Energy Resources
35. State Council Directive on Economizing on Electricity
36. State Council Directive on Economizing on Oil
37. Industrial and Commercial Management Regulations
38. State Council (Policy) Regulations on Non-Agricultural Individual Economy in Urban Areas
39. Regulations on Special Economic Zones
40. Provisional Regulations on Registration of Enterprises in the Special Economic Zones of Guangdong Province
41. Provisional Regulations on Land Management in the Shenzhen Special Economic Zone
42. Regulations on Environmental Protection

Section III: Monographic Studies

1. Complete the Task of Readjustment and Strive for a Basic Improvement in the National Economy
2. Heavy Industry Must Advance Amidst Readjustment
3. Stressing the Development of the Consumer Goods Industry Is an Important Component of China's Economic Construction
4. China's Communications and Transport: The Present Situation and Prospects for Future Development
5. Focussing on Methods of Creating, Collecting and Using Funds and Accelerating the Socialist Four Modernizations
6. The Scientific and Technological Reform of Existing Enterprises Is of Strategic Importance in China's Economic Development
7. Resolutely Carry Out the Reform of the Economic System

Section IV: Survey of China's Economy

1. China's Economy in 1981

Agriculture, Forestry and Fishing

2. China's Agriculture in 1981
3. China's Grain Cultivation
4. China's Industrial Crop Cultivation
5. Sideline Occupations of Commune Members in China's Countryside
6. China's Land Reclamation in 1981
7. The New Look of Xinjiang's Reclaimed Areas
8. China's Forestry in 1981
9. China's Fishing in 1981
10. How the Dalian Sea-Fishing Company Improved Its Economic Results

11. China's Animal Husbandry in 1981
12. China's Meteorology

Industry

13. China's Industry in 1981

Light Industry

14. China's Light Industry in 1981
15. China's Paper Industry
16. China's Sewing Machine Industry
17. China's Bicycle Industry
18. China's Clock Industry
19. China's Wine Industry
20. China's Confectionery Industry
21. China's Tobacco Industry
22. China's Salt Industry
23. China's Handicrafts Industry
24. China's Leather Industry
25. China's Garments Industry
26. China's Cosmetics Industry
27. Shanghai's Household Chemical Products Industry
28. China's Textile Industry
29. China's Commune- and Brigade-Run Industries

Energy and Power

30. Survey of China's Energy Resources Industry
31. China's Petroleum Industry
32. China's Coal Mining Industry
33. China's Electric Power Industry

Heavy Industry

34. China's Machinery Industry
35. China's Heavy Machinery Industry
36. China's Instrument and Meter Industry
37. China's Electrical Machinery Industry
38. China's Automobile Industry
39. China's Bearings Industry
40. China's Machine Tool Industry
41. China's Tool Industry
42. China's Shipbuilding Industry
43. China's Agricultural Machinery Industry and New Developments in Agricultural Mechanization
44. China's Electronics Industry in 1981
45. China's Electronics Calculator Industry
46. China's Broadcasting Industry
47. China's Aviation Industry
48. China's Chemical Industry in 1981
49. China's Iron and Steel Industry in 1981
50. China's Non-Ferrous Metals Industry
51. China's Building Materials Industry in 1981
52. China's Cement Industry
53. China's Plate-Glass Industry
54. China's Construction Engineering in 1981
55. China's Urban Construction
56. China's Pharmaceuticals Industry
57. China's Production of Traditional Medicine

Transport and Communications

58. China's Communications and Transport in 1981
59. China's Railway Transportation
60. China's Newly Constructed Railways
61. China's Highway Traffic
62. China's Water Transport
63. China's Ocean Shipping
64. China's Civil Aviation
65. China's Posts and Telecommunication in 1981

Domestic Commerce

66. Distribution of Commodities in 1981
67. State-Owned Commerce in 1981
68. China's Large State-Owned Department Stores
69. Grain Distribution and Management in China
70. China's Supply and Marketing Cooperatives
71. Trade at China's Country Fairs

Foreign Trade

72. China's Foreign Trade in 1981
73. Reform of China's Foreign Trade System
74. China's Importation of Technology
75. China's Customs

Construction

76. China's Capital Construction in 1981
77. Construction of Rural Houses in China
78. China's Project Planning
79. Construction in China's Small Towns
80. China's Water Conservancy Projects in 1981
81. Environmental Protection in China in 1981

Banking and Finance

82. China's Finance in 1981
83. China's Taxation in 1981
84. China's Banking in 1981
85. China's Rural Banking in 1981

86. The Development of Insurance in China
87. The Active Role of China's Banking in the Four Modernizations
88. Work of the People's Construction Bank
89. China's Tourism in 1981

Science and Technology, Education, Culture

90. Science and Technology in China in 1981
91. Work in China's Scientific Institutes in 1981
92. Standardization in China in 1981
93. Measurement in China

Labour

94. Labour Employment and Management in China's Urban Areas in 1981
95. Labour Protection in China in 1981
96. Wages, Labour Insurance and Welfare for China's Staff and Workers in 1981
97. Work of China's Trade Unions in 1981
98. China's Economic Legislation

Section V: Survey of Economic Development in China's Counties, Municipalities and Autonomous Regions

1. Survey of Beijing's Economy
2. Survey of Tianjin's Economy
3. Survey of the Economy of Hebei Province
4. Survey of the Economy of Shanxi Province
5. Survey of the Economy of Inner Mongolia Autonomous Region
6. Survey of the Economy of Liaoning Province
7. Survey of the Economy of Jilin Province
8. Survey of the Economy of Heilongjiang Province
9. Survey of Shanghai's Economy
10. Survey of the Economy of Jiangsu Province
11. Survey of the Economy of Zhejiang Province
12. Survey of the Economy of Anhui Province
13. Survey of the Economy of Fujian Province
14. Survey of the Economy of Jiangxi Province
15. Survey of the Economy of Shandong Province
16. Survey of the Economy of Henan Province
17. Survey of the Economy of Hubei Province
18. Survey of the Economy of Hunan Province
19. Survey of the Economy of Guangdong Province
20. Survey of the Economy of Guangxi Zhuang Autonomous Region
21. Survey of the Economy of Sichuan Province
22. Survey of the Economy of Guizhou Province
23. Survey of the Economy of Yunnan Province
24. Survey of the Economy of Shaanxi Province
25. Survey of the Economy of Gansu Province
26. Survey of the Economy of Ningxia Hui Autonomous Region.
27. Survey of the Economy of Xinjiang Uygur Autonomous Region

Addenda:

A. Economic Survey of Taiwan Province
B. Economic Survey of Hong Kong
C. Economic Survey of Macao

Section VI: Research in Economic Theory

The Past Year's Progress and Future Trends in China's Research in Economic Theory

Section VII: Economic Statistical Data

1. Selected Economic Statistical Data
2. National Economic Statistics Over the Years
3. Report by the State Statistical Bureau of the People's Republic of China on the Results of National Economic Planning in 1981
4. Selected Statistical Data on the World Economy

Section VIII: Chronology of Major Economic Events

Section IX: Appendix

1. The Four Research Centres of the State Council
2. Listing of China's Major Economic Research Institutes
3. China's Major Economic Periodicals
4. China's Economics Societies
5. Listing of China's Colleges and Universities Specializing in Finance and Economics and Other Institutions with Departments and Specializations in Finance, Economics and Management

CONTENTS OF 1982 ALMANAC

6. China's Publications in Economics in 1981
7. New Industrial Products
8. China's Top-Quality Industrial and Handicrafts Prooducts in 1981
9. China's Arts and Handicrafts
10. China's Traditional Arts and Crafts
11. China's Foreign Trade Corporations and Their Organization
12. Exchange-Rate Table for *Renminbi* and Other Currencies in 1981

BANK OF CHINA

A Bank of the People's Republic of China Specializing in International Banking

We offer a full range of international banking services:
- Settlement of international trade and non-trade transactions.
- International inter-bank deposits and loans.
- Foreign currency deposits and loans.
- Renminbi import and export credits.
- Buying and selling of foreign exchange.
- International remittances.
- Issuance of foreign currency bonds and other securities.
- Traveller's cheques.
- Trust and consultancy services.
- Our overseas branches offer local banking services.

Branch offices in China's major cities and ports.

Overseas branches in London, Singapore, Hongkong, New York and Luxembourg. Representative Offices in Paris and Tokyo.

Correspondent banks in more than 146 countries and regions.

Head office address: Xijiao Minxiang 17, Beijing, China.   Telephone: 33.8521
Cable address: HOCHUNGKUO or CHUNGKUO, Beijing
Telex: 22254 22289 22321 BCHO CN

Dresdner Bank – One of the leading banks in the world.
Dresdner Bank AG · Head Office: 1 Jürgen-Ponto-Platz, 6 Frankfurt/Main, Federal Republic of Germany.
Representative Office for the People's Republic of China
Dr. Erich Brogl, Manager and Representative
Beijing Office: Suite 3101-3, Beijing Exhibition Hall Hotel, Xi Wai Da Jie, Beijing, V.R. China, Tel. 89 60 80, Telex 22627 Dreba CN.
Hong Kong Office: World Wide House, 19 Des Voeux Road C., G.P.O. Box 9910, Hong Kong.

SHANGHAI FOREIGN TRADE CORPORATION

Address; 27 Chung Shan Road, (E.1) Shanghai, China
Cable: "SHANTRA" Shanghai   Telex: 33034 SIMEX CN

This Corporation is pleased to develop business with economic and Trade circles in the world. For particular business, please contact the following Corporations:

IMPORT & TRUST BUSINESS HANDLED BY THE FOLLOWING DEPARTMENTS:

Shanghai Foreign Trade Corporation, Import Department.

Shanghai Foreign Trade Corporation, Trust Department.

**EXPORT
HANDLED BY THE FOLLOWING BRANCHES OF THE CHINA NATIONAL IMPORT & EXPORT CORPORATIONS:**

China National Cereals, Oils & Foodstuffs Import & Export Corporation, Shanghai Cereals & Oils Branch

China National Cereals, Oils & Foodstuffs Import & Export Corporation, Shanghai Foodstuffs Branch

China National Native Produce & Animal By-Products Import & Export Corporation, Shanghai Animal By-Proucts Branch

China National Native Produce & Animal By-Products Import & Export Corporation, Shanghai Native Produce Branch

China National Native Produce & Animal By-Products Import & Export Corporation, Shanghai Tea Branch

China National Textiles Import & Export Corporation, Shanghai Branch

China National Textiles Import & Export Corporation, Shanghai Silk Branch

China National Textiles Import & Export Corporation, Shanghai Garments Branch

China National Light Industrial Products Import & Export Corporation, Shanghai Branch

China National Arts & Crafts Import & Export Corporation, Shanghai Branch

China National Chemicals Import & Export Corporation, Shanghai Branch

China National Machinery Import & Export Corporation, Shanghai Branch

China National Machinery & Equipment Export Corporation, Shanghai Branch

China National Metals & Minerals Import & Export Corporation, Shanghai Branch

Shanghai Toys Import & Export Corporation

China Jinshan Associated Trading Corporation

China National Packaging Import & Export Corporation, Shanghai Branch

**OTHERS
HANDLED BY THE FOLLOWING CORPORATIONS:**

China Export Bases Development Corporation, Shanghai Branch

China National Foreign Trade Transportation Corporation, Shanghai Branch

China National Chartering Corporation, Shanghai Sub-Branch

China National Foreign Trade Storage Corporation, Shanghai Branch

Shanghai Advertising Corporation

HEILONGJIANG FUR PRODUCTS

- SUPERB WORKMANSHIP
- FASHIONABLE DESIGNS
- TOP QUALITY
- ORDERS ACCORDING TO BUYERS' SAMPLES AND DESIGNS ARE WELCOME

China National Native Produce & Animal By-Products Import & Export Corporation

HEILONGJIANG BRANCH

55, Heping Road, Harbin, China.
Cable: "HNAIEC" Harbin

HEILONGJIANG FLAX

HEILONGJIANG PROVINCE IS THE CHIEF FLAX GROWING AREA IN CHINA AND HAS A LONG HISTORY OF FLAX PLANTING. WITH REFINED PROCESSING AND ADVANCED PACKING TECHNIQUES, THE PRODUCTS ARE OF SUPERIOR QUALITY AND ALL SPECIFICATIONS ARE AVAILABLE. FLAX EXPORTED FROM HEILONGJIANG IS RETTED EITHER IN LUKE-WARM WATER OR IN RAIN AND DEW. BOTH ARE SOFT IN TEXTURE, HIGH IN BREAKING STRENGTH, TENSILE, OF UNIFORM CONSISTENCY AND EXCELLENT FOR SPINNING AND WEAVING.
HEILONGJIANG EXPORTED FLAX FLUFF IS OF SUPERIOR QUALITY, IDEAL FOR MAKING HIGH-QUALITY PAPER.
STOCKS OF FLAX AND FLAX FLUFF ARE NOW AVAILABLE. ORDERS ARE WELCOME.

China National Native Produce & Animal By-Products Import & Export Corporation
HEILONGJIANG BRANCH
55, Heping Road, Harbin, China.
Cable: "HNAIEC", Harbin

BEIJING FOREIGN TRADE CORP

Address: 190 Chaoyangmennei Street, Beijing, China Tel.: 55.4871

Beijing Foreign Trade Corporation is pleased to establish and develop business relations with trade circles and manufacturers from all parts of the world. For particular import/export business and specific projects, please contact the following branches:

China National Textiles Import and Export Corporation, Beijing Branch
Cotton fabrics; garments; knitwear; woollen blankets, etc.
Tel.: 89.3203 Cable: PEKITEX Beijing Telex: 22148 PKTEX CN

China National Light Industrial Products Import and Export Corporation, Beijing Branch
Stationeries; sports goods; musical instruments; general merchandise; leather shoes and leather products; building materials; photographic equipment; electrical materials.
Address: 76 West Changan Ave., Beijing, China
Tel.: 33.5906 Cable: INDUSPK Beijing Telex: 22142 LITPK CN

China National Arts and Crafts Import and Export Corporation, Beijing Branch
Drawn work and embroidered articles; ivory, jade and semiprecious stone carvings; lacquer and cloisonne wares; furniture; antiques and imitations; painting and calligraphy; artistic handicrafts and other handicrafts for daily use.
Address; Bldg. No. 16 Yongandongli, Jianguomenwai, Beijing, China
Cable Address: "PEKARTCO" BEIJING Telex: 22334 BJART CN

China National Arts and Crafts Import and Export Corporation, Beijing Jewellery Branch
Gold and silver jewellery; pearl and gem; diamond jewellery; enamel wares; petit-point articles.
Address: 22 Fuwai Street, Beijing, China
Tel.: 89.1315 Cable: PEKJEWECO Beijing Telex: 22188 PEKJW CN

China National Native Produce and Animal By-products Import and Export Corporation, Beijing Branch
Fur coats; hides; leather; feathers and feather products; native produce; patent drugs and medicinal herbs.
Address: 52 Xijiaominxiang, Beijing, China
Tel.: 33.4998 Cable: TUHSUBRAN Beijing Telex: 22317 TSPB CN

China National Cereals, Oils and Foodstuffs Import and Export Corporation, Beijing Branch
Canned goods; confectionery; liquors and wines; frozen meat; preserved and dried fruits; fresh fruits; vegetables.
Address: 22 Fuwai Street, Beijing, China
Tel.: 89.3258 Cable: CIFCPB Beijing Telex: 22472 PFOOD CN

China National Metals and Minerals Import and Export Corporation, Beijing Branch
Metal products and semi-products; metal ores; marble; tarrazzo etc.
Address: 190 Chaoyangmennei Street, Beijing, China
Tel.: 55.1454 Cable: MINMET Beijing Telex: 22470 BFTCC-D CN

China National Chemicals Import and Export Corporation, Beijing Branch
Chemicals; plastic raw materials; petrochemical products; chemical reagents; pharmaceuticals; medical instrucments and supplies.
Address: 190 Chaoyangmennei Street, Beijing, China
Tel.: 55.1316 Cable: SINOCHEMIP Beijing Telex: 22470 BFTCC-A CN

China National Machinery Import and Export Corporation, Beijing Branch
Tools; agricultural machinery; equipment; meters; watches; electronic equipment and materials; measuring devices; mechanical processing equipment.
Address: 190 Chaoyangmennei Street, Beijing, China
Tel.: 55.3504 Cable; MACHBRANCH Beijing Telex: 22470 BFTCC-B CN

北京市對外貿易總公司

Telex: 22470 BFTCC CN Cable: JINGTRA Beijing

China National Machinery and Equipment Import and Export Corporation, Beijing Branch
Machine tools; lathes; vehicles and accessories; electric meters and watches.
Address: A1, Xi Hai Dong Yan, De Sheng Men Nei Street, Beijing, China
Cable Add.: "EQUIBRANCH" BEIJING   Telex: 22470 BFTCC CN

China National Packaging Import and Export Corporation, Beijing Branch
Packaging materials, containers and machinery.
Address: 190 Chaoyangmennei Street, Beijing, China
Tel.: 55.6727 Cable: PACKBRANCH Beijing Telex: 22470 BFTCC-C CN

Beijing Advertising Corporation
Local advertising for foreign products and overseas advertising for China's export commodities.
Address: 190 Chaoyangmennei Street, Beijing, China
Tel.: 55.3326 Cable: ADVERCORP Beijing Telex: 22470 BFTCC-C CN

China National Arts & Crafts Import & Export Corp. Beijing Embroidery Branch.
Available for export now: Table-cloth, Pillow cases, Bedsheet sets, Aprons. Toast covers. Guests towels. Breakfast sets, etc.
Add.: 30 Shatan Houjie, Beijing China. Cable: PEKEMB TELEX: 22495 BJEMB
Tel.: 44.1121

China National Native Produce and Animal By-Products I/E Corporation, Beijing Carpets Branch
Chinese Super Woollen Carpets, Hand-made. Peking PM90 & P90 Carpets Hand-made.
Peking Antique Finished Carpets, Peking PNB & Blossom Carpets, etc.
Add.: 52 Xijiaominxiang, Beijing China. Tel.: 33.6628 Cable: CARPETBRAN BEIJING
Telex: 22317 TSPE CN

Joint Ventures

China Resource Products (U.S.A) Ltd.
1133 Ave. of The Americas, New York, N.Y. 10036
Tel.: (212) 398-1748 Cable: PROCREPCO Telex: 5200029

Peking Macau Co., Ltd.
101-103, RUA DA PRAIA GRANDE 2 Fl. Macau
Tel: 89888 89355 Cable Add.: "PMCO" MACAU Telex: OM-349-PMCO.

Beijing Seibu Co., Ltd.
SUNSHINE 60 BLDG 1-1, 3-chome, Higashi-Ikebukuro
Toshima-ku, Tokyo, 170 JAPAN

Kuwait Beijing Trade Centre
Tel.: 616411 616413 Tex.: 22151 LUNA
P.O.Box 2954 Safat KUWAIT

We wish to take this opportunity to express our sincere appreciation to the trade circles as well as manufacturers, at home and abroad, for their friendly cooperation extended to the various Beijing branches over the past years.

Mount Elephant

BRAND

MUSHROOMS

- Superior Quality
- Uniform Size
- Brilliant Texture
- Available in various specifications

GREEN BEANS

- Springless and tender
- Delicious and Nutritious
- Available in all sizes
- Amazingly Affordable

CHINA NATIONAL CEREALS, OILS & FOODSTUFFS IMPORT & EXPORT CORPORATION GUANGXI BRANCH

ADDRESS : HONG XING LU WEI, NANNING
CABLE   : CEROILFOOD NANNING
TEL   : NANNING 3629
TELEX   : 48102 FOODS CN

徵求

中國經濟年鑑

日、德、法、西、阿拉伯文版 的出版發行

中　文　版 世界各地的廣告代理

（廣告在中文國內版及中文海外版同時刊登）

中文海外版 世界各地發行代理

（中文國內版與中文海外版的內容全部相同
而中文國內版不向港澳及海外發行）

洽談處：中國經濟年鑑有限公司
香港銅鑼灣新寧道2-4號三樓
電話：5-8910493
電傳：71942 MCTDP HX
電報掛號：4718

INVITATION

ALMANAC OF CHINA'S ECONOMY

invites application for:

a) Publisher of the Japanese, French, Spanish and Arabic Edition;
b) Worldwide Advertising Agent for the Chinese Edition;
c) Worldwide Distribution of the Chinese Edition other than in China, Hong Kong and Macau.

Interesting parties please write to Economic Management Monthly,
Institute of Industrial Economics,
Almanac of China's Economy Co. Ltd.
3/F., 2-4 Sunning Road, Causeway Bay, Hong Kong.
Tel: 5-8910493
Telex: 71942 MCTDP HX
Cable: 4718

Can you afford

- Abundant natural resources
- Extensive trading experience
- Competitive prices

A golden opportunity

LIAONING TRADE FO

135 Stalin Road, Dalian, China   Telephone: 23041

Import

Handled by the Import Department of Liaoning Foreign Trade Corporation, including:

1. All import business for domestic enterprises.

2. Agency and distribution for foreign manufacturers and enterprises.

3. Consignment business and exhibition sales, repair and maintenance services on behalf of enterprises and manufacturers of various countries.

Export

Handled by the following branches of the China National Import & Export Corporations:

China National Cereals, Oils and Foodstuffs Import & Export Corporation, Liaoning Cereals & Oils Branch.
145 Stalin Road, Dalian, China. Tel: 27289
Cable: DALCEROIL DALIAN
TELEX: 86159 DACOF CN
   Cereals, Edible Vegetable Oils and Vegetable Oils for industrial use, Oil Seeds, Seeds, Oil Cakes and other Feed Stuffs, etc.

China National Cereals, Oils and Foodstuffs Import & Export Corporation, Liaoning Foodstuffs Branch.
145 Stalin Raod, Dalian, China. Tel: 27940
Cable: DALFOOD DALIAN
TELEX: 86159 DACOF CN
   Salt, Livestock and Meat, Animal Fats, Eggs, Fresh Fruits, and Fruits Products, Fresh and Dried Vegetables, Salted and Preserved Vegetables, Aquatic and Marine Products, Canned Goods, Sugar and Sweets, Wines and Spirits, Beverages, Dairy Products, Condiments, etc.

China National Native Produce and Animal By-products Import & Export Corporation, Liaoning Native Produce Branch.
139 Stalin Road, Dalian, China.
Cable: PRODAIREN DALIAN
TELEX: 86155 PRO CN
   Black Melon Seeds, Pumpkin Seeds, Bee Honey, Dried Chillies, Bitter Apricot Kernels, Pinenut Kernels, Hazelnut Kernels, Wild Vegetables, Ginseng, Deer's Antler, Tobacco, "ANCIENT PORCELAIN" and "GOLDEN FLOWERS" Brand Cigarettes, Gummy Bags, Polypropylene Woven Bags, Feed Stuffs, Gelatine, Bone Glue, Hide Glue, Beeswax, "GOLDEN PINE" Brand Candles, etc.

China National Native Produce and Animal

to miss Liaoning?

- Comprehensive product lines
- Excellent port facilities
- Superior quality

for all foreign traders!

REIGN CORPORATION

TELEX: 86151 LFTC CN   Cable: LIAOTRA DALIAN

By-products Import & Export Corporation, Liaoning Animal By-products Branch.
139 Stalin Road, Dalian, China.
Cable: BYPRODUCTS DALIAN
TELEX: 86155 PRO CN

"PEACOCK FEATHER" Brand Fur Products and Leather Products, Various Kinds of Fur Plates, "GREAT WALL" Brand Carpets and Tapestries, Northeast China Bristles, "FLYING HORSE" Brand Horse Tail Hairs, Mixed Animal Hairs, Casings, "POLAR BEAR" Brand Brushes, Feed and Fertilizer, Woollen Felt, etc.

China National Textiles Import & Export Corporation, Liaoning Branch.
139, Stalin Road, Dalian, China.
Cable: GARMENTS DALIAN
TELEX: 86154 LDTEX CN

Cotton Fabrics, Polyester/Cotton Yarn & Fabrics, Woollen Piece Goods, Tussah Silk, Tussah Silk Pongee, Knitted Goods, Cotton Manufactured Goods, Blankets, Sewing Threads, Spun Rayon Yarn, etc.

China National Textiles Import & Export Corporation, Liaoning Garments Branch.
139 Stalin Road, Dalian, China.
Cable: GARMENTS DALIAN
TELEX: 86154 LDTEX CN

Clothing and Caps made of different materials such as woollen fabrics, cotton fabrics as well as blended fabrics.

China National Chemicals Import & Export Corporation, Liaoning Petroleum Branch.
139 Stalin Road, Dalian, China.   Tel: 27379
Cable: SINOCHEMIR DALIAN
TELEX: 86152 CHEMD CN

Various Lubricant Oils, Lubricant Grease, Lubricant Base Oil, Naphtha Decant Oil, Oil for Coating Agricultural Pharmaceutical Oil, Aromatics Petroleum by Products, Solvent and Paraffin Wax, Floor Wax, Petroleum Coke, etc.

China National Chemicals Import & Export Corporation, Liaoning Chemicals and Pharmaceuticals Branch.
139 Stalin Road, Dalian, China.   Tel: 24689 26717
Cable: SINOCHEMIR DALIAN
TELEX: 86152 CHEMD CN

Various Organic & Inorganic Chemicals, Agricultural Chemicals & Insecticides, Dyestuffs, Rubber & Plastic Products, Various Pharmaceuticals, Pharmaceutical Preparations, Medical Instruments, Chemicals of Feed Grade, Medicines for Poultry & Livestock Use, etc.

China National Light Industrial Products Import & Export Corporation, Liaoning Branch.
110 Stalin Road, Dalian, China.
Cable: INDUSTRY DALIAN
TELEX: 86156 YASHU CN

Glasswares, Enamel Wares, Aluminium Wares, Vacuum Flasks, Sewing Machines & Parts, Bicycles

& Parts, Bicycle Tyres & Tubes, Shoes, Leather Products, Canvas & Imitation Leather Products, Clocks & Watches, Detergent Powder, Plastic Products, Paper & Boards, Stationery, Musical Instruments, Sporting Goods, Building Materials, Electric Appliances, etc.

China National Arts and Crafts Import & Export Corporation, Liaoning Branch.

2 Hong Yan Street, Dalian, China.
Cable: ARTS DALIAN
TELEX: 86160 DAC CN

Jade Carvings, Stone Carvings, Wood Carvings, different kinds of Pictures and Artifical Flowers, Porcelainware, Drawnworks, Embroidery Products, Furnitures, Willow Articles, Grass Articles, etc.

China National Metals and Minerals Import & Export Corporation, Liaoning Minerals Branch

145 Stalin Road, Dalian. Chian. Tel: 23981
Cable: MINMETALS DALIAN
TELEX: 86153 MIMET CN

Talc Lump & Talc Powder, Agate Ball, Agate Mortar and Pestle, Bentonite, Dead Burned Magnesite, Calcined Magnesite, Crystalline Flake Graphite, Marble, Terrazzo, Granite Block, Stone Carving, etc.

China National Metals and Minerals Import & Export Corporation, Liaoning Metals Branch.

145 Stalin Road, Dalian, China. Tel: 23981
Cable: MINMETALS DALIAN
TELEX: 86153 MIMET CN

Foot Controlled Door Holders, Spring Tower Bolts, Flat Iron Washers, Window Grilles, Chain Link Fence, Link Chain, Flanges, Cast Iron Products, Wire Rope Fittings, Brass Gate Valves, Door Locks, Hinges, Nuts and Bolts, Wire Netting, Door Pulls, Wire Rope, etc.

China National Machinery Import & Export Corporation, Liaoning Branch.

145 Stalin Road, Dalian, China.
Cable: MACHIMPEX DALIAN
TELEX: 86157 DCMC CN

Rubber Machinery, Building Machinery, Textile Machinery, Hand Tools, Agricultural Implements, Electronic Components & Parts, Graphite Electrodes, Instruments, etc.

China National Machinery and Equipment Import & Export Corporation, Liaoning Branch.

145 Stalin Road, Dalian, China.
Cable: EQUIMPEX DALIAN
TELEX: 86158 CMEDB CN

Metallurgical Equipment, Cranes, Electric & Manual Chain Blocks, Jacks, Belt Conveyors, Coal Unloaders, Coal Casting Machines, Scraping Blade Conveyors. Dampers, Electric Flat Carriages. Bulldozers, Material Pile-up and Pick-off Machines. Mining Cars. Pneumatic Tools, Machine Tools, Water Conservancy Control Facilities, Rubber Processing Machinery, Refrigerating Equipment, Valves, Cooling & Heating Blowers, Air Compressors, Filtering Press, Water-electrolytic Hydrogen Making Equipment, Plastics Processing Machines, Gas Steel Cylinders, Pumps, Gas Compressors, Wood Working Machinery, Gauges & Cutters, Griding Tools, Abrasives, Artificial Diamonds, Attachment for Machine Tools, Electric Equipment for Machine Tools, Bench Drills, Fasteners, Universal Auto Parts, Bearings, A C Motors, DC Motors, Miniature Motors, Transformers, Induction Voltage Regulators & Phaseshifters, Low & High Tension Electric Equipment, Electric Wires, Cables, Bare Copper Wir, Bore Aluminium Wire, Steel Core Aluminium Strand Wire, Enamel Wire, Electric Wire (Cotton Covered), Electric Welding Machines, Welding Electrodes, Electric Wires, Low and High Tension Porcelain insulators, Storage Batteries, Electro-carbon Products, Insulating Materials, Electric Locomotives for Mines, Storage Battery Cars, Electric Engineering Instruments & Meters, Optical Instruments, Flaw Detectors, Material Testing Machines, Cinematographic Machinery & Supplies, Cameras & Supplies, Packaged Air Conditioners, Diesel Engines and Generating Sets, Agricultural Machinery, Building Machinery, Ice Making Plant, Complete Refrigerating Plant for Cold Storage Room, Combined Cold Storage Room, Complete Rolling Equipment, Air Separation Plant, Complete Plant for Galvanize Steel Sheet, Complete Equipment for Dinner Set, etc.

Besides the above-mentioned articles we also undertake manufacturing business with trade mark, design or material supplied.

Others

Handled by the following Corporations:

China National Foreign Trade Transportation Corporation, Liaoning Branch.

135 Stalin Road, Dalian, China.
Cable: ZHONGWAIYUN DALIAN

China National Foreign Trade Transportation Corporation, Liaoning Truck Transportation Branch.

135 Stalin Road, Dalian, China.

China National Chartering Corporation, Dalian Sub-branch.

135 Stalin Road, Dalian, China.
Cable: ZHONGZU DALIAN

China National Packaging Import & Export Corporation, Liaoning Branch.

2 Hong Yan Street, Dalian, China. Tel: 35952
Cable: CHINAPACK DALIAN

China National Foreign Trade Storage Corporation, Liaoning Branch.

Hou Gezhenpu, Ganjingzi District, Dalian, China.

Liaoning Advertising Corporation

2 Hong Yan Street, Dalian, China. Tel: 32342
Cable: LIAOAVT DALIAN
TELEX: 86151 LFTC CN

Nantong No. 2 Cotton Mill

CHAOYANG

- 60 years' experience
- First class technical level
- Modernized equipment

- Strict inspection
- Stable quality
- Prompt delivery

Chaoyang Grey Cloth, praised as a trustworthy product by users at home and abroad, sells well in five continents.

Chaoyang Brand Grey Cloth
- Winner of National Quality Medal and Silver Medal
- Winner of state certificate for famous trademark
- Winner of the title "National Famous Brand Product"

Chaoyang Grey Cloth

Glossy, thick, smooth, with straight edges Acclaimed as the "All-Purpose Cloth", it meets the required standards of the dyeing, bleaching and printing processes.

Distributor:
The Chinese Textiles Import-Export Corporation
Address of Manufacturer:
Gongnong St., Nantong, Jiangsu Province, P.R.C.
Telephone: 3151 (Switchboard) Cable Address: 1260

Xinguang Brand Miner's Lamp

Winner of National Silver Medal for

Model KS-8 Xinguang Brand Miner's Lamp using Lead-acid batteries is portable and designed for miners in the pit. Electrolyte is injected outside the box; there is no acid leakage. The batteries are charged through the lamp-holder, the safety of which cuts off current once the single- or double-filament bulb is broken. Light of the double-filament bulb is converged.

Sold at home and abroad for years, the lamp is a favourite among its users.

Specification: Model KS-8

Number	Parameter		Unit	Amount			Remarks
				Single-Filament Bulb	Double-Filament Bulb		
					A	B	
1	Maximum Voltage		Volt	4	4	4	
2	Maximum Capacity		Ampere-hour	8	8	8	
3	Lighting Time		Hour	11	11	9	
4	Bulb	Voltage	Volt	4	4	4	Single-filament bulb is charged with argon; double-filament bulb is charged with krypton.
		Current	Ampere-hour	0.7	0.7/0.7	0.9/0.9	
		Luminous Flux	Lumen	22	29	37	
5	Size	Length	mm.	151	151	151	
		Width	mm.	64	64	64	
		Height	mm.	194	194	194	
6	Weight (Electrolyte Included)		Kilogram	2.3	2.3	2.3	

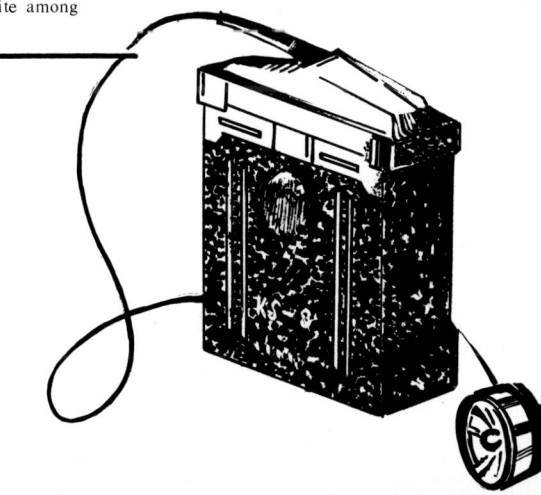

Manufacturer: Meishan Miner's Lamp Plant of the Coal Industry
Address: Meishan Town, Changxin County, Zhejiang Province, P.R.C.
Cable Address: 3597

Chifeng Pharmaceutical Plant

Registered Trademark

Hongma Brand

The plant uses domestic and foreign advanced technical equipment, modern testing instruments and methods of chemical testing to extract the following three products from wild ephedra:

- EPHEDRINE HYDROCHLORIDE
- ISOEPHEDRINE HYDROCHLORIDE
- L-METHYLEPHEDRINE HYDROCHLORIDE

- Fine quality
- Winner of National Silver Medal

Address: Chifeng, Inner Mongolia, P.R.C.
Cable Address: 5673   Telephone: 2227

FAMOUS PRODUCT OF BENXI IRON & STEEL Co.
—— FOUNDRY PIG IRON

Our company is an iron and steel complex with a history of over 60 years, now with several giant blast furnaces in operation. The pig iron produced is great in quantity and superior in quality. We can supply a variety of pig irons. Through the use of high grade raw materials from our own mines, through the adoption of advanced technology and through careful operation, the pig iron produced is characterized by being low-phosphorous, low-sulphurous, stable in chemical composition, low in detrimental impurities, good in casting, uniform in piecesize and by having a smooth surface. In 1979 a national gold medal was won for its superiority in quality. This product is well-known as "Ginseng spirit iron" and has been on sale at home and abroad. Our products are well known and much in favor of our customers. We abide by contracts and goods are prompt in delivery. Customers are welcome to make orders with us through negotiation or correspondence.

Symbol and Chemical Composition Piece Wt. 3~7kg

Designation	Symbol	Si %	Mn %			P %	S %	
			Group 1	Group 2	Group 3		Class 1	Class 2
Zhu 35	Z 35	3.25~3.75	<0.50	>0.50~0.90	>0.90~1.30	<0.10	<0.03	<0.04
Zhu 30	Z 30	2.75~3.25						
Zhu 25	Z 25	2.25~2.75						
Zhu 20	Z 20	1.75~2.25						
Zhu 15	Z 15	1.25~1.75					<0.04	<0.05

Add: Renmin Rd., Benxi city, Liaoning Province, P.R.C. Cable: 3561 Tel: 5455

Founded in January 1980, China Metallurgical Import & Export Corporation holds the "business license" No. 01005 (Import) and "business certificates" Nos. 0079 to 0083 issued to industrial and commercial enterprises by the Industrial and Commercial Administration Bureau of the P.R.C. This corporation is a state-owned enterprise integrating industry and trade and combining technology with trade. With the backing of metallurgical industrial enterprises throughout the country, it is well able to supply its customers' needs.

Major Tasks of the Corporation:

1) Export of metallurgical products (including metals and minerals, iron and steel, nonferrous metals, rare metals and rare-earth metals, ferroalloy, metallurgical cokes and their chemical products, refractory materials, graphite electrode);

2) Engage in compensatory trade between metallurgical industrial enterprises and foreign companies and in joint ventures with Chinese and foreign capital;

3) Import of metallurgical epuipmennt (including equipment for iron and steel plants, nonferrous smelting works, metal mines and nonmetal mines), spare parts and instruments and meters;

4) Export of metallurgical technical patents and special skills;

5) Joint manufacture of metallurgical equipment (including equipment for mines) and machine parts, and processing of materials and samples of various iron and steel casting supplied by foreign businessmen;

6) Process materials for metallurgical products supplied by foreign businessmen.
We are willing to develop various forms of trade and cooperation with factories and business circees of friendly countries and regions on the basis of cquality and mutual benefit and helping supply each other's needs. We welcome foreign businessmen to sign individual as well as long-term trade agreements and contracts. We will do our best to satisfy our customers' specifications.

China Metallurgical Import & Export Corp.
Address: 46 Xidajie, Dongsi, Beijing P.R.C.
Tel: 550197 or 557431-760
Cable Address: (Beijing) 2250 Telex: 22461   MIEC CN

經 濟 管 理
"ECONOMIC MANAGEMENT"
MONTHLY

歡 迎 訂 閱

※ 內 容 簡 介 ※

《經濟管理》月刊以基層經濟單位領導與管理幹部為對象，主要內容是：宣傳黨和國家的方針政策，探討有關管理的理論與實踐問題，介紹國內外先進管理經驗，普及有關管理的基本知識。

編輯者：《經濟管理》編輯委員會
出版者：經濟管理雜誌社
社　址：北京埠外月壇北小街2號（郵政編號100037）電　話：89-1013
Address: No. 2 Yuetan Beixiaojie, Beijing ・ Tel: 89-1013

國外總發行：**中國國際書店**（北京399信箱）
Oversea Distributor:
GUOJI SHUDIAN (CHINA PUBLICATIONS CENTRE)
P.O. Box 399, Beijing, China.

國內期刊代號：2-839
國外期刊代號：M107
國　內　定　價：0.30元

"三乐牌" 历史古酒 "杜康酒"
"Trio-happiness" Brand Historic "Du-kang" Wine

天下美酒　唯有杜康
古今一品　饮之寿长

The only good wine in the world through all ages! To enjoy a long life, drink Du-kang!

追溯历史，流传两千五百多年的杜康酒，素称"进贡仙酒"，以杜康始做秫酒得名。它独具风格，解忧、助欢、延年益寿。魏武帝曹操曰："何以解忧，唯有杜康。"杜甫曾吟："杜康频劳劝，张梨不外求。"予以称颂。在国宾宴上，日本前首相田中角荣曾向周恩来总理点名欢饮杜康酒，传为历史佳话。

杜康酒颇具历史遗风，自然的醇香，清澈透明，回味悠长。古今中外美名远扬。

Du-kang wine, which dates back over two thousand five hundred years, is usually called "Immortal Tribute Wine". It has been so called since Du Kang initiated to brew millet wine. It possesses a unique character, dissipated sorrow, helps increasing pleasure and prolongs life. "Du-kang wine is the only means of dissipating sorrow", said Emperor Wei Wu, Tsao Tsao. "Du-kang used to recommend it, and nothing else would Zhang Li seek", recited Du Pu once to compliment the wine. At a state banquet, former Japanese premier Tanaka requested Chinese late premier Zhou Enlai to designate Du-kang wine as the wine for the banquet, and the incident has since become famous.

Du-kang wine, being rich in historical customs, naturally fragrant, clear and lucid and abundant in after-taste, is famous far and wide.

经　销　者：中国粮油食品进出口公司
　　　　　　河南省分公司
地　　　址：中国郑州文化路六十九号
电　　　话：32620
电报挂号：YUFOOD ZHENGZHOU

CHINA NATIONAL CEREALS, OILS AND FOODSTUFFS IMPORT & EXPORT CORP. HENAN BRANCH

ADDRESS: 69, WENHUA ROAD, ZHENGZHOU
TEL: 32620　CABLE: YUFOOD ZHENGZHOU

Shanghai Electrochemical Works

上海电化厂

OFFER THE CHEMICALS BOTH INLAND AND ABROAD

LARGEST PRODUCER IN CHINA
P.T.F.E. RESIN

All sorts of grades of medium, fine, superfine grain without oils and high strength, suitable for manufacturing all kinds of films, spacers, tubes, plates, bearings and valves etc.

Refrigerants
FLUOROCARBON-11, 12, 13, 22

Provide these products in time and in series and serve the customers for packing.

OTHER PRODUCTS
Caustic Soda (45%)
Liquid Chlorine
Carbon Tetrachloride
Ammonium Chloride
White Carbon
(Silicon dioxide in fine state)

EXCELLENT QUALITY LOWER PRICE

ADDRESS: WUJING, SHANGHAI, CHINA. PHONE: 379380 CABLE: SHANGHAI 8407
THE SUPPLY & MARKETING AGENCY: 170 JIANGXI ROAD (CENTRAL). PHONE: 210885

Holder of national prize for quality

Famous Brand · Quality First
Wide Variety ·
Sold Throughout the World

"Golden Cock" Alarm Clock

Tianjin Clock and Watch Plant

Address: 2 Xizhuang Road,
Heping District, Tianjin
Tel: 20527
Cable Address: 5430

"FRIENDLY" BRAND FOOTWEAR

"FRIENDLY" brand footwear
Available in all sizes
Fashionable in styles
Attractive in designs
Comfortable in wearing
Moderate in prices

Orders are welcome

中国轻工业品进出口公司江苏省分公司
中国南京中华路 50 号

CHINA NATIONAL LIGHT INDUSTRIAL PRODUCTS IMPORT & EXPORT CORP. JIANGSU BRANCH

50 Zhong Hua Road,
Nanjing China
TEL: 24769

Cable Address:
"INDUSTRY" NANJING
TELEX: 34105 INDNK CN

CHINA NATIONAL METALS & MINERALS IMPORT & EXPORT CORPORATION BEIJING BRANCH

中国五金矿产进出口公司北京市分公司

经营项目 TRADING ITEMS

黄 铜 棒：	BRASS RODS
铝 卷 片：	ALUMINIUM MILL SHEETS IN COILS
普 通 园 钉：	COMMON ROUND IRON WIRE NAILS
制 钉 丝：	BRIGHT HARD DRAWN NAIL WIRE
镀 锌 丝：	GALVANIZED IRON WIRE
圆 油 桶：	METAL DRUM
扁 油 桶：	METAL PETROL CAN
机 螺 钉：	MILD STEEL MACHINE SCREWS
（德制、美制）	(DIN STANDARD、AMERICAN IFI STANDARD)
六 角 螺 丝 帽：	BRIGHT MILD STEEL HEXAGONAL NUTS
（德制、美制）	(DIN STANDARD、AMERICAN IFI STANDARD)
道 钉：	TRACK SPIKE
马 蹄 铁：	HORSESHOES
窗 纱：	IRON WIRE NETTING
门 锁：	DOOR LOCKS
厚 铁 合 页：	BRIGHT HEAVY IRON HINGES, FIXED PIN
薄 铁 合 页：	BRIGHT LIGHT IRON HINGES, FIXED PIN
A 型 门 拉 手：	DOOR PULLS TYPE "A"
大 理 石：	MARBLE TILES
水 磨 石：	TERRAZZO TILES
板 石：	SLATE TILES
大 理 石 米：	MARBLE CHIPS
生 石 灰 粉：	QUICK LIME POWDER
粘 土 砖：	FIRE BRICK
高 铝 砖：	HIGH ALUMINA BRICK
轻 质 保 温 砖：	INSULATING BRICK
电 炉 顶 砖：	ELECTRIC FURNACE ROOFING BRICK
矾 土 骨 料：	CALCINED BAUXITE AGGREGATE
矾 土 细 粉：	CALCINED BAUXITE POWDER
多 晶 硅：	POLYCRYSTALLINE SILICON
三 氧 化 钨：	TUNGSTEN TRIOXIDE
硅 铁：	FERRO-SILICON
电 阻 发 热 丝：	ELECTRIC RESISTANCE & HEATING WIRE
焊 缝 管：黑管和镀锌管	WELDED STEEL PIPES: BLACK & GALVANIZED
法 兰 盘：	FLANGES
铸 铁 制 品：	CAST IRON PRODUCTS
元 钢：	MILD STEEL ROUND BARS
扁 钢：	MILD STEEL FLAT BARS
带 钢：	MILD STEEL STRIP
角 钢：	MILD STEEL EQUAL ANGLES
盘 条：	MILD STEEL WIRE RODS
钢 丝：	STEEL WIRE
各 种 优 质 钢：	HIGH QUALITY STEEL
螺 纹 钢：	HIGH TENSILE DEFORMED STEEL BARS
钢 锭 模：	STEEL INGOT MOULD

Address: 190 Chao Nei Street, Beijing China.
Telephone: 55.1454
地址：北京朝内大于190号
电话：55.1454

Telex: 22470 BFTCC–C CN
Cable: MINMET Beijing
电传：22470 BFTCC–C CN
电报挂号：北京 MINMET

SHANGHAI DYESTUFFS INDUSTRIAL COMPANY STRIVES TO BRING BRIGHTNESS AND COLOUR TO THE WORLD!

Major products:
 dyes: reactive dyes, disperse dyes
  positive ion dyes, azoic dyes
  vat dyes, sulphur dyes
  acid dyes, direct dyes
  edible pigments

dyestuffs: organic dyestuffs (phthalocyanine, azo)
textile auxiliaries
industrial chemicals and dyestuff
 intermediates:
  pathalic anhydride,
  phenol, maleic
  anhydride

SDC
上染

A long history
Wide assortment of goods
High quality
Our choicest products
await your selection!

Address: 107 Fuzhou Road, Shanghai
Tel: 213866
Cable Address: 0208

POLAR BEAR BRAND
MENTHOL CRYSTALS

- A long history
- Top quality
- Meets the needs of customers from many countries
- Famous on the international market

"Polar Bear Brand" Menthol Crystals produced by Shanghai perfumery is handled by the Shanghai Branch, Chinese Tea and Native Products Import & Export Lorp

This product, refined from mint oil, is colourless, transparent, pleasantly cool, and less oily, with big crystals, a heavy aroma, high purity and a melting point of 42°–44°. It is used in large quantities for articles of everyday use — tooth paste, tooth powder, beverages, gargles, cigarettes, foodstuffs and medicinal products

Address:
1 Nanzhangjiabang Road, Tangqiao, Pudong, Shanghai
Tel: 840126, 840674   Cable Address: 5267

溝通中外商品的媒介
Popular maganizes having a high circulation both in China and overseas

審美 Hair & Beauty
亞洲版（雙月刊）
(ASIA) BIMONTHLY

健康家庭 HEALTHY FAMILY
月刊 MONTHLY

Producted & Published by:
TAI DAO PUBLISHING CO. (Hong Kong) 香港大道文化公司
Address: 115 Wanchai Road, 13/F., Block D, Hong Kong.
Cable: 4718   Telex: 71942 MCTDP

地球上飞起一隻天鹅!
Exciting Trading Opportunities in Northern China!

中国轻工业品进出口公司黑龙江省分公司
CHINA NATIONAL LIGHT INDUSTRIAL PRODUCTS IMPORT & EXPORT CORPORATION HEILONGJIANG BRANCH

(H. L.)

我公司经营的商品有日用百货、文教体育用品、纸张、建材、家用电器、鞋类和皮革制品等数百个规格品种,行销世界一百多个国家和地区,享有良好信誉。欢迎世界各国贸易界人士洽谈生意。

The main scope of business of our corporation is the import and export of general merchandise, stationery, paper, sports goods, construction materials, household electrical appliances, shoes and leather articles, etc., totalling several hundred varieties and models. Heilongjiang products have been exported to more than a hundred countries, and have gained a world-wide reputation for quality and variety.

We welcome foreign traders from all countries to come to China to negotiate business.

地址: 哈尔滨市大成街36号	ADD. NO. 36 DACHENG STR. HARBIN CHINA
电话: 35549	TEL. 35549
电报: 6110	CAB. INDUSTRY
电传: 80072 HFTBI CN INDUSTRY	TELEX: 80072 HFTBI CN INDUSTRY